*The Consumer Credit and Sales*
*Legal Practice Series*

CREDIT AND BANKING LIBRARY



# CONSUMER CREDIT REGULATION

## Credit Cards, Payday Loans, Auto Finance, and Other Non-Mortgage Credit

**First Edition**

WITH COMPANION WWW WEBSITE

See *page ix* for information about the companion website.

Carolyn L. Carter
Andrew G. Pizor
Jonathan Sheldon

Contributing Authors: Elizabeth Renuart, Lauren K. Saunders, Chi Chi Wu, Alys I. Cohen, Persis S. Yu, Arielle Cohen, John W. Van Alst, Jeremiah Battle, Jr.

**National Consumer Law Center®**
7 Winthrop Square, 4th Floor Boston, MA 02110 www.nclc.org

| | |
|---|---|
| *About NCLC®* | The National Consumer Law Center®, a nonprofit corporation founded in 1969, assists consumers, advocates, and public policy makers nationwide who use the powerful and complex tools of consumer law to ensure justice and fair treatment for all, particularly those whose poverty renders them powerless to demand accountability from the economic marketplace. For more information, go to www.nclc.org. |
| *Ordering NCLC Publications* | Order securely online at www.nclc.org, or contact Publications Department, National Consumer Law Center, 7 Winthrop Square, 4th Floor, Boston, MA 02110, (617) 542-9595, FAX: (617) 542-8028, e-mail: publications@nclc.org. |
| *Training and Conferences* | NCLC participates in numerous national, regional, and local consumer law trainings. Its annual fall conference is a forum for consumer rights attorneys from legal services programs, private practice, government, and nonprofit organizations to share insights into common problems and explore novel and tested approaches that promote consumer justice in the marketplace. Contact NCLC for more information or see our website. |
| *Case Consulting* | Case analysis, consulting and co-counseling for lawyers representing vulnerable consumers are among NCLC's important activities. Administration on Aging funds allow us to provide free consulting to legal services advocates representing elderly consumers on many types of cases. Massachusetts Legal Assistance Corporation funds permit case assistance to advocates representing low-income Massachusetts consumers. Other funding may allow NCLC to provide very brief consultations to other advocates without charge. More comprehensive case analysis and research is available for a reasonable fee. See our website for more information at www.nclc.org. |
| *Charitable Donations and* Cy Pres *Awards* | NCLC's work depends in part on the support of private donors. Tax-deductible donations should be made payable to National Consumer Law Center, Inc. For more information, contact Gerald Tuckman of NCLC's Development Office at (617) 542-8010 or gtuckman@nclc.org. NCLC has also received generous court-approved *cy pres* awards arising from consumer class actions to advance the interests of class members. For more information, contact Robert Hobbs (rhobbs@nclc.org) or Rich Dubois (rdubois@nclc.org) at (617) 542-8010. |
| *Comments and Corrections* | Write to the above address to the attention of the Editorial Department or e-mail consumerlaw@nclc.org. |
| *About This Volume* | This is the First Edition of *Consumer Credit Regulation*. This book includes a companion website. Continuing developments can be found in periodic supplements to and revised editions of this volume, on the companion website, and in NCLC eReports. |
| *Cite This Volume As* | National Consumer Law Center, Consumer Credit Regulation (2012). |
| *Attention* | *This publication is designed to provide authoritative information concerning the subject matter covered. Always use the most current edition and supplement, and use other sources for more recent developments or for special rules for individual jurisdictions. This publication cannot substitute for the independent judgment and skills of an attorney or other professional. Non-attorneys are cautioned against using these materials to conduct a lawsuit without advice from an attorney and are cautioned against engaging in the unauthorized practice of law.* |
| *Copyright* |  |

ISBN: 978-1-60248-106-0 (this volume)
ISBN: 978-0-943116-10-5 (Series)

Library of Congress Control Number: 2012942743

# About the Authors

**Carolyn L. Carter** is NCLC's deputy director for advocacy and was formerly co-director of Legal Services, Inc., in Gettysburg, Pennsylvania, and director of the Law Reform Office of the Cleveland Legal Aid Society. She is co-author of *Mortgage Lending, Collection Actions*, *Unfair and Deceptive Acts and Practices*, *Consumer Warranty Law* and *Automobile Fraud*, author of *Repossessions*, and a contributing author to *Truth in Lending*, *Fair Debt Collection,* and *Fair Credit Reporting*. She is a past member of the Federal Reserve Board Consumer Advisory Council and a recipient of the Vern Countryman Consumer Law Award.

**Andrew G. Pizor** is a staff attorney in NCLC's Washington, D.C., office, a co-author of *Mortgage Lending,* and a contributing author to *Foreclosures* and *Truth in Lending*. He was formerly an attorney at the Connecticut Fair Housing Center, Consumer Law Group L.L.C., and Legal Services Corp. of Delaware, where he worked on housing and consumer protection issues, focusing on defending foreclosures and fighting predatory lending.

**Jonathan Sheldon** has been an NCLC staff attorney writing and consulting on a number of consumer law topics since 1976. Previously he was a staff attorney with the Federal Trade Commission. His other publications include *Unfair and Deceptive Acts and Practices*, *Consumer Warranty Law*, *Consumer Arbitration Agreements, Automobile Fraud*, and *Repossessions*, and is a contributing author to a number of other NCLC publications.

**Elizabeth Renuart** is an associate professor of law at Albany Law School and formerly an NCLC staff attorney, and is co-author of *Truth in Lending, The Cost of Credit,* and *Stop Predatory Lending*. She is a former member of the Federal Reserve Board Consumer Advisory Council. She was the managing attorney of a legal services office in Baltimore, Maryland, where she litigated cases involving Truth in Lending, usury, deceptive practices, and fraud.

**Chi Chi Wu** is an NCLC staff attorney working on consumer credit, credit reporting, and medical debt issues. She is a co-author of *Fair Credit Reporting* and *Collection Actions* and a contributing author to *Truth in Lending* and *Credit Discrimination.* She was formerly an assistant attorney general with the Massachusetts attorney general's office and an attorney with Greater Boston Legal Services.

**John W. Van Alst** is an NCLC staff attorney and formerly was an attorney at Legal Aid of North Carolina and adjunct clinical professor at the University of North Carolina School of Law. He is co-author of *Automobile Fraud*, *Consumer Warranty Law*, and *Consumer Rights for Domestic Violence Survivors*, and a contributing author to *Foreclosures* and *Unfair and Deceptive Acts and Practices*.

**Arielle Cohen** is an NCLC staff attorney focusing on class action litigation and other advocacy. She is a co-author of the seventh edition of *Consumer Class Actions* and contributes to several other NCLC treatises. She was formerly a Skadden Fellow at the New Jersey Institute for Social Justice.

**Jeremiah Battle, Jr.** is an NCLC staff attorney and a contributing author to several NCLC publications. Previously, he was a staff attorney with Northeast New Jersey Legal Services, and a managing attorney with what is now Disability Rights New Jersey.

**Persis S. Yu** is an NCLC staff attorney and works on the Fair Credit Reporting Act, student loans, and on other consumer advocacy issues. Prior to joining NCLC, Persis was a Hanna S. Cohn Equal Justice Fellow at Empire Justice Center in Rochester, New York.

**Lauren K. Saunders** is the managing attorney of NCLC's Washington office, and co-author of *Consumer Banking and Payments Law* and *Combating Foreclosure Rescue Scams* and a contributing author to *Fair Debt Collection* and *Fair Credit Reporting*. She previously directed the Federal Rights Project of the National Senior Citizens Law Center, was deputy director of litigation at Bet Tzedek Legal Services in Los Angeles, and was an associate at the public interest firm Hall & Phillips.

**Alys I. Cohen** is a staff attorney at NCLC's Washington office, author of *Credit Discrimination*, co-author of *Stop Predatory Lending*, and a contributing author to *Truth in Lending*. Formerly, she was an attorney in the Federal Trade Commission's Bureau of Consumer Protection, Division of Financial Practices.

## Acknowledgments

This treatise largely draws upon and supersedes NCLC's *The Cost of Credit.* That work in turn drew heavily from *Consumer Usury and Credit Overcharges* (1982) and *Usury and Consumer Credit Regulation* (1989). Thus, the authors are indebted to Mark Leymaster, the author of the 1982 volume (who also contributed the credit math program found on the companion website), to Kathleen Keest and Kevin Brown for the 1989 volume, to Kathleen Keest for the first edition of *The Cost of Credit,* and to Elizabeth Renuart and Kathleen Keest for the second, third and fourth editions of *The Cost of Credit*. And of course, we are also indebted to the many people who contributed to all of those volumes—too many to list here.

Special thanks to Birny Birnbaum for substantive contributions; Denise Lisio for editorial supervision; Kim Calvi for editorial assistance; Margot Saunders for her substantive contributions; Shirlron Williams for cite checking; Mary Kingsley, Emily Green Caplan, Bryant Jirvisitcul, Kurt Terwilliger, and Allen Agnitti for legal research and writing; Shannon Halbrook for the companion website; Microsearch for website services; Xylutions for typesetting services; and Mary McLean for indexing.

# What Your Library Should Contain

***The Consumer Credit and Sales Legal Practice Series*** contains 19 titles, updated annually, arranged into four libraries, and designed to be an attorney's primary practice guide and legal resource in all 50 states. Titles are available individually or as part of the complete 19-volume series. Each title includes free access to a companion website containing sample pleadings, primary sources, and other practice aids, allowing pinpoint searches and the pasting of text into a word processor. Access remains free as long as purchasers keep their titles current.

## *Debtor Rights Library*

*2009 Ninth Edition (Two Volumes), 2011 Supplement, and Companion Website.*

**Consumer Bankruptcy Law and Practice:** the definitive personal bankruptcy manual, from the initial interview to final discharge, including consumer rights when a company files for bankruptcy. This practice package contains the leading expert analysis of individual bankruptcy law and such practice aids as over 150 pleadings and forms, a client questionnaire and handout, the latest Bankruptcy Code, Rules, and fee schedules, a date calculator, software to compute the initial forms, and means test data.

*2011 Seventh Edition (Two Volumes), 2012 Supplement, and Companion Website*

**Fair Debt Collection:** the basic reference covering the Fair Debt Collection Practices Act and common law, state statutory and other federal debt collection protections. Thousands of unique case summaries cover reported and unreported FDCPA cases by category. The companion website contains sample pleadings and discovery, the FTC Commentary, an index to and the full text of *all* FTC staff opinion letters, and other practice aids.

*2012 Fourth Edition and Companion Website*

**Foreclosures:** examines RESPA and other federal and state requirements placed on mortgage loan servicers, and details loan modification and mediation programs implemented by federal and state governments. The volume features standing and other substantive and procedural defenses to foreclosure and tactics after the foreclosure sale. Special chapters cover tax liens, land installment sales contracts, manufactured home and condominium foreclosures, and other topics.

*2010 Seventh Edition, 2011 Supplement, and Companion Website*

**Repossessions:** a unique guide to motor vehicle and mobile home repossessions, threatened seizures of household goods, statutory liens, and automobile lease and rent-to-own default remedies. The volume examines UCC Article 9 and hundreds of other federal and state statutes regulating repossessions.

*2010 Fourth Edition, 2011 Supplement and Companion Website*

**Student Loan Law:** collection harassment; closed school, disability, and other discharges; tax intercepts, wage garnishment, and offset of social security benefits; and repayment plans, consolidation loans, deferments, and non-payment of loan based on school fraud.

*2011 Fifth Edition and Companion Website*

**Access to Utility Service:** consumer rights as to regulated and unregulated utilities, including telecommunications, terminations, billing errors, low-income payment plans, utility allowances in subsidized housing, LIHEAP, and weatherization.

## *Credit and Banking Library*

*2010 Seventh Edition (Two Volumes), 2011 Supplement, and Companion Website*

**Truth in Lending:** detailed analysis of *all* aspects of TILA, the Consumer Leasing Act, the Fair Credit Billing Act, the Home Ownership and Equity Protection Act (HOEPA), and the Credit CARD Act, including the major 2010 amendments. Appendices and the website contain the Acts, Reg. Z, Reg. M, and their official staff commentaries, numerous sample pleadings, rescission notices, two programs to compute APRs, TIL legislative history, and a unique compilation of *all Federal Register* notices and supplementary information on Regulation Z since 1969.

*2010 Seventh Edition, 2011 Supplement, and Companion Website*

**Fair Credit Reporting:** the key resource for handling any type of credit reporting issue, from cleaning up blemished credit records to suing reporting agencies and creditors for inaccurate reports. Covers the new FACTA changes, identity theft, creditor liability for failing to properly reinvestigate disputed information, credit scoring, privacy issues, the Credit Repair Organizations Act, state credit reporting and repair statutes, and common law claims.

*Superseded*

**The Cost of Credit** is replaced by two new titles, *Mortgage Lending* and *Consumer Credit Regulation*. Responding to major changes in the nature and regulation of mortgage lending and other consumer credit, these two new titles expand upon, update, and re-organize *The Cost of Credit* material.

*2012 First Edition and Companion Website, replacing* The Cost of Credit

**Mortgage Lending:** covers federal and state regulation (and federal preemption of state regulation) of the origination and the terms of mortgage loans, including ability to pay, steering, churning, flipping, appraisals, loan broker compensation, insurance, adjustable rates, negative amortization, interest rate limitations, late fees, reverse mortgages, holder-in-due course, mortgage litigation, and claims against failed banks.

*2012 First Edition and Companion Website, replacing* The Cost of Credit

**Consumer Credit Regulation:** examines federal and state regulation (and federal preemption of state regulation) concerning credit cards, payday loans, automobile and manufactured home finance and installment sales, auto title pawns, rent-to-own, refund anticipation loans, "sale" of the consumer's future income stream and other non-mortgage lending. Special chapters on credit math, what is interest, and credit insurance.

*2009 Fourth Edition, 2012 Supplement, and Companion Website*

**Consumer Banking and Payments Law:** covers checks, telechecks, electronic fund transfers, electronic check conversions, money orders, and credit, debit, payroll, unemployment, and stored value cards. The title also covers banker's right of setoff, electronic transfers of federal and state benefit payments, and a special chapter on electronic records and signatures.

*2009 Fifth Edition, 2012 Supplement, and Companion Website*

**Credit Discrimination:** analysis of the Equal Credit Opportunity Act, Fair Housing Act, Civil Rights Acts, and state credit discrimination statutes, including reprints of all relevant federal interpretations, government enforcement actions, and numerous sample pleadings.

## *Consumer Litigation Library*

*2011 Second Edition, 2012 Supplement, and Companion Website*

**Collection Actions:** a complete guide to consumer defenses and counterclaims to collection lawsuits filed in court or in arbitration, with extensive discussion of setting aside default judgments and limitations on a collector's post-judgment remedies. Special chapters include the rights of active duty military, and unique issues involving medical debt, government collections, collector's attorney fees, and bad check laws.

*2011 Sixth Edition and Companion Website*

**Consumer Arbitration Agreements:** successful approaches to challenge arbitration agreements' enforceability and waivers of class arbitration, the interrelation of the Federal Arbitration Act and state law, class actions and punitive damages in arbitration, implications of NAF's withdrawal from consumer arbitrations, the right to discovery, and other topics.

*2010 Seventh Edition, 2012 Supplement, and Companion Website*

**Consumer Class Actions:** makes class litigation manageable even for small offices, including numerous sample pleadings, class certification memoranda, discovery, class notices, settlement materials, and much more. Includes a detailed analysis of the Class Action Fairness Act, class arbitration, state class action rules and case law, and other topics.

*Website and 2011 Index Guide: ALL pleadings from ALL NCLC treatises, including* Consumer Law Pleadings Numbers One through Seventeen

**Consumer Law Pleadings:** over *2000* notable pleadings from all types of consumer cases, including predatory lending, foreclosures, automobile fraud, lemon laws, debt collection, fair credit reporting, home improvement fraud, student loans, and lender liability. Finding aids pinpoint desired pleading in seconds, ready to paste into a word processor.

## *Deception and Warranties Library*

*2008 Seventh Edition, 2011 Supplement, and Companion Website*

**Unfair and Deceptive Acts and Practices:** the only practice manual covering all aspects of a deceptive practices case in every state. Special sections on automobile sales, the federal racketeering (RICO) statute, unfair insurance practices, the FTC Holder Rule, telemarketing fraud, attorney fees, and many other topics.

*2011 Fourth Edition and Companion Website*

**Automobile Fraud:** examination of title law, "yo-yo" sales, odometer tampering, lemon laundering, sale of salvage and wrecked cars, undisclosed prior use, and prior damage to new cars. The website contains numerous sample pleadings and title search techniques.

*2010 Fourth Edition, 2012 Supplement, and Companion Website*

**Consumer Warranty Law:** comprehensive treatment of new and used car lemon laws, the Magnuson-Moss Warranty Act, UCC Articles 2 and 2A, manufactured home, new home, and assistive device warranty laws, FTC Used Car Rule, tort theories, car repair and home improvement statutes, service contract and lease laws, with numerous sample pleadings.

## *NCLC's Companion Websites*

*Newly redesigned and upgraded*

Every NCLC manual includes a companion website, allowing rapid access to appendices, pleadings, primary sources, and other practice aids. Search for documents by category or with a table of contents or various keyword search options. All documents can be downloaded, printed, and copy-pasted into a word processing document. Pleadings are also available in Word format. Web access is free with each title ordered and remains free as long as a title is kept current.

*Website continually subject to update*

**Consumer Law on the Web:** combines *everything* from the 19 other NCLC companion websites. Using *Consumer Law on the Web*, instead of multiple individual companion websites, is often the fastest and most convenient way to pinpoint and retrieve key documents among the thousands available on our individual companion websites.

## *Other NCLC Publications for Lawyers*

*Over 100 articles a year on current topics*

**NCLC eReports:** over 100 online articles a year (currently free to those on automatic subscription to updates to NCLC treatises, paid subscriptions for others), with not just the latest consumer law developments, but also novel ideas, innovative tactics, and key insights from NCLC's experienced consumer law attorneys. Articles can be copy-pasted into a word processor, web links are live, and past articles are easily searchable. Optional free e-mail alerts announce new articles and list just-released regulations, statutes, and key court decisions.

*First Edition and Companion Website*

**Bankruptcy Basics: A Step-by-Step Guide for Pro Bono Attorneys, General Practitioners, and Legal Services Offices:** provides everything attorneys new to bankruptcy need to file their first case, with a companion website that contains software, sample pleadings, and other practice aids that greatly simplify handling a bankruptcy case.

*Second Edition and Companion Website*

**Foreclosure Prevention Counseling: Preserving the American Dream:** explains how to obtain a workout, with advice specifically tailored for Fannie Mae, Freddie Mac, subprime, FHA-insured, VA, and Rural Housing Service loans. The book also details new loan modification initiatives from federal and state governments and industry.

*Second Edition with CD-Rom*

**STOP Predatory Lending: A Guide for Legal Advocates:** provides a roadmap and practical legal strategy for litigating predatory lending abuses, from small loans to mortgage loans. How to analyze the documents, spot issues, raise legal claims, select defendants, and even craft a community response.

*First Edition*

**Instant Evidence: A Quick Guide to Federal Evidence and Objections:** facilitates objection by rule number and includes common objections and motions at every stage of a case—all in under 20 pages! Spiral-bound to lay flat, all pages are laminated, allowing new notations for each trial with a dry-erase pen.

*Second Edition with CD-Rom*

**The Practice of Consumer Law: Seeking Economic Justice:** contains an essential overview to consumer law and explains how to get started in a private or legal services consumer practice. Packed with invaluable sample pleadings and practice pointers for even experienced consumer attorneys.

***National Consumer Law Center Guide Series*** are books designed for consumers, counselors, and attorneys new to consumer law:

*2010 Edition*

**NCLC Guide to Surviving Debt:** a great overview of consumer law. Everything a paralegal, new attorney, or client needs to know about home foreclosures and mortgage modifications, debt collectors, managing credit card debt, whether to refinance, credit card problems, evictions, repossessions, credit reporting, utility terminations, student loans, budgeting, and bankruptcy.

*First Edition*

**NCLC Guide to the Rights of Utility Consumers:** explains consumer rights concerning electric, gas, and other utility services: shut off protections, rights to restore terminated service, bill payment options, weatherization tips, rights to government assistance, and much more.

*First Edition*

**NCLC Guide to Consumer Rights for Domestic Violence Survivors:** provides practical advice to help survivors get back on their feet financially and safely establish their economic independence.

*First Edition*

**NCLC Guide to Mobile Homes:** what consumers and their advocates need to know about mobile home dealer sales practices and an in-depth look at mobile home quality and defects, with 35 photographs and construction details.

*First Edition*

**Return to Sender: Getting a Refund or Replacement for Your Lemon Car:** find how lemon laws work, what consumers and their lawyers should know to evaluate each other, investigative techniques and discovery tips, how to handle both informal dispute resolution and trials, and more.

Visit **www.nclc.org** to order securely online or for more information on all NCLC publications and companion websites, including the full tables of contents, indices, and **web-based searches of the publications' full text**.

# About the Companion Website, Other Search Options

## *The Companion Website*

Purchase of any title in NCLC's consumer law practice series includes free access to its companion website. Access remains free if you subscribe or continue to purchase updates to that title. Frequently updated, NCLC companion websites offer the treatises' appendices plus hundreds of additional documents in PDF and Microsoft Word formats—pleadings, forms, statutes, regulations, agency interpretations, legislative and regulatory history, and much more—all easily located with flexible, powerful search tools. Documents can be electronically searched, printed, downloaded, and copy-pasted into a word processor.

### Accessing the Companion Website

One-time registration is required to access the companion website. Once registered, a user subsequently logging in will be granted immediate access to all the companion websites he or she is authorized to use.

To register for the first time, go to **www.nclc.org/webaccess** and click on the "New users click here to register" link. Enter the Companion Website Registration Number[1] found on the packing statement or invoice accompanying this book. Then enter the requested information and click on "Login." An e-mail address may be used for the user name, or a different user name may be chosen.

**Users do *not* need to register more than once.**[2] If you subsequently purchase additional NCLC titles, you will automatically be given access to the corresponding companion websites. Registering a second time with the same registration number overrides a prior user name and password.

Once registered, click on the log-in link at **www.nclc.org/webaccess**, enter the user name and password, and select a website from the list of authorized websites.

An alternative log-in method may be particularly useful for libraries, legal aid offices, or law firms that subscribe to the entire set of NCLC treatises. Simply send an e-mail to publications@nclc.org with a list or range of static IP addresses for which access should be permitted. Users from those addresses can then go to www.nclc.org/ipaccess to be granted access *without* entering a user name and password.

1 If you cannot locate this number, contact NCLC Publications at (617) 542-9595 or publications@nclc.org.

2 If you have not updated *any* of your NCLC treatises for some time, your account may be deleted; if this happens, you must re-register if you subsequently purchase a book.

Once logged in, users can click the "My Account" link located on the toolbar to change their personal information.

### Locating Documents on the Companion Website

The companion website provides three options to locate documents.

**1. The search page** (the home page) offers keyword searches to find documents—either all documents' full text or only the documents' titles.

- Narrow the search to documents of a certain type (such as federal statutes or pleadings) by making a selection from the "Document Type" menu, and then perform a full text or document title search.
- To locate a specific appendix section, select the appendix section number (e.g., A.2.3) or a partial identifier (e.g., A) in the search page's "Appendix" drop-down fields.
- Click Search Hints for a quick reference to special search operators, wildcards, shortcuts, and complex searches. Read this closely, as syntax and search operators may be slightly different from those of other websites.

**2. The contents page** (click on the "Contents" tab at the top of the page) is a traditional nested table of contents. Click a branch to expand it into a list of sub-branches or documents. Each document appears once on this contents tree.

**3. The pleading finder page** (click on the "Pleading Finder" tab at the top of the page, *if available*) allows pleadings to be located using one or more menus, such as "Type of Pleading" or "Subject." **Select more than one item from a menu, or deselect items, by holding the Ctrl key while clicking.** For example, make one selection from "Type of Pleading–General," one from "Subject," and three from "Legal Claims" to locate all pleadings of that type and subject that contain one or more of the three legal claims selected. If this search produces insufficient results, simply broaden the search by deselecting "Subject" and/or "Legal Claims" to find pleadings of that type in any subject area or based upon any legal claim. This page also includes optional fields to specify terms to be found in the documents' text or titles, to further narrow search results.

### How to Use the Documents, Find Microsoft Word Versions, and Locate Additional Features

Click a document title in your search results or on the contents page to view the document in your web browser. Text may be copy-pasted directly from the page or the full document may be downloaded as a PDF file. (You will need a PDF reader to open PDF documents; the free Adobe Reader is available at www.adobe.com.) Additionally, pleadings and certain other documents can be downloaded in Microsoft Word format, enabling the opening of entire documents in a word processing program. Icons to download PDF and Word versions are found at the top of the page.

Links on the left-hand toolbar bring you to credit math software, search tips, other websites, tables of contents and indices of all NCLC treatises, and other practice aids. Links to especially important new developments will be placed toward the bottom of the "Search" page.

### Documents Found on the Website

The companion website to *Consumer Credit Regulation* includes a guide to analyzing a loan flipping case, a large number of sample complaints and discovery requests, and sample affidavits and expert witness testimony. Other pleadings include sample briefs, class certification materials, settlements, injunctive orders, jury instructions, and judgments.

The website also includes key federal statutes with updates, retail installment sales acts summarized and citations to other state lending statutes. Also included are federal agency regulations with recent updates, the full text of numerous other hard-to-find statements of policy, interpretation letters, opinion letters, and guidelines from HUD, NCUA, OCC, OTS, and FDIC.

## *Locating Topics in This Treatise*

NCLC offers a handy online utility to search the full text of our publications. This free search utility is found at www.nclc.org/keyword and requires no registration or log-in. While the chapters' text is not available online, this web-based search engine will find a word or phrase, which can then easily be located in this printed treatise. Select this book, enter a search term or combination of search terms—such as a case name, a regulation citation, or other keywords—and the page numbers containing those terms will be listed. Search results are shown in context, enabling selection of the most relevant pages.

## *Locating Topics in Other NCLC Manuals or NCLC eReports*

The search utility found at www.nclc.org/keyword can also be used to search other NCLC publications, including NCLC eReports. Simply perform the search as described above and select the publication to be searched.

Current tables of contents, indices, and other information for all nineteen titles in the NCLC *Consumer Credit and Sales Legal Practice Series* can be found at www.nclc.org/shop. Click the "For Lawyers" link and scroll down to the book you are interested in. The PDF-format documents found there can be quickly searched for a word or phrase.

The Quick Reference, found at www.nclc.org/qr, is an alphabetical index spanning all nineteen NCLC treatises. It lists over 1000 subjects and indicates the book(s) and section(s) where each subject is discussed.

## *Finding Pleadings*

Pleadings relating to this title are found in PDF and Word format on the companion website; search options are discussed above at "Locating Documents on the Companion Website." Over 2000 pleadings are also available at NCLC's *Consumer Law Pleadings* website using the same search techniques discussed above. Pleadings can also be located using *Consumer Law Pleadings*' index guide, which lists pleadings organized by type, subject area, legal claim, title, and other categories identical to those on the website.

# Summary Contents

# Contents

## Chapter 4 Interest, Points, Fees, and Delinquency Charges

## Chapter 5 Credit Math: Calculating Interest and Rebates

Chapter 7

# Litigation

## Part II Specific Types of Credit

### Chapter 8 Credit Cards: Abuses, Regulation, and State Law Claims

## Chapter 9 Payday Loans

## Chapter 10 Motor Vehicle, Manufactured Home and Other Installment Sales

## Chapter 12 Rent-to-Own



## Chapter 13 "Sale" of Future Payment Streams



## Chapter 14 Refund Anticipation Loans (RALs) and Tax Refund Schemes

# Chapter 1 Background

## 1.1 About This Treatise

### *1.1.1 Topics Covered and Relation to Other NCLC Treatises*

This treatise examines federal and state restrictions on consumer credit transactions, and federal preemption of the state restrictions. It focuses on interest rates, fees, third-party charges, rebates of unearned interest, late charges and other credit terms for non-mortgage credit. Other NCLC treatises detail limits on creditor remedies where a consumer defaults on a credit obligation—debt collection, collection lawsuits, repossessions, credit reporting, and garnishment. This treatise focuses on the origination of the credit obligation and its terms.

*Consumer Credit Regulation* Part I analyzes issues of general applicability, including a survey of applicable legal claims, an analysis of what state law applies and federal preemption, an examination of interest, the basics of credit math, credit insurance, and litigation issues. Part II focuses on particular forms of consumer credit:

- Credit cards;
- Payday loans and credit union small loans;
- Automobile sales financing;
- Manufactured home sales financing;
- Other installment sales;
- Rent to own transactions;
- Auto title pawns;
- "Sales" of future income streams;
- Refund anticipation loans.

Of note are the topics not covered in this treatise. Most significantly, home mortgages, home equity lines of credit, and other loans taking a home as security are covered in another NCLC treatise in this series, *Mortgage Lending*.[1] Other books in this series also cover certain specialized forms of consumer credit. Student loans are analyzed in NCLC's *Student Loan Law*.[2] *Consumer Banking and Payments Law*[3] covers bank charges where a bank processes a check or a debit, ATM, or stored value card transaction, even though there are insufficient funds in the consumer's bank account. *Access to Utility Service*[4] examines credit related to the provision of gas, electric, water, telephone, and other utilities.

1 (2012).
2 (4th ed. 2010 and Supp.).
3 (4th ed. 2010 and Supp.).
4 (5th ed. 2011).

*Consumer Credit Regulation* focuses only on the substantive limits on interest rates and other credit terms. Disclosure requirements are detailed in NCLC's *Truth in Lending*.[5] Consumer claims for discrimination in the extension of credit are detailed in NCLC's *Credit Discrimination*.[6]

Separate treatises in this series address consumer rights where a debt is disputed or the creditor claims the loan is in default. *Fair Debt Collection*[7] sets out consumer rights concerning debt collection contacts; *Collection Actions*[8] concerns collection lawsuits, garnishment, and other post-judgment remedies; and *Fair Credit Reporting*[9] concerns a creditor's furnishing of negative information to reporting agencies. Credit card dispute rights and claims for unauthorized charges are set out in *Truth in Lending*. Consumer rights concerning repossessions of motor vehicles, manufactured homes and other personal property are set out in NCLC's *Repossessions*,[10] while issues of mortgage servicing and home foreclosures are detailed in NCLC's *Foreclosures*.[11] The right to discharge secured and unsecured debts in bankruptcy is set out in NCLC's *Consumer Bankruptcy Law and Practice*.[12]

### *1.1.2 This Treatise Supersedes* Cost of Credit

*Consumer Credit Regulation* is a successor to NCLC's *The Cost of Credit*.[13] Since that treatise was first written, there have been profound changes in the nature of consumer credit, in the federal and state regulation of that credit, and in federal preemption of state credit law. Non-traditional mortgage loans, origination abuses, and lax mortgage lending underwriting have helped create a major national crisis, resulting in significant federal statutory and regulatory changes to the way mortgage lending is regulated. This has all pointed to the need for a separate treatise on mortgage lending.

At the same time, there have been dramatic shifts in the nature of non-mortgage credit offered to consumer, and to the regulation of that credit. Small finance company loans and other older forms of small loans have been replaced by payday loans, auto title loans, and refund anticipation loans. Retail

5 (7th ed. 2010 and Supp.).
6 (5th ed. 2010 and Supp.).
7 (7th ed. 2011 and Supp.).
8 (2d ed. 2011 and Supp.).
9 (7th ed. 2010 and Supp.).
10 (7th ed. 2010 and Supp.).
11 (4th ed. 2012).
12 (9th ed. 2009 and Supp.).
13 (4th ed. 2009 and 2011 Supp.).

installment sales of furniture and electronics have been outpaced by rent-to-own transactions. Credit cards are now the dominant form of consumer credit (other than home mortgages and student loans). The Credit CARD Act now addresses many substantive terms of credit cards and new forms of state legislation have been enacted to either legitimize some of the new forms of credit or to seek to regulate it where traditional general usury limits no longer apply.

In response to these trends, NCLC has now replaced *The Cost of Credit* with two new treatises: *Mortgage Lending* and *Consumer Credit Regulation.* Between these two volumes, we have attempted to retain all material from *The Cost of Credit* still relevant and useful today, while adding much that is new. The two volumes now organize the existing and new information in a more accessible and useable format, that is also much more reflective of the issues presented by today's consumer credit transactions. Current subscribers to *The Cost of Credit* are being sent both *Mortgage Lending* and *Consumer Credit Regulation* as a revision to the 2009 edition of *The Cost of Credit.*

## 1.1.3 Treatise's Organization and Appendices

*Consumer Credit Regulation*'s chapters are divided into two parts. Part I (Chapters 1–7) includes topics of general application to the regulation of consumer credit. Chapter 1 provides background information, including how to use this treatise, the history of consumer credit regulation, why regulate consumer credit, and general information about different types of creditors and credit.

Chapter 2 surveys federal and state laws that limit the terms of consumer credit. Chapter 3 analyzes federal preemption of state law, federal and state standards as to which state's law applies to a credit transaction, which credit statute in a state applies, and whether an amendment to a credit statute should be applied retroactively.

Chapter 4 covers general concepts as to interest, points, fees and delinquency charges, including what is interest, hidden interest, third-party charges, document preparation fees, and late fees. Chapter 5 develops credit math concepts, particularly calculation of interest and rebates.

Chapter 6 analyzes credit insurance and non-insurance products that serve essentially the same purposes as credit insurance. Chapter 7 deals with litigation about substantive credit restrictions, including construction of state usury statutes, right to a jury trial, arbitration requirements, elements of a prima facie usury case, and usury claims in deregulated states. The chapter also covers creditor defenses, consumer remedies, and jurisdiction.

Each of the chapters in Part II (Chapters 8–14) focuses on a particular form of non-mortgage lending found in the marketplace today. Chapter 8 covers credit cards, Chapter 9 payday lending, and Chapter 10 retail installment sales, automobile finance, and manufactured home credit-sales. Chapter 11 addresses auto title loans, and Chapter 12 considers rent-to-own transactions. Chapter 13 examines upfront payments in return for assignment or sale of such future income streams as military pensions, structured litigation settlements, and potential litigation recoveries. Chapter 14 covers refund anticipation loans and other tax refund lending schemes.

Appendix A sets out federal statutes and regulations that substantively limit consumer credit. Appendix B provides citations for the state credit statutes found in each of the fifty states, while Appendix C is a state-by-state analysis of retail installment sales acts.

Appendix D provides federal statutes, regulations, and agency interpretations concerning depository institutions' right to export their home state interest rates. Appendix E sets out federal statutes, regulations, and agency interpretations concerning preemption of the application of state law to national banks and federal savings associations. Appendix F provides materials concerning federal preemption of state interest rate caps on manufactured home loans. Appendix G reprints federal material concerning regulation of federal credit union loans.

Appendix H details how to use the companion website. These are followed by the index to this treatise.

## 1.1.4 Companion Website and Web-Based Finding Aids

Subscribers to this book receive free access to the book's companion website as long as they keep the book current with its annual update. Information on registering for the website is found at page ix, *supra*. How to best use the website is described at Appendix H, *infra*.

The website includes two different software programs to calculate APRs and create amortization tables. One is simpler to use, but is appropriate only for regular transactions or those with minimal irregular terms. The other program works for any irregularity.

The website also includes all the material in the appendices plus a number of sample complaints, discovery requests, affidavits, expert witness testimony, briefs, settlements, jury instructions, and additional pleadings. Also included is the full text of scores of federal banking agency interpretations and federal statutes and regulations.

All the material can be searched, downloaded, printed, and cut and pasted into a Microsoft Word document. Most pleadings are also available in Microsoft Word format. Over 2000 additional pleadings are available at NCLC's companion website for *Consumer Law Pleadings With Index Guide.*

This book's website does *not* include the book chapters. The book chapters can be searched electronically using keywords or combinations of keywords at www.nclc.org/keyword. All pages that match those search terms will be listed, showing the search terms in context. In addition, to locate a particular topic, reference can be made to this volume's detailed table of contents or its index.

### 1.1.5 How to Use This Treatise

The authors recommend a three-step approach to using this treatise. First identify and review the Part II chapter that matches the type of credit transaction at issue. Based upon a review of that chapter, step 2 would be to identify and read related discussions in other NCLC treatises that are cross-referenced in that chapter. Step 3 is to refer then to general issues discussed in *Consumer Credit Regulation's* Part I that have specific relevance to the particular case at hand.

More particularly, steps 1 and 2 for the following types of credit would include:

- *Credit cards*: Go to Chapter 8, *infra*. Also review NCLC's *Truth in Lending* for more detail as to the Truth in Lending Act's substantive requirements, remedies, scope, and defenses as they relate to credit cards. Refer only to that treatise for issues as to credit card disclosures, unauthorized use, credit billing, and disputed credit card charges. For debit and stored value card issues, refer only to NCLC's *Consumer Banking and Payments Law.*
- *Payday Loans:* Go to Chapter 9, *infra*. For more information on the relationship of payday loans to the law of check payments, electronic transfers, and related banking issues, see NCLC's *Consumer Banking and Payments Law.*
- *Auto Loans:* Go to Chapter 10, *infra*. For more information on Truth in Lending Act claims, see NCLC's *Truth in Lending.* For more on the FTC Holder Notice, see NCLC's *Unfair and Deceptive Acts and Practices.* For auto dealer deceptive practices, see NCLC's *Unfair and Deceptive Acts and Practices* and also *Automobile Fraud.* For warranty issues, see NCLC's *Consumer Warranty Law.* For repossession issues, see NCLC's *Repossessions.*
- *Manufactured Home Loans*: Go to Chapter 10, *infra*. For more information on Truth in Lending Act claims, see NCLC's *Truth in Lending.* For more on the FTC Holder Notice, see NCLC's *Unfair and Deceptive Acts and Practices.* For warranty issues, see NCLC's *Consumer Warranty Law.* For seizure of the home, see both NCLC's *Repossessions* and *Foreclosures.*
- *Other Retail Installment Sales:* Go to Chapter 10, *infra*. For more information on Truth in Lending Act claims, see NCLC's *Truth in Lending.* For more on the FTC Holder Notice, see NCLC's *Unfair and Deceptive Acts and Practices.*
- *Auto Title Loans*: Go to Chapter 11, *infra*. For more on the lender's ability to enforce its security interest in the title, see NCLC's *Repossessions.*
- *Rent-to-Own Transactions:* Go to Chapter 12, *infra*. For disclosure issues, see NCLC's *Truth in Lending.* For a discussion of RTO termination issues, see NCLC's *Repossessions.*
- *Cash Payments for Assignment of Military Pensions, Income from Structured Settlements, or Potential Litigation Recoveries:* Go to Chapter 13, *infra*.
- *Refund Anticipation Loans and Other Tax Refund Lending Schemes*: Go to Chapter 14, *infra.*
- *Mortgage Lending*: go instead to NCLC's *Mortgage Lending.* For foreclosure and servicing issues, see NCLC's *Foreclosures.*
- *Student Loans:* go instead to NCLC's *Student Loan Law.*

Step 3 will depend on the facts of a case. If a case rests on a federal claim, that claim may be discussed in more detail at Chapter 2, *infra*. If the case instead involves a state claim, reference should also be made to Chapter 3, *infra*, which discusses whether federal law preempts that state claim. Chapter 2 also details which state's law applies, which state law within a state applies, and whether an amended statute should be applied retroactively.

Reference should be made to Chapter 4, *infra*, if a case involves issues as to what is considered interest, how points are to be treated, and whether third-party charges or late fees are legitimate. Chapter 5 should be consulted where a case involves the calculation of interest, rebates of unearned interest, or other charges. Reference should be made to Chapter 6 if credit insurance or a credit card "debt protection" product is involved. Finally, Chapter 7 should be consulted in shaping a litigation concerning a violation of a consumer credit regulation requirement.

### 1.1.6 Other Resources

Few treatises on substantive limits to the interest rate and terms of consumer credit exist, which is one of the reasons that this treatise has been written. Apart from this treatise, the most comprehensive treatments of usury issues are probably contained in the *Corpus Juris Secundum* (C.J.S.)[14] and *American Jurisprudence, Second Series* (Am. Jur. 2d)[15] articles on interest and usury.

A number of topics in this treatise are examined in more detail in other NCLC treatises. Of particular note is NCLC's *Truth in Lending*, which goes into greater depth regarding the Truth in Lending Act's regulation of credit cards, including scope, remedies, creditor defenses, disclosure requirements, and the substantive requirements themselves. NCLC's *Consumer Arbitration Agreements* is devoted to challenges to the enforceability of arbitration clauses, while this treatise just provides an overview of that topic in one section in the litigation chapter. State deceptive practices law (UDAP) challenges to credit abuses are considered in this treatise, but far more detail on UDAP statutes' scope, remedies, defenses, and prohibitions is found in NCLC's *Unfair and Deceptive Acts and Practices.*

A good source for summaries of state credit laws is the loose-leaf service *Consumer Credit Guide* published by Commerce Clearinghouse, Inc. More concise summaries can be

14 47 C.J.S. *Interest & Usury; Consumer Credit* (2005).

15 17 Am. Jur. 2d *Consumer & Borrower Protection* (2004); 44B Am. Jur. 2d *Interest & Usury* (2007).

found in *The Cost of Personal Borrowing in the United States* (Financial Publishing Co./Carleton, Inc.). The latter source contains numerous rate tables tailored to individual state usury and credit insurance statutes and can be very helpful with rate calculation issues, but unfortunately it lacks statutory citations. Appendix A, *infra*, provides many of those statutory citations, as does the *Consumer Credit Guide*.

### 1.1.7 Why This Treatise

There is a widespread belief that regulation of consumer credit is minimal—that federal law offers few protections, that state limits have been deregulated, and that those state limits that do exist can be avoided through federal preemption, rate exportation, or other means. The true picture today is far more complex. Federal restrictions are now in place concerning credit cards; federal protections concerning payday; auto title and refund anticipation loans apply to military servicemembers and their dependents; and federal law regulates the rebate of unearned interest. Federal rate ceilings apply to federal credit union loans. Federal banking agencies have been active in limiting tax refund anticipation loans.

The extent of state regulation of consumer credit today also is extremely varied, differing not only by state but by type of consumer credit. For example, automobile installment sales in a state may have meaningful interest rate ceilings while direct loans in the same state may not. For loans originated by banks and savings associations, federal law allows these entities to utilize interest rates allowed for the most favored lender in their home state, instead of the applicable law where the loan is made. But the bank must still comply with all material restrictions of that particular state law, and non-banks cannot take advantage of this ability to export rates. The ability to export rates does not apply to the non-interest aspects of state credit regulation, and federal preemption of those non-interest aspects is now limited by the Dodd-Frank Consumer Protection and Wall Street Reform Act.

This treatise seeks to sort out the interplay of federal preemption and federal and state restrictions on consumer credit. Every attempt is made to ensure the discussion is relevant to a particular form of credit and to a particular state where the loan is made or the creditor resides. This is a challenging undertaking because of the complexities and uncertainties of federal preemption and the extremely varied forms of state credit regulation, not only among the states but even within a state. We know of no other treatise that seeks to meet this challenge, which is reason enough to produce this publication intended to help attorneys sort through the intricacies of consumer credit regulation.

## 1.2 Historical Development of Usury Laws

### 1.2.1 Early Attitudes Toward Interest

The lending of money or commodities such as grain in return for interest has been documented as early as 3000 B.C.[16] From its inception, the practice seems to have caused controversy in many societies. In part, the charging of interest was condemned on moral and religious grounds; it was considered ungodly and uncharitable for one man to profit from the need of another. In hard times, a borrower could lose all his property and be sold into slavery to pay his debts. The evils caused by usury were very real, and money lending was at times banned outright. For example, under the laws of the Old Testament, one Jew was forbidden to lend at interest to another.[17]

16 The records are Sumerian. *See* Homer, A History of Interest Rates 25 (1963). Those interested in more detail about the history of usury regulation should consult the following sources: Bodfish, History of Building and Loan Associations in the U.S. (1931); Cobb, Federal Regulation of Depository Institutions: Enforcement Powers and Procedures (1984); The Consumer Finance Industry: Its Costs and Regulation (Chapman & Shea, Eds., 1967); 1 Credit Union Law Service Ch. 1 (Matthew Bender 1987); Curran, Trends in Consumer Credit Legislation (1966); Homer, A History of Interest Rates (1963); Hubachek, Annotations on Small Loan Laws (1938); Kawaja, Regulation of the Consumer Finance Industry: A Case Study of Rate Ceilings and Loan Size Limits in New York State (1971); Bruce M. McCall, Unprofitable Lending: Modern Credit Regulation and the Lost Theory of Usury, 30 Cardozo Law Rev. 549 (2008); J.B.C. Murray, History of Usury (1866); Saulnier, Industrial Banking Companies and Their Banking Practices (1940); Sherman, Modern Story of Mutual Savings Banks (1934); Welfling, Mutual Savings Banks (1968); *Combating the Shark*, 8 Law & Contemp. Prob. 1-205 (Winter 1941) (series of articles on usury, small loan laws, and loan sharking); Curran, *Legislative Controls As a Response to Consumer-Credit Problems*, 8 B.C. Ind. & Com. L. Rev. 409 (1966–1967); Lynn Drysdale & Kathleen Keest, *The Two-Tiered Consumer Financial Services Marketplace: The Fringe Banking System and Its Challenge to Current Thinking About the Socio-Economic Role of Usury Laws in Today's Society*, 51 S.C. L. Rev. 589 (2000); David J. Gerber, *Prometheus Born: The High Middle Ages and the Relationship Between Law and Economic Conduct*, 38 St. Louis L. J. 673 (1994); Edward L. Glaeser & Jose Scheinkman, *Neither a Borrower Nor a Lender Be: An Economic Analysis of Interest Restrictions and Usury Laws*, 41 J. Law & Econ. 1 (1998); Note, *Interest Rates and the Law: A History of Usury*, 1981 Ariz. St. L.J. 61; Jordan & Warren, *A Proposed Uniform Code for Consumer Credit*, 8 B.C. Ind & Com. L. Rev. 441 (1966–1967); Littlefield, *Parties and Transactions Covered By Consumer-Credit Legislation*, 8 B.C. Ind. & Com. L. Rev. 463 (1966–1967); Christopher L. Peterson, *Truth, Understanding, and High-Cost Consumer Credit: The Historical Context of the Truth in Lending Act*, 55 Fla. L. Rev. 807 (2003); Redfield, *Savings Banks and Savings and Loan Associations: The Past and the Future*, 16 Bus. Law 170 (1960); Roster, *Modern Role of Thrifts*, 18 Loyola L.A. L. Rev. 1099 (1985); Vincent D. Rougeau, *Rediscovering Usury: An Argument for Legal Controls on Credit Card Interest Rates*, 67 U. Colo. L. Rev. 1 (1996); John D. Skees, *The Resurrection of Historic Usury Principles for Consumption Loans in a Federal Banking System*, 55 Cath. U. L. Rev. 1131, 1140–1148 (2006); James J. White, *The Usury Trompe l'Oeil*, 51 S.C. L. Rev. 445 (Spring 2000).

17 *Exodus* 22:25; *Leviticus* 25:35–25:37; *Deuteronomy* 23:19–23:20.

The complete abolition of money lending at interest is not, however, a realistic solution to the problems that lending can cause or exacerbate. If one person has money or some commodity that another needs, the self-interest of the lender and the desire of the would-be borrower align powerfully. Loan contracts are, after all, consensual agreements, even if not always even-handed ones. Nor do loans at interest invariably spell doom for the borrower. They can and do benefit both parties in most cases, especially in commercial transactions. Not surprisingly, early commercial societies were tolerant of money lending, although they frequently limited the permissible interest rates. Conversely, societies that nominally prohibited loans at interest created exceptions, particularly for commercial lending.[18] To give one example, while the Old Testament condemned usurers and forbade one Jew from collecting interest from another, it allowed the collection of interest from foreigners.[19]

Medieval Europe, under the powerful influence of the Catholic church, followed a similar path.[20] The church repeatedly condemned the assessment of "usury" (i.e., interest),[21] but Jews were permitted to operate pawnshops. As trade gradually increased through the centuries, Christian merchants developed various schemes to avoid the prohibitions, such as assignments of rents, "investments," and the use of bills of exchange. In England, it was not until 1545 that Parliament legalized charging interest in the modern sense.[22] This statute was repealed during the reign of Queen Mary, only to be reenacted in 1570 under Queen Elizabeth. Although interest was legalized, the rate remained capped at or below ten percent.

In 1713, the Statute of Anne was enacted, voiding all contracts for interest at more than five percent.[23] The Statute of Anne applied to both direct loans and to forbearances, or creditors' agreements to postpone collection of a preexisting debt in exchange for interest payments. The Statute of Anne has remained the basic template for Anglo-American usury laws, although the rate ceiling chosen varies.

In 1787, the English philosopher Jeremy Bentham published an influential essay, *Letters in Defense of Usury*, in which he argued that usury ceilings limited the credit available to those who could not offer security, violated the principle of freedom of contract, and therefore should be abolished. According to Bentham's view, interest rates should be governed by free market rules of supply and demand. This utilitarian reframing of the debate over usury contributed to the repeal of English usury statutes in 1854 and continues to influence the debate over credit regulation.

### 1.2.2 General Usury Statutes in the United States

English usury statutes were adopted by the American colonies prior to independence.[24] Variations on these statutes remain in effect to this day in many states, and are commonly referred to as "general" usury laws because they purport to set a ceiling for all loans of money in a jurisdiction, not just for particular types of lenders or credit transactions. With very few exceptions, general usury laws were the only statutes regulating credit costs in the United States prior to the twentieth century.

The importation of the English statutes was accompanied by the importation of the preexisting English case law. The understanding of credit regulation developed in the English case law was adopted by American courts and represents an important source of authority in the interpretation of modern usury statutes. It is, at least in effect, a common law of usury. In the absence of express statutory treatment, this case law governs issues such as the elements of proof of a usury case and the definition of interest.

Many of the inconsistencies and irrationalities that exist in current credit laws can be traced to English case law and, through it, to even earlier origins in common law or canon law.

---

*See* Commonwealth v. Donoghue, 63 S.W.2d 3 (Ky. Ct. App. 1933) (quoting a fourth century Christian theologian's views of usury and referring to Old Testament prohibitions).

18 *See* John D. Skees, *The Resurrection of Historic Usury Principles for Consumption Loans in a Federal Banking System*, 55 Cath. U. L. Rev. 1131, 1142–1148 (2006) (arguing that, under historic Christian teachings governing usury, there was a distinction between commercial lending, where usury was permitted, and consumer lending to the poor, where usury was forbidden).

19 *See Deuteronomy* 23:19–23:20. *Cf.* Walid S. Hegazy, *Contemporary Islamic Finance: From Socioeconomic Idealism to Pure Legalism*, 7 Chi. J. Int'l L. 581 (2007) (discussing Islamic law prohibitions on usury and different responses to those prohibitions); Theodore Karasik, Frederic Wehrey & Steven Strom, *Islamic Finance in a Global Context: Opportunities and Challenges*, 7 Chi. J. Int'l L. 379 (2007).

20 *See* Brian McCall, *Unprofitable Lending: Modern Credit Regulation and the Lost Theory of Usury*, 30 Cardozo L. Rev. 549 (2008) (discussing in detail the thinking of the Catholic church during the middle ages on usury).

21 In medieval terms the word "usury," derived from the Latin "usera," equated with what we would call "interest" today. The prohibition of usury was essentially a prohibition of charging for the use of money. However, common law distinguished reimbursement for a loss associated with a loan from charges for the use of money and permitted the former while forbidding the latter. This legal compensation for loss was known as "interesse" from the Latin "intereo" meaning "to be lost." Thus legal charges associated with a loan appear to have evolved to the modern notion of "interest," while illegal charges eventually came to be called "usury." *See* Homer, A History of Interest Rates 73–74 (1963).

For a discussion of Mormon and Christian scriptural views of usury, see Steven M. Graves & Christopher L. Peterson, *Usury Law and the Christian Right: Faith-Based Political Power and the Geography of American Payday Loan Regulation*, 57 Cath. U. L. Rev. 637 (Spring 2008).

22 37 Hen. 8, C. 9 (1545). The statute was entitled "An Act Against Usury," doublespeak apparently having preceded George Orwell by several centuries. *See also* Commonwealth v. Donoghue, 63 S.W.2d 3 (Ky. Ct. App. 1933) (discussing the development of English usury law).

23 J. B. C. Murray, History of Usury 50–51 (1866).

24 *See generally* Christopher L. Peterson, *Usury Law, Payday Loans, and Statutory Sleight of Hand: Salience Distortion of American Credit Pricing Limits*, 92 Minn. L. Rev. 1110 (Apr. 2008) (discussing the adoption of the Statute of Anne by the colonies and the usury statutes in existence at independence).

For example, the English courts ruled that a sale of goods on credit did not constitute a loan or forbearance and was thus exempt from the interest limitations of usury statutes.[25] This rule, known as the time-price doctrine, was adopted by American courts[26] and, despite much criticism, is still recognized in some states today. The time-price doctrine is the source of the separate regulation of loans and credit sales in virtually all states.

Another example of the ancient roots of modern usury law principles is the distinction between interest on a loan and "penalties," such as late fees, which can be assessed on overdue accounts without usury limitations. While many modern consumer statutes separately regulate late fees, most states codified the general distinction between interest and fees. This distinction between interest and fees appears to have come to American law, through English case law, from a canon law rule that one could not exact gain from a loan (i.e., charge any interest), but that one could be compensated for loss incurred through a loan, including the loss suffered when the loan was not promptly repaid.[27] This convenient doctrine appears to have been used in the Middle Ages to evade the church's prohibition against interest,[28] just as it is used today to evade laws which limit the amount of interest that a lender may charge.[29]

Beginning with the small loan laws adopted in the early years of the twentieth century, states created numerous "special" usury laws to govern particular types of lenders. These special usury laws, discussed in the next subsections, have displaced general usury laws for large parts of the consumer credit market. General usury laws remain relevant, however, for creditors—primarily fringe creditors—that do not fit under one of the special usury laws or that choose not to comply with the licensing requirements and substantive restrictions of those laws.

### 1.2.3 The Development of "Special" Usury Laws

Consumer credit as we know it today did not exist, for practical purposes, prior to the twentieth century.[30] Pawn broking, of course, had been around for millennia, and personal loans secured by real estate were not unknown. Yet the vast majority of credit transactions were commercial. The total amount of credit available in the nineteenth century United States was limited, and most of it was directed towards industrial development where the profits available were higher and the risks lower than for individual loans. Furthermore, demand for individual credit was lower than it is today. Not only was individual borrowing socially frowned upon, but the economy was not oriented toward the production of consumer durable goods. In the days before automobiles, televisions, refrigerators, and other modern appliances, there was less for an individual to buy on credit.

This is not to say that individual Americans had no need to borrow for personal expenses prior to the twentieth century, or that there was no demand for goods, but rather that the official credit system simply did not extend to the average wage-earner. Given interest ceilings under general usury statutes in the neighborhood of six percent, and the proportionately higher administrative expense in small personal loans than in large commercial loans, banks could make more money lending to businesses. Thus, individuals in need of personal loans had to resort to loan sharks or "salary lenders." The typical arrangement seems to have been a loan for $5 on a Monday, repayable on Friday (payday) for $6—an annual interest rate of 1040%.[31]

The problem of loan sharking was pervasive in the nineteenth century,[32] leading to increased recognition of both the financial plight of wage earners and their need for a legitimate source of credit. Early attempts to reform were small-scale, informal and uncoordinated, but seemed to follow one of three basic strategies. First, cooperative societies were formed, generally following models pioneered in Europe, in which individuals pooled their money for their mutual benefit. The earliest of these societies took the form of mutual savings banks, organized under existing banking laws, but catering to and owned by small depositors. As the name implies, however, mutual savings banks were primarily concerned with encouraging thrift rather than providing credit. Building and loan associations, on the other hand, were cooperative organizations established primarily to provide mortgage money to members. Both of these institutions, precursors of modern savings banks and savings and loan associations respectively, had become widespread by the turn of the century.[33] A later model of the cooperative society, which did not emerge in the United States until the first decade of the twentieth century, was the credit

25 *See* Beete v. Bidgood, 7 B. & C. 453, 108 Eng. Rep. 792 (K.B. 1827).

26 *See* Hogg v. Ruffner, 66 U.S. (1 Black) 115 (1861).

27 The common law rule in turn seems to derive from Roman law. *See* Homer, A History of Interest Rates 73–74 (1963).

28 J.B.C. Murray, History of Usury (1866).

29 *See* § 5.7, *infra* (discussing the treatment of late fees under modern usury law).

30 *See generally* Curran, *Legislative Controls As a Response to Consumer Credit Problems*, 8 B.C. Ind. & Com. L. Rev. 409 (1966–1967); Note, *Interest Rates and the Law: A History of Usury*, 1981 Ariz. St. L.J. 61.

31 *See* Commonwealth v. Donoghue, 63 S.W.2d 3 (Ky. Ct. App. 1933) (discussing the 1930s versions of salary lenders); Lynn Drysdale & Kathleen Keest, *The Two-Tiered Consumer Financial Services Marketplace: The Fringe Banking System and Its Challenge to Current Thinking About the Socio-Economic Role of Usury Laws in Today's Society*, 51 S.C. L. Rev. 589 (2000) (fuller discussion of the historical antecedents of today's fringe lenders); § 2.5, *infra* (discussing modern incarnations of salary lenders).

32 *See generally Combating the Loan Shark*, 8 Law & Contemp. Prob. 1-205 (Winter 1941) (issue devoted to articles on usury, small loan laws, and loan sharking).

33 *See generally* Bodfish, History of Building and Loan Associations in the U.S. (1931); Cobb, Federal Regulation of Depository Institutions: Enforcement Powers and Procedures (1984); Sherman, Modern Story of Mutual Savings Banks (1934); Welfling, Mutual Savings Banks (1968); Redfield, *Savings Banks and Savings and Loan Associations: The Past and the Future*, 16 Bus. Law 170 (1960).

union. Like its predecessors, credit unions emphasized the pooling of resources, but further required the existence of some common bond among the members, typically a common employer.[34] Credit unions took off during the 1920s, due largely to the lobbying efforts of a Massachusetts businessman, who pushed for the introduction of enabling statutes at the state and federal level.[35]

A second response to the loan shark problem was more strictly philanthropic.[36] Organizations supported by donated funds made small loans at no charge except administrative expenses. Some employers apparently followed the same route. The money available through such organizations does not appear to have been sufficient enough to make much of a dent in the demand for small loans.

The third and latest strategy aimed at combating loan sharking was to attract credit, previously extended only to businesses, to the consumer credit market by making consumer lending a profitable prospect. Primarily, this was done by creating exceptions to the general usury law for small, unsecured loans with the aim of making these loans attractive to legitimate, mainstream creditors. The small loan and industrial bank laws, as well as early credit union laws, all first adopted in the early twentieth century, aimed to increase the amount of consumer credit available by increasing the legal yield on consumer credit.

The small loan laws, pioneered by the Russell Sage Foundation[37] and the research that it supported, took a direct approach to attracting capital to the consumer market. The Uniform Small Loan Law, the first draft of which was issued in 1916, created a licensed class of small loan lenders authorized to charge rates significantly in excess of the general usury ceilings. In return, these lenders accepted regulation, the risk involved in personal lending, and the higher administrative expense of small loans. For example, the fourth draft of the uniform law[38] allowed the charging of 3.5% *monthly* on loans of $300 or less. This rate was much higher than the general usury ceiling, but was nevertheless vastly lower than the rates charged by loan sharks.[39]

Industrial banks, first organized under regular state banking laws early in the twentieth century, took a less direct approach to increasing the yields on consumer credit.[40] These institutions accepted individual deposits and made loans secured by those deposits. Arthur Morris devised a plan which treated loans as repayable in a single lump sum at the end of the agreed term and computed interest accordingly. However the Morris Plan required the borrower to make regular "deposits" in the bank which were calculated to equal the total amount of principal and interest due at the end of the term. Essentially, the Morris Plan allowed industrial banks to increase yields by charging interest on sums the borrower had already repaid (i.e., by ignoring the declining principal balance on the loan). Although this device was an evasion of existing general usury laws, many states adopted statutory exceptions to general usury laws to validate the practice, and industrial banks came to serve a market of consumers seeking loans in excess of the $300 limits set for small loan licensees.

Carving out statutory exceptions to the general usury laws proved an effective means of increasing consumer credit. Not surprisingly, it also proved to be difficult to limit. Although credit laws developed differently in each state, statutory usury exceptions were soon made, not only for small loan lenders, but also for industrial banks, as discussed above, credit unions, mortgage lenders such as savings banks and building and loan associations, and eventually, banks making "installment loans" to finance consumer purchases.[41]

### 1.2.4 The Treatment of Sales

Under English common law, usury restrictions did not apply to the price that a merchant could charge for goods. A seller could charge one price for the goods if the buyer paid immediately, and another, higher price if the buyer chose to pay over some agreed time. The difference between the "time price" and the "cash price" was not counted against the usury ceiling. This so-called "time-price doctrine" was adopted by American courts interpreting American general usury laws. Consequently, the charges associated with the credit sale of goods were generally not considered interest and were unregulated until specific statutory controls were adopted in the middle of the twentieth century.[42]

This treatise treats retail installment sales acts (RISAs) and motor vehicle retail installment sales acts (MVRISAs) as a subclass of special usury laws, since a credit sale is merely a secured loan in different legal clothing. The historical distinctions between loans and credit sales still occasionally crop up in modern consumer credit cases, however, and practitioners should remain alert for those distinctions.[43]

---

34 *See* 1 Credit Union Law Service Ch. 1 (Matthew Bender 1987) (discussing the evolution of credit unions); § 3.1.2.3, *infra* (discussing credit unions).

35 Credit Union Nat'l Ass'n, Cooperative Activity in America, *available at* www.creditunion.coop/history/wakeup.html.

36 *See* Kawaja, Regulation of the Consumer Finance Industry: A Case Study of Rate Ceilings and Loan Size Limits in New York State 23 (1971).

37 *See generally* Curran, Trends in Consumer Credit Legislation (1966); Hubachek, *The Development of Regulatory Small Loan Laws*, 8 Law & Contemp. Prob. 108 (1941).

38 *Reprinted in* Hubachek, Annotations on Small Loan Laws (1938).

39 *Cf.* Christopher L. Peterson, *Usury Law, Payday Loans, and Statutory Sleight of Hand: Salience Distortion of American Credit Pricing Limits*, 92 Minn. L. Rev. 1110 (Apr. 2008) (arguing that the enactment of the small loan laws eroded the consensus for a uniform and relatively low usury cap).

40 *See generally* Curran, Trends in Consumer Credit Legislation 52 (1966); Saulnier, Industrial Banking Companies and Their Banking Practices (1940).

41 *See* Curran, Trends in Consumer Credit Legislation 65 (1966) (discussing the varying scope of installment loan laws).

42 *See* § 7.5.2, *infra* (discussing the definition of interest).

43 *See* §§ 2.3, 3.9.4, 7.5.2, 10.6, *infra*.

## 1.2.5 Deregulation of Usury Law

The late 1970s and early 1980s were watershed years for usury law. As a result of anti-inflation federal monetary policy, short-term commercial market interest rates rose above twenty percent, far above general usury ceilings and many special usury law ceilings. Because lenders themselves borrow the money they lend, lenders' profits were squeezed as their interest expenses rose. There was a fear that creditors would be understandably reluctant to lend money at rates below their cost of funds and that mortgage loans and other kinds of consumer credit would dry up as creditors cut back on their volume of lending. Legislators and the credit industry agreed that something had to be done about usury laws, and action was taken at both the federal and state levels.

In 1980, in response to the tension between usury ceilings and rising market interest rates, the federal government preempted many, but not all, state usury limitations.[44] Congress allowed all federally insured depository lenders and, temporarily, all creditors issuing business or agricultural credit in excess of $1,000, to operate under a variable interest ceiling, which had previously been reserved for national banks.[45] Congress also preempted all interest ceilings for most major lenders for credit secured by first mortgages on borrower's homes, including manufactured homes.[46] Congress did not replace the state usury caps it preempted with a federal usury cap; the federal framework presumed that no credit regulation was good credit regulation. States could "opt out" of any of these preemptions by legislative proclamation. This statutory structure shifted the legislative burden to the proponents of usury laws; if a state failed to adopt new usury provisions or to reenact its old ones, most usury restrictions in the state were, by default, repealed.

Some federal preemption is conditioned on the creditor's compliance with federal regulations. Thus, preempted state statutes that remain on the books may still have some teeth when the creditor fails to comply with federal regulations.[47] These preempted state statutes may also have teeth against small, individual, hard-money lenders.[48]

Because of the federal usury preemptions, state legislatures were forced to consider what role, if any, usury statutes should play in a modern economy. This was not exactly a new issue,[49] yet there was no consensus on the correct balance between consumer protection and credit availability or if, indeed, there was a necessary tradeoff between those two desirable ends.[50] Most states had in place a fairly complex set of general and special usury statutes, some of which, such as the small loan acts and RISAs, were relatively uncontroversial, and some of which, such as fixed-rate general usury statutes, were clearly unworkable in the face of sizeable fluctuations in market interest rates.

Most states responded by raising their interest ceilings to a point not constricting on traditional lenders. Other states modified their general usury laws so that the ceilings would fluctuate with some published market interest rate. For example, several states set their ceilings to five or six percentage points above the federal discount rate. Some states repealed general usury ceilings completely, allowing parties who were not regulated by special usury statutes to contract for the payment of any agreed rate.[51]

Generally, states retained their special usury statutes, only raising or repealing the interest rate ceilings.[52] In retaining the special usury statutes, the states tacitly recognized the need for some regulation of the credit market.

Federal preemption of state consumer regulation was not limited to interest rate caps. Beginning in the 1980s,[53] federal banking regulators aggressively preempted state restrictions on the origination and terms of consumer credit for lenders they regulated, without adopting any meaningful regulatory framework in its place.[54] Commentators warned that the scope of

44 *See* Ch. 3, *infra* (detailed discussion of federal usury preemption). *See also* Patricia A. McCoy & Elizabeth Renuart, *The Legal Infrastructure of Subprime and Nontraditional Home Mortgages, in* Borrowing to Live: Consumer and Mortgage Credit Revisited 110, 112 (Nicolas P. Retsinas & Eric S. Belsky ed. 2008); Cathy Lesser Mansfield, *The Road to Subprime "HEL" Was Paved with Good Congressional Intentions: Usury Deregulation and the Subprime Home Equity Market*, 51 S.C. L. Rev. 473 (2000); James J. White, *The Usury Trompe l'Oeil*, 51 S.C. L. Rev. 445 (Spring 2000); Ch. 3, *infra*.

45 The temporary business and agricultural preemption expired Apr. 1, 1983.

46 12 U.S.C. § 1735f-7a. *See* § 3.7.2, *infra*.

47 *See* § 3.7.2, *infra*.

48 *See, e.g.*, Abir v. Malky, Inc., 873 N.Y.S.2d 350 (N.Y. App. Div. 2009) (finding foreclosure rescue loan made at interest in excess of 25% usurious).

49 *Cf. In re* Coxson, 43 F.3d 189 (5th Cir. 1995) (noting that Texas had abolished usury laws during Reconstruction, but "credit abuses arose in the absence of usury laws," and they were reintroduced). *See generally* § 1.2.1, *supra* (summarizing the evolution of usury regulation in England).

50 *See generally* Christopher L. Peterson, *Usury Law, Payday Loans, and Statutory Sleight of Hand: Salience Distortion of American Credit Pricing Limits*, 92 Minn. L. Rev. 1110 (Apr. 2008) (describing the "decompression" of usury regulation in the states and the lack of consensus or uniformity on how to regulate the cost of credit).

51 *See* § 7.6, *infra* (discussing the interpretation of "agreed rate" statutes); Christopher L. Peterson, *Usury Law, Payday Loans, and Statutory Sleight of Hand: Salience Distortion of American Credit Pricing Limits*, 92 Minn. L. Rev. 1110 (Apr. 2008) (listing seven states without any interest rate cap); Leah A. Plunkett & Ana Lucia Hurtado, *Small Dollar Loans, Big Problems: How States Protect Consumers from Abuses and How the Federal Government Can Help*, 44 Suffolk U. L. Rev. 31 (2011).

52 *See* Appx. A, *infra*.

53 *See* Ch. 3, *infra*.

54 *See Wall Street and the Financial Crisis: The Role of Bank Regulators: Hearing Before the Subcomm. on Investigations of S. Comm. on Homeland Security and Governmental Affairs*, 111th Cong. 2d Sess. (2010) (memorandum by Sen. Carl Levin, Chair, & Sen. Tom Coburn, Ranking Minority Member) (discussing failure of Office of Thrift Supervision and Federal Deposit Insurance Corporation to exercise regulatory authority over Washington Mutual before the bank imploded); *Modernizing Bank Supervision and Regulations: Hearing Before the S. Comm. on Banking, Housing, and Urban Affairs*, 111th Cong. (Mar. 2009) (statement of Sheila C. Bair,

deregulation posed a threat to federalism and the dual banking system[55] and enabled destructive and discriminatory credit practices.[56] The reach of federal deregulation was extended by state parity laws, which treat state licensed entities comparably with federally regulated lenders.[57]

## *1.2.6 Steps Toward Reregulation to Address the Resurgence of Abusive Lending*

By the mid-1990s, the growth of abusive home equity lending prompted Congress to take a small step toward reregulation. The Home Ownership and Equity Protection Act of 1994 forbade a few particularly abusive terms and practices in a small subset of very high-cost home equity loans.[58] Irresponsible mortgage lending continued to grow, however, ultimately leading to the 2007 market collapse and the failure or near-failure of most of the nation's largest lenders, including many banks and savings associations.

In the area of non-mortgage credit, the situation facing the policy-makers who designed the Uniform Small Loan Laws at the beginning of the twentieth century had resurfaced by its end. Many of the finance companies that grew out of that effort[59] had themselves moved out of the genuinely small loan business into larger-balance, home-secured lending. A variety of alternate sources with effective rates that would make a loan shark jealous sprang up to fill the void left by conventional lenders.[60] Payday loans, which operate with remarkable similarity to the old salary lenders,[61] are now offered (legally or not) in many states. These loans, in small amounts, for terms of only a week or so at a time, may have effective interest rates of 700% to 2000%.[62] Pawnbrokers are with us still, but some have developed new variations, such as the "auto-pawn," in which the borrower "pawns the title, and keeps the car." This is essentially an auto-secured loan at pawnbrokers' rates of over 900%.[63] Rent-to-own companies provide a species of retail sales credit for household goods at effective rates which can reach triple digits.[64]

Abuses in credit card lending also grew. In 2009, Congress enacted the Credit Card Accountability Responsibility and Disclosure Act, providing some meaningful regulation of credit cards.[65]

In 2010, Congress dramatically restructured the credit marketplace by enacting the Dodd-Frank Wall Street Reform and Consumer Protection Act (hereinafter the Dodd-Frank Act).[66] The Dodd-Frank Act represents the culmination of a series of hearings that documented the dangers, instability, and need for regulation in the credit marketplace.[67] Among the major features of the Dodd-Frank Act are:

---

Chairman, Fed. Deposit Ins. Corp) (stating that federal preemption of state consumer protection laws "resulted in a 'race-to-the-bottom' mentality" and advocating for abandonment of preemption of more protective state credit regulation); Patricia A. McCoy & Elizabeth Renuart, *The Legal Infrastructure of Subprime and Nontraditional Home Mortgages, in* Borrowing to Live: Consumer and Mortgage Credit Revisited 110, 132–133 (Nicolas P. Retsinas & Eric S. Belsky ed. 2008); Christopher L. Peterson, *Preemption, Agency Cost Theory, and Predatory Lending by Banking Agents: Are Predatory Lenders Biting Off More Than They Can Chew?*, 56 Am. U. L. Rev. 515 (2007); Lloyd T. Wilson, *Sometimes Less Is More: Utility, Preemption, and Hermeneutical Criticisms of Proposed Federal Regulation of Mortgage Brokers*, 59 S.C. L. Rev. 61 (2007) (discussing the failure of existing and proposed federal regulation to grapple with broker abuses); Ctr. for Community Capital, The Preemption Effect: The Impacts of State Anti-Predatory Lending Laws on the Foreclosure Crisis (2010), *available at* www.ccc.unc.edu/documents/Preemption.Effect.RELEASE.3.23.10.pdf (finding that OCC preemption of state anti-predatory lending laws led to increased risky refinance lending by regulated lenders); Ctr. for Responsible Lending, National Bank Regulator Enabled Overdraft Abuses (Feb. 2010), *available at* www.responsiblelending.org/overdraft-loans/policy-legislation/regulators/National-Bank-Regulator-Enabled-Overdraft-Abuses.html (cataloging abusive features of overdraft loans and Office of Comptroller of the Currency's failure to address effectively those abuses); Ch. 3, *infra*.

55 *See, e.g.*, Baher Azmy, *Squaring the Predatory Lending Circle: A Case for States As Laboratories of Experimentation*, 57 Fla. L. Rev. 295 (2005); Christopher L. Peterson, *Federalism and Predatory Lending: Unmasking the Deregulatory Agenda*, 78 Temp. L. Rev. 1 (2005); Arthur E. Wilmarth, Jr., *The OCC's Preemption Rules Exceed the Agency's Authority and Present a Serious Threat to the Dual Banking System*, 23 Ann. Rev. Bank. L. 288 (2004).

56 *See, e.g.*, Cassandra Jones Havard, *Democratizing Credit: Examining the Structural Inequities of Subprime Lending*, 55 Syracuse L. Rev. 233 (2006).

57 *See* § 3.6, *infra*.

58 *See* National Consumer Law Center, Truth in Lending § 9.6 (7th ed. 2010 and Supp.).

59 *See* § 1.2.3, *supra*.

60 *See, e.g.*, Jessica Silver-Greenberg, *Payday Lenders Go Hunting: Operations Encroach on Banks During Loan Crunch; "Here, I Feel Respected,"* Wall St. J., Dec. 24, 2010 (describing how payday lenders have increased lending as banks have decreased lending).

61 *See* § 1.2.3, *supra*.

62 *See* Creola Johnson, *Payday Loans: Shrewd Business or Predatory Lending?*, 87 Minn. L. Rev. 1 (Nov. 2002) (analyzing survey data that vividly portrays the payday lending industry's abuses); Ch. 9, *infra* (discussing payday lending generally).

63 Ch. 11, *infra*.

64 Ch. 12, *infra*. *See* Creola Johnson, *Welfare Reform and Asset Accumulation: First We Need a Bed and a Car*, 2000 Wis. L. Rev. 1221 (2000) (describing the reasons welfare recipients are forced into RTO transactions to acquire basic necessities).

65 Pub. L. No. 111-24, 123 Stat. 1734 (May 22, 2009). *See* § 8.2, *infra*; National Consumer Law Center, Truth in Lending Ch. 7 (7th ed. 2010 and Supp.) (full discussion CARD Act).

66 Pub. L. No. 111-203, 124 Stat. 1376 (July 21, 2010) (hereinafter cited as Dodd-Frank).

67 *See, e.g.*, S. 566, 111th Cong. (2009) (proposing a national financial products safety commission); *Modernizing Bank Supervision and Regulations, Parts I & II: Hearing Before the S. Comm. on Banking, Housing, and Urban Affairs*, 111th Cong. (Mar. 2009); *Consumer Protections in Financial Services: Past Problems, Future Solutions: Hearing Before the S. Comm. on Banking, Housing, and Urban Affairs*, 111th Cong. (Mar. 2009); *Federal and State Enforcement of Financial Consumer and Investor Protection Laws: Hearing Before the H. Comm. on Financial Serv.*, 111th Cong. (Mar. 2009); *Staff of the Joint Economic Comm., State by State Figures: Foreclosure and Housing Wealth Losses*, 110th Cong., 2d Sess. (Apr. 2008), *available at* http://jec.senate.gov/index.cfm?FuseAction=Reports.Reports&ContentRecord_id=392cb915-9c45-fa0d-5a46-f61f6e619381&Region_id=&Issue_id=; *Staff of the Joint Economic Comm., State*

- Significant narrowing of the authority of federal banking regulators to preempt state law, creating substantially more room for states to regulate consumer credit.[68]
- Abolition of the Office of Thrift Supervision and consolidation of oversight of both national banks and federal savings and loan associations in the Office of the Comptroller of the Currency.[69]
- Addition to the Truth in Lending Act of a host of substantive restrictions on mortgage loan and servicing abuses.[70]
- Expansion of the remedies under the Truth in Lending Act.[71]
- Expansion of the enforcement authority of state attorneys general and banking regulators.[72]
- Creation of the Consumer Financial Protection Bureau (CFPB), with authority to write rules prohibiting unfair, deceptive, and abusive practices.[73]

The CFPB also has authority to ban mandatory arbitration clauses after conducting a study[74] and the authority, transferred from a variety of other agencies, to write rules under a number of key federal statutes such as the Truth in Lending Act.[75] The CFPB does not, however, have authority to impose a usury cap.[76]

## 1.3 Purpose of Consumer Credit Regulation

### 1.3.1 Unfettered Consumer Credit Market Leads to Extensive Abuse

As indicated by the history of credit regulation, discussed at § 1.2, *supra*, there is a constant tension between those favoring efforts to prevent credit abuses and those who favor the unfettered working of a free market. What is clear, though, is that an unfettered consumer credit marketplace leads to massive fraud, abuse, overcharges, and oppressive credit terms. This much is evident looking at the actual facts of the first decade of this century. Consumer credit regulation is necessary, regardless of the claimed efficiencies gained through a deregulated market.[77]

There are many reasons why creditors left to their own will take unfair advantage of consumers. Credit transactions by their very nature are complicated, beyond most consumers' ability to understand.[78] Take the typical credit card agreement that goes on for pages of fine print, whose terms are never read, and that

*by State Foreclosure Analysis*, 110th Cong., 2d Sess. (Mar. 2008), *available at* http://jec.senate.gov/index.cfm?FuseAction=Reports.Reports&ContentRecord_id=29b87995-d13a-3419-d0f6-c6338f111706&Region_id=&Issue_id=; *Staff of the Joint Economic Comm., The Subprime Lending Crisis: The Economic Impact on Wealth, Property Values and Tax Revenues, and How We Got Here*, 110th Cong., 1st Sess. (2007), *available at* http://jec.senate.gov/index.cfm?FuseAction=Reports.Reports&ContentRecord_id=c6627bb2-7e9c-9af9-7ac7-32b94d398d27&Region_id=&Issue_id=; *Staff of the Joint Economic Comm., Sheltering Neighborhoods from the Subprime Foreclosure Storm*, 110th Cong., 1st Sess. (2007), *available at* http://jec.senate.gov/Documents/Reports/subprime11apr2007revised.pdf; *Subprime Mortgage Market Turmoil: Examining the Role of Securitization: Hearings Before the Senate Comm. on Banking, Housing, and Urban Development*, 110th Cong., 1st Sess. (2007), *available at* http://banking.senate.gov/index.cfm?Fuseaction=Hearings.Detail&HearingID=256; *Preserving the American Dream: Predatory Lending Practices and Home Foreclosures: Hearings Before the Senate Comm. on Banking, Housing, and Urban Development*, 110th Cong., 1st Sess. (2007), *available at* http://banking.senate.gov/index.cfm?Fuseaction=Hearings.Detail&HearingID=248; *Mortgage Market Turmoil: Causes and Consequences: Hearings Before the Senate Comm. on Banking, Housing, and Urban Development*, 110th Cong., 1st Sess. (2007), *available at* http://banking.senate.gov/index.cfm?Fuseaction=Hearings.Detail&HearingID=254; *Possible Responses to Rising Mortgage Foreclosures: Hearings Before the House Comm. on Financial Services*, 110th Cong., 1st Sess. (2007), *available at* www.house.gov/apps/list/hearing/financialsvcs_dem/ht041707.shtml; *Subprime and Predatory Mortgage Lending: New Regulatory Guidance, Current Market Conditions and Effects on Regulated Financial Institutions: Hearings Before the House Comm. on Financial Services*, 110th Cong., 1st Sess. (2007), *available at* www.house.gov/apps/list/hearing/financialsvcs_dem/ht032707.shtml; *Foreclosure, Predatory Mortgage and Payday Lending in America's Cities Hearings Before the Domestic Policy Subcomm. of the House Comm. on Oversight and Government Reform*, 110th Cong., 1st Sess. (2007), *available at* http://oversight.house.gov/story.asp?ID=1218. *Cf.* S. 500, 111th Cong. (2009) (proposing federal usury limit for all consumer credit transactions).

68 *See* § 3.2, *infra*; Arthur E. Wilmarth, Jr., *The Dodd-Frank Act's Expansion of State Authority to Protect Consumers of Financial Services*, 36 J. Corp. L. 893 (Summer 2011).

69 Dodd-Frank tit. III, §§ 311–313.

70 National Consumer Law Center, Truth in Lending Ch. 9 (7th ed. 2010 and Supp.) (full discussion of these provisions).

71 *See* National Consumer Law Center, Truth in Lending Chs. 9, 11 (7th ed. 2010 and Supp.) (full discussion of these provisions).

72 *See* Lauren Saunders, National Consumer Law Center, The Role of the States under the Dodd-Frank Wall Street Reform and Consumer Protection Act of 2010 (Dec. 2010), *available at* www.nclc.org.

73 *See* § 2.2.6.2, *infra*.

74 Dodd-Frank tit. X, § 1028.

75 Dodd-Frank tit. X, §§ 1002(12), 1022.

76 Dodd-Frank tit. X, § 1027(o).

77 *See, e.g.*, Steven Mercatante, *The Deregulation of Usury Ceilings, Rise of Easy Credit, and Increasing Consumer Debt*, 53 S.D. L. Rev. 37 (2008).

78 *See* Till v. SCS Credit Corp., 541 U.S. 465, 124 S. Ct. 1951, 1962–1964, 158 L. Ed. 2d 787 (2004) (recognizing that the subprime auto finance market is not "perfectly" competitive and that creditors have much more information about the market than do consumers); Richard Lord, American Nightmare: Predatory Lending and the Foreclosure of the American Dream (Common Courage Press 2005); Patricia A. McCoy, *Rethinking Disclosure in a World of Risk-Based Pricing*, 44 Harv. J. on Legis. 123, 139–149 (2007) (discussing lack of price transparency); Elizabeth Renuart, *An Overview of the Predatory Lending Process*, 15 Housing Pol'y Debate 467 (2004); Kathleen C. Engel & Patricia A. McCoy, *A Tale of Three Markets: The Law and Economics of Predatory Lending*, 80 Tex. L. Rev. 1255 (2002). *Cf.* Sumit Agarwal, John C. Driscoll, Xavier Gabaix, & David Laibson, The Age of Reason: Financial Decisions Over the Lifecycle 37 (Feb. 11, 2008), *available at* http://ssrn.com/abstract=973790 (finding that older and younger borrowers pay more for credit than midlife borrowers across a range of credit products, perhaps because older and younger borrowers do not understand "shrouded attributes," such as the relationship between higher LTVs and higher APRs).

exhibits pricing sufficiently complex that it can puzzle economics professors.[79]

Car buyers never understand that the car dealer, who they think is finding the best deal for them, is actually marking up the risk-based interest rate that the lender is offering. Consumers may not understand that a creditor is seeking out the most expensive credit insurance product to sell, because that product will offer the highest return for the creditor. Consumers are in no position to shop around or even compare a credit insurance price with that offered by other insurers.

Often fees and other charges come into play after the credit is extended, and in ways never understood by the consumer. Computing rebates for unearned interest using the Rule of 78s is one example. So is a card issuer raising the card interest rate because the consumer is disputing a credit obligation completely unrelated to the credit card issuer. The true cost of credit can also be hidden in fees, charges, and other costs not included in the APR.

This complexity of a credit transaction exacerbates the inability of many Americans to understand credit terms. Roughly 40% of the U.S. population lacks the literacy to fill out correctly job applications or a bank deposit slip.[80] The overwhelming majority of the U.S. population does not understand how to calculate interest, given the amount borrowed on a loan and the number and amount of payments. The 1992 National Assessment of Adult Literacy used a typical advertisement for a home equity loan as one of its measures of "quantitative literacy," and only 4% of the adults sampled could calculate how much interest would be charged.[81] Deficiencies in quantitative literacy are particularly pronounced for non-whites and older consumers,[82] precisely those groups most often targeted by abusive lenders. Unsurprisingly, consumers with the worst quantitative literacy are the most likely to default on risky products like subprime mortgages and the most likely to engage in multiple cash-out refinancings on their homes.[83]

Many, if not most, consumers make systematic errors of judgment in evaluating credit.[84] Most consumers, even edu-

79 *See, e.g.*, Michael LaCour-Little & Cynthia Holmes, *Prepayment Penalties in Residential Contracts: A Cost-Benefit Analysis,* 19 Housing Pol'y Debate 631, 631–632 (2008) ("Given the embedded options they contain, mortgages are among the most complex of financial instruments."); Ronald J. Mann, *Boilerplate in Consumer Contract: "Contracting" for Credit*, 104 Mich. L. Rev. 899, 900 (2006) (arguing that credit card contracts are particularly complex in economic terms, since they aggregate multiple small transactions that occur over differing economic circumstances).

80 U.S. Dep't of Educ., National Ctr. for Educ. Statistics, Adult Literacy in America (Sept. 1993) (available from the U.S. Gov't Printing Office, GPO stock number 065-000-00588-3), *discussed in, e.g.*, Alan M. White & Cathy Lesser Mansfield, *Literacy and Contract*, 13.2 Stan. L. & Pol'y Rev. 233, 235–242 (2002); Mary Jordan, *Literacy of 90 Million Is Deficient*, Washington Post, Sept. 9, 1993, at A1. *Cf.* Mark Kutner, Elizabeth Greenberg, Ying Jin, Bridget Boyle, Yung-Chen Hsu, Eric Dunleavy & Sheida White, Literacy in Everyday Life: Results from the 2003 National Assessment of Adult Literacy 13 (2007), *available at* http://nces.ed.gov/Pubs2007/2007480.pdf (22% of the U.S. population has less than basic proficiency in quantitative literacy).

81 U.S. Dep't of Educ., National Center for Educ. Statistics, Adult Literacy in America 100 (Sept. 1993). (The ad included all the information necessary to make the calculation: number and amount of monthly payments, and loan principal.) *Cf.* Annamaria Lusardi & Olivia S. Mitchell, *Baby Boomer Retirement Security: The Roles of Planning, Financial Literacy, and Housing Wealth*, 54 J. Monetary Econ. 205, 207, 216 (2007) (finding that less than 18% of surveyed adults between the ages of fifty-one and fifty-six could calculate compound interest at 10% on $200 over two years); Macro Int'l, Inc., Design and Testing of Effective Truth in Lending Disclosures 52 (2007), *available at* www.federalreserve.gov/dcca/regulationz/20070523/Execsummary.pdf ("[V]ery few participants could accurately describe how interest charges were accurately calculated"); Annamaria Lusardi & Olivia S. Mitchell, Financial Literacy and Planning: Implications for Retirement Wellbeing 4, 7 (Pension Research Council, Working Paper No. 1, 2006), *available at* www.dartmouth.edu/~alusardi/Papers/FinancialLiteracy.pdf (noting that only 67% of surveyed adults, many over fifty, could correctly determine whether, after five years of interest at 2% on $100, they would have less than, more than, or exactly $102); Danna Moore, Wash. St. U., Soc. & Econ. Sci. Research Ctr., Survey of Financial Literacy in Washington State: Knowledge, Behavior, Attitudes, and Experiences (Tech. Rep. 03-39, 2003), *available at* www.dfi.wa.gov/news/finlitsurvey.pdf (finding approximately 30% of respondents do not understand that if interest compounds, it builds on itself).

82 Mark Kutner, Elizabeth Greenberg, and Justin Baer, U.S. Dep't of Educ., National Center for Education Statistics, A First Look at the Literacy of America's Adults in the 21st Century 1, 10 (Dec. 2005), *available at* http://nces.ed.gov/NAAL/PDF/2006470.PDF.

83 Kristopher Gerardi, Lorenz Goette, & Stephan Meier, *Financial Literacy and Subprime Mortgage Delinquency: Evidence from a Survey Matched to Administrative Data* 4–5, 17 (Fed. Reserve Bank of Atlanta, Working Paper No. 2010-10, 2010), *available at* www1.gsb.columbia.edu/mygsb/faculty/research/pubfiles/3615/wpmeier.pdf (finding a strong and statistically significant correlation between interviewees holding subprime mortgages who defaulted and those who had difficulty with simple math questions such as finding 10% of 1,000, holding constant for income, education, credit score at time of origination, and other factors; interviewees in the bottom quartile of quantitative literacy were fifteen percentage points more likely to experience foreclosure or be behind in their payments than those in the top quartile).

84 *E.g.*, Elizabeth Renuart & Diane E. Thompson, *The Truth, the Whole Truth and Nothing but the Truth: Fulfilling the Promise of Truth in Lending*, 25 Yale J. on Reg. 181 (2008); Oren Bar-Gill, *The Behavioral Economics of Consumer Contracts,* 92 Minn. L. Rev. 749, 761–765 (2008); Oren Bar-Gill, *Bundling and Consumer Misperception*, 73 U. Chi. L. Rev. 33, 45 (2006); Susan Block-Lieb, *The Myth of the Rational Borrower: Rationality, Behavioralism, and the Misguided "Reform" of Bankruptcy Law,* 84 Tex. L. Rev. 1481 (2006); Lauren E. Willis, *Decisionmaking and the Limits of Disclosure: The Problem of Predatory Lending: Price* 65 Md. L. Rev. 707 (2006); Matthew A. Edwards, *Empirical and Behavioral Critiques of Mandatory Disclosure: Socio-Economics and the Quest for Truth in Lending*, 14 Cornell J.L. & Pub. Pol'y 199, 221–223 (2005); Jason J. Kilborn, *Behavioral Economics, Overindebtedness & Comparative Consumer Bankruptcy: Searching for Causes and Evaluating Solutions,* 22 Emory Bankr. Dev. J. 13, 18–19 (2005); Patricia A. McCoy, *Elder Law: A Behavioral Analysis of Predatory Lending*, 38 Akron L. Rev. 725, 734 (2005) (detailing the difficulties faced by shoppers for subprime mortgage loans); Oren Bar-Gill, *Seduction by Plastic*, 98 Nw. U. L. Rev. 1373 (2004); Jeff Sovern, *Toward a Theory of Warranties in Sales of New Homes: Housing the Implied Warranty Advocates, Law and Economics Mavens, and Consumer Psychologists Under One Roof*, 1993 Wis. L. Rev. 13 (1993); Ren S. Essene & William Apgar, Joint Ctr. for Housing

cated consumers, focus on the payment to estimate the cost of a loan.[85] This focus on the payment works fine as a short-cut if the loans being compared are fixed-rate loans of the same time to repay, but it gravely misleads borrowers comparing loans of different lengths or with adjustable-rate periods. Worse, virtually all consumers, when given a payment stream, underestimate the effective interest, on average by as much as thirty-eight percentage points.[86]

Added to consumers' difficulty understanding credit terms is the fact that creditors, not borrowers, draft loan documents, and that the terms of credit contracts offered to consumers are basically non-negotiable. A potential borrower can "take it or leave it" and go elsewhere, though sometimes the "elsewhere" is not so easy to find. Thus not only are oppressive credit terms not easy to understand, but they are buried in a take it or leave it contract.

Most credit contracts are written in language far beyond what the average American can read and understand. The Government Accountability Office, as part of its study of credit cards, retained a usability expert to review credit card agreements and disclosures, who found that credit card agreements required reading at a 15th grade level—or three years of college. By comparison, nearly half of American consumers read at no more than an 8th grade level, the level at which most credit card *solicitations* are written.[87]

An unregulated free market system rewards creditors who hide the real cost of credit.[88] Little wonder then that too many creditors understate or obscure the real cost of credit.[89] The experience of the first decade of the twenty-first century has taught us if nothing else that there are many many individuals and even large banks and other major corporations who are tempted by such easy profits.

The ease with which a creditor can take unfair advantage can lead to extreme abuse when the consumer also is desperate to borrow money. Without adequate credit regulation, consumers are easily exploited where their financial circumstances require an immediate loan no matter the long-term cost.[90] Matters can

---

Studies, Harvard Univ., Understanding Mortgage Market Behavior: Creating Good Mortgage Options for All Americans (2007).

85 *See, e.g.*, Lauren E. Willis, *Decisionmaking and the Limits of Disclosure: The Problem of Predatory Lending: Price* 65 Md. L. Rev. 707 (2006); Ren S. Essene & William Apgar, Joint Ctr. for Housing Studies, Harvard Univ., Understanding Mortgage Market Behavior: Creating Good Mortgage Options for All Americans (2007).

86 The median underestimation was twenty-five percentage points. Victor Stango & Jonathan Zinman, How a Cognitive Bias Shapes Competition: Evidence from Consumer Credit Markets 3–4 (Sept. 5, 2006), *available at* http://papers.ssrn.com/sol3/papers.cfm?abstract_id=928956.

87 Government Accountability Office, Credit Cards: Increased Complexity in Rates and Fees Heightens Need for More Effective Disclosure to Consumers, GAO-06-929, at 38 (2006), *available at* www.gao.gov/new.items/d06929.pdf.

88 *See* Oren Bar-Gill, *The Law, Economics, and Psychology of Subprime Mortgage Contracts*, 94 Cornell L. Rev. 1073, 1083–1084 (2009) ("enhanced competition" likely increases prevalence of complexity and cost deferral in subprime mortgages); Oren Bar-Gill, *The Behavioral Economics of Consumer Contracts*, 92 Minn. L. Rev. 749, 789 (2008) (arguing that consumer misperceptions cause market distortions in pricing and other attributes of credit).

89 *See, e.g.*, Miller v. Americor Lending Group, Inc., 2007 WL 107664 (W.D. Mich. Jan. 9, 2007) (broker offers to arrange fixed-rate, non-negatively amortizing, pick-a-payment 2% interest rate loan and provides initial Truth in Lending Act disclosures, although knew no such loan existed); Complaint at 4, Fed. Trade Comm'n v. Chase Fin. Funding, Inc., No. SACV04-549 (C.D. Cal. May 12, 2004), *available at* www.ftc.gov/os/caselist/0223287/040602comp0223287.pdf (adjustable-rate mortgage with initial minimum payment, based on interest at 3.5% amortized over thirty years, which results in negative amortization, since actual interest rate is much higher, advertised as "3.5% fixed payment 30 year loan"); Nationscapital Mortgage Corp. v. State Dep't of Fin. Inst., 137 P.3d 78, 83–84 (Wash. Ct. App. 2006) (broker apparently had pattern of representing on Truth in Lending Act disclosures that borrower not responsible for broker fee); John R. Wilke, *Hidden Fees in Most Mortgages Bring Scrutiny to Fannie, Freddie*, Wall St. J., Jan. 14, 2005, at A1 (reporting on guarantee fees paid by lenders to Fannie Mae and Freddie Mac that are packaged in the interest rate and undisclosed to borrowers; averaging two-tenths of a percent of the loan amount per month); Gov't Accountability Office, Alternative Mortgage Products: Impact on Defaults Remains Unclear, but Disclosure of Risks to Borrowers Could Be Improved, GAO No. 06-1021, at 22 (2006), *available at* www.gao.gov/new.items/d061021.pdf (describing advertisement for payment option ARM that promised 45% reduction in monthly mortgage payments and interest rate of 1.25%; interest rate of 1.25% only applied for first month, and this fact disclosed in "much smaller print" on second page). *Cf.* Patricia A. McCoy, *Rethinking Disclosure in a World of Risk-Based Pricing*, 44 Harv. J. on Legis. 123, 128–138, 142–143 (2007) (discussing limitation of current disclosure regime to provide relevant, binding information in a timely and useful manner).

90 *See, e.g.*, Ghirardo v. Antonioli, 883 P.2d 960 (Cal. 1994) (purpose of usury law is " 'to protect the necessitous, impecunious borrower who is unable to acquire credit from the usual sources and is forced by his economic circumstances to resort to excessively costly funds to meet his financial needs.' "); Jersey Palm-Gross, Inc. v. Paper, 658 So. 2d 531, 534 (Fla. 1995) (purpose of usury laws is to "protect borrowers from paying unfair and excessive interest to overreaching creditors"; and "to bind the power of creditors over necessitous debtors and prevent them from extorting harsh and undue terms in the making of loans"); Nelson v. Associates Fin. Servs. Co., 659 N.W.2d 635 (Mich. Ct. App. 2002) (purpose of restrictions on prepayment penalties is to protect loan customers from being locked in to high interest rates); Trapp v. Hancuh, 530 N.W.2d 879 (Minn. Ct. App. 1995) (purpose of usury laws is "to protect the weak and necessitous from being taken advantage of by lender who can unilaterally establish the terms of the loan transaction"; distinguishing position of corporations, presumed to be in an equal bargaining position); Watkins v. Mississippi Bar, 589 So. 2d 660 (Miss. 1991) (central purpose of usury law is to protect borrowers from overreaching creditors); Scarr v. Boyer, 818 P.2d 381, 383 (Mont. 1991) ("Usury statutes protect borrowers who lack real bargaining power against overreaching by creditors"); Schneider v. Phelps, 359 N.E.2d 1361, 1365 (N.Y. 1977) ("The purpose of usury laws, from time immemorial, has been to protect desperately poor people from the consequences of their own desperation. Law-making authorities in almost all civilizations have recognized that the crush of financial burdens causes people to agree to almost any conditions of the lender and to consent to even the most improvident loans. Lenders, with the money, have all the leverage; borrowers, in dire need of money have none."); Seidel v. 18 East 17th St. Owners, 598 N.E.2d 7 (N.Y. 1992) (same); Smith v. Mitchell, 616 A.2d 17 (Pa. Super. Ct. 1992) (purpose of usury law, which applied to business loans under $10,000, "to protect the citizenry . . . from being exploited at the hands of unscrupulous individuals seeking to circumvent the law at the expense of *unsuspecting* borrowers who

get even worse where the consumer is unable to repay the high-cost loan and thus is forced to find yet additional high-cost credit to pay off the first loan. This spiral of debt makes consumers even more vulnerable and open to exploitation. Consumers who are illiterate, uneducated, frail, or less than fluent in English are especially vulnerable.[91] Worse, abusive sellers and lenders frequently target borrowers who are perceived as vulnerable, including members of racial groups historically excluded from mainstream credit, on the belief that the borrowers are, in some sense, still a captive market.[92]

### 1.3.2 Does Regulation Increase the Cost of Consumer Credit?

Creditors often argue against consumer credit regulation by alleging that an unregulated market increases competition that brings credit costs to a competitively low rate. They argue counter-intuitively that interest-rate ceilings actually increase the cost of credit.[93] Yet competition among lenders does not appear to drive down rates as more players enter the fringe lending business.[94]

For example, in the area of payday loans, competition has resulted in excessive solicitation and overlending, but loan pricing has increased due to deregulation of small loan rates. In Colorado, where payday lenders operated for several years without an interest rate cap, the situation for consumers worsened substantially. The number of payday loan stores and loans per store increased, but the average APR did not fluctuate—competition did not drive down rates.[95]

### 1.3.3 Does Regulation Limit the Supply of Credit?

Proponents of deregulation assert that regulation deprives needy borrowers of credit. This assumption, too, appears faulty. Dire predictions that over-regulation will deprive consumers of access to credit are not new. Virtually every existing consumer credit protection, when enacted, was criticized as limiting the supply of credit.[96] These predictions almost invariably lack credible empirical support and fail to materialize once the legislation is adopted.[97]

---

may have no other avenue to secure backing for a, for example, business venture."); Whitworth & Yancy v. Adams, 5 Rand 333, 335, 26 Va. 333 (1827) ("These statutes were made to protect needy and necessitous persons from the oppression of usurers and monied men, who are eager to take advantage of the distress of others; while they, on the other hand, from the pressure of their distress, are ready to come to any terms; and with their eyes open, not only break the law, but complete their ruin."); Paulman v. Filtercorp, 899 P.2d 1259 (Wash. 1995) (usury laws' aim is "to protect vulnerable borrowers from oppression"; the evil at which they are directed "is oppression of the borrower 'who by adversity and necessity of economic life [is] driven to borrow money at any cost.' "); Demopolis v. Galvin, 786 P.2d 804, 807 (Wash. Ct. App. 1990) (purpose is to protect desperate borrowers "driven to borrow money at any cost").

91 *See, e.g.*, Martinez v. Freedom Mortgage Team, Inc., 527 F. Supp. 2d 827 (N.D. Ill. 2007) ("Supplying Martinez with the loan contract disclosing the true terms of the agreement in English does nothing to vitiate the fraud, because Martinez was unable to read the contract. . . . '[D]isclosing' the true terms of a document written in a foreign language is tantamount to no disclosure at all."). *Cf.* Kristopher Gerardi, Lorenz Goette, & Stephan Meier, *Financial Literacy and Subprime Mortgage Delinquency: Evidence from a Survey Matched to Administrative Data* 17 (Fed. Reserve Bank of Atlanta, Working Paper No. 2010-10, 2010), *available at* www1.gsb.columbia.edu/mygsb/faculty/research/pubfiles/3615/wpmeier.pdf (finding that rate of cash-out refinancing increased among subprime borrowers, holding constant for income and education, as basic quantitative literacy declined).

92 *See, e.g.*, Carlisle v. Whirlpool Fin. Nat'l Bank, Civil Action No. CV 97-068, Clearinghouse No. 52,516 (Circuit Court, Hale County Ala. Aug. 25, 1999) (post trial order) (jury verdict in two satellite sale and financing cases for $580 million in punitive damages reduced $300 million though judge found defendants behavior "alarming" and "reprehensible," in part due to the evidence of sales practice designed to target and take advantage of the poor, under-educated, older, and African-American citizens); McGlawn v. Pa. Human Relations Comm'n, 891 A.2d 757 (Pa. Commw. Ct. 2006) (finding that brokerage firm targeted African Americans through advertising in sources "oriented toward African American audiences"). *See generally* National Consumer Law Center, Credit Discrimination Ch. 8 (5th ed. 2009 and Supp.).

93 *See, e.g.*,1981 Ariz. St. L.J. 1 (entire issue devoted to discussion of usury law and usury deregulation in Arizona; the authors of these articles go to great length to demonstrate that usury statutes do not set interest rates in Arizona, but they ignore that usury laws are not intended to set market rates); T. Durkin, *An Economic Perspective on Interest Rate Limitations*, 9 Ga. St. U. L. Rev. 821 (1993); H. Nathan, *Economic Analysis of Usury Laws*, 10 J. Bank Research 200 (1980); Note, *Usury Legislation—Its Effects on the Economy and a Proposal for Reform*, 33 Vand. L. Rev. 199 (1980); R. Shay, *The Impact of State Rate Ceilings upon the Availability and Price of Credit*, 4 National Commission on Finance Technical Studies (1973).

94 *See, e.g.*, Robert DeYoung & Ronnie J. Phillips, Federal Reserve Bank of Chicago, Strategic Pricing of Payday Loans: Evidence from Colorado, 2000–2005, at 20, 22 (July 14, 2006), *available at* www.chicagofed.org/digital_assets/others/events/2007/financing_community_development/paper_payday_loans.pdf.

95 Lynn Drysdale & Kathleen Keest, *The Two-Tiered Consumer Financial Services Marketplace: The Fringe Banking System and Its Challenge to Current Thinking About the Socio-Economic Role of Usury Laws in Today's Society*, 51 S.C. L. Rev. 589 (2000). *See also* Robert DeYoung & Ronnie J. Phillips, Strategic Pricing of Payday Loans: Evidence from Colorado, 2000–2005, at 20 (July 14, 2006), *available at* www.chicagofed.org/digital_assets/others/events/2007/financing_community_development/paper_payday_loans.pdf.

In preliminary results, the researchers found that, after rate regulation by Colorado's legislature, the price of payday lending was higher in markets more thoroughly saturated by payday lenders and by banks.

96 For example, when the Federal Trade Commission proposed the elimination of the holder-in-due-course doctrine from consumer credit sales, the industry sounded widespread alarms. In the thirty-five years since, consumer credit has continued to grow.

97 George J. Benston, An Analysis of Maine's 36-Month Limitation on Finance Company Small Loans, 33–41 (Dec. 1972), *reprinted in* the National Commission on Consumer Finance, Technical Studies, vol. II (Maine rate cap on refinanced loans resulted in many high-rate borrowers finding alternative and often lower-rate alternatives and others viewed themselves as better off not having high rate credit); R. Peterson & G. Falls, Credit Research Center, Purdue Univ., Impact of a Ten Percent Usury Ceiling: Empirical Evidence (1981) (credit more available in Arkansas with 10% usury limit than

Usury limits by definition restrict the supply of credit for loans carrying an interest rate above that usury limit. Thus the allegation that regulation limits the supply of credit in this context relates to those whose credit risk requires an interest rate above the usury limit. Nevertheless, it is a myth that high credit pricing is closely related to a consumer's high credit risk. More often than not, limiting the cost of credit means that the consumer will obtain credit elsewhere at a lower cost. There are at least three reasons why those who pay interest rates above a proposed usury cap are not such bad risks as would require such a high rate, and instead would find credit at lower rates if such a cap is instituted.

First, the high price of credit is often a function not of the consumer's high risk, but rather of the dynamics of reverse competition. In many consumer credit transactions, an auto dealer or other seller, a loan broker or some other party controls the consumer's choice for credit and credit-related items such as credit insurance. Creditors, credit insurers, and others seeking to market these products will not do so by offering a competitively low price reflective of the consumer's risk, but will instead compete to offer the greatest possible reward to the auto dealer, loan broker or other party controlling the consumer's decision. Typically, they will compete as to who will offer the *highest* priced credit or credit product, so that there is the most amount of room above cost to reward the auto dealer, broker, or other third party. Where all creditors are subject to the same usury ceiling, creditors will compete just as aggressively for the dealer or broker's business, but within that ceiling. Creditors will not make less profit—only the dealer or broker will receive lower profits.

Other times credit is sold by predatory lenders that take advantage of vulnerable consumers and charge exorbitant rates, irrespective of the consumer's credit risk. Often underwriting is not even part of the credit transaction. The predatory lender does not offer a lower rate if it discovers the consumer in fact is a good credit risk.[98] In a study of subprime lending in four cities in California, twenty-five percent of borrowers took out loans from a subsidiary or affiliate of a regulated financial institution, yet none were referred to the prime lender for lower-cost loans, even though most of the surveyed homeowners self-reported their credit as good or excellent.[99] In another study in five large cities, payday lenders concentrated their high-cost loan business around elder housing because such individuals had such steady income—their Social Security checks—and thus were good credit risks.[100]

A Freddie Mac study found that 10% to 30% of homeowners in the subprime mortgage market would be eligible for prime-market mortgages.[101] Fannie Mae opined that almost half of all subprime borrowers could qualify for lower-cost conventional financing.[102] Studies have found borrowers in the subprime market had FICO scores between 600 and 700.[103] Lenders describe the credit characteristics of their subprime borrowers as "excellent" with FICO scores above 700.[104]

Predatory lenders have a business plan of using aggressive sales tactics to offer credit at exorbitant rates even though many of their customers are good credit risks and could obtain credit at much lower rates elsewhere.[105] In this context, instituting a usury cap will just reduce the extent of predatory lending, and not deprive consumers of access to credit.

Even when lenders purport to price loans based on risk, there is little evidence that consumers labeled as high risk are in fact high risk,[106] and thus little evidence that lenders know who should only be offered high-rate credit. Use of a credit score is the most common method to evaluate risk for car loans, credit cards, and other supposed risk-based loans. But recent evidence suggests that credit scores have become less predictive of default risk, with a difference perhaps as small as ten points between borrowers who default and those who continue pay-

in other states); Raphael W. Bostic et al., *State and Local Anti-Predatory Lending Laws: The Effect of Legal Enforcement Mechanisms*, 60 J. Econ. & Bus. 47 (2008); Wei Li and Keith Ernst, The Best Value in the Subprime Market: State Predatory Lending Reform (Feb. 23, 2006), *available at* www.responsiblelending.org/mortgage-lending/research-analysis/StateEffectsToolkit.pdf.

98 *Wall Street and the Financial Crisis: The Role of High Risk Home Loans: Hearing Before the Subcomm. on Investigations of S. Comm. on Homeland Security and Governmental Affairs*, 111th Cong. 2d Sess. (2010) (memorandum by Sen. Carl Levin, Chair, & Sen. Tom Coburn, Ranking Minority Member).

99 Kevin Stein & Margaret Libby, California Reinvestment Committee, Stolen Wealth: Inequities in California's Subprime Mortgage Market 41, 47, 50 (Dec. 2001).

100 Ellen E. Schulz & Theo Francis, *High-Interest Lenders Tap Elderly, Disabled*, Wall St. J., Feb. 12, 2008.

101 Automated Underwriting: Making Mortgage Lending Simpler and Fairer for American Families (Freddie Mac Pub. No. 259 Sept. 1996).

102 Press Release, Fannie Mae (Mar. 2, 2000).

103 Marsha J. Courchane, *The Pricing of Home Mortgage Loans to Minority Borrowers: How Much of the APR Differential Can We Explain?*, 29 J. Real Est. Res. 399, 415, 417 (2007).

104 Paul Muolo, *Subprime Lending Starting to Attract Interest Again*, Am. Banker, July 14, 2010.

105 *See, e.g.*, Richard R.W. Brooks, *Credit Past Due*, 106 Colum. L. Rev. 994, 1003–1006 (2006); Cassandra Jones Havard, *Democratizing Credit: Examining the Structural Inequities of Subprime Lending*, 56 Syracuse L. Rev. 233 (2006); Elvin K. Wyly, Mona Atia, Holly Foxcroft, Daniel J. Hamme, Kelly Phillips-Watts, *American Home: Predatory Mortgage Capital and Neighbourhood Spaces of Race and Class Exploitation in the United States*, 88 Geografiska Annaler, Series B: Human Geography 105 (2006); Ronald J. Mann, *"Contracting" for Credit*, 104 Mich. L. Rev. 899, 914–915 (2005–2006); Ronald H. Silverman, *Toward Curing Predatory Lending*, 122 Banking L.J. 483, 531–544 (2005); Michelle A. Danis & Anthony Pennington-Cross, The Delinquency of Subprime Mortgages 7 (Fed. Res. Bank St. Louis, Working Paper 2005-022A Mar. 2005), *available at* http://research.stlouisfed.org/wp/2005/2005-022.pdf; Kathleen C. Engel & Patricia A. McCoy, *A Tale of Three Markets: The Law and Economics of Predatory Lending*, 80 Tex. L. Rev. 1255, 1271–1283 (2002).

106 *See, e.g.*, Howard Lax, Michael Manti, Paul Raca & Peter Zorn, *Subprime Lending: An Investigation of Economic Efficiency*, 15 Housing Pol'y Debate 533 (2004); Clifford V. Rossi, Mortgage Bankers' Ass'n, Anatomy of Risk Management Practices in the Mortgage Industry: Lessons for the Future (2010), *available at* www.housingamerica.org/RIHA/RIHA/Publications/72939_9946_Research_RIHA_Rossi_Report.pdf.

ing.[107] Some studies find no correlation between low credit scores and subsequent risk of foreclosure.[108]

The linkage between price and risk is further weakened by the extensive evidence that, among those with the *same* credit risk, there is wide variation in price based upon race. African Americans, Latinos, and Native Americans pay more for all kinds of credit, including car loans,[109] home mortgages,[110] and credit cards.[111] Where broker, dealer, or lender discretion exists, minority consumers are overcharged.[112] The effect of a usury ceiling in this context then is to reduce the amount of racial discrimination in credit pricing.

High risk of default is frequently cited as the reason for high rates. Yet this can be a self-fulfilling prophecy. Borrowers for whom fairly priced products and market-rate credit are within their ability to pay may become unable to pay the "sucker surcharge." Low-income consumers may be particularly unable to withstand the effect of increased pricing, and yet low-income consumers are particularly likely to be subjected to increased pricing.[113] Thus usury ceilings can help to reduce credit losses.

---

107 Kurt Eggert, *The Great Collapse: How Securitization Caused the Subprime Meltdown,* 41 Conn. L. Rev. 1257, 1289–1291 (2009).

108 *See, e.g.,* J. M. Collins & C.K. Reid, Who Receives a Loan Modification? Race and Income Differentials in Loan Workouts 11 (Jan. 2011), http://papers.ssrn.com/sol3/papers.cfm?abstract_id=1743159; Sumit Agarwal, John C. Driscoll, Xavier Gabaix, & David Laibson, The Age of Reason: Financial Decisions Over the Lifecycle 4, 16, 17 (Feb. 11, 2008), *available at* http://ssrn.com/abstract=973790.

109 *See, e.g.,* Coleman v. General Motors Acceptance Corp., 196 F.R.D. 315 (M.D. Tenn. 2000), *vacated and remanded on other grounds,* 296 F.3d 443 (6th Cir. 2002) (reversing class certification); Mark A. Cohen, Imperfect Competition in Auto Lending: Subjective Markups, Racial Disparity, and Class Action Litigation (Jan. 14, 2007), *available at* http://ssrn.com/abstract=951827; Consumer Fed'n of Am., African Americans Pay Higher Auto Loan Rates, but Can Take Steps to Reduce This Expense (Feb. 15, 2006), *available at* www.consumerfed.org/pdfs/African_American_Auto_Financing_Rates_021506.pdf; Ian Ayers, Expert Report (June 2004), *available at* www.nclc.org/images/pdf/litigation/closed/ahfc-cohen-report-appendix-f.pdf.

110 *See, e.g.,* Marsha J. Courchane, *The Pricing of Home Mortgage Loans to Minority Borrowers: How Much of the APR Differential Can We Explain?*, 29 J. Real Est. Res. 399, 415, 417 (2007); Thomas P. Boehm, Paul D. Thistle, Alan Schlottmann, *Rates and Race: An Analysis of Racial Disparities in Mortgage Rates*, 17 Housing Pol'y Debate 109, 126 (2006); First Nations Dev. Inst., Borrowing Trouble: Predatory Lending in Native American Communities 14–16 (2008), *available at* www.aecf.org/~/media/Pubs/Topics/Special%20Interest%20Areas/Other/BorrowingTroublePredatoryLendinginNativeAmeri/borrowing%20trouble.pdf; Carsey Institute, Subprime and Predatory Lending in Rural America: Mortgage Lending Practices That Can Trap Low-Income Rural People, Pol'y Brief No. 4 (2006), *available at* www.carseyinstitute.unh.edu/publications/PB_predatorylending.pdf.

111 José Garciá & Tamara Draut, The Plastic Safety Net: How Households Are Coping in a Fragile Economy: Findings from a 2008 National Household Survey of Credit Card Debt Among Low- and Middle-Income Households 5 (2009), *available at* http://demos.org/pubs/PSN_low.pdf.

112 *See* Howell E. Jackson & Laurie Burlingame, *Kickbacks or Compensation: The Case of Yield Spread Premiums*, 12 Stan. J.L. Bus. & Fin. 289, 350 (2007); Susan Wharton Gates, Vanessa Gail Perry & Peter M. Zorn, *Automated Underwriting in Mortgage Lending: Good News for the Underserved*, 13 Housing Pol'y Debate 369, 380 (2002);Robert B. Avery, Kenneth P. Brevoort, & Glenn B. Canner, *The 2007 HMDA Data*, Fed. Reserve Bull. A107, A141 (2008), *available at* www.federalreserve.gov/pubs/bulletin/2008/pdf/hmda07final.pdf; Robert B. Avery & Glenn B. Canner, *New Information Reported Under HMDA and Its Application in Fair Lending Enforcement*, Fed. Reserve Bulletin 344, 380, 394 (Summer 2005), *available at* www.federalreserve.gov/pubs/bulletin/2005/3-05/hmda.pdf; Debbie Gruenstein Bocian, Keith S. Ernst & Wei Li, Ctr. for Responsible Lending, Unfair Lending: The Effect of Race and Ethnicity on the Price of Subprime Mortgages 21–23 (May 31, 2006), *available at* www.responsiblelending.org/mortgage-lending/research-analysis/unfair-lending-the-effect-of-race-and-ethnicity-on-the-price-of-subprime-mortgages.html; Press Release, Office of the New York State Attorney General, Countrywide Agrees to New Measures to Combat Racial and Ethnic Disparities in Mortgage Loan Pricing (Dec. 5, 2006), *available at* www.ag.ny.gov/press-release/countrywide-agrees-new-measures-combat-racial-and-ethnic-disparities-mortgage-loan. *See also* Rakesh Kochar, Ana Gonzalez-Barrera, Daniel Dockterman, Pew Hispanic Center, Through Boom and Bust: Minorities, Immigrants, and Homeownership, at v (May 12, 2009), *available at* http://pewhispanic.org/files/reports/109.pdf; Paul S. Calem, Jonathan E. Hershaff & Susan M. Wachter, *Neighborhood Patterns of Subprime Lending: Evidence from Disparate Cities*, 15 Housing Pol'y Debate 603 (2004); William Apgar, Amal Bendimerad & Ren S. Essene, Joint Ctr. for Hous. Studies, Harvard Univ., Mortgage Market Channels and Fair Lending: An Analysis of the HMDA Data 9, 27, 37 (2007), *available at* www.jchs.harvard.edu/sites/jchs.harvard.edu/files/mm07-2_mortgage_market_channels.pdf; Jim Campen, Saara Nafici, Adam Rust, Geoff Smith, Kevin Stein & Barbara van Kerkhove, Neighborhood Econ. Dev. Advocacy Project, Paying More for the American Dream: A Multi-State Analysis of Higher Cost Home Purchase Lending 10 (2007), *available at* www.nedap.org/resources/documents/2007_Report-2005_HMDA.pdf; Jim Campen, Mass. Community & Banking Council, Changing Patterns XIII: Mortgage Lending to Traditionally Underserved Borrowers & Neighborhoods in Boston, Greater Boston and Massachusetts, 1990–2005, at 7 (Nov. 2006), *available at* www.masscommunityandbanking.org; Geoff Smith, Woodstock Institute, Key Trends in Chicago Area Mortgage Lending: Analysis of Data from the 2004 Chicago Area Community Lending Fact Book (2006); Geoff Smith, Woodstock Institute, Key Trends in Chicago Area Mortgage Lending: Analysis of Data from the 2004 Chicago Area Community Lending Fact Book (2006); Janis Bowdler, Nat'l Council of La Raza, Jeopardizing Hispanic Homeownership: Predatory Practices in the Homebuying Market 9 (May 2005), *available at* www.radicalmath.org/docs/PredatoryLendingHispanics.pdf; Calvin Bradford, Center for Community Change, Risk or Race? Racial Disparities and the Subprime Refinance Market (May 2002); Ken Zimmerman, Elvin Wyly & Hilary Btein, N.J. Inst. for Social Justice, Predatory Lending in New Jersey: The Rising Threat to Low-Income Homeowners 5, 6 (Feb. 2002), *available at* www.njisj.org/reports/predatory_lending.pdf; U.S. Dep't of Housing and Urban Dev., Unequal Burden: Income and Racial Disparities in Subprime Lending in America (Apr. 2000).

113 *See* Robert B. Avery, Kenneth P. Brevoort, & Glenn B. Canner, *The 2007 HMDA Data*, Fed. Reserve Bull. A107, A111 (2008), *available at* www.federalreserve.gov/pubs/bulletin/2008/pdf/hmda07final.pdf (reporting that borrowers with high cost mortgages in 2007 had incomes 20% lower than borrowers whose mortgages were not high cost).

### 1.3.4 *Is Limiting the Supply of High-Priced Credit a Bad Thing?*

As examined at § 1.3.3, *supra*, the industry claim that credit regulation limits the supply of consumer credit is dramatically overstated, and has a more profound effect on the extent of reverse competition and predatory lending found in the marketplace. Moreover, even if consumer credit regulation does restrict the availability of very high-priced credit, this is not a bad thing.[114] High-cost credit will not solve consumers' financial problems, but will only make matters worse when the first payment is due.[115] Some credit regulation can be seen as preventing debtors in desperate financial straits from making unwise credit decisions that will just make matters worse.[116] High-risk borrowers, who are already up to their necks in debt, do not need the freedom to go in over their heads.[117] It is, after all, not only those individual borrowers and their families who may end up drowning in debt, but the entire economic system.

Thus some credit restriction may be a good thing, particularly where it is high rate and often predatory lending.[118] Usury caps may be a better way to combat predatory lending than directly suing the lenders for fraud or other law violations. If recent experience is any guide, government and private enforcement against widespread predatory lending is far from adequate to either stop the lending or to remedy defrauded consumers.

## 1.4 Types of Creditors

### 1.4.1 *Distinctions Between Depository and Non-Depository Creditors*

The most basic division between types of creditors is the distinction between depository lenders, such as banks and savings and loan associations, which accept deposits, usually interest-bearing, and non-depository creditors, such as finance companies, which do not accept demand deposits from the public. Both depository and non-depository creditors act as intermediaries in the sense that they obtain funds from disparate investors and lend them at a profit to those who want money.

The acceptance of funds from the general public results in depositories traditionally being regulated by either federal or state government to ensure the safety of the public's deposits. Regulation of non-depositories is generally both more recent and more limited. Another distinction between depositories and non-depositories is that federal law allows most depository institutions to "export rates," that is to take advantage of the interest rate regulation of the depository's home state instead of that where the loan is made. Non-depository lenders do not share that right.

Other distinctions between depository and non-depository lenders have decreased over time. For example, while high-rate loans were traditionally the sole province of non-depositories, this is no longer the case. Some banks in fact are offering payday loans. Meanwhile, many non-depository creditors made conscious and generally successful attempts to branch out into middle-income consumer markets, particularly the market for home equity loans.[119] Aggressive preemption of state regulations by federal regulators overseeing depository institutions up through 2010[120] and the increase in large financial holding companies that own both depository and non-depository institutions further blurred these distinctions. It is no longer strictly true that poor people go to finance companies while wealthier borrowers do business with banks and other depository lenders.

Unfortunately, the result of this blurring of the lines has been an increase in abusive practices by depository institutions, not a decrease in abuse by non-depositories. Moreover, it is often the depositories that are funding or entering into other relationships with non-depositories offering payday loans, auto title

---

114 *See, e.g.*, McGlawn v. Pa. Human Relations Comm'n, 891 A.2d 757 (Pa. Commw. Ct. 2006).

115 *See, e.g.*, Jean Braucher, *Theories of Overindebtedness: Interaction of Structure and Culture*, 7 Theoretical Inquiries L. 323, 326 (2006); Jason J. Kilborn, *Behavioral Economics, Overindebtedness Comparative Consumer Bankruptcy: Searching for Causes and Evaluating Solutions*, 22 Bank. Dev. J. 13 (2005). *Cf.* Angela Littwin, *Beyond Usury: A Study of Credit Card Use and Preference Among Low-Income Consumers*, 86 Tex. L. Rev. 451 (2008); Paige Marta Skiba & Jeremy Tobacman, Do Payday Loans Cause Bankruptcy? (Sept. 8, 2008), *available at* http://papers.ssrn.com/sol3/papers.cfm?abstract_id=1266215.

116 *See, e.g.*, Eric A. Posner, *Contract Law in the Welfare State: A Defense of the Unconscionability Doctrine, Usury Laws, and Related Limitations on the Freedom to Contract*, 24 J. Legal Stud. 283 (1995).

117 G. Wallace, *The Uses of Usury: Low Rate Ceilings Reexamined*, 56 B.U. L. Rev. 451 (1976). *See also* Diane Ellis, Bank Trends—The Effect of Consumer Interest Rate Deregulation on Credit Card Volumes, Charge-Offs, and the Personal Bankruptcy Rate (1999), *available at* www.fdic.gov/bank/analytical/bank/bt_9805.html (attributing rise in personal bankruptcies to deregulation of credit card interest rates).

118 *See, e.g.*, John D. Skees, *The Resurrection of Historic Usury Principles for Consumption Loans in a Federal Banking System*, 55 Cath. U. L. Rev. 1131 (2006); Roberto G. Quercia, *Assessing the Impact of North Carolina's Anti-Predatory Lending Law*, 15 Hous. Policy Debate 546, 584–590 (2004) (decline in lending is largely confined to "predatory refinancing"); Vincent D. Rougeau, *Rediscovering Usury: An Argument for Legal Controls on Credit Card Interest Rates*, 67 U. Colo. L. Rev. 1 (1996); Ctr. for Community Capital, The Preemption Effect: The Impacts of State Anti-Predatory Lending Laws on the Foreclosure Crisis (2010), *available at* www.ccc.unc.edu/documents/Preemption.Effect.RELEASE.3.23.10.pdf (finding that OCC preemption of state anti-predatory lending laws led to increased risky refinance lending by regulated lenders with increased defaults); Lei Ding, et al., Ctr. for Community Capital, The APL Effect: The Impacts of State Anti-Predatory Lending Laws on Foreclosures 5 (2010), *available at* www.ccc.unc.edu/documents/APL.effect.RELEASE.3.23.10.pdf ("If anti-predatory lending laws have curbed so-called predatory practices while permitting non-abusive subprime lending to develop, the laws have done what they were intended to do.").

119 *See* Cathy Lesser Mansfield, *The Road to Subprime "HEL" Was Paved with Good Congressional Intentions: Usury Deregulation and the Subprime Home Equity Market*, 51 S.C. L. Rev. 473 (2000) (detailed analysis of the growth of subprime home equity lending by non-depository institutions).

120 *See generally* § 3.2, *infra*.

loans, refund anticipation loans, and rent-to-own transactions.[121] For example, until federal regulators ended the practice, banks also lent their names—and the ability to preempt state law—to payday lenders through "rent-a-bank" relationships.[122] Depositories also have directly entered the arena of small loans via credit cards, a relatively expensive form of credit,[123] or overdraft loans, which cover bounced checks at effective annual percentage rates in excess of those charged by payday lenders.[124]

## *1.4.2 Banks*

Commercial banks, by far the oldest form of depository institutions, significantly predate the founding of the United States. For example, the Bank of England, itself preceded by major Italian and Dutch international banking enterprises, was founded in 1694.

In the United States, banks were first chartered and regulated, to the extent that they were regulated at all, by state law.[125] The system was chaotic; the federal government held the power of coinage, but any state bank could issue paper notes, and numerous kinds of paper notes were simultaneously in circulation. After a few abortive attempts and much political ado, the National Bank Act established a permanent federal banking system in 1864. Upon application, qualifying institutions were granted federal banking charters and special lending rights. In return, they agreed to maintain specified reserves and to comply with other federal regulations. Thus a dual state and federal banking system was established, with state banks regulated by state law and national banks regulated by federal law.[126]

The federal banking system has been significantly modified since its inception. In 1913, a true central banking system was created with the establishment of the Federal Reserve System. Then, in 1933 the Federal Deposit Insurance Corporation was created, and all federal banks were required to participate in the FDIC's insurance program. Qualifying state banks have the option of joining the FDIC. By the 1980s, virtually all state and federal banks were insured by the FDIC. Through their insurance by the FDIC, even state banks are subject to some federal regulation on issues such as reserve requirements and the percentage of funds which may be issued to any one borrower. Although consumer protection regulation of state banks, including usury and other substantive consumer credit restrictions, nominally remains a matter of state law, the extent of federal preemption[127] under interstate banking and deregulation legislation has undermined the ability of states to regulate state banks and threatened the existence of the dual banking system.[128]

The laws of some states authorize the charter of more than one kind of state bank. The mutual savings banks, organized in many eastern states in the nineteenth century under existing banking laws to provide banking service to small depositors,[129] may technically be "banks," but the applicable state regulations may be distinct from those governing regular commercial banks. Similarly, "industrial banks," which were first organized in the early twentieth century under state banking laws, soon obtained separate regulation in most states and may most accurately be viewed as variants of consumer finance companies.[130]

Banks as a whole were slow to enter the field of consumer credit, becoming significantly involved only after the depression. Modern banks frequently issue mortgage loans or other well-secured consumer installment credit such as automobile loans. Banks also have been leaders in promoting high-priced, unsecured consumer credit in the form of open-end credit card accounts and overdraft protection. Banks, in particular, are

121 *See* Lynn Drysdale & Kathleen Keest, *The Two-Tiered Consumer Financial Services Marketplace: The Fringe Banking System and Its Challenge to Current Thinking About the Socio-Economic Role of Usury Laws in Today's Society*, 51 S.C. L. Rev. 589 (2000) (providing a comprehensive overview of high-cost lending to poor families).

122 *See* § 9.6.1, *infra.*

123 *See generally* Ch. 8, *infra* (credit card abuses).

124 *See* Donald P. Morgan & Michael R. Strain, Fed. Reserve Bank of N.Y., Staff Rep. No. 309, Payday Holiday: How Households Fare after Payday Credit Bans 5–6 (Feb. 2008), *available at* www.newyorkfed.org/research/staff_reports/sr309.pdf (arguing that in the absence of payday lending, consumers substitute costlier overdraft protection loans); Leslie Parrish, Ctr. for Responsible Lending, Overdraft Explosion: Bank Fees Increase 35% in Two Years (2009), *available at* www.responsiblelending.org/overdraft-loans/research-analysis/crl-overdraft-explosion.pdf (reporting increase in overdraft fee income of 35% between 2006 and 2008); Eric Halperin, Lisa James & Peter Smith, Ctr. for Responsible Lending, Debit Card Danger: Banks Offer Little Warning and Few Choices As Customers Pay a High Price for Debit Card Overdrafts (Jan. 25, 2007), *available at* www.responsiblelending.org/overdraft-loans/research-analysis/Debit-Card-Danger-report.pdf. *Cf.* Gov't Accountability Office, GAO No. 08-281, Bank Fees: Federal Banking Regulators Could Better Ensure That Consumers Have Required Disclosure Documents Prior to Opening Checking or Savings Accounts 13 (Jan. 2008), *available at* www.gao.gov/new.items/d08281.pdf (overdraft fees increased 13% between 2000 and 2007). *See generally* Owen B. Asplundh, *Consumer Protection Issues: Bounce Protection: Payday Lending In Sheep's Clothing?*, 8 N.C. Banking Inst. 349 (2004); § 9.5.1, *infra.*

125 *See generally* Cobb, Federal Regulation of Depository Institutions: Enforcement Powers and Procedures (1984); Homer, A History of Interest Rates (1963); Hutchinson, Money, Banking, and the United States Economy (1967).

126 *See* Arthur E. Wilmarth, Jr., *The Expansion of State Bank Powers, the Federal Response, and the Case for Preserving the Dual Banking System*, 58 Fordham L. Rev. 1133 (1990) (providing a good overview of the history of the dual banking system).

127 *See generally* Ch. 3, *infra.*

128 *See, e.g.*, Arthur E. Wilmarth, Jr., *The Dodd-Frank Act's Expansion of State Authority to Protect Consumers of Financial Services*, 36 J. Corp. L. 893 (Summer 2011); Arthur E. Wilmarth, Jr., *The OCC's Preemption Rules Exceed the Agency's Authority and Present a Serious Threat to the Dual Banking System*, 23 Ann. Rev. Bank. L. 288 (2004).

129 *See generally* Sherman, Modern Story of Mutual Savings Banks (1934); Welfling, Mutual Savings Banks (1968).

130 *See generally* Curran, Trends in Consumer Credit Legislation 52 (1966); Saulnier, Industrial Banking Companies and Their Banking Practices (1940); § 3.1.2.4, *infra.*

well-positioned to profit from credit card lending, since they can afford major marketing campaigns and national banks and federally insured state banks can avoid the consumer's home state restrictions on interest rates, late charges, and other fees through rate exportation—the bank's ability to use its home state interest rate instead of that of the consumer's. The profitability of the credit card business has led to the formation of specialized banks concentrating in that business.[131]

### 1.4.3 Savings and Loan Associations

Savings and loan associations (S&Ls) are also known as "thrifts" or "thrift institutions." In the federal banking system they are officially called "savings associations."

S&Ls are descendants of the building and loan associations of the nineteenth century.[132] These were private cooperative organizations in which each of the members contributed periodic payments on his "share" in the organization in return for receiving a mortgage loan as sufficient funds became available to the cooperative. Early building and loan associations generally dissolved once houses had been built for all members. Yet by the turn of the century, building and loan associations had evolved to permanent organizations, chartered and regulated by many states, in which the accounts of shareholders and borrowers were separately maintained.

A parallel system of state and federal S&Ls, somewhat comparable to the dual state and federal banking system, was established during the depression when many S&Ls faced severe financial problems. In 1932, the Federal Home Loan Bank System was created, modeled after the Federal Reserve System. Twelve regional federal home loan banks were established, under one board, the Federal Home Loan Bank Board (FHLBB). The regional federal home loan banks extend short- and long-term credit to member S&Ls.[133] In 1933, the Home Owners' Loan Act provided for the chartering of federal S&Ls, subject to a 6% rate cap.[134] The Home Owners' Loan Act mandated the participation of federal S&Ls in the Federal Home Loan Bank System. In 1934, the Federal Savings and Loan Insurance Corporation (FSLIC) was created, and deposits in all federal S&Ls and many state S&Ls were federally insured.

In the high interest rate environment of the late 1970s, the lending authority of federal S&Ls and many state S&Ls was expanded from long-term, low-yield mortgages to other forms of credit.[135] Federal S&Ls, for example, were authorized to issue consumer loans, home improvement loans, commercial real estate loans, credit cards, student loans, and many other forms of credit, although the percentage of an S&L's assets which may be invested in some of these forms of credit is limited.[136] The lending authority of state S&Ls is generally specified by state law. As with banks, federal savings associations, and federally insured S&Ls can export their home state interest rate to other states.[137]

This expanded lending authority did not prove to be a boon for the savings and loan industry. In fact, it resulted in failure for an unprecedented number of thrifts, placing financial strains on the thrift insurer, FSLIC.[138] As a result, Congress passed the Financial Institutions Reform, Recovery and Enforcement Act of 1989 (FIRREA),[139] a general overhaul of the federal regulatory structure for thrifts. The Federal Home Loan Bank Board was abolished, and many of its supervisory functions were transferred to the Office of Thrift Supervision (OTS).

Nor did OTS prove to be an effective regulator. It encouraged irresponsible lending by offering lax regulation as a way of competing for the business of lending institutions that might otherwise operate under national bank charters or state charters.[140] Starting in 2007, all of the major OTS-regulated thrifts failed. The Dodd-Frank Wall Street Reform and Consumer Protection Act of 2010 abolished the OTS, consolidating oversight of both national banks and federal savings and loan associations in the Office of the Comptroller of the Currency.[141]

### 1.4.4 Credit Unions

The third major type of depository creditor is the credit union. Credit unions are generally nonprofit cooperatives with membership open to a limited group of people who have some common bond. For example, employees of a single employer, members of a union, or residents of a specific region might be eligible to join a credit union organized for one of these groups. Depositors in a credit union are technically shareholders, and the funds deposited in the credit union are used to provide credit to the credit union's members.

---

131 *See* Lynn Drysdale & Kathleen Keest, *The Two-Tiered Consumer Financial Services Marketplace: The Fringe Banking System and Its Challenge to Current Thinking About the Socio-Economic Role of Usury Laws in Today's Society*, 51 S.C. L. Rev. 589 (2000); Ch. 8, *infra*.

132 *See generally* Bodfish, History of Building and Loan Associations in the U.S. (1931); Sherman, Modern Story of Mutual Savings Banks (1934).

133 Mutual savings banks and insurance companies were also permitted to join the federal home loan bank system, although there have been no insurance company members since 1959. *See* Welfling, Mutual Savings Banks 92–94 (1968).

134 Patricia A. McCoy & Elizabeth Renuart, *The Legal Infrastructure of Subprime and Nontraditional Home Mortgages*, *in* Borrowing to Live: Consumer and Mortgage Credit Revisited 110, 112 (Nicolas P. Retsinas & Eric S. Belsky ed. 2008).

135 *See* Anchor Sav. Bank v. United States, 81 Ct. Cl. 1 (2008).

136 *See* 12 U.S.C. § 1464; 12 C.F.R. pt. 545.

137 *See* § 3.4, *infra*.

138 Even a brief overview of the S&L crisis is beyond the scope of this treatise. One interesting and readable treatment of the S&L crisis is Kathleen Day, S&L Hell: The People and the Politics Behind the $1 Trillion Savings and Loan Scandal (1993). The jacket art alone is worth the price of the book.

139 Pub. L. No. 101-73, 103 Stat. 183 (Aug. 9, 1989).

140 *See* Arthur E. Wilmarth, Jr., *The Dodd-Frank Act's Expansion of State Authority to Protect Consumers of Financial Services*, 36 J. Corp. L. 893 (Summer 2011).

141 Pub. L. No. 111-203, tit. III, §§ 311–313, 124 Stat. 1376 (July 21, 2010). *See* § 3.1.2.2, *infra*.

The first American credit unions were established in New England at the turn of the last century and were based on European and Canadian models.[142] Massachusetts passed the first state statute authorizing the charter of credit unions in 1909. By 1930, following a substantial private publicity campaign funded primarily by the Boston merchant Edward A. Filene, credit union statutes modeled on the Massachusetts statute had been adopted in thirty-two states.

In 1934, the Federal Credit Union Act,[143] also based in part on the original Massachusetts statute, authorized the federal charter of credit unions, and a dual state and federal credit union system, similar to the dual banking and S&L systems, was established. Federal insurance, through the National Credit Union Share Insurance Fund, was required for deposits in federal credit unions and was made available to qualifying state credit unions. Today, virtually all credit unions are federally insured.

By their nature, credit unions are usually small, consumer-oriented institutions. Because of their nonprofit status and their selective membership standards, credit unions are often able to provide more favorable terms than other institutions on both member deposits and loans. They may also be subject to more exacting regulation. However, some credit unions have grown significantly beyond their consumer-oriented roots with an attendant growth in abuses. In particular, the lending practices of credit unions have come in for criticism.[144]

## *1.4.5 Finance Companies and Other Licensed Lenders*

Licensed lenders are corporations or individuals who have received a state license to issue consumer credit, frequently at high interest rates, under one or more of the numerous state special usury statutes. For example, small loan laws, industrial bank laws, and pawnbroker statutes generally require that a creditor receive a state license and comply with state regulations in order to lend at the generous rates that these statutes usually authorize. Creditors that purport to operate under a special usury statute but fail to obtain the proper license may face serious penalties for violations of the state's general usury law.[145]

Probably the most common example of a licensed lender in the past was the consumer finance company. These companies, the descendants of small loan lenders, have, in many cases, expanded their operations to include a more middle-class consumer market.[146] Many finance companies have made substantial profits through the cross-selling of credit insurance and other services in conjunction with their loans, through the repeated refinancing of outstanding consumer debt, and through questionable extensions of credit to insolvent borrowers on over-secured loans. Some states also authorize payday lending or auto title lending, usually requiring licensure but typically imposing only minimal substantive regulation.[147]

Although some states required licensing for second mortgage lenders, first mortgage lenders that were not depository institutions were historically not licensed lenders. As previously unregulated mortgage companies became the source of some abusive lending practices in the 1980s, some states added these to the list of lenders subject to licensing and regulation.[148] The federal SAFE Act[149] requires individual mortgage loan brokers to be licensed, but whether mortgage lenders themselves must be licensed is still a question of state law.

## *1.4.6 Retail Sellers*

Another major class of non-depository creditor consists of retailers of consumer durable goods. Many consumers cannot afford to purchase big-ticket goods such as automobiles, furniture, refrigerators, and other appliances in cash. Retailers offer credit plans to boost sales and sometimes as an independent profit center. The terms of the installment credit sales contracts, including the maximum interest rate[150] and other charges on the contract, are regulated in many states by retail installment sales acts or motor vehicle retail installment sales acts. However, most states have by statute exempted rent-to-own transactions from their retail installment sales acts, even though these transactions are equivalent in all essential respects to retail installment sales.[151]

Major retailers such as department stores often offer revolving credit plans represented by "charge cards." These revolv-

142 *See generally* 1 Credit Union Law Service Ch. 1 (Matthew Bender 1987).

143 12 U.S.C. §§ 1751–1795k. *See* § 3.3, *infra* (discussing federal usury preemption for credit unions).

144 *See* National Consumer Law Center, Stopping the Payday Loan Trap: Alternatives That Work, Ones That Don't (June 2010), *available at* www.nclc.org/images/pdf/high_cost_small_loans/payday_loans/pr-stopping-payday-trap.pdf (documenting high-cost payday-style lending by certain credit unions); Letter from Lauren K. Saunders, National Consumer Law Center, to Michael E. Fryzel, Nat'l Credit Union Admin. (Jan. 27, 2009), *available at* www.nclc.org/images/pdf/high_cost_small_loans/payday_loans/letter-ncua-payday-0109.pdf (discussing involvement of credit unions in high cost payday lending); National Community Reinvestment Coalition, Credit Unions: True to Their Mission? 3 (2005), *available at* www.ncrc.org/media-a-resources-mainmenu-118/press-releases-mainmenu-75/514-are-credit-unions-serving-their-mission ("[B]anks consistently exceed credit unions' performance in lending to women, minorities, and low- and moderate-income borrowers and communities.").

145 *See* § 7.8, *infra.*

146 *See* Lynn Drysdale & Kathleen Keest, *The Two-Tiered Consumer Financial Services Marketplace: The Fringe Banking System and Its Challenge to Current Thinking About the Socio-Economic Role of Usury Laws in Today's Society*, 51 S.C. L. Rev. 589 (2000).

147 *See* Chs. 9 (payday lending), 11 (auto title pawn), 12 (rent-to-own), *infra.*

148 *See, e.g.,* Mass. Gen. Laws ch. 255E (Licensing of Certain Mortgage Lenders and Brokers) (enacted 1991).

149 *See* National Consumer Law Center, Mortgage Lending § 3.3 (2012).

150 Because the transaction is a sale rather than a loan, the charge assessed may be described as "time-price differential" or "finance charge" instead of "interest," but the difference is purely semantic. § 1.2.4, *supra.*

151 *See* § 12.3.2.2, *infra.*

ing credit accounts are usually regulated separately from installment credit under state law.

Retailers often sell or assign installment sales contracts soon after they are signed. They transfer them to other creditors, typically banks, finance companies, or "acceptance" companies, at a discount from the amount that the consumer is obligated to pay over the term of the contract. For example, if a consumer has contracted to pay a retailer $100 over a period of a year, the retailer might sell the contract to a finance company in return for an immediate payment of $85. The retailer and the finance company generally enter into a "master contract" under which the finance company agrees to purchase some or all of the retailer's contracts on stated terms.

The assignment of a retail installment contract may or may not significantly affect the credit buyer. At the least, the buyer may receive a notice that payments should be made to the assignee rather than the retailer. If the buyer falls behind in payments, the effect may be greater. Depending on the terms of the master contract, either the assignee may sue the buyer on the contract or the contract will be reassigned to the retailer, which will have to enforce the contract itself.[152] Alternatively, finance companies use assigned consumer contracts as a source of new customers, and if a buyer is not seriously in default, the finance company might use the opportunity of delinquency to convince the consumer to refinance the debt. Such refinancings can be extremely profitable for creditors, with the borrower's obligation growing larger with each refinance. The costs of refinancing are explored at §§ 5.8, 5.9, *infra*.

### *1.4.7 Convenience Creditors*

Convenience creditors, a third category of non-depository creditors, are sellers who forbear the collection of existing debts in return for installment payments with interest. Such creditors include doctors, lawyers, hospitals, utilities, oil companies, farm supply companies, and other businesses that have no formal charge account plan but are willing to finance debts either to increase their volume of business or in order to avoid the collection process as long as their customers are making payments. These credit agreements are often evidenced merely by a sales receipt that states that a monthly charge will be imposed if the debt is not paid within thirty days.

Determining which statute controls a transaction with a convenience creditor may require a careful analysis of state law. In some states, such a transaction is considered a "detention" of money to which the usury laws do not apply.[153] Other states have separate interest ceilings for goods sold on open accounts. Yet others may treat convenience creditors under retail installment sales acts (RISAs),[154] although RISAs do not always reach sellers that extend credit only infrequently. Alternately, usury statutes may apply to sales on account on the theory that interest is being charged for the seller's forbearance of debt.[155] In any case, charges assessed by convenience creditors should be examined closely. Such creditors frequently violate credit statutes, either out of ignorance of the controlling law or because they fail to take credit limitations seriously.

## 1.5 Types of Credit

### *1.5.1 Loans vs. Credit Sales*

The distinction between loans and credit sales has a long history and is embedded in most states' laws even though it has little theoretical basis.[156] Many courts, often using the fiction of the time-price doctrine, have interpreted general usury statutes to regulate only loans or forbearances of debt and not sales of goods on credit.[157] Consequently, consumer credit sales were largely unregulated by state legislatures, but were governed only by regular contract law, until after the Second World War.

Starting in the 1950s, most states adopted retail installment sales acts (RISAs) to regulate the terms and the charges imposed in credit sales of goods and services. However, even in states that have adopted RISAs, the time-price doctrine may continue to apply to sales transactions that fall outside the scope of the RISA.[158]

A credit sale is not just any credit which is eventually used to buy goods; rather, it is credit extended specifically by the seller in conjunction with the sale of specific goods.[159] Thus, if a consumer gets a finance company loan for the express purpose of buying furniture, the transaction, in most circumstances, is still a loan subject to loan, not sale, regulations.[160] Similarly, if the buyer charges the purchase on a bank credit card, the credit is a loan. Yet, if the furniture store directly offers the consumer separate cash and time prices for the same goods, the transaction is a credit sale that general usury laws do not reach, but that will be controlled by retail installment sales acts (RISAs) in most states.[161]

### *1.5.2 Open-End vs. Closed-End Credit*

The consumer credit laws of most states distinguish closed-end or installment credit from open-end or revolving credit.[162]

152 Contracts between sellers and the assignees that purchase consumer paper such as retail installment contracts are divided into "recourse" contracts, in which the assignee may force the credit seller to buy back the paper if the consumer defaults, "non-recourse" contracts in which the assignee has no such right, and "limited recourse" contracts in which the repurchase of the consumer contract can be compelled only for debts above a stated amount, for specified types of default, or for specified categories of transactions.

153 *See* § 7.5.2.3, *infra*.

154 *See* § 10.2, *infra*.

155 *See* § 7.5.2.3, *infra*.

156 *See* § 3.9.4, *infra*.

157 *See* §§ 1.2.4, *supra*.

158 *See* §§ 7.5.2.2, 10.2.1, *infra*.

159 *See generally* § 10.2.1, *infra* (discussing the time-price doctrine in detail, including other limitations, such as the required disclosure of the separate credit and cash prices prior to the sale).

160 *See generally* § 3.9.4, *infra*.

161 *See* §§ 7.5.2.2, 10.2, *infra*.

162 *See* Seibert v. Sears, Roebuck & Co., 120 Cal. Rptr. 233 (Cal. Ct. App. 1975) (comparing open-end and closed credit).

Generally, closed-end credit statutes address a single extension of credit between a creditor and a debtor that the debtor agrees to pay off in a fixed number of periodic installments of a specified amount. The credit sale of an automobile is a good example of such a transaction because any one sale will almost invariably represent the entire debt outstanding between the two parties. Although the consumer might go back to the same dealer over many years to purchase more automobiles, each credit sale would be viewed as an isolated transaction, to be paid for individually.

Open-end credit statutes, on the other hand, contemplate frequent transactions between the parties in which the debt from each individual transaction is merged into the larger outstanding debt. A typical example of this arrangement is a bank credit card or a charge account at a department store. The debt from each purchase by a consumer is added to an outstanding balance, and the consumer receives a monthly statement giving the total outstanding balance, the accrued finance charge from the preceding month, and the minimum payment due. There is no set number of payments that the consumer will make on the account, and there is no expectation that the size of each payment will be equal. The consumer is required to pay only a stated minimum amount which will vary with the outstanding balance and which will, in most cases, at least equal the accrued finance charge for the previous month.[163] The consumer is free to pay off the entire balance whenever he or she wishes. Under the terms of most card agreements, finance charges may be avoided altogether if the full account balance is paid on time every month,[164] although annual fees are sometimes imposed regardless of the consumer's payment record.

The separate regulation of installment credit and open-end credit makes some sense because the two arrangements raise different concerns. For example, calculation of the monthly finance charge or the minimum amount due does not cause much problem in installment credit where the principal is paid down on a regular basis, but does not otherwise fluctuate. Conversely, rebates of unearned interest are not an issue in open-end accounts because the interest on such accounts is not precomputed.[165]

The interest rate on both fixed-term or open-end credit may be either a fixed rate or a variable rate. Yet it is much more common for closed-end transactions to be at a fixed rate and open-end transactions to be at a variable rate. The charges on closed-end non-mortgage credit are often precomputed while charges on open-end credit are computed monthly. Open-end accounts thus lend themselves to a frequently changing interest rate.

While the distinction between closed-end and open-end credit is generally clear-cut, this is not always the case. If open-end credit allows creditors a higher interest ceiling, fewer restrictions, or fewer disclosures, some creditors will try to structure single transactions as lines of credit that fall under the open-end statutes.[166]

A related gray area between closed-end and open-end credit is a finance company practice of repeatedly refinancing its customers' outstanding loans.[167] The process works approximately as follows. A finance company either loans consumer money or, more often, acquires preexisting debt through assignment or debt consolidation. This initial transaction looks like regular installment debt: a fixed number of usually equal payments is required to retire the debt and there is no obligation or even expectation that the creditor will give the borrower any more loans. Yet, before the initial obligation is paid off, the debt is refinanced. The new loan also appears to be a closed-end transaction, but its principal includes not only the outstanding principal from the previous loan, but also unpaid interest, various non-interest fees such as credit insurance premiums, and often a small new cash advance to the borrower. In effect, new charges have been added to the consumer's account. With each subsequent refinancing, the process is repeated and the consumer's debt is extended. Repeated refinancing creates a highly remunerative form of an open-end account composed of a series of closed-end transactions.

### *1.5.3 Security Taken in Credit Transactions*

The law commonly distinguishes between secured and unsecured credit generally and among secured credit by the type of collateral. Collateral may be either real or personal property of the debtor. The security interest, given by contract, grants the creditor the right to seize the collateral to satisfy the remaining debt if the debtor defaults. For example, credit sales contracts usually give the seller and its assignees a security interest in the goods purchased. If the buyer defaults on the payments and the security interest is valid, the creditor can repossess the goods and sell them to satisfy the outstanding debt.[168] A creditor that has no security interest can ultimately collect on its debt by

163 If the minimum payment is less than the monthly finance charge, the result of making the minimum payment every month is negative amortization, and the debtor owes progressively more and more money, even if no additional charges (i.e., credit purchases) are made on the account. *See* Ch. 8, *infra*.

164 Many cards have a "grace period" during which the amount billed in the previous month can be paid without finance charge provided that the customer had entered the month with an account balance of zero. Some cards, however, provide no grace period, and interest is assessed from the day a purchase is recorded (i.e., "posted") by the creditor. *See* § 8.6, *infra* (discussing grace periods and credit cards).

165 In a precomputed contract, all interest charges are determined at the time the contract is entered into, and a fixed monthly payment size is set at a level sufficient to pay off both the interest charges and the principal debt over the term stated in the contract. This is the traditional format for a small loan or credit sale. *See* § 5.8.2, *infra*.

166 *See* § 3.9.3, *infra*; National Consumer Law Center, Truth in Lending § 6.2 (7th ed. 2010 and Supp.) (spurious open-end credit).

167 *See, e.g.*, Porter v. Ace Cash Express, Inc., 2000 U.S. Dist. LEXIS 15996 (E.D. La. Oct. 25, 2000) (payday lender did not fall within revolving credit statute; insufficient evidence that parties contemplated repeat transactions), *aff'd*, 277 F.3d 1372 (5th Cir. 2001). *See generally* §§ 3.9.3 (discussing the distinction between open-end and closed-end credit), 5.9 (discussing refinancing), *infra*.

168 *See* National Consumer Law Center, Repossessions (7th ed. 2010 and Supp.).

obtaining a judgment on the debt and attaching the debtor's property pursuant to the judgment. However, this process is generally more costly and time-consuming than self-help repossession. Moreover, much of a debtor's property may be immune to attachment because of state exemption statutes.[169]

The existence of security on a credit contract is largely independent of other credit terms. Both fixed-term and open-end credit generally may be secured, as may both loans and credit sales. Moreover, unless prohibited by law, any kind of creditor may require security. Yet the kind of security that may be required legally frequently depends on the type of transaction involved.[170] For example, a small loan licensee or a retailer operating under a RISA may be prohibited from taking a security interest in real estate.

Security interests are important because they shift the parties' risks. A creditor that obtains a valuable security interest, such as a lien on a motor vehicle, faces a much lower risk of nonpayment than does an unsecured creditor, and well-secured loans such as automobile loans frequently carry a lower interest rate than unsecured credit such as the average credit card account. Conversely, the consequences for a debtor of defaulting on a loan are much greater if the loan is secured. A borrower who defaults on a home or automobile loan may lose the car in short order. Faced with such consequences, a borrower may make payments on a loan even if meeting the payments leads to severe privation. Indeed, prior to legal restrictions on the practice, small loan lenders and retailers frequently took security interests in household goods of negligible cash value *simply* because of the threat of repossession was effective in obtaining payment.[171]

Special usury statutes are often aimed at transactions involving a particular kind of collateral. Many states have special RISAs that address only the sale of motor vehicles. Other statutes apply only to manufactured home sales.

169 *See generally* National Consumer Law Center, Fair Debt Collection (7th ed. 2011 and Supp.).

170 *See, e.g.*, Ohio Rev. Code § 1321.12 (prohibiting small loan licensees from taking security interest in real estate); Pa. Stat. tit. 69, §§ 1401(k) (prohibiting creditor under state RISA from taking security interest in residential real estate), 1403 (restricting security interest to goods sold).

171 *See* 16 C.F.R. pt. 444 (effective Mar. 1, 1985) (forbidding creditors from taking a non-purchase money security interest in most household goods); National Consumer Law Center, Unfair and Deceptive Acts and Practices § 6.2.1 (7th ed. 2008 and Supp.); Richard R.W. Brooks, *Credit Past Due*, 106 Colum. L. Rev. 994, 1003–1006 (2006) (discussing fringe lender's motivations in taking a security interest).

# Chapter 2 Statutes Restricting Credit Terms

## 2.1 Introduction

This chapter provides overviews of federal and state laws that apply to non-mortgage consumer credit. The application of these laws to particular types of credit transactions is analyzed in more detail in later chapters.

Section 2.2 addresses federal laws and regulations that regulate the terms of consumer credit. The discussion is summary, except for the Talent-Nelson Military Lending Act, which is analyzed in detail.

Section 2.3 describes state laws that prescribe or limit the terms of consumer credit. In reviewing state law, it should be remembered that federal law preempts the application of state law in some circumstances, primarily where a federally related creditor is involved. Preemption of state consumer credit law is discussed in detail at Chapter 3, *infra*.

Section 2.4 gives overviews of state and federal statutes that are not directly aimed at consumer credit terms but set general standards—UDAP statutes, state and federal fair lending laws, fraud, unconscionability, and other statutes and common law doctrines. The chapter concludes with a discussion at § 2.5 of the state and federal laws that address electronic consumer credit transactions. The application of the federal Racketeer Influenced and Corrupt Organizations Act (RICO) to consumer credit transactions is discussed at § 7.8.6.2, *infra*.

## 2.2 Federal Statutes and Rules Regulating Credit Terms

### *2.2.1 Regulation of Federal Depository Institutions*

The National Bank Act allows national banks to abide by either a federal interest rate ceiling or their home state's ceiling, which they can export to other states. Supreme Court case law and OCC regulations define "interest" broadly for purposes of rate exportation, allowing national banks to export a wide variety of fees and charges. The statutory scheme for federal savings associations is similar and they are now also regulated by the OCC.

By contrast, federal law caps the interest rate for federal credit unions at 15%, but the National Credit Union Administration Board (NCUA) has authority to authorize a higher cap for periods of up to eighteen months if justified by money market rates.[1] In April 2011, the NCUA extended its then current 18% cap through September 2012.[2] Effective October 25, 2010, federal credit unions—if the loan meets certain conditions—may also charge an interest rate on "short-term, small amount loans" that is up to ten points higher than the rate allowed by the general rate cap (resulting, effectively, in a 28% cap), plus a single application fee up to $20.[3]

As to loan terms other than the broad definition of interest, the OCC has asserted the right to preempt state requirements and restrictions, but the OCC generally has not adopted requirements or restrictions in their place. One exception is an OCC regulation that requires national banks not to make consumer loans based predominantly on the bank's realization of the foreclosure or liquidation value of the borrower's collateral, without regard to the borrower's repayment ability.[4] OCC regulations also generally prohibit unfair or deceptive practices as defined by the Federal Trade Commission Act.[5] Regulation of interest rates for national banks, federal savings associations, and credit unions is discussed in detail §§ 3.3, 3.4, *infra*.

### *2.2.2 The Truth in Lending Act*

#### 2.2.2.1 Disclosure and Substantive Protections for Non-Mortgage Lending

The federal Truth in Lending Act (TILA)[6] was adopted in 1968. TILA requires creditors to give consumers a standardized disclosure statement before a transaction is consummated.[7] Among other disclosures, this statement must contain the "Amount Financed," which is the amount of money of which the consumer will have actual use, the "Finance Charge," which is the total dollar cost of the credit, and the "Annual Percentage Rate" (APR), which expresses the cost of the credit

1 12 U.S.C. § 1757. *See also* 12 C.F.R. § 701.21(c)(7) (stating that, every eighteen months, Board will determine whether to authorize rates in excess of 15%).

2 Letter from National Credit Union Admin. to Federal Credit Unions No. 11-FCU-04 (Apr. 2011).

3 75 Fed. Reg. 58,285 (Sept. 24, 2010), *to be codified at* 12 C.F.R. § 701.21(c)(7)(iii). This assumes the application fee does not meet TILA's definition of a finance charge.

4 12 C.F.R. § 7.4008(b).

5 12 C.F.R. § 7.4008(c).

6 15 U.S.C. §§ 1601 to 1666j.

7 The discussion here of TILA requirements is cursory at best and is intended only as an overview of the statute. *See* National Consumer Law Center, Truth in Lending (7th ed. 2010 and Supp.) (thorough treatment TILA).

on a yearly basis. All of these figures must be calculated according to detailed regulations.[8]

Congress has recognized, at least implicitly, the inadequacy of disclosures to rein in abusive lending, and has steadily added substantive protections to TILA. TILA's substantive protections for non-mortgage credit apply primarily to credit cards and other open-end credit. Prior to 2009, the major protections were billing error procedures for open-end credit, the right to dispute charges on credit cards, protection against liability for unauthorized use of a credit card, and a prohibition against the unsolicited issuance of credit cards.[9] TILA also prohibits offsetting a consumer's deposit account to repay credit card debt, and addresses some aspects of the creditor-merchant-cardholder relationship.[10]

The Credit Card Accountability, Responsibility and Disclosures (CARD) Act of 2009 (hereinafter the Credit CARD Act),[11] effective February 22, 2010,[12] added many substantive protections for credit cards. TILA now also prohibits certain types of increases in the annual percentage rate (APR) and certain fees or charges for a credit card account.[13] The Credit CARD Act gives the consumer the right to cancel a credit card account as a way of rejecting reject certain changes that a credit card issuer makes to the terms of the account,[14] and prohibits "double cycle billing," a method of calculating interest on a credit card account.[15] It requires penalty fees to be reasonable and proportional,[16] and provides some protections against aggressive solicitation and improvident lending, particularly involving college students and other younger consumers.[17] TILA also requires credit card lenders to refund credit balances, prohibits the termination of credit cards for failure to incur a finance charge, imposes record retention requirements, and requires timely settlement of claims by card issuers against decedents' estates.[18] TILA also provides substantive protections for mortgage loans, which are discussed elsewhere in this series of treatises.[19]

TILA is an important and complex statute that is supplemented by detailed and technical regulations. Advocates facing a consumer credit case should always analyze the case for Truth in Lending issues, and should refer to NCLC's *Truth in Lending* (7th ed. 2010 and Supp.).

### 2.2.2.2 TILA Remedies

TILA gives consumers a private cause of action to enforce most of its protections. Consumers can bring suit for actual damages caused by violations of most of TILA's disclosure requirements and substantive protections.[20] Statutory damages are available for a subset of violations.[21] The statutory damage award varies depending on the type of credit transaction, but for most non-mortgage transactions it is double the finance charge with a minimum award of $100 or $200 and a maximum award of $2,000 or $4,000.[22] Statutory damages in class actions are limited to $1 million or 1% of the creditor's net worth, whichever is less.[23]

In some circumstances, TILA gives consumers the right to rescind credit transactions, but this right applies only to credit that is secured by the consumer's principal dwelling.[24] TILA also provides for enhanced damages for violation of its provisions regarding certain high-cost mortgage loans.[25]

A consumer who brings a successful action under TILA is entitled to an award of reasonable attorney fees and costs.[26]

### 2.2.2.3 Relationship Between TILA and State Law

TILA preempts state disclosure laws only to the extent they are inconsistent with TILA's requirements.[27] In general, TILA does not preempt or alter state usury ceilings or other cost caps, nor does it affect the way that interest rates are calculated for the purposes of state usury law.[28] Indeed, many consumer credit contracts currently state two interest rates—one on the contract or note which is calculated as required or permitted by state law, and one on the TILA disclosure statement which contains the APR and other disclosures as calculated under federal law. Further, an accurate TILA disclosure does not legitimize the imposition of interest or fees that are not authorized by the contract.[29]

8 12 C.F.R. pt. 1026 [pt. 226].

9 National Consumer Law Center, Truth in Lending §§ 7.9–7.12 (7th ed. 2010 and Supp.).

10 National Consumer Law Center, Truth in Lending §§ 7.13, 7.14 (7th ed. 2010 and Supp.).

11 Pub. L. No. 111-24, 123 Stat. 1735 (May 22, 2009).

12 *Id.* § 3.

13 15 U.S.C. § 1666i-1(a). *See* National Consumer Law Center, Truth in Lending § 7.2 (7th ed. 2010 and Supp.).

14 15 U.S.C. § 1637(i)(3). *See* National Consumer Law Center, Truth in Lending § 7.3 (7th ed. 2010 and Supp.).

15 15 U.S.C. § 1637(j)(1)(A). *See* National Consumer Law Center, Truth in Lending § 7.4 (7th ed. 2010 and Supp.).

16 15 U.S.C. § 1665d(a). *See* National Consumer Law Center, Truth in Lending § 7.5 (7th ed. 2010 and Supp.).

17 15 U.S.C. §§ 1665e, 1637(c)(8). *See* National Consumer Law Center, Truth in Lending § 7.6 (7th ed. 2010 and Supp.).

18 National Consumer Law Center, Truth in Lending § 7.15 (7th ed. 2010 and Supp.).

19 National Consumer Law Center, Truth in Lending Ch. 9 (7th ed. 2010 and Supp.).

20 15 U.S.C. § 1640(a)(1). *See* National Consumer Law Center, Truth in Lending § 11.5 (7th ed. 2010 and Supp.).

21 15 U.S.C. § 1640(a)(2). *See* National Consumer Law Center, Truth in Lending § 11.6 (7th ed. 2010 and Supp.).

22 15 U.S.C. § 1640(a)(2)(A).

23 15 U.S.C. § 1640(a)(2)(B).

24 15 U.S.C. § 1635. *See* National Consumer Law Center, Truth in Lending Ch. 10 (7th ed. 2010 and Supp.).

25 15 U.S.C. § 1640(a)(4). *See* National Consumer Law Center, Truth in Lending § 9.6.11 (7th ed. 2010 and Supp.).

26 15 U.S.C. § 1640(a)(3). *See* National Consumer Law Center, Truth in Lending § 11.9 (7th ed. 2010 and Supp.).

27 15 U.S.C. § 1610(a).

28 15 U.S.C. § 1610(b). *See* Tavares v. Sprunk (*In re* Tavares), 298 B.R. 195 (Bankr. D. Mass. 2003) (distinguishing between usury laws, which shield debtors from high interest rates, and TILA and similar state statutes, which provide credit disclosures and enable comparison shopping).

29 *See* Payday Today, Inc. v. Defreeuw, 903 N.E.2d 1057 (Ind. Ct. App. 2009) (disclosure of annualized rate in APR as required by

## 2.2.3 *Federal Rebate Statute*

The federal rebate statute was adopted in 1992 to address the failure of some creditors to make proper rebates of unearned interest when a consumer credit transaction was prepaid, refinanced, or accelerated. It requires that unearned interest be rebated. In addition, for transactions with terms longer than sixty-one months, it requires that a method at least as favorable to the consumer as the actuarial method be used to calculate the rebate. It is discussed in detail at § 5.8.6.1.2, *infra*.

## 2.2.4 *Servicemembers Civil Relief Act*

The Servicemembers Civil Relief Act (formerly titled the Soldiers and Sailors Civil Relief Act) regulates interest rates in some situations. The Act provides that the interest rate on any obligation that was incurred by a person before entering into military service must be reduced to 6%.[30] The rate reduction lasts as long as the person is in active duty, plus, for mortgages, it continues for a year after active duty ends.[31] The interest rate must be reduced on the entire obligation, so both the servicemember and any cosigners are benefited.[32] The creditor can avoid this result by applying to a court for a determination that the debtor's ability to pay a higher rate is not materially affected by military service.

In order to obtain the interest reduction, the sevicemember must, no later than 180 days after release from active duty, give the creditor written notice of his or her entry into active duty and a copy of the relevant order.[33] This requirement also applies to any subsequent orders extending the servicemember's initial call to active duty.

When a creditor lowers the interest rate on a loan the interest must be forgiven, not just deferred.[34] Additionally, the periodic payment due from the servicemember must be reduced by the amount of the forgiven interest; creditors cannot require the same payment but simply apply a greater portion toward principal.[35] Other aspects of the Servicemembers Civil Relief Act are discussed in a different treatise in this series and should be reviewed closely in cases to which the Act may apply.[36]

The 36% cap set by the Talent-Nelson Military Lending Act, described in the following subsection, applies only to certain short-term loans extended to servicemembers *after* they enter active military status and does not affect the limit on interest rates set by the Servicemembers Civil Relief Act for *pre*-active duty obligations.[37] Thus, the 6% cap under the Servicemembers Civil Relief Act will continue to apply to obligations the servicemember incurred *before* active duty began.

## 2.2.5 *Talent-Nelson Military Lending Act*

### 2.2.5.1 Overview

The Talent-Nelson Military Lending Act (MLA), enacted in 2006,[38] imposes a 36% interest rate cap, bans mandatory arbitration, and imposes other restrictions on "consumer credit," other than residential mortgages and purchase money loans, that are extended to active duty members of the military and their dependents. It effectively bans payday loans and auto title loans, as defined by the statute and regulations.

The MLA applies only to an individual who, at the time he or she becomes obligated on a consumer credit transaction, is an active duty member of the armed forces or a dependent of an active duty member.[39] (By contrast, the Servicemembers Civil Relief Act applies to credit taken out *before* an individual enters active duty.[40]) The loan must be made on or after October 1, 2007, the date when both the statute and the regulations issued by the Department of Defense (DOD) went into effect.[41]

### 2.2.5.2 Covered Loans Generally

The main provisions of the Act apply only to "consumer credit" as defined by regulations issued by the Department of Defense (DOD). Those regulations limit "consumer credit" to payday loans, auto title loans, and refund anticipation loans. The MLA does not restrict other kinds of credit. In particular, open-end or purchase money loans of any kind are excluded

TILA did not authorize imposition of interest when contract only provided for single finance charge). *See also* 15 U.S.C. § 1610(d) (except for its provisions regarding rescission, consumer causes of action, and return of goods charged to a credit card, TILA does not affect validity or enforceability of any contract).

30 50 U.S.C. app. § 527; Rodriguez v. American Express, 2006 WL 908613 (E.D. Cal. Apr. 7, 2006) (interest must be reduced as of date servicemember enters military, not as of date of notice of entry to creditor); Cathey v. First Republic Bank, 2001 U.S. Dist. LEXIS 13150 (W.D. La. July 6, 2001) (magistrate's report), *adopted by* 2001 U.S. Dist. LEXIS 13195 (W.D. La. Aug. 13, 2001); Koenig v. Waukesha State Bank, 2006 WL 2334841 (E.D. Wis. Aug. 10, 2006) (noting that "interest" subject to the § 527 limitation includes service charges and late payment fees related to the obligation).

31 50 U.S.C. app. § 527(a)(1)(a).

32 Linscott v. Vector Aerospace, 2006 WL 1310511 (D. Or. May 12, 2006) (applying 6% interest cap to corporation's obligation personally guaranteed by servicemember); Cathey v. First Republic Bank, 2001 U.S. Dist. LEXIS 13150 (W.D. La. July 6, 2001) (magistrate's report), *adopted by* 2001 U.S. Dist. LEXIS 13195 (W.D. La. Aug. 13, 2001).

33 50 U.S.C. app. § 527(b)(1).

34 50 U.S.C. app. § 527(a)(2).

35 50 U.S.C. app. § 527(a)(3).

36 National Consumer Law Center, Collection Actions Ch. 7 (2008 and Supp.).

37 10 U.S.C. § 987(g).

38 Sen. John Warner National Defense Authorization Act (Talent-Nelson Amendment), Pub. L. No. 109-364, § 670, 120 Stat. 2266 (2006) (codified at 10 U.S.C. § 987 (Talent-Nelson Military Lending Act (MLA)).

39 10 U.S.C. § 987(i)(1); 32 C.F.R. § 232.3(c).

40 *See* § 2.2.4, *supra*.

41 72 Fed. Reg. 50,580 (Aug. 31, 2007), *codified at* 32 C.F.R. pt. 232. The final regulations differ little from the draft regulations, issued in April 2007. 72 Fed. Reg. 18,157 (Apr. 11, 2007). DOD did not address the loopholes identified by consumer advocates. *Consumer Groups Disappointed at Draft Regulations on Military Lending Act, Comments Sought*, NCLC REPORTS *Consumer Credit and Usury Ed.* 18 (Mar./Apr. 2007).

from coverage.[42] As discussed below, as a practical matter, payday loans and auto title loans are banned (unless the term of the payday loan exceeds 91 days or the amount financed exceeds $2000, or the term of the auto title loan exceeds 181 days).[43] Thus, of the three kinds of regulated consumer credit—payday loans, refund anticipation loans, and auto title loans—only refund anticipation loans may be made, so the Act's restrictions regarding specific loan terms are relevant only to refund anticipation loans.

A court might find that the regulations' narrow definition of "consumer credit" exceeds DOD's regulatory authority. The statute permits DOD to define "consumer credit" and to impose "criteria or limitations" that DOD determines appropriate.[44] However, the definition and the limitations must be "consistent with the provisions" of the statute.[45] The statute by its terms makes it clear that the drafters had in mind a broader definition of consumer credit than that adopted by DOD.

Congress adopted the MLA in response to the DOD's report on predatory lending targeted at servicemembers. That report covered far more lending than the three narrow classes covered by DOD's regulations. In particular, the report raised concerns about military installment loans, a high-cost, short-term, unsecured form of lending targeted at servicemembers. According to the report, military installment lenders were able to avoid state laws, including state interest caps.[46] Any sensible interpretation of the statute results in the conclusion that Congress meant to cover at least military installment loans in addition to payday loans, auto title loans, and refund anticipation loans.

There are at least three textual bases for believing Congress meant to cover more consumer credit than did the DOD. First, Congress imposed restrictions on covered loans;[47] the restrictions on covered credit make little sense if Congress only intended them to apply to refund anticipation loans as they now do, given DOD's narrow definition of consumer credit and the de facto banning of covered payday loans and auto title loans. Second, Congress forbade states from excluding nonresident servicemembers from coverage under state consumer protection statutes.[48] Again, the expansive wording of this provision makes no sense if Congress was only concerned about protecting servicemembers from refund anticipation loans. And third, Congress included credit insurance premiums in the calculation of the interest cap of 36%.[49] Credit insurance is not a common feature of the only covered loans that may be made under the regulations—refund anticipation loans—but it is a common feature of military installment loans. The exclusion of these loans is inconsistent with the statutory provisions aimed directly at them.

### 2.2.5.3 Covered Payday Loans

The MLA defines a payday loan as "consumer credit" that is subject to the MLA's restrictions only if it includes all of the following elements:

- It is closed-end credit;[50]
- It has a term of 91 days or fewer;[51]
- The amount financed does not exceed $2,000;[52] and
- The borrower, contemporaneously with receipt of funds, provides a check or other payment instrument or debit authorization that is deferred for more than one day.[53]

The 91-day and $2,000 requirements appear to be strict; a 92-day or $2,001 loan is likely exempt. The closed-end requirement is discussed separately below.[54]

An agreement allowing a depository institution to offset fees against deposited funds, consistent with the depository's legal offset rights, is not considered a deferred payment instrument.[55] Thus loans made as advances from bank accounts, such as direct deposit account advances or overdraft loans, are likely not covered, regardless of the interest rate. Moreover, any transaction not considered consumer credit under the Truth in Lending Act (TILA) or not subject to TILA's disclosure requirements (such as an overdraft loan) is excluded.[56]

Payday lenders may manipulate the paperwork in order to avoid the requirement that a deferred check or payment instrument be given "contemporaneously" with the loan proceeds. The regulations do not define "contemporaneously," but the term should certainly cover any agreement that is an integral part of the loan contract, even if the loan proceeds are not paid out immediately.

### 2.2.5.4 Covered Vehicle Title Loans

A vehicle title loan is defined as "consumer credit" that is subject to the MLA's restrictions only if it meets all of the following requirements:

- It is closed-end;
- It has a term of 181 days or less;

42 *See* Goodwin v. H.M. Brown & Assocs., Inc., 2011 WL 820025 (D. Colo. Mar. 2, 2011) (MLA's ban on mandatory arbitration inapplicable because auto loans not covered).

Loans secured by a qualified retirement account or exempt from the TILA's disclosure requirements are also excluded. 10 U.S.C. § 987(i)(6); 32 C.F.R. § 232.3(b)(2).

43 *See* §§ 2.2.5.3, 2.2.5.4, *infra*.

44 10 U.S.C. § 987(h)(2)(D), (E), 987(i)(6).

45 10 U.S.C. § 987(h)(2)(D), (E).

46 Department of Defense, Report on Predatory Lending Practices Directed at Members of the Armed Forces and Their Dependents 18–19, 51–52 (2006), *available at* www.defenselink.mil/pubs/pdfs/Report_to_Congress_final.pdf.

47 10 U.S.C. § 987(e). *See generally* § 2.2.5.7, *infra* (discussing the restrictions).

48 10 U.S.C. § 987(d)(2).

49 10 U.S.C. § 987(i)(4).

50 32 C.F.R. § 232.3(b)(1)(i), *incorporating* 12 C.F.R. § 226.2(a)(10), (20) [§ 1026.2(a)(10), (20)] (TILA definition).

51 32 C.F.R. § 232.3(b)(1)(i).

52 32 C.F.R. § 232.3(b)(1)(i). "Amount financed" is not defined, but is expected to follow the TILA definition. *See* 32 C.F.R. § 232.3(i); 72 Fed. Reg. 50,580 (Aug. 31, 2007).

53 32 C.F.R. § 232.3(b)(1)(i)(B).

54 *See* § 2.2.5.9, *infra*.

55 32 C.F.R. § 232.3(b)(1)(i)(B).

56 32 C.F.R. § 232.3(b)(2)(v).

- It is secured by title to a registered motor vehicle owned by a covered borrower; and
- It is not a purchase-money loan.[57]

The regulations do not define "secured." Any arrangement that allows the lender to acquire the car in the event of default or otherwise use the car to secure repayment should be covered.

Some vehicle title lenders may use a sale-leaseback transaction to attempt to fit within the exemption for purchase money loans. If the borrower previously owned the car, however, a look at the entire transaction will show that the loan was not truly made "to finance the purchase or lease of a motor vehicle" as required under the exemption.[58]

### 2.2.5.5 Covered Refund Anticipation Loans

The regulations define a refund anticipation loan as:

- Closed-end credit
- That is "expressly" repaid with a tax refund.[59]

This definition excludes loans made by tax preparers if the terms of the agreement do not expressly require it to be repaid by the anticipated tax refund. The commentary explains that loans are not covered if the borrower merely notes that the source of the repayment is the tax refund.[60]

### 2.2.5.6 Identification of Covered Members and Dependents; Safe Harbor

The MLA covers credit that is extended to an individual who, at the time he or she becomes obligated, is an active duty member of the military or the spouse, child or dependent of an active duty member.[61] Active duty includes Active Guard and Reserve duty.[62] The member must be serving on active duty under an order or call that does not specify a period of thirty or fewer days.[63] "Dependent" is defined as the member's spouse or child, or an individual for whom the member provided more than one-half of the individual's support for 180 days immediately preceding the credit extension.[64]

The regulations provide a safe harbor to a creditor that unwittingly makes a loan that violates the MLA when the creditor does not realize that the borrower is a covered borrower. To fall within this safe harbor, two conditions must be met. First, the applicant must have signed a statement in the form provided in the regulations stating that he or she is not a covered borrower.[65] Second, the creditor must not have determined, pursuant to an optional verification procedure set forth in the regulation, that any such applicant is a "covered borrower."[66] This safe harbor also applies to renewals or refinancings if the borrower was not a covered borrower at the time of the original credit transaction.[67]

The optional verification procedure to which the safe harbor refers[68] permits creditors to verify military status by a military leave and earning statement, military identification card, military orders, or the military's website. Predatory lenders may argue that the safe harbor applies even if the lender is aware that the borrower's signed statement is false, as long as that knowledge comes from a source other than those specified in the verification procedure. They might argue, for example, that they can ignore the applicant's military uniform, oral disclosure of military status, or provision of a bank statement showing a military direct deposit.

DOD's commentary preceding the regulations states that creditors lose the protection of the safe harbor if the creditor "recognizes the applicant is a covered borrower as a result of the documents presented as part of the credit transaction."[69] The commentary does not indicate that creditors can ignore sources of information other than those in specified in the verification procedure, and states that this caveat to the safe harbor "prevents creditors from using the declaration to allow covered borrowers to waive their right to the protections provided by the regulation."[70] But it may be difficult to pierce this safe harbor if the borrower falsifies his or her status unless it is clear from the documents that the creditor knew or should have known the borrower's status.

### 2.2.5.7 Requirements for Covered Loans

Once a credit transaction is covered by the MLA, several rules apply:

- The military APR (MAPR) may not exceed 36%.[71]
- The credit may not be secured with a check, title to a personal vehicle, access to a financial account, or military allotment, though credit at or under 36% may require electronic payment, direct deposit, or a security interest in funds deposited after and in connection with the credit.[72]
- The MAPR must be disclosed orally and in writing (though it need not be disclosed in advertisements).[73]
- Mandatory arbitration clauses are banned.[74]
- The credit may not be rolled over or renewed except on terms more favorable to the borrower.[75]

57 10 U.S.C. § 987(i)(6); 32 C.F.R. § 232.3(b)(2)(ii).

58 32 C.F.R. § 232.3(b)(2)(ii).

59 32 C.F.R. § 232.3(b)(1)(iii).

60 72 Fed. Reg. 50,580, 50,586 (Aug. 31, 2007).

61 10 U.S.C. § 987(i)(1); 32 C.F.R. § 232.3(c).

62 10 U.S.C. § 987(i)(1)(B).

63 10 U.S.C. § 987(i)(1); 32 C.F.R. § 232.3(c).

64 10 U.S.C. § 987(i)(2); 32 C.F.R. § 232.3(c)(2); 72 Fed. Reg. 18,168 (Apr. 11, 2007).

65 32 C.F.R. § 232.5(a)(1).

66 32 C.F.R. § 232.5(a)(2).

67 32 C.F.R. § 232.5(d).

68 32 C.F.R. § 232.5(b).

69 72 Fed. Reg. 50,580, 50,588 (Aug. 31, 2007).

70 *Id.*

71 10 U.S.C. § 987(b); 32 C.F.R. § 232.4(b).

72 10 U.S.C. § 987(e)(5), (6); 32 C.F.R. § 232.8(a)(5), (6).

73 10 U.S.C. § 987(c); 32 C.F.R. § 232.6.

A toll-free telephone number may be provided for Internet and mail transactions. 32 C.F.R. § 232.6(b)(2). The disclosures must also include a statement about assistance available to servicemembers. 32 C.F.R. § 232.6(a)(4).

74 10 U.S.C. § 987(e)(3), (f)(4); 32 C.F.R. §§ 232.8(a)(3), 232.9(d).

75 10 U.S.C. § 987(e)(1); 32 C.F.R. § 232.8(a)(1).

- Prepayment penalties are banned.[76]
- Waivers of legal rights and onerous notice requirements in case of disputes are banned.[77]

In practice, this list of protections applies only to refund anticipation loans. Payday loans and auto title loans by definition are secured in violation of the MLA; therefore, creditors may not make covered payday or auto title loans to active duty servicemembers or their families.

### 2.2.5.8 Calculating the Cap

The Military Lending Act imposes a 36% cap on the "annual percentage rate of interest." This hybrid term incorporates the Truth in Lending Act (TILA) concept of "annual percentage rate" (APR), but adds in the term "interest," which the statute defines more broadly than the "finance charge" that is used to calculate the TILA APR. The regulations characterize this hybrid APR as the "military annual percentage rate" or MAPR and make clear that it includes charges not in the TILA APR.[78] The MAPR includes the costs specified in the statute and regulations but otherwise is calculated and disclosed following the rules for closed-end credit under the TILA.[79]

The MAPR includes and subjects to the 36% cap the following costs "if they are financed, deducted from the proceeds of the consumer credit, or otherwise required to be paid as a condition of the credit":[80]

- Interest, fees, credit service charges, credit renewal services;[81]
- Credit insurance premiums and debt cancellation or suspension fees;[82]
- Fees for credit-related ancillary products sold in connection with and either at or before consummation of the credit transaction.[83]

The statute also includes a catch-all category of "any other charge or premium with respect to the extension of consumer credit," though this category is not specifically listed in the regulations.

This definition is broader than TILA's APR. The supplementary information accompanying the final regulations makes clear that the MAPR includes "fees associated with origination, membership, administration, or other cost that may not be captured in the TILA definition of APR."[84] Voluntary credit insurance and the cost of ancillary products such as Internet access or catalog sales—regardless of whether they are always included in the TILA APR—are also included in the MAPR definition.[85] Thus, annual or other participation fees, such as a $150 monthly participation fee charged by one payday lender, should be included in the MAPR regardless of how they are treated under TILA. The MAPR may also be broader than state definitions of interest. For example, although Texas does not include broker fees in its definition of interest,[86] such fees should be included in the MAPR as "credit service charges."

The MAPR excludes only the following fees:

- Fees or charges for actual unanticipated late payments or other defaults;[87]
- Legally required taxes or fees paid to public officials related to security interests;[88] and
- Tax return preparation fees.[89]

Predatory lenders may attempt to structure their products to encourage late payments or other defaults, and thus shift the interest costs to late or default fees outside of the 36% cap. Practitioners should examine whether such fees are truly "unanticipated." If the fees were reasonably foreseeable, they should be included in the MAPR.

### 2.2.5.9 Attacking Spurious Open-End Credit

Only closed-end credit is covered by the MLA. Some predatory lenders may try to avoid the MLA by structuring their loans as open-end credit, as they have done in attempting to avoid state usury laws.

The regulations follow TILA's definition of closed-end credit, which is defined as all credit that does not meet TILA's definition of open-end credit. Open-end credit requires a plan that:

- Reasonably contemplates repeated transactions;
- Imposes a finance charge computed from time to time on an outstanding unpaid balance; and
- Provides a replenishable credit line that is reusable without further approvals.[90]

The label of a plan or account is not determinative,[91] and courts have sometimes found credit to be spurious open-end credit.[92] Most case law dealing with spurious open-end credit relates to purchase financing (excluded from the MLA) and may not be especially helpful. Nonetheless, analysis of a loan agreement or usage pattern may show that supposedly open-

76 10 U.S.C. § 987(e)(7); 32 C.F.R. § 232.8(a)(7).
77 10 U.S.C. § 987(e)(2), (3), (4); 32 C.F.R. § 232.8(a)(2), (3), (4).
78 32 C.F.R. § 232.3(h).
79 32 C.F.R. § 232.3(h).
80 32 C.F.R. § 232.3(h)(1).
81 32 C.F.R. § 232.3(h)(1)(i).
82 32 C.F.R. § 232.2(h)(1)(ii).
83 32 C.F.R. § 232.2(h)(1)(iii).
84 72 Fed. Reg. 50,580, 50,587 (Aug. 31, 2007).
85 72 Fed. Reg. 50,580, 50,587 (Aug. 31, 2007).
86 *See* Lovick v. Ritemoney Ltd., 378 F.3d 433 (5th Cir. 2004) (finding that broker fees were not interest under state law).
87 32 C.F.R. § 232.3(h)(2)(i).
88 32 C.F.R. § 232.3(h)(2)(ii), (iii).
89 32 C.F.R. § 232.3(h)(2)(iv).
90 15 U.S.C. § 1602(i); Reg. Z, 12 C.F.R. § 1026.2(a)(20) [§ 226.2(a)(20)]; Reg. Z, Official Commentary § 1026.2(a)(20) [§ 226.2(a)(20)]; National Consumer Law Center, Truth in Lending § 6.2.2 (7th ed. 2010 and Supp.).
91 Reg. Z, Official Commentary § 1026.2(a)(20)-6 [§ 226.2(a)(20)-6].
92 National Consumer Law Center, Truth in Lending § 6.2.3 (7th ed. 2010 and Supp.) (discussing spurious open-end credit under the TILA). *See also* § 3.9.3, *infra* (discussing the distinction between open-end and closed-end credit under usury laws generally).

end payday or auto title loans do not meet the regulatory definition.[93]

The payment structure may make it unlikely that the credit line will be replenished, so that repeat transactions are not reasonably contemplated. Repayments must generally replenish the credit line for the plan to qualify as open-end credit.[94] The borrower may not have full access to the credit line initially or subsequently without new approvals. A credit line is reusable, and thus open-end credit, only if new approvals are not needed.[95] Or the loan may be due in full, or virtually in full, in a finite period of time, so that it is actually a closed-end loan and not a plan permitting a balance that fluctuates, can rise and fall, and can be carried over time.

Payday borrowers returning for new loans may not satisfy the "repeat transactions" requirement for open-end loans. New loans require new approvals and new fees not included in the original credit plan, and are not repeat transactions under an original open-end credit plan.

Refund anticipation lenders should have a hard time using the open-end loophole. If the loan agreement contains an express requirement that the loan will be repaid with the tax refund—a one-time annual event—repeat transactions would not be reasonably contemplated, and the finance charge will not be based on a fluctuating balance over time. Any new credit extensions after repayment of the tax refund are a new loan.

### 2.2.5.10 Enforcement

The DOD expresses a desire for state regulators to assist in enforcing the MLA,[96] and nothing in the MLA preempts them from doing so. Any credit agreement that violates the statute or the regulations is void from its inception.[97] The DOD commentary makes clear that the Department expects this provision to be enforced in private litigation.[98] Both the statute and regulations explicitly preserve other remedies, including contract law claims.[99]

Congress did not include the MLA in the list of enumerated statutes transferred to the newly created Consumer Financial Protection Bureau (CFPB), so regulatory authority over the MLA remains with the DOD.[100] The CFPB is, nevertheless, probably able to enforce the provisions of the MLA under its general UDAAP authority.[101] The CFPB has established an Office of Servicemember Affairs that will work with the DOD to address financial issues affecting servicemembers, including complaints, financial education, and coordinating federal and state consumer protection measures for military families.[102]

### 2.2.5.11 Application of State Protections to Military

The MLA and its regulations preempt only inconsistent state laws and expressly permit state laws that provide greater protection to servicemembers.[103] Thus states are free to adopt laws that target predatory credit excluded from the MLA, to the extent that other laws do not preempt them.

The MLA prohibits states from permitting credit to nonresident servicemembers that would violate state interest caps or consumer lending protections if made to a resident of the state.[104] The impact of this nondiscrimination provision is unclear since the regulations narrowly restrict the definition of covered "consumer credit." However, the nondiscrimination provision in the MLA is not dependent on the adoption of regulations and does not use the term "consumer credit."[105] The definition of "covered member" in the MLA also does not incorporate that term.[106] Further, the nondiscrimination provision in the MLA indicates its broad scope by prohibiting the violation or waiver of "*any* State consumer lending protections" on the basis of nonresident or military status of a covered servicemember.[107] Thus, a plain reading of the statute suggests that Congress intended to give nonresident servicemembers the full benefit of all the consumer lending statutes in the states where the servicemembers happen to find themselves. Accordingly, it appears that the nondiscrimination provision of the statute reaches all credit extended to covered military borrowers, regardless of whether the credit at issue is "consumer credit" within the meaning of the MLA regulations.

## *2.2.6 The Dodd-Frank Act*

### 2.2.6.1 Key Features of the Act

In 2010, Congress dramatically restructured the credit marketplace by enacting the Dodd-Frank Wall Street Reform and Consumer Protection Act (hereinafter the Dodd-Frank Act).[108] The Dodd-Frank Act represents the culmination of a series of hearings that documented the dangers, instability, and need for regulation in the credit marketplace.[109] Among the major features of the Dodd-Frank Act are:

93 National Consumer Law Center, Truth in Lending § 6.2.2 (7th ed. 2010 and Supp.).

94 Reg. Z, Official Commentary § 1026.2(a)(20) [§ 226.2(a)(20)].

95 *See* National Consumer Law Center, Truth in Lending § 6.2.2.4 (7th ed. 2010 and Supp.).

96 72 Fed. Reg. 50,580, 50,589–50,590 (Aug. 31, 2007).

97 10 U.S.C. § 987(f)(3); 32 C.F.R. § 232.9(c).

98 72 Fed. Reg. 50,580, 50,590 (Aug. 31, 2007).

99 10 U.S.C. § 987(f)(2); 32 C.F.R. § 232.9(b).

100 *See* Pub. L. No. 111-203, tit. X, § 1002(12), 124 Stat. 1376 (July 21, 2010) (enumerated consumer laws).

101 *See* § 2.2.6.2, *infra*.

102 Elizabeth Warren, *Welcoming Holly Petraeus to the Consumer Financial Protection Bureau Implementation Team*, White House Blog (Jan. 6, 2011, 5:30 a.m.), www.whitehouse.gov/blog/2011/01/06/welcoming-holly-petraeus-consumer-financial-protection-bureau-implementation-team.

103 10 U.S.C. § 987(d)(1); 32 C.F.R. § 232.7(a).

104 10 U.S.C. § 987(d)(2); 32 C.F.R. § 232.7(b).

105 10 U.S.C. § 987(d)(2); 32 C.F.R. § 232.7(b).

106 10 U.S.C. § 987(i)(1).

107 10 U.S.C. § 987(d)(2); 32 C.F.R. § 232.7(b) (emphasis added).

108 Pub. L. No. 111-203, 124 Stat. 1376 (July 21, 2010) (hereinafter cited as Dodd-Frank).

109 *See, e.g.*, S. 566, 111th Cong. (2009) (proposing a national financial products safety commission); *Modernizing Bank Supervision and Regulations, Parts I & II: Hearing Before the S. Comm. on Banking,*

- Significant narrowing of the authority of federal banking regulators to preempt state law.[110]
- Abolition of the Office of Thrift Supervision and consolidation of oversight of both national banks and federal savings and loan associations in the Office of the Comptroller of the Currency.[111]

Housing, and Urban Affairs*, 111th Cong. (Mar. 2009); *Consumer Protections in Financial Services: Past Problems, Future Solutions: Hearing Before the S. Comm. on Banking, Housing, and Urban Affairs*, 111th Cong. (Mar. 2009); *Federal and State Enforcement of Financial Consumer and Investor Protection Laws: Hearing Before the H. Comm. on Financial Serv.*, 111th Cong. (Mar. 2009); *Staff of the Joint Economic Comm., State by State Figures: Foreclosure and Housing Wealth Losses*, 110th Cong., 2d Sess. (Apr. 2008), *available at* http://www.jec.senate.gov/public/index.cfm?p=StateByStateArchives&ContentRecord_id=392cb915-9c45-fa0d-5a46-f61f6e619381&ContentType_id=efc78dac-24b1-4196-a730-d48568b9a5d7; *Staff of the Joint Economic Comm., State by State Foreclosure Analysis*, 110th Cong., 2d Sess. (Mar. 2008), *available at* http://www.jec.senate.gov/public/index.cfm?p=StateByStateArchives&ContentRecord_id=29b87995-d13a-3419-d0f6-c6338f111706&ContentType_id=efc78dac-24b1-4196-a730-d48568b9a5d7; *Staff of the Joint Economic Comm., The Subprime Lending Crisis: The Economic Impact on Wealth, Property Values and Tax Revenues, and How We Got Here*, 110th Cong., 1st Sess. (2007), *available at* http://www.jec.senate.gov/archive/Documents/Reports/10.25.07OctoberSubprimeReport.pdf; *Staff of the Joint Economic Comm., Sheltering Neighborhoods from the Subprime Foreclosure Storm*, 110th Cong., 1st Sess. (2007), *available at* http://www.jec.senate.gov/archive/Documents/Reports/subprime11apr2007revised.pdf; *Subprime Mortgage Market Turmoil: Examining the Role of Securitization: Hearings Before the Senate Comm. on Banking, Housing, and Urban Development*, 110th Cong., 1st Sess. (2007), *available at* http://banking.senate.gov/public/index.cfm?FuseAction=Hearings.Hearing&Hearing_ID=a14998f7-0b7d-4deb-8e2b-ce11fa95d79f; *Preserving the American Dream: Predatory Lending Practices and Home Foreclosures: Hearings Before the Senate Comm. on Banking, Housing, and Urban Development*, 110th Cong., 1st Sess. (2007), *available at* http://banking.senate.gov/public/index.cfm?FuseAction=Hearings.Hearing&Hearing_ID=2053fdd2-9832-4731-802d-fa9c18772267; *Mortgage Market Turmoil: Causes and Consequences: Hearings Before the Senate Comm. on Banking, Housing, and Urban Development*, 110th Cong., 1st Sess. (2007), *available at* http://banking.senate.gov/public/index.cfm?FuseAction=Hearings.Hearing&Hearing_ID=4ccca4e6-b9dc-40b1-bab5-137b3a77364d; *Possible Responses to Rising Mortgage Foreclosures: Hearings Before the House Comm. on Financial Services*, 110th Cong., 1st Sess. (2007), *available at* www.house.gov/apps/list/hearing/financialsvcs_dem/ht041707.shtml; *Subprime and Predatory Mortgage Lending: New Regulatory Guidance, Current Market Conditions and Effects on Regulated Financial Institutions: Hearings Before the House Comm. on Financial Services*, 110th Cong., 1st Sess. (2007), *available at* www.house.gov/apps/list/hearing/financialsvcs_dem/ht032707.shtml; *Foreclosure, Predatory Mortgage and Payday Lending in America's Cities Hearings Before the Domestic Policy Subcomm. of the House Comm. on Oversight and Government Reform*, 110th Cong., 1st Sess. (2007), *available at* http://oversight.house.gov/story.asp?ID=1218. *Cf.* S. 500, 111th Cong. (2009) (proposing federal usury limit for all consumer credit transactions).

110 *See* § 3.2, *infra*; Arthur E. Wilmarth, Jr., *The Dodd-Frank Act's Expansion of State Authority to Protect Consumers of Financial Services*, 36 J. Corp. L., Issue 4 (2011).

111 12 U.S.C. § 5411–5413. *See* §§ 3.1.2.2, *infra*.

- Addition to the Truth in Lending Act of a host of substantive restrictions on mortgage loan and servicing abuses, discussed in detail elsewhere in this series.[112]
- Expansion of the Truth in Lending Act's scope and remedies.[113]
- Expansion of the enforcement authority of state attorneys general and banking regulators.[114]
- Creation of the Consumer Financial Protection Bureau (CFPB), with authority to write rules prohibiting unfair, deceptive, and abusive practices.[115]
- Transfer of rulemaking authority under a number of key federal statutes such as the Truth in Lending Act from a variety of other agencies to the CFPB.[116]

The CFPB also has authority to ban mandatory arbitration clauses after conducting a study.[117] The CFPB does not, however, have authority to impose a usury cap.[118]

### 2.2.6.2 CFPB and FTC UDAAP Rulemaking Authority

The Dodd-Frank Act gives the CFPB authority to write rules to prevent unfair, deceptive, or abusive acts or practices (UDAAP authority) in connection with a broad array of consumer financial products and services.[119]

The Act's definition of "unfair" incorporates the definition found in the FTC Act:

> (A) the act or practice causes or is likely to cause substantial injury to consumers which is not reasonably avoidable by consumers; and
>
> (B) such substantial injury is not outweighed by countervailing benefits to consumers or to competition.[120]

The meaning and interpretation of this standard is discussed in detail at § 4.3.2, *infra*. The Act provides that the CFPB may consider established public policies in determining whether an act or practice is unfair, but public policy cannot be the primary basis for a determination.[121]

The Act does not include a definition of "deception," but the FTC[122] and a large body of decisions under state UDAP statutes

112 *See* National Consumer Law Center, Truth in Lending Ch. 9 (7th ed. 2010 and Supp.) (full discussion of these provisions).

113 *See* National Consumer Law Center, Truth in Lending Chs. 2, 9, 11 (7th ed. 2010 and Supp.) (full discussion of these provisions).

114 *See* Lauren Saunders, National Consumer Law Center, The Role of the States under the Dodd-Frank Wall Street Reform and Consumer Protection Act of 2010 (Dec. 2010), *available at* www.nclc.org; National Consumer Law Center, Unfair and Deceptive Acts and Practices § 15.1a (2011 Supp.).

115 *See* § 2.2.6.2, *infra*.

116 12 U.S.C. §§ 5481(12), 5512.

117 12 U.S.C. § 5518.

118 12 U.S.C. § 5517(o).

119 *Id.* § 5531. Products and services covered by the Act are generally set forth in 12 U.S.C. § 5481(15).

120 12 U.S.C. § 5531(c)(1).

121 12 U.S.C. § 5531(c)(2).

122 *See In re* Cliffdale Assocs., Inc., 103 F.T.C. 110 (1984) (including, in an appendix, an analysis of the meaning of deception).

have refined and applied this term.[123]

The Act's grant of authority over abusive acts and practices does not have a counterpart in the FTC Act. To ban an act as abusive, the CFPB must find that the act or practice:

(1) materially interferes with a consumer's ability to understand a term or condition of a consumer financial product or service; or
(2) takes unreasonable advantage of—
  (A) a consumer's lack of understanding of the material risks, costs, or conditions of the product or service;
  (B) a consumer's inability to protect his or her own interests when selecting or using a product or service; or
  (C) the consumer's reliance on a covered person.[124]

The CFPB's rulemaking authority extends to virtually everyone in the financial services area, including banks, credit unions, mortgage lenders, credit bureaus, auto finance companies, debt collectors, student lenders, and payday lenders. Most dealers of automobiles, motorcycles, boats, recreational vehicles, and motor homes are exempt and stay under FTC authority, however.[125] Effective July 21, 2011, the FTC gained streamlined authority to write rules preventing unfair or deceptive practices by dealers exempted from the CFPB's jurisdiction.[126] The FTC also retains enforcement power over these dealers.

Certain credit from "merchants, retailers or sellers" is also exempt from the CFPB's UDAAP jurisdiction (but not from its authority under certain enumerated consumer protection statutes such as the Truth in Lending Act). To be exempt, the credit must be offered by the merchant directly, for its own nonfinancial good or service; must not be assigned or conveyed; cannot exceed the market value of the good or service or be used as an evasion; and must be offered by a merchant who does not regularly extend credit subject to a finance charge, unless the merchant is a small business or does not significantly engage in offering consumer financial products or services.[127]

The CFPB lacks UDAAP authority over insurers, including credit insurers, but has authority over lenders who offer or sell such insurance. Less clear is whether it has UDAAP rulemaking authority over rent-to-own transactions.[128]

The CFPB has the authority to issue UDAAP rules applicable to attorneys who offer or provide "consumer financial products or services."[129] This term is defined to include not just extensions of credit but also credit counseling, debt management, debt settlement, loan modification, foreclosure avoidance, and debt collection.[130] Nonetheless, the CFPB cannot enforce UDAAP rules against attorneys for conduct that constitutes the practice of law and occurs exclusively within the scope of the attorney-client relationship with a consumer.[131] It can enforce UDAAP rules against attorneys if the consumer is not the attorney's client.

While the CFPB, federal banking regulators, state attorneys general, and state banking regulators share enforcement authority,[132] the Dodd-Frank Act does not provide a private cause of action for violations of CFPB UDAAP rules.[133] But UDAP or other state causes of action may be available.[134] The Dodd-Frank Act also makes it unlawful "to offer or provide to a consumer any financial product or service not in conformity with Federal consumer financial law" (including CFPB rules).[135] Illegality is generally a defense to a contract,[136] and consumers may be able to assert this defense to void or enjoin enforcement of non-conforming agreements.

The effective date of the CFPB's UDAAP rulemaking authority is somewhat unclear. It is part of Title X of the Act, which became effective on July 21, 2011.[137] However, the Act also gave the Treasury Department the temporary authority to exercise the CFPB's authority until a permanent CFPB director was appointed.[138] A strained reading of the details of this provision has led some to conclude that the CFPB could not exercise UDAAP rulemaking authority until a permanent director was appointed.[139] In any event, a permanent director was

123 *See generally* National Consumer Law Center, Unfair and Deceptive Acts and Practices § 4.2 (7th ed. 2008 and Supp.).

124 12 U.S.C. § 5531(d).

125 *Id.* § 5519. The exemption for motor vehicle dealers does not extend to dealers that retain financing or sell or assign financing to a related entity, such as many buy-here, pay-here dealers. *See id.* § 5519(b)(2). However, such dealers are likely exempt through the merchant exception, discussed below, if they are a small business.

126 The FTC generally must follow the lengthy and cumbersome "Magnuson-Moss" procedures when writing rules, but for motor vehicle dealers it now can use the more streamlined Administrative Procedure Act process.

127 12 U.S.C. § 5517(a).

128 Rent-to-own transactions likely do not fall within the definition of leases subject to the CFPB's jurisdiction, 12 U.S.C. § 5481(15)(A)(2), though the CFPB does have jurisdiction if rent-to-own transactions are considered credit. Notably, the Dodd-Frank Act defines the term "credit" more broadly than the TILA definition at 15 U.S.C. § 1602(e). In addition, TILA's restrictive definition of "creditor" (15 U.S.C. § 1602(f)) is not carried over into the Dodd-Frank Act.

129 12 U.S.C. §§ 5481(6) (definition of "covered person"), 5481(15) (definition of "financial product or service"), 5517(e) (exception for practice of law), 5531 (general authority to adopt UDAAP rules for "covered persons").

130 *Id.* § 5481(15)(A)(viii), (x).

131 *Id.* § 5517(e)(2).

132 *See* Lauren Saunders, National Consumer Law Center, The Role of the States under the Dodd-Frank Wall Street Reform and Consumer Protection Act of 2010 (Dec. 2010), *available at* www.nclc.org.

133 *See* National Consumer Law Center, Consumer Banking and Payments Law § 8.2.5 (4th ed. 2009 and Supp.) (discussing difficulties of implying private cause of action to enforce federal statutes and rules).

134 *See In re* TJX Companies Retail Sec. Breach Litig., 564 F.3d 489 (1st Cir. 2009) (finding FTC guidelines and consent decrees instructive as to whether conduct is unfair under Massachusetts law). *See generally* National Consumer Law Center, Unfair and Deceptive Acts and Practices § 3.4.5 (7th ed. 2008 and Supp.).

135 12 U.S.C. § 5536(a)(1)(A).

136 *See, e.g.*, Rugemer v. Rhea, 957 P.2d 184, 187 n.1 (Or. Ct. App. 1998) ("Illegal contracts may be rescinded by the party not at fault.").

137 12 U.S.C. § 5301 note; Dodd-Frank § 4.

138 12 U.S.C. § 5586.

139 *See* National Consumer Law Center, Issue Brief: The CFPB Received Its Full Power on July 21, 2011—Challengers to Recess

appointed on January 4, 2012.[140] Since the CFPB did not issue any UDAAP rules prior to that date, the question whether it could have issued such rules before then is academic.

### 2.2.7 Credit Practices Rule

The Credit Practices Rule Rule[141] restricts several credit terms:

- Confessions of judgment, *cognovits*, and other waivers of the right to notice and opportunity to be heard in the event of suit;
- Waiver of exemptions from execution on personal or real property, such as waiver of a homestead exemption, unless the waiver applies only to property that is the subject of a security interest granted in that credit transaction;
- Most irrevocable wage assignments;
- Non-purchase money security interests in certain household goods;
- Pyramiding late charges by assessing more than one delinquency charge for one late payment (pyramiding late charges for a *missed* payment is not prohibited); and
- Failure to provide cosigners with a specified warning indicating the potential obligations of a cosigner.

These prohibitions are discussed in detail in National Consumer Law Center, *Unfair and Deceptive Acts and Practices* § 6.11 (7th ed. 2008 and Supp.).

The FTC's version of the rule applies to lenders and retail installment sellers who extend credit to consumers.[142] Lease-purchase contracts are included as long as the consumer is obligated to pay a specified amount and is permitted to become the owner of the property for little or no additional consideration.[143]

The FTC rule applies to finance companies, retailers, and other creditors within the FTC's jurisdiction, but does not apply to most banks. Nevertheless, the Office of the Comptroller of the Currency (OCC) and the Federal Reserve Board (FRB) have adopted analogous rules for savings and loan institutions[144] and for all other banks,[145] respectively. (The OCC rule was formerly issued by the Office of Thrift Supervision (OTS) until it was abolished in 2011 by the Dodd-Frank Act). Credit unions are covered by a comparable rule adopted by the National Credit Union Administration (NCUA).[146]

While the rules enacted by these other agencies closely track the FTC rule, there are a number of differences. For example, while the FTC rule is silent on its applicability to real estate loans, the FRB and OCC/OTS rules do not apply to credit extended for the purchase of real property. The FRB and OCC/OTS rules, however, do apply to credit extended to improve a home or to purchase a manufactured home deemed to be personalty under state law. The NCUA, OCC/OTS and FRB rules also give the creditor the added option of including the cosigner notice in the contract and not just in a separate document, and of modifying the notice in some respects. In addition, the definition of "cosigner" and "household goods" have been clarified and limited. The FRB and OCC/OTS rules do not prohibit certain types of cognovits, and the FRB rule allows refinancing of purchase money loans without losing their purchase money characterization.

The most important difference is that the FRB, OCC/OTS and NCUA rules only prohibit banks and credit unions from entering into credit agreements containing or enforcing the prohibited creditor remedies. The FRB, OCC/OTS and NCUA rules do not prohibit a bank or credit union from purchasing consumer credit agreements containing the prohibited terms as long as the financial entity does not enforce the prohibited creditor remedy.

## 2.3 State Statutes Regulating Credit

### 2.3.1 Introduction

Until the 1980s, state law was the primary source of regulation of non-mortgage consumer credit. The wave of deregulation that began in the 1980s, coupled with the expansion of federal preemption, significantly reduced the impact of state law. Nonetheless, state law is still the primary source of regulation of non-mortgage credit that is not extended by a federally related lender. State law is particularly important in its application to motor vehicle finance and predatory fringe lenders.[147]

The structure of credit statutes in many states today is a general usury ceiling riddled with statutory exceptions for particular creditors or transactions. These statutory exceptions are known as "special" usury laws because of their individually limited scopes. However, special usury laws have proliferated to such an extent that to view them as exceptions to a general usury ceiling is misleading. Today, the average credit transaction is governed, if at all, by a special usury statute. Indeed, to some extent, special usury statutes have replaced general usury laws.[148]

Appointment May Be Kicked Out of Court (Feb. 2, 2012), *available at* http://www.nclc.org/issues/regulatory-reform.html.

140 http://www.whitehouse.gov/the-press-office/2012/01/04/president-obama-announces-recess-appointments-key-administration-posts.

141 16 C.F.R. pt. 444.

142 16 C.F.R. § 444.1. The prohibition against pyramiding of late charges applies to collection of these extensions of credit. *See* 16 C.F.R. § 444.4.

143 16 C.F.R. § 444.1(b). *See* Green, FTC Informal Staff Opinion Letter (Mar. 16, 1985) (rule covers lease-purchase contracts where consumer is obligated to pay specified amount and is permitted to become owner of the property for little or no additional consideration).

144 Former 12 C.F.R. § 535.

145 12 C.F.R. § 227.11–227.16.

146 12 C.F.R. § 706.

147 *See, e.g.*, Cash America Net of Nev., L.L.C. v. Commw., Dep't of Banking, 8 A.3d 282 (Pa. 2010) (applying state general usury law and small loan act to payday lender).

148 *See* Christopher L. Peterson, *Usury Law, Payday Loans, and Statutory Sleight of Hand: Salience Distortion of American Credit Pricing Limits*, 92 Minn. L. Rev. 1110 (Apr. 2008) (arguing that the enactment of the small loan laws eroded the consensus for a uniform and relatively low usury cap); § 1.2.5, *infra* (discussing survival of special usury statutes after general usury statutes were largely dismantled during the 1980s).

Some states have attempted to consolidate the rules into one, presumably simplified statute. The most widely recognized attempt at such simplification is the Uniform Consumer Credit Code (UCCC), forms of which have been adopted in approximately ten states.[149] However, while such codes are more clearly written and internally consistent than the statutes they replace, they nevertheless maintain preexisting distinctions between creditors or loan types as often as they abolish them. Furthermore, state attempts at simplification are inherently limited because they cannot untangle overlapping state and federal regulation.

The deregulation wave that began in the 1980s affected state consumer credit statutes in two ways. First, a number of states simply repealed statutory restrictions on consumer credit. Often this was accomplished by replacing a state interest rate ceiling with a provision allowing any rate to which the parties agreed.[150] Second, federal preemption enabled many lenders to avoid state consumer credit statutes. For example, national banks could locate in low-regulation states and export credit to other states without regard to restrictions in effect in the borrower's home state.[151] The Office of the Comptroller of the Currency also asserted authority to preempt other state restrictions on credit terms as applied to national banks, federal savings associations, and their subsidiaries. The Office of Thrift Supervision went even farther and asserted authority to occupy "the entire field of lending regulation for federal savings associations."[152] The 2010 Dodd-Frank Act cut back significantly on federal preemption, leaving a greater scope for state law. These preemption issues are discussed in detail at Chapter 3, *infra*.

## 2.3.2 General and Criminal Usury Laws

English usury statutes were adopted by the American colonies prior to independence.[153] Variations on these statutes remain in effect to this day in many states, and are commonly referred to as "general" usury laws because they purport to set a ceiling for all loans of money in a jurisdiction, not just for particular types of lenders or credit transactions. In a few states the state constitution contains a general usury cap.

Some but not all states have criminal usury laws. These laws typically criminalize the charging of interest above a relatively high cap, such as 25%.[154] Some states, when deregulating their civil usury statutes, nonetheless retained their criminal usury ceilings, which may act as an outer limit on high-cost credit.[155]

With very few exceptions, general usury laws were the only statutes regulating credit costs in the United States prior to the twentieth century. At that point, states began to adopt "special" usury statutes, such as the small loan laws, industrial loan laws, and installment loan laws discussed in the next subsections. Special usury statutes create exceptions to the general usury law for specific classes of transactions. They typically allow a higher rate of interest, but impose other restrictions such as limits on the loan term, the amount, and the type of security.

## 2.3.3 Small Loan Laws and Their Progeny

Small loan laws were first adopted in the early twentieth century in response to the widespread problem of loan sharking. They were largely the product of the research and promotional efforts of the Russell Sage Foundation. Between 1916 and 1942, the Russell Sage Foundation published seven drafts of a Uniform Small Loan Law. This uniform law was widely adopted by the states, and language from the uniform statute appears in numerous consumer finance statutes today.[156]

Small loan laws were designed to drive loan sharks out of business by making it profitable for regular business enterprises to make small loans to individuals.[157] The uniform law created a class of licensed lenders that, in return for compliance with requirements regarding such matters as bookkeeping, security interests, and collection practices, were authorized to issue loans of less than $300 at interest rates in the neighborhood of 3% per month or 60% per annum.[158] The uniform law strictly

149 Some other states adopted portions of the U.C.C.C. and another model act, the National Consumer Act. *See* § 2.3.10, *infra*.

150 *See* §§ 1.2.5, *supra*, 7.6, *infra*.

151 *See* § 3.4, *infra*.

152 12 C.F.R. § 560.2(a) (2010).

153 *See generally* Christopher L. Peterson, *Usury Law, Payday Loans, and Statutory Sleight of Hand: Salience Distortion of American Credit Pricing Limits*, 92 Minn. L. Rev. 1110 (Apr. 2008) (discussing the adoption of the Statute of Anne by the colonies and the usury statutes in existence at independence).

154 *See* Appx. A, *infra*.

155 *See* Yaldu v. Bank of Am. Corp., 700 F. Supp. 2d 832, 846–847 (E.D. Mich. 2010) (recognizing that 25% criminal usury cap remains in effect after adoption of agreed rate provision for first mortgage loans); Lawyers Title Ins. Corp. v. Wells, 881 So. 2d 668 (Fla. Dist. Ct. App. 2004) (criminal usury statute made debt unenforceable so lender had no insurable interest in it and title insurer was not obliged to cover it); Nelson v. Associates Fin. Servs. Co. of Ind., Inc., 659 N.W.2d 635, 641–642 (Mich. Ct. App. 2002) (25% criminal usury cap continues to apply to first mortgage loans after deregulation); Perez v. Rent-A-Center, 892 A.2d 1255, 1270–1272 (N.J. 2006) (criminal usury statute continues to act as cap on retail installment contracts after deregulation); People v. Farrell, 630 N.Y.S.2d 791 (N.Y. App. Div. 1995) (upholding criminal usury conviction; terms at issue 3% weekly). *See also* Leah A. Plunkett & Ana Lucia Hurtado, *Small Dollar Loans, Big Problems: How States Protect Consumers from Abuses and How the Federal Government Can Help*, 44 Suffolk U. L. Rev. 31 (2011) (state-by-state report on interest rate caps on payday loans and other small-dollar extensions of credit).

156 An invaluable source of information about the interpretation of small loan laws is Hubachek, Annotations on Small Loan Laws (Russell Sage Found. 1938). *See also* Curran, Trends in Consumer Credit Legislation (1966); Hubachek, *The Development of Regulatory Small Loan Laws*, 8 Law & Contemp. Prob. 108 (1941).

157 *See* Austin v. Alabama Check Cashers Ass'n, 2005 Ala. LEXIS 197, at *30–35 (Ala. Nov. 18, 2005) (discussing the history and purpose of small loan laws); Berger v. State Dep't of Revenue, 910 P.2d 581 (Alaska 1996); Beneficial New York, Inc. v. Stewart, 884 N.Y.S.2d 643, 645 (N.Y. Sup. Ct. 2009) (discussing the tension between "the virtually limitless opportunity conferred upon licensed lenders to extract exorbitant rates of interest" and the desire to encourage responsible lending to borrowers "who may pose repayment risks.").

158 Later drafts of the uniform law authorized split rates under which the interest rate applied to the first $100 of the outstanding balance

limited the charges or fees other than interest that a lender could assess, and provided harsh penalties, including loss of principal, for statutory violations.[159]

The original small loan laws have been substantially modified in many states. Most significantly, the size of the loan to which these laws apply has been greatly increased, in many states to $25,000 or more.[160] Other states have authorized discount or add-on interest calculation methods,[161] which were prohibited by the uniform law. Finally, small loan laws have sometimes been combined with industrial loan laws and other credit statutes, and have been renamed "consumer finance" laws.

In some states, small loan laws have the effect of prohibiting high-rate payday and auto title loans.[162] However, lenders have convinced some state legislatures to enact special legislation permitting payday or auto title lending to operate outside the restraints of the small loan law.[163]

Because small loan laws were based on a uniform statute, the terminology employed in the modern small loan and consumer finance statutes of different states may be similar or identical. Practitioners interested in the interpretation of particular provisions of these statutes may be able to find precedent in the decisions of courts in other states.

### *2.3.4 Industrial Loan Laws*

Industrial loan laws are special usury statutes which, like the small loan laws, were first enacted to attract credit to a consumer market dominated by loan sharks. However, instead of straightforwardly raising interest rates for licensed lenders as the small loan laws did, the industrial loan laws raised yields on consumer loans by authorizing mathematical subterfuge.[164] In particular, industrial loan laws adopted "Morris Plan" banking, under which a prospective borrower and a lender entered into supposedly separate loan and investment contracts. The loan would be repayable in one lump sum at the end of an agreed-upon term, and interest would be deducted in advance. Simultaneously, the borrower would make periodic deposits, pursuant to the investment agreement, which would total the amount of the lump sum when the loan came due. Industrial "banks" were thus authorized, in effect, to charge discount interest[165] at the general usury ceiling. Separate service charges, apart from the stated interest, were also permitted by most industrial loan laws.[166]

Industrial bank acts were adopted in only about half of the states. The development of industrial banks was limited by competition from small loan lenders and by commercial banks, especially in states that did not authorize industrial banks to accept demand deposits.[167] Nevertheless, industrial banks became established in many states as consumer lenders able to offer loans above the small loan limits.

Seven states have active industrial loan company charters.[168] Operating under charters granted in those seven states, industrial loan companies now engage in a wide spectrum of consumer lending across the United States, including automotive, retail, and credit card lending.[169] To the uninitiated, an industrial loan company can look identical to a mainstream lender, although the regulatory structure is usually quite different. The main reason for the continued existence of industrial loan companies is that industrial loan companies are the only financial institution that can currently be owned and controlled by another entity whose primary business is not financial.[170]

---

may exceed the rate charged on the remainder of the principal balance. *See* § 5.3.4, *infra.*

159 *See* § 7.8, *infra.*

160 *See, e.g.,* Beneficial New York, Inc. v. Stewart, 884 N.Y.S.2d 643, 645 (N.Y. Sup. Ct. 2009) (discussing history of New York's act and $25,000 cap).

161 These methods enable a creditor to understate, relative to an actuarial calculation such as the Truth in Lending Act's "APR," the interest rate it is charging. *See* §§ 5.3.1–5.3.3, 5.4, *infra.*

162 *See, e.g.,* NCAS of Del., L.L.C. v. Pa. Dep't of Banking, 948 A.2d 752 (Pa. 2008); Leah A. Plunkett & Ana Lucia Hurtado, *Small Dollar Loans, Big Problems: How States Protect Consumers from Abuses and How the Federal Government Can Help*, 44 Suffolk U. L. Rev. 31 (2011) (listing the permissible APR on a typical small loan of six months and a year, payday loan, and title loan).

163 *See, e.g.,* Cash in a Flash, Inc. v. McCullough, 853 N.E.2d 533, 536–537 (Ind. Ct. App. 2006) (legislature enacted a small loan act to permit payday lending not subject to interest rate caps imposed on other consumer loans); Steven M. Graves & Christopher L. Peterson, *Usury Law and the Christian Right: Faith-Based Political Power and the Geography of American Payday Loan Regulation*, 57 Cath. U. L. Rev. 637 (Spring 2008) (discussing legislation authorizing payday lending in Alabama and Mississippi that has higher effective caps than the state's small loan laws). *See generally* Chs. 9, 11, *infra.*

164 *See* 1 Consumer Credit Guide (CCH) ¶ 560 (industrial loan laws and the variations among the states' laws).

165 *See* § 5.3.3, *infra* (discussing discount interest).

166 *See* § 7.5.4.3, *infra* (discussing the usury law distinctions between "interest" and "other charges").

167 Under federal law, industrial banks cannot accept demand deposits. 12 U.S.C. § 1841(c)(2)(H)(I). Nonetheless, they may offer nonbusiness NOW (negotiable order of withdrawal) accounts—checking accounts that retain the legal right to require advance notice of the withdrawal, which allows them to function very much like a bank when they choose to. 12 U.S.C. § 1832.

168 The seven states are California, Colorado, Hawaii, Indiana, Minnesota, Nevada, and Utah. *Advisory Committee on Banking and Policy, Industrial Loan Companies* (Feb. 26, 2009), *available at* http://www.fdic.gov/about/learn/advisorycommittee/ilc060204.html.

169 Among the present day industrial loan companies (ILCs) are automotive lenders (BMW), retailers (Target), and credit card lenders (American Express). All of these are chartered in Utah, which has the most active ILCs of any state. Gov't Accountability Office, Industrial Loan Corporations: Recent Asset Growth and Commercial Interest Highlight Differences in Regulatory Authority 19 (2005), *available at* www.gao.gov/new.items/d05621.pdf. A list of Utah chartered industrial banks is available at www.dfi.utah.gov/IBSList.htm; a list by asset size as of December 2004 is in the Economic Development Corporation of Utah's report on industrial banks. Economic Development Corp. of Utah, Utah Industrial Banks Profile 3 (2005), *available at* www.edcutah.org/documents/UtahDataCenterIndustry_052611.pdf.

170 12 U.S.C. § 1841(c)(2)(H).

### 2.3.5 Installment Loan Laws

Installment loan laws are a diverse collection of statutes that authorize banks, and frequently other lenders, to issue standard installment-payment loans at interest rates higher than those authorized by the general usury statute.[171] Installment loan laws have usually been constructed to allow banks to make loans similar to those made by small loan lenders, industrial banks, credit unions, or other lenders with statutory authority to lend at rates above the general usury ceiling. For example, some installment loan statutes apply only to credit below a stated principal amount or to loans with terms of less than five or ten years. Installment loan statutes also focus on interest calculation methods that might give competing lenders undue advantages. For example, they frequently authorize the use of add-on or discount interest and address the rebate issues that arise when such precomputed loans are prepaid.

Although installment loan laws may be seen primarily as a special usury law for banks, other lenders may be covered as well. Typically, these other lenders are savings and loan associations or thrifts, mutual savings banks, or other state-regulated creditors that do not have their own special usury statutes.

A danger of installment loan laws is the possibility that they may be used by any lender to avoid the general usury ceiling, thus creating a significant usury exception. For example, payday lenders in Illinois avoided that state's payday loan law by operating under the installment loan law until that loophole was closed in 2010.[172] In order to take advantage of an installment loan law, the lender must comply with its requirements regarding such matters as equal periodic payments, rebates upon prepayment, other credit terms, and disclosure; if it does not, the general usury law's rate caps and remedies are likely to apply.

### 2.3.6 Retail Installment Sales Acts

Retail installment sales acts (RISAs) were adopted by most states in the 1940s and 1950s. These statutes regulate traditional fixed-term credit sales of consumer goods, which, prior to the adoption of these statutes, had generally been free from interest ceilings due to the time-price doctrine.[173] In general, these statutes only cover financing extended by sellers and do not cover loans made directly by third-party lenders.[174]

171 *See* 1 Consumer Credit Guide (CCH) ¶ 570 (installment loan laws and the variations among them); Appx. A, *infra*. *See also* Tom Feltner & Sarah Duda, Woodstock Inst., Beyond Payday Loans: Consumer Installment Lending in Illinois (2009) (documenting the types of lending done under Illinois' Consumer Installment Loan Act, ranging from near-payday lending to used car loans and personal lines of credit).

172 Ill. Pub. Act 96-936, H.B. 537, 2010 Ill. Legis. Serv. 96-936 (West) (amending 205 Ill. Comp. Stat. 670/1 to 670/24.5 (2000) and 815 Ill. Comp. Stat. 122/1-10).

173 *See* §§ 1.2.4, *supra*, 7.5.2.2, *infra* (discussing the time-price doctrine).

174 *See, e.g.*, Asset Acceptance, L.L.C. v. Witten, 2008 WL 2837304 (Ohio Ct. App. July 24, 2008). *See generally* §§ 1.5.1, *supra*, 3.9.4, *infra*.

The scope of RISAs varies significantly from state to state.[175] Some RISAs cover the installment sale of all goods or services. Some cover only goods. Frequently a state will have special RISAs which apply exclusively to the credit sale of particular kinds of goods such as motor vehicles or manufactured homes. A few states have special RISA-type statutes for home improvement transactions.[176] States that have enacted special motor vehicle RISAs may or may not have parallel statutes that govern the credit sale of all other goods or services. Many states exempt rent-to-own transactions from RISA coverage on the pretext that they are not credit sales.[177]

The substance of RISAs also varies among the states. Generally, all RISAs emphasize the disclosure of contract terms and the need to inform purchasers of their legal rights. They require all credit sale contracts to be written and, usually, to contain an itemization of charges. However, other RISA provisions are less consistent between jurisdictions. Most motor vehicle RISAs establish maximum rates for interest charges and frequently authorize add-on interest calculations. RISAs governing the credit sale of "other goods," however, often contain no rate ceiling. Most RISAs do address late charges, prepayment rights, insurance disclosures, and penalties for statutory violations. Some RISAs also limit co-signor liability or require a special notice to co-signors.[178] Other RISAs prohibit the taking of a security interest in property other than the goods sold or serviced.[179]

Appendix C, *infra* summarizes state RISAs, and they are discussed in detail at Chapter 10, *infra*.

175 *See* 1 Consumer Credit Guide (CCH) ¶ 520 (cataloging the state RISAs). *Cf.* Williams v. Empire Funding Corp., 109 F. Supp. 2d 352 (E.D. Pa. 2000) (interpreting the conflicting cancellation rights of Truth in Lending and Pa. home improvement financing statute); Gonzalez v. Old Kent Mortgage Co., 2000 U.S. Dist. LEXIS 14530 (E.D. Pa. Sept. 19, 2000) (applying Pa. statute to home improvement loan); *In re* Barber, 266 B.R. 309 (Bankr. E.D. Pa. 2001) (applying state statute to home improvement loan); Westside Health & Racquet Club, Inc. v. Jefferson Fin. Servs., Inc., 19 S.W.3d 796 (Tenn. Ct. App. 1999) (applying Tennessee RISA to member contracts with health spa).

176 Fla. Stat. §§ 520.60 to 520.98; Mich. Comp. Laws §§ 445.1101 to 445.1431; N.J. Stat. Ann §§ 17:16C-62 to 17:16C-94 (West); 73 Pa. Stat. Ann. §§ 501-101 to 501-602 (West); Tenn. Code Ann. § 45-3-705.

AARP has published a model home improvement finance law. Margot Saunders & Elizabeth Renuart, AARP Public Policy Institute Publication # D1765, Home Improvement Financing: A Model State Law (Oct. 2000), *available at* http://research.aarp.org.

177 *But see* Perez v. Rent-A-Center, Inc., 892 A.2d 1255 (N.J. 2006) (holding that New Jersey's RISA applies to rent-to-own contracts). *See generally* § 12.3.2.2, *infra*.

178 Lee v. Nationwide Cassell, L.P., 675 N.E.2d 599 (Ill. 1996) (holding co-signor liable under Illinois law only if he or she has physically received the car or is a parent or spouse of the buyer).

179 *E.g.*, Ohio Rev. Code Ann. § 1317.071 (West); Parker Fin. v. Matthews, 1999 Ohio App. LEXIS 338 (Feb. 3, 1999) (finding no remedy under Ohio's RISA for taking a prohibited security interest). *See* National Consumer Law Center, Repossessions § 3.4.3 (7th ed. 2010 and Supp.).

### 2.3.7 *Insurance Premium Finance Statutes*

The credit sale of insurance is regulated by insurance premium financing statutes in many jurisdictions.[180] Most premium financing is initiated by insurance agents, who assign the contracts to specialized finance companies. The financing of automobile insurance premiums is particularly common when the consumer cannot afford to pay the entire annual premium in one installment.

The structure of insurance premium financing invites consumer exploitation. If a borrower defaults in the payments, the insurance policy is cancelled, often with little or no notice,[181] and the creditor receives the rebate for the unearned portion of the policy.[182] Because credit sellers require a down payment of, perhaps, 30% of the premium, the amount of the rebate invariably exceeds the balance of the debt, and the creditor loses nothing. Despite this "perfect security," creditors frequently charge rates for insurance premium financing that are at or near the ceilings set by these statutes.

### 2.3.8 *Open-End Credit Laws*

Open-end or "revolving" credit is regulated separately from fixed-term credit in most states. Within the open-end category, open-end *loan* accounts, typically offered by banks, may fall under a different statute from open-end credit *sales* accounts, such as the charge accounts available at many department stores.[183] Most open-end accounts, whether constituting loans or credit sales, are associated with plastic "credit cards."[184]

Statutes governing open-end credit require monthly statements to be sent to the borrower showing the debits, credits, and finance charges assessed on the account during the previous billing cycle. They often set a ceiling on the monthly interest rate that can be assessed on the outstanding balance of the account, and specify how that outstanding balance may be calculated.[185] Finally, open-end credit statutes may limit the imposition of periodic (usually annual) "membership" fees as well as other fees such as late fees and fees for exceeding the authorized credit limit.

The effect of the consumer's state statutes on credit card accounts issued by depository lenders, as opposed to retail charge card accounts issued directly by merchants, has been significantly limited by federal law allowing for "rate exportation." National banks, federal savings associations, and federally-insured state-chartered banks, savings associations, and credit unions can charge interest rates and certain other fees as determined by the institution's home state law, even if the rate or charge would not be allowed in the consumer's home state.[186]

Depository institutions that issue credit cards typically charter themselves in states with minimal regulation of credit cards. This has enabled major credit card issuers to do business by mail, phone, or the Internet from states which have high or non-existent interest ceilings and, in effect, to ignore the low ceilings in the borrowers' home states. It also led to a "race to the bottom" in terms of consumer protection laws as local banks convinced legislatures that they must become more "creditor friendly" or risk losing businesses to states that were.[187]

State limits on open-end credit remain relevant for payday lenders and other high-cost predatory lenders who are not federal or federally insured depositories. Effective restrictions on open-end credit can prevent these lenders from avoiding state usury laws by structuring their credit products as open-end credit.

### 2.3.9 *Pawnbroker Statutes*

Pawnbroking is a form of secured lending that usually involves a small principal, a short term, and a high interest rate.[188] It differs from small loan lending in that the pawnbroker takes physical possession of the security pledged by the borrower at the time the loan is made.[189] When the loan is repaid, usually in a lump sum, but occasionally in installments, the collateral is

180 *See generally* § 6.4.4, Appx. A, *infra*.

181 *See* Barnett v. Funding Plus of Am., Inc., 740 So. 2d 1069 (Ala. 1999) (upholding premium finance company's use of power of attorney from borrower to cancel her insurance without statutory advance notice after she missed a payment).

182 Technically, the creditor takes a security interest in the rebate. This procedure is expressly authorized by insurance premium financing statutes.

183 Major credit cards such as Visa, MasterCard, or American Express, are loan accounts. The creditor is the card issuer, although the credit is used to pay off debts to retailers. On the other hand, the creditor on a department store charge account is the retailer itself, and the transactions are generally considered credit sales rather than loans.
*See* State v. Allied Mktg. Group, 949 S.W.2d 816 (Tex. App. 1997) (discussing whether a nationwide mail-order company's use of gold card giving a customer a $10,000 line of credit created a retail credit card arrangement under Texas law).

184 Not all plastic cards are credit cards; some are debit cards linked to a consumer's bank account, or a stored value card, with a preloaded amount often linked to a single retailer. A credit card is a card associated with a true line of credit from a bank or other creditor. For such a line of credit to exist, the borrower should not have to deposit any money with the creditor, although in practice some banks may only issue credit cards to their depositors. A debit card acts more like a bank check. As soon as a "charge" on a debit card is received by the bank, the cardholder's bank account is debited by the amount of the purchase. Banks may extend credit to depositors who overdraw their accounts via debit cards just as they do with depositors who bounce checks. *See* § 7.5.6, *infra* (discussing overdraft loans). A full discussion of these various plastic methods of payment, their definitions, and applicable statutes and regulations is contained in National Consumer Law Center, Consumer Banking and Payments Law (4th ed. 2009 and Supp.).

185 *See* § 5.3.5, *infra*.

186 *See* § 3.4, *infra*.

187 *See* Greenwood Trust Co. v. Massachusetts, 776 F. Supp. 21 (D. Mass. 1991), *rev'd* 971 F.2d 818 (1st Cir. 1992) (discussing the history, policy and problems surrounding legislatures' desire to be creditor friendly). *See generally* §§ 3.4 (exportation), 3.6 (state parity laws), *infra*.

188 *See* John P. Caskey, Fringe Banking (1994) (reviewing pawnbroking in detail).

189 *See* Agapitov v. Lerner, 133 Cal. Rptr. 2d 837 (Cal. Ct. App. 2003).

returned to the borrower. If the borrower fails to repay the loan within a set time, the pawnbroker is permitted to sell the collateral to recover its debt.

Most states have a special usury statute which exempts licensed pawnbrokers from the general usury ceiling and permits them to charge rates comparable to small loan lenders. An exemption may apply only to statutory pawn transactions, rather than all activities by a pawnbroker. Depending on the state, unlicensed pawnbrokers are either prohibited or must operate under the state's general usury law.

Debt collection is not a big issue with pawnbrokers, because the value of the collateral they accept invariably exceeds the debt they are owed. However, pawnbrokers must keep records to demonstrate that they are not fencing stolen property,[190] and state laws or regulations usually restrict the manner in which a pawnbroker can dispose of pledged property.[191] For example, many states require public sales and insist that any surplus from such a sale be turned over to the borrower. State law may also restrict the charges apart from "interest" that a pawnbroker may impose. For example, storage charges for holding the borrower's pledged property may be forbidden. In addition to state regulation, some localities may require licensing or registration, or impose record-keeping requirements.[192] Pawnshop lending is being increasingly replaced by payday lending,[193] which is less regulated and more expensive. Most pawnbrokers are small operations, with one or two stores, but a handful of publicly traded companies run stores across the country.[194]

Some lenders have pushed the standard definition of pawnbroking by taking as security the title to a car. Such loans straddle the normal definition of pawnbroking and secured small loan lending. Unsurprisingly, these loans are extremely high-cost and prone to abuse.[195] Nonetheless, about twenty states either have no significant limits on the interest rates or substantive terms of these transactions, or have passed special title pawn laws authorizing them.[196] These laws are summarized at Appendix B, *infra*, and are discussed at Chapter 11, *infra*.

### 2.3.10 Comprehensive Consumer Credit Codes

Several states have rewritten and consolidated all or parts of their various special usury statutes in the form of consumer credit codes. Among these jurisdictions are Alabama, Colorado, Idaho, Iowa, Indiana, Kansas, Maine, Oklahoma, South Carolina, Texas, Utah, West Virginia, Wisconsin, and Wyoming. Some of these states have adopted statutes that are unique to the adopting state. However, most of these jurisdictions have enacted comprehensive consumer codes adapted from some form of the Uniform Consumer Credit Code (UCCC).

The UCCC is a model statute, approved by the National Conference of Commissioners on Uniform State Laws and the American Bar Association. Two basic versions of the UCCC exist, one from 1968 and a revision from 1974.[197]

The original 1968 draft was funded and written predominantly by representatives of the consumer credit industry. It relied primarily on competition rather than rate ceilings to restrain excessive charges for credit, although the statute did contain ceilings that vary with the class of loan or credit involved.[198] The adoption of this draft was opposed by many consumer groups on the grounds that it provided insufficient consumer protection. Seven states adopted some form of the 1968 draft.[199]

In response to the deficiencies of the UCCC, the National Consumer Law Center issued an alternative consumer credit code, the National Consumer Act (NCA), in 1970. This statute

190 *See, e.g., In re* Schwabl, 347 B.R. 726, 736 (D. Nev. 2006) ("Pawnbrokers are regulated in a manner designed to deter personal property theft"); Pawnmart, Inc. v. Gwinnett County, 608 S.E.2d 639 (Ga. 2005) (upholding county regulation of pawnbrokers designed to prevent the sale of stolen property through pawnbrokers); Gessner v. Gregg's Pawn Shop, Inc., 908 N.E.2d 948 (Ohio Ct. App. 2009) (finding statute requires return of stolen property to rightful owner without charge).

191 *See, e.g.,* Cash America v. Prado, 413 B.R. 599 (S.D. Tex. 2008) (discussing Texas law requirement that the pawnshop document the forfeiture of the pawned goods prior to sale); S.C. Code Ann. § 40-39-110 (requiring notice of forfeiture on loans greater than $50, and a sixty-day redemption period). *Cf.* Mickens v. The Pawn Store, 723 N.W.2d 450 (Iowa Ct. App. 2006) (upholding trial court's finding that pawnshop customer had given pawnshop implicit authority to permit third party to redeem pledged collateral).

192 Robin A. Prager, *Determinants of the Locations of Payday Lenders, Pawnshops, and Check-Cashing Outlets* 9 (Fin. & Econ. Discussion Series, Div. of Research & Statistics & Monetary Affairs, Fed. Res. Board, Paper No, 2009-33, 2009), *available at* www.federalreserve.gov/pubs/feds/2009/200933/200933pap.pdf.

193 Donald P. Morgan, Fed. Reserve Bank of New York, Defining and Detecting Predatory Lending, Staff Report No. 273, at 5–6 (Jan. 2007), *available at* www.newyorkfed.org/research/staff_reports/sr273.pdf.

194 Robin A. Prager, *Determinants of the Locations of Payday Lenders, Pawnshops, and Check-Cashing Outlets* 5–6 (Fin. & Econ. Discussion Series, Div. of Research & Statistics & Monetary Affairs, Fed. Res. Board, Paper No, 2009-33, 2009), *available at* www.federalreserve.gov/pubs/feds/2009/200933/200933pap.pdf.

195 *See* Lynn Drysdale & Kathleen Keest, *The Two-Tiered Consumer Financial Services Marketplace: The Fringe Banking System and Its Challenge to Current Thinking About the Socio-Economic Role of Usury Laws in Today's Society*, 51 S.C. L. Rev. 589 (2000) (reporting interest rates of 80–900% in auto pawn lending. *See generally* Ch. 11, *infra*.

196 Leah A. Plunkett & Ana Lucia Hurtado, *Small Dollar Loans, Big Problems: How States Protect Consumers from Abuses and How the Federal Government Can Help*, 44 Suffolk U. L. Rev. 31 (2011). *See also* Mark S. Edelman, Robert A. Aitken, & Raechelle C. Yballe, *The Road Ahead: Emerging Trends in Personal Property Finance*, 63 Bus. Law. 597 (2008).

197 The 1968 model U.C.C.C. is published in 7 Uniform Laws Annotated (West 1985). The 1974 model U.C.C.C. is published in 7A Uniform Laws Annotated (West 1985).

198 *See* Luttenegger v. Conseco Fin. Servicing Corp., 671 N.W.2d 425 (Iowa 2003) (distinguishing between fees with and without caps under the U.C.C.C.).

199 These states are Colorado, Indiana, Oklahoma, South Carolina, Utah, Wisconsin, and Wyoming. The 1968 draft has also been adopted in Guam. The Wisconsin statute is actually a combination of the 1968 U.C.C.C. draft and the National Consumer Act. Utah technically repealed the U.C.C.C. in 1985, but the statute was replaced by a consumer code containing many U.C.C.C. provisions.

and a subsequent abbreviated draft of the NCA, known as the Model Consumer Credit Act (MCCA), included significantly more comprehensive consumer protections than the 1968 UCCC.[200] For example, the NCA abolished the traditional distinction between loans and credit sales, restricted security interests and credit insurance commissions, and addressed credit bureau abuses and deceptive trade practices.[201] The NCA was not adopted in its entirety by any state. Yet many states incorporated individual NCA provisions in their credit laws.[202]

The NCA served as a counterpoint to the 1968 UCCC, and significantly influenced the second draft of the UCCC, which was issued in 1974. The 1974 draft went farther than its predecessor towards abolishing unnecessary distinctions among types of credit. It also improved upon the consumer protections of the 1968 draft and, accordingly, received much less industry support. The 1974 UCCC draft was adopted to varying degrees by four states.[203]

As suggested by the fact that there are two outstanding drafts of the UCCC, the statute is somewhat less than uniform in practice. State legislatures exacerbated the differences between the 1968 and 1974 drafts by declining to adopt either version in its entirety, exempting specific transactions from UCCC coverage, and otherwise amending the statute of their own accord. Nevertheless, significant similarities among UCCC jurisdictions remain, and practitioners in one UCCC state should consult decisions from other UCCC jurisdictions on unclear points of law.

## *2.3.11 State Laws Regarding Specific Fringe Lenders*

### 2.3.11.1 Overview

In recent years, many state legislatures have adopted laws aimed at specific types of fringe lending: payday lending, auto title pawns, and rent-to-own transactions. These statutes have typically been promoted by fringe lenders and place few limits on these high-rate transactions. However, some have been vehicles for reform, and have been amended over the years to rein in at least some of the abusive aspects of these transactions.

### 2.3.11.2 Payday Loan Laws

A number of states have laws addressing payday lending. Most of these laws legalize triple-digit interest rates for these loans, and impose few meaningful restrictions. In response to abuses, however, some state legislatures have tightened their payday loan laws, for example by reducing the allowable interest rate.

Payday lenders typically respond to a tighter cap by seeking ways to restructure their loans to avoid it. Failing that, they may leave the state or go underground, maintaining a concealed presence in the state while purporting to be operating from another state.

Payday loan laws are listed at Appendix B, *infra*, and discussed in detail at Chapter 9, *infra*.

### 2.3.11.3 Auto Title Pawn Laws

About twenty states have special auto title pawn laws. Most of these statutes legalize high-rate auto title lending, and were enacted in response to industry pressure, but a few of them have effective limits on auto title lending. These statutes are listed at Appendix A, *infra*, and discussed at Chapter 11, *infra*.

In the absence of a special auto title pawn law, auto title lending is likely to violate state law. Auto title lenders have difficulty fitting their operations under state pawnshop laws since the borrower does not turn over possession of the car to the lender.[204]

### 2.3.11.4 Rent-to-Own Laws

All but a few states have laws directed at rent-to-own transactions. These laws typically carve out rent-to-own transactions from the state retail installment sales act (RISA). As a result, the RISA interest rate cap does not apply to rent-to-own transactions, and the consumer's interest in the property cannot be treated as a security interest that is entitled to certain protections under bankruptcy law and Article 9 of the Uniform Commercial Code.

The application of consumer credit statutes to rent-to-own transactions is discussed at detail in Chapter 12, *infra*. Issues regarding repossession and the application of Article 9 are discussed in another treatise in this series.[205]

## *2.3.12 State Credit Services Laws*

### 2.3.12.1 Introduction

A number of states have laws regulating "credit services organizations."[206] These laws typically deal with abuses by credit repair organizations, a topic discussed in another treatise in this series.[207] They are relevant for this book because most also apply to organizations that assist or offer to assist consumers in obtaining extensions of credit. Often they are referred to as "state credit repair laws," but in this subsection they will be referred to as state credit services laws.

200 Copies of the National Consumer Act and the Model Consumer Credit Code are available at www.nclc.org/images/pdf/high_cost_small_loans/usury/national-consumer-act.pdf.

201 For comparisons of the U.C.C.C. and NCA, see generally Rothschild & Carroll, Consumer Protection: Text and Materials § 19.06E (2d ed. 1977); Boyd, The U3C and the NCA: A Comment and Comparison in Consumer Viewpoints: Critique of the Uniform Consumer Credit Code 663 (1971).

202 The NCA had the greatest influence in Wisconsin, which adopted a combined version of the NCA and U.C.C.C.

203 These states are Idaho, Iowa, Kansas, and Maine.

204 *See* § 2.3.9, *supra,* § 11.3, *infra.*

205 National Consumer Law Center, Repossessions § 14.3 (7th ed. 2010 and Supp.).

206 *See* National Consumer Law Center, Fair Credit Reporting Appx. H (7th ed. 2010 and Supp.).

207 *Id.* Ch. 15.

State credit services laws impose significant restrictions on the organizations they cover. Entities that operate on the fringes of the credit market and arrange extensions of credit for financially pressed borrowers may run afoul of these laws. However, as discussed at § 9.6.5, *infra*, there is a danger that high-rate fringe lenders may obtain licenses under state credit services laws, recast their activities as obtaining credit from other organizations, and argue that they may charge enormous fees for obtaining credit notwithstanding state usury laws.

### 2.3.12.2 Coverage

The state credit services laws that apply to organizations that assist or offer to assist consumers in obtaining extensions of credit are usually limited to credit for personal, family, or household use. Typically they apply to an organization only if it provides its services in return for the payment of money or other consideration.

Entities potentially covered by the "obtaining credit" branch of these laws include credit card "finders" that claim to be able to procure credit cards for consumers;[208] tax preparers who offer, for a fee, to arrange refund anticipation loans for their clients;[209] and loan brokers and mortgage brokers.[210] A key question for coverage under these statutes is whether the organization has arranged the loan in return for the payment of money or other consideration. Even if the organization does not charge a special fee for this service, it may receive a fee in the form of a kickback of part of the borrower's payment to the lender. Even sellers of goods and services who arrange credit for their customers may be covered by these statutes, although courts have differed on this question.[211]

State statutes vary in the parties they exempt, but most exempt non-profit organizations; licensed real estate brokers and attorneys when acting within the scope of their licenses;[212] broker-dealers registered with the SEC or CFTC; consumer reporting agencies; credit unions; banks eligible for FDIC insurance; banks and other lenders authorized under federal or state law; and lenders approved by HUD for participation in federal mortgage insurance.[213] These exemptions will exclude most licensed institutional lenders but will not exclude fringe lenders who lack state or federal licenses.

### 2.3.12.3 Substantive Prohibitions

Typical requirements of state credit services statutes include:

- Registration and bonding.
- A signed written contract with specified provisions, including a description of the services to be provided.
- A prohibition against charging the consumer for a referral to a retail seller who will or may extend credit to the consumer on the same terms as those available to the general public.
- A three- or five-day right to cancel.[214]

Most also prohibit certain misrepresentations and deceptive acts. A number of state statutes explicitly prohibit waivers of the statutory protections.

Some state credit services organization statutes prohibit organizations from accepting payment from the buyer before performing services. Many allow advance payment once the organization has posted a bond, however.

---

208 *See* State v. Schlosser, 681 N.E.2d 911 (Ohio 1997) (affirming conviction of credit card finder under state RICO statute based on predicate offense of operating unlicensed credit services organization); State v. New Beginning Credit Ass'n, 2006 WL 1472284 (Tenn. Ct. App. May 25, 2006) (statute covers company that offered to help people reestablish their credit with an unsecured credit card).

209 *See, e.g.*, Fugate v. Jackson Hewitt, Inc., 347 S.W.3d 81 (Mo. Ct. App. 2011); Harpter v. Jackson Hewitt, Inc., 706 S.E.2d 63 (W. Va. 2010). *But see* Gomez v. Jackson Hewitt, Inc., 16 A.3d 261 (Md. Ct. Spec. App. 2011) (tax return preparer not credit services organization under Maryland law where it does not charge separate fee specifically for arranging refund anticipation loan), *review granted*, 30 A.3d 193 (Md. 2011).

210 *See, e.g.*, Lovick v. Ritemoney Ltd., 378 F.3d 433 (5th Cir. 2004) (state credit services law covers loan broker and authorizes it to charge fees); Sherzer v. Homestar Mortgage Servs., 2010 WL 1947042 (E.D. Pa. May 7, 2010) (magistrate recommended decision) (refusing to dismiss claim that Pennsylvania credit repair law applies to state-licensed mortgage brokers), *adopted by* 2010 WL 2649852 (E.D. Pa. July 1, 2010); Lewis v. Delta Funding Corp. (*In re* Lewis), 290 B.R. 541, 556 (E.D. Pa. 2003) (loan broker meets Pa. definition of credit services organization); *In re* Bell, 309 B.R. 139 (Bankr. E.D. Pa. 2004) (mortgage loan broker meets Pennsylvania definition of credit services organization), *on reconsideration in part*, 314 B.R. 54 (Bankr. E.D. Pa. 2004) (dealing with damages issues); Barker v. Altegra Corp. (*In re* Barker), 251 B.R. 250 (Bankr. E.D. Pa. 2000) (finding that loan broker was covered under Pa. credit repair statute, but basing decision on language that does not appear in most states' statutes); Arnold v. United Companies Lending Corp., 511 S.E.2d 854 (W. Va. 1998) (loan broker meets definition of "credit services organization").

211 *Compare* Midstate Siding & Window Co. v. Rogers, 789 N.E.2d 1248 (Ill. 2003) (credit services law inapplicable to retailer), *and* Cannon v. William Chevrolet/Geo, Inc., 794 N.E.2d 843 (Ill. App. Ct. 2003) (car dealership not a credit repair organization even though it charged consumer a $46.88 documentary fee and required consumer to pay 4.5% higher interest rate than bank charged), *and* Snook v. Ford Motor Co., 755 N.E.2d 380 (Ohio Ct. App. 2001) (interpreting somewhat differently-worded statute; consumer must show either payment of a fee specifically for the service of arranging credit or that the cost of this service was included in the price of the product sold), *with* Premium Air, Inc. v. Luchinski, 735 N.W.2d 194 (Wis. Ct. App. 2007) (table, text at 2007 WL 1345839) (statute inapplicable to retailer). *See generally* National Consumer Law Center, Fair Credit Reporting § 15.3.4 (4th ed. 2009 and Supp.) (detailed discussion of this issue).

212 *See* King v. Rubin, 35 Phila. 571, 1998 Phila. Cty. Rptr. LEXIS 73 (Pa. Ct. Com. Pl. July 1, 1998) (licensed real estate brokers were exempt even when holding credit workshops, as this was related to their real estate business).

213 *See* Brown v. Mortgagestar, Inc., 194 F. Supp. 2d 473 (S.D. W. Va. 2002) (HUD-approved lender exempt even though it was acting as broker in transaction with plaintiff).

214 Lewis v. Delta Funding Corp. (*In re* Lewis), 290 B.R. 541 (Bankr. E.D. Pa. 2003) (broker's failure to include notice of right to cancel in broker agreement violated state credit repair law, and this claim can be asserted against lender who prepared the agreement and presented it to borrower).

#### 2.3.12.4 Private Causes of Action

Almost all state credit services statutes provide a private right of action to consumers. Some do so both by making a violation actionable under the state UDAP statute[215] and by creating a special cause of action. Many authorize minimum damages, punitive damages, and attorney fees. Many set as minimum damages the total amount paid by the consumer.[216] In addition, a number of state laws make non-complying contracts void and unenforceable.

#### 2.3.12.5 High-Rate Lenders' Use of Credit Services Laws to Evade State Usury Caps

In some states, there is a danger that high-rate fringe lenders will use the state credit services law as a way of evading state usury statutes. In Texas, an organization, CPCWA Co., registered under the state's weak credit services organization law. That law did not place any cap on the fee a licensed credit services organization could charge for arranging an extension of credit. CPCWA Co. then, for a $1,500 fee, "arranged" a title pawn loan with proceeds of $500. The loan itself carried interest at just 10%, so on the surface appeared to comply with the state's general usury statute. The Fifth Circuit fell for this ruse, holding that the $1,500 fee was not interest under the state usury statute because it was charged by an broker that was independent of the lender.[217]

Discovery, had it been allowed, would probably have shown that the lender and the credit services organization were not independent entities, that some of the $1,500 fee made its way to the lender, or that the credit services organization was the true lender and was therefore doing more than its credit services organization license allowed. Facts along these lines, and differences in statutory language, may distinguish the Fifth Circuit decision if high-rate lenders try the same tactic in other states.

Until 2010, payday lenders in Maryland operated under a similar scheme, setting themselves up as credit services organizations and charging broker fees to arrange payday loans.[218] The legislature closed this loophole by prohibiting broker fees that, when added to the interest charged on a loan, exceed the applicable interest cap.[219]

215 *See* Illinois v. Nat'l Credit Mgmt. Group, 1996 U.S. Dist. LEXIS 8722 (N.D. Ill. June 20, 1996) (violation of state credit repair law is UDAP violation); Barker v. Altegra Corp. (*In re* Barker), 251 B.R. 250 (Bankr. E.D. Pa. 2000) (any violation of state credit repair law is UDAP violation).

216 *See* Bell v. Parkway Mortgage, Inc. (*In re* Bell), 309 B.R. 139 (Bankr. E.D. Pa. 2004) (awarding as damages the amount consumer paid to mortgage loan broker, including yield spread premium), *reconsideration granted in part,* 314 B.R. 54, 60 (Bankr. E.D. Pa. 2004) (addressing questions regarding UDAP damages); Barker v. Altegra Corp. (*In re* Barker), 251 B.R. 250 (Bankr. E.D. Pa. 2000) (amount paid must be awarded regardless of amount of actual damages).

217 Lovick v. Ritemoney, 378 F.3d 433 (5th Cir. 2004).

218 Leah A. Plunkett & Ana Lucia Hurtado, *Small Dollar Loans, Big Problems: How States Protect Consumers from Abuses and How the Federal Government Can Help,* 44 Suffolk U. L. Rev. 31, 42 (2011).

219 Md. Code, Comm. Law § 14-1902(7).

## 2.4 Other Statutes and Theories of Liability Relevant to Consumer Credit

### *2.4.1 State UDAP Statutes*

#### 2.4.1.1 Introduction

Overreaching consumer credit transactions can often be challenged under state unfair and deceptive acts and practices (UDAP) statutes, which are the subject of a separate treatise in this series.[220] In many states, violation of another consumer protection statute is a per se UDAP violation,[221] so the UDAP statute may provide a remedy for violation of a state credit statute that does not itself provide a private cause of action.[222]

#### 2.4.1.2 Does the State UDAP Statute Cover Credit Transactions and Creditors?

An initial question that must be addressed in any UDAP challenge is whether the statute covers credit transactions and creditors. There are a number of different ways in which this issue presents itself.

The statute may explicitly exclude certain types of financial institutions, such as banks. In addition, some statutes exempt other actors who may be involved in deceptive loan schemes, such as real estate agents, attorneys, and insurers.

In other states the UDAP statute limits itself, or limits its private cause of action, to transactions involving sales of goods or services. These statutes may be interpreted to cover credit that is extended in connection with a sale of goods or services, but not straight loans of money. However a number of states have interpreted this language more broadly and concluded that an extension of credit is a service.[223]

Another way the issue arises is through an exemption for entities, transactions, or practices that are regulated by other law. Many UDAP statutes have an exemption along these lines, but there is a great deal of variation in the phrasing of these exemptions and in courts' interpretations of them. Some courts interpret these exemptions to exclude regulated entities such as most creditors from the state UDAP statute altogether, regardless of the unfair or deceptive nature of the entity's acts. Other

220 National Consumer Law Center, Unfair and Deceptive Acts and Practices (7th ed. 2008 and Supp.). *See also* § 6.4.6, *infra* (application of UDAP statutes to credit insurance problems).

221 *See* National Consumer Law Center, Unfair and Deceptive Acts and Practices § 3.2.7 (7th ed. 2008 and Supp.).

222 *See, e.g.,* Barnes v. Fleet Nat'l Bank, 370 F.3d 164 (1st Cir. 2004) (violation of Truth in Savings Act is Mass. UDAP violation); Pierce v. Novastar Mortgage, Inc., 238 F.R.D. 624 (W.D. Wash. 2006) (by statute, violation of Consumer Loan Act is per se unfair or deceptive act occurring in trade or commerce); Thompson v. 10,000 RV Sales, Inc., 31 Cal. Rptr. 3d 18 (Cal. Ct. App. 2005) (violation of Cal. Automobile Sales Finance Act's disclosure requirements is UDAP violation).

223 *See* National Consumer Law Center, Unfair and Deceptive Acts and Practices § 2.2.1.3 (7th ed. 2008 and Supp.).

courts interpret this type of exemption more in keeping with the rule that UDAP statutes are to be liberally construed, and hold that the exemption merely means that a creditor or other entity cannot be held liable under the state UDAP statute for an act that was required or specifically permitted by other law.

UDAP coverage issues are discussed in detail in National Consumer Law Center, *Unfair and Deceptive Acts and Practices* Ch. 2 (7th ed. 2008).[224] That book includes a state-by-state survey of the coverage of credit transactions and creditors under each state's UDAP statute.

### 2.4.1.3 UDAP Statutes' Substantive Prohibitions

#### *2.4.1.3.1 Overview*

The typical state UDAP statute prohibits unfair (or unconscionable) and deceptive acts and practices in broad terms, and includes a non-exhaustive list of specific prohibitions. Some, however, include a broad prohibition only of deception, not unfair acts, and some prohibit only a closed list of specific practices, without any broad, general prohibitions.

In about half the states, the UDAP statute gives a state agency the authority to adopt regulations prohibiting additional specific practices. Some states have made use of this authority and have adopted a number of specific regulations.

A detailed analysis of UDAP statutes' substantive prohibitions may be found in another treatise in this series.[225] UDAP claims regarding credit card abuses are discussed at § 8.11.3, *supra*, and claims regarding vehicle financing at § 10.3.3.3.4, *infra*.

#### *2.4.1.3.2 Overreaching, unfairness*

The broad prohibitions against unfairness or unconscionability found in many UDAP statutes are particularly well-suited to challenging overreaching credit terms.[226] One way to frame the UDAP claim is as failure to disclose the disadvantageous cost or nature of the loan.[227]

It may be an unfair practice to use a faulty and unreliable automated property valuation system to reduce a line of credit.[228] Failure to translate important written information into the same language as principally used in the transaction can also give rise to a UDAP claim, even in the absence of a statute mandating the translation.[229] But a court held that a lender did not commit an unfair or deceptive act by making a commercial loan that had a variable interest rate that was solely in the lender's control, when the rate was fully disclosed and a high rate was in effect only for such a short period that it did not cause the borrower substantial injury.[230]

#### *2.4.1.3.3 Loan padding, excess charges, and violation of other consumer protection statutes*

An allegation of "loan-padding"—structuring a loan to increase its size without advancing additional funds to borrowers, thereby increasing lender profit or enabling the creditor to reach

224 *See also* Carolyn Carter, National Consumer Law Center, Consumer Protection in the States: A 50-State Report on Unfair and Deceptive Acts and Practices Statutes (Feb. 2008), *available at* www.nclc.org/images/pdf/udap/report_50_states.pdf (summary of features of state UDAP statutes, including detailed state-by-state appendix).

225 National Consumer Law Center, Unfair and Deceptive Acts and Practices (7th ed. 2008 and Supp.). *See also* Carolyn Carter, National Consumer Law Center, Consumer Protection in the States: A 50-State Report on Unfair and Deceptive Acts and Practices Statutes (Feb. 2008), *available at* www.nclc.org/images/pdf/udap/report_50_states.pdf (summarizing features of state UDAP statutes, including detailed state-by-state appendix).

226 *See, e.g.*, Williams v. First Gov't Mortgage & Investors Corp., 225 F.3d 738 (D.C. Cir. 2000); Gutierrez v. Wells Fargo & Co., 622 F. Supp. 2d 946 (N.D. Cal. 2009) (jury question whether bank violated the U.C.C. standard of good faith and the state UDAP statute by manipulating the order in which it processed debit card transactions in order to maximize overdraft fees); O'Donovan v. Cashcall, Inc., 2009 WL 1833990 (N.D. Cal. June 24, 2009) (refusing to dismiss claim that high-rate, payday-type Internet loan was unconscionable and therefore violated Unfair Competition Law); Hendrickson v. Popular Mortgage Servicing, Inc., 2009 WL 1455491 (N.D. Cal. May 21, 2009) (denying motion to dismiss UDAP claim that lender violated UDAP statute by giving consumers a loan that did not benefit them); Lieberman v. Emigrant Mortgage Co., 436 F. Supp. 2d 357 (D. Conn. 2006) (denying motion to dismiss claim that imposition of 18% penalty interest rate on mortgage loan was unfair practice that violated UDAP statute); Phillips v. Dukes (*In re* Dukes), 24 B.R. 404 (Bankr. E.D. Mich. 1982). *But see* Strong v. Option One Mortgage Corp. (*In re* Strong), 356 B.R. 121 (Bankr. E.D. Pa. 2004) (loan not unconscionable in violation of UDAP statute when material terms were disclosed to consumers in advance and they failed to inquire about disadvantageous features), *aff'd on other grounds*, 2005 WL 1463245 (E.D. Pa. June 20, 2005). *But cf.* Martin v. GMAC, 825 N.E.2d 1138 (Ohio Ct. App. 2005) (upholding summary judgment for car dealer; consumer was not especially vulnerable and had shopped around for credit and affirmatively chosen this dealer).

227 *See, e.g.*, Besta v. Beneficial Loan Co., 855 F.2d 532 (8th Cir. 1988) (unconscionability); *In re* Milbourne, 108 B.R. 522 (Bankr. E.D. Pa. 1989) (UDAP). *See also* Fed. Trade Comm'n v. Stewart Fin. Co. Holdings, Inc., Civ. No. 1:03-CV-2648-JTC (N.D. Ga. filed Sept. 2003) (complaint, temporary restraining order), (Oct. 28, 2003) (consent orders for preliminary injunction), *available at* www.ftc.gov/os/2003/09/stewartcmp.shtm (failure to inform borrowers that separate loan would be less expensive than refinancing); Smoot v. Physicians Life Ins. Co., 87 P.3d 545 (N.M. Ct. App. 2003) (affirming denial of motion to dismiss claim that UDAP statute imposes duty on insurer to disclose dollar amount and effective annual percentage rate of the extra costs imposed for paying premium monthly instead of annually; detrimental reliance need not be alleged); Azar v. Prudential Ins. Co., 68 P.3d 909 (N.M. Ct. App. 2003) (insurer may have duty to disclose APR representing extra costs imposed for paying premium in monthly installments instead of annually). *See generally* National Consumer Law Center, Unfair and Deceptive Acts and Practices §§ 2.2.1, 2.2.5, Ch. 6 (7th ed. 2008 and Supp.).

228 Hickman v. Wells Fargo Bank, N.A., 683 F. Supp. 2d 779 (N.D. Ill. 2010) (denying motion to dismiss).

229 *See* National Consumer Law Center, Unfair and Deceptive Acts and Practices § 5.6.1 (7th ed. 2008 and Supp.) (compiling decisions finding that failure to translate is a UDAP violation, and state statutes that require translations).

230 3525 North Reta, Inc. v. Federal Deposit Ins. Corp., 2011 WL 62128 (N.D. Ill. Jan. 6, 2011).

more collateral—has been held to state a cause of action under a state UDAP statute.[231] Similarly, packing a loan with worthless products states a UDAP claim.[232] Falsely representing that credit insurance is required is a UDAP violation.[233] A lender may commit an unfair and deceptive act by leading borrowers to believe that it is merely passing through third-party charges when in fact it is charging significantly more than its costs.[234]

A UDAP statute has been held applicable in an action seeking recovery of excess interest charged upon prepayment[235] or charging an illegal prepayment penalty.[236] Collecting fees in excess of those allowed by state usury laws or by the contract may state a UDAP claim.[237] (A UDAP challenge to the price of credit per se may be preempted by the National Bank Act or other federal laws, however, depending on the identity of the lender.[238])

Trying to cut off a borrower's rights against assignees or related lenders under the FTC holder rule by omitting the required notice from its contracts also gives rise to a UDAP claim against the lender.[239] Where the assignee of a financing contract containing the FTC holder notice fails to acknowledge liability under the FTC rule, this behavior, in and of itself, can constitute a UDAP violation.[240]

#### 2.4.1.3.4 Deception and nondisclosure

Failure to specify the rate of interest on a loan, at least where required, can also violate a UDAP statute.[241] The First Circuit, in upholding a jury verdict to that effect, noted that laws requiring full disclosure of the rate of interest take on added significance in the wake of the elimination of usury laws.[242]

---

231 Knapp v. Americredit Fin. Serv., Inc., 245 F. Supp. 2d 841 (S.D. W. Va. 2003) (practice of adding hidden acquisition fees into the cash price with intent to deceive consumers states UDAP violation; injury is at least the increased sales tax paid by the consumer on the higher cash price); Therrien v. Resource Fin. Group, 704 F. Supp. 322 (D.N.H. 1989) (lender required payment escrow which it advanced as part of the loan, adding nearly $12,000 to the principal at 20.25% interest, placed the payment escrow in an interest-bearing account on which it credited borrowers with 5.00% interest and retained any excess; also lender double-charged for closing costs). *See also* Fed. Trade Comm'n v. Stewart Fin. Co. Holdings, Inc., Civ. No. 1:03-CV-2648-JTC (N.D. Ga. filed Sept. 2003) (complaint, temporary restraining order) (Oct. 28, 2003) (consent orders for preliminary injunction), *available at* www.ftc.gov/os/2003/09/stewartcmp.shtm (charging small loan lender with packing loans with expensive add-on products, such as insurance and car club membership, soliciting customers to engage in costly refinancings, and urging customers to participate in a direct deposit program that triggers fees for the lender, despite representations that it is a free service); Siemer v. Associates First Capital Corp., 2000 U.S. Dist. LEXIS 21244 (D. Ariz. Dec. 14, 2000) (granting class certification on claims of UDAP, breach of contract, negligent supervision, and unjust enrichment regarding credit insurance loan packing scheme), *adopted by*, 2001 U.S. Dist. LEXIS 12810 (D. Ariz. Mar. 30, 2001); Fidelity Fin. Servs. v. Hicks, 574 N.E.2d 15 (Ill. App. Ct. 1991) (home improvement RISA contract of $6,000 at 18% and $106 payments refinanced by 26%, $22,000 contract with $525 payments; allegation that deceptive practices used to make an unaffordable loan in order to acquire the equity in home stated a UDAP claim).

232 Taylor v. Bob O'Connor Ford, Inc., 2000 U.S. Dist. LEXIS 11486 (N.D. Ill. June 29, 2000). *But see* Butler v. Sterling, Inc., 210 F.3d 371 (6th Cir. 2000) (table, text at 2000 WL 353502) (affirming dismissal of credit insurance packing claims based on consumer's inability to show causation under Ohio UDAP statute).

233 Cruz v. Household Fin. Consumer Discount Co., 441 B.R. 23 (Bankr. E.D. Pa. 2004).

234 McKell v. Washington Mut., Inc., 49 Cal. Rptr. 3d 227 (Cal. Ct. App. 2006).

235 McTeer v. Provident Life & Accident Ins., 712 F. Supp. 512 (D.S.C. 1989). *See also* MacDonell v. PHH Mortgage Corp., 846 N.Y.S.2d 223 (N.Y. App. Div. 2007) (allowing claim to go forward that lender committed UDAP violation by charging fee for payoff statement in excess of amount allowed by state law). *But see* Stutman v. Chemical Bank, 731 N.E.2d 608 (N.Y. 2000) (collecting a $275 attorney fee for the simultaneous transfer of funds to allow the consumers' collateral to be available to secure the new loan at the time of prepayment of the current loan when the loan note permitted the consumers to repay without any prepayment charge does not state a UDAP claim; not clear that the fee constituted a prepayment charge, so no deception).

236 Nelson v. Associates Fin. Serv. Co. of Ind., 659 N.W.2d 635 (Mich. Ct. App. 2002). *But see* Puentes v. Wells Fargo Home Mortgage, Inc., 72 Cal. Rptr. 3d 903 (Cal. Ct. App. 2008).

237 Cohen v. JP Morgan Chase & Co., 498 F.3d 111, 126–127 (2d Cir. 2007) (reversing dismissal of UDAP claim; charging of illegal fee may constitute deception even if it was disclosed); Siradas v. Chase Lincoln First Bank. N.A., 1999 U.S. Dist. LEXIS 15593 (S.D.N.Y. Sept. 30, 1999) (miscalculation of interest due using the wrong index in variable rate transactions states a UDAP claim); Fielder v. Credit Acceptance Corp., 19 F. Supp. 2d 966 (W.D. Mo.), *remanded to state court*, 188 F.3d 1031 (8th Cir. 1998); Tavares v. Sprunk (*In re* Tavares), 298 B.R. 195 (Bankr. D. Mass. 2003) (violation of criminal usury statute by exceeding 20% cap when making a mortgage loan is a per se UDAP violation); Perez v. Rent-A-Center, 892 A.2d 1255, 1274–1275 (N.J. 2006) (reinstating claim that rent-to-own seller violated UDAP statute by exceeding criminal usury cap); Kidd v. Delta Funding Corp., 704 N.Y.S.2d 66 (N.Y. App. Div. 2001) (lender practice of charging and collecting illegal processing fees and impliedly representing that it was entitled to do so states UDAP claim); Odell v. Legal Bucks, L.L.C., 665 S.E.2d 767 (N.C. Ct. App. 2008) (violating public policies embodied in usury laws, and failing to inform borrower that contract is illegal, may be UDAP violations). *See also* Tomlin v. Dylan Mortgage Inc. (N.C. Super. Ct. June 12, 2000), *available at* www.nclc.org/unreported (charging fees in excess of that allowed by other provisions of state law can state a UDAP claim). *But see* Miller v. Pacific Shore Funding, 224 F. Supp. 2d 977 (D. Md. 2002) (charging fees in excess of state law without more does not necessarily state a UDAP claim; dismissing claim under Maryland UDAP statute since no explicit representation was made about the legality of the fee), *aff'd on other grounds*, 92 Fed. Appx. 933 (4th Cir. 2004).

238 *See* Ch. 3, *supra*. *See also* National Consumer Law Center, Unfair and Deceptive Acts and Practices § 2.5.3 (7th ed. 2008 and Supp.).

239 *See* Brown v. LaSalle Northwest Nat'l Bank, 820 F. Supp. 1078 (N.D. Ill. 1993) (bank's scheme to avoid putting FTC holder notice on its car financing paper stated consumer fraud act and RICO claims).

240 Jaramillo v. Gonzales, 50 P.3d 554 (N.M. Ct. App. 2002).

241 Chroniak v. Golden Inv. Corp., 983 F.2d 1140 (1st Cir. 1993).

242 Chroniak v. Golden Inv. Corp., 983 F.2d 1140, 1147 (1st Cir. 1993) (that the note specified the interest charge in a dollar amount did not salvage it; the second mortgage statute places the burden of disclosure on the lender, as the average consumer would find it difficult to compute the rate).

In the payday loan context, disguising a small loan as check cashing, and failing to disclose the interest rate and charges, constitutes a UDAP violation.[243] Disclosing a charge but listing it as a "carrying charge" rather than as "interest" states a UDAP claim.[244] Describing a credit card interest rate as "fixed" in advertisements and TILA disclosures may be a UDAP violation when the creditor in fact reserved the right to increase it.[245]

Deception in advertising or closing an extension of credit can be the basis of a UDAP claim.[246] Misleading or false telemarketing or high-pressured sales tactics in the credit card context also state a UDAP claim.[247] Providing a credit card with a *de minimis* credit limit, after having advertised a more generous limit, is a UDAP violation.[248] Inducing a borrower to pay a non-refundable fee through assurances that a loan in the requested amount would be forthcoming, and then relying on nebulous contract language to offer a loan only in a reduced amount, may be a UDAP violation.[249]

#### 2.4.1.4 UDAP Remedies and Limitations

All states authorize a private cause of action under the state UDAP statute.[250] Many states allow consumers to recover not only actual damages, but also statutory damages, minimum damages, multiple damages, equitable relief, or attorney fees.[251]

A consumer is entitled to only one recovery for a single injury, so may not recover the same actual damages on both a UDAP claim and a contract or tort claim.[252] But if an unfair trade practices claim is not based solely upon the defendant's usurious conduct, recovery can occur under both causes of

243 Burden v. York, Civ. Action No. 98-268, Clearinghouse No. 52,502 (E.D. Ky. Sept. 29, 1999) (granting summary judgment to consumer). *See also* O'Donovan v. Cashcall, Inc., 2009 WL 1833990 (N.D. Cal. June 24, 2009) (misrepresentation and failure to make clear disclosure of terms of high-rate Internet loan). *See generally* Ch. 9, *infra* (payday lending).

244 Delaware *ex rel.* Brady v. 3-D Auto World, Inc., 2000 Del. Super. LEXIS 17 (Del. Super. Ct. Jan. 19, 2000) (granting partial summary judgment; reserving for trial question whether dealer intended that others rely on the omission).

245 Rubio v. Capital One Bank, 613 F.3d 1195 (9th Cir. 2010) (California law).

246 Hauk v. JP Morgan Chase Bank USA, 552 F.3d 1114 (9th Cir. 2009) (denying motion to dismiss UDAP claim that lender promised 4.99% rate for transferred balance but imposed 28.74% because of late payment on another account, where it knew or should have known of the late payment before the consumer accepted the offer); Rush v. American Home Mortgage, Inc., 2009 WL 4728971 (D. Md. Dec. 3, 2009) (denying motion to dismiss claim that disclosure that option ARM interest rate "may" increase was UDAP violation when it was certain to increase); Martinez v. Freedom Mortgage Team, Inc., 527 F. Supp. 2d 827 (N.D. Ill. 2007) (refusing to dismiss UDAP claim against broker for misrepresenting loan terms and amount of monthly payment); Johnson v. Equity Title & Escrow Co., 476 F. Supp. 2d 873 (W.D. Tenn. 2007) (denying motion to dismiss when consumer alleged misstatement of loan terms and other deceptive acts); Marks v. Chicoine, 2007 WL 1056779 (N.D. Cal. Apr. 6, 2007) (allegation that broker misstated interest rate and failed to disclose that loan had forty-year term states UDAP claim); Morris v. Novastar Mortgage, Inc., 2006 WL 2707349 (W.D. Mo. Sept. 19, 2006) (question of fact whether broker was lender's agent, making lender liable for its bait-and-switch tactics); Szczubelek v. Cendant Mortgage Corp., 215 F.R.D. 107 (D.N.J. 2003) (UDAP claim survives motion for summary judgment where mortgage lender misrepresented or intentionally concealed the fact that the appraisal fee contained charges for ordering the appraisal and for processing, as well as for the appraisal itself); *In re* First Alliance Mortgage Co., 298 B.R. 652 (C.D. Cal. 2003) (finding that lender trained its employees to use various methods, including deception, to sell its services; similar findings may be found in *Pagter v. First Alliance* (Cal. Ct. App. Feb. 5, 1999), *available at* www.nclc.org/unreported), *aff'd in relevant part, vacated in part on other grounds*, 471 F.3d 977 (9th Cir. 2006); Christakos v. Intercounty Title Co., 196 F.R.D. 496 (N.D. Ill. 2000) (UDAP claim stated where settlement company represented that it would record a release of a mortgage, but did not, and collected a fee to perform this activity), *further proceedings*, 2001 U.S. Dist. LEXIS 1933 (N.D. Ill. Feb. 15, 2001); Heastie v. Community Nat'l Bank, 690 F. Supp. 716 (N.D. Ill. 1988) (denying motion to dismiss claim that broker violated state UDAP statute by misrepresenting itself as lender); *In re* Partners Group Fin., L.L.C., 394 B.R. 68 (Bankr. E.D. Pa. 2008) (misrepresentation that loan had been obtained); *In re* Balko, 382 B.R. 717 (Bankr. W.D. Pa. 2008) (borrowers stated UDAP claim against lender's president by alleging that he condoned or encouraged lender's failure to give them loan documents, acquisition of fraudulent appraisal, and misrepresentation that they could refinance in two years); Stuart v. Decision One Mortgage Co., 367 B.R. 541, 557 (Bankr. E.D. Pa. 2007) (allowing UDAP claim to go to trial when plaintiff alleged that lender and assignee engaged in concerted plan to provide financial services contrary to representations and to misrepresent that services were needed); Hawaii Cmty. Fed. Credit Union v. Keka, 11 P.3d 1 (Haw. 2000) (UDAP claim stated where mortgage loan officer promised 7.25% interest rate but it turned into 9.00% at settlement, whereupon homeowners were told not to worry as they could refinance later; when "later" came, loan company refused to refinance); Welch v. Centex Home Equity Co., 178 P.3d 80 (Kan. Ct. App. 2008) (table, text at 2008 WL 713690) (upholding UDAP judgment for borrower where lender issued loan with higher payment and longer term than she had agreed to, and knew her signature had been forged). *See also* Rossman v. Fleet Bank (R.I.) Nat'l Ass'n, 280 F.3d 384 (3d Cir. 2002) (baiting a consumer with advertisements and a credit card agreement stating that there will be no annual fee and subsequently imposing an annual fee within the first year states a claim under TILA; UDAP claim also pleaded but not addressed); Complaint, Fed. Trade Comm'n v. Chase Fin. Funding, Inc., Case No. SACV04-549 GLT (ANx) (C.D. Cal. May 12, 2004), *stipulated preliminary injunction entered* (May 28, 2004), *available at* www.ftc.gov/opa/2004/06/chasefinancial.htm (broker misrepresented that it was offering fixed-rate thirty-year mortgage loans).

247 Sims v. First Consumers Nat'l Bank, 758 N.Y.S.2d 284 (N.Y. App. Div. 2003) (high-pressure sales tactics allegedly lured consumers into accepting credit cards with hidden fees); People *ex rel.* Spitzer v. Telehublink Corp., 756 N.Y.S.2d 285 (N.Y. App. Div. 2003) (upholding permanent injunction against telemarketing company that misrepresented to consumers that they were pre-approved for a low interest rate credit card upon payment of $220).

248 People *ex rel.* Spitzer v. Applied Card Sys., Inc., 834 N.Y.S.2d 558 (N.Y. App. Div. 2007), *aff'd on other grounds,* 863 N.Y.S.2d 615 (N.Y. 2008).

249 Professional Cleaning and Innovative Bldg. Servs., Inc. v. Kennedy Funding, Inc., 245 Fed. Appx. 161 (3d Cir. 2007) (unpublished).

250 National Consumer Law Center, Unfair and Deceptive Acts and Practices § 12.2.1 (7th ed. 2008 and Supp.).

251 *Id.* Ch. 13.

252 *See* National Consumer Law Center, Unfair and Deceptive Acts and Practices § 13.3.9 (7th ed. 2008 and Supp.).

action.[253] Further, a consumer may recover actual damages on one claim and statutory damages, attorney fees, or penalties on another claim.[254]

Some UDAP statutes impose certain preconditions to suit. Most require some showing of injury or loss on the part of the plaintiff;[255] a few require the plaintiff to send notice to the defendant prior to suit;[256] and a few require the plaintiff to show that the defendant's acts impact the public.[257]

If the acts complained of are specifically authorized by other state or federal law, the state UDAP act may not be violated.[258] For example, Illinois courts have held that a UDAP claim cannot be based on disclosures that comply with the Truth in Lending Act.[259] But where the practices complained of are not specifically governed or authorized by TILA, a UDAP claim should survive a motion to dismiss.[260] And when TILA is violated, a UDAP claim may also flow from the violation.[261]

## 2.4.2 State and Federal Fair Lending Laws

The Equal Credit Opportunity Act (ECOA)[262] applies to every stage of a credit transaction, including the application, the evaluation of the application, the decision to grant or deny credit, and various activities that follow the granting of credit. It sets out a general rule that creditors cannot discriminate against any applicant in any stage of a credit transaction on the basis of:

- Race;
- Color;
- Religion;
- National origin;
- Sex;
- Marital status;
- Age;
- Public assistance income; or
- The exercise of rights under the Consumer Credit Protection Act (the Act that includes the Truth in Lending Act, the ECOA itself, the Fair Debt Collection Practices Act, and several other major federal consumer protection statutes).[263]

The ECOA also sets out various specific actions that creditors must or must not take. For example, it prohibits creditors from taking certain factors into account in determining credit-worthiness, and it regulates the way in which information is reported to credit reporting agencies concerning spouses. It also imposes notice requirements on a creditor when a loan application is approved or denied.

The ECOA gives consumers a private cause of action to enforce its requirements, including actual damages, punitive damages, costs, and attorney fees, as well as equitable and declaratory relief.[264] The ECOA is discussed in detail in another treatise in this series.[265]

Almost every state has its own fair lending law. In some states the only state fair lending law is confined to real estate transactions, but many states have a fair lending law that, like the ECOA, applies broadly to all types of credit transactions. State fair lending laws may define more protected classes than

---

253 *See, e.g.*, Williams v. First Gov't Mortgage and Investors Corp., 176 F.3d 497 (D.C. Cir. 1999) (compliance with TILA does not shield defendant from a UDAP claim where statutes have different purposes and requirements). *But see* Hardwick v. Austin Gallery of Oriental Rugs, Inc., 779 S.W.2d 438 (Tex. App. 1989) (applying provision of Texas UDAP statute which precluded recovery thereunder for the same act for which a usury penalty is awarded). *See generally* National Consumer Law Center, Unfair and Deceptive Acts and Practices § 13.3.9 (7th ed. 2008 and Supp.).

254 *See* National Consumer Law Center, Unfair and Deceptive Acts and Practices § 13.3.9 (7th ed. 2008 and Supp.).

255 *See* National Consumer Law Center, Unfair and Deceptive Acts and Practices § 12.5.2 (7th ed. 2008 and Supp.).

256 *See id.* § 12.5.3.

257 *See, e.g.*, Cashmere Valley Bank v. Brender, 116 P.3d 421 (Wash. Ct. App. 2005) (business loan did not have requisite effect on public interest where lender did not advertise to the public and all wrongful acts took place behind closed doors), *aff'd on other grounds*, 146 P.3d 928 (Wash. 2006). *See generally* National Consumer Law Center, Unfair and Deceptive Acts and Practices § 12.5.3 (7th ed. 2008 and Supp.).

258 *See, e.g.*, MacDermid v. Discover Fin. Servs., 488 F.3d 721 (6th Cir. 2007) (UDAP claim cannot be based on credit card issuer's Internet application process that complied with federal law). *See generally* National Consumer Law Center, Unfair and Deceptive Acts and Practices §§ 2.3.3, 2.5.3 (7th ed. 2008 and Supp.).

259 *See, e.g.*, Jackson v. South Holland Dodge, Inc., 755 N.E.2d 462 (Ill. 2001) (where assignee is not liable under TILA solely because the TILA violation was not apparent on the face of the documents, no liability under Illinois UDAP act); Lanier v. Associate Fin., Inc., 499 N.E.2d 440 (Ill. 1986); Price v. FCC Nat'l Bank, 673 N.E.2d 1068 (Ill. App. Ct. 1996). *See also* Graham v. RRR, L.L.C., 202 F. Supp. 2d 483 (E.D. Va. 2002), *aff'd*, 55 Fed. Appx. 135 (4th Cir. 2003) (applying this rule to the Virginia UDAP statute). *But cf.* Fed. Trade Comm'n v. OSI Fin. Serv., Inc., 2003 WL 1904013 (N.D. Ill. Apr. 17, 2003) (UDAP claims based upon misrepresentations related to balloon payments and as to whether the payments would include an escrow for taxes and insurance were not destroyed by TILA disclosures, especially when the consumers alleged they did not receive complete or timely TILA disclosures); Chandler v. American Gen. Fin., Inc., 768 N.E.2d 60 (Ill. App. Ct. 2002) (bait-and-switch claim takes this case out of the *Lanier* rule). *See generally* National Consumer Law Center, Unfair and Deceptive Acts and Practices § 2.2.1.6.3 (7th ed. 2008 and Supp.).

260 *See* Williams v. First Gov't Mortgage & Investors Corp., 176 F.3d 497 (D.C. Cir. 1999) (compliance with TILA does not shield defendant from a UDAP claim where statutes have different purposes and requirements); *In re* First Alliance Mortgage Co., 280 B.R. 246 (C.D. Cal. 2002); Parish v. Beneficial Illinois, Inc., 1996 WL 172127 (N.D. Ill. Apr. 10, 1996) (where fraud claim reaches beyond the scope of the loan documents, UDAP claim survives).

261 Meyer v. Argent Mortgage Co. (*In re* Meyer), 379 B.R. 529, 554 (Bankr. E.D. Pa. 2007) (TILA violation is also UDAP violation). *Cf.* Horvath v. Adelson, Golden & Loria, Prof'l Corp., 773 N.E.2d 478 (Mass. App. Ct. 2002) (table) (text available at 2002 WL 1931997) (consumer, however, failed to show causal connection for damages).

262 15 U.S.C. §§ 1691 to 1691f.

263 15 U.S.C. § 1691(a).

264 15 U.S.C. § 1691e.

265 National Consumer Law Center, Credit Discrimination (5th ed. 2009 and Supp.).

the ECOA. These statutes are discussed in National Consumer Law Center, *Credit Discrimination* (5th ed. 2009 and Supp.). Appendix F to that book consists of state-by-state summaries of these laws.

## 2.4.3 Fraud

### 2.4.3.1 Elements of a Fraud Claim; Parties Liable

Common law fraud is a powerful claim against those arranging or extending abusive credit. Fraud claims are decided by juries, whose judgments about truthfulness and deceit will reflect general community standards. Punitive damages are available, and can be substantial even with the constitutional caps the Supreme Court has imposed.[266] A fraud claim has stricter elements than a UDAP claim, and in many jurisdictions requires a higher standard of proof, but it avoids the restricted scope and preconditions to suit that limit many state UDAP statutes.

The traditional elements of fraud are:

- A false representation of material fact;
- Scienter, the defendant's knowledge or belief that the representation is false, or the defendant's lack of a sufficient basis on which to make the representation;
- An intent to induce the plaintiff to act in reliance upon the representation;
- Justifiable or reasonable reliance by the plaintiff; and
- Damages.[267]

Fraud can be by fraudulent concealment as well as affirmative misstatements. The elements of fraudulent concealment are often stated as: (1) the intentional concealment or suppression of a material fact; (2) a duty to disclose; (3) intent to defraud; (4) actual and justifiable reliance; and (5) damages.[268]

Another benefit of a fraud claim is that it can be used to reach lenders and other parties who facilitate the fraud even if they do not deal directly with the consumer. Theories on which fraud liability can be extended include:

- The initial party was the financier's employee or acted as its agent;
- The lender participated directly in the fraud;
- The lender aided and abetted or conspired with the tortfeasor;
- The lender participated in a joint venture;
- The lender knowingly obtained at least some of the fruits of the fraud;
- The lender induced the broker to breach its fiduciary duty to the borrower; or
- Special circumstances required the lender to disclose to the borrower information it knew about the seller and failed to reveal.

These theories are developed in more detail in National Consumer Law Center, *Mortgage Lending* Ch. 10 (2012)

### 2.4.3.2 Misrepresentation of Loan Terms

A fraud theory can be used to challenge a creditor's misrepresentation of loan terms. In *Hutchinson v. Delaware Sav. Bank F.S.B.*, the borrowers were held to have sufficiently raised a fraud claim by alleging that the lender stated falsely that the loan was beneficial, that the fees were usual and customary, that fees were part of the finance charge or amount financed, and that certain amounts were due and owing.[269] Importantly, the court held that the plaintiffs satisfied Federal Rule of Civil Procedure 9(b)'s particularity requirements even though they did not identify individuals making misrepresentations by name.

Misrepresenting the amount of credit life insurance coverage necessary to pay off the loan in the event of the borrower's death may constitute fraud.[270] However, a car dealer's statement that he would try to get a "better deal" was held not to be a misrepresentation but only an opinion based upon a statement about a future event.[271]

It often happens that oral misrepresentations made to a borrower are glaringly contradicted by documents in the loan package, and some courts have barred fraud claims on this ground.[272] Quite often, the borrower has not read these docu-

266 *See* § 2.4.3.5, *supra*.

267 *See generally* National Consumer Law Center, Automobile Fraud Ch. 8 (4th ed. 2007 and Supp.) (detailed discussion of common law fraud).

268 *See, e.g.*, Amparan v. Plaza Home Mortgage, Inc., 678 F. Supp. 2d 961 (N.D. Cal. 2008) (denying motion to dismiss allegation of fraudulent concealment based on TILA disclosure violations; gravamen of allegation was that defendant failed to disclose in manner required by TILA, rendering disclosures that were made incomplete or deceptive).

269 Hutchinson v. Delaware Sav. Bank F.S.B., 410 F. Supp. 2d. 374 (D.N.J. 2006). *See also* Miller v. Americor Lending Group, Inc., 2007 WL 107664 (W.D. Mich. Jan. 9, 2007) (denying motion to dismiss fraud claim where documents sent to borrower indicated fixed 2% loan with no negative amortization, but the loan at closing had interest rate of 6.7%); Washington v. Ameriquest Mortgage Co., 2006 WL 1980201 (N.D. Ill. July 11, 2006) (denying motion to dismiss fraud claim based on lender's statement that monthly payments would be lower than those on existing mortgage, but closing paperwork indicated higher payments and higher interest rate). *But see* Hanning v. Homecomings Fin. Networks, 436 F. Supp. 2d 865 (W.D. Mich. 2006) (dismissing for failing to state fraud claim with particularity including failure to identify the party or parties alleged to have committed the fraudulent conduct).

270 McCullar v. Universal Underwriters Life Ins. Co., 687 So. 2d 156, 164 (Ala. 1996).

271 Graham v. RRR, L.L.C., 202 F. Supp. 2d 483 (E.D. Va. 2002), *aff'd mem.*, 55 Fed. Appx. 135 (4th Cir. 2003).

272 *See, e.g.*, Davis v. G.N. Mortgage Corp., 396 F.3d 869 (7th Cir. 2005) (borrowers' failure to read and compare two stacks of documents presented to them at closing negates justifiable reliance on lender's misrepresentation that prepayment penalty only applied for two years); Jacob v. Home Sav. & Loan Co. of Youngstown, Ohio, 679 F. Supp. 2d 837, 841 (N.D. Ohio 2010) ("It is axiomatic that if a person can read and is not prevented from reading what he signs, he alone is responsible for his omission to read what he signs.") (quotations and citations omitted); Gorham-DiMaggio v. Countrywide Home Loans, Inc., 592 F. Supp. 2d 283, 297 (N.D.N.Y. 2008) (not reasonable to rely on "oral assertions of a payment amount

ments. Indeed, research has shown that consumers are unlikely to understand contemporary consumer contracts even if they attempt to read them.[273]

While the person signing a document is generally presumed to have read and understood its contents, a consumer may overcome that assumption by showing that another party prevented the consumer from reading the document.[274] If the lender uses fraud or misrepresentation to induce the borrower to sign the documents without reading them, and the borrower exercised due care under the circumstances, that may constitute part of the fraud.[275] Where a lack of education, inability to read the language, or a disability makes it impossible for a borrower to read or understand the documents, that simply may bolster claims of the lender's fraud.[276]

The parol evidence rule does not bar evidence of fraud, at least fraud in the factum.[277] Inducing a consumer to sign a loan document in reliance on misrepresentations regarding its nature or essential terms is fraud in the factum.[278]

#### 2.4.3.3 Hidden Fees and Other Credit Practices

Hidden charges and other hard-to-detect methods of increasing the cost of credit have also been challenged successfully on fraud theories. For example, a fraud claim may be stated by allegations that a car dealer misrepresented that payments to a third-party service contract provider and to an insurance company were accurate.[279] The Alabama Supreme Court upheld a jury verdict against a lender and insurer for knowingly selling credit insurance to ineligible borrowers.[280] The jury had awarded a general verdict of $5 million, covering both compensatory and punitive damages. After a remand from the U.S. Supreme Court, the Alabama Supreme Court upheld $1 million of this verdict.

Loan flipping, the practice of frequently refinancing debt, particularly debt laden with insurance premiums and extra charges,[281] can be challenged as fraudulent.[282] As the manner in

---

contradicting the written bill without requiring adequate written assurances"), *aff'd*, 421 Fed. Appx. 97 (2d Cir. 2011); Yoder v. Waterfield Fin. Corp., 2007 WL 614200 (W.D. Mich. Feb. 23, 2007) (fraud cannot be based on misrepresentation that is clearly contradicted by loan documents); Clark v. U.S. Bank N.A., 2004 WL 1380166 (E.D. Pa. June 18, 2004) (no justifiable reliance where borrower signed multiple documents at closing that guided him not to rely on oral representations and that stated that only loan terms were those contained in the documents); Moore v. Mortgagestar, Inc., 2002 U.S. Dist. LEXIS 27457 (S.D. W. Va. Dec. 18, 2002) (granting summary judgment to lender on fraud claim; borrowers cannot show justifiable reliance on oral misrepresentations about loan terms where they did not review the documents they signed; denying summary judgment on other fraud claims and unconscionability claim); Peabody v. Northgate Ford, Inc., 794 N.Y.S.2d 452 (N.Y. App. Div. 2005) (no justifiable reliance to support fraud claim where borrower admitted that she signed agreement without reading it); Dunn v. Northgate Ford, Inc., 794 N.Y.S.2d 449 (N.Y. App. Div. 2005).

273 Cathy Lesser Mansfield & Alan White, *Literacy and Contract*, 13 Stan. L. & Policy Rev. 503 (2003).

274 *See* Jones v. Adams Fin. Servs., 84 Cal. Rptr. 2d 151, 155 (Cal. Ct. App. 1999) ("A party does not have 'a reasonable opportunity' to discover the true nature of the writing if the party is prevented from doing so by some physical or other impairment."); Gray v. First Nat'l Mortgage Co., of Evansville, 2003 WL 1343470 (Ky. Ct. App. Feb. 21, 2003) ("evidence that another has prevented the complainant from reading the contract" is "an exception to the general rule that one will be deemed to know the contents of a writing one signs").

275 *See, e.g.*, Rodriguez v. Lynch Ford, 2004 WL 2958772 (N.D. Ill. Nov. 18, 2004) (allegations that car dealer engaged in "spot delivery" preclude summary judgment on plaintiff's fraud claim); Holveck v. Ameriquest Mortgage Co., 2003 WL 21149085 (N.D. Ill. May 19, 2003) (denying motion to dismiss when borrowers alleged that they were induced to sign a note based upon representations that it did not contain a prepayment penalty); Young v. First Am. Fin. Servs., 977 F. Supp. 38 (D.D.C. 1997) (denying defendant lender's motion to dismiss fraud claim where homeowners alleged that lender refinanced in an amount double the existing mortgage with the false promise of another refinancing in a year to reduce significantly the monthly payment); Hanson v. American Nat'l Bank & Trust, 844 S.W.2d 408 (Ky. 1992), *vacated and remanded on other grounds*, 509 U.S. 918 (1993), *on remand*, 865 S.W.2d 302 (Ky. 1993).

276 *See* Smith v. Jenkins, 718 F. Supp. 2d 155 (D. Mass. 2010) (allegation that broker committed fraud by having illiterate, schizophrenic consumer sign loan application containing false information survives summary judgment motion); Gonzalez v. Ameriquest Mortgage Co., 2004 WL 2472249 (N.D. Cal. Mar. 1, 2004) (justifiable reliance and other elements of fraud pleaded sufficiently where oral representations made in Spanish contradicted final agreement written in English); Perez v. Hempstead Motor Sales, Ltd., 662 N.Y.S.2d 184 (N.Y. Dist. Ct. 1997) (denying automobile dealer's motion for summary judgment based in part on plaintiff's allegation that Spanish speaking salesperson falsely read agreement to plaintiff who had limited ability to speak or read English), *aff'd*, 674 N.Y.S.2d 564 (N.Y. App. Term. 1998).

277 *See, e.g.*, Davis v. G.N. Mortgage Corp., 396 F.3d 869 (7th Cir. 2005) (parol evidence may be considered in fraud claim but not breach of contract claim); Jeffries v. Ameriquest Mortgage Co., 543 F. Supp. 2d 368 (E.D. Pa. 2008) (parol evidence is admissible when integrated contract is ambiguous or when party alleges that a term was omitted because of accident, mistake, or fraud in the execution (but not fraud in the inducement); O'Brien v. Cacciatore, 591 N.E.2d 1384, 1390 (Ill. App. Ct. 1992). *See generally* National Consumer Law Center, Automobile Fraud § 7.7.2 (3d ed. 2007 and Supp.).

278 *See* Juergens v. Urban Title Servs., Inc., 533 F. Supp. 2d 64, 77 (D.D.C. 2008) (refusing to dismiss claim that lender's agent misrepresented the nature of the documents borrower was signing).

279 Sutton v. Viking Oldsmobile Nissan, Inc., 2001 WL 856250 (Minn. Ct. App. July 31, 2001) (denying dealer's motion for summary judgment), *later op. at* 2004 WL 26595 (Minn. Ct. App. Jan. 6, 2004) (affirming jury verdict against consumer).

280 Union Sec. Life Ins. Co. v. Crocker, 667 So. 2d 688 (Ala. 1995), *vacated on other grounds*, 116 S. Ct. 1872 (1996) (remanding $2 million punitive damage award to Alabama Supreme Court for further consideration in light of BMW of N. Am., Inc. v. Gore, 517 U.S. 559, 116 S. Ct. 1589 (1996)), *upon remand from Supreme Court*, 709 So. 2d 1118 (Ala. 1997) (upholding $1 million of punitive damages award where acts of insurance company's agent, while reprehensible and economically devastating to the plaintiff, were an "aberration for the company").

281 *See* § 5.9, *infra*.

282 Stewart v. Associates Consumer Discount Co., 183 F.R.D. 189 (E.D. Pa. 1998) (granting class certification where allegations involved a scheme targeting borrowers who had difficulty obtaining credit from banks, sending them "live" checks, charging exorbitant

which this practice insidiously ratchets up the cost of credit works mostly outside the APR disclosure, it is an almost inherently deceptive practice. A reported Seventh Circuit decision has held that a well-pleaded claim of loan flipping can state a claim for mail fraud sufficient to withstand a motion to dismiss a RICO claim.[283] A bankruptcy court held that the lender's failure to inform the borrowers of the effects of converting unsecured debt to secured debt and failure to disclose that payments on secured debt would extend for a longer period of time than payments on unsecured debt could support a fraud through omission claim.[284]

On the other hand, the Kansas Supreme Court upheld summary judgment against the borrower in a flipping case where the borrower alleged that the lender failed to tell him material facts about the cost of repeated refinancings in the context of the lender's "campaign" to get customers flip loans.[285] Though conceding that loan flipping, under certain circumstances, could rise to the level of fraud, the court found no theory to support a duty on the lender's part to disclose the effect of refinancing on the borrower's overall picture. The dissent, in contrast, looked to *The Restatement of Torts*, which creates a duty to exercise reasonable care in order to prevent partial or ambiguous statements of facts from being misleading.[286]

### 2.4.3.4 Falsification and Forgery

Complaints by consumers and homeowners about car dealers and mortgage brokers inflating their income and falsifying credit applications are common.[287] Courts may be reluctant to believe the consumer that these parties perpetrated the fraud, instead blaming the consumer. An Illinois decision should add credibility to these complaints.[288] The decision outlines a "massive pattern of fraud" alleged by an assignee who bought retail installment contracts and leases from a car dealer. In another case, a court denied defendants' summary judgment motion on claims of conspiracy and joint venture based on testimony that the lender trained the dealer to create false pay stubs and false down payments.[289] Many other sources document the frequency of falsification by lenders and sellers.[290] In addition to fraud claims, this conduct may violate federal or state credit repair statutes.[291] Furthermore, falsifying a loan application or inflating an appraisal is a federal criminal offense.[292]

In cases involving falsified credit applications or inflated appraisals, defendants often argue that the consumer cannot make out a fraud claim because, if anyone relied on the falsified document it was the lender rather than the consumer.[293] In the

---

points, upselling the loans from consumer loans to home-secured loans, promising to consolidate other debt but failing to do so, and repeatedly refinancing existing loans; claims raised under fraud, conspiracy, RICO, UDAP, TILA, and unjust enrichment theories). *See also* Reynolds v. American Gen. Fin, Inc., 1999 Ala. Civ. App. LEXIS 858 (Ala. Ct. Civ. App. Dec. 3, 1999) (reversing summary judgment for lender in flipping case where lender stated that interest rate was 20% but it was actually higher; issue was whether statute of limitations was tolled due to alleged fraud), *addressed on appeal*, 795 So. 2d 685 (Ala. 2000) (statute of limitations not tolled).

283 Emery v. American Gen. Fin., Inc., 71 F.3d 1343 (7th Cir. 1995).

284 *In re* Miner, 369 B.R. 655 (Bankr. D. Kan. 2007) (denying, in part, lender's motion to dismiss fraud claim).

285 Gonzales v. Associates Fin. Serv., 967 P.2d 312 (Kan. 1998). *See also Ex parte* Ford Motor Credit Co., 717 So. 2d 781 (Ala. 1997) (denying fraudulent suppression claim where consumer who was experienced in purchasing, selling, and financing used cars asked dealer why loan rate was so high but made no specific inquiry about existence of commission agreement between dealer and credit company; also finding no justifiable reliance in misrepresentation claim given customer's level of sophistication); Brown v. Norwest Fin. Ala., Inc., 723 So. 2d 97 (Ala. Ct. Civ. App. 1998) (though acknowledging that a fraudulent suppression cause of action could arise from the practice of flipping, in Alabama the borrower must show that the lender had a duty to communicate, arising either from a confidential relationship or a request for information, neither of which existed in this case; contention that lender fraudulently suppressed the existence of the mortgage placed on her home also failed).

286 Restatement (Second) of Torts § 551(2)(b), (c), (e) (1965).

287 *See, e.g.*, United States v. Ford, 558 F.3d 371 (5th Cir. 2009) (title company employee convicted of preparing false real estate documents for closings to support inflated loans); Whitley v. Taylor Bean & Whitacker Mortgage Corp., 607 F. Supp. 2d 885 (N.D. Ill. 2009) (refusing to dismiss fraud claim based on issuance of inflated appraisal); Juergens v. Urban Title Servs., Inc., 533 F. Supp. 2d 64, 79–80 (D.D.C. 2008) (refusing to dismiss fraud claim alleging that lender misrepresented nature of documents consumer was signing, created documents to disguise the nature of the loan, and possibly falsified documents); Farlow v. Barbarino Bros., Inc., 2006 WL 3755219 (Conn. Super. Ct. Dec. 1, 2006) (finding that consumer's allegation that car dealer's inflation of her income on loan application led to foreseeable and avoidable injury would reasonably support a finding of causation and stated a legally sufficient claim); Premium Air, Inc. v. Luchinski, 735 N.W.2d 194 (Wis. Ct. App. 2007) (table) (text available at 2007 WL 1345839) (vendor submitted forged loan application).

288 Gelco Corp. v. Duval Motor Co., 2002 WL 31875537 (N.D. Ill. Dec. 26, 2002).

289 Knapp v. Americredit Fin. Serv., Inc., 245 F. Supp. 2d 841 (S.D. W. Va. 2003). *See also* First Nat'l Bank v. Cincinnati Ins. Co., 485 F.3d 971 (7th Cir. 2007) (addressing insurance issues in case in which car dealer forged customers' names on fabricated and altered leases and submitted them to bank).

290 *See also* Mortgage Review Board; Administrative Actions, 72 Fed. Reg. 35,249 (June 27, 2007) (listing settled administrative actions against mortgage brokers/lenders many of whom were alleged to have used falsified or unverified loan applications or documentation); Michael Hudson, *Lending a Hand: How Wall Street Stoked The Mortgage Meltdown*, Wall St. J., June 27, 2007, *available at* http://online.wsj.com/article/SB118288752469648903.html (subscription required) (describing allegations that front-line workers and managers exaggerated borrowers' creditworthiness by falsifying tax forms, pay stubs, and other information or ignoring inaccurate data submitted by independent mortgage brokers).

291 *See, e.g.*, Premium Air, Inc. v. Luchinski, 735 N.W.2d 194 (Wis. Ct. App. 2007) (table; text available at 2007 WL 1345839) (vendor who arranged financing was "credit services organization" under Wisconsin Consumer Act and violated Act by submitting forged loan application; violation rendered contract unenforceable). *See generally* National Consumer Law Center, Fair Credit Reporting § 15.2.7 (7th ed. 2010 and Supp.).

292 18 U.S.C. § 1014.

293 *See, e.g.*, Dunn v. Northgate Ford, Inc., 794 N.Y.S.2d 449 (App. Div. 2005) (auto dealership's misrepresentations to a lender on a credit application did not constitute fraud on the customer, where she did not read or rely on those misstatements); Peabody v.

case of a falsified credit application, one approach to this problem is to find out whether the defendant misrepresented to the consumer that the credit application the consumer signed contained the same information the consumer provided. The consumer may have relied on that misrepresentation. In addition, even if the consumer never saw the falsified document, the misrepresentation to others may have enabled the fraud to succeed, and may form the basis for joint venture or civil conspiracy liability.[294]

### 2.4.3.5 Constitutional and Statutory Restrictions on Punitive Damages

One of the benefits of a fraud claim is that punitive damages are available in most jurisdictions. In a number of states, however, punitive damages for some or most torts are capped by statute either at a fixed multiple of compensatory damages or at a dollar amount.[295]

In addition, the U.S. Supreme Court has held that the Due Process Clause prohibits a state from imposing grossly excessive punitive damages on a tortfeasor. The Court has identified three guideposts for determining whether a punitive damage award is grossly excessive:

- The degree of reprehensibility on the part of the defendant;
- The disparity between the harm or potential harm suffered and the punitive damages awarded;
- The difference between the punitive damages awarded and the civil penalties authorized or imposed in comparable cases.[296]

Factors that courts should consider when weighing the reprehensibility of a defendant's conduct include:

- Whether the harm is physical as opposed to economic;
- Whether the tortious conduct shows an indifference to or reckless disregard of the health or safety of others;
- Whether the target of the conduct had financial vulnerability;
- Whether the conduct involved repeated actions or was only an isolated incident;
- Whether the harm resulted from intentional malice, trickery, or deceit, or mere accident.[297]

Some of these factors are likely to be pronounced in consumer credit cases. The harm will usually be economic rather than physical, but the creditor's actions may involve some threat to the consumer's health or safety, particularly if loss of a home, loss of utility service, or faulty home repairs are involved. The targets of fraud in consumer credit cases typically are financially vulnerable, and fraudulent creditors often specifically seek out these vulnerable consumers. Showing repetition and malicious intent is also often possible.

As to the ratio of punitive to compensatory damages, "few awards exceeding a single-digit ratio between punitive and compensatory damages, to a significant degree, will satisfy due process."[298] Nonetheless, the Supreme Court held that a higher ratio may be consistent with due process if an egregious act causes only a small amount of economic harm.[299] Many courts have applied this principle, upholding punitive damages well in excess of a single-digit ratio to compensatory damages where the compensatory damage award was relatively small.[300]

The constitutional standards for punitive damages are discussed in detail in another treatise in this series.[301]

## *2.4.4 Negligent Misrepresentation*

Negligent misrepresentation, which does not require proof of intent to deceive, has also been held to apply in some instances to the debtor-creditor relationship.[302] The *Restatement* defines this tort as the provision of false information to guide others in their business transactions by someone "in the course of his business, profession, or employment, or in any other transaction in which he has a pecuniary interest" who fails to exercise reasonable care or competence in obtaining or communicating the information.[303] Representations by retail sellers (car dealers, home improvement contractors) and loan brokers about the nature of the financing they will arrange may lead to claims for negligent misrepresentation. While a claim of negligent mis-

---

Northgate Ford, Inc., 794 N.Y.S.2d 452 (App. Div. 2005) (rejecting fraud claim where consumer did not read or rely on false statements in credit application).

294 *See* National Consumer Law Center, Mortgage Lending § 10.6 (2012).

295 *See* National Consumer Law Center, Automobile Fraud § 7.10.4 (3d ed. 2007 and Supp.).

296 State Farm Mut. Auto. Ins. Co. v. Campbell, 538 U.S. 408, 123 S. Ct. 1513, 155 L. Ed. 2d 585 (2003); BMW of N. Am., Inc. v. Gore, 517 U.S. 559, 116 S. Ct. 1589, 134 L. Ed. 2d 809 (1996).

297 State Farm Mut. Auto. Ins. Co. v. Campbell, 538 U.S. 408, 123 S. Ct. 1513, 1521, 155 L. Ed. 2d 585 (2003).

298 *Id.*, 123 S. Ct. at 1524.

299 *Id.*

300 *See generally* National Consumer Law Center, Automobile Fraud § 7.10.6.3.6 (3d ed. 2007 and Supp.).

301 National Consumer Law Center, Automobile Fraud § 7.10.6 (3d ed. 2007 and Supp.).

302 *See, e.g.,* Richter, S.A. v. Bank of Am. Nat'l Trust & Sav. Ass'n, 939 F.2d 1176 (5th Cir. 1991) (bank's negotiating with debtor over restructuring debt without informing him it had decided to "disengage" from credit relationship supported jury finding of negligent misrepresentation, though bank had legal right to refuse loan); Fidler v. Central Coop. Bank (*In re* Fidler), 210 B.R. 411 (Bankr. D. Mass. 1997) (allegations that lender negligently misrepresented the nature and terms of the loan stated a claim); Frame v. Boatmen's Bank, 824 S.W.2d 491 (Mo. Ct. App. 1991) (bank's oral representation that it would fund a loan to purchase real estate without informing debtor of all contingencies which must be met prior to approval held subject to claim; bank knew debtor relying on its professional judgment on the matter, and loan officer had duty of due care in providing information and advice); Federal Land Bank v. Sloane, 825 S.W.2d 439 (Tex. 1991) (negligent misrepresentation that it had approved loan application).

303 Restatement (2d) of Torts § 552 (1977). *See* Birt v. Wells Fargo Home Mortgage, Inc., 75 P.3d 640, 651–657 (Wyo. 2003). *See generally* National Consumer Law Center, Automobile Fraud § 7.4.3.5 (3d ed. 2007 and Supp.); National Consumer Law Center, Consumer Warranty Law § 11.4.3 (4th ed. 2010 and Supp.).

representation has a lower standard of proof than fraud, some jurisdictions may subject it to the same requirement to plead with particularity.[304] This means a creditor's vague promise of favorable loan terms may not be sufficient to state a claim for negligent misrepresentation.[305] A consumer's reliance on the creditor's statements must also be reasonable under the circumstances.[306]

## 2.4.5 *Breach of Fiduciary Duty*

### 2.4.5.1 Existence of a Fiduciary Relationship

#### *2.4.5.1.1 Special circumstances in debtor-creditor relationship can give rise to fiduciary duty*

Traditionally, a credit transaction has been considered an arm's length transaction in which there is no special duty read into the creditor-debtor relationship.[307] Most courts, however, have held that the presence of certain factors in the creditor-debtor relationship may give rise to a fiduciary duty.[308]

For example, a fiduciary relationship can arise when a party—generally a "weaker" party in the sense of the ability to protect himself or herself—places trust and confidence in another.[309] Such a duty can arise if a lender acts in the role of advisor and knows or should have known of the borrower's trust.[310]

304 Meridian Project Sys., Inc. v. Hardin Constr. Co., L.L.C., 404 F. Supp. 2d 1214, 1219 (E.D. Cal. 2005) ("It is well settled in the Ninth Circuit that misrepresentation claims are a species of fraud, which must meet Rule 9(b)'s particularity requirement."). *But see* General Elec. Capital Corp. v. Posey, 415 F.3d 391 (5th Cir. 2005) (negligent misrepresentation claim not subject to heightened pleading requirements of Rule 9(b)).

305 *See, e.g.*, Delino v. Platinum Community Bank, 628 F. Supp. 2d 1226, 1235 (S.D. Cal. 2009) ("representation that very favorable terms are available" is insufficient to put defendant on notice of what misrepresentations were made).

306 Jacob v. Home Sav. & Loan Co. of Youngstown, Ohio, 679 F. Supp. 2d 837, 841 (N.D. Ohio 2010), *aff'd*, 428 Fed. Appx. 523 (6th Cir. 2011).

307 Sallee v. Fort Knox Nat'l Bank (In *re* Sallee), 286 F.3d 878 (6th Cir. 2002) (ordinarily no fiduciary duty on bank to act in borrower's interest; but business borrower's fraud claim is actionable where bank kept one appraisal secret while revealing another, as duty to disclose arises from partial disclosure by one with superior knowledge); Dicicco v. Willow Grove Bank, 2004 WL 2150980 (E.D. Pa. Sept. 21, 2004) (lender not fiduciary of borrower—law presumes the relationship between lender and borrower is conducted at arms-length and the parties are each acting in their own interest); Strong v. First Family Fin. Servs., Inc. 202 F. Supp. 2d 536 (S.D. Miss. 2002) (lenders and borrowers typically not in a fiduciary relationship); Landreneau v. Fleet Fin. Group, 197 F. Supp. 2d 551 (M.D. La. 2002) (no duty by lender, though this is not a per se rule); Baldwin v. Laurel Ford Lincoln-Mercury, Inc., 32 F. Supp. 2d 894 (S.D. Miss. 1998) (ordinarily, no fiduciary relationship between creditor and debtor; no special facts alleged by consumer to find such a relationship with car dealer who obtained financing through the car manufacturer); Citibank, N.A. v. Gifesman, 773 A.2d 993 (Conn. App. Ct. 2001); Geiger v. Crestar Bank, 778 A.2d 1085 (D.C. App. Ct. 2001) (relationship between bank and depositor is governed by the written agreement; ordinarily no fiduciary duty owed by the bank); Huntington Mortgage Co. v. DeBrota, 703 N.E.2d 160 (Ind. Ct. App. 1998) (no fiduciary duty between creditor and borrower absent special circumstances); Morton v. Bank of the Bluegrass, 18 S.W.3d 353 (Ky. Ct. App. 1999); Holmes v. Peoples State Bank, 796 So. 2d 176 (La. Ct. App. 2001) (relationship between bank and depositor is governed by the written agreement; ordinarily no fiduciary duty owed by the bank); Rossbach v. FBS Mortgage Corp., 1998 Minn. App. LEXIS 374 (Apr. 7, 1998); GMAC v. Baymon, 732 So. 2d 262 (Miss. 1999); Koch v. First Union Corp., 2002 WL 372939 (Pa. Ct. Com. Pl. Jan. 10, 2002); Hutson v. Wenatchee Fed. Sav. & Loan Ass'n, 588 P.2d 1192, 1198 (Wash. Ct. App. 1979).

308 *See* Brewer v. Indymac Bank, 609 F. Supp. 2d 1104, 1121 (E.D. Cal. 2009) (allegation that lender held itself out as mortgage broker sufficient to support claim that lender owed fiduciary duty); Rennick v. Provident Bank, 2008 WL 696893 (S.D. Ohio Mar. 12, 2008) (debtor-creditor relationship does not establish fiduciary relationship unless special circumstances exist; special circumstances found when parties agree in writing that fiduciary relationship exists); Frye v. Am. Gen. Fin., Inc., 307 F. Supp. 2d 836 (S.D. Miss 2004) (special circumstances between lender and borrower may create fiduciary duty); Watson v. CBSK Fin. Group, Inc., 2002 WL 598521 (N.D. Ill. Apr. 18, 2002) (pleading that contractor and broker acted as financial advisors and actively sought to inspire confidence that they would act in the consumer's interest); Birt v. Wells Fargo Home Mortgage, Inc., 75 P.3d 640, 660–662 (Wyo. 2003) (fiduciary duty may arise between lender and borrower, but not shown here).

309 *See* Smith v. Jenkins, 626 F. Supp. 2d 155, 171 (D. Mass. 2009) (borrower with mental illness sufficiently pleaded claim for breach of fiduciary duty where defendants knew he was novice at real estate transactions and could not understand underlying details, and took advantage of his trust); Garrett v. BankWest, 459 N.W.2d 833 (S.D. 1990); Mark Budnitz, *The Sale of Credit Life Insurance: The Bank as Fiduciary*, 62 N.C. L. Rev. 295 (1984).

310 Smith v. Jenkins, 626 F. Supp. 2d 155, 171 (D. Mass. 2009) (mentally disabled consumer stated claim for breach of fiduciary duty by alleging defendants lured him into transaction with representation that they would act in his best interest and where defendants were aware of consumer's inability to understand transaction); Ellipso, Inc. v. Mann, 541 F. Supp. 2d 365 (D.D.C. 2008) (borrower failed to allege facts that would give rise to special circumstances); Frye v. American Gen. Fin., Inc., 307 F. Supp. 2d 836 (S.D. Miss. 2004) (acknowledging special circumstances may give rise to fiduciary duty between lender and borrower; such circumstances not sufficiently alleged); Stewart v. Phoenix Nat'l Bank, 64 P.2d 101, 106 (Ariz. 1937) (confidential relationship adequately alleged, but claim barred by res judicata); Boatmen's Nat'l Bank v. Ward, 595 N.E.2d 622 (Ill. App. Ct. 1992) (upholding finding that bank had fiduciary duty toward customer whose mental health was declining and who relied on bank to help him manage his financial affairs); First Nat'l Bank v. Brown, 181 N.W.2d 178, 182 (Iowa 1970); First Am. Nat'l Bank v. Mitchell, 359 So. 2d 1376 (Miss. 1988) (mortgagor and mortgagee are in relationship of trust; mortgagee had duty to disclose higher price was available when it forced sale of collateral); Deist v. Wachholz, 678 P.2d 188 (Mont. 1984). *See also* Watson v. CBSK Fin. Group, Inc., 2002 WL 598521 (N.D. Ill. Apr. 18, 2002) (consumer pleaded that the contractor and broker acted as financial advisors and actively sought to inspire confidence that they would act in the consumer's interest); Capital Bank v. MVB, Inc., 644 So. 2d 515 (Fla. Dist. Ct. App. 1994) (commercial transaction); Irvin v. American Gen. Fin., Inc., 2005 WL 1607460 (Ohio Ct. App. June 30, 2005) (whether special circumstances exist giving rise to fiduciary relationship between lender and borrower is question of fact precluding dismissal). *But cf.* Fridenmaker v. Valley Nat'l Bank, 534 P.2d 1064 (Ariz. Ct. App. 1975) (mortgagor's consultation with competent counsel mili-

As lenders go beyond giving a borrower what he or she has asked for, by offering extra services, a "quasi-fiduciary relationship of trust and confidence" may be created,[311] which at least gives rise to a duty of disclosure.[312] Such a relationship has been found where a lender gave a borrower advice about such things as qualifying for a special lending program, whether to finance a remodeling or a new house, and whether the consumer could afford a certain type of credit insurance.[313]

It might be arguable that aggressive marketing techniques used by lenders create a "trust and confidence" relationship. Some lenders' advertising campaigns invite consumers to view them as trustworthy financial advisors. One lender's letter to a new borrower read "[t]here are many ways we can help . . . not only by lending money—but by giving you sound money management when you need it."[314] If a borrower succumbs to such pitches—entering into an unaffordable home equity loan because the lender touted the tax advantages, engaging in expensive and disadvantageous flipping or loan consolidations at the lender's suggestion, or getting an insurance-packed loan—the facts should be viewed carefully in the light of these cases. In a decision in a case with a long history, a Pennsylvania appellate court held that carefully orchestrated and pervasive advertising intended to create confidence and trust can establish the prima facie elements of a confidential relationship.[315]

Entities that arrange refund anticipation loans (RALs) typically not only arrange the loan but also assist the consumer in preparing and filing a tax return. Some courts have held that a fiduciary duty arises in this context, either because the RAL provider is the consumer's agent[316] or because the lender solicits the trust and confidence of consumers.[317] Other courts have held that a tax preparation/RAL transaction is too short and isolated to create a fiduciary relationship.[318]

There may be an argument that a lender or car dealer creates a fiduciary relationship when it requires the consumer to sign a power of attorney for some purpose in the transaction. A power of attorney may be signed, for example, when actual title to a car is not readily available and the dealer wishes to transfer title. A car dealer may also have a fiduciary relationship to a consumer in regard to credit insurance sold by the dealer to the

---

tates against finding that confidential relationship existed); Mans v. Peoples Bank of Imboden, 10 S.W.3d 885 (Ark. 2000) (husband's twenty-three-year relationship with bank and widow's lack of sophistication insufficient to create fiduciary duty such that bank had duty to inform widow of lapse in credit life insurance policy); Bloomfield v. Nebraska State Bank, 465 N.W.2d 144 (Neb. 1991) (no fiduciary relationship between bank and agricultural borrower in absence of evidence of special relationship or opportunity to influence borrower; noting borrower's failure to present evidence of disparity in bargaining power, although stating that superior bargaining power alone does not create a fiduciary duty); Victoria Bank & Trust Co. v. Brady, 779 S.W.2d 893, 902 (Tex. App. 1989) (mere subjective trust on part of borrower will not alone create fiduciary relationship), *aff'd in part, rev'd in part on other grounds*, 811 S.W.2d 931 (Tex. 1991); Birt v. Wells Fargo Home Mortgage, Inc., 75 P.3d 640, 660–662 (Wyo. 2003) (fiduciary duty may arise between lender and borrower, but not shown here).

311 Johnson v. Robinson (*In re* Johnson), 292 B.R. 821 (Bankr. E.D. Pa. 2003) (acknowledging that lender could have fiduciary responsibilities to borrower under certain circumstances not present here); Morton v. Bank of Bluegrass, 18 S.W.3d 353 (Ky. Ct. App. 1999) (where bank loan officer was also agent of credit insurance company, fiduciary duty to disclose material facts about eligibility arose; reversing summary judgment for lender); Hutson v. Wenatchee Fed. Sav. & Loan Ass'n, 588 P.2d 1192, 1199 (Wash. Ct. App. 1979); Birt v. Wells Fargo Home Mortgage, Inc., 75 P.3d 640 (Wyo. 2003) (recognizing that lender can create fiduciary relationship with borrower, but not on these facts).

312 Restatement (Second) of Torts § 551 (1977). *See also* Deist v. Wachholz, 678 P.2d 188 (Mont. 1984) (where confidential relationship existed between bank and customer, bank employee had duty of disclosure and duty to do nothing which would place customer at a disadvantage). *But cf.* Jenkins v. Hyundai Motor Fin. Co., 389 F. Supp. 2d 961 (S.D. Ohio 2005) ("touting" and "selling" credit disability insurance not sufficient to create fiduciary duty).

313 Hutson v. Wenatchee Fed. Sav. & Loan Ass'n, 588 P.2d 1192 (Wash. Ct. App. 1979) (lender therefore had duty to disclose that the mortgage insurance purchased was not the credit life insurance requested by borrowers). *See also* Camp v. First Fed. Sav. & Loan, 671 S.W.2d 213 (Ark. Ct. App. 1984) (fact question whether construction lender had duty to disclose facts it knew which diminished the value of the house borrower was purchasing); First Nat'l Bank & Trust Co. v. Pack, 789 So. 2d 411 (Fla. Dist. Ct. App. 2001) (fiduciary relationship created when consumer asked bank to help with builder and to make sure construction moved forward; bank undertook this responsibility and told consumer that it would be present at walk-through and that defects would be corrected); Tomaszewski v. McKeon Ford, Inc., 573 A.2d 501 (N.J. Super. Ct. App. Div. 1990) (auto dealer who advised purchaser about how to qualify for credit approval from financier also had duty to advise her concerning credit insurance purchase, and insuring herself instead of co-buyer, who was the principal income earner); Glascock v. City Nat'l Bank of W. Va., 576 S.E.2d 540 (W. Va. 2002) (construction loan lender creates special relationship with borrower by overseeing or intervening in construction process; had duty to disclose information critical to project). *But see* Mans v. Peoples Bank of Imboden, 10 S.W.3d 885 (Ark. 2000) (no fiduciary relationship between bank and customer regarding credit insurance; ignoring fact that the bank acted as agent for the insurance company).

314 Examples of such advertisements are found in Mark Budnitz, *The Sale of Credit Life Insurance: The Bank As Fiduciary*, 62 N.C. L. Rev. 295, 318 n.126 (1984).

315 Basile v. H&R Block, Inc., 777 A.2d 95 (Pa. Super. Ct. 2001). *See also* Green v. H&R Block, Inc., 735 A.2d 1039 (Md. 1999) (tax preparer found to be agent of consumer thus creating fiduciary duty to advise the consumer that it receives payments and other benefits from the lender for facilitating the making of the loan).

316 Green v. H&R Block, Inc., 735 A.2d 1039 (Md. 1999). *But see* Basile v. H& R Block, Inc., 761 A.2d 1115, 1120 (Pa. 2000).

317 Basile v. H&R Block, Inc., 777 A.2d 95 (Pa. Super. Ct. 2001).

318 Peterson v. H&R Block Tax Servs., Inc., 971 F. Supp. 2d 1204, 1213–1214 (N.D. Ill. 1997) (fiduciary relationship can be imposed on *ad hoc* basis, but not here, where tax preparer had no close, long-term relationship with borrower or influence over management or investment of her assets); Beckett v. H&R Block, Inc., 714 N.E.2d 1033 (Ill. App. Ct. 1999) (tax preparer not an agent; no duty to disclose secret profit to consumer); Carnegie v. H&R Block, Inc., 703 N.Y.S.2d 27 (N.Y. App. Div. 2000) (no fiduciary duty where refund anticipation loan transaction was arms-length, isolated transaction that did not occur in context of a broader relationship of trust and confidence). *Cf.* Hunter v. Jackson Hewitt, Inc., 2007 WL 3376841 (S.D. W. Va. Nov. 6, 2007) (even if taxpayer had confidential relationship with tax preparer as to preparation of taxes, it did not extend to refund anticipation loan transaction).

consumer when the dealer is responsible for handling a refund of the insurance premium in the event the insurance is denied or terminated.[319]

A fiduciary relationship may also be created by statute. For example, a number of state mortgage broker laws specify that the broker owes a fiduciary duty to the borrower.[320]

#### *2.4.5.1.2 Principal-agent relationship*

The relationship of agent to principal is a fiduciary relationship.[321] The parties must consent to an agency relationship, but consent may be found either in an express agreement or by inference from the parties' acts.[322]

The highest court in Maryland has cited three factors to consider in determining whether a principal-agent relationship exists: (1) whether the agent has the power to alter the legal relations of the principal; (2) whether the agent has a duty to act primarily for the benefit of the principal; and (3) whether the principal has the right to control the agent.[323] Illinois decisions list two components of an agency relationship: (1) the principal has the right to control the manner and method in which the agent performs the work; and (2) the agent has the power to subject the principal to personal liability.[324] The Pennsylvania Supreme Court lists the elements of an agency relationship as "the manifestation by the principal that the agent shall act for him, the agent's acceptance of the undertaking and the understanding of the parties that the principal is to be in control of the undertaking."[325]

Some courts hold that the principal must exercise control only over the result or ultimate objectives of the agency relationship, and that direct supervisory control of the agent's work need not be shown.[326] When the facts otherwise demonstrate an agency relationship, the highest court in Maryland held that the fact that the principal ultimately signs any contract that is negotiated does not establish that the agent lacks the power to alter the principal's legal relationships.[327] However, the Pennsylvania Supreme Court held that a tax preparer was not the taxpayer's agent because it could not file a tax return or arrange a refund anticipation loan without the taxpayer's signature.[328]

### 2.4.5.2 Duties of a Fiduciary

A fiduciary owes its principal a duty of loyalty.[329] As the agent in a principal-agent relationship, the fiduciary has a duty to act in the best interests of the principal.[330] The existence of a fiduciary or quasi-fiduciary duty also gives rise to a duty of fair and honest disclosure of all facts which might be presumed to influence the consumer in regard to his or her actions,[331] including those favorable to the creditor or a third party and adverse to the borrower's interest.[332]

One court held that, where a fiduciary duty arose between bank and borrower after the initial negotiation of the loan terms, the bank breached that duty by providing inaccurate, untimely, and incomplete information to the borrowers.[333] Another court held that where the lender made a construction loan to the borrowers and maintained oversight of the construction process, it created a special relationship and duty to disclose information that would be critical to the integrity of the project.[334] A bank that has a fiduciary duty to a customer breaches that duty by steering the customer into a transaction

---

319 Crow v. Fred Martin Motor Co., 2003 WL 1240119 (Ohio Ct. App. Mar. 19, 2003).

320 *See* National Consumer Law Center, Mortgage Lending § 7.2.3.4 (2012).

321 Restatement (Second) of Agency § 1 (1958). *See* Green v. H&R Block, Inc., 735 A.2d 1039, 1047 (Md. 1999).

322 First Nat'l Bank & Trust Co. v. Pack, 789 So. 2d 411 (Fla. Dist. Ct. App. 2001) (fiduciary relationship implied in law based upon lender's behavior); Green v. H&R Block, Inc., 735 A.2d 1039, 1047 (Md. 1999); Basile v. H&R Block, Inc., 777 A.2d 95 (Pa. Super. Ct. 2001) (confidential relationship can arise between tax preparer and customer depending on the circumstances, even where no agency exists). *See also* Poskin v. TD Banknorth, N.A., 687 F. Supp. 2d 530 (W.D. Pa. 2009) (fact question whether manufactured home broker was agent for lender); Crow v. Fred Martin Motor Co., 2003 WL 1240119 (Ohio Ct. App. Mar. 19, 2003).

323 Green v. H&R Block, Inc., 735 A.2d 1039, 1049 (Md. 1999).

324 Peterson v. H&R Block Tax Servs., Inc., 971 F. Supp. 2d 1204 (N.D. Ill. 1997); Knapp v. Hill, 657 N.E.2d 1068, 1071 (Ill. App. Ct. 1995).

325 Basile v. H& R Block, Inc., 761 A.2d 1115, 1120 (Pa. 2000).

326 Green v. H&R Block, Inc., 735 A.2d 1039, 1050 (Md. 1999). *See also* Hunter v. Jackson Hewitt, Inc., 2007 WL 3376841 (S.D. W. Va. Nov. 6, 2007). *But see* Peterson v. H&R Block Tax Servs., Inc., 971 F. Supp. 2d 1204, 1213 (N.D. Ill. 1997) (principal must control the manner or method in which agent performs services; tax preparer that arranged refund anticipation loan was not borrower's agent); Beckett v. H&R Block, Inc., 714 N.E.2d 1033 (Ill. App. Ct. 1999) (borrower failed to allege facts showing that she had control over the manner and method by which tax preparer performed its services).

327 Green v. H&R Block, Inc., 735 A.2d 1039, 1051 (Md. 1999). *See also* Hunter v. Jackson Hewitt, Inc., 2007 WL 3376841 (S.D. W. Va. Nov. 6, 2007) (jury is to determine degree of control exercised and nature of relationship thereby created).

328 Basile v. H& R Block, Inc., 761 A.2d 1115, 1122 (Pa. 2000).

329 *See, e.g.*, Frey v. Fraser Yachts, 29 F.3d 1153 (7th Cir. 1994).

330 *Id. See also* MIC Life Ins. Co. v. Hicks, 2001 Miss. LEXIS 296 (Oct. 31, 2001) (insurance company's failure to refund unearned insurance premium in a timely way can constitute a breach of this duty; upholding jury award of actual damages plus $6 million in punitive damages against the insurance company in light of evidence of a pattern of failing to refund unearned premiums), *op. withdrawn, reh'g granted*, 825 So. 2d 616 (Miss. 2002) (remanding for new trial on amount of punitive damages).

331 Stewart v. Phoenix Nat'l Bank, 64 P.2d 101, 106 (Ariz. 1937); Green v. H&R Block, Inc., 735 A.2d 1039, 1056 (Md. 1999) (borrowers alleged sufficient facts to show that tax preparer was their agent so had duty to disclose money it received from lender for arranging refund anticipation loan); Basile v. H& R Block, Inc., 761 A.2d 1115, 1120 (Pa. 2000).

332 Barrett v. Bank of Am., 229 Cal. Rptr. 16 (Cal. Ct. App. 1986). *See also* Frey v. Fraser Yachts, 29 F.3d 1153, 1156 (7th Cir. 1994) (undisclosed dual agency of yacht broker, receiving commission from buyer as well as seller, breached fiduciary duty to seller).

333 Callahan v. First Merit Mortgage Corp. 2005 WL 3867346 (Ohio Mun. Ct. Sept. 22, 2005) (lender created relationship of trust and confidence by assuring borrowers that they would receive specified loan terms).

334 Glasock v. City Nat'l Bank of W. Va., 576 S.E.2d 540 (W. Va. 2002).

with another party that it knows is in financial distress and unlikely to be able to perform.[335] For example a bank improved its own position and reduced the likelihood that a troubled bank customer would default by encouraging prospective borrowers to contract with that customer.[336]

When a fiduciary duty creates a duty to disclose, failure to do so should give rise to a tort action for nondisclosure,[337] or the silence may qualify as misrepresentation.[338] One who knowingly aids and abets a fiduciary in a breach of its duty is also liable.[339]

## 2.4.6 *Breach of Duty of Due Care As Negligence*

In some circumstances, a negligence claim will be possible if the plaintiff can identify a duty of care owed by the defendant.[340] Some courts hold that a financial institution generally owes no duty of care to a borrower, but they recognize that this rule does not apply if the financial institution exceeds the scope of its conventional role as a mere lender.[341] Falsifying a borrower's income and the value of the collateral goes beyond a lender's conventional role and may amount to a breach of a duty of care.[342]

A bank, by virtue of agreeing to process a mortgage loan application and lock in a specified interest rate for ninety days in exchange for a $144 payment for an appraisal and credit report fee, entered into a relationship which gave rise to a tort duty of due care in processing the application.[343] In this case, the court suggested that the duty might be measured by looking at industry standards, such as credit underwriting standards established by the Federal Home Loan Mortgage Corporation, in the case of mortgage lending.[344] A mortgage holder which held a pay-off check from a third party too long, with the result that the check bounced when the issuer went out of business, breached a duty of care to the borrower.[345]

A negligence claim may also be viable against a party who owes the consumer a fiduciary duty, as such a party has a duty of care toward the consumer.[346] The elements of and defenses to negligence claims are discussed in more detail in National Consumer Law Center, *Consumer Warranty Law* § 12.2 (4th ed. 2010 and Supp.).

## 2.4.7 *Unconscionability*

### 2.4.7.1 Statutory and Common Law Sources of Prohibition Against Unconscionability

Unconscionability is a useful theory for protecting consumers from egregious overreaching. It may also operate as an outer limit on the price of credit.

The doctrine of unconscionability is embodied in common law,[347] UCC § 2-302, non-UCC statutory unconscionability

335 *See, e.g.*, Security Pac. Nat'l Bank v. Williams, 262 Cal. Rptr. 260 (Cal. Ct. App. 1989) (unpublished) (bank breached fiduciary duty by fraudulently inducing plaintiff to purchase failing car dealership in which bank had significant investment at stake); Barnett Bank v. Hooper, 498 So. 2d 923 (Fla. 1986); Capital Bank v. MVB, Inc., 644 So. 2d 515 (Fla. Dist. Ct. App. 1994) (bank breached fiduciary duty to loan customer where loan officer induced customer to purchase malfunctioning equipment from another bank customer in financial distress); First Nat'l Bank v. Brown, 181 N.W.2d 178 (Iowa 1970). *But cf.* Tokarz v. Frontier Fed. Sav. & Loan, 656 P.2d 1089 (Wash. Ct. App. 1983) (finding no special circumstances that would create fiduciary duty, so no duty to disclose to borrowers that home improvement contractor was having financial problems which impaired its ability to perform).

336 Capital Bank v. MVB, Inc., 644 So. 2d 515 (Fla. Dist. Ct. App. 1994) (bank breached fiduciary duty to loan customer where loan officer induced customer to purchase malfunctioning equipment from another bank customer in financial distress).

337 Restatement (Second) of Torts § 551. *See also* Green v. H&R Block, Inc., 735 A.2d 1039, 1056 (Md. 1999) (where agent breaches duty of disclosure and profits from the breach, principal may maintain action to recover those profits).

338 First Nat'l Bank v. Brown, 181 N.W.2d 178, 182 (Iowa 1970) (if the misrepresentation amounts to fraud in the inducement "whether innocent or not," the defrauded party may have the right to avoid the contract in an action in equity).

339 Jackson v. Smith, 254 U.S. 586, 589 (1921). *But see* Lum v. New Century Mortgage Corp., 800 N.Y.S.2d 408 (N.Y. App. Div. 2005) (dismissing claim of inducement of breach of fiduciary duty for yield spread premium where no showing of fiduciary duty between broker and borrower).

340 *See, e.g.*, Jacques v. First Nat'l Bank, 515 A.2d 756, 758 (Md. Ct. Spec. App. 1986) (elements of negligence action are a duty owed to the plaintiff or to a class of which the plaintiff is a part, a breach of that duty, causation, and damages). *But cf.* Bojorquez v. Gutierrez, 2010 WL 1223144 (N.D. Cal. Mar. 25, 2010) (as general rule, financial institution owes no duty of care to borrower when its role does not exceed conventional role as mere lender of money).

341 Watkinson v. MortgageIT, Inc., 2010 WL 2196083 (S.D. Cal. June 1, 2010) (listing factors to weigh in determining whether lender owes duty of care to borrower).

342 *Id.*; Sullivan v. JP Morgan Chase Bank, N.A., 725 F. Supp. 2d 1087 (E.D. Cal. 2010) (no duty of care not to misinform borrower about loan modification process, but lender may have violated duty of care by falsifying borrower's income and the appraisal during loan application process).

343 Jacques v. First Nat'l Bank, 515 A.2d 756, 761 (Md. Ct. Spec. App. 1986). *See also* High v. McLean Fin. Corp., 659 F. Supp. 1561 (D.D.C. 1987). *Cf.* Ferleger v. First Am. Mtg. Co., 662 F. Supp. 584 (N.D. Ill. 1987) (broker allegedly offered locked-in terms without disclosing the time limit, and would delay processing past expiration date, borrowers alleged RICO and UDAP claims; denying defendant's motion to dismiss).

344 Jacques v. First Nat'l Bank, 515 A.2d 756, 764 (Md. Ct. Spec. App. 1986). *But see* Whitley v. Taylor Bean & Whitacker Mortgage Corp., 607 F. Supp. 2d 885 (N.D. Ill. 2009) (dismissing negligence claim; lender has no duty to refrain from making unaffordable loan). *But cf. In re* Figard, 382 B.R. 695 (Bankr. W.D. Pa. 2008) (gist of claim for breach of duty arising from contract is contractual, so negligence claim not available).

345 *See* Family Fed. Sav. & Loan v. Davis, 172 B.R. 437 (Bankr. D.D.C. 1994).

346 *See, e.g.*, Watkinson v. MortgageIT, Inc., 2010 WL 2196083 (S.D. Cal. June 1, 2010); Carillo v. Countrywide Home Loans, 2010 WL 1904883 (S.D. Cal. May 12, 2010). *See generally* § 2.4.5, *supra*.

347 *See* Earl of Chesterfield v. Jansen, 28 Eng. Rep. 82 (Ch. 1751) (enunciating equitable concept of an unconscionable contract as one no person in her senses would make and no fair and honest person

provisions,[348] and some UDAP statutes that either explicitly prohibit unconscionability or that meld unfairness or deception standards into unconscionability standards.[349] Because there is considerable overlap,[350] case law as to what type of conduct or contract terms may be unconscionable should be helpful irrespective of which of the above vehicles was used. Whether the claim is based on statute or common law, thorough investigation and command of the facts of the case are critical to an unconscionability claim.[351]

### 2.4.7.2 Elements of a Claim of Unconscionability

There are two forms of unconscionability: procedural and substantive. Procedural unconscionability involves the bargaining process when the contract was made. Substantive unconscionability focuses on the content of the contract.[352] Some courts hold that both procedural and substantive unconscionability must be shown to invalidate a contract term.[353]

A court will find substantive unconscionability if the contract unfairly and unjustifiably "reallocates the risks of the bargain in an objectively unreasonable or unexpected manner."[354] The

---

would accept). *See also* Besta v. Beneficial Loan Co., 855 F.2d 532 (8th Cir. 1988); *In re* Maxwell, 281 B.R. 101 (Bankr. D. Mass. 2002); Williams v. E.F. Hutton Mortgage Corp., 555 So. 2d 158 (Ala. 1989). *See also* Hume v. United States, 132 U.S. 406, 410 (1889). *See generally* National Consumer Law Center, Consumer Warranty Law § 11.2 (4th ed. 2010 and Supp.) (U.C.C. unconscionability); Spanogle, *Analyzing Unconscionability Problems*, 117 U. Pa. Rev. 931, 936–941 (1968–1969).

348 *See, e.g.*, Ala. Code § 5-19-16 (consumer credit transactions); Alaska Stat. § 45.12.108 (leases); Cal. Civ. Code § 1670.5 (West); Cal. Fin. Code § 22302 (West) (consumer loans by finance lenders); Colo. Rev. Stat. § 5-5-109 (U.C.C.C.); D.C. Code § 28-3812 (consumer credit transactions or direct installment loans); Idaho Code Ann. § 28-45-106 (U.C.C.C.); Ind. Code § 24-4.5-5-108 (U.C.C.C.); Iowa Code § 537.5108 (U.C.C.C.); Kan. Stat. Ann. §§ 16a-4-106, 16a-6-111 (U.C.C.C.); La. Rev. Stat. Ann. § 9:3551 (consumer credit transactions); Me. Rev. Stat. tit. 9-A, §§ 5-108, 9-402 (U.C.C.C.); N.C. Gen. Stat. § 25A-43 (consumer credit sales); Okla. Stat. tit. 14A, §§ 4-106, 5-108, 6-111 (U.C.C.C.); S.C. Code Ann. §§ 37-4-106, 37-5-108, 37-10-105 (U.C.C.C.); Tenn. Code Ann. § 47-14-117(c); Utah Code Ann. § 70C-7-106 (U.C.C.C.); W. Va. Code §§ 46A-2-121 (U.C.C.C. hybrid), 46B-2-2 (rent-to-own); Wis. Stat. § 425.107 (UCCC); Wyo. Stat. Ann. §§ 40-14-106, 40-14-508.

349 *See* National Consumer Law Center, Unfair and Deceptive Acts and Practice § 4.4 (7th ed. 2008 and Supp.).

350 *See, e.g.*, U.C.C.C. § 5.108 cmts. ¶¶ 1, 3; Perdue v. Crocker Nat'l Bank, 702 P.2d 503, 511 n.10 (Cal. 1985).

351 The fact intensive nature of the unconscionability inquiry should preclude summary judgment unless there are no factual disputes. *See* Knapp v. American Gen. Fin. Inc., 111 F. Supp. 2d 758 (S.D. W. Va. 2000); Mallory v. Mortgage Am., Inc., 67 F. Supp. 2d 601 (S.D. W. Va. 1999) (summary judgment cannot be based on documents alone; factual issues ordinarily abound); Herrod v. First Republic Mortgage Corp., Inc., 625 S.E.2d 373 (W. Va. 2005). *See also* Cazares v. Pacific Shore Funding, 2006 WL 149106, at *6 n.4 (C.D. Cal. Jan. 3, 2006) ("determination of whether contract is unconscionable requires consideration of facts beyond scope of a motion to dismiss").

352 *See generally* Soltani v. Western & Southern Life Ins. Co., 258 F.3d 1038 (9th Cir. 2001); A&M Produce v. FMC Corp., 186 Cal. Rptr. 114 (Cal. Ct. App. 1982); National Consumer Law Center, Consumer Warranty Law § 11.2 (4th ed. 2010 and Supp.); Steven W. Bender, *Rate Regulation at the Crossroads of Usury and Unconscionability: The Case for Regulating Abusive and Commercial Interest Rates Under the Unconscionability Standard*, 31 Hous. L. Rev. 721 (1994); Leff, *Unconscionability and the Code—The Emperor's New Clause*, 115 U. Pa. L. Rev. 485, 509, 539 (1967); Note, *Reviving the Law of Substantive Unconscionability, Applying the Covenant of Good Faith and Fair Dealing to Excessively Priced Consumer Credit Contracts*, 33 UCLA L. Rev. 940, 944, 946 (1986).

353 M&T Mortgage Corp. v. Miller, 323 F. Supp. 2d 405 (E.D.N.Y. 2004) (both procedural and substantive unconscionability required; sufficiently alleged here where defendants baited consumers with one home, then switched them to another highly overpriced and unaffordable home at last minute, presented inflated appraisal, and steered them to lender and attorney they chose); Carboni v. Arrospide, 2 Cal. Rptr. 2d 845 (Cal. Ct. App. 1991) (both procedural and substantive unconscionability must be present; however, the greater the degree of substantive unconscionability, the less the degree of procedural unconscionability that is required). *See also In re* Allen, 174 B.R. 293 (Bankr. D. Or. 1994) (RTO transaction not unconscionable; noting that Oregon courts typically balance both procedural and substantive unconscionability). *But see* Luna v. Household Fin. Corp., 236 F. Supp. 2d 1166 (W.D. Wash. 2002) (plaintiff need only show procedural or substantive unconscionability under Washington law); Maxwell v. Fidelity Fin. Servs., Inc., 907 P.2d 51, 59 (Ariz. 1995) (unconscionability can be established with a showing of substantive unconscionability alone, especially in cases involving either price-cost disparity or limitation of remedies). *See generally* National Consumer Law Center, Consumer Warranty Law § 11.2.4.5 (4th ed. 2010 and Supp.).

354 *See* Maxwell v. Fairbanks Capital Corp. (*In re* Maxwell), 281 B.R. 101 (D. Mass. 2002) (standard is whether the terms of the loan drive too hard of a bargain); Luna v. Household Fin. Corp., 236 F. Supp. 2d 1166 (W.D. Wash. 2002) (standard is whether terms of arbitration rider were one-sided or overly harsh); Williams v. First Gov't Mortgage & Investors Corp., 974 F. Supp. 17 (D.D.C. 1997), *aff'd in part*, 176 F.3d 497 (D.C. Cir. 1999), *remanded after jury verdict*, 225 F.3d 738 (D.C. Cir. 2000) (upholding jury verdict for consumer on UDAP unconscionability claim; remanding trial court's rejection of common law unconscionability claim for further consideration); A&M Produce v. FMC Corp., 186 Cal. Rptr. 114 (Cal. Ct. App. 1982); Family Fin. Servs. v. Spencer, 677 A.2d 479 (Conn. App. Ct. 1996) (upholding trial court's finding of substantive unconscionability where second mortgage loan contained balloon payment which borrower had no means of paying and borrower had no opportunity to understand the terms of the contract); Howard v. Diolosa, 574 A.2d 995 (N.J. Super. Ct. App. Div. 1990) (standard is whether there was patent unfairness in the contract such that no reasonable person would accept its terms unless acting out of compulsion or necessity; case involved sale-leaseback of home). *See also* Beneficial Mortgage Co. of Ohio v. Leach, 2002 WL 926759 (Ohio Ct. App. May 9, 2002) (reversing summary judgment for defendant where genuine issue of material fact existed as to whether term of refinance agreement was substantively unconscionable); Sosa v. Paulos, 924 P.2d 357 (Utah 1996) (holding clause substantively unconscionable where it required patient to pay all costs incurred by physician to defend medical malpractice arbitration and all costs of the arbitration itself if the arbitrator awarded patient less than half of the amount she sought). *But see* Gruber v. Fed. Nat'l Mortgage Ass'n, 2003 WL 1091046 (Cal. Ct. App. Mar. 13, 2003) (loan assumption fee not unconscionable due to full disclosure that such fee could be imposed and disclosure of the actual amount of the fee prior to the assumption); Shadoan v. World Sav. & Loan Ass'n, 268 Cal. Rptr. 207 (Cal. Ct. App. 1990) (using

most typical type of procedural unconscionability involves oppression or surprise in the bargaining process.[355] Oppression occurs when there is a disparity in bargaining power between the parties.[356] For example, a form contract in which one party has no choice in the matter and cannot obtain better terms elsewhere might be oppressive.[357] Surprise occurs when creditors hide contract terms from the consumer in fine print or unusually complex clauses.[358] Negotiation of a loan transaction in a language other than English can be a factor.[359]

Thus a New Mexico court found a small, unsecured loan with a very high interest rate to be procedurally unconscionable based upon the absence of meaningful choice, the borrower's lack of sophistication, and the presence of deceptive practices.[360] The lender took unfair advantage of the borrower's low educational level and low income. The court relied in part on the testimony of an expert in behavioral economics that showed how the lender's marketing efforts made the loan's cost appear nominal (for example, one dollar a day), and how it used information "overload" to direct the consumer away from the loan's true cost. The court did not find the loan substantively unconscionable because allowable interest rates were more of a legislative function. But it did find the loans to be procedurally

unconscionability standard to evaluate UDAP claim; contract combining a unilateral call provision and a prepayment penalty did not impermissibly reallocate risk, where prepayment penalty would not attach if lender exercised call option). *But cf.* Emigrant Mortgage Co. v. Crismara, 2008 WL 2551039, at *8 (D. Conn. June 27, 2008) (18% default interest rate did not make loan substantively unconscionable, where such an interest rate was permissible in other contexts such as for tax debts).

355 *See* A&M Produce v. FMC Corp., 186 Cal. Rptr. 114 (Cal. Ct. App. 1982) (" 'Oppression' arises from an inequality of bargaining power which results in no real negotiation and absence of meaningful choice. . . . 'Surprise' involves the extent to which the supposedly agreed-upon terms of the bargain are hidden in a prolix printed form drafted by the party seeking to enforce the disputed terms."); Sosa v. Paulos, 924 P.2d 357 (Utah 1996) (listing six factors it will weigh: (1) whether each party had reasonable opportunity to understand the terms and conditions of the agreement; (2) whether there was a lack of opportunity for meaningful negotiation; (3) whether agreement was boilerplate form drafted solely by the party in the stronger bargaining position; (4) whether the terms of the agreement were explained to the weaker party; (5) whether the aggrieved party had a meaningful choice; (6) whether the stronger party employed deceptive practices to obscure key contractual provisions). *See generally* Note, *Reviving the Law of Substantive Unconscionability, Applying the Covenant of Good Faith and Fair Dealing to Excessively Priced Consumer Credit Contracts*, 33 UCLA L. Rev. 940, 944 n. 456 (1986).

356 *See also* Luna v. Household Fin. Corp., 236 F. Supp. 2d 1166 (W.D. Wash. 2002) (contract of adhesion meets this standard); Knapp v. American Gen. Fin. Inc., 111 F. Supp. 2d 758 (S.D. W. Va. 2000); Williams v. E.F. Hutton Mortgage Corp., 555 So. 2d 158 (Ala. 1989) (gross inequality of bargaining power); Howard v. Diolosa, 574 A.2d 995 (N.J. Super. Ct. App. Div. 1990). *But cf.* Taylor v. Bob O'Connor Ford, Inc., 2000 U.S. Dist. LEXIS 11486 (N.D. Ill. June 29, 2000) (allegations of lack of education and sophistication alone are not enough to state an unconscionability claim in this auto packing case); Marshall v. Mercury Fin. Co., 550 So. 2d 1026 (Ala. Civ. App. 1989) (unconscionability is an extraordinary remedy reserved for parties who are uneducated and unsophisticated; plaintiff who had college education and understood transaction did not establish claim of unconscionability). *See generally* Speidel, *Unconscionability, Assent and Consumer Protection*, 31 U. Pitt. L. Rev. 359 (1970).

357 *See* Johnson v. Long Beach Mortgage Loan Trust 2001-4, 451 F. Supp. 2d 16 (D.D.C. 2006) (defendant adequately alleged lack of meaningful choice as basis for common law unconscionability); Luna v. Household Fin. Corp., 236 F. Supp. 2d 1166 (W.D. Wash. 2002) (arbitration rider was offered on a take it or leave it basis and the disparity in bargaining power between the homeowner and a major financial institution was vast); Landreneau v. Fleet Fin. Group, 197 F. Supp. 2d 551 (M.D. La. 2002) (denying summary judgment for credit card company where credit card agreement may be a contract of adhesion); Carboni v. Arrospide, 2 Cal. Rptr. 2d 845 (Cal. Ct. App. 1991); Beneficial Mortgage Co. of Ohio v. Leach, 2002 WL 926759 (Ohio Ct. App. May 9, 2002); Kripke, *Gesture and Reality in Consumer Credit Reform*, 44 N.Y.U. L. Rev. 1, 7 (1969) ("The ghetto shopper is not a comparison shopper and does not have access to the lowest prices").

358 A&M Produce v. FMC Corp., 186 Cal. Rptr. 114 (Cal. Ct. App. 1982). *See also* Emigrant Mortgage Co. v. Crismara, 2008 WL 2551039 (D. Conn. June 27, 2008); M&T Mortgage Corp. v. Miller, 323 F. Supp. 2d 405 (E.D.N.Y. 2004) (finding procedural and substantive unconscionability sufficiently alleged in property flipping scheme where defendants baited consumers with one home, then switched them to another highly overpriced and unaffordable home at last minute, presented inflated appraisal, and steered them to lender and attorney chosen by defendants); Moore v. Mortgagestar, Inc., 2002 U.S. Dist. LEXIS 27457 (S.D. W. Va. Dec. 18, 2002) (denying lender's motion for summary judgment on unconscionability claim where one borrower was illiterate, the other could read but could not understand mortgage documents' complex, confusing, inconsistent, and substantively unconscionable terms, lender misrepresented loan terms, and closing was rushed); Knapp v. American Gen. Fin. Inc., 111 F. Supp. 2d 758 (S.D. W. Va. 2000) (though contract terms may have been clear, lender misrepresented the contents of the documents to consumers who could not read); Williams v. E.F. Hutton Mortgage Corp., 555 So. 2d 158 (Ala. 1989) (it is relevant whether, considering education or lack of it, there was a reasonable opportunity to understand terms of contract or whether important terms were "hidden in a maze of fine print and minimized by deceptive sales practices"); Razor v. Hyundai Motor Am., 854 N.E.2d 607 (Ill. 2006) (upholding trial court's determination that limitation on consequential damages in warranty agreement was procedurally unconscionable where plaintiff never saw the agreement until after she purchased the vehicle). *See generally* Steven W. Bender, *Rate Regulation at the Crossroads of Usury and Unconscionability: The Case for Regulating Abusive and Commercial Interest Rates Under the Unconscionability Standard*, 31 Hous. L. Rev. 721 (1994).

359 *See, e.g.*, Prevot v. Phillips Petroleum Co., 133 F. Supp. 2d 937 (S.D. Tex. 2003) (involving arbitration agreement); Family Fin. Servs. v. Spencer, 677 A.2d 479 (Conn. App. Ct. 1996) (upholding trial court's finding that second mortgage loan was unconscionable, in part, based on plaintiff limited knowledge of English). *See also In re* Turner Bros. Trucking, Inc., 8 S.W.3d 370 (Tex. App. 1999) (arbitration agreement unconscionable because employee who signed it was illiterate and had no one to explain it to him). *But cf.* Emigrant Mortgage Co. v. Crismara, 2008 WL 2551039 (D. Conn. June 27, 2008) (18% default interest rate for mortgage loan not procedurally unconscionable where borrower was educated businesswoman represented by counsel she had chosen, even though she was in desperate financial situation, the loan documents were given to her only at closing and were not explained to her, and default interest rate was never drawn to her attention).

360 State v. B&B Inv. Group, Inc. (N.M. Dist. Ct. Dec. 3, 2010), *available at* www.nclc.org/unreported.

unconscionable and thus in violation of the state deceptive practices statute.

It is important for practitioners to remember that special vulnerabilities such as financial distress or limited education should be relevant in evaluating unconscionability.[361] The fact that consumer contracts are not only non-negotiable but also unreadable by the majority of consumers argues in favor of a liberal application of the unconscionability doctrine.[362]

In its enumeration of examples of unconscionability, the 1974 version of the UCCC includes such substantive standards as gross price disparity, contracting for insurance charges with the effect of making the transaction unconscionable, entering into a transaction knowing the consumer could not receive a substantial benefit from it, or entering into a transaction knowing there was no reasonable probability of payment in full by the consumer, as well as examples of procedural unconscionability.[363]

When an unconscionability claim is brought against a national bank, questions arise as to whether the National Bank Act and federal regulation preempt the state law unconscionability claim. One federal court, in considering such preemption, determined that there was no black-and-white answer, and it depended on whether the conduct being challenged was authorized by federal regulation. Thus an unconscionable inducement claim was not preempted but a challenge that an adjustable rate mortgage (ARM) was unconscionable was preempted because federal law explicitly allowed for such mortgages.[364] Preemption issues are discussed in detail at Chapter 3, *infra*, and in National Consumer Law Center, *Mortgage Lending* Ch. 5 (2012).

### 2.4.7.3 Unconscionability As Outer Limit on Price of Credit

In the absence of legislatively prescribed usury ceilings, unconscionability can serve as an outer limit on the price of credit.[365] Idaho, for example, removed its statutorily defined interest rate caps in 1983,[366] but retained the prohibition on unconscionable consumer transactions.[367] Similarly, Massachusetts, by regulation, sets the outer limits on mortgage rates or terms at those which "significantly deviate from industry-wide

361 *See, e.g.*, Johnson v. Long Beach Mortgage Loan Trust 2001-4, 451 F. Supp. 2d 16 (D.D.C. 2006) (denying motion to dismiss claim that defendants violated unconscionability prohibition of UDAP statute by taking unfair advantage of plaintiff's age, limited education, limited ability to comprehend the nature of loans, limited economic resources and lack of business sophistication); *In re* Fleet, 95 B.R. 319 (E.D. Pa. 1989); Kugler v. Romain, 279 A.2d 640 (N.J. 1970). *Cf.* Sosa v. Paulos, 924 P.2d 357 (Utah 1996) (physician's behavior in giving patient arbitration agreement regarding medical malpractice minutes before surgery was procedurally unconscionable where patient, who was nervous and vulnerable, had no "meaningful choice" with respect to signing document).

362 Cathy Lesser Mansfield & Alan White, *Literacy and Contract*, 13 Stan. Law & Policy Rev. 233 (2003).

363 Uniform Consumer Credit Code (U.C.C.C.) § 5.108 (1974), and comments thereto. *See also* Idaho Code Ann. §§ 28-44-106, 28-45-106, 28-46-111; Iowa Code § 537.5108; S.C. Code Ann. § 37-5-108.

364 Watkins v. Wells Fargo Home Mortgage, 631 F. Supp. 2d 776 (S.D. W. Va. 2008).

365 *See* 1 Arthur L. Corbin, Corbin on Contracts § 129, at 556 (1963) (noting that, absent a usury statute, a contractual interest rate will be enforced "up to the point at which 'unconscionability' becomes a factor"); Van Jackson v. Check 'N Go of Illinois, Inc., 193 F.R.D. 544 (N.D. Ill. 2000), *further proceedings*, 123 F. Supp. 2d 1079 (N.D. Ill. 2000) (granting summary judgment for consumer on TILA claims); Davis v. Cash for Payday, Inc., 193 F.R.D. 518 (N.D. Ill. 2000) (certifying class on price unconscionability claim in payday loan context where state law does not provide an outer limit on interest rates); Donnelly v. Illini Cash Advance, Inc., 2000 WL 1161076 (N.D. Ill. Aug. 16, 2000); Sharp v. Chartwell Fin. Servs. Ltd., 2000 U.S. Dist. LEXIS 3143, 2000 WL 283095 (N.D. Ill. Mar. 6, 2000); Johnson v. Tele-Cash, Inc., 82 F. Supp. 2d 264 (D. Del. 1999) (refusing to dismiss price unconscionability claim in payday loan case (APR of 917%) even though Delaware does not have any applicable usury caps), *rev'd on other grounds sub nom.* Johnson v. West Suburban Bank, 225 F.3d 366 (3d Cir. 2000); Hartke v. Illinois Payday Loans, Inc., 1999 U.S. Dist. LEXIS 14937 (C.D. Ill. Sept. 15, 1999) (denying lender's motion for summary judgment; Illinois recognizes substantive unconscionability); Family Fin. Servs. v. Spencer, 677 A.2d 479 (Conn. App. Ct. 1996) (loan unconscionable where it called for balloon payment exceeding the principal, payment of a year's interest in advance, and a monthly payment of $733.33 for borrower who had first mortgage payment of $1,011.00 and monthly income of $1,126.67); Gonzales v. Associates Fin. Serv., 967 P.2d 312 (Kan. 1998) (observing that a loan origination fee, though legal in amount under Kansas U.C.C.C., may be unconscionable given the totality of a particular creditor's conduct, but in this case unconscionability can only be raised defensively). *See also In re* Wernly, 91 B.R. 702 (Bankr. E.D. Pa. 1988) (check-cashing fee of over 10% of face value is unconscionable where normal fee in the industry is 2%). *Cf.* Paulman v. Filtercorp, 899 P.2d 1259, 1263 (Wash. 1995) (business loan "would have made a loan shark proud," but is subject to the commercial exemption to the state's usury laws; suggesting in dissent that an argument "that this transaction [was] so outrageous as to be unconscionable and against public policy" might have been well taken, had it been made). *But see* Porter v. Ace Cash Express, Inc., 2000 WL 1610632 (E.D. La. Oct. 26, 2000) (where fees charged in a payday loan transaction were permitted by law, transaction cannot be unconscionable on that basis), *aff'd without opinion*, 277 F.3d 1372 (5th Cir. 2001); Black v. Barnes Auto Group, Inc., 390 B.R. 357 (Bankr. N.D. Ill. 2008) (as a matter of law, 44% interest rate for car finance is not unconscionable where state retail installment sales act states "there shall be no limit on the finance charges which may be charged, collected, or received"); *In re* Allen, 174 B.R. 293 (Bankr. D. Or. 1994) (RTO transaction not unconscionable). *But cf.* Emigrant Mortgage Co. v. Crismara, 2008 WL 2551039, at *8 (D. Conn. June 27, 2008) (18% default interest rate did not make loan substantively unconscionable, where such an interest rate was permissible in other contexts such as for tax debts). *See generally* Cathy Lesser Mansfield & Alan White, *Literacy and Contract*, 13 Stan. L. & Policy Rev. 233, 254–256 (2003) (arguing in favor of an approach to unconscionability that takes unreadability of modern consumer credit contracts into account); Steven W. Bender, *Rate Regulation at the Crossroads of Usury and Unconscionability: The Case for Regulating Abusive and Commercial Interest Rates Under the Unconscionability Standard*, 31 Hous. L. Rev. 721, n.258 (1994) (arguing that an unconscionability standard is preferable to usury ceilings; extensively reviewing statutory and common law unconscionability).

366 Idaho Code Ann. § 28-42-201.

367 Idaho Code Ann. § 28-45-106. *See also* Idaho Dep't of Finance, Policy Statement 84-5 (Dec. 6, 1994) (former guideline advising that 45% was prima facie unconscionable; as of 2009, however, the Idaho Department of Finance has indicated that this policy is no longer in effect due to changes in federal and state laws).

standards or which are otherwise unconscionable."[368] North Carolina prohibits fees for refund anticipation loans in amounts that the state regulator has determined to be unconscionable.[369]

A California court, analogizing to retail sales price unconscionability cases, had no trouble finding a 200% loan unconscionable.[370] Recognizing that both substantive and procedural unconscionability must be present, it held there is a "sliding scale" relationship—the greater one is, the less of the other is needed. In ruling for the borrower, the court also turned around the usual excuse high-rate, "last-resort" lenders advance for their conduct. The borrower had been unable to obtain a loan elsewhere, which the court held established unequal bargaining power and an absence of meaningful choice—the procedural unconscionability in this transaction.

Not all unconscionability challenges to interest rates succeed,[371] and such cases are fact-intensive.[372] "Lack of borrower sophistication, financial necessity, lender sharp practices, and lack of choice are deemed relevant in most of the interest pricing cases."[373] It is critical to develop the facts extensively and to piece together all information which illustrates the "smell" factor of the transaction. One other factor which enters into these cases, but is rarely mentioned, is the "eye of the beholder" factor.[374] It is worth considering taking the determination of unconscionability to a jury, if jury trial is allowed.

The more outrageous the facts, the more likely it is that the court will find causes of action under a variety of statutes and common law theories. In Illinois, a lender made installment small loans to poor, unsophisticated borrowers. The interest rates ranged from 179.66% to 557.15%, which resulted in finance charges that were about equal to or exceeded the principal borrowed.[375] The creditor then engaged in what was alleged to be "extortionate collection of credit" efforts. The court refused to dismiss the unconscionability count when it looked at the borrowers' lack of access to credit, the creditor's alleged tortious and criminal conduct, and the high interest rates charged.

### 2.4.7.4 Improvident Lending As Unconscionable

Improvident lending may also be attacked using unconscionability theories. In Connecticut, a court found both substantive and procedural unconscionability in a second mortgage loan. The loan terms required a monthly payment of $733.33 for a borrower with monthly income of $1,126.67 and a first mortgage payment of $1,011.00. It also required the borrower to pay a year's interest in advance and contained a balloon payment which exceeded the principal.[376] Another court refused to

368 940 Mass. Code Regs. § 8.06(6). *See* United Cos. Lending Corp. v. Sargeant, 20 F. Supp. 2d 192 (D. Mass. 1998) (upholding validity of regulation). *See also* Massachusetts v. First Alliance Mortgage Co., 1998 Mass. Super. LEXIS 712 (Mass. Super. Ct. Nov. 27, 1998) (preliminarily enjoining FAMCO from making mortgage loans in Massachusetts in which the points charged exceeded five, citing this regulation), *aff'd*, Clearinghouse No. 52,512, No. 98-J-0857 (Mass. App. Ct. Jan. 7, 1999).

369 N.C. Gen. Stat. § 53-250(4).

370 Carboni v. Arrospide, 2 Cal. Rptr. 2d 845 (Cal. Ct. App. 1991). *See also* O'Donovan v. CashCall, Inc., 2009 WL 1833990 (N.D. Cal. June 24, 2009) (allegation of 98% rate in conjunction with other onerous features states claim for substantive unconscionability).

371 *See, e.g.*, Brown v. Investors Mortgage Co., 121 F.3d 472 (9th Cir. 1997) (rejecting challenge to 15% and 16% interest rates ); Emigrant Mortgage Co. v. Crismara, 2008 WL 2551039 (D. Conn. June 27, 2008) (18% default interest rate not unconscionable where borrower, although financially desperate and inexperienced in mortgage borrowing, was an educated businesswoman); Harris v. Howell, 739 F. Supp. 565 (N.D. Ala. 1989) (20% rate was not unconscionable), *aff'd*, 902 F.2d 959 (11th Cir. 1990); *In re* Kohls, 2007 WL 130323 (Bankr. N.D. W. Va. Jan. 11, 2007) (insufficient indicia of unconscionability at the time loan was made); *In re* Glaser, 2002 WL 32375007 (Bankr. E.D. Va. Oct. 25, 2002) (pawn transaction by sophisticated businessman not unconscionable); *In re* Moorhous, 180 B.R. 138 (Bankr. E.D. Va. 1995) (business loan involving knowledgeable, sophisticated debtor, and private investor/creditor; 22% was not unconscionable "under the circumstances of this case"); Family Fed. Sav. & Loan v. Davis, 172 B.R. 437 (Bankr. D.D.C. 1994) (educated person who demonstrated basic understanding of the loan terms did not succeed in challenging second mortgage in which more than 50% was for a disclosed finders fee, in a very complicated factual context); Bramlett v. Adamson Ford, 717 So. 2d 772 (Ala. Civ. App. 1996) (interest rate of 15.49% on auto loan not unconscionable), *rev'd on other grounds*, 717 So. 2d 781 (Ala. 1997); Marshall v. Mercury Fin. Co., 550 So. 2d 1026 (Ala. Civ. App. 1989) (car loan at 30% under "as agreed" statute not so excessive as to be unconscionable where debtor had a college education and understood the documents); Capitol Furniture & Appliance Co. v. Morris, 8 U.C.C. Rep. 321 (D.C. Ct. Gen. Sess. 1970), *aff'd*, 280 A.2d 775 (D.C. 1971) (sale price on furniture marked up more than 100% over wholesale with 17.9% interest rate on the credit not unconscionable); Mobile Am. Corp. v. Howard, 307 So. 2d 507, 16 U.C.C. Rep. 625 (Fla. Dist. Ct. App. 1975) (11.75% APR on manufactured home sale not unconscionable).

372 Equity Mortgage v. Johnson, 149 B.R. 284, 288 (Bankr. D. Conn. 1993).

373 Steven W. Bender, *Rate Regulation at the Crossroads of Usury and Unconscionability: The Case for Regulating Abusive and Commercial Interest Rates Under the Unconscionability Standard*, 31 Hous. L. Rev. 721 (1994).

374 For example, the facts as portrayed by the majority opinion in Cheshire Mortgage Serv. v. Montes, 612 A.2d 1130 (Conn. 1992) look very different from the facts as portrayed by the dissent. *See also* Judge Posner's decision in Emery v. American Gen. Fin., Inc., 71 F.3d 1343 (7th Cir. 1995).

375 Brown v. CIL, Inc., 1996 WL 164294 (N.D. Ill. Apr. 1, 1996).

376 Family Fin. Servs. v. Spencer, 677 A.2d 479 (Conn. App. Ct. 1996). *See also* Williams v. First Gov't Mortgage & Investors Corp., 225 F.3d 738 (D.C. Cir. 2000) (affirming UDAP verdict that loan was unconscionable where lender knew that there was no reasonable probability of payment in full and knowingly took advantage of a borrower's inability to protect his interest, but finding that trial court failed to consider all factors when it rejected common law unconscionability claim); Matthews v. New Century Mortgage Corp., 185 F. Supp. 2d 874 (S.D. Ohio 2002) (denying motion to dismiss in case involving falsified application and income information, larger loans than anticipated, inability to repay); Maxwell v. Fairbanks Capital Corp. (*In re* Maxwell), 281 B.R. 101 (D. Mass. 2002) (finding refinance loan unconscionable where homeowner received nothing of value but principal and monthly payment increased and loan did not amortize); Beneficial Mortgage Co. of Ohio v. Leach, 2002 WL 926759 (Ohio Ct. App. May 9, 2002) (refinancing of fixed rate 9% loan into 14% adjustable rate loan may be unconscionable in light of other circumstances; revering summary judg-

dismiss an unconscionability claim where the homeowners alleged that the substantive terms of the loan were one-sided, they were charged ten points, the lender and broker held themselves out as experts, the borrowers had no choice as to the terms offered, and the defendants contrived to trap the borrowers into making a loan that would inevitably default.[377]

### 2.4.7.5 Challenging Terms Other Than Interest Rate As Unconscionable

Unconscionability may be well-suited to challenge the non-interest rate tools used to quietly extract an excessive price for credit. It is especially appropriate to apply the unconscionability doctrine to these transactions since so few consumers are able to detect, much less understand, these methods of increasing the cost of credit.[378]

Unconscionability was successfully invoked in *Besta v. Beneficial Loan Co.* to challenge a creditor's subtle manipulation of the non-interest rate terms of a loan, with the result that the cost of the loan more than doubled, though there was no additional benefit to the consumer.[379] The lender accomplished this by stretching the repayment term to six years, and then packing the loan with insurance premiums for a six-year loan. The insurance packing also took the amount financed over the statutory threshold necessary to enable the creditor to take a security interest in the borrower's residence.[380] (Real estate closing fees were then added, as well.)

The Eighth Circuit found the loan "substantively unfair" because there was no reasonable basis for a six-year repayment period. However, it based its decision on a finding of procedural unconscionability, holding there was lack of fair notice and unfair surprise in the creditor's failure to tell the borrower that she could have repaid the same loan for less money with lower monthly payments in half the time if the loan had been structured differently. Thus, in essence, the procedural unconscionability lay in the creditor's failure to tell the consumer that a much cheaper alternative was available to her. The court specifically stated that this ruling was not based on a quasi-fiduciary duty of disclosure of disadvantageous terms, but it noted that the average borrower could not have ascertained the existence of more advantageous options even by careful reading of the contract. Though Iowa codified unconscionability standards in its consumer credit code, the court specifically predicated its ruling upon both common law and statutory unconscionability. *Besta* thus should be good precedent even in states without a statutory unconscionability provision.[381]

Loan flipping—the refinancing of an old loan into a new one, generally by the existing creditor[382]—can be expensive for the consumer (and lucrative for the lender). Unconscionability can be one way to attack this problem. In one case, a door-to-door salesman sold a homeowner a solar water heater for $6,512 which never functioned properly and was subsequently declared a hazard. The solar heater company's sales were financed by a finance company that charged 19.5% interest over a ten-year period, resulting in a total finance charge of almost $9,000. To make matters worse, a security interest was taken in the home as well as the water heater. During the course of the term of this loan, the homeowner approached the finance company to borrow $800 for unrelated purposes. Instead of adding this sum to the outstanding balance of the existing loan or making a separate small loan, the lender refinanced the existing loan, added the $800, and sold the homeowner a $313 term life insurance policy. The term of the new loan was six years at 19.5% interest per year. An Arizona court found that such a transaction presents a question of grossly excessive price since the homeowner could end up paying half of $40,000, the value of her home, for a non-functioning water heater.[383] The "apparent injustice and oppression" in placing a mortgage on her home as security may also constitute substantive unconscionability.

---

ment for lender); City Fin. Servs. v. Smith, 2000 WL 288469 (Ohio Mun. Ct., Cuyahoga County Jan. 4, 2000) (finding $3,000 mortgage loan at 22.5% interest unconscionable and unenforceable where it exceeded borrower's ability to pay; criticizing lender's underwriting guidelines which grossed up her disability income based on the fact that it was tax-free). *But cf.* Cheshire Mortgage Serv. v. Montes, 612 A.2d 1130 (Conn. 1992) (concluding that facts did not support claim that loan, although imprudent, was unconscionable).

377 Young v. First Am. Fin. Servs., 977 F. Supp. 38 (D.D.C. 1997). *See also* Fidler v. Central Coop. Bank (*In re* Fidler), 210 B.R. 411 (Bankr. D. Mass. 1997) (borrowers survived summary judgment by alleging only that there was a gross disparity between the cost of the loan to the borrowers and the benefit given); Herrod v. First Republic Mortgage Corp., Inc., 625 S.E.2d 373 (W. Va. 2005) (reversing summary judgment in favor of lender and finding that evidence of fees in excess of 10% of the loan amount and an inflated appraisal created fact questions with respect to unconscionability claim).

378 Cathy Lesser Mansfield & Alan White, *Literacy and Contract*, 13 Stan. L. & Policy Rev. 233 (2003).

379 855 F.2d 532 (8th Cir. 1988). *See also* Knapp v. American Gen. Fin. Inc., 111 F. Supp. 2d 758 (S.D. W. Va. 2000) (packing loan with several credit insurance products may be unconscionable due to fraudulent representation by lender that insurance was required when it was not); Vance v. National Benefit Ass'n, 1999 U.S. Dist. LEXIS 13846 (N.D. Ill. Aug. 26, 1999) (denying motion to dismiss unconscionability claim by consumer who purchased $1,209 membership in an association and was entitled to certain "benefits" including an unsecured credit card with 19.9% interest rate and starting limit of $300, of which $219 was consumed by down payment on membership fee); Johnson v. Cash Store, 68 P.3d 1099 (Wash. Ct. App. 2003) (refusing to vacate default judgment of unconscionability against payday lender who rolled over customer's loan fourteen times even though lender complied with the letter of state anti-rollover law).

380 *See* § 5.9, *infra* (discussing this case further).

381 Common law unconscionability may be limited to a defensive shield, though.

382 *See* § 5.9, *infra*.

383 Maxwell v. Fidelity Fin. Servs., Inc., 907 P.2d 51 (Ariz. 1995). *See also* Hager v. American Gen. Fin., Inc., 37 F. Supp. 2d 778 (D. W. Va. 1999) (denying lender's motion for summary judgment on unconscionability claim where borrowers alleged that defendants induced them to enter into and refinance high interest rate loans and to mortgage their residence without realizing the magnitude of the debt they were incurring or the ramifications of these transactions).

Padding the non-interest charges tacked onto credit is a common tool for exacting extra profit from consumers,[384] and these, too, may be vulnerable. Price unconscionability cases in retail credit sales,[385] for example, may help in challenging the price of loan add-ons inflated to hide interest.[386] Some charges for credit-related services, such as broker fees, appraisal fees, and attorney fees, may be so far above market price as to subject them to challenge.[387] Applying a statutory definition, a Tennessee court held that a creditor that imposed substantial late charges with no contractual authority in order to pressure repayment engaged in unconscionable conduct.[388]

Bank fees, unrelated to credit, have been challenged under California's unconscionability provisions. In *Perdue v. Crocker National Bank*,[389] the California Supreme Court held that a bank's charge for its expenses—in this case its insufficient funds check charge—could be unconscionable. The ruling came in a motion to dismiss, so no determination on the merits was made. But the court looked at the law on price unconscionability, and found that such factors as the market price for the service or good, the cost of the goods or services to the seller, the inconvenience imposed on the seller, and the true value of the product or service should be considered.[390]

In *Perdue*, the check charge was six dollars, while plaintiff alleged the actual cost to the bank to be between thirty cents and one dollar—at least a 600% profit margin.[391] Combined with the procedural unconscionability factors—that the contracts were essentially adhesion contracts, and there was an absence of equal bargaining power, full disclosure, or open negotiations—the court held that an evidentiary hearing should be allowed to determine whether a fee so far in excess of its cost was unconscionable.[392] In contrast, a mark-up from a $1.50 cost to a $3.00 charge did not shock an appellate court's conscience, particularly as that was at the low end of the scale charged by other banks for the same fee.[393]

---

384 *See* Ch. 4, *infra*.

385 For example, in Frostifresh Corp. v. Reynoso, 274 N.Y.S.2d 757 (N.Y. Dist. Ct. 1966), *rev'd as to damages*, 281 N.Y.S.2d 964 (N.Y. App. Term 1967), the sellers used an installment sale contract written in English to sell a refrigerator to Spanish-speaking buyers. The refrigerator cost the seller $348, but the sale price, including the credit payments, was $1,145.80. The court declared the contract unconscionable because of the excessive price. The opinion in dicta also stressed the language barrier as procedural unconscionability, but did not make it clear whether procedural unconscionability was a necessary prerequisite to the finding that the purchase price was excessive.

In Lefkowitz v. ITM, Inc., 275 N.Y.S.2d 303 (N.Y. Sup. Ct. 1966), a merchant sold exorbitantly priced items in a fraudulently deceptive manner. The court held that retail installment contracts in which the prices charged ranged from two to six times the cost per unit were unconscionable as a matter of law.

Toker v. Pearl, 247 A.2d 701 (N.J. Super. Ct. Law Div. 1966), *aff'd*, 260 A.2d 244 (N.J. Super. Ct. App. Div. 1970) found that the seller had charged an exorbitant price and held that the contract was unconscionable. On appeal, the appellate division affirmed on the grounds of fraud, specifically expressing no opinion on the trial court's finding that the excessive price alone made the contract unenforceable.

In Jones v. Star Credit Corp., 298 N.Y.S.2d 264 (N.Y. Sup. Ct. 1969), a welfare recipient entered into an installment sales contract with a door-to-door salesman for a freezer. The contract price, $1,234.80, was more than four times the retail value of $300. The court found the price charged unconscionable as a matter of law.

In Toker v. Westerman, 274 A.2d 78 (N.J. Dist. Ct. 1970), a New Jersey court held that a purchase price of $1,229.76 for a freezer worth between $350 and $400 was unconscionable, even though no misconduct took place in the bargaining process. The buyer had already paid $655.87 toward the freezer. Given the market value of approximately $400, the court regarded the amount paid as fair compensation for the freezer, relieving the buyer of the duty to pay the remaining balance, but failing to return to the buyer any of the amount paid.

In Kugler v. Romain, 279 A.2d 640 (N.J. 1971), the defendants sold books worth approximately $110 for $279.95. The court held that when a seller charged a price two and one half times the reasonable market value and when the goods were defective, the excessive price alone rendered the contract unconscionable.

*See also In re* Wernly, 91 B.R. 702 (Bankr. E.D. Pa. 1988) (check-cashing fee of over 10% of face value is unconscionable where normal fee in the industry is 2%); Assocs. Home Equity Servs., Inc. v. Troup, 778 A.2d 529 (N.J. Super. Ct. App. Div. 2001) (reversing dismissal of unconscionability claim where allegations revealed that the higher interest rates and points charged the borrowers may not have been warranted).

386 *See* §§ 4.5, 4.6, *infra*.

387 *See, e.g., In re* Dukes, 24 B.R. 404 (Bankr. E.D. Mich. 1982); U.S. Home & Realty Corp. v. Lehnartz (Mich. Dist. Ct. Sept. 30, 1987), *available at* www.nclc.org/unreported. *See also In re* Fleet, 95 B.R. 319 (E.D. Pa. 1989) (fees of $195–$260 to a purported credit counseling service for referring consumers to a bankruptcy lawyer, a service available for free elsewhere, was an unconscionable price; noting that consumers were financially troubled and distraught, many unemployed, disabled, and facing foreclosure). *But see* Fanning v. Fritz's Pontiac-Cadillac-Buick, Inc., 472 S.E.2d 242 (S.C. 1996) ($87 "procurement fee" added to the sales price of cars by a dealer was not unconscionable; the definition of unconscionability in consumer credit sales is limited by South Carolina statute to "gross disparity" between price charged and price at which similar property or services are readily obtainable by like consumers; court also believed that the disclosure of the fee gave the consumer the ability to negotiate it; consumer claims attacking the fee on grounds of fraud, misrepresentation, unfair trade practices survived summary judgment, however).

388 Bank of Crockett v. Cullipher, 752 S.W.2d 84 (Tenn. Ct. App. 1988) (late charge increased obligation by $933 every ten days; applying Tenn. Code Ann. § 47-14-117 which defines knowing imposition of excess charges, among other things, as unconscionable conduct).

389 702 P.2d 503 (Cal. 1985), *interpreting* Cal. Civ. Code § 1670.5.

390 Perdue v. Crocker Nat'l Bank, 702 P.2d 503, 512 (Cal. 1985).

With respect to the market price, the defendant bank had contended that the charge was at market price, and therefore could not be held unconscionable. The court said that, "[w]hile it is unlikely that a court would find a price set by a freely competitive market to be unconscionable [*citation omitted*], the market price set by an oligopoly should not be immune from scrutiny," and that the other "price justification" factors should be reviewed as well.

391 *Id.* at 513.

392 *Id.* at 513–514. *But see* Best v. United States Nat'l Bank, 739 P.2d 554 (Or. 1987) (unconscionability doctrine did not apply because NSF check charge was not a term of the contract; duty of good faith, which arises with respect to performance of an existing contract, did apply).

393 California Grocers Ass'n v. Bank of Am., 27 Cal. Rptr. 2d 396 (Ct. App. 1994) (the "DIR" fee, charged to a depositor who had the

A credit card contract under which the issuer charged the cardholder over-the-limit fees for more than six years was found to be unconscionable by an Ohio trail court.[394] The evidence showed that, although the consumer made almost no use of her credit card after a certain point, her balance continued to grow because of monthly debits for credit insurance and because some of her payments were late. In May 1997, three months after her final use of the card, the accrual of finance charges and late fees pushed her balance to $1,962.82—slightly more than her $1,900 credit limit, so the creditor started charging her over-the-limit fees. Over the next six years she continued to make payments, but her balance never dropped below $1,900 because of all the over-the-limit fees, late charges, and finance charges being added every month. Thus, despite paying Discover $3,492 between May 1997 and May 2003, the consumer owed $5,564.28 in May 2003. The court found, in part, that the card member agreement as applied to the consumer was "manifestly unconscionable." After noting the "widespread financial exploitation of the urban poor by overbearing credit-card companies," the court invoked its equitable powers to grant judgment in favor of the consumer on the creditor's suit for the debt.

Other substantive provisions of the loan may be unconscionable. For example, a cross-collateralization clause which gives a security interest in the consumer's property to secure all past and future debts may not pass scrutiny where the clause is shuffled in among other boilerplate provisions and the consumer had no prior knowledge or understanding of the provision's effect.[395] A concurrence in a case involving a non-credit contract matter suggests that contracts with one-sided attorney fees provisions may be unconscionable.[396] Failure to properly disclose a balloon payment as required by state law can be unconscionable.[397] Courts are increasingly turning to the unconscionability doctrine to strike down arbitration clauses.[398]

misfortune to have someone else's check bounce, ranged from $4 to $10 at other institutions).

394 Discover Bank v. Owens, 822 N.E.2d 869 (Ohio Mun. Ct. 2004).

395 *Cf.* Williams v. Walker-Thomas Furniture Co., 350 F.2d 445 (D.C. Cir. 1965). *But see* Alcantar v. Windsor-Orange County Credit Union, 2000 Tex. App. LEXIS 1576 (Mar. 9, 2000) (where the new advance or cross-collateralization clause is allowed under Texas law, its mere presence in the contract does not render it unconscionable); Bastaich v. Kenworth Northwest, Inc., 1997 Wash. App. LEXIS 635 (Wash. Ct. App. Apr. 28, 1997) (cross-collateralization clause not unconscionable because buyer knew of its existence, negotiated to change it, and, having failed, signed the contract).

396 HILB, Rogal & Hamilton Agency of Dayton, Inc. v. Reynolds, 610 N.E.2d 1102 (Ohio Ct. App. 1992) (concurring op.) (the contract provided for reimbursement of employer's attorney fees to enforce an anti-piracy provision, but none for employees who prevailed).

397 Mallory v. Mortgage Am., Inc., 67 F. Supp. 2d 601 (S.D. W. Va. 1999); Malik v. Bernitt, 800 N.Y.S.2d 349 (N.Y. Sup. Ct. 2005) (table) (denying plaintiff's summary judgment motion against homeowners; homeowners, who were not represented by counsel, claimed they were induced to sign mortgage and one-year note with balloon payment in order to save their down payment).

398 *See* National Consumer Law Center, Consumer Arbitration Agreements (5th ed. 2007 and Supp.).

### 2.4.7.6 Remedies for Unconscionability

The remedy for unconscionability under the common law and the UCC is usually limited to a defense against the enforcement of the unconscionable contract or terms, and may not support an affirmative claim for restitutionary damages.[399] Despite this general rule, courts have allowed affirmative common law unconscionability claims for declaratory judgment in which the consumer seeks to delete or limit the application of unconscionable contract provisions and does not seek to recover damages or obtain other affirmative relief except under the contract itself.[400]

State UDAP statutes that prohibit unconscionability offer affirmative relief,[401] and non-UCC codifications of unconscionability may do so as well.[402] Common law or UCC unconscionability can also be the basis of another cause of action, such as unjust enrichment or a UDAP claim.[403]

## *2.4.8 Unjust Enrichment*

Unjust enrichment is a theory of legal liability based not on contract or statute, but upon equity and justice. Thus, a person who has been unjustly enriched at the expense of another is required to make restitution to the other. The elements of an unjust enrichment claim vary by state, but generally are: (1) a benefit conferred on the defendant by the plaintiff; (2) an appreciation or knowledge by the defendant of the benefit; and (3) the acceptance or retention by the defendant of the benefit under such circumstances as to make it inequitable for the

399 Rubio v. Capital One Bank, 613 F.3d 1195, 1205–1206 (9th Cir. 2010) (California law); Cowin Equip. Co. v. General Motors Corp., 734 F.2d 1581 (11th Cir. 1984); Williams v. E.F. Hutton Mortgage Corp., 555 So. 2d 158 (Ala. 1989); Gonzales v. Associates Fin. Serv., 967 P.2d 312 (Kan. 1998) (unconscionability can only be raised defensively under Kansas law); Best v. United States Nat'l Bank, 714 P.2d 1049 (1986), *aff'd on other grounds*, 739 P.2d 554 (Or. 1987). *But see* Johnson v. Tele-Cash, Inc., 82 F. Supp. 2d 264, 278–279 (D. Del. 1999) (court should not require the consumer to breach the loan agreement in order to become subject to the lawsuit so that she can then raise the defense of unconscionability), *rev'd on other grounds sub nom.* Johnson v. West Suburban Bank, 225 F.3d 366 (3d Cir. 2000). *See generally*, Steven W. Bender, *Rate Regulation at the Crossroads of Usury and Unconscionability: The Case for Regulating Abusive and Commercial Interest Rates Under the Unconscionability Standard*, 31 Hous. L. Rev. 721 (1994).

400 *See* Carey v. Lincoln Loan Co., 125 P.3d 814 (Or. Ct. App. 2005), *aff'd on other grounds*, 157 P.3d 775 (Or. 2007). *See also* Eva v. Midwest Nat'l Mortgage Banc, Inc. 143 F. Supp. 2d 862, 895 (N.D. Ohio 2001) (denying motion to dismiss and holding unconscionability may support affirmative claim for declaratory judgment); Vockner v. Erickson, 712 P.2d 379 (Alaska 1986) (upholding trial court's reformation of unconscionable land sale contract between seventy-three-year-old seller of apartment building and buyer who was a professional real estate agent); Restatement of Contracts (Second) § 208.

401 *See, e.g.*, D.C. Code § 28-3904(r).

402 *See, e.g.*, Iowa Code § 537.5108 (court may refuse to enforce unconscionable agreement in whole or in part, consumer may be awarded actual damages and attorney fees).

403 *In re* First Alliance Mortgage Co., 280 B.R. 246 (C.D. Cal. 2002).

defendant to retain the benefit without making restitution.[404] Various types of predatory lending or debt collection may be actionable.[405] Unjust enrichment may also be used as a theory of recovery against the beneficiary of fraudulent conduct even if the beneficiary did not participate in the fraud.[406]

An example of an unjust enrichment claim is *Discover v. Owens*,[407] in which the court granted judgment in favor of the consumer debtor based, in part, on the fact that Discover, the credit card issuer, had continued to allow her balance to accumulate long after it had become clear that she would be unable to pay it. The court noted that if the account had been charged off within a reasonable period, the debt would have been approximately $2,000. Instead, the card issuer held the account open for an additional six years after the defendant last used her card, thereby allowing fees and charges to accumulate. As a result and despite having received nearly $3,500 in payments, the defendant's $2,000 balance increased to more than $5,500. The court held that the card issuer would be unjustly enriched if judgment was granted in its favor where it failed to even minimally pay attention to the defendant's circumstances and allowed the debt to accumulate unchecked.

The existence of a valid express contract does not necessarily preclude the possibility of an unjust enrichment claim.[408] However, unjust enrichment cannot be predicated on the defendant's failure to fulfill contractual terms.[409]

Unjust enrichment as a cause of action is discussed in more detail in National Consumer Law Center, *Unfair and Deceptive Acts and Practices*.[410]

## 2.4.9 Contract Claims

In some circumstances, a breach of contract claim can provide reasonably useful remedies for lender overreaching. Breach of contract claims have the advantage of likely avoiding federal preemption.[411] Contract claims also avoid the scope issues that can make UDAP and other statutory claims inapplicable to certain lenders. Contract claims are often suitable for class action treatment, as lenders are likely to use form contracts with identical clauses for large groups of consumers.

Some states have statutes that provide for fee-shifting in contract actions or that allow a fee award to a prevailing consumer if the contract makes the consumer liable for the creditor's fees when the creditor prevails.[412] In addition, a contract claim that is pursued as a class action may result in a large enough common fund to pay attorney fees.

One court refused to dismiss a claim that a broker and lender had contracted to assist the borrower in obtaining a loan and to provide the borrower with a loan commitment on affordable terms.[413] The borrower alleged that the defendants had breached this contract by failing to exercise due diligence as promised, by making false representations regarding the borrower's qualification for the loan and the availability of refinancing, and by failing to secure a loan with the promised payment and interest rate. Another court allowed a contract claim to proceed on the theory that the lender owed a contractual duty to make responsible loans and to decline to make loans when there was an obvious risk of default.[414]

## 2.4.10 Duty of Good Faith and Fair Dealing

### 2.4.10.1 Nature of the Duty

The duty of good faith and fair dealing between parties to a contract is based both in common law[415] and the

404 Restatement (First) of Restitution § 1 (2005). *See* Pierce v. Emigrant Mortgage Co., 2007 WL 4800725 (D. Conn. Dec. 27, 2007) (unjust enrichment when lender unreasonably delayed foreclose resulting in significant increase in default interest due to lender), *amended in part by* 2008 WL 349191 (D. Conn. Feb. 6, 2008); Orser v. Select Portfolio Serv., Inc., 2005 WL 3478126 (W.D. Wash. Dec. 20, 2005).

Generally unjust enrichment will not be found when the borrower has an adequate remedy at law. *See In re* Vincent, 381 B.R. 564 (Bankr. D. Mass. 2008) (borrower has adequate remedy under state UDAP statute).

405 *See, e.g.*, Treadway v. Nations Credit Fin. Servs. Corp., 892 N.E.2d 534 (Ill. App. Ct. 2008) (trial court erred in dismissing dismissal of unjust enrichment claim on preemption grounds when lender allegedly failed to give loan discount despite charging loan discount fee, but dismissal proper on res judicata grounds).

406 *See* Poskin v. TD Banknorth, N.A., 687 F. Supp. 2d 530 (W.D. Pa. 2009) (lender may raise unjust enrichment by equitable recoupment in defense of borrower's suit); Collier v. Batiste, 2006 WL 1560739 (E.D. La. May 23, 2006).

407 822 N.E.2d 869 (Ohio Mun. Ct. 2004).

408 *See* Orser v. Select Portfolio Serv., Inc., 2005 WL 3478126 (W.D. Wash. Dec. 20, 2005) (unjust enrichment claim for collecting $50 payoff fee not precluded by existence of valid mortgage loan where loan documents did not expressly authorize fee). *But see* Hassler v. Sovereign Bank, 374 Fed. Appx. 341 (3d Cir. 2010) (bank's manipulation of order in which it paid checks, as way of maximizing overdraft fees, not unjust enrichment when contract allowed this); Curley v. Allstate Ins. Co., 289 F. Supp. 2d 614 (E.D. Pa. 2003) (doctrine of unjust enrichment unavailable where relationship of the parties is founded on a written agreement or express contract); Lum v. New Century Mortgage Corp., 800 N.Y.S.2d 408 (N.Y. App. Div. 2005).

409 *See* Guinn v. Hoskins Chevrolet, 361 Ill. App. 3d 575 (Ill. App. Ct. 2005) (dismissing claim of unjust enrichment where plaintiff incorporated allegations that defendant violated contract into unjust enrichment claim). *See also In re* Glaser, 2002 WL 32375007 (Bankr. E.D. Va. Oct. 25, 2002) (recovery for unjust enrichment against pawnbroker precluded where express agreement provided that property would be forfeited if loan was not paid at maturity).

410 National Consumer Law Center, Unfair and Deceptive Acts and Practices § 14.6 (7th ed. 2008 and Supp.).

411 *See, e.g.*, Davis v. Chase Bank, 650 F. Supp. 2d 1073, 1086 (C.D. Cal. 2009) (contract claim seeks only to force creditor to adhere to the contracts it creates, which has at most an incidental effect on its lending powers). *See generally* Ch. 3, *supra*.

412 *See* National Consumer Law Center, Consumer Warranty Law § 13.9 (4th ed. 2010 and Supp.).

413 Falcocchia v. Saxon Mortgage, Inc., 709 F. Supp. 2d 873 (E.D. Cal. 2010).

414 Smith v. Jenkins, 718 F. Supp. 2d 155 (D. Mass. 2010).

415 Restatement (Second) of Contracts § 205 (1979). *See also* Smith v. Jenkins, 626 F. Supp. 2d 155, 170 (D. Mass. 2009) (duty of good faith and fair dealing applies to oral contracts); Frye v. American

UCC.[416] Unlike unconscionability, which is ordinarily determined by looking at contract terms at the time the contract was made, the duty of good faith is imposed on parties to an existing contract "to prohibit improper behavior in the performance and enforcement" of that contract.[417] For example, a bank's decision to reorder charges posted to a consumer's account in a manner that would maximize overdraft penalties could be found to be an abuse of discretion that violates the implied covenant of good faith and fair dealing.[418]

Thus, while onerous contract terms might be subject to challenge under other theories, such as unconscionability, UDAP, or fraud, the duty of good faith and fair dealing may be useful to challenge creditor overreaching in later stages of the relationship.[419] The line may be quite fine at times.[420]

Many courts hold that the duty of good faith does not extend contract rights beyond the terms of the contract and cannot be used to require a lender to surrender contractual rights.[421]

---

Gen. Fin., Inc., 307 F. Supp. 2d 836 (S.D. Miss. 2004) (duty of good faith and fair dealing implied in every contract but only arises between parties to the contract; dismissing claim against officers of lender); Carreau & Co. v. Security Pac. Bus. Credit, Inc., 272 Cal. Rptr. 387, 398 (Cal. Ct. App. 1990); Cadle Co. v. Vargas, 771 N.E.2d 179 (Mass. App. Ct. 2002); Am. Bankers' Ins. Co. v. Wells, 819 So. 2d 1196, 1206–1207 (Miss. 2001) (lender's purchase of force-placed insurance on gross rather than net balance may be a violation); GMAC v. Baymon, 732 So. 2d 262, 269 (Miss. 1999) (duty exists in all contracts, but lender's purchase of force-placed insurance here was not a breach); Noonan v. First Bank Butte, 740 P.2d 631 (Mont. 1987) (tortious breach of covenant of good faith and fair dealing requires action which is arbitrary, capricious or unreasonable and exceeds plaintiff's justifiable expectations); Kirke La Shelle Co. v. Paul Armstrong Co., 188 N.E. 163, 167 (N.Y. 1933) ("in every contract there exists an implied covenant of good faith and fair dealing"); Southface Condo. Owners Ass'n, Inc. v. Southface Condo. Ass'n, 733 A.2d 55, 58 (Vt. 1999). *Cf.* Cable & Assocs. Ins. Agency v. Commercial Nat'l Bank, 875 A.2d 361 (Pa. Super. Ct. 2005) (lender has duty of good faith, but negotiating loan terms favorable to itself is not a violation; heightened duty applies to legal relationships such as insurer-insured); Arnold v. National County Mut. Fire Ins. Co., 725 S.W.2d 165 (Tex. 1987) (duty of good faith and fair dealing arises as a result of special relationship between contracting parties or agreed to in contract; such relationship exists between insurer and insured). *But see* Lovell v. Western Nat'l Life Ins. Co., 754 S.W.2d 298 (Tex. 1988) (no duty of good faith and fair dealing between mortgagor and mortgagee absent special relationship of trust and confidence or express language in contract); Victoria Bank & Trust Co. v. Brady, 779 S.W.2d 893, 902 (Tex. App. 1989) (while Texas courts recognize duty of good faith and fair dealing in cases where a special relationship exists, the debtor-creditor relationship does not give rise to such a duty; "However laudatory the concept may be, a duty of good faith and fair dealing does not arise in every contract or business transaction."), *aff'd in relevant part, rev'd in part on other grounds*, 811 S.W.2d 931 (Tex. 1991). *But cf.* Jordan v. Paul Financial, L.L.C., 644 F. Supp. 2d 1156, 1170 (N.D. Cal. 2009) (no liability for tortious breach of implied covenant of good faith and fair dealing without special relationship with fiduciary characteristics). *See generally* Symons, *The Bank-Customer Relation: Part II—The Judicial Decisions*, 100 Banking L.J. 325, 346–353 (1983); Johnson & Gaffney, *Lender Liability: Perspectives on Risk and Prevention*, 105 Banking L.J. 325 (1988); Annotation, *Bank's Liability for Breach of Implied Contract of Good Faith and Fair Dealing*, 55 A.L.R.4th 1026 (1987).

416 U.C.C. § 1-203.

417 Alan's of Atlanta, Inc. v. Minolta Corp., 903 F.2d 1414 (11th Cir. 1990) (implied covenant of good faith and fair dealing is not an independent contract term, but a doctrine governing the performance of the explicit contract terms); Biggins v. Wells Fargo & Co., 266 F.R.D. 399 (N.D. Cal. 2009) (duty of good faith does not apply to pre-contract negotiations); Baldwin v. Laurel Ford Lincoln-Mercury, Inc., 32 F. Supp. 2d 894 (S.D. Miss. 1998) (recognizing the duty but finding it inapplicable to a claim that consumer did not get the best terms available; the duty concerns the performance of the contract, not the negotiation leading to the agreement); 201 Forest St. L.L.C. v. LBM Fin., L.L.C. (*In re* 201 Forest St. L.L.C.), 409 B.R. 543, 591–592 (Bankr. D. Mass. 2009) (covenant of good faith and fair dealing applies to performance but not enforcement of contract); Best v. United States Nat'l Bank, 739 P.2d 554 (Or. 1987) (bank must use good faith in exercising its discretion to set NSF fees; reversing summary judgment for bank because of fact questions). *See also* Continental Bank v. Modansky, 997 F.2d 309 (7th Cir. 1988) (no duty of good faith and fair dealing in contract negotiations); Birt v. Wells Fargo Home Mortgage, Inc., 75 P.3d 640 (Wyo. 2003) (duty does not arise until the parties have reached an agreement and does not bind them during earlier negotiations). *Cf.* LLMD of Michigan v. Marine Midland Realty Credit, 789 F. Supp. 657 (E.D. Pa. 1992) (Michigan law) (implied duty of good faith and fair dealing includes a duty of good-faith negotiation where parties are already subject to a binding commitment agreement); Teachers Ins. & Annuity Ass'n of Am. v. Butler, 626 F. Supp. 1229 (S.D.N.Y. 1986) (implied duty of good faith and fair dealing includes a duty of good-faith negotiation where parties are already subject to a binding commitment agreement).

418 Gutierrez v. Wells Fargo & Co., 622 F. Supp. 2d 946, 953–954 (N.D. Cal. 2009). *But see* Hassler v. Sovereign Bank, 374 Fed. Appx. 341 (3d Cir. 2010) (bank's manipulation of order in which it paid checks, as way of maximizing overdraft fees, not breach of duty of good faith when contract explicitly allowed this).

419 Fisher v. American Gen. Fin. Co., 52 Fed. Appx. 601 (4th Cir. 2002) (taking a security interest in a larger parcel of land than the parties agreed upon can subject the creditor to this duty, but not breached here where the evidence of other dishonest acts of the creditor was not admissible).

420 *Compare* Perdue v. Crocker Nat'l Bank, 702 P.2d 503 (Cal. 1985) (both unconscionability and duty of good faith implicated in the bank's imposition of NSF charges), *with* Best v. United States Nat'l Bank, 739 P.2d 554 (Or. 1987) (unconscionability doctrine not applicable to bank's NSF charges, because the specific fee was not part of agreement; duty of good faith and fair dealing was applicable).

421 Brazell v. First Nat'l Bank & Trust, 982 F.2d 206 (7th Cir. 1992) (Illinois law) (good faith is a "gap-filler," and does not apply to contingencies expressly provided for in the contract); Deerman v. Federal Home Loan Mortgage Corp., 955 F. Supp. 1393 (N.D. Ala. 1997) (interpreting New York and Alabama common law to hold that covenant of good faith cannot expand contract rights beyond the terms of the contract; no breach of duty where mortgage contracts did not require FHLMC to notify the borrowers of any right to cancel private mortgage insurance but required borrowers to maintain insurance until the entire indebtedness was repaid); Citibank, N.A. v. Gifesman, 773 A.2d 993 (Conn. App. Ct. 2001) (the implied duty cannot be applied to achieve a result contrary to the clear expressed contract terms, unless those terms are contrary to public policy); Azar v. Prudential Ins. Co., 68 P.3d 909 (N.M. Ct. App. 2003) (implied covenant cannot be used to challenge charges expressly authorized by insurance contract); Cable & Assoc. Ins.

However, it imposes duties of reasonableness and good faith in the performance and enforcement of those rights.[422]

The policy behind the doctrine is to exclude conduct which "violate[s] community standards of decency, fairness or reasonableness."[423] While the doctrine applies to business contracts, it is stronger in some respects in the consumer context, where there is generally not equal bargaining power, many of the terms are not subject to negotiation, and the borrower is usually less sophisticated than business borrowers.[424]

A number of courts have held that a creditor's decision to accelerate and foreclose on collateral is subject to the duty of good faith and fair dealing.[425] Creditor behavior which thwarts a consumer's ability to file for and obtain benefits under a credit disability policy may also state a cause of action under this theory.[426] Similarly, an insurance company has a duty to deal fairly and act in good faith with its insureds. This duty is breached where, in the credit insurance context or otherwise, the creditor or insurer deliberately and willfully engages in a pattern of canceling insurance policies as soon as claims are filed without determining whether it has good cause to do so.[427]

The assignee of a bank breached the duty of good faith when it tried to force the debtor's wife to pay a loan that the debtor took out to fund a divorce settlement with her. The wife had signed an open-ended guarantee during the marriage, guaranteeing any and all debts to the bank that the debtor might incur, but the bank did not rely on the guarantee when it made the loan for the divorce settlement.[428]

In the credit card context, the duty of good faith may not apply to the unilateral cancellation of the card by the creditor where the credit card agreement permits the termination for any reason.[429] However, one court has held that prior notice of the cancellation is required regardless of whether the card agree-

---

Agency v. Commercial Nat'l Bank, 875 A.2d 361 (Pa. Super. Ct. 2005) (lender not required to surrender rights granted by statute or conferred by contract; no breach where lender refused to release security interest to allow borrower to secure additional credit); Farm Credit Servs. of Am. v. Dougan, 704 N.W.2d 24 (S.D. 2005) (use of remedies expressly provided for in contract—foreclosure—does not give rise to breach of duty).

422 Duffield v. First Interstate Bank, 13 F.3d 1403 (10th Cir. 1993) (duty of good faith and fair dealing limits right to act unreasonably even if express terms of contract appear to permit unreasonableness; upholding $6 million jury verdict for failure to act in good faith in workout arrangements upon default); Littlejohn v. Parrish, 839 N.E.2d 49 (Ohio Ct. App. 2005) (reversing summary judgment in favor of mortgagee who refused to permit prepayment of loan and finding good faith and fair dealing requires not only honesty but also reasonableness in the enforcement of the contract).

423 Restatement (Second) of Contracts § 205, cmt. a (1979).

424 Restatement (Second) of Contracts § 205, cmt. a (1979) (listing "abuse of power to specify terms" as one factor in a laundry list of "bad faith" conduct).

425 *See, e.g.*, Duffield v. First Interstate Bank, 13 F.3d 1403 (10th Cir. 1993) (duty of good faith and fair dealing limits right to act unreasonably even if express terms of contract appear to permit unreasonableness; upholding $6 million jury verdict for failure to act in good faith in workout arrangements upon default); Bank One, Texas, N.A. v. Taylor, 970 F.2d 16 (5th Cir. 1992) (acceleration of ostensible demand note subject to U.C.C. duty of good faith when fair reading of all documents suggests intention that demand clause would only be invoked in event of default); Knapp v. American Gen. Fin. Inc., 111 F. Supp. 2d 758 (S.D. W. Va. 2000) (claim for breach of duty of good faith and fair dealing is stated where lender-insurance broker defendants tried to repossess personal property based upon an allegedly invalid security agreement and by employing a repossession agent and directing him to harass the consumers; genuine issue of material fact as to whether repo man was defendants' employee with regard to the repossessions); *In re* Peterson, 93 B.R. 323 (Bankr. D. Vt. 1988) (refusing to dismiss claim for breach of covenant and good faith dealing arising out of purported unlawful declaration of acceleration and overreaching in obtaining modification of original agreement); *In re* Martin Specialty Vehicles, Inc., 87 B.R. 752 (Bankr. D. Mass. 1988), *rev'd on jurisdictional grounds*, 97 B.R. 721 (D. Mass. 1989) ($500,000 contract damages for bad faith foreclosures where default was minor and could have been cured by ordinary practice of bank set-off); Farmers & Merchants Bank v. Hancock, 506 So. 2d 305, *modified*, 510 So. 2d 201 (Ala. 1987) (U.C.C. duty of good faith); Am. Bankers' Ins. Co. v. Wells, 819 So. 2d 1196, 1206–1207 (Miss. 2001) (jury question whether lender violated duty of good faith by force-placing insurance on gross rather than net balance for borrowers whose own insurance lapsed); Noonan v. First Bank Butte, 740 P.2d 631 (Mont. 1987) (holding that U.C.C. duty and common law duty both may apply to a transaction, but reversing because of improper jury instructions); First Nat'l Bank v. Twombly, 689 P.2d 1226 (Mont. 1984) (punitive damages for bad faith acceleration); State Nat'l Bank v. Farah Mfg. Co., 678 S.W.2d 661 (Tex. App. 1984) (dismissed by agreement Mar. 6, 1985) (acceleration clauses do not permit acceleration when the facts make its use unjust or oppressive); Monahan v. GMAC Mortgage Corp., 893 A.2d 298 (Vt. 2005) (servicer-lender breached duty by pursuing foreclosure when its own breach of contract and lack of assistance in remedying breach were at least partly responsible for borrower's inability to pay). *But see* Price v. Wells Fargo Bank, 261 Cal. Rptr. 735, 742 (Cal. Ct. App. 1989) (contractual duty of good faith does not impose affirmative duty of moderation in enforcing creditor's legal rights); Affiliated Capital v. Commercial Fed. Bank, 834 S.W.2d 521 (Tex. App. 1992) (no breach of duty of good faith where creditor acted in accord with terms of contract in commercial loan). *See generally* National Consumer Law Center, Repossessions § 4.2.3 (7th ed. 2010 and Supp.); Johnson & Gaffney, *Lender Liability: Perspectives on Risk and Prevention*, 105 Banking L.J. 325, 498 (1988) (promising to work with borrowers during periods of financial distress, getting additional collateral, then "mov[ing] in for the kill" is a classic example of "bad faith"); Note, *Mortgage Lender Liability to the Purchasers of New or Existing Homes*, 1988 U. Ill. L. Rev. 191, 211–214; Annotation, *Bank's Liability for Breach of Implied Contract of Good Faith and Fair Dealing*, 55 A.L.R.4th 1026 (1987).

426 *Cf.* Chandler v. General Motors Acceptance Corp., 426 N.E.2d 521 (Ohio Ct. App. 1980) (denying summary judgment to GMAC in deficiency suit where GMAC refused to complete its portion of credit disability insurance claim form but later repossessed the car; while only breach of contract and wrongful repossession claims were raised, a breach of the duty of good faith and fair dealing could have been raised). *But see* Rouse v. Household Fin. Corp., 156 P.3d 569 (Idaho 2007) (lender and credit life disability insurer did not breach duty to deal fairly, honestly and in good faith with borrowers where lender encouraged borrowers to refinance, refinance cancelled borrowers' credit disability insurance, and new policy was declined).

427 *See, e.g.*, Vining v. Enterprise Fin. Group, Inc., 148 F.3d 1206 (10th Cir. 1998).

428 Cadle Co. v. Vargas, 771 N.E.2d 179 (Mass. App. Ct. 2002).

429 Shwartz v. American Express Travel Co., 2002 WL 1684440 (E.D. La. July 22, 2002).

ment calls for it.[430] With respect to bank fees, one court has held that banks must use good faith in exercising their discretion to set insufficient funds fees.[431]

### 2.4.10.2 Remedies for Violation of Duty of Good Faith

Since the duty of good faith is an implied contract term, most jurisdictions allow a contract claim for violation of this duty.[432] Tort liability may require a showing of some special relationship, beyond that of lender and customer, such as special circumstances giving rise to a fiduciary or quasi-fiduciary relationship or other indicia of a heightened duty.[433]

## *2.4.11 Other Theories of Liability*

### 2.4.11.1 Financial Abuse and Older Consumers

California's broad Elder Abuse Act[434] applies to persons sixty-five years of age or older.[435] It covers financial abuse as well as other types of abuse,[436] and provides a private cause of action to redress violations.[437] A loan broker violates this statute when it brokers a loan for an older consumer and obtains a fee by misrepresenting the terms of the loan.[438] At least one court has found the Act to have been preempted by HOLA when applied to the lending practices of a federal savings association, however.[439]

### 2.4.11.2 Estoppel

The elements of an estoppel claim include that the party estopped must have engaged in conduct which amounted to a false representation or concealment of material facts, must have had an intention that such conduct would be acted upon by the other party, and must have known the real facts. The party asserting estoppel must show that he or she lacked knowledge of the true facts, relied upon the conduct of the party estopped,[440] and prejudicially changed her position in reliance thereon.[441] For example, an estoppel claim may be available if a consumer relied on a lender's oral non-contractual assurances.[442] In a yo-yo car case,[443] in which the dealer accepted and sold the consumer's trade-in and assured her that financing had gone through for her new purchase, only to tell her the next day that financing had not been approved, a court held that the dealer was estopped from denying that the original purchase order was valid when the consumer had relied upon it in good faith to her detriment.[444]

### 2.4.11.3 Conversion

Conversion is the wrongful exercise of dominion over personal property.[445] As a general rule, conversion involves a specific chattel rather than money.[446] However, courts have recognized an exception to this rule where money is specifically identifiable and subject to an obligation to be returned or treated

430 *Id.*

431 Best v. United States Nat'l Bank, 739 P.2d 554 (Or. 1987). *See also* Wallace v. Nat'l Commerce Bancorporation, 1993 WL 44600 (Tenn. Ct. App. Feb. 23, 1993). *But see* Tolbert v. First Nat'l Bank, 823 P.2d 965 (Or. 1991) (while duty to fairly exercise discretion existed, initial agreement to allow unilateral discretion in setting fees coupled with notice of fee increase satisfied duty as a matter of law).

432 National Consumer Law Center, Consumer Warranty Law § 11.3.4 (4th ed. 2010 and Supp.). *But see* Johnstone v. Bank of Am., 173 F. Supp. 2d 809 (N.D. Ill. 2001) (no independent cause of action even in contract); Voyles v. Sandia Mortgage Co., 751 N.E.2d 1126 (Ill. 2001) (Illinois does not recognize an independent cause of action for the breach of the duty of good faith and fair dealing).

433 *See, e.g.*, Sullivan v. JP Morgan Chase Bank, N.A., 725 F. Supp. 2d 1087 (E.D. Cal. 2010); Falcocchia v. Saxon Mortgage, Inc., 709 F. Supp. 2d 873 (E.D. Cal. 2010); Block v. Pre-Paid Legal Servs., Inc., 2008 WL 723775 (W.D. Okla. Mar. 14, 2008) (tort claims for the breach of the duty of good faith and fair dealing limited to insurance-related contracts); Williams v. Wash. Mut. Bank, 2008 WL 115097 (E.D. Cal. Jan. 11, 2008) (Nev. law) (tort action for breach of the implied covenant of good faith and fair dealing requires a special element of reliance); Foley v. Interactive Data Corp., 765 P.2d 373 (Cal. 1988) (tort for breach of implied covenant of good faith and fair dealing not available in employment contract cases; suggesting tort will only be recognized in insurance cases); Mitsui Mfrs. Bank v. Superior Court, 260 Cal. Rptr. 793 (Cal. Ct. App. 1989) (no tort liability for breach of duty of good faith). *But cf. In re* Figard, 382 B.R. 695 (Bankr. W.D. Pa. 2008) (gist of claim for breach of duty arising from contract is contractual, so tort claim not available). *See generally* § 2.4.5, *supra* (discussing fiduciary duty).

434 Cal. Welf. & Inst. Code §§ 15600–15675 (West).

435 Cal. Welf. & Inst. Code § 15610.27 (West).

436 Cal. Welf. & Inst. Code § 15610.30 (West) (defining financial abuse of older consumers).

437 Cal. Welf. & Inst. Code § 15657.5 (West).

438 Zimmer v. Nawabi, 566 F. Supp. 2d 1025, 1033–1034 (E.D. Cal. 2008); Toscano v. Ameriquest Mortgage Co., 2007 WL 3125023, at *6 (E.D. Cal. Oct. 24, 2007) (financial abuse of older consumer is actionable even if defendant did not have fiduciary relationship with the consumer).

439 Cosio v. Simental, 2009 WL 201827 (C.D. Cal. Jan. 27, 2009).

440 *See* Fridenmaker v. Valley Nat'l Bank of Arizona, 534 P.2d 1064 (Ariz. Ct. App. 1975) (no estoppel where mortgagor failed to demonstrate reliance, i.e., he would not have signed the mortgage except for the bank's promises).

441 First Union Nat'l Bank v. Tecklendburg, 769 N.Y.S.2d 573 (N.Y. App. Div. 2003).

442 First Nat'l Bank of Logansport v. Logan Mfg. Co., 577 N.E.2d 949 (Ind. 1991); Bittel v. Farm Credit Servs. of Cent. Kan., 962 P.2d 491 (Kan. 1998) (estoppel claim based on lender's promise to extend farm loan not barred under promissory estoppel, even though promise was unenforceable as a credit agreement). *But see* Greuling v. Wells Fargo Home Mortgage, Inc., 690 N.W.2d 757 (Minn. Ct. App. 2005) (estoppel claim based on mortgagee's oral promise to refinance barred by state statute requiring that "new credit agreements" be in writing); Ford v. City State Bank of Palacios, 44 S.W.3d 121 (Tex. App. 2001) (absent promise to reduce to writing oral promise to renew and extend promissory note, estoppel argument barred by statute of frauds).

443 *See* National Consumer Law Center, Automobile Fraud Ch. 4 (4th ed. 2011).

444 Heltzel v. Mecham Pontiac, 730 P.2d 235 (Ariz. 1986).

445 *See* Restatement (Second) of Torts § 222A (2005).

446 *See, e.g.*, Calvetti v. Antcliff, 346 F. Supp. 2d 92 (D.C. Cir. 2004); Biermann v. Gus Shaffar Ford, Inc., 805 S.W.2d 314 (Mo. Ct. App. 1991).

in a particular manner. For example, a conversion claim may lie when a consumer pays money for a specific purpose, such as a payment into an escrow account or a payment on a specific obligation, but the creditor fails to apply the payment properly.[447]

## 2.5 Electronic Credit Transactions and the Interplay Between State and Federal Law

### 2.5.1 Introduction

Paperless lending is a developing issue in consumer credit. While electronic credit transactions offer new convenience for borrowers, they also create new opportunities for fraud. When borrowing is accomplished over the Internet, there are often a series of preliminary issues to be addressed. For example, the issue of which state's law applies—the state in which the borrower lives, or the state in which the lender is domiciled—can be complicated, and is addressed at § 3.8, *infra*. Additionally the issues related to long-arm jurisdiction are discussed at § 7.9.2, *infra*.

This section discusses the rules for complying with the documentation requirements for credit when it is processed electronically. There are both federal and state laws applicable. Electronic transactions of all sorts are examined in detail in Chapter 11 of NCLC's *Consumer Banking and Payments Law* (4th ed. 2009 and Supp.).

This section sketches out the rules to determine whether state or federal law governs the documentation requirements for an electronic credit transaction. It also provides an overview of three issues in electronic consumer credit transactions: consumer consent requirements; timing and format requirements; and validity and enforceability.

### 2.5.2 Overview of E-Sign and UETA

Congress gave an impetus to electronic transactions by passing the Electronic Signatures in Global and National Commerce Act (E-Sign), effective October 1, 2000.[448] It provides that neither a signature nor a contract can be denied legal effect, validity, or enforceability solely because it is in electronic form.[449] It also provides that "if a statute, regulation, or other rule of law requires that information relating to a transaction or transactions in or affecting interstate or foreign commerce be provided or made available to a consumer in writing," the information can be provided electronically, as long as certain conditions are met.[450]

The federal statute applies not only to transactions that the consumer initiates electronically, but also to transactions conducted in person where the documents are delivered electronically. It authorizes creditors to provide information electronically in transactions that are otherwise conducted entirely on paper, as long as the federal statute's requirements are satisfied. For consumer transactions, the key requirement is that the consumer must consent in a very specific way to receive electronic disclosures.[451]

Many state credit laws require that the credit contract be in writing. Because of E-Sign, a contract cannot be invalidated solely because it is electronic rather than written, or solely because it was electronically signed.[452] These same credit laws also typically require that the consumer be given a copy of the written contract. E-Sign will override the requirement that delivery of the information be in writing rather than electronic format, but only if the consumer has followed E-Sign's specific electronic consent procedures and the transaction meets the other requirements of E-Sign.[453] Even if the consumer consents, however, E-Sign does not authorize electronic provision of certain important notices such as foreclosure notices.[454]

The federal statute allows states to supersede some of its provisions, including its key consumer protection provisions, only if the state passes the exact version of the Uniform Electronic Transactions Act (UETA)[455] after E-Sign's 2000 enactment date or passes another state law that is both technologically neutral and consistent with the federal statute.[456] By 2012, most states had adopted some form of UETA. The complex question of whether a state's adoption of UETA has superseded portions of E-Sign is summarized at § 2.5.3, *infra*, and discussed in detail in National Consumer Law Center, *Consumer Banking and Payments Law* § 11.4 (4th ed. 2009 and Supp.).

Like E-Sign, UETA provides that contracts, other records, and signatures cannot be denied legal effect because they are in electronic form.[457] It also echoes E-Sign in providing that elec-

447 *See, e.g.*, Johnson v. Citimortgage, Inc., 351 F. Supp. 2d 1368 (N.D. Ga. 2004) (receiving mortgage payments but failing to apply them to the mortgage loan); Johnson v. GMAC Mortgage Corp., 162 S.W.3d 110 (Mo. Ct. App. 2005) (failure to apply escrow payments to escrow account).

448 Pub. L. No. 106-229, 114 Stat. 464 (June 30, 2000), *codified at* 15 U.S.C. §§ 7001–7031.

449 15 U.S.C. § 7001(a). *See* Roger Edwards, Ltd. Liab. Co. v. Fiddes & Son, Ltd., 245 F. Supp. 2d 251 (D. Me. 2003) (e-mails may be sufficient to meet statute of frauds), *aff'd on other grounds*, 387 F.3d 90 (1st Cir. 2004); Med. Self Care, Inc. v. National Broad. Co., 2003 WL 1622181 (S.D.N.Y. Mar. 28, 2003) (e-mail satisfies contractual requirement of a writing; court states this result is arguably mandated by E-Sign).

450 15 U.S.C. § 7001(c). *See In re* Cafeteria Operators, Ltd. P'ship, 299 B.R. 411 (Bankr. N.D. Tex. 2003) (e-mails satisfied federal regulation's requirement of a writing).

451 *See* § 2.5.4, *supra*; National Consumer Law Center, Consumer Banking and Payments Law Ch. 11 (4th ed. 2009 and Supp.).

452 15 U.S.C. § 7001(a).

453 *See* National Consumer Law Center, Consumer Banking and Payments Law Ch. 11 (4th ed. 2009 and Supp.).

454 *See* National Consumer Law Center, Consumer Banking and Payments Law Ch. 11 (4th ed. 2009 and Supp.).

455 The text of UETA is posted on the website of the National Conference of Commissioners on Uniform State Laws, www.uniformlaws.org, along with a list of the states that have adopted it.

456 15 U.S.C. § 7002(a).

457 UETA § 7. *See, e.g.*, Polyad Co. v. Indopco, Inc., 2007 WL 2893638 (N.D. Ill. Sept. 25, 2007) (an e-mail containing the sender's name and confirming a contract can satisfy the statute of frauds).

tronic documents and electronic signatures satisfy state laws that require writings.[458] But UETA is different in many ways from the federal statute. First, it does not require E-Sign's specific consent procedures before information that must otherwise be provided in writing can be provided electronically. It merely requires that the parties agree to conduct transactions by electronic means.[459] Second, UETA does not make exceptions for important documents like foreclosure notices. Third, UETA allows tape recordings and other electronic records of oral communications to serve as a writing,[460] while under E-Sign an oral communication or a recording of an oral communication does not qualify as an "electronic record."[461] UETA's document integrity requirements are also significantly weaker than E-Sign's.[462] States that displace E-Sign by enacting UETA have the option of preserving E-Sign's consumer protections, however.[463]

Except for those aspects of laws that require physical signatures or written documents, both E-Sign and UETA leave state consumer protection and credit statutes unchanged. E-Sign provides that it does not "limit, alter, or otherwise affect any requirement imposed by a statute, regulation, or rule of law relating to the rights and obligations of persons under such statute, regulation, or rule of law other than a requirement that contracts or other records be written, signed, or in nonelectronic form."[464] UETA does not have such a specific savings clause, but states "[a] transaction subject to this Act is also subject to other applicable substantive law."[465] The official comments to UETA clarify that "the substantive rules of contracts remain unaffected by UETA,"[466] and that the uniform act takes a "minimalist" approach, leaving to other law the question whether a contract or signature has any effect.[467]

However the ease with which a person can be deemed to have agreed to a contract electronically has allowed some courts to find contract formation where the consumer may not have understood the consequences of the electronic activity or had any real choice regarding agreeing to the contract. For example, the act of typing in one's e-mail address at a weblink has been interpreted by a court to be equivalent to a signature, used to signify agreement to an onerous contract detailed on another weblink on-line.[468] Additionally, clicking through a link on an e-mail has been found to be equivalent to signing a contract.[469]

Both E-Sign and UETA also clear the way for electronic promissory notes.[470] As to secured transactions, neither the federal statute nor UETA applies to a contract or other record (electronic document) "to the extent that it is governed by" Article 9 of the Uniform Commercial Code,[471] but the 1999 revision to Article 9, which all states have adopted, has its own provisions allowing electronic documents in secured transactions.[472]

### 2.5.3 What Rules Apply to an Electronic Credit Contract?

The federal E-Sign law always applies when federally required writings are replaced with electronic records.[473] So if the question is whether the requirements to provide federally required disclosures—such as Truth in Lending disclosures—have been met, then compliance with E-Sign's consumer consent provisions is the test to determine the answer.

However, if the issue is whether state law writings—such as those required to satisfy the statute of frauds, or disclosures required under state law—have been provided, determining the answer is a bit more complicated, as some states opted out of E-Sign.

If the E-Sign consent process[474] has been complied with, and the consumer received the required E-Sign disclosures, and has consented to receive electronic records pursuant to E-Sign, that should be the end of the inquiry regarding whether state disclosures have been properly provided. No state requires more to determine a consumer's consent than the federal E-Sign law.

However, if E-Sign's consent process was not followed, and the argument is whether a writing required under state law has been provided or signed by the consumer, then one needs to engage in the analysis of which law applies. E-Sign has an unusual provision that allows states to opt out of certain of its provisions by passing a uniform version of UETA or another state law that is consistent with E-Sign and does not favor any

458 UETA § 7.

459 UETA § 5(b).

460 UETA § 2 cmt. 6, 7.

461 15 U.S.C. § 7001(c)(6).

462 *See* National Consumer Law Center, Consumer Banking and Payments Law Ch. 11 (4th ed. 2009 and Supp.).

463 *See* § 2.5.3, *infra* (discussing states that have adopted UETA after E-Sign's passage); National Consumer Law Center, Consumer Banking and Payments Law Ch. 11 (4th ed. 2009 and Supp.).

464 15 U.S.C. § 7001(b)(1). *See* Comments of Sen. Leahy, 106th Cong., 2d Session, 146 Cong. Rec. S. 5221 (June 15, 2000) ("the bill does not limit any legal requirement or prohibition other than those involving the writing, signature, or paper form of a contract").

465 UETA § 3(d).

466 UETA Prefatory note, ¶ 3.

467 UETA Prefatory note, § B.

468 *In re* Vistaprint Corp Mktg. & Sales Practices Litig., 2009 WL 2884727 (S.D. Tex. Aug. 31, 2009) (plaintiffs had typed e-mail address below box and clicked "yes" signifying agreement with contract.), *aff'd sub nom.* Bott v. Vistaprint USA Inc., 2010 WL 3303692 (5th Cir. Aug. 23, 2010). *See also* National Consumer Law Center, Consumer Banking and Payments Law §§ 11.3.7.3 and 11.4 (4th ed. 2009 and Supp.).

469 Sherman v. Travelers Indem. Co., 2011 WL 1628011 (D. Conn. Apr. 28, 2011) (plaintiff electronically signed the Arbitration Policy and Code of Conduct by clicking through a link on an e-mail received from her employer). *See also* Vergara Hermosilla v. Coca-Cola Co., 2011 WL 744098 (S.D. Fla. Feb. 23, 2011) (e-mail exchange considered a contract even while both parties were discussing terms of separate, attached contract).

470 15 U.S.C. § 7021; UETA § 16.

471 15 U.S.C. § 7003(a)(3); UETA § 3(b).

472 *See* National Consumer Law Center, Repossessions §§ 3.2.3, 10.4.3 (7th ed. 2010 and Supp.).

473 15 U.S.C. § 7001; National Consumer Law Center, Consumer Banking and Payments Law § 11.1.2 (4th ed. 2009 and Supp.).

474 *See* § 2.5.4, *infra*.

particular electronic technology.[475] What law or laws apply depends on whether and when the state implemented one of these options. This complex issue is only summarized here, and is analyzed in detail in National Consumer Law Center, *Consumer Banking and Payments Law* § 11.4 (4th ed. 2009 and Supp.).

In most states, the consumer protection provisions of E-Sign are *not* preempted by state law. But even if a state has preempted E-Sign, the preemption only applies to state law requirements, and E-Sign's consumer protections continue to apply when a creditor makes federally mandated disclosures or delivers federally mandated documents to the consumer.[476]

The only states that have clearly displaced the consumer protection provisions of E-Sign are Arkansas and Louisiana. These two states adopted a uniform version of UETA and specifically indicated an intent to override E-Sign.[477] In these two states, it is possible that requirements for a writing under state law, or signature, could be considered to be met with an electronic record or an electronic signature, even without compliance with E-Sign's consent process.[478] However, federal disclosures would not be considered provided without compliance with E-Sign.

In every state except Arkansas and Louisiana, E-Sign's consumer consent requirements apply either because E-Sign was not displaced, or because the state specifically adopted the consumer consent requirements explicitly in its own law, or by reference.[479]

## 2.5.4 Consumer Consent Requirements in Electronic Transactions

### 2.5.4.1 E-Sign

E-Sign overrides the requirement in many state credit statutes that the consumer be given a copy of the contract or other information in writing, but only if the consumer consents.[480] The consumer's consent must meet a set of strict requirements:

- Prior to consenting, the consumer must be given a clear and conspicuous statement of:
  - Any right or option to get the copy of the contract in non-electronic form;
  - The right to withdraw consent and the procedures for and consequences of doing so;
  - What transactions the consumer's consent applies to;
  - The procedures for updating the information needed to contact the consumer electronically; and
  - How, after consenting to electronic provision of the information, the consumer may get a paper copy, and whether any fee will be imposed.[481]
- The consumer must also be given a statement of the hardware and software requirements for access to and retention of electronic records.[482]
- The consumer must either give consent electronically to receive the copy of the contract electronically, or must confirm consent electronically.[483] In either case, the consent or confirmation of consent must be done "in a manner that reasonably demonstrates that the consumer can access information in the electronic form that will be used to provide the information that is the subject of the consent."[484]

This final requirement means that the consumer must demonstrate, not just affirm, that he or she has access to the equipment and programs necessary to receive, open, and read electronic documents from the creditor.[485] Unscrupulous creditors may to try to evade this requirement through use of creditor-owned in-house terminals, but this would hardly meet the requirement of "reasonably demonstrat[ing] that the consumer can access information in electronic form." Merely consenting on the creditor's computer should not be sufficient since the consumer cannot independently access the disclosure.

E-Sign also provides that the legal effect, validity, or enforceability of an electronic record may be denied if it is not in a form that is capable of being retained and accurately reproduced.[486] Thus, posting information on a website in a way that

475 15 U.S.C. § 7002(a). E-Sign also requires that such companion provisions make specific reference to E-Sign if they are passed after E-Sign was adopted. 15 U.S.C. § 7002(a)(2)(B).

476 *See* National Consumer Law Center, Consumer Banking and Payments Law Ch. 11 (4th ed. 2009 and Supp.).

477 Ark. Code Ann. §§ 25-32-101 to 25-32-120; La. Rev. Stat. Ann. §§ 9:2601 to 9:2620.

478 *See* National Consumer Law Center, Consumer Banking and Payments Law, § 11.4 (4th ed. 2009 and Supp.).

479 *See* National Consumer Law Center, Consumer Banking and Payments Law, § 11.4 (4th ed. 2009 and Supp.).

480 15 U.S.C. § 7001(c)(1)(A). *See also* Collins v. Missouri Elec. Coops. Employees Credit Union, 2006 WL 2189693 (E.D. Mo. July 26, 2006) (Electronic Funds Transfer Act does not require periodic statements to be in writing, so creditor need not comply with consumer consent requirements), *aff'd*, 2008 WL 3270900 (8th Cir. Aug. 11, 2008). *See generally* National Consumer Law Center, Consumer Banking and Payments Law Ch. 11 (4th ed. 2009 and Supp.) (full discussion of these requirements).

481 15 U.S.C. § 7001(c)(1)(B).

482 15 U.S.C. § 7001(c)(1)(C)(i).

483 15 U.S.C. § 7001(c)(1)(C)(ii).

484 *Id. See Statement of Sens. Hollings, Wyden and Sarbanes*, 106th Cong., 2d Session, 146 Cong. Rec. S. 5224 (June 15, 2000) ("The Act requires that consumers consent electronically—or confirm their consent electronically—in either case, in a manner that allows the consumer to test his capacity to access and retain the electronic records that will be provided to him.").

485 *See Comments of Sen. Wyden*, 106th Cong., 2d Session, 146 Cong. Rec. S. 5216 (June 15, 2000) ("Reasonably demonstrates means just that. It means the consumer can prove his or her ability to access the electronic information that will be provided. It means the consumer, in response to an electronic vendor enquiry, actually opens an attached document sent electronically by the vendor and confirms that ability in an e-mail response. . . . It is not sufficient for the consumer merely to tell the vendor in an e-mail that he or she can access the information in the specified formats.") *See generally* National Consumer Law Center, Consumer Banking and Payments Law § 11.3.5.4 (4th ed. 2009 and Supp.).

486 15 U.S.C. § 7001(e).

precludes downloading or printing will not satisfy a state law requirement that the information be provided to the consumer in writing.

### 2.5.4.2 UETA

UETA lacks E-Sign's specific consumer consent protections (although most states preserved them when adopting UETA). However, it does leave considerable room for evaluation of whether the consumer actually agreed to conduct the transaction electronically.

UETA allows electronic transactions only if the parties agree to conduct transactions by electronic means, which is determined "from the context and surrounding circumstances, including the parties' conduct."[487] Unlike E-Sign, UETA does not establish a separate standard for consumer consent to receive disclosures electronically, but the fact that agreement is to be determined by the context means that different standards should be applied to consumer transactions and commercial ones. The comments to UETA § 5 are particularly explicit about the need to go behind the documents to determine whether there is actual consent.

## *2.5.5 Effect of E-Sign and UETA on Timing and Format Requirements*

E-Sign states that it does not affect requirements regarding the content or timing of disclosures.[488] In addition, it states more generally that it has no effect on any state laws other than those requiring that contracts or other documents be written, signed, or in nonelectronic form.[489] The legislative history shows that Congress considered format requirements, such as a requirement that disclosures be clear and conspicuous, to be an example of a requirement that was unaffected by E-Sign.[490]

Some state credit statutes require that contracts, or portions of contracts, be printed in a certain size type. While it is not entirely clear how such a format requirement will be translated to electronic format, it is reasonable to interpret it as requiring that the words appear at least as large to a person sitting an average distance from a computer screen as words printed in the required type size would appear to the average reader.

Other state credit statutes require contract provisions to be "clear and conspicuous." To meet these standards, electronic disclosures should be easily readable from a monitor, organized logically, and free from distracting stimuli such as flashing advertisements or sounds. The FTC has issued detailed guidelines for evaluating whether an electronic disclosure is clear and conspicuous that may be useful in evaluating this question.[491]

UETA provides that if a state law requires a document to contain information that is formatted in a certain manner, an electronic version must be formatted in that same manner.[492] This requirement cannot be waived.[493] UETA does not provide guidance about how format requirements are to be translated to electronic documents, but leaves this question to the courts or the legislature.[494]

## *2.5.6 Validity and Enforceability of Electronic Contracts and Signatures Under E-Sign and UETA*

E-Sign and UETA contain functionally identical language about the validity and enforceability of electronic contracts. E-Sign provides:

> Notwithstanding any statute regulation, or other rule of law . . . with respect to any transaction in or affecting interstate or foreign commerce (1) a signature, contract, or other record relating to such transaction may not be denied legal effect, validity, or enforceability *solely* because it is in electronic form; and (2) a contract relating to such transaction may not be denied legal effect, validity, or enforceability *solely* because an electronic signature or electronic record was used in its formation.[495]

UETA provides:

> (a) A record or signature may not be denied legal effect or enforceability *solely* because it is in electronic form.
>
> (b) A contract may not be denied legal effect or enforceability *solely* because an electronic record was used in its formation.
>
> (c) If a law requires a record to be in writing, an electronic signature satisfies the law.
>
> (d) If a law requires a signature, an electronic

487 UETA § 5(b).

488 15 U.S.C. § 7001(c)(2)(A). *See also* 15 U.S.C. § 7001(b)(1) (E-Sign does not undermine any statutory or regulatory requirements other than those that require contracts or other records to be written, signed, or in nonelectronic form).

489 15 U.S.C. § 7001(b)(1).

490 *Accord* Statement of Rep. Dingell, 106th Cong., 2d Session, 146 Cong. Rec. H. 4358 (June 14, 2000). *See* Statement of Sens. Hollings, Wyden, and Sarbanes, 106th Cong., 2d Session, 146 Cong. Rec. S. 5230 (June 15, 2000) ("if a statute requires that a disclosure . . . include specific language set forth *clearly and conspicuously*, [t]hat requirement could be met by an electronic disclosure . . . which . . . included the specified language, set forth *clearly and conspicuously*").

491 FTC, Dot Com Disclosures 5-14 (2000), available on the FTC's website at www.ftc.gov. *See* National Consumer Law Center, Consumer Banking and Payments Law Ch. 11 (4th ed. 2009 and Supp.) (detailed discussion of standards of conspicuousness in electronic transactions).

492 UETA § 8(b)(3).

493 *Id.*

494 *See* UETA § 8 cmt. 4 ("If those legal requirements can be satisfied in an electronic medium, e.g., the information can be presented in the equivalent of 20 point bold type as required by other law, this Act will validate the use of the medium, leaving to the other applicable law the question of whether the particular electronic record meets the other legal requirements.").

495 15 U.S.C. § 7001(a) (emphasis added). *See* National Consumer Law Center, Consumer Banking and Payments Law Ch. 11 (4th ed. 2009 and Supp.).

signature satisfies the law.[496]

The drafters of UETA envisioned it as taking a "minimalist and procedural" approach, deferring to existing substantive law.[497]

Neither E-Sign nor UETA limits the range of electronic signatures. An electronic signature could consist of a name typed at the end of an e-mail by a sender, a PIN number, a mouse click, pressing a number on a touch-tone telephone, or biometrics.[498]

The term "solely" in both E-Sign and UETA is of great significance. Even if an electronic contract or signature meets all the requirements of E-Sign or UETA or both, the contract is not automatically valid and enforceable.[499] Neither E-Sign[500] nor UETA[501] requires the use or acceptance of electronic contracts or signatures. The practitioner should still evaluate all the usual questions about the contract. For example, do its substantive terms violate a state or federal law? Is it unconscionable? Does the creditor have any licenses the jurisdiction requires? Did the creditor commit fraud or violate the state deceptive practices statute in inducing the consumer to agree to the contract, or to agree to conduct the transaction electronically?

There are also particular issues regarding the validity of electronic contracts that the practitioner should evaluate. First, electronic documents are easily altered. Is the document that the creditor has produced the same as the document the consumer agreed to? When the consumer electronically signed the document, was the action creating the signature attached to or logically associated with the contract or other record? Can the seller prove that the document it has produced is the same as the one the consumer signed? E-Sign provides that an electronic contract or document may be denied legal effect, validity, or enforceability if it is not in a form that is capable of being retained and accurately reproduced for later reference by all parties or persons who are entitled to retain it.[502] In other words, the document must be change-proof and tamper-proof. UETA has similar, although weaker protections.[503]

Second, was there a true meeting of the minds as to the terms of the contract, including the agreement that it could be conducted electronically? UETA makes it particularly clear that "[w]hether the parties agree to conduct a transaction by electronic means is determined from the context and surrounding circumstances, including the parties' conduct,"[504] not just by the contract. This implies much less reliance on the language of the contract than is usual. Indeed, the comments to UETA give an example of the absence of true agreement: a standard form contract in which an agreement to receive all notices electronically is buried in fine print.[505] Electronic transactions raise additional questions about whether the consumer's mouse click was actually an expression of consent to the contract, or whether it was, for example, a misplaced attempt to link to a different page.

In addition, forgery or fraudulent assumption of the consumer's identity is particularly easy in an electronic environment. Thus it must also be determined whether the consumer in fact, rather than some unauthorized person, took whatever action was necessary to create the electronic signature.

496 UETA § 12 (emphasis added).

497 Prefatory Note to UETA, § B.

498 *See* International Casings Group v. Premium Standard Farms, Inc., 358 F. Supp. 2d 863, 873 (W.D. Mo. 2005) (e-mail header may constitute signature).

499 *In re* Piranha, Inc., 297 B.R. 78 (N.D. Tex. 2003), *aff'd*, 2003 WL 22922263 (5th Cir. Dec. 9, 2003).

500 15 U.S.C. § 7001(b)(2). *See* Prudential Ins. Co. v. Prusky, 413 F. Supp. 2d 489 (E.D. Pa. 2005); DWP Pain Free Med. P.C. v. Progressive Northeastern Ins. Co., 831 N.Y.S.2d 849 (N.Y. Dist. Ct. 2006).

501 UETA § 5(a). *See* Epco Carbon Dioxide Prods., Inc. v. JP Morgan Chase Bank, 467 F.3d 466 (5th Cir. 2006) (party relying on electronic signature on credit agreement must prove that other party agreed to conduct transaction electronically); DWP Pain Free Med. P.C. v. Progressive Northeastern Ins. Co., 831 N.Y.S.2d 849 (Dist. Ct. 2006).

502 15 U.S.C. § 7001(e).

This requirement applies where state law would otherwise require the contract to be in writing. *See* National Consumer Law Center, Consumer Banking and Payments Law § 11.3.6.1 (4th ed. 2009 and Supp.).

503 UETA § 12. *See* National Consumer Law Center, Consumer Banking and Payments Law § 11.3.6.1 (4th ed. 2009 and Supp.).

504 UETA § 5. *See* EPCO Carbon Dioxide Prods, Inc. v. JP Morgan Chase Bank, 467 F.3d 466, 469 (5th Cir. 2006) (proof that parties agreed to conduct transactions electronically is "significant evidentiary burden," but plaintiff's notice pleading was sufficient to withstand motion to dismiss), *on remand*, 2007 WL 1347785 (W.D. La. May 8, 2007) (concluding that the parties did not agree to conduct the transaction electronically); Audi AG v. D'Amato, 381 F. Supp. 2d 644, 663 (E.D. Mich. 2005) (e-mails did not create contract in absence of evidence that parties agreed to conduct transaction electronically), *aff'd on other grounds*, 469 F.3d 534 (6th Cir. 2006); International Casings Group v. Premium Standard Farms, Inc., 358 F. Supp. 2d 863, 875 (W.D. Mo. 2005) (parties' extended negotiation by e-mail is evidence that they consented to conduct transaction electronically); Hepfinger v. White, 2005 WL 2219445 (Mich. Ct. App. Sept. 13, 2005) (UETA does not apply in absence of evidence that parties agreed to conduct a transaction by electronic means); Crestwood Shops, L.L.C. v. Hilkene, 197 S.W.3d 641 (Mo. Ct. App. 2006) (upholding finding that parties agreed to conduct transaction electronically, where they both expressed preference for e-mail).

505 UETA § 5 cmt. 5(A).

# Chapter 3 Federal Preemption and the Applicable State Statute

## 3.1 Getting Started

### *3.1.1 Overview*

The "normal" operation of state law is that when a consumer enters into a transaction, the transaction must comply with the law of the state where the transaction took place. But there is nothing normal about the operation of state credit statutes, particularly where a loan is originated by a depository institution, such as a bank, savings association, or credit union.

Federal law provides for "rate exportation" whereby a national bank or federal savings association's home state's interest rate applies when it makes a loan in another state, not the law of the state where the loan is made.[1] Moreover, as a "most favored lender," the depository often can utilize an interest rate cap that does not even apply to banks, but to other types of creditors in its home state.[2]

Similar rules apply even to federally-insured *state*-chartered banks, savings associations, and credit unions. Such institutions can even choose between their home state's interest cap and that of the state where the loan is made. Moreover, state "parity laws" may even offer similar options to state depositories that are *not* federally insured.[3]

An entirely different regime applies to federal credit unions. Maximum interest rates are set by federal statute and regulation.[4] By operation of state "parity laws," state credit unions may be able to avail themselves of the same federal interest caps as federal credit unions.[5]

These federal rules determine the applicability of state interest rate ceilings, but do not determine the applicability of state law regulating the "non-interest" portion of a credit transaction. Office of the Comptroller of the Currency (OCC) regulations seek to preempt much "non-interest" state credit regulation as it applies to national banks and federal savings associations.[6] State parity laws and other legal theories may mean that OCC preemption of state law applies indirectly to loans originated by state-chartered banks and savings associations.[7]

The applicability of state law becomes even more complex in the case of manufactured home credit sales and loans. Several federal statutes preempting state law as applied to mortgage lending also apply to manufactured home credit, adding additional layers of preemption for such credit.[8]

While federal law and regulation thus have a profound impact on the applicability of a consumer's state law to a loan originated by a depository institution, this generally is not the case where a non-depository creditor originates the loan. Nevertheless, financial transactions today often implicate a number of different states and it will still be unclear which state's law regulates the loan. For example, a payday lender headquartered in one state may offer a loan over the Internet to a consumer residing in a different state, payments are received in a third state, and the credit agreement specifies the law of a fourth state is applicable.

Section 3.8, *infra* examines *state* law that determines which state's law applies to loans originated by non-depositories. That discussion will also be relevant to the "non-interest" terms of a loan originated by a depository institution, if OCC regulation does not preempt that state law.

In both these contexts, determining which *state's* law applies is only half the battle. The next step is to determine which statute within a particular state applies to a particular type of credit transaction. As considered at § 3.9, *infra*, different statutes within a state may apply to consumer vs. business loans, to open-end credit vs. closed-end credit, to credit sales vs. straight loans, to small loans vs. larger loans, and to those regularly extending credit vs. those who do not. States may also have special licensing statutes applicable to certain types of creditors and credit may have to comply not only with civil but also criminal usury statutes.

Section § 3.10 considers a final issue—which *version* of a particular credit statute in the applicable state governs a loan, the version of the statute in effect when the loan was made or the version of the statute in effect at the time litigation is instituted. This question of the retroactive application of a statutory change has practical significance because state legislatures with surprising frequency either weaken or strengthen credit statutes.

1 *See* § 3.4, *infra.*
2 *See* § 3.5, *infra.*
3 *See* § 3.6, *infra.*
4 *See* § 3.3, *infra.*
5 *See* § 3.6, *infra.*
6 *See* § 3.2, *infra.*
7 *See* § 3.2.3, *infra.*
8 *See* § 3.7, *infra.*

## 3.1.2 Identifying the Nature of the Originating Lender

### 3.1.2.1 Introduction; Depository vs. Non-Depository Lenders

The first step in determining the applicable law regulating credit is to identify the nature of the originating creditor—not the lender presently holding the loan, but the creditor that first originated the loan. The assignee steps into the shoes of the assignor, and it is the nature of the originating lender that typically determines the applicable law.

Of particular importance is whether the originating creditor is a depository institution, such as a bank, savings association, or credit union. This determines whether federal law preempts state law and which state's interest rate applies to a transaction. Very different rules apply to credit originated by depository vs. non-depository creditors.

Even if a depository institution is involved, in multi-party transactions the financial institution may not be the lender. For example, if credit is made available on a prepaid card issued by a bank, the credit may be extended by the prepaid card program manager or another party and not necessarily by the bank. Similarly, a payday lender may purport to offer credit that is extended under a contract with a bank. In either situation, examine the transaction to determine who the actual lender is. If the payday lender or prepaid card program manager makes eligibility determinations and purchases the loans from the bank, or indemnifies the bank from loss, a court may find that the bank is not the actual lender and that bank preemption rules do not apply.

### 3.1.2.2 Banks and Savings Associations

Different rules may also apply to federally vs. state chartered banks and savings associations. The banking system consists of two parallel tracks for depository institutions—those that operate under federal charters and are federally regulated and those that operate under state charters and are primarily state regulated. Those with state charters can opt for certain forms of federal regulation and preemption of state law by opting for federal insurance of their deposits.

The FDIC reports that as of the end of 2011 there were 1,931 *federally* chartered banks and savings associations holding over $9.6 trillion in assets and 5,426 *state*-chartered banks and savings associations holding assets of over $4.2 trillion.[9]

A depository institution can choose the nature of federal preemption and rate exportation that is applicable to the institution by selecting a state or federal charter and, if state-chartered, deciding whether to opt for federal deposit insurance.[10] The FDIC website, www2.fdic.gov/idasp/main_bankfind.asp, is a useful resource to determine whether a depository is federally or state chartered, in what state the charter is granted, and whether a depository is federally insured. Type in the name and location information about the institution, and the site will indicate the type of institution, its regulator, its branches, and other information.

National banks have a federal charter, are regulated by the Office of the Comptroller of the Currency (OCC), and typically will include either "N.A." or "National Bank" in their legal name. Some of the nation's largest banks are national banks.

Federal savings banks and federal savings associations also have federal charters. Federal savings banks typically will have the term "F.S.B." or Federal Savings Bank in their legal name, while federal saving associations will typically have F.A. or Federal Savings in their name. Both of these types of savings entities, formerly regulated by the Office of Thrift Supervision (OTS), are now regulated by the OCC. The OTS preemption standards, which have now been superseded, only apply to contracts entered into before July 21, 2010.[11] Those standards are discussed in another NCLC treatise, *Mortgage Lending* (2012).

State-chartered depositories are regulated primarily by the state banking commissioner. If a state-chartered bank is a member of the Federal Reserve System, it is also subject to Federal Reserve Board oversight. If a state-chartered bank is not part of the Federal Reserve System, but is federally insured, it is also subject to certain regulation by the Federal Deposit Insurance Corporation (FDIC). Banks are insured under the FDIC's Bank Insurance Fund and savings associations are insured under the FDIC's Savings Association Fund.[12]

State-chartered banks will have either "State Bank" or "Bank" (without the word "National") in their legal name. State-chartered savings banks will have either "Savings Bank" or "S.S.B" in their name. State savings associations will have "Savings" or "S.A." in their name (without either "Federal" or "Bank" in the name).

### 3.1.2.3 Credit Unions

Credit unions are depository institutions. Federal credit unions have federal charters and are regulated by the National Credit Union Association (NCUA). State credit unions have state charters and are subject to state banking supervision. If they are federally insured, it is through the National Credit Union Share Insurance Fund, administered by the NCUA. The NCUA has some regulatory control over state-chartered credit unions through their participation in the insurance fund.

---

9 *See* www2.fdic.gov/SDI/main.asp.

10 *See* Patricia A. McCoy, Banking Law Manual Ch. 3 (Lexis Pub. 2d ed. 2003) (discussing the history of the dual banking system, the choices among charters, and suggests that the dual banking system should be scrapped). *See also* Binyamin Appelbaum, *By Switching Their Charters, Bank Skirt Supervision*, Wash. Post, Jan. 22, 2009, at A1 (reporting on the number of charter conversions since 2000 and providing examples of when conversions occurred to avoid regulatory oversight); Patricia A. McCoy & Elizabeth Renuart, *The Legal Infrastructure of Subprime and Nontraditional Home Mortgages*, *in* Borrowing to Live 128–129 (Nicolas P. Retsinas & Eric S. Belsky, eds. 2008) (describing the factors an institution considers when picking a charter and its primary supervisor or converting its charter and changing its supervisor).

11 *See* § 3.2.4.2, *infra*.

12 12 U.S.C. § 1821(a)(5)–(a)(6).

As of the end of 2011, the NCUA reported that there were 7,094 federal or federally-insured state credit unions. They served over 91 million members with deposits exceeding $960 billion and loans over $571 billion.[13]

A federal credit union is a nonprofit, cooperative financial institution owned and run by its members. Members pool their funds to make loans to each other. A customer's account is called a share account, rather than a deposit or checking account. To join a credit union, a potential customer must be eligible for membership. Each institution decides who it will serve. Most credit unions are organized to serve people in a particular community, group or groups of employees, or members of an organization or association. Low-income designated credit unions are a unique form of credit union, serving primarily low-income members in distressed and financially underserved area.

#### 3.1.2.4 Industrial Loan Companies

Seven states charter industrial loan companies (ILCs) or industrial banks—California, Colorado, Hawaii, Indiana, Minnesota, Nevada, and Utah.[14] They may, depending on state law, use in their name the word "Bank" or "Savings Bank" or "Industrial Loan Company" or "Thrift."[15] An ILC need not have any particular words in its name that identify its legal status.[16]

Since ILCs are creatures of state law, state law generally applies to most of their activities. In addition, the state in which they are chartered will determine whether or not ILCs are different from a bank in any functional manner. For most purposes, ILCs can function as banks, but they cannot offer business checking accounts.[17] ILCs can be owned by any business corporate entity, and there is generally no limitation on their ability to own subsidiaries. If an ILC is federally insured, the FDIC regulates the ILC to some extent, but ILCs remain state-chartered and state-regulated financial institutions.

In 2011, iBanknet reported that there were thirty-six ILCs with assets over $125 billion, including such entities as UBS Bank, American Express Centurion Bank, GE Capital Financial, BMW Bank of North America, and Sallie Mae Bank, all with assets over $7 billion.[18]

13 *See* www.ncua.gov/DataApps/Documents/CRS2011-12.pdf.

14 FDIC, The FDIC's Supervision of Industrial Loan Companies: A Historical Perspective (Summer 2004), *available at* www.fdic.gov/regulations/examinations/supervisory/insights/sisum04/industrial_loans.html.

15 *See, e.g.*, Utah Code Ann. § 7-1-701. *See also* Cal. Fin. Code § 18101.6 (West).

16 *See* Utah Department of Financial Institutions, What Is a Utah Industrial Bank?, *available at* www.dfi.state.ut.us/whatisIB.htm.

17 12 U.S.C. § 1841(c)(2)(H)(I).

Technically, ILCs cannot offer any demand deposit accounts, but they may offer nonbusiness NOW (negotiable order of withdrawal) accounts—checking accounts that retain the legal right to require advance notice of the withdrawal. 12 U.S.C. § 1832.

18 *See* www.ibanknet.com.

#### 3.1.2.5 Bank Subsidiaries and Finance Companies

National banks have "operating" subsidiaries and "financial" subsidiaries. Operating subsidiaries are those that can engage solely in activities that national banks are permitted to engage in directly. Subsidiaries that can engage in other activities are financial subsidiaries.

An aid in determining if an entity is an operating subsidiary of a national bank is the list found at www.helpwithmybank.gov/national-banks/operating-subsidiaries/national-banks-subsidiaries-a-m.html. Another place to check is the state's appropriate regulatory agency to see if the lender is a licensed lender.

### *3.1.3 Checklist: When to Read Each Section*

- For credit originated by national banks or federal savings associations, first go to §§ 3.2, 3.4, and 3.5, *infra*. Also for a manufactured home credit sale or loan, go to § 3.6a. Then to the extent that state law is applicable, go to §§ 3.8–3.10.
- For credit originated by state-chartered banks or savings associations, first go to §§ 3.2.3 and 3.4–3.6, *infra*. Also for a manufactured home credit sale or loan, go to § 3.7. Then if OCC preemption is applicable, go to the remainder of § 3.2 and to the extent that state law is applicable, go to §§ 3.8–3.10.
- For credit originated by federal credit unions, first go to § 3.3, *infra*. Also for a manufactured home credit sale or loan, go to § 3.7. Then to the extent that state law is applicable, go to §§ 3.8–3.10.
- For credit originated by state-chartered credit unions, first go to §§ 3.3 and 3.6, *infra*. Also for a manufactured home credit sale or loan, go to § 3.7. Then to the extent that state law is applicable, go to §§ 3.8–3.10.
- For credit originated by non-depository lenders, go to §§ 3.7–3.9, *infra*. If federal preemption is alleged, also review §§ 3.2.2, 3.4.2.6, and 3.4.3. Also if a manufactured home credit sale or loan, go to § 3.7.

## 3.2 OCC Preemption of State Law Regarding Matters Other Than Interest

### *3.2.1 Scope of This Section*

The Office of Comptroller of the Currency (OCC) regulates national banks and federal savings associations. It has adopted a set of regulations that preempt state law in certain areas as applied to those depositories. A former OCC regulation provided that these preemption rules applied equally to national banks' operating subsidies.[19] However, the Dodd-Frank Act abolished preemption for subsidiaries, affiliates, and agents of

19 12 C.F.R. § 7.4006 (2004).

national banks and federal savings associations, effective for contracts entered into after July 21, 2010.[20] The preemption standards for older contracts are discussed in another NCLC treatise, *Mortgage Lending* (2012).

OCC preemption of state law does not apply directly to other creditors not regulated by the OCC, and the burden is on the party claiming preemption to prove it is a national bank or a federal savings association.[21] Nevertheless, there are exceptions (discussed at § 3.2.3, *infra*) where OCC preemption applicability to federal depositories is extended by operation of federal or state law to *state chartered* depositories.[22] That is, OCC regulation of federal depositories may cause certain state law not to apply to state chartered depositories.

Separate OCC regulations examined at §§ 3.4–3.5, *infra*, implement the federal statutes that specify that national banks and federal savings associations may charge the higher of a federal cap or the maximum rate (often unlimited) specified by the institution's home state. OCC regulation does not directly affect the home state interest caps, but the National Bank Act does permit depositories to take broad advantage nationally of permissive home state laws.

This section examines OCC preemption of state laws governing matters other than interest, as it applies to banks and savings associations. Federal preemption issues are different for credit unions, and those are examined at § 3.3, *infra*.

Prior to the Dodd-Frank Wall Street Reform and Consumer Protection Act (hereinafter the Dodd-Frank Act), enacted July 21, 2010, OTS had its own preemption regulations, applicable to federal savings associations. The Dodd-Frank Act not only limited the preemption authority of OCC, but it also transferred supervision of federal savings banks and savings associations to OCC.[23]

The Dodd-Frank preemption standards went into effect on July 21, 2011. They appear to apply to contracts entered into after July 21, 2010, because the statute states that the changes do not apply to contracts entered into before that date.[24]

This section focuses solely on OCC preemption standards, as specified by the Dodd-Frank Act, and not OCC and OTS standards applicable to earlier contracts. For a detailed discussion of OTS and OCC standards for contracts entered into prior to July 21, 2010, see another NCLC treatise, *Mortgage Lending* (2012).

That treatise also deals with OCC preemption in a more detailed fashion, even for loans extended after July 21, 2010. For example, the case law is confused as to the application of OCC preemption where a national bank or federal savings association purchases a loan from an entity not regulated by the OCC. That issue is examined only in *Mortgage Lending* (2012).

20 *See* § 3.2.2, *infra*.

21 *See* Jara v. Aurora Loan Servs., L.L.C., 2011 WL 6217308 (N.D. Cal. Dec. 14, 2011).

22 *See* § 3.2.3, *infra*.

23 Dodd-Frank Wall Street Reform and Consumer Protection Act, Pub. L. No. 111-203, tit. III, §§ 312, 313, 124 Stat. 1376 (July 21, 2010) (hereinafter cited as Dodd-Frank).

24 *See* 12 U.S.C. 5553 (changes do not apply to contracts entered into before July 21, 2010 effective date). *See also* § 3.2.4.2, *infra*.

### 3.2.2 *OCC Preemption Does Not Apply to Subsidiaries, Affiliates, or Agents*

OCC preemption of state law applies only to credit originated by national banks and federal savings associations, and not to credit originated by their subsidiaries, affiliates, or agents. Prior to the Dodd-Frank Act, OCC regulations preempted state law as applied not just to national banks but also to national bank operating subsidiaries (but not financial subsidiaries[25]).[26] The OCC also preempted any state laws that affected national banks' "incidental powers,"[27] which includes the power to use agents.[28]

However, the Dodd-Frank Act amended the National Bank Act to explicitly state that national bank subsidiaries, affiliates, or agents are not entitled to the advantages of OCC preemption of state law, unless that entity is also a national bank.[29] The Dodd-Frank Act also applies the same standards to subsidiaries, affiliates or agents of savings banks and savings associations.[30] These changes apply to any credit originated after July 21, 2010.[31]

The Dodd-Frank Act defines subsidiaries and affiliates as having the same meaning as in 12 U.S.C. § 1813.[32] Subsidiary is defined there as any company which is owned or controlled directly or indirectly by another company.[33] Subsidiary includes any service corporation owned in whole or in part.[34] Affiliate is defined as any company that controls, is controlled by, or is under common control with another company.[35]

Following passage of the Dodd-Frank Act, the OCC rescinded its incidental powers preemption rule.[36] Consequently, any cases based on that rule, or more generally applying

25 *See* § 3.1.2.5, *supra* (distinguishing between operating and financial subsidiaries).

26 Watters v. Wachovia Bank, N.A., 550 U.S. 1 (2007); 12 C.F.R. § 7.4006, *removed by* 76 Fed. Reg. 43,549 (July 21, 2011).

27 *See* former 12 C.F.R. § 7.4009 (repealed by 76 Fed. Reg. 43,566 (July 21, 2011)) ("A national bank may exercise all powers authorized to it under Federal law, including conducting any activity that is part of, or incidental to, the business of banking, subject to such terms, conditions, and limitations prescribed by the Comptroller of the Currency and any applicable Federal law.").

28 12 U.S.C. § 24, Seventh (giving national banks the power "To exercise by its board of directors or duly authorized officers or agents, subject to law, all such incidental powers as shall be necessary to carry on the business of banking . . ."); SPGGC, L.L.C. v. Ayotte, 488 F.3d 525 (1st Cir. 2007).

29 12 U.S.C. § 25b(e), (h)(2).

30 12 U.S.C. § 1465(a). *See also* 76 Fed. Reg. 43,565 (July 21, 2011) (whereby the OCC removed 12 C.F.R. § 7.4006 that had previously applied state law to operating subsidiaries to the same extent that it applied to parent national banks); 12 C.F.R. § 34.6 (OCC regulation: "Federal savings associations and their subsidiaries shall be subject to the same laws and legal standards, including regulations of the OCC, as are applicable to national banks and their subsidiaries, regarding the preemption of state law.").

31 U.S.C. § 5553.

32 U.S.C. § 25b(h)(1) (referring to 12 U.S.C. § 1813).

33 12 U.S.C. § 1813(w)(4)(A).

34 *Id.* § 1813(w)(4)(B).

35 *Id.* § 1813(w)(6) (referencing 12 U.S.C. § 1841(k)).

36 *See* 76 Fed. Reg. 43,566 (July 21, 2011) (repealing 12 C.F.R. § 7.4009).

preemption to bank subsidiaries, affiliates, or agents may no longer be good law.

## *3.2.3 OCC Preemption's Indirect Effect on State-Chartered Depositories*

The OCC does not regulate state-chartered banks or savings banks, so that OCC preemption does not apply directly to these entities. Although the FDIC has limited regulatory authority over federally-insured state-chartered depositories, that regulation is not enough to preempt state law.[37] Federal regulation of state-chartered depositories is minimal,[38] and states retain primary authority over state banks and savings associations.

In addition, federal law that allows *state*-chartered banks and savings associations to export interest rates applies only to interest rates and related fees, and not to licensing laws, loan terms unrelated to the interest rate, or most other state consumer credit laws.[39] Thus a FDIC letter states that federal authority to export rates "does not prevent states from enforcing consumer protection and lending laws other than interest-rate related limitations."[40]

Nevertheless, OCC preemption *does* indirectly preempt state law's application to state-chartered banks. First, a federal statute provides that a branch of an out-of-state state-chartered bank can comply with its home state's law and not the host state's law, if OCC regulation preempts the application of the host state's law to a national bank.[41] For example, consider where a national bank operates in Massachusetts and OCC regulation preempts a Massachusetts law that prohibits credit cards being secured by a cardholder's home. Then a Massachusetts branch of a New York state-chartered bank need not comply with that Massachusetts statute either. Instead, New York law will govern the legality of this practice.

OCC preemption affects state-chartered banks and savings associations in another way, as well. State parity statutes, in effect in most states, provide state-chartered banks and savings associations with the same rights as national banks and federal savings associations.[42] If a national bank does not have to comply with state law, but only with OCC standards, then, under the state parity law, state-chartered banks in that state may not have to comply with state law either, but only with the same standards as the national banks must meet.

## *3.2.4 Statutory Standards for OCC Preemption*

### 3.2.4.1 General

The Dodd-Frank Wall Street Reform and Consumer Protection Act of 2010 (hereinafter the Dodd-Frank Act)[43] makes sweeping changes in the authority of federal banking regulators to preempt state law. These changes apply to both national banks and federal savings associations.[44]

The Dodd-Frank Act amends the National Bank Act (NBA) and Home Owners Loan Act (HOLA) to provide that state "consumer financial laws" are preempted only if one of three specific criteria is met. Two of the criteria are of less importance—that the state law discriminates against national banks on behalf of state banks, or some other law preempts state law.[45] The key Dodd-Frank standard is that a state consumer financial laws is preempted if "in accordance with the legal standard for preemption in . . . *Barnett Bank of Marion County, N. A. v. Nelson, Florida Insurance Commissioner et al.*, 517 U.S. 25 (1996), the State consumer financial law prevents or significantly interferes with the exercise by the national bank of its powers."[46]

"State consumer financial law" is defined as a law "that does not directly or indirectly discriminate against national banks and that directly and specifically regulates the manner, content, or terms and conditions of any financial transaction (as may be authorized for national banks to engage in), or any account related thereto, with respect to a consumer)."[47]

### 3.2.4.2 Dodd-Frank Act's Effective Date and Impact on Prior Law

The Dodd-Frank Act amendments concerning OCC preemption took effect on July 21, 2011.[48] The Dodd-Frank Act provides that Title X, which encompasses the preemption amendments, "shall not be construed to alter or affect the applicability of [any OCC regulation, order, guidance or interpretation] regarding the applicability of State law under Federal

37 Thomas v. U.S. Bank Nat'l Ass'n N.D., 575 F.3d 794 (8th Cir. 2009); BankWest, Inc. v. Baker, 411 F.3d 1289 (2005), *reh'g granted, op. vacated*, 433 F.3d 1344 (11th Cir. 2005), *op. vacated due to mootness*, 446 F.3d 1358 (11th Cir. 2006). *See also* FDIC General Counsel Letter 02-96 (Dec. 19, 2002) (Michigan retail installment act was not preempted except for the interest rates), *available on the companion website to this treatise*.

38 *See, e.g.*, FDIC Senior Deputy General Counsel Letter (Sept. 12, 2003) ("The FDIC, however, does not routinely examine institutions for compliance with state laws, and the enforcement of state laws is not a primary focus of the FDIC's supervisory activities."), *available on the companion website to this treatise*.

39 *See* § 3.4.2.3, *infra*. *See also* BankWest, Inc. v. Baker, 411 F.3d 1289 (2005), *reh'g granted, op. vacated*, 433 F.3d 1344 (11th Cir. 2005), *op. vacated due to mootness*, 446 F.3d 1358 (11th Cir. 2006).

40 FDIC Chairman Powell Letter to North Carolina Attorney General Roy Cooper (Apr. 27, 2005), *available on the companion website to this treatise*.

41 12 U.S.C. § 1831a(j).

42 *See* § 3.6, *infra*.

43 Pub. L. No. 111-203, 124 Stat. 1376 (July 21, 2010) (hereinafter cited as Dodd-Frank).

44 12 U.S.C. § 1465(a) (making National Bank Act preemption standards applicable to federal savings associations).

45 12 U.S.C. §§ 25b(b)(1) (NBA), 1465(a) (HOLA, incorporating NBA standard).

46 12 U.S.C. §§ 25b(b)(1) (NBA), 1465(a) (HOLA, incorporating NBA standard).

47 12 U.S.C. § 25b(a)(2).

48 Dodd-Frank § 1100G specifies an effective date for Title X provisions (including the provisions on OCC preemption standards) as of the "designated transfer date." 75 Fed. Reg. 57,252 (Sept. 20, 2010) sets the designated transfer date as July 21, 2011.

banking law to any contract entered into on or before [July 21, 2010] by . . . national banks, . . . or subsidiaries thereof. . . ."[49] Thus, the preemption amendments apply to contracts entered into after July 21, 2010, but not before that date.[50]

The Dodd-Frank Act however does not prohibit courts from using the Dodd-Frank Act to *interpret* whether the NBA and OCC regulation preempts state law applicable to a contract entered into prior to July 21, 2010. Since Dodd-Frank preemption provisions are explicitly termed "clarifications" rather than changes to the law, courts should take them into account in interpreting OCC preemption for cases that arose prior to the Dodd-Frank Act's enactment.[51]

This section focuses solely on OCC preemption standards for contracts entered into starting on July 22, 2010. For transactions before that date, reference should be made to NCLC's *Mortgage Lending* (2012) which has a detailed discussion of the pre-Dodd-Frank federal agency preemption standards. Note that older cases that upheld state laws are still very relevant, as laws that withstood preemption before standards were tightened should not be preempted under the more strict preemption standards.

### 3.2.4.3 The *Barnett Bank* "Significantly Interferes" Standard

The Dodd-Frank Act specifies use of the *Barnett Bank* "significantly interferes" standard to determine if OCC regulation preempts state credit statutes. The *Barnett Bank* case was a narrow Supreme Court decision, preempting a state law that completely forbade an activity that Congress explicitly authorized for national banks: acting as an insurance agent in towns of less than 5,000.[52] State laws are preempted if they "forbid or impair significantly, the exercise of a power that Congress explicitly granted." The Court emphasized that its ruling "is not to deprive States of the power to regulate national banks, where (unlike here) doing so does not prevent or significantly interfere with the national bank's exercise of its powers."[53]

The *Barnett Bank* standard is a strict conflict preemption standard.[54] As one court described the Dodd-Frank standard, "the targeted state statute is irreconcilably in conflict with the NBA."[55]

The reinstatement of the *Barnett Bank* "prevent or significantly interfere" standard should be interpreted as effectively reversing OCC's broad 2004 regulations that purported to preempt ten broad categories of state laws. This regulation was a significant departure from the *Barnett Bank* standard and highly controversial.[56] The Dodd-Frank Act's legislative history is clear that the Act intended to undo the OCC's 2004 preemption standards:

> The standard for preempting State consumer financial law would return to what it had been for decades, those recognized by the Supreme Court in *Barnett Bank v. Nelson*, 517 U.S. 25 (1996), undoing broader standards adopted by rules, orders, and interpretations issued by the OCC in 2004.[57]

### 3.2.4.4 Other Supreme Court Cases Comport with the *Barnett Bank* Standard

Other Supreme Court cases provide guidance as to the *Barnett* standard. Cases in which the Supreme Court has held that state laws are preempted involve specific contexts:

- State taxes on national banks;[58]
- Laws that intrude on federal bank regulators' exclusive statutory power to exercise visitation on federal depositories[59] and to resolve an insolvent bank;[60]
- Interest rates,[61] an area of preemption directly authorized in the National Bank Act[62] and preserved by the Dodd-Frank Act;[63] and

49 12 U.S.C. § 5553.

50 *See* Copeland-Turner v. Wells Fargo Bank, N.A., 2011 WL 2650853 (D. Or. July 6, 2011).

51 *See* Cline v. Bank of Am., N.A., 2011 WL 4857934 (S.D. W. Va. Oct. 13, 2011).

52 12 U.S.C. § 92.

53 Barnett Bank v. Nelson, 517 U.S. 25, 34 (1996).

54 *See* Baptista v. JPMorgan Chase Bank, 640 F.3d 1194 (11th Cir. 2011).

55 Meluzio v. Capital One Bank (USA), N.A., 2012 WL 847324 (N.D. W. Va., Mar. 12, 2012); Cline v. Bank of Am., N.A., 2011 WL 4857934 (S.D. W. Va. Oct. 13, 2011).

56 *See generally* Arthur E. Wilmarth, Jr., *The OCC's Preemption Rules Exceed the Agency's Authority and Present a Serious Threat to the Dual Banking System*, 23 Ann. Rev. Banking & Fin. L. 225 (2004).

57 S. Rep. No. 111-176, at 175 (2010). *See* Arthur E. Wilmarth, Jr., *The Dodd-Frank Act's Expansion of State Authority to Protect Consumers of Financial Services*, 36 J. Corp. L 803. (2011).

The Librarians' Society of Washington, D.C., has compiled a comprehensive legislative history of the Dodd-Frank Act entitled *Dodd-Frank Wall Street Reform and Consumer Financial Protection Act: A Brief Legislative History with Links, Reports and Summaries*. It is available at www.llsdc.org/dodd-frank-act-leg-hist/.

58 *See, e.g.*, First Agric. Nat'l Bank of Berkshire County v. State Tax Comm'n, 392 U.S. 339, 88 S. Ct. 2173, 20 L. Ed. 2d 1138 (1968); Laurens Fed. Sav. & Loan Ass'n v. South Carolina Tax Comm'n, 365 U.S. 517, 81 S. Ct. 719, 5 L. Ed. 2d 749 (1961); M'Culloch v. Maryland, 17 U.S. 316, 4 L. Ed. 579, 4 Wheat. 316 (1819). *But see* First Nat'l Bank v. Commonwealth, 76 U.S. 353, 362, 19 L. Ed. 701, 9 Wall. 353(1869) (holding that state taxes on bank stock are not preempted).

59 Cuomo v. Clearing House Ass'n, L.L.C., 129 S. Ct. 2710 (2009). *See also* Watters v. Wachovia Bank, N.A., 550 U.S. 1, 127 S. Ct. 1559, 167 L. Ed. 2d 389 (2007).

60 Anderson v. Abbott, 321 U.S. 349, 64 S. Ct. 531, 88 L. Ed. 793 (1944); Easton v. Iowa, 188 U.S. 220, 23 S. Ct. 288, 47 L. Ed. 452 (1903); Earle v. Conway, 178 U.S. 456, 20 S. Ct. 918, 44 L. Ed. 1149 (1900); Earle v. Pennsylvania, 178 U.S. 449, 20 S. Ct. 915, 44 L. Ed. 1146 (1900); Davis v. Elmira Sav. Bank, 161 U.S. 275, 287, 16 S. Ct. 502, 40 L. Ed. 700 (1896).

61 Beneficial Nat'l Bank v. Anderson, 539 U.S. 1, 123 S. Ct. 2058, 156 L. Ed. 2d 1 (2003); Smiley v. Citibank (S.D.), N.A., 517 U.S. 735, 116 S. Ct. 1730, 135 L. Ed. 2d 25 (1996); Marquette Nat'l Bank of Minneapolis v. First of Omaha Serv. Corp., 439 U.S. 299, 99 S. Ct. 540, 58 L. Ed. 2d 534 (1978).

62 *See* §§ 3.4.2–3.4.5, *supra*.

63 *See* Dodd-Frank tit. X, § 1044(a), *codified at* 12 U.S.C. § 25b(f).

- State laws that discriminate against national banks in favor of state institutions[64] (another preemption category preserved by the Dodd-Frank Act).

Outside these contexts, the Supreme Court rarely finds that federal regulation of national banks and federal thrifts preempts state law.[65] State laws that are preempted are ones that, as in *Barnett Bank* itself, flatly prohibit exercise of a power explicitly granted to national banks,[66] that irreconcilably conflict with federal law,[67] or that impose an especially serious interference with such a power.[68] A state law can severely limit a national bank's powers, as long as those powers are not authorized by federal law.[69]

The Supreme Court has distinguished between state laws that effectively prevent a bank from exercising its powers and laws that merely condition or regulate the exercise of those powers. In the 1896 case *McClellan v. Chipman Traders' National Bank*, the Supreme Court rejected the bank's claim that a state law voiding preferential transfers by insolvent debtors was preempted.[70] The bank's power under the NBA to take real estate as security for or in satisfaction of debts did not conflict with state law that "provides that it cannot be done under particular and exceptional circumstances. . . . No function of [national] banks is destroyed or hampered by allowing the banks to exercise the power to take real estate, provided only they do so under the same conditions and restriction to which all the other citizens of the state are subjected. . . ."[71] The Court found "no conflict between the special power conferred by congress upon national banks to take real estate for certain purposes and the general and undiscriminating law of the state of Massachusetts subjecting the taking of real estate to certain restrictions, in order to prevent preferences in case of insolvency. . . ."[72]

Similarly, in the escheat area, the Court has upheld laws that impose duties on national banks to turn over funds that are subject to escheatment[73] as long as the laws do not go so far as to threaten improper confiscation of depositors' funds.[74] Though both types of laws affect the power to accept deposits, only the latter was found to significantly interfere with that power. The Court has also upheld state laws that are stricter on national banks than applicable federal laws.[75]

#### 3.2.4.5 Case-by-Case Preemption Determinations; Repudiation of Field Preemption

The Dodd-Frank Act requires that OCC regulations preempting state consumer financial laws determine, *on a case-by-case basis*, that a particular state law, or one with substantially equivalent terms, meets the *Barnett* standard.[76] "Case-by-case basis" is defined as "a determination concerning the impact of a particular State consumer financial law on any national bank that is subject to that law, or the law of any other State with substantively equivalent terms."[77] The OCC cannot preempt broad categories of state laws, but can only preempt a "particular" state law that "prevents or significantly interferes"

64 Franklin Nat'l Bank of Franklin Square v. People, 347 U.S. 373, 74 S. Ct. 550, 98 L. Ed. 767 (1954) (state law preempted where it prevented banks not chartered in New York from using the word "savings" in their name).

65 *See, e.g.*, Atherton v. Federal Deposit Ins. Corp., 519 U.S. 213, 222, 117 S. Ct. 666, 136 L. Ed. 2d 656 (1997) (federal law setting forth gross negligence standard for directors or officers of federally insured savings institutions provides only a floor and does not stand in the way of a stricter state law standard); Anderson Nat'l Bank v. Luckett, 321 U.S. 233, 248, 64 S. Ct. 599, 88 L. Ed. 692 (1944) (upholding state law requiring all banks to transfer dormant bank accounts to the state so that the state could initiate escheat proceedings); Lewis v. Fidelity & Deposit Co., 292 U.S. 559, 564–566, 54 S. Ct. 848, 78 L. Ed. 1425 (1934) (state law requiring bank, in accepting deposits of state funds, to provide surety bond not preempted); First Nat'l Bank in St. Louis v. Missouri, 263 U.S. 640, 44 S. Ct. 213, 68 L. Ed. 486 (1924) (state statute prohibiting bank from operating branches not preempted); McClellan v. Chipman, 164 U.S. 347, 356–359, 17 S. Ct. 85, 41 L. Ed. 461 (1896) (state law prohibiting insolvent debtors from making preferential transfers of property to any creditor was not preempted by national bank's power to accept conveyances of real estate as security for debts; the purpose of the NBA "was to leave such banks as to their contracts in general under the operation of the state law").

66 Missouri *ex rel.* Burnes Nat'l Bank of St. Joseph v. Duncan, 265 U.S. 17, 44 S. Ct. 427, 68 L. Ed. 881 (1924).

67 Van Reed v. People's Nat'l Bank of Lebanon, 198 U.S. 554, 25 S. Ct. 775, 49 L. Ed. 1161 (1905).

68 *See* Fidelity Fed. Sav. & Loan Ass'n v. De la Cuesta, 458 U.S. 141, 153–154, 102 S. Ct. 3014, 73 L. Ed. 2d 664 (1982) (state law prohibiting due-on-sale clauses preempted because such clauses are essential to the financial security and stability of savings association; First Nat'l Bank of San Jose v. California, 262 U.S. 366, 368–369, 43 S. Ct. 602, 67 L. Ed. 1030 (1923) (state law that escheated bank accounts to the state interfered with national banks' ability to exercise their express authority to accept deposits). *But cf.* Anderson Nat'l Bank v. Luckett, 321 U.S. 233, 248, 64 S. Ct. 599, 88 L. Ed. 692 (1944) (upholding state law requiring all banks to transfer dormant bank accounts to the state).

69 First Nat'l Bank in St. Louis v. Missouri, 263 U.S. 640, 44 S. Ct. 213, 68 L. Ed. 486 (1924) (state statute prohibiting banks from establishing branches did not frustrate the purpose for which bank was created or interfere with the discharge of its duties to the government or impair its efficiency as a federal agency).

70 164 U.S. 347, 17 S. Ct. 85, 41 L. Ed. 461 (1896).

71 164 U.S. at 358.

72 164 U.S. at 360.

73 Anderson Nat'l Bank v. Luckett, 321 U.S. 233, 248, 64 S. Ct. 599, 88 L. Ed. 692 (1944) (upholding state law requiring all banks to transfer dormant bank accounts to the state so that the state could initiate escheat proceedings).

74 First Nat'l Bank of San Jose v. California, 262 U.S. 366, 368–369, 43 S. Ct. 602, 67 L. Ed. 1030 (1923) (state law that escheated bank accounts to the state upon mere dormancy for a specified period and without any proof of abandonment threatened a "possible confiscation" of depositors' funds and thereby significantly interfered with national banks' ability to exercise their express authority to accept deposits).

75 *See* Atherton v. Federal Deposit Ins. Corp., 519 U.S. 213, 222, 117 S. Ct. 666, 136 L. Ed. 2d 656 (1997) (federal law setting forth gross negligence standard for directors or officers of federally insured savings institutions provides only a floor and does not stand in the way of a stricter state-law standard).

76 12 U.S.C. § 25b(b)(1)(A).

77 12 U.S.C. § 25b(b)(3)(A).

with a bank power. While the OCC has some ability to extend that preemption determination to substantially equivalent laws, it must start with a case-by-case assessment of the impact of a particular law.

The Dodd-Frank Act also provides that neither the National Bank Act[78] nor HOLA[79] "occup[ies] the field in any area of State law."[80] Unlike the OTS, the OCC never explicitly purported to occupy the field of lending regulation for national banks, but both its pre- and post-Dodd-Frank regulations preempt ten broad categories of state credit regulation,[81] and some courts have read the OCC's preemption regulations so broadly as to amount to field preemption.[82] The Dodd-Frank Act thus also repudiates the OCC's authority to preempt entire areas of state law.

### 3.2.4.6 Procedures for Adoption of Preemption Rules

The Dodd-Frank Act sets out the procedures for any OCC preemption determination. The OCC can make *Barnett Bank* conflict preemption determinations only by regulation or order, not by opinion letter.[83] The determination can be made only by the comptroller and cannot be delegated to any other OCC employee.[84]

"Substantial evidence, made on the record of the proceeding," must support the OCC's finding that the *Barnett Bank* standard has been met as to a "particular" state law.[85] The "substantial evidence" standard means that the OCC cannot merely assert, as it has in the past, that a state law interferes with federal regulation of banking. It must produce clear evidence of that conflict.

Once it has determined that a "particular" state law is preempted, the OCC may extend preemption to other state laws with "substantially equivalent terms."[86] But the OCC must consult with the Consumer Financial Protection Bureau (CFPB) before making a determination that a state law is substantively equivalent to one that the OCC has preempted on a case-by-case basis.[87]

Every determination that federal law preempts a state consumer financial law, whether issued under the *Barnett Bank* conflict preemption standard or some other criteria, must be reviewed every five years.[88] The OCC must publish a list of preemption determinations every quarter,[89] presumably in the *Federal Register*. Moreover, by statute, any OCC preemption determination is subject to rigorous judicial review that need not defer to the agency's expertise.[90]

### 3.2.4.7 Limited OCC Preemption of State Laws of General Applicability

Dodd-Frank authority for the OCC to preempt state law applies only to a "State consumer financial law," defined as a law that "directly and specifically regulates the manner, content, or terms and conditions of any financial transaction . . . or any account related thereto, with respect to a consumer."[91] There should be even less preemption as to state laws of more general applicability.[92]

The Supreme Court consistently endorses application of state laws of general applicability to national banks. For example, in *Cuomo v. Clearing House Ass'n*, the Supreme Court stated: "States . . . have always enforced their general laws against national banks—and have enforced their banking-related laws against national banks for at least 85 years. . . ."[93] Even the OCC and OTS, when they aggressively asserted a broad preemption standard, excluded general state laws from the full scope of preemption.[94] It makes no sense to interpret the Dodd-Frank Act's silence regarding the preemption standard for laws of general applicability as providing the OCC with greater authority to preempt such laws than it has to preempt specific consumer credit legislation.

The 2004 OCC and OTS regulations and the 2011 revised OCC regulations do not address whether state laws against unfair or deceptive acts or practices (UDAP statutes) are preempted. They are not listed as preempted or as not preempted.[95] Courts generally find that federal banking regulation does not preempt state UDAP statutes when they are used to challenge deception, although it is unclear whether such regulation preempts use of a UDAP statute to prohibit as unfair certain allowed banking practices.[96] UDAP statutes are not "State consumer financial laws" as defined by the Dodd-Frank Act, as they do not "directly and specifically regulat[e] the manner, content, or terms and conditions of any financial transaction . . . or any account related thereto, with respect to a consumer."[97] UDAP statutes should be treated like other laws of general

78 12 U.S.C. § 25b(b)(4).

79 12 U.S.C. § 1465(b).

80 *See also* Arevalo v. Bank of Am. Corp., ___ F. Supp. 2d ___, 2011 WL 1195973, at *12 n.5 (N.D. Cal. Mar. 29, 2011) (interpreting Dodd-Frank Act to be consistent with Watters v. Wachovia Bank, 550 U.S. 1, 127 S. Ct. 1559, 167 L. Ed. 2d 389 (2007), in rejecting field preemption).

81 *See* § 3.2.5, *infra*.

82 *See* National Consumer Law Center, Mortgage Lending § 5.6 (2012).

83 12 U.S.C. § 25b(b)(1)(B).

84 12 U.S.C. § 25b(b)(6).

85 12 U.S.C. § 25b(c).

86 12 U.S.C. § 25b(b)(3).

87 12 U.S.C. § 25b(b)(3)(B).

88 12 U.S.C. § 25b(d)(1).

89 12 U.S.C. § 25b(g). This requirement applies to all preemption determinations under any standard and regarding any law.

90 *See* § 3.2.6.1, *infra*.

91 12 U.S.C. § 25b(a)(2).

92 *See* Arthur E. Wilmarth, Jr., *The Dodd-Frank Act's Expansion of State Authority to Protect Consumers of Financial Services*, 36 J. Corp. L 803 (2011).

93 129 S. Ct. 2710, 2720, 174 L. Ed. 2d 464 (2009).

94 *See* 12 C.F.R. §§ 7.4007(c), 7.4008(e), 7.4009(c), 34.4(b).

95 *See* 12 C.F.R.§ 7.4008(d), (e).

96 *See generally* National Consumer Law Center, Unfair and Deceptive Acts and Practices §§ 2.5.3.2, 2.5.3.3 (7th ed. 2008 and Supp.).

97 Dodd-Frank tit. X, § 1044, *codified at* 12 U.S.C. § 25b(a)(2) (definition of "State consumer financial law").

applicability and should be preempted only under standard Supremacy Clause principles.

Moreover, even if the *Barnett Bank* "prevent or significantly interfere" standard applies to state UDAP laws, UDAP laws should withstand scrutiny, unless they operate to prohibit practices explicitly allowed by federal regulators. Federal law prohibits national banks and federal savings associations from engaging in unfair, deceptive, or abusive conduct,[98] and state law prohibitions thus do not prevent or significantly interfere with a power authorized by federal law.[99]

### 3.2.5 OCC Preemption Regulations

Several OCC regulations govern preemption. OCC preemption regulations concerning non-mortgage lending are found at 12 C.F.R. § 7.4008(d) and (e). Deposit-taking activities, such as activities related to checking and savings accounts, are governed by 12 C.F.R. § 7.4007. Another regulation, 12 C.F.R. § 7.4002, authorizes national banks and federal savings associations to charge their customers non-interest charges and fees, including deposit account service charges, and discusses the application of state law to those activities.[100]

A separate NCLC treatise, *Mortgage Lending* (2012) considers preemption regulations concerning mortgage lending, found at 12 C.F.R. § 34.4.

On July 21, 2011, the OCC revised its non-mortgage lending and deposit-taking preemption regulations, allegedly to respond to the Dodd-Frank changes. (The OCC also repealed its subsidiary preemption regulation and its preemption of laws restricting national banks' incidental powers.[101])

Surprisingly, the OCC did not make any change to its *enumeration* of state laws that were or might not be preempted, and only amended its *general standards* as to when a state law might or might not be preempted.

The prior OCC non-real-estate lending regulation stated that "state laws that obstruct, impair, or condition a national bank's ability to fully exercise its Federally authorized non-real estate lending powers are not applicable to national banks."[102] The deposit-taking regulation had identical language.[103]

Responding to the fact that the Dodd-Frank Act enunciates a different standard—"prevents or significantly interferes"[104]—the OCC, effective July 21, 2011, removed the "obstruct, impair, or condition" language from both regulations.[105] It also stated "to the extent that an existing preemption precedent is exclusively reliant on the phrase 'obstructs, impairs or conditions' as the basis for a preemption determination, we believe that validity of the precedent would need to be reexamined to ascertain whether the determination is consistent with the *Barnett* conflict preemption analysis."[106]

Nevertheless, the OCC made no change at all in the laundry list of ten state lending laws that are preempted, including any state laws concerning:

- Licensing, registration, or reports;
- The bank's ability to require or obtain insurance for collateral or other credit enhancements or risk mitigants;
- Loan-to-value ratios;
- Credit terms, including repayment schedules, amortization of loans, balance, payments due, minimum payments, or term to maturity of the loan;
- Escrow and similar accounts;
- Security property;
- Access to and use of credit reports;
- Disclosure and advertising; and
- Disbursements and repayments.[107]

Similarly, the OCC deposit-taking rule continues to preempt state laws concerning:

- Abandoned and dormant accounts;[108]
- Checking accounts;
- Disclosure requirements;
- Funds availability;
- Savings account orders of withdrawal;
- State licensing or registration requirements (except for purposes of service of process); and
- Special purpose savings services.[109]

The 2011 OCC rules also change the general standard as to what state lending or deposit-taking laws are *not* preempted. The old standard stated that state laws were not preempted "to the extent to which they only incidentally affect the exercise of national banks' " deposit-taking or non-real-estate lending pow-

98 *See* Dodd-Frank tit. X, § 1031; 15 U.S.C. §§ 45(a)(1), 57a(f).

99 *See* Meluzio v. Capital One Bank (USA), N.A. 2012 WL 847324 (N.D. W. Va. Mar. 12, 2012); First Nat'l Bank in St. Louis v. Missouri, 263 U.S. 640, 44 S. Ct. 213, 68 L. Ed. 486 (1924) (state statute prohibiting banks from establishing branches not preempted when court interpreted federal law to prohibit establishment of branches as well).

100 Charges and fees that are "interest" within the meaning of 12 U.S.C. 85 are governed by 12 C.F.R. § 7.4001 and not by § 7.4002. *See* §§ 3.4, 3.5, *infra*.

101 *See* § 3.2.2, *supra*.

102 12 C.F.R. § 7.4008(d)(1), *deleted by* 76 Fed. Reg. 43,565 (July 21, 2011).

103 12 C.F.R. § 7.4007(b)(1), *deleted by* 76 Fed. Reg. 43,565 (July 21, 2011).

104 12 U.S.C. § 25b(b)(1)(B).

105 76 Fed. Reg. 43,565 (July 21, 2011).

106 76 Fed. Reg. 43,556 (July 21, 2011).

107 *See* 76 Fed. Reg. 43,565 (July 21, 2011) (leaving unchanged 12 C.F.R. § 7.4008(d)(2)(i)–(x) but re-designating it as § 7.4008(1)–(10)).

With respect to rates of interest on loans, the tenth subject listed, the regulation makes reference in a footnote to § 85 of the National Bank Act, which allows national banks the choice of abiding by a federal rate cap or exporting their home state's interest rate ceiling.

108 The regulation includes a footnote stating that "This does not apply to state laws of the type upheld by the United States Supreme Court in Anderson Nat'l Bank v. Luckett, 321 U.S. 233 (1944), which obligate a national bank to 'pay [deposits] to the persons entitled to demand payment according to the law of the state where it does business.' *Id.* at 248–249." 12 C.F.R. § 7.4007(b)(1) n.3.

109 *See* 76 Fed. Reg. 43,565 (July 21, 2011) (leaving unchanged 12 C.F.R. § 7.4007(b)(2)(i)–(vii) but re-designating it as § 7.4007(b)(1)–(7)).

ers.[110] Instead, state laws now are not preempted "to the extent consistent with the decision of the Supreme Court in *Barnett Bank*. . . ."[111]

While the 2011 rules change the general standard as to when a state law affecting lending or deposit-taking is not preempted, the OCC's list of specific laws that are *not* automatically preempted is unchanged:

- Contracts;
- Torts;
- Criminal law;
- Rights to collect debts;
- Acquisition and transfer of property;
- Taxation;
- Zoning.[112]

Some courts relied on the former version this savings clause to reject preemption challenges to common law claims, debt collection laws, and other laws of general applicability.[113] This conclusion is certainly clearer in light of the Dodd-Frank amendments and the removal of the "incidentally affects" standard from OCC's rules.[114] Although courts have been inconsistent, there are compelling arguments that state laws banning unfair and deceptive practices should be treated as falling within this list of non-preempted general laws.[115]

The OCC did not change the regulation authorizing a national bank to charge its customers non-interest charges and fees, including deposit account service charges.[116] The regulation specifies that "the establishment of non-interest charges and fees, their amounts, and the method of calculating them are business decisions to be made by each bank, in its discretion, according to sound banking judgment and safe and sound banking principles."[117] The regulation has a general preemption provision stating that the OCC "applies preemption principles derived from the United States Constitution, as interpreted through judicial precedent, when determining whether State laws apply that purport to limit or prohibit charges and fees described in this section."[118] Some, but not all,[119] courts have found that this regulation preempts state laws governing fees and charges.[120]

The OCC regulations are now applicable not only to national banks, but also to federal savings associations. Current OCC regulations state: "Federal savings associations and their subsidiaries shall be subject to the same laws and legal standards, including regulations of the OCC, as are applicable to national banks and their subsidiaries, regarding the preemption of state law."[121]

This treatise does not generally discuss the case law under the OCC preemption regulations prior to the Dodd-Frank changes, though some of the recent cases cited may involve pre-Dodd-Frank facts. That case law, which is discussed in NCLC's *Mortgage Lending* treatise, may still be applicable in interpreting or determining the validity of the current OCC regulations, particularly cases that upheld state laws before preemption standards were tightened.

---

110 12 C.F.R. §§ 7.4007(c), 7.4008(e), prior to their amendment by 76 Fed. Reg. 43,565 (July 21, 2011).

111 *Id.* §§ 7.4007(c), (c)(8), 7.4008(e), (e)(8), *as amended by* 76 Fed. Reg. 43565 (July 21, 2011).

112 *Id.* §§ 7.4007(c)(1)–(7), 7.4008(e)(1)–(7).

113 *See, e.g.,* Larin v. Bank of Am., N.A., 2012 WL 1131542 (9th Cir. Apr. 5, 2012) (claim that bank violated UDAP statute by affirmatively misrepresenting the value of its overdraft protection program, rather than by operating the program as it did, not preempted as general state laws aimed at misrepresentations are not preempted); Epps v. JP Morgan Chase Bank, __ F.3d __, 2012 WL 1134065 (4th Cir. Apr. 5, 2012) (state laws governing automobile repossessions fall within savings clause for debt collection laws and only incidentally affect national banks); Aguayo v. U.S. Bank, 653 F.3d 912 (9th Cir. 2011); *In re* Checking Account Overdraft Litig., 797 F. Supp. 2d 1312 (S.D. Fla. 2011) (refusing to dismiss contract and tort law claim that banks charged excessive overdraft fees on debit card transactions, where customers only sought recovery for manner in which banks manipulated their debit and checking charges, rather than manner in which overdraft fees were computed); Lombino v. Bank of Am., N.A., 797 F. Supp. 2d 1078 (D. Nev. 2011) (rejecting challenge to jury verdict in favor of consumer on tort claims of negligent misrepresentation and negligence arising from overdraft due to forged check that was deposited by customer into his account). *See also In re* Bate, 454 B.R. 869 (M.D. Fla. 2011) (rejecting preemption notwithstanding OCC interpretive letter stating that savings clause in preemption regulation for "right to collect debts" only preserved state laws regarding national banks' rights to collect debts, not state laws regarding debt collection).

114 *See* Meluzio v. Capital One Bank (USA), N.A., 2012 WL 847324 (N.D. W. Va. Mar. 12, 2012) (taking Dodd-Frank amendments into account and finding state debt collection and common law claims not preempted because they do not significantly interfere with bank powers under *Barnett* standard).

115 *See* § 3.2.4, *supra*; National Consumer Law Center, Unfair and Deceptive Acts and Practices § 2.5.3 (7th ed. 2008 and Supp.).

116 12 C.F.R. § 7.4002.

117 12 C.F.R. § 7.4002(b)(2). The regulation specifies several factors that banks should consider. *See id.* § 7.4002(b)(2)(i)–(iv).

118 12 C.F.R. § 7.4002(d).

119 *See In re* Checking Account Overdraft Litig., 797 F. Supp. 2d 1312 (S.D. Fla. 2011) (refusing to dismiss contract and tort law claim that banks charged excessive overdraft fees on debit card transactions, where customers only sought recovery for manner in which banks manipulated their debit and checking charges, rather than manner in which overdraft fees were computed).

120 *See, e.g.,* Baptista v. JPMorgan Chase Bank, N.A., 640 F.3d 1194 (11th Cir. 2011) (preempting state law restricting check-cashing fees charged to nonaccount holders, relying on OCC regulation defining such persons as "customers" within the regulation); Martinez v. Wells Fargo Home Mortgage, Inc., 598 F.3d 549 (9th Cir. 2010) (unfairness challenge to $800 underwriting fee preempted); Robinson v. Bank of Am., 2011 WL 5870541 (C.D. Cal. 2011) (finding preempted common law and unfair and deceptive claims that bank failed to disclose that consumers have the ability to avoid account maintenance fees). *See also* Collier v. National Penn Bank, 2012 WL 1214325 (E.D. Pa. Apr. 11, 2012) (finding significant federal issue and refusing to remand challenge to overdraft fees to state court because unconscionability claim turned on whether bank's conduct conformed with standards in § 7.4002(b)).

121 12 C.F.R. § 34.6.

## *3.2.6 Are the 2011 OCC Rules Legal?*

### 3.2.6.1 Judicial Review Standards

The Dodd-Frank Act states that "a court in reviewing any determinations by the Comptroller regarding preemption . . . shall assess the validity of such determinations, depending on the thoroughness evident in the consideration of the agency, the validity of the reasoning of the agency, the consistency with other valid determinations made by the agency, and other factors which the court finds persuasive and relevant to its decision."[122] This language is taken from the Supreme Court's decision *Skidmore v. Swift & Co.*[123] The Dodd-Frank Act also states that an OCC rule cannot preempt a state consumer financial law "unless substantial evidence, made on the record of the proceeding, supports the specific finding regarding the preemption of such provision in accordance with the legal standard of the decision" in *Barnett Bank.*[124]

Unlike deference that courts typically give to other agency determinations, a court will not defer to the OCC's expertise in making preemption determinations. A court considering challenges to OCC preemption determinations cannot use the deferential *Chevron*[125] standard (which has led some courts to rubber stamp OCC regulations). Instead, the court must use the more rigorous *Skidmore* standard described in the preceding paragraph.[126]

Even when the Dodd-Frank Act's explicit adoption of the *Skidmore* standard did not control, one court has refused to defer to the OCC's position, "whether formal or informal, on preemption issues because a preemption determination involves matters more within the expertise of the courts than within the expertise of the agency."[127]

### 3.2.6.2 Do OCC Preemption Regulations Comply with the Dodd-Frank Act?

The Dodd-Frank Act sets out three grounds for preempting state law.[128] Its preemption regulations are based on the second of these three grounds—the *Barnett Bank* standard. (The other two grounds are that the state law has a discriminatory effect on national banks in comparison with state-chartered banks,[129] or that the state law conflicts with some federal statute other than the National Bank Act.)[130]

The *Barnett Bank* standard allows preemption of a state law that prevents or significantly interferes with the exercise by a national bank of its powers.[131] This finding must be made on a case-by-case basis, defined as the impact of a particular state law on a national bank.[132] The OCC can also make the same determination for another state's law that has substantially equivalent terms, but only if the OCC consults with the CFPB and takes the CFPB's views into consideration when making the determination.[133]

As described at § 3.2.5, *supra*, the OCC non-mortgage-lending regulation lists ten categories of state law that are preempted. This part of the regulation seems inconsistent with the Dodd-Frank standards. The CFPB was not consulted, no determination was made on a case-by-case basis, and the *Barnett* standard should not invalidate every aspect of all state laws relating to "escrow accounts" or "security property" or "insurance for collateral or other credit enhancements," to list just a few.

The OCC regulations do not even require that these ten categories of laws be preempted only to the extent to which they meet the *Barnett* standard. There is no qualifier at all to the preemption of these categories of state laws. Nor is the preemption of these ten categories of laws supported by any, let alone substantial, evidence on the record. They amount to a continuation of *de facto* field preemption. Indeed, when the OCC issued those rules in 2004, it said that it was identifying state laws for preemption "in a more generic way."[134] Moreover, it was this very part of the OCC regulations that Congress was limiting by its Dodd-Frank preemption language. In response, the OCC has not in any way restricted the preemption of the ten categories of state law.

The OCC defends its position by stating that the Dodd-Frank Act's requirement for a case-by-case determination only applies to future OCC preemption determinations and not existing ones.[135] This is a stunning statement in that these regulations were rejected by Congress. The OCC is arguing that since the regulations were enacted before Congress rejected them, they stay in force. The OCC is not arguing that these old determinations apply to old contracts, but that they continue to apply to new contracts even though Congress explicitly stated that new contracts are governed by new standards, and not the standards that formed the basis for the old regulations.

The OCC also states that its preemption of these ten categories of state laws is not field preemption. Instead, its position is that every possible example of the listed types of state laws is

122 12 U.S.C. § 25b(b)(5)(A).

123 Skidmore v. Swift & Co., 323 U.S. 134, 65 S. Ct. 161, 89 L. Ed. 124 (1944).

124 12 U.S.C. § 25b(c).

125 Chevron U.S.A., Inc. v. Natural Res. Def. Council, Inc., 467 U.S. 837, 104 S. Ct. 2778, 81 L. Ed. 2d 694 (1984).

126 12 U.S.C. § 25b(b)(5). *See* Arthur E. Wilmarth, Jr., *The Dodd-Frank Act's Expansion of State Authority to Protect Consumers of Financial Services*, 36 J. Corp. L. 803 (2011) (more detailed discussion of *Skidmore* standard).

127 *In re* Bate, 454 B.R. 869, 877 n.46 (M.D. Fla. 2011) (rejecting preemption notwithstanding OCC interpretive letter stating that savings clause in preemption regulation for "right to collect debts" only preserved state laws regarding national banks' rights to collect debts are not state laws regarding debt collection; applying *Skidmore* deference standard even though Dodd-Frank's adoption of it was not controlling in this case).

128 12 U.S.C. § 25b(1).

129 *See* 12 U.S.C. § 25b(b)(1)(A).

130 *Id.* § 25b(b)(1)(C).

131 *Id.* § 25b(b)(1)(B). *See* 76 Fed. Reg. 43,549 (July 21, 2011).

132 *Id.* § 25b(b)(3)(A).

133 *Id.* § 25b(b)(3)(B).

134 69 Fed. Reg. 1904, 1911 (Jan. 13, 2004).

135 76 Fed. Reg. 43,557 (July 21, 2011).

preempted by the *Barnett* conflict preemption standard.[136] This is an equally stunning proposition, that there can be no state law of any kind relating to any aspect of ten areas of credit that does not significantly interfere with OCC regulation. The OCC is claiming for example, that there is significant interference from any state law of any nature dealing with escrow accounts, security property, access to and use of credit reports, advertising, or repayments.

The OCC also states that it has re-reviewed these ten categories, and found all laws in these categories to fall under the *Barnett* preemption standard.[137] Its justification for this outlandish conclusion is the conclusory statement that all state laws fitting into these ten categories "would meaningfully interfere with fundamental and substantial elements of the business of national banks and with their responsibilities to manage that business and those risks."[138] The OCC provides no evidence or further specification of its reasoning for this conclusion.

It may be possible to interpret the OCC rule to be consistent with the Dodd-Frank Act and the *Barnett Bank* standard. A number of courts, both before and after the OCC's 2011 revision of the rule, have treated the list of subjects on which state laws are preempted as something far less than an absolute rule. These courts interpret the revised OCC rules as limiting preemption to the *Barnett Bank* standard.[139] A state law is not preempted just because it affects one of the subject areas listed in the OCC rule; instead, the state law must prevent or significantly interfere with the bank's statutory powers in that area.[140] If the rule is interpreted in this manner, it would not be invalid on substantive grounds, but OCC's failure to proceed on a case-by-case basis and its failure to consult with the CFPB would still be contrary to the Dodd-Frank Act.

## 3.3 Preemption Applicable to Federal (and State) Credit Unions

National Credit Union Administration (NCUA) regulations provide that the NCUA has exclusive authority to regulate the "rates, terms or repayment and other conditions of Federal credit union loans and lines of credit (including credit cards) to members."[141] The regulations specifically preempt states laws that limit or affect:

—Rates of interest and amounts of finance charges, including, terms related to variable rate loans and late charges;[142]
—Closing costs, application, origination, or other fees;
—Terms of repayment, including, maturity of loans and lines of credit; the amount, uniformity, and frequency of payments; balloon payments; and prepayment limits;
—Conditions related to the amount or purpose of the loan or line of credit and the type or amount of security;
—The imposition and enforcement of liens on the shares (deposits) of borrowers and accommodating parties.[143]

The NCUA states that this list is exclusive.[144] State laws that do not affect rates, terms of repayment, and other conditions specified in NCUA regulations are *not* preempted.[145] The NCUA also identifies certain state laws that are not preempted, including: insurance laws; laws relating to the transfer of and security interests in real and personal property (except relating to due-on-sale clauses); laws relating to collection costs and attorney fees; requirements that documents be in plain English; laws addressing the circumstances in which a borrower may be in default; and cure statutes.[146] A court has also found that the Federal Credit Union Act does not preempt a state law limiting the maximum attorney fees that a lender can recover.[147]

The regulation also states that the NCUA does not intend to preempt state laws affecting aspects of credit transactions that are primarily regulated by other federal laws, for example, those state laws concerning credit cost-disclosure requirements, credit discrimination, credit reporting practices, unfair credit practices, and debt collection practices.[148] When these types of state laws are at issue, the agency will determine the applicability of such laws according to the preemption standards of the relevant federal law and regulations.

Further guidance as to whether state laws are preempted is found in numerous NCUA preemption letters.[149] These letters

136 76 Fed. Reg. 43,556 (July 21, 2011).

137 76 Fed. Reg. 43,557 (July 21, 2011).

138 *Id.*

139 *See, e.g.*, Smith v. BAC Home Loans Servicing, LP, 769 F. Supp. 2d 1033, 1044 (S.D. W. Va. 2011) (treating pre-2011 rule as merely a distillation of conflict preemption rules); Cline v. Bank of Am., 2011 WL 4857934 (S.D. W. Va. Oct. 13, 2011) (applying 2011 rule). *See also* Scott v. Wells Fargo Bank, 2011 WL 3837077 (D. Minn. Aug. 29, 2011) (all state laws that affect a subject listed in 12 C.F.R. § 34.4(a) are not preempted; here, state law claims arising out of lender's refusal to acknowledge its receipt of homeowner's loan modification documentation are not preempted even though they relate to terms and servicing of mortgages).

140 *See, e.g.* Williams v. Wells Fargo Bank, 2011 WL 4901346 (S.D. Fla. Oct. 14, 2011) (applying pre-2011 version of rule; even though unconscionability, good faith, and unjust enrichment claims touch on area of insurance, a subject listed in the rule as preempted, these claims are preempted only if they meet conflict preemption standards).

141 12 C.F.R. § 701.21(b)(1).

142 *See also Ex parte* Davis, 401 So. 2d 52 (Ala. 1981); Neal v. Redstone Fed. Credit Union, 447 So. 2d 805 (Ala. Civ. App. 1984); Christian v. Atlanta Army Depot Fed. Credit Union, 231 S.E.2d 7 (Ga. Ct. App. 1976); Brooklyn Jenapo Fed. Credit Union v. Schucher, 245 N.Y.S.2d 637 (N.Y. Sup. Ct. 1963); McAnally v. Ideal Fed. Credit Union, 428 P.2d 322 (Okla. 1967).

143 12 C.F.R. § 701.21(b)(1). *See* E53 Fed. Credit Union v. Perez (*In re* Perez), 440 B.R. 634 (Bankr. D.N.J. 2010); *In re* Cabrera, 2009 WL 4666460 (Bankr. S.D. Fla. Dec. 8, 2009) (FCUA preempts state exemption law).

144 12 C.F.R. § 701.21(b)(2).

145 *See also Ex parte* Davis, 401 So. 2d 52 (Ala. 1981). *See also* McAnally v. Ideal Fed. Credit Union, 428 P.2d 322 (Okla. 1967).

146 *Id.*

147 *Ex parte* Davis, 401 So. 2d 52 (Ala. 1981).

148 12 C.F.R. § 701.21(b)(3).

149 The letters issued by the NCUA since 1992 are summarized at Appx. G.3, *infra*. These letters are available on the companion website to this treatise.

are somewhat evenly divided between those approving and those disapproving the applicability of state laws to federal credit unions. For example, registration requirements in certain situations, laws relating to the deposits of a decedent, laws regulating the advertising of loans, state debt collection requirements, and prohibitions on fees for use of ATMs by nonmembers are *not* preempted.[150] On the other hand, state usury laws, restrictions on changing the terms in open-end credit, laws relating to grace periods, minimum payment disclosure requirements relating to credit card plans, restrictions on establishing ATM machines in a state, conditions to the refinancing of a balloon payment, and state anti-predatory lending laws *are* preempted.[151]

One area where the NCUA has flip-flopped regarding preemption relates to installment sales contracts that are originated by car dealers and then purchased by credit unions ("indirect" loans). In 1992, the NCUA opined that state motor vehicle retail installment sales laws are not preempted where the car dealer originates the credit sale and sells the contract to a federal credit union.[152] It reasoned that the FCUA preemption only applies to loans originated by the credit union regardless of the fact that all parties contemplate that the loan will be assigned immediately to the credit union. In 1999, the NCUA reversed itself, without discussing the 1992 letter.[153]

Even if the FCUA preempts an installment sales act where a consumer's loan is sold to a credit union, this should only be the case where the consumer qualifies for credit union membership.[154] Car dealers may play fast and loose with the membership criteria of the credit unions to whom they wish to sell car loans.

In addition, FCUA preemption should not be applicable to credit union service organizations (CUSOs). Federal credit unions can invest in and make loans to CUSOs, subject to certain funding limits and other regulatory restrictions.[155] CUSOs are creatures of state law and subject to applicable federal, state, and local laws.[156] Unlike national banks, states may "visit" the CUSOs and access their books and records.[157]

While FCUA preemption only applies to federal credit unions, state-chartered credit unions may be able to benefit indirectly from this preemption. State parity statutes may provide that state-chartered credit unions can benefit from the same rights as federal credit unions. If federal credit unions need comply only with federal and not state restrictions, then state credit unions may be able to do the same. State parity statutes are examined at § 3.6, *infra*.

## 3.4 Rate Exportation: Federal Law Specifying Which State's Usury Cap Applies

### 3.4.1 General

Federal law provides that most banks, savings associations, and state credit unions can utilize the interest rate allowed by the institution's home state, not the rate allowed by the state where the loan is made. Moreover, quite often the depository can choose between the rate cap of its home state and the cap of the state where the loan is extended.

This "federal choice of state law" provision, commonly referred to as rate exportation, applies only to depository institutions,[158] and only to loans originated by a depository institution and not loans later assigned to the depository.[159] Although often confused with the most favored lender doctrine, rate exportation is a separate concept. When a depository through rate exportation uses its home state interest rate, the most favored lender doctrine, if applicable, allows the depository to charge the highest rate that any lender in the home state could charge for that class of loans—called the most favored lender rate.

Rate exportation may have more impact than the most favored lender doctrine because depositories often select as their home state a jurisdiction that has few if any limits on interest rates. The most favored lender doctrine has an impact where, in a depository's home state, banks can only charge a low rate, but some other lender in the state can charge a higher rate for the same class of loans. Rate exportation and the most favored lender doctrine when combined can produce startling results, as where a state-chartered bank in state A making a loan in state B need only comply with state A's rate ceiling for finance companies even though state A's ceiling for state-charted banks is much lower.

Federal law not only specifies which state's usury cap applies, but also provides federal remedies for violations of the applicable state usury law. Where rate exportation makes the depository's home state usury cap the applicable law, then federal law provides federal remedies for violating that state cap.[160]

---

150 *See* NCUA Letters: Nov. 26, 2003; Jan. 29, 1996; July 7, 1992; June 11, 1992; May 18, 1992; Apr. 25, 1992.

151 *See* NCUA Letters: Mar. 12, 2004; Jan. 28, 2004; Nov. 10, 2003; May 23, 2003; Oct. 4, 2002; Oct. 3, 2002; July 29, 2002; June 26, 2002; Mar. 2, 2001; Feb. 1, 1999; Sept. 4, 1997. *See also* American Bankers Ass'n v. Lockyer, 239 F. Supp. 2d 1000 (E.D. Cal. 2002) (upholding NCUA's letter opining that California's minimum payment disclosure law was preempted).

152 NCUA Letter (June 24, 1992).

153 NCUA Letter (Feb. 1, 1999).

154 12 U.S.C. §§ 1757(5) (credit union powers to make loans to members), 1759 (definition of membership), 1761b (credit union board must review all applications for membership or delegate to membership officers; board must appoint loan officers to approve loans and lines of credit to members).

155 12 U.S.C. § 1757(7)(I). *See also* 63 Fed. Reg. 10,743 (Mar. 5, 1998).

156 12 C.F.R. § 712.3(e).

157 12 C.F.R. § 741.222; 73 Fed. Reg. 79,307, 79,313 (Dec. 29, 2008).

158 Fleming v. Dollar Tree Stores, Inc., 2006 WL 2975581 (N.D. Cal. Sept. 15, 2006) (NBA does not apply to retail stores); Goldman v. Simon Prop. Group, 818 N.Y.S.2d 245 (N.Y. App. Div. 2006) (NBA does not apply to non-bank); Cohen v. Eisenberg, 697 N.Y.S.2d 625 (N.Y. App. Div. 1999) (potential usury violation where originating lender entitled to export rates was substituted at closing for lender not entitled to export rates).

159 *See* § 3.4.3, *infra*.

160 *See* § 3.4.6, *infra*.

As succeeding subsections will detail, the applicable allowed interest rate under federal law for a depository is not as simple as the previous paragraphs imply. National banks and federal savings associations, instead of their home state interest rate caps, may be able to charge rates established by the state where a branch is located, or even the higher of the branch state's rate or that of the bank's home state.[161] For federal credit unions, a separate maximum federal rate applies irrespective of the rate applicable in a credit union's home state.[162] For federally-insured, state-chartered depository institutions, the allowed rate is that of the institution's home state or that of the borrower's state, whichever is higher.[163] Federally insured Arkansas state banks can charge rates set by other states as long as a bank in that other state has a branch in Arkansas.[164]

Moreover, depository institutions alternatively can charge up to 1% above the federal discount rate.[165] Since discount rates today are close to zero, the alternative federal rate allowance is under 2% and has no practical application.[166] Even if the discount rate increased dramatically to, for example, 5%, few lenders would be interested in 6% rates outside the mortgage context. To simplify an overly complex area, this chapter largely ignores the alternative federal rate of 1% over the discount rate and focuses instead on the other applicable state rate ceilings.

Nevertheless, in claiming that a rate exceeds that allowed by the state where a bank or other depository is located, the borrower may be required to establish the controlling federal discount rate to show that it too is below the rate charged by the creditor.[167] The federal discount rate in effect at the time and place of a transaction can be found at the Federal Reserve Board's statistical data on-line.[168]

## *3.4.2 Rate Exportation Rules Vary by Type of Depository*

### 3.4.2.1 National Banks and Federal Savings Associations

The allowed interest rate for national banks is that specified by the bank's home state.[169] The bank's home state interest cap is exported to the state where the loan is made. The same is the case for federal savings associations.[170] Nevertheless, banking agency interpretations suggest even more flexibility as to the maximum rate. As described at § 3.4.4, *infra*, these interpretations suggest that if a national bank or federal savings institution opens a branch in the borrower's state, in some cases the depository can charge the higher of the rate allowed in its home state or in the borrower's state.

### 3.4.2.2 Federal Credit Unions

Federal credit unions (as opposed to federally insured state credit unions) are not entitled to rate exportation, but instead must comply with a federal interest cap that preempts state interest limits. The allowable interest rate is capped at 15% or at some other temporary rate set by the National Credit Union Administration (NCUA) if economic conditions so require.[171] In April 2011, the NCUA extended its then current 18% cap through September 2012.[172] In April 2011, the NCUA also allowed a 28% cap for its payday-like short-term small loan program.[173]

### 3.4.2.3 State-Chartered Depositories: Banks, Savings Associations, and Credit Unions

#### *3.4.2.3.1 General*

The Depository Institutions Deregulation and Monetary Control Act of 1980 (DIDA) provides that federally-insured state-chartered depositories (banks, savings banks, and credit unions) can charge the higher of the rate allowed by the state where a loan is made and the rate allowed by the institution's home state.[174] The FDIC interprets this choice of law provision as also applying to a state's common law usury rate restrictions.[175]

Rate exportation applies to state-chartered federally-insured "banks" as defined by the Federal Deposit Insurance Act,[176] which requires that a "bank" receives deposits. A federal court in *Heaton* refused to grant deference to an FDIC letter claiming that the defendant was a state "bank" for preemption and exportation purposes. The consumer proved that the bank was not engaged in the business of taking deposits because its only depositor was its parent company.[177] However, in response, the

161 § 3.4.4, *infra*.

162 § 3.4.2.2, *infra*.

163 § 3.4.2.3, *infra*.

164 § 3.4.2.5, *infra*.

165 12 U.S.C. §§ 85 (national banks), 1463(g)(10) (federal savings associations), 1831d(a) (state banks and savings associations), 1785(g) (state credit unions).

166 The alternative federal rate is 1% above the discount rate on ninety-day commercial paper in effect at the federal reserve bank in the district where the national bank is located. 12 U.S.C. § 85.

167 *See e.g.* Kerper v. NCMB Nat'l Bank of Fla., 496 So. 2d 199 (Fla. Dist. Ct. App. 1986).

168 Current and historical discount rates are found at www.federalreserve.gov/pubs/supplement/statsupdata/statsupdata.htm and click on "1.14 Federal Reserve Bank Interest Rates."

169 15 U.S.C. § 85.

170 12 U.S.C. § 1463(g)(1). *See also* Gavey Properties/762 v. First Fin. Sav. & Loan Ass'n, 845 F.2d 519 (5th Cir. 1988); Cappalli v. Nordstrom, F.S.B., 155 F. Supp. 2d 339 (E.D. Pa. 2001), *aff'd*, 28 Fed. Appx. 160 (3d Cir. 2002).

171 12 U.S.C. § 1757(5)(A)(vi)(I).

172 Letter from National Credit Union Admin. to Federal Credit Unions No. 11-FCU-04 (Apr. 2011).

173 *Id.*

174 12 U.S.C. §§ 1831d(a) (banks and savings associations), 1785(g) (credit unions).

175 FDIC Letter (July 12, 1992), *reprinted on the companion website to this treatise*.

176 12 U.S.C. § 1813(a)(2).

177 Heaton v. Monogram Credit Card Bank of Ga., 1999 WL 1789422 (E.D. La. Nov. 22, 1999), *appeal dismissed*, 231 F.3d 994 (5th Cir. 2000), *remand following appeal*, 2001 WL 15635 (E.D. La. Jan. 5,

FDIC enacted a regulation defining "being in the business of receiving deposits,"[178] sticking to its position articulated in the letter discredited in *Heaton*, i.e., a bank need only maintain one or more non-trust deposit accounts in the minimum aggregate amount of $500,000.

#### *3.4.2.3.2 State's right to opt out of rate exportation for state-chartered depositories*

DIDA provides that states can opt out of the federal provision allowing state-chartered depositories to export their home state interest cap.[179] A state opts out by adopting a law stating explicitly that the state does not want the federal rate exportation provisions to apply to loans made in that state.[180] There is no deadline for a state to exercise this opt-out right. Jurisdictions presently opting out of rate exportation for state-chartered depositories are Iowa and Puerto Rico.[181]

#### *3.4.2.3.3 State's right to opt out applies to loans "made" in that state*

A state can opt out of rate exportation by state-chartered depositories for loans "made" in that state.[182] This leads to the question where a loan was "made" if several different states are involved in the transaction. For example, a depository may handle virtually all aspects of a loan in its own home state and the consumer's payments may be mailed to the depository's home state, while the consumer applies for the loan and receives the credit in the consumer's state of residence.

One court has decided that where a loan is "made" is a matter of state law, and that state law in that case indicates that the loan is made where the card issuer resides, not where the consumer resides.[183] Thus in that case a Delaware state bank issued a credit card to a Colorado consumer, and could export Delaware's interest rate limits even though at the time Colorado had opted out of rate exportation.[184] Of course, this also means that if state law determines a credit card contract is made where the consumer resides, then a state-chartered bank cannot export its home state rates into a state that has opted out of rate exportation.

The question of where a loan is "made" is ordinarily analyzed using the law of the forum state. Section 3.7, *infra*, discusses state choice of law issues. Nevertheless, federal banking agencies have weighed in on the issue as well.[185]

### 3.4.2.4 FDIC-Insured Industrial Loan Companies/ Industrial Loan Banks

If an industrial loan company (ILC) or an industrial loan bank[186] is federally insured, it is treated like any other federally-insured state-chartered bank. It is subject to the higher of the usury caps of its home state or where the loan is made.[187] This means that Utah-chartered ILCs can export Utah's usury laws anywhere in the country, even without branches in other states. Since Utah has no interest rate caps,[188] a Utah ILC can lend money in any other state at whatever rate it chooses. As of 2011, ILCs controlling the overwhelming majority of ILC assets were chartered in Utah.[189]

### 3.4.2.5 Special Rule for Arkansas State Banks

12 U.S.C. § 1831u(f) has a special rate provision applying only to states with a constitutional provision limiting the maximum lawful rate of interest on a contract to no more than 5% above the discount rate for ninety-day commercial paper in effect at the federal reserve bank for the federal reserve district in which such state is located. This provision applies only to Arkansas.[190]

---

2001) (remanding to state court despite new FDIC opinion letter and change in Georgia law, finding that, while the bank had a deposit, it was not in the business of receiving deposits and, therefore, not entitled to preemption), *subsequent proceedings*, 297 F.3d 416 (5th Cir. 2002) (remand to state court denied).

178 12 C.F.R. § 303.14(a); 66 Fed. Reg. 54,645 (Oct. 30, 2001).

179 DIDA § 525, *reprinted at* Appx. F.1, *infra*. DIDA § 525 is found as a subsidiary note to 12 U.S.C. § 1785. It is also referenced as a note at 12 U.S.C. § 1831d. It was found as a subsidiary note to 12 U.S.C. § 1730g, but that statute was repealed along with the rest of National Housing Act Title IV. Repeal of the National Housing Act has no effect on DIDA's opt out provision. Pub. L. No. 101-73, tit. IV, § 407, 103 Stat. 183 (1989).

*For additional discussion of DIDA opt-out the provision see* S. Rep. No. 96-368, at 18, *reprinted in* 1980 U.S.C.C.A.N. 236, 254 (emphasis added). *See also* Fed. Deposit Ins. Corp., Opinion Letter, FDIC No. 88-45, *reprinted in* [1988-1989 Transfer Binder] Fed. Banking L. Rep. (CCH) ¶ 88,110 (Jones, Jan. 29, 1988) ("in an effort to preserve principles of federalism, . . . Congress enacted [a provision permitting states to "opt out" of these DIDA provisions] in order to enable States to recover authority [the preemption] had taken away.").

180 *See* DIDA § 525.

181 Iowa Code § 537 preamble (1980 Iowa Acts 1156 § 32); P.R. Laws Ann. tit. 10 § 9881.

182 DIDA § 525. *See also* Stoorman v. Greenwood Trust Co., 888 P.2d 289 (Colo. App. 1994), *aff'd on other grounds*, 908 P.2d 133 (Colo. 1995).

183 Stoorman v. Greenwood Trust Co., 888 P.2d 289 (Colo. App. 1994), *affirmed on other grounds*, 908 P.2d 133 (Colo. 1995).

184 *Id.*

185 OCC Interpretive Letter No. 822 (Feb. 17, 1998) (which state law applies depends on where the loan is approved, credit is extended, and funds are disbursed); FDIC General Counsel Op., 63 Fed. Reg. 27,282 (May 18, 1998) (adopting the OCC's definition). *But see* Fed. Home Loan Bank Bd. Opinion Letter No. 581 (June 14, 1983) (Doyle) (where a contract is made depends on a state's choice of law principles).

186 *See* § 3.1.2.4, *supra*.

187 12 U.S.C. § 1831d(a); Pub. L. No. 97-320, 96 Stat. 1469 (1982); 12 U.S.C. §§ 1815(a) (any "depository institution" may apply for FDIC insurance), 1813(c)(1) (references the definition of "bank" at § 1813(a)(2) that includes ILCs).

188 Utah Code Ann. § 15-1-1.

Utah law also does not limit the amount of late fees that may be charged by depository institutions, including ILCs. Utah Code Ann. § 70C-2-102(1)(b).

189 www.iBanknet.com.

190 *See* Johnson v. Bank of Bentonville, 122 F. Supp. 2d 994 (W.D. Ark. 2000), *aff'd*, 269 F.3d 894 (8th Cir. 2001) (recognizing that Arkansas is the only state which has such a constitutional provision;

The statute allows federally-insured Arkansas state depositories to use the higher of the Arkansas rate or *another* state's interest cap, even when making loans in Arkansas. The Arkansas depository can use the rate cap set by any other state where a bank that has a branch in Arkansas is chartered. The provision allows Arkansas state banks to charge the same interest rates as out-of-state banks that export their rates into Arkansas.[191]

A court applied this provision to hold that a Texas consumer who received a credit card from an Arkansas-chartered bank could not complain of usury under Arkansas law.[192] Because a branch of an Alabama-chartered bank existed in Arkansas, the Arkansas bank need not comply with the Arkansas usury cap because Alabama law permitted the parties to contract for any interest rate.

### 3.4.2.6 Operating Subsidiaries of Depositories

Rate exportation should not apply to operating subsidiaries of depositories. The Supreme Court prior to the Dodd-Frank Act interpreted federal law as allowing national bank operating subsidiaries (as opposed to financial subsidiaries[193]) to be treated the same as the national banks,[194] and this implies that a national bank's operating subsidiary could export its home state rate caps. But the Dodd-Frank Act specifies that "a State consumer financial law shall apply to a subsidiary or affiliate of a national bank (other than a subsidiary or affiliate that is chartered as a national bank) to the same extent that the State consumer financial law applies to any person, corporation or other entity subject to such State law."[195]

Thus the Dodd-Frank Act explicitly states that bank subsidiaries are subject to "state consumer financial law" the same as any non-depository creditor. Non-depository creditors are subject to the interest rate ceiling of the state where the loan is made so that national bank subsidiaries are too.

The only question about this analysis is whether the interest rate ceiling is a state consumer financial law. State consumer financial law is defined as one that directly "regulates the manner, content, or terms and conditions of any financial transaction" with respect to a consumer.[196] A state law setting a maximum interest rate certainly fits within this definition. Accordingly, the consumer's own state's interest cap, not the bank's home state interest rate cap, should apply to national bank subsidiaries and affiliates.

The Dodd-Frank Act also states that the same preemption standards apply to federal savings associations as to national banks,[197] so that rate exportation also should not be available to operating subsidiaries of federal savings associations.

## 3.4.3 Federal Provisions Apply Where Depositories Originate, Not Purchase Loans

The status of the lender originating the loan, not the statute of an assignee, determines whether rate exportation is applicable.[198] Rate exportation does not apply where a loan is originated by a non-depository and then sold to a national bank, a federal savings bank, a state-chartered bank, or another depository.[199] A bank cannot purchase a usurious note and then claim that the note is no longer usurious on the theory that the laws of the bank's home state should control. The parties to a contract have the right to expect that the contract terms and the laws governing them are fixed as of the time the contract is consummated.

Similarly, where a depository originates a loan and then assigns the loan to a second depository, it is the first depository's status that determines rate exportation, not that of the second depository.[200] Where a depository entitled to rate ex-

Congress has the power under the Commerce Clause to enact this preemption provision).

191 H.R. Rep. No. 106-434, at 184 (1999), *reprinted in* 1999 U.S.C.C.A.N. 245, 277; Johnson v. Bank of Bentonville, 122 F. Supp. 2d 994, 999 (W.D. Ark. 2000), *aff'd*, 269 F.3d 894 (8th Cir. 2001).

192 Jessup v. Pulaski Bank, 327 F.3d 682 (8th Cir. 2003).

193 *See* § 3.1.2.5, *supra* (distinguishing between the two).

194 *See* Watters v. Wachovia Bank, N.A., 550 US 1 (2007). *Cf.* Higginbottom v. US Bancorp, 2011 WL 1558681 (N.D. Cal. Apr. 25, 2011).

195 12 U.S.C. 25b(e).

196 12 U.S.C. 25b(a)(2).

197 12 U.S.C. § 1465(a).

198 *See, e.g.*, Fed. Deposit Ins. Corp. v. Lattimore Land Corp., 656 F.2d 139 (5th Cir. 1981); Fed. Nat'l Mortgage Ass'n v. Lefkowitz, 390 F. Supp. 1364 (S.D.N.Y. 1975); *In re* Harrington, 6 B.R. 655 (Bankr. D.R.I. 1980); OTS Unofficial Letter (July 14, 2006); Letter from the Virginia Attorney General 3 n.7 (June 1, 2007), *available on the companion website to this treatise*. *See also* Miller v. Pacific Shore Funding, 224 F. Supp. 2d 977 (D. Md. 2002), *aff'd on other grounds*, 92 Fed. Appx. 933 (4th Cir. 2004) (assignees stand in the shoes of the assignors and are subject to the same claims and defenses unless the holder-in-due-course defense applies). *But see* Dannewitz v. Equicredit Corp. of Am., 839 N.E.2d 1060 (Ill. App. Ct. 2005) (forum state's law preempted where loan made by non-bank assigned to bank).

199 Thomas v. U.S. Bank Nat'l Ass'n N.D., 575 F.3d 794 (8th Cir. 2009); *In re* Cmty. Bank of N. Va., 418 F.3d 277 (3d Cir. 2005); Phipps v. Federal Deposit Ins. Corp., 417 F.3d 1006, 1013 (8th Cir. 2005); Munoz v. Pipestone Fin., L.L.C., 513 F. Supp. 2d 1076 (D. Minn. 2007); Discover Bank v. Vaden, 409 F. Supp. 2d 632 (D. Md. 2006), *subsequent proceedings*, 489 F.3d 594 (4th Cir. 2007) (addressing federal court jurisdiction), *rev'd*, 556 U.S. 49, 129 S. Ct. 1262, 173 L. Ed. 2d 206 (2009) (reversal concerns question of federal jurisdiction); Terry v. Community Bank of N. Va., 255 F. Supp. 2d 817 (W.D. Tenn. 2003); Thomas v. CitiMortgage (*In re* Thomas), 447 B.R. 402, 407 (Bankr. D. Mass. 2011); Viereck v. Peoples Sav. & Loan Ass'n, 343 N.W.2d 30 (Minn. 1984); Garrison v. First Fed. Sav. & Loan Ass'n of S.C., 402 S.E.2d 25 (Va. 1991);OTS Unofficial Letter (July 14, 2006). *But see* Dannewitz v. Equicredit Corp. of Am., 839 N.E.2d 1060 (Ill. App. Ct. 2005); OTS Chief Counsel Letter P-2002-4 (May 14, 2002) (preemption of state law applies whether bank makes leases directly or purchases leases from car dealers), *available on the companion website to this treatise*.

200 Khan v. World Sav. Bank, F.S.B., 2011 WL 90765 (N.D. Cal. Jan. 11, 2011) (action governed by HOLA because originator was federal savings bank, even though holder is national bank).

portation assigns the obligation to a non-depository, most courts hold that the loan does not become usurious because of the assignment.[201]

These rules may be more complicated in the case of open-end credit where an account is assigned to a depository and then the depository issues additional credit. In that case, rate exportation may apply to the new credit.[202]

Payday lenders may try to "rent-a-bank" and claim that a loan is originated by a bank when in fact the payday lender is the party originating the loan and just uses the bank's name and financing. Such loans are not subject to rate exportation.[203]

There are also issues as to whether a bank has originated a loan, or is just an assignee where the bank table-funds the loan. A table-funded transaction is one where a nominal lender is originating the loan for an entity whose money is used to fund the loan. The loan is transferred immediately to the actual lender. In that case, the OCC considers the table-funding bank to be the originator, so that rate exportation would apply.[204] Where a bank, though, is merely the trustee of a pool of loans and did not originate the loan and did not fund the loan at inception, the bank cannot export its home state interest rate.[205]

## *3.4.4 Identifying a Depository's Home State; Branch Banking*

### 3.4.4.1 General

A depository's home state for purposes of rate exportation is where the depository is chartered.[206] In *Marquette*, the Supreme Court held that the fact that a bank in one state extends credit by mail to a consumer in a second state does not make the second state the bank's home state.[207] The Court reasoned that this was no different from an out-of-state customer coming across a state line to obtain a loan in the second state.

201 Olvera v. Blitt & Gaines, 431 F.3d 285 (7th Cir. 2005); Discover Bank v. Vaden, 409 F. Supp. 2d 632 (D. Md. 2006), *rev'd*, 556 U.S. 49, 129 S. Ct. 1262, 173 L. Ed. 2d 206 (2009) (addressing issue of the jurisdiction of the federal court to hear a motion to compel arbitration in a case filed in state court); PRA III, L.L.C. v. Hund, 846 N.E.2d 965 (Ill. App. Ct. 2006). *But see* Citibank (South Dakota), N.A. v. Martin, 807 N.Y.S.2d 284 (N.Y. Civ. Ct. 2005).

202 Krispin v. The May Dep't Stores Co., 218 F.3d 919 (8th Cir. 2000).

203 *See* § 9.6.1, *infra*. *See also* Community State Bank v. Strong, 651 F.3d 1241 (11th Cir. 2011).

204 OCC Interpretive Letter No. 1000 (Apr. 2, 2004); OCC Interpretive Letter No. 1002 (May 13, 2004), *reprinted on the companion website to this treatise*. *But cf.* Adkison v. First Plus Bank, 143 S.W.3d 29 (Mo. Ct. App. 2004) (bank was the lender since it was listed on the documents; implying disapproval of the claim that the table-funding "lender," technically the assignee, is the lender).

205 OCC Interpretive Letter No. 1016 (Jan. 14, 2005), *reprinted on the companion website to this treatise*.

206 Marquette Nat'l Bank v. First of Omaha Corp., 439 U.S. 299 (1978).

207 Marquette Nat'l Bank v. First of Omaha Corp., 439 U.S. 299 (1978). *See also* Phipps v. Federal Deposit Ins. Corp., 417 F.3d 1006 (8th Cir. 2005).

### 3.4.4.2 Impact of Branches Outside Depository's Home State

*Marquette* did not deal with a depository with branches outside the state where it holds its charter and thus does not answer the question whether a loan made by a branch of an out-of-state bank is subject to the interest rate limit of the state where the branch is located, the state where the bank is chartered, or the higher of the two.[208] The *Marquette* analogy of the out-of-state customer coming into the second state for a loan no longer holds, because instead the bank is bringing an office to the consumer, not the consumer going to the bank.

Until 1992, banks were prevented from establishing branches interstate,[209] so that branch banking was not on Congress's mind when it enacted the National Banking Act's rate exportation provision. Today, the Interstate Banking and Branching Efficiency Act of 1994 (IBBEA), also known as the Riegle-Neal Act, makes interstate branch banking legal,[210] and banks frequently have branches in other states.

The IBBEA indicates that Congress did not intend, by its passage, to tip the balance of existing law on preemption one way or the other. It leaves the judicial process to continue to take its course.[211] Its Conference Report even states that the federal banking regulatory agencies have been "inappropriately

208 *See* Elizabeth R. Schiltz, *The Amazing, Elastic, Ever-Expanding Exportation Doctrine and Its Effects on Predatory Lending Regulations*, 88 Minn. L. Rev. 518 (2004) (discussing *Marquette* and interstate banking).

209 The McFadden Act, 12 U.S.C. § 36, limited the national banks' right to establish branches in other states.

210 Pub. L. No. 103-328, 108 Stat. 2338 (Sept. 29, 1994), *codified at* 12 U.S.C. § 36.

211 Pub. L. No. 103-328, § 102(b)(1), 108 Stat. 2338, *codified at* 12 U.S.C. § 36(f)(1) (national bank branches are subject to laws of host state regarding consumer protection, CRA, fair lending, and establishment of intrastate branches except when federal law preempts such state laws with respect to national banks). *See also* Pub. L. No. 103-328, § 102(b)(3), 108 Stat. 2338, *codified at* 12 U.S.C. § 1831a(j) (out-of-state state bank branches are subject to laws of host state regarding consumer protection, CRA, fair lending, and establishment of intrastate branches.

The Conference Committee Report states:

> States have a strong interest in the activities and operations of depository institutions doing business within their jurisdictions, regardless of the type of charter an institution holds. In particular, States have a legitimate interest in protecting the rights of their consumers, businesses, and communities. . . . Congress does not intend that [this Act] alter this balance and thereby weaken States' authority to protect the interests of their consumers, businesses, or communities.

It goes on to reiterate the standard judicial principles of interpretation: state law applies unless there is a direct conflict, or federal law is so comprehensive as to evidence congressional intent to occupy the field, or state law stands as an obstacle to accomplished the federal law's purposes. Thus safe and soundness is one factor to consider, but, on the other hand, courts usually "use a rule of construction which avoids finding a conflict where possible. This title does not change these judicially established principles." H.R. Conf. Rep. No. 103-651, at 53 (1994), *reprinted in* 1994 U.S.C.C.A.N. 2068.

aggressive" in preempting state law "in situations where the federal interest did not warrant that result."[212]

Nevertheless, two subsequent OCC Interpretive Letters ignore this congressional intent. In the first letter, the OCC stated that a bank can export the interest rates of its home state to other states despite the anticipated location of branches in those states.[213] Then the OCC chief counsel's Interpretive Letter of February 17, 1998,[214] indicated that a national bank may be located in *both* its home state and its host (or branch) state for purposes of exportation:

> [A]n interstate national bank may charge interest permitted by the laws of its home state unless the loan is made—that is, the loan is approved, credit is extended, and funds are disbursed—in a branch or branches of the bank in a single host state. If one or two of these three functions occur in a host state, the bank may, alternatively, charge the interest permitted by that state if, based on an assessment of all the facts and circumstances, the loan has a clear nexus to that state.[215]

Under this interpretation, national banks can utilize the higher of the home state or branch state rate if the loan has a clear nexus to the branch state and one or two of the listed functions occur in the branch state—the decision to extend credit and the communication of that decision, the extension of credit itself, or the disbursal of loan proceeds. If all three functions are performed in the branch state, then only the branch state's maximum rates apply to the loan. These letters create a roadmap that shows national banks with branches in other states how to design their business so their branches can utilize either the bank's home state interest cap or that of the state where the branch is located.

An FDIC opinion states that the same rules that apply to national banks also apply to branches of federally-insured state-chartered banks.[216] This result follows from language in the IBBEA that the same rules apply to branches of out-of-state state-chartered banks as branches of out-of-state national banks.[217]

Nevertheless, the bank, not the consumer should have the burden of establishing which non-ministerial acts occurred in the bank's home state or at the branch in the host state.[218] To hold otherwise would place an unfair burden on the consumer, who would have to discover where each activity occurred: the decision to extend credit and communicate the decision, the extension itself, and the disbursal of funds.[219]

An OTS letter is even more permissive than the OCC and FDIC in providing options for branches of federally chartered savings associations. Such branches can charge a rate allowed by the association's home state rate wherever the loan is made and even if all aspects of the loan take place where its out-of-state branch is located; alternatively the branch can charge the rate allowed by the state where it is located, if the loan is "booked" where the branch is located.[220] Nevertheless, the OCC standards are more likely now to apply to federal savings associations because OTS responsibilities have now been transferred to the OCC[221] and current OCC regulations state: "Federal savings associations and their subsidiaries shall be subject to the same laws and legal standards, including regulations of the OCC, as are applicable to national banks and their subsidiaries, regarding the preemption of state law."[222]

### 3.4.4.3 What Constitutes a Branch

To take advantage of the added interest rate options provided by an out-of-state branch, the bank's office located out of state must qualify as a "branch." Branch is defined as a location "at which deposits are received, or checks paid, or money lent. The term 'branch,' as used in this section, does not include an automated teller machine or a remote service unit."[223]

The Fourth Circuit holds that the H&R Block office in South Carolina (where Beneficial National Bank made tax refund anticipation loans) was not a branch,[224] since the office merely collected and transmitted information to the bank and the bank made its credit decisions and lent the money from its main office. Similarly, a federal court found that an out-of-state office of a national bank was not a branch and could not use the interest rate where the office was located, when the office merely processed home equity loans.[225]

### 3.4.4.4 Electronic Banking

An OCC regulation addresses where a bank is located when it maintains technology out-of-state. A national bank is not located in a state solely because it physically maintains tech-

212 H.R. Conf. Rep. No. 103-651, at 53, 54 (1994), *reprinted in* 1994 U.S.C.C.A.N. 2068.

213 OCC Interpretive Letter No. 776 (Mar. 18, 1997).

214 OCC Interpretive Letter No. 822 (Feb. 17, 1998). *See also* OCC Interpretive Letter No. 995 (June 22, 2004) (national bank may export the state fiduciary law of any state in which it conducts fiduciary services to any other state; a state's law that restricts foreign national banks from providing fiduciary services in its state unless certain conditions are met is preempted).

215 OCC Interpretive Letter No. 822, at 14, 15 (Feb. 17, 1998).

216 FDIC General Counsel Opinion No. 11, 63 Fed. Reg. 27,282 (May 18, 1998), *reprinted on the companion website to this treatise*.

217 12 U.S.C. § 1831a(j).

218 *See, e.g.*, Citibank (SD) N.A. v. Hansen, 902 N.Y.S.2d 299, 300–302 (N.Y. Dist. Ct. 2010).

219 A good example of this problem arose in MorEquity, Inc. v. Naeem, 118 F. Supp. 2d 885 (N.D. Ill. 2000), where the court found that the consumers failed to allege where the non-ministerial acts occurred and dismissed their usury claim.

220 OTS Letter No. P-2004-8 (Sept. 17, 2004); Fed. Home Loan Bank Bd., General Counsel Opinion No. 588 (Raiden, Dec. 11, 1984).

221 Dodd-Frank tit. X, §§ 312, 313.

222 12 C.F.R. § 34.6.

223 12 U.S.C. 36(j). *See also* OCC Interpretive Letter No. 980 (Dec. 24, 2003) (UPS drop box at various non-bank offices of a national bank do not constitute branches given the particular facts).

224 Cades v. H&R Block, Inc., 43 F.3d 869 (4th Cir. 1994). *See also* Christiansen v. Beneficial Nat'l Bank, 972 F. Supp. 681 (S.D. Ga. 1997); OCC Amendment to Interpretive Ruling § 7.1012 Addressing "Messenger Services," 64 Fed. Reg. 60,092 (Nov. 4, 1999).

225 Flannick v. First Union Home Equity Bank, 134 F. Supp. 2d 389 (E.D. Pa. 2001), *vacated without discussion*, 2004 WL 1218600 (E.D. Pa. Mar. 8, 2004).

nology in that state, such as a server or automated loan center; nor is it located in a state because the bank's products or services are accessed through electronic means by consumers located in the state.[226]

OCC regulations also state that where a national bank operates exclusively through the Internet, its "main" office is the office relevant for rate exportation.[227] The main office may be little more than an office suite and a call center. The leeway this regulation provides to Internet-only banks has been criticized as not consistent with the National Bank Act.[228]

## 3.4.5 *Definition of "Interest Rate" for Rate Exportation Purposes*

### 3.4.5.1 Introduction

Federal statutes provide that a depository can charge "interest" at the rate set by the institution's home state. These statutes provide no authority for a depository to export state law provisions dealing with matters *other* than interest. The definition of "interest" thus determines whether a particular state statutory provision can be exported.

If an aspect of credit does *not* involve interest, a state law regulating that aspect of the credit can still be preempted by federal law, but the preemption will be via federal agency regulation of federal depositories. OCC and NCUA preemption regulations do more than just specify which state's law applies, but preempt the applicability of *any* state's law to certain aspects of the federal depositories. Preemption based upon federal agency regulation is examined at §§ 3.2 and 3.3, *supra*.

Creditors pressing for a broad interpretation of the term interest want a "heads-I-win-tails-you-lose" result. For exportation purposes, they want "interest" defined broadly to include as many fees as possible; for usury purposes, they want interest defined narrowly, to exclude as many fees as possible from being counted as interest.[229]

How successful banks have been in achieving this "heads-I-win-tails-you-lose" result can be seen in federal regulations governing rate exportation. Interest is broadly defined to cover late charges and other fees not usually considered interest for usury purposes,[230] and the same regulation states that this broad definition does not change state law definitions of interest for purposes of state law.[231] Thus a home state's limit (or lack of a limit) on late fees is exported, but then is not counted for purposes of an interest rate limit if state law would not count it as such. Thus what is interest for purposes of rate exportation is a matter of federal law, but calculation of a state's usury limit is a matter of state law.[232]

### 3.4.5.2 OCC Definition of Interest

OCC regulations define interest for purposes of national bank and federal savings association rate exportation as "any payment compensating a creditor or prospective creditor for an extension of credit, making available a line of credit, or any default or breach by a borrower of a condition upon which credit was extended."[233] The regulations pointedly state that this definition does not affect state law definitions of interest for purposes of state law interest rate limits.[234]

The regulations list the following as interest:

- Numerical periodic rates;
- Late fees;
- Creditor-imposed NSF fees when a check payment on a debt has insufficient fees[235]
- Over-the-limit fees;
- Annual fees;
- Cash advance fees; and
- Membership fees.[236]

The regulations further state that interest ordinarily does *not* include:

- Appraisal fees;
- Premiums and commissions attributable to insurance guaranteeing repayment;
- Finders' fees;
- Document preparation or notarization fees;
- Fees to obtain credit reports.[237]

FDIC interpretation letters follow the OCC's definition of "interest" for purposes of rate exportation by federally-insured state-chartered institutions.[238]

226 12 C.F.R. § 7.5008.

227 12 C.F.R. § 7.5009.

228 *See* discussion of these issues in Elizabeth R. Schiltz, *The Amazing, Elastic, Ever-Expanding Exportation Doctrine and Its Effects on Predatory Lending Regulations*, 88 Minn. L. Rev. 518, 558–559 (2004) (suggesting that even the OCC thought it was pushing the envelope with this regulation).

229 Mazaika v. Bank One, 653 A.2d 640 (Pa. Super. Ct. 1994), *rev'd*, 680 A.2d 845 (Pa. 1996) (applying the holding in *Smiley*) (noting that the fees the bank wished to export under Ohio law as "interest" would have made its contracts usurious if they were considered interest under Ohio's usury ceiling).

230 12 C.F.R. §§ 7.4001(a), 560.110(a).

231 12 C.F.R. §§ 7.4001(c), 560.110(c).

232 *See, e.g.*, Lewis v. Wells Fargo Bank, N.A., 2011 WL 5374575 (D. Minn. Nov. 4, 2011); Taft v. Wells Fargo Bank, 2011 WL 5237785 (D. Minn. Nov. 1, 2011).

233 12 C.F.R. §§ 7.4001(a), 560.110(a).

234 12 C.F.R. §§ 7.4001(c), 560.110(c).

235 This applies only to NSF charges linked to a payment on a debt. Fees that a bank charges for its deposit account services, including overdraft and returned check charges, are not "interest." 66 Fed. Reg. at 34,786. *See* Terrell v. Hancock Bank, 7 F. Supp. 2d 812 (S.D. Miss. 1998). *See also* Video Trax, Inc. v. NationsBank, N.A., 33 F. Supp. 2d 1041 (S.D. Fla. 1998), *aff'd*, 205 F.3d 1358 (11th Cir. 2000) (table) (honoring checks on an overdrawn account is not an extension of credit and fees related to honoring such checks do not constitute interest); Nicolas v. Deposit Guarantee Nat'l Bank, 182 F.R.D. 226 (S.D. Miss. 1998) (at issue was a NSF fee imposed on deposit account that did not include an overdraft feature).

236 12 C.F.R. §§ 7.4001(a), 560.110(a).

237 *Id.*

238 FDIC General Counsel Opinion No. 10, 63 Fed. Reg. 19,258 (Apr. 17, 1998); FDIC Letter (July 8, 1992); FDIC Letter (Oct. 20, 1983).

OCC Interpretive Letter No. 744 states that prepayment penalties constitute interest for purposes of national bank rate exportation,[239] because they compensate the lender for relinquishing its right to receive the anticipated earnings on the loan over its projected life. OCC Interpretive Letter No. 803 determines that the following fees charged in connection with home equity open-end accounts are interest:[240] an "account opening fee," a "fixed-rate option fee,"[241] fees for prepaying a fixed rate option and for early closure of the account, and some "rejected item" fees.

Not addressed by OCC regulations and interpretations and which should *not* be considered interest for rate exportation purposes are attorney fees and collection costs assessed because of a default, insurance charges, other fees paid to third parties who guarantee or insure repayment of loans in the event of default, credit card replacement fees, copy and delivery fees, security interest filing and release or termination fees, and other types of secured loan closing and post-closing costs and fees.

Another issue is whether a bank can export not only its home state interest rate, but also the home state rule that corporate borrowers cannot raise usury defenses. The OCC states that where the bank's home state law so provides, the national bank can charge the corporate borrower any rate of interest agreed upon by a corporate borrower.[242]

#### 3.4.5.3 The Supreme Court's *Smiley* Decision and Subsequent Court Rulings

Support for the OCC definition of interest is found in the Supreme Court's *Smiley* decision, where the Court found the OCC interpretation to be reasonable and also gave deference to an OCC ruling finding late fees to be interest.[243] The Court drew a distinction between "payment compensating a creditor or prospective creditor for an extension of credit, making available of a line of credit, or any default or breach by a borrower" and all other payments. "All other payments" consist essentially of payments made to third parties who perform services that assist in the making or guaranteeing of the loan.

The Eighth Circuit after *Smiley* held that insurance premiums attributable to force-placed insurance covering loss of the purchased automobile were not interest.[244] The premiums were akin to insurance guaranteeing repayment of any extension of credit (therefore, not interest under the OCC ruling) than to charges compensating a creditor for a default or breach by a borrower (therefore, interest). Similarly, courts have found that credit insurance premiums are not interest.[245] One court found that a deception claim did not involve interest where it was alleged that the lender charged for discount fees for a loan that was not discounted.[246] Similarly, allegations of fraudulent and deceptive practices related to inducing consumers to incur over-the-limit fees do not involve the level of interest.[247]

One trial court has found that credit card interest rates as high as 50% could be struck down as unconscionable under the consumer's state unconscionability standards. This is the case even though the court recognized that generally the bank's home state interest rate cap would apply—which in this case had no ceiling.[248]

On the other hand, courts find that loan origination and discount fees constitute interest.[249] So do over-the-limit charges.[250] Courts have even found underwriting and application fees to be interest.[251]

### 3.4.6 *Remedies Where Rate Exceeds Depository's Home State Cap*

If a national bank, federal savings association, or state-chartered depository can charge a higher rate because of rate exportation, yet still exceeds that rate, the consumer's remedy is under federal law. Where the violation is knowingly done, the consumer can recover a forfeiture of the entire amount of interest that the debt carries with it or that is agreed to be paid.[252] The consumer can also recover double the amount of interest already paid.[253] There is a two-year statute of limitations for such an action.[254]

---

239 OCC Interpretive Letter No. 744 (Aug. 21, 1996), *available on the companion website to this treatise*. *See also* Minnett v. Commerce Bank, N.A., 2005 WL 2447969 (N.J. Super. Ct. App. Div. Oct. 3, 2005) (state law claim based on a national bank chartered in New Jersey charging origination fees and prepayment penalties in excess of that permitted under state law dismissed as this is a federal claim only).

240 OCC Interpretive Letter No. 803 (Oct. 7, 1997), *available on the companion website to this treatise*.

241 A fee allowing the consumer the option to obtain fixed-rate advances payable in regular monthly installments over a fixed term.

242 12 C.F.R. § 7.4001(d).

243 Smiley v. Citibank (S.D.), N.A., 517 U.S. 735, 116 S. Ct. 1730, 135 L. Ed. 2d 25 (1996).

244 Doe v. Norwest Bank Minn., N.A., 107 F.3d 1297 (8th Cir. 1997). *See also* Richardson v. National City Bank of Evansville, 141 F.3d 1228 (7th Cir. 1998); Gutter v. Bank One, La., N.A., 1997 WL 722952 (E.D. La. Nov. 17, 1997).

245 Brown v. Nationscredit Fin. Servs., 647 F. Supp. 2d 1314 (M.D. Fla. 2008).

246 Bumpers v. Community Bank of Northern Virginia, 2011 WL 3904084 (N.C. Ct. App. Sept. 6, 2011).

247 State v. Capital One Bank (USA) N.A., 2011 WL 3516149 (S.D. W. Va. Aug. 11, 2011).

248 Citibank (South Dakota) N.A. v. Decristoforo, 28 Mass. L. Rptr. 139 (Mass. Super. Ct. 2011).

249 Phipps v. Federal Deposit Ins. Corp., 417 F.3d 1006 (8th Cir. 2005). *But see* Bumpers v. Community Bank of Northern Virginia, 2011 WL 3904084 (N.C. Ct. App. Sept. 6, 2011).

250 Kent v. Bank of Am., 2003 WL 327465 (Cal. Ct. App. Feb. 11, 2003).

251 *Id.*

252 12 U.S.C. §§ 86 (national banks), 1463(g)(2) (federal savings associations), 1785(g)(2) (state-chartered credit unions), 1831d(b) (state chartered banks and savings associations).

253 12 U.S.C. §§ 86 (national banks), 1463(g)(2) (federal savings associations), 1785(g)(2) (state-chartered credit unions), 1831d(b) (state chartered banks and savings associations).

254 12 U.S.C. §§ 86 (national banks), 1463(g)(2) (federal savings associations), 1785(g)(2) (state-chartered credit unions), 1831d(b) (state chartered banks and savings associations).

The consumer's usury remedies under state law are preempted.[255] Even though the action is based upon the depository's violation of a state usury limit, the consumer's only cause is this one based upon federal law and there is federal court jurisdiction for the cause of action.[256]

The operation of the remedy is more complicated in the case of state-chartered depositories, since they can charge the higher of their home state rate (via rate exportation) or the applicable rate where the loan is made. If the rate cap is higher in the state where the loan is made than in the depository's home state, then the remedy is under that state's usury law.[257] But if the rate cap is higher in the state depository's home state, then the remedy is only under federal law.[258]

## 3.5 Most Favored Lender Doctrine

### *3.5.1 General*

The most favored lender doctrine provides that a depository uses as its applicable home state interest rate ceiling the highest rate that any lender in the state can utilize for a particular class of loans. For example, if a California finance company can charge a higher rate for the same type of loan as a California-chartered state bank, then a national bank whose home state is California can charge the California finance company rate for that type of loan, not the state-chartered bank rate.

Unlike rate exportation, which is explicitly authorized by statute, the most favored lender doctrine is not found in a statute, but was developed through case law and now by federal regulation.[259] For example, the National Bank Act simply specifies "the rate allowed by the laws of the State,"[260] and does not specify what that rate is and certainly does not state that it is the highest allowable rate. While a long line of court cases find the most favored lender doctrine applies to national banks,[261] applying the doctrine to state-chartered institutions is not so evident—there are arguments why it should not apply to state-chartered institutions, as described at § 3.5.2, *infra*.

### *3.5.2 Depositories That Can Take Advantage of the Most Favored Lender Doctrine*

OCC regulations provide that "a national bank located in a state may charge interest at the maximum rate permitted to any state-chartered or licensed lending institution by the law of that state."[262] Federal regulations provide the same right to federal savings associations.[263] These regulations are based not upon language in federal statutes, but upon court decisions applicable to national banks.[264]

Less certain is whether the most favored lender doctrine applies to state-chartered depositories. To do so would have the odd result that the legislature of a bank's home state would select an applicable interest cap for its state-chartered banks, but the applicable rate would be one the same legislature chose for different types of lenders.

Because the language in DIDA extending rate *exportation* to federally insured state-chartered depositories closely matches language creating rate *exportation* in the National Bank Act,[265] lenders argue that by analogy, they are similarly granted most favored lender status. The federal banking agencies agree,[266] as do some courts.[267]

The contrary argument is that national bank most favored lender status is designed so that states cannot treat national banks differently than its own lenders. This is not a concern with a state regulating its own financial institutions, and there is no reason why a state should not differentiate among the state's own lenders if that is what the state legislature determines. There is nothing in DIDA's legislative history to support extension of the most favored lender doctrine to state-chartered depositories. DIDA's rate exportation language was adopted as a last-minute compromise.

Nevertheless, the issue is moot in many states, because state parity statutes allow state depositories to charge the same rates as federal depositories in that state. If a national bank can charge the most favored lender's rate, then a state bank in the same state may be able to charge that rate under the state parity statute.[268]

255 *See* Beneficial Nat'l Bank v. Anderson, 539 U.S. 1, 123 S. Ct. 2058, 156 L. Ed. 2d 1 (2003).

256 *See* Beneficial Nat'l Bank v. Anderson, 123 S. Ct. 2058 (2003).

257 *See* Giner v. Synovus Bank, 2011 WL 358429 (N.D. Ga. July 22, 2011).

258 12 U.S.C. §§ 1785(g)(2) (state credit unions), 1831d(b) (state chartered banks and savings associations).

259 *See* § 3.5.2, *infra*.

260 12 U.S.C. § 85.

261 *See* § 3.1.2.2, *supra* (describing national banks).

262 12 C.F.R. § 7.4001(b).

263 12 C.F.R. § 560.110(b).

264 *See* Tiffany v. National Bank of Missouri, 85 U.S. 409 (1873); Fisher v. First National Bank of Omaha, 548 F.2d 255 (8th Cir. 1977); Northway Lanes v. Hackley Union Nat'l Bank & Trust Co., 464 F.2d 855 (6th Cir. 1972). *See also* Marquette Nat'l Bank of Minneapolis v. First Omaha Serv. Corp., 439 U.S. 299, 314 n.26 (1978).

265 *Compare* 12 U.S.C. §§ 1436(g), 1785(g), 1831d(a), *with* 12 U.S.C. § 85.

The remedies also match. *Compare* 12 U.S.C. § 86, *with* 12 U.S.C. §§ 1463(g)(2), 1831d(b).

266 *See, e.g.*, Fed. Home Loan Bank Bd., General Counsel Opinion No. 4 (Sept. 19, 1980) (FHLBB interpretation giving most favored lender status to an FSLIC-insured "thrift"); Fed. Banking L. Rep. (CCH) ¶ 81,635 and Consumer Cred. Guide (CCH) ¶ 95,511 (FDIC opinion letter applying it to an FDIC-insured state-chartered bank); Letter from Douglas H. Jones, Deputy Gen. Counsel, FDIC-93-27 (July 12, 1993), *reprinted on the companion website to this treatise*; Letter of Oct. 20, 1983, *reprinted on the companion website to this treatise*; FDIC General Counsel's Op., 63 Fed. Reg. 27,282 (May 18, 1998), *reprinted on the companion website to this treatise*; NCUA Statement of Interpretation and Policy (IRPS 81-31), 46 Fed. Reg. 24,153 (Apr. 30, 1981), *amending*, IRPS 80-11, 45 Fed. Reg. 78,624 (Nov. 26, 1980) (NCUA opinion as to federally insured credit unions).

267 *See* VanderWeyst v. First State Bank of Benson, 425 N.W.2d 803 (Minn. 1988).

268 *See* § 3.6, *infra*.

### 3.5.3 Where Lender's Home State Specifies No Interest Cap

Where lenders in a state can charge for a class of loans any rate agreed to by the parties to the loan, then national banks and federal savings associations located in that state can also charge any rate agreed to by the parties.[269] This result, while consistent with most favored lender analysis, appears to contradict NBA language which establishes a 7% rate in the absence of a state ceiling: "when no rate is fixed by the laws of the State . . ., the bank may . . . charge a rate not exceeding 7 per centum."[270] A 1900 Supreme Court decision resolved this conflict by holding that the 7% cap applies only where the national bank's home state prohibits the charging of any interest.[271]

### 3.5.4 Does the Doctrine Apply Only to the Most Favored State Lender?

National banks may only adopt the rates of competing *state* lenders in their home state and not those of other *federal* lenders with whom they compete in their home state, such as federal credit unions that may be able to charge rates in excess of those available to state lenders.[272] The NBA, for example, allows a national bank to charge the rate permitted of a "state-chartered or licensed lending institution by the laws of that state."[273]

The intent of the most favored lender doctrine is to prevent discriminatory state regulation in favor of state institutions, not to provide equality among federal lenders. Thus, a national bank cannot use the most favored lender doctrine to charge a rate available to federal credit unions.[274]

This is, however, not the end of the story, because state parity laws (discussed in more detail at § 3.6, *infra*), in conjunction with most favored lender analysis, may provide national banks with an indirect path to the federal credit union rates. For example, a state-chartered credit union may be entitled by virtue of a state "parity" statute to charge the same rate as federal credit unions.[275] The national bank under the most favored lender doctrine can use the state credit union rate. Because the state credit union can invoke the federal credit union rate ceiling under the state's parity statute, the national bank may argue that it too has the right to charge the federal credit union rate.[276]

Using a state parity statute in this manner is neither what Congress nor the state legislature intended. Congress intended that national banks and federal credit unions have different rate ceilings from each other. And yet the national bank claims the benefit of the federal credit union rate ceiling by virtue of a state law intended to create parity only between state and federal credit unions.

Similarly, a 2004 OCC Interpretive Letter opines that a national bank may charge prepayment penalties, even though not authorized by OCC regulations nor permitted under state law.[277] State savings banks can charge prepayment penalties because the state parity statute puts them on equal footing with federal savings banks, and OTS allows federal savings banks to charge such penalties. If state savings banks can charge prepayment penalties, then the national bank can under the most favored lender doctrine. Again, Congress intended national banks to follow OCC regulations, not OTS regulations. And the state's only interest was to create parity between federal and state savings banks and had no interest in extending rights to national banks.

### 3.5.5 State Rate Cap Must Be for Same Type of Loan

Depositories that invoke the most favored lender doctrine cannot charge the highest interest rate that any lender is permitted to charge, but only the rate which competing lenders may use *when issuing the same type of loan*.[278] A bank may not use finance company rates if it is making a type of loan that finance companies are not authorized to make, because the finance companies do not compete with the bank for that type of loan.[279]

One element to be used in defining a class of loans is any limitation placed on the total amount of the loan by the "borrowed" statute.[280] If the depository wishes to make loans that are larger than those finance companies are allowed to make, the depository may not use the state finance company rate ceiling.

269 *See* Hiatt v. San Francisco Nat'l Bank, 361 F.2d 504 (9th Cir. 1966); Hawkins v. Citicorp Credit Servs., Inc., 665 F. Supp. 2d 518 (D. Md. 2009), *aff'd*, 405 Fed. Appx. 789 (4th Cir. 2010);Keresey v. Nevada Nat'l Bank, 646 P.2d 1224 (Nev. 1982); Patten v. Md. Bank, N.A., 126 S.W.3d 532 (Tex. App. 2003); Moore v. United Nat'l Bank, 821 S.W.2d 409 (Tex. App. 1991); 12 C.F.R. § 7.4001. *See also* Begala v. PNC Bank, Ohio, N.A., 214 F.3d 776 (6th Cir. 2000).

270 12 U.S.C. § 85.

271 Daggs v. Phoenix Nat'l Bank, 177 U.S. 549, 20 S. Ct. 732, 44 L. Ed. 882 (1900). *See also* Hiatt v. San Francisco Nat'l Bank, 361 F.2d 504 (9th Cir. 1966) (7% rate cap may be ignored).

272 *See* § 3.3, *supra*.

273 12 U.S.C. § 85.

274 OCC Letter, Consumer Cred. Guide (CCH) ¶ 96,744 (Jan. 19, 1983).

275 *See* § 3.6, *infra*.

276 *See* First Bank of Cadillac v. Miller, 347 N.W.2d 715 (Mich. Ct. App. 1984).

277 OCC Interpretive Letter No. 1004 (Aug. 4, 2004), *available on the companion website to this treatise*.

278 United Mo. Bank v. Danforth, 394 F. Supp. 774 (W.D. Mo. 1975); Att'y Gen. v. Equitable Trust Co., 450 A.2d 1273 (Md. 1982). *See also* Saul v. Midlantic Nat'l Bank S., 572 A.2d 650 (N.J. Super. Ct. App. Div. 1990). *Cf.* Shaner v. Chase Bank, USA, N.A., 587 F.3d 488 (1st Cir. 2009).

279 OCC Interpretive Letter No. 178, Consumer Cred. Guide (CCH) ¶ 97,239 (1981). Relevant letters from 1992 forward are available on the companion website to this treatise and are summarized at Appx. D.1.3, *infra*.

280 12 C.F.R. § 7.4001(b); OCC Interpretive Letter No. 178, Consumer Cred. Guide (CCH) ¶ 97,239 (1981).

Relevant letters from 1992 forward are available on the companion website to this treatise. *See also* VanderWeyst v. First State Bank of Benson, 425 N.W.2d 803, 809 (Minn. 1988).

Another limitation may be where a statute provides a rate cap only for closed-end accounts. Courts have split on whether a national bank can invoke a state's small loan ceiling in connection with its credit card accounts. Some courts have allowed the use of the small loan ceiling, despite the structural differences between open-end accounts and traditional small loans, on the grounds that both small loans and credit cards are used to finance similar consumer purchases and that both may be repaid in installments.[281] Other courts have reasoned that the use of small loan ceilings for credit cards would lead to an obliteration of state distinctions between classes of credit.[282]

### 3.5.6 Most Favored Lender Must Comply with "Material" State Restrictions

A depository institution that exports a rate cap found in a home state statute must comply with any statutory restrictions which are "material" to determination of the interest rate on that type of loan.[283] If state law permits finance companies to issue high interest loans, but restricts their associated loan fees, a national bank cannot adopt only the state interest rate without complying with the fee restrictions, because these restrictions are "material" to the interest rate allowed on the loan.

The materiality requirement can force depositories to comply with numerous state loan regulations if they want to adopt a particular state interest rate. Courts have found regulations concerning compounding of interest,[284] maximum loan charges,[285] attorney fees,[286] and requirements that credit terms be in writing[287] to be material to the interest rates allowable. In one of the most comprehensive discussions of the materiality issue, Maryland's highest court in *Attorney General v. Equitable Trust Co.*[288] specified that state regulations governing loan duration, fees, wage assignments, service charges, loan-splitting, post-default interest rate reductions, refinancing, compounding of interest, credit insurance, part payment bookkeeping, non-sufficient fund fee limitations, and prepayment penalties were all material to the interest rate allowed under the state small loan law.

In contrast, the same opinion held that a small loan provision prohibiting holder-in-due-course status for a lender financing a sale was not material to the interest rate permitted by the statute. Similarly, regulations governing licensing,[289] capital requirements, reporting requirements, or the supervision of state-regulated lenders may not be material to the interest rate allowed on a class of loans.[290] Some dispute exists over the materiality of state disclosure requirements.[291] However, if a state requires greater disclosure on high-rate consumer loans than on other classes of loans, these disclosure requirements should logically be deemed material to the higher rate.

The Minnesota Supreme Court has defined materiality as (1) pertaining to the manner in which the numerical rate of interest is calculated or (2) defining the "class of loans in such a way (as by size, type of borrower, or maturity)" as to affect the borrowed rate.[292] Licensing requirements would not be material, for example. The court specifically declined to decide whether attorney fees or loan-splitting provisions were material, as neither of these were part of the state statute the court chose to borrow.[293]

The interest calculation method used to determine the most favored lender rate is the method set by state law. The use of state law for interest calculation has not always been the rule. In *Evans v. National Bank of Savannah*,[294] the Supreme Court used a state's numerical interest ceiling, not its method of calculation, in setting the most favored lender rate. A state 8% usury ceiling was read to permit an 8% discount rate for a national bank even though no state lender could charge an equivalent rate under state law.

The Eighth Circuit has limited *Evans* to its facts, holding that state calculation methods apply except on short-term single-installment notes.[295] The Eighth Circuit's approach is more

281 *See* Fisher v. First Nat'l Bank of Omaha, 548 F.2d 255 (8th Cir. 1977); United Mo. Bank v. Danforth, 394 F. Supp. 774 (W.D. Mo. 1975); *See also* OCC Interpretive Letter No. 178, Consumer Cred. Guide (CCH) ¶ 97,239 (1981) (invocation of RISA ceiling for credit card account under most favored lender doctrine).

Relevant letters from 1992 forward are available on the companion website to this treatise. *Cf.* Commissioner of Small Loans v. First Nat'l Bank, 300 A.2d. 685 (Md. 1973) (card issuer could charge small loan rate for card cash advances in amounts under small loan law maximum).

282 Att'y Gen. v. Equitable Trust Co., 450 A.2d 1273 (Md. 1982).

283 12 C.F.R. § 7.4001(b). *See also* Kent v. Bank of Am., N.A., 2003 WL 327465 (Cal. Ct. App. Feb. 11, 2003) (bank is subject to state laws material to the determination of late payment and over-the-limit fees). *Cf.* Sherman v. Citibank (S.D.), N.A., 668 A.2d 1036 (N.J. 1995), *vacated and remanded on other grounds*, 517 U.S. 1241, 116 S. Ct. 2493, 135 L. Ed. 2d 86 (1996).

284 *See, e.g.*, Haas v. Pittsburgh Nat'l Bank, 526 F.2d 1083 (3d Cir. 1975), *aff'd*, 627 F.2d 677 (3d Cir. 1980); Partain v. First Nat'l Bank of Montgomery, 467 F.2d 167 (5th Cir. 1972).

285 *See, e.g.*, Northway Lanes v. Hackley Union Nat'l Bank & Trust Co., 464 F.2d 855 (6th Cir. 1972).

286 *See, e.g.*, Rockland-Atlas Nat'l Bank of Boston v. Murphy, 110 N.E.2d 638 (Mass. 1953).

287 *See, e.g.*, Landau v. Chase Manhattan Bank, N.A., 367 F. Supp. 992 (S.D.N.Y. 1973).

288 450 A.2d 1273, 1292 (Md. 1982).

289 *See* 12 C.F.R. § 7.4001(b).

290 *See* OCC Interpretive Letter No. 178 (Jan. 12, 1981) Consumer Cred. Guide (CCH) ¶ 97,239 (RISA disclosure requirements not material).

291 Burke & Kaplinsky, *Unraveling the New Federal Usury Law*, 37 Bus. Law. 1079, 1102, 1103 (1981–1982). *See also* Finkelstein, *Most Favored Lender Status for Insured Banks*, 42 Bus. Lawyer 915 (1987).

292 VanderWeyst v. First State Bank of Benson, 425 N.W.2d 803, 810 (Minn. 1988).

293 *Id.* at 810, 811.

294 251 U.S. 108, 40 S. Ct. 58, 64 L. Ed. 171 (1919). *See* Annotation, 81 A.L.R.2d 1280 (1962).

295 First Nat'l Bank v. Nowlin, 509 F.2d 872 (8th Cir. 1975). *See also* Magnotta v. Stearns Bank, N.A., 2007 WL 2406847 (D. Minn. Aug. 20, 2007) (applying both the state's rate cap and its method of calculating a rebate in the event of prepayment to a national bank; construing state law to mean that lenders must only reimburse a borrower who prepays when that prepayment results in an interest rate in excess of the cap and dismissing the case). *Cf. In re* Late Fee

consistent with both the most favored lender doctrine and the modern lending environment than the *Evans* decision. Reading an 18% state usury ceiling as a discount rate for national banks, for example, would permit 200% simple interest on a five-year, $5,000 transaction.[296]

### 3.5.7 *Other Lenders Need Not Have Made Loans Under the Applicable State Law*

It is the legal authority, rather than the actual practice of the potentially "competing" state lenders that determines whether a state lender is a competitor for purposes of the most favored lender analysis.[297] For example, in order to invoke an interest ceiling normally applicable to finance companies, a national bank need not prove that finance companies actually make the type of loan which the bank has made, but only that finance companies in the relevant state could legally make such loans if they chose to. Similarly, an OCC staff letter indicates that state-chartered credit unions are competitors of a national bank for most favored lender purposes, even if no credit unions are located in the county or geographic banking market of the national bank.[298]

## 3.6 State "Parity" Statutes: State Depository Use of Federal Depository's Interest Caps

### 3.6.1 *The Surprising Reach of State Parity Statutes*

Nearly every state has enacted a state parity law that seeks to create competitive equality between a state depository and its federal counterpart.[299] These parity statutes in some states are referred to as "wild card" statutes. A state's parity statute might provide, for example, that a state-chartered bank can extend consumer credit under the same rate ceiling or under the same terms and conditions as a national bank. Similarly, state credit unions may be given authority to make loans under the same terms as federal credit unions, or state savings associations under the same terms as federal savings associations. State parity statutes may provide these benefits to state depositories, whether or not that depository is federally insured.

Parity statutes can also set off domino effects that allow for rate exportation or federal agency preemption in ways not foreseen by either Congress or the state legislature enacting the parity laws. For example, Tennessee allowed state-chartered savings associations, but not state-chartered banks to charge interest as high as 24%. Nevertheless, a Tennessee appellate court allowed a state chartered bank to charge 24%, because Tennessee national banks under the most favored lender doctrine can charge the state savings association rate of 24%. In turn, the state parity statute was interpreted as allowing state-chartered banks to charge the same 24% rate as national banks.[300]

Consider another possible example. Federal credit unions now can charge 28% on certain small loans, and a state parity statute may allow state credit unions to do the same. A national bank located in that state, under the most favored lender doctrine, could then use the same 28% rate as state credit unions. Since the national bank in that state could charge 28%, then a state-chartered bank in that state under a state parity statute might be able to do the same.[301]

These domino effects likely surprised federal and state legislators. Congress probably had no intention to allow national banks to make loans on the same terms as federal credit unions. Similarly, the state legislature in allowing state credit unions to make loans on the same terms as federal credit unions may be surprised to learn that at the same time it allowed state banks to make loans on the same terms as credit unions.

Going one step further, a national bank in Delaware might export Delaware's lack of any usury limit to Massachusetts consumers. A Massachusetts parity statute might allow a Massachusetts state bank to make similar loans in Massachusetts with no usury limit. Then a federally insured Massachusetts state bank under rate exportation might be able to use Delaware's lack of a usury statute in loans it makes in California. It is hard to believe that Congress in authorizing rate exportation or Massachusetts enacting a state parity statute envisioned Massachusetts banks being able to export Delaware interest rates to California.

---

& Over-Limit Fee Litig., 528 F. Supp. 2d 953 (N.D. Cal. 2007) (refusing to read a constitutional restriction on "punitive" fees into § 85 that would have limited the amount of late and over-limit fees imposed by a bank upon its credit card customers).

296 An 18% discount on a sixty-month transaction takes $4,500 in interest, leaving only $500 as the financed amount. *See* § 5.3.3, *infra*.

297 *See* United Mo. Bank v. Danforth, 394 F. Supp. 774 (W.D. Mo. 1985); VanderWeyst v. First State Bank of Benson, 425 N.W.2d 803 (Minn. 1988). *See also* Fisher v. First Nat'l Bank of Omaha, 548 F.2d 255 (8th Cir. 1977); First Bank of Cadillac v. Miller, 347 N.W.2d 715 (Mich. Ct. App. 1984).

298 OCC Letter, Apr. 16, 1985, *discussed in* 44 Wash. Fin. Rep. (BNA) 800, 801 (May 6, 1985).

299 *See* Finance Comm'n of Texas and Credit Union Comm'n of Texas, Legislative Report: Preemption of Financial Services Study 12–13 (Dec. 2006), *available at* www.fc.state.tx.us/Studies/preemption.pdf; John J. Schroeder, *"Duel" Banking System? State Bank Parity Laws: An Examination of Regulatory Practice, Constitutional Issues, and Philosophical Questions*, 36 Ind. L. Rev. 197, 202 (2003).
This article contains a chart of the state parity laws. *Id.* at 223–227. Only two states, Iowa and North Carolina, have not. However, another banking provision in Iowa permits state banks to exercise all powers necessary to effect any and all of the purposes for which the bank is organized. Iowa Code §§ 524.801(10). North Carolina law grants to state banks "powers conferred by law upon private corporations." N.C. Gen. Stat. § 53-43.

300 Foster Bus. Park, L.L.C. v. J & B Inv., L.L.C., 269 S.W.3d 50 (Tenn. Ct. App. 2008); J & B Inv., L.L.C. v. Surti, 258 S.W.3d 127 (Tenn. Ct. App. 2007).

301 *See, e.g.*, First Bank of Cadillac v. Miller, 347 N.W.2d 715 (Mich. Ct. App. 1984).

### 3.6.2 *Limits to the Impact of State Parity Statutes*

There are limits to the impact of state parity statutes—the exact language of a statute must be carefully parsed. There are a few "super parity" statutes that provide state depositories with rights on a par with *any* lender doing business in the state. More typically, statutes provide parity only to one type of depository with the analogous federal depository.

For example, a statute will only provide state credit unions with rights enjoyed by federal credit unions. The statute will not give state credit unions the same rights as national banks, and the statute will give no rights to state-chartered banks. The state typically enacts a separate statute for state-chartered banks. Thus while virtually every state has enacted parity statutes, a state may not have enacted statutes covering all types of state depositories—banks, savings associations, and credit unions.

When the statute provides parity between a state and federal depository, what is the scope of activities of that parity? Does it include interest rates? Does it extend to other terms and conditions of lending? Does a state parity statute allow a depository to engage in activity specifically prohibited by state law? One commentator argues that a parity statute that allows a state bank to engage in activities not otherwise authorized may not cover activities that are specifically prohibited.[302]

State parity statutes also typically require a state depository to obtain approval from the state banking agency before it can ignore state law, or at least provide notice to the banking agency. It is important to determine whether the depository obtained the required approval or provided the appropriate notice.

State parity laws may also be subject to constitutional challenge, particularly when utilized in ways not foreseen by the state legislature. A federal court has found a Utah parity statute to violate the Utah Constitution.[303] The state statute giving state savings and loans parity with federal savings and loans embodied an unconstitutional delegation of the state's legislative authority to Congress and federal agencies.[304] The court distinguished the situation in which the state legislature adopts existing federal law from the unconstitutional adoption of prospective federal law as state law.

302 John J. Schroeder, *"Duel" Banking System? State Bank Parity Laws: An Examination of Regulatory Practice, Constitutional Issues, and Philosophical Questions*, 36 Ind. L. Rev. 197, 203, 204 (2003).

303 *See, e.g.*, Utah League of Insured Sav. Ass'n v. State, 555 F. Supp. 664 (D. Utah 1983). *See also* cases discussed in John J. Schroeder, *"Duel" Banking System? State Bank Parity Laws: An Examination of Regulatory Practice, Constitutional Issues, and Philosophical Questions*, 36 Ind. L. Rev. 197, 209–214 (2003).

304 Utah League of Insured Sav. Ass'n v. State, 555 F. Supp. 664, 673–675 (D. Utah 1983).

## 3.7 Manufactured Home Credit Preemption

### 3.7.1 *Introduction*

Manufactured home credit and loans present special preemption issues. Two federal statutes that preempt state law for mortgage loans extend their coverage to manufactured homes, even if the home is sold from a dealership and is not sited on real estate at the time of the loan. Where state law treats a manufactured home credit sale as covered by an installment sales act applying to personal property, federal mortgage loan preemption statutes still apply. In addition, federal agencies insure manufactured home loans, and this also raises special preemption issues. The federal mortgage loan preemption statutes are discussed in more detail in National Consumer Law Center, *Mortgage Lending* Ch. 8 (2012).

### 3.7.2 *DIDA Interest Rate Preemption*

The Depository Institutions Deregulation and Monetary Control Act of 1980 (DIDA) preempts state laws limiting interest rates on *first* mortgage loans,[305] and this DIDA provision applies to manufactured home credit.[306] For preemption to be applicable, the manufactured home creditor must either be a "qualified lender" or the manufactured home creditor must sell the loan to a qualified lender. Qualified lenders include federally insured depositories, lenders approved for FHA insured loans, lenders who make or invest in at least $1 million in residential real estate loans or manufactured home credit sales in excess of $1 million per year, or the home's prior occupant.[307] In addition, there is a qualified lender if the loan is eligible for resale on the federal secondary mortgage market.[308] Generally, this means that the loan originator must have been approved by Fannie Mae or Freddie Mac and that the loan terms and structure must meet the federal purchaser's requirements.

DIDA first lien preemption only applies to a manufactured home loan or credit sale if it complies with certain federal consumer protection regulations.[309] These regulations govern the refund of pre-computed finance charges; prepayment penalties; late charges; deferral fees; balloon payments; and the consumer's right to notice before repossession, foreclosure, or acceleration.[310]

305 U.S.C. § 1735f-7a.

306 12 U.S.C. § 1735f-7a(a)(1)(A), (B).

307 12 U.S.C. § 1735f-7a(a)(1)(C). *See also* 12 U.S.C. § 1735f-5(b)(2).

308 12 U.S.C. § 1735f-5(b)(2)(C) (incorporated by 12 U.S.C. § 1735f-7a(a)(1)(C)).

309 DIDA § 501(c), 12 U.S.C. § 1735f-7a. *See also* Quiller v. Barclay's American/Credit, Inc.,764 F.2d 1400 (11th Cir. 1985), *reinstating* 727 F.2d 1067 (11th Cir. 1984); Livingston v. Vanguard Fed. Sav. Bank, 563 A.2d 175, 180 (Pa. Super. Ct. 1989) (DIDA does not apply where manufactured home lender's contract did not comply with applicable regulations). *But see* Nelson v. River Valley Bank & Trust, 971 S.W.2d 777 (Ark. 1998).

310 12 C.F.R. 190.4 (OCC interim final rule, replacing 12 C.F.R. § 590.4 enacted by the OTS). *See* 76 Fed. Reg. 49,152 (Aug. 9,

There is no direct remedy if a manufactured home lender fails to comply with the consumer protection regulations. Instead, DIDA first mortgage preemption is not applicable, and the lender is left to comply with any applicable state law. If the remaining applicable state law is a usury cap, and the loan exceeds that cap, then failure to comply with the consumer protection regulations leads to *state* usury remedies.[311] But there is no remedy for failure to comply with the consumer protection regulations if the lender has not otherwise violated state law, since the lender is not relying on DIDA preemption.

If the manufactured home creditor complies with the consumer protection regulations, then DIDA applies to any first mortgage liens, including non-purchase-money mortgages.[312] One notable exception is Texas, where DIDA does not preempt provisions of the Texas Constitution limiting interest rates on non-purchase money mortgages.[313] In addition, federal law allows states to opt out of DIDA first mortgage preemption, and opt-out states include Colorado, Georgia, Hawaii, Idaho, Iowa, Kansas, Maine, Massachusetts, Minnesota, Nebraska, North Carolina, Puerto Rico, South Carolina, and South Dakota, and to a lesser extent Nevada.[314] For more on DIDA first mortgage preemption and manufactured homes, see National Consumer Law Center, *Mortgage Lending* § 8.4.5 (2012).

### *3.7.3 AMTPA Preemption of State Restrictions on Loan Structure*

The Alternative Mortgage Transaction Parity Act (AMTPA) preempts certain state restrictions *not* on interest rates, but on the *structure* of manufacture home credit sales and loans.[315] AMTPA is a complex statute examined in more detail at National Consumer Law Center, *Mortgage Lending* § 8.6 (2012).

AMTPA applies to "alternative mortgage transactions," which is a defined term in the statute. This term's definition and thus AMTPA's scope has changed over time. Effective for any loan made on or after July 21, 2011,[316] AMTPA preempts any state law that limits a lender's ability "to make, purchase and enforce" adjustable rate mortgages.[317] Because of AMTPA, states cannot prohibit lenders from making adjustable rate mortgage loans, but states can regulate or restrict the terms of such mortgages as long as they do not prevent lenders from making, purchasing, and enforcing them.

AMTPA applies to "housing creditors,"[318] defined as depository institutions, HUD-approved lenders, or any person who "regularly makes" loans or credit sales or advances secured by residential realty, dwellings, or manufactured homes, and any transferee of these lenders.[319] AMTPA gives state-regulated housing creditors a choice whether to comply with state laws relating to "alternative mortgage transactions" or with federal agency regulations.[320]

Effective for any mortgage loan where the creditor received the application on or after July 22, 2011, state creditors who opt to avoid state law concerning adjustable rate mortgages must then comply with Consumer Financial Protection Bureau (CFPB) Regulation D.[321] Effective July 22, 2012, all creditors must comply with the CFPB's Regulation D.[322] For mortgage loans where the application was received prior to July 22, 2011, state-chartered banks had the option to comply with applicable OCC regulations, state credit unions with NCUA regulations, and all other "housing creditors" with applicable OTS regulations. OTS's AMTPA regulations formerly preempted state restrictions on prepayment penalties and late fees, but OTS narrowed these regulations effective July 1, 2003.[323]

AMTPA does not apply where a state through legislation opted out of AMTPA by 1985.[324] Maine, Massachusetts, New York, South Carolina and Wisconsin opted out.[325] In addition, by federal statute, AMTPA applies in Texas only to purchase money mortgages.[326]

---

2011). *Cf.* Burris v. First Fin. Corp., 928 F.2d 797 (8th Cir. 1991) (holding an "acquisition charge" not refunded upon prepayment is not a prepayment penalty within 12 C.F.R. § 590.4).

311 Quiller v. Barclay's American/Credit, Inc.,764 F.2d 1400 (11th Cir. 1985), *reinstating* 727 F.2d 1067 (11th Cir. 1984). *Cf.* Burris v. First Fin. Corp., 928 F.2d 797 (8th Cir. 1991) (no violation of consumer protection regulations, so not state usury claim); Atkinson v. General Elec. Credit Corp.,866 F.2d 396 (11th Cir. 1989); Moyer v. Citicorp Homeowners, Inc.,799 F.2d 1445 (11th Cir. 1986); Grant v. General Elec. Credit Corp.,764 F.2d 1404 (11th Cir. 1985); Chambliss v. Oakwood Acceptance Corp. (*In re* Chambliss), 315 B.R. 166 (Bankr. S.D. Ga. 2004).

312 *See* National Consumer Law Center, Mortgage Lending § 8.4.5 (2012).

313 *Id.* § 8.4.3.2.

314 Colo. Rev. Stat. §§ 5-13-101 to 5-13-103; Ga. Code Ann. § 7-4-20; Haw. Rev. Stat. § 478-9 (nevertheless, Hawaii exempts first lien mortgages from state usury caps under Haw. Rev. Stat. § 478-8); Idaho Code Ann. § 28-49-105; Iowa Code § 537 preamble (1980 Iowa Acts 1156, § 32); Kan. Stat. Ann. § 16-207a; Me. Rev. Stat. tit. 9A, § 1-110; Mass. Gen Laws ch. 183, § 63 note (1980 Mass. Acts 385); Minn. Stat. § 47.203; Neb. Rev. Stat. § 45-1,104; N.C. Gen. Stat. § 24-2.3; P.R. Laws Ann. tit. 10, § 9881; 1982 S.C. Acts 385, § 1 (*see* note to S.C. Code § 29-3-40); S.D. Codified Laws § 54-3-15. *See also* 1981 Nev. Stat. 668, § 11 (overriding DIDA § 501(a)(1) with respect to business or agricultural loans in amounts of $1,000 or more; *see* note to Nev. Rev. Stat. § 97.285).

Wisconsin originally opted out. *See* 1981 Wis. Laws 45, § 50, but in 1998 Wisconsin repealed its opt-out. 1997 Wis. Laws 142. *See generally* National Consumer Law Center, Mortgage Lending § 8.4.6 (2012).

315 12 U.S.C. §§ 3801–3806.

316 Dodd-Frank tit. X, § 1083(b), *codified at* 12 U.S.C. § 3802 note.

317 12 U.S.C. §§ 3802(1), 3803(a).

318 12 U.S.C. § 3803.

319 12 U.S.C. § 2802(2).

320 *See* 12 U.S.C. § 3803.

321 *See* 76 Fed. Reg. 44,226 (July 22, 2011) (enacting interim final rule 12 C.F.R. 1004, Alternative Mortgage Transaction Parity (Regulation D)). *See also* 12 U.S.C. §§ 3802 note, 3803.

322 *See* 76 Fed. Reg. 44,226 (July 22, 2011) (enacting interim final rule 12 C.F.R. 1004, Alternative Mortgage Transaction Parity (Regulation D)).

323 67 Fed. Reg. 60,542 (Sept. 26, 2002).

324 *See* 12 U.S.C. § 3804.

325 Me. Rev. Stat. tit. 9A, § 1-110 (West); 1985 Mass. Acts 224; N.Y. Banking Law § 6-g (McKinney) (did not opt out with respect to residential manufactured homes); 1984 S.C. Acts 355, § 1 (not codified); 1983 Wis. Laws 389, § 11(1) (non-statutory).

326 12 U.S.C. § 1462a. *See also* H.R. Conf. Rep. No. 103-651, at 57

### 3.7.4 FHA- and VA-Insured Manufactured Home Loans

The Federal Housing Administration (FHA) and the Department of Veterans Affairs (VA) are authorized to insure loans for the purchase or improvement of manufactured homes,[327] and state interest ceilings are preempted for these loans.[328] For FHA-insured loans, the preemption of state law applies to the "amount of interest"[329] while the VA preemption applies to statutes that limit the rate or amount of interest, the manner of calculating that interest (including the prohibition of charging interest on interest), or that require a minimum amortization of principal.[330]

Currently, both the VA[331] and the FHA[332] permit borrowers and lenders to agree to any interest rate. As a result, unless a state opts out of VA and FHA preemption, there is no interest ceiling on FHA-insured or VA-insured loans.

States may opt out of this FHA- and VA-insured loan preemption of state law. A state can opt out of FHA preemption by enacting a statute after December 21, 1979 that limits interest, points, or other charges for such loans.[333] The opt-out is applicable for loans extended after the state statute's enactment.

A federal statute indicates that if state law is preempted for FHA loans, then it is also preempted for VA loans.[334] The Eleventh Circuit interprets this as also stating the contrary—that if a state law acts to opt out of FHA preemption, then it also opts out of VA preemption.[335] For more on state opt-outs of VA- and FHA-insured loan preemption, see National Consumer Law Center, *Mortgage Lending* § 8.2.2 (2012).

In addition to the explicit statutory preemption of state interest rate regulation for VA and FHA loans, state law is preempted if it conflicts with VA or FHA regulations. VA regulations set out requirements as to prepayment penalties,[336] how a loan is amortized,[337] charges and fees that can and cannot be charged,[338] discount points,[339] late charges,[340] and as to adjustable rate mortgages.[341] FHA regulations for manufactured home loans include provisions concerning loan maturities,[342] payments,[343] late charges,[344] and prepayment penalties.[345] These regulations are described in more detail in National Consumer Law Center, *Mortgage Lending* Ch. 8 (2012).

### 3.7.5 RHS Direct and Guaranteed Manufactured Home Loans

The Rural Housing Service (RHS), an agency of the United States Department of Agriculture, administers two different loan programs: direct loans and guaranteed loans. Both programs allow loans to purchase manufactured homes.

Section 502 direct single-family housing loans provide for direct loans from RHS to low-income individuals for the purchase, construction, or rehabilitation of single family homes located in rural areas. RHS sets the interest rate, term, and payment arrangements for these thirty-year, low-interest, fixed rate loans.[346] As loans directly from a federal agency, state law will not apply to the interest rate or structure of the loans.

The Section 502 guaranteed loan program assists rural residents with modest incomes obtain housing through conventional financing.[347] The federal regulations require that the mortgages be thirty-year fixed rate, and that interest rates comply with state limits on interest rates and also be at or below the "Fannie Mae rate" as described in its regulations and as set out in RHS instructions.[348] Late fees are limited by the percentage allowed by "HUD or Fannie Mae or Freddie Mac."[349]

## 3.8 State Choice of Law Standards

### 3.8.1 Introduction

The preceding sections discuss whether federal law displaces state consumer credit law,[350] or allows a depository institution to export one state's law to another state.[351] Unless one of these exceptions applies, state law determines which state's law applies to a credit transaction (assuming that federal law does not preempt all state law).

The forum state's law will apply if the consumer and lender both reside in the forum state and the credit transaction took place in that state. But often the borrower's residence, the lender's residence, and the place the loan was extended are not all located in the same state. The credit contract may also specify which state's law applies to the transaction. In any of these cases,

(1994), *reprinted in* 1994 U.S.C.C.A.N. 2068. *See* National Consumer Law Center, Mortgage Lending § 8.6.3 (2012).

327 *See* 12 U.S.C. § 1703; 38 U.S.C. § 3703.

328 *See* 12 U.S.C. § 1709-1a; 38 U.S.C. § 3728.

329 12 U.S.C. § 1709-1a.

330 38 U.S.C. § 3728.

331 *See* 38 C.F.R. §§ 36.4311, 36.4312; 60 Fed. Reg. 38,256 (July 26, 1995).

332 12 U.S.C. § 1709(b)(5); 24 C.F.R. §§ 201, 203.20(a).

HUD removed the 1% cap on certain origination and closing costs charged by lenders when making FHA-insured loans. Instead, HUD will rely upon its policy statements addressing lender-paid broker compensation, to ensure that the total origination costs on all loans, including FHA loans be reasonable. 73 Fed. Reg. 68,204, 68,227 (Nov. 17, 2008). This change was effective on January 1, 2010.

333 12 U.S.C. § 1735f-7(b).

334 38 U.S.C. § 3728.

335 *See* Doyle v. Southern Guar. Corp. 795 F.2d 907 (11th Cir. 1986).

336 38 C.F.R. § 36.4311.

337 38 C.F.R. § 36.4310.

338 38 C.F.R. § 36.4313.

339 38 C.F.R. § 36.4312(b).

340 38 C.F.R. § 36.4312(c).

341 38 C.F.R. § 36.4312(d).

342 24 C.F.R. § 201.11.

343 24 C.F.R. § 201.14.

344 24 C.F.R. § 201.15.

345 24 C.F.R. § 201.17.

346 7 C.F.R. §§ 3550.66, 3550.67.

347 42 U.S.C. § 1472(h).

348 7 C.F.R. §§ 1980.320, 1980.321. *See also* 7 C.F.R. § 1980.302 (definition of "Fannie Mae rate").

349 7 C.F.R. § 1980.324(b).

350 *See* § 3.2, 3.3, 3.7, *supra*.

351 *See* § 3.4, *supra*.

courts typically utilize the forum state's choice of law rules to determine which state's law applies to the credit transaction.[352]

State choice of law rules are often complex when it comes to credit transactions. To begin with, many states have a "general" usury statute, several "special" usury statutes, and a "criminal" usury statute. General usury statutes, sometimes found in the state constitution, create a generally-applicable cap on interest rates. "Special" usury statutes make exceptions for particular types of transactions, such as second mortgage loans and bank installment loans. These special usury statutes allow higher rates, but also place additional restrictions on the loans. Some states also have a criminal usury statute, with a higher cap than the general usury statute. In the 1980s and 1990s, some states repealed some or all of their caps, often replacing them with a provision allowing the parties to agree to any rate. However, many of these caps remain on the books.

States often have different choice of law standards for general, special, and criminal usury statutes.[353] In addition, most of the case law involving choice of law concerning general and even criminal usury statutes is in a commercial setting where one business extends credit to another business. It is questionable whether such precedent should be binding on consumer lending.[354]

Special usury statutes in particular will often explicitly provide for a choice of law standard right in the statute.[355] Moreover, consumer contracts typically specify the state's law that is applicable to the contract, and questions arise as to whether that choice is binding.[356] Finally, special issues apply as to whether a state's laws apply to servicemembers at a military installation in that state, because the servicemembers are not residents of that state.[357]

### 3.8.2 Contractual Choice of Law Clauses

Consumer credit contracts typically include a clause stating that the contract will be governed by a particular state's laws. Uniform Commercial Code (UCC) § 1-301 validates a choice of law clause as long as the transaction bears a "reasonable relation" to the state whose law is chosen, and the UCC applies to the transaction.[358]

But at least in the consumer context, much law is to the contrary. Such a choice of law will not be given effect if a statute in the forum state prohibits such a clause for the types of loan contracts at issue,[359] or state law requires that the law of that state be chosen.[360] Under the *Restatement of Conflict of Laws*, such a clause also will not be upheld if the chosen state does not have a substantial relation to the transaction.[361] Nor will the clause be given effect if the result would be contrary to a fundamental policy of the state with the most significant relation to the transaction, as long as that state also has a materially greater interest in the issue.[362] Courts may also look at the provision as an unfair adhesion contract and find it unenforceable on that basis.[363]

352 *See, e.g.*, Klaxon Co. v. Stentor Elec. Mfg. Co., 313 U.S. 487, 61 S. Ct. 1020, 85 L. Ed. 1477 (1941); *In re* Presque Isle Apts., L.P., 118 B.R. 332 (Bankr. W.D. Pa. 1990); Fu v. Fu, 733 A.2d 1133, 1152 (N.J. 1999); Vanderbilt Mortgage & Fin., Inc. v. Posey, 146 S.W.3d 302 (Tex. App. 2004); Waddoups v. Amalgamated Sugar Co., 54 P.3d 1054 (Utah 2002). *But see* Olympic Coast Inv., Inc. v. Wright (*In re* Wright), 256 B.R. 626, 631–632 (Bankr. D. Mont. 2000) (bankruptcy court must apply federal choice of law rules, not those of forum state, in core matters); Committee of Unsecured Creditors v. RG Fin., Ltd. (*In re* Powerburst), 154 B.R. 307 (Bankr. E.D. Cal. 1993).

353 *See* §§ 3.8.4, 3.8.5, *infra*.

354 *See* § 3.8.5.1, *infra*.

355 *See* § 3.8.3, *infra*.

356 *See* § 3.8.2, *infra*.

357 *See* § 3.8.6, *infra*.

358 *See also* Anderson v. Chainani (*In re* Kemper), 263 B.R. 773, 781 n.15 (E.D. Tex. 2001) (upholding clause selecting state where debtor lived, signed the notes, and generated payments); Jett Racing & Sales, Inc. v. Transamerica Commercial Fin. Corp., 892 F. Supp. 161 (S.D. Tex. 1995) (commercial case).

A revised version of Article 1's choice of law rules was approved by the Uniform Law Commission (formerly the National Conference of Commissioners on Uniform Laws, or NCCUSL) in 2001 for consideration by state legislatures, would have loosened these standards except in consumer transactions. Almost no jurisdictions adopted these revised choice of law rules, however, and the Uniform Law Commission withdrew them in 2008. *See* William H. Henning & Fred H. Miller, Report on the UCC: 2008—Part 1, UCC Bull. 1 n.2 (Jan. 2009).

359 *See, e.g.*, Minn. Stat. § 47.601, subdiv. 2 ("No contract or agreement between a consumer short-term loan lender and a borrower residing in Minnesota may contain . . . a provision selecting a law other than Minnesota law under which the contract is construed or enforced").

360 Whitaker v. Spiegel, Inc., 623 P.2d 1147, *amended*, 637 P.2d 235 (Wash. 1980).

361 Restatement of Conflict of Laws 2d § 187. *See* Am. Honda Fin. Corp. v. GloMc, Inc., 820 F. Supp. 1157 (E.D. Ark. 1993) (clause upheld where substantial connection to chosen state's law and borrower was sophisticated businessman); Brock v. First Fid. Acceptance Corp. (*In re* Brock), 214 B.R. 877 (Bankr. E.D. Ark. 1997) (clause upheld where substantial connection to chosen state); Culbert v. Rols Capital Co., 585 N.Y.S.2d 67 (N.Y. App. Div. 1992) (connection to New Jersey may be a sham to avoid New York usury laws); American Express Travel Related Servs. Co., 26 Misc. 3d 1016 (N.Y. Civ. Ct. 2009); Cook v. Frazier, 765 S.W.2d 546 (Tex. App. 1989) (Texas borrowers' formation of Utah partnership was sham device). *See also* Gulfcoast Hospitality, Inc. v. Amstat Corp. (*In re* Gulfcoast Hospitality, Inc.), 305 B.R. 341 (Bankr. M.D. Fla. 2003) (question of fact).

362 Restatement of Conflict of Laws 2d § 187(2). *See* Orix Credit Alliance, Inc. v. CIT Group/Equip. Fin., Inc. (*In re* Hughes), 230 B.R. 213 (Bankr. M.D. Ga. 1998) (upholding choice of law clause in absence of "overwhelming public policy"); Washington Mut. Bank v. Superior Court, 15 P.3d 1071 (Cal. 2001); Brack v. Omni Loan Co., 80 Cal. Rptr. 3d 275 (Cal. Ct. App. 2008) (state Finance Lenders Law represents fundamental policy of state, and California has materially greater interest in enforcing this law than Nevada, the state named in the choice-of-law clause, has in enforcing its law); American Express Travel Related Servs. Co., 26 Misc. 3d 1016 (N.Y. Civ. Ct. 2009); Dep't of Banking v. NCAS of Del., L.L.C., 948 A.2d 752, 759 n.9 (Pa. 2008) (agreeing in dictum that choice of law clause would not be effective to subject Pennsylvania debtors to exploitive payday loan interest rates authorized in state where lender was incorporated); State *ex rel.* Meierhenry v. Spiegel, Inc., 277 N.W.2d 298 (S.D. 1979).

363 *Cf.* Washington Mut. Bank v. Superior Court, 15 P.3d 1071 (Cal. 2001) (choice of law clause in consumer contract is not per se

But where there is a substantial relationship with the state specified in the clause, courts have generally enforced such clauses.[364] A number of these decisions, however, stress that the parties were sophisticated business negotiators, and suggest that boilerplate choice of law clauses in consumer contracts will be subjected to closer scrutiny.[365]

When determining whether a state's law represents a fundamental policy of the state, the court looks at the law as a whole, not just the specific substantive provisions that differ from the law of the chosen state.[366] In general, a state's special usury statutes represent such a fundamental policy.

Thus, a California appellate court held that its Finance Lenders Law, which requires lenders to be licensed, renders loan obligations void if made by unlicensed lenders, and gives the state various enforcement remedies, represents a fundamental policy of the state.[367] This is so even though there were only minimal differences in the substantive requirements between California and Nevada, the state named in the choice of law clause. By immunizing a lender operating in California from the California regulatory scheme, the choice of Nevada's law violated a fundamental policy of California. The court also held that California had a greater interest in enforcing this law, without which a substantial segment of the public would be deprived of the protections California affords all other consumers, than Nevada had in enforcing its laws.

A choice of law clause in the contract between a payday lender and an out of state "rent-a-bank" has no effect on the authority of state regulators to apply their state law to the payday lender.[368] Nor does a choice of law clause between a payday lender and its borrowers prevent a state agency from enforcing state usury laws against the lender.[369] While lenders usually insert choice of law clauses to protect themselves from usury claims, a clause that subjects a contract to laws of a state under which it is usurious may also be upheld.[370]

### *3.8.3 State Statutes Explicitly Governing Choice of Law*

A state's courts will almost always follow the forum's statutory provision requiring that the law of that state apply. For example, a Washington statute provides:

> Whenever a loan or forbearance is made outside Washington state to a person then residing in this state the usury laws found in chapter 19.52 RCW, as now or hereafter amended, shall be applicable in all courts of this state to the same extent such usury laws would be applicable if the loan or forbearance was made in this state.[371]

In other states, a rule about what state's law applies may be incorporated into a special usury statute. For example, a state law may require all companies doing business in the state to comply with the state's licensing requirements.[372] Or a state

unenforceable, but may be invalidated if superior power was unfairly used in imposing it or if enforcing it would cause substantial injustice).

364 *See, e.g.*, Aetna Life Ins. Co. v. Great Nat'l Corp., 818 F.2d 19 (8th Cir. 1987) (commercial transaction); Consolidated Jewelers, Inc. v. Standard Fin. Corp., 325 F.2d 31 (6th Cir. 1963) (Kentucky law) (commercial case); Abat v. Chase Bank USA, N.A., 738 F. Supp. 2d 1093 (C.D. Cal. 2010); L'Arbalete, Inc. v. Zaczac, 474 F. Supp. 2d 1314 (S.D. Fla. 2007); Petters Co. v. BLS Sales Inc., 2005 WL 2072109 (N.D. Cal. Aug. 26, 2005); Jones v. First Fid. Acceptance Corp. (*In re* Jones), 231 B.R. 66 (E.D. Ark. 1999); Jett Racing & Sales, Inc. v. Transamerica Commercial Fin. Corp., 892 F. Supp. 161 (S.D. Tex. 1995); Superior Funding Corp. v. Big Apple Capital Corp., 738 F. Supp. 1468 (S.D.N.Y. 1990); Rieser v. Todd (*In re* Chari), 2005 WL 4030034 (Bankr. S.D. Ohio Sept. 2, 2005); *In re* Wright, 256 B.R. 626 (Bankr. D. Mont. 2000); Committee of Unsecured Creditors v. RG Fin., Ltd. (*In re* Powerburst), 154 B.R. 307 (Bankr. E.D. Cal. 1993); *In re* Mickler, 20 B.R. 346 (Bankr. M.D. Fla. 1982); Continental Mortgage Inv. v. Sailboat Key, Inc., 395 So. 2d 507 (Fla. 1981) (upholding contractual choice of law clause in commercial case; recognizing that in consumer cases courts give them less deference); Jackson v. Pasadena Receivables, Inc., 921 A.2d 799 (Md. 2007); Kronovet v. Lipchin, 415 A.2d 1096 (Md. 1980) (commercial case); Goodwin Bros. Leasing, Inc. v. H&B Inc., 597 S.W.2d 303 (Tenn. 1980) (commercial case); Cook v. Frazier, 765 S.W.2d 546 (Tex. App. 1989); Hi Fashion Wigs Profit Sharing Trust v. Hamilton Inv. Trust, 579 S.W.2d 300 (Tex. Civ. App. 1979) (commercial case). *See also* Moyer v. Citicorp Homeowners, Inc., 799 F.2d 1445 (11th Cir. 1986); Evans v. Harry Robinson Pontiac Buick, 983 S.W.2d 946 (Ark. 1999); Settlement Funding, L.L.C. v. Von Neumann-Lillie, 645 S.E.2d 436 (Va. 2007).

365 Continental Mortgage Inv. v. Sailboat Key, Inc., 395 So. 2d 507 (Fla. 1981) (recognizing that in consumer cases courts give choice of law clauses less deference); Goodwin Bros. Leasing, Inc. v. H&B Inc., 597 S.W.2d 303 (Tenn. 1980) ("This is not a case of the victimizing of an uninformed consumer by an avaricious finance company"). *See also* Washington Mut. Bank v. Superior Court, 15 P.3d 1071 (Cal. 2001) (choice of law clause in consumer contract is not per se unenforceable, but may be invalidated if superior power was unfairly used in imposing it or if enforcing it would cause substantial injustice).

366 Brack v. Omni Loan Co., 80 Cal. Rptr. 3d 275 (Cal. Ct. App. 2008).

367 *Id.*

368 Bankwest, Inc. v. Oxendine, 598 S.E.2d 343 (Ga. Ct. App. 2004).

369 Dep't of Banking v. NCAS of Del., L.L.C., 948 A.2d 752, 759 (Pa. 2008).

370 Moyer v. Citicorp Homeowners, Inc., 799 F.2d 1445 (11th Cir. 1986); Pro v. Hertz Equip. Rental Corp., 67 U.C.C. Rep. Serv. 2d 626 (D.N.J. 2008); Rieser v. Todd (*In re* Chari), 2005 WL 4030034 (Bankr. S.D. Ohio Sept. 2, 2005); Committee of Unsecured Creditors v. RG Fin., Inc.(*In re* Powerburst Corp.), 154 B.R. 307 (Bankr. E.D. Cal. 1993); *In re* Mickler, 20 B.R. 346 (Bankr. M.D. Fla. 1982).

371 Wash. Rev. Code § 19.52.034. *See* Whitaker v. Spiegel, Inc., 623 P.2d 1147 (1981), *amended*, 637 P.2d 235 (Wash. 1981) (Washington law controls), *appeal dismissed*, 454 U.S. 958 (1981); Falk v. Riedel, 2000 Wash. App. LEXIS 1889 (Sept. 29, 2000) (applying Washington law); Golden Horse Farms, Inc. v. Parcher, 629 P.2d 1353 (Wash. Ct. App. 1981) (Washington law applies).

372 *See* Gorman v. Marcon Capital Corp., 274 B.R. 351 (D. Vt. 2002); People v. Fairfax Family Fund, Inc., 47 Cal. Rptr. 812 (Cal. Ct. App. 1964), *appeal dismissed*, 382 U.S. 1 (1965). *See also* HIMC Inv. Co. v. Siciliano, 246 A.2d 502 (N.J. Super. Ct. Law Div. 1968); Oxford Consumer Discount Co. v. Stefanelli, 246 A.2d 460 (N.J. Super. Ct. App. Div. 1968), *supplemental op. at* 250 A.2d 593 (N.J. Super. Ct. App. Div. 1969) (New Jersey second mortgage statute indicates legislative intent that New Jersey law apply to all contracts involving second mortgage on New Jersey real estate), *modified and*

may specify that its laws apply to contracts made by out-of-state companies with state residents.[373] A state may also have a statute that sets a general choice of law standard for contracts.[374]

If a state has a choice of law statute, it will be binding on courts of that state.[375] Those courts will not need to analyze the other choice of law factors.[376] Courts have upheld the authority of states to enforce choice of law statutes against challenges based on due process, the Full Faith and Credit Clause, and the Commerce Clause of the Constitution.[377]

However, the Seventh Circuit found unconstitutional the application of an Indiana statute that required an Illinois auto title lender who advertised or solicited transactions in Indiana to obtain an Indiana license and abide by Indiana statutory limits on interest if it made loans to Indiana residents.[378] The court granted that Indiana had a colorable interest in protecting its residents from these loans. Some language in the opinion suggests that Indiana might have been allowed to apply its law if there had been evidence that the lender had moved to the border area of a neighboring state, or opened an office there, with the specific intent to evade Indiana law while lending to Indiana consumers.

### 3.8.4 *Rule for Special Usury Statutes*

As long as a transaction bears a substantial relationship to the forum state, courts of that state will typically apply that state's special usury statutes, such as the small loan laws, installment sales acts, and second mortgage statutes.[379] This is consistent with the typical state choice of law rule for contract cases (*other* than for general usury statutes) that the law of the state with the most significant relationship to the parties and the transaction should apply.[380]

Special usury laws are supported by strong and explicit public policies. States have a strong interest in protecting particularly vulnerable classes of borrowers. Special usury statutes, which as a whole are comparatively modern enactments, reflect legislative concern about abuses in modern credit markets which harmed such borrowers. Special usury laws also often incorporate their own choice of law provisions.[381]

States may even enact special usury statutes in part with the specific intent of controlling foreign lenders who do business in the state. Courts have enforced such legislation even though the regulated transactions may have a substantial relation to another state.[382]

### 3.8.5 *Rule for General Usury Statutes*

#### 3.8.5.1 General

For most states, the choice of law rule for contract cases (and for special usury statutes) is that the law of the state with the

*aff'd*, 262 A.2d 874 (N.J. 1970), *appeal dismissed*, 400 U.S. 808, 923 (1970). *Cf.* Pilcher v. Direct Equity Lending, 189 F. Supp. 2d 1198 (D. Kan. 2002) (denying summary judgment on question whether Kan. U.C.C.C. licensure requirement applies to out-of-state lender; lender's out-of-state assignees, which had no contact with Kan., are exempt from licensure).

373 *See, e.g.*, Kan. Stat. Ann. § 16a-1-201 (specifying when consumer credit transaction is considered made in Kansas; Consumer Credit Code applies to all such loans); N.C. Gen. Stat. § 24-2.1 (any extension of credit is deemed to have been made in North Carolina and subject to its laws if borrower accepts or makes loan offer in North Carolina).

374 *See* Shannon-Vail Five Inc. v. Bunch, 270 F.3d 1207 (9th Cir. 2001); Cal. Civ. Code § 1646 (West) (applying law of place of performance).

375 *See* Restatement of Conflict of Laws 2d § 6; Resolution Trust Co. v. Northpark Joint Venture, 958 F.2d 1313 (5th Cir. 1992); McCorhill Publishing, Inc. v. Greater New York Sav. Bank (*In re* McCorhill Publishing, Inc.), 86 B.R. 783 (Bankr. S.D.N.Y. 1988).

376 Whitaker v. Spiegel, Inc., 623 P.2d 1147 (1981), *amended*, 637 P.2d 235 (Wash. 1981) (Washington courts will not engage in conflict of law analysis because state statute says Washington law controls), *appeal dismissed*, 454 U.S. 958 (1981).

377 Aldens, Inc. v. Miller, 610 F.2d 538 (8th Cir. 1979); Aldens, Inc. v. LaFollette, 552 F.2d 745 (7th Cir. 1977); Aldens, Inc. v. Packel, 524 F.2d 38 (3d Cir. 1975). *See also* Quik Payday, Inc. v. Stork, 549 F.3d 1302 (10th Cir. 2008) (state law regulating out-of-state, Internet payday lender does not violate dormant Commerce Clause); Valley Bank v. Plus Sys., Inc., 914 F.2d 1186 (9th Cir. 1990) (upholding state law that regulated agreements regarding ATM charges); Underhill Assocs., Inc. v. Bradshaw, 674 F.2d 293 (4th Cir. 1982) (requiring out-of-state securities broker-dealers to register with state before transacting business there does not violate Commerce Clause or due process). *Cf.* Arab African Int'l Bank v. Epstein, 10 F.3d 168 (3d Cir. 1993) (remanding for determination whether state law prohibiting foreign banks from doing business there is excessive burden on interstate commerce). *But cf.* Pioneer Military Lending, Inc. v. Manning, 2 F.3d 280 (8th Cir. 1993) (Commerce Clause prevents Missouri from regulating out-of-state lender that had branch office in Missouri but made loans only to non-Missouri residents).

378 Midwest Title Loans, Inc. v. Mills, 593 F.3d 660 (7th Cir. 2010).

379 *See* American Sec. & Trust Co. v. Equitable Life Ins. Co. (*In re* Parkwood, Inc.), 461 F.2d 158, 194 n.78 (D.C. Cir. 1971); Lyles v. Union Planters Nat'l Bank, 393 S.W.2d 867 (Ark. 1965); People v. Fairfax Family Fund, Inc., 47 Cal. Rptr. 812 (Cal. Ct. App. 1964) (interstate commerce analysis), *appeal dismissed*, 382 U.S. 1 (1965); Johnson v. Ronamy Consumer Credit Corp., 515 A.2d 682 (Del. 1986); HIMC Inv. Co. v. Siciliano, 246 A.2d 502 (N.J. Super. Ct. Law Div. 1968); Oxford Consumer Discount Co. v. Stefanelli, 246 A.2d 460 (N.J. Super. Ct. App. Div. 1968), *supplemental op. at* 250 A.2d 593, *modified and aff'd*, 262 A.2d 874 (N.J. 1970), *appeal dismissed*, 400 U.S. 808, 923 (1970); State *ex rel.* Meierhenry v. Spiegel, Inc., 277 N.W.2d 298 (S.D. 1979), *appeal dismissed*, 444 U.S. 804 (1979); Whitaker v. Spiegel, Inc., 623 P.2d 1147 (1981), *amended*, 637 P.2d 235 (Wash. 1981), *appeal dismissed*, 454 U.S. 958 (1981).

380 Restatement of Conflict of Laws 2d § 188.

381 *See* § 3.8.5, *infra*.

382 *See* Oxford Consumer Discount Co. v. Stefanelli, 246 A.2d 460 (N.J. Super. Ct. App. Div. 1968), *supplemental op. at* 250 A.2d 593, *modified and aff'd*, 262 A.2d 874 (N.J. 1970), *appeal dismissed*, 400 U.S. 808, 923 (1970); Whitaker v. Spiegel, Inc., 623 P.2d 1147, *amended*, 637 P.2d 235 (Wash. 1981), *appeal dismissed*, 454 U.S. 958 (1981). *See also* Johnson v. Ronamy Consumer Credit Corp., 515 A.2d 682 (Del. 1986) (Delaware's law applies because it has interest in preventing predatory second mortgage lending). *See generally* R. Leflar, *Choice-Influencing Considerations in Conflicts Law*, 41 N.Y.U. L. Rev. 267 (1966).

most significant relationship to the parties and the transaction should apply,[383] such as where the contract requires repayment to be made.[384] But this choice of law rule often does not apply for general usury statutes, at least in the commercial context.

While a minority of courts also follow the most significant relationship approach for general usury cases,[385] the majority rule concerning *general* usury statutes is that the law of the state with the highest usury cap applies, as long as the state that has some substantial relationship to the transaction, even if it does not have the most significant relationship.[386] Similarly, where a loan exceeds both states' general usury caps, some courts will use the same standard to pick the state with the weakest remedy for the usury violation.[387] (These rules though generally do not apply to special usury statutes.[388])

An explanation for this special rule for general usury statutes is that commercial cases dominate conflicts between states' usury laws, and courts bend over backwards to uphold credit contracts in commercial cases, provided that the contracts bear some reasonable relationship to a state under whose laws they are legal.[389] This proclivity should not apply to consumer transactions and commercial usury precedent should be largely inapplicable. There are special public policy arguments that support application of a particular state's consumer usury law that may be inapplicable to a commercial usury law.[390]

Nevertheless, the majority rule is succinctly stated in *Restatement of Conflict of Laws* § 203:

> The validity of a contract will be sustained against the charge of usury if it provides for a rate of interest that is permissible in a state to which the contract has a substantial relationship and is not greatly in excess of the rate permitted by the general usury law of the state of the otherwise applicable law. . . .[391]

Many states follow this rule or a variant of it.[392] A court will apply the state's law with the highest cap if the state has a substantial relationship to the transaction and that rate is not greatly in excess of the other state's rate. Such factors are not matters of law, but rather issues of fact requiring evidentiary hearings.[393]

The *Restatement*'s formula will not apply if a statute in the forum state overrides these principles and dictates the choice of law.[394] In addition, more traditional conflict of law analysis may be applied to challenges to credit charges that are based on grounds other than usury, such as UDAP violations, breach of contract, or breach of the duty of good faith.[395]

Uniform Commercial Code (UCC) § 1-301 provides that if there is no choice of law clause, the court is to apply the forum state's UCC law to transactions bearing "an appropriate relation" to the forum state.[396] Most usury cases apply the *Restatement*'s choice of law rules rather than the UCC's. Nonetheless, a number of cases apply the UCC choice of law rules to usury questions when the transaction involves a negotiable instrument or a contract governed by the UCC.[397]

### 3.8.5.2 Substantial Relationship Test Under the *Restatement of Conflict of Laws*

The *Restatement* test for general usury statutes requires a "substantial relationship" between the contract and the state whose laws are adopted (i.e., the state with the highest usury ceiling). The comments to Restatement § 203 suggest that a "substantial" relationship requires a "normal and natural" relationship to the contract and parties, which "is unlikely to be based solely upon contacts purposely located in . . . [a] . . . state . . . in an attempt to gain the benefit of that state's usury statute."[398] The borrower's state of residence has a substantial

383 Restatement of Conflict of Laws 2d § 188.

384 Restatement of Conflict of Laws 2d § 195. *See* Shannon-Vail Five Inc. v. Bunch, 270 F.3d 1207 (9th Cir. 2001) (law of place of performance applies unless location of repayment was selected to circumvent usury laws or has a very tangential relation to the contract); C.I.O.S. Found. v. Berkston Ins. A.V.V., 2000 U.S. Dist. LEXIS 2337 (N.D. Miss. Feb. 1, 2000).

385 *See, e.g.*, Am. Equities Group, Inc. v. Ahava Dairy Prods. Corp., 2004 WL 870260 (S.D.N.Y. Apr. 23, 2004); U.S. Trust Co. v. LTV Steel Co. (*In re* Chateaugay Corp.), 150 B.R. 529 (Bankr. S.D.N.Y. 1993), *aff'd*, 170 B.R. 551 (S.D.N.Y. 1994); Marder v. Levin, 664 N.Y.S.2d 344 (N.Y. App. Div. 1997); Commercial Credit Corp. v. West, 677 S.W.2d 669 (Tex. App. 1984).

386 Restatement of Conflict of Laws 2d § 203 cmt. c. *See In re* Wright, 256 B.R. 626 (Bankr. D. Mont. 2000) (comparing § 188 to § 203). *But see* Rieser v. Todd (*In re* Chari), 2005 WL 4030034 (Bankr. S.D. Ohio Sept. 2, 2005) (applying § 188 to usury issue).

387 *See, e.g.*, W. Heller & Co. v. Chopp-Wincraft Printing Specialties, 587 F. Supp. 557 (S.D.N.Y. 1982) (choice of law favors lightest penalty for credit sale disguised as lease); Wood v. Sadler, 468 P.2d 42 (Idaho 1970). *But see* Speare v. Consolidated Assets Corp., 367 F.2d 208 (2d Cir. 1966) (criticizing approach of seeking out lower penalties).

388 *See* § 3.8.4, *infra*.

389 *See* Continental Mortgage Investors v. Sailboat Key, Inc., 395 So. 2d 507 (Fla. 1981) (stressing commercial setting of case).

390 *See* Continental Mortgage Investors v. Sailboat Key, Inc., 395 So. 2d 507 (Fla. 1981); State *ex rel.* Meierhenry v. Spiegel, Inc., 277 N.W.2d 298 (S.D. 1979), *appeal dismissed*, 444 U.S. 804 (1979).

391 Restatement of Conflict of Laws 2d § 203 (ALI 1971).

392 *See* Superior Funding Corp. v. Big Apple Capital Corp., 738 F. Supp. 1468 (S.D.N.Y. 1990).

393 *In re* Rexplore, Inc. Sec. Litig., 685 F. Supp. 1132 (N.D. Cal. 1988) (California law); Mencor Enters., Inc. v. Hets Equities Corp., 235 Cal. Rptr. 464 (Cal. Ct. App. 1987).

394 *See* § 3.8.3, *supra*.

395 *See* Washington Mut. Bank v. Superior Court, 15 P.3d 1071 (Cal. 2001) (challenge to forced placement of insurance at excessive rates).

396 U.C.C. § 1-105.

397 *See, e.g.*, Admiral Ins. Co. v. Brinkcraft Dev., Ltd., 921 F.2d 591 (5th Cir. 1991); Davidson Oil Country Supply Co. v. Klockner, Inc., 908 F.2d 1238 (5th Cir. 1990); Woods-Tucker Leasing Corp. of Ga. v. Hutcheson-Ingram Dev. Co., 642 F.2d 744 (5th Cir. 1981); Jett Racing & Sales, Inc. v. Transamerica Commercial Fin. Corp., 892 F. Supp. 161 (S.D. Tex. 1995); Nevins v. Tinker, 429 N.E.2d 332 (Mass. 1981).

398 Restatement of Conflict of Laws 2d § 203 cmt. c. *See also* A. Conner General Contracting, Inc. v. Rols Capital Co., 535 N.Y.S.2d 420 (N.Y. App. Div. 1988) (if New York partnership only nominally operating in New Jersey to avoid New York usury laws, New Jersey has no significant contacts).

relationship to the contract, as does the state where the loan is to be repaid.[399]

The *Restatement* suggests that other "significant" contacts, such as the place where the loan was made, the lender's principal place of business, and the place where the contract was principally negotiated, as well as "lesser" contacts such as the place where the note was drawn and dated, the place where the money is to be used, and the situs of land given as security, may not individually constitute a substantial relationship, but may do so in conjunction with other contacts.[400] When there is doubt, courts considering conflict issues in usury cases tend to find such a substantial relationship where application of that state's usury laws would uphold the disputed contract.[401]

### 3.8.5.3 The *Restatement's* "Not Greatly in Excess" Requirement; Public Policy Considerations

The second limitation on the *Restatement's* rule adopting the general usury statute of the state that would uphold a contract is concern that such a rule undermines the public policy of the state whose laws are not followed. Generally, state courts have not found the application of a sister state's usury law to violate public policy.[402] But public policy does underpin the *Restatement's* rule that the law of a higher-rate state is to be used only if the resulting contract rate is not greatly in excess of the ceiling in the state whose laws would normally apply.[403]

Since Restatement § 203 requires a comparison between the rate charged and the rate permitted by the law of the state that would be "otherwise applicable," the court must determine which state's law would normally apply to the transaction.[404] This requires an analysis of which state has the "most significant relationship" to the transaction.[405] After this analysis, the court will be in a position to compare the law of the high-rate state with the law that would normally apply.

Some idea of what is meant by greatly in excess is found in the *Restatement's* comments: "[o]rdinarily, the permissible rate of interest will vary only slightly from state to state," and that, therefore, applying the law of the high-rate state "can hardly affect adversely the interests of another state when the stipulated interest is only a few percentage points higher than would be permitted by the local law . . ."[406] A number of decisions that uphold contracts explicitly rely on the fact that the interest rate was only slightly higher than that allowed by the state whose law would normally apply.[407]

However, in the current partially deregulated market, in which some states maintain usury ceilings and others have none, the "not greatly in excess" language becomes a significant limitation on the scope of the basic rule.[408] In addition, if the contract provides for a variable rate which has the potential to exceed the local rate by a substantial amount, the local law may be enforced even though the actual rate charged under the contract only slightly exceeds the local usury ceiling.[409] Public policy concerns may also dominate if the otherwise permissible interest rate shocks the conscience of the court.[410]

399 *See, e.g.*, Direct Mail Specialist, Inc. v. Brown, 673 F. Supp. 1540 (D. Mont. 1987) (law of place where note is payable applies); Acorn Partners II v. Kiley, 597 N.Y.S.2d 63 (N.Y. App. Div. 1993).

400 Restatement of Conflict of Laws 2d § 203 cmt. c.

401 *See, e.g.*, McHenry Cty. Credit Co. v. Feuerhelm, 720 F.2d 525 (8th Cir. 1983); Tiffany Indus. v. Commercial Grain Bin Co., 714 F.2d 799 (8th Cir. 1983); Bice Constr. v. CIT Corp., 700 F.2d 465 (8th Cir. 1983); International City Bank v. Morgan Walton Properties, Inc., 675 F.2d 666 (5th Cir. 1982); Lockwood Corp. v. Black, 669 F.2d 324 (5th Cir. 1982); Roofing & Sheet Metal Serv. v. La Quinta Motor Inns, 689 F.2d 982 (11th Cir. 1982); Federal Deposit Ins. Corp. v. Lattimore Land Corp., 656 F.2d 139 (5th Cir. 1981); Weiss v. Federal Deposit Ins. Corp., 654 F.2d 453 (6th Cir. 1981); L'Arbalete, Inc. v. Zaczac, 474 F. Supp. 2d 1314 (S.D. Fla. 2007); *In re* Crabtree, 48 B.R. 528 (Bankr. E.D. Tenn. 1985); Easton State Bank v. Winn, 19 B.R. 218 (Bankr. E.D. Ark. 1982); GiantValley v. Meneley Motors, 14 B.R. 457 (Bankr. D. Nev. 1981); Stacey v. St. Charles Custom Kitchens, 683 S.W.2d 225 (Ark. 1985); Grogg v. Colley Home Ctr., Inc., 671 S.W.2d 733 (Ark. 1984); McMillen v. Winona Nat'l & Sav. Bank, 648 S.W.2d 460 (Ark. 1983) (accepted seller financing in Minnesota, where note not usurious); Snow v. CIT Corp., 647 S.W.2d 465 (Ark. 1983); Peragallo v. Sklat, 466 A.2d 1200 (Conn. Super. Ct. 1983); Finance Am. Corp. v. Moyler, 494 A.2d 926 (D.C. Ct. App. 1985); Morgan Walton Properties, Inc. v. International City Bank & Trust, 404 So. 2d 1059 (Fla. 1981); Nevins v. Tinker, 429 N.E.2d 332 (Mass. 1981); Burrill v. First Nat'l Bank of Shawnee Mission, 668 S.W.2d 116 (Mo. Ct. App. 1984); Mostek Corp v. Chemetron Corp., 642 S.W.2d 20 (Tex. App. 1982); Hammel v. Ziegler Fin. Corp., 334 N.W.2d 913 (Wis. Ct. App. 1983).

402 *See, e.g.*, L'Arbalete, Inc. v. Zaczac, 474 F. Supp. 2d 1314 (S.D. Fla. 2007); Gamer v. duPont Walston, Inc., 135 Cal. Rptr. 230 (Cal. Ct. App. 1976); Ury v. Jewelers Acceptance Corp., 38 Cal. Rptr. 376 (Cal. Ct. App. 1964); Santoro v. Osman, 174 A.2d 800 (Conn. 1961); Continental Mortgage Investors v. Sailboat Key, Inc., 395 So. 2d 507 (Fla. 1981); Big Four Mills, Ltd. v. Commercial Credit Co., 211 S.W.2d 831 (Ky. 1948); Kronovet v. Lipchin, 415 A.2d 1096 (Md. 1980); Exchange Bank & Trust Co. v. Tamerius, 265 N.W.2d 847 (Neb. 1978); Grady v. Denbech, 251 N.W.2d 864 (Neb. 1977); Ferdie Sievers & Lake Tahoe Land Co. v. Diversified Mortgage Investors, 603 P.2d 270 (Nev. 1979).

403 Restatement of Conflict of Laws 2d § 203. *See Id.* § 203 cmt. b (discussing the interests of states in enacting usury laws to protect debtors against extortion).

404 Shannon-Vail Five Inc. v. Bunch, 270 F.3d 1207 (9th Cir. 2001) (finding the high-rate state to be the state with the most substantial relationship to the transaction, thereby making analysis under § 203 unnecessary).

405 Restatement of Conflict of Laws 2d §§ 188, 195.

406 Restatement of Conflict of Laws 2d § 203 cmt. b.

407 Peragallo v. Sklat, 466 A.2d 1200 (Conn. Super. Ct. 1983); Shull v. Dain, Kalman & Quail, Inc., 267 N.W.2d 517 (Neb. 1978).

408 *See, e.g.*, Securities & Exch. Comm'n v. Elmas Trading Corp., 683 F. Supp. 743 (D. Nev. 1987) (500% return wildly in excess of the 13% return allowed under Arkansas law), *aff'd*, 865 F.2d 265 (9th Cir. 1988) (table); North Am. Bank, Ltd. v. Schulman, 474 N.Y.S.2d 383 (N.Y. Co. Ct. 1984) (court might allow "somewhat higher ceiling," but will not apply law of jurisdiction that has rejected usury laws altogether).

If the contract rate exceeded that permitted by local law by only a small amount, the absence of any ceiling in another state would not seem to invoke the "not greatly in excess" exception. *See* Restatement of Conflict of Laws 2d § 203 cmt. a.

409 *See* O'Brien v. Shearson, Hayden, Stone, Inc., 586 P.2d 830 (1978), *on reconsideration* 605 P.2d 779 (Wash. 1980).

410 Trinidad Indus. Bank v. Romero, 466 P.2d 568 (N.M. 1970). *Cf.* Ferdie Sievers & Lake Tahoe Land Co. v. Diversified Mortgage

### 3.8.6 Military Small Loan Companies

Lenders may target personnel at military bases who are not legal residents of the state where the base is located. Since many state credit laws apply only to state residents, these lenders argue that those laws do not apply, allowing the lender to export interest rates and credit regulation of the state where the lender is headquartered or licensed.

The Eighth Circuit held that the forum state could not enforce its small loan laws against such a lender making loans to military personnel whose residences were out of state. The forum state's interest in protecting non-residents from usurious rates and oppressive lending was insufficient to outweigh the burden on interstate commerce.[411] After this decision, many state regulators issued opinion letters stating that their state credit laws did not apply to military lenders who made loans to non-resident military personnel.[412]

Some regulators, however, have refused to exempt military lenders from their laws when the lender has a significant state presence, even if it is only lending to non-resident military.[413] Moreover, the lender's representation that it only lends to non-resident military personnel may be spurious.

The federal Military Lending Act addresses this loophole in state lending laws,[414] prohibiting different treatment under state law of servicemembers and dependents from other state residents. The Act gives the Department of Defense (DOD) authority to issue implementing regulations. Unfortunately, those regulations limit many of the Act's protections by defining "consumer credit" covered by the Act to include only payday loans, auto title loans, and refund anticipation loans.[415]

Nevertheless, it is unclear whether DOD's limitation as to "consumer credit" restricts the scope of the Act's discriminatory treatment provision, because that provision does not use the term "consumer credit." Whereas the Act's 36% interest rate cap and other provisions apply only to transactions within the narrow scope of "consumer credit," the different treatment provision refers instead only to "loans" and "consumer lending protections."

> States shall not—
>
> (A) authorize creditors to charge covered members and their dependents annual percentage rates of interest for loans higher than the legal limit for residents of the State; or
>
> (B) permit violation or waiver of any State consumer lending protections for the benefit of residents of the State on the basis of nonresident or military status of a covered member or dependent of such a member, regardless of the member's or dependent's domicile or permanent home of record.[416]

Subsection (A), *supra*, does refer to "creditors," and "creditors" is defined with reference to "consumer credit."[417] But subsection (B), *supra*, does not refer to creditors or to consumer credit.

## 3.9 Which Usury Statute in the Applicable State Applies?

### 3.9.1 Substance Rather Than Form Controls; Opting In

Once it is determined which state's law applies to a transaction, the next step is to determine under state law which statute in that state is applicable, because most states have a number of different statutes regulating credit. In determining the applicable statute, the creditor's characterization of the loan's nature is not always controlling. For example, credit sales may be disguised as loans to take advantage of higher rates; loans may be disguised as sale-repurchase or sale-leaseback transactions; or closed-end credit may be designated as open-end. Courts look behind the face of documents to ascertain the actual nature of the transaction; substance, not form dictates what statute governs.[418]

---

Investors, 603 P.2d 270 (Nev. 1979) (contract rate not sufficient to shock conscience of court).

411 Pioneer Military Lending, Inc. v. Manning, 2 F.3d 280 (8th Cir. 1993). *See also* Pioneer Military Lending, Inc. v. DuFauchard, 2006 WL 2053486 (E.D. Cal. July 21, 2006).

412 *See* Pioneer Military Lending, Inc. v. DuFauchard, 2006 WL 2053486, at *3 n.5 (E.D. Cal. July 21, 2006) (stating that more than twenty-five states adopted rationale of Pioneer Military Lending v. Manning).

413 *See* Brack v. Omni Loan Co., Ltd., 80 Cal. Rptr. 3d 275, 278 (Cal. Ct. App. 2008) (quoting regulator's letter declining to exempt Omni from licensing requirements: "Under the [Finance Lenders Law], California has a number of state interests in licensing finance lending activities beyond the protection of its citizens; therefore, any expansion of the business presence and business activities in California related to loans to non-resident military personnel could impact the state's interests and thus the Department would require licensure under the [Finance Lenders Law]").

414 10 U.S.C. § 987(d)(2). The law was an amendment to the John Warner National Defense Authorization Act for Fiscal Year 2007, but it is commonly referred to as the Talent-Nelson Military Lending Act (MLA).

415 72 Fed. Reg. 50,580 (Aug. 31, 2007), *codified at* 32 C.F.R. pt. 232. *See generally* § 2.2.5, *supra* (detailed discussion of Military Lending Act).

416 10 U.S.C. § 987(d)(2)(A), (B).

417 The statute defines "creditor" as "one who is engaged in the business of extending consumer credit." 10 U.S.C. § 987(i)(5). And the regulations add "with respect to a consumer credit transaction covered by this part." 32 C.F.R. § 232.3(e).

418 *See, e.g.*, Easter v. Am. West Fin., 381 F.3d 948 (9th Cir. 2004); ECE Technologies, Inc. v. Cherrington Corp., 168 F.3d 201 (5th Cir. 1999); Aaron v. Mattikow, 146 F. Supp. 2d 263 (E.D.N.Y. 2001), *aff'd*, 2003 WL 1973353 (2d Cir. Apr. 22, 2003) (table); Cashback Catalog Sales v. Price, 102 F. Supp. 2d 1375 (S.D. Ga. 2000); Hamilton v. York, 987 F. Supp. 953 (E.D. Ky. 1997); Khalif v. Khalif, 308 B.R. 614 (Bankr. N.D. Ga. 2004); Brown v. Courtesy Consumer Discount Co., 134 B.R. 134 (Bankr. E.D. Pa. 1991); Carter v. Four Seasons Funding Corp., 97 S.W.3d 387, 395 (Ark. 2003); Luebbers v. Money Store, Inc., 40 S.W.3d 745 (Ark. 2001); McElroy v. Grisham, 810 S.W.2d 933 (Ark. 1991); Smith v. Eisen, 97 Ark. App. 130 (Ark. Ct. App. 2006); Ghirardo v. Antonioli, 883 P.2d 960 (Cal. 1994); Sheehy v. Franchise Tax Bd., 100 Cal. Rptr. 2d 760 (Cal. Ct. App. 2000);

On the other hand, a creditor may be stuck with its characterization of a loan where the creditor so describes the transaction's nature to the consumer's benefit. A creditor may "opt in," or provide by contract that a specific regulatory statute will apply to the transaction, even though it would, in absence of that contractual provision, fall outside the scope of that statute. For example, a business-purpose loan may become subject to a consumer credit code, though otherwise excluded, because the contract so provides.[419] If the creditor opts in, as a matter of contract law, it then must comply with the requirements of that statute.

This rule applies only where a creditor alters the nature of the loan for the *consumer's benefit*. Thus an unlicensed lender cannot acquire the right to charge a higher interest rate allowed to licensed creditors by including a clause in its adhesion contract that the parties agree the transaction will be governed by that statute.[420]

## 3.9.2 Is the Loan for Consumer or Business Purposes?

### 3.9.2.1 General

Usury laws frequently distinguish business from consumer credit, allowing higher interest rates or completely eliminating usury ceilings for business transactions. The distinction may be accomplished by limiting the scope of a usury law to "consumer" credit. For example, the Uniform Consumer Credit Code applies only to credit extended "primarily for a personal, family, household, or agricultural purpose."[421]

More frequently, business loans are treated as a specific exception to a usury law which would cover business transactions but for the exclusion. Under such a statutory scheme, the precise language of the usury exception is critical. The exception may be limited to corporate loans, or might include partnerships, joint ventures, or individuals seeking credit for business purposes.[422] In California, a loan to a borrower who has assets over $2 million is exempt from the state constitution's usury ceiling if the borrower has a preexisting relationship with the lender or the lender and the borrower are financially sophisticated.[423] Yet another statutory approach is to limit the power of a company to assert usury as a claim or defense.[424]

Business credit may be excluded from some of a statute's provisions, but not from others. In Pennsylvania, residential mortgage transactions with a business purpose are exempted from the rate cap, but other provisions apply, such as the prohibition against prepayment penalties.[425]

Business exceptions in usury statutes may be written to apply only to loans over a set principal amount, on the assumption that businesses obtaining larger loans have the wherewithal to protect themselves from bad bargains.[426] Business or corporate exceptions can also be drafted so that the usury statute still

Hernandez v. Atlantic Fin., 164 Cal. Rptr. 279 (Cal. Ct. App. 1980); Browner v. District of Columbia, 549 A.2d 1107, 1114 (D.C. App. Ct. 1988); Pinchuck v. Canzoneri, 920 So. 2d 713 (Fla. Dist. Ct. App. 2006); Oregrund Ltd. P'ship v. Sheive, 873 So. 2d 451, 457 (Fla. Dist. Ct. App. 2004); Low Cost Auto Pawn, Inc. v. Greco, 851 So. 2d 768 (Fla. Dist. Ct. App. 2003); Party Yards, Inc. v. Templeton, 751 So. 2d 121 (Fla. Dist. Ct. App. 2000); Antonelli v. Neumann, 537 So. 2d 1027 (Fla. Dist. Ct. App. 1988); Bankwest, Inc. v. Oxendine, 598 S.E.2d 343 (Ga. Ct. App. 2004); Williams v. Powell, 447 S.E.2d 45 (Ga. Ct. App. 1994); Jackson v. Commercial Credit Corp., 83 S.E.2d 76 (Ga. Ct. App. 1954); Bednar v. Provident Bank, 937 A.2d 210 (Md. 2007); Wilcox v. Moore, 93 N.W.2d 288 (Mich. 1958); Aple Auto Cash Express of Okla., Inc. v. State *ex rel.* Oklahoma Dep't of Consumer Credit, 78 P.3d 1231 (Okla. 2003); Income Tax Buyers, Inc. v. Hamm, 1992 WL 12092431 (S.C. Com. Pleas Jan. 14, 1992); Pacific E. Corp. v. Gulf Life Holding Co., 902 S.W.2d 946 (Tenn. Ct. App. 1995); Sturm v. Muens, 224 S.W.3d 758, 764 (Tex. App. 2007); Swank v. Sverdlin, 121 S.W.3d 785 (Tex. App. 2003); Bantuelle v. Williams, 667 S.W.2d 810 (Tex. App. 1983); Kjar v. Brimley, 497 P.2d 23, 25 (Utah 1972); Zachman v. Whirlpool Acceptance Corp., 841 P.2d 27 (Wash. 1992). *Cf.* First USA Mgmt., Inc. v. Esmond, 960 S.W.2d 625 (Tex. 1997) (substance rather than form controls, but arrangement here did not create usurious interest). *See generally* Singer & Singer, 3A Sutherland Statutory Construction § 70.7 (7th ed. 2010); 44B Am. Jur. 2d *Interest and Usury* § 84 (2007); 47 C.J.S. *Interest and Usury; Consumer Credit* § 144 (2005).

419 *See, e.g.*, Mack Fin. Corp. v. Crossley, 550 A.2d 303 (Conn. 1988); First Northwestern Nat'l Bank v. Crouch, 287 N.W.2d 151 (Iowa 1980); Farmers State Bank v. Haflich, 699 P.2d 553 (Kan. 1985); Kan. Bank & Trust Co. v. Rixner, 610 P.2d 116 (Kan. Ct. App. 1980), *aff'd*, 619 P.2d 1156 (Kan. 1980); Bank of Barron v. Gieske, 485 N.W.2d 426 (Wis. Ct. App. 1992).

420 *See* Floyd v. Baton Rouge Sash & Door Co., 502 So. 2d 1073 (La. 1987).

421 U.C.C.C. §§ 2.104, 2.106, 3.104 (1968); U.C.C.C. §§ 1.301(12), 1.301(14), 1.301(15) (1974). *See also* Edwards v. Alabama Farm Bureau Mut. Cas. Ins. Co., 453 So. 2d 746 (Ala. Ct. App. 1983) (definition of consumer credit transaction under Alabama "Mini-Code"); *See generally* Hall v. Owen Cty. State Bank, 370 N.E.2d 918 (Ind. Ct. App. 1978); Decision Point, Inc. v. Reece & Nichols Realtors, Inc., 144 P.3d 706 (Kan. 2006); Bill Brown Mfg. Inc. v. Crane, 589 P.2d 708 (Okla. Civ. App. 1978).

422 *See, e.g.*, Bank of Am., N.A. v. Shelbourne Dev. Group, Inc., 732 F. Supp. 2d 809 (N.D. Ill. 2010) (Ill. statute excludes corporations); GWC Restaurants, Inc. v. Hawaiian Floor Mills, Inc., 691 F. Supp. 274 (D. Haw. 1988) (Hawaii statute excludes merchants); Havens v. Woodfill, 266 N.E.2d 221 (Ind. Ct. App. 1971) (discussing extension of corporate usury exemption to trusts, partnerships, joint ventures etc.); Walker, Tooke & Lyons v. Sapp, 862 So. 2d 414 (La. Ct. App. 2003) (exclusion for "commercial or business purposes"); Krause v. Griffis, 443 N.W.2d 444 (Mich. Ct. App. 1989) (business entity exception); Ludlum Corp. Pension Plan Trust v. Matty's Superservice, Inc., 548 N.Y.S.2d 292 (N.Y. App. Div. 1989) (usury exemption applied to a de facto corporation). *See also* Borowski v. Falleder, 744 N.Y.S.2d 177 (N.Y. App. Div. 2002) (corporation exception does not apply where loan to individual in personal capacity even if borrower owned a business and put the loan to corporate use).

423 Cal. Corp. Code § 25118. *See* Raceway Props., L.L.C. v. LSOF Carlsbad Land L.P., 157 Fed. Appx. 959 (9th Cir. 2005) (finding borrower to be financially sophisticated).

424 *See, e.g.*, Bridges Fin. Group, Inc. v. Beech Hill Co., 2010 WL 3946529 (D.N.J. Oct. 5, 2010); Sogeti, U.S.A., L.L.C. v. Whirlwind Bldg. Sys., Inc., 496 F. Supp. 2d 380, 382 (S.D.N.Y. 2007); Rieser v. Todd (*In re* Chari), 2005 WL 4030034 (Bankr. S.D. Ohio Sept. 2, 2005).

425 *In re* Jungkurth, 74 B.R. 323 (Bankr. E.D. Pa. 1987).

426 *See, e.g.*, *In re* Moorhous, 180 B.R. 138 (Bankr. E.D. Va. 1995) (Pa. law); *In re* Schlag, 60 B.R. 749 (Bankr. W.D. Pa. 1986); Tides Edge Corp. v. Central Fed. Sav., F.S.B., 542 N.Y.S.2d 763 (N.Y. App. Div. 1989); Smith v. Mitchell, 616 A.2d 17 (Pa. Super. Ct. 1992).

applies if the borrower is a close corporation with a small number of shareholders,[427] or where the incorporation looks to be an evasive device.[428]

In general, if a loan is usurious on its face, the lender has the burden of proving the business purpose, rather than the debtor having to prove a nonbusiness purpose.[429] The absence of an exemption to the usury statute is not an element of usury that the consumer must plead.[430]

### 3.9.2.2 Criteria for Business vs. Personal Purpose

Typically, loans used for direct investment or to finance a profit-making enterprise are business loans.[431] The absence of any profit-making enterprise suggests personal purposes,[432] but even if a borrower is engaged in a business, a loan has a non-business purpose if it is used primarily for medical expenses, household expenses, and other personal expenses.[433]

The borrower's intended purpose at the inception of the loan controls: a loan originally intended for business purposes does not lose that character if the borrower subsequently changes his mind and uses the proceeds for personal purposes.[434] On the other hand, the character of a loan may change upon refinancing.[435]

A contract to purchase land to live on is not a business transaction merely because the land had been classified as agricultural until the sale.[436] Smaller loans will more likely be treated as personal,[437] as will loans which are expected to be repaid through income unrelated to the loan.[438] Where the majority of a loan is for business purposes, it may have a business purpose even where a minority of the loan is for personal purposes.[439] Useful precedent can also be found in cases interpreting similar exclusions for Truth in Lending and other consumer protection statutes.[440]

### 3.9.2.3 Consumer's Incorporation or Affidavit of Business Purpose

Creditors may require borrowers to incorporate or sign affidavits of business purpose before credit is issued, so that business interest rates may be charged. A majority of courts follow what is sometimes called the New York rule that a lender can require a borrower to incorporate to receive a loan under a corporate usury exception, *provided that* the loan is made for a bona fide business purpose.[441] Incorporation of a true business operation is merely a matter of legal form, and requiring a business to incorporate to obtain a loan is an attempt to comply with usury statutes rather than an attempt to evade them. On the other hand, incorporation of individuals who have no bona fide business goals is a sham transaction which will not be recognized for usury purposes.[442]

Courts may also treat a loan as a legitimate business loan where the lender requires a major stockholder in a close corporation to give a personal guarantee of corporate debt before

---

427 *See* Federal Deposit Ins. Corp. v. Caledonia Inv. Corp., 725 F. Supp. 90, 92–93 (D. P.R. 1989).

428 *See, e.g.,* N.Y. Gen. Oblig. Law. § 5-521(2); Millerton Properties v. Brescia Ent., 584 N.Y.S.2d 660 (N.Y. App. Div. 1992). *See generally* § 3.9.2.3, *infra* (false contractual business purpose statements).

429 Hommel v. Thweatt, 834 P.2d 1058 (Wash. Ct. App. 1992); Marashi v. Lannen, 780 P.2d 1341 (Wash. Ct. App. 1989); Aetna Fin. Co. v. Darwin, 691 P.2d 581 (Wash. Ct. App. 1985).

430 Aetna Fin. Co. v. Darwin, 691 P.2d 581 (Wash. Ct. App. 1985).

431 *See, e.g.,* Whirlpool Fin. Corp. v. Sevaux, 96 F.3d 216 (7th Cir. 1996); *In re* LeBlanc, 622 F.2d 872 (5th Cir. 1980); Ross v. Lake Equity Fin. Co., 425 F.2d 1 (7th Cir. 1970); Allen v. Mainway Fin. Corp., 446 F. Supp. 26 (N.D. Ill. 1977); *In re* Stipetich, 294 B.R. 635 (Bankr. W.D. Pa. 2003) (Md. law); Briggs v. Capital Sav. & Loan Ass'n, 597 S.W.2d 600 (Ark. 1980); United Cent. Bank v. Kruse, 439 N.W.2d 849 (Iowa 1989); Krause v. Griffis, 443 N.W.2d 444 (Mich. Ct. App. 1989); Galloway v. Travelers Ins. Co., 515 So. 2d 678 (Miss. 1987); Selengut v. Ferrara, 496 A.2d 725 (N.J. Super. Ct. App. Div. 1985); Bollag v. Dresdner, 495 N.Y.S.2d 560 (N.Y.C. Civ. Ct. 1985); Pacesetter Real Estate, Inc. v. Fasules, 767 P.2d 961 (Wash. Ct. App. 1989); Conrad v. Smith, 712 P.2d 866 (Wash. Ct. App. 1986); Wayne Cty. Bank v. Hodges, 338 S.E.2d 202 (W. Va. 1985).

432 *See* Havens v. Woodfill, 266 N.E.2d 221 (Ind. Ct. App. 1971).

433 Decision Point, Inc. v. Reece & Nichols Realtors, Inc., 144 P.3d 706 (Kan. 2006).

434 Revocable Living Trust v. Wel-Co Group, Inc., 86 P.3d 818 (Wash. Ct. App. 2004); Jansen v. Nu-West, Inc., 6 P.3d 98 (Wash. Ct. App. 2000); Falk v. Riedel, 2000 Wash. App. LEXIS 1889 (Sept. 29, 2000); Hommel v. Thweatt, 834 P.2d 1058 (Wash. Ct. App. 1992). *See also In re* Stipetich, 294 B.R. 635 (Bankr. W.D. Pa. 2003) (Md. law).

435 *See* § 3.9.2.5, *infra*.

436 Beltz v. Dings, 6 P.3d 424 (Kan. Ct. App. 2000).

437 *Compare* Allen v. Mainway Fin. Corp., 446 F. Supp. 26 (N.D. Ill. 1977) ($100,000 loan size suggests business purpose), *with* Havens v. Woodfill, 266 N.E.2d 221 (Ind. Ct. App. 1971) (three separate $100 loans; concurrence suggests loan size indicates non-business purpose).

438 *See* Schneider v. Phelps, 359 N.E.2d 1361 (N.Y. 1977).

439 *See* Damron v. Associates Fin. Servs. Co., 701 So. 2d 1146 (Ala. Civ. App. 1997).

440 *See* National Consumer Law Center, Truth in Lending §§ 2.2.3, 2.4.2 (7th ed. 2010 and Supp.) (nevertheless, TILA excludes credit extended for agricultural purposes from its definition, unlike many state usury laws); National Consumer Law Center, Fair Debt Collection § 4.14.2 (6th ed. 2008 and Supp.); National Consumer Law Center, Unfair and Deceptive Acts and Practices § 2.1.8 (7th ed. 2008 and Supp.).

441 *See, e.g., In re* LeBlanc, 622 F.2d 872 (5th Cir. 1980); Briggs v. Capital Sav. & Loan Ass'n, 597 S.W.2d 600 (Ark. 1980); Jones v. Nelson, 432 N.W.2d 792 (Minn. Ct. App. 1988); Galloway v. Travelers Ins. Co., 515 So. 2d 678 (Miss. 1987); Schneider v. Phelps, 359 N.E.2d 1361 (N.Y. 1977); Jenkins v. Moyse, 172 N.E. 521 (N.Y. 1930); Republicbank Dallas NA v. Shook, 653 S.W.2d 278 (Tex. 1983); Skeen v. Glenn Justice Mortgage Co., 526 S.W.2d 252 (Tex. Civ. App. 1975).

442 *See, e.g.,* Sloan *ex rel.* Juergens v. Urban Title Servs., Inc., 652 F. Supp. 2d 51 (D.D.C. 2009) (fact question whether loan was a consumer loan disguised as a commercial loan); *In re* Seisay, 49 B.R. 354 (S.D.N.Y. 1985), *aff'd*, 1986 WL 2826 (S.D.N.Y. Feb. 28, 1986); *In re* King, 68 B.R. 569 (Bankr. D. Minn. 1986); Rutter v. Troy Mortgage Servicing Co., 377 N.W.2d 846 (Mich. Ct. App. 1985); Allan v. M&S Mortgage Co., 359 N.W.2d 238 (Mich. Ct. App. 1984); Schneider v. Phelps, 359 N.E.2d 1361 (N.Y. 1977); Essex v. Newman, 655 N.Y.S.2d 595 (N.Y. App. Div. 1997). *See also* Metcoff v. Mutual Trust Life Ins. Co., 339 N.E.2d 440 (Ill. App. Ct. 1975); Havens v. Woodfill, 266 N.E.2d 221 (Ind. Ct. App. 1971).

credit will be extended to the corporation. Courts generally uphold such requirements either on the grounds that guarantors fall within statutory corporate usury exceptions or on the broader grounds that guarantors as a group lack standing to assert usury.[443]

The breadth of the usury loophole created by the combination of the New York rule and the ability of creditors to obtain personal guarantees of business debt has lead a minority of courts, most notably New Jersey courts, to take a different approach. Under the New Jersey rule, whether a corporate loan is bona fide or merely a concealed individual loan is a question of fact which will not be determined merely by the existence of a business purpose.[444] The New Jersey rule gives more effect to the basic policy behind usury limitations and greater protection to small businesses at the price of some uncertainty about how any particular personally guaranteed business loan will be treated.

Lenders may require the borrower to represent that the loan is for business purposes, and normally such representations determine the loan's nature. But if the lender manipulated the loan's structure or rigged its documentation, then the borrower's subjective intent should be examined.[445] Borrowers' affidavits of business purpose are given effect where the lender had no reason to doubt that the loan was really a business loan.[446] Such affidavits have also been dispositive when the borrowers' oral representations were inconclusive.[447] However, statements or affidavits of business purposes that the lender knew or should have known to be false should be given no effect.[448]

### 3.9.2.4 Intermediaries

It is unclear whether borrowers who act as intermediaries for the true borrowers (typically for relatives who could not obtain a loan) have business purposes just because the true borrowers do.[449] However, a debtor who signs a genuine business purpose loan as surety is bound by the business characterization of the transaction just as the principal is.[450]

### 3.9.2.5 Refinancing

Whether loans refinancing preexisting business debts continue to be treated as business debts may depend upon a combination of the borrower's motivation in seeking the refinancing and what the lender knows of the borrower's purpose.

Some courts look at the "primary" purpose of the loan, and if the bulk of the proceeds are business-related, it will be considered a business loan.[451] Other courts make a determination after evaluating all the circumstances. If a delinquent business debt was secured by the borrower's residence, and refinancing seeks to prevent foreclosure on the home, of which the lender is aware, the second loan may be viewed as a personal loan.[452] Paying off a second mortgage personal loan

443 *See* § 7.7.1, *infra* (standing to assert usury). *But see* Trapp v. Hancuh, 530 N.W.2d 879 (Minn. Ct. App. 1995) rule regarding standing of guarantors not applicable where individual has direct and primary liability).

444 *See, e.g.*, Sun Bank of Tampa Bay v. Spigrin Properties, 469 So. 2d 240 (Fla. Dist. Ct. App. 1985) (sham incorporation of partnership); *In re* Greenberg, 121 A.2d 520 (N.J. 1956); Gelber v. Kugel's Tavern Inc., 89 A.2d 654 (N.J. 1952); Gottesfeld v. Kaminski, 524 A.2d 872 (N.J. Super. Ct. App. Div. 1987) (corporation set up by broker was shell); Walnut Discount Co. v. Weiss, 208 A.2d 26 (Pa. Super. Ct. 1965).

445 *Compare* Brown v. Giger, 757 P.2d 523 (Wash. 1988) (borrower signed documents stating specific business purpose), *with* Marashi v. Lannen, 780 P.2d 1341 (Wash. Ct. App. 1989) (borrowers' certificate stating business purpose in general, conclusory language was not dispositive).

446 *See, e.g.*, Anglin v. J&G Assocs., Consumer Cred. Guide (CCH) ¶ 96,677 (D.D.C. 1983); *In re* Stipetich, 294 B.R. 635 (Bankr. W.D. Pa. 2003) (Md. law); Briggs v. Capital Sav. & Loan Ass'n, 597 S.W.2d 600 (Ark. 1980); Revocable Living Trust v. Wel-Co Group, Inc., 86 P.3d 818 (Wash. Ct. App. 2004); Castronuevo v. General Acceptance Corp., 905 P.2d 387 (Wash. Ct. App. 1995); Stevens v. Security Pac. Mortgage Co., 768 P.2d 1007 (Wash. Ct. App. 1989); Conrad v. Smith, 712 P.2d 866 (Wash. Ct. App. 1986).

447 Falk v. Riedel, 2000 Wash. App. LEXIS 1889 (Sept. 29, 2000) (loan documents stated business purpose, and borrower's contrary evidence was unpersuasive); Marashi v. Lannen, 780 P.2d 1341, 1343 (Wash. Ct. App. 1989).

448 *See, e.g.*, Sheffield Commercial Corp. v. Clemente, 792 F.2d 282 (2d Cir. 1986); *In re* Seisay, 49 B.R. 354 (S.D.N.Y. 1985), *aff'd*, 1986 WL 2826 (S.D.N.Y. Feb. 28, 1986), *later opinion at* 61 B.R. 940 (Bankr. S.D.N.Y. 1986); Family Fed. Sav. & Loan v. Davis, 172 B.R. 437 (Bankr. D.D.C. 1994); *In re* King, 68 B.R. 569 (Bankr. D. Minn. 1986); Barco Auto Leasing Corp. v. House, 520 A.2d 162 (Conn. 1987); Commercial Mtg. & Fin. Co. v. Life Savs. of Am., 541 N.E.2d 661 (Ill. 1989); *In re* Estate of Backofen, 404 N.W.2d 675 (Mich. Ct. App. 1987); Thelma Sanders & Assoc. v. Friedman, 524 N.Y.S.2d 768 (N.Y. App. Div. 1988); Halco Fin. Servs., Inc. v. Foster, 770 S.W.2d 554 (Tenn. Ct. App. 1989); Brown v. Giger, 757 P.2d 523 (Wash. 1988); Jansen v. Nu-West, Inc., 6 P.3d 98 (Wash. Ct. App. 2000); McGovern v. Smith, 801 P.2d 250 (Wash. Ct. App. 1990); Marashi v. Lannen, 780 P.2d 1341 (Wash. Ct. App. 1989). *See also* Faison v. Nationwide Mortgage Corp., 839 F.2d 680 (D.C. Cir. 1987) ($100,000 damages for extracting a business purpose statement for loan without explaining that had the effect of depriving borrower of protections); Metcoff v. Mutual Trust Life Ins. Co., 339 N.E.2d 440 (Ill. App. Ct. 1975).

449 *Compare* Metcoff v. Mutual Trust Life Ins. Co., 339 N.E.2d 440 (Ill. App. Ct. 1975) (loan to parents was not a business loan), *with* Simpson v. Aetna Fin. Co., 523 N.E.2d 762 (Ind. Ct. App. 1988) (where parents gave loan proceeds to son for "investment," loan was for business purpose), *and* Brown v. Giger, 757 P.2d 523 (Wash. 1988) (loan was a business loan), *and* Castronuevo v. General Acceptance Corp., 905 P.2d 387 (Wash. Ct. App. 1995) (business loans where parents borrowed money to finance son's business ventures), *and* Conrad v. Smith, 712 P.2d 866 (Wash. Ct. App. 1986) (parents borrow money to start son in siding business).

450 *In re* Jungkurth, 74 B.R. 323 (Bankr. E.D. Pa. 1987); Simoni v. Time-Line, Ltd., 708 N.Y.S.2d 142 (N.Y. App. Div. 2000). *See also* Holland v. Michigan Nat'l Bank-West, 420 N.W.2d 173 (Mich. Ct. App. 1988); McGovern v. Smith, 801 P.2d 250 (Wash. Ct. App. 1990).

451 Toy Nat'l Bank v. McCarr, 286 N.W.2d 376 (Iowa 1979). *Accord In re* Stipetich, 294 B.R. 635 (Bankr. W.D. Pa. 2003) (Md. law).

452 *See* Anderson v. Lester, 382 So. 2d 1019 (La. Ct. App. 1980). *See also* National Consumer Law Center, Truth in Lending § 2.4.2.2.3 (7th ed. 2010 and Supp.). *Compare* McGovern v. Smith, 801 P.2d 250 (Wash. Ct. App. 1990) (a loan refinancing a business loan that is a personal obligation may not be for a business purpose), *and In re* Jackson, 42 B.R. 76 (Bankr. D.D.C. 1984) (consolidation loan of previous business debts by new creditor to prevent foreclosure on homes was not business debt), *with In re* Stipetich, 294 B.R. 635 (Bankr. W.D. Pa. 2003) (Md. law) (if purpose of original loan was

with proceeds of a loan specifically obtained to start a business has been held to be a business loan.[453]

### 3.9.3 Open-End vs. Closed-End Credit

Open-end credit is extended under a plan in which repeated transactions are contemplated. Credit cards and lines of credit are common examples of open-end credit. Closed-end credit examples include car loans and other installment sales. Where regulation of open-end credit is more favorable for a lender than closed-end, lenders may label as open-end what is really closed-end credit. This is called "spurious open-end credit."

Whether a lender's characterization of credit as open-end is legal will depend on a state statute's definition of open-end credit. Often the definition requires that repeated transactions be reasonably contemplated,[454] which is similar to the Truth in Lending Act standard.[455] For example, a credit seller of funeral goods and services cannot reasonably contemplate repeated transactions.[456]

One indication that repeat transactions are not contemplated is if there is a fixed due date to repay the extension of credit.[457] Another is if the maximum available line of credit approximates the initial purchase price. An extreme case would be where the initial extension is at the line's maximum, and the "minimum" monthly payments reduce the principal only minimally, leaving little room for an additional credit extension on the credit line.[458] The purchase of big ticket items, such as cars,[459] satellite dishes,[460] or furniture[461] financed by a supposed revolving line of credit may not meet the standard that repeated transactions are contemplated.

On the other hand, the Seventh Circuit held in the Truth in Lending context that repeated transactions could reasonably be contemplated where twenty percent of cardholders made additional purchases and the bank aggressively advertised repeat purchases.[462] Since the determination of whether repeat transactions are reasonably contemplated is uniquely within the competence of juries, plaintiffs who seek a trial on this issue should be granted one unless no rational jury could conclude that the lender acted unreasonably.[463]

Other indicia of a spurious open-end home equity loan include refinancing of closed-end loans into open-end or open-end into open-end, especially by the same creditor.[464] Additional indicia are a prepayment penalty;[465] a call provision;[466] or a term-limited draw provision coupled with a non-amortizing payment period.[467]

Other approaches to challenging spurious open-end credit are fraud and UDAP claims. For example in *Carlisle v. Whirlpool Fin. Nat'l Bank*,[468] the court upheld a jury award of $580

business, refinance is also business loan), *and* Jansen v. Nu-West, Inc., 6 P.3d 98 (Wash. Ct. App. 2000) (original purpose clings to transaction through all refinancings), *and* Conrad v. Smith, 712 P.2d 866 (Wash. Ct. App. 1986) (though purpose of refinancing was to prevent foreclosure, business characterization retained where borrower emphasized the business purpose). *Cf. In re* Jackson, 42 B.R. 76, 79–81 (Bankr. D.D.C. 1984) (discussing the lack of compelling authority on whether refinancing a business loan to save a home converts it to a personal loan).

453 Anderson v. Foothill Indus. Bank, 674 P.2d 232 (Wyo. 1984).

454 Groth Lumber Co. v. Dahl, 2006 WL 1738048 (Minn. Ct. App. June 27, 2006); Premier Fed. Credit Union v. Douglas, 465 S.E.2d 338 (N.C. Ct. App. 1996); Zachman v. Whirlpool Acceptance Corp., 841 P.2d 27 (Wash. 1992).

455 15 U.S.C. § 1602(i); Reg. Z § 226.2(a)(20). *See generally* National Consumer Law Center, Truth in Lending § 6.2 (7th ed. 2010 and Supp.).

456 *See, e.g.*, American Accounts Advisors, Inc. v. Hendrickson, 460 N.W.2d 83 (Minn. Ct. App. 1990).

457 Ag Acceptance Corp. v. Glinz, 684 N.W.2d 632 (N.D. 2004).

458 *See* American Accounts Advisors, Inc. v. Hendrickson, 460 N.W.2d 83 (Minn. Ct. App. 1990). *But see* Roper v. Associates Fin. Servs., 533 So. 2d 206 (Ala. 1988); Smith v. Citicorp Person-to-Person Fin. Ctrs., Inc., 477 So. 2d 308 (Ala. 1985).

459 Premier Fed. Credit Union v. Douglas, 465 S.E.2d 338 (N.C. Ct. App. 1996).

460 Perry v. Household Retail Servs., Inc., 953 F. Supp. 1370 (M.D. Ala. 1996), 180 F.R.D. 423 (M.D. Ala. 1998) (granting motion for class certification for TILA statutory damages), *rev'd. on reconsideration*, 119 F. Supp. 2d 1258 (M.D. Ala. 2000), *aff'd without op.*, 268 F.3d 1067 (11th Cir. 2001).

461 Wise Furniture v. Dehning, 343 N.W.2d 26 (Minn. 1984).

462 Benion v. Bank One, Dayton, 144 F.3d 1056 (7th Cir. 1998).

463 Long v. Fidelity Water Sys., Inc., 2000 U.S. Dist. LEXIS 3982 (N.D. Cal. Mar. 16, 2000); Maes v. Motivation for Tomorrow, Inc., 356 F. Supp. 47 (N.D. Cal. 1973); Premier Fed. Credit Union v. Douglas, 465 S.E.2d 338 (N.C. Ct. App. 1996).

464 Refinancing an open-end account is essentially an oxymoron. A consumer needing additional cash simply obtains a cash advance under the current account up to the credit line limit. There is no need to close one credit line and open another with a higher limit. The creditor could also raise the credit line limit to allow a borrower to finance any arrears. For example, under Truth in Lending § 1602(i), Congress intended that there be one plan under which repeated transactions occur. The repeated transactions include the financing of *new* purchases or *new* cash advances under the *same* account. To equate the concept of "repeated transactions" under one preexisting plan with refinancing is to obliterate all distinctions between open-end and closed-end loans.

465 Prepayment penalties are inconsistent with open-end credit, where borrowers can pay off the obligation immediately or over time. *See, e.g.*, Sears, Roebuck & Co. v. Oszajca (*In re* Oszajca), 207 B.R. 41, 47 (B.A.P. 2d Cir. 1997). "Prepaying" has no meaning since there is no fixed term.

466 A call provision gives the creditor the right to close the account and require payment of the balance for any or no reason even when the account is current. The call provision turns the concept of open-end lending on its head. Borrowers no longer have the right to repay over whatever period of time they choose.

467 Some equity line accounts contain a provision which limits the period during which a consumer can draw additional monies on the account to, e.g., the first ten years of the account. If the initial draw was equal or close to the account limit, it is very unlikely that the account would replenish itself through monthly payments so that a consumer could actually draw additional sums during the draw period. The replenishing aspect inherent in a true open-end transaction is absolutely eliminated where a limited draw provision is coupled with a required payment amount that does not result in the loan amortizing during the same time-frame.

468 Civ. Action No. CV-97-068, Clearinghouse No. 52,516 (Ala. Circuit Court, Hale County Aug. 25, 1999) (post-trial order).

Although the post-trial order is unreported, the jury's verdict is mentioned in Davis v. Carl Cannon Chevrolet-Olds, Inc., 182 F.3d 792, 799 n.3 (11th Cir. 1999).

million punitive damages, reduced to $300 million, grounded squarely upon fraud and deception.

In a twist, a lender may characterize open-end credit as closed-end to avoid state credit restrictions that are tougher on open-end credit. In one case, each time a consumer made a purchase by providing the account number, the company required the member to sign a new closed-end credit agreement. A court had little trouble finding this to be open-end credit.[469]

## 3.9.4 Loans vs. Credit Sales; Body-Dragging

A seller of goods or services offering financing with the sale is governed in most states by a retail installment sales act (RISA), even if the credit seller immediately assigns the obligation to a lender.[470] Where a consumer independently arranges a loan from a bank or other lender, even with the express purpose of purchasing goods or services, the transaction is typically governed by a separate statute applicable to direct consumer loans.[471]

A seller, instead of making a credit sale, may arrange for a loan directly with a lender connected to the seller. Sellers may have an incentive to structure the credit in this fashion where the state's direct loan legislation has a higher usury limit than the state's installment sales act.[472] In a classic scenario called "body-dragging," sellers—particularly used car dealers and home improvement contractors—take their buyer over to a finance company or other lender with whom they routinely do business. Instead of financing the purchase with an installment sales contract, the closely-connected lender writes a "direct, third-party loan" at a higher rate, the proceeds of which are used to pay off the seller.

Courts may find body-dragging to be an impermissible effort to evade the rate ceiling and other RISA requirements, and find the finance company's loan therefore usurious.[473] That is not always the case, however.[474]

## 3.9.5 Statutes Applying Only to Those "In the Business" of Extending Credit

Some state credit statutes apply only to lenders who extend credit with a certain frequency (e.g., who "regularly extend credit"[475]) or who are in the business of making loans. Lending is an integral part of the business of most lenders and credit sellers, so that this requirement only presents an issue where an individual or other entity infrequently makes loans. Someone who makes a single loan as an investment, or makes a loan to a friend, may not be considered to "regularly" extend credit, and therefore may fall outside the scope of a particular usury statute that so limits its scope.

On the other hand, a lender may be "in the business" if he makes only a single loan, at least if done as a business proposition as opposed to a personal accommodation for the borrower.[476] One court looked to a standard found in the federal Truth in Lending Act and a state counterpart and held that a creditor was "regularly engaged in the business of making loans" for the purposes of the state usury law if it made more than twenty-five loans, or more than five loans secured by a dwelling, in the preceding calendar year.[477]

469 State v. Allied Mktg. Group, 949 S.W.2d 816 (Tex. App. 1997).

470 *See, e.g.*, Bell v. Muller, 118 P.3d 405 (Wash. Ct. App. 2005).

If a sales transaction for some reason falls outside the scope of a RISA, the time-price usury exception may then come into play. *See, e.g.*, Southwest Concrete Co. v. Gosh Constr., 798 P.2d 1247 (Cal. 1990); Saul v. Midlantic Nat'l Bank/South, 572 A.2d 650 (N.J. Super. Ct. App. Div. 1990).

471 De La Rosa v. Western Funding, Inc., 24 P.3d 637 (Colo. App. 2001); Micro-Switch Employee's Credit Union v. Collier, 530 N.E.2d 595 (Ill. App. Ct. 1988); Collins v. Horizon Hous., Inc., 519 S.E.2d 534 (N.C. Ct. App. 1999). On the other hand, the Uniform Consumer Credit Code governing credit sales applies across the board to any type of creditor subject to the Act extending purchase-money credit.

472 In some circumstances, there may be a higher ceiling for credit sales than for certain loans, which creates an incentive to disguise the transaction as a credit sale. *See* De La Rosa v. Western Funding, Inc., 24 P.3d 637 (Colo. App. 2001).

473 Gonzalez v. Old Kent Mortgage Co., 2000 U.S. Dist. LEXIS 14530 (E.D. Pa. Sept. 19, 2000); Barber v. Fairbanks Capital Corp. (*In re Barber*), 266 B.R. 309 (Bankr. E.D. Pa. 2001); Brown v. Courtesy Consumer Discount Co., 134 B.R. 134 (Bankr. E.D. Pa. 1991); Hernandez v. Atlantic Fin., 164 Cal. Rptr. 279 (Cal. Ct. App. 1980). *See also* Johnson v. Household Mortgage Servs., 2004 WL 2188111 (E.D. Pa. Sept. 9, 2004); Prudential Dev. Co. Pension Plan Trust v. Rebector (*In re* Rebector), 208 B.R. 867 (W.D. Tex. 1997) (fact question as to borrower's understanding about whether home improvement company was financing the work as opposed to a third-party lender and as to whether she was offered a cash price and a credit price by the seller).

474 Kinzel v. Southview Chevrolet, 892 F. Supp. 1211 (D. Minn. 1995); Mullen v. Fifth Third Bank, 539 N.E.2d 683 (Ohio Ct. App. 1988); Briercroft Serv. Corp. v. de Los Santos, 776 S.W.2d 198 (Tex. App. 1988).

475 *See, e.g.*, Ala. Code § 5-19-1(3), *interpreted in In re* Crotzer, 147 B.R. 252 (Bankr. N.D. Ala. 1992) (creditor who extended real estate secured credit twenty-six times during the year prior to transaction and twenty-four times during the year of transaction, as shown by county records, fell within that definition); D.C. Mun. Regs. tit. 16, § 299; Iowa Code § 537.1301 (14)(a)(1) ("regularly engaged in the business of making loans"). *See also* Chen v. Bell-Smith, 768 F. Supp. 2d 121 (D.D.C. 2011).

476 *See, e.g.*, Gorman v. Marcon Capital Corp., 274 B.R. 351 (D. Vt. 2002) (out-of-state lender that proposed business loan to state resident was in business of making loans); Gottesfeld v. Kaminski, 524 A.2d 872, 875 (N.J. Super. Ct. App. Div. 1987). *See also In re* Rose, 266 B.R. 192 (Bankr. N.D. Cal. 2001) (lender who made 5 loans over ten years and two commercial loans within one-year period was engaged in the business). ***But see*** Rivera v. Schlick, 887 A.2d 492 (D.C. 2005) (lender was not in business of lending money so not covered by loan shark law even though he made three loans, where they were all part of a single real estate rehabilitation endeavor by a former business partner). ***But cf.*** White v. Coors Distrib. Co. (*In re* White), 260 B.R. 870 (B.A.P. 8th Cir. 2001) (company not in the business of purchasing installment contracts where its primary business was unrelated to financing but it had accepted assignment of three installment contracts from a related company).

477 Bunch v. Terpenning, 229 P.3d 574 (Okla. Civ. App. 2009).

## 3.9.6 Licensed Lenders

### 3.9.6.1 General

Credit statutes often apply to specific types of creditors, such as finance companies operating under small loan acts, pawnbrokers, insurance premium finance companies, home improvement sellers, and finance or motor vehicle sales finance companies. In many states, these creditors may not engage in their particular business without complying with state licensing or registration requirements, unless a statutory exemption applies.[478] Alternatively, the lender cannot take advantage of a higher rate ceiling available under a special usury law unless it is licensed and subjects itself to regulation and supervision.[479] There may also be a local ordinance that requires a license or permit.[480]

Unlicensed lenders cannot take advantage of higher-rate special usury statutes by use of a contractual clause providing that the parties agree that the transaction will be subject to such a statute.[481] Though the failure to obtain a license when necessary has serious ramifications for creditors, no license is required if the creditor is not engaging in regulated activity,[482] or if the entity does not fall within the scope of coverage of the statute in question.[483]

A number of licensing statutes require that licenses be posted at the place of business,[484] and a visit to the creditor's office will reveal the nature of the license. The same information can often be obtained by calling the state regulatory agency with supervisory authority under the applicable special usury act. Many agencies publish annual reports which list the names and addresses of licensees. Some post this information on their websites.

In states with both small loan and industrial loan acts, most finance companies will be licensed under both acts. Where a lender is a dual licensee, identifying the relevant statute will require a determination as to which hat the lender was wearing when writing the loan in question. Typically, the finance company will write a loan under whichever statute allows it the highest return. If the amount borrowed is under the small loan maximum, a lender typically writes the loan pursuant to its small loan license, as that license generally allows the highest yield to the creditor for that loan amount.

Special usury statutes governing licensed creditors usually specify the permissible terms of individual credit transactions and include significant penalties if they fail to obtain a required license or violate their licenses by ignoring statutory consumer protections. Licensees generally must comply with the statute's requirements in order to retain their licenses.[485] Since obtaining the requisite license may be a precondition to lending under some special usury statutes, failure to do so may give rise to a usury claim under the statute.[486] Moreover, the failure to obtain a license may itself void the transaction.[487]

The special licensing statute supplants the general usury statute where there is a conflict.[488] A licensed lender who engages in transactions outside the scope of the license may not be able to claim the exemption from the general usury law that the licensing statute creates, however.[489]

In Arizona, the legislature repealed the ceiling on interest rates in the general usury statute at the same time as it reenacted the Small Loan Act with its own rate ceilings. For a period of four years, until the legislature resolved the ambiguity,[490] this left the question whether lenders licensed under the Small Loan Act were bound by its interest rate ceilings or could take advantage of the unlimited interest rates permitted by the general usury statute. The Arizona Supreme Court concluded that the legislature would not have intended to do a futile act by reenacting a Small Loan Act that did not apply to any lenders, and held that licensees had to comply with the Small Loan Act ceilings.[491]

478 Special usury licensing statutes often exempt creditors subject to other regulatory statutes. Absent a specific statutory exception, such entities are not exempt from the licensing requirements. *In re* Parkwood, Inc., 461 F.2d 158 (D.C. Cir. 1971).

In fact a lender may have to comply with both its own licensing statute and the one governing the type of transaction at issue. *See* Attorney Gen. of Md. v. Equitable Trust, 450 A.2d 1273, 1285 (Md. Spec. Ct. App. 1982); Schmidt v. Beneficial Fin. Co., 400 A.2d 1124 (Md. Spec. Ct. App. 1979); Columbus Mortgage, Inc. v. Morton, 2007 WL 1748142 (Ohio Ct. App. June 19, 2007).

479 *See, e.g.*, Vt. Stat. Ann. tit 8, § 2201; Dep't of Banking v. NCAS of Del., L.L.C., 948 A.2d 752 (Pa. 2008); U.C.C.C. § 3.502 (1968); U.C.C.C. § 2.301 (1974).

480 Malish v. City of San Diego, 101 Cal. Rptr. 2d 18 (Cal. Ct. App. 2000); Circle D Pawn #2, Inc. v. Norman, 956 P.2d 931 (Okla. Civ. App. 1998).

481 Floyd v. Baton Rouge Sash & Door Co., 502 So. 2d 1073 (La. 1987).

482 Hernandez v. Atlantic Fin., 164 Cal. Rptr. 279 (Cal. Ct. App. 1980); Dilleree v. Devoe, 724 P.2d 171 (Mont. 1986); Albers v. Overland Nat'l Bank, 324 N.W.2d 396 (Neb. 1982); Pattavina v. Pignotti, 128 N.W.2d 817 (Neb. 1964).

483 *See, e.g.*, Casey v. Travelers, 531 So. 2d 846 (Ala. 1988); Goldstein v. Betty Ginsburg Interior Design, Inc., 519 So. 2d 645 (Fla. Dist. Ct. App. 1987); Terrebonne Bank & Trust Co. v. Lacombe, 464 So. 2d 753 (La. Ct. App. 1984); Eriksen v. Fisher, 421 N.W.2d 193 (Mich. Ct. App. 1988); First Nat'l Bank v. Dickinson, 308 N.W.2d 910 (Wis. Ct. App. 1981).

484 *See, e.g.*, Ohio Rev. Code Ann. § 1321.05 (West); Or. Rev. Stat. § 725.160; Vt. Stat. Ann. tit 8, § 2206.

485 *See, e.g.*, Iowa Code § 536.9; Ohio Rev. Code Ann. § 1321.08 (West); Vt. Stat. Ann. tit 8, § 2210; U.C.C.C. § 3.504 (1968); U.C.C.C. § 2.303 (1974).

486 *See* § 7.8.5.1, *infra*.

487 *See id.*

488 Benoit v. United Cos. Mortgage, 504 So. 2d 196 (Miss. 1987).

489 Agapitov v. Lerner, 133 Cal. Rptr. 2d 837 (Cal. Ct. App. 2003). *But cf.* Thrasher v. Homecomings Fin. Network, Inc., 838 A.2d 392 (Md. Spec. Ct. App. 2003) (interpreting statute to create private cause of action only against lender who is completely unlicensed, not one who makes loans at locations other than those allowed by the license).

490 In 1984, the legislature amended the Act to require all consumer lenders to be licensed and thus regulated by the Act. *See* Aros v. Beneficial Arizona, Inc., 977 P.2d 784, 785 n.1 (Ariz. 1999). The statute was rewritten again in 1997.

491 Aros v. Beneficial Arizona, Inc., 977 P.2d 784 (Ariz. 1999).

### 3.9.6.2 Licensing Requirement's Relationship to Assignees

In some states, finance companies or other entities which purchase retail installment contracts (but do not originate them) need not obtain a license.[492] However, licensure may be required if the assignee is in the business of taking assignments of such loans and directly collects the payments.[493] Generally, an assignee of a debt is subject to the same interest rate restrictions as the assignor.[494]

### 3.9.6.3 Creditor's Efforts to Evade Licensing Requirements

Creditors may seek to evade state credit requirements by arguing that they need not be licensed because they are making the type of loans prohibited for licensed lenders. That is, the creditor fails to obtain a license, makes loans of a type prohibited for licensed lenders, and argues that the license requirement does not apply because the creditor is making loans of a type prohibited for licensed lenders. Courts will not agree with this sophistry, since the creditor falls within the statute's explicit scope and the creditor is engaging in precisely the sort of evasion that the act was designed to prevent.[495]

Failure to obtain a license does not insulate the creditor from liability for such subterfuges, for the "inhibitory provisions" of special usury licensing statutes apply to both licensees and non-licensees.[496] Many versions of the state small loan acts and other credit statutes contain prohibitions against circumventing or evading the act, thus further weakening the creditor's argument.[497]

Other lenders may retain a small loan license for use with normal small loans, while creating a theoretically distinct corporate identity, unlicensed under the act, to make real estate secured loans. But small loan statutes often forbid licensees from conducting any unregulated business at their registered location unless authorized to do so by the regulatory agency. Such permission is not to be given if the nature of the other business would "conceal or facilitate violation or evasion" of the act.[498]

A lender may argue that no license is required because it is not regularly engaged in the business of making loans. Under New Jersey's Secondary Mortgage Act, however, making a single second mortgage loan "may constitute engaging in the secondary loan business."[499] The threshold number is larger in other states.[500]

Another argument to evade licensing requirements is that the originating lender is only table-funded by the true lender and is

492 *See, e.g.*, Niemiec v. NCO Fin. Sys., Inc., 2006 WL 1763643 (N.D. Ind. June 27, 2006); Ala. Code § 5-19-22; Farmer v. Hypo Holdings, Inc., 675 So. 2d 387 (Ala. 1996); Galatti v. Alliance Funding Co., 644 N.Y.S.2d 330 (N.Y. App. Div. 1996). *See also* (licensure requirement applies only if assignee is both in the business of taking assignments and undertaking direct collection of payments). *But see* Gaspard v. Vanguard Acceptance Corp., 689 So. 2d 1352 (La. 1997) (applying former La. Rev. Stat. § 6:951(9) (1985) which required the assignee of retail installment contracts to be licensed).

493 Walters v. PDI Mgmt. Servs., 2004 WL 2137513 (S.D. Ind. June 14, 2004), *modifying* 2004 WL 1622217 (S.D. Ind. Apr. 6, 2004); Rainey v. National Check Bur., Inc., 849 N.E.2d 776 (Ind. Ct. App. 2006).

494 Olvera v. Blitt & Gaoines, P.C., 431 F.3d 285 (7th Cir. 2005); Niemiec v. NCO Fin. Sys., Inc., 2006 WL 1763643 (N.D. Ind. June 27, 2006); PRA III v. Hund, 846 N.E.2d 965 (Ill. App. Ct. 2006).

495 Rhodes v. City of Hartford, 513 A.2d 124, 126 (Conn. 1986) (one cannot "avoid a tax on shoes by calling shoes slippers"); Valley Acceptance Corp. v. Glasby, 337 S.E.2d, 291, 295 (Va. 1985).

496 Robertson v. Burnett, 109 N.W.2d 716 (Neb. 1961), *vacated on other grounds sub nom.* Michigan Nat'l Bank v. Robertson, 372 U.S. 591 (1963) (vacating and remanding for further consideration of whether venue in Nebraska was proper); State *ex rel.* Beck v. Associates Discount Corp., 77 N.W.2d 215 (1956), *further proceedings*, 96 N.W.2d 55 (Neb. 1959). *See also* Murphy v. Citizens Discount Corp., 90 N.E.2d 622, 626 (Ohio Ct. Com. Pleas 1950).

Of course, if the loan would not be subject to the statute in any case, this principle does not act to bring non-licensees within its scope. Albers v. Overland Nat'l Bank, 324 N.W.2d 396 (Neb. 1982); Pattavina v. Pignotti, 128 N.W.2d 817 (Neb. 1964).

497 *See, e.g.*, Ariz. Rev. Stat. Ann. § 6-603(B); Ohio Rev. Code Ann. § 1321.02 (West); Va. Code Ann. § 6.1-251.

498 *See, e.g.*, Ariz. Rev. Stat. Ann. § 6-606(F) (amended following litigation); Iowa Code § 536.12; Va. Code Ann. § 6.1-267. *See also* U.C.C.C. §§ 3-512 (1968), 2-309 (1974) (other business permitted unless for purpose of evasion or violation of the act); Transamerica Fin. Corp. v. Superior Court, 761 P.2d 1019 (Ariz. 1988) (if evidence establishes that loans made by unlicensed lender should be attributable to its licensed alleged alter ego, loans would be void, *dicta*), *but see on remand sub nom.* Ranscon v. Transamerica Fin. Corp., 812 P.2d 1019 (Ariz. Ct. App. 1990) (holding that a loophole existed for four-year period during which licensed lenders were permitted to charge a deregulated rate in excess of rates applicable to licensees); Murphy v. Citizens Discount Corp., 90 N.E.2d 622 (Ohio Ct. Com. Pleas 1950) (holding that small loan prohibitions and remedy apply to lender in business of loaning amounts under the ceiling whether done as licensee, private person, or corporation; rejecting lender's argument that the loans were made under its general corporate power to lend money, not as small loan licensee).

Even where a licensee has sought and obtained permission to engage in real estate lending, the transaction should be closely scrutinized to see if the lender has complied with any applicable restrictions. One small loan licensee sought permission to engage in mortgage lending at its small loan location, and obtained permission on the conditions that such mortgage lending neither take additional personal property as collateral, nor include the sale of property insurance. Nonetheless, the licensee did both. Beneficial v. State Corp. Comm., 339 S.E.2d 192 (Va. 1986).

499 Gottesfeld v. Kaminski, 524 A.2d 872, 875 (N.J. Super. Ct. App. Div. 1987) (test is apparently whether the loan is made as a business proposition or a personal accommodation).

500 *See, e.g.*, Maine Consumer Credit Code, Me. Rev. Stat. tit. 9-A, § 1-301 (coverage is triggered if more than five mortgage loans in the preceding calendar year); Maryland Mortgage Lender Law, Md. Code Ann., Fin. Inst. § 11-502 (more than three mortgage loans per calendar year). *See also* Gorman v. Marcon Capital Corp., 274 B.R. 351 (D. Vt. 2002) (lender's negotiation and preliminary agreement amounted to engaging in business of making loans, so license was required). *But cf.* White v. Coors Distrib. Co. (*In re* White), 260 B.R. 870 (B.A.P. 8th Cir. 2001) (company not in the business of purchasing installment contracts where its primary business was unrelated to financing, but it had accepted assignment of three installment contracts from a related company).

not, therefore, the true lender for licensing purposes. Table-funding means that the lender listed on the loan documents was given all of the funds by the assignee and did not actually extend its own funds to the borrower. The loan is immediately assigned to the funding lender.

A federal court rejected this argument, noting that the loan was initially payable to the originating lender, not the funding lender.[501] In addition, the debt was only assigned to the funding lender after the loan was made. Thus, the originating lender must be licensed. On the other hand, a Ninth Circuit decision, interpreting Washington law, holds that a mortgage broker need not be licensed if it is engaging only in "table-funded" transactions in which it lends another party's funds, but if it is lending its own funds it must be licensed.[502]

Persons who engage in sale-leaseback schemes may engage in unlicensed lending,[503] which may make the transactions void.[504] Car dealers that finance the consumer's negative equity in a trade-in vehicle may also be considered to be lending money without a license in some states.

## *3.9.7 Distinctions Based on Loan Size: Loan Splitting and Loan Packing*

### 3.9.7.1 Loan Splitting

A state's usury law may have a higher ceiling for small loans than for loans above a specified dollar value. To take advantage of the higher ceiling, lenders may split a large loan into several small ones. This practice of "loan-splitting" may be specifically prohibited by the small loan law.[505]

Loan splitting is also attractive to lenders who operate under a statute that allows per-loan fees. For example, a payday loan law may allow a minimum finance charge of a certain dollar amount regardless of the size of the loan. Splitting a loan into two smaller loans allows the lender to double these fees without extending any additional credit.[506]

Lenders may also engage in loan splitting to avoid giving the borrower meaningful information about the cost and terms of the loan. Borrowers will have more difficulty calculating a composite interest rate for two loans issued on the same day. In the Truth in Lending context, courts determine if a transaction should be treated as one loan by whether "the debtor wants, requests, and expects to get a single loan consummated in a single transaction, but the lender instead documents and makes disclosures for the loan as if it were two separate transactions."[507]

### 3.9.7.2 Loan Packing

In some states, usury restrictions only apply if a loan's principal is *under* a certain amount. Under such circumstances, creditors want to *increase* the size of the loan instead of splitting it into smaller loans. The practice of adding fees to the face amount of a loan note in order to reach the minimum loan size to avoid a usury statute is sometimes known as "packing" or "padding" the principal. Packing the loan principal may be legal because most states recognize as valid non-interest expenses which a lender may properly finance as part of the loan principal reasonable third-party fees, such as credit insurance premiums, and sometimes fees for lender services. However, fees should not be added to the principal if they should be treated under state law as part of the loan's interest.[508]

A lender may also pad a loan by requiring or encouraging the borrower to consolidate other debts,[509] or by the added incremental costs that come with frequent refinancings.[510] Such practices might be challenged under non-usury theories, such as unconscionability or state UDAP statutes.

A loan's size can be increased if several small loans, which do not individually reach the statutory threshold, are treated as one loan. Whether this is permissible depends on the specific language of the relevant usury statute, but most statutes apply a

501 St. Jean v. Racal Mortgage, 952 F. Supp. 22 (D. Me. 1997), *questions certified to Maine Supreme Court*, 135 F.3d 37 (1st Cir. 1998) (concurring with district court on merits, but certifying questions as to penalties), *vacated on other grounds sub nom.* Reagan v. Racal Mortgage Inc., 155 F.3d 6 (1st Cir. 1998) (remanding for determination of bona fide error).

502 Easter v. American W. Fin., 381 F.3d 948 (9th Cir. 2004).

503 Browner v. District of Columbia, 549 A.2d 1107 (D.C. 1988) ("foreclosure specialists" engaging in sale-leasebacks were making unlicensed loans under Loan Sharking Act). *See generally* National Consumer Law Center, Foreclosures Ch. 17 (4th ed. 2012).

504 Browner v. District of Columbia, 549 A.2d 1107 (D.C. 1988). *See also* § 7.8.5.1, *infra*.

505 *See* Uniform Small Loan Law, Seventh Draft § 15 (as revised June 1, 1942), *reprinted in* Curran, Trends in Consumer Credit Legislation (1966) (restricting use of small loan rates where aggregate debt to one borrower or married couple, either as principal borrower(s) or as guarantor(s), exceeds $300). *See also* Securities Inv. Co. v. Pearson, 143 S.E.2d 36 (Ga. Ct. App. 1965); Decision Point, Inc. v. Reece & Nichols Realtors, Inc., 144 P.3d 706 (Kan. 2006).

Loan-splitting also may be used improperly to increase the yield under split-rate usury statutes, § 5.3.4, *infra*. *But see* Kinzel v. Southview Chevrolet Co., 892 F. Supp. 1211 (D. Minn. 1995) (no loan splitting issue where consumer financed down payment on a car purchase with loan from a finance company and financed remaining balance through the dealer; no allegation that this constituted scheme to avoid usury limits).

506 *See* Bellizan v. Easy Money of La., 2002 WL 1611648 (E.D. La. July 19, 2002) (practice not found to involve RICO violation).

507 *See, e.g.*, Kane v. Equity One, Inc., 2003 WL 22939377 (E.D. Pa. Nov. 21, 2003) (loan splitting as TILA violation can go forward to trial). *See generally* National Consumer Law Center, Truth in Lending §§ 5.15.3.2 (7th ed. 2010 and Supp.).

508 *See* Aetna Fin. Co. v. Darwin, 691 P.2d 581 (Wash. Ct. App. 1984); Sparkman & McLean Income Fund v. Wald, 520 P.2d 173 (Wash. Ct. App. 1974).

The Seventh Draft of the Uniform Small Loan Act § 2 (as revised June 1, 1942), *reprinted in* Curran Trends in Consumer Credit Legislation (1966) provides: "For the purpose of this section, a loan shall be deemed to be in the amount of $300 or less if the net amount or value advanced to or on behalf of the borrower, after deducting all payments for interest, principal, expenses, and charges of any nature taken substantially contemporaneously with the making of the loan, does not exceed $300."

509 *See* Wolf v. Kian, 2000 Minn. App. LEXIS 963 (Aug. 16, 2000).

510 *See* § 5.9, *infra* (explaining how refinancings add to the cost of a loan).

transactional approach. If a borrower and lender signed a contract under which the lender agreed to advance, in several installments, an aggregate sum, this series of advances is treated as a single loan, based on a single transaction.[511] However, the advances will be viewed as individual loans if the individual advances are not interrelated, i.e., the creditor, having advanced money, is not obligated to make further advances.[512]

Courts narrowly construe these usury exceptions and are reluctant to allow a series of loans to qualify for a large loan exemption.[513] Nevertheless, the existence of several payees on a single loan note may not indicate the presence of several smaller loans to which usury ceilings would apply.[514] Similarly, when a valid debt clearly in excess of a statutory threshold was replaced, pursuant to a settlement of insurance litigation, by a note for less than the threshold, a court determined that the usury exemption still applied because the new note was a "partial renewal and extension" of the original debt.[515]

### 3.9.8 Where Loan Includes a Home As Security

A small consumer loan that includes a home as security may be covered by two different lending statutes, such as a small loan law and a second mortgage statute. In such situations, courts protect the borrower by applying the most restrictive statute which is relevant to the transaction. Where a small loan law and second mortgage statute both apply, but the mortgage statute has the stricter provisions, that statute has been found to apply.[516] On the other hand, a court has found a violation where a creditor made small loans but sought to avoid the small loan law (that prohibited real estate security) by claiming it was complying with the state's second mortgage statute.[517]

### 3.9.9 Criminal Usury Statutes

Some states, even when deregulating their civil usury statutes, retain their criminal usury ceilings.[518] Similarly, even if a civil usury statute exempts business loans, a criminal usury ceiling may apply.[519] Criminal usury statutes are typically found in the state criminal code. They are listed in Appendix B, *infra*, and analyzed in an NCLC report on small dollar loans.[520]

New York[521] and Florida[522] courts hold that loans taken in violation of a criminal usury ceiling are void, and thus unenforceable. The Georgia Supreme Court also holds that loans made in violation of the criminal usury statute are illegal, and subject to usury penalties in a civil action.[523] Massachusetts has a criminal usury statute, but it allows lenders to exceed the cap if they first register with the Massachusetts Attorney General.[524]

511 *See* Mohr, Inc. v. Bank of California, 443 F. Supp. 370 (D. Or. 1978), *aff'd*, 622 F.2d 594 (9th Cir. 1980); Irving Trust Co. v. Smith, 349 F. Supp. 146 (S.D.N.Y. 1972) (treating series of cross-collateralized demand notes as one loan); Negaard v. Miller Constr. Co., 396 N.W.2d 833 (Minn. Ct. App. 1986); American Bank & Trust Co. v. Lichtenstein, 369 N.Y.S.2d 155 (N.Y. App. Div. 1975), *aff'd mem.*, 352 N.E.2d 132 (N.Y. 1976); Sparkman & McLean Income Fund v. Wald, 520 P.2d 173 (Wash. Ct. App. 1974).

512 *See* Henson v. Columbus Bank & Trust, 770 F.2d 1566 (5th Cir. 1985); Citizens & Southern South DeKalb Bank v. Watkins, 225 S.E.2d 266 (Ga. 1976); Western Auto Supply v. Vick, 277 S.E.2d 360, *reaff'd on rehearing*, 283 S.E.2d 101 (N.C. 1981); Magee v. Dyrdahl, 926 P.2d 319 (Or. Ct. App. 1996); Olson v. Froslee, 2000 Minn. App. LEXIS 795 (Aug. 1, 2000); Dean Vivian Homes v. Sebera's Plumbing & Appliances, Inc., 615 S.W.2d 921 (Tex. Civ. App. 1981).

513 *See* Citizens & Southern S. DeKalb Bank v. Watkins, 225 S.E.2d 266 (Ga. 1976); Sparkman & McLean Income Fund v. Wald, 520 P.2d 173 (Wash. Ct. App. 1974).

514 *See* Peterson v. Harville, 445 F. Supp. 16 (D. Or. 1977), *aff'd*, 623 F.2d 611 (9th Cir. 1980); Salzman v. Cole, 567, 254 S.E.2d 888 (Ga. Ct. App. 1979).

515 Sulton v. General Elec. Credit Corp., 268 S.E.2d 789 (Ga. Ct. App. 1980).

516 *See, e.g.*, Schmidt v. Beneficial Fin. Co., 400 A.2d 1124 (Md. 1979);

517 Valley Acceptance Corp. v. Glasby, 337 S.E.2d 291 (Va. 1985). *See also* Girard Acceptance Corp. v. Wallace, 388 A.2d 582 (N.J. 1978) (RISA prohibited real estate security and second mortgage statute did not clearly apply). *But see* Corrigan v. Insilco Corp., 439 N.W.2d 350 (Mich. Ct. App. 1989) (where goods sold were construction materials for a new home, RISA applied despite fact that seller also took a mortgage on the home); Ott v. Peppertree Resort Villas, Inc., 716 N.W.2d 127 (Wis. Ct. App. 2006) (transaction was a mortgage loan and not installment sale).

518 *See* Yaldu v. Bank of Am. Corp., 700 F. Supp. 2d 832, 846–847 (E.D. Mich. 2010); Lawyers Title Ins. Corp. v. Wells, 881 So. 2d 668 (Fla. Dist. Ct. App. 2004); Nelson v. Associates Fin. Servs. Co. of Ind., Inc., 659 N.W.2d 635, 641–642 (Mich. Ct. App. 2002); Perez v. Rent-A-Center, 892 A.2d 1255, 1270–1272 (N.J. 2006); People v. Farrell, 630 N.Y.S.2d 791 (N.Y. App. Div. 1995).

519 Hufnagel v. George, 135 F. Supp. 2d 406 (S.D.N.Y. 2001); Resolution Trust Corp. v. Minassian, 777 F. Supp. 385 (D.N.J. 1991); Committee of Unsecured Creditors v. RG Fin., Ltd. (*In re* Powerburst), 154 B.R. 307 (Bankr. E.D. Cal. 1993); Norris v. Sigler Daisy Corp., 392 S.E.2d 242 (Ga. 1990); Tower Funding, Ltd. v. David Berry Realty, Inc., 755 N.Y.S.2d 413 (N.Y. App. Div. 2003); Nikezic v. Balaz, 585 N.Y.S.2d 86 (N.Y. App. Div. 1992); Transmedia Restaurant Co. v. 33 E. 61st St. Restaurant Corp., 710 N.Y.S.2d 756 (N.Y. Sup. Ct. 2000).

520 Consumers Union, National Consumer Law Center, and Consumer Federation of America, Small Dollar Loan Products Scorecard (Aug. 2008), *available at* www.nclc.org.

521 *See, e.g.*, Hammelburger v. Foursome Inn Corp., 431 N.E.2d 278 (N.Y. 1980); Fareri v. Rain's Int'l Ltd., 589 N.Y.S.2d 579 (N.Y. App. Div. 1992). *See also* Funding Group, Inc. v. Water Chef, Inc., 852 N.Y.S.2d 736 (N.Y. Sup. Ct. 2008) (unenforceable but not void, so no affirmative recovery). *But see* Brodie v. Schmutz (*In re* Venture Mortgage Fund), 282 F.3d 185 (2d Cir. 2002) (questioning whether loan that violates N.Y. criminal usury statute is void); American Equities Group, Inc. v. Ahava Dairy Prods. Corp., 2004 WL 870260 (S.D.N.Y. Apr. 23, 2004) (same).

522 Fla. Stat. § 687.071(7).

523 Norris v. Sigler Daisy Corp., 392 S.E.2d 242 (Ga. 1990) (penalty in Georgia is forfeiture of interest and other charges). *See also* Moore v. Comfed Sav. Bank, 908 F.2d 834 (11th Cir. 1990), *rehearing denied*, 917 F.2d 570 (11th Cir. 1990); S&A Indus., Inc. v. Bank Atlanta, 543 S.E.2d 743 (Ga. Ct. App. 2000).

524 Cannarozzi v. Fiumara, 371 F.3d 1 (1st Cir. 2004) (notifying attorney general at time of refinancing was sufficient to invoke exemption for new loan even though original loan also exceeded cap); Clean Harbors, Inc. v. John Hancock Life Ins. Co., 833 N.E.2d 611 (Mass. App. Ct. 2005) (filing with attorney general a few hours after making the loan is a violation, but may be *de minimis*).

## 3.10 Retroactive Amendment of Usury Statutes

### 3.10.1 General

Legislative amendments may strengthen or weaken existing state usury statutes, and the question arises whether transactions taking place before that amendment are governed by the old or new statute. States can specify whether a statute is to be applied retroactively or not. The U.S. Constitution's prohibition of *ex post facto* laws[525] applies only to criminal statutes.[526] Congress and the states may adopt civil statutes with retrospective effect as long as other constitutional limitations are respected. Most notably among those limits, retrospective statutes may not impair the obligation of existing contracts,[527] and may not deny due process.[528]

Retroactive application is limited where a new statute regulates activity that had not previously been regulated, or that prohibits transactions that had not previously been prohibited.[529] The same may be the case where a usury cap is lowered or a previously permissible fee is prohibited. Retroactive application might impair the existing contractual obligation.[530]

On the other hand, a legislature may have authority to retroactively repeal a usury ceiling. The leading decision on this point is *Ewell v. Daggs*,[531] in which the U.S. Supreme Court in 1883 gave retroactive effect to an amendment to the Texas Constitution which abolished certain usury statutes. Such a retroactive application did not deprive the borrower of vested rights or impair the obligation of contract because the statute merely removed the borrower's right to avoid an otherwise valid contractual obligation. Despite the declaration in the previously existing Texas usury statute that usurious obligations were "void" as to interest, such language indicated to the Court that the contract was merely voidable.[532]

Moreover, the Court found the statute to be penal in nature, and stated that where a statute is penal in nature, the retroactivity of its repeal should be presumed in the absence of a savings clause. Thus, a borrower's statutory right to usury forfeitures and penalties remains vulnerable to legislative action until that right is reduced to final judgment,[533] which means that a judgment could even be undone by a legislative change while an appeal is pending.[534]

The *Ewell* decision continues to be widely followed, so that most courts find that legislatures have the authority to retroactively raise usury caps or eliminate usury statutes, since the borrower has no vested right in penalties or forfeitures.[535] Some courts though hold to the contrary.[536] Maryland's highest court

525 U.S. Const. art. 1, § 10, cl. 1.

526 *See generally* Annotation, 53 L. Ed. 2d 1146 (1978).

527 U.S. Const. art. 1, § 10, cl. 1.

528 U.S. Const. amends. V, XIV.

529 *See, e.g.*, Givens v. Rent-A-Center, Inc., 720 F. Supp. 160 (S.D. Ala. 1988), *aff'd mem.*, 885 F.2d 879 (11th Cir. 1989) (Alabama Rental Purchase Agreements Act).

530 *See* Hoyne v. Prudential Sav. & Loan Ass'n, 711 S.W.2d 899 (Mo. Ct. App. 1986); Garrett v. Citizens Sav. Ass'n, 636 S.W.2d 104 (Mo. Ct. App. 1982); Weinstein v. Investors Sav. & Loan Ass'n, 381 A.2d 53 (N.J. Super. Ct. 1977).

531 108 U.S. 143 (1883).

532 It is possible to argue that *Ewell* is not applicable to usury statutes that void interest and principal. Usury statutes which invalidate only interest implicitly recognize that the remainder of the usurious contract—the obligation to repay principal—is legally sound and enforceable. If, however, a statute declares a transaction completely void from its inception and never recognizes that any contractual obligation of the borrower ever existed, then the reasoning in *Ewell* (i.e., a contractual obligation remains in effect during the term of the usurious contract, but that this obligation is merely unenforceable due to the usury statute), would not apply.

Moreover, some state courts have specifically held that the complete voiding of a loan is not a "penalty," Szerdahelyi v. Harris, 490 N.E.2d 517 (N.Y. 1986), which knocks down another of the underpinnings of the *Ewell* decision. *But see* Moran v. Am. Funding, Ltd., 569 A.2d 841 (N.J. Super. Ct. Ch. Div. 1989) (prior legislation which declared usurious loan void as unenforceable was amended to provide for lesser penalty; court held the amendment retroactive).

Despite the theoretical limitations in the reasoning of *Ewell*, it is unlikely at this late date that the *Ewell* decision will be limited in any significant way by modern courts. The decision has already been widely accepted and broadly applied. Furthermore, the void and voidable distinction between various usury statutes has been criticized by at least one court. *See* American Sav. Life Ins. Co. v. Financial Affairs Mgmt. Co., 513 P.2d 1362 (Ariz. Ct. App. 1973).

533 *See, e.g.*, Jacobson v. General Fin. Corp., 592 N.E.2d 1121 (Ill. App. Ct. 1992) (amendment legalizing use of Rule of 78s applied retroactively); Clouse v. Heights Fin. Corp., 510 N.E.2d 1 (Ill. App. Ct. 1987) (amendment solely affecting remedies for violation of Consumer Installment Loan Act, with no savings clause, applied retroactively); L.E. Marlowe & Sons, Ltd. v. Farner, 406 N.W.2d 273 (Mich. Ct. App. 1987) (amendment expanding business exemption enacted five years after transaction extinguished borrower's usury defense to obligation).

534 *See* Chapman v. Farr, 183 Cal. Rptr. 606 (Cal. Ct. App. 1982). *See also* Dorsey v. West, 311 S.E.2d 816 (Ga. 1984) (no retroactive application because judgment could no longer be appealed).

535 *See, e.g.*, Johnson v. Countrywide Home Loans, Inc., 434 Fed. Appx. 693 (9th Cir. 2011); *In re* Lara, 731 F.2d 1455 (9th Cir. 1984) (California law); Wight v. Agristor Leasing, 652 F. Supp. 1000 (D. Kan. 1987) (little discussion); American Sav. Life Ins. Co. v. Financial Affairs Mgmt. Co., 513 P.2d 1362 (Ariz. Ct. App. 1973); Orden v. Crawshaw Mortgage & Inv. Co., 167 Cal. Rptr. 62 (Cal. Ct. App. 1980); Ward v. Hudco Loan Co., 328 S.E.2d 729 (Ga. 1985); Fountain v. Dixie Fin. Co., 314 S.E.2d 906 (Ga. 1984); Ehrman v. Manning, 339 S.E.2d 652 (Ga. Ct. App. 1986); Wasser v. Citizens & So. Nat'l Bank, 318 S.E.2d 518 (Ga. Ct. App. 1984); Sweeney v. Citicorp Fin., 510 N.E.2d 93 (Ill. App. Ct. 1987); Duff v. Bank of Louisville & Trust Co., 705 S.W.2d 920 (Ky. 1986); Krause v. Griffis, 443 N.W.2d 444 (Mich. Ct. App. 1989); Paul v. U.S. Mut. Fin. Corp., 389 N.W.2d 487 (Mich. Ct. App. 1986); First Fed. Sav. & Loan Ass'n v. Guildner, 295 N.W.2d 501 (Minn. 1980); United Realty Trust v. Prop. Dev., 269 N.W.2d 737 (Minn. 1978); Farmland Enters. v. Schuemann, 322 N.W.2d 665 (Neb. 1982); Davis v. G.M.A.C., 127 N.W.2d 907 (Neb. 1964); Bokum v. First Nat'l Bank, 740 P.2d 693 (N.M. 1987); Vaughan v. Kalyvas, 342 S.E.2d 617 (S.C. Ct. App. 1986); Cazzanigi v. General Elec. Credit Corp., 938 P.2d 819 (Wash. 1997). *See also* Moran v. American Funding, Ltd., 569 A.2d 841 (N.J. Super. Ct. Ch. Div. 1989).

536 Dua v. Comcast Cable, 805 A.2d 1061 (Md. 2002); Merritt v. Knox, 380 S.E.2d 160, 162 (N.C. Ct. App. 1989); Arguelles v. Kaplan, 736 S.W.2d 782 (Tex. App. 1987).

held that retroactive authorization of late fees for cable television service violated the state constitution.[537]

Even if a legislature has the authority to apply an amendment retroactively, the amendment will only be so applied if this is the legislative intent. If a usury statute states that its application is prospective only, or that it should not affect pending litigation, then that statute clearly will not be given retroactive effect.[538]

State constitutions and statutes may have other limitations as to the state legislature's ability to apply a statutory change retroactively. Alabama's constitution prohibits retroactive application of a statutory change to any suits that have been filed before the passage of the change.[539] Maine has a general "savings statute" that preserves remedies in effect at the time of any amendment for behavior which occurred prior to the amendment.[540]

Legislative intent that the amendment be applied prospectively only can be determined even if the statute's savings clause is not explicit on the subject.[541] Despite the statement in *Ewell* that retrospective effect should be presumed, state courts often presume the opposite in non-usury cases, and in some states this presumption is sufficiently strong to refute in usury cases the opposite presumption stated in *Ewell*[542]—which is, after all, merely persuasive authority on the issue of legal presumptions under state law.

537 Dua v. Comcast Cable, 805 A.2d 1061 (Md. 2002).

538 *See* Mickler v. Maranatha Realty Assoc., 20 B.R. 346 (Bankr. M.D. Fla. 1982); Credit Alliance Corp. v. Timmco Equip. Co., 507 So. 2d 657 (Fla. Dist. Ct. App. 1987); Hamm v. St. Petersburg Bank & Trust Co., 379 So. 2d 1300 (Fla. Dist. Ct. App. 1980), *rev'd on other grounds*, 414 So. 2d 1071 (Fla. 1982); Farmland Enters. v. Schuemann, 322 N.W.2d 665 (Neb. 1982); Hazen v. Cook, 637 P.2d 195 (Or. Ct. App. 1981), *rev'd in part on other grounds*, 646 P.2d 33 (Or. 1982).

539 Ala. Const. Art. IV, § 95. *See also* Smith v. Alfa Fin. Corp., 762 So. 2d 850 (Ala. 1999); United Companies Lending Corp. v. Autrey, 723 So. 2d 617 (Ala. 1998).

540 Me. Rev. Stat. tit. 1, § 302; Reagan v. Racal Mortgage, Inc., 715 A.2d 925 (Me. 1998).

541 *See* Southern Guar. Corp. v. Doyle, 353 S.E.2d 510 (Ga. 1987); Norstar Bank v. Pickard & Anderson, 547 N.Y.S.2d 734 (N.Y. 1989); Hardwick v. Austin Gallery of Oriental Rugs, Inc., 779 S.W.2d 438 (Tex. App. 1989).

542 *See* Mapes v. Palo Alto Town & Country Vill., Inc., 584 F. Supp. 508 (D. Nev. 1984); U.S. Trust Co. v. LTV Steel Co. (*In re* Chateaugay Corp.), 150 B.R. 529 (Bankr. S.D.N.Y. 1993), *aff'd*, 170 B.R. 551 (S.D.N.Y. 1994); Walker v. Pliss, 34 B.R. 432 (Bankr. D. Or. 1983); Broussard v. Crochet Broussard & Co., 477 So. 2d 166 (La. Ct. App. 1985); U.S. Life Title Ins. Co. v. Brents, 676 S.W.2d 839 (Mo. Ct. App. 1984); Hazen v. Cook, 637 P.2d 195 (Or. Ct. App. 1981) (statutory increase in interest ceiling was not retroactive, but forfeiture of loan principal to the state was penal and was repealed retroactively), *rev'd in part on other grounds*, 646 P.2d 33 (Or. 1982).

## *3.10.2 Variable or Floating Usury Ceilings Distinguished*

A legislative amendment to a usury statute must be distinguished from a mere temporary change in the usury cap found in a floating or variable interest ceiling statute. In a variable or floating interest rate ceiling statute, the usury ceiling goes up or down in relation to a specified market rate, called the index. The index and the margin are set by statute, but the actual numerical ceiling will change without any change in statute.

Generally, under variable rate statutes, the interest ceiling which applies to any given transaction is fixed on the date the transaction is consummated. If the statutory ceiling later increases or decreases, due to a change in a market interest rate to which the statute is pegged, the existing transaction must continue to respect the limit in effect when that transaction was consummated.[543] Only new loans are governed by the new cap.

Nevertheless, some floating rate statutes are not fixed as of the date of the transaction, and allow the interest rate charged under a variable rate contract to rise above the ceiling which existed on the date the contract was consummated, so long as the rate assessed at any point during the contract term does not exceed the usury ceiling which exists at that time. In addition, a refinancing or a new loan forbearance agreement may trigger application of the interest rate in effect at that later time.[544] A forbearance after a default may be treated as a new transaction, and the usury ceiling in effect on the date of the forbearance will control what may be charged for the forbearance.[545] However, the rate permitted for the forbearance or renewal may not be applied retroactively to increase the rate charged on the original loan or on earlier forbearances.[546]

543 *See* Eikenberry v. Adirondack Spring Water Co., 480 N.E.2d 70 (N.Y. 1985); Bookman v. First Bank of Marietta, 1983 Ohio App. LEXIS 13566 (Ohio Ct. App. Feb. 18, 1983); Reagan v. City Nat'l Bank, N.A., 714 S.W.2d 425 (Tex. App. 1986).

544 Heuberger v. Rounsefell, 776 P.2d 596 (Or. Ct. App. 1989). *But see* Reagan v. City Nat'l Bank, N.A., 714 S.W.2d 425 (Tex. App. 1986) (subsequent addition of co-maker was not alteration or renewal which would change the applicable ceiling).

545 *See* Cent. Flying Serv., Inc. v. Cain, 686 S.W.2d 432 (Ark. 1985); Eikenberry v. Adirondack Spring Water Co., 480 N.E.2d 70 (N.Y. 1985).

546 *Id.*; Bank of Evening Shade v. Lindsey, 644 S.W.2d 920 (Ark. 1983).

# Chapter 4 Interest, Points, Fees, and Delinquency Charges

## 4.1 Introduction

This chapter deals with the interpretation of state law restrictions on interest and other charges in credit transactions. In the wave of deregulation that started in the 1980s, some states reduced or even eliminated their restrictions on the cost of credit. However, in many states such statutes remain in force and are the key bulwark against predatory non-mortgage lending. Moreover, even states that repealed most of their caps on interest and other charges often proceeded piecemeal, leaving some restrictions on the books for some types of extensions of credit.

The interpretation of state restrictions on the cost of credit can be complex. State statutes and constitutional provisions vary widely in the way they describe the charges they cap. Some cap "interest," without defining it, so courts fall back on common law to determine what is interest.[1] Other statutes that cap "interest" define it to include or exclude various types of charges. Yet other statutes restrict "finance charges," or specify a set of charges that are authorized and ban all others. Some statutes specifically authorize lenders to charge origination charges, late charges, and third-party fees, and specifically exclude these charges from "interest."

This chapter first analyzes the terms "interest" and "finance charges." It then examines the treatment of specific kinds of charges: points, commitment fees, and other one-time percentage-based fees; other ways of inflating the principal; third-party fees; document preparation fees; non-cash compensation and side agreements; and delinquency charges. The chapter pays particular attention to methods creditors use to hide the cost of credit, for example by folding fees into the principal. Other chapters also discuss hidden interest in the context of particular credit products such as payday loans and refund anticipation loans.[2]

Because of the differences in consumer credit laws from state to state, and even within a state, the advocate must always start with a close review of the language of the specific state statute that is applicable to the consumer's transaction. This chapter pulls together courts' resolution of typical questions, but a decision from one state will have little value in another state that has foreclosed the issue through statutory language. Even within a state, a decision that appears to be dispositive may be based on an earlier version of the statute. Finally, the effect of federal preemption should always be considered when evaluating the application of a state usury law to a transaction.[3]

Of course, restrictions on interest are relevant only if there is a loan or other credit transaction. Some states accept the fiction that an installment sale does not involve credit, and that the "time-price differential"—the difference between the cash price and the credit price—is not interest.[4] In some states, the usury laws are inapplicable to credit sales,[5] although many states have adopted installment sales statutes or other laws to fill this void.[6] Many courts also hold usury statutes inapplicable to interest or fees imposed when a buyer fails to pay a bill when due, unless the seller has agreed to allow payment over time.[7] However, usury statutes that apply to "detention" of money may be applicable in this situation.[8]

## 4.2 What Is "Interest"

### *4.2.1 General Interpretation of "Interest"*

Where a law restricts the costs of credit by imposing a restriction on "interest," the key question is what constitutes interest. As this chapter discusses, if interest were narrowly defined as the application of a percentage rate over a period of time, a cap that restricted only interest would have little effect, as the lender could hide all the cost of credit in other fees and charges.

When faced with laws that cap "interest" but do not explicitly address what charges are included in interest, courts generally adopt a broad definition of the term, thus including a

1 *See, e.g.* Vanderweyst v. First State Bank, 425 N.W.2d 803, 811 (Minn. 1988).

2 *See* Chs. 9, 14, , *infra*.

3 *See* Chs. 3, *supra*, 8, *infra*.

4 *See* § 7.5.2.2, *infra*.

5 *See, e.g.*, Southwest Concrete Co. v. Gosh Constr., 798 P.2d 1247 (Cal. 1990) (because of time-price doctrine, late charges imposed when buyer did not pay invoice on due date are not subject to usury laws); Ruminant Nitrogen Prods. v. Zittle, 433 N.Y.S.2d 644 (N.Y. App. Div. 1980). *But cf.* Butler v. Holt Machinery Co., 741 S.W.2d 169, 173 (Tex. App. 1987), *as corrected on denial of rehearing by* 739 S.W.2d 958 (1987) (contract that consolidated and refinanced balances due on several credit sales is not protected by time-price doctrine; late charges that were imposed without borrower's agreement are interest). *See generally* §§ 1.2.2 (ancient roots of this approach), 1.2.4, *supra*.

6 *See* § 2.3, *supra*.

7 *See* § 7.5.2.3, *infra*.

8 *See* Scarr v. Boyer, 818 P.2d 381 (Mont. 1991) (Montana's usury statute applies to compensation for detention of money, thus it includes post-default interest within definition of interest). *See generally* § 7.5.2.3, *infra* (discussing forbearance and detention).

wide variety of flat-fee and one-time charges. A typical definition is that interest is the compensation paid to a lender for the use of money or the forbearance of a debt.[9]

Sometimes a definition along these lines has been incorporated into a usury statute.[10] Often these statutes signal their broad scope by stating that the term includes compensation "however denominated" or "whether paid directly or indirectly." Some definitions include charges for "detention" of money, not just "use or forbearance."[11] The Supreme Court has noted the long history of a broad definition of "interest," one that is not tied exclusively to the application of a rate over a period of time.[12]

When interpreting a statute that does not define interest, or that defines it only in general terms, some courts hold that a charge is interest if it is profit for the lender, compensation for overhead, or compensation for the general costs of doing business.[13] These courts generally conclude that compensation for services incidental to setting up and making a loan is interest.[14] This is so even though an up-front fee for the administrative costs of setting up a loan may represent a legitimate expense.[15] Even these courts, though, may draw a distinction between fees that amount to compensation for the lender, and fees for legitimate services of a sort that are not normally incidental to lending or that are paid to third parties, such as title insurance costs, recording fees, or fees paid to a government agency for guaranteeing the loan.[16]

On the other hand, some courts interpret "interest" to exclude the reasonable expenses incurred by the lender in making a loan.[17] This approach is fundamentally unsound, as it allows creditors to pass many of their costs on to borrowers, increasing their profits with no ostensible increase in interest rate. Typically, the separate services are tied to the loan transaction and are only "purchased" by the borrower so that the credit may be obtained. The fees generally benefit the lender by securing collateral for the loan, enabling the lender to evaluate the borrower's creditworthiness, or reducing the consequences to

---

9 *See, e.g.*, Kenty v. Bank One, Columbus, N.A., 1992 WL 170605, at *3 (S.D. Ohio Apr. 23, 1992) ("compensation allowed by law or fixed by the parties for the use or forbearance of money"), *aff'd in part and rev'd in part*, 92 F.3d 384 (6th Cir. 1995) (though excessive premium may be interest, usury cap not applicable by virtue of state law and the most favored lender doctrine); McGhee v. Ark. State Bd. of Collection Agencies, 289 S.W.3d 18, 25 (Ark. 2008) ("[t]he compensation which is paid by the borrower of money to the lender for its use, and generally, by a debtor to his creditor in recompense for his detention of the debt"); Wombold v. Associates Fin. Serv. Co., 104 P.3d 1080, 1088 (Mont. 2004) (although not defined by statute, interest is generally defined as "a charge made for the use, forbearance, or detention of money"). *See also* Vanderweyst v. First State Bank, 425 N.W.2d 803, 811 (Minn. 1988) ("compensation for the use of the money loaned"); Garrison v. First Fed. Saving & Loan Ass'n, 402 S.E.2d 24, 29 (Va. 1991) ("any charge that cannot be attributed to principal or to an allowable charge for collateral service"). *But cf.* Barnett Bank v. Abramowitz, 419 So. 2d 627 (Fla. 1982); Begelfer v. Najarian, 409 N.E.2d 167, 182 (Mass. 1980) ("compensation fixed by the parties or allowed by law for the use of money or as damages for its detention"); Black's Law Dictionary (7th ed. 1999).

10 *See, e.g.*, Dikeou v. Dikeou, 928 P.2d 1286, 1291 (Colo. 1997) ("the sum of all charges payable directly or indirectly by a debtor and imposed directly or indirectly by a lender as an incident to or as a condition of the extension of credit to the debtor, whether paid or payable by the debtor, the lender, or any other person on behalf of the debtor to the lender or to a third party"); B.F. Saul Co. v. West End Park N., Inc., 246 A.2d 591 (Md. 1968) ("any compensation imposed directly or indirectly by a lender for the extension of credit for the use or forbearance of money"); Scarr v. Boyer, 818 P.2d 381, 382 (Mont. 1991) ("the compensation allowed by law or fixed by the parties for the use or forbearance or detention of money"); First USA Mgmt., Inc. v. Esmond, 960 S.W.2d 625, 627 (Tex. 1997) ("Interest is compensation for the use, forbearance, or detention of money").

11 *See* § 7.5.2.3, *infra* (distinction between forbearance and detention).

12 Smiley v. Citibank (South Dakota), N.A., 517 U.S. 735, 745–746, 116 S. Ct. 1730, 135 L. Ed. 2d 25 (1996).

13 Johnston v. Citizen's Bank & Trust, 659 F.2d 865 (8th Cir. 1981) (Ark. law); Modern Pioneers Ins. Co. v. Nandin, 437 P.2d 658, 664–665 (Ariz. 1968) (charges for lender's ordinary overhead expenses are interest); First Nat'l Mortgage Co. v. Arkmo Lumber & Supply Co., 641 S.W.2d 31 (Ark. 1982) (fee charged to borrower that covers part of lender's cost of doing business must be treated as interest); Ark. Sav. & Loan Ass'n v. Mack Truck of Ark., Inc., 566 S.W.2d 128 (Ark. 1978) (service charge, commitment fee, points, and the like are interest); Sparkman & McLean Income Fund v. Wald, 520 P.2d 173 (Wash. Ct. App. 1974) (fee to lender is interest where it is not for any services beyond those for making the loan and for the use of the money). *See also* O'Connor v. Lamb, 593 S.W.2d 385 (Tex. Civ. App. 1979) (charge for services provided by lender as part of making loan is interest).

14 O'Connor v. Lamb, 593 S.W.2d 385 (Tex. Civ. App. 1979) (fee to compensate lender for borrowing the money that he then loaned to the borrower is interest); Cuevas v. Montoya, 740 P.2d 858 (Wash. Ct. App. 1987); Aetna Fin. Co. v. Darwin, 691 P.2d 581 (Wash. Ct. App. 1984). *But cf.* Barnett Bank v. Abramowitz, 419 So. 2d 627 (Fla. 1982) (bank's 1% "service fee" not interest and not subject to statutory cap where it was compensation for "several functions," not identified by the court, beyond those for a straight loan transaction).

15 Cuevas v. Montoya, 740 P.2d 858 (Wash. Ct. App. 1987) (attorney fees and "set-up" fee were charges for services normally incidental to making a loan, thus were interest); Aetna Fin. Co. v. Darwin, 691 P.2d 581 (Wash. Ct. App. 1984) ($1,000 "loan funding fee" to prepare documents, arrange payoffs, etc. was interest; "[c]harges for making a loan and for the use of money are interest; charges are not interest if they are for services actually provided by the lender, reasonably worth the price charged, and for which the borrower agreed to pay.").

16 *See, e.g.*, Johnston v. Citizen's Bank & Trust, 659 F.2d 865 (8th Cir. 1981) (Ark. law) (reasonable fee, paid in good faith to third party—here a fee to Small Business Administration for guaranteeing a loan—is not interest); Modern Pioneers Ins. Co. v. Nandin, 437 P.2d 658, 664–665 (Ariz. 1968) (reasonable fees for specific services are not interest if they are not a device for exacting extra profit or compensation for ordinary overhead expenses; appraisal fee, title search fee, and credit report fee are not interest, but other fees are); Harris v. Guaranty Fin. Corp., 424 S.W.2d 355 (Ark. 1968) (title insurance premium is not interest); Aetna Fin. Co. v. Darwin, 691 P.2d 581 (Wash. Ct. App. 1984) (title insurance fees and recording fees paid to third parties are not interest).

17 *See, e.g.*, Vanderweyst v. First State Bank, 425 N.W.2d 803 (Minn. 1988) (reasonable expenses excluded as a matter of common law; fact question whether 1.5% origination fee is interest); Collins v. Union Fed. Sav. & Loan Ass'n, 662 P.2d 610 (Nev. 1983) (actual and reasonable expenses are not interest; accepting lender's affidavit that application fee and other fees covered expenses to establish and service the loan).

the lender if the borrower defaults. All of these charges can easily be classified as the ordinary costs of doing business.

Sometimes lenders purport to provide services that are wholly independent of the loan transaction. For example, the loan contract may say that the lender is also providing investment advice, and it may include a charge for this advice. Or the contract may oblige the consumer to pay for loan-related steps that the creditor does not in fact take. These ploys would be an easy cloak for usury if courts allowed them. Whether or not the statute treats expenses incurred by the lender in making the loan as interest, charges for services that the lender does not in fact perform are interest.[18]

### *4.2.2 Statutes That Exclude Enumerated Charges from Interest or the Finance Charge*

Some statutes that cap "interest" set forth a general definition of the term, and then specify charges that are excluded from the definition.[19] Statutes that cap the "finance charge" for a transaction rather than capping "interest" are often structured this way as well.[20] (The term "finance charge" is more clearly intended as an all-inclusive term than "interest," so there is less likely to be controversy about whether the term includes charges that are not based on application of a percentage rate over a period of time.) The federal Truth in Lending Act follows this pattern in its definition of the components of the finance charge for purposes of disclosure.[21]

Whether the statute caps "interest" or the "finance charge," if it enumerates charges that can be excluded from the cap, then non-enumerated charges have to be included.[22] Imposing a non-enumerated charge may not be illegal in and of itself, but the requirement to treat that charge as part of the finance charge may push the finance charge over the statutory cap.[23]

Some statutes do not enumerate the charges that can be excluded from interest or the finance charge, but simply allow "reasonable" expenses to be excluded.[24] Whether an expense is reasonable is a fact question.[25] In evaluating whether a particular fee amounts to interest under such a statute, the advocate should ask whether the fee covers specific expenses related to the consumer's specific loan? Fees covering only overhead or profit might be challenged as hidden interest.[26] Second, were the fees actually incurred? Fees for appraisals which were never performed or filing fees for documents which were never filed are good examples of concealed interest.[27] Finally, was the size of the fee reasonably related to the costs of the services involved? Excessive charges for otherwise valid services are not actually attributable to those services to the extent they are excessive, and should be considered interest to that extent.[28] If a fee is unreasonable under the facts of an individual case, it may be usurious even if it is below a statutory maximum.[29] Kickbacks to the lender from third-party service fees may also be interest.[30]

## 4.3 Points, Commitment Fees, and Other Percentage Fees

### *4.3.1 General*

One type of ostensibly non-interest charge that is often used and misused by lenders is a fee calculated as a percentage of loan principal. Depending on the type of lender and loan

18 *See* § 4.5.2, *infra.*

19 *See, e.g.*, Md. Code Ann., Com. Law §§ 12-105 (general cap on interest), 12-105 (specifying charges excludable from interest on most loans), 12-306 (capping interest for consumer loans), 12-307 (fees on consumer loans).

20 *See, e.g.*, *In re* Ferris, 764 F.2d 1475 (11th Cir. 1985) (interpreting Ga. Motor Vehicle Sales Finance Act's cap on "finance charge"); Grantham v. First Union Home Equity Bank, 685 So. 2d 748 (Ala. Civ. App. 1996).

21 15 U.S.C. § 1605.

22 *See, e.g.*, Garrison v. First Fed. Saving & Loan Ass'n, 402 S.E.2d 24 (Va. 1991) ("risk management fee" was interest where it was not specifically authorized by statute; appraisal charge in excess of actual cost was interest). *Compare* Opinion of the Mich. Att'y Gen., No. 6594, 5 Consumer Cred. Guide (CCH) § 95,775 (July 17, 1989) (documentary fees, services fees or inspection fees imposed on installment buyer as part of cash price or amount financed were not specifically provided for in MVRISA and therefore violated the statute's limitation on charges), *with* Opinion of the Tenn. Att'y Gen., No. 87-192, 5 Consumer Cred. Guide § 95,918 (CCH) (Dec. 16, 1987) (in response to question about whether document preparation fees could be assessed, opinion says "yes, but . . .," federal law prohibits charging for preparation of RESPA or TILA statements, and other document preparation fees would generally fall within guidelines for loan charges or similar provisions applicable under relevant state or federal general or special usury statute). *But see* Grantham v. First Union Home Equity Bank, 685 So. 2d 748 (Ala. Civ. App. 1996) (cost of appraisal performed by creditor's employee was properly included in the finance charge under Ala. Code § 5-19-1; section 5-19-1 merely defines the charges to be included in the finance and does not prohibit the charging of any particular fee).

23 Luttenegger v. Conseco Fin. Servs. Corp., 671 N.W.2d 425 (Iowa 2003).

24 *See* Fikes v. First Fed. Sav. & Loan Ass'n, 533 P.2d 251, 265 (Alaska 1975) (commitment fee may be interest under statute that caps interest but allows "reasonable expenses"); Freeman v. Gonzales Cty. Sav. & Loan Ass'n, 526 S.W.2d 774 (Tex. App. 1975), *aff'd*, 534 S.W.2d 903 (Tex. 1976).

25 VanderWeyst v. First State Bank of Benson, 425 N.W.2d 803 (Minn. 1988); Gonzales Cty. Sav. & Loan Ass'n v. Freeman, 534 S.W.2d 903 (Tex. 1976).

26 *See* Eskridge, *One Hundred Years of Ineptitude: The Need for Mortgage Rules Consonant with the Economic and Psychological Dynamics of the Home Sale and Loan Transaction*, 70 Va. L. Rev. 1083, 1092 (1984).

27 *See* § 4.5.2, *infra.*

28 *In re* Bogan, 281 F. Supp. 242, 249–250 (W.D. Tenn. 1968) (repeated imposition of investigation or loan fee for series of loans was excessive and amounted to usury); Fikes v. First Fed. Sav. & Loan of Anchorage, 533 P.2d 251 (Alaska 1975); Altherr v. Wilshire Mortgage Corp., 448 P.2d 859 (Ariz. 1969).

29 *See In re* Bogan, 281 F. Supp. 242 (W.D. Tenn. 1968) (repeated assessment of investigation fee in a series of refinancing transactions was unreasonable and usurious).

30 *See* § 4.5.2.2, *infra.*

involved, this fee may be variously described as an "origination fee," "commitment fee," "service charge," or "loan fee," but is perhaps best known as "points" or "discount points," with one point being a sum equal to one percent of the loan principal.

Regardless of the precise name used or the precise manner of calculation, points are essentially a "bonus": an additional incentive or inducement supposedly offered to the lender to convince it to issue a loan. As such, it is logically very difficult to characterize points as anything but interest, both because they are clearly compensation to the lender for the use of money, and because it is extremely hard for a lender to identify any separate service, apart from general overhead expense or risk assumed, which varies with the size of the loan and can thus justify a non-interest percentage fee.[31]

For example, points on home mortgages have been alternately described as compensation to the lender for the costs of packaging a loan for resale on the secondary mortgage market ("origination fees"), or as compensation for the discounted price at which the mortgage must be resold. However, the first justification fails when one realizes that the costs of "originating" a mortgage either have already been passed on to the borrower in the form of appraisal fees, attorney fees, etc., or are just overhead costs. The second justification similarly fails because compensating the lender for the discount on resale is no different from guaranteeing its profit margin.[32]

Whatever the theoretical justification, points are particularly subject to abuse by high rate lenders for two reasons. First, they offer an effective way for creditors to understate the real cost of credit (and thereby undercut legitimate competitors) when trying to sell the credit to prospective borrowers.

Consider this scenario: A borrower needs $5,000; she and the loan officer discuss the monthly payments for a five-year term.[33] The loan officer explains that her monthly payments at 15% will be $146.76. And indeed, 15% is the interest rate specified in the promissory note, but the stated principal is $6,169, not $5,000. The lender has capitalized (treated as principal, not interest) 19 points in drafting the note and making the calculations.[34] The lender's compensation for that $5,000 loan is $3,805.60: $2,636.60 "interest" (15% for five years on the proceeds plus points), plus $1,169 (the 19 points). Somewhere in the mound of loan papers there should be a Truth in Lending disclosure statement which, if properly done, discloses the cost of credit more accurately as an APR of 25%.[35] But the borrower may not notice this buried document, or understand its significance if she does, and the lender encourages (or at least does not discourage) the impression that this is a 15% loan.[36]

The second reason that points are subject to abuse is the potential windfall to the lender in the event of prepayment, by refinancing, outright pay-off, or acceleration in the event of default. Because lenders treat points as "earned" at consummation, they generally do not treat points as subject to rebate.[37] To see how that affects the borrower, assume the above five-year loan is paid off after twenty-four months. If treated simply as a $5,000, 25% loan, the lender would have earned $2,213.22 in interest upon prepayment after two years. When treated as a $6,169 loan (including the $1,169 in points) at 15%, the lender will have earned $1,586.86 in regular interest, plus the $1,169 in points, for a total of $2,755.86. The use of points instead of a higher interest rate thus costs the borrower an extra $540, creating an effective interest rate of 29 ½% for those two years. Given the frequency of refinancing, particularly in some segments of the consumer credit industry, such an example makes clear the impetus to abuse the concept of points.[38]

The significant added cost imposed by points, and their inherent capacity for deception, create a number of potential issues apart from whether or not they are characterized as interest. General calculation issues are discussed at § 5.6.1, *infra*, the special rebate questions they present are discussed at § 5.8.4.2, *infra,* and the distortions they cause in refinancing are discussed at § 5.9, *infra*.

### 4.3.2 Legal Considerations

When statutes do not specifically address the treatment of points and similar fees, lenders carry the burden of demonstrat-

31 *See* Fikes v. First Fed. Sav. & Loan of Anchorage, 533 P.2d 251, 265 (Alaska 1975) (among other considerations listed, the variation of a "loan fee" with the amount or risk of a loan suggests interest).

Under a Financial Accounting Standards Board standard, lenders must recognize income received from origination or similar fees over the entire loan term rather than at the consummation of the loan because, as a matter of generally accepted accounting practice, originating a loan is not a separate income-producing activity apart from the lending of money itself. If originating a loan is an integral part of the over-all lending process, then expenses incurred through loan origination are part of a lender's overhead expense which cannot be compensated by non-interest fees. FASB Statement No. 91, Accounting for Nonrefundable Fees and Costs Associated with Originating or Acquiring Loans and Initial Direct Costs of Leases, *available at* www.fasb.org/st/summary/stsum91.shtml.

32 *See* Bernhardt v. Atlantic Fin. Corp., 40 A.2d 713 (Mass. 1942) (discount was interest).

33 The conventional wisdom is that most consumer borrowers focus foremost on the amount of the monthly payment. That is one reason that lenders can manipulate the other loan terms without the borrower's being aware of it in many cases.

34 The points ($1,169) amount to almost 19% of the $6,169 principal shown on the note. The $1,169 figure actually amounts to more than 23 points if $5000—the amount actually made available to the borrower—is treated as the principal. *See* § 5.6.1, *infra* (calculating points).

35 Points, service charges, etc., are considered a part of the finance charge, and hence calculated in the APR, for purposes of the Truth in Lending Act. As a result, the amount financed would be disclosed as $5,000 and the finance charge as $3,805.60, which includes the points as a $1,169 prepaid finance charge. 15 U.S.C. § 1605(a)(1), (3); Reg. Z § 1026.4(b)(3). *See* National Consumer Law Center, Truth in Lending §§ 3.7.5, 3.8 (7th ed. 2010 and Supp.).

36 *See, e.g., In re* First Alliance Mortgage Co., 298 B.R. 652 (C.D. Cal. 2003) (describing how FAMCO loan officers were trained to give sales presentations designed to obfuscate loan origination fees (points) and other fees.).

37 *See* § 5.8.4.2, *infra.*

38 *See* §§ 5.8.4.2, 5.9, *infra* (discussing both the mathematics and legal considerations surrounding points and early termination).

ing that points are justified by actual recognized costs associated with a loan and are not merely extra profit or compensation for overhead expense.[39] This is a burden that lenders can seldom carry, and numerous courts have found points and similar fees to constitute hidden interest.[40]

More commonly, the relevant state statute specifically permits the exclusion of points, often allowing one or two points to be excluded from interest.[41] The existence of such statutes is helpful to consumers in at least one way: by specifying how many points and other fees may be excluded from interest, these statutes clearly imply that any additional fees are to be treated as interest.[42]

Practitioners should check statutes which permit the exclusion of a percentage fee from interest to see how this fee may be calculated. Equitably, fees should be calculated as a percentage of the sum received by the borrower. Yet, lenders often collect a percentage of every sum that they finance, including previously assessed fees and the points themselves. Depending on the precise statutory language, this practice of assessing fees on fees may be usurious.[43]

---

39 *See, e.g.*, Ark. Sav. & Loan Ass'n v. Mack Trucks of Arkansas, 566 S.W.2d 128 (Ark. 1978); United-Bilt Homes, Inc. v. Teague, 432 S.W.2d 1 (Ark. 1968); VanderWeyst v. First State Bank of Benson, 425 N.W.2d 803 (Minn. 1988) (origination fee is interest if not related to expenses; affidavit of bank officer making that assertion not adequate); Freeman v. Gonzales Cty. Sav. & Loan Ass'n, 526 S.W.2d 774 (Tex. App. 1975), *aff'd*, 534 S.W.2d 903 (Tex. 1976) (2% "loan fee" not proven reasonable and thus constituted usury under statute). *See also* Moore v. Comfed Sav. Bank, 908 F.2d 834 (11th Cir. 1990); Norris v. Sigler Daisy Corp., 392 S.E.2d 242 (Ga. 1990) (interpreting Georgia's criminal usury statute, Ga. Code Ann. § 7-4-18, as not excluding points from the definition of interest, so the effect of points would be considered in determining whether the criminal usury ceiling was violated even though the civil usury code excludes points from definition of usury).

40 *See, e.g.*, Smith v. Anderson, 801 F.2d 661 (4th Cir. 1986) (applying Virginia law); Perry v. Stewart Title Co., 756 F.2d 1197 (5th Cir. 1985) (front end charges were interest, but "spreading" of interest avoids usury violation); Johnston v. Citizen's Bank & Trust, 659 F.2d 865 (8th Cir. 1981) (applying Arkansas law); Imperial Corp. of Am. v. Frenchman's Creek Corp., 453 F.2d 1338 (5th Cir. 1972) (applying Texas law); Bowen v. Mt. Vernon Sav. Bank, 105 F.2d 796 (D.C. Cir. 1939); *In re* Perry, 425 B.R. 323, 371 (Bankr. S.D. Tex. 2010) (front end charge, here an administrative fee to lender, is interest); First Nat'l Mortgage Co. v. Arkmo Lumber & Supply Co., 641 S.W.2d 31 (Ark. 1982); Pazianos v. Schenker, 366 A.2d 440 (D.C. Ct. App. 1976); Montgomery Fed. Sav. & Loan Ass'n v. Baer, 308 A.2d 768 (D.C. Ct. App. 1973); First Fed. Sav. v. Norwood Realty Co., 92 S.E.2d 763 (Ga. 1956); Eisenstein v. Diprimo, 2000 Ga. App. LEXIS 1140 (Ga. Ct. App. Sept. 15, 2000); Saskill v. 4-B Acceptance, 453 N.E.2d 761 (Ill. Ct. App. 1983); Luttenberger v. Conseco Fin. Servs. Corp., 671 N.W.2d 425 (Iowa 2003) (holding loan origination and processing fees included in Iowa U.C.C.C. definition of "finance charge" for consumer loans; such fees permissible so long as resulting finance charge does not exceed 21% cap); B.F. Saul Co. v. West End Park N., Inc., 246 A.2d 591 (Md. 1968) (excellent discussion); Bernhardt v. Atlantic Fin. Corp., 40 A.2d 713 (Mass. 1942) (discount was interest); Hilal v. Lipton, 642 N.Y.S.2d 78 (N.Y. App. Div. 1996); Hope v. Contemporary Funding Group, 513 N.Y.S.2d 171 (N.Y. App. Div. 1987) (discount retained by lender is additional interest); Vee Bee Serv. Co. v. Household Fin. Corp., 51 N.Y.S.2d 590 (N.Y. Sup. Ct. 1944), *aff'd*, 55 N.Y.S.2d 590 (N.Y. 1945); Gonzales County Sav. & Loan Ass'n v. Freeman, 534 S.W.2d 903 (Tex. 1976); Tarver v. Sebring Capital Credit Corp., 69 S.W.3d 708 (Tex. App. 2002) (Texas constitutional 3% cap on fees does not apply to discount points paid in exchange for a lower rate; such points are considered interest); Riverdale Mall Inc. v. Larwin Mortgage Invs., 515 S.W.2d 5 (Tex. App. 1975); Garrison v. First Fed. Sav. & Loan Ass'n, 402 S.E.2d 24 (Va. 1991) (points, or loan discount fee, are interest); Aetna Fin. Co. v. Darwin, 691 P.2d 581 (Wash. Ct. App. 1984). *But see* Wombold v. Associates Fin. Serv. Co., 104 P.3d 1080 (Mont. 2004) (points were not interest; however, lender's charging of points violated Montana Consumer Loan Act's restriction on fees not authorized by statute). *But cf.* Concord Realty Co. v. Continental Funding Corp., 776 P.2d 1114 (Colo. 1989) (lender withheld portion of proceeds of commercial loan to cover interest payment that would come due during loan term, and placed this amount in reserve account; this was principal, not interest).

41 *See, e.g.*, Kan. Stat. Ann. § 16a-2-401(9) (five points authorized in real estate loans; two points on other closed-end loans); Md. Code Ann., Com. Law § 12-405 (West); Winn v. Ameriquest Mortgage Co., 2006 WL 1229755 (Conn. Super. Ct. Apr. 12, 2006) (discussing Connecticut law limiting the amount of any prepaid finance charges that may be charged in connection with a first mortgage loan to the greater of $2,000 or 5% of the original loan amount plus 5% of any additional proceeds received by the borrower in the refinancing). *See also* Hafford v. Equity One, Inc., 2008 WL 906015 (D. Md. Mar. 31, 2008) (interpreting state Secondary Mortgage Loan Law to permit lenders to charge a variety of fees related to the loan origination provided that they do not exceed the cap in the aggregate).

42 *See, e.g.,* Smith v. Anderson, 801 F.2d 661 (4th Cir. 1986) (applying Virginia law); Miller v. Pac. Shore Funding, 224 F. Supp. 2d 977 (D. Md. 2002) (lender exceeded Maryland's 10% cap on loan origination fees for secondary mortgages by charging both origination fee and "non-interest, non-recording" fees that, when combined, were greater than 10% of "net proceeds"), *aff'd on other grounds,* 92 Fed. Appx. 933 (4th Cir. 2004) (affirming dismissal of claims based on statute of limitations and standing grounds); United Companies Lending Corp. v. Autrey, 723 So. 2d 617 (Ala. 1998) (points equal finance charge and excess over 5% cap violates Alabama's Mini-Code; issue arose in context of resolving which of two possible remedy provisions apply); Bandas v. Citizens State Bank, 412 N.W.2d 818 n.1 (Minn. Ct. App. 1987) (controlling statute designates permitted charges which are not interest; loan origination fee is not listed, therefore is interest), *rev'd and remanded on other grounds sub nom.* VanderWeyst v. First State Bank, 425 N.W.2d 803 (Minn. 1988) (concluding that the statute interpreted by the intermediate appellate court did not apply to the transaction); Aetna Fin. Co. v. Darwin, 691 P.2d 581 (Wash. Ct. App. 1984). *Cf.* Marketic v. U.S. Bank, N.A., 436 F. Supp. 2d 842 (N.D. Tex. 2006) (under the Texas Constitution, discount "points" are interest, not fees subject to the cap); Fidelity Fin. Servs. v. Hicks, 574 N.E.2d 15 (Ill. App. Ct. 1991) (denying motion to dismiss claim that creditor that charged thirteen points violated statute limiting loan to three points; rejecting creditor's argument that statute deregulating interest rates had impliedly repealed limitation on points).

43 *See In re* Bogan, 281 F. Supp. 242 (W.D. Tenn. 1968); Cheshire Mortgage v. Montes, 612 A.2d 1130, 1142 n.29 (Conn. 1992); Md. Code Ann., Com. Law § 12-107. *Cf.* Miller v. Pac. Shore Funding, 224 F. Supp. 2d 977 (D. Md. 2002) (Maryland's 10% cap on loan origination fees for secondary mortgages is calculated based upon "net proceeds" of loan; statute provides formula for calculating net proceeds), *aff'd on other grounds,* 92 Fed. Appx. 933 (4th Cir. 2004) (affirming dismissal of claims based on statute of limitations and standing grounds). *But cf.* Nilsen v. Long Beach Mortgage Co.,

It is arguable that even when the points imposed fall within a statutorily authorized amount, there is an implicit reasonableness standard that must be met. In assessing a series of refinancings in which service charges (which, like points, were designed to compensate for the lender's expenses and services) were repeatedly assessed, the Tennessee Supreme Court said that a charge within the authorized maximum was merely prima facie valid, but the borrower might show that the charges did not bear a reasonable relation to those costs.[44] The logic is equally persuasive whether the fee is denominated points or service charges.

Even if a state statute specifically excludes points from interest without any numerical limitation, there may be another statutory restriction. For example, in Georgia, though the civil usury statute excludes points from interest without limit,[45] the criminal statute does not.[46] Points were also what took a nominal 15% loan over New York's 25% criminal usury cap.[47]

Points may be vulnerable to attack even in states that do not cap interest. A Montana decision, interpreting a statute that allowed any interest rate agreed to by the parties, held that points were not interest.[48] Instead, they were fees. Since the statute prohibited any fees that were not specifically authorized by the statute, the lender violated the statute by charging the points. Another court held that a lender violated an agreed-rate statute by charging points on top of the agreed interest rate, as this was a *sub rosa* way of charging interest in excess of the agreed rate.[49]

An excessive number of points is also a clue that the transaction may be vulnerable a more broad fairness-based challenge.[50]

### 4.3.3 Commitment Fees

Where a statute does not prevent it, a few courts have allowed the exclusion of a percentage-based commitment fee from interest. Commitment fees are assessed when a lender agrees to hold open a line of credit for a certain time, at a given interest rate. Some courts view commitment fees as non-interest compensation to the lender for granting the borrower an ongoing option to borrow money,[51] although there is authority for the position that the fee must be reasonable to be excluded from "interest."[52] Other courts have held that commitment fees merely compensate the lender for normal overhead risk involved in lending, and are therefore interest.[53]

---

2006 WL 2469141 (Wash. Ct. App. Aug. 28, 2006) (fee paid to independent broker does not count towards statutory origination fee cap even though fee was listed as origination fee on settlement statement). *See generally* § 5.6.2, *infra*.

44 Cumberland Capitol Corp. v. Patty, 556 S.W.2d 516 (Tenn. 1977). *See also In re* Bogan, 281 F. Supp. 242 (W.D. Tenn. 1968). *But see* Hathaway v. First Family Fin. Servs., Inc., 1 S.W.3d 634 (Tenn. 1999) (describing a change in Tennessee's constitution in response to the *Cumberland* decision and the enactment of a statute allowing a 4% service charge; unclear whether the *Cumberland* "reasonable" standard survived).

45 *See In re* Curtis, 83 B.R. 853 (Bankr. S.D. Ga. 1988); *In re* Cleveland, 67 B.R. 144 (Bankr. M.D. Ga. 1986).

46 *See* Moore v. Comfed Sav. Bank, 908 F.2d 834 (11th Cir. 1990); Norris v. Sigler Daisy Corp., 392 S.E.2d 242 (Ga. 1990); Eisenstein v. Diprimo, 2000 Ga. App. LEXIS 1140 (Ga. Ct. App. Sept. 15, 2000).

47 Fareri v. Rain's Int'l Ltd., 589 N.Y.S.2d 579 (N.Y. App. Div. 1992) (15% loan with $30,000 origination fee resulted in an effective rate of 26.14%, which violated criminal usury ceiling, thus loan was void ab initio). *See also* Kidd v. Delta Funding Corp., 2000 N.Y. Misc. LEXIS 29 (N.Y. Sup. Ct. Feb. 22, 2000) (processing fee which was not identified as a permitted "application" fee violates N.Y. Banking regulation for motion to dismiss purposes) , *later op. at* 751 N.Y.S.2d 267 (N.Y. App. Div. 2002) (affirming denial of lender's motion for summary judgment on fraud, unjust enrichment, and UDAP claims based on charging of illegal processing fees).

48 Wombold v. Associates Fin. Serv. Co., 104 P.3d 1080 (Mont. 2004) (points were not interest; however, lender's charging of points violated Montana Consumer Loan Act's restriction on fees not authorized by statute). Note that Montana's restrictions on non-interest fees no longer apply to first lien mortgages.

49 Garrison v. First Fed. Saving & Loan Ass'n, 402 S.E.2d 24 (Va. 1991).

50 *See* §§ 2.4, *supra*, 7.8, *infra*. *See also* National Consumer Law Center, Truth in Lending Ch. 9 (7th ed. 2010 and Supp.) (excessive points and fees as trigger for applicability of Home Ownership and Equity Protection Act provisions of Truth in Lending Act).

51 *See, e.g.*, Mims v. Fidelity Funding, Inc. (*In re* Auto Int'l Refrigeration), 275 B.R. 789 (Bankr. N.D. Tex. 2002) (bona fide commitment fee not interest if reasonable and supported by "separate and additional consideration"); St. Petersburg Bank & Trust Co. v. Hamm, 414 So. 2d 1071 (Fla. 1982); People v. Central Fed. Sav. & Loan Ass'n, 385 N.E.2d 555 (N.Y. 1978); Stedman v. Georgetown Sav. & Loan Ass'n, 595 S.W.2d 486 (Tex. 1979) (bona fide commitment fee not interest); Rollingbrook Inv. Co. v. Texas Nat'l Bank of Baytown, 790 S.W.2d 375 (Tex. App. 1990) (bona fide commitment fee may be charged for renewal option where commercial borrower had no right to renew and fee in fact was consideration for an option to borrow in the future; under circumstances, fact that no new money was advanced in the renewal was immaterial); Gibson v. Drew Mortgage Co., 696 S.W.2d 211 (Tex. App. 1985). *But see* Reiser v. Todd (*In re* Chari), 2005 WL 4030034 (Bankr. S.D. Ohio Sept. 2, 2005) (fee paid as compensation for the lender's commitment to make a loan was for the use or forbearance of money paid and, therefore, constituted interest). *But cf.* Brazosport Bank v. Oak Park Townhouses, 837 S.W.2d 652 (Tex. App. 1992) (evidence inconclusive that up-front fee was a bona fide commitment fee or authorized interest, so court upheld trial finding that it was an unauthorized fee for making loan; appellate court held appropriate penalty under relevant statute was disallowance of fee rather than a usury violation), *rev'd on other grounds*, 851 S.W.2d 189 (Tex. 1993). *See generally* Annotation, 93 A.L.R.3d 1156 (1979).

52 *See* Mims v. Fidelity Funding, Inc. (*In re* Auto Int'l Refrigeration), 275 B.R. 789 (Bankr. N.D. Tex. 2002) (commitment fee must be reasonable to be excluded from interest); Altherr v. Wilshire Mortgage Corp., 448 P.2d 859 (Ariz. 1968) (*reasonable* commitment fee); First Am. Bank & Trust v. Windjammer Time Sharing Resort, Inc., 483 So. 2d 732 (Fla. Dist. Ct. App. 1986) (reasonableness depends on market conditions and industry practice; 20% commitment fee was clearly unreasonable when industry norm was between 1.5% and 5%).

53 *See* Henslee v. Madison Guar. Sav. & Loan, 760 S.W.2d 842 (Ark. 1988); First Nat'l Mortgage Co. v. Arkmo Lumber & Supply Co., 641 S.W.2d 31 (Ark. 1982). *See also* Johnston v. Citizens Bank & Trust, 659 F.2d 865 (8th Cir. 1981) (applying Arkansas law); *In re* Feldman, 259 F. Supp. 218 (D. Conn. 1966) ("commitment fee" was interest).

The latter view should prevail in consumer cases because, in the average consumer credit transaction, only one loan is sought and the borrower will almost certainly exercise his or her "option" to borrow as soon as the lender allows it. Under such circumstances, the notion of payment for an option loses all credibility.[54]

An exception may be the annual fee imposed on many credit card users. Such fees closely resemble commitment fees since the cardholder obtains a true line of credit which may or may not be used. Credit card lenders invariably take advantage of federal preemption to avoid state statutory restrictions on annual fees.[55]

A variation on commitment fees is the "rate lock fee," which consumers pay to obtain a certain interest rate for a mortgage.[56] However, this fee is different in that it does not guarantee the option to borrow, but instead guarantees the price of borrowing if the loan is approved.

## 4.4 Hidden Interest When Principal Amount Is Overstated

### *4.4.1 Introduction*

Interest can be hidden by exaggerating the amount of principal which a borrower has received. The idea behind inflating the principal amount is essentially a variation on the use of discount interest.[57] To use a simplistic example, a borrower might receive $100 from a lender while signing a note obliging him or her to pay back $120 in "principal" a year later. The $20 difference is clearly interest, although such arrangements are occasionally touted as no-interest loans.[58] Similarly, a check casher may "defer presentment" of a check with a face amount of $120, give the consumer $100, and require the consumer to cover the check in two weeks. The $20 difference is a finance charge which translates into a 520% annual percentage rate.[59]

Of course, the "hiding" of the interest in these examples is quite transparent and may be questioned even by unsophisticated consumers. However, if some justification is given for the $20 increase in principal, the transaction begins to look reasonable. Even though it is more expensive than the loan described above, a borrower might be less likely to question a transaction in which the lender gave him or her $100, added a $20 "processing fee," and then charged 10% interest on the $120. Similarly, the borrower might not question a transaction in which a retail seller took what would normally be a $300 television set, marked the price up to $360, and then offered it on "easy credit" terms. Yet, in essence, all of these transactions are the same; the creditor in some manner inflates the principal amount of the loan or the price of the goods sold, and then charges interest on the inflated total.

### *4.4.2 Fees Added to Principal; General Methods of Overstating Principal*

The most common technique used to inflate loan principal is the inclusion of various fees in the face amount of the note.[60] Assume that a borrower applies for a $1,000 loan. The lender approves the loan, but tells the borrower that she will have to pay a $10 credit investigation fee, a $20 service charge, and $70 for credit property insurance on her car which, by the way, she will have to provide as security. The borrower is unlikely to have $100 in cash for the fees, and the finance company lends the borrower the $100 for the fees as well as the $1,000 that she wanted originally. The borrower signs a $1,100 note which provides for interest at the statutory maximum, the lender deducts $100 for the fees, and the borrower keeps $1,000.

At least two usury issues are raised by such transactions. First, as discussed at § 4.2, *supra,* is whether the fees fall within the definition of interest under state law. If the controlling statute allows the exclusion of credit insurance premiums from interest, but makes no such provision for credit investigation or service charges, then the contract contains $30 of hidden interest, even if the borrower pays the fees out of his or her pocket. If the note already carries an interest rate at the statutory maximum, then the addition of the $30 renders the contract usurious.

The usury in this contract, however, does not stop at the $30.[61] The fact that the lender financed the hidden interest fees means that the face amount of the note signed by the borrower includes interest charges. The interest rate should be calculated on the basis of the principal actually received by the borrower, without the hidden interest, not on the face amount of the

54 *See* Mims v. Fidelity Funding, Inc. (*In re* Auto Int'l Refrigeration), 275 B.R. 789 (Bankr. N.D. Tex. 2002) (commitment fee was not bona fide and thus was interest when it was paid, not to hold option open, but at closing after loan was entered into and as a condition of receiving the funds); Gonzales Cty. Sav. & Loan Ass'n v. Freeman, 534 S.W.2d 903 (Tex. 1976) (distinguishing bona fide commitment fee for option permitting borrower to enter into loan in future from fee arising after parties had entered into loan agreement).

55 *See* § 3.4, *supra.*

56 *See, e.g.,* Jones v. E*Trade Mortgage, 397 F.3d 810 (9th Cir. 2005) (rate-lock fee must be refunded when consumer exercises right of rescission under Truth in Lending Act).

57 *See generally* § 5.3.3, *infra.*

58 *See, e.g.,* National Travis Inc. v. Gialousakis, 466 N.Y.S.2d 624 (N.Y. Sup. Ct. 1983). *See also* Wilner v. O'Donnell, 637 S.W.2d 757 (Mo. Ct. App. 1982) ($25,000 is true loan principal when lender receives immediate $5,000 kickback from $30,000 loan); Clausing v. Virginia Lee Homes, 384 P.2d 644 (Wash. 1963) (loan was usurious where promissory note stated loan amount was $67,500, but borrowers only received $56,000 in cash.).

59 *See generally* Ch. 9, *infra* (payday loans).

60 *See generally* § 4.5, *infra* (third-party fees).

61 *See* Kenty v. Bank One, Columbus, N.A., 1992 WL 170605 (S.D. Ohio Apr. 23, 1992) (if force-placed insurance includes unnecessary and unauthorized coverage, excess premium is interest, as is interest charged on it), *aff'd in part and rev'd in part*, 92 F.3d 384 (6th Cir. 1995) (though excessive premium may be interest, usury cap not applicable by virtue of state law and the most favored lender doctrine).

note.[62] Since the lender has been charging interest on the full face amount of the note including the $30 of hidden interest, it obviously has been assessing interest on interest, i.e., compounding. This compounding leads to a second overcharge in addition to the $30.[63] Specifically, if the contract rate were 10% add-on interest, the compounding would create a $3 annual overcharge. Given a two-year loan term, the total overcharge would be $36.

If the compounding raises the effective rate above the usury ceiling, usury will result.[64] But the presence of compounding also raises issues beyond the legality of the effective interest rate charged by the lender. Courts traditionally frown upon the use of compound interest, and the mere presence of compounding may be treated as a contract overcharge in some jurisdictions, even when the usury ceiling has not been breached.[65] Similarly, the inclusion of interest charges in the face amount of a note amounts to the assessment of discount interest, at least in part, on the credit contract.[66] While most usury statutes limit only the effective interest rate charged by a creditor and do not regulate the precise method by which a creditor may calculate contract interest, a few statutes do prohibit the assessment of discount interest.[67] The inclusion of hidden interest fees in the face amount of a note could thus violate a statutory prohibition of discounting and could, depending on the statute, lead to usury penalties even if the effective interest ceiling had not been exceeded.

The practice of deducting fees from the proceeds paid to the borrower is particularly profitable since many of the fees will not represent out-of-pocket expenses to the lender. Even the credit insurance premium, which must be paid to an insurance company, contains a significant commission that will be returned to the lender. Thus, the creditor can exclude from interest sums which largely represent overhead expense or profit, but it can simultaneously charge interest on those sums. A few statutes, however, do prohibit lenders from charging interest on certain financed costs.[68]

A creditor may inflate the loan principal in ways other than padding it with fees. For example, where a creditor erroneously required the borrower to make the first payment on the date of consummation, rather than thirty days later, the payment should have been treated as a down payment, rather than a part of the principal upon which interest was charged.[69] In addition, charging interest on the full amount of the loan from the date of consummation when some of it was withheld by the creditor in escrow for later disbursal may improperly inflate the principal.[70]

Another scheme from Illinois involved a creditor that required its customers to deposit $250 in order to obtain a loan for $750. The lender placed the cash money in its general operating account to return to the consumers after they made all of the payments on the $750 loan. However, the lender disclosed the amount financed as $750, not $500, even though the net effect of the transaction was that the consumers received a $500 loan. The Seventh Circuit confirmed the consumers' TILA claims and reversed the lower court's denial of class certification which included an unfair and deceptive practices claim.[71]

Some of these devices can be extraordinarily expensive. One device, seen in several variations, might be called "the prepaid payment pyramid." In its most extreme form, a lender writes a one-payment, one-year balloon note, but deducts up-front the equivalent of twelve monthly interest-only payments from the face amount of the note. As this is, in effect, discount interest,[72] the real interest rate on this purported 24% loan is 66.67%.[73]

---

62 *See, e.g.*, Rollins v. Odom, 519 So. 2d 652, 656 (Fla. Dist. Ct. App. 1988) (for purpose of statute on computing effective rate of interest, the principal is the "actual amount of money which the lender turns over to the borrower"). *See also* Sparkman & McLean Income Fund v. Wald, 520 P.2d 173, 175–176 (Wash. Ct. App. 1974) (lender cannot evade usury laws by using note that is non-usurious on its face while actually disbursing less than the principal amount of the note).

63 *See* Westervelt v. Gateway Fin. Serv., 464 A.2d 1203, 1207 (N.J. Super. Ct. App. Div. 1983). *See also* Kenty v. Bank One, Columbus, N.A., 1992 WL 170605 (S.D. Ohio Apr. 23, 1992) (if force-placed insurance includes unnecessary and unauthorized coverage, excess premium is interest, as is interest charged on excess premium), *aff'd in part and rev'd in part*, 92 F.3d 384 (6th Cir. 1995) (though excessive premium may be interest, usury cap not applicable by virtue of state law and the most favored lender doctrine); Clark v. Aetna Fin. Corp., 340 N.W.2d 747 (Wis. Ct. App. 1983) (interest charged on funds never received by borrower).

64 *See* Giventer v. Arnow, 372 N.Y.S.2d 63 (N.Y. App. Div. 1975).

65 *See* § 5.5.1, *infra*.

66 *See* § 5.3.3, *infra*. This form of discount is a one-time charge, however, and includes no time factor in its calculation as does traditional "discount interest."

67 Discounting was prohibited under the Uniform Small Loan Law, upon which many existing small loan and consumer loan statutes are based. *See* Uniform Small Loan Law, Seventh Draft § 13(b) (1942), *reprinted in* Curran, Trends in Consumer Credit Legislation (1966) (charges "shall not be paid, deducted, or received in advance").

68 *See* Brown v. Nowlin, 570 P.2d 1246, 1250–1251 (Ariz. 1977). *But cf.* Dietrich v. Camargo Cadillac Co., 504 N.E.2d 1201 (Ohio Ct. App. 1986) (sales tax could be included in "cash price" and could be financed by seller); Fanning v. Fritz's Pontiac-Cadillac-Buick, Inc., 472 S.E.2d 242 (S.C. 1996) (procurement fee was legitimately part of sales price of car because it was charged to cash and credit customers alike and was disclosed to buyer).

69 Edwards v. Alabama Farm Bureau Mut. Cas. Ins. Co., 509 So. 2d 232 (Ala. Civ. App. 1986) (creditor failed to carry burden that this was a bona fide computation error).

70 *See* Danziger v. San Jacinto Sav. Ass'n, 732 S.W.2d 300 (Tex. 1987). *But see* McPherson Ent. v. Producers Co-op., 827 S.W.2d 94 (Tex. App. 1992) (interest rate applied to improper principal held not usury. [*Ed. Note*: The court for inscrutable reasons did not deal with this as a bona fide error case (*see* § 7.5.5.2, *infra*), which would have made sense in the circumstances. As it is, this intermediate court case looks to be at odds with *Danziger*]).

71 Williams v. Chartwell Fin. Servs., Ltd., 204 F.3d 748 (7th Cir. 2000).

72 *See* § 5.3.3, *infra*. *But see* Concord Realty Co. v. Continental Funding Corp., 776 P.2d 1114 (Colo. 1989) (lender withheld portion of proceeds of commercial loan to cover interest payment that would come due during loan term, and placed this amount in reserve account; this was principal, not interest).

73 The proceeds to the borrower amounted to $24,000. The note was for $40,000, and $9,600 in prepaid payments was deducted along

### 4.4.3 Indexing Loan Principal

A less common method of inflating loan principal is to adjust the principal periodically to compensate for currency inflation or some other factor, for example by pegging the principal to the consumer price index.[74] If the consumer price index shows a 5% inflation rate for each of several years, and the contract provides for annual adjustments, the outstanding loan principal would be multiplied by a factor of 1.05 at the end of each year. Payments for the subsequent year would be calculated using this adjusted principal amount.

The few courts which have directly considered the indexing of loan principal have agreed that the amount of an upward adjustment in principal is, in fact, hidden interest which may render the loan usurious.[75] The risk of inflation is inherent in the act of lending money, and the lender is compensated for this risk through the payment of interest. Interest rates at the time a contract is consummated reflect the level of inflation anticipated over the term of the loan. Additional loan payments, made possible by an indexed principal, are additional payments for a risk the lender has already incurred and, as such, are interest.

### 4.4.4 Compensating Balances

Another method through which a creditor may overstate the principal amount of a loan and, thereby, understate the true interest rate on the loan is to require that the borrower maintain an account with the lender with a minimum deposit of, perhaps, ten percent of the stated amount of the loan. This "compensating balance," which remains in the lender's control, is frequently described as "security" which is supposed to guarantee payments on the loan. In fact, it is just another form of discount because the borrower is paying interest on a larger sum than he or she is actually receiving. Frequently, no formal account will be maintained, but the lender's books will simply be adjusted to show a higher principal amount than the amount actually disbursed.

Compensating balance requirements have a long history in usury law, and it is generally recognized by the courts that a credit contract is usurious if a borrower is required to maintain a compensating balance as a condition of receiving the loan, and if the resulting interest rate, based on the principal actually received by the borrower, exceeds the state's interest ceiling.[76] The critical question is whether the lender requires the deposit and maintains control over it.[77] Such control is strongly suggested when a lender commingles the deposit with its own funds.[78]

The Tennessee Supreme Court, considering a variant in which the lender required the borrower to purchase an investment certificate as a condition of receiving the loan, sensibly observed that the borrower is, in effect, funding his own loan to the extent of the required investment. Since interest is, in theory, payment for the use of the lender's money, this creates a conceptual problem. In a case in which the lender required the purchase of a $50,000 investment certificate to secure a $100,000 loan, the court explained it this way: The borrower was paying 9.5% on $50,000 of the bank's money and $50,000 of his own money, while receiving only a 5.5% return on his investment certificate. The bank thus netted 4% on the borrower's $50,000, effectively receiving 13.5% interest on its money, a usurious return under applicable law.[79]

However, courts have refused to find usury when the evidence failed to establish that the lender *required* the borrower to maintain the compensating balance.[80] Similarly, deposits in escrow accounts which are not controlled by the lender may not be usurious.[81] Finally, a few courts have declined to find usury

with other interesting closing costs. The effective rate is 66.67%. Such machinations are the reason the Home Ownership and Equity Protection Act provisions of the Truth in Lending Act limits prepaid payments.

74 *See generally* Note, *Indexed Principal: A Way Around Usury Laws?*, 31 Ark. L. Rev. 141 (1977); Note, *Purchasing-Power Adjusted Loans*, 45 U. Mo. K.C. L. Rev. 140 (1976–1977); Note, *Indexing The Principal: The Usury Laws Hang Tough*, 37 U. Pitt. L. Rev. 755 (1976).

75 Olwine v. Torrens, 344 A.2d 655 (Pa. Super. Ct. 1975); Aztec Properties v. Union Planters Nat'l Bank of Memphis, 530 S.W.2d 756 (Tenn. 1975).

76 *See, e.g.*, American Timber & Trading Co. v. First Nat'l Bank, 690 F.2d 781 (9th Cir. 1982); Harris v. McCann, 319 S.W.2d 832 (Ark. 1959); Tri-County Fed. Sav. & Loan Ass'n v. Lyle, 371 A.2d 424 (Md. 1977); Grundel v. Bank of Craig, 515 S.W.2d 177 (Mo. Ct. App. 1974). *See generally* Annotation, 92 A.L.R.3d 769 (1970).

77 American Timber & Trading Co. v. First Nat'l Bank, 690 F.2d 781 (9th Cir. 1982). *See generally* Annotation, 92 A.L.R.3d 769 (1979).

78 *See* American Acceptance Corp. v. Schoenthaler, 391 F.2d 64 (5th Cir. 1968); *In re* Montagne, 421 B.R. 65 (Bankr. D. Vt. 2009) (holding that lender violated applicable state usury cap by (1) charging commercial borrower interest on entire face amount of loan when part of loan was held by lender in "suspense account" upon which borrower could draw and (2) co-mingling "suspense account" with other funds in lender's own interest-earning investment account; loan found unenforceable going forward but lender not required to disgorge earned interest); Bank of Lumpkin v. Farmers' State Bank, 132 S.E. 221 (Ga. 1926); Lyle v. Tri-County Fed. Sav. & Loan Ass'n, 363 A.2d 642 (Md. Ct. Spec. App. 1976), *aff'd*, 371 A.2d 424 (Md. 1977); Miller v. First State Bank, 551 S.W.2d 89 (Tex. Civ. App. 1977), *modified on other grounds*, 563 S.W.2d 572 (Tex. 1978). *But cf.* Starness v. Guaranty Bank, 634 S.W.2d 325 (Tex. App. 1982) (ignoring commingling of funds when interest-bearing certificate of deposit required by lender was not purchased with loan proceeds).

79 Continental Bankers Life Ins. Co. v. Bank, 578 S.W.2d 625, 636 (Tenn. 1979), *quoted* in Brabson v. Valentine, 804 S.W.2d 451 (Tenn. Ct. App. 1990).

80 *See, e.g.*, Rebman v. Flagship First Nat'l Bank, 472 So. 2d 1360 (Fla. Dist. Ct. App. 1985) (no-interest escrow account was not compensating balance because not required by contract); Swanson v. Gulf W. Int'l Corp., 429 So. 2d 817 (Fla. Dist. Ct. App. 1983); Reid v. National Bank of Georgia, 256 S.E.2d 82 (Ga. Ct. App. 1979).

81 *See also In re* Curtis, 83 B.R. 853 (Bankr. S.D. Ga. 1988) (where required escrow bears realistic relationship to charges it is designed to cover, it is a permissible charge, distinguishing Knight v. First Fed. Sav. & Loan, 260 S.E.2d 511 (Ga. Ct. App. 1979)); Concord Realty Co. v. Continental Funding Corp., 776 P.2d 1114, 1122 (Colo. 1989) (en banc) (reserve accounts for payment of prior encumbrances and interest during one-year term of note constituted principal; commercial transaction, but U.C.C.C. used as guide in

when a loan commitment required the lender to release loan proceeds on a certain date, but the lender instead placed the proceeds in an account pending the borrower's completion of some contract requirement.[82] Such lender delays in the disbursal of loan proceeds are only justified, however, when the delay is caused by the borrower.[83]

### 4.4.5 Inflating the Sale Price

Interest can be hidden in the price of goods purchased on credit in the same manner that it is concealed in the principal amount of a loan. For example, a seller can offer low-rate financing, but then simply jack up the price of the product for buyers who take advantage of the offer.

At least in theory, the concealment of interest in an inflated cash price should cause a usury violation, if the true interest rate exceeds the statutory limit.[84] However, some states still recognize the traditional "time-price exception" to state usury laws.[85] These states allow the seller to charge whatever price it can extract, short of unconscionability, for installment sales of goods. In these jurisdictions, the time-price doctrine will preclude usury unless the purchaser can convince a court that the seller's failure to state an accurate cash price removes the transaction from the time-price usury exception.[86]

However, the time-price doctrine has been abolished in many states, and has been replaced by Retail Installment Sales Acts or other statutes which limit the finance charge that a seller can collect in a credit sale.[87] In such situations, the difference between the stated sale price and the actual value of the goods purchased is a clear example of hidden interest which, when included in the rate calculations, may cause usury. Hiding interest in the cash price, and the difficulties of proving the actual value of the goods, are discussed in more detail in the context of auto financing at § 10.3.6, *infra*.

### 4.4.6 Seller's Points

A special method by which interest costs may be hidden in the sale price of goods or real estate is the use of "seller's points." Seller's points occur most frequently in real estate transactions when the real estate seller, typically a builder, pays points to a bank or other lender in return for the lender's commitment to issue "low-interest" loans to qualified buyers. Such an arrangement might appear to be a boon to buyers and, indeed, seller's points would not be deceptive or usurious, if the seller did not recover its expense by raising the selling price of the real estate. In real life, however, seller's points are frequently, if not invariably, just a sales gimmick whose cost is passed on to the buyer in the form of an inflated sale price.[88]

---

determining principal and interest). *Compare In re* Bryant, 39 B.R. 313 (Bankr. D. Nev. 1984) ("undisbursed principal" was not usurious when held by broker and available to lenders only with restrictions), *and* Knight v. First Fed. Sav. & Loan Ass'n, 260 S.E.2d 511 (Ga. Ct. App. 1979), *with* Hoffman v. Key Fed. Sav. & Loan Ass'n, 416 A.2d 1265 (Md. 1979) (borrower stated usury claim when interest assessed on escrow account if all or part of it was under sole control of lender), *and* Danziger v. San Jacinto Sav. Ass'n, 732 S.W.2d 300 (Tex. 1987) (when borrower did not receive all of loan proceeds, practice of charging interest on all of proceeds and periodically rebating excess charges to escrow account was usurious).

82 *E.g.*, Bettum v. Montgomery Fed. Sav. & Loan Ass'n, 277 A.2d 600 (Md. 1971).

83 *See* Williamson v. Clark, 120 So. 2d 637 (Fla. Dist. Ct. App. 1960). *See also* Danziger v. San Jacinto Sav. Ass'n, 732 S.W.2d 300 (Tex. 1987) (when borrower did not receive all of loan proceeds, practice of charging interest on all of proceeds and periodically rebating excess charges to escrow account was usurious).

84 *See In re* Stewart, 93 B.R. 878 (Bankr. E.D. Pa. 1988) (goods priced at $2,000 which were readily available at a retail price of $900 concealed a finance charge of over 80% instead of the disclosed 18%, thus violating state RISA); Riley v. Red River Marine, Inc., 664 S.W.2d 200 (Ark. 1984) (where car price raised by $200 from price on original bill of sale to price on subsequent retail installment sale agreement, the $200 inflated price constituted interest and rendered the transaction usurious); United-Bilt Homes, Inc. v. Elder, 615 S.W.2d 367 (Ark. 1981) (usury in inflated price of insulation and cabinets in prefabricated home revealed when buyers were required to obtain their own installation); Rowe Auto & Trailer Sales, Inc. v. King, 517 S.W.2d 946 (Ark. 1975) (allegations of TILA and usury violations in inflated price of used car). *See also* American Sav. Life Ins. Co. v. Fin. Affairs Mgmt. Co., 474 P.2d 51 (Ariz. Ct. App. 1970) (loan principal included deliberately over-valued stock); Mutual Home Dealers Corp. v. Alves, 258 N.Y.S.2d 786 (N.Y. App. Div. 1965) (allegation of inflated cash price as cloak for usury in credit sale was meritorious defense sufficient to vacate default judgment). *But see* King v. Western United Assurance Co., 997 P.2d 1007 (Wash. Ct. App. 2000) (discount that consumer could have gotten in the sale price of real estate if she paid in cash is not interest where the financed price was no higher than the appraised price).

85 *See* § 7.5.2.2, *infra* (discussing more completely the time-price doctrine).

86 Generally speaking, a transaction will not fall within the time-price doctrine if it looks too much like a loan. This may happen if the niceties of quoting separate cash and time prices are not observed. Daniel v. First Nat'l Bank of Birmingham, 227 F.2d 353 (5th Cir. 1955).

If the seller appears to be a mere front for a lender to whom the credit sale contract is immediately sold. Hare v. General Contract Purchase Corp., 249 S.W.2d 973 (Ark. 1952); Midland Guardian Co. v. Thacker, 314 S.E.2d 26 (S.C. Ct. App. 1984).

Or if the goods being sold are a sham. W.T. Grant Co. v. Walsh, 241 A.2d 46 (N.J. Dist. Ct. 1968) (coupons/script); Tuition Plan, Inc. v. Zicari, 335 N.Y.S.2d 95 (N.Y. Dist. Ct. 1972) (retail installment contract for tuition money was loan).

Also where a seller raises its sale price based on the reasonable assurance of discounting its credit contracts to a finance company, the transaction may be in substance a loan subject to usury laws rather than a bona fide credit sale. *See* Hare v. Gen. Contract Purchase Corp., 249 S.E.2d 973 (Ark. 1952). *See also* Butler v. Holt Machinery Co., 741 S.W.2d 169 (Tex. App. 1987), *corrected on denial of rehearing*, 739 S.W.2d 958 (1987) (where creditor added interest charges which were neither agreed to nor disclosed to the time-sale price in what was really a lending transaction rather than a credit sale, such charges should be deducted from the price).

It may also be fraud. *See* Johnson v. Mercury Fin., Clearinghouse No. 50,407, Case No. CV 93-952 (Ala. Cir. Ct. Aug. 1994) (jury verdict); § 12.10, *infra*.

87 *See* §§ 2.3.6, *supra*, 10.2, *infra*.

88 *See* William N. Eskridge, Jr., *One Hundred Years of Ineptitude: The Need for Mortgage Rules Consonant with the Economic and Psy-*

The few usury statutes that specifically consider payments by sellers to lenders usually treat them the same as points paid directly by buyers.[89] Some statutes, however, legitimize seller's points provided that they are not passed on to buyers,[90] which leaves open the question of what amounts to passing the points on to the buyer.

In the absence of express statutory treatment, practitioners should examine the underlying structure of the usury statute. If the statute defines interest as payments received by the lender without discussing who makes the payments, then a strong argument can be made that any payment to the lender, including seller's points, are interest.[91]

If the relevant statutory language is inconclusive, it is possible to argue that seller's points should always be seen as interest because they inherently involve the inflation of the sale price beyond what it would be in their absence. Despite the appeal of this argument, for which at least some support exists,[92] practitioners should recognize that there is a strong predisposition among the courts to rule that a seller can name whatever price it wants for its property without usury becoming an issue. To overcome this predisposition, it may be necessary to prove that the seller literally raised its price to compensate for points.[93] Such a proof might be established by evidence that preliminary sale negotiations, before seller's points were involved, contemplated a lower price than the final agreement; by evidence that the buyers were offered a better sale price on the condition that they obtained their own financing; or by evidence that cash buyers of the seller's property in general received better prices than credit buyers who used seller's points financing.

## 4.5 Payments for Third-Party Services

### *4.5.1 General Principles*

Credit contracts frequently contain not only fees which are assessed for various lender services, but also fees collected by the lender on behalf of third parties who have, in fact or theory, provided some service to the borrower in connection with the contract. Third-party payments may cover a myriad of services: broker fees, appraisal fees, recording fees, credit insurance, inspection fees, and attorney fees, to name but a few. The type of services provided by third parties can overlap with services which lenders themselves at times provide and charge for, the only difference being the identity of the party that does the work and ultimately receives the fee.

Some state statutes expressly limit the amount or types of fees that can be charged in a particular transaction: regardless of whether the fee is treated as principal or interest, it simply cannot be charged.[94] For example, some small loan laws prohibit lenders from selling insurance other than certain types, regardless of whether the premium is treated as interest or as principal.[95] In addition, if the insurance is required as part of the credit transaction, the fee may be illegal under state law for this reason.[96]

Other statutes, instead of specifying the type of fees that can be charged, specify whether they must be treated as interest for purposes of a usury cap. A few states include third-party fees in

---

*chological Dynamics of the Home Sale and Loan Transaction*, 70 Va. L. Rev. 1083, 1136, n.167 (1984).

89 Mich. Comp. Laws § 438.31c(2)(b) (prohibiting lender from imposing discount or points on purchaser or seller except as specified); Ohio Rev. Code Ann. § 1343.011 (West) (capping discount points whether paid by seller or buyer); W. Va. Code § 47-6-5b(g) (defining points to include sums received by lender "from whatever source"). *See also* B.F. Saul Co. v. West End Park N., Inc., 246 A.2d 591 (Md. 1968) (statutory language—"extracted by a lender from either the borrower or any other person"—covers sellers points). *But see* 10 Pa. Code § 7.2 (excluding seller's points from definition of "discount points").

90 *See* Md. Code Ann., Com. Law § 12-105(f) (seller's points are not interest; may not be charged to home purchaser unless they are charged as interest). *See also* Maine Bureau of Consumer Credit Protection Advisory Ruling No. 56, Consumer Cred. Guide (CCH) ¶ 97,083 (Aug. 11, 1981); Opinion of the Wisconsin Attorney General, No. OAG 116-79 Consumer Cred. Guide (CCH) ¶ 97,537 (Nov. 30, 1979).

91 *See* Yasner v. Commercial Mortgage Co., 295 A.2d 209 (N.J. Essex Cty. Ct. 1972). *See also* B.F. Saul Co. v. West End Park N., Inc., 246 A.2d 591 (Md. 1968). *But see* McArthur v. Schenck, 31 Wis. 673 (1873).

92 *See* Johnson v. Federal Nat'l Mortgage Ass'n, 609 S.W.2d 60 (Ark. 1980) (Smith, J. concurring). In his concurring opinion, Judge Smith succinctly describes the essence of a seller's points transaction. The buyer, seller, and lender sit down at a table. The lender gives the buyer, say, $100,000 in return for a promissory note. The buyer hands over the $100,000 to the seller for the purchase price, and the seller then gives perhaps $2,000 back to the lender (two points). Seen in this light, it is difficult to consider the two seller's points to be anything but discount interest, paid by the buyer. This approach to seller's points is effectively ratified by the numerous statutes which treat all seller's points as interest.

93 *See* Johnson v. Federal Nat'l Mortgage Ass'n, 609 S.W.2d 60 (Ark. 1980); Maynard v. England, 538 P.2d 551 (Wash. Ct. App. 1975).
The idea that a buyer must prove that the seller literally raised an earlier price to recover the cost of seller's points does not make much sense because there is no real difference between that situation and one in which the seller sets the original price in contemplation of recovering its seller's points, or one in which the seller agrees to pay points instead of lowering the sale price. *Compare* Johnson v. Federal Nat'l Mortgage Ass'n, 609 S.W.2d 60 (Ark. 1980), *with* Hare v. General Contract Purchase Corp., 249 S.W.2d 973 (Ark. 1952) (price inflated in anticipation of discount).

94 *See, e.g.*, Hawkins v. Thorp Credit & Thrift Co., 441 N.W.2d 470 (Minn. 1989) (small loan law prohibits licensees from selling insurance other than credit insurance); Turner v. First Union Nat'l Bank, 740 A.2d 1081 (N.J. 1999) (interpreting state statute that prohibited imposition of document preparation fee in some circumstances, but finding it permissible here).

95 *See, e.g.*, Hawkins v. Thorp Credit & Thrift Co., 441 N.W.2d 470 (Minn. 1989) (small loan law prohibits licensees from selling insurance other than credit insurance).

96 *See* Compton v. Altavista Motors, Inc., 121 F. Supp. 2d 932, 940 (W.D. Va. 2000) (denying summary judgment on whether GAP insurance was voluntary; if required, the premium was an unlawful finance charge under state law); Aclin Ford Co. v. Cordell, 625 S.W.2d 459 (Ark. 1981) (credit insurance premium was interest and caused interest rate to exceed state cap where it was required by creditor).

the calculation of the finance charge,[97] in effect capping them, at least in the aggregate. Generally, however, case law and statutes exclude reasonable, bona fide third-party payments from interest or the finance charge on credit contracts.[98]

The rationale for excluding third-party fees from the definition of interest is essentially the same as that which allows lenders to assess some non-interest fees directly; the services provided are regarded as separate from the extension of credit and, therefore, as separately compensable.[99] The argument for excluding fees from interest is stronger, however, in the case of third-party payments than in the case of direct lender fees. The lender presumably does not retain the fee, so it is not compensation to the lender, although the creditor may in fact attempt to reduce its overhead expense by contracting out work that would otherwise be done by its employees.

In addition, third-party services are typically more concrete and easily distinguished from the extension of credit than many lender "services." In some cases, though, this rationale fails almost entirely. For example, appraisal fees and title-related costs are commonly excluded from characterization as interest in real-estate-secured transactions.[100] In purchase-money mortgages, such services do provide some benefit to both parties—assuring the borrowers they will obtain clear title to property worth the sales price, and the lenders that they are adequately protected by the collateral. In non-purchase-money mortgages, however, they have little relevance to the homeowners, and almost exclusively serve the lenders' interest in adequate protection.

## 4.5.2 Subterfuges

### 4.5.2.1 Sham Third Parties

Despite the general rule that bona fide third-party payments are not interest or components of the finance charge, usury laws could easily be circumvented if a subsidiary or agent of the lender could collect non-interest payments on the lender's behalf. Accordingly, courts have held that payments to a creditor's agents or employees are not bona fide third-party payments.[101]

### 4.5.2.2 Upcharges, Kickbacks, Unexpended Fees, and Fees for Products Different from Those Represented

A third-party fee for an item or service that the lender does not actually acquire from the third party is interest.[102] Third-party payments may also involve hidden interest when the third party kicks back a percentage of its fee to the lender,[103] or the

97 *See, e.g.*, Tavares v. Sprunk (*In re* Tavares), 298 B.R. 195 (Bankr. D. Mass. 2003) (fees to third parties included in calculation of interest rate for purposes of determining whether loan violates Massachusetts criminal usury statute); Luttenegger v. Conseco Fin. Servs. Corp., 671 N.W.2d 425 (Iowa 2003) (courier fee was included in Iowa U.C.C.C. definition of "finance charge" for consumer loans; such fees permissible so long as resulting finance charge does not exceed 21% cap); Gardin v. Long Beach Mortgage Co., 661 N.W.2d 193 (Iowa 2003) (Iowa's 2% cap on loan processing fees for home-secured loans applies to fees paid to third parties for credit reports, appraisal, and broker fees, if they are collected by lender; however, cap does not apply to fees directly charged by third party).

98 *See, e.g.*, *In re* Richards, 272 F. Supp. 480 (D. Me. 1967) (credit insurance); Grantham v. First Union Home Equity Bank, 685 So. 2d 748 (Ala. Civ. App. 1996) (interpreting Ala. Code §§ 5-19-1 and 5-19-4(b)); Cooprider v. Security Bank, 890 S.W.2d 240 (Ark. 1994) (reasonable fees, "made in good faith," to third parties "for something appropriate to establishing or protecting the lender's security"; title insurance at issue); Lockhart v. G.M.A.C., 481 S.W.2d 350 (Ark. 1972) (declining to treat vendor's single interest insurance as interest); Concord Realty Co. v. Continental Funding Corp., 776 P.2d 1114 (Colo. 1989) (*en banc*) (appraisal fee, inspection fee, credit reports, federal express charges, legal fees at closing); Swanson v. Gulf W. Int'l Corp., 429 So. 2d 817 (Fla. Dist. Ct. App. 1983) (broker fee); Palmer v. Bank of Louisville & Trust Co., 682 S.W.2d 789 (Ky. Ct. App. 1985) (appraisal fees, title insurance fees, title search fees actually paid to third parties were not interest); Goldring v. Texas Commercial Bank, 665 S.W.2d 103 (Tex. 1984) (attorney fee); Durias v. Boswell, 791 P.2d 282 (Wash. Ct. App. 1990) (a reasonable fee for actual services performed is not interest; whether it is so is a question of fact (broker fee at issue)). *See also* 12 C.F.R. § 7.4001 (interest for purposes of National Bank Act § 85 does not include several enumerated charges typically payable to third parties, though not couched in terms of third-party payments).

99 *See generally* Ch. 6, *infra*.

100 *See, e.g.*, Capparelli v. Amerifirst Home Improvement Fin., 535 F. Supp. 2d 554 (E.D.N.C. 2008) (charges for document preparation, appraisal, and title search services fall within statutory list of fees for loan-related services that can be excluded from interest).

101 *See, e.g.*, *In re* Vehm Eng'g Corp., 521 F.2d 186 (9th Cir. 1975) (fee paid to lender's sister corporation was usurious interest); *In re* Dukes, 24 B.R. 404 (Bankr. E.D. Mich. 1982) (broker was not bona fide third party); Winston v. Personal Fin. Co., 249 S.W.2d 315 (Ark. 1952) (fees for services performed by lender's employees); Howes v. Curtis, 661 P.2d 729 (Idaho 1983) (no independent broker); Equitable Life Assurance Soc'y v. Ins. Comm'r, 246 A.2d 604 (Md. 1968); B.F. Saul v. West End Park N. Inc., 246 A.2d 591 (Md. 1968) (appraisal fees, fees for title work, and commission for credit insurance are interest when work was performed by lender's staff and lender retained the fees).

102 *See* United-Bilt Homes v. Teague, 432 S.W.2d 1 (Ark. 1968) (credit insurance premium was interest where lender collected it from borrower in advance but did not pay it in advance); United-Bilt Homes v. Knapp, 396 S.W.2d 40 (Ark. 1965) (usury when charges for credit life insurance and appraisals not expended); Cheshire Mortgage v. Montes, 612 A.2d 1130, 1142–1143 (Conn. 1992) (fee for recording future assignment of mortgage must be treated as part of prepaid finance charge, not principal, where lender never actually assigned the mortgage); Westervelt v. Gateway Fin. Serv., 464 A.2d 1203 (N.J. Super. Ct. Ch. Div. 1983) ($3,000 for credit life insurance which was not procured) *Cf.* Capparelli v. Amerifirst Home Improvement Fin., 535 F. Supp. 2d 554 (E.D.N.C. 2008) (document preparation, appraisal, and title search services were performed and therefore were bona fide and not interest under North Carolina law). *But see* Durante Bros. & Sons Inc. v. Flushing Nat'l Bank, 652 F. Supp. 101, 105 (E.D.N.Y. 1986) (exaggeration of lender's own costs in connection with loan supports claim of fraud rather than usury).

103 *See, e.g.*, Kenty v. Bank One, Columbus, N.A., 1992 WL 170605, at *4 (S.D. Ohio Apr. 23, 1992) (kickbacks or rebates from force-placed property insurance premium charged to consumer's account constitute interest), *aff'd in part and rev'd in part*, 92 F.3d 384 (6th Cir. 1995) (though excessive premium may be interest, usury cap not applicable by virtue of state law and the most favored lender doctrine); Stubbs v. Security Consumer Discount, 426 A.2d 1014

lender charges the borrower more than the amount paid.[104]

Consider the commission which lenders or their employees receive from insurance companies for selling credit insurance to borrowers. These payments often exceed half the insurance premium.[105] Logically, commissions should be interest because they are either direct income to the lender from the loan transaction or a significant supplement to its employees' incomes and, therefore, to its overhead, and sometimes are so held.[106] However, courts usually find insurance commissions to be hidden interest only when the borrower was required to purchase insurance from the creditor, or when evidence suggested either overpricing or the sale of unnecessary insurance.[107] On the other hand, kickbacks other than insurance commissions have been held to be hidden interest.[108]

Another issue is whether the fees actually purchase the intended product or service.[109] For example, some creditors that take personal property as collateral routinely purchase "non-filing insurance" to protect their secured party status as against other secured parties who may later acquire an interest in the same collateral. Discovery in litigation[110] may unearth a purported "non-filing insurance," that actually resembles a default reserve, whereby most of the "premium" fees are returned to the creditor to compensate for bad debt losses—bankruptcies, skips, and so forth.[111] Since this clearly is not non-filing insurance, it should be subject to challenge as hidden interest.

Similarly, premiums for property insurance, which creditors may require to protect collateral, may purchase coverage beyond that authorized by the contract or by law. A number of lawsuits have alleged that some "force-placed" insurance policies (purchased by creditors when borrowers fail to provide insurance or allow theirs to lapse) included additional coverage such as conversion, embezzlement and secretion, mechanics liens, premium deficiency, repossession expense, repossession storage expense, and repossessed vehicle coverage. The premium costs attributable to charges that are unauthorized and unnecessary to protect the collateral are interest.[112]

### 4.5.2.3 Services That Primarily Benefit the Lender

Another hidden interest issue in third-party payments is whom the services really benefit. Some services provided by third parties benefit both the creditor and the borrower. Credit insurance, for example, guarantees payment of outstanding debt if the debtor becomes ill or if the collateral is damaged. If both the creditor and the debtor benefit from the guarantee, the existence of some lender benefit will not alone demonstrate hidden interest.[113]

However, as the services become less beneficial to the borrower, the services begin to resemble non-cash compensation to the lender. For example, if a borrower pays for a credit report to be given to the lender, this payment should logically be treated as interest, even if the credit reporting company is a bona fide third party which retains all of the fee, because the report solely benefits the lender.[114] (However, such fees may be statutorily excluded from the definition of interest or finance charge.[115]) Courts and statutes often deal with this problem by requiring third-party expenses to be "reasonable" or "neces-

(N.J. 1980). *But see* Durante Bros. & Sons Inc. v. Flushing Nat'l Bank, 652 F. Supp. 101, 105 (E.D.N.Y. 1986) (exaggeration or misrepresentation of lender's own costs in connection with loan support claim of fraud rather than usury).

104 Garrison v. First Fed. Saving & Loan Ass'n, 402 S.E.2d 24 (Va. 1991) (appraisal fee in excess of actual charge was interest).

105 *See* Federal Deposit Ins. Corp. v. Gulf Life Ins. Co., 737 F.2d 1513 (11th Cir. 1984) (65% commission); United Fin. & Thrift Corp. v. Smith, 387 S.W.2d 752 (Tex. Civ. App. 1965) (85% commission). *See generally* § 6.2.2, *infra*.

106 *See, e.g.*, Kenty v. Bank One, Columbus, N.A., 1992 WL 170605 (S.D. Ohio Apr. 23, 1992) (rebates or kickbacks to creditor from force-placed property insurance premium is interest), *aff'd in part and rev'd in part*, 92 F.3d 384 (6th Cir. 1995) (though excessive premium may be interest, usury cap not applicable by virtue of state law and the most favored lender doctrine). *See also* § 6.4.5.2, *infra*.

107 *See* Bailey v. Defenbaugh & Co., 513 F. Supp. 232 (N.D. Miss. 1981); Aclin Ford Co. v. Cordell, 625 S.W.2d 459 (Ark. 1981) (citing Arkansas cases); Equitable Life Assurance Soc'y v. Ins. Comm'r, 246 A.2d 604 (Md. 1968); B.F. Saul v. West End Park N. Inc., 246 A.2d 591 (Md. 1968) (credit insurance commission is interest when retained by lender); North Am. Acceptance Corp. v. Warren, 451 S.W.2d 921 (Tex. App. Ct. 1970). *But see* Equitable Life Assurance Soc'y of U.S. v. Scali, 232 N.E.2d 712 (Ill. 1967) (required life insurance generally not interest). *See generally* Annotation, 91 A.L.R.2d 1344; §§ 6.5 (compulsory credit insurance), 6.6, 6.7 (excessive credit insurance cost and coverage), *infra*.

108 *See* Stubbs v. Security Consumer Discount Co., 426 A.2d 1014 (N.J. 1980). *Cf.* Kovian v. Fulton Nat'l Bank & Trust Co., 647 F. Supp. 830 (N.D.N.Y. 1986) (kickback of finder's fees; insufficient allegations to state usury claim).

109 *See, e.g.*, Whittemore Homes, Inc. v. Fleishman, 12 Cal. Rptr. 235 (Cal. App. Ct. 1961) (loan usurious where lender charged fee for sham services that were not in fact provided).

110 *See* Edwards v. Your Credit, Inc., 148 F.3d 427 (5th Cir. 1998); Walmsley v. Mercury Fin. Co. (S.D. Fla. Sept. 10, 1993), *available at* www.nclc.org/unreported (order on motions to dismiss); Dixon v. S&S Loan Serv. of Waycross, 754 F. Supp. 1567, 1572–1574 (S.D. Ga. 1990).

111 Edwards v. Your Credit, Inc., 148 F.3d 427 (5th Cir. 1998) (reversing grant of summary judgment to creditor, fact question whether policy was really a general default policy cloaked in nonfiling garb). *See also* Adams v. Plaza Fin. Co., 168 F.3d 932 (7th Cir. 1999). *See generally* § 6.7, *infra* (discussing insurance packing).

112 Kenty v. Bank One, Columbus, N.A., 1992 WL 170605 (S.D. Ohio Apr. 23, 1992), *aff'd in part and rev'd in part*, 92 F.3d 384 (6th Cir. 1995) (though excessive premium may be interest, usury cap not applicable by virtue of state law and the most favored lender doctrine). *But cf.* Doe v. Norwest Bank, 107 F.3d 1297, 1303 (8th Cir. 1997) (premium for force-placed insurance is not interest as defined by National Bank Act; rejecting consumer's contention that it included additional coverage); Sunwest Bank v. Gutierrez, 819 S.W.2d 673 (Tex. App. 1992) (fee for force-placed insurance, even if unauthorized, is not interest because it is for separate and additional consideration). *See generally* National Consumer Law Center, Unfair and Deceptive Acts and Practices § 10.5.10 (7th ed. 2008 and Supp.) (discussing further these cases).

113 *See* Lockhart v. General Motors Acceptance Corp., 481 S.W.2d 350 (Ark. 1972).

114 Winston v. Personal Fin. Co., 249 S.W.2d 315 (Ark. 1952) (obtaining credit report was solely for lender's benefit, so its cost must be treated as interest).

115 *See, e.g.*, W. Va. Code § 46A-3-109(a)(4).

sary and incidental" to the loan.[116] The benefit received from third-party services is at least one factor to be considered in determining whether payments are interest.[117]

### 4.5.2.4 Sham Services

Lenders may also increase the cost of credit surreptitiously by charging borrowers for sham services that are not in fact provided. Charges for services that the lender does not in fact perform are interest.[118] For example, courts have held payments to lenders under sham consulting contracts to be interest.[119]

## 4.5.3 Broker Fees

### 4.5.3.1 Where Broker Is Related to the Lender

Loan broker commissions added to the principal may often be hidden interest. While loan brokers represent that they provide a service to the consumer by finding the best loan, often they have a relationship with just one lender and steer consumers to that lender, who does not offer the best deal.

Fees to bona fide third-party brokers are valid third-party expenses in most jurisdictions.[120] Yet precisely because they are nominally valid, broker fees have provided a convenient artifice for lenders attempting to collect excessive interest.[121] Less sophisticated lenders may impose the fee directly, paying themselves a broker fee assuming that it will go unchallenged. As with other third-party payments, fees which are collected when no third party exists,[122] which are never forwarded to a third party,[123] or which are kicked back to the lender[124] are interest.

More frequently, the fee will be paid to a supposedly independent party which is in fact associated with the lender in some way. In either situation, the fees are hidden interest and should be challenged as such.

Numerous courts have held that broker fees are interest on a loan when the broker is an agent of the lender and hence is not a bona fide third party.[125] However, no universal test exists for

116 *See, e.g.*, Va. Code Ann. § 6.2-326 (fees charged in connection with residential mortgage loans must be reasonable and necessary); Fikes v. First Fed. Sav. & Loan Ass'n Anchorage, 533 P.2d 251 (Alaska 1975) (interpreting Alaska Stat. § 06.30.590, now repealed); U.C.C.C. § 2.501 (1974 Model Act) (charges "reasonable" in relation to benefits received).

117 *See* United-Bilt Homes, Inc. v. Teague, 432 S.W.2d 1 (Ark. 1968) (appraisal fee); Winston v. Personal Fin. Co., 249 S.W.2d 315 (Ark. 1952); Sparkman & McLean Income Fund v. Wald, 520 P.2d (Wash. Ct. App. 1974). *See also In re* Marill Alarm Sys., Inc., 68 B.R. 399 (Bankr. S.D. Fla. 1986), *aff'd*, 81 B.R. 119 (S.D. Fla. 1987) ("consulting fees" paid third party in conjunction with loan were interest where no documentation reflecting basis for consulting arrangement and no satisfactory explanation of services provided to earn the fee). *See also* S.C. Code Ann. § 37-2-202(e) (creditors may impose charges for "other benefits" in credit sales if they are of value to the buyer and meet other requirements); U.C.C.C. § 2.501 (1974 Model Act).

118 Anderson v. Chainani (*In re* Kemper), 263 B.R. 773 (Bankr. E.D. Tex. 2001) ("consulting fee" will be interest if the alleged services—finding investors for a corporation with which borrower was involved—were not actually performed); Modern Pioneers Ins. Co. v. Nandin, 437 P.2d 658, 664–665 (Ariz. 1968) (sham broker fee was interest); Whittemore Homes, Inc. v. Fleishman, 12 Cal. Rptr. 235 (Cal. 1961) (fee for non-existent "other services and things of value" was interest); First Fed. Sav. v. Norwood Realty Co., 93 S.E.2d 763 (Ga. 1956) (service charge was interest if no service is to be rendered to borrower).

119 *See, e.g., In re* Marill Alarm Sys., Inc., 68 B.R. 399 (Bankr. S.D. Fla. 1986); *In re* Mickler, 50 B.R. 818 (Bankr. M.D. Fla. 1985); *In re* Rosner, 48 B.R. 538 (Bankr. E.D.N.Y. 1985); Antonelli v. Neumann, 537 So. 2d 1027 (Fla. Dist. Ct. App. 1988) (landscape consulting contract with lender held to be subterfuge to conceal usurious transaction: lender had letter indicating desire to extract 2% excess interest; the "landscape consulting fees" were coincidentally 2% payments made contemporaneously with each loan payment, rather than for work as performed; lender never testified the 2% payments were credited to the consulting fee).

120 *See* Family Fed. Sav. & Loan v. Davis, 172 B.R. 437 (Bankr. D.D.C. 1994); *In re* Bryant, 39 B.R. 313 (Bankr. D. Nev. 1984); Walker v. Pliss, 34 B.R. 432 (Bankr. D. Or. 1983); *In re* Verdini Enters., 13 B.R. 739 (Bankr. S.D. Fla. 1981); Swanson v. Gulf W. Int'l Corp., 429 So. 2d 817 (Fla. Dist. Ct. App. 1983); Gardin v. Long Beach Mortgage Co., 661 N.W.2d 193 (Iowa 2003) (Iowa's 2% cap on loan processing fees for home-secured loans does not apply to broker fees, because broker fees are not "collected" by lender); Ashland Nat'l Bank v. Conley, 22 S.W.2d 270 (Ky. 1929). *See also* Wood v. Froerer Corp., 611 P.2d 193 (Nev. 1980) (broker was bona fide third party to loan transaction where lenders had no knowledge of and did not share in commission; promissory note was made payable to broker only as convenience to multiple lenders). *But see* Tavares v. Sprunk (*In re* Tavares), 298 B.R. 195 (Bankr. D. Mass. 2003) (all loan expenses, including broker fees, are explicitly included in calculation of interest rate for purposes of determining whether loan violates Massachusetts criminal usury statute). *See generally* Annotation, 52 A.L.R.2d 703 (1957).

121 *See, e.g.* Lovick v. Ritemoney, Ltd., 378 F.3d 433 (5th Cir. 2004) (holding that state Credit Services Organization Act allows storefront lender to charge $1,500 fee for "brokering" a $2,000 auto title loan, even though it undertook many tasks usually handled by lender, such as performing credit checks, arranging for the agreement and note to be signed, issuing the loan principal check, and collecting payments).

122 *See In re* Mickler, 50 B.R. 818 (Bankr. M.D. Fla. 1985) (sham referral fee); Howes v. Curtis, 661 P.2d 729 (Idaho 1983); Henderson v. Security Mortgage & Fin. Co., 160 S.E.2d 39 (N.C. 1968); Terry v. Teachworth, 431 S.W.2d 918 (Tex. Civ. App. 1968).

123 *Cf.* United-Bilt Homes v. Knapp, 396 S.W.2d 40 (Ark. 1965) (credit life insurance and appraisal fees not actually expended).

124 *See* Stubbs v. Security Consumer Discount Co., 426 A.2d 1014 (N.J. 1980); National Am. Life Ins. Co. v. Bayou Country Club, Inc., 403 P.2d 26 (Utah 1965). *See also* Kenty v. Bank One, Columbus, N.A., 1992 WL 170605 (S.D. Ohio Apr. 23, 1992) (insurance kickbacks), *aff'd in part and rev'd in part*, 92 F.3d 384 (6th Cir. 1995). *Cf.* Kovian v. Fulton Nat'l Bank & Trust Co., 647 F. Supp. 830 (N.D.N.Y. 1986) (insufficient factual allegations to state claim); *In re* Salzman, 83 B.R. 233 (Bankr. S.D.N.Y. 1988) (in absence of evidence that brokerage fee inured to benefit of creditor in any way, brokerage fee paid to brother of one of the creditors was not interest).

125 *See, e.g., In re* Dukes, 24 B.R. 404 (Bankr. E.D. Mich. 1982); Browne v. Nowlin, 570 P.2d 1246 (Ariz. 1977); Bayne v. Jolley, 38 Cal. Rptr. 873 (Cal. Ct. App. 1964); North Am. Investors v. Cape San Blas Joint Venture, 378 So. 2d 287 (Fla. 1978); Feemster v. Schurkman, 291 So. 2d 622 (Fla. Dist. Ct. App. 1974); Applebaum v. Laham, 161 So. 2d 690 (Fla. Dist. Ct. App. 1964); Williamson v. Clark, 120 So. 2d 637 (Fla. Dist. Ct. App. 1960); Howes v. Curtis, 661 P.2d 729 (Idaho 1983); Coner v. Morris S. Berman, Unlimited,

determining when a broker is actually the lender's agent, and courts typically view the issue as a question of fact which must be examined on a case-by-case basis.[126] A few state statutes do specify that when a broker acts as agent for both the lender and borrower, it will be deemed to be the agent of the lender.[127]

When broker fees have been paid to apparently independent brokers, practitioners should examine the relationship between the broker and lender. If the lender or its officers hold a financial interest in the broker, there may be an agency relationship.[128] Agency is also suggested if the broker arranges loans largely or exclusively for one lender,[129] or if the broker uses the lender's forms or offices to conduct its business.[130] Where the broker and lender are related by family ties, the possibility of the creditor sharing the benefits of the broker fees should be explored.[131]

The broker's agreement with the borrower may claim that the broker is not the agent of any lender. Where such an agreement exists, close scrutiny of the actual relationship between the lender and broker as discussed is essential to overcome the written disclaimer. The parol evidence rule is inapplicable to usury claims, so would not prevent a court from looking behind the documents.[132]

Some courts look to the relative benefits that the broker provides to the borrower and lender. If the broker takes care of the loan application paperwork for the lender or otherwise performs as the lender's employee, the broker fee may actually be a device to shift the lender's overhead expenses to the borrower and would therefore constitute hidden interest in some jurisdictions.[133]

---

501 A.2d 458 (Md. Ct. Spec. App. 1985) (violation of state secondary mortgage and finder's fees laws); Duckworth v. Bernstein, 466 A.2d 517 (Md. Ct. Spec. App. 1983); Julian v. Burrus, 600 S.W.2d 133 (Mo. Ct. App. 1980); De Lee v. Hicks., 611 P.2d 211 (Nev. 1980); United Mortgage Co. v. Hildreth, 559 P.2d 1186 (Nev. 1977); O'Connor v. Lamb, 593 S.W.2d 385 (Tex. Civ. App. 1979) (purported broker was the actual lender); Terry v. Teachworth, 431 S.W.2d 918 (Tex. Civ. App. 1968); Busk v. Hoard, 396 P.2d 171 (Wash. 1964); Durias v. Boswell, 791 P.2d 282 (Wash. Ct. App. 1990) (broker fee is interest where broker is agent of lender); Sparkman & McLean Income Fund v. Wald, 520 P.2d 173 (Wash. Ct. App. 1974). *See also* Goldome Credit Corp. v. Burke, 923 So. 2d 282 (Ala. 2005) (suggesting that if the broker is an agent of the lender, the broker fee could constitute points); Hicki v. Choice Capital Corp., 694 N.Y.S.2d 750 (N.Y. App. Div. 1999) (whether broker fee constituted interest is fact question). *But cf.* Mills v. State Nat'l Bank, 329 N.E.2d 255 (Ill. App. Ct. 1975) (bank's inclusion of brokers' commission as "service charge" on finance charge disclosure form did not, absent other indicia of bank's authority or control over brokers, create agency relationship); Farrell v. Lincoln Nat'l Bank, 320 N.E.2d 208 (Ill. App. Ct. 1974) (listing of broker fee as "service charge" on truth in lending disclosure form did not give rise to inference of principal-agent relationship between bank and brokers where there was no other evidence of agency); Nilsen v. Long Beach Mortgage Co., 2006 WL 2469141 (Wash. Ct. App. Aug. 28, 2006) (fee paid to independent broker even though fee was listed as origination fee on settlement statement does not count towards the statutory origination fee cap). *See generally* Annotation, 52 A.L.R.2d 703 (1957).

126 *See, e.g.*, Hicki v. Choice Capital Corp., 694 N.Y.S.2d 750 (N.Y. App. Div. 1999); Argo Air, Inc. v. Scott, 197 S.E.2d 256 (N.C. App. Ct. 1973) (fact question whether broker was agent for lender, in which case broker fee would make loan usurious).

127 *See, e.g.*, Neb. Rev. Stat. § 45-105; N.M. Stat. Ann. § 56-8-12; Wash. Rev. Code Ann. § 19.52.030(2), *interpreted in* Durias v. Boswell, 791 P.2d 282 (Wash. Ct. App. 1990) (broker fee is interest where broker is agent of lender; factors relevant to determining agency include lender's reliance on broker for information concerning creditworthiness of borrower, preparation of documents necessary to close and adequately secure the loan, and performing record keeping functions; not relevant whether lender knew of broker fee, as Washington law provides that where broker acts as agent for both borrower and lender, it is deemed lender's agent for purposes of usury statute).

128 Modern Pioneers Ins. Co. v. Nandin, 437 P.2d 658 (Ariz. 1968); Kamrath v. Great Southwestern Trust Corp., 551 P.2d 92 (Ariz. Ct. App. 1976); Coner v. Morris S. Berman, Unlimited, 501 A.2d 458 (Md. Ct. Spec. App. 1985) (secondary mortgage law violated where brokerage actually run by lender although nominally owned by lender's wife). *Cf.* Bourgeois v. Mortgage Funding Corp., No. 95-1541 (Bankr. D. Mass. Mar. 6, 1998), *available at* www.nclc.org/unreported (TILA case; lender made about 90% of its loans through the broker; payment of the broker fee was a condition of settlement; broker and lender were owned, in whole or in part, by the same person); *In re* Whitley, 177 B.R. 142 (Bankr. D. Mass. 1995) (TILA case; broker and lender shared business address and parent company); Vezzani v. Tallant, 172 S.E.2d 858 (Ga. Ct. App. 1970) (allegation that lender controlled corporation to which borrower paid brokerage fee insufficient to uphold defense of usury on motion to dismiss). *But cf.* Thunderbird Inv. Corp. v. Rothschild, 97 Cal. Rptr. 112 (Cal. Ct. App. 1971) (fact that loan broker split commission with attorney employed by lender to investigate and advise lender of real estate investments did not render transaction usurious where lender did not know of or share in payment).

129 *In re* Dukes, 24 B.R. 404 (Bankr. E.D. Mich. 1982); *In re* Mandell, 6 B.R. 961 (Bankr. D.R.I. 1980). *But see* Lovick v. Ritemoney, Ltd., 378 F.3d 433 (5th Cir. 2004) (special agency relationship between lender and broker, in which lender made all its loans through broker, did not transform broker fees into interest; relying on state credit services organization act as allowing unlimited broker fee arrangements).

130 Modern Pioneers Ins. Co. v. Nandin, 437 P.2d 658 (Ariz. 1968) (corporate lenders and broker shared same suite in office building, same receptionist and same telephone number); Kamrath v. Great Southwestern Trust Corp., 551 P.2d 92 (Ariz. Ct. App. 1976) (corporate lender and brokers had interlocking directors and officers and offices were linked by an intercom system); Wheeler v. Superior Mortgage Co., 17 Cal. Rptr. 291 (Cal. Ct. App. 1961) (corporate lender and broker did business in same building, at same location and shared telephone number; broker's offices had no identification to distinguish them from lender's). *Cf. In re* Dukes, 24 B.R. 404 (Bankr. E.D. Mich. 1982) (broker completed all paper work).

131 Bayne v. Jolley, 38 Cal. Rptr. 873 (Cal. Ct. App. 1964) (commission to lender's broker daughter was usurious; she was lender's agent); Rollins v. Odom, 519 So. 2d 652 (Fla. Dist. Ct. App. 1988) (brokerage fee went to lender's wife, who kept books for herself and her husband); Miller v. York, 548 P.2d 941 (Nev. 1976) (brokerage commission paid to lender's son-in-law was interest, rendering loan usurious). *But cf. In re* Salzman, 83 B.R. 233 (Bankr. S.D.N.Y. 1988) (no evidence lender benefited from broker fee paid to his brother).

132 Aclin Ford Co. v. Cordell, 625 S.W.2d 459 (Ark. 1982). *See generally* § 7.5.1.4, *infra*.

133 *See In re* Dukes, 24 B.R. 404 (Bankr. E.D. Mich. 1982); Busk v. Hoard, 396 P.2d 171 (Wash. 1964) (mortgage broker was individual lender's agent where broker, without charge to lender, checked title,

### 4.5.3.2 Where Lender and Broker Split the Broker Fee

Where the lender and the broker split an interest rate up-charge, this is often called a "yield spread premium."[134] The Alabama Supreme Court permitted a case that alleged this arrangement to be a concealed device to evade the state's 5% cap on points to go to the jury.[135] However, to the extent the decision held that a yield spread premium constituted "points" under a state law capping the number of points a lender can charge, the court overruled itself in a later decision.[136] The court held, instead, that a yield spread premium cannot constitute "points" because points are defined in the statute as paid in cash at the time of the loan or deducted from the proceeds and included in the original principal balance.

Effective for loan applications received after April 1, 2011, regulations under the Truth in Lending Act prohibit the payment of yield spread premiums to loan originators, but only for loans secured by a dwelling.[137] The 2010 Dodd-Frank Wall Street Reform and Consumer Protection Act includes a similar prohibition.[138]

### 4.5.3.3 State Statutes Regulating Brokers

The 2008 SAFE Mortgage Licensing Act requires all states to have at least a basic licensing system for mortgage loan brokers.[139] Non-mortgage loan brokers are also expressly regulated in most states. Some of these states also cap the fees that loan brokers may charge.[140] However, these statutes frequently contain broad loopholes.[141] But where a fee is illegal, and the lender knows the fee is illegal, courts will treat the fee as interest.[142]

A number of states regulate non-mortgage loan brokers through their state credit services organization acts.[143] While these statutes do provide for some consumer protections, such as a cooling-off period, they do not cap broker fees. One court held that the lack of a fee cap in a state credit services organization act permitted a broker to charge whatever fee it wanted, and that the act insulated broker fees from challenge under state usury laws.[144]

## 4.6 Document Preparation Fees

### *4.6.1 Statutory Caps on Document Preparation Fees*

Some state statutes cap the amount that sellers can charge for document preparation.[145] Some of these caps are part of retail installment sales acts, so apply only to credit sales, while others apply to cash sales as well, or set different caps for cash sales and credit sales. The statute may specify a remedy for violations, but even if it does not a consumer who pays a charge exceeding the cap is likely to have a cause of action for unjust enrichment or under the state UDAP statute.[146]

---

prepared legal instruments for loan and mortgage on borrower's home, collected loan payments, maintained records regarding payments and made remittances to lender; brokers' knowledge of usury imputed to lender based on agency principles); Durias v. Boswell, 791 P.2d 282 (Wash. Ct. App. 1990) (broker fee is interest where broker is agent of lender; factors relevant to determining agency include lender's reliance on broker for information concerning creditworthiness of borrower, preparation of documents necessary to close and adequately secure the loan, and performing record keeping functions; not relevant whether lender knew of broker fee, as Washington law provides that where broker acts as agent for both borrower and lender, it is deemed lender's agent for purposes of usury statute); Sparkman & McLean Income Fund v. Wald, 520 P.2d 173 (Wash. Ct. App. 1974). *But see* Lovick v. Ritemoney, Ltd., 378 F.3d 433 (5th Cir. 2004) (fact that broker performed many services of behalf of lender—such as performing credit checks, arranging for the agreement and note to be signed, issuing the loan principal check, and collecting payments—was insufficient to make broker fee "interest"); Mills v. State Nat'l Bank, 329 N.E.2d 255 (Ill. App. Ct. 1975) (rejecting borrowers' claim that brokers who prepared loan application were agents of lender bank). *But cf.* Farrell v. Lincoln Nat'l Bank, 320 N.E.2d 208 (Ill. App. Ct. 1974) (brokers who handled loan application paperwork on behalf of lender bank were not bank's agents where bank had no role in brokers' decision to submit applications, brokers submitted loan applications on behalf of customers to other banks, bank accepted applications through other brokers, brokers had no authority over bank's decision to grant loans, brokers did not service loans after they were made, and bank did not control or receive any portion of broker fees; under these circumstances, inclusion of broker fee as "service charge" on Truth in Lending finance charge disclosure form did not make broker fee interest for purpose of usury law).

134 *See* § 10.3.5, *infra*.

135 Smith v. First Family Fin. Servs., Inc., 626 So. 2d 1266 (Ala. 1993).

136 Goldome Credit Corp. v. Burke, 923 So. 2d 282 (Ala. 2005). *See also* Maluski v. U.S. Bank, 2008 WL 5102013 (S.D. Tex. Dec. 1, 2008) (holding that yield spread premium paid by lender to broker was not a fee for purposes of state constitutional cap on closing fees for home equity loan because it was not paid directly by the borrower, even though it was arguably passed on to the borrower in the form of a higher interest rate charged by lender), *aff'd*, 349 Fed. Appx. 971 (5th Cir. 2009).

137 12 C.F.R. § 1026.36(d).

138 15 U.S.C. § 1639b. *See* National Consumer Law Center, Truth in Lending §§ 3.7.4.5, 9.3.2 (7th ed. 2010 and Supp.).

139 *See* National Consumer Law Center, Mortgage Lending § 3.3, Appx. H.4 (2012).

140 *See, e.g.*, Diane Inc. v. Kapnison, 667 P.2d 450 (N.M. 1983) (interpreting N.M. Stat. Ann. § 56-8-7 (1978)).

141 *See, e.g.*, Neb. Rev. Stat. §§ 45-190, 45-191.10 (excluding, *inter alia*, attorneys, real estate brokers, real estate salespeople, accountants, investment advisors, and most lenders).

142 *See* Pease v. Taylor, 496 P.2d 757 (Nev. 1972) (where lender either charged purported broker fee himself or ratified charge, agency established and fee treated as interest under usury law); Hubschman v. Broda, 247 A.2d 698 (N.J. Super. Ct. App. Div. 1968); National Am. Life Ins. Co. v. Bayou Country Club, Inc., 403 P.2d 26 (Utah 1965) (lender and broker shared an illegal additional charge; broker's share also attributed to lender as interest).

143 *See* National Consumer Law Center, Fair Credit Reporting § 15.3 (7th ed. 2010 and Supp.).

144 Lovick v. Ritemoney, Ltd., 378 F.3d 433 (5th Cir. 2004).

145 *See* National Consumer Law Center, Unfair and Deceptive Acts and Practices § 7.2.8.5 (7th ed. 2008 and Supp.).

146 Negrin v. Norwest Mortgage, Inc., 700 N.Y.S.2d 184 (N.Y. App. Div. 1999) (allegation that mortgage lender imposed unlawful fax fee and fabricated recording fee during the payoff or refinancing of

Even if the state retail installment sales act does not specifically cap document preparation charges, it may contain an exclusive list of the types or amounts of fees which the lender may impose. If it does not specifically list a document preparation fee, imposing such a fee may violate the statute.[147]

### 4.6.2 *Are Document Preparation Fees Interest?*

If a state does not specifically regulate document preparation fees, the fee might still be treated as a component of interest or the finance charge. In that case, it will be subject to any overall cap that the state imposes on interest or the finance charge.

States that treat charges representing the ordinary costs of extending credit as interest[148] may treat document preparation fees as interest. However, Truth in Lending cases hold that document preparation fees are not part of the finance charge if they are imposed equally on both cash and credit customers.[149] If a state follows this reasoning,[150] it may still treat the fee as part of interest rather than the cash price if the amount of the fee is higher for credit customers. The state might also treat a document preparation charge as interest if the document preparation services are not actually performed or the dealer is reimbursed by another party for the same service.[151] For example, manufacturers may reimburse dealers for some or all of the services performed for a "delivery and handling" fee.[152]

### 4.6.3 *Whether Charging a Document Preparation Fee Amounts to Unauthorized Practice of Law*

A lender or other entity that charges a fee for preparing or filling in the blanks on legal documents may be engaged in the unauthorized practice of law.[153] If a fee is illegal for this reason, then charging it in a credit transaction may violate a state usury statute. Even in a cash transaction the consumer may be able to recover the fee on a UDAP or unjust enrichment theory.

## 4.7 Non-Cash Compensation and Side Agreements

Lenders may exact non-cash bonuses in consideration for the extension of credit, and these may constitute hidden interest in the same manner as cash payments.[154] For example, a lender's requirement that the borrower assume a third party's debt to the

a loan states UDAP claim); Motzer Dodge Jeep Eagle, Inc. v. Ohio Atty. Gen., 642 N.E.2d 20 (Ohio Ct. App. 1994) (fee violated Ohio UDAP statute where delivery and handling fee, supposedly optional, was actually mandatory, where dealer failed to itemize the activities performed for the fee, and where manufacturer actually reimbursed dealer for some of the services).

147 *See* Washington v. Countrywide Home Loans, Inc., 655 F.3d 869 (8th Cir. 2011) (Mo. Law) (while document preparation fee is allowed by statute, document processing/delivery fee is not, so borrower can proceed on claim of statutory violation). *See generally* §§ 2.3, *supra*, 10.3, *infra*.

148 *See* § 4.2.1, *supra* (general definition of "interest").

149 *In re* Ferris, 764 F.2d 1475 (11th Cir. 1985).

150 *Cf.* Fanning v. Fritz's Pontiac-Cadillac-Buick, Inc., 472 S.E.2d 242 (S.C. 1996) (procurement fee was legitimately part of sales price of car because it was charged to cash and credit customers alike and was disclosed to buyer).

151 *See* § 4.5.2, *supra*.

152 *See, e.g.*, Motzer Dodge Jeep Eagle, Inc. v. Ohio Atty. Gen., 642 N.E.2d 20 (Ohio Ct. App. 1994) (noting that some of services covered by a non-optional $95 "delivery and handling" fee were paid for by the manufacturer).

153 *See, e.g.*, Lawson v. First Union Mortgage Co., 786 N.E.2d 279 (Ind. Ct. App. 2003) (reversing trial court's dismissal of a consumer's equitable claim for return of a document preparation fee; holding that while a lender's lay employees did not commit the unauthorized practice of law by preparing mortgage loan documents, the lender could not charge a separate fee for such documents); Carpenter v. Countrywide Home Loans, Inc., 250 S.W.3d 697 (Mo. 2008) (mortgage lender engaged in unauthorized practice of law by preparing mortgage documents and charging a document preparation fee); Eisel v. Midwest BankCentre, 230 S.W.3d 335 (Mo. 2007) (bank employees who fill in preprinted mortgage related documents engage in the unauthorized practice of law when the bank charges a separate fee). *See also In re* Van Dyke, 296 B.R. 591 (Bankr. D. Mass. 2003) (real estate settlement services provided by non-attorney could be unauthorized practice of law); Doe v. McMaster, 585 S.E.2d 773 (S.C. 2003) (preparation of mortgage documents, as well as title search and documentation, constitutes practice of law). *But see* Newman v. Ed Bozarth Chevrolet, Inc., 714 F. Supp. 2d 1114 (D. Colo. 2010) (dealer's completion of vehicle sales documents is not unauthorized practice of law); King v. First Capital Fin. Servs. Corp., 798 N.E.2d 118 (Ill. App. Ct. 2003) (lender did not commit unauthorized practice of law by preparing mortgage documents for its own use, because it was acting *pro se*), *aff'd*, 828 N.E.2d 1155 (Ill. 2005) (upholding the "*pro se*" exception to the unauthorized practice of law where the document preparer is not a party to the transaction; the lenders and their employees would be parties and not subject to the exception); Charter One Mortgage Corp. v. Condra, 865 N.E.2d 602 (Ind. 2007) (holding no unauthorized practice of law when the plaintiff did not allege that lender offered legal services to the public or represented that its non-lawyers were qualified to perform legal tasks, or that the loan documents were prepared incorrectly); Dressel v. Ameribank, 664 N.W.2d 151 (Mich. 2003) (bank did not engage in unauthorized practice of law by preparing mortgage documents using standard form documents, because it did not require the use of legal discretion or "profound legal knowledge"); Cardinal v. Merrill Lynch Realty/Burnet, Inc., 433 N.W.2d 864 (Minn. 1988) (finding no unauthorized practice of law); Perkins v. CTX Mortgage Co., 969 P.2d 93 (Wash. 1999) (finding no unauthorized practice of law). *See generally* Michael C. Ksiazek, Note, *The Model Rules of Professional Conduct and the Unauthorized Practice of Law: Justification for Restricting Conveyancing to Attorneys*, 37 Suffolk U. L. Rev. 169 (2004); Joyce Palomar, *The War Between Attorneys and Lay Conveyancers—Empirical Evidence Says "Cease Fire!"* 31 Conn. L. Rev. 423 (1999); Fed. Trade Comm'n & United States Dep't of Justice, Comments on the American Bar Association's Proposed Model Definition of the Practice of Law (Dec. 20, 2002) (taking position that permitting non-lawyers to prepare mortgage loan documents is consumer-friendly because it increases competition and reduces costs).

154 *See, e.g.*, Pacific E. Corp. v. Gulf Life Holding Co., 902 S.W.2d 946 (Tenn. Ct. App. 1995) (where insurance company was a lender, question of fact whether life insurance policy required as collateral on life of a principal in a commercial loan was pretext for usury).

lender constitutes interest on the loan to the borrower.[155] A provision giving the lender a share of the rents from the mortgaged property may be interest.[156]

Similarly, borrowers who are forced to enter side contracts, favorable to the lender and supposedly independent of the extension of credit, may in fact be paying hidden interest.[157] For example, requiring the borrower to purchase services from the lender that are of no value or which the lender does not in fact provide may amount to hidden interest.[158] On the other hand, some courts have found no additional interest present when the obligations undertaken by the borrower are supported by independent consideration and are therefore not given as payment for the loan.[159]

A non-cash bonus may be held not to be hidden interest if the benefit to the lender is contingent[160] or if the value of the bonus cannot be quantified.[161] This problem arises most frequently

155 *See, e.g.*, Curtiss Nat'l Bank of Miami Springs v. Solomon, 243 So. 2d 475 (Fla. Dist. Ct. App. 1971); Ferdon v. Zarriello Bros. Inc., 208 A.2d 186 (N.J. Super. Ct. App. Div. 1965); First USA Mgmt., Inc. v. Esmond, 960 S.W.2d 625 (Tex. 1997) (lender's requirement that borrower assume a third party's debt to lender is interest); Alamo Lumber Co. v. Gold, 661 S.W.2d 926 (Tex. 1983). *Cf.* Durante Bros. & Sons, Inc. v. Flushing Nat'l Bank, 652 F. Supp. 101, 104 (E.D.N.Y. 1986) (assumption or repayment of third-party debt usurious only if lender acted with usurious intent, for example with knowledge that the third party could not or would not pay); Standard Sav. Ass'n v. Greater New Canaan Missionary Baptist Church, 786 S.W.2d 774 (Tex. App. 1990) (payment of third-party debt is interest only when required as condition of making loan; fact question); Dodson v. Citizens State Bank of Dalhart, 701 S.W.2d 89 (Tex. App. 1986) (assumption of third-party debt is interest only when it is a condition for the extension of credit). *But cf.* Victoria Bank & Trust Co. v. Brady, 811 S.W.2d 931 (Tex. 1991) (amount of third-party debt owed to a *different* lender that borrower was required to assume is not interest; it was third-party expense to protect priority as to creditor's security, which is not necessarily interest). *See generally* Annotation, 31 A.L.R.3d 763 (1970).

156 *See* Bagri v. Desai, 349 S.E.2d 309 (N.C. Ct. App. 1986) (loan for purchase of motel; profits from motel shared with lender were additional charges that rendered loan usurious). *See generally* Annotation, 16 A.L.R.3d 475 (1967) (sharing earnings from property as usurious).

157 *See* Boyles v. Smith, 759 P.2d 518 (Alaska 1988) (side-sale agreement held to be hidden interest); Brabson v. Valentine, 804 S.W.2d 451 (Tenn. Ct. App. 1990) (where lending bank required borrower to purchase an investment certificate from it, the transaction was usurious; applying the common sense perspective that where the loan proceeds were $126,340, and the bank required the borrower purchase a $100,000 investment certificate, the bank only loaned $26,340 of its money); Glover v. Buchman, 104 S.W.2d 66 (Tex. Civ. App. 1937) (borrower forced to buy cash discount coupons from lender). *See also* Ransom v. S&S Food Ctr., Inc., 700 F.2d 670 (11th Cir. 1983) (mandatory service contract is TILA finance charge); Carney v. Worthmore Furniture, Inc., 561 F.2d 1100 (4th Cir. 1977) (mandatory service policy tied with credit sale was Truth in Lending "finance charge"). *See generally* Annotation, 81 A.L.R.2d 1280 (1962).

158 *See* § 4.5.2.4, *supra*.

159 *See, e.g.*, Zer-Ilan v. Frankford (*In re* CPDC, Inc.), 337 F.3d 436 (5th Cir. 2003) (consulting agreement payments did not constitute usurious interest because agreement was with third-party company, not lender, and services were actually provided—despite the fact that lender owned the third-party company and the agreed price was over eighteen times the real worth of the services); Durante Bros. & Sons, Inc. v. Flushing Nat'l Bank, 652 F. Supp. 101, 105 (E.D.N.Y. 1986); Feinberg v. Old Vestal Road Assocs., 550 N.Y.S.2d 482 (N.Y. App. Div. 1990) (though courts may look beyond form of transaction to ascertain its real nature, in this commercial loan, a separate agreement with an individual lender for a finder's fee to the lender was not a front for a usurious loan where the lender's own collateral was tied up by the loan, the borrower sought advice and assistance, and the borrower's attorneys drafted the agreements); Goldring v. Texas Commercial Bank, 665 S.W.2d 103 (Tex. 1984) (attorney fee based on consideration apart from loan); Sunwest Bank of El Paso v. Gutierrez, 819 S.W.2d 673 (Tex. App. 1991) (creditor's purchase of VSI insurance on collateral was not "unauthorized," usurious charge, but was a charge for separate and additional consideration, which allows creditors to pass on expenses for protection of collateral); Moody v. Main Bank of Houston, 667 S.W.2d 613 (Tex. App. 1984) (separate consideration for guarantee of third-party debt). *See also* S.C. Dep't of Consumer Affairs Adm. Interp., No. 2 110-8701, Consumer Cred. Guide (CCH) 95,911 (Dec. 30, 1987) (bona fide and optional sale of service contract in conjunction with auto sale is properly considered part of cash price of transaction, and hence amount financed, but if such collateral sales are not offered to cash customers or arranged so that cash sales are rarely or never made, may be interest "incident to extension of credit"; Department will make determination on case by case basis, looking at substance, not form of transaction). *Cf.* Heine v. Schendel, 797 S.W.2d 278 (Tex. App. 1990) (borrower who agreed to perform work for the creditor at one-half borrower's usual price failed to establish that was device to give creditor additional interest).

160 *See* D-Beam Ltd. P'ship v. Roller Derby Skates, 366 F.3d 972 (9th Cir. 2004) (when promissory notes limited repayment to borrower's interest in royalty payments, loans were not usurious because of contingency); Dopp v. Yari, 927 F. Supp. 814 (D.N.J. 1996) (following Kraft v. Mason); Kraft v. Mason, 668 So. 2d 679 (Fla. Dist. Ct. App. 1996) (fact that payment of interest depended on contingency of successful lawsuit showed lack of corrupt intent to render loan usurious); First USA Mgmt., Inc. v. Esmond, 911 S.W.2d 100 (Tex. App. 1995) (where both obligation to make the payment and its amount are dependent on occurrence of contingency, contract is not usurious unless debtor shows that it is a subterfuge for usury; this payment was contingent, but fact question whether it was a device to evade usury laws), *rev'd on other grounds*, 960 S.W.2d 625 (Tex. 1997) (no fact question; this charge—forfeiture of unpaid salary when debtor was terminated from his job with lender—is not interest as a matter of law); Beavers v. Taylor, 434 S.W.2d 230 (Tex. Civ. App. 1968) ("no interest" contract that gave lender a percentage of business' gross receipts was not usurious because payments were contingent on existence and quantity of any gross receipts). *But cf.* Najarro v. SASI Int'l, Ltd., 904 F.2d 1002 (5th Cir. 1990) (Tex. law) (finding usury where series of notes for purchase of goods for resale each required commission, calculated as 25% per year for the number of days outstanding; since amount is fixed, this is usury even if commission was due only if borrower made a profit on resale; contract is usurious if there is any contingency by which lender can receive more than lawful interest rate); Jersey Palm-Gross, Inc. v. Paper, 658 So. 2d 531 (Fla. 1995) (treating 15% equity interest in business partnership, which lender demanded, as interest to the extent of its value on date of transaction).

161 First USA Mgmt., Inc. v. Esmond, 960 S.W.2d 625, 627 (Tex. 1997) (forfeiture of unpaid salary when debtor was terminated from his job with lender not interest because its value in comparison with value of his services was uncertain). *See also* Swank v. Sverdlin, 121 S.W.3d 785 (Tex. App. 2003) (evidence of their value is necessary before assignment of patent rights can be considered interest).

when a loan contract grants the lender a share of the profits from the borrower's business or investment in consideration for making the loan. Contracts of this nature were traditionally structured as partnerships or joint ventures, but they have branched into the home mortgage market in the form of "lender participation" mortgages in which lenders and borrowers share any appreciation in the value of the mortgaged property.[162] In either case, the relevant usury question is whether the lender's return is truly contingent on the success of the borrower's enterprise, and is consequently an investment, or whether instead the lender's return is guaranteed and is thus potentially usurious interest.

Transactions which grant a lender equity participation in the borrower's enterprise vary widely in their structure, and usury issues are easily answered only in the more extreme cases. When an investor risks its capital and is rewarded only upon the success of the enterprise in which it has invested, its ultimate return is not interest subject to usury limits.[163] On the other hand, a lender whose loan is absolutely repayable and who receives interest payments at the statutory limit should not additionally receive equity participation under the guise of a purported investment even if the value of its equity is uncertain.[164]

Equity participation is most likely to be held to be interest when the evidence indicates that the parties intended the transaction to be a loan, when a large difference exists between the proceeds advanced by the lender and the fair market value of the equity, when little or no additional consideration is given to the borrower for the equity, and when unequal bargaining power was evident.[165] Statutes in a few states control whether equity participation may be interest.[166]

## 4.8 Delinquency Charges

### *4.8.1 The Nature of Late Fees*

The typical credit contract requires the borrower to pay off the debt in installments, with each installment being due on a particular date, such as the first day of each month. Credit contracts usually provide a grace period, e.g., ten days, beyond the due date of an installment, within which the borrower may pay an installment without penalty.[167] However, if an installment is paid after expiration of the grace period, credit contracts generally authorize the creditor to impose a "late fee" or "delinquency fee." Late charges may be imposed only if the contract authorizes it.[168]

The imposition of a late fee does not mean that a borrower is in default, although the contract may technically grant the lender the right to declare default on the basis of a single missed payment. Subject to notice requirements,[169] once a lender declares default it is entitled to pursue remedies such as acceleration of the debt, repossession of collateral, and collection. In practice, however, consumer credit payments are frequently late, and creditors are content to collect generous late charges unless and until accounts become seriously overdue.

One justification for the imposition of late fees is that they compensate creditors for expenses incurred when payments are made late, such as dunning costs[170] and loss of use of the principal which was due. However, at least in the case of lenders using interest-bearing bookkeeping, interest continues to accrue on a payment until it is received, and a lender which additionally imposes a fee on late payments is receiving double compensation. Such lenders should not be allowed to claim that some other expenses, such as dunning costs, justify the imposition of late fees unless they can demonstrate that these costs are actually incurred when payments are made late. However, some statutes are interpreted as authorizing both interest and late fees.[171]

162 *See, e.g.,* Jones v. Wells Fargo Bank, 5 Cal. Rptr. 3d 835 (Cal. Ct. App. 2003) (example of a "classic shared appreciation loan arrangement" in real estate investment context; no usury because California law exempted from usury cap national banks acting as a fiduciary for a trust). *See generally* Kiefer, *Participating Mortgages: The Risk for Lenders*, 14 Real Estate L.J. 218 (Winter 1986); Burnes, *The Shared Appreciation Mortgage—A Joint Venture, A Relationship Between Debtor and Creditor, or Both?*, 12 J. Real Estate Tax'n 195 (1985) (tax analysis concluding that debtor-creditor relation prevails in shared appreciation mortgages).

163 *See, e.g.,* Securities & Exch. Comm'n v. First Sec. Co., 507 F.2d 417 (7th Cir. 1974).

164 *See, e.g.,* Thomas v. Estes, 229 S.E.2d 538 (Ga. Ct. App. 1976); Kessing v. National Mortgage Corp., 180 S.E.2d 823 (N.C. 1971); Bagri v. Desai, 349 S.E.2d 309 (N.C. Ct. App. 1986) (loan for purchase of motel; 15% interest and one-sixth of motel's profits plus one-sixth of any gain on resale was usurious); Johns v. Jaeb, 518 S.W.2d 857 (Tex. Civ. App. 1974).

165 *See* Comment, *Equity Participation in Texas: A Lender's Dream or a Usurious Nightmare?*, 34 S.W.L.J. 877 (1980).

166 *See, e.g.,* Fla. Stat. § 687.03(4) (loans exceeding $500,000).

167 However, the economic reality is that a penalty does, in fact, exist if the lender uses interest-bearing bookkeeping, because interest may continue to accrue through the grace period. As a result, more of the next payment will be allocated to interest and less to principal.

168 *See* Bank of Crockett v. Cullipher, 752 S.W.2d 84 (Tenn. Ct. App. 1988) (imposing substantial late charges in absence of contractual authorization to pressure repayment was unconscionable conduct under state statute); Bowman Plumbing, Heating & Elec. v. Logan, 59 Va. Cir. 446 (Va. Cir. Ct. 2002) (Virginia late payment statute requires late payment fee to be specified in the contract).

169 *See generally* National Consumer Law Center, Repossessions § 4.2.3 (7th ed. 2010 and Supp.) (state law requirements that creditor give written notice of default and provide opportunity for debtor to cure before pursuing remedies such as acceleration or repossession).

170 *See, e.g., In re* Graboyes, 371 B.R. 113 (Bankr. E.D. Pa. 2007) (recognizing this rule in Pennsylvania); Gaddis v. Stardust Hills Owners Ass'n, 804 N.E.2d 231 (Ind. Ct. App. 2004) (late fee of 1% per day or 365% annually was justified because association was required to incur expenses due to homeowner's delinquency). *Cf.* Opinion of the Kansas Att'y General No. 88-30, Consumer Cred. Guide (CCH) § 95,908 (Mar. 3, 1988) (reasonable late charge assessed by cable television company is not interest, so long as actual efforts to collect are made and delinquent users are not offered alternative options for payment).

171 *See, e.g.,* Iowa Code § 537.2502 (late fee permitted on interest-bearing transactions); Opinion of the Attorney General of Michigan, No. 5486, 1979 WL 36818 (Apr. 30, 1979), *summarized at* Consumer Cred. Guide (CCH) ¶ 97,758; Harrell v. Chrysler Fin. Co., 811 A.2d 597 (Pa. Super. Ct. 2002) (interpreting motor vehicle

Late fees, like any other payments made to a lender, are a potential source of hidden interest and should be closely scrutinized. A lender's ability to exclude late charges from interest on a contract varies widely from state to state, and reference to the relevant state's statutes and case law is essential to the analysis of any particular case.[172]

### *4.8.2 Late Fees As Interest; Contingency*

To the extent that a common law treatment of late fees exists, the general rule is that late fees are excluded from interest because the fees are avoidable or, more precisely, are contingent on the performance of the borrower.[173] Courts frequently view late payment as a voluntary act of the borrower and the late fee as a consequence of the borrower's voluntary act. These courts are reluctant to allow the borrower to transform an otherwise valid contract into a usurious one through voluntary late payment, and therefore exclude the late fee from interest,[174] typically describing it instead as a "penalty" designed to encourage prompt payment.[175]

The logic of this common law approach is questionable in many consumer credit cases because the late payment is often not so much a matter of the borrower's voluntary decision as one of economic necessity.[176] Furthermore, although a late fee provides an incentive for prompt payment when the borrower actually has the ability to make a payment, the notion of incentive loses its value when the borrower has no money.

The view that late fees are contingent and not interest is not universal. A number of courts hold that, in the absence of an express statutory exception, late fees are interest and are therefore subject to the state usury law's limits on interest.[177] Some courts reach this result on the theory that failure to make a payment when due is a "detention" of money, the compensation for which constitutes interest in some states.[178]

Courts that generally refuse to treat late charges as interest may reach a different conclusion when it can be shown that the parties expected late fees to be imposed at the time the contract was created and that the fees are therefore not contingent.[179] Such expectations may be difficult to prove, but numerous courts applying the common law approach have at least paid lip

installment sales act to allow both daily interest on unpaid payments plus late fees).

172 *See* § 7.2, *infra* (statutory construction).

173 *See, e.g.*, Alston v. Crown Auto, Inc., 224 F.3d 332 (4th Cir. 2000) (Va. law); Camilla Cotton Oil Co. v. Spencer Kellogg & Sons, Inc., 257 F.2d 162 (5th Cir. 1958); Hayes v. First Nat'l Bank, 507 S.W.2d 701 (Ark. 1974); Southwest Concrete Co. v. Gosh Constr., 798 P.2d 1247 (Cal. 1990); Barbour v. Handlos Real Estate & Bldg. Corp., 393 N.W.2d 581 (Mich. Ct. App. 1986); Lew v. Goodfellow Chrysler Plymouth, Inc., 492 P.2d 258 (Wash. Ct. App. 1971); Union Bank v. Kruger, 463 P.2d 273 (Wash. Ct. App. 1969); Randall v. Home Loan & Inv. Co., 12 N.W.2d 915 (Wis. 1944). *But see* Fisher v. Westinghouse Credit Corp., 760 S.W.2d 802, 805 (Tex. App. 1988) (note is usurious if there is any contingency by which lender can extract usurious interest).

174 *See, e.g.*, Nolen v. Nucentrix Broadband Networks, 293 F.3d 926 (5th Cir. 2002) (Tex. law) (cable television provider's late fee of up to 30% per month was not interest and thus not usurious); Alston v. Crown Auto, Inc., 224 F.3d 332 (4th Cir. 2000) (Va. law) (late fee that exceeds statutory cap is not interest because debtor could avoid it by making timely payments); Camilla Cotton Oil Co. v. Spencer Kellogg & Sons, Inc., 257 F.2d 162 (5th Cir. 1958) (Ga. law) (late charge not interest because debtor can avoid it); *In re* Borum, 60 B.R. 516 (Bankr. E.D. Ark. 1986); Tackett v. First Sav. of Arkansas, 810 S.W.2d 927 (Ark. 1991); Hayes v. First Nat'l Bank, 507 S.W.2d 701 (Ark. 1974); Union Bank v. Kruger, 463 P.2d 273 (Wash. Ct. App. 1969).

175 Smith v. Figure World Plus, Inc., 705 S.W.2d 432 (Ark. 1986) (100% late fee was not usurious interest, but rather was penalty, because charge was a fixed amount and was a one-time fee).

176 *See* Begelfer v. Najarian, 409 N.E.2d 167 (Mass. 1980). *See also* Scarr v. Boyer, 818 P.2d 381, 383 (Mont. 1991) ("Usury statutes protect borrowers who lack real bargaining power against overreaching by creditors." Default does not alter this public policy, and in fact increases the need; "a debtor who cannot retire a debt compounded by legal interest certainly lacks the resources to pay usurious interest.").

177 Bunn v. Weyerhauser Co., 598 S.W.2d 54 (Ark. 1980) (1.5% monthly service charge if open account balance is not paid within thirty days is interest); Dikeou v. Dikeou, 928 P.2d 1286 (Colo. 1997) (late charges fall within non-consumer usury statute's definition of interest as "all charges payable directly or indirectly by a debtor and imposed directly or indirectly by a lender as an incident to or as a condition of the extension of credit to that debtor," where this definition, unlike the consumer usury statute's, did not explicitly exclude late fees, but this loan is non-usurious because the late charges do not push the interest above the cap); Wright Ins. Agency v. Scott, 371 So. 2d 1207 (La. Ct. App. 1979); Begelfer v. Najarian, 409 N.E.2d 167 (Mass. 1980); Fisher v. Westinghouse Credit Corp., 760 S.W.2d 802 (Tex. App. 1988) (if balance was not properly accelerated, then lender could charge maximum legal interest rate only on past-due installments, so charging it on accelerated balance would render loan usurious).

178 *See, e.g.*, *In re* Brummer, 147 B.R. 552 (Bankr. D. Mont. 1992) ("reinvestment premium" due to satisfy the accelerated amount due after a default is a charge for the detention of money, and therefore interest); Scarr v. Boyer, 818 P.2d 381 (Mont. 1991) (Montana's usury statute applies to compensation for detention of money, thus it includes post-default interest within definition of interest); Swindell v. Federal Nat'l Mortgage Ass'n, 409 S.E.2d 892 (N.C. 1991), *modifying and aff'g* 387 S.E.2d 220 (N.C. Ct. App. 1990) (to extent that late fee compensates lender for delay it is interest on the detention of money or for forbearance in collection); Hardwick v. Austin Gallery of Oriental Rugs, Inc., 779 S.W.2d 438, 443 (Tex. App. 1989) (late fees fall within statutory definition of interest, although not common law definition); Dixon v. Brooks, 604 S.W.2d 330 (Tex. Civ. App. 1980). *See also* Butler v. Holt Machinery Co., 741 S.W.2d 169, 174 (Tex. App. 1987), *as corrected on denial of rehearing by* 739 S.W.2d 958 (1987) (late charges imposed without disclosure or borrower's agreement are interest, but no usury here since the resultant increase did not exceed the legal maximum). *See generally* § 7.5.2.3, *infra* (difference between forbearance and detention).

179 *See* Landon v. Mapco, Inc., 405 N.W.2d 825 (Iowa 1987) (interest imposed on overdue payments for propane deliveries was finance charge, not default charge for unanticipated late payments); Metric Constr., Inc. v. Great Plains Props., 344 N.W.2d 679 (N.D. 1984) (late payment is not "unanticipated" where contract provided 1.5% monthly charge on overdue amounts, so the charge is interest and is subject only to state's usury cap, not to special requirements for imposition of late charges); Metro Hauling, Inc. v. Daffern, 723 P.2d 32 (Wash. Ct. App. 1986) (addition of a default interest rate to a contract after the consumer has already defaulted is usury if rate exceeds usury cap, as there is no contingency at that point).

service to the idea that the rule should not control if evidence exists that the late fees have been imposed with an intent to avoid usury law.[180]

Sometimes, however, treating late fees as interest reduces protections for consumers. For example, it will not help the borrower to treat late fees as interest in a state that no longer caps interest rates but caps other charges.[181] Late fees are also considered interest for purposes of federal preemption and the rate exportation rights of depository institutions,[182] which means that these lenders can ignore the laws of the consumer's home state regulating late fees.

### 4.8.3 Late Fee Statutes

Statutes governing late fees are generally more advantageous for consumers than the common law rule. A common statutory formula allows the lender to collect the lesser of $5 or 5% of the regular installment as a late fee, and restricts the lender to one late fee per installment no matter how late the installment is paid.[183] Some statutes also specify a minimum grace period which must be allowed before a late fee may be imposed.[184]

If a late fee statute specifies the limits of the permissible fees, then late fees may be considered interest to the extent that they exceed the statutory limit.[185] This added interest may be enough to make the loan in violation of state usury caps. In addition, a borrower will be entitled to the usury statute's remedies if the creditor imposes fees prior to the expiration of a statutory grace period,[186] in an amount exceeding the statutory maximum,[187] or in violation of other statutory requirements.[188] Finally, an excessive late fee may be challengeable under contract or other theories.[189]

### 4.8.4 Approaches When Usury Statute Is Inapplicable; Challenging Late Fees As Penalties

Additional issues arise when late fees are imposed by sellers of goods or services. In some states, because of the time-price doctrine, usury laws are inapplicable to credit sales,[190] so late charges will not be treated as interest. Many of these states, though, have adopted installment sales statutes that place limits on late charges.[191]

---

180 *See, e.g.*, Camilla Cotton Oil Co. v. Spencer Kellogg & Sons, Inc. 257 F.2d 162 (5th Cir. 1958); Hayes v. First Nat'l Bank, 507 S.W.2d 701 (Ark. 1974); Loigman v. Keim, 594 A.2d 1364 (N.J. Super. Ct. Law Div. 1991) (dicta) (usury statute does not apply to interest on defaulted obligations, but that narrow exception does not apply where default is expected); Lew v. Goodfellow Chrysler Plymouth, Inc., 492 P.2d 258 (Wash. Ct. App. 1971); Randall v. Home Loan & Inv. Co., 12 N.W.2d 915 (Wis. 1944). *See also* Administrative Interpretation #10, Maine Department of Business Regulation, Bureau of Consumer Protection Consumer Cred. Guide (CCH) § 98,617 (Jan. 29, 1975) (late charges on open account may be finance charge subject to Maine Consumer Credit Code if creditor continues to extend credit to debtor and fee is actually a periodic charge for delaying payment).

181 *See, e.g.*, Cantrell v. Walker Builders, Inc., 678 So. 2d 169 (Ala. Civ. App. 1996) (approving of Alabama attorney general's opinion that late fee falls within statutory definition of "interest" as "all direct and indirect charges imposed as an incident to a loan, forbearance of money or credit sale;" as a result, the only limit on the size of the late fee under § 8-8-5 is whether the fee is unconscionable).

182 Smiley v. Citibank (South Dakota), N.A., 517 U.S. 735, 745–746, 116 S. Ct. 1730, 135 L. Ed. 2d 25 (1996). *See generally* § 3.4.5, *supra*.

183 *See, e.g.*, Cal. Civ. Code § 1803.6 (Retail Installment Act); U.C.C.C. § 2.502 (1974 Model Code). *See also* Bowman Plumbing, Heating & Elec. v. Logan, 59 Va. Cir. 446 (Va. Cir. Ct. 2002) (Virginia late payment statute caps fees at 5%).

184 *See, e.g.*, 24 C.F.R. § 203.25 (FHA-insured loans; 4% late fee allowed on installments more than fifteen days late); 38 C.F.R. § 36.4212 (VA-insured loans, 4% late fee allowed on installments more than fifteen days late); Cal. Civ. Code § 1803.6 (West) ($10 if less than ten days late; $15 if less than fifteen days late); U.C.C. § 2.502(1) (1974 Model Code) (ten days).

185 *See, e.g.*, Miller v. Parker McCurley Props., L.L.C., 36 So. 3d 1234 (Miss. 2010) (amount of late fee that exceeds statutory cap is finance charge, but not usurious since law allows parties to agree to any finance charge they choose). *But see* Alston v. Crown Auto, Inc., 224 F.3d 332 (4th Cir. 2000) (Va. law) (late fee that exceeds statutory cap is not interest because debtor could avoid it by making timely payments).

186 *See* Bumpus v. Vandeford, 2002 U.S. Dist. LEXIS 20062 (N.D. Miss. Mar. 27, 2002) (late fee is finance charge where it is imposed prior to end of statutory fifteen-day grace period; state law allows borrower to recover these illegal fees from the lender); Reliable Credit Corp. v. Smith, 418 So. 2d 1311 (La. 1982) (allowing borrower to invoke statutory usury remedies for improperly imposed extension fee). *See also* Steves Sash & Door Co. v. Ceco Corp., 751 S.W.2d 473 (Tex. 1988) (awarding usury penalties where creditor charged interest during grace period when none was due).

187 Swindell v. Federal Nat'l Mortgage Ass'n, 409 S.E.2d 892 (N.C. 1991) (charging late fees in excess of those permitted by state law subjects lender to usury penalty; penalty is forfeiture of all late fees, not all interest). *See also In re* Crotzer, 147 B.R. 252 (Bankr. N.D. Ala. 1992) (imposing late fees in excess of statutory maximum resulted in creditor's forfeiture of *all* late fees; to rule otherwise by permitting creditor to retain the legal amount would give creditors an incentive to break the law).

188 *See, e.g.*, Reliable Credit Corp. v. Smith, 418 So. 2d 1311 (La. 1982) (lender is liable for statutory usury penalty where it failed to obtain debtor's written agreement to imposition of deferral charge as required by deferred charge statute); Aldrich v. Ellis, 52 P.3d 388 (Mont. 2002) (seller failed to meet requirements of Montana statute governing imposition of late payment charges for accounts receivable; buyer permitted to amend complaint to add usury claim); Bowman Plumbing, Heating & Elec. v. Logan, 59 Va. Cir. 446 (Va. Cir. Ct. 2002) (Virginia late payment statute requires late payment fee to be specified in the contract between seller and consumer; failure to include fee in contract bars seller from collecting late fee).

189 For example, in a case involving a UDAP claim, rather than a usury claim, a careful parsing of contract language setting the amount of a permissible charge showed the creditor overcharged on late fees. Depending on the language of the statute involved, a similar analysis may prove fruitful. *See In re* Andrews, 78 B.R. 78 (Bankr. E.D. Pa. 1987) (mortgage contract called for late charge of 4% on installment—interpreted to be the principal and interest amount, but creditor calculated charges on basis of aggregate monthly payment amount which also included insurance and tax escrow). *Contra* Moore v. Lomas Mtg. USA, 796 F. Supp. 300 (N.D. Ill. 1992).

190 *See* §§ 1.2.4, *supra*, 7.5.2.2, 10.3.6.3, *infra*.

191 *See* § 10.2.8, *infra*.

Many courts also hold usury statutes inapplicable to fees imposed when a buyer fails to pay a bill when due, unless the seller has agreed to allow payment over time.[192] However, usury statutes that apply to "detention" of money may be applicable in this situation.[193]

Even if late fees are not treated as interest, and no statute caps them, they are not necessarily immune from challenge. A number of states view late fees as liquidated damages.[194] Contract provisions calling for liquidated damages may be valid if they represent a good faith effort of the parties at the time of the creation of the contract to assess and compensate for the damage which will be caused by a specified breach of contract.[195] However, liquidated damages provisions which go beyond the mere compensation of the injured party, and which act as punishment for the breach are unenforceable.[196] Apply-

192 *See, e.g.*, Johnston v. Palmer, 158 P.3d 998 (Mont. 2007); *In re* City of Binghamton, 521 N.Y.S.2d 140 (N.Y. 1987) (rejecting usury claim on ground that no "loan or forbearance" was involved in a statutorily authorized late fee on overdue sewer and water assessments); O'Connor v. Televideo Sys., Inc., 267 Cal. Rptr. 237 (Cal. Ct. App. 1990) (no forbearance involved where past due accounts subject to 18% annual late charge; court noted that this was commercial transaction between parties of equal bargaining power and no evidence it was a device to evade usury laws); Irwin Rogers Ins. Agency v. Murphy, 833 P.2d 128 (Idaho Ct. App. 1992) (late charges were not interest; usury required excessive compensation for loan, forbearance or extension of payment on existing debt, and there was no evidence of agreement for extended time for payment in consideration for late charges); Widmark v. Northrup King Co., 530 N.W.2d 588 (Minn. Ct. App. 1995); Alaskan Fireplace, Inc. v. Everett, 667 N.W.2d 378 (Wis. Ct. App. 2003) (table) (text available at 2003 WL 21397747); Garcia v. Tex. Cable Partners, Ltd. P'ship, 114 S.W.3d 561 (Tex. App. 2003) (cable television late fee not interest because no use, forbearance, or detention of money involved). *See also* Gaddis v. Stardust Hills Owners Ass'n, 804 N.E.2d 231 (Ind. Ct. App. 2004) (late fee of 1% per day or 365% annually on unpaid homeowner association dues not usurious interest); Domizio v. Progressive County Mut. Ins. Co., 54 S.W.3d 867 (Tex. App. 2001) (payment of insurance premiums in installments does not equal credit, as consumer receives insurance for a new period only upon payment for that period; therefore, late fees are not subject to usury claim). *But see* Bunn v. Weyerhauser Co., 598 S.W.2d 54 (Ark. 1980) (1.5% monthly service charge if open account balance is not paid within thirty days is interest); Rea v. Breakers Ass'n, 674 So. 2d 496 (Miss. 1996) (applying Mississippi usury and late fee limitations apply when condo association assesses late fee on monthly assessment, as condo owner is personally liable and condo association has power to foreclose).; Seaton v. City of Lexington, 97 S.W.3d 72 (Mo. Ct. App. 2002) (late payment fee designed to ensure prompt payment of municipal sewer bill is not the equivalent of interest charged for the use of money).

193 *See* Scarr v. Boyer, 818 P.2d 381 (Mont. 1991) (Montana's usury statute applies to compensation for detention of money, thus it includes post-default interest within definition of interest). *See generally* § 7.5.2.3, *infra* (discussion of forbearance and detention).

194 *See, e.g.*, *In re* Union Square Dev., 140 B.R. 544 (D. Colo. 1992) (Colorado test is whether parties intend to liquidate damages; damages must be uncertain or difficult to prove, and late fee must be a reasonable amount not grossly disproportionate to presumed loss); Garrett v. Coast & So. Fed. Sav. & Loan Ass'n, 511 P.2d 1197 (Cal. 1973); Utility Consumers' Action Network v. AT&T Broadband, 37 Cal. Rptr. 3d 827 (Cal. Ct. App. 2006); Beasley v. Wells Fargo Bank, N.A., 1 Cal. Rptr. 2d 446 (Cal. Ct. App. 1991); O'Connor v. Televideo Sys., Inc., 267 Cal. Rptr. 237 (Cal. Ct. App. 1990); MetLife Capital Fin. Corp. v. Washington Avenue Ass'n, L.P., 732 A.2d 493 (N.J. 1999). *But see But see* Perez v. Capital One Bank, 522 S.E.2d 874 (Va. 1999) (common law rule that excessive late fee is unenforceable as a penalty is abrogated by statute allowing any fee agreed to by the parties, even though it does not cap the amount of the fee). *See generally* Annotation, 63 A.L.R.3d 50 (1975).

195 Norwest Bank v. Blair Road Assocs., 252 F. Supp. 2d 86 (D.N.J. 2003) (holding that late fee, plus default interest rate increase of 3%, plus a "prepayment premium" of at least 3% of the principal remaining, were enforceable as reasonable in commercial transaction); Gaddis v. Stardust Hills Owners Ass'n, 804 N.E.2d 231 (Ind. Ct. App. 2004) (late fee of 1% per day on unpaid homeowner association dues not unenforceable as a penalty); MetLife Capital Fin. Corp. v. Washington Avenue Ass'n, L.P., 732 A.2d 493 (N.J. 1999) (test is whether amount is reasonable in light of the anticipated or actual loss caused by the breach and difficulties of proof of loss; 5% late fee is not an unenforceable penalty in commercial loan); MONY Life Ins. Co. v. Paramus Parkway Bldg., Ltd., 834 A.2d 475 (N.J. Super. Ct. App. Div. 2003); Westmark Commercial Mortgage Fund IV v. Teenform Assocs., Ltd. P'ship, 827 A.2d 1154 (N.J. Super. Ct. App. Div. 2003); Stuchin v. Kasirer, 568 A.2d 907 (N.J. Super. Ct. App. Div. 1990) (remanding case to determine whether 15% increase in post-maturity rate was unenforceable penalty); Waterbury v. City of Oswego, 674 N.Y.S.2d 530 (N.Y. App. Div. 1998) (late fees not unenforceable penalty imposed by a municipality operating its own water supply).

196 *See, e.g.*, N. Bloom & Son (Antiques), Ltd. v. Skelly, 673 F. Supp. 1260 (S.D.N.Y. 1987) (sales invoices called for interest at 2% per month on balances unpaid for more than thirty days; given amounts involved this was an impermissible penalty and thus void); 201 Forest Street L.L.C. v. LBM Fin. L.L.C. & Marcello Mallegni (*In re* 201 Forest Street L.L.C.), 409 B.R. 543 (Bankr. D. Mass. 2009) (41% default interest rate and 10% late fee unenforceable in commercial transaction because they were not reasonably tied to lender's forecast and actual damages, respectively); *In re* Hein, 60 B.R. 769 (Bankr. S.D. Cal. 1986) ($500/day late fee was unenforceable penalty); Garrett v. Coast & So. Fed. Sav. & Loan Ass'n, 511 P.2d 1197 (Cal. 1973) (liquidated damages analysis; late fee was unrelated to actual damages incurred); Beasley v. Wells Fargo Bank, N.A., 1 Cal. Rptr. 2d 446 (Cal. Ct. App. 1991) (late charge calculated to include indirect costs and collection agency expenses did not constitute good faith effort to compensate for damage caused by a specific default. *Note*: case is informative on methodology in setting fees; that bank seemed to have viewed late and over-the-limit fees as a revenue source probably was a factor in result). *See also In re* Graboyes, 371 B.R. 113 (Bankr. E.D. Pa. 2007) (agreeing that a penalty provision that assesses a charge disproportionate to the injury that occurred will be treated as an unenforceable penalty; interpreting the contract late fee provision to prohibit the compounding of late fees and the capitalization of late fees or the charging of late fees after the contract's maturity date; disallowing the lender's claim to the extent based upon violations of these provisions); Begelfer v. Najarian, 409 N.E.2d 167, 186 (Mass. 1980) (finding late charge usurious on other grounds; it would also be unenforceable as an unreasonable, unconscionable, and oppressive penalty); Funding Group, Inc. v. Water Chef, Inc., 852 N.Y.S.2d 736 (N.Y. Sup. Ct. 2008) (late fee provision awarding the equivalent of 120% per year penalty unreasonable and "confiscatory" in light of public policy of the criminal usury statute; business case). *See also* Crest Sav. & Loan Ass'n v. Mason, 581 A.2d 120 (N.J. Super. Ct. Ch. Div. 1990) (late charges on installment payments cannot be imposed after mortgage debt has been accelerated and creditor has filed foreclosure complaint, because by these acts creditor repudiates borrower's right to make installment payments). *Cf. In re* Late Fee

ing this approach, a late fee calculated as a percentage of the outstanding loan balance, rather than as a percentage of the delinquent amount, may be void as a penalty.[197] Similarly, a 5% late fee was unenforceable as a penalty, when it was applied to a balloon payment and there was also a default interest rate.[198]

In general, borrowers bear the burden of demonstrating that late fees have no relationship to creditors' collection expenses.[199] If a court finds that a liquidated damages clause is actually a penalty clause, it may simply refuse to enforce the penalty clause, rather than grant the remedies of the usury statute. An affirmative action for damages may lie, however.[200]

Another theory for challenging the amount of a late charge is the common law rule that the damages collectible for failure to pay a sum of money are limited to interest at the legal rate. A Maryland decision,[201] later overruled by statute,[202] accepted this theory.

### 4.8.5 Pyramiding Late Charges

The "pyramiding" of late charges is one method that creditors use to assess multiple late charges on an account after as little as one late payment. Pyramiding is accomplished by attributing a borrower's current payments first to outstanding late charges or overdue amounts and only second to the installment which is currently due. For example, if a borrower must make $100 monthly payments on a loan, due on the first of each month, and the borrower makes her January payment of $100 after the grace period has expired, on January 20th, a $5 late fee will be assessed for the late January payment.

When the borrower makes a $100 February payment, even if that payment is properly made on February 1st, the first $5 of the payment will be attributed to the January late charge rather than to the February installment. As a result, the borrower will be $5 short in her February payment, unless she has thought to include an extra $5 with the February payment to cover the outstanding late fee. If the February payment is short by $5, the lender will add another late fee for the February payment, and the account will now have a $10 outstanding balance before the March payment comes due. The process will repeat with a late fee being added in March and every subsequent month even if all these payments are made on time.

The pyramiding of late charges presents a hidden interest problem in that the monthly addition of late charges to a debtor's account, when only one or two payments may actually have been late, constitutes a *de facto* increase in the interest rate. However, proving hidden interest through pyramiding may not be an easy case in many states, at least in the absence of a statute prohibiting the practice.[203] One court did hold that pyramiding or "compounding" late fees was unlawful under a statute that did not directly address this issue.[204] But a challenge to pyramiding based on a statutory prohibition against charging more than one late fee for each delinquent payment—rather than on the amount of the late fees being charged—fared less well.[205]

A Federal Trade Commission (FTC) rule prohibits certain types of late charge pyramiding. The FTC Credit Practices Rule[206] declares that various credit contract practices, including

& Over-Limit Fee Litig., 528 F. Supp. 2d 953 (N.D. Cal. 2007) (recognizing the consumer's argument that excessive contract damages, in this case the $39 late fee permitted in the credit card agreement, could be "punitive" and, therefore, penalties, but finding that the common law description of "punitive" does not transform the charges into "punitive damages" that trigger constitutional due process concerns).

197 *See* Garrett v. Coast & So. Fed. Sav. & Loan Ass'n, 511 P.2d 1197 (Cal. 1973). *See also In re* Jordan, 91 B.R. 673 (Bankr. E.D. Pa. 1988) (1.5% monthly late fee calculated on full amount of delinquency impermissible for a variety of reasons, *inter alia* late charges excessive in relation to creditor's damage an unenforceable penalty; particularly so here, where APR was already over 24%); Johnnycake Mountain Assocs. v. Ochs, 2006 WL 538109 (Conn. Super. Ct. Jan. 18, 2006) (calculating late fee as percentage of balloon payment was so disproportionate as to be a penalty and was thus unenforceable), *aff'd in part, rev'd in part on other grounds*, 932 A.2d 472 (Conn. Ct. App. 2007); Velenchik v. First Union Nat'l Bank, 2003 WL 21152967 (Conn. Super. Ct. May 7, 2003) (calculating late fee on balloon payment was penalty and thus unenforceable).

198 *In re* Market Ctr. E. Retail Prop., Inc., 433 B.R. 335 (Bankr. D.N.M. 2010). *But cf.* MetLife Capital Fin. Corp. v. Washington Avenue Ass'n, L.P., 732 A.2d 493 (N.J. 1999) (upholding 5% late fee in commercial contract even though it was applied to balloon payment).

199 *See* Smith v. Figure World Plus, Inc., 705 S.W.2d 432 (Ark. 1986); Metlife Capital Fin. Corp. v. Washington Avenue Assocs. L.P., 732 A.2d 493 (N.J. 1999) (commercial transaction).

200 *See, e.g.*, United Cable TV of Baltimore Ltd. v. Burch, 732 A.2d 887 (Md. 1999), *legislative abrogation on other grounds noted by* Dua v. Comcast Cable, 805 A.2d 1061 (Md. Ct. Spec. App. 2002) (noting legislature's adoption of late fee statute).

201 United Cable TV of Baltimore, L.P. v. Burch, 732 A.2d 887 (Md. 1999) (5% late fee assessed by cable television company for bill for service is an unlawful penalty because it exceeds 6% legal interest rate).

202 *See* Dua v. Comcast Cable, 805 A.2d 1061 (Md. Ct. App. 2002). *But cf.* McDaniel v. Am. Honda Fin. Corp., 926 A.2d 757 (Md. 2007) (late fee can exceed legal interest rate and does not constitute interest if statute allows it to be imposed).

203 Such prohibitions do exist. *See, e.g.*, 24 C.F.R. § 203.25 (FHA loans); 38 C.F.R. § 36.4212 (VA loans); U.C.C.C. § 2.502(3) (1974 Model Code).

204 Waterman Convalescent Hosp., Inc. v. Jurupa Cmty. Servs. Dist., 62 Cal. Rptr. 2d 264 (Cal. Ct. App. 1996) (statute at issue allowed for a 10% penalty for late payments and an additional penalty not exceeding 0.5% per month for nonpayment of the charges and the basic penalty; charging 10% on the 10% penalty violated the clear language).

205 Davis v. Ford Motor Credit Co., 101 Cal. Rptr. 3d 697 (Cal. Ct. App. 2009) (upholding trial court decision that prohibition in California's auto finance statute on assessing more than one late fee for each delinquent payment not violated when lender applied borrower's payment to outstanding delinquent amount instead of amount owed in current month).

206 16 C.F.R. § 444.4. *See also* 49 Fed. Reg. 7740 (Mar. 1, 1984) (statement of basis and purpose).

Other regulatory agencies have adopted parallel rules. *See* 12 C.F.R. § 560.33 (OTS). *See also* Reg. Z, 12 C.F.R. § 226.36(c)(1)(ii) [§ 1026.36(c)(1)(ii)], *adopted by* 73 Fed. Reg. 44,522, 44,604 (July 30, 2008) (parallel rule covering servicers of most mortgages), *discussed in* National Consumer Law Center, Truth in Lending § 9.4 (7th ed. 2010 and Supp.).

late fee pyramiding, are "unfair" under section 5 of the Federal Trade Commission Act.[207] Under the FTC Rule, it is an "unfair act or practice" for a creditor to impose a late charge "when the only delinquency is attributable to late fee(s) or delinquency charge(s) assessed on earlier installments."[208]

Thus, the FTC Rule would prohibit the type of pyramiding described in the example at the beginning of this section. However, it does not reach pyramiding which results from a skipped payment rather than a late payment.[209] For example, if a borrower makes no January payment on a loan, the creditor may validly attribute the February 1st payment to the outstanding January debt, and may later attribute the March 1st payment to the February debt, etc. Under this accounting method, every payment is viewed as one month late and late charges are validly assessed every month.[210] This practice is prohibited if the loan is precomputed in those states which have adopted the 1974 draft of the UCCC.[211]

## 4.8.6 Other Charges Imposed Upon Default

### 4.8.6.1 Deferral Charges

Late fees should be distinguished from "deferral fees," which are payments that a debtor may be permitted to make to delay the date when a payment is due and, thereby, to avoid default.[212] When a creditor charges a deferral fee, the result is that the consumer skips a payment and the maturity date of the loan is extended.

Some credit statutes specifically authorize deferral charges and specify how they are to be calculated and when they can be imposed.[213] A creditor was liable for statutory usury penalties where it collected a deferral charge from a debtor at a time when the payment was not yet delinquent, without getting the borrower's agreement in writing as required by the statute.[214]

If a state statute does not specifically address deferral fees, a court may treat them as interest and therefore subject to the state usury cap. In one case, a business borrower executed a note, and then obtained 203 thirty-day extensions of the due date, each time paying a forbearance fee. The court treated the forbearance fees as interest subject to the state usury cap.[215]

207 15 U.S.C. § 45(a).

208 16 C.F.R. § 444.4.

209 *See* FTC Staff Advisory Letter (June 21, 1985) *reprinted in* Consumer Cred. Guide (CCH) ¶ 96,257; FTC Staff Advisory Letter (May 31, 1985), *reprinted in* Consumer Cred. Guide (CCH) ¶ 96,309.

210 *See* National Consumer Law Center, Unfair and Deceptive Acts and Practices §§ 3.4.5, 6.1.1, 6.12 (7th ed. 2008 and Supp.).

211 U.C.C.C. § 2.502 (1974). *See* § 2.3.10, *supra* (discussing U.C.C.C.).

212 *See generally* Hayes v. First Nat'l Bank, 507 S.W.2d 701 (Ark. 1974); Watson v. Avco Fin. Servs. Int'l, Inc., 401 N.W.2d 485 (Neb. 1987).

213 *See* § 10.2.7, *infra.*

214 *See* Reliable Credit Corp. v. Smith, 418 So. 2d 1311 (La. 1982).

215 Sunburst Bank v. Keith, 648 So. 2d 1147 (Miss. 1995). *But cf.* Watson v. Avco Fin. Servs. Int'l, Inc., 401 N.W.2d 485 (Neb. 1987) (nothing in installment sales act prevented creditor from renegotiating contract to extend maturity in return for a charge, even though statute did not specifically authorize deferral charges).

### 4.8.6.2 Property Inspection Fees

Many credit contracts are written broadly to allow creditors to impose both late fees after a delinquency and "property inspection fees" for home-secured loans. A California decision holds that property inspection fees are not late fees, and may be charged in addition to late fees, which are capped by California law.[216] This analysis would appear to undermine the concept of late fees as a form of liquidated damages. The reason for treating late fees as liquidated damages is to compensate the creditor for expenses from a delinquency that are impractical to quantify; thus, the creditor is permitted a single flat charge to compensate for the expenses. Once the creditor is permitted to pile on additional fees for discrete expenses, it becomes apparent that the late fee is simply a penalty.

### 4.8.6.3 Attorney Fees upon Default

It is common for consumer credit contracts to make the debtor liable for attorney fees that the creditor incurs in collecting the debt if the debtor defaults. Attorney fee contractual provisions and statutory limitations are discussed in National Consumer Center, *Collection Actions* §§ 6.2, 6.3 (2d ed. 2011 and Supp.).

There seems to be general agreement that contractual provisions for the payment of attorney fees in the event of default are exempt from usury restrictions unless they are somehow used as a "cloak" for usury.[217] The most frequently mentioned reason for this rule is that a charge for attorney fees upon default is not a charge for the use of the creditor's money and hence is not "interest."[218] In addition, the charge is contingent on the borrower's performance and thus should not be included in the interest calculation for usury purposes.[219]

### 4.8.6.4 Default Interest Rates

Consumer credit contracts sometimes provide for a default interest rate, i.e., a provision by which the interest rate is increased if the borrower defaults. Some courts hold that an interest rate cap in a usury law does not apply to a default interest rate, at least as long as the parties, when they entered into the transaction, contemplated that the loan would be repaid

216 Walker v. Countrywide Home Loans, 121 Cal. Rptr. 2d 79 (Cal. Ct. App. 2002).

217 In a few cases, creditors that have assessed usurious charges have retroactively attempted to justify them as valid charges for attorney fees. This gambit has not held up in court. *See* Ganus v. Jopes, 470 So. 2d 237 (La. Ct. App. 1985); Coppedge v. Colonial Sav. & Loan Ass'n, 721 S.W.2d 933 (Tex. App. 1986).

218 *See* Community Credit Union v. Connors, 105 A.2d 772 (Conn. 1954); Armin Corp. v. Kullman, 318 A.2d 448 (N.J. Super. Ct. App. Div. 1974). *Cf.* Oyster Creek Fin. Corp. v. Richwood Invs. II, Inc., 176 S.W.3d 307 (Tex. App. 2004) (upholding jury's finding that lender did not charge usurious interest in demanding amount that included principal, interest, and attorney fees.).

219 *See* Powell v. Sowell 145 So. 2d 168, *suggestion of error overruled* 146 So. 2d 576 (Miss. 1962); Annotation, 17 A.L.R.2d 228 (1951).

when due.[220] However, usury caps that apply not just to loans and forbearances but also to the "detention" of money[221] may apply to default interest rates, as the default interest rate applies if the borrower detains the loan proceeds after the loan has matured by the passage of time or acceleration.[222]

In addition, a default interest rate may be unenforceable as a penalty.[223] A number of courts have found that it is an unenforceable penalty to charge both a late fee and to assess a default interest rate.[224]

A related question is the effect of a state credit law that explicitly limits delinquent charges.[225] A Colorado decision holds that a default interest rate is a default or delinquency charge, so its imposition violated a state credit statute that specified the only default charges that were permissible.[226]

The Truth in Lending Act prohibits default interest rates for certain high-cost mortgage loans.[227] The Credit CARD Act amendments to the Truth in Lending Act and implementing regulations prohibit a credit card issuer from imposing a penalty rate on an existing balance unless the consumer makes a payment over sixty days late and the issuer sends a notice. The former rate must be reinstated after six months of on-time payments.[228] An issuer may impose a penalty rate on future transactions with forty-five days' notice. Other limitations and details are discussed in another treatise in this series.[229]

220 Stuchin v. Kasirer, 568 A.2d 907 (N.J. Super. Ct. App. Div. 1990); Klapper v. Integrated Agricultural Mgmt. Co., 539 N.Y.S.2d 812 (N.Y. App. Div. 1989); Metro Hauling, Inc. v. Daffern, 723 P.2d 32 (Wash. Ct. App. 1986). *See also* Pierce v. Emigrant Mortgage Co., 2005 WL 2406007 (D. Conn. Sept. 29, 2005) (default interest rate is within borrower's control so does not render loan usurious). *See generally* J.D. Perovich, *Provision for Interest After Maturity at a Rate in Excess of Legal Rate As Usurious or Otherwise Illegal*, 28 A.L.R. 3d 449 (1969).

221 *See* § 7.5.2.3, *infra*.

222 Scarr v. Boyer, 818 P.2d 381, 383 (Mont. 1991). *See also* T.F. James Co. v. Vakoch, 604 N.W.2d 459 (N.D. 2000) (interest after maturity is compensation for detention of money so is governed by legal interest statute, not usury statute, and usury penalties do not apply).

223 *See, e.g.*, Inland Bank & Trust v. Knight, 927 N.E.2d 777 (Ill App. Ct. 2010) (default interest rate is measured by liquidated damages standards, but this one is reasonable so is not a penalty); Stuchin v. Kasirer, 568 A.2d 907 (N.J. Super. Ct. App. Div. 1990) (default interest rate must be viewed as liquidated damages clause and will be unenforceable as a penalty if it is unconscionable). *See also In re* Kalian, 178 B.R. 308 (Bankr. D.R.I. 1995) (evaluating 36% default rate under bankruptcy law; noting in *dicta* that default interest rate also may be unenforceable penalty under state law). *Cf.* MetLife Capital Fin. Corp. v. Washington Avenue Ass'n, L.P., 732 A.2d 493 (N.J. 1999) (applying liquidated damages analysis to default interest rate but finding it not to be unenforceable as a penalty). *But cf.* Norwest Bank v. Blair Road Assocs., 252 F. Supp. 2d 86 (D.N.J. 2003) (holding that late fee, plus default interest rate increase of 3%, plus a "prepayment premium" of at least 3% of the principal remaining, were enforceable as reasonable in commercial transaction).

224 *In re* Market Ctr. E. Retail Prop., Inc., 433 B.R. 335 (Bankr. D.N.M. 2010); Cliftondale Oaks, L.L.C. v. Silver Lake Enter., 357 B.R. 883 (Bankr. N.D. Ga. 2006); *In re* AE Hotel Venture, 321 B.R. 209 (Bankr. N.D. Ill. 2005). *See also* First Bank of Ohio v. Brunswick Apartments of Trumbull County, Ltd., 169 F.3d 333 (6th Cir. 1999).

225 *See* § 4.8.3, *supra*.

226 First Nat'l Bank v. Union Tavern Corp., 794 P.2d 261 (Colo. App. 1990).

227 15 U.S.C. § 1639(d). *See* National Consumer Law Center, Truth in Lending § 9.6.9.3 (7th ed. 2010 and Supp.).

228 15 U.S.C. § 1666i-1(b)(4); 12 C.F.R. § 1026.55. *See* National Consumer Law Center, Truth in Lending § 7.2.3 (7th ed. 2010 and Supp.).

229 National Consumer Law Center, Truth in Lending § 7.2.3 (7th ed. 2010 and Supp.).

# Chapter 5 Credit Math: Calculating Interest and Rebates

## 5.1 Introduction

The other chapters in this treatise focus on the interpretation and application of usury statutes and other state restrictions on the cost and terms of non-mortgage credit. By contrast, this chapter focuses on mechanics: on how to make sense of—and check—the numbers in individual consumer credit transactions.

In order to simplify the discussion, the authors have made several assumptions about the reader's knowledge. First, the reader is assumed to have done some preliminary research and to know which statute, such as a state RISA, applies to the transaction in question. Second, having looked at the statute, the reader is assumed to know the relevant maximum interest rate. Finally, the reader is assumed to know how the statute defines "principal" and "interest" payments. In other words, this chapter generally assumes that the "principal" in a loan is the amount of cash received by the borrower and that all payments except those attributable to repayment of principal are "interest." A more detailed and realistic assessment of "interest" and "principal" is found in Chapter 4, *supra*.

What is not assumed is that the reader knows how to calculate the 8% "add-on interest" allowed by the RISA or the differences between, for example, add-on interest and actuarial interest. By carefully reading this chapter, and § 5.3.2, *infra*, in particular, the reader should fairly quickly understand how to make "add-on" interest rate calculations.

Readers are urged to keep a pencil and paper (or a calculator) handy as they go through this chapter. The best way to understand the calculations presented is to try to duplicate the examples given. Before the mathematically faint-of-heart give up, let it be said that the mathematics of this chapter would not challenge a reasonably bright, well-educated sixth grade student. The only skills required are addition, subtraction, multiplication, and division. Almost any calculator, if it is easy to use and easy to read, can do the job.

But let there be no mistake: the emphasis here is on the numbers, the dollars and cents, of consumer usury, and there is no way to avoid these simple arithmetic calculations. The authors have tried diligently to make the text and the examples simple and understandable. A careful reading of this chapter should intellectually enrich the reader and, more importantly, financially benefit the client.

This chapter includes a detailed discussion of interest rate calculations, rebates of unearned charges, and the mathematics of flipping. A separate treatise, NCLC's *Mortgage Lending* (2012), discusses several credit math issues that arise almost exclusively in mortgage lending, including biweekly mortgage payment plans, daily interest (including the use of the 365/360-day method), progress payments, and negatively amortizing "option" adjustable rate mortgages.

## 5.2 Interest Calculations: Single Payment Transactions

### 5.2.1 Calculation Rules

Nearly every schoolchild (even those who grow up to be lawyers) learns that the formula for savings account interest is I = P × R × T, where I = Interest ($), P = Principal ($), R = Rate of interest (%), and T = Time. The following example will illustrate the application of this formula.[1]

Suppose a depositor places $1,000 in a savings account that pays 8% simple interest on an annual basis. If the depositor does not withdraw any of the $1,000 for a year, how much interest will have been earned by the end of the year?[2] In this example, the principal, P = $1,000; the rate of interest, R = 8% per year; and the time, T = one year. Therefore I = $1,000 × 8% × 1 = $80. At the end of the year, this prudent depositor will have $80 interest plus the original principal of $1,000, for a total of $1,080 in her account.

Another depositor puts her $1,000 in a savings account in the same bank at the same 8%, annual interest rate. This depositor, however, leaves the $1,000 in her account for three years. How much interest will have been earned by the end of three years?

Again, P = $1,000 and R = 8%. This time, however, T = three years. Therefore, I = $1,000 × 8% × 3 = $240. At the end of the three years, the depositor will have $240 in interest, plus the original $1,000 principal, for a total of $1,240.

At this point, impatient readers will point out that this discussion may be nostalgic and possibly even interesting, but of little relevance, since this treatise is concerned with the problems of consumer borrowers, not consumer depositors. But turn the tables and think of a situation where a consumer, instead of enjoying the luxury of a $1,000 savings account, needs to *borrow* $1,000 for one year from the same bank that

1 The numbers used, however, may reflect only the experience of a very affluent schoolchild growing up in an inflationary, deregulated economy.

2 In both this and the next example, the discussion assumes that interest is not compounded, or added to principal, at any point except at the end of the particular time period in question.

is lending money at the same annual interest rate of 8%. Instead of the bank "borrowing" the consumer's money and paying her interest, as in the first examples, now the consumer is borrowing the bank's money and paying the bank interest.

The bank uses the same formula for calculating interest, I = P × R × T. If the consumer needs to borrow $1,000 for one year at 8% annual interest, then P = $1,000; R = 8%; and T = 1. Then, I = $1,000 × 8% × 1 = $80. At the end of one year, the consumer will owe the bank $80 interest plus $1,000 principal for a total of $1,080.

If another consumer needs to borrow $1,000 at the same 8% rate from the same bank, but for three years, instead of one year, then P = $1,000; R = 8%; and T = 3. Therefore, I = $1,000 × 8% × 3 = $240. The consumer will owe the bank a total of $240 in interest. The bank may allow the consumer to pay all the interest at the end of the three-year term, at which point the consumer will owe $240 in interest plus $1,000 in principal, for a total of $1,240.[3]

This is the essence of simple-interest, one-payment transactions. As can be seen above, the maximum interest is relatively easy to calculate[4] and the method is relatively unambiguous.

### 5.2.2 *Payday Loan Interest and APR Calculations*

Most types of consumer credit do not involve single-payment loans. For example, it would be unheard-of for a lender to make a consumer mortgage loan whereby the consumer borrowed $200,000, paid nothing for thirty years, and then repaid the principal plus thirty years of interest.

However, single-payment loans predominate in payday lending. Since the term of a payday loan is usually one month or less, the interest rate calculations described in the preceding subsection have to be adjusted to take account of this shortened term. But otherwise, the calculations described in the preceding subsection can be used for payday loans.

For example, assume a consumer borrows $100 from a payday lender. If the interest rate is 180% and repayment is due exactly one month later, the amount of interest the consumer will have to pay is Principal × Rate × Time, i.e., $100 × 180% × 1/12 = $15. One-twelfth is used as the term of the loan because a month is one-twelfth of a year.

Usually payday lenders do not calculate the amount of interest to charge by applying a percentage rate to the principal for the amount of time the loan is outstanding. Instead, they charge a flat amount per $100 borrowed, regardless of the length of time the loan will be outstanding. The interest rate then depends on the length of the loan. For example, if a payday lender charges $15 for a $100 loan, the effective interest rate is 780% if the consumer repays the loan in one week, 390% if the consumer repays in two weeks, and 180% if the consumer repays in one month.

The formula for finding the interest rate for a single-payment loan when the amount of the finance charge is known and the term is a certain number of days is:

$$\text{Rate} = \frac{\text{finance charge} \times 365 \times 100}{\text{principal} \times \text{number of days in the term}}$$

If the loan term is a certain number of weeks, the formula is:

$$\text{Rate} = \frac{\text{finance charge} \times 52 \times 100}{\text{principal} \times \text{number of weeks in the term}}$$

If the loan term is a certain number of months, the formula is:

$$\text{Rate} = \frac{\text{finance charge} \times 12 \times 100}{\text{principal} \times \text{number of months in the term}}$$

Note that the annual percentage rate (APR) for Truth in Lending purposes will not always be the same as the interest rate produced by these calculations. The reason is that, in some cases, the Truth in Lending regulations allow the lender to ignore some components of the cost of the loan when calculating the APR.[5]

## 5.3 Interest Formulae for Installment Credit: Actuarial Interest, Add-On Interest, and Discount Interest

### 5.3.1 *Introduction*

The explosive growth of consumer credit after World War II was marked by an almost exclusive reliance on *installment* credit[6] and by a bewildering array of methods to calculate consumer installment interest. Installment interest is premised on the assumption that the consumer will make payments on a periodic basis (usually monthly) and that if every payment is made on time, all of the principal, as well as all of the interest that has been earned over the life of the transaction, will have been paid to the lender by the end of the loan term. This section will try to demystify the various interest methods: actuarial (simple), add-on, and discount.

As a preview, consider whether an auto loan from a dealership at 6% is cheaper than the same loan from a credit union at

3 Or the bank may require the consumer to pay interest as it is earned every year. Therefore the consumer will pay $80 interest at the end of the first year; $80 interest at the end of the second year; and $80 interest plus the $1,000 principal at the end of the third year.

4 Usury issues, such as compounding or rounding, may still arise, however, in simple interest, one-payment transactions. *See* §§ 5.5.1, 5.5.5, *infra*. *See also* Fried v. Bolanos, 629 N.Y.S.2d 538 (N.Y. App. Div. 1995) (a determination of the loan term was necessary to establish whether the interest charge in a single payment loan was usurious; repayment date tied to an uncertain, contingent event was not sufficiently definite).

5 *See* § 5.4, *infra*.

6 As opposed to the one-payment transactions discussed at § 5.2, *supra*.

10%. The answer might seem obvious, but compare the following results on a three-year, $2,000 personal loan.

- 10% actuarial = $323.24 interest
- 6% add-on = $360 interest
- 6% discount = $439.02 interest

That anomalous result—the 10% loan is cheaper than two 6% loans, which themselves are not equal in cost—is, in short, why the Truth in Lending annual percentage rate (APR) was developed as a standard basis for comparison shopping for installment credit.[7] The next subsections explore these different ways to express interest rates, and the calculations behind them.

#### 5.3.1.1 Amortizing Credit Explained; Actuarial or Simple Interest Calculations

N.B.: The following discussion of actuarial interest must be mastered in order to understand the rest of this section. This section should not be difficult to comprehend, and it is particularly important for credit math novices.

The reader will recall one of the examples from the discussion of simple interest[8] in which the consumer wanted to borrow $1,000 at 8% annual simple interest, repayable in one payment at the end of the year. Using the formula $I = P \times R \times T$, it became clear that interest was $80 and at the end of the year the consumer would owe $80 interest and $1,000 principal, for a total of $1,080.

Now imagine that same consumer returned to the same bank that was still advertising the same "8% interest rate." Having once again been asked to lend another $1,000 for a year, the bank readily agreed, with one small, but very critical, change in terms. It would indeed give the consumer $1,000 for one year and would only charge the same $80 interest. This time, however, the bank would like the consumer to pay back the total amount owed ($1,080, of which $1,000 is principal and $80 is interest) in twelve monthly installments of $90 each.[9]

A smart consumer would not accept the bank's offer without first thinking about the difference between the two loans. The loans are remarkably similar: they are both "8%" loans of $1,000 for one year. However, in the first loan, the consumer had the full use of the $1,000 for a full year. She could use the loan proceeds any way she wanted: she could invest the $1,000; spend it; or put it under her mattress. As long as she paid the bank the $1,080 at the end of the year, she had the full use of the $1,000 for a year.

In the second loan, there are more restrictions. First and foremost, the consumer will not be able to use the $1,000 for the full year. Instead, she will have to give the bank $90 one month after receiving the $1,000 loan, and then $90 every month thereafter, until all twelve $90 payments have been made. Each payment will be applied in some fashion partly to interest and partly to principal. Therefore, beginning with the very first payment of $90, each payment reduces the amount of principal the consumer has at her disposal. Intuitively, the consumer will realize that the first loan is much more economically attractive than the second loan. Each loan charges the same amount of interest, but the first loan gives her full use of the $1,000 for the full year. In order to make the two loans economically equivalent, the bank would have to charge less interest for the second loan.

The consumer's insights are correct. Indeed, applying the $80 simple interest for a one-year, one-payment $1,000 loan to a one-year, twelve-payment $1,000 loan almost doubles the *effective* annual interest rate.[10] The effective annual interest rate for the first loan is obviously 8%, while the effective annual interest rate of the second is, not so obviously, 14.45%. Conversely, in order for the second loan's effective annual interest rate to be 8%, the same as that of the first loan, the monthly payments would have to be reduced from $90 to $86.99.[11] The interest charge for this transaction would only be $43.86, slightly more than half of the $80 charge in the other transaction.

All of the above is just a long way of saying that while there is more than one way of skinning the "8% interest" cat, there is essentially only one way to calculate simple or "actuarial" interest. *Actuarial interest is calculated by applying a periodic interest rate to the outstanding balance of the unpaid principal every repayment period for the term of the loan. The reduction over time of the outstanding balance, to produce "declining balances," is known as "amortization."* If we return once again to the two previous examples, the application of the actuarial method will become clearer.

The first example is the $1,000 loan for one year at 8% simple annual interest, with one payment at the end of the year. In this example, the repayment period is one year, so the periodic rate is 8%. Therefore, at the end of the one-year period, the 8% periodic rate is applied to the $1,000 outstanding balance of the unpaid principal, which produces $80 in interest. The consumer now owes the original principal of $1,000, plus $80, for a total of $1,080. If the consumer makes an $1,080 payment at that point, she will have completely satisfied her debt to the bank.

---

7 *See* § 5.4, *infra* (more detailed explanation of APR). *See also* National Consumer Law Center, Truth in Lending § 1.1.1 (7th ed. 2010 and Supp.).

8 *See* § 5.2, *supra*.

9 Since $1,080 ÷ 12 = $90.

10 For the purpose of the general discussion of credit math in this chapter, the word "effective" is properly understood to have its everyday, common meaning. It is not employed as a term of art. However, in the context of open-end credit transactions, the term "effective Annual Percentage Rate (APR)" is a term of art. As discussed in National Consumer Law Center, Truth in Lending § 6.7.6.4 (7th ed. 2010 and Supp.), the Truth in Lending rules formerly required credit card lenders to disclose the effective APR.

11 The twelfth final payment would be $86.97, $0.02 less than the first eleven payments.

**CHART 1**

**Amortization of $1,000 Loan at 8% Simple (Actuarial) Interest**

Principal = $1,000
12 monthly payments
Regular payment (#1 − #11) = $86.99
Final payment (#12) = $89.98
Total interest = $43.86
Simple Interest rate = 8%
Annual Percentage Rate = 8%

| *Payment #* | *Unpaid Balance* + | *Monthly Interest* − | *Payment* = | *New Balance* | *Total Interest To Date* |
|---|---|---|---|---|---|
| 1 | $1000.00 | $6.67 | $86.99 | $919.68 | $ 6.67 |
| 2 | $ 919.68 | $6.13 | $86.99 | $838.82 | $12.80 |
| 3 | $ 838.82 | $5.59 | $86.99 | $757.42 | $18.39 |
| 4 | $ 757.42 | $5.05 | $86.99 | $675.48 | $23.44 |
| 5 | $ 675.48 | $4.50 | $86.99 | $592.99 | $27.94 |
| 6 | $ 592.99 | $3.95 | $86.99 | $509.95 | $31.89 |
| 7 | $ 509.95 | $3.40 | $86.99 | $426.36 | $35.29 |
| 8 | $ 426.36 | $2.84 | $86.99 | $342.21 | $38.13 |
| 9 | $ 342.21 | $2.28 | $86.99 | $257.50 | $40.41 |
| 10 | $ 257.50 | $1.72 | $86.99 | $172.23 | $42.13 |
| 11 | $ 172.23 | $1.15 | $86.99 | $ 86.39 | $43.28 |
| 12 | $ 86.39 | $0.58 | $86.97 | $ 0.00 | $43.86 |

Contrast this example with the example of borrowing $1,000at 8% simple (or actuarial) annual interest for one year, repayable in twelve monthly installments, which is the basis for Chart 1. In this example, the monthly payment is $86.99. Since the repayment period is one *month*, the periodic rate is 8% ÷ 12 (as there are twelve months in a year) or .6667% or .006667. Therefore, at the end of the first one month period, the .6667% periodic rate is applied to the $1,000 outstanding balance of the unpaid principal, which produces $6.67 in interest.[12] If the consumer wanted to pay off her loan on this date, she would then owe the $1,000 principal plus the $6.67 interest, for a total of $1,006.67. However, the consumer is only contractually obligated to make a payment of $86.99. This payment is first applied to the $6.67 interest that has been earned. The remaining $80.32[13] is subtracted from the $1,000 principal to produce a new balance of $919.68. This process (called "amortization") is repeated every month, so that each month the outstanding balance declines until the unpaid balance has been reduced to zero.

The next month the process is repeated, except that interest will only be earned on a principal of $919.68. This month the loan will earn $6.13 in interest. This is calculated by multiplying the $919.68 unpaid principal times 8% annual rate and dividing that by 12, since only one of twelve months has passed. $919.68 × .08 ÷ 12 = $6.13. The $86.99 payment is applied first to the $6.13 accrued interest. The remainder of the payment, $80.86 ($86.99 − $6.13 = $80.86), is applied to the principal. The unpaid balance is now $838.82 since $919.68 − $80.86 = $838.82.

Whenever an installment payment is made, the payment is applied first to interest; this includes both interest that has accrued since the last payment was made and any interest that remained unpaid when the last payment was credited. The remaining portion of any payment that is not applied to interest is then applied to the unpaid principal.

Chart 1 (Amortization of $1,000 Loan at 8% Simple Interest) illustrates this process. It also demonstrates that because the unpaid balance declines after every monthly payment, then the amount of interest earned on the unpaid balance declines every month as well.[14] If the payments are calculated correctly, then the final payment will equal the unpaid principal balance plus the interest earned over the last period, thereby reducing the unpaid balance to zero.

At this point, the impatient, pragmatic reader will protest "all of this theory is very interesting, but how do we calculate actuarial interest for installment transactions? We have the formula for simple or actuarial interest for one payment transactions (I = P × R × T). Now give us the formula for actuarial interest for installment transactions."

The unhappy answer is that there is no simple formula for calculating actuarial interest for installment transactions. As will be discussed in the subsection on annual percentage rate,[15] there are both complicated formulas[16] and tables[17] that can be used to calculate actuarial interest for installment transactions. There are also hand-held calculators, web-based calculation tools, and computer programs, including one on the companion website to this treatise, which can precisely calculate actuarial interest rates, particularly when all the payment periods and payment amounts are identical.[18] Nonetheless, there is no relatively unsophisticated formula that creditors or consumer law-

12 *See* Chart 1, Amortization of $1,000 Loan at 8% Simple Interest, third column.

13 $86.996 − 6.67 = $80.32.

14 If this were not true, then $6.67, that is the monthly interest earned on the full $1,000 principal, would be earned every month; over twelve months, $80.00 in interest would be earned (12 × $6.67 = $80.00). This would create the obvious anomaly of the two loans generating the same amount of interest, despite the borrower getting less use of the principal in the second loan example.

15 *See* § 5.4, *infra.*

16 *See, e.g.*, Reg. Z, 12 C.F.R. pt. 226, app. J.

17 *See, e.g.*, Fed. Reserve Board Annual Percentage Rate Tables. There are two volumes. Volume I is suitable for the overwhelming majority of consumer credit transactions, and Volume II is used when less common, irregular transactions are involved. Consumer law practitioners would rarely need Volume II. The tables may be ordered for $5.00 each from the FRB. Prepaid orders should be sent to: Publications Fulfillment, Mail Stop 127, Board of Governors of the Federal Reserve System, Washington, D.C. 20551, (202) 452-3245. The tables may also be ordered on-line at www.newyorkfed.org/publications/frame1.cfm. They may also be found on the companion website to NCLC's Truth in Lending treatise.

18 *See, e.g.*, Financial Publishing Co. in South Bend, Indiana (800-247-3214) will also calculate actuarial interest rates. For more information, see § 5.4.2, *infra*.

yers can use to obtain quickly the actuarial interest rate or the maximum actuarial interest allowable in any transaction.[19]

However, it is helpful to have an understanding of the basic procedure employed in calculator and computer programs that determine the rate being charged in a transaction. Basically, they use the same trial and error technique anyone would use.[20] They take an educated guess at the actuarial interest rate needed to amortize a given loan amount at a given term with a given payment schedule. The final unpaid balance should be $0.00 after the final payment. If the final balance is higher than $0.00 (a positive number), then the interest rate should be reduced (so that the loan is amortized more quickly). On the other hand, if the final balance is less than $0.00 (a negative number), then the interest rate should be increased (so that the loan is not amortized so quickly). By trial and error, eventually an interest rate is found that creates a final unpaid balance of $0.00 and that is the true, actuarial rate for that transaction.

By way of illustration, let us return to Chart 1, where the $1,000, one-year loan, with eleven monthly payments of $86.99 and a 12th, final payment of $86.97 is amortized exactly at 8%. Let us assume for a moment, however, that we do not know what the true, actuarial interest rate is, but that we would like to find out.

**CHART 2**

**Trial Amortization of $1,000 Loan at 10% Simple Interest**

Principal = $1,000

12 monthly payments

Regular payment (#1 – #11) = $86.99

Final payment (#12) = $86.97

Total interest = $55.52

Simple Interest rate = 10%

| Payment # | Unpaid Balance + | Monthly Interest – | Payment = | New Balance | Total Interest To Date |
|---|---|---|---|---|---|
| 1 | $1000.00 | $8.33 | $86.99 | $921.34 | $ 8.33 |
| 2 | $ 921.34 | $7.68 | $86.99 | $842.03 | $16.01 |
| 3 | $ 842.03 | $7.02 | $86.99 | $762.06 | $23.03 |
| 4 | $ 762.06 | $6.35 | $86.99 | $681.42 | $29.38 |
| 5 | $ 681.42 | $5.68 | $86.99 | $600.11 | $35.06 |
| 6 | $ 600.11 | $5.00 | $86.99 | $518.12 | $40.06 |
| 7 | $ 518.12 | $4.32 | $86.99 | $435.45 | $44.38 |
| 8 | $ 435.45 | $3.63 | $86.99 | $352.09 | $48.01 |
| 9 | $ 352.09 | $2.93 | $86.99 | $268.03 | $50.94 |
| 10 | $ 268.03 | $2.23 | $86.99 | $183.27 | $53.17 |
| 11 | $ 183.27 | $1.53 | $86.99 | $ 97.81 | $54.70 |
| 12 | $ 97.81 | $0.82 | $86.97 | $ 11.66 | $55.52 |

Then let us assume that we make an educated guess that the actuarial interest rate for this transaction is 10%. We, therefore, carefully prepare an amortization of the above loan at 10% (reproduced at Chart 2, Trial Amortization of $1,000 Loan at 10% Simple Interest). That is, the first month we multiply the unpaid balance of $1,000 times the periodic rate of 10% ÷ 12 or .8333% and we get $8.33 interest. The $86.99 payment is applied first to the $8.33 interest, with the remaining $78.66 subtracted from the $1,000 unpaid balance, to create a new unpaid balance of $921.34. This process is repeated until all 12 payments have been made. As can be seen, in Chart 2, the final unpaid balance is $11.66. Since this is *higher* than zero, it means the actuarial interest rate must be *lower* than 10%.

**CHART 3**

**Trial Amortization of $1,000 Loan at 6% Simple Interest**

Principal = $1,000

12 monthly payments

Regular payment (#1 – #11) = $86.99

Final payment (#12) = $86.97

Total interest = $32.50

Simple Interest rate = 6%

| Payment # | Unpaid Balance + | Monthly Interest – | Payment = | New Balance | Total Interest To Date |
|---|---|---|---|---|---|
| 1 | $1000.00 | $5.00 | $86.99 | $918.01 | $ 5.00 |
| 2 | $ 918.01 | $4.59 | $86.99 | $835.61 | $ 9.59 |
| 3 | $ 835.61 | $4.18 | $86.99 | $752.80 | $13.77 |
| 4 | $ 752.80 | $3.76 | $86.99 | $669.57 | $17.53 |
| 5 | $ 669.57 | $3.35 | $86.99 | $585.93 | $20.88 |
| 6 | $ 585.93 | $2.93 | $86.99 | $501.87 | $23.81 |
| 7 | $ 501.87 | $2.51 | $86.99 | $417.39 | $26.32 |
| 8 | $ 417.39 | $2.09 | $86.99 | $332.49 | $28.41 |
| 9 | $ 332.49 | $1.66 | $86.99 | $247.16 | $30.07 |
| 10 | $ 247.16 | $1.24 | $86.99 | $161.41 | $31.31 |
| 11 | $ 161.41 | $0.81 | $86.99 | $ 75.23 | $32.12 |
| 12 | $ 75.23 | $0.38 | $86.97 | –$ 11.36 | $32.50 |

Therefore we try the lower actuarial interest rate of, for example, 6% and carefully prepare an amortization of the above loan at the 6% rate. As can be seen in Chart 3 (Trial Amortization of $1,000 Loan at 6% Simple Interest), the final unpaid balance is -$11.36. Since this is *less* than zero, it means that the actuarial interest rate for this transaction is *higher* than 6%.

At this point, then, we know that the true actuarial interest rate lies somewhere between 6% and 10%. Therefore we would try other interest rates within that range until we found one that worked exactly; that is, the amortization would produce a final unpaid balance of $0.00. As can be seen in Chart 1, the precise actuarial interest rate for this transaction is 8%. The computer would have arrived at this answer in a matter of seconds, while a paper and pencil calculation takes considerably longer. Nonetheless, the trial and error process would be the same.

19 Indeed, as is explained at § 5.3.1.1, *infra*, these computational difficulties explain the growth of simplified calculation methods, such as add-on interest.

20 The critical difference is that the computer is much faster and unlikely to make the arithmetical mistakes that pass unnoticed by mere mortals.

The same process can be used to determine the proper monthly payment in an actuarial transaction. Someone or something takes an educated guess at the size of the payment needed to amortize a given loan amount at a given actuarial interest rate with a given number of periodic payments. The final unpaid balance should be $0.00 after the final payment. If the final balance is *higher* than $0.00, then the payment size should be increased (so that the loan is amortized more quickly). On the other hand, if the final balance is less than $0.00, then the payment size should be decreased (so that the loan is not amortized so quickly). By trial and error, eventually a payment size (or sizes) will be found that creates a final unpaid balance of $0.00.

By way of illustration, let us return to Chart 1, where the $1,000, one-year loan is amortized at 8% with eleven monthly payments of $86.99 and a 12th, final payment of $86.97. Let us assume for a moment, however, that we do not know (but would like to) what size monthly payments are needed to amortize this loan at 8% over twelve months.

**CHART 4**
**Trial Amortization of $1,000 Loan at 8% Simple Interest with $85 Payments**

Principal = $1,000
12 monthly payments
Regular payment (#1 – #12) = $85.00
Simple Interest rate = 8%

| *Payment #* | *Unpaid Balance* | + | *Monthly Interest* | – | *Payment* | = | *New Balance* | *Total Interest To Date* |
|---|---|---|---|---|---|---|---|---|
| 1 | $1000.00 | | $6.67 | | $85.00 | | $921.67 | $ 6.67 |
| 2 | $ 921.67 | | $6.14 | | $85.00 | | $842.81 | $12.81 |
| 3 | $ 842.81 | | $5.62 | | $85.00 | | $763.43 | $18.43 |
| 4 | $ 763.43 | | $5.09 | | $85.00 | | $683.52 | $23.52 |
| 5 | $ 683.52 | | $4.56 | | $85.00 | | $603.52 | $28.08 |
| 6 | $ 603.08 | | $4.02 | | $85.00 | | $522.10 | $32.10 |
| 7 | $ 522.10 | | $3.48 | | $85.00 | | $440.58 | $35.58 |
| 8 | $ 440.58 | | $2.94 | | $85.00 | | $358.52 | $38.52 |
| 9 | $ 358.52 | | $2.39 | | $85.00 | | $275.91 | $40.91 |
| 10 | $ 275.91 | | $1.84 | | $85.00 | | $192.75 | $42.75 |
| 11 | $ 192.75 | | $1.29 | | $85.00 | | $109.04 | $44.04 |
| 12 | $ 109.04 | | $0.73 | | $85.00 | | $ 24.77 | $44.77 |

Then let us assume that we make an educated guess that $85 monthly payments will amortize this transaction at 8%. We, therefore, carefully prepare an amortization of the above loan with monthly payments of $85 (reproduced at Chart 4, Trial Amortization of $1,000 Loan at 8% Simple Interest with $85 Payments). As can be seen, the final unpaid balance is $24.77. Since this is *higher* than zero, it means the payment size must be higher than $85.00.

**CHART 5**
**Trial Amortization of $1,000 Loan at 8% Simple Interest with $90 Payments**

Principal = $1,000
12 monthly payments
Regular payment (#1 – #12) = $90.00
Simple Interest rate = 8%

| *Payment #* | *Unpaid Balance* | + | *Monthly Interest* | – | *Payment* | = | *New Balance* | *Total Interest To Date* |
|---|---|---|---|---|---|---|---|---|
| 1 | $1000.00 | | $6.67 | | $90.00 | | $916.67 | $ 6.67 |
| 2 | $ 916.67 | | $6.11 | | $90.00 | | $832.78 | $12.78 |
| 3 | $ 832.78 | | $5.55 | | $90.00 | | $748.33 | $18.33 |
| 4 | $ 748.33 | | $4.99 | | $90.00 | | $663.32 | $23.32 |
| 5 | $ 663.32 | | $4.42 | | $90.00 | | $577.74 | $27.74 |
| 6 | $ 577.74 | | $3.85 | | $90.00 | | $491.59 | $31.59 |
| 7 | $ 491.59 | | $3.28 | | $90.00 | | $404.87 | $34.87 |
| 8 | $ 404.87 | | $2.70 | | $90.00 | | $317.57 | $37.57 |
| 9 | $ 317.57 | | $2.12 | | $90.00 | | $229.69 | $39.69 |
| 10 | $ 229.69 | | $1.53 | | $90.00 | | $141.22 | $41.22 |
| 11 | $ 141.22 | | $0.94 | | $90.00 | | $ 52.16 | $42.16 |
| 12 | $ 52.16 | | $0.35 | | $90.00 | | –$ 37.49 | $42.51 |

Therefore we try the higher payment size of $90 and carefully prepare an amortization of the above loan at the 8% rate. As can be seen in Chart 5 (Trial Amortization of $1,000 Loan at 8% Simple Interest with $90 Payments), the final unpaid balance is -$37.49. Since this is *less* than zero, it means that the payment size must be *lower* than $90.

At this point, then, we know that the actual payment size lies somewhere between $85 and $90. Therefore we would try other payment sizes within that range until we found one that worked exactly; that is, the amortization would produce a final unpaid balance of $0.00. As can be seen in Chart 1, the payments required to amortize this loan at 8% are 11 payments of $86.99 and a final payment of $86.97. Therefore, the total interest earned in this transaction (assuming there are 12 regular payments), is $43.86.[21]

The companion website to this treatise includes a software program that calculates APRs and prepares amortization tables.

## 5.3.1.2 Negative Amortization; Non-Amortizing Credit; Balloon Payments

### *5.3.1.2.1 How negative amortization works*

As discussed above, one of the principal features of amortization of actuarial interest transactions is "declining balances," in which the unpaid principal balance declines or decreases as payments are made. The more time that has passed, and the more payments that have been made, the faster the rate of decline; with successive payments, less interest is earned every period, so that a larger portion of each payment is applied to principal.

Not every actuarial transaction runs true to this form. In some transactions, either by design or by accident, there is a "negative amortization" in which the outstanding obligation (including the unpaid principal) increases over time, rather than

21 (11 × $86.99) + (1 × $86.97) = $1,043.86. $1,043.86 – $1,000 = $43.86.

declines over time. This process is called "negative amortization" because it is the opposite of regular amortization: instead of the outstanding obligation moving towards zero over time, it actually increases over time. The practical results for the consumer may be, at best, quite astounding and, at worst, financially disastrous. (For this reason, Congress has limited the right of creditors to use negatively amortizing loans in certain high-cost home equity credit.[22])

A few examples may help to illustrate "negative amortization." Suppose a bank agrees to lend a consumer $1,000 at an 8% annual interest rate and the consumer agrees to repay the loan in eleven monthly payments of $5.00 each and a twelfth payment of the outstanding unpaid principal and interest.

**CHART 6**
**Negative Amortization of $1,000 Loan at 8% Actuarial Interest—Actuarial Rule**

Principal = $1,000 12 monthly payments
Regular payment (#1 − #11) = $5.00
Final payment (#12) = $1,025.75
Actuarial interest Rate = 8%

| *Payment #* | *Unpaid Balance* | + | *Monthly Interest* | − | *Payment* | = | *New Balance* | *Total Interest To Date* |
|---|---|---|---|---|---|---|---|---|
| 1 | $1000.00 | | $6.67 | | $5.00 | | $1001.67 | $ 6.67 |
| 2 | $1001.67 | | $6.68 | | $5.00 | | $1003.35 | $13.35 |
| 3 | $1003.35 | | $6.69 | | $5.00 | | $1005.04 | $20.04 |
| 4 | $1005.04 | | $6.70 | | $5.00 | | $1006.74 | $26.74 |
| 5 | $1006.74 | | $6.71 | | $5.00 | | $1008.45 | $33.45 |
| 6 | $1008.45 | | $6.72 | | $5.00 | | $1010.17 | $40.17 |
| 7 | $1010.17 | | $6.73 | | $5.00 | | $1011.90 | $46.90 |
| 8 | $1011.90 | | $6.75 | | $5.00 | | $1013.65 | $53.65 |
| 9 | $1013.65 | | $6.76 | | $5.00 | | $1015.41 | $60.41 |
| 10 | $1015.41 | | $6.77 | | $5.00 | | $1017.18 | $67.18 |
| 11 | $1017.18 | | $6.78 | | $5.00 | | $1018.96 | $73.96 |
| 12 | $1018.96 | | $6.79 | | $1025.75 | | $ 0.00 | $80.75 |

That consumer may well be shocked to find out how much she will owe for that final payment. She would be less shocked if she made a few simple calculations before agreeing to the terms of the loan. If the annual interest rate is 8%, then during the first month, the $1,000 will earn $6.67 in interest.[23] Her $5.00 monthly payment will not even cover the $6.67 interest that has been earned over the first month. Therefore nothing remains of her payment to be applied to principal. With nothing to be applied to principal, the $1,000 unpaid principal balance is not going to decline. In fact, depending on how the bank treats the unpaid interest every month, the unpaid principal balance may actually *increase*.

The bank may use the "actuarial rule,"[24] adding the unpaid interest every month to the unpaid principal balance, so that the unpaid principal balance increases every month. The results can be seen in Chart 6 (Negative Amortization of $1,000 Loan at 8% Actuarial Interest—Actuarial Rule). Every month, as the unpaid principal balance increases, the amount of interest earned on that balance will also increase.

For example, since $6.67 in interest was earned the first month, there was $1.67 in unpaid interest after the $5.00 payment was made.[25] $1.67 unpaid interest is added to the $1,000 unpaid principal balance to create a new unpaid balance of $1,001.67.

The next month, since the unpaid balance is slightly higher, the amount of interest earned is also slightly higher. Now $6.68 interest is earned, and after subtracting the $5.00 payment, $1.68 interest is unpaid. The $1.68 is added to the previous unpaid balance to create a new unpaid balance of $1,003.35. This process is repeated every month.

At the end of the 11th month, the unpaid balance has increased to $1,018.96. Since that balance will generate $6.79 in interest over the 12th month, the consumer will then owe a "balloon payment"[26] of $1,025.75,[27] which is more than the amount originally borrowed.

If the bank takes a more consumer-oriented view and follows the "U.S. Rule"[28] and does not add unpaid interest to the unpaid principal balance each month, there will still be a negative amortization; at the end of the 12th month, the consumer will still owe more than the $1,000 she borrowed. The results of this negative amortization can be seen in Chart 7 (Negative Amortization of $1,000 Loan at 8% Simple Interest—U.S. Rule).

**CHART 7**
**Negative Amortization of $1,000 Loan at 8% Simple Interest—U.S. Rule**

Principal = $1,000 12 monthly payments
Regular payment (#1 − #11) = $5.00
Final payment (#12) = $1,025.04
Simple interest Rate = 8%

| *Payment #* | *Unpaid Balance* | + | *Monthly Interest* | − | *Payment* | = | *New Balance* | *Total Interest To Date* | *Total Unpaid Interest To Date* |
|---|---|---|---|---|---|---|---|---|---|
| 1 | $1000.00 | | $6.67 | | $5.00 | | $1000.00 | $ 6.67 | $ 1.67 |
| 2 | $1000.00 | | $6.67 | | $5.00 | | $1000.00 | $13.34 | $ 3.34 |
| 3 | $1000.00 | | $6.67 | | $5.00 | | $1000.00 | $20.01 | $ 5.01 |
| 4 | $1000.00 | | $6.67 | | $5.00 | | $1000.00 | $26.68 | $ 6.68 |
| 5 | $1000.00 | | $6.67 | | $5.00 | | $1000.00 | $33.35 | $ 8.35 |
| 6 | $1000.00 | | $6.67 | | $5.00 | | $1000.00 | $40.02 | $10.02 |
| 7 | $1000.00 | | $6.67 | | $5.00 | | $1000.00 | $46.69 | $11.69 |
| 8 | $1000.00 | | $6.67 | | $5.00 | | $1000.00 | $53.36 | $13.36 |
| 9 | $1000.00 | | $6.67 | | $5.00 | | $1000.00 | $60.03 | $15.03 |
| 10 | $1000.00 | | $6.67 | | $5.00 | | $1000.00 | $66.70 | $16.70 |
| 11 | $1000.00 | | $6.67 | | $5.00 | | $1000.00 | $73.37 | $18.37 |
| 12 | $1000.00 | | $6.67 | | $1025.04 | | $ 0.00 | $80.04 | $ 0.00 |

22 15 U.S.C. § 1639(f). *See also* 15 U.S.C. § 1602(aa) (definition of covered loans). *See generally* National Consumer Law Center, Truth in Lending Ch. 9 (7th ed. 2010 and Supp.).

23 $1,000 × 8% ÷ 12 (since there are twelve months per year) = $6.67.

24 *See* § 5.5.1, *infra*.

25 $6.67 − $5.00 = $1.67.

26 *See* § 5.3.1.2.2, *infra*.

27 $1,018.96 + 6.79 = $1,025.75.

28 *See* § 5.4.2, *infra*.

For example, since $6.67 in interest was earned the first month, there was $1.67 in unpaid interest after the $5.00 payment was made. The $1.67 in unpaid interest is *not* added to the $1,000 unpaid principal balance (as in the actuarial method), but instead is kept separate in an unpaid interest column. No interest, under the U.S. Rule method, is earned on unpaid interest. The $1,000 unpaid principal balance remains the same.

The next month, and indeed every month (except for the last month), the same process is repeated. The $1,000 balance always remains the same; it always generates $6.67 in interest, of which only $5.00 is paid; and the $1.67 in unpaid interest is added to the unpaid interest column.

After eleven months, there is $18.37 in the unpaid interest column. In the 12th month, another $6.67 in interest is earned on the $1,000 unpaid principal balance. Therefore, to pay off the loan, the consumer must pay $1,000 + $6.67 interest + $18.37 unpaid interest for a total of $1,025.04. Again, there has been a negative amortization, in that the balance owed at the end of the loan is higher than that owed at the beginning.

#### *5.3.1.2.2 Balloon payments*

Balloon payments can be produced in a number of situations. A negatively amortizing loan produces a balloon payment that is larger than the original principal, because it includes some of the interest that accrued while the principal was outstanding. With an interest-only loan, at the end of the term the borrower owes a balloon payment consisting of the full principal plus the final installment of interest.

A loan can also be partially amortizing. In that case, part of each payment is applied to principal, but not enough to repay the loan fully within the loan term. With such a loan, a balloon payment is due at the end of the loan term, consisting of the remaining unpaid principal.

Balloon payments can create major problems for average wage-earners who do not have a lot of flexibility in their budget. For this reason, consumer credit statutes, for example RISAs, often limit or prohibit balloon payments, or require that the consumers be given the opportunity to refinance the loan on the same terms, absent changed circumstances.[29]

## *5.3.2 Add-On Interest*

### 5.3.2.1 Basic Calculations

Creditors, particularly before the widespread use of computers, were troubled by the complexities of calculating simple or actuarial interest for installment transactions, as demonstrated by the discussion in § 5.3.1.1, *supra*. If a consumer, for example, wanted to borrow $960.11 and to repay it in eighteen monthly installments and the maximum legal interest rate was 8.5%, without a computer or a chart from a consumer finance publishing firm, there was no easy way to compute the maximum interest charge or the monthly payments.[30] What creditors needed was an easy way of calculating maximum interest charges, preferably one that drew upon their experience with the I = P × R × T formula.[31]

One method that became very popular was the add-on interest method. Add-on interest is used only for installment transactions, yet add-on interest is calculated as if there were no installments. It takes the I = P × R × T formula (which is traditionally used only for one-payment, simple-interest transactions) and uses it to calculate installment interest.

State retail installment sales acts (RISAs) often specify the maximum interest rate as an add-on rate. However, many add-on interest rate statutes do not use the words "add-on" to describe the rates therein. They may, for example, use such terms as "$8.00 per $100 per annum" to describe an 8% add-on rate.[32]

Add-on interest is a method for calculating "precomputed" interest[33] in which the consumer agrees to pay the total of payments, which includes both interest and principal, as opposed to agreeing to pay the principal plus interest as it accrues at a certain rate. Because add-on interest is precomputed, the note or contract should contain an agreement as to how unearned interest will be rebated in the event of prepayment.[34]

With installment payments, the average unpaid balance is only slightly more than one-half of the original principal.[35] With simple (actuarial) interest, the interest calculated when each payment is credited will decline, because the principal is declining.[36] In contrast, add-on interest is calculated at the outset of the loan on the full amount for the full term, as if the principal did not decline over the course of the loan. Compare the total interest earned on a one-year, $1,000 loan at 8% actuarial interest, $43.86 (Chart 1) with that earned at 8% add-on interest, $79.98 (Chart 8). Thus, the 8% add-on interest means more than $36 extra in earnings for this creditor[37] than for 8% actuarial interest. To earn an equivalent dollar amount, the creditor would obviously have to charge a higher *actuarial interest* rate. Chart 9

29 *See, e.g.*, Utah Code Ann. § 70C-3-102 (right to refinance closed-end consumer debt on same terms if consumer creditworthy); W. Va. Code Ann. § 46A-4-110a (balloon payments prohibited in supervised loans).

30 The maximum interest would be $65.89 and the monthly payments would be $57.00 each. (We have a computer.)

31 *See* § 5.2, *supra*.

32 Restaurant Dev., Inc. v. Cananwill, Inc., 80 P.3d 598 (Wash. 2003) ("$10 per $100 per year" states add-on rate). *See* Corcoran v. TranSouth Fin. Corp. (*In re* Corcoran, 268 B.R. 882) (Bankr. M.D. Fla. 2001) (interpreting "$17 per $100 per year" as add-on rate).

33 *See* § 5.3.2, *infra*.

34 *See* § 5.8, *infra*. *See also* Restaurant Dev., Inc. v. Cananwill, Inc., 80 P.3d 598 (Wash. 2003) (citing statutory provision for rebate of unearned charges as evidence that legislature intended interest rate to be an add-on rate).

35 *See, e.g.*, Chart 8 (Amortization of $1,000 Loan at 8% Add-On Interest). Note that after six payments, the unpaid balance is only $517.93, slightly more than half of the original unpaid balance of $1,000. The average unpaid balance for this transaction is $554.74, again slightly more than half of the original unpaid balance of $1,000.

36 *See* § 5.3.1.1, *supra*.

37 $79.98 – $43.86 = $36.12.

(Simple Interest Rates Equivalent to Add-On Rates on Loans with Equal Payments) illustrates the contrast between the nominal add-on rate and the effective simple interest rate. As the chart shows, add-on rates always dramatically understate the effective simple or actuarial interest rate.[38]

**CHART 8**
**Amortization of $1,000 Loan at 8% Add-On Interest (14.45% Actuarial Interest)**

Principal = $1,000
12 monthly payments
Regular payment (#1 − #11) = $90.00
Final payment (#12) = $89.98
Total interest = $79.98
Add-on Interest rate = 8%
Annual Percentage Rate = 14.45%

| *Payment #* | *Unpaid Balance* | + | *Monthly Interest* | − | *Payment* | = | *New Balance* | *Total Interest To Date* |
|---|---|---|---|---|---|---|---|---|
| 1 | $1000.00 | | $12.04 | | $90.00 | | $922.04 | $12.04 |
| 2 | $ 922.04 | | $11.10 | | $90.00 | | $843.14 | $23.14 |
| 3 | $ 843.14 | | $10.15 | | $90.00 | | $763.29 | $33.29 |
| 4 | $ 763.29 | | $ 9.19 | | $90.00 | | $682.48 | $42.48 |
| 5 | $ 682.48 | | $ 8.22 | | $90.00 | | $600.70 | $50.70 |
| 6 | $ 600.70 | | $ 7.23 | | $90.00 | | $517.93 | $57.93 |
| 7 | $ 517.93 | | $ 6.24 | | $90.00 | | $434.17 | $64.17 |
| 8 | $ 434.17 | | $ 5.23 | | $90.00 | | $349.40 | $69.40 |
| 9 | $ 349.40 | | $ 4.21 | | $90.00 | | $263.61 | $73.61 |
| 10 | $ 263.61 | | $ 3.17 | | $90.00 | | $176.78 | $76.78 |
| 11 | $ 176.78 | | $ 2.13 | | $90.00 | | $ 88.91 | $78.91 |
| 12 | $ 88.91 | | $ 1.07 | | $89.98 | | $ 0.00 | $79.98 |

**CHART 9**
**Simple Interest Rates Equivalent to Add-On Rates on Loans with Equal Monthly Payments**

| *Loan Duration (Months)* | *6% Add-on* | *8% Add-on* | *12% Add-on* |
|---|---|---|---|
| 12 | 10.90% | 14.45% | 21.46% |
| 18 | 11.08% | 14.65% | 21.64% |
| 24 | 11.13% | 14.68% | 21.57% |
| 30 | 11.12% | 14.63% | 21.41% |
| 36 | 11.08% | 14.55% | 21.20% |
| 48 | 11.97% | 14.35% | 20.75% |
| 60 | 10.85% | 14.13% | 20.31% |

Thus, an added benefit of add-on rates for creditors is that add-on rates can be used in a deceptive fashion to understate the true simple rate of interest. Not only may consumers be misled as to the true interest rates for their loans and sales transactions, but legislators may also be misled. For example, if legislators are asked to raise rates for a particular class of transactions from 6% add-on to 8% add-on, they may not realize that (1) the former rates are the equivalent of nearly 12% simple interest for some transactions and (2) the new rates would be the equivalent of nearly 15% for some transactions.

The calculation of add-on rates is relatively simple. The *principal* is multiplied by the (annual) add-on *rate* times the number of *years* in the transaction. This produces the maximum amount of interest allowable under the add-on rate statute. P × R × T = I where P = Principal, R = Rate (annual add-on rate), T = Time (number of years), and I = Interest. For example, if a consumer borrows $1,000 and agrees to pay the loan in twelve monthly installments, what is the maximum amount of interest that can be charged under an 8% add-on rate? In this example:

P = $1,000
R = .08 (or 8%)
T = 1 year

P × R × T = $1,000 × .08 × 1 = $80. Therefore, I = $80.

The consumer will have to pay a total of $1,000 principal + $80 interest, or $1,080. Each month, the consumer will have to pay $90.00 ($1,080 ÷ 12 = $90). Chart 8 (Amortization of $1,000 Loan at 8% Add-On Interest) shows the actuarial amortization of this loan.[39]

This was a comparatively easy example, although no add-on interest rate example is very difficult since add-on interest was designed to be easy to use. A more complicated example: if a consumer borrows $3,890.99 and agrees to repay the loan in thirty monthly installments, what is the maximum amount of interest that can be charged under an 8.25% add-on rate? In this example:

P = $3,890.98
R = .0825 (or 8.25%)
T = 2.5 years (or 30 ÷ 12 months)

P × R × T = $3,890.98 × .0825 × 2.5 = $802.51.
Therefore, I = $802.51.

The consumer will have to pay a total of $3,890.98 principal plus $802.51 interest, or $4,693.49. Each month, the consumer will have to pay $156.45.[40] Again, it is important to remember that the true simple interest rate, or annual percentage rate, for this transaction is 15.06%, or almost twice the nominal add-on rate of 8.25%.

38 *See, e.g., In re* Pena, 397 B.R. 566 (B.A.P. 1st Cir. 2008) (noting that creditor's use of add-on methodology to calculate 18% interest meant that effective APR exceeded 35%); *In re* Pokrzywinski, 311 B.R. 846 (Bankr. E.D. Wis. 2004) (noting differences between add-on interest and actuarial interest; 11.5% add-on rate sought by creditor here would equal an actuarial rate of 20%).

39 This is the same formula as the single-payment transaction described at § 5.2.2, *supra*, in both cases yielding $80 in interest earned over one year. A three-year, 8% add-on installment loan likewise would yield the same amount as a comparable-term, single-payment loan: $1,000(P) × 0.08(8%) × 3 (years) = $240 (I), for a total indebtedness of $1,240. *See* Corcoran v. TranSouth Fin. Corp. (*In re* Corcoran), 268 B.R. 882 (Bankr. M.D. Fla. 2001) (giving examples of calculation of add-on rates).

40 More precisely, the final payment will be $156.44, since 29 × $156.45 = $4,537.05; 1 × $156.44 = $156.44; and $4,537.05 + $156.44 = $4,693.49.

#### 5.3.2.2 Add-On Interest in Split Rate Transactions

A still more complicated example would involve "split rates" in which two or more add-on rates would apply to the transaction. For example, a usury statute might allow a creditor to apply an add-on rate of 10% to the first $500 of principal and an add-on rate of 8% to any original principal balance above $500. If a consumer borrows $748.28 and agrees to repay the loan in twenty-four monthly installments, what is the maximum amount of interest that can be charged under these add-on rates?

In this example, it makes the calculations easier if the loan principal is divided into two parts, P(1) or $500, to which the 10% add-on rate applies, and P(2) or $248.28, to which the 8% add-on rate applies. Therefore, P = $748.28 = P(1) $500.00 + P(2) $248.28.

The next step is to calculate the maximum interest that can be charged on each part of the principal.

P(1) = $500
R(1) = .10 (or 10%)
T(1) = 2 years (or 24 months)

P(1) × R(1) × T(1) = $500.00 × .10 × 2 = $100.00.
Therefore, I(1) = $100.00.

P(2) = $248.28
R(2) = .08 (or 8%)
T(2) = 2 years (or 24 months)

P(2) × R(2) × T(2) = $248.28 × .08 × 2 = $39.72
Therefore I(2) = $39.72

The total interest (I) = $100 + $39.72 = $139.72. The consumer will have to pay a total of $748.28 principal plus $139.72 interest, or $888. Each month, the consumer will have to pay $37 ($888 ÷ 12 = $37). Remember, again, that the true simple interest rate, or annual percentage rate, for this transaction is 17.01%, much higher than either of the "split" add-on rates of 8% and 10%.

#### 5.3.2.3 Irregular Payment Periods and Other Computational Issues

Other computational problems, such as odd payment periods, rounding, and counting days,[41] may need to be considered, as with all interest methods. A careful look at the relevant add-on interest usury statute should be the very first step, as the statute itself may directly address these issues.[42]

Generally, however, add-on interest statutes require all payments to be equal in size, with slight variations allowed in the first payment (particularly if the first payment period is longer than one month). If the payment sizes are not similar, particularly if the initial payments are considerably larger than the later payments, the effective annual interest rate is significantly increased.[43]

### 5.3.3 *Discount Interest*

#### 5.3.3.1 Description of Discount Interest

The method for calculating discount interest is similar to that for calculating add-on interest. Discount interest, like add-on interest, is a method for calculating "precomputed" interest[44] in which the consumer agrees to pay the total of payments, which includes both interest and principal, as opposed to agreeing to pay the principal plus interest as it accrues at a certain rate. Because discount interest, like add-on interest, is precomputed, the note or contract should contain an agreement as to how unearned interest will be rebated in the event of prepayment.[45]

As with add-on interest, discount interest is calculated as if there were no installment payments. Instead, interest is calculated as if only one simple interest payment were going to be made at the end of the loan term. With discount interest, however, the interest is subtracted, or discounted, from the "face amount."[46] The remainder, or principal, is given to the consumer, who is obligated to repay the "face amount" (which consists of principal and interest). The net result of discount interest is to create an effective interest rate that is not only higher than the nominal simple interest rate but also higher than the effective add-on interest rate.[47]

#### 5.3.3.2 Examples of Discount Interest Calculations

A few examples will help clarify the discount interest method. Suppose a consumer takes out a one-year loan with a $1,000 "face amount" at 8% discount interest. The simple interest charge on a one-year loan with a $1,000 "face amount," if only one payment is made at the end of the term, is $80 ($80 = $1,000 × 8% × 1). However, the $80 interest charge is "discounted" or deducted from the $1,000 "face amount," leaving only $920 in principal which is given to the consumer. At the end of the year,

41 *See* §§ 5.5.2, 5.5.4, 5.5.5, *infra*.

42 For example, many add-on interest usury statutes allow a creditor to charge a full month's interest if an odd payment period is longer than fifteen days. Under such a statute, if a loan is consummated on March 1 and the first payment is due on April 22, or one month and twenty-two days later, then the creditor may charge two full months of interest. *See* § 5.3.2, *supra*. *See also* Parten v. General Motors Acceptance Corp., 370 S.E.2d 778 (Ga. Ct. App. 1988) (ruling against the borrower's usury claim based on an add-on transaction because the borrower failed to consider the special statutory section on irregular payments; failing, however, to give enough detail to determine whether the court's analysis is correct).

43 Indeed, some add-on statutes allow creditors to require irregular payments, as long as the effective interest rate is not higher than it would be if all payments were the same size.

44 *See* §§ 5.3.3.2, 5.3.3.3, *infra*.

45 *See* § 5.8, *infra*.

46 Sometimes referred to as "statutory principal."

47 At this point, it should be noted that some usury statutes have been interpreted to prohibit discount or "capitalized" interest. Other statutes allow it in limited form. *See, e.g.*, Grigg v. Robinson Furniture, 260 N.W.2d 898 (Mich. Ct. App. 1977). *But cf.* Durant v. Olympic Sav. & Loan Ass'n, 582 F.2d 1090 (7th Cir. 1978) (interpreting Illinois statute to allow points to be deducted from face amount of note, but interest to be calculated on original amount).

the consumer is obliged to pay $1,000 to the lender. The effective annual interest rate is 8.7%. This interest rate is higher than the nominal interest rate of 8%, because $80 interest is being charged on a principal of only $920, and not $1,000.[48]

The next example is identical to the first example, except that the loan is repayable in twelve monthly installments. (Installment, discount interest is sometimes referred to as "discount per annum.") The amount of interest is again calculated the same way, as if there were a $1,000 simple interest 8% loan repayable in one payment at the end of one year. The interest charge, therefore, is again $80 ($1,000 × 8% × 1 = $80). The $80 interest charge is deducted or "discounted" from the "face amount" of $1,000, leaving the consumer with $920 principal. This time, however, the consumer must make twelve monthly payments of $83.33 each ($1,000 ÷ 12).[49] The effective annual interest rate (APR) for this discount installment loan is 15.68%. This rate is not only almost twice the nominal interest rate of 8%, but it is also even higher than the effective interest rate (APR) of 14.45% for a one-year 8% add-on transaction. (In both the 8% add-on and 8% discount interest scenarios, the borrower pays $80 for her one-year loan, but the discount borrower is paying the same dollar amount of interest ($80) for less money. The effective rate is higher because paying $80 of interest for a $920 loan is more expensive credit than $80 of interest for a $1,000 loan.)

Furthermore, the longer the term of a discount interest installment transaction, the higher the effective annual interest rate (APR). For example, a $1,000 "face amount" loan at 8% discount interest repayable in thirty-six monthly installments (three years) of $27.78 each[50] would produce $240 of interest ($1,000 × 8% × 3 = $240). Therefore, the consumer would receive only $760 in principal ($1,000 − 240 = $760). The effective annual interest rate (APR) for this transaction would be 18.79%.

For this reason, discount interest rates, unlike most other interest rate methods, can only be used in relatively short-term loans. Otherwise, the effective annual interest rates for longer term, discount interest loans become extremely high; for example, the APR for a 120-month (ten-year) 8% discount loan is almost 50%.

In addition, at some point for each discount interest rate, the amount of interest will exceed the amount of the loan. Since interest is deducted or "discounted" from the "face amount," in such a situation the consumer would receive nothing as principal but would be compelled to pay interest, at an infinite rate of interest, over the life of the loan. This would clearly be an absurd result. For example, if a consumer took out a ten-year loan with a face amount of $1,000, at 10% discount interest, he would owe $1,000 interest, which would immediately be "discounted" from the "face amount" of $1,000, leaving him with a principal of $0, but an obligation to repay the $1,000 over the next ten years.

48 *See* Corcoran v. TranSouth Fin. Corp. (*In re* Corcoran), 268 B.R. 882 (Bankr. M.D. Fla. 2001) (giving example of discount interest calculations).

49 More precisely, the consumer must make eleven monthly payments of $83.33 each and a twelfth, final payment of $83.37.

50 More precisely, the consumer must make thirty-five payments of $27.78 each and a thirty-sixth final payment of $27.70.

### 5.3.3.3 Calculating Discount Interest for a Given Principal

Readers who want to calculate maximum discount interest charges in real-life consumer finance situations may object to the above formulas, which start with the total amount of the obligation rather than the amount the consumer wants to borrow. If a consumer wants to receive $1,000 in cash as a loan, the discount loan company (and the consumer law practitioner) must be able to calculate quickly discount interest on the principal and not the "face amount" which includes both principal and interest.

As the footnote below explains,[51] the formula for finding discount installment interest (I) on a principal (P) at a given discount interest rate (R) over a given time (T) is

$$I = \frac{P \times R \times T}{1-(R \times T)}$$

For example, if a consumer borrows $1,000 principal at 8% discount interest repayable in 12 monthly installments (one year), then

$$P = \$1,000$$
$$R = 8\% = .08$$
$$T = 1$$
$$I = \frac{\$1,000 \times .08 \times 1}{1-(0.8 \times 1)}$$
$$= \frac{\$80}{.92}$$
$$= \$86.96.$$

Therefore, the maximum interest that can be charged is $86.96, and the face amount of the loan note will be $1,086.96. The consumer would repay the loan in 12 installments of $90.58 each and the effective interest rate (APR) for this loan, as it is for all one-year 8% discount installment loans, is 14.45%. In this loan, it is important to remember that the consumer will receive the full $1,000 principal. He will generally be unaware that the $86.96 interest has been "discounted" from the "face amount" of $1,086.96.

In a similar example, if a consumer borrows $1,000 principal at 8% discount interest repayable in 36 monthly installments (three years), then

$$P = \$1,000$$
$$R = 8\% = .08$$
$$T = 3$$
$$I = \frac{\$1,000 \times .08 \times 3}{1-(0.8 \times 3)}$$
$$= \frac{\$240}{.76}$$
$$= \$315.79.$$

51 Discount interest is calculated on the "face amount" which includes both interest (I) + principal (P). Therefore:

$$I = (P + 1) \times R \times T$$
$$I = PRT + IRT$$
$$I - IRT = PRT$$
$$I(1 - RT) = PRT$$
$$I = \frac{PRT}{1-RT}$$

Therefore, the maximum interest that can be charged is $315.79, and the face amount of the note will be $1,315.79. The consumer would repay the loan in 36 installments of $36.55 each[52] and the effective interest rate (APR) for this loan, as it is for all three-year, 8% discount installment loans, is 18.79%. Note that the maximum interest for a three-year loan ($315.79) is more than three times (indeed, it is nearly four times) the maximum interest for a one-year loan ($86.95).

## 5.3.4 Split Rate Interest—Graduated Rates

Consumer credit laws sometimes authorize lenders to charge "split" or graduated interest rates on some loans.[53] In a split rate loan, one actuarial interest rate is applied to one part of the loan and a different actuarial interest rate is applied to the remaining part of the loan.[54] The overall interest charge for each payment on a split rate loan is the aggregate of the interest charges for each step. Usually, the highest interest rate is applied to the lowest part of the loan amount. The second highest interest rate is applied to the second lowest part of the loan amount, and so on.

For example, a small loan law may authorize a lender to charge an annual interest rate of 24% (or a monthly interest rate of 2%) on the first $500 of the loan and an annual interest rate of 18% (or a monthly interest rate of 1.5%) on the portion of the loan exceeding $500, up to $2,000.

52 More precisely, the consumer must make thirty-five payments of $36.55 each and a thirty-sixth, final payment of $36.54.

53 *See, e.g., In re* Williams, 330 B.R. 534 (Bankr. M.D. La. 2005) (discussing Louisiana's consumer credit law, limiting contract interest rates to 36% on the first $1,400 loaned, up to 27% on the next amount up to $4,000, up to 24% on the next amount up to $7,000, and up to 21% on the money loaned after the first $7,000).

54 *See* § 5.3.1.1, *supra*.

**CHART 10**
**Amortization of $1,000 Split Rate Loan**

Principal = $1,000.00
24 monthly payments
Regular payment (#1 − #23) = $52.00
Final payment (#24) = $51.85
Split rate structure:
$0–$500: 2%/month or 24%/year
$500–$2000: 1.5%/month or 18%/year
Annual Percentage Rate = 22.24%

| *Payment #* | *Unpaid Balance* | + | *2% Monthly Interest* | + | *1.5% Monthly Interest* | − | *Payment* | *(Paid to Principal)* | = | *New Monthly Balance* | *Total Monthly Interest* | *Interest To Date* |
|---|---|---|---|---|---|---|---|---|---|---|---|---|
| 1 | 1000.00 | | 10.00 | | 7.50 | | $52.00 | (34.50) | | 965.50 | (17.50 | 17.50) |
| 2 | 965.50 | | 10.00 | | 6.98 | | $52.00 | (35.02) | | 930.48 | (16.98 | 34.48) |
| 3 | 930.48 | | 10.00 | | 6.46 | | $52.00 | (35.54) | | 894.94 | (16.46 | 50.94) |
| 4 | 894.94 | | 10.00 | | 5.92 | | $52.00 | (36.08) | | 858.86 | (15.92 | 66.86) |
| 5 | 858.86 | | 10.00 | | 5.38 | | $52.00 | (36.62) | | 822.24 | (15.38 | 82.24) |
| 6 | 822.24 | | 10.00 | | 4.83 | | $52.00 | (37.17) | | 785.07 | (14.83 | 97.07) |
| 7 | 785.07 | | 10.00 | | 4.28 | | $52.00 | (37.72) | | 747.35 | (14.28 | 111.35) |
| 8 | 747.35 | | 10.00 | | 3.71 | | $52.00 | (38.29) | | 709.06 | (13.71 | 125.06) |
| 9 | 709.06 | | 10.00 | | 3.14 | | $52.00 | (38.86) | | 670.20 | (13.14 | 138.20) |
| 10 | 670.20 | | 10.00 | | 2.55 | | $52.00 | (39.45) | | 630.75 | (12.55 | 150.75) |
| 11 | 630.75 | | 10.00 | | 1.96 | | $52.00 | (40.04) | | 590.71 | (11.96 | 162.71) |
| 12 | 590.71 | | 10.00 | | 1.36 | | $52.00 | (40.64) | | 550.07 | (11.36 | 174.07) |
| 13 | 550.07 | | 10.00 | | 0.75 | | $52.00 | (41.25) | | 508.82 | (10.75 | 184.82) |
| 14 | 508.82 | | 10.00 | | 0.13 | | $52.00 | (41.87) | | 466.85 | (10.13 | 194.95) |
| 15 | 466.95 | | 9.34 | | 0.00 | | $52.00 | (42.66) | | 424.29 | ( 9.34 | 204.29) |
| 16 | 424.29 | | 8.49 | | 0.00 | | $52.00 | (43.51) | | 380.78 | ( 8.49 | 212.78) |
| 17 | 380.78 | | 7.62 | | 0.00 | | $52.00 | (44.38) | | 336.40 | ( 7.62 | 220.40) |
| 18 | 336.40 | | 6.73 | | 0.00 | | $52.00 | (45.27) | | 291.13 | ( 6.73 | 227.13) |
| 19 | 291.13 | | 5.82 | | 0.00 | | $52.00 | (46.18) | | 244.95 | ( 5.82 | 232.95) |
| 20 | 244.95 | | 4.90 | | 0.00 | | $52.00 | (47.10) | | 197.85 | ( 4.90 | 237.85) |
| 21 | 197.85 | | 3.96 | | 0.00 | | $52.00 | (48.04) | | 149.81 | ( 3.96 | 241.81) |
| 22 | 149.81 | | 3.00 | | 0.00 | | $52.00 | (49.00) | | 100.81 | ( 3.00 | 244.81) |
| 23 | 100.81 | | 2.02 | | 0.00 | | $52.00 | (49.98) | | 50.83 | ( 2.02 | 246.83) |
| 24 | 50.83 | | 1.02 | | 0.00 | | $51.85 | (50.83) | | 0.00 | ( 1.02 | 247.85) |

Each month, the different interest rates are applied to the relevant parts of the loan principal. The amortization of a $1,000 loan, repayable over twenty-four months, under the above terms is set forth in Chart 10 (Amortization of $1,000 Split Rate Loan). As can be seen, the amortization of a split rate loan is similar to the amortization of a simple, single interest rate loan. The basic difference is that each month the different interest rates are applied to different parts of the unpaid balance.

For example, look at the first month. The $1,000 principal is divided into two parts, $500 (to which the 2% monthly rate is applied) and the remaining $500 (to which the 1.5% monthly rate is applied). On the first $500, the interest for that month is $10 ($500 × 2% = $10). On the second $500, the interest for that month is $7.50 ($500 × 1.5% = $7.50). Therefore the total interest for the first month is $17.50 ($10.00 + 7.50 = $17.50). After the $17.50 interest is subtracted from the $52.00 payment, the remaining $34.50 is applied to principal, thereby reducing the unpaid principal to $965.50 ($1,000 – 34.50 = $965.50).

This process is repeated the next month. The $965.50 unpaid balance is divided into two parts, $500 (to which the 2% monthly interest rate is applied to produce $10.00 interest) and $465.50 (to which the 1.5% monthly interest rate is applied to produce $6.98 interest). The total interest for that month is $16.98 ($10.00 + 6.98 = $16.98).

This process is repeated each month until the unpaid balance is reduced to less than $500. At this point, only the higher monthly interest rate of 2% is applied to the unpaid balance. The lower monthly interest rate of 1.5% is *not* applied to any portion of the unpaid balance because there is no balance above $500.

For example, look at payment number 15 on Chart 10. At that point, the unpaid balance is $466.95. Applying the 2% monthly interest rate to this balance produces $9.34 in interest. The 1.5% monthly interest rate is not applied because the unpaid balance is less than $500. This process is repeated every month, until the 24th payment reduces the unpaid balance to $0.00.[55]

It is important to remember that the amortization of a split rate loan, as discussed above and in Chart 10, is—like all other amortizations—the amortization of a single loan of $1,000. It is not the amortization of two loans, one of $500 at 2% per month, and a separate loan of $500 at 1.5% per month.[56] To amortize those two loans concurrently over twenty-four months would require monthly payments of, respectively, $26.43 and $24.96, for a total of $51.39; contrast this with the fact, as illustrated in Chart 10, that monthly payments of $52.00 would be required to amortize the single split rate loan of $1,000.

55 These actuarial split rate loans should be distinguished from "add-on" split rate loans. The latter are described in different statutory terms (usually as two or more add-on or $__ per $100 per annum) and are much easier to calculate. *See* § 5.3.2, *supra*.

56 Watson v. Avco Fin. Servs. Int'l, 401 N.W.2d 485 (Neb. 1987).

This is not to suggest that the separate amortization of two loans always produces lower maximum payments than those produced by the correct, integrated amortization of a single loan. Sometimes the dual amortizations produce higher maximum payments.

For example, consider a small loan, split rate statute that allows lenders to charge 2.5% monthly interest on the first $500 and 2% interest on the balance above $500. The maximum monthly payment on a $1,200 loan repayable over twenty-four months at the split rates is $57.84. However, to amortize loans of $500 and $700 concurrently over twenty-four months at the respective monthly interest rates of 2.5% and 2% would require monthly payments, respectively, of $27.96 and $37.01, for a total of $64.97 per month.

Another important point to remember is that split rate loans, like all loans, bear an effective annual interest rate (called annual percentage rate or APR)[57] that must be determined independently of the method used to calculate maximum interest under the state usury law.[58] For example, the APR for the transaction described at Chart 10 is 22.24%.

However, it is also important to recognize that the APR, intuitively, should fall between the two split rates if the maximum allowable interest has been charged. Every month, the effective interest rate in a split rate amortization will never exceed the highest interest rate nor will it fall below the lowest interest rate. Therefore, it makes sense that the true, effective rate, or annual percentage rate, will fall between the two split rates.

For example, in the transaction described at Chart 10, the two split rates are 24% per year and 18% per year. The fact that the APR is 22.24% is a rough indicator that the interest charged was near or at the statutory maximum. An annual percentage rate of 25% would be a good indicator that the interest charged exceeded the maximum lawful interest (assuming that the "finance charge" used to compute the annual percentage rate is synonymous with the interest charged).[59]

The final point is that the amortization of a transaction at the split rates is different from the amortization of the identical transaction at the annual percentage rate. Generally, the unpaid balance is reduced more slowly in the latter amortization.

57 *See* § 5.4, *infra*.

58 *See, e.g.*, Wilson v. St. Charles Mortgage & Loan, Inc., 756 So. 2d 514 (La. Ct. App. 2000) (noting difference between split rates and effective annual percentage rate).

59 "Finance charge" and "annual percentage rate" are both terms defined by the federal Truth in Lending Act, 15 U.S.C. § 1605. TILA requires that certain types of credit-related charges in addition to "interest," as that term is commonly used (and as it is used in this chapter), be considered a "finance charge" and factored into the calculation of the APR. For some types of credit, the TILA definition of "finance charge" encompasses charges that state law often does not consider "interest." *See* § 5.4, *infra*. *See also* National Consumer Law Center, Truth in Lending Ch. 3 (7th ed. 2010 and Supp.).

**CHART 11**
**Amortization of Loan at 22.24% Annual Percentage Rate**

Amount Financed = $1,000.00
24 monthly payments
Regular payment (#1 – #23) = $52.00
Final payment (#24) = $51.83
Annual Percentage Rate = 22.24%

| *Payment #* | *Unpaid Balance* | + | *Monthly Interest* | – | *Payment* | = | *New Balance* | *Total Interest To Date* |
|---|---|---|---|---|---|---|---|---|
| 1 | $1000.00 | | $18.53 | | $52.00 | | $966.53 | $ 18.53 |
| 2 | $966.53 | | $17.91 | | $52.00 | | $932.44 | $ 36.44 |
| 3 | $932.44 | | $17.28 | | $52.00 | | $897.72 | $ 53.72 |
| 4 | $897.72 | | $16.63 | | $52.00 | | $862.35 | $ 70.35 |
| 5 | $862.35 | | $15.98 | | $52.00 | | $826.33 | $ 86.33 |
| 6 | $826.33 | | $15.31 | | $52.00 | | $789.64 | $101.64 |
| 7 | $789.64 | | $14.63 | | $52.00 | | $752.27 | $116.27 |
| 8 | $752.27 | | $13.94 | | $52.00 | | $714.21 | $130.21 |
| 9 | $714.21 | | $13.23 | | $52.00 | | $675.44 | $143.44 |
| 10 | $675.44 | | $12.52 | | $52.00 | | $635.96 | $155.96 |
| 11 | $635.96 | | $11.78 | | $52.00 | | $595.74 | $167.74 |
| 12 | $595.74 | | $11.04 | | $52.00 | | $554.78 | $178.78 |
| 13 | $554.78 | | $10.28 | | $52.00 | | $513.06 | $189.06 |
| 14 | $513.06 | | $ 9.51 | | $52.00 | | $470.57 | $198.57 |
| 15 | $470.57 | | $ 8.72 | | $52.00 | | $427.29 | $207.29 |
| 16 | $427.29 | | $ 7.92 | | $52.00 | | $383.21 | $215.21 |
| 17 | $383.21 | | $ 7.10 | | $52.00 | | $338.31 | $222.31 |
| 18 | $338.21 | | $ 6.27 | | $52.00 | | $292.58 | $228.58 |
| 19 | $292.58 | | $ 5.42 | | $52.00 | | $246.00 | $234.00 |
| 20 | $246.00 | | $ 4.56 | | $52.00 | | $198.56 | $238.56 |
| 21 | $198.56 | | $ 3.68 | | $52.00 | | $150.24 | $242.24 |
| 22 | $150.24 | | $ 2.78 | | $52.00 | | $101.02 | $245.02 |
| 23 | $101.02 | | $ 1.87 | | $52.00 | | $ 50.89 | $246.89 |
| 24 | $ 50.89 | | $ 0.94 | | $51.83 | | $ 0.00 | $247.83 |

For example, compare the split rate amortization at Chart 10 with the annual percentage rate amortization of the identical loan at Chart 11 (Amortization of $1,000 Split Rate Loan at 22.24% Annual Percentage Rate). Applying the split interest rates to the original unpaid balance of $1,000 creates a new balance after the first payment of $965.50. However, applying the APR to the same original unpaid balance produces a new balance of $966.53. The unpaid balance after the 12th payment is $550.07 on the split rate amortization and $554.78 on the annual percentage rate amortization.

This difference becomes important in the event of prepayment, refinancing, or acceleration after default. In the absence of state law requiring the computation of the unpaid balance by one method or the other, the consumer's attorney should argue that the unpaid balance should be calculated by the use of the split rates.[60]

The companion website to this treatise includes a software program that will calculate APRs and prepare amortization tables for split rate loans.

60 *See* § 5.8.6.4.3, *infra.*

## 5.3.5 *Open-End Credit*

### 5.3.5.1 Calculation Distinctions Between Open- and Closed-End Credit

The preceding discussions of interest calculation methods focused on closed-end credit: a single advance of credit, repayable in fixed payments over a fixed term. Interest may be calculated at the outset because all three variables in our formula—principal (P), rate (R) and time (T)—are known at the outset.

Open-end credit, however, presents a different situation because two of the variables—principal (P) and time (T)—are not known at the outset.[61] Open-end credit anticipates repeated use of the credit, so the principal balance will fluctuate, depending on the borrower's use of the account.[62] There also is not a fixed term for repayment of an open-end credit account,[63] and installment payments vary. (Typically, the contract requires minimum payments set at a specified percentage of the account balance.[64])

The response is to calculate the interest due at the time each installment payment is due. That may be simple, if a borrower only uses the credit card once each month, preferably on the first day of the billing cycle (to give the creditor a full thirty days of interest). That is not, however, a typical usage pattern for open-end credit, and consequently a variety of methods have been devised for calculating the "P" from which "I" is determined on open-end accounts.

### 5.3.5.2 Methods of Calculating Interest on Open-End Credit

The Truth in Lending Act requires the Consumer Financial Protection Bureau to list up to five of the most commonly used methods of computing a balance on open-end credit for purposes of calculating interest.[65] Regulation Z lists the following four methods of calculation:[66]

(1) *Average Daily Balance (including new purchases) or (excluding new purchases).* This balance is figured by adding the outstanding balance (including or excluding new pur-

61 Open-end credit is also referred to as revolving credit. Examples include credit cards and home equity lines of credit (HELOCs).

62 *See* § 3.9.3, *supra.*

63 Some open-end credit contracts, home-equity lines of credit (HELCs), for example, do not have an indefinite life. The contract may have a "call provision," where the piper must be fully paid when the creditor exercises it. Some may provide that it can be exercised in as little as three years, others in fifteen years. Other HELCs may divide the account into, for example, a ten-year "draw" period, and then a fifteen-year "repayment" period, during which payment amounts will be set high enough to repay the entire debt.

64 *See* § 8.6.8, *infra* (guidance by banking regulators regarding size of required minimum payments on credit card accounts).

65 15 U.S.C. § 1637(c)(1)(A)(iv). *See* National Consumer Law Center, Truth in Lending § 6.5.3.7 (7th ed. 2010 and Supp.).

66 12 C.F.R. § 1026.5a(g).

chases and deducting payments and credits) for each day in the billing cycle, and then dividing by the number of days in the billing cycle

(2) *Adjusted Balance*. This balance is figured by deducting payments and credits made during the billing cycle from the outstanding balance at the beginning of the billing cycle.

(3) *Previous Balance*. This balance is the outstanding balance at the beginning of the billing cycle.

(4) *Daily Balance (also frequently called "true" or "actuarial" average daily balance)*. For each day in the billing cycle, this balance is figured by taking the beginning balance each day, adding any new purchases, and subtracting any payment and credits.

If a creditor uses one of these methods, it may only disclose the name of the method in the application disclosures;[67] otherwise the creditor must include a detailed description of the method.[68] Regulation Z similarly permits disclosure of only the name of the balance computation method, and not the actual method, in the account opening disclosure table.[69] Thus, the contract, and sometimes the creditor's actual practice, must be consulted to determine exactly how it is computing the balance.

Previously, one of the most prevalent methods of computing interest was the Two-Cycle Average Daily Balance, also known as "double-cycle billing."[70] However, the Credit Card Accountability, Responsibility, and Disclosures Act of 2009 (the Credit CARD Act) amended TILA to prohibit double-cycle billing on credit card accounts.[71]

One of the most common methods of balance calculation is the Daily Balance method. The following example highlights how this method works. Assume that a consumer, who has a revolving credit/credit card account that authorizes the creditor to charge interest at 18% APR (which is a monthly rate of 1.5% and a daily rate of .05%), enters into the following transactions:

| Dates | Transaction | Amount |
|---|---|---|
| May 1 | Previous balance | 0 |
| May 12 | Purchase | $1,000 |
| May 31 | Ending balance | $1,000 |
| June 1 | Previous balance | $1,000 |
| June 10 | Purchase | $1,000 |
| June 25 | Payment | $ 500 |
| June 30 | Ending balance | $1,500 |

Under the Daily Balance method, no interest is assessed if the previous balance is zero, or if payments and credits equal the previous balance. However, if there is a previous balance and it is not paid in full, then an interest charge is made on the previous balance, plus purchases minus payments and credits, all weighted as of the date they occurred.

The formula for this method is: Sum of (interest rate ÷ 360 × daily balance) for each day in the billing cycle.[72] Interest would accumulate as follows:

| Date | Balance | Daily Periodic Rate | Daily Interest Accrued | Month-to-Date Interest (sum) |
|---|---|---|---|---|
| 1-May | 0 | 0.050% | $— | $— |
| 2-May | 0 | 0.050% | $— | $— |
| 3-May | 0 | 0.050% | $— | $— |
| 4-May | 0 | 0.050% | $— | $— |
| 5-May | 0 | 0.050% | $— | $— |
| 6-May | 0 | 0.050% | $— | $— |
| 7-May | 0 | 0.050% | $— | $— |
| 8-May | 0 | 0.050% | $— | $— |
| 9-May | 0 | 0.050% | $— | $— |
| 10-May | 0 | 0.050% | $— | $— |
| 11-May | 0 | 0.050% | $— | $— |
| 12-May | 1,000 | 0.050% | $0.50 | $ 0.50 |
| 13-May | 1,000 | 0.050% | $0.50 | $ 1.00 |
| 14-May | 1,000 | 0.050% | $0.50 | $ 1.50 |
| 15-May | 1,000 | 0.050% | $0.50 | $ 2.00 |
| 16-May | 1,000 | 0.050% | $0.50 | $ 2.50 |
| 17-May | 1,000 | 0.050% | $0.50 | $ 3.00 |
| 18-May | 1,000 | 0.050% | $0.50 | $ 3.50 |
| 19-May | 1,000 | 0.050% | $0.50 | $ 4.00 |
| 20-May | 1,000 | 0.050% | $0.50 | $ 4.50 |
| 21-May | 1,000 | 0.050% | $0.50 | $ 5.00 |
| 22-May | 1,000 | 0.050% | $0.50 | $ 5.50 |
| 23-May | 1,000 | 0.050% | $0.50 | $ 6.00 |
| 24-May | 1,000 | 0.050% | $0.50 | $ 6.50 |
| 25-May | 1,000 | 0.050% | $0.50 | $ 7.00 |
| 26-May | 1,000 | 0.050% | $0.50 | $ 7.50 |
| 27-May | 1,000 | 0.050% | $0.50 | $ 8.00 |
| 28-May | 1,000 | 0.050% | $0.50 | $ 8.50 |
| 29-May | 1,000 | 0.050% | $0.50 | $ 9.00 |
| 30-May | 1,000 | 0.050% | $0.50 | $ 9.50 |
| 31-May | 1,000 | 0.050% | $0.50 | $10.00 |
| 1-June | 1,000 | 0.050% | $0.50 | $ 0.50 |
| 2-June | 1,000 | 0.050% | $0.50 | $ 1.00 |
| 3-June | 1,000 | 0.050% | $0.50 | $ 1.50 |
| 4-June | 1,000 | 0.050% | $0.50 | $ 2.00 |
| 5-June | 1,000 | 0.050% | $0.50 | $ 2.50 |
| 6-June | 1,000 | 0.050% | $0.50 | $ 3.00 |

67 12 C.F.R. § 1026.60(b)(6); Official Commentary to Reg. Z, 12 C.F.R. § 1026.60(b)(6)-1. *See* Hale v. MBNA Am. Bank, 2000 U.S. Dist. LEXIS 13403 (S.D.N.Y. Sept. 18, 2000) (creditor need not disclose details of method of computing balance).

68 12 C.F.R. § 1026.60(b)(6).

69 74 Fed. Reg. 5244, 5408 (Jan. 29, 2009) (new 12 C.F.R. § 1026.6(b)(2)(vi)).).

70 For a review of the varied types of interest calculation methods formerly used by credit card issuers, see Historic Methods of Computing Interest on Revolving Credit on the companion website to this treatise.

71 15 U.S.C. § 1637(j)(1)(A). *See* National Consumer Law Center, Truth in Lending § 7.4 (7th ed. 2010 and Supp.). (discussion of prohibition on double cycle billing).

72 This calculation could be done by dividing the rate by 360 or 365. *See* § 5.5.4, *infra* (discussing these two approaches).

| Date | Balance | Daily Periodic Rate | Daily Interest Accrued | Month-to-Date Interest (sum) |
|---|---|---|---|---|
| 7-June | 1,000 | 0.050% | $0.50 | $ 3.50 |
| 8-June | 1,000 | 0.050% | $0.50 | $ 4.00 |
| 9-June | 1,000 | 0.050% | $0.50 | $ 4.50 |
| 10-June | 2,000 | 0.050% | $1.00 | $ 5.50 |
| 11-June | 2,000 | 0.050% | $1.00 | $ 6.50 |
| 12-June | 2,000 | 0.050% | $1.00 | $ 7.50 |
| 13-June | 2,000 | 0.050% | $1.00 | $ 8.50 |
| 14-June | 2,000 | 0.050% | $1.00 | $ 9.50 |
| 15-June | 2,000 | 0.050% | $1.00 | $10.50 |
| 16-June | 2,000 | 0.050% | $1.00 | $11.50 |
| 17-June | 2,000 | 0.050% | $1.00 | $12.50 |
| 18-June | 2,000 | 0.050% | $1.00 | $13.50 |
| 19-June | 2,000 | 0.050% | $1.00 | $14.50 |
| 20-June | 2,000 | 0.050% | $1.00 | $15.50 |
| 21-June | 2,000 | 0.050% | $1.00 | $16.50 |
| 22-June | 2,000 | 0.050% | $1.00 | $17.50 |
| 23-June | 2,000 | 0.050% | $1.00 | $18.50 |
| 24-June | 2,000 | 0.050% | $1.00 | $19.50 |
| 25-June | 1,500 | 0.050% | $0.75 | $20.25 |
| 26-June | 1,500 | 0.050% | $0.75 | $21.00 |
| 27-June | 1,500 | 0.050% | $0.75 | $21.75 |
| 28-June | 1,500 | 0.050% | $0.75 | $22.50 |
| 29-June | 1,500 | 0.050% | $0.75 | $23.25 |
| 30-June | 1,500 | 0.050% | $0.75 | $24.00 |

Accordingly, this method produces $24 interest for the month of June.[73]

## 5.3.6 *Variable Rates*

### 5.3.6.1 Variable Rate Transactions Described

In a traditional consumer loan, a borrower contracts to pay a fixed interest rate and/or a specified amount of interest. Assuming that the credit calculations are correctly made, and that all installments are paid on time,[74] then the size of the borrower's payments can be predicted with absolute certainty before credit is extended.

In contrast, in a variable rate loan, no rate of interest is guaranteed over the term of the loan. Instead, the rate may increase or decrease periodically and, absent special contract terms, the size of the borrower's payments will fluctuate with the rate. Because the contract rate and payments may change, variable rate loans cannot be precomputed; they are inherently interest-bearing transactions.[75] They may or may not be structured as open-end credit. Credit card accounts and home equity lines of credit are typical examples of open-end credit which have variable rates. Purchase money mortgages, on the other hand, are usually as closed-end, with a fixed term of ten, fifteen, or thirty years regardless of whether they employ variable interest rates.

A variable rate transaction is perhaps most easily viewed as a series of short-term fixed-rate transactions, the lengths of which depend upon the frequency with which the interest rate on the variable loan can change.[76] For example, consider an open-end account on which the rate may change monthly. This is essentially a series of renewable one-month fixed-rate loans. The rate assessed during any one month does not change, although the rates charged during different months may be different. Similarly, a fifteen-year variable-rate mortgage on which the rate may change annually is comparable to a series of fifteen one-year balloon notes,[77] the first fourteen of which the creditor is obliged to refinance upon maturity at the current market interest rate. Indeed, the similarity between a long-term variable rate loan and a series of short-term fixed-rate loans is so great that some creditors that would normally extend long-term credit have evaded statutes that prohibit interest variations during the term of a loan by employing short-term loans that are renewable at a renegotiated interest rate.[78]

73 Many thanks to Mark Furletti at the Federal Reserve Bank of Philadelphia for helping us with this analysis and chart.

74 Late payments on interest-bearing debt will increase the interest earned by the creditor. The extra interest will throw off the anticipated repayment schedule and may cause compounding of the interest. *See* § 5.5.1, *infra*.

With precomputed debt, late charges are often imposed for tardy payments, and these fees obviously increase the borrower's total payments. *See* §§ 4.8, *supra*, 5.7, *infra*.

75 *See* § 5.8.2, *infra* (discussing interest-bearing and precomputed transactions).

76 This view implies that the legality of a variable rate loan for usury purposes is determined by the rate charged in any one or more of the payment periods in the loan term. Thus, a variable loan under a fixed 10% simple interest ceiling would be usurious if the rate assessed in any one month exceeded an annualized 10% return, even if the rate charged during all the other months was well below the ceiling. Other views of variable transactions exist, however. Most importantly, it is possible to look only at the effective rate charged over the whole term of a variable rate loan, rather than at the rates assessed in individual payment periods. This approach presumes that interest payments can be "spread" across different payment periods. *See* § 5.5.6, *infra*.

77 Each of the fifteen loans would have to partially amortize the loan principal in order for the analogy to be precise.

78 *See* Barck v. Grant State Bank, 357 N.W.2d 872 (Mich. Ct. App. 1984); Shebuski v. Lakeland State Bank, 345 N.W.2d 898 (Wis. Ct. App. 1984).

A series of fixed-term balloon notes may have to be disclosed as a variable rate transaction under TILA, however. *See* Official Commentary to Reg. Z, 12 C.F.R. § 1026.17(c)(1)-11.

Another way that a creditor may obtain the advantages of a variable rate loan in a purportedly fixed-rate transaction is to add a "demand clause" to a traditional fixed term transaction. Demand clauses authorize the creditor to require the borrower to pay the full balance on the loan. They often can be invoked by the creditor at any point in the loan term. Their purpose is not so much to give a creditor the power to compel the repayment of a loan, as it is to enable the creditor to compel the refinancing of the debt if interest rates increase significantly. As such, demand clauses are a hidden variable rate feature that can be more disadvantageous to borrowers than normal variable rate terms, because they will never be invoked

Recent decades have witnessed the dramatic growth of variable rate contracts. The early growth of these contracts was traceable to the dramatic increase in interest rates in the late 1970s. Lenders that had entered into long-term, fixed-rate transactions, such as traditional thirty-year mortgages, incurred serious losses, and some went bankrupt. The dramatic increase in the volume of variable rate lending reflected an attempt by creditors, generally with the blessing of their government regulators, to avert future losses by shifting the risk of interest fluctuations onto borrowers. In the early years of the 21st century, adjustable rate loans came to dominate the subprime mortgage market.[79]

### 5.3.6.2 Determining the Current Rate

The interest rates charged under variable rate contracts normally do not fluctuate arbitrarily.[80] Rather, they vary according to a formula that is specified in each credit contract. Typically, such formulae tie the contract rate to an external interest rate or "index"[81] such as the prime lending rate at a specified bank, the federal discount rate,[82] a treasury bill rate, or sometimes a rate that represents the creditor's cost of funds.[83] The contract also specifies a "margin" that is added to the index rate to arrive at the contract rate. The contract may also provide for rounding of the rate up or down in some circumstances. Rounding to the nearest 1/8th or 0.125% is common.

Regardless of the precise formula used to set a variable rate, the method must be disclosed to the consumer in accordance with Truth in Lending rules, which vary, depending on the type of credit, the nature of the security, and the length of the term.[84] These disclosures, together with the contract itself, and a publication source for the index,[85] should enable the consumer or the practitioner to determine the appropriate rate.

In addition to the basics (identifying the index and establishing the margin), the contract should specify the frequency with which the rate may change, the reference date to use in identifying the index rate,[86] and any rounding rules.[87]

For example, a variable rate mortgage may specify that the rate will change semi-annually on the anniversary date of the first payment (the "change" date), the index will be that of the most recent yield at auction on six-month treasury bills, measured as of thirty days prior to the "change" date, and the margin is 3%. If that yield, as of the reference date, was 8.5%, the contract rate would be 11.5% for at least the next six months.

Some variable rate contracts also set "caps" and "floors" on the interest rate that may be charged, so that the rate may fluctuate only within a specified range. Other provisions limit the speed with which the contract rate may change. For example, a contract interest rate might be permitted to increase or decrease no more than one percent annually. Such limitations on the variation of rates are discussed at § 5.3.6.4, *infra*.

Calculation errors on adjustable rate loans are not uncommon.[88] A bank that originates loans using Index A, measured thirty days before the change date, may purchase on the secondary market other loans, that may use Index B, or use Index A, but are measured as of forty-five days before the change date. The bank may nonetheless use the same computer program, geared to its own product, for all loans, irrespective of what the contract says. Such errors, of course, do not always work to the consumer's disadvantage. Unless the error is one that is systematically biased against borrowers, they may have been undercharged instead of overcharged. (Examples of errors that would systematically result in overcharges are consistently

---

if interest rates decline. Special (and ineffectual) TILA disclosure rules apply to demand obligations. *See* 12 C.F.R. §§ 1026.17(c)(5), 1026.18(i).

79 Ellen Schloemer, Wei Li, Keith Ernst and Kathleen Keest, Center for Responsible Lending, Losing Ground: Foreclosures in the Subprime Market and Their Cost for Homeowners 26 (Dec. 2006), *available at* www.responsiblelending.org/mortgage-lending/research-analysis/foreclosure-paper-report-2-17.pdf (over 80% of subprime mortgages originated in 2006 were adjustable-rate mortgages).

80 Some variable rate loans, especially open-end accounts such as credit cards, are structured so that creditors may change the interest rate at will. As of February 22, 2010, the Credit Card Accountability Responsibility and Disclosure Act of 2009 (Credit CARD Act), Pub. L. No. 111-24, § 102(a), 123 Stat. 1738 (May 22, 2009), imposes some limits on credit card issuers' ability to make changes to borrowers' interest rates without warning. *See* National Consumer Law Center, Truth in Lending Ch. 7 (7th ed. 2010 and Supp.) (details about the Credit CARD Act).

81 *See* 15 U.S.C. § 1647(a); Reg. Z, 12 C.F.R. § 1026.40(f)(1) (requiring that variable-rate home-equity lines of credit use an external index). *See generally* National Consumer Law Center, Truth in Lending § 8.6.3 (7th ed. 2010 and Supp.).

82 *See* § 3.4.1, *supra* (federal discount rate).

83 *See* § 5.3.6.5, *infra* (legal issues when creditor uses internal index).

84 15 U.S.C. § 1637a (HELCs); Reg. Z, 12 C.F.R. §§ 1026.60(b) (credit and charge card solicitations), 1026.40(d)(12) (HELCs), 1026.18(f) (closed-end, not secured by a residence, or with a term of one year or less), 1026.19(b) (closed-end, residence-secured with term longer than one year). *See generally* National Consumer Law Center, Truth in Lending §§ 5.12, 8.3.5.12 (7th ed. 2010 and Supp.).

85 The *Wall Street Journal* generally publishes rates on indices commonly used, or they may be found in the Federal Reserve Bulletin. In some states, where there is a usury cap that floats with an index, the regulatory agency may publish the index rates in a state administrative bulletin. (The TILA disclosure statement must disclose a source of information about the index for home-secured ARMs. Reg. Z, 12 C.F.R. §§ 1026.40(d)(12)(iii), 1026.19(b)(2)(ii).) LIBOR rates, often used as the index for subprime mortgages, can be found at www.bbalibor.com; however, there are fees associated with historical information older than six months. LIBOR rates going back to 1990 are available free of charge at http://mortgage-x.com.

86 Since those rates change, it is necessary to fix a point in time that will be the one used. *See, e.g.*, Hubbard v. Fidelity Fed. Bank, 824 F. Supp. 909 (C.D. Cal. 1993), *aff'd in part, rev'd in part*, 91 F.3d 75 (9th Cir. 1996) (lender changed its method of determining what date to use, with the result that the rate stayed higher in a time of falling rates).

87 A contract may provide that the rate will be rounded to the nearest one-eighth percent, for example. If the index was 4.73%, and the margin was 3%, the contract rate would be 7.75%.

88 *See* Whitford v. First Nationwide Bank, 147 F.R.D. 135, 140 (W.D. Ky.) (magistrate's recommendation) (recommending approval of class action settlement; noting that lender had found errors in ARM calculations for 65,617 borrowers), *adopted by* 1992 WL 442864 (W.D. Ky. Nov. 17, 1992) (approving class action settlement).

rounding the rate up to the next one-eighth, instead of rounding to the nearest one-eighth as the contract may provide; conscientiously following upward index rate adjustments, but not downward ones; or using a somewhat fluid identification of the index rate (e.g., "most recent"), and then looking for the index's highest point among several of the "most recent" announcements.)

### 5.3.6.3 Amortizing Variable Rate Loans over Fixed Time Periods

In many ways, amortizing a variable rate loan is similar to the amortization calculation in a regular interest-bearing loan.[89] Each month (or other payment period), the current interest rate must be applied to the currently outstanding loan balance to determine the interest that has accrued. This accrued interest is deducted from the borrower's payment, and the remainder of the payment, if any, is used to pay down the loan balance.

The problem with a variable rate loan is that, because of the possibility of interest rate fluctuation, the amount of interest that will be accruing at any point in the loan cannot be predicted ahead of time. Consequently, the size of the monthly payment that will be needed to pay this interest and to retire the loan principal over a stated term cannot be known ahead of time either.[90] In short, in order to amortize a variable rate loan over a fixed period of time, the borrower's payments must be allowed to fluctuate to match the periodic interest rate changes.

To determine the size of the periodic payment necessary to repay a loan when the interest rate changes requires reamortization of the loan. For example, assume a thirty-year variable rate mortgage of $100,000 with an initial interest rate of 12%. The borrower's initial payments would be set at $1,028.61 just as if this were a fixed-rate loan.[91] After one year of regular payments, the balance on the loan would be $99,637.14 and twenty-nine years would be left on the loan term. If, at that point, the interest rate increased to 13%, the loan would be reamortized as a $99,637.14 loan for twenty-nine years at 13% annual interest. The new monthly payments would increase to $1,105.41. Whenever the interest rate changed thereafter, the loan would be reamortized in the same manner, given the then-existing loan balance, interest rate, and remaining loan term.

89 *See* § 5.3.1.1, *supra*.

90 Of course, not all variable rate transactions have a stated term. In open-end transactions, the monthly minimum payment is usually a percentage of the outstanding balance. So long as this percentage exceeds the monthly interest rate, borrowers who pay the minimum amount each month will eventually pay off any outstanding balance, even if the precise interest rate varies. Open-end contracts in which the minimum payments merely meet the currently accrued interest (i.e., which allow interest-only payments) or which do not meet the currently accrued interest (i.e., which allow negative amortization) should be approached cautiously since they can leave a borrower in a state of perpetual and, in the latter case, increasing debt.

91 In other words, equal monthly payments of $1,028.61 over thirty years would precisely amortize a $100,000 loan at 12% annual interest.

If the interest rate on a variable rate loan increases but the lender does not increase the required payment, the loan will become non-amortizing. For example, the "option ARM" loans that became widespread in the early 2000s were structured in this way, so the principal increased rather than decreased. These issues are discussed at § 5.3.6.4.2, *infra*.

### 5.3.6.4 Caps and Floors in Variable Rate Transactions; Explanation and Requirements

#### *5.3.6.4.1 Caps and floors on variable rates*

A loan with an unlimited variable rate can be quite risky for a borrower, especially if it is a large mortgage loan that consumes a high percentage of the borrower's income. Relatively small increases in the interest rate can significantly raise the monthly payment, and larger rate increases can force borrowers into default. In order to allay these risks, federal law has required all new variable rate home mortgages since 1987 to include interest rate caps, though the creditor may set the cap as high as it chooses,[92] unless there is an applicable state ceiling.

In theory, a variable rate also gives the consumer the benefit of falling rates. However, some creditors have set contract floors as a way of limiting their risk in a climate of falling rates. Adjustable rate mortgages in early 2000s often set the initial rate as the floor, so the rate had the potential to adjust upward but would never be reduced below the initial level.[93]

#### *5.3.6.4.2 Payment caps and their relationship to adjustable rates*

Caps are essentially contractual limitations on the extent that the interest rate or the payments may vary during the loan term. They can provide borrowers with valuable safeguards against major fluctuations in market interest rates. However, all caps are not alike, and some may provide borrowers with little or no real protection. It is critical for attorneys who are reviewing proposed variable rate contracts to examine carefully the contractual language that defines the cap.

The most important distinction among contractual caps is whether a cap restricts the interest *rate* that may be charged or only the monthly *payment*. A cap that limits the contract interest rate to a maximum of, say, 15% annual interest prevents the creditor from earning any more than 15% interest, regardless of how high the loan's index rate may go. Thus, if the contract rate is normally the six-month treasury bill rate plus 3%, but the rate is capped at 15%, the interest earned on the loan would remain at 15% even if the T-bill rate rose higher than 12%. This is the kind of "cap" that is required for all variable rate home mortgage transactions.[94]

92 12 U.S.C. § 3806. Reg. Z, 12 C.F.R. § 1026.30 requires all "creditors," who regularly extend credit for personal, family, or household purposes, to include a limitation on the maximum interest rate that can be charged on an adjustable-rate mortgage loan.

93 *See also* § 5.3.6.4.3, *infra* (discussion of recapture, whereby creditors recoup interest lost due to a cap when rates later decline).

94 12 U.S.C. § 3806.

A cap that restricts the size of the borrower's monthly *payment*, however, can spell trouble for the borrower because it does not limit the amount of interest that the creditor may earn. Instead, it limits only the amount of interest and principal that the borrower can currently be required to pay. If interest rates rise to the point where the payments needed to amortize the debt exceed the maximum monthly payment, then the amount of the monthly payment being used to pay down principal will be too small to retire the debt over the stated loan term, and the borrower will be left with a balloon payment at the end of the term.

If interest rates go higher, the situation can get worse. If the interest that the creditor is earning on the debt rises so that it equals the payment that the borrower is making, then the borrower will not pay down the debt at all. When the accruing interest exceeds the borrower's maximum payment, the debt balance actually will increase.[95]

Thus, if interest rates rise sufficiently, a mortgage borrower with a capped monthly payment, but without a capped interest rate, or with a cap too high to prevent negative amortization, can wind up losing equity in the home, despite making all of the required monthly payments as they come due. In the worst case, at the end of the loan term, the borrower may face a balloon payment that exceeds the amount of money originally borrowed. Payment option ARMs, discussed in detail in NCLC's *Mortgage Lending* (2012) typically allow the borrower to select a payment amount that produces negative amortization until the principal increases by a certain amount. Once that negative amortization cap is reached, the borrower's payment amount jumps, often dramatically, to the amount necessary to pay the loan in full in the remaining months of the term.

##### *5.3.6.4.3 Recapture clauses*

An important issue regarding the interpretation of caps is what happens when interest rates decline after the rate cap or the monthly maximum payment has been reached. Some credit contracts authorize the creditor to recapture or "carry over" any interest that it would have earned or collected but for the cap, by refusing to lower the borrower's payments when market interest rates decline. The precise recapture mechanism will depend on the type of cap in the contract. Generally a contract with an interest rate cap might permit a recapture by authorizing the creditor to refuse to lower its rates, while a contract with a maximum payment provision might require the borrower to continue making the maximum payment until the loan could be amortized by reduced payments. Either of these mechanisms would prevent the borrower's payments from declining, but the interest due to the carry-over in the former system would be charged as it was earned, thus avoiding compounding.

A variation of a recapture clause appears in a California case involving a disputed mortgage.[96] The contract in question capped the interest rate at 2.5% above the initial rate and limited any change in the contract rate to 0.25% during any six-month period. Rate increases were optional with the creditor while decreases were described as mandatory. However, the contract also provided that the contract rate should maintain the same margin above its index rate as existed when the contract was consummated. On the basis of this last provision, and on the basis of a clause that stated that the failure of the creditor to invoke an increase did not constitute a waiver of its right to do so later, the creditor claimed the right to carry over rate increases, including apparently both increases that it voluntarily waived and those that it was precluded from invoking by either the 2.5% cap or the 0.25% maximum six-month increase. Thus, when the market index, to which the contract rate was pegged, rapidly increased, the creditor built up a large reserve of "unapplied interest increases." When the index subsequently declined, the creditor refused to lower the contract rate, despite the mandatory decrease provision, but instead offset the decrease against its previously unused increases.

After a careful analysis of the mortgage contract, the California Court of Appeals determined that the creditor's actions were contractually permissible and did not violate a state lending regulation. Yet it is clear that this contractual interpretation was not anticipated by the borrower, and given the vagueness of the contract and the "mandatory decrease" language that it contained, it is not obvious that even a careful, intelligent borrower could have deciphered the terms of the caps in the contract.[97]

### 5.3.6.5 Legal Issues in Variable Rate Credit

In many types of consumer transactions, creditors are statutorily authorized to set variable rates. For example, statutes regulating open-end credit generally allow variable rates, and because of federal preemption of mortgage regulations, creditors may contract for variable rates in almost any mortgage transaction.[98] However, as noted at § 5.3.6.2, *supra*, calculation errors in ARMs have been relatively common, engendering litigation, enhanced regulatory attention, and more self-audits by industry. Moreover, it is important for attorneys who are examining consumer transactions to remember that variable rates are a fairly recent phenomenon in consumer credit, and older statutes may explicitly or implicitly prohibit variable transactions.

A few states have adopted explicit variable rate controls. Yet, even ignoring the effects of federal preemption, creditors may

95 In other words, negative amortization would occur. *See* § 5.3.1.2, *supra*.

96 Gabbard v. American Sav., 233 Cal. Rptr. 610 (Cal. Ct. App. 1986) (unpublished).

97 *See also* Mayne v. Bank of Am., 242 Cal. Rptr. 357 (Cal. Ct. App. 1987) (unpublished) (even though lender informed borrower, that rate would generally rise and fall with the index, and the documents explaining the recapture mechanism were difficult to understand, the documents contained an accurate explanation of the formula and therefore there was no violation of statutes prohibiting false, deceitful or misleading representations).

98 *See* National Consumer Law Center, Mortgage Lending § 8.6 (2012) (AMTPA).

The 2010 Dodd-Frank Act dramatically narrowed the preemptive scope of AMTPA, but it still prevents states from denying "housing creditors," a term that includes many state-chartered lenders and non-bank lenders, the right to make adjustable rate loans.

find it easy to circumvent such statutes if they are not well written. For example, if a statute prohibits variable rates, but not balloon notes, a creditor can simulate variable rates by issuing a series of short-term fixed-rate balloon notes to a borrower.[99] The rate on each individual note may be fixed, but if different notes have different rates, the over-all transaction is effectively variable.

The most widespread prohibition of variable rates is in those statutes that require debts to be paid off in substantially equal monthly installments over a fixed term. Variable rate contracts cannot meet these requirements because a change in interest rate will require either a change in the monthly payments, a final balloon payment, or a change in the loan term to compensate for the altered interest charges. The statutes that most commonly require a fixed loan term and equal monthly installments are installment sales acts (RISAs) and small loan laws. Consumer law practitioners should be particularly suspicious of variable rate contracts that otherwise seem to fall within the scope of these statutes.

Most importantly, a variable rate transaction should also be assessed for compliance with the contract itself, as well as with applicable statutes, for adjustment errors have been quite common. For example, some variable rate contracts tie the interest rate charged to an internal, rather than external index.[100] An internal index could be the bank's own "prime rate," often defined as the lowest rate regularly charged by the bank to its commercial customers with the highest credit rating, rather than the prime rate charged by a nonparty bank or a federal index. Sometimes a borrower may find that a "prime rate" within the creditor's control is a rather fluid concept, and that the bank may be charging the borrower a higher rate than other commercial borrowers.[101] (Readers should be aware that some real-estate-secured adjustable-rate mortgages must be tied to an index that is beyond the lender's control.[102])

More basically, errors occur when the wrong index is used, or the wrong reference date for valuing the index, and so forth.[103] The typical claims raised are Truth in Lending, breach of contract, negligence, and fraud.[104]

If the contract specifies as the index the prime rate of a bank that fails, the question may arise as to what index should then be used. The Fifth Circuit has allowed the substitution of an analogous rate.[105] Many variable rate contracts provide for such a contingency.

Variable rate contracts may be subject to an absolute statutory ceiling. Most courts have held that the interest rate may never exceed the cap even if on average it is below the ceiling.[106] To hold otherwise would require the borrower to pay excess interest during the term of the transaction, not knowing whether the payments were legal until the end of the payment period.

Where the contract contains a rate escalator clause that has no limits or reference to an index by which an interest charge may be determined, the contract may be subject to challenge. In *Preston v. First Bank of Marietta*,[107] borrowers signed a note that simply allowed the bank to raise the interest rate on thirty days' notice. The court held that the clause, with neither limit nor definition, was too uncertain to be enforceable. Moreover, while the contract allowed for a decrease in rates, the borrower had no right to force a decrease when the bank's cost of money declined. To enforce such contracts, which lacked mutuality and definition, would have been unconscionable. The court ordered that the notes be calculated at their original rates.[108] (But similar provisions, when agreed to by an astute business person for whom refinancing is a viable escape from such an agreement, may be held to be enforceable.[109]) Finally, if the

99 *See, e.g.*, Barck v. Grant State Bank, 357 N.W.2d 872 (Mich. Ct. App. 1984); Shebuski v. Lakeland State Bank, 345 N.W.2d 898 (Wis. Ct. App. 1984). *See also* Lage v. Pan Am. Bank, 529 So. 2d 1242 (Fla. Dist. Ct. App. 1988) (where statute required special disclosure of balloon payments in transaction with "regular payment," payments under variable-rate contract at fixed intervals were "regular"); Manufacturers Nat'l Bank v. Pink, 341 N.W.2d 181 (Mich. Ct. App. 1983) (contract with integral variable rate does not violate statute forbidding changes in credit contract rates where index is beyond control of lender).

100 *See* § 5.3.6.2, *supra* (identification of common external indices used to calculate the applicable rate).

101 *See, e.g.*, Briggs Transp. Co. v. Second Northwestern Nat'l Bank, 406 N.W.2d 7 (Minn. Ct. App. 1987) (issue of fact precluding summary judgment where borrower alleged banks made loans to their commercial customers at lower rate than the announced prime upon which his rate was based).

102 *See* 15 U.S.C. § 1647 (home equity lines of credit); 12 C.F.R. § 1007.22 [§ 34.22] (OCC regulations governing national banks).

103 *See* § 5.3.6.2, *supra.*

104 *See, e.g.*, Hubbard v. Fidelity Fed. Bank, 824 F. Supp. 909 (C.D. Cal. 1993) (TILA violated, but claim time-barred), *aff'd in part and rev'd in part*, 91 F.3d 75, 78 (9th Cir. 1996) (a consumer can state a claim for breach of contract if the loan documents require notice of periodic rate changes and the lender does not provide proper notice; if such a breach occurred, Truth in Lending Act could be violated as well); Whitford v. First Nationwide Bank, 147 F.R.D. 135, 140 (W.D. Ky.) (magistrate's recommendation) (recommending approval of class action settlement; noting that lender had found errors in ARM calculations for 65,617 borrowers), *adopted by* 1992 WL 442864 (W.D. Ky. Nov. 17, 1992) (approving class action settlement). *See generally* National Consumer Law Center, Truth in Lending § 5.13 (7th ed. 2010 and Supp.) (TILA variable-rate disclosure requirements).

105 Ginsberg 1985 Real Estate P'ship v. Cadle Co., 39 F.3d 528 (5th Cir. 1994).

106 *See* § 5.5.6, *infra* (more detailed discussion of spreading).

107 473 N.E.2d 1210 (Ohio Ct. App. 1983). *See also In re* Computer Optics, 126 B.R. 664, 669 n.9 (Bankr. D.N.H. 1991) (noting in *dictum* that bank's unfettered discretion to raise or lower the interest rate without reference to a contractual formula would not be enforceable).

108 Preston v. First Bank of Marietta, 473 N.E.2d 1214–1215 (Ohio Ct. App. 1983) (holding that trial court's remedy was authorized both as actual damages under TILA, and under the common law contract rule that a court may enforce part of a contract and refuse to enforce other parts). *See also* Baxter v. First Bank of Marietta, 1992 WL 330252 (Ohio Ct. App. 1992).

109 Bank of New Hampshire v. Scanlon, 743 A.2d 842 (N.H. 1999) (allowing bank to recover deficiency on commercial loan even though variable rate was discretionary rather than tied to some external index; holding that this did not violate statute requiring

lender misrepresents the nature of a variable rate provision, the court may refuse to enforce it.[110]

## 5.4 Truth in Lending APR and Finance Charge Distinguished

### 5.4.1 *Purpose of the Truth in Lending APR; Finance Charge Explained, Distinguished from Interest*

As was noted in the discussion at §§ 5.3.1.1, 5.3.2.1, *supra*, when one creditor advertises that it lends money at "8% interest," and another creditor advertises "12% interest," the consumer would ordinarily have no way of knowing which creditor was offering a better deal. For example, an 8% "add-on" rate[111] is considerably more expensive than a 12% "actuarial" or "simple interest" rate.[112]

Theoretically, a consumer could ask each creditor how large the payments would be as a basis of comparison. However, assuming that both creditors disclosed accurate information, the 8% add-on creditor might disclose that the consumer would have to pay $48.33 a month for twenty-four months, while the 12% actuarial creditor might disclose that the consumer would have to pay $88.84 a month for twelve months. Would arming the consumer with that information make it possible to make a more rational decision as to which offer was more financially attractive? At best, the theoretical consumer would still be comparing apples and oranges, with no common standard for evaluating the two loans.

With the explosive growth of consumer credit after World War II, Congress was concerned about the need for a standard basis of comparison for the costs of credit. Better-informed consumers presumably would choose creditors who offered the lowest costs, thus encouraging competition among creditors and theoretically lowering costs for consumer credit. Thus, Congress passed the Truth in Lending Act (TILA) in 1968,[113] requiring creditors to disclose the costs of consumer credit using a standardized format and terminology.

Creditors must make numerous disclosures under TILA, most of which are not discussed in this treatise.[114] However, the two most important TILA disclosures will be briefly discussed here. They are the "finance charge" and the "annual percentage rate" or APR. Basically, the finance charge is the cost of credit on a dollar basis. It is conceptually comparable to the total interest charge on a credit contract, except that the finance charge is more broadly defined[115] and generally includes charges that are often excluded from the definition of interest under state usury laws. The APR, on the other hand, is essentially an actuarial rate.

Because it accurately reflects the effective cost of credit when declining balances are taken into account, unlike add-on or discount notes, the APR "truthfully" discloses the cost of credit. In most fixed term transactions, the APR is the rate which amortizes the finance charge and the "amount financed" (in TILA terminology) at the scheduled repayment terms. (The amount financed is conceptually comparable to the loan principal. However, as TILA defines the finance charge more broadly than state usury law defines interest, the amount financed conversely is more narrowly defined than principal is defined for state usury law purposes.)

These distinctions between TILA finance charge and state-law-defined interest, and TILA amount financed and state-law-defined principal are critical to remember.

The TILA finance charge includes not only that which is classified as "interest" under state usury law, but many of the numerous fees imposed by the lender that state laws often exclude from "interest," and that are instead frequently included in the face amount of the note, or principal.[116] For example, many usury statutes allow creditors to exclude points[117] or a "service charge" or "processing charge," which is often one or two percent of loan proceeds, from "interest" on a loan. Such provisions enable creditors to increase their return without exceeding the express "interest" ceilings of usury laws. These loopholes also permit creditors to understate the actual cost of credit to the borrower, a problem that TILA was specifically designed to cure. Thus, even though state law excludes a service charge from the law's definition of interest, under TILA's general definition, the service charge is a charge payable by the consumer and imposed by the creditor as a condition of the extension of credit and therefore must be included in the finance charge.[118]

By using an actuarial calculation method and a more realistic, inclusive definition of the cost of credit (the finance charge), the APR is the more accurate measure of the cost of credit.

---

disclosure of rate); Murello Constr. Co. v. Citizens Home Sav. Co., 505 N.E.2d 637 (Ohio Ct. App. 1985) (distinguishing *Preston*).

110 *See* Baxter v. First Bank of Marietta, 1992 WL 330252 (Ohio Ct. App. 1992) (loan officer's statement to homeowners that loan was a fixed-rate loan and they should ignore variable rate provision was "inconsistent additional information" which violated Truth in Lending; proper remedy is refusal to enforce variable rate provision).

111 *See* § 5.3.2, *supra*.

112 *See* §§ 5.3.1, 5.3.2, *supra*.

113 15 U.S.C. § 1601. *See also* 12 C.F.R. pt. 1026 (Regulation Z); National Consumer Law Center, Truth in Lending (7th ed. 2010 and Supp.).

114 The TILA discussion in this treatise is greatly simplified. It is designed to give practitioners the basic concepts behind TILA and, in particular, its APR disclosure. Attorneys who need to know about TILA in any detail, or who want to calculate an APR, should consult National Consumer Law Center, Truth in Lending (7th ed. 2010 and Supp.).

115 The finance charge includes any charge payable directly or indirectly by the consumer, imposed directly or indirectly by the creditor, as an incident to or a condition of the extension of credit. 15 U.S.C. § 1605(a); 12 C.F.R. § 1026.4(a). *See generally* National Consumer Law Center, Truth in Lending Ch. 3 (7th ed. 2010 and Supp.).

116 *See, e.g.*, Am. Gen. Fin. v. Bauer, 2001 Ohio App. LEXIS 2228 (May 4, 2001) (explaining difference between "interest" as defined by state mortgage loan act and "finance charge" as defined by TILA). *See also* Ch. 4, *supra* (definition of "interest" under state usury law, and treatment of various fees).

117 *See* § 4.3, *supra*.

118 *See* 12 C.F.R. § 1026.4(b)(2), (3).

(However, the accuracy of the TILA-defined APR as a measure of the cost of credit has been undermined by regulations allowing many cost items to be excluded from the finance charge on which the APR is calculated.[119] In addition, in 2010, the Federal Reserve Board revised its TILA regulations to allow just the interest component of the finance charge to be disclosed as the APR for open-end credit.[120])

Because the TILA finance charge in a credit contract thus often exceeds the "interest" as defined by state law, the APR, which uses the finance charge as one component of its calculation, in turn, will often exceed the "interest rate" shown on the contract, even if the contract interest rate is computed actuarially.[121] For purposes of examining a transaction for usury violations, however, it is the state law definitions of interest and interest rate that are dispositive, not the TILA-defined APR and finance charge.[122]

Let us return to the example given at the beginning of this section. Which loan is more advantageous to the consumer, an 8% add-on loan for two years or a 12% actuarial loan for one year? Assuming that there are no costs of credit other than interest, the former loan has an APR of 14.68% while the latter loan has an APR of 12%. Assuming the total cost of the credit is the most important consideration for the consumer, the 12% actuarial loan for one year is better for the consumer, who would save $93.84. (However, if monthly cash flow is the most critical factor for the borrower, he or she may consider saving $40.51 in payments for each of twelve months' worth paying an extra $93.84 over the life of the loan.)

Since the state law definitions of interest and interest rate are the relevant ones for a usury analysis, is the APR of any relevance to an analysis of a contract for state law claims? Assuming the creditor has properly calculated the APR, a great disparity between the note interest rate and the APR may indicate that excessive points were charged, or the loan was otherwise padded. Some difference is to be expected, but, for example, an 18% note rate and 28% APR suggests excessive prepaid finance charges that should be closely scrutinized.[123]

## 5.4.2 *Calculation and Accuracy of the Annual Percentage Rate*

As suggested in the preceding subsection, the APR is basically an actuarial rate that states the cost of credit as a yearly percentage rate. However, Regulation Z, which implements TILA[124] allow the APR to be calculated either on a strict actuarial basis, or through the use of the "United States Rule" (U.S. Rule).[125] The two methods are similar in that each requires the application of an interest rate to an unpaid balance to produce the interest accrued during each payment period. In most fixed term transactions the two methods will produce identical results. The use of the U.S. Rule, however, prevents the compounding of interest charges when interest accrues faster than it is paid off.

Unfortunately for both creditors and consumers, just as there is no formula for calculating actuarial rates in general, there is no simple formula to calculate the annual percentage rate using either the strict actuarial method or the U.S. Rule. Appendix J of Regulation Z sets out in great detail "instructions and equations for the actuarial method."[126] These instructions and equations will probably intimidate, rather than enlighten most creditors and consumers. One alternative is to turn to experts who have produced computer programs, spreadsheets, programmable and programmed calculators, on-line calculation tools, and charts that can calculate annual percentage rates.[127]

Another alternative is to use the Truth in Lending Annual Percentage Rate Tables. Volume I of these Tables can be used to compute annual percentage rates for "regular" transactions and for transactions with irregular first payments, irregular first periods, and irregular final payments.[128]

Volume II of the Annual Percentage Rate Tables can be used to calculate annual percentage rates for "irregular" transactions. An "irregular" transaction is one that includes one or more of the following features: multiple advances, irregular payment periods, or irregular payment amounts (other than an irregular first period or an irregular first or final payment).[129]

119 Elizabeth Renuart and Diane Elizabeth Thompson, *The Truth, the Whole Truth, and Nothing But the Truth: Fulfilling the Promise of Truth in Lending*, 25 Yale J. on Reg. 181 (Summer 2008).

120 *See* National Consumer Law Center, Truth in Lending § 6.7.6.4 (7th ed. 2010 and Supp.).

121 *See, e.g.*, Am. Gen. Fin., Inc. v. Bauer, 2001 Ohio App. LEXIS 2228 (May 4, 2001) (noting differences between TILA APR and rate under state mortgage loan act).

122 Some state statutes utilize the TILA rules in their definitions, in which case the properly calculated APR would be the relevant figure. *See also* Olympic Coast Inv. v. Wright (*In re* Wright), 256 B.R. 626 (Bankr. D. Mont. 2000) (accepting APR as persuasive indication of compliance with Montana usury law). *Cf.* Matlock v. Atomic Pawn, Inc., 2005 WL 2456963 (E.D. Tenn. Oct. 5, 2005) (because of differences in calculation rules, TILA APR differs slightly from statutory interest rate even for single payment loan), *aff'd*, 191 Fed. Appx. 411 (6th Cir. 2006).

123 *See* Ch. 4, *supra* (points).

124 The TILA regulations, known as Regulation Z, and the Official Commentary to Regulation Z are found at 12 C.F.R. pt. 1026.

125 *See* 12 C.F.R. § 1026.22(a) (Regulation Z). The U.S. Rule is discussed in greater detail at § 5.5.1.1, *infra*.

126 12 C.F.R. pt. 1026, App. J.

127 For example, Financial Publishing Co., 1251 North Eddy St., Ste. 202, South Bend, IN 46617-1478 (800-247-3214) publishes many such charts and will calculate APRs for a nominal fee; the National Consumer Law Center will also calculate APRs at a nominal fee; many spreadsheet programs, on-line programs, and hand-held calculators will compute APRs for many transactions. An APR program is also included on the companion website to this treatise.

128 The tables may be ordered for $5.00 each from the FRB. Prepaid orders should be sent to: Publications Fulfillment, Mail Stop 127, Board of Governors of the Federal Reserve System, Washington, D.C. 20551, (202) 452-3245. The tables may also be ordered on-line at www.newyorkfed.org/publications/frame1.cfm. They may also be found on the companion website to NCLC's Truth in Lending treatise.

129 12 C.F.R. § 1026.22(a)(3).

Very few transactions subject to TILA will require the use of Volume II.

Creditors are allowed to use the Annual Percentage Rate Tables in calculating annual percentage rates but are not required to do so. They may use any other computation tool to calculate the annual percentage rate as long as the tool determines an annual percentage rate equal to the precise actuarial or U.S. Rule annual percentage rate, within the required degree of accuracy.[130] Therefore, the fact that an annual percentage rate computed with the Annual Percentage Rate Tables is different from the disclosed annual percentage rate is only an indication that the annual percentage rate has not been disclosed accurately, not conclusive proof, since the creditor may have used one of the other approved methods of calculation.

Another caveat is that creditors have the option of disregarding some payment schedule irregularities that arise from an irregular first payment period.[131] Since a creditor need not disclose whether it has disregarded the irregularity, the annual percentage rate in those situations should be calculated both ways, once disregarding the irregularity and once taking it into account.

Finally, TILA defines an "accurately" disclosed APR to allow some leeway. For most consumer credit transactions, there is an allowable tolerance of 1/8 of 1% (.125%).[132] For those who wish a more detailed explanation of TILA standards for calculating the APR, see NCLC's *Truth in Lending.*[133]

## 5.5 Special Calculation Problems

### *5.5.1 Compound Interest*

#### 5.5.1.1 When Does Compounding Occur?

Most attorneys are probably familiar with the concept of compound interest. In essence, compounding is the practice of charging interest on interest, or in other words, of adding accrued interest to the principal amount of a debt and making subsequent interest calculations on the basis of this new, increased principal amount. The effect of compounding is to increase the effective interest rate paid on the debt. Note that compounding often is not permitted under the terms of the contract and is frowned upon by public policy.[134]

A common example of the compounding of interest can be found in the typical bank savings account. Interest on such accounts is computed at some stated interval: daily, monthly, or quarterly. At the end of each interval, the amount of interest earned during that interval is calculated and credited to the account. In subsequent intervals, the interest payments that have previously been credited to the account themselves bear interest, just like cash deposited in the account. For example, if a depositor opens a savings account with a $1,000 deposit, and the account pays 5% interest, compounded monthly, then the following calculations would apply. First, the *monthly* interest rate is 5/12% or .0041666. Thus, after the first month, if there have been no new deposits or withdrawals, the account will have earned $1,000 × 0.0041666 = $4.17 (rounded) in interest. This $4.17 is credited to the account and bears interest in subsequent months. Therefore, the interest earned in the second month will be slightly higher: $1,004.17 × 0.0041666 = $4.18 (rounded). The balance after two months is $1,008.35. As a result of the monthly compounding, the effective annual interest rate paid will be 5.116% rather than 5.0%. In general, the more frequently interest on an account is compounded, the more the compounding increases the effective interest rate.

Interest can compound on an interest-bearing loan[135] in essentially the same manner that it compounds in a savings account. Indeed, a bank account can be regarded as a variety of interest-bearing loan, repayable on demand, in which the depositor is the creditor and the bank is the debtor. Compounding in interest-bearing consumer loans is, however, not a certainty. Rather, it depends first on whether interest on the loan is charged faster than it is paid off and, second, on how any excess interest is treated after it accrues.

In order for compounding to occur, interest must in some fashion be charged on a loan more rapidly than it is paid off.[136] This can happen in several ways. For example, if interest on a loan is calculated and charged daily while payments are due only monthly, then the interest cannot be paid as rapidly as it accrues and compounding may occur, even if all payments are made as scheduled.[137] Compounding will occur whenever interest is calculated more frequently than it is paid, provided that the interest is added to the outstanding principal balance as soon as it is computed. Alternatively, if the amount of interest that accrues during a payment interval is larger than the payment due in that interval,[138] then the excess accrued interest will probably be

130 12 C.F.R. § 1026.22(b)(2).

131 *See* 12 C.F.R. § 1026.17(c)(4).

132 15 U.S.C. § 1606(c); 12 C.F.R. § 1026.22(a)(2).

133 National Consumer Law Center, Truth in Lending §§ 5.5.6.2, 5.6.4.6 (7th ed. 2010 and Supp.).

134 *See* § 5.5.1.2, *infra*.

135 The discussion in this subsection is limited to interest-bearing transactions except where otherwise indicated. For a discussion of the distinction between interest-bearing and precomputed transactions, see § 5.8.2, *supra*.

136 The assumption made here is that payments on a loan are attributed first to the interest that accrued in the previous interval and subsequently to the principal debt. This is the standard procedure in actuarial calculation. *See, e.g.*, 12 C.F.R. § 226, app. J(a) (actuarial calculations under Regulation Z). Compare, however, the methods used to calculate damages in usury cases (§ 7.8.2.2, *infra*).

137 The difference can be significant in a long-term loan. For example, consider a manufactured home purchase, purportedly at 24% annual interest, which is actually computed with daily compounding. The effective yield thus will be 24.234% per annum. Over a thirty-year loan of $40,000, the borrower would pay $248,231 for the 24% simple-interest loan, but $251,021 for the same loan with daily compounding. The compounding costs the borrower $2,790.

138 The periodically accruing interest can exceed the scheduled periodic payment in several situations. In some variable rate mortgages, the size of the monthly payment is capped, but the interest rate that may be charged did not have to be capped until 1987, and even after 1987 the cap can be set at any level. Under such contracts, the interest charged will exceed the monthly payment if the contract

added to the outstanding loan balance, causing compounding in subsequent interest calculations. Finally, and perhaps most commonly, excess interest will accrue when a borrower makes late payments or misses payments on an interest-bearing debt.[139]

The second prerequisite for compounding interest on an interest-bearing debt is that any accrued, unpaid interest be added to the outstanding principal balance of the debt and treated as principal in subsequent interest calculations.[140] The addition of accrued interest to the principal debt in this manner is known as the "actuarial rule" and is widely employed, especially in open-end credit accounts.[141] However, the actuarial rule is not the only way to handle excess interest. In fact, the U.S. Supreme Court has ruled that overdue interest generally should *not* be added to principal to allow compounding.

> The correct rule in general is, that the creditor shall calculate interest whenever a payment is made. To this interest the payment is first to be applied; and if it exceed the interest due, the balance is to be applied to diminish the principal. If the payment fall short of the interest, the balance of interest is not to be added to the principal so as to produce interest. This rule is equally applicable whether the debt be one which expressly draws interest, or on which interest is given in the name of damages.[142]

This latter approach to accounting for accrued interest, which has become known as the "U.S. Rule," essentially requires creditors to maintain separate accounts for principal and unpaid interest and allows the assessment of interest only on the principal account.[143]

An example may help to illustrate the differences between the actuarial rule and the U.S. Rule. Assume that the outstanding principal balance of a mortgage loan is $50,000, that all payments are up to date, that the interest rate is 1% monthly, and that the interest which consequently accrues on the debt in the current month is $500. Assume further that the normal monthly mortgage payment is $800. If the borrower makes this regular $800 payment, or indeed if the borrower makes any payment that meets or exceeds the accrued interest of $500, the results under the actuarial rule and U.S. Rule will be the same; the first $500 of the payment will be attributed to the accrued interest and any remainder will be used to pay down the $50,000 principal balance. If, however, the borrower for some reason makes a lower payment, say $400, there will be accrued but unpaid interest of, in this example, $100, and the difference between the actuarial rule and U.S. Rule comes into play.

Under the actuarial rule, the $100 in unpaid interest will be added to the $50,000 balance, and the sum of $50,100 will be used to compute the following month's interest which, at the 1% monthly rate, will be $501. If the normal $800 payment is made the next month, the first $501 of that payment is attributed to interest and the remaining $299 is used to pay down the principal debt, leaving a balance of $49,801.

Under the U.S. Rule, the $100 of accrued but unpaid interest is not added to the $50,000 balance but is kept separately and does not bear interest. Thus, the $50,000 balance is unchanged and the following month's interest remains $500. If the normal $800 payment is then made the next month, $100 of the payment will first be used to pay off the existing accrued interest, $500 of the payment will be attributed to the interest that has just accrued, and the remaining $200 will be used to pay down principal, leaving a balance of $49,800. The use of the U.S. Rule has left the borrower with a balance that is one dollar lower than the balance computed with the actuarial rule. The borrower's savings are not just one dollar, however. Rather, the borrower will continue to save money, initially at the rate of one cent per month,[144] throughout the loan term because his balance will always be slightly lower than it would have been under the actuarial rule. Thus, slightly less interest will accrue every month and the principal will be paid down slightly faster. Depending on the time the loan remains outstanding, the savings from the U.S. Rule to the borrower in this example could

---

rate goes high enough, and negative amortization will occur. Similarly, accruing interest can exceed the required monthly payment on an open-end account if the minimum payment is not set high enough. *Cf.* Grunbeck v. Dime Sav. Bank, 74 F.3d 331 (1st Cir. 1996) (allegation that negative amortization resulting from similar circumstances in variable rate loans violated state simple interest statute; issue on appeal was preemption).

139 Compounding is most readily justified in this latter situation because the creditor suffers a loss due to the late payment and the compounding may compensate for this loss if it is not otherwise compensated by special late fees. *See* § 4.8, *supra*. *Cf.* Norman v. Norman, 506 N.W.2d 254 (Mich. Ct. App. 1993) (simple interest mandated in absence of statute, explicit agreement or "special circumstances dictating otherwise;" speculating in *dicta* that equitable compound interest may be appropriate if a debt arising out of a divorce judgment was significantly delinquent, requiring the creditor-spouse to seek court aid in enforcing judgment).

However, at least one court has held that an erratic and incomplete payment history is no defense to a usury challenge to compounding. A.J. Reynolds v. Succession of Williams, 628 So. 2d 1 (La. Ct. App. 1993).

In contrast, compounding that cannot be avoided by the borrower's timely payment of installments is merely a ruse for charging more than the stated contact rate.

140 *See, e.g.*, Niggeling v. Michigan Dep't of Transp., 488 N.W.2d 791, 792 (Mich. Ct. App. 1992). *Cf.* Pentico v. Mad-Wayler, Inc., 964 S.W.2d 708, 717-8 (Tex. App. 1998) (charging interest on unpaid interest is compounding, but charging interest on unpaid late fees is not).

141 Estate of Baxter v. Shaw Assocs., Inc., 797 So. 2d 396 (Miss. Ct. App. 2001) (construing statute allowing "actuarial" interest as allowing compounding).

142 Story v. Livingston, 38 U.S. (13 Pet.) 359, 371 (1839).

143 All payments are attributed first to paying off any accrued interest. Only after all accrued interest in the interest "account" is paid off are payments attributed to principal. *See* 12 C.F.R. § 226, app. J(a) (Federal Reserve Board explanation of U.S. Rule).

144 At a 1% monthly interest rate, the mortgage balance under the actuarial rule, which is $49,801, will earn one cent more in one month than the U.S. Rule balance of $49,800. Thus, after an additional month, the difference between the balances will increase from $1.00 to $1.01. Due to the effects of continued compounding, the difference between the balances will increase for as long as the debt is outstanding.

be several dollars. The difference would be much greater if there were multiple missed, partial, or late payments.[145]

Although compound interest is most often thought of in conjunction with interest-bearing accounts, the two components of compounding—a charge of interest in excess of any concurrent payment, and the addition of this excess to the principal balance—are by no means so limited. Indeed, compounding is an element in many credit practices that are commonly used to increase yield on all kinds of consumer loans. For example, discount interest,[146] which is invariably associated with precomputed debt, employs compounding because the borrower is assessed interest on a greater sum than is actually received and because, under most usury statutes, the difference between the amount the borrower receives and the amount on which the interest is calculated is, itself, interest. Similarly, when creditors charge "points" or other fees at the consummation of a loan,[147] and then "finance" those charges by including them in the face amount of a loan note instead of demanding immediate cash payment, compound interest is being assessed. Conceptually, the fees themselves are usually interest payments (although a statute may define them otherwise[148]), and once these fees are added to loan principal, they themselves bear interest. In general, any time a creditor includes interest charges in the face amount of a loan note, it is assessing compound interest.

### 5.5.1.2 Legal Restrictions on Compounding

#### *5.5.1.2.1 Whether state law prohibits compounding*

The law traditionally has taken a dim view of the compounding of interest. The courts have recognized that compounding increases the yield that a creditor receives, and have questioned the use of compounding even when the ultimate yield that it provides is below the usury ceiling.[149] The basic concern seems to be that compounding is deceptive, so that "an improvident debtor is not likely to realize the extent to which the interest will accumulate."[150] Of course, this concern could just as well be voiced (and sometimes is) about myriad other practices that creditors use to increase yield. Nevertheless, perhaps because the effects of compounding are easy to perceive, the courts have been especially vigorous in its condemnation. Sufficient case law exists to make compounding open to challenge in many jurisdictions if it is not expressly authorized by statute.[151]

Many cases that discuss the validity of compound interest are not usury cases. Rather they are cases argued under common law contract principles that have challenged compounding on public policy grounds. In some jurisdictions, agreements requiring the payment of compound interest have been held to violate public policy.[152] However, some of these courts distinguish agreements to compound interest in connection with debts not yet owed, from agreements to pay interest on interest obligations that have already come due, and have declared that the latter do not involve "compounding."[153] For example, a

145 *See, e.g.*, American Bank v. Wegener, 776 S.W.2d 922, 923 (Mo. Ct. App. 1989) (compounding would have added $40,804.17 in interest).

146 *See* § 5.3.3, *supra*. Of course, if discount interest is authorized by statute, then the compounding is probably legal.

147 *See* §§ 4.3, *supra*, 5.6, *infra*.

148 In general, the statutory definition of "interest" must be addressed before the presence of compounding, at least from a legal standpoint, can be determined. If "points" or other fees are interest under the controlling statute, but are treated as loan principal in a credit contract, then compounding is inevitable. If the creditor may legally exclude points or other up-front fees from "interest," then compounding may not technically be present, although the economic consequences are the same.

149 *See* Citizens Nat'l Bank v. Donnell, 195 U.S. 369 (1904); Acker v. Provident Nat'l Bank, 512 F.2d 729 (3d Cir. 1975).

150 Household Fin. Corp. v. Goldring, 33 N.Y.S.2d 514 (N.Y. App. Div.), *aff'd*, 43 N.E.2d 715 (N.Y. 1942).

151 *See, e.g.*, Iowa Sup. Ct. Bd. of Prof'l Ethics & Conduct v. McKittrick, 683 N.W.2d 554 (Iowa 2004) (compound interest generally not permitted without agreement between parties and specifically not permitted on finance charge for accounts receivable); A.J. Reynolds v. Succession of Williams, 628 So. 2d 1 (La. Ct. App. 1993) (creditor compounded in a transaction not subject to one of Louisiana's statutory exceptions to general rule against compounding); Imperial Cas. & Indemnity Co. v. Bellini, 947 A.2d 886 (R.I. 2008) (compounding disfavored unless specifically authorized by legislature; "12% per annum" authorizes only simple interest); Dodd v. Potomac Riverside Farm, Inc., 664 S.E.2d 184 (W. Va. 2008) (interest is simple in absence of statutory authorization or express written agreement). *See generally* Annotation, 10 A.L.R.3d 421 (1966) (definition of compound interest in statutes prohibiting compounding); Annotation, 57 A.L.R.2d 630 (1958) (interest taken in advance as usury); Annotation, 37 A.L.R. 325 (1925) (validity of agreement to pay interest on interest) *supplemented at* 76 A.L.R. 1484 (1932).

152 *See, e.g.,* Debentureholders Protective Comm. v. Continental Inv. Corp., 679 F.2d 264 (1st Cir. 1982) (interpreting New York law); *In re* Rosner, 48 B.R. 538 (Bankr. E.D.N.Y. 1985); *In re* Webb, 29 B.R. 280 (Bankr. E.D.N.Y. 1983); Giventer v. Arnow, 333 N.E.2d 366 (N.Y. 1975). *Cf. In re* Graboyes, 223 Fed. Appx. 112 (3d Cir. 2007) (loan note and public policy do not allow capitalization of late fees when calculating interest; noting that Pennsylvania "frowns upon compound interest" and thus it only is permitted when parties expressly have provided for it in the contract or a statute allows for it). *But see* Elliott Assocs. v. Banco De La Nacion, 194 F.R.D. 116 (S.D.N.Y. 2000) (applying statutory amendment allowing compound interest); Spodek v. Park Prop. Dev. Assocs., 759 N.E.2d 760 (N.Y. 2001) (allowing post-judgment interest on judgment that represented both principal and interest); Steinberg v. Williams, 558 N.Y.S.2d 188 (N.Y. App. 1990) (negative amortization in mortgage was not compounding; also, loan was a purchase money mortgage to which usury law did not apply); Harris v. Coles, 60 S.W.3d 848 (Tenn. Ct. App. 2001) (compound interest allowed, but only if parties have agreed to it). *See generally* Annotation, 37 A.L.R. 325 (1925), *supplemented at* 76 A.L.R. 1484 (1932).

153 *See* Smith v. MRCC P'ship, 792 S.W.2d 301 (Ark. 1990) (not usury to add accrued, unpaid interest on antecedent debt to principal on new debt and write new contract with maximum rate of interest on whole amount); Coupounas v. Madden, 514 N.E.2d 1316 (Mass. 1987); Beneficial Fin. Co. v. Fusco, 203 A.2d 457 (Me. 1964); Giventer v. Arnow, 333 N.E.2d 366 (N.Y. 1975); Household Fin. Co. v. Goldring, 33 N.Y.S.2d 514 (N.Y. App. Div.), *aff'd*, 43 N.E.2d 715 (N.Y. 1942). *See also* Bryant Motors, Inc. v. Blue Bird Body Co., 2009 WL 1796001 (M.D. Ga. June 22, 2009) (federal law allows creditor to recover post-judgment interest on unpaid interest, but state law prohibits pre-judgment interest on interest); *In re*

provision in a loan agreement to charge interest on any future interest installments that the borrower does not pay on time might be void, while an agreement made after an installment was overdue to pay interest on the overdue installment might be valid. The reason for this somewhat unlikely distinction appears to be a belief that the former transaction allows debts to mount without the borrower's knowledge while the latter merely compensates the creditor for its loss.[154]

##### *5.5.1.2.2 Framing compounding as a usury violation*

Although contract law arguments against the imposition of compound interest are worth considering in many consumer transactions, they have one major drawback. Specifically, the remedy for an impermissible agreement to compound interest may be limited to the voiding of the improper contract clause. Thus, whenever possible, it is to a consumer's advantage to argue that compounding is prohibited not only by contract law, but also by a usury statute which contains more expansive remedies.

There are two ways in which compounding can lead to a usury violation. First, compounding can violate a usury statute if the effect of the compounding is to raise the creditor's yield above the statutory ceiling. Thus, a 7.5% simple interest ceiling is violated when a lender charges interest at 7.5%, compounded quarterly, because the actual return is 7.72%.[155] This argument can be made in deregulated states, too, where the statute provides that the permissible rate is that "agreed to" by the parties.[156] Unless the contract itself specifically provides for compounding, it can be argued that the effect of compounding is to charge more than the "agreed-to" cap.

The second situation in which compounding of interest may violate usury laws occurs when a usury statute prohibits compounding, either explicitly or implicitly, regardless of the resulting yield.[157] The most significant examples of such statutes were the earlier drafts of the Uniform Small Loan Law which provided that: "Interest shall not be paid, deducted, or received in advance. Interest shall be computed and paid only on unpaid principal balances and shall not be compounded."[158]

This clause clearly prohibits compounding through the use of open-end credit accounts.[159] It has also been read by many courts to prohibit a creditor from refinancing an existing debt and adding the unpaid interest that had accrued under the existing loan to the principal of the new obligation.[160] Some courts, however, have permitted such *de facto* compounding through refinancing, despite the small loan law provisions, by reading into the act the common law distinction between agree-

Rosner, 48 B.R. 538 (Bankr. E.D.N.Y. 1985) (compounding by prior agreement void); *In re* Estate of Jackson, 508 N.Y.S.2d 671 (N.Y. App. Div. 1986).

154 Giventer v. Arnow, 333 N.E.2d 366, 368 (N.Y. 1975) ("it is considered against public policy to encourage creditors to silently permit debts to progressively mount at the expense of debtors who, often unaware of the consequences of the prior agreement, tend to confuse forbearance with indulgence"). *See also* North Dade Church of God v. JM Statewide, 851 So. 2d 194 (Fla. Dist. Ct. App. 2003) (allowing the payment of interest on past-due interest because such payment "supplies the place of prompt payment and indemnifies the creditor for his or her forbearance"); Boatmen's First Nat'l Bank v. Bogina Petroleum Engineers, 794 S.W.2d 703 (Mo. Ct. App. 1990). *See generally* § 5.9.5.2, *infra* (addition of unpaid interest to new principal when loan is refinanced).

155 Strawn Furniture Co. v. Austin, 655 S.W.2d 397 (Ark. 1983) (10/12% per month compounds to 10.76% annually, exceeding 10% usury ceiling). *Cf.* Haider v. Montgomery, 423 N.W.2d 494 (N.D. 1988) (though compounding prohibited, forfeiture penalty inapplicable; forfeiture penalty only applies where interest exceeds maximum allowable rate (in this case 13.854%) and effective rate resulting from compounding herein was 13.497%); Ervin v. Muller, 2003 WL 21744332 (Wash. Ct. App. July 29, 2003) (contract, which allowed for compound interest, was permissible; effective rate did not exceed statutory usury ceiling). *But cf.* Urban Communicators PCS Ltd. P'ship v. Gabriel Capital, L.P., 394 B.R. 325 (S.D.N.Y. 2008) (compounding that ultimately resulted in interest rate in excess of 25% usury cap did not make loan usurious where it occurred only after default, as N.Y. usury laws do not apply to defaulted obligations); OCM Principal Opportunities Fund v. CIBC World Mkts. Corp., 85 Cal. Rptr. 3d 350 (Cal. Ct. App. 2008) (compounding that resulted from renewal of judgment as allowed by statute did not violate constitutional usury cap where cap was expressed as "per annum" and renewal was allowed only every five years).

156 *See* § 7.6, *infra*.

157 *Cf.* Grunbeck v. Dime Sav. Bank, 74 F.3d 331 (1st Cir. 1996) (involving allegation that negative amortization resulting from minimum payments too low to pay accrued interest on variable rate mortgage increases violated New Hampshire's simple interest statute; issue on appeal was preemption); A.J. Reynolds v. Succession of Williams, 628 So. 2d 1 (La. Ct. App. 1993) (finding implied contract for usury where creditor's accounting method on erratically paid loan compounded interest annually, in violation of general rule against compounding, over twenty-three year life of transaction; fact that amount paid was less than would have been paid had loan been fully paid according to terms did not negate the usury inherent in the compounding, nor did the fact that debtor still may have owed something in true principal when usury was asserted).

158 Uniform Small Loan Law, 6th Draft, § 13 (1935), *reprinted in* Hubachek, Annotations On Small Loan Laws (Russell Sage Found. 1938). Earlier drafts contained similar prohibitions against compounding. The seventh draft, however, gives creditors a limited right to compound when refinancing small loans:

> [c]harges shall not be compounded; provided that, if part or all of the consideration for a loan contract is the unpaid principal balance of a prior loan, then the principal amount payable under such loan contract may include any unpaid charges on the prior loan that have accrued within sixty days before the making of such loan contract.

Uniform Small Loan Law, 7th Draft, § 13 (1942), *reprinted in* Curran, Trends In Consumer Credit Legislation (Univ. of Chicago Press 1966).

159 *See* Partain v. First Nat'l Bank, 467 F.2d 167 (5th Cir. 1972).

160 *See* Madison Personal Loan, Inc. v. Parker, 124 F.2d 143 (2d Cir. 1941) (applying New York law) (excellent discussion, but its authority in New York is questionable due to later state court decisions); Vann v. Accounts Supervision Co., 88 So. 2d 548 (Fla. 1956); Lanier v. Consolidated Loan & Fin. Co., 170 S.E. 99 (Ga. Ct. App. 1933); Securities Fin. Co. v. Maranto, 119 So. 2d 120 (La. Ct. App. 1966); Vaughn v. Graham, 121 S.W.2d 222 (Mo. Ct. App. 1938); Commonwealth v. State Loan Corp., 176 A. 516 (Pa. Super. Ct. 1935).

ments that automatically compound interest and those that provide only for the payment of interest on interest that has already accrued.[161]

In addition to small loan laws, other usury statutes may limit or prohibit compounding.[162] In some jurisdictions, usury statutes allow compounding only if the parties expressly agree to the practice.[163] Case decisions suggest that courts will require any such agreement to be explicit, so the practitioner should carefully review the contract language where the creditor has compounded interest.[164] Usury violations have been found where no specific agreement existed.[165]

Finally, consumer law practitioners should consider whether any provisions of a usury statute may impliedly prohibit compounding of interest. For example, the Third Circuit held that a Pennsylvania installment sales act that authorized the assessment of "simple" interest was violated by compounding even though the effective yield received by the creditor did not exceed the simple interest ceiling.[166] In general, the distaste that courts have shown for compounding suggests that statutes must

161 *See* Beneficial Fin. Co. v. Fusco, 203 A.2d 457 (Me. 1964); Rouse v. Jennings, 249 N.W. 10 (Mich. 1933); Household Fin. Corp. v. Goldring, 33 N.Y.S. 514 (N.Y. App. Div.), *aff'd*, 43 N.E.2d 715 (N.Y. 1942).

162 *See, e.g.*, D.A.N. Joint Venture III, L.P. v. Turk, 138 P.3d 1253 (Kan. Ct. App. 2006) (Kansas U.C.C.C. prohibits charging judgment interest on interest); American Bank v. Wegener, 776 S.W.2d 922 (Mo. Ct. App. 1989) (statute limits compounding to once annually); N.D. Cent. Code § 47-14-09; Haider v. Montgomery, 423 N.W.2d 494 (N.D. 1988) (finding violation of statutory prohibition of compounding; compounded interest forfeited but not all interest because compounding did not raise interest rate above usury limit); Northwestern Equip., Inc. v. Badinger, 403 N.W.2d 8 (N.D. 1987) (reversing summary judgment in favor of seller that compounded interest on account receivable, because it failed to prove that it fell within an exception to the prohibition against compounding).

163 Fielder v. Credit Acceptance Corp., 19 F. Supp. 2d 966 (W.D. Mo. 1998) (interpreting Mo. Rev. Stat. § 408.080) (parties did not contract to collect compound interest; creditor practice of compounding interest in connection with its repossession and deficiency actions subjects it to the penalty provisions of the state Motor Vehicle Time Sales Act), *vacated on jurisdictional grounds*, 188 F.3d 1031 (8th Cir. 1999) (ordering interest overcharge portion of case severed and remanded to state court). *But cf. In re* 201 Forest Street L.L.C., 409 B.R. 543 (Bankr. D. Mass. 2009) (refusing to enforce provision in commercial loan contract for compound interest; although explicit, provision was key component of default interest rates held to be unenforceable penalties).

164 *See, e.g.*, Pennsylvania Truck Lines, Inc. v. Solar Equity Corp., 127 F.R.D. 127 (N.D. Ill. 1988) (compounding would render inconsistent parties' agreement to "1.5% per month (18% per annum)"), *aff'd on other grounds*, 882 F.2d 221 (7th Cir. 1989); *In re* Kosinski, 409 B.R. 268 (Bankr. D. Mass. 2009) (rejecting creditor's argument that compound rather than simple interest should accrue on debtor's obligation; applying general Massachusetts rule that without express agreement of parties—absent in this case—or statutory basis, presumption of simple interest applies), *aff'd in part, rev'd in part and remanded*, __ B.R.__, 2010 WL 706059 (B.A.P. 1st Cir. Mar. 1, 2010) (not addressing interest issue but reversing debtor's underlying obligation); *In re* Brummer, 147 B.R. 552 (Bankr. D. Mont. 1992) (under Montana statute, contract must unequivocally provide for compounding; parties' intent or market practice will not suffice); *In re* Charleston Med. Ctr., Ltd., 100 B.R. 962 (Bankr. S.D. Ohio 1989) (contract provision that interest is to be computed and payable "on a monthly basis" does not expressly allow compounding of interest, since it speaks merely to periodicity rather than to method of computation); Ninety Five Ten v. Crain, 282 Cal. Rptr. 141 (Cal. Ct. App. 1991) (note calling for interest "per annum-monthly" calls for simple, not compound interest; creditor could not circumvent requirement for agreement to compound by seeking prejudgment interest); Haughton v. Namano, Inc., 476 S.E.2d 31 (Ga. Ct. App. 1996) (may be usurious to charge interest on interest on an open account, in absence of agreement); Weigel Broad. Co. v. Smith, 682 N.E.2d 745 (Ill. App. Ct. 1996) (compound interest disfavored; available only when no statutory bar and the parties specifically agree); Helland v. Helland, 573 N.E.2d 357 (Ill. App. Ct. 1991) ("8% per annum" specified in contract did not permit compounding); Norman v. Norman, 506 N.W.2d 254 (Mich. Ct. App. 1993) (in absence of statute, explicit agreement of parties or special circumstances dictating otherwise, rule is to calculate interest on simple, not compound basis); Lincoln Lumber Co. v. Fowler, 533 N.W.2d 898 (Neb. 1995) (in absence of statute or contract, compound interest not allowed; documents signed by guarantor did not specify compound interest, so creditor limited to simple interest); Campbell v. Lake Terrace, Inc., 905 P.2d 163 (Nev. 1995) (compound interest disfavored; allowed only if statute or agreement specifically provides); Mayer v. Medancic, 919 N.E.2d 721 (Ohio 2009) (upon default of written instrument, absent express agreement or statutory authorization, only simple interest accrues, but post-judgment simple interest accrues both on unpaid principal and interest outstanding at time of default); Christensen v. Munns, 812 P.2d 69 (Utah Ct. App. 1991) (compound interest not authorized where contract specified the variable rate to be applied to the principal until maturity, and specified no post-maturity rate); Mountain States Broad. v. Neale, 776 P.2d 643 (Utah Ct. App. 1989) (note providing that unpaid interest would "bear like interest as the principal" did not explicitly allow monthly compounding). *Cf.* Southfield W., Inc. v. City of Southfield, 520 N.W.2d 721 (Mich. 1994) (construing statute to allow prejudgment interest to be included in amount on which post-judgment interest is charged, since statute made a distinction between pre- and post-judgment); American Bank v. Wegener, 776 S.W.2d 922 (Mo. Ct. App. 1989) (finding agreement to compound interest in provision that note and all installments were to bear interest after maturity, since installments included interest; compounding limited by statute to once annually); Ervin v. Muller, 2003 WL 21744332 (Wash. Ct. App. July 29, 2003) (upholding mortgage contract provision providing that unpaid interest will be added to the principal).

165 *See* McConnell v. Merrill Lynch, Pierce, Fenner, & Smith, 578 P.2d 1375 (Cal. 1978), *later op. at* 662 P.2d 916 (Cal. 1983) (form contract that authorized interest charges in accordance with broker's "usual custom" did not constitute agreement to compound); Crest Sav. & Loan Ass'n v. Mason, 581 A.2d 120 (N.J. Super. Ct. Ch. Div. 1990). *See also* Acker v. Provident Nat'l Bank, 512 F.2d 729 (3d Cir. 1975); Helland v. Helland, 573 N.E.2d 357 (Ill. App. Ct. 1991) (compounding authorized only when parties specifically agree to it and no statute bars it); Coupounas v. Madden, 514 N.E.2d 1316 (Mass. 1987) (in absence of express agreement to pay compound interest on interest-bearing account invoices due, creditor cannot compound interest); William C. Dear & Assocs., Inc. v. Plastronics, Inc., 913 S.W.2d 251 (Tex. App. 1996) (commercial case where parties did not agree to any interest rate; in absence of written agreement Tex. Civ. Code Ann. § 5069-1:03 applied; statute does not expressly allow compounding so it is prohibited).

166 Acker v. Provident Nat'l Bank, 512 F.2d 729 (3d Cir. 1975). *See also* Stovall v. Illinois Cent. Gulf R.R., 722 F.2d 190 (5th Cir. 1984) ("actuarial method" allows compounding only annually).

clearly authorize the practice before it will be permitted.[167] For example, the Vermont Supreme Court has held that, without further expression of legislative intent, the use of the phrase "computed by the actuarial method" in the statute on judgment interest was not sufficient to change the common law rule that required computing by simple interest and prohibited compounding.[168]

## 5.5.2 *Odd Payment Periods and Odd Payment Amounts*

### 5.5.2.1 General

Most of the discussion thus far of installment interest methods and calculations has rested on the assumption that in any particular transaction all of the payment periods are equal[169] and all of the payment amounts are also equal.[170] This assumption holds true for most consumer credit installment transactions. Indeed, many consumer credit laws, particularly add-on interest usury laws,[171] require creditors to impose payment schedules with equal payment periods and/or equal payment amounts.

The reason for these requirements is that unequal periods or amounts can affect the effective interest rate (and, of course, the annual percentage rate).[172] Generally, *higher* effective interest rates will be created by relatively shorter initial payment periods and higher initial payments because the consumer must repay the loan more quickly. (For this reason, it is not uncommon for used car dealers to run afoul of both usury laws and TILA when they require repayment periods shorter than one month, as is discussed in more detail in § 5.5.2.2, *infra*.)

167 Stovall v. Illinois Cent. Gulf R.R., 722 F.2d 190 (5th Cir. 1984) (no compounding in absence of express statutory authorization); Acker v. Provident Nat'l Bank, 512 F.2d 729 (3d Cir. 1975) (same); Westbrook v. Fairchild, 9 Cal. Rptr. 2d 277 (Cal. Ct. App. 1992) (statute permitting post-judgment interest of 10% per annum on the principal construed to prohibit compounding; similar provision in state constitution construed in same way); Simon v. CNA Ins. Co., 543 A.2d 110 (N.J. Super. Ct. App. Div. 1988) (omission of word "simple" from amended statute on rate of judgment interest did not permit compounding); William C. Dear & Assocs., Inc. v. Plastronics, Inc., 913 S.W.2d 251 (Tex. App. 1996) (no compounding in absence of express statutory authorization). *But cf.* American Milling Co. v. Brennan Marine, Inc., 623 F.3d 1221 (8th Cir. 2010) (rule requiring party to pay "interest at the rate of 6% per annum" gives court equitable discretion to order compound interest); Grigg v. Robinson Furniture Co., 260 N.W.2d 898 (Mich. Ct. App. 1978) (general state prohibition of compound interest does not prevent compounding of time-price differentials).

168 Greenmoss Builders v. Dun & Bradstreet, 543 A.2d 1320 (Vt. 1988).

169 Indeed, every example so far has used equal monthly payment periods.

170 Sometimes, the last payment had to be adjusted by a few cents due to rounding, and the discussion of balloon payments obviously, does not rest on that assumption.

171 *See* § 5.3.2, *supra*.

172 *See* § 5.4, *supra*.

Conversely, *lower* effective interest rates will be created by relatively longer initial payment periods, lower initial payments, and larger final payments, because the consumer repays the loan more slowly.

For example, suppose a creditor agrees to lend a consumer $1,000 repayable in twelve monthly installments and charges $80 interest. This loan is identical to the $1,000 8% add-on loan illustrated in Chart 8, except that the first payment is due only ten days after the loan is consummated and all other payments are due monthly. This change in terms, without affecting the amount of principal, the amount of interest, or the number or size of the payments, raises the effective annual interest rate (APR) from 14.45% to 16.16%.

Similarly, another creditor might extend the same loan with equal payment periods but requiring a first payment of $145 and 11 more payments of $85. Again, it is the same total of payments as the original loan, but this payment schedule would also raise the effective interest rate, this time from 14.45% to 15.20%.

While both of these examples might violate a state's add-on interest usury law, it is not unusual for consumers to enter credit agreements with unequal ("odd") payment periods or payment amounts. Sometimes, transactions are structured this way for the convenience of the consumer. For example, a consumer who obtains a loan on August 16 may not receive her first paycheck until October 1. Changing the first monthly payment due date from September 16 to October 1 will certainly help the consumer get off to a good start.

This change will also benefit the creditor. First, the creditor will usually be able to charge more interest for the first payment period since it is longer than a month. Second, many consumer credit usury statutes (particularly add-on interest statutes) allow a creditor to charge two full months' interest for the first payment period if that period is at least one month and fifteen days (or 1.5 months) long. The same $1,000, one-year, 8% add-on loan, but with an August 16 to October 1 first payment period, would allow the lender to charge interest as if the loan had 13 payments rather than 12. Because of the "odd" first period of one month and fifteen days, it could charge an extra $6.67 in interest[173] without exceeding the maximum interest charge allowable under the statute. At the same time, however, the effective annual interest rate (APR) would be raised slightly from 14.45% to 14.47%.

The same creditor could, of course, ignore the odd first period and merely charge the same interest as if all the payment periods were equal. Since the odd first period is longer than the others, the effective annual interest rate (APR) would be lowered from 14.45% to 13.39%.

Other credit statutes may also give creditors the option of ignoring odd payment periods or odd payment amounts. For example, in calculating and disclosing annual percentage rates, for Truth in Lending purposes, creditors may ignore first periods up to eleven days shorter or twenty-one days longer than a

173 $\$1,000 \times 8\% \times 13 \div 12 = \$86.67$. $\$1,000 \times 8\% \times 12 \div 12 = \$80.00$. $\$86.67 - 80.00 = \$6.67$.

regular period in transactions with terms between one and ten years.[174]

Reducing the size of the initial payments can have a significant financial impact on the consumer, as it may require the consumer to make a "balloon" payment—a final payment that is significantly larger than the other payments. At a constant interest rate, the lower the initial payments, the higher the "balloon" payment. If the balloon payment is very high and the creditor does not guarantee refinancing on reasonable terms, the consumer may be unable to make the payment and may be compelled to default or to refinance the debt on very expensive terms.

For an illustration of a balloon payment, see Chart 6.[175] The first 11 payments are very low and do not even cover interest. As a consequence, the 12th payment of $1,025.75 is a "balloon" payment and is even higher than the original principal. A consumer who originally needed to borrow $1,000 is unlikely to be able to make a $1,025.75 payment only one year later.

The consumer lawyer should ask the following questions if there are any irregular payment periods or payment amounts in a particular consumer credit transaction:

- Does any relevant law prohibit that irregularity (or require all payment periods or payment amounts to be equal)?
- If the irregularity is allowed or not prohibited, does the law establish special rules for the adjustment of interest charges to reflect the effect of the irregularity?
- Has the creditor accurately adjusted the interest charges to reflect the effect of the irregularity?
- Has the creditor correctly disclosed the APR, keeping in mind the tolerance allowed by Regulation Z?[176]

APRs for transactions with irregular payment amounts can be calculated with the APR program on the companion website to this treatise.

### 5.5.2.2 Weekly, Bi-Weekly Payment Periods; Legal Issues

The most common regular repayment period in consumer transactions is monthly. However, other periods are sometimes used. Used car financing contracts, for example, may call for weekly, bi-weekly, or semi-monthly repayment periods. Absent some specific prohibition, such shorter periods are legitimate. However, practitioners have found that it is relatively common for the dealer to run afoul of usury laws or TILA (or both) in doing so.

The common mistake is a simple one. As noted in the preceding section, a shorter repayment term results in a higher APR. Take, as an example, a $2,000 loan, repayable in 24 installments of $105.75, for a total repayment obligation of $2,538.

- Monthly installments—24% APR[177]
- Semi-monthly installments—48% APR[178]
- Bi-weekly installments—52% APR[179]
- Weekly installments—104% APR[180]

If the dealer (not having read this chapter), uses the computer program or charts for twenty-four *monthly* repayment periods, while the contract calls for shorter repayment periods, the APR, as is evident above, will be seriously understated, and hence a TILA violation.[181]

It may also be a usury violation. If the statutory limit is 28% actuarial interest,[182] any repayment period other than monthly will result in an overcharge. Even in deregulated states, where there is no rate cap other than the one "agreed-to" by the parties, the *agreed rate* on this loan is probably disclosed as 24%, so that cap, too, is violated.[183] Some statutes may specifically allow repayment on other than a regular monthly basis, but nonetheless provide that the yield cannot exceed the yield in a monthly payment contract. Thus, in the above example, a payment schedule more frequent than monthly would make this a usurious transaction.[184]

174 12 C.F.R. § 1026.17(c)(4)(ii). Section 1026.17(c)(4) also lists the rules for shorter and longer transactions.

175 Negative Amortization of $1,000 Loan at 8% Actuarial Interest—Actuarial Rule. *See generally* § 5.3.1.2, *supra*.

176 *See* 12 C.F.R. §§ 1026.17(c)(4), 1026.22(a).

177 Thirty-day period, 12 periods per year.

178 Fifteen-day period, twenty-four periods per year. (Calculated on the basis of a thirty-day month. *See generally* § 5.5.4.3, *infra*.)

179 Fourteen-day periods, twenty-six periods per year.

180 Seven-day periods, fifty-two periods per year.

181 15 U.S.C. § 1638(a)(4); Reg. Z, 12 C.F.R. §§ 1026.18(e), 1026.22; National Consumer Law Center, Truth in Lending § 5.5 (7th ed. 2010 and Supp.).

182 It is fairly common for a state to have tiered rate caps, with older cars subject to significantly higher rates than new cars. *See, e.g.*, Fla. Stat. § 520.08.

183 *See* § 7.6, *infra*.

If the statute provides that the parties agree to a *rate*, the disclosure of the $538 finance charge is not an effective defense. *See* Chroniak v. Golden Inv. Corp., 983 F.2d 1140 (1st Cir. 1993) (note that specified interest in dollar amount, but no rate, violated an as-agreed statute, invoked statutory penalties; this is also a UDAP violation, as full disclosure of interest rates takes on added significance with the elimination of usury ceilings).

184 *See, e.g.*, Fla. Stat. § 520.08 (Motor Vehicle Retail Installment Sales Act). Subsection (1) states the maximum add-on rates. (*See* § 5.3.2, *supra*.) Subsection (2) says that the maximum finance charge allowable "shall be computed . . . on contracts payable in successive monthly payments substantially equal in amount." Subsection (3) states that when the contract calls for unequal or irregular installment payments, "the finance charge may be at a rate which will provide the same yield as is permitted on monthly payment contracts under subsections (1) and (2) *having due regard for the schedule of payment*." (Emphasis added.)

Thus, for example, on a five-year-old car, the maximum rate is 17% add-on, which on a twenty-four-installment monthly repayment basis has an actuarial equivalent of 29.85%. If the twenty-four installments in the same amount were repayable more frequently than monthly the finance charge would have a much higher yield than 29.85%, as shown in the text, and so, "having due regard" for the payment schedule, such a loan would be usurious.

## 5.5.3 Date Finance Charge Can Begin to Accrue

Another calculation issue is the date on which the creditor is allowed to start charging interest. In many credit transactions, there is a delay between the time the consumer becomes obliged on the contract and the time the creditor actually parts with the loan funds or the item being sold. Can the creditor begin charging interest on the date the contract is signed, or only upon disbursement of the funds or delivery of the goods?

An Illinois decision holds that the Motor Vehicle Retail Installment Sales Act allows a dealer to begin charging interest as of the date of the transaction, even though financing was approved only after that date.[185] Similarly, an Ohio decision holds that a bank could charge interest on the proceeds of a mortgage refinancing during the three-day period before it disbursed the proceeds.[186] The Ohio court concluded that, although the state second mortgage and small loan acts prohibited the charging of interest prior to the date of disbursement, the laws governing the bank did not.

The Ninth Circuit has held that federal law does not preempt a California statute regulating the date on which interest could begin to be charged in mortgage loans.[187] The statute formerly prohibited the charging of interest until the day before recordation of the deed of trust, but was amended in 2003 to refer instead to the day before disbursement of the proceeds.[188] The California Attorney General's Office also has clarified that a mortgage lender may not charge the borrower interest from the date its funds are paid into escrow, but rather must wait until the date the funds are disbursed from the escrow for the borrower's use.[189]

## 5.5.4 Daily Interest Rates and the 365/360 Method

### 5.5.4.1 General

Lenders with interest-bearing accounts sometimes choose to ignore (within certain limits) the exact date a payment is made. If a consumer makes a payment a few days before the payment due date or a few days after the payment due date, the lender may nonetheless charge interest as if the payment were made exactly when due.[190] Many mortgage lenders, for example, follow this practice, which benefits consumer borrowers who make their payments a few days late.

Other lenders, particularly those with more sophisticated computer programs, charge their borrowers a daily rate of interest. The general effect of applying daily rates undoubtedly increases the yield of their loans, since payments are more likely to be made after their due dates than before their due dates.[191] An argument should be made that lenders should clearly disclose that the application of daily interest rates could cost borrowers more money in interest charges and could lengthen their repayment schedules, or result in a higher final payment.[192] However, the application of daily interest rates, in itself, does not pose special usury problems.[193]

The use of daily interest rates can pose computational problems. There are two basic, intertwined issues: one is how to compute the daily rate and the other is how to count the number of days in a particular payment period.

**Chart 12**

**DAY COUNTING METHODS**

Principal = $1,000 (remains unchanged)

Annual interest rate = 18%

Date of transaction: March 1, 2009

| *Date of Interest-Only Payments* | *365 day Method Interest*[1] | *360 day Method Interest*[2] | *365/360 day Method Interest*[3] |
|---|---|---|---|
| April 1, 2009 | $15.28 (31 days) | $15.00 (30 days) | $15.50 (31 days) |
| May 1, 2009 | $14.79 (30 days) | $15.00 (30 days) | $15.00 (30 days) |
| June 15, 2009 | $22.18 (45 days) | $22.00 (44 days) | $22.50 (45 days) |
| *Total Interest* | $52.25 | $52.00 | $53.00 |

1 Daily interest rate: 18%/365 = .0493%
2 Daily interest rate: 18%/360 = .05%
3 Daily interest rate: 18%/360 = .05%

For the purposes of illustrating the different methods, assume that a consumer borrows $1,000 at 18% on March 1, 2009 and makes interest-only payments on April 1, 2009; May 1, 2009; and June 15, 2009. The results of the different methods are explained below and summarized at Chart 12, Day Counting Methods.

185 Guinn v. Hoskins Chevrolet, 836 N.E.2d 681, 701 (Ill. App. Ct. 2005).

186 Wixom v. Union Sav. Bank, 848 N.E.2d 569, 771–772 (Ohio Ct. App. 2006).

187 Quicken Loans, Inc. v. Wood, 449 F.3d 944 (9th Cir. 2006). *Accord* Wells Fargo Bank v. Boutris, 419 F.3d 949, 969 (9th Cir. 2005).

188 Cal. Civ. Code § 2948.5.

189 Opinion Letter, Office of the California Attorney General, 1999 WL 1249545 (Cal. Att'y Gen. Dec. 22, 1999) (unfair practice to charge the borrower interest before the close of escrow).

190 Of course, the lender may impose a late charge or accelerate the loan if the payment is made too many days late.

191 *See* Haynes v. Homeq Servicing Corp., 2006 WL 2167375 (M.D. Tenn. Aug. 1, 2006) (detailing how plaintiffs were left owing $2,206.50 after making all payments on daily simple interest loan for $41,365, due to late payments and interest charged during a "payment holiday" in which plaintiffs moved the due date for the first payment, and all subsequent payments, ahead by two weeks).

192 *See, e.g.*, Colo. Rev. Stat. § 5-3-106 (requiring disclosure that application of daily interest rate may cause borrower to owe additional and substantial money at end of credit transaction). *But cf.* Haynes v. Homeq Servicing Corp., 2006 WL 2167375 (M.D. Tenn. Aug. 1, 2006) (no duty under Truth in Lending Act to disclose that interest would be calculated on daily basis).

193 *Cf.* § 5.5.4.4, *infra* (issues presented by 365/360 calculation method).

### 5.5.4.2 365-Day Method

The most obvious solution to these issues is to divide the relevant annual interest rate by 365 (the number of days in a year)[194] and then simply to count the exact number of days that have elapsed in each period. For example, consider the first payment on April 1, 2009. The daily interest rate is .0493% (18% ÷ 365 = .0493%). The number of days between March 1 and April 1 is 31. Therefore, the interest that is earned during that period is $15.28 ($1,000 × .0493% × 31 days = $15.28).

If the consumer made a second payment on May 1, the same process would be repeated. The daily interest rate is .0493%. The number of days between April 1 and May 1 is 30. Therefore, the interest that is earned during that period (assuming that the unpaid principal remains unchanged at $1,000), is $14.79 ($1,000 × .0493% × 30 days = $14.79).

If the consumer made a third payment on June 15, the same process would again be repeated. The number of days between May 1 and June 15 is 45. Therefore, the interest that is earned is $22.18 ($1,000 × .0493% × 45 days = $22.18). The total interest earned between March 1 and June 15 is $52.25.

Some Capital One credit card holders filed a class action suit against the lender for failing to account for leap years properly. The cardholders alleged that calculating the daily periodic rate based on a 365-day year—when leap years are 366 days—amounted to a breach of the covenant of good faith and fair dealing. The Eleventh Circuit upheld the trial court's dismissal of the suit on the grounds that the credit card contracts clearly set forth this methodology and the relevant state law did not provide for the alteration of express contract terms based on an implied covenant.[195]

### 5.5.4.3 360-Day Method

Another method, that many creditors prefer because it is easier to apply, is to divide the annual interest rate by 360 and to assume that all monthly periods have thirty days. This assumption is maintained regardless of whether the actual number of days in a monthly period is 28, 29, 30 or 31.

In the first example, of a payment period between March 1 and April 1 at an annual rate of 18% and a principal of $1,000, the daily interest rate is .05% (18% ÷ 360 = .05%). While the exact number of days between March 1 and April 1 is 31, under the 360-day method, it is assumed that this monthly period is thirty days. Therefore, the interest that is earned during that period is $15.00.

If the consumer made another payment on May 1, the same process would be repeated. The daily interest rate is .05%. It is another monthly period so the number of days again is 30 (although this time, the thirty days coincides with the exact number of days). Therefore, the interest earned during that period is again $15.00 ($1,000 × .05% × 30 days = $15.00).

If the consumer made a third payment on June 15, the same process would again be repeated. The monthly period between May 1 and June 1 is considered thirty days (even though the exact number of days is 31). The period between June 1 and June 15 is considered fourteen days, for a total of forty-four days. Therefore, the interest earned during that period is $22.00 ($1,000 × .05% × 44 days = $22.00). The total interest earned between March 1 and June 15 is $52.00, or slightly less than the 365-day method.

This comparison between the 365-day method and the 360-day method is typical. If both methods are correctly applied, then they will generate approximately the same amount of interest, particularly over the long term. Indeed, if a consumer made every monthly payment exactly on time over a year, then each method would produce the exact same amount of interest.

### 5.5.4.4 365/360-Day Method: "The Bankers' Year"

A third method, the 365/360-day method, however, not only combines aspects of the first two methods but consistently generates interest higher than that produced by the other methods. The 365/360 method uses a 360-day year to calculate the daily interest rate, so that each day earns more interest. However, it also uses a 365-day year to count the number of days in any given payment period; it does not assume that each monthly payment period has thirty days, regardless of the actual number of days in a particular payment period. As a result, a lender who uses the 365/360 method will collect an extra five days of interest every year. This has the effect of increasing the interest rate by 1.39% (5 ÷ 360 = .0139). For example, in the 18% annual interest rate example discussed above, the effective interest rate under the 365/360 method would be 18.25% (18% × 1.0139 = 18.25%).

The application of the 365/360 method to the above example is summarized at Chart 12. In each instance, the daily interest rate is .05% (18% ÷ 360 = .05%). In the first payment period between March 1 and April 1, there are thirty-one days. Therefore, the interest generated is $15.50 ($1,000 × .05% × 31 = $15.50). This method produced $.50 more interest than that generated by 360-day method which assumed that there were only thirty days in a monthly payment period.

The second payment period produced $15.00 in interest, the same as that produced by the 360-day method, because the number of actual days in the period (30) is the same as the assumed number of days in the monthly period (30). Therefore, the interest generated during that period is $15.00 ($1,000 × .05% × 30 days = $15.00).

However, the third payment period again illustrates the discrepancies between the 365/360 method and the 360-day method. Counting the exact number of days between May 1, 2009 and June 15, 2009 produces forty-five days. Therefore, the interest generated during this period is $22.50 ($1,000 × .05% × 45 days = $22.50). Again this method produced $.50

194 Scientific purists may point out that a year actually has 365.25 days; however, more practical, but no less precise, observers may also point out that a *calendar* year, with the exception of a leap year, has exactly 365 days.

195 Renslow v. Capital One Servs., Inc., 343 Fed. Appx. 457 (11th Cir. 2009) (unpublished). *See also* Duru v. HSBC Bank Nevada, N.A., 411 Fed. Appx. 240 (11th Cir. 2011) (affirming dismissal of similar suit).

more interest than that generated by the 360-day method which assumed that there were only thirty days between May 1 and June 1 and counted fourteen days between June 1 and June 15, for a total of forty-four days. The total interest earned between March 1 and June 15 is $53.00, that is more than 1% higher than the 365-day method and nearly 2% higher than the 360-day method.

The 365/360 method of interest calculation has been widely used in the banking industry for the past two centuries. A 1971 Federal Reserve Board study indicated that 82% of all commercial banks used this method on at least some loans. In 1971 Congressman Wright Patman estimated that of the total amount of interest collected annually in the United States, $145 million was due to the difference between stated and actual rates that results from use of the 365/360 method.[196]

Borrowers charged interest computed by means of the 365/360 method at the maximum rate allowed by law have frequently brought usury actions against their lenders. In the first such reported case, *New York Firemen Insurance Co. v. Ely & Parsons*,[197] the court found the challenged loan usurious. Throughout the remainder of the nineteenth century and the first half of the twentieth century, however, the vast majority of courts rejected the *Ely & Parsons* view.[198]

The courts that rejected the *Ely & Parsons* rationale usually found that established banking custom and the need for easy calculation justified the use of the 365/360 method. It was said that computation of interest under the 365/365 method was far more difficult than under the 365/360 method. In addition, some courts found that there was no legislative intent to interfere with this long-established custom. Other courts dismissed the problem as insignificant, because each borrower suffers only slight harm.[199]

In recent years, with the advent of computerized banking, the rationale of these earlier cases has been carefully reconsidered. As one commentator noted,

> [i]nterest is now calculated, not by uneducated bank clerks, but by computers that can easily be programmed to use any method of calculation. The advanced technology would seem to support an inference that the lender using the 365/360 method does so in order to collect the excess interest rather than to promote convenience.[200]

The Ninth Circuit, applying Oregon law, agreed with this rationale in *American Timber & Trading Co. v. First National Bank of Oregon*.[201] It held that the usury statute "should be construed with regard to its net effect upon the borrower rather than upon the bookkeeping burden, custom, or convenience of the lender."[202] It was especially skeptical of the defendant bank's convenience argument in view of the fact that the bank used the 365/365 method to compute interest it paid to its depositors.[203]

*American Timber* has been received enthusiastically.[204] More importantly, the decision has been expressly followed by most of the courts that subsequently considered the issue.[205] The California Supreme Court relied on *American Timber* in reaching its conclusion that use of the 365/360 method constitutes false and misleading advertising.[206]

Not all courts have followed *American Timber*, however. In *Beazley v. Georgia Railroad Bank & Trust Co.*,[207] a Georgia intermediate court followed a 1906 decision of the Georgia

196 *See* Comment, *Legal Aspects of the Use of "Ordinary Simple Interest,"* 40 U. Chi. L. Rev. 141, 142–143 (1972). *See also* Republic of France v. Amoco Transp. Co., (*In re* Oil Spill by Amoco Cadiz Off the Coast of France on Mar. 16, 1978), 4 F.3d 997 (7th Cir. 1993) (table) (describing calculations and policy arguments; upholding trial court's discretion to use 360/360 method to calculate pre-judgment interest).

197 2 Cow. 678 (N.Y. 1824).

198 *See generally* Comment, *Legal Aspects of the Use of "Ordinary Simple Interest,"* 40 U. Chi. L. Rev. 141, 145–152 (1972); Annotation, 35 A.L.R.2d 842, 843–850 (1954).

199 *See* cases cited in Comment, *Legal Aspects of the Use of "Ordinary Simple Interest,"* 40 U. Chi. L. Rev. 141, 145–150 (1972); Annotation, 35 A.L.R.2d 842, 843–848 (1954).

200 Comment, *Legal Aspects of the Use of "Ordinary Simple Interest,"* 40 U. Chi. L. Rev. 141, 148 (1972).

201 511 F.2d 980, 983–984 (9th Cir. 1974).

202 *Id.* at 983.

203 *Id.* at 983–984.

204 *See, e.g.*, Comment, *Legal Aspects of the Use of "Ordinary Simple Interest,"* 40 U. Chi. L. Rev. 141, 148–149 (1972); Note, 6 U. Tol. L. Rev. 541, 559 (1975).

205 *See In re* Rosner, 48 B.R. 538 (Bankr. E.D.N.Y. 1985) (loan nominally at maximum legal interest rate made usurious by use of 365/360 method); Ellis Nat'l Bank v. Davis, 359 So. 2d 466 (Fla. 1978); Perlman v. First Nat'l Bank, 305 N.E.2d 236 (Ill. App. Ct. 1978), *appeal dismissed*, 331 N.E.2d 65 (Ill. 1975) (rejecting defense of "customary practice"); Nicoladze v. Lomas & Nettleton Mortgage Investors, 679 S.W.2d 671 (Tex. App. 1984) (finding usury on one of several loans because of undisclosed 365/360 calculations), *aff'd in relevant part, rev'd in part on other grounds sub nom.* Lawler v. Lomas & Nettleton Mortgage Investors, 691 S.W.2d 593 (Tex. 1985); O'Brien v. Shearson Hayden Stone, Inc., 586 P.2d 830, 836 (Wash. 1978). *See also* Hamilton v. Ohio Sav. Bank, 694 N.E.2d 442 (Ohio 1998) (ordering certification of class action challenging lender's use of 365/360 method); S.C. Dep't of Consumer Affairs Admin. Interp. No. 3.508-7702, Consumer Cred. Guide (CCH) ¶ 98,214 (1977); Servicing Guide, pt. II, ch. 5, § 501, pt. VI, ch. 1, § 102.01, *available at* www.allregs.com (for mortgages held by Fannie Mae, interest for a partial month must be calculated on the basis of a 365-day year; instructions for accessing the Fannie Mae Servicing Guide and ordering print copies are available at www.efanniemae.com/sf/guides/ssg/#pv). *But cf.* Federal Deposit Ins. Corp. v. Fox Creek Holding, L.L.C., 2010 WL 2667336 (D. Idaho July 2, 2010) (365/360 interest calculation method not usurious when state does not have usury ceiling; even when contract is silent, not deceptive to use 365/360 method when sophisticated commercial borrower should have known that it was widely used).

206 Chern v. Bank of Am., 544 P.2d 1310 (Cal. 1976) (en banc). *Cf.* South Bay Chevrolet v. General Motors Acceptance Corp., 85 Cal. Rptr. 2d 301 (Cal. Ct. App. 1999) (financially sophisticated automobile dealer that knew its floor plan financer used 365/360 method could not assert UDAP claim). *See generally* National Consumer Law Center, Unfair and Deceptive Acts and Practices § 6.6.1 (7th ed. 2008 and Supp.).

207 241 S.E.2d 39, 40 (Ga. Ct. App. 1977). *See also* Mom Corp. v. Chattahoochee Bank, 418 S.E.2d 74 (Ga. Ct. App. 1992) ("daily charge equal to annual percentage rate divided by 360 is not usurious *per se*"; method of counting days not at issue).

Supreme Court and found that a loan which yielded interest at the maximum legal rate was not usurious, even though the 365/360 method was used. And the Arkansas Supreme Court, with one justice dissenting, concluded with "no hesitancy" that "for practical, legal, and historical reasons, . . . the use of the 360-day year is lawful even when the interest is [the legal maximum]."[208] Some courts have recognized the defense of mistake in 365/360 cases.[209] Finally, some state statutes seem to authorize the use of 365/360 method.[210]

On a more elementary level, a creditor who casually counts the days that a loan is outstanding may find that it has committed usury. For example, in *Ex Parte Underwood*,[211] a contract was executed on August 26, 1982, with a final payment due on August 15, 1984. The exact time period was one year and 354 days, but the creditor charged interest on a two-year basis. This slight overcharge violated the Alabama Mini-Code.

Additionally, a lender that calculates interest based on the 365/360 method will face a legal challenge if the loan contract contains an interest rate based on a less expensive calculation method.[212] Moreover, where the contract indicates the percentage interest per annum, collection of more than that amount constitutes a violation of the contract. Such a practice also could support a UDAP claim based on the federal rebate statute,[213] which does not allow a lender to keep more interest than has been earned.

### 5.5.4.5 Effect of Late Posting of Payments

If the lender intentionally delays posting the payments, more interest may accrue over the term of the loan than contracted for or allowed by law. For example, assume a $1,000 simple interest loan made on April 1, with a monthly payment of $86.99 at 8%. See loan in Chart 6, *supra*. Assume that the lender calculates interest on a 365-day year, so the daily rate is .0219%. If the borrower pays the scheduled amount of $86.99 on time each month but the lender fails to post the payment for 15 additional days, the interest charges would look like this:

**Chart 13**
**Simple Interest One-Year Loan With 8% Simple Interest Computed on Daily Basis, Showing Effect of Late Posting of Payments**

| Payment | Due Date[214] | Unpaid Balance | # of Days of Interest[215] | Interest | Payment | New Balance |
|---|---|---|---|---|---|---|
| | | | | | | |
| 1 | 5/1 | $1,000.00 | 45 | 9.86 | 86.99 | 922.87 |
| 2 | 6/1 | $ 922.87 | 31 | 6.27 | 86.99 | 842.15 |
| 3 | 7/1 | $ 842.15 | 30 | 5.72 | 86.99 | 760.88 |
| 4 | 8/1 | $ 760.88 | 31 | 5.17 | 86.99 | 679.06 |
| 5 | 9/1 | $ 679.06 | 31 | 4.61 | 86.99 | 596.68 |
| 6 | 10/1 | $ 596.68 | 30 | 3.92 | 86.99 | 513.61 |
| 7 | 11/1 | $ 513.61 | 31 | 3.49 | 86.99 | 430.11 |
| 8 | 12/1 | $ 430.11 | 30 | 2.82 | 86.99 | 345.95 |
| 9 | 1/1 | $ 345.95 | 31 | 2.35 | 86.99 | 261.31 |
| 10 | 2/1 | $ 261.31 | 31 | 1.77 | 86.99 | 176.09 |
| 11 | 3/1 | $ 176.09 | 28 | 1.08 | 86.99 | 90.18 |
| 12 | 4/1 | $ 90.18 | 31 | 0.61 | 86.99 | 3.80 |

The total interest earned is $47.67, as compared to $43.86 if the payments had been credited on time, plus the borrower still owes $3.80 after twelve months of payments. While the additional interest is certainly a small amount in this example, in a

208 Martin v. Moore, 601 S.W.2d 838, 839 (Ark. 1980). *But see* Cagle v. Boyle Mortgage Co., 549 S.W.2d 474 (Ark. 1977).

209 *See, e.g.*, First Am. Nat'l Bank v. Booth, 606 S.W.2d 70 (Ark. 1980); Libowsky v. Lake Shore Commercial Fin. Corp., 330 N.W.2d 248 (Wis. Ct. App. 1982) (charged 365/360 by error of programmer).

210 *See, e.g.*, Voitier v. First Nat'l Bank of Commerce, 514 F. Supp. 585 (E.D. La. 1981); Asset Exch. II, L.L.C. v. First Choice Bank, 953 N.E.2d 446 (Ill. App. 2011) (noting legislature's amendment of Interest Act to provide that 365/360 calculation method is not a violation).

211 496 So. 2d 46 (Ala. 1986). *Cf.* Yates Ford, Inc. v. Ramirez, 692 S.W.2d 51 (Tex. 1985) (agreeing with administrative ruling allowing creditor to use either of two methods to count the number of extra days in payment periods that were longer than one month).

212 Hamilton v. Ohio Sav. Bank, 694 N.E.2d 442 (Ohio 1998) (certifying class action where lender calculated interest with the 365/360 method and consumers' interest payments exceeded the agreed rate; one subclass of plaintiffs also had loans that would not fully amortize within agreed loan terms and thus would face a balloon payment); JNT Props., L.L.C. v. Keybank, 2011 WL 2566510 (Ohio App. June 30, 2011) (fact question whether lender breached loan contract where it provided for 8.93% per annum but also provided for 365/360 calculation method); Ely Enters., Inc. v. FirstMerit Bank, N.A., 2010 WL 125960 (Ohio Ct. App. Jan. 14, 2010) (allowing breach of contract claim by commercial borrower to proceed where alleged breach was based on lender's use of the 365/360 method, resulting in higher effective interest rate than provided for by loan agreement). *But cf.* Kreisler & Kreisler, L.L.C. v. Nat'l City Bank, 657 F.3d 729 (8th Cir. 2011) (contract provisions for "per annum" interest rate and for 365/360 calculation method are not inconsistent); Bank of Am., N.A. v. Shelbourne Dev. Group, Inc., 732 F. Supp. 2d 809 (N.D. Ill. 2010) (holding that 365/360 method conformed to contractual clause that interest "will be computed on the basis of a 360-day year and the actual number of days elapsed"); *In re* Market Ctr. East Retail Prop., Inc., 433 B.R. 335, 354–335 (Bankr. D.N.M. 2010) (finding commercial loan contract's description of 365/360 method unambiguous); Asset Exch. II, L.L.C. v. First Choice Bank, 953 N.E.2d 446 (Ill. App. 2011) (rejecting claim that lender deviated from terms of note by using 365/360 method of calculation, where note provided for "per annum" rate and 365/360 method); RBS Citizens, N.A. v. RTG-Oak Lawn, L.L.C., 943 N.E.2d 198 (Ill. App. Ct. 2011) (contract language specifying that interest would be calculated on basis of 360-day year, using actual number of days, authorized 365/360 method despite other references to interest rate "per annum"); Hubbard Street Lofts L.L.C. v. Inland Bank, 2011 WL 6344377 (Ill. App. Ct. Dec. 13, 2011) (note not ambiguous despite references to both a per annum rate and a 365/360 calculation method).

213 15 U.S.C. § 1615(a).

214 In this example it is assumed that the borrower makes every payment on time, so the due date is the same as the date of receipt of the payment.

215 In this example, the lender charged interest for forty-five days (the thirty days from April 1 to May 1, plus the fifteen days during which posting was delayed) for the first payment period. For the second payment period, the lender charged interest for the thirty-one days from May 15 to June 15. The number of days in succeeding periods varies depending on the number of days in the month.

thirty-year $40,000 second mortgage loan at 8.23% simple interest per year, a pattern of posting payments fifteen days late will cost the borrower $370.80 in interest.

Creditors may also post payments late as a means of generating revenue in the form of late charges.[216] This practice is prohibited by the Truth in Lending Act for open-end credit,[217] but creditors may still attempt to manipulate grace periods and due dates to evade this prohibition. A major credit card bank entered into a $300 million settlement in 2000 with the Office of the Comptroller of the Currency and the San Francisco District Attorney's Office that required it, *inter alia*, to refund late fees it had charged due to delayed posting of payments.[218] Some states also have laws requiring prompt crediting of payments.[219]

### 5.5.5 Rounding

Attorneys calculating interest rates and payments will inevitably encounter the issue of rounding. Specifically, rounding is necessary whenever the product of a multiplication operation or the quotient (i.e., the result) of a division operation cannot be expressed precisely within some specified number of decimal places.

Perhaps the two most common examples of rounding problems in interest calculations are the determination of a periodic interest rate, and the multiplication of the balance of a debt by this periodic rate to obtain a borrower's monthly payments. For example, assume that an interest-bearing loan states a 10% annual interest rate. The first step in determining the borrower's monthly payment is to find the monthly interest rate, which will be the annual rate divided by twelve.[220] But 10 ÷ 12% cannot be expressed precisely in decimal form; on an eight-digit calculator it is rounded (down) to 0.0083333.

The next step in determining the monthly payment is to multiply the outstanding balance, which for simplicity we will say is $1,000, by the monthly rate, here 0.0083333, to obtain the interest earned in the month, which will be $8.3333. The problem is that the borrower cannot pay $8.3333, but must pay either $8.33 or $8.34. In the former case, the creditor is losing a third of a cent which it has earned, while in the latter case, the creditor will be receiving two-thirds of a cent which it did not earn. This may not seem significant, but over a long-term transaction, the difference can amount to a few dollars.[221]

There are basically three ways in which rounding can be handled: numbers can be rounded up, down, or to the nearest digit. The fairest technique is rounding to the nearest digit.[222] Using this method over a series of calculations, charges which are slightly too high because of rounding error tend to be offset by charges that have been rounded down, and rounding error is thus minimized. Some creditors, however, consistently round payments up one penny to maximize their profits.

Usury statutes are generally silent as to permissible rounding practices, as they are with many calculation techniques. However, rounding can be a usury issue because a creditor that consistently rounds earned interest up a penny is slightly increasing the effective interest rate it is charging. If a credit contract is already set at the maximum rate permitted by statute, then any increase in effective rate, no matter how small, exceeds the usury ceiling. Of course, such small overcharges may be subject to a *de minimis* defense in some jurisdictions.[223] Yet, overcharges due to a systematic practice of rounding up a penny should not be lightly dismissed. There is no justification for this practice other than maximizing profits, and if creditors are permitted to maximize profits despite statutory prohibitions, the law will rapidly lose meaning.

With variable rate notes, the interest rate itself may involve rounding issues, as the index rates commonly used may be odd numbers, e.g., 7.56%. Often, the variable rate contracts will provide for rounding the rate to the nearest one-eighth percent. As noted at § 5.3.6.2, *supra*, a creditor may sometimes use a rate obtained by rounding up, instead of rounding down to a nearer mark. Section 5.3.6.2, *supra*, discusses some claims that may arise from such a contract violation.

216 *See* MassPIRG Education Fund, A Road Map to Avoiding Credit Card Hazards (Mar. 2001).

217 15 U.S.C. § 1666c. *See* National Consumer Law Center, Truth in Lending §§ 7.7.2, 7.7.3 (7th ed. 2010 and Supp.).

218 *In re* Providian Nat'l Bank, #2000-53 (U.S. Dep't of Treas., Office of the Comptroller of the Currency), *available at* www.occ.treas.gov/ftp/release/2000-49.txt. *See also In re* Providian Fin. Corp. Sec. Litig., 152 F. Supp. 2d 814 (E.D. Pa. 2001) (denying motion to dismiss claims by investors who alleged that credit card bank concealed fact that its high returns were based on misrepresentations to consumers); Mangone v. First USA Bank, 206 F.R.D. 222 (S.D. Ill. 2001) (approving settlement of class action involving late posting of payments); Capital One Bank v. Rollins, 106 S.W.3d 286 (Tex. App. 2003) (reversing certification of class challenging manipulation of payment crediting dates in order to impose late charges; remanding for further analysis of existence of individual issues).

219 *See, e.g.*, Iowa Code § 535.14.

220 This assumes all months are of equal length. Some creditors recognize the different lengths of months, in which case the answer is slightly different. *See* § 5.5.4.3, *supra*.

221 If a creditor rounded up on all payments in a 360 payment loan and gained, on average, an extra half cent from each payment, it would earn an extra $1.80 directly. The actual extra earnings would be higher due to compounding.

222 Specifically, earnings of 0.5¢ and above are rounded to 1.0¢ while earnings below 0.5¢ are rounded to 0.0¢. This is the technique used in the charts in this treatise. Whatever method is employed should be used consistently. When checking the interest calculations in the credit contract, it may be advisable for a consumer's attorney to round up on all calculations. This method gives the creditor its highest possible earnings. If the creditor is claiming an even higher amount, the attorney can be certain that the difference is not due to rounding error.

223 *See* § 7.7.7, *infra*.

## 5.5.6 Spreading

### 5.5.6.1 A Calculation Defense to Usury Claims in Fixed Term Loans

The rate of interest charged on many loans fluctuates during the term of the credit. This fluctuation may be obvious, as in the case of loans in which the interest rates are pegged to some market rate such as the federal discount rate, or it may be concealed, as in the case of apparent fixed rate loans in which the borrower must pay various one-time fees at the outset of the transaction as well as the constant monthly payments.[224] In either situation, a tricky usury issue may arise. Specifically, it is possible that the interest rate will exceed the usury ceiling for one or more payment periods during the loan without exceeding the ceiling for the loan term as a whole. For example, consider a variable rate account, over a six-month period, with a constant outstanding balance, in a state with a 10% simple interest ceiling. If interest is charged on the account at an annual rate of 9% for the first five months, but the rate then jumps to 11% for the last month before the debt is paid off, is the transaction usurious? The answer obviously depends on whether each monthly payment period is viewed individually, in which case a usury violation occurs in the last month of the loan, or whether the loan is viewed as a whole and the interest charges are averaged, in which case the overall contract rate is 9.33%, significantly below the usury ceiling.[225]

Or consider an 18% second mortgage loan, with 20 points charged, in theory earned at consummation. During the first month of the loan, those 20 points[226] added to the regular 18% interest for one month, will result in a significantly higher yield than 1.5% (.18% ÷ 12 = 1.5%). As in the previous example, whether the loan is usurious or not depends upon whether the court looks at the return for one month, or the life of the loan.

Courts reviewing traditional fixed-term loans have generally applied usury ceilings to the overall rate of return for credit transactions and have done so through a doctrine which is often called "spreading."[227] Although it may be stated differently in different jurisdictions, the spreading doctrine essentially instructs a court to calculate the maximum charges that a creditor could assess on a credit transaction and to compare this figure with the charges actually assessed. If the actual charges do not exceed the permitted charges for the over-all transaction, then fluctuations in the effective rate of return during the loan term are ignored. Conceptually, the interest overcharges during some payment periods are "spread" over other payment periods and are offset by the amounts of extra interest that the creditor might legally have charged,[228] but did not actually charge, during those other payment periods.

The notion of spreading interest seems fairly reasonable at first glance, and it clearly makes calculations easier for courts reviewing usury cases. Nevertheless, the doctrine may allow

224 Because of the one-time fees, the *effective* interest rate will usually be higher at the beginning of the transaction than later in the loan term even though the contract describes the interest rate as fixed.

225 This example assumes that the accrued interest is paid off monthly with no monthly payments to principal. The assumption of a constant principal balance is a bit unrealistic since the balances of most accounts fluctuate; however, it is made here to simplify the example. If the monthly balances in the example varied, it would not be sufficient merely to average the monthly rates, as this example does. Instead, the maximum charge for each month, given its particular outstanding balance, would have to be computed. Under the "spreading" rule, the sum of these monthly maximum charges would be compared to the actual charge. *See* § 5.5.6.2, *infra* (spreading in open-end, variable-rate transactions).

For a discussion of Texas law and calculation issues in the spreading context, see Frank A. St. Claire, *The "Spreading of Interest" Under the Actuarial Method*, 10 St. Mary's L.J. 753 (1979), *cited in* Groseclose v. Rum, 860 S.W.2d 554 (Tex. App. 1993), a rather odd case involving graduated interest rates and a court that seemingly forced a usury theory into the case in order to invoke the spreading doctrine.

226 *See* §§ 4.3, *supra,* 5.6, *infra* (discussion of points).

227 *See, e.g.*, Perry v. Stewart Title Co., 756 F.2d 1197 (5th Cir. 1985) (Texas law); Kissell Co. v. Gressley, 591 F.2d 47 (9th Cir. 1979) (Arizona law) (transaction usurious despite spreading); C.I.O.S. Fdn. v. Berkston Ins. A.V.V., 2000 U.S. Dist. LEXIS 2337 (N.D. Miss. Jan. 28, 2000) (applying Texas spreading law to find loan not usurious); *In re* Auto Int'l Refrigeration, 275 B.R. 789, 809–816 (Bankr. N.D. Tex. 2002), *aff'd,* 307 B.R. 849 (N.D. Tex. 2002); Olympic Coast Inv. v. Wright (*In re* Wright), 256 B.R. 626 (Bankr. D. Mont. 2000) (origination fees and similar charges must be spread over full term of loan); Wooten v. Davis, 739 S.W.2d 669 (Ark. 1987) (invoking concept, though not by name, to determine no usurious overcharge); White v. Sweeney, 291 P.2d 77 (Cal. 1955); St. Petersburg Bank & Trust Co. v. Hamm, 414 So. 2d 1071 (Fla. 1982); Fleet Fin., Inc. v. Jones, 430 S.E.2d 352 (Ga. 1993) (invoking doctrine, though not by name); Ransom v. Fleet Fin., Inc., 466 S.E.2d 686 (Ga. Ct. App. 1996) (invoking doctrine, though not by name); Mayfield v. Oklahoma State Bank, 460 P.2d 414 (Okla. 1969) (following the doctrine without using the term); Danziger v. San Jacinto Sav. Ass'n, 732 S.W.2d 300, 303 (Tex. 1987); Tanner Dev. Co. v. Ferguson, 561 S.W.2d 777 (Tex. 1977) (lengthy discussion); Pentico v. Mad-Wayler, Inc., 964 S.W.2d 708 (Tex. App. 1998); R.V. Indus. v. Urdiales, 851 S.W.2d 306 (Tex. App. 1992) (interpreting Tex. Rev. Civ. Stat. Ann. § 5069-1.07 that mandates use of spreading doctrine to determine whether real-estate-secured loan is usurious), *rev'd in part on other grounds*, 851 S.W.2d 216 (Tex. 1993); Nicoladze v. Lomas & Nettleton Mortgage Inv., 679 S.W.2d 671 (Tex. App. 1984). *But cf. In re* Brummer, 147 B.R. 552 (Bankr. D. Mont. 1992) (under Montana law, spreading doctrine does not apply where transaction facially usurious, but does where usurious interest due to borrower's action; i.e., prepayment or default); Hoffman v. Key Fed. Sav. & Loan Ass'n, 416 A.2d 1265, 1271 (Md. 1979) (statutory allowance of "yield to maturity" allowed spreading only of points or other charges made at loan inception; not applicable if creditor improperly charged interest on progress payments in advance of disbursement; spreading is much like "reasoning that if one who must travel 600 miles drives 375 m.p.h. in the first hour and 25 m.p.h. for each of the next nine hours, a permissible rate of 60 m.p.h. has been achieved"); Benchmark Land Dev., Inc. v. Wooley, 2001 Tex. App. LEXIS 8390 (Dec. 20, 2001) (usurious interest cannot be saved by spreading it out over three subsequent signed notes).

228 This reference is to the amount that the creditor might legally have charged under the usury ceiling, not the amount it might permissibly charge under the terms of the contract. *See, e.g.*, Rent Am., Inc. v. Amarillo Nat'l Bank, 785 S.W.2d 190 (Tex. App. 1990) (using spreading doctrine to find that interest calculation sought in court pleading did not exceed statutory usury ceiling, though it did include unearned interest in excess of rate agreed upon in contract).

creditors to obtain an effective yield in excess of the usury ceiling because it ignores the timing of payments that the creditor receives. Essentially, payments made early in a loan term are more valuable to a creditor than later payments because the creditor has use of the money for a longer time. This is one reason that creditors often require one-time interest payments in the form of points, commitment fees, service charges, and other charges, at the outset of a credit transaction.[229] To the extent that the spreading doctrine ignores the time value of payments in a credit transaction, it can be a loophole in the usury ceiling.

An example may help to show the potential effect of spreading. Assume a twelve-month $1,000 loan, repayable in equal monthly installments, under a 10% simple interest ceiling. The permissible interest charge over the term of this loan is $55.[230] Under the spreading doctrine, it theoretically does not matter when the creditor imposes this $55 charge. In the extreme case, the creditor could require that the borrower pay the $55 at the outset of the transaction, in which case the borrower is effectively receiving not $1,000 in loan proceeds, but only $945.[231] However, the simple interest yield on a twelve-month loan of $945 with equal monthly payments and total interest charges of $55 is approximately 10.57%. Thus, in this example, spreading could increase the yield of the loan by 0.57%.

It should be emphasized that this example is a bit extreme in that all the interest charges were imposed at the outset of the transaction. Many courts that recognize the spreading doctrine would treat this transaction as a $945 loan. For example, under Texas law, it is clear that the "true principal" of a transaction must be determined before spreading is applied,[232] and that the $55 deducted at the outset of the loan would not be treated as principal. However, an interpretation of a Florida spreading statute by that state's Supreme Court suggests that one Florida usury statute would permit a creditor to increase its yield, under the guise of spreading, in precisely the manner that the example indicates.[233] The increase in yield illustrated by the example would occur, albeit to a lesser extent, in any transaction where apparent overcharges early in the term of the loan are spread over later payment periods.[234]

Another example of the application of the spreading doctrine involves extraordinarily expensive home equity loans that flooded Georgia when it repealed its civil usury ceiling. These loans had more than 20 points. Lenders claimed that these points were earned at the outset of the loan, so the yield in the first month was well in excess of 5%. Nonetheless, in *Fleet Finance, Inc. v. Jones*,[235] the Georgia Supreme Court invoked the spreading doctrine (although not by name) to hold that the contracts did not violate a criminal usury cap of "5% per month."

However, it may be that even the *Jones* decision should not be the final word as to whether spreading is available where the statute clearly sets a "*per month*" cap. An earlier decision interpreted similar language in Georgia's small loan act exactly as the *Jones* borrowers argued.[236] It is possible that the fact that it was a criminal statute may have been the critical factor that led the *Jones* court to use the spreading doctrine in the face of the statutory language and long-standing precedent. The court noted that the statute was susceptible of multiple interpretations, and as a criminal statute, it must be construed most favorably to the potentially liable party. It may be that a civil statute, particularly a special usury statute such as a small loan act or its successor, would still be interpreted as in the earlier decision.[237]

#### 5.5.6.2 Spreading in Open-End, Variable-Rate Transactions

Although numerous courts have applied the spreading doctrine in fixed-term transactions, several courts have refused to extend spreading to open-end, variable-rate transactions.[238] The reason seems to be the tenet of usury law that a transaction is usurious at its inception if it is usurious at all. Courts considering the application of spreading to open-end accounts have recognized that usury in such accounts could never be determined until the account was terminated if spreading were

229 *See* § 4.3, *supra* (discussing attraction of points for creditors).

230 Actually it's $55.04, but the amounts are rounded in this example.

231 The process amounts to charging a form of discount interest. *See* § 5.3.3, *supra*.

232 *See, e.g.*, Perry v. Stewart Title Co., 756 F.2d 1197 (5th Cir. 1985) (applying Texas law); Tanner Dev. Co. v. Ferguson, 561 S.W.2d 777 (Tex. 1977).

233 St. Peterburg Bank & Trust Co. v. Hamm, 414 So. 2d 1071 (Fla. 1982) (using face amount of note, including "interest" charges, to calculate contract rate under state spreading statute).

234 In most cases where spreading is an issue, the creditor has collected interest payments throughout the loan term, but has exacted more interest at the beginning of the loan than later in the term. To some extent, of course, this practice of collecting more interest early in the loan term is actuarially justified because the outstanding principal balance is greater than it is later in the term. Yet the size of the interest payments that lenders collect in the form of points and other "up-front" fees more than compensates for this actuarial effect and raises the effective interest rate at the beginning of the loan term. The increase in effective yield occurs even when the one-time fees are quite small, although the smaller the fee, the smaller the increase.

235 430 S.E.2d 352 (Ga. 1993).

236 Hartsfield Co. v. Fulwiler, 200 S.E. 309 (Ga. 1938).

237 *See* § 7.2, *infra* (statutory construction).

238 *See* Connell v. Merrill, Lynch, Pierce, Fenner, & Smith, 578 P.2d 1375 (Cal. 1978), *later opinion at* 662 P.2d 916 (Cal. 1983); Arneill Ranch v. Petit, 134 Cal. Rptr. 456 (Cal. Ct. App. 1976). *See also* Voitier v. First Nat'l Bank of Commerce, 514 F. Supp. 585 (E.D. La. 1981) (rejecting spreading argument although "spreading" terminology not used); Superior Improvement v. Mastic Corp., 604 S.W.2d 950 (Ark. 1980) (same); Sailboat Apartment Corp. v. Chase Manhattan Mortgage & Realty Trust, 363 So. 2d 564 (Fla. Dist. Ct. App. 1978); Norstar Bank v. Pickard & Anderson, 529 N.Y.S.2d 667 (N.Y. App. Div. 1988) (cannot "average" the return on a variable-rate loan over life of loan for purposes of determining usury; to rule otherwise would compel borrowers to pay excessive interest and not seek relief until end of term; creditor, on other hand, could have avoided problem by use of caps or an index that would have avoided usury). *See generally* Annotation, *Usury in Connection with Loan Calling for Variable Interest Rate*, 18 A.L.R.4th 1068.

allowed, because any monthly overcharges could theoretically be spread to later payment periods in which the maximum rate was not charged.

Conversely, any apparently non-usurious account could be made usurious by later overcharges. Faced with the possibility that the presence of usury in an open-end account might depend entirely on the date that the account terminated, some courts seem to have concluded that spreading is unworkable in open-end transactions, and that these transactions are better viewed as a series of (monthly) loans or forbearances which must be individually examined for usury. Other courts, however, have had no problem with the idea of testing for usury at the time an open-end account is terminated and have applied the spreading doctrine to open-end transactions.[239]

### 5.5.6.3 Spreading in Special Situations

A final issue raised by the concept of spreading is the term over which interest payments may be spread. This issue can arise in two basic situations: when the term of the credit is shortened, usually by default or prepayment; and when there is more than one credit transaction between the same debtor and creditor.

As suggested earlier in this discussion, a creditor that assesses one-time fees at the beginning of the term of a loan is charging a higher effective interest rate at the beginning of the term than later in the loan. Under the spreading doctrine, this practice is permissible if the over-all contract rate is below the usury ceiling. Yet what happens when the term of the loan is cut short, perhaps by prepayment? Logically, even under the spreading doctrine, the lender will have charged a higher rate of interest than it would have if the loan had remained in effect for the originally anticipated term, because there will now be fewer payment periods over which the one-time fees can be spread.[240] If the contract interest rate exceeds the statutory limit when the fees are spread over the shortened loan term, usury should result.[241]

There is, however, a major limitation on the argument that the premature termination of credit can cause usury: courts are reluctant to find usury violations based on contingencies within the control of the borrower.[242] Most courts view prepayment and default as contingencies within the borrower's control. Thus, it is probable that the premature termination of a loan through acceleration or prepayment will not in itself cause usury even if the effective interest rate charged on the shortened loan exceeds the usury ceiling.[243] (Yet acceleration caused by the lender's wrongdoing can trigger a usury violation if the effective contract rate caused by the shortened loan term is too high.[244]) Moreover, many modern credit statutes require the creditor to rebate enough interest to the borrower upon early loan termination to ensure that the effective interest rate over the shortened contract term does not exceed the usury ceiling.[245] Failure to provide these rebates may be usurious even if the early termination is caused by the borrower.[246]

The second situation in which the term of a loan can be an issue under the spreading doctrine arises when there is more than one transaction between the debtor and creditor. If some, but not all of the obligations between the parties are usurious when viewed individually, creditors may attempt to spread the excess interest in the apparently usurious notes across the non-usurious obligations to defeat a usury claim. This tactic presumes, of course, that the over-all interest charge when the notes are aggregated is below the maximum permissible for a loan of the size of the aggregated debts.

The validity of spreading interest across two or more notes appears to depend on the relationship, if any, between the notes. Clearly, interest cannot be spread across unrelated debts.[247] However, if a series of notes is created pursuant to a single

239 *See* American Timber & Trading Co. v. First Nat'l Bank, 690 F.2d 781 (9th Cir. 1982); S & A Indus., Inc. v. Bank Atlanta, 543 S.E.2d 743 (Ga. Ct. App. 2000) (applying spreading to line of credit even though term of repayment period not defined); O'Brien v. Shearson, Hayden, Stone, Inc., 586 P.2d 830 (Wash. 1978), *on reconsideration* 605 P.2d 779 (Wash. 1980). *See also In re* Auto Int'l Refrigeration, 275 B.R. 789, 817–818 (Bankr. N.D. Tex. 2002) (using total amount borrower could have borrowed under line of credit, rather than smaller amount actually borrowed), *aff'd,* 307 B.R. 849 (N.D. Tex. 2002).

240 *See* § 4.3.1, *supra.*

241 *See* Kissell v. Gressley, 591 F.2d 47 (9th Cir. 1979) (applying Arizona law).

242 *See* § 4.8.2, *supra.*

243 *See, e.g., In re* Brummer, 147 B.R. 552 (Bankr. D. Mont. 1992) (under Montana law, spreading doctrine applies where usurious interest results from borrower's action, i.e., prepayment or default, though does not apply where transaction facially usurious); French v. Mortgage Guarantee Co., 104 P.2d 655 (Cal. 1940). *But see In re* Auto Int'l Refrigeration, 275 B.R. 789, 809–816 (Bankr. N.D. Tex. 2002) (acceleration of note would have meant that interest was to be spread over shortened term, but not shown here), *aff'd,* 307 B.R. 849 (N.D. Tex. 2002); *In re* Abramoff, 92 B.R. 698 (Bankr. W.D. Tex. 1988) (allowing spreading over actual period borrower had use of funds, but lender's acceleration itself precludes spreading over the original contract term); Armstrong v. Steppes Apts., Ltd., 57 S.W.3d 37 (Tex. App. 2001) (finding loan usurious after spreading charges only over the shortened term after lender accelerated); Financial Sec. Servs. v. Phase I Elecs., 998 S.W.2d 674 (Tex. App. 1999) (an advance payment of interest can be spread only over actual period borrower had use of funds where lender accelerated debt and borrower paid accelerated amount after one year of five-year loan).

244 *See* Kissell v. Gressley, 591 F.2d 47 (9th Cir. 1979); Foster v. Universal CIT Credit Corp., 330 S.W.2d 288 (Ark. 1959) (involuntary prepayment). *Cf. In re* Abramoff, 92 B.R. 698 (Bankr. W.D. Tex. 1988) (spreading over actual period borrower had use of funds, but lender's acceleration itself precludes spreading over the original contract term).

245 *See, e.g.,* Danziger v. San Jacinto Sav. Ass'n, 732 S.W.2d 300 (Tex. 1987) (referring to statute now codified as Tex. Fin. Code § 302.101); Coppedge v. Colonial Sav. & Loan Ass'n, 721 S.W.2d 933 (Tex. App. 1986).

246 *See, e.g.,* Danziger v. San Jacinto Sav. Ass'n, 732 S.W.2d 300 (Tex. 1987) (referring to statute now codified as Tex. Fin. Code § 302.101); Coppedge v. Colonial Sav. & Loan Ass'n, 721 S.W.2d 933 (Tex. App. 1986). *See generally* § 5.8, *infra* (discussing rebates of unearned interest apart from the context of spreading).

247 *See* American Timber & Trading Co. v. First Nat'l Bank, 690 F.2d 781, 790 (9th Cir. 1982).

financing agreement, the notes apparently may be aggregated and the interest spread among them.[248] Similarly, if two notes represent the same debt spreading may be permissible, although determining when a renewal note represents the same debt as its predecessor can be a tricky problem.[249] For example, one Texas court allowed the spreading of interest across a refinancing transaction on the grounds that the old debt was never extinguished,[250] while a bankruptcy court in California refused to spread interest across a transaction in which a credit sale contract (in the guise of a lease) was rewritten as a forbearance at usurious rates.[251]

#### 5.5.6.4 Contract Argument Against Spreading

Consumer law practitioners should observe that spreading usually appears as a defense in a usury action. It is rarely mentioned in the contract itself and may not be closely considered when the contract is drafted. Therefore, creditors may unwittingly insert clauses in the credit contract that are inconsistent with a spreading defense.

For example, one of the justifications for the spreading of loan fees over the term of a loan is that these charges are related to the entire term of the loan and should not be attributed entirely to any one payment period.[252] Yet, to avoid rebates of unearned charges, creditors usually claim that various loan fees are earned at the outset of the loan transaction. Such claims are clearly incompatible with a spreading defense, although whether they would defeat the defense in a jurisdiction that recognizes spreading is unclear.[253] While the argument was unsuccessful in the Georgia Supreme Court, that case involved a criminal usury statute "susceptible of multiple interpretations," which the court said must be construed strictly in favor of the creditor.[254] In the civil context, a court might be more willing to hold the creditor—who drafted the contract—to its own words.[255]

### *5.5.7 Minimum Finance Charges or Service Charges*

Some credit statutes, like the Indiana version of the UCCC, authorize a minimum finance charge. The interrelationship between this charge and a statutory interest rate cap can be confusing. In Indiana, payday lenders argued that the $30 minimum finance charge provision meant that they could charge $30 for any transaction, no matter how short, even if it pushed the APR far above the statutory cap of 36%. The Indiana Supreme Court disagreed, holding that the minimum finance charge merely represented the amount that the lender was entitled to retain out of the finance charge if the borrower prepaid the loan.[256] The finance charge for the full term of the loan as written still had to be within the 36% cap. (Since this decision, the Indiana legislature adopted a separate statute that exempts payday loans from these limits.[257])

## 5.6 Points and Origination Charges

### *5.6.1 Calculation of Points*

Often, the charges that a borrower must pay to obtain credit are not limited to monthly interest payments. Points are a prime example. Especially in real estate transactions, borrowers normally are assessed one-time fees at the consummation of a transaction, in addition to their regular monthly installments. Some of these fees directly compensate the creditor for specific third-party expenses, such as filing fees or appraisal fees, and generally do not present problems in calculation. Other fees, however, are not directly connected to expenses that the creditor has incurred and are expressed in terms of a percentage of the loan that the borrower is receiving. Such fees are called points, discount points, origination fees, commitment fees, service charges, or just loan fees.[258] Throughout most of this treatise, they are referred to simply as "points." In normal

---

248 *See id.* at 789 (9th Cir. 1982); Mayfield v. Oklahoma State Bank, 460 P.2d 414 (Okla. 1969); § 3.9.7, *supra* (discussing a closely related issue, the aggregation of debt for purposes of determining loan size).

249 The issue is similar to the question of whether a renewal note represents the same debt as a preceding usurious note and is therefore tainted with the preexisting usury. *See* § 7.8.4, *infra.*

250 Nicoladze v. Lomas & Nettleton Mortgage Investors, 679 S.W.2d 671 (Tex. App. 1984).

251 Fox v. Peck Iron & Metal, 25 B.R. 674 (Bankr. S.D. Cal. 1982).

252 *See* Arneill Ranch v. Petit, 134 Cal. Rptr. 456 (Cal. Ct. App. 1976).

253 The issues of spreading and rebates are closely related. (For a discussion of rebates, see § 5.8, *infra.*) If a loan fee is "earned" at the outset of a transaction and is therefore exempt from rebate calculations, it would be inconsistent to spread the fee over the term of the loan for rate calculation purposes because the former theory presumes that the whole fee is earned at once, while the latter presumes that part of the fee is earned in each payment period. A creditor that invokes the spreading doctrine, while denying that the fees that it wants to spread are rebateable, is trying to have its cake and eat it too. However, if statutes authorize both spreading and the treatment of points or other fees as earned upon the consummation of a transaction, challenging the inconsistency may be difficult. If the statutes are worded permissively (i.e., points *may* be treated as earned at consummation), then it might be argued that the contractual choice to treat the points as earned should constitute a waiver of a subsequent spreading defense.

254 Fleet Fin., Inc. v. Jones, 430 S.E.2d 352 (Ga. 1993). *See* § 5.5.6.1, *supra.*

For statutory construction rules in civil usury statutes, see § 7.2, *infra. Cf.* Fisher v. Westinghouse Credit Corp., 760 S.W.2d 802 (Tex. App. 1988) (lender cannot spread illegal late charge interest over term of underlying note).

255 At the very least, it might consider the contract to be ambiguous, and as such, should be construed against the drafter.

256 Livingston v. Fast Cash USA, Inc., 753 N.E.2d 572 (Ind. 2001).

257 Ind. Code Ann. § 24-4.5-7-411.

258 Though these are clearly compensation to the creditor, whether they are legally characterized as interest varies, dependent upon state law. *See* § 4.3, *supra.* Points are always treated as "finance charge" under the federal Truth in Lending Act, even when they are not "interest" under state usury law. *See* 12 C.F.R. § 1026.4(b)(3) (Regulation Z).

industry usage, one point is equal to one percent of the face amount of the loan note that the borrower signs.[259]

Although points are often described by creditors as a fee which a borrower must pay, this is not precisely the way they normally work. Instead, points are usually treated as a "discount"[260] withheld from the loan, thus reducing the amount that the borrower receives. For example, assume that a borrower goes to a bank seeking a $100,000 mortgage. The bank offers to make the loan at 10% simple interest, plus three points. Since one point is 1% of the nominal loan amount, in this case one point will equal $1,000. Therefore the bank is demanding $3,000 (three points) in addition to the 10% stated interest. If the borrower agrees to these terms, he will sign a note for $100,000 and will pay 10% on this amount, but he will receive only $97,000 in loan proceeds because of the points.[261]

It does not take great insight to see that the use of points increases a creditor's yield on a loan, and that the stated 10% contract rate in the example is misleading.[262] The precise increase in yield depends on the term of the loan; the shorter the term, the greater the increase.[263] If the loan in the example is a thirty-year fixed-rate mortgage which is not paid off early, the lender's yield will be 10.3657% simple interest, or more than a third of a percentage point higher than the stated rate.[264] Most mortgage loans are retired early, however, so in practice the increase in the loan yield may be significantly higher.[265]

An alternate method of calculating points exists, although it is less often used than the practice just described. This alternative is to calculate points as a percentage of the loan proceeds that the borrower actually receives, rather than as a percentage of the face amount of the loan note. The points are then added on to the proceeds to calculate the amount of the note. Thus, if the borrower wants a $100,000 loan and must pay three points, he would sign a note for $103,000. The yield to the lender under this system, although still above the 10% rate stated on the note, is lower than when the same number of points are treated as a discount,[266] and the disparity may explain why the discount system is more frequently used.

## 5.6.2 *Legal Issues Arising in Calculation of Points*

The legal characterization of points and similar charges as interest generally is discussed at § 4.3, *supra*. This discussion focuses on legal issues that may arise regarding the *calculation* of points.

Usury statutes frequently limit themselves to restricting the effective interest rate that a creditor may charge and may not dictate the manner in which a creditor can calculate its fees. Under these statutes, creditors may calculate points however they please, so long as the resulting interest rate, including the charges for points, does not surpass the usury ceiling. On the other hand, some states have specific limitations on points. These limits should be investigated carefully, since they may continue to apply even if the state eliminates the interest rate ceiling applicable to a transaction.[267]

Specific limitations on points come in several forms. First, some statutes prohibit "paying, adding, or deducting interest in advance," which arguably is violated when points are charged.[268]

---

259 Miner v. Beneficial Mortgage Co. of Kan. (*In re* Miner), 369 B.R. 655, 659 n.4 (Bankr. D. Kan. 2007) (agreeing that one point equals 1% of the loan amount but characterizing "points" to mean "discount points").

As discussed later in this section, points may also be calculated as a percentage of the sum that the borrower actually receives.

260 This discount is technically not "discount interest," discussed at § 5.3.3, *supra*, because there is no time factor in the calculation. Three points on a short-term loan is the same dollar amount as three points on a long-term loan of the same principal, although the charging of points on a short-term loan will increase a lender's yield more than the charging of the same number of points on a long-term loan.

261 If the borrower needs the full $100,000 in cash, the creditor will probably just increase the amount of the loan note so that $100,000 will remain after three points have been subtracted. Specifically, if the borrower signed a note for $103,092.78, 3% of this amount (i.e., three points) would be $3,092.78, and the borrower would be left with exactly $100,000 after the points were subtracted.

262 The Truth in Lending Act disclosures should accurately reflect the interest rate being charged because the points must be included in the TILA finance charge and APR.

263 *See, e.g.*, Bandas v. Citizens State Bank, 412 N.W.2d 818 (Minn. Ct. App. 1987) (stated APR was 14.25%, not including a 1.5% loan origination fee; since note due in fourteen days, including loan origination fee as interest raised effective interest rate to a usurious rate of 51.52%), *rev'd and remanded on other grounds sub nom.* VanderWeyst v. First State Bank, 425 N.W.2d 803 (Minn. 1988).

264 The yield can be calculated in the following manner. First, the monthly payment required to amortize a 10% simple interest loan of $100,000 in equal monthly installments is $877.57, so this is the payment the borrower will be making. However, the borrower is receiving only $97,000, not $100,000, because of the points. The APR on a thirty-year loan of $97,000 with equal monthly payments of $877.57 is 10.3657%, and this is the correct yield. Note, however, that state "spreading" statutes may dictate different methods for calculating the increase in yield due to points. These methods generally understate the increase. Spreading is discussed at § 5.5.6, *supra*.

265 This assumes that the points are not subject to statutory rebate requirements. If points must be rebated upon prepayment, and there is a serious argument that they should be (*see* § 5.8.4.2, *infra*), then prepayment would not increase the loan yield.

266 Specifically, the actuarial yield from this method of calculating points is 10.3548%, which is 0.0109% lower than the yield when points are discounted. The calculation works as follows. The borrower signs a note for $103,000 bearing 10% simple interest. Amortization of this note over thirty years will require equal monthly payments of $903.90. However, the borrower is only getting $100,000, not $103,000. The APR for a $100,000 loan with equal monthly payments of $903.90 over thirty years (which, again, is the payment that the borrower will actually be making) is 10.3548%.

267 *See* Watley v. Transamerica Fin. Servs. (*In re* Watley), 708 So. 2d 890 (Ala. 1997) (statutory cap on points continues to apply even though interest rate is deregulated). *See generally* § 4.3, *supra* (treatment of points as interest or non-interest).

268 *See, e.g.*, *In re* Peterson, 93 B.R. 323 (Bankr. D. Vt. 1988) (allegation that prepaid interest was charged states a viable cause of action, interpreting Vt. Stat. Ann. tit. 9, § 41a(d)(1)).

Second, if a usury statute either restricts the absolute number of points that a creditor may assess or excludes a stated number of points from the statute's definition of "interest," then the manner in which these points are calculated is clearly significant, and the consumer's attorney must read the statutory language very carefully. One critical question is what amount to base the calculation of points on. For example, if a statute allows a creditor to charge only three points, and if points are described as a percentage of loan "principal,"[269] the definition of principal must be checked. Generally, "principal" does not include interest charges such as points, so under these circumstances the points would have to be calculated on the basis of the money actually received by the borrower or paid on his behalf for non-interest expenses. The calculation of points as a discount in this example could be usurious.[270]

Unfortunately, when usury statutes do restrict points, they are often imprecise. Consider, for example, a Missouri statute permitting a lender to charge "a fee not to exceed one percent of the loan amount. . . ."[271] What is the loan amount? Is it the amount of the note? Is it the amount the borrower receives? The answer is not immediately obvious, although a dissection of Missouri case law, or perhaps a closer reading of the statute, might provide some clues. For an example of the differing approaches taken to bring some clarity to these statutes, compare *In re Bogan*,[272] in which "principal amount loaned" was interpreted to exclude the percentage-based loan fee in question, with *Lee v. Beneficial Finance Co.*,[273] in which "face amount of contract" was interpreted to include the loan fee.

Another issue that can arise when a statute restricts the number of points that can be charged is whether excess points are buried among other costs. This issue has been raised in connection with "yield spread premiums," a device whereby the creditor charges a higher rate than it would otherwise impose on a loan, and gives the difference, or some portion of it, to a referring broker.

Among other challenges to the practice, plaintiffs in *Smith v. First Family Financial Services, Inc.*[274] alleged that the table-funding[275] arrangement between a broker and lender was a device to circumvent Alabama's five-point cap. The Alabama Supreme Court held that "[i]t is a part of the origination fee paid to the mortgage broker on the front end of the loan," and that it was a question of fact whether the arrangement was designed to evade the statutory point cap.[276] However in 2005, the Alabama Supreme Court in *Goldome Credit Corp. v. Burke,*[277] overruled its decision in *Smith v. First Family Fin. Services.* The court held that yield spread premiums did not constitute "points" for purposes of calculating the five-point limit on points, finding that a yield spread premium differs from points because it is not charged to or collected from the borrower under a contract, is not fully earned on the date of the loan, and does not, in a prepayment situation, entitle the borrower to a refund or credit. In addition, the court noted that after the court's holding in *Smith*, the state legislature amended the state code to remove any uncertainty regarding whether yield spread premiums require a separate finance charge disclosure. (Yield spread premiums raise a number of other issues as well, and are discussed further at §§ 7.3.4, 9.6, *infra* and in NCLC's *Mortgage Lending* (2012).)

Determining the principal amount on which points can be based raises even more questions when the new loan refinances an old loan from the same lender. Some states allow points to be assessed only on the new funds advanced, i.e., the difference between the principal of the new loan and the unpaid balance of the old loan.[278] A Tennessee Supreme Court decision holds that the net payoff amount of the old loan, not the full balance including unearned interest, should be used in making this calculation.[279] In *Gonzales v. Associates Fin. Servs.*,[280] however, the Kansas Supreme Court interpreted its statute to allow a 2% origination fee to be imposed upon the whole principal of the new loan, not just the new money.

269 *See, e.g.*, 815 Ill. Comp. Stat. § 205/4.1a, which, unfortunately, nowhere defines principal amount.

270 *See, e.g.*, Cheshire Mortgage v. Montes, 612 A.2d 1130 (Conn. 1992) (calculating 10% prepaid finance charge on principal amount including the prepaid finance charge impermissible; effective prepaid finance charge was thus 11%, which exceeded statutory maximum). *See also In re* Bogan, 281 F. Supp. 242 (W.D. Tenn. 1968) (statute allowing loan fee of 4% of "principal amount loaned" interpreted to mean principal *before* loan fee added; fee could not be based on fee itself; since creditor did so, it constituted usury). *But see* Watley v. Transamerica Fin. Servs., 708 So. 2d 890 (Ala. 1997) (points can be included in the "original principal balance" on which points are calculated, where statute also provided that points could be "deducted from the proceeds and included in the original principal"; change in law to add a reference to "original amount financed" may, however, require different interpretation in future).

271 Mo. Rev. Stat. § 408.052 (1990).

272 281 F. Supp. 242 (W.D. Tenn. 1968). *See also* Cheshire Mortgage v. Montes, 612 A.2d 1130 (Conn. 1992) (calculating prepaid finance charge on amount including prepaid finance charge is impermissible).

273 282 S.E.2d 770 (Ga. Ct. App. 1981).

274 626 So. 2d 1266 (Ala. 1993).

275 A table-funded loan is one in which a broker, or "correspondent lender," with no money, closes the loan *in his or her name* with funds supplied by a genuine lender, and immediately assigns the loan to the lender. (Note that for purposes of the Real Estate Settlement Procedures Act (RESPA), the "assignee" is considered the creditor, and the correspondent lender is considered a broker. *See* National Consumer Law Center, Mortgage Lending §§ 3.2, 7.4 (2012).)

276 Smith v. First Family Fin. Servs., Inc., 626 So. 2d 1266, 1271 (Ala. 1993).

277 Goldome Credit Corp. v. Burke, 923 So. 2d 282 (Ala. 2005).

278 *See* § 5.9, *infra* (discussing in detail the calculations involved in refinancing).

279 Hathaway v. First Family Fin. Servs., 1 S.W.3d 634 (Tenn. 1999).

280 967 P.2d 312 (Kan. 1998).

## 5.7 Calculation of Late Charges and Deferral Charges

### 5.7.1 *Late Charges*

Usury statutes often allow creditors to contract for the payment of late charges on delinquent credit accounts. Generally these charges may be imposed only after the expiration of a grace period, frequently ten days, which runs from the date on which an installment payment is contractually due.[281] The legal status of late charges as interest or non-interest charges is discussed at § 4.8, *supra*.

In most transactions, the calculation of late charges is straightforward. They are typically expressed as a percentage of the overdue installment, provided that they do not exceed some amount specified by statute. For example, a usury statute might allow a creditor to assess a late fee of 5% of an overdue installment, not to exceed $5.00.[282] Under this formula, the charge on an overdue installment of $50 would be $2.50 (i.e., 5% of $50), but the fee for an overdue $150 installment would be only $5.00, not $7.50, because of the fixed $5.00 limit in the statute.

Both usury statutes and credit contracts should be carefully read to determine the size of the late fee that may be imposed when a debtor pays only part of the monthly installment on time. The issue in this situation is whether the late fee is calculated as a percentage of the full installment, even though the debtor has actually paid some of this amount on time, or as a percentage of only that part of the installment that is actually late. For example, if a debtor pays only $30 of a regular $50 installment, is the late fee $2.50 (i.e., 5% of $50) or only $1.00 (i.e., 5% of the unpaid portion, $20)? Most usury statutes seem to take the latter approach and limit the late charge to a percentage of the amount actually overdue.[283] This approach makes sense because it provides the debtor with an incentive to make a timely partial payment, rather than no payment at all, and because it reflects the lesser damages incurred by a creditor when a partial payment is made.

If a usury statute does permit a creditor to follow the more lucrative technique of ignoring partial payments in the calculation of late fees, a consumer's attorney should pay close attention to the contractual description of late charges. Late fees may be imposed only as authorized by contract.[284] Furthermore, a Truth in Lending violation may exist if a consumer credit contract does not unambiguously describe the method to be used to calculate a late fee in the event of a partial payment.[285]

A second calculation issue related to late fees is the manner in which a borrower's regular payments are treated once a late charge has been imposed. Most usury statutes limit a creditor to one late charge per installment. However, a single late payment can be transformed into multiple late charges if a borrower's regular installment payments are attributed first to any outstanding late fees and only second to the installment(s) which have come due. This practice, that is known as the "pyramiding" of late charges, is discussed in detail at § 4.8.5, *supra*.

Another issue is whether a creditor who is charging interest on a daily basis can also charge a late charge for a payment that is paid late. The answer will probably depend on the exact language of the statute. A Pennsylvania court found both authorized by its Motor Vehicle Sales Finance Act.[286] Even though the daily interest should be full compensation to the lender for the delay in payment, lenders will seek to justify the late charge in the name of deterrence.

In addition to calculation issues, questions often arise as to whether the creditor had the right to impose the late charge. The statute may require a written agreement[287] or at least a disclosure,[288] and may mandate a grace period. Some creditors have been charged with deliberately posting payments late in order to maximize their revenue from late charges.[289] The loan note and public policy also may disallow the capitalization of late fees when calculating interest.[290]

### 5.7.2 *Deferral Charges*

In addition to allowing late charges, many consumer credit statutes permit creditors to collect a deferment charge (sometimes called an extension or forbearance charge) when monthly payments are deferred for a period of time, extending the maturity date of the loan. Where deferral charges are not specifically addressed by statute, a court may treat such charges as separate forbearance agreements, subject to the relevant usury ceiling.[291]

281 Note that, if the transaction is interest-bearing, the grace period does not affect the accumulation of interest, which accrues during the grace period.

282 *See, e.g.*, Metlife Capital Fin. Corp. v. Washington Avenue Assocs., 732 A.2d 493 (N.J. 1999) (reciting New Jersey statutes allowing late fees as percentage of overdue installment and upholding a similar late fee clause in a contract between two sophisticated commercial parties).

283 *See, e.g.*, U.C.C.C. § 2.502(1) (1974 Model Act).

284 *See* Metro Hauling, Inc. v. Daffern, 723 P.2d 32 (Wash. Ct. App. 1986). *See also* § 4.8.3, *supra* (case law on improperly calculated late charges as interest or overcharge).

285 *See In re* Whitley, 772 F.2d 815 (11th Cir. 1985); Watts v. Key Dodge Sales, Inc., 707 F.2d 847 (5th Cir. 1983). *See generally* National Consumer Law Center, Truth in Lending § 5.9.7 (7th ed. 2010 and Supp.).

While statutory damages are not available for failure to disclose late charges, this violation may be suitable for actual damages. *Id.* §§ 8.5, 8.6.5.2.

286 Harrell v. Chrysler Fin. Co., 811 A.2d 597 (Pa. Super. Ct. 2002).

287 Aldrich & Co. v. Ellis, 52 P.3d 388 (Mont. 2002) (merchant must have written agreement to collect late payment charges on retail installment sales and retail charge accounts but it is unnecessary for accounts receivable).

288 *See* § 10.3.2.2, *infra*.

289 *See* § 5.5.4.5, *supra*.

290 *See, e.g.*, *In re* Graboyes, 371 B.R. 113 (Bankr. E.D. Pa. 2007) (loan note and public policy do not permit capitalization of late fees when calculating interest). *See generally* § 5.5.1, *supra* (further discussion of compounding).

291 *Cf.* Sunburst Bank v. Keith, 648 So. 2d 1147 (Miss. 1995) (oral

Deferral charge provisions generally apply only to *precomputed* consumer loans repayable in substantially equal monthly installments.[292] On interest-bearing accounts, the interest continues to accrue during the deferred period, so there is automatically an adjustment to compensate the creditor for the delay. Precomputed interest, by contrast, is fixed at consummation, on the assumption that the loan will be paid as originally scheduled. Any delay, therefore, requires some adjustment if the creditor is to be compensated for it.[293]

Typical consumer credit statutes provide that a deferral agreement must be in writing[294] or the original loan contract must specifically allow the imposition of a deferral charge.[295] Some state laws specify that the creditor cannot impose or retain a late charge if a deferral charge is applied to the delinquency period.[296] Other aspects of statutory deferral provisions a consumer's attorney should check include: whether deferral of partial monthly installments is allowed and, if so, how it is to be calculated;[297] whether appropriate additional charges (e.g., official fees and taxes, insurance charges, annual credit card fees) may be added to the amount deferred for purposes of computing the deferral charge;[298] whether the statute allows the original loan contract to provide that the creditor may unilaterally grant a deferral and impose related charges where a monthly payment is not made within a set period of time from its due date;[299] and whether the deferment charge is partially refundable if the loan is prepaid during that period.[300]

A sampling of statutes addressing deferral fees shows three methods—which are harder to read than to calculate—for calculating deferral charges. Assume that Carl's job got downsized soon after he took out a precomputed $1,000 loan at 10% for one year on February 1. After making only the first payment of $87.92 on March 1,[301] he finds he needs to ask for a deferral. A partial amortization chart for his loan would show that the interest earned during his second payment interval, due April 1, is $7.67.

| Balance | Interest | – Payment | = New Bal | Due Date |
|---|---|---|---|---|
| $1,000.00 | $8.33 | $87.92 | $920.41 | Mar. 1 |
| $ 920.41 | $7.67 | $87.92 | $840.16 | Apr. 1 |

We can use Carl's request to see how much a deferral would cost him under each of the three sample statutory methods.

1. "*The deferment charge for a one month period may not exceed the applicable interest for the installment period immediately following the due date of the last undeferred payment.*"[302]

Under this method, Carl's charge to defer the April payment one month, until May 1, is $7.67. The "due date of the last undeferred payment" is March 1, and the interest due for the period between March 1 and April 1 is $7.67, according to the amortization chart.[303] He is in effect buying the right to keep his outstanding principal at $920.41 for two months, instead of one, and is paying an extra month's interest at the contract rate to do so.

2. The lender may collect "*a charge not exceeding the rate previously stated to the consumer pursuant to the provisions on disclosure . . . applied to the amount or amounts deferred for the period of deferral. . . .*"[304]

If the disclosed APR in Carl's loan was 10%, one month's deferral would be $7.67 by this method, as well: $920.41 × 10% ÷ 12 (monthly rate) × 1 (month) = $7.67.[305]

3. "*The interest for deferment . . . may not exceed . . . the difference between the refund that would be required for prepayment in full as of the date of deferment and the refund that would be required for prepayment in full one month before the date of deferment . . . multipl[ied] . . . by the number of months in the deferment period.*"[306]

deferral agreements entered into on business loans were separate forbearance agreements subject to maximum annual interest allowed by statute, to be calculated by statutorily required actuarial method; lender exceeded ceiling by using a pro rata calculation in arriving at deferral charge, which failed to take into account the decline in principal balance at time of deferral).

292 *See, e.g.*, Cal. Fin. Code § 22400(a)(4) (West); 205 Ill. Comp. Stat. § 670/15(f)(5); Tex. Fin. Code Ann. § 342.204 (West).

293 *See generally* § 5.8.2, *infra*.

294 *See, e.g.*, Colo. Rev. Stat. § 5-2-204(1); Iowa Code § 537.2503(1); Mass. Gen. Laws ch. 140, § 100; 209 Mass. Code Regs. § 26.01(4)(d) (small loans).

295 *See, e.g.*, Cal. Fin. Code § 22400(a)(4) (West); N.Y. Banking Law § 351(5)(c) (McKinney).

296 *See, e.g.*, Colo. Rev. Stat. § 5-2-204(4); Iowa Code § 537.2503(4); 209 Mass. Code Regs. § 26.01(4)(d).

Since the borrower is essentially buying the right to not make the payment, it is not a late payment.

297 *Compare, e.g.*, Colo. Rev. Stat. § 5-2-204(1) (deferral of part of unpaid installments allowed), *with* 205 Ill. Comp. Stat. § 670/15(f)(5) (allowing only deferment of wholly unpaid installments, though allowed proportionally for partial months).

298 *See, e.g.*, Colo. Rev. Stat. § 5-2-204(2); Iowa Code § 537.2503(2).

299 *See, e.g.*, Colo. Rev. Stat. § 5-2-204(3); Iowa Code § 537.2503.

300 *See, e.g.*, 205 Ill. Comp. Stat. § 670/15(f)(5); Tex. Fin. Code § 342.204(d).

301 The lender used the actuarial method, assuming all payments would be made as scheduled, to precompute the interest. *See, e.g.*, 205 Ill. Comp. Stat. § 670/15(b).

His monthly payments are $87.92, and the total finance charge for the twelve month period would be $55.04. *See generally* § 5.3.1, *supra*.

302 205 Ill. Comp. Stat. § 670/15(f)(5). *See also* Cal. Fin. Code § 22400(a)(4) (West).

303 $920.41 (principal) × 10%/12 (monthly rate) × 1 (month) = $7.67. *See* § 5.3.1, *supra*.

For the aficionado of mathematical minutiae, there is arguably an ambiguity in the Illinois statute used in this example. On the one hand, it says that the precomputed loan includes interest "computed actuarially in advance, assuming all payments will be made when scheduled." 205 Ill. Comp. Stat. 670/15(b). Yet in the same section, it defines "applicable interest" in language that seems to describe the sum of the balances method, a variant on the Rule of 78s. (*See* § 5.8.6.3.4, *infra*.) As is discussed below in connection with the third type of sample deferral formula, that can be a bit more expensive for the borrower.

304 Colo. Rev. Stat. § 5-2-204(1). *Cf.* Iowa Code § 537.2503(1) (1.5% per month, not to exceed the disclosed APR applied to the amount deferred for the time deferred).

305 *See* § 5.3.1, *supra*.

306 Tex. Fin. Code Ann. § 342.204 (West). *See also* N.Y. Banking Law § 351(5)(c) (McKinney).

Carl is a little confused here, because he has not read § 5.8, *infra*, about rebates upon prepayment yet, and does not understand why rules for paying a loan off early should have anything to do with paying to make a loan last longer. But he forges ahead. Taking a detour to that chapter, he sees that there are two customary ways to calculate a rebate upon prepayment: the actuarial method[307] and the Rule of 78s.[308] The second method, the Rule of 78s, has an inherent bias that overcompensates the creditor upon prepayment, and that bias can carry over into deferral fee calculations if the Rule of 78s is the refund rule that serves as the point of reference for the deferral charge calculation.

If the statute governing Carl's loan calls for actuarial rebates, those are, as he sees at § 5.8, *infra*, calculated by subtracting the interest as computed by the actuarial method at the time of prepayment from the total precomputed interest, and refunding the difference. The refund that would be due on Carl's loan if there were a prepayment one month prior to deferral (March 1) would be: $55.04[309] – $8.33 = $46.71. The refund that would be due if there were a prepayment on the date of deferral (April 1) would be: $55.04 – ($8.33 + $7.67) = $39.04. The difference between those two refunds is—voilà—$7.67.[310] The deferral charge by this method is the same as the previous two.

However, if the relevant statute would permit a prepayment rebate calculated by the Rule of 78s (not all do), it is a different story. Using the formula he learns from peeking at § 5.8.6.3, *infra*, he calculates the rebate as of March 1 to be $46.57.[311] As of April 1, it would be $38.81.[312] The difference, and hence the deferral fee, would be $7.76—a bit more than a deferral fee calculated without using rebates as a reference. Not by much, but pennies can add up across a lot of customers and a lot of deferrals.

## 5.8 Rebates of Unearned Charges

### *5.8.1 Overview*

A distinct form of overcharge often appears when credit is retired early by prepayment of the debt (including by refinancing) or when a debt matures early because of default and acceleration. Since the amount of interest due is in part a function of the time the credit is outstanding,[313] shortening the time should, as a matter of logic and fairness, reduce the amount of interest the borrower pays. But that may not always happen. The creditor may impose hidden charges, consisting of any unearned amount of insurance premiums and precomputed interest that it retains upon the early termination of credit.

An example may help to explain how unearned interest is extracted when precomputed credit is paid off early. If a consumer receives a $1,000 loan that is to be paid off over two years with precomputed add-on interest of 24% per year, the total amount repayable will be $1,000 principal + $480 interest = $1,480. In a precomputed transaction, the note would obligate this consumer to pay the full $1,480, typically in equal monthly installments.

After one year of regular payments, the consumer will have paid off half the debt, leaving a balance of $740. At this point, assume that the consumer wins the lottery and wants to pay off the debt. Or assume, more realistically, that the lender accelerates the debt and demands full payment because the consumer has been laid off and defaulted on the payments. Or assume, most realistically, that the lender hears of the consumer's unemployment and sympathetically agrees to refinance the debt with a new loan, most of the proceeds of which will be used to pay off the old debt. In any of these situations, the remaining obligation to be paid off is apparently $740. Yet, if the consumer pays this amount, two years' interest ($480) will have been paid for a loan that actually lasted only one year. This would be an effective add-on interest rate of 48%, caused by the lender's retaining the second year's unearned interest charges.

Similarly, if the borrower purchases a two-year credit life insurance policy, it is common for the lender to deduct the entire two-year premium from the proceeds of the loan.[314] If the loan is then paid off after only one year, the consumer will have received only part of the coverage paid for. The premium for the second year is unearned and, if not rebated, will constitute a hidden overcharge.[315] Note that insurance premium rebates will be necessary even if the loan is interest-bearing and not precomputed, because, regardless of the method of interest calculation, the insurance premium often is calculated and prepaid on the assumption of a two-year credit repayment period. In other words, the insurance premium may be precomputed even if the loan is not.[316]

The subsections that follow discuss the legal mandates regarding rebates and explain the necessary formulae to make the calculations to assess a consumer credit transaction for this kind of an overcharge. Prepayment penalties are conceptually distinct, but, like unrebated charges, they economically penalize consumers who want to retire their debt early. They are men-

307 *See* § 5.8.6.4, *infra.*

308 *See* § 5.8.6.3, *infra.*

309 Remember that the interest on $1,000 at 10% actuarial for twelve months is $55.04. *See* note 301, *supra.*

310 $46.71 – $39.04 = $7.67

311 ($55.04) × (0.8462) = $46.57.

312 ($55.04) × (0.7051) = $38.81.

313 *See* §§ 5.2, 5.3.1.1, *supra.*

314 In open-end credit, by contrast, the credit insurance premium is usually paid month-by-month, for one month of coverage at a time. Because of pressure from consumers and regulators, some closed-end lenders are also now charging for credit insurance on a month-by-month basis, rather than deducting the entire premium for the full term of the loan from the loan proceeds.

315 *See, e.g.*, Varner v. Century Fin. Co., 738 F.2d 1143 (11th Cir. 1984) (interest and charges forfeited under Georgia Industrial Loan Act when loan agreement failed to provide for rebate of unearned insurance premium); Clyde v. Liberty Loan Co., 287 S.E.2d 551 (Ga. 1982) (usury for failure to rebate insurance premiums); Brown v. Associates Fin. Servs. Corp., 346 S.E.2d 873 (Ga. Ct. App. 1986). *See generally* § 6.10, *supra.*

316 *See* § 8.6, *infra.*

tioned here but are discussed in more detail in NCLC's *Mortgage Lending* § 8.11 (2012).

For consumers who refinance their debt, unrebated charges (whether legal or not) become part of the principal of the new loan, and, in turn, inflate the cost of the new loan. The interaction of prepayment costs with refinancing costs can make the cost of the credit spiral upward all out of proportion to its nominal cost. These techniques for increasing the cost of credit—the mathematics of loan flipping—are discussed at § 5.9, *infra*.

The windfall that a creditor would receive if it could retain unearned charges upon prepayment or acceleration of precomputed debt has been widely recognized, and rebates are required by state credit laws or the federal rebate law[317] in all or almost all consumer credit transactions. Even in the absence of a specific statute or contract provision requiring a rebate, a court may impose such a requirement based on an equitable principle that unearned interest must be deducted upon acceleration and payment of a debt prior to maturity.[318]

Thus, although the proper formula for calculating the rebate varies,[319] and there are questions about what charges are subject to rebate,[320] it is almost universally recognized that a consumer who prepays a credit obligation is entitled to a rebate of unearned interest.

The calculations and other details of the required rebate are analyzed in the next subsections and will address:

- Whether a transaction is structured so that interest is precomputed (in general, a rebate is required only in precomputed transactions);
- What constitutes prepayment and how to determine the date of prepayment;
- The particular charges that are subject to rebate;
- Which rebate calculation formula is required;
- How to calculate a rebate by each of the standard rebate methods;
- The point at which a creditor has charged illegal unearned interest.

317 15 U.S.C. § 1615. *See* § 5.8.6.1.2, *infra.*

318 *See In re* Coxson, 43 F.3d 189 (5th Cir. 1995) (Texas follows equitable rule requiring surrender of unearned interest to obtain a foreclosure; rule invoked to avoid usurious construction of contract silent about rebate upon acceleration); Aardwoolf Corp. v. Nelson Capital Corp., 861 F.2d 46 (2d Cir. 1988); Denley v. Peoples Bank, 553 So. 2d 494 (Miss. 1989) (even though statute was silent as to prepayment rebate method, use of Rule of 78s was usurious when it caused lender's yield to exceed statutory ceiling stated as actuarial rate; that implies a requirement of an actuarial rebate on precomputed loans).

319 *See* § 5.8.6.1, *infra.*

320 *See* § 5.8.4, *infra.*

## 5.8.2 *When Are Charges Unearned? Distinction Between Precomputed and Interest-Bearing Credit*

### 5.8.2.1 Introduction

There are two basic ways of structuring consumer credit transactions: "interest bearing" and "precomputed." The distinction between these is critical to understanding rebates, as a rebate of unearned interest is required only if the transaction is precomputed.

An interest bearing transaction is one in which the borrower agrees to pay the principal, plus interest as it accrues during the course of the loan. Interest is added to the debt only as it is earned.[321] Thus as a general rule, there is no unearned interest involved in interest-bearing credit, though, as is discussed below, that is not an absolute.

A precomputed transaction, in contrast, folds into the borrower's legal obligation at the outset all the interest to be earned over the originally scheduled life of the loan. The borrower agrees to pay a "total of payments" that includes both the principal and all the interest that is scheduled to be earned. As payments are made, they are subtracted from the "total of payments" and not allocated between interest and principal,[322] so at any point prior to the scheduled maturity, the remaining debt (the sum of the remaining payments due) will include some interest not yet earned. It is primarily this context in which rebate issues arise.

The following hypothetical illustrates the differences between these two ways of structuring a credit transaction. Consumer A and Consumer B each borrow $1,000 at an actuarial interest rate of 14.45% and are obligated to make eleven monthly payments of $90.00 each and a final, 12th monthly payment of $89.98. However, assume that both consumers make five monthly payments of $90 exactly as scheduled and then, having shared a lottery win, both prepay their loans. If A's loan is "interest bearing" and B's loan is "precomputed," the consequences that follow from prepayment will be very different, as explained in detail in the next two subsections. If A and B had each made all 12 payments exactly on time, there would have been no discernible difference between the two loans.

321 At any given time, the amount due on an interest-bearing contract is the unpaid principal balance plus accrued interest. *See, e.g., In re* Curtis, 83 B.R. 853 (Bankr. S.D. Ga. 1988); Wombold v. Associates Fin. Servs. Co., 104 P.3d 1080, 1089 (Mont. 2004) (rebate formula only applies to add-on loans, not interest-bearing loans); Foster v. Centrex Capital Corp., 80 S.W.3d 140 (Tex. App. 2002) (finding that finance charge was precomputed, so statutory rebate formula applied); Myles v. Resolution Trust Corp., 787 S.W.2d 616 (Tex. App. 1990) (no usury contracted for in acceleration clause of interest-bearing contract).

322 *See* § 5.8.2.3, *infra*; James H. Hunt, *The Rule of 78: Hidden Penalty for Prepayment in Consumer Credit Transactions*, 55 B.U. L. Rev. 331, n.2 (1975).

#### 5.8.2.2 Interest Bearing

The traditional way to compute interest is on an "interest-bearing" basis. In an interest-bearing transaction, the consumer agrees to pay the principal (or amount financed, etc.) plus interest as it accrues at a certain periodic rate. Usually, the consumer signs a note agreeing to pay the principal "together with interest thereon at an annual rate of _______%."

With an "interest-bearing" note, the lender sets up the loan on a "declining balance" basis.[323] Every time a periodic payment is made, a periodic interest rate (the annual rate divided by the number of periods) is applied to the outstanding balance. The interest that is produced (plus late charges, if any) is subtracted from the payment; the remainder of the payment is applied to the outstanding balance, thereby reducing it. Each time a payment is made, the same process is repeated, until the outstanding balance is reduced to zero.

If at any time the amortization is interrupted (because of prepayment, acceleration, refinancing, etc.), the outstanding balance can be quickly determined by adding any interest (and other charges) that have accrued since the last payment to the previous outstanding balance. Ordinarily, no "rebates" of unearned interest charges have to be calculated, since the consumer is only being charged for interest that has been earned.[324] Likewise, if the consumer makes additional payments toward principal, the principal balance on which interest is computed will be reduced, and the consumer will pay less interest.[325]

In our hypothetical, Consumer A has signed an "interest-bearing" note because she has agreed to pay "$1,000 together with interest thereon at the annual rate of 14.45%." She has also agreed to the payment schedule described above. Once the loan has been consummated, the lender sets up its books or computer on a declining balance method at an annual actuarial interest rate of 14.45%, a monthly periodic rate of 1.204% (14.45% divided by 12), or on a daily rate, using a 365-day year, of .0396% (14.45% divided by 365).[326] Assuming that Consumer A makes monthly payments exactly as scheduled, every time Consumer A makes a payment, the outstanding balance is multiplied by the monthly periodic rate of 1.204% to produce the interest earned during the previous month. The interest is subtracted from the payment, the remainder of which reduces the outstanding balance.

Chart 8[327] (Amortization of $1,000 Loan at 8% Add-on Interest) illustrates the process. For example, with the first monthly payment, the 1.204% periodic monthly rate is multiplied by the $1,000 unpaid balance to produce $12.04 interest. This interest is subtracted from the $90 payment and the $77.96 remainder is applied to the $1,000 unpaid balance, thereby reducing it to $922.04.[328] Every month the same process is repeated. If Consumer A made every $90 payment (and the final $89.98 payment) exactly on time, at the end of the twelve months, the balance would be zero.

However, under the hypothetical, Consumer A decides to pay off her loan immediately after making the fifth $90 payment. As can be seen, the new unpaid balance *after* the fifth payment is credited is $600.70. Assuming that there are no prepayment penalties, other additional charges, or any unearned charges that would have to be rebated (for example, unearned credit insurance premiums),[329] Consumer A need only pay the lender $600.70 to pay off the loan completely. Consumer A has been charged only for interest that has been earned. As noted on Chart 8, after five months $50.70 in interest has been earned.[330]

Since, in an interest-bearing transaction, a consumer is charged interest only as it is earned, there is generally no need to rebate unearned interest if the consumer prepays the obligation. However, rebate issues can arise in interest-bearing transactions, as contract interest may not be the only type of charge imposed. Most commonly, both precomputed and interest-bearing loans may contain other charges that are priced in relation to time, such as credit insurance premiums. These will need to be rebated upon early termination.[331] Arguments may arise about other charges, such as points, origination fees, or service charges, which may be imposed in both precomputed and interest-bearing transactions. Creditors argue that these kinds of charges are "earned at consummation" and therefore are not subject to rebate.[332]

Finally, an examination of some lenders' amortization schedules for interest-bearing loans may show that the "interest earned" figures have been calculated upon the infamous Rule of 78s, rather than the true, actuarial method of calculation. The Rule of 78s is discussed in detail at § 5.8.6.3, *infra*, but for now, suffice it to say that it is neither an accurate nor a fair method of determining earned interest. Rather, it is a shorthand formula devised in "the pre-electronic world"[333] to *approximate* earned interest in short term loans with low rates,[334] and one that is always biased in the creditor's favor.[335] In longer term or higher

323 *See* § 5.3.1.1, *supra*.

324 *See, however*, § 5.8.4.2, *infra* (rebates and points).

325 *See* § 5.8.3.2, *infra* (discussion of partial prepayments).

326 For a case dealing with the details of converting a daily rate to an annual rate under a state statute that incorporated TILA's calculation methods, see Hooks v. Cobb Ctr. Pawn & Jewelry Brokers, Inc., 527 S.E.2d 566 (Ga. Ct. App. 1999) (where statute allowed 25% interest "per 30 day period," annual rate was to be computed by dividing 25% by 30 to get a daily rate, and then multiplying the daily rate by 365, rather than by multiplying the thirty-day rate by 12).

327 *See* § 5.3.2.1, *supra*.

328 $1,000.00 – $77.96 = $922.04.

329 *See* § 6.10, *infra*.

330 This is the sum of $12.04, $11.10, $10.15, $9.19, and $8.22, the interest earned each month during the first five months.

331 *See* §§ 5.8.4.1, 6.10, *infra*.

332 *See* § 5.8.4.2, *infra*.

333 Kedziora v. Citicorp Nat'l Servs., 780 F. Supp. 516, 525 (N.D. Ill. 1991), *quoting* Peter Canellos & Edward Kleinbard, *The Miracle of Compound Interest: Interest Deferral and Discount after 1982*, 38 Tax. L. Rev. 565, 566 (1983).

334 Peter Canellos & Edward Kleinbard, *The Miracle of Compound Interest: Interest Deferral and Discount after 1982*, 38 Tax. L. Rev. 565, 566, 581 (1983); James H. Hunt, *The Rule of 78: Hidden Penalty for Prepayment in Consumer Credit Transactions*, 55 B.U. L. Rev. 331–332, 338, 344 (1975).

335 "This is always true; the 78's method favors the lender." Financial Publishing Co., Financial 78's Method Handbook 6 (Pub. No. 841

rate transactions, the distortion is "absurd"[336] and should not be used.

If the Rule of 78s would not otherwise be permitted in connection with the transaction, a creditor's effort to extract its extra profit from the consumer upon early payment by the artifice of "earning" it each period prior to pay-off on an interest-bearing contract should be viewed as an impermissible device to evade the law.[337] It is difficult for a creditor to offer a legitimate reason to use it when "address[ing] the issue from first principles" and "as a matter of logic and statutory construction."[338] Generally accepted accounting principles do not permit interest to be imputed by the rule except where the result is "not materially different" from the interest method.[339] The IRS takes the position that, even when a loan agreement provides that interest shall be earned by the Rule of 78s, "no deduction for interest will be allowed for any year in excess of the economic accrual of interest,"[340] because of the high degree of distortion it creates.[341] And courts have generally disfavored the rule except when it was *explicitly* sanctioned by statute or administrative rule.[342] Consequently, absent express authorization, any use of the Rule of 78s—whether to calculate rebates in precomputed transactions, or to accrue interest in interest-bearing transactions—should be challenged.

### 5.8.2.3 Precomputed

The other principal way of structuring consumer credit transactions is on a "precomputed" basis. Until fairly recently, almost all consumer credit installment transactions, with the notable exception of mortgages, were structured on a "precomputed" basis.

"Precomputed" is clearly a term of art, because in both "interest-bearing" and "precomputed" transactions, the interest that would be earned if every payment were made on time is precomputed in the sense that it is calculated in advance. However, "precomputed" transactions are called such because the interest for the transaction has been included in the amount the consumer *contractually* agrees to pay.

In a "precomputed" transaction, the consumer agrees to pay the *total of payments*, which includes both principal and all anticipated interest.[343] At the beginning of a precomputed transaction, the creditor calculates the interest that will be earned over the course of the transaction. However, during the life of the transaction, the creditor will not calculate the interest earned during each periodic payment interval. The creditor will not set up the loan on a "declining balances" basis and indeed, unless the loan is prepaid in some fashion, the creditor need not ever make any "interest" calculations. Instead, every time a periodic payment is made, the creditor will subtract the pay-

---

Rev. Apr. 1982). *See also* James H. Hunt, *The Rule of 78: Hidden Penalty for Prepayment in Consumer Credit Transactions*, 55 B.U. L. Rev. 331, 338, 345–346 (1975).

336 Financial Publishing Co., Yields If Prepaid, vi (1970), *quoted in* James H. Hunt, *The Rule of 78: Hidden Penalty for Prepayment in Consumer Credit Transactions*, 55 B.U. L. Rev. 331, 338 (1975).

For examples of the unfairness of the use of the rule in long-term loans, see Draper v. American Funding, Ltd., 285 Cal. Rptr. 640 (Cal. Ct. App. 1991) (use of Rule of 78s instead of actuarial method cost borrower $17,410); Pysh v. Security Pac. Hous. Serv., 610 A.2d 973 (Pa. Super. Ct. 1992) (use of Rule of 78s would result in early pay-off balance approximately $3,000 greater than actuarial method); Livingston v. Vanguard Fed. Sav. Bank, 563 A.2d 175 (Pa. Super. Ct. 1989) (manufactured home buyers, despite making payments for 4.5 years on a fifteen-year contract, would have had a pay-off of about $700 more than they borrowed).

337 *See* § 3.9.1, *supra* (courts look to substance, not form of transaction).

338 Kedziora v. Citicorp Nat'l Servs., 780 F. Supp. 516, 524 (N.D. Ill. 1991) (refusing to dismiss claim that the use of the rule upon early termination of a lease was an unenforceable penalty).

339 Financial Accounting Standards Board, FASB Accounting Standards, § I.69.108 (2008–2009 ed.).

340 Rev. Rul. 83-84, 1983-1 CB97, 1983 IRB LEXIS 390.

341 *See* Prabel v. Commissioner, 882 F.2d 820 (3d Cir. 1989); Mulholland v. United States, 22 F.3d 1105 (table), 1994 U.S. App. LEXIS 5109 (Fed. Cir. 1994); LaVerne v. Commissioner, 94 F.T.C. 637 (1990), *aff'd on other grounds*, 956 F.2d 274 (9th Cir. 1992) (table); Levy v. Commissioner, 92 F.T.C. 1360 (1989). *See also* German v. Commissioner, 1993 WL 42850 (U.S. Tax. Ct. Feb. 22, 1993), *aff'd*, 46 F.3d 1141 (9th Cir. 1995).

There was formerly an exception for short-term consumer loans, Rev. Proc. 83-40, 1983-1 CB 774, 1983 IRB LEXIS 481. This exception has been eliminated, however, and "the Rule of 78s is no longer an acceptable method of accounting for federal income tax purposes." § 5.04 of Rev. Proc. 99-49, 1999 IRB LEXIS 456 (Dec. 27, 1999). *See also* Rev. Proc. 97-37, 1997 IRB LEXIS 241 (Aug. 18, 1997).

A borrower who actually pays a "78s penalty" (*see* § 5.8.6.3, *infra*) upon prepayment may deduct it. Rev. Rul. 86-42, 1986-1 CB82; 6-1b. The Third Circuit, in *Prabel*, though, stated that in the event of prepayment, the difference between the economic accrual interest owed and that determined to be owed under the Rule of 78s "should be considered a prepayment penalty." 882 F.2d at 827. *See also* Peter Canellos & Edward Kleinbard, *The Miracle of Compound Interest: Interest Deferral and Discount after 1982*, 38 Tax. L. Rev. 565, 566, 585 (1983) (78s "should be viewed as a hidden prepayment penalty, not an accurate measure of the interest cost per period.").

342 *See In re* Jungkurth, 74 B.R. 323 (Bankr. E.D. Pa. 1987) (where statute prohibits prepayment penalties but does not specify a method of calculating rebates, the actuarial method must be used; unless expressly authorized by statute, use of the Rule of 78s would constitute a prepayment penalty); Dechow v. Sko-Fed Credit Union, 536 N.E.2d 1382 (Ill App. Ct. 1989) ("it is untenable to suggest that interest 'accrues' according to the Rule of 78s"); Denley v. Peoples Bank, 553 So. 2d 494 (Miss. 1989) (even though statute was silent as to prepayment rebate method, use of Rule of 78s was usurious when it caused lender's yield to exceed statutory ceiling stated as actuarial rate; that implies a requirement of an actuarial rebate on precomputed loans). *See also* Kedziora v. Citicorp Nat'l Servs., 780 F. Supp. 516 (N.D. Ill. 1991). *But see* Ortegel v. ITT Thorp Corp., 569 N.E.2d 586 (Ill. App. Ct. 1991) (use of Rule of 78s is not a prepayment penalty and was not prohibited in a 1983 mortgage in excess of $25,000. *Note*: It is clear from the court's discussion that it was confused about the nature of the rule (e.g., "the borrower must pay the interest even if the loan is not prepaid," *id.* at 590), so this case should be viewed as an anomaly).

343 Contrast this with an "interest-bearing" transaction in which the consumer agrees to pay the *principal* plus interest as it accrues. *See* Foster v. Centrex Capital Corp., 80 S.W.3d 140 (Tex. App. 2002) (construing contract as a precomputed transaction).

ment from the original total of payments. If the consumer makes every payment on time, the total of payments will be reduced to zero and the loan will be fully paid.

If the consumer makes a late payment, clearly the creditor cannot charge extra interest, since interest calculations are not made during the life of the precomputed transaction. That is not to say, however, that a lender will not be compensated for the late payment. First, the relevant law and contract will usually authorize the lender to impose a late charge.[344] This late charge often exceeds the amount of interest that would be earned in an interest-bearing transaction.

Second, the lender may also be allowed to impose a "deferral" fee, the payment of which allows the consumer to make one or more payments later than originally scheduled. Again, the deferral fee often exceeds the amount of interest that would be earned in an interest-bearing transaction. Finally, the lender has various debt collection techniques, ranging from simple moral suasion to threats of acceleration or repossession, that may discourage the consumer from making late payments.

Precomputed transactions clearly offer creditors a simple bookkeeping method. Instead of being concerned about declining balances, periods between payments, interest earned during each period, etc., the creditor need only keep a simple record or ledger of the account. It starts with the total of payments. Then, each payment is subtracted from the total of payments (and late charges are added to the total of payments). Assuming that the creditor's records and addition/subtraction are accurate, the loan will be fully paid when the total of payments has been reduced to zero.

Prepayment poses some difficulty, however. It would be unfair to require the consumer to simply pay the unpaid total of payments, since that includes interest that would have been earned over the full loan term, but has not yet been earned at the time of prepayment. Hence most state laws governing consumer credit transactions have long required that unearned interest and other unearned charges be rebated when a precomputed contract is terminated early, and in 1992 Congress mandated rebates of unearned interest in all consumer credit transactions.[345]

The simplicity inherent in bookkeeping for precomputed transactions is directly related to the inherent simplicity of the add-on and discount methods of calculating interest.[346] Just as the difficulty of calculating actuarial interest for installment transactions led to the widespread use of add-on and discount interest, so the relative complexity of keeping books on an interest-bearing basis has led to the widespread use of precomputed transactions.

In the hypothetical, we know that Consumer B signed a "precomputed" note because she has agreed to pay $1,079.98 (total of payments) in eleven monthly installments of $90 each and a twelfth monthly installment of $89.98. This total of payments includes $1,000 principal and $79.98 precomputed interest. The promise-to-pay portion of the note need not refer to any interest rate, because the interest has been "precomputed" and already included in the total of payments.

Once the loan has been consummated, the lender sets up its books or computer on a declining total of payments method, beginning with a total of payments of $1,079.98. Every time Consumer B makes a $90 payment, the payment is subtracted from the unpaid total of payments. For example, after Consumer B has made her first $90 payment, the lender subtracts $90 from the $1,079.98 unpaid total of payments for a new balance of $989.98.[347] The lender will also *add* to the unpaid total of payments any late charge or other charges that have been earned since the last payment.

Every month the same process is repeated. If Consumer B makes every $90 payment (and the final $89.98 payment) exactly on time (or at least does not make any late payments and thereby avoids late charges), at the end of the twelve months, the balance will be zero.[348] As mentioned previously, there are no practical differences between interest-bearing and precomputed transactions when every payment is made on time and all payments are made.

However, under the hypothetical, Consumer B decides to pay off her loan immediately after making her fifth $90 payment. The unpaid balance after five payments of $90 is $629.98,[349] assuming that no late charges or other charges have been added on. If the lender asked Consumer B to pay $629.98, Consumer B would point out that this would be unfair. The $629.98 unpaid total of payments includes interest that would have been earned if the loan went the full twelve months, but only five months' interest has been earned. In other words, not all of the $979.98 precomputed interest has been earned after five months, and some of it should be rebated.

At this point, the lender suddenly remembers his legal, contractual, and moral obligation to rebate unearned interest in the event of prepayment.[350] The lender calculates the rebate by using the Rule of 78s, which, as is explained at § 5.8.6.3, *infra*, gives it a rebate percentage of 35.90% or .3590.[351] Multiplying 35.90% times the precomputed interest of $79.98 produces a rebate of unearned interest of $28.71.[352] (This means that *earned* interest = $79.98 − $28.71 = $51.27.) The *unearned* interest of $28.71 is subtracted from the unpaid total of payments of $629.98 to produce a "payoff" balance of $601.27.[353]

Note that this figure is slightly higher than the $600.70 "payoff" balance for the interest-bearing loan. The difference resulted because in the interest-bearing transaction, only $50.70 in interest was earned after the fifth payment, while in the

344 *See* §§ 4.8, *supra*, 5.7, *infra*.

345 15 U.S.C. § 1615(a)(1). How rebates of unearned charges are calculated is discussed at § 5.8.6, *infra*.

346 *See* §§ 5.3.2, 5.3.3, *supra*. Indeed those two methods are generally used only in precomputed transactions.

347 $1,079.98 − $90.00 = $989.98.

348 $1,079.98 − (11 × $90 + 1 × $89.98) = 0.

349 5 × $90 = $450.00. $1,079.98 − $450.00 = $629.98.

350 *See* §§ 5.8.3, 5.8.6, *infra*.

351 (7 × 8) ÷ (12 × 13) = 0.3590.

352 $79.98 × 0.3590 = $28.71.

353 $629.98 − $28.71 = $601.27.

precomputed transaction, $51.27 was considered "earned" after the fifth payment.[354]

## 5.8.3 What Constitutes Prepayment

### 5.8.3.1 Early Termination

A rebate is required only if the borrower repays the loan early. The key word is "early." If a borrower defaulted on the last two payments of a loan that was scheduled to mature on April 1, 2009, but the creditor did not seek payment until June 1, 2009, there will be no rebate issues. Since the loan went to (and past) maturity, all the precomputed interest would have been fully earned, as would any credit insurance premiums.[355]

Also related to the "early termination" prerequisite is how rebates are to be handled when the transaction is *involuntarily* terminated prior to scheduled maturity. In the event of default, the loan may mature early through acceleration. Involuntary early termination of a consumer credit transaction triggers rebate requirements, under both the 1992 federal rebate law[356] and the Home Ownership and Equity Protection Act's absolute prohibition against the Rule of 78s in high-cost mortgages.[357] State law often mandates rebates upon involuntary early termination, as well.[358] (However, as will be seen at § 5.8.5, *infra*, fixing the precise date to use in making the calculations is not as obvious as it is when a voluntary pay-off has occurred.)

### 5.8.3.2 Partial Prepayments

Federal law and most state laws typically do not require rebates for "partial prepayments."[359] These are early payments that are too small to retire the consumer's total debt. If, for example, a borrower took out a loan repayable in twenty-four equal monthly installments and then paid both the fifth and sixth installments when only the fifth had come due, the borrower would have made a partial prepayment on the loan. If the lender in this example were using interest-bearing bookkeeping,[360] the partial prepayment would work to the borrower's advantage because the extra payment would be used to pay down the outstanding principal balance of the loan. Subsequent monthly interest payments would be calculated using this reduced principal amount, and the borrower would save on interest charges.[361]

In a precomputed transaction, on the other hand, the borrower will frequently receive no economic benefit from a partial prepayment unless the contract provides for some interest adjustment.[362] The reason is that the total amount of interest due on the contract has been predetermined, and despite the fact that the partial prepayment will render some of this interest unearned, most usury laws require no rebates of unearned interest in the case of partial prepayments. To the extent that any justification exists for this legal omission, it is that creditors do not want to have to recalculate precomputed debts whenever a partial prepayment is made, and partial prepayments can conceivably occur many times in the term of a single loan.

Practitioners representing borrowers who have made partial payments in precomputed transactions should check the language of both the state usury statutes and the credit contract to see how partial payments are treated. A few state statutes do require that the consumer receive credit for partial prepayment by some mechanism.[363] The federal act requires rebates only in the event of complete prepayment,[364] but that is a minimum standard. It should not preempt more protective state laws,[365] and certainly parties can contract for a more favorable rule.[366]

354 The Rule of 78s, used in this hypothetical, is a short-cut formula for calculating interest that has a consistent bias in favor of the creditor. For this reason, there are legal restrictions on its use. *See* § 5.8.6.1, *infra*.

355 There may be another issue, however, as to how the creditor calculated any interest due after maturity and before the legal action. Some contracts provide for lower post-maturity rates (though rarely these days), others provide for continuing at the original rate, and yet others provide for a higher "default" rate. Some predatory home equity lenders have contracted for default rates of 36–42% on fully secured loans. As a consequence Congress prohibited increasing the interest rate upon default for high-cost mortgages. Home Ownership and Equity Protection Act, 15 U.S.C. § 1639(d). Some state statutes may regulate default rates, as well. *See, e.g.*, Ala. Code § 5-18-15(j) (small loan maximum interest reduced to 8% six months after maturity). *See generally* § 4.8.4, *supra* (delinquency penalties as liquidated damages).

356 15 U.S.C. § 1615(a)(3). *See* § 5.8.6.1.2, *infra*.

357 15 U.S.C. § 1639(d). *See* § 5.8.6.1.3, *infra*; National Consumer Law Center, Truth in Lending § 9.6.9.2 (7th ed. 2010 and Supp.).

358 *See, e.g.*, Iowa Code § 537.2510(6). *See also* Union Trust Co. v. Tyndall, 428 A.2d 428 (Md. 1981); First Va. Bank v. Settles, 588 A.2d 803 (Md. Ct. Spec. App. 1991) (equating repossession sale with prepayment).

359 *See, e.g.*, 15 U.S.C. § 1615(a); Neb. Rev. Stat. § 45-1024(2)(b), (c) (requiring rebates for "prepayment in full"). *But see* Cal. Fin. Code § 22400(a)(3) (West) (recomputation required for partial prepayment of three or more installments).

360 *See* § 5.8.2.2, *supra*.

361 On the other hand, the borrower receives no benefit from prepayment under a purportedly interest-bearing system used by a few lenders that treats prepayments as prepaid interest instead of crediting them against the principal balance. Such manipulative bookkeeping could be usurious if it raised a lender's yield above the usury ceiling. Otherwise it might be challenged as a breach of contract or as a violation of state statutes prohibiting unfair or deceptive acts and practices. Another technique some lenders use is to hold a prepayment in a suspense account until the next regularly scheduled payment date arrives. These lenders may, however, apply the prepayment to reduce the principal if the borrower so specifies when making the payment.

362 Of course, the borrower would gain some benefit if he or she made a partial prepayment of at least the amount of one installment and then continued to make regular payments. Under this scenario, the debtor would ultimately make a full prepayment one or more installment periods before the loan had been scheduled to be retired, and the debtor would receive some rebate at that point.

363 *See, e.g.*, Cal. Fin. Code § 22400(a)(3) (West) (contract must be recomputed when a prepayment of three installments or more is made); Md. Code Ann., Com. Law § 12-308(c)(2) (West) (partial prepayments must be applied first to accrued interest, then to reduce the principal balance).

364 15 U.S.C. § 1615(a).

365 § 5.8.6.1.7, *infra*.

366 *Cf.* Sanders v. Lincoln Serv. Corp., 1993 WL 112543 (N.D. Ill.

Typically, however, usury statutes will neither require nor prohibit rebates for partial prepayment, and the contract language will therefore control.[367] If the contract does not specifically distinguish full and partial prepayments, contract provisions providing rebates of unearned interest may arguably apply to both types of prepayment. However, most precomputed credit contracts expressly deny any creditor obligation to give rebates for partial prepayments, and absent the mandate of a state statute, consumers who have voluntarily made partial prepayments are not entitled to any rebates.

## 5.8.4 *What Charges Are Subject to Rebate?*

### 5.8.4.1 General: Contract Interest in Precomputed Transactions; Other Charges and Fees

In all consumer credit transactions, the creditor must "promptly refund any unearned portion of the interest charge to the consumer."[368] In precomputed transactions, by definition there will be unearned interest when the loan is fully prepaid,[369] and so a refund is necessary. Creditors usually charge debtors not just the stated contract interest but also numerous fees.[370] This practice enables a creditor to understate the actual interest rate it is charging, but it is also attractive to creditors because it may allow them to limit the size of the rebates they must give upon acceleration or prepayment. (A graphic example of how this can increase the creditor's actual yield upon prepayment is described at § 4.3.1, *supra*.)[371] The trick stems from the theory that rebates apply only to charges that are unearned as a result of the early termination of credit. Creditors typically claim that fees are earned at the consummation of the credit contract and need not be rebated because they are unrelated to the term of the credit. The validity of this argument depends on the particular type of fee that has been assessed and the language of the controlling statute.

The argument that a fee is earned at the outset of a credit transaction makes no sense in the case of fees that are clearly related to the term of credit. Credit insurance premiums, for example, usually vary with the term of credit, and the difference between a two-year premium and a one-year premium is unearned if prepayment occurs after one year.[372] The same principle may apply to other types of fees. One court has held that a broker fee had to be reduced upon the involuntary prepayment of a note when the broker's services were supposed to extend over the full term of the loan.[373]

Service contracts on cars, which are both expensive and sold for a particular time period, also may present rebate issues. If a consumer wanted to pay off the car loan early, but wanted both to keep the vehicle and to continue the service contract on it in force, there is no reason for a rebate on the service contract. However, if during the period it is in force, the car is repossessed or traded in, the service contract should be cancelled, and the unearned portion of the cost rebated; the borrower should not have to subsidize coverage for a subsequent owner.[374] Separate charges associated with credit sales for repair contracts on appliances might similarly be rebatable, particularly if one assumes that more repairs would be likely at the end of the contract term, after the appliance has been subjected to normal wear and tear, than at the beginning of the contract when the appliance is new.

The logical relationship between a fee and the term of credit is, however, only part of the rebate story. As with other usury issues, whatever fee the controlling statute says is rebatable is rebatable, and whatever fee the statute excuses from rebates need not be rebated, common sense notwithstanding. Thus, a one-time appraisal fee that a statute treats as part of the finance charge must be rebated if the statute requires the rebate of "finance charges,"[375] and a service charge need not be if the statute so specifies.[376]

Statutes can and frequently do exclude all or part of various fees, including basic interest charges, from rebate requirements with no apparent reason. For example, many statutes provide for the subtraction of an acquisition fee from the total finance charge before a rebate is calculated.[377] Similarly, statutes fre-

1993) (two-month cap for mortgage escrow funds under RESPA is a cap, not a floor; parties can contract for smaller cushion).

367 *See, e.g.*, Saul v. Midlantic Nat'l Bank/South, 572 A.2d 650 (N.J. Super. Ct. App. Div. 1990).

368 15 U.S.C. § 1615(a).

369 *See* §§ 5.8.2.3, *supra*, 5.11, *supra* (tips on how to identify a precomputed transaction).

370 *See* Chs. 4, *supra*, 6, infra.

371 *See also* § 5.9, *infra*.

372 *See* Varner v. Century Fin. Co., 738 F.2d 1143 (11th Cir. 1984); Clyde v. Liberty Loan Co., 287 S.E.2d 551 (Ga. 1982) (maintenance charges and credit insurance premiums must be rebated if unearned); Brown v. Associates Fin. Servs. Corp., 346 S.E.2d 873 (Ga. Ct. App. 1986).

But note that some types of credit may charge for credit insurance on a monthly installment basis, as is typically the case with credit cards, rather than on a precomputed basis. *See generally* § 6.10.2, *infra*.

373 Jackson Inv. Co. v. Bates, 366 So. 2d 225 (Miss. 1978).

374 *See* § 10.3.4.2, *infra*; National Consumer Law Center, Unfair and Deceptive Acts and Practices § 7.2.6.7 (7th ed. 2008 and Supp.). *Cf.* Jackson Inv. Co. v. Bates, 366 So. 2d 225 (Miss. 1978). *See generally* National Consumer Law Center, Consumer Warranty Law Ch. 19 (4th ed. 2010 and Supp.).

375 *See* S.C. Dep't of Consumer Affairs Interp. 3.210-8109, Consumer Cred. Guide (CCH) ¶ 97,043 (Sept. 8, 1981).

376 *In re* Tucker, 74 B.R. 923 (Bankr. E.D. Pa. 1987) (though persuasive authority and public policy suggest a "service charge" *should* be rebated, the controlling statute is clear that no such rebate is required).

377 *See, e.g.*, Alaska Stat. § 45.10.070 ($10 except for $25 for automobile credit sale under state RISA); Ga. Code Ann. § 10-1-3 ($20); Foster v. Centrex Capital Corp., 80 S.W.3d 140 (Tex. App. 2002) (creditor need not rebate acquisition charge even though contract does not specifically allow this, since statute allows it); Restaurant Dev., Inc. v. Cananwill, Inc., 80 P.3d 598 (Wash. 2003) (construing provision of insurance premium finance law to require rebate of unearned finance charges but not acquisition fee). *See generally* James H. Hunt, *The Rule of 78: Hidden Penalty for Prepayment in Consumer Credit Transactions*, 55 B.U. L. Rev. 331, 339 (1975).

quently allow creditors to ignore rebates that would be less than one dollar.[378]

### 5.8.4.2 Rebates of Points and Other Origination Charges

#### *5.8.4.2.1 Are points and other prepaid finance charges "earned at consummation"?*

One potential area of dispute is whether the federal law or a relevant state law governing the transaction requires the rebate of points, service charges, origination charges or other one-time fees charged at the time the loan is consummated.[379] Some state statutes, particularly ones regulating real-estate-secured loans, explicitly permit the exclusion of points and other prepaid finance charges from the rebate by denominating them as "nonrefundable" or stating that they are to be considered earned at consummation.[380] Other states may specifically curtail the practice.[381]

On other occasions, statutes are silent on the matter. Even within a state, the statutory treatment may not be consistent. There may be an express provision denominating points as nonrefundable in real estate transactions, with no similar provision regarding points or origination fees in other types of credit. Where not expressly addressed, a mandate to rebate points may nevertheless follow directly from standard statutory rebate language. Statutes may simply require the rebate of "unearned interest" or the "unearned finance charge" according to a particular rebate formula.[382] Where points or similar fees fall within the definition of "interest" or "finance charge," whichever the statute uses, one element of that test is met.[383] Where a statute requires actuarial computation, it also can be argued that points are inconsistent with that requirement.[384]

The next question, then, is whether those charges are "earned" at the outset of the transaction. In the absence of any controlling statute or case law, the need to rebate points may depend on the underlying economic validity of the creditor's argument that they are.[385] This argument depends on the existence of some separate service that the creditor provides at the beginning of a credit transaction and for which it may claim immediate compensation. Some courts considering the nature of points and similar fees have found no such separate service and have held instead that these fees merely constitute profit or compensation for overhead expense.[386] Such decisions suggest that points should be subject to rebate because there is no reason to consider income designated as profit or compensation for overhead expense to be earned at the outset of a transaction.[387]

Additional authority for this proposition is found in generally accepted accounting principles. The Financial Accounting Standards Board (FASB), a trade association council that sets generally accepted accounting standards, issued an accounting standard in 1987 that requires origination fees, commitment fees, and other loan fees to be recognized as income to the lender over the life of the loan.[388] Thus, if the lender's books

378 *See, e.g.*, Ala. Code §§ 5-19-4 ($1), 8-8-14 ($25); Alaska Stat. §§ 06.40.150, 45.10.070; Mich. Comp. Laws § 445.858(2); 69 Pa. Stat. Ann. § 1603 (West).

379 *See* §§ 4.3 (discussion of points as interest), 5.6 (calculation of points), *supra*.

380 *See, e.g.*, Ga. Code Ann. § 7-4-2(a)(3) (points and origination fees on mortgage loans excluded from both definition of "interest" and rebate calculations). *See also In re* Tucker, 74 B.R. 923 (Bankr. E.D. Pa. 1987) (though persuasive authority and public policy suggest a "service charge" *should* be rebated, the controlling statute is clear that no such rebate is required).

381 Ala. Code § 8-8-14 (pro rata refund of 6% interest surcharge for prepayment within ninety days); La. Rev. Stat. Ann. § 9-3532(B) (rebate of prepaid finance charge in simple interest transaction unless amount financed exceeds $10,000, scheduled term of credit is thirty-six months or more, and prepaid finance charge is less than 5% of amount financed).

382 *See* § 5.8.6, *infra* (discussion of rebate formulae).

383 *See, e.g.*, S.C. Dep't of Consumer Affairs, Admin. Interp. No. 3.109-8010 (Sept. 3, 1980) (rebate of "unearned portion of the loan finance charge," that includes points within its definition under Consumer Protection Code). *Cf.* 1989 S.C. Op. Atty. Gen., No. 89-25, 1989 WL 406115 (Feb. 28, 1989) (no refund of points required upon payment of first mortgage not subject to Consumer Protection Code); Cumberland Capital Corp. v. Patty, 556 S.W.2d 516 (Tenn. 1977) (treating service charge as interest).

384 State of Kansas, Consumer Credit Commissioner, Admin. Interp. No. 107 (Jan. 2, 1985) (limit of three points on mortgage loans; points prohibited for other consumer transactions by Kan. Stat. Ann. § 16a-2-401 because inconsistent with actuarial computation requirement (Kansas law has since been amended to allow two points on non-real estate loans, so this interpretation is no longer effective, but the analysis might apply in other states)).

385 *Cf. In re* Tucker, 74 B.R. 923 (Bankr. E.D. Pa. 1987) (though persuasive authority and public policy suggest a "service charge" *should* be rebated, the controlling statute is clear that no such rebate is required).

It is interesting to note the inconsistency between the creditor argument in rebate cases that interest fees such as points are earned at the outset of a transaction and the doctrine of "spreading" frequently advocated by creditors in rate calculation disputes. (*See* § 5.5.6, *supra,* for a discussion of spreading.) It is not at all clear why a creditor should be able to claim that points are earned at the consummation of a transaction, but that the effective interest rate should be calculated by treating the points as being earned throughout the term of the loan. *Cf.* Williams v. Seeley (*In re* Williams), 2001 U.S. App. LEXIS 13246 (4th Cir. June 13, 2001) (points are not considered "paid" at outset of the transaction when the lender merely reserves them from the proceeds of the loan); Fleet Fin. Inc. v. Jones, 430 S.E.2d 352 (Ga. 1993) (adopting spreading doctrine when points would have exceeded usury cap if attributed to first month; court notes it was not called upon to decide whether usury might result if loan period shortened by acceleration); Danziger v. San Jacinto Sav. Ass'n, 708 S.W.2d 1 (Tex. App. 1986) (discussing Texas rebate rules when spreading doctrine applied), *rev'd on other grounds*, 732 S.W.2d 300 (Tex. 1987).

386 *See* § 4.3, *supra*.

387 *Cf.* Smith v. Anderson, 801 F.2d 661 (4th Cir. 1986) (Va. law) (distinguishing "service charge," compensation for investigating and processing a loan, from points).

388 *See* FASB Statement No. 91, Accounting for Nonrefundable Fees and Costs Associated With Originating or Acquiring Loans and Initial Direct Costs of Leases (effective for fiscal years beginning

are prepared in accord with generally accepted accounting standards, its own records may belie the notion that points are earned at the outset of a loan.

One final problem concerning the rebate of points should be mentioned. Many rebate statutes require rebates of unearned charges solely in "precomputed transactions," because as discussed above, theoretically there is no unearned interest in an interest-bearing loan.[389] Points and similar charges are in fact "precomputed *charges*," but they are often imposed on interest bearing transactions, particularly mortgage loans.[390] Even assuming that these prepaid charges are really earned over the term of the credit and not at consummation of the transaction, these mixed transactions might nevertheless escape rebate if the rebate statute addresses only "precomputed transactions" and does not define a precomputed transaction broadly enough to cover points on interest-bearing debt.[391] For example, Colorado follows the rule that a transaction is precomputed only if at least 50% of the finance charge is precomputed,[392] and under such an approach, points on nominally interest-bearing debt will rarely be rebatable. Recognizing this problem, other states have either limited the number of points that may be assessed or have expanded their rebate requirements so that they are no longer limited to "precomputed" credit.[393]

#### *5.8.4.2.2 Treatment of points under the federal rebate statute*

As discussed above, in the absence of specific language excluding points and similar charges from rebate requirements, the need to rebate them may be inferred from the rebate statute—if it requires that "unearned interest" be rebated, then the argument depends on whether points are interest, and whether they are earned at consummation.

The federal rebate statute requires that "[i]f a consumer prepays in full the financed amount under any consumer credit transaction, the creditor shall promptly refund any unearned portion of the interest charge to the consumer."[394] Whether points are "interest" for purposes of this statute is a particularly interesting issue.

One might think (wrongly) that the answer would be easy: since it is codified amidst the Truth in Lending Act, Truth in Lending definitions apply, and interest, for Truth in Lending purposes, has a separate identity from points.[395] (Both, though, are part of the broader category "finance charge."[396]) However, it is by no means clear that TILA definitions do—or should—apply, for the rebate statute is not part of TILA despite its location in the code books. Rather, it was a free-standing part of the Housing and Urban Development Act of 1992, and is specifically denominated as *not* being part of TILA.[397] The decision as to where it would be codified was made subsequently by a House body called the Office of the Law Revision Counsel.[398]

No federal agency has official interpretive authority for this statute.[399] However, outside of the TILA context, there has grown up what one court has termed the "federal common law" definition of interest,[400] and an appealing argument can be made that this definition should be the relevant one. Much litigation over the definition of interest has arisen in the context of federal preemption and exportation, and most favored lender status, where the majority of courts have interpreted the term broadly.[401] Among the charges courts have held to be interest are late charges,[402] over-the-limit fees on credit cards,[403] a compensating balance requirement,[404] cash

---

after Dec. 15, 1987), *printed in* FASB Original Pronouncements, vol. I (2008–2009 ed.). *See generally* FASB Statement of Accounting Concepts No. 7, App. B (Feb. 2000); FASB Accounting Standards, § L20 (2004–2005 ed.).

389 *See* § 5.8.2.1, *supra*. *See* Wombold v. Associates Fin. Servs. Co., 104 P.3d 1080, 1089 (Mont. 2004) (rebate formula only applies to add-on loans, not interest-bearing loans, but charging points violated another portion of the statute).

Some statutes and regulations avoid the problem of unearned interest and rebates by forbidding precomputation, at least for long-term debt. *See, e.g.*, 38 C.F.R. § 36.4310 (FHA-insured manufactured home loans with term over five years); Cal. Civ. Code § 2981.7 (West) (motor vehicle credit sales with term over sixty-two months).

390 *Compare* Colorado Dep't Law, Admin. Interp. Nos. 2.201, 3.201, 3.508-8301 (Oct. 14, 1983) (no rebate of prepaid finance charges required in non-precomputed transactions; note that a Colorado statute, Colo. Rev. Stat. § 5-2-207(2)(b), and regulation, 4 Colo. Code Regs. 902-1 Rule 13, now require such a rebate if refinancing occurs within the first year), *with* Mass. Gen. Laws Ann. ch. 255, § 13L (requiring rebate of all "precomputed charges").

391 *See* Colorado Dep't Law, Admin. Interp. Nos. 2.201, 3.201, 3.508-8301 (Oct. 14, 1983). This might be argued as a prepayment penalty. *See* § 5.8.2, *supra*.

392 *See, e.g.*, Colo. Rev. Stat. § 5-1-301(35).

393 La. Rev. Stat. Ann. § 9:3532(B) (limiting nonrebatable prepaid finance charge on simple interest transactions).

394 15 U.S.C. § 1615(a)(1).

395 Reg. Z, 12 C.F.R. § 1026.4(b)(1), (3).

396 15 U.S.C. § 1605(a)(1); Reg. Z, 12 C.F.R. § 1026.4(b).

397 15 U.S.C. § 1615, Historical Note on Codification. *See also* Davis v. Pacific Capital Bank, 550 F.3d 915 (9th Cir. 2008) (noting that language that would have made the rebate statute an amendment to TILA was removed from the bill before enactment).

398 Roland E. Brandel, Joseph E. Terraciano, & Barry A. Abbott, Truth in Lending (2d ed.) ¶ 33.02*[1] (1994 Supp.).

399 In fact, the FRB, when it had interpretive authority over TILA, took the view that it had no interpretive authority over the federal rebate statute, and as such, could not issue any clarifying rules. *See* Davis v. Pacific Capital Bank, 550 F.3d 915 (9th Cir. 2008) (noting that no agency has interpreted the unearned interest provision of the rebate statute).

400 Greenwood Trust Co. v. Massachusetts, 971 F.2d 818, 829 (1st Cir. 1992).

401 *See* Ch. 3, *supra*.

402 *See, e.g.*, Smiley v. Citibank (South Dakota), N.A., 517 U.S. 735, 116 S. Ct. 1730, 135 L. Ed. 2d 25 (1996) (approving of and giving deference to the definition of interest contained in the 1996 OCC Interpretative Ruling); Greenwood Trust Co. v. Massachusetts, 971 F.2d 818 (1st Cir. 1992) (DIDA § 521).

403 *See, e.g.*, Watson v. First Union Nat'l Bank, 837 F. Supp. 146 (D.S.C. 1993) (NBA § 85).

404 *See, e.g.*, McAdoo v. Union Nat'l Bank, 535 F.2d 1050 (8th Cir. 1976) (NBA § 85 based on Arkansas law).

advance fees,[405] bonus or commissions paid to lenders,[406] and closing costs.[407] One of the federal banking agencies has issued a regulation defining interest to include many of these charges.[408] It has also been held to encompass the method of calculating interest, as that affects the effective yield.[409] Using this body of law as the relevant definition, then, would mean that a great many kinds of charges, such as points, would be "interest charges" subject to the federal rebate mandate. It certainly has the appeal of fairness that a federal common law definition of "interest" should be interpreted with consistency irrespective of whether it benefits the creditor or the borrower.[410]

In a 2008 decision, however, the Ninth Circuit confined the definition of "interest" in the federal rebate statute to charges that vary according to the length of time the extension of credit is outstanding.[411] It therefore held that a flat fee imposed for a refund anticipation loan did not have to be rebated when the loan was repaid earlier than expected. The court gave weight to the fact that a section of the original bill, which would have required creditors to refund unearned portions not only of interest but also of any "finance charge," was removed before enactment. Inconsistently, the court also gave weight to the TILA definition of "finance charge" as something separate from interest, even though the bill had also been amended before enactment to delete language that would have made it an amendment to TILA. Another flaw in the court's reasoning is that its construction of the statute makes the requirement of a rebate easy for creditors to evade, simply by moving the cost of credit into fixed-fee finance charges.

Assuming that a charge falls within the federal rebate statute's definition of "interest," there remains the question of whether a given item in that broad category of charges is "unearned." For some charges under the federal definition, it should not be a difficult determination: late fees, for instance, are not imposed except where a payment is late, and so those charges would be earned. For points and similar prepaid finance charges, the analysis should be the same as was mentioned in the preceding section.[412]

## 5.8.5 *What Is the Date of Prepayment?*

### 5.8.5.1 Fixing the Date for the Rebate Calculation

That the size of a rebate depends on the time when the debt is prepaid or otherwise matured makes intuitive sense. If a borrower pays off a two-year loan after only one month, the creditor has earned less interest and should have to refund more money than if the consumer paid off the same loan after twenty-two months. The reason is that the borrower who prepays early in the term of the loan has had the use of the borrowed principal for less time than the borrower who prepays near the end of the term of the loan.

The first step in any rebate calculation is to determine the precise date from which the rebate must be calculated. If a loan is prepaid, either directly by the borrower or through refinancing, the controlling date will be the date of prepayment, although as discussed at § 5.8.5.2, *infra*, that date may be rounded to the nearest regular payment date preceding or following the actual date of prepayment. If a debt is matured through acceleration rather than voluntary prepayment, however, determining the date when a rebate must be credited is more complicated.[413]

In some states acceleration is simply treated as a form of prepayment and the controlling date for rebate calculations is the date on which the creditor accelerates the debt.[414] Some courts have held that rebates are required when a post-repossession sale is held.[415] In other states, however, acceleration is not viewed as terminating the credit, and the creditor continues to earn interest until some later date, such as the date the creditor files an action on the debt, or the date of final judgment on the debt.[416] If the date of filing or the judgment date, as the case may be, is later than the date on which the debt was

405 *See, e.g.*, Fisher v. First Nat'l Bank, 548 F.2d 255 (8th Cir. 1977) (NBA § 85).

406 *See, e.g.*, Cronkleton v. Hall, 66 F.2d 384 (8th Cir. 1933) (NBA § 85, 86).

407 *See, e.g.*, Northway Lanes v. Hackley Union Nat'l Bank & Trust, 464 F.2d 855 (6th Cir. 1972) (NBA § 85).

408 12 C.F.R. § 7.4001(a).

409 First Nat'l Bank in Mena v. Nowlin, 509 F.2d 872 (8th Cir. 1975) (discount interest prohibited for national banks, as it was for all state lenders). *But cf.* Grunbeck v. Dime Sav. Bank, 74 F.3d 331 (1st Cir. 1996) (DIDA does not preempt state simple interest statute).

410 Readers should be aware that an industry representative obtained a post-enactment letter from the bill's sponsor, Congressman Torres, indicating that it was not intended to require a rebate of points. *See* Roland E. Brandel, Joseph E. Terraciano, & Barry A. Abbott, Truth in Lending ¶ 33.03*[2] n.3 (2d ed. Supp. 1994).

However, general rules of statutory construction do not give much weight to the post-enactment statements of a single legislator, and they are not part of the legislative history. Singer, Sutherland Statutory Construction ¶ 48.16 (6th ed. 2000).

411 Davis v. Pacific Capital Bank, 550 F.3d 915 (9th Cir. 2008).

412 *See* § 5.8.4.2.1, *supra*.

413 Of course, accelerating an interest-bearing debt, instead of a precomputed debt, will not require any rebates, as there is no unearned interest to rebate. *See In re* Curtis, 83 B.R. 853 (Bankr. S.D. Ga. 1988); Myles v. Resolution Trust Corp., 787 S.W.2d 616 (Tex. App. 1990) (no usury contracted for in acceleration clause of interest-bearing contract). *See generally* §§ 5.8.2.2, 5.8.4.1, *supra*.

414 *See, e.g.*, Iowa Code § 537.2510(6) (if judgment is obtained, rebate is calculated as of date of acceleration); N.Y. Pers. Prop. Law § 408(5) (McKinney); N.C. Gen. Stat. § 25A-32 (the earlier of date judgment obtained or fifteen days after repossession); 69 Pa. Stat. Ann. § 622(B) (West); Va. Code Ann. § 6.2-401. *See also* Palace Indus., Inc. v. Craig, 339 S.E.2d 313 (Ga. Ct. App. 1985); Berman v. Schwartz, 298 N.Y.S.2d 185 (N.Y. Sup. Ct. 1968), *aff'd*, 305 N.Y.S.2d 1019 (N.Y. App. Div. 1969); General Motors Acceptance Corp. v. Uresti, 553 S.W.2d 660 (Tex. Civ. App. 1977).

415 Union Trust Co. v. Tyndall, 428 A.2d 428 (Md. 1981); First Va. Bank v. Settles, 588 A.2d 803 (Md. Ct. App. 1991).

416 For example, both the 1968 and 1974 versions of the U.C.C.C. provide that "[i]f the maturity is accelerated for any reason and judgment is entered, the consumer is entitled to the same rebate as if payment had been made on the date judgment is entered." U.C.C.C. §§ 2.210(8), 2.510(7), 3.210(8).

originally scheduled to terminate, the creditor will have earned all the interest due under the contract, and no rebate will be required.

### 5.8.5.2 Intervals: Rounding the Time Calculation

The next complication in calculating the time that a precomputed loan has been outstanding occurs when contractually interest is "earned" and payments are due at specific intervals, usually monthly, during the term of the loan, but prepayments and accelerations generally do not occur exactly on a payment date. Rather than giving the borrower a partial rebate for the days remaining in the payment interval,[417] lenders have traditionally rounded up to the next payment date (rarely back to the previous payment date). Thus a borrower who prepaid a twelve month loan after only four months and two days would receive a rebate for only the last seven months of interest, not for seven months and twenty-eight days.[418]

Such self-serving calculations are profitable for lenders because consumer credit is frequently refinanced, and with each refinancing a lender that follows this practice may retain nearly one full month's worth of unearned interest and insurance premiums while charging interest on it under the new contract—in effect "double-dipping."[419] Moreover, prepayment shortly after a regular payment date, when the rebate calculation most favors the lender, is often guaranteed by lenders who stall for a few days before processing prepayments received late in the monthly payment period. By such simple expedients, creditors can minimize rebates and maximize profits.

The practice of rounding payment intervals in a lender's favor has traditionally been sanctioned by state law. Many small loan acts, for example, require rebates of unearned charges based on the installment date scheduled to follow prepayment.[420] As consumers and regulators have become more sophisticated, however, more and more statutes have prohibited the rounding of intervals in the creditor's favor during the first fifteen days of the payment period,[421] and improper rounding has been challenged in court.[422] Specific statutory rounding rules, even if they still favor creditors, provide clear standards against which a creditor's calculations may be measured. Creditors who claim excess interest through improper rounding will be charging illegal hidden interest.[423]

The difficulty with statutes controlling the rounding of payment intervals is two-fold. First, the statutes are frequently unenforced because they are poorly understood by many practitioners. Second, creditors can still avoid the effect of the statutes by refusing to accept prepayments during the first half of the month. Such a manipulation of the rebate provisions could, however, be revealed by an examination of a creditor's account records. A pattern of prepayment in the second half of the month, if sufficiently dramatic, might support a claim alleging a systematic effort to evade the statute, and thus state a usury claim.[424] (Moreover, if there is also a statute prohibiting prepayment penalties, one could argue that refusal to accept prepayment when tendered violates that statute.[425])

## *5.8.6 Rebate Formulae*

### 5.8.6.1 Determining Which Formula to Use

#### *5.8.6.1.1 Introduction*

Once the particular charges that are subject to rebate are identified and the duration of the credit has been determined, the final step in computing the amount of the rebate is to apply to these figures one of the three rebate formulae that are generally used: the pro rata formula, the actuarial formula, or the Rule of 78s. Which formula to apply is partly a question of state law, with a significant overlay of federal law.

When challenging the rebate formula that the creditor used, it is helpful to show the dollar amount difference between the rebate produced by that formula and an actuarial rebate.[426] A commercially published volume, the *78's Method Handbook*,[427]

417 Such partial rebates may be required only for prepayments in the first thirty or sixty days of a loan. *See, e.g.*, Ohio Rev. Code Ann. §§ 1321.13 (small loans), 1321.57 (second mortgages) (if payment is made before first installment is due, lender may keep 1/30 of monthly finance charge per day loan was outstanding).

418 *See* Steele v. Ford Motor Credit Co., 783 F.2d 1016 (11th Cir. 1986) (Truth in Lending case; unrebated interest due to improper rounding is finance charge in refinanced loan); Fitch v. General Motors Acceptance Corp., 351 S.E.2d 215 (Ga. Ct. App. 1986) (pro rata rebate need not be calculated on a daily basis) (is it just coincidence that the creditor chose to accelerate this note two days into a payment period?); Beaty v. Land of Lincoln Sav. & Loan, 468 N.E.2d 1259 (Ill. App. Ct. 1984) (entire month's interest earned on first day of month under mortgage contract).

419 *See* § 5.9.4, *infra* (case study of costs to consumers of this and other "frequent flipping" practices).

420 *See, e.g.*, Ariz. Rev. Stat. Ann. § 6-634 (rebate applicable to all fully unexpired months . . . which follow the installment date nearest the date of prepayment; rounding in creditor's favor thereby guaranteed).

421 *See, e.g.*, Ala. Code § 5-19-4; Neb. Rev. Stat. § 45-1024(2)(c); Ohio Rev. Code Ann. §§ 1321.13, 1321.57 (West); S.C. Dep't of Consumer Affairs 3.210-7609 Consumer Cred. Guide (CCH) ¶ 98,318 (Oct. 21, 1976) (one day cannot be treated as one month for rebate purposes). *See also* Tex. Fin. Code Ann. § 342.352 (West) (pro rata earnings for odd days when prepayment is not on installment date). *But cf.* Webster v. International Harvester Credit Corp., 367 N.E.2d 924 (Ohio Ct. App. 1977) (rounding in creditor's favor allowed after first ten days of payment period).

422 *See, e.g.*, Steele v. Ford Motor Credit Co., 783 F.2d 1016 (11th Cir. 1986) (Truth in Lending case). *Cf. In re* Jones, 79 B.R. 233 (Bankr. E.D. Pa. 1987) (state law permits use of Rule of 78s and rounding forward to allow a fraction of a month to be considered a full month).

423 *Cf.* Steele v. Ford Motor Credit Co., 783 F.2d 1016 (11th Cir. 1986) (hidden finance charge under Truth in Lending Act).

424 *See* § 3.9.1, *supra.*

425 *Cf.* Grosedlose v. Rum, 860 S.W.2d 554 (Tex. App. 1993) (contract clause prohibiting prepayment is a penalty or charge, violative of statute prohibiting prepayment penalties).

426 *See, e.g.*, *In re* Milbourne, 108 B.R. 522 (Bankr. E.D. Pa. 1989).

427 Financial Publishing Co., 1251 North Eddy Street, South Bend, IN 46617-1478 (800-247-3214). While this book is currently out of print, it may still be available in libraries, or calculations can be

pinpoints the dollar amount difference, as well as the effective interest rate obtained by the lender when a Rule of 78s rebate is calculated. These calculations can also be performed using the programs on this treatise's companion website.[428]

### *5.8.6.1.2 Federal rebate statute*

For consumer credit transactions with terms longer than sixty-one months consummated after September 30, 1993, federal law prohibits the use of the Rule of 78s. It requires instead the use of a formula at least as favorable to the borrower as the actuarial method.[429] This federal law preempts any contrary state law.[430]

The federal rebate law incorporates the Truth in Lending Act's definition of consumer credit transaction, except that "creditor" includes any assignee.[431] Since, however, the federal rebate law is not part of the Truth in Lending Act (even though it is codified there[432]), TILA's exemption of various types of transactions does not affect the scope of the rebate law.[433] The scope of the rebate law is also unaffected by the exemptions from portions of TILA that the Federal Reserve Board has given to five states.[434]

### *5.8.6.1.3 The Truth in Lending Act's rebate requirements for mortgage loans*

The Home Ownership and Equity Protection Act of 1994 (HOEPA) prohibits prepayment penalties in certain closed-end high-cost home equity loans consummated on or after October 1, 1995.[435] It defines a prepayment penalty to include a rebate calculated by a method that is less favorable to the consumer than the actuarial method.[436] As originally enacted, HOEPA included a complicated five-part exception to this prohibition, allowing less favorable rebate calculation methods during the first five years (reduced by a 2008 regulation to two years) of a loan in certain circumstances.[437] The Dodd-Frank Wall Street Reform and Consumer Protection Act, enacted July 21, 2010, repeals this exception.[438] As of late 2011, however, the regulations implementing this section of HOEPA had not been amended to reflect the Dodd-Frank Act.[439]

In addition, in 2008 the Federal Reserve Board adopted a rule prohibiting prepayment penalties, including rebates of precomputed interest less favorable to the consumer than the actuarial method, for a defined set of non-HOEPA subprime mortgage loans (referred to in the regulation as "higher-priced" mortgage loans), with a somewhat less demanding exception.[440]

The Dodd-Frank Act also includes some general restrictions and prohibitions regarding prepayment penalties that are potentially applicable to all mortgage loans, but their scope and substance will not be defined until the Consumer Financial Protection Bureau issues rules implementing them.[441] These restrictions are discussed in other treatises in this series.[442]

### *5.8.6.1.4 Rebate requirements for manufactured home financing*

The Depository Institutions Deregulation and Monetary Control Act of 1980 (DIDA)[443] preempts state interest rate ceilings for credit secured by a first lien on a residential manufactured home. To take advantage of this preemption, however, the creditor must comply with certain consumer protections set forth in a federal banking agency rule.[444] Two key requirements of the rule are that there can be no prepayment penalties in such credit,[445] and all rebates must be computed by the actuarial method.[446]

The rule does not mean that prepayment penalties and non-actuarial rebates are prohibited, but a creditor that does not comply with the rule cannot take advantage of federal preemption so is subject to state usury law and its penalties. The rule is discussed in detail at § 3.7, *supra.*

### *5.8.6.1.5 Bankruptcy law*

Bankruptcy law is an overlay upon federal and state rebate law. Section 502(b) of the Bankruptcy Code requires the bankruptcy court to determine the amount of each claim filed by a creditor that will be allowed. This determination is to be made as of the date the bankruptcy petition was filed, and claims cannot include "unmatured interest."[447] This means that interest on a debt is collectible from the bankruptcy estate only to

purchased from Financial Publishing Co.

428 *See also* §§ 5.8.6.3, 5.8.6.4, *infra.*

429 15 U.S.C. § 1615. *See* §§ 5.8.6.1.2, 5.8.7.4, *infra.*

430 *See* § 5.8.6.1.7, *infra.*

431 15 U.S.C. § 1615(d)(3).

432 *See* § 5.8.7.4, *infra.*

433 15 U.S.C. § 1603 (stating that "this subchapter does not apply" to certain specified transactions; the federal rebate law is not part of the subchapter that includes TILA).

434 15 U.S.C. § 1633; Official Commentary § 1026.29(a)-4 (granting exemptions to Connecticut, Maine, Massachusetts, Oklahoma, and Wyoming).

435 15 U.S.C. § 1639. *See* National Consumer Law Center, Truth in Lending § 9.6.1.1 (7th ed. 2010 and Supp.).

436 15 U.S.C. § 1639(c).

437 15 U.S.C. § 1639(c)(2).

438 Pub. L. No. 111-203, §§ 1432, 1083, 124 Stat. 1376 (July 21, 2010). *See* National Consumer Law Center, Truth in Lending § 1.3 (7th ed. 2010 and Supp.) (discussion of effective date of these amendments).

439 12 C.F.R. § 1026.32(d)(5), (6), (7).

440 12 C.F.R. § 1026.35(b)(2).

441 15 U.S.C. § 1639c(c).

442 *See* National Consumer Law Center, Truth in Lending Ch. 9 (7th ed. 2010 and Supp.).

443 Pub. L. No. 96-221, tit. v, 94 Stat. 164, § 501(c) (1980), 12 U.S.C. § 1735f-7a.

444 12 U.S.C. § 1735f-7a(c).

445 12 C.F.R. § 190.4(d). *See* 76 Fed. Reg. 48,950, 49,152 (Aug. 9, 2011) (adopting and renumbering former 12 C.F.R. § 590.4 without substantive change as an interim final rule of the Office of the Comptroller of the Currency, to replace the rule originally adopted by the Office of Thrift Supervision, which was abolished effective July 21, 2011).

446 12 C.F.R. § 190.4(c) (formerly 12 C.F.R. § 590.4(c)).

447 11 U.S.C. § 502(b)(2). *See also* National Consumer Law Center,

the extent it is earned before the filing of the bankruptcy petition.[448]

Some courts have construed this language to prohibit use of the Rule of 78s to compute the rebate of interest on a debt in bankruptcy, even if the contract and state or federal rebate law would allow use of the rule.[449] These courts have reasoned that application of the Rule of 78s formula provides only an approximation of the amount of unearned interest and always favors the lender.[450] This error in favor of the lender can be viewed as a penalty charge,[451] which is detrimental to the debtor, the estate, and the other creditors because it causes less money to be distributed to other creditors.[452] In addition, the Rule of 78s, which computes rebates on a monthly basis, is inconsistent with the Bankruptcy Code's mandate that the court determine the amount of the claim as of the date the bankruptcy petition is filed.[453] Further, some state statutes authorize Rule of 78s rebates only in the event of prepayment.[454] The bankruptcy court may be willing to make a distinction between prepayment and the acceleration that occurs when a bankruptcy petition is filed, and hold that an actuarial rebate is required for the latter.[455]

### *5.8.6.1.6 State rebate law*

For transactions consummated prior to the effective date of these federal statutes, and for transactions not subject to them, the appropriate rebate formula remains a matter of state law[456] or a matter of contract law, in the absence of applicable state law.[457] State credit statutes often authorize the use of the Rule of 78s, also known as the "sum of the digits" formula, because it maximizes the amount of interest and other charges that the creditor can claim to be earned, and can therefore exclude from the rebate, when prepayment occurs. (However, the applicable statute should be checked carefully to ensure that the statute in fact allows it. Where the statute describes a system, rather than naming it, creditors may improperly interpret it to their benefit.[458])

In many states, the rebate formula that should be used will vary from statute to statute. It may depend on the originally anticipated duration of the credit. Some states mandate actuarial rebates for mortgage loans, but allow Rule of 78s rebates for small loans or credit sales.[459] Similarly, some states require

---

Consumer Bankruptcy Law and Practice § 12.6.2 (9th ed. 2009 and Supp.).

448 *See, e.g.*, Gass v. Mid-State Homes, Inc. (*In re* Gass), 57 B.R. 109 (Bankr. E.D. Tenn. 1985). *See also* S. Rep. No. 989, 95th Cong., 2d Sess. at 62–63 (1978), *reprinted in* 1978 U.S.C.C.A.N. 5787, 5848–5849 (legislative history supporting this general rule).

Note that in certain circumstances, post-petition interest may be charged and collected by creditors. *See* National Consumer Law Center, Consumer Bankruptcy Law and Practice §§ 11.6.1.3.3.4, 12.6.2 (9th ed. 2009 and Supp.).

449 *In re* McMurray, 218 B.R. 867 (Bankr. E.D. Tenn. 1998); Gass v. Mid-State Homes, Inc. (*In re* Gass), 57 B.R. 109 (Bankr. E.D. Tenn. 1985); General Motors Acceptance Corp. v. Willis (*In re* Willis), 6 B.R. 555 (Bankr. N.D. Ill. 1980). *But see* Meeker v. Bloomington Fed. Sav. & Loan Ass'n (*In re* Hughes), 61 B.R. 400 (Bankr. C.D. Ill. 1986); *In re* Watson, 32 B.R. 491 (Bankr. W.D. Wis. 1983); *In re* Clausel, 32 B.R. 805 (Bankr. W.D. Tenn. 1983). *See generally* National Consumer Law Center, Consumer Bankruptcy Law and Practice § 14.4.3.4.3 (9th ed. 2009 and Supp.).

450 *See* § 5.8.6.3.1, *infra*.

451 James H. Hunt, *The Rule of 78: Hidden Penalty for Prepayment in Consumer Credit Transactions*, 55 B.U. L. Rev. 331, 339 (1975).

452 *In re* McMurray, 218 B.R. 867 (Bankr. E.D. Tenn. 1998).

453 *Id.*

454 *See, e.g.*, Tenn. Code Ann. § 45-5-402(b).

455 *See In re* McMurray, 218 B.R. 867 (Bankr. E.D. Tenn. 1998).

The legislative history of section 502(b) indicates that: "bankruptcy operates as the 'acceleration' of the principal amount of the claims against the debtor." S. Rep. No. 989, 95th Cong., 2d Sess. at 62–63 (1978), *reprinted in* 1978 U.S.C.C.A.N. 5787, 5848–5849.

456 Certain transactions may be subject to other federal law that may also prohibit the use of the Rule of 78s, such as federally related loans secured by first liens on manufactured homes. *See* 12 C.F.R. § 190.4 (former 12 C.F.R. § 590.4); § 5.8.6.1.4, *supra*.

457 Zwayer v. Ford Motor Credit Co., 665 N.E.2d 843 (Ill. App. Ct. 1996) (rebates computed by the Rule of 78s are not allowed where contract terms are ambiguous).

458 *See, e.g.*, Dechow v. Sko-Fed Credit Union, 536 N.E.2d 1382 (Ill. App. Ct. 1989) (statute providing that interest could not be "computed, calculated, charged or collected for any period of time occurring after the date on which the total indebtedness [except late charges] is paid in full" requires actuarial calculation; rejecting creditor argument that Rule of 78s is method of calculating interest accruing prior to prepayment); Denley v. Peoples Bank, 553 So. 2d 494 (Miss. 1989) (use of Rule of 78s rebate improper and usurious under applicable statute that was silent as to rebate method but provided that parties could agree to "pay a finance charge which will result in a yield not to exceed [specified percentages] each calculated according to the actuarial method"; though contract rate was legal on its face if loan paid according to original terms, where there is prepayment, the "yield" must be recalculated to account for the altered term so that the yield does not exceed the specified rate according to the actuarial method). *See also In re* Jungkurth, 74 B.R. 323 (Bankr. E.D. Pa. 1987) (where statute prohibits prepayment penalties but does not specify a method of calculating rebates, actuarial method must be used; unless expressly authorized by statute, use of the Rule of 78s would constitute a prepayment penalty). *But see* Dennis v. Old Republic Ins. Co., 578 N.E.2d 1010 (Ill. App. Ct. 1991) (appearing to question *Dechow's* interpretation in *dicta*).

459 *See, e.g.*, Dechow v. Sko-Fed Credit Union, 536 N.E.2d 1382 (Ill. App. Ct. 1989) (interpreting statute governing transactions secured by residential real estate to preclude use of Rule of 78s); Denley v. Peoples Bank, 553 So. 2d 494, 501 n.6 (Miss. 1989). *Cf.* Draper v. American Funding, Ltd., 285 Cal. Rptr. 640 (Cal. Ct. App. 1991) (applicable statute was personal property brokers law, which at the time authorized Rule of 78s, not statute governing residential property loans). *But see* Jacobson v. General Fin. Corp., 592 N.E.2d 1121 (Ill. App. Ct. 1992) (sorting out morass remaining after amendments to interest statutes that followed *Dechow* decision, and finding use of rule acceptable. *Ed. Note*: Illinois borrowers—and bewildered attorneys—can be grateful that the new federal legislation prohibiting the use of the Rule of 78s on long-term consumer loans make it unnecessary to sort out the Illinois scheme for loans consummated after Sept. 30, 1993); Dennis v. Old Republic Ins. Co., 578 N.E.2d 1010 (Ill. App. Ct. 1991) (appearing to question *Dechow's* interpretation in *dicta*, but avoiding direct conflict by holding different statute applicable. (*Ed. Note*: the case appears to be rather result-oriented, as it invokes the statutory construction principle that the more specific statute governs over the more

pro rata rebates when a debt is accelerated, but allow the Rule of 78s if the debt is voluntarily prepaid.[460] Finally, separate regulations often cover insurance premium rebates, so an insurance premium may be rebated under the Rule of 78s, while the other charges are rebated actuarially.

##### *5.8.6.1.7 Relationship between federal and state rebate requirements*

In some cases, federal law will provide greater protections to borrowers than they would otherwise have under state or other federal law. In other states, though, state law may provide greater protection.

HOEPA is explicit about preemption. Even in the limited circumstances where a creditor is permitted to impose a prepayment penalty or make less than an actuarial rebate under that statute, it can only do so if otherwise applicable law also permits it.[461] Further, the law's disclosure and substantive prohibitions do not affect state law "except to the extent that those State laws are inconsistent, and then only to the extent of the inconsistency,"[462] by which Congress intended "to allow states to enact more protective provisions than those in this legislation."[463]

The restrictions on prepayment penalties in non-HOEPA "higher-priced mortgage loans,"[464] are structured in a way that is similar to HOEPA. A creditor is allowed to impose a prepayment penalty only if it is "otherwise permitted by law."[465] Thus, if a state law prohibits a prepayment penalty, it cannot be imposed in a covered loan even if the prepayment penalty meets the other requirements of the federal rule.

The federal rebate statute does not include any preemption language, so it should not preempt state laws more protective of the consumer. Consumer protection statutes are to be liberally construed to effectuate their purposes.[466] The purpose of this legislation was to assure that consumers were given rebates, and were not financially harmed by the gross distortions of the Rule of 78s in long-term loans.[467]

While the odd history of the placement of the rebate statute in the code books muddies the waters,[468] in this case the end should be the same whether TILA preemption language or general preemption principles apply. TILA is explicit that it does not affect state laws relating to "types, amounts or rates of charges, or any element or elements of charges,"[469] except to the extent of the inconsistency. A state statute that would permit a creditor to keep unearned interest is preempted, as such a statute is inconsistent with the federal rebate law's requirement that unearned interest be rebated. By the same reasoning, the federal rebate statute preempts state statutes that would allow use of the Rule of 78s in long-term transactions, as a creditor could not limit a rebate to the Rule of 78s calculation without violating the federal act. In contrast, it is not inconsistent to protect consumers from overcharges created by skewed methods of calculating rebates.

Even if the TILA preemption language is inapplicable, more protective state statutes are not preempted. Preemption may be found where language in the federal statute reveals an explicit intent to preempt state law. It may also be found where the federal statute's structure and purpose, or nonspecific statutory language, reveal an implicit preemptive intent, either because the federal regulatory scheme is so pervasive as to make it reasonable to infer Congress intended to occupy the field, or because the federal law is in irreconcilable conflict with the state law.[470] An irreconcilable conflict may be found if compliance with both the federal and the state law is physically impossible, or if the state law stands as an obstacle to the accomplishment of Congress's purpose.[471]

These limited congressional forays into providing minimum standards of consumer protection cannot be reasonably assumed to occupy the field of the substantive regulation of consumer credit, particularly since credit regulation has historically been an area of state concern. Finally, more protective state laws supplement, rather than conflict with, the rights given under the federal law. A creditor can comply with state statutes giving greater protection to consumers without running afoul of the federal law.[472] The federal statute thus sets the minimum consumer protection, not the maximum.

---

general in the case of a conflict. It proceeds to find that a statute governing all secured or unsecured installment loans except certain purchase money mortgages is *more* specific than the statute applying to loans secured by residential real estate. That is a judgment call about which reasonable minds may differ.)).

460 *See* Varner v. Century Fin. Corp., Inc., 317 S.E.2d 178 (Ga. 1984) (Rule of 78s may be used for rebates pursuant to refinancing or voluntary prepayment, but pro rata rebate must be given if debt is accelerated pursuant to a default); Carter v. First Fed. Sav. & Loan Ass'n, 347 S.E.2d 264 (Ga. Ct. App. 1986) (MVRISA).

461 15 U.S.C. § 1639(c)(2)(D). *See* H.R. Conf. Rep. No. 652, 103d Cong., 2d Sess. 1, at 162 (1994).

462 15 U.S.C. § 1610(b).

463 H.R. Conf. Rep. No. 652, 103d Cong., 2d Sess. 1, at 162 (1994).

464 *See* § 5.8.6.1.3, *supra.*

465 12 C.F.R. § 1026.35(b)(2)(i).

466 Singer, Sutherland Statutory Construction ¶ 73.1 (6th ed. 2003). *See* § 7.2.1, *infra*; National Consumer Law Center, Truth in Lending § 1.5.2.3 (7th ed. 2010 and Supp.).

467 *Mortgage Refinancing Reform Act of 1992: Hearings on H.R. 5170 Before the House Subcommittee on Consumer, Affairs and Coinage of the Committee on Banking, Finance and Urban Affairs*, 102d Cong. 2d Sess. (May 27, 1992). The rebate provision of H.R. 5170 resurfaced as § 933 of the Housing and Community Development Act of 1992, Pub. L. No. 102-550.

468 *See* § 5.8.7.4, *infra.*

469 15 U.S.C. § 1610(b). The preemption language of § 1610(a) speaks only to disclosures.

470 Barnett Bank v. Nelson, 517 U.S. 25, 31, 116 S. Ct. 1103, 134 L. Ed. 2d 237 (1996). *See* Ch. 3, *supra.*

471 *Id.*

472 Hillsborough County v. Automated Med. Labs, 471 U.S. 707, 105 S. Ct. 2371, 85 L. Ed. 2d 714 (1985) (FDA and state health ordinances imposing more requirements can co-exist).

### 5.8.6.2 Pro Rata Rebates

The simplest but least used rebate formula is the pro rata method. This formula assumes that interest is earned in direct proportion to the time that a loan or credit has been outstanding. If a prepayment occurs four months into the term of a precomputed loan that was scheduled to be repaid in twelve months, the pro rata method provides that 4/12 of the interest has been earned. Consequently, the remaining 8/12 of the interest is unearned and must be rebated. If the total finance charge subject to rebate had been $1,000, then 8/12 × $1,000 = $666.67 should be rebated to the consumer.

The pro rata rebate method is simple to apply, but it is mathematically very crude because it fails to consider the effect of a declining principal balance on the earning of interest. Because a borrower has the use of all or most of the loan principal at the beginning of the term of a loan, the interest earned in the earlier payment intervals is greater than that earned in later intervals when much of the principal has already been paid back. About two thirds of the total interest on an amortization schedule is earned before the midpoint of the term of an installment loan. By ignoring the effect of the declining principal balance, the pro rata method recognizes less interest as "earned" at any given point in the loan term than would otherwise be the case. When a prepayment occurs, the lender is deemed to have earned less interest and must pay a larger rebate under the pro rata method than if a formula recognizing the effect of declining balances had been used.

Not because of its mathematical inaccuracy, but because the pro rata method yields larger rebates for borrowers than either the Rule of 78s or the actuarial method, it is rarely used. The fundamental mathematical flaw in the pro rata calculation method is its failure to recognize declining principal balances. Yet, add-on and discount interest calculations have exactly the same flaw,[473] and these methods are widely authorized and used, supposedly for their simplicity, but actually for their profitability.

Statutes requiring pro rata rebates do, nevertheless, crop up at times, particularly for rebates required when a creditor accelerates a debt because of default or some other contingency,[474] or in the event of a quick-flip on a loan.[475] Practitioners should be sure that these rebates are properly calculated and credited to the consumer's account. Furthermore, in any add-on or discount interest transaction for which a rebate formula is not statutorily or administratively specified, practitioners should argue that pro rata rebates are appropriate. If interest is earned in precomputed transactions without regard to declining balances, fairness and consistency demand it should be rebated in the same fashion.[476]

### 5.8.6.3 Rule of 78s

#### *5.8.6.3.1 Background and legal status*

As the reader who has been introduced to the Rule of 78s in other parts of this treatise may have gathered,[477] this method of calculating rebates is a bane to consumers and a boon to creditors. It is also an anachronism; since the advent of widely available computers, there is no reason for it other than to maximize income for creditors.[478]

In the pre-computer era, it was a tedious task to calculate how much interest was earned at a given point prior to maturity on a precomputed loan. If a borrower wanted to terminate a loan thirty-six months into a forty-eight-month term, determining the actual interest earned to that point would require that an amortization table be prepared for the loan, calculating the interest due at each payment interval on the declining principal balance. While not a difficult task, it was time-consuming and labor-intensive, requiring in the above example thirty-six separate three-step calculations.[479] The Rule of 78s is nothing more than a shorthand formula designed to *approximate* the results of an actual amortization with a single, simple five-step formula, which is all the more efficient because it can be applied to all transactions irrespective of term or interest rate. There is, however, a hitch in this shorthand approximation: it has an inherent bias in the creditor's favor. There will always be a smaller rebate to the consumer when the Rule of 78s is used than when the actuarial method is used, so the borrower always loses.[480] The difference between the two amounts can be termed a "78s penalty."[481]

In short-term, small balance loans, the degree of error is relatively small. For example, in a $1,000, one-year, 10% loan prepaid at six months, the 78s penalty the borrower pays is only 25 cents. At that scale, the lender bias might have been economically rationalized in the 1930s, when it was first legally sanctioned,[482] by arguing that the bias cost the consumer less

473 *See* §§ 5.3.2–5.3.3, *supra*.

474 *See, e.g.*, Walter E. Heller & Co. v. Mall, Inc., 267 F. Supp. 343 (E.D. La. 1967) (pro rata refund of discount interest upon acceleration under Louisiana law); Varner v. Century Fin. Corp., Inc., 317 S.E.2d 178 (Ga. 1984) (interpreting Ga. Code Ann. § 7-4-2(b)(1)); Fitch v. General Motors Acceptance Corp., 351 S.E.2d 215 (Ga. Ct. App. 1986) (pro rata rebate required, but calculation need not be on a daily basis, only a monthly basis); Bozeman v. Tifton Fed. Sav. & Loan Ass'n, 297 S.E.2d 49 (Ga. Ct. App. 1982) (pro rata rebate required by motor vehicle special usury law upon acceleration).

475 *See, e.g.*, Ala. Code § 5-19-4(d) (pro rata rebate if refinanced by same creditor or affiliate with 120 days).

476 *See In re* Lowell, Clearinghouse No. 30,955 (S.D. Me. 1972).

477 *See, e.g.*, §§ 5.8.2.2, *supra*, 5.111, *infra*.

478 *See* § 5.8.4.1, *supra*.

479 (1) Calculate the interest due for the payment period; (2) allocate a portion of the payment to the accrued interest; and (3) apply the remaining payment to the principal balance to obtain the new principal balance. The process is repeated for each payment period. *See* § 5.3.1.1, *supra*.

480 Bonker, *The Rule of 78*, XXXI Journal of Finance 877, 885 (No. 3, June 1976); Hunt, *The Rule of 78: Hidden Penalty for Prepayment in Consumer Credit Transactions*, 55 B.U. L. Rev. 331 (1975).

481 *In re* McMurray, 218 B.R. 867 (Bankr. E.D. Tenn. 1998).

482 Financial Publishing Co., 78's Method Handbook 5 (Pub. No. 841 Rev. Apr. 1982). While this book is out of print, it may be available in a library, or calculations can be purchased from Financial Publishing Co., 1251 South Eddy Street, Ste. 202, South Bend, IN 46617-1478 (800-247-3214).

than the increased operational expenses that would have been passed onto borrowers if the labor-intensive actuarial calculations were required.

However, the longer the term, the higher the rate, and, of course, the higher the balance, the greater the distortion. The use of the rule on a fifteen-year, $30,000, 16% manufactured home contract, prepaid at the sixtieth month, penalizes the consumer to the tune of almost $4,600.[483] When Congress first examined the rule in 1979, it was estimated that its use cost consumers as much as half a billion dollars.[484] In light of the widespread availability of computers and programs that can do amortizations in a matter of seconds, there is no longer any legitimate reason for the use of the rule.[485] However, theories challenging the rule, such as alleging it violates UDAP statutes or statutes limiting prepayment penalties, have met with mixed success.[486]

483 Even at a more modest 10% rate on a twenty-year, $37,000 manufactured home contract, prepaid in year eight, the interest earned by the actuarial method is $27,157.84; by the Rule of 78s $31,106.52—nearly a $3,950 Rule of 78s penalty. *See also* Draper v. American Funding, Ltd., 285 Cal. Rptr. 640 (Ct. App. 1991) (interpreting former Cal. Fin. Code § 22482 (West), governing personal property brokers; that provision, requiring actuarial rebates, was passed too late to save the plaintiff the $17,410 excess cost caused by the use of the Rule of 78s). *See generally* Financial Publishing Co., 78's Method Handbook (Pub. No. 841 Rev. Apr. 1982) (charting the augmented returns resulting from the use of the Rule of 78s; for example, a 24%, 120-month loan prepaid after twenty-four months means the true interest paid is 28.75%).

484 *Restrict the Use of the Rule of 78: Hearings Before the Subcommittee on Consumer Affairs of the Senate Comm. on Banking, Housing, and Urban Affairs on S. 2002*, 96th Cong., 1st Sess. (1979) (statement of Willard Ogburn and Bonnie Freeman at 118–119).

485 Kedziora v. Citicorp Nat'l Servs., 780 F. Supp. 516, 525 (N.D. Ill. 1991). *See also* Draper v. American Funding, Ltd., 285 Cal. Rptr. 640 (Ct. App. 1991) (Consumer Leasing Act case; programmed calculators and computers reduce ease-of-use factor to *de minimis* proportions, and weight of independent thinking tips toward view of it as penalty "unrelated to real economic interest"; FRB view otherwise "looks more and more like the result of lender lobbying rather than thoughtful analysis").

486 *Prepayment penalties*: *Compare In re* Jungkurth, 74 B.R. 323 (Bankr. E.D. Pa. 1987) (unless specifically authorized by statute, use of rule would constitute a prepayment penalty), *with* Jacobson v. General Fin. Corp., 592 N.E.2d 1121 (Ill. App. Ct. 1992) (declining to rule, but appearing to disfavor argument), *and* Pysh v. Security Pac. Hous. Serv., 610 A.2d 973 (Pa. Super. Ct. 1992) (use of Rule of 78s would result in early pay-off balance approximately $3,000 greater than actuarial method; borrowers alleged use of rule violated MVSFA's prohibition against prepayment penalty, but since MVSFA and banking regulations also specifically authorized use of rule to calculate rebate, court reconciled two provisions by allowing use of rule to calculate unearned interest, but prohibiting imposition of separate charge or penalty for prepayment). *See generally* Kedziora v. Citicorp Nat'l Servs., 780 F. Supp. 516 (N.D. Ill. 1991) (historical perspective).

*UDAP*: *See In re* Milbourne, 108 B.R. 522 (Bankr. E.D. Pa. 1989); *In re* Tucker, 74 B.R. 923 (Bankr. E.D. Pa. 1987) (dicta). *But see* Lanier v. Assocs. Fin., Inc., 499 N.E.2d 440 (Ill. 1986) (rejecting UDAP claim because of TILA disclosure rules, and declining to address public policy issues; concurrence suggests claim under disclosure provisions of Illinois Interest Act may have met with more success).

*Other*: Drennan v. Security Pac. Nat'l Bank, 621 P.2d 1318 (Cal. 1981) (rejecting argument that use of Rule of 78s in adhesion contract makes it ambiguous and therefore void; discussing fairness and policy issues but declining to reach them).

### *5.8.6.3.2 Calculating a Rule of 78s rebate: a simplified step-by-step guide for mathphobes*

When Congress enacted the federal rebate law in 1992,[487] it did not prohibit use of the rule for transactions with terms up to sixty-one months, so it is still necessary to know how to calculate a Rule of 78s rebate. Fortunately, as you may recall from high school, if you know the formula, you can get the right answer even if you do not know how the formula was derived.[488] So, herewith, the formula:

$$\text{rebate} = \frac{R(R+1)}{N(N+1)} \times FC$$

where

N = originally scheduled number of installments;

R = number of scheduled installments remaining after date of prepayment (use rounding formula specified in statute);

FC = total finance charge (i.e., total interest subject to rebate).

Applying that formula is a simple matter (honestly), as can be seen from working through an example. Bob Borrower signed a loan on December 1, 1992, with the following terms: $5,000 principal, 18% interest, and forty-eight monthly payments of $146.87.[489] The $5,000 principal does not include any points, service charge, or other prepaid finance charge. It does include credit insurance premiums in the amount of $215. A late charge of five dollars may be imposed if a payment is more than ten days late. On March 17, 1994, Bob refinanced. To determine the proper amount to be rebated under the rule, follow this step by step guide.

*1. Determine which charges are subject to rebate requirements. (§ 5.8.4, supra)*

Examining the documents, we determine that this is a precomputed contract,[490] so there is unearned interest to be rebated. As there are no prepaid finance charges,[491] the $215 credit insurance premiums are the only other charges that should be rebated.[492]

We can obtain the precomputed interest figure in a number of ways: if the documents list a loan principal and an interest charge, it's handed to us. If it lists a loan principal only, we can subtract that amount from the total of payments to come up with the interest. Or if there are no prepaid finance charges or other non-interest finance charges, as in this case, we can just

487 15 U.S.C. § 1615. *See* § 5.8.6.1.2, *supra*.

488 For those who enjoy that sort of thing, the derivation is explained in the next subsection. For those who do not enjoy that sort of thing, the next subsection can be safely ignored.

489 The last payment should be adjusted to account for rounding.

490 *See* §§ 5.8.2.3, *supra*, 5.11.4, *infra*.

491 *See* § 5.8.4.2, *supra*.

492 *See* §§ 5.8.4, *supra*, 6.10, *infra*.

use the "finance charge" as disclosed on the TILA disclosure statement. In Bob's loan, we find that the disclosed finance charge is $2,049.76.[493]

*2. Determine how the statute authorizing the Rule of 78s rebate defines which payment dates and intervals to use.[494] (§ 5.8.5, supra)*

Assume the applicable statute requires rounding to the regular payment due date nearest to the date of prepayment. Following that rounding rule, the April 1, 1994 payment due date is the closest to the March 17 refinancing.

Having determined that April 1 is the appropriate date, we calculate that 16 payment intervals have "fully elapsed" on that date.[495] (January 1, 1993 to April 1, 1994 = 16 fully elapsed payment periods.)

*3. Determine how many months are remaining in the scheduled loan term: number of months originally scheduled (n) minus number of elapsed months = number of months remaining (r):*

Forty-eight months (originally scheduled term) minus 16 elapsed months = 32. (Or, you can just count them up.) This number is called "r" in the formula (for "remaining"—clever, eh?).

*4. Determine the rebate fraction (or rebate factor), by use of the formula set out at the beginning of this subsection.*

$$\frac{r(r+1)}{n(n+1)}$$

$$r = 32,\ n = 48$$

$$\frac{32(32+1)}{48(48+1)} = \frac{32(33)}{48(49)} = .4490$$

*5. Multiply the charges subject to the Rule's rebate by the rebate factor.*

As we determined in step 1, in Bob's loan FC = $2,049.76 interest subject to rebate + $215 credit insurance premiums subject to rebate = $2,264.76.

| | |
|---|---|
| ($2,049.76) × (.4490) | = $920.34 unearned interest to be rebated.[496] |
| ($215) × (.4490) | = $96.54 unearned insurance to be rebated. |
| | $1,016.88 total unearned charges to be rebated. |

To determine the actual payoff amount on Bob's loan, we must also credit all payments made, and add all late charges which he may have incurred. In Bob's case, if he made all payments timely through February 1, he would have paid 14 payments, for a total of $2,056.18. As the March 1 payment would have been late on the date of refinancing, Bob incurred one $5 late charge.

| | |
|---|---|
| Total of payments | $7,049.76 (48 @ $146.87) |
| Minus Payments made | –2,056.18 (14 @ $146.87) |
| Minus Rebates | –1,016.88 |
| Plus Late charge | + 5.00 (1 @ $5.00) |
| Pay off balance | $3,981.70 |

If the creditor is asking for a larger payoff than this, there is an overcharge.

For mathphobes, this is all that is necessary; you may safely ignore the next section. For those who are curious, the theory behind it is explained there.

#### 5.8.6.3.3 The explanation of the Rule of 78s for those who care (optional reading for the practitioner)

So how does the Rule of 78s work? Like the pro rata method, the Rule of 78s calculates the fraction or percentage of the finance charge that has been earned at any point in the loan. Unlike the pro rata method, however, the Rule of 78s does not assume that the interest earned in each month (or other interval) of the loan is equal. Instead, it weights the earliest months in the loan term most heavily and attributes progressively less interest to later months. As a general approach, this concept of attributing more interest to months early in the loan term than to months later in the term is correct because of the declining principal balance owed on the loan. However, the method used by the Rule of 78s weights the early months too heavily and the later months too lightly and thus, when a loan is prepaid, credits the lender with more earned interest than it is actuarially due.[497]

The method by which the Rule of 78s weights the income earned in each payment interval of a loan is as follows. First, the total number of payment intervals (usually months) in the originally anticipated loan term is counted. In a one-year loan

493 Remember that the TILA finance charges may include some charges that under state law may not need to be rebated, such as points. *See* § 5.4, *supra*. So if we are using only the disclosure statement on a loan with prepaid finance charges, we may need to make an adjustment.

For example, if there had been a 2% origination fee on Bob's loan (2% of $5,000 principal = $100), the TILA disclosure statement would have listed the finance charge as $2,149.76. (The interest on $5,000 at 18% for four years, plus the $100 origination fee.)

If, under applicable state law, origination fees are considered "earned at consummation," and do not need to be rebated (*see* § 5.8.4.2, *supra*) then we must subtract that fee from the TILA finance charge in order to obtain the interest charge subject to rebate. $2,149.76 (TILA finance charge) minus $100 (origination fee) = $2,049.76 interest subject to rebate.

494 If the statute does not specify rounding rules, the banking department or other regulatory agency may have rules that do so. Administrative regulations should be reviewed, or simply call the regulator and ask.

495 That language commonly appears in statutes or regulations governing rules for rounding intervals.

496 Compare this to the actuarial rebate of $1,020.57, over $100 more to consumer. *See* § 5.8.6.4, *infra*.

497 *See* Hunt, *The Rule of 78: Hidden Penalty for Prepayment in Consumer Credit Transactions*, 55 B.U. L. Rev. 331 (1975). *See also* Kedziora v. Citicorp Nat'l Servs., 780 F. Supp. 516 (N.D. Ill. 1991); Denley v. Peoples Bank, 553 So. 2d 494, 498–499 (Miss. 1989) (discussion of how Rule of 78s "skews the accrual" of finance charges); IRS Rev. Ruling 83-84, 1983-1 CB97.

with payments due monthly, there will be twelve payment intervals. In a similar two-year loan, there will be twenty-four intervals.

Second, the denominator of the rebate fraction is determined by adding up all of the integers from one to the number of payment intervals originally anticipated for the loan. For the one year loan mentioned above, this sum is: 1+2+3+4+5+6+7+8+9+10+11+12 = 78. This sum of 78s is the origin of the name of the Rule of 78s, but the sum is 78 only for a loan with twelve equal repayment intervals. For the two-year loan, for example, the denominator of the rebate fraction will be 1+2+3+4+ . . . +21+22+23+24 = 300. In general, the formula for determining the sum of the digits from one to the number of payment intervals is: sum = $[N \times (N + 1)] \div 2$ where N represents the number of payments originally anticipated for the loan.

Third, each month is given a weight that is the opposite of its order of repayment. Thus, the first month of a one-year loan with equal monthly installments is given a weight of twelve, the second month is given a weight of eleven, the third ten, etc. The final month of any loan, regardless of the length of the term, will always be given a weight of one. Each month's weight represents the amount of interest that is earned in that month according to the rule. Remembering that the denominator of the rebate fraction for a one-year loan is 78, the amount of interest earned in the first month of the loan is 12/78ths or about 15.38% of the total interest.[498] Similarly, the amount of interest earned during the second month of the loan is 11/78ths of the total or about 14.1%. The interest credited to the third month will be 10/78ths of the total, and so on. As a result, the amount of interest earned during the first three months of this one-year loan would be 12/78 + 11/78 + 10/78 = 33/78ths of the total contract interest, or about 42.3%. At the same time, the amount of unearned interest that must be rebated is the fraction attributed to the last nine scheduled months which is, starting with the interest earned in the twelfth month: 1/78 + 2/78 + . . . + 8/78 + 9/78 = 45/78 or about 57.7% of the total interest charge.[499]

From this is derived the rebate formula used in the preceding section.

#### *5.8.6.3.4 Sum of the balances method: a variant on the Rule of 78s*

An important variant of the Rule of 78s, or sum of the digits method, is the "sum of the balances" method. Its impact lies in loans where the scheduled payments are unequal, particularly where a final balloon payment is called for. It provides that the fraction of the total contract interest that must be rebated at any given time in the loan term is the sum of the monthly loan balances for the months remaining in the originally scheduled loan term divided by the sum of the monthly balances for all the months in the scheduled loan term.[500] Thus, for a six-month loan of $600 that is scheduled to be repaid in $100 monthly installments, the rebate fraction after two months would be:

$$\frac{400+300+200+100}{600+500+400+300+200+100} = \frac{1000}{2100} = \frac{10}{21} = 0.476 \text{ (rounded).}$$

This fraction would be multiplied by the finance charge (i.e., the total contract interest subject to rebate) to obtain the actual dollar amount of unearned interest. If $40 of that $600 total of payments was the interest, the amount rebated would be $19.04.[501]

The rebate fraction obtained with the sum of the balances formula in the example above is identical to the fraction that would be produced by the Rule of 78s.[502] For any loan that is paid off in equal monthly installments, the sum of the balances method and the Rule of 78s will provide identical rebates. However, if a loan schedule contains unequal payments, and especially if the loan is scheduled to be retired by a final balloon installment, the rebates under the sum of the balances method and the Rule of 78s are *not* the same. Instead, the more the repayment schedule is loaded with large payments near the end of the loan term, the more the sum of the balances method will favor the borrower in comparison with the Rule of 78s. Creditors that give standard Rule of 78s rebates on balloon note transactions when the statute prescribes the sum of the balances method are probably violating the state law.

The only way to calculate a sum of the balances rebate on a transaction with several unequal monthly payments is to laboriously add up all the monthly balances. However, if all the payments are the same size except for a final balloon payment, the sum of the balances rebate can be calculated by the following formula:

$$\text{rebate} = \left[(R \times B) + \left(\frac{R(R-1)}{2} \times P\right)\right] \times FC \div \left[(N \times B) + \left(\frac{N(N-1)}{n} \times P\right)\right]$$

where

N = originally scheduled number of installments;

R = number of scheduled installments remaining after date of prepayment (use rounding formula specified in statute);

FC = total finance charge (i.e., total interest subject to rebate);

498 The interest earned in the first month of a two-year, 24-installment loan would, in contrast, be 24/300ths of the total interest or 8%.

499 Note that you can use the formula previously given, sum = $[N \times (N + 1)] \div 2$, to figure out that the sum of the integers from one to nine is forty-five, i.e., $[9 \times (9 + 1)] \div 2 = 90 \div 2 = 45$. Thus the numerator of the rebate fraction can be calculated as easily as the denominator. All you have to do is to decide how many intervals (usually months) remain after the date of prepayment, and then apply the formula.

500 Statutes that call for a sum of the balances rebate are often difficult to decipher. The typical language might provide for a rebate of "at least as great a proportion of the finance charge as the sum of the monthly balances after the date of prepayment bears to the sum of all the monthly balances under the schedule in the contract." The average statute also has language describing the rounding method for determining the number of remaining installments.

501 (0.476) × ($40) = $19.04.

502 The rebate fraction calculated by the Rule of 78s would be:

$$\frac{4+3+2+1}{6+5+4+3+2+1} \times \frac{10}{21}$$

B = balloon payment due as last installment;

P = regular payment amount.

As an example of the use of this formula, consider the same six-month loan for $600 that was mentioned earlier in this section, but assume that instead of equal monthly payments of $100, the loan is repayable in five installments of $60 and a final $300 balloon installment. Following the formula, the rebate upon prepayment after two months is:

$$\left[(4 \times 300) + \left(\frac{4 \times 3}{2} \times 60\right)\right] \times FC \div \left[(6 \times 300) + \left(\frac{6 \times 5}{2} \times 60\right)\right]$$

$$= \frac{1200+360}{1800+900} \times FC$$

$$= \frac{1560}{2700} \times FC$$

$$= 0.578 \text{ (rounded)} \times FC$$

Thus the difference between the sum of the balances rebate and the Rule of 78s rebate on this loan is more than one tenth of the total finance charge.[503] Again assuming that $40 of the $600 total of payments was the interest subject to rebate, the amount of the rebate is $23.12,[504] compared to the $19.04 rebate yielded by a straight Rule of 78s method. On large loans with high finance charges this difference can be thousands of dollars.

### 5.8.6.4 Actuarial Rebates

#### *5.8.6.4.1 Legal status*

The most accurate and the fairest way to balance creditor and debtor interests in a rebate calculation is to determine the actuarial interest that the creditor has earned at the time of prepayment and to refund to the borrower the difference between the total contract interest and this actuarially earned amount. Generally accepted accounting principles consider this the economic reality.[505]

The extreme distortion caused by the Rule of 78s, particularly for contracts with longer terms and high principal amounts, has led many states to require the actuarial method, at least in long-term loans. In addition, the 1992 Federal rebate law mandates it for all consumer credit transactions with terms longer than sixty-one months.[506] The Truth in Lending Act also contains several provisions prohibiting or restricting use of the Rule of 78s for certain mortgage loans regardless of the length of the term.[507]

#### *5.8.6.4.2 Calculation of actuarial rebates*

The computation of an actuarial rebate requires the construction of an amortization schedule. There is no easy formula to calculate the rebate. At the time each payment is made from the beginning of the loan to the point of prepayment, the interest earned during the preceding period or fractional period must be computed by multiplying the outstanding principal balance by the periodic interest rate, and the payments received must be used, first to pay off the accrued interest and, second, to reduce the outstanding principal balance. The process may be tedious, especially in precomputed transactions where no amortization schedule is otherwise needed, but it is the most economically accurate and fairest of the three rebate methods: the lender receives income for the actual use of its funds and the borrower does not overpay interest.

The companion website to this treatise includes two programs that will prepare and print amortization schedules so that actuarial rebates can be determined. Practitioners using the program should also be familiar with the manual calculations necessary to check the amortization schedule that are discussed in this subsection and at § 5.3.1.1, *supra*. When presenting the amortization schedule to a court, it is important to be able to demonstrate its accuracy by doing the simple arithmetic necessary to check it.[508]

The calculation of actuarial interest has previously been discussed in this treatise,[509] but a brief example of the use of an actuarial calculation to compute the size of a rebate will nevertheless be given here. Assume that a consumer takes out a precomputed one-year loan of $1,000 repayable in equal monthly installments with 14% add-on interest and an APR of 24.91%. The total amount repayable will be $1,000 principal + ($1,000 × 0.14) interest = $1,140. The monthly installment will be $1,140 ÷ 12 = $95. If the consumer prepays the loan after exactly three months and the relevant statute calls for an actuarial rebate of the unearned interest, then the amount of interest that the lender has earned in the three months that the loan was outstanding must be calculated. The difference between the total interest of $140 and the amount that the lender has earned will be the amount of the rebate.

The following partial amortization table shows the appropriate actuarial earnings.[510] Note that the periodic (here, monthly) rate is 24.91 ÷ 12 = 2.07583%.[511]

503 The difference is 0.578 − 0.476 = 0.102.

504 (0.578) × ($40) = $23.12.

505 James H. Hunt, *The Rule of 78: Hidden Penalty for Prepayment in Consumer Credit Transactions*, 55 B.U. L. Rev. 331 (1975). *See* § 5.8.4, *supra*.

506 15 U.S.C. § 1615(b) (Rule of 78s prohibited on precomputed consumer credit transactions consummated after September 30, 1993 with term longer than sixty-one months; method at least as favorable to consumer as actuarial method must be used). *See* §§ 5.8.4, *supra*, 5.8.7.4, *infra*.

507 *See* § 5.8.6.1.3, *supra*.

508 *See also* § 5.10, *infra*.

509 § 5.3.1.1, *supra*.

510 This table rounds fractions of cents to the nearest penny.

511 24.91% is the actuarial equivalent of 14% add-on rate for twelve months.

| | *Old Periodic Balance* | + | *2.07583% Monthly Interest* | − | *Monthly Installment Payment* | = | *New Periodic Balance* | *Monthly Paid To Principal* | *Cumulative Interest Earned* |
|---|---|---|---|---|---|---|---|---|---|
| Jan. | $1,000.00 | | $20.76 | | $95.00 | | $925.76 | $74.24 | $20.76 |
| Feb. | $925.76 | | $19.22 | | $95.00 | | $849.98 | $75.78 | $39.98 |
| Mar. | $849.98 | | $17.64 | | $95.00 | | $772.62 | $77.36 | $57.62 |
| Apr. | $772.62 | | | | | | | | |

The interest earned each month is calculated by multiplying the current principal balance by the periodic interest rate. This earned interest is deducted from the monthly payment and the remainder of the payment is used to reduce the balance of the loan. The following month's interest is calculated using this new, reduced balance.

In this example, the lender has earned $57.62 in interest over the three months of the loan, and the borrower is entitled to a rebate of: $140 total precomputed interest − $57.62 earned interest = $82.38. The total amount repayable of $1,140 minus the amount that the borrower has already paid (3 × $95 = $285) equals $855, the amount the lender shows as due after three months.[512] When the rebate of $82.38 is subtracted, the balance is $772.62, which is the amount that the borrower will have to pay to retire the loan at this point.

The example given here assumes that the first three installments of the loan were paid on time. If a payment had been missed or paid late, additional portions of the borrower's payments would be attributed to interest or late fees, and the rebate would be reduced. On the other hand, if some of the payments had been made early, the lender would have earned less interest and the rebate would increase. However, many statutes allow actuarial rebates to be calculated using the assumption that all installments were paid on time.[513]

Whenever a debt is accelerated or prepaid on any day other than the scheduled monthly payment date, the effect of the fractional payment interval must be taken into account. For example, if the borrower had prepaid the loan after three months and one day instead of after exactly three months, the lender would have earned an extra day's interest. That one day's interest would be: $772.62 (the loan balance after three months) × 0.0207583 (the monthly rate) × 1/30 (assuming one day to be one thirtieth of a month) = $0.53. Therefore, after three months and one day, the lender would have earned $57.62 + $0.53 = $58.15, and the borrower would be entitled to a rebate of $140 − $58.15 = $81.85.

Lenders may attempt to round fractional intervals in their favor. Thus, when prepayment occurs after three months and a day, a lender might claim four months of interest. Although this practice may be permitted by some rebate statutes,[514] it is important to recognize that such rounding is not actuarial. Actuarially, a lender can earn only one day's interest in one day, not a whole month's interest.[515] Therefore, the very fact that a statute requires an "actuarial" rebate should preclude such rounding unless the statute specifically permits it.

#### 5.8.6.4.3 *Actuarial rebates under actuarial split rate statutes*

A special rebate calculation issue arises under actuarial "split rate" usury statutes, which apply one interest rate to part of the outstanding balance and another rate, to the rest.[516] Such statutes do not produce a simple interest amortization pattern. Yet, when calculating rebates for precomputed transactions under actuarial split rate statutes,[517] creditors frequently assume simple interest amortization, using one twelfth of the APR as the monthly interest rate. Such an assumption changes the earnings pattern mandated by the split rate statute, and, assuming that the rate permitted for the first part of the outstanding balance is higher than the rate permitted for the rest, causes lower rebates.[518] An example may help to illustrate this point.

512 Note that the balance due under the loan contract is $855 after three months, while the amortization table shows $772.62 in principal remaining at that point. The reason for the difference is that the remaining balance due under the loan contract includes interest that has not yet been earned (which is why a rebate is necessary). The $772.62 figure shown on the amortization table does not include any unearned interest, but represents only the remaining principal, after an actuarial allocation of payments between principal and interest.

513 *See, e.g.*, Ariz. Rev. Stat. Ann. § 6-634.

514 *See* § 5.8.5.2, *supra*. *Cf.* Beaty v. Land of Lincoln Sav. & Loan, 468 N.E.2d 1259 (Ill. App. Ct. 1984) (where contract provided that interest for the month was earned on first day of the month, and state law allowed collection of interest in advance, lender's collection of interest for full month when borrower prepaid on second day of month did not violate state law and was not prepayment penalty).

515 *See* Financial Publishing Co., The Cost of Personal Borrowing in the United States 32 (2004).

516 The issue arises only under actuarial split rate statutes as opposed to split rate statutes that allow add-on or discount interest calculations. The reason is that only actuarial computation takes the declining principal balance of the credit into account and, thus, causes the effective interest rate to rise during the term of the transaction as the part of the principal balance to which the lower rate applies is paid off. Split rate calculations are discussed at § 5.3.4, *supra*.

517 The concept of precomputed actuarial interest may seem contradictory, but actually it need not be. If permitted by the applicable statute, a creditor may simply calculate actuarial interest with an amortization table by assuming that payments are made on the scheduled installment dates. It then adds this precomputed actuarial interest to the principal amount and requires the borrower to sign a note for the total amount.

518 The difference between the earnings pattern under a simple interest rate, such as the APR, and the pattern created by a split rate statute can be viewed in the following manner. A simple interest amortization assumes that a single unchanging rate is applied, usually monthly, to the total outstanding balance at the time of each installment payment. Under a split rate statute, however, two or more different rates may apply simultaneously to different portions

Assume a split rate debt of $1,000 where the actuarial interest rate is 2% per month on the first $500 of credit and 1.5% per month on the remaining $500, creating a total precomputed interest charge of $247.99 over twenty-four months. The regular monthly payment is $52. The first three months' amortization of the loan is shown in the following chart, where "Interest 1" is the interest generated by the first incremental rate (2% on the first $500) and "Interest 2" is generated by the second incremental rate (1.5% on the balance over $500):

| *Old Balance* | + | *Interest 1* | + | *Interest 2* | – | *Payment* | = | *New Balance* |
|---|---|---|---|---|---|---|---|---|
| $1,000.00 | | $10.00 | | $7.50 | | $52.00 | | $965.50 |
| $965.50 | | $10.00 | | $6.98 | | $52.00 | | $930.48 |
| $930.49 | | $10.00 | | $6.46 | | $52.00 | | $894.94 |

The total interest earned (adding the Interest 1 and Interest 2 columns) in three months is $50.94. The rebate at this point would be $197.05 ($247.99 – 50.94 = $197.05).

The APR for this transaction is 22.2267%. But if the APR is used to work out the amortization at 1.852% per month (22.226% ÷ 12 = 1.852%), the same total interest is earned overall but the pattern in which interest is earned is different:

| *Old Balance* | + | *Interest* | – | *Payment* | = | *New Balance* |
|---|---|---|---|---|---|---|
| $1,000.00 | | $18.52 | | $52.00 | | $966.52 |
| $966.52 | | $17.90 | | $52.00 | | $932.42 |
| $932.42 | | $17.27 | | $52.00 | | $897.69 |

The total interest earned by the creditor after three months using this amortization is $53.69, or $2.75 more than would be generated using the split rate. Using the APR for amortization, the rebate would only be $194.30 ($247.99 – $53.69 = $194.30).

State laws and regulations must be consulted to determine which of these two actuarial rebates is correct. In a few states the problem has been directly addressed by statute.[519] However, if the applicable statute simply requires an "actuarial" rebate and does not specify that a simple interest amortization may be used for the rebate calculation, practitioners should argue that the very existence of the split rate statute constitutes a statutory specification that interest may only be earned in accordance with a split rate amortization pattern. The use of a simple interest amortization under such circumstances should be recognized as no more than a self-serving method of retaining illegal unearned interest.

## 5.8.7 Remedies for Rebate Violations

### 5.8.7.1 Failure to Give a Required Rebate As a Usury Violation

A number of decisions recognize that failure to give a required rebate, or to calculate the rebate correctly, gives rise to a usury or overcharge claim[520] and entitles the borrower to the remedies the usury law provides.[521] As discussed in the next subsection, older decisions holding that a contract cannot be made usurious by a "contingency" have largely been rendered irrelevant to rebate issues by the incorporation of rebate requirements into consumer credit laws. Whether intent must be shown, and what acts demonstrate intent, remains an issue, however, as discussed at § 5.8.7.3, *infra*.

### 5.8.7.2 Usury upon a Contingent Event

Until the 1960s, it was common for usury statutes to neglect the issue of rebates upon the early termination of precomputed debt. With the exception of small loan laws or other special usury statutes, most usury laws simply provided interest ceilings, and many courts, adopting a strict construction of usury provisions, held that these ceilings applied only to the terms of

of the outstanding balance. Usually a higher rate applies to the first $500 or $1,000 of the outstanding balance, and one or more progressively lower rates apply to any additional portions of the outstanding balance. The critical point to recognize is that the "upper" portion(s) of the principal balance, to which the lower rate(s) apply, are paid off first. Thus, the lower rate(s) apply only during the beginning of the loan term while the higher incremental rate that applies to the first $500 or $1,000 will apply throughout the entire loan term. Consequently, under a split rate statute, the effective interest rate on the outstanding balance is higher later in the loan term.

If a single flat interest rate, specifically the APR, is substituted for the split interest rate, the total amount of interest earned over the entire loan term will be the same, but the effective interest rate and the interest earned at the beginning of the loan term will be exaggerated, while the effective rate and the interest earned at the end of the term will be understated. Therefore, a creditor that uses the APR in a rebate calculation will be claiming more earnings early in the credit term than it is due under a split rate amortization, and will provide a lower rebate than that to which the borrower may be entitled.

519 *See* Cal. Fin. Code § 22308 (West).

520 *See, e.g.*, Clyde v. Liberty Loan Co., 287 S.E.2d 551 (Ga. 1982) (contract was usurious where it allowed acceleration without a rebate); Palace Indus., Inc. v. Craig, 339 S.E.2d 313 (Ga. Ct. App. 1985) (acceleration without rebate is usurious); Jim Walter Homes v. Schuenemann, 668 S.W.2d 324 (Tex. 1984) (acceleration clause that would call for payment of unearned time-price differential was usurious); Dryden v. City Nat'l Bank, 666 S.W.2d 213 (Tex. App. 1984) (demand for full amount, without rebate of unearned interest, is usurious); Commercial Credit Corp. v. Chasteen, 565 S.W.2d 342 (Tex. Ct. App. 1978) (accelerating debt and demanding unearned interest is usurious). *See also* Brookshire v. Longhorn Chevrolet, Inc., 788 S.W.2d 209 (Tex. App. 1990) (acceleration clause in contract rendered it usurious on its face where it expressly entitled creditor, upon happening of the contingency of default and acceleration, to exact greater than lawful interest by demanding the unpaid balance of the "Total of Payments," which includes the finance charges). *Cf.* Greeley Nat'l Bank v. Sloan, 677 P.2d 409 (Colo. App. 1983) (rebate required, but declining to impose penalty where creditor voluntarily adjusted its claim before judgment). *But cf.* Horton v. Middle Georgia Bank, 380 S.E.2d 749 (Ga. Ct. App. 1989) (method of acceleration and rebate could not give rise to usury claim because there was no interest rate ceiling for this type of loan, so the unearned interest did not push the effective rate above the ceiling).

521 *See* § 7.8, *infra*.

a contract at the time of its execution.[522] Thus, a contract that would not have been usurious if its anticipated payment schedule had been met could not be made usurious by some "contingency," such as the "voluntary" action of the debtor in prepaying or defaulting on the debt.[523]

The rule against the creation of usury through contingencies can be criticized on its own terms. The notion that contractual default and acceleration is caused by the voluntary action of the debtor is, to say the least, strained.[524] Similarly, the position that voluntary prepayment is unanticipated at the time a credit contract is executed lacks credibility, given the high percentage of consumer loans that are prepaid or refinanced.[525] Such common sense arguments aside, it is critical for practitioners to recognize that the rule against the existence of usury in contingencies is simply a rule of construction developed by courts interpreting statutes that were silent on the need for rebates.[526] If a statute specifically requires the rebate of unearned interest or premiums, as do almost all modern statutes regulating precomputed consumer credit, then the failure of the creditor to provide such rebates triggers whatever remedies that statute provides. These remedy provisions often apply even absent intent,[527] but in any case, the intentional failure of the creditor to provide required rebates is usurious.[528] The question then is: when does a creditor manifest an intent to deny the rebate to which the consumer is entitled?

522 This result may still hold if a statute regulates only the interest "contracted for," as opposed to the interest "contracted for or received," especially if the legislature used the latter language in another statute. Concord Realty Co. v. Continental Funding Corp., 776 P.2d 1114, 1120 (Colo. 1989) (*en banc*). *See also* § 5.8.7.3, *infra*.

523 *See, e.g.*, Lederman Enters., Inc. v. Westinghouse Credit Corp., 347 F. Supp. 1291 (D. Colo. 1972) (prepayment penalty); Winkle v. Grand Nat'l Bank, 601 S.W.2d 559 (Ark. 1980); Valliappan v. Cruz, 917 So. 2d 257 (Fla. Dist. Ct. App. 2005) (loan not usurious where obligation to repay more than principal was contingent upon outcome of business negotiation); Jackson Inv. Co. v. Bates, 366 So. 2d 225 (Miss. 1978) (relying on contingency rule to decline to impose usury remedies where failure to make rebate pushed effective interest rate above statutory cap); B.F. Saul Co. v. West End Park North, Inc., 246 A.2d 591 (Md. 1968) (prepayment); Industrial Nat'l Bank v. Stuard, 318 A.2d 452 (R.I. 1974) (default and acceleration). *But see* C.I.O.S. Found. v. Berkston Ins. A.V.V., 2000 U.S. Dist. LEXIS 2337 (N.D. Miss. 2000) (Texas law) (usury penalties apply if any contingency would make loan usurious, but applying spreading doctrine to avoid usury); Dixon v. Brooks, 604 S.W.2d 330 (Tex. Ct. App. 1980) (usury exists as a matter of law when any contingency exists under which the creditor can receive more than the maximum rate).

524 *See* Begelfer v. Najarian, 409 N.E.2d 167 (Mass. 1980) (late fees). *Cf.* Texas Airfinance Corp. v. Lesikar, 777 S.W.2d 559 (Tex. App. 1989) (upon acceleration borrower has not sought privilege of early payment and therefore prepayment penalty is impermissible).

525 *See* § 5.9.1, *infra*.

526 *See* B.F. Saul Co. v. West End Park North, Inc., 246 A.2d 591 (Md. 1968) (distinguishing loans to which rebate statute applies).

527 *See* § 5.8.7.3.1, *infra*.

528 *See, e.g.*, *In re* Sprouse, 577 F.2d 989 (5th Cir. 1978); Aetna Fin. Co. v. Brown, 323 S.E.2d 720 (Ga. Ct. App. 1984); Union Trust Co. of Md. v. Tyndall, 428 A.2d 428 (Md. 1981); Jim Walter Homes, Inc. v. Schuenemann, 668 S.W.2d 324 (Tex. 1984).

The rule against usury through contingencies nevertheless may allow creditors to avoid making rebates in some credit transactions that are nominally interest-bearing but which include significant prepaid finance charges, such as points. If a rebate statute applies only to precomputed transactions and the definition of "precomputed" does not encompass such mixed transactions, the traditional rule against usury in contingency situations could be invoked to excuse the failure to rebate the prepaid charges.[529]

### 5.8.7.3 Intent; What Constitutes "Charging," or "Collecting" Unearned Charges

#### *5.8.7.3.1 Whether intent is required*

Under some consumer credit statutes, specific remedies are authorized wherever finance charges (or simply charges) in excess of those allowed are charged, or more generally where provisions of the act are violated.[530] Any time the statute provides for a specific remedy for imposing charges in excess of those allowed, a provision requiring rebates should be considered to be encompassed by that language.

In other cases, given a statute that requires the rebate of unearned charges upon prepayment or acceleration, proof of usury may depend primarily on a demonstration of the creditor's intent to collect unearned charges in violation of the statute. Interpretations of usurious intent vary significantly from jurisdiction to jurisdiction, and the subject as a whole is treated elsewhere in this treatise.[531] Nevertheless, the intent to collect unearned charges presents some special issues that will be mentioned here.

#### *5.8.7.3.2 Does the contract show the creditor's intent to charge unearned interest?*

There are two ways in which a creditor may violate usury law rebate requirements: either the creditor can provide a contract that on its face fails to provide for the appropriate rebate, or it can neglect in actual practice to give a rebate that it is both contractually and statutorily required to give. Where intent is required, demonstrating a usury violation in the first situation may be considerably easier than in the second because the contract itself can show the creditor's intent. In many jurisdictions, it is usurious merely to "contract for" usurious payments. Any contract calling for the collection of unearned charges upon acceleration or prepayment is therefore facially usurious and justifies statutory sanctions even if the contingency of acceleration or prepayment never occurs.[532]

529 *See* Colorado Dep't of Law, Admin. Interp. Nos. 2.201, 3.201 and 3.508-8301 (Oct. 14, 1983) (interpreting Colorado U.C.C.C. not to require rebate for prepaid finance charges in nonprecomputed transactions unless prepayment was originally anticipated. Note that Colorado statute and regulations now require such a rebate if refinancing occurs within the first year); Colo. Rev. Stat. § 5-2-207(2)(b); 4 Colo. Code Regs. § 902-1 Rule 13.

530 *See generally* §§ 7.5.5, 7.8, *infra*.

531 *See* § 7.5.5, *infra*.

532 *See, e.g.*, G.A.C. Fin. Corp. v. Hardy, 208 S.E.2d 453 (Ga. 1974);

This rule has led to considerable litigation in some states, especially Georgia and Texas, over the construction of acceleration clauses, and the courts involved have drawn some very fine lines. For example, in Georgia, contract clauses permitting the acceleration of "all installments,"[533] "the entire balance,"[534] and "all remaining payments"[535] were usurious, as was a contract requiring payment of "the entire debt," stated as the face amount of the note.[536] On the other hand, contracts allowing the acceleration of "the note"[537] or "all liabilities"[538] were not. Similarly, in Texas acceleration of an entire "note" has been held to be usurious when the note includes unearned interest, while the acceleration of "debt" has been held not to violate usury law because the "debt" can be construed not to include unearned interest.[539]

In jurisdictions where case law has not already determined the standard for interpreting acceleration and prepayment clauses, practitioners should argue that such clauses should be read as an average consumer would read them.[540] It is important to recognize that the reason that dozens of judicial interpretations of acceleration clauses have been necessary is not that the consumer credit industry is incapable of drafting an acceleration clause that clearly and unambiguously provides for the rebate of unearned interest. The only conclusion that can be drawn from the amount of litigation construing acceleration clauses is that the drafting of consumer contracts is often deliberately opaque and designed to convince lay debtors that a creditor has greater rights than the law actually allows.

The muddying of consumers' clear statutory rights through the use of vague contract language should be combated by construing these clauses as debtors would interpret them rather than through the construction of fine legal distinctions that would never occur to the average consumer. Thus practitioners should argue that if a debtor reading an acceleration clause would believe that the creditor could retain or collect unearned charges, the clause should be so interpreted and the contract held to be illegal.[541]

#### *5.8.7.3.3 Has the creditor failed to give the rebate the contract requires?*

If a credit contract properly provides for a rebate upon the early termination of a precomputed debt, the next question is whether, when the prepayment or acceleration finally occurs, the creditor actually gives the rebate properly. Often the issue will be whether the creditor's acts violate a statutory prohibition against "charging," "collecting," or "receiving" usurious interest.[542]

Generally, the "charging" of unearned interest involves some demand by the creditor for the payment of a sum in excess of that to which it is entitled at the time of the demand. Illegal charging has been found in demand letters,[543] in statements of account,[544] and in court pleadings.[545] However, courts have at times allowed creditors to amend apparently usurious court pleadings, and thereby to avoid usury, by removing unearned charges from the judgment originally sought.[546] This practice is extremely unwise, as some courts have recognized, because it enables unscrupulous creditors to circumvent the usury law.[547] Because defaults on consumer credit are rarely contested, such a rule allows a creditor to charge and collect unearned interest

Coastal Cement Sand Inc. v. First Interstate Credit Alliance, Inc., 956 S.W.2d 562 (Tex. App. 1997) (commercial case applying *Schuenemann* holding); Jim Walter Homes, Inc. v. Schuenemann, 668 S.W.2d 324 (Tex. 1984); Commercial Credit Corp. v. Chasteen, 565 S.W.2d 342 (Tex. Ct. App. 1978).

533 Lewis v. Termplan, Inc., 184 S.E.2d 473 (Ga. Ct. App. 1971).

534 Hardy v. G.A.C. Fin., 205 S.E.2d 526 (Ga. Ct. App. 1974), *aff'd*, 208 S.E.2d 453 (Ga. 1974).

535 Frazier v. Courtesy Fin. Co., 208 S.E.2d 175 (Ga. Ct. App. 1974).

536 Clyde v. Liberty Loan Co., 287 S.E.2d 551 (Ga. 1982) (also holding contract usurious that provided for rebate of unearned interest but not unearned maintenance charges and credit insurance premiums upon acceleration).

537 Plant v. Blazer Fin. Servs., 598 F.2d 1357 (5th Cir. 1979) (construing clause allowing acceleration of "the note" in light of other provisions referring to rebates).

538 Goodwin v. Trust Co. of Columbus, 242 S.E.2d 302 (Ga. Ct. App. 1978).

539 Jim Walter Homes v. Schuenemann, 668 S.W.2d 324 (Tex. 1984) (citing Texas cases). *See also* Mack v. Newton, 737 F.2d 1345 (5th Cir. 1984) (discussing Texas law). Interestingly, the acceleration of a "note" may not call for the collection of unearned interest under Georgia law, at least when proper language exists elsewhere in the contract.

540 *See In re* Sprouse, 577 F.2d 989 (5th Cir. 1978) (discussing effect of overreaching contract language on consumers in transactions that are not litigated).

541 *See id.*

542 *See* § 7.5.4.2, *infra*.

543 *See* Palace Indus., Inc. v. Craig, 339 S.E.2d 313 (Ga. Ct. App. 1985) (demand letters and complaint seeking unearned interest amount to illegal charge in violation of RISA); Dryden v. City Nat'l Bank, 666 S.W.2d 213 (Tex. App. 1984) (demand letters were "charge" even though debtor's account properly credited with rebate). *See generally* § 7.5.4.2, *infra*.

544 *See* Danziger v. San Jacinto Sav. Ass'n, 732 S.W.2d 300 (Tex. 1987) (inclusion of excess interest in pay-off quote constituted "charging" illegal interest); Cigna Ins. Co. v. TPG Store, Inc., 894 S.W.2d 431 (Tex. App. 1995) (statement including unrebated interest constituted usurious "charging"; subsequent credit cannot purge the usury). *But cf.* Mack v. Newton, 737 F.2d 1345 (5th Cir. 1984) (telephone conversation). *See generally* § 7.5.4.2, *infra*.

545 *See* Bell v. Loosier of Albany, Inc., 229 S.E.2d 374 (Ga. 1976) (filing suit for unearned interest violates usury statute); Palace Indus., Inc. v. Craig, 339 S.E.2d 313 (Ga. Ct. App. 1985). *But see* George A. Fuller Co. v. Carpet Serv., Inc., 823 S.W.2d 603 (Tex. 1992) (filing suit for unlawful unearned interest does not make pleader liable for statutory usury penalties). *See generally* § 7.5.4.2, *infra*.

546 *See* Greeley Nat'l Bank v. Sloan, 677 P.2d 409 (Colo. App. 1983); Northwestern Bank v. Barber, 339 S.E.2d 452 (N.C. Ct. App. 1986). *See also* Gergora v. Goldstein Prof'l Ass'n, 500 So. 2d 695 (Fla. Dist. Ct. App. 1987) (finding that lender complies with statutory "purge" provision by dismissing action that claimed usurious interest; sending letter reducing note rate to legal rate, and then refiling lawsuit). *But cf.* Carter v. First Fed. Sav. & Loan Ass'n, 347 S.E.2d 264 (Ga. Ct. App. 1986) (statute violated despite amendment of amount sought).

547 *See* Thomas v. Universal Guardian Corp., 243 S.E.2d 101, 102 (Ga. Ct. App. 1978). *Cf.* Danziger v. San Jacinto Sav. Ass'n, 732 S.W.2d 300 (Tex. 1987) (once usurious sum is charged, usury cannot be cured by rebate of excess charges to debtor's account). *See generally* § 7.7.9, *infra* (usury saving clauses).

as a general policy, amending its complaint and providing proper rebates only in the rare instances when it is challenged.[548] It thus keeps the illegal gains and completely avoids any sanction in the majority of cases where it is not caught.

### 5.8.7.4 Special Issues Regarding Remedies for Violation of the Federal Rebate Statute

The federal rebate statute does not include any provisions for a specific remedy in the event a creditor violates it. Its codification in the midst of a statute of which it is not officially a part creates confusion as to applicable remedies.[549] Nonetheless, there are several viable theories that the consumer can assert in the event a creditor violates the statute.

***Truth in Lending***: Given its location, the immediate thought would be to look to Truth in Lending Act remedies. However, irrespective of whether it is considered part of TILA, a violation of the federal rebate statute probably does *not directly* lead to a viable claim for private TILA remedies.[550] Nonetheless, a violation may lead *indirectly* to a TILA violation. If a creditor[551] refinances its own loan (or a holder or servicer refinances a loan it is holding or servicing),[552] and calculates the prior loan's payoff in violation of the federal rebate statute—either by failing to give rebates or by using the Rule of 78s when the actuarial method is required—the new loan will include an "unearned portion of the old finance charge that is not credited to the existing obligation."[553] Under TILA rules, that is to be considered part of the finance charge in the new loan.[554] Thus, the disclosed amount financed, finance charge, and APR on the new loan all will be inaccurately disclosed. Depending on whether the amount of the error exceeds certain tolerances,[555] Truth in Lending remedies such as statutory damages may be available for this violation.[556]

***UDAP***: Failure to comply with the rebate law should also state a UDAP claim, where the transaction and lender are subject to the statute: the amount of the improperly calculated rebate would be actual damages.[557] The mere presence of a contract clause that indicates no rebate would be made, or that the Rule of 78s would be used in violation of the statute, might be considered a UDAP violation even if never invoked.[558]

***Contract law***: Common law contract principles may also be invoked to seek a remedy, as applicable law is an implied term of every contract.[559]

### 5.8.7.5 Framing Rebate Issues As Prepayment Penalty Questions

A number of state statutes specifically prohibit prepayment penalties.[560] In these states, it may be advantageous to frame a rebate issue as a prepayment penalty. For example, where not specifically authorized, a creditor's use of the Rule of 78s to calculate rebates upon prepayment may be challenged as an illegal prepayment penalty.[561]

Early Truth in Lending cases discussed, but did not resolve, the issue of whether the rule was a prepayment penalty which should have been disclosed as such under TILA.[562] The federal legislation regulating certain high-cost home equity loans specifically labels any rebate method less favorable than the actuarial method a prepayment penalty.[563]

---

548 *See In re* Sprouse, 577 F.2d 989 (5th Cir. 1978).

549 *See* § 5.8.4.2.2, *supra*.

550 Civil liability applies to violations of parts B, D, and E of TILA. 15 U.S.C. § 1640. The rebate statute was codified in Part A, 15 U.S.C. § 1615.

551 *See* 15 U.S.C. § 1615(d) (defining "creditor" by reference to TILA's definition, but specifically including assignees as well).

552 Official Commentary on Regulation Z § 1026.20(a)-5.

553 Reg. Z, 12 C.F.R. § 1026.20(a). *See, e.g.*, Steele v. Ford Motor Credit Co., 783 F.2d 1016 (11th Cir. 1986). *See generally* National Consumer Law Center, Truth in Lending § 3.7.2.3.3 (7th ed. 2010 and Supp.). Note that this would also be the case when a creditor used the rule in violation of any other applicable statute.

554 Reg. Z, 12 C.F.R. § 1026.20(a).

555 National Consumer Law Center, Truth in Lending § 5.4.3 (7th ed. 2010 and Supp.).

556 15 U.S.C. § 1640; National Consumer Law Center, Truth in Lending §§ 11.5, 11.6 (7th ed. 2010 and Supp.).

557 *See* § 2.4.1, *supra* (scope, substantive prohibitions, and remedies of UDAP statutes in credit transactions); National Consumer Law Center, Unfair and Deceptive Acts and Practices (7th ed. 2008 and Supp.).

558 National Consumer Law Center, Unfair and Deceptive Acts and Practices § 7.5.2 (7th ed. 2008 and Supp.); Leardi v. Brown, 474 N.E.2d 1094 (Mass. 1985).

559 National Consumer Law Center, Unfair and Deceptive Acts and Practices § 5.6.3.3 (7th ed. 2008 and Supp.); 17A Am. Jur. 2d, *Contracts* § 371 (2004).

560 *See* National Consumer Law Center, Mortgage Lending § 8.11 (2012) (regulation of prepayment penalties in mortgage loans).

561 *See In re* Jones, 79 B.R. 233 (Bankr. E.D. Pa. 1987); *In re* Jungkurth, 74 B.R. 323 (Bankr. E.D. Pa. 1987) (ordering actuarial rebate; failure to provide a fair rebate constitutes prepayment penalty). *See also* Livingston v. Vanguard Fed. Sav. Bank, 563 A.2d 175 (Pa. Super. Ct. 1989) (challenging use of Rule of 78s as contravening state statute prohibiting prepayment penalties in manufactured home contracts; case decided on other grounds). *Cf.* Prabel v. Commissioner, 882 F.2d 820, 827 (3d Cir. 1989) (IRS case; noting that in event of prepayment, the difference between the economic accrual of interest owed and that owed under the Rule of 78s "should be considered a prepayment penalty"); Kedziora v. Citicorp Nat'l Servs., 780 F. Supp. 516 (N.D. Ill. 1991) (discussing Rule of 78s as method of determining early termination penalty in auto lease under Consumer Leasing Act); *In re* Tucker, 74 B.R. 923, 927 (Bankr. E.D. Pa. 1987) (non-actuarial formula would be usurious prepayment penalty, but here state law allows it). *But see* Ortegel v. ITT Thorp Corp., 569 N.E.2d 586 (Ill. App. Ct. 1991) (use of Rule of 78s was not a prepayment penalty. *Note*: the precedential value of this case should be limited, as the court's analysis suggests it was confused as to the nature of the problem, e.g., ". . . the borrower must pay the interest even if the loan is not prepaid," and "plaintiffs would have paid [interest charges] regardless of early payment." *Id.* at 590, 588 respectively. That begs the question, which is the 78s penalty upon prepayment. *See* § 5.8.6.3, *supra*).

562 *Compare* Bone v. Hibernia Bank, 493 F.2d 135 (9th Cir. 1974), *and* Drennan v. Security Pac. Nat'l Bank, 621 P.2d 1318 (Cal. 1981) (no TILA violation), *with* Ballew v. Associates Fin. Servs. Co. of Neb., 450 F. Supp. 253 (D. Neb. 1976) (TILA violation). *See also* Kedziora v. Citicorp Nat'l Servs., 780 F. Supp. 516 (N.D. Ill. 1991) (discussion and criticism of the TILA treatment of the rule as a prepayment penalty).

563 *See* § 5.8.6.1.3, *supra*.

Despite these similarities, it would be a mistake to regard rebate requirements and prepayment penalty prohibitions as interchangeable. The most obvious difference is that statutes prohibiting prepayment penalties typically are invoked when debt is retired through voluntary prepayment,[564] while rebate requirements apply to precomputed debt regardless of whether it is prepaid, accelerated, or otherwise matured.[565] As one court viewed it, a statutory Rule of 78s rebate authorization deals with the calculation of unearned interest, while a prepayment penalty prohibition forbids imposing a separate charge or penalty "simply for the privilege of prepaying."[566] Another court distinguished between voluntary prepayment and acceleration to decide whether the Rule of 78s could be used by a creditor upon acceleration when the contract clause in the loan regarding acceleration was silent as to the method of rebate but the clause regarding prepayment allowed the rebate to be computed using the Rule of 78s. The court held that the contract was ambiguous, so would be construed against the maker, and therefore the use of the Rule of 78s was prohibited.[567]

A second significant difference between the prohibition of prepayment penalties and rebate requirements is that rebates apply only to precomputed debt whereas statutes forbidding prepayment penalties usually encompass interest-bearing transactions, such as the typical mortgage. As a result, a lender's failure to rebate points or other prepaid finance charges on nominally interest-bearing debt may be better attacked as a prepayment penalty (assuming that the debt is retired through prepayment) than as a rebate violation.

Even if a state does not explicitly prohibit prepayment penalties, it may view a prepayment penalty as the assessment of interest. In that case, the prepayment penalty may cause the loan to exceed the usury cap. However, some courts hold that a prepayment penalty is not interest, but a charge for the option of prepayment.[568] However, there may be a question as to whether the payment is contingent upon the voluntary choice of the borrower to prepay the debt, and courts generally refuse to find usury in contingencies.[569]

## 5.9 The Mathematics of Loan Flipping

### *5.9.1 Overview*

Refinancing, in the right circumstances, and with the right lender, is a good deal for both parties. For example, many consumers replaced the 10% to 11% purchase money mortgages written in the 1980s with 7% to 8% mortgages when interest rates dipped to surprising lows in the early 1990s.

But refinancing is not always so mutually beneficial. It can be a trap for unwary consumers, and it is on the hidden costs that can attend refinancing that this section focuses. Being a repeat customer at the neighborhood finance company or mortgage lender, for example, frequently is not quite the same thing as being a repeat customer at the neighborhood grocery store. At the grocery store, the price of a loaf of bread marked $1.29

564 *See In re* LHD Realty Corp., 726 F.2d 327 (7th Cir. 1984); *In re* Planvest Equity Income Partners IV, 94 B.R. 644 (Bankr. D. Ariz. 1988) (prepayment penalty not allowed upon liquidation or acceleration); Broadway Bank v. Star Hospitality, Inc., 2004 WL 2677658 (Iowa Ct. App. Nov. 24, 2004) (prepayment penalty not available when lender accelerates debt); Texas Airfinance Corp. v. Lesikar, 777 S.W.2d 559 (Tex. App. 1989) (prepayment penalty is unenforceable with acceleration because borrower is not seeking privilege of early payment). *See also* Clean Harbors, Inc. v. John Hancock Life Ins. Co., 833 N.E.2d 611 (Mass. App. Ct. 2005) (rejecting attempt by borrower to avoid prepayment penalty by voluntarily defaulting so that debt would be accelerated). *Cf. In re* Imperial Coronado Partners, Ltd., 96 B.R. 997 (B.A.P. 9th Cir. 1989) (prepayment penalty not available where creditor accelerates, but if borrower opted to sell the property and pay off the loan after acceleration instead of exercising right of reinstatement under state law or deacceleration under bankruptcy, prepayment was voluntary and penalty could be collected ); LaSalle Bank v. Mobile Hotel Props., L.L.C., 367 F. Supp. 2d 1022 (E.D. La. 2004) (lender not entitled to collect prepayment fee upon acceleration unless contract explicitly provides). *But see* Katzenstein v. VIII SV5556 Lender, L.L.C. (*In re* St. Vincent's Catholic Med. Ctrs. of N.Y.), 440 B.R. 587, 597 (Bankr. S.D.N.Y. 2010); Financial Ctr. Assocs. v. TNE Funding Corp. (*In re* Financial Ctr. Assocs.), 140 B.R. 829 (Bankr. E.D.N.Y. 1992) (prepayment penalty may be charged upon acceleration if note so provides); Westmark Commercial Mortgage Fund IV v. Teenform Assocs., 827 A.2d 1154 (N.J. Super. Ct. App. Div. 2003) (prepayment penalty is available upon acceleration of commercial loan unless it is unreasonable).

565 The existence of a statute requiring rebates upon prepayment, in the absence of a statute compelling rebates upon default and acceleration, need not, however, be read as allowing the retention of unearned interest upon acceleration. *See* Glacier Lincoln-Mercury, Inc. v. Freeman, Consumer Cred. Guide (CCH) ¶ 99,567 (Alaska Dist. Ct. 1970).

566 Pysh v. Security Pac. Hous. Serv., 610 A.2d 973 (Pa. Super. Ct. 1992) (recognizing that use of Rule of 78s results in an early pay-off balance some $3,000 greater than actuarial method, but applicable statute specifically authorized rule while prohibiting prepayment penalties, so reconciling the two provisions).

567 Zwayer v. Ford Motor Credit Co., 665 N.E.2d 843, 846 (Ill. App. Ct. 1996) (also noting that Illinois Motor Vehicle Resale Installment Sales Act permits but does not require use of Rule of 78s). *See also* *In re* Deep River Warehouse, Inc., 2005 WL 1513123 (Bankr. M.D.N.C. June 22, 2005) (construing contract against drafter to hold that prepayment penalty did not become due upon default and acceleration). *But see* Charley v. Franklin Capital Corp., 2010 WL 4162550 (N.M. Ct. App. June 17, 2010) (refusing to construe contract's silence about method of calculating rebate of unearned insurance premiums as requiring actuarial calculation), *cert. granted*, 242 P.3d 1289 (N.M. 2010).

568 *See, e.g.*, C.C. Port, Ltd. v. Davis-Penn Mortgage Co., 61 F.3d 288 (5th Cir. 1995) (Texas law) (prepayment premium is charge for option of prepayment, not interest; commercial case); Texas Airfinance Corp. v. Lesikar, 777 S.W.2d 559 (Tex. App. 1989); Boyd v. Life Ins. Co. of the Southwest, 546 S.W.2d 132 (Tex. Civ. App. 1977). *See also* Achee Holdings, L.L.C. v. Silver Hill Fin., L.L.C., 2009 WL 347751 (S.D. Tex. Feb. 9, 2009) (Texas statute provides that prepayment penalty is not interest, so seeking it was not usury), *aff'd*, 342 Fed. Appx. 943 (5th Cir. 2009). *Cf.* Affiliated Capital v. Commercial Fed. Bank, 834 S.W.2d 521 (Tex. App. 1992) (apparently treating prepayment penalty as interest, but applying spreading doctrine to find loan not usurious).

569 *See* Lederman Enters., Inc. v. Westinghouse Credit Corp., 347 F. Supp. 1291 (D. Colo. 1972); Winkle v. Grand Nat'l Bank, 601 S.W.2d 559 (Ark. 1980). *See also* B.F. Saul Co. v. West End Park North, Inc., 246 A.2d 591 (Md. 1968). *See generally* § 5.8.7.2, *supra*.

really is $1.29 for everybody, every time. A $1,000 loan at 30% for two years should be marked to sell for $342 in interest.[570] But a customer refinancing to borrow an extra $1,000 at 30% can pay a lot more than $342 for that extra $1,000.

That is why some segments of the consumer credit industry encourage refinancing. They urge borrowers to combine medical, dental, credit card, and utility bills into a single debt for the "ease of a single monthly payment," or they promise that refinancing a mortgage loan will produce lower payments or provide needed cash. Solicitous letters arrive regularly to existing customers asking if they would like more money.[571]

The "flipping penalty"—the added cost of borrowing that can result from refinancing—can be substantial. Refinancing also usually lengthens the amount of time the borrower remains indebted, and it may put the borrower's home on the line if it becomes collateral on the new loan. Repeated refinancing of mortgage loans is a way for the lender to strip the equity out of a home.[572] Payday lenders also rely on repeat lending, which enables them to charge a flat fee for each of a series of loans, at much greater profit than a single loan for a longer term.[573]

When a loan is flipped, the creditor has many opportunities to violate the terms of the credit contract or the applicable credit statute. But even if a creditor does not impose any illegal overcharges—that is, it calculates each individual charge correctly, and calculates all rebates correctly—the overall transaction may nonetheless be so overreaching that other legal claims may be available.[574]

### *5.9.2 Refinancing, Consolidation, and Flipping Defined*

At the outset, it may be helpful to define some of the terms used to describe different kinds of credit renewals. While "refinancing" is seldom statutorily defined, it means to "finance something new," usually after a renegotiation of credit terms.[575] On paper, a "refinancing" is a new loan, generally between an existing creditor and debtor, the proceeds of which are used to pay off the preexisting debt.

"Consolidation" converts several debts into one new debt. The greatest abuse of consolidation occurs when several short-term, low-interest loans are consolidated into one very expensive loan, secured by the equity in the borrower's home. Consolidation may also occur when a preexisting debt with the same lender is refinanced and a new advance is made. Whether the amount of a new advance is sufficient to change its character as refinanced debt may be important, for there are instances in which there are limits on the charges that can be imposed on a refinanced loan.[576]

The term "flipping" may be used to describe refinancing in general, though it is sometimes used more restrictively to describe situations in which new credit is extended at a higher rate than the refinanced credit. This chapter generally uses the former, broader meaning.

In examining a refinanced or consolidation loan, practitioners must look for overcharges in the same manner as examining an original loan. However, unlike an original loan, the analysis cannot stop there; the credit agreements being refinanced or consolidated must also be examined, for the earlier loans themselves may give rise to a usury claim, tainting any subsequent loan. Additionally, the subsequent loan also may exceed applicable cost limitations if the outstanding balance from the earlier loan was improperly calculated, or if improper finance charges are imposed on the preexisting balance. If renewals are done improperly there may be usury.[577]

Much of the discussion in the following subsections applies to credit transactions between parties with an existing debtor-creditor relationship, in which one or more preexisting credit obligations are replaced by new debt. The calculation issues, however, are the same irrespective of whether the same creditor refinances the earlier debt.

### *5.9.3 The Elements of the Price Escalator*

In assessing a series of refinancings, it is useful to keep both a micro and macro viewpoint. Illegal overcharges can occur even if the transaction as a whole does not breach standards of ethical dealing. Conversely, the creditor's dealings may well violate community standards even if no specific illegal overcharge was imposed. This subsection discusses the charges to evaluate for proper treatment in a series of refinancings. But do so keeping in mind the true value the consumer received out of the transactions. What is the cumulative amount from the whole

570 $341.91, to be more precise. *See generally* § 5.3.1.1, *supra*.

571 *See* Emery v. American Gen. Fin., Inc., 71 F.3d 1343 (7th Cir. 1995) (one such letter).

572 Office of Thrift Supervision, Final Rule, 67 Fed. Reg. 60,542, 60,548 (Sept. 26, 2002).

573 *Cf.* Emery v. American Gen. Fin., Inc., 71 F.3d 1343 (7th Cir. 1995) (noting similarity to twisting).

574 *See, e.g.*, Besta v. Beneficial Loan Co., 855 F.2d 532 (8th Cir. 1988); *In re* Milbourne, 108 B.R. 522 (Bankr. E.D. Pa. 1989); Villegas v. Transamerica Fin. Servs., 708 P.2d 781 (Ariz. Ct. App. 1985). *See also* Emery v. American Gen. Fin., Inc., 71 F.3d 1343 (7th Cir. 1995); Hager v. American Gen. Fin., Inc., 37 F. Supp. 2d 778 (S.D. W. Va. 1999) (denying lender's motion for summary judgment on unconscionability and fraud claims where consumers were in immediate financial need due to fire; lender allegedly misrepresented that credit insurance was required, and lender began flipping the loan just nine days after the original transaction); Maxwell v. Fidelity Fin. Servs., Inc., 907 P.2d 51 (Ariz. 1995) (reversing grant of summary judgment for lender on unconscionability claim where inoperable water heater costing over $6,500 was financed at 19.5%, then refinanced along with a $800 cash advance to create a total deferred price of over $17,000); § 12.10, *infra*. *But see* Gonzales v. Associates Fin. Serv., 967 P.2d 312 (Kan. 1998). *See generally* § 2.4, *supra*.

575 Bar Harbor Bank & Trust v. Supt. of Bureau of Cons. Prot., 471 A.2d 292 (Me. 1984) (construing U.C.C.C. reference to refinancing to include post-maturity renewal of the obligation); Moore v. Canal Nat'l Bank, 409 A.2d 679, 684 (Me. 1979). *Cf.* Springhill Lake Investors Ltd. v. Prince George's County, 690 A.2d 535 (Md. Spec. Ct. App. 1997) (citing various definitions of refinancing in context of interpretation of county transfer tax ordinance).

576 *See* § 5.9.5.5, *infra*.

577 *See* § 7.8.4, *infra*.

series that actually formed the consideration to the borrower: proceeds; payoffs of legitimate debts; purchase price of goods and services?[578] Then consider how the other costs imposed grow in relation to that sum over the course of the borrowers' history with the company.

- *Unearned interest in prior loans*: Precomputed loans will raise questions of proper rebates.[579] In some states, even interest-bearing transactions may raise questions, as there may be a limit on how much accrued, but unpaid interest can be included in a refinancing.[580]
- *Insurance premiums*: Rebates are required for unearned premiums and they most commonly use the more expensive Rule of 78s. (A favored tool for padding loans, these create such a wide array of potential issues that an entire chapter (Chapter 6, *infra*) is devoted to credit insurance.)
- *Non-rebatable charges*: Points, origination fees, and service charges, if unusually high, are a good sign of trouble in a series of refinancings, because of the way they skew the yield.[581] Closing costs work the same way.
- *Invoking prepayment penalty clauses in refinancing*: This is another warning sign. Since the ostensible purpose of such clauses is to compensate the creditor for the loss of its intended bargain,[582] it has no place in a same-creditor refinancing, which is essentially an extension of the bargain.
- *Delinquency costs*: If a borrower is delinquent in paying the refinanced loan, earned, unpaid interest will also be added to the principal of the new loan, along with any deferral charges or late fees that may have been imposed. These charges, many of which are considered "interest" on the old loan, will become principal on the new loan, again increasing the interest cost on the new loan.

Having calculated the pay-off on the existing loan to its maximum profit, the lender is likely to add more charges to the new loan. In addition to more interest on a higher principal (usually for a longer term), and more insurance premiums (on a larger loan, for a longer term),[583] other charges may be repeated: service charges, filing fees, title opinions or title searches (if the credit is secured by real estate), document preparation fees and other such charges. In real estate loans (and to some extent in non-real-estate loans as well), a new set of points, origination fees, and broker fees is typically added at each refinancing, and these fees are the key mechanism by which loan flippers strip away the homeowner's equity.

Repeated refinancings compound these hidden costs. Borrowers are encouraged to refinance when they show signs of having trouble making their scheduled payments on time. They may be encouraged to rewrite a loan to lower their payments, but the payments may be reduced only minimally (or not at all), while the total cost to the borrower is greatly increased.[584] As the loan size rises, the APR may even decline, though the real cost to the borrower rises. This works simply because so much of the cost is now buried in the loan principal.

In addition to directly increasing the total amount due, the lender may have other incentives to increase the principal on a new loan. Where statutes prohibit using real estate as security on loans under certain dollar amounts, refinancing can be an effective way of padding the principal past the magic threshold, so that the lender can take the borrower's home as collateral.[585] In states where interest rates are deregulated except for small loans,[586] inflating the principal through refinancing also may enable the lender to enter a deregulated lending arena.

### 5.9.4 Small Loan Example

Here is an example of how it works.[587] A Pennsylvania consumer made a retail purchase for $747 on a "90-day same as cash" basis. The seller assigned the paper to a finance company, a common introduction to finance company borrowing. Over the course of the next six years, the consumer received approximately $6,000 from eleven separate loans. Each of the advances was a small sum, less than $1,000. Had these advances been written as eleven separate loans, giving equal value to the consumer, while allowing the lender maximum legal interest rates and prepaid finance charges, and the same credit insurance protection, the cumulative total of payments the consumer would have been obligated to pay was $6,926. In contrast, his total obligation for the series of refinanced loans was $16,000. Same benefit to the customer; comparable return and insurance protection for the lender in both cases, but over $9,000 difference in cost!

How does that happen? A variety of factors converge to create a flipping penalty, not all of which are present in every case, but this example illustrates most of them.

*The Rule of 78s Penalty*: As was discussed earlier in this chapter, the pay-off balance on a loan being refinanced is artificially inflated when the Rule of 78s is used to calculate the rebate of unearned interest.[588] Both the unearned insurance premiums and unearned interest were calculated by the rule on each of these refinancings.

To add insult to injury, this series of loans illustrates one of the glosses on the Rule of 78s—double-dipping. Recall that the rule does not use fractional time intervals.[589] So, for example, when one loan with a due date on the first of the month was refinanced on April 6, the lender rounded forward to the May 1 due date. By virtue of the Rule of 78s, the lender "earned"

578 But note that cash prices, too, can be inflated. *See* § 4.4, *supra*.

579 *See* § 5.8, *supra*.

580 *See, e.g.*, Fla. Stat. § 516.031(5).

581 *See* §§ 4.3, 5.8.4.2, *supra*.

582 *See* National Consumer Law Center, Mortgage Lending § 8.5 (2012).

583 *See* § 6.6, *infra* (explaining the relation of the cost of insurance to the loan size and term).

584 *Cf.* Villegas v. Transamerica Fin. Servs., 708 P.2d 781 (Ariz. Ct. App. 1985).

585 *See* Besta v. Beneficial Loan Co., 855 F.2d 532 (8th Cir. 1988) (example of padding for such a purpose).

586 *See* § 3.9.7, *supra*.

587 This example is taken from a Pennsylvania legal services client's experience with a nationally known finance company. The case was settled (NCLC files).

588 *See* §§ 5.8.1, 5.8.6.3, *supra*.

589 *See* §§ 5.8.5.1, 5.8.6.3.2, *supra*.

interest and calculated it into the old loan's pay-off balance (at 25.8%) for twenty-four days *after* it was paid off. At the same time, it also charged interest on the old-loan portion of the new loan principal (at 25.8%) for the same twenty-four days.[590]

*Service Charges*: Pennsylvania's consumer discount law permits a service charge of $1 per $50 of the loan.[591] Obviously, as the total obligation grows, the amount of that fee grows. With the unflipped loan series, the service charge never gets above $20 per loan, since no individual loan exceeds $1,000. With the series of flipped loans, the service charge reaches a $100 statutory cap half-way through the flipping sequence and stays there. As written, the consumer was charged $944.79 in service charges. Without flipping, the total of eleven maximum allowable service charges would have been $138.50. These prepaid finance charges are useful to the creditor in two ways other than their face value: the interest clock gets to tick on them;[592] and they are considered "earned" at consummation, so they generally are not subject to any rebate requirement when the next refinancing occurs.[593]

*Credit Insurance*: Like the service charges, credit insurance is calculated on the total of payments, so burgeoning loans make for bigger premiums, which in turn, further bloat the loans.[594] Credit life insurance protection for the borrower cost $374.26 in the refinanced series, ten times more than equally full protection in an unflipped series ($34.62).[595]

*Stretching the Loan Term*: Since interest and credit insurance premiums are time-sensitive components of the cost of credit, the longer the loan term, the higher both those figures are. In Pennsylvania, which authorizes a 9.5% discount rate ceiling for these loans,[596] the problem is exacerbated by the nature of discount interest. Recall from § 5.3.3, *supra,* that discount interest is deducted in advance, so the longer the term, the greater the amount deducted, and the higher the effective yield to the creditor.[597]

The initial $817 loan started at thirty-six months, for which the equivalent yield is 23.27%. The first seven loans were for thirty-six months, and the last four were for forty-eight months, a period that has an equivalent yield of 25.8%. Since these advances were all for less than $1,000, there was no reason to write thirty-six-month loans.[598] A twelve-month loan term would be more appropriate. The yield on a twelve-month 9.5% discount loan is "only" 18.84%—a full 4.50% lower than writing the same loan for thirty-six months, and 7% lower than writing it for forty-eight months.

Along with lower effective interest rates, the principal to which those rates are applied is also lower when not inflated by the repeated flippings. Hence the dramatic savings between writing eleven separate 9.5% discount loans and writing eleven flipped 9.5% discount loans.

The following chart summarizes the way the cost of the $1.29 loaf of credit rises beyond its price tag.[599]

| | **11 no-flip, no-stretch loans** | **11 flipped & stretched loans (as written)** |
|---|---|---|
| Proceeds to Borrower (including debt consolidation) | $ 6,094.88 | $ 5,977.61 |
| Credit Life Premium ($ .50/$100) | $ 34.62 | $ 1,117.30 Charged<br>– 743.04 Rebates Made*<br>$ 374.26 |
| Service Charge/ Prepaid Finance Charge ($1/$50) | $ 138.50 | $ 944.79 |
| Interest (Max. 9.5% discount) | $ 657.56 | $ 18,533.69 Charged<br>– 12,464.79 Rebates Made*<br>$ 6,068.90 |
| Cumulative Total of Payments | $ 6,925.56 | $ 7,440.00 **<br>+ 8,561.00 ***<br>$ 16,001.00 |

Total "*Besta/Milbourne*"[600] Penalty = $9,075.44
($16,001.00 – $6,925.56)

*According to creditor's accounting records
**The total obligation on the final loan to maturity
***The sum of all payments made on loans 1 to 10, prior to the time each was refinanced, according to creditor's accounting

590 When a refinancing occurs late in the monthly cycle, this "double dipping" effect is minimized, but several of these loans seemed to happen early in the cycle. Pennsylvania law requires that credit insurance premium rebates be rounded to the nearest due date, but has no such requirement for interest rebates.

591 The allowable service charge under Pennsylvania law was increased in 1998 to $1.50 for every $50.00, with a maximum of $150.00, 7 Pa. Stat. Ann. § 6213(F) (West), so the costs of refinancing would have been even higher after 1998.

592 For Truth in Lending purposes, they are considered a finance charge and are considered in calculating the TILA-APR. But authorized points, service charges and the like are generally permitted to be included in the loan principal for usury purposes under state law, so the note interest rate is applied to that amount. *See generally* § 4.3, *supra.*

593 *See* § 5.8.4, *supra. See also* § 5.9.5.3, *infra.*

594 *See* Ch. 6, *infra.* (In addition, this lender sold the insurance products of its own insurance affiliates, thus further bolstering corporate profits on each loan).

595 The problem is even worse when disability, unemployment and property insurance are also packed into a loan. *See* § 6.7, *infra.*

596 7 Pa. Stat. Ann. § 6213(E) (West).

597 For example, a 9.5% discount rate equals:
18.84% APR at 12 months
21.11% APR at 24 months
23.27% APR at 36 months
25.80% APR at 48 months
The Cost of Personal Borrowing in the United States T132–133 (Financial Publishing Co. 1986 with loose-leaf supplements).

598 *Cf.* Besta v. Beneficial Loan Co., 855 F.2d 532 (8th Cir. 1988).

599 To calculate the total cost for the flipped series, the total of payments made on all the prior loans was added to the total obligation on the final loan in the series. Compare that with the cumulative total of payments due on the series of unflipped loans. The difference is the hidden penalty.

600 Besta v. Beneficial Loan Co., 855 F.2d 532 (8th Cir. 1988); *In re* Milbourne, 108 B.R. 522 (Bankr. E.D. Pa. 1989). *See* § 5.9.1, *supra.*
For another example of the cost of repeated refinancings, see the affidavit found on the companion website to this treatise, which was prepared for the consumer's counsel in Hager v. American Gen. Fin., Inc., 37 F. Supp. 2d 778 (S.D. W. Va. 1999).

## 5.9.5 Evaluating the Calculations When a Loan Is Refinanced

### 5.9.5.1 Calculating Proper Rebates

The example in the previous subsection illustrates the numerous computational steps in which a lender can err in determining the cost of a new loan to the borrower. The first step for the practitioner is to check the regulatory statute applicable to the transaction to determine two things: the charges that must be rebated from the prior loan,[601] and the formula to be used in computing those rebates.[602] All states require that credit insurance be cancelled and rebates given upon refinancing.[603] Precomputed interest also must be rebated.[604] If refunds are not made or if the wrong formula is used—one that would result in a higher "earned" premium or interest figure than the prescribed formula—the transaction is subject to challenge for illegal overcharge.[605]

Even a lender who uses the proper rebate formula may apply it improperly. In the example in the preceding subsection, the loan was refinanced on the 13th day of the loan's 21st month. Even if the applicable statute authorizes use of the Rule of 78s to compute the insurance rebates, the statute may not permit the lender to consider the insurance earned for the 21st period. A number of states provide that no insurance premium charge may be made if fifteen days or less in a month have elapsed, though a full month's charge may be imposed if 16 or more days have elapsed. Under such a statute, the insurance premium in the example would have been improperly calculated, giving the lender an excessive charge. The number of months remaining in the loan term should have been 40, instead of 39. Thus the Rule of 78s rebate factor to be applied to the insurance should have been 44.81% ((40 × 41) ÷ (60 × 61)) instead of 42.62%. The insurance rebate should have been $69.90 ($156 × 44.81), instead of $66.49 ($156 × 42.62%), for an insurance overcharge of $3.41. When a loan being refinanced is packed with very high insurance premiums,[606] substantial overcharges can result from improper calculations of insurance rebates.

Similarly, the statute applicable to interest rebates may prohibit the rounding of the final thirteen days to a full month for rebate purposes. If the lender rounds up to a full month anyway, an overcharge occurs.[607] Note that some statutes prescribe different rules for calculating rebates where the transaction is refinanced after a short term.[608]

601 *See* § 5.8.4, *supra*.

602 *See* § 5.8.6, *supra*.

603 *See* § 6.10, *infra*. Usually, rebates of less than $1.00 need not be made.

604 *See generally* § 5.8.5.2, *supra*.

605 *See In re* Jungkurth, 74 B.R. 323 (Bankr. E.D. Pa. 1987); *In re* Tucker, 74 B.R. 923, 927 (Bankr. E.D. Pa. 1987) ("any formula other than the 'actuarial method' of calculating rebates, unless such a formula is specifically authorized by state law, would constitute the imposition of a prepayment penalty and hence be usurious").

606 *See* § 6.7, *infra* (insurance packing).

607 *See* § 5.8.5.2, *supra*.

608 *See, e.g.*, Ala. Code § 5-19-4(d) (pro rata refund if renewed or refinanced by same creditor or affiliate within 120 days of original loan); Colo. Rev. Stat. § 5-2-207(2) (where prepaid finance charge was imposed on loan being refinanced or consolidated within one year, creditor must either limit new prepaid finance charge to new advance, or must rebate prepaid finance charge on old loan according to actuarial method).

### 5.9.5.2 Compounding

The calculations in a refinancing transaction should be checked to see whether, in determining the pay-off on the prior loan, the lender improperly compounded interest. One of the reasons it is so expensive for borrowers to bring delinquent accounts current via refinancing is that earned, but unpaid, interest from the delinquent account is added to the principal in the new account, thus swelling the basis upon which interest on the new account is calculated. Ordinarily, absent the refinancing, no interest can be imposed on earned but unpaid interest.[609]

The general rule about compounding is that interest may be charged on accrued unpaid interest by an agreement made after the interest becomes due.[610] However, the applicable statute should be carefully reviewed. Though the courts are divided, a line of cases holds that including earned, unpaid interest in the principal of a refinanced loan constitutes illegal compounding under a state's small loan act. The rationale of these cases is that small loan acts prohibit compounding interest, and further prohibit taking excess charges "directly or indirectly."[611] Other states' small loan acts specifically provide that only unpaid interest that accrued within the sixty days prior to refinancing may be included in the new loan principal.[612] Consequently, the inclusion of any unpaid interest beyond sixty days in the new principal would result in illegal interest.

### 5.9.5.3 Non-Rebatable Charges on Old Loan

A practice that should act as a red flag for practitioners is the characterization of portions of the finance charge as non-rebatable fees, such as service charges, points, or loan origination fees. If the statute does not specifically categorize a charge as non-rebatable, the failure to rebate it should be viewed as a "device or subterfuge" to exact usury, and an effort to circumvent or evade the law's requirement that interest be rebated.[613] This argument should be especially persuasive in the context of statutes that prohibit directly or indirectly taking charges not specifically authorized.[614]

The inclusion of unrebated charges in the principal of the new loan has a two-fold effect: the borrower not only fails to receive the rebate, but will also pay interest on the unrebated

609 *See* § 5.5.1.2 *supra*.

610 *Id.*

611 *See, e.g.*, Securities Fin. Co. v. Maranto, 119 So. 2d 120 (La. Ct. App. 1960).

612 *See, e.g.*, Fla. Stat. § 516.031(5); N.H. Rev. Stat. Ann. § 399-A:11(IV). This is the provision in the seventh draft of the Uniform Small Loan Act, *reprinted in* Curran, Trends in Consumer Credit Legislation 30 (1965).

613 *See* §§ 3.9.1 (devices to evade usury restrictions), 5.8.4.2 (detailed discussion of points as rebatable charges), *supra*.

614 *See* § 7.2, *infra* (statutory construction).

amount. For example, assume that a lender charged a $210 loan origination fee for a sixty-month loan. If the loan is refinanced after twenty-one months, the Rule of 78s requires a rebate of 42.62% of the unearned charges. If this rebate factor is applied to the loan origination fee of $210, the interest rebate would be $89.50 in addition to the rebate applied to the scheduled interest.[615] If, on the other hand, the lender does not rebate any portion of the origination fee, it will retain an extra $89.50. Furthermore, because the $89.50 was not credited to the pay-off balance, the principal of the new loan will be improperly increased by that amount, and will generate additional interest at the new loan rate. If the new loan is written at 12% add-on interest for five years, the additional interest will be $89.50 × .12 × 5 = $53.70. Thus the total overcharge to the borrower arising simply from the lender's failure to rebate the "origination fee" is $143.20.

#### 5.9.5.4 Imposition of Additional Charges on the New Loan

The practitioner should examine the new, refinancing transaction and check the legitimacy of any new charges imposed. For example, some regulatory statutes explicitly prohibit imposing any points, service charges, or administrative fees on loans that are refinanced within a specified amount of time, commonly six months to one year.[616] Other statutes, while allowing non-rebatable acquisition charges at the time of the initial transaction, may disallow them altogether at refinancing.[617] Statutes may also prohibit assessing service charges, and other such charges, on that portion of a loan used to pay off a prior loan, irrespective of time limits.[618] If the lender ignores this prohibition, the excess service charge is interest, and if, when added to the other interest charged, the total exceeds the allowable amount, the loan is usurious.[619]

Even where there are no specific limitations on such charges for refinanced loans, they still may be subject to challenge. The Tennessee Supreme Court, interpreting a state statute in light of a former provision of the state constitution, articulated a series of standards against which statutorily authorized service charges should be measured. Such charges must bear a reasonable relation to the expenses and services of the lender, and may not include compensation for overhead expenses, such as rents, salaries, and loan losses.[620] The legislative definition of a maximum permissible charge should not be construed as granting creditors permission to automatically charge that maximum amount to all borrowers. Rather, when the fee is within the statutory limits, it is considered to be prima facie valid, and the burden shifts to the borrower to show that the charge does not bear a reasonable relation to expenses and services rendered.[621] When a lender repeatedly refinances loans over a relatively short interval, imposing new charges each time, no legitimate justification for such charges exists. Repeated, unnecessary charges such as investigation fees for each of a series of flipped loans should be considered a device to obtain excessive interest.[622]

#### 5.9.5.5 Is the New Rate Proper?

The economic injury caused by refinancing or consolidation is compounded when the new loan is written at a higher rate than the loan being refinanced. In some cases, the rate increase can be challenged.

A few states explicitly restrict the right of a lender to raise the interest rate on a refinanced loan. For example, in Iowa, if the rate on the original loan exceeded 18%, the rate cannot be increased on the refinancing of the unpaid balance.[623]

More common than such general rate restrictions on refinancing are provisions in Retail Installment Sales Acts (RISAs) that refinanced sales contracts retain their character as sales contracts, subject to the terms of the RISA.[624] Many of these statutes apply this restriction to all *holders* of retail sales contracts, not just to the original seller. Historically, one of the notable abuses in refinancing occurred when retail sales contracts were assigned to finance companies. Because the rate limitations applicable to loans made by finance companies were often considerably higher than those applicable to credit sales, the assignee-finance companies would flip the assigned credit sale into one of its own loans, using the higher small loan or industrial loan rate. Requiring that refinanced contracts con-

615 *See* § 5.9.6, *infra*.

616 *See, e.g.*, Cal. Fin. Code § 18212.2 (West) (Industrial Loan Act). *See also* Colo. Rev. Stat. § 5-2-207(2) (where prepaid finance charge is imposed on loan being refinanced or consolidated within one year, creditor must either limit new prepaid finance charge to new advance or must rebate prepaid finance charge on old loan according to actuarial method); Ohio Rev. Code Ann. § 1321.57(G) (West) (cannot either charge new points on refinancing real-estate secured loan within one year where prior loan had points charged, or impose a prepayment penalty).

617 *See* Independent Fin. Inst. v. Clark, 990 P.2d 845 (Okla. 1999) (interpreting pre-1997 version of Oklahoma's Consumer Credit Code to prohibit non-rebatable acquisition fees upon refinancing, even for loans that qualified for these fees when initially made; statute was subsequently amended to allow acquisition fees upon refinancing of some very small loans, but to make these fees subject to rebate).

618 *See, e.g.*, Tenn. Code Ann. § 45-5-403 (industrial loan).

619 Coleman v. Allstate Loan & Inv. Co., Consumer Cred. Guide (CCH) ¶ 97,322 (E.D. Tenn. June 23, 1980).

620 Cumberland Capital Corp. v. Patty, 556 S.W.2d 516, 535–536 (Tenn. 1977).

The state constitution was amended soon after *Cumberland Capital* to give more discretion to the state legislature. *See In re* Henley, 228 B.R. 425 (Bankr. E.D. Ark. 1998) (interpreting current version of Tenn. constitution not to limit legislature's authority to set interest rates).

621 Cumberland Capital Corp. v. Patty, 556 S.W.2d 516, 535–536 (Tenn. 1977).

622 *In re* Bogan, 281 F. Supp. 242, 250 (W.D. Tenn. 1968).

623 Iowa Code Ann. § 537.2504.

624 *See, e.g.*, Cal. Civ. Code §§ 1807.2 (West) (explicitly regulating refinancing), 1807.3; Mass. Gen. Laws ch. 255D, § 17; 69 Pa. Stat. Ann. § 1702 (West). *But cf.* Mich. Comp. Laws § 445.861(d)(2) (holder who refinances retail installment contract may charge rate of interest or finance charge under Credit Reform Act, Mich. Comp. Laws § 445.1854).

tinue to be treated under the terms of the RISA when refinanced by a "holder" prevents the finance company from treating it as a loan regulated by the small loan law. (The same incentive to flip applies when the RISA is rate regulated, but a consumer loan is not.)

### 5.9.6 Refinancing Calculations in Action: Another Walk-Through Case Study[625]

This subsection examines a finance company loan, secured by a second mortgage, and the calculations that the lender would make to prepare the refinanced loan. By highlighting the numerous calculations that must be made in deriving the figures for the new loan, this example demonstrates the myriad opportunities for improperly calculating rebates, or ignoring rebates, that may give rise to a usury claim. The example thus suggests information that should be sought through discovery in cases involving refinanced loans. While the complexity of the information needed may seem intimidating, pattern interrogatories are easily designed to elicit the necessary facts.

Assume a loan statement[626] shows the following components:

| | | |
|---|---|---|
| Principal $3,250 | | |
| Includes: | $2,685 | proceeds to borrower |
| | 156 | credit life insurance |
| | 150 | real property fees |
| | 9 | filing fees |
| | 40 | service charge |
| | 210 | loan origination fees |
| Scheduled Interest | | $1,550[627] |
| Total of Payments | | $4,800 |
| Rate of Charge | | 16.56%[628] |

This precomputed loan is to be repaid over five years, in sixty monthly installments of $80 each. The contract authorizes a late charge of $4 per late installment. The applicable usury statute authorizes a 12% add-on rate.[629]

Assume that, after seventeen months of prompt payment, this borrower had trouble making payments. The 18th and 19th payments were a week late, and then he was unable to make the 20th payment at all. Thirteen days after the due date for the 20th payment, the lender calls to ask about it. The lender suggests refinancing to bring the account current. The borrower inquires about getting an additional $200 cash advance, as he needs to pay a medical bill.

Because this was a precomputed loan, the current balance showing on the ledger is simply the Total of Payments ($4,800) less the sum of the payments actually paid, $1,520 ($80 × 19), for a current balance of $3,280 ($4,800 – 1,520 = $3,280). To determine the pay-off balance, the lender will add any accrued charges not already reflected, such as late charges. It must also credit any required rebates to the consumer's balance.

Unless applicable law clearly prohibits it, both interest rebates and credit insurance will likely be calculated according to the Rule of 78s. Because the refinancing takes place thirteen days into the 21st month of the loan, the lender decides to count the 21st month as a full month for purposes of computing the earned interest and insurance premiums. Thus, when using the Rule of 78s formula[630] the lender considers the number of remaining months in the loan term to be 39 (60 – 21 = 39). Next, it derives a rebate factor of 42.62% ((39 × 40) ÷ (60 × 61)). Because the lender characterized $250 ($40 service charge + $210 loan origination fee) as charges earned at the time this loan was consummated, it does not consider that amount to be subject to the rebate requirements. Therefore, it only applies the rebate factor to the "scheduled interest" of $1,550. So the borrower is credited with an unearned interest rebate of $660.61 ($1,550.00 × 42.62% = $660.61).[631]

625 *See* §§ 5.9.4, *supra* 5.11.4, *infra* (others).

626 The Truth in Lending Act does not require an itemization of the finance charge, even though it might have several components, see, e.g., 12 C.F.R. § 1026.4(b). However, many creditors do itemize such charges. Creditors are required to disclose the components of the amount financed on a closed-end transaction, or to notify the borrower of the right to obtain such an itemization, 12 C.F.R. § 1026.18(c). If the borrower does not have an itemization, that should be obtained through formal or informal discovery as quickly as possible. (RESPA settlement statements or disbursal statements also may contain the necessary itemization.) Though the characterization of interest and finance charges is not always the same for TILA and usury laws, see § 5.4, *supra*, the disclosure statement is nonetheless an invaluable starting point for any usury analysis because it reveals what charges the creditor has imposed.

627 The TILA disclosure statement would break down the charges differently:

| | |
|---|---|
| Amount Financed | $3,000 |
| Finance Charge | $1,800 |
| Total of Payments | $4,800 |
| APR | 20.31% |

TILA requires the service charges and loan origination fee to be considered part of the finance charge, while the lender included these fees in the "principal" to which it applied a 16.56% (rounded) rate to derive the "scheduled interest." *See* § 5.4, *supra*.

628 Rate of charge rounded; actual charge 16.5577% (actuarial). Note the distinction between the APR and the "rate of charge" as this creditor uses that term. The creditor here applied a "rate of charge" to a "principal" that includes both the elements of the amount financed and the prepaid finance charges (service charge and loan origination fee) to derive the interest earned over time. In practice, the creditor probably selected a "rate of charge" that yields a "scheduled interest amount," which, when added to the prepaid finance charges (generally considered interest) will result in a total interest yield equivalent to 12% add-on for $3,000. The creditor's use of the term "principal" to refer to the $3,250 is somewhat misleading, because $250 of that sum is a prepaid finance charge, generally considered interest, but the creditor is financing it. *See* § 4.3, *supra*.

629 *See* § 5.3.2, *supra*.

630 *See* § 5.8.6.3, *supra*.

631 *See* § 5.8.5.2, *supra* (rounding intervals).

Notice the impact of a Rule of 78s calculation. Though the loan is only one-third into its scheduled term, over 57% of the "scheduled interest" ($889.39) is considered earned ($1,550 – 660.61 = $889.39). Compare this to an actuarial rebate, which would have resulted in a rebate of $738.49 of scheduled interest; only 52.35% ($811.51) of the interest would have been "earned." (The actuarial calculation includes forty-three days of daily interest on a 360-day year earned after the last payment was made in the nineteenth month.) Thus the borrower paid a Rule of 78s penalty of $77.88.

The credit life insurance rebate is determined by the same formula,[632] so the rebate credited to the account balance is: $156.00 × 42.62% = $66.49

Having determined the rebates that must be credited to the current balance, the lender then determines whether there are additional charges to be added to the current balance. Assume two $4 late charges are added. (Although three payments were late, the first two may have been made within a contractual grace period, in which case it may be improper to impose a late charge on one of those payments.)

Thus, the current pay-off is:

$3,280.00 (current balance)
+ 8.00 (late charges)
– 660.61 (interest rebate)
– 66.49 (insurance rebate)

$2,560.90 NET PAY-OFF

To this pay-off of the current loan, the lender will add the $200 that the consumer wants to borrow to pay a medical bill. Then the lender determines what other charges to add onto this loan. Theoretically, the insurance charges will only be added if the debtor chooses to purchase the insurance. As a practical matter, however, many lenders automatically include such charges in the documents before the borrower arrives.[633]

If the lender continues to insure the loan,[634] and again writes it for a five-year term at the same interest rate used in the prior loan,[635] the critical loan components are as follows:

| Amount Financed | $3,080.06 |
|---|---|
| Includes: | |
| Net pay-off prior loan | $2,560.90 |
| Amount given to borrower | 200.00 |
| Real Estate Fees | 150.00 |
| Filing Fees | 9.00 |
| Credit Life Insurance | 160.16 |
| Finance Charge | 1,848.04 |
| Total of Payments | 4,928.10 |

The refinancing does not lower the monthly payment for this borrower, but raises it slightly to $82.14.[636] In fact, refinancing from this lender and borrowing $200 extra turns out to be very expensive for the borrower. A simple comparison of the first loan to the second is ample demonstration of how adversely refinancing can affect borrowers.

The borrower is again charged fees totaling $159 in connection with the security, along with interest on those repeat fees. This artificially inflated pay-off in turn inflates the interest yield on the new loan. The use of the Rule of 78s, instead of the actuarial method, to calculate the interest rebate due on the first loan cost the borrower an extra $77.88.[637] Failure to rebate any of the loan origination fee cost the borrower another $89.50.[638] Together, these rebate bonuses, now part of the new principal, increase the interest yield on the new loan by $100.43 ($167.38 at 12% add-on for five years), thus costing the borrower an extra $267.81. However, it is even more dramatic to compare this to the cost of a $200 loan as the borrower probably imagined it. Since a $200 loan would probably be unsecured, there would be no filing fees, real estate fees, or property insurance, as there likely would be on a real estate secured loan. Even borrowing that amount separately at high Small Loan Act rates,[639] and spreading payment out over two years, the loan would consist of:

| Proceeds to borrower | $199.49[640] |
|---|---|
| Credit Life | 3.74 |
| Amount Financed | 203.23 |
| Finance Charge | 84.77 |
| Total of Payments | 288.00 |
| Monthly Payment | 12.00 |

The combined monthly payments on the two loans would be $92, just $12 more over two years. The gross cost, however, would be $1,360.10 less. This can be seen by comparing the total of payments due on the two separate loans ($4,800 + $288 = $5,088) to the total of payments due on the new loan plus payments already made on the earlier loan ($4,928.10 + $1,520.00 = $6,448.10).[641]

The cost of a non-refinanced loan for $200 could further be reduced by repaying it over a shorter period, or by borrowing from a lower rate lender. Merely paying off the medical bill at the 1.5% per month on outstanding balances often charged by

632 It is likely that the insurance company issuing the policy considers premiums earned on an actuarial basis. If that is the case, then figuring the borrower's premium rebate by the Rule of 78s allows the lender to retain an insurance bonus, as well.

633 *See* § 6.5, *infra*.

634 In this hypothetical case, the legal credit life insurance rate is 65¢/$100/year. *See* § 6.6.1, *infra* (providing further details on credit insurance calculations).

635 The add-on rate on the prior loan was 12%, with an actuarial equivalent of 20.31%. For the sake of simplicity, the finance charge is not further broken down into a service charge, loan origination fee, and scheduled interest, as was done on the original loan. *See* notes 627–628, *supra*, for explanation of the difference in the way the first loan was structured.

636 $4,928.10 ÷ 60 = 59 at $82.14 and 1 at $81.84. To lower the payments, the lender may stretch the term yet longer, further increasing the total cost. A lender also may structure the loan with a balloon payment at the end in order to "lower" the monthly payments on a refinanced loan.

637 *See* note 631, *supra*.

638 *See* § 5.9.5.3, *supra*. This actually understates the rebate bonus, because the $89.50 rebate of the loan origination fee was calculated by the Rule of 78s, not the actuarial method.

639 Assume the state has a split rate small loan ceiling authorizing 36% per year on an amount financed up to $250 of amount financed, and 24% per year on the excess to $400. The actuarial equivalent APR on this loan would be 36%.

640 As is often the case with real loans, the components of this loan are in odd amounts to reflect the way the creditors' computational charts are constructed.

641 The comparison, of course, is not a direct one because the separate $200 advanced with the refinancing of the previous balance was financed over five years. However, it is a legitimate cost comparison, because it illustrates one of the pitfalls borrowers face in refinancing: the repayment period is lengthened, thus making the

service providers would be cheaper in the long run, and would be an unsecured debt. In short, a borrower who chooses refinancing in order to obtain additional credit, such as the $200 in this example, is paying far too much for the credit and may be putting his or her home at risk to boot.

Making the effort to work through the calculations in a refinancing can be very persuasive. It was the mathematical consequences to the borrower ($3,000 more than obtaining new, separate loans for new advances) that led one court to hold that it was opportunistic conduct rising to the level of an unfair practice to fail to disclose the lender's advantage and the borrower's disadvantage in choosing a refinancing option.[642] This followed a similar analysis also showing a hidden penalty of about $3,000, that led another court to declare the transaction unconscionable.[643] Sample expert reports showing these costs can be found on this treatise's companion website.

## 5.10 Proving Mathematical Issues in Court

Once computations have been made that suggest usury claims, the next question is how to prove the mathematical issues to the court. The first step is to translate the words of the relevant statute into the proper formula. If the statute uses a phrase commonly understood, such as Rule of 78s rebate, or "add-on" interest, that translation is not difficult. However, sometimes no clarifying words are used, and it is a question of law as to what formulation is authorized, which may be determined by ordinary rules of statutory construction.[644] Sometimes a statute describes a computational method, and it becomes an issue as to precisely what formula those words describe.[645] Banking department regulations should always be checked, as they may clarify the statute.[646]

The question of what the statute requires or permits is a question of law. However, as a practical matter, the statutory language may be technical, readily understandable by those experienced in the area but less accessible to those who are not—including judges who may not frequently hear such cases. Therefore, there may be confusion as to what computational system is authorized, and it may be useful to make that clear for the court. In some cases, the parties (both presumably familiar with the state's scheme) will not disagree, and a request for admission or stipulation will avoid the problem. If it becomes an issue, affidavits from the Banking Department or other relevant regulatory authority may be useful,[647] and could be the basis for a motion for partial summary judgment.

Once the statutorily prescribed method is established—actuarial rebate or Rule of 78s rebate; simple interest or add-on interest, etc.—the next step is to determine the proper formula which expresses that system. A number of sources that discuss financial mathematics may be used to provide the proper formula.[648] Reference to such treatises as authority for a formulaic expression of the method of calculation should be adequate. Arguably, this, too, is a question of law, although even if it is viewed as a factual question, it may be viewed as a type of "verifiable fact" of which courts may take judicial notice.[649]

---

loan more expensive, often providing little or no advantage to the borrower. Further, a lengthened term renders this borrower vulnerable to external events that may interrupt income and make him subject to foreclosure for a total of 80.5 months, instead of sixty months.

642 *In re* Milbourne, 108 B.R. 522 (Bankr. E.D. Pa. 1989). *See also* Hager v. American Gen. Fin., Inc., 37 F. Supp. 2d 778 (S.D. W. Va. 1999) (denying lender's motion for summary judgment on unconscionability claim); *In re* Tucker, 74 B.R. 923, 927 (Bankr. E.D. Pa. 1987) (noting the lopsided math in dicta and suggesting that failure of a usury claim would not forestall a UDAP claim).

643 Besta v. Beneficial Loan Co., 855 F.2d 532 (8th Cir. 1988). *See also* Hager v. American Gen. Fin., Inc., 37 F. Supp. 2d 778 (S.D. W. Va. 1999) (denying lender's motion for summary judgment on unconscionability claim).

644 *See, e.g.*, Skolnick v. Ford Motor Credit Co., 465 A.2d 1064 (Pa. Super. Ct. 1983) (interpreting MVRISA's interest rate cap as add-on interest), *appeal dismissed*, 482 A.2d 275; Dear v. Holly Jon Equip. Co., 423 A.2d 721 (Pa. Super. Ct. 1980) (interpreting MVRISA's "7 ½% per year" cap to allow add-on calculation).

645 *See, e.g.*, Kenney v. Landis Fin. Group, Inc., 349 F. Supp. 939 (N.D. Iowa 1972) (holding, on motion for summary judgment, that state small loan rebate provision mandates use of actuarial method), *subsequent proceeding*, 376 F. Supp. 852 (N.D. Iowa 1974) (holding, after trial, upon defendant's presentation of expert testimony and exhibits regarding state department of banking interpretation, that relevant provision states the Rule of 78s); Watson v. Avco Fin. Servs., Int'l, 401 N.W.2d 485 (Neb. 1987) (manner of computing split-rate interest at issue). *See also* Dechow v. Sko-Fed Credit, 536 N.E.2d 1382 (Ill. App. Ct. 1989) (statute precluding interest for any time period after payment in full precluded use of Rule of 78s rebate); Denley v. Peoples Bank, 553 So. 2d 494 (Miss. 1989) (use of Rule of 78s rebate improper under applicable statute that provided that parties could agree to "pay a finance charge which will result in a yield not to exceed [specified percentages] each calculated according to the actuarial method"; though contract rate was legal on its face if loan paid according to original terms, where there is prepayment, the "yield" must be recalculated to account for the altered term so that the yield does not exceed the specified rate according to the actuarial method).

646 *See, e.g.*, Skolnick v. Ford Motor Credit Co., 465 A.2d 1064 (Pa. Super. Ct. 1983) (relying in part on state banking department's interpretation).

647 *See, e.g.* Dear v. Holly Jon Equip. Co., 423 A.2d 721 (Pa. Super. Ct. 1980) (relying in part on affidavit from state banking department staff that department interpreted statute as setting add-on interest rate cap).

648 This source, for example. Some formulae are also described in Comment, *Usury: Issues in Calculation*, 34 Ark. L. Rev. 442 (1980); Financial Publishing Co., The Cost of Personal Borrowing (1986 loose-leaf with supplements). *See also* David Thorndike, Encyclopedia of Banking & Financial Tables, Thomson Financial/Pratt (2001 with yearbooks) (general reference).

649 *See, e.g.*, Fed. R. Evid. 201(b)(2) (provides that courts may take judicial notice of facts not subject to reasonable dispute, such as ones verifiable "by resort to sources whose accuracy cannot reasonably be questioned"). *See also In re* Jungkurth, 74 B.R. 323, 328 n.1 (Bankr. E.D. Pa. 1987) (taking judicial notice of rebate calculations pursuant to Fed. R. Evid. 201(b)); *In re* Russell, 72 B.R. 855, 860, 865–866 n.1 (Bankr. E.D. Pa. 1987). *Cf.* Besse v. Burlington-N., Inc., 79 F.R.D. 623 (D. Minn. 1978) (court may take judicial notice of a present value table when valuing damages in a personal injury case).

Requests for admission, interrogatories or stipulations are also simple means of presenting the proper formula to the court.

Of course, disputes are likely to arise as to how to treat irregularities in the transaction, such as whether odd days may be rounded in calculating a prepayment rebate, and if so, should they be rounded up or down. Such issues, of course, are ones of law. Again, banking department regulations should be checked, since the department may have promulgated rules to deal with accounting details such as rounding, 360/365 day years and other similar issues.

The final step is to carry out the computations in accordance with the relevant formula. Since this is no more than multiplication, division, subtraction, and addition, the calculations themselves are facts of which courts certainly may take notice.[650]

In order to establish whether there is a usurious overcharge, a number of courts simply calculate the maximum allowable charge under the statute, and compare that to the charge actually imposed.[651] That is a simple, straightforward method of establishing an overcharge, and one that avoids the necessity of "proving" the rate actually charged. While some parties have used experts such as CPAs to testify as to the effective rate of return on the transaction,[652] that does not appear to be necessary. The same information can be developed by use of spreadsheet programs, on-line calculation tools, or financial calculators,[653] which are widely used and accepted. The companion website to this treatise includes a program that will also calculate APRs and prepare an amortization table. Calculations so derived may simply constitute judicially noticed mathematics that may be spelled out in the memorandum of law.[654]

Requests for admissions as to specific computations are another useful method of establishing numbers, particularly if the jurisdiction has a sanctions rule similar to Federal Rule of Civil Procedure 37(c), which provides that a party failing to admit the truth of any matter as requested may be required, in certain circumstances, to pay the opposing party the expenses incurred in establishing the proof of such matter. (See the companion website to this treatise for a sample request for admission.) The practitioner who does wish to present expert evidence, either as a convenient method to prove the calculations or to establish more complex mathematical analysis, may do so either through the use of affidavits or testimony. The companion website to this treatise contains a sample affidavit and portions of sample expert testimony.

## 5.11 Practical Tips

### *5.11.1 Developing a System for Analyzing Consumer Credit Issues*

Generally, clients do not complain to their attorneys about specific usury issues. For example, it would be fairly unusual for a client to waltz into a law office saying, "I think the bank overcharged me $0.39 for credit insurance which is arguably interest and possibly a usury violation." More likely a client will appear after the transaction has gone sour for one reason or another. It then becomes the attorney's job to analyze the facts and issues relevant to the transaction.

The beginning of this chapter should give the reader insight into some of the more common legal and computational usury issues that arise in consumer credit transactions. The consumer lawyer, however, needs more than this raw knowledge. He or she also needs to take a methodical approach to every consumer credit case, in order to uncover potential overcharge issues. The following discussion represents the author's approach to gathering and analyzing the numbers in a consumer credit transaction, as illustrated by a hypothetical used car credit transaction. This approach works for the author, but it may not work for other lawyers. The important thing is not which method the lawyer adopts but the fact that the lawyer has a method. Every

650 Miller v. Federal Land Bank, 587 F.2d 415, 422 (9th Cir. 1978) (the amount of interest saved by a reduction of principal and shortening of the amortization period is a question of mathematics, of which the court can and should take judicial notice). *See also In re* Jungkurth, 74 B.R. 323, 328 n.1 (Bankr. E.D. Pa. 1987) (taking judicial notice of rebate calculations pursuant to Fed. R. Evid. 201 (b)); *In re* Russell, 72 B.R. 855, 860, 865–866 n.1 (Bankr. E.D. Pa. 1987); Dillon v. Resolution Trust Corp., 811 S.W.2d 765, 766–767 (Ark. 1991) ("It requires no expert testimony to compute the interest which would be owed at 13% per annum"); Parks v. E.N. Beard Hardwood Lumber, Inc., 565 S.W.2d 615 (Ark. 1978); Vela v. Yates Ford, 675 S.W.2d 232 (Tex. App. 1984), *rev'd on other grounds sub nom.* Yates Ford, Inc. v. Ramirez, 692 S.W.2d 51 (Tex. 1985) (court simply goes through equations, apparently taking judicial notice of arithmetic principles; dissent opines that complex calculations from Reg. Z app. J should "be supported by expert testimony and explanations of the mathematical intricacies involved," but notes that consumers did not challenge calculations or results. *Id.* at 57); Cuevas v. Montoya, 740 P.2d 858, 861 n.1 (Wash. Ct. App. 1987) (court apparently prepared its own calculations).

651 *See, e.g.,* Williams v. Seeley (*In re* Williams), 241 B.R. 387 (Bankr. E.D. Va. 1999) (court did its own calculations, using business calculator), *rev'd in part on other grounds*, 11 Fed. Appx. 344 (4th Cir. 2001); *In re* Russell, 72 B.R. 855, 860, 865–866 (Bankr. E.D. Pa. 1987); Parks v. E.N. Beard Hardwood Lbr., Inc., 565 S.W.2d 615 (Ark. 1978); Cappaert v. Bierman, 339 So. 2d 1355 (Miss. 1976); Butler v. Holt Machinery Co., 741 S.W.2d 169 (Tex. App. 1987), *corrected on denial of rehearing*, 739 S.W.2d 958 (1987). *See also* A.J. Reynolds v. Succession of Williams, 628 So. 2d 1 (La. Ct. App. 1993) (where creditor calculated charge annually and added it to the balance, court calculated maximum annual interest charge to establish compounding, which rendered transaction usurious).

652 *See, e.g.,* Olympic Coast Inv., Inc. v. Wright (*In re* Wright), 256 B.R. 626 (Bankr. D. Mont. 2000) (finding mortgage banker's and accountant's expertise more persuasive re interest rate calculation than that of economist who did not have experience in financial industry); Smith v. MRCC P'ship, 792 S.W.2d 301 (Ark. 1990); Wooten v. Davis, 739 S.W.2d 669 (Ark. 1987); Cappaert v. Bierman, 339 So. 2d 1355 (Miss. 1976); Equilease Corp. v. Belk Hotel Corp., 256 S.E.2d 836 (N.C. Ct. App. 1979).

653 The practitioner should make sure that the calculator performs amortizations.

654 Submitting amortization schedules from recognized publishers may also be adequate. *See* Hoffman v. Key Fed. Sav. & Loan Ass'n, 416 A.2d 1265 (Md. 1979) (utilizing schedule published by Financial Publishing Co., "relied upon by many lenders").

consumer lawyer who wants to represent the client vigorously must develop his or her own approach.

The hypothetical situation is far less complicated than most consumer credit transactions. However, it will help to illustrate a methodical approach to documentary analysis. On January 1, 2000, the client, Connie Consumer ("Consumer"), bought a used car from C.R. Pyle Clean Used Cars ("Pyle") which provided financing. After Consumer made only three payments, Pyle repossessed the car, sold it at auction, and sent Consumer a letter demanding payment of a $3,800 deficiency balance. This transaction will suggest many consumer law issues, such as Truth in Lending violations, wrongful repossession, and deceptive practices, but the primary focus of this discussion will be the overcharge issues.

## *5.11.2 Gathering Information from the Client*

The first step is to gather as much information as possible directly from the client. Obviously the client must be carefully and methodically interviewed, to get the entire story, from the beginning to the end of the transaction. As explained below, the client must also be asked to give the lawyer all of the relevant documents from the transaction.

In the hypothetical, the following questions suggest possible lines of inquiry for the client interview:

- Why did Consumer go to Pyle (previous transactions; advertising; recommendation of a friend)?
- What representations were made by Pyle about the cost of the car and the cost of the financing?
- What representations were made about non-interest charges in connection with the transaction (e.g., official fees, insurance premiums, service contracts, etc.)?
- What charges did Consumer think were compulsory, what charges did she think were optional, and of what charges did she only later become aware?
- What oral representations, if any, induced client to enter into the transaction with Pyle?
- What, if any, down payment did Consumer make, in cash and/or a trade-in?
- What documents did Consumer receive from Pyle or third parties, and when did she receive them?[655]
- What payments did Consumer make and when did she make them?
- What communications, oral or written, did she receive from Pyle after default, repossession, or the sale of her car at auction?

In addition to a methodical interview, the consumer lawyer should ask the client to produce all of the relevant documents in her possession, since the simplest and cheapest way to obtain the relevant documents is through the client. As all lawyers know, there is no way to predict what documents the client will show up with at the initial interview: possibilities range from shopping bags filled with every scrap of paper to nothing at all, not even the notice of the foreclosure sale scheduled for that afternoon. Regardless of that range, the lawyer must stress to the client how important it is to bring in the documents, and must give the client direction as to what documents to look for.

In the hypothetical, the following documents should be obtained, if possible, from the client:[656]

- Newspaper advertisement by Pyle;
- Purchase order;
- Bill of sale;
- Contract;
- Truth in Lending disclosure statement, including, if given, itemization of Amount Financed;
- Odometer disclosures;
- Insurance documents (credit insurance, physical damage insurance, liability insurance, etc.);
- Warranty documents;
- FTC Used Car Notice;
- Service contract;
- Title and registration;
- Receipts (down payment; regular payments);
- Payment book;
- Correspondence from Pyle or third parties (dunning notices, repo notices, deficiency claim notices, etc.);
- Legal documents (e.g., complaint, notice of judgment, etc.).

After the documents have been obtained (both from the client and from third parties), the lawyer must compare the information in the documents with that obtained from the client interview; the client should then be asked to explain, if possible, any disparities.

## *5.11.3 Gathering Information from Creditor and Other Parties*

Not only is there a wide range of documents that clients will bring to the initial interview, but everyone has different record-keeping habits. Therefore, few clients will have all of the documents listed above. Since these documents can be very important in a consumer credit case, other sources must be explored, particularly the creditor.

There are also important documents that can only be obtained from the creditor or other parties. These documents are records of the creditor's financial transactions with the client, as well as with third parties, such as insurance companies, state title agencies, repossession companies, etc.

There are a variety of ways these documents can be obtained. Obviously, one way is to file suit and obtain the documents through formal discovery. However, since these documents generally are necessary to evaluate the case at the outset, formal discovery is not an efficient method. Moreover, if one does not have other facts suggesting the existence of colorable claims, it

655 *See* discussion at § 5.11.3, *infra*.

656 If the documents cannot be obtained from the client, then the lawyer or client should try to obtain them from the creditor and third parties. *See* § 5.11.3, *infra*.

is of dubious ethics. Nor may it be strategically advisable (if there are documents that might be destroyed after a claim has been filed), or financially feasible (considering the costs of litigating unsuccessful claims).[657]

But there are other, informal approaches to obtaining the desired documents from the creditor. For example, depending on the client's or lawyer's relationship with the creditor, the lawyer could be very straightforward with the creditor. He or she could say, "I am trying to advise my client what to do about your claim against him. I cannot properly advise her as to either her rights or her responsibility to you without having this information. It would be helpful to get your side of the story, including copies of your records." Another more aggressive approach would be to tell the creditor that litigation is being considered but that, if the creditor provides the relevant documents, it would not be filed until the lawyer has had a chance to review those records.

Third parties may be another source of records. It can be helpful to get records from the attorney general or consumer protection agency, if the client has already filed a complaint; from other state agencies, such as the title bureau; and from insurance companies.

657 *See also* Fed. R. Civ. P. 11 (sanctions for filing unwarranted claims).

In the hypothetical, the following documents, possibly available from Pyle and other parties, would be helpful:

- Pyle's ledger or account that records payments, late charges, and other charges;
- Master group credit insurance and automobile insurance policies;
- Title or other documents with information on liens and other security interests on the client's car.

## 5.11.4 Calculations and Analysis

Once all the available documents have been gathered, the consumer law practitioner can begin the calculations and analysis necessary to uncover the client's potential usury claims. For purposes of the hypothetical, we have gathered only (because this is an imperfect world) four documents: the Truth in Lending disclosure statement;[658] portions of the sales contract and itemization of the Amount Financed;[659] Pyle's ledger;[660] and a letter from Pyle to Consumer following the repossession sale of her car.[661]

658 *See* Chart 14, Truth in Lending Disclosure Statement.
659 *See* Chart 15, Sales Contract.
660 *See* Chart 16, Ledger Card.
661 *See* Chart 17, Deficiency Collection Letter.

**CHART 14**
**Truth in Lending Disclosure Statement**
**C.R. Pyle Clean Used Cars**

| ANNUAL PERCENTAGE RATE The cost of your credit as a yearly rate 21.48% | FINANCE CHARGE The dollar amount the credit will cost you. $1535.51 | Amount Financed The amount of credit provided to you or on your behalf. $4196.05 | Total of Payments The amount you will have paid after you have made all payments as scheduled. $5731.56 | Total Sale Price The total cost of your purchase on your downpayment of $653.88. $5385.44 |
|---|---|---|---|---|

You have the right to receive at this time an itemization of the Amount Financed.

☒ I want an itemization. ☐ I do not want an itemization.

Your Payment schedule will be:

| Number of Payments | Amount of Payments | When Payments Are Due |
|---|---|---|
| 36 | $159.31 | Montly beginning 2/1/2010 |
| | | |

**Insurance**
Credit life insurance and credit disability insurance are not required to obtain credit, and will not be provided unless you sign and agree to pay the additional cost.

| Type | Premium | Signature | |
|---|---|---|---|
| Credit life | $103.17 | I want credit life insurance | ________ Signature |
| Credit Disability | $186.58 | I want credit disability insurance | ________ Signature |
| Credit Life and Disability | | I want credit life and disability insurance | ________ Signature |

You may obtain property insurance from anyone you want that is acceptable to (Creditor). If you get the insurance from (Creditor). You will pay $ *N.A.*

**Security:** You are giving a security interest in:

☒ the goods or property being purchased.
☐ (brief description of other property).

**Filing fees:** $ 46.30 Non-filing insurance $ —

**Late Charge:** If a payment is more than ten days late, you will be charged $ 5.00 / 5 % of the payment, whichever is less.

**Prepayment:** If you pay off early, you

☐ may ☐ will not have to pay a penalty
☒ may ☐ will not be entitled to a refund of part of the finance charge.

See your contract documents for any additional information about nonpayment, default, any required repayment in full before the scheduled date, and prepayment refunds and penalties.

---

@ means an estimate

**CHART 15**
**Sales Contract**

| *BUYER* | *SELLER* |
|---|---|
| CONNIE CONSUMER | C.R. PYLE<br>CLEAN USED CARS |

You, the Buyer, may buy the vehicle described below for cash or on credit. The cash price is shown below as "Cash Price." The credit price is shown below as "Total Sale Price". By signing this contract, you choose to buy the vehicle on credit under the agreements on the front and back of this contract.

| New or Used | Year and Make | Series (Model) | Body Style | No. Cyl. | M Truck Ton Capacity | Vehicle Identification Number | Use For Which Purchased |
|---|---|---|---|---|---|---|---|
| USED | 2005 HONDA | ESCORT | 4/DR | 6 | | 123456789 | ☐ Personal<br>☐ Agricultural<br>☐ Commercial<br>☐ |

INCLUDING:

☐ Radio ☐ Air Conditioner ☐ Automatic Transmission ☐ Power Steering ☐ ________ ☐ ________

| TRADE-IN | 2002 Toyota | $ 2,000 | $ 1,546.12 |
|---|---|---|---|
| | Year and Make | Gross Allowance | Amount Owing |

ITEMIZATION OF AMOUNT FINANCED

| | | | |
|---|---|---|---|
| Cash Price | | $ 3727.50 | (1) |
| Down Payment | | | |
| (a) Cash Paid | $ 200.00 | | |
| (b) Pickup Payment due ________ 19____ | $ N.A. | | |
| (c) Cash Down Payment (a plus b) | $ 200.00 | | |
| (d) Trade-in (Description Above) | $ 453.88 | | |
| Total Down Payment (c plus d) | | $ 653.88 | (2) |
| Unpaid Balance of Cash Price (1 minus 2) | | $ 3073.62 | (3) |
| Amounts Paid on Your Behalf | | | |
| To Public Officials (i) for license, title & registration fees $40.00<br>(ii) for official fees $ N.A. .<br>(iii) for documentary stamps $ 6.30 .<br>(iv) for taxes (not in Cash Price) $ 186.38 | $ 232.68 | | |
| To Insurance Companies for | | | |
| Vehicle Insurance | $ N.A. | | |
| Credit Life Insurance | $ 103.17 | | |
| Credit Disability Insurance | $ 286.58 | | |
| ________ | $ N.A. | | |
| To ________ for ________ | $ N.A. | | |
| To ________ for ________ | $ 500.00 | | |
| To TOW MOTOR CO. for EXTENDED SERVICE PLAN | $ N.A. | | |
| TOTAL | | $ 1122.43 | (4) |
| Amount Financed (3 plus 4) | | $ 4196.05 | (5) |

**CHART 16**
**Ledger**
**C.R. Pyle Clean Used Cars**

Total of Payments: $5731.56
Payment Schedule: 36 × $159.31 Due Date: 1st
First Payment 2/1/10
LC: $7.97

| *Date* | *Payment* | *LC* | *New Balance* |
|---|---|---|---|
| 2/1/10 | $159.31 | — | $5573.25 |
| 3/9/10 | $159.31 | $7.97 | $5421.91 |
| 4/11/10 | $ 79.88 | $7.97 | $5350.00 |
| 5/12/10 | Call — will send check | | |
| 6/12/10 | Repo. | | |
| 6/28/10 | Sale — $3000.00 | | |

**CHART 17**
**Deficiency Collection Letter**

July 18, 2010

Connie Consumer
11 Beacon Street
Boston, MA 02108

Dear Ms. Consumer:

As you can see from the attached report, your car has been sold and you now are obligated for a deficiency of $3,800.

| | |
|---|---|
| Amount Owed | $5350 |
| Repossession Expenses | 300 |
| Storage Charges | 150 |
| Sales Expenses | 200 |
| Reconditioning Expenses | 300 |
| Attorney's Fees | 500 |
| | $6800 |
| Less Sale Price of | 3000 |
| | $3800 |

Please forward this amount to us immediately.

Yours truly,

C.R. PYLE CLEAN USED CARS

The first step is to examine the documents generally to get an overall sense of the transaction and to look for numbers or other data that are not consistent with the client's story or with the lawyer's knowledge of the facts. The relevant numbers should also match on all documents. Not all discrepancies will necessarily be important, relevant, or actionable, especially after further investigation, but some may reveal overcharges or fraud. The basic question to ask is: "Do these numbers make sense?"

For example, in the hypothetical, the lawyer makes note of the following observations:

1. *Trade-in*: Consumer traded in her 2002 Toyota and only received a gross $2,000 credit for it.[662] The lawyer might investigate the approximate value of a 2002 Toyota on January 1, 2010, the date of the trade-in. The lawyer might discover that the Toyota had just been "totaled" in an accident or perhaps that Pyle unconscionably took advantage of Consumer's ignorance of the Toyota's value. Perhaps Pyle would also be liable to a claim for "hidden interest" in the amount of the undervaluation.[663]
2. *Service contract*: The lawyer notices a $500 charge to Tow Motor Co. for an "Extended Service Plan." Consumer did not mention this plan, which may well be a form of service contract; indeed, Consumer provided quite a long narrative about all the car repairs she had to pay for on the 2005 Honda Civic she purchased from Pyle. In addition to obvious contract and warranty claims, Consumer may well have paid $500 for a non-existent contract or for illusory warranty coverage, either of which may also be "hidden interest."[664]
3. *Credit disability insurance*: The itemization of the Amount Financed shows that the premium for credit disability ("A&H") insurance is $286.58, while the Truth in Lending disclosure statement, in the credit insurance authorization section, shows a premium of only $186.58, a $100 difference. If Consumer were truly charged the higher figure, this would probably be a Truth in Lending violation. In addition, she may have a claim that the $100 "overcharge" was actually interest for usury purposes, since she only "contracted" (via the authorization) to pay the lower premium.
4. *Missing payment*: Consumer told the lawyer that she paid Pyle $80 in cash at the end of April (to make up a partial payment earlier in the month) but did not get a receipt. This payment does not appear on the ledger. If this issue of fact can be resolved in Consumer's favor, not only

662 After subtracting the $1,546.12 pay off on the debt secured by the Toyota, Consumer only received a $453.88 net credit for her trade-in. Another question is whether the payoff figure was accurately calculated. *See* §§ 5.9.5, *supra*, 6.10, *infra*.

663 The hidden interest claim would depend on whether Pyle would have given Consumer a better deal on the trade-in or the Honda's sales price if Consumer had paid cash. The client should be asked how the price of the trade-in and new purchase was set. *See* §§ 4.4.5, *supra*, 10.3.6, *infra*.

There is evidence that prices may be routinely hiked for certain categories of consumers, such as older consumers, Native Americans, African Americans, and women. In addition to hidden interest claims, such differential pricing based on race, age, gender, ethnicity, etc. may violate UDAP laws, civil rights laws, and may arguably implicate fair lending laws, where the purchase is financed. *See* National Consumer Law Center, Credit Discrimination (5th ed. 2009 and Supp.).

664 *Id.*

would Consumer save at least $80, but she might also have a usury claim.[665]

The next step is to see whether the numbers are internally and mathematically consistent: do the numbers bear a mathematical relationship to each other, is the arithmetic correct? In the hypothetical, for example, the lawyer would look at the itemization of the Amount Financed[666] to make sure the numbers add and subtract properly; the payment schedule on the Truth in Lending disclosure statement[667] to make sure that the payments equal the "Total of Payments"; the ledger[668] to make sure that payments are subtracted properly from the running balance and the late charges are properly added thereto; and at the July 18 collection letter[669] to make sure that the numbers are added and subtracted correctly.

After examining these documents, the lawyer might make note of the following problems:

- *Payment schedule*: According to the Truth in Lending disclosure statement, Consumer was supposed to pay thirty-six monthly payments of $159.31 each. However, the product of 36 × $159.31 is $5,735.16, or $3.60 higher than the disclosed Total of Payments. Not only is this a possible Truth in Lending violation, it may also provide a usury claim for the client.[670]
- *Late charges*: The lawyer uncovers several problems with the late charges. First, according to the Truth in Lending disclosure statement, the maximum late charge is supposed to be $5.00 or 5% of the payment, whichever is *less*. Consumer was twice charged $7.97, which may not only be a violation of the contract, but may also violate state usury laws; the overcharge may be considered "interest."[671] Another problem with the late charges is that, again according to the Truth in Lending disclosure statement, late charges should only be imposed "if a payment is more than ten days late." Yet Pyle imposed a late charge on Consumer when she made her March 1, 2010 payment on March 9, 2010, only eight days after it was due. Similar contractual and usury claims may also arise from this problem.

The third step in the analysis is to determine which state and federal laws apply to this transaction and to decide whether any of these laws have been violated. While many states have "deregulated" some consumer credit transactions, one of the basic tenets of consumer law still holds true: nearly every charge and every term of a consumer credit contract is specifically regulated, controlled, or limited by a statute or regulation, *even if the statute or regulation merely says that a charge may be set by agreement between the parties*.[672]

Therefore it is important for the consumer lawyer to become familiar with the relevant laws and regulations. In addition, the lawyer must carefully check the charges and terms of each transaction. In the hypothetical, the following charges should be carefully scrutinized:

- Interest and finance charge;
- Annual percentage rate;
- Credit insurance charges;
- Documentary fees (license, title, registration);
- Taxes;
- Late charges;
- Rebates (in the event of prepayment, acceleration, repossession, etc.);
- Attorney fees.

Having looked at these charges and the relevant laws, the lawyer might make note of the following:

1. *Interest*: Interest rates for financing used cars is governed by the state's Motor Vehicle Retail Installment Sales Act (MVRISA). MVRISA states that the maximum rate of charge for financing a used car between three and five model years old[673] is "$12 per $100 per annum" or 12% add-on.[674] Multiplying $4,196.05 (principal or Amount Financed) × 12% (maximum add-on rate) × 3 (years) produces a maximum charge of $1,510.58. However, Pyle charged Consumer $1,535.51, for an overcharge of $24.93,[675] which could implicate the statutory usury penalties.
2. *Credit life insurance*: By state regulation, the maximum charge for credit life insurance on the borrower is $.50/$100/year. Multiplying $.50 × $5,731.56 ÷ 100 (Total of Payments divided by 100) × 3 (years) produces a maximum premium charge of $85.97.[676] However, Pyle charged Consumer $103.17, for an overcharge of $17.20.[677] Depending on the various statutes and regulations, this overcharge may also invoke usury

665 Failure to credit payments properly will lead to an excessive balance on the consumer's account. When the overcharge is treated as interest, it will increase the effective rate charged by the creditor, possibly causing usury. The consumer should be aware of the possibility of a good faith error defense, however. *See* § 7.5.5.2, *infra*.

666 *See* Chart 15.

667 *See* Chart 14.

668 *See* Chart 16.

669 *See* Chart 17.

670 If the creditor were already charging the highest permissible interest rate, a $3.60 overcharge would be usurious. A misstatement of the number or amount of payments is a TILA violation for which statutory damages are available, and TILA does not provide any tolerance for minor inaccuracies in the payment schedule. However, the creditor might try to recharacterize this misstatement as an inaccuracy in the total of payments, for which statutory damages are not available. 15 U.S.C. §§ 1638(a)(6), 1640(a). *See* National Consumer Law Center, Truth in Lending § 5.6 (7th ed. 2010 and Supp.).

671 *See* § 4.8, *supra*.

672 *See* § 7.6, *infra* (on interpreting deregulated statutes).

673 This provision applies because Consumer purchased in 2010 a 2005 Honda, a car that was five model years old.

674 *See* § 5.3.2, *supra*.

675 $1,535.51 − 1,510.58 = $24.93.

676 *See* § 6.6.1, *infra* (discussing calculating credit insurance premiums).

677 $103.17 − $85.97 = $17.20. Apparently, Pyle charged Consumer $0.60/$100/year, instead of $0.50/$100/year. $0.60 × $5,731.56 ÷ 100 × 3 = $103.17.

penalties.[678] At the very least, Consumer will save $17.20 plus interest less the rebate.[679]

3. *Fees*: Consumer paid $40 for license, title, and registration fees, yet the maximum fees under state law are only $37.50. The $2.50 overcharge may be a form of "hidden interest."[680]

4. *Late charges*: Under the MVRISA, as well as under the contract, the maximum late charge is $5.00 or 5% of the payment, whichever is *less*. As noted above, Pyle has overcharged on two late charges (by exceeding the $5.00 ceiling) and has also imposed a late charge when a payment was less than ten days late. In addition, Pyle also imposed a full late charge on April 11, even though a partial payment of $79.88 was made. The question of whether Pyle could charge a full late charge (that is, up to the $5.00 legal maximum), a partial late charge, or no late charge at all, should be investigated further.[681]

5. *Rebates*: Under the applicable MVRISA, the creditor must rebate unearned interest when a precomputed transaction is prepaid or otherwise "terminated" before the final payment. The statute authorizes the use of the Rule of 78s to calculate the rebate of unearned precomputed interest.[682] Obviously, one must first determine whether this is a "precomputed" transaction, as opposed to an interest-bearing transaction.[683] Since the Truth in Lending statement refers to prepayment rebates, rather than penalties, and the ledger shows that the account was not kept on an interest-bearing basis, this appears to be a precomputed transaction. Another sign is that add-on interest was charged, which is generally precomputed.[684] The use of add-on interest generally binds the consumer to pay the total of payments. To be completely sure, the rest of the contract, not yet available, must be examined. If it says that Connie Consumer agrees to pay the "total of payments listed above, $5,731.56" or some variant, it is precomputed. If, under the contract, Connie Consumer promises to pay "the amount financed together with interest thereon . . ." or "$4,196.05 together with interest thereon. . . ." or similar language, it is interest-bearing, and no interest rebate is required.[685]

The lawyer notes that the "Amount Owed" on the July 18 letter ($5,350) is the same as the April 11 "New Balance" on the Ledger ($5,350). Therefore, the lawyer is fairly certain that the unearned interest has not been rebated or otherwise credited to Consumer's account, but is less certain about the amount of the rebate to which Consumer is entitled. (That's because he hasn't yet read § 5.8.6.3, *supra,* which unveils the mysteries of the Rule of 78s. But, if he makes a quick detour there now, he can confidently go forward with his analysis of Consumer's case.) There are at least two issues that have to be resolved before the exact amount of the rebate can be determined:

- Which event triggers the rebate: the last payment (April 11), the date of acceleration (date unknown), the repossession (June 12), the repossession sale (June 28), the date of the demand letter (July 18)?[686]
- Since none of the above events took place on a payment due date (the 1st of every month), should the rebate be calculated as of the nearest payment date, the previous payment date, or the next payment date?[687]

Without yet knowing the answers to those questions, the lawyer can still calculate the rebate on the terms most favorable to the creditor. It is to the creditor's advantage to calculate the rebate on the latest possible date, since that produces the smallest rebate. Therefore, the lawyer uses the July 18 letter as the triggering event and uses the next payment date, August 1, as the rebate date.

As of August 1, seven payment dates have passed,[688] so 29 payments remain.[689] The rebate fraction would then equal $(29 \times 30) \div (36 \times 37) = 65.32\%$ or .6532. Multiplying $65.32\% \times$ $1,535.51 (interest charge) = $1,003. The lawyer knows that the client, Consumer, is entitled to a rebate of $1,003 at the very least.

In addition, the lawyer knows that Consumer is entitled to a Rule of 78s rebate of the unearned portion of the $389.75 credit insurance premiums.[690] Again using the most conservative assumptions, the lawyer multiplies 65.32% × $389.75 to get a $254.58 credit insurance rebate.

Therefore, even without raising usury issues relating to initial charges,[691] and using conservative assumptions, the lawyer has reduced Pyle's claim by $1,257.58.[692]

678 *See* § 6.6.2, *infra*.
679 *See* § 6.10, *infra* (discussing further rebates of credit insurance premiums).
680 *See* § 4.5, *supra*.
681 *See* § 4.8, *supra*.
682 *See* § 5.8.6.3, *supra*.
683 *See* § 5.8.2, *supra*.
684 *Id.*
685 *Id.* Rebates of credit insurance, however, may still be required. *See* § 6.10, *infra*.
686 Pyle might argue that no rebate is due until judgment or payment of judgment. *See* § 5.8.5, *supra*.
687 *See* § 5.8.5, *supra*.
688 February, March, April, May, June, July, August.
689 36 – 7 = 29.
690 $103.17 (credit life) + $286.58 (credit disability) = $389.75. *See* § 6.10, *infra* (as to when insurance rebates are required).
691 Indeed, the failure to rebate interest and/or credit insurance premiums itself gives rise to usury claims. *See* §§ 5.8.7, *supra*, 6.10, *infra*.
692 $1,003.00 + 254.58 = $1,257.58.

# Chapter 6 Credit Insurance and Debt Protection Products

## 6.1 Introduction

One of the most remunerative methods for imposing extra costs on a credit transaction (open- or closed-end) is through the sale of credit insurance. The most common basic types of credit insurance include:

- Credit life, which protects the account against the loss of the borrower's life;
- Credit disability or accident and health (A&H), which is an indemnity insurance to cover payments in the event the borrower's income is interrupted for health reasons;
- Credit property, which protects the collateral;
- Credit family leave, which covers expenses associated with family leave; and
- Loss of income, an indemnity policy to provide limited payments in the event of involuntary loss of employment.

In addition, a related product, the debt cancellation or suspension agreement, is a newer entrant into the market. It works like the credit life, disability, and loss of income insurances described above from the consumer's perspective but is not considered "insurance" under many state laws. A report by the U.S. Government Accountability Office found that in 2009 consumers paid approximately $2.4 billion for debt protection products on credit cards.[1] The report found that the annual cost often exceeded 10% of the cardholder's average monthly balance on a credit card account; cardholders received twenty-one cents in tangible financial benefits for every dollar spent in debt protection fees while card issuers retained over fifty cents for every dollar as pretax earnings.[2]

Although total credit insurance net written premiums (the dollar amount of premiums sold) have decreased substantially over the last few years, this is attributable in part to the rise of debt cancellation products, which are also costly and much less regulated. Credit insurance is still commonly found on loans from auto dealers, finance companies and some credit unions and small banks.

Debt cancellation agreements are analyzed at § 6.3.2, *infra*, including their cost, regulation, and abuses practices related to the topic. The rest of this chapter focuses on credit insurance, including a series of common problems with the product and consumer remedies to deal with each of those problems.

Because it is so profitable for creditors and the insurance industry, the pressures to sell credit life, disability, property, and loss of income products are enormous. As a consequence, consumers spend billions of dollars per year on credit insurance, often with little understanding of what they have bought.[3] This volume of business conceals annual overcharges in the billions[4] where "overcharge" is defined in an economic sense rather than a legal sense.

For many years advisors outside the credit industry have recommended that most consumers do not purchase these products.[5] One of the exceptions is when a credit union is the

1 United States Government Accountability Office, Credit Cards: Consumer Costs for Debt Protection Products Can Be Substantial Relative to Benefits but Are Not a Focus of Regulator Oversight (Mar. 2011), *available at* www.gao.gov/products/GAO-11-311. The report notes that, because debt protection products, unlike insurance products, clearly fall within federal regulatory jurisdiction, they could be the subject of future regulator action by the Consumer Financial Protection Bureau.

2 *Id.*

3 Center for Economic Justice & Consumer Federation of America, Letter to National Association of Insurance Commissioners (Oct. 13, 2009) (relying on data submitted by insurers to state insurance regulators, countrywide credit insurance loss ratios hovered in the 40% vicinity for a decade), *available at* www.cej-online.org/cfacejcfpb091013.pdf; Center for Economic Justice and Consumer Federation of America, Letter to Senator Dodd, et al. (July 29, 2009) (detailing credit insurance abuses and supporting creation of federal consumer financial protection agency; noting loss ratios in 2008 of 44% for credit life, 38% for credit disability, 13% for credit unemployment, 7.8% for credit property, and 0.2% for credit family leave insurance), *available at* www.consumerfed.org/elements/www.consumerfed.org/file/CFPA_insurance_letter_7-29-09.pdf; The Fact Book of Credit-Related Insurance, 2007 Credit-Related Insurance Experience Data 5 (Nov. 30, 2008) (showing that consumers paid $6.46 billion in 2007 and total premium payments increased by 16% over the previous year); Jack Gillis, James Hunt, D.J. Powers & Birny Birnbaum, Consumer Federation of America and Center for Economic Justice, Credit Insurance Overcharges Hit $2.5 Annually (Nov. 2001), *available at* www.cej-online.org/creditinsurance.php (in 2000, consumers paid about $6 billion for the traditional credit insurance products). *See also* Mary Griffin & Birny Birnbaum, Consumers Union and the Center for Economic Justice, Credit Insurance: The $2 Billion a Year Rip-Off (Mar. 1999) (from 1995 to 1997, more than $17 billion of credit insurance was sold in the U.S., excluding private mortgage insurance).

4 Jack Gillis, James Hunt, D.J. Powers & Birny Birnbaum, Consumer Federation of America & Center for Economic Justice, Credit Insurance Overcharges Hit $2.5 Annually (Nov. 2001), *available at* www.cej-online.org/creditinsurance.php.

5 *E.g.*, *Credit Life Insurance: Oversold and Overpriced*, Changing Times 62 (Mar. 1980); *Credit Insurance: The Quiet Overcharge*, Consumer Reports 415 (July 1979); Jack Gillis, James Hunt, D.J. Powers & Birny Birnbaum, Consumer Federation of America and Center for Economic Justice, Credit Insurance Overcharges Hit

creditor. That credit insurance typically meets the recommended standards for price-to-value.

Though credit insurance is regulated to varying degrees in every state and to some extent by federal rules regarding its sale in connection with credit, neither the state regulatory bodies nor competitive pressures successfully control the problems.[6] This lack of control, combined with the product's profitability, leads to great potential for abuse. Indeed, a former chair of the California Senate Insurance Committee took bribes from the credit insurance industry to push (successfully) for legislation which helped hike the price of the product. A consumer's RICO action against the legislator was blocked by a finding of legislative immunity.[7]

## 6.2 Economic Incentives; Market Failures

### *6.2.1 Background*

Credit life insurance initially was sold in connection with Morris Plan Bank loans in 1917, its purpose admittedly to protect the creditor in the event of the borrower's death, and the premium cost was paid by the creditor.[8] Today, most lenders sell insurance for which the borrower pays a separate premium charge.

Credit insurance may be written as an individual policy, sold directly to the borrower. More often, however, it is a group policy, issued by the insurer to the creditor. The actual terms of the policy are set forth in the master policy between the creditor and the insurer. The group eligible to be insured under this policy is the creditor's borrowers, who are "enrolled" as members of the group if they purchase the insurance. Instead of receiving an insurance policy, a borrower receives a certificate of insurance.

The use of group policies, by which the creditor merely enrolls a borrower, may allow the creditor to avoid licensing or other regulatory requirements of a state insurance department. Group insurance also has administrative economies which should make it cheaper than individual policies, as there is less administrative work for the insurer. However, because of market structures promoting substantial creditor and insurer profits from credit insurance and due to lack of transparency, group credit insurance provides no cost advantage for consumers.

### *6.2.2 Benefits to Creditor*

#### 6.2.2.1 Creditor Compensation from Sale of Insurance

Because the lender receives commissions at a specified percentage of each premium dollar, sometimes as much as 40–50%, the lender has a strong financial incentive to sell the most expensive insurance to borrowers, rather than the cheapest. One company's 1998 SEC Form 10-K filing revealed both its philosophy of reverse competition as well as the commissions paid:

> The Company used contracts which allowed the Company's clients [i.e., creditors] to participate in the underwriting results of policies they marketed to their customers. The "Retro Plan" contract linked a client's overall commission to the claims experience on policies marketed to its customers, so that low loss-ratios result in higher commissions for the client and the high loss-ratios resulted in lower commissions. Another form of participation was a profit sharing contract under which the client earns up to 50% of the profits generated from its insurance business. The Company also reinsured premiums generated by certain clients to the clients' own captive insurance companies or to reinsurance subsidiaries in which clients have an ownership interest.[9]

---

$2.5 Annually (Nov. 2001), *available at* www.cej-online.org/creditinsurance.php; Credit Life Insurance: The Nation's Worst Insurance Rip Off, Statement of Consumer Federation of America and National Insurance Consumer Organization (June 4, 1990) (updated May 20, 1992) (updated again July 25, 1995) (updated again Jan. 29, 1997, *available on the companion website to this treatise*).

6 Jack Gillis, James Hunt, D.J. Powers & Birny Birnbaum, Consumer Federation of America and Center for Economic Justice, Credit Insurance Overcharges Hit $2.5 Annually (Nov. 2001), *available at* www.cej-online.org/creditinsurance.php.

7 Chappell v. Robbins, 73 F.3d 918 (9th Cir. 1996). It is unclear why the bribers were not sued, instead of the bribee.

8 *See* Gary Fagg, *When Worlds Converge*, Contingencies (Jan./Feb. 2003) (historical look at credit insurance and the onset of debt cancellation products; noting that credit insurance was modeled on Morris Plan banks, which extended credit to working class people based on borrower earning capacity, and that credit insurance policies were developed as group policies because one rate could be charged to all borrowers, regardless of risk), *available at* www.contingencies.org/janfeb03/worlds.pdf. *See also* College of Bus. Adm., Ohio Univ., Consumer Credit Life and Disability Insurance 7–8 (C. Hubbard, ed. 1973); National Ass'n of Ins. Comm'rs, A Background Study of the Regulation of Credit Life and Disability Insurance 3 (1970); Dobson, *Credit Insurance: The Hidden Insurance*, 65 Mich. Bar J. 166, 167 (Feb. 1986).

Arthur Morris and the Morris Plan Banks may merely have brought about the rebirth of the concept. There is apparently reference to credit insurance in the Code of Hammurabi.

9 *See* American Bankers Ins. Group, 1998 10-K Filing (Mar. 30, 1999), *available at* www.sec.gov. *See also* Spears v. Colonial Bank of Alabama, 514 So. 2d 814 (Ala. 1987) (car dealer, who received a 50% commission from each premium, earned profits of nearly a quarter million dollars in one year from his insurance sales); Higgins v. Harold-Chevrolet-GEO, 2004 WL 2660923 (Minn. Ct. App. Nov. 23, 2004) (car dealer retained almost one-half of the cost of credit insurance premiums and the commission was not disclosed to the consumer); Credit Life Insurance Revisited II (second update of Consumer Federation of America/National Insurance Consumer Organization, Clearinghouse No. 45,773B, at n.12 (July 25, 1995)) (commission and other compensation to creditors from credit life averages 45% nationally; range is from 20% or less in NY to *70% or more in LA*; this excludes additional finance charge on premiums; return also varies with type of creditor, with auto dealers receiving the largest margin), *updated again Jan. 29, 1997, available on the companion website to this treatise*).

The benefits to the lender increase when the loan is flipped or refinanced several times over, especially if the Rule of 78s is used to rebated unearned insurance premiums.[10]

In fact, cheaper providers may be driven out of the market. Prudential Insurance explained in one proceeding that it lost "millions of dollars in credit insurance, millions of it" because it "indulge[d] in the sin of not charging enough for its coverage."[11] This financial stake in the credit insurance sale, coupled with market deficiencies which prevent consumers from exerting countervailing pressures,[12] sets the stage for reverse competition. Instead of competing to offer the cheapest insurance, insurers compete "in reverse" to offer the most expensive insurance so they can offer the highest commissions.

In addition to commissions, creditors may receive compensation in other forms. The insurer may also pay dividends or retrospective rate credits to the lender if the insurer has a favorable claims experience.[13] Further, many of the larger finance companies market the policies of a "captive insurer"—one which is affiliated with or wholly owned by the finance company. ITT Financial (formerly Thorp Finance and Aetna Finance), for example, sold the insurance products of its affiliates ITT Lyndon Life and ITT Lyndon Property, among other affiliates. Beneficial sold insurance through its subsidiary, Central National Life of Omaha.

The same funneling of the insurance profits to other relatives in the creditor's corporate family may occur through reinsurance agreements. In these arrangements, the creditor initially purchases policies from an independent insurer, which then shares the risk, by reinsuring with an insurer affiliated with the creditor. For example, one SEC filing described it this way: "A substantial portion of Assurant Solutions and Assurant Specialty Property's reinsurance activities are related to agreements to reinsure premiums and risks related to business generated by certain clients to the clients' own captive insurance companies or to reinsurance subsidiaries in which the clients have an ownership interest."[14] It should be noted, too, that individual employees may receive some form of incentive or bonuses based on their insurance sales,[15] thus giving an individual loan officer economic pressures to sell insurance which are personal, as well as institutional.

Creditors also profit from investment income. Even though the borrower theoretically pays a single premium in advance for the entire loan term, the lender frequently does not forward the premium to the insurer. Rather, it is placed in escrow, and the creditor computes a monthly group premium due (after subtracting any premium refunds and creditor compensation) and then remits the insurer's share to the insurer.[16] The result is that the creditor may get investment interest earnings on the borrower's premium in addition to the interest the borrower pays directly.

#### 6.2.2.2 Creditor Benefits from the Insurance Coverage

Quite simply, the insurance is added security on the account. Though the borrower or the family may be protected from the hardships of a delinquent debt in the event of death or other misfortune, the major function "is to protect the lender, not the borrower, by insuring that a loan will be repaid despite destruction of collateral or impairment of the borrower's earning ability."[17]

#### 6.2.2.3 Creditor Receives Interest on the Premium

If the purchase of the credit life or A&H is voluntary, or if the borrower has a choice of providers on required property insurance on collateral, the Truth in Lending Act and most state credit laws[18] permit the cost of the premium to be included in the principal or amount financed. Obviously, the larger the principal, the greater the dollar yield to the creditor in interest; while the larger the portion of a debt attributed to the principal, the lower the interest rate will appear. (The same impact occurs with the Truth in Lending calculations.) Given the trend toward longer terms and larger loans, the premiums can significantly inflate the cost of the loan, by several thousand dollars in a manufactured home loan. Consider this example where the credit insurance premium was financed as part of the principal in a manufactured home loan. The credit life insurance premium added $10,000 to the loan principal.

---

10 *See, e.g.*, Hager v. American Gen. Fin., Inc., 37 F. Supp. 2d 778 (S.D. W. Va. 1999).

11 *Testimony of W.L. Skinner, Sept. 4, 1964 Before the Comm. to Investigate All Insurance Rates and Practices Concerning Credit Life, Credit Accident and Health, Credit Property Insurance Sold in South Carolina, cited in Hearings on the Consumer Credit Industry (Credit Insurance) Before the Subcomm. on Antitrust and Monopoly of the Comm. on the Judiciary of the U.S. Senate*, 90th Cong., 1st Sess. 96, n.19 (1967).

12 *See, e.g.*, Spears v. Colonial Bank of Alabama, 514 So. 2d 814, 817–818 (Ala. 1987) (special concurrence). *See generally* § 6.2.3.1, *infra*.

13 Fagg, Credit Life and Disability Insurance 94–99 (1986); College of Bus. Adm., Ohio Univ., Consumer Credit Life and Disability Insurance 29–31 (C. Hubbard, ed. 1973). *See, e.g.*, Kenty v. Bank One, Columbus, N.A., 92 F.3d 384 (6th Cir. 1996).

14 *See, e.g.*, SEC Form 10-K, Assurant, Inc. and Subsidiaries, at F-58 (Dec. 31, 2011). *See generally* College of Bus. Adm., Ohio Univ., Consumer Credit Life and Disability Insurance 30 (C. Hubbard, ed. 1973). *See* Alinco Life Ins. Co. v. United States, 373 F.2d 336 (Ct. Cl. 1967) (describing reinsurance arrangements).

15 *See Equity Predators: Stripping, Flipping and Packing Their Way to Profits: Hearing Before the Spec. Comm. on Aging United States Senate*, 105th Cong. 2d Sess. 33–34, Serial No. 105-18 (Mar. 16, 1998) (statement of Jim Dough, former employee of predatory lender); Fagg, Credit Life and Disability Insurance 50 (1986).

16 College of Bus. Adm., Ohio Univ., Consumer Credit Life and Disability Insurance 35 (C. Hubbard, ed. 1973). *See generally* Fagg, Credit Life and Disability Insurance 94–100, 106–108 (1986).

17 Bailey v. Defenbaugh & Co. of Cleveland, Inc., 513 F. Supp. 232, 243 (N.D. Miss. 1981).

18 *See* § 6.5, *infra*. *See also Hearing on Equity Predators: Stripping, Flipping and Packing Their Way to Profits: Hearing Before the Spec. Comm. on Aging United States Senate*, 105th Cong. 2d Sess. 33–34, Serial No. 105-18 (Mar. 16, 1998) (statement of Jim Dough, former employee of predatory lender).

| | WITH CREDIT INSURANCE | WITHOUT CREDIT INSURANCE |
|---|---|---|
| Principal | $68,593 | $58,366 |
| Note Rate | 14.79% | 14.79% |
| Monthly Payment | 239 @ $856 plus 1 @ $54,327 | 240 @ $759.52 |
| Total of Payments | $258,866 | $182,280 |

The total cost difference between these two loans, one with and one without the credit insurance, is over $96 per month plus the final balloon payment of $76,586.[19] The loan would have amortized in full over 240 months but for the credit insurance premium! It accounts for the balloon payment.

This inflation is exacerbated by the fact that most states permit insurance premiums to be calculated on the total of payments, which, in turn, includes the cost of the premiums and the finance charge, thus spiraling the cost.[20]

## 6.2.3 *Excessive Cost of Credit Insurance*

### 6.2.3.1 Reverse Competition; Market Failures

Credit insurance, for the most part, is an overpriced insurance product.[21] As the previous section suggests, the price the consumer pays for this insurance goes as much for additional profits to the creditor and insurer as it does for the protection it provides the borrower. In the absence of more stringent regulation than has occurred in the past, credit insurance is likely to remain overpriced.

The phenomenon of reverse competition is the primary explanation for the excessive cost of credit insurance. Reverse competition is the result of two intertwined factors: the financial incentives to the creditor to sell the most expensive insurance to its customers on the one hand; and the inability of consumers, for a variety of reasons, to force the price down by their market behavior on the other. For example, in 2009, the United Kingdom's Competition Commission published an extensive survey of "payment protection insurance," finding that there is little or no competition for sale of such products at point of sale. As a result, the commission will introduce measures to enhance competition, including a ban on sales of such products at the credit sale and for seven days following, as well as a total ban on single premium products.[22]

The economic impetus for creditors to push hard the sale of credit insurance is largely explained by how much profit they make from credit insurance sales. Evidence in a Virginia rate-setting hearing for small loan companies showed that those companies received *one-third* of their net income from credit insurance.[23] Other studies show credit insurance constituting 30%–50% of pre-tax income for some lenders.[24] Insurance profits can even exceed the profits creditors make from their credit business.[25] Another way to measure the excessive compensation earned by lenders is to review the compensation ratio, the relationship of the commissions paid to the lenders to the total premiums charged for the product. For one major credit insurance company, the ratio was in the 40% range during the height of the credit insurance boom in the 1990s.[26]

One startling example of the degree of the inflation in the cost of credit insurance due to the reverse competition effect is discussed in an Eleventh Circuit decision in which an insurer sought to avoid paying the FDIC the cost of rebates on unearned insurance premiums for approximately 300 prematurely terminated mortgage loans.[27] The insurance company defended on the ground that it had received only 35% of the premiums, the other 65% having been paid to the creditors' officers and employees or distributed to the creditors' stockholders![28] Ten years later, the picture had little improved. A 1994 CFA/NICO study reported that creditor compensation, *exclusive* of extra finance charge income, averages nearly 45% of the insurance cost.[29] In 2008, loss ratios were 44% for credit life, 38% for

19 *Hearing on Predatory Mortgage Lending: The Problem, Impact and Responses, Hearing Before the S. Comm. on Banking, Housing, and Urban Affairs* (July 26, 2001), *available at* www.senate.gov/%7Ebanking/01_07hrg/072601/miller.htm (this example appeared in Appendix B of the written testimony of Attorney General Thomas J. Miller of Iowa).

20 *See* § 6.6.1, *infra*.

21 *See, e.g.*, Carter v. Citigroup Inc., 938 So. 2d 809 (Miss. 2006) (describing credit insurance sold to borrowers who had not finished high school and with single premiums that ranged from $3,000 to $8,000 per loan; the decision addressed statutes of limitations issues, however the facts of the underlying transactions are instructive).

22 Market Investigation into Payment Protection Insurance, Competition Commission of the United Kingdom (Jan. 29, 2009), *available at* www.competition-commission.org.uk/rep_pub/reports/2009/fulltext/542.pdf.

23 *Credit Life Insurance Hearing Before the Subcomm. on Antitrust, Monopoly and Business Rights of the S. Comm. on the Judiciary*, 96th Cong, 1st Sess. 48 (1979) (statement of Robert Sable). *See also Equity Predators: Stripping, Flipping and Packing Their Way to Profits: Hearing Before the Spec. Comm. on Aging United States Senate*, 105th Cong. 2d Sess., 33–34, Serial No. 105-18 (Mar. 16, 1998) (statement of Jim Dough, former employee of predatory lender); Spears v. Colonial Bank of Alabama, 514 So. 2d 814 (Ala. 1987) (car dealer, who received a 50% commission from each premium, earned profits of nearly a quarter million dollars in one year from his insurance sales).

24 *Credit Life Insurance Hearing Before the Subcomm. on Antitrust, Monopoly and Business Rights of the S. Comm. on the Judiciary*, 96th Cong, 1st Sess. 48 (1979) (statement of Robert Sable).

25 Dobson, *Credit Insurance: The Hidden Insurance*, 65 Mich. Bar J. 167 (Feb. 1986).

26 American Banker's Insurance Group, 1998 10-K Filing 37 (Mar. 30, 1999), *available at* www.sec.gov.

27 Fed. Deposit Ins. Corp. v. Gulf Life Ins., 737 F.2d 1513 (11th Cir. 1984).

28 *Id.* The insurance company lost on this issue, but it did recover a $36,349 judgment for overpaid commissions from a former employee of the creditor.

29 Credit Life Insurance Revisited II (second update of Consumer Federation of America/National Insurance Consumer Organization July 25, 1995, Clearinghouse No. 45,773B) (ranging from a low of 20% to less in New York to high of 70% or more in Los Angeles), *updated again Jan. 29, 1997, available on the companion website to this treatise.*

credit disability, 13% for credit unemployment, 7.8% for credit property, and 0.2% for credit family leave insurance.[30]

This loading of hidden creditor-profit into the costs of the product helps explain why credit insurance is no bargain for consumers. A comparison with regular term life insurance is telling; the premium for a credit life policy on a $10,000 car loan at 13% for four years might cost $438.64 (including interest), while a term life policy for the same amount might cost $229.[31]

The financial benefits of expensive insurance explains creditors' failure to seek the lowest cost insurance, but consumers' failure to bring competitive pressures to bear must also be explained. Quite simply, the matter of insurance is of peripheral concern to most borrowers. The absolute dollar cost of the premium may seem small in comparison to their total obligation; the *idea* of credit insurance seems sound, and consumers have no way of knowing what a genuinely reasonable cost for the protection would be. While the industry has pointed to studies showing a lack of buyer resentment as to credit insurance,[32] the survey questionnaires did not fully set the stage for the respondents. No survey has prefaced its questions with an explanation that the product is as much as four times more expensive than comparable non-credit insurance, or other relevant information consumers likely do not know. If the consumer does any comparison shopping, it is for the primary product—the credit—not an ancillary product such as insurance.[33] Further, all too often, borrowers are unaware that they purchased insurance, or felt coercion in purchasing the insurance.[34]

### 6.2.3.2 Low Loss-Ratios Demonstrate Excessive Cost

That credit insurance is overpriced can be demonstrated by reviewing what is called the "loss-ratio" of credit insurers. This is a key term for understanding the value, or lack thereof, of credit insurance (or any insurance). A loss-ratio is the percentage of each premium dollar which is paid out to insureds in claims benefits. In other words, if an insurer has a 35% loss-ratio, then 35% of each premium dollar is paid out to insureds for claims. The other 65% is retained for the insurer's expenses and profit and the creditor's compensation. Insurance with a "high" loss-ratio means that most of the premium dollar is spent for the benefit of insureds, and that the insurance may be a good buy for consumers.

Credit insurance, however, historically has had low loss-ratios. Congress found that data indicated that typical loss-ratios were in the 35% to 40% range for credit life insurance.[35] The 1979 average compared unfavorably with the 80% loss-ratio then required in Canada[36] or sometimes found in group life insurance plans sold to employers.[37] By 1990, the loss-ratio had only progressed to a 41.5% average nationwide.[38] In the wake of negative publicity, some states responded by lowering rates resulting in another incremental advance to an estimated 44% average loss-ratio nationally,[39] though by 1997, the national average was only 41.6%.[40] By 2000, the national average declined to 40.7%.[41] The ten-year average for loss ratios between 2000 and 2010 were 43% for credit life and 44.5% for credit accident and health.[42] These loss-ratios compare unfavorably with the 60% minimum loss-ratio recommended by the National Association of Insurance Commissioners.[43]

30 Center for Economic Justice and Consumer Federation of America, Letter to Senator Dodd, et al. (July 29, 2009), *available at* www.consumerfed.org/elements/www.consumerfed.org/file/CFPA_insurance_letter_7-29-09.pdf.

31 Dobson, *Credit Insurance: The Hidden Insurance*, 65 Mich. Bar J. 167 (Feb. 1986).

32 *See, e.g.*, Fagg, Credit Life and Disability Insurance 463–470 (1986).

33 Alinco Life Ins. Co. v. United States, 373 F.2d 336, 338 n.3 (Ct. Cl. 1967); Spears v. Colonial Bank of Alabama, 514 So. 2d 814, 818 (Ala. 1987) (special concurrence).

34 *See* § 6.5, *infra*.

35 *Credit Life Insurance Hearing Before the Subcomm. on Antitrust, Monopoly and Business Rights of the Senate Comm. on the Judiciary*, 96th Cong, 1st Sess. 3 (1979).

36 Credit Life Insurance Revisited: A Continuing Consumer Ripoff, Statement of Consumer Federation of America and National Insurance Consumer Organization, Clearinghouse No. 45,773A (May 20, 1992), *updated Jan. 29, 1997, available on the companion website to this treatise*.

37 Fonseca, 2 Handling Consumer Credit Cases § 12:10, at 497 (3d ed. 1986 with 2012 Supplement).

38 Credit Life Insurance Revisited: A Continuing Consumer Ripoff, Statement of Consumer Federation of America and National Insurance Consumer Organization, Clearinghouse No. 45,773A (May 20, 1992) (this updates a report issued June 4, 1990, available as Clearinghouse No. 45,773), *updated again Jan. 29, 1997, available on the companion website to this treatise. See also In re* Universal Underwriters Life Ins. Co., 685 N.W.2d 44 (Minn. Ct. App. 2004) (upholding state's action disallowing as excessive an insurer's credit life and disability rates, where the insurer's average loss ratio was significantly below 50%, even though the rates were within the prima facie range).

39 Credit Life Insurance Revisited II (second update of Consumer Federation of America/National Insurance Consumer Organization July 25, 1995, Clearinghouse No. 45,773B), *updated again Jan. 29, 1997, available on the companion website to this treatise*.

40 Mary Griffin & Birny Birnbaum, Consumers Union and the Center for Economic Justice, Credit Insurance: The $2 Billion a Year Rip-Off (Mar. 1999).

41 Jack Gillis, James Hunt, D.J. Powers & Birny Birnbaum, Consumer Federation of America and Center for Economic Justice, Credit Insurance Overcharges Hit $2.5 Annually 3 (Nov. 2001). This report lists the loss-ratios per type of credit insurance by state.

42 National Association of Insurance Commissioners, Credit Life Insurance and Credit Accident & Health Insurance Experience 2006-2010 (2011).

43 In 1997, only New York exceeded that 60% mark by posting a loss-ratio of 67.6%. Mary Griffin & Birny Birnbaum, Consumers Union and the Center for Economic Justice, Credit Insurance: The $2 Billion a Year Rip-Off 7 (Mar. 1999). *See also* Lopez v. Associates Fin. Servs. of Hawaii, Inc. (D. Haw. Oct. 29, 1998) (motion for summary judgment), *available on the companion website to this treatise* (Associates answers to interrogatories showed that in 1995, it made 689 mortgage loans in Hawaii, 408 of which included credit life [59%]; in 1996, it made 628 mortgage loans, 341 of which included credit life [54%]; and in 1997, it made 530 mortgage loans, 197 of which included credit life [37%]. The number of claims filed

Credit disability insurance fares slightly better in loss-ratios. In 1997, the national loss-ratio was 48.6%.[44] Six states and Puerto Rico exceeded the 60% benchmark.[45] However, by 2000, the loss-ratio dropped to 46.1%, with only five states reaching or exceeding the 60% mark.[46] Between 2004 and 2008 seven states maintained loss ratios below 40%, with one as low as 16%.[47]

Credit property insurance, which is generally not rate-regulated, has even lower loss-ratios (though the NAIC passed a model credit property act containing a 60% loss-ratio requirement in 2001). An early credit property insurance study found loss-ratios ranging between 7% and 25%.[48] A 1997 investigation revealed that the average loss-ratio was 26.3%.[49] By 2000, however, that ratio declined to 14.7%.[50] In 2008, it was down further to 7.8%.[51]

Unemployment insurance posted a dismal 12.6% national loss-ratio in 1997.[52] By 2000, this ratio had dropped to 5.8%.[53] In 2008, it was only back up to 13%.[54]

in 1995 was only 46; in 1996, 63, in 1997, 66. The loss-ratios were not obtained in discovery. Employee bonus programs were associated with the sale of these products.

44 Mary Griffin & Birny Birnbaum, Consumers Union and the Center for Economic Justice, Credit Insurance: The $2 Billion a Year Rip-Off 3 (Mar. 1999).

45 *Id.* at 7. These states were Maine, New Jersey, New York, Pennsylvania, Vermont, and West Virginia.

46 Jack Gillis, James Hunt, D.J. Powers & Birny Birnbaum, Consumer Federation of America and Center for Economic Justice, Credit Insurance Overcharges Hit $2.5 Annually 3 (Nov. 2001). These states are West Virginia (80%), South Carolina (60%), Maine (78%), Pennsylvania (63%), and New Jersey (64%).

47 Center for Economic Justice &Consumer Federation of America, Letter to National Association of Insurance Commissioners, Oct. 13, 2009 (relying on data submitted by insurers to state insurance regulators), *available at* www.cej-online.org/cfacejcfpb091013.pdf .

48 *Credit Life Insurance Hearing Before the Subcomm. on Antitrust, Monopoly and Business Rights of the S. Comm. on the Judiciary*, 96th Cong, 1st Sess. 43 (1979) (statement of Robert Sable).

49 Mary Griffin & Birny Birnbaum, Consumers Union and the Center for Economic Justice, Credit Insurance: The $2 Billion a Year Rip-Off 3 (Mar. 1999) (this loss-ratio relates only to credit property insurance sold in conjunction with closed-end loans; on the other hand the loss-ratio drops to only 11.6% for credit property sold to credit card holders).

50 Jack Gillis, James Hunt, D.J. Powers & Birny Birnbaum, Consumer Federation of America and Center for Economic Justice, Credit Insurance Overcharges Hit $2.5 Annually 3 (Nov. 2001).

51 Center for Economic Justice and Consumer Federation of America, Letter to Senator Dodd, et al. (July 29, 2009), *available at* www.consumerfed.org/elements/www.consumerfed.org/file/CFPA_insurance_letter_7-29-09.pdf.

52 Mary Griffin & Birny Birnbaum, Consumers Union and the Center for Economic Justice, Credit Insurance: The $2 Billion a Year Rip-Off 3 (Mar. 1999).

53 Jack Gillis, James Hunt, D.J. Powers & Birny Birnbaum, Consumer Federation of America and Center for Economic Justice, Credit Insurance Overcharges Hit $2.5 Annually 3 (Nov. 2001).

54 Center for Economic Justice and Consumer Federation of America, Letter to Senator Dodd, et al. (July 29, 2009), *available at* www.consumerfed.org/elements/www.consumerfed.org/file/CFPA_insurance_letter_7-29-09.pdf.

In theory, rate regulation focuses on loss-ratios in an effort to assure that the cost of credit insurance is reasonable in relation to the benefits.[55] For a number of reasons, rate regulation has not made credit insurance a cost-effective purchase for consumers. First, where rates are set by reference to a targeted, or "benchmark" loss-ratio, the benchmark is most often 50% or 60%.[56] This probably is overly generous, given much lower loss ratios. Second, the set insurance rates are the result of an estimate as to what rate would result in achieving the benchmark loss-ratio. However, it is an estimating process that is often wrong and rarely re-examined. Finally, credit property insurance generally is not rate regulated at all and the loss-ratio therefore is likely to be very low.[57] A trend toward closer scrutiny and reasonable pricing would be welcome news for consumers.

The convergence of all the above factors makes the credit insurance area one ripe for abuse, so much so that it has been called "The Tail That Wags the Dog."[58] Consequently, any responsible evaluation of a consumer credit transaction must include an in-depth assessment of the facts and circumstances surrounding the sale of credit insurance. The National Association of Insurance Commissioners (NAIC) compiles raw data which it translates into loss-ratios. This information is available for credit life and disability insurance.[59]

# 6.3 Types of Credit and Credit-Related Insurance Products

## *6.3.1 Credit Insurance*

### 6.3.1.1 Overview

The two most commonly sold types of credit insurance are credit life and credit accident and health (credit A&H), designed to make payments on the account in the event of the borrower's death or disability.[60] Credit property protects collateral for the account. Another type of credit insurance began

55 *See* § 6.4.2, *infra*.

56 Consumer Credit Insurance Association Info. Bull., vol. XXXV, no. 61 (July 16, 1986). *See also* Fagg, Credit Life and Disability Insurance Appx. D (1986).

57 *See* Mary Griffin & Birny Birnbaum, Consumers Union and the Center for Economic Justice, Credit Insurance: The $2 Billion a Year Rip-Off 3 (Mar. 1999) (26.3% loss-ratio for property insurance; 12.6% for unemployment insurance; study also shows loss-ratios for these products by state).

58 Fonseca, Handling Consumer Credit Cases Ch. 12 (3d ed. 1986).

59 Practitioners can contact the publications department at NAIC at (816) 374-7259. NAIC's website is located at www.naic.org. *See* David Birnbaum, Center for Economic Justice, A Consumer Advocate's Guide to Getting, Understanding, and Using Insurance Data (Aug. 1999), *available at* www.cej-online.org/intro.php (helpful guide to understanding insurance data).

60 Insurance generally should cover balloon payments as well as regular monthly payments. *See* Wallace v. First Assurance Life of Am., 862 So. 2d 374 (La. Ct. App. 2003). Note that decreasing life policies and those that list a specific monthly payment will not cover balloon payments.

to be aggressively marketed in the mid-1980s: a loss-of-income coverage which makes limited payments on an account in the event of the borrower's involuntary unemployment. The latest type of credit insurance covers family and medical leave.

The National Association of Insurance Commissioners now makes information regarding consumer complaints about credit insurance available by state, by type of insurance, and by insurance company.[61] Sections 6.4, *infra* to the end of this chapter detail various credit insurance abuses and consumer remedies to challenge those abuses.

### 6.3.1.2 Credit Life

Credit life pays off an outstanding obligation in the event of the borrower's death. There are two types of credit life. The most commonly sold type of credit life is *decreasing or declining term credit life insurance.* "Decreasing term" means that the amount of coverage decreases as the balance on the loan declines because of the installment payments. Theoretically, the benefits payable in the event of death will cover only the outstanding balance on the loan at the time the death occurs.[62]

In most states the amount of coverage is based on the remaining monthly payments at the time of death.[63] This coverage, called "gross coverage," overinsures the loan because it includes unearned interest. A few states require "net coverage," which covers only the remaining principal excluding unearned interest.[64] If gross coverage is prohibited, the sale of such insurance would also raise the possibility of a claim based on the excess charge, as net coverage should be cheaper. The method of determining the benefits payable at a given time may vary according to the policy terms.[65] These terms should be carefully reviewed to determine whether the policy will pay off the indebtedness in full in the event of death. The allegations in one case describe how the named plaintiff was told that the policy would always pay off the mortgage, though this was not the case based upon a standardized form.[66]

The second type of credit life insurance is *level term credit life insurance,* where the amount of coverage or benefits payable does not decrease despite the fact that the installment payments reduce the account balance. The benefits payable remain level over the entire term of the policy.

Because the coverage does not decline with the loan balance, a level life policy overinsures the loan even more than gross coverage decreasing insurance; it provides excessive coverage for which the borrower pays. It is more expensive than declining term; premium rates may be over 50% higher. For these reasons, it is illegal to write level term credit life on amortized loans in most states. Creditors may wish to sell level term because financing the higher premium will result in a greater interest yield. If it is sold impermissibly, an overcharge claim may be raised.[67]

Level term insurance may be justified and legally permitted where it is written in conjunction with interest-only loans, with the coverage on the policy set at the principal amount of the loan. In this type of loan, the monthly payments pay only the interest accrued each month, the principal never declines. The principal is due in one lump-sum "balloon" payment at the end of the loan term.

There are also credit life variations depending on the debtors covered. Single life protects only one named debtor. Joint life protects two debtors who are obligated on an account. Most often, joint life is sold where two spouses are both obligated on an account. Joint coverage, however, means only that the policy will pay if *either* borrower dies. If both borrowers die, there are no additional benefits. The premium rate for joint life is more expensive than single life. While this higher premium is attractive to creditors, the extra benefit to consumers may be marginal if repayment of the loan depends on the earning capacity of only one spouse.[68]

State law may restrict the insurer from selling credit insurance products with terms longer than ten years or from selling insurance in conjunction with loans having a term in excess of ten years.[69] For longer term loans, such as manufactured home loans or mortgage loans, these restrictions result in lenders marketing "truncated" insurance policies, i.e., policies with terms that are shorter than the term of the loan. Even where no such restriction exists, lenders commonly sell five- or ten-year policies in conjunction with loans of fifteen- or thirty-year terms.

In these situations, the consumers pay the premium over the full term of the loans, often at high interest rates on subprime loans, even though the coverage ends well before the loan term ends. Even if these loans are prepaid, much of the truncated policy premiums are "earned" by that point, so that much of the principal reduction during the life of the loan simply paid off the over-priced insurance premiums. While this practice may not be illegal per se, practitioners should scrutinize the written and oral representations made about the policy. Some lenders may lead consumers to believe that the insurance policy will pay off the loan . . . and fail to state that this is true for only a portion of the loan term.

61 *See* https://eapps.naic.org/cis/.

62 *See* Pena v. Associates Fin. Life Ins. Co., 77 Fed. Appx. 259 (5th Cir. 2003) (holding that amount payable upon insured's death was limited to mortgage balance, not the $100,000 listed as the maximum coverage offered by the policy).

63 *See, e.g.,* Printis v. Bankers Life Ins. Co., 583 S.E.2d 22 (Ga. 2003).

64 *See* § 6.6.1.2, *infra.* The NAIC consumer credit insurance model act would mandate net coverage. NAIC Consumer Credit Insurance Model Act § 4(A) (1994).

65 *See* § 6.8, *infra.* Fagg, Credit Life and Disability Insurance 14–15 (1986).

66 Siemer v. Associates First Capital Corp., 2000 U.S. Dist. LEXIS 21244 (D. Ariz. Dec. 14, 2000) (magistrate recommended class certification), *aff'd,* 2001 U.S. Dist. LEXIS 12810 (D. Ariz. Mar. 30, 2001).

67 *See* § 6.6.3.1, *infra.*

68 *Cf.* Tomaszewski v. McKeon Ford, Inc., 573 A.2d 501 (N.J. Super. Ct. App. Div. 1990) (breach of fiduciary duty to fail to inform borrower of significance of failing to insure the principal wage earner).

69 *See, e.g.,* Ga. Code Ann. § 33-31-2(c).

### 6.3.1.3 Credit Disability/Accident and Health

Credit disability insurance developed later than credit life insurance, but in much the same manner and for the same purpose. Creditors were looking to borrowers' wages to repay debt; death and disability are two major unforeseen circumstances that could interrupt wages. The purpose of credit disability insurance is to insure that payments on a loan or credit sale will still be made should sickness or accident cause a significant unanticipated interruption in income. Credit disability is indemnity coverage, which makes the monthly payments while the insured borrower is unable to work due to a disability covered under the policy—a "covered loss."

Two critical terms determine what type of credit disability insurance is offered: "waiting period" and "elimination period." The waiting period is the number of continuous days a person is required to be "disabled" by sickness or accident before the disability comes within the coverage provisions of the policy. The elimination period is the initial number of days in the period of disability for which there are no benefits payable by the policy. The waiting period is an essential element indicating to the policyholder if there is a covered disability or not. The elimination period, if there is one, operates like a deductible.

The following waiting periods are generally used for credit disability insurance: seven days, fourteen days, and thirty days. The elimination periods will be stated by using one of two terms, "retroactive" or "non-retroactive." The elimination period will be either the same length of time as the waiting period (non-retroactive), or there will be no elimination period (retroactive). For example, an insured debtor with a fourteen-day non-retroactive policy must be sick or injured continuously for more than fourteen days to have a covered disability; benefits begin to accrue on the fifteenth day. With a fourteen-day retroactive policy, the insured debtor still must be sick or injured continuously for more than fourteen days to have a covered disability, but benefits are payable effective back to the first day of the disability.

Retroactive insurance is more expensive than non-retroactive, and the shorter the waiting period the more expensive the insurance. Since creditor profits are greatest with the largest insurance premium, finance companies historically sold the most expensive type of credit disability insurance—seven day retroactive. However, seven day retroactive policies are no longer approved by state insurance departments in many states. The most popular policy now in the consumer finance industry is the second most expensive—fourteen day retroactive.

Other restrictions may apply and insurance policies and information provided to the consumer should be carefully reviewed. For example, in some policies there is a shifting definition of "total disability," whereby for the first year benefits are available when the insured cannot perform duties of the insured's current occupation, and thereafter benefits only continue if the insured cannot perform duties of any occupation.[70]

### 6.3.1.4 Involuntary Unemployment Insurance

Loss-of-income or involuntary unemployment insurance is aimed primarily at loss of income caused by lay-offs, though some policies will also make monthly payments on a credit account if, in certain circumstances, the borrower goes out on strike or is fired. Unemployment insurance may be sold separately, or in combination with credit disability coverage. This combination coverage may raise special cost and voluntariness questions which should be explored.[71]

As with other types of credit insurance, the actual premium cost of involuntary unemployment insurance will seem to be a small portion of most loans, and so will not be likely to raise questions from consumers. The premium amount, considered in a vacuum, may even seem small enough to be attractive protection. However, two factors suggest that its cost may be very expensive in relation to the benefits.

- *Low loss-ratio*: As of 2007, the highest loss ratio (57%) was attributed to Pennsylvania, New Jersey, and Maine while the lowest (13%) was awarded to Nevada. More dramatically, all states except Nevada had loss ratios above 20%.[72] In 2008, the average loss ratio nationally was 13%.[73]
- *Limited benefits*: Most policies provide protection only against short-term unemployment. The insurer will pay only a limited number of monthly payments on an account during each period of unemployment.[74] California, among only a few states thus far to establish an standards on involuntary unemployment insurance requires a minimum benefit period of only four loan installments,[75] and Tennessee sets the minimum at one-third the number of months covered by the policy.[76]

In addition to the limited number of monthly payments, the policy is likely to have a maximum ceiling on the total benefits or a maximum duration. The duration of a policy sold in connection with a closed-end loan may be shorter than the term of the loan, further reducing the statistical odds that a covered loss will occur within the policy term and that the policy will provide a benefit to the borrower.

Finally, when sold in conjunction with open-end credit, such as a credit card, the monthly benefit may be limited to the

70 *See* Meyer v. CUNA Mut. Group, 2007 WL 2907276 (W.D. Pa. Sept. 28, 2007) (interpreting such a provision).

71 *See* § 6.5, *infra*.

72 Consumer Credit Industry Association, The Fact Book of Credit-Related Insurance, 2007 Credit Life Insurance Experience By State (Nov. 30, 2008).

73 Center for Economic Justice and Consumer Federation of America, Letter to Senator Dodd, et al. (July 29, 2009), *available at* www.consumerfed.org/elements/www.consumerfed.org/file/CFPA_insurance_letter_7-29-09.pdf.

74 Some policies permit the insured to re-qualify for benefits after being re-employed for a specified period of time.

75 Cal. Fin. Code §§ 18292.5(d) (West) (industrial loan companies), 22321 (property-brokers loans). Maryland, North Carolina and New York also have established minimum benefit standards by rule. Most states establish minimum standards through policy form approval.

76 Tenn. Code Ann. § 45-5-305(3)(D) (industrial loans).

*minimum* monthly payment established by the creditor. This can be as little as ten dollars, depending on the outstanding balance of the account. If a policy provides six months' maximum benefits, and is limited to a ten dollar minimum monthly payment, the maximum benefit of the policy could be sixty dollars, whether the borrower was continuously unemployed for six months or two years. In addition, products sold in conjunction with credit card accounts may limit coverage to the number of months that the consumer paid in or if the consumer is self-employed and may deny claims if the consumer's account was not current or over-limit, if the consumer paid more than the minimum payment to any credit card account other than the bank's, and if the consumer accessed credit from any credit card other than the bank's.[77] Others may fail to pay the minimum monthly payment due on the credit card.[78]

### 6.3.1.5 Credit Property

Credit property insurance insures the borrower's property, rather than health or life. The coverage is designed to protect the creditor against loss to the collateral taken as security on the insured loan. Such collateral could include furniture, jewelry, or home repair supplies. However, it is not unknown for credit property insurance to be written on property unrelated to the loan, or for coverage to be written in amounts greater than the loan despite the fact that this practice may be illegal in many states.[79]

Further, the creditor may sell insurance that may not bear a reasonable relation to the risk of loss. For example, a policy may cover loss or damage caused by fire and lightning but only if certain conditions unrelated to these occurrences also exists (i.e., the insured had defaulted in payment, the property has been repossessed, and the interest of the insured creditor has become impaired as a result of a loss covered by the policy). A policy could cover a "collision or overturn while being transported by land" without covering the more common occurrence of theft or vandalism.

Related to credit property insurance is force-placed property insurance, where the contract calls for the lender to purchase property insurance covering the collateral if the consumer does not purchase such insurance or the consumer's insurance lapses. Since this is most typically found in automobile and mortgage loans, force-placed insurance is discussed at § 10.3.8.3, *infra* and also in National Consumer Law Center, *Mortgage Lending* (2012).

Credit property insurance is less thoroughly regulated than credit life and A&H, and generally is not rate regulated at all. Such rate regulation as exists may be vague, such as that it must be sold "at standard rates."[80] Some credit property insurance may be subject to a state's general property insurance laws, but credit property is often classified as "inland marine," which is subject to little or no meaningful regulation.[81]

In 2001, the National Association of Insurance Commissioners adopted a credit personal property insurance model act.[82] Where enacted, this act curbs some of the abuses in this market, most especially its excessive cost. Its key provisions include requirements that: gross debt not be used in calculating the premium; benefits provided by the credit insurance be reasonable in relation to the premium charged, which is met if the loss-ratio is at least 60%; rebates be made by the pro rata method; for closed-end loans, the credit insurance cannot exceed the amount of the underlying debt, and the credit insurance cannot be sold unless the loan amount exceeds a minimum amount set by each state; the insurance cannot be bundled with other types of insurance; it must be an option and not a condition of obtaining credit approval; consumers receive a pre-purchase disclosure describing certain rights; consumers receive a certificate of insurance. The NAIC model has been adopted in Arizona and West Virginia, while the following states have adopted some other form of credit property statute or regulation: Alabama, Colorado, Florida, Kansas, Missouri, New York, North Carolina, North Dakota, Oklahoma, Pennsylvania, South Carolina, Virginia.[83]

This historical lack of regulation has made credit property insurance even more lucrative for creditors and insurers than credit life and disability. Though there is less data available on credit property, the lack of regulation seems to result in exorbitant pricing compared to the benefits. One early study found credit property loss ratios of only 7% to 25%, with commissions to creditors as high as 60%.[84] A 1997 report revealed the national loss-ratio to be only 22.3% for credit property sold in conjunction with closed-end accounts and 11.6% for insurance sold to credit card holders.[85] A review of loss-ratios showed that the national credit property loss-ratio logged in at an abysmal 14.7% in 2000.[86] By 2008, it reached 7.8%.[87]

77 *See In re* Providian Nat'l Bank, Department of Treasury, Consent Order #2000-53 (June 28, 2000), *available at* www.occ.gov/static/enforcement-actions/ea2000-53.pdf.

78 *See, e.g.*, Hammett v. Am. Bankers Ins. Co. of Florida, 203 F.R.D. 690 (S.D. Fla. Nov. 19, 2001) (nationwide class action denied on RICO claim due to reliance issues and on state breach of contract claim due to the possibility of variances in the laws of fifty states).

79 *See* § 6.6.4, *infra*.

80 *E.g.*, Cal. Fin. Code § 18294 (West) (industrial loans).

81 Insurance on motor vehicles, however, will not fall into the inland marine category.

82 *See* NAIC Credit Personal Property Insurance Model Act, *available on the companion website to this treatise*.

83 National Association of insurance Commissioners Model Regulation Service, 2010.

84 National Consumer Law Center, Limitation and Regulation of Credit Property Insurance 41 (U.S. Dep't of Housing & Urban Development, Office of Federal Insurance Administration 1978); *Credit Life Insurance Hearing Before the Subcomm. on Antitrust, Monopoly and Business Rights of the S. Comm. on the Judiciary*, 96th Cong, 1st Sess. 42 (1979) (statement of Robert Sable).

85 Mary Griffin & Birny Birnbaum, Consumers Union and the Center for Economic Justice, Credit Insurance: The $2 Billion a Year Rip-Off 3 (Mar. 1999).

86 Jack Gillis, James Hunt, D.J. Powers & Birny Birnbaum, Consumer Federation of America and Center for Economic Justice, Credit Insurance Overcharges Hit $2.5 Annually 3 (Nov. 2001).

87 Center for Economic Justice and Consumer Federation of America, Letter to Senator Dodd, et al. (July 29, 2009), *available at*

Probably because of this profitability, credit property insurance has played a central role in the phenomenon of "insurance-packing," the loading of loans with unnecessary insurance which has been the subject of frequent litigation.[88] As a result of changes to standard reporting forms, practitioners may be better able to determine loss-ratios for a credit property insurance company. The information may be on file with the state insurance commission, in the Credit Insurance Supplement, Experience Exhibit, or it may be available through the NAIC's database.

## 6.3.2 Credit Card Debt Suspension and Debt Cancellation Products

### 6.3.2.1 Overview of Industry

The most common types of credit insurance found with credit cards are debt cancellation or suspension agreements (collectively "debt protection products").[89] These products are sometimes called "payment protection" plans. All nine of the largest credit card issuers offer debt protection products.[90] This product also is associated with open- and closed-end credit from credit unions as well as certain closed-end bank loans.

In 2009, about 7% of the credit card accounts for these nine issuers carried debt protection, or around 24 million accounts.[91] Lenders sold 6 million debt protection products in 2009; 73% of these were for existing accounts and 27% were for newly opened accounts.[92] About half of all direct mail credit card solicitations contained an offer for debt protection.[93]

In contrast to the brisk sales of debt protection products, the sale of traditional credit insurance for credit card accounts has plummeted. By 2002, most new credit card solicitations had made the shift, containing an offer for debt protection products rather than credit insurance.[94] In 2009, three of the largest credit insurance providers reported that they sold only 44,114 new packages for credit cards.[95]

One reason for the shift from credit insurance to debt protection is that states have been hindered in regulating the latter, or have chosen not to, under the theory that they are "banking products" and thus do not constitute "insurance."[96] In addition, federal banking agencies have given banks a green light to sell debt protection products with minimal regulation.[97]

There have been a number of criticisms of debt protection products. First, a U.S. Government Accountability Office study and other evidence indicate that debt protection products are overpriced and provide relatively few benefits in proportion to their expense.[98] Second, there have been allegations that credit card issuers have involuntarily enrolled cardholders in these programs, or have engaged in deceptive or unfair practices when soliciting cardholders to enroll.[99]

### 6.3.2.2 Nature of Debt Protection Products

Both credit insurance and debt cancellation agreements eliminate some or all of the consumer's indebtedness. Credit insurance, however, usually involves a third-party insurer, whereas debt protection products are sold by the lender directly to the consumer. The absence of a third-party insurer is part of the reason these products are more profitable for lenders.[100]

From where the consumer stands, however, a debt protection product functions much like traditional credit insurance.[101] For a fee (akin to a premium), the lender agrees to cancel payment on the consumer's loan or forgive or defer monthly payments for some period of time in the event of death, serious illness or injury, unemployment, or to suspend payments for some of these same events as well as when there is a divorce, family leave from work, military relocation, disaster, or even incarceration of a spouse. The fee for debt protection is usually paid as a monthly charge.

From the creditor's perspective, the primary purpose of a debt protection product is to protect the creditor from a risk of income loss (the monthly or periodic payments the consumer owes on the account) caused by a particular covered event. The fees collected are used to create reserves to cover the creditor's interest in the loan should the indebtedness be reduced, deferred, or canceled by an enumerated contingency. In the alternative, the creditor can use the funds to transfer all or some of the risk to an insurance company through a contractual liability insurance policy. In the latter case, the obligation to pay the potential benefit is removed from the lender's balance sheet.[102]

---

www.consumerfed.org/elements/www.consumerfed.org/file/CFPA_insurance_letter_7-29-09.pdf.

88 *See* § 6.7, *infra*.

89 *See* Gary Fagg, *When Worlds Converge*, Contingencies 26 (Jan./Feb. 2003), *available at* www.contingencies.org/janfeb03/worlds.pdf (historical information and an industry perspective on the development of debt protection products). *See also* Center for Economic Justice, The Impact of Debt Cancellation Contracts on State Insurance Regulation (July 2003), *available at* www.cej-online.org/cej%20first%20dcc%20report%20no%20app.pdf (comprehensive review of debt protection products).

90 *See* U.S. Gov't Accountability Office, Credit Cards: Consumer Costs for Debt Protection Products Can Be Substantial Relative to Benefits but Are Not a Focus of Regulator Oversight, GAO-11-311, at 3 (Mar. 2011), *available at* www.gao.gov/products/GAO-11-311.

91 *Id.* at 6.

92 *Id.* at 7.

93 *See* Victoria Finkle and Jeff Horwitz, *Consumer Bureau Threatens Banks; Credit Card Protection Profits*, Am. Banker, Feb. 6, 2012 (citing data from Mintel Comperemedia).

94 *See* Gary Fagg, *When Worlds Converge*, Contingencies 26 (Jan./Feb. 2003), *available at* www.contingencies.org/janfeb03/worlds.pdf.

95 *Id.* at 7.

96 *See* § 6.3.2.4, *infra*.

97 *See id.*

98 *See* § 6.3.2.3, *infra*.

99 *See* § 6.3.2.5, *infra*.

100 U.S. Gov't Accountability Office, Credit Cards: Consumer Costs for Debt Protection Products Can Be Substantial Relative to Benefits but Are Not a Focus of Regulator Oversight, GAO-11-311, at 8 (Mar. 2011), *available at* www.gao.gov/products/GAO-11-311.

101 *Id.* at 14.

102 *See* Robert T. Watterson, Using Risk Retention Groups to Insure Contractual Liability Arising from Debt Cancellation Products Offered by National Banks and Other Consumer Lenders, 17.2 Risk Retention Rep. (Feb. 2003).

### 6.3.2.3 Debt Protection Products May Be Overpriced

Debt protection products have been criticized for being overpriced.[103] This can be demonstrated by reviewing data that is comparable to the "loss-ratio" for these products.[104] For example, a report by the U.S. Government Accountability Office (GAO) found that in 2009, consumers paid approximately $2.4 billion for debt protection products on credit cards.[105] Yet cardholders only received twenty-one cents in tangible financial benefits for every dollar spent in debt protection fees,[106] a "loss-ratio" of only 21%. In contrast, other insurance products pay out 90% of premiums in benefits, according to industry experts.[107] NAIC's Consumer Credit Insurance Model Regulation specifies that benefits provided must be reasonable in relation to the premiums charged and notes that the requirement is met if the loss ratio is 60% or more[108]—nearly three times the loss ratio of 21% for debt protection products.

The GAO report found that credit card lenders kept an astounding 55% of the $2.4 billion in fees as pretax earnings—or $1.3 billion as pure profit.[109] Lenders also spent 24% on administrative expenses, i.e., they spent more on administrative costs than they paid out in benefits.[110] Thus, debt protection products are extremely profitable,[111] especially after the Credit CARD Act[112] took effect because that law did not affect them.[113]

Debt protection products are expensive on an individual basis as well. The GAO report found that the annual cost of these products often exceeded 10% of the cardholder's average monthly balance on a credit card account.[114] Only 5.3% of consumers who bought debt protection and carried a balance on their credit cards received a benefit in 2009, with an average amount of $607.[115]

Because it is so profitable for credit card lenders, the pressure to sell debt protection products is enormous. This may be part of the reason why lenders have been accused of deceptive practices in selling these products, or even enrolling consumers without their permission.[116] As a consequence, consumers spend billions of dollars per year on these products, often with little benefit or understanding as to what they have bought.

For example, consumer testing of disclosures for debt protection products on home equity lines of credit revealed that consumers could not correctly calculate the monthly fee based on the disclosures, and were surprised to learn of the exclusions from eligibility.[117]

Furthermore, although similar in structure, debt cancellation and suspension products generally offer far fewer benefits than credit insurance due to differences in covered or triggering events and the types of benefits provided. For example, unlike credit insurance, death benefits under most debt cancellation products generally apply only in case of accidental death. As a result, only about ten percent of the eligible claims under a credit life insurance policy would result in a payment of benefits under a debt cancellation agreement.

A debt suspension agreement provides even more limited benefits than those provided by a debt cancellation agreement. Instead of canceling payment of interest and principal, it simply waives the monthly finance charge for the covered months. Most credit card lenders now primarily offer these limited debt suspension agreement programs.[118]

A look at some statistics shows the drastic loss suffered by consumers when credit insurance is replaced with a debt cancellation or suspension product.[119]

---

103 Consumer advocates are not the only ones to question the value of debt protection products. *See* William H. Ryan, Portales Partners, *Alliant Data Systems Corp*., Mar. 21, 2011 (noting with respect to World Financial Network Bank's debt protection product that "we fail to understand how offering products of questionable value (see details in the lawsuit), especially relative to the price paid by the borrower, will stand the test of time or go unnoticed by regulators.").

104 This is a term that also must be understood in order to appreciate the regulatory scheme for credit insurance. *See* § 6.4, *infra*.

105 U.S. Gov't Accountability Office, Credit Cards: Consumer Costs for Debt Protection Products Can Be Substantial Relative to Benefits but Are Not a Focus of Regulator Oversight, GAO-11-311, at 29 (Mar. 2011), *available at* www.gao.gov/products/GAO-11-311.

106 *Id.*

107 Carter Dougherty, *JP Morgan Debt-Protection Fees May Drop on Consumer Bureau Rules*, Bloomberg News, May 2, 2011 (quoting Edward Graves, Associate Professor of Insurance at the American College in Byrn Mawr, PA).

108 U.S. Gov't Accountability Office, Credit Cards: Consumer Costs for Debt Protection Products Can Be Substantial Relative to Benefits but Are Not a Focus of Regulator Oversight, GAO-11-311, at 23 (Mar. 2011), *available at* www.gao.gov/products/GAO-11-311.

109 *Id.* at 30.

110 *Id.*

111 *See, e.g.,* Andrew Johnson, *Discover Shares Drop of News of FDIC Review*, Am. Banker, July 1, 2011 (noting that debt protection and other fee-based products generated $412.5 million in income for Discover Financial Services in 2010, up 40% from the previous year).

112 *See* § 8.2.2, *infra* (credit cards).

113 *See* Victoria Finkle and Jeff Horwitz, *Consumer Bureau Threatens Banks; Credit Card Protection Profits*, Am. Banker, Feb. 6, 2012 (noting that revenue from debt protection took on increased importance after the Credit CARD Act).

114 U.S. Gov't Accountability Office, Credit Cards: Consumer Costs for Debt Protection Products Can Be Substantial Relative to Benefits but Are Not a Focus of Regulator Oversight, GAO-11-311, at 27 (Mar. 2011), *available at* www.gao.gov/products/GAO-11-311.

115 *Id.* at 29.

116 *See* § 6.3.2.5, *infra*.

117 U.S. Gov't Accountability Office, Credit Cards: Consumer Costs for Debt Protection Products Can Be Substantial Relative to Benefits but Are Not a Focus of Regulator Oversight, GAO-11-311, at 33 (Mar. 2011), *available at* www.gao.gov/products/GAO-11-311.

118 *See* Center for Economic Justice, The Impact of Debt Cancellation Contracts on State Insurance Regulation (July 2003), *available at* www.cej-online.org/cej%20first%20dcc%20report%20no%20app.pdf.

119 This information is based on a chart which available from the Center for Economic Justice report on Debt Cancellation Contracts. *See* Center for Economic Justice, The Impact of Debt Cancellation Contracts on State Insurance Regulation (July 2003), *available at* www.cej-online.org/cej%20first%20dcc%20report%20no%20app.pdf.

**What the Shift from Credit Insurance to Debt Protection Products Means for Credit Card Consumers**

| | Credit Insurance | Debt Protection | Difference |
|---|---|---|---|
| Premiums/Fees Annually | $2,000,000,000 | $2,500,000,000 | 25.0%* |
| Benefit Ratios | 40% | 5% | -84.4%** |
| Benefit Dollars | $800,000,000 | $125,000,000 | $650,000,000*** |

*Accordingly debt protection product costs are 25% more expensive than credit insurance.

**Accordingly debt protection product benefits are over 84% less than credit insurance benefits, keeping fees constant.

* * *Accordingly debt protection products provide $675,00,000 less in benefits than does credit insurance, keeping fees constant.

In contrast, creditors have tremendous incentives to replace credit insurance with debt protection products because of lower business costs and higher profits.[120] Many of these lower business costs are due to the unregulated nature of these products.

Finally, when sold in conjunction with credit cards, the monthly benefit may be limited to the *minimum* monthly payment established by the creditor. This can be as little as twenty dollars, depending on the outstanding balance of the account.[121] If a policy provides six months' worth of maximum benefits,[122] and is limited to a twenty dollar minimum monthly payment, the maximum benefit of the policy could be one hundred twenty dollars, whether the borrower was continuously unemployed for six months or two years.

In addition, products sold in conjunction with credit card accounts may limit coverage to the number of months that the consumer paid in or if the consumer is self-employed. They may deny claims if the consumer's account was not current or over-the-limit, if the consumer paid more than the minimum payment to any credit card account other than the bank's, and if the consumer accessed credit from any credit card other than the bank's.[123] Others may simply fail to pay the minimum monthly payment due on the credit card.[124] And with debt suspension products, the lender does not even pay the minimum monthly payment, but simply defers it until a later date.

### 6.3.2.4 Regulation of Debt Protection Products

One reason for the shift from credit insurance to debt protection products is the relative lack of regulation of these products. Initially, some states decided not to regulate these products, or courts barred them from regulating the products, deciding that debt protection products are "banking products" and thus did not constitute "insurance."[125] However, some states still expressly regulate debt protection products as insurance,[126] although these state provisions face preemption issues as discussed below.

Lack of regulation by state insurance agencies provides multiple benefits for the industry, such as: no need to license employees selling debt protection products; no need to maintain insurance rate tables and benefit adjustments; no existing state regulations to raise compliance issues; freedom to create an unending array of new products (such as "divorce in process" protection and products for the newly married) and full power to select rates.[127]

120 Gary Fagg, State of the Payment Protection Industry (powerpoint presentation June 7, 2007) (demonstrating growth of debt cancellation products including plans to expand into the mortgage market), *available at* www.cimro.org/CIMRO_2007/1__Gary_Fagg_CIMRO_2007_060707.pdf.

121 The method for determining the minimum monthly payment will vary. It can be as low as 1% of the outstanding balance, plus finance charges and fees, or a minimum of $20, whichever is greater. *See* § 8.6.8, *infra*. *See also* U.S. Gov't Accountability Office, Credit Cards: Consumer Costs for Debt Protection Products Can Be Substantial Relative to Benefits but Are Not a Focus of Regulator Oversight, GAO-11-311, at 30 (Mar. 2011), *available at* www.gao.gov/products/GAO-11-311 (noting minimum payment is typically only 1% to 2% of the balance).

122 For example, the GAO Report noted that most debt protection products have time limits, such as a six to twenty-four month limit for benefits triggered by involuntary unemployment. *Id* at 31.

123 *See In re* Providian Nat'l Bank, Dep't of Treasury, Consent Order #2000-53 (June 28, 2000), *available at* www.occ.treas.gov/ftp/eas/ea2000-53.pdf.

124 *See, e.g.*, Hammett v. Am. Bankers Ins. Co. of Florida, 203 F.R.D. 690 (S.D. Fla. Nov. 19, 2001) (nationwide class action denied on RICO claim due to reliance issues and on state breach of contract claim due to the possibility of variances in the laws of fifty states).

125 *See, e.g.*, First Nat'l Bank of E. Arkansas v. Eubanks, 740 F. Supp. 1427 (E.D. Ark. 1989) (sale of debt cancellation products does not constitute business of insurance and thus is not subject to regulation by state insurance department; department had sought to regulate such products); Auto. Funding Group Inc. v. Garamendi, 7 Cal. Rptr. 3d 912 (Cal. Ct. App. 2003); Md. Att'y Gen. Op. No. 94-051, 1994 Md. AG LEXIS 50 (Oct. 17, 1994) (debt cancellation agreements do not constitute contracts of insurance).

In Texas, the state Finance Commission adopted a rule expressly authorizing the sale by state-charted banks of debt protection products on consumer loans and allowing the financing of such premiums. 7 Tex. Admin. Code § 12.33. Similarly, the South Dakota Legislature adopted a provision allowing state-charted banks to sell debt protection products. S.D. Codified Laws §§ 51A-4 to 51A-46.

126 *See* Justice v. Branch Banking & Trust Co., 2009 WL 853993 (S.D. W. Va. Mar. 24, 2009) (declining to conclude that debt cancellation contracts are not insurance under state law and noting that some states expressly regulate such contracts as insurance).

A few states are explicitly retaining the power to regulate debt protection products as insurance for some classes of financial institutions. *See, e.g.*, Utah Code Ann. § 7-1-324 (debt protection products fall within definition of insurance in insurance code, but depository institutions are exempt from such regulation); Utah Admin. Code r. 331-25; Opinion Letter Regarding Regulation of National Banks Offering Debt Cancellation Contracts and Debt Suspension Agreements (Nevada Div. of Ins. Apr. 2, 2003), *available on the companion website to this treatise* (state regulation of national banks is preempted under Gramm-Leach-Bliley, but other types of financial institutions are subject to insurance regulation for sales of debt protection products).

127 *See* Consumer Credit Insurance Association, The 2005 Fact Book of Credit-Related Insurance 33 (Apr. 2005), *1997, available on the companion website to this treatise*; Bob Reilley, *Debt Cancellations: The Preferred Alternative to Credit Insurance*, ABA Banking Journal (Oct. 2001), *available at* www.promsoft.com/techltr/aba_debt_cancellation.pdf. *See also* Robert T. Watterson, *Using Risk Retention Groups to Insurance Contractual Liability Arising from Debt Cancellation Products Offered by National Banks and Other*

Regulations issued by the Office of Comptroller of Currency (OCC) also hinder state regulation of debt protection products.[128] These regulations have opened the floodgates for the sale of debt protection products. The OCC codified its long-held view that debt protection products are not insurance.[129] Because of preemption under the Gramm-Leach Bliley Act,[130] state provisions that limit fees or treat debt protection products as insurance appear to no longer apply to national banks.[131]

The OCC debt protection regulations provide only minimal substantive consumer protections, predominately in the mortgage context.[132] Unlike state insurance regulators, the OCC and other federal banking regulators do not address the reasonableness of the pricing of debt protection products.[133] The OCC primarily relies on disclosure of the terms of the agreement to protect consumers. These include mandatory "short-form" disclosures—which may be provided orally at the time of solicitation, including telephone sales—and "long-form" disclosures, which are generally provided in writing before the consumer completes the purchase.[134]

The short-form disclosures must state that consumers will receive additional information before they pay for the product and that certain eligibility requirements, conditions, and exclusions may apply.[135] The long-form disclosures must provide further information regarding these requirements, conditions, and exclusions; they also state, among other things, that consumers have the right to cancel the product.[136]

The OCC's rule also includes a ban on misleading advertisements or practices.[137] In addition, it prohibits lenders from modifying product features unilaterally unless the modification benefits the consumer without an additional charge, or the consumer is allowed to cancel the product without a penalty.[138] The rule also prohibits national banks from tying the approval of credit to the consumer's purchase of a debt protection product, i.e., the bank cannot make its approval contingent on the consumer's purchase of a debt protection product.[139]

The Truth in Lending Act contains provisions regarding the disclosure of debt suspension, debt cancellation, and credit insurance products, all three of which are treated the same for purposes of disclosure requirements.[140] Under these rules, mandatory debt protection or credit insurance fees are treated as finance charges, whereas voluntary products are not.[141] In order

---

*Consumer Lenders*, 17.2 Risk Retention Rep. (Feb. 2003) (describing industry benefits from the demise of state regulation of these products).

128 12 C.F.R. pt. 37 (OCC).

129 *See, e.g.*, OCC Interpretative Letter No. 903 (Jan. 2001) (stating that debt protection products are part of lending function of national banks). *See also* First Nat'l Bank v. Taylor, 907 F.2d 775 (8th Cir. 1990) (state insurance commissioner could not prohibit national bank from entering into debt cancellation agreements because National Bank Act gave national banks "incidental" powers to conduct business; since contracts do not require the bank to take investment risk or to make payment to the borrower's estate, thus are not "insurance"); Opinion Letter from Sheila A. Albin, Assoc. Gen. Counsel, National Credit Union Admin. to Barbara Means, AVP, Aon Integramark (Jan. 28, 2004), *available at* www.ncua.gov/Legal/OpinionLetters/OL2003-1039.pdf (a federal credit union may offer debt cancellation agreements to its members as an exercise of incidental powers without having to comply with state law; this does not constitute the business of insurance); OTS Chief Counsel Letter (Dec. 18, 1995), *available at* www.ots.treas.gov/docs/5/56521.pdf; 12 C.F.R. § 721.3(g) (National Credit Union Administration).

130 *See* § 6.4.8, *infra* (discussing the Gramm-Leach-Bliley Act).

131 *See* DeCohen v. Abbassi, L.C.C., 2011 WL 3438625 (D. Md. July 26, 2011) (OCC regulations preempted restrictions in state closed-end credit law regarding GAP debt cancellation even though bank did not did not extend credit directly but was an assignee of the retail installment contract). *See also* Opinion Letter Regarding Banks Sales of Debt Suspension Agreements and Debt Cancellation Contracts, Clearinghouse No. 54,591 (New York State Ins. Dep't Apr. 4, 2003) (national banks selling debt protection products in New York are not subject to regulation by the state insurance department, although it is generally the department's position that "debt cancellation contracts are considered insurance under New York Insurance Law").

It is still an open question whether states that historically have treated debt protection products as insurance will be influenced by the OCC's regulations to allow lenders other than national banks to sell them without substantial state regulation. Approximately forty states have "parity statutes" that give state chartered financial institutions the same rights as federally chartered counterparts. These laws potentially could serve as a basis for state chartered banks to argue that they have the right to sell debt protection products free of any state regulation. Center for Economic Justice, The Impact of Debt Cancellation Contracts on State Insurance Regulation 21 (July 2003).

132 The regulations prohibit the use of single-premium financing for debt protection products sold in connection with residential mortgage loans, and require lenders offering lump-sum payment products to also offer a bona fide periodic payment option. 12 C.F.R. §§ 37.3(c)(2) and 37.5. However, the regulations do not set limits on fees. They also allow the lender to offer contracts that do not provide for a refund of a lump-sum premium (on loans other than residential mortgages) in the event of prepayment or refinancing, so long as the bank also offers a comparable contract that does provide for a refund. 12 C.F.R. § 37.4(a).

Perhaps ironically, the OCC modeled its regulations on those requirements that apply to banks' insurance sales. *See* 67 Fed. Reg. 58,963 (Sept. 19, 2002).

133 U.S. Gov't Accountability Office, Credit Cards: Consumer Costs for Debt Protection Products Can Be Substantial Relative to Benefits but Are Not a Focus of Regulator Oversight, GAO-11-311, at 20–22 (Mar. 2011), *available at* www.gao.gov/products/GAO-11-311.

134 12 C.F.R. § 37.6(a), (b).

135 12 C.F.R. pt. 37, app. A.

136 12 C.F.R. pt. 37, app. B.

137 12 C.F.R. § 37.3(b).

138 12 C.F.R. § 37.3(c).

139 12 C.F.R. § 37.3(a). *See also* OCC Interpretative Letter No. 1028 (May 9, 2005) (discussing the tying prohibition in 12 C.F.R. § 37.3(a) and finding that financing of a GAP feature sold by the same national bank does not constitute a violation of that provision).

This letter is summarized at Appx. D.1.3, *infra*, and appears in full on the companion website to this treatise.

140 *See* 15 U.S.C. § 1605(b); Reg. Z, 12 C.F.R. §§ 1026.4(b)(7), (10) and 1026.4(d)(1), (3) [§§ 226.4(b)(7), (10) and 226.4(d)(1), (3)]; Reg. Z, Official Commentary §§ 1026.4(b)(10) and 1026.4(d)(3) [§§ 226.4(b)(10) and 226.4(d)(3)]. *See also* § 6.5, *infra*; National Consumer Law Center, Truth in Lending § 3.9.4 (7th ed. 2010 and Supp.).

141 *See* 15 U.S.C. § 1605(b)(1); Reg. Z, 12 C.F.R. § 1026.4(b)(7), (10) [§ 226.4(b)(7), (10)].

to qualify as voluntary, lenders must make certain disclosures.[142]

The Consumer Financial Protection Bureau (CFPB) has jurisdiction under the Dodd-Frank Act to issue regulations governing disclosures or other requirements for debt protection products.[143] The CFPB has stated it may consider such an action.[144]

### 6.3.2.5 Abusive or Deceptive Practices in the Sale of Debt Protection Products

In addition to concerns over the pricing and benefits of debt protection products, there have been allegations of abusive or deceptive practices in the sale of these products to consumers. These include allegations that cardholders were involuntarily enrolled into these programs, and that they were enrolled using deceptive or misleading representations. The GAO report on debt protection products noted that nearly half of all sales resulted when consumers spoke via telephone with a lender's customer service representative on another matter, such as an inquiry or request.[145] Thus, it appears that lenders' representatives are trained to promote these ancillary products as part of their response to other matters.

The Minnesota attorney general filed a lawsuit in 2010 against Discover Bank, alleging that telemarketers for Discover Bank used deception to sell debt protection to credit card customers. These allegations including enrolling customers after a quick recital of terms and conditions and by manipulating phone conversations such that anytime a consumer said "okay" to a seemingly benign statement during the call, the consumer was presumed to have agreed to enroll in the plan.[146] A California lawsuit similarly alleged that consumers were involuntary enrolled in debt protection products.[147]

Another frequent problem is the sale of debt protection products to consumers who will not benefit or only minimally benefit from them. Consider the infamous case of Ruth Owens, an older consumer in Cleveland who was the textbook example of credit card abuses.[148] Ms. Owens was charged approximately $10 per month (totaling about $370) for a Discover card debt protection product called CreditSafe Plus.[149] This product purported to provide for a suspension of payments and finance charges if Ms. Owens became unemployed, hospitalized, or disabled. Since Ms. Owens was already on Social Security disability and unemployed, the CreditSafe product presumably would apply only if she became hospitalized. Ms. Owens was no doubt paying for a product that would likely never benefit her.

Indeed, the GAO report noted a number of restrictions that would make consumers ineligible for benefits, such as exclusion of unemployment coverage for consumers with part-time or seasonal employment.[150] Other restrictions include thirty-day waiting periods and caps on how much cardholders could receive in benefits.[151] The GAO report found that lenders denied about 24% of benefits requests in 2009, and approved 70% of them.[152]

The West Virginia Attorney General's Office has sued Capital One for selling debt protection products to consumers who were ineligible for the coverage, as well as other practices that were unfair and deceptive. Capital One agreement to pay $14.5 million in restitution and attorney fees, and to forgive up to $3 million in debt for West Virginia consumers.[153] A number of private lawsuits have also been filed alleging deception and unfair practices in the sale of debt protection products, although courts in some of the cases have held that the claims are preempted by the OCC regulations.[154]

The CFPB has begun examining debt protection products as well. The CFPB and FDIC have informed Discover Bank that they plan to take joint enforcement action against Discover's marketing of debt protection products.[155]

142 *See* 15 U.S.C. §§ 1605(b)(1) and (3); Reg. Z § 1026.4(d)(1), (3) [§ 226.4(d)(1), (3)].

143 U.S. Gov't Accountability Office, Credit Cards: Consumer Costs for Debt Protection Products Can Be Substantial Relative to Benefits but Are Not a Focus of Regulator Oversight, GAO-11-311, at app. II (Mar. 2011), *available at* www.gao.gov/products/GAO-11-311.

144 *Id.* Carter Dougherty, *JPMorgan Debt-Protection Fees May Drop on Consumer Bureau Rules*, Bloomberg News, May 2, 2011.

145 U.S. Gov't Accountability Office, Credit Cards: Consumer Costs for Debt Protection Products Can Be Substantial Relative to Benefits but Are Not a Focus of Regulator Oversight, GAO-11-311, at 13 (Mar. 2011), *available at* www.gao.gov/products/GAO-11-311.

146 Press Release, Minnesota Att'y Gen., Attorney General Lori Swanson Files Suit Against Discover Bank: Lawsuit Alleges That Credit Card Company Deceptively Charged Customers for Pricey Financial Products Marketed As a Way for People to Protect Themselves from Fraudulent Charges and Financial Instability (Dec. 6, 2010), *available at* www.ag.state.mn.us/consumer/pressrelease/120610 discoverbank.asp.

147 Arevalo v. Bank of America Corp., ___ F. Supp. 2d ___, 2011 WL 1195973 (N.D. Cal. Mar. 29, 2011) (declining to dismiss state law UDAP claims as preempted).

148 *See* § 6.3.2.3, *supra*.

149 Discover Bank v. Owens, 822 N.E.2d 869 (Ohio Mun. Ct. 2004).

150 U.S. Gov't Accountability Office, Credit Cards: Consumer Costs for Debt Protection Products Can Be Substantial Relative to Benefits but Are Not a Focus of Regulator Oversight, GAO-11-311, at 11–12 (Mar. 2011), *available at* www.gao.gov/products/GAO-11-311.

151 *Id.* at 12.

152 *Id.*

153 Final Order of Dismissal, State v. Capital One Bank (USA), N.A., Civ. Ac. No. 10C-7-N (W. Va. Cir. Ct. Jan. 10, 2012).

154 *See* Denton v. Department Stores National Bank, 2011 WL 3298890 (W.D. Wash. Aug, 1, 2011) (dismissing state law claims as preempted); Thomas v. Bank of Am. Corp., 711 S.E.2d 371 (Ga. Ct. App. 2011) (dismissing state law claims as preempted). *But see* Arevalo v. Bank of Am. Corp., ___ F. Supp. 2d ___, 2011 WL 1195973 (N.D. Cal. Mar. 29, 2011) (declining to dismiss state law UDAP claims as preempted). *See generally* Victoria Finkle and Jeff Horwitz, *Lawyers Face Uphill Climb in Challenging Payment Protection*, Am. Banker, Feb. 6, 2012.

155 Donal Griffin and Carter Dougherty, *Discover Financial Says CFPB Probe May Have "Adverse Impact" on Net Income*, Bloomberg News, Jan. 27, 2012. *See also* Andrew Johnson, *Discover Shares Drop of News of FDIC Review*, Am. Banker, July 1, 2011 (noting that debt protection and other fee-based products generated $412.5 million in income for Discover Financial Services in 2010, up 40% from the previous year).

In 2009, the United Kingdom's Competition Commission published an extensive survey of "payment protection insurance," finding that there is little or no competition for sale of such products at point of sale. As a result, the commission announced it would introduce measures to enhance competition, including a ban on sales of such products at the credit sale and for seven days following, as well as a total ban on single premium products.[156]

### 6.3.3 Non-Credit Insurance Distinguished

Creditors, particularly finance companies, may offer to sell ancillary insurance, unrelated to the debt itself. This insurance does not protect the creditor against any risk relating to the account, unlike credit insurance where the beneficiary is the creditor or the debtor's account. However, the creditor will finance the premium for this "separately" purchased product. The creditor may sell cancer insurance, accidental death and dismemberment insurance,[157] or level term non-credit life insurance (in addition to the credit life). Insurance packing schemes frequently involve abusive sales techniques in the offering of these forms of non-credit insurance.[158]

The Minnesota Supreme Court took note of the distinction between credit life and non-credit life insurance sold by lenders in that state. It ruled that the state Regulated Loan Act[159] authorized only the sale of credit insurance, so the sale of a non-credit life insurance policy was prohibited.[160] The policy in question could not be categorized as credit insurance because it did not provide for the indemnity of the creditor and the policy term is unrelated to the loan.[161]

Like Minnesota, the North Carolina Consumer Finance Act prohibits covered lenders from soliciting or transacting any business other than making loans and selling credit insurance. The banking commissioner denied a lender's request for permission to sell a non-credit form of insurance known as (euphemistically) "Liberator Income Protector Plan" (LIPP) based, in part, upon the testimony of a legal service attorney.[162] LIPP is income replacement disability insurance. In the event of disability, LIPP would not pay off the balance of the loan but, rather, would make a payment directly to the borrower. Thus, the indebtedness of the loan would not be reduced. Since the insurance premium was to be financed as part of the loan, interest would be earned on the premium. Practitioners should be mindful of the administrative advocacy opportunities that may exist to prevent lenders from introducing new non-credit products into their repertoire especially where they drive up the cost of credit.

156 Market Investigation into Payment Protection Insurance, Competition Commission of the United Kingdom (Jan. 29, 2009), *available at* www.competition-commission.org.uk/rep_pub/reports/2009/fulltext/542.pdf.

157 These types of specialized insurance policies have often been criticized by insurance professionals. They are expensive for the protection they buy and because they cover only specialized risks, are less likely to be of benefit than comprehensive health coverage or regular life insurance. *See, e.g., Cancer Insurance: Exploiting Fear for Profit (An Examination of Dread Disease Insurance), Select Comm. on Aging*, 97th Cong. 1st Sess. 2d Ed. (Comm. Print Oct. 1981).

158 *See* § 6.7.3, *infra*.

159 Minn. Stat. ch. 56.

160 Hawkins v. Thorp Credit & Thrift Co., 441 N.W.2d 470 (Minn. 1989). *See generally* § 6.7.3, *infra*.

161 *Cf.* Reg. Z, Official Commentary § 1026.4(d)-6 [§ 226.4(d)-6] ("Insurance is not credit life, accident, health or loss of income insurance if the creditor or the credit account of the consumer is not the beneficiary of the insurance coverage").

162 Beneficial North Carolina, Inc. v. State, 484 S.E.2d 808 (N.C. Ct. App. 1997).

## 6.4 Overview of Regulation and Consumer Claims

### 6.4.1 Introduction

Regulation of credit insurance involves restrictions on both the creditor and the insurer. Some provisions may regulate only the conduct of the insurer, while others may regulate only the conduct of the creditor. Similarly, the administrative agency responsible for enforcing and administering the rules will differ. The state insurance department has authority over the insurers; the creditors are subject to oversight by the relevant state licensing authority, such as the state banking department.

Most states specifically designate in their insurance codes chapters devoted to credit insurance. The majority of these are based on the Model Credit Life, Accident and Health Insurance Act, developed by the National Association of Insurance Commissioners (NAIC) in 1960.[163] Even where that Act is not specifically adopted in a state, the Act often influences the substance of the state's credit insurance regulation.[164]

163 Model Bill to Provide for the Regulation of Credit Life Ins. and Credit Accident and Health Ins., Nat'l Ass'n of Ins. Comm'rs, Model Regulatory Service, 360-1, 370-1, and 375-1 (NIARS Corp. 1984); Alaska Stat. §§ 21.57.010 to 21.57.160; Ariz. Rev. Stat. Ann. §§ 20-1602 to 20-1616.01; Ark. Code Ann. §§ 23-87-101 to 23-87-119; Cal. Ins. Code §§ 779.1 to 779.36 (West); Colo. Rev. Stat. §§ 10-10-101 to 10-10-119; Conn. Gen. Stat. §§ 38a-645 to 38a-658; Del. Code Ann. tit 18, §§ 3701 to 3713; Ga. Code Ann. §§ 33-31-1 to 33-31-12; Haw. Rev. Stat. §§ 431:10B-101 to 431:10B-114; Idaho Code Ann. §§ 41-2301 to 41-2316; 215 Ill. Comp. Stat. §§ 5/155.51 to 5/155.65; Ind. Code §§ 27-8-4-1 to 27-8-4-14; Ky. Rev. Stat. Ann. §§ 304.19-010 to 304.19-140 (West); Me. Rev. Stat. tit. 24-A, §§ 2851 to 2865; Md. Code Ann., Ins. §§ 13-101 to 13-117 (West); Mich. Comp. Laws §§ 550.601 to 550.624; Minn. Stat. §§ 62B.01 to 62B.14; Mo. Rev. Stat. §§ 385.010 to 385.080; Mont. Code Ann. §§ 33-21-101 to 33-21-207; Neb. Rev. Stat. §§ 44-1701 to 44-1713; Nev. Rev. Stat. §§ 690A.010 to 690A.280; N.H. Rev. Stat. Ann. §§ 408-A:1 to 408-A:15; N.J. Stat. Ann. §§ 17B:29-1 to 17B:29-13 (West); N.M. Stat. Ann. §§ 59A-25-1 to 59A-25-14; N.C. Gen. Stat. §§ 58-57-1 to 58-57-115; N.D. Cent. Code §§ 26.1-37-01 to 26.1-37-16; Ohio Rev. Code Ann. §§ 3918.01 to 3918.99 (West); Or. Rev. Stat. §§ 743.371 to 743.380; 40 Pa. Stat. Ann. §§ 1007.1 to 1007.15 (West); Tex. Ins. Code Ann. §§ 1153.001 to 1153.703 (West); Utah Code Ann. §§ 31A-22-801 to 31A-22-809; Vt. Stat. Ann. tit. 8, §§ 4101 to 4115; Va. Code Ann. §§ 38.2-3717 to 38.2-3738; Wash. Rev. Code §§ 48.34.010 to 48.34.900; Wyo. Stat. Ann. §§ 26-21-101 to 26-21-114. *See also* N.Y. Ins. Law § 3201.

164 *E.g.*, Tenn. Code Ann. §§ 56-7-901 to 56-7-914.

In 2001, the NAIC adopted a credit personal property insurance model act,[165] although it has not been widely adopted. Only two states have adopted this model act, Arizona and West Virginia, although over ten other states had adopted some form of regulation.[166]

Another source of insurance legislation dealing with credit insurance, in addition to the state's special chapter on credit insurance, is the state's general group insurance laws.[167] Additionally, the state insurance department may promulgate administrative rules pursuant to either the credit insurance or group insurance statutes to further interpret and implement those statutes. The NAIC has developed model regulations to flesh out the Model Credit Insurance Act, but they have not been widely adopted.[168]

## 6.4.2 Rate Regulation

### 6.4.2.1 General

Most states have a prescribed mechanism for establishing authorized rates for credit life and disability insurance, but most states do not do so for credit property and credit involuntary unemployment insurance (IUI). Credit property and credit IUI rates are more typically subject to department review and approval or department review and disapproval—depending on the regulatory structure (prior approval, file and use, etc.). Consequently, this discussion relates primarily to credit life and disability rates.

With respect to credit life, a few states have established maximum rates by statute or regulation.[169] These are generally cast as x cents per $100 of the initial indebtedness per year, e.g., 60¢/$100/yr.[170] The more common approach for both credit life and disability, however, is not an inflexible statutory maximum ceiling, but the more fluid concept of *prima facie* rates, as set out in the 1960 NAIC Model Act.[171] The NAIC model act governing credit property insurance establishes the same 60% loss-ratio benchmark as the 1960 act, but it is not widely adopted by the states.

Under the NAIC Model Act, insurers are required to file "all policies, certificates of insurance, notices of proposed insurance, applications for insurance, endorsements and riders and the schedules of premium rates pertaining thereto" with the state insurance commission, which has the authority to disapprove any forms or premium schedule. The Act *requires* the Commissioner to disapprove the form if "the benefits provided therein are not reasonable in relation to the premium charge."[172] Similar language has been interpreted to give the insurance department the authority, in effect, to set rate standards.[173]

The generally used method of determining what premium rate would be "reasonable in relation to the benefits" is to adopt a "benchmark loss-ratio," and then to attempt to establish rates expected to produce that benchmark loss-ratio. A loss-ratio is that portion of each premium dollar paid out in claims to insureds. The rates are purportedly chosen on the basis of actual experience, derived from determining the ratio of "incurred claims" to "earned premiums" for a given period. This information is found in filings insurance companies must provide annually to insurance departments in states where they do business.[174] Of course, authorized rates cannot be established retroactively, as using actual loss-ratios would suggest, so insurance commissions are authorized to establish prima facie rates, which they anticipate will meet the loss-ratio benchmark. The prima facie "reasonable" rate, derived by this system, becomes the "authorized" premium rate.

The NAIC recommends a benchmark standard for a "reasonable charge" to be a 60% loss-ratio for both credit life and credit A & H.[175] However, most states utilize a 50% benchmark loss-ratio. The applicable benchmark may be established by statute, by administrative regulation, or by letters or bulletins issued by the insurance department. Some states set different benchmark loss-ratios for life than for disability insurance.

The NAIC modified the credit insurance model regulation and statute in the mid-1990s to allow insurers to use a pricing system that justifies lower loss ratios than the NAIC model loss ratio standards. While many states still have statutes based on the earlier model, some states have updated their laws to reflect this greater flexibility for insurers (and creditors).[176]

---

165 *See* NAIC Credit Personal Property Insurance Model Act, *available on the companion website to this treatise*.

166 Ariz. Rev. Stat. Ann. §§ 20-1621 to 20-1621.11; W. Va. Code R. §§ 114-61-1 to 114-61-9.

State rules with some protections, but that fall short of adopting all of the major provisions of the NAIC model act include: Ala. Admin. Code r. 482-1-093-.01 to 482-1-093-.14; 4 Colo. Code Regs. §§ 902-1:1 to 1:17; Fla. Stat. § 624.605(j); Fla. Admin. Code Ann. § 69O-184.006; Kan. Stat. Ann. §§ 16a-4-301, 16a-4-302, 16a-4-304; Kan. Stat. Ann. § 16a-2-501; Kan. Admin. Regs. § 75-6-9; Kan. Op. Att'y Gen. No. 86-42 (1986), 1986 WL 238275 (Kan. A.G.); Mo. Rev. Stat. §§ 385.010 to 385.080; Mo. Code Regs. Ann. tit. 20, § 1140-3.041; N.Y. Ins. Law § 2340 (McKinney); N.Y. Banking Law § 357 (McKinney); N.Y. Comp. Codes R. & Regs. tit. 11, §§ 186.1 to 186.13; N.C. Gen. Stat. § 58-57-90; N.D. Cent. Code §§ 26.1-37-01 to 26.1-37-16; Okla. Stat. tit. 14A, §§ 4-301, 4-302, 4-304; 31 Pa. Code §§ 112.1 to 112.12; Va. Code Ann. § 38.2-233. *See also* NAIC Model Regulation Service (Oct. 2010).

167 *E.g.*, Iowa Code §§ 509.1 to 509.19; Vt. Stat. Ann. tit. 8, §§ 3805, 3806.

168 Fonseca, Handling Consumer Credit Cases 484–485 (3d ed. 1986).

169 In Texas, the maximum fee is 30% above the "presumptive" rate. *See* Service Life & Cas. Ins. Co. v. Montemayor, 150 S.W.3d 649 (Tex. App. 2004).

170 *E.g.*, Ky. Rev. Stat. Ann. § 304.19-080 (West); Mo. Rev. Stat. § 385.070; Tenn. Code Ann. § 56-7-908(a).

171 *See* note 163, *supra*.

172 Model Bill to Provide for the Regulation of Credit Life Ins. and Credit Accident and Health Ins., National Ass'n of Ins. Comm'rs, Model Regulatory Service § 7B (NIARS Corp. 1984).

173 Old Republic Life Ins. Co. v. Wikler, 175 N.E.2d 147 (N.Y. 1961).

174 *See* David Birnbaum, Center for Economic Justice, A Consumer Advocate's Guide to Getting, Understanding, and Using Insurance Data (Aug. 1999), *available at* www.cej-online.org/intro.php (guide which assists in this information gathering process).

175 Fagg, Credit Life and Disability Insurance 382–383 (1986).

176 State by state information can be found in the NAIC Model Regulation Service. *See e.g.*, NAIC Model Regulation Service (Oct. 2010).

### 6.4.2.2 Problems with Prima Facie Rates

One problem with prima facie rates is that they result from a guess as to what will achieve the benchmark loss-ratio, though past experience is supposed to guide the process. The guessing historically has been on the high side. The original prima facie rate for credit life insurance in many states was $1 or more per hundred per year.[177] By 1994, forty-five states had established a prima facie rate for single decreasing credit life rates of 65¢ or less per hundred per year.[178] In addition, the *actual* experience of many insurers shows that even the authorized prima facie rates often result in loss ratios far lower than the targeted loss ratio.[179]

### 6.4.2.3 Deviations

As the term indicates, the prima facie rate is a presumptive standard of reasonable benefits. An insurer may request that the insurance department grant an "upward deviation," which then allows it to charge a higher premium. Theoretically, the insurer must present actuarial evidence to the department to establish that the prima facie rate is insufficient. Only a few states have mandatory downward deviations if the rates charged do not meet the benchmark loss-ratio.[180]

One problem with the upward deviation process is that some insurers may look upon the loss-ratio benchmark as a guaranteed return, and may seek a deviation even if the loss-ratio exceeds the benchmark by only a little. Since many consumer experts in the field argue that a loss-ratio of 70–80% provides ample return to insurers and creditors,[181] granting a deviation in such circumstances excessively burdens consumers. For this reason, some states authorize upward deviations only if the insurer's loss-ratio exceeds a specified "loss-ratio corridor." For example, if a state has a 50% benchmark, an upward deviation may not be granted unless the insurer's loss-ratio is over 60%.[182] Or there may be a "no-action corridor," where no change is implemented if the new rate would be within a specified "corridor" from the current rate.[183]

### 6.4.2.4 Challenging Prima Facie Rates

The NAIC Model Act specifies in mandatory terms that the insurance commissioner require rates that are reasonable in relation to benefits. Therefore, a commissioner who has authorized prima facie rates which result in loss-ratios lower than the state's target benchmark loss-ratio may be vulnerable to a mandamus challenge from consumers. This rarely has been done, though consumers were ultimately successful in Ohio and Illinois when this approach was tried.[184]

In Georgia, a different litigation approach was taken to challenge rates which exceed target loss-ratios. The insurers themselves were sued in a series of related cases.[185] The plaintiffs contended that the prima facie reasonable rate set an *outside* limit, and that a state administrative regulation required insurers to further reduce rates annually to an amount which would result in at least a 50% loss-ratio. The regulation also created a presumption that a commission in excess of 40% operates to prevent the insurer from reaching that 50% target loss-ratio.

The defending insurers lost important preliminary rounds in the litigation. In denying one insurer's motion to dismiss,[186] the court held that the regulations have the force of law and form a part of the contract. It further found that Georgia law would recognize a private cause of action to provide a remedy: acting contrary to a legal duty constitutes actionable fraud;[187] a state statute provides that "for every right there shall be a remedy;"[188] and, of course, breach of contract, since lawful regulations are an implied term of every contract.

In a companion case, *Shellman v. Investors National Life Insurance Co.*,[189] the insurer argued that the target loss-ratio was simply a mechanism to assure the financial solvency of the insurers, and placed no burden on it to lower rates to meet that. It further argued that there was an implied approval of its rates by virtue of its filings with the Insurance Department, and that an insurer indeed is not *permitted* to charge less than the maximum rates set by regulation. The court rejected all those arguments in denying the defendants' motion to dismiss.[190] Though this liti-

177 National Ass'n of Ins. Comm'rs, A Background Study of the Regulation of Credit Life and Disability Insurance 70 (1970).

178 The Cost of Personal Borrowing published by Financial Publishing Company, contains state-by-state charts of credit insurance rates. Increased public attention has led to more attention by insurance commissions. *See* § 6.2, *supra*.

179 *See* § 6.2.3.2, *supra* (discussing loss ratios).

180 *E.g.*, Ohio Admin. Code 3901-1-14(C)(8).

181 E.g., *Credit Life Insurance Hearing Before the Subcomm. on Antitrust, Monopoly and Business Rights of the Senate Comm. on the Judiciary*, 96th Cong, 1st Sess. 12, 52–53 (1979).

182 Fagg, Credit Life and Disability Insurance 181 (1986).

183 The NAIC Model Regulation uses 5% as the "no-action corridor." Thus if the indicated new rate is within 5% of the old rate, no deviation will be authorized. Fagg, Credit Life and Disability Insurance 181 (1986).

184 Madrigal v. O'Connor, No. 81 L 27570, Clearinghouse No. 41,268 (Ill. Cir. Ct. Cook Cty. Mar. 4, 1987); State *ex. rel.* Consumers League v. Ratchford, 457 N.E.2d 878 (Ohio Ct. App. 1982).

185 For example, see Griffin v. American Life Ins. Co. (Super. Ct., Richmond Cty., filed Aug. 23, 1989), *available on the companion website to this treatise* in which the plaintiffs sued the insurer for paying commissions to its creditor/agents in excess of the commission caps authorized under state regulations and exceeding lawful premiums. Causes of action alleged were: fraud (seeking a constructive trust on the excess fund); breach of contract, in that each contract incorporates existing law and regulations into its terms; unconscionability; and the state RICO Act. The matter was ultimately resolved when the state insurance commission lowered the rates.

186 Colvin v. Citizens & S. Life Ins. Co., Clearinghouse No. 45,775 (Super. Ct., Richmond Cty., motion to dismiss denied Jan. 8, 1990). *Accord* Shellman v. Investors Nat'l Life Ins. Co., Clearinghouse No. 45,774 (Ga. Super. Ct., Richmond Cty. Aug. 16, 1990) (defendant's motion for summary judgment denied).

187 Ga. Code Ann. § 23-2-51(b).

188 Ga. Code Ann. § 9-2-3.

189 Clearinghouse No. 45,774 (Super. Ct., Richmond Cty. Aug. 16, 1990) (denying defendant's motion for summary judgment).

190 These and a number of related cases were subsequently settled after parallel hearings before the state Insurance Commissioner resulted

gation was only one of several factors, the result of bringing attention to bear in Georgia was to improve dramatically the situation for consumers, who will save an estimated $32.8 million annually as a result of the 40% rate reduction.[191]

In a West Virginia challenge to prima facie rates, where the plaintiff claimed the rates were excessive and unreasonable, the state supreme court found that this was an administrative, rather than a judicial matter, because the legislature had given the state insurance commission such jurisdiction when establishing the rate making procedure, and because otherwise the judiciary would be involved in rate setting.[192] This opinion may be limited, however, because in West Virginia the state code expressly provides the right to a hearing before the insurance commissioner for the purpose of challenging approved insurance rates.

### 6.4.2.5 Filed-Rate Doctrine

Where insurance companies (or other entities) file and seek approval for their rates from a state regulatory body, the filed-rate doctrine[193] requires courts to accord state administrative and regulatory bodies deference regarding approved rates.[194]

The doctrine bars claims for monetary relief where the plaintiff seeks to enforce a rate other than that filed with the state.[195] A consumer is presumed to have suffered no monetary loss if she paid a filed rate, even if she claims that the amount was obtained through a misrepresentation.[196] Additionally, other types of claims against regulated entities may be limited or dismissed because consumers are presumed to have constructive knowledge of the filed rate and thus could not have relied upon misrepresentations or other fraud perpetrated by the regulated entity.[197]

The doctrine is limited, however, to where the court decision would have an impact upon state regulatory procedures and rate determinations. Thus, a rescission claim or a claim that insurance was sold without the consumer's knowledge does not implicate the filed-rate doctrine.[198] It also should not apply when the claim challenges inducements for referrals paid to third parties, such as developers, lenders, brokers, or real estate agents.[199]

The artificial nature of this doctrine presuming consumer knowledge is apparent in light of the doctrine's failure to bar similar claims against an unregulated entity, such as a bank, selling the regulated product.[200] Moreover, where the industry in question is not closely regulated by a particular state, the court, where it chooses to apply this doctrine, is providing deference to a hollow process that can gravely harm consumers.[201]

## *6.4.3 Non-Rate Insurance Regulation*

### 6.4.3.1 NAIC Model Act Governing Credit Life and Disability Insurance

The NAIC Model Act governing credit life and disability covers more than just ratemaking. It limits the term of coverage.[202] Relying upon a similar provision in Georgia law, the

in the credit life rate being lowered to $0.45/$100.00. *See* Aldrich v. Georgia Int'l Life Ins. Co., Clearinghouse No. 50,417 (Va. Super. Ct. Richmond Cty. Apr. 14, 1994) (stipulation of settlement filed).

191 *See* Credit Life Insurance Revisited II (second update of Consumer Federation of America/National Insurance Consumer Organization July 25, 1995, Clearinghouse No. 45,773B), *updated again Jan. 29, 1997, available on the companion website to this treatise.*

192 State *ex rel.* Citifinancial, Inc. v. Madden, 672 S.E.2d 365 (W. Va. 2008).

193 Many jurisdictions apply the filed-rate doctrine to insurance rates. *See, e.g.,* Kirksey v. Am. Bankers Ins. Co. of Fla., 114 F. Supp. 2d 526 (S.D. Miss. 2000); Allen v. State Farm Fire & Cas. Co., 59 F. Supp. 2d 1217 (S.D. Ala. 1999); Morales v. Attorneys' Title Ins. Funds, Inc., 983 F. Supp. 1418 (S.D. Fla. 1997); Horwitz v. Bankers Life & Cas. Co., 745 N.E.2d 591 (Ill. Ct. App. 2001); Amundson & Assoc. Art Studio, Ltd. v. National Council on Compensation Ins., Inc., 988 P.2 1208 (Kan. Ct. App. 1999).

At least one court has held that when the state statute establishing the filed-rate doctrine in that state explicitly does not grant any private recourse, a plaintiff is barred from bringing a private cause of action alleging a violation of the rates filed with the state. *See* Morrisette v. Novastar Home Mortgage, 484 F. Supp. 2d 1227 (S.D. Ala. 2007), *aff'd on other grounds*, 284 Fed. Appx. 729 (11th Cir. 2008).

194 In Richardson v. Standard Guar. Ins. Co., 853 A.2d 955 (N.J. Super. Ct. App. Div. 2004), a consumer class action alleging that a credit card bank fraudulently induced consumers to purchase credit insurance policies, the court acknowledged the controversial nature of the filed-rate doctrine, yet it still found that it is bound by it. Even the U.S. Supreme Court has noted that it "may seem harsh in some circumstances." American Tel. & Tel. Co. v. Central Office Tel., Inc., 524 U.S. 214, 222 (1998). The Court however explained that, at least in the communications context, the strict application of the filed-rate doctrine is important to prevent carriers from offering shippers rebates or discounts and to ensure that all consumers pay the same price. In the credit insurance context, however, the problem is that consumers are all held to noncompetitive, high prices and fraud can be used to hold a consumer to a higher price than she reasonably could have expected to pay.

195 *See, e.g.,* Smith v. Tower Loan of Mississippi, Inc., 216 F.R.D. 338 (S.D. Miss. 2003) (filed-rate doctrine bars allegation of excessive rates; court approved a class action settlement alleging other credit insurance abuses).

196 Richardson v. Standard Guar. Ins. Co., 853 A.2d 955 (N.J. Super. Ct. App. Div. 2004).

197 In addition to barring consumer claims, the nondiscrimination strand also has been found to bar antitrust claims. Square D Co. v. Niagara Frontier Tariff Bureau, Inc., 476 U.S. 409 (1986).

198 *See, e.g.,* Gulf States Util. Co. v. Alabama Power Co., 824 F.2d 1465 (5th Cir.), *op. amended,* 831 F.2d 557 (5th Cir. 1987); Nordlicht v. New York Tel. Co., 617 F. Supp. 220 (S.D.N.Y. 1985); Richardson v. Standard Guar. Ins. Co., 853 A.2d 955 (N.J. Super. Ct. App. Div. 2004).

199 *See, e.g.,* Blaylock v. First Am. Title Ins., 504 F. Supp. 2d 1091 (W.D. Wash. 2007) (rejecting insurers' argument that state law claims by plaintiffs challenging inducements paid for referrals, when state law prohibited such inducements, should be barred by the filed-rate doctrine).

200 Smith v. SBC Comm. Inc., 839 A.2d 850 (N.J. 2004). An agent, but not a retailer, can avail itself of the filed-rate doctrine in this context. This rule creates an incentive for purveyors of insurance to fashion themselves as agents in order to shield themselves from a broad array of legal claims.

201 *See* Allan Kanner, *The Filed Rate Doctrine and Insurance Fraud Litigation*, 76 N.D. L. Rev. 1 (2000).

202 The NAIC Model Act applies only to credit life and disability policies of less than ten years duration. Longer term insurance is subject to general insurance laws. State versions may vary.

Georgia Insurance Commissioner brought an enforcement proceeding against a lender who sold credit insurance in connection with loans whose terms exceeded ten years.[203] Following a hearing, the Commissioner ordered the lender to cease selling such insurance on loans with a duration of more than ten years.

In addition, the Model Act limits initial coverage to the initial indebtedness,[204] interpreted to mean the total of payments.[205] Many states require that credit life be written on a declining-term basis to reflect the fact that the balance declines as payments are made.[206]

The Model Act prohibits charging for a policy the term of which extends more than fifteen days beyond the scheduled maturity date of the transaction.[207] If a credit transaction is refinanced, the old insurance must be canceled and required rebates made before writing new insurance, thus prohibiting the practice of "pyramiding" insurance.[208]

The Model Act specifies the information which must be disclosed to the borrower in the policy or certificate of insurance, such as the identity and address of the insurer, the premium cost, a description of the coverage, any applicable restrictions, and the distribution of any surplus.[209] This information is to be given to the debtor at the time of the consummation, either in the policy or certificate or, somewhat abbreviated, in a copy of the application or notice of proposed insurance.[210] In any event, a copy of the policy or certificate must be delivered within thirty days from the date of consummation.[211]

Whether the required disclosures were in fact given prior to consummation is a question of fact.[212] Evidence concerning non-compliance could be obtained by deposing a loan officer as to whether the insurance certificates are included in loan sets. If they are, the order of the documents can be important; if not, ask whether the certificates are given to the borrower when the completed documents (note, security agreement, TILA disclosure) are signed. The certificate of insurance, unlike the other loan documents, does not generally include the borrower's signature. The certificate may therefore be at the bottom of the pile of papers, or not given to the borrower prior to obtaining the signature—which would ordinarily be the "consummation of the loan."

The Model Act requires that all policies and other forms be submitted to the insurance commissioners for approval. The commissioner may disapprove a policy if it contains provisions which are "unjust, unfair, inequitable, misleading, deceptive, or encourage misrepresentation of the coverage, or are contrary to any provision of the Insurance Code. . . ."[213] It is illegal for an insurer to use a disapproved form.[214]

It is also unlawful under the Model Act for an insurer to charge premium rates which exceed that on file with, and

203 *In re* Associates Fin. Life Ins. Co., Case No. 99C-014B (Ga. Office of Insurance and Safety Fire Commissioner Jan. 31, 2000), *available at* www.nclc.org/unreported (decision based upon Ga. Code Ann. § 33-31-2(c)). *See also* Darden v. Ford Consumer Fin. Co. (Ga. Super. Ct. Aug. 20, 2001) (settlement agreement), *available on the companion website to this treatise* (class action filed claiming that the lender and its insurance company sold credit life and health and accident insurance policies in connection with loans of more than ten years in duration certified for settlement purposes; class members to receive a refund of entire insurance premium plus a $300 or $500 cash payment plus a 0.5% reduction in the loan interest rate depending upon whether the class members cancel the insurance, the loan is still held by the lender, and other factors).

204 Model Bill to Provide for the Regulation of Credit Life Ins. and Credit Accident and Health Ins., National Ass'n of Ins. Comm'rs, Model Regulatory Service § 4 (NIARS Corp. 1984).

Under the revised NAIC model act, net coverage would be mandated. NAIC Consumer Credit Insurance Model Act § 4(A) (1994).

205 Winkle v. Grand Nat'l Bank, 601 S.W.2d 559, 571 (Ark. 1980). *See* Gall v. American Heritage Life Ins. Co., 3 F. Supp. 2d 1344 (S.D. Ala. 1998) (stating it is not bound by plurality in *McCullar* and, agreeing with the dissent, finding that insurance can be calculated on the total of payments); Liberty Bank & Trust Co. v. Splane, 959 P.2d 600 (Okla. Civ. App. 1998) (construing provision in U.C.C.C. restricting the amount of the permissible credit insurance to that which does not "exceed the debt" and another provision in Oklahoma insurance law restricting the amount of such insurance to "the approximate unpaid balance of the loan" to allow insurance premiums to be calculated on the total of payments; specifically rejecting the plurality in *McCullar*). *See also* Gartman v. The Indep. Life & Accident Ins. Co., 1998 U.S. Dist. LEXIS 22069 (S.D. Ala. Oct. 9, 1998) (class certified, by consent, in case challenging insurance charges based on total of payments, relying on *McCullar* decision); Singleton v. Protective Life Ins. Co., 857 So. 2d 803 (Ala. 2003) (applying *McCullar* in finding that borrowers failed to establish sale of excess insurance where net coverage was sold; also finding that state rate requirements were followed). *But cf.* McCullar v. Universal Underwriters Life Ins. Co., 687 So. 2d 156 (Ala. 1996) (plurality) (interpreting Alabama regulation limiting coverage to "approximate unpaid balance of the loan" to require net coverage, despite agency interpretation that gross coverage was permissible).

206 Model Bill to Provide for the Regulation of Credit Life Ins. and Credit Accident and Health Ins., National Ass'n of Ins. Comm'rs, Model Regulatory Service § 4(A)(1) (NIARS Corp. 1984). *Cf.* NAIC Consumer Credit Insurance Model Act § 4(A)(1) (1994) (which would mandate net debt coverage).

207 Model Bill to Provide for the Regulation of Credit Life Ins. and Credit Accident and Health Ins., National Ass'n of Ins. Comm'rs, Model Regulatory Service § 5(A)(1) (NIARS Corp. 1984).

208 *Id. See also In re* Associates Fin. Life Ins. Co., Case No. 99C-014A, Clearinghouse No. 52,508 (Ga. Office of Insurance and Safety Fire Commissioner Jan. 31, 2000) (when lender sold multiple policies, it incorrectly calculated unearned premium for each insurance product separately and failed to rebate when each rebate was lower than the $10 floor per Ga. Comp. R. & Regs. 120-2-27-.18, e.g., if each rebate was less than $10 but, combined, exceeded $10, both must be refunded); MIC Life Ins. Co. v. Hicks, 825 So. 2d 616 (Miss. 2002) (affirming the lower court's ruling that state law requires a refund of unearned insurance premiums within thirty days of termination of the policy).

209 Model Bill to Provide for the Regulation of Credit Life Ins. and Credit Accident and Health Ins., National Ass'n of Ins. Comm'rs, Model Regulatory Service §§ 5B, 6B (NIARS Corp. 1984).

210 Model Bill To Provide For The Regulation Of Credit Life Ins. And Credit Accident And Health Ins., National Ass'n Of Ins. Comm'rs, Model Regulatory Service § 6D (NIARS Corp. 1984).

211 *Id.*

212 *See, e.g.,* Bair v. Public Serv. Emp. Credit Union, 709 P.2d 961, 962 (Colo. App. 1985).

213 Model Bill To Provide For The Regulation Of Credit Life Ins. And Credit Accident And Health Ins., National Ass'n Of Ins. Comm'rs, Model Regulatory Service § 7B (NIARS Corp. 1984).

214 *Id.* § 7C.

approved by, the commissioner,[215] and the premium amount charged to a debtor cannot exceed the premiums charged by the insurer.[216] If the policy is terminated before its scheduled maturity, rebates are required.[217] Finally, the Model Act has an anti-tie-in or anti-coercion provision which requires that borrowers be given a choice of insurers.[218]

### 6.4.3.2 NAIC Model Act Governing Credit Property Insurance

The NAIC credit personal property insurance model act does not cover insurance on motor vehicles designed for highway use and manufactured homes, insurance written in connection with a credit transaction that is secured by a real estate mortgage or deed of trust, force-placed insurance, non-filing insurance, or insurance for which no identifiable charge is made or collected from the consumer.[219] The Act's key non-rate provisions include a prohibition against using gross debt in calculating the premium,[220] a significant improvement over the model credit life and disability act.

Insurance premium rebates must be made by the pro rata method.[221] For closed-end loans, the credit insurance cannot exceed the amount of the underlying debt, unless otherwise required by state law, nor can the insurer sell insurance with a term that exceeds the scheduled term of the underlying credit transaction.[222]

The credit insurance cannot be sold unless the loan amount exceeds a minimum amount to be set by each adoptive state.[223] The insurance cannot be bundled with other types of insurance and it must be optional and not a condition of obtaining credit approval.[224] Consumers must receive a pre-purchase clear and conspicuous disclosure describing certain rights contemporaneously with the extension of credit (or, if the insurance is sold after the initial extension of credit, within ten days after the election or the date any written material is provided to the consumer).[225] The insurer must provide consumers with certificates of insurance that shall contain certain information.[226]

Like the life and disability model act, all policies, certificates of insurance, application forms, endorsements and riders must be filed with the state insurance commissioner before being used. Only approved rates and forms may be used.[227]

215 *Id.* § 8A.
216 *Id.* § 8D.
217 *Id.* § 8B. *See also* § 6.10, *infra*.
218 Model Bill to Provide for the Regulation of Credit Life Ins. and Credit Accident and Health Ins., National Ass'n of Ins. Comm'rs, Model Regulatory Service § 11 (NIARS Corp. 1984).
219 NAIC Credit Personal Property Insurance Model Act § 2, *available on the companion website to this treatise*.
220 *Id.* § 4(G).
221 *Id.* § 10.
222 *Id.* § 4(B), (C).
223 *Id.* § 4(A).
224 *Id.* §§ 4(F), 5(a)(2).
225 *Id.* § 5(A), (B).
226 *Id.* § 5(D), (E).
227 *Id.* § 6.

No claim may be denied because the consumer was ineligible for coverage later than ninety days after the initiation of coverage unless the consumer misrepresented a material fact. If a claim is denied because the consumer misrepresented a material fact or was ineligible for coverage within ninety days of the initiation of coverage, the insurer must refund all of the premium paid *and* the creditor must refund any finance charge paid on the premium.[228]

### 6.4.3.3 State Licensing Requirements

State insurance laws often require that the insurer obtain a certificate of authority or license before soliciting insurance applications or transacting insurance in the state or from offering insurance in other states from an office in that state.[229] If the insurer does not obtain the necessary permission from the state insurance agency to operate, the insurance contract may be void.[230]

## *6.4.4 Insurance Premium Financing Laws*

Insurance premium financing laws do *not* regulate the sale of credit insurance, even though that sale is financed as part of the loan it insures. Instead, these laws regulate the financing of ordinary insurance premiums, often allowing high interest rates on these transactions, which are actually credit sales. Insurance premium financing statutes commonly apply to automobile insurance premiums, where the insured cannot afford to pay the entire amount in a single installment. However, these statutes may also apply, in some instances, to a lender's sale of extraneous insurance, such as cancer policies, level term non-credit-life, or accidental death and dismemberment policies, as are often sold in insurance-packing schemes. Some of these statutes do not apply to traditional lenders, however. Consequently, it is important to be aware of the scope and requirements of insurance premium financing statutes in those states which currently have them.[231]

## *6.4.5 State Credit Statutes*

### 6.4.5.1 General Restrictions

State credit statutes, such as small loan acts, consumer loan acts, industrial loan acts, second mortgage laws or general credit statutes, including retail installment sales acts, may contain important limitations on the *creditor's* sale of credit insur-

228 *Id.* § 11(D).
229 *See, e.g.*, Fla. Stat. § 624.401.
Note that in limited instances insurance companies selling credit insurance have been exempted from state regulation under a special charter. *See, e.g.*, Indiana Dep't of Ins. v. Vernon Gen. Ins. Co., 784 N.E.2d 556 (Ind. Ct. App. 2003).
230 *See* Fabricant v. Sears Roebuck, 202 F.R.D. 310 (S.D. Fla. 2001) (class certified on this type of claim).
231 *E.g.*, Ala. Code §§ 27-40-1 to 27-40-18; Alaska Stat. §§ 06.40.010 to 06.40.080; Ariz. Rev. Stat. Ann. §§ 6-1401 to 6-1419; Idaho Code Ann. § 28-43-205; Ky. Rev. Stat. Ann. §§ 304.30-020 to 304.30-120; Minn. Stat. §§ 59A.01 to 59A.15.

ance.[232] Unlike most credit insurance codes, credit and licensing statutes often provide viable consumer remedies for violations. Remedies often are the same as for any other violation of the credit statute, so that if a small loan act provides that loans will be void if any consideration or charge in excess of that permitted by the statute is assessed, insurance charges not in compliance with applicable insurance law provisions can void the loan.[233]

Consumer credit statutes covering credit insurance usually establish limitations on the premium cost, often by providing that insurance must be written in compliance with the credit insurance code,[234] or by otherwise referring to the insurance department rate limitations.[235] State credit statutes also may impose disclosure requirements in addition to those of the Truth in Lending Act.[236] They may also specify what type of insurance may be sold in conjunction with a covered transaction, thus rendering premiums for any type of unlisted insurance an unauthorized additional charge.[237]

Restrictions on credit property insurance may include standards for the premium cost,[238] and limitations on the kinds of loans on which property insurance may be written.[239] Such statutes may require that credit property insurance be written only on collateral,[240] and that coverage be limited to either the loan amount or the value of the property.[241] Further, there may be a limitation on writing property insurance in connection with loans below a specified amount.[242] Some states also prohibit the financing of credit insurance or debt cancellation coverage.[243]

Many credit statutes require that credit insurance must be sold by a licensed agent.[244] The statutes often reiterate the requirement that borrowers be given a choice of insurers, thus making this requirement applicable to *creditors*,[245] or do so implicitly by requiring that all insurance written comply with the credit insurance code. These statutes may also impose additional disclosure requirements, such as information regarding whether insurance is compulsory.[246]

States adopting comprehensive consumer credit codes generally have detailed provisions regarding credit insurance in transactions subject to the credit code.[247] Article 4 of the Uniform Consumer Credit Code (UCCC) is the primary example of such a statute and it in turn is derived in part from the NAIC Model Act.[248] However, the 1960 NAIC Model Act governs only credit life and A&H, while the UCCC model also regulates credit property insurance[249] and it governs creditor conduct, rather than insurer conduct.

### 6.4.5.2 Can a Credit Insurance Premium Lead to a Usury Claim?

As a general rule, credit insurance is considered to benefit borrowers as well as creditors, and therefore premium charges are not considered interest for usury purposes.[250] However, for nearly two centuries, it has been recognized that insurance schemes can be a pretext for usury.[251] This is particularly true with credit insurance, and thus transactions involving its sale should be carefully scrutinized.[252]

---

232 *But see* Brown v. Protective Life Ins. Co., 135 Fed. Appx. 647 (5th Cir. 2005) (challenge to sale of excessive credit insurance by car dealer rejected where insurance company could not be held vicariously liable under the state motor vehicle sales finance act because the auto finance company is not a licensing agent of the insurer for lending purposes under the state law).

233 *See* § 6.6.2, *infra*.

234 *E.g.*, Fla. Stat. Ann. § 516.35; N.H. Rev. Stat. Ann. § 399-A:11 (lender licensing).

235 *E.g.*, Del. Code Ann. tit. 6, § 4307 (RISA); Ga. Code Ann. § 7-3-14(3) (ind. loan); Vt. Stat. Ann. tit. 9, § 2355(g).

236 *E.g.*, Conn. Gen. Stat. § 36a-566; N.D. Cent. Code § 51-13-02; Vt. Stat. Ann. tit. 9, § 2355(f)(1)(D).

237 *Cf. Ex Parte* New Fin. Ltd, 225 So. 2d 782, 784 (Ala. 1969) (Small Loan Acts strictly inclusive as to permissible charges); Hawkins v. Thorp Credit & Thrift Co., 441 N.W.2d 470 (Minn. 1989) (non-credit insurance not an authorized charge; its sale violated licensing act). *See also* § 6.6.2, *infra*.

238 *E.g.*, Ala. Code § 5-19-20(b); Ariz. Rev. Stat. Ann. § 6-636; Cal. Fin. Code § 18294 (West) (industrial loan); U.C.C.C. § 4-301 (1968 and 1974).

239 Some states require that the amount financed and the value of the insured collateral meet a minimum floor in order for property insurance to be written, e.g., Ala. Code § 5-19-20(g); Colo. Rev. Stat. § 5-4-301.

240 *E.g.*, Ariz. Rev. Stat. Ann. § 6-636 (consumer loans); Iowa Code §§ 536.27, 536A.23(3), 537.2501(2); Miss. Code Ann. § 75-67-121 (small loans); U.C.C.C. § 4-301(1) (1968 and 1974).

241 *E.g.*, Ariz. Rev. Stat. Ann. § 6-636(E); S.C. Code Ann. Regs. 69-11.1(C)(1)(d).

242 *E.g.*, Ala. Code § 5-19-20(g) (no property insurance unless loan amount exclusive of charges is $300 or over and value of property is $300 or more); Colo. Rev. Stat. § 5-4-301 (same provisions, but with amounts of $1,000 in each case).

243 *See, e.g.*, N.J. Stat. Ann § 46:10B-26 (West); N.M. Stat. Ann. §§ 58-21A-1 to 58-21A-14; Ohio Rev. Code Ann. § 1345.031(11) (West).

244 *E.g.*, Ariz. Rev. Stat. Ann. § 6-636(D); Iowa Code §§ 536.1, 536.26. *See also* Bailey v. Defenbaugh & Co. of Cleveland, Inc., 513 F. Supp. 232, 243 (N.D. Miss. 1981); *In re* Associates Fin. Life Ins. Co., Case No. 99C-014A (Ga. Office of Insurance and Safety Fire Commissioner Jan. 31, 2000), *available at* www.nclc.org/unreported (also check state insurance law for a similar requirement as the Insurance Commissioner in this case brought an enforcement proceeding for, among other reasons, the lender could not show that only licensed agents in the lender's shop were selling the credit insurance).

245 *E.g.*, Miss. Code Ann. § 63-19-33 (MVRISA).

246 *Compare* U.C.C.C. §§ 202(2), 3-202(2) (1968) (requiring disclosure that life and A&H insurance is not a factor in approval of extension of credit; otherwise creditor may not impose the charge), *and* U.C.C.C. § 2-501(2) (1974) (notice of voluntary nature of life and A&H must be given in order to exclude premiums from finance charge), *with* Tex. Fin. Code Ann. § 348.204 (West) (clear and conspicuous notice mandated if insurance is required).

247 *E.g.*, La. Rev. Stat. §§ 9:3542 to 9:3550; U.C.C.C. §§ 4-101 to 4-304 (1968 and 1974).

248 U.C.C.C. § 4-102 cmt. 1 (1974).

249 U.C.C.C. §§ 4.301–4.304 (1968 and 1974).

250 *See* § 6.5.4, *infra*.

251 *See* Vernon, *Regulated Credit Life and Disability Insurance and the Small Loan*, 29 N.Y.U.L. Rev. 1098, 1100–1101 (1954).

252 *See, e.g.*, Robinson v. Rebsamen Ford, Inc., 530 S.W.2d 660, 662 (Ark. 1975); Tribble v. State, 80 S.E.2d 711 (Ga. Ct. App. 1954).

There is an argument that insurance charges are interest if the circumstances strongly suggest they were not imposed in good faith, but rather as a pretext for usury. "It is impossible to wink so hard as not to see what [is] expected by the contract—that its end [is] more interest on the money advanced than the law authorize[s]."[253]

Careful attention must be paid to presenting evidence regarding the circumstances: the full extent of the creditor's profit; evidence regarding the borrower's level of sophistication or education; the borrower's impression of implicit or explicit coercion; or the borrower's special relationship of confidence with the lender.[254] A number of cases declined to find usury where there was no indication the insurance was more expensive than if purchased elsewhere, or no circumstances of compulsion, duress, or fraud.[255] Lacking such specific evidence of overreaching, the court may view the premiums as a legitimate charge passed on to a third party, and may also view commissions as compensation for services in connection with the insurance just as any other agent commission is treated.[256] Where the credit insurance is hidden interest, any specific statutory remedy for excessive charge, or the more general array of traditional usury remedies should be available.[257]

Credit statutes often specify, implicitly or explicitly, the conditions which must be met in order for the insurance premiums to be excluded from the finance charge, such as that the insurance must be voluntary,[258] or that the charges must be imposed in compliance with specified statutory provisions.[259] If the insurance's sale is not in accordance with applicable law, the premiums, or any excess portion of them, may be considered interest.[260] If, when added to other interest charged, the yield exceeds the ceiling, the borrower has a usury claim. This is even the case where a state statute allows the parties to agree to any interest rate, because excess insurance charges can be argued to result in the interest rate exceeding the agreed-upon rate.[261] Further, some statutory language suggests that improper insurance practices give rise to a claim for statutory penalties, irrespective of whether the total interest exceeds the maximum usury limit.[262]

## 6.4.6 Unfair and Deceptive Acts and Practices

### 6.4.6.1 General UDAP Statutes

Every state has a state deceptive practices (UDAP) statute that typically provides strong remedies and attorney fees for any unfair or deceptive act or practice.[263] UDAP statutes usu-

253 Wilson v. Whitworth, 125 S.W.2d 112, 113–114 (Ark. 1939), *quoting* Heytle v. Archibald Logan, 1 A.K. Marsh, Ky, 529 (lender had required a $3,500 life insurance policy for a $150 loan from a borrower who earned 22 cents an hour working five to eight hours a day). *Contra* Lemelledo v. Beneficial Mgmt., 674 A.2d 582 (N.J. Super. Ct. App. Div. 1996) (finding that insurance charges are not interest, citing state statutes excluding certain charges from the definition of interest), *aff'd on other grounds*, 696 A.2d 546 (N.J. 1997).

254 *See* § 6.4.7, *infra*.

255 *Compare* the Arkansas Supreme Court's analysis in Poole v. Bates, 520 S.W.2d 273 (Ark. 1975), *with* its analyses in Robinson v. Rebsamen Ford, Inc., 530 S.W.2d 660 (Ark. 1975), *and* Aclin Ford v. Cordell, 625 S.W.2d 459 (Ark. 1982). *See also* Coner v. Morris S. Berman Unlt'd, 501 A.2d 458 (Md. Ct. Spec. App. 1985) ($25,000 coverage on a small loan not improper where there was no evidence that the excess coverage added cost to the premium).

256 *See, e.g.*, Anthony v. Community Loans & Inv. Corp., 559 F.2d 1363 (5th Cir. 1977); Poole v. Bates, 520 S.W.2d 273 (Ark. 1975). *See also* § 6.6.2, *infra*. *But see* Kenty v. Bank One, Columbus, N.A., 1992 WL 170605 (S.D. Ohio Apr. 23, 1992) (commissions, kickbacks or rebates paid by insurer to creditor from premium charged to borrower's account are interest), *aff'd in part rev'd in part* 92 F.3d 384 (6th Cir. 1996) (without disturbing holding that those costs constitute interest, court held national bank defendant authorized under most favored lender status to charge unlimited interest under Ohio law, therefore no usury found).

257 *See, e.g.,* Car Now Acceptance Co. v. Block, 2002 WL 32001272 (Ohio Ct. Com. Pl. Nov. 25, 2002) (certifying class action in part based on usury claim where consumer asserted that the $35 he paid for VSI insurance should have been included in the finance charge rather than the amount financed, thus bringing the interest rate above the state usury ceiling), *aff'd*, 2003 WL 21714583 (Ohio Ct. App. July 24, 2003). *See generally* § 7.8, *infra* (discussing usury claims more fully).

258 *E.g.*, Ala. Code § 5-19-20; Iowa Code § 537.2501(2); La. Rev. Stat. § 9:3542(A).

259 *E.g.*, Ala. Code § 5-19-1(1); Ga. Code Ann. § 7-3-14(3). *See also* Gartman v. The Indep. Life & Accident Ins. Co., 1998 U.S. Dist. LEXIS 22069 (S.D. Ala. Oct. 9, 1998) (class certified, by consent, in case challenging insurance charges based on total of payments, relying on McCullar decision); Singleton v. Protective Life Ins. Co., 857 So. 2d 803 (Ala. 2003) (applying *McCullar* and finding that borrowers failed to establish sale of excess insurance where net coverage was sold and finding that state rate requirements were followed); McCullar v. Universal Underwriters Life Ins. Co., 687 So. 2d 156 (Ala. 1996) (plurality) (regulatory language requiring that when repayment is in substantially equal installments, the credit insurance can "never exceed approximate unpaid balance of the loan" prohibits gross coverage notwithstanding contrary agency interpretations; question of fact whether creditor's telling consumers that gross amount of insurance was needed to pay off debt in event of death constituted fraud). *But see* Gall v. American Heritage Life Ins. Co., 3 F. Supp. 2d 1344 (S.D. Ala. 1998) (stating it is not bound by plurality in *McCullar* and, agreeing with the dissent, finding that insurance can be calculated on the total of payments); Liberty Bank & Trust Co. v. Splane, 959 P.2d 600 (Okla. Civ. App. 1998) (construing provision in U.C.C.C. restricting the amount of the permissible credit insurance to that which does not "exceed the debt" and another provision in Oklahoma insurance law restricting the amount of such insurance to "the approximate unpaid balance of the loan" to allow insurance premiums to be calculated on the total of payments; court specifically rejects the plurality in *McCullar*.).

260 *But see* Lemelledo v. Beneficial Mgmt., 674 A.2d 582 (N.J. Super. Ct. App. Div. 1996) (New Jersey law excludes credit life insurance premiums from its definition of interest; no discussion, however, of whether the coercive sale of credit insurance transforms the premiums into a usury claim), *aff'd on other grounds*, 696 A.2d 546 (N.J. 1997).

261 *See* § 7.6.1, *infra*.

262 *E.g.*, U.C.C.C. § 4-104(2) (1968 and 1974); Attorney General of Md. v. Equitable Trust Co., 450 A.2d 1273, 1292 (Md. Spec. Ct. App. 1982).

263 *See generally* National Consumer Law Center, Unfair and Deceptive Acts and Practices (7th ed. 2008 and Supp.).

ally are well suited to challenge credit insurance abuses,[264] but some state statutes exclude credit or insurance transactions from their coverage, or find that a state's regulation of unfair insurance practices prevents a private UDAP claim.[265]

Deceptive practices include the use of misleading statements, partial truths, or the omission of material facts[266]—again all practices which are likely to be involved in insurance abuse cases. For example, allegations that a credit disability insurer defrauded its insureds by promising benefits it did not intend to pay, calculating benefits on a daily (instead of monthly basis), and prematurely terminating coverage stated a claim under the state UDAP and federal RICO statutes.[267] Additionally, allegations in an FTC case that a creditor violated the FTC Act by failing to disclose cost and terms of credit insurance provided a basis in part for a temporary restraining order and two preliminary injunctions, as well as a freezing of the company owner's assets.[268]

UDAP statutes can also be used to challenge creditor practices which undermine the written voluntariness disclosures. Courts have specifically held that failure to disclose the availability of cheaper credit insurance is a UDAP violation.[269] Most insurance packing cases have raised UDAP claims and one court found sufficient probability of success on the merits to issue a preliminary injunction.[270] Most of the insurance packing cases to date have settled so there are few decisions. Breach of fiduciary duty and UDAP claims have survived motions to dismiss where the insurance premium finance company and the insurance company were connected and failed to disclose this information to the consumer.[271] One court suggested in dicta that a viable UDAP claim might be stated if the borrower alleges the insurance is overpriced or that substantial undisclosed commissions unfairly increase insurance costs.[272]

#### 6.4.6.2 UNIP Statutes

In addition to general UDAP statutes, every state has adopted some version of an "unfair insurance trade practices" (UNIP) act,[273] based on a NAIC Model Act. These statutes may squarely address some of the marketing abuses often involved in credit insurance sales. Among these abuses are coercive sales tactics,[274] and the sale of insurance which may be worthless to borrowers who are clearly ineligible for benefits.[275]

The UNIP statutes generally prohibit debtor coercion through tie-in arrangements, whereby creditors require that insurance be purchased from particular insurers or agents.[276] Additionally, UNIP statutes generally prohibit misrepresentation concerning the "terms, conditions and extent of insurance policy coverage."[277] Usually there is no explicit private right of action under

---

264 *E.g.*, Schroeder v. Acceleration Life, 972 F.2d 41 (3d Cir. 1992); *In re* Dickson, 432 F. Supp. 752 (W.D.N.C. 1977); Washington Mut. Bank v. Superior Court, 82 Cal. Rptr. 2d 564 (Cal. Ct. App. 1999), *rev'd and remanded*, 15 P.3d 1071 (Cal. 2001) (reversing class certification in class action involving allegations of kickback between lender and insurance companies and requiring the lower court to address the effect of the choice of law provision in the contract); Fox v. Industrial Cas. Ins. Co., 424 N.E.2d 839 (Ill. App. Ct. 1981); Browder v. Hanley-Dawson Cadillac, 379 N.E.2d 1206 (Ill. App. Ct. 1978); Marshall v. Citicorp Mtg., Inc., 601 So. 2d 669 (La. Ct. App. 1992); State v. Ralph Williams North West Chrysler Plymouth, Inc., 553 P.2d 423 (Wash. 1976).

265 *See generally* National Consumer Law Center, Unfair and Deceptive Acts and Practices, §§ 2.2.1, 2.3.1 (7th ed. 2008 and Supp.).

266 *Id.* §§ 4.2.13, 4.2.14.

267 Schroeder v. Acceleration Life, 972 F.2d 41 (3d Cir. 1992) (credit disability contract provided that insurance would terminate upon discharge of debt, but also provided that termination would be without prejudice to previously originating claims; provision interpreted by state court in a breach of contract action to require benefits paid from onset of disability to loan's scheduled maturity. This case alleged fraudulent promise to pay excess benefits upon early termination and schemes to reduce benefits as UDAP and RICO violations). *Cf.* Fort Worth Mortgage Corp. v. Abercrombie, 835 S.W.2d 262 (Tex. App. 1992) (mortgagee's cancellation of policy and substituting one with less benefits without borrower's notice or consent was UDAP violation and unconscionable).

268 Fed. Trade Comm'n v. Stewart Fin. Co., Civ. No. 103CV-2648 (N.D. Ga. Nov. 9, 2005) (stipulated final judgment and order), *available at* www.ftc.gov/os/2005/11/051109stewartstipa103cv2648.pdf.

269 Browder v. Hanley-Dawson Cadillac, 379 N.E.2d 1206 (Ill. App. Ct. 1978); State v. Ralph Williams North West Chrysler Plymouth Inc., 553 P.2d 423 (Wash. 1976).

270 Balderos v. Illinois Vehicle Premium Fin. Co., 1997 WL 627650 (N.D. Ill. 1997) (certifying class action where lender added a purported hospitalization policy premium into the financing of the consumer's purchase of auto insurance without informing the customer; value of additional "insurance" speculative in light of allegation that $85 of the $100 "premium" was kept as a commission; lack of disclosure about this supposed policy would likely result in a low loss ratio; claims raised include TILA, UDAP, breach of fiduciary duty, and RICO); State v. Aetna Fin. Co., Case No. 84 CV0103, Clearinghouse No. 36,151 (Wis. Cir. Ct. Dane Cty. Feb. 20, 1984). *See also* Urbina v. Aetna Fin. Co., Civ. 83-452 TUC-ACM (D. Ariz. filed June 30, 1983); Samorano v. Aetna Fin. Co., No. 213316 (Ariz. Super. Ct. Pima Cty. filed Dec. 8, 1983); Fox v. Industrial Cas. Ins. Co., 424 N.E.2d 839 (Ill. App. Ct. 1981) (complaint regarding packing credit insurance sale with non-credit insurance stated a UDAP claim). *See generally* § 6.7, *infra*.

271 *See, e.g.*, Harris v. Illinois Vehicle Premium Fin. Co., 2000 U.S. Dist. LEXIS 13763 (N.D. Ill. Sept. 7, 2000). *But see* Hobson v. Lincoln Ins. Agency, Inc., 2001 WL 55528, 2001 U.S. Dist. LEXIS 476 (N.D. Ill. Jan. 22, 2001) (breach of fiduciary duty claim dismissed pursuant to an Illinois statute that expressly negates the existence of a fiduciary duty).

272 *In re* Milbourne, 108 B.R. 522, 540, 543 n.8 (Bankr. E.D. Pa. 1989). *See also* Balderos v. Illinois Vehicle Premium Fin. Co., 1997 WL 627650 (N.D. Ill. 1997) (certifying class action where lender added a purported hospitalization policy premium into the financing of the consumer's purchase of auto insurance without informing the customer; value of additional "insurance" speculative in light of allegation that $85 of the $100 "premium" was kept as a commission; lack of disclosure about this supposed policy would likely result in a low loss ratio; claims raised include TILA, UDAP, breach of fiduciary duty, and RICO).

273 *See* National Consumer Law Center, Unfair and Deceptive Acts and Practices § 10.5.2 (7th ed. 2008 and Supp.).

274 *See* § 6.5, *infra*.

275 *See* § 6.8, *infra*.

276 National Consumer Law Center, Unfair and Deceptive Acts and Practices § 10.5.5.7 (7th ed. 2008 and Supp.).

277 *Id.* Misrepresentations in the sales of credit insurance also can be challenged using state fraud statutes. *See* Byrd v. Metropolitan Corp. (Minn. Dist. Ct. Apr. 29, 2002), *available on the companion*

UNIP statutes, although a private right of action may be implied, or a UNIP violation may constitute a violation of a state UDAP statute.[278] Similarly, if a special licensing statute provides generally that an insurance charge "made in violation of the law," implicates the remedies authorized by that law, a UNIP violation may make that statute's penalty provisions applicable.[279]

### 6.4.7 *Breach of Fiduciary Duty; Bank Holding Company Act*

Creditors may have a fiduciary duty to borrowers, which they may breach if they impose disadvantageous credit insurance charges. Ordinarily, debtors do not have a fiduciary relationship with creditors,[280] but one may be extrapolated with respect to credit insurance from a number of sources. It is a question of fact whether the creditor owes a fiduciary duty to any given borrower.[281] A borrower also may have a claim for breaching the duty of good faith and fair dealing.[282]

Creditors that are part of a bank holding company have a fiduciary obligation when they sell credit insurance to borrowers.[283] The Federal Reserve Board grants bank holding companies authority to act as insurance agents and brokers, selling credit life insurance, but requires lenders utilizing that authority to exercise a fiduciary responsibility to the insured borrower. Lenders utilizing this authority must make their best effort to obtain insurance at the "lowest practicable cost to the consumer."[284] While the Board later liberalized its rules concerning other bank underwriting activities, it did not change its position concerning banks *selling* credit insurance, since coercion is "more likely to be exerted by an agent at the point of sale," rather than by the underwriter.[285] These regulations were overhauled in 1997 and renumbered, but the Board stated that the current regulation is unchanged.[286] In *In re Dickson*,[287] that fiduciary duty was violated by selling insurance at inflated premiums, receiving a 25% commission and failing to disclose such facts.[288]

A source of a creditor's fiduciary duty where the creditor is not a bank holding company is that credit insurance sales are generally required to be made by licensed agents;[289] and state insurance laws may give rise to a fiduciary obligation on the creditor's part. At a minimum, a fiduciary relationship creates a duty to disclose the availability of cheaper insurance.[290]

Other cases have found the source of a fiduciary relationship in the "trust and confidence" which the borrower has reposed in the creditor, at least with respect to terms raised as part of "loan processing," after the central terms are agreed upon through arms' length negotiation. In *Stone v. Davis*,[291] an Ohio court found a fiduciary relationship to have arisen, after a mortgage had been arranged, when the lender purportedly broached the subject of mortgage insurance.[292] Another court found a quasi-fiduciary relationship in *Hutson v. Wenatchee Federal Savings and Loan Ass'n*[293] where the lender had advised the borrower on a number of things, giving rise at a minimum to a duty of disclosure. Both of these factors were present in another case finding a fiduciary duty on the part of an auto dealer with respect to the sale of credit insurance.[294]

One commentator has suggested that a creditor, when selling credit insurance, acts as the borrower's agent, thus giving rise to a fiduciary relationship.[295] This source of fiduciary respon-

---

*website to this treatise* (jury finding in a class action that a car dealer used false statements in the retail installment contract when the dealer kept as profit almost half of a credit insurance premium it had agreed to pay to the insurer on behalf of the consumer).

278 National Consumer Law Center, Unfair and Deceptive Acts and Practices §§ 5.3.6, 10.5.5.7 (7th ed. 2008 and Supp.).

279 *E.g.*, Iowa Code § 537.4101(2).

280 *See* Ross v. Citifinancial, 344 F.3d 458 (5th Cir. 2003); Hutson v. Wenatchee Fed. Sav. & Loan Ass'n, 588 P.2d 1192, 1198 (Wash. Ct. App. 1979). *Cf.* Younker v. Citizens Commercial Bank & Trust Co., 2004 WL 1770439 (Ohio Ct. App. Aug. 9, 2004) (creditor does not have fiduciary duty to offer credit insurance).

281 Browder v. Hanley-Dawson Cadillac, 379 N.E.2d 1206, 1210–1211 (Ill. App. Ct. 1978).

282 Pate v. Guarantee Trust Life Ins. Co., 2010 WL 987090 (N.D. Ohio Mar. 15, 2010) (finding that the duty of good faith arose from a legal duty created by the relationship between the parties).

283 *In re* Dickson, 432 F. Supp. 752 (W.D.N.C. 1977), *interpreting* 12 C.F.R. § 225.4(a)(1), *now appearing at* 12 C.F.R. § 225.28(b)(11) (1999).

284 *Id. citing* 36 Fed. Reg. 15,526 (Aug. 17, 1971).

285 51 Fed. Reg. at 36,204 (Oct. 9, 1986).

286 "Several commenters urged the Board to take a variety of steps to authorize broader insurance activities. The Board will continue to consider these suggestions in light of the specific terms of the BHC [Bank Holding Company] Act." 62 Fed. Reg. 9,290 (Feb. 28, 1997).

287 432 F. Supp. 752 (W.D.N.C. 1977).

288 *Id.* at 760.

289 Model Bill to Provide for the Regulation of Credit Life Ins. and Credit Accident and Health Ins., National Ass'n of Ins. Comm'rs, Model Regulatory Service § 9 (NIARS Corp. 1984).

290 *See, e.g.*, Robinson v. Rebsamen Ford, Inc., 530 S.W.2d 660 (Ark. 1975); Browder v. Hanley-Dawson Cadillac, 379 N.E.2d 1206, 1211–1212 (Ill. App. Ct. 1978).

Note that in Robinson v. Rebsamen Ford, *supra*, the court stated that it was "influenced," but not "controlled" by state insurance laws requiring good faith. 530 S.W.2d at 662. Thus *Rebsamen Ford* may be used as precedent even in the absence of a similar statutorily imposed duty of good faith.

291 419 N.E.2d 1094 (Ohio 1981). *Cf.* Blon v. Bank One, Akron, N.A., 519 N.E.2d 363 (Ohio 1988) (cites factors which led court to conclude no fiduciary relationship existed, hence no duty to disclose that finance charge included a finder's fee, and that finder's fee was on sliding scale which increased with higher interest rates. (*Ed. note*: It should be noted that the finder's fee was included in the disclosed APR, so there was no question of a "hidden" finance charge included in the loan principal as sometimes happens with brokers' fees or finders' fee. *See* § 4.5.3, *supra*)).

292 *See also* Crow v. Fred Martin Motor Co., 2003 WL 1240119 (Ohio Ct. App. Mar. 19, 2003) (finding a fiduciary duty where the consumer applied for credit insurance in connection with her car purchase and "entrusted Appellee to process and forward the signed paperwork and insurance premium payment" to the insurer; the consumer subsequently was rejected for coverage but was not informed until she sought to file a claim).

293 588 P.2d 1192 (Wash. Ct. App. 1978).

294 Tomaszewski v. McKeon Ford, Inc., 573 A.2d 501 (N.J. Super. Ct. App. Div. 1990).

295 Budnitz, *The Sale of Credit Life Insurance: The Bank As Fiduciary*, 62 N.C. L. Rev. 295 (1984). *See also* Harris v. Illinois Vehicle

sibility, of course, is broader than the two previously discussed, as it would apply to all creditors who sell credit insurance to their customers.

Once a fiduciary relationship is established, whatever its source, there are a number of duties implicated: a duty of loyalty, the duty to use care and skill, to provide the borrower with information he or she "would desire to have," and to disclose any adverse interests the agent might have.[296] A breach of fiduciary duty claim would be particularly appropriate in insurance packing cases, as they often involve a breach of most duties a fiduciary has. The claim would also be appropriate in most other situations involving abuses discussed in this chapter. Breach of fiduciary duty claims have survived motions to dismiss where the insurance premium finance company and the insurance company were connected and failed to disclose this information to the consumer.[297]

## 6.4.8 Gramm-Leach-Bliley Regulation of Banks and Preemption of State Law

### 6.4.8.1 Joint Banking Agency Regulations

The Gramm-Leach-Bliley Act requires the various federal banking agencies to publish customer protection regulations that apply to the retail sales practices, solicitations, advertising, or offers of any insurance products by a depository institution or affiliate.[298] In response, the Office of the Comptroller of the Currency, the Federal Reserve Board, the Federal Deposit Insurance Corporation, and the Office of Thrift Supervision issued joint regulations under this provision of the Act,[299] effective date October 1, 2001.[300] The regulations cover prohibited practices, disclosures, restrictions on where insurance activities may take place, and insurance sales personnel licensing requirements and qualifications.

Regarding prohibited acts, any covered person[301] may not lead a consumer to believe that an extension of credit is conditional upon either: (1) the purchase of an insurance product or an annuity from the bank or any of its affiliates or (2) an agreement by the consumer not to obtain, or a prohibition on the consumer from obtaining, any insurance product or annuity from an unaffiliated entity. Further, covered persons may not mislead any person into believing that the insurance product or annuity is backed by the federal government or insured by the FDIC, or that any product which involves investment risk does not have such risk or cannot lose its value. Finally, covered persons may not consider the fact that a consumer is a victim of domestic violence in the underwriting, pricing, renewal, or scope of coverage or with regard to the payment of claims except as required or expressly permitted under state law.[302]

Banks and covered persons must disclose to consumers several pieces of information related to the above-described prohibited practices. Such disclosures must state that: the insurance product or annuity is not a deposit, or other obligation of or guaranteed by the bank or an affiliate; such product is not insured by the FDIC or any other agency; and if the product involves investment risk, that the risk exists, including the possibility of loss.[303] These disclosures must be provided both orally and in writing before the completion of the initial sale of an insurance product or annuity.[304] Further, the bank must disclose that it cannot condition the purchase of an insurance product on the extension of credit or that the consumer agree not to obtain an insurance product or annuity from an unaffiliated entity. This information must be provided orally and in writing at the time the consumer applies for an extension of credit.[305] The disclosures must be "readily understandable," clear and conspicuous, and designed to call attention to the nature and significance of the information provided.[306] In

Premium Fin. Co., 2000 U.S. Dist. LEXIS 13763 (N.D. Ill. Sept. 7, 2000); Hobson v. Lincoln Ins. Agency, Inc., 2000 U.S. Dist. LEXIS 13314 (N.D. Ill. Sept. 7, 2000) (breach of fiduciary duty and UDAP claims survived motions to dismiss where the insurance premium finance company and the insurance company were connected and failed to disclose this fact to the consumer; note that RICO claims were dismissed but with leave to amend in these cases); Robinson v. Rebsamen Ford, Inc., 530 S.W.2d 660 (Ark. 1975). *But see* Frye v. American Gen. Fin., 307 F. Supp. 2d 836 (S.D. Miss. 2004) (no fiduciary duty between creditor and borrower because insufficient course of dealing); Knapp v. American Gen. Fin. Inc., 111 F. Supp. 2d 758 (S.D. W. Va. 2000); Mans v. Peoples Bank of Imboden, 10 S.W.3d 885 (Ark. 2000) (no fiduciary relationship between bank and customer regarding credit insurance; bank acted as agent for insurance company); The Huntington Mortgage Co. v. DeBrota, 703 N.E.2d 160 (Ind. Ct. App. 1998) (no fiduciary duty between creditor and borrower absent special circumstances); Rossbach v. FBS Mortgage Corp., 1998 Minn. App. LEXIS 374 (Apr. 7, 1998); Green v. Paradise Pontiac, 483 N.E.2d 1213 (Ohio Ct. App. 1984) (where debtor admitted creditor was not his agent, and credit insurance was not required, but debtor requested it, there was no fiduciary relationship and no duty to disclose the creditor's commission).

296 Budnitz, *The Sale of Credit Life Insurance: The Bank As Fiduciary*, 62 N.C. L. Rev. 322–323 (1984).

297 *See, e.g.,* Harris v. Illinois Vehicle Premium Fin. Co., 2000 U.S. Dist. LEXIS 13763 (N.D. Ill. Sept. 7, 2000). *But see* Hobson v. Lincoln Ins. Agency, Inc., 2001 WL 55528 (N.D. Ill. Jan. 22, 2001) (breach of fiduciary duty claim dismissed pursuant to an Illinois statute that expressly negates the existence of a fiduciary duty).

298 Gramm-Leach-Bliley § 305, *amending* Federal Insurance Deposit Act at 12 U.S.C. § 1831x.

299 65 Fed. Reg. 75,822 (Dec. 4, 2000).

300 66 Fed. Reg. 15,345 (Mar. 19, 2001).

301 A covered person is defined as a bank or "any other person only when the person sells, solicits, advertises, or offers an insurance product or annuity to a consumer at an office of the bank or on behalf of a bank." 12 C.F.R. § 1007.82(j) [§ 208.82(j)] (the regulation also discusses what are activities performed on behalf of a bank) (CFPB regulations).

302 12 C.F.R. § 1007.83 [§ 208.83] (CFPB regulations).

303 12 C.F.R. § 1007.84(a), (b) [§ 208.84(a), (b)] (CFPB regulations).

304 12 C.F.R. § 1007.84(c)(1) [§ 208.84(c)(1)] (CFPB regulations) (if a sale is conducted by mail, oral disclosures need not be provided; if a sale is conducted or application is taken by telephone, the timing rules for the provision of the written disclosure change, see §§ 208.84(2) and (3)).

305 *Id.*

306 12 C.F.R. § 1007.84(c)(5) [§ 208.84(c)(5)] (CFPB regulations) (the regulation provides some examples of statements that could be used in advertisements which are simple, direct, readily understandable, and formatted in a way to call attention to the nature and signifi-

addition, the disclosures must be given in a "meaningful" form.[307]

If disclosures are provided electronically, the consent requirements set forth in the Electronic Signatures in Global and National Commerce Act apply.[308] The bank may provide the mandated written disclosures electronically "if the consumer affirmatively consents to receiving the disclosures electronically and if the disclosures are provided in a format that the consumer may retain or obtain later, for example, by printing or storing electronically (such as by downloading)."[309] If the information is provided electronically, oral disclosures need not be given. Electronic disclosures are not meaningfully provided if the consumer can bypass the visual text before purchasing the insurance product or annuity.[310]

Significantly, the regulations require that the consumer acknowledge receipt of the mandated disclosures in writing or electronically.[311] The consumer is not specifically entitled to a copy of this acknowledgment, however.

Two additional substantive restrictions apply to these types of transactions. First, where practicable, the bank must physically separate its insurance business from where it conducts its retail deposit business. The insurance product or annuity sales section of the bank must be "clearly delineated" and "distinguished" from the other bank functions. However, bank personnel employed in the deposit section of the bank may refer consumers to the insurance or annuity portion of the bank only if that person received no more than a "nominal" fee of a fixed dollar amount for each referral.[312] Second, a bank may not allow any person who sells or offers for sale any such products to do so in its offices or to act on its behalf unless that person is qualified and licensed under applicable state insurance licensing rules regarding the specific products being recommended or sold.[313]

### 6.4.8.2 Preemption of State Regulation

The Gramm-Leach-Bliley Act prohibits the states, by way of statute, regulation, or other action, from preventing or significantly interfering with the ability of an insured depository institution (or a subsidiary or affiliate thereof) from engaging in any insurance sales, solicitations, or cross-marketing activity.[314] This preemption is subject to thirteen exceptions that preserve the states' rights to regulate a bank's insurance sales so long as the restrictions are no more burdensome or restrictive than the provisions outlined in the Act and do not discriminate against or impose a disparate burden on banks and their affiliates.[315] These thirteen areas that the states may regulate include referral fees, licensing, regulatory inspection of books, release of information and privacy issues, conditioning extension of credit upon purchase of insurance, disclosures regarding choice of providers if the insurance is required, disclosures regarding the fact that the insurance is not insured by the FDIC, and financing of the premium.[316]

The OCC has acted on requests that it determine that certain Massachusetts and West Virginia state insurance laws are preempted by Gramm-Leach-Bliley.[317] The OCC opined that some provisions of West Virginia insurance law are preempted and some are not,[318] and found that all of the sections of Massachusetts law at issue are preempted.[319] Both West Virginia and Massachusetts challenged the legality of these letters in federal

cance of the information as well as a list of the types of methods that could be used to satisfy this requirement, see § 208.84(c)(5), (c)(6)).

307 12 C.F.R. § 1007.84(c)(6) [§ 208.84(c)(6)] (CFPB regulations).

308 12 C.F.R. § 1007.84(c)(4) [§ 208.84(c)(4)] (CFPB regulations).

The Electronic Signatures in Global and National Commerce Act, 15 U.S.C. §§ 7001–7031, is discussed at § 2.5.4.1, *supra*.

309 12 C.F.R. § 1007.84(c)(4) [§ 208.84(c)(4)] (CFPB regulations).

310 12 C.F.R. § 1007.84(c)(6)(iii) [§ 208.84(c)(6)(iii)] (CFPB regulations).

311 12 C.F.R. § 1007.84(c)(7) [§ 208.84(c)(7)] (CFPB regulations) (special rules apply if the transaction is conducted by telephone).

312 12 C.F.R. § 1007.85 [§ 208.85] (CFPB regulations) (and the payment of the fee cannot depend on whether the referral results in a sale).

313 12 C.F.R. § 1007.86 [§ 208.86] (CFPB regulations).

314 15 U.S.C. § 6701(d). *See* Association of Banks in Ins., Inc. v. Duryee, 270 F.3d 397 (6th Cir. 2001) (Ohio's licensing laws and restrictions on solicitations of customers were preempted by Gramm-Leach-Bliley); TD Banknorth Ins. Agency v. Kofman, 2008 WL 2967644 (D. Me. Aug. 1, 2008) (magistrate recommendation finding that a waiting period rule under Maine law is preempted by Gramm-Leach-Bliley because it prevents or significantly interferes with insurance cross marketing, despite the fact that factual information proffered did not support such a conclusion).

315 15 U.S.C. § 6701(d)(2)(B), (e).

316 15 U.S.C. § 6701(d)(2)(B)(i)–(xiii).

317 65 Fed. Reg. 57,427 (Sept. 22, 2000) (Rhode Island Financial Institutions Insurance Sales Act); 65 Fed. Reg. 43,827 (July 14, 2000) (certain provisions of the Massachusetts bank insurance sales statute and regulations); 65 Fed. Reg. 35,420 (June 2, 2000) (West Virginia Insurance Sales Commission Protection Act).

318 66 Fed. Reg. 51,502 (Oct. 9, 2001).

*Preempted* were provisions: (1) requiring financial institutions to use separate employees' for insurance solicitations; (2) restricting the timing of bank employees' referral or solicitation of insurance business from customers who have loan applications pending with the bank; (3) restricting the sharing of information with bank affiliates acquired by a financial institution in the course of a loan transaction to solicit or offer insurance; (4) requiring that financial institutions segregate the place of solicitation or sale of insurance so that it is readily distinguishable from deposit-taking and lending areas.

*Not preempted* were provisions: (1) prohibiting a requirement or implication that the purchase of an insurance product is required as a condition of a loan; (2) prohibiting a financial institution from offering an insurance product in combination with other products unless all of the products are available separately; (3) requiring that, where insurance is required as a condition of credit, the insurance and credit transactions be completed independently and through separate documents.

319 67 Fed. Reg. 13,405 (Mar. 22, 2002).

The affected provisions prohibited non-licensed bank personnel from referring prospective customers to a licensed insurance agent except upon an inquiry initiated by the customer; prohibited non-licensed bank personnel from receiving any additional compensation for making a referral; prohibited banks from telling loan applicants that insurance products are available through the bank until the application is approved and, in the case of a loan secured by a mortgage on real property, until after the customer has accepted the bank's written commitment to extend credit.

appellate courts. The Fourth Circuit upheld the OCC's preemption of the West Virginia provisions.[320] The court ruled that the OCC has the authority to interpret Gramm-Leach-Bliley and that the OCC's reasoning in finding the West Virginia provisions to be preempted was valid.[321] This was the first time a federal court had ruled on the OCC's preemption of state law under Gramm-Leach-Bliley. Unlike the Fourth Circuit, the First Circuit held that it had no jurisdiction under Article III of the Constitution because the OCC's opinion letter had no legal effect and was not coercive, and thus did not give rise to a "case or controversy."[322] Subsequently, a group of lenders challenged in district court the Massachusetts laws relating to sales, solicitations, and marketing of insurance products (thus providing an actual case). The court held that all four challenged provisions were preempted by Gramm-Leach-Bliley.[323] Applying a *Barnett*[324] analysis, the court found that the state law substantially burdened a lender's ability to cross-market and sell insurance products by significantly decreasing marketing opportunities, impeding lenders from offering insurance until after a consumer is likely to have purchased it elsewhere, and imposing "more costs" in its requirement for separate insurance-related space.

## 6.5 Voluntariness

### *6.5.1 General: The Law and the Practice*

A first step in examining a credit insurance transaction is to determine whether the insurance purchase was voluntary. Few lenders explicitly require borrowers to purchase insurance from the lender. State law rarely authorizes such a requirement. Even if it does, Truth in Lending only allows exclusion of financed insurance premiums from the TILA finance charge if their purchase is voluntary.[325] The question of whether the purchase of insurance was voluntary is a question of fact.[326]

However, the existence of a signed "voluntary" insurance authorization as required by the TILA does not end the inquiry. A consumer may be able to claim under state law that the contract is illegal.[327] Clients must be questioned to ascertain whether they knew they purchased credit insurance, whether they were orally informed that the insurance was required, or whether the creditor implied that the insurance was necessary.

It is also worthwhile to check whether the initials on the credit insurance authorization are forged.[328] Beyond the conventional notions of coercion and voluntariness, there is also an argument that credit insurance is not voluntary when the insurance is valueless. This argument might apply when the consumer cannot recover any benefits because of ineligibility.[329]

Other evidence is the portion of a creditor's transactions which include credit insurance sales (called the penetration rate). Company targets for insurance and other products sales also are important evidence.[330]

If the purchase of credit insurance is not voluntary, then it is likely that there are remedies for violation of a number of federal and state statutes. In addition, the insurance cost may be considered interest for usury purposes, making the loan usurious.

### *6.5.2 Truth in Lending and Usury Distinguished*

Truth in Lending Act (TILA) analysis must be distinguished from usury analysis. TILA requires that credit life, A&H, or loss of income premiums be included in the TILA-defined finance charge unless there is a disclosure of the cost of the credit and of the fact that the insurance is not a factor in the approval of the credit. Additionally, the consumer must give a "specific, affirmative written indication of [the] desire to purchase the insurance after receiving the disclosure."[331]

Similarly, property insurance on collateral may be excluded from the TILA finance charge even though required, so long as there is a written disclosure of the cost if the creditor's proffered

320 Cline v. Hawke, 51 Fed. Appx. 392 (4th Cir. 2002).

321 *Id.*

322 Bowler v. Hawke, 320 F.3d 59 (1st Cir. 2003).

One judge on the Fourth Circuit panel dissented from the majority on the same basis, arguing that the matter did not meet the "case or controversy" requirement of Article III of the Constitution. Cline v. Hawke, 51 Fed. Appx. 392, 2002 WL 31557392 (4th Cir. 2002) (King, J., dissenting).

323 Massachusetts Bankers Ass'n v. Bowler, 392 F. Supp. 2d 24 (D. Mass. 2005).

The provisions at issue: prohibit bank employees who are not licensed insurance agents from referring a bank customer to a licensed insurance agent unless the customer inquires about insurance; forbids banks from paying insurance referral fees; allows banks to solicit loan applicants for insurance sales only after written approval and disclosures have been provided; and requires insurance solicitation to be physically separate from other bank functions.

324 Barnett Bank of Marion County v. Nelson, 517 U.S. 25 (1996) (where state law forbids or significantly impairs a congressional grant of authority, state law is preempted).

325 The limited exception is property insurance. *See* § 6.5.2, *infra*.

326 *See* § 6.5.3, *infra*.

327 London v. Wal-Mart Stores, Inc., 340 F.3d 1246 (11th Cir. 2003). The court, which retained supplemental jurisdiction after TILA claims were settled, held that a credit card applicant who obtained related credit insurance had suffered "injury in fact," even though he knew the insurance was not required and the enrollment form stated it was optional. The creditor, however, did not comply with a state law requirement to disclose to an applicant that purchasing the insurance is not a prerequisite to obtaining the loan. The court ruled that the applicant suffered injury per se by paying consideration for an illegal contract.

328 *See* Vickers v. Interstate Dodge, 882 So. 2d 1236 (La. Ct. App. 2004) (because buyer's initials were forged by dealership, premium amount should have been disclosed as a finance charge).

329 *See* § 6.8.1, *infra* (discussing post-claim underwriting).

330 Fed. Trade Comm'n v. Stewart Fin. Co., Civ. No. 103CV-2648 (N.D. Ga. Nov. 9, 2005) (stipulated final judgment and order) (settlement based on complaint alleging that company set a goal of having 40% of the total amount customer repays comprised of add-on products), *available at* www.ftc.gov/os/2005/11/051109 stewartstipa103cv2648.pdf.

331 15 U.S.C. § 1605(b); 12 C.F.R. §§ 1026.4(b)(7), (10), 1026.4(d)(1), (3) [§§ 226.4(b)(7), (10), 226.4(d)(1), (3)]. Note that regulations regarding debt cancellation fees apply whether or not it is treated as insurance under applicable law.

insurance is purchased, and disclosure of the borrower's choice of providers.[332] Even if insurance premiums may be considered interest for purposes of state usury law, they may not be a finance charge for TILA purposes if they meet the criteria for exclusion set forth in the Act.[333]

Of course, the converse is true as well. A proper exclusion of premiums from the finance charge under TILA does not necessarily insulate the insurance component of the transaction from usury claims. State law, not TILA, must be the controlling reference as to when insurance premiums are interest for purposes of state usury claims.

### 6.5.3 Truth in Lending

A lender may exclude the credit life and accident insurance premium cost from the calculation of the TILA finance charge,[334] but only if the insurance is not a factor in approving the credit, and the consumer is so informed.[335] Further, the cost of any such insurance must be disclosed, and the borrower must give specific affirmative written indication of a desire to purchase it.[336] Otherwise, credit insurance charges are treated as part of the finance charge.

Credit property insurance may be excluded from the TILA finance charge if the borrower is informed that he or she may choose the insurance provider, and the cost of the insurance, if purchased through the creditor, is disclosed.[337] In order to be excluded from the finance charge, single interest force-placed property insurance must comply with regular property insurance disclosures, and the insurer must also waive all subrogation rights against the consumer.[338]

The Fifth Circuit has addressed the issue of *actual* coercion in the sale of credit insurance as a TILA claim, holding that TILA is only a disclosure law. Technical compliance with the disclosure requirements is all that is necessary. Parole evidence is inadmissible to contradict the written disclosures, absent allegations of illiteracy, fraud or duress.[339] Though even under this approach, a TILA claim apparently would still be allowed if it can be proven that the lender specifically and unequivocally required the insurance despite the proper disclosures.[340]

The Fifth Circuit approach has been roundly criticized as ignoring the statutory purpose of the TILA insurance requirement, which is to assure that the credit insurance purchase is the result of a genuinely free and informed choice. The analysis also ignores TILA's remedial purposes, the sounder reasoning of contrary judicial authority, and the expressed opinion of the Federal Reserve Board to the contrary.[341]

The precedential effect of the Fifth Circuit approach is open to question because of the Supreme Court's subsequent decision in *Ford Motor Credit Co. v. Milhollin*[342] that opinions of the Federal Reserve Board (and now the Consumer Financial Protection Bureau) interpreting TILA are to be given great deference unless "demonstrably irrational."[343] The FRB position in its Official Commentary to TILA Regulation Z states that "whether the insurance is in fact required or optional is a factual question."[344] Thus, despite the old Fifth Circuit opinion, evidence that a creditor engaged in conduct undermining or contradicting the voluntariness disclosure should give rise to a TILA claim.[345]

Ten years after the *USLIFE* decision, the Federal Trade Commission initiated an enforcement complaint which further underscored its position that the voluntariness of the insurance is a factual issue not determinable solely by reference to the written disclosure. The complaint in *In re Tower Loan of Mississippi*[346] alleged that the creditor violated TILA by re-

332 15 U.S.C. § 1605(c); 12 C.F.R. § 1026.4(b)(8), (d)(2) [§ 226.4(b)(8), (d)(2)].

333 Hickman v. Cliff Peck Chevrolet, 566 F.2d 44 (8th Cir. 1977). *See generally* National Consumer Law Center, Truth in Lending § 3.9.4 (7th ed. 2010 and Supp.).

334 Calculating the finance charge for TILA purposes is different than calculating interest for purposes of the state usury law. *See* § 6.5.2, *supra*.

335 15 U.S.C. § 1605(b)(1); 12 C.F.R. § 1026.4(d)(1) [§ 226.4(d)(1)].

336 15 U.S.C. § 1605(b)(2); 12 C.F.R. § 1026.4(d)(1) [§ 226.4(d)(1)].

337 15 U.S.C. § 1605(c); 12 C.F.R. § 1026.4(d)(2) [§ 226.4(d)(2)].

338 12 C.F.R. § 1026.4(d)(2) n.5 [§ 226.4(d)(2) n.5]. *See* National Consumer Law Center, Truth in Lending § 3.9.4 (7th ed. 2010 and Supp.) (detailing TILA requirements relating to credit insurance disclosures).

339 USLIFE Credit Corp. v. Federal Trade Comm'n, 599 F.2d 1387 (5th Cir. 1979); Anthony v. Community Loan & Inv. Corp., 559 F.2d 1363 (5th Cir. 1977).

340 Mims v. Dixie Fin. Co., 426 F. Supp. 627, 631 (N.D. Ga. 1976).

341 Sheffey, *Credit Life and Disability Insurance Disclosures Under Truth in Lending: The Triumph of Form over Substance*, 8 Fla. St. U.L. Rev. 463, 477–490 (1980).

342 444 U.S. 555 (1980).

343 *Id.*

344 Reg. Z, Official Commentary § 1026.4(d)(5) [§ 226.4(d)(5)].

345 *See In re* Milbourne, 108 B.R. 522, 541 (Bankr. E.D. Pa. 1989) (coercion could be a TILA violation if proven, but not on the facts of this case). *See also* Hager v. American Gen. Fin., Inc., 37 F. Supp. 2d 778 (S.D. W. Va. 1999) (disagreeing with *USLIFE* finding that if a lender misrepresents to its customers that insurance is required, even though the loan contracts unequivocally state that the purchase of insurance is optional, a violation of the TILA may be established; denying lender's motion for summary judgment); Kaminski v. Shawmut Credit Union, 494 F. Supp. 723, 729 (D. Mass. 1980) (100% penetration rate among borrowers under 70 established required insurance purchase, notwithstanding the signed voluntariness disclosures, therefore, was a finance charge as to all class members; however named plaintiff lost out because he testified he knew he bought it and would have done so even if not required); Cruz v. Household Fin. Consumer Disc. Co. (*In re* Cruz), 441 B.R. 23 (Bankr. E.D. Pa. 2004) (borrower's oral testimony that she was told to sign the papers, though self-serving, was adequate to rebut assertion that insurance was voluntary). *Cf.* Wojcik v. Courtesy Auto Sales, Inc., 2002 WL 31663298 (D. Neb. Nov. 25, 2002) (credit insurance was properly included as part of amount financed rather than finance charge because consumer signed documents stating the insurance was optional, even though consumer had not read the loan documents and was told by the lender that the insurance was required). *But see* Dixon v. S&S Loan Serv. of Waycross, 754 F. Supp. 1567 (S.D. Ga. 1990) (holding *USLIFE* binding on it; no indication from published opinion as to whether these arguments were advanced).

346 Consumer Cred. Guide Rpt. No. 579; FTC Docket No. 9241 (filed July 5, 1990).

quiring credit insurance and failing to include premiums in the finance charge.

## 6.5.4 Compulsory Insurance and Usury

### 6.5.4.1 General

Prior to the development of credit insurance, insurance companies, when acting as lenders, sometimes required borrowers to purchase life insurance from them as a condition of receiving the loan. Courts generally considered such mandatory insurance premiums to be interest, constituting usury if this interest payment combined with the loan's other interest charges exceeded state limits.[347] Compulsory premiums were either per se interest, or the requirement created a presumption that the intention was to circumvent the usury laws.[348]

A minority view, however, considered this insurance to be a collateral transaction to provide the lender with additional security. Under this view, compulsory insurance premiums were not interest unless the premium charge or amount of coverage was excessive.[349] As credit insurance in its modern incarnation became more prevalent, this became the majority view.[350]

By the middle of the twentieth century, at least in the absence of specific statutory provisions, creditors generally were permitted to require insurance as a condition of obtaining credit, unless there were factors indicating that the insurance requirement was a pretext for circumventing usury laws instead of as loan security.[351] Among the factors which courts considered in determining whether the premiums should be considered interest were:[352]

- Whether the lender retained commission or profit from the premiums; and if so, how much;
- Whether the premiums exceeded the fair rate;
- Whether the loan was amply secure without it;
- Whether the amount of insurance was excessive;
- Whether there was a choice of insurers; and
- Whether an insurance policy was actually purchased.

Where the relevant consumer credit statutes do not specifically address the voluntariness issue, these cases still provide sound precedent for making a usury claim in such circumstances.

However, today the regulation of credit insurance is much more pervasive, and relevant statutes and rules in many states specifically address the voluntariness issue. The UCCC, for example, specifically prohibits compulsory credit life or disability insurance. It incorporates the TILA requirement that the borrower be informed that such purchase is not a factor in obtaining the credit, as well as TILA's cost disclosure and signature requirements.[353] Premiums must be included as interest for the purposes of the state usury ceiling if *all* these conditions are not met.[354] Many other consumer credit statutes also prohibit compulsory credit life and disability insurance.[355]

### 6.5.4.2 Choice of Insurers

Some credit statutes do not specifically address compulsory insurance, but do prohibit the creditor from tying the extension of credit to purchase of insurance from a particular insurer. The Model NAIC Credit Life and Disability Act provides that borrowers must have the option of supplying required insurance through an insurer of their choice.[356] The NAIC's Model Unfair Insurance Practices Act also prohibits the tie-in of credit to the purchase of insurance from particular providers.[357] Even in the absence of a statutory provision, the failure to give the borrower a choice of providers "converts the premiums into interest."[358]

Most states permit creditors to require credit personal property insurance on collateral as long as the borrower has a choice of providers,[359] although the purchase of the insurance is not usually "required" in the traditional sense. Some states may prohibit property insurance on loans under a specified dollar amount,[360] or limit the amount of required coverage.[361]

347 Vernon, *Regulated Credit Life and Disability Insurance and the Small Loan*, 29 N.Y.U.L. Rev. 1098, 1105 (1954). *Cf.* Cochran v. Alabama *ex rel.* Gallion, 119 So. 2d 339 (Ala. 1960) (charging and retaining exorbitant credit insurance premiums is attempt to evade usury law); Pacific E. Corp. v. Gulf Life Holding Co., 902 S.W.2d 946 (Tenn. Ct. App. 1995) (question of fact whether life insurance policy required as collateral on life of a principal in a commercial loan was pretext for usury; insurer was one of lenders).

348 Vernon, Regulated Credit Life and Disability Insurance and the Small Loan, 29 N.Y.U.L. Rev. 1098, 1106 (1954).

349 *Id.* at 1106–1107.

350 *Id.*; *Credit Insurance: Abuse and Reform*, 10 B.C. Ind. & Com. L. Rev. 439, 454 n.87 (1969).

351 Vernon, *Regulated Credit Life and Disability Insurance and the Small Loan*, 29 N.Y.U.L. Rev. 1098, 1106–1107 (1954); Annotation, 91 A.L.R.2d 1344 (1963). *Cf.* Farber v. Republic Pension Serv., 553 N.Y.S.2d 179 (N.Y. App. Div. 1990) (invoking principle that mandatory life insurance not interest so long as policy issued at same rate and on same terms as policies issued to non-borrowers).

352 Annotation, 91 A.L.R.2d at 1348. *See also* Standard Sav. Ass'n v. Greater New Canaan Missionary Baptist Church, 786 S.W.2d 774 (Tex. App. 1990) (noting Texas law holds insurance to be interest when it is required as a condition of accepting the loan and the borrower shows he or she had no role in selecting the insurance).

353 U.C.C.C. §§ 2-202(2), 3-202(2) (1968); U.C.C.C. § 2-501(2) (1974).

354 U.C.C.C. §§ 2-202(2), cmt. ¶ 2, 3-202(2) (1968). *See also* Compton v. Altavista Motors, Inc., 121 F. Supp. 2d 932 (W.D. Va. 2000) (summary judgment to creditor on usury claim due to alleged lack of choice in purchasing the protection plan denied where credit insurance "protection plan" form not given to car buyer until after the credit contract was signed).

355 *E.g.*, Ala. Code § 5-19-20(a) (all consumer credit); Cal. Fin. Code § 18291(b) (West) (industrial loans); Cal. Fin. Code § 22314 (West) (consumer loans); Conn. Gen. Stat. § 36a-566 (small loans).

356 Model Bill to Provide for the Regulation of Credit Life Ins. and Credit Accident and Health Ins., National Ass'n of Ins. Comm'rs, Model Regulatory Service § 11 (NIARS Corp. 1984).

357 NAIC Model Unfair Insurance Practices Act § 5.

358 North Am. Acceptance Corp. v. Warren, 451 S.W.2d 921, 925 (Tex. Civ. App. 1970).

359 *E.g.*, Ala. Code § 5-19-20(a), (e); U.C.C.C. §§ 2-202(2)(a), 3-202(2)(a) (1968); U.C.C.C. § 2-501(2)(a) (1974); U.C.C.C. § 4-109 (1968 and 1974).

360 *E.g.*, Ala. Code § 5-19-20(g); U.C.C.C. § 4-301(3) (1968); U.C.C.C. § 4-301(3) (1974) (same, but exempting open-end credit).

361 *See* §§ 6.4.5, *supra*, 6.6.4, *infra*.

As a practical matter, though, with the exception of property insurance, it is very difficult for a borrower to purchase credit insurance from someone other than the creditor. Credit insurance is not sold independently of the credit transaction it insures. A finance company borrower, for example, could not insure her loan with the cheaper credit insurer used by credit unions. A borrower would have to purchase a regular life or disability policy.

## *6.5.5 UDAP*

A potentially successful way to challenge coercion in the sale of credit insurance is a claim under a state UDAP statute.[362] This claim will be available in most states, but not be available in certain states where either insurance or credit is outside the scope of the state UDAP statute.[363]

In some states a violation of another statute designed to protect the public is a per se UDAP violation.[364] Because both the NAIC's Model UNIP statute[365] and the NAIC Model Credit Insurance Act,[366] both adopted in some form in most states, prohibit at least the tie-in of credit to particular providers, a coerced sale to the lender's insurer is arguably a per se UDAP violation in those states.

But a safer approach to challenging credit insurance coercion as a UDAP violation is to allege that the creditor has made misrepresentations, that it failed to disclose important information, or that its conduct was unfair. Evidence of oral misrepresentations in the sales pitch is admissible despite any subsequent written disclosures in the loan documents themselves.[367]

Overtly misrepresenting or intimating that the credit will not be granted without insurance is certainly deceptive,[368] in violation of a state UDAP statute. Conduct undermining the borrower's sense of a free choice is likely to be a UDAP violation as well.[369] The FTC administrative law judge in the *USLIFE* case noted that the same facts alleged to create a TILA violation as to the genuine voluntariness of the insurance purchase may be an unfair and deceptive practice, though the FTC had not pleaded such a violation.[370]

In other cases, the FTC has used its authority to stop unfair and deceptive practices to issue cease and desist orders prohibiting a creditor from misrepresenting that credit would be unavailable without credit insurance and from pre-including insurance charges on the contracts.[371] In another case, the FTC alleged that a finance company engaged in an unfair and deceptive practice by obtaining false statements from consumers that the insurance was voluntary.[372] The FTC also settled a case in which the creditor automatically included the insurance in the monthly payment amounts for the loan.[373]

One court articulated its test for establishing allegations of coerced credit insurance purchases as a UDAP claim: 1) the lender affirmatively represented, by words or conduct, that insurance was required in fact, and 2) the borrower purchased insurance as a result of the lender's action which he or she otherwise would not have done. The borrower further should be permitted to introduce evidence to prove those elements, despite the existence of a signed voluntariness disclosure executed pursuant to TILA or a similar state law.[374]

362 *See* § 6.4.6.1, *supra*.

363 National Consumer Law Center, Unfair and Deceptive Acts and Practices §§ 2.2.1 (credit), 2.3.1 (insurance) (7th ed. 2008 and Supp.).

364 *See* National Consumer Law Center, Unfair and Deceptive Acts and Practices § 3.2.7 (7th ed. 2008 and Supp.).

365 *See* § 6.4.6.1, *supra*.

366 *See* § 6.4.3.1, *supra*.

367 *See* National Consumer Law Center, Unfair and Deceptive Acts and Practices § 4.2.19 (7th ed. 2008 and Supp.). *See also* Macheda v. Household Fin. Realty Corp. of N.Y., 2009 WL 113474 (N.D.N.Y. Jan. 15, 2009) (consumer's signature on the loan documents does not prevent inquiry into the circumstances in which the loan was sold); *In re* Milbourne, 108 B.R. 522, 541 (Bankr. E.D. Pa. 1989).

368 *See, e.g., In re* Tower Loan of Mississippi, Consumer Cred. Guide Rpt. No. 579, FTC Docket No. 9241 (filed July 5, 1990) (FTC alleges that the creditor violated the FTC unfair and deceptive practices act by obtaining false statements from consumers stating that the purchase of credit insurance was voluntary, when the creditor was in fact requiring the purchase and failing to include the premiums in the finance charge in violation of TILA). *But see* Credithrift of Am., Inc. v. Whitley, 380 S.E.2d 489 (Ga. Ct. App. 1989) (holding that creditors' statement that "although they were not required by law to purchase certain insurance . . . as a practical matter they would probably not be approved for the loan unless the insurance was purchased" did not constitute fraudulent misrepresentation or a violation of the state fair business practices act. *Note*: the court's reasoning is viable only if creditors are free under state law to deny credit if consumers refuse to buy insurance. But in many, if not most states, consumer credit regulation laws do not permit creditors to require credit life or disability insurance as a condition of receiving the loan, in which case decision is inapposite).

369 *See e.g.,* Fox v. Industrial Cas. Ins. Co., 424 N.E.2d 839 (Ill. App. Ct. 1981) (state Consumer Fraud Act designed to protect plaintiffs sold credit auto insurance without having been advised of additional cost, term of policy, and that less expensive policies available).

370 *In re* USLIFE Credit Corp. & USLIFE Corp., 91 F.T.C. 984, 1015–1016, Consumer Cred. Guide CCH ¶ 97,938 (1978), *modified on other grounds*, 92 F.T.C. 353 (1978), *rev'd on other grounds*, 599 F.2d 1387 (5th Cir. 1979). The case was brought solely pursuant to the FTC's enforcement authority over Truth in Lending.

*Note*: the ALJ's recommended decision, to the effect that *USLIFE* did not violate TILA, was not adopted by the full commission. 91 F.T.C. at 1017–1046.

371 *See In re* The Money Tree, Inc., 62 Fed. Reg. 7232 (Feb. 18, 1997) (notice of proposed order), 62 Fed. Reg. 35,819 (July 2, 1997) (notice of final order); *In re* Peacock Buick, Inc., 86 F.T.C. 1532, 1558, 1567 (1975).

372 *In re* Tower Loan of Mississippi, Consumer Cred. Guide Rpt. No. 579; FTC Docket No. 9241 (filed July 5, 1990).

373 Complaint, FTC v. Associates First Cap. Corp., Civil Action No. 1:01-CV-00606-JTC, (N.D. Ga. Mar. 6, 2001), *available at* www.ftc.gov/os/2001/03/citigroupcmp.pdf. *See also* Settlement Order, Sept. 19, 2002, *available at* www.ftc.gov/os/2002/09/associates.pdf.

374 Cruz v. Household Fin. Consumer Disc. Co. (*In re* Cruz), 441 B.R. 23 (Bankr. E.D. Pa. 2004) (finding UDAP violation; borrower could rely on oral representations to show insurance was not voluntary); *In re* Milbourne, 108 B.R. 522 (Bankr. E.D. Pa. 1989). *See* § 6.5.8, *infra*. *Cf.* Agnew v. Washington Mut. Fin. Group, 244 F. Supp. 2d 672 (N.D. Miss. 2003); Harrison v. Commercial Credit Corp., 2003

## 6.5.6 Antitrust Challenges

### 6.5.6.1 Sale of Credit Insurance As an Unlawful Tie-In

Perhaps because of its complexity, antitrust law has not been frequently invoked as a private remedy for coercion in the sale of credit insurance. An antitrust claim may arise when there is explicit or implied[375] coercion in the sale of credit insurance. Tie-in arrangements, in which the sale of one product is tied to the sale of a second product, are generally condemned under the antitrust laws.[376] The high penetration rates of credit insurance, an expensive insurance product for the coverage purchased, suggest that the insurance purchase may in fact be tied to the sale of the credit. In addition, some creditors sell credit insurance as a package deal, i.e., to get any one type of insurance, the consumer must purchase two or more.[377]

It seems well-established now that credit can be the tying (the desired) product under the Sherman Act.[378] A tie-in requires evidence of at least three case elements:

- A tie of two products (here arguably, the credit and the credit insurance);
- The challenged conduct has "affected a not insubstantial amount of commerce in the market for the tied product" (the tied product being credit insurance);
- "The defendant has substantial economic power in the market for the tying product" (the tying product here being credit).

A showing of coercion may also be required.[379]

The elements regarding economic power may be the most difficult ones to prove. One commentator suggests that the penetration rate itself is evidence of economic power, especially when coupled with the high price of credit insurance in relation to comparable ordinary insurance.[380] Further, though a defendant is likely to argue that the credit marketplace is competitive, and that market dominance is lacking, a number of factors can limit consumers' choices.

One of the most fundamental is the extent of borrower sophistication required if he or she is to perceive the full implications of the tie-in arrangement. Most borrowers focus on the credit, not the ancillary insurance product.[381] Only a very small portion of the borrowing public is likely to understand the cost of credit insurance in relation to its benefits.[382] The fact that the relevant credit market may be segmented as a result of geographic or income factors may suggest that a defendant has sufficient economic power despite the presence of other types of creditors serving other geographic or income markets.[383] Because of the complexity of this issue, the practitioner may wish to seek expert assistance.

There are also other tie-ins in credit insurance. Though credit life insurance may be sold alone, rarely is credit disability made available separately. Rather, it must be purchased with credit life coverage. For example, a borrower with standard life

---

WL 1844464 (S.D. Miss. Mar. 20, 2003) (one of a series of cases holding that a lender's omission or misrepresentation regarding the terms and conditions of credit insurance does not constitute fraudulent concealment—and thus does not toll the statute of limitations—where the loan documents disclose the insurance information, whether or not the consumer has read the papers); Singleton v. Protective Life Ins. Co., 857 So. 2d 803 (Ala. 2003). *But see* Strong v. First Family Fin. Servs., Inc., 202 F. Supp. 2d 536 (S.D. Miss. 2002) (clear and conspicuous TILA disclosures regarding credit insurance preclude plaintiffs' argument that lender failed to disclose material terms of the insurance); Hayes v. Osterman Jewelers, 2002 WL 1608445 (Ohio Ct. App. Apr. 19, 2002) (although plaintiff did not discuss the credit insurance with the creditor and did not read the document that she signed accepting credit insurance, the court presumed she had read and understood the terms of the agreement and held that the creditor had not committed a deceptive act by selling the insurance).

375 Though the legal issues are generally the same, the factual issues establishing the claim are more difficult in cases of implicit coercion.

376 As a practical matter, § 1 of the Sherman Act, 15 U.S.C. §§ 1–39, would be the applicable statute, as the Clayton Act, though forbidding tying arrangements, does not apply to intangibles such as credit or insurance. Polden, *The Antitrust Implications of Credit Insurance Tying Arrangements*, 32 Drake Law Rev. 862, 882 n.78 (1982–1983) (much of this discussion is derived from this article).

377 For an example of this phenomenon, see Fabricant v. Sears Roebuck & Co., 202 F.R.D. 310 (S.D. Fla. 2001) (certifying class in case of retailer selling credit card plan that automatically includes package of credit life, disability, property, and unemployment insurance without properly advising consumer that the package was optional) (no antitrust claim raised), *subsequent history*, Order on Motions for Summary Judgment (S.D. Fla. Mar. 5, 2002), *available on the companion website to this treatise* (granting summary judgment on two of plaintiffs' counts and voiding the contracts as unenforceable on public policy grounds); Baron v. Best Buy Co., 75 F. Supp. 2d 1368 (S.D. Fla. 1999) (same but Best Buy calls the package the "Payment Maker Protection Plan"; court found arbitration clause unenforceable), *rev'd and vacated*, 260 F.3d 625 (11th Cir. 2001) (reversing denial of motions to compel arbitration).

378 Fortner Enters., Inc. v. United States Steel Corp., 394 U.S. 495 (1969); Homestead M. Homes, Inc. v. Foremost Corp. of Am., 603 F. Supp. 767 (N.D. Tex. 1985) (where manufactured home financing arrangements tied to insurance, conduct not exempt from antitrust as business of insurance. Further, because insurer acted in concert with a non-exempt entity, exemption would have been forfeited in any case).

379 Polden, *The Antitrust Implications of Credit Insurance Tying Arrangements*, 32 Drake Law Rev. 862, 880 (1982–1983).

This treatise does not address the distinction between pleading and proving a per se tying case and a tying case analyzed under the rule of reason, as that is beyond the scope of this treatise. The concepts, however, are important in litigating an antitrust tie-in case. *See generally id.* at 881; Jefferson Parish Hosp. Dist. No. 2 v. Hyde, 466 U.S. 2 (1984).

380 Polden, *The Antitrust Implications of Credit Insurance Tying Arrangements*, 32 Drake Law Rev. 862, 895–896 (1982–1983).

381 *See* § 6.2.3.1, *supra*.

382 *Id.*

383 Polden, *The Antitrust Implications of Credit Insurance Tying Arrangements*, 32 Drake Law Rev. 862, 984–992 (1982–1983).

In a rural area, there are likely to be fewer choices as to credit providers. During a farm recession, which may cause rural banks with a high volume of troubled agricultural credit to restrict their lending to lower-income consumers, for example, the finance company segment of the lending market may assume greater economic control, at least in relation to that class of borrowers.

insurance adequate to cover all expenses and debts in the event of death may view credit life as superfluous, and wish to insure only against disability. Many lenders would provide such a borrower only with a choice between both credit life and credit disability or neither. Policies cast as loss-of-income policies covering both disability and involuntary-unemployment also in effect, present a tie-in.[384]

The issues involved in the tying of one type of credit insurance to another type of credit insurance apparently have been little explored in cases or commentary.[385] Arguably most of the analysis of that type of tie-in would be similar to that in situations where the insurance is tied to the purchase of credit. However, it is conceivable that the "business of insurance" factor may be weighed differently where insurance is both the tying and tied product, or where the *insurer*, rather than a creditor, creates the tied package.[386]

### 6.5.6.2 McCarran-Ferguson Act's Impact on Antitrust, Other Challenges to Credit Insurance Practices

The McCarran-Ferguson Act[387] provides that a state insurance law can displace the application of the three major federal anti-trust statutes to insurance practices—the Clayton Act, the Sherman Act, and the FTC Act. Every state, generally at the behest of the insurance industry, has enacted a state unfair insurance practices act in an attempt to specifically supplant these anti-trust statutes. But there are at least six ways in which anti-trust or related claims can be raised concerning coercion in the sale of credit insurance, despite the McCarran-Ferguson Act.

First, despite McCarran-Ferguson, the Sherman Act still applies to insurance practices involving "any agreement to boycott, coerce, or intimidate, or act of boycott, coercions, or intimidation."[388] Thus Sherman Act claims may still be available where a creditor forces the consumer to purchase credit insurance as a condition of obtaining credit.

Second, McCarran-Ferguson displaces the Clayton, Sherman, and FTC Acts only where they are "applicable to the business of insurance."[389] The mere fact that a practice involves an insurance policy does not place the practice within the "business of insurance."[390] For example, the Fifth Circuit

384 California requires that loss of income (LOI) insurance and disability insurance must be offered separately, even if a combination plan is offered. Cal. Fin. Code § 18292.5(e) (West) (industrial loan).

385 *Compare* Kenty v. Bank One, Columbus, N.A., 1992 WL 170605, 1992 U.S. Dist. LEXIS 16645 (S.D. Ohio Apr. 23, 1992), *aff'd in relevant part* 92 F.3d 384 (6th Cir. 1996) (claim under anti-tying provision of Bank Holding Co. Act, 12 U.S.C. § 1972, dismissed where allegation that credit loss endorsements were tied to force-placed property insurance purchase), *with* Boyd v. Society Bank & Trust, Clearinghouse No. 47,939A (Ohio Ct. Com. Pleas Oct. 29, 1991) (order on motion to dismiss) (same claim survived motion to dismiss).

For an example of this phenomenon but where antitrust claims have not been raised, see Baron v. Best Buy Co., 75 F. Supp. 2d 1368 (S.D. Fla. 1999) (same but Best Buy calls the package the "Payment Maker Protection Plan"), *rev'd*, 260 F.3d 625 (11th Cir. 2001) (reversing denial of motions to compel arbitration); Fabricant v. Sears Roebuck & Co., 1999 U.S. Dist. LEXIS 16574 (S.D. Fla. Sept. 30, 1999) (Sears card "credit plan" is sold as a package which automatically includes credit life, disability, property, and unemployment insurance) (antitrust claim not raised).

386 *See* Kintner, Bauer & Allen, *Application of the Antitrust Laws to the Activities of Insurance Companies*, 63 N.C. L. Rev. 431, 465 (1985).

387 15 U.S.C. §§ 1012, 1013. The McCarran-Ferguson exclusion provision reads in its entirety as follows:

> (b) Federal regulation. No Act of Congress shall be construed to invalidate, impair, or supersede any law enacted by any State for the purpose of regulating the business of insurance, or which imposes a fee or tax upon such business, unless such Act specifically relates to the business of insurance: *Provided, That after June 30, 1948, the Act of July 2, 1890, as amended, known as the Sherman Act* [15 U.S.C. §§ 1–39], and the Act of Oct. 15, 1914, as amended, known as the Clayton Act, and the Act of Sept. 26, 1914, known as the Federal Trade Commission Act, as amended [15 U.S.C. §§ 41–58], shall be applicable to the business of insurance to the extent that such business is not regulated by State law.

15 U.S.C. § 1012(b) (emphasis added).

Congress expressed the intent behind the exclusion as follows:

> Congress hereby declares that the continued regulation and taxation by the several States of the business of insurance is in the public interest, and that silence on the part of the Congress shall not be construed to impose any barrier to the regulation or taxation of such business by the several States.

15 U.S.C. § 1011.

388 12 U.S.C. § 1013(b). *See also* Hartford Fire Ins. Co. v. Calif., 509 U.S. 764, 802–806 (1993) (sufficient allegation of boycott, making McCarran-Ferguson inapplicable).

389 12 U.S.C. § 1012(b). *See* Sec. & Exch. Comm'n v. Nat'l Sec., Inc., 393 U.S. 453, 460 (1969).

390 To determine whether particular conduct falls within "the business of insurance," courts have used a three part test derived from three Supreme Court decisions: Union Labor Life Ins. Co. v. Pireno, 458 U.S. 119 (1982); Group Life & Health Ins. Co. v. Royal Drug Co., 440 U.S. 205 (1979); Securities and Exch. Comm'n v. National Sec., Inc., 393 U.S. 453 (1969).

This test asks: whether the practice has the effect of transferring or spreading a policyholder's risk; whether the practice is an integral part of the policy relationship between the insurer and the insured; and whether the practice is limited to entities within the insurance industry. *See, e.g.*, U.S. Dep't of Treasury v. Fabe, 508 U.S. 491, 501–502 (1993) (to the extent a state law furthers the interests of policyholders, it regulates the business of insurance, to the extent it furthers the interests of others, it does not, therefore portion of state bankruptcy priority statute that gave priority to policyholders regulated business of insurance, but portion that gave priority to other creditors did not and therefore that portion was not protected by the McCarran-Ferguson Act from preemption by federal statute that granted priority to the government); O'Connor v. Unum Life Ins. Co., 146 F.3d 959, 962 (D.C. Cir. 1998); Autry v. Northwest Premium Servs., 144 F.3d 1037, 1044 (7th Cir. 1998) (a statute is enacted for the purpose of regulating the "business of insurance" if "it possesses the end, intention or aim of adjusting, managing, or controlling the relationship between the insurance company and the policyholder, directly or indirectly") (holding that an Illinois statute requiring insurance premium finance agreements to disclose certain

has held that the McCarran-Ferguson Act did not bar the FTC from investigating whether finance companies were violating the Federal Trade Commission Act[391] by misrepresenting to borrowers that they must purchase credit insurance to obtain credit.[392] The court reasoned that the appropriate focus is not on the sale of the insurance, but on the extension of credit, which is not "the business of insurance," and accordingly falls outside of the McCarran-Ferguson Act.[393] Similar reasoning should preserve federal antitrust law challenges to such credit practices as well, because the specific practice is not the "business of insurance" because it arises from a creditor-borrower relationship, not an insurer-insured relationship.[394]

Moreover, the Supreme Court has drawn a distinction between the broad category of laws enacted for the purpose of regulating the business of insurance and the narrower concept of the business of insurance.[395] McCarran-Ferguson's displacement of the three anti-trust statutes applies only to the business of insurance regulated to state law, and not to the broader category specified elsewhere in the Act of state laws enacted for the purpose of regulating the business of insurance.

Third, federal antitrust laws *do* apply to the business of insurance to the extent that such business is "not regulated by State law."[396] While lines of authority differ as to the degree of state regulation necessary to invoke the exemption,[397] the more thoroughly reasoned view requires that the state both specifically authorize the conduct at issue *and* actively regulate it.[398] Since many states prohibit creditors from requiring insurance in credit transactions,[399] and all states require creditors to give the consumer a choice of provider in any case,[400] no state has expressed a policy of allowing credit insurance tie-ins, and thus the exemption should not apply.[401]

Fourth, McCarran-Ferguson does not limit federal claims where the federal statute "specifically relates to the business of insurance,"[402] such as where the statute specifically mentions insurance. For example, the Real Estate Procedures Settlement Act (RESPA) specifically mentions mortgage insurance, so that such RESPA claims are not displaced by state law, and the federal statute should preempt any state law that conflicts with it.[403]

A fifth approach is to bring a federal claim not based on the Sherman, Clayton, or FTC Act, but based upon RICO, TILA, or any federal statute other than the three anti-trust statutes. For such other federal statutes, the application of McCarran-Ferguson is very different than for the Clayton, Sherman, and FTC Acts. Any other federal statute (e.g., TILA or RICO) applies unless it would "invalidate, impair, or supersede" the state law.[404] (As mentioned in the prior paragraph, the federal

information did not regulate the business of insurance, and therefore McCarran-Ferguson did not bar TILA claim, because the law addressed the relationship between a creditor and debtor, not the relationship between an insurance company and a policyholder, that the money borrowed ultimately paid insurance premiums was "incidental"); Perry v. Fidelity Union Life Ins. Co., 606 F.2d 468, 471 (5th Cir. 1979) (where defendant insurance company acted as a creditor, not as an insurer, its premium financing was not the "business of insurance" and therefore Act did not bar TILA; focus is on the nature of the activity itself, not the type of business that is conducting it). *See also* Ruthardt v. United States, 303 F.3d 375, 380 (1st Cir. 2002) (even when antitrust is not involved, "business of insurance" should be read restrictively, focusing on the insurance contract and protection of policyholders). *But see* Arroyo-Melecio v. Puerto Rican Am. Ins. Co., 398 F.3d 56, 68 (1st Cir. 2005) (dismissing one of plaintiffs' antitrust claims against insurer on the grounds that the decision to use or not use agents to market and solicit for policies is within the "business of insurance" and therefore exempt from antitrust challenge pursuant to the antitrust clause of the McCarran-Ferguson Act), Standard Sec. Life Ins. Co. v. West, 267 F.3d 821, 823 (8th Cir. 2001) (McCarran-Ferguson barred application of Federal Arbitration Act because state statute prohibiting arbitration clauses in insurance contracts involved the business of insurance).

391 15 U.S.C. § 45(a)(2).

392 Federal Trade Comm'n v. Dixie Fin. Co., 695 F.2d 926, 930 (5th Cir. 1983).

393 *Id.*

394 *See, e.g.,* Homestead M. Homes, Inc. v. Foremost Corp. of Am., 603 F. Supp. 767, 771–772 (N.D. Tex. 1985) (where manufactured home financing arrangements tied to insurance, conduct not exempt from antitrust as business of insurance; further, because insurer acted in concert with a non-exempt entity, exemption would have been forfeited in any case). *But see* Gilchrist v. State Farm Mut. Auto. Ins. Co., 390 F.3d 1327, 1333 (11th Cir. 2004) (holding that automobile policy holder's antitrust claim based on allegations that insurers had lowered the quality and cost of repairs by specifying inferior parts and had further failed to pass the savings onto policy holders was barred; court reasoned that the heart of Gilchrist's complaint is that claim went "to the heart of 'the relationship between insurer and insured' and attack[ed] the 'reliability, interpretation, and enforcement' of the insurance policy itself") (quoting Securities & Exch. Comm'n v. National Sec., Inc., 393 U.S. 453, 460 (1969)). *See generally* Kintner, Bauer, & Allen, *Application of the Antitrust Laws to the Activities of Insurance Companies*, 63 N.C. L. Rev. 431, 461–465 (1985); Polden, *The Antitrust Implications of Credit Insurance Tying Arrangements*, 32 Drake Law Rev. 862, 903–905 (1982–1983).

395 *See* U.S. Dep't of Treasury v. Fabe, 508 U.S. 491, 504 (1993).

396 15 U.S.C. § 1012(b).

397 *See* Polden, *The Antitrust Implications of Credit Insurance Tying Arrangements*, 32 Drake Law Rev. 862, 906, nn.183–84 (1982–1983), *discussing* Klamath-Lake Pharm. Ass'n v. Klamath Med. Serv. Bureau, 701 F.2d 1276 (9th Cir. 1983), *and* Dexter v. Equitable Life Assurance Soc'y, 527 F.2d 233 (2d Cir. 1975).

398 *See* Polden, *The Antitrust Implications of Credit Insurance Tying Arrangements*, 32 Drake Law Rev. 862, 906–908 (1982–1983), *discussing, inter alia*, United States v. Crocker Nat'l Corp., 656 F.2d 428 (9th Cir. 1981), *rev'd on other grounds*, BankAmerica Corp. v. United States, 462 U.S. 122 (1983).

399 *See* § 6.5.4, *supra.*

400 *Id.*

401 Polden, *The Antitrust Implications of Credit Insurance Tying Arrangements*, 32 Drake Law Rev. 862, 907, 910–911 (1982–1983).

402 12 U.S.C. § 1012(b). *See also* Merchants Home Delivery Servs. v. Frank B. Hall & Co., 50 F.3d 1486, 1488–1489 (9th Cir. 1995).

403 *See, e.g.*, Patton v. Triad Guar. Ins., 277 F.3d 1294, 1298 (11th Cir. 2002). *See also* Barnett Bank of Marion County v. Nelson, 517 U.S. 25, 38–39 (1996) (holding that federal statute granting national banks in small towns the authority to sell insurance preempted state law prohibiting such banks from selling insurance).

404 *See* Humana Inc. v. Forsyth, 525 U.S. 299, 307 (1999) ("invalidate" means "to render ineffective, generally without providing a replacement rule or law"; "supersede" ordinarily means "to displace (and thus render ineffective) while providing a substitute rule"; "im-

statute is even applicable if it impairs state law if the federal statute specifically relates to the business of insurance.)

The U.S. Supreme Court has defined "impair" in *Humana v. Forsyth* to mean " '[t]o weaken, to make worse, to lessen in power, diminish, or relax, or otherwise affect in an injurious manner.' "[405] In that case, a health care insurer sought to use McCarran-Ferguson to evade a federal RICO claim that alleged that the insurer failed to pass cost discounts it received from service providers on to its consumers. The Court upheld the RICO claim, reasoning that it did not impair Nevada's Unfair Insurance Practices Act because the state's many remedies to victims of insurance fraud showed that the federal statute would complement and advance state policy, rather than impair it.[406]

Nevertheless, there are other situations where the federal statute does conflict with state insurance law. In those cases, the application of the federal statute is displaced by the state insurance law.[407]

Sixth, McCarran-Ferguson does not prevent a consumer from asserting a *state* claim, including a state anti-trust claim. It is a matter of state law whether a consumer can bring an anti-trust claim under the state's unfair insurance practices act or other insurance law, whether there is a separate state anti-trust statute, and whether that anti-trust statute applies to insurance practices.

### 6.5.7 Banking Holding Act and Regulation Y

The insurance-related activities of banks and bank holding companies are subject to the requirements of the Bank Holding Company Act and Regulation Y.[408] The Act prohibits tying credit to the purchase of credit insurance from the bank, holding company, or an affiliate.[409] It also limits the right of regulated banks and bank holding companies to underwrite insurance to those circumstances where the underwriter's performance could "reasonably be expected to produce benefits to the public."[410]

### 6.5.8 Proving Coercion

Creditors today rarely openly admit that they require insurance. Most credit documents include a boiler-plate insurance

pair" means a direct conflict with state regulation and the frustration of state policy or interference with a state's administrative regime) (using these definitions, the Court held that RICO did not invalidate, supersede, or impair Nevada's Unfair Insurance Practices Act); American Chiropractic Ass'n v. Trigon Healthcare, Inc., 367 F.3d 212, 231 (4th Cir. 2004) (McCarran-Ferguson Act did not bar application of federal RICO statute because RICO furthered state policy in policing insurance fraud, did not frustrate any declared state policy, and did not interfere with state's administrative scheme even though RICO's damages provisions were more severe than many of the state's laws); Dehoyos v. Allstate Corp., 345 F.3d 290, 298 (5th Cir. 2003) (McCarran-Ferguson Act did not bar civil rights action arising from insurers' use of credit scoring system to price insurance policies, rejecting argument that such actions would frustrate states' ability to regulate insurance pricing policies); Ruthardt v. United States, 303 F.3d 375, 382–383 (1st Cir. 2002) (while state's bankruptcy priority statute's provision granting priority to guaranty funds was not preempted by federal priority statute, its one-year claims deadline was because it was not sufficiently directed to policyholder protection to fall within McCarran-Ferguson's protection); Highmark, Inc. v. UPMC Health Plan, Inc., 276 F.3d 160, 168 (3d Cir. 2001) (Lanham Act not overridden by state insurance law because it did not invalidate, impair or supersede the state law, notwithstanding that state law imposed a different standard of liability and provided for administrative enforcement without private remedies); Moore v. Liberty Nat'l Life Ins. Co., 267 F.3d 1209, 1221–1222 (11th Cir. 2001) (McCarran-Ferguson did not bar application of civil rights laws to insurer because they neither frustrated any state regulation nor conflicted with any statute enacted to regulate insurance); Lander v. Hartford Life & Annuity Ins. Co., 251 F.3d 101, 115–116 (2d Cir. 2001) (McCarran-Ferguson did not prevent application of Securities Litigation Uniform Standards Act to insurance companies); BancOklahoma Mortgage Corp. v. Capital Title Co., 194 F.3d 1089, 1099–1100 (10th Cir. 1999) (upholding RICO claim against McCarran-Ferguson preemption argument); LaBarre v. Credit Acceptance Corp., 175 F.3d 640, 643–644 (8th Cir. 1999) (RICO claim against RISC assignee arising from assignee's purchase of vendor-single-interest insurance not barred by McCarran-Ferguson, though plaintiff's claims against insurers were so barred because they fell within a state insurance provision); Edwards v. Your Credit, Inc., 148 F.3d 427, 434 (5th Cir. 1998) (McCarran-Ferguson did not protect finance company from alleged TILA violation arising from failure to include "nonfiling insurance premium" in disclosed amount financed); Autry v. Northwest Premium Servs., 144 F.3d 1037, 1044–4105 (7th Cir. 1998) (McCarran-Ferguson did not bar TILA claim based on alleged misstatements in premium financing agreement for automobile insurance policy); Sabo v. Metropolitan Life Ins. Co., 137 F.3d 185, 192–193 (3d Cir. 1998) (RICO not overridden by state unfair insurance practices statute because it did not invalidate, supersede, or impair the statute); Kenty v. Bank One, Columbus, N.A., 92 F.3d 384, 392–393 (6th Cir. 1996) (McCarran-Ferguson did not protect bank from RICO claim with respect to forced-place insurance, but did protect insurer); Garcia v. Island Program Designer, Inc., 4 F.3d 57, 62 (1st Cir. 1993) (state's bankruptcy filing deadline not protected from preemption by McCarran-Ferguson because it was not reasonably necessary to further the goal of protecting policyholders); National Consumer Law Center, Truth in Lending § 3.9.4.2 (7th ed. 2010 and Supp.).

405 525 U.S. 299, 309–310 (1999) (quoting Black's Law Dictionary 752 (6th ed. 1990)).

406 *Id.* at 311–312.

407 *See, e.g.*, Brown v. Cassens Transp. Co., 409 F. Supp. 2d 793, 811 (E.D. Mich. 2005) (McCarran-Ferguson Act barred application of RICO claim in case where employees alleged that employers had fraudulently denied them benefits under state's worker's compensation act because allowing the claim would undermine policy of state act), *aff'd on other grounds*, 492 F.3d 640 (6th Cir. 2007), *cert. granted, judgment vacated, and case remanded*, 128 S. Ct. 2936 (2008); Standard Sec. Life Ins. Co. v. West, 267 F.3d 821, 823 (8th Cir. 2001) (in case against insurer, McCarran-Ferguson barred application of Federal Arbitration Act because it would invalidate, impair or supersede state arbitration act with conflicting provisions); Moon v. Harrison Piping Supply, 375 F. Supp. 2d 577, 608 (E.D. Mich. 2005) (same), *aff'd in part, rev'd in part on other grounds*, 465 F.3d 719 (6th Cir. 2006).

408 12 U.S.C. § 1843(c)(8); 12 C.F.R. § 225.28(b)(11) (1999). *See* Hinkle, *Insurance Activities of National Banks and Bank Holding Companies*, 105 Banking L.J. 137 (1988).

409 12 U.S.C. § 1972.

410 12 U.S.C. § 1843(c)(8).

authorization containing the TILA disclosure that life and disability is not required, and that there is a choice of providers if property insurance is required. However, a signature on such an authorization is not the end of the analysis.

The mere fact that a borrower did not read the insurance authorization form indicating the purchase is voluntary, before signing it, is unlikely to warrant a finding that the insurance was compulsory.[411] Claims and defenses which arise independently of the contract, such as the state UDAP statute, misrepresentation, unconscionability, or the duty to disclose should not be subject to the parole evidence rule in any event,[412] nor should a claim for usury,[413] at least where there are allegations of fraud, illiteracy or duress.[414] A class action case based on such a claim, however, will face the additional hurdle of demonstrating to the court that the oral representations were not so individualized as to defeat class certification.[415]

Marketing and training materials to establish a pattern may support a class claim.[416] Because a case alleging coercion may result in a swearing contest,[417] it is often helpful to depose individual loan officers to find out what their sales practices are, what training or instruction they receive, and what their employer's performance expectations are.[418]

The subtle coercion of a customer can begin at the initial inquiry stage. Most lenders automatically assume the transaction will include insurance. When a prospective borrower calls to ask the terms on a loan, the quotes given by the lender

411 Payne v. First Nat'l Bank of Clarksdale, 2005 WL 3481484 (N.D. Miss. Dec. 20, 2005) (signature on forms precludes argument that credit life insurance was not voluntary); Universal C.I.T. Credit Corp. v. Lackey, 305 S.W.2d 858 (Ark. 1957); Swyters v. Motorola Employees Credit Union, 535 S.E.2d 508 (Ga. Ct. App. 2000) (consumer is bound to read the contract in absence of illiteracy; summary judgment granted to creditor on whether insurance was required); Andrus v. Ellis, 887 So. 2d 175 (Miss. 2004) (consumer generally is assumed to have read documents; failure to read loan documents does not support claim for fraudulent concealment and therefore statute of limitations was not tolled at loan closing); Morgan v. Citizens Bank, 912 So. 2d 1133 (Miss. Ct. App. 2005) (signed documents prevent argument that person did not know content of contract for credit life insurance policy; plaintiff's alleged mental capacity prevented such understanding but court found that while consumer was not "a proficient reader, he can indeed read"); Irvin v. American Gen. Fin., 2005 WL 1607460 (Ohio Ct. App. June 30, 2005) (slip op.) (parol evidence rule precluded claim that finance company misrepresented that insurance was required where signed paperwork indicated it was voluntary, although it did not preclude other claims for breach of fiduciary duty, negligence, or alleged violations of a state mortgage lending statute). *See also* Anthony v. Community Loans & Inv. Corp., 559 F.2d 1363 (5th Cir. 1977).

412 See §§ 6.5.3, 6.5.5, *supra*, 6.7, *infra*, and National Consumer Law Center, Consumer Warranty Law (4th ed. 2010 and Supp.) for discussions of other potential claims which should be unaffected by the parol evidence rule.

413 Cruz v. Household Fin. Consumer Disc. Co. (*In re* Cruz), 441 B.R. 23 (Bankr. E.D. Pa. 2004) (borrower could rely on oral representations to show insurance was not voluntary); Aclin Ford v. Cordell, 625 S.W.2d 459 (Ark. 1982). *See also* Fisher v. Beneficial Fin. Co. of Hoxsie, 383 F. Supp. 895 (D.R.I. 1974) (borrower could introduce evidence that defendant actually required insurance by its conduct). *But see* Dixon v. S&S Loan Serv. of Waycross, 754 F. Supp. 1567 (S.D. Ga. 1990) (parol evidence rule invoked to bar borrower's claim of coerced non-credit accidental death and dismemberment insurance where contract form stated purchase is voluntary; court invoked rule despite damning memorandum obtained in discovery instructing that "all new and former borrower's [sic] are to have AD&D on this loan."); Irvin v. American Gen. Fin., 2005 WL 1607460 (Ohio Ct. App. June 30, 2005) (parol evidence rule precluded claim that finance company misrepresented that insurance was required where signed paperwork indicated it was voluntary, although it did not preclude other claims for breach of fiduciary duty, negligence, or alleged violations of a state mortgage lending statute).

414 Anthony v. Community Loans & Inv. Corp., 559 F.2d 1363, 1369 (5th Cir. 1977); Knapp v. American Gen. Fin Inc., 111 F. Supp. 2d 758 (S.D. W. Va. 2000); Cruz v. Household Fin. Consumer Disc. Co. (*In re* Cruz), 441 B.R. 23 (Bankr. E.D. Pa. 2004); Wiegand v. Walser Auto. Groups, 683 N.W.2d 807 (Minn. 2004).

415 *See* Frelin v. Oakwood Homes Corp., 2002 WL 31863487 (Ark. Cir. Ct. Nov. 25, 2002) (declining to certify "false insurance class" primarily because the case requires "individualized transaction-by-transaction showing" of the oral presentations made to consumers; the court did note that plaintiff's counsel had failed to provide sample jury forms or other documents to demonstrate how this issue could be overcome).

416 *See, e.g.,* Complaint, FTC v. Associates First Cap. Corp., Civil Action No. 1:01-CV-00606-JTC (N.D. Ga. Mar. 6, 2001), *available at* www.ftc.gov/os/2001/03/citigroupcmp.pdf. *See also* Settlement Order, FTC v. Associates First Cap. Corp., Civil Action No. 1:01-CV-00606-JTC (N.D. Ga. Sept. 19, 2002), *available at* www.ftc.gov/os/2002/09/associates.pdf.

417 *Cf.* Porter v. Nationscredit Consumer Discount Co., 2006 WL 851307 (E.D. Pa. Mar. 31, 2006) (genuine issue of material fact as to whether client signed affirmative request to buy credit insurance when plaintiff received a postcard at her home from the defendants stating that she had not purchased credit insurance and offering her such coverage and plaintiff testified that she did not sign for any credit life insurance, even though court found that the TILA disclosure statement and credit life insurance application appeared to be signed and dated by plaintiff, and company had met other requirements regarding voluntary nature of the product); Miller v. Dobbs Mobile Bay, Inc., 661 So. 2d 203 (Ala. 1995) (denying creditor and insurer's motions for summary judgment where deceased borrower's representative alleged auto dealer said purchase of insurance was required and ill health did not matter; case challenging insurer's failure to pay, not the coercion). *But cf.* Standard Sav. Ass'n v. Greater New Canaan Missionary Baptist Church, 786 S.W.2d 774 (Tex. App. 1990) (borrower's affidavit that insurance purchase was required was insufficient evidence to warrant finding of usury on motion for summary judgment; "stricter standard of proof" required because of "harshness and finality of summary judgments").

418 At least two wrongful discharge cases have been brought by former finance company employees alleging they were fined for failure to push insurance hard enough. Laws v. Aetna Fin., 667 F. Supp. 342 (N.D. Miss. 1987) (Aetna's motion for summary judgment denied, court holding that plaintiff stated a cognizable cause of action for wrongful discharge where the alleged ground for discharge was a refusal to engage in illegal acts for the employer); Zimmer v. Thorp Credit, Civ. No. 33,073 (Iowa Dist. Ct., Marion County filed Dec. 1984) (case dismissed upon negotiated settlement). (Apart from that stick, carrots of free trips to Aruba may also lead to excessive sales pressure on consumers.) *But cf.* *In re* Milbourne, 108 B.R. 522 (Bankr. E.D. Pa. 1989) (refusing to interpret creditor's internal memorandum to its loan closers telling them to explain insurance as evidence that it was sent in response to a previous problem with employees requiring insurance).

automatically (and often without explanation) include the price of insurance premiums in the quotation on monthly payments.[419] Typically, the documents are generally typed up beforehand, ready for the borrower's signature, with all the figures reflecting an insured loan.[420] It is possible that nothing will be said concerning the insurance; the borrower may simply be told what lines to sign, including the insurance authorization. In the industry, this is called "sliding."

The allegations in one case are instructive. Borrowers desperate for money, were given a "negative" option to buy insurance since all loans offered by the lender were packaged with credit insurance even if not requested by borrowers. The loan documents were prepared before the borrowers arrived to sign and already included credit insurance. If the borrowers questioned or objected to the unrequested insurance, the salesperson implied that the borrowers would not be given the loan proceeds at that time but would have to return (presumably because the documents would have to be re-done).[421] In such a case the insurance is compulsory, and the premium is considered interest.[422]

The creditor may even contradict the written voluntariness disclosure, and orally inform the borrower that the insurance is required.[423] In addition, if the evidence indicates the borrower is unable to read the authorization he or she signed, and its provisions were not explained, it should be considered compulsory, and may therefore constitute interest.[424]

419 *See Equity Predators: Stripping, Flipping and Packing Their Way to Profits: Hearing Before the Special Committee on Aging United States Senate*, 105th Cong. 2d Sess. 33–34, Serial No. 105-18 (Mar. 16, 1998) (statement of Jim Dough, former employee of predatory lender).

420 This is usually treated as a positive practice by management. *See Credit Life Insurance Hearing Before the Subcomm. on Antitrust, Monopoly and Business Rights of the Senate Comm. on the Judiciary*, 96th Cong, 1st Sess. 47 (1979). *See also Equity Predators: Stripping, Flipping and Packing Their Way to Profits: Hearing Before the Special Committee on Aging United States Senate*, 105th Cong. 2d Sess. 33–34, Serial No. 105-18 (Mar. 16, 1998) (statement of Jim Dough, former employee of predatory lender); Lemelledo v. Beneficial Mgmt., 674 A.2d 582 (N.J. Super. Ct. App. Div. 1996) (named plaintiff in this class action sought a loan of $2,000 to pay her daughter's college tuition, but was given a loan for $2,538.17 of which $335.28 was for credit insurance. This insurance charge added 15.2% to the cost of her loan.), *aff'd on other grounds*, 696 A.2d 546 (N.J. 1997).

421 Lemelledo v. Beneficial Mgmt., 674 A.2d 582 (N.J. Super. Ct. App. Div. 1996), *aff'd on other grounds*, 696 A.2d 546 (N.J. 1997).

422 Aclin Ford v. Cordell, 625 S.W.2d 459, 461 (Ark. 1982); § 6.5.4, *supra*.

423 Knapp v. American Gen. Fin Inc., 111 F. Supp. 2d 758 (S.D. W. Va. 2000); Cruz v. Household Fin. Consumer Disc. Co. (*In re* Cruz), 441 B.R. 23 (Bankr. E.D. Pa. 2004). *See* allegations in Hager v. American Gen. Fin., Inc., 37 F. Supp. 2d 778 (S.D. W. Va. 1999) (lender's motion for summary judgment denied on the TILA credit insurance claim based upon disputes of fact regarding the voluntary nature of the insurance). *But see* Irvin v. Am. Gen. Fin. Inc., 2005 WL 1607460 (Ohio Ct. App. June 30, 2005) (applying parol evidence rule to exclude evidence of oral misrepresentations that insurance was required).

424 *In re* Bogan, 281 F. Supp. 242, 251 (W.D. Tenn. 1968).

Because credibility likely will be an issue in such cases, it is important to have buttressing evidence. A good source for suggestions as to the type of corroborative evidence which may be probative is found in *In re USLIFE* and other Federal Trade Commission enforcement cases.[425] Among the factors considered by the FTC, as well as other courts and regulators looking at coerced insurance sales are:

- The creditor's penetration rate (i.e., that portion of loans which include insurance). In the case of USLIFE, the penetration rate on credit life was 80–90%.[426] The penetration rate has been a factor in usury cases, as well.[427]
- The creditor's pecuniary interest in making the sale.[428]
- A practice of including insurance in quoting monthly repayment figures to prospective borrowers.[429]
- The automatic pre-inclusion of premiums in loan documents.[430]

425 *In re* USLIFE Credit Corp. & USLIFE Corp., 91 F.T.C. 984, Consumer Cred. Guide CCH ¶ 97,938 (1978), *modified on other grounds*, 92 F.T.C. 353 (1978), *rev'd on other grounds* 599 F.2d 1387 (5th Cir. 1979).

426 *In re* USLIFE Credit Corp. & USLIFE Corp., 91 F.T.C. 984, 996, Consumer Cred. Guide CCH ¶ 97,938 (1978), *modified on other grounds*, 92 F.T.C. 353 (1978), *rev'd on other grounds* 599 F.2d 1387 (5th Cir. 1979).

427 Aclin Ford v. Cordell, 625 S.W.2d 459 (Ark. 1982) (salesman denied telling consumer insurance was required, but had a 100% penetration rate on his credit sales). *But cf. In re* Milbourne, 108 B.R. 522 (Bankr. E.D. Pa. 1989) (in case alleging coerced life and disability insurance purchase as TILA and UDAP violation, court declined to find a 99.55% penetration rate of credit life as per se proof of required purchase without knowing why it was not sold on the other 0.45% of loans; court also troubled by a complete lack of data on penetration rate concerning credit disability insurance).

428 *In re* USLIFE Credit Corp. & USLIFE Corp., 91 F.T.C. 984, 1027, Consumer Cred. Guide CCH ¶ 97,938 (1978), *modified on other grounds*, 92 F.T.C. 353 (1978), *rev'd on other grounds* 599 F.2d 1387 (5th Cir. 1979); Aclin Ford v. Cordell, 625 S.W.2d 459, 461 (Ark. 1982).

One court has suggested in dicta that a consumer alleging coerced insurance purchases made a strategic error in failing to plead causes of action predicated upon the creditor's profit from the insurance. *In re* Milbourne, 108 B.R. 522, 540, 543 n.8 (Bankr. E.D. Pa. 1989).

*Note*: when doing discovery on this element, it is important to learn *all* of the profit sources, not just front-end commissions, and to ask about both corporate profit and profit to individual loan officers. *See* § 6.2, *supra*. Counsel for borrowers in Hawkins v. Thorp Credit & Thrift Co., 441 N.W.2d 470 (Minn. 1989) (*see* § 6.7.3, *infra*) calculated that the creditor made almost 100% profit on $48 million worth of sales on one insurance product when increased interest return, commissions, and profits received through reinsurance agreements were considered.

429 *In re* USLIFE Credit Corp. & USLIFE Corp., 91 F.T.C. 984, 1024–1025, Consumer Cred. Guide CCH ¶ 97,938 (1978), *modified on other grounds*, 92 F.T.C. 353 (1978), *rev'd on other grounds* 599 F.2d 1387 (5th Cir. 1979). *See also Equity Predators: Stripping, Flipping and Packing Their Way to Profits: Hearing Before the Special Committee on Aging United States Senate*, 105th Cong. 2d Sess. 33–34, Serial No. 105-18 (Mar. 16, 1998) (statement of Jim Dough, former employee of predatory lender).

430 *In re* USLIFE Credit Corp. & USLIFE Corp., 91 F.T.C. 984, 1024–1025, Consumer Cred. Guide CCH ¶ 97,938 (1978), *modified on other grounds*, 92 F.T.C. 353 (1978), *rev'd on other grounds* 599

- Placing a "x" by the authorization signature line or otherwise indicating the borrower should sign it.[431]
- Presenting pre-typed loan agreements for signature without disclosing the purpose of the signature.[432]
- Suggesting the loan may be delayed if the borrower does not purchase the insurance.[433]

The training given by the company to loan officers as to how to make insurance sales may stress just such factors as the FTC considered coercive in *USLIFE*. Employees may feel pressured to achieve high penetration rates. In *USLIFE*, loan officers testified that they were under standing orders not to write uninsured loans.[434] Former employees of companies involved in some insurance packing investigations have reported pressure on the job to achieve high penetration rates.[435] Some said they were fired because they did not meet insurance sales performance standards.[436] A fertile ground for disaffected ex-employees is to look for wrongful discharge lawsuits brought against the creditor. Seeking discovery of any job evaluations of the loan officer who closed the loan may be helpful, as it may indicate whether he or she was under pressure which could lead to coercive selling tactics.

A creditor's "going over" loan documents with the borrower, that is, explaining the insurance charges pre-included in the documents, does not negate the inherent coercion, but may reinforce the notion that the insurance is required.[437] One court held that a TILA[438] or UDAP[439] claim predicated upon an allegation that the credit insurance purchase was compulsory required proof of two elements: 1) the lender affirmatively represented, by words or conduct, that insurance was required in fact, and 2) the borrower purchased insurance as a result of the lender's action which he or she otherwise would not have done. The borrower further should be permitted to introduce evidence to prove those elements, despite the existence of a signed voluntariness disclosure executed pursuant to TILA or a similar state law.[440]

Before seeking production of documents or doing a deposition, the consumer's attorney should perform some informal investigation. Annual reports filed by the companies can be informative about the corporate relationship between the creditor and insurer, if any, and, in gross terms, about the relative profitability of the various corporate entities. These reports may be filed with the state insurance agency or may be available at university or public libraries.

Corroborative evidence of coercive sales practices also may be found in the testimony of borrowers other than the client. The client may know of other borrowers who may have had a similar experience with the same creditor. Attorneys who specialize in consumer matters may hear the same complaints from several clients regarding a particular lender.

---

F.2d 1387 (5th Cir. 1979); FRB Letter No. 1286, excerpts published in Truth in Lending, Special Releases—Correspondence, Apr. 1969 to Oct. 1978, ¶ 31,777 (CCH) (1979). *See also* Lemelledo v. Beneficial Mgmt., 674 A.2d 582 (N.J. Super. Ct. App. Div. 1996), *aff'd on other grounds*, 696 A.2d 546 (N.J. 1997); *Equity Predators: Stripping, Flipping and Packing Their Way to Profits: Hearing Before the Special Committee on Aging United States Senate*, 105th Cong. 2d Sess. 33–34, Serial No. 105-18 (Mar. 16, 1998) (statement of Jim Dough, former employee of predatory lender).

431 *In re* USLIFE Credit Corp. & USLIFE Corp., 91 F.T.C. 984, 1029–1030, Consumer Cred. Guide CCH ¶ 97,938 (1978), *modified on other grounds*, 92 F.T.C. 353 (1978), *rev'd on other grounds* 599 F.2d 1387 (5th Cir. 1979); W.T. Grant Co., 83 F.T.C. 1328, 1337 (1974) (consent order). *But cf.* Credithrift of Am., Inc. v. Whitley, 380 S.E.2d 489 (Ga. Ct. App. 1989) (holding that creditors' statement that "although they were not required by law to purchase certain insurance . . . as a practical matter they would probably not be approved for the loan unless the insurance was purchased" did not constitute fraudulent misrepresentation or a violation of the state fair business practices act. *Note*: the court's reasoning is viable only where creditors are legally free to deny credit if consumers refuse insurance, as Georgia law may have done. But in many, if not most jurisdictions, consumer credit regulation laws do not permit creditors to require credit life or disability insurance as a condition of receiving the loan, in which case this decision would be inapposite).

432 *In re* USLIFE Credit Corp. & USLIFE Corp., 91 F.T.C. 984, 1024, Consumer Cred. Guide CCH ¶ 97,938 (1978), *modified on other grounds*, 92 F.T.C. 353 (1978), *rev'd on other grounds* 599 F.2d 1387 (5th Cir. 1979).

433 FRB Letter No. 1286, excerpts published in Truth in Lending, Special Releases—Correspondence, Apr. 1969 to Oct. 1978, ¶ 31,777 (CCH) (1979). *See also* Lemelledo v. Beneficial Mgmt., 674 A.2d 582 (N.J. Super. Ct. App. Div. 1996), *aff'd on other grounds*, 696 A.2d 546 (N.J. 1997); *Equity Predators: Stripping, Flipping and Packing Their Way to Profits: Hearing Before the Special Committee on Aging United States Senate*, 105th Cong. 2d Sess. 33–34, Serial No. 105-18 (Mar. 16, 1998) (statement of Jim Dough, former employee of predatory lender).

434 *In re* USLIFE Credit Corp. & USLIFE Corp., 91 F.T.C. 984, 1026, Consumer Cred. Guide CCH ¶ 97,938 (1978), *modified on other grounds*, 92 F.T.C. 353 (1978), *rev'd on other grounds*, 599 F.2d 1387 (5th Cir. 1979). *But see* Dixon v. S&S Loan Serv. of Waycross, 754 F. Supp. 1567 (S.D. Ga. 1990) (parol evidence rule invoked to prevent claim of coerced non-credit insurance where preprinted contract form stated purchase is voluntary, despite discovery of internal memorandum stating all new loans must have it).

435 *See Equity Predators: Stripping, Flipping and Packing Their Way to Profits: Hearing Before the Special Committee on Aging United States Senate*, 105th Cong. 2d Sess. 33–34, Serial No. 105-18 (Mar. 16, 1998) (statement of Jim Dough, former employee of predatory lender).

436 Bogdanich, *Unwanted Extras: Irate Borrowers Accuse ITT's Loan Companies of Deceptive Practices*, Wall St. J., Feb. 26, 1985 at 1, col. 1, 22.

437 *In re* USLIFE Credit Corp. & USLIFE Corp., 91 F.T.C. 984, 1028, Consumer Cred. Guide CCH ¶ 97,938 (1978), *modified on other grounds*, 92 F.T.C. 353 (1978), *rev'd on other grounds*, 599 F.2d 1387 (5th Cir. 1979).

438 *See* § 6.5.3, *supra*.

439 *See* § 6.5.5, *supra*.

440 *In re* Milbourne, 108 B.R. 522 (Bankr. E.D. Pa. 1989). *Note*: It is arguable that, at least as to the UDAP claim, that second element imposes a reliance requirement, though most UDAP statutes use a tendency to deceive standard. *See* National Consumer Law Center, Unfair and Deceptive Acts and Practices § 4.2.2 (7th ed. 2008 and Supp.). *See also* Hager v. American Gen. Fin., Inc., 37 F. Supp. 2d 778 (S.D. W. Va. 1999) (disagreeing with *USLIFE* finding that if a lender misrepresents to its customers that insurance is required, even though the loan contracts unequivocally state that the purchase of insurance is optional, a violation of the TILA may be established; unconscionability claim raised on other grounds).

# 6.6 Excessive Cost of Credit Insurance

## *6.6.1 Calculating Credit Insurance Charges*

### 6.6.1.1 Introduction

There are at least three ways in which a creditor can overcharge for credit insurance. One is to charge a premium rate higher than that permitted by law or regulation.[441] Another is to purchase insurance coverage in excess of that allowable under the law or necessary to protect the loan. Finally, a level life policy may be sold where a decreasing life policy is required.

To check for an overcharge of these types, it is necessary to understand how the premium amount on any given credit insurance policy is calculated. The formulas discussed in subsequent sections apply where the insurance rates are expressed as x¢ per $100 per annum (life) or x¢ per $100 (A&H) in the regulation or statute, and the borrower pays a single premium charge. They will not work in certain states where the rates are determined by more complicated formulas.[442] Nor will they work with an outstanding balance rate, usually expressed as a " 'per thousand dollars per month' rate,"[443] or where the coverage provided by the insurance provides only net payoff coverage.[444]

### 6.6.1.2 Credit Life

The statute, regulation, or other administrative ruling establishing the approved rates for credit life insurance will usually couch the rate in terms of the cost per $100 of the obligation per year, e.g., 65¢/$100/year. The insurance is usually written to insure the total of payments on a closed-end loan, which includes both the anticipated interest and the insurance premiums themselves.

This in itself is an overcharge in an economic sense, though legal in most states. It is excessive because more insurance is sold than is needed. At any time before the last payment is made, the outstanding balance includes unearned interest, which must be rebated if the account is paid before maturity.[445] If the borrower dies before the loan matures, the loan is prepaid. The coverage thus includes the unearned interest, coverage the borrower does not need. The policies, and many state laws, require that the difference be paid to the estate of the borrower. Often the family does not realize that there is extra money due and creditors or insurance companies do not voluntarily pay back this difference. The practice of writing insurance on the total of payments (called "gross coverage") is, however, valid in most states, though some require net coverage.[446] The Vermont Supreme Court upheld the validity of such a regulation under Vermont's revision of the NAIC Model Credit Insurance Act.[447]

The Model NAIC Act provides that the initial amount of credit life insurance cannot exceed the total amount repayable under the contract of indebtedness,[448] and indebtedness is further defined to mean the total amount repayable.[449] Thus the formula below uses the term "total of payments," as TILA defines it, because that generally is equal to the initial insured indebtedness.

---

441 *See, e.g.*, Smith v. Tower Loan of Miss., Inc., 216 F.R.D. 338 (S.D. Miss. 2003) (discussing the filed-rate doctrine in approving a class action settlement for various credit insurance abuses and holding that the doctrine bars allegations of excessive rates), *aff'd*, 91 Fed. Appx. 952 (5th Cir. 2004).

442 Such as the decremental rate. *See* Financial Publishing Co., The Cost of Personal Borrowing 44–45 (1998).

443 *Id.* at 43–44.

This method of calculation is commonly used in connection with open-end credit. Fagg, Credit Life and Disability Insurance 487 (1986).

444 Net payoff coverage covers net indebtedness plus accrued interest. Fagg, Credit Life and Disability Insurance 14 (1986). *See also* Financial Publishing Co., The Cost of Personal Borrowing 46–49 (1998).

445 *See generally* § 5.8, *supra*.

446 Mary Griffin & Birny Birnbaum, Consumers Union and the Center for Economic Justice, Credit Insurance: The $2 Billion a Year Rip-Off 23 (Mar. 1999). *See, e.g.*, Me. Rev. Stat. tit. 24-A, § 2855(1)(A); N.Y. Comp. Codes R. & Regs. tit. 11, § 185.6(2)(1); 21-020-006 Vt. Code R. § 3(10); Wash. Rev. Code § 48.34.060 (for group coverage). *See also* Dixon v. Ford Motor Credit, 2000 U.S. Dist. LEXIS 7934 (E.D. La. May 31, 2000) (allegations that Louisiana law mandates net coverage, that the terms of the insurance were not properly disclosed, and that excessive commissions were paid to sell the insurance product warrants denial of motion for summary judgment on RICO claim), *subsequent proceedings*, 137 F. Supp. 2d 702 (E.D. La. 2000) (RICO claim dismissed; supplemental state law claims dismissed); Gartman v. The Indep. Life & Accident Ins. Co., 1998 U.S. Dist. LEXIS 22069 (S.D. Ala. Oct. 9, 1998) (class certified, by consent, in case challenging insurance charges based on total of payments, relying on McCullar decision); Singleton v. Protective Life Ins. Co., 857 So. 2d 803 (Ala. 2003) (applying *McCullar* and finding that borrowers failed to establish sale of excess insurance where net coverage was sold and finding that state rate requirements were followed); McCullar v. Universal Underwriters Life Ins. Co., 687 So. 2d 156 (Ala. 1996) (plurality) (Alabama law requires net coverage, though regulatory agencies had been interpreting it to permit gross coverage). *But see* Gall v. American Heritage Life Ins. Co., 3 F. Supp. 2d 1344 (S.D. Ala. 1998) (stating it is not bound by plurality in *McCullar* and, agreeing with the dissent, finding that insurance can be calculated on the total of payments); Robertson v. PHF Life Ins. Co., 702 So. 2d 555 (Fla. Dist. Ct. App. 1997) (Florida law permitted calculation based on the total of payments); Liberty Bank & Trust Co. v. Splane, 959 P.2d 600 (Okla. Civ. App. 1998) (construing provision in U.C.C.C. restricting the amount of the permissible credit insurance to that which does not "exceed the debt" and another provision in Oklahoma insurance law restricting the amount of such insurance to "the approximate unpaid balance of the loan" to allow insurance premiums to be calculated on the total of payments; court specifically rejects the plurality in *McCullar*).

447 Consumer Credit Ins. Admin. v. Vermont, 544 A.2d 1159 (Vt. 1988).

448 Model Bill to Provide for the Regulation of Credit Life Ins. and Credit Accident and Health Ins., National Ass'n of Ins. Comm'rs, Model Regulatory Service § 4A(1) (NIARS Corp. 1984). *But cf.* NAIC Consumer Credit Insurance Model Act § 4(A) (1994) (NAIC model act now would mandate net coverage).

449 Model Bill to Provide for the Regulation of Credit Life Ins. and Credit Accident and Health Ins., National Association of Ins. Commissioners, Model Regulatory Service § 2B(5) (NIARS Corp. 1984). *See* Winkle v. Grand Nat'l Bank, 601 S.W.2d 559 (Ark. 1980).

However, in some cases, the initial insured indebtedness will differ from the total of payments. In that situation the initial insured indebtedness should be substituted for the total of payments in the formula. This may occur, for example, if the loan is for a term longer than a legally permissible term for credit insurance, or if the loan amount exceeds the amount of permissible coverage under group insurance laws. Another example is if the full term of the loan takes the borrower past his or her 66th birthday, an age beyond which many credit insurers will not insure debtors. The certificate of insurance will state the amount of initial insured indebtedness.

Where credit life rates are expressed in dollars or cents per $100 per year, the rate may be calculated for a particular transaction by dividing the premium (that is, the amount charged for credit life insurance in that transaction) by the number of years in the transaction. That number (or premium per year) is then divided by the total amount repayable. Finally, that figure (or the premium per dollar per year) is multiplied times 100, resulting in the rate per hundred per year. This computation may be expressed by the following formula:[450]

$$\text{Rate per \$100 per year} = \frac{\text{Premium}}{\text{Years in a Transaction}} \times \frac{100}{\text{Total of Payments}}.$$

It is important to check the certificate of insurance to confirm the term of the insurance. For instance, a forty-five-day first payment period on a two year loan under some state laws may be charged as a twenty-five-month transaction. Where, as in such a case, the transaction involves parts of years, substitute for years the number of months divided by 12. Therefore, the formula may be written:[451]

$$\text{Rate per \$100 per year} = \frac{\text{Premium} \times 12}{\text{Months in Transaction}} \times \frac{100}{\text{Total of Payments}}.$$

An example may be helpful. The state authorizes a credit life rate of 65¢/$100/year for single, declining term coverage. A $210.60 credit life premium was charged on a six year loan with a Total of Payments of $5,400. To determine the propriety of that premium, the calculation would be:

$$\frac{\text{\$210.60 (Premium)}}{\text{6 (Years of Transaction)}} \times \frac{100}{\text{\$5,400 (Total of Payments)}} = 65¢/\$100/\text{year}.$$

The rate charged is at the maximum rate allowed.

One might also wish to use an alternative formula to calculate what the maximum allowable premium would be for a given transaction. That formula is:[452]

$$\text{Maximum Premium} = \frac{\text{Legal Max. Rate} \times \text{Yrs. of Transaction} \times \text{Total of Payments}}{100}$$

The answer is then compared to the premium actually charged to derive the amount of an overcharge, if any. In the example above, the maximum legal premium could be derived as follows:

$$\frac{65¢ \times 6 \times \$5,400}{100} = \$210.60.$$

As that was the amount actually charged, there was no overcharge.

In comparing the premium rate actually charged to the legally allowable rate, it is, of course necessary to be sure one is comparing the appropriate rate. Thus one must check the certificate of insurance to see if the insurance is single or joint, declining or level.[453] The legal rate for joint life may be separately established at a specific amount, e.g., $1.07/$100/year, or it may be listed as an adjustment factor to be derived from the single life coverage. If the latter, one must do yet another calculation. To check the authorized rate for joint life, where an adjustment factor is given, multiply the factor times the legal single coverage rate. For example, if the legal rate for single life is 60¢/$100/yr., and the adjustment factor for joint life is 1.50%, the allowable joint life rate is:

$$60¢ \times 1.50 = 90¢/\$100/\text{year}.$$

If the insurance sold is a level life policy, there may be an overcharge even if the rate per se is authorized, as many states do not permit level credit life in consumer transactions.[454]

### 6.6.1.3 Credit Accident and Health

Approved rates for credit accident and health, also called credit disability insurance, are generally derived from estimates as to what rate will result in a specified target loss-ratio.[455] There are different kinds of disability coverage: retroactive and non-retroactive; seven-, fourteen-, or thirty-day waiting periods or elimination periods,[456] each with its own approved rate. If these rates are not published in the state administrative code, they are likely to be the subject of an insurance department bulletin or directive, which can be obtained from the insurance department. Financial Publishing Company, *The Cost of Personal Borrowing* summarizes credit insurance rates for all states.[457]

It is important to know what type of coverage was written in order to compare the rate charged with the applicable legal rate. That information usually can be obtained from the certificate of insurance. The policy most commonly sold is fourteen-day retroactive policy, and this may be used as a first guess because

450 Substitute "initial insured indebtedness" if that amount is different from the loan "total of payments." That figure may be obtained by checking the certificate of insurance, which should have been given to the borrower.

451 Model Bill to Provide for the Regulation of Credit Life Ins. and Credit Accident and Health Ins., National Association of Ins. Commissioners, Model Regulatory Service § 2B(5) (NIARS Corp. 1984).

452 *Id.*

453 *See* § 6.3.1.2, *supra.*

454 *See* § 6.6.3.1, *infra.*

455 *See* § 6.4.2, *supra.*

456 *See* § 6.3.3, *supra.*

457 *See* § 1.1.6, *supra.*

it has the highest allowable premium in most states. (A seven-day, or even three-day, retroactive policy is more expensive, but it is rarely sold because many states do not allow it). Of course, later the consumer attorney will have to confirm through discovery or otherwise what coverage was actually sold to the client.

Disability policies, and the approved rates, are based on the full term of the transaction, not on a yearly basis. The rates are set on a sliding scale which establishes a maximum rate per hundred dollars for loans of various lengths; the longer the loan, the higher the rate, though the increase generally is not proportional.[458] In most states the rates are expressed in dollars per $100 of loan. The formula below will not work in states with more complex rate structures.

As with credit life, the amount of coverage usually is based on the total of payments as TILA defines the term. To find the rate charged, the disability premium is divided by the total of payments, and that figure is multiplied by 100.

$$\frac{\text{A \& H Premium}}{\text{Total of Payments}} \times = \text{Rate Charged}$$

An example may be helpful. Consider a disability premium of $53.28 on a three-year loan with a total of payments of $1,296.00. To determine the rate that was charged, the calculation is:

$$\frac{\$53.28}{\$1{,}296.00} \times 100 = \$4.11.$$

Assume the state has in effect a rate schedule as described in note 458, *supra*. The appropriate rate for a fourteen-day retroactive policy on a three-year loan would then be $3.80. Therefore, there appears to be an overcharge.

To determine the amount of the apparent excess charge, one can use this formula to determine the maximum legal premium:

$$\text{Max. Premium} = \frac{\text{Legal Max. Rate} \times \text{Total of Payments}}{100}$$

In this example, the calculation would be:

$$\frac{\$3.80 \text{ (legal Max. Rate)} \times \$1{,}296 \text{ (Total of Payments)}}{100} = \$49.25.$$

Therefore, there may have been an overcharge of $4.03 ($53.28–$49.25).

However, there is one more step to take before determining if there is an excess charge. If the calculations reveal an overcharge, contact the insurance department to see if that insurer has been granted an upward deviation. If so, the rate as authorized by the deviation is the maximum allowable rate, not the rate on the regular schedules. To see if it is within the authorized deviated rate, the authorized deviation rate is substituted for the "legal maximum rate" in the above formula.

The insurance department, upon inquiry about an upward deviation, simply may supply the authorized rate for that type of coverage, saying, for example, that Calm Yourself Insurance Co. may charge $4.02/$100 for fourteen-day retroactive coverage on a three-year loan. Or, the insurance department may force the practitioner back to the calculator by authorizing a uniform percentage increase to all the authorized rates on the standard chart. For example, a 125% upward deviation, applied to fourteen-day retro coverage on a three-year loan in the state described in note 458, *supra,* would be calculated as follows:

$$3.80 \times 1.25 = \$4.75.$$

Insurance could charge $4.75/$100 for this coverage on this three year loan.

It may turn out that the approval of that deviation is subject to challenge, if it results in a return that exceeds the target loss ratio.[459] That is a separate legal challenge and probably would not support a usury claim on a transaction written while it was authorized by the insurance department.[460]

### 6.6.1.4 Credit Property Insurance

Credit property insurance generally is not subject to rate regulation. However, the borrower may have purchased excess coverage,[461] which could give rise to an overcharge claim. It may be a simple matter to determine the amount of coverage by referring to the certificate of property insurance. However, if the certificate of insurance is unavailable, or if it does not contain the amount of coverage, the practitioner may have to try to calculate the amount of coverage sold.

Unlike credit life or disability, there may be two unknowns in the mathematical equation for credit property insurance, so some preliminary inquiries must be made. Since there usually is no rate regulation, a rate must be determined to use in the formula. A call to the insurance department staffer who works with credit insurance can yield information about the most common rates used in the state for credit property. If the practitioner knows the name of the insurer, the insurance department probably can supply the rate used by that company.[462] The certificate of insurance or the master policy may also state the rate on its face, and this rate should then be used.

458 For example, a state may have approved a rate scale of fourteen-day retroactive coverage similar to the following:

| Length of Loan | Max. Rate Per $100 of Total of Payments |
|---|---|
| 1–12 months | $2.20/$100 |
| 13–24 months | $3.00/$100 |
| 25–36 months | $3.80/$100 |
| 37–48 months | $4.30/$100 |
| 49–60 months | $4.70/$100 |

For longer terms, the insurance department rule usually will specify the adjustment factor.

459 *See* § 6.4.2, *supra.*

460 Keniston v. American Nat'l Ins. Co., 107 Cal. Rptr. 583, 588 (Cal. Ct. App. 1973).

461 *See* § 6.6.4, *infra.*

462 The insurance department may even know which insurance is with a particular transaction simply from the identity of the creditor.

The second unknown is the amount of coverage. Unlike credit life and A&H, one should not assume that the coverage is equivalent to the total of payments, though it may be. Because some insurers have a minimum amount of coverage available, e.g., $1,000, a borrower may pay for $1,000 of insurance coverage even though the total of payments on the loan may be only $750.

After having obtained from the client's insurance documents or from the insurance department the rate/$100/year charged by the company, the formula to determine the amount of coverage is:

$$\text{Amount of coverage} = \frac{\text{Premium} \times 100}{\text{Rate} \times \text{Number of years}}.$$

Consider an example: a charge for household contents insurance of $60 was made on a two-year loan with a total of payments of $576. The insurance policy stated that the rate was $2 per $100 per year. To determine the amount of coverage the consumer purchased, the formula is:

$$\frac{\$60\text{ (premium)} \times 100}{\$2\text{ (rate)} \times 2\text{ (term of loan)}} = \$1{,}500\text{ Amount of Coverage.}$$

This consumer purchased $1,500 of property insurance coverage on a total of payments of $576. Though the insurance department does not regulate the property insurance rate, state credit laws may in some fashion require property insurance to relate to the loan amount. If that is the case, this property insurance may be an excessive charge.[463]

## 6.6.2 Excess Premium Charges As Usury

### 6.6.2.1 General

In most circumstances, the statutory foundation for a claim for an excessive credit insurance charge is found in the credit statute applicable to the credit transaction in question rather than in the credit insurance code. The NAIC Model Act provides that insurers shall not issue a policy "for which the premium rate exceeds that determined by the schedules of such insurer as then on file with the Commissioner,"[464] and that the amount then charged to a debtor "shall not exceed the premiums charged by the insurer."[465] However, in most states the credit insurance code regulates the insurers, not the creditors, and there is usually no direct private remedy granted to insured debtors under the credit insurance codes.[466]

When read together with the law governing the credit transaction, however, most state statutory schemes should support a claim against the creditor under the consumer credit statute. Many of the comprehensive consumer credit codes which govern creditors, for example, include some variation on language that limits the charge to the debtor to the authorized premium permitted for such coverage,[467] or exclude from the definition of finance charge only premiums for "permissible" or "authorized" insurance.[468] Some statutes specifically provide that an excess premium charge is subject to the penalties prescribed for excess charges generally.[469]

Small loan, industrial loan or consumer loan acts may specifically authorize the imposition of credit insurance premiums only under specified conditions.[470] Since many such special usury statutes prohibit any charges except "as authorized,"[471] if all the prescribed conditions are not met, including any incorporated rate or coverage limitations or voluntariness requirements, the premiums should be an unauthorized charge.[472] Most RISA[473] and industrial loan[474] statutes are similarly structured to prohibit creditors from charging debtors for insurance premiums in excess of the rates authorized by the insurance department.

If a special usury statute is silent as to whether insurance premiums are authorized, an argument can be made that the debtor cannot be charged at all for insurance premiums,[475]

463 *See* §§ 6.4.5, *supra*, 6.6.3, *infra*.

464 Model Bill to Provide for the Regulation of Credit Life Ins. and Credit Accident and Health Ins., National Ass'n of Ins. Comm'rs, Model Regulatory Service § 8(A) (NIARS Corp. 1984).

465 *Id.* § 8(D).

466 *See, e.g.,* Cope v. Aetna Fin. Co. of Maine, 412 F.2d 635, 640 (1st Cir. 1969); Jennings v. Globe Life & Accident Ins. Co., 922 P.2d 622 (Okla. 1996) (also rejecting the creative argument that the Oklahoma version of the U.C.C.C. provided a private right of action to enforce violations of regulations promulgated by the Insurance Commissioner; the U.C.C.C. is specifically limited to "creditor" not "insurer" violations).

467 *E.g.*, Ala. Code § 5-19-20; Colo. Rev. Stat. § 5-4-107(1); Kan. Stat. Ann. § 16a-4-107(1); La. Rev. Stat. Ann. § 9:3545; U.C.C.C. § 4-107(1) (1968 and 1974).

468 *E.g.*, Ala. Code § 5-19-1(1). *Cf.* Kenty v. Bank One, Columbus, N.A., 1992 WL 170605 (S.D. Ohio Apr. 23, 1992), *aff'd in part, rev'd in part on other grounds*, 92 F.3d 384 (6th Cir. 1996) (cost in force-placed insurance premium for unauthorized coverage and coverage unnecessary to protect the collateral is interest under the National Bank Act (*NB*: This type of insurance is not subject to credit insurance statute. Court relied on common law principles.)).

469 U.C.C.C. § 4-104(2) (1968 and 1974); Colo. Rev. Stat. § 5-4-104(2); Kan. Stat. Ann. § 16a-4-104; La. Rev. Stat. Ann. § 9:3552 (penalties for violating the provisions of Consumer Credit Law).

Under the U.C.C.C., there are additional requirements which must be met as well to insulate insurance premiums from a usury claim §§ 2-202 (1968), 3-202 (1968), 2-501 (1974).

470 *E.g.*, Ariz. Rev. Stat. Ann. § 6-636; Conn. Gen. Stat. § 36a-566.

471 *E.g.*, Conn. Gen. Stat. § 36a-563(h).

472 Dickinson v. Buck, 220 So. 2d 48, 51 (Fla. Dist. Ct. App. 1969) (insurance commissions authorized only under circumstances authorized by law).

473 *E.g.*, Alaska Stat. § 45.10.130; Del. Code Ann. tit. 6, § 4307.

474 *E.g.*, Iowa Code § 536A.23.

475 *Ex parte* New Fin., Ltd., 225 So. 2d 784 (Ala. 1969) (small loan act); Sunderland v. Day, 145 N.E.2d 39 (Ill. 1957); Home Fin. Co. v. Padgett, 54 So. 2d 813, 817 (La. Ct. App. 1951); Hawkins v. Thorp Credit & Thrift Co., 441 N.W.2d 470 (Minn. 1989) (non-credit life insurance not authorized under state regulated loan act, see § 6.7.3, *infra*, for further discussion of this case). *See also* Moran v. American Funding, Ltd., 569 A.2d 841, 842 (N.J. Super. Ct. Ch. Div. 1989) (at issue a prior version of New Jersey's second mortgage act under which title insurance was not a specifically authorized charge and therefore was prohibited by the catch-all provision preventing the creditor from receiving anything other than "charges authorized by this Act"); Garrison v. First Fed. Saving &

though the majority of courts have allowed them, in the absence of lender profit, as a third-party expense.[476] Since most special usury statutes now specifically refer to credit life, disability, and property, this issue may arise only with respect to non-traditional insurances, such as involuntary unemployment insurance, or non-credit insurance policies, such as term life or accidental death and dismemberment policies not insuring the debt.[477]

Usury claims must be developed through discovery, and evidence should be presented as to the lender's profit and role in selecting the insurer. In some instances, courts refuse to hold creditors liable for improper or unauthorized credit insurance charges on the grounds that the creditor merely passes through the premiums to a third party—the insurer. In this view, premiums do not represent compensation retained by the creditor.[478] Similarly, at least one court has implied that creditors might not be liable for excess premiums if the insurer sets the premiums.[479] In addition, claims of excessive insurance premiums may first have to be raised administratively with the Insurance Commissioner rather than through judicial channels.[480]

There are several flaws in such analyses. First, many special usury statutes focus on those charges which the borrower must pay, rather than on what charges the lender receives.[481] For example, if the statute prohibits a licensed lender from "charging, collecting or receiving" any charges except those specifically authorized, then merely "charging" the borrower the unauthorized amount is a violation of the statute. This interpretation is recognized in a number of cases under small loan acts which find usury even where the illegal amounts were never paid, because the act prohibits "charging" or "contracting for" any charges not specifically authorized.[482]

In addition, to look at credit insurance premiums simply as a charge passed through to a third party, while ignoring compensation retained by the lender, is to ignore the realities of the substantial profit accruing to lenders in the sale of insurance.[483] The consumer's attorney, to be safe, should always present evidence concerning the full extent of creditor compensation.

Similarly, cases which suggest that the creditor should have no liability where an excess rate is set by the insurer also ignore the business realities of the creditor-insurer relationship. The First Circuit, recognizing the ease with which such a dichotomous view could facilitate an evasion of the law, held that the creditor was liable where there was essentially a joint decision because of a captive insurer relationship.[484] The evidence showed that "in essence, the [parent company] commanded its wholly owned insurance subsidiary to set a rate and its own wholly owned loan company to pass it on."[485]

Even outside the captive insurer (or captive lender) situation, the creditor is not isolated from the decision making. The creditor chooses the insurance it sells to its customers. The reverse competition phenomenon is a large part of the reason a creditor selects among the independent insurers competing for its business: the higher the premium, the higher the creditors' commission.[486] Since corporate lenders are well aware of the prevailing legal limits on credit insurance charges, they should not escape liability for choosing non-compliant insurers, especially since the lender retains the consequent excessive commissions.

Normal usury analysis supports this view. "Reasonable" third-party expenses may not be considered interest.[487] However, it is not a "reasonable" expense if it is in excess of that authorized by law. Use discovery to determine why the creditor chose or retained a particular insurer, and what efforts the creditor routinely makes to be sure the insurer is operating within the law.

---

Loan Ass'n of S.C., 402 S.E.2d 24 (Va. 1991) (risk management fee was not specifically authorized, and thus constituted excess interest); Opinion of the Michigan Att'y Gen., No. 6594, 5 Consumer Cred. Guide (CCH) ¶ 95,775 (July 17, 1989) (MVRISA statute did not authorize any charges other than those specifically itemized, therefore documentary fees, service fees or inspection fees imposed on installment buyers of cars as part of cash price of car were prohibited charges).

476 *See* cases cited in *In re* Richards, 272 F. Supp. 480, 485 n.12 (D. Me. 1967), *rev'd on other grounds and remanded*, 412 F.2d 635 (1st Cir. 1969), *on remand* 304 F. Supp. 817 (1969). *Cf.* Jones v. Jones, 301 S.W.2d 737 (Ark. 1957) (credit insurance premium charge in excess of actual cost of insurance purchased was interest).

477 *See* § 6.5.6, *supra*. After initially running into trouble with at least two states for selling involuntary unemployment credit insurance in the absence of authorizations, the industry has been successful in getting it statutorily authorized in a number of states.

478 *E.g.*, *In re* Galea'i, 31 B.R. 629 (Bankr. D. Haw. 1981); Universal C.I.T. Credit Corp. v. Lackey, 305 S.W.2d 858, 862 (Ark. 1957). *See also* General Motors Acceptance Corp. v. Baymon, 732 So. 2d 262 (Miss. 1999) (jury verdict for consumer for $35,000 in compensatory damages and $5 million in punitive damages reversed and remanded for new trial; grounds for mistrial to allow evidence of excessive profits, that rates amounted to "gouging" and that GMAC had manipulated the rate approval process).

479 Cope v. Aetna Fin. Co. of Maine, 412 F.2d 635, 642 (1st Cir. 1969) (dicta).

480 *See, e.g.*, State of W. Va. *ex rel.* Citifinancial, Inc. v. Madden, 672 S.E.2d 365 (W. Va. 2008) (granting a writ of prohibition preventing enforcement of lower court decision finding insurance rates were excessive because any such challenge must be brought before the state insurance commissioner).

481 Sunderland v. Day, 145 N.E.2d 39 (Ill. 1957). *See also* Vernon, *Regulated Credit Life and Disability Insurance and the Small Loan*, 29 N.Y.U.L. Rev. 1098, 1109 (1954).

482 *E.g.*, Clyde v. Liberty Loan Corp., 287 S.E.2d 551 (Ga. 1982); Danziger v. San Jacinto Sav. Ass'n, 732 S.W.2d 300, 303–304 (Tex. 1987) (pay-off quotation containing excessive interest constituted "charging" usurious interest); Nationwide Fin. Corp. v. English, 604 S.W.2d 458 (Tex. Civ. App. 1980). *See also* Kaiser Agr. Chems., Inc. v. Peters, 417 N.W.2d 437 (Iowa 1987) (general usury statute providing that no one shall "receive" excess interest does not require that the borrower actually pay it to establish a violation of the statute; "it is the agreement to exact and pay usurious interest," not the performance which renders it usurious). *See generally* § 7.6.1, *infra*.

483 *See* § 6.2, *supra*.

484 Cope v. Aetna Fin. Co. of Maine, 412 F.2d 635 (1st Cir. 1969), *on remand* 304 F. Supp. 817 (D. Me. 1969).

485 *Id.* 412 F.2d at 641.

486 *See* § 6.2.3.1, *supra*.

487 *See* § 4.5, *supra*.

Many times an excess premium amount is charged on a transaction not because the insurer has set an unauthorized rate, but because the creditor's calculations include an excess amount. In such cases, it is the creditor's liability, not the insurers.

#### 6.6.2.2 Creditor Compensation As Interest

A number of early cases considered whether credit insurance premiums constituted usury under state small loan acts. As phrased in the Uniform Small Loan Law:

> In addition to the interest herein provided for, no further or other charge or amount for any examination, service, brokerage, expense, fee, or bonus or otherwise shall be directly or indirectly charged, contracted for, or received.[488]

The Small Loan Act was generally construed strictly, and such language precluded the imposition of any charge not specifically authorized, including credit insurance premiums.[489] This strict language, moreover, raised the related question of whether small loan licensees could retain commissions, even assuming the insurance sale was authorized. One early court allowed the creditor to require insurance as security, but held that it must be purchased from an outside insurer.[490] Some states permitted tie-in sales, but prohibited commissions;[491] others authorized them as compensation for services rendered.[492]

Perhaps in reaction to adverse legal developments, small loan acts were amended specifically to authorize credit life, disability and property insurance charges, to provide that the premiums were not considered interest, and that profit to the creditor from the insurance sale should not be considered interest.[493] However, this was also the era when regulation of credit insurance was strengthening, as with the adoption of the NAIC Model Credit Insurance Act, which required approval of premium rates. Such statutes must be read in *pari materia*, so that the rate regulation is not rendered meaningless. Thus the language of statutes which exclude insurance profits from the definition of interest can only be rationally interpreted to mean that authorized commissions from authorized insurance premiums are excluded from interest.[494]

Some states provided that the authorized premium was limited to the "actual cost of any premium paid."[495] Such language has been interpreted to mean the cost of insurance to the small loan licensee, exclusive of the licensee's profit.[496] One court noted that the authorized interest rate for small loan licensees is quite high as it is, and the legislature would have authorized additional commissions if it so desired.[497] Two state supreme courts have rejected that view, however, holding that premiums commonly encompass commissions, and creditors may charge the maximum premium rate irrespective of the commissions.[498]

Other states specifically regulate creditor profit; some clearly designate retained commissions as interest.[499] Nearly one half the states now have set limits on creditor compensation.[500] In a California case, the state's authority to impose such caps was

488 Sixth Draft of Uniform Small Loan Law § 13, *reprinted in* Hubacheck, Annotations on Small Loan Laws 70–80 (1938).

489 *Ex parte* New Fin., Ltd., 225 So. 2d 782, 784 (Ala. 1969); Sunderland v. Day, 145 N.E.2d 39 (Ill. 1957); Home Fin. v. Padgett, 54 So. 2d 813, 817 (La. Ct. App. 1951). *See also* Hawkins v. Thorp Credit & Thrift Co., 441 N.W.2d 470 (Minn. 1989) (interpreting Minnesota Regulated Loan Act, which evolved from the state's small loan act; court interpreted language restricting insurance sales to prohibit the sale of non-credit insurance). *See generally* § 7.2.1, *infra*.

A minority of states, however, allowed credit insurance premiums under the rationale that credit insurance was a collateral transaction for security.

490 Martorano v. Capitol Fin. Co., 43 N.E.2d 705 (N.Y. 1942). *See generally* Vernon, *Regulated Credit Life and Disability Insurance and the Small Loan*, 29 N.Y.U. L. Rev. 1098, 1109–1110 (1954); *Credit Insurance: Abuse and Reform*, 10 B.C. Ind. & Com. L. Rev. 439, 441–442 (1969).

491 *See* Mors, Small Loan Laws and Credit Insurance, 1954 Ins. L.J. 778, 792; Vernon, Regulated Credit Life and Disability Insurance and the Small Loan, 29 N.Y.U. L. Rev. 1098, 1117 n.80 (1954).

492 *Credit Insurance: Abuse and Reform*, 10 B.C. Ind. & Com. L. Rev. 439, 442 (1969).

493 *E.g.*, Ariz. Rev. Stat. Ann. § 6-636(H).

494 Cope v. Aetna Fin. Co. of Maine, 412 F.2d 635, 642 (1st Cir. 1969); Bank of Winnfield & Trust v. United States, 540 F. Supp. 219 (W.D. La. 1982) (fact that creditor is authorized to sell insurance does not implicitly authorize it to retain commissions from sales where such is prohibited); Hatridge v. Home Life & Accident Ins. Co., 246 S.W.2d 666 (Tex. Civ. App. 1951). *See also* Bailey v. Defenbaugh & Co. of Cleveland, Inc., 513 F. Supp. 232 (N.D. Miss. 1981); Browder v. Hanley-Dawson Cadillac, 379 N.E.2d 1206, 1212 (Ill. App. Ct. 1978) (claim survived motion to dismiss). *Cf.* Hawkins v. Thorp Credit & Thrift Co., 441 N.W.2d 470 (Minn. 1989) (sale of non-credit life insurance, not specifically authorized by the Regulated Loan Act, is prohibited).

495 *E.g.*, Miss. Code Ann. § 75-67-121.

496 Bailey v. Defenbaugh & Co. of Cleveland, Inc., 513 F. Supp. 232 (N.D. Miss. 1981). A similar claim survived a motion to dismiss in Browder v. Hanley-Dawson Cadillac, 379 N.E.2d 1206, 1212 (Ill. App. Ct. 1978).

497 Bailey v. Defenbaugh & Co. of Cleveland, Inc., 513 F. Supp. 232, 242, 243 (N.D. Miss. 1981).

498 Spears v. Colonial Bank of Alabama, 514 So. 2d 814 (Ala. 1987) (Ala. Code § 5-10-20 provides "[t]he charge to the debtor for any such insurance shall not exceed the authorized premium permitted for such coverages." Where premiums charged were within lawful maximum established by state banking department, fact that creditors received 50% commission from the premium did not violate § 5-19-20); Tew v. Dixieland Fin. Co., 527 So. 2d 665 (Miss. 1988) (creditor may charge maximum authorized premium rate under Small Loan Regulatory Law regardless of commission paid to creditor; premiums allowable are those "usually and customarily paid for life insurance" and it is customary for sellers in state to charge the maximum premium; also definition of premium may include commission to seller). *But cf. In re* Milbourne, 108 B.R. 522, 540, 543 n.8 (Bankr. E.D. Pa. 1989) (indicating in dicta that it was a strategic error on the borrower's part to fail to allege lender's receipt of substantial commissions as improper finance charges).

499 *See* Equitable Life Assurance Soc. of U.S. v. Ins. Comm., 246 A.2d 604 (Md. 1968).

500 California, Colorado, Georgia, Illinois, Indiana, Maine, Maryland, Massachusetts (only state chartered banks), Michigan, Mississippi, Missouri, Montana, Nebraska, Nevada, New York, Ohio, Oklahoma, Pennsylvania, South Dakota, Tennessee, Utah, Washington, Wyoming; Arkansas. *See* Fagg, Credit Life and Disability Insurance 534–536 (1986).

upheld.[501] The court held that the reverse compensation and captive market factors create influences "detrimental to insureds if left uncontrolled," and that limiting compensation is an appropriate means to assure that the insurance cost is reasonable in relation to the benefits.[502]

Apparently only a few states strictly enforce compensation caps,[503] so it is not improbable that these ceilings are being violated. If so, the excess commission would be unauthorized, and thus should be considered interest,[504] subject to whatever penalties are provided for excess charges.[505] If excessive compensation is retained by a small loan licensee, even a provision holding that profit from insurance sales is not deemed a violation of any other law would not immunize the lender. That provision must be read *in pari materia* with statutes regulating the cost of the insurance to mean that only authorized benefits from an authorized premium is excluded from interest.[506] Examining charges for force-placed property insurance (not a rate-regulated insurance), one court has held that the commissions, kickbacks or rebates given to the creditor from the premium are interest under the National Bank Act, as is interest on the excess premium.[507]

Another possible source of limitation on creditors' commissions may be found in insurance laws. The Mississippi insurance code, for example, prohibited acceptance of a commission by one not licensed as an insurance agent. Since a corporate-creditor could not be licensed as an insurance agent, the creditor could not retain the commissions. (The creditors generally had one or more employees licensed as agents, but it was the corporate creditor that retained the commissions, not the licensed individual agents, thereby violating the law). However, the court recognized that the legislature created a conflict in other legislation recognizing that corporate creditors do receive commissions from the sale of credit insurance. The court resolved the conundrum by holding that it was illegal for the unlicensed corporate creditor to receive the commissions, but making its ruling prospective, thus giving the legislature and administrative agencies time to adjust to the ruling.[508]

## 6.6.3 Excess Coverage As Illegal Overcharge

### 6.6.3.1 Level Term Credit Life Insurance

Even if premium rates are properly calculated, a usury claim may lie if the insurance coverage exceeds that permitted by law. Most states prohibit the writing of level term credit life insurance. The NAIC Model Act, for example, provides that where the debt "is repayable in substantially equal installments, the amount of insurance shall at no time exceed the scheduled or actual amount of unpaid indebtedness, whichever is greater."[509] Where a state prohibits level life policies, a creditor charging the borrower the higher level life premium would be charging in excess of that permitted by law, and thus would be vulnerable to a usury claim under the same analysis as if it were engaged in a rate overcharge.[510] If, however, the statute does not specifically prohibit level term, the courts are unlikely to infer such a prohibition.[511]

### 6.6.3.2 Amount of Coverage

Courts have long recognized that usury may exist when lenders charge borrowers for coverage in an amount "greater than the amount of the loan with a purpose of increasing the proportion of charges to the amount of money lent."[512] Some regulations similarly restrict credit life and disability coverage to the amount and term of the indebtedness.[513] This limitation is found in both the credit insurance codes,[514] and often in the special credit

501 Credit Ins. Gen. Agents Assoc. v. Payne, 148 Cal. Rptr. 141 (Cal. Ct. App. 1978).

502 *Id.* at 148 Cal. Rptr. 143–144. The captive market factor results because the borrower cannot shop for credit insurance. It is not sold separately from its related credit transaction, and the creditor generally offers only a single insurer. Furthermore, the borrower may be a poor credit risk with limited options. *Id.* at 143–144 n.2.

503 Fagg, Credit Life and Disability Insurance 377 (1986). *Cf.* Shellman v. Investors Nat'l Life Ins. Co., Clearinghouse No. 45,774 (Ga. Super. Ct., Richmond Cty. Aug. 16, 1990) (defendants' motion for summary judgment denied) (though Georgia has a 40% commission cap, evidence in connection with this summary judgment showed the defendant insurer paid 55% to 90% commissions to one of its creditors. The case and companion cases are discussed in more detail at § 6.4.2.4, *supra*).

504 *See* Bank of Winnfield & Trust v. United States, 540 F. Supp. 219 (W.D. La. 1982) (fact that creditor is authorized to sell insurance does not implicitly authorize it to retain commissions from sales where such is prohibited); Hatridge v. Home Life & Accident Ins. Co., 246 S.W.2d 666 (Tex. Civ. App. 1951). *See also* Bailey v. Defenbaugh & Co. of Cleveland, Inc., 513 F. Supp. 232 (N.D. Miss. 1981); Browder v. Hanley-Dawson Cadillac, 379 N.E.2d 1206, 1212 (Ill. Ct. App. 1978) (claim survived motion to dismiss).

505 In some jurisdictions, however, a violation of a regulation may not offer the same remedies as a statutory violation. *See, e.g.*, Robinson v. Central Loan & Fin. Corp., 609 F.2d 170 (5th Cir. 1980). *See generally* § 6.4.2.4, *supra* (another approach to challenging insurance charges with excessive commissions).

506 *Cf.* Cope v. Aetna Fin., 412 F.2d 635, 641–643 (1st Cir. 1969).

507 Kenty v. Bank One, Columbus, N.A., 1992 WL 170605 (S.D. Ohio Apr. 23, 1992), *aff'd in part, rev'd in part on other grounds*, 92 F.3d 384 (6th Cir. 1996).

The latter point recognizes that, since the capitalized premium contains hidden interest, the effect is to compound interest. *See* § 4.4, *supra*.

508 Tew v. Dixieland Fin., Inc., 527 So. 2d 665 (Miss. 1988).

509 Model Bill to Provide for the Regulation of Credit Life Ins. and Credit Accident and Health Ins., National Ass'n of Ins. Comm'rs, Model Regulatory Service § 4A(1) (NIARS Corp. 1984).

510 *See* § 6.6.2, *supra*.

511 Mason v. Service Loan & Fin. Co., 198 S.E.2d 391 (Ga. Ct. App. 1973).

512 Western Guar. Loan Co. v. Dean, 309 S.W.2d 857, 862 (Tex. Civ. App. 1957); Industrial Fin. Şerv. Co. v. Riley, 295 S.W.2d 498, 506 (Tex. Civ. App. 1956), *rev'd in part on other grounds*, 302 S.W.2d 652 (Tex. 1957).

513 *See, e.g.*, Richardson v. Bank of Am., 643 S.E.2d 410 (N.C. Ct. App. 2007) (upholding trial court finding that sale of single-premium credit insurance on loan with term beyond fifteen years violated state UDAP law and breached duty of good faith and fair dealing).

514 *E.g.*, Model Bill to Provide for the Regulation of Credit Life Ins. and Credit Accident and Health Ins., National Ass'n of Ins. Comm'rs,

regulatory laws.[515] Charges for any greater coverage would be in excess of that authorized by law, and therefore subject to penalties for excess charges applicable under the statute governing the transaction,[516] or common law claims.[517]

It is clear that the creditor, not the insurer is responsible for excessive coverage, unlike the situation with respect to excessive rates, where there is an argument that the insurer is responsible.[518] This is because the creditor is the one who determines the amount of coverage.

Model Regulatory Service §§ 4(A) (Life), 4(B) (A&H), 5 (Term) (NIARS Corp. 1984).

515 *E.g.*, Ala. Code §§ 5-18-17 (small loan), 5-19-20 (Credit Code). *See also* Gartman v. The Indep. Life & Accident Ins. Co., 1998 U.S. Dist. LEXIS 22069 (S.D. Ala. Oct. 9, 1998) (class certified, by consent, in case challenging insurance charges based on total of payments, relying on *McCullar* decision); McCullar v. Universal Underwriters Life Ins. Co., 687 So. 2d 156 (Ala. 1996) (plurality) (interpreting Ala. law to mandate net coverage, not gross coverage, as agencies had interpreted it) (the original opinion found at 1995 WL 577025 (Ala. 1995) was withdrawn upon rehearing; the substituted opinion affirms the earlier decision and, in addition, rejects the defendants' argument that the decision should not have retroactive effect; the lengthy dissent claims the retroactive application will damage the Alabama economy "beyond estimate" and "only allows for predatory attacks on legitimate businesses. . . . The termites are swarming" (meaning that the consumer bar will feed on such creditors: what a rare reversal!); the dissent includes an appendix listing every other state's definition of total indebtedness for purposes of calculating credit insurance premiums). *But see* Dixon v. Ford Motor Credit, 2000 U.S. Dist. LEXIS 7934 (E.D. La. May 31, 2000) (allegations that Louisiana law mandates net coverage, that the terms of the insurance were not properly disclosed, and that excessive commissions were paid to sell the insurance product warrants denial of motion for summary judgment on RICO claim), *subsequent proceedings*, 137 F. Supp. 2d 702 (E.D. La. 2000) (RICO claim dismissed; supplemental state law claims dismissed); Gall v. American Heritage Life Ins. Co., 3 F. Supp. 2d 1344 (S.D. Ala. 1998) (stating it is not bound by plurality in *McCullar* and, agreeing with the dissent, finding that insurance can be calculated in total of payments); Liberty Bank & Trust Co. v. Splane, 959 P.2d 600 (Okla. Civ. App. 1998) (construing provision in U.C.C.C. restricting the amount of the permissible credit insurance to that which does not "exceed the debt" and another provision in Oklahoma insurance law restricting the amount of such insurance to "the approximate unpaid balance of the loan" to allow insurance premiums to be calculated on the total of payments; court specifically rejects the plurality in *Mccullar*); Robertson v. PHF Life Ins. Co., 702 So. 2d 555 (Fla. Dist. Ct. App. 1997) (with no discussion, court holds that Florida law allows credit life insurance to be calculated based upon the total of payments rather than the principal amount of the loan).

516 An insurance charge may purchase some hidden *types* of additional coverage, which may not be authorized, and would, therefore constitute interest. *See, e.g.*, the discussion of force-placed insurance at § 10.3.8.3, *infra*.

517 *See, e.g.*, Brown v. Protective Life Ins. Co., 135 Fed. Appx. 647 (5th Cir. 2005) (alleging that amount of coverage on credit life insurance sold in connection with financed vehicle purchase exceeded the financed amount and included coverage for unearned interest in violation of the state motor vehicle sales finance act; claim against insurer rejected because the auto finance company is not a licensing agent of the insurer for lending purposes under the state law); McCullar v. Universal Underwriters Life Ins. Co., 687 So. 2d 156 (Ala. 1996).

518 *See* § 6.6.2.1, *supra*.

Defining the appropriate limits of coverage for an open-end credit account, in which the amount of debt varies, is more difficult. The UCCC provides that coverage on an open-end account should be "reasonably commensurate with the amount of debt as it exists from time to time."[519] An opinion of the Kansas Attorney General defines open-end credit to include lines of credit.[520] Thus, if a borrower has opened a $10,000 line of credit to have available in case of emergencies, but generally carries a balance of less than $2,000, any credit insurance should relate to the $2,000 balance. If the borrower's line of credit has been suspended, for example, due to a decrease in property value, then the homeowner has no available credit and a balance of zero, and the insurance should be terminated.[521]

## 6.6.4 *Special Credit Property Issues*

### 6.6.4.1 Scope of Insurable Interest

Excess property insurance may be manifested in a number of different ways. The creditor may sell it in transactions where it is not permitted by law; it may sell coverage for an amount greater than the collateral (or the debt) is worth; it may insure property which is not collateral; it may add additional types of coverage beyond that which is authorized or necessary; or it may insure a phantom risk.

While state insurance regulation of credit property insurance is somewhat minimal, a number of states' *credit* statutes limit the sale of credit property insurance. Some states prohibit creditors from requiring credit property insurance in conjunction with very small loans.[522] Other states prohibit writing credit property insurance at all unless the amount financed (exclusive of insurance charges) and the value of the collateral each exceed a specified minimum.[523] Other credit statutes more generally require that credit property insurance charges be "reasonable" in relation to both the value of the insured property and the amount of the loan[524] or, depending on the

519 U.C.C.C. § 4-202 (1968 and 1974).

520 Opinion of Kansas Att'y Gen., No. 88-13, Consumer Cred. Guide (CCH) ¶ 95,910 (Feb. 2, 1988).

The opinion includes lines of credit within the scope of the definition of "open-end credit," or revolving credit, and distinguishes them from "credit commitments," in which the appropriate insurance coverage may combine both the current debt and the limits of the commitment.

521 *Cf.* Hofstetter v. Chase Home Fin., L.L.C., 2010 WL 3259773 (N.D. Cal. Aug. 16, 2010) (no flood insurance was required under the National Flood Insurance Act when the home equity line of credit had been suspended due to a decrease in property value and no credit was available).

522 Ga. Comp. R. & Regs. §§ 120-1-11-.04(3) and 120-1-14-.17(3); Robinson v. Central Loan & Fin. Corp., 609 F.2d 170, 175 (5th Cir. 1980).

523 *E.g.*, Ala. Code § 5-19-20(g); U.C.C.C. § 4-301 (1968); U.C.C.C. § 4-301(3) (1974) (same, but exempting open-end credit).

524 *E.g.*, Ga. Code Ann. § 7-3-14(3) (industrial loan); U.C.C.C. § 4-301 (1968); (1968); U.C.C.C. § 4-301(3) (1974) (same, but open-end credit is governed not by the statute but by rules consistent with the statutory principles to be adopted by administrator).

statute, to the greater[525] or lesser[526] of these two amounts. Some states require that coverage be reasonable in relation to the risk, not to exceed the loan amount.[527]

The UCCC prohibits property insurance charges unless the insurance covers: a) a substantial risk of loss or damage to property related to the transaction; b) the amount, terms and conditions of the insurance are reasonable in relation to the character and value of the property, and c) the term is reasonable in relation to the terms of credit, i.e., if it is customary and closely coincides with the term of the credit transaction.[528] Read together with the UCCC's general credit insurance provisions limiting credit insurance coverage generally to the value of the debt, the statute requires that the amount of property insurance coverage is limited to *the lesser of* the amount of the debt or the value of the property.[529]

A number of statutes specify that property insurance can only be written on collateral. The UCCC provides that property insurance can be written on property "related to the credit transaction."[530] Thus, property insurance written on non-collateral property should be an excessive charge where a statute limits the specified authorized charges to an inclusive list.[531] Interpreting UCCC language permitting property insurance to cover a risk of loss on "property related to the credit transaction," and requiring that insurance be of benefit to the borrower, the Kansas Attorney General has ruled that a creditor cannot sell property insurance on household goods unless there is a purchase-money security interest in the household goods which would be valid under the FTC Credit Practices Rule;[532] if there is no valid security interest, it cannot be property "related to the credit transaction." Further, a creditor cannot shortcut this requirement by taking a valid purchase money-security interest in *some* household goods, and then naming itself as loss payee on a policy insuring *all* household goods.[533]

Property insurance cannot be "required"—either explicitly or implicitly—where the lender has no interest in the insured property, as in an unsecured loan,[534] or where the coverage extends beyond the collateral.[535] Other statutes authorize credit property on security if it is sold at "standard" rates, reasonably insuring against loss considering the circumstances, and if sold through licensed agents.[536] Generally, charging premiums for excess coverage should constitute usury,[537] though only if it is established that the excess coverage added cost to the premium charged the borrower.[538]

### 6.6.4.2 Phantom Coverage

Excess coverage may also be argued in situations where the coverage buys illusory benefits. This may occur, for example, in connection with open-end accounts, where the account balance reflects non-durable purchases, such as lunches at the department store restaurant, tune-ups at the auto-center, or cosmetics.

Phantom coverage may also occur where the property insured is worth less than the total of payments. Coverage in the amount of the total of payments may be illusory if the policy limits liability to the value of the property. In such a case, coverage in the full loan amount would not meet a statutory requirement that the insurance be reasonable in relation to the risk, even if the statute would otherwise permit coverage to equal the total amount of the obligation.[539]

Even in states where the statute specifically authorizes property insurance coverage related to either the value of the property or the amount of the loan, whichever is greater,[540] excess coverage should be argued in this situation. Such a provision can only rationally be interpreted to allow full coverage of the property's value even if it exceeds the total of

525 *E.g.*, Ariz. Rev. Stat. Ann. § 6-636(E) (consumer loan act). *But see* § 6.6.4.2, *infra* ("phantom coverage").

526 *E.g.*, Bailey v. Defenbaugh & Co. of Cleveland, Inc., 513 F. Supp. 232, 241 (D. Miss. 1981) (interpreting Miss. Code Ann § 75-67-121 (Regs. VI(A)(2)).

527 *E.g.*, Tenn. Code Ann. § 45-5-305(3)(C). *See also* § 6.6.4.2, *infra* ("phantom coverage").

528 U.C.C.C. § 4-301 (1968); U.C.C.C. § 4-301 (1974) (same, but open-end credit is governed not by the statute but by rules consistent with the statutory principles to be adopted by administrator).

529 Opinion of Kansas Att'y Gen., No. 87-3, Consumer Cred. Guide (CCH) ¶ 95,980 (Jan. 9, 1987), *modified by* opinion of Kansas Att'y Gen., No. 87-47, Consumer Cred. Guide (CCH) ¶ 95,981 (Mar. 12, 1987).

530 U.C.C.C. § 4-301(1)(a) (1968 and 1974). *See* Department of Fin. Inst. v. Beneficial Fin. Co. of Madison, 426 N.E.2d 711, 713 (Ind. Ct. App. 1981).

531 *See* § 6.6.2, *supra*. *See also* § 6.7.4, *infra*.

532 Opinion of Kansas Attorney General, No. 87-3, Consumer Cred. Guide (CCH) ¶ 95,980 (Jan. 9, 1987), *modified by* Opinion of Kansas Att'y Gen., No. 87-47, Consumer Cred. Guide (CCH) ¶ 95,981 (Mar. 12, 1987). *See* § 6.7.4, *infra* (discussing briefly what may constitute a valid security interest under the FTC rule).

533 Opinion of Kansas Attorney General, No. 87-3, Consumer Cred. Guide (CCH) ¶ 95,980 (Jan. 9, 1987), *modified by* Opinion of Kansas Att'y Gen., No. 87-47, Consumer Cred. Guide (CCH) ¶ 95,981 (Mar. 12, 1987).

534 *In re* Bogan, 281 F. Supp. 242, 251 (W.D. Tenn. 1968).

535 Opinion of Kansas Att'y Gen., No. 87-3, Consumer Cred. Guide (CCH) ¶ 95,980 (Jan. 9, 1987), *modified by* Opinion of Kansas Att'y Gen., No. 87-47, Consumer Cred. Guide (CCH) ¶ 95,981 (Mar. 12, 1987).

Selling property insurance to cover non-collateral property is one of the insurance packing tricks. *See* § 6.7.4, *infra*.

536 Cal. Fin. Code § 22313 (West) (consumer loans).

537 Bailey v. Defenbaugh & Co. of Cleveland, 513 F. Supp. 232, 241–242 (N.D. Miss. 1981). *See also* Western Guar. Loan Co. v. Dean, 309 S.W.2d 857 (Tex. Civ. App. 1957).

538 *See* Coner v. Morris S. Berman, Unltd., 501 A.2d 458, 462 (Md. Ct. Spec. App. 1985).

539 *See* Opinion of Kansas Att'y Gen., No. 87-3, Consumer Cred. Guide (CCH) ¶ 95,980 (Jan. 9, 1987), *modified by* Opinion of Kansas Att'y Gen., No. 87-47, Consumer Cred. Guide (CCH) ¶ 95,981 (Mar. 12, 1987) (where value of property is less than the debt, coverage should be limited to property value, even if policy would pay in excess of value of property, resulting in surplus; public policy forbids this result, as creditor could benefit in excess of its rights under security interest; even if borrower received surplus, public policy should forbid this, as borrower may have unknowingly contracted for insurance neither needed or desired).

540 *E.g.*, Ariz. Rev. Stat. Ann. § 6-636(E).

payments, as, for example, where a $5,000 car is offered as security on a $1,000 loan. To hold otherwise would require the assumption that the legislature intended to authorize the sale of phantom insurance, an irrational result not lightly to be reached under principles of statutory construction.

## 6.7 Insurance Packing

### *6.7.1 Overview*

Insurance packing refers to increasing a consumer's debt by padding or "packing" the amount financed through the sale of expensive, unnecessary and often unwanted products, such as insurance.[541] A number of claims can be raised to challenge packing practices: usury, UDAP, breach of fiduciary duty, RICO. In addition, coercive sales practices described at § 6.5, *supra,* often are utilized in connection with insurance packing, so the theories and evidentiary suggestions discussed in that section should also be considered in challenging packing schemes. The excessive charge challenges discussed at § 6.6, *supra,* are also often relevant.

### *6.7.2 Packing to Exceed Critical Statutory Thresholds*

The primary motivation for insurance packing is increased profits through the sale of additional profitable products.

One of the more subtle mechanisms by which insurance packing can be maximized is to stretch a loan's term, since the cost of the premiums increases with the term of the loan. Consider the following actual fact situation:[542] a customer wished to borrow approximately $1,400, and informed the lender she could afford a $75 per month payment. The creditor could have written the loan for a three-year term, a common term for such a small amount. In a three-year loan at the lender's already ample 28.09% rate, the borrower's loan would have looked like this:

| | |
|---|---|
| Net Proceeds to Borrower | $1,440.22 |
| Credit Life Insurance | 49.42 |
| Credit Disability | 96.31 |
| Property Insurance | 114.05 |
| AMOUNT FINANCED | $1,700.00 |
| 36 Mo. Payments @ | 70.40 |
| Finance Charge | 834.43 |
| TOTAL OF PAYMENTS | $2,543.43 |

Such a loan would have served the customer's needs: $1,400 to her with less than a $75 monthly payment. The lender would have had a fully insured loan, and a very high return of 28.09%.

Consider, though if the lender decided to write the loan for a six-year term, to look like this:

| | |
|---|---|
| Net Proceeds to Borrower | $1,442.23 |
| Credit Life Insurance | 210.60 |
| Credit Disability Insurance | 275.40 |
| Property Insurance | 486.00 |
| Real Estate Security Fees | 184.00 |
| AMOUNT FINANCED | $2,598.23 |
| 72 Mo. Payment @ | 75.00 |
| Finance Charge | $2,801.77 |
| TOTAL OF PAYMENTS | $5,400.00 |

For two dollars more in loan proceeds than she would have in a three-year transaction, the customer received slightly higher monthly payments, was obligated to make those monthly payments twice as long, and more than doubled her debt.

This example shows the need to look behind the mere numbers on a document. Just computing the credit insurance charged does not reveal a higher rate per $100 than allowed under applicable law. But the unusually long term and high fees in relation to the borrower's proceeds should raise suspicions. The extra interest and extra commissions on higher premiums may be ample motivation alone, but in this case, there was a further reason for padding the amount financed with huge insurance premiums. The state in which this loan took place prohibited security interests in consumers' residences unless the amount financed exceeded $2,000. The padding of the amount financed took the borrower's loan over the magic threshold, from $1,700 to $2,598, and placed the borrower's home at risk for $1,440 in loan proceeds. The insurance padding took place to provide the creditor with excessive collateral—excessive as defined by the legislature in enacting such a threshold.[543]

There may be other statutory thresholds which a lender may try to cross by packing a loan with insurance premiums. For example, the UCCC permits a seller to take a purchase-money security interest in goods sold, but in no other personalty unless the debt meets a minimum amount.[544] Such padding may also be desirable to creditors in states which have deregulated all lending except for small loans. The lender might wish to pad the amount financed in order to increase the loan beyond the maximum small loan size, thus allowing the creditor freedom to charge whatever interest rate it chooses.

While a number of theories are appropriate for this kind of overreaching, courts should look behind a facially proper transaction to see if otherwise legitimate charges are imposed in bad

541 *See, e.g.,* Miner v. Beneficial Mortgage Co. of Kan. (*In re* Miner), 369 B.R. 655 (Bankr. D. Kan. 2007) (describing a series of loan refinancings containing credit insurance and culminating in a one-time, financed fee of almost $10,000 for credit life and credit disability insurance on a loan of almost $75,000; ultimately, the credit insurance application was denied and the premiums were refunded).

542 *See* Besta v. Beneficial Loan Co., 855 F.2d 532 (8th Cir. 1988).

543 Besta v. Beneficial Loan Co., 855 F.2d 532 (8th Cir. 1988).

544 U.C.C.C. § 2-407 (1968); U.C.C.C. § 3-301(1) (1974). Note also that the FTC Credit Practices Rule restricts the right of most lenders to take non-purchase money security interests in household goods, irrespective of amounts.

faith, to serve as a pretext for usury. In the six-year loan described above, it is hard to think of a "good faith" rationale for the lender's actions. In the past, courts have found charges, including insurance premiums, to be unreasonable and evasive in intent when viewed in relation to the *real* consideration to the borrower.[545] Courts, in finding usury in insurance coverage which exceeded the loan, have noted that the purpose and effect of such is to increase the proportion of the charges to the amount of money lent,[546] an impact and purpose similarly found in this kind of loan padding.

### 6.7.3 Packing with Sales of Non-Credit Insurance and Other Ancillary Products

Some creditors pack into loans non-credit insurance, club memberships and similar fee-generating extras. Creditors profit from these sales and often have set employee quotas for inclusion of the products. The insurance packing practices of ITT Financial provides an example. Debtors would request a loan in a specified amount. The lender would telephone back that the loan plus optional insurance had been approved with a stated monthly payment, never mentioning the total loan amount. When the debtor arrived at the lender's offices for the closing, all loan and insurance documents had been typed and intermingled, making them look like one transaction.

Actually, what many ITT Financial customers had purchased in addition to the loan was some combination of: credit life insurance and credit accident and health insurance; "Unipay," a single premium policy covering certain types of accidental death and dismemberment until age 65; "SPT-5," a five-year term, single premium life insurance policy, again totally unrelated to the credit life policy; "ITT Thrift Club" giving the debtor discounts on hotels, rental cars, and other purchases; credit property insurance on household goods taken as collateral for the personal loan, even if the debtor already had property insurance on those goods, and often when the consumer had no idea that household goods would be required as collateral on the loan; and credit property insurance on household goods that were *not* collateral on the loan (in effect, "non-credit property insurance"); or excessive property insurance on collateral, the value of which had been artificially inflated.

Collateral contracts, such as those involved in the sale of non-credit insurance items in packing cases, can be viewed as "a device to extract an exorbitant rate of interest," even if the theoretically independent contract is not "illegal, improper, or illusory, nor totally lacking in substance."[547] The questionable value of the types of ancillary products sold in packing cases, combined with the implicitly coercive or deceptive sales tactics which often accompany such sales should make these kinds of packing cases fall within the definition of a device to extract an exorbitant rate of interest[548] thus subject to challenge.

Furthermore, it is worth looking carefully at the scope of the authority granted a licensee under a special usury statute to make such sales. Such statutes, like small loan acts, may specifically authorize the licensee to sell credit insurance and impose premium charges, but make no mention of non-credit insurance charges. Such statutes are to be interpreted strictly, and charges not specifically authorized should not be permitted.[549]

Moreover, the relevant licensing statute may contain a provision similar to that from the Uniform Small Loan Act, which prohibits conducting other business at the same location as its lending business, unless authorized by the regulatory authority upon a finding that "the granting of such authority would not facilitate evasions" of the statute.[550] The sale of products, including insurance products not specifically listed as authorized, should constitute "conducting other business" that is not permitted. Certainly, the profits to the lender or its affiliates from insurance packing, accompanied by the frequently coercive or deceptive sales practices, suggest this "other business" tends to circumvent or evade the special usury statutes.[551] The strict interpretation of Minnesota's version of the small loan statute led the state supreme court to rule that the sale of non-credit life insurance by a finance company licensed under the Minnesota Regulated Loan Act[552] was prohibited in *Hawkins v. Thorp Credit and Thrift Co.*[553]

One challenge to an ancillary accidental death and dismemberment (AD&D) insurance product, predicated on the assertion that it was coerced, and thus a finance charge under state and TILA law, failed.[554] However, the facts described as to one of the named plaintiffs raise some intriguing "what if" questions: what if the economic impact of these policies had been demonstrated in the context of an insurance packing and/or loan flipping challenge?[555] Loading up frequently refinanced loans with non-rebated charges plays a significant role in artificially inflating the debt. Unlike credit insurance policies, which are required to be cancelled and to have the unearned premiums

545 Home Fin. Co. v. Padgett, 54 So. 2d 813, 814–815 (La. Ct. App. 1951).

546 Western Guar. Loan Co. v. Dean, 309 S.W.2d 857 (Tex. Civ. App. 1957); Industrial Fin. Serv. Co. v. Riley, 295 S.W.2d 498 (Tex. Civ. App. 1956), *rev'd in part on other grounds*, 302 S.W.2d 652 (Tex. 1957). *See also* Strickler v. State Auto Fin. Co., 249 S.W.2d 307 (Ark. 1952) (premiums were 10% of principal); Wilson v. Whitworth, 125 S.W.2d 112 (Ark. 1939) ($150 real proceeds, $3,500 insurance required); Tribble v. State, 80 S.E.2d 711 (Ga. Ct. App. 1954).

547 *In re* Rosner, 48 B.R. 538, 550 (Bankr. E.D.N.Y. 1985).

548 *See also* § 6.5, *supra* (discussing voluntariness, which will often be a factual issue in packing cases).

549 *See* § 7.2.1, *infra*.

550 Uniform Small Loan Act § 12.

551 *Cf.* Beneficial Fin. Co. v. State Corp. Comm., 339 S.E.2d 192 (Va. 1986).

552 Minn. Stat. ch. 56 (regulated loans).

553 441 N.W.2d 470 (Minn. 1989).

554 Mitchell v. Industrial Credit Corp., 898 F. Supp. 1518 (N.D. Ala. 1995).

555 Statements of fact in reported opinions, are, of course, always truncated. It is possible such evidence was presented, but the judge found it not important enough to mention.

rebated upon refinancing, premiums for these non-credit ancillary policies generally are not rebated.

### 6.7.4 Unnecessary Collateral, Duplicative Insurance

Another feature of packed loans may be unnecessary collateral taken as security in order to write profitable property insurance. A creditor may, for example, take a superfluous non-purchase money security interest in the borrower's old car which has little or no market value, and write property insurance for it into the loan. The most common example of unnecessary collateral is household goods, despite the legal restrictions on a creditor's right to take household goods as security.

The FTC restricts the right of creditors to take non-purchase money security interest in household goods.[556] The policy behind the prohibition is that ordinary household goods have little genuine value as security—they are generally taken for their *in terrorem* usefulness in debt collection and, perhaps more importantly, to justify writing property insurance on them. Because of the profitability of the insurance, some creditors aggressively attempt to take this security despite the legal restrictions.

One exception to the rule is for purchase-money security interests, which are permitted. A creditor may attempt to improperly extend the purchase-money status of a security interest through cross-collateral clauses and refinancing.[557] A second exception arises in the definition of household goods provided in the FTC and related rules. Some items which either tend to have greater value, or are less necessary for daily living are excluded from the rule's scope.[558] Some creditors have developed form contracts which purport to comply by taking a security interest in the excluded items. In some instances, a creditor may flatly overshoot its mark, and list a protected item. In other cases, it may use fuzzy contract language to try to comply. Depending upon the way the contract is written, it may be subject to challenge as well. An FTC Informal Staff Letter took the position that a contract which took a non-purchase money security interest in household goods, but included an exclusion for consumer transactions as to items covered by the FTC Rule, violates the rule.[559]

The property insurance arising from the security interest must be scrutinized as carefully as the security interest itself.[560] In insurance packing cases, property insurance can arguably be viewed as a pretext for usury: the collateral may be unnecessary because the loan is otherwise amply secured;[561] the collateral itself may be impermissible; the collateral may be of so little intrinsic value that as a practical matter it adds no security; or security may be listed with inflated values so as to increase the insurance sold.[562] The statutory provisions setting standards for the sale of credit property may dictate that property insurance is improper if it does not bear the required relationship to the risk, as the statute defines that relationship.[563] Where the statute requires that property insurance be written only on collateral, or that it bear a relationship to the creditor's risk, a creditor cannot sell property insurance on household goods unless there is a purchase-money security interest in the household goods which would be valid under the FTC Credit Practices Rule.[564] Further, a creditor cannot shortcut this requirement by taking a valid purchase money-security interest in some household goods, and then be named loss payee on a policy insuring all household goods.[565]

Another factor in a number of insurance packing cases is that the property insurance on the collateral is duplicative of existing homeowner's or renter's policies.[566] In the *Beneficial* case, an Indiana state regulatory agency challenged the sale of duplicative property insurance, on the grounds that there was no risk of loss to the creditor, and the insurance thus was improper under the statute.[567] But the court noted that the relevant statute specifically referred to risk of loss to the property, not the creditor. The court also pointed out a few respects in which the creditor's insurance did not duplicate the consumer's own policy. The court therefore failed to find a violation of the statute.

This case should not be dispositive of the issue of duplicative insurance, however. The court decision does not indicate that this insurance was sold in an insurance-packing context which might suggest unfair and deceptive acts and practices or un-

---

556 16 C.F.R. pt. 444. *See generally* National Consumer Law Center, Unfair and Deceptive Acts and Practices §§ 6.11–6.12 (7th ed. 2008 and Supp.).

557 *See* National Consumer Law Center, Repossessions § 3.8 (7th ed. 2010 and Supp.) (discussing duration of purchase money security interests).

558 *E.g.*, VCRs, a second television, artwork, jewelry other than wedding rings. 16 C.F.R. § 444.1(i).

559 FTC Informal Staff Letter, Wilmore, Clearinghouse No. 44,824 (Sept. 27, 1988).

560 Many of the abuses discussed in this section concerning the sale of property insurance on unnecessary collateral and excessive or duplicative property insurance were alleged in the California insurance-packing case, California v. ITT Fin. Corp., Clearinghouse Nos. 44,801S and T, No. 656038-0 (Cal. Super. Ct. Alameda Cty. Sept. 21, 1989) (complaint and settlement filed). *See also* Hawkins v. Thorp; Hohn v. Thorp, Clearinghouse No. 44,801V (D. Minn. 1991) (consolidated complaint), 44,801W (D. Minn. 1991) (settlement); Arizona v. Associates Fin. Servs. Co., CV 92-21853, Clearinghouse No. 44,801Z (Dec. 16, 1992) (stipulated judgment filed), Clearinghouse No. 44,801Y (Dec. 16, 1992) (complaint).

561 *Cf.* Wilson v. Whitworth, 125 S.W.2d 112 (Ark. 1939) ($3,500 insurance required on $150 proceeds).

562 California v. ITT Consumer Fin. Corp., Clearinghouse No. 44801S ¶ 11-M, No. 656038-0 (Cal. Super. Ct. Alameda Cty. Sept. 31, 1989) (complaint filed) (California attorney general alleged in packing case that security interests were taken in personal property as a pretext to sell household contents insurance, and that was unfair competition in violation of Cal. Bus. & Prof. Code § 17200). *See* § 6.7.3, *supra* (further discussion of this case).

563 *See* § 6.6.4, *supra*.

564 Opinion of Kansas Att'y Gen., No. 87-3, Consumer Cred. Guide (CCH) ¶ 95,980 (Jan. 9, 1987), *modified by* Opinion of Kansas Att'y Gen., No. 87-47, Consumer Cred. Guide (CCH) ¶ 95,981 (Mar. 12, 1987).

565 *Id.*

566 Department of Financial Institutions v. Beneficial Fin. Co. of Madison, 462 N.E.2d 711 (Ind. Ct. App. 1981).

567 Ind. Code § 24-4.5-4-301 (1)(a) (U.C.C.C. 4-301(1)(a) (1968)).

conscionable practices, a breach of fiduciary duty, or conduct designed to circumvent interest ceilings. Indeed, there were a number of other statutory provisions relevant to that case itself which were not addressed at all by the court, such as the creditor's need for the insurance protection (which, in effect, does require insurance to relate to the creditor's risk of loss), the relation between the amount and terms of the credit and the insurance benefits, the potential benefits to the consumer[568] and the cost of the insurance in relation to its benefits.[569] A packing case involving duplicative insurance may utilize a large number of different statutory provisions and doctrines.

Interpreting its similar version of the UCCC, the Kansas Attorney General did look at the other provisions of the statute ignored by the Indiana court in the *Beneficial* case. The attorney general opinion noted that if the credit insurance policy had a *pro rata* clause, that would deny the consumer any benefit from the insurance sale, and would be unconscionable if the creditor did it knowingly.[570]

## 6.7.5 Non-Filing Insurance

Ordinarily, a creditor taking a security interest in personal property files a record of its security interest in a county recorder's office as a means of protecting its interest in the collateral against other creditors.[571] However, sometimes creditors find it easier to purchase non-filing insurance than to perfect the security interest.

Non-filing insurance is simply a way for the creditor to avoid the cost and effort of filing the security interest with the county recorder's office as a means of establishing its priority over later creditors on the collateral. In theory, it pays the lender if the lender cannot repossess its collateral upon default, if the loss is occasioned by the fact that the lender did not file its security interest.[572] As a practical matter, that is only going to happen when another secured party gets priority as a result of the creditor's failure to record its lien.[573]

The cost of non-filing premiums is generally fairly small, since Truth in Lending regulations require that the cost not exceed the actual cost of filing with the public officials in order for the insurance to be excluded from the TILA finance charge.[574] However, it is impermissible to both file and charge for the non-filing insurance.[575]

A pair of cases from Alabama with conflicting results suggests that it is key how the facts are developed and presented. A federal court in *Mitchell* found non-filing insurance not in violation of either the Alabama Mini-Code or TILA.[576] In contrast, a thoughtful and detailed opinion by the Alabama Supreme Court in *Whitson* distinguished *Mitchell* because it did not involve purchase money security interests in consumer goods.[577] Instead the Alabama Supreme Court found three arguments to be persuasive in its case. First, there was no insurance involved at all. Two necessary characteristics of insurance are risk-shifting, and distribution of risk among similarly situated persons. In the arrangement at issue, the creditor's "claims" are paid simply by returning the premiums it pays in, less an administrative fee, so there is no risk shifted at all, nor is there any distribution of risk. Second, even if it were insurance, it was not "in lieu of perfecting a security interest": it was, instead, default insurance. The insurer paid on losses due to bankruptcy, skips, and destroyed goods—none of which relate to risks created by non-filing. Finally, since the contracts in question were all purchase-money security interests in non-automotive consumer goods, the creditor's security interest was automatically perfected under the UCC, as noted above. The premium was not, therefore, "in lieu of perfecting."

This "non-filing insurance" premium therefore failed to qualify for the finance charge exemption in Alabama's mini-code, meaning the charge was considered interest. Since the admitted interest charged was at or very near the statutory maximum, this hidden interest took the contracts over the usury ceiling, with the prescribed result being forfeiture of the entire finance charge.[578]

The Alabama Supreme Court, however, reversed the trial court's grant of summary judgment on the issue of whether the imposition of the charges was deliberate which, if so, triggered the remedy of voiding the usurious loans. Instead, the court held that whether the charging of the non-filing fee was done with deliberateness was a question of fact to be decided by the jury.

An earlier decision from Florida outlined a similar variation of non-filing "insurance."[579] There the seller-creditor charged $7 for non-filing insurance every time a customer purchased goods in excess of $20. In lieu of filing a security interest statement, the entire charge was sent to American Bankers Ins. Co. pursuant to an agreement. American Bankers issued a non-filing insurance policy which limited the insurer's liability for losses to 90% of the premiums. American Bankers retained 10% of the premiums paid and returned the remaining 90% to the creditor to cover any losses that could occur. Since a purchase money security interest

568 Ind. Code § 24-4.5-4-106 (U.C.C.C. § 4-106 (1968)).

569 Ind. Code § 24-4.5-5-108 (U.C.C.C. § 5-108 (1968)).

570 Opinion of Kansas Att'y Gen., No. 87-3, Consumer Cred. Guide (CCH) ¶ 95,980 (Jan. 9, 1987), *modified by* Opinion of Kansas Att'y Gen., No. 87-47, Consumer Cred. Guide (CCH) ¶ 95,981 (Mar. 12, 1987).

571 *See* U.C.C. art. 9, pts. 3 and 4.

572 *See* Fagg, Credit Life and Disability Insurance 522–523 (1986).

573 *See, e.g.*, White & Summers, Uniform Commercial Code § 33-4 (5th ed. 2002).

574 15 U.S.C. § 1605(d)(2); Reg. Z, 12 C.F.R. § 1026.4(e)(2) [§ 226.4(e)(2)]. *See generally* National Consumer Law Center, Truth in Lending § 3.9.7.3 (7th ed. 2010 and Supp.).

575 *See* Mitchell v. Industrial Credit Corp., 898 F. Supp. 1518 (N.D. Ala. 1995).

576 Mitchell v. Industrial Credit Corp., 898 F. Supp. 1518 (N.D. Ala. 1995).

577 Warehouse Home Furnishing Distribs., Inc. v. Whitson, 709 So. 2d 1144 (Ala. 1997) (noting that the *Mitchell* court held that the insurance premium did constitute a finance charge for the one plaintiff against whose property a security interest had been perfected).

578 Ala. Code § 5-19-19.

579 W.S. Badcock Corp. v. Myers, 696 So. 2d 766 (Fla. Dist. Ct. App. 1996).

in consumer goods is perfected automatically without filing, the "losses" to the creditor would be few or none. The court held that this scheme was not insurance because there was no insurable interest since perfection occurred automatically. Further there was no risk of loss. Since this arrangement was not insurance, the court found that the creditor's behavior was subject to Florida's UDAP statute and upheld summary judgment in favor of the consumers on the merits.

Even if the evidence does not support a finding that the purported non-filing insurance is really a reserve fund, the insurance policy may, in fact, be a general default policy and not non-filing insurance. If so, the charge may be illegal under the state usury and/or credit insurance laws. For example, discovery in a case that reached the Fifth Circuit revealed that as many as 84.5% of the claims paid by the insurance company were based on losses not covered by the non-filing policy.[580]

## 6.8 Post-Claim Underwriting, Ineligibility

### *6.8.1 Challenging the Sale of Insurance to Borrowers Unlikely to Benefit*

Credit insurance may be sold to borrowers who are ineligible for the insurance coverage under the terms of the policies that they buy. Unlike ordinary insurance sales, creditors rarely ask borrowers for information, such as medical histories, relating to their eligibility for benefits under credit insurance policies.[581] Only after a claim is filed are eligibility factors such as health, age, and employment checked to see if grounds exist for denying coverage. Many policies simply provide that the policy will be canceled and the premium refunded if ineligibility is determined. The result of this arrangement is that creditors and insurance companies keep the premiums paid by ineligible debtors who never file an insurance claim, while refusing to pay on the same policies if claims are ever filed.[582]

Most credit life policies have age restrictions, and many have preexisting condition exclusions as well. Many disability policies have exclusionary periods whereby they will not pay for disabilities traceable to preexisting conditions which occur within the first six months of coverage. Refinancing may begin a new exclusionary period, and repeated refinancings result in rolling periods of ineligibility.[583] Thus, the odds of becoming disabled during a period of eligibility are reduced. Such a practice may lead to a finding that an insurance sale is just a pretext for usury.[584] Currently, a number of states restrict the use of preexisting condition exclusions on refinanced loans, at least where the same group policy is used to insure the refinanced loan.[585]

Another abuse is the sale of insurance to protect against unforeseen loss of income (accident and health or involuntary unemployment) to people whose ability to repay will not be jeopardized by such loss because they are on a fixed income, such as Social Security or AFDC.[586] The benefit to such a borrower is utterly illusory, as most disability policies have some form of "actively at work" clause which effectively excludes people with a non-wage income from benefits. The same problem may also arise with the sale of involuntary unemployment insurance to unemployed borrowers. Such insurance also has an actively at work clause, and usually excludes self-employed workers. Involuntary unemployment insurance policies also may be sold to those who are highly unlikely to be laid off, such as those in the military.

In general, claims concerning these abuses should be brought against the creditor, not the insurer. The creditor is responsible for the insurance sale and the creditor knows the borrower's employment situation from the credit application. While most insurance contracts limit the insurer's liability to a return of the premium if it is determined the borrower was ineligible for coverage, litigation may be required to recover from the creditor the interest charged on the premium.

Sales of insurance without a benefit to the consumer may be viewed as a pretext for usury.[587] Other possible consumer claims include the contract defense of failure of consideration, UDAP, unconscionability, negligence,[588] bad faith,[589] or even

580 Edwards v. Your Credit Inc., 148 F.3d 427 (5th Cir. 1998). *Accord* Adams v. Plaza Fin. Co., 168 F.3d 932 (7th Cir. 1999).

581 *See, e.g.*, Justus v. Mountain Life Ins. Co., 1999 Tenn. App. LEXIS 702 (Tenn. Ct. App. Oct. 15, 1999) (bank employee took no application but represented that a credit life insurance policy was in full force and effect). *See generally* Rita G. Pereira, *Credit Insurance: Obtaining Relief for Postclaim Ineligibility Determinations*, 28 Clearinghouse Rev. 891 (Dec. 1994).

582 *See, e.g.*, Taylor v. American Bankers Ins. Group, Inc., 700 N.Y.S.2d 458 (N.Y. App. Div. 1999) (class certification granted in case where consumers allege practice of rejecting insurance claims on grounds that customers had not been paying for the appropriate type of insurance after disclosing the nature of the insurance in small, inconspicuous type); Osborne v. Mountain Life Ins. Co., 130 S.W.3d 769 (Tenn. 2004) (insurer not estopped from asserting policy exclusion by failure to inquire about insured's health, where insured's medical situation, if known when insurance was purchased as part of credit contract, would have made insured ineligible for the insurance). *Cf. In re* Sprouse, 577 F.2d 989 (5th Cir. 1978) (discussing effect of overreaching contract language on consumers in transactions which are not litigated).

583 Dobson, *Credit Insurance: The Hidden Insurance*, 65 Mich. Bar J. 168, 169 (Feb. 1986). *See generally* § 5.9, *supra* (incidence of refinancing).

584 *Cf.* Peebles v. State, 75 S.E.2d 35 (Ga. Ct. App. 1953).

585 Fagg, Credit Life and Disability Insurance 117 (1986). *See also* Founders Life Assurance Co. v. Poe, 251 S.E.2d 247 (Ga. 1978) (relating exclusionary period back to original transaction, though loan refinanced four times; court ordered recovery under the policy).

586 National Ass'n of Ins. Comm'rs, A Background Study of the Regulation of Credit Life and Disability Insurance 51 (1970).

587 *See* § 6.6.3, *supra*. *See also* § 4.5.2.3, *supra*.

588 *See, e.g.*, Estate of Carr v. Circle S Enters., 664 S.E.2d 83 (S.C. Ct. App. 2008) (car dealer accepted payments for credit life insurance, failed to inform consumers that older buyer was uninsurable; negligence claim stated; seller who accepted premium payments had duty to purchase insurance or inform buyers he could not; consumers damaged when after buyer's death daughter stopped making payments in belief that insurer would pay, and car was repossessed).

589 *See, e.g.*, Vining v. Enterprise Fin. Group, 148 F.3d 1206 (10th Cir. 1998) (upholding jury verdict of bad faith and associated award of damages where insurer rescinded a credit life insurance policy sold in connection with a car loan after insured's death; court cites insurer's

fraud.[590] In its laundry list of factors which are relevant to determining unconscionability, the UCCC lists a sale of services where the seller knows the consumer could not receive substantial benefits from the services sold.[591] Such a sale also should be a breach of fiduciary duty[592] or a breach of the common law duty of disclosure.[593] The Bank Holding Company Act and Regulation Y[594] limit the right of regulated banks and bank holding companies to underwrite insurance to those circumstances where the underwriter's performance could "reasonably be expected to produce benefits to the public."[595]

## 6.8.2 Incomplete Coverage

A credit insurance abuse involves the sale of coverage represented to be full but is only partial coverage. As consumer loan balances grow larger, and terms longer, it is becoming more common for creditors to sell credit insurance which does not completely insure the loan. For example, a ten-year, $10,000 policy may be sold in connection with a fifteen-year, $15,000 loan. If the benefits of such a policy are misrepresented as being full coverage, the consumer should have a UDAP or a common law fraud claim.[596]

In a major enforcement action, the OCC accused Providian National Bank with unfair and deceptive behavior for, among other things, failing to tell its customers that a "credit protection plan" (CPP) (a package of credit insurances) sold in conjunction with credit cards accounts was limited to the number of months that the consumer paid in, rather than the eighteen months claimed by telemarketers; that the involuntary unemployment insurance was unavailable if the consumer was self-employed and did not commence until the consumer had paid in three months of premiums; that the hospitalization, illness, or disability coverage was unavailable for preexisting conditions unless the consumer had paid six months of premiums; that CPP could be denied if the consumer's account was not current or over-the-limit; that CPP could be denied if the consumer paid more than the minimum payment to any credit card account other than Providian's; that CPP could be denied if the consumer accessed credit from any credit card other than Providian's. The matter settled and Providian was required to compensate consumers nationwide.[597]

Another possible actionable non-disclosure is that the insurer will cancel a policy if the lender declares the consumer in default on a loan. But the consumer should insist on payment under the policy if the consumer's claim is made prior to the insurer delivering notice of cancellation of the policy.[598]

## 6.8.3 Collecting the Benefits of the Insurance Bargain

### 6.8.3.1 Types of Improper Denial of Coverage

There are any number of reasons why a credit insurance claim will be improperly denied. The consumer's pre-existing medical condition may be a disqualification and the creditor knew of the condition (or should have known), but does not inform the insurer.[599] The creditor may simply not inquire about relevant facts, such as health. In some cases, there is no

practices aimed at maximizing profits by overstating premiums costs and routinely denying claims on policies sold in previous two years; while consumer had a heart condition the decade before he died, he had been in good health since then and had answered all questions truthfully regarding previous twelve months of health, and the stated policy of the company was to only underwrite based on the previous twelve months; the court noted in a footnote that the insurer's practices somewhat resembled the practices of the fictional insurance company in John Grisham's novel The Rainmaker).

590 *See, e.g.*, Union Sec. Life Ins. Co. v. Crocker, 709 So. 2d 1118 (Ala. 1997) (punitive damages award for fraud in sale of credit life insurance coverage to plaintiff and her husband when he was known to have disqualifying health problems; award was reduced after U.S. Supreme Court concluded that a higher amount would violate due process, see 517 U.S. 1230 (1996)); Lucas v. Cont'l Cas. Co., 170 S.E.2d 856 (Ga. Ct. App. 1969) (jury question existed regarding waiver of exclusion for prior illness where insured questioned auto dealer about whether prior heart condition would limit credit insurance availability). *But see* Southards v. Cent. Plains Ins. Co., 441 P.2d 808 (Kan. 1968) (plaintiff denied coverage under credit disability policy where he did not know at the time of purchase that he had a certain degenerative disease, although a medical expert could have detected it if the plaintiff would have been examined); S. Branch Valley Nat'l Bank v. Williams, 155 S.E.2d 845 (W. Va. 1967) (credit insurer was not liable under policy where cashier for bank processed insurance application for insured who was ineligible based on age).

591 U.C.C.C. § 5-108(4)(b) (1974).

592 § 6.4.7, *supra*.

593 *See* Suburban State Bank v. Squires, 427 N.W.2d 393 (Wis. Ct. App. 1988) (where borrower had heart attack and collected on disability insurance and loan was refinanced, court upheld finding that creditor was negligent in not advising borrower that new disability policy would bar recovery if borrower had another heart attack).

594 12 U.S.C. § 1843(c)(8); 12 C.F.R. § 225.28(b)(11) (1999). *See* Hinkle, *Insurance Activities of National Banks and Bank Holding Companies*, 105 Banking L.J. 137 (1988).

595 12 U.S.C. § 1843(c)(8).

596 *Cf.* Ginocchio v. American Bankers Life Assur. Co., 889 F. Supp. 1078 (N.D. Ill. 1995) (credit disability insurance sold with fifteen-year mortgage ambiguous as to meaning of thirty-six-month truncated term; insurer's motion for summary judgment on breach of contract, UDAP, and improper claims practices denied); Marshall v. Citicorp Mortgage 601 So. 2d 669 (La. Ct. App. 1992).

597 Consent Order in *In re* Providian Nat'l Bank, Dep't of Treasury, #2000-53 (June 28, 2000), *available at* www.occ.treas.gov/ftp/eas/ea2000-53.pdf.

598 Smith v. Liberty Life Ins. Co., 2005 WL 2445430 (W.D. La. Sept. 30, 2005) (where borrower with credit insurance covering accidental death died in auto accident almost two months after receiving a formal notice of default, court found that insurance company was required to pay claim because it had not provided notice of policy cancellation to the borrower).

599 *See, e.g.*, Union Sec. Life Ins. Co. v. Crocker, 667 So. 2d 688 (Ala. 1995), *vacated on other grounds*, 116 S. Ct. 1872 (1996) ($2 million punitive damage award was sent back to Alabama Supreme Court for further consideration in light of BMW of N. Am., Inc. v. Gore, 517 U.S. 559, 116 S. Ct. 1589 (1996)), *upon remand from Supreme Court*, 709 So. 2d 1118 (Ala. 1997) (creditor knew of consumer's bad health but filled out the credit insurance application listing no prior illnesses); Miller v. Dobbs Mobile Bay, Inc., 661 So. 2d 203 (Ala. 1995).

instruction from the insurer to do so. On occasion, the creditor deliberately misstates information on the insurance application.

Other claims are denied when the creditor does not properly process the borrower's insurance application, such as where the creditor never obtains insurance or forwards the premium to an insurer.[600] Creditors may continue to collect insurance payments from a borrower who was eligible for coverage at loan origination but who becomes ineligible due to age, even when the creditor reasonably has knowledge of the insured's ineligibility.[601] Another abuse occurs where the lender hinders processing of a claim.[602]

Nor can a claim be denied based on an eligibility requirement not found in the insurance contract. Where an eligibility requirement is not specified or express, it may not be implied in law.[603]

### 6.8.3.2 Theories of Recovery Against the Insurer

Where the consumer's insurance claim is denied, any resulting litigation must decide whether to sue the creditor-seller, or the insurance company, or both. Legal claims leading to liability may differ depending on the defendant. This section examines theories of recovery against the insurer and the next against the lender.

Since credit insurance is sold only through creditors, never directly by the insurer, the insurer's liability may depend upon whether the creditor-seller is viewed as the insurer's agent, or the borrower's agent, about which there is a divergence of judicial opinion. If the creditor acts as the insurer's agent, its knowledge of disqualifying factors, or misrepresentations may be attributed to its principal, the insurer.

Though the division appears to be too close for these labels to be accurate, they have been denominated as a majority rule and minority rule. The "majority" rule holds that a creditor acts as the agent of the insured borrower, so the insurer cannot be bound by the creditor's knowledge.[604] But about half the cases follow the "minority" rule, and conclude that the creditor is the insurer's agent.[605]

Where the creditor is viewed as the insurer's agent, the insurer can be liable for both actual and punitive damages. For example, the Alabama Supreme Court upheld a jury verdict for $2 million punitive damages (later reducing the award to $1 million after remand from the United States Supreme Court) for fraud against both the creditor and insurer in a case involving sale of credit life insurance to a borrower in ill health. In *Union Security Life Insurance Co. v. Crocker*,[606] a creditor, knowing of the borrower's ill-health (and consequent ineligibility for insurance) nonetheless filled out an application for credit insurance indicating no history of prior illnesses. When the borrower died, the claim for credit life benefits was denied. The widow brought a successful action for fraud, concealment, and a scheme to defraud against both the creditor and insurer. The lender, acting as a knowledgeable agent for the insurer has a duty to disclose that benefits might not be payable. The widow

600 Card v. Chase Manhattan Bank, 669 N.Y.S.2d 117 (N.Y. Civ. Ct. 1996) (holding bank liable for false advertising).

601 *See* Eaves-Leanos v. Assurant, 2008 WL 80155 (W.D. Ky. Jan. 8, 2008) (plaintiff brought UDAP and fraud claims challenging the collection of premiums after insured became ineligible for coverage due to age). *Cf.* Bauer v. Beneficial Consumer Discount Co., 2007 WL 4269804 (W.D. Pa. Dec. 3, 2007) (when the borrower died before the three-day rescission period had ended, the creditor did not fund the transaction and claimed that no insurance could have been processed; denying defendants' motion to dismiss and allowed the plaintiff (the deceased's spouse) to proceed with her claim for breach of contract and breach of fiduciary duty).

602 *See, e.g.*, Jenkins v. Hyundai Motor Fin., 389 F. Supp. 2d 961 (S.D. Ohio 2005) (borrower financed credit disability insurance with a car purchase and alleged that when she became disabled one year later and filed a claim with the insurer, the lender hindered the processing of the claim by failing to provide relevant paperwork; after repossessing vehicle for lack of payment lender then tried to apply insurance rebate to loan balance).

603 *See, e.g.*, First Federated Life Ins. Co. v. Citizen's Bank & Trust, 593 S.W.2d 97 (Ky. Ct. App. 1979). *See also* Justus v. Mountain Life Ins. Co., 1999 Tenn. App. LEXIS 702 (Tenn. Ct. App. Oct. 15, 1999) (bank employee took no credit insurance application information and represented that credit life insurance policy was in full force and effect).

604 *See, e.g.*, Sadtler v. John Hancock Mut. Life Ins. Co., 291 A.2d 500 (D.C. App. Ct. 1972) (decision based on Michigan statute, Mich. Comp. Laws § 500.4416, and on master policy clause denying agency); National Life Ins. Co. v. Harriott, 268 So. 2d 397 (Fla. Dist. Ct. App. 1972); Merchants Bank v. Gill, 1999 Tex. App. LEXIS 3252 (Tex. App. Apr. 29, 1999); South Branch Valley Nat'l Bank v. Williams, 155 S.E.2d 845 (W. Va. 1967) . *See also* Palmer v. Newport Trust Co., 245 A.2d 438 (Me. 1968); Martinson v. North Cent. Life Ins. Co., 222 N.W.2d 611 (1974), *rehearing denied*, 225 N.W.2d 604 (Wis. 1975).

605 *See, e.g.*, Ginocchio v. American Bankers Life Assur. Co., 889 F. Supp. 1078 (N.D. Ill. 1995); Union Sec. Life Ins. Co. v. Crocker, 667 So. 2d 688 (Ala. 1995), *vacated on other grounds*, 116 S. Ct. 1872 (1996), *upon remand*, 709 So. 2d 1118 (Ala. 1997); Miller v. Dobbs Mobile Bay, Inc., 661 So. 2d 203 (Ala. 1995); Grimm v. USLIFE Credit Life Ins. Co., 1999 Ohio App. LEXIS 2445 (Ohio Ct. App. May 19, 1999 (Ohio statute makes the person who solicits and procures insurance the agent of the company issuing the insurance); Hardy v. American S. Life Ins. Co., 211 So. 2d 559 (Fla. 1968); Key v. Cherokee Credit Life Ins. Co., 298 So. 2d 892 (La. Ct. App. 1974); Simonson v. Michigan Life Ins. Co., 194 N.W.2d 446 (Mich. Ct. App. 1971); McDaniel v. Ins. Co. of Oregon, 410 P.2d 814 (Or. 1966); Justus v. Mountain Life Ins. Co., 1999 Tenn. App. LEXIS 702 (Tenn. Ct. App. Oct. 15, 1999) . *See also* Barnes v. First Franklin Fin. Corp., 313 F. Supp. 2d 634 (S.D. Miss. 2004) (assuming lender is agent of insurer); Hayes Truck Lines, Inc. v. Investors, Ins. Corp., 525 P.2d 1289 (Or. 1974). *Cf.* Vining v. Enterprise Fin. Group, Inc., 148 F.3d 1206 (10th Cir. 1998) (plaintiff proved the insurers' deliberate, willful pattern of rescinding life insurance policies as soon as claims were made without determining whether it had good cause to do so).

606 667 So. 2d 688 (Ala. 1995), *vacated on other grounds*, 116 S. Ct. 1872 (1996), *upon remand from Supreme Court*, 709 So. 2d 1118 (Ala. 1997) (reducing punitive damages award to $1 million by weighing reprehensible conduct of insurance company's agent (though an apparently isolated instance) coupled with the "catastrophic" economic injury to Mrs. Crocker facing foreclosure of her manufactured home in the wake of her husband's death against percentage of $2 million award to insurance companies' net worth). *Cf.* Miller v. Dobbs Mobile Bay, Inc., 661 So. 2d 203 (Ala. 1995) (similar facts, but fraud claim dismissed because deceased borrower was sole obligor and credit insurance did not list widow or children as secondary beneficiary; fraud claim did not survive his death).

alleged that the insurer's failure to pay benefits was part of a scheme to defraud.[607]

Factors which courts consider in holding a creditor to be the insurer's agent are its role in issuing and accepting applications, collecting and paying the premiums, and its receipt of a percentage of the premium.[608] Without expressly discussing agency theory, other courts have invoked waiver or estoppel theory to decide the issue, though this implicitly accepts the "minority" view of agency.

For example, in *Larr v. Minnesota Mutual Life Ins. Co.*[609] the debtor had reached the cutoff age of seventy within nine months of purchasing the insurance with the loan, though the insurer accepted payment of three monthly premiums after that date. The court held the acceptance of the premiums after the cutoff age waived the contract provision establishing an age limitation. The creditor's knowledge was attributed to the insurer, thus implicitly accepting the creditor's agency.

Where age is the ineligibility factor, actual or constructive knowledge should be easy to establish, as most credit applications and credit insurance applications ask for age or a date of birth. While a credit insurance premium appears as a single-payment, upfront charge on a closed-end loan, the creditor's payments to the insurer on the customers' loans may be in monthly installments.[610]

Some cases, however, hold that waiver and estoppel may avoid forfeiture of a policy, but cannot change, rewrite, or enlarge the contract's insured risks.[611] Moreover, the insured borrower's certain knowledge of a disqualifying condition will preclude application of waiver and estoppel.[612] But the consumer's vague awareness of some health problems which may or may not cause disability or death may not constitute adequate knowledge on the debtor's part.[613] Moreover, an innocent misrepresentation may not be a basis to infer "intent to deceive" nor to preclude application of waiver and estoppel doctrines.[614]

In some circumstances, UDAP statutes[615] or even RICO may be used. For example, the Third Circuit reversed summary judgment in favor of the insurer and remanded a case where borrowers had alleged that the insurer failed to pay excess disability benefits as provided for in their policies.[616] As with other insurance matters, claims for breach of contract and bad faith are also available when a claim has been purportedly denied based on policy exclusions.[617] Some states also have incontestability clauses, limiting the rights of the insurer to contest the validity of the policy in some specified circumstances.[618]

#### 6.8.3.3 Theories of Recovery Against the Creditor

Fraud claims against a creditor may be appropriate in challenging the denial of benefits.[619] Thus, knowingly selling credit

607 *Cf.* § 6.8.1, *supra* (renumerability of post-claim underwriting).

608 *See* Ford Life Ins. Co. v. Jones, 563 S.W.2d 399 (Ark. 1978); Vulcan Life & Accident Ins. Co. v. United Banking Co., 162 S.E.2d 798 (Ga. Ct. App. 1968); Justus v. Mountain Life Ins. Co., 1999 Tenn. App. LEXIS 702 (Tenn. Ct. App. Oct. 15, 1999). *Cf.* Union Sec. Life Ins. Co. v. Crocker, 667 So. 2d 688 (Ala. 1995), *vacated on other grounds*, 116 S. Ct. 1872 (1996), *upon remand from Supreme Court*, 709 So. 2d 1118 (Ala. 1997); Miller v. Dobbs Mobile Bay, Inc., 661 So. 2d 203 (Ala. 1995) (noting auto dealer/agent also allegedly told borrower he could not buy the car without purchasing the credit life insurance).

609 567 So. 2d 239 (Miss. 1990), and 924 F.2d 65 (5th Cir. 1991). *See also* Commonwealth of Puerto Rico v. Pan Am. Life Ins. Co., 307 F. Supp. 1065 (D. P.R. 1969) (master policy between creditor and insurer contained a clause stating that all borrowers "whom the creditor believes to be in good health" were eligible for insurance; court held this clause implied no affirmative duty on the creditor to investigate the health of borrowers, and since the company had accepted the premiums, it was estopped from denying coverage); Keller v. First Nat'l Bank, 403 S.E.2d 424, 427 (W. Va. 1991) ("[m]ost people expect insurance once they pay the premium," therefore, acceptance of premium payments by the seller, or an agent, after ineligibility becomes ascertainable was found to be a waiver of any ineligibility clause in the policy by virtue of creating a reasonable expectation of insurance).

610 *See* § 6.2, *supra*.

611 *See, e.g.*, Great Am. Reserve Ins. Co. v. Mitchell, 335 S.W.2d 707 (Tex. Civ. App. 1960) (where insurer accepted premiums beyond age termination date, insured only entitled to refund of premium).

*Great American* was not a credit insurance case, but two subsequent Texas cases explicitly followed *Great American*. Minnesota Mut. Life Ins. Co. v. Morse, 487 S.W.2d 317 (Tex. 1972); Hocutt v. Prudential Ins. Co., 501 S.W.2d 347 (Tex. Civ. App. 1973). *See also* Currie v. Occidental Life Ins. Co. of North Carolina, 194 S.E.2d 642 (N.C. 1973) (age-limitation clause); Sharp v. Richmond Life Ins. Co., 183 S.E.2d 132 (Va. 1971) (preexisting illness clause). *But cf.* Ginocchio v. American Bankers Life Assur. Co., 889 F. Supp. 1078 (N.D. Ill. 1995) (where credit disability insurance contract's term was ambiguous, creditor-agent's representation may fill the void).

612 *See* National Life Ins. Co. v. Harriott, 268 So. 2d 397 (Fla. 1972) (husband's purchase of credit life insurance on car loan clearly motivated by his wife's impending death, which he failed to disclose).

613 See, for example, Security Southwest Life Ins. Co. v. Gomez, 768 S.W.2d 505 (Tex. App. 1989), in which the court upheld a jury verdict finding that the debtor's representation on a credit insurance application that he was "in good health," despite treatment for ischemic heart disease, was not made with an intent to deceive. Here, the court observed that Mr. Gomez was a farmer who had an elementary education. He had been seen by his doctor over the years for various ailments, but never hospitalized or unable to work. Moreover, it was clear that his purpose in going to the bank was to obtain a loan for his farming operations, not for insurance to provide for his family upon his death. *See also* Gatlin v. World Serv. Life Ins. Co., 616 S.W.2d 606 (Tenn. 1981).

614 *See* Carter v. Service Life & Cas. Ins. Co., 703 S.W.2d 349 (Tex. App. 1985) (insurer had burden not only to plead and prove debtor's answers in application for credit insurance are false, but that debtor gave answers knowing them to be false).

615 *See generally* § 6.4.6, *supra*; National Consumer Law Center, Unfair and Deceptive Acts and Practices § 10.5.7 (7th ed. 2008 and Supp.).

616 Schroeder v. Acceleration Life, 972 F.2d 41 (3d Cir. 1992).

617 *See, e.g.*, Jewell v. Household Life Ins. Co., 2006 WL 1228831 (W.D. Ky. May 5, 2006) (discussing breach of contract, state UDAP, and bad faith claims for denial of credit life insurance claim when borrower suffered an amputation as a result of a blood clot and the insurer denied the claim based on the argument that it was not part of the dismemberment coverage).

618 *E.g.*, Ala. Code § 27-18-4 (group life).

619 Note that general claims of fraud regarding the terms of the insurance often will face the argument that a plaintiff has a duty to read the contract and cannot rely on oral misrepresentations regarding a

insurance to a borrower unlikely to be eligible for benefits has been found to be fraudulent under Alabama law.[620] One intriguing case raises the question of whether selling excessive insurance coverage may be fraudulent. The Alabama Supreme Court has held it is a factual question whether an automobile dealer fraudulently misrepresented the amount of insurance needed to pay off the debt in the event of death.[621]

The *Restatement of Torts* describes a common law duty to disclose facts basic to a transaction if one party knows the other is about to enter into the agreement under a mistake as to the facts and if the other party, because of the relationship involved, the customs of the trade or other objective circumstances, would reasonably expect disclosure of those facts.[622] The Colorado Court of Appeals has applied that doctrine in a situation in which the borrower testified he would not have purchased a credit disability policy had he known the monthly benefit did not fully cover his monthly obligation.[623] At least one court has found a duty to disclose factors which may indicate that the insurance may not provide the protection anticipated.[624] Certainly a lender has a duty to disclose to a borrower that he or she may be ineligible for benefits under the credit insurance policy being sold, particularly where the insurance agent, i.e., the creditor, is the agent of the insured.[625]

Some courts have held that, with respect to the sale of credit insurance, the creditor stands in a fiduciary or quasi-fiduciary relationship to the borrower.[626] Negligence or misrepresentation has also been used successfully.[627] Unconscionability may be appropriate in some circumstances,[628] as is a potential usury claim.[629]

An important cause of action is a state UDAP claim, where the state allows UDAP claims against creditors.[630] For ex-

---

written contract. *See, e.g.,* Ross v. Citifinancial, 344 F.3d 458 (5th Cir. 2003).

620 Union Sec. Life Ins. Co. v. Crocker, 667 So. 2d 688 (Ala. 1995) *vacated on other grounds*, 116 S. Ct. 1872 (1996), *upon remand from Supreme Court*, 709 So. 2d 1118 (Ala. 1997). *See also* Cordell v. Greene Fin. of Georgetown, Ga., 953 F. Supp. 1391 (M.D. Ala. 1996) (misrepresentation claim which involved the selling of disability insurance including a provision which excluded from coverage anyone not working at least thirty hours per week on the effective date to a borrower whose only source of income was Social Security (and, therefore, not working) survived creditor's and insurer's motion for summary judgment) (interpreting Georgia law). *But see* Amerson v. Gardner, 681 So. 2d 570 (Ala. Civ. App. 1996) (claim for fraud not stated where borrower was simply asked if he wanted credit disability insurance, where creditor had no knowledge of any preexisting conditions, and where borrower failed to read the insurance application prior to signing which informed him of the conditions of eligibility).

621 McCullar v. Universal Underwriters Life Ins. Co., 687 So. 2d 156 (Ala. 1996). Subsequently, the Alabama Supreme Court held that in evaluating the factual question of whether the premium calculation method was fraudulently suppressed, a claim will fail where the method for calculating the premiums is contained in the loan documents signed by the borrowers. *See* Singleton v. Protective Life Ins. Co., 857 So. 2d 803 (Ala. 2003). Moreover, where plaintiffs brought a purported class action alleging a common course of conduct in the sale of gross, rather than net, coverage of credit insurance, the Alabama Supreme Court found that a class cannot be certified for claims of negligent supervision/hiring that led to fraudulent suppression because the allegations of oral misrepresentations do not allow for common questions of law and fact to predominate. Voyager v. Whitson, 867 So. 2d 1065 (Ala. 2003).

622 Restatement (Second) of Torts § 551(2) (1977).

623 *See, e.g.,* Bair v. Public Serv. Emp. Credit Union, 709 P.2d 961, 962 (Colo. App. 1985). *But see* Blon v. Bank One, Akron, N.A., 519 N.E.2d 363 (Ohio 1988) (bank had no duty to disclose details of its financing fee arrangement with auto dealer whereby dealer's finder's fee was on sliding scale which increased with higher rates. (*Note*: the finder's fee was included in the interest rate calculation, so there was no allegation of "hidden" interest padding the principal.)).

624 *Compare* Merchants Bank v. Gill, 1999 Tex. App. LEXIS 3252 (Tex. App. Apr. 29, 1999) (bank had duty to tell insured that insurance company was insolvent), *and* Suburban State Bank v. Squires, 427 N.W.2d 393 (Wis. Ct. App. 1988) (where borrower had heart attack and collected on disability insurance prior to refinancing loan, court upheld finding that creditor was negligent in not advising borrower that new disability policy would bar recovery if borrower had another heart attack), *with* First United Bank of Poplarville v. Reid, 612 So. 2d 1131 (Miss. 1992) (bank was borrower's agent for purposes of processing credit insurance, owing duty of good faith and reasonable care. Court found no breach of that duty in bank's failure to inform borrowers that loan could not be renegotiated upon expiration if one were in poor health; no substantial credible evidence they would have sought other life insurance had they known it was not renewable).

625 *See, e.g.,* Union Sec. Life Ins. Co. v. Crocker, 667 So. 2d 688 (Ala. 1995), *vacated*, 116 S. Ct. 1872 (1996), *upon remand*, 709 So. 2d 1118 (Ala. 1997); Suburban State Bank v. Squires, 427 N.W.2d 393 (Wis. Ct. App. 1988) (where borrower had heart attack and collected on disability insurance under a prior loan, court upheld finding that creditor was negligent in not advising borrower that new disability policy sold at refinancing would bar recovery if borrower had another heart attack). *See also* Smoot v. Physicians Life Ins. Co., 87 P.3d 545 (N.M. Ct. App. 2003) (allegation of failure to disclose that monthly life insurance premiums are more costly than an annual premium states a claim for statutory and common law duty to disclose a material fact); Merchants Bank v. Gill, 199 Tex. App. 3252 (Tex. App. Apr. 29, 1999) (bank had duty to notify insured of insurer's insolvency).

626 *See* § 6.4.7, *supra*. In jurisdictions where the creditor is considered the agent of the borrower, instead of the insurer, a fiduciary duty should naturally flow from that.

627 *See, e.g.*, Beiter v. Decatur Fed. Sav. & Loan Ass'n, 150 S.E.2d 687 (Ga. 1966) (where a creditor undertakes to procure insurance and fails to do so due to its own fraud or misrepresentation, it is liable for the debtor's loss to the limit of the agreed-upon policy); American Bank and Trust Co. of Houma v. Deroche, 357 So. 2d 1176 (La. Ct. App. 1978) (using the reasoning in *Beiter* to find the creditor liable); Robichaud v. Athol Credit Union, 225 N.E.2d 347 (Mass. 1967); Musgrave v. Mutual Sav. & Loan Ass'n, 174 S.E.2d 820 (N.C. Ct. App. 1970) (where there was a question as to whether a loan had been insured, bank's "custom and usage" of insuring loans indicated to the borrower that this loan was insured; court further stated that this custom and usage, viewed alongside the bank's disorganized system of handling insurance applications, supported the finding of negligence by the bank); Park Fed. Sav. & Loan Ass'n v. Lillie, 265 N.E.2d 339 (Ohio Ct. C.P. Franklin Cty. 1970) (using the reasoning in *Beiter* to find the creditor liable). *See also* Strickler v. Neff Trailer Sales, Inc., 542 F.2d 890 (4th Cir. 1976) (recovery of punitive damages allowed from a creditor who "maliciously" disregarded debtor's application for credit insurance and retained premium payments).

628 *See* § 6.8.2, *supra*.

629 *See* § 6.8.1, *supra*.

630 *See* § 6.4.6, *supra*.

ample, a class was certified where a UDAP claim related to the defendant's practice of offering "easily available" credit insurance coverage in prominent print, relegating to small, inconspicuous print the precise terms of the insurance, and then rejecting claims on the ground that the customers had not been paying for the appropriate type of insurance.[631] A UDAP claim would also be appropriate where a consumer is denied credit life insurance coverage for health reasons where state law requires coverage to be provided notwithstanding health condition for coverage under a certain dollar amount. In one case the plaintiff used a UDAP theory to challenge the defendant's denial of insurance benefits, when the denial was based on the insured being past the maximum age permitted to be insured but when the defendant continued to collect premiums even after the insured reached the maximum age.[632]

A breach of contract claim may also be useful in certain circumstances. For example, by charging for and collecting insurance premiums, the creditor assumes a contractual obligation to purchase the insurance,[633] and to do so properly.[634] If it did not, it is liable for the full amount of the consumer's insurance claim. At least one court has held that an affirmative insurance authorization on the loan[635] may create a contractual duty to purchase the insurance.[636]

No matter the theory, actual direct damages may be calculated as if the insurer were liable on the policy, that is the benefit of the reasonably anticipated bargain.[637]

Courts have also denied a creditor's claim for a post-repossession deficiency where the creditor had failed to provide the consumer with claim forms necessary to apply for the disability insurance[638] and where the contract allowed repossession "to extent permitted by law" but state law regarding pending credit insurance claims was violated.[639]

## 6.9 Surpluses, Secondary Beneficiaries

Because the purpose of credit life insurance is to protect the account from default in the event the borrower dies, the named primary beneficiary will be the creditor. However, any surplus should be distributed to a secondary beneficiary. While there is no reliable data, many people question whether insurance companies actually distribute any surplus to a secondary beneficiary.

There are several reasons why these funds are not likely to be distributed, the most important of which is that a borrower's beneficiaries will not realize there is excess insurance. Creditors over-insure the loan by insuring the total of payments to give the creditor better protection and provide a larger premium base for collection. When the survivors are notified that the loan is paid off by insurance, they do not expect to receive or ask for extra cash benefits. In addition, in many transactions there is no secondary beneficiary designated who would have standing to file a claim.

A surplus will virtually always occur if a level life policy is written on a transaction, as it by definition over-insures the loan.[640] A surplus also will usually result even in the case of declining term life, unless the borrower was in default at the time of death. If the policy provides, for example, that the insurance "shall at no time exceed the scheduled or actual amount of unpaid indebtedness whichever is *greater*," there should be a surplus if the borrower was ahead in his or her scheduled payments at the time of death.[641] A similar issue may arise with respect to disability insurance.[642] A surplus may also

---

631 Taylor v. American Bankers Ins. Group, Inc., 700 N.Y.S.2d 458 (N.Y. App. Div. 1999). *But see* Vickers v. Interstate Dodge, 882 So. 2d 1236 (La. Ct. App. 2004) (plaintiff alleging forgery of election of purchase credit life insurance did not present evidence of actual damages under state's UDAP law).

632 *See* Eaves-Leanos v. Assurant, 2008 WL 80155 (W.D. Ky. Jan. 8, 2008). *See generally* § 6.8, *supra* (discussing challenges to post-claims underwriting).

633 Pernell v. First Sav. & Loan Ass'n, 336 So. 2d 764 (Miss. 1976); Watkins v. Valley Fid. & Trust Co., 474 S.W.2d 915 (Tenn. 1971).

634 *E.g.*, Barnett v. First Nat'l Bank, 253 So. 2d 480 (Fla. Dist. Ct. App. 1971) (creditor liable for damages equal to the benefits under the policy when it had insured the wrong person); *In re* Estate of Carter, 116 N.W.2d 419 (Iowa 1962) (creditor held liable when it did not insure all of the loans involved).

635 *See* § 6.5.3, *supra*; National Consumer Law Center, Truth in Lending § 3.9.4.5.5 (7th ed. 2010 and Supp.).

636 Allied Elevator, Inc. v. East Texas State Bank of Buna, 965 F.2d 34 (5th Cir. 1992) (decedent initialed request on face of note for credit life insurance and premium charge included in loan; court remands for consideration of whether that was a material term, the breach of which would excuse the debtor's estate from paying the balance).

In the absence of a contract, though, the creditor may have no obligation to procure the insurance. *E.g.*, Burgess v. Charlottesville Sav. & Loan Ass'n, 349 F. Supp. 133 (W.D. Va. 1972), *rev'd on jurisdictional grounds*, 477 F.2d 40 (4th Cir. 1973); Peer v. First Fed. Sav. & Loan Ass'n of Cumberland, 331 A.2d 299 (Md. 1975). However, in neither case did the creditor collect premiums, and in both cases it was not clear that an application for insurance had been made.

637 *E.g.*, Barnett v. First Nat'l Bank, 253 So. 2d 480 (Fla. Dist. Ct. App. 1971) (creditor liable for damages equal to the benefits under the policy when it had insured the wrong person).

638 Cincinnati Cent. Credit Union v. Harper, 652 N.E.2d 10 (Ohio Mun. Ct. 1995) ("had the employee assisted in the application for disability, there may have been no delinquency."). *See also* Chandler v. General Motors Acceptance Corp., 426 N.E.2d 521 (Ohio Ct. App. 1980) (denying summary judgment to creditor in a deficiency suit where the facts revealed that the creditor refused to complete its portion of a credit disability insurance claim which the consumer needed to file for payment but later repossessed the car!).

Oregon courts have interpreted U.C.C. Article 9 to mandate that creditors check to determine whether a consumer is eligible for purchased credit insurance benefits before repossessing collateral. *See* National Consumer Law Center, Repossessions § 4.2.1 (7th ed. 2010 and Supp.).

639 McManis v. San Diego Postal Credit Union, 71 Cal. Rptr. 2d 617 (Cal. Ct. App. 1998).

640 *See* § 6.3.1.2, *supra.*

641 *See* Dublinske v. Pacific Fid. Life Ins. Co., 230 N.W.2d 924 (Iowa 1975).

642 *See* Schroeder v. Acceleration Life, 972 F.2d 41 (3d Cir. 1992) (credit disability insurance contract which provided that insurance would terminate upon discharge of indebtedness, but also that termination would be without prejudice to any claim originating

result from the combined effect of different forms of credit insurance, as where there is property and credit life insurance on an automobile loan, and the borrower dies in an accident involving the insured auto.

The NAIC Model Act requires that each individual policy or certificate of insurance must state that benefits "shall be paid to the creditor to reduce or extinguish the unpaid indebtedness and, whenever the amount of insurance may exceed the unpaid indebtedness, that any such excess shall be payable to a beneficiary, other than the creditor, named by the debtor or to his estate."[643] Thus, failure to distribute the surplus would be a breach of the insurance contract. The NAIC Model Act language has been interpreted to impose a duty on the creditor to apply the benefits to the borrower's account and distribute the surplus. That may create a fiduciary duty on the creditor's part toward the borrowers, at least upon the insurer's payment of benefits.[644] Should the creditor retain the surplus, it should constitute compensation which the creditor is not authorized by law to receive, thus an illegal overcharge.

# 6.10 Rebate of Unearned Insurance Premiums

## *6.10.1 The Requirement of a Rebate*

Upon prepayment, refinancing, or default leading to cancellation of insurance, the unearned portion of the premium must be rebated.[645] At the outset of any litigation, practitioners should take care to ensure that insurers retain information regarding policy termination dates so that subsequent review of rebate issues is possible.[646]

The NAIC Model Act requires that each credit life or A&H insurance policy provide for a prompt refund or credit "to the person entitled thereto" in the event of termination of *insurance* prior to the scheduled maturity date of indebtedness.[647] The Model Act also requires that the insurance be terminated when the account is prepaid by renewal or otherwise.[648] The two provisions together thus mandate a refund any time the debt is prepaid by refinancing or otherwise.[649] This Credit Insurance Code provision is often reiterated in the applicable credit statutes.[650]

Failure to comply with these requirements may be widespread. For example, the Texas Attorney General reached nine settlements against credit insurers and auto dealers for failure to rebate credit insurance premiums upon refinancing or prepayment.[651] Some policies require written notice requiring the insured to notify the insurer of prepayments triggering rebates.[652] Such boilerplate language in the contract is not suffi-

---

prior to termination, was interpreted to mean that monthly benefits would be paid from date of disability to scheduled maturity date, even if loan actually satisfied earlier. According to a prior state court decision, company's failure to do so constituted breach of contract. Those facts formed basis for RICO and state UDAP claims in federal court, and appellate court denied insurer's motion for summary judgment).

643 Model Bill to Provide for the Regulation of Credit Life Ins. and Credit Accident and Health Ins., National Ass'n of Ins. Comm'rs, Model Regulatory Service § 6(B) (NIARS Corp. 1984).

644 Wilson v. Household Fin. Corp., 182 Cal. Rptr. 590, 593 (Cal. Ct. App. 1982). A UDAP claim should also be warranted.

645 For example, in the Federal Trade Commission's case against Stewart Finance, the company allegedly failed to rebate unearned insurance premiums upon refinancing of a consumer's loan. Fed. Trade Comm'n v. Stewart Fin. Co., Civ. No. 103CV-2648 (N.D. Ga. Nov. 9, 2005) (stipulated final judgment and order), *available at* www.ftc.gov/os/2005/11/051109stewartstipa103cv2648.pdf. *See also* Amoche v. Guarantee Trust Life Ins. Co., 556 F.3d 41 (1st Cir. 2009) (denying removal and affirming the trial court's certification of a class in action where consumers with automobile loans paid off the loans early but did not receive a refund of the unearned portion of the prepaid premium); JMIC Life Ins. Co. v. Toole, 634 S.E.2d 123 (Ga. Ct. App. 2006) (certifying class in case alleging failure to rebate and allowing insured to assert tort claim against insurer).

In some states, a borrower may be obligated to notify the insurance company directly of the loan's termination. *See id.* at 126 (finding that insured had satisfied requirement to notify insurer of loan termination). *See also* Baker v. Am. Heritage Life Ins. Co., 2006 WL 2536460 (M.D. Ga. Sept. 1, 2006) (class action alleging insurance company failed to rebate premiums upon loan termination, when state law requires borrower to notify insurance company directly).

646 Lawson v. Life of the S. Ins. Co., 738 F. Supp. 2d 1376 (M.D. Ga. 2010) (plaintiffs in putative class action sought to preserve insurer's records on termination dates when claim related to failure to rebate unearned premiums upon prepayment; district court found it had no such jurisdiction once the appeal had been filed).

647 Model Bill to Provide for the Regulation of Credit Life Ins. and Credit Accident and Health Ins., National Ass'n of Ins. Comm'rs, Model Regulatory Service § 8B (NIARS Corp. 1984).

648 *Id.* § 5.

649 The Supreme Court of Mississippi has ruled that an undue delay of a premium refund supports an award for punitive damages. MIC Life Ins. Co. v. Hicks, 825 So. 2d 616 (Miss. 2002) (finding that a punitive damages award is appropriate for a two-year delay, but holding that a $1 million award for failure to refund $637.99 is unconstitutionally excessive and that trial and evidentiary errors in this particular case preclude a punitive damage award against the insurer).

650 *E.g.*, Iowa Code § 537.2510.

It may also be incorporated by a general reference in the credit statute to the applicability of the credit insurance code. It also may be provided for in the contract. *See* Amoche v. Guarantee Trust Life Ins. Co., 556 F.3d 41 (1st Cir. 2009) (denying removal in class action regarding failure to rebate unearned credit insurance premiums for borrowers who paid off early and affirming the trial court's granting of summary judgment in favor of consumers, holding that the insurance company's failure to provide rebate violated the express terms of the contract).

651 *See* State of Texas v. Resource Life Ins. Co., No., D-1-GV-07-000408 (Mar. 2, 2010), *available at* www.oag.state.tx.us/newspubs/releases/2010/030310rlic_avc.pdf (agreed order approving assurance of voluntary compliance); Press Release, Resource Life Ins. Co. to Refund $2 Million to Auto Credit Insurance Policyholders (Mar. 4, 2010), *available at* www.oag.state.tx.us/oagnews/release.php?id=3235 (stating that nine settlements totaling $37 million in refunds to Texas consumers had been reached). *See also* America Gen. Fin. Servs. v. Griffin, 685 F. Supp. 2d 729 (N.D. Ohio 2010) (class action counterclaim alleging that insurance companies routinely failed to properly refund credit insurance premiums).

652 *See, e.g.*, Santana v. Union Fidelity Life Ins. Co., 2009 WL 4799376 (N.D. Ohio July 1, 2009) (dismissing insured's complaint because

cient to establish a condition precedent to a rebate, however, and thus the rebate still must be provided.[653] Moreover, such language often will violate state law and public policy.[654]

Another way in which creditors may try to evade the requirement to rebate unearned insurance premiums is to use boilerplate language taking a security interest in insurance. Any purported security interest in insurance should be carefully examined: contract language giving a security interest in specified property "and insurance or other proceeds thereon" was held in one case to give rise to a security interest only in property insurance on the collateral. Neither it, nor any other provision in the contract, gave the creditor any right to retain refunds on the credit life and disability insuring the loan.[655]

## *6.10.2 Rebates upon Default and Acceleration of the Debt*

Some state statutes require that all unearned charges, including insurance, be rebated on prepayment, and further require that acceleration be treated as prepayment.[656] Also review carefully the terms of the master policy between the lender and the insurer, if group insurance, or the borrower's policy if individually insured. The insurance contract may require the rebate.

The lender, however, may not credit the account with a refund upon acceleration, arguing the policy will remain in force until the originally scheduled maturity, and that the insurance premium is therefore an "earned" charge not subject to the rebate requirement. Theoretically, leaving insurance policies in effect after default may not seem to be unfair to borrowers, but for the fact that borrowers, many of whom may not even know the account is insured in the first place, are unlikely to think about submitting insurance claims once the debt has been reduced to judgment. More importantly, the insurance in fact may not remain in force, depending on the terms of the policy. That, of course, would deprive the creditor's argument of any semblance of validity.

One Georgia case states that there is no general requirement that a lender cancel insurance upon acceleration. The court held that there is thus no violation of a statute requiring insurance refunds upon cancellation of the insurance when the creditor accelerates the debt in accordance with a properly drafted acceleration clause, without giving an insurance refund because the insurance is still in effect.[657] However, such a requirement may be implied by the general rebate statute, or a rebate may be required because the insurance was in fact canceled.

If a state statute specifically provides that all required rebates must be made upon acceleration as if there was prepayment, the argument that the policy can remain in force and therefore is not an "unearned" charge has little force. First, the clear legislative intent is to treat acceleration as if it were prepayment by any other means, and the creditor cannot leave the insurance in force in those circumstances. Further, the argument that credit insurance could remain in force until the end of the originally scheduled term proves too much: it would suggest that creditors do not need to rebate interest until a debt is actually paid, irrespective of when acceleration occurred, an interpretation that would render the rebate statute a nullity, and thus an interpretation which the courts should not adopt.[658]

Irrespective of state law regarding how rebates upon acceleration are to be handled, whether the insurance policy remains "in force" is a question of fact. Even if state law does not mandate termination of the policy, it may terminate upon default by its own terms, which then triggers the rebate requirement. The actual policy must be reviewed to see how it defines termination events. If the insurance is group insurance, the borrower's certificate will probably not include the relevant terms. Instead, the master policy issued to the creditor must be reviewed. The master policy may be obtained from the creditor or the insurer. It also will be on file at the state insurance department.

Some policies include default-related events as events triggering the automatic termination of the loan. Such events may relate to the repossession of the loan's collateral, to a specified kind of default in payment on the loan (e.g., six month's nonpayment), or to entry of judgment on the debt.[659]

If the policy calls for automatic termination of the policy at a specific default-related time, the refund must be made as of the date of that termination, even if the creditor took no action at that time to cause the cancellation. This is because the refund language in use in most states requires a "prompt" refund upon termination of the *insurance*.[660] In fact, even if the creditor thinks the policy is still in force and continues to forward

policy clearly required notice, which had not been provided); Bishop's Property Invs., L.L.C. v. Protective Life Ins. Co., 255 F.R.D. 619 (M.D. Ga. 2009) (denying class certification to plaintiffs seeking rebates of unearned credit insurance premiums because some but not all policies required notice of prepayment).

653 Resource Life Ins. Co. v. Buckner, 698 S.E.2d 19 (Ga. Ct. App. 2010) (affirming class certification on the rebate issue and finding that sanctions were not unreasonable due to creditor's conduct in the discovery process).

654 *See id.*

655 *In re* Williams, 92 B.R. 761 (Bankr. S.D. Ohio 1988) (*N.B.*: the right to a rebate of credit life and disability rebates arose because the insurance contract automatically terminated coverage upon repossession of collateral securing the loan).

656 *E.g.*, Iowa Code § 537.2510(1), (6).

657 Williams v. Charter Credit Co., 347 S.E.2d 635 (Ga. Ct. App. 1986).

658 Singer and Singer, 2A Sutherland on Statutory Construction § 46.6 (7th ed. 2007). *But see* Central Budget Corp. v. Blackett, 349 N.Y.S.2d 577 (N.Y. Civ. Ct. 1973) (acceleration accelerates maturity date, therefore no credit due if paid or accelerated "before maturity").

659 *See, e.g.*, *In re* Williams, 92 B.R. 761 (Bankr. S.D. Ohio 1988) (terms of credit insurance agreement between insurer and creditor provided that repossession of the collateral terminated the insurance coverage and gave rise to right to refund for unearned premiums, and borrower was to be given refund or credit on his account if insurance terminated before term expired); Carl v. General Motors Assurance Corp., 199 N.E.2d 452 (Ill. App. Ct. 1964).

660 Model Bill to Provide for the Regulation of Credit Life Ins. and Credit Accident and Health Ins., National Ass'n of Ins. Comm'rs, Model Regulatory Service § 8B (NIARS Corp. 1984).

monthly premium installments on that account to the insurer, the policy still may have been automatically terminated,[661] thus triggering the refund requirement.

In addition to automatic termination situations under the insurance policy, the creditor may overtly take some action resulting in the cancellation of the insurance. The creditor will sometimes cancel the insurance when the borrower is in default even if the policy itself does not list default as a ground for termination.[662]

Determine through formal or informal discovery how the creditor forwards to the insurer the premiums on insurance in force. On open-end accounts, the borrower usually pays the insurance periodically, so that it is most likely to be forwarded from the creditor to insurer on a periodic basis as well. In closed-end credit, while the premium usually is assessed to the borrower as a single up-front charge, the creditor may nonetheless forward to the insurer the premium payments on policies in force on a monthly outstanding-balance basis. This permits the creditor, who in the interim may retain the unearned portion of the premium, to obtain additional investment income. If the creditor uses the monthly outstanding balance premium payment method, and the consumer's policy premium is not forwarded after default, acceleration, or judgment, the policy has been terminated and the refund should be credited as of the date of termination. On the other hand, forwarding the premiums will not keep the policy in force contrary to automatic termination provisions in the policy.

In addition to the issue of whether the insurance policy as a matter of *fact* remained in force after default or acceleration, the credit contract language should be examined. Some usury statutes prohibit not only receiving excess charges, but also merely "contracting for" charges greater than that allowed by law.[663] If the contract on its face provides that the lender will accelerate insurance premiums, this contractual provision may violate such a statute, thus automatically implicating the penalties for usury, including forfeiture of interest.[664] This is true even if the policy form has been approved by the insurance department.[665] Furthermore, filing suit for an amount which includes unrebated insurance, if rebates are required, may constitute "charging" an illegal charge.[666]

## 6.10.3 Calculating the Rebate

State insurance departments generally prescribe the method by which a rebate must be calculated, usually authorizing the generous Rule of 78s formula. Even in states where interest rebates must be calculated by the actuarial method, the Rule of 78s may be authorized for credit insurance rebates. Other authorized methods are the pro rata method, an average of the Rule of 78s and pro rata methods, or the Rule of Anticipation.[667] There may be a minimum amount below which rebates need not be made.[668] For information on how to check the mathematical accuracy of a rebate, see § 5.8, *supra,* on rebates.

## 6.10.4 Consumer Remedies

Failure to provide a rebate is a breach of contract.[669] In addition, if the lender has retained greater compensation than that to which it is entitled, the amount retained would be interest.[670] Similarly, where a contract term provide that insurance premium refunds will be applied to the last maturing installments, and not to the principal remaining unpaid or to currently maturing installments, such a provision contains "the seeds of usury" and may render the transaction usurious.[671] The reason such a provision unfairly and illegally benefits the creditor is that the scheduled installments are calculated to retire the principal at a predicted rate. Since the premium cost is ordinarily a part of the principal, if initially imposed in accord with all applicable laws, the refund should reduce the principal immediately, thus reducing the base upon which earned interest is to be calculated for the remainder of the term. By applying it to the last due installments, the creditor deprives the borrower of the earlier (and consequently cheaper) retirement of principal.

661 *See* Palmer v. Newport Trust Co., 245 A.2d 438 (Me. 1968).

662 *See, e.g.*, Federal Deposit Ins. Corp. v. Gulf Life Ins. Co., 737 F.2d 1513, 1518 n.4 (11th Cir. 1984).

663 *See generally* § 4.2.2, *supra*.

664 Brown v. Associates Fin. Servs. Corp., 346 S.E.2d 873 (Ga. Ct. App. 1986). *See also* Varner v. Century Fin. Co., 738 F.2d 1143, 1149–1150 n.10 (11th Cir. 1984).

665 Brown v. Associates Fin. Servs. Corp., 346 S.E.2d 873, 874 (Ga. Ct. App. 1986).

666 *See* § 5.8.6, *supra*.

667 *See* Fagg, Credit Life and Disability Insurance 182–184 (1986).

668 Model Bill to Provide for the Regulation of Credit Life Ins. and Credit Accident and Health Ins., National Ass'n of Ins. Comm'rs, Model Regulatory Service § 8B (NIARS Corp. 1984).

669 *See* Adams v. Monumental Gen. Cas. Co., 2007 WL 2071252 (M.D. Ga. July 19, 2007) (dismissing claims regarding insurance rebate under tort theories but allowing claim to proceed for breach of contract).

Often, this problem is widespread and conducive to class litigation. *See, e.g.*, Resource Life Ins. Co. v. Buckner, 698 S.E.2d 19 (Ga. Ct. App. 2010) (affirming class certification on the rebate issue and finding that discovery was not unreasonable due to creditor's conduct in the discovery process). *See also* American Gen. Fin. Servs. v. Griffin, 685 F. Supp. 2d 729 (N.D. Ohio 2010) (holding that class action for failure to rebate could not be removed under Class Action Fairness Act and remanding to state court); Eldridge v. Cardif Life Ins. Co., 266 F.R.D. 173 (N.D. Ohio 2010) (failing to certify class on basis that plaintiff had not shown that putative class was so numerous as to make joinder impracticable).

670 For reasons which are unclear, a case appears to have challenged the insurer, rather than the creditor for routinely failing to rebate unearned credit insurance premiums unless asked by the borrowers. Though a district court judge condemned the practice as "reprehensible," he held it did not constitute mail fraud sufficient to state a RICO claim. Richards v. Combined Ins. Co., 55 F.3d 247 (7th Cir. 1995). A UDAP claim, consequently dismissed on jurisdictional grounds, may be more successful if it is refiled.

671 Ford Motor Credit v. Yarbrough, 567 S.W.2d 96 (Ark. 1978).

# Chapter 7 Litigation

## 7.1 Introduction

This chapter addresses litigation issues: principles for construing usury statutes; whether there is a right to a jury trial; whether creditors can impose mandatory arbitration; what elements are necessary to establish a prima facie case for the borrower; establishing usury in a state that has eliminated the relevant interest rate ceiling; typical creditor defenses; typical remedies available upon a finding of usury or other types of illegal overcharges; and two jurisdictional issues—whether the doctrine of complete preemption allows a creditor to remove a state lawsuit against a federally related lender to federal court, and the circumstances under which courts can exercise long-arm jurisdiction over out-of-state lenders and trusts.

## 7.2 Construction of State Usury Statutes

### *7.2.1 Broad vs. Narrow Construction of Usury Statutes*

#### 7.2.1.1 Introduction

Usury is a statutory offense rather than an infraction of common law, and principles of statutory construction come into play in the many cases where the controlling usury statutes are vague or ambiguous. Unfortunately, the misunderstood history of usury has created confusion as to how one important principle of statutory construction applies—that statutes in derogation of common law are to be strictly construed. Moreover, two other basic tenets of statutory construction—the broad construction of remedial statutes, and the strict construction of penal statutes—conflict when applied to the typical usury statute.[1]

Statutory construction is an issue only when some ambiguity exists for a court to construe. If statutory language is clear it must be applied as written.[2]

Additional principles may come into play when a usury provision is part of a state constitution. California recognizes a presumption in favor of interpreting a state constitutional usury provision in a way that will uphold a state statute adopted pursuant to it.[3]

#### 7.2.1.2 Invoking the History and Purpose of Usury Statutes

The fact that specific usury ceilings did not exist at common law can be misleading: to some it suggests that the interest restrictions contained in modern usury statutes are novel restrictions on previously unregulated lending and thus these restrictions should be narrowly construed because they would be in derogation of common law.[4] In fact, at early common law it was forbidden to charge *any* interest at all, and common law recognized an action to recover usury (i.e., interest) paid.[5] The first usury statutes legalized the previously prohibited practice of charging interest on loans.

Thus, usury statutes are actually in derogation of common law only to the extent that they *allow* the charging of interest, *not* to the extent that they restrict interest charges. Therefore, when applying the rule that statutes in derogation of common law should be strictly construed, one must conclude that it is the right to *charge* interest in modern usury statutes which should be strictly construed. Conversely, restrictions on that right should be broadly interpreted.[6]

---

1 *See generally* Singer & Singer, 3A Sutherland Statutory Construction § 70.7 (7th ed. 2010).

2 *See* Rhodes v. Hartford, 513 A.2d 124 (Conn. 1986); Ponca Fin. Co. v. Esser, 132 S.W.3d 930 (Mo. Ct. App. 2004) (reading agreed rate statute to be unambiguous and to override statute limiting judgment interest rate).

3 OCM Principal Opportunities Fund v. CIBC World Mkts. Corp., 85 Cal. Rptr. 3d 350 (Cal. Ct. App. 2008).

4 *See, e.g.,* Cullen v. Bragg, 350 S.E.2d 798 (Ga. Ct. App. 1986); Jacobson v. General Fin. Corp., 592 N.E.2d 1121 (Ill. App. Ct. 1992); Schuran, Inc. v. Walnut Hill Assocs., 606 A.2d 885 (N.J. Super. Ct. Law Div. 1991); C & K Invs. v. Fiesta Group, Inc., 248 S.W.3d 234 (Tex. App. 2007).

5 *See* § 7.8.2.2, *infra.*

6 *See generally* Dennis v. Bradbury, 236 F. Supp. 683 (D. Colo. 1964), *aff'd*, 368 F.2d 905 (10th Cir. 1966); Federal-Mogul Corp. v. Dep't of Treasury, 411 N.W.2d 169 (Mich. Ct. App. 1987) (statutes allowing interest are in derogation of common law, thus court strictly construes statute to deny authority of Tax Tribunal to award interest on franchise fee refund in absence of specific statutory grant of such authority); Smith v. Mitchell, 616 A.2d 17 (Pa. Super. Ct. 1992) ("At common law the taking of any interest whatever was illegal, and the right to charge it, being a privilege granted by statute, is subject to legislative control"); Whitworth & Yancy v. Adams, 5 Rand. 333, 26 Va. 415 (1827) (no interest could be charged under common law); Note, *Interest Rates and the Law: A History of Usury*, 1981 Ariz. St. L.J. 61; Horack, *A Survey of the General Usury Laws*, 8 Law and Contemp. Probs. 7 (1941).

### 7.2.1.3 Remedial vs. Penal Purposes

The conflict between the broad construction of remedial statutes and the narrow construction of penal statutes also may cloud statutory construction issues. Specifically, usury statutes seek to protect necessitous debtors from the exploitation of avaricious lenders[7] and to compensate debtors for the damages they have incurred through the payment of usurious interest. These remedial purposes are a reason to construe ambiguous provisions broadly to protect consumers.[8]

On the other hand, many usury statutes go beyond compensating the victims of usury and impose penalties and forfeitures upon creditors who are guilty of usury. For example, many usury statutes prohibit a lender from collecting *any* interest on a usurious loan, and some forbid the recovery of principal. Such penalties or forfeitures are designed for their deterrent effect.[9] Without these penalties, a lender could charge usurious interest as a matter of course and simply refund the excess over the legal rate if challenged. Consequently, these remedies are penal, and their presence suggests that usury statutes should be strictly construed.[10] (Of course, some usury statutes carry greater penalties than others. As the degree of the penalty decreases, any need to construe usury statutes in favor of lenders also decreases.[11]) Similarly, a criminal usury statute, if susceptible

7 *See, e.g.*, Ghirardo v. Antonioli, 883 P.2d 960 (Cal. 1994) (purpose of usury law is "to protect the necessitous, impecunious borrower who is unable to acquire credit from the usual sources and is forced by his economic circumstances to resort to excessively costly funds to meet his financial needs"); Jersey Palm-Gross, Inc. v. Paper, 658 So. 2d 531, 534 (Fla. 1995) (purpose of usury laws is to "protect borrowers from paying unfair and excessive interest to overreaching creditors"; and "to bind the power of creditors over necessitous debtors and prevent them from extorting harsh and undue terms in the making of loans"); Nelson v. Associates Fin. Servs. Co., 659 N.W.2d 635 (Mich. Ct. App. 2002) (purpose of restrictions on prepayment penalties is to protect loan customers from being locked in to high interest rates); Watkins v. Mississippi Bar, 589 So. 2d 660 (Miss. 1991) (central purpose of usury law is to protect borrowers from overreaching creditors); Scarr v. Boyer, 818 P.2d 381, 383 (Mont. 1991) ("Usury statutes protect borrowers who lack real bargaining power against overreaching by creditors"); Seidel v. 18 E. 17th St. Owners, 598 N.E.2d 7 (N.Y. 1992); Schneider v. Phelps, 359 N.E.2d 1361, 1365 (N.Y. 1977) ("The purpose of usury laws, from time immemorial, has been to protect desperately poor people from the consequences of their own desperation. Law-making authorities in almost all civilizations have recognized that the crush of financial burdens causes people to agree to almost any conditions of the lender and to consent to even the most improvident loans. Lenders, with the money, have all the leverage; borrowers, in dire need of money have none."); Car Now Acceptance Co. v. Block, 2003 WL 21714583 (Ohio Ct. App. July 14, 2003); Smith v. Mitchell, 616 A.2d 17 (Pa. Super. Ct. 1992) (purpose of usury law, which applied to business loans under $10,000, "to protect the citizenry . . . from being exploited at the hands of unscrupulous individuals seeking to circumvent the law at the expense of *unsuspecting* borrowers who may have no other avenue to secure backing for a, for example, business venture"); Whitworth & Yancy v. Adams, 5 Rand 333, 335, 26 Va. 333 (1827) ("These statutes were made to protect needy and necessitous persons from the oppression of usurers and monied men, who are eager to take advantage of the distress of others; while they, on the other hand, from the pressure of their distress, are ready to come to any terms; and with their eyes open, not only break the law, but complete their ruin"); Demopolis v. Galvin, 786 P.2d 804, 807 (Wash. Ct. App. 1990) (purpose is to protect desperate borrowers "driven to borrow money at any cost"). *See also* Trapp v. Hancuh, 530 N.W.2d 879 (Minn. Ct. App. 1995) (purpose of usury laws is "to protect the weak and necessitous from being taken advantage of by lenders who can unilaterally establish the terms of the loan transaction"); Paulman v. Filtercorp, 899 P.2d 1259 (Wash. 1995) ("The evil at which the usury laws are aimed . . . is the oppression of the borrower 'who by adversity and necessity of economic life [is] driven to borrow money at any cost' "; protecting vulnerable borrowers from oppression is the objective). *Cf.* Sunburst Bank v. Keith, 648 So. 2d 1147 (Miss. 1995) (purpose of usury statutes and its remedy of forfeiture "is to discourage exorbitance"; business loans at issue). *See generally* Steven W. Bender, *Rate Regulation at the Crossroads of Usury and Unconscionability: The Case for Regulating Abusive and Commercial Interest Rates Under the Unconscionability Standard*, 31 Houston L. Rev. 721 (1994).

8 *See, e.g.*, General Motors Acceptance Corp. v. Mid-West Chevrolet Co., 66 F.2d 1 (10th Cir. 1933); *In re* Feldman, 259 F. Supp. 218 (D. Conn. 1966); Agapitov v. Lerner, 133 Cal. Rptr. 2d 837, 838 (Cal. Ct. App. 2003); State v. Weiner, 28 A.2d 16 (Del. 1942); Liberty Fin. Co. v. Catterton, 158 A. 16 (Md. 1932) (small loan law); Williams v. Standard Fed. Sav. & Loan Ass'n, 545 A.2d 708 (Md. Ct. Spec. App. 1988) (state usury statute interpreted as remedial and not penal for purpose of applying statute of limitations); Nelson v. Associates Fin. Servs. Co., 659 N.W.2d 635 (Mich. Ct. App. 2002) (restrictions on prepayment penalties); Mitchell v. Residential Funding Corp., 334 S.W.3d 477 (Mo. Ct. App. 2010); Pease v. Taylor, 496 P.2d 757 (Nev. 1972); Perez v. Rent-A-Center, 892 A.2d 1255, 1268 (N.J. 2006) (RISA must be liberally construed); Tilley v. Pacesetter Corp., 585 S.E.2d 292, 298 (S.C. 2003) (applying pre-1997 version of statute); Income Tax Buyers, Inc. v. Hamm, 1992 WL 12092431 (S.C. Ct. Com. Pl. Jan. 14, 1992); Valley Acceptance Corp. v. Glasby, 337 S.E.2d 291 (Va. 1985) (small loan law); Radford v. Community Mortgage & Inv. Corp., 312 S.E.2d 282 (Va. 1984); Dunlap v. Friedman's, Inc., 582 S.E.2d 841 (W. Va. 2003) (state Consumer Credit and Protection Act); State v. J.C. Penny Co., 179 N.W.2d 641 (Wis. 1970). *See also* Pakay v. Davis, 367 Ark. 421 (Ark. 2006) (applying general rule that provisions of state constitution should be liberally construed; giving continued effect to constitutional usury cap by substituting different FRB rate for one that FRB discontinued). *Cf.* Sunburst Bank v. Keith, 648 So. 2d 1147 (Miss. 1995) (remedy of forfeiture of "all interest" includes interest paid before note became usurious). *See generally* Annotation, 43 A.L.R.4th 675 at §§ 3–4 (1986) (construction and application of second mortgage statutes).

9 *See, e.g.*, Seidel v. 18 E. 17th St. Owners, 598 N.E.2d 7 (N.Y. 1992) (New York's severe penalty of voiding the loan reflects legislative view that severe "consequences are necessary to deter the evils of usury").

10 *See, e.g.*, Thrift v. Hubbard, 44 F.3d 348 (5th Cir. 1995); Allied Chem. Corp. v. Jack MacKay, 695 F.2d 854 (5th Cir. 1983); Anderson v. Chainani (*In re* Kemper) 263 B.R. 773 (E.D. Tex. 2001); Morosani v. First Nat'l Bank of Atlanta, 539 F. Supp. 1171 (N.D. Ga. 1982), *rev'd on other grounds*, 703 F.2d 1220 (11th Cir. 1983); Indian Springs State Bank v. Kelley's Auto Supply, Inc., 675 P.2d 379 (Kan. Ct. App. 1984); Ranson v. C.A. Snyder, 75 So. 2d 738 (Miss. 1954); Crisman v. Corbin, 128 P.2d 959 (Or. 1942); Maners v. Lexington County Sav. & Loan Ass'n, 267 S.E.2d 422 (S.C. 1980); Swank v. Sverdlin, 121 S.W.3d 785 (Tex. App. 2003); Domizio v. Progressive County Mut. Ins. Co., 54 S.W.3d 867 (Tex. App. 2001); Standard Sav. Ass'n v. Greater New Canaan Missionary Baptist Church, 786 S.W.2d 774 (Tex. App. 1990).

11 *See In re* Russell, 72 B.R. 855 (Bankr. E.D. Pa. 1987) (distinguishing penalty of three times the excess charges actually paid from

of multiple interpretations, may be strictly construed in favor of the party facing liability.[12]

The conflict between these two principles of statutory construction, when applied to usury statutes, promotes a standard litigation posture in usury cases in which the borrower emphasizes the remedial purposes of usury laws, the lender claims strict construction, and each side cites plentiful authority to support its position. The result is a legal deadlock which effectively leaves the court free to construe usury statutes as it wishes, and usury decisions which involve any degree of statutory construction frequently seem based as much on the equities of the case or the predisposition of the court as on any compelling logical reason for choosing one rule of construction over another.

### 7.2.1.4 The Purpose of Special Usury Laws

Regardless of the nature of usury laws in general, there are sound reasons to argue that the particular usury statutes most often involved in consumer cases—small loan laws, installment sales acts, second mortgage acts, and consumer credit codes—are distinguishable from general usury statutes and should be more liberally construed.[13] General usury statutes were, for the most part, adopted prior to the twentieth century at a time when consumer credit was limited, almost to the point of nonexistence.[14] The consumer loans that did exist were made by loan sharks, and the limited number of consumer credit sales which existed were beyond the scope of usury laws because of the time-price doctrine.

Instead, usury statutes were primarily concerned with commercial transactions which, both then and now, have many different characteristics from consumer credit. Most significantly, commercial transactions are far more likely than consumer transactions to occur after detached consideration and after arm's length bargaining over both interest rates and other credit terms.[15] Furthermore, the payment of usurious interest by a business, while serious, will not directly cause the same individual loss or hardship that may be suffered by a consumer who is the victim of usury. Consequently, it is not surprising that nineteenth and early twentieth century courts, interpreting general usury statutes in a commercial setting, construed those statutes narrowly, preferring to limit the government's role in private contracts, especially in light of the serious consequences of a usury violation for the lender.

So-called special usury laws, such as small loan laws, industrial bank acts, retail installment sales acts, and second mortgage acts, almost all of which have been enacted since the 1920s, are clearly distinguishable. Small loan laws, for example, were specifically aimed at protecting individual borrowers.[16] As originally structured, they attempted to displace the monopoly of the loan sharks by luring commercial investors to the small loan market. The general approach was to allow interest rates that, especially by the standards of the day, were extremely generous to lenders, in return for strict licensing and regulation to prevent the recurrence of loansharking.[17]

The structure and purposes of many special usury statutes such as small loan laws can enable practitioners to distinguish commercial usury cases decided under general usury statutes, and to argue that the more carefully targeted special usury laws should be broadly construed to give effect to their remedial purposes, despite their penal provisions. Typically, the best way to evaluate the purposes of any one special usury statute is to examine the language of the statute itself. Such statutes frequently contain statements of legislative purpose which reveal remedial goals.

For example, the declaration of legislative intent in the Seventh Draft of the Uniform Small Loan Law, which regulated loans of $300 or less, discusses the inadequacy of previously existing usury laws in governing small loans, recognizes the exorbitant charges, fraud, and oppressive collection practices prevalent among such loans, and specifies that legislation to control this class of loans is necessary to protect the public welfare.[18] This statute remains at the core of many contemporary consumer loan acts and that statement of purpose likewise remains. Similarly, the Uniform Consumer Credit Code contains a statement of purpose which, although vastly more qualified than that of the Uniform Small Loan Law, inherently recognizes the need for special consumer credit legislation. It specifies that one purpose of the UCCC is "to protect consumers against unfair practices by some suppliers of consumer credit, having due regard for the interest of legitimate and scrupulous creditors,"

---

more severe penalties of automatic forfeiture of principal and/or interest).

12 Cannarozzi v. Fiumara, 371 F.3d 1, 5 (1st Cir. 2004) (Mass. law); Glinton v. And R, Inc., 524 S.E.2d 481 (Ga. 1999); Fleet Fin., Inc. v. Jones, 430 S.E.2d 352 (Ga. 1993); Marshall v. Speedee Cash of Ga., 665 S.E.2d 888 (Ga. Ct. App. 2008) (invoking rule of strict construction to hold that provision of pawn statute allowing thirty-day term overrode provision creating criminal penalty if term was less than a calendar month, which would sometimes be thirty-one days). *Cf.* Hartsfield Co. v. Fulwiler, 200 S.E. 309 (Ga. 1938) (interpreting identical language in the Small Loan Act, but reaching opposite result in a civil collection case, though the remedy therein was the "penal" one of voiding the loan. See the dissent in *Fleet Finance* for a discussion of the seeming inconsistency).

13 *See* Chroniak v. Golden Inv. Corp., 577 A.2d 1209, 1213 (N.H. 1990) (purpose of act is to protect homeowners finding themselves "forced to go into a second mortgage"). *See generally* Annotation, 43 A.L.R.4th 675, at §§ 3–4 (1986) (construction and application of second mortgage statutes).

14 *See also* Curran, Trends in Consumer Credit Legislation (1966); Curran, *Legislative Controls as a Response to Consumer-Credit Problems*, 8 B.C. Ind. & Comm. L. Rev. 409 (1966–1967). *See generally* § 1.2, *supra* (discussing development of consumer credit legislation).

15 *See* Curran, *Legislative Controls as a Response to Consumer-Credit Problems*, 8 B.C. Ind. & Com. L. Rev. 409, 427 (1966–1967).

16 *See, e.g.*, Aros v. Beneficial Arizona, Inc., 977 P.2d 784 (Ariz. 1999).

17 Curran, *Legislative Controls as a Response to Consumer-Credit Problems*, 8 B.C. Ind. & Com. L. Rev. 409, 410–412 (1966–1967).

18 Seventh Draft of the Uniform Small Loan Law § 1(a) (as revised June 1, 1942), *reprinted in* Curran, Trends in Consumer Credit Legislation 144 (1966). *See also In re* Rose, 266 B.R. 192 (Bankr. N.D. Cal. 2001) (applying liberal construction mandate of California's Finance Lenders Law).

and instructs that the Act "be liberally construed and applied to promote its underlying purposes and policies."[19]

Some special usury laws say that they are remedial and should be broadly construed. In such cases, it is a simple matter to argue that this legislative intent should be respected. Even without such a provision, special usury laws inherently recognize the existence of special classes of transactions or borrowers, and should be interpreted as reaching all of the transactions or borrowers in the protected class unless an exception was clearly intended by the legislature.[20]

In addition, the enactment of special usury laws when a general usury statute is already in force clearly indicates the inadequacy of the preexisting law either as written or as applied. Thus, rules of construction applied to preexisting usury statutes need not automatically control the construction of the new statute. Finally, in the case of credit sales, it may be possible to argue that installment sales acts are technically not "usury" statutes and should not be interpreted as such because usury laws did not historically apply to credit sales under the time-price doctrine.[21]

## 7.2.2 Expressio Unius Est Exclusio Alterius: *Limiting the Creditor's Ability to Add Extra Charges Not Specifically Authorized*

Creditors may try to increase their return by adding non-interest fees to a loan.[22] The statutory construction principle *expressio unius est exclusio alterius*[23] is especially useful in challenging these fees as hidden interest, particularly under special usury statutes with roots in Small Loan Acts. Current versions of small loan acts (also called regulated loan acts or consumer loan acts), second mortgage laws, and some retail installment sales acts often have provisions similar to one in the Uniform Small Loan Act:

> In addition to the interest [or charges] herein provided for, no further or other charge or amount for any examination, service, brokerage, expense, fee, or bonus or otherwise shall be directly or indirectly charged, contracted for, or received.[24]

The statutes then specifically list certain types of charges which the creditor can impose on the transaction. The principle that the express mention of one thing implies the exclusion of others dictates that the list of authorized charges is an exhaustive list, and no other costs are permitted.[25]

## *7.2.3 Deference to Administrative Interpretations*

Another principle of statutory construction that arises in usury cases is that courts will defer to the interpretation of a

19 U.C.C.C. § 1.102 (1974 Model Code); Idaho Code Ann. § 28-41-102; Iowa Code § 537.1102; S.C. Code Ann. § 37-1-102. *See* State *ex rel.* Salazar v. Cash Now Store, Inc., 31 P.3d 161 (Colo. 2001) (citing and applying rule of liberal construction); Bar Harbor Banking & Trust Co. v. Superintendent of Bur. of Consumer Prot., 471 A.2d 292 (Me. 1984) (citing U.C.C.C.'s requirement of liberal construction; rejecting lender's claim that restrictions on increasing interest rate did not apply to post-maturity renewals).

20 *See* Rhodes v. Hartford, 513 A.2d 124 (Conn. 1986) (broad construction of pawnbroker statute to protect those who must have recourse to pawnbrokers). *Cf.* Browner v. District of Columbia, 549 A.2d 1107 (D.C. 1988) (rejecting argument that criminal provisions of Loan Sharking Statute should not apply to sale-leaseback transactions because some borrowers were relatively well-educated; purpose of usury and loan-sharking laws is to protect persons from the consequences of their financial desperation).

21 *See, e.g.*, Barco Auto Leasing Corp. v. House, 520 A.2d 162 (Conn. 1987) (liberal construction of Installment Sales Financing Act to promote its remedial purpose).

22 *See* §§ 3.9.7, 4.4.6.4.7 (hidden interest), Ch. 6 (credit insurance), *supra*.

23 Expression of one thing is the exclusion of another. Bryan A. Garner, Black's Law Dictionary 661–662 (9th ed. 2009). *See generally* Singer & Singer, Sutherland Statutory Construction §§ 47.23 to 47.25 (7th ed. 2007).

24 Sixth Draft of Uniform Small Loan Law § 13, *reprinted in* Hubachek, Annotations on Small Loan Laws 79–93 (1941). *See, e.g.*, Alaska Stat. § 06.20.260; Ohio Rev. Code Ann. § 1321.13(G) (West); Va. Code Ann. § 6.2-1523.

25 *See, e.g.*, *Ex parte* New Fin., Ltd., 225 So. 2d 784 (Ala. 1969); Sunderland v. Day, 145 N.E.2d 39 (Ill. 1957); Home Fin. Co. v. Padgett, 54 So. 2d 813 (La. Ct. App. 1951); Hawkins v. Thorp Credit & Thrift Co., 441 N.W.2d 470 (Minn. 1989) (where statute specifically authorized only sale of credit insurance, creditor was not authorized to sell noncredit life insurance policies as part of credit transactions); Wombold v. Associates Fin. Servs. Co., 104 P.3d 1080 (Mont. 2004) (where statute allowed any interest rate but no other charges, creditor could not charge points); Moran v. American Funding, Ltd., 569 A.2d 841 (N.J. Super. Ct. Ch. Div. 1989) (title insurance was not a specifically authorized charge under prior version of New Jersey's second mortgage act and was therefore prohibited by the Act); Garrison v. First Fed. Saving & Loan Ass'n of S.C., 402 S.E.2d 25 (Va. 1991) (risk management fees not listed as a permissible charge for junior mortgage loans, and therefore was an illegal charge); Byrd v. Crosstate Mortgage & Invs., Inc., 1994 WL 1031124 (Va. Cir. Ct. 1994); Opinion of the Kansas Att'y Gen. No. 87-3, 1987 WL 290401 (Kan. A.G. Jan. 9, 1987), *modified by* Opinion of the Kansas Att'y Gen., No. 87-47, 1987 WL 290444 (Kan. A.G. Mar. 12, 1987) (cannot sell property insurance except on property subject to valid security interest under statute); Opinion of the Michigan Att'y Gen., No. 6594 (Mich. A.G. July 17, 1989) (documentary fees, service fees or inspection fees added to cash price on installment car purchase not specifically enumerated as authorized charge, and were therefore prohibited; note that the specific provisions regarding documentary charges have since been repealed). *But cf.* Alston v. Crown Auto, Inc., 224 F.3d 332 (4th Cir. 2000) (only charges imposed up front, not late charges, are interest); Mayo v. GMAC Mortgage, L.L.C., 763 F. Supp. 2d 1091, 1108–1109 (W.D. Mo. 2011) (statute allowing "bona fide closing costs . . . which shall include" certain enumerated items does not create exclusive list); Luttenegger v. Conseco Fin. Servicing Corp., 671 N.W.2d 425 (Iowa 2003) (where Iowa U.C.C.C. capped finance charges at 21% and finance charge was defined broadly rather than limited to certain types of charges, creditor could assess a charge that was not listed as long as total charge was within the cap); S.C. Dep't of Consumer Affairs v. Rent-A-Center, Inc., 547 S.E.2d 881 (S.C. Ct. App. 2001) (where RTO statute does not specify allowable charges, creditor may impose other charges).

statute by an agency that is charged with administering it.[26] This principle sometimes helps consumers but sometimes hurts them. If the state agency that regulates financial institutions is overly friendly to the industry, its interpretations may be unhelpful to consumers.

In dealing with unhelpful agency interpretations, it should be remembered that the court should defer to an agency's interpretation only if the statute is ambiguous.[27] There is also authority that a court engaged in constitutional scrutiny will not defer to an agency's interpretation.[28] This limitation is particularly important in states that include a usury ceiling in their state constitutions. In addition, where an agency has been inconsistent in its interpretation of a statute, its opinion will be entitled to less deference.[29] Finally, inaction by a regulatory agency, such as failure to prohibit a creditor's practice, is not entitled to any deference as an administrative interpretation.[30]

Some states have codified the deference to agency interpretations by giving lenders a safe harbor if they rely on an agency interpretation.[31] A lender can only rely on an agency interpretation that is in existence, so one issued after the transaction in question cannot protect the lender.[32]

26 *See, e.g.*, Babbitt v. Sweet Home Chapter, 515 U.S. 687, 115 S. Ct. 2407, 132 L. Ed. 2d 597 (1995); Chevron U.S.A., Inc. v. National Res. Defense Council, 467 U.S. 837, 104 S. Ct. 2778, 81 L. Ed. 2d 694 (1984); Cash. Am. Net of Nevada, L.L.C. v. Commw., Dep't of Banking, 8 A.3d 282 (Pa. 2010) (court is bound by plain language of statute, not by administrative agency's prior interpretations); Hathaway v. First Family Fin. Servs., 1 S.W.3d 634 (Tenn. 1999) (agency's interpretation of state usury law would be persuasive if statute were ambiguous). *But see* Luttenegger v. Conseco Fin. Servicing Corp., 671 N.W.2d 425 (Iowa 2003) (giving no deference to chart published by agency showing what fees were allowed, where chart did not reveal agency's analysis and contained disclaimer that it was not the law).

27 Food and Drug Admin. v. Brown & Williamson Tobacco Co., 529 U.S. 120, 120 S. Ct. 1291, 146 L. Ed. 2d 121 (2000) ("[a]lthough agencies are generally entitled to deference in the interpretation of statutes that they administer, a reviewing court, as well as the agency, must give effect to the unambiguously expressed intent of Congress"); Bednar v. Provident Bank, 937 A.2d 210 (Md. 2007) (declining to defer to administrative agency's interpretation when statute was not ambiguous); Hathaway v. First Family Fin. Servs., 1 S.W.3d 634 (Tenn. 1999).

28 Miller v. Johnson, 515 U.S. 900, 115 S. Ct. 2475, 132 L. Ed. 2d 762 (1995).

29 Good Samaritan Hosp. v. Shalala, 508 U.S. 402, 113 S. Ct. 2151, 124 L. Ed. 2d 368 (1993). *Cf.* Indep. Fin. Inst. v. Clark, 990 P.2d 845 (Okla. 1999) (agreeing with agency's new interpretation of statute, based on attorney general opinion, which departed from interpretation it had accepted for twenty-seven years, but making its ruling effective only from date agency issued its new interpretation). *But cf.* Smiley v. Citibank (South Dakota), N.A., 517 U.S. 735, 116 S. Ct. 1730, 135 L. Ed. 2d 25 (1996) (according deference to newly minted agency interpretation even though it was inconsistent with prior less formal expressions of agency's views).

30 Wombold v. Associates Fin. Servs. Co., 104 P.3d 1080 (Mont. 2004).

31 *See, e.g.*, Alexander v. PSB Lending Corp., 800 N.E.2d 984 (Ind. Ct. App. 2003) (interpreting Ind. U.C.C.C. § 24-4.5-6-104).

32 *Id.*

## 7.3 Right to Jury Trial

Assuming that a case is not forced into arbitration, the question arises whether trial by jury is available. The right to a trial by jury in a state court is not addressed by the Seventh Amendment to the United States Constitution and is therefore a matter of state law, at least in civil cases.[33] Most states follow the federal approach: in the absence of express statutory treatment, juries are available by right in civil actions which were recognized at common law and in their modern statutory counterparts, while no right to a jury exists in actions previously recognized only in courts of equity.[34]

The right to a jury in usury cases is seldom litigated because in the average usury case the presence of the right is obvious. Usury is usually raised as a debtor defense or counterclaim in the creditor's action on a debt. Such a creditor action is a suit seeking the recovery of money damages for breach of contract, which is the epitome of an action recognized at common law.[35] The debtor can thus request a jury by right as the defendant in the creditor's suit.

Obtaining a jury is similarly seldom a problem in affirmative usury actions. In many states,[36] a common law action for the recovery of usurious interest paid was recognized, and modern statutory usury remedies are thus just a continuation of common law rights. Even in the absence of a specific common law predecessor, most usury statutes provide the debtor with an action to recover money which inherently resembles an action at law more than a suit in equity.[37] A state may also treat the existence of a bona fide credit sale as an issue of fact to be decided by a jury.[38]

The one circumstance in which a debtor may have trouble obtaining a jury to hear a usury claim exists when the creditor

33 *See* City of Monterey v. Del Monte Dunes at Monterey, Ltd., 526 U.S. 687 (1999); Gasperini v. Center for Humanities, Inc., 518 U.S. 415 (1996); Hawkins v. Czarnecki, 1998 WL 57333 (6th Cir. Feb. 2, 1998); Elliott v. City of Wheat Ridge, 49 F.3d 1458 (10th Cir. 1995).

34 *See generally* Burlington N. R.R. Co. v. Warren, 574 So. 2d 758 (Ala. 1990) (ordinarily an action in equity does not provide a right to a jury trial); State v. Dutch Harbor Seafoods, Ltd., 965 P.2d 738 (Alaska 1998) (state constitution preserves right to jury to same extent as at common law, i.e., civil cases when the amount in controversy exceeds $250); Riggin v. Dierdorff, 790 S.W.2d 897 (Ark. 1990) (right to jury trial does not extend to equity); Claudio v. State, 585 A.2d 1278 (Del. 1991) (state constitution preserves, *inter alia*, common law right to jury for civil claims); Dickeman v. Millwood Gold & Racquet Club, Inc., 67 S.W.3d 724 (Mo. Ct. App. 2002) (no right to jury trial on rescission claim).

35 *See generally* Dairy Queen v. Wood, 369 U.S. 469, 82 S. Ct. 894, 8 L. Ed. 2d 44 (1962) (action to collect debt for breach of contract); Raedeke v. Gibraltor Sav. & Loan Ass'n, 517 P.2d 1157 (Cal. 1974); Whitfield v. Cornelius, 554 S.W.2d 870 (Ky. Ct. App. 1977).

36 *See* § 7.8.2.3.4, *infra*.

37 *See* Rowell v. Kaplan, 235 A.2d 91 (R.I. 1967) (usury action for monetary damages was action at law, but allegations insufficient to state a claim).

38 *See* Dehart v. R/S Fin. Corp., 337 S.E.2d 94 (N.C. Ct. App. 1985); Carper v. Kanawha Banking & Trust Co., 207 S.E.2d 897 (W. Va. 1974).

is attempting to foreclose on property given as security for the debt and the debtor is raising usury as a defense to the foreclosure. In most states foreclosure is recognized as an equitable remedy.[39] The existence of an equitable action will generally not preclude the jury trial of legal claims arising from the same transaction.[40] Nonetheless, the debtor may have to demonstrate more clearly the presence of a significant legal issue. Thus, an Oklahoma court denied a jury request in a creditor's suit for foreclosure and recovery on a promissory note when the usury defense did not dispute the amount of the debt.[41] Similarly, a debtor's suit in Rhode Island for the cancellation and rescission of notes and mortgages did not merit a jury when the complaint contained insufficient allegations to raise a claim for a monetary recovery.[42] The Florida Supreme Court held that, in a foreclosure action, there is no right to a jury trial of a counterclaim that seeks a statutory usury penalty, although there would be for an action that sought return of usurious interest already paid plus statutory penalties.[43]

Even when there is a right to a jury trial, some issues will be questions of law. For example, a Washington court has held that it is for the jury to decide what the borrower told the lender about the purpose of a loan, but whether these facts make it a business loan is a question of law for the court.[44] But a Texas decision holds that whether a charge is a device to conceal usury is a question of fact.[45]

## 7.4 Arbitration Requirements

### *7.4.1 Introduction*

Mandatory arbitration provisions are nearly universal in consumer credit contracts. Creditors insist on this requirement because it significantly limits their exposure to class-wide damages, punitive damages awards, discovery, publicity, and even individual damage claims. As a general rule, consumer litigants will want to avoid arbitration requirements for these very reasons.

The enforceability of mandatory arbitration clauses is treated in detail in another NCLC treatise, *Consumer Arbitration Agreements* (6th ed. 2011). Its companion website also includes a large number of briefs and other pleadings that can be cut and pasted into a word processor. This section summarizes many of the topics examined in detail in that treatise, particularly those of relevance to consumer credit litigation. For the most part, the section cites only to Supreme Court case law and to the relevant subsection of *Consumer Arbitration Agreements*, where a complete and updated listing of case law can be found.

### *7.4.2 Is an Arbitration Clause Prohibited?*

#### 7.4.2.1 Settlement Binds Banks Not to Require Arbitration

Bank of America, JP Morgan Chase, Capital One, and HSBC have settled an antitrust case by agreeing that, until November

39 *See* Songer v. Civitas Bank, 771 N.E.2d 61 (Ind. 2002) (where essential point of case is lender's attempt to take possession of collateral, and legal claims are merely incidental, case is equitable and jury trial not required); First Nat'l Bank v. Clark, 602 P.2d 1299 (Kan. 1979) (defense in foreclosure action that note was not yet due is essentially equitable); Oliver-Mercer Elec. Co-op, Inc. v. Davis, 678 N.W.2d 757 (N.D. 2004) (action to foreclose on collateral is equitable even if it includes claim for deficiency, so no right to jury trial). *Cf.* General Elec. Credit Corp. v. Richman, 338 N.W.2d 814 (N.D. 1983) (action to foreclose on chattel mortgage would be equitable, but jury trial is required here because this suit seeks money damages and possession of specific personal property). *But see* Cheatham v. Bynum, 568 P.2d 649 (Okla. Civ. App. 1977) (jury right in suit to recover judgment on note and to foreclose security). *But cf.* Pernell v. Southall Realty, 416 U.S. 363 (1974) (right to recover possession of rental property was recognized at common law, so Seventh Amendment requires opportunity for jury trial in District of Columbia); *Ex parte* Moore, 880 So. 2d 1131 (Ala. 2003) (tenant has right to jury trial in eviction action since this was an action at law at time of adoption of state constitution).

40 *See* Dairy Queen, Inc. v. Wood, 369 U.S. 469, 82 S. Ct. 894, 8 L. Ed. 2d 44 (1962); Marseilles Hydropower L.L.C. v. Marseilles Land & Water Co., 299 F.3d 643 (7th Cir. 2002) (right to jury trial arose when landowner counterclaimed for back rent in tenant's suit for injunction and declaratory judgment); Eldredge v. Gourley, 505 F.2d 769 (3d Cir. 1974); Prudential Ins. Co. v. Bonney, 299 F. Supp. 794 (W.D. Okla. 1969); Eason v. Bynon, 781 So. 2d 238 (Ala. Civ. App. 2000) (homeowner entitled to jury trial on claim of fraud asserted in foreclosure action); Poston v. Gaddis, 335 So. 2d 165 (Ala. Civ. App. 1976); Barth v. Florida State Constructors Serv., 327 So. 2d 13 (Fla. 1976); David Steed & Assocs., Inc. v. Young, 766 P.2d 717 (Idaho 1988); Songer v. Civitas Bank, 771 N.E.2d 61 (Ind. 2002); State *ex rel.* Leonardi v. Sherry, 137 S.W.3d 462 (Mo. 2004) (jury trial available on counterclaims asserted in response to suit seeking primarily equitable relief); Welsh v. Case, 43 P.3d 445 (Or. Ct. App. 2002) (if borrower raises legal defenses or counterclaims in foreclosure action, right to jury trial is available, but not here where borrower raised claims only by way of recoupment); Rowell v. Kaplan, 235 A.2d 91 (R.I. 1967); North Carolina Fed. Sav. & Loan Ass'n v. Dav Corp., 381 S.E.2d 903 (S.C. 1989); Gardner v. Travis, 450 S.E.2d 54 (S.C. Ct. App. 1994); First Western Bank v. Livestock Yards Co., 466 N.W.2d 853 (S.D. 1991); Green Spring Farms v. Spring Green Farms Assocs., 492 N.W.2d 392 (Wis. Ct. App. 1992). *See also* Williams Elec. Games, Inc., 366 F.3d 569 (7th Cir. 2004) (if both legal and equitable remedies are sought, legal issues should be tried first, and jury's findings will bind judge who tries the equitable issues); Nwosu v. Uba, 19 Cal. Rptr. 3d 416 (Cal. Ct. App. 2004) (where case involved mixed legal and equitable claims, equitable claims should be tried first; note that jurisdictions split on this issue). *But see* Morris v. Bank One, 789 N.E.2d 68 (Ind. Ct. App. 2003) (where bank's foreclosure and replevin claims were essentially equitable, no right to jury trial on counterclaims); Vanier v. Ponsoldt, 833 P.2d 949 (Kan. 1992); Oliver-Mercer Elec. Co-op, Inc. v. Davis, 678 N.W.2d 757 (N.D. 2004) (counterclaim seeking money damages does not give right to jury trial if damage claim is incidental to and dependent upon primary claim where jury trial is not allowed). *See generally* Annotation, 17 A.L.R.3d 1321 (1968) (right in equity suit to jury trial of legal counterclaim).

41 McCrary v. Stephens, 94 P.2d 532 (Okla. 1938). *But cf.* Cheatham v. Bynum, 568 P.2d 649 (Okla. Ct. App. 1977) (right to jury in suit to recover judgment on note and foreclose security).

42 *See* Rowell v. Kaplan, 235 A.2d 91 (R.I. 1967).

43 *See* Cerrito v. Kovitch, 457 So. 2d 1021 (Fla. 1984).

44 Jansen v. Nu-West, Inc., 6 P.3d 98 (Wash. Ct. App. 2000).

45 Sturm v. Muens, 224 S.W.3d 758 (Tex. App. 2007).

1, 2013, they will delete their arbitration clauses from existing consumer credit agreements and will not enforce existing arbitration agreements.[46] PNC Bank, TD Bank, Regions Bank, and other card issuers have also abandoned arbitration requirements for various reasons, although they are free to re-institute the requirement.

Do not assume that a bank's credit card agreement includes an arbitration clause. The only way to determine this is to examine the credit agreement that applies to a particular consumer and also recent amendments to that agreement. If the agreement is found in a Bank of America, JP Morgan Chase, Capital One, or HSBC contract, that arbitration requirement will not be enforced, at least until November 1, 2013.

### 7.4.2.2 No Arbitration Requirement for Manufactured Home Loans

The Truth in Lending Act requires that no manufactured home loan include an arbitration requirement.[47] The provision applies to residential mortgage loans, which are defined to include a consumer credit transaction that includes a security interest in a consumer's principal dwelling,[48] and dwelling is defined as including a manufactured home.[49] This TILA provision also provides that no other agreement between the consumer and the creditor shall bar a consumer from bringing an action in court.[50]

The effective date of this provision is unclear. As set out in in NCLC's *Truth in Lending* § 1.3,[51] the provision will almost certainly be in effect by January 21, 2013, and may have already gone into effect on July 22, 2010.

Whatever the provision's effective date, the question arises whether it should be applied retroactively to arbitration agreements in effect before that date. A federal court, interpreting a related provision prohibiting mandatory arbitration where a whistleblower brings an action, found the provision to be retroactively applied.[52] Congress did not evidence an intent one way or another, so that the determinative question is whether the provision is procedural or substantive. Since the Supreme Court has stated that arbitration does not affect substantive rights, but is just an alternative forum, the provision only affects procedure and is to be applied retroactively.[53] But since that decision was issued, three other federal courts have come to the opposite conclusion.[54]

46 Final Judgment and Order of Dismissal with Respect to Enumerated Defendants, Ross v. Bank of Am., N.A., MDL No. 1409 (S.D.N.Y. July 22, 2010), *available at* www.nclc.org/unreported.

47 15 U.S.C. § 1639c(e)(1).

48 15 U.S.C. § 1602(cc)(5).

49 15 U.S.C. § 1602(w).

50 15 U.S.C. § 1639c(e)(3).

51 (7th ed. 2009 and Supp.).

52 Pezza v. Investors Capital Corp., 767 F. Supp. 2d. 225 (2011).

53 *Id.*

54 Taylor v. Fannie Mae, 2012 WL 928170 (D. D.C. Mar. 20, 2012); Holmes v. Air Liquide USA, L.L.C., 2012 WL 267194 (S.D. Tex. Jan. 30, 2012); Henderson v. Masco Framing Corp., 2011 WL 30222535 (D. Nev. July 22, 2011).

### 7.4.2.3 State Insurance Law Can Prohibit Arbitration

Although the general rule is that the Federal Arbitration Act (FAA) preempts state laws limiting the enforceability of an arbitration agreement,[55] state insurance laws are an exception. The federal McCarran-Ferguson Act provides that where there is a conflict between a federal statute (such as the FAA) and a state insurance law, the state law prevails, unless the federal statute explicitly applies to insurance (which the FAA does not).[56] To the extent that state insurance law limits the application of an arbitration requirement for a particular type of insurance claim, then the state law prevails over the FAA.[57]

### 7.4.2.4 Limits on Arbitration Involving Military Personnel

Federal law prohibits arbitration clauses in consumer credit agreements with military personnel or their dependents, or the enforcement of such a consumer credit agreement.[58] Nevertheless, Department of Defense regulations define consumer credit narrowly as applying only to payday loans, auto title loans, and refund anticipation loans.[59]

### 7.4.2.5 Potential CFPB Limits on Arbitration

The Consumer Financial Protection Bureau (CFPB) has the authority to limit consumer arbitration agreements after it conducts a study.[60] The regulation will apply to any contract entered into 180 days after the regulation's effective date.[61] The CFPB has not yet completed its study.

### 7.4.2.6 Arbitration Is Consistent with CROA

The Credit Repair Organizations Act (CROA)[62] contains provisions that appeared to some courts as inconsistent with an arbitration requirement, but the U.S. Supreme Court has resolved that question by finding that CROA claims can be forced into binding arbitration.[63]

### 7.4.2.7 Arbitration When Consumer Files Bankruptcy

When a consumer, as part of the consumer's bankruptcy proceeding, litigates core bankruptcy matters, the bankruptcy

55 National Consumer Law Center, Consumer Arbitration Agreements § 3.2.1 (6th ed. 2011).

56 See *Id.* § 3.3.4.

57 *Id.*

58 10 U.S.C. § 987(e), (f).

59 32 C.F.R. § 232.

60 12 U.S.C. § 5518.

61 12 U.S.C. § 5518(d).

62 *See* National Consumer Law Center, Fair Credit Reporting Ch. 15 (7th ed. 2010 and Supp.) (discussion of CROA claims in consumer credit cases).

63 Compucredit Corp. v. Greenwood, 132 S. Ct. 665 (2012).

court has discretion whether to require the matter to be removed to arbitration or be heard before the bankruptcy judge.[64]

## *7.4.3 Is There a Binding Contract?*

### 7.4.3.1 Defendant Must Produce the Arbitration Agreement

Arbitration is a matter of agreement between the parties. If there is no agreement, then there is no arbitration requirement. Before a creditor or the creditor's assignee can force a litigation into arbitration, it must produce an agreement that applies to the particular consumer plaintiff, and that agreement must contain an arbitration clause. In some cases, the creditor or its assignee may not be able to produce the actual contract entered into by the particular consumer.

### 7.4.3.2 Was the Agreement Properly Formed?

An arbitration requirement is a matter of contract, and like any contract, it is not binding on the parties unless the contract is properly formed. This requires assent from both parties, usually by valid signatures. The consumer must have the capacity to assent, and any amendment to the consumer credit contract adding the arbitration agreement (such as in a bill stuffer) must be shown to be binding on the parties.[65] Agreements cannot be reached unilaterally; the arbitration clause cannot be presented to the consumer after the overall agreement has been consummated; and the agreement cannot be illusory, such as where the creditor has the right to change any aspect of the agreement unilaterally at will.[66]

### 7.4.3.3 Where NAF Is the Sole Designated Arbitration Forum

Arbitration agreements typically specify one or more arbitration forums that will administer the arbitration. The National Arbitration Forum (NAF) has been listed in millions of consumer credit agreements as the sole designated forum, but a law enforcement action prevents the NAF from acting as the arbitration forum in any consumer dispute. Courts must consider whether NAF designation is integral to the agreement or ancillary. If integral, then the courts will not enforce the agreement. A majority of courts looking at standard language designating the NAF and NAF rule find designation of the NAF to be integral to the agreement.[67]

### 7.4.3.4 Has the Arbitration Agreement Been Superseded by Another Contract?

Since arbitration is a matter of agreement between the parties, an arbitration requirement is not effective if found in an agreement that is superseded by a later agreement that does not contain the arbitration requirement. This may occur where the buyer's order contains the arbitration requirement, but an arbitration agreement is not present in the installment sales agreement, or where early payday loan agreements contain the arbitration requirement, but the consumer has replaced those obligations with new payday loans not containing the arbitration requirement.[68]

### 7.4.3.5 Where Usury Voids the Contract

One might think that a usurious or illegal contract that is unenforceable under state law would also mean that the arbitration requirement is unenforceable. But the Supreme Court has stated that this is not the case, that the arbitration clause must be looked at independently from the rest of the contract.[69]

### 7.4.3.6 Has the Creditor Waived the Arbitration Requirement?

A creditor cannot participate in court litigation on a matter and then suddenly change its mind and require the case to be sent to arbitration. This is particularly the case where this prejudices the consumer.[70]

### 7.4.3.7 Is the Arbitration Agreement Unconscionable

One of the most common ways to challenge an arbitration agreement is by showing that it is unconscionable. The FAA states that an arbitration agreement is enforceable "save upon such grounds as exist at law or in equity for the revocation of any contract."[71] Unconscionability is one such ground.

Courts find an arbitration agreements unconscionable and unenforceable where there is an adequate showing of procedural unconscionability (e.g., small print, lack of choice, uneven bargaining power, take-it-or-leave-it negotiation) and substantive unconscionability. Such substantive unconscionability can be based upon the arbitration clause requiring: the consumer to bear unaffordable costs (arbitrators cost hundreds of dollars an hour); only the consumer, not the creditor to arbitrate; the consumer to forgo statutory remedies; the consumer to arbitrate in an inconvenient venue; the consumer to use a biased arbitrator or arbitration forum; the consumer to forgo necessary discovery; a non-prevailing consumer to pay all arbitration costs; and that the proceedings be secret.[72]

64 National Consumer Law Center, Consumer Arbitration Agreements § 4.3.3 (6th ed. 2011).

65 *Id.* at Ch. 5.

66 *Id.*

67 *Id.* § 5.8.

68 *Id.* § 6.8.4.2.

69 Buckeye Check Cashing, Inc. v. Cardegna, 546 US 440 (2006).

70 National Consumer Law Center, Consumer Arbitration Agreements Ch. 8 (6th ed. 2011).

71 9 U.S.C. § 2.

72 National Consumer Law Center, Consumer Arbitration Agreements Ch. 6 (6th ed. 2011).

### 7.4.4 Does the Arbitration Agreement Apply to the Dispute and to the Parties?

In general, only the parties to the arbitration agreement are bound by the agreement.[73] While the creditor's assignees and agents may be able to invoke the arbitration requirement, other third parties, such as independent contractors or insurance companies, should not be able to do so.[74] Similarly, consumers (such as family members) who do not sign an arbitration agreement are generally not bound by it.[75]

By the same token, the arbitration agreement will specify what disputes must be arbitrated, and those are the only disputes that must go to arbitration.[76] For example, if the arbitration clause applies only to contract disputes, then it may not apply to a dispute not based upon the contract.

### 7.4.5 Does the Court or Arbitrator Determine Arbitrability?

A preliminary matter in any challenge to the enforceability of an arbitration clause is whether the enforceability determination is to be made by a court or by the arbitrator. In *Rent-A-Center, West, Inc. v. Jackson,*[77] the Supreme Court held that, "ordinarily," issues about whether parties have agreed to a valid arbitration clause are for a court—not an arbitrator—to decide. This rule is "based on an assumption about the parties' expectations"—the fact that most individuals would think that a court would be the one to decide if an arbitration clause was enforceable before one could be forced into arbitration.[78]

The Court recognized one exception to this rule: if an arbitration clause clearly and unmistakably delegates to the arbitrator the issue of whether the arbitration clause is valid (a so-called "delegation clause"),[79] and the delegation clause itself is not subject to challenge under a law that would revoke any contract, then the challenge is for the arbitrator, not the court, to decide.

Accordingly, who decides a challenge to an arbitration agreement's enforceability—the court or the arbitrator—will depend upon three factors. First, does the arbitration clause contain a delegation clause? If not, the issue is for the court.

Second, if there is a delegation clause, is it "clear and unmistakable"? If not, the court still decides.[80] When there is a clear and unmistakable delegation clause, the third factor is whether that delegation clause itself is enforceable. The court decides whether the clause is valid. If the delegation clause is not enforceable, then the court also decides the enforceability of the whole arbitration requirement.

The Supreme Court held that delegation clauses—like other types of arbitration clauses—are subject to the normal rules of contract law, including defenses to contracts.[81] One consequence of *Rent-A-Center*, then, will be litigation over the validity, under ordinary state law, of particular delegation clauses. When there is a delegation clause, the consumer's court challenge to an arbitration agreement must focus, at least initially, not on the enforceability of the arbitration agreement as a whole but on the enforceability of the delegation clause.

A prime example would be when a party argues that an arbitration clause is unconscionable because it imposes prohibitive costs of arbitration upon individuals. If the arbitration contract delegates this issue to the arbitrator to decide, there is an argument that the delegation clause is unconscionable, in part because of the inherent conflict of interest in letting an arbitrator evaluate the reasonableness of her or his own fees.

Similarly, a number of courts have struck down as unconscionable arbitration clauses that would require individuals to travel long distances to have their claims heard in arbitration. A delegation clause providing that an individual can only challenge such a clause by traveling to a far-away arbitration would be invalid for the same reasons as the broader arbitration clause would be.

### 7.4.6 Class Arbitration

Where an arbitration clause prohibits class-wide relief, an arbitrator is unlikely to allow such relief, and a court would almost certainly overturn such an award. A recent Supreme Court decision has made it quite difficult to challenge as unconscionable such a prohibition against class-wide relief. The Court in *Concepcion* overturned a California ruling that the class arbitration ban was unconscionable, holding that the California ruling was inconsistent with the FAA.[82]

Perhaps the best challenge to a ban on class-wide arbitration is one based on the Second Circuit's ruling in *In re American Express Merchants' Litigation*,[83] issued after *Concepcion*. The Second Circuit held that a class arbitration ban was unenforceable as conflicting with federal statutory rights where expert witness and other litigation costs make it impossible to enforce those federal statutory rights individually.

Not all arbitration clauses prohibit class-wide relief and some of them are silent on the issue. Where an arbitration clause does not prohibit class arbitration, it is for the arbitrator, not the court

73 *Id.* §§ 7.4, 7.5.

74 *Id.* §§ 7.4, 7.5.

75 *Id.* § 7.4.

76 *Id.* § 7.3.

77 130 S. Ct. 2772 (2010).

78 *Id.*

79 Rent-A-Center's delegation clause reads as follows: "The Arbitrator, and not any federal, state, or local court or agency, shall have exclusive authority to resolve any dispute relating to the interpretation, applicability, enforceability or formation of this Agreement including, but not limited to any claim that all or any part of this Agreement is void or voidable." *Id.* at 2775.

80 *See also* Granite Rock Co. v. International Bhd. of Teamsters, 130 S. Ct. 2847 (2010) (citing First Options of Chicago, Inc. v. Kaplan, 514 U.S. 938 (1995) and AT&T Technologies, Inc. v. Communication Workers, 475 U.S. 643 (1986)).

81 *See* Rent-A-Center, West, Inc. v. Jackson, 130 S. Ct. 2772, 2776 (2010) ("generally applicable contract defenses, such as fraud, duress, or unconscionability" may be applied to invalidate an arbitration clause, including a delegation clause).

82 AT&T Mobility L.L.C. v. Concepcion, 2011 WL 1561956 (U.S. Apr. 27, 2011).

83 667 F.3d 204 (2d Cir. 2012).

to decide whether, consistent with the parties' intent, the silent arbitration clause should be construed as allowing class arbitration.[84] While the Supreme Court has said the arbitrator cannot make such a ruling on public policy grounds, the arbitrator can do so based upon an interpretation of the contract.[85] A number of arbitrators have interpreted a silent clause as allowing class arbitration, and courts generally uphold such rulings.[86]

The ability to seek class-wide relief in arbitration is significant because many creditors fear class arbitration more than class actions. An arbitrator's construction of a silent clause as allowing class-wide arbitration dramatically strengthens the consumer's position, perhaps more so than if the arbitration clause were found unenforceable, allowing a class action to be brought in court.

## 7.4.7 *Punitive Damages*

While an arbitrator may be less likely to award punitive damages than a jury, this is partially offset by the fact that there is must less court review of an arbitrator's punitive damages award.[87] Instead of a judge remitting the jury award and appellate courts reviewing the resulting award, an arbitrator's award is only subject to very narrow judicial review.[88] In fact, the defendant may not even have a due process claim concerning the size of the award, since the arbitration is a nongovernmental action.[89]

Moreover, if the arbitration agreement seeks to limit the availability of punitive damages, this may be enough to find the arbitration agreement to be unenforceable. The limitation may be unconscionable,[90] and it may also be inconsistent with federal statutory rights where a federal statute provides for punitive damages (such as the Equal Credit Opportunity Act and the Fair Credit Reporting Act).[91]

# 7.5 Elements of a Prima Facie Case

## 7.5.1 *General*

### 7.5.1.1 Overview of Elements

In the traditional usury case there are four elements which a borrower must establish:[92] 1) the existence of a loan or forbearance; 2) an absolute obligation to repay principal; 3) an interest overcharge; and 4) the usurious intent of the lender.

These elements exist expressly or by judicial inference in most usury statutes, and serious attention should be paid to their proof in most cases. Yet, they are neither universal nor exclusive. Usurious intent, for example, need not be demonstrated under some statutes.[93] On the other hand, many statutes contain elements beyond these four, such as the existence of "consumer" credit, the size of the loan principal, or the type of security taken. The statute may also grant the borrower a private cause of action only if certain additional facts, such as payment of a portion of the usurious charge, are shown.[94]

In general, a consumer's attorney should examine with specificity the reasons that a particular usury statute applies, and the reasons why it has been violated. Evidence to support each of these reasons should be introduced in court. With this basic approach in mind, the four most common elements of a prima facie usury case will be examined in more detail in the next subsections.

The proof of usury need not be complicated. Merely the introduction of the credit contract may suffice in some cases if the stated interest rate exceeds the limit in an undisputedly applicable statute. However, the sufficiency of the contract as proof of usury should never be assumed. Credit contracts are usually drafted by creditors, and frequently contain recitations

84 *See* National Consumer Law Center, Consumer Arbitration Agreements § 9.2 (6th ed. 2011).

85 Stolt-Nielsen S.A. v. AnimalFeeds Int'l Corp., 130 S. Ct. 1758 (2010).

86 *See* National Consumer Law Center, Consumer Arbitration Agreements § 9.2 (6th ed. 2011).

87 *Id.* § 10.7.

88 *Id.*

89 *Id.*

90 *Id.* § 6.6.4.1.

91 *Id.* § 4.4.2.4.

92 *See, e.g.*, Rae v. Estate of Van Buren (*In re* Rae), 2002 WL 832203 (4th Cir. May 2, 2002) (Fla. law); Henson v. Columbus Bank & Trust, 770 F.2d 1566 (11th Cir. 1985) (Georgia law); Cashback Catalog Sales, Inc. v. Price, 102 F. Supp. 2d 1375 (S.D. Ga. 2000); *In re* Bogan, 281 F. Supp. 242 (W.D. Tenn. 1968); *In re* Hoberg, 300 B.R. 752 (Bankr. C.D. Cal. 2003); Varr v. Olimpia, 2002 WL 1425373 (Cal. Ct. App. July 1, 2002); Bryer v. Green-Venable, 2001 WL 1580963 (Cal. Ct. App. Dec. 12, 2001); Oregrund Ltd. P'ship v. Sheive, 873 So. 2d 451 (Fla. Dist. Ct. App. 2004) (similar but slightly different list); Bermil Corp. v. Sawyer, 353 So. 2d 579 (Fla. Dist. Ct. App. 1977); Dang v. F&S Land Dev. Corp., 618 P.2d 276 (Haw. 1980); Tyrcha v. Wesolek, 543 N.E.2d 222, 224 (Ill. App. Ct. 1989) ("loan must be of money or something circulating as money"); Wolf v. Kian, 2000 WL 1281109 (Minn. Ct. App. Sept. 12, 2000); St. Paul Bank for Coops. v. Ohman, 402 N.W.2d 235 (Minn. Ct. App. 1987); Western Auto Supply Co. v. Vick, 277 S.E.2d 360, *on reh'g* 283 S.E.2d 101 (N.C. 1981); Odell v. Legal Bucks, L.L.C., 665 S.E.2d 767 (N.C. Ct. App. 2008); Liebergesell v. Evans, 613 P.2d 1170 (Wash. 1980); King v. Western United Assurance Co., 997 P.2d 1007 (Wash. Ct. App. 2000) (adds "money or its equivalent constituting the subject matter of the loan or forbearance" as a fifth element); Marashi v. Lannen, 780 P.2d 1341, 1343 (Wash. Ct. App. 1989). *See also* Sheehy v. Franchise Tax Bd., 100 Cal. Rptr. 2d 760 (Cal. Ct. App. 2000) (listing only three elements, omitting absolute obligation to repay); Pinchuck v. Canzoneri, 920 So. 2d 713 (Fla. Dist. Ct. App. 2006) (requiring an "understanding" that the money lent shall be repaid, rather than an absolute obligation); Valliappan v. Cruz, 917 So. 2d 257, 258 (Fla. Dist. Ct. App. 2005) (requiring an "understanding" that the money lent shall be repaid, rather than an absolute obligation); North Carolina *ex rel.* Cooper v. NCCS Loans, Inc., 624 S.E.2d 371 (N.C. Ct. App. 2005) (requiring an "understanding" that the money lent shall be repaid, rather than an absolute obligation); Oyster Creek Fin. Corp. v. Richwood Invs. II, Inc., 176 S.W.3d 307 (Tex. App. 2004) (first three listed, intent required as part of evaluating "substance" of contract).

93 *See* § 7.5.5.1, *infra*.

94 Egge v. Healthspan Servs. Co., 115 F. Supp. 2d 1126 (D. Minn. 2000). *See generally* § 7.8.2.4, *infra*.

of business purposes or other factual admissions which, if unrebutted by other evidence, may preclude a finding of usury. Furthermore, the applicability of a particular usury statute is often disputed, and it may be necessary or appropriate to introduce evidence showing that a statute which the creditor claims to be controlling is really inapposite. Another concern is that some courts construe ambiguous credit contracts to avoid usury.[95] Finally, many usury violations, such as the collection of unearned interest upon the acceleration of a debt[96] or the imposition of hidden interest charges, are not revealed by the terms of the credit contract and so must be separately proven.[97]

### 7.5.1.2 Burden of Proof

Courts generally presume the validity of contracts, and a party who claims that a contract is usurious therefore carries the burden of proving the usury, whether the claim is being asserted as an independent cause of action or as an affirmative defense.[98] Each of the statutory elements must be proved in court. If usury is being raised defensively,[99] usury may be an affirmative defense which must be pleaded or lost.[100] The major exception to this rule is that once a facially usurious interest rate has been demonstrated by the debtor, the burden may shift to the creditor to rebut the allegation of usury. Thus, a creditor who has assessed charges apparently in excess of the usury ceiling, but who claims that some of the charges are excluded from "interest" as reasonable transaction fees, may be required to demonstrate the reasonableness of those fees.[101] Similarly, if a debtor has shown that a general usury ceiling has been exceeded, but the creditor claims to be within a statutory exception to that ceiling, some courts have indicated that the burden of proof shifts to the creditor to demonstrate that the transaction fell within the scope of the exception.[102] Finally, in many jurisdictions usurious intent will be presumed if the contract on its face violates the statutory ceiling, and it is therefore up to the creditor to show any absence of intent.[103]

### 7.5.1.3 Standard of Proof

The precise standard of proof by which usury must be demonstrated varies significantly from jurisdiction to jurisdiction, and splits of authority within individual states are common.[104] Nevertheless, the most frequently applied standards in

95 *See* § 7.5.1.4, *infra*.

96 Remember, however, that some jurisdictions recognize a rule against the creation of usury through contingencies, so there may be issues about the treatment of agreements that impose charges only if the borrower defaults on the debt. *See* §§ 4.8.2 (late charges), 5.8.7.2 (acceleration), *supra*.

97 Introducing evidence outside of the credit contract generally does not cause parol evidence problems in usury cases because courts widely recognize the need to examine all the facts and circumstances of a transaction to determine whether usury may be concealed. *See* §§ 3.9.1, *supra*, 7.5.1.4, *infra*.

98 *See, e.g.*, OMP v. Security Pac. Bus. Fin. Inc., 716 F. Supp. 239 (N.D. Miss. 1989) ("no 'presumption of usury'; one claiming usury must furnish clear, positive, and certain proof of usury"); *In re* Perry, 425 B.R. 323, 370–301 (Bankr. S.D. Tex. 2010) (party claiming usury has burden of proof, so must show that particular charge should be recharacterized as interest); *In re* Borum, 60 B.R. 516 (Bankr. E.D. Ark. 1986) (burden of proof on debtor when contract not usurious on its face); Costello v. F&M Enters., 34 B.R. 211 (Bankr. M.D. Fla. 1983) (burden of proving intent on debtor); Smith v. MRCC P'ship, 792 S.W.2d 301 (Ark. 1990) (where usury not apparent on face of document, burden of proving intent on debtor); Rhode v. Kremer, 655 S.W.2d 410 (Ark. 1983); Valliappan v. Cruz, 917 So. 2d 257, 259 (Fla. Dist. Ct. App. 2005) (defendant who raises usury as affirmative defense bears burden of proof); Naples Cay Dev. Corp. v. Ferris, 555 So. 2d 1272 (Fla. Dist. Ct. App. 1989) (burden of proof on debtor to affirmatively plead and prove usury where contract not usurious on face); Transmedia Restaurant Co. v. 33 East 61st St. Restaurant Corp., 710 N.Y.S.2d 756 (N.Y. Sup. Ct. 2000) ("strong presumption against the finding of usury"); Ervin v. Muller, 2003 WL 21744332, at *5 (Wash. Ct. App. July 29, 2003) (borrower has burden of proof unless usury is apparent on face of contract); Durias v. Boswell, 791 P.2d 282 (Wash. Ct. App. 1990) (party alleging usury has burden of proof where usury is not apparent on face of transaction); Carper v. Kanawha Banking & Trust Co., 207 S.E.2d 897 (W. Va. 1974). *See also* Burge v. Pack, 785 S.W.2d 207 (Ark. 1990) (as an affirmative defense, usury must be pleaded and proved); Comstock v. Steinbergh, 18 Mass. L. Rep. 573 (Mass. Super. Ct. 2004) (debtor has burden). *See generally* Annotation, 51 A.L.R.2d 1087 (1957).

99 Some state usury claims may only be raised defensively. *See* George v. Capital South Mortgage Invs., Inc., 961 P.2d 32 (Kan. 1998) (construing Kan. Stat. Ann. § 16-207(a)).

Kansas recognizes an affirmative claim for usury, however, under its common law. *Id.*

100 *See* Arnold Machinery Co. v. CSL Bldg. Corp., 733 P.2d 115 (Or. 1987). *See also* Apodaca v. Rios, 163 S.W.3d 297 (Tex. App. 2005) (failure to raise usury as affirmative defense defeats usury claim).

101 *See* Kissell Co. v. Gressley, 591 F.2d 47 (9th Cir. 1979) (Arizona law); Bunn v. Weyerhauser Co., 598 S.W.2d 54 (Ark. 1980) (burden on lender to show that late charge was not interest); United-Bilt Homes, Inc. v. Teague, 432 S.W.2d 1 (Ark. 1968); Freeman v. Gonzales County Sav. & Loan Ass'n, 526 S.W.2d 774 (Tex. Civ. App. 1975), *aff'd*, 534 S.W.2d 903 (Tex. 1976).

102 *See In re* Russell, 72 B.R. 855 (Bankr. E.D. Pa. 1987) (lender carries burden of proving applicability of federal usury preemption); Colter v. Consol. Credit Corp., 157 S.E.2d 812 (Ga. Ct. App. 1967) (burden shifted to lender to show it was operating under and had complied with Industrial Loan Act); Revocable Living Trust of Harold G. Strand v. Wel-Co Group, Inc., 86 P.3d 818, 821 (Wash. Ct. App. 2004); Hommel v. Thweatt, 834 P.2d 1058 (Wash. Ct. App. 1992); Marashi v. Lannen, 780 P.2d 1341 (Wash. Ct. App. 1989); Stevens v. Security Pac. Mortgage Corp., 768 P.2d 1007 (Wash. Ct. App. 1989); Brown v. Giger, 738 P.2d 312 (Wash. Ct. App. 1987) (elements of usury apparent on face of loan; burden shifted to lender to prove it fell within business exemption), *rev'd on other grounds*, 757 P.2d 523 (Wash. 1988); Aetna Fin. Co. v. Darwin, 691 P.2d 581 (Wash. Ct. App. 1984) (lender bore burden of showing that transaction fell within usury exception for business loans over $50,000). *See also* Pierce v. Emigrant Mortgage Co., 2005 WL 2406007 (D. Conn. Sept. 29, 2005) (burden of proving that mortgage was bona fide and therefore qualified for mortgage exception for usury statute on defendant lender). *But see* American Century Mortgage Investors v. Reg'l Ctr., Ltd., 529 S.W.2d 578 (Tex. Civ. App. 1975).

103 *See* Easton State Bank v. Winn, 19 B.R. 218 (Bankr. E.D. Ark. 1982); Carper v. Kanawha Banking & Trust Co., 207 S.E.2d 897 (W. Va. 1974). *See generally* § 7.5.5, *infra* (usurious intent).

104 *See* Annotation, *Quantum, Degree, or Weight of Evidence to Sustain Usury Charge,* 51 A.L.R.2d 1087 (1957) (comprehensive annotation).

civil usury cases are "clear and convincing"[105] evidence and "preponderance of the evidence"[106] or some variation of these tests.[107] Courts are more likely to apply a standard of proof higher than a preponderance of the evidence if usury is not apparent on the face of the documents[108] or criminal usury is alleged.[109]

### 7.5.1.4 Contract Construction

Issues of contract construction typically arise in usury cases in connection with the proof of some of the elements of usury. Most notably, a court's interpretation of a contract may determine its finding of usurious intent, the absolute obligation of the debtor to repay principal, or the presence of an overcharge.

Construction of a credit contract becomes an issue only if the contract is ambiguous on some relevant point.[110] A contract which unambiguously calls for usurious payments cannot be cured by a forgiving "interpretation."[111] (Indeed, even if the contract was usurious due to mutual mistake, a creditor may not be able to salvage it by seeking reformation.[112]) Conversely, a borrower may prove usury which is not evident on the face of the contract even if the contract is unambiguous. It is black letter law that a court will consider all the facts and circumstances surrounding a transaction to determine whether usury is concealed.[113] Thus the parol evidence rule will not exclude evidence of usury.[114]

The main problem for borrowers when facing questions of contract interpretation is the widely accepted principle that the terms of a contract should be construed as non-usurious if the language of the contract as a whole is fairly susceptible to that construction.[115] This rule is obviously not important if a creditor has already demanded or accepted usurious payments, but if a statute forbids "contracting" for usury and the "contracting" is the sole issue before the court, the construction of the contract itself becomes critical. For example, when an acceleration clause in a precomputed credit contract does not specify the treatment of unearned interest upon acceleration, courts construing the acceleration clause often assume that the parties intend a legal transaction to avoid finding usury.[116]

---

105 *See, e.g.*, Bellagio Ins., Ltd. v. Digital Broad. Corp., 2005 WL 677223 (W.D. Va. Mar. 23, 2005) (under either New York or Virginia law, burden of proof by "clear and convincing" or "clear and cogent" evidence on debtor), *aff'd*, 201 Fed. Appx. 917 (4th Cir. 2006); *In re* Transcapital Fin. Corp., 433 B.R. 900, 907 (Bankr. S.D. Fla. 2010); Hickman v. Courtney, 203 S.W.3d 632 (Ark. 2005); Carter v. Four Seasons Funding Corp., 97 S.W.3d 387 (Ark. 2003); Smith v. MRCC P'ship, 792 S.W.2d 301 (Ark. 1990); Hochman v. LaRea, 789 N.Y.S.2d 300 (N.Y. App. Div. 2005) (debtor has "heavy burden" of showing usury by "clear and convincing" evidence); Goldstein v. CIBC World Mkts. Corp., 776 N.Y.S.2d 12 (N.Y. App. Div. 2004); Transmedia Restaurant Co. v. 33 East 61st St. Restaurant Corp., 710 N.Y.S.2d 756 (N.Y. Sup. Ct. 2000).

106 *See, e.g.*, El Paso Ref., Inc. v. Spurlock Permian Corp., 77 S.W.3d 374 (Tex. App. 2002).

107 *See, e.g.*, Rae v. Estate of Van Buren (*In re* Rae), 2002 WL 832203 (4th Cir. May 2, 2002) (Fla. law) ("clear and satisfactory" evidence necessary); Valliappan v. Cruz, 917 So. 2d 257, 259–260 (Fla. Dist. Ct. App. 2005) ("clear and satisfactory evidence"); Naples Cay Dev. Corp. v. Ferris, 555 So. 2d 1272 (Fla. Dist. Ct. App. 1989) (borrower has burden to establish usury by clear and satisfactory evidence when contract is not usurious on its face); Standard Sav. Ass'n v. Greater New Canaan Missionary Baptist Church, 786 S.W.2d 774 (Tex. App. 1990) (holding borrowers to "a stricter standard of proof"; borrower's affidavit that insurance purchase and third-party loan pay-off were required, thus constituting hidden interest, was insufficient evidence to warrant finding of usury on motion for summary judgment).

108 *See, e.g.*, Carper v. Kanawha Banking & Trust Co., 207 S.E.2d 897, 917–918 (W. Va. 1974) (distinguishing between usury on the face of the document, which requires only a preponderance of the evidence, and in the conduct of the parties, which requires "a clear and satisfactory preponderance of the evidence").

109 *See, e.g.*, Rumbaut v. Reinhart, 628 N.Y.S.2d 75 (N.Y. App. Div. 1995); Feinberg v. Old Vestal Road Assocs., Inc., 550 N.Y.S.2d 482 (N.Y. App. Div. 1990).

110 Zwayer v. Ford Motor Credit Co., 665 N.E.2d 843 (Ill. App. Ct. 1996) (holding contract ambiguous and therefore construing it against the maker where it contained a clause allowing the use of the Rule of 78s to rebate upon prepayment but was silent if acceleration occurred).

111 *See* Giventer v. Arnow, 372 N.Y.S.2d 63 (N.Y. 1975); *In re* Estate of Dane, 390 N.Y.S.2d (N.Y. App. Div. 1976); Brookshire v. Longhorn Chevrolet, Inc., 788 S.W.2d 209 (Tex. App. 1990) (where contract called for payment upon acceleration of the "unpaid balance of the total of payments," which latter term had a contractual definition calculating it to include the finance charges, creditor could not save it from usury claim by arguing that it meant "Unpaid Balance-Amount Financed"); Gemperle v. Crouch, 724 P.2d 375 (Wash. Ct. App. 1986); Gemperle v. Crouch, 724 P.2d 375 (Wash. Ct. App. 1986) (traditional rule, that if contract can be construed lawfully as well as unlawfully the lawful construction should be used, does not apply if usury is apparent on face); Aetna Fin. Co. v. Darwin, 691 P.2d 581 (Wash. Ct. App. 1984). *See also* C.I.O.S. Found. v. Berkston Ins., 2000 U.S. Dist. LEXIS 2337 (N.D. Miss. Jan. 28, 2000) (where usurious contract was unambiguous, parol evidence was not admissible).

112 *See* § 7.8.3.3, *infra*.

113 *See, e.g.*, Beausejour Corp., N.V. v. Offshore Dev. Co., 802 F.2d 1319 (11th Cir. 1986) (Florida law); Blessing v. Zeffero, 386 N.W.2d 590 (Mich. Ct. App. 1986); Lowell & Austin, Inc. v. Traux, 507 A.2d 949 (Vt. 1985); Gemperle v. Crouch, 724 P.2d 375 (Wash. Ct. App. 1986). *See also* § 3.9.1, *supra*.

114 *See* Kennedy Funding, Inc. v. Shelton, __ S.W.3d __, 2010 WL 1988276, at *4 (Ark. Ct. App. May 19, 2010) ("Parol evidence has long been considered admissible for the purpose of showing usury."). *But cf.* Sturm v. Muens, 224 S.W.3d 758, 762–763 (Tex. App. 2007) (parol evidence rule does not bar evidence to show that loan is usurious, but bars evidence to show that an agreement that does not appear to be a loan is in fact a loan). *See generally* § 3.9.1, *supra* (substance not form dictates nature of the transaction).

115 *See, e.g.*, *In re* Casbeer, 793 F.2d 1436 (5th Cir. 1986) (Texas usury law); Wall v. East Texas Teachers Credit Union, 533 S.W.2d 918 (Tex. 1976). *See also* Rockstad v. Erikson, 113 P.3d 1215, 1223 (Alaska 2005) (rejecting testimony that two loans created instead of one since to do so would be to make the contract usurious); Hoxie Implement Co. v. Baker, 65 S.W.3d 140 (Tex. App. 2001) (if ambiguous, creditor's demand letter should be interpreted not to "charge" usurious interest).

116 *See* § 5.8.7.3, *supra*. *See also* Coxson v. Commonwealth Mortgage Co. (*In re* Coxson), 43 F.3d 189 (5th Cir. 1995); Watson v. Avco Fin. Servs., Int'l, 401 N.W.2d 485 (Neb. 1987) (lender did not illegally contract for attorney fees where contractual clause for such fees prefaced by words, "to the extent permitted by law"). *Cf.* Myles v.

There are essentially two ways for debtors to combat the tendency of courts to construe contracts in favor of creditors, both of which depend on a recognition of the fact that creditors write consumer credit contracts. First, because of this fact, a consumer's attorney should not rely on the contract alone to prove a usury case if there is any conceivable ambiguity in the contract terms. Instead, remembering that a court should consider all the facts and circumstances around a transaction when considering usury, a debtor's attorney should attempt to build a record showing the intent of the parties at the time the transaction was consummated and, if a form contract is at issue, the manner in which the creditor has applied the disputed contract provision in other transactions.

The second method of dealing with unfavorable rules of contract construction is to attack them head-on, at least insofar as they apply to consumer credit contracts. It is widely recognized that a contract should be construed against its drafter.[117] Consumer credit contracts are not only written by creditors, but they are almost uniformly contracts of adhesion which are offered to the consumer on a take-it-or-leave-it basis.[118] One court, observing that ambiguous contract language can mislead consumers about their rights and dissuade them from asserting their rights, suggested that consumer credit contracts should be construed as the average consumer would interpret them.[119]

## 7.5.2 *Loan or Forbearance*

### 7.5.2.1 Introduction

The first element of almost all usury violations is the existence of a "loan" or "forbearance" of money. Although the definition of these terms may vary from statute to statute, a loan (often referred to as the "use of money" in usury statutes[120]) may generally be thought of as a temporary transfer of money or its equivalent from a creditor to a debtor or to a third party on the debtor's behalf.[121] A forbearance, on the other hand, is an agreement between an existing debtor and creditor under which the debtor gives consideration (i.e., pays interest) in return for the creditor's agreement to refrain from demanding immediate payment of a preexisting debt which has come due.[122] Most usury statutes treat loans and forbearances interchangeably.[123]

Some state usury statutes apply to more than loans and forbearances. For example, a court interpreted a North Carolina usury statute that applies to "advances" to encompass transactions where the repayment obligation was not absolute.[124] In addition, some usury statutes apply to the "detention" of money as well as to loans and forbearances. (The difference between forbearance and detention is that in the former the creditor grants the debtor the right to pay a debt over time, while in the latter the debtor fails to pay a debt when due without any agreement on the part of the creditor.[125]) A Pennsylvania usury statute provides a treble damages recovery whenever excess charges are paid, regardless of whether the charges were imposed in connection with a loan.[126] In Arkansas, where the usury ceiling is found in the state constitution, the courts have the role of determining whether a transaction is a loan; the legislature does not have the authority to define a type of transaction as a non-loan.[127]

Courts have held the following types of transactions to be loans or forbearances that are governed by the usury laws, even when structured in a way that disguises their nature:

- Payday loans, in which the lender cashes a check for less than its face value, and holds off on depositing it for a

---

Resolution Trust Corp., 787 S.W.2d 616, 618 (Tex. App. 1990) (court will construe acceleration clause as non-usurious unless its express and positive terms require unearned interest to be collected in all events).

117 *See, e.g.*, Zwayer v. Ford Motor Credit Co., 665 N.E.2d 843 (Ill. App. Ct. 1996) (contract was ambiguous and should be construed against the maker where it contained a clause allowing the use of the Rule of 78s to rebate upon prepayment but was silent if acceleration occurred).

118 *See* Drennan v. Security Pac. Nat'l Bank, 621 P.2d 1318 (Cal. 1981) (discussing the interpretation of adhesive contracts).

119 *See In re* Sprouse, 577 F.2d 989, 993–994 (5th Cir. 1978) (Ga. law).

120 *See* Tygrett v. University Gardens Home Ass'n, 687 S.W.2d 481 (Tex. App. 1985).

121 *See generally* Eikenberry v. Adirondack Spring Water Co., 480 N.E.2d 70 (N.Y. 1985) (distinguishing loan and forbearance).

122 *See* Sunburst Bank v. Keith, 648 So. 2d 1147 (Miss. 1995) (oral agreements to extend loan term accompanied by payment of foreclosure fee were forbearance agreements); Eikenberry v. Adirondack Spring Water Co., 480 N.E.2d 70 (N.Y. 1985) (agreement was a forbearance); Clark v. Darby, 639 N.Y.S.2d 549 (N.Y. App. Div. 1996) (acceptance of a bond and mortgage by an employer from an employee who embezzled funds and an agreement to defer the employer's right to pursue legal remedies as long as employee paid back the amount owed with interest of 13.5% constituted a forbearance that was subject to New York's usury statute limiting interest to 11%); Carper v. Kanawha Banking & Trust Co., 207 S.E.2d 897 (W. Va. 1974) (no reversible error in usury verdict where debtor's attorney claimed usurious "loan" in opening argument but later proved usurious "forbearance"). *But cf.* Kenty v. Bank One, Columbus, N.A., 92 F.3d 384 (6th Cir. 1996) (force-placed insurance premium was not a forbearance); Henson v. Columbus Bank & Trust Co., 770 F.2d 1566 (11th Cir. 1985) (refraining from calling a demand note is not a forbearance); Smith Machinery Co. v. Jenkins, 654 F.2d 693 (10th Cir. 1981) (N.M. law) (transaction is detention, not forbearance); Anderson v. Nextel Partners, Inc., 745 N.W.2d 464 (Iowa 2008) (one-year cell phone subscriber agreement not credit even though vendor required credit check, contract referred to transaction as an extension of credit, and consumer was required to pay fee if she terminated early, as consumer was not allowed to defer payment of monthly charges); Lowell & Austin, Inc. v. Traux, 507 A.2d 949 (Vt. 1985) (no forbearance).

123 *See, e.g.*, Edwards v. Alabama Farm Bureau Mut. Cas. Ins. Co., 509 So. 2d 232 (Ala. Civ. App. 1986) (no distinction between treatment of loan and forbearance in Alabama Mini-Code); Ott v. Peppertree Resort Villas, Inc., 716 N.W.2d 127 (Wis. Ct. App. 2006) (time-share seller's acceptance of installment payments constitutes a forbearance so qualifies as a loan).

124 Odell v. Legal Bucks, L.L.C., 665 S.E.2d 767 (N.C. Ct. App. 2008).

125 *See* § 7.5.2.3, *infra*.

126 Roethlein v. Portnoff Law Assocs., Ltd., 25 A.3d 1274 (Pa. Commw. Ct. 2011) (allowing recovery of excess charges imposed by collector of delinquent taxes).

127 Luebbers v. Money Store, Inc., 40 S.W.3d 745 (Ark. 2001).

period of time,[128] even if the loan fee is disguised as payment for goods or services;[129]
- Sale-leaseback schemes for vehicles or other items of personal property;[130]
- Refund anticipation loans;[131]
- A conveyance of real estate with a buyback option;[132]
- Sales of future income, in some circumstances.[133]

On the other hand, courts have held the following types of transactions not to be loans:

- Transactions in which the customer receives the goods or services over time, and pays for them only as received;[134]
- Sales of accounts receivable;[135]
- Transactions that fall through before they are consummated.[136]

### 7.5.2.2 Credit Sales and the Time-Price Doctrine

#### *7.5.2.2.1 Time-price exception to usury laws*

Absent specific statutory guidance, the chief uncertainty about the definition of a loan is whether this term includes credit extended in connection with the installment sale of goods or services. When interpreting a statute that applies only to loans, not to the forbearance of an obligation or the detention of money, courts may require the debtor to show that the transaction involved a transfer of money that was to be repaid, thereby excluding purchase and sale transactions.[137]

Some jurisdictions follow the time-price doctrine, a legal fiction that results in the exclusion of credit sales from usury laws. These jurisdictions apply the doctrine when a buyer and seller agree to separate "cash" and "time" prices, the former being the price which would be paid if the buyer used cash or its equivalent, and the latter being the (invariably higher) price which the buyer will pay in return for the ability to pay in installments.[138] The difference between the time price and the cash price is not legally recognized as interest, but is instead

---

128 *See, e.g.*, Turner v. E-Z Check Cashing, Inc., 35 F. Supp. 2d 1042 (M.D. Tenn. 1999) (deferred presentment of check constitutes a loan); Hamilton v. York, 987 F. Supp. 953 (E.D. Ky. 1997) (deferred presentment of check); McGhee v. Ark. State Bd. of Collection Agencies, 289 S.W.3d 18 (Ark. 2008) (payday loan transaction is a loan); Betts v. McKenzie Check Advance of Fla., L.L.C., 928 So. 2d 1204 (Fla. 2006). *But see* Betts v. Advance Am., 213 F.R.D. 466 (M.D. Fla. 2003) (relying on now-overruled state court decision to hold that payday loan is not an extension of credit). *See generally* Ch. 9, *supra*.

129 Cashback Catalog Sales v. Price, 102 F. Supp. 2d 1375 (S.D. Ga. 2000) (denying lender's motion for summary judgment; payday lender's agreement not to cash post-dated checks until borrower's payday was a forbearance; fact that lender gave borrower gift certificates equal to face value of checks did not fool the court); Short On Cash.Net of New Castle, Inc. v. Dep't of Fin. Inst., 811 N.E.2d 819 (Ind. Ct. App. 2004) (sale of Internet service with cash back is loan). *See generally* § 4.5.2, *supra* (sham services and other subterfuges), Ch. 9 (payday lending), *infra*.

130 *See, e.g.*, SAL Leasing, Inc. v. Arizona *ex rel.* Napolitano, 10 P.3d 1221 (Ariz. Ct. App. 2000) (vehicle sale-leaseback scheme is loan); Aple Auto Cash Express, Inc. v. State *ex rel.* Oklahoma Dep't of Consumer Credit, 78 P.3d 1231 (Okla. 2003) (sale-leaseback). *But see* People v. Lee, 526 N.W.2d 882 (Mich. 1994) (sale of expensive watch with repurchase option not loan because no obligation to repay; criminal usury prosecution; note dissent). *But cf.* Human Res. Dev. Press, Inc. v. IKON Office Solutions Co., 2006 WL 149043 (D. Mass. Jan. 12, 2006) (commercial equipment lease not loan). *See generally* § 11.2, *infra*.

131 *See, e.g.*, State *ex rel.* Salazar v. The Cash Now Store, Inc., 31 P.3d 161 (Colo. 2001) (tax refund assignments are loans). *See generally* § 14.5, *infra*.

132 *See, e.g.*, Oregrund Ltd. P'ship v. Sheive, 873 So. 2d 451 (Fla. Dist. Ct. App. 2004) (reversing dismissal of complaint; land conveyance with repurchase option may be loan). *See generally* National Consumer Law Center, Foreclosures Ch. 17 (4th ed. 2012).

133 *See* § 13.3, *infra*.

134 *See, e.g.*, Mackey v. Bristol W. Ins. Servs., 130 Cal. Rptr. 2d 536, 552 (Cal. Ct. App. 2003) (financing of auto insurance policy not a credit transaction when insured was under no obligation to pay for full term, but could cancel after paying for any number of months). *See also* Anderson v. Nextel Partners, Inc., 745 N.W.2d 464 (Iowa 2008) (one-year cell phone agreement not credit where consumer was required to pay monthly charges upon billing and could cancel at any time, even though she would have to pay substantial fee on early termination).

135 *See, e.g.*, Carter v. Four Seasons Funding Corp., 97 S.W.3d 387 (Ark. 2003) (sale of accounts receivable by sophisticated business entity not a loan even though buyer had recourse against seller if accounts proved uncollectible); Korrody v. Miller, 126 S.W.3d 224 (Tex. App. 2003) (upholding factual finding that sale of accounts receivable not a loan even though parties never signed factoring agreement and account debtor was never notified of assignment); Ravkind v. Mortgage Funding Corp., 881 S.W.2d 203 (Tex. App. 1994) (assignment of payments due on contract for deed not a loan even though assignee had recourse against assignor). *But see* Decision Point, Inc. v. Reece & Nichols Realtors, Inc., 144 P.3d 706 (Kan. 2006) (applying U.C.C.C. definition of loan as "creation of debt by the lender's payment of or agreement to pay money to the debtor"; advancing money to real estate agents in return for their agreement to repay it either through assignment of specific anticipated commissions or repurchase of the account creates loans); Baxter v. Stevens, 773 P.2d 890 (Wash. Ct. App. 1989) (sale of payment obligation, a promissory note, for an amount less than its face value was loan where transferor had absolute obligation of repayment if the obligor on the note defaulted).

136 Rhode v. Kremer, 655 S.W.2d 410 (Ark. 1983) (manufactured home sale with contingent financing never completed so no "credit"); Miro v. Allied Fin. Co., 650 S.W.2d 938 (Tex. App. 1983) (no loan when loan instrument cancelled shortly after signing and never funded).

137 *See, e.g.*, Tyrcha v. Wesolek, 543 N.E.2d 222 (Ill. App. Ct. 1989) (though preamble to usury statute refers to "sales on credit," penalty section applies only to a "loan of money" so does not apply to a sale); McComb v. McWilliams, 505 N.E.2d 1378 (Ill. App. Ct. 1987) (interpreting Illinois Interest Act not to apply to obligation on promissory note that arose from exchange of property); Carey v. Lincoln Loan Co., 998 P.2d 724 (Or. Ct. App. 2000) (land sale contract not loan for purposes of statute requiring lender to allow prepayment).

138 *See, e.g.*, General Motors Acceptance Corp. v. Mackrill, 122 N.W.2d 742 (Neb. 1963); Carper v. Kanawha Banking & Trust Co., 207 S.E.2d 897 (W. Va. 1974). *Cf.* Leasing Serv. Corp. v. Simpkins Metal Bldgs., Inc., 638 F. Supp. 896 (S.D.N.Y. 1986) (Texas law; even if purported lease was a credit sale, the charge was a time-price difference and was excludable from interest even if separate cash and time prices were not stated).

labeled a "time-price differential" which is not regulated by traditional usury laws.[139]

It is important for attorneys to recognize that the time-price doctrine is merely a legal fiction. A modern credit sale is not logically distinguishable from either a forbearance by the seller or a loan from the seller to the buyer, which the buyer must use to pay for the goods being purchased. Nevertheless, several states continue to follow the common law distinction between these two fundamentally identical transactions, and this adherence has given creditors a significant motivation to restructure credit in the form of credit sales. Instead of arranging a car loan from a lender subject to usury limitations, for example, an auto dealer that is not subject to usury ceilings may extend credit directly to the consumer. The dealer then sells the consumer's credit contract or note to a bank or finance company which might otherwise have given the consumer a direct loan. The outcome is identical to a direct loan transaction—the consumer purchases a car; the dealer receives cash; and the third-party financier holds the consumer's debt. Nonetheless, under the time-price doctrine, usury law does not apply because the form of the transaction is legally a credit sale, not a loan.[140]

In jurisdictions where the time-price doctrine remains in force, a buyer's attorney should closely examine any credit sale transaction to be certain that the exception actually applies. The time-price exception does not apply to sham sales where the "buyer" obtains coupons or scrip that can be used as cash.[141] Nor can a loan be disguised as a sale if the services or goods sold are of little or no value.[142] Moreover, usury ceilings will apply to credit sales when the seller fails to go through the formalities of stating a separate cash price for the purchased goods and disclosing the time-price differential.[143] Whether the seller computes sales tax on the cash price or the time price may be another factor.[144] Further, an extension of credit to refinance or consolidate an earlier credit sale does not itself arise out of a credit sale, and therefore is not subject to the time-price exception.[145]

A final limitation on the time-price usury exception arises from the contradictions between the traditional application of the doctrine to seller-financed sales, and the widespread commercial practice of assigning consumer credit contracts or notes to third-party creditors. As mentioned previously in this section, the distinction between a direct purchase money loan from a bank or finance company to a consumer and the financing of a sale directly by the seller is one of form over substance, particularly when, in the latter transaction, the seller discounts

139 *See, e.g.,* Bartholomew v. Northampton Nat'l Bank, 584 F.2d 1288 (3d Cir. 1978); Wilkins v. M&H Fin. Inc., 476 F. Supp. 212 (D. Ark. 1979), *aff'd*, 621 F.2d 311 (8th Cir. 1980); Agristor Credit Corp. v. Lewellen, 472 F. Supp. 46 (N.D. Miss. 1979); Credit Alliance Corp. v. David O. Crump Sand & Fill Co., 470 F. Supp. 489 (S.D.N.Y. 1979); Scientific Prods. v. Cyto Med. Lab., Inc., 457 F. Supp. 1373 (D. Conn. 1978); Cavazos v. Mid-State Trust II (*In re* Hillsborough Holdings Corp.), 267 B.R. 882 (Bankr. M.D. Fla. 2001) (sale of home); *In re* Craft, 120 B.R. 84 (Bankr. E.D. Mich. 1989) (2% per month service charge on unpaid balance was a time-price differential not governed by any specific Michigan statutes); Southwest Concrete Co. v. Gosh Constr., 798 P.2d 1247 (Cal. 1990) (utilizing time-price doctrine in evaluating late charge on credit sale); Boerner v. Colwell Co., 577 P.2d 200 (Cal. 1978); Varr v. Olimpia, 2002 WL 1425373 (Cal. Ct. App. July 1, 2002) (even after it was restructured, debt for accounting services was still exempted from usury laws by time-price doctrine); Phillips v. Allis-Chalmers Credit Corp., 339 S.E.2d 302 (Ga. Ct. App. 1985); Walker v. Fingerhut Corp., 2000 WL 136096 (Minn. Ct. App. Jan. 28, 2000); Woods v. Evans Prods. Co., 574 S.W.2d 488 (Mo. Ct. App. 1978); Servpro Indus., Inc. v. Pizzillo, 2001 WL 120731 (Tenn. Ct. App. Feb. 14, 2001) (sale of franchise); Anchor, Inc. v. Laguna Enters., Inc., 2002 WL 287706 (Tex. App. Feb. 7, 2002) (discount given by seller for prompt payment is not interest); Mid State Homes v. Sullivan, 592 S.W.2d 29 (Tex. Civ. App. 1979). *But cf.* Thelen v. Ducharme, 390 N.W.2d 264 (Mich. Ct. App. 1986) (time-price differential was interest where usury statute definition of interest incorporated all amounts defined as "finance charge" under Truth in Lending Act).

140 *See* Bell v. Muller, 118 P.3d 405 (Wash. Ct. App. 2005) (car financing that was structured as retail installment contract is governed by state RISA, not Consumer Loan Act, even though seller immediately assigned the contract so did not actually provide financing). *See generally* Hare v. General Contract Purchase Corp., 249 S.W.2d 973 (Ark. 1952) (examining use of credit sale format for loans).

141 *See* W.T. Grant Co. v. Walsh, 241 A.2d 46 (N.J. Dist. Ct. 1968) (coupons-scrip); Tuition Plan, Inc. v. Zicari, 335 N.Y.S.2d 95 (N.Y. Dist. Ct. 1972) (retail installment contract for tuition money was a loan). *See generally* Austin v. Alabama Check Cashers Ass'n., 936 So. 2d 1014 (Ala. 2005) (finding deferred presentment checks to be loans).

142 People v. JAG NY, L.L.C., 794 N.Y.S.2d 488 (N.Y. App. Div. 2005) (sale of gift certificates disguised usurious loans); North Carolina *ex rel.* Cooper v. NCCS Loans, Inc., 624 S.E.2d 371 (N.C. Ct. App. 2005) (a few hours of Internet service a month at lender's offices had little or no monetary value). *See generally* § 4.5, *supra*.

143 *See, e.g.,* Daniel v. First Nat'l Bank of Birmingham, 227 F.2d 353 (5th Cir. 1955); Pollice v. National Tax Funding, 59 F. Supp. 2d 474 (W.D. Pa. 1999) (time-price doctrine does not apply where buyer did not make conscious decision to pay for goods on credit at a higher price than cash price), *aff'd in part, rev'd in part on other grounds*, 225 F.3d 379 (3d Cir. 2000); General Motors Acceptance Corp. v. Mackrill, 122 N.W.2d 742 (Neb. 1963); Western Auto Supply Co. v. Vick, 268 S.E.2d 842 (N.C. Ct. App. 1980), *aff'd*, 277 S.E.2d 360 (1981), *reh'g* 283 S.E.2d 101 (N.C. 1981); Davenport v. Unicapital Corp., 230 S.E.2d 905 (S.C. 1976); Kinerd v. Colonial Leasing Co., 800 S.W.2d 187 (Tex. 1990); El Paso Dev. Co. v. Berryman, 769 S.W.2d 584 (Tex. App. 1989) (inflated sales price of real estate constituted interest instead of valid time-price differential); Commercial Credit Equip. Corp. v. West, 677 S.W.2d 669 (Tex. App. 1984); Whitaker v. Spiegel, Inc., 623 P.2d 1147 (Wash.), *amended on other grounds*, 637 P.2d 235 (Wash. 1981); Carper v. Kanawha Banking & Trust Co., 207 S.E.2d 897, 911–912 (W. Va. 1974) (convenient general summary of the factors to be considered in determining whether the time-price doctrine applies to a particular sales transaction). *See also* Walker v. Fingerhut Corp., 2000 WL 136096 (Minn. Ct. App. Jan. 28, 2000) (seller established separate cash and time prices so fell within time-price doctrine except in cases where it rebated credit charges upon prepayment, which is inconsistent with existence of separate time-price; remanding case for determination of usurious intent issue).

144 *Cf.* Walker v. Fingerhut Corp., 2000 WL 136096 (Minn. Ct. App. Jan. 28, 2000) (other factors outweighed fact that seller computed sales tax on cash price rather than time price; time-price doctrine applied).

145 Butler v. Holt Machinery Co., 741 S.W.2d 169 (Tex. App. 1987), *corrected on denial of reh'g*, 739 S.W.2d 958 (1987).

the consumer paper to the bank or finance company shortly after the sale. At times the distinctions between the two characterizations of the transaction become so transparent that courts in jurisdictions which generally recognize the time-price exception have decided that transactions are not "true" credit sales but are merely disguised loans or forbearances to which usury limitations apply.[146] Such rulings are most common with open-end sales accounts or when a seller, immediately after a sale, assigns the credit contract to a third-party creditor with whom it regularly deals and whose forms it may use. Generally, evidence that the third-party financing was pre-arranged is evidence that the transaction was not a "true" credit sale.[147]

If the equities of a credit sale transaction favor the consumer and the seller has close connections to a finance company to which it assigns its contracts, it may be appropriate for a practitioner to argue that a true credit sale does not exist. However, a word of caution is in order. Cases deciding whether a true credit sale or a concealed loan exist often seem result oriented. Courts have not developed any rigorous tests to distinguish valid assignments of consumer paper from concealed loans, simply because there is no real difference beyond the speed or frequency with which the seller discounts the contracts it obtains.

At least with respect to consumer credit sales, most jurisdictions have abolished the time-price doctrine, often by adopting a retail installment sales act that explicitly regulates the terms and charges for credit sales.[148] Courts may still, however, interpret the term "loan" in state credit statutes to exclude credit sales.[149]

##### 7.5.2.2.2 *The erosion of the time-price doctrine: direct regulation of consumer credit sales and RISAs*

The time-price usury exception has been rendered irrelevant to consumer credit transactions in most jurisdictions by the enactment of installment sales acts or consumer credit codes.[150] Although some states amended their statutes in the 1980s to permit any interest rate to which the parties agreed, most of these laws impose ceilings on the charges that may be assessed in connection with consumer credit sales. In a few jurisdictions the doctrine has been put to rest judicially by courts which have recognized its illogic or which have simply applied usury statutes at their face value.[151]

Many of the jurisdictions which now regulate credit sales still nominally distinguish credit sales and loans, and may still employ terminology such as the "time-price differential" which originated in the time-price doctrine.[152] For example, a credit sale might be regulated by an installment sales act, while a loan could fall under a corresponding small loan act, and a consumer claiming an installment sales act violation might well be required to establish the existence of a "credit sale" or "installment sale" rather than a "loan" as an element of the statutory violation.[153] Yet such distinctions are as much a matter of form as of substance,[154] and practitioners should not assume that a jurisdiction applies the time-price usury exception merely because the terminology associated with the doctrine remains in

146 *See, e.g.*, Hare v. General Contract Purchase Corp., 249 S.W.2d 973 (Ark. 1952); Lloyd v. Gutgsell, 124 N.W.2d 198 (Neb. 1963); State Wholesale Supply, Inc. v. Allen, 227 S.E.2d 120 (N.C. Ct. App. 1976) (open-end account); Midland Guardian & Co. v. Thacker, 314 S.E.2d 26 (S.C. Ct. App. 1984). *See also* Perez v. Rent-A-Center, Inc., 892 A.2d 1255 (N.J. 2006) (finding time-price equivalent to interest). *Cf.* Scientific Prods. v. Cyto Med. Lab., Inc., 457 F. Supp. 1373 (D. Conn. 1978); First Nat'l Bank of Ottawa v. Larkins, 444 N.E.2d 818 (Ill. App. Ct. 1983) (manufactured home financing was bona fide sale); St. Paul Bank for Coops. v. Ohman, 402 N.W.2d 235 (Minn. Ct. App. 1987) (contract was a forbearance, not a time-price sale; use of "time-price" language and similarity of transaction to automobile installment sales or revolving credit plans was not controlling); Woods v. Evans Prods. Co., 574 S.W.2d 488 (Mo. Ct. App. 1978); Kinerd v. Colonial Leasing Co., 800 S.W.2d 187 (Tex. 1990).

147 Daniel v. First Nat'l Bank of Birmingham, 227 F.2d 353 (5th Cir. 1955); Hare v. General Contract Purchase Corp., 249 S.W.2d 973 (Ark. 1952); Miller v. Diversified Loan Serv. Co., 382 S.E.2d 514 (W. Va. 1989); Carper v. Kanawha Banking & Trust Co., 207 S.E.2d 897 (W. Va. 1974).

148 *See* Perez v. Rent-A-Center, Inc., 892 A.2d 1255 (N.J. 2006) (reciting history and abrogation of doctrine); Note, *Interest Rates and the Law: A History of Usury*, 27 Ariz. St. L.J. 61 (1981). *See generally* §§ 1.2.4, *supra*, 7.5.2.2.2, *infra*.

149 *See, e.g.*, Carey v. Lincoln Loan Co., 998 P.2d 724 (Or. Ct. App. 2000) (land sale contract not loan for purposes of statute requiring lender to allow prepayment).

150 *See, e.g.*, Perez v. Rent-A-Center, 892 A.2d 1255, 1264–1265 (N.J. 2006) (reciting history of RISAs); Bell v. Muller, 118 P.3d 405 (Wash. Ct. App. 2005) (installment sale of car is regulated under RISA and thereby excluded from usury regulation), *amended on other grounds*, 2005 Wash. App. LEXIS 3111 (Wash. Ct. App. Dec. 8, 2005). *But cf.* Saul v. Midlantic Nat'l Bank/South, 572 A.2d 650 (N.J. Super. Ct. App. Div. 1990) (legislature's adoption of RISA is endorsement of time-price doctrine even though this car sale falls outside RISA's scope).

151 *See* Foreign Commerce v. Tonn, 789 F.2d 221 (3d Cir. 1986); Sloan v. Sears, Roebuck & Co., 308 S.W.2d 802 (Ark. 1957); State *ex rel.* Turner v. Younker Bros., 210 N.W.2d 550 (Iowa 1973); Rollinger v. J.C. Penny Co., 192 N.W.2d 699 (S.D. 1971); Cloud v. Whitley, 1996 WL 626270 (Tex. App. Oct. 30, 1996) (home improvement contract which provided that the homeowner need not pay for the work until fifteen days following completion constituted a loan subject to state usury limits); Whitaker v. Spiegel, Inc., 623 P.2d 1147 (Wash. 1981); State v. J.C. Penny Co., 179 N.W.2d 641 (Wis. 1970). *See also* Perez v. Rent-A-Center, Inc., 892 A.2d 1255 (N.J. 2006) (recognizing that interest and time-price differential are indistinguishable; applying criminal usury statutes to rent-to-own contracts); Ott v. Peppertree Resort Villas, Inc., 716 N.W.2d 127 (Wis. Ct. App. 2006) (time-share seller's acceptance of installment payments constitutes a forbearance so qualifies as a loan).

152 *See, e.g.*, Tauber v. Johnson, 291 N.E.2d 180 (Ill. App. Ct. 1972) (excessive time-price differential charged under motor vehicle retail installment sales act). *See also* U.C.C. § 9-625(c)(2) (specifying statutory damages for certain violations of U.C.C. Article 9 in terms of "time-price differential").

153 *See, e.g.*, Briercroft Serv. Corp. v. de Los Santos, 776 S.W.2d 198 (Tex. App. 1988) (borrower could not establish violation of statute governing retail installment transactions because contract was a loan with interest, rather than a retail installment sale with a time-price differential; statute therefore did not apply).

154 *See* Girard Acceptance Corp. v. Wallace, 388 A.2d 582 (N.J. 1978).

use. Distinctions between statutes regulating credit sales and "usury" statutes regulating loans may, however, be important under some circumstances. For example, courts often strictly construe "usury" statutes, but may be inclined to distinguish installment sales acts as remedial legislation which must be broadly construed.

Another issue that arises under state retail installment sales acts is whether a particular sale involves credit. The Iowa Supreme Court held that a one-year cell phone subscriber agreement was not credit even though the vendor required a credit check, the contract referred to the transaction as an extension of credit, and the consumer was required to pay a substantial fee if she terminated early. The court held that it was not credit because the consumer was not charged for a year of service in advance, and then allowed to pay this amount in monthly installments. Instead, she had the option of canceling service, albeit with an early termination fee. The contract did not allow her to defer payment of monthly charges, but required those charges to be paid each month upon billing.[155]

### 7.5.2.3 Forbearance and Detention

Usury statutes generally apply not only to loans but also to forbearances. A forbearance is an agreement between a creditor and debtor under which the creditor defers the enforcement of a debt which has come due in return for the debtor's payment of interest on that debt.[156] For example, if a balloon payment came due on a mortgage and the debtor was unable to make the payment, the lender might agree to forbear collection of the balloon payment for a year in return for continued or increased interest payments.

The fact that most usury statutes cover forbearances means that many transactions which are not normally considered extensions of credit may be subject to usury limitations. All that is needed is a debt which has come due and an agreement between the parties allowing the debt to be paid off over time. The underlying debt often need not have been a loan. Thus, an agreement between an attorney and client for the payment of overdue bills for legal services may be a forbearance subject to usury law.[157] A payment plan for delinquent taxes and water and sewer charges is a forbearance.[158] Even a judicial settlement which provides for the payment of interest on an agreed liability may be a forbearance.[159] Moreover, debts which are created through credit sales that are exempt from usury limitations may provide the basis for forbearances to which usury ceilings do apply.[160] The Mississippi Supreme Court has held that credit transactions which were not usurious at their inception may become tainted by a subsequent forbearance agreement allowing for unlawful interest.[161]

The chief limitation on the definition of a forbearance is that a forbearance usually requires an agreement between the parties under which the creditor agrees to forego the collection of the existing debt at least temporarily.[162] In most transactions, however, when a debt such as an oil bill comes due but is not paid, the creditor simply starts assessing interest on the outstanding debt, often in the name of late charges, but does not agree to forego collection. Consequently, no forbearance exists. Instead, this situation technically constitutes the "detention" of money,

155 Anderson v. Nextel Partners, Inc., 745 N.W.2d 464 (Iowa 2008).

156 *See* Pollice v. National Tax Funding, 225 F.3d 379 (3d Cir. 2000) (installment payment agreement for preexisting debt was forbearance, but interest was not consideration for the forbearance because creditor charged debtors the same rate they had paid before entering into the agreements); Cashback Catalog Sales v. Price, 102 F. Supp. 2d 1375 (S.D. Ga. 2000) (denial of lender's motion for summary judgment) (payday lender's agreement not to cash post-dated check until borrower's payday is a forbearance); Sunburst Bank v. Keith, 648 So. 2d 1147 (Miss. 1995); Eikenberry v. Adirondack Spring Water Co., 480 N.E.2d 70 (N.Y. 1985); Clark v. Darby, 639 N.Y.S.2d 549 (N.Y. App. Div. 1996) (acceptance of a bond and mortgage by an employer from an employee who embezzled funds and an agreement to defer the employer's right to pursue legal remedies as long as employee paid back the amount owed with interest of 13.5% constituted a forbearance that was subject to New York's usury statute limiting interest to 11%); Western Auto Supply Co. v. Vick, 277 S.E.2d 360 (1981), *reh'g* 283 S.E.2d 101 (N.C. 1981); Tygrett v. University Gardens Home Ass'n, 687 S.W.2d 481 (Tex. App. 1985); Whitaker v. Spiegel, Inc., 623 P.2d 1147 (Wash.) *amended on other grounds*, 637 P.2d 235 (Wash. 1981). *Cf.* Ott v. Peppertree Resort Villas, Inc., 716 N.W.2d 127 (Wis. Ct. App. 2006) (treating installment sale of time-share as forbearance and therefore covered by loan provisions of Wisconsin Consumer Credit Transaction Act).

157 Eikenberry v. Adirondack Spring Water Co., 480 N.E.2d 70 (N.Y. 1985).

158 Pollice v. National Tax Funding, 225 F.3d 379, 396–397 (3d Cir. 2000). *Cf.* Sheehy v. Franchise Tax Bd., 100 Cal. Rptr. 2d 760 (Cal. Ct. App. 2000) (no agreement to forbear collection of unpaid taxes, so usury laws did not apply).

159 Clifford v. Clifford, 453 N.W.2d 675 (Mich. 1990) (usury statute applies to judgment interest rate entered by consent in divorce case, but remedy is correction of order rather than forfeiture of interest); Farley v. Fischer 358 N.W.2d 34 (Mich. Ct. App. 1984) (applying usury statute to divorce settlement that required wife to pay interest in excess of 7% usury cap on payment owed to husband for conveyance of home). *But see In re* Hoberg, 300 B.R. 752, 766 (Bankr. C.D. Cal. 2003) (husband's obligation to pay money to satisfy spousal support and division of property claims not loan or forbearance). *But cf.* Ghirardo v. Antonioli, 883 P.2d 960 (Cal. 1994) (usury statute inapplicable to credit sale, so also inapplicable to notes executed in settlement of litigated dispute regarding the sale); Wiley-Reiter Corp. v. Groce, 693 S.W.2d 701 (Tex. App. 1985) (settlement contained no loan or charge for the use/detention of money).

160 *See In re* Pillon-Davey & Assocs., 52 B.R. 455 (Bankr. N.D. Cal. 1985). *But see* Ghirardo v. Antonioli, 883 P.2d 960 (Cal. 1994) (notes executed in settlement of litigated dispute regarding an exempt credit sale constituted a modification, not a non-exempt loan or forbearance).

Some statutes, however, limit forbearances to the forbearance of debt arising from a loan. *See* U.C.C.C. § 3.106(4) (1968 Act), U.C.C.C. § 1.301(25) (1974 Act).

161 Sunburst Bank v. Keith, 648 So. 2d 1147 (Miss. 1995).

162 *See* Smith Machinery Co. v. Jenkins, 654 F.2d 693 (10th Cir. 1981) (N.M. law); Terrell Inc. v. DeShazo Builders, 661 P.2d 303 (Idaho 1983). *Cf.* Rollingbrook Inv. Co. v. Texas Nat'l Bank, 790 S.W.2d 375 (Tex. App. 1990) (bank's renewal of note was not forbearance where it did not grant additional time for performance, but extended a ninety-day offer to renew, collected a higher rate of interest during commitment period, and executed new note with differing interest rate and payments as well as amount due and maturity date).

and in many jurisdictions charges for the detention of money are not within the scope of usury laws.[163]

Generally speaking, the detention of money is the failure to pay a debt when it comes due without obtaining the agreement of the creditor. The majority view is that charges on overdue debt, without a specific agreement to forbear, are simply penalties designed to encourage tardy debtors to pay up.[164] Courts frequently state that nonpayment is a "voluntary" act of the debtor,[165] and that usury will not result from the occurrence of a contingency within the control of the debtor, even if the debtor ends up paying charges which, if treated as interest, would exceed the legal rate.[166] In other words, charges for the detention of money, even if computed at a monthly rate instead of a one-time assessment,[167] are treated the same as late fees, and are not subject to usury limitations, unless it can be shown that the nonpayment which gave rise to the detention was anticipated by the parties at the time the transaction was consummated, and that the supposed "detention" is thus a ruse to escape the usury laws.[168]

Nevertheless, some usury statutes do address the "detention" of money as well as the forbearance of a debt, and under these statutes charges assessed on overdue accounts must respect usury ceilings.[169] This general approach makes sense. As

163 *See, e.g.*, Pollice v. National Tax Funding, 225 F.3d 379, 393–396 (3d Cir. 2000) (nonpayment of taxes and water and sewer charges was detention and was exempt from Pennsylvania usury laws, though payment plan could be forbearance); Sogeti, U.S.A., L.L.C. v. Whirlwind Bldg. Sys., Inc., 496 F. Supp. 2d 380, 382 (S.D.N.Y. 2007); Resolution Trust Corp. v. Oaks Apt. Joint Venture, 753 F. Supp. 1332, 1338 (N.D. Tex. 1990) (demand for payment of five times amount of principal and interest due is not a demand for compensation for the use forbearance or detention of money), *aff'd in relevant part, vacated in part on other grounds*, 966 F.2d 995 (5th Cir. 1992); Sheehy v. Franchise Tax Bd., 100 Cal. Rptr. 2d 760 (Cal. Ct. App. 2000) (no agreement to forbear collection of unpaid taxes); Butler v. Target, Inc., 601 So. 2d 1276 (Fla. Dist. Ct. App. 1992) (bill for legal services not a loan, so usury laws inapplicable to 1-1/2% monthly charge if unpaid after thirty days); Widmark v. Northrup King Co., 530 N.W.2d 588 (Minn. Ct. App. 1995) (no agreement to forbear, and "unlike typical credit arrangements," did not encourage to pay late to receive additional charges; commercial transaction); Protection Indus. Corp. v. Kaskel, 691 N.Y.S.2d 457 (N.Y. App. Div. 1999); T.F. James Co. v. Vakoch, 604 N.W.2d 459 (N.D. 2000) (nonpayment of rent is detention, and charges are covered by legal interest rate statute rather than usury law); Lowell & Austin, Inc. v. Traux, 507 A.2d 949 (Vt. 1985) (no agreement to forbear); Alaskan Fireplace, Inc. v. Everett, 667 N.W.2d 378 (Wis. Ct. App. 2003) (not a credit transaction when seller did not grant buyers the right to defer payment, but imposed 1.5% monthly late charge as means of dissuading late payment); Opinion of the Kansas Att'y Gen., No. 88-30, 1988 WL 429668 (Kan. A.G. Mar. 3, 1988) (reasonable late fees charged by cable television company are not interest, as they are not in consideration for forbearance as long as actual efforts to collect are undertaken and delinquent users are not given payment options). *See also* Pierce v. Emigrant Mortgage Co., 2005 WL 2406007 (D. Conn. Sept. 29, 2005) (default interest rate not subject to usury regulation); Griffin v. Georgia-Pacific Corp., 341 S.E.2d 499 (Ga. Ct. App. 1986) (specific statutory rate authorized for unpaid commercial accounts). *But cf.* Overboe v. Brodshaug, 751 N.W.2d 177 (N.D. 2008) (upholding trial court's finding that attorney agreed to extend credit, where payment was due only upon completion of services but he charged monthly service charges on balance before then, so usury statute applies); Forest Point Venture #703 v. Forest Point Owners Ass'n, 2001 WL 1160995 (Tex. App. Oct. 3, 2001) (detention of lender's money is within scope of Texas usury statute, but not shown here). *See generally* Annotation, 28 A.L.R. 3d 449 (1969) (interest after maturity as usurious or otherwise illegal); § 4.8, *supra* (treatment of late fees under state credit statutes).

164 *See*, e.g., Smith Machinery Co. v. Jenkins, 654 F.2d 693 (10th Cir. 1981) (N.M. law) (usury statute that does not apply to detention is inapplicable to post-maturity interest rate); Pierce v. Emigrant Mortgage Co., 2005 WL 2406007 (D. Conn. Sept. 29, 2005) (citing principle that usury laws do not apply to detention as one ground for holding that post-default interest rate not subject to usury laws); Scientific Prods. v. Cyto Med. Lab., 457 F. Supp. 1373 (D. Conn. 1978) (interest imposed if invoice not paid within thirty days is not governed by usury statute); Southwest Concrete Prods. v. Gosh Constr. Co., 263 Cal. Rptr. 387 (Cal. Ct. App. 1989) (1.5% monthly charge on bill not paid in full when due was not charge for forbearance and thus was not subject to usury laws, rather it was charge imposed to encourage prompt payment and compensate seller for delay; further, seller did not agree not to enforce its claim so there was no forbearance); Terrell Inc. v. DeShazo Builders, 661 P.2d 303 (Idaho 1983) (late charge imposed when invoice not paid when due is not usury because no agreement to extend time for payment); Rangen, Inc. v. Valley Trout Farms, Inc., 658 P.2d 955 (Idaho 1983) (no forbearance where seller did not agree to forego collection; Kelso Oil Co. v. East West Truck Stop, Inc., 102 S.W.3d 655 (Tenn. Ct. App. 2002) (late charges not governed by usury statute where creditor never agreed to extend due date). *Cf.* T.F. James Co. v. Vakoch, 604 N.W.2d 459 (N.D. 2000) (monthly charges on overdue rent are governed by legal interest rate statute but do not constitute usury so usury penalties do not apply). *But see* A.Y. McDonald Mfg. Co. v. Shackelford, 652 S.W.2d 9 (Ark. 1983); Bunn v. Weyerhauser Co., 598 S.W.2d 54 (Ark. 1980); Mark McDowell Corp. v. LSM 128, 263 Cal. Rptr. 310 (Cal. Ct. App. 1989) (holding charge usurious); Crestwood Lumber Co. v. Citizens Sav. & Loan Ass'n, 148 Cal. Rptr. 129 (Cal. Ct. App. 1978); Thrift Funds of Baton Rouge, Inc. v. Jones, 274 So. 2d 150 (La. 1973); Begelfer v. Najarian, 409 N.E.2d 167 (Mass. 1980). *See generally* Annotation, 28 A.L.R. 3d 449 (1969) (interest after maturity as usurious).

165 Smith Machinery Co. v. Jenkins, 654 F.2d 693 (10th Cir. 1981) (N.M. law).

166 Corvetti v. Hudson, 676 N.Y.S.2d 263 (N.Y. App. Div. 1998) (commercial case); Bowman Plumbing, Heating & Elec., Inc. v. Logan, 59 Va. Cir. 446 (2002).

167 The expression of a late charge as a monthly rate has often not been considered relevant to its status as an interest or non-interest charge. *See, e.g.*, Scientific Prods. v. Cyto Med. Lab., Inc., 457 F. Supp. 1373 (D. Conn. 1978).

However, at least in Arkansas, a late charge seems more likely to be held to be a non-interest "penalty" if it is a one-time assessment, rather than a monthly charge. *Compare* Bunn v. Weyerhauser Co., 598 S.W.2d 54 (Ark. 1980) (monthly "service charge"), *with* Smith v. Figure World Plus, 705 S.W.2d 433 (Ark. 1986) (large one-time late charge).

168 *See* Union Mortgage Banking & Trust Co. v. Hagood, 97 F. 360 (4th Cir. 1899); Davis v. Rider, 53 Ill. 416 (Ill. 1870); Osborn v. McCowen, 25 Ill. 218 (Ill. 1860); Carroll County Sav. Bank v. Strother, 6 S.E. 313 (S.C. 1888); Metro Hauling, Inc. v. Daffern, 723 P.2d 32 (Wash. Ct. App. 1986) (modification of contract after default; no contingency).

169 *See* Iowa Supreme Court Bd. of Prof'l Ethics & Conduct v. McKittrick, 683 N.W.2d 554, 560 (Iowa 2004) (interpreting and ap-

one court has stated: "If a borrower is to be protected from the extortion of an excessive rate for the use of money, there is no apparent reason why . . . [the protection] . . . should be limited to the term of the loan."[170] Furthermore, creditors clearly expect and tolerate late payment on accounts, at least to a limited extent. In addition, default charges may be separately regulated and subject to statutory penalties.[171]

## 7.5.3 Absolute Obligation to Repay Principal; Joint Ventures

The second element of a traditional usury case is the debtor's absolute obligation to repay the principal amount of the money transferred to him or her.[172] In a way this second element is closely intertwined with the first, i.e., the existence of a loan, because in the absence of an absolute obligation to repay, it is quite plausible to argue that a transfer of money is a gift or an investment rather than a loan. Nevertheless, most courts treat the obligation to repay as a distinct element in a usury case, and so it is separately discussed here.

The requirement that the repayment obligation be absolute means that it cannot be contingent. An example of a transaction that is not credit because the repayment obligation is contingent is a joint venture investment where the investor (lender) provides cash to a business enterprise, typically in return for a share of any profits made by the enterprise.[173] The investor's return may be very large, but it is contingent on the success of the enterprise and is thus, in a true joint venture, exempt from usury law.[174] Even if there is an absolute obligation to repay the principal, a court may conclude that the transaction is not a loan if the profit is uncertain.[175]

The joint venture begins to look more like a high-interest loan, however, as the investor's risk of losing its investment decreases. An "investment" which is absolutely repayable is, in fact, a loan rather than an investment.[176] Courts have found joint ventures to be usurious credit transactions when the investor's return on its funds is guaranteed by the contract,[177] or

plying Iowa limits on finance charges and compounding of interest on accounts receivable); Walker, Tooke & Lyons v. Sapp, 862 So. 2d 414 (La. Ct. App. 2003) (interpreting usury cap to apply to contract that set interest rate if client did not make timely payment of legal fees); Scarr v. Boyer, 818 P.2d 381 (Mont. 1991); 271 Truck Repair & Parts, Inc. v. First Air Express, Inc., 2008 WL 2387630 (Tex. App. June 11, 2008) (Texas usury statute covers suppliers of goods and services when they charge interest on past-due amounts); C.K. Oil Props., Inc. v. Hrubetz Operating Co., 2002 WL 32344609 (Tex. App. Apr. 25, 2002); Hardwick v. Austin Gallery of Oriental Rugs, Inc., 779 S.W.2d 438, 443 (Tex. App. 1989); Letter from David H. Bleicken, Deputy Chief Counsel, Pennsylvania Dep't of Banking 27 (Nov. 19, 2001), *available at* www.portal.state.pa.us/portal/server.pt/document/700916/011119-issues_under_the_cdca_and_branch_location_under_cdca_pdf (taking position that Pennsylvania Consumer Discount Company Act regulates all charges, including charges for detention of money). *Cf.* Domizio v. Progressive County Mut. Ins. Co., 54 S.W.3d 867 (Tex. App. 2001) (Texas usury laws apply to charges for detention of money only if the debt arises from a loan transaction; not applicable to charges imposed for late payment of insurance premiums); Tygrett v. Univ. Gardens Homeowners' Ass'n, 687 S.W.2d 481 (Tex. App. 1985) (late charges may be interest, but no lending relationship here between condominium owner and condominium association with respect to condominium assessments). *But see* Garcia v. Tex. Cable TV Partners, 114 S.W.3d 561 (Tex. App. 2003) (late charge on cable television bill is not for forbearance or detention). *But cf.* Hoxie Implement Co. v. Baker, 65 S.W.3d 140, 155–156 (Tex. App. 2001) (alleged debtor did not detain creditor's money where court found that no debt was owed; creditor's demand for interest on this non-existent debt is therefore not usury).

170 Ulvиden v. Sorken, 237 N.W. 565 (S.D. 1931). *Accord* Scarr v. Boyer, 818 P.2d 381, 383 (Mont. 1991) (usury statute that applies to "detention" governs post-default interest rate; a debtor who cannot pay a debt with legal interest certainly "lacks the resources to pay usurious interest").

171 *See, e.g.*, T.F. James Co. v. Vakoch, 604 N.W.2d 459 (N.D. 2000) (late charges on lease are governed by legal rate of interest statute). *See generally* § 4.8, *supra*.

172 *See* Berger v. State Dep't of Revenue, 910 P.2d 581 (Alaska 1996) (sale of state-issued certificates for dividends from pension fund not loans even though sellers guaranteed payment; dissent argues that guarantee was unconditional repayment obligation); Lawsuit Fin., L.L.C. v. Curry, 683 N.W.2d 233 (Mich. Ct. App. 2004); Goffney v. O'Quinn, 2004 WL 2415067 (Tex. App. Oct. 28, 2004) (contracts obliging clients, if litigation is successful, to reimburse attorneys for litigation expenses, including interest the attorneys paid on loans to finance those expenses, do not create an absolute obligation to repay and so are not usurious). *See also* Meklir v. J.C. Penney Co., 2005 WL 1579658 (Mich. Ct. App. July 5, 2005).

173 *See, e.g.*, Burge v. Pack, 785 S.W.2d 207 (Ark. 1990) (discussing evidence necessary to establish a joint venture). *See generally* *Existence of Joint Venture*, 12 Proof of Facts 2d 295 (1977).

174 Securities & Exch. Comm'n v. First Sec. Co., 507 F.2d 417 (7th Cir. 1974); L'Arbalete, Inc. v. Zaczac, 474 F. Supp. 2d 1314 (S.D. Fla. 2007) (investment interest not a loan as it was a substantial risk); *In re* York Furniture Co., 32 B.R. 211 (Bankr. S.D.N.Y. 1983) (transaction constituted joint venture, not loan); Donatelli v. Siskind, 565 N.Y.S.2d 224 (N.Y. App. Div. 1991) (finding arrangement to be joint venture, not loan). *Cf.* D-Beam Ltd. P'ship v. Roller Derby Skates, 366 F.3d 972 (9th Cir. 2004) (when promissory notes limited repayment to borrower's interest in royalty payments, loans were not usurious because of contingency). *See generally* § 4.7, *supra* (regarding whether a loan is usurious when part of the compensation is a contingent share of profits).

175 *See, e.g.*, Concord Realty Co. v. Continental Funding Corp., 776 P.2d 1114 (Colo. 1989) (en banc) (usury law does not apply if return of principal is guaranteed but profit is uncertain); Valliappan v. Cruz, 917 So. 2d 257 (Fla. Dist. Ct. App. 2005) (loan not usurious where obligation to repay more than principal was contingent upon outcome of business negotiation); Comstock v. Steinbergh, 2004 WL 3120554 (Mass. Super. Ct. Dec. 16, 2004) (finding shared-appreciation/wrap-around mortgage that required payment of 48% of the net sale proceeds beyond repayment of principal and interest not usurious since bargained for and contingent).

176 *See, e.g.*, Najarro v. SASI Int'l Ltd., 904 F.2d 1002, 1007 (5th Cir. 1990) (Tex. law) (advance of money with absolute obligation to repay was loan, not investment, regardless of parties' intent); Beausejour Corp., N.V. v. Offshore Dev. Co., 802 F.2d 1319 (11th Cir. 1986) (Fla. law) (loan was usurious where absolute repayment obligation was evidenced by mortgage note); Pinchuck v. Canzoneri, 920 So. 2d 713 (Fla. Dist. Ct. App. 2006).

177 Hufnagel v. George, 121 F. Supp. 2d 305 (S.D.N.Y. 2000) (agreement creates a loan, not a joint venture, where advanced money was repayable on a date certain; no profits existed to pay the interest or return on the investment), *subsequent proceeding at* 135 F. Supp. 2d

where the contingency under which the business may avoid repayment is a practical impossibility.[178] For example, in a Florida case, a contract supposedly for the construction and purchase of a condominium complex was found to be a usurious loan when the developer (i.e., borrower) received a $372,800 "preconstruction purchase price" minus a $36,200 "finder's fee" and was obliged to complete the condominiums in twenty months or, alternatively, to repay $559,200. The court determined that the complex could not have been constructed in the allotted twenty months and that usury law applied regardless of the outward appearance of the transaction.[179]

Whether there is an absolute obligation to repay is occasionally an issue in complex business transactions.[180] In the average consumer credit case, however, proving the existence of an absolute obligation to repay principal is not a problem; the obligation is stated on the face of the note or credit contract and can be established by the introduction of these documents into evidence. The obligation to repay is something creditors care a great deal about, so credit contracts are rarely ambiguous on this point. A loan will not be considered contingent unless the lender, by the terms of the loan, is subjected to some greater hazard than that the borrower will fail to repay the loan or that the security will depreciate in value.[181]

However, occasionally creditors attempt to evade laws regulating credit and credit charges by constructing a transaction in a way in which this element appears to be missing. Courts typically will look behind the facade to determine the true nature of the agreement.[182] Some courts hold that economic facts may make the agreement to pay binding even though it is expressed as conditional.[183] Some of the most common subterfuges, and applicable case law, are discussed in more detail in Part II of this treatise (Chapters 8–14): investments; sale-repurchase or sale-leaseback agreements; leases, including rent-to-own (RTO) transactions; various post-dated check cashing schemes; refund anticipation loans; and pawn arrangements. Some courts have held that purchase of a stake in litigation does not involve usury where there is no repayment obligation if the suit is unsuccessful.[184]

---

406 (S.D.N.Y. 2001) (affirming that agreement creates a loan and voiding loan for violation of N.Y. criminal usury statute); Peterson v. Harville, 455 F. Supp. 16 (D. Or. 1977), *aff'd*, 623 F.2d 611 (9th Cir. 1980) (also emphasizing intent of parties); Dennis v. Bradbury, 236 F. Supp. 683 (D. Colo. 1964), *aff'd*, 368 F.2d 905 (10th Cir. 1966); WRI Opportunity Loans II L.L.C. v. Cooper, 65 Cal. Rptr. 3d 205 (Cal. Ct. App. 2007) (finding that the shared appreciation provisions did not subject the plaintiff to any real risk and, thus, did not fall within the statutory exemption from the usury law); Maze v. Sycamore Homes, Inc., 41 Cal. Rptr. 338 (Cal. Ct. App. 1964); Whittemore Homes, Inc. v. Fleishman, 12 Cal. Rptr. 235 (Cal. Ct. App. 1961); Oregrund Ltd. P'ship v. Shieve, 873 So. 2d 451 (Fla. Dist. Ct. App. 2004) (sale-option transaction held to be a disguised loan given the disparity in the "sale" amount and the true value of property); Dang v. F & S Land Dev. Corp., 618 P.2d 276 (Haw. 1980); Grotjohn Precise Connexiones Int'l, S.A. v. JEM Fin., Inc., 12 S.W.3d 859 (Tex. App. 2000); Ravkind v. Mortgage Funding Corp., 881 S.W.2d 203 (Tex. App. 1994) (assignment of payments due on contract for deed not a loan even though assignee had recourse against assignor only if obligor prepaid or defaulted or assignor breached a warranty); Johns v. Jaeb, 518 S.W.2d 857 (Tex. Civ. App. 1974). *See also In re* Venture Mortgage Fund, Ltd. P'ship, 245 B.R. 460 (Bankr. S.D.N.Y. 2000) (religious document creating a joint venture to avoid a religious ban on charging interest has no effect on whether the transaction is a usurious loan; finding business loan violated the New York criminal usury law), *aff'd*, 282 F.3d 185 (2d. Cir. 2002). *Cf.* Jones v. Wells Fargo Bank, 5 Cal. Rptr. 3d 835 (Ct. App. 2003) (holding no usury because California law exempted national banks acting as a fiduciary for a trust from usury cap where the parties did not dispute that shared appreciation mortgage arrangement was a loan). *But see* Florida Trading & Inv. Co. v. River Constr. Servs., 537 So. 2d 600 (Fla. Dist. Ct. App. 1988) (fact that agreement did not explicitly provide for sharing losses does not preclude its characterization as investment, where entity supplying capital was fully integrated into the operation). *But cf.* Junkin v. Golden West Foreclosure Serv., Inc., 103 Cal. Rptr. 3d 582 (Cal. App. Ct. Jan. 5, 2010) (balancing various factors and concluding that transaction was a joint venture).

178 Schwartz v. Lincoln Constr. & Dev. Corp., 455 So. 2d 612 (Fla. Dist. Ct. App. 1984).

179 *Id. Cf.* L'Arbalete, Inc. v. Zaczac, 474 F. Supp. 2d 1314, 1324 (S.D. Fla. 2007) (holding an "equity investment" not a loan when the investment was "clearly" at substantial risk, and the parties intended that the advance was an investment, citing factors in Estate of Mixon v. United States, 464 F.2d 394, 402 (5th Cir. 1972)).

180 *See* D-Beam Ltd. P'ship v. Roller Derby Skates, Inc., 366 F.3d 972 (9th Cir. 2004) (repayment obligation was contingent where it was to come from royalty payments); Valliappan v. Cruz, 917 So. 2d 257 (Fla. Dist. Ct. App. 2005) (loan not usurious where obligation to repay more than principal was contingent upon outcome of business negotiation); Dublin v. Veal, 341 S.W.2d 776 (Ky. 1960) (usury laws inapplicable to transaction that obliged obligor to repay principal amount invested in business plus portion of profits); Meklir v. J.C. Penney Co., 2005 WL 1579658 (Mich. Ct. App. July 5, 2005) (investment transaction was loan because contract created absolute obligation to repay principal); Olson v. Froslee, 2000 WL 1052007 (Minn. Ct. App. Aug. 1, 2000) (lease of equipment with option to buy was not loan because no absolute obligation to pay option price); Transmedia Restaurant Co. v. 33 East 61st St. Restaurant Corp., 710 N.Y.S.2d 756 (N.Y. Sup. Ct. 2000) (money that network gave to restaurant would be repaid only if and when cardholders bought meals at restaurant; since network bore risk of loss, transaction was not a loan). *See also* Zoo Holdings, L.L.C. v. Clinton, 814 N.Y.S.2d 893 (table), 2006 WL 297730 (N.Y. Sup. Ct. Jan. 24, 2006). *Cf.* WRI Opportunity Loans II L.L.C. v. Cooper, 65 Cal. Rptr. 3d 205 (Cal. Ct. App. 2007) (interest contingency and shared appreciation exceptions inapplicable when repayment of loan to develop condos was not subject to any significant risk).

181 Britz v. Kinsvater, 351 P.2d 986 (Ariz. 1960).

182 *See* § 3.9.1, *supra*.

183 *See, e.g.*, Oregrund Ltd. P'ship v. Sheive, 873 So. 2d 451 (Fla. Dist. Ct. App. 2004) (option to repurchase can be considered an unconditional obligation where there is a great disparity between sale price and true value).

184 Dopp v. Yari, 927 F. Supp. 814 (D.N.J. 1996); *In re* Transcapital Fin. Corp., 433 B.R. 900, 907 (Bankr. S.D. Fla. 2010) (financing provided to company to enable it to continue litigation was not loan because repayment contingent on success); Anglo-Dutch Petroleum Int'l, Inc. v. Haskell, 193 S.W.3d 87 (Tex. App. 2006). *See also* Kraft v. Mason, 668 So. 2d 679 (Fla. Dist. Ct. App. 1996) (no usury where borrower had duty to repay principal, but the usurious interest was contingent on litigation success); Anglo-Dutch Petroleum Int'l, Inc. v. Haskell, 193 S.W.3d 87 (Tex. App. 2006) (loan that was only to be paid back at the successful completion of litigation created no absolute obligation to repay and was not

When dealing with an arguably non-absolute repayment obligation, it is important to check the exact language of the usury statute. If the statute extends to "advances" as well as loans, for example, it may cover transactions where the repayment obligation is not absolute.[185]

## 7.5.4 Interest Overcharge

### 7.5.4.1 General

The heart of every usury case is an overcharge of interest. Logically, this element of proof can be divided into three parts:

- The creditor exacted or attempted to exact payments from the debtor.
- The payments were "interest" under the relevant usury statute.
- The total of payments exceeded the statutory limit.[186]

### 7.5.4.2 Charging, Contracting For, or Receiving Excess Interest

The precise wording of usury statutes varies, but generally creditors may not "contract for," "collect," "exact," "receive," or "charge" payments in excess of those specifically permitted by statute. Under statutes which forbid a creditor to "contract for" excessive payments, merely the signing of an offending contract may constitute a usury violation even if the lender never attempts to collect the excessive charges.[187] Even a usury statute providing only that no one shall "receive" greater interest than permitted by law has been interpreted to render a credit transaction usurious where the contract provides for excess interest but the debtor has not yet paid it. The Iowa Supreme Court said it is "the agreement to exact and pay" excess interest which renders the transaction usurious.[188]

In these circumstances, simply the introduction of a credit contract into evidence can show the violation.[189] (Relying solely on introducing the contract is risky, however, as some courts construe contracts to avoid usury.[190]) However, usurious payments may not always be revealed by the contract itself. For example, the lender might require the borrower to pay fees not mentioned by the contract.[191] Similarly, the lender might not give the borrower the full amount of principal stated in the contract or might not give the borrower the use of all the principal for the full loan term.[192] It may manipulate the

therefore usurious); Goffney v. O'Quinn, 2004 WL 2415067 (Tex. App. Oct. 28, 2004) (contingency contracts between attorneys and clients for repayment of litigation expenses upon successful completion of case do not create an absolute obligation to repay and so are not usurious). *But cf.* Lawsuit Fin., L.L.C. v. Curry, 683 N.W.2d 233 (Mich. Ct. App. 2004) (repayment obligation was not contingent where borrower signed agreement after tortfeasor had admitted liability and jury had returned $27 million verdict); Rancman v. Interim Settlement Funding Corp., 789 N.E.2d 217 (Ohio 2003) (declining to decide whether nonrecourse advance of funds secured solely by interest in a pending lawsuit and at 180% interest is a loan; contract is void as champerty and maintenance). *See generally* § 13.6, *infra*.

185 Odell v. Legal Bucks, L.L.C., 665 S.E.2d 767 (N.C. Ct. App. 2008).

186 Some statutes, however, may impose liability for imposing any charge in excess of that authorized, irrespective of whether the overall yield to the creditor would breach an applicable ceiling. *See* § 7.5.4.4, *infra*.

187 *See, e.g.*, First Nat'l Mortgage Co. v. Arkmo Lumber Supply Co., 641 S.W.2d 31 (Ark. 1982) (contract that called for usurious commitment fee was usurious though lender never charged it; cannot purge usury by dropping charge when suit is filed, and option to impose it remained with lender); Equity Mortgage, Inc. v. Niro, 690 A.2d 407 (Conn. App. Ct. 1997) (taking unusual step of addressing usury apparent on the face of the loan on appeal even though not raised below; holding contract unenforceable based upon the note which listed 15% as the contract rate when Connecticut law only permitted 12%); Overboe v. Brodshaug, 751 N.W.2d 177 (N.D. 2008); Jim Walter Homes v. Schuenemann, 668 S.W.2d 324 (Tex. 1984); C & K Invs. v. Fiesta Group, Inc., 248 S.W.3d 234 (Tex. App. 2007) (analyzing "contract for" liability separately from "charging and receiving" liability); Brookshire v. Longhorn Chevrolet, Inc., 788 S.W.2d 209 (Tex. App. 1990) (acceleration clause in contract rendered it usurious on its face where it expressly entitled creditor, upon happening of the contingency of default and acceleration, to exact greater than lawful interest by demanding balance without rebating unearned finance charges); Myles v. Resolution Trust Corp., 787 S.W.2d 616 (Tex. App. 1990). *See also* Washburn v. Michailoff, 613 N.W.2d 405 (Mich. Ct. App. 2000) (usury law applies if lender seeks to enforce contract, even if it does not seek the usurious interest; lender would have avoided usury if it had filed action to reform the contract). *But see* Power Equip., Inc. v. Tschiggfrie, 460 N.W.2d 861 (Iowa 1990) (invoices with excessive interest were not "contracted for" sufficient to warrant penalty when borrower never agreed to the charges and refused to pay them); Opella v. Opella, 896 A.2d 714 (R.I. 2006) (affirming ruling that intra-family loan was not usurious where trial court disregarded face amount of note and allowed interest at legal rate only on actual amount loaned).

188 Kaiser Agr. Chems., Inc. v. Peters, 417 N.W.2d 437 (Iowa 1987) (open-end account statement and court petition listing interest greater than allowed by statute constituted an exaction of greater profit than was allowed by law).

189 Equity Mortgage, Inc. v. Niro, 690 A.2d 407 (Conn. App. Ct. 1997) (taking unusual step of addressing usury apparent on the face of the loan on appeal even though not raised below; holding contract unenforceable based upon the note which listed 15% as the contract rate when Connecticut law only permitted 12%); Brookshire v. Longhorn Chevrolet, Inc., 788 S.W.2d 209 (Tex. App. 1990). *But cf.* Farmland Enters. v. Schuemann, 322 N.W.2d 665 (Neb. 1982) (usury not shown where variable rate loan's interest rate did not exceed cap at consummation, even though future rate increases could occur).

190 *See* § 7.5.1.4, *supra*.

191 *In re* McCorhill Pub., Inc., 86 B.R. 783, 793–794 (Bankr. S.D.N.Y. 1988) (contract provided for no pre-default interest, but creditor imposed a flat fee for the use of the money).

192 *See, e.g.*, *In re* Montagne, 421 B.R. 65 (Bankr. D. Vt. Nov. 13, 2009) (lender should not have charged interest on portion of loan funds held in lender's account even though available to borrower); Edwards v. Alabama Farm Bureau Mut. Cas. Ins. Co., 509 So. 2d 232 (Ala. Civ. App. 1986) (payment collected on date of loan consummation, rather than thirty days later, should have been treated as down payment and principal amount upon which finance charge assessed reduced accordingly); Hoffman v. Key Fed. Sav. & Loan, 416 A.2d 1265 (Md. 1979); Danziger v. San Jacinto Sav. Ass'n, 732 S.W.2d 300, 302–303 (Tex. 1987) (lender contracted for usurious interest when it contracted for interest on entire principal

calculation of a variable rate in a way that increases the interest charged.[193] Or, in the case of prepayment, the lender might not credit the borrower with a rebate which it was contractually, as well as legally obligated to give.[194] In these circumstances, evidence beyond the contract itself would be necessary to show the payments that the creditor actually charged or received. Such evidence might include the borrower's testimony of the sum actually received as loan proceeds, checks given by the borrower for fees, or the creditor's payment records.

Statutes that prohibit "charging" usurious interest have also been broadly construed. Account statements, the creditor's demand letters or similar communications,[195] affidavits, and court pleadings[196] have all been held to evidence the "charging" of usurious payments. The Texas Supreme Court has held, however, that a demand for interest found solely in a pleading does not constitute "charging" usurious interest.[197] Notwithstanding this decision, a demand in a pleading should still be relevant to prove usury in many consumer cases. For example, a contract may not specify that the creditor will use the Rule of 78s, but the amount of the demand in the pleading may show that it did use that accounting method in a transaction where it was prohibited.[198] In that case, though the overcharge appeared "solely" on the pleadings, it arose directly out of the consumer transaction, and should constitute a "charging" of excess interest.[199] The demand in the pleading shows the creditor actually construed the clause to allow the excess charge.

The broad language used in usury statutes means that consumers can reach entities other than the original lender. For example, even if an assignee has not "contracted" for usurious interest, it may have "received" or "charged" it. The assignee of a mortgage loan was liable under a statute that prohibited directly or indirectly charging, contracting for, or receiving an illegal charge, even though the illegal charges were closing costs that had been imposed by the loan originator.[200]

### 7.5.4.3 "Interest" or Regulated Charge

Once the payments charged or received by a creditor have been identified, the next question is which of those payments constitute "interest" or an excess charge under the relevant statute. Most obviously, the creditor may simply calculate the interest erroneously.[201] For example, an auto financing loan which calculates interest at a 15% add-on rate would violate a statute which caps such loans at a 15% actuarial rate.[202] Failing to rebate unearned charges may be considered excess interest in

---

though contract called for multiple disbursements; lender's practice of crediting back the overcharge upon disbursement of the principal in portions does not purge the usury); C & K Invs. v. Fiesta Group, Inc., 248 S.W.3d 234 (Tex. App. 2007) (loan was usurious when lender required borrower to turn over 10% of principal).

193 *See* Siradas v. Chase Lincoln First Bank, 1999 WL 787658 (S.D.N.Y. Sept. 30, 1999) (denying lender's motion for judgment on the pleadings on claim that banker's use of improper method to adjust interest rates was UDAP violation).

194 *See* § 5.8, *supra.*

195 Najarro v. SASI Int'l Ltd., 904 F.2d 1002, 1007–1008 (5th Cir. 1990) (Tex. law) (cover letters, attached to promissory notes, promising to pay "commission" in addition to repayment of principal were evidence of a charge for the use of money, especially where commissions were paid directly to lender); Kaiser Agr. Chems., Inc. v. Peters, 417 N.W.2d 437 (Iowa 1987) (open-end account statement and court petition constituted exaction of excess interest); Danziger v. San Jacinto Sav. Ass'n, 732 S.W.2d 300, 303–304 (Tex. 1987) (payment of loan not necessary; mere inclusion of excess interest in pay-off quote constituted "charging" illegal interest); Allen v. Am. Gen. Fin., Inc., 251 S.W.3d 676 (Tex. App. 2007) (demand letter amounts to charging of excess interest even if debtor never received or read it); Strasburger Enters., Inc. v. TDGT Ltd. P'ship, 110 S.W.3d 566, 579 (Tex. App. 2003) (letter demanding debt plus interest at usurious rate was "charge"); Hoxie Implement Co. v. Baker, 65 S.W.3d 140 (Tex. App. 2001) (demand letter that enclosed copy of petition creditor intended to file in court constituted "charging," but an intent to seek interest on another debt was not a charge when it was never communicated to debtor); Torres v. Overby, 2000 WL 382417 (Tex. App. Apr. 17, 2000) (letter demanding late fee charged that fee, but its threat to assess future late fees did not); Pentico v. Mad-Wayler, Inc., 964 S.W.2d 708 (Tex. App. 1998) (amortization schedule attached to a demand letter constituted a "charge" of interest); Karg v. Strickland, 919 S.W.2d 722 (Tex. App. 1996) (excess interest demanded in letter constitutes charging interest). *But cf.* Thrift v. Hubbard, 44 F.3d 348 (5th Cir. 1995) (Texas law) (interpreting demand letter to avoid usurious claim); Cavazos v. Mid-State Trust II (*In re* Hillsborough Holdings Corp.), 267 B.R. 882 (Bankr. M.D. Fla. 2001) (form filed with IRS does not constitute a charge); Lairsen v. Slutzky, 80 S.W.3d 121, 127 (Tex. App. 2002) (construing demand letter's reference to note as limiting demand to amount allowed by note); Varel Mfg. Co. v. Acetylene Oxygen Co., 990 S.W.2d 486 (Tex. App. 1999) (statement on invoice that interest will be charged if payments are late is not "charging"); Heine v. Schendel, 797 S.W.2d 278 (Tex. App. 1990) (demand letter did not constitute charging usurious interest when drafted by creditor's lawyer without creditor's knowledge; lawyer acting beyond scope of his employment); White v. Groco Corp., 783 S.W.2d 24 (Tex. App. 1990) (original invoice which had printed notation that 1.5% per month would be charged on amount not paid after thirty days did not constitute charging or demanding excess interest where demand letter and court petition did not include amount greater than permitted by law).

196 *See, e.g.*, Kaiser Agr. Chems., Inc. v. Peters, 417 N.W.2d 437 (Iowa 1987) (open-end account statement and court petition constituted exaction of excess interest).

197 George A. Fuller Co. v. Carpet Servs., Inc., 823 S.W.2d 603, 604 n.1, 605–606 (Tex. 1992). *See also In re* CPDC, Inc., 337 F.3d 436 (5th Cir. 2003) (amending pleading to delete usurious charge precludes usury liability); Briones v. Solomon, 842 S.W.2d 278 (Tex. 1992); Hoxie Implement Co. v. Baker, 65 S.W.3d 140 (Tex. App. 2001) (testimony in court about amount sought does not constitute charging).

198 *See* § 5.8.6.3, *supra.*

199 The *Fuller* court specifically stated it was not addressing the question of pleadings claiming interest based on underlying documents. 823 S.W.2d at 604 n.1. *Cf.* Cigna Ins. Co. v. TPG Store, Inc., 894 S.W.2d 431 (Tex. App. 1995) (statement sent which failed to reflect rebate of unearned interest constituted usurious "charging"; subsequent credit of the excess amount will not purge the usury).

200 Mitchell v. Residential Funding Corp., 334 S.W.3d 477, 500–501 (Mo. Ct. App. 2010) (noting assignee's detailed specifications of requirements for the loans it purchased). *Accord*, Mayo v. GMAC Mortgage, L.L.C., 763 F. Supp. 2d 1091, 1108–1109 (W.D. Mo. 2011) (assignees are liable but non-holder servicers are not).

201 *See generally* § 5.2, *supra.*

202 *See* §§ 5.3.1, 5.3.2, *supra.*

the loan being terminated,[203] or, if refinanced by the same creditor, in the new loan.[204] Chapters 4 to 6 of this treatise discuss various calculation issues relevant to examining a transaction for excess charges.

Beyond the obvious charge for the use of money, the definition of "interest" sometimes is a complicated issue which varies from statute to statute, and to which Chapter 4 of this treatise is devoted. Nevertheless, most statutes classify all payments made by a borrower as either principal, interest, or non-interest fees in the following manner. First, non-interest fees are charges, such as insurance premiums or late fees, which are expressly excluded from interest by statute, or excluded by judicial interpretation.[205] However, such charges are often subject to separate regulation by consumer credit statutes, and may be among the types of charges for which statutory liability attaches if limits are exceeded.[206] Next, "principal" generally includes loan proceeds given to the borrower or paid on the borrower's behalf and often may include any non-interest fees which the lender pays on the borrower's behalf.[207] Finally, "interest" is any payment not attributable to the repayment of principal or to non-interest fees.[208]

Those payments which a contract defines as interest will generally require no proof, beyond the introduction of the contract, in order to be identified as interest.[209] However, whether various "fees" should be included in or excluded from interest frequently requires careful scrutiny, which sometimes requires examination of evidence beyond the contract.[210]

First, the applicable provision should be examined closely. Though third-party fees may be excluded from interest under general usury principles,[211] the relevant statute may be drafted restrictively, so that any charge—irrespective of the recipient—may constitute interest if it is not among those specifically authorized.[212] Second, even if the type of charge is authorized, it should be examined to assure that it meets standards necessary to exclude it. For example, charges may be excluded from interest only to the extent they are "actually" charged or are "bona fide and reasonable," qualifications which must be verified.[213] Some third-party fees may be excluded if they are unreasonably high.[214] Credit and ancillary non-credit insurance premiums may be in amounts[215] or of a type[216] which will make them subject to challenge,[217] or they may never have been forwarded to the insurer, which may turn an otherwise authorized charge into interest.[218] Chapters 4 and 6 of this treatise discuss in detail the various types of fees and charges which often are challenged as illegal overcharges, and relevant case law. Even amounts which would appear to be clearly non-interest charges, such as payments made to the borrower, cannot always be taken for granted.[219]

The larger the portion of the note principal that ends up in the lender's or third parties' pockets, or the more exorbitant the overall cost, the more closely the practitioner should examine

203 *See* § 5.8.7, *supra*.

204 *See* §§ 5.9.5.1, 5.9.5.3, *supra*.

205 *See* Ch. 4, *supra*.

206 *See, e.g.*, Alston v. Crown Auto, Inc., 224 F.3d 332 (4th Cir. 2000) (excessive late fees do not make loan usurious, but penalties in late fee statute apply); Smith v. Khalif (*In re* Khalif), 308 B.R. 614 (Bankr. N.D. Ga. 2004) (treating late charges as violating criminal usury cap); S&A Indus., Inc. v. Bank Atlanta, 543 S.E.2d 743 (Ga. Ct. App. 2000) (concurring opinion for half of equally divided court) (late charge is considered a fee under criminal usury statutes but did not exceed limits); Garrison v. First Fed. Sav. & Loan Ass'n of S.C., 402 S.E.2d 25 (Va. 1991) (risk management fee not listed among permissible charges and therefore was an illegal charge; only "actual" appraisal cost authorized, excess constituted interest). *See also* Wombold v. Assocs. Fin. Servs. Co. of Mont., Inc., 104 P.3d 1080 (Mont. 2004) (points and fees not interest and not among permitted fees; therefore, charged in violation of Consumer Loan Act). *Cf.* Mayo v. Key Fin. Servs., Inc., 1994 Mass. Super. 549 (June 22, 1994) (implied private right of action for violation of statute limiting points; assertable by a suitable common law remedy; borrowers choose to assert common law restitution), *aff'd, as modified, on other issues*, 678 N.E.2d 1311 (Mass. 1997). *See generally* §§ 4.8.3 (late fee statutes), 6.6 (credit insurance charges), *supra*.

207 *See* §§ 4.3–4.6, 5.4.1, *supra*.

208 *See, e.g.*, Yazzie v. Ray Vicker's Special Cars, Inc., 12 F. Supp. 2d 1230 (D.N.M. 1998) (pawn service fee exceeded legal limit); Rieser v. Todd (*In re* Chari), 2005 WL 4030034 (Bankr. S.D. Ohio Sept. 2, 2005) (fees were interest even though termed loan commitment fees where they were consideration for the loan; extension fees also interest to extent they exceeded reasonable late fees); Fryer v. Easy Money Title Pawn, Inc., 183 B.R. 322 (Bankr. S.D. Ga. 1995) (pawnbroker's 23% per month "service charge" was not to reimburse it for any specific expenses, and was therefore interest); McGhee v. Ark. State Bd. of Collection Agencies, 289 S.W.3d 18 (Ark. 2008) (check-casher's charge for "operational costs" for payday loan is interest); Dep't of Banking v. NCAS of Del., L.L.C., 948 A.2d 752 (Pa. 2008) (payday lender's monthly participation fee, which was required before borrower could access line of credit, must be included in calculating whether interest rate exceeds Consumer Discount Company Act's aggregate cap); Dunnam v. Burns, 901 S.W.2d 628 (Tex. App. 1995) (additional sum to be repaid with principal was interest, even though not denominated as such); Byrd v. Crosstate Mortgage & Invs., Inc., 34 Va. Cir. 17 (1994). *But cf.* Nicolas v. Deposit Guarantee Nat'l Bank, 182 F.R.D. 226 (S.D. Miss. 1998) (NSF fee not interest under Mississippi law because it was not charged in connection with a credit transaction).

209 *See, e.g.*, Dillon v. Resolution Trust Corp., 811 S.W.2d 765 (Ark. 1991) (contract defined payments as interest; rejecting creditor's after-the-fact attempt to allocate portion of payments to principal).

210 *See* Swank v. Sverdlin, 121 S.W.3d 785 (Tex. App. 2003) (fact question is raised when there is dispute in the evidence as to whether a charge in addition to interest is actually for additional consideration).

211 *See* § 4.5, *supra*.

212 *See* §§ 4.5.1, 7.2.2, *supra*.

213 *See, e.g.*, Garrison v. First Fed. Sav. & Loan Ass'n of S.C., 402 S.E.2d 25 (Va. 1991) (only "actual" appraisal cost authorized; excess is interest). *See generally* § 4.5, *supra*.

214 *See* Fikes v. First Fed. Sav. & Loan of Anchorage, 533 P.2d 251 (Alaska 1975); Altherr v. Wilshire Mortgage Corp., 448 P.2d 859 (Ariz. 1969).

215 *See* § 6.6, *supra*.

216 *See, e.g.*, §§ 6.6.4, 6.7.3, 6.7.4, *supra*.

217 *See also* §§ 6.5.3–6.5.6, *supra* (UDAP and other challenges to credit insurance), 7.8, *infra*.

218 *See* United-Bilt Homes v. Knapp, 396 S.W.2d. 40 (Ark. 1965). *See generally* § 4.5.2.2, *supra*.

219 *See* § 4.4, *supra*.

each component of the loan. Loan padding or high rates are signs of a creditor who is trying to maximize profits and stretch the limits of the law, and who may cross the line in doing so. Even if specific statutes regulating charges are not breached, overreaching may nonetheless be attacked under other legal theories discussed at § 2.4, *supra*.

#### 7.5.4.4 Proving the Charge Is Excessive

Once the amount of interest charged or collected in connection with a contract has been determined, the last step in proving an interest overcharge is to show that the interest is excessive. Since most usury ceilings are expressed as rates, normally the easiest way to demonstrate an overcharge is to calculate the highest permissible interest charge under the controlling statutory rate formula, given the principal amount properly determined,[220] and the length of time the loan or credit has been outstanding[221] or was scheduled to be outstanding.[222] For common interest calculation formulae, such as simple interest, add-on interest, or discount interest, parties can frequently stipulate to the accuracy of a published rate chart which will show the permissible finance charge for any given principal amount (or amount financed) and rate.[223] Requests for admission might also be used.[224]

If the amount of interest assessed by the creditor exceeds this statutory maximum, then a usurious overcharge is present regardless of the precise manner in which the creditor calculated or exacted the interest.[225] As a matter of proof, using an expert to make these calculations is always helpful, if not essential to proving the existence of usury.[226] At the very least, such an expert may be necessary to rebut the creditor's claim that the loan is not usurious.[227]

Keep in mind that, as part of the borrower's proof, it is necessary to establish what maximum that particular creditor can charge for that particular kind of transaction.[228] It is also important to establish that no preemption questions are involved.[229] Which party bears the burden of proof on these issues is discussed at § 7.5.1.2, *supra*.

### *7.5.5 Intent*

#### 7.5.5.1 When Proof of Intent Is Required

Typically the final element of a usury claim is the usurious intent of the lender. Generally, intent requirements are not expressly stated in usury statutes, but have been inferred by the courts. Some courts have inferred an intent requirement from the existence of a bona fide error defense.[230] However, the better view is that the existence of a bona fide error defense shows that intent is not an element that the plaintiff must prove, but is a defense that the lender has the burden of raising and proving.

---

220 *See* § 7.5.4.3, Chs. 4, 6 *supra*.

221 *But cf.* § 5.8.7.2, *supra* (early termination).

222 *See* § 5.10, *supra* (proof of mathematical issues).

223 A common source is The Cost of Personal Borrowing in the United States, published by the Financial Publishing Company, Boston, MA.

224 *See* the companion website to this treatise.

225 *See* Pena v. Gonzalez (*In re* Pena), 397 B.R. 566 (B.A.P. 1st Cir. 2008) (18% add-on interest calculated as 35% effective rate violated 20% per annum interest rate cap); Ogier v. Johnson (*In re* Healing Touch, Inc.), 2005 WL 6488238 (Bankr. N.D. Ga. May 6, 2005) (calculating interest rate by "taking the total amount of interest charged under the loan and dividing by the number of months in the loan" and then comparing that to the permissible rate); Smith v. Khalif (*In re* Khalif), 308 B.R. 614 (Bankr. N.D. Ga. 2004) (loan was usurious where maximum allowable interest per month was $1,250 but note required $1,562.50); Corcoran v. TranSouth Fin. Corp. (*In re* Corcoran), 268 B.R. 882 (Bankr. M.D. Fla. 2001); Wellman v. Bank One, 2005 WL 2291741 (Mich. Ct. App. Sept. 20, 2005) (calculating simple interest rate, lender had to know rate was usurious); C & K Invs. v. Fiesta Group, Inc., 248 S.W.3d 234 (Tex. App. 2007) (citing testimony of borrower's expert as to effective interest rate when lender required borrower to pay over a portion of proceeds); Strasburger Enters., Inc. v. TDGT Ltd. P'ship, 110 S.W.3d 566, 579 (Tex. App. 2003); Pentico v. Mad-Wayler, Inc., 964 S.W.2d 708 (Tex. App. 1998) (determining maximum allowable interest by multiplying the principal by the rate of interest and multiplying that amount by the term of repayment and then comparing that amount to the sum of the actual interest charged plus late fees [considered "interest" under state law]). *But cf.* Aikens v. Wagner, 498 S.E.2d 766 (Ga. Ct. App. 1998) (simply comparing the rate specified in the contract and payment history to the maximum rate allowed by law at the time the contract was consummated). *See generally* § 5.10, *supra* (proving mathematical issues in court).

226 C & K Invs. v. Fiesta Group, Inc., 248 S.W.3d 234 (Tex. App. 2007) (citing testimony of borrower's expert as to effective interest rate when lender required borrower to pay over a portion of proceeds). *Cf.* Columbus Mortgage, Inc. v. Morton, 2007 WL 1748142 (Ohio Ct. App. June 19, 2007) (trial court properly relied on defense expert's calculation of interest rate with and without origination fee; dissent correctly notes that majority failed to resolve question whether origination fee should have been included in finance charge for purposes of determining whether interest rate was usurious).

The companion website to this treatise includes several sample expert affidavits, reports, and testimony: Sample Expert Affidavit re Broker Fee As Hidden Charge; Expert Witness Testimony re Loan Splitting from Besta v. Beneficial Finance; Expert Witness Testimony re Economic Cost of Debt Consolidated; Expert Witness Testimony re Spiraling Costs, Profits from Multiple Refinancings.

227 Britt v. Jones, 472 S.E.2d 199 (N.C. Ct. App. 1996) (relying on borrower's expert to find that all payments made should be attributed to each of four loans in chronological order, i.e., not until the first was paid off would subsequent payments be attributed to the later loans; thus, loans would never be paid in full due to negative amortization). *Cf. In re* Williams, 330 B.R. 534 (Bankr. M.D. La. 2005) (relying on lender's testimony that rate was calculated correctly in absence of evidence from borrowers); Rivera v. Schlick, 887 A.2d 492 (D.C. 2005) (borrower failed to prove interest rate or provide information from which the court could calculate the interest rate; conclusory allegations of interest rate insufficient); Perez v. Rent-A-Center, Inc., 892 A.2d 1255 (N.J. 2006) (citing borrowers' expert witness on the interest rate of the rent-to-own contracts).

228 *See generally* § 3.9, *supra*.

229 *See* §§ 3.3–3.5, *supra*.

230 *See* Kendrick v. Jim Walter Homes, 545 F. Supp. 541 (S.D. Ind. 1981) (reading intent requirement into U.C.C.C. because of bona fide error defense). *See generally* § 7.5.5.2, *infra* (bona fide error defense).

Courts interpret some statutes, particularly those regulating charges in consumer credit transactions, not to require a showing of intent.[231] Some statutes narrow defenses or enhance remedies when the violations are intentional or in reckless disregard,[232] thereby making it quite clear there is no intent requirement.

The difficulty of establishing an intent element frequently depends on whether the usury is created by a facially improper contract interest rate or is instead apparent only when hidden interest, disguised credit, or improper collection practices are exposed.

### 7.5.5.2 Usury Apparent on Face of Contract; Bona Fide Error

Except in one or two states,[233] if usury appears on the face of a credit contract, the requisite usurious intent is merely the intent of the lender to charge the interest rate which, in fact, was contracted for. This intent may be presumed from the contract.[234] Thus, the courts widely agree that if an overcharge is facially apparent, a lender need not have known that the interest rate was legally usurious and need not have had any intent to violate the law, provided that the interest which it intended to charge in fact exceeded the statutory limit.[235]

---

231 *See, e.g.*, *In re* Swartz, 37 B.R. 766 (Bankr. D.R.I. 1984) (small loans); Beneficial Fin. Co. v. Administrator of Loan Laws, 272 A.2d 649 (Md. 1971) (no intent requirement under Small Loan Act); Duckworth v. Bernstein, 466 A.2d 517 (Md. Ct. Spec. App. 1983) (lender can recover no more than principal if loan violates second mortgage law, regardless of intent, but for treble damages must show that violation was knowing; arranger was lender's agent so his knowledge can be attributed to lender); Thelen v. Ducharme, 390 N.W.2d 264 (Mich. Ct. App. 1986); Sturm v. Muens, 224 S.W.3d 758 (Tex. App. 2007) (listing elements, without including intent); Commercial Credit Equip. Corp. v. West, 677 S.W.2d 669 (Tex. App. 1984). *See also* §§ 5.8.7.3.1, 7.5.5.1, *supra*.

232 *See, e.g.*, Ala. Code § 5-19-19 (greater penalty for deliberate or reckless violations); Ky. Rev. Stat. Ann. § 371.990(4) (West) (no correction of error permitted for willful and intentional failure to comply); W. Va. Code § 46A-5-101 (in no event does consumer have to pay excess charges, and has right to recover them; creditor contracting for or receiving excess charge additionally liable for statutory penalty, absent correction of error or successful defense of bona fide error notwithstanding maintenance of procedures reasonably adopted to avoid error).

233 An exception is Florida which generally requires a showing of "corrupt intent." *See, e.g.*, Robertson v. Strickland (*In re* Robertson), 333 B.R. 894 (Bankr. M. D. Fla. 2005) (foreclosure "rescue" loan by broker does not demonstrate corrupt intent); Dixon v. Sharp, 276 So. 2d 817 (Fla. 1973) (fact that lender actually gets more than law permits is insufficient; must show purpose to get more than legal interest); Oregrund Ltd. P'ship v. Sheive, 873 So. 2d 451 (Fla. Dist. Ct. App. 2004) (shown by intent to charge more than law allows); Gergora v. Goldstein Prof'l Ass'n Defined Benefits Plan Pension & Trust, 500 So. 2d 695 (Fla. Dist. Ct. App. 1987) (must show corrupt intent to take more than the law allows; not shown here). *See also* Jersey Palm-Gross, Inc. v. Paper, 658 So. 2d 531 (Fla. 1995) (ill will or malevolent intent unnecessary; intent to extract excessive rate of interest shown where lender actively sought and received the usurious amounts and knew that borrowers were in urgent need); North Am. Mortgage Investors v. Cape San Blas Joint Venture, 378 So. 2d 287 (Fla. 1979) (corrupt intent demonstrated); § 7.5.5.3, *infra* (further discussion of Florida standards).

New Mexico also requires a showing of "corrupt intent" for forfeiture. Maulsby v. Magnuson, 755 P.2d 67 (N.M. 1988) (the court overturned Hays v. Hudson, 514 P.2d 31 (N.M. 1973) (limiting lender to legal interest rate, but refusing to order forfeiture where all parties were experienced in business, and the borrowers suggested the interest rate; must show "some usurious intent to exploit")).

234 *See* Henson v. Columbus Bank & Trust Co., 770 F.2d 1566 (11th Cir. 1985); Duderwicz v. Sweetwater Sav. Ass'n, 595 F.2d 1008 (5th Cir. 1979) (Georgia law); *In re* Venture Mortgage Fund, 245 B.R. 460, 474 (Bankr. S.D.N.Y. 2000), *aff'd on other grounds*, 282 F.3d 185 (2d Cir. 2002); *In re* McCorhill Pub., Inc., 86 B.R. 783 (Bankr. S.D.N.Y. 1988) (N.Y. law); *In re* Rosner, 48 B.R. 538 (Bankr. E.D.N.Y. 1985) (New York law); Fikes v. First Fed. Sav. & Loan Ass'n, 533 P.2d 251 (Alaska 1975); Citizen's Nat'l Bank of Willmar v. Taylor, 368 N.W.2d 913 (Minn. 1985); Fareri v. Rain's Int'l Ltd., 589 N.Y.S.2d 579 (N.Y. App. Div. 1992) (also invoking parol evidence rule to deny admission of creditor's evidence that it did not retain all of offending charge where contract unambiguously stated it was payable to the lender); *In re* Estate of Dane, 390 N.Y.S.2d 249 (N.Y. App. Div. 1976); Cook v. Frazier, 765 S.W.2d 546 (Tex. App. 1989); Kollman v. Hunnicutt, 385 S.W.2d 600 (Tex. Civ. App. 1964); Cuevas v. Montoya, 740 P.2d 858 (Wash. Ct. App. 1987). *See also* Fogie v. Thorn Americas, Inc., 95 F.3d 645 (8th Cir. 1996) (Minnesota law).

235 *See, e.g.*, Brodie v. Schmutz (*In re* Venture Mortgage Fund), 282 F.3d 185 (2d Cir. 2002) (N.Y. law) (loan is usurious if lender intends to take and receive interest in excess of that allowed by law even though lender has no specific intent to violate usury laws; loans made by victims to Ponzi scheme operator because of promised high returns are void); Najarro v. SASI Int'l Ltd., 904 F.2d 1002, 1009 (5th Cir. 1990) (Tex. law) (where evidence showed intent to enter into usurious bargain, a specific intent to charge usury is irrelevant); Henson v. Columbus Bank & Trust Co., 770 F.2d 1566 (11th Cir. 1985); American Timber & Trading v. First Nat'l Bank of Oregon, 690 F.2d 781 (9th Cir. 1982); Duderwicz v. Sweetwater Sav. Ass'n, 595 F.2d 1008 (5th Cir. 1979); Kissell Co. v. Gressley, 591 F.2d 47 (9th Cir. 1979); Gillivan v. Austin, 640 F. Supp. 1325 (D. V.I. 1986); *In re* Rosner, 48 B.R. 538 (Bankr. E.D.N.Y. 1985); Southland Mobile Home Corp. v. Webster, 563 S.W.2d 430 (Ark. 1978); Smith v. Eisen, 245 S.W.3d 160 (Ark. Ct. App. 2006) (test is not whether lender intended to violate usury laws but whether lender knowingly entered into usurious contract intending to profit by the methods employed); Varr v. Olimpia, 2002 WL 1425373 (Cal. Ct. App. July 1, 2002); Mark McDowell Corp. v. LSM 128, 263 Cal. Rptr. 310 (Cal. Ct. App. 1989) (intent is material to a determination of what terms the parties agreed to, but otherwise is "more or less immaterial"; creditor is presumed to intend what he actually does); McClung v. Saito, 83 Cal. Rptr. 44 (Cal. Ct. App. 1970); Dang v. F&S Land Dev. Co., 618 P.2d 276 (Haw. 1980); Kaiser Agric. Chem., Inc. v. Peters, 417 N.W.2d 437 (Iowa 1987); Citizen's Nat'l Bank of Willmar v. Taylor, 368 N.W.2d 913 (Minn. 1985); Trapp v. Hancuh, 530 N.W.2d 879 (Minn. Ct. App. 1995); Scarr v. Boyer, 818 P.2d 381 (Mont. 1991) (intent required is to charge a rate that is usurious in fact; lack of knowledge that the rate is illegal or intent to violate the law is irrelevant); Freitas v. Geddes Sav. & Loan Ass'n, 471 N.E.2d 436 (N.Y. 1984) (plurality opinion stating rule for facially usurious contract); Norstar Bank v. Pickard & Anderson, 547 N.Y.S.2d 734 (N.Y. App. Div. 1989); Angelo v. Brenner, 457 N.Y.S.2d 630 (N.Y. App. Div. 1982) (even without specific intent to do usury, usurious note is void); Funding Group, Inc. v. Water Chef, Inc., 852 N.Y.S.2d 736 (N.Y. Sup. Ct. 2008);

There is some room for disagreement about when a contract is usurious on its face.[236] Logically, usury on the face of a contract should include any transaction in which excess interest or other statutory violations are the necessary consequence of the signing or enforcement of the contract.[237] Some courts, however, may implicitly employ a narrower definition, especially when more "technical" violations are involved.[238]

A lender's only defense to usury on the face of the contract is to rebut the presumption of usurious intent by demonstrating that a bona fide error occurred in the preparation of the contract and that the lender therefore did not intend to charge the stated rate. The defense of mistake or bona fide error is a narrow one which must be proven by the lender.[239] It is generally limited to non-recurring errors such as numerical transpositions or a non-recurring mathematical error.[240] Repeated "errors" such as overcharges caused by the use of an improper rate calculation method or an improperly programmed computer will not establish a bona fide error defense.[241] Moreover, a mistake in law

---

Babcock v. Berlin, 475 N.Y.S.2d 212 (N.Y. Sup. Ct. 1984); Western Auto Supply Co. v. Vick, 277 S.E.2d 360 (N.C. 1981), *aff'd on reh'g*, 283 S.E.2d 101 (1981); Odell v. Legal Bucks, L.L.C., 665 S.E.2d 767 (N.C. Ct. App. 2008); Swindell v. Overton, 342 S.E.2d 391 (N.C. Ct. App. 1986); Jim Walter Homes v. Schuenemann, 668 S.W.2d 324, 328 (Tex. 1984) (intent to reach the bargain made is sufficient); Alamo Lumber Co. v. Gold, 661 S.W.2d 926 (Tex. 1983); Cochran v. American Sav. & Loan Ass'n of Houston, 586 S.W.2d 849 (Tex. 1979); Hoxie Implement Co. v. Baker, 65 S.W.3d 140 (Tex. App. 2001); Brookshire v. Longhorn Chevrolet, Inc., 788 S.W.2d 209 (Tex. App. 1990) (only intent required is to make the bargain made); Hardwick v. Austin Gallery of Oriental Rugs, Inc., 779 S.W.2d 438 (Tex. App. 1989) (usurious intent means intent to make the agreement that was made); Cuevas v. Montoya, 740 P.2d 858 (Wash. Ct. App. 1987); Cuevas v. Montoya, 740 P.2d 858 (Wash. Ct. App. 1987) (intent need not be culpable, merely intent to enter a transaction which in fact carries unlawful rate of interest); Metro Hauling, Inc. v. Daffern, 723 P.2d 32 (Wash. Ct. App. 1986) (no intent to violate usury statute necessary). *See also* SAL Leasing, Inc. v. State *ex rel.* Napolitano, 10 P.3d 1221 (Ariz. Ct. App. 2000) (unlawful intent is shown by mere fact of intentionally doing what is forbidden by statute).

236 *See* Freitas v. Geddes Sav. & Loan Ass'n, 471 N.E.2d 436 (N.Y. 1984) (mislabeling of fee not facially usurious).

237 *See, e.g.*, Kish v. Van Note, 692 S.W.2d 463 (Tex. 1985) (failure to disclose that credit insurance premium was not fixed or approved by the state is apparent on face of contract; court can take judicial notice of statutes setting premium rates).

238 *See* Kissell Co. v. Gressley, 591 F.2d 47 (9th Cir. 1979) (Arizona law) (usury due to commitment fee and acceleration does not appear on face of contract); *In re* Rosner, 48 B.R. 538 (Bankr. E.D.N.Y. 1985) (apparently regarding usury as appearing on face of note only when stated contract rate exceeds usury ceiling); Medford v. Wholesale Elec. Supply Co., 691 S.W.2d 857 (Ark. 1985) (given variable rate ceiling, contract cannot be usurious on its face); Allied Supplier & Erection, Inc. v. A. Baldwin & Co., 688 S.W.2d 156 (Tex. App. 1985).

239 *See* Cochran v. American Sav. & Loan Ass'n of Houston, 586 S.W.2d 849 (Tex. 1979); Grotjohn Precise Connexiones Int'l, S.A. v. JEM Fin., Inc., 12 S.W.3d 859 (Tex. App. 2000); Commerce Crowdus & Canton, Ltd. v. DKS Constr., Inc., 776 S.W.2d 615, 618–619 (Tex. App. 1989) (" 'bona fide error' defense is only available when the evidence shows that the charge of usury results from the ignorance of a material fact or from other unintentional mishaps in office practice or routine which may be fairly characterized as 'clerical' errors"). *See also* Commercial Credit Equip. Corp. v. West, 677 S.W.2d 669 (Tex. App. 1984); Perez v. Hernardez, 658 S.W.2d 697 (Tex. App. 1983) (pleading of defense). *Cf.* Jones v. Jones, 301 S.W.2d 737 (Ark. 1957) (creditor failed to prove mistake in overcharging for insurance premium where he failed to offer testimony corroborating his claim that insurance agent misinformed him of cost, and he never informed borrower of the overcharge); Lupo v. Equity Collection Serv., 808 S.W.2d 122 (Tex. App. 1991) (defendant's pleading bona fide error did not constitute summary judgment proof; thus creditor presented no evidence sufficient to defeat debtor's motion for summary judgment); §§ 7.7.7 (de minimis violations), 10.6.9 (industry custom and usage), 7.7.10 (correction of error), *infra*.

240 *See, e.g.*, Walters v. First Tennessee Bank, 855 F.2d 267 (6th Cir. 1988) (mistake in computation is defense under National Bank Act, 12 U.S.C. § 86); Rhode v. Kremer, 655 S.W.2d 410 (Ark. 1983) (typographical error); Szeray v. Schaub, 496 So. 2d 883 (Fla. Dist. Ct. App. 1986) (error in calculations alleged); Sumner v. Adel Banking Co., 259 S.E.2d 32 (Ga. 1979) (mistake in calculation or by inadvertence which is not part of a usurious design or otherwise intentional); Harlow v. Walton Loan Corp., 329 S.E.2d 616 (Ga. Ct. App. 1985) (clerical error in complaint); Huddleston v. Bossier Bank & Trust Co., 475 So. 2d 1082 (La. 1985) (clerical error); Fidelity Funds, Inc. v. Price, 491 So. 2d 681 (La. Ct. App. 1986) (error in hand calculation—no bad faith); United Companies Mortgage & Inv. v. Lester, 394 So. 2d 1350 (Miss. 1981); Wycoff v. Commerce Bank, 561 S.W.2d 399 (Mo. Ct. App. 1977); Hanson v. Bonner, 661 P.2d 421 (Mont. 1983) (lawyer representing both parties who miscalculated interest and tried to correct error had no intent to commit usury); Freitas v. Geddes Sav. & Loan Ass'n, 471 N.E.2d 436 (N.Y. 1984) (plurality opinion) (erroneous description of otherwise valid fee); Heelan v. Security Nat'l Bank, 343 N.Y.S.2d 417 (N.Y. Dist. Ct. Suffolk Cty. 1973) (bank had no usurious intent when borrower's excessive overdrafts caused computer to assess improper late charges and bank refunded the overcharge); Swindell v. Federal Nat'l Mortgage Ass'n, 409 S.E.2d 892, 895–896 (N.C. 1991) (only the intent to charge a rate in excess of the statutory limit need be shown); North Shore Auto Fin., Inc. v. Block, 934 N.E.2d 381 (Ohio Ct. App. 2010) (holding trial court misapplied law by focusing on whether auto dealer willfully violated retail installment act rather than whether it willfully imposed questionable fee); Tyra v. Bob Carroll Constr. Co., 639 S.W.2d 690 (Tex. 1982) (usury in creditor pleadings excused as attorney error); Mayfield v. San Jacinto Sav. Ass'n, 788 S.W.2d 119 (Tex. App. 1990) (bona fide error defense established where creditor presented evidence that transposition error created an overcharge); Martinez v. Teachers Credit Union, 758 S.W.2d 946 (Tex. App. 1988) (bona fide error where contract called for usurious daily rate, but non-usurious annual rate and total of payments); Ervin v. Muller, 2003 WL 21744332, at *6 (Wash. Ct. App. July 29, 2003) (computation errors in lender's hand-kept ledgers did not establish usury). *But cf.* Miller v. Soliz, 648 S.W.2d 734 (Tex. App. 1983) (failure to credit $465 down payment violates usury statute; not a bona fide error); Clark v. Aetna Fin. Corp., 340 N.W.2d 747 (Wis. Ct. App. 1983) (loan officer stole part of loan; given apparent authority, company answerable in usury for unrefunded interest overcharges even though principal returned; no bona fide error defense). *See generally* Annotation, *Usury As Affected by Mistake in Amount or Calculation of Interest or Service Charges for Loan,* 11 A.L.R. 3d 1498 (1967).

241 *See* Ford Motor Credit Co. v. Hutcherson, 640 S.W.2d 96 (Ark. 1982) (usury because of shorter initial installment interval is not excusable error); Southland Mobile Home Corp. v. Webster, 563 S.W.2d 430 (Ark. 1978) (incorrect interest formula used in computer program); Ford Motor Credit Co. v. Catalani, 383 S.W.2d 99

does not negate a lender's intent to charge the contract rate and is not a valid usury defense.[242] (Nor will a mistake in law as to the maximum rate support a creditor's effort to reform a usurious contract.[243]) Finally, a bona fide error defense cannot be maintained in some states unless the creditor proves that it had maintained procedures designed to prevent error.[244]

(Ark. 1964) (mistaken use of wrong interest rate did not negate usurious intent); Lawler v. Lomas & Nettleton Mortgage Investors, 691 S.W.2d 593 (Tex. 1985) (charging per diem rate based on 360-day year not accidental or bona fide error); Mackie's Auto., Inc. v. Parks, 2004 WL 213716 (Tex. App. Feb. 4, 2004). *See also* Norstar Bank v. Pickard & Anderson, 529 N.Y.S.2d 667 (N.Y. App. Div. 1988) (computer error could be defense to usury, but affidavit from bank officer insufficient evidence). *But see* Jordan v. Tri County Ag, Inc., 546 S.E.2d 528 (Ga. Ct. App. 2001) (creditor not liable for usury where overcharges were caused by software and creditor corrected them upon discovery); Libowsky v. Lakeshore Commercial Fin. Corp., 330 N.W.2d 248 (Wis. Ct. App. 1982) (lender lacked intent when 365/360 interest charged because of programmer error). *See generally* Annotation, *Usury As Affected by Mistake in Amount or Calculation of Interest or Service Charges for Loan,* 11 A.L.R.3d 1498 (1967).

242 *See, e.g.*, American Timber & Trading Co. v. First Nat'l Bank of Oregon, 690 F.2d 781 (9th Cir. 1982); LaPetina v. Metro Ford Truck Sales, 648 F.2d 283 (5th Cir. 1981) (wrong rate class chosen in motor vehicle usury law); Household Fin. Co. v. Swartz, 37 B.R. 776 (Bankr. D.R.I. 1984) ($4 recording fee usurious where not permitted separately under statute; no good-faith error defense allowed); Edwards v. Alabama Farm Bureau Mut. Cas. Ins. Co., 509 So. 2d 232 (Ala. Civ. App. 1986) (payment collected date loan was executed should have been treated as a down payment, rather than principal; this was error of law, and not a computational error, which is the only type of error subject to the statutory bona fide error defense); Ford Motor Credit Co. v. Catalani, 383 S.W.2d 99 (Ark. 1964); Varr v. Olimpia, 2002 WL 1425373 (Cal. Ct. App. July 1, 2002) (lender had usurious intent despite reliance on exemption to usury law that court later struck down); McClung v. Saito, 84 Cal. Rptr. 44 (Cal. Ct. App. 1970); Sunburst Bank v. Keith, 648 So. 2d 1147 (Miss. 1995) (usurious forbearance agreements; mistake as to legal effect of purposeful act binds creditor); Vee Bee Serv. Co. v. Household Fin. Co., 51 N.Y.S.2d 590 (N.Y. Sup. Ct. 1944), *aff'd without op.*, 55 N.Y.S.2d 870 (N.Y. App. Div. 1944); Commerce, Crowdus & Canton, Ltd. v. DKS Constr., Inc., 776 S.W.2d 615, 618–619 (Tex. App. 1989) (mistaken interpretation of contract provision was not bona fide error); Hardwick v. Austin Gallery of Oriental Rugs, Inc., 779 S.W.2d 438, 443 (Tex. App. 1989) (trial court's finding that lender acted upon "mistaken and unfounded belief" regarding contract provision could not be interpreted as finding bona fide error). *See also* Danziger v. San Jacinto Sav. Ass'n, 732 S.W.2d 300, 302–303 (Tex. 1987) (creditor cannot purge a usurious charge by a subsequent credit). *Cf.* Aetna Fin. Co. v. Brown, 323 S.E.2d 720 (Ga. Ct. App. 1984) (regulatory agency's approval of loan contract form filed with it does not enable lender to claim statutory defense for contracts made in good faith conformity with rule, regulation or appellate judicial interpretation); Walker v. Fingerhut Corp., 2000 WL 136096 (Minn. Ct. App. Jan. 28, 2000) (remanding case for determination whether precautions creditor took to avoid violating state usury laws negated usurious intent; trial court had found usurious intent but that precautions established a good faith defense). *But see* Pilcher v. Direct Equity Lending, 189 F. Supp. 2d 1198 (D. Kan. 2002) (statute provides defense for bona fide error of law or fact). *See generally* National Consumer Law Center, Truth in Lending §§ 7.4.2.1, 7.4.2.2., 7.4.3 (7th ed. 2010 and Supp.) (discussing an analogous statutory defense in TILA).

243 *See* Olsen v. Porter, 539 N.W.2d 523 (Mich. Ct. App. 1995). *See generally* § 7.8.3.3, *infra*.

### 7.5.5.3 Usury Not Apparent on Face of Contract

In many cases, a credit contract is not usurious on its face. The usury may be based on the exposure of "hidden interest," the occurrence of some contingency such as acceleration, or the revelation of the extension of credit in a disguised credit contract. In such situations, the courts apply a broad spectrum of approaches to determine the existence of usurious intent. Although decisions within most jurisdictions show some inconsistency, three overall approaches seem to exist.

First, in at least one state, Texas, the courts draw no distinction between facially usurious contracts and other forms of usury, and look only at the lender's objective intent to make the loan. The Supreme Court of Texas held that usurious intent was established, despite a jury finding that a bank had no subjective intent to charge excess interest, when a borrower showed that the bank had required her to assume a debt of her son's in order to obtain a refinancing of her loan.[245] The borrower's proof, that the bank had required the assumption of her son's debt as a condition for the extension of credit, established that the assumed debt was interest on the refinanced loan under Texas law, and the lender's intent to exact this interest was presumed. Because the true interest rate on the new loan exceeded the statutory limit, usury was demonstrated.

A second and more common approach to cases where usury is not facially apparent is to deny the borrower the presumption of intent otherwise granted, and to regard the existence of intent as a question of fact.[246] Given the same facts which existed in

244 *See* Trapp v. Hancuh, 530 N.W.2d 879 (Minn. Ct. App. 1995); Sumrall v. Navistar Fin. Corp., 818 S.W.2d 548 (Tex. App. 1991) (where there was no procedure to verify the calculation, nor if it existed, was the procedure used in the case where the collection supervisor "just skimmed" statement, the creditor did not meet statutory requirement of maintaining procedures designed to avoid bona fide errors); Moore v. White Motor Credit Corp., 708 S.W.2d 465 (Tex. App. 1985). *See also* Chrysler Fin. Co. v. Bergstrom, 703 N.W.2d 415 (Iowa 2005) (finding requirements of bona fide error defense under Iowa's Consumer Credit Code less than under TILA). *See generally* National Consumer Law Center, Truth in Lending § 7.4.4 (7th ed. 2010 and Supp.) (statutory bona fide error defense to TILA liability); National Consumer Law Center, Fair Debt Collection § 7.2 (7th ed. 2011 and Supp.) (statutory bona fide error defense to FDCPA liability).

245 Alamo Lumber Co. v. Gold, 661 S.W.2d 926 (Tex. 1983). *See also* Najarro v. SASI Int'l Ltd., 904 F.2d 1002, 1009 (5th Cir. 1990) (Tex. law) (usurious intent irrelevant); Brookshire v. Longhorn Chevrolet, Inc., 788 S.W.2d 209 (Tex. App. 1990) (only intent required is to make the bargain made).

246 *See, e.g.*, Greglon Industries, Inc. v. Bowman, 572 A.2d 369 (Conn. App. Ct. 1990); Dang v. F&S Land Dev. Co., 618 P.2d 276 (Haw. 1980); A&M Dev. v. Sherwood & Roberts, Inc., 457 P.2d 439 (Idaho 1969); Freitas v. Geddes Sav. & Loan Ass'n, 471 N.E.2d 436 (N.Y. 1984) (plurality opinion); Norstar Bank v. Pickard & Anderson, 547 N.Y.S.2d 734 (N.Y. App. Div. 1989); Western Auto Supply v. Vick, 277 S.E.2d 360 (N.C. 1981), *reaff'd on reh'g*, 283 S.E.2d 101 (1981). *See also* Cashback Catalog Sales v. Price, 102 F. Supp.

the Texas case described above, courts following this approach would require proof not only of the fact that the lender required the assumption of the son's debt, but also that it did so with the intent to exact more interest. Note, however, that such a showing is not the same as the demonstration of a knowing violation of the usury law.[247] If the lender intended to exact more interest through the borrower's assumption of third-party debt, it need not have known that the addition of this interest would cause the true rate to exceed the statutory limit and, thereby, to violate state usury law. Thus, the real difference between this approach and the one taken in Texas is not the intent which must be proved, but rather the presumptions which aid the proof.

The third approach, taken by only a small minority of courts, to usury which is not apparent on the face of the contract is to require proof that the lender subjectively intended to evade the usury laws by structuring the contract as it did.[248] Thus, a lender who entered a contract in "good faith" or without "corrupt intent" may not have committed usury even if it intended to charge interest at a rate which, in fact, exceeds the statutory limit.[249] (However, at least as the Florida courts interpret their "corrupt intent" requirement, it is not always clear that the borrower need prove any more than that the creditor consciously intended to make the charges which result in usury and did so.[250]) The "good faith" approach is particularly favored in a line of California cases in which challenged overcharges were based on the occurrence of some contingency.[251] This approach clearly places a heavy burden of proof on borrowers.

### 7.5.5.4 Inference of Intent

In the majority of consumer transactions, a court's decision to view usurious intent as a question of fact should not preclude a finding of usury even if subjective intent is at issue. The court will examine all the circumstances surrounding the transaction in deciding whether to infer intent. Consequently, the inference is more likely to be drawn in standard consumer cases involving experienced lenders and distressed borrowers than in transactions exhibiting arm's length bargaining or inexperienced lenders.[252] Usurious intent has been found even when the only direct testimony on this point was the lender's denial of any intended usury.[253]

## 7.6 Usury Claims in "Deregulated" States

### *7.6.1 Exceeding an "Agreed Rate" Cap*

In the late 1970s and early 1980s, numerous state legislatures decided to remove interest ceilings on some or all types of

2d 1375 (S.D. Ga. 2000) (intent to charge unlawful interest may be inferred from other facts, but lender can attempt to rebut it); Hickman v. Courtney, 203 S.W.3d 632 (Ark. 2005) (lender, CPA, filed tax returns demonstrating interest at usurious rate and testified that he wanted the rate to be above 7%; lender's knowledge that rate exceeded the usury threshold sufficient); Smith v. MRCC P'ship, 792 S.W.2d 301 (Ark. 1990) (where usury is not apparent on face, borrower must show lender intent to exact usurious interest; intent will not be inferred or imputed where opposite result can be fairly and reasonably reached).

247 *See* Western Auto Supply v. Vick, 277 S.E.2d 360 (N.C. 1981), *reaff'd on reh'g*, 283 S.E.2d 101 (1981).

248 *See, e.g.*, Handi Inv. Co. v. Mobil Oil Corp., 550 F.2d 543 (9th Cir. 1977) (California law); McDermott v. Strauss, 678 S.W.2d 334 (Ark. 1984) (value of debtor's services did not constitute additional interest absent showing of usurious intent); McConnell v. Merrill, Lynch, Pierce, Fenner, & Smith, 578 P.2d 1375 (Cal. 1978); Arneill Ranch v. Petit, 134 Cal. Rptr. 456 (Cal. Ct. App. 1976); Argento v. Reynolds, 452 So. 2d 135 (Fla. Dist. Ct. App. 1984) (error to limit testimony regarding intent); Steward v. Nangle, 103 So. 2d 649 (Fla. Dist. Ct. App. 1958) (corrupt intent); Lockhart Co. v. Naef, 693 P.2d 1090 (Idaho Ct. App. 1984) ((evidence must show that lender charged usurious rate "knowingly and with corrupt intent" where lender's failure to sign note made otherwise permissible rate unlawful); Walker v. Fingerhut Corp., 2001 WL 506952 (Minn. Ct. App. May 15, 2001) (defendant's good faith efforts to comply with states' laws demonstrated lack of intent). *See also* Warehouse Home Furnishing Distribs., Inc. v. Whitson, 709 So. 2d 1144 (Ala. 1997) (holding that it was fact question whether lender's imposition of an illegal non-filing insurance fee was "deliberate," but without specifying whether standard is subjective).

249 *See* McConnell v. Merrill, Lynch, Pierce, Fenner, & Smith, 578 P.2d 1375 (Cal. 1978); Gergora v. Goldstein Prof'l Ass'n, 500 So. 2d 695 (Fla. Dist. Ct. App. 1987) (Florida law). *See also* Washington Fed. Sav. & Loan v. Baker, 374 N.W.2d 786 (Minn. Ct. App. 1985). *See generally* Comment, *Usury's Intent Requirement: Should There Be a Good Faith Defense?*, 1985 B.Y.U.L. Rev. 789 (generally advocating good faith standard and suggesting that burden of proving good faith be placed on lender).

250 *See, e.g.*, Rollins v. Odom, 519 So. 2d 652 (Fla. Dist. Ct. App. 1988). *See also* Jersey Palm-Gross, Inc. v. Paper, 658 So. 2d 531 (Fla. 1995) (ill will or malevolent intent unnecessary; intent to extract excessive rate of interest shown where lender actively sought and received the usurious amounts and knew that borrowers were in urgent need). *But cf.* Polakoff v. State, 586 So. 2d 385 (Fla. Dist. Ct. App. 1991) (in criminal usury and RICO case, state's failure to allege in information that usurious acts were willful and knowing was fatal defect).

251 *See* McConnell v. Merrill, Lynch, Pierce, Fenner, & Smith, 578 P.2d 1375 (Cal. 1978). *See also* Handi Inv. Co. v. Mobil Oil Corp., 550 F.2d 543 (9th Cir. 1977) (California law); Arneill Ranch v. Petit, 134 Cal. Rptr. 456 (Cal. Ct. App. 1976). *But cf. In re* Pillon-Davey & Assocs., 52 B.R. 455 (Bankr. N.D. Cal. 1985) (good faith not relevant if note usurious as matter of law and usury not dependent on a contingency); McClung v. Saito, 84 Cal. Rptr. 44 (Cal. Ct. App. 1970) (usury despite belief contract was legally proper).

252 Dixon v. Sharp, 276 So. 2d. 817 (Fla. 1973) (borrower distress is factor in "corrupt intent"). *See also* Valliappan v. Cruz, 917 So. 2d 257, 258 (Fla. Dist. Ct. App. 2005) (finding no usurious intent since lender was "an unsophisticated lender trying to help out his friends" with handwritten note); Howes v. Curtis, 661 P.2d 729 (Idaho 1983) (finding usurious intent where borrower was distressed and lender engaged in real estate transactions and mortgage brokering business for several years). *Cf.* Meridian Bowling Lanes, Inc. v. Brown, 412 P.2d 586 (Idaho 1966) (finding enforceable land sale contract rather than usurious loan where experienced parties dealt at arm's length, no party was a necessitous debtor, and creditor not a professional lender).

253 Howes v. Curtis, 661 P.2d 729 (Idaho 1983) (inferring usurious intent from lender's business background and borrower's dire straits despite lender's uncontroverted testimony denying intent); Rollins v. Odom, 519 So. 2d 652 (Fla. Dist. Ct. App. 1988). *See also* Ford Motor Credit Co. v. Catalani, 383 S.W.2d 99 (Ark. 1964).

credit transactions.[254] However, even in deregulated states, there usually remain benchmarks which provide a consumer with possible claims or defenses if a creditor violates them. Two such benchmarks, unconscionability standards and criminal usury statutes, are discussed at §§ 2.4.7.3 and 3.9.9, *supra*. This section will discuss another possible benchmark which may be breached—the credit agreement itself.

In some deregulating states, the approach taken was a simple repeal which removed a usury statute from the books entirely. But a greater number of "deregulated" states found it expedient to leave most of an existing usury statute intact and to alter only that portion of the statute which set a numerical interest rate ceiling. For example, a statute which had previously authorized any rate of interest, not to exceed ten percent, might be modified to permit any "agreed rate." Such an amendment raises interesting usury questions because many lenders in the state will assume that they no longer need worry about usury regulations, while in fact they may still face serious sanctions if they assess charges which exceed the "agreed rate."

The most obvious way that a creditor could violate an "agreed rate" usury statute would be to assess charges to which the borrower had not agreed. A threshold issue may be whether there was an *agreement* to pay any specified rate at all. If the statute allows an agreed *rate*, but there is no *rate* agreed to in the note, then the lender's receipt of interest charges may also violate the cap, even if the note specifies the finance charges in some other way.[255] However, contracts that call for interest payments at a bank's prime rate appear to be sufficiently specific to satisfy an agreed rate requirement, so long as the rate charged is indeed the bank's prime rate.[256] If the borrower did not actually agree to the rate, because of fraud, incapacity, or some other factor, the agreed rate statute may likewise be inapplicable.[257]

254 *See* § 1.2.5, *supra*.

255 Chroniak v. Golden Inv. Corp., 983 F.2d 1140 (1st Cir. 1993) (second mortgage statute required disclosure of rate of interest and set cap at agreed-upon rate of interest; note which specified the interest in a dollar amount, but no rate, violated the statute, thus invoking statutory penalty of forfeiture of interest). *But see* Dunnam v. Burns, 901 S.W.2d 628 (Tex. App. 1995) (agreed interest rate does not have to be specified as a numeric rate; adequate if it can be determined from terms of note. *N.B.*: This case may be distinguished by the fact that it was a business loan and the borrower drafted the terms).

256 *See* Pappas v. NCNB Nat'l Bank, 653 F. Supp. 699 (M.D.N.C. 1987) (agreed rate existed despite borrowers' claim that they did not understand the meaning of the term prime rate; misunderstanding was the unilateral mistake of the borrowers); 1600 Capital v. Bankers First Fed. Savs. & Loan, 370 S.E.2d 668 (Ga. Ct. App. 1988) (setting rate in reference to bank's "base" rate, which was rate set by committee of bank officers, was sufficient to satisfy statutory requirement of agreement in writing expressed in "simple interest terms"); Holmes v. Dallas Int'l Bank, 718 S.W.2d 59 (Tex. App. 1986).

257 *Cf.* Hanning v. Homecomings Fin. Networks, 436 F. Supp. 2d 865 (W.D. Mich. 2006) (finding it unnecessary to decide this theory, because borrower in fact agreed to the rate). *But see* Wilson v. Homecomings Fin. Network, 407 F. Supp. 2d 893 (N.D. Ohio 2005) (fraud did not vitiate borrower's agreement to rate).

In other cases, the critical issue may be whether the lender in fact imposed charges at the agreed rate. For example, a lender might contract to charge twelve percent interest while in fact charging a somewhat higher rate due to its use of a 365/360 interest calculation.[258] Similarly, a creditor might contract to charge a borrower its "prime rate" while in fact charging a higher rate.[259] A lender may charge more interest than allowed by the contract by calculating the interest due on late payments using the daily interest accruing on the note balance times the number of days since the last payment as opposed to calculating the interest on the amount of the monthly payment in arrears.[260] Or a lender may delay posting the borrowers' payments, thus extracting a few more days of interest each month than the contract allows,[261] or manipulate a variable rate contrary to the contract.[262] In these instances, an "agreed rate" statute may automatically convert a contract overcharge to a usury violation.

Some statutes set a low interest rate ceiling unless the parties agree to a higher rate.[263] Under many such statutes the agree-

258 *See* § 5.5.4.4, *supra*.

259 *Cf.* Briggs Transp. Co. v. Second Northwestern Nat'l Bank, 406 N.W.2d 7 (Minn. Ct. App. 1987) (breach of contract claim where borrower allegedly was charged higher rate than the lender's actual prime lending rate to most creditworthy commercial borrowers). *But cf.* NCNB Nat'l Bank v. Tiller, 814 F.2d 931 (4th Cir. 1987).

260 Karg v. Strickland, 919 S.W.2d 722 (Tex. App. 1996). *But cf.* Miller v. Parker McCurley Props., L.L.C., 36 So. 3d 1234 (Miss. 2010) (concluding, without explanation, that imposition of additional finance charges in the form of illegal late charges did not make interest rate usurious under agreed rate statute).

261 *See* § 5.5.4.5, *supra*.

262 *See* Siradas v. Chase Lincoln First Bank, 1999 WL 787658 (S.D.N.Y. Sept. 30, 1999) (denying lender's motion for judgment on pleadings on UDAP claim that it miscalculated variable rates).

263 A series of cases has interpreted a Texas statute which sets a low interest ceiling for transactions in which the parties do not agree to a specified interest rate. The issue of what constitutes an agreement therefore has been frequently litigated. These opinions have been fairly generous in finding agreements.

*FINDING AGREEMENT*: Ginsberg 1985 Real Estate P'ship v. Cadle Co., 39 F.3d 528 (5th Cir. 1994) (Texas law) (finding implicit agreement to substitute an analogous prime rate where benchmark bank specified in variable rate contract failed); Luttenegger v. Conseco Fin. Serv. Corp., 671 N.W.2d 425 (Iowa 2003) (HUD-1 settlement statement was "written agreement" on which charge could be based, even though lender did not sign it); Preston Farm & Ranch Supply v. Bio-Zyme Enters., 625 S.W.2d 295 (Tex. 1981) (continued use of open-end commercial account after imposition of finance charge constituted agreement to rate charged; expressly distinguishing consumer accounts); Rent Am., Inc. v. Amarillo Nat'l Bank, 785 S.W.2d 190 (Tex. App. 1990) (contract for interest tied to the prime rate of a third-party bank sufficiently stated a rate of interest); Broady v. Johnson, 763 S.W.2d 832 (Tex. App. 1988) (Texas law allows 6% where no contract rate specified); Augusta Dev. Co. v. Fish Oil Well Serv., 761 S.W.2d 538 (Tex. App. 1988) (work tickets authorizing maximum amount permitted by law sufficient to permit 18% interest); Campbell v. First Bank & Trust of Cleveland, 714 S.W.2d 363 (Tex. App. 1986) (APR listed on face of note sufficiently specifies rate when "interest" space on note left blank); Holmes v. Dallas Int'l Bank, 718 S.W.2d 59 (Tex. App. 1986) (contract providing for interest at 2% over bank's prime rate sufficiently stated a rate of interest); Dodson v. Citizens State Bank

ment must be in writing. Oral agreements for a higher rate would then be usurious or, at least, unenforceable.[264]

Another issue in an agreed rate jurisdiction is exactly what components of the cost of credit have been deregulated. For example, a Montana statute exempted certain lenders from all limitations on the "rate of interest" they may charge. The Montana Supreme Court held that points were not interest for purposes of this statute.[265] Thus, while a lender could charge any interest rate it chose, it cannot charge points. The court held:

> the points charged on the loans in question are not interest; that is, they are not charged for the use, forbearance, or detention of money. Under the circumstances of this case and the provisions of the [Consumer Loan Act], the imposition of a flat fee, computed as a percentage of the loan, bearing no direct relation to actual costs of specific services performed, front-loaded into the loan, which did not constitute a charge for the use of the lender's money over time, is not interest.[266]

The court declined to interpret the state Consumer Loan Act "in such a way that it contains a loophole whereby predatory lenders may add points onto the beginning of an interest-bearing loan and thereby escape the requirement that such points be at least partially refunded if the loan is prepaid or refinanced."[267]

## 7.6.2 Hidden Interest in Agreed Rate Transactions

Because these statutes are pegged to an agreed rate, issues of hidden interest are just as relevant as with statutorily defined numerical rate caps. In fact, they may be more relevant, as the prospect of lending in a deregulated environment may make some lenders feel more comfortable taking chances at the margins of acceptable practices.

The theory behind deregulation was that market forces would drive the interest rates. Thus these "as agreed" statutes do not limit the amount of interest a lender can charge; a 100% annual rate, if agreed upon, would theoretically be permissible under an agreed rate usury statute, although it might be unconscionable.[268] But the rate has to be the one agreed upon,[269] and creditors that charge rates in excess of the market may not wish to be very forthcoming about those rates. Accordingly, a creditor may charge an above-market interest rate while stating a lower rate. One way to accomplish this is to inflate the loan principal through the inclusion of various "fees," such as points, service charges, commitment or other fees, or sham closing costs. These artifices have long been used by lenders to circumvent fixed usury ceilings, but they are equally useful in understating effective interest rates in an unrestricted market. Some of these devices, such as phony closing costs or unauthorized charges, have never been legitimately excluded from calculation of the interest rate, but others—particularly points—have been in certain circumstances, and so are commonly counted as part of the note's principal.[270] This fact goes a long

---

of Dalhart, 701 S.W.2d 89 (Tex. App. 1986) (contract provided for interest at "highest legal rate" after maturity of debt; this specified a rate sufficiently to avoid the 6% ceiling in effect when no rate is specified); Morgan v. Amarillo Nat'l Bank, 699 S.W.2d 930 (Tex. App. 1985) (post-maturity interest at "highest lawful rate" specified a definite interest rate).

*REFUSING TO FIND AGREEMENT*: *In re* Charter Co., 913 F.2d 1575 (11th Cir. 1990) (buyer's failure to object to interest charged on invoices sent by seller did not establish agreement to pay interest); Tubelite v. Risica & Sons, Inc., 819 S.W.2d 801 (Tex. 1991) (unilateral addition of late charges on acknowledgments and invoices did not constitute agreement to modify the contract which had no provision regarding late charges; purchaser's failure to object did not constitute implied modification; 6% statutory rate applicable and the 18% rate imposed was twice the legal rate); Triton Oil & Gas Corp. v. Marine Contractors & Supply, Inc., 644 S.W.2d 443 (Tex. 1982) (unilateral charges imposed by one joint venture partner on another were not agreed upon where never paid despite deduction of amount equal to charged interest from proceeds owed to debtor partner); Strasburger Enters., Inc. v. TDGT Ltd. P'ship, 110 S.W.3d 566, 579 (Tex. App. 2003) (borrower entitled to usury penalty when creditor demanded interest in excess of legal rate on a contract that was silent as to interest); Baker v. Howard, 799 S.W.2d 450 (Tex. App. 1990) (amortization chart not signed by either party and used as evidence of completed oral contract did not constitute the necessary written agreement).

The issue has been litigated under other statutes, as well. *See also* Redmond v. McClelland, 2000 WL 1015774 (Minn. Ct. App. July 25, 2000) (construing facts to have created equitable mortgage and loan; since no interest rate was ever agreed to, creditor's attempt to charge more than the cap was usurious); Northwestern Equip., Inc. v. Badinger, 403 N.W.2d 8 (N.D. 1987) (written agreement met by merely mailing unsigned invoices to borrower; statute specifically provided that, as between merchants, that constituted a written agreement unless the borrower objected to it in writing); Lawler v. Lomas & Nettleton Mortgage Invs., 691 S.W.2d 593 (Tex. 1985) (different Texas statute) (would be usurious to charge a corporation more than 10% interest unless corporation agrees to pay higher rate; finding agreement in this case). *Cf.* Power Equip., Inc. v. Tschiggfrie, 460 N.W.2d 861 (Iowa 1990) (remanding to trial court to sort out whether written agreement existed: factors suggesting agreement were invoices reciting the existence of the charge, creditor's billing in accordance with invoice, debtor's employees signing the invoices, and debtor's continued dealings with creditor; factors suggesting no agreement were that creditor did not always require signed invoices, nor assess charges in accord with invoices, and debtor consistently denied liability for them and refused to pay them).

264 *See In re* Bradford Realty, Inc., 55 B.R. 218 (Bankr. D.N.H. 1985) (oral agreement unenforceable); Northwestern Equip., Inc. v. Badinger, 403 N.W.2d 8 (N.D. 1987) (written agreement met by merely mailing unsigned invoices to borrower; statute specifically provided that, as between merchants, that constituted a written agreement unless the borrower objected to it in writing). *See also* Gus T. Handge & Son Painting Co. v. First Bank & Trust Co., 756 S.W.2d 652 (Mo. Ct. App. 1988) (statute requiring written agreement as to rate of interest complied with by precomputed note calling for specified payments of principal and interest totaling the precomputed face amount of note).

265 Wombold v. Associates Fin. Servs. Co., 104 P.3d 1080 (Mont. 2004).

266 *Id.* at 1089.

267 *Id.*

268 *See* § 2.4.7.3, *supra.*

269 *See* § 7.6.1, *supra.*

270 *See* Chs. 3, 4, *supra.*

way towards explaining why points and other such fees are so prevalent in "deregulated" credit markets where lenders can charge whatever rate the market will bear.

Depending on the precise wording of a deregulated state's agreed rate statute, an answer to an understated interest rate accomplished through the use of one-time fees may lie in the apparently emasculated usury statute. The usury statute sets the usury ceiling at a *rate* agreed upon by the parties, and under both normal usage and statutory definition, a rate is a percentage figure, not a total charge.[271] The rate stated on the face of the loan note will be lower than the effective interest rate if the lender has charged hidden interest fees, such as points or other charges. Since the rate stated on the face of the note is arguably the only *rate* to which the parties have agreed, then this rate is the usury ceiling for the transaction. By charging a higher effective rate, the lender has exceeded the usury ceiling, and the frequently serious sanctions that the legislature left on the books when it "deregulated" the usury statute can be invoked.

The Virginia Supreme Court adopted this approach in *Garrison v. First Federal Savings and Loan Association*,[272] holding that a second mortgage was null, void and unenforceable, the penalty authorized for a violation of the usury statute,[273] though the rate ceiling on such loans had been removed. Virginia's deregulation provision permitted junior mortgage loans to be "lawfully enforced at the interest rate stated therein on the principal amount of the loan. . . ."[274] At the time Ms. Garrison's loan was made, the statute authorized a 2% service charge, but there was no limitation on points. As is most frequently the case in mortgage loans, the points—26 of them—were included in the $9,200 note principal and the agreed-upon interest rate was 18%.[275]

Conventional practice notwithstanding, the "economic reality" is that points are interest,[276] and the lender in *Garrison* conceded as much. Yet Ms. Garrison's twenty-six points were not included within the stated 18% interest rate. The court refused to "allow a second tier of interest to be collected" by way of points that were not reflected in the rate disclosed on the note.[277] In other words, points are interest, not principal, and an agreed-upon interest rate must be calculated accordingly. Otherwise, the rate, which, theoretically, is to be set by market forces, will be understated, which is inherently deceptive and anticompetitive. As the court stated, "[n]othing could be more confusing or deceptive to the borrower than reciting an 'agreed' interest rate on one line and then adding additional interest on another."[278]

In addition to the points, there were other challenged charges which had been included in the note principal: a "risk management fee," which was not a type of charge authorized to be imposed in these loans; and an appraisal fee greater than was actually incurred. These hidden finance charges in excess of those authorized by statute were also interest, thus further distorting the agreed rate of interest.[279]

Following its common sense approach in *Garrison*, the Virginia court torpedoed another subterfuge when it refused to recognize the accounting fiction behind a wraparound note, and held that the transaction was really a usurious $4,300, 31.20% loan, rather than a 13.25%, $50,000 loan.[280] In the absence of an accurately stated rate in the note, the general usury ceiling of 8% applied.

Similarly, in *Howes v. Curtis*,[281] the Idaho Supreme Court interpreted a usury statute which exempted commercial loans from a 10% usury ceiling by allowing parties, who "agree in writing which clearly sets forth the rate of interest charged, to pay any rate of interest. . . ." The lender in *Howes* obtained a note for $44,600 at a stated 10% interest rate but, because of sham broker fees and funds never advanced, the actual loan principal was only $37,500 with an effective interest rate in excess of 17%. The court ruled that:

> In such a posture, the note lost efficacy as a valid disclosure of the rate of interest which would bar the issue of usury. Only by reference to extrinsic evi-

271 Chroniak v. Golden Inv. Corp., 983 F.2d 1140 (1st Cir. 1993).

272 402 S.E.2d 25 (Va. 1991). The borrower's brief is available through National Clearinghouse for Legal Servs., Clearinghouse No. 46,421. *See also* Anderson v. Federal Nat'l Mortgage Ass'n, Civ. No. 87-0236 (E.D. Va. 1988), *available on the companion website to this treatise* (plaintiffs' brief in opposition to defendants' motion to dismiss).

273 Va. Code Ann. § 6.1-330.47(A).

Following the state's notoriously bad experience with deregulated second mortgages, it re-regulated them. Va. Code Ann. § 6.1-330.71. The statute was amended to weaken the penalty in 1987, but the legislature specifically provided that the former law applied to subordinate mortgages closed prior to July 1, 1986. Acts 1987, c. 622, cl. 3. Second mortgage loans in Virginia are now regulated by Va. Code Ann. § 6.2-327.

274 Va. Code Ann. § 6.1-330.16E (1983).

275 This loan was originated by Landbank Equity, which went on to achieve some notoriety before collapsing into bankruptcy and criminal prosecutions. *See, e.g., High Rate Mortgage Lending Can Violate Georgia's Criminal Usury Law*, 9 NCLC REPORTS *Consumer Credit & Usury Ed.* 1 (July/Aug. 1990) (discussing Moore v. Comfed Sav. Bank, 908 F.2d 834 (11th Cir. 1990)).

276 Smith v. Anderson, 801 F.2d 661 (4th Cir. 1986); Garrison v. First Fed. Sav. & Loan Ass'n, 402 S.E.2d 25 (Va. 1991). *See generally* § 4.3.2, *supra* (legal characterization of points).

277 Garrison v. First Fed. Sav. & Loan Ass'n, 402 S.E.2d 25, 30 (Va. 1991).

278 *Id.* at 30. *See also* Fidelity Fin. Servs., Inc. v. Hicks, 574 N.E.2d 15, 19 (Ill. App. Ct. 1991) (statutorily limiting points in agreed-rate transactions "helps prevent an unscrupulous lender from luring an unsophisticated borrower with low interest rates that may undercut legitimate competition, only to impose additional, onerous, or undisclosed fees to compensate for the artificially low interest rate").

279 In those states which, by statute, specifically authorize a specified number of points, charging those points may be permissible in agreed rate transactions, just as here, the 2% statutorily authorized service charge was not considered part of the note interest. *See, e.g.*, Fidelity Fin. Servs., Inc. v. Hicks, 574 N.E.2d 15, 19 (Ill. App. Ct. 1991) (construing statutory limit on points to apply to agreed rate transactions). *Cf.* Norris v. Sigler Daisy Corp., 392 S.E.2d 242 (Ga. 1990) (question of statutory interpretation: points excluded from interest in civil usury statute; included as interest in criminal usury statute). *See generally* § 4.3.2, *supra*.

280 Skinner v. Cen-Pen Corp., 414 S.E.2d 824 (Va. 1992).

281 661 P.2d 729 (Idaho 1983).

> dence could the total amount of interest charged or the rate of interest be determined. Therefore, the disclosure did not comport with the statutory condition requiring a writing which clearly sets forth the rate of interest charged, . . . and a claim of usury could be properly raised.[282]

The *Howes* court held that an agreed rate usury statute can be violated by the inclusion of hidden interest fees in the face amount of a loan note, and by the corresponding understatement of the actual interest rate.[283]

A Missouri appellate decision reached a similar conclusion.[284] The Missouri Second Mortgage Loan Act had been amended to replace an interest rate cap with the rate agreed to by the parties, but it kept restrictions on fees. The court held that a lender that charges fees beyond those specifically allowed by the Act cannot take advantage of the lack of an interest rate cap but is bound by the legal interest rate. It upheld the consumers' recovery of the interest as compensatory damages.

Applying a different agreed rate statute to an otherwise similar transaction, however, a middle-level Arizona appeals court in *Layne v. Transamerica Financial Services, Inc.*,[285] refused to rule that the charging of points constituted a *per se* violation of an Arizona statute setting a ten percent annual interest ceiling "unless a different rate is contracted for in writing, in which event any rate of interest may be agreed to." The note in *Layne* stated that the "Agreed Rate of Charge is 19.9% per annum interest on the Total Amount of the Loan, plus a Prepaid Finance Charge of 10% of the Total Amount of Loan." The borrower contended that since the points were not included in the 19.9% interest rate they constituted a charge in excess of the agreed-upon rate, and were therefore usurious. However, the court construed the statute to allow the parties to agree to any *effective* rate of interest, so it validated the parties' agreement to pay interest plus points.

While the *Howes* and *Layne* decisions illustrate how subtle distinctions in statutory analysis and legislative history can affect a court's analysis, the Virginia Supreme Court's decision in *Garrison* persuasively states the case for putting substance over form, and giving teeth to the agreed rate language. There are also policy arguments which support such a reading. First, if legislatures had intended to abolish usury statutes through deregulation they could easily have done so. Their decision to leave most of the text of deregulated statutes intact suggests that it is still meaningful, and agreed rate language should be construed in a way that will avoid rendering these parts of the statute meaningless.

Second, the deregulation of interest rates in those states which have removed usury ceilings has generally been explained as a decision to allow the free market to govern a lender's return. Yet, the use of points and other hidden interest fees is inherently deceptive and anti-competitive. The anti-competitive effect of points is particularly pronounced if the lender takes the position, as many do, that points are not subject to rebate if the borrower refinances.[286] This makes it uneconomical for the borrower to refinance, and immunizes the lender from the market forces that at least theoretically might drive rates down, as other lenders compete for the borrower's business by offering to refinance at lower rates. Thus, interpreting agreed rate statutes as forbidding points that are not included in the stated rate is consistent with the fundamental theories on which they are based. Agreed rate statutes should be construed as allowing the lender any effective rate of return that the market will bear, so long as that *rate* is knowingly agreed upon.[287] Any other approach merely encourages inefficient lenders and deceptive lending practices.

## 7.7 Creditor Defenses

### *7.7.1 Standing to Assert Usury*

#### 7.7.1.1 Requirement of Standing

Noting that usury statutes are designed to protect needy borrowers rather than to penalize lenders, courts have widely viewed usury as a claim that is personal to the borrower.[288] This

282 *Id.* at 661 P.2d 732.

283 A creditor in another state might find it a bit awkward to try to distinguish *Howes* on the basis that the Idaho statute required the rate to be stated "clearly." The absence of the word "clearly" or its equivalent certainly would not suggest legislative approval of unclear disclosure.

284 Mitchell v. Residential Funding Corp., 334 S.W.3d 477 (Mo. Ct. App. 2010).

285 707 P.2d 963 (Ariz. Ct. App. 1986). *See also* Scavenger Sale Investors L.P. v. Bryant, 2000 WL 360118 (N.D. Ill. Mar. 22, 2000) (assuming that loan fees in a commercial case would be part of agreed rate).

286 *See* § 5.8.4.2, *supra*.

287 *See also* Chroniak v. Golden Inv. Corp., 983 F.2d 1140 (1st Cir. 1993) (specifying only dollar amount of interest where statute required disclosure of rate of interest and set cap at agreed upon rate of interest violates that statute and also is a UDAP violation; noting that full disclosure of interest rates takes on added significance with the elimination of usury ceilings); Fidelity Fin. Servs. v. Hicks, 574 N.E.2d 15 (Ill. App. Ct. 1991) (in ruling that statute deregulating interest rates did not implicitly repeal a statutory limitation on points; noting notes possibility of misuse of points to gouge consumers, undercut legitimate competition and discriminate against disfavored borrowers).

288 *See, e.g.*, Manohara v. Medifax, Inc., 2002 WL 1376212 (Cal. Ct. App. June 26, 2002) (debtor's limited partner does not have standing); Ideal Loan & Fin. Corp. v. Little, 457 S.E.2d 274 (Ga. Ct. App. 1995) (judge could not exclude award of interest on grounds of usury in default judgment, as usury defense is personal to the borrower); Midwest Fed. Sav. v. West Bend Mut. Ins., 407 N.W.2d 690 (Minn. Ct. App. 1987) (insurance company could not assert usury claim because claim was personal to borrower-insureds and because usury defense is unavailable to corporations); LaBarre v. Gold, 520 So. 2d 1327 (Miss. 1988); General Elec. Credit Corp. v. Best Refrigerated Express, Inc., 385 N.W.2d 81 (Neb. 1986); All Seasons Window & Door Mfg. v. Red Dot Corp., 181 S.W.3d 490 (Tex. App. 2005) (company for whose use funds were advanced cannot claim usury since only its president was a party to the contract); Smart v. Crawford Bldg. Material Co., 638 S.W.2d 228 (Tex. App. 1982).

rule is frequently raised by creditors as a defense in usury actions where the party seeking to assert usury is not the same party who received the credit proceeds. The issue is often framed as one of standing to assert usury. Standing is a question of law for the court.[289]

It is fairly clear that any maker or obligor on a note has standing to assert usury. Thus, a co-signer can plead usury.[290] Furthermore, a person whose interest in the litigation derives from the borrower may be able to assert usury on the borrower's behalf, but the extent to which such derivative rights exist can vary significantly with the plaintiff and the state.[291] A receiver or bankruptcy trustee can generally maintain a usury action on behalf of a debtor.[292] Some courts hold that the estate of a deceased borrower has standing to assert usury on the borrower's behalf.[293]

#### 7.7.1.2 Guarantors and Sureties

Most cases where creditors dispute a plaintiff's standing to assert usury involve guarantors or sureties to a debt, and most courts hold that guarantors and sureties do not have standing to assert usury.[294] Litigation regarding guarantors typically involves loans to close corporations secured by the individual guaranty of a major stockholder. In such cases the corporate borrower may be unable to claim usury because of a high or non-existent corporate usury ceiling, and the addition of the rule denying standing to guarantors essentially exempts the entire transaction from usury limitations.

One danger with denying guarantors the right to assert usury is that creditors may force individuals who are seeking personal loans to receive their loans through a shell corporation and to add their personal guaranty to the corporation's note. It is somewhat reassuring, therefore, that courts examining individually guaranteed loans to close corporations have frequently recognized the potential for usury evasion and have specifically looked at the purposes of such loans before upholding them.[295]

---

289 El Paso Ref., Inc. v. Scurlock Permian Corp., 77 S.W.3d 374 (Tex. App. 2002).

290 *See* Bizzoco v. Chintz, 476 A.2d 572 (Conn. 1984); Fidelcor Mortgage Co. v. Tyroff, 302 S.E.2d 96 (Ga. 1983) (individual co-maker had standing to assert usury but lost claim because of business purpose usury exception); Ciminelli v. Ford Motor Credit Co., 624 S.W.2d 903 (Tex. 1981); Williams v. Security Sav. & Loan Ass'n, 355 N.W.2d 370 (Wis. Ct. App. 1984).

291 *See, e.g.*, Family Fed. Sav. & Loan v. Davis, 172 B.R. 437 (Bankr. D.D.C. 1994) ("purchaser of equity of redemption in real estate who is in privity of estate or contract with the mortgagor and grantor can plead usury"); Eisenstein v. DiPrimio, 2000 WL 1300452 (Ga. Ct. App. Sept. 15, 2000) (law firm had standing to claim usury as defense when its client's creditor sought to impose constructive trust over money in client trust account); Nogueras v. Maisel & Assocs. of Mich., 369 N.W.2d 492 (Mich. Ct. App. 1985) (individual partners can assert usury, if at all, only after partnership fails to pay debt and partner is called upon to repay the loans himself); Seidel v. 18 East 17th St. Owners, 598 N.E.2d 7 (N.Y. 1992) (original borrower's corporate transferee was essentially same people, and transfer occurred as a result of building's conversion to a co-op, not a sale to an independent third party, so transferee could assert usury); Williams v. Macchio, 329 N.Y.S.2d 405 (N.Y. Sup. Ct. 1972) (wife can assert usury in note signed solely by husband when she satisfied the usurious note under duress because of lender's threats to harm her husband). *See also* Russell v. Fin. Capital Equities, 158 Fed. Appx. 953 (10th Cir. 2005) (cousin of borrower who had ownership interest in mortgaged property, possibly acquired after execution of the note, lacked standing to assert claims against lender); Weisfeld v. Tex. Land Fin. Co. II, 162 S.W.3d 379 (Tex. App. 2005) (purchaser of property at foreclosure sale not obligor and cannot assert usury in defense of lien).

292 *See, e.g.*, McCollum v. Hamilton Nat'l Bank, 303 U.S. 245 (1938) (trustee in bankruptcy); Rieser v. Todd (*In re* Chari), 2005 WL 4030034 (Bankr. S.D. Ohio Sept. 2, 2005); *In re* Giorgio, 62 B.R. 853 (Bankr. D.R.I. 1986); *In re* Pair, 14 B.R. 732 (Bankr. N.D. Ga. 1981) (trustee could assert usury on behalf of named bankrupt but not on behalf of another debtor); North v. Cecil B. De Mille Productions, Inc., 39 P.2d 199 (Cal. 1934) (receiver); Scott v. Hollingsworth, 9 P.2d 836 (Cal. 1932) (receiver). *See also* Sheehan v. Richardson, 315 B.R. 226 (D.R.I. 2004) (trustee has standing to pursue assigned claim), *aff'd*, 185 Fed. Appx. 11 (1st Cir. 2006); *In re* Colad Group, Inc., 324 B.R. 208 (Bankr. W.D.N.Y. 2005) (debtor's waiver of defense of usury does not bind bankruptcy estate).

293 *See, e.g.*, Barnes v. Hartman, 54 Cal. Rptr. 514 (Cal. Ct. App. 1966) (death of plaintiff did not abate usury cause of action, although plaintiff lacked standing for other reasons); Chandlee v. Tharp, 137 So. 540 (Miss. 1931); Tilley v. Pacesetter Corp., 585 S.E.2d 292, 310 (S.C. 2003) (usury claim based on statute survives borrower's death). *Cf.* McNish v. Gen. Credit Corp., 83 N.W.2d 1 (Neb. 1957) (standing of estate not contested). *But see* Orr v. International Bank of Commerce, 649 S.W.2d 769 (Tex. App. 1983) (usury does not survive death of either the liable party or the party entitled to a penalty); Snodgrass v. Sisson's Mobile Home Sales, Inc., 244 S.E.2d 321 (W. Va. 1978) (no common law survivability).

294 *See, e.g.*, Superior Funding Corp. v. Big Apple Capital Corp., 738 F. Supp. 1468 (S.D.N.Y. 1990) (guarantor of corporate debt cannot assert usury as defense); *In re* Perry, 425 B.R. 323, 372 (Bankr. S.D. Tex. 2010); Bizzoco v. Chintz, 476 A.2d 572 (Conn. 1984); Snyder v. Woxo, Inc., 177 N.W.2d 281 (Neb. 1970); Colonial Acceptance Corp. v. Northeastern Printcrafters, 330 S.E.2d 76 (N.C. Ct. App. 1985); El Paso Ref., Inc. v. Scurlock Permian Corp., 77 S.W.3d 374 (Tex. App. 2002); Williams v. Security Sav. & Loan Ass'n, 355 N.W.2d 370 (Wis. Ct. App. 1984). *See also* Ginsberg 1985 R.E. P'ship v. Cadle Co., 39 F.3d 528 (5th Cir.1994) (Texas law); First South Sav. Ass'n v. First South Partners, II, Ltd., 957 F.2d 174 (5th Cir. 1992) (Texas law) (denying guarantor's usury claim on the ground that there was no compensation demanded for the guarantor's use, forbearance or detention of money); Mayo v. GMAC Mortgage, L.L.C., 763 F. Supp. 2d 1091, 1108-9 (W.D. Mo. 2011) (wife who signed mortgage but not note does not have standing to assert claim that loan terms violated state usury statute); Marrone v. Meecorp Capital Mkts., L.L.C., 2004 WL 2677175 (E.D. Pa. Nov. 19, 2004) (dismissing guarantor's claim against creditor; borrower is indispensable party); Houston Sash & Door, Inc. v. Heaner, 577 S.W.2d 217 (Tex. 1979). *Cf.* Foster Bus. Park, L.L.C. v. J & B Invs., L.L.C., 269 S.W.3d 50 (Tenn. Ct. App. 2008) (debtor corporation does not have standing to assert usury claim on behalf of guarantors). *But see* Martin v. Ajax Constr. Co., 269 P.2d 132 (Cal. Ct. App. 1954) (usury in business loan may be asserted by guarantors as well as by principal obligor); Johnson v. Ronamy Consumer Credit Corp., 515 A.2d 682 (Del. 1986) (second mortgage statute covered guarantors); First Nat'l Consumer Discount Co. v. Fuller, 419 A.2d 940 (Del. 1980). *But cf.* Skeen v. Slavik, 555 S.W.2d 516 (Tex. Civ. App. 1977) (corporation's guarantor, who later executes personal note to lender assuming the debt of the corporation, may assert usury). *See generally* Annotation, *Statute Denying Defense of Usury to a Corp.*, 63 A.L.R.2d 924 (1959).

295 *See, e.g.*, Bizzoco v. Chintz, 476 A.2d 572 (Conn. 1984) (no proof that debt was not corporate); Brint v. Ellin Express Corp., 273

The result of this judicial approach is that individual loans through close corporations probably cannot be attacked as usurious if the loans have a business purpose, even if they are actually loans to individuals, but individual guarantors can challenge usurious personal or consumer loans that are structured in this manner.[296] Thus, the rule against guarantor standing effectively creates a usury exception similar to the business purpose exception that already exists in many states.

A second potential problem created by the rule against the standing of guarantors to assert usury is that a guaranty or surety agreement can be structured so that there is really no difference between the duties of the guarantor and those of the maker or obligor. It seems a triumph of form over substance to give usury protection to a borrower and then to deny it to a surety whose liability is "primary, direct and unconditional," and who may be sued prior to any action against the primary borrower, but this is the law in many states.[297] This rule may encourage creditors to obtain guarantors rather than co-signers in order to limit the number of potential usury plaintiffs.

Fortunately, such a scenario has not developed with any frequency in consumer transactions. The main reason may be that there must always be at least one obligor on a note and in a consumer transaction, unlike a corporate loan, that obligor will usually be able to assert any usury claim. In addition, sometimes the reason that a guarantor lacks standing is that a statute denies the protections of the state's usury laws to corporations, and the court extends this statute to guarantors of a corporate debt.[298] This rationale will not apply to the guarantor of a non-corporate debt.

Furthermore, a few usury statutes specifically extend to guarantors or sureties on consumer credit contracts.[299] Finally, there is some precedent for finding parties that are liable on consumer debt to be obligors rather than guarantors when doubt about their status exists.[300]

Some statutes absolutely bar the lender from recovering any interest if the loan is usurious. Even if a guarantor does not have standing to assert an affirmative claim for usury remedies, this language may allow the guarantor to prevent the lender from recovering the usurious interest.[301]

N.Y.S.2d 860 (1966), *aff'd*, 282 N.Y.S.2d 450 (N.Y. App. Div. 1967); Micrea Inc. v. Eureka Life Ins. Co., 534 S.W.2d 348 (Tex. Ct. App. 1976); Allied Supplier & Erection Inc. v. A. Baldwin & Co., 688 S.W.2d 156 (Tex. App. 1985). *Cf.* Raceway Props., L.L.C. v. LSOF Carlsbad Land L.P., 157 Fed. Appx. 959 (9th Cir. 2005) (unpublished) (California statutory law limits the sophisticated borrower exception to usury to cases where there are no individual guarantors).

296 *See also* § 3.9.2.3, *supra* (sham corporate loans).

297 *See* Colonial Acceptance Corp. v. Northeastern Printcrafters, 330 S.E.2d 76 (N.C. Ct. App. 1985). *See also* Dahmes v. Industrial Credit Co., 110 N.W.2d 484 (Minn. 1961).

298 *See, e.g.*, Colonial Acceptance Corp. v. Northeastern Printcrafters, 330 S.E.2d 76 (N.C. Ct. App. 1985).

299 *See* 69 Pa. Cons. Stat. Ann § 603(3) (motor vehicle sales).

300 *See* Ciminelli v. Ford Motor Credit Corp., 624 S.W.2d 903 (Tex. 1981).

301 Washburn v. Makedonsky, 718 N.W.2d 842 (Mich. Ct. App. 2006).

### 7.7.1.3 Assignees

Another party whose standing to assert usury may be questioned is the assignee of a credit buyer—i.e., the person who purchases used goods and who, in so doing, assumes the original buyer's rights and obligations under the original credit contract. While borrowers who have paid usurious interest do not lose their right to recover the penalty by assigning their interest in the contract to a third party,[302] several courts have held that usury claims may not be assigned.[303] The reasoning is that the assignee should not be able to step into the assignor's shoes and reap a windfall through a usury claim.

Although denying usury claims to assignees might make sense if the assignment were viewed as a form of champerty, denying usury claims can lead to hardship for an innocent consumer who, instead of arranging his own financing, simply assumes the payments of the previous owner, only to discover later that the payments are usurious. Such arrangements invariably require the permission of the creditor, and the failure of a court to recognize a new extension of credit, from the original creditor to the new owner, that would give the new owner standing to assert usury, seems unnecessarily narrow-minded. Nevertheless, this is the position taken by some courts.[304]

Other courts, however, have developed somewhat more evenhanded rules. A New York decision, for example, allowed an assignee to claim usury after tendering the principal and legal interest to the creditor.[305] Another New York decision held that

302 Mangold v. Wilson, 695 F. Supp. 841 (D. V.I. 1988).

303 *See* Eposti v. Rivers Bros. Inc., 279 P. 423 (Cal. 1929); General Elec. Credit Corp. v. Best Refrigerated Express, Inc. 385 N.W.2d 81 (Neb. 1986); Radner v. Burnett, 122 N.W.2d 747 (Neb. 1963); Smart v. Crawford Bldg. Material Co., 638 S.W.2d 228 (Tex. App. 1982). *See also* Lenart v. Ragsdale, 385 N.W.2d 282 (Mich. Ct. App. 1986) (an undisclosed principal may raise usury but not an assignee); Moore v. Plaza Commercial Corp., 192 N.Y.S.2d 770 (N.Y. App. Div. 1959), *aff'd*, 168 N.E.2d 390 (N.Y. 1960) (restrictions on assignee standing); Snodgrass v. Sisson's Mobile Home Sales, Inc., 244 S.E.2d 321 (W. Va. 1978) (action to collect a statutory penalty generally not assignable in absence of statute allowing assignment). *Cf.* Demopolis v. Galvin, 786 P.2d 804 (Wash. Ct. App. 1990) (one who purchases encumbered property from original borrower but does not assume liability on underlying note is not in privity and cannot assert usury; one exception is where original debtor joins in the claim or gives purchaser permission to pursue it).

304 *See* General Elec. Credit Corp. v. Best Refrigerated Express, Inc., 385 N.W.2d 81 (Neb. 1986). *See also* Nesbitt v. Citicorp Sav. of Florida, 514 So. 2d 371 (Fla. Dist. Ct. App. 1987) (denying standing to subsequent property owners who apparently assumed mortgage).

305 Moore v. Plaza Commercial Corp., 192 N.Y.S.2d 770 (N.Y. App. Div. 1959), *aff'd*, 168 N.E.2d 390 (N.Y. 1960). *See also* Benser v. Independence Bank, 735 S.W.2d 566 (Tex. App. 1987) (suggesting in dicta that one in privity with the borrower may have a right to challenge a usurious contract if claim is derived from the borrower's right); Demopolis v. Galvin, 786 P.2d 804 (Wash. Ct. App. 1990) (one who purchases encumbered property from original borrower but does not assume liability on underlying note is not in privity and cannot assert usury, but there is an exception is where original debtor joins in the claim or gives purchaser permission to pursue it; original borrower's assignment to subsequent purchaser of "all causes of action arising from the loans" was ineffective as to

parties who bought real estate that was subject to a usurious loan could assert the usury claim, where the original agreement contemplated that the real estate would be transferred to them.[306] A Rhode Island case permitted assignment of a usury claim from the borrower to the trustee of a bankrupt corporation.[307] The court thought it was relevant that funds from the bankrupt corporation had been used to make payments on the loan and that the original purpose of the loan was the acquisition of the corporation. Finally, some retail installment sales acts extend to a buyer's legal successors in interest and therefore should protect a buyer who assumes another buyer's installment sale contract.[308]

#### 7.7.1.4 Other Standing Issues

One case holds that a borrower seeking an affirmative usury remedy under section 86 of the National Bank Act does not have standing unless she paid the challenged charges.[309] This issue is usually analyzed in terms of whether one of the necessary elements of a prima facie usury claim has been met, rather than as a standing question, however.[310]

Standing issues can affect those not obligated on the debt, as well. Junior lienholders seeking to void a senior lien may run afoul of the general rule that only immediate parties to the transaction may raise usury.[311] Texas courts have distinguished between assertion of a statutory usury penalty and assertion of a common law usury claim that the principal indebtedness should be reduced by the payments of usurious interest, and have allowed junior lienholders to assert the latter claim.[312]

A title insurer was permitted to use usury to deny coverage on its policy to the overcharging lender on the theory that the lender does not have an insurable interest if the underlying transaction is usurious.[313] A Maryland appellate court rejected the use of the juridical link doctrine as a way of allowing class action plaintiffs to sue lenders with whom they had not contracted, but who had made loans similar to those made by the plaintiffs' lenders.[314] A federal court has held that California's Unfair Competition Law does not give a loan guarantor standing to assert violations of the FDIC's safety and soundness regulations, regarding real estate lending, as a defense to a debt collection action.[315]

## 7.7.2 Estoppel and Waiver

#### 7.7.2.1 Overview

Estoppel is a loosely defined equitable doctrine under which a party may be barred from asserting legal or factual claims in court for any one of numerous reasons including fraud, misrepresentation, previous judicial rulings (i.e., "collateral estoppel"), or waiver. In what is probably the most common application of the doctrine in usury cases, a party may be estopped from denying the truth of facts that it previously asserted, if the party seeking the estoppel reasonably relied, to its detriment, on the earlier assertion.[316] So, for example, lenders may seek to estop borrowers from claiming usury because of various real or supposed misrepresentations made by the borrower in obtaining the disputed loan.[317] However, a review of the relevant decisions demonstrates that the doctrine is inapplicable to most consumer usury cases.

#### 7.7.2.2 Borrower's Knowledge

The most common reason for estoppel asserted by lenders is that the borrower knew that the terms of the loan were usurious at the time of the transaction and induced the lender to issue a loan that the borrower knew would not have to be repaid. In fact, there are cases involving inexperienced individuals lending money to street-wise small businessmen where usury claims

statutory usury claims because damages were penal and therefore not assignable, but was effective as to common law usury claim, which is remedial and therefore assignable).

306 Seidel v. 18 East 17th St. Owners, Inc., 598 N.E.2d 7 (N.Y. 1992).

307 Sheehan v. Richardson, 315 B.R. 226 (D.R.I. 2004) (trustee has standing to pursue assigned claim), *aff'd*, 185 Fed. Appx. 11 (1st Cir. 2006).

308 *See* 69 Pa. Cons. Stat. Ann. § 603(3) (motor vehicle sales).

309 Ament v. PNC Nat'l Bank, 849 F. Supp. 1015 (W.D. Pa. 1994), *aff'd without op. sub nom.* Deffner v. Corestates Bank, 92 F.3d 1170 (3d Cir. 1996).

310 *See* § 7.5.4.2, *supra*.

311 LHC Corp. v. Primecap Mortgage Fund, 2008 WL 2447739 (Ariz. Ct. App. June 12, 2008). *See also* Henslee v. Madison Guar. Sav. & Loan, 760 S.W.2d 842 (Ark. 1988) (discussing impact of change in usury penalties on statute permitting rival lienholder to gain priority when other lienholder's rights are tainted by usury).

312 Allee v. Benser, 779 S.W.2d 61 (Tex. 1988).

313 Focus Invs. Ass'n, Inc. v. American Title Ins. Co., 992 F.2d 1231 (1st Cir. 1993) (Rhode Island law).

314 Master Fin., Inc. v. Crowder, 972 A.2d 864, 877–881 (Md. 2009).

315 Intervest Mortgage Inv. Co. v. Skidmore, 632 F. Supp. 2d 1005 (E.D. Cal. 2009).

316 The precise statement of the rule varies from court to court. *See* First State Bank of Bedford v. Miller, 551 S.W.2d 89 (Tex. Ct. App. 1977), *modified on other grounds and aff'd as modified*, 563 S.W.2d 572 (Tex. 1978) (elements of estoppel are (1) false representation or concealment of material fact, (2) made with knowledge of facts, (3) to person ignorant of truth, (4) with intent that innocent person rely, and (5) person induced to act by false representation). *See also* Rieser v. Todd (*In re* Chari), 2005 WL 4030034 (Bankr. S.D. Ohio Sept. 2, 2005); Cook v. Frazier, 765 S.W.2d 546 (Tex. App. 1989) (borrowers relying on contract for six years and claiming interest as tax deduction until IRS disallowed did not estop usury claims; only if lender deceived by borrower can it claim estoppel). *Cf.* Perlman v. First Nat'l Bank, 305 N.E.2d 236 (Ill. App. Ct. 1973) (bank overcharges) (statement or conduct must cause another to do something he would not have done but for statements or conduct, and person relying on statement or conduct had no knowledge or convenient means of knowing true facts); Murphy v. Hagan, 271 S.E.2d 311 (S.C. 1980) (party asserting estoppel must show lack of knowledge and means of knowing true facts, and detrimental reliance upon conduct of party asserting usury).

317 *See, e.g.*, Rieser v. Todd (*In re* Chari), 2005 WL 4030034 (Bankr. S.D. Ohio Sept. 2, 2005) (borrower estopped from asserting usury where he misrepresented encumbrances on property securing loan, lender provided loan based on misrepresentation, and documents were primarily drafted by borrower's agents).

have been estopped on precisely those grounds.[318] Thus, there is a line of cases holding that in some unusual circumstances a borrower who initiates the usurious aspects of the transaction is then estopped from raising usury as a defense.[319]

Yet such circumstances are the exception. Most lenders are in the business of lending money. They know or can find out what the usury laws are, and they do not rely on any representation of the borrower that the contract is legal.[320] The courts have widely ruled that no estoppel against usury can exist when the lender knew or should have known what the usury law was, even though the borrower was also aware of the usury.[321]

318 *See* Holt v. Rickett, 238 S.E.2d 706 (Ga. Ct. App. 1974); Broaddus v. National Bank of Lancaster, 709 S.W.2d 461 (Ky. Ct. App. 1986) (professional banker with expertise in commercial transactions estopped from asserting usury); Olson v. Froslee, 2000 WL 1052007 (Minn. Ct. App. Aug. 1, 2000) (recognizing estoppel defense if borrower knows of usury, but finding it not shown here); LaBarre v. Gold, 520 So. 2d 1327 (Miss. 1988) (invoking estoppel in context of Byzantine set of facts); Angelo v. Brenner, 457 N.Y.S.2d 630 (N.Y. App. Div. 1982) (estoppel is issue of fact precluding summary judgment); Schylander v. Tsaruchas, 409 N.Y.S.2d 932 (N.Y. City Civ. Ct. 1978); Gilbert v. Otterson, 550 A.2d 550 (Pa. Super. Ct. 1988) (where employer borrowed money from employee, the documents were prepared by borrower-employer's attorney, and borrower may have suggested the interest rate, estoppel was a permissible defense to the treble damage claim for violation of usury statute); Liebergesell v. Evans, 613 P.2d 1170 (Wash. 1980). *Cf.* Gillivan v. Austin, 640 F. Supp. 1325 (D. V.I. 1986) (estoppel appeared appropriate but could not be raised as defense by court *sua sponte*).

319 *Borrower estopped*: Massie v. Rubin, 270 F.2d 60 (10th Cir. 1959) (attorney who obtained money by drafting transaction in form of trust but which may have been loan at usurious interest could be estopped from raising usury defense); Holden v. Nevergall, 526 N.E.2d 928 (Ill. App. Ct. 1988) (daughter who insisted on usurious rate of interest when borrowing money from parents was estopped from raising usury defense and note was enforceable according to its terms); Cohn v. Receivables Fin. Co., 260 N.E.2d 67 (Ill. App. Ct. 1970) (where attorney borrowed money from client, prepared the loan documents and made payments for twenty-five years, he was estopped from asserting usury); Russo v. Carey, 706 N.Y.S.2d 760 (N.Y. App. Div. 2000) (lender could raise defense of estoppel where he and borrower were friends, borrower prepared note and set interest rate, and some evidence suggested that borrower deliberately inserted usurious interest rate to avoid repayment); Abramovitz v. Kew Realty Equities, Inc., 580 N.Y.S.2d 269 (N.Y. App. Div. 1992) (experienced and sophisticated businessmen who induced a friend to loan them money as an investment and knowingly prepared loan documents with usurious rates were estopped from asserting usury as a defense); Berry v. Martens, 58 Va. Cir. 315 (2002) (borrower who proposed the interest rate is estopped from claiming usury). *See also* Keezing v. Rodriguez, 765 N.Y.S.2d 196 (N.Y. Sup. Ct. 2003) (reducing interest to legal rate but refusing to void loan when debtor initiated and structured the transaction and prepared the documents).

*Borrower not estopped*: Hufnagel v. George, 135 F. Supp. 2d 406 (S.D.N.Y. 2001) (no estoppel without special relationship, which is limited to attorney-client, fiduciary, trustee, or long-standing relationship or its equivalent; borrower's suggestion of interest rate is not a defense); Hornblower & Weeks, Inc. v. Blue Marlin Breweries, Inc., 2000 WL 1371329 (S.D.N.Y. Sept. 22, 2000) (borrower not estopped from raising criminal usury as defense even if it knew loan was usurious and its agent prepared documents), *aff'd without op.*, 2003 WL 21369246 (2d Cir. June 10, 2003); Mangold v. Wilson, 695 F. Supp. 841 (D. V.I. 1988) (estoppel unavailable if lender was represented by counsel who reviewed the agreement); *In re* Perry, 425 B.R. 323, 374–376 (Bankr. S.D. Tex. 2010) (borrower obtained and gave lender two opinion letters that loans were not usurious, but no estoppel in absence of evidence that borrower intended to disavow these opinions later); *In re* Venture Mortgage Fund, 245 B.R. 460 (Bankr. S.D.N.Y. 2000) (lender must show special relationship with borrower, a representation by borrower that the transaction is legal, intent to induce reliance, actual reliance, and injury; not shown here), *aff'd on other grounds*, 282 F.3d 185 (2d Cir. 2002); Van Carr Enters. v. Hamco, Inc., 232 S.W.3d 427 (Ark. 2006) (debtor's transcription of the loan agreement is insufficient basis for estoppel); McElroy v. Grisham, 810 S.W.2d 933 (Ark. 1991) (borrower in dire financial straits who proposed deed with option to purchase as means of obtaining temporary financial relief was not estopped from asserting usury; creditors were aware of his situation and received an unfair advantage from it); Commercial Mtg. & Fin. Co. v. Life Savs. of Am., 541 N.E.2d 661 (Ill. 1989) (where creditor initiated idea of having borrower sign false business purpose affidavit and borrower cooperated, borrower was not estopped from asserting usury; noting distinction between borrower initiating transaction, which is virtually always the case, and borrower initiating the usurious terms); Lane v. Fabert, 533 N.E.2d 546 (Ill. App. Ct. 1989) (rejecting pawnbroker's argument that customer was estopped from asserting usury because she initiated the pawn transaction, where she did not suggest a usurious rate, but merely initiated the transaction and paid the pawnbroker's going rate); Seidel v. 18 East 17th Street Owners, Inc., 598 N.E.2d 7 (N.Y. 1992) (no estoppel where lender did not detrimentally rely on borrower's representation); Funding Group, Inc. v. Water Chef, Inc., 852 N.Y.S.2d 736 (N.Y. Sup. Ct. 2008) (no estoppel in absence of special relationship with lender, even if borrower suggested the interest rate); Marashi v. Lannen, 780 P.2d 1341 (Wash. Ct. App. 1989) (borrowers not estopped from asserting usury by their certificate stating business purpose in general, conclusory language; lender told borrowers that certificate was "just a formality" and did not explain its significance). *See also* Lenart v. Ragsdale, 385 N.W.2d 282 (Mich. Ct. App. 1986) (failure to raise usury defense for thirteen years does not estop borrower; no lender reliance); Lucas v. Beco Homes, Inc., 494 S.W.2d 417 (Mo. Ct. App. 1973) (no estoppel when debtor paid installments for two years; no reliance or prejudice); Seidel v. 18 East 17th St. Owners, 598 N.E.2d 7 (N.Y. 1992) (essential element of estoppel is that conduct or representation was intended to and did influence the other party to his or her injury; not established in this case); Dunnam v. Burns, 901 S.W.2d 628 (Tex. App. 1995) (if there is an absolute obligation to pay, usury law is not concerned with which party might have originated the usurious terms; though borrower had drafted the document, creditor agreed to receive usurious interest). *Cf.* Watkins v. Mississippi Bar, 589 So. 2d 660 (Miss. 1991) (reversing state bar's reprimand of attorney who, as a borrower, proposed to pay usurious interest on loan from an individual; borrower does not break the law by agreeing to pay usurious interest, and he had not "practiced deceit" by entering into an unenforceable contract, since he had never raised usury as a defense to his debt). *See generally* 47 C.J.S. *Interest and Usury* § 207, at 351–352.

320 Brodie v. Schmutz (*In re* Venture Mortgage Fund), 282 F.3d 185 (2d Cir. 2002) (estoppel not shown because no special relationship and no reliance); *In re* King, 68 B.R. 569 (Bankr. D. Minn. 1986) (holding loan usurious where lender failed to show reliance on borrower's misrepresentations of loan purpose).

321 *See, e.g., In re* General Am. Communications Corp., 63 B.R. 534 (Bankr. S.D.N.Y. 1986); *In re* Seisay, 61 B.R. 940 (Bankr. S.D.N.Y. 1986), *aff'd*, 1986 WL 2826 (S.D.N.Y. Feb. 28, 1986); LaBarr v. Tombstone Territorial Mint, 580 P.2d 744 (Ariz. Ct. App.), *adopted*,

Indeed, this position is the only one that can uphold the fundamental purpose of usury statutes—that of protecting desperate "borrowers 'driven to borrow money at any cost.' "[322] If courts estopped usury claims merely because the borrower knew of the usury, any lender could evade the usury statutes simply by informing the borrower of the usury at the time of the transaction.[323]

California's corporation code excludes some commercial loans from usury if the borrower could "reasonably be expected to protect [its] own interests," thus, in some contexts creating a "sophisticated borrower" exception from usury.[324] However, the California Supreme Court held that there was no sophisticated borrower exemption to the usury prohibition in the state constitution.[325]

### 7.7.2.3 False Contractual Statements

A second situation in which creditors raise estoppel as a usury defense centers upon contract clauses through which the borrower purportedly attests to the existence of facts which may exclude the transaction from the scope of usury statutes. For example, a loan contract executed in a jurisdiction that does not regulate interest rates on business loans may state that the borrower intends to use the loan proceeds for business purposes. Lenders have claimed that such a clause estops the borrower from asserting that the transaction was actually a personal loan at a usurious interest rate.

As with cases involving the borrower's knowledge of the usury, courts have occasionally estopped usury claims because of a borrower's contractual misrepresentations of fact, but they have done so only after examining the substance of the transaction. For example, one court sustained a "business loan" usury defense after observing that the borrower had apparently made repeated representations of his business purposes to the lender, and that nothing in the record suggested that the lender knew otherwise.[326]

It is, of course, possible to quarrel with a court's factual findings regarding the "voluntary" action of a debtor who signs a paper acknowledging a fictitious business purpose. The important point, however, is that even courts that invoke estoppel because of a borrower's misrepresentations do so only after looking at the facts of the case. This approach is entirely appropriate both because of the equitable nature of estoppel, and because of the widely recognized need to foil any legal artifice that is designed to evade usury statutes.[327] A court will not estop a borrower from asserting usury simply because a contract states some "agreed" fact which, if true, would preclude a usury claim.[328] Moreover, in examining the facts behind allegedly false contractual statements of business purpose, courts have often found the disputed loans to be personal in nature and have given no effect to the clearly adhesive statements of loan purpose.[329] If the lender induced the borrower to make the false

---

582 P.2d 639 (Ariz. 1978) (en banc); McIlroy Bank & Trust v. Seven Day Builders, 613 S.W.2d 837 (Ark. Ct. App. 1981); Bjornstad v. Perry, 443 P.2d 999 (Idaho 1968); Gudgel v. Kaelin, 551 S.W.2d 803 (Ky. Ct. App. 1977); Murphy v. Hagan, 271 S.E.2d 311 (S.C. 1980); First State Bank of Bedford v. Miller, 563 S.W.2d 572 (Tex. 1978); Arguelles v. Kaplan, 736 S.W.2d 782 (Tex. App. 1987) (no estoppel where debtor's attorney prepared note; creditor was attorney who could have easily discovered what applicable rate ceiling was). *See also* Marashi v. Lannen, 780 P.2d 1341 (Wash. Ct. App. 1989) (party claiming estoppel must show justified reliance on business purpose certification and thus cannot have known or had means to know true purpose; knowledge of lender's agent is imputed to lender and will defeat estoppel claim). *See generally* Annotation, *Borrower's Initiation of or Fraud Contributing to Usurious Transaction As Affecting Rights or Remedies of the Parties,* 16 A.L.R.3d 510 (1967).

322 Demopolis v. Galvin, 786 P.2d 804, 807 (Wash. Ct. App. 1990). *See also* Schneider v. Phelps, 359 N.E.2d 1361, 1365 (N.Y. App. Div. 1977) ("The purpose of usury laws, from time immemorial, has been to protect desperately poor people from the consequences of their own desperation. Law-making authorities in almost all civilizations have recognized that the crush of financial burdens causes people to agree to almost any conditions of the lender and to consent to even the most improvident loans. Lenders, with the money, have all the leverage; borrowers, in dire need of money have none."); Whitworth & Yancy v. Adams, 5 Rand 333, 335, 26 Va. 333 (1827) ("These statutes were made to protect needy and necessitous persons from the oppression of usurers and monied men, who are eager to take advantage of the distress of others; while they, on the other hand, from the pressure of their distress, are ready to come to any terms; and with their eyes open, not only break the law, but complete their ruin."). *See generally* § 7.2, *supra.*

323 *See* Gudgel v. Kaelin, 551 S.W.2d 803 (Ky. Ct. App. 1977) (invoking estoppel even when a lender knows of usury would enable lenders to circumvent usury laws); *In re* Estate of Dane, 390 N.Y.S.2d 249 (N.Y. App. Div. 1976) (if usury law did not apply when the borrower set the interest rate, lenders would avoid usury by requiring the borrower to set the rate).

324 *See* Raceway Props., L.L.C. v. LSOF Carlsbad Land L.P., 157 Fed. Appx. 959 (9th Cir. 2005) (unpublished).

325 Ghirardo v. Antonioli, 883 P.2d 960 (Cal. 1994) (creditor prevailed on other grounds).

326 Conrad v. Smith, 712 P.2d 866 (Wash. Ct. App. 1986). *See also* Ross v. Lake City Equity Fin. Co., 425 F.2d 1 (7th Cir. 1970) (affirming summary judgment for lender where borrower's summary judgment materials did not dispute the facts in the business purpose affidavit); Anglin v. J&G Assocs., Consumer Cred. Guide (CCH) ¶ 96,677 (D.D.C. 1983) (applying estoppel to preclude borrower from denying the business purpose of a loan after signing an affidavit voluntarily and without duress or undue influence).

327 § 3.9.1, *supra.*

328 *See* Sheffield Commercial Corp. v. Clemente, 792 F.2d 282 (2d Cir. 1986) (protections of Motor Vehicle Retail Installment Sales Act are non-waivable, so business purpose clause has no effect; fact question whether consumer had business purpose); Metcoff v. Mutual Trust Life Ins. Co., 339 N.E.2d 440 (Ill. App. Ct. 1975) (letter from borrower to land trustee contains statement of business purpose, but no estoppel because statement not made to lender, no reliance was present, and no detail was given about the purported business); Allan v. M&S Mortgage Co., 359 N.W.2d 238 (Mich. Ct. App. 1984) (reversing summary judgment); Hammelburger v. Foursome Inn Corp., 431 N.E.2d 278 (N.Y. 1980) (estoppel certificate invalid if signed under duress; remanding for factual determination).

329 *See, e.g., In re* Seisay, 49 B.R. 354 (S.D.N.Y. 1985), *aff'd,* 1986 WL 2826 (S.D.N.Y. Feb. 28, 1986), *later op. at* 61 B.R. 940 (Bankr. S.D.N.Y. 1986); Sun Bank v. Spigrin, 469 So. 2d. 240 (Fla. Dist. Ct. App. 1985) (sham incorporation); Gelber v. Kugel's Tavern, Inc., 89 A.2d 654 (N.J. 1952) (no estoppel when no evidence that borrower knew purpose of incorporation); Marashi v. Lannen, 780 P.2d 1341

statement, or knew or had reason to know the truth, it is unlikely to be able to make out a claim of estoppel.[330]

### 7.7.2.4 Waiver

A lender defense related to estoppel is the claim that the borrower has waived the right to assert usury. A waiver is a knowing surrender of legal rights. It is possible for a borrower to waive a usury claim, for example, through a settlement agreement, negotiated at arm's length.[331] A usury claim may also be waived by failing to raise it in litigation.[332] However, it is not possible for the borrower to waive a usury defense through a provision in the usurious contract or related documents.[333] The reason for this restriction is obvious: if usury claims could be waived in this manner, all credit contracts would contain waiver provisions, and usury laws would be rendered meaningless.

A more difficult question regarding the waiver of usury defense occurs when usurious credit agreements are renewed or refinanced at non-usurious rates. Creditors have argued that such renewals constitute waivers or settlements of any usury claims which arose from the original agreement. The merits of this argument are discussed at § 7.8.4, *infra*. Similarly, a creditor may argue that participating in workout arrangements and delaying in filing suit is a waiver. However, that is not evidence of a waiver of a known right.[334] On the other hand, if the obligation is voluntarily satisfied without renewal or refinancing, the borrower may be held to have waived a usury defense, thus defeating a claim for restitution.[335]

## 7.7.3 Res Judicata

Closely related to the defense of equitable estoppel is the doctrine of res judicata, which prohibits the relitigation of issues previously decided by the courts. Essentially, a judgment

---

(Wash. Ct. App. 1989) (borrowers' certificate stating business purpose in general, conclusory language was not dispositive; lender told borrowers that certificate was "just a formality" and did not explain its significance). *See generally* § 3.9.2.3, *supra* (sham incorporation).

330 Marketic v. U.S. Bank, 436 F. Supp. 2d 842, 853 (N.D. Tex. 2006) (no estoppel if lender had means of knowing the truth); Kredietbank N.V. v. E.S.I.C. Capital Corp. (*In re* Rosner), 48 B.R. 538, 549–550 (Bankr. E.D.N.Y. 1985) (borrower's fulfillment of condition of the loan, which required letter from borrower's attorney stating the loan was legal, does not create estoppel); Commercial Mortgage & Fin. Co. v. Life Saving of Am., 541 N.E.2d 661 (Ill. 1989) (creditor could not claim estoppel where it had suggested to borrower that loan be falsely characterized as having business purpose). *See generally* §§ 3.9.1, 3.9.2.3, *supra*.

331 *See, e.g.*, Gunn Plumbing, Inc. v. Dania Bank, 252 So. 2d. 1 (Fla. 1971); Blanco v. Kinas, 936 So. 2d 31 (Fla. Dist. Ct. App. 2006) (agreement settling litigation is effective waiver of usury); Thompson v. First Nat'l Bank, 300 S.E.2d 529 (Ga. Ct. App. 1983); Bokum v. First Nat'l Bank in Albuquerque, 740 P.2d 693 (N.M. 1987) (accord and satisfaction agreement between bank and sophisticated, experienced businessman-borrower who was represented by counsel purged previous series of refinanced loans of usury); Biggs v. ABCO Props., Inc., 2006 WL 414919 (Tex. App. Feb. 23, 2006) (giving effect to waiver of usury claims as part of agreement that settled lawsuit); Vordenbaum v. Rubin, 611 S.W.2d 463 (Tex. Civ. App. 1980); Dunbabin v. Brandenfels, 566 P.2d 941 (Wash. Ct. App. 1977). *See also* Higgins v. Erickson (*In re* Higgins), 270 B.R. 147 (Bankr. S.D.N.Y. 2001) (borrowers waived usury defense by signing confession of judgment after default). *But cf. In re* Vehm Eng'g, 521 F.2d 186 (9th Cir. 1975) (narrow construction of release; usury claim not waived); *In re* Giorgio, 62 B.R. 853 (Bankr. D.R.I. 1986) (settlement binds debtor but does not later bind debtor's trustee in bankruptcy); Aspeitia v. California Trust Co., 322 P.2d 265 (Cal. Ct. App. 1958) (statement purporting to waive claims and defenses was not compromise or settlement of borrowers' usury claim, but was renewal of original agreement to pay debt); Victoria Bank & Trust Co. v. Brady, 779 S.W.2d 893 (Tex. App. 1989) (upholding jury's finding that release was invalid on various grounds, including borrower's ignorance of usury claim and failure of consideration), *aff'd in part and rev'd in part on other grounds*, 811 S.W.2d 931 (Tex. 1991) (finding no usury, but holding release ineffective as to borrower's other claims).

332 REG, Inc. v. Rayho, 2000 WL 1218423 (Neb. Ct. App. Aug. 29, 2000); Holdgate v. Acton, 764 A.2d 187 (R.I. 2000). *Cf.* Van Carr Enters. v. Hamco, Inc., 232 S.W.3d 427 (Ark. 2006) (usury not waived by requesting specific performance of contract in same suit; relying on fact that in Arkansas only the excess interest was void, not the entire contract).

333 *See, e.g.*, Aaron v. Mattikow, 146 F. Supp. 2d 263 (E.D.N.Y. 2001) (giving effect to contractual waiver would run counter to court's duty to uncover true nature of transaction), *aff'd*, 2003 WL 1973357 (2d Cir. Apr. 22, 2003); Kredietbank N.V. v. E.S.I.C. Capital Corp. (*In re* Rosner), 48 B.R. 538 (Bankr. E.D.N.Y. 1985) (no estoppel when lender requires letter from borrower's attorney stating that contract is legal); Transworld Telecomms., Inc. v. Pacific Mezzanine Fund, Inc. (*In re* Transworld Telecommunications, Inc.), 260 B.R. 204 (Bankr. D. Utah 2000), *rev'd and remanded on other grounds*, 309 F.3d 744 (10th Cir. 2002) (indemnification and limitation of liability provisions in loan contract are ineffective); LaBarr v. Tombstone Territorial Mint, 580 P.2d 744 (Ariz. Ct. App. 1978), *adopted* 582 P.2d 639 (Ariz. 1978) (usury cannot be waived at inception of loan, and making payments on usurious loan does not constitute waiver); WRI Opportunity Loans II L.L.C. v. Cooper, 65 Cal. Rptr. 3d 205 (Cal. Ct. App. 2007) (guarantor may not waive usury); HIMC Inv. Co. v. Siciliano, 246 A.2d 502 (N.J. Super. Ct. Law Div. 1968) (waiver provision is contrary to public policy as expressed in second mortgage statute and has no effect even if borrowers signed with full knowledge of contract provisions and with intent to be bound by them). *See also* Sheffield Commercial Corp. v. Clemente, 792 F.2d 282 (2d Cir. 1986) (express statutory prohibition of waivers).

334 El Paso Dev. Co. v. Berryman, 769 S.W.2d 584 (Tex. App. 1989) (waiver is intentional relinquishment of known right or intentional conduct inconsistent with claiming it; borrower's delay in filing suit and executing reinstatement agreements and modifications not evidence of waiver where borrower appeared to simply be foregoing claim as long as creditor was working with him, and he pursued claim only when foreclosure imminent).

335 *See, e.g.,* Thelen v. Ducharme, 390 N.W.2d 264 (Mich. Ct. App. 1986) (holding, however, that payment after judgment was rendered on note is not a voluntary payment, therefore usury defense was not waived). *Cf. In re* Estate of Backofen, 404 N.W.2d 675 (Mich. Ct. App. 1987) (usury defense not waived here; waived only to extent usurious interest is voluntarily repaid); § 7.8.2.3, *infra*. *But cf.* Hardwick v. Austin Gallery of Oriental Rugs, Inc., 779 S.W.2d 438 (Tex. App. 1989) (stating common law rule that voluntary payment of usury can be recovered and granting such recovery in addition to statutory usury penalty of three times the usurious interest charged; borrower here, however, made payments out of necessity to free property of lien so that it could be sold).

estops the parties to that judgment, outside of the normal appeals process, from continuing to contest any issues decided by the judgment. Judicial settlements, if negotiated at arm's length, may constitute a similar bar although technically they may operate as a release or waiver rather than res judicata.[336]

In most states, a borrower may assert usury either as a defense to the lender's collection or foreclosure action or as an independent cause of action for statutory penalties. (While the independent cause of action is typically brought as a counterclaim to the lender's action on the debt, it can also be brought separately, in the absence of any lender action.) Borrowers who fail to raise the defense of usury in a lender's action may argue that, while they have forfeited their usury *defense*,[337] they retain the right to bring an *action* for statutory usury forfeitures or penalties. Lenders, on the other hand, argue that the original judgment precludes any subsequent usury action because it inherently affirms the validity of the debt and therefore the absence of usury. The question is whether the usury counterclaim which the borrowers could have brought in response to the lender's action is a compulsory counterclaim, which is forfeited if not asserted, or a permissive counterclaim, which may be asserted subsequently.

As a general rule, a defendant who could raise a claim as a counterclaim, but who fails to do so, is precluded from raising that claim subsequently in two situations: (1) the counterclaim is required to be imposed by a compulsory counterclaim statute or rule of court; or (2) the relationship between the counterclaim and the plaintiff's claim is such that the successful prosecution of the second action would nullify the initial judgment or would impair rights established in the initial action.[338] Compulsory counterclaim statutes, to the extent that they exist, vary significantly from state to state and are not thoroughly treated here. Nevertheless, it is worth noting that Federal Rule of Civil Procedure 13 makes counterclaims compulsory, with some exceptions, if they arise out of the transaction or occurrence that is the subject matter of the opposing party's claim, and if they do not require for their adjudication the presence of third parties over whom the court cannot obtain jurisdiction. This rule arguably makes usury a compulsory counterclaim to an action on a note.[339]

In the absence of a controlling compulsory counterclaim statute, most decisions hold that a judgment for a creditor in a foreclosure action or an action on a note necessarily affirms the validity of a debt and would be undermined if subsequent usury claims were permitted. Consequently, usury is generally barred by res judicata if not asserted when a creditor's action on a debt is litigated.[340] Some authority to the contrary does exist, but much of it seems questionable in light of its age, later case law, or special circumstances.[341]

Despite the prevailing view that a judgment on a debt, whether directly or through a foreclosure action, bars a subsequent usury action on the same debt, practitioners should be careful in defining exactly what that "same debt" is. When a debtor and creditor have executed a series of notes, several courts have held that a judgment on one note need not preclude the assertion of usury against the remaining notes,[342] even if they are only extensions of the note on which judgment had been given.[343]

Federal courts must not only give the same preclusive effect to a state court judgment as the judgment would be given in courts of the state that rendered it, but also lack jurisdiction to review state court judgments.[344] Thus, a federal court lacked jurisdiction to order a creditor to petition to amend state court judgments to delete usurious post-judgment interest.[345]

Whether a potential usury defense is a basis for reopening a default judgment is a separate question. New York courts find usury to be a "meritorious defense" which may justify the reopening of a default judgment.[346] On the other hand, Georgia courts have limited attempts to reopen judgments on the basis of usury because, under Georgia law, a judgment will not be set

336 *See* § 7.7.2, *supra*.

337 *See, e.g.*, Federal Deposit Ins. Corp. v. Ramirez-Rivera, 869 F.2d 624 (1st Cir. 1989).

338 Restatement (Second) of Judgments § 22 (1982). *See also* Circle v. Jim Walter Homes, 654 F.2d 688 (10th Cir. 1981).

339 *Cf.* John R. Alley & Co. v. Federal Nat'l Bank of Shawnee, 124 F.2d 995 (10th Cir. 1942).

340 *See, e.g.*, Circle v. Jim Walter Homes, 654 F.2d 688 (10th Cir. 1981); Andrews v. Reidy, 60 P.2d 832 (Cal. 1936); Madden v. Harlandale Bank, 574 SW.2d 590 (Tex. Ct. App. 1978). *See also* Fielder v. Credit Acceptance Corp., 188 F.3d 1031 (8th Cir. 1999) (claim that state court judgments included impermissible post-judgment interest cannot be raised in federal court because it is inextricably intertwined with claims adjudicated in state court). *See generally*, Annotation, *Judgment As Res Judicata of Usury Notwithstanding Question As to Usury Not Raised,* 98 A.L.R. 1027 (1935).

341 *See* Flint v. Kimbrough, 115 P.2d 84 (N.M. 1941) (court in the underlying foreclosure action had not obtained personal jurisdiction over the borrower); Murphy v. Fidelity Inv. Co., 17 P.2d 472 (Okla. 1932); Weaver v. White, 164 S.W.2d 48 (Tex. Civ. App. 1942) (questionable authority after Madden v. Harlandale Bank, 574 S.W.2d 590 (Tex. Civ. App. 1978)); McDonald v. Smith, 53 Vt. 33 (1880).

342 *See* Alston v. Goodwin, 343 P.2d 993 (Cal. Ct. App. 1959); Yager v. Rubymar Corp., 216 N.Y.S.2d 577 (N.Y. Sup. Ct. Special Term 1961) (interpreting New Jersey Law). *See also* Heine v. Albin Gustafson Co., 461 N.Y.S.2d 934 (N.Y. Sup. Ct. 1983). *Cf.* Sunbelt Sav., F.S.B. v. Barr, 824 S.W.2d 600 (Tex. App. 1991) (a note and a guaranty are separate transactions; prior suit against individual in his capacity as guarantor was not res judicata as to suit against him as a partner on the partnership's note).

343 *See* Yager v. Rubymar Corp., 216 N.Y.S.2d 577 (N.Y. Sup. Ct. Special Term 1961) (N.J. law).

344 District of Columbia Court of Appeals v. Feldman, 460 U.S. 462 (1983); Rooker v. Fidelity Trust Co., 263 U.S. 413 (1923). *See also* Lance v. Dennis, 546 U.S. 459, 126 S. Ct. 1198 (2006) (narrowing the *Rooker-Feldman* doctrine). *See generally* National Consumer Law Center, Foreclosures § 11.6.4 (4th ed. 2012) (discussing *Rooker-Feldman* doctrine).

345 Fielder v. Credit Acceptance Corp., 188 F.3d 1031 (8th Cir. 1999).

346 *See* Mutual Home Dealers Corp. v. Alves, 258 N.Y.S.2d 786 (N.Y. App. Div. 1965); National Travis, Inc. v. Gialousakis, 466 N.Y.S.2d 624 (N.Y. Sup. Ct. 1983), *aff'd mem.*, 471 N.Y.S.2d 1023 (N.Y. App. Div. 1984). *See also In re* Hamlett, 63 B.R. 492 (Bankr. M.D. Fla. 1986) (usury is type of defense which allows Bankruptcy Court to look behind state court default judgment notwithstanding principles of res judicata).

aside unless it is void on its face or unless the pleadings affirmatively show that the plaintiff had no claim.[347]

## 7.7.4 Voluntary Payment Defense

### 7.7.4.1 Nature and Origin of the Voluntary Payment Doctrine

A borrower who has already made payments on a usurious loan may have to contend with an ancient, sporadically recognized defense, the voluntary payment doctrine. The doctrine developed in tax cases, and was created to prevent those who had paid illegally imposed taxes from recouping their payments from the tax collector.[348] The basis for the doctrine lies in the fiscal concerns of a government that may need to be certain of the amount of funds available for disbursement. The doctrine protects it from having to refund collected taxes that it may have already spent in a previous year.[349]

The justification of the doctrine is the fiction that every person is supposed to know and understand the law and the limits it places on taxing authorities, and therefore a person who voluntarily makes a demanded but unauthorized payment may not later use ignorance of the law to justify a refund.[350] The doctrine has limits, though: it will not apply when the payment was not "voluntary," that is, when it was made under some compulsion.[351] Formal notice of protest will also deflect the doctrine, so taxes paid after filing a complaint are not considered voluntary.[352] The degree of compulsion necessary for a taxpayer to avoid the doctrine has been relaxed over the years by some courts, and it may be sufficient to show that serious consequences would ensue from failing to pay.[353] Nonetheless, the doctrine continues to be applied occasionally.[354]

### 7.7.4.2 Does the Voluntary Payment Doctrine Apply Beyond Tax Payments?

In some states, the voluntary payment doctrine has been extended not just to payments to taxing authorities, but payments to private businesses as well.[355] As with the taxing authority version, the voluntary payment defense is rationalized on the basis that it allows one who receives payment to rely upon those funds, and that it operates as a means to settle disputes without resort to courts by requiring the person asserting an overcharge to notify the payee before payment.[356] These are, essentially, arguments of economic and judicial efficiency, concerns that should not trump a legitimate claim that one was tricked, defrauded, or otherwise overcharged by a party that knew or should have known that it was not entitled to the sums demanded.

Furthermore, it is not at all obvious that the justifications for the doctrine in the tax collecting context extend to charges

---

347 *See* Hyman v. Plant Imp. Co., 260 S.E.2d 531 (Ga. Ct. App. 1979) (denying motion to set aside default judgment where nothing in record showed that liquidated damages provision of rental agreement on its face violated Georgia law, or that late fees charged for nonpayment of rent constituted usurious interest as a matter of law). *See also* Ideal Loan & Fin. Corp. v. Little, 457 S.E.2d 274 (Ga. Ct. App. 1995)(court is not authorized to raise usury defense *sua sponte* when entering default judgment); Clark v. Kaiser Agricultural Chems., 274 S.E.2d 648 (Ga. Ct. App. 1980)(defendant may not move to set aside default judgment where usury defense was known but not pressed while case was pending, or could have been discovered through reasonable diligence).

348 *See, e.g.*, City of Little Rock v. Cash, 644 S.W.2d 229 (Ark. 1982); Sullivan v. Bd. of Comm'rs of Oak Lawn Park Dist., 743 N.E.2d 1057 (Ill. Ct. App. 2001); Louisville & N. Ry. Co. v. Hopkins County, 9 S.W. 497 (Ky. Ct. App. 1888); Quaker Oats Co. v. Stanton, 96 S.W.3d 133 (Mo. Ct. App. 2003); Shenango Furnace Co. v. Fairfield Township, 78 A. 937 (Pa. 1911); G. Heileman Brewing Co. v. City of LaCrosse, 312 N.W.2d 875 (Wis. Ct. App. 1981). *See also* Time Warner Entertainment Co. v. Whiteman, 802 N.E.2d 886 (Ind. 2004) (distinguishing between voluntary payment to government agency and voluntary payment to private business). *Cf.* City of Laredo v. South Tex. Nat'l Bank, 775 S.W.2d 729 (Tex. App. 1989) (doctrine did not apply to taxes paid into court registry pursuant to an agreement between the taxing authority and the taxed). *See generally* BMG Direct Mktg. v. Peake, 178 S.W.3d 763, 768–771 (Tex. 2005) (discussing history of voluntary payment doctrine; asserting that it has only been applied "infrequently" to illegal taxes); National Consumer Law Center, Unfair and Deceptive Acts and Practices §§ 4.2.19.5, 14.6.4.3 (7th ed. 2008 and Supp.).

349 Quaker Oats Co. v. Stanton, 96 S.W.3d 133, 143 (Mo. Ct. App. 2003) (taxing authority needs to have certainty so that collector can disburse collected taxes); Putnam v. Time Warner Cable of Southeastern Wis., Ltd., 649 N.W.2d 626, 637 (Wis. 2002) (government needs to have stability and certainty over funds that have been transferred without dispute).

350 *See, e.g.*, City of Little Rock v. Cash, 644 S.W.2d 229, 232 (Ark. 1982); Yates v. Royal Ins. Co., 65 N.E. 726, 727 (Ill. 1902).

351 Getto v. City of Chicago, 426 N.E.2d 844, 849 (Ill. 1981) (doctrine will not apply where payments made under duress or compulsion or if plaintiff did not have knowledge of the facts on which to frame a protest). *See also* Balmoral Racing Club, Inc. v. Gonzales, 788 N.E.2d 269 (Ill. Ct. App. 2003) (doctrine also does not apply when the tax statute authorizes recovery).

352 Worth v. City of Rogers, 14 S.W.3d 471 (Ark. 2000) (reversing and remanding judgment for taxing authority). *See also* Conrad v. Home & Auto Loan Co., 385 N.Y.S.2d 979 (N.Y. App. Div. 1976) (construing statutory remedy for usury not to preclude recovery of payments made under a reservation of rights and without prejudice after suit filed).

353 *See, e.g.*, Getto v. City of Chicago, 426 N.E.2d 844 (Ill. 1981) (risk of losing phone service if the tax was not paid was sufficient compulsion); Dreyfus v. Ameritech Mobile Communications, Inc., 700 N.E.2d 162 (Ill. Ct. App. 1988) (a payment is involuntary if payor either lacked knowledge of the facts or paid under duress; sufficient duress exists where taxpayer pays to prevent injury to himself, his business, or property without adequate opportunity to effectively resist the demand); State v. Conn. Gen. Life Ins. Co., 382 S.W.2d 745 (Tex. 1964) (risk that a business would lose its license established sufficient duress). *But cf.* City of Little Rock v. Cash, 644 S.W.2d 229 (Ark. 1982) (discretionary power of municipal waterworks to terminate service for failure to pay did not constitute sufficient distress where it had no such termination policy and none of the taxpayers testified that they had paid the tax out of coercion).

354 BMG Direct Mktg. v. Peake, 178 S.W.3d 763, 771 n.3 (Tex. 2005).

355 *See, e.g.*, King v. First Capital Fin. Servs. Corp., 828 N.E.2d 1155, 1170–1174 (Ill. 2005) (discussing history of voluntary payment doctrine in Illinois).

356 Putnam v. Time Warner Cable of Southeastern Wis., Ltd., 649 N.W.2d 626, 633 (Wis. 2002).

made by private parties. Unlike a taxing entity, which may well have to collect and disburse all sums within one fiscal period, businesses have the flexibility to plan for contingent funds. If a business wants to be certain that it will be able to keep the sums it has collected, it can ensure that it is fully entitled to them before charging them. The voluntary payment doctrine puts the burden of understanding the applicable laws, regulations and contract terms on the consumer, which can only encourage unscrupulous businesses to attempt to overcharge their customers in the hope that consumers will pay the excess before realizing the error.

The rule can lead to inequitable results for consumers. In one case, home sellers sued a mortgage company that assessed recording and tax service fees against them even though the services had been provided to the buyers, not the sellers. The mortgage company did not notify them of the fees until just before closing, and the sellers paid them in order for the closing to proceed, then sued for money wrongfully had and received *in assumpsit.* Their claim was dismissed on the grounds that regardless of whether the fees were appropriate, the plaintiffs relinquished their claim by paying them.[357] The court rejected their argument that they were compelled to pay the illegitimate charge because the mortgage company would have shut down the closing had they refused.[358] In *Dallas County Cmty. College Dist. v. Bolton*, the Texas Supreme Court ruled that students at a community college had voluntarily paid an increase in student service and technology fees.[359] Students who did not pay the fees could be barred from registering for classes or from receiving credit for completed coursework. The majority held that payment was voluntary since students could seek "other educational opportunities," namely, taking fewer credit hours and thus incurring lower fees. These cases show how the rule can catch overcharged consumers unaware, essentially imposing an instant statute of limitations on their claim, before they have had time to fully assess the charge and its legitimacy.

### 7.7.4.3 Usury Cases

Though lenders have asserted the voluntary payment defense in usury cases, the majority of jurisdictions addressing the issue have refused to apply it in those circumstances.[360] Even where the voluntary payment doctrine is accepted in other contexts, courts have recognized that strong policy reasons argue against applying it in usury cases. First, allowing the defendant to retain the usurious interest would thoroughly undermine the purpose of usury laws, which seek to protect borrowers from overreaching lenders.[361] Lenders would be encouraged to make usurious loans in the hope of ultimately being able to retain the illicit profit. Second, the voluntary payment rule fails to recognize the imbalance of power between most lenders and their borrowers. A few states reject or limit the common law doctrine by statute.[362] In addition, usury statutes that give the borrower a cause of action to recover illegally paid interest[363] implicitly reject the doctrine.

Nonetheless, a number of jurisdictions have applied the voluntary payment doctrine to bar a consumer from recovering usurious interest paid to a lender.[364] Even states that do not

357 Butitta v. First Mortgage Corp., 578 N.E.2d 116, 119 (Ill. App. Ct. 1991).

358 Butitta v. First Mortgage Corp., 578 N.E.2d 116 (Ill. App. Ct. 1991). *See also* Putnam v. Time Warner Cable of Southeastern Wis., Ltd., 649 N.W.2d 626, 631 (Wis. 2002) (voluntary payment doctrine precluded cable television customers' restitution claim arising from allegedly illegal late payment fees). *But cf.* King v. First Capital Fin. Servs. Corp., 828 N.E.2d 1155, 1173 (Ill. 2005) (suggesting that voluntary payment doctrine might not have precluded recovery of allegedly illegal document fees if plaintiffs had alleged that they were compelled to either pay the fee or forgo the loans; here, they could have had their own lawyers prepare the documents).

359 Dallas County Cmty. College Dist. v. Bolton, 185 S.W.3d 868 (Tex. 2005).

360 *See, e.g.*, LaBarr v. Tombstone Territorial Mint, 580 P.2d 744 (Ariz. Ct. App.) (rejecting *in pari delicto* argument), *op. adopted by* 582 P.2d 639 (Ariz. 1978); Stock v. Meek, 221 P.2d 15 (Cal. 1950); Baruch Inv. Co. v. Huntoon, 65 Cal. Rptr. 131 (Cal. Ct. App. 1967); Richlin v. Schleimer, 7 P.2d 711 (Cal. Ct. App. 1932); Babcock v. Olhasso, 293 P. 141 (Cal. Ct. App. 1930); Morgan v. Shepherd, 154 S.E. 780 (Ga. 1930); Young v. Barker, 342 P.2d 150, 159 (Kan. 1959) (arguing that it would be futile to declare usury to be criminal while allowing the lender to keep the "fruits of [its] crime"); Kline v. Robinson, 428 P.2d 190, 194 (Nev. 1967) (overruling earlier authority that precluded recovery of usurious interest voluntarily paid on grounds that "the wiser and more just result" was to allow such recovery); Damico v. Mayer, 158 A. 847 (N.J. Sup. Ct. 1932) (plaintiff could recover usurious interest on mortgage contract that had been paid in full; interpreting the right as arising from an implied promise of the lender to repay the usurious interest); Hardwick v. Austin Gallery of Oriental Rugs, Inc., 779 S.W.2d 438 (Tex. App. 1989). *See also* Dougherty v. North Fork Bank, 753 N.Y.S.2d 130 (N.Y. App. Div. 2003) (voluntary payment of illegal fees for payoff quotes is not a defense); Siefkes v. Clark Title Ins. Co., 215 N.W.2d 648 (S.D. 1974) (citing with approval the majority rule allowing borrowers to recover usurious interest that they paid). *But see* Gawry v. Countrywide Home Loans, Inc., 640 F. Supp. 2d 942, 956–957 (N.D. Ohio 2009) (payment of illegal prepayment penalty subject to voluntary payment defense), *aff'd*, 395 Fed. Appx. 152 (6th Cir. 2010).

361 *See, e.g.*, Stock v. Meek, 221 P.2d 15, 20 (Cal. 1950) (rejecting *in pari delicto* reasoning on grounds that applying voluntary payment doctrine would vitiate the usury law); Baruch Inv. Co. v. Huntoon, 65 Cal. Rptr. 131 (Cal. Ct. App. 1967) (noting that usury laws are designed to protect society); Mitchell v. Residential Funding Corp., 334 S.W.3d 477 (Mo. Ct. App. 2010) (allowing voluntary payment of closing costs as defense to usury claim "would negate the [second mortgage act's] provision for consumer protection").

362 *See, e.g.*, Chakford v. Sturm, 65 So. 2d 864 (Fla. 1953) (under Fla. Stat. Ann. § 687.03, immaterial that usurious interest was paid voluntarily); BMG Direct Mktg. v. Peake, 178 S.W.3d 763, 770, 776 (Tex. 2005) (Texas usury statute and tax code limit reach of voluntary payment doctrine); Ostiguy v. A.F. Franke Constr., Inc., 347 P.2d 1049 (Wash. 1959) (citing Wash. Rev. Code § 19.52.030).

363 *See* § 7.8.2.3.2, *infra*.

364 *See, e.g.*, Lincoln Nat'l Bank v. Kaufman, 406 F. Supp. 448 (E.D. Mich. 1976); *In re* Goehring, 23 B.R. 323 (Bankr. W.D. Mich. 1982); Bell v. Barnes, 190 So. 273 (Ala. 1939); Bizzoco v. Chinitz, 476 A.2d 572 (Conn. 1984) (based on Conn. Gen. Stat. § 37-2); Jenkins v. Concorde Acceptance Co., 828 N.E.2d 1155 (Ill. 2005); Christian v. Filbert, 249 Ill. App. 230 (Ill. App. Ct. 1928); Wright v. First Nat'l Bank of Monroe, 297 N.W. 505 (Mich. 1941); Bebee v.

apply the voluntary payment doctrine to usury cases may reach the same result in some situations if they allow borrowers to assert usury only defensively.[365]

### 7.7.4.4 Exceptions to the Doctrine

Even where accepted, there are exceptions to the voluntary payment doctrine. For example, while a payment made under a mistake of law is considered voluntary in many states,[366] one made under a mistake of fact is considered involuntary.[367] Other courts have distinguished cases where the loan has been only partially paid from those where the loan has been completely paid, allowing a borrower to recover usurious interest in the former case, but not the latter.[368]

As with the tax version, compulsion precludes application of the doctrine.[369] Payments considered involuntary, such as those made only after judgment was rendered against a borrower, may be recovered.[370] A payment may not in fact have been voluntary if nonpayment would have put the borrower at risk of losing the security for the loan.[371] Money obtained through fraud is also not considered voluntarily paid.[372]

In addition, the doctrine does not apply where there is a statutory right to recover.[373] Nor should it apply when it would thwart the legislature's intent in adopting a consumer protection statute.[374] Some courts may also distinguish between criminal usury, with its stiffer penalties, and civil usury.[375] Finally, if the consumer made any form of protest before or simultaneously with making a payment on an illegal loan, the payment may be "involuntary" for purposes of the doctrine.[376]

The more facts that show the plaintiff was pressured to accede to the usurious interest payments, the less likely a court will allow the lender to use the voluntary payment defense to shield itself from its own illegal acts. The voluntary payment doctrine is fundamentally an equitable doctrine that requires a factual inquiry.[377]

## 7.7.5 *Statutes of Limitations*

Usury, like other causes of action, is subject to statutes of limitations, so that affirmative usury claims must be filed within a set period after they mature. The length of time allotted varies from state to state, but typically ranges from one to three years

---

Grettenberger, 266 N.W.2d 829 (Mich. Ct. App. 1978); Farmers' Bank & Trust Co. v. Redwine, 167 S.E. 687 (N.C. 1933). *See also* Wakefield v. Goldstein, 644 F.2d 707 (8th Cir. 1981) (usurious contract was voidable, not void, and by releasing security to lender debtor voluntarily fulfilled the contract). *See generally* § 7.8.2.3.4, *infra* (effect of "voluntary" payment on right to recover payments made).

365 *See* § 7.8.2.3, *infra*.

366 BMG Direct Mktg., Inc. v. Peake, 178 S.W.3d 763 (Tex. 2005) (voluntary payment doctrine applies where debtor pays late charge with knowledge of its amount and the circumstances in which it is imposed, even though debtor does not know whether amount so exceeds creditor's damages that it is illegal as a penalty). *But see* Time Warner Entertainment Co. v. Whiteman, 802 N.E.2d 886, 891–892 (Ind. 2004); Criterion Ins. Co. v. Fulgham, 247 S.E.2d 404 (Va. 1978).

367 *See, e.g.*, Robinson v. Fountainhead Title Group Corp., 447 F. Supp. 2d 478, 493–494 (D. Md. 2006); Durant v. Servicemaster, 159 F. Supp. 2d 977, 981 (E.D. Mich. 2001); Luebke v. Moser, 598 N.E.2d 760 (Ohio Ct. App. 1991) (allowing defense where plaintiff paid usurious interest due to a mistake of law).

368 *See, e.g.*, Lincoln Nat'l Bank v. Kaufman, 406 F. Supp. 448 (E.D. Mich. 1976) (allowing plaintiff to recover prepaid interest where loan had not yet been fully repaid); *In re* Goehring, 23 B.R. 323, 325–326 (Bankr. D. Mich. 1982) (allowing debtor to recoup interest paid on unfulfilled note, but barring claim based on fully paid note, on grounds payment was "voluntary"); Waldorf v. Zinberg, 307 N.W.2d 749 (Mich. Ct. App. 1981) (defendant must apply collected usurious interest against principal due on matured loan); Bebee v. Grettenberger, 266 N.W.2d 829 (Mich. Ct. App. 1978); Sienkiewicz v. Leonard Mortgage Co., 229 N.W.2d 352 (Mich. Ct. App. 1975).

369 *See, e.g.*, Jenkins v. Mercantile Mfg. Co., 231 F. Supp. 2d 737 (N.D. Ill. 2003) (refusing to dismiss claim of borrower who sought to recover fees assessed by title company at closing which title company misrepresented as necessary to pay governmental charges); Raintree Homes, Inc. v. The Vill. of Long Grove, 906 N.E.2d 751 (Ill. App. Ct. 2009). *Cf.* Jenkins v. Concorde Acceptance Corp., 828 N.E.2d 1155, 1173 (Ill. 2005) (citing plaintiffs' failure to plead facts demonstrating compulsion as reason transaction did not fall within exception to voluntary payment doctrine); BMG Direct Mktg., Inc. v. Peake, 178 S.W.3d 763 (Tex. 2005) (consumers did not pay late fee under duress, as they could have bought the merchandise from other vendors). *See generally* Dallas County Cmty. College Dist. v. Bolton, 185 S.W.3d 868 (Tex. 2005) (discussing duress and compulsion).

370 Thelen v. Ducharme, 390 N.W.2d 264 (Mich. Ct. App. 1986).

371 *See* Aubertin v. Fairbanks Capital Corp., 2005 WL 331351 (D.N.H. Feb. 11, 2005) (payment of prepayment penalty in order to sell home was under duress); Gonzalez v. Codilis & Assocs., P.C., 2004 WL 719264 (N.D. Ill. Mar. 31, 2004) (payment of lenders' attorney fees by borrower in foreclosure done under duress). *See also* Raintree Homes, Inc. v. The Vill. of Long Grove, 906 N.E.2d 751, 770–771 (Ill. App. Ct. 2009) (finding business compulsion to pay improper municipal impact fee a defense to voluntary payment doctrine). *But see* King v. First Capital Fin. Servs. Corp., 828 N.E.2d 1155, 1170–1174 (Ill. 2005) (rejecting argument that document preparation fee paid at closing was paid under duress).

372 Lawson v. First Union Mortgage Co., 786 N.E.2d 279, 284 (Ind. Ct. App. 2003) (reversing dismissal in favor of mortgage company that had charged borrowers a documentation fee prohibited by state statute; voluntary payment rule does not apply when the payee was induced by fraud or improper conduct).

373 BMG Direct Mktg. v. Peake, 178 S.W.3d 763, 776 n.9 (Tex. 2005). *Cf.* Gonzalez v. Codilis & Assocs., P.C., 2004 WL 719264 (N.D. Ill. Mar. 31, 2004) (FDCPA preempts voluntary payment doctrine).

374 Huch v. Charter Commc'ns, Inc., 290 S.W.3d 721 (Mo. 2009) (purpose of statute was to protect consumers; application of voluntary payment doctrine would nullify legislative intent); Mitchell v. Residential Funding Corp., 334 S.W.3d 477 (Mo. Ct. App. 2010) (allowing voluntary payment of closing costs as defense to claim under second mortgage act "would negate the MSMLA's provision for consumer protection").

375 Wellman v. Bank One, 2005 WL 2291741 (Mich. Ct. App. Sept. 20, 2005).

376 *See* Aubertin v. Fairbanks Capital Corp., 2005 WL 331351 (D.N.H. Feb. 11, 2005).

377 BMG Direct Mktg. v. Peake, 178 S.W.3d 763, 776 (Tex. 2005). *See also* Siegel v. Shell Oil Co., 480 F. Supp. 2d 1034, 1049–1050 (N.D. Ill. 2007) (whether voluntary payment defense applies usually cannot be determined on a motion to dismiss).

after the usury action accrues.[378] If a state recognizes a common law action for the recovery of usurious interest paid, the statute of limitations for it may differ from that for the state's statutory cause of action for usury.[379] In most states, statutes of limitations are tolled under special circumstances, such as incompetence.[380]

At least as important as determining the time period provided by a statute of limitations is determining when the relevant period begins to run. If a one year statute of limitations were to begin to run on the day the loan agreement is consummated, many causes of action would be time-barred before the borrower discovered the usury. Although some courts hold that a usury claim arises at closing,[381] most courts rule that statutes of limitations do not begin to run against usury actions until the date of final payment on the usurious note.[382] Normally this is the date on which the loan was originally scheduled to terminate, but an earlier termination, such as the satisfaction of a debt through a foreclosure on secured property, may trigger the statute earlier.[383] Likewise, a later termination, through some form of extension agreement, may start the clock later.[384]

The language of the statute on which the substantive claim is based may be determinative as to when the statute of limitations begins to run. If it forbids *collection* of unlawful charges, or gives the borrower a private cause of action only upon *payment* of those charges, then it is difficult for a lender to argue that the statute of limitations should run from closing—a point at which some of the elements of a claim will not have occurred. A number of courts, dealing with statutes like this, hold that the statute of limitations begins to run anew each time the borrower makes a payment.[385] Accordingly, with a three-year statute of

378 *See, e.g.*, M. Nahas & Co. v. First Nat'l Bank, 930 F.2d 608 (8th Cir. 1991) (two years under National Bank Act; rejecting plaintiff's argument that DIDA permitted state opt-out of National Bank Act's statute of limitation, and Arkansas did not opt-out in any event); Durante Bros. v. Flushing Nat'l Bank, 755 F.2d 239 (2d Cir. 1985) (two years under National Bank Act; three years under borrowed New York law for civil RICO collection of unlawful debt); Van Cleef v. Aeroflex Corp., 657 F.2d 1094 (9th Cir. 1981) (three years under Arizona usury statute); Johnson v. Long Beach Mortgage Loan Trust 2001-4, 451 F. Supp. 2d 16 (D.D.C. 2006) (two years for DC usury law); Kendrick v. Jim Walter Homes, Inc., 545 F. Supp. 538 (S.D. Ind. 1980) (one year under Indiana U.C.C.C.); Henson v. Columbus Bank & Trust Co., 240 S.E.2d 284 (Ga. Ct. App. 1977) (one year); Master Fin. Inc. v. Crowder, 972 A.2d 864 (Md. 2009) (claim for civil penalties for violation of Secondary Mortgage Act are subject to twelve-year statute of limitations but common law remedy of declaring voiding loans void or voidable based on violation of Act is subject to three-year limitations period); Scott v. Forest Lake Chrysler-Plymouth Dodge, 637 N.W.2d 587 (Minn. Ct. App. 2002) (two-year statute for penalty applies to MVRISA claim); Trapp v. Hancuh, 1997 WL 396234 (Minn. Ct. App. July 15, 1997) (two-year statute for actions upon a statute for a penalty applies); Schwartz v. Bann-Cor Mortgage, 197 S.W.3d 168 (Mo. Ct. App. 2006) (six-year statute of limitations for claims against "moneyed corporations" applies to usury claim against mortgage lender); Arrowhead, Inc. v. Safeway Stores, Inc., 587 P.2d 411 (Mont. 1978) (two years); Englishtown Sportswear Ltd. v. Marine Midland Bank, 467 N.Y.S.2d 693 (N.Y. App. Div. 1983) (one year for usury, but six years for recovery of contract overcharge below usury ceiling); Henderson v. Security Mortgage & Fin. Co., 160 S.E.2d 39 (N.C. 1968) (two years); Car Now Acceptance Co. v. Block, 2003 WL 21714583 (Ohio Ct. App. July 14, 2003) (six-year period for action upon liability created by statute other than a forfeiture or penalty applies to retail installment sales act claim, as it is a remedial statute); Mackey v. Maurer, 220 P.3d 1235 (Wash. Ct. App. 2009) (six-month limitations period for asserting statutory usury penalty for common law usury; UDAP statute has longer limitations period but requires additional proof); Dunlap v. Friedman's, Inc., 582 S.E.2d 841 (W. Va. 2003) (construing statute liberally to apply four-year statute of limitations to credit sales); Snodgrass v. Sisson's Mobile Home Sales, 244 S.E.2d 321 (W. Va. 1978) (one year). *See also* U.C.C.C. § 5.202(1), (2) (1968 Model Code) (one year and two years respectively); U.C.C.C. § 5.201 (1974 Model Code) (one or two years depending on transaction).

379 *See* Easter v. Am. West Fin., 381 F.3d 948 (9th Cir. 2004) (different limitation periods and periods run from different events); Dennis v. Bradbury, 236 F. Supp. 683 (D. Colo. 1964), *aff'd*, 368 F.2d 905 (1966); Westman v. Dye, 4 P.2d 134 (Cal. 1931); § 7.8, *infra*.

380 *See* Bassett v. Ruggles, 2009 WL 2982895, at *12 (E.D. Cal. Sept. 14, 2009) (limitations period tolled because lender refused to provide information necessary to identify potential claim); Galindo v. Financo Fin., Inc., 2008 WL 4452344 (N.D. Cal. Oct. 3, 2008) (limitations period tolled where consumer illiterate and broker orally misrepresented loan terms at closing). *But cf.* Carter v. Zachary, 418 S.W.2d 787 (Ark. 1967) (insufficient evidence of fraudulent concealment to toll usury statute of limitation); Henson v. Columbus Bank & Trust Co., 240 S.E.2d 284 (Ga. Ct. App. 1977) ("renewal statute" did not toll statute of limitations when federal court declined pendant jurisdiction over usury claim).

381 *See* Miller v. Pacific Shore Funding, 92 Fed. Appx. 933 (4th Cir. 2004) (Md. law) (cause of action based on closing costs accrues at closing, even if those costs are financed, but for interest it accrues when each payment is made); Boland v. Crum (*In re* Brown), 363 B.R. 591 (Bankr. D. Mont. 2007) (cause of action for points assessed at closing accrues at closing). *See also* Mayfield v. San Jacinto Sav. Ass'n, 788 S.W.2d 119 (Tex. App. 1990) (interpreting Tex. Rev. Stat. Ann. art 5069-8.04(a) (now Tex. Fin. Code § 349.402), statute of limitations runs from later of date notes were signed or occurrence of violation; also holding that though one transaction can have multiple violations of "contracting for," "charging" and "receiving" usurious interest, no new limitations period runs from each event).

382 *See* Easter v. Am. West Fin., 381 F.3d 948 (9th Cir. 2004) (statute of limitations for statutory usury claim runs from date when loan is paid in full or when final payment is due; for common law usury claim, from date of each payment); *In re* Giorgio, 862 F.2d 933 (1st Cir. 1988) (R.I. law); Wenck v. Ins. Agents Fin. Corp., 99 So. 2d 883 (Fla. Dist. Ct. App. 1958); Miller v. York, 548 P.2d 941 (Nev. 1976); Snodgrass v. Sisson's Mobile Home Sales, 244 S.E.2d 321 (W. Va. 1978). *See also* Kendrick v. Jim Walter Homes, Inc., 545 F. Supp. 538 (S.D. Ind. 1980) (citing Indiana U.C.C.C.; Ind. Code § 24-4.5-5-202(1)).

383 *See* Van Cleef v. Aeroflex Corp., 657 F.2d 1094 (9th Cir. 1981); Shelton v. Chrysler First Fin. Servs. Corp., 676 So. 2d 591 (La. 1996) (if borrower prepays, "date of final payment" under statute of limitations means the date of prepayment, not date of maturity of loan); Fidelity Funds, Inc. v. Price, 491 So. 2d. 681 (La. Ct. App. 1986) (interpreting date of acceleration as date of "final payment").

384 *See* Gemperle v. Crouch, 724 P.2d 375 (Wash. Ct. App. 1986). *See also* Pacific Eastern Corp. v. Gulf Life Holding Co., 902 S.W.2d 946 (Tenn. Ct. App. 1995) (paying off a note is not a final payment if note is one of a series of notes that are part of a continuing transaction; however, it is a final payment if it is a novation, which extinguishes the existing contract and substitutes a new one).

385 Easter v. Am. West Fin., 381 F.3d 948 (9th Cir. 2004) (statute of limitations for common law usury claim runs from date of each

limitations, the borrower can recover the overcharge that was included in that payment, and any overcharges paid in the prior three years. This approach sometimes leads to elusive questions about when the consumer paid an illegal charge.

It is important to recognize that the statutes of limitations discussed in this section apply only to a borrower's affirmative action under a usury statute. Statutes of limitations normally do not bar the debtor's assertion of usury as a defense to a creditor's action on the relevant debt.[386] Even if a borrower's affirmative cause of action to recover penalties for usury is time-barred, the borrower can still offset by way of recoupment the amount the lender seeks on the usurious note. In states allowing extrajudicial foreclosures, a "defensive" use of a claim relating to overcharges beyond the statute of limitations arguably may be used despite the fact that the borrowers must file suit in order to stop a foreclosure.[387]

### 7.7.6 Whether Usury Can Be Asserted Against a Holder in Due Course

If a creditor claims that it is protected from a usury claim by holder-in-due-course status, the first question is whether it really is a holder in due course. If it has not met a series of requirements set forth in Article 3 of the Uniform Commercial Code, it will not be a holder in due course.[388]

In addition, if the underlying transaction involves the sale of goods or services, the FTC Holder Rule subjects almost any holder of the note or contract to any claims or defenses that the consumer could raise against the seller, up to a cap. Many states also have laws that restrict the holder-in-due-course doctrine in consumer transactions. The federal Homeownership and Equity Protection Act (HOEPA) also subjects assignees of certain high-cost mortgage loans to claims and defenses the consumer could raise against the loan originator, up to a cap. These restrictions on holder-in-due-course status are discussed in detail in other treatises in this series.[389]

But, more fundamentally, under UCC § 3-305, even a holder in due course is subject to the defense of the "illegality of the transaction, which, under other law, nullifies the obligation of the obligor."[390] Although there is some questionable authority to the contrary,[391] and although a few states have special

---

payment; for statutory usury claim, from date when loan is paid in full or when final payment is due); Faircloth v. Fin. Asset Secs. Corp., 87 Fed. Appx. 314 (4th Cir. 2004) (N.C. law) (usury claims accrue on date of payment; for closing costs claim accrues at closing even if they are financed, but for interest it accrues when each payment is made); Beltz v. Dings, 6 P.3d 424 (Kan. Ct. App. 2000) (cause of action for usury accrues with each payment made on a continuing contract); Henderson v. Security Mortgage & Fin. Co., 160 S.E.2d 39 (N.C. 1968) (each payment of usurious interest gives rise to separate cause of action, and statute of limitation runs from each payment date, but unallocated payments attributed first to principal, so most interest payments occur at end of loan term and can be recovered); Merritt v. Knox, 380 S.E.2d 160 (N.C. Ct. App. 1989) (statute of limitation runs from date of payment for remedy providing double recovery of interest, from date of contract for interest forfeiture remedy); Skinner v. Cen-Pen Corp., 414 S.E.2d 824 (Va. 1992) (Virginia treats each payment of an installment of interest as a usurious payment; since pay-off included usurious interest, action brought within two years of pay-off was not barred). *See also* McCarthy v. First Nat'l Bank, 223 U.S. 493, 32 S. Ct. 240, 56 L. Ed. 523 (1912) (statute of limitations under National Bank Act runs from date usurious interest is paid, not from date of final payment); Garver v. Brace, 55 Cal. Rptr. 2d 220 (Cal. Ct. App. 1996) (cause of action does not accrue until borrower actually pays excess interest; since payments on usurious note are deemed to apply first to principal, statute of limitations does not begin to run until debtor has paid the entire principal amount of the debt); Cook v. Frazier, 765 S.W.2d 546 (Tex. App. 1989) (payment of interest under usurious contract triggers limitation, not just payment of excess interest). *But cf.* Shepard v. Ocwen Fed. Bank, 638 S.E.2d 197 (N.C. 2006) (cause based on payment of origination fee accrues at closing even when the fee is deducted from loan proceeds so is rolled into the loan balance that is paid over time; decision was overruled in 2007 by an amendment to N.C. Gen. Stat. § 1-53 that provides that the two-year statute of limitations accrues with each payment made and accepted on the loan).

386 *See, e.g., In re* Bishop, 79 B.R. 94 (Bankr. D.D.C. 1987); Simmons v. Patrick, 27 Cal. Rptr. 347 (Cal. Ct. App. 1962); Young v. Wilder, 77 So. 2d. 604 (Fla. 1955); Adamson v. Trust Co. Bank, 271 S.E.2d 899 (Ga. Ct. App. 1980); Thrift Funds of Baton Rouge, Inc. v. Jones, 274 So. 2d. 150 (La. 1973); Fidelity Funds, Inc. v. Price, 491 So. 2d. 681 (La. Ct. App. 1986) (consumer credit law); Miley v. Steedley, 269 So. 2d. 522 (La. Ct. App. 1972); Miller v. York, 548 P.2d 941 (Nev. 1976); Rebeil Consulting Corp. v. Levine, 617 N.Y.S.2d 830 (N.Y. App. Div. 1994) (affirmative defenses such as usury not subject to statute of limitations). *Cf.* Merritt v. Knox, 380 S.E.2d 160 (N.C. Ct. App. 1989) (since limitation period for interest forfeiture had run, lender was awarded interest at statutory "legal" rate from date of contract; interest reduced from contract rate on theory that contract interest provisions were illegal and void). *But cf.* Valley View State Bank v. Caulfield, 731 P.2d 316 (Kan. Ct. App. 1987) (series of notes; borrower cannot assert defenses in earlier notes in action to enforce later note) (narrow reading of U.C.C.C.); Negaard v. Miller Constr. Co., 396 N.W.2d 833 (Minn. Ct. App. 1986) (usury defense must arise from same debt that creditor is attempting to enforce).

387 Hill v. Hawes, 144 F.2d 511 (D.C. Cir. 1944) (usury claim raised affirmatively beyond statute of limitations); *In re* Bishop, 79 B.R. 94 (Bankr. D.D.C. 1987) (a "defensive use" of a usury claim permitted beyond statute of limitations in extrajudicial foreclosure jurisdiction); Richlin v. Schleirer, 7 P.2d 711 (Cal. 1932) (usury case; immaterial that due to nature of foreclosure proceedings under a deed of trust, debtor must act as plaintiff to seek to enjoin threatened foreclosure rather that asserting a defense in an action initiated by the creditor); King v. Kitchen Magic, Inc., 391 A.2d 1184 (D.C. 1978) (suit to nullify mortgage based on fraud was an equitable action filed as a defensive measure against the foreclosure; allowed despite statute of limitations).

388 *See, e.g.*, Creative Ventures, L.L.C. v. Jim Ward & Assocs., 126 Cal. Rptr. 3d 564, 576–578 (Cal. Ct. App. 2011) (investors in usurious loan not holders so cannot be holders in due course).

389 National Consumer Law Center, Unfair and Deceptive Acts and Practices §§ 11.6, 11.7 (7th ed. 2008 and Supp.); National Consumer Law Center, Mortgage Lending § 10.7 (2012).

390 *See generally* National Consumer Law Center, Unfair and Deceptive Acts and Practices § 11.7.2 (7th ed. 2008 and Supp.).

391 *See* Beatty v. Franklin Inv. Co., 319 F.2d 712 (D.C. Cir. 1963); Pilcher v. Direct Equity Lending, 189 F. Supp. 2d 1198 (D. Kan. 2002) (treating usurious loans as voidable despite statutory language that they are void); Katz v. Simcha Co., 246 A.2d 555 (Md. 1968) (dictum, citing *Beatty, supra*). *See also* Hatton v. Money Lenders & Assocs., Ltd., 469 N.E.2d 360 (Ill. App. Ct. 1984) (granting summary judgment to note holder once good faith and absence of notice of usury defense established; no discussion of possibility that usury is defense against a holder in due course).

rules,[392] it seems clear that a usury violation or a fraud that renders an obligation void under state law is an "illegality" that renders the obligation a "nullity" under the UCC and may thus be asserted as a defense against a holder in due course of the obligation.[393] Further, if a note is void because it was issued by an unlicensed lender in violation of a state credit statute,[394] it will remain void when transferred to an innocent assignee, even if that assignee holds a license which would have authorized it to originate the loan.[395]

A more difficult question is the status of a usury defense when the existence of usury under state law voids only part of the obligation by, for example, voiding the interest on the obligation while allowing the creditor to recover principal. Some support exists for the argument that usury is a defense under the UCC to a holder in due course to the extent that it voids the obligation even if the obligation is not rendered entirely void.[396] However, courts interpreting the Negotiable Instruments Law were split on the issue, with some courts concluding that usury was not a defense to a holder in due course if the usury statute merely forbids the collection of the illegal portion of the interest.[397]

## *7.7.7* De Minimis *Violations*

The *de minimis* defense to usury is the argument that penalties should not be assessed for trivial usury violations. This defense is rejected in some states on the grounds that its recognition by the courts in the face of mandatory statutory penalties would constitute judicial legislation beyond the courts' authority.[398] Nevertheless, the *de minimis* defense is recognized in other states,[399] and in these jurisdictions it can cause problems for usury claimants.

Where the *de minimis* defense is recognized, there are few standards as to which violations can confidently be described as trivial and not worthy of judicial attention. The dollar amount of an overcharge clearly influences the court, but it is unclear how large a *de minimis* overcharge may be. The nature of the violation—for example, a disclosure violation as opposed to an interest overcharge—may also influence some courts,[400] but other courts have rejected such distinctions.[401] Similarly, some suggestion has been made that the collection of an excessive but otherwise legal charge may be *de minimis*, while the imposition of a completely unauthorized charge may not, but this approach too has been rejected by some courts.[402]

---

392 *See* Michigan Nat'l Bank v. Mattingly, 212 S.E.2d 754 (W. Va. 1975); Carper v. Kanawha Banking & Trust Co., 207 S.E.2d 897 (W. Va. 1974) (West Virginia usury statute amended to preclude recovery from holder in due course).

393 *See, e.g.*, Bank of North Carolina v. Rock Island Bank, 630 F.2d 1243 (7th Cir. 1980); Andrews v. Martin, 436 S.W.2d 285 (Ark. 1969); Fuller v. Universal Acceptance Corp., 264 A.2d 506 (D.C. 1970); Lucas v. Beco Homes, Inc., 494 S.W.2d 417 (Mo. Ct. App. 1973); Westervelt v. Gateway Fin. Serv., 464 A.2d 1203 (N.J. Super. Ct. Ch. Div. 1983); Robinson v. Rudy, 666 S.W.2d 507 (Tex. App. 1984); Michigan Nat'l Bank v. Mattingly, 212 S.E.2d 754 (W. Va. 1975) (transaction prior to statutory amendment). *See also* Mayo v. GMAC Mortgage, L.L.C., 763 F. Supp. 2d 1091, 1111 n.11 (W.D. Mo. 2011) (noting that holder in due course may be subject to usury defense if it extinguishes obligation to pay interest); National Consumer Law Center, Unfair and Deceptive Acts and Practices § 11.7.2 (7th ed. 2008 and Supp.).

394 *See* § 7.8.5, *infra*.

395 *See In re* Harrington, 6 B.R. 655 (Bankr. D.R.I. 1980).

396 *See* Lucas v. Beco Homes, Inc., 494 S.W.2d 417 (Mo. Ct. App. 1973). *See also* Fuller v. Universal Acceptance Corp., 264 A.2d 506 (D.C. 1970) (usury precludes holder-in-due-course status; assignee forfeits interest). *But cf.* Cromwell v. All State Credit Corp., 10 U.C.C. Rep. 403 (D.C. Sup. Ct. 1971) (usury renders debt voidable, not void, and so is not defense to holder in due course).

397 *See* Hall v. Mortgage Sec. Corp., 192 S.E. 145 (W. Va. 1937) (good discussion); Annotation, 95 A.L.R. 735 (1935) (NIL as affecting defense of usury). *See also* Lydick v. Stamps, 316 S.W.2d 107 (Tex. Civ. App. 1958) (contract void as to interest even in the hands of an innocent purchaser; debtor recovers twice the usurious interest).

398 *See, e.g.*, *In re* Ferris, 42 B.R. 374 (S.D. Ga. 1984) ($16.56 overcharge was not *de minimis*), *rev'd on other grounds*, 764 F.2d 1475 (11th Cir. 1985) (finding no substantive violation); *In re* Swartz, 37 B.R. 776 (Bankr. D.R.I. 1984) (loan void for $4 overcharge; amount of overcharge is irrelevant); Georgia Inv. Corp. v. Norman, 204 S.E.2d 740 (Ga. 1974) ($1 notary fee not *de minimis*); Kelly v. Sylvan Motors, 287 S.E.2d 359 (Ga. Ct. App. 1981) ($1.27 overcharge not *de minimis*); Gray v. Quality Fin. Co., 204 S.E.2d 483 (Ga. Ct. App. 1974) (loan term exceeded statutory maximum by one day; not *de minimis*); Scott v. Forest Lake Chrysler-Plymouth Dodge, 637 N.W.2d 587 (Minn. Ct. App. 2002) (*de minimis* exception does not apply to cases involving statutory interpretation); Dickey v. Bank of Clarksdale, 184 So. 314 (Miss. 1938) (overcharges between $0.50 and $1.00).

399 *See* Yates Ford v. Ramirez, 692 S.W.2d 51 (Tex. 1985) (monthly overcharges of $0.074 and $0.002 from improper odd day calculations were *de minimis*); Buendia v. Advanta Mortgage Corp.-USA, 2003 WL 21982321 (Tex. App. Aug. 21, 2003) ($2.36 overcharge is *de minimis*); Gawlik v. Padre Staples Auto Mart, 666 S.W.2d 161 (Tex. App. 1983) ($1.62 overcharge in purchase and sale of two cars was *de minimis*); Wayne Strand Pontiac-GMC v. Molina, 653 S.W.2d 45 (Tex. App. 1983) ($5.53 "license plate fee" plus $2.50 "official fees" were *de minimis*); Thornhill v. Sharpstown Dodge Sales, 546 S.W.2d 151 (Tex. Civ. App. 1976) ($0.24 overcharge on $5,300 credit was *de minimis*). *Cf. In re* Cadillac Wildwood Dev. Corp., 138 B.R. 854 (Bankr. W.D. Mich. 1992) ($3 overcharge on closing costs was "mistake of fact" needing correction, but was not a usurious overcharge); Clean Harbors, Inc. v. John Hancock Life Ins. Co., 833 N.E.2d 611 (Mass. App. Ct.) (failure to notify attorney general of rate until the afternoon when loans funded in the morning, although a violation of the statute, will not support a finding of usury). *But cf.* Bendele v. Tri-County Farmers Coop., 635 S.W.2d 459 (Tex. App.) (*de minimis* argument does not apply under statute that imposed serious penalties for overcharges in excess of twice the permissible rate, when creditor exceeded twice the permissible rate by only a small amount), *aff'd*, 641 S.W.2d 208 (Tex. 1982); Ceco Corp. v. Steve's Sash & Door Co., 714 S.W.2d 322 (Tex. App. 1986), *aff'd as modified*, 751 S.W.2d 473 (Tex. 1988) ($245.69 was not *de minimis* on total contract price of $71,702.95).

400 *See* Georgia Inv. Corp. v. Norman, 204 S.E.2d 740 (Ga. 1974). *See also* Jenkins v. Commercial Credit Plan, Inc., 419 S.E.2d 484 (Ga. Ct. App. 1992).

401 *See, e.g.*, Anguianao v. Jim Walters Homes, 561 S.W.2d 249 (Tex. Civ. App. 1978) (refusing to find that failure of a creditor to use the term "retail installment contract" is *de minimis*).

402 *See* Wayne Strand Pontiac-GMC v. Molina, 653 S.W.2d 45 (Tex. App. 1983) (compare majority and dissenting opinions).

In fact it may be impossible for courts to develop coherent principles regarding the *de minimis* defense because to do so would effectively dismantle whatever usury requirement was labeled *de minimis*. For example, if courts predictably ruled that a $1 overcharge was *de minimis*, creditors could uniformly charge the maximum interest plus $1 with impunity, and the state's usury ceiling would effectively have been raised. Courts refusing to recognize the *de minimis* defense find that its recognition would constitute judicial legislation.

Because of the absence of predictable standards, consumer attorneys in jurisdictions which recognize a *de minimis* defense should attempt to change the focus of the argument, rather than to debate precisely what size overcharge is *de minimis*. A court looking at a single $1 overcharge in one solitary case may be inclined to tell the usury claimant that it has more important matters to worry about. However, overcharges not involving bona fide error usually result from a systematic practice of the creditor. With a little effort, the borrower's attorney can show that the overcharge was not just $1, but was really $1 per customer. Courts looking at the $1 overcharge from this perspective may well be willing to follow the reasoning of the Supreme Court of Mississippi which, in rejecting the contention that overcharges of $1 or $0.50 were *de minimis*, stated: "[i]f these charges are so trifling that the court should close its eyes to them, they are so trifling that banks should not insist upon them as conditions of making small loans. . . ."[403]

## 7.7.8 Industry Custom and Usage

A less commonly raised usury defense is the argument that long-standing and widely accepted financial industry practices should not be deemed usurious or otherwise illegal. For example, in an Illinois case borrowers claimed that a bank had overcharged them by calculating interest on the basis of a 360-day year, and the bank replied that the banking industry universally calculated interest in this manner, that the borrowers should have known this (unpublicized) fact, and that this should be a defense to the borrower's challenge. The court disagreed with the bank's defense.[404]

The primary justification for the industry-practice defense arises from the common law principle that ambiguous contracts should be construed in the light of general customs and usage.[405] Yet, whatever the merits of this doctrine as a matter of contract construction, it is black letter law that industry practice may not contravene a statute, and the courts have universally held that industry practice is no defense to usury.[406] Furthermore, evidence of industry practice is inadmissible if offered to validate an otherwise usurious transaction.[407]

Despite the rule that industry practice is no defense to usury violations, widespread financial customs may occasionally affect the outcome of usury cases. If, after the application of the standard principles of statutory construction, a usury statute is ambiguous regarding the legality of some practice, a court may well be reluctant to find that practice usurious in the face of long-standing custom. This judicial tendency is hard to quantify, but it is often expressed in terms of the narrow construction of usury statutes.[408] Courts may hesitate to impose significant usury penalties unless there are firm statutory grounds for holding a widespread practice usurious.

On the other hand, if the statute is ambiguous, some courts have recognized the equally valid policy grounds to refuse to give much deference to industry usage, particularly in the consumer credit context:

> It is not surprising that interested, sophisticated lenders consistently interpret ambiguous laws to their own advantage and to the disadvantage of their obviously less-sophisticated customers. This data only highlights the need of the disinterested courts to be vigilant to prevent industry-wide overreaching.[409]

The related issue of deference to an administrative agency's interpretation is discussed at § 7.2.3, *supra*.

## 7.7.9 Usury Saving Clauses

Many credit contracts contain boilerplate "saving clauses" which, in one form or another, recite that the parties to the contract intend to comply with applicable usury laws, and that

403 Dickey v. Bank of Clarksdale, 184 So. 314 (Miss. 1938) (stating that the aggregate gain to the creditor from its overcharges is the same as the aggregate loss to the borrowers, and that the legal wrong is no less wrong when its effect is diffused among many borrowers). *See also In re* Ferris, 42 B.R. 374 (S.D. Ga. 1984) (recognizing the impact of repeated, small overcharges), *rev'd on other grounds*, 764 F.2d 1475 (11th Cir. 1985); Georgia Inv. Corp. v. Norman, 204 S.E.2d 740 (Ga. 1974). *Cf. In re* Sprouse, 577 F.2d 989 (5th Cir. 1978) (discussing effect of overreaching contract language on consumers in transactions which are not litigated); Sander v. Lincoln Serv. Corp., 1993 WL 112543 (N.D. Ill. Apr. 5, 1993) (lender with many customers can realize substantial profit from small individual overcharges; RESPA case). *But see* HSAM Inc. v. Gatter, 814 S.W.2d 887 (Tex. App. 1991) (recognizing that excess late charges on thousands of contracts would not be *de minimis*, but finding this argument unpersuasive where creditor appeared to have been "set-up" for the usury claim and, by court's calculation, borrower's loss was only a hypothetical two cents).

404 Perlman v. First Nat'l Bank, 305 N.E.2d 236 (Ill. App. Ct. 1973).

405 *Id. See also* Cohen v. District of Columbia Nat'l Bank, 382 F. Supp. 270 (D.D.C. 1974).

406 *See* Cohen v. District of Columbia Nat'l Bank, 382 F. Supp. 270 (D.D.C. 1974) (custom of ignoring declining balance in interest calculation); Harmon v. Lehmann, 5 So. 197 (Ala. 1888) (sales commission); Perlman v. First Nat'l Bank, 305 N.E.2d 236 (Ill. App. Ct. 1973) (360-day year); Beneficial Fin. Co. v. Administrator of Loan Laws, 272 A.2d 649 (Md. 1971) (alleged custom of correcting errors discovered in lender's books without imposing penalty); Dickey v. Bank of Clarksdale, 184 So. 314 (Miss. 1938) (custom of imposing service charge on small loans); Cowgill v. Jones, 73 S.W. 995 (Mo. Ct. App. 1903) (sales commissions); Kollman v. Hunnicutt, 385 S.W.2d 600 (Tex. Civ. App. 1964) (car dealer floor plan financing). *See also* Barclay Kitchen, Inc. v. Calif. Bank, 25 Cal. Rptr. 383 (Cal. Ct. App. 1962) (bank deposits).

407 *See* Kollman v. Hunnicutt, 385 S.W.2d 600 (Tex. Civ. App. 1964).

408 *See* § 7.2.1, *supra*.

409 *In re* Jordan, 91 B.R. 673, 688 (Bankr. E.D. Pa. 1988). *See also* § 7.2.1, *supra*.

the contract should not be interpreted as providing for usurious interest rates. Saving clauses frequently specify that any charge above the usury ceiling should be deemed a mistake, and that the overcharge should either be refunded to the borrower or credited against the outstanding principal balance.

The aim of usury saving clauses is to convert apparently usurious overcharges to mere contract violations and thereby to avoid the statutory penalties associated with usury. Saving clauses attempt to negate usurious intent by denying the presence of any such intent. In addition, savings clauses purport to reclassify any interest overcharge as a principal payment or as money in some manner held by the creditor on the debtor's behalf. If a charge above the usury ceiling occurs, but the savings clause is given effect, the interest overcharge element of a usury violation is negated.

If saving clauses were broadly construed, they would circumvent the enforcement of usury statutes.[410] Whenever a borrower challenged an apparently usurious contract, the creditor either would deny any intent to assess overcharges which the contract provided for but which had not yet occurred, or would simply rebate excessive charges without penalty. The incentive to comply with usury statutes would be greatly reduced because the majority of their contracts would never be challenged, and creditors could retain the excessive charges from them.[411]

Courts have given saving clauses only limited effect.[412] A saving clause will normally be given no effect where any reasonable interpretation of the contract clearly calls for the payment of usurious charges or such charges have already been demanded.[413] Nor will a savings clause be given effect where the lender has not attempted to implement it but has persisted in demanding unlawful interest.[414]

410 Transworld Telecomms., Inc. v. Pacific Mezzanine Fund, Inc. (*In re* Transworld Telecommunications, Inc.), 260 B.R. 204 (Bankr. D. Utah 2000), *rev'd and remanded on other grounds*, 309 F.3d 744 (10th Cir. 2002); Eisenstein v. DiPrimio, 2000 WL 1300452 (Ga. Ct. App. Sept. 15, 2000) (savings clause would be a "win-win proposition" for unscrupulous lenders); Swindell v. Federal Nat'l Mortgage Ass'n, 409 S.E.2d 892, 896 (N.C. 1991), *modifying and aff'g* 387 S.E.2d 220 (N.C. Ct. App. 1990) (if valid, savings clause would shift onus onto borrower, contravening policy and depriving borrower of statute's protections). *See also* Jersey Palm-Gross, Inc. v. Paper, 658 So. 2d 531 (Fla. 1995) (if savings clause were to be absolute bar to usury claim, lender could relieve himself of legal penalties for his conduct by writing into the contract a disclaimer of any intent to do what he plainly did).

411 *See In re* Sprouse, 577 F.2d 989, 993 (5th Cir. 1978) (Ga. law) (without usury remedies, creditors could invoke illegal clauses against borrowers who did not know of the illegality). *See also* Swindell v. Federal Nat'l Mortgage Ass'n, 409 S.E.2d 892, 896 (N.C. 1991) ("A lender cannot charge usurious rates with impunity by making that rate conditional upon its legality and relying upon the illegal rate's automatic rescission when discovered and challenged by the borrower").

412 *See, e.g.*, Kissell Co. v. Gressley, 591 F.2d 47 (9th Cir. 1979) (acceleration due to lender's misconduct; giving no effect to savings clause); Rieser v. Todd (*In re* Chari), 2005 WL 4030034 (Bankr. S.D. Ohio Sept. 2, 2005) (giving no effect to savings clause where transaction was usurious on its face); Jersey Palm-Gross, Inc. v. Paper, 658 So. 2d 531 (Fla. 1995) (upholding finding of usury; savings clause is not absolute bar to usury claim, but rather one factor in determining creditor's intent; other factors include how narrow the usurious margin, whether it is complex transactions in which a mathematical error made, whether the usury was contingent, and lender's knowledge of the urgency of borrower's need); Lawrimore v. Sun Fin. Co., 205 S.E.2d 110 (Ga. Ct. App.), *aff'd*, 208 S.E.2d 454 (Ga. 1974) (boilerplate clause stating that contract provisions will be ineffective to extent of any illegality could not be given effect, because to do so would nullify the regulatory statute); Swindell v. Federal Nat'l Mortgage Ass'n, 409 S.E.2d 892 (N.C. 1991) (holding savings clause not to protect creditor even though no excess charge collected and creditor offered to reduce charge to legal maximum); Okla. Preferred Fin. & Loan Corp. v. Morrow, 497 P.2d 221 (Okla. 1972) (prospectively repudiating earlier decision that gave effect to saving clauses). *But see In re* Perry, 425 B.R. 323, 376–377 (Bankr. S.D. Tex. 2010) (giving effect to savings clause in large commercial loan, when parties did their best to draft the contracts to avoid usury violations); Lairsen v. Slutzky, 80 S.W.3d 121, 127 (Tex. App. 2002) (relying on savings clause without discussion); S&J Invs. v. Am. Star Energy & Minerals Corp., 2001 WL 1380027 (Tex. App. Nov. 7, 2001) (giving effect to savings clause in open-end credit agreement that contemplated a succession of debts).

413 *See* ECE Technologies, Inc. v. Cherrington Corp., 168 F.3d 201 (5th Cir. 1999); Mack v. Newton, 737 F.2d 1343 (5th Cir. 1984) (mere presence of savings clause cannot rescue transaction that is necessarily usurious by its explicit terms); Kissell Co. v. Gressley, 591 F.2d 47 (9th Cir. 1979) (savings clause cannot save contract which is usurious on its face); Mims v. Fid. Funding, Inc., 307 B.R. 849 (N.D. Tex. 2002) (savings clause did not save contract that was usurious on its face; hypothetical possibility that conditions for charging usurious fees would not occur did not make savings clause effective); Nevels v. Harris, 102 S.W.2d 1046 (Tex. 1937); Armstrong v. Steppes Apts., Ltd., 57 S.W.3d 37 (Tex. App. 2001). *See also* Hardwick v. Austin Gallery of Oriental Rugs, Inc., 779 S.W.2d 438, 442–443 (Tex. App. 1989) (disclaimer of intent to contract for usury is immaterial if usury has actually been charged). *But see* Federal Sav. & Loan Ins. v. Kralj, 968 F.2d 500 (5th Cir. 1992) (Tex. law) (giving effect to savings clause where usury claim was based on allegation that one of two alternate rates specified by note was usurious, and lender had never invoked that rate); First South Sav. Ass'n v. First South Partners, II, Ltd., 957 F.2d 174 (5th Cir. 1992) (commercial loan to sophisticated businessmen; savings clause remedied demand for excess amount in demand letters and original judicial complaint); Poulsen's, Inc. v. Wood, 756 P.2d 1162 (Mont. 1988) (finding no usury in commercial case where contract on its face provided for excess interest, but contract also had savings clause and demand letter properly calculated interest at non-usurious rate); Woodcrest Assocs. Ltd. v. Commonwealth Mortgage Corp., 775 S.W.2d 434 (Tex. App. 1989) (lender's demand letter for specific, excessive amount was a "charge" under the usury statute but savings clause in loan rendered excess unenforceable and avoided usury; large commercial transaction). *But cf.* Szenay v. Schaub, 496 So. 2d. 883 (Fla. Dist. Ct. App. 1986) (saving clause along with allegation of actual mistake supports finding of no intent despite usurious rate of interest in note; observe that Florida follows a minority rule on usurious intent, see § 7.5.5, *supra*); Watson v. Avco Fin. Servs., Int'l, 401 N.W.2d 485 (Neb. 1987) (lender did not illegally contract for attorney fees where contractual clause for such fees prefaced by words "to the extent permitted by law"); Robert Joseph Phillips Living Trust v. Scurry, 988 S.W.2d 418 (Tex. App. 1999) (giving effect to savings clause where note was not usurious on its face and lender was unaware of preexisting first mortgage, making new loan a junior mortgage loan subject to a lower rate cap).

414 Armstrong v. Steppes Apts., Ltd., 57 S.W.3d 37 (Tex. App. 2001). *See also* C & K Invs. v. Fiesta Group, Inc., 248 S.W.3d 234 (Tex.

The one situation in which a saving clause may carry some weight is in an ambiguous contract which can plausibly be interpreted as either usurious or non-usurious. For example, two notes might be construed as a single loan at a legal rate or as two loans, one of which was usurious.[415] Similarly, a precomputed contract might be unclear about whether the creditor was required to rebate unearned interest charges upon prepayment or acceleration.[416] Under such circumstances, saving clauses are frequently cited by courts as support for their choice of the non-usurious construction of the transaction.[417] Consequently, saving clauses can make it more difficult for debtors to prove the element of usurious intent in ambiguous contracts which are not usurious on their face, especially when the overcharge has not yet been assessed.

## 7.7.10 Correction of Error As a Defense

In the absence of a statute so providing, creditors cannot rebut usurious intent or otherwise avoid usury statutes simply by rebating excessive charges that the debtor has already paid.[418] However, allowing a creditor a period of time to avoid liability by correcting an error is a common feature of usury statutes.[419] Texas gives a lender a statutory defense if it corrects a violation, including paying interest on any overcharge at the contract rate, within sixty days after discovering it and gives written notice of the violation to the obligor. The lender must take these steps before the obligor gives written notice of the violation or files an action alleging the violation.[420] The creditor's notice to the obligor must acknowledge the specific usury violation.[421] Sending a demand letter asking only for the non-usurious portion of the obligation, without explicitly releasing the usurious portion, is probably insufficient.[422]

Another Texas provision allows a lender another sixty days to correct an error after receiving notice of the violation.[423] Responding to the obligor's notice by arguing that there was no usury violation is insufficient.[424] The pre-suit notice is mandatory,[425] but a bankruptcy court declined to dismiss a usury claim on this ground where the parties had already been through pre-trial mediation that served the same purpose.[426] Cure pur-

App. 2007) (declining to give effect to savings clause when creditor never attempted to make the refund it required).

415 *See, e.g.*, Spanish Vill. Ltd. v. American Mortgage Co., 586 S.W.2d 195 (Tex. Civ. App. 1979). *See also* Rockstad v. Erikson, 113 P.3d 1215, 1223 (Alaska 2005) (rejecting testimony that two loans created, not one, since to do so would be to make the contract usurious).

416 *See, e.g.*, Mack v. Newton, 737 F.2d 1343 (5th Cir. 1984). *See also* Myles v. Resolution Trust Corp., 787 S.W.2d 616 (Tex. App. 1990) (superfluously invoking savings clause against borrower's challenge to acceleration provision in an interest-bearing contract, where acceleration would not have resulted in charging of unearned interest in any event). *See generally* § 5.8.7.3, *supra*.

417 *See, e.g.*, *In re* Casbeer, 793 F.2d 1436 (5th Cir. 1986); Mack v. Newton, 737 F.2d 1343 (5th Cir. 1984); Rickman v. Modern Am. Mortgage Corp., 583 F.2d 155 (5th Cir. 1978); Imperial Corp. v. Frenchman's Creek Corp., 453 F.2d 1338 (5th Cir. 1972); Rebman v. Flagship First Nat'l Bank, 472 So. 2d. 1360 (Fla. Dist. Ct. App. 1985); Nevels v. Harris, 102 S.W.2d 1046 (Tex. 1937); Pentico v. Mad-Wayler, Inc., 964 S.W.2d 708 (Tex. App. 1998) (contract is not explicitly usurious, therefore, savings clause is effective; usury only apparent after the total interest charges over the loan term at the non-usurious contract rate are added to excessive late fees considered "interest" under state law); Parhms v. B&B Ventures, Inc., 938 S.W.2d 199 (Tex. App. 1997) (giving effect to savings clause where collection of usurious interest was contingent solely upon the borrower making late payments and the extent of the tardiness of those payments, and contract was ambiguous as to whether interest was charged in excess of that allowed by law); Edmondson v. First State Bank, 819 S.W.2d 605 (Tex. App. 1991) (giving effect to savings clause where no evidence of usurious rate charged; debtor apparently had alleged that the mere existence of multiple prime rates at the bank resulted in usury); Spanish Vill. Ltd. v. American Mortgage Co., 586 S.W.2d 195 (Tex. Civ. App. 1979). *See also* R.V. Indus. v. Urdiales, 851 S.W.2d 306 (Tex. App. 1992) (savings clause reflects an intent to comply with usury laws and indicates spreading should be used to avoid charge of usury).

418 *See* Duderwicz v. Sweetwater Sav. Ass'n, 595 F.2d 1008 (5th Cir. 1979) (cancellation of usurious escrow account does not moot usury claim); Szerdahelyi v. Harris, 490 N.E.2d 517 (N.Y. 1986) (loan void despite tender of excess payments); Danziger v. San Jacinto Sav. Ass'n, 732 S.W.2d 300, 302 (Tex. 1987) (creditor's practice of crediting back overpaid interest is insufficient to avoid usury); Coppedge v. Colonial Sav. & Loan Ass'n, 721 S.W.2d 933 (Tex. App. 1986) (refund of usurious overcharge did not preclude finding of usury despite language in Texas "spreading" statute). *Cf.* Dillon v. Resolution Trust Corp., 811 S.W.2d 765 (Ark. 1991) (contract defined payments as interest; creditor's subsequent unilateral effort to reallocate excess interest to principal cannot purge contract of usury, nor can subsequent modification agreement, as usury is determined as of inception of contract (no savings clause at issue)).

419 *See, e.g.*, Colo. Rev. Stat. § 5-5-502(2); Fla. Stat. Ann. § 687.04.

420 Tex. Fin. Code Ann. § 305.103(a) (West). *See In re* CPDC, Inc., 337 F.3d 436 (5th Cir. 2003) (sixty days run from lender's subjective discovery that lender has violated usury prohibition); Rieser v. Todd (*In re* Chari), 2005 WL 4030034 (Bankr. S.D. Ohio Sept. 2, 2005) (letter ineffective where sent more than sixty days after lender should have discovered overcharge); Strasburger Enters., Inc. v. TDGT Ltd. P'ship, 110 S.W.3d 566 (Tex. App. 2003) (no defense when complaint that did not seek usurious interest was delivered to debtor only after creditor received usury notice).

421 Tex. Fin. Code Ann. § 305.103(a)(creditor must give "written notice to the obligor of the violation"). *See* Pagel v. Whatley, 82 S.W.3d 571 (Tex. App. 2002) (attachment to complaint acknowledging possibility of usury violation was sufficient where debtor first raised usury issue after receiving complaint).

422 Anderson v. Chainani (*In re* Kemper), 263 B.R. 773 (Bankr. E.D. Tex. 2001).

423 Tex. Fin. Code § 305.006(c) (West). *See, e.g.*, Rieser v. Todd (*In re* Chari), 2005 WL 4030034 (Bankr. S.D. Ohio Sept. 2, 2005) (remedy for failure to send pre-suit notice is abatement, not dismissal); Bair Chase Prop. Co. v. S & K Dev. Co., 260 S.W.3d 133 (Tex. App. 2008) (finding lender's corrective actions sufficient to avoid liability). *See also* Ohio Rev. Code Ann. § 1317.08 (West) (similar provision allowing refund within ten days after receiving notice); Sotelo v. Interstate Fin. Corp., 224 S.W.3d 517 (Tex. App. 2007) (lender has sixty days after notice to correct the usury; notice sent while suit was abated is treated same as pre-suit notice).

424 Anderson v. Chainani (*In re* Kemper), 263 B.R. 773 (Bankr. E.D. Tex. 2001).

425 Rieser v. Todd (*In re* Chari), 2005 WL 4030034, at *14 (Bankr. S.D. Ohio Sept. 2, 2005); Anderrson v. Chainani (*In re* Kemper), 263 B.R. 773, 784 (Bankr. E.D. Tex. 2001).

426 Rieser v. Todd (*In re* Chari), 2005 WL 4030034 (Bankr. S.D. Ohio Sept. 2, 2005).

suant to this provision has been construed as precluding all usury remedies, whether statutory or common law.[427] In addition, a Texas constitutional provision makes a lender liable for certain violations only if it fails to correct an error within a reasonable time after receiving notice from the borrower.[428]

The Minnesota MVRISA was amended in 1996 to allow dealers a 120-day period to cure violations of the requirement to provide the buyer with a signed copy of the contract. Sending the buyer a letter stating that the buyer can request a copy is insufficient.[429]

In a state with a correction of error statute, a borrower should be extremely careful about revealing the presence of a usury claim to the creditor prior to the filing of some formal notice such as the debtor's answer. For example, in a Florida case, counsel for a debtor made the mistake of informing the creditor's counsel of the debtor's usury claim before the debtor filed an answer to the creditor's action on a debt. The creditor immediately withdrew its complaint, sent the debtor a "purge" letter, and then refiled the action on the debt. The court held that the creditor lacked the "corrupt intent" which, under Florida law, the debtor must prove to establish usury.[430]

The existence of a correction of error statute can benefit the borrower in some circumstances. A court cited a Louisiana statute that provides a right to cure as a reason for rejecting the lender's claim that the violation was merely technical and did not warrant a refund.[431] Having failed to take advantage of the opportunity to correct the error, the lender could not complaint that the remedy was too severe.

### *7.7.11 Exhaustion of Administrative Remedies*

In a 2005 Texas case, *Meekey v. Rick's Cabaret International, Inc.*, the defendant argued that the consumers were required to exhaust their administrative remedies.[432] The case involved an illegal surcharge in violation of the Texas Finance Code. The defendant argued that the code was part of a pervasive regulatory scheme and that the Texas Finance Commission had either exclusive or primary jurisdiction of the dispute. The appellate court held that, since the administrative process did not provide any remedy for an illegal surcharge, the agency did not have exclusive jurisdiction. Nor did the Finance Commission have primary jurisdiction, since it did not have special expertise in the disputed questions of law and fact.[433]

### *7.7.12 Special Defenses When FDIC Becomes Receiver for Failed Bank*

The rash of bank failures caused by the subprime mortgage crisis has inserted a number of new issues into borrower litigation. First are procedural hurdles: when a bank fails, the FDIC sets up an administrative claims process that applies to almost all claims against the bank.[434] If a litigant does not exhaust the administrative claims process, the court lacks subject matter jurisdiction over the claim.[435] Most courts recognize an exception to the exhaustion requirement for affirmative defenses, but there is disagreement about whether the exhaustion requirement applies to an affirmative defense that could also have been raised as an independent claim.[436]

Second are special substantive defenses that the FDIC can assert. These special defenses are collectively but somewhat imprecisely known as the *D'Oench* doctrines. Roughly speaking, in at least some circumstances, they preclude claims that are based on secret, unwritten, or unrecorded agreements, including claims of fraudulent inducement, with the failed bank. These issues are discussed in detail in another treatise in this series.[437]

## 7.8 Remedies for Illegal Overcharges; Traditional Usury Remedies

### *7.8.1 Introduction*

The remedies available to victims of illegal overcharges are primarily determined by individual state statutes. Consequently, attorneys who are concerned about the remedies available in an individual overcharge case must first pay close attention to the statute under which the action is brought or the defense raised. Remedies for exceeding authorized cost ceilings vary widely from statute to statute, so an earlier case decided under a different statute may have little precedential value.

Despite the preeminence of state statutes in determining what remedies are available for illegal overcharges in the consumer credit context, other sources of law should also be considered. For example, an action at common law for recovery of the usurious interest already paid to a lender is recognized in many states and, in the absence of statutory provisions addressing this topic, a common law action may be the sole means to obtain such a recovery.[438] (If there is a statute providing a

427 Bair Chase Prop. Co. v. S & K Dev. Co., 260 S.W.3d 133, 140 n.4 (Tex. App. 2008).

428 *See* Vincent v. Bank of Am., 109 S.W.3d 856 (Tex. App. 2003) (requirement of notice and opportunity to cure bars class action).

429 Scott v. Forest Lake Chrysler-Plymouth Dodge, 637 N.W.2d 587 (Minn. Ct. App. 2002).

430 Gergora v. Goldstein Prof'l Ass'n Defined Benefits Pension Plan Trust, 500 So. 2d 695 (Fla. Dist. Ct. App. 1987). *But cf.* Beausejour Corp., N.V. v. Offshore Dev. Co., 802 F.2d 1319 (11th Cir. 1986) (statutory cure provisions not satisfied where creditor's letter did not state that transaction was usurious, did not refund any portion of sum paid under contract, and did not make formal adjustments to the contract).

431 Vickers v. Interstate Dodge, 882 So. 2d 1236 (La. Ct. App. 2004).

432 Meekey v. Rick's Cabaret Int'l, Inc., 171 S.W.3d 394 (Tex. App. 2005).

433 *See generally* National Consumer Law Center, Unfair and Deceptive Acts and Practices § 2.3.3.6 (7th ed. 2008 and Supp.).

434 12 U.S.C. § 1821(d).

435 *See* National Consumer Law Center, Mortgage Lending § 11.3 (2012).

436 12 U.S.C. § 1821(d)(13)(D).

437 National Consumer Law Center, Mortgage Lending §§ 11.4–11.13 (2012).

438 *See* § 7.8.2.3.4, *infra*.

remedy for the usury violation, it should be checked to make sure that it does not displace these common law remedies.[439]) Similarly, a usury statute may apply only to actions on a debt, and a borrower may be forced to seek equitable intervention to prevent the foreclosure of a usurious mortgage. Finally, federal law provides statutory remedies for usurious loans made by lenders operating under federal interest ceilings, for overcharges resulting from contract terms that are illegal under the federal high-cost mortgage legislation, and for many other loans if the interest exceeds twice the enforceable rate.[440] These topics are discussed in the following subsections.

Apart from the remedies available specifically for usury or violations of other limitations on charges, practitioners should investigate related non-usury causes of action and remedies. Usury claims do not exist in a vacuum, and usurious transactions frequently involve other illegalities. For example, fraud and unfair or deceptive practices often go hand in hand with usury, and statutes prohibiting such practices should be considered.[441] Even if the failure to disclose information required under the state usury statute is not actionable under that law,[442] the failure to disclose may state a claim under the state's UDAP statute.[443] Similarly, invalid security interests may be taken in usurious transactions which can lead to claims under the UCC.[444]

Last, but not least, basic contract theories and remedies should be kept in mind. The voiding of interest or principal for usury may lead to contract claims such as failure of consideration in a renewal note,[445] and questionable lender practices, such as compounding of interest, may constitute breach of contract even if usury ceilings are not violated.[446] A lender's conduct may be unconscionable, or violate the duty of good faith and fair dealing that all parties to a contract owe the others.[447]

## 7.8.2 *State Statutory Remedies*

### 7.8.2.1 Overview; Implying a Remedy When Statute Is Silent

At first glance, there seems to be little consistency among state laws that provide usury remedies. Ignoring for the moment cases decided in equity, usury remedies nonetheless vary from the mere forfeiture of the usurious portion of the contract interest[448] to the requirement that the creditor return all of the payments on the contract and pay additional statutory penalties.[449] Some measure of order can be imposed on this chaos, however, if one recognizes that the outcome in any one case depends on the interaction of several variables that are common to almost all the statutes. Specifically, a debtor's obligation to repay principal on a usurious contract may be treated differently from the obligation to pay interest; payments already made on the contract may be treated differently from amounts still owed; and the portion of the interest in excess of the permissible amount may be treated differently from the remainder of the contract interest.

Some consumer credit statutes may not include specific provisions for individual remedies. Some of the equitable remedies discussed at § 7.8.3, *infra*, particularly reformation of the contract, may be available to a debtor in this situation. In addition, the consumer may argue that such statutes create an implied private right of action.[450] Where a statute declares

439 *See, e.g.*, Bair Chase Prop. Co. v. S & K Dev. Co., 260 S.W.3d 133 (Tex. App. 2008) (construing usury penalty statute as displacing common law remedy, i.e., voiding of usurious interest, for violation of state constitution's usury restrictions).

440 *See* § 7.8.6.2, *infra* (federal RICO statute).

441 Cuevas v. Montoya, 740 P.2d 858 (Wash. Ct. App. 1987) (usury is a per se violation of state Consumer Fraud Act; awarding attorney fees, costs, and damages based on usurious contract). *But see* Hathaway v. First Family Fin. Servs., 1 S.W.3d 634 (Tenn. 1999) (if statute creates a new right and remedy, then the prescribed remedy is exclusive; state usury statute created exclusive remedy, so cannot use state UDAP act to create additional remedies, at least for the usury violation). *See generally* §§ 12.5, 12.10, *infra*; National Consumer Law Center, Unfair and Deceptive Acts and Practices (7th ed. 2008 and Supp.).

442 Cazzanigi v. General Elec. Credit Corp., 938 P.2d 819 (Wash. 1997) (holding no cause of action to enforce any violation of the state RISA other than the charging of excess interest (called a "service fee") even though statute states: "any person . . . who does not comply with the provisions of this chapter . . . shall be barred from the recovery of any service charge. . . .").

443 *See* National Consumer Law Center, Unfair and Deceptive Acts and Practices §§ 2.2.1.2, 6.4, 6.6.7 (7th ed. 2008 and Supp.).

444 *See generally* National Consumer Law Center, Repossessions Chs. 3, 13 (7th ed. 2010 and Supp.).

445 *See generally* National Consumer Law Center, Repossessions (7th ed. 2010 and Supp.); National Consumer Law Center, Foreclosures (4th ed. 2012).

446 *See* Giventer v. Arnow, 372 N.Y.S.2d 63 (N.Y. 1975).

447 *See* §§ 2.4.7, 2.4.10, *supra*.

448 *See, e.g.*, Conde v. O.F.S. Equities, Inc., 492 So. 2d 1153 (Fla. Dist. Ct. App. 1986) (under Colorado law, only effect of criminal usury violation is reduction of interest to maximum permissible rate, not cancellation of the transaction).

449 *See* Szerdahelyi v. Harris, 490 N.E.2d 517 (N.Y. 1986) (excellent discussion of distinctions between "forfeitures," "penalties," and voiding of a loan).

450 Bailey v. Defenbaugh & Co., 513 F. Supp. 232 (N.D. Miss. 1981); Transamerica Fin. Corp. v. Superior Court, 761 P.2d 1019 (Ariz. 1988), *rev'g*, 746 P.2d 497 (Ariz. Ct. App. 1987) (consumer loan act voiding usurious loans implied a right of action to seek that remedy). *See also* Mayo v. Key Fin. Servs., Inc., 1994 WL 879676 (Mass. Super. Ct. June 22, 1994), *aff'd on other grounds*, 678 N.E.2d 1311 (Mass. 1997) (implied private right of action for violation of statute limiting points; assertable by a suitable common law remedy; borrowers choose to assert common law restitution); Tew v. Dixieland Fin., Inc., 527 So. 2d 665 (Miss. 1988); Wombold v. Assocs. Fin. Servs. Co. of Mont., Inc., 104 P.3d 1080 (Mont. 2004) (finding implied private right of action under Montana's Consumer Loan Act, since enacted to benefit borrowers). *But see* Taylor v. Citizens Fed. Savs. & Loan, 846 F.2d 1320 (11th Cir. 1988) (no private right of action to enforce FHLBB regulations promulgated pursuant to Home Owner's Loan Act of 1933, 12 U.S.C. § 1461); Moroz v. Alexico Corp., 2008 WL 109090 (E.D. Pa. Jan. 8, 2008) (refusing to imply private cause of action for violation of Motor Vehicle Sales Finance Act's restrictions on markups); Miller v. Pacific Shore Funding, 224 F. Supp. 2d 977 (D. Md. May 17, 2002) (no private cause of action to enforce provision of licensing statute that limits lender's operations to certain loca-

usurious loans void or bars the creditor from collecting usurious charges, a number of courts have implied a private cause of action to seek that remedy.[451] There may also be a common law action for recovery of usurious interest that the borrower has paid.[452] If the lender violated a licensing statute, the consumer may be able to invoke the common law doctrine that contracts made by a party who lacks a required license are unenforceable.[453]

Generally speaking, illegal contracts are unenforceable as a matter of common law, but whether a particular usurious contract fits into this category depends on the nature of the violation and public policy considerations.[454] Depending on the surrounding facts, a loan contract may be void if it violates a criminal usury statute.[455] Usury cases have extended this principle even to the situation in which the criminal violation in question had no express civil penalty but other types of criminal violations did.[456] Or a court, finding a contract to be illegal due to a violation of a criminal usury statute, may order that interest and other charges be forfeited.[457]

### 7.8.2.2 Forfeiture of Creditor's Right to Recover Principal, Interest, Other Illegal Overcharges, or to Collect Attorney Fees

#### *7.8.2.2.1 Statutes that void the contract interest or other charges*

A most basic distinction made by many usury statutes is the difference between a debtor's obligation to repay the principal amount of a usurious loan and the obligation to pay the contract interest or other charges. Very often a statute will declare a usurious loan void as to all or part of the interest, while leaving the principal obligation intact.[458] Under such statutes, the widely

tions), *aff'd on other grounds*, 92 Fed. Appx. 933 (4th Cir. 2004); Staley v. Americorp Credit Corp., 164 F. Supp. 2d 578 (D. Md. 2001) (no private cause of action to enforce requirement that lender may operate only out of specific location); Luckett v. Alpha Constr. & Dev., Inc., 2001 WL 1286815 (N.D. Ill. Oct. 23, 2001) (no private right of action under Ill. Residential Loan Act where there was no evidence of legislative intent to create private remedy and court found criminal penalty sufficient for enforcement); Doubet v. USA Fin. Servs., Inc., 714 F. Supp. 980 (C.D. Ill. 1987) (no implied private right of action for violations of disclosure provisions of installment loan act; improper disclosures omitted in list of violations that trigger interest forfeiture penalty); Pattans Ventures, Inc. v. Williams, 959 So. 2d 115 (Ala. Civ. App. 2006) (no consumer remedy for violation of statutory requirement that auto title pawn lender keep vehicle on premises for twenty-one days); Lane v. Fabert, 533 N.E.2d 546 (Ill. App. Ct. 1989) (no implied private right of action under pawnbroker licensing statute; court, however, weighed fact that consumer had other remedies in so finding); Couture v. G.W.M., Inc., 2002 WL 31962752 (N.H. Super. Ct. Dec. 3, 2002).

451 Transamerica Fin. Corp. v. Superior Court, 761 P.2d 1019 (Ariz. 1988); Wombold v. Assocs. Fin. Servs. Co., 104 P.3d 1080 (Mont. 2004) (implying private cause of action where statute said loan was void but was silent as to private cause of action); Couture v. G.W.M., Inc., 2002 WL 31962752 (N.H. Super. Ct. Dec. 3, 2002). *See* § 7.8.2.3, *infra*.

452 *See* § 7.8.2.3, *infra*.

453 *See* § 7.8.5, *infra*.

454 *See* Siner v. Am. Gen. Fin., Inc., 2004 WL 2441185 (E.D. Pa. Oct. 28, 2004) (home improvement contract that included forbidden cash loan is illegal as an essential term violates public policy); Mincks Agri Ctr., Inc. v. Bell Farms, Inc., 611 N.W.2d 270 (Iowa 2000) (spelling out policy considerations, in non-usury case). *But cf.* Lloyd Capital Corp. v. Pat Henchar, Inc., 544 N.Y.S.2d 178 (N.Y. App. Div. 1989), *aff'd*, 603 N.E.2d 246 (N.Y. 1992) (violation of SBA regulations insufficient to render contract unenforceable). *See generally* § 3.9.6.3, *supra*, § 7.8.5, *infra*.

455 Norman Singer and J.B. Shambie Singer, 2B Sutherland Statutory Construction § 55.7 (7th ed. 2008). *See* Comtois v. MAK Invs., L.L.C. (*In re* Comtois), 363 B.R. 336 (Bankr. D.N.H. Feb. 16, 2007) (loan made in disregard of state lending laws may be void, depending on the surrounding facts).

456 Walker v. Peoples Fin. & Thrift Co., 49 P.2d 1005 (Ariz. 1935); G. Nicotera Loan Corp. v. Gallagher, 160 A. 426 (Conn. 1932); Hartsfield Co. v. Roberston, 173 S.E. 201 (Ga. Ct. App. 1934); Burque v. Brodeur, 158 A. 127 (N.H. 1932). *See also* Patchell v. Option One Mortgage Corp. (*In re* Patchell), 334 B.R. 492 (Bankr. D. Mass. 2005) (loan may be avoided or rescinded, even though no civil penalties available). *But see* Walters v. PDI Mgmt. Servs., 2004 WL 2137513 (S.D. Ind. June 14, 2004) (violation of requirement of U.C.C.C. that carries only criminal penalty does not make loan void), *modifying* 2004 WL 1622217 (S.D. Ind. Apr. 6, 2004).

457 Moore v. Comfed Sav. Bank, 908 F.2d 834 (11th Cir. 1990); Norris v. Sigler Daisy Corp., 392 S.E.2d 242 (Ga. 1990). *See also* Schuran, Inc. v. Walnut Hill Assocs., 606 A.2d 885 (N.J. Super. Ct. Law Div. 1991) (where criminal usury statute was silent as to penalty, only excessive interest was illegal, not contract, so creditor may recover loan principal).

458 *See, e.g., In re* Vehm Eng'g Corp., 521 F.2d 186 (9th Cir. 1975); Speare v. Consolidated Assets Corp., 367 F.2d 208 (2d Cir. 1966); Walters v. PDI Mgmt. Servs., 2004 WL 2137513 (S.D. Ind. June 14, 2004) (applying U.C.C.C. to reduce interest rate to statutory maximum unsupervised lender could charge), *modifying* 2004 WL 1622217 (S.D. Ind. Apr. 6, 2004); Daenzer v. Wayland Ford, Inc., 193 F. Supp. 2d 1030 (W.D. Mich. 2002) (finance charges void where seller does not give copy of contract to buyer at time buyer signs, but civil penalties under separate Motor Vehicle Sales Finance Act apply only if seller has sought prohibited charges); Smith v. Khalif (*In re* Khalif), 308 B.R. 614, 625 (Bankr. N.D. Ga. 2004); *In re* Rose, 266 B.R. 192 (Bankr. N.D. Cal. 2001) (voiding of entire loan is penalty only for consumer loans; for commercial loan, court merely disallows interest); Cantrell v. Walker Builders, Inc., 678 So. 2d 169 (Ala. Civ. App. 1996) (discussing changes to the Alabama Mini-Code); Patterson v. Green, 474 So. 2d. 725 (Ala. Civ. App. 1985); Metcalf v. Bartrand, 491 P.2d 747 (Alaska 1971); Dillon v. Resolution Trust Corp., 811 S.W.2d 765 (Ark. 1991) (state constitution makes usurious contract "void as to unpaid interest"; since void from inception, all interest paid is unlawful); Westman v. Dye, 4 P.2d 134 (Cal. 1931); Brown v. Fenner, 757 P.2d 184 (Colo. App. 1988) (lender on note at usurious rate could recover principal and interest at maximum legal rate); Centrust Sav. Bank v. Springs Cmty. Ass'n, Inc., 580 So. 2d 654 (Fla. Dist. Ct. App. 1991) (where creditor contracts for excess interest, the penalty is forfeiture of all interest, and only principal can be enforced); Southern Discount Co. v. Ector, 268 S.E.2d 621 (Ga. 1980); Cornelius v. Auto Analyst, Inc., 476 S.E.2d 9 (Ga. Ct. App. 1996) (citing to *Pave Way*); Pave Way Constr. Co. v. Parrish, 370 S.E.2d 495 (Ga. Ct. App. 1988) (interest is forfeited in usurious loan but principal may be collected because usury does not make the loan void and unenforceable as illegal contract); Bjornstad v. Perry, 443 P.2d 999 (Idaho 1968); Route 50 Auto Sales, Inc. v. Muncy, 771 N.E.2d 635 (Ill. App. Ct. 2002) (credit seller whose contract did not include items required by MVRISA cannot recover interest, late charges, or repos-

accepted rule is that all payments already made on the contract, unless the parties have specifically agreed otherwise,[459] will be applied to the principal debt until that debt has been paid off.[460] If the applicable statute voids the interest, then the maximum amount that a debtor may owe upon judgment is the original principal amount minus the payments made on the contract.[461] The creditor should not be able to fall back on the legal rate of interest.[462]

Another question is what portion of the interest is forfeited when a loan is made usurious by acts subsequent to the initial extension of credit. The Mississippi Supreme Court has held that an unlawful forbearance agreement, executed well after the initial extension of credit, tainted the entire transaction, making all interest on the original note subject to the forfeiture remedy.[463]

Usury statutes allowing the creditor to collect only principal, less the usury penalty, may be interpreted to preclude an award of attorney fees and costs to a creditor suing on the usurious note, even if the contract provides for it.[464] Similarly, where non-interest charges such as late charges are limited by statute, a creditor which imposes excess charges may forfeit the right to collect any such fees,[465] for to merely reduce fees to the

session fees, but debt for principal is not void); Saskill v. 4-B Acceptance, 452 N.E.2d 771 (Ill. App. Ct. 1983); Bonfanti v. Davis, 487 So. 2d. 165 (La. Ct. App. 1986); Patrick v. Shaw, 739 N.W.2d 365 (Mich. Ct. App. 2007) (when original loan was not usurious but an extension of it was, interest on the latter is forfeited), *aff'd*, 743 N.W.2d 897 (Mich. 2008); Meklir v. J.C. Penney Co., 2005 WL 1579658 (Mich. Ct. App. July 5, 2005) (usurious loan is not void, but collection of usurious interest is barred); Waldorf v. Zinberg, 307 N.W.2d 749 (Mich. Ct. App. 1981); Trapp v. Hancuh, 530 N.W.2d 879 (Minn. Ct. App. 1995) (interpreting Minn. Stat. § 334.011, subdiv. 2, regarding usury on business and agricultural loans under $100,000); Thomas Lakes Owners Ass'n v. Riley, 612 N.W.2d 529 (Neb. Ct. App. 2000) (obligation to pay interest is void, and creditor cannot replace usurious interest with interest at legal rate); *In re* Castillian Apartments, Inc., 190 S.E.2d 161 (N.C. 1972); Pennsylvania Dep't of Banking v. NCAS of Del., L.L.C., 995 A.2d 422 (Pa. Commw. Ct. 2010) (under Loan Interest and Protection Law, usurious interest rate does not void note; only makes voidable the interest specified beyond lawful rate); Tilley v. Pacesetter Corp., 585 S.E.2d 292 (S.C. 2003) (applying pre-1997 version of statute) (finance charge is forfeited and loan is non-interest-bearing when lender violated provision of usury statute unrelated to interest rate); First State Bank of Bedford v. Miller, 563 S.W.2d 572 (Tex. 1978). *See also* First Bus. Credit Co. v. Grayboyes (*In re* Grayboyes), 2006 WL 437546 (E.D. Pa. Feb. 22, 2006) (where interest capped by statute, interest reduced to statutory rate cap); Walters v. PDI Mgmt. Serv., 2004 WL 2137513 (S.D. Ind. June 14, 2004) (under Ind. U.C.C.C., debtor is not required to pay usurious interest and may recover any amount already paid); Patzka v. Viterbo College, 917 F. Supp. 654 (W.D. Wis. 1996) (creditor not entitled to any interest where it failed to make cost of credit disclosures required by Wisconsin Consumer Protection Act); Ring v. Jeziorski (*In re* Jeziorski), 428 B.R. 18 (Bankr. W.D.N.Y. 2010) (even if note for balance due for professional services were usurious and void, borrower would be liable for the cost of the professional services, and mortgage securing that amount is enforceable); Van Carr Enters., Inc. v. Hamco, Inc., 232 S.W.3d 427 (Ark. 2006) (contract with usurious rate of interest is void as to unpaid interest, but remaining provisions are enforceable); Badalamento v. Blonde, 57 U.C.C. Rep. Serv. 2d (Callaghan) 186 (Mich. Ct. App. 2005) (interest void on loan); Meklir v. J.C. Penney Co., 2005 WL 1579658 (Mich. Ct. App. July 5, 2005) (loan void as to interest, late fees, and attorney fees).

459 *See* Stacks v. East Dallas Clinic, 409 S.W.2d 842 (Tex. 1966) (rule that, in a usury case, payments are applied first to principal does not apply where, as here, the parties designated payments as interest). *See also* Cherry v. Berg, 508 S.W.2d 869 (Tex. Civ. App. 1974) (payment originally designated by parties as interest cannot be retroactively designated by borrower as principal, but may be applied to principal of void usurious loan); Barach Inv. Co. v. Huntoon, 65 Cal. Rptr. 131 (Cal. Ct. App. 1967) (all payments allocated to principal where no actual application to interest shown by creditor); Credit Alliance Corp. v. Timmco Equip. Co., 507 So. 2d 657 (Fla. Dist. Ct. App. 1987) (interest payments already made applied to principal); Hubschnan v. Broda, 247 A.2d 698 (N.J. Super. Ct. Ch. Div. 1968) (payments attributed to principal where lender's unilateral application to interest and principal was not made at time of payment). *But see In re* Vehm Eng'g Corp., 521 F.2d 186 (9th Cir. 1975) (payments under usurious agreement, although denominated as interest, will be deemed payment on principal until principal amount is exceeded).

460 *See, e.g.*, *In re* Vehm Eng'g Corp., 521 F.2d 186 (9th Cir. 1975) (California law); Speare v. Consolidated Assets Corp., 367 F.2d 208 (2d Cir. 1966) (New Jersey law); *In re* Bogan, 281 F. Supp. 242 (W.D. Tenn. 1968) (Tennessee law); Westman v. Dye, 4 P.2d 134 (Cal. 1931); Gibbo v. Berger, 19 Cal. Rptr. 3d 829 (Cal. Ct. App. 2004); Marino v. Whitney, 2000 WL 1687540 (Conn. Super. Oct. 12, 2000); Route 50 Auto Sales, Inc. v. Muncy, 771 N.E.2d 635 (Ill. App. Ct. 2002); Tauber v. Johnson, 291 N.E.2d 180 (Ill. App. Ct. 1972) (decision under MVRISA); *In re* Castillian Apartments, Inc., 190 S.E.2d 161 (N.C. 1972); Magee v. Dyrdahl, 926 P.2d 319 (Or. Ct. App. 1996) (this principle is also applicable to a business loan which violated Oregon's usury statute); Packer v. Wardwell, 744 P.2d 1312 (Or. Ct. App. 1987) (where statute provides for forfeiture of interest in usurious contracts, payments made will be applied solely to principal). *But see* Negaard v. Miller Constr. Co., 396 N.W.2d 833 (Minn. Ct. App. 1986) (payments are applied first to interest as a matter of law).

461 Metcalf v. Bartrand, 491 P.2d 747 (Alaska 1971) (both the stated interest and the interest hidden in the principal are void).

462 Bjornstad v. Perry, 443 P.2d 999 (Idaho 1968); Thomas Lakes Owners Ass'n v. Riley, 612 N.W.2d 529 (Neb. Ct. App. 2000).

463 Sunburst Bank v. Keith, 648 So. 2d 1147 (Miss. 1995) (business loans at issue). *But see* McCullough v. Jeziorski (*In re* Jeziorski), 428 B.R. 18 (Bankr. W.D.N.Y. 2010) (subsequent modification of loan agreement may be illegal but cannot render usurious original, lawful agreement).

464 *See, e.g.*, Dent v. Associates Fin. Servs. of Am., Inc., 137 B.R. 78 (Bankr. S.D. Ga. 1992) (if contract is usurious, creditor may not add attorney fees to its secured claim in bankruptcy); Hansen v. Doerflein, 757 P.2d 997 (Wash. Ct. App. 1988); Cuevas v. Montoya, 740 P.2d 858 (Wash. Ct. App. 1987). *See also* First Bus. Credit Co. v. Grayboyes (*In re* Grayboyes), 2006 U.S. Dist. LEXIS 6671 (E.D. Pa. Feb. 22, 2006) (denying attorney fees in adversary bankruptcy proceeding to creditor where creditor failed to comply with statute although attorney fees authorized by note and mortgage), *aff'd*, 223 Fed. Appx. 112 (3d Cir. Feb. 14, 2007); Meklir v. J.C. Penney Co., 2005 WL 1579658 (Mich. Ct. App. July 5, 2005) (loan void as to interest, late fees, and attorney fees). *But see* Suncrete Corp. v. Glusman (*In re* Suncrete Corp.), 100 B.R. 102 (Bankr. M.D. Fla. 1989) (usury penalty limited to forfeiture of interest and does not prevent recovery of attorney fees); Hazen v. Cook, 646 P.2d 33 (Or. 1982) (where judgment granted creditor for principal only on usurious note, it was a prevailing party entitled to attorney fees).

465 *See, e.g.*, *In re* Crotzer, 147 B.R. 252 (Bankr. N.D. Ala. 1992) (creditor which imposed excess late fees forfeited right to collect

statutorily allowed amount would give creditors an incentive to break the law.[466]

#### 7.8.2.2.2 Statutes that void the entire obligation

Although many usury statutes limit usury remedies to a forfeiture of interest, harsher sanctions are also found.[467] Numerous statutes declare usurious obligations to be completely void and prohibit any creditor recovery whether or not the principal has been repaid.[468] This sanction is most common in small loan laws and consumer loan laws derived from them. They often deny the lender the right to "collect or receive" any principal or interest charges whatsoever.[469] Second mortgage laws commonly provided for similar relief, at least prior to the general loosening of statutory standards in the deregulation wave of the 1980s.[470] The loan is also void under the UCCC when credit is extended by an unlicensed lender,[471] and in some states, where double or treble the amount of legal interest was charged.[472]

---

any; interpreting "actual damages" for violating Ala. Mini-Code's late fee limitation); LaBarr v. Tombstone Territorial Mint, 580 P.2d 744 (Ariz. Ct. App.), *adopted*, 582 P.2d 639 (Ariz. 1978) (en banc); Swindell v. Federal Nat'l Mortgage Ass'n, 409 S.E.2d 892 (N.C. 1991) (interpreting late fees as "interest" on detained money; statute calling for forfeiture of interest therefore called for forfeiture of all late charges). *Cf.* Bagri v. Desai, 349 S.E.2d 309 (N.C. Ct. App. 1986) (usurious loan for purchase of motel; lender could not recover share of profits from operation and resale of motel as provided in the usurious agreement).

466 *See, e.g., In re* Crotzer, 147 B.R. 252 (Bankr. N.D. Ala. 1992) (creditor which imposed excess late fees forfeited right to collect any; interpreting "actual damages" for violating Ala. Mini-Code's late fee limitation); Mitchell v. Residential Funding Corp., 334 S.W.3d 477 (Mo. Ct. App. 2010) (remedy for violation of fee restrictions includes bar on recovering any interest on contract; limiting penalty to unlawful fees and interest thereon would enable wrong-doing lender to profit from usury). *Cf. In re* Sprouse, 577 F.2d 989 (5th Cir. 1978) (discussing effect of overreaching contract language in transactions which are not litigated).

467 *See, e.g.,* Williams v. Seeley (*In re* Williams), 227 B.R. 83 (Bankr. E.D. Va. 1998) (Virginia's secondary mortgage loan law provides for the recovery of the total amount of interest paid in excess of that permitted plus twice the total amount of interest paid during the two years immediately preceding the filing of the action plus court costs and attorney fees).

468 *See, e.g., In re* Montagne, 421 B.R. 65 (Bankr. D. Vt. Nov. 13, 2009) (loan declared prospectively unenforceable where excess interest charged); Robertson v. Strickland (*In re* Robertson), 333 B.R. 894 (Bankr. M.D. Fla. 2005) (under Florida law, entire principal obligation is voided); Equity Mortgage, Inc. v. Niro, 690 A.2d 407 (Conn. App. Ct. 1997) (applying Conn. Gen. Stat. § 37-8; taking unusual step of addressing usury apparent on face of contract on appeal even though not raised below); Rea v. Breakers Ass'n, 674 So. 2d 496 (Miss. 1996) (finance charge in excess of amount allowed by 100% triggers forfeiture of principal and interest as well as repayment of any amounts paid); Seidel v. 18 East 17th St. Owners, 598 N.E.2d 7 (N.Y. 1992) (New York Gen. Obligations Law § 5-511(2) voids usurious loans; borrower relieved of further interest and principal payment and mortgages securing the loan are canceled); Borowski v. Falleder, 744 N.Y.S.2d 177 (N.Y. App. Div. 2002) (loan void where made to individual and interest rate exceeded 15%); Hilal v. Lipton, 642 N.Y.S.2d 78 (N.Y. App. Div. 1996) (usury of one of two individual investors who made the loan taints the entire loan and renders it unenforceable under New York Gen. Obligations Law § 5-511(2)); Malespin v. AB, 814 N.Y.S.2d 562 (N.Y. Civ. Ct. Dec. 7, 2005) (table, text at 2005 WL 3360900) (under New York law, entire loan is void and borrower can "walk away" from the loan with no obligation and recover amounts paid); North Carolina *ex rel.* Cooper v. NCCS Loans, Inc., 624 S.E.2d 371 (N.C. Ct. App. 2005) (North Carolina law requires voiding usurious loan and return of all payments); Ferrari v. Howard, 2002 WL 1500414 (Ohio Ct. App. July 11, 2002) (contract that included illegal charge is unenforceable under former version of Ohio RISA); Commerce, Crowdus & Canton Ltd. v. DKS Constr., Inc., 776 S.W.2d 615 (Tex. App. 1989) (interest in excess of twice amount legally allowed results in forfeiture of principal as well as interest, in addition to penalty of three times amount of usurious interest). *But see* Southern Discount Co. v. Ector, 268 S.E.2d 621 (Ga. 1980) (interpreting Ga. law to require forfeiture of interest and charges but not voiding of obligation to pay principal). *But cf.* Brodie v. Schmutz (*In re* Venture Mortgage Fund), 282 F.3d 185 (2d Cir. 2002) (questioning whether loan that violates N.Y. criminal usury statute is void); Brest v. Kleidman, 751 N.Y.S.2d 473 (N.Y. App. Div. 2002) (original non-usurious loan is not void even though post-default extension agreement is usurious and void).

469 *See* Bailey v. Defenbaugh & Co., 513 F. Supp. 232 (N.D. Miss. 1981); *In re* Perry, 272 F. Supp. 73 (D. Me. 1967); *In re* Tavares, 298 B.R. 195 (Bankr. D. Mass. 2003); *In re* Harrington, 6 B.R. 655 (Bankr. D.R.I. 1980); McNish v. General Credit Corp., 83 N.W.2d 1 (Neb. 1957) (statute since amended); Conrad v. Home & Auto Loan Co. 385 N.Y.S.2d 979 (N.Y. App. Div. 1976); Smashed Ice v. Lee, 200 N.W.2d 236 (S.D. 1972). *Cf.* Aikens v. Wagner, 498 S.E.2d 766 (Ga. Ct. App. 1998) (usury can be a defense to a foreclosure action but applicable statute forfeits interest only; transaction not void). *But cf.* Miller v. Pacific Shore Funding, 224 F. Supp. 2d 977 (D. Md. May 17, 2002) (loan made in violation of Second Mortgage Loan Law not void or voidable where statute did not explicitly provide that remedy), *aff'd on other grounds*, 92 Fed. Appx. 933 (4th Cir. 2004); Ferrigno v. Cromwell Dev. Ass'n, 708 A.2d 1371 (Conn. 1998) (suit for deficiency judgment after mortgage foreclosure falls within statutory exception to prohibition against suit on usurious loan). *See generally* Hubachek, Annotations on Small Loan Laws (Russell Sage Found. 1938) (complete compilation of small loan act cases decided through 1938); Hubachek, *The Development of Regulatory Small Loan Laws*, 8 Law & Contemporary Problems 108 (1941) (including supplemental list of small loan cases through 1941).

470 *See, e.g.,* Garrison v. First Fed. Sav. & Loan Ass'n of S.C., 402 S.E.2d 25 (Va. 1991) (usurious second mortgage null and void and unenforceable under Virginia's second mortgage act, since revised in 1987); Moran v. American Funding, Ltd., 569 A.2d 841 (N.J. Super. Ct. Ch. Div. 1989) (the words "void and unenforceable" mean just that in New Jersey's second mortgage act, since amended in 1987). *But see* Thoreson v. Shaffer, 683 A.2d 1153 (Md. Ct. Spec. App. 1996) (Maryland secondary mortgage loan law provides that any violation of the statute prevents the lender from collecting "any interest, costs, or other charges with respect to the loan": broker fee is not a charge with respect to the loan, and thus, collectible by the lender, unless the lender has a direct pecuniary interest or managerial influence or control over the broker).

471 *See* United Kansas Bank & Trust v. Rixner, 610 P.2d 116 (Kan. Ct. App.), *aff'd*, 619 P.2d 1156 (Kan. 1980) (1974 draft of U.C.C.C.); Kuykendall v. Malernee, 516 P.2d 558 (Okla. Ct. App. 1973) (1968 draft of U.C.C.C.). *See also* Edwards v. Alabama Farm Bureau Mut. Cas. Ins. Co., 509 So. 2d 232 (Ala. Civ. App. 1986) (loan by unlicensed lender voided under Alabama Mini-Code; borrower also entitled to refund of payments under statute). *See generally* §§ 3.9.6.3, *supra*, 7.8.5, *infra* (remedies for unlicensed lending).

472 *See, e.g.,* Tex. Fin. Code § 305.002 (West); Risica & Sons, Inc. v. Tubelite, 794 S.W.2d 468 (Tex. App. 1990), *aff'd*, 819 S.W.2d 801 (Tex. 1991) (awarding forfeiture of principal, return of borrower's

### 7.8.2.3 Borrower's Recovery of Payments Made

#### *7.8.2.3.1 Introduction*

A critical question which often arises when a loan is declared usurious is: what happens to the money already paid to the creditor? The answer will depend partly on whether the statute voids the entire obligation or merely the interest. If only interest is forfeited, it is fairly clear, as mentioned at § 7.8.2.2.1, *supra*, that all payments made under the contract will be credited to the principal debt until that debt is satisfied, unless the parties have specifically attributed some of those payments to interest. Less clear is what happens if the loan is completely void so that no principal debt technically ever existed, if payments exceed the amount of the principal originally extended to the borrower, or if the payments were expressly deemed to be interest payments by the parties.

#### *7.8.2.3.2 Statutes allowing recovery*

Some statutes which declare usurious loans to be completely void spell out the debtor's right to recover payments made, in which case the problem is solved.[473] For example, some versions of the uniform small loan act have denied the creditor the right to "retain" payments, so a refund is obviously required.[474] Small loan acts which declare usurious loans void and deny the creditor's right to "collect or receive" any charges on the contract have generally been interpreted as requiring a refund of all payments made, including principal.[475] A federal court in Michigan allowed buyers to recover finance charges from a dealer under this type of statutory provision in a state installment sales law even though the dealer had sold and assigned the credit contracts to finance companies.[476] The court reasoned that the finance company's payment to the dealer was based at least in part on the present value of the interest payments the buyers were expected to make, so the dealer had received a benefit from those finance charges.

#### *7.8.2.3.3 Implying the right to recover payments made*

In the absence of statutory authority, there are difficulties in arguing that payments to principal or interest may be recovered simply because the obligation is declared "void" by statute. The problem is multifaceted. First, strictly speaking, if a contract is "void," a court will generally refuse to recognize its existence and will leave the parties where it finds them.[477] This suggests that while a lender could not sue the debtor on the purported debt, neither could the debtor recover payments back without specific statutory authorization, although courts have sometimes rejected this reasoning because of the intent of usury statutes to protect borrowers.[478]

Second, courts frequently reason that even though a statute declares a usurious debt to be "void," the debt is actually voidable at the option of the debtor.[479] This position has led some courts to hold that a borrower can waive the usury by "voluntary" payment,[480] and having so waived his rights, may not recover the payments.[481] Third, some usury statutes are

---

payments, and penalty of three times the amount of excess interest charged, where lender charged more than double the amount of legal interest).

473 *See, e.g.*, U.C.C.C. § 5.202(2) (1968 Model Code); Edwards v. Alabama Farm Bureau Mut. Cas. Ins. Co., 509 So. 2d 232 (Ala. Civ. App. 1986) (loan by unlicensed lender voided under Alabama Mini-Code; borrower also entitled to refund of payments made); Rea v. Breakers Ass'n, 674 So. 2d 496 (Miss. 1996) (applying statute forfeiting all interest on usurious loan and allowing debtor to recover it back); Ferrari v. Howard, 2002 WL 1500414 (Ohio Ct. App. July 11, 2002) (interpreting former version of retail installment sales act; when violation was willful, consumer has no further obligation on the contract, need not return the collateral, and is entitled to refund of all payments).

474 *See* Young v. Barker, 342 P.2d 150 (Kan. 1959) (Kansas has since adopted a version of the U.C.C.C.). *See also* Ganus v. Jopes, 470 So. 2d. 237 (La. Ct. App. 1985) (statutory "forfeiture" required return of all interest payments).

475 *See* Bailey v. Defenbaugh & Co. of Cleveland, 513 F. Supp. 232 (N.D. Miss. 1981); *In re* Harrington, 6 B.R. 655 (Bankr. D.R.I. 1980); McNish v. General Credit Corp., 83 N.W.2d 1 (Neb. 1957); Smashed Ice v. Lee, 200 N.W.2d 236 (S.D. 1972). *See also In re* Capobianco, 73 B.R. 101 (Bankr. D.R.I. 1987) (ordering return of payments where Secondary Mortgage Loan Act voided usurious loans and provided that lender has no right to receive "any principal, interest or charges whatsoever"); Kinerd v. Colonial Leasing Co., 800 S.W.2d 187 (Tex. 1990) (awarding refund of amounts paid, cancellation of debt, and penalty of three times the usurious interest, where interest charged was more than twice that allowed by Texas' general usury statute); Risica & Sons, Inc. v. Tubelite, 794 S.W.2d 468 (Tex. App. 1990), *aff'd*, 819 S.W.2d 801 (Tex. 1991) (awarding forfeiture of principal, return of borrower's payments, and penalty of three times the amount of excess interest charged, where lender charged more than double the amount of legal interest; statute provided for forfeiture of "all principal"). *But see* Conrad v. Home & Auto Loan, Inc., 385 N.Y.S.2d 979 (N.Y. App. Div. 1976) (no refund of payments "voluntarily" made).

476 Daenzer v. Wayland Ford, Inc., 210 F.R.D. 202 (W.D. Mich. 2002).

477 *See In re* Montagne, 421 B.R. 65 (Bankr. D. Vt. Nov. 13, 2009) (loan prospectively unenforceable but statute does not provide for disgorgement); Szerdahelyi v. Harris, 490 N.E.2d 517 (N.Y. 1986) (voiding is neither penalty nor forfeiture). *See also* Siner v. Am. Gen. Fin., Inc., 2004 WL 2441185 (E.D. Pa. Oct. 28, 2004) (home improvement contract that included forbidden cash loan is illegal as an essential term violates public policy; it is therefore unenforceable, but consumer cannot recover payments already made). *But cf.* Kowalski v. Cedars of Portsmouth Condo. Ass'n, 769 A.2d 344 (N.H. 2001) (allowing recovery on unjust enrichment theory of payments made to unlicensed real estate broker).

478 *See In re* Harrington, 6 B.R. 655 (Bankr. D.R.I. 1980); Kuykendall v. Malernee, 516 P.2d 558 (Okla. Civ. App. 1973).

479 Elwell v. Daggs, 108 U.S. 143 (1883) (interpreting Texas statute); Wakefield v. Goldstein, 644 F.2d 707 (8th Cir. 1981) (Arkansas law); Pilcher v. Direct Equity Lending, 189 F. Supp. 2d 1198 (D. Kan. 2002); Chandlee v. Tharp, 137 So. 540 (Miss. 1931).

480 The precise distinction between the voluntary and involuntary payment of usury is far from obvious. It is apparently a question of fact. *See* Conrad v. Home & Auto Loan Co., 385 N.Y.S.2d 979 (N.Y. App. Div. 1976) (remand for factual determination). *See also* Thelen v. Ducharme, 390 N.W.2d 264 (Mich. Ct. App. 1986) (payment by borrowers after judgment rendered against them is not voluntary payment which would waive usury); § 7.7.4, *supra*.

481 *See, e.g.*, Wakefield v. Goldstein, 644 F.2d 707 (8th Cir. 1981); Bizzoco v. Chintz, 476 A.2d 572 (Conn. 1984) (interpreting statute that expressly prohibited recovery of voluntary payments of interest); Waldorf v. Zinberg, 307 N.W.2d 749 (Mich. Ct. App. 1981); Sienk-

structured so that usury remedies are exclusively defensive. For example, a statute might declare a usurious loan "void" but then proceed to provide merely that the creditor may not collect on the debt.[482]

One implication could be that no debtor recovery is available except by recoupment in a creditor's action. However, it is possible to argue that, in the absence of clear statutory language making it solely defensive, such statutes create an implied private right of action to enforce the borrower's rights under the usury statute. The Arizona Supreme Court, interpreting its Consumer Loan Act which, in common with other statutes based upon the Uniform Small Loan Act, voided usurious loans by licensees and prohibited the collection of principal, interest or other charges, held that the statute created a private right of action.[483] The court also noted that the provisions of a licensing act are part of a loan contract by operation of law, and are thus enforceable in a contract action.[484] A New Hampshire trial court has also concluded that a borrower can sue affirmatively to recover finance charges and other charges that the usury statute bars the creditor from collecting.[485] The court reasoned that it would be illogical to require a buyer to stop making payments, and wait to be sued, in order to take advantage of this right.

#### 7.8.2.3.4 *Common law action for recovery of usurious interest that has been paid*

A significant exception to the rule against the debtor's recovery of payments made, apart from statutes which specifically provide a recovery remedy, is that many states recognize a common law action for the recovery of the usurious portion of interest payments made on a contract.[486] Such a claim has particular potential in very high-rate credit such as payday loans, where the finance charges often exceed the principal after a few rollovers. Such an action can be invaluable to debtors if litigation occurs only after most of a loan is paid off because the creditor's forfeiture of future payments means little at this point. A common law recovery can also help debtors who have statute of limitations problems, because the time limit for the common law claim may exceed that in the usury statute.[487]

Not all states recognize the common law action, and in some states which formerly recognized the action, it has been abrogated by statute.[488] A number of courts, though, have held that

---

iewicz v. Leonard Mortgage Co., 229 N.W.2d 352 (Mich. Ct. App. 1975); Luebke v. Moser, 598 N.E.2d 760 (Ohio Ct. App. 1991) (Ohio common law is that usurious interest may not be recovered if voluntarily paid); Cherry v. Berg, 508 S.W.2d 869 (Tex. Civ. App. 1974) (borrower can have all payments applied to reduce principal of usurious loan, but voluntary payments made after principal has been fully repaid cannot be recovered). *See also* Chandlee v. Tharp, 137 So. 540 (Miss. 1931) (property sold pursuant to foreclosure at which no usury was alleged cannot be recovered because of waiver, although purchase price may be recovered); Conrad v. Home & Auto Loan Co., 385 N.Y.S.2d 979 (N.Y. App. Div. 1976) (construing statutory usury remedy not to allow recovery of voluntary payments). *But see* Kline v. Robinson, 428 P.2d 190 (Nev. 1967); Dougherty v. North Fork Bank, 753 N.Y.S.2d 130 (N.Y. App. Div. 2003) (voluntary payment of illegal fees for pay-off quotes is not a defense); Siefkes v. Clark Title Co., 215 N.W.2d 648 (S.D. 1974). *See generally* § 7.7.4, *supra*; National Consumer Law Center, Unfair and Deceptive Acts and Practices §§ 4.2.19.5, 14.6.4.3 (7th ed. 2008 and Supp.).

482 *See* Olsen v. Porter, 539 N.W.2d 523 (Mich. Ct. App. 1995) (Michigan law requiring prior interest paid be applied to principal applies only in defense to creditor's action to enforce usurious contract; creditor's action to reform the contract was not enforcement action, so remedy unavailable to borrowers); Michigan Mobile Homeowners Ass'n v. Bank of Commonwealth, 223 N.W.2d 725 (Mich. Ct. App. 1974) (discussing former Michigan law). *Cf.* Bank of Guam v. Demapan, 839 F.2d 1344 (9th Cir. 1988) (where statute merely limits the amount of interest a lender can recover when suing on the contract and does not otherwise provide for voiding the contract or punishing the lender, court will not enforce the contract for the excess, but borrower cannot recover interest paid); Scantek Mecial, Inc. v. Sabella, 582 F. Supp. 2d 472 (S.D.N.Y. 2008) (criminal usury is affirmative defense only); Funding Group, Inc. v. Water Chef, Inc., 852 N.Y.S.2d 736 (N.Y. Sup. Ct. 2008) (loan made in violation of criminal usury statute is unenforceable but not void, so borrower cannot obtain affirmative recovery).

483 Transamerica Fin. Corp. v. Superior Court, 761 P.2d 1019 (Ariz. 1988). *But see* Taylor v. Citizens Fed. Savs. & Loan, 846 F.2d 1320 (11th Cir. 1988) (no private right of action implied by the Home Owner's Loan Act of 1933 to seek damages for violations of FHLBB regulations promulgated pursuant thereto; state law claims for breach of contract, conversion and breach of fiduciary duty could be prosecuted in proper forum). *See also* §§ 7.8.3, 7.8.5, *infra*.

484 Transamerica Fin. Corp. v. Superior Court, 761 P.2d 1019, 1022 (Ariz. 1988).

485 Couture v. G.W.M., Inc., 2002 WL 31962752 (N.H. Super. Ct. Dec. 3, 2002).

486 *See* Dennis v. Bradbury, 236 F. Supp. 683 (D. Colo. 1964), *aff'd*, 368 F.2d 905 (10th Cir. 1966); Westman v. Dye, 4 P.2d 134 (Cal. 1931); Beltz v. Dings, 6 P.3d 424 (Kan. Ct. App. 2000); Flannery v. Bishop, 504 P.2d 778 (Wash. Ct. App. 1972). *See also* Gibbo v. Berger, 19 Cal. Rptr. 3d 829 (Cal. Ct. App. 2004) (where state usury law barred lender from collecting any interest, borrower was entitled to refund on unjust enrichment theory of amount by which her payments exceeded the principal); Mayo v. Key Fin. Servs, Inc., 1994 WL 879676 (Mass. Super. Ct. June 22, 1994), *aff'd on other grounds*, 678 N.E.2d 1311 (Mass. 1997) (implied private right of action for violation of statute limiting points; assertable by a suitable common law remedy; borrowers choose to assert common law restitution). *But see* Marker v. Pacific Mezzanine Fund, 309 F.3d 744 (10th Cir. 2002) (provision for forfeiture of interest does not create right to recover interest already paid); Anderson v. Chainani (*In re* Kemper) 263 B.R. 773, 781 n.15 (Bankr. E.D. Tex. 2001) (noting Texas legislature's 1999 abolition of common law remedies for usury); Luebke v. Moser, 598 N.E.2d 760 (Ohio Ct. App. 1991) (Ohio common law is that borrower cannot recover usurious interest voluntarily paid, at least if payment involved mistake of law rather than mistake of fact). *But cf.* Taylor v. Citizens Fed. Savs. & Loan Ass'n, 846 F.2d 1320 (11th Cir. 1988) (federal common law does not give borrower a right to recover excess charges imposed in violation of FHLBB regulations, but consumer may have viable claims under state common law).

487 *See* § 7.8.2.4, *infra* (discussing the attribution of contract payments to principal, interest, or usurious interest for purposes of a statute of limitation).

488 *See* Anderson v. Chainani (*In re* Kemper) 263 B.R. 773, 781 n.15 (Bankr. E.D. Tex. 2001) (noting Texas legislature's 1999 abolition of common law remedies for usury); Smith v. Barnett Bank of Murray Hill, 350 So. 2d. 358 (Fla. Dist. Ct. App. 1977), *overruled on other grounds*, 457 So. 2d. 1021 (Fla. 1984); Schlattman v. Stone, 511 P.2d 959 (Wyo. 1973). *See generally* Annotation, 59 A.L.R.2d 522 (1958) (right, in absence of statute expressly so providing, to recover back usurious payments).

the common law action has not been repealed by the enactment of specific statutory remedies, but that the common law action supplements them.[489]

Consumer attorneys should be careful to plead a common law action, if available in their jurisdiction, separately in their complaint or counterclaim so that it will not be deemed waived.

#### 7.8.2.4 Statutory Penalties

Beyond providing restitution to a borrower who has proved usury, usually in the form of a credit for or recovery of usurious interest paid, usury statutes often impose penalties on the creditor involved. The penalties frequently take the form of an award to the borrower of double or triple either the interest or the usurious portion of the interest paid on the contract.[490] (These penalties are often limited to that paid within a year or two of the filing of the suit.[491]) It is difficult to generalize about the interpretation or effect of penalty provisions because the terms of the statutes vary significantly. Nevertheless, a few issues arise with regularity.

The first issue is one of accounting. If the penalty only reaches *interest payments made* within a year or two of the date of filing suit, it is obviously important to figure out what portion of the payments made during that period should be attributed to interest. If the contract does not specifically address which payments will be credited to interest and which to principal,[492] most courts will first credit payments to principal.[493] This rule can be either advantageous or disadvantageous to borrowers depending on the circumstances. If the total payments made on the contract do not exceed the principal debt and they are all credited against that debt, then no interest will have been paid for purposes of the penalty provision.[494] However, if the total payments made exceed the principal debt, then the rule attributing payments first to principal suggests that the last payments made on the contract—i.e., the payments on which the statute of limitations for the penalty has not yet expired—are exclusively interest payments.[495]

For example, if a statute provided a penalty of twice the interest paid within a year of the date suit was filed, all of the payments made within that year should be doubled to calculate the penalty, so long as previous payments on the contract had satisfied the principal debt. Similarly, if the recovery is calculated solely on the basis of the usurious portion of the interest paid, then unallocated contract payments will be attributed first to principal, next to any unforfeited legal interest, and only last to usurious interest. Again, the statute of limitations begins to run from the date the borrower's payments were first applied to the usurious portion of the interest.[496]

If the statute provides for a penalty of two or three times the amount of excess interest "*charged or contracted for*," the question of allocating payments made is avoided. The amount of excess interest is determined by the charge imposed or contracted for, not the payments made.[497] However, if the loan

489 Westman v. Dye, 4 P.2d 134 (Cal. 1931); Commercial Credit Equip. Corp. v. West, 677 S.W.2d 669 (Tex. App. 1984); Flannery v. Bishop, 504 P.2d 778 (Wash. 1972); Demopolis v. Galvin, 786 P.2d 804, 808 (Wash. Ct. App. 1990) ("statutory usury remedies do not abrogate the common law action to recover usurious interest"). *Cf.* Auto Refinance Source, Inc. v. HSBC N. Am. Holdings Inc., 584 F. Supp. 2d 899 (E.D. La. 2008) (existence of Motor Vehicle Sales Finance Act remedy does not preclude contract claim or other state or federal claims, but statutory remedy may be exclusive if claim involves violation of interest rate caps).

490 *See, e.g.*, Trapp v. Hancuh, 530 N.W.2d 879 (Minn. Ct. App. 1995) (interpreting Minn. Stat. § 334.011 subdiv. 2 (small business/agricultural loans), providing for forfeiture of all interest plus recovery of twice interest actually paid); Britt v. Jones, 472 S.E.2d 199 (N.C. Ct. App. 1996) (applying statute allowing award of double the amount of usurious interest paid during the preceding two years). *See also* Creative Ventures, L.L.C. v. Jim Ward & Assocs., 126 Cal. Rptr. 3d 564, 576–578 (Cal. Ct. App. 2011) (where total amount of interest exceeded state's 10% usury cap, defendant has "received" usurious interest and is liable for statutory remedies even though another payee received a portion of the borrower's interest payments, so this payee's portion did not exceed the cap); Roethlein v. Portnoff Law Assocs., Ltd., 25 A.3d 1274 (Pa. Commw. Ct. 2011) (plaintiff can recover three times the unlawful charges paid even where underlying transaction involved collection of delinquent taxes rather than a loan); C & K Invs. v. Fiesta Group, Inc., 248 S.W.3d 234 (Tex. App. 2007) (denying recovery of treble the interest charged because borrowers failed to prove how much each of two holders had received in interest). *Cf.* Tilley v. Pacesetter Corp., 585 S.E.2d 292 (S.C. 2003) (denying recovery of double the excess finance charge when violation of usury law related to loan closing procedures rather than interest, even though as a result of that violation lender forfeited the finance charge).

491 *See, e.g.*, Williams v. Seeley (*In re* Williams), 227 B.R. 83 (Bankr. E.D. Va. 1998) (Virginia's secondary mortgage loan law provides for the recovery of the total amount of interest paid in excess of that permitted plus twice the total amount of interest paid during the two years immediately preceding the filing of the action plus court costs and attorney fees), *on remand*, 241 B.R. 387 (Bankr. E.D. Va. 1999), *rev'd on other grounds*, 2001 WL 652028 (4th Cir. June 13, 2001); Skinner v. Cen-Pen Corp., 414 S.E.2d 824 (Va. 1992) (interpreting former Va. Code § 6.1-330.46 to allow recovery of twice all interest paid within limitations period).

492 *See, e.g., In re* Grigsby, 127 B.R. 759 (E.D. Pa. 1990) (where contract provided that payments would be applied first to interest, Pennsylvania law mandates award of three times amount of excess interest due on any given payment).

493 *See* § 7.8.2.2.1, *supra*. *But cf.* C & K Invs. v. Fiesta Group, Inc., 248 S.W.3d 234, 248–251 (Tex. App. 2007) (treating each payment as allocated partly to principal and partly to interest for purposes of calculating penalty of treble the interest charged, and requiring evidence showing how much interest was paid to each of two holders of note).

494 *See In re* Vehm Eng'g, 521 F.2d 186 (9th Cir. 1975).

495 *See* Henderson v. Security Mortgage & Fin. Co., 160 S.E.2d 39 (N.C. 1968).

496 *See* Baruch. Inv. Co. v. Huntoon, 65 Cal. Rptr. 131 (Cal. Ct. App. 1967).

497 *See, e.g.*, Strasburger Enters., Inc. v. TDGT Ltd. P'ship, 110 S.W.3d 566, 579 (Tex. App. 2003) (penalty is based on difference between legal rate and interest creditor demanded, even though not paid); Risica & Sons, Inc. v. Tubelite, 794 S.W.2d 468 (Tex. App. 1990), *aff'd*, 819 S.W.2d 801 (Tex. 1991) (awarding three times the amount of excess interest charged as penalty, even though no payments to interest had been made; determining the amount of excess interest charged from statements of account).

has gone past maturity, there may be a question whether to use the interest up to the date of trial or just up to the maturity date.[498]

Accounting issues can also arise, at least in cases involving open accounts, where the statute provides for the forfeiture of principal. The Texas Supreme Court held in one case that the principal to be forfeited was that part of the open account upon which the usurious interest was charged.[499]

A second issue that may arise is the effect of statutory penalty provisions in the absence of an express statutory forfeiture of the lender's right to receive future interest payments on the contract. Some creditors have argued that statutes which require the creditor to pay a penalty of, say, twice the interest contracted for, do not preclude the creditor from simultaneously recovering interest at the legal rate which would then be offset against the penalty. Courts have generally rejected this argument on the grounds that it would undermine the effectiveness of the penalty provision.[500] Moreover, at least under some penalty provisions, a lender may not treat the penalty that it owes the borrower as an offset against any principal balance still outstanding, but instead must pay the full amount of the penalty to the borrower.[501]

A third issue may arise where a statute authorizes a penalty based on the "excess" over the "lawful rate": what statute applies to define the "lawful rate"? In a Pennsylvania case, the debtor argued that the lawful rate should be equated with the general usury statute's "legal" rate of 6%. The court rejected that argument, holding that the lawful rate was determined instead by reference to the special usury statute with which the court believed the creditor should have complied.[502]

Finally, it should be argued that the imposition of statutory penalties is mandatory,[503] at least in the absence of clear language to the contrary. If the law provides, for example, that the creditor "shall forfeit" a triple damage penalty to the borrower, that is mandatory on the court: such a penalty is "meant to punish and deter those who charge usuriously."[504] Moreover, statutory damages may be assessed against each separate entity guilty of usury.[505]

#### 7.8.2.5 Attorney Fees

Usury statutes that provide explicit causes of action for consumers often provide for awards of attorney fees if the consumer prevails.[506] A fee award is mandatory under the U.C.C.C. if the consumer prevails.[507] A decision that a loan is usurious may also prevent the creditor from recovering its fees under a contract clause.[508]

## *7.8.3 Equitable Remedies*

### 7.8.3.1 Courts' Authority to Impose Equitable Remedies

Although most remedies for usury and other overcharges exist under statutes or common law, there are circumstances when a debtor's appropriate remedy for usury is in equity.[509]

---

498 *See* Confederated Tribes v. Quantum Five, Inc., 91 P.3d 1255 (Mont. 2004) (discussing competing rationales, but using lesser amount here because of unique facts and equitable principles).

499 Steves Sash & Door Co. v. Ceco Corp., 751 S.W.2d 473 (Tex. 1988).

500 *See* Bjornstad v. Perry, 443 P.2d 999 (Idaho 1968) (no interest whatever on the principal can be charged or offset against the penalties); Commercial Credit Equip. Corp. v. West, 677 S.W.2d 669 (Tex. App. 1984). *See also* Bonfanti v. Davis, 487 So. 2d 165 (La. Ct. App. 1986) (forfeiture of interest means all interest, not just the difference between the contract rate and the legal rate); Thomas Lakes Owners Ass'n v. Riley, 612 N.W.2d 529 (Neb. Ct. App. 2000) (where usurious contract is not void, but recovery is limited to principal without interest, creditor cannot fall back on legal rate of interest). *But cf.* Mark McDowell Corp. v. LSM 128, 263 Cal. Rptr. 310 (Cal. Ct. App. 1989) (usury resulted in note payable at maturity in principal amount only, but did not prevent creditor from earning post-maturity interest at legal rate); Merritt v. Knox, 380 S.E.2d 160 (N.C. Ct. App. 1989) (lender allowed to collect "legal" rate of interest, generally the lowest rate of various allowable ones, from contract date because limitation period for interest forfeiture had expired).

501 *See* McCollum v. Hamilton Nat'l Bank, 303 U.S. 245 (1938) (National Bank Act penalties).

502 *In re* Russell, 72 B.R. 855 (Bankr. E.D. Pa. 1987). *See also In re* Marshall, 1998 Bankr. LEXIS 515 (Bankr. M.D.N.C. Mar. 2, 1998) (amount over rate cap of 16% in RISA is forfeited); Addison v. Jester, 758 S.W.2d 454 (Mo. Ct. App. 1988) (using higher of statute's two alternate rates to calculate penalty that was based on interest rate "permitted by law," but using legal rate for penalty that was based on "legal interest"); Stringer v. Perales, 2003 WL 1848594 (Tex. App. Apr. 10, 2003) (any interest charged in an interest-free period is in excess of twice the legal rate of zero). *Cf.* Avila v. Cmty. Bank, 2003 WL 22002779 (Mo. Ct. App. Aug. 26, 2003) (bank that charged interest allowed by its home state and federal laws was in compliance with statute limiting it to "lawful" interest rates); Dunnam v. Burns, 901 S.W.2d 628 (Tex. App. 1995) (Texas cap for agreed rates is 18%, 6% if no agreed rate; where loan specified a dollar amount of interest and terms from which the rate could be determined, the 18% ceiling applied. *N.B.*: compare § 7.6, *supra*).

503 McElroy v. Grisham, 810 S.W.2d 933 (Ark. 1991) (provision that borrower "may recover" twice the amount of interest paid was mandatory; to read it otherwise would defeat purpose of discouraging usurious contracts).

504 Berryman v. El Paso Natural Gas, 838 S.W.2d 610 (Tex. App. 1992) (holding debtor entitled to recover full penalty even though he pleaded an incorrect amount).

505 *Id.*

506 *See, e.g.*, Smith v. Eisen, 245 S.W.3d 160 (Ark. Ct. App. 2006) (award of fees is mandatory in usury cases involving consumer loans and credit sales); Washburn v. Michailoff, 613 N.W.2d 405, 410 (Mich. Ct. App. 2000) (treating attorney fee award as mandatory where lender attempts to enforce usurious contract, but only borrower, not guarantor, may recover fees); Robinson & Harrison Poultry Co. v. Galvan, 323 S.W.3d 236 (Tex. App. 2010) (attorney fee award proper under statute despite jury finding of no damages); Hoxie Implement Co. v. Baker, 65 S.W.3d 140, 150 (Tex. App. 2001) (treating fee award as mandatory).

507 U.C.C.C. § 5.201. *See* D.A.N. Joint Venture III v. Turk, 138 P.3d 1253 (Kan. Ct. App. 2006).

508 *See* § 7.8.2.2.1, *supra*.

509 Clean Harbors, Inc. v. John Hancock Life Ins. Co., 833 N.E.2d 611 (Mass. App. Ct. 2005) (Massachusetts law permits judge to fashion equitable remedies for usury).

The most common occasion is when the creditor is attempting to foreclose upon security, often the borrower's home, given in conjunction with the usurious loan. Borrowers who want to enjoin foreclosures must typically invoke the court's equitable powers. Equity may also control if a borrower wants to rescind an illegal credit sale contract, although rescission of consumer sales contracts is often controlled by statute.[510]

### 7.8.3.2 Rescission

Seeking rescission as an equitable remedy for usury can present serious problems for borrowers. The main obstacle is the rule that a party seeking equity must do equity. In the case of a borrower facing foreclosure of a usurious mortgage, this requirement may mean tendering the principal balance owed on the debt,[511] sometimes with legal interest,[512] and sometimes with amounts expended by the lender to maintain the security.[513] Tender may be avoided if a statute declares the underlying debt to be void or if the payments already made on the contract exceed the principal originally lent, because in either case the principal balance owed is zero.[514] Yet, if principal is still owed, the debtor will have the difficult task of producing a large sum of money quickly. Such a requirement, in the face of demonstrated wrongdoing on the part of the creditor, hardly seems equitable.

The courts have some discretion to delay the time when tender must be made.[515] In addition, immediate payment of the full amount of principal might not be necessary if for some reason the payments were not yet due under the contract. For example, in a North Carolina case, a senior mortgagee foreclosed on a parcel of land, leaving a surplus. The second mortgage note was held usurious, so the second mortgage lender was entitled to recover only its principal. The court held that because the borrower had never defaulted on the second mortgage note, no event had occurred to enable the second mortgage lender to accelerate its debt, and that the second mortgage lender was thus entitled only to periodic payments of principal from the surplus amount.[516]

A second problem with equitable usury remedies is that the debtor may be unable to obtain in a foreclosure proceeding all the offsets or penalties which might be available in a creditor's action on the debt. While there are not always problems,[517] the precise language of the statutes varies greatly, and can sometimes create difficulties. Prior to an amendment to Michigan law, that state's usury statute provided the borrower with a defense to the creditor's action on a note, but if the creditor instead attempted foreclosure, the borrower could be forced to tender principal plus legal interest.[518]

Practitioners should note that home equity credit transactions which include illegal overcharges frequently also violate the Truth in Lending Act's disclosure requirements, and TILA rescission may be a separate remedy available.[519] As TILA has both its own tender rules, which differ from those for equitable rescission under common law, and its own rules regarding credits, offsets and penalties, a home foreclosure case should always be evaluated for TILA rescission rights, in addition to relief under state law.

510 *See* Barco Auto Leasing Corp. v. House, 520 A.2d 162 (Conn. 1987) (implied right of rescission under Retail Installment Sales Financing Act).

511 Speare v. Consolidated Assets Corp., 367 F.2d 208 (2d Cir. 1966) (New Jersey law); Metcalf v. Bartrand, 491 P.2d 747 (Alaska 1971); Winnett v. Roberts, 225 Cal. Rptr. 82 (Cal. Ct. App. 1986) (proper tender made; foreclosure sale set aside); Feemster v. Schurkman, 291 So. 2d. 622 (Fla. Dist. Ct. App. 1974); Citizens & Southern DeKalb Bank v. Watkins, 225 S.E.2d 266 (Ga. 1976); I.D.S. Homes Corp. v. Lucas, 186 S.E.2d 745 (Ga. 1972); Kawauchi v. Tabata, 413 P.2d 221 (Haw. 1966); Michigan Mobile Homeowners Ass'n v. Bank of Commonwealth, 223 N.W.2d 725 (Mich. Ct. App. 1974); Naumburg v. Pattison, 711 P.2d 1387 (N.M. 1985); Bohlinger v. Am. Credit Co., 594 S.W.2d 710 (Tenn. Ct. App. 1979).

512 *See* Kawauchi v. Tabata, 413 P.2d 221 (Haw. 1966) (emphasizing the equities in this particular case); Bohlinger v. Am. Credit Co., 594 S.W.2d 710 (Tenn. Ct. App. 1979).

513 *See* Metcalf v. Bartrand, 491 P.2d 747 (Alaska 1971) (tender must include amount lender paid for real estate tax where loan transaction included borrower's agreement to repay lender); Feemster v. Schurkman, 291 So. 2d. 622 (Fla. Dist. Ct. App. 1974) (lender can recover expenses related to prior lease and first mortgage); Pisaro v. Rand, 291 N.Y.S.2d 82 (N.Y. App. Div. 1968) (under unjust enrichment theory, lender can recover sums spent for taxes and payments on outstanding senior mortgages). *But see* Kuykendall v. Malernee, 516 P.2d 558 (Okla. Civ. App. 1973) (lender cannot recover voluntary payment for excise taxes and expenses on automobile when borrower rescinds and lender was not required to make payments under loan transaction). *But cf.* Barco Auto Leasing Corp. v. House, 520 A.2d 162 (Conn. 1987) (creditor that violated Retail Installment Sales Financing Act is not entitled to offset for fair rental value of automobile when buyer rescinds contract).

514 *See* I.D.S. Homes Corp. v. Lucas, 186 S.E.2d 745 (Ga. 1972) (borrower must tender amount admittedly due; complete failure of consideration could obviate tender in proper case); Bjornstad v. Perry, 443 P.2d 999 (Idaho 1968) (recovery by borrowers exceeds remaining principal due); Pisaro v. Rand, 291 N.Y.S.2d 82 (N.Y. App. Div. 1968) (mortgage was void). *See also* Williams v. Macchio, 329 N.Y.S.2d 405 (N.Y. Sup. Ct. 1972) (no tender necessary when usurious contract signed under duress).

515 *See* Speare v. Consolidated Assets Corp., 367 F.2d 208 (2d Cir. 1966) (bankruptcy case).

516 *In re* Castillian Apartments, Inc., 190 S.E.2d 161 (N.C. 1972).

517 *See, e.g.*, Johnson v. Ronamy Consumer Credit Corp., 515 A.2d 682 (Del. 1986) (invalidation of second mortgage pursuant to second mortgage statute also reaches personal guarantees executed by debtors); Colter v. Consol. Credit Corp., 154 S.E.2d 713 (Ga. Ct. App.) (allowing borrower to assert statutory claim of forfeiture of interest as defense to foreclosure), *later appeal,* 157 S.E.2d 812 (Ga. Ct. App. 1967); El Paso Dev. Co. v. Berryman, 769 S.W.2d 584 (Tex. App. 1989), *further proceedings*, 838 S.W.2d 610 (Tex. App. 1992) (debtor can obtain both statutory penalties and common law remedy of cancellation of deed of trust). *See also* Enell Corp. v. Longoria, 834 S.W.2d 132 (Tex. App. 1992) (debtor may obtain invalidation of lien plus statutory penalties).

518 *See* Michigan Mobile Homeowners Ass'n v. Bank of Commonwealth, 223 N.W.2d 725 (Mich. Ct. App. 1974).

519 15 U.S.C. § 1635. *See generally* National Consumer Law Center, Truth in Lending Ch. 10 (7th ed. 2010 and Supp.).

#### 7.8.3.3 Reformation of Contract

A final equitable issue that may arise in usury cases is the question of reformation. Creditors have sometimes sought to avoid usury penalties by requesting that usurious contracts be reformed to non-usurious rates.[520] Such reformation has occasionally been granted on grounds of mutual mistake of the parties or fraud by the borrower.[521] However, outside of these narrow circumstances, courts have viewed statutory usury remedies as mandatory and have refused to resort to equity.[522]

The one situation in which reformation may benefit a borrower arises when a transaction is declared usurious, perhaps by a criminal usury statute, but no civil statutory remedies are provided. In this circumstance, it is within the equitable power of a court at least to reform the contract to a legal rate,[523] possibly to void the loan if the facts warrant such an action,[524] or to invoke the clean hands doctrine to refuse an offending lender's claim for relief.[525] The court might also imply a right of action from a criminal usury ceiling, and limit a creditor's right to recover solely to principal, forfeiting interest and charges.[526]

Another basis for a reformation-like remedy is any usury savings clause by which the lender agrees to refund any excess interest.[527] While typically consumers seek to avoid the effect of these clauses so they can recover usury penalties, such a clause can form the basis of a contract claim if no other remedy is available.[528]

520 *See also* § 7.7.9 *supra* (usury savings clauses).

521 *See* Turney v. Roberts, 501 S.W.2d 601 (Ark. 1973); Beach Assocs., Inc. v. Fauser, 401 N.E.2d 858 (Mass. App. Ct. 1980). *See generally* Annotation, 74 A.L.R.3d 1239 (1976) (Reformation of Usurious Contracts); § 7.7.2, *supra* (creditor's defense of estoppel).

522 *See* Varr v. Olimpia, 2002 WL 1425373 (Cal. Ct. App. July 1, 2002) (confining reformation of contract to cases of scrivener's error); Bjornstad v. Perry, 443 P.2d 999 (Idaho 1968) (court cannot reform contract after action to enforce contract is brought and usury defense is raised); Olsen v. Porter, 539 N.W.2d 523 (Mich. Ct. App. 1995) (noting that reformation is generally not granted for errors of law; if it were permitted, unscrupulous lenders could collect "ill-gotten" interest when not discovered, and then simply seek reformation if it were, without any deterrent force in the law); Szerdahelyi v. Harris, 490 N.E.2d 517 (N.Y. 1986) (loan is void despite tender of excess interest to borrower); *In re* Dane's Estate, 390 N.Y.S.2d 249 (N.Y. App. Div. 1976) (cannot invoke equity when statute mandates penalty).

523 *But cf.* Lieberman v. Emigrant Mortgage Co., 436 F. Supp. 2d 357, 365 (D. Conn. 2006) (noting decisions holding that contracts can be reformed only for fraud or mistake, not for usury).

524 *See* Begelfer v. Najarian, 409 N.E.2d 167 (Mass. 1980); Allegheny Int'l Credit Corp. v. Bio-Energy of Lincoln, Inc., 485 N.E.2d 965 (Mass. App. Ct. 1985); Beach Assocs., Inc. v. Fauser, 401 N.E.2d 858 (Mass. App. Ct. 1980).

525 *See, e.g.*, Brabson v. Valentine, 804 S.W.2d 451 (Tenn. Ct. App. 1990).

526 *See* § 7.8.2.1, *supra.*

527 *See* § 7.7.9, *supra.*

528 *See* Lieberman v. Emigrant Mortgage Co., 436 F. Supp. 2d 357, 365 (D. Conn. 2006).

### *7.8.4 Usurious Taint in Refinanced Obligations*

#### 7.8.4.1 Continuation of Taint in Renewal Transactions

Because consumer debt is frequently refinanced, it is important to consider the extent to which the presence of usury in one obligation affects the validity of a subsequent agreement between the same parties when they renew or extend the outstanding debt. The question is particularly significant when the new agreement calls for interest at a legal rate and would be valid but for the previous usury. For example, assume that a borrower takes out a loan at the maximum legal interest rate, but that the transaction is usurious because the lender exacts a hidden interest fee in addition to the stated interest. If this loan is later renewed at the same rate, but no new fees are assessed, is the renewal note valid?

The short answer to this question is no. The rule followed by almost all courts is that once a debt is tainted by usury, the usury will follow the debt through any number of renewal transactions.[529] Depending on the state, the taint may invalidate the new obligation to the same extent that it invalidated the original transaction.[530]

529 *See, e.g.*, Bowen v. Mt. Vernon Sav. Bank, 105 F.2d 796 (D.C. Cir. 1939); Aaron v. Mattikow, 146 F. Supp. 2d 263 (E.D.N.Y. 2001); *In re* Feldman, 259 F. Supp. 218 (D. Conn. 1966); Family Fed. Sav. & Loan v. Davis, 172 B.R. 437 (Bankr. D.D.C. 1994); Sanders v. Barron, 282 So. 2d 237 (Ala. 1973); American Sav. Life Ins. Co. v. Financial Affairs Mgmt. Co., 474 P.2d 51 (Ariz. Ct. App. 1970); Westman v. Dye, 4 P.2d 134 (Cal. 1931); Coral Gables First Nat'l Bank v. Constr. of Fla., 119 So. 2d 741 (Fla. Dist. Ct. App. 1960); Henson v. Dixie Fin. Corp., 296 S.E.2d 593 (Ga. 1982); McNair v. Gold Kist, Inc., 305 S.E.2d 478 (Ga. Ct. App. 1983); Gold Kist v. McNair, 303 S.E.2d 290 (Ga. Ct. App. 1983); Harrison v. Arrendale, 147 S.E.2d 356 (Ga. Ct. App. 1966); Dickey v. Bank of Clarksdale, 184 So. 314 (Miss. 1938); Nelson v. Gen. Credit Corp., 90 N.W.2d 799 (Neb. 1958); State *ex rel.* Beck v. Associates Discount Corp., 77 N.W.2d 215 (Neb. 1956); Manufacturer Hanover Trust v. Meadowdale Dev. Co., 458 N.Y.S.2d 700 (N.Y. App. Div. 1983) (rejecting argument that general release, executed in connection with modification and extension of original loan agreement, bars usury claim); Henderson v. Security Mortgage & Fin. Co., 160 S.E.2d 39 (N.C. 1968); Crabb v. Cole, 84 S.W.2d 597 (Tenn. Ct. App. 1935); Wallace v. D.H. Scott & Son, 127 S.W.2d 447 (Tex. 1939); Lentino v. Cullen Ctr. Bank & Trust, 919 S.W.2d 743 (Tex. App. 1996). *See also* L'Arbalete, Inc. v. Zaczac, 474 F. Supp. 2d 1314 (S.D. Fla. 2007) (usury will taint refinancing unless all excess interest in original note is expunged). *See generally* 47 C.J.S. *Interest & Usury* §§ 267–273 (2005).

530 *See, e.g., In re* Feldman, 259 F. Supp. 218 (D. Conn. 1966) (both principal and interest uncollectible); Henson v. Dixie Fin. Corp., 296 S.E.2d 593 (Ga. 1982) (interest and charges on original usurious loan forfeited, but lender may recover legal interest on new cash advanced upon refinancing); Dickey v. Bank of Clarksdale, 184 So. 314 (Miss. 1938) (interest on renewal notes void); Highway Equip. & Supply Co. v. Jones, 153 N.W.2d 859 (Neb. 1967) (interest forfeiture); Nelson v. Gen. Credit Corp., 90 N.W.2d 799 (Neb. 1958) (renewal note void); Wallace v. D.H. Scott & Son, 127 S.W.2d 447 (Tex. 1939) (creditor can charge interest on new money advanced in refinancing but not on tainted principal); Lentino v.

Courts have recognized that usury laws would be seriously undermined if the mere renewal of a usurious obligation could purge the debt of usury.[531] To regard renewal notes as valid as long as they state a legal interest rate would be to ignore the inflation of the principal of the renewal note at least by the amount of the usurious charges in the previous transaction, and additionally by the amount of any void principal or interest carried over from the previous loan.[532]

Furthermore, allowing renewals to purge usury would give borrowers significant problems with usury statutes of limitations. In many states the usury statute of limitations runs from the date of the last payment.[533] Since renewal of an obligation involves paying off the old obligation and replacing it with a new one, the statute of limitations for the old obligation may run from the date of renewal, i.e., the final payment date.[534] If the new obligation was considered free from the taint of usury, the borrower could be left without a usury remedy after a few years, even though the usurious charges from the old loan were part of the new, ongoing obligation.

### 7.8.4.2 No Taint If First Debt Forms No Part of Consideration

Despite the general rule against the purging of usury through renewal or replacement contracts, courts do recognize circumstances under which the usury in one obligation will not taint a subsequent transaction between the parties. If the debt created by the first transaction forms no part of the consideration for the second obligation, then the two notes will be viewed as distinct, and usury in one note will not affect the legality of the other, unless the two are actually parts of a single usurious scheme.[535] (Similarly, a valid obligation will not be tainted by subsequent usurious agreements between the parties.)

This exception to the general rule of taint, however, is merely a statement that a second note between two parties will not be affected by usury in the prior note if in fact it is not a renewal of the previous note. Since refinancing transactions by definition involve the renewal of outstanding debt, this exception should seldom be of concern to practitioners considering taint in refinanced obligations.

### 7.8.4.3 Novation and Waiver

#### *7.8.4.3.1 Purging of usury through a novation*

There is a more serious limitation to the rule that the taint of usury will follow a debt through a renewal transaction. It is widely recognized that a usurious obligation may be purged of its usury by a subsequent agreement between the parties through which the usurious contract is completely abandoned with the "full knowledge and consent" of the borrower, and "new or independent" consideration is provided for the new contract.[536] In other words, courts allow usury to be purged through a "novation," which they regard as distinct from a mere "renewal." Yet because the continuation of at least some portion of the old debt as part of the consideration in a new credit contract apparently does not preclude the existence of a novation, figuring out the real difference between a renewal and a novation for usury purposes can be a problem. Despite the plethora of opinions which state that usury may be purged by a novation but not by a renewal, only a few courts have attempted to provide any general guidelines for distinguishing the two transactions.

The most logical rule for distinguishing between renewals and novations is that a refinancing may not be seen as a novation which purges a debt of usury unless the transaction in some manner credits the borrower with the amount of the usurious charges assessed in the previous transaction. Thus, any transaction which rolls over the full amount of an outstanding usurious obligation into a new note would be a renewal, not a novation, because the debt quite literally has not been purged of usurious charges.

A few courts have expressly stated the requirement that an agreement must at least credit the borrower with all usurious charges assessed on the preexisting debt in order to purge the debt of usury.[537] Moreover, this proviso is consistent with many

---

Cullen Ctr. Bank & Trust, 919 S.W.2d 743 (Tex. App. 1996); Cherry v. Berg, 508 S.W.2d 869 (Tex. Civ. App. 1974) (interest forfeiture).

531 *See* Bowen v. Mt. Vernon Sav. Bank, 105 F.2d 796 (D.C. Cir. 1939); Family Fed. Sav. & Loan v. Davis, 172 B.R. 437 (Bankr. D.D.C. 1994).

532 *See In re* Feldman, 259 F. Supp. 218 (D. Conn. 1966) (borrower owed nothing when refinanced debt was void).

533 *See* § 7.7.5, *supra*.

534 *See* Crabb v. Cole, 84 S.W.2d 597 (Tenn. Ct. App. 1935). *See also* Valley View State Bank v. Caulfield, 731 P.2d 316 (Kan. Ct. App. 1987) (series of refinancing agreements evidenced by as many as forty-seven notes over seven years; court's extremely narrow reading of U.C.C.C. bars consumer defendants from asserting claims based on earlier notes as setoff against obligation represented by most recent note).

535 *See* Dichter v. Viking Office Prods., Inc., 501 N.Y.S.2d 420 (N.Y. App. Div. 1986). *Compare* Brookshire v. Coffman, 696 S.W.2d 748 (Ark. 1985) (single usurious scheme), *and* Johnson v. Ronamy Consumer Credit Corp., 515 A.2d 682 (Del. 1986) (second mortgage and collateral guarantees were parts of single unenforceable transaction), *with* Thomas v. Estes, 229 S.E.2d 538 (Ga. Ct. App. 1976) (separate transactions).

536 *See* American Sav. Life Ins. Co. v. Fin. Affairs Mgmt. Co., 474 P.2d 51 (Ariz. Ct. App. 1970); Kogan v. Bergman, 53 Cal. Rptr. 371 (Cal. Ct. App. 1966) (obligation was purged of usury when lender obtained and accepted a memo from borrower showing a credit to the account that brought it within usury ceiling). *See also* Ronen v. Teer, 498 P.2d 1284 (Idaho 1972); *In re* Estate of Jackson, 508 N.Y.S.2d 671 (N.Y. App. Div. 1986) (lender's acceptance of repayment in non-usurious amount as full settlement of usurious note purged note of usury). *Cf.* Cannarozzi v. Fiumara, 371 F.3d 1, 5–6 (1st Cir. 2004) (high-interest loan that complied with Mass. requirement of notice to attorney general was not usurious even though it was a refinance of loan that did not comply).

537 *See* Bowen v. Mt. Vernon Sav. Bank, 105 F.2d 796 (D.C. Cir. 1939); Family Fed. Sav. & Loan v. Davis, 172 B.R. 437 (Bankr. D.D.C. 1994) (lender not only did not purge original loan of usury, but condoned further unscrupulous activity by third parties in the process of settling litigation over the original loan); *In re* Bishop, 79 B.R. 94 (Bankr. D.D.C. 1987); Kogan v. Bergman, 53 Cal. Rptr. 371

less explicit opinions which have found transactions that provided no such credit to be mere renewals.[538] It should nevertheless be observed that courts take a more metaphysical approach to the question of novation, and seem to worry a great deal about whether the usurious agreement has been "abandoned" or whether the new agreement is truly distinct from the old.[539] Clauses in refinancing agreements which reaffirm the former debt or which adopt the provisions of the original agreement have frequently been brandished as evidence of the entirely obvious fact that the new credit contracts are mere continuations of the old.[540]

In a slightly different vein, some courts emphasize the intent of the parties in entering the new transaction to see whether usury was purged,[541] although it may not be entirely clear what type of intent the court is examining. It has been stated that a specific intent to purge usury is unnecessary,[542] which suggests that the courts are looking exclusively at the intent of the parties to retire old debt and form an entirely new contract. But looking for such intent is a bit unrealistic. In the real world, if they think about the subject at all, debtors and creditors almost invariably view refinancing agreements as modifications of existing agreements and extensions of existing debt. Furthermore, one can question whether the intent of the parties to form a completely new contract, even if demonstrated, should be allowed to purge usury from the new note unless the refinancing agreement has been negotiated at arm's length. Otherwise, borrowers could be compelled upon refinancing to waive rights that could not be waived at the consummation of the original transaction.[543]

It is critical to note that some agreement is required before any purging of usury is possible. Unless expressly authorized by statute,[544] a creditor cannot purge a debt of usury through its own unilateral action.[545]

#### 7.8.4.3.2 Waiver as an alternate approach

Rather than considering whether a refinancing agreement constitutes a novation which may purge usury, a few courts have framed the question as whether the refinancing agreement constitutes a settlement and release of the parties' outstanding claims against each other, including usury.[546] It is generally recognized that the parties to a usurious agreement may enter into a settlement of a usury claim provided that the agreement is negotiated at arm's length.[547] Thus, it is possible to view the issue of the purging of usury through refinancing as a question of whether the borrower released his or her usury claim pursuant to an arm's length settlement in the form of a refinancing

(Cal. Ct. App. 1966); Whittemore Homes, Inc. v. Fleishman, 12 Cal. Rptr. 235 (Cal. Ct. App. 1961); Henson v. Dixie Fin. Corp., 296 S.E.2d 593 (Ga. 1982); Ronen v. Teer, 498 P.2d 1284 (Idaho 1972) (usury was eliminated from the transaction when lender released the obligation in exchange for payments and transfer of property with total value less than principal plus legal interest). *But see* Negaard v. Miller Constr. Co., 396 N.W.2d 833 (Minn. Ct. App. 1986) (holding that payments on note applied first to interest, including usurious interest, so renewal note consists entirely of principal and is free of usury).

538 *See, e.g.*, Rollins v. Odom, 519 So. 2d 652 (Fla. Dist. Ct. App. 1988) (usury becomes part of subsequent agreement unless all usurious elements of original loan abandoned and borrower voluntarily agrees to new obligation); Coral Gables First Nat'l Bank v. Constructors of Fla., 119 So. 2d 741 (Fla. Dist. Ct. App. 1960) (new contract must be free from the vice of the old); Gemperle v. Crouch, 724 P.2d 375 (Wash. Ct. App. 1986) ("new, clean, and different transaction" required).

539 *See, e.g.*, Highway Equip. & Supply Co. v. Jones, 153 N.W.2d 859 (Neb. 1967).

540 *In re* Feldman, 259 F. Supp. 218 (D. Conn. 1966); Maze v. Sycamore Homes, Inc., 41 Cal. Rptr. 338 (Cal. Ct. App. 1964); Henderson v. Security Mortgage & Fin. Co., 160 S.W.2d 39 (N.C. 1968); Lawler v. Lomas & Nettleton Mortgage Invs., 691 S.W.2d 593 (Tex. 1985); Cherry v. Berg, 508 S.W.2d 869 (Tex. Ct. App. 1974).

541 *See* Wallace v. D.H. Scott & Son, 127 S.W.2d 447 (Tex. 1939) (no intent to purge contract of usury). *See also In re* Estate of Jackson, 508 N.Y.S.2d 671 (N.Y. App. Div. 1986) (borrower failed to prove usurious intent behind consolidated note). *Cf.* Lawler v. Lomas & Nettleton Mortgage Inv., 691 S.W.2d 593 (Tex. 1985) (question of intent does not entirely resolve issue; citing differences in terms of the two notes and fact that new note paid off old note); Cherry v. Berg, 508 S.W.2d 869 (Tex. Civ. App. 1974).

542 *See* Ronen v. Teer, 498 P.2d 1284 (Idaho 1972). *But cf.* Carter v. Warde Capital Corp., 838 P.2d 327 (Idaho Ct. App. 1992) (must show intent to eliminate usury from the transaction, not intent to waive claim of usury); Henderson v. Security Mortgage & Fin. Co., 160 S.E.2d 39 (N.C. 1968) (renewal of note was not settlement of usury claim when issue of usury had not arisen at time of renewal).

543 *See* Bowen v. Mt. Vernon Sav. Bank, 105 F.2d 796 (D.C. Cir. 1939). *See generally* § 7.7.2.4, *supra* (validity of waivers as usury defense).

544 *See* § 7.7.10, *supra* (statutes that allow creditor to purge contract of usury by notifying debtor and providing a credit).

545 *See, e.g.*, Duderwicz v. Sweetwater Sav. Ass'n, 595 F.2d 1008 (5th Cir. 1979); Riley v. Red River Marine, Inc., 664 S.W.2d 200 (Ark. 1984); Cigna Ins. Co. v. TPG Store, Inc., 894 S.W.2d 431 (Tex. App. 1995)Davidson v. Commercial Credit Equip. Corp., 499 S.W.2d 68 (Ark. 1973) (subsequent disclaimer); United-Bilt Homes, Inc. v. Teague, 432 S.W.2d 1 (Ark. 1968) (suit for legal interest only does not purge usury); State *ex rel.* Beck v. Associates Discount Corp., 77 N.W.2d 215 (Neb. 1956); Yakutsk v. Alfino, 349 N.Y.S.2d 718 (N.Y. App. Div. 1973); Danziger v. San Jacinto Sav. Ass'n, 732 S.W.2d 300 (Tex. 1987); (subsequent credit of the excess amount will not purge the usury); Fin. Commerce, Inc. v. McLean, 435 P.2d 932 (Wash. 1968). *See also* Dillon v. Resolution Trust Corp., 811 S.W.2d 765 (Ark. 1991) (contract defined payments as interest; rejecting creditor's after-the-fact attempt to allocate portion of payments to principal).

546 *See* Gunn Plumbing, Inc. v. Dania Bank, 252 So. 2d 1 (Fla. 1971) (giving effect to stipulation in collection action withdrawing all defenses and agreeing to a new promissory note in a compromise amount). *See also* Duderwicz v. Sweetwater Sav. Ass'n, 595 F.2d 1008 (5th Cir. 1979) (view of purging as settlement with new contract); LaBarr v. Tombstone Territorial Mint, 580 P.2d 744 (Ariz. Ct. App. 1978), *adopted* 582 P.2d 639 (Ariz. 1978) (settlement did not cover usury claim); Munilla v. Perez-Cobo, 335 So. 2d 584 (Fla. Dist. Ct. App. 1976) (following *Gunn Plumbing*, *supra*); McNair v. Gold Kist, Inc., 305 S.E.2d 478 (Ga. Ct. App. 1983) (note in payment of an open-end account did not cut off usury defense despite rules applicable to other contract defenses such as failure of consideration); Ronen v. Teer, 498 P.2d 1284 (Idaho 1972) (settlement purges usury); Henderson v. Security Mortgage & Fin. Co., 160 S.E.2d 39 (N.C. 1968) (renewal note was not a settlement).

547 *See* § 7.7.2.4, *supra.*

agreement. The cases suggest that such a release may occur provided that the agreement actually contained a release clause, and provided that the borrower was represented by counsel during the negotiations.[548] It seems that neither a specific waiver of usury claims nor a credit for usurious payments is a prerequisite for a valid release, apparently because the representation of the borrower by counsel is presumed (rightly or wrongly) to ensure that the borrower's interests have been protected.[549]

Predicting whether a court will follow a "purging" or a "release" line of reasoning in any refinancing case can be difficult, especially since some jurisdictions profess to recognize both doctrines. Generally, the concept of release seems aimed at the settlement of ongoing disputes where both parties are adequately represented, while the concept of purging seems better suited to modifications prior to any litigation, although the line between these two situations can be difficult to draw.[550]

It is important to recognize that under either line of reasoning, the average consumer refinancing will not terminate preexisting usury. If the court applies the "purging" doctrine, there is a strong argument that the usurious taint will infect the refinanced note unless the lender has taken the unusual step of crediting the borrower with the usurious charges. If, on the other hand, the court looks for a valid release in a consumer refinancing, it will not usually find one because consumers are rarely represented by counsel in such transactions, and thus the purported settlement will probably not have been reached through arm's length negotiations.

## 7.8.5 *Consumer Remedies for Creditor's Failure to Obtain a License*

### 7.8.5.1 Unlicensed Lending

The effects of failure to obtain a proper license vary.[551] Many licensing statutes clearly specify the impact of failure to obtain a required license. Sometimes the specified result is to void the transaction in which the unlicensed lender has participated.[552] This is the case with many small loan acts[553] as well as one version of the UCCC.[554] Furthermore, though a loan from an unlicensed lender under the UCCC may be void as to the lender's right to collect, it still gives the borrower the right to collect statutory penalties under the Act for other violations.[555] Other states may provide lesser penalties.[556]

Operating without a required license is a UDAP violation in many states.[557] A court may be willing to require an unlicensed entity to refund any money the consumer has already paid, on an unjust enrichment theory.[558]

One question is whether an assignee of a loan must be licensed in its own right or whether it can depend upon the status of the originating lender.[559] Some states require an assignee of a supervised loan to be licensed; if it is not, the loan

548 *See* Gunn Plumbing, Inc. v. Dania Bank, 252 So. 2d 1 (Fla. 1971); Munilla v. Perez-Cobo, 335 So. 2d 584 (Fla. Dist. Ct. App. 1976); Victoria Bank & Trust Co. v. Brady, 779 S.W.2d 893 (Tex. App. 1989) (upholding jury's finding that release was invalid on various grounds, including borrower's ignorance of usury claim and failure of consideration), *rev'd on other grounds*, 811 S.W.2d 931 (Tex. 1991) (finding no usury). *Cf.* Henderson v. Security Mortgage & Fin. Co., 160 S.E.2d 39 (N.C. 1968) (no attorney representation).

549 *But see* Family Fed. Sav. & Loan v. Davis, 172 B.R. 437 (Bankr. D.D.C. 1994) (waiver not a knowing or deliberate relinquishment of usury defense where debtor, though represented by counsel, did not believe he had claims, so thought waiver a moot point); *In re* Bishop, 79 B.R. 94 (Bankr. D.D.C. 1987) (whether settlement of earlier action bars claim presents complex questions of law and fact not susceptible to determination on summary judgment).

550 *See* Gunn Plumbing, Inc. v. Dania Bank, 252 So. 2d 1 (Fla. 1971) (compare majority and dissenting opinions).

551 *See generally* Annotation, 29 A.L.R.4th 884 (1984).

552 Beneficial Hawaii, Inc. v. Kida, 30 P.3d 895 (Haw. 2001) (loan arranged by unlicensed broker is void and unenforceable pursuant to Hawaii statute; holder may have equitable lien but only in amount of consideration it paid for the obligation); Moran v. American Funding, Ltd., 569 A.2d 841 (N.J. Super. Ct. Ch. Div. 1989); Gottesfeld v. Kaminski, 524 A.2d 872 (N.J. Super. Ct. App. Div. 1987) (second mortgage made by unlicensed lender voided the obligation under New Jersey Secondary Mortgage Act); Rancman v. Interim Settlement Funding Corp., 2001 WL 1339487 (Ohio Ct. App. Oct. 31, 2001) (loan made by unlicensed lender void under Small Loan Act); Bunch v. Terpenning, 229 P.3d 574 (Okla. Civ. App. 2009) (per Okla. Consumer Credit Code § 3-502, supervised loan by unlicensed lender is void). *See also* Rivera v. Schlick, 887 A.2d 492 (D.C. 2005).

553 *See, e.g.*, Ariz. Rev. Stat. § 6-613(B); Ohio Rev. Code Ann. § 1321.02 (West). *See also* Currier v. Tuck, 287 A.2d 625 (N.H. 1972); Smashed Ice v. Lee, 200 N.W.2d 236 (S.D. 1972).

554 U.C.C.C. § 5.202(2) (1968).

555 Kuykendall v. Malernee, 516 P.2d 558 (Okla. Civ. App. 1973). *See also* United Kansas Bank & Trust Co. v. Rixner, 610 P.2d 116 (Kan. Ct. App.), *aff'd*, 619 P.2d 1156 (Kan. 1980).

556 *See, e.g.*, Niemiec v. NCO Fin. Sys., Inc., 2006 WL 1763643 (N.D. Ind. June 27, 2006) (construing Indiana U.C.C.C. section not to provide consumer remedy for non-licensure); Smith v. Alfa Fin. Corp., 762 So. 2d 850 (Ala. 1999) (Alabama's mini-code was amended several times, first replacing the ultimate penalty of voiding the loan with recovery of actual damages, and then, in 1996, completely eliminating a cause of action for failure to obtain a license); Dixon v. Mercury Fin. Co., 694 N.E.2d 693 (Ill. App. Ct. 1998) (Illinois law allows recovery of actual damages only; distinguishing cases voiding contracts in absence of required license as limited to licensing requirements which could have a significant impact on public health or safety or where licensing statute does not contain a lesser penalty). *See also* Gaspard v. Vanguard Acceptance Corp., 689 So. 2d 1352 (La. 1997) (Louisiana's Sales Finance Companies Licensing Law requires the payment of twice the interest and charges originally computed on the loan); Me. Rev. Stat. tit. 9-A, § 9-405 (stripping finance charges from loan if lender is unlicensed).

557 *See* National Consumer Law Center, Unfair and Deceptive Acts and Practices § 5.4.8.2 (7th ed. 2008 and Supp.).

558 Kowalski v. Cedars of Portsmouth Condo. Ass'n, 769 A.2d 344 (N.H. 2001) (unlicensed real estate broker).

559 *Compare* PRA III, L.L.C. v. Hund, 846 N.E.2d 965 (Ill. App. Ct. 2006) (holding that an assignee can rely on the status of the originating lender), *and* Bobby D. Assocs. v. McDonald, 2004 WL 831179 (Cal. Ct. App. Apr. 19, 2004) (holding that an assignee can rely on the status of the originating lender), *with* Walters v. PDI Mgmt. Servs., 2004 WL 2137513 (S.D. Ind. June 14, 2004) (finding that unlicensed assignee cannot collect interest above statutory maximum).

is not void, but the unlicensed assignee is barred from enforcing it.[560]

Transactions with lenders who are not licensed, but should be, may be void even in the absence of a special statutory provision to that effect. The common law principle that "contracts made in violation of regulatory statutes enacted for the protection of the public [are] rendered null and unenforceable" has been applied where creditors failed to comply with appropriate licensing requirements.[561] This general rule applies to licensing statutes enacted for the protection of the public, rather than those enacted merely to raise revenue. Special usury licensing statutes are clearly in the former category, as they are designed to protect borrowers "through the strict regulation and supervision of the creditors themselves."[562]

560 Independent Fin., Inc. v. Wanna, 186 P.3d 196 (Kan. Ct. App. 2008); Bunch v. Terpenning, 229 P.3d 574 (Okla. Civ. App. 2009) (even if loan made by licensed originator, unlicensed assignees may not attempt direct collection or foreclosure). *See also* § 3.9.6.2, *supra*.

561 Derico v. Duncan, 410 So. 2d 27, 29 (Ala. 1982) (loan of money was void as to principal and interest where defendant made loan at supervised lending rate without having obtained a license); Edwards v. Alabama Farm Bureau Mut. Cas. Ins., 509 So. 2d 232 (Ala. Civ. App. 1986) (note obtained by casualty insurer from uninsured motorist on subrogation claim was consumer loan, requiring that insurer be licensed under Mini-Code; failure to obtain license voided the loan); Solomon v. Gilmore, 731 A.2d 280 (Conn. 1999) (mortgage taken by unlicensed lender is unenforceable); Family Constr. v. District of Columbia Dep't of Cons. & Regulatory Affairs, 484 A.2d 250 (D.C. 1984) (home improvement contractor who was engaged in retail installment sales transactions was required to register; failure to register voided the transaction, and contractor was required to return the down payment). *See also* Gorman v. Marcon Capital Corp., 274 B.R. 351 (D. Vt. 2002) (even if statute's explicit voiding provision did not apply to pre-loan agreement with unlicensed lender, common law may make it unenforceable); RCDI Constr., Inc. v. Spaceplan/Architecture, Planning & Interiors, 148 F. Supp. 2d 607 (W.D.N.C. 2001) (contract with unlicensed construction firm is unenforceable), *aff'd on other grounds*, 29 Fed. Appx. 120 (4th Cir. 2002). *But see* Raceway Props., L.L.C. v. LSOF Carlsbad Land L.P., 157 Fed. Appx. 959 (9th Cir. 2005) (unpublished) (failure to obtain a license does not deprive lender of protection of usury exception for sophisticated borrowers); Dixon v. Mercury Fin. Co., 694 N.E.2d 693 (Ill. App. Ct. 1998); Bennett v. Bourne, 5 S.W.3d 124 (Ky. 1999); Bell v. Muller, 118 P.3d 405 (Wash. Ct. App. 2005) (citing state agency interpretation that licensing is "voluntary" and that lending without a license may but need not violate state usury laws). *But cf.* Walters v. PDI Mgmt. Servs., 2004 WL 2137513 (S.D. Ind. June 14, 2004) (declining to void assignment of obligation since Indiana U.C.C. had other explicit remedies for violations). *See generally* cases collected in Annotation, 29 A.L.R.4th 884, § 4[b].

562 Derico v. Duncan, 410 So. 2d 27, 31 (Ala. 1982). *Accord* Solomon v. Gilmore, 731 A.2d 280 (Conn. 1999) (secondary mortgage act imposes comprehensive set of rules, going far beyond lender's personal qualifications; mortgage by unlicensed lender is unenforceable). *See also* Vermont Dev. Credit Corp. v. Kitchel, 544 A.2d 1165 (Vt. 1988) (development credit corporations not specifically exempt under statute requiring license in order to make loans at greater than 12% interest; fact that purpose of corporation is to promote general welfare of state does not mean it can never charge excessive interest or engage in unfair practices); § 7.2.1, *supra*.

Some courts may not be willing to adopt an absolute rule that contracts made by unlicensed parties are void, but may apply a balancing test, weighing the interest in enforcing the contract against the public policy behind the licensing requirement.[563] This balancing approach is espoused by the *Restatement (Second) of Contracts* § 181. The factors that the *Restatement* lists as weighing in favor of enforcing the contract or contract term are:

- The parties' justified expectations;
- Any forfeiture that would result if enforcement were denied; and
- Any special public interest in the enforcement of the particular term.

The *Restatement* factors that weigh against enforcement are:

- The strength of the public policy, as manifested by legislation or judicial decisions;
- The likelihood that a refusal to enforce the term will further that policy;
- The seriousness of any misconduct involved and the extent to which it was deliberate; and
- The directness of the connection between that misconduct and the term.[564]

The fact that the unlicensed party will suffer a forfeiture should not be a decisive factor. As the *Restatement* notes, it is usually the case that the unlicensed party will have already performed, so will typically face a forfeiture.[565]

Applying these factors to the case of an unlicensed lender, the existence of any criminal penalty for unlicensed lending, and any legislative history showing the reasons behind the licensing requirement, will help demonstrate the strength of the public policy. The practitioner should stress that the licensing requirement is designed to protect the public rather than just raise revenue.[566] Common indications that the purpose goes beyond revenue are, according to the *Restatement*, provisions for examination to ensure minimum standards, a bond requirement, or procedures for license revocation to ensure that standards are maintained.[567]

It also should not be difficult to show that refusing to enforce the loan contract would further the statute's public policies by providing a financial disincentive for unlicensed lending. To allow unlicensed lenders to reap the profits of illegal transactions would only encourage others to enter the business. As to the parties' justified expectations, a lender will have a difficult time

563 *See* Fabricant v. Sears Roebuck (S.D. Fla. Mar. 5, 2002), *available at* www.nclc.org/unreported (citing *Restatement*; failure to obtain license to sell credit insurance makes contract void), *class certified*, 202 F.R.D. 310, 320 (S.D. Fla. 2001) (reiterating that unlicensed sale of credit insurance makes contracts void); Mincks Agri Ctr., Inc. v. Bell Farms, Inc., 611 N.W.2d 270 (Iowa 2000).

564 Restatement (Second) of Contracts § 178.

565 Restatement (Second) of Contracts § 181 cmt. c.

566 *See* Restatement (Second) of Contracts § 181 cmt. b (contract not unenforceable if purpose of licensing requirement is merely to raise revenue).

567 *Id.*

arguing that it was justified in expecting repayment of an unlicensed loan at extortionate rates. A loan contract is unlikely to have any special impact on the public, so a court is unlikely to find any special public interest in enforcing it. How the other factors play out would depend on the facts of the particular case.

The failure to obtain a necessary license need not be willful to invoke a penalty.[568] However, statutory language providing for a bona fide error defense may be construed to insulate a creditor who reasonably and in good faith failed to obtain a license upon the advice of counsel.[569]

### 7.8.5.2 Remedies Where Licensed Creditor Violates Conditions of Licensure Statute

Even if a creditor has obtained a required license, it may not have complied with all the other requirements necessary to enable it to charge a particular rate. Thus, a South Carolina licensed creditor who neglected to file an annual rate schedule with the state as required was limited to an 18% APR and ordered to refund or credit any excess interest charged to borrowers while it was out of compliance.[570] Where the lender has not complied with the statute's requirements for licensed lenders, the loan may not qualify for the protections of the special usury law, making it subject to a lower general usury ceiling.[571]

The fact that a lender has a license does not mean that any loan it makes can take advantage of the higher usury ceiling in the licensing statute. If a licensee makes a loan that does not conform to the requirements of the licensing law, the loan will be subject to the general usury ceiling.[572] The borrower may also be able to make the violation the basis of a UDAP claim, assuming that causation and damages can be shown,[573] or assert an implied cause of action.[574]

On the other hand, some courts have viewed the question as whether a statutory cause of action is available for a lender's non-compliance with licensing requirements. A series of decisions from Maryland find no private cause of action to enforce a provision of a licensing statute that limits the lender's operations to certain locations.[575]

## 7.8.6 *Federal Remedies*

### 7.8.6.1 Remedies Under National Bank Act and DIDA

The National Bank Act establishes the remedy for a usurious loan issued by a national bank: the lender forfeits the entire contract interest, and the borrower may recover a penalty of twice the interest paid.[576] The action must be commenced within two years of the occurrence of the usurious transaction.[577] Similar, but not identical remedies apply to federal savings associations and federal credit unions, and to state banks, state savings and loan institutions, and state credit unions that claim federal preemption of state usury laws under the alternative ceiling provisions of the Depository Institutions Deregulation and Monetary Control Act of 1980 (DIDA).[578] If the alternative ceiling exceeds the interest rate allowed by the state, and the state ceiling is thereby preempted, but the lender charges a rate even higher than allowed by the DIDA alternative ceiling, then the lender forfeits the entire contract interest and the borrower may recover twice the amount of the interest paid within two years of the commencement of the action. If the state interest ceiling exceeds the DIDA alternative ceiling or if for some other reason, such as a state opt-out, the alternative ceiling preemption does not apply, the wording of DIDA suggests that state usury remedies control.

### 7.8.6.2 RICO

#### *7.8.6.2.1 Overview of RICO*

The Racketeer Influenced and Corrupt Organizations Act (RICO)[579] provides powerful civil remedies,[580] including attorney fees and treble damages, to victims of a broadly defined

568 Derico v. Duncan, 410 So. 2d 27, 31 (Ala. 1982); Edwards v. Alabama Farm Bureau Mut. Cas. Ins. Co., 509 So. 2d 232 (Ala. Civ. App. 1986) (failure to obtain license rendered loan void, whether willful or not; state banking department had advised insurer no license was necessary).

569 Rea v. Wichita Mortgage Corp. 747 F.2d 567 (10th Cir. 1984).

570 Bell Fin. v. Dep't of Consumer Affairs, 374 S.E.2d 918 (S.C. Ct. App. 1988).

571 *See, e.g.,* Agapitov v. Lerner, 133 Cal. Rptr. 2d 837 (Cal. Ct. App. 2003).

572 Agapitov v. Lerner, 133 Cal. Rptr. 2d 837 (Cal. Ct. App. 2003).

573 *See* § 2.4.1, *supra*. *But see* Rivera v. Grossinger Autoplex, Inc., 2000 WL 796158 (N.D. Ill. June 19, 2000) (consumer does not have private cause of action against creditor for engaging in conduct which the licensing agency can consider as grounds to deny a license), *aff'd on other grounds*, 274 F.3d 1118 (7th Cir. 2001).

574 *See* § 7.8.2.1, *supra.*

575 Miller v. Pacific Shore Funding, 224 F. Supp. 2d 977 (D. Md. 2002) (no private cause of action to enforce provision of licensing statute that limits lender's operations to certain locations), *aff'd on other grounds*, 92 Fed. Appx. 933 (4th Cir. 2004) (table); Staley v. Americorp Credit Corp., 164 F. Supp. 2d 578 (D. Md. 2001) (no private cause of action to enforce requirement that licensed lender operate only out of specific location).

576 12 U.S.C. § 86. *See, e.g.,* Beneficial Nat'l Bank v. Anderson, 539 U.S. 1, 8, 123 S. Ct. 2058, 156 L. Ed. 2d 1 (2003) (noting the nature of the federal cause of action and holding that it completely preempts state usury claims); McCollum v. Hamilton Nat'l Bank, 303 U.S. 245 (1938); American Timber & Trading v. First Nat'l Bank of Or., 690 F.2d 781 (9th Cir. 1982) (subclass recovers double interest paid on usurious loans, but prejudgment interest denied); First Nat'l Bank in Mena v. Nowlin, 509 F.2d 872 (8th Cir. 1975) (state remedies preempted); Bokum v. First Nat'l Bank, 740 P.2d 693 (N.M. 1987) (National Bank Act claim disallowed where not filed within two years). *See generally* § 7.9.1.3, *infra* (complete preemption of usury claims under National Bank Act).

577 12 U.S.C. § 86.

578 The remedy provisions are found at 12 U.S.C. §§ 1463(g)(2) (thrifts), 1785(g) (credit unions), 1831d (state banks). *See* § 3.7.2, *supra* (DIDA preemption).

579 18 U.S.C. §§ 1961–1968.

For a detailed analysis of RICO, see National Consumer Law Center, Unfair and Deceptive Acts and Practices §§ 14.2, 14.3, Appx. C.2 (7th ed. 2008 and Supp.) (summaries of state RICO statutes).

580 *See* 18 U.S.C. § 1964.

range of "racketeering activity" and to those who have been subjected to the collection of an "unlawful debt." "Unlawful debt" includes any usurious debt bearing interest of at least twice the "enforceable rate."[581] RICO prohibits four activities:

> (a) It shall be unlawful for any person who has received any income derived, directly or indirectly, from a pattern of racketeering activity or through collection of an unlawful debt in which such person has participated as a principal within the meaning of section 2, title 18, United States Code, to use or invest, directly or indirectly, any part of such income, or the proceeds of such income, in acquisition of any interest in, or the establishment or operation of, any enterprise which is engaged in, or the activities of which affect, interstate or foreign commerce. . . .
>
> (b) It shall be unlawful for any person through a pattern of racketeering activity or through collection of an unlawful debt to acquire or maintain, directly or indirectly, any interest in or control of any enterprise which is engaged in, or the activities of which affect, interstate or foreign commerce.
>
> (c) It shall be unlawful for any person employed by or associated with any enterprise engaged in, or the activities of which affect, interstate or foreign commerce, to conduct or participate, directly or indirectly, in the conduct of such enterprise's affairs through a pattern of racketeering activity or collection of unlawful debt.
>
> (d) It shall be unlawful for any person to conspire to violate any of the provisions of subsection (a), (b), or (c) of this section.[582]

RICO is by no means limited to organized crime, but is broadly written to encompass a myriad of fraudulent activities conducted by theoretically "legitimate" organizations such as banks and other creditors. Especially in light of the Supreme Court's decisions in *Sedima S.P.R.L. v. Imrex Company, Inc.*,[583] and *American National Bank and Trust Company of Chicago v. Haroco, Inc.*,[584] which overruled lower court attempts to limit the breadth of civil RICO, practitioners whose clients have been the victims of either fraudulent overcharging (indicating racketeering activity) or overcharging of at least twice the civil usury rate (indicating the collection of an unlawful debt) may wish to consider a RICO claim.

The essential elements of a civil RICO action depend upon which of the four subsections of section 1962 is alleged to have been violated. The following elements are common to any civil RICO cause of action:

- An enterprise must exist;
- The enterprise must be engaged in or affect interstate or foreign commerce;
- The defendant must have engaged in one or more of the four prohibited enumerated in section 1962; and
- The prohibited conduct must have caused injury to the plaintiff's business or property, a requirement discussed in more detail at § 10.8.5.3.4, *infra*.

For the purposes of a RICO action, an "enterprise" includes almost any business organization, whether or not formally incorporated.[585] No criminal conviction is required before a RICO defendant may be pursued civilly, and the plaintiff need show no injury beyond that caused by the racketeering activity or the unlawful debt collection.[586]

In addition to these elements, every RICO violation must involve either "collection of an unlawful debt" or a "pattern of racketeering activity" that relates to the enterprise in the manner proscribed by the particular subsection of section 1962.[587] Section 1962(c) generally requires that the plaintiff plead and prove an enterprise that is separate and distinct from the defendant person, while subsections (a), (b), and (d) do not necessarily have that same requirement.[588]

#### 7.8.6.2.2 *Racketeering activity and the pattern requirement*

A "racketeering activity" is conduct that violates any of a list of state and federal statutes. Most notably for consumer purposes, this list includes mail fraud, wire fraud, and extortion.[589] A "pattern" is a *minimum* of two incidents of racketeering activity.[590] A pattern of racketeering activity need not involve organized crime, cannot be shown merely by proving two predicate acts, and does not require predicate acts that are part of separate illegal schemes.[591] When alleging predicate acts founded on fraud, practitioners should be alert to complying with Federal Rule of Civil Procedure 9(b)'s particularity requirements, which must be met as to each alleged act.[592]

In *H.J. Inc. v. Northwestern Bell Telephone Co.*,[593] the Supreme Court held that the concept of "pattern" has two separate properties that must be established: relationship and continuity.[594] Acts meet the relationship test if they have "the same or similar purposes, results, participants, victims, or methods of commission, or are otherwise interrelated."[595] As for

581 18 U.S.C. § 1961(6) (also including gambling debts that either arose from illegal gambling activity or are unenforceable due to state or federal usury laws).

582 18 U.S.C. § 1962(a)–(d).

583 473 U.S. 479, 105 S. Ct. 3275, 87 L. Ed. 2d 346 (1985).

584 473 U.S. 479, 105 S. Ct. 3291, 87 L. Ed. 2d 437 (1985).

585 18 U.S.C. § 1961(4).

586 *See* Sedima, S.P.R.L. v. Imrex Co., 473 U.S. 479, 105 S. Ct. 3275, 87 L. Ed. 2d 346 (1985).

587 *See* 18 U.S.C. § 1961.

588 *See* National Consumer Law Center, Unfair and Deceptive Acts and Practices § 14.2.3.4.5 (7th ed. 2008 and Supp.).

589 18 U.S.C. § 1961(1).

590 18 U.S.C. § 1961(5). *See* Sedima, S.P.R.L. v. Imrex Co., 473 U.S. 479, 105 S. Ct. 3275, 3285, 87 L. Ed. 2d 346, 358–359 (1985) (requirement of two incidents is only a minimum).

591 H.J. Inc. v. Northwestern Bell Tel. Co., 492 U.S. 229 (1989).

592 *See, e.g.*, Vandenbroeck v. CommonPoint Mortgage Co., 210 F.3d 696 (6th Cir. 2000) (federal RICO). *See generally* National Consumer Law Center, Unfair and Deceptive Acts and Practices § 14.2.6.2 (7th ed. 2008 and Supp.).

593 492 U.S. 229 (1989).

594 *Id.* at 239.

595 *Id.* at 240 (quoting 18 U.S.C. § 3575(e)).

continuity, although the Court declined to express a specific test, it roughed out the requirement by providing that a plaintiff could meet it by showing either closed-ended or open-ended continuity.[596] A plaintiff could show closed-ended continuity "by proving a series of related predicates extending over a substantial period of time."[597] Alternatively, a plaintiff could show "open-ended" continuity by proving a threat of continued racketeering activity.[598] Courts have differed in their application of these tests, particularly where identical fraudulent representations are made to a large number of individuals, or where a scheme directed at a single person involves multiple predicate acts.[599]

For cases alleging a conspiracy under section 1962(d) to violate one of the other subsections of section 1962, the Supreme Court, relying on traditional conspiracy law, has ruled that RICO does not require that the defendant must commit or agree to commit two or more predicate acts. Instead, the defendant need only "intend to further an endeavor which, if completed, would satisfy all of the elements of a substantive criminal offense."[600]

#### 7.8.6.2.3 *Alleging a RICO claim based on the collection of an unlawful debt*

An unlawful debt is either an illegal gambling debt or a debt incurred through the "business of lending money or a thing of value" at a usurious rate, provided that any part of the principal or interest is unenforceable under state or federal usury law and the rate charged is at least twice the enforceable rate.[601] The plaintiff must be able to point to a federal or state usury statute that sets the rate that the transaction exceeded.[602]

Consequently, the key to proving a RICO violation based on collection of an unlawful debt is showing that a creditor collected a debt where the interest rate exceeded twice the enforceable rate.[603] Violating a lending law is not enough—the law must set a maximum amount of interest that can be charged and the creditor must have charged more than twice that set amount. Collection of an unlawful debt thus cannot be based merely on violations of laws dealing with the method of collecting interest or the kind of property that can be received for a loan.[604]

A RICO claim has been disallowed based on a mortgage lender's practice of charging more than twice the legally allowable points on a mortgage loan, because the total amount charged was not more than twice the legally permissible interest rate of 24%.[605] The court held that charging more than twice the allowable points was not twice the allowable "rate." It is actionable if the total of all interest-related charges is twice the allowable rate, not just a component of the total interest charge.[606]

Interest that is disguised as some other type of charge or payment—for example, in a payday loan[607] or rent-to-

596 *Id.* at 241.

597 *Id.* at 242.

598 *Id.* at 242.

599 National Consumer Law Center, Unfair and Deceptive Acts and Practices § 14.2.2.4 (7th ed. 2008 and Supp.).

600 Salinas v. United States, 522 U.S. 52, 118 S. Ct. 469, 139 L. Ed. 2d 232 (1997).

601 18 U.S.C. § 1961(6). *See* Merly v. D'Arcangelo, 1992 WL 11182 (Conn. Super. Ct. Jan. 16, 1992) (sufficient to allege "that the plaintiff was associated with the Gambino crime family, that each defendant was engaged in interstate commerce, and that the notes called for usurious interest (104%)"). *But cf.* Bellizan v. Easy Money of Louisiana, Inc., 2002 WL 1611648 (E.D. La. July 19, 2002) (rejecting argument that where loan was illegally split into two transactions to avoid interest rate limitations, allowable interest on second loan was zero for purposes of RICO's interest rate element); Porter v. Ace Cash Express, Inc., 2000 WL 1610632, at *4–7 (E.D. La. Oct. 26, 2000) (dismissing action; because term of loans made to plaintiff exceeded those defined by state payday loan act by five days, they fell outside its interest limitations; since loans were not usurious under state law they did not meet RICO's definition of an unlawful debt), *aff'd*, 277 F.3d 1372 (5th Cir. 2001).

602 Blount Fin. Servs. v. Walter E. Heller & Co., 632 F. Supp. 240 (E.D. Tenn. 1986) (complaint must specify rate charged and controlling usury statute), *aff'd*, 819 F.2d 151 (6th Cir. 1987).

603 Bellizan v. Easy Money of Louisiana, Inc., 2002 WL 1611648, at *6 (E.D. La. July 19, 2002) (rejecting argument that where loan was illegally split into two transactions to avoid interest rate limitations, allowable interest on second loan was zero for purposes of RICO's interest rate element).

604 Sundance Land Corp. v. Cmty. First Fed. Sav. & Loan Ass'n, 840 F.2d 653, 666–667 (9th Cir. 1988). *See also* Montclair v. L.O.I., Inc., 246 Fed. Appx. 535, 537 (9th Cir. Sept. 4, 2007) (affirming dismissal of RICO claim based on collection agency's pursuit of bad check charges, ruling that collection agency was not subject to statutory restrictions on bad check penalties that applied to payday lenders, notwithstanding that the agency took the assignment of the debt from a payday lender). *But see* Rivera v. AT&T Corp., 141 F. Supp. 2d 719, 723–725 (S.D. Tex. 2001) (since late fee was not interest under state law, no usury that would establish collection of an unlawful debt), *aff'd without op.*, 2002 WL 663707 (5th Cir. Mar. 25, 2002).

605 Reidy v. Meritor Sav., 888 F.2d 898 (table), 1989 WL 132673, at *1 (D.C. Cir. 1989); Sundance Land v. Community First Fed. Sav. & Loan, 840 F.2d 653 (9th Cir. 1988) (where borrower claimed it was required to put up motels as security, no RICO claim for collection of unlawful debt stated because FHLBB regulations allegedly violated did not relate to amount of interest lender can charge). *See also* Johnson v. Fleet Fin., Inc., 785 F. Supp. 1003, 1010 (S.D. Ga. 1992) (dismissing federal and state RICO claims by mortgagors against lenders because, although the first month's interest rate exceeded the permitted percentage, the interest calculated over the life of the loan did not).

606 *See* Nolen v. Nucentrix Broadband Networks, Inc., 293 F.3d 926, 929 (5th Cir. 2002) (late fee not interest under Texas law).

607 *See* Cook v. Easy Money of Ky., Inc., 196 F. Supp. 2d 508 (W.D. Ky. 2001) (interpreting now-repealed version of state small loan law, refusing to dismiss § 1962(a) and (c) claims arising from interest and fees charged on payday loans); Cashback Catalog Sales, Inc. v. Price, 102 F. Supp. 2d 1375, 1380 (S.D. Ga. 2000) (denying summary judgment to defendant who took post-dated checks in return for a reduced amount of cash plus an allegedly valueless certificate to a mail-order catalog company for the difference); Arrington v. Colleen, Inc., 2000 WL 34001056, at *6 (D. Md. Aug. 7, 2000) (denying lender's motion for summary judgment); Burden v. York, Civil Action No. 98-268 (E.D. Ky. Sept. 29, 1999), *available at* www.nclc.org/unreported; Hamilton v. HLT Check Exch., 987 F. Supp. 953, 957–958 (E.D. Ky. 1997) (denying the motion of the defendant, a check cashing business, to dismiss RICO

own[608] transaction—can meet the requirement of being twice the lawful rate. A Maryland bankruptcy court described as a loan a transaction that was structured as a sale from distressed homeowners to a foreclosure-rescue firm.[609] The court based the conclusion on a provision that called for the homeowners to pay to the firm a certain sum from proceeds of an anticipated settlement, a sum that the court construed as interest.[610] That sum, measured against the amount of the disguised loan, exceeded the state's maximum rate for secondary mortgages by more than twice the legal amount, and accordingly, the court concluded, the transaction called for the collection of an unlawful debt under RICO.

In another case, a foreclosure rescue arrangement nominally transferred title from the sellers to the foreclosure rescue firm, allowed the sellers to stay in the home in exchange for rent, and required the sellers to "repurchase" the home at the end of one year or face eviction.[611] In a class action brought in Maryland, a federal district court construed the arrangement as creating an equitable mortgage under Maryland law, so the rent was interest.[612] Accordingly, the sellers stated a class action RICO claim for collection of an unlawful debt by alleging that the loans made entailed interest in excess of twice Maryland's usury limit.[613] A foreclosure rescue scheme may alternatively be pleaded as a pattern RICO case, with phone calls and wire transfers of funds giving rise to predicate acts of mail and wire fraud.[614]

Because the collection of an unlawful debt is a separate and distinct RICO violation from a "pattern of racketeering activity," a plaintiff does not have to demonstrate a "pattern" of collecting unlawful debts: collection of a single unlawful debt meets the statute's requirement.[615] However, the plaintiff must demonstrate that the unlawful debt (if not from gambling) was "incurred in connection with . . . the business of lending money or a thing of value, at a rate usurious under State or Federal law, where the usurious rate is at least twice the enforceable rate."[616] Two courts have interpreted this provision as requiring the plaintiff to show that the defendant was not just in the business of lending money, but in the business of lending money at a usurious rate.[617]

#### 7.8.6.2.4 The "injury" element

In the early years of RICO litigation, some lower courts required plaintiffs to establish a special "racketeering injury" apart from the injury directly caused by the individual predicate acts of racketeering activity. This strained interpretation was expressly rejected by the Supreme Court in 1992, which held that a RICO plaintiff making a claim under section 1962(c) need only demonstrate injury from the predicate acts of racketeering.[618] That same year the Supreme Court also held that a borrower could state a claim under section 1962(c) by alleging an injury caused by the predicate act itself, a fraudulent interest overcharge.[619]

Nevertheless, seven years later, in *Holmes v. Securities Investor Protection Corp.*,[620] the Supreme Court somewhat narrowed RICO's injury element, holding that a RICO plaintiff must demonstrate that the injuries were directly and proxi-

claim alleging the collection of an unlawful debt). *See also* Henry v. Cash Today, Inc., 199 F.R.D. 566, 572–573 (S.D. Tex. 2000) (class certification granted in cash back ad sale case). *See generally* Chs. 4, *supra*, 9, *infra*.

608 *See* Starks v. Rent-A-Center, 1994 WL 577974 (D. Minn. May 16, 1990), *aff'd on other grounds*, 58 F.3d 358 (8th Cir. 1995); Miller v. Colortyme, Inc., 518 N.W.2d 544, 548 (Minn. 1994) (Minnesota's usury statute applies to rent-to-own contracts); Fogie v. Rent-A-Center, Inc., 518 N.W.2d 544, 548 (Minn. 1994) (rent-to-own contracts are consumer credit sales under Minnesota law). *See generally* Ch. 12, *infra*.

609 *In re* Eyler, 2008 WL 4833096, at *4–5 (Bankr. D. Md. Oct. 28, 2008) (amended proposed findings of fact and conclusions of law submitted to the United States District Court for the District of Maryland), *adopted in relevant part, rejected in part on other grounds*, 2008 WL 4844962 (D. Md. Aug. 26, 2008) (rejecting Bankruptcy Court's conclusion that plaintiff must show pattern).

610 *Id.* at *4.

611 Proctor v. Metropolitan Money Store Corp., 645 F. Supp. 2d 464, 481–482 (D. Md. 2009) (citing Md. Code Ann., Real Prop. § 7-101(a)).

612 *Id.* at 482.

613 *Id. See also* Day v. DB Capital Group, L.L.C., 2011 WL 887554, at *14 (D. Md. Mar. 11, 2011) (dismissing foreclosure rescue scheme victim's RICO claim on the grounds that while he had pleaded the prevailing legal rate, he had failed to plead the rate that the defendants imposed, necessary to determine whether the loan was usurious).

614 *See* Brock v. Thomas, 782 F. Supp. 2d 133, 142 (E.D. Pa. Apr. 14, 2011) (denying the defendants' motion to dismiss RICO claim that alleged that defendants misrepresented sale as home improvement loan, and then stripped away plaintiff's equity).

615 *See* United States v. Oreto, 37 F.3d 739 (1st Cir. 1994) (unlawful debt section does not require pattern—that does not render the statute unconstitutional); Ballen v. Prudential Bache Sec., 23 F.3d 335 (10th Cir. 1994); Davis v. Mutual Life Ins. Co. of New York, 6 F.3d 367 (6th Cir. 1993); United States v. Weiner, 3 F.3d 17 (1st Cir. 1993); United States v. Giovanelli, 945 F.2d 479 (2d Cir. 1991) (only single collection of unlawful debt need be proved); Eyler v. 3 Vista Court L.L.C., 2008 WL 4844962, at *3 (D. Md. Aug. 26, 2008) (need not demonstrate pattern of collection of an unlawful debt); United States v. Megale, 363 F. Supp. 2d 359, 363 (D. Conn. 2005).

616 18 U.S.C. § 1961(6)(B). *See also* United States v. Megale, 363 F. Supp. 2d 359, 364 (D. Conn. 2005).

617 Wright v. Sheppard, 919 F.2d 665 (11th Cir. 1990) (a single, isolated use of force by a law enforcement officer in trying to collect a debt owed a private creditor, which did not result in financial gain for the officer, not actionable under RICO, which does not extend to occasional usurious transactions by one not in the business of loansharking); Durante Bros. & Sons, Inc. v. Flushing Nat'l Bank, 755 F.2d 239 (2d Cir. 1985) (must allege that defendant was in business of making usurious loans); Weisel v. Pischel, 197 F.R.D. 231, 241 (E.D.N.Y. 2000) (reasoning that RICO's legislative history justified limiting the statute to loan sharkers, not ordinary businessmen who might make a usurious loan (quoting S. Rep. No. 91-617, 91st Cong., 1st Sess. 158 (1969)); VanderWeyst v. First State Bank of Benson, 425 N.W.2d 803 (Minn. 1988) (must show defendant was in business of lending money at usurious rate).

618 Sedima, S.P.R.L. v. Imrex Co., 473 U.S. 479 (1985).

619 American Nat'l Bank & Trust Co. v. Haroco, Inc., 473 U.S. 606, 105 S. Ct. 3291, 87 L. Ed. 2d 437 (1985).

620 503 U.S. 258 (1992).

mately caused by a defendant's racketeering activity. Most courts have construed *Holmes* as requiring that when alleging a section 1962(a) claim, the plaintiff must show more than simply injury from a predicate act; the plaintiff must show injury from the use or investment of the racketeering income.[621] However, when the claim arises from section 1962(c), which prohibits a person from conducting an enterprise's affairs through a pattern of racketeering activity or collection of an unlawful debt, simply showing injury from a predicate act may suffice.[622]

In *Beck v. Prupis*,[623] the Supreme Court continued to narrow the injury element, holding that when a claim arises from section 1962(d), which prohibits any person from conspiring to violate any of sections 1962(a)–(c), the plaintiff must show an injury that was caused by an overt act that is an act of racketeering or otherwise wrongful under RICO. The Court affirmed the dismissal of the case of a former employee who alleged that his firing was part of the defendant's conspiracy to violate RICO. Since the firing itself was not an overt act of racketeering or otherwise prohibited by the statute, the claim failed to meet RICO's injury requirement.[624]

Similarly, a plaintiff advancing a claim based on the collection of an unlawful debt, rather than a pattern of racketeering activity, may have to show injury from the violation of the particular subsection. The Eighth Circuit ruled that plaintiffs injured by reason of usurious interest in a rent-to-own transaction, construed as the collection of an unlawful debt, must also demonstrate that they were injured by reason of the subsection of RICO they claimed.[625] Because they brought their claim under 18 U.S.C. § 1962(a), they had to show that they were injured by the use or investment of racketeering income, and not just from the unlawful debt collection.[626]

Aside from causation, to maintain standing under RICO a plaintiff must show not just an injury, but an injury to the plaintiff's business or property.[627] In a recent predatory lending case, a plaintiff brought a RICO claim after she ended up with an unaffordable loan product sold by a loan officer who had inflated the plaintiff's income on the loan application. The court concluded that the plaintiff could not establish RICO standing based on the impending, but not yet realized, loss of the borrower's home.[628] In contrast, two other plaintiffs in the case were able to establish standing because they plausibly pleaded that the home equity line of credit loan that the defendants sold to them caused them to lose $200,000 in equity in their home.[629]

#### 7.8.6.2.5 RICO and creditor overcharges

Several RICO cases involving allegedly fraudulent creditor overcharges have been litigated.[630] One common situation in-

621 *See, e.g.*, Fogie v. Thorn Americas, Inc., 190 F.3d 889 (8th Cir. 1999). *See generally* National Consumer Law Center, Unfair and Deceptive Acts and Practices § 14.2.5.2.1 (7th ed. 2008 and Supp.).

622 *See* First Nationwide Bank v. Gelt Funding Corp., 27 F.3d 763 (2d Cir. 1994); Lester v. Percudani, 556 F. Supp. 2d 473, 483–487 (M.D. Pa. 2008); Ruiz v. Stewart Assocs., Inc., 171 F.R.D. 238 (N.D. Ill. 1997) (plaintiffs raised issue of fact as to injury suffered by reason of misrepresentation as to force-placed insurance; also certifying class); Red Ball Interior Demolition Corp. v. Palmadessa, 874 F. Supp. 576 (S.D.N.Y. 1995) (plaintiff must show direct relationship between plaintiff's injury and defendant's conduct). *But cf.* Bonilla v. Volvo Car Corp., 150 F.3d 62 (1st Cir. 1998) (defendant's excise fraud, which presumably lowered the cost of cars purchased by plaintiffs, could not support a RICO claim because plaintiffs were not injured by reason of the fraud).

623 529 U.S. 494 (2000).

624 *Id.* at 507. However, the Court expressly declined to decide whether "whether a plaintiff suing under § 1964(c) for a RICO conspiracy must allege an actionable violation under § 1962(a)–(c), or whether it is sufficient for the plaintiff to allege an agreement to complete a substantive violation and the commission of at least one act of racketeering that caused him injury." *Id.* at 506, n.10. Based on dicta, it does not appear that a plaintiff must necessarily have a claim under § 1962(c) in order to allege a violation of § 1962(d), which would functionally render § 1962(d) superfluous: "a plaintiff could, through a § 1964(c) suit for a violation of § 1962(d), sue co-conspirators who might not themselves have violated one of the substantive provisions of § 1962." The Third Circuit subsequently upheld such an interpretation, ruling that a defendant alleged to have conspired to violate § 1962(c) did not have to commit or agree to commit predicate acts to be liable for conspiracy under § 1962(d), so long as he knowingly agreed to facilitate a scheme that included operation or management of a RICO enterprise. Smith v. Berg, 247 F.3d 532 (3d Cir. Apr. 13, 2001).

625 Fogie v. Thorn Americas, Inc., 190 F.3d 889, 895 (8th Cir. 1999) (siding with majority of circuits that have addressed the issue, see cases cited therein).

626 *Id. See also* Yates v. All Am. Abstract Co., 487 F. Supp. 2d 579, 582–583 (E.D. Pa. 2007) (dismissing section 1962(a) claim arising from allegedly predatory loan on the grounds that the plaintiff had failed to plead an investment injury distinct from the injury from the predicate acts themselves).

627 18 U.S.C. § 1964(c).

628 Pradhan v. Citibank, N.A., 2011 WL 90235, at *6 (N.D. Cal. Jan. 10, 2011).

629 *Id.* (but dismissing complaint for failure to comply with pleading requirements of Fed. R. Civ. P. 9(b)). *See also* Proctor v. Metropolitan Money Store Corp., 645 F. Supp. 2d 464, 484 (D. Md. 2009) (loss of home equity due to foreclosure rescue scam is sufficient injury).

630 *See* American Nat'l Bank & Trust Co. v. Haroco, Inc., 473 U.S. 606, 105 S. Ct. 3291, 87 L. Ed. 2d 437 (1985), *aff'g*, 747 F.2d 384 (7th Cir. 1984) (fraudulent overcharging stated RICO claim); Emery v. American Gen. Fin. Corp., 71 F.3d 1343 (7th Cir. 1995) (well-pleaded allegation of loan flipping may state a claim of RICO predicate act of mail fraud sufficient to withstand a motion to dismiss); Raceway Props., L.L.C. v. LSOF Carlsbad Land L.P., 157 Fed. Appx. 959, 964 (9th Cir. 2005) (refusing to dismiss RICO claim based on alleged bait-and-switch lending scheme); Johnson v. Equity Title & Escrow Co., 476 F. Supp. 2d 873 (W.D. Tenn. 2007) (denying motion to dismiss in case alleging predatory lending scheme targeted toward African-American homeowners); Carr v. Home Tech Co., 476 F. Supp. 2d 859 (W.D. Tenn. 2007); Beard v. Worldwide Mortgage Corp., 354 F. Supp. 2d 789, 800–808 (W.D. Tenn. 2005) (denying motion to dismiss § 1962(c) claim against title company and attorney based on alleged predatory lending scheme); Matthews v. New Century Mortgage Corp., 185 F. Supp. 2d 874 (S.D. Ohio 2002) (plaintiffs adequately alleged pattern in state RICO claim brought against defendants who had allegedly been part of a fraudulent home improvement loan scheme targeting older women); Faircloth v. Certified Fin. Inc., 2001 WL 527489 (E.D. La. May 16, 2001) (accepting settlement in class action that

volves a bank that, after contracting to lend to a business at the "prime rate" that it charges its most creditworthy customers, in fact lends at a higher rate. Plaintiffs have alleged that the mailing of interest statements assessing excessive interest constitutes mail fraud and provides the underlying "predicate offense" to support the RICO action.[631]

A group of homeowners used the predicate offense of mail fraud to bring RICO claims against a real estate developer, an appraiser, and a mortgage lender, claims that alleged that the defendants had developed a scheme to overvalue residential real estate in the Pocono Mountains, leading to oversized mortgages with monthly payments that exceeded those originally advertised.[632] The plaintiffs alleged that the defendants worked together to create and use artificially inflated appraisals and to evade accepted lending standards in order to conceal the inability of the borrowers to repay the mortgages.[633] The Pennsylvania district court denied the defendants' motion for summary judgment on the plaintiffs' RICO claims, ruling that the plaintiffs had produced adequate evidence of a pattern of racketeering activity and injury.[634] However, another court construed a lender's representation that its loans were the "best available" or "ideal" as mere puffery, not actionable under the mail fraud statute.[635]

Mail fraud is not the only predicate act that might appear in a creditor-borrower relationship. Where a creditor, as part of extending or collecting a debt, threatens to use overreaching means to collect on the debt, it may violate the federal loansharking statute,[636] which is a RICO predicate act.[637] That statute prohibits extortionate extensions of credit, those made with the understanding that failure to repay "could result in the use of violence or other criminal means to cause harm to the person, reputation, or property of any person."[638] It further prohibits collecting a debt with the implicit or explicit threat to use violence or other criminal means to cause such harm.[639] One court liberally read collection letters sent to a plaintiff to find that they could suggest the threat of criminal means to collect the debt, and that the plaintiff thereby stated a class-action RICO claim based on loansharking against a consumer lender.[640] Another court sustained a RICO claim by a plaintiff who claimed that a bank threatened to jail his wife and call in the FBI unless he mortgaged his farm to secure an overdrawn account of his wife's employer.[641]

Many usurious consumer transactions are named not as the loans they are, but as sales or leases. An example of a common consumer transaction that may violate RICO through the collection of an unlawful debt in violation of RICO is the rent-to-own (RTO) appliance sale, discussed at length at Chapter 12, *infra*. These transactions resemble credit sales at exorbitant interest rates, but are disguised as leases with an option to purchase. Most states have legalized these high-rate transactions, but a few still place effective limits on their charges. In these states, if a practitioner can establish that the RTO contract in fact involves a credit sale under state usury law rather than a true lease,[642] the disguised interest will likely be more than double the enforceable rate, and should serve to satisfy the "collection of an unlawful debt" element of RICO.[643]

alleged that defendant had lent funds to plaintiffs with pending personal injury actions and then flipped the loans to create unlawful interest); Kerby v. Mortgage Funding Corp., 992 F. Supp. 787 (D. Md. 1998) (denying motion to dismiss RICO claim arising from allegedly fraudulent mortgage refinancing scheme); Hastings v. Fidelity Mortgage Decisions Corp., 984 F. Supp. 600 (N.D. Ill. 1997) (granting leave to plaintiffs to amend complaint alleging fraudulent yield spread premium payment so as to meet particularity requirements). *See also* Dixon v. Ford Motor Credit, 2000 WL 713259 (E.D. La. May 31, 2000) (allegations that auto dealer failed to disclose commissions on credit life insurance sales could present predicate act of mail fraud sufficient to avoid dismissal of RICO claim).

631 *See* American Nat'l Bank & Trust Co. v. Haroco, Inc. 473 U.S. 606, 105 S. Ct. 3291, 87 L. Ed. 2d 437 (1985) (allowing RICO claim to proceed against bank that lied about its prime rate, on which rates to customers were based; injury from the predicate acts is sufficient to meet injury requirement); Charing Cross Inc. v. Riggs Nat'l Bank, 1983 WL 2193 (D.D.C. Oct. 7, 1983) (denying motion to dismiss RICO claim based on bank's use of mails to send monthly statements that concealed true interest rate).

632 Lester v. Percudani, 556 F. Supp. 2d 473 (M.D. Pa. 2008) (denying defendants' motion for summary judgment).

633 *Id.* at 475–478.

634 *Id.* at 483–487. *See also* Meeks-Owens v. Indymac Bank, 557 F. Supp. 2d 566, 569, 574 (M.D. Pa. 2008) (denying lender's motion to dismiss RICO claim where plaintiff alleged that mortgage loan exceeded property's market value by over 30% and that defendant misrepresented it as a conventional loan, made loan without investigating plaintiff's repayment ability, and accepted incomplete mortgage application and "patently defective" inflated appraisal).

635 *In re* Countrywide Fin. Corp. Mortgage Mktg. & Sales Practices Litig., 601 F. Supp. 2d 1201, 1217 (S.D. Cal. 2009).

636 18 U.S.C. §§ 891–894.

637 18 U.S.C. § 1961(6).

638 18 U.S.C. §§ 891(6), 892.

639 18 U.S.C. §§ 891(7), 894.

640 Brown v. C.I.L., Inc., 1996 U.S. Dist. LEXIS 4917, at *40–41 (N.D. Ill. Jan. 28, 1996) (magistrate's report and recommendation) (statements examined by the court included: "We can be reached at . . . any time should you wish to repay your debt in full without any damge [sic] to you or your credit"; "My 'ass' is being hung out to dry by you and I would like you to be man enough to tell me why? After you begged for us to loan you money, not once! but twice! My good Friends are interested to [sic]!"; and "Your attitude about this money you begged for is almost unbelievable. Our people in Mr. Carpenter's Office are watching with great interest. Stop being a coward, Big Man!"), *adopted by* 1996 U.S. Dist. LEXIS 4053, 1996 WL 164294 (N.D. Ill. Apr. 1, 1996).

641 Ford v. Citizens & Southern Nat'l Bank, 700 F. Supp. 1121 (N.D. Ga. 1988) (allegations of blackmail sufficed to meet statute's requirement of "the use, or an express or implicit threat of use, of violence or other criminal means to cause harm to the person, reputation, or property of any person").

642 *See* Miller v. Colortyme, Inc., 518 N.W.2d 544 (Minn. 1994) (Minnesota's usury statute applies to rent-to-own contracts); Fogie v. Rent-A-Center, Inc., 518 N.W.2d 544 (Minn. 1994) (rent-to-own contracts are consumer credit sales under Minnesota law).

643 *See* Fogie v. Rent-A-Center, Inc., 1995 WL 649575 (D. Minn. 1995) (implicit interest in RTO contracts was usurious under state law and was more than twice the applicable rate; RICO predicate element of "unlawful debt" therefore established), *aff'd sub nom.*, Fogie v. Thorn Americas, Inc., 95 F.3d 645 (8th Cir. 1996) (declining to address RICO issue).

This approach should similarly provide RICO remedies for other hidden interest or mislabeled transactions such as the sham corporate loan or the sham real estate sale and repurchase.[644]

A RICO claim may also be based on a payday loan that is disguised to conceal its nature. A court denied summary judgment to a defendant that, though denying any lending activity, took post-dated checks in return for cash in an amount well under the face value of the check, along with an allegedly valueless gift certificate to an obscure catalog company in the amount of the difference.[645] Whether the gift certificate was actually "interest" under the usury statute, said the court, was for a trier of fact to decide.

The fact that an interest rate is unconscionable is not sufficient to make out a RICO claim for collection of an unlawful debt if state law authorizes the interest rate. For example, after ruling that the structure of payday loans allowed them to escape the usual limits, a Louisiana court dismissed a RICO claim that was based on the exorbitant charges collected for cashing post-dated checks.[646] Similarly, the Fifth Circuit dismissed a RICO claim based on a loan broker's $1,500 fee assessed on a $2,000 loan on the grounds that the Texas Credit Services Organization Act permitted such fees and therefore they could not be characterized as disguised interest.[647] The First Circuit allowed a lender to escape a RICO claim through a loophole in the Massachusetts criminal usury law that precludes criminal liability for loans bearing interest above the established ceiling if the lender simply notifies the state attorney general that it intends to charge such excess interest.[648]

#### *7.8.6.2.6 State RICO statutes*

At least twenty-two states[649] have state RICO statutes that afford consumers a private cause of action in state court. In addition, a state RICO statute may offer the alternative of equitable relief.[650] Where state court is a preferable forum to federal court, claims under state RICO statutes should be considered.

Many of these statutes explicitly list fraud and usury as predicate offenses,[651] and some list violations of specific consumer protection laws, such as those prohibiting equity skimming or telemarketing fraud. Some parallel the federal RICO statute by prohibiting collection of an unlawful debt.[652] These statutes demonstrate the legislative intent to treat consumer fraud as organized crime, and to afford victimized consumers the powerful remedies of the RICO laws. Several of these state RICO statutes allow for or mandate multiple damages.

### *7.8.7 Class Actions*

Usury cases are well-suited to class action treatment.[653] Lenders who overcharge typically do so systematically, so there are common issues of law and fact. Often each borrower is entitled to a relatively small recovery, such as double the amount of the overcharge. A primary purpose of class actions is to provide a way to recover damage awards that are too small to make individual suits economically feasible.[654]

Usury class actions produce other benefits as well. As the California Supreme Court has noted, such actions often produce "several salutary by-products, including a therapeutic

644 *See, e.g.*, *In re* Eyler, 2008 WL 4833096 (Bankr. D. Md. Oct. 28, 2008). *See generally* § 3.9.2.3, *supra*; National Consumer Law Center, Foreclosures Ch. 17 (4th ed. 2012).

645 Cashback Catalog Sales, Inc. v. Price, 102 F. Supp. 2d 1375 (S.D. Ga. Mar. 20, 2000).

646 Bellizan v. Easy Money of Louisiana, Inc., 2002 WL 31115249 (E.D. La. July 19, 2002) (because "overlapping" loans made by payday lender did not violate state laws prohibiting "rollover" or "renewal" loans, plaintiff failed to establish that defendant collected an unlawful debt). *See also* Porter v. ACE Cash Express, Inc., 2000 WL 1610632 (E.D. La. Oct. 26, 2000) (because term of loans made to plaintiff exceeded those defined by state payday loan act by five days, they fell outside its interest limitations; since loans were not usurious under state law they did not meet RICO's definition of an unlawful debt, action dismissed), *aff'd*, 277 F.3d 1372 (5th Cir. 2001) (table).

647 Lovick v. Ritemoney Ltd., 378 F.3d 433, 44 (5th Cir. 2004).

648 Cannarozzi v. Fiumara, 371 F.3d 1, 5 (1st Cir. 2004).

649 Arizona, Colorado, Delaware, Florida, Georgia, Hawaii, Idaho, Indiana, Iowa, Louisiana, Mississippi, Nevada, New Jersey, New Mexico, North Carolina, North Dakota, Ohio, Oregon, Rhode Island, Utah, Washington, and Wisconsin. *See generally* National Consumer Law Center, Unfair and Deceptive Acts and Practices § 14.3, Appx. C.2 (7th ed. 2008 and Supp.).

650 *See, e.g.*, Bowcutt v. Delta North Star Corp., 976 P.2d 643 (Wash. Ct. App. 1999) (ruling homeowners could seek injunction against foreclosure pursuant to state RICO statute).

651 *See also* Check 'N Go of Fla., Inc. v. State, 790 So. 2d 454 (Fla. Dist. Ct. App. 2001) (concluding that attorney general had sufficient grounds to believe that payday lender was violating state RICO statute by making rollover loans in violation of state usury law). *But see* State v. Roderick, 704 So. 2d 49 (Miss. 1997) (finding state RICO statute unconstitutionally vague in case against payday lenders because it criminalized usury without providing fair warning).

652 *See In re* Giorgio, 62 B.R. 853 (Bankr. D.R.I. 1986) ("unlawful debt" under state RICO statute is any debt that is unenforceable in whole or in part due to usury), *rev'd*, 81 B.R. 766 (D.R.I. 1988) (debt could not be considered unenforceable where state court had entered non-collusive judgment on it two years earlier), *aff'd*, 862 F.2d 933 (1st Cir. 1988) (suggesting interpretation that would confine unlawful debt to gambling debts); *In re* Marill Alarm Sys., Inc., 68 B.R. 399 (Bankr. S.D. Fla. 1986) (usury in sham consulting fees triggers state RICO statute), *adopted by* 81 B.R. 119 (S.D. Fla. 1987), *aff'd*, 861 F.2d 725 (11th Cir. 1988) (table).

653 *See, e.g.*, Violette v. P.A. Days, Inc., 214 F.R.D. 207 (S.D. Ohio 2003) (certifying class on claim that interest charge exceeded RISA limits); Tomlin v. Dylan Mortgage Inc., 2002 WL 32986130 (N.D. Super. Ct. Feb. 1, 2002) (certifying class on usury claim); Car Now Acceptance Co. v. Block, 2002 WL 32001272 (Ohio Ct. Com. Pl. Nov. 25, 2002), *aff'd*, 2003 WL 21714583 (Ohio Ct. App. July 14, 2003). *But see* Vincent v. Bank of Am., 109 S.W.3d 856 (Tex. App. 2003) (class certification would undermine statutory provision that usury remedy was available only if creditor failed to cure within reasonable time after receiving notice).

Sample class action pleadings, including a complaint, class certification memos, and notices to the class, may be found on the companion website to this treatise.

654 *See, e.g.*, Linder v. Thrifty Oil Co., 2 P.3d 27, 38 (Cal. 2000) (class action challenging surcharge imposed on customers who paid with credit card).

effect upon those sellers who indulge in fraudulent practices, aid to legitimate business enterprises by curtailing illegitimate competition, and avoidance to the judicial process of the burden of multiple litigation involving identical claims."[655] Even an unconscionability claim that requires examination of the comparative bargaining positions of the lender and consumers may be appropriate for class treatment where the consumers as a group share material characteristics.[656]

Individual issues are likely to be minimal in a usury class action. Some usury statutes apply only to non-business loans, but, since in most cases the purpose of the loan is determined by the written representations the borrower made to the lender,[657] this can easily be determined from the lender's records. If there are individual factual questions about the purpose of the loan, they can be resolved through the claims process or by bifurcating the proceedings.[658] Damages can usually be determined from the lender's own records.[659] For nationwide class actions, however, the court will either have to find a basis for applying the law of a single state, or conclude that variations among the states' laws are not so significant as to make the class action unmanageable.[660] Class action issues are addressed in detail in another NCLC treatise.[661]

655 *Id.* (quoting from Vasquez v. Superior Court, 484 P.2d 964 (Cal. 1971)).

656 Dienese v. McKenzie Check Advance, 2000 WL 34511333 (E.D. Wis. Dec. 11, 2000).

657 *See* § 3.9.2, *supra*.

658 *See* Fed. R. Civ. P. 23(c)(4)(A). *See also* Tay-Tay, Inc. v. Young, 80 S.W.3d 365 (Ark. 2002) (affirming certification of usury class action); Luttenegger v. Conseco Fin. Serv., 671 N.W.2d 425, 439–440 (Iowa 2003) (claims process can be used to determine nature of loans; individual damage issues do not preclude class certification when liability involves common questions). *See generally* 3 Newberg on Class Actions §§ 9.53, 9.64 (4th ed. 2002).

659 *See* National Consumer Law Center, Consumer Class Actions § 10.5.3.6 (7th ed. 2010 and Supp.).

660 *See* Cassese v. Washington Mut., Inc., 255 F.R.D. 89, 97–98 (E.D.N.Y. 2009) (variations among state laws do not preclude certification of class involving excess fees charged in connection with loan payoff), *later op. at* 711 F. Supp. 2d 261 (E.D.N.Y. 2010) (decertifying class action against failed bank because of FDIC administrative claim requirement, but noting that class action against its holding company remains certified), *later op. at* 743 F. Supp. 2d 148 (E.D.N.Y. 2010) (refusing to decertify class action against bank holding company; class is not limited to those who file claims through FDIC administrative claims process); Washington Mut. Bank v. Superior Court, 15 P.3d 1071 (Cal. 2001). *See generally* National Consumer Law Center, Unfair and Deceptive Acts and Practices § 13.5.5 (7th ed. 2008 and Supp.); National Consumer Law Center, Consumer Class Actions Ch. 3 (7th ed. 2010 and Supp.).

661 National Consumer Law Center, Consumer Class Actions § 10.5.3.6 (7th ed. 2010 and Supp.).

# 7.9 Jurisdiction

## *7.9.1 Federal Jurisdiction and Removal of Consumer Suits to Federal Court*

### 7.9.1.1 Introduction

Sometimes a consumer prefers to litigate a claim in federal court. Even if the consumer files in state court, the creditor may have the right to remove the case to federal court. This subsection outlines issues regarding federal jurisdiction in consumer credit cases, including unique issues that apply to usury claims and claims against federally-chartered banks.

There are several routes to federal jurisdiction. This subsection analyzes federal question jurisdiction, the complete preemption doctrine, diversity jurisdiction, and jurisdiction under the Class Action Fairness Act. Jurisdictional issues when a bank is in FDIC receivership are discussed in another treatise in this series.[662] The Federal Courts Jurisdiction and Venue Clarification Act of 2011[663] made a number of changes to federal jurisdiction statutes effective for new federal cases filed on or after January 6, 2012.

### 7.9.1.2 Federal Question Jurisdiction in Consumer Credit Cases

Federal jurisdiction is proper when a claim arises under the Constitution, laws, or treaties of the United States.[664] If a case that would come within federal question jurisdiction is filed in state court, it can be removed to federal court.[665]

A plaintiff who prefers state court can usually avoid removal on federal question grounds by pleading state law claims only.[666] The mere presence of a federal issue embedded in a state claim does not automatically create federal question jurisdiction.[667] For example, citing a violation of a federal standard as an element of a state claim does not usually create federal question jurisdiction.[668] In 2005, however, the Supreme Court re-interpreted its prior rulings on this question and held that a state law claim is removable if it presents a disputed and substantial question of federal law that a federal court may

662 National Consumer Law Center, Mortgage Lending § 11.3 (2012).

663 Pub. L. No. 112-63, 125 Stat. 758 (Dec. 7, 2011). *See generally* National Consumer Law Center, Consumer Class Actions Ch. 2 (2011 Supp.) (discussing in greater detail the 2011 amendments).

664 28 U.S.C. § 1331.

665 28 U.S.C. § 1441.

666 Rivet v. Regions Bank of La., 522 U.S. 470, 475, 118 S. Ct. 921, 139 L. Ed. 2d 912 (1998); Hill v. Chem. Bank, 799 F. Supp. 948 (D. Minn. 1992).

667 Merrell Dow Pharms., Inc. v. Thompson, 478 U.S. 804, 808, 106 S. Ct. 3229, 92 L. Ed. 2d 650 (1986).

668 *See, e.g.*, Caampued v. First Fed. Bank of California, 2010 WL 963080 (N.D. Cal. Mar. 16, 2010) (remanding state fraud and negligence claims that incorporate HOEPA for standard of care; insufficient federal interest in resolution of tort claim); Wertz v. Washington Mut. Bank, 2008 WL 1882843 (E.D. Cal. Apr. 24, 2008) (granting remand even though some of the state claims were based upon duties created by OTS regulations).

decide without disturbing any congressionally approved balance of federal and state judicial responsibilities.[669] At the same time, however, it reiterated an earlier holding that a federal question embedded in a state tort claim was insufficient for removal, because otherwise there would be a tremendous increase in "garden variety" tort cases in federal court.[670] If a state claim can be supported by alternative federal or state theories, removal will not be appropriate because the federal issue is not a necessary element.[671]

For federal question jurisdiction, the federal question must appear on the face of the complaint; the existence of a defense or counterclaim rooted in federal law is not grounds for removal.[672] Except in the rare case of complete preemption, discussed in the next subsection, the fact that federal law may preempt the state laws on which the consumer's claim is based is a defense that does not create federal question jurisdiction.[673]

### 7.9.1.3 Complete Preemption and *Beneficial Bank*

The doctrine of complete preemption is a rare but important exception to the rule that a case raising only state law claims cannot be removed to federal court simply because federal law might preempt those claims. When a federal statute completely preempts a state law cause of action, then a claim which comes within the scope of the federal statute, even if pleaded solely in terms of state law, is in reality a federal claim and is removable.[674]

The Supreme Court has carved out one portion of the National Bank Act as completely preempting state law: usury claims raised against national banks.[675] The Court held that sections 85 and 86 of the National Bank Act provide the exclusive cause of action for these claims. Thus, any case raising a state-law usury claim against a national bank is removable to federal court.

In applying *Beneficial Bank*, the first question is what is a usury claim. Courts have construed the decision to reach claims that any fee defined as interest by the OCC is usurious.[676] However, a corollary is that, if a fee is not encompassed within OCC's definition of interest, then a claim that the fee is excessive is not completely preempted.[677]

Further, even if a fee is interest, the National Bank Act completely preempts only usury claims. A non-usury claim, i.e., a claim based on grounds other than that an interest charge is excessive in and of itself, is not completely preempted.[678] Thus, a claim that a bank charged fraudulent fees rather than excessive fees,[679] or fraudulently induced the consumer to enter into a high-cost loan,[680] is not completely preempted. Likewise, a claim

---

669 Grable & Sons Metal Prods., Inc. v. Darue Eng'g & Mfg., 545 U.S. 308, 125 S. Ct. 2363, 162 L. Ed. 2d 257 (2005).

670 *Id.*, 125 S. Ct. at 2370. *Accord* Empire Healthchoice Assurance, Inc. v. McVeigh, 126 S. Ct. 2121 (2006) (federal courts do not have "arising under" jurisdiction over health insurer's claim for reimbursement from federal employee's state court tort settlement).

671 Rains v. Criterion Sys., Inc., 80 F.3d 339, 346 (9th Cir. 1996).

672 *See, e.g.*, Vaden v. Discover Bank, 556 U.S. 49 (2009); Beneficial Nat'l Bank v. Anderson, 539 U.S. 1, 123 S. Ct. 2058, 156 L. Ed. 2d 1 (2003); Holmes Group, Inc. v. Vornado Air Circulation Sys., Inc., 535 U.S. 826, 122 S. Ct. 1889, 153 L. Ed. 2d 13 (2002) (involving counterclaim in a patent infringement case); Rivet v. Regions Bank of La., 522 U.S. 470, 118 S. Ct. 921, 139 L. Ed. 2d 912 (1998).

673 Beneficial Nat'l Bank v. Anderson, 539 U.S. 1, 6, 123 S. Ct. 2058, 156 L. Ed. 2d 1 (2003) ("Thus, a defense that relies on . . . the pre-emptive effect of a federal statute . . . will not provide a basis for removal"). *Accord* King v. Homeside Lending, Inc., 2007 WL 1009383 (S.D. W. Va. Mar. 30, 2007) (ordinary preemption is a defense and is not a basis for removal); Beard v. Aurora Loan Servs., 2006 WL 1350286 (S.D. Tex. May 17, 2006).

674 Beneficial Nat'l Bank v. Anderson, 539 U.S. 1, 8, 123 S. Ct. 2058, 156 L. Ed. 2d 1 (2003).

675 Beneficial Nat'l Bank v. Anderson, 539 U.S. 1, 123 S. Ct. 2058, 156 L. Ed. 2d 1 (2003).

676 *See, e.g.*, Phipps v. Guar. Nat'l Bank, 417 F.3d 1006 (5th Cir. 2005) (since OCC defines origination and loan discount fees as interest, claim that national bank imposed them in violation of state law is completely preempted).

677 Brown v. Nationscredit Fin. Servs., 647 F. Supp. 2d 1314 (M.D. Fla. 2008) (since OCC defines fees and charges attributed to credit insurance not to be interest, then claim that bank fraudulently charged such fees is not a usury claim and is not completely preempted); Jacobs v. ABN AMRO Bank N.V., 2004 WL 869557 (E.D.N.Y. Apr. 21, 2004) (fax fees are not in the nature of interest, so claims based on charging them in violation of state law is not completely preempted); Hancock v. Bank of Am., 272 F. Supp. 2d 608 (W.D. Ky. 2003) (OCC does not define fax fee as interest, so claim that charging it violated state law is not completely preempted).

678 *In re* Community Bank, 418 F.3d 277, 296 (3d Cir. 2005); California v. H&R Block, Inc., 2006 WL 2669045 (N.D. Cal. Sept. 18, 2006) (no complete preemption of claim that lender fraudulently marketed and sold high-cost refund anticipation loans, where plaintiffs did not claim that costs were wrongful in and of themselves). *See also* Bumpers v. Community Bank, 2008 WL 203343 (W.D. Pa. Jan. 24, 2008); Freunscht v. Banknorth, NA, 2004 WL 540693 (D.N.H. Mar. 17, 2004) (no complete preemption of claim that bank violated state law by failing to notify credit insurer that consumer had paid car loan off early, so that insurer would give consumer a refund); West Virginia *ex rel.* McGraw v. Parrish Auto. Training Co., 147 F. Supp. 2d 470 (N.D. W. Va. 2001) (pre-*Beneficial Bank* case; where claim is that defendant failed to disclose the charges, not that the charges were excessive in and of themselves in violation of state law, no complete preemption).

679 Bumpers v. Community Bank, 2008 WL 203343 (W.D. Pa. Jan. 24, 2008).

680 California v. H&R Block, Inc., 2006 WL 2669045 (N.D. Cal. Sept. 18, 2006) (no complete preemption of claim that lender fraudulently marketed and sold high-cost refund anticipation loans); Anderson v. Ocwen Fin. Corp., 2006 WL 1515682 (N.D. Miss. May 26, 2006) (reference to excessive charges as part of fraud and negligence claims is not a usury claim, so no complete preemption); Cortazar v. Wells Fargo & Co, 2004 WL 1774219 (N.D. Cal. Aug. 9, 2004) (claim that bank used bait-and-switch tactics to put consumers into loans with exorbitant interest rates is not a usury claim so is not completely preempted); Delaney v. Bank of Am. Corp. 2004 WL 1553518 (N.D. Miss. June 16, 2004) (no complete preemption where claim is not that rates were inherently excessive in light of state law, but rather than bank fraudulent charged them); Wilson v. Bank of Am. Corp., 2004 WL 443881 (S.D. Miss. Feb. 20, 2004) (no completely preemption where claim was that bank fraudulently induced plaintiffs to agree to high-cost loans, not that the charges were greater than those allowed by state law); Cavette v. MasterCard Int'l, Inc., 282 F. Supp. 2d 813 (W.D. Tenn. 2003) (claims based on non-disclosure and negligent misrepresentation of a fee are

that a bank charged more than it represented it would charge is a contract-based claim, not a usury claim, so is not completely preempted.[681] Even if a claim against a third party is based on violation of the state's usury law, a claim against a national bank for aiding and abetting that violation is not a usury claim, but is a tort claim, so again is not completely preempted.[682] Holding claims along these lines completely preempted would be inconsistent with OCC's preemption regulations, which carve out a role for state law contract and tort claims.[683]

Courts have generally held that HOLA,[684] AMTPA,[685] and the appraisal fraud provisions of FIRREA[686] do not completely preempt state law claims. Some of the language in the Depository Institutions Deregulation and Monetary Control Act (DIDA) is similar to the National Bank Act, leading some courts to conclude that DIDA completely preempts state usury claims.[687] However, the differences are significant enough that the better view is that DIDA does not completely preempt state usury claims against federally-insured state-chartered banks that are subject to DIDA.[688]

The National Bank Act does not completely preempt usury claims against a non-bank purchaser of loans, even loans originated by national banks.[689] While one decision concludes that usury claims against national banks' operating subsidiaries are completely preempted,[690] *Beneficial Bank* involved a claim only against the bank itself so does not support this position. Another decision holds the complete preemption doctrine inapplicable to claims against non-banks such as payday lenders, even when a bank is involved in the transactions, at least where the plaintiff does not allege that the bank was the true lender.[691]

The National Bank Act does not completely preempt claims against state-chartered banks.[692] The issue is more completed, though, when a national bank merges into the state bank. In one case, a court held that a case against a state bank was not completely preempted where the complaint expressly disavowed any claims arising from the acts of the predecessor national banks that had merged into the state bank.[693]

#### 7.9.1.4 Diversity Jurisdiction

For diversity jurisdiction, the action must be between citizens of different states and the amount in controversy must exceed $75,000.[694] The Supreme Court has held that a bank is located for diversity jurisdiction purposes in the state where its main office is located, as set forth in its articles of incorporation.[695] This definition permits national banks to sue under the diversity provision or to remove state court actions in every other state. In contrast, a federal credit union is not considered to be a citizen of any state, so diversity jurisdiction cannot be based on its presence as a party.[696]

#### 7.9.1.5 Jurisdiction under the Class Action Fairness Act

The Class Action Fairness Act relaxes the requirements for diversity jurisdiction over class actions.[697] It allows a class action to be filed in or removed to federal court in certain circumstances even if the parties do not meet the usual standards for diversity of citizenship. The total amount sought by the class must exceed $5 million. The Class Action Fairness Act is discussed in detail in another treatise in this series.[698]

### *7.9.2 Long-Arm Jurisdiction over Out-of-State Lenders*

#### 7.9.2.1 Constitutional and Statutory Standards

The proliferation of interstate and e-commerce transactions increases the importance of long-arm jurisdiction. Whether a court can exercise jurisdiction over an out-of-state creditor is a separate question from the question of which state's law to

not completely preempted); West Virginia *ex rel.* McGraw v. Parrish Auto. Training Co., 147 F. Supp. 2d 470 (N.D. W. Va. 2001) (pre-*Beneficial Bank* case; where claim is that defendant failed to disclose the charges, not that the charges were excessive in and of themselves in violation of state law, no complete preemption).

681 Levitanksy v. FIA Card Servs., N.A., 492 F. Supp. 2d 758 (N.D. Ohio 2007); Patterson v. Regions Bank, 2006 WL 3407852 (S.D. Ill. Nov. 27, 2006). *See also* Fornshell v. FirstMerit Corp., 2006 WL 3545134 (N.D. Ohio Dec. 8, 2006) (no completely preemption of claim that bank knew or should have known of Ponzi scheme).

682 California *ex rel.* Herrera v. Check 'N Go of Cal., Inc., 2007 WL 2406888 (N.D. Cal. Aug. 20, 2007).

683 12 C.F.R. §§ 7.4007(c), 7.4008(e), 34.4(b).

684 Bolden v. KB Home, 618 F. Supp. 2d 1196 (C.D. Cal. 2008); King v. Homeside Lending, Inc., 2007 WL 1009383 (S.D. W. Va. Mar. 30, 2007) (HOLA does not provide an exclusive cause of action, so no complete preemption); Beard v. Aurora Loan Servs., 2006 WL 1350286, at *4 (S.D. Tex. May 17, 2006) (HOLA does not create complete preemption because HOLA provides no private right of action for the wrongs alleged, and OTS regulations make clear that state law applies in certain circumstances); McKenzie v. Ocwen Fed. Bank, 306 F. Supp. 2d 543 (D. Md. 2004).

685 Ansley v. Ameriquest Mortgage Co., 340 F.3d 858 (9th Cir. 2003); Arnold v. First Greensboro Home Equity, Inc., 327 F. Supp. 2d 1022 (E.D. Mo. 2004).

686 Bolden v. KB Home, 618 F. Supp. 2d 1196 (C.D. Cal. 2008).

687 *See, e.g., In re* Community Bank, 418 F.3d 277, 295–296 (3d Cir. 2005).

688 *See* Thomas v. US Bank, 575 F.3d 794 (8th Cir. 2009); Griner v. Synovus Bank, 2011 WL 3581429 (N.D. Ga. July 22, 2011) (analyzing opposing circuit court opinions); Saxton v. Capital One Bank, 392 F. Supp. 2d 772 (S.D. Miss. 2005). *See generally* § 3.5.2, *supra* (equivalence between § 85 of the NBA and § 521 of DIDA).

689 *In re* Community Bank, 418 F.3d 277, 296 (3d Cir. 2005).

690 Taylor v. Wells Fargo Home Mortgage, Inc., 2004 WL 856673 (E.D. La. Apr. 20, 2004).

691 Flowers v. EZPawn Oklahoma, Inc., 307 F. Supp. 2d 1191 (N.D. Okla. 2004).

692 Griner v. Synovus Bank, 2011 WL 3581429 (N.D. Ga. July 22, 2011).

693 *Id.*

694 28 U.S.C. § 1332.

695 Wachovia Bank v. Schmidt, 546 U.S. 303, 126 S. Ct. 941 (2006).

696 Northern Virginia Foot & Ankle Assocs., L.L.C. v. Pentagon Fed. Credit Union, 2011 WL 280983 (D. Md. Jan. 26, 2011).

697 28 U.S.C. § 1332(d).

698 National Consumer Law Center, Consumer Class Actions § 2.4 (7th ed. 2010 and Supp.).

apply, which is discussed at § 3.8, *supra*. Nonetheless, both questions turn at least to some extent on similar factual issues relating to the out-of-state party's contacts with the forum state. Long-arm jurisdiction also affects the choice of law issue because courts generally follow the choice of law rules of the state where they sit.[699]

Courts must consider both the state's long-arm statute and due process principles when determining whether they can exercise jurisdiction over out-of-state defendants. Due process requires that a defendant, if not present in the state, have certain minimum contacts with it such that maintaining the suit does not offend traditional notions of fair play and substantial justice.[700] Since many long-arm statutes state that they are intended to allow jurisdiction to the maximum extent allowed by the Constitution, the analysis of statutory issues tends to merge with that of constitutional issues.

In analyzing constitutional issues, courts draw a conceptual distinction between "general jurisdiction" and "specific jurisdiction." Courts have general or all-purpose jurisdiction over a defendant who has substantial or continuous and systematic contacts with the forum state.[701] If a court has general jurisdiction, the constitution allows it to hear any cause of action against that defendant, regardless of whether the claim arose from the defendant's activities in the state.[702] For example, a company has continuous and systematic contact with the state where its headquarters are located, so can be sued there on any claim.[703] Some courts describe the standard for general jurisdiction as "exacting."[704] Registering to do business in a state and appointing an agent for service of process are helpful, although not conclusive, indications of general jurisdiction.[705]

Even if a defendant does not have continuous and systematic contact with a state, the constitution allows a court to exercise "specific" or case-linked jurisdiction over a cause of action that arises directly from the defendant's contacts with the forum state.[706] Specific jurisdiction is permissible if the defendant has purposefully availed itself of the privilege of conducting activities in the forum state.[707] The court must also determine that the exercise of jurisdiction would comport with fair play and substantial justice.[708] Random, fortuitous, or attenuated contacts are insufficient, but specific jurisdiction is permissible if a defendant has deliberately engaged in significant activities within a state or created continuing obligations with members of the forum state.[709]

A forum selection clause in a contract can also establish long-arm jurisdiction, as long as the clause is freely negotiated and is not unreasonable or unjust.[710]

The unique jurisdictional issues that arise in tribal payday loan cases are discussed at § 9.6.3, *infra*.

### 7.9.2.2 Jurisdiction over Internet-Based Lenders

In some situations, a lender's contacts with state residents through the Internet can meet the "minimum contacts" test,[711] so that courts in the borrower's home state can assert jurisdiction over the lender. The fact that a company does business in a state without being physically present there does not defeat jurisdiction.[712]

---

699 *See* § 3.8.1, *supra*.

700 International Shoe v. Washington, 326 U.S. 310, 66 S. Ct. 154, 90 L. Ed. 95 (1945). *See also* Burger King Corp. v. Rudzewicz, 471 U.S. 462, 476, 105 S. Ct. 2174, 85 L. Ed. 2d 528 (1985) (jurisdiction can be exercised over defendant who never physically entered the forum state).

701 Goodyear Dunlop Tires Operations, S.A. v. Brown, 131 S. Ct. 2846, 2850, 180 L. Ed. 2d 796 (2011).

702 Heliocopteros Nacionales de Colombia v. Hall, 466 U.S. 408, 414 nn.8–9, 104 S. Ct. 1868, 80 L. Ed. 2d 404 (1984); Burger King Corp. v. Rudzewicz, 471 U.S. 462, 473 n.15, 105 S. Ct. 2174, 85 L. Ed. 2d 528 (1985); Lakin v. Prudential Sec., Inc., 348 F.3d 704, 707 (8th Cir. 2003); Davis v. Nordstrom F.S.B., 2006 WL 2479002 (S.D. Tex. Aug. 25, 2006) (general allegations that credit card issuer has customers and does business in forum state insufficient to establish general jurisdiction; must allege quantity and frequency).

703 Goodyear Dunlop Tires Operations, S.A. v. Brown, 131 S. Ct. 2846, 2853–2854, 180 L. Ed. 2d 796 (2011); J. McIntyre Machinery, Ltd. v. Nicastro, 131 S. Ct. 2780, 2787, 180 L. Ed. 2d 765 (2011) (plurality op.).

704 CollegeSource, Inc. v. AcademyOne, Inc., 653 F.3d 1066, 1074 (9th Cir. 2011). *See also* ALS Scan v. Digital Serv. Consultants, Inc., 293 F.3d 707 (4th Cir. 2002) (standard for general jurisdiction is more demanding than for specific jurisdiction).

705 Perkins v. Benguet Consol. Mining Co., 342 U.S. 437, 444–448, 72 S. Ct. 413, 96 L. Ed. 485 (1952); Miller v. Robertson, 2008 WL 270761 (D. Utah Jan. 29, 2008).

706 Goodyear Dunlop Tires Operations, S.A. v. Brown, 131 S. Ct. 2846, 2855, 180 L. Ed. 2d 796 (2011) (flow of manufacturer's products into forum state may bolster claim of specific jurisdiction); Burger King Corp. v. Rudzewicz, 471 U.S. 462, 473 n.15, 105 S. Ct. 2174, 85 L. Ed. 2d 528 (1985); Heliocopteros Nacionales de Colombia v. Hall, 466 U.S. 408, 414 nn.8–9, 104 S. Ct. 1868, 80 L. Ed. 2d 404 (1984). *See also*. J. McIntyre Machinery, Ltd. v. Nicastro, 131 S. Ct. 2780, 2787–2788, 180 L. Ed. 2d 765 (2011) (plurality op.) (targeting the forum state by directing goods or agents there can support specific jurisdiction, but placing goods into stream of commerce insufficient in itself even if defendant is aware that they will reach forum state).

707 Burger King v. Rudzewicz, 471 U.S. 462, 473 n.15, 105 S. Ct. 2174, 85 L. Ed. 2d 528 (1985).

708 Burger King Corp. v. Rudzewicz, 471 U.S. 462, 476, 105 S. Ct. 2174, 2183–2184, 85 L. Ed. 2d 528 (1985). *See also* Bird v. Parsons, 289 F.3d 865 (6th Cir. 2002) (must show that exercise of jurisdiction is reasonable); Panavision Int'l v. Toeppen, 141 F.3d 1316 (9th Cir. 1998) (exercise of jurisdiction must be reasonable).

709 Burger King Corp. v. Rudzewicz, 471 U.S. 462, 105 S. Ct. 2174, 2183–2184, 85 L. Ed. 2d 528 (1985). *See also* Pebble Beach Co. v. Caddy, 453 F.3d 1151 (9th Cir. 2006) (may establish specific jurisdiction by showing that defendant either purposely availed itself of privilege of conducting activities in the forum or purposely directed itself toward forum; claim must also arise from these activities, and exercise of jurisdiction must be reasonable); Vanderbilt Mortgage & Fin., Inc. v. Flores, 789 F. Supp. 2d 750 (S.D. Tex. 2011) (specific jurisdiction proper over manufacturer that sold manufactured homes to Texas residents and promoted the financing program out of which plaintiff's fraud claims arise).

710 Burger King Corp. v. Rudzewicz, 471 U.S. 462, 473 n.14, 105 S. Ct. 2174, 85 L. Ed. 2d 528 (1985).

711 *See* § 7.9.2.1, *supra*.

712 uBid, Inc. v. GoDaddy Group, Inc., 623 F.3d 421, 429 (7th Cir. 2010).

In analyzing whether Internet-based contacts are sufficient for specific jurisdiction, some courts have followed the seminal case *Zippo Mfg. Co. v. Zippo Dot Com*,[713] and divided websites into three categories.[714] On one end of the scale are passive websites that do no more than post advertisements that are accessible by people in the forum state. Courts uniformly find that this sort of website is insufficient to give the forum state jurisdiction.[715] On the other end of the scale are websites by which a defendant conducts business with residents of the forum state, for example by entering into contracts and exchanging files. Courts generally find that this activity meets the minimum contacts test, as it shows that the defendant is targeting forum state residents or deliberately engaging in transactions with them.[716] In this case, specific jurisdiction may be established as long as there is a sufficient nexus between the plaintiff's injury and the Internet transaction.[717]

In the middle are websites that are interactive in that the user can exchange information with the host computer, for example by ordering product information or sending e-mail to sales representatives. Whether maintaining such a website meets the minimum contacts test usually depends on the level of interactivity and the commercial nature of the exchange of information.[718]

Some courts find the *Zippo* three-category analysis unsuited to the determination of general jurisdiction.[719] However, general jurisdiction may be established where a company maintains a sophisticated website that is clearly and deliberately structured to operate as a virtual store or office in the forum state.[720]

---

713 952 F. Supp. 1119 (W.D. Pa. 1997).

714 Revell v. Lidov, 317 F.3d 467 (5th Cir. 2002) (applying *Zippo*, but interactive website insufficient where it was not aimed at forum state); ALS Scan v. Digital Serv. Consultants, Inc., 293 F.3d 707 (4th Cir. 2002) (upholding specific jurisdiction over person who directs electronic activity into forum state with manifest intention of engaging in business or other transactions there and that activity creates a cause of action for a person in that state; passively placing information on the Internet insufficient); Bird v. Parsons, 289 F.3d 865 (6th Cir. 2002) (citing *Zippo* favorably). *See also* Mink v. AAAA Dev. L.L.C., 190 F.3d 333 (5th Cir. 1999) (applying *Zippo* analysis to general jurisdiction; website here insufficiently interactive to allow jurisdiction). *But cf.* Shrader v. Biddinger, 633 F.3d 1235, 1242 (10th Cir. 2011) (declining to take position on *Zippo*); Metcalf v. Lawson, 802 A.2d 1221 (N.H. 2002) (where sale by defendant occurs through an on-line auction site, *Zippo* test "not particularly helpful . . . because the majority of cases using it are based upon a defendant's conduct over its own website").

715 *See, e.g.*, Jennings v. AC Hydraulic A/S, 383 F.3d 546 (7th Cir. 2004) (passive website does not create specific jurisdiction because defendant is not directing its activities toward forum state residents in particular); GTE New Media Servs. Inc. v. Bellsouth Corp., 199 F.3d 1343 (D.C. Cir. 2000) (maintaining a website that is accessible to residents of the jurisdiction is insufficient).

716 *See, e.g.*, Bridgeport Music, Inc. v. Still N the Water Publishing, 327 F.3d 472, 483 (6th Cir. 2003) (operating an interactive website that reveals specifically intended interaction with forum state residents may create specific jurisdiction, but not shown here); ALS Scan v. Digital Serv. Consultants, Inc., 293 F.3d 707 (4th Cir. 2002) (merely posting information insufficient because it does not show intent to engage in business in the state); Bird v. Parsons, 289 F.3d 865 (6th Cir. 2002) (doing business over Internet with residents of forum statute sufficient for specific jurisdiction although not for general jurisdiction); Stuart v. Hennesey, 214 F. Supp. 2d 1198 (D. Utah 2002); Arnold v. Goldstar Fin. Sys., Inc., 2002 WL 1941546, at *6 (N.D. Ill. Aug. 22, 2002) (credit repair company's acceptance of payment on web page is "roughly analogous to . . . setting up a twenty-four hour storefront" in the forum state; this plus other contacts sufficient for specific jurisdiction); Alitalia-Linee Aeree Italiane S.P.A. v. Casinoalitalia.com, 128 F. Supp. 2d 340 (E.D. Va. 2001) (allowing forum state residents to place bets through out-of-state website sufficient for specific jurisdiction over claim that website infringed on plaintiff's trademark); Thompson v. Handa-Lopez, Inc., 998 F. Supp. 738 (W.D. Tex. 1998) (website through which Texas resident purchased game tokens and gambled gave Texas jurisdiction); Zippo Mfg. Co. v. Zippo Dot Com, Inc., 952 F. Supp. 1119 (W.D. Pa. 1997) (sale of services to forum state residents by credit card through website gave forum state jurisdiction over trademark infringement case). *But cf.* Metcalf v. Lawson, 802 A.2d 1221 (N.H. 2002) (no specific jurisdiction where defendant was seller on Internet auction site and winning bidder could potentially reside in any state).

717 Bird v. Parsons, 289 F.3d 865 (6th Cir. 2002); Bell v. Imperial Palace Hotel/Casino, Inc., 200 F. Supp. 2d 1082 (E.D. Mo. 2001) (plaintiff showed no connection between hotel's website and slip and fall accident at hotel).

718 Carefirst of Md., Inc. v. Carefirst Pregnancy Ctrs., Inc., 334 F.3d 390 (4th Cir. 2003) (generally accessible, semi-interactive website did not target forum state so insufficient for specific jurisdiction); Panavision Int'l v. Toeppen, 141 F.3d 1316 (9th Cir. 1998) (maintaining non-interactive website that diverted potential customers, plus attempt to extort money from trade name holder, gave court specific jurisdiction over cybersquatter); iAccess, Inc. v. WEBcard Techs., Inc., 182 F. Supp. 2d 1183 (D. Utah 2002) (website where user could send e-mail to WEBcard, subscribe to receive regular e-mails, and view the progress of the transaction on-line was insufficient); Biometrics, L.L.C. v. New Womyn, Inc., 112 F. Supp. 2d 869 (E.D. Mo. 2000) (specific jurisdiction established where website contained a "sales rep. locator" feature with a box labeled "Missouri" for the user to check off).

719 FC Inv. Group LC v. IFX Mkts., Ltd., 529 F.3d 1087 (D.C. Cir. 2008) (interactive website insufficient for jurisdiction without showing that forum residents used it in continuous and systematic way); Lakin v. Prudential Sec., Inc., 348 F.3d 704 (8th Cir. 2003) (*Zippo* interactivity criteria insufficient for general jurisdiction analysis; must also analyze quantity of contacts with forum state); Revell v. Lidov, 317 F.3d 467 (5th Cir. 2002) (finding three-category analysis not well adapted to general jurisdiction questions); Bird v. Parsons, 289 F.3d 865 (6th Cir. 2002). *Cf.* Dennis T. Yokoyama, *You Can't Always Use the Zippo Code: The Fallacy of a Uniform Theory of Internet Personal Jurisdiction*, 54 DePaul L. Rev. 1147 (2005). *But see* Gator.com Corp. v. L. L. Bean, Inc., 341 F.3d 1072 (9th Cir. 2003) (applying *Zippo* analysis to general jurisdiction question), *appeal dismissed upon rehearing en banc*, 398 F.3d 1125 (9th Cir. 2005) (no case or controversy after settlement); Mink v. AAAA Dev. L.L.C., 190 F.3d 333 (5th Cir. 1999) (applying *Zippo* analysis to general jurisdiction; website here insufficiently interactive to allow jurisdiction).

720 Lakin v. Prudential Sec., Inc., 348 F.3d 704 (8th Cir. 2003) (substantial and continuous Internet contacts may support general jurisdiction if quantity is high enough); Gorman v. Ameritrade, 293 F.3d 506 (D.C. Cir. 2002) (general jurisdiction could be established by brokerage firm's twenty-four-hour website that allowed residents to enter into contracts, pay commissioners, exchange information, etc., but court lacks jurisdiction for other reasons); Coremetrics, Inc. v. Atomic Park.com, L.L.C., 370 F. Supp. 2d 1013 (N.D. Cal. 2005). *See also* Shrader v. Biddinger, 633 F.3d 1235, 1243-4 (10th Cir. 2011) (acknowledging that selling products to residents of a state

When the claim is that the defendant used a website to commit an intentional tort, many courts apply criteria based on the Supreme Court's decision *Calder v. Jones*,[721] finding specific jurisdiction if the defendant engaged in intentional conduct that was expressly aimed at the forum state and the defendant knew that the effects would be felt in the forum state.[722] This analysis tends to converge with the *Zippo* analysis, as a passive website is unlikely to meet these criteria.[723]

Making a loan to a consumer through the Internet is likely to create at least specific jurisdiction over causes of action arising directly from that loan.[724] On the other hand, if the consumer merely gets information about a potential consumer credit transaction from a website, but then travels to the creditor's home state to enter into the transaction, the fact that the website was accessible in the consumer's home state is unlikely to meet the minimum contacts test.[725] A state statute may define the location of a consumer credit transaction as within the forum state if the creditor solicited the transaction by Internet.[726]

### 7.9.2.3 Personal Jurisdiction over Securitization Trusts

#### *7.9.2.3.1 Overview*

Whether courts can exercise personal jurisdiction over a securitization trust that is located in another state is a significant question as more and more obligations are securitized.[727] In analyzing the question, it is important to separate the question of general jurisdiction from specific jurisdiction.[728] If a defendant has continuous and systematic contacts with the forum state, the U.S. Constitution allows the courts of that state to exercise *general jurisdiction*. Then the courts in that state can hear any case against that defendant regardless of whether the case arose from the defendant's contacts with the state. Even when general jurisdiction is unavailable, a state can exercise *specific jurisdiction* over a defendant who has purposefully directed its activities at state residents if the litigation arises out of or relates to those activities.[729] In many cases against securitization trusts, specific jurisdiction will be a more fruitful possibility to pursue than general jurisdiction.

Another important question is whether the trust has a security interest in real or personal property located in the forum state. If it does, it is more likely that the state will have jurisdiction. A final question is the litigation context in which the claim is presented: whether the debtor seeks to assert an affirmative suit or a counterclaim to a collection suit, and whether the matter arises in bankruptcy court.

In evaluating the defendant's contacts with the forum state, it is important to consider both the acts of the defendant itself and the acts of its agents. The latter can be sufficient to give the forum state jurisdiction.[730] It may also be easier to get jurisdiction over the trustee than over the trust.[731]

#### *7.9.2.3.2 General jurisdiction*

General jurisdiction allows a court to can hear any case, even one that is unrelated to the defendant's activities in the forum state. A court may constitutionally exercise general jurisdiction over a defendant who has continuous and systematic contacts with the forum state.[732] For example, courts have general

through the Internet can be basis for general jurisdiction, but sales not substantial enough here).

721 465 U.S. 783, 104 S. Ct. 1482, 79 L. Ed. 2d 804 (1984).

722 *See, e.g.*, CollegeSource, Inc. v. AcademyOne, Inc., 653 F.3d 1066 (9th Cir. 2011); Tamburo v. Dworkin, 601 F.3d 693 (7th Cir. 2010). *Cf.* Mobile Anesthesiologists Chicago v. Anesthesia Assocs. of Houston Metroplex, P.A., 623 F.3d 440 (7th Cir. 2010) (maintaining website in Texas that infringed on Illinois competitor's trademark is insufficient); Johnson v. Arden, 614 F.3d 785 (8th Cir. 2010) (posting defamatory statements on passive website insufficient).

723 *See, e.g.*, Johnson v. Arden, 614 F.3d 785 (8th Cir. 2010) (reaching same conclusion after *Zippo* analysis as *Calder* analysis).

724 Brannon v. Fin. Am., L.L.C., 483 F. Supp. 2d 1136 (M.D. Ala. 2007) (Alabama has jurisdiction over lender that made home-secured loan through Internet to Alabama consumers after learning of their interest in a loan through a loan application website to which it had access); Asmar v. Benchmark Literacy Group, Inc., 2005 WL 2562965 (E.D. Mich. Oct. 11, 2005) (interactive website that allows out-of-state consumers to enroll in credit repair program sufficient for courts in consumer's home state to exercise long-arm jurisdiction).

725 Bell v. Imperial Palace Hotel/Casino, Inc., 200 F. Supp. 2d 1082 (E.D. Mo. 2001) (hotel website allowing customers to make reservations on-line insufficient for specific jurisdiction, as no money or anything of intrinsic value was transmitted on-line, and travel to outside state was required to actually transact business).

726 *See* Colo. Rev. Stat. § 5-1-201 ("[f]or purposes of this code, a consumer credit transaction is made in this state if . . . (b) A consumer who is a resident of this state enters into the transaction with a creditor who has solicited or advertised in this state by any means, including . . . internet, or other electronic means").

727 *See* National Consumer Law Center, Mortgage Lending §§ 1.2.3, 1.7 (2012) (describing securitization).

728 The distinction between general and specific jurisdiction is described in Burger King Corp. v. Rudzewicz, 471 U.S. 462, 472, 105 S. Ct. 2174, 85 L. Ed. 2d 528 (1985) and Helicopteros Nacionalies de Columbia, S.A. v. Hall, 466 U.S. 408, 414, 415 n.9, 104 S. Ct. 1868, 80 L. Ed. 2d 404 (1984). *See also* Lakin v. Prudential Sec., Inc., 348 F.3d 704, 707 (8th Cir. 2003); § 7.9.2.1, *supra*.

729 *See, e.g.*, Hallmark Cards, Inc. v. Monitor Clipper Partners, L.L.C., 757 F. Supp. 2d 904(W.D. Mo. 2010) (allegedly harmful communications by non-resident defendant, sent in response to plaintiff's inquiries, were sufficient basis for specific jurisdiction because they were voluntary and purposefully directed into state).

730 Daynard v. Ness, Motley, Loadholt, Richardson & Poole, 290 F.3d 42 (1st Cir. 2002); Gilmor v. Preferred Credit Corp., 2011 WL 111238 (W.D. Mo. Jan. 13, 2011). *See also* ACORN v. Household Int'l, Inc., 211 F. Supp. 2d 1160 (N.D. Cal. 2002) (court may exercise jurisdiction over holding company based on actions in forum state of its subsidiary, which was its general agent). *Cf.* Ross v. Thousand Adventures, 675 N.W.2d 812 (Iowa 2004) (rejecting jurisdiction over nonresident investor banks in pool of retail installment sales contracts, where banks lacked authority to collect payments and few of the contracts had any connection to Iowa).

731 *Cf.* Appleberry v. DDH, Inc., No. CV 03-01-0162 (Ohio Ct. C.P. Butler Cty. Mar. 6, 2006) (finding jurisdiction over the trustee, in part because the trustee, a national bank, was doing business in the state), *available at* www.nclc.org/unreported.

732 Burger King Corp. v. Rudzewicz, 471 U.S. 462, 473 n.15, 105 S. Ct. 2174, 85 L. Ed. 2d 528 (1985); Helicopteros Nacionalies de Co-

jurisdiction over a bank that has branch bank locations in the forum state and that forecloses upon and acquires ownership of property there.[733]

In cases against securitization trusts, or against any defendant that does business on a nationwide basis, the defendant is likely to point to the small percentage of its business that relates to the forum state. However, the Third and Eighth Circuits have held that the that fact that only a small percentage of a company's sales occurs in a given state is generally irrelevant.[734] The more relevant inquiry is whether the percentage of a company's contacts with the forum state is substantial for the forum.[735] The trust's lack of employees or offices in the forum state is also not dispositive.[736]

Several district court decisions have held that general jurisdiction is not established by a trust's purchase of loans originated in the forum state and its holding of mortgages secured by property in the forum state.[737] To justify this conclusion, these cases cite Supreme Court decisions that say that jurisdiction cannot be based on the "unilateral activity of another party or a third person."[738] But those Supreme Court cases involve markedly different factual contexts. In one case, a third party sent the out-of-state defendant checks drawn on a forum state bank account.[739] Obviously, the defendant had no control over where the third party did its banking. The defendant's acceptance of these checks did not give the forum state jurisdiction.

Another case dealt with a New York vehicle dealer who sold a car to a New York resident in New York. The buyer then drove the car to Oklahoma and had an accident.[740] The Supreme Court held that "the fortuitous circumstance that a single Audi automobile, sold in New York to New York residents, happened to suffer an accident while passing through Oklahoma," was insufficient to give Oklahoma jurisdiction over the buyer's suit.[741] Other cases in which the Supreme Court has applied this principle have similarly involved acts over which the defendant had no control.[742]

By contrast, a trust has complete control over the states from which it will acquire obligations. It can purposefully avail itself of that state's business or choose not to. In fact, the pooling and servicing agreement will probably specify the states from which obligations will be acquired. If the trust does not want to take obligations from these states, it can choose not to enter into that agreement.[743]

The Third Circuit approved general jurisdiction over an out-of-state bank that had purchased a number of loans on the secondary market that arose in the forum state.[744] The bank's ownership of loans secured by property in the forum state, plus its maintenance of a bank account there, amounted to continuous and systematic contacts with the forum state. The reasoning

lumbia, S.A. v. Hall, 466 U.S. 408, 414, 415 n.9, 104 S. Ct. 1868, 80 L. Ed. 2d 404 (1984). *See generally* § 7.9.2.1, *supra*.

733 Williams v. FirstPlus Home Loan Owner Trust 1998-4, 310 F. Supp. 2d 981, 996 (W.D. Tenn. 2004).

734 Lakin v. Prudential Sec., Inc., 348 F.3d 704, 709 (8th Cir. 2003); Provident Nat'l Bank v. Cal. Fed. Sav. & Loan Ass'n, 819 F.2d 434 (3d Cir. 1987).

735 Lakin v. Prudential Sec., Inc., 348 F.3d 704, 709 (8th Cir. 2003); Gilmor v. Preferred Credit Corp., 2011 WL 111238 (W.D. Mo. Jan. 13, 2011) (finding jurisdiction over securitization trusts, intervening assignees, and mortgage servicers after extensive discussion of contacts with forum state, but without specifying general or specific jurisdiction).

736 Burger King v. Rudzewicz, 471 U.S. 462, 476, 105 S. Ct. 2174, 85 L. Ed. 2d 528 (1985); Lakin v. Prudential Sec., Inc., 348 F.3d 704, 709 (8th Cir. 2003) (Arkansas had general jurisdiction even though defendant's only physical office was located in Georgia).

737 Mull v. Alliance Mortgage Banking Corp., 219 F. Supp. 2d 895 (W.D. Tenn. 2002); Williams v. FirstPlus Home Loan Trust, 209 F.R.D. 404 (W.D. Tenn. 2002); Brooks v. Terra Funding, 2002 WL 1797785 (W.D. Tenn. July 31, 2002); Street v. PSB Lending Corp., 2002 WL 1797773 (W.D. Tenn. July 31, 2002). *See also* Easter v. Am. West Fin., 381 F.3d 948 (9th Cir. 2004) (finding specific jurisdiction but not general jurisdiction where trust acquired forum state mortgage loans but had no offices, employees, bank accounts, or business operations in forum state); Johnson v. Long Beach Mortgage Loan Trust 2001-4, 451 F. Supp. 2d 16, 34 (D.D.C. 2006) (holding mortgages in forum state insufficient for general jurisdiction, but finding specific jurisdiction); Williams v. FirstPlus Home Loan Owner Trust, 310 F. Supp. 2d 981 (W.D. Tenn. 2004) (following *Barry*; holding notes secured by mortgages in forum state insufficient for general jurisdiction); Pilcher v. Direct Equity Lending, 189 F. Supp. 2d 1198, 1209 (D. Kan. 2002) (not distinguishing between general and specific jurisdiction); Lobatto v. Berney, 1999 WL 672994 (S.D.N.Y. Aug. 26, 1999) (court does not have jurisdiction over assignee of unsecured obligations simply because the assignor was subject to personal jurisdiction); Barry v. Mortgage Servicing Acquisition Corp., 909 F. Supp. 65, 74, 75 (D.R.I. 1995) ("where the property is completely unrelated to the plaintiff's cause of action, the presence of the defendant's property in the forum will not alone support the exercise of jurisdiction").

738 Helicopteros Nacionalies de Columbia, S.A. v. Hall, 466 U.S. 408, 417, 104 S. Ct. 1868, 80 L. Ed. 2d 404 (1984). *See also* Burger King Corp. v. Rudzewicz, 471 U.S. 462, 475, 105 S. Ct. 2174, 85 L. Ed. 2d 528 (1985).

739 Helicopteros Nacionalies de Columbia, S.A. v. Hall, 466 U.S. 408, 411, 416, 417, 104 S. Ct. 1868, 80 L. Ed. 2d 404 (1984).

740 World-Wide Volkswagen Corp. v. Woodson, 444 U.S. 286, 100 S. Ct. 559, 62 L. Ed. 2d 490 (1980).

741 *Id.* at 295.

742 Kuklo v. Super. Ct., 436 U.S. 84, 93, 94, 98 S. Ct. 1690, 56 L. Ed. 2d 132 (1978) (mother's choice of state in which to live with the children did not give that state jurisdiction over other parent); Hanson v. Denckla, 357 U.S. 235, 78 S. Ct. 1228, 2 L. Ed. 2d 1283 (1958) (fact that person who created trust later moved to Florida did not give Florida courts jurisdiction over Delaware trustee).

743 *See* National Consumer Law Center, Mortgage Lending §§ 1.2.3, 1.7 (2012) (discussing securitization, pooling and servicing agreements, and how to locate pooling and servicing agreements). *But cf.* Williams v. FirstPlus Home Loan Owner Trust 1998-4, 310 F. Supp. 2d 981, 995 (W.D. Tenn. 2004) (fact that loan pools included mortgage loans in forum state insufficient for general or specific jurisdiction over trust; court does not consider whether terms of pooling and servicing agreement specified that obligations from forum state would be acquired).

744 Provident Nat'l Bank v. Cal. Fed. Sav. & Loan Ass'n, 819 F.2d 434 (3d Cir. 1987). *See also* Bondi v. Citigroup, 2006 WL 1933319 (N.J. Super. Ct. App. Div. July 14, 2006) (foreign company's purchase of New Jersey business's receivables, which it then securitized, and its conduct of due diligence in New Jersey, is sufficient for specific jurisdiction). *But cf.* Hyams v. Halifax P.L.C., 2005 WL 3441230 (N.J. Super. Ct. App. Div. Dec. 16, 2005) (distinguishing *Provident Bank* because defendant here did not maintain bank account in forum state).

of this decision could subject a securitization trust to jurisdiction in any state in which property securing a substantial number of its loans is located. In another case, the Eighth Circuit cited the defendant's liens on hundreds to thousands of real properties in the forum state as a factor favoring general jurisdiction.[745]

#### *7.9.2.3.3 Specific jurisdiction when claim relates to property in forum state*

Often a debtor's suit relates to a security interest held by the trust in real or personal property that is located in the forum state. For example, a consumer may have entered into a loan transaction in his or her home state, and given the creditor a mortgage on real estate or a security interest in a manufactured home located in that same state. If a trust later acquires the mortgage or security agreement and note, can the consumer bring a suit arising out of the loan in the state where the loan originated and the secured property is located? Because the suit in this situation arises out of the trust's contacts with the forum state,[746] the forum state may have specific jurisdiction over the case.

Specific jurisdiction requires a showing only that the defendant has purposefully directed its activities at forum state residents, not that the defendant has maintained continuous and systematic contacts with the forum state. As the Supreme Court has stated, parties who "reach out beyond one state and create continuing relationships and obligations with citizens of another state" are subject to jurisdiction in the other state for the consequences of their activities.[747]

A United States Supreme Court decision strongly suggests that the consumer's home state will have jurisdiction over a securitization trust to which the note and mortgage are assigned, as long as the consumer's claim relates to the mortgaged property. In *Shaffer v. Heitner*, the Supreme Court stated: "[W]hen claims to the property itself are the source of the underlying controversy between the plaintiff and the defendant, it would be unusual for the State where the property is located not to have jurisdiction. . . . The State's strong interests in assuring the marketability of property within its borders and in providing a procedure for peaceful resolution of disputes about the possession of that property would also support jurisdiction, as would the likelihood that important records and witnesses will be found in the State."[748] This decision supports jurisdiction in the state where property is located whenever the claim relates to the existence or amount of a secured debt.[749]

The leading case is *Easter v. American West Financial*.[750] There, the Ninth Circuit held that a federal court could assert specific jurisdiction over trusts that acquired mortgage loans in the forum state, even though they had no offices, employees, or bank accounts in the forum state, conducted no business there, and had not contracted with any forum state resident. The court held that the trusts "have availed themselves of the protections of Washington law because they are beneficiaries of deeds of trust, which hypothecate Washington realty to secure payments on notes" they own.[751] According to the court, simply holding a deed of trust represents a significant contact with the forum state. When combined with the income stream from those loans, it demonstrates that the trusts "have purposefully availed themselves of the privilege of doing business" in the forum state.[752] Because the trial court had specific jurisdiction, it could hear a suit by borrowers arising out of allegedly excessive interest they paid on their notes.

Likewise, a district court held that Illinois had jurisdiction over an out-of-state bank that acquired an Illinois mortgage loan and then assigned the servicing rights to another entity. The court pointed out that "a party who holds a mortgage agreement with an Illinois resident on Illinois property is on notice that it might be sued in Illinois."[753] Such a party "should reasonably anticipate being haled into court there."[754]

Another district court reached the same conclusion, even though the trust had no offices, bank accounts, or employees in the forum state, did not own, lease, or use any real estate there, had not made contracts there, did not originate the plaintiff's mortgage loan, did not solicit mortgage loans, did not collect payments directly from borrowers, and did not have physical

745 Lakin v. Prudential Sec., Inc., 348 F.3d 704, 710 (8th Cir. 2003). *See also* Gilmor v. Preferred Credit Corp., 2011 WL 111238 (W.D. Mo. Jan. 13, 2011) (finding jurisdiction over securitization trusts after extensive discussion of contacts with forum state, but without specifying general or specific jurisdiction).

746 *See, e.g.*, Gilmor v. Preferred Credit Corp., 2011 WL 111238 (W.D. Mo. Jan. 13, 2011) (finding jurisdiction over securitization trusts, intervening assignees, and mortgage servicers after extensive discussion of contacts with forum state, but without specifying general or specific jurisdiction); Johnson v. Long Beach Mortgage Loan Trust 2001-4, 451 F. Supp. 2d 16, 30 (D.D.C. 2006) (suit seeking declaration that security interest in home was void, and seeking to hold assignee trust liable for wrongdoing in connection with creation of the security interest, arises out of trust's contacts with forum).

747 Burger King Corp. v. Rudzewicz, 471 U.S. 462, 473, 105 S. Ct. 2174, 85 L. Ed. 2d 528 (1985) (quoting Travelers Health Ass'n v. Virginia, 339 U.S. 643, 647, 70 S. Ct. 927, 94 L. Ed. 2d 1154 (1950)).

748 433 U.S. 186, 208, 97 S. Ct. 2569, 53 L. Ed. 2d 683 (1977).

749 *See also* Johnson v. Long Beach Mortgage Loan Trust 2001-4, 451 F. Supp. 2d 16, 31 (D.D.C. 2006) (citing *Shaffer* in support of jurisdiction over trust for claims regarding the mortgaged property); Abernathy v. Abernathy, 482 S.E.2d 265 (Ga. 1997) (action to resolve ownership of Georgia property can be brought in Georgia against non-resident).

750 381 F.3d 948, 960–961 (9th Cir. 2004).

751 *Id.* at 961.

752 *Id. But cf.* Henderson v. MetLife Bank, 2011 WL 1897427 (N.D. W. Va. May 18, 2011) (fact that lender acquired security interest in real property in W. Va. does not give W. Va. jurisdiction over title company to which buyer transferred funds before closing, as suit seeks return of those funds and does not challenge validity of security interest); GD Deal Holdings, L.L.C. v. Lotus Bus. Group, 20009 WL 2971795 (W.D. Tenn. Sept. 10, 2009) (merely holding mortgage on forum state real estate insufficient where claim does not arise from those liens).

753 Newman v. 1st 1440 Inv., Inc., 1990 WL 125369, at *2 (N.D. Ill. Aug. 22, 1990).

754 *Id.* at *3.

custody of the mortgage notes.[755] The court held that the minimum contacts requirement was satisfied by the fact that the trust held a security interest in the homeowner's real property in the forum state, had taken assignment of her mortgage note, and drew a revenue stream from her payments.

A 2011 district court decision's analysis is particularly persuasive.[756] Consumers brought claims under the Missouri Second Mortgage Loan Act against securitization trusts that held their loans. The trusts owned the mortgages but did not collect payments or directly enforce rights against borrowers. They did not have offices, employees, or bank accounts in Missouri.

In finding jurisdiction in Missouri over the trusts, the court stressed that the trusts knew in advance that they were assuming contracts with Missouri residents and that the loans were secured by Missouri real estate. Accordingly, the trusts could reasonably expect to be involved in litigation in Missouri to enforce their rights under the mortgages. The trusts also accepted loan payments from the Missouri residents, and the fact that servicers collected the borrowers' payments for the trusts made no difference: "whether on their own or through others acting on their behalf, the trusts have purposely directed activity into Missouri to collect and enforce the loans."[757] The court also rejected the argument that ownership of interests in the loans had been divided among so many entities that no one of them had sufficient contact with Missouri.

The loan servicers were likewise subject to Missouri jurisdiction because they directed communications into Missouri to collect on the loans, received money from Missouri residents, and took other actions to enforce the loans. Finally, the court held that it had jurisdiction over the entities that purchased the loans from the loan originator and then transferred them to various trusts, even though they held the loans only for a short period.

Several district court opinions are sometimes cited for the proposition that an out-of-state securitization trust that acquires loans secured by property in the forum state is not subject to that state's long-arm jurisdiction. However, most of these cases are entirely inapposite. *Barry v. Mortgage Servicing Acquisition Corp.*,[758] involves a highly unusual fact pattern because the plaintiff obtained a loan in Rhode Island that was secured by a home mortgage on property in a different state. When the plaintiff filed suit in Rhode Island to assert Truth in Lending claims against a bank to which the mortgage and note had been transferred, the bank objected to jurisdiction. The court held that the bank's status as assignee of 138 mortgages secured by Rhode Island real property was insufficient to give Rhode Island general jurisdiction over the bank. The opinion suggests, however, that as the plaintiff's claims related to the mortgaged property, the state where the property was located would have had jurisdiction over the claim.[759] Thus this decision supports specific jurisdiction over a trust in the state where the mortgaged property is located, as long as the claim relates to the property.

Another frequently cited case, *Rogers v. 5-Star Management, Inc.*,[760] also arose in a very atypical context. The debtor there had signed a note secured by real estate in four states: New Mexico, Arizona, California, and New York. The note was assigned to a Texas corporation that brought suit in New York to foreclose on the New York real estate. The debtor then brought suit in New Mexico to enjoin the New York foreclosure. The court held that the fact that the debtor had signed the note in New Mexico with the original creditor was insufficient to give New Mexico jurisdiction over the assignee. The court stressed that the action did not concern whether the defendant "properly possesses or could properly foreclose the New Mexico lien,"[761] thus suggesting, as in *Barry*, that there would have been jurisdiction in New Mexico if the suit had related to the New Mexico property.

Six cases from Tennessee also involve unusual facts.[762] In each case the plaintiffs sued a host of securitization trusts, but did not allege that any one of them held their loans. Thus, there was no tenable claim that the forum state had specific jurisdiction over the plaintiffs' claims. The courts also held that the fact that the trusts owned other mortgage loans in the forum state was insufficient to give the forum state general jurisdiction.

Only a few cases decline to find jurisdiction where debtors entered into credit transactions in the forum state and gave mortgages on homes in the same state. In the first case, *Pilcher v. Direct Equity Lending*,[763] a court in the debtors' home state held that it did not have long-arm jurisdiction over an out-of-state trust to which the mortgages and notes had been assigned. The court held that the trust's interests in the real estate in the forum state were insufficient to confer jurisdiction because the trusts were not attempting to foreclose and the "essence" of the plaintiffs' case was not the lien but the loan interest and fees. *Pilcher* did not discuss or even cite the United States Supreme Court's ruling in *Shaffer v. Heitner* discussed above, so cannot be regarded as sound precedent. Further, the court erred in characterizing the plaintiffs' claim as unconnected to the trust's interest in the real property. The plaintiffs' claims went to the dollar amount of the trust's liens, and could have resulted in voiding of the entire debt.

755 Johnson v. Long Beach Mortgage Loan Trust 2001-4, 451 F. Supp. 2d 16, 29–30 (D.D.C. 2006).

756 Gilmor v. Preferred Credit Corp., 2011 WL 111238 (W.D. Mo. Jan. 13, 2011).

757 *Id.* at *4.

758 909 F. Supp. 65 (D.R.I. 1995).

759 909 F. Supp. at 73, 74. *See also* Johnson v. Long Beach Mortgage Loan Trust 2001-4, 451 F. Supp. 2d 16, 30 (D.D.C. 2006) (citing *Barry* in support of jurisdiction over trust for claims relating to the mortgaged property).

760 946 F. Supp. 907 (D.N.M. 1996).

761 *Id.* at 911.

762 Mull v. Alliance Mortgage Banking Corp., 219 F. Supp. 2d 895 (W.D. Tenn. 2002); Williams v. FirstPlus Home Loan Trust, 209 F.R.D. 404 (W.D. Tenn. 2002); Brooks v. Terra Funding, 2002 WL 1797785 (W.D. Tenn. July 31, 2002); Street v. PSB Lending Corp., 2002 WL 1797773 (W.D. Tenn. July 31, 2002). *See also* Frazier v. Preferred Credit, 2002 WL 31039856 (W.D. Tenn. July 31, 2002); Berry v. GMAC-Residential Funding Corp., 2002 WL 1797779 (W.D. Tenn. July 31, 2002).

763 189 F. Supp. 2d 1198 (D. Kan. 2002).

In the second case, *Williams v. FirstPlus Home Loan Owner Trust 1998-4*,[764] a federal district court held that a trust that acquired a loan pool that "happened" to include loans secured by Tennessee real estate did not thereby give Tennessee courts specific jurisdiction over it. If the court had before it a pooling and servicing agreement that showed the trust's specific intent to acquire the Tennessee loans, it might have reached a different conclusion.[765]

In *Skinner v. Preferred Credit*,[766] a bare majority of the North Carolina Supreme Court refused to find jurisdiction over a trust, although it was undisputed the trust held the plaintiffs' mortgages. The court focused on the small number of North Carolina loans in the pool (less than 3%) and the fact that the trust was not involved in the origination of the loans but a passive recipient of the payments made by North Carolina residents through a servicer. It described the trust's interest in the plaintiffs' North Carolina real estate as merely a beneficial interest that was insufficient to confer jurisdiction. The court relied on *Frazier v. Preferred Credit*[767] in arriving at these conclusions, but did not address the fact that in *Frazier* there was no showing that the plaintiffs' loans were actually held by the trust. Three of the seven justices dissented, noting that the majority's decision "aids in the exploitation of our state's most vulnerable citizens" by placing the trusts beyond the reach of the state long-arm statute.[768] A year later, the state legislature overruled this decision by amending a state credit statute to provide that an assignee of a loan made to a North Carolina resident and secured by North Carolina real estate is deemed to have consented to jurisdiction in North Carolina's courts regarding any usury action or claim related to the loan.[769]

If consumers sue a securitization trust in the state where the collateral is located, they should frame the complaint to make it clear that the relief they are seeking relates to the collateral. For example, the complaint could seek a declaratory judgment reducing or voiding the security interest, and an order requiring the trust to file documents in the local recording office to reflect the reduction or release of the security interest.[770]

#### 7.9.2.3.4 *Specific jurisdiction when unsecured debts have been assigned to a trust*

Even when the obligations at issue are not secured by property in the forum state, there are good arguments in favor of jurisdiction over the trust that holds the obligation, when the plaintiff's claim arises out of that obligation. By taking assignment of a contract, the trust purposely avails itself of the benefits of the forum state's law.[771]

In *McGee v. International Life Insurance Co.*,[772] a California resident bought life insurance from an Arizona insurance company. Then a Texas company assumed the Arizona insurance company's obligations. The United States Supreme Court held that California had jurisdiction over the Texas company in a suit for policy benefits, even though the Texas company had no office or agent in California and this insurance policy was the only one it held for a California resident. While this case dates from 1957, the Supreme Court has cited it with approval in more recent decisions.[773]

An Iowa Supreme Court decision is consistent with *McGee* and suggests that the state where the obligations were created has jurisdiction over a securitization trust to which the obligations have been assigned, as long as the claims arise out of those obligations. In *Ross v. First Savings Bank of Arlington*,[774] the Iowa Supreme Court dealt with retail installment contracts that the original seller had assigned to a bank. That bank then pooled them and sold fractional interests in the pools to other banks. The court held that the banks that bought the fractional interests—who would be the equivalent of investors who buy shares in a securitization trust—did not have sufficient contacts with Iowa to be subject to the jurisdiction of the Iowa courts. But its language strongly suggests that the bank to which the contracts were actually assigned—which would be the equivalent of a securitization trust—would be subject to Iowa jurisdiction.[775] That bank holds the contracts, has contractual relationships with the debtors, has the right to assert contractual

764 310 F. Supp. 2d 981, 995 (W.D. Tenn. 2004).

765 *See generally* National Consumer Law Center, Mortgage Lending §§ 1.2.3, 1.7 (2012) (discussion of securitization, including pooling and servicing agreements and how to locate them).

766 Skinner v. Preferred Credit, 638 S.E.2d 203 (N.C. 2006).

767 Frazier v. Preferred Credit, 2002 WL 31039856 (W.D. Tenn. July 31, 2002).

768 Skinner v. Preferred Credit, 638 S.E.2d 203, 213 (N.C. 2006) (J. Timmons-Goodson, dissenting).

769 N.C. Gen. Stat. § 24-2.1. *See also* N.C. Gen. Stat. § 1-75.4(6) (state long-arm statute; a loan is deemed to be made in the state, regardless of the situs of the lender, assignee, or holder, and regardless of whether payments on the loan are made through a servicer, as long as the loan was made to a resident of the state for personal, family or household purposes and is secured by a one-to-four family home in the state).

770 *See* Johnson v. Long Beach Mortgage Loan Trust 2001-4, 451 F. Supp. 2d 16 (D.D.C. 2006) (suit seeking declaration that security interest in home was void, and seeking to hold assignee trust liable for wrongdoing in connection with creation of the security interest, arises out of trust's contacts with forum).

771 Johnson v. Long Beach Mortgage Loan Trust 2001-4, 451 F. Supp. 2d 16, 32 (D.D.C. 2006) (mortgage notes).

772 355 U.S. 220, 78 S. Ct. 199, 2 L. Ed. 2d 223 (1957). *See also* Kelly Inv., Inc. v. Basic Capital Mgmt., Inc., 85 S.W.3d 371 (Tex. App. 2002) (Texas courts have jurisdiction over California corporation that bought notes signed in Texas, where debtors had already sued original payee; notes were secured by out-of-state realty).

773 *See, e.g.*, Burger King Corp. v. Rudzewicz, 471 U.S. 462, 105 S. Ct. 2174, 85 L. Ed. 2d 528 (1985) (citing *McGee* throughout).

774 675 N.W.2d 812 (Iowa 2004).

775 *See also* Hyams v. Halifax P.L.C., 2005 WL 3441230 (N.J. Super. Ct. App. Div. Dec. 16, 2005) (institution's ongoing contacts with depositors in New Jersey, including mailing of periodic statements and newsletters, sufficient for specific jurisdiction even though accounts were opened elsewhere). *But cf.* Ross v. Thousand Adventures of Iowa, Inc., 723 N.W.2d 449 (Iowa Ct. App. 2006) (Iowa does not have jurisdiction over out-of-state bank that received assignments of class members' retail installment contracts as security for loan to originator; liability under FTC Holder Rule insufficient to create jurisdiction); Appleberry v. DDH, Inc., No. CV 03-01-0162 (Ohio Ct. C.P. Butler Cty. Mar. 6, 2006) (FTC Holder rule cannot overrule Due Process clause of constitution and create jurisdiction), *available at* www.nclc.org/unreported.

claims against the debtors, has the right to control collection, and is subject to liability for the debtors' claims under the FTC Holder Rule.[776] On the other hand, the Seventh Circuit has held, in a commercial case, that an assignee of a business contract does not automatically step into the shoes of the assignor for jurisdictional purposes.[777]

#### *7.9.2.3.5 Jurisdiction in bankruptcy court and over counterclaims*

If the debtor is litigating claims against a securitization trust in bankruptcy court, long-arm jurisdiction is not an issue. Nationwide service of process is allowed in bankruptcy court,[778] without regard to whether the defendant has minimum contacts with the state in which the bankruptcy court is located.[779]

Long-arm jurisdiction and due process issues are also not a concern if the trust voluntarily submits itself to the jurisdiction of the forum state's courts. For example, if the trust brings suit or joins in a suit in the forum state against the consumer, it subjects itself to the consumer's counterclaims or even the consumer's affirmative claims in a related suit, regardless of whether it has minimum contacts with the forum state.[780]

### 7.9.2.4 Jurisdiction over Parent Companies and Holding Companies

Another question that may arise is whether the consumer can obtain jurisdiction over an out-of-state parent company or holding company that is related to an in-state company that dealt with the consumer. Sometimes it is important to join the parent or holding company because the local corporation is thinly capitalized.

In order to exercise jurisdiction over an out-of-state corporation, courts generally require the plaintiff to show that it controls the activities of the in-state corporation.[781] In general, the independent activities of the parent corporation will not establish jurisdiction over a subsidiary, even a wholly owned subsidiary.[782]

An Oklahoma Supreme Court decision examined this issue in detail in an abusive loan case.[783] The court held that Oklahoma had jurisdiction over the parent company because it had continuous, systemic contacts with the in-state company, exercising significant day-to-day control over it. The parent company paid the expenses of certain on-site supervisors who visited the Oklahoma offices, and it helped the in-state offices set their yearly objectives. The Oklahoma company referred to the parent company as the "home office," and the parent company referred to the Oklahoma company as one of its 500 nationwide offices. On the other hand, the court held that Oklahoma did not have jurisdiction over three holding companies that owned stock in the Oklahoma company, shared some board members with the Oklahoma company, filed consolidated tax returns with the Oklahoma company, and signed a management agreement with the parent company. This decision highlights the importance of detailed development of the facts in any challenge to jurisdiction.[784]

776 16 C.F.R. § 433.2.

777 Purdue Research Found. v. Sanofi-Synthelabo, S.A., 338 F.3d 773 (7th Cir. 2003). *See also* Pilcher v. Direct Equity Lending, 189 F. Supp. 2d 1198, 1209 (D. Kan. 2002) (not distinguishing between general and specific jurisdiction); Lobatto v. Berney, 1999 WL 672994 (S.D.N.Y. Aug. 26, 1999) (court does not have jurisdiction over assignee of unsecured obligations simply because the assignor was subject to personal jurisdiction); Hammond v. Fla. Asset Fin. Corp., 695 N.W.2d 1 (Iowa 2005) (irrelevant for purposes of personal jurisdiction analysis that court had jurisdiction over assignor).

778 Fed. R. Bankr. P. 7004(b). *See* National Consumer Law Center, Consumer Bankruptcy Law and Practice § 13.3.2.1 (9th ed. 2009 and Supp.).

779 *In re* Fed. Fountain, Inc., 165 F.3d 600 (8th Cir. 1999).

780 Gen. Contracting & Trading Co. v. Interpole, Inc., 940 F.2d 20 (1st Cir. 1991); Threlkeld v. Tucker, 496 F.2d 1101 (9th Cir. 1974); Nobel Floral, Inc. v. Pasero, 130 Cal. Rptr. 2d 881 (Cal. Ct. App. 2003).

781 Negron-Torres v. Verizon Communications, Inc., 478 F.3d 19 (1st Cir. 2007); Stubbs v. Wyndham Nassau Resort & Crystal Palace Casino, 447 F.3d 1357, 1361 (11th Cir. 2006) (jurisdiction proper over out-of-state parent company if its separate corporate status is formal only); Epps v. Stewart Info. Servs. Corp., 327 F.3d 642 (8th Cir. 2003) (must show that parent company so dominated and controlled subsidiary that that latter's corporate existence was disregarded and it was the parent company's alter ego); Dickson Marine, Inc. v. Panalpine, Inc., 179 F.3d 331, 338 (5th Cir. 1999).

782 Keeton v. Hustler Magazine, Inc., 465 U.S. 770, 104 S. Ct. 1473, 79 L. Ed. 2d 790 (1984); Freudensprung v. Offshore Tech. Servs., 379 F.3d 327 (5th Cir. 2004). *Cf.* Bondi v. Bank of Am. Corp. (*In re* Parmalat Sec. Litig.), 381 F. Supp. 2d 283 (S.D.N.Y. 2005) (finding general jurisdiction, but no specific jurisdiction, over subsidiary because subsidiary was integrated into the operations of resident parent corporation).

783 Gilbert v. Security Fin. Corp., 152 P.3d 165 (Okla. 2006).

784 *See, e.g.*, Harris v. Option One Mortgage Corp., 261 F.R.D. 98, 108–110 (D.S.C. 2009) (discussing detailed affidavit showing lack of sufficient basis for personal jurisdiction).

# Chapter 8 Credit Cards: Abuses, Regulation, and State Law Claims

## 8.1 Introduction

### 8.1.1 Background and Historical Perspective

The use of credit cards is pervasive in American society, and they have become an increasingly integral part of American lives. Seventy-two percent (72.2%) of all households have at least one credit card, and 40.3% of cardholders carry credit card debt from month to month.[1] There are almost 1.2 billion cards in circulation—over ten credit cards for every household in the country.[2] The amount of credit card debt outstanding as of January 2012 was over $800 billion,[3] nearly three times as much as in 1993.[4]

Yet the widespread use of credit cards dates back less than sixty years. Charge cards were introduced in about 1914 by department stores, hotels, oil companies, and Western Union.[5] These cards could only be used to purchase the lender's goods and services, and the balance had to be paid in full each month. In the 1950s, Diners' Club and American Express began issuing general purpose cards that could be used at a variety of vendors. Banks followed several years later with credit cards, which allowed balances to be carried over from one month to the next. In the 1960s, groups of banks created the national credit card transaction processing networks under the names VISA and MasterCard.[6]

A great explosion in credit card lending occurred after the Supreme Court ruled in 1978 that national banks could export interest rates from their home states by issuing credit cards to residents of other states.[7] In effect, this removed any usury caps from credit card lending, and banks rushed to locate in states without interest rate limits. The growth in credit cards, and credit card debt, continued after the Supreme Court's 1996 decision that similarly removed state law limits on fees.[8] The federal banking regulators expanded the scope of federal preemption in the early 2000s to allow credit card lenders greater ability to exploit consumers without the need to comply with state consumer protection laws.[9]

### 8.1.2 The Massive Credit Card Debt Burden

The explosion of credit card debt placed an enormous burden on millions of American consumers. Consumers experienced dramatically increased credit card debt, rising from an average of $630 in 1970 to over $4,000 in 2001, and to $7,300 in 2007,[10] before declining slightly after the Great Recession to an average of $6,800 per household in 2012.[11] The percentage of American families with credit card debt has also grown substantially. By 2009, 72% of American families held credit cards and 59.8% of these families reported outstanding balances.[12]

---

1 Kevin Foster, Erik Meijer, Scott Schuh, & Michael A. Zabek, *The 2009 Survey of Consumer Payment Choice*, Fed. Reserve Bank of Boston Public Policy Discussion Paper No. 11-1 (Apr. 2011).

2 United States Census Bureau, Statistical Abstract of the United States: 2012, at 740 (Table 1188): Credit Cards—Holders, Number, Spending and Debt, 2000 and 2009, and Projections, 2012, *available at* www.census.gov/compendia/statab/2012/tables/12s1188.pdf; United States Census Bureau, 2010 Housing Characteristics Census Briefs (Oct. 2011), *available at* www.census.gov/prod/cen2010/briefs/c2010br-07.pdf (117 million households in 2010).

3 Federal Reserve Board, Statistical Release No. G.19, Consumer Credit (Jan. 2012), *available at* www.federalreserve.gov/releases/g19/hist/cc_hist_sa.html.

4 *Id.*

5 This summary of the development of the credit card industry is based on Diane Ellis, Bank Trends—The Effect of Consumer Interest Rate Deregulation on Credit Card Volumes, Charge-Offs, and the Personal Bankruptcy Rate (1999), *available at* www.fdic.gov/bank/analytical/bank/bt_9805.html.

6 VISA and MasterCard are not themselves creditors or card issuers; the bank or store retains that status. National Consumer Law Center, Truth in Lending § 6.2.4.4.5 (7th ed. 2010 and Supp.).

7 *See* § 3.4, *supra*.

8 *See* § 3.4.5.3, *supra*.

9 *See* § 3.2, *supra*.

10 Brian K. Bucks, Arthur B. Kennickell, Traci L. Mach & Kevin B. Moore, *Changes in U.S. Family Finances from 2004 to 2007: Evidence from the Survey of Consumer Finances*, 95 Fed. Reserve Bull. A40, A46 (Feb. 12, 2009).

Figures vary somewhat, and self-reported balance data may result in understated debts. *See generally* David S. Evans, *The Growth and Diffusion of Credit Cards in Society*, 2 Payment Card Economics Review 59, 64–66 (2004); Tamara Draut & Javier Silva, Demos, Borrowing to Make Ends Meet: The Growth of Credit Card Debt in the '90s, at 9–11 (Sept. 2003), *available at* www.aecf.org/upload/publicationfiles/fe3679k534.pdf.

11 Federal Reserve Board, Statistical Release No. G.19, Consumer Credit (Jan. 2012), *available at* www.federalreserve.gov/releases/g19/hist/cc_hist_sa.html.

12 Kevin Foster, Erik Meijer, Scott Schuh, & Michael A. Zabek, The 2009 Survey of Consumer Payment Choice, Fed. Reserve Bank of Boston Public Policy Discussion Paper No. 11-1 (Apr. 2011); Jesse Bricker, Brian Bucks, Arthur Kennickell, Traci Mach, & Kevin Moore, Surveying the Aftermath of the Storm: Changes in Family Finances from 2007 to 2009, Finance and Economics Discussion

The debt burden is greatest on families with annual incomes under $10,000.[13] For families in this category carrying ongoing debt, the debt load quadrupled from 1989 to 2004—from an average of $622 to $2,750—reaching an average debt load of 31% of total gross income.[14] Low- and middle-income older Americans experienced a further 26% increase in credit card debt from 2005 to 2008.[15]

Credit card debt has grown fastest among older Americans, with a 194% increase in average credit card debt from 1989 to 2004.[16] Medical expenses made up over one-third of older Americans' credit card debt in 2008.[17] While median credit card balances for older Americans ages 65 to 74 decreased slightly from $3,200 in 2007 to $2,900 in 2009, it increased from $800 to $2,000—a whopping 150%—for older Americans ages 75 and above during that same time period.[18]

For young adults aged 25–34, credit card debt increased 47% to an average of $4,358 from 1989 to 2004.[19] In 2004, young adults spent nearly 25% of their monthly income on debt service, more than twice what young adults spent as a proportion of their income in 1989.[20] Low- and middle-income young adults are particularly burdened by debt, with an average credit card debt of nearly $10,000 for those adults in debt.[21]

The negative consequences of this escalating mountain of debt on individual consumers as well as the American economy cannot be minimized. Credit card debt created enormous pressure on families.[22] In the most recent recession, approximately 6.6% of credit cards were thirty or more days past due—the highest delinquency rate in eighteen years.[23] Credit card debt also contributed to the foreclosure crisis. For example, a 2005 study found that 40% of low- and middle-income homeowners surveyed had refinanced or gotten a second mortgage during the past three years, and half of those homeowners had used the proceeds from the new home-secured loan to pay down credit card debt.[24] The substantially worsening of the credit card consumer's condition was accompanied by credit card earnings that have been consistently higher than returns on all commercial bank activities,[25] even after the Great Recession and the passage of the Credit CARD Act.[26]

### 8.1.3 Escalating Debt Loads Caused by Industry Practices

The credit card industry bears a significant portion of the responsibility for this explosion in credit card debt. For one thing, credit card lenders aggressively solicited consumers. The number of direct mail solicitations peaked in 2005 at 6 billion, before dropping in the Great Recession to 3.9 million,[27] then making a comeback, as consumers received 5 billion credit card offers in 2011.[28] This means more than forty-two mailings went out to every American household last year—not counting Internet or telephone solicitations.[29]

More importantly, a significant amount of debt load was caused, not by consumer borrowing, but by the punitive tactics of the credit card industry. Many overburdened consumers

Series (Dec. 11, 2011), *available at* www.federalreserve.gov/pubs/feds/2011/201117/201117pap.pdf (discussing data from the 2009 Panel Survey of Consumer Finances).

13 José A. García, Borrowing to Make Ends Meet: The Rapid Growth of Credit Card Debt in America 7 (2007), *available at* www.demos.org/publication/borrowing-make-ends-meet-rapid-growth-credit-card-debt-america.

14 José A. García, Borrowing to Make Ends Meet: The Rapid Growth of Credit Card Debt in America 7 (2007), *available at* www.demos.org/publication/borrowing-make-ends-meet-rapid-growth-credit-card-debt-america.

15 José Garciá & Tamara Draut, The Plastic Safety Net: How Households Are Coping in a Fragile Economy: Findings from a 2008 National Household Survey of Credit Card Debt Among Low- and Middle-Income Households 4 (2009), *available at* www.nyc.gov/html/ofe/downloads/pdf/fenforum_plastic_safety_net.pdf.

16 José A. García, Borrowing to Make Ends Meet: The Rapid Growth of Credit Card Debt in America 9 (2007), *available at* www.demos.org/publication/borrowing-make-ends-meet-rapid-growth-credit-card-debt-america.

17 *Id.* at 8.

18 Jesse Bricker, Brian Bucks, Arthur Kennickell, Traci Mach, & Kevin Moore, Surveying the Aftermath of the Storm: Changes in Family Finances from 2007 to 2009, Finance and Economics Discussion Series (Dec. 11, 2011), *available at* www.federalreserve.gov/pubs/feds/2011/201117/201117pap.pdf (discussing data from the 2009 Panel Survey of Consumer Finances).

19 Demos, Generation Debt: Student Loans, Credit Cards, and Their Consequences 3 (2007), *available at* www.demos.org/sites/default/files/publications/DemosYoungAdultEconSeries_Debt.pdf.

20 *Id.*

21 José Garciá & Tamara Draut, The Plastic Safety Net: How Households Are Coping in a Fragile Economy: Findings from a 2008 National Household Survey of Credit Card Debt Among Low- and Middle-Income Households 4 (2009), *available at* www.nyc.gov/html/ofe/downloads/pdf/fenforum_plastic_safety_net.pdf.

22 *See* Elizabeth Warren & Amelia Warren Tyagi, The Two-Income Trap: Why Middle-Class Mothers and Their Families Are Going Broke (Basic Books 2003).

23 Government Accountability Office, Credit Cards: Fair Debt Collection Practices Act Could Better Reflect the Evolving Debt Collection Marketplace and Use of Technology, GAO-09-748 (Sept. 2009), *available at* www.gao.gov/assets/300/295588.pdf.

24 Tamara Draut, Ansel Brown, Lisa James, Kathleen Keest, Jabrina Robinson & Ellen Schloemer, DEMOS & Center for Responsible Lending, The Plastic Safety Net: The Reality Behind Debt in America (Oct. 2005), *available at* www.demos.org/publication/plastic-safety-net-reality-behind-debt-america.

25 Board of Governors of the Federal Reserve System, Report to Congress on the Profitability of Credit Card Operations of Depository Institutions 4 (June 2011), *available at* www.federalreserve.gov/boarddocs/rptcongress/creditcard/2011/ccprofit2011.pdf.

Profitability dipped in 2009, when credit card banks as a group experienced negative net earnings for the first time since the Federal Reserve Board began tracking this data in 1986, but quickly rebounded in 2010. *Id.* at 3–4.

26 *Id. See also* Harry Terris, *After Sound and Fury, Post-CARD Act Revenues Hold*, Am. Banker, Nov. 3, 2010.

27 Cardtrak.com, Card Mail (Jan. 30, 2009), *available at* www.cardtrak.com/news/2009/01/30/card_mail.

28 Mintel Comperemedia, Plain Vanilla Cards the Flavor of the Month, (Feb. 2012) *available at* www.mintel.com/press-centre/press-releases/823/plain-vanilla-cards-the-flavor-of-the-month-reports-mintel-comperemedia.

29 United States Census Bureau, 2010 Housing Characteristics Census Briefs (Oct. 2011), *available at* www.census.gov/prod/cen2010/briefs/c2010br-07.pdf (117 million households in 2010).

struggled to pay their obligations, but credit card lenders keep consumers on a treadmill of debt, paying fees and charges, for as long as possible.

Consider the classic case of Ruth Owens, a consumer from Cleveland, Ohio who did try to repay her debt, but was driven hopelessly into default by her credit card lender.[30] In May 1997, Ms. Owens stopped using her credit card, made no further purchases or cash advances, and tried to pay off her debt to her credit card lender. At that time, she owed $1,963. Over the next six years, Ms. Owens made $3,492 in payments to this lender. One might assume this was enough to pay off her debt. After all, if Ms. Owens had made the same payments on a $2,000 loan with interest at 21% annual percentage rate (the usury limit in many states), her debt would be paid off.

From May 1997 until her account was sent for collection in May 2003, not one penny of Ms. Owens' $3,492 in payments went to reduce her balance. During this time, the credit card lender charged Ms. Owens various fees that consumed all of her payments and caused her debt to grow even larger. The following fees and interest were charged to Ms. Owens' account:

*Fees and Interest*

| | |
|---|---|
| *Over-the-Limit Fees* | $1,518.00 |
| *Late Fees* | $1,160.00 |
| *Credit Insurance* (CreditSafe)[31] | $ 369.62 |
| *Interest and Other Fees* | $6,008.66 |
| | |
| Total | $9,056.28 |

Despite having received substantial payments for six years, the lender claimed that Ms. Owens still owed $5,564 when it filed a collection lawsuit against her. In other words, after having paid $3,492 on a $1,963 debt, Ms. Owens' balance grew to $5,564.

The court held that Ms. Owens was not liable for this debt on the basis that her credit card lender would be unjustly enriched by a judgment in its favor. The court also held that the accumulation of fees was "manifestly unconscionable," stating "[t]his court is all too aware of the widespread financial exploitation of the urban poor by overbearing credit-card companies. [Ms. Owens] has clearly been the victim of plaintiff's unreasonable, unconscionable and unjust business practices."[32]

Another example of how credit card practices drive consumers into overwhelming debt comes from the bankruptcy case of Josephine McCarthy.[33] Ms. McCarthy had two accounts with one credit card lender. On one account, she made $3,058 in payments over a two-year period during which her balance on the account increased from $4,888 to $5,357. She had made only $218.16 (net of store credit) in purchases during this time. All of her payments went to pay finance charges (at a 29.99% interest rate), late charges, over-the-limit fees, bad check fees, and phone payment fees. On the other card, she made $2,008 in payments over the same period and the account balance increased from $2,020.90 to $2,607.66. During this time, she added only $203.06 in purchases.

| | Total Payments | Purchases | Balance Increase | Total Interest and Fees in 2-Year Period |
|---|---|---|---|---|
| Account 1 | $3,058.00 | $218.16 | $469.00 | $3,308.84 |
| Account 2 | $2,008.00 | $203.06 | $586.76 | $2,391.79 |

Other bankruptcy decisions shed further light on how high finance charges and junk fees, not irresponsible spending, may be the root cause of overwhelming credit card debt. In one proceeding, a bankruptcy court forced a major credit card lender to break out principal versus interest and fees in its claims against thirty-one separate debtors. The bankruptcy court's order reveals that on average, 57% of the debts consisted of interest and fees.[34]

### *8.1.4 Disparate Impact of High Rates and Fees*

The punitive interest rates and fees charged by credit card lenders disproportionately impact minorities, women, and low-income consumers. An analysis of data from the Federal Reserve Board and CardData (an on-line database of credit card industry information) found that:[35]

- African-American and Latino credit card holders who carry a balance are more likely than whites to be paying an interest rate over 20% (which is likely to be penalty rates[36]). Nearly 15% of African-American and 13% of Latino holding revolving credit accounts pay these rates, versus 7% of whites. In addition, 40% of African-American card holders and 26% of Latino card holders reported paying late, potentially triggering a late fee.

30 Discover Bank v. Owens, 822 N.E.2d 869 (Ohio Mun. Ct. 2004).

31 Like many card customers, Ms. Owens was being charged for one of the numerous products sold by card companies known as debt protection, which are notorious for abuse. In this case, Ms. Owens was charged approximately $10 per month for a Discover card product called CreditSafe Plus, which apparently provided for a suspension of payments and finance charges if Ms. Owens became unemployed, hospitalized, or disabled. Since Ms. Owens was already on Social Security disability and unemployed, the CreditSafe product presumably would apply only if she became hospitalized. Ms. Owens was no doubt paying for a product that would likely never benefit her. *See* § 6.3.2, *supra* (discussion of credit card debt protection products).

32 Discover Bank v. Owens, 822 N.E.2d 869, 875 (Ohio Mun. Ct. 2004).

33 *In re* Josephine McCarthy, No. 04-10493-SSM (Bankr. E.D. Va. filed 2004), *available on the companion website to this treatise*.

34 Amended Order Overruling Objection to Claims, *In re* Blair (W.D.N.C. Feb. 10, 2004), *available on the companion website to this treatise*. *See* National Consumer Law Center, Consumer Bankruptcy Law and Practice §§ 14.4.3.5, 15.4.3.2.3.2 (9th ed. 2009 and Supp.) (discussing credit-card-related bankruptcy issues).

35 Jennifer Wheary & Tamara Draut, Demos, Who Pays? The Winners and Losers of Credit Card Deregulation (Aug. 1, 2007), *available at* www.demos.org/publication/who-paysthe-winners-and-losers-credit-card-deregulation.

36 *See* §§ 8.3.1.2.1, 8.4.2, *infra* (discussing penalty rates).

- Low-income revolvers (incomes below $25,000) are twice as likely as middle-income revolvers (incomes of $50,000–$100,000) and five times as likely as upper-income revolvers (income over $100,000) to pay an interest rate over 20%. Nearly 12% of low-income revolvers pay a rate in excess of 20% versus only 2.7% of upper-income revolvers. More than 20% of low-income borrowers also reported a late payment.
- Single women revolvers are almost twice as likely as single male revolvers to pay an interest rate over 20%: 11% versus 5.8%. In addition, 22% of single women card holders reported paying late.

In 2006, the Boston Federal Reserve Bank published a study that found significant differences in credit card terms based on racial makeup of the cardholder's neighborhood, when comparing cardholders with identical risk profiles living in different areas.[37]

## 8.2 Overview: Regulation of Credit Card Lending

### 8.2.1 *From Regulation to the Wild West and Back*

Credit card companies were not always so free to engage in reprehensible behavior. Credit card deregulation, and the concomitant spiraling credit card debt of Americans, began in 1978, with the Supreme Court's decision in *Marquette National Bank of Minneapolis v. First of Omaha Service Corp.*[38] This case gave national banks the ability to take the most favored lender status from their home state across state lines, and preempt the law of the borrower's home state.[39] As a result, national banks and other depositories established their headquarters in states that eliminated or raised their usury limits, giving them free rein to charge whatever interest rate they wanted.[40]

After the *Marquette* decision, credit card debt increased dramatically. As of 1978, credit card debt was $50 billion.[41] From 1978 to 1995, credit card debt increased six-fold to $378 billion.[42]

In 1996, the Supreme Court paved the way for credit card banks to increase their income stream even more dramatically. In *Smiley v. Citibank (South Dakota), N.A.*,[43] the court approved of the Office of the Comptroller of the Currency's (OCC) definition of interest that included a number of credit card charges, such as late payment, over-the-limit, cash advance, returned check, annual fees, and membership fees.[44] As a result, national banks and other depositories could charge fees in any amount to their customers as long as their home-state laws permitted the fees and so long as the fees were "interest" under the OCC definition.

The preemption of state laws went even further for credit card lenders. Most of these lenders, and certainly the top ten lenders, are national banks or other federally chartered depository institutions. Regulations issued by the Office of Comptroller of Currency allowed national banks to ignore state laws governing lending practices even if the state law did not set interest or rate caps.[45] In some cases, even state consumer protection laws prohibiting unfair or deceptive acts or practices were held to be preempted.[46] Thus, for several decades, there had been little regulation of credit card practices due to this sweeping expansion of federal bank preemption.

In addition to preemption, another reason that credit card lenders were able to impose high interest rates and fees and engage in abusive practices was the lack of competition due to the predominance of the largest credit card lenders, plus the Visa and Mastercard networks. At the end of 2010, the top nine credit card lenders accounted for 85% of the outstanding credit card loans nationwide.[47] Commentators have opined that the hegemony of the top lenders and VISA and MasterCard networks has stifled competition between the lenders on pricing and product development.[48] Several antitrust cases have been brought by cardholders alleging collusion in developing abusive practices.[49]

---

37 Ethan Cohen-Cole, *Credit Card Redlining*, Fed. Reserve Bank of Bos., Working Paper No. QAU08-1, Feb. 26, 2008, *available at* www.bos.frb.org/bankinfo/qau/wp/2008/qau0801.pdf.

38 439 U.S. 299, 99 S. Ct. 540, 58 L. Ed. 2d 534 (1978).

39 It is worth noting that there was no interstate banking when the National Bank Act was passed.

40 Other depository institutions obtained the same most favored lender status when Congress enacted § 521 of the Depository Institutions Deregulation and Monetary Control Act of 1980 (codified at 12 U.S.C. § 1831d). *See* § 3.4, *supra*.

41 Diane Ellis, FDIC—Division of Insurance, *The Effect of Consumer Interest Rate Deregulation on Credit Card Volumes, Charge-Offs, and in the Personal Bankruptcy Rate*, Bank Trends, 98-05 (Mar. 1998), *available at* www.fdic.gov/bank/analytical/bank/bt_9805.html.

42 *See* Federal Reserve Board, Statistical Release, Consumer Credit Historical Data (Revolving), *available at* www.federalreserve.gov/releases/g19/hist/cc_hist_mt.txt.

43 517 U.S. 735, 116 S. Ct. 1730, 135 L. Ed. 2d 25 (1996).

44 The OCC definition of interest is found in 12 C.F.R. § 7.4001(a). *See* § 3.4.5.2, *supra*.

45 *See* § 3.2, *supra*.

46 *But see* § 3.2.4.7, *supra*.

47 Government Accountability Office, Credit Cards: Consumer Costs for Debt Protection Products Can be Substantial Relative to Benefits but Are Not a Focus of Regulatory Oversight, GAO-11-311 (Mar. 2011).

48 Duncan MacDonald, *Issuers Should Innovate on Their Own*, Am. Banker, Aug. 19, 2005, at 11. *See also* Michael Simkovic, Credit Card Reform and Bankruptcy Reform, Norton Bankruptcy Law Adviser, Issue No. 10 (Oct. 2009) (rise in prices and lender profits after Bankruptcy Abuse Prevention and Consumer Protection Act showed lack of competitiveness and transparency in credit card industry).

49 *See, e.g.*, Ross v. Bank of Am., N.A., 524 F.3d 217 (2d Cir. 2008) (reversing dismissal of antitrust claims brought by cardholders alleging illegal collusion by lenders that resulted in near unanimous use of mandatory arbitration agreements); *In re* Currency Conversion Fee Antitrust Litig., 773 F. Supp. 2d 351 (S.D.N.Y. 2011) (denying summary judgment to lenders on claims brought under the Sherman Act for price fixing of currency conversion fees).

The Department of Justice and state attorneys general have also brought antitrust cases against Visa, MasterCard, and American

As a result of these forces, abuses by credit card lenders spun out of control, creating enormous hardships for consumers. It was not until January 2009—thirteen years after the *Smiley* decision and over thirty years after the *Marquette* decision—that banking regulators issued the first substantive federal regulations governing credit card practices.

In January 2009, the Federal Reserve Board, Office of Thrift Supervision, and National Credit Union Administration issued a new rule that prohibited certain unfair or deceptive practices (UDAP) by credit card lenders.[50] This rule was issued pursuant to the agencies' authority under the Federal Trade Commission Act,[51] and thus was not privately enforceable.[52]

A few months later, Congress enacted the Credit Card Accountability Responsibility and Disclosure Act of 2009 (hereinafter the Credit CARD Act).[53] This law finally established substantive federal statutory protections for credit card consumers.

## 8.2.2 The Credit CARD Act: Scope, Rulemaking, Private Enforcement

The Credit CARD Act addresses some (but not all) of the worst abuses by credit card lenders. It prohibits rate increases for existing balances,[54] caps penalty fees,[55] protects cardholders in making payments,[56] and prohibits harmful practices such as double cycle billing.[57] The Credit CARD Act primarily amends the Truth in Lending Act (TILA), and thus is discussed in detail in another treatise in this series.[58] This chapter provides summaries of the Credit CARD Act's protections.

Most of the Credit CARD Act's provisions became effective on February 22, 2010.[59] The FRB issued a number of rules as required by the Credit CARD Act.[60] The FRB also withdrew the UDAP rule it had issued pursuant to the FTC Act.[61]

Effective July 21, 2011, the Dodd-Frank Wall Street Reform and Consumer Protection Act of 2010 (hereinafter the Dodd-Frank Act) transferred rule writing authority for the Truth in Lending Act, including that for the Credit CARD Act, to the Consumer Financial Protection Bureau (CFPB).[62] Thus, any changes to the Credit CARD Act regulations after that date will be the CFPB's responsibility.

The vast majority of the Credit CARD Act provisions specifically apply to "credit cards under an open-end (not home-secured) consumer credit plan." The FRB defined this term to exclude two specific types of credit cards:[63]

1. Credit cards that access a home-equity line of credit subject to the disclosure requirements of section 1026.40 [section 226.5b] of Regulation Z.[64]
2. An overdraft line of credit accessed by a debit card.

This section will indicate when a particular Credit CARD Act provision has a broader scope (as applying to all types of credit cards or even all open-end credit). Otherwise, it may be assumed that the provision only applies to "credit cards under an open-end (not home-secured) consumer credit plan" as defined above.

Because the Credit CARD Act is part of TILA, the private remedies for the latter are available to address violations.[65] Actual damages, statutory damages, and attorney fees are available for any violation of the Credit CARD Act requirements discussed in this section, *except* for:[66]

- Mandatory re-evaluation of rate increases;[67]
- Requirement for reasonable and proportional penalty fees;[68]
- General requirement for consideration of ability to repay.[69]

Statutory damages are available regardless of the existence or non-existence of actual damages.[70] Statutory damages are twice the finance charge with a minimum of $500 and a maximum of $5,000, respectively.[71] The maximum can be even greater in the case of an established pattern or practice of failure to comply with TILA.[72]

---

Express for rules that these networks imposed on merchants accepting credit cards. *See* Order Approving Final Judgment, United States v. American Express Co., 10-cv-4496 (E.D.N.Y. July 20, 2011), *available on the companion website to this treatise*. *See also* Kendall v. Visa, 518 F.3d 1042 (9th Cir. 2008) (upholding dismissal of antitrust claims brought by merchants against credit card networks and lenders for imposition of interchange fees).

50 74 Fed. Reg. 5498 (Jan. 29, 2009) (issuing former 12 C.F.R. §§ 227.21 to 227.26 (FRB Regulation AA); 12 C.F.R. §§ 535.21 to 535.26 (OTS); 12 C.F.R. §§ 706.21 to 706.26 (NCUA)).

51 15 U.S.C. § 57a(f).

52 *See* National Consumer Law Center, Unfair and Deceptive Acts and Practices § 14.1 (7th ed. 2008 and Supp.).

53 Pub. L. No. 111-24, 123 Stat. 1734 (May 22, 2009).

54 *See* § 8.3.2, *infra*.

55 *See* § 8.4.2, *infra*.

56 *See* § 8.6, *infra*.

57 *See* § 8.3.4, *infra*.

58 National Consumer Law Center, Truth in Lending Ch. 7 (7th ed. 2010 and Supp.).

59 Pub. L. No. 111-24, 123 Stat. 1735 (May 22, 2009).

60 75 Fed. Reg. 7658 (Feb. 22, 2010).

61 75 Fed. Reg. 7925 (Feb. 22, 2010). The NCUA similarly removed the credit card provisions of its FTC Act rule, 75 Fed. Reg. 6558 (Feb. 10, 2010), as did the Office of Thrift Supervision, 75 Fed. Reg. 23,565 (May 4, 2010).

62 Pub. L. 111-203, § 1100A, 124 Stat. 1376 (July 21, 2010). *See* National Consumer Law Center, Truth in Lending, § 1.2.11 (7th ed. 2010 and Supp.).

63 12 C.F.R. § 1026.2(a)(15)(ii) [§ 226.2(a)(15)(ii)]. *See* National Consumer Law Center, Truth in Lending §§ 6.2.4.2, 7.1.2.2 (7th ed. 2010 and Supp.); *id.* § 6.2.4.1 (broader, more general definition of "credit card").

64 These disclosure requirements are discussed at National Consumer Law Center, Truth in Lending Ch. 8 (7th ed. 2010 and Supp.).

65 *Id.* at Ch. 11 (discussing private remedies for TILA).

66 15 U.S.C. § 1640(a)(1). National Consumer Law Center, Truth in Lending Ch. 11 (7th ed. 2010 and Supp.).

67 *See* § 8.3.3, *infra*.

68 *See* § 8.4.2, *infra*.

69 *See* § 8.7.2.2, *infra*.

70 Krutchkoff v. Fleet Bank, 960 F. Supp. 541 (D. Conn. 1996). *See* National Consumer Law Center, Truth in Lending § 11.6.2 (7th ed. 2010 and Supp.).

71 15 U.S.C. § 1640(a)(2)(A)(iii). *See* National Consumer Law Center, Truth in Lending § 11.6.3 (7th ed. 2010 and Supp.).

72 15 U.S.C. § 1640(a)(2)(A)(iii). *See* National Consumer Law Center,

Greater detail on the TILA's private remedies provided in another treatise in this series.[73]

## 8.2.3 Benefits of the Credit CARD Act

The Credit CARD Act has resulted in enormous benefit for consumers. Americans are the most satisfied that they have been with their credit cards since 2008, due in part to the protections and disclosures mandated by the Act.[74] The majority of consumers familiar with the Act have reported that it has been good for them, and 60% of consumers in general believe that they monthly statements have been clearer and easier to read.[75] Interest rate hikes were dramatically curtailed, the amount of late fees were substantially reduced, and over-the-limit fees have virtually disappeared.[76]

## 8.2.4 Industry's Response

### 8.2.4.1 The "Democratization of Credit"

The credit card industry defended its practices by arguing that deregulation benefited many consumers, with fewer annual fees, lower interest rates, and rich reward programs.[77] In addition, the industry touted the "democratization of credit," with credit cards available to the vast majority of Americans. It predicted that re-regulating rates and fees would raise costs and limit credit for the majority of consumers in order to help financially distressed borrowers.[78]

However, the problem with excessive penalty rates and fees is that they permit credit card lenders to "hide the ball" on the real price of a credit card. Consumers shop for credit cards based information in the solicitation—non-penalty annual percentage rates, credit card rewards, and annual fees. Consumers never shop based on penalty rates or late fees because they never expect to incur them, a phenomenon called "hyperbolic discounting."

More importantly, these arguments proved to be hollow after the passage of the Credit CARD Act. Lenders raised annual fees by only a modest amount,[79] and credit card solicitations were no less favorable[80] or abundant than before the Credit CARD Act.[81] While interest rates increased prior to the Act's effective date, they actually dropped after the effective date.[82] Credit card companies remain highly profitable.[83]

### 8.2.4.2 New Abuses: Business Credit Cards

The credit card industry responded to the passage of the Credit CARD Act with new tactics as well.[84] Some lenders also continued to engage in prohibited practices.[85]

Another tactic was to promote credit cards that were ostensibly "professional" or business cards.[86] Business credit cards are not subject to the Credit CARD Act or TILA.[87] American households receive 10 million offers every month for business credit cards,[88] and there is some question as to whether all of these credit cards are truly offered or intended for business purposes.[89] Advocates and others have urged that the protections of the Credit CARD Act be extended to credit cards used by small businesses or for which the individual can be held personally liable.[90] A study by the Pew Charitable Trust found

---

Truth in Lending § 11.6.3 (7th ed. 2010 and Supp.).

73 National Consumer Law Center, Truth in Lending Ch. 11 (7th ed. 2010 and Supp.).

74 Maria Aspan, *Americans Are Happier with Their Credit Cards, Thanks to CARD Act*, Am. Banker, Aug. 18, 2011 (citing J.D. Power and Assoc. survey).

75 Synovate, Consumer Perceptions and Reactions to the CARD Act (Feb. 22, 2011), *available at* http://files.consumerfinance.gov/f/2011/01/Synovate_FINAL.pdf.

76 Jennifer Faulkner, Office of the Comptroller of Currency, The CARD Act—One Year Later: Impact on Pricing and Fees (Feb. 22, 2011).

77 Jonathan Orszag & Susan Manning, COMPASS, An Economic Assessment of Regulating Credit Card Fees and Interest Rates 14–15 (Sept. 2007). This report was commissioned by the American Bankers Association.

78 *Id.* at 5.

79 *See* Nick Bourke & Ardie Hollifield, Pew Health Group, Two Steps Forward: After the Credit CARD Act, Credit Cards are Safer and More Transparent—But Challenges Remain (July 2010), *available at* www.pewtrusts.org/uploadedFiles/wwwpewtrustsorg/Reports/Credit_Cards/PEW-CreditCard%20FINAL.PDF.

80 Andrea McKenna, *Increased Competition, Less Fallout from CARD Act Than Expected, Mintel Says*, PaymentsSource.com (Aug. 4, 2010), *available at* www.paymentssource.com/news/mintel-less-fallout-card-act-3002807-1.html.

81 Josh Frank, Center for Responsible Lending, Credit Card Clarity: CARD Act Reform Works (Feb. 16, 2011), *available at* www.responsiblelending.org/credit-cards/research-analysis/FinalCRL-CARD-Clarity-Report2-16-11.pdf.

82 *Id.*

83 Federal Deposit Ins. Corp., Quarterly Bank Profile—Fourth Quarter 2010, Table III-A: Full Year 2010, All FDIC-Insured Institutions, *available at* www2.fdic.gov/qbp/2010dec/all3a1.html (showing that in 2010, all but two of the twenty-two credit card banks were profitable and their return on assets was 1.8%, nearly triple that of all banks in general). *See also* Harry Terris, *After Sound and Fury, Post-CARD Act Revenues Hold*, Am. Banker, Nov. 3, 2010.

84 *See* Josh Frank, Center for Responsible Lending, Dodging Reform: As Some Credit Card Abuses Are Outlawed, New Ones Proliferate (Dec. 10, 2009), *available at* www.responsiblelending.org/credit-cards/research-analysis/CRL-Dodging-Reform-Report-12-10-09.pdf.

85 *See* Letter from National Consumer Law Center et al. to Comptroller of Currency re Potential Credit CARD Act Violations (July 7, 2010), *available at* www.nclc.org/images/pdf/credit_cards/letter-occ-card-act-enforcement-07-10.pdf.

86 *Id.*; Pew Charitable Trusts, U.S. Households at Risk from Business Credit Cards, May 2011, at 1, available at www.pewtrusts.org/uploadedFiles/wwwpewtrustsorg/Reports/Credit_Cards/Pew_Business_Credit_Cards_Report.pdf. *See also* Jessica Silver-Greenberg, *Beware That New Credit-Card Offer*, Wall St. J., Aug. 28, 2010.

87 *See* National Consumer Law Center, Truth in Lending § 2.4.2 (7th ed. 2010 and Supp.).

88 Pew Charitable Trusts, U.S. Households at Risk from Business Credit Cards, May 2011, at 1, *available at* www.pewtrusts.org/uploadedFiles/wwwpewtrustsorg/Reports/Credit_Cards/Pew_Business_Credit_Cards_Report.pdf.

89 *Id.*; Jessica Silver-Greenberg, *Beware That New Credit-Card Offer*, Wall St. J., Aug. 28, 2010.

90 Pew Charitable Trusts, U.S. Households at Risk from Business

that business credit cards continue to be subject to potentially harmful practices.[91] The problem is exacerbated by the fact that in many cases, credit card lenders require the individual using the credit card to become individually liable for the account, leaving employees on the hook for large debts if the company cannot pay them.[92]

## *8.2.5 Other Federal Regulation*

Prior to the enactment of the Credit CARD Act, TILA primarily regulated credit cards through disclosure, although there were a handful of dispute resolution and substantive protections specifically for credit cards. Another treatise in this series discusses TILA's disclosure requirements for credit cards and open-end credit in general.[93]

Other parts of the Consumer Credit Protection Act (the umbrella act that encompasses many of the important federal consumer protection statutes) may also apply to credit card lenders. For example, the Fair Credit Reporting Act (FCRA) governs "furnishers" of information to consumer reporting agencies, which include almost all credit card lenders.[94] The FCRA also includes a provision specifically governing credit card numbers on receipts issued by merchants, requiring that the credit card number be truncated, that is, only the last five digits be displayed.[95] The Equal Credit Opportunity Act prohibits discrimination by lenders, including credit card lenders.[96]

Credit Cards, May 2011, at 1, *available at* www.pewtrusts.org/uploadedFiles/wwwpewtrustsorg/Reports/Credit_Cards/Pew_Business_Credit_Cards_Report.pdf; Alexandra Alper, Small Firms Say Captive to Credit Card Changes, Reuters, Mar. 8, 2012, *available at* www.reuters.com/article/2012/03/08/us-usa-creditcards-idUSBRE8270U620120308; Andrew Johnson, *CardHub.com Calls for CARD Act Rules to Apply to Small-Business Cards*, Am. Banker, Apr. 13, 2011.

91 Pew Charitable Trusts, U.S. Households at Risk from Business Credit Cards, May 2011, at 2–3, *available at* www.pewtrusts.org/uploadedFiles/wwwpewtrustsorg/Reports/Credit_Cards/Pew_Business_Credit_Cards_Report.pdf.

92 *Id.* at 8, n.3 (ten of the twelve surveyed lenders explicitly required business credit card applicants to be personally liable for all business account expenses). *See, e.g.*, *In re* Fairfield, 455 B.R. 849 (Bankr. E.D. Pa. 2011) (individual owner of medical practice was personally liable for practice's credit card debt); Cosmas v. American Express Centurion Bank, 757 F. Supp. 2d 489 (D.N.J. 2010) (lender hired collection agency to pursue non-principal employee for company's credit card debt); Eze v. JP Morgan Chase Bank, N.A., 2010 WL 3189813 (E.D.N.Y. Aug. 11, 2010) (principal of business was personally liable for business credit card debt); American Express Bank, F.S.B. v. Kayatta, 118 Cal. Rptr. 3d 462 (Cal. Ct. App. 2010) (individual was personally liable for business credit card debt).

93 National Consumer Law Center, Truth in Lending Ch. 6 (7th ed. 2010 and Supp.).

94 National Consumer Law Center, Fair Credit Reporting Ch. 6 (7th ed. 2010 and Supp.).

95 *Id.* § 9.2.5.1.

96 *See* National Consumer Law Center, Credit Discrimination (5th ed. 2009 and Supp.).

# 8.3 Interest Rate Increases

## *8.3.1 Pricing and Interest Rate Abuses*

### 8.3.1.1 Introduction

One of the biggest problems with credit pricing that occurred prior to the Credit CARD Act was that lenders are not required to abide by a fundamental contract principle—that a "deal is a deal." Credit card lenders were permitted to raise the interest rate for any reason, or no reason at all, by simply mailing a notice to consumers.

The Credit CARD Act prohibits certain types of repricing. In general, creditors are prohibited from increasing the interest rate applicable to the existing or "outstanding" balance on account unless a specific exception applies.[97] After the first year of an account, the lender can increase the interest rate for future transactions by sending a notice forty-five days in advance.[98] These prohibitions have led to a dramatic decrease in interest rate hikes, according to the data from the OCC.[99]

### 8.3.1.2 Common Repricing Abuses

#### *8.3.1.2.1 Penalty rates*

A penalty rate is an increase in a credit card account's APR triggered by the occurrence of a specific event, such as the consumer's making a late payment or exceeding the credit limit. Penalty rates are a relatively recent phenomenon, first appearing in the 1990s.[100] A Government Accountability Office study found that the average penalty rate for the six major credit card lenders was about 27% APR, and that twenty-seven out of the most popular twenty-eight credit cards carried them.[101]

The existence of penalty rates for minor transgressions alone would be enough to draw criticism. Raising an APR from the mid-teens to 30% or higher, simply on the basis of a single transgression, itself is unjustified. After all, the credit card lender has already collected a one-time charge in the form of a penalty fee. Increasing the consumer's APR simply allows the lender to reap additional profit.

Even worse, though, is that prior to the Credit CARD Act, lenders would apply the new terms to the existing balance—leaving consumers stuck with paying for already completed transactions at interest rates far higher than was originally agreed. This practice was uniquely abusive, as no other industry in the country is allowed to increase the price of a product once it is purchased.

97 *See* § 8.3.2, *infra*.

98 *Id.*

99 Jennifer Faulkner, Office of the Comptroller of Currency, The CARD Act—One Year Later: Impact on Pricing and Fees (Feb. 22, 2011).

100 Government Accountability Office, Credit Cards: Increased Complexity in Rates and Fees Heightens Need for More Effective Disclosures to Consumers, GAO-06-929, at 24 (Sept. 2006), *available at* www.gao.gov/new.items/d06929.pdf.

101 *Id.*

Lenders justified penalty rates as necessary to price for risks. They point out that credit cards constitute an open line of credit available for future extensions of credit. However, such reasoning is not applicable when it comes to repricing existing balances. Credit card lenders had already assessed a consumer's risk of not repaying when the credit was first extended, and presumably offered an interest rate based on that risk.

Indeed, if a consumer is truly risky, the responsible action would be to terminate or reduce the credit line so that no more credit could be extended. Instead, lenders chose to keep extending credit, but at exorbitant prices. In one especially egregious case, a credit card lender doubled the consumer's credit line despite obvious signs of financial distress as shown by fifteen late payments during a three-year period. After the consumer increased her balance, the lender then reduced her credit limit and doubled the interest rate, presumably as a penalty rate.[102]

#### 8.3.1.2.2 *Universal default*

Universal default is an especially criticized form of credit card repricing. With universal default, credit card lenders impose penalty rates on consumers, not for late payments or any behavior with respect to the consumer's account with that particular lender, but for late payments to any of the consumer's other creditors. In some cases, lenders will impose penalties simply if the credit score drops below a certain number, whether or not the drop was due to a late payment or another factor.[103]

A survey of credit card banks found that 45% admitted they had a universal default policy.[104] More importantly, customer services representatives of the banks surveyed admitted the following circumstances could trigger a penalty rate hike: credit score drops (90%); late payment to any creditor (86%); going over limit (57%); bouncing a payment check (52%); too much debt (43%); too much available credit (33%); getting a new credit card (33%); inquiring about car loan or mortgage (24%).[105]

The Credit CARD Act did not entirely eliminate universal default, but it did prohibit its application to existing balances, ban it during the first year of an account, and require advance notice for its application to future balances.[106] At least one state also bans a variation of universal default. Nevada prohibits a lender from increasing the interest rate on a credit card account based upon the consumer's late payment to another creditor unaffiliated with the lender.[107] Note that federal banking law may preempt the application of the Nevada anti-universal default statute to federally chartered depository institutions.[108] However, a major card lender at one point apparently included a provision choosing Nevada law,[109] and there is a potential argument that a violation of Nevada law could constitute a breach of contract.[110]

#### 8.3.1.2.3 *Any time, any reason repricing*

Penalty rates and universal default are not the only forms of credit card repricing. Lenders use change-in-terms notices[111] to raise a card holder's rates for any reason, or for no reason at all.[112] Lenders have raised rates because card holders used too much of their credit line (despite the fact the card holders did not exceed their credit limits) or simply to make up for losses in the lender's other business lines.[113]

## 8.3.2 *Limits on Price Increases for an* Outstanding *Balance*

### 8.3.2.1 Overview

The Credit CARD Act contains significant limits for lenders seeking to raise the annual percentage rate (APR) applicable to the existing or "outstanding balance" on an account. This protection also applies to certain fees and charges.

It prohibits a lender from increasing the APR or certain fees and charges on an outstanding balance,[114] except pursuant to four exceptions:[115]

---

102 Citibank, S.D., N.A. v. Palma, 646 S.E.2d 635 (N.C. Ct. App. 2007) (finding imposition of penalty rate not unconscionable).

103 *See, e.g.*, Barrer v. Chase Bank USA, N.A., 566 F.3d 883 (9th Cir. 2009) (describing practice of "adverse action repricing," where lender would increase rates by sending Fair Credit Reporting Act notices that would cite decline in factors used to calculate credit scores, such as ratio of credit used to credit available).

104 Linda Sherry, Consumer Action, *2005 Credit Card Survey*, Consumer Action News (Summer 2005), *available at* www.consumer-action.org/news/articles/2005_credit_card_survey.

105 *Id.*

106 *See* § 8.3.2, *infra*.

107 Nev. Rev. Stat. § 97A.200.

108 *See* § 3.4, *supra* (explaining why federal law would preempt the Nevada anti-universal default statute).

109 Gillespie v. HSBC North Am. Holdings, Inc., 2006 WL 2735135, at *8 (M.D. Fla. Sept. 25, 2006).

110 *See* Wells v. Chevy Chase Bank, F.S.B., 832 A.2d 812 (Md. 2003) (plaintiffs could bring breach of contract claim against bank, where bank's credit card agreement stated that the interest rate would never exceed 24% and that it was governed by Maryland law, despite federal Home Loan Owners Act's preemption of state restrictions on interest rates). *But see* Flagg v. Yonkers Sav. & Loan Ass'n, 396 F.3d 178 (2d Cir. 2005) (general choice of law provision selecting New York law was not specific enough to incorporate into contract New York's requirement to pay interest on an escrow account).

111 *See* § 8.9, *infra*.

112 *See* Consumer Action, *2008 Credit Card Survey*, Consumer Action News (July 22, 2008), *available at* www.consumer-action.org/downloads/english/2008_Summary.pdf (seventeen of twenty-two banks or 77% stated they could change a cardholder's interest rate at any time, for any reason).

113 *Id.* at 18 (four of the top credit card lenders cited factors that might cause an interest rate increase such as: "market conditions," "the economy," and "business strategies."); David Lazarus, *What Rate Cuts? Use of Plastic Gets Pricier*, Los Angeles Times 1, Feb. 10, 2008 (citing industry observers who believed that lenders raised credit card rates in part to generate new revenue after suffering billions of dollars in losses from the subprime mortgage crisis). *See, e.g.*, Rubio v. Capital One Bank (USA), N.A., 572 F. Supp. 2d 1157 (C.D. Cal. 2008) (lender increased APR "[i]n light of rising interest rates over the past few years"), *aff'd in part, rev'd in part*, 613 F.3d 1195 (9th Cir. 2010).

114 15 U.S.C. § 1666i-1(a).

115 15 U.S.C. § 1666i-1(b).

- Promotional APRs where an increase in the APR is disclosed ahead of time and which will occur upon expiration of a disclosed period of time;
- Where the APR is a variable one;
- If the consumer makes a payment over sixty days late; or
- If the consumer has completed or failed to comply with a workout or temporary hardship arrangement.

Regulation Z adds another exception to this list:

- If an APR has been decreased pursuant to the Servicemembers Civil Relief Act, and the protections of that Act no longer apply.[116]

This section and the ones that follow provide a brief summary of these five exceptions. Much greater detail is provided in another treatise in this series.[117]

Lenders are permitted to increase the APR, a fee, or a charge pursuant to one of the exceptions above, even if the increase would not be permitted under a different section of the Credit CARD Act.[118] In other words, the list of exceptions is not mutually exclusive. However, unless specifically permitted by one of these exceptions, a lender is not permitted to increase an APR on an outstanding balance, even if the circumstances under which the increase will occur are disclosed in advance.[119]

While the protections apply only to outstanding balances, the Credit CARD Act also prohibits increasing the APR on even future transactions during the first year, subject to the same four exceptions. This limitation is discussed at § 8.3.2.4, *infra*. After the first year, lenders may increase the APR, fee or charge that will be applied to future transactions, with forty-five days' notice.[120] Regulation Z refers to this provision as the "advance notice exception."

## 8.3.2.2 Allowable Rate Increases

### *8.3.2.2.1 Promotional rate exception*

The Credit CARD Act permits a lender to increase an APR applicable to an outstanding balance at the expiration of a specified period of time, if:

- The increased APR and the time period are both clearly and conspicuously disclosed, in writing, prior to the commencement of that period.[121]
- After the specified time period expires, the lender increases the APR only up to the APR as previously disclosed.[122]

The primary application of this exception would be to "promotional" rates. Promotional rates that are offered at the opening of an account, i.e., "teaser" or "introductory" rates, are also subject to special disclosure requirements under TILA.[123] The increased rate after the promotional period is called the "post-promotional rate."

The Credit CARD Act requires that all promotional rates have a minimum period of six months.[124] However, the lender is permitted to limit the promotional rate to a particular category of transactions, e.g., balances transfers over $100.[125]

The promotional rate exception does not permit a lender to disclose and apply a rate increase that is conditioned on a contingent circumstance or is at the lender's discretion.[126] Permitting a contingent or discretionary rate increase would create a loophole to the general prohibition against rate increases for outstanding balances and during the account's first year.

The exception for promotional rates is applicable to deferred interest programs.[127] This permits a lender to offer deferred interest plans, which would otherwise run afoul of the prohibition on APR increases for an outstanding balance. Deferred interest programs are discussed in detail at § 8.8, *infra*.

### *8.3.2.2.2 Variable rate exception*

A lender may increase an APR on an outstanding balance due to the operation of a variable rate.[128] Variable rates are generally computed by adding a margin to an index.[129] If the index increases, the rate increases correspondingly.

In order to qualify for this exception, the index must not be under the lender's control.[130] It must also be a publicly available rate.[131]

A fixed maximum rate, or "ceiling," is permitted.[132] However, a fixed minimum rate or "floor" is banned, e.g., prime plus 5% but not lower than 15% APR.[133]

The variable rate exception permits a lender to increase the APR only if there is an increase in the index.[134] A lender is not permitted to increase the APR by changing the method or

116 Reg. Z, 12 C.F.R. § 1026.55(b)(6) [§ 226.55(b)(6)].

117 National Consumer Law Center, Truth in Lending § 7.2 (7th ed. 2010 and Supp.).

118 Reg. Z, 12 C.F.R. § 1026.55(b) [§ 226.55(b)].

119 Official Commentary to Reg. Z, 12 C.F.R. § 1026.55(a)-1 [§ 226.55(a)-1].

120 *See* § 8.3.2.2.4, *infra*.

121 15 U.S.C. § 1666i-1(b)(1)(A); Reg. Z, 12 C.F.R. § 1026.55(b)(1)(i) [§ 226.55(b)(1)(i)]. *See* National Consumer Law Center, Truth in Lending § 6.6.5.5 (7th ed. 2010 and Supp.) (discussing promotional rate disclosures).

122 15 U.S.C. § 1666i-1(b)(1)(B); Reg. Z, 12 C.F.R. § 1026.55(b)(1)(ii)(C) [§ 226.55(b)(1)(ii)(C)].

123 *See* National Consumer Law Center, Truth in Lending § 6.6.5.5 (7th ed. 2010 and Supp.).

124 15 U.S.C. § 1666i-2(b); Reg. Z, 12 C.F.R. § 1026.55(b)(1) [§ 226.55(b)(1)].

125 Official Commentary to Reg. Z, 12 C.F.R. § 1026.55(b)(1)-2 [§ 226.55(b)(1)-2].

126 Official Commentary to Reg. Z, 12 C.F.R. § 1026.55(b)(1)-4 [§ 226.55(b)(1)-4].

127 Official Commentary to Reg. Z, 12 C.F.R. § 1026.55(b)(1)-4.i [§ 226.55(b)(1)-4.i].

128 15 U.S.C. § 1666i-1(b)(2).

129 *See* National Consumer Law Center, Truth in Lending § 6.5.3.2.5 (7th ed. 2010 and Supp.).

130 15 U.S.C. § 1666i-1(b)(2); Reg. Z, 12 C.F.R. § 1026.55(b)(2)(i) [§ 226.55(b)(2)(i)].

131 15 U.S.C. § 1666i-1(b)(2); Reg. Z, 12 C.F.R. § 1026.55(b)(2)(i) [§ 226.55(b)(2)(i)].

132 *Id.*

133 Official Commentary § 1026.55(b)(2)-2.ii [§ 226.55(b)(2)-2.ii].

134 Reg. Z, 12 C.F.R. § 1026.55(b)(2)(ii) [§ 226.55(b)(2)(ii)].

formula used to determine the APR, e.g., by increasing the margin.[135]

### *8.3.2.2.3 Sixty days' delinquency exception*

A lender may increase an APR, fee, or charge if it does not receive the consumer's required minimum payment within sixty days after the due date for that payment.[136] This increase may apply to the outstanding balance.

In order to rely on this exception, a lender must require monthly minimum payments and must not have received two consecutive required minimum payments. The lender must also provide a notice forty-five days in advance.[137] Finally, the consumer is entitled to have the former rate reinstated if he or she makes six months of on-time payments on the account.[138] Regulation Z specifies that the six months of minimum payments must be consecutive, and must begin immediately with the first payment due following the effective date of the increase.[139]

### *8.3.2.2.4 Rate increases permitted on future transactions—advanced notice exception*

Lenders are prohibited from increasing the APR, fees, or charges for *any* transactions during the first year of an account, even for new transactions.[140] After the first year of an account, a lender may apply an increased APR, fee, or charge to transactions that occur fourteen days after giving notice of the increase.[141] Regulation Z refers to this ability as "the advanced notice exception."[142]

The lender may also increase a fee that applies to the account as a whole using this exception.[143] For example, after the first year following account opening, a lender generally may add or increase a monthly maintenance fee that applies to the whole account, even though there are protected balances in that account.[144] Furthermore, the lender cannot impose an increased fee or charge if the consumer has rejected the increase.[145]

Note that the increased APR, fee, or charge itself will not become effective until forty-five days after the notice is given.[146] For example, a lender gives a notice of an increase in the APR from 15% to 18% on March 15. The lender may apply the 18% APR to all transactions occurring after March 29 (fourteen days after the notice). However, the 18% APR will not take effect until May 1 (forty-five days after the notice).[147] Furthermore, the 18% APR cannot be applied to any balances outstanding prior to March 29, unless one of the other exceptions described in this section applies.

### *8.3.2.2.5 Workout or temporary hardship arrangement exception*

In some cases, a lender will reduce an APR for a delinquent or financially distressed consumer pursuant to a workout or temporary hardship arrangement. A lender is permitted to increase an APR, fee, or finance charge if the consumer fails to comply with the terms of the workout or temporary arrangement, or after the consumer has completed the arrangement.[148]

No advance notice of the increase is required when it is imposed.[149] Before the commencement of the workout or hardship arrangement, however, the lender must provide a disclosure of the terms, including the increase in APR at the completion or due to the failure of the arrangement.[150]

### *8.3.2.2.6 Servicemembers Civil Relief Act exception*

Regulation Z creates an exception not found in the Credit CARD Act to the prohibitions against increases in an APR for an outstanding balance.[151] The exception addresses accounts for which an APR has been reduced pursuant to the Servicemembers Civil Relief Act (SCRA), 50 U.S.C. app. § 527, and was created pursuant to the FRB's authority under the Truth in Lending Act.[152]

In general, the SCRA requires a creditor to reduce the APR on an account to 6% while a servicemember is on active duty. However, this protection ceases to apply once the servicemember is no longer on active duty.[153]

Regulation Z permits a lender to increase the APR for an account that had been previously reduced pursuant to the SCRA, once the SCRA no longer applies.[154] The lender must

---

135 Official Commentary to Reg. Z, 12 C.F.R. § 1026.55(b)(2)-1 [§ 226.55(b)(2)-1].

136 15 U.S.C. § 1666i-1(b)(4); Reg. Z, 12 C.F.R. § 1026.55(b)(4) [§ 226.55(b)(4)].

137 *See* National Consumer Law Center, Truth in Lending § 7.2.3.5.2 (7th ed. 2010 and Supp.).

138 15 U.S.C. § 1666i-1(b)(4)(B). *See* National Consumer Law Center, Truth in Lending § 7.2.3.4.3 (7th ed. 2010 and Supp.).

139 Reg. Z, 12 C.F.R. § 1026.55(b)(4)(i) [§ 226.55(b)(4)(i)].

140 *See* § 8.3.2.4, *infra.*

141 Reg. Z, 12 C.F.R. § 1026.55(b)(3) [§ 226.55(b)(3)].

142 *Id.*

143 Official Commentary to Reg. Z, 12 C.F.R. § 1026.55(c)(1)-3 [§ 226.55(c)(1)-3].

144 *Id.* However, the lender cannot add or increase a fee if the account is closed or suspended. Reg. Z, 12 C.F.R. § 1026.55(b)(3)(iii) [§ 226.55(b)(3)(iii)].

145 Official Commentary to Reg. Z, 12 C.F.R. § 1026.55(b)(3)-1 [§ 226.55(b)(3)-1]. *See* § 8.9.3.2, *infra* (discussing right to reject changes to an account).

146 *See* National Consumer Law Center, Truth in Lending §§ 6.8.4.1, 6.8.5.5 (7th ed. 2010 and Supp.).

147 This is a simplified version of the example in Official Commentary to Reg. Z, 12 C.F.R. § 1026.55(b)(3)-4.i [§ 226.55(b)(3)-4.i].

148 15 U.S.C. § 1666i-1(b)(3). Reg. Z, 12 C.F.R. § 1026.55(b)(5) [§ 226.55(b)(5)].

149 15 U.S.C. § 1637(i)(1). Reg. Z, 12 C.F.R. § 1026.55(b)(5)(i) [§ 226.55(b)(5)(i)]. *See also* Reg. Z, 12 C.F.R. § 1026.9(c)(2)(v)(D) [§ 226.9(c)(2)(v)(D)].

150 Reg. Z, 12 C.F.R. § 1026.55(b)(5)(i) [§ 226.55(b)(5)(i)].

151 Reg. Z, 12 C.F.R. § 1026.55(b)(6) [§ 226.55(b)(6)].

152 *See* National Consumer Law Center, Truth in Lending § 1.5.3.3 (7th ed. 2010 and Supp.) (discussing FRB's authority to promulgate regulations).

153 *See* National Consumer Law Center, Collection Actions Ch. 7 (2d ed. 2011 and Supp.) (describing in full SCRA protections).

154 Reg. Z, 12 C.F.R. § 1026.55(b)(6) [§ 226.55(b)(6)].

send a forty-five-day notice pursuant to Regulation Z in order to increase the rate pursuant to this exception.[155]

#### 8.3.2.3 Repayment Protections for Outstanding or "Protected" Balances

To prevent the lender from requiring accelerated payment of the outstanding balance, also called a "protected" balance, the lender is limited in how much it can change the repayment terms of that balance. The lender must use one of the following formulas for repaying the outstanding balance, or a method that is no less favorable:[156]

- The same payment method or formula that the lender used before the effective date of the increase;
- An amortization period of no less than five years starting from the effective date of the increase;[157] or
- A minimum payment that includes no greater than twice the percentage of the balance that was required to be paid off prior to the effective date of the increase.

#### 8.3.2.4 Protections for the First Year of an Account

Generally, a credit card lender may increase an APR for future transactions pursuant to a change-in-terms or penalty rate notice.[158] However, even for future transactions, the lender is not permitted to increase the APR during the first year after an account is opened.[159]

### *8.3.3 Mandatory Re-Evaluation of Rate Increases*

If the interest rate on a credit card account has been increased based on risk, market conditions, or other factors, the Credit CARD Act requires the lender to re-evaluate that account every six months to determine whether the rate should be reduced.[160] Lenders must have reasonable written policies and procedures to conduct these re-evaluations.[161]

The rate re-evaluation requirement is located in Part C of TILA, so that there is no private right of action.[162] If a lender fails to re-evaluate the rate at all, practitioners could consider a state UDAP claim, however, a re-evaluation that leaves the rate unchanged may be difficult to challenge. The Credit CARD Act specifically states that the re-evaluation requirement "shall not be construed to require a reduction in any specific amount."[163]

The re-evaluation requirements applies both to: (1) APR increases based on an individual consumer's credit risk or other circumstances specific to that consumer and (2) APR increases based on non-individualized factors, such as changes in market conditions or the lender's cost of funds.[164] However, increases due to a variable rate[165] or expiration of a promotional rate[166] do not require re-evaluation. Also exempted are rate increases pursuant to the exception for the Servicemembers Civil Relief Act,[167] and accounts that have been charged-off.[168]

Greater detail on the requirement for re-evaluation of APR increases is provided in another treatise in this series.[169]

### *8.3.4 Double Cycle Billing*

Double cycle billing is a method of calculating interest on credit cards that assesses the interest based on the account balance for the past two billing cycles.[170] This method results in significantly higher interest being charged to the cardholder. In addition, it eliminates the benefit of the grace period if a cardholder moves from non-revolving to revolving status. In other words, if a cardholder with no previous balances does not pay off the entire balance by the end of the grace period, even by a few dollars, the credit card lender will compute interest on the entire balance, not just on the few dollars carried over to the next billing cycle. A GAO study found that two out of the six major credit card lenders use double cycle billing.[171]

The Credit CARD Act eliminates double cycle billing. It prohibits credit card lenders from imposing finance charges as a result of the loss of a grace period based on balances from a previous billing cycle.[172] In other words, when the consumer ceases to be eligible for a grace period, the lender cannot compute the finance charge based on any days in a billing cycle that preceded the most recent billing cycle.[173]

Greater detail on the prohibition against double cycle billing is provided in another treatise in this series.[174]

---

155 Official Commentary to Reg. Z, 12 C.F.R. § 1026.55(b)(6)-2 [§ 226.55(b)(6)-2].

156 15 U.S.C. § 1666i-1(c); Reg. Z, 12 C.F.R. § 1026.55(c)(2) [§ 226.55(c)(2)].

157 The five-year period begins from the date on which the increase in the APR, fee, or charge becomes effective. Official Commentary to Reg. Z, 12 C.F.R. § 1026.55(c)(2)(ii)-1 [§ 226.55(c)(2)(ii)-1].

158 *See* § 8.3.2.2.4, *supra* (describing advance notice exception).

159 15 U.S.C. § 1666i-2(a); Reg. Z, 12 C.F.R. § 1026.55(b)(3)(iii) [§ 226.55(b)(3)(iii)].

160 15 U.S.C. § 1665c; Reg. Z, 12 C.F.R. § 1026.59 [§ 226.59].

161 Reg. Z, 12 C.F.R. § 1026.59(b) [§ 226.59(b)].

162 *See* National Consumer Law Center, Truth in Lending § 11.6.5.4 (7th ed. 2010 and Supp.).

163 15 U.S.C. § 1665c(c).

164 Reg. Z, 12 C.F.R. § 1026.59(a) [§ 226.59(a)]; Official Commentary to Reg. Z, 12 C.F.R. § 1026.59(a)(1)-1 [§ 226.59(a)(1)-1].

165 *See generally* § 8.3.2.2.2, *supra.*

166 *See generally* § 8.3.2.2.1, *supra.*

167 Reg. Z, 12 C.F.R. § 1026.59(h)(1) [§ 226.59(h)(1)]. *See generally* § 8.3.2.2.6, *supra.*

168 Reg. Z, 12 C.F.R. § 1026.59(h)(2) [§ 226.59(h)(2)].

169 National Consumer Law Center, Truth in Lending § 7.2.5 (7th ed. 2010 and Supp.).

170 Government Accountability Office, Credit Cards: Increased Complexity in Rates and Fees Heightens Need for More Effective Disclosures to Consumers, GAO-06-929, at 28 (Sept. 2006), *available at* www.gao.gov/new.items/d06929.pdf.

171 *Id.*

172 15 U.S.C. § 1637(j)(1)(A).

173 Reg. Z, 12 C.F.R. § 1026.54(a)(1)(i) [§ 226.54(a)(1)(i)].

174 National Consumer Law Center, Truth in Lending § 7.4 (7th ed. 2010 and Supp.).

# 8.4 Credit Card Fee Abuses

## 8.4.1 Background

### 8.4.1.1 Skyrocketing Fees

The Supreme Court's decision in *Smiley v. Citibank (South Dakota), N.A.*,[175] which uncapped fee amounts,[176] resulted in the rapid growth of and reliance on fee income by credit card lenders. It also contributed significantly to the snowballing credit card debt of American consumers.

After *Smiley*, penalty fee revenue increased nearly nine-fold from $1.7 billion in 1996 to $18 billion in 2007.[177] Penalty fees constituted about 10% to 13% of profits for credit card lenders.[178] The income from just three fees—penalty fees, cash advance fees, and annual fees—reached $29 billion in 2007.[179] Fee income topped $30 billion if balance transfer fees, foreign exchange, and other fees were added to this total.[180]

In the decade prior to the Credit CARD Act, lenders grew fee income by making fees higher in amount, imposing them more quickly, and assessing them more often. After *Smiley*, banks rushed to increase fee amounts. The average late payment fee soared from $12.83 in 1995 to over $33.64 in 2005, an increase of 115% adjusted for inflation.[181] Over-the-limit fees similarly jumped from $12.95 in 1995 to over $30.81 in 2005, an increase of 95% adjusted for inflation.[182] In contrast, prior to *Smiley*, few credit card lenders charged late or over-the-limit fees in the late 1980s and early 1990s, and if they did, it was for amounts such as $5 to $10.[183]

Part of the reason for this explosion of fees was that credit card lenders were no longer imposing penalty fees as a way to curb undesirable behavior from consumers, which previously was the primary justification for imposing high amounts. Instead, these fees constituted a significant source of revenue for lenders. The problem was that penalty fees, especially in combination with the penalty interest rates, exacerbated the problems of consumers who had hit hard times.

In contrast, one fee that became less frequent was the annual fee, perhaps due in part because of its prominent disclosure in Truth in Lending disclosures.[184] A GAO study in 2005 found that almost 75% of credit cards did not carry an annual fee.[185] The need to compensate for the reduction of annual fees to all cardholders might also have explained in part the eagerness of lenders to impose back-end penalty fees.

### 8.4.1.2 Fee Proliferation

Not only did the size of fee income for credit card lenders grown enormously, the types of fees mushroomed as well. Some common fees include:

- Annual fee;
- Cash advance fee;
- Balance-transfer fee;
- Late fee or late-payment fee;
- Over-the-limit or over-the-credit-limit fee;
- Returned-item fee.

But the universe of fees is unlimited, restricted only by the imagination of credit card lenders. A plethora of other fees exist, such as:

- *Credit-limit-increase fee.*[186] Charged if the consumer asks for and receives an increase in the credit limit.
- *Set-up (or account opening) fee.*[187] Charged when a new credit card account is opened.
- *Participation or membership fee.*[188] A monthly or yearly fee charged for having the credit card.
- *Application fee.*[189] Charged when the consumer applies for a credit card.
- *Expedited-delivery fee.* Charged when the consumer requests an additional credit card and requests that it be delivered in an expedited way.
- *Replacement card fee.* Charged when the consumer's credit card is lost, stolen, damaged, or otherwise needs to be replaced.
- *Additional card fee.* Charged when the consumer requests a card for a family member or otherwise wishes an additional card.
- *Wire transfers, lottery tickets, and casino chips fees.*[190]
- *"Early pay down fee."* Assessed if the consumer's account falls below a certain amount during a certain time period.[191]

---

175 517 U.S. 735, 116 S. Ct. 1730, 135 L. Ed. 2d 25 (1996).

176 *See* § 3.4.5.3, *supra*.

177 Jennifer DeWalt, *Card Fees*, CardTrak.com (Jan. 18, 2008), *available at* www.cardtrak.com/news/2008/01/18/card_fees.

178 Government Accountability Office, Credit Cards: Increased Complexity in Rates and Fees Heightens Need for More Effective Disclosures to Consumers, GAO-06-929, at 67, 72 (Sept. 2006), *available at* www.gao.gov/new.items/d06929.pdf.

179 Jennifer DeWalt, *Card Fees*, CardTrak.com (Jan. 18, 2008), *available at* www.cardtrak.com/news/2008/01/18/card_fees.

180 *Id.*

181 Government Accountability Office, Credit Cards: Increased Complexity in Rates and Fees Heightens Need for More Effective Disclosures to Consumers, GAO-06-929, at 20–21 (Sept. 2006), *available at* www.gao.gov/new.items/d06929.pdf. The GAO also found that many lenders now use a tiered structure for fees, imposing higher late fees on higher balances.

182 *Id.*

183 *Id.* at 14.

184 National Consumer Law Center, Truth in Lending §§ 6.5.2.3.1, 6.5.2.3.2, 6.5.2.4.1, 6.5.3.3.1, 6.5.3.3.3, 6.4.3.3.4 (7th ed. 2010 and Supp.).

185 Government Accountability Office, Credit Cards: Increased Complexity in Rates and Fees Heightens Need for More Effective Disclosures to Consumers, GAO-06-929, at 23 (Sept. 2006), *available at* www.gao.gov/new.items/d06929.pdf.

186 Described in Federal Reserve Board, A Consumer's Guide to Credit Cards: Fees (June 15, 2010), *available at* www.federalreserve.gov/creditcard/fees.html.

187 *Id.*

188 *Id.*

189 *Id.*

190 USPIRG, The Credit Card Trap: How to Spot It, How to Avoid It 8–9 (Apr. 2001), *available at* https://pincdn.s3.amazonaws.com/assets/2uC8i5-gbx0EBcOu0cH_pw/Credit_Card_Trap.pdf.

191 Forrest v. Universal Sav. Bank, F.A., 507 F.3d 540 (7th Cir. 2007).

### 8.4.1.3 Potential Challenges to Abusive Fees

The Credit CARD Act establishes a requirement that penalty fees be reasonable and proportional to the violation,[192] as discussed at § 8.4.3, *infra*. Prior to the Credit CARD Act, there were few limitations on penalty fees. Because of the *Smiley* decision, state law challenges to the amount of a fee are difficult, and state law limits of the amount of fees are preempted.

One commentator had suggested challenging credit card penalty fees as excessive punitive damages in violation of the Due Process Clause of the U.S. Constitution.[193] However, the first lawsuit to raise this constitutional challenge was dismissed.[194]

Regulators in the United Kingdom also imposed a cap on credit card penalty fees, restricting them to an amount that a default can reasonably be expected to cost the lender.[195] The U.K. Office of Fair Trading declared that penalty fees greater than £12 (or about $19) are presumptively unfair.[196]

## *8.4.2 Requirement for Reasonable and Proportional Penalty Fees*

### 8.4.2.1 General

In response to penalty fee abuses, the Credit CARD Act established a requirement that penalty fees be "reasonable and proportional" to the consumer's omission or violation.[197] The Act required the Federal Reserve Board to establish regulations to assess whether a penalty fee is reasonable and proportional, which the Board did.[198] The Dodd-Frank Act transferred this rulemaking authority to the CFPB.[199]

TILA private remedies do not apply to the penalty fee section, as it is located in TILA Part C, which is not included in the list of TILA provisions that are privately enforceable.[200] Practitioners may, nevertheless, be able to challenge penalty fees that violate the reasonable and proportional requirement by using state laws that prohibit unfair or deceptive acts or practices, especially if the fee violates one of the bright-line prohibitions of the rule.

This subsection and the ones that follow provide a brief summary of the penalty fee restrictions in Regulation Z. Much greater detail is provided in another treatise in this series.[201]

### 8.4.2.2 Rules to Determine If a Fee Is Reasonable

#### *8.4.2.2.1 General*

Credit card lenders are prohibited from imposing penalty fees unless the dollar amount of the fee is either (1) a reasonable proportion of the lenders' total costs as a result of that type of violation or (2) is within the safe harbors that Regulation Z establishes.[202]

The FRB has established safe harbors. Lenders may charge $25 for the first violation of a particular type.[203] For the second violation of the same type during the same billing period or during the next six billing periods, the fee may be $35,[204] but only if a penalty fee has been imposed for the first violation of the same type.[205] Both amounts are subject to annual adjustment by the FRB (now CFPB) based on the Consumer Price Index.[206]

#### *8.4.2.2.2 Prohibited fees*

Penalty fees are also subject to certain bright-line limits or prohibitions.[207] Even if a penalty fee is properly determined on the basis of costs, or is within the safe harbor amounts, these prohibitions apply regardless.[208]

A penalty fee cannot exceed the dollar amount associated with the violation or omission.[209] For example, despite the $25 safe harbor, the lender can only charge a $15 late fee if a $15 minimum payment is late. Similarly, the lender can only charge a $15 over-the-limit fee if the credit limit is exceeded by only $15.

No penalty fee may be charged if there is no dollar amount associated with the violation,[210] even if based on costs or the safe harbor rules are followed.[211] Regulation Z specifies that the following events have no dollar amount associated with them, and thus no penalty fee may be charged for:

- Declined transactions;
- Account inactivity; and

192 15 U.S.C. § 1665(d) (TILA).

193 Seana Valentine Shiffrin, *Are Credit Card Late Fees Unconstitutional?*, 15 Wm. & Mary Bill Rts. J. 457 (2006).

194 *In re* Late & Over-Limit Fee Litig., 528 F. Supp. 2d 953 (N.D. Cal. 2007).

195 United Kingdom Office of Fair Trading, Calculating Fair Default Charges in Credit Card Contracts (Apr. 2006), *available at* www.oft.gov.uk/shared_oft/reports/financial_products/oft842.pdf.

196 *Id.*

197 15 U.S.C. § 1665d(a).

198 Reg. Z, 12 C.F.R. § 1026.52(b).

199 *See* § 2.2.2, *supra*.

200 *See* National Consumer Law Center, Truth in Lending § 11.6.5.4 (7th ed. 2010 and Supp.).

201 National Consumer Law Center, Truth in Lending § 7.5 (7th ed. 2010 and Supp.).

202 Reg. Z, 12 C.F.R. § 1026.52(b)(1) [§ 226.52(b)(1)].

203 Reg. Z, 12 C.F.R. § 1026.52(b)(1)(ii)(A) [§ 226.52(b)(1)(ii)(A)].

204 Reg. Z, 12 C.F.R. § 1026.52(b)(1)(ii)(B) [§ 226.52(b)(1)(ii)(B)].

205 Official Commentary to Reg. Z, 12 C.F.R. § 1026.52(b)(1)(ii)-1.i [§ 226.52(b)(1)(ii)-1.i]. If a lender has imposed a penalty fee but then waived or rebated all or part of it, the lender is permitted to charge $35 for the next violation. *Id.*

206 Reg. Z, 12 C.F.R. § 1026.52(b)(1)(ii)(D) [§ 226.52(b)(1)(ii)(D)]; Official Commentary to Reg. Z, 12 C.F.R. § 1026.52(b)(1)(ii)-2 [§ 226.52(b)(1)(ii)-2].

207 Reg. Z, 12 C.F.R. § 1026.52(b)(2) [§ 226.52(b)(2)]. *See* National Consumer Law Center, Truth in Lending § 7.5.2.4 (7th ed. 2010 and Supp.).

208 Official Commentary to Reg. Z, 12 C.F.R. § 1026.52(b)(1)-1.ii, (b)(2)-1 [§ 226.52(b)(1)-1.ii, (b)(2)-1].

209 Reg. Z, 12 C.F.R. § 1026.52(b)(2)(i)(A) [§ 226.52(b)(2)(i)(A)]; Official Commentary to Reg. Z, 12 C.F.R. § 1026.52(b)(2)(i) [§ 226.52(b)(2)(i)].

210 Reg. Z, 12 C.F.R. § 1026.52(b)(2)(i)(B) [§ 226.52(b)(2)(i)(B)].

211 Official Commentary to Reg. Z, 12 C.F.R. § 1026.52(b)(2) [§ 226.52(b)(2)].

- The closure or termination of an account.[212]

Note that the ban on declined transaction fees does not include a declined credit access check, for which a penalty fee may be charged.[213]

In addition, lenders may not impose multiple penalty fees based on a single event or transaction.[214] For example, if a check is returned, making the payment late, the lender can charge a late fee or a returned check fee but not both.[215] The lender may comply with this prohibition, at its option, by imposing only one penalty fee per billing cycle.[216] Over-the-limit fees are not subject to this prohibition, because the Credit CARD Act specifically permits lenders to charge three over-the-limit fees based on the same transaction.[217]

## *8.4.3 Specific Penalty Fees*

### 8.4.3.1 Late Fees

#### *8.4.3.1.1 Background*

Late fees are the most common type of penalty fee. One estimate is that they constitute about 70% of the $18 billion imposed in penalty fees in 2007.[218] Credit card lenders reported that 35% of their active U.S. accounts were assessed late fees in 2005.[219]

In the decades before the Credit CARD Act, lenders aggressively increased the amount of late fees. They were quicker and more assertive in imposing them. In years past, credit card lenders gave consumers a leniency period of a few days before imposing late fees.[220] Now, credit card lenders will impose late fees if the consumer is even one day over the due date. In fact, some lenders had imposed late fees for payments received on the payment due date but after a certain cut-off time, a practice discussed more fully at § 8.6.4, *infra*.

The exorbitant late fees imposed by credit card lenders appeared to violate the common law doctrine that liquidated damages provisions which go beyond the reasonable anticipated costs of a breach of contract, and which act as a punishment, are void.[221] However this common law doctrine has been held preempted by section 85 of the National Bank Act, as interpreted in the *Smiley* decision.[222]

The penalty fee provisions of the Credit CARD Act have resulted in a substantial reduction in the amount of late fees imposed on consumers.[223]

#### *8.4.3.1.2 Restrictions on late fees*

Under Regulation Z, any late fee is capped at the amount of the late minimum periodic payment that was due immediately prior to assessment of the fee, regardless whether any portion was paid.[224] Thus, if a minimum payment of $15 is due on September 25, the late fee is capped at $15, even if $10 of the minimum payment was made.[225]

The late fee is capped by the amount of the minimum payment even if other rules would justify a higher fee.[226] For example, in the previous example, the late fee cannot exceed $15, even if the consumer was late the previous month and the safe harbor rule would justify a $35 fee.

Regulation Z's penalty rate provisions prohibit a credit card lender from charging a second late fee based on a single missed or late payment. Thus, if payment is due on March 25, a late fee can be imposed on March 26 but a second late fee cannot be charged if payment is not received by a subsequent date (such as March 31).[227] However, the next month's minimum payment is considered an independent event, which may justify another late fee.

Lenders can charge either a late fee or a returned payment fee, but not both, if a returned payment causes the payment to be late.[228] Nor can it charge both fees if the same check is both late *and* is returned.[229]

212 Reg. Z, 12 C.F.R. § 1026.52(b)(2)(i)(B) [§ 226.52(b)(2)(i)(B)]. These transactions are discussed in more detail at National Consumer Law Center, Truth in Lending §§ 7.5.2.5.5 to 7.5.2.7 (7th ed. 2010 and Supp.).

213 *Id.* § 7.5.2.5.4.

214 Reg. Z, 12 C.F.R. § 1026.52(b)(2)(ii) [§ 226.52(b)(2)(ii)]; Official Commentary to Reg. Z, 12 C.F.R. § 1026.52(b)(2)(ii) [§ 226.52(b)(2)(ii)].

215 Official Commentary to Reg. Z, 12 C.F.R. § 1026.52(b)(2)(ii)-1.ii.A, -1.ii.B [§ 226.52(b)(2)(ii)-1.ii.A, -1.ii.B].

216 Reg. Z, 12 C.F.R. § 1026.52(b)(2)(ii) [§ 226.52(b)(2)(ii)].

217 Official Commentary to Reg. Z, 12 C.F.R. § 1026.52(b)(1)(ii)-1.ii [§ 226.52(b)(1)(ii)-1.ii]. *See* § 8.4.3.2.1, *infra* (discussing the three over-the-limit fee rule).

218 Jennifer DeWalt, *Card Fees*, CardTrak.com (Jan. 18, 2008), *available at* www.cardtrak.com/news/2008/01/18/card_fees (visited Apr. 7, 2009).

219 Government Accountability Office, Credit Cards: Increased Complexity in Rates and Fees Heightens Need for More Effective Disclosures to Consumers, GAO-06-929, at 33 (Sept. 2006), *available at* www.gao.gov/new.items/d06929.pdf.

220 *The Role of FCRA in the Credit Granting Process: Hearing Before the Subcommittee on Financial Institutions and Consumer Credit* 7 (June 12, 2003) (statement of Dr. Robert D. Manning, Caroline Werner Gannett Professor of Humanities, Rochester Institute of Technology), *available at* www.creditcardnation.com/pdfs/061203rm.pdf.

221 *See* § 4.8, *supra*.

222 *In re* Late & Over-Limit Fee Litig., 528 F. Supp. 2d 953 (N.D. Cal. 2007).

223 Jennifer Faulkner, Office of the Comptroller of Currency, The CARD Act—One Year Later: Impact on Pricing and Fees (Feb. 22, 2011).

224 Official Commentary to Reg. Z, 12 C.F.R. § 1026.52(b)(2)(i)-1 [§ 226.52(b)(2)(i)-1].

225 Official Commentary to Reg. Z, 12 C.F.R. § 1026.52(b)(2)(i)-1.i, -1.ii [§ 226.52(b)(2)(i)-1.i, -1.ii].

226 Official Commentary to Reg. Z, 12 C.F.R. § 1026.52(b)(2)(i)-1.i, -1.ii, -1.iii [§ 226.52(b)(2)(i)-1.i, -1.ii, -1.iii].

227 Official Commentary to Reg. Z, 12 C.F.R. § 1026.52(b)(2)(ii)-1.i [§ 226.52(b)(2)(ii)-1.i].

228 Official Commentary to Reg. Z, 12 C.F.R. § 1026.52(b)(2)(ii)-1.ii.A [§ 226.52(b)(2)(ii)-1.ii.A].

229 Official Commentary to Reg. Z, 12 C.F.R. § 1026.52(b)(2)(ii)-1.ii.B [§ 226.52(b)(2)(ii)-1.ii.B].

### 8.4.3.2 Over-the-Limit Fees

#### *8.4.3.2.1 How over-the-limit fees work*

Over-the-limit fees are particularly unfair because the card lender technologically has the ability to decline over-the-limit transactions, but chooses to permit them and then reap penalty fee income.[230] A few decades ago, credit card lenders did not require specific authorization of transactions under a certain amount due to costs.[231] Thus, a cardholder had the ability to exceed his or her limit without the lender's knowledge or permission.

However, for the last fifteen to twenty years electronic authorizations have been employed on effectively *all* card-based transactions originated in the United States.[232] Thus, lenders have the ability to deny all transactions that would exceed a credit limit.

Prior the Credit CARD Act, credit card lenders typically "padded" the nominal credit limit.[233] For example, a consumer enters into a credit card agreement that specifies a credit limit of $2,000. Usually, after a relatively brief period during which the customer manages the account in an acceptable manner, the *pad* is instituted. The card lender may increase the *effective* credit limit up to $2,500. The *effective* credit limit has become $2,500, even though the consumer may still believe the credit limit is the *nominal* amount of $2,000.

The original ostensible purpose of this pad was to avoid customer relations problems stemming from denials for proposed charges that would have resulted in a balance exceeding the nominal credit limit only by a relatively modest amount.[234] However, with the proliferation of fees, an additional impetus arose for credit card lenders, namely, to generate substantial over-the-limit fees. In fact, one major credit card lender had a practice of offering multiple low-limit credit cards to overextended borrowers in order to maximize over-the-limit fees.[235]

The Credit CARD Act addresses over-the-limit abuses by requiring that a consumer expressly elect or "opt in" to permitting the creditor to complete over-the-limit transactions before the lender can charge any over-the-limit fees.[236] The Credit CARD Act also prohibits lenders from charging more than one over-the-limit fee per billing cycle and from charging the fee in more than two subsequent billing cycles unless the consumer obtains an additional extension of credit or goes below the limit and subsequently exceeds it.[237]

The Credit CARD Act's restrictions on over-the-limit fees greatly reduced their prevalence. In 2005, about 75% of card lenders impose over-the-limit fees.[238] Lenders reported that 13% of their active U.S. accounts were assessed over-the-limit fees in that year.[239] After the Credit CARD Act took effect, a study by the Pew Health Group reported that fewer than 25% of credit cards surveyed by Pew imposed an over-the-limit fee.[240] A study by the OCC found that over-the-limit fees have virtually disappeared.[241]

During the economic recession of the late 2000s, credit card lenders significantly reduced credit limits to protect themselves from losses and in response to tightened credit availability.[242] Credit card lenders have been known to reduce a consumer's credit card limit for reasons such as having a late payment, going over the limit, a drop in the consumer's credit score, a higher debt-to-income ratio, or the consumer "becomes a risk."[243]

Credit card lenders have also been known to lower customers' credit limits during the middle of the billing cycle, then charge over-the-limit fees when unsuspecting consumers exceed the new limit at the end of the cycle.[244] Regulation Z now

230 *See National Consumer Law Center,* et al., *Comments to the Federal Reserve Board's Advance Notice of Proposed Rulemaking—Review of the Open-End (Revolving) Credit Rules of Regulation Z,* Docket No. R-1217, at 40-32 (Mar. 28, 2004), *available at* www.nclc.org. The over-the-limit fee discussion in this document was drafted by Professor James Brown, Center for Consumer Affairs, University of Wisconsin at Milwaukee.

231 *Id.*

232 *Id.*

233 *Id.*

234 *Id.*

235 *See* Van Slyke v. Capital One Bank, 2007 WL 2874417 (N.D. Cal. Sept. 28, 2007) (Van Slyke III) (alleging that Capital One offered subprime cards with $250 to $300 credit limits, expecting that cardholders would go over-the-limit on at least one account, allowing lender to charge high fees). *See also* Robert Berner, *Cap One's Credit Trap,* Business Week, Nov. 6, 2006.

236 15 U.S.C. § 1637(k)(1).

237 *Id.*

238 Government Accountability Office, Credit Cards: Increased Complexity in Rates and Fees Heightens Need for More Effective Disclosures to Consumers, GAO-06-929 (Sept. 2006), *available at* www.gao.gov/new.items/d06929.pdf.

239 *Id.*

240 Nick Bourke & Ardie Hollifield, Pew Health Group, Two Steps Forward: After the Credit CARD Act, Credit Cards Are Safer and More Transparent—But Challenges Remain, (July 2010), *available at* www.pewtrusts.org/uploadedFiles/wwwpewtrustsorg/Reports/Credit_Cards/PEW-CreditCard%20FINAL.PDF.

241 Jennifer Faulkner, Office of the Comptroller of Currency, The CARD Act—One Year Later: Impact on Pricing and Fees, Feb. 22, 2011.

242 Larry Abramson, Credit Card Companies Lowering Borrowers' Limits, National Public Radio, Apr. 13, 2009, Robin Sidel, *Card Issuers Get Personal to Check Credit,* Wall St. J., June 19, 2008, D1.

In addition to putting consumers at risk of exceeding the lower limits, this action also lowers their credit scores. *See* National Consumer Law Center, Fair Credit Reporting § 14.5.2.1.3 (7th ed. 2010 and Supp.) (30% of credit score based on ratio of credit used to credit available).

243 Consumer Action, *2007 Credit Card Survey,* Consumer Action News (Spring 2007), *available at* www.consumer-action.org/downloads/english/CA_News_CC_07.pdf.

One subprime lender lowered credit limits if cardholders used them at certain businesses, such as tire and retreading shops, massage parlors, bars, billiard parlors, and marriage counseling offices. Jessica Silver-Greenberg, *Your Lifestyle May Hurt Credit Score,* Businessweek.com, Aug. 9, 2008.

244 Consent Order and Order to Pay, *In re* World's Foremost Bank, Sidney, Nebraska, FDIC-10-775b, FDIC-10-777k (Dep't of Treasury, Federal Deposit Ins. Corp. Mar. 8, 2011) (FDIC consent order in which bank agreed to refrain from imposing over-the-limit fee

requires lenders to provide notice forty-five days before they can lower a credit limit that results in the imposition of a penalty fee or rate.[245]

### *8.4.3.2.2 Opt-in requirement*

The Credit CARD Act addresses over-the-limit abuses by requiring that a consumer expressly elect or "opt in" to permitting the lender to complete over-the-limit transactions before the lender can charge any over-the-limit fees.[246] Specifically, the lender must:[247]

1. Provide the consumer with an initial notice describing the consumer's right to opt in to the lender's payment of over-the-limit transactions;[248]
2. Provide a reasonable opportunity for the consumer to opt in;[249]
3. Obtain the consumer's affirmative consent to opt-in;
4. Provide the consumer with confirmation of the opt-in;[250] and
5. Provide the consumer with notice of the right to revoke that opt-in following the assessment of an over-the-limit fee.[251]

If a lender does not have a policy or practice of permitting over-the-limit transactions, it is not required to comply with these requirements.[252] However, if the lender does not comply and ends up paying an over-the-limit transaction, it cannot impose a fee for the transaction.[253] This prohibition applies even if the lender is unable to avoid paying the over-the-limit transaction, such as when a transaction is not submitted for authorization.[254]

An "over-the-limit transaction" is defined as an "extension of credit by a card issuer to complete a transaction that causes a consumer's credit card account balance to exceed the credit limit."[255] The above requirements only apply to over-the-limit fees, and do not apply other types of fees that might be caused by an over-the-limit transaction.[256] For example, a lender is not required to obtain the consumer's opt-in to impose a balance transfer fee, even if the balance transfer causes the consumer to exceed the account's limit.[257]

### *8.4.3.2.3 Prohibited over-the-limit practices*

In addition to requiring the consumer to consent or opt in to payment of over-the-limit transactions, the Credit CARD Act prohibits two other over-the-limit fee practices.[258] The Credit CARD Act also required the FRB to issue regulations to prevent unfair or deceptive acts or practices in connection with the manipulation of credit limits designed to increase over-the-limit fees.[259] The FRB issued three other restrictions pursuant to this authority and its general rulemaking authority under TILA. Together, the Act and Regulation Z prohibit:

(1) Charging more than one over-the-limit fee per billing cycle;[260]
(2) Charging an over-the-limit fee in more than two subsequent billing cycles unless the consumer obtains an additional extension of credit or goes below the limit and subsequently exceeds it.[261] This means the lender may not charge more than three over-the-limit fees for the same over-the-limit transaction;[262]
(3) Charging an over-the-limit fee resulting from a failure to promptly replenish a credit line;[263]
(4) Conditioning the amount of the consumer's credit limit on whether the consumer consents to over-the-limit transaction payment;[264] and
(5) Imposing an over-the-limit fee because fees or interest caused the consumer to exceed the credit limit.[265]

Greater detail on these prohibitions is provided in another treatise in this series.[266]

Lenders may only impose the fee if the credit limit is actually exceeded during the billing cycle.[267] Thus, the lender cannot impose recurring or periodic fees for paying over-the-limit transactions, such as a monthly "over-the-limit protection" service fee, even if the consumer agrees to it.[268]

---

after reducing credit limit and applying lowered limit to balances that preceded the date of decrease). *See also* Complaint, State of Minnesota v. Capital One Bank (Minn. Dist. Ct.—2d Jud. Dist. Dec. 30, 2004), *available on the companion website to this treatise*. *See also* Kelli B. Grant, *How to Blow Your Credit Limit—Without Spending*, SmartMoney, Mar. 11, 2009.

245 Reg. Z, 12 C.F.R. § 1026.9(c)(2)(vi) [§ 226.9(c)(2)(vi)]. *See* National Consumer Law Center, Truth in Lending §§ 6.8.4.6.2 and 6.8.5.5 (7th ed. 2010 and Supp.).

246 15 U.S.C. § 1637(k)(1).

247 Reg. Z, 12 C.F.R. § 1026.56(b)(1)(i)–(v) [§ 226.56(b)(1)(i)–(v)]. *See* National Consumer Law Center, Truth in Lending § 7.5.3.2 (7th ed. 2010 and Supp.) (detailing these requirements).

248 15 U.S.C. § 1637(k)(2).

249 15 U.S.C. § 1637(k)(3); Reg. Z, 12 C.F.R. § 1026.56(c) [§ 226.56(c)].

250 15 U.S.C. § 1637(k)(4).

251 15 U.S.C. § 1637(k)(2).

252 Official Commentary to Reg. Z, 12 C.F.R. § 1026.56(b)-1 [§ 226.56(b)-1].

253 *Id.*

254 Official Commentary to Reg. Z, 12 C.F.R. § 1026.56(b)(2)-1 [§ 226.56(b)(2)-1].

255 Reg. Z, 12 C.F.R. § 1026.56(a) [§ 226.56(a)].

256 Official Commentary to Reg. Z, 12 C.F.R. § 1026.56(b)(2)-2 [§ 226.56(b)(2)-2].

257 *Id.*

258 15 U.S.C. § 1637(k)(7).

259 15 U.S.C. § 1637(k)(5)(B).

The rulemaking authority under this provision has been transferred to the Consumer Financial Protection Bureau effective July 21, 2011.

260 15 U.S.C. § 1637(k)(7).

261 *Id.*

262 Reg. Z, 12 C.F.R. § 1026.56(j)(1)(i) [§ 226.56(j)(1)(i)].

263 Reg. Z, 12 C.F.R. § 1026.56(j)(1)(iii) [§ 226.56(j)(1)(iii)].

264 Reg. Z, 12 C.F.R. § 1026.56(j)(1)(iv) [§ 226.56(j)(1)(iv)].

265 Reg. Z, 12 C.F.R. § 1026.56(j)(1)(v) [§ 226.56(j)(1)(v)].

266 National Consumer Law Center, Truth in Lending § 7.5.3.3 (7th ed. 2010 and Supp.).

267 Reg. Z, 12 C.F.R. § 1026.56(j)(1)(i) [§ 226.56(j)(1)(i).

268 Official Commentary to Reg. Z, 12 C.F.R. § 1026.56(j)-1 [§ 226.56(j)-1].

##### *8.4.3.2.4 Other restrictions on over-the-limit fees*

Over-the-limit fees are subject to the same requirement that they be reasonable and proportional in amount, i.e., that they be reasonably related to cost or within the safe harbors set by Regulation Z.[269] Furthermore, Regulation Z caps over-the-limit fees at the total amount of credit extended by the lender in excess of the credit limit during the billing cycle in which the fee is imposed.[270] Thus, if the credit limit is exceeded by $10 in one transaction and then by another $5 in another transaction (at which point the account is $15 over the credit limit), the over-the-limit fee is capped at $15.[271] A $15 fee is permitted in that situation even if the consumer makes a payment and reduces the balance below the limit before the end of the billing cycle.[272]

A lender may charge both a late fee and an over-the-limit fee if they are based on different events or transactions. Thus, if the consumer's balance is $970 and credit limit is $1,000, if the minimum payment of $35 has not been received by March 25, and a $70 transaction on March 31 causes the balance to rise to $1,040, the lender may charge both a late payment fee of $25 and an over-the-limit fee of $25.[273] However, if a late fee of $35 was what caused the account to exceed the credit limit, an over-the-limit fee cannot be charged, both because two fees would be based on the same event (the late payment) and it would violate the prohibition against fees or finance charges triggering an over-the-limit fee.[274]

The FDIC has taken enforcement actions under the Federal Trade Commission Act against banks for assessing two consecutive over-the-limit fees.[275] The banks would assess an over-the-limit fee during the billing cycle in which the consumer went over his or her limit, then assess a second over-the-limit fee on the first day of next billing cycle, before the consumer had a chance to make a payment in order to get back under the limit.[276] The FDIC also cited one of these banks for setting minimum payments too low to avoid recurring over-the-limit fees and for imposing over-the-limit fees after reducing the consumer's credit limit to below the current balance on the account.[277]

## *8.4.4 Other Fees*

### 8.4.4.1 Balance Transfer Fees

Balance transfer fees can be insidious because they often involve consumers who have been carrying a large balance from month to month. Credit card lenders lured these consumers into transferring large balances by heavily advertising low or 0% APRs, but not disclosing the balance transfer fee as prominently. For example, a credit card solicitation would trumpet a "low 2.9% Fixed APR" for balance transfers using large type, but only disclose the balance transfer fee of 3% on the reverse page in 8-point type. Changes to Regulation Z require disclosure of the balance transfer fee in the mandatory table for credit card applications and solicitations, which improved its visibility.[278]

With a 3% balance transfer fee, a consumer transferring a balance of $2,000 would be faced with $60 in additional costs. As a result of a balance transfer, this consumer would add more to her debt burden, yet card lender's advertising would have led her to believe that a balance transfer would save her money. To add insult to injury, the lender would sometimes treat this balance transfer fee as a "purchase" and charge its "purchase" APR on this fee, not the low or 0% APR advertised for a balance transfer.[279]

### 8.4.4.2 Currency Conversion Fees

Currency conversion fees constitute a double whammy, in that they are imposed in many cases twice—once by the card lender and once by the MasterCard or VISA network. These fees were previously hidden by deceptively "padding" the exchange rate, i.e., giving the consumer a worse exchange rate than that obtained by the card lender.[280] Regulation Z now requires lenders to disclose currency conversion fees, termed "foreign transaction" fees, in the mandatory table included in application/solicitation and account opening disclosures.[281]

---

269 *See* § 8.4.2, *supra*.

270 Official Commentary to Reg. Z, 12 C.F.R. § 1026.52(b)(2)(i)-3 [§ 226.52(b)(2)(i)-3].

271 Official Commentary to Reg. Z, 12 C.F.R. § 1026.52(b)(2)(i)-3.i [§ 226.52(b)(2)(i)-3.i].

272 Official Commentary to Reg. Z, 12 C.F.R. § 1026.52(b)(2)(i)-3.ii [§ 226.52(b)(2)(i)-3.ii].

273 Official Commentary to Reg. Z, 12 C.F.R. § 1026.52(b)(2)(ii)-1.iv [§ 226.52(b)(2)(ii)-1.iv].

274 *See* § 8.4.3.2.3, *supra*.

275 Consent Order and Order to Pay, *In re* World's Foremost Bank, Sidney, Neb., FDIC-10-775b, FDIC-10-777k (Dep't of Treasury, Federal Deposit Ins. Corp. Mar. 8, 2011); Consent Order and Order to Pay, *In re* 1st Fin. Bank USA Dakota Dunes, South Dakota, FDIC-09-s07b, FDIC-09-309k (Dep't of Treasury, Federal Deposit Ins. Corp. Dec. 30, 2009).

In *In re* World's Foremost Bank, the bank agreed to pay $10.1 million in restitution to injured consumers and $250,000 in penalties. In *In re* 1st Fin. Bank USA, the bank agreed to pay $10 million in restitution to injured consumers and $140,000 in penalties.

276 Consent Order and Order to Pay, *In re* World's Foremost Bank, Sidney, Neb., FDIC-10-775b, FDIC-10-777k (Dep't of Treasury, Federal Deposit Ins. Corp. Mar. 8, 2011); Consent Order and Order to Pay, *In re* 1st Fin. Bank USA Dakota Dunes, South Dakota, FDIC-09-s07b, FDIC-09-309k (Dep't of Treasury, Federal Deposit Ins. Corp. Dec. 30, 2009).

277 Consent Order and Order to Pay, *In re* World's Foremost Bank, Sidney, Neb., FDIC-10-775b, FDIC-10-777k (Dep't of Treasury, Federal Deposit Ins. Corp. Mar. 8, 2011).

278 National Consumer Law Center, Truth in Lending § 6.5.3.11 (7th ed. 2010 and Supp.).

279 *See also Examining the Billing, Marketing, and Disclosure Practices of the Credit Card Industry, and Their Impact on Consumers: Hearing Before the Senate Committee on Banking, Housing, and Urban Affairs*, 110th Cong. (2007), *available at* www.nclc.org/images/pdf/credit_cards/archive/written_testimony.pdf (statement of Michael D. Donovan, Partner, Donavan Searles, L.L.C.).

280 *See In re* Currency Conversion Fee Antitrust Litig., 265 F. Supp. 2d 385 (S.D.N.Y. 2003).

281 Official Commentary to Reg. Z, 12 C.F.R. § 1026.60(b)(4)-2 [§ 226.5a(b)(4)-2]. National Consumer Law Center, Truth in Lending §§ 6.5.3.5.2, 6.6.6.2.4 (7th ed. 2010 and Supp.).

A number of lawsuits were filed against both card lenders and credit card networks over currency conversion fees. These cases brought claims under the TILA, state UDAP statutes, unjust enrichment, and antitrust laws.[282] A global settlement that resolved a number of these cases provided for $336 million in compensation, roughly 10–15% of the currency conversion fees received by the lenders and the Visa/MasterCard networks during the relevant time period.[283]

# 8.5 Subprime and Secured Credit Cards

## *8.5.1 Background*

### 8.5.1.1 Introduction

There are a number of credit card products targeted at the "subprime market," which generally means consumers with lower credit scores and/or impaired credit histories. These include fee-harvester and secured credit cards.[284]

"Fee-harvester" cards are particularly abusive.[285] Prior to the Credit CARD Act, they often imposed hundreds of dollars in fees and extend minimal available credit—sometimes as little as $50. For example, one fee-harvester card offered by First Premier Bank of South Dakota ostensibly provided a credit limit of $250.[286] However, when the account was opened or soon thereafter, First Premier automatically imposed a $95 program fee, a $29 account set-up fee, a $6 monthly participation fee, and a $48 annual fee—a total of $178 in fees and available credit of only $72.[287] The Credit CARD Act addresses fee-harvester cards by limiting the amount of fees that can be charged to a credit card to 25% or less of the card's limit.[288] However, First Premier has manage to evade the intent of the protections by charging fees ostensibly before the account is opened.[289]

Another product targeted at consumers with poor or nonexistent credit histories is the secured credit card. A secured credit card requires the consumer to maintain a deposit with the lender, which serves as collateral for the line of credit.[290] The Truth in Lending Act generally prohibits a credit card lender from exercising a right of set-off against a consumer's deposit account, but allows a consensual security interest if certain requirements are met.[291] Before the Credit CARD Act, there was a fee-harvester variation of secured cards in which the lender charged the deposit to the card, where, along with fees, it consumed almost the entire available line of credit.

### 8.5.1.2 Common Abuses

The limited number of consumer protection actions taken by the federal banking regulators against credit card lenders have primarily focused on subprime cards and have targeted practices such as:

- "Downselling" consumers by prominently marketing one package of credit card terms, but then approving consumers only for accounts with less favorable terms, and touting the approved account in a fashion designed to mislead the customer about the fact he or she had has received a more expensive card with less favorable terms.[292]

282 Bildenstein v. MasterCard Int'l, Inc., 2005 WL 1324972 (S.D.N.Y. June 6, 2005) (claims for violation of N.Y. UDAP law and unjust enrichment; denying motion to dismiss); Rubin v. MasterCard Int'l, L.L.C., 342 F. Supp. 2d 217 (S.D.N.Y. 2004) (claims under Florida UDAP law; motion to remand granted); *In re* Currency Conversion Fee Antitrust Litig., 265 F. Supp. 2d 385 (S.D.N.Y. 2003) (claims under the Sherman Act, TILA, and South Dakota UDAP law); Fischer v. MasterCard Int'l, Inc., 2003 WL 22110169 (S.D.N.Y. Sept. 11, 2003) (claims under N.Y. UDAP law and for fraud; motion to remand granted); Schwartz v. Visa Int'l Corp., 34 Cal. Rptr. 3d 449 (Cal. Ct. App. 2005) (California UDAP claim; reversing judgment for plaintiffs on basis that private attorney general actions under California's UDAP statute were retroactively barred by California Proposition 64).

283 *In re* Currency Conversion Fee Antitrust Litig., 2006 WL 3247396 (S.D.N.Y. Nov. 8, 2006).

A similar case brought against American Express resulted in a $75 million settlement. LiPuma v. American Express Co., 406 F. Supp. 2d 1298 (S.D. Fla. 2005).

284 A related scam targeting credit-impaired consumers is the "credit card finder" operation, which promises the consumer a credit card but is really a ruse to get the consumer to pay a fee for a nonexistent or useless credit card. These scams are discussed in National Consumer Law Center, Unfair and Deceptive Acts and Practices § 6.8.2 (7th ed. 2008 and Supp.).

285 *See* Rick Jurgens & Chi Chi Wu, National Consumer Law Center, Fee-Harvesters: Low-Credit, High-Cost Cards Bleed Consumers 3 (Nov. 2007), *available at* www.nclc.org/images/pdf/credit_cards/fee-harvesters-report.pdf. These cards have also been described as "sub-sub-prime." *See also* Freedom Card, Inc. v. JP Morgan Chase & Co., 432 F.3d 463 (3d Cir. 2005) (fee-harvester card was blatantly targeted at minority communities, featuring advertisements with prominent African-American entertainer Queen Latifah).

286 This example is featured in Rick Jurgens & Chi Chi Wu, National Consumer Law Center, Fee-Harvesters: Low-Credit, High-Cost Cards Bleed Consumers 3 (Nov. 2007), *available at* www.nclc.org/images/pdf/credit_cards/fee-harvesters-report.pdf.

287 *Id.* at 3–4.

288 15 U.S.C. § 1637(n)(1). *See* National Consumer Law Center, Truth in Lending § 7.8.2 (7th ed. 2010 and Supp.).

289 *See* § 8.5.1.3, *infra.*

290 *See* National Consumer Law Center, Consumer Banking and Payments Law § 6.1.3.3 (4th ed. 2009 and Supp.) (discussing secured credit cards).

291 *See* National Consumer Law Center, Truth in Lending § 7.13.2 (7th ed. 2010 and Supp.).

292 *In re* Direct Merchants Credit Card Bank, No. 2001-24 (Dep't of Treasury, Office of the Comptroller of Currency May 3, 2001), *available at* www.occ.gov/static/enforcement-actions/ea2001-24.pdf (consent order); Press Release, Federal Trade Commission, Subprime Credit Card Marketer to Provide At Least $114 Million in Consumer Redress to Settle FTC Charges of Deceptive Conduct (Dec. 19, 2008), *available at* www.ftc.gov/opa/2008/12/compucredit.shtm (CompuCredit advertised card with "up to" $3,250 credit limit but failed to adequately disclose that half of the available credit would be withheld for the first ninety days). *See also* Jewett v. Capitol One Bank, 2006 WL 1085895 (Cal. Ct. App. Apr. 26, 2006) (similar facts, but finding no UDAP violation because Capital One did not violate FCRA in making solicitation); People v. Applied Card Sys., 894 N.E.2d 1 (N.Y. 2008) (Cross Country Bank marketed cards with "up to" $2,500 credit limit but issued cards

- Fee-harvester practices.[293]
- Deceptively marketing credit "protection" products.[294]

Prior to the Credit CARD Act, fee-harvester cards relied heavily on penalty fees, especially over-the-limit fees given that the available credit lines are so limited on these cards.[295] One fee-harvester lender posted a surprise loss in 2007 due to its cardholders incurring $22 million less in over-the-limit and late fees than the lender had expected.[296] Fee-harvester card issuers have also engaged in plain old deception, such as advertising "no annual fee [or] other extraneous charges" but then imposing an annual fee of $49 plus other fees totaling $124.[297]

Subprime credit card lenders often engage in debt collection abuse. For example, Cross County Bank (now known as Applied Card Bank) is a major subprime credit card lender that has had a controversial history.[298] A number of state attorneys general sued Cross County Bank for debt collection abuse and electronically withdrawing payments from consumers' bank accounts without their permission.[299]

Indeed, subprime credit card debt is partly responsible for the explosion of debt collection cases filed in state small claims or lower courts. For example, a study by the Urban Justice Center found that 320,000 collection lawsuits seeking to collect almost $1 billion were filed in New York City Civil Courts in 2006—almost as many as the sum total of all criminal and civil cases brought that year in federal courts in the entire nation.[300] Subprime credit card debt was the basis of nearly 30% of these lawsuits that were brought by debt buyers.[301]

Finally, subprime cards are often marketed as a means to build or improve a credit history.[302] However, their effectiveness in so doing is limited. One study commissioned by the industry found that 37% of fee-harvester cardholders improved their credit scores within one year after opening the account; however, this means the other 63% experienced a decline or no change in their scores.[303] This is not surprising, since one third of new fee-harvester cardholders default and over 75% of them do so immediately, causing further damage to their credit histories.[304]

### 8.5.1.3 Fee Harvester Cards After the Credit CARD Act

After the Credit CARD Act's limitations on account fees took effect, First Premier, a prominent subprime issuer, responded by raising interest rates to a startling 79.9% APR, which it subsequently dropped to 59.9%.[305] This actually dem-

---

with credit limit as low as $350); Press Release, Attorney General Darrell McGraw Sues Capital One Bank and Capitol One Services, Inc. (July 7, 2005) (Capitol One's credit card solicitations offer card "up to" $5,000 in credit limit, but consumers received cards with $200 or $300 limit), *available from Westlaw at* 2005 WLNR 10881649.

293 *In re* First Nat'l Bank in Brookings, No. 2003-1 (Dep't of the Treasury, Office of the Comptroller of the Currency Jan. 17, 2003), *available at* www.occ.gov/static/enforcement-actions/ea2003-1.pdf; *In re* First Nat'l Bank of Marin, No. 2001-97 (Dep't of the Treasury, Office of the Comptroller of the Currency Dec. 3, 2001), *available at* www.occ.gov/static/enforcement-actions/ea2001-97.pdf; Complaint for Permanent Injunction and Other Equitable Relief, Federal Trade Commission v. Low Pay, Inc., Case No. CV-09-1265 (D. Or. Oct. 28, 2009) (lender deceptively offered credit card that could only be used to purchase catalog items at inflated prices, and deducted $199 in advance fees plus $199 annual fee from consumer's bank account); Press Release, Federal Trade Commission, Subprime Credit Card Marketer to Provide at Least $114 Million in Consumer Redress to Settle FTC Charges of Deceptive Conduct (Dec. 19, 2008), *available at* www.ftc.gov/opa/2008/12/compucredit.shtm (credit card with $300 limit immediately reduced by $185 in fees).

294 *In re* Providian Nat'l Bank, No. 2000-53 (Dep't of the Treasury, Office of the Comptroller of the Currency June 28, 2000), *available at* www.occ.gov/static/enforcement-actions/ea2000-53.pdf. *See* § 6.3.2.5, *supra* (discussion of credit card debt suspension products).

295 *See, e.g.*, Van Slyke v. Capital One Bank, 2007 WL 2874417 (N.D. Cal. Sept. 28, 2007) (Van Slyke III) (alleging that Capital One offered subprime cards with $250 to $300 credit limits, expecting that cardholders would go over-the-limit on at least one account, allowing lender to charge high fees).

296 Harry Terris, *New Card Mix, New Issues at CompuCredit*, Am. Banker, May 10, 2007.

297 Akpan v. First Premier Bank, 2010 WL 917886 (D. Md. Mar. 8, 2010).

298 Mitchell Pacelle, *Pushing Plastic Combative Banker Faces State Suits Over Credit Cards*, Wall St. J., Nov. 5, 2004, at A1.

299 State v. Cross Country Bank, 703 N.W.2d 562 (Minn. Ct. App. 2005); People v. Applied Card Sys., 894 N.E.2d 1 (N.Y. 2008); Cross County Bank v. McGraw, No. 04-C-464 (W. Va. Cir. Ct. Kanawa County Dec. 9, 2004), *available at* www.wvs.state.wv.us/wvag/press/2004/dec/CrossCountryorder.htm. *See also Lautenschlager Suing Delaware Credit Card Issuer*, Greater Milwaukee Bus. J., Nov. 21, 2003, *available at* www.bizjournals.com/milwaukee/stories/2003/11/17/daily40.html.

Consumers have also brought private class actions against Cross Country Bank. *See, e.g.*, Forness v. Cross County Bank, 2006 WL 726233 (S.D. Ill. Mar. 20, 2006) (compelling arbitration of consumers' claim under the Illinois Fraud and Deceptive Practices Act); Klussman v. Cross Country Bank, 36 Cal. Rptr. 3d 728 (Cal. Ct. App. 2005) (denying motion to compel arbitration of state UDAP claims for misrepresenting payoff charges, imposing unauthorized fees, charging late fees for timely payments, automatically subscribing card holders to costly programs, and using abusive collection tactics); Coady v. Cross Country Bank, 729 N.W.2d 732 (Wis. Ct. App. 2007) (denying motion to compel arbitration of claims under Wisconsin Consumer Act for illegal debt collection practices such as abusive, derogatory, and obscene language and threats).

300 Anika Singh, Urban Justice Ctr., Debt Weight: The Consumer Credit Crisis in New York City and Its Impact on the Working Poor 1 (Oct. 2007).

301 *Id.* at 15–16.

302 *See, e.g.*, Greenwood v. CompuCredit, 132 S. Ct. 665 (2012) (alleging fee-harvester lender's claims for improving credit history violated Credit Repair Organizations Act; Supreme Court held claims subject to mandatory arbitration).

303 TransUnion, Summary of Results for Citizens for Equal Access to Credit (July 2008), *available at* www.equalaccesstocredit.org/Documents/NewsArticles/TU%20Data%20Survey%20FINAL.pdf.

304 74 Fed. Reg. 5498, 5541 (Jan. 29, 2009).

305 Candace Choi, *Credit Card's Newest Trick: 79.9 Percent Interest*, Associated Press, Dec. 17, 2009. *See also* Blake Ellis, *My Credit Card Had a 79.9% APR*, CNNMoney.com (Feb. 14, 2011), *avail-*

onstrates that the Credit CARD Act was effective in one of itsZ central purposes—to increase transparency in credit card costs. Instead of obscuring the high costs of a subprime card by charging fees that are not included in the APR, First Premier was forced to include those costs in the pricing information that is most transparent—the APR.

Unfortunately, the transparency was short-lived for First Premier, as it also began charging a $95 processing fee that it claimed was not subject to the Credit CARD Act's limitation on fees because it was charged before the account was opened.[306] In response, the FRB revised Regulation Z to apply the 25% limit to fees that the consumer is required to pay before account opening, as well as fees during the first year of the account.[307] However, First Premier successfully obtaining a preliminary injunction to postpone the effective date of this provision,[308] and the CFPB has proposed withdrawing the requirement that pre-account opening fees be included in the 25% limit.[309]

Another tactic used by First Premier was to charge a "credit limit increase fee" after the first year of the account. This fee consists of 25% of the amount by which the limit is increased.[310]

Applied Bank, formerly Cross Country Bank, also responded to the 25% limitation in a similarly less transparent manner. Applied Bank began offering a credit card promoting 0% interest but then charging a monthly $10 fee for a credit line of $500.[311]

## 8.5.2 *Limits on Fees Charged to a Subprime Credit Card Account*

### 8.5.2.1 Prohibition on Fees and Security Deposits That Exceed 25% of the Credit Limit

The Credit Card Act limits the percentage of an account's credit limit that can be consumed by fees and security deposits charged to the account. The Act provides that the total amount of fees that a consumer is required to pay with respect to the account during the first year must not exceed 25% of the account's credit limit.[312] For purposes of this restriction, a security deposit charged to a credit card account is considered a fee.[313]

This 25% limit applies to both fees that the lender charges to the account, as well as fees that the lender requires the consumer to pay through other means.[314] Thus, the lender cannot avoid the 25% limit by requiring the consumer to pay an amount above 25% by direct payments to the lender, such as from the consumer's asset account or another credit account provided by the lender.[315] The CFPB has proposed withdrawing the requirement that pre-account opening fees be included in the 25% limit;[316] if finalized, this change would permit fees charged and paid before the account is opened to exceed 25% of the credit limit.

The Credit CARD Act provides that if the fees exceed 25% of the credit limit, the lender cannot assess ANY of the fees to the account's credit limit.[317] However, the Commentary permits a lender who has imposed fees over the 25% limit to comply by waiving or removing the fees that exceed the limit, and any associated interest charges.[318]

The 25% limitation applies to the account's initial credit limit, i.e., the limit in effect when the credit card account is first opened.[319] If the lender increases the account's limit during the year, the increase does not permit the lender to charge additional fees or security deposits.[320] However, if the lender decreases the account's credit limit, the lender must waive or remove any fees charged to the account that exceed 25% of the reduced credit limit.[321]

This subsection and the ones that follow provide a summary of 25% limit on fees for a credit card account. Much greater detail is provided in another treatise in this series.[322]

### 8.5.2.2 Types of Fees Counted Toward the Limit

#### *8.5.2.2.1 Included fees*

The 25% limit includes all fees that a lender will or may require with respect to the account, unless specifically excluded.[323] Included fees are:

- Fees for the issuance or availability of credit, including any fee based on account activity or inactivity[324] and any fee required to receive a particular credit limit.[325] Examples

*able at* http://money.cnn.com/2011/02/07/pf/credit_card_interest_rate/index.htm.

306 Carolyn Carter, Leah Plunkett, & Lauren Saunders, National Consumer Law Center, Stopping the Payday Loan Trap, Alternatives That Work, Ones That Don't 27 (June 2010), *available at* www.nclc.org/images/pdf/high_cost_small_loans/payday_loans/report-stopping-payday-trap.pdf.

307 Reg. Z, 12 C.F.R. § 1026.52(a)(1) [§ 226.52(a)(1)].

308 First Premier Bank v. Consumer Fin. Prot. Bur., __ F. Supp. 2d __ 2011 WL 4458785 (D.S.D. Sept. 23, 2011).

309 77 Fed. Reg. 21,875 (Apr. 12, 2012).

310 Blake Ellis, First Premier's $400-a-year credit card, CNNMoney, Feb. 9, 2012.

311 *America's Worst Credit Card*, Consumer Reports, Nov. 2010, at 14.

312 15 U.S.C. § 1637(n)(1).

313 Official Commentary to Reg. Z, 12 C.F.R. § 1026.52(a)(2)-3 [§ 226.52(a)(2)-3].

314 Reg. Z, 12 C.F.R. § 1026.52(a)(1) [§ 226.52(a)(1)]; Official Commentary to Reg. Z, 12 C.F.R. § 1026.52(a)(1)-1 [§ 226.52(a)(1)-1].

315 Official Commentary to Reg. Z, 12 C.F.R. § 1026.52(a)(1)-1 [§ 226.52(a)(1)-1].

316 77 Fed. Reg. 21,875 (Apr. 12, 2012).

317 15 U.S.C. § 1637(n)(1).

318 Official Commentary to Reg. Z, 12 C.F.R. § 1026.52(a)(1)-2 [§ 226.52(a)(1)-2].

319 15 U.S.C. § 1637(n)(1).

320 Official Commentary to Reg. Z, 12 C.F.R. § 1026.52(a)(1)-3.i.

321 Official Commentary to Reg. Z, 12 C.F.R. § 1026.52(a)(1)-3.ii [§ 226.52(a)(1)-3.ii].

322 National Consumer Law Center, Truth in Lending § 7.8.2 (7th ed. 2010 and Supp.).

323 Official Commentary to Reg. Z, 12 C.F.R. § 1026.52(a)(2)-1 [§ 226.52(a)(2)-1].

324 Note that another provision of Regulation Z prohibits inactivity fees. Reg. Z, 12 C.F.R. § 1026.52(b)(2)(i)(B)(2) [§ 226.52(b)(2)(i)(B)(2)]. *See* § 8.4.2.2.2, *supra*.

325 Official Commentary to Reg. Z, 12 C.F.R. § 1026.52(a)(2)-1.i [§ 226.52(a)(2)-1.i].

would be annual fees, application fees, and participation fees.[326]

- Fees for required credit insurance, debt cancellation, or debt suspension coverage.[327]
- Transaction fees, such as cash advance, balance transfer, or foreign transaction fees.[328]
- Fixed finance charges;[329]
- Minimum interest charges;[330] and
- Penalty fees[331] unless specifically excluded.[332]

##### *8.5.2.2.2 Excluded fees*

The Credit CARD Act excludes certain fees from the 25% limit. These include late payment fees, over-the-limit fees, and fees for a returned payment.[333] The Act itself only excludes fees for a payment returned for insufficient funds, but Regulation Z expands that exclusion to a fee for a payment returned for any reason.[334]

Also excluded are fees that the consumer is not required to pay.[335] These include fees for making an expedited payment, to the extent permitted under Regulation Z;[336] fees for travel insurance; fees for reissuing a lost or stolen card; or statement reproduction fees.[337]

##### *8.5.2.2.3 Security deposits charged to the account*

One type of abusive fee-harvester card involves a "secured" card in which the security deposit is charged to the card's credit line, consuming most of the available credit for the account. To address this abuse, the Official Commentary to Regulation Z provides that a security deposit that is charged to a credit card account is a fee for purposes of the 25% limit.[338] Thus, these faux security deposits are now limited to 25% of the credit line.

However, a security deposit that is not charged to the account is not limited to the 25% limit.[339] For example, a lender is permitted to require the consumer to provide a $400 security deposit to obtain a credit card with a $400 credit line, if the $400 is not charged to that credit card. This permits lenders to provide secured credit cards in which the consumer actually deposits her or her own funds in a bank account that secures extensions from the credit card.

#### 8.5.2.3 Intersection with Other Fee Prohibitions

The Credit CARD Act provides that its 25% limitations should not be interpreted to permit the imposition of fees otherwise prohibited by law.[340] The Commentary cites as example certain advance fees that FTC Telemarketing Rule[341] prohibits a telemarketer from charging for helping a consumer obtain credit in certain circumstances.[342] This provision should also apply to certain advance fees prohibited by some state laws, such as for credit repair.[343]

### *8.5.3 Prior Regulatory Guidance on Subprime Credit Cards*

Prior to the Credit CARD Act, the OCC had issued an advisory letter identifying a number of practices that were potentially unfair or deceptive under the Federal Trade Commission Act, such as promoting credit cards with credit limits "up to" a specified dollar amount when the "up to" amount is essentially illusory, and offering promotional rates without disclosing significant limitations on those rates.[344]

A second OCC advisory letter addressed potentially unfair or deceptive practices in the marketing of secured credit cards.[345] This letter especially disapproves of the variation of the secured cards in which the lender charges the security deposit to the

326 National Consumer Law Center, Truth in Lending § 6.5.3.3 (7th ed. 2010 and Supp.).

327 Official Commentary to Reg. Z, 12 C.F.R. § 1026.52(a)(2)-1.ii [§ 226.52(a)(2)-1.ii].

328 Official Commentary to Reg. Z, 12 C.F.R. § 1026.52(a)(2)-1.iii [§ 226.52(a)(2)-1.iii].

329 Official Commentary to Reg. Z, 12 C.F.R. § 1026.52(a)(2)-1.v [§ 226.52(a)(2)-1.v].

330 Official Commentary to Reg. Z, 12 C.F.R. § 1026.52(a)(2)-1.vi [§ 226.52(a)(2)-1.vi].

331 Official Commentary to Reg. Z, 12 C.F.R. § 1026.52(a)(2)-1.iv [§ 226.52(a)(2)-1.iv].

332 Excluded fees include late, over-the-limit, returned payment, and optional fees. Reg. Z, 12 C.F.R. § 1026.52(a)(2) [§ 226.52(a)(2). *See* § 8.5.2.2.2, *infra*.

333 15 U.S.C. § 1637(n)(1); Reg. Z, 12 C.F.R. § 1026.52(a)(2)(i) [§ 226.52(a)(2)(i).

334 75 Fed. Reg. 7658, 7726 (Feb. 22, 2010).

335 Reg. Z, 12 C.F.R. § 1026.52(a)(2)(ii) [§ 226.52(a)(2)(ii)].

336 *See* National Consumer Law Center, Truth in Lending § 7.7.6 (7th ed. 2010 and Supp.) (discussing limitations for expedited payment fees).

337 Official Commentary to Reg. Z, 12 C.F.R. § 1026.52(a)(2)-2 [§ 226.52(a)(2)-2].

338 Official Commentary to Reg. Z, 12 C.F.R. § 1026.52(a)(2)-3 [§ 226.52(a)(2)-3].

339 *Id.*

340 15 U.S.C. § 1637(n)(2); Reg. Z, 12 C.F.R. § 1026.52(a)(3) [§ 226.52(a)(3)].

341 16 C.F.R. § 310.4(a)(4). *See generally* National Consumer Law Center, Unfair and Deceptive Acts and Practices § 9.6.4.7.3 (7th ed. 2008 and Supp.).

342 Official Commentary to Reg. Z, 12 C.F.R. § 1026.52(a)(3)-1 [§ 226.52(a)(3)-1].

343 *See generally* National Consumer Law Center, Unfair and Deceptive Acts and Practices § 6.2.2 (7th ed. 2008 and Supp.); National Consumer Law Center, Fair Credit Reporting § 15.3.5 (7th ed. 2010 and Supp.).

344 OCC Advisory Letter AL 2004-10 (Sept. 14, 2004), *available at* www.occ.gov/static/news-issuances/memos-advisory-letters/2004/advisory-letter-2004-10.pdf.

A further discussion of this letter is in National Consumer Law Center, Unfair and Deceptive Acts and Practices § 6.8.1.2 (7th ed. 2008 and Supp.). *See also* OCC Advisory Letter AL 2002-3 (Mar. 22, 2002), *available at* www.occ.gov/static/news-issuances/memos-advisory-letters/2002/advisory-letter-2002-3.pdf (discussing unfair or deceptive acts or practices with respect lending and marketing practices).

345 OCC Advisory Letter AL 2004-4 (Apr. 28, 2004), *available at* www.occ.gov/static/news-issuances/memos-advisory-letters/2004/advisory-letter-2004-4.pdf.

card,[346] which along with fees consumes almost the entire available line of credit.[347]

## 8.6 Abuses Involving Payments

### 8.6.1 Overview of Abuses

Prior to the Credit CARD Act, some lenders had deliberately instituted practices that resulted in greater imposition of late payment fees. These abuses included:

- Decreasing the amount of time between the mailing of the billing statement and the payment due date, and thus increasing the chance that the consumer would send in a payment that would be received past the due date.[348]
- Setting an early hour cut-off time, such as 9:00 or 10:00 a.m., for crediting payments received that day.[349] Consequently, if a consumer's payment is received on the payment due date, it will be considered late because in all likelihood, the U.S. Postal Service will not have delivered the mail so early in the morning.
- Failing to post an electronic[350] or in-person payment at a bank branch[351] on the date the payment is made, instead posting the payment several days later.
- Treating the payment as late if not received on the prior business day when due dates fell on a weekend or holiday.[352]
- Providing only a post office box as an acceptable payment address, effectively prevented consumers from making timely payments late in the billing cycle by using overnight and other forms of high-speed mail that will not deliver to post offices boxes.
- Changing mailing addresses, which may trigger late payments by consumers who use electronic bill payment services through their own bank. Since these programs sometimes physically mail a check, the check could be mailed to the wrong address.[353]

The Credit CARD Act has a number of provisions that specifically counter these abuses. The subsections that follow provide a summary of these provisions. Much greater detail is provided in another treatise in this series.[354]

### 8.6.2 Twenty-One Day Requirement for Mailing Statements

The Credit CARD Act specifically mandates that the credit card billing statements be mailed or delivered twenty-one days before the due date.[355] If the lender provides a grace period, there is a similar requirement that the periodic statement be mailed or delivered to the consumer twenty-one days before the expiration of the grace period.[356]

If the lender fails to provide this twenty-one-day period, it is prohibited from treating the consumer's payment as late.[357] Regulation Z modifies this prohibition to apply to only those payments received within twenty-one days after the mailing or delivery of the periodic statement.[358] Thus, if the lender fails to provide twenty-one days but the payment is received forty-five days after the mailing of the statement, the lender is permitted to treat the payment as late.[359]

Treating a payment as late for any purposes includes the following actions:[360]

---

346 For more detail about this variation, see § 8.5.1.2, *supra*.

347 OCC Advisory Letter AL 2004-4 (Apr. 28, 2004), *available at* www.occ.gov/static/news-issuances/memos-advisory-letters/2004/advisory-letter-2004-4.pdf.

348 USPIRG, The Credit Card Trap: How to Spot It, How to Avoid It 12 (Apr. 2001), *available at* https://pincdn.s3.amazonaws.com/assets/2uC8i5-gbx0EBcOu0cH_pw/Credit_Card_Trap.pdf.

349 *See, e.g.*, Lawrence v. Household Bank, 343 F. Supp. 2d 1101 (M.D. Ala. 2004) (9:00 a.m. cut-off for payment posting); Landreneau v. Fleet Fin. Group, 197 F. Supp. 2d 551 (M.D. La. 2002) (9:00 a.m. cut-off for payment posting); Bond v. Fleet Bank, 2002 WL 31500393 (D.R.I. Oct. 10, 2002); Schwartz v. Citibank (S.D.), Nat'l Ass'n (C.D. Cal. May 5, 2000), *available at* www.nclc.org/unreported (class action settlement notice in case challenging 10:00 a.m. cut-off); Marsh v. First U.S.A. Bank, N.A., C.N. 3-99CV0783-T (N.D. Tex. Apr. 8, 1999). *Cf.* Johnson v. Capital One Bank, 15 Cal. Rptr. 3d 917 (Cal. Ct. App. 2004) (breach of contract claim for failing to promptly post payments; summary judgment granted for defendant on basis that Virginia state law limits defendant's liability to TILA for conduct that could be subject of TILA claim).

350 *See, e.g.*, Jaffe v. Capital One Bank, 2010 WL 691639 (S.D.N.Y. Mar. 1, 2010) (consumer charged late fee despite electronic payment made one day prior to due date; consumer failed to adequately pleaded claims for fraud, conversion, or unjust enrichment).

351 *See, e.g.*, Trombley v. Bank of Am. Corp., 715 F. Supp. 2d 290 (D.R.I. 2010) (consumer charged late fee despite making payment at Bank of America branch on due date); Pownall v. PNC Bank, 2010 WL 3515661 (N.D. Ohio Aug. 31, 2010).

352 Consumer Action, *2007 Credit Card Survey*, Consumer Action News (Spring 2007), *available at* www.consumer-action.org/downloads/english/CA_News_CC_07.pdf (seven of twenty credit card lenders would consider payment late if not received by prior business date when due date falls on a holiday or weekend).

A challenge to this practice under California's "holiday statute," which provides that if an act is required to be performed on a holiday it can be performed the next day without adverse consequence, was held to be preempted under federal banking law. Miller v. Bank of Am., 88 Cal. Rptr. 3d 723 (Cal. Ct. App. 2009).

353 Ruhi Maker, Greater Rochester Community Reinvestment Coalition, Testimony in Opposition to the Proposed Merger of Bank of America and MBNA (Sept. 27, 2005).

354 National Consumer Law Center, Truth in Lending § 7.7 (7th ed. 2010 and Supp.).

355 15 U.S.C. § 1666b(a); Reg. Z, 12 C.F.R. § 1026.5(b)(2)(ii)(A)(1) [§ 226.5(b)(2)(ii)(A)(1)].

356 15 U.S.C. § 1666b(b); Reg. Z, 12 C.F.R. § 1026.5(b)(2)(ii)(B)(1) [§ 226.5(b)(2)(ii)(B)(1)].

357 15 U.S.C. §§ 1666b(a), 1666b(b).

358 Reg. Z, 12 C.F.R. § 1026.5(b)(2)(ii)(A)(2) [§ 226.5(b)(2)(ii)(A)(2)].

359 Official Commentary to Reg. Z, 12 C.F.R. § 1026.5(b)(2)(ii)-2 [§ 226.5(b)(2)(ii)-2].

360 Official Commentary to Reg. Z, 12 C.F.R. § 1026.5(b)(2)(ii)-2 [§ 226.5(b)(2)(ii)-2].

Note, however, that if prior payments to the account have been late, the lender is permitted to continue to treat the account as late. Official Commentary to Reg. Z, 12 C.F.R. § 1026.5(b)(2)(ii)-4.ii [§ 226.5(b)(2)(ii)-4.ii].

- Imposing a penalty rate;
- Reporting the consumer as delinquent to a credit reporting agency;
- Assessing a late fee;
- Initiating collection activities;
- Terminating benefits (such as rewards on purchases); or
- Assessing finance charges for failure to pay within the grace period if this twenty-one-day period is not provided.[361]

Regulation Z implements this provision by requiring creditors to have "reasonable procedures" designed to ensure that periodic statements are mailed or delivered twenty-one days prior to the payment due date and end of the grace period.[362] Thus, a lender is not required to determine the specific date on which a statement is mailed or delivered; rather, the lender will comply with the rule if it has adopted "reasonable procedures."[363]

## *8.6.3 Prompt Crediting of Consumer Payments*

TILA requires credit card lenders to promptly credit consumer payments, if the creditor has received the payment in a readily identifiable form in the amount, manner, location, and time indicated by the creditor.[364] Payment must be credited as of (although not necessarily on) the day of receipt unless a delay in posting does not result in a finance charge or other charge.[365]

Credit card lenders may impose specific requirements for the manner of payment, but these requirements must be "reasonable,"[366] i.e., most consumers should be able to make conforming payments.[367] The creditor can specify, *inter alia*:

- That the payment be accompanied by the account number or payment stub.
- That mail payment be made only by check or money order and not in cash.
- That payment be made in U.S. dollars.
- That payment be made to a specific address, such as a post office box.[368] However, there are specific rules regarding a change in payment addresses.[369]
- That payment be received by 5:00 p.m. or a later cut-off times.[370]

If the creditor accepts a payment made in a different manner than that specified, it need not credit the payment as of the date of receipt, but must credit the payment within five days of receipt.[371]

If the creditor promotes a particular method of payment, it must treat any payments made using that method as conforming payments. Such payments must be credited as of the date of receipt, unless a delay in crediting does not result in a finance or other charge.[372] Thus, if a creditor promotes electronic payment on its website, including disclosing that payments may be made via the website, any payments so made would generally be considered conforming payments.[373]

In general, payments made via a creditor's website must be credited as of the date on which the consumer authorizes the creditor to deduct the payment, not the date when the consumer makes the authorization or the date the payment is affected.[374] Furthermore, the Electronic Fund Transfers Act prohibits creditors from *requiring* that recurring payments be made by electronic fund transfer.[375]

## *8.6.4 Payment Due Date Restrictions*

### 8.6.4.1 No Cut-Off Time Before 5:00 p.m.

In response to the practice of lenders setting early hour cut-off times, such as 9:00 or 10:00 a.m., the Credit CARD Act established a requirement that payment cut-off times must be specifically set for 5:00 p.m.[376] Regulation Z specifies that the relevant time zone is the one for the location specified by the creditor for the receipt of payments.[377] Regulation Z also permits the creditor to set a payment cut-off time later than 5:00 p.m.[378]

### 8.6.4.2 Same Due Date Each Month

The Credit CARD Act requires that the payment due date must be the same day of each month for credit card accounts.[379] That means that the due date must be the same numerical date each month, e.g., the 25th of every month.[380] A due date that is the same relative date but not the same numerical date each month, such as the third Tuesday of the month, generally would

361 15 U.S.C. § 1666b(b); Reg. Z, 12 C.F.R. § 1026.5(b)(2)(ii)(B)(2) [§ 226.5(b)(2)(ii)(B)(2)].

362 Reg. Z, 12 C.F.R. § 1026.5(b)(2)(ii)(A), (B) [§ 226.5(b)(2)(ii)(A), (B)].

363 Official Commentary to Reg. Z, 12 C.F.R. § 1026.5(b)(2)(ii)-1 [§ 226.5(b)(2)(ii)-1].

364 15 U.S.C. § 1666c(a).

365 Reg. Z, 12 C.F.R. § 1026.10(a) [§ 226.10(a)].

366 Reg. Z, 12 C.F.R. § 1026.10(b)(1) [§ 226.10(b)(1).

367 *Id.* The disclosure of the creditor's payment requirements does not need to be in a form that the consumer may keep, which inhibits the consumer's ability to comply with payment specifications. Reg. Z, 12 C.F.R. § 1026.5(a)(1)(ii)(B) [§ 226.5(a)(1)(ii)(B)].

368 Reg. Z, 12 C.F.R. § 1026.10(b)(2)(v) [§ 226.10(b)(2)(v)].

369 *See* § 8.6.5.1, *infra.*

370 *See* § 8.6.4.1, *infra.*

371 Reg. Z, 12 C.F.R. § 1026.10(b)(4) [§ 226.10(b)(4)].

372 Reg. Z, 12 C.F.R. § 1026.10(b)(4)(ii) [§ 226.10(b)(4)(ii)].

373 Official Commentary to Reg. Z, 12 C.F.R. § 1026.10(b)-2.i [§ 226.10(b)-2.i].

374 Official Commentary to Reg. Z, 12 C.F.R. § 1026.10(a)-2.iv [§ 226.10(a)-2.iv].

375 Official Commentary to Reg. Z, 12 C.F.R. § 1026.10(b)-1 [§ 226.10(b)-1] (cross-reference to 15 U.S.C. § 1693k). *See* National Consumer Law Center, Consumer Banking and Payments Law § 4.11.5 (4th ed. 2009 and Supp.).

376 15 U.S.C. § 1666c(a); Reg. Z, 12 C.F.R. § 1026.10(b)(2)(ii) [§ 226.10(b)(2)(ii)].

377 Reg. Z, 12 C.F.R. § 1026.10(b)(2)(ii) [§ 226.10(b)(2)(ii)].

378 *Id.*

379 15 U.S.C. § 1637(o)(1); Reg. Z, 12 C.F.R. § 1026.7(b)(11)(i) [§ 226.7(b)(11)(i)].

380 Official Commentary to Reg. Z, 12 C.F.R. § 1026.7(b)(11)-6 [§ 226.7(b)(11)-6].

not comply, except the due date can be the last day of each month, even though it would not be the same numerical date.[381]

### 8.6.4.3 Weekend and Holiday Due Dates

If the payment due date falls on a day on which the creditor does not receive or accept payments by mail, it may not treat as late any payment received by mail on the next "business day."[382] The "next business day" is the next day on which the creditor accepts or receives payments by mail.[383] This provision addresses the practice of lenders, when due dates fell on a weekend or holiday, of treating payments as late if they not received on the prior business day.

A creditor must not treat a payment under these circumstances as late "for any purpose."[384] This includes imposing a penalty rate, reporting the consumer as delinquent to a credit reporting agency, or assessing a late fee.[385] It does not include imposition of interest charges when the account is not eligible for a grace period.[386]

This prohibition against treating a payment as late if the due date falls on weekend or holiday does not apply to payments made by other methods, such as electronic or telephone payments.[387] However, the creditor must accept or receive payments made on the weekend or holiday due date by these other methods.[388]

Note that if the due date does fall on a weekend or holiday, the creditor is still required to disclose the due date as that weekend or holiday date. For example, if the due date for an account is the 4th of every month, the creditor must disclose the due date as July 4, even though the creditor may not treat a mailed payment received on the next business day (e.g., July 5) as late for any purpose.[389]

## 8.6.5 *Address for Payment*

### 8.6.5.1 Change in Address

If a credit card lender makes a material change in the address for receiving payments or procedures for handling payments, and the change causes a material delay in the crediting of a payment during a sixty-day period after the change, the lender is prohibited from assessing late fees or finance charges for late payment.[390]

Essentially, a "material change" means any change that causes a delay in the crediting of a payment resulting in the imposition of a late fee or finance charge.[391] Thus, a change that does not result in a late fee or finance charge would be immaterial.[392]

### 8.6.5.2 In-Person Payments

If a credit card lender is a financial institution that maintains branches or offices, and the consumer makes a payment in person at a branch or office at which credit card payments are accepted in person, the date on which the consumer makes a payment at the branch or office must be considered to be the date on which the payment is made.[393]

In order to be credited as of the date of payment, the consumer must make the payment prior to the close of business of that branch or office.[394] If the branch or office closes earlier than 5:00 p.m., a lender may impose a cut-off time as of the close of business even if it is earlier than 5:00 p.m.[395]

This requirement applies to a bank, savings association, or credit union,[396] but does not include the location of a retailer, even if the credit card is a store-branded credit card and the consumer is able to make a payment on the account at the retailer's location.[397] It does include the affiliate of the lender that is a financial institution and shares a name with the lender, such as "Citibank," if the affiliate accepts in-person payments on the lender's accounts.[398]

For the payment to be considered "in person," the payment must be made to or with the direct assistance of a branch or office employee, such a teller at a bank branch.[399] Payments made without the direct assistance of a branch or office employee, such as those placed in a mail slot (or presumably an ATM), are not considered payments made "in person."[400]

## 8.6.6 *Limit on Fees Related to Method of Payment*

The Credit CARD Act limits fees that some lenders previously charged for services such as accepting a payment by telephone or at an Internet website. Lenders may not impose a separate fee to allow the cardholder to make a payment on a credit card account, regardless of whether the payment is made

381 *Id.*
382 15 U.S.C. § 1637(o)(2); Reg. Z, 12 C.F.R. § 1026.10(d)(1) [§ 226.10(d)(1)].
383 Reg. Z, 12 C.F.R. § 1026.10(d)(1) [§ 226.10(d)(1)].
384 Reg. Z, 12 C.F.R. § 1026.10(d)(1) [§ 226.10(d)(1)].
385 Official Commentary to Reg. Z, 12 C.F.R. § 1026.10(d)-2 [§ 226.10(d)-2].
386 Official Commentary to Reg. Z, 12 C.F.R. § 1026.10(d)-2 [§ 226.10(d)-2].
387 Reg. Z, 12 C.F.R. § 1026.10(d)(2) [§ 226.10(d)(2)].
388 *Id.*
389 Official Commentary to Reg. Z, 12 C.F.R. § 1026.7(b)(11)-9 [§ 226.7(b)(11)-9].
390 15 U.S.C. § 1666c(c); Reg. Z, 12 C.F.R. § 1026.10(f) [§ 226.10(f)].
391 Official Commentary to Reg. Z, 12 C.F.R. § 1026.10(f)-2 [§ 226.10(f)-2].
392 *Id.*
393 15 U.S.C. § 1637(b)(12)(C); Reg. Z, 12 C.F.R. § 1026.10(b)(3)(i) [§ 226.10(b)(3)(i)].
394 Reg. Z, 12 C.F.R. § 1026.10(b)(3)(i) [§ 226.10(b)(3)(i)].
395 *Id.*
396 Reg. Z, 12 C.F.R. § 1026.10(b)(3)(ii) [§ 226.10(b)(3)(ii)].
397 Official Commentary to Reg. Z, 12 C.F.R. § 1026.10(b)-5 [§ 226.10(b)-5].
398 Official Commentary to Reg. Z, 12 C.F.R. § 1026.10(b)-7 [§ 226.10(b)-7].
399 Official Commentary to Reg. Z, 12 C.F.R. § 1026.10(b)-6 [§ 226.10(b)-6].
400 *Id.*

by mail, electronic transfer, telephone authorization, or other means, unless the payment involves an expedited service by a customer service representative of the lender.[401]

Thus, the lender cannot charge a fee for an automated means of making payment that does not involve a live person, such as a voice response unit or interactive voice response system, although an automated system can be used for a portion of the transaction if a live person is also involved.[402] The term "separate fee" means a fee imposed for making a payment to the account. It does not include a late fee or other charge imposed if payment is made after the due date.[403]

## *8.6.7 Payment Allocation Order*

Many credit card companies heavily advertise low APRs in their solicitations that are only applicable to one category of transactions. Previously, one tactic used by these lenders to increase profitability was to allocate payments first to the balances with lower APRs, thus leaving the higher balance APRs to accrue finance charges. A GAO study found that for twenty-three out of the twenty-eight most popular credit cards, the lenders allocated payments to the balance with the lowest rate of interest.[404] Private class actions were brought challenging this abuse as deceptive.[405]

The Credit CARD Act addressed this payment allocation abuse by requiring that credit card lenders allocate payments in excess of the minimum using a high-to-low method.[406] That is, lenders must allocate payments first to the balance with the highest APR and any remaining portions to other balances in descending order based on APR.

The payment allocation rule does not govern the lender's ability to allocate the minimum payment.[407] The lender may apply the minimum payment to the balance with the lowest APR, which is a significant weakness.

If a deferred interest program is involved,[408] special rules apply during the last two billing cycles immediately preceding the expiration of the deferred interest period. During these last two cycles, the creditor must allocate the entire payment in excess of the minimum to the balance on which interest is deferred.[409] However, the lender may at its option allocate payments in excess of the minimum among the balances on the account in the manner requested by the consumer.[410]

If the consumer has exercised the right to withhold payment based on a billing error dispute or claims or defenses against a merchant, the lender must allocate in a manner that avoids or minimizes any reduction in the amount of that claim or defense.[411]

Greater detail on the payment allocation rules is provided in another treatise in this series.[412]

## *8.6.8 Tiny Minimum Monthly Payments*

### 8.6.8.1 Background

In the early to mid-2000s, many credit card lenders decreased the minimum monthly payments from 4% to 2% or 3% of the consumer's balance.[413] With lowered monthly minimum payments, consumers who pay only the minimum will take much longer to pay off the credit card debt and will pay substantially more in finance charges.

For example, it would take a consumer nearly twenty years to pay off a $1,000 balance with an 18% APR if the consumer makes only the minimum payment of 2% of the balance. Additional examples are shown below. Many consumers did not realize how much more time and money paying only the minimum will cost.[414]

In some cases, the combination of the minimum monthly payments and the penalty interest rates result in negatively amortizing debt, i.e., the minimum payments do not pay off the accrued interest and fees, so that the debt increases even when payments are made. Federal banking regulators issued guidance to discourage minimum payments that are so low as to create negative amortization.[415]

---

401 15 U.S.C. § 1637(l); Reg. Z, 12 C.F.R. § 1026.10(e) [§ 226.10(e)].

402 *Id.*

403 Official Commentary to Reg. Z, 12 C.F.R. § 1026.10(e)-1 [§ 226.10(e)-1].

404 Government Accountability Office, Credit Cards: Increased Complexity in Rates and Fees Heightens Need for More Effective Disclosures to Consumers, GAO-06-929, at 27 (Sept. 2006), *available at* www.gao.gov/new.items/d06929.pdf.

405 Davis v. Chase Bank USA, N.A., 650 F. Supp. 2d 1073 (C.D. Cal. 2009) (plaintiff brought breach of contract and UDAP claims challenging payment allocation abuse).

Cases alleging payment allocation abuses occurred even after the Credit CARD Act required payments to be applied to the highest rate balance. Complaint, Vosko v. Capital One, 2:11-cv-12513 (Ed. Mich. June 10, 2011), *available on the companion website to this treatise*.

406 15 U.S.C. § 1666c(b)(1); Reg. Z, 12 C.F.R. § 1026.53(a) [§ 226.53(a)].

407 15 U.S.C. § 1666c(b)(1).

408 A "deferred interest program" is defined in Reg. Z, 12 C.F.R. § 1026.16(h)(2) [§ 226.16(h)(2)]. *See* § 8.8, *infra*.

409 15 U.S.C. § 1666c(b)(2); Reg. Z, 12 C.F.R. § 1026.53(b)(1)(i) [§ 226.53(b)(1)(i)].

410 Reg. Z, 12 C.F.R. § 1026.53(b)(1)(ii) [§ 226.53(b)(1)(ii)].

411 Official Commentary to Reg. Z, 12 C.F.R. § 1026.53-3 [§ 226.53-3] (cross-referencing Reg. Z, 12 C.F.R. §§ 1026.12(c) and 1026.13 [§§ 226.12(c) and 226.13]).

412 National Consumer Law Center, Truth in Lending § 7.7.7 (7th ed. 2010 and Supp.).

413 Linda Sherry, *Annual Credit Card Survey 2004*, Consumer Action (Spring 2004), *available at* www.consumer-action.org/news/articles/2004_credit_card_survey.

414 In consumer education programs conducted by one attorney general's office, even college-educated consumers consistently underestimated how long it would take to pay off credit card balances. Center for Responsible Lending, Comments to Advance Notice of Proposed Rulemaking—Regulation Z, Subpart B: Open-End Credit, Docket No. R-1217, at 22–23 (Mar. 28, 2004), *available on the companion website to this treatise*.

415 Federal Financial Institutions Examination Council, Credit Card Lending Account Management and Loss Allowance Guidance (Jan. 2003), *available at* www.federalreserve.gov/BoardDocs/press/bcreg/2003/20030108/attachment.pdf.

According to media reports, regulators advised lenders to use a formula for minimum payments that would pay off fees and accrued finance charges, plus 1% of the principal.[416] Note that at lower periodic APRs, this 1% plus finance charges and fees formula produces results close to the same 2% formula that credit card lenders previously used. This formula is better for consumers at higher interest rates; however, it is still far inferior to requiring a 4% payment, unless perhaps the account incurs substantial fees, e.g., late, over-the-limit, cash advance fees. The following chart shows how long it will take to pay of a $4,500 balance (assuming no additional extensions of credit or fees incurred) using different minimum payment formulas:

| Balance | Periodic APR | Minimum Payment Formula | # Months to Pay | Total Interest |
|---|---|---|---|---|
| $4,500 | 12% | 1% plus interest & fees | 291 | $ 4,327 |
| $4,500 | 12% | 2% | 289 | $ 4,196 |
| $4,500 | 12% | 4% | 124 | $ 1,455 |
| $4,500 | 18% | 1% plus interest & fees | 307 | $ 6,459 |
| $4,500 | 18% | 2% | 532 | $12,431 |
| $4,500 | 18% | 4% | 146 | $ 2,615 |

Conversely, at least one credit card lender has increased minimum payments, from 2% to 5%, for cardholders who had favorably low interest rates, in order to pressure to them to accept a higher interest rate.[417] The Credit CARD Act prohibits dramatic increases in the minimum payment, but only when the protections against raising the interest rate on an outstanding balance apply.[418]

### 8.6.8.2 Minimum Payment Repayment Disclosures

In response to the problem of low minimum payments, the Credit CARD Act added a requirement that lenders disclose the actual number of months that it will take to pay off the balance on an account if the consumer makes only the minimum payment.[419] Lenders are required to provide the following warning in periodic statements using the exact language below:[420]

> Minimum Payment Warning: If you make only the minimum payment each period, you will pay more in interest and it will take you longer to pay off your balance.

In addition, the lender must disclose the following information regarding repayment of the outstanding balance:

(1) An estimate of the length of time that it would take to pay off the balance, if the consumer makes only the minimum monthly payment.[421]
(2) An estimate of the total cost for paying off the balance in full making only minimum monthly payments.[422]
(3) An explanation that the estimates described in (1) and (2), *supra*, are based on the current outstanding balance shown on the periodic statement, and on the assumption that only minimum payments are made and no other amounts are added to the balance.[423]
(4) A toll-free number at which the consumer may receive information about credit counseling services.[424]
(5) An estimate of the monthly payment that would be required to pay off the outstanding balance in thirty-six months and an estimate of the total cost for such a payoff.[425]

These disclosures appear to be having a salutary effect, as one study found that fewer consumers are paying only the minimum amount, and more consumers are paying the amount disclosed that would pay off the balance in thirty-six months.[426] Greater detail on the minimum payment repayment disclosures is provided in another treatise in this series.[427]

## 8.7 Abuses in the Opening of Accounts

### 8.7.1 *Deceptive Marketing*

Some credit card lenders have engaged in questionable marketing practices when soliciting consumers. "Bait and switch" tactics were common. For example, some credit card lenders marketed "no annual fee" credit cards, then imposed an annual fee six months later using a change-in-terms notice.[428] They heavily advertised low "fixed" rates, but subsequently raised rates through change-in-terms notices and penalty pricing.[429]

416 Kathy Chu, *Banks Raise Credit Card Payments*, USA Today, Dec. 20, 2005, at 1A. *See also* Mara Der Hovanesian, *Tough Love for Debtors*, BusinessWeek, Apr. 25, 2006.

417 *In re* Chase Bank USA, N.A. "Check Loan" Contract Litig., 2009 WL 4063349 (N.D. Cal. Nov. 20, 2009).

418 *See* National Consumer Law Center, Truth in Lending § 7.2.3.5 (7th ed. 2010 and Supp.).

419 15 U.S.C. § 1637(b)(11).

420 15 U.S.C. § 1637(b)(11)(A); Reg. Z, 12 C.F.R. § 1026.7(b)(12)(i)(A) [§ 226.7(b)(12)(i)(A)].
The language in the Credit CARD Act was modified by the Federal Reserve Board, which had authority to establish different language pursuant to consumer testing. 15 U.S.C. § 1637(b)(11)(A).

421 15 U.S.C. § 1637(b)(11)(B)(i); Reg. Z, 12 C.F.R. § 1026.7(b)(12)(i)(B) [§ 226.7(b)(12)(i)(B)].

422 15 U.S.C. § 1637(b)(11)(B)(ii); Reg. Z, 12 C.F.R. § 1026.7(b)(12)(i)(C) [§ 226.7(b)(12)(i)(C)].

423 Reg. Z, 12 C.F.R. § 1026.7(b)(12)(i)(D) [§ 226.7(b)(12)(i)(D)].

424 15 U.S.C. § 1637(b)(11)(B)(iv); Reg. Z, 12 C.F.R. § 1026.7(b)(12)(i)(E) [§ 226.7(b)(12)(i)(E)].

425 15 U.S.C. § 1637(b)(11)(B)(iii); Reg. Z, 12 C.F.R. § 1026.7(b)(12)(i)(F) [§ 226.7(b)(12)(i)(F)].

426 Dennis Campbell et al., Harvard Bus. Sch., Reframing Behavior: The Impact of the CARD Act on Cardholder Repayment Rates (Feb. 2011), *available at* www.consumerfinance.gov/wp-content/uploads/2011/03/Gartenberg-Presentation-Revised-Final.pdf.

427 National Consumer Law Center, Truth in Lending § 6.7.11.4 (7th ed. 2010 and Supp.).

428 Rossman v. Fleet Bank (R.I.) Nat'l Ass'n, 280 F.3d 384 (3d Cir. 2002).

429 Roberts v. Fleet Bank (R.I.), Nat'l Ass'n, 342 F.3d 260 (3d Cir. 2003); Gaynoe v. First Union Direct Bank, Nat'l Ass'n, 571 S.E.2d 24 (N.C. Ct. App. 2002); Chavers v. Fleet Bank (R.I.), N.A., 844 A.2d 666 (R.I. 2004).

Subprime credit card lenders are particularly notorious for their deceptive marketing.[430] One lender prominently marketed cards with a $300 limit, but failed to adequately disclose that $185 in fees that would be immediately charged to the card.[431] Another subprime credit card lender marketed "no annual fee" credit cards without disclosing that the consumer was required to purchase credit protection at $156 a year.[432]

## 8.7.2 Aggressive Solicitation and Account Opening

### 8.7.2.1 Background

Until recently, lenders often offered credit cards based solely on a consumer's credit score.[433] Credit scores supposedly measure the consumer's propensity to repay a debt, but they do not measure whether the consumer's income is adequate to take on new debt, or show if the consumer is already carrying too much debt.[434] As a result, credit card lenders often granted new credit cards to consumers who were already overextended.[435] Federal regulators issued guidance urging credit card lenders to consider repayment capacity when granting new credit,[436] but this guidance was not mandatory. With the last economic downturn, lenders finally began examining other factors in deciding whether to grant credit, or as Bank of America's CEO put it, adding "an overlay of a human being looking at the credit."[437]

In addition to creating enormous burdens on financially distressed consumers, aggressive opening of new accounts was responsible for some of the other abuses discussed in this section. Instead of granting credit on the basis of a front-end analysis of the consumer's ability to pay, lenders engaged in "back end" underwriting. After the consumer receives the credit card and runs up a debt, if the consumer's account exhibits signs of trouble, the credit card lender raised the account's interest rate. Lenders justified the increase on the basis of the "newly discovered" high risk of nonpayment, instead of initially denying credit to consumers who could not afford the credit in the first place.[438]

The eagerness of credit card lenders to open new accounts and their failure to adequately screen applications also contributed to the problem of identity theft.[439] For example, the Sixth Circuit expressed concern over the ease with which a credit card account could be opened online, including without a consumer's authorization, stating:

> It may well be true that credit card applications—and in particular, on-line credit card applications—are too lightly regulated. For example, maybe it should be more difficult for an applicant to subject a co-signator to substantial debt liability (as appears to have happened here) without express authorization from the co-signator. . . . Likewise, maybe it should take more than just the click of a mouse for an individual who has recently emerged from personal bankruptcy, and who has a mental disorder that manifests itself in bouts of excessive spending on exotic pussycats, to be able to obtain a credit card in the first place.[440]

---

For an interesting analysis of the alleged deceptiveness of Capital One's heavy promotion including its prolific television ad campaign, see Complaint, State of Minnesota v. Capital One Bank (Minn. Dist. Ct.—2d Jud. Dist. Dec. 30, 2004), *available on the companion website to this treatise*.

430 *See* § 8.5.1.2, *supra*.

431 Complaint, Federal Trade Comm'n v. CompuCredit, Civ. No. 1:08-CV-1976 (N.D. Ga. June 10, 2008), *available at* www.ftc.gov/os/caselist/0623212/080610compucreditcmplt.pdf. *See also* Order to Cease and Desist and Order to Pay, In the Matter of Columbus Bank and Trust Co., FDIC-08-033b (Dep't of the Treasury, Federal Deposit Insurance Corp. June 9, 2008).

432 Consent Order, *In re* Providian Nat'l Bank, No. 2000-53 (Dep't of the Treasury, Office of the Comptroller of the Currency June 28, 2000), *available at* www.occ.gov/static/enforcement-actions/ea2000-53.pdf.

433 National Consumer Law Center, Fair Credit Reporting § 14.3 (7th ed. 2010 and Supp.); Federal Reserve Board, Report to the Congress on Practices of the Consumer Credit Industry in Soliciting and Extending Credit and Their Effects on Consumer Debt and Insolvency 19–22 (June 2006), *available at* www.federalreserve.gov/boarddocs/rptcongress/bankruptcy/bankruptcybillstudy200606.pdf.

434 Unfortunately, regulators appear to accept that the industry's heavy reliance on credit scores adequately prevents lenders from offering credit indiscriminately. Federal Reserve Board, Report to the Congress on Practices of the Consumer Credit Industry in Soliciting and Extending Credit and Their Effects on Consumer Debt and Insolvency 19–22 (June 2006), *available at* www.federalreserve.gov/boarddocs/rptcongress/bankruptcy/bankruptcybillstudy200606.pdf.

435 *See, e.g.,* Universal Card Servs. Corp. v. Akins (*In re* Akins), 235 B.R. 866 (W.D. Tex. 1999) (card lender approved consumer to use convenience check up to her full $4,000 credit limit based on acceptable FICO score even though she had two other credit cards totaling approximately $30,000 in debt, or 150% of her gross income); AT&T Universal Card v. Ellingsworth (*In re* Ellingsworth), 212 B.R. 326 (Bankr. W. D. Mo. 1997) (consumer sent pre-approved credit card with credit limit of $4,000 based on her FICO score of 759 even though she had sixteen other credit cards).

436 Federal Financial Institutions Examination Council, Credit Card Lending Account Management and Loss Allowance Guidance (Jan. 2003), *available at* www.federalreserve.gov/BoardDocs/press/bcreg/2003/20030108/attachment.pdf.

437 Robin Sidel, *Card Issuers Get Personal to Check Credit*, Wall St. J., June 19, 2008, at D1.

438 Some investment analysts have pointed out the same problem and theorized that this model of lending is not sustainable in the long term, at least not during economic downturns. Gregory Larkin and Laura Nishikawa, Innovest, Credit Cards at a Tipping Point (Oct. 2008).

439 *See* National Consumer Law Center, Fair Credit Reporting Ch. 9 (7th ed. 2010 and Supp.) (discussing identity theft).

440 MacDermid v. Discover Fin. Servs., 488 F.3d 721 (6th Cir. 2007). *See also* Wolfe v. MBNA Am. Bank, 485 F. Supp. 2d 874 (W.D. Tenn. 2007) (holding that, under state negligence law, bank has a duty to verify the authenticity and accuracy of a credit card application before issuing a card). *But see* Chinners v. General Elec. Capital Corp., 2010 WL 2595308 (D.S.C. June 23, 2010) (summary judgment to creditor; consumer who was wrongfully added as a co-applicant on a credit card application without his consent); Harmon v. GE Money Corp., 2010 WL 2219345 (E.D. Cal. June 1, 2010) (uncle listed nephew as co-borrower without nephew's knowledge; no FDCPA violation because lender was not "debt collector"). *See generally* National Consumer Law Center, Fair Credit Reporting § 9.5.2 (7th ed. 2010 and Supp.).

### 8.7.2.2 Credit CARD Act's Ability-to-Pay Requirement

The Credit CARD Act, for the first time, imposes underwriting requirements on credit card lenders. The Act sets forth a general requirement, applicable to all consumers, that a lender may not open a credit card account or increase a credit limit unless the lender considers the ability of the consumer to make the required minimum payments.[441] The lender's consideration of ability-to-pay must be based on both the consumer's income or assets, and the consumer's current obligations.[442]

The requirement to consider ability-to-pay applies to both an application for a new credit card account, and an increase in the credit line for an existing account.[443] For credit limit increases, the requirement applies whether the consumer requested the increase or the lender initiated it.[444]

The lender is not required to consider ability-to-pay to the exclusion of other factors. It may also consider the consumer's credit history or credit score and any other factor consistent with Regulation B,[445] which implements the Equal Credit Opportunity Act.[446]

The Credit CARD Act's ability-to-pay provision is in Part C of TILA, which is not privately enforceable except potentially through state UDAP statutes.[447] The provision might also be used as a defense in a collection lawsuit brought against the consumer.[448]

Greater detail on the ability-to-pay provision is provided in another treatise in this series.[449]

### 8.7.2.3 Marketing to Younger Consumers

#### *8.7.2.3.1 Introduction*

College students are a favorite target of credit card lenders.[450] One study found that 70% of undergraduates had one credit card and 90% of these students carried a balance.[451] In 2008, the average college senior had credit card debt of $4,100.[452] In response, a number of states passed laws regulating credit card marketing on college campuses.[453]

The Credit CARD Act establishes a number of protections for consumers under the age of twenty-one, discussed below in summary. Greater detail on the protections for younger consumers is provided in another treatise in this series.[454]

#### *8.7.2.3.2 Consideration of ability to repay for young consumers*

In addition to the generally applicable requirement to consider ability to repay,[455] the Credit CARD Act imposes specific underwriting requirements for consumers under the age of twenty-one.[456] The Act establishes two alternative methods to determine a young consumer's ability to pay, as discussed in the next subsection.

The first alternative requires the young consumer to submit financial information "indicating an independent means of repaying" the credit.[457] While this language would seem to set a higher standard than the generally applicable requirement to "consider the ability of the consumer" to pay, Regulation Z permits lenders to use the same analysis for both requirements.[458]

The second alternative requires that the application must be co-signed by an individual over twenty-one years old who has the means to repay debts incurred on the account and accepts joint liability for debts.[459] While the Credit CARD Act only requires the co-signor to agree to joint liability for the account before the consumer turns twenty-one,[460] the FRB staff permitted lenders to require the cosigner to assume liability for debts incurred after the young consumer reaches twenty-one.[461]

The biggest difference between the generally applicable requirement and the requirements for young consumers is that the

441 15 U.S.C. § 1665e; Reg. Z, 12 C.F.R. § 1026.51(a)(1)(i) [§ 226.51(a)(1)(i)].

442 Reg. Z, 12 C.F.R. § 1026.51(a)(1)(i) [§ 226.51(a)(1)(i)].

443 15 U.S.C. § 1665e; Reg. Z, 12 C.F.R. § 1026.51(a)(1)(i) [§ 226.51(a)(1)(i)].

444 Official Commentary to Reg. Z, 12 C.F.R. § 1026.51(a)(1)-3 [§ 226.51(a)(1)-3].

445 Official Commentary to Reg. Z, 12 C.F.R. § 1026.51(a)(1)-1 [§ 226.51(a)(1)-1].

446 15 U.S.C. §§ 1691–1691f. *See generally* National Consumer Law Center, Credit Discrimination (5th ed. 2009 and Supp.).

447 *See* National Consumer Law Center, Truth in Lending § 11.6.5.4 (7th ed. 2010 and Supp.).

448 *See, e.g.*, Citibank (South Dakota), N.A. v. Mazzarella, 2010 WL 5610861 (Conn. Super. Ct. Dec. 14, 2010) (consumer raised violation of ability-to-pay requirement as a special defense in collection action; defense struck because consumer failed to allege violation occurred after effective date of Credit CARD Act).

449 National Consumer Law Center, Truth in Lending § 7.6.2 (7th ed. 2010 and Supp.).

450 Tamara Draut, Strapped: Why America's 20- and 30-Somethings Can't Get Ahead 106–110 (2005).

451 Marty Ludlum, et al., Financial Literacy and Credit Cards: A Multi Campus Survey, 3 Intl J. of Bus. and Social Science 25, 27–28 (2012).

452 Sandra Block, *Credit Card Reform Swipes Easy Plastic from College Students*, USA Today, May 26, 2009 (citing Sallie Mae statistics).

453 *See, e.g.*, Ark. Code Ann. § 4-104-202; Cal. Educ. Code § 99030 (West); Conn. Gen. Stat. § 10a-446; 110 Ill. Comp. Stat. 26/1 to 26/97; La. Rev. Stat. Ann. §§ 9:3577.1 to 9:3577.5, and 17:3351.2; Md. Code, Educ. § 15-111 (West); Minn. Stat. § 135A.145; N.Y. Educ. Law § 6437 (McKinney); 24 Pa. Stat. Ann. § 23-2302-A (West); Tenn. Code Ann. § 49-7-143; Wash. Rev. Code § 28B.10.618; W. Va. Code § 18B-14-10.

454 National Consumer Law Center, Truth in Lending § 7.6.3 (7th ed. 2010 and Supp.).

455 *See* § 8.7.2.2, *supra*.

456 15 U.S.C. § 1637(c)(8).

457 *Id.*

458 Reg. Z, 12 C.F.R. § 1026.51(b)(1)(i) [§ 226.51(b)(1)(i)] (cross-referencing Reg. Z, 12 C.F.R. § 1026.51(a) [§ 226.51(a)]).

459 15 U.S.C. § 1637(c)(8); Reg. Z, 12 C.F.R. § 1026.51(b)(1)(ii) [§ 226.51(b)(1)(ii)].

460 15 U.S.C. § 1637(c)(8).

461 Official Commentary to Reg. Z, 12 C.F.R. § 1026.51(b)-2 [§ 226.51(b)-2].

latter provisions are found in Part B of TILA and thus are privately enforceable.[462]

If an over-twenty-one consumer is a co-signor for a credit card account for a younger consumer, the lender must obtain the co-signor's agreement before the credit limit for that account may be increased.[463] This agreement must be in writing, and the co-signor must agree to assume liability for the increase.[464]

In general, a lender is permitted to issue a credit card only upon the consumer's request, but such a request may be made either in writing or orally.[465] For younger consumers, the Credit CARD Act requires that a credit card be issued only in response to a written application.[466]

#### *8.7.2.3.3 Restrictions on marketing of credit cards to college students*

The Credit CARD Act prohibits credit card lenders from offering any tangible item to induce a student at an institution of higher education to apply for an open-end credit plan.[467] To be prohibited, the offer must be made:

- On or near the campus;[468]
- At an event sponsored by the school;
- Where the event is related to the school;[469] *or*
- Through a physical mailing sent to the college student at an address on or near the campus[470] (but the FRB stated this does not include e-mails sent to the student[471]).

The inducement is that the item will be provided if the person applies for a card—the Act is not violated if the item (such as refreshments) is offered irrespective if the consumer applies for a card.[472]

Because the restrictions on marketing is in TILA Part B (and is not in or related to 15 U.S.C. §§ 1637 or 1638), a consumer is entitled to actual damages, statutory damages, and attorney fees for any violation of the marketing restrictions.[473]

462 National Consumer Law Center, Truth in Lending §§ 11.6.5, 11.6.6 (7th ed. 2010 and Supp.).

463 15 U.S.C. § 1637(p); Reg. Z, 12 C.F.R. § 1026.51(b)(2) [§ 226.51(b)(2)].

464 Reg. Z, 12 C.F.R. § 1026.51(b)(2) [§ 226.51(b)(2)].

465 National Consumer Law Center, Truth in Lending § 7.12.1 (7th ed. 2010 and Supp.).

466 15 U.S.C. § 1637(c)(8)(A); Reg. Z, 12 C.F.R. § 1026.51(b)(1) [§ 226.51(b)(1)].

467 15 U.S.C. § 1650(f)(2).

468 Near is defined as within 1,000 feet of the border of the campus, as defined by the college. Official Commentary to Reg. Z, 12 C.F.R. § 1026.57(c)-3 [§ 226.57(c)-3]. If a bank or other retail creditor has a permanent location falling within this definition and thus is near the campus, the Regulation applies to marketing at that location. Section-by-Section Analysis, 75 Fed. Reg. 7757 (Feb. 22, 2010).

469 15 U.S.C. § 1650(f)(2); Reg. Z, 12 C.F.R. § 1026.57(c) [§ 226.57(c)].

470 Official Commentary to Reg. Z, 12 C.F.R. § 1026.57(c)-4 [§ 226.57(c)-4].

471 75 Fed. Reg. 7658, 7758 (Feb. 22, 2010).

472 Official Commentary to Reg. Z, 12 C.F.R. § 1026.57(c)-2 [§ 226.57(c)-2.

473 15 U.S.C. § 1640(a).

Related to this prohibition, the Credit CARD Act added a provision to the Fair Credit Reporting Act (FCRA) prohibiting a consumer reporting agency from providing consumer reports for a prescreened offer of consumer credit or insurance where the consumer report indicates that they consumer is under twenty-one years of age, unless the consumer opts in to such offer.[474] Thus a prescreened offer of any form of consumer credit or insurance to anyone under twenty-one may result in private FCRA remedies against both the consumer reporting agency and the user of the report—the creditor or insurer sending out the prescreened offer.

## 8.8 Deferred Interest Plans

### *8.8.1 Background*

"Deferred interest" plans are credit card accounts that promote "no interest" or "no payments" until a certain date, but then retroactively assess interest starting from the purchase date if the consumer does not pay off the entire balance by the specified date.[475] The problem is that many consumers do not understand that they could be charged interest retroactively for the entire deferred interest period if they do not pay off the balance at the end of the period.[476]

Lenders do not tout this retroactive assessment of interest as prominently as the enticements of "no interest," "no interest until X date," or "0% interest." Clearer disclosure, however, would not solve the problem. The enticing statements of "no interest" are inherently deceptive given that fact there will be retroactive interest charged if the balance is not paid in full by the end of the deferred interest period. The complexity of these plans makes it almost impossible to formulate a short, simple disclosure necessary to adequately prevent consumers from being deceived.

Even if some consumers realize that they must pay the balance in full by a certain date, they may still get trapped by these schemes. They may forget or miscalculate the critical date for payoff, or they may expect to be able to pay the balance in full but for a variety of reasons (such as job loss or other financial emergency) find that they cannot. In any of these circumstances, the consumer is hit with an enormous, retroactive application of interest, something that lenders count on in making deferred interest offers.

Furthermore, deferred interest plans are often pitched to consumers when they purchase big ticket items, such as electronics or furniture. These are the same types of purchases often involved in spurious open-end credit schemes.[477] In some

474 15 U.S.C. § 1681b(c)(1)(B). *See* National Consumer Law Center, Fair Credit Reporting § 7.3.4 (7th ed. 2010 and Supp.).

475 The term is defined in Reg. Z, 12 C.F.R. § 1026.16(h)(2).

476 Allie Johnson, *Deferred Interest, Same as Cash: Play the Game Right or Lose*, CreditCards.Com, Dec. 9, 2008, *available at* www.creditcards.com/credit-card-news/deferred-interest-pros-and-cons-1267.php.

477 *See* National Consumer Law Center, Truth in Lending § 6.2.3 (7th ed. 2010 and Supp.).

cases, merchants have been known to inflate the purchase price of goods financed with a deferred interest plan.[478]

## 8.8.2 Rules Governing Deferred Interest Plans

### 8.8.2.1 Summary of Disclosures for Deferred Interest Plans

Regulation Z requires special disclosures for deferred interest programs. These include:

- Special disclosures for advertisements, including promotional materials accompanying applications or solicitations;[479]
- A special APR disclosure for the application/solicitation table;[480]
- A special APR disclosure for periodic statements;[481]
- A special disclosure of the balance for periodic statements;[482]
- A disclosure of accrued interest for periodic statements; and[483]
- A mandatory warning for periodic statement.[484]

These disclosures are discussed in detail in another treatise in this series.[485]

### 8.8.2.2 Credit CARD Act Provisions for Deferred Interest Plans

Deferred interest plans are a creation of Regulation Z, as they would violate several provisions of the Credit CARD Act if not for the exceptions carved out to permit them. In fact, at one point, the FRB had banned deferred interest plans in the Credit CARD UDAP Rule, citing the fact "the assessment of accrued interest [from these plans] causes substantial injury to consumers."[486]

The exceptions that permit the existence of deferred interest plans include:

- Promotional rates to deferred interest programs.[487] This permits lender to offer deferred interest plans, which would otherwise run afoul of the prohibition on APR increases for an outstanding balance.
- Double cycle billing for deferred interest programs. Otherwise, the language of the double cycle billing prohibition literally bans deferred interest programs. Outside of this exception, the double cycle billing prohibition prohibits imposing a finance charge as a result of the loss of any time period provided by the creditor in which the consumer may repay a portion of the balance without incurring a finance charge.

In addition, there is a special provision for deferred interest plans in the payment allocation rules. During the last two billing cycles immediately preceding the expiration of the deferred interest period, the creditor must allocate the entire payment in excess of the minimum to the balance on which interest is deferred.[488]

### 8.8.2.3 Minimum Payment Requirements for Deferred Interest Plans

Another problem with deferred interest plans is that the lenders may set the minimum payment as less than the amount that would pay off the balance during the deferred interest period. Thus, a consumer making only the minimum payment will inevitably be retroactively assessed interest for the entire balance for the entire deferred interest period. In fact, some plans did not require any minimum payment during the deferred interest period, and were promoted as "no payment" programs. Federal regulators, however, have required banks under their supervision to have minimum payments for credit card accounts, including for deferred interest plans,[489] of at least 1% of the balance plus any assessed monthly interest and finance charges.[490]

# 8.9 Unilateral Change-in-Terms

## 8.9.1 Expansive Change-in-Terms Provisions in Credit Card Contracts

Many lenders place extremely expansive change-in-terms provisions in their credit card agreements, which allow the lenders to change any of the terms in the agreement at any time.[491] Change-in-terms provisions are the mechanism that

478 *See, e.g.*, Villasenor v. American Signature, Inc., 2007 WL 2025739 (N.D. Ill. July 9, 2007) (merchant charged $705 more for customers who paid using deferred interest plan).

479 Reg. Z, 12 C.F.R. § 1026.16(h) [§ 226.16(h)]. National Consumer Law Center, Truth in Lending § 6.4.6 (7th ed. 2010 and Supp.).

480 National Consumer Law Center, Truth in Lending § 6.5.3.2.7 (7th ed. 2010 and Supp.).

481 *Id.* § 6.7.6.3.

482 *Id.* § 6.7.7.5.

483 *Id.* § 6.7.8.3.2.

484 *Id.* § 6.7.14.

485 National Consumer Law Center, Truth in Lending Ch. 6 (7th ed. 2010 and Supp.).

486 74 Fed. Reg. 5498, 5528 (Jan. 29, 2009).

487 Official Commentary to Reg. Z, 12 C.F.R. § 1026.55(b)(1)-4.i [§ 226.55(b)(1)-4.i].

488 15 U.S.C. § 1666c(b)(2); Reg. Z, 12 C.F.R. § 1026.53(b)(1)(i) [§ 226.53(b)(1)(i)].

489 Timothy Ward, Deputy Director of Examinations, Supervision and Consumer Protection, Office of Thrift Supervision, Memorandum for Chief Executive Officers re: "No Interest, No Payment" Credit Card Programs (Sept. 24, 2009), *available at* www.occ.gov/static/news-issuances/ots/ceo-memos/ots-ceo-memo-321.pdf.

490 *See* § 8.6.8, *supra*.

491 A typical change-in-terms agreement provides:

> We may amend or change any part of your Agreement, including the periodic rates and other charges, or add or remove requirements at any time. If we do so, we will give you notice if required by law of such amendment or change. Changes to the annual percentage rate(s) will apply to your account balance from the effective date of

permits credit card lenders to engage in the abusive practices discussed in this chapter. Some states even permit changes in the terms of a credit agreement without a change-in-terms reservation in the credit card agreement.[492]

Other states require that the credit card agreement reserve the right to change the terms[493]—which the agreements almost certainly do.[494] Consumers are considered to have accepted the lenders change in terms if they use the card or if they do not send a notice of rejection, despite the fact as discussed below, the overwhelming majority of consumers never even read the change-in-terms notice, let alone reach a "meeting of the minds" with the creditors in accepting them.[495] Furthermore, the creditor is only required to establish that it sent the change-in-terms notice, and need not prove that the consumer actually received it.[496]

## 8.9.2 *Problems Created by Unilateral Changes-in-Terms*

There are at least two problems with these notices. First, these expansive change-in-terms provisions deprive consumers of any "benefit of bargain." They make a mockery of contract law because the terms of the "bargain" are illusory. They also undermine the Truth in Lending Act's purpose in ensuring effective disclosure. One court has described change-in-terms provisions as "an Orwellian nightmare, trapped in agreements that can be amended unilaterally in ways they never envisioned."[497]

Second, the vast majority of consumers probably do not read or understand change-in-terms notices. According to the GAO, very few cardholders opt out of changes in terms, and the GAO has questioned the ability of consumers to really exercise a meaningful choice.[498]

While not involving credit cards, the case of *Ting v. AT&T*[499] is instructive. Before mailing out an agreement containing a mandatory arbitration provision, AT&T conducted research designed to predict how consumers would react to the mailing. AT&T then designed its mailing to ensure that consumers would be less likely to read and understand the details of the agreement.

For instance, AT&T's research found that only 25% of customers would actually open up the envelope for the mailing if it was sent separately from the monthly bill. For those customers who did open the envelope, AT&T's research found that only 30% of them would read the entire agreement.

Other research confirms that consumers are unlikely to review the entire notice. One study provided a three page consent form to ninety-one college students to see if they would read the form. The form included a provision in the fifth paragraph that:

> committed participants to administering electric shocks to fellow participants, if instructed to do so,

---

> the change, whether or not the account balance included items billed to the account before the change date and whether or not you continue to use the account. Changes to fees and other charges will apply to your account from the effective date of the change.

Stone v. Golden Wexler & Sarnese, P.C., 341 F. Supp. 2d. 189, 191 (E.D.N.Y. 2004).

492 *See, e.g.*, Del. Code Ann. tit. 5, § 952(a); Va. Code Ann. § 6.1-330.63.

Some courts have justified unilateral changes in terms under the theory that credit card agreements by nature are unilateral contracts. As one court described it:

> When an issuer of a credit card, like MasterCard, Visa or American Express, sends to the holder the card and the form describing the terms for its use, it makes an offer for the formation of a number of contracts by successive acceptances from time to time as the card is used. . . . The credit card relationship, properly analyzed, should be viewed as an offer by the issuer to create the opportunity for a series of unilateral contracts which are actually formed when the holder uses the credit card to buy goods or services or to obtain cash.

Taylor v. First North Am. Nat'l Bank, 325 F. Supp. 2d 1304 (M.D. Ala. 2004) (quoting *In re* Ward, 857 F.2d 1082, 1086–1087 (6th Cir. 1988)).

493 *E.g.*, S.D. Codified Laws § 54-11-10.

494 However, it may be worth parsing the provision in the original agreement which authorized the change in terms. Some of these provisions were not written broadly enough to encompass a change that adds a significant new term (e.g., arbitration). *See, e.g.*, Stone v. Golden Wexler & Sarnese, 341 F. Supp. 2d 189 (E.D.N.Y. 2004) (collection of cases on this issue); Perry v. FleetBoston Fin. Corp., 2004 WL 1508518 (E.D. Pa. July 6, 2004); Badie v. Bank of Am., 79 Cal. Rptr. 2d 273 (Cal. Ct. App. 1998). *See generally* National Consumer Law Center, Consumer Arbitration Agreements § 5.6.4 (6th ed. 2011).

Delaware law permits a change in terms whether or not they are new terms. Del. Code Ann. tit. 5, § 952(a).

495 *See generally* National Consumer Law Center, Consumer Arbitration Agreements § 5.6.4 (6th ed. 2011). *But see* Robertson v. J.C. Penney Co., 484 F. Supp. 2d 561, 567 (S.D. Miss. 2007) (card holder had not "voluntarily and knowingly" agreed to new mandatory arbitration provision in contract, thus provision was not enforceable; noting that waiver of right to access courts was "much more significant and of a different character than changing the terms and conditions of a bank account, assent for which can be obtained simply be the continued use of the account").

In some states, the consumer will not be bound by the change in terms if she does not use the card after receiving the notice. McIntyre v. Household Bank, 2004 WL 1088228 (N.D. Ill. May 14, 2004) (consumer never used credit card, so agreement never became effective).

496 Lawrence v. Household Bank, 343 F. Supp. 2d 1101 (M.D. Ala. 2004); Taylor v. First North Am. Nat'l Bank, 325 F. Supp. 2d 1304 (M.D. Ala. 2004); Kurz v. Chase Manhattan Bank, 319 F. Supp. 2d 457 (S.D.N.Y. 2004). *See also* National Consumer Law Center, Truth in Lending § 6.8.4.9 (7th ed. 2010 and Supp.).

497 Perry v. FleetBoston Fin. Corp., 2004 WL 1508518, at *4 n.5 (E.D. Pa. July 6, 2004).

This court went on to say that it was "reminded of George Orwell's 1946 work, Animal Farm, in which the pigs assume power and change the terms of the animals' social contract, reducing the original Seven Commandments, which included 'All animals are equal,' to one—'All animals are equal, but some animals are more equal than others.' "

498 Government Accountability Office, Credit Cards: Increased Complexity in Rates and Fees Heightens Need for More Effective Disclosures to Consumers, GAO-06-929, at 26 (Sept. 2006), *available at* www.gao.gov/new.items/d06929.pdf.

499 319 F.3d 1126 (9th Cir. 2003).

> even if that participant screamed, cried, and asked for medical assistance. It also required participants to do push-ups, if the experimenter instructed them to do so. Contrary to human-subject protection guidelines, the form required participants to remain in the laboratory until and unless the experimenter allowed them to leave.[500]

An astounding 96% of the college students—eighty-seven of out ninety-one—signed this consent form. The authors reported that: "Very few read any provisions or even skimmed enough to get a vague idea of those provisions. The average time that these participants spent looking at the bogus consent form was 2.0 seconds."[501]

Finally, even if a consumer is savvy enough to read change-in-terms notices, the notices can be full of dense, impenetrable legal jargon that even seasoned practitioners have difficulty understanding.[502] The vast majority of consumers do not have the ability to read and comprehend complex notices.[503] The print in these notices can be small, and even miniscule.[504]

The Credit CARD Act and changes to Regulation Z have somewhat improved change-in-terms notices by mandating that the notices be sent forty-five days in advance for certain changes.[505] For changes in certain critical terms, these notices must be in a particular format,[506] which helps improve readability. However, one of the most frequent changed terms—the addition of a mandatory arbitration clause—is not included in the list of changes for which a forty-five-day notice is required.

## 8.9.3 Credit CARD Act Provisions Relevant to Changes-in-Terms

### 8.9.3.1 Changes-in-Terms Notices

The Credit CARD Act specifically requires credit card lenders to provide forty-five days' notice for any increases in the APR[507] and any significant changes in terms for credit card accounts.[508] Lenders are required to disclose a summary of the changes using a table format similar to credit card application/solicitation table and account-opening table.[509]

Regulation Z limits the requirement to send a change-in-terms notice forty-five days in advance to "significant changes in account terms."[510] Changes to terms that are not significant do not require any advance notice.[511]

The significant terms for which changes require forty-five days' advance notice are:[512]

- Any annual percentage rates.
- Fees for the issuance or availability of credit. This includes annual fees, other periodic fees, and any fees based on account activity or inactivity.
- Fixed finance charges or a minimum interest charge exceeding $1.
- Transaction charges.
- Grace period.
- Balance computation method.
- Cash advance fee or balance transfer fee.
- Late payment fee, over-the-limit fee, or returned-payment fee.
- Fees for required insurance, debt cancellation, or debt suspension coverage.
- Increase in the minimum periodic payment required.[513]

---

500 Debra Pogrund Stark and Jessica M. Choplin, *A License to Deceive: Enforcing Contractual Myths Despite Consumer Psychological Realities*, N.Y.U. J.L. & Bus. 29–30 (Spring 2009).

501 *Id.* at 31.

502 For example, a sample change-in-terms notice states:

> Your Daily Periodic Rate and corresponding APR may increase or decrease from time to time according to the movements up or down of the Index, which is the highest Prime Rate published in the "Money Rates" section of the Midwest Edition of The Wall Street Journal in the last ninety days, before the date on which the billing cycle closed (in other words, the "statement date"). Any variable rate adjustment based on an Index change will be effective as of the first day of the billing cycle, and will apply to the new and outstanding Account balances and transactions subject to that variable rate.

Using the Flesch Reading Ease score built into Microsoft Word, this text rates at a mere 29.7 out of 100 (the higher the better, standard documents score around 60 to 70), and requires a 12th grade reading level. In addition, this particular change-in-terms agreement was written in 4 1/2-point type, in a bill stuffer consisting of sixteen folded panels.

503 *See* Elizabeth Renuart and Diane Thompson, *The Truth, the Whole Truth, and Nothing but the Truth: Fulfilling the Promise of Truth in Lending*, 25 Yale J. on Reg. 181, 207–211 (Summer 2008); Alan M. White & Cathy Lesser Mansfield, *Literacy and Contract*, 13 Stan. L. & Pol'y Rev. 233 (2002) (according to National Adult Literacy Survey, only 3–4% of the American adult population has the documentary literacy skills necessary to utilize a table comparing the features of two credit cards, so as to identify two differences between the cards).

504 *See, e.g.*, Spann v. American Express Travel Related Servs. Co., 224 S.W.3d 698 (Tenn. Ct. App. 2006) (noting in dicta that most of the text in American Express's change in terms notices were "incredibly small," "miniscule," necessitated the use of a magnifying glass, and appeared ill-designed to provide information to large numbers of consumers whose eyesight "falls over a wide range of acuity"); Government Accountability Office, Credit Cards: Increased Complexity in Rates and Fees Heightens Need for More Effective Disclosures to Consumers, GAO-06-929, at 41 (Sept. 2006), *available at* www.gao.gov/new.items/d06929.pdf (documenting numerous problems with credit card disclosures including "mice type" and condensed fonts).

505 *See* § 8.3.2.2.4, *infra*.

506 *Id.*

507 15 U.S.C. § 1637(i)(1).

508 15 U.S.C. § 1637(i)(2).

509 Reg. Z, 12 C.F.R. § 1026.9(c)(2)(iv)(D)(1) [§ 226.9(c)(2)(iv)(D)(1)]. *See* National Consumer Law Center, Truth in Lending § 6.8.4.3.1 (7th ed. 2010 and Supp.).

510 Reg. Z, 12 C.F.R. § 1026.9(c)(2)(i) [§ 226.9(c)(2)(i)].

511 Reg. Z, 12 C.F.R. § 1026.9(c)(2)(iii) [§ 226.9(c)(2)(iii)].

512 Reg. Z, 12 C.F.R. § 1026.9(c)(2)(ii) [§ 226.9(c)(2)(ii)].

513 The minimum payment is not a required disclosure in the account-opening table, but it is a significant term that requires a change-in-terms notice.

• Acquisition of a security interest.[514]

In addition, lenders must provide forty-five days' notice of a decrease in an account's credit limit, if such reduction may result in imposition of an over-the-limit fee or penalty rate.[515] The credit limit reduction can be effective immediately, but no penalty rate or fee can be imposed for exceeding that limit for forty-five days after the notice is given.[516]

Greater detail on change-in-terms notices is provided in another treatise in this series.[517]

### 8.9.3.2 Limited Right to Reject Changes

The Credit CARD Act requires lenders to provide, in any notice of a change in account terms or an increase in APR, a brief statement of the consumer's right to cancel the account before the changes take effect.[518] However, Regulation Z limits this requirement to only certain account terms,[519] and does not require it for increases in the APR.[520]

The FRB interpreted this Credit CARD Act provision to substantively provide consumers with a right to reject changes to a credit card account.[521] The right to reject changes to an account generally applies whenever the lender is required to send a change-in-terms notice that discloses the right to reject.[522]

The Act and Regulation Z also provide that a consumer's rejection of the change or cancellation of the account cannot constitute a default of the cardholder agreement, nor can it trigger an obligation to repay the account in full, i.e., an acceleration of the debt.[523] However, the lender is permitted to increase the minimum payment within certain limits.[524]

Greater detail on the consumer's right to reject changes to an account is provided in another treatise in this series.[525]

## 8.10 Other Credit Card Abuses

### *8.10.1 Debt Collection Abuses*

Credit card lenders, like many creditors, have been known to engage in plain old debt collection abuse—harassment, deception, and unfair practices.[526] However, there are a few practices that are unique to credit card companies and their collectors.

Most important is the fact that credit card companies, or the debt buyers to whom they sell the debt, often initiate collection cases against consumers without any documentation of a credit card agreement signed by the consumer or periodic statements to show transaction activity.[527] Instead, they simply offer up an affidavit from an employee in their loss recovery department and/or sue on an account-stated theory.[528] This deprives the consumer of the ability to challenge erroneous transactions or demonstrate how much of their debt is due to purchases versus finance charges and junk fees. One state has addressed collection practices for credit card debt by forbidding creditors or collectors from contacting the cardholder if the cardholder disputes the debt or any fees or charges, and is represented by a lawyer.[529]

Another practice peculiar to credit card debt is "debt transfer"[530] or "zombie debt" credit cards where credit card lenders buy old credit card debts, and then offer the debtors new credit cards to revive the old debt.[531] Often, the debts are time-barred by the statute of limitations and would constitute stale information on the consumer's credit report under the Fair Credit Reporting Act.[532] Of course, the debt-buying credit card lenders

514 An addition of a security interest is not a required disclosure in the account-opening table, but it is a significant term that requires a change-in-terms notice.

515 Reg. Z, 12 C.F.R. § 1026.9(c)(2)(vi) [§ 226.9(c)(2)(vi)].

516 *See* § 8.3.2.2.4, *supra* (notice of credit limit decreased required to impose penalty rate).

517 National Consumer Law Center, Truth in Lending § 6.8.4 (7th ed. 2010 and Supp.).

518 15 U.S.C. § 1637(i)(3). The rulemaking authority under this provision will be transferred to the Consumer Financial Protection Bureau effective July 21, 2011.

519 Reg. Z, 12 C.F.R. § 1026.9(c)(2)(iv)(B) [§ 226.9(c)(2)(iv)(B)].

520 *Id. See* National Consumer Law Center, Truth in Lending § 7.3.2.2 (7th ed. 2010 and Supp.).

521 Reg. Z, 12 C.F.R. § 1026.9(h)(1) [§ 226.9(h)(1)].

522 Reg. Z, 12 C.F.R. § 1026.9(h)(1) [§ 226.9(h)(1)] (right to reject changes limited to when § 1026.9(c)(2)(iv)(B) [§ 226.9(c)(2)(iv)(B)] requires disclosure of that right). *See also* Official Commentary to Reg. Z, 12 C.F.R. § 1026.h(3)-1 [§ 226.h(3)-1].

523 15 U.S.C. § 1637(i)(4).

524 *Id.* National Consumer Law Center, Truth in Lending § 7.3.4 (7th ed. 2010 and Supp.).

525 National Consumer Law Center, Truth in Lending § 7.3 (7th ed. 2010 and Supp.).

526 *See, e.g.*, MacDermid v. Discover Fin. Servs., 488 F.3d 721 (6th Cir. 2007) (credit card debt collector's accusation of fraud driving consumer to suicide); State v. Cross Country Bank, 703 N.W.2d 562 (Minn. Ct. App. 2005) (listing debt collection abuses by subprime credit card lender).

A credit card lender might be held liable for the harassment and abuse of a collection agency, if the consumer can show that the lender was negligent in the selection or supervision of the collector. Colorado Capital v. Owens, 227 F.R.D. 181 (E.D.N.Y. 2005) (holding that credit card lenders owe duty of reasonable care to their customers, including in the collection of its debts).

527 *See* National Consumer Law Center, Collection Actions Ch. 4 (20011 and Supp.).

528 *Id.* § 4.7.

529 Vt. Stat. Ann. tit. 8, § 14304.

530 This is the Federal Trade Commission's term for these types of cards. Press Release, Federal Trade Commission, Subprime Credit Card Marketer to Provide at Least $114 Million in Consumer Redress to Settle FTC Charges of Deceptive Conduct (Dec. 19, 2008), *available at* www.ftc.gov/opa/2008/12/compucredit.shtm.

531 *See, e.g.*, Complaint, Federal Trade Commission v. CompuCredit, Civ. No. 1:08-CV-1976 (N.D. Ga. June 10, 2008), *available at* www.ftc.gov/os/caselist/0623212/080610compucreditcmplt.pdf (describing "debt transfer" program in which consumers were pitched new credit cards, but in fact did not qualify for the new cards until they paid 25–50% of their old debt balances).

532 *See, e.g.*, Clark v. Pinnacle Credit Serv., 697 F. Supp. 2d 995 (N.D. Ill. 2010) (debt buyer and MetaBank allegedly used debt transfer credit card to collect debt that was time-barred or otherwise legally unenforceable); Deaville v. Capital One Bank, 425 F. Supp. 2d 744 (W.D. La. 2006) (bank used credit card solicitation in attempt to

deceptively omit this critical fact or bury it in fine print.[533] In addition, the debt buyer/credit card lenders may fail to provide required disclosures as debt collectors under the Fair Debt Collection Practices Act.[534] They may also fail to disclose that the seller of the debt only receives a fraction of the amount that is charged to the new credit card account.[535]

Credit card collections are now often sold to debt buyers, often for pennies on the dollar.[536] One issue posed by the practice of credit card debt buying is whether the debt buyer can continue to assess the same rate of interest as permitted to the original credit card lender. The Seventh Circuit has permitted debt buyers to take advantage of the credit card lender's ability to exceed certain interest rate caps under Illinois law.[537]

## 8.10.2 Use of Mandatory Arbitration Clauses

At least at one point in time, almost all credit card lenders have inserted mandatory arbitration provisions into their agreements.[538] Many of these mandatory arbitration provisions have been added using the change-in-terms notices discussed at § 8.9.3.1, *supra*. Courts have held that an arbitration agreement even protects third parties, such as the Visa and MasterCard networks, despite the fact that they are not signatories to the arbitration agreement.[539]

Another treatise in this series discusses mandatory arbitration in depth.[540] In short, mandatory arbitration in credit card disputes is consumer unfriendly because the consumer's only option for relief is an expensive arbitration proceeding (often conducted by arbitration providers that are biased against consumers).[541] As a result of an antitrust case against credit card companies alleging they colluded to include arbitration provisions in their agreements,[542] several of the largest companies have agreed to cease using arbitration agreements until late 2013.[543] Consequently, one study found that only 10% of card agreements included a mandatory arbitration clause, down from 68% in July 2009.[544]

Credit card lenders have even used arbitration provisions offensively, as a lopsided method to obtain judgments against unsuspecting consumers.[545] Some of these consumers include victims of unauthorized use and identity theft.[546]

Many credit card agreements had specified the National Arbitration Forum (NAF) as the arbitration forum provider, and

---

revive and collect time-barred debt); Brink v. First Credit Res., 185 F.R.D. 567 (D. Ariz. 1999).

533 Jessica Silver-Greenberg, *Bringing Expired Debt Back to Life*, Wall St. J., Dec. 21, 2011 (consumers had no knowledge they were paying off expired debt using debt transfer card; West Virginia Attorney General calling one program "abusive").

534 Deaville v. Capital One Bank, 425 F. Supp. 2d 744 (W.D. La. 2006) (dismissing FDCPA claim as time-barred); Carbajal v. Capitol One, F.S.B., 2003 WL 22595265 (N.D. Ill. Nov. 10, 2003). *Cf.* Hernandez v. Midland Credit Mgmt., 2007 WL 2874059 (N.D. Ill. Sept. 25, 2007) (granting summary judgment to consumer; finding debt collector violated FDCPA in making certain statements in solicitation for debt transfer credit card).

535 *See, e.g.*, Clark v. Pinnacle Credit Serv., 697 F. Supp. 2d 995 (N.D. Ill. 2010) (allowing FDCPA and TILA claims to go forward for failure to disclose similar split); Large v. LVNV Funding, L.L.C., 2010 WL 3069409 (W.D. Mich. Aug. 2, 2010) (TILA and FDCPA did not require debt buyer to disclose it was settling plaintiff's debt for twenty cents on each dollar transferred to new credit card account); Miller v. NCO Portfolio Mgmt., 2010 WL 2671910 (S.D. Ind. June 29, 2010) (dismissing FDCPA claims for similar split).

536 *See* National Consumer Law Center, Collections Actions § 1.4 (2011 and Supp.); National Consumer Law Center, Fair Debt Collection § 1.5.4 (6th ed. 2011 and Supp.).

537 Olvera v. Blitt & Gaines, P.C., 431 F.3d 285 (7th Cir. 2005) (assignee debt buyer permitted to collect same interest as original creditor under Illinois Interest Act); PRA III, L.L.C. v. Hund, 846 N.E.2d 965 (Ill. App. Ct. 2006).

However, state law may vary on this point. *See, e.g.,* Tully v. Citibank (South Dakota), N.A., 173 S.W.3d 212 (Tex. App. 2005) (creditor could not recover interest charges because the original contract did not specify the interest rate, and no evidence of rate increase notices introduced into evidence).

538 *See* Ross v. Bank of Am., N.A., 524 F.3d 217 (2d Cir. 2008) (reversing dismissal of antitrust claims brought by cardholders alleging illegal collusion by lenders that resulted in near unanimous use of mandatory arbitration agreements).

539 *In re* Currency Conversion Fee Antitrust Litig., 361 F. Supp. 2d 237 (S.D.N.Y. 2005), *interlocutory review granted*, 2005 WL 1871012 (S.D.N.Y. Aug. 9, 2005). *See generally* National Consumer Law Center, Consumer Arbitration Agreements §§ 7.4, 7.5 (6th ed. 2011).

540 National Consumer Law Center, Consumer Arbitration Agreements §§ 5.2.3, 5.6.4 (6th ed. 2011).

541 In cases handled by the National Arbitration Forum , the creditor or business prevailed over the consumer 94.7% of the time! *Id.* § 12.1.

542 Ross v. Bank of Am., N.A., 524 F.3d 217 (2d Cir. 2008).

543 Final Judgment and Order of Dismissal with Respect to Defendants [Bank of America, JPMorgan Chase, Capital One Bank, and HSBC Bank Nevada, N.A.], Ross v. Bank of Am., N.A., MDL No. 1409 (S.D.N.Y. July 22, 2010).

544 Nick Bourke & Ardie Hollifield, Pew Health Group, Two Steps Forward: After the Credit CARD Act, Credit Cards are Safer and More Transparent—But Challenges Remain (July 2010), *available at* www.pewtrusts.org/uploadedFiles/wwwpewtrustsorg/Reports/Credit_Cards/PEW-CreditCard%20FINAL.PDF.

545 National Consumer Law Center, Consumer Arbitration Agreements Ch. 11 (6th ed. 2011). *See also* Steve Tripoli & Paul Bland, National Consumer Law Center & Trial Lawyers for Public Justice, New Trap Door for Consumers: Card Issuers Use Rubber-Stamp Arbitration to Rush Debts into Default Judgments (Feb. 27, 2005), *available at* www.nclc.org/images/pdf/preemption/archive/fdic_comments-05.pdf.

546 *See, e.g.*, Wolfe v. MBNA Am. Bank, 485 F. Supp. 2d 874 (W.D. Tenn. 2007) (credit card lender commenced arbitration against consumer despite his dispute that he was identity theft victim; notice of arbitration was sent to thief's address even though lender had victim's actual address); Boran v. Columbia Credit Serv., 2006 WL 3388400 (D. Conn. Nov. 21, 2006) (National Arbitration Forum award in favor of credit card lender for $10,640, despite consumer's assertion that she was victim of identity theft by son's girlfriend who was arrested for fraud); MBNA Am. Bank, N.A. v. Cornock, Civ. No. 03-0018 (N.H. Super. Ct. Mar. 20, 2007), *available at* www.nclc.org/unreported (denying petition to enforce arbitration award where consumer alleged that ex-wife opened MBNA credit card account in his name without his permission, and MBNA could not produce credit card application signed by consumer that contained arbitration agreement). *See generally* National Consumer Law Center, Consumer Arbitration Agreements § 11.4.4.1 (6th ed. 2011).

creditors often used NAF to collect credit card debts. In a stunning development, the Minnesota Attorney General obtained a consent order against NAF in which NAF agreed to cease administering any consumer arbitrations nationwide.[547] Thus, the use of arbitration to collect debts has ceased for the short-term future. Other treatises in this series discuss the fallout from the NAF consent order in further detail.[548]

## 8.11 State Claims Challenging Credit Card Abuse

### *8.11.1 Introduction*

Even with the scope of federal preemption, there is still room to bring state law claims against credit card lenders. If an abusive practice is outside of the scope of the Credit CARD Act or violates a provision without a private remedy, practitioners may want to consider claims for breach of contract or the duty of good faith and fair dealing, or under state laws prohibiting unfair or deceptive acts or practices (UDAP statutes).

### *8.11.2 Breach of Contract*

A breach of contract claim is probably one of the first theories that comes to mind when analyzing an abusive credit card practice for legal violations.[549] Obtaining and understanding the underlying contract, however, may not be as easy as it sounds—and not just because the contractual language is obscure. Many consumers do not keep their credit card contracts. Even if they do, it may not be the contract governing the transaction, given the ability of credit card lenders to make unilateral changes in terms.[550] Furthermore, determining which documents are part of the contract, and which are not, may not be an easy task.[551]

Thus, it may be possible that the consumer is legally being charged a 15% interest rate even though the original credit contract provided for a fixed rate of 12%.[552] This possibility must be considered before pursuing any contract claim. Even if the lender's ability to make unilateral changes in terms precludes a breach of contract claim, it may not preclude a claim for breach of the implied covenant of good faith and fair dealing.[553]

Without obtaining the initial credit card agreement and any changes in terms notices, it is thus difficult to evaluate the merits of any claim. If the client does not have everything needed and the creditor will not send the necessary documentation voluntarily, it is available in discovery.

The quandary with planning a case around a discovery strategy is, of course, that it is difficult to determine the initial violation justifying commencing the case at all. One potential way around this problem is to look for a legal claim of any type based on the available documentation. For example, state unfair and deceptive practices arguments may be easier to identify then a breach of contract violation. The UDAP claim then provides a platform to file a case and pursue discovery. Other appropriate claims can then be raised by amending the initial pleadings.

Breach of contract claims can be brought to challenge conduct that violates a contract even if the applicable law permits it. For example, the plaintiffs in *Wells v. Chevy Chase Bank* alleged that the bank violated its agreement, which stated that the interest rate would never exceed 24% and that it was governed by Maryland law.[554] The court held that, despite the fact that the federal Home Owners Loan Act preempts state restrictions on interest rates, the plaintiffs could bring a breach of contract action when the bank did raise its rates over 24%.[555]

As part of the contractual relationship, card lenders may owe their cardholders a duty of good faith and fair dealing.[556] The

---

547 Consent Judgment, State v. National Arbitration Forum, No. 27-CV-09-18550 (Minn. Dist. Ct.—Hennepin Cnty. July 17, 2009), *available in* National Consumer Law Center, Collection Actions Appx. 0.2 (2012 Supp.).

548 National Consumer Law Center, Collection Actions § 8.1a (2012 Supp.).

549 *See, e.g.*, Acosta v. Target, 728 F. Supp. 2d 968 (N.D. Ill. 2010) (declining to dismiss UDAP and breach-of-contract claims); Pownall v. PNC Bank, 2010 WL 3515661 (N.D. Ohio Aug. 31, 2010) (declining to dismiss breach of contract claim); Davis v. Chase Bank USA, N.A., 650 F. Supp. 2d 1073 (C.D. Cal. 2009) (permitting claim for breach of contract to go forward); Chavers v. Fleet Bank (R.I.), N.A., 844 A.2d 666 (R.I. 2004) (dismissing UDAP claim but permitting breach of contract claim to go forward).

One state prohibits breach of contract and other state law claims against a lender, if the conduct challenged could be the subject of an action under the Truth in Lending Act. Johnson v. Capital One Bank, 15 Cal. Rptr. 3d 917 (Cal. Ct. App. 2004) (breach of contract claim for failing to promptly post payments; summary judgment granted for defendant on basis that Virginia state law limits defendant's liability to TILA for conduct that could be subject of TILA claim).

550 *See* § 8.9, *supra*.

551 Holt v. Macy's Retail Holdings, Inc., 719 F. Supp. 2d 903 (W.D. Tenn. 2010) (credit card brochure promising 180-day "hassle-free" return policy did not create a contractual obligation by retailer/creditor).

552 *See* § 8.3.1.2.3, *supra*.

553 *See, e.g.*, *In re* Chase Bank USA, N.A. "Check Loan" Contract Litig., 2009 WL 4063349 (N.D. Cal. Nov. 20, 2009). *See also* Rockwell v. Chase Bank, 2011 WL 2292353 (W.D. Wash. June 7, 2011) (following *In re* Chase Bank USA, N.A. "Check Loan" Contract Litigation); Barrer v. Chase Bank, USA, N.A., 2011 WL 11421 (D. Or. Jan. 4, 2011); Trombley v. Bank of Am. Corp., 715 F. Supp. 2d 290 (D.R.I. 2010).

554 Wells v. Chevy Chase Bank, F.S.B., 832 A.2d 812 (Md. 2003).

555 *Id. See also* Pownall v. PNC Bank, 2010 WL 3515661 (N.D. Ohio Aug. 31, 2010) (Regulation Z may have permitted delay in crediting payment when consumer made payment at branch on due date, but lender may have been violated Cardholder Agreement by charging interest for those five days); *In re* Chase Bank USA, N.A. "Check Loan" Contract Litigation, 2009 WL 4063349 (N.D. Cal. Nov. 20, 2009) (lender's selection of Delaware law made it subject to that state's implied covenant of good faith and fair dealing; rejecting lender's claim that National Bank Act preempted Delaware law).

556 Davis v. Chase Bank USA, N.A., 650 F. Supp. 2d 1073 (C.D. Cal. 2009) (permitting claims for breach of covenant of good faith and fair dealing to go forward); *In re* Chase Bank USA, N.A. "Check Loan" Contract Litigation, 2009 WL 4063349 (N.D. Cal. Nov. 20, 2009) (lender's selection of Delaware law made it subject to that state's implied covenant of good faith and fair dealing); Badie v. Bank of Am., 79 Cal. Rptr. 2d 273 (Cal. Ct. App. 1998); Broder v. MBNA

United Kingdom Office of Fair Trading, which regulates credit cards for that country, has reiterated that credit card practices are subject to a standard of good faith.[557] Another source of contractual duties could be the agreements between banks and merchants; however, cardholders have been unsuccessful in bringing actions claiming they were third-party beneficiaries of these contracts.[558]

### 8.11.3 State UDAP Statutes

Consumers may have claims against credit card lenders under their state's unfair and deceptive acts and practices (UDAP) statute.[559] Private class actions have asserted UDAP claims against credit card lenders for deceptive and unfair practices when charging fees.[560]

Regulators have brought enforcement actions under the Federal Trade Commission Act, which similarly prohibits unfair or deceptive acts or practices. The Office of the Comptroller of the Currency took several enforcement actions under the FTC Act against credit card lenders that committed allegedly unfair or deceptive acts against consumers.[561] The FDIC has taken action against a credit card bank under the FTC Act for sending convenience checks to cardholders, then lowering the cardholders' credit limit causing the checks to be dishonored when the cardholders attempted to use them.[562]

Some state UDAP statutes or regulations provide that a violation of a federal or state consumer protection statute is a violation of the state UDAP statute.[563] Thus, a violation of the Credit CARD Act or other federal rules might constitute a violation of these statutes. Prior to the Credit CARD Act, the OCC had issued two advisory letters identifying a number of potential unfair and deceptive credit card marketing practices.[564] A practice that contravenes one of the OCC advisory letters should be challengeable under a state UDAP statute.

Note that some states may exempt lenders from the scope of their UDAP statutes.[565] In other states, mere breach of contract cannot be brought as a UDAP action.[566]

Furthermore, the issue of preemption must be considered when using UDAP statutes against federally chartered institutions. A UDAP challenge to the size of a fee or its existence will probably be preempted.[567] A challenge to a credit card practice as deceptive or unfair may or may not be.[568] Any

---

Corp., 722 N.Y.S.2d 524 (N.Y. Sup. Ct. 2001) (under Delaware law, every contract carries an implied duty to perform in good faith). *See also* Rockwell v. Chase Bank, 2011 WL 2292353 (W.D. Wash. June 7, 2011) (following *In re* Chase Bank USA, N.A. "Check Loan" Contract Litigation); Barrer v. Chase Bank, USA, N.A., 2011 WL 11421 (D. Or. Jan. 4, 2011); Trombley v. Bank of Am. Corp., 715 F. Supp. 2d 290 (D.R.I. 2010). *But see* McCoy v. Chase Manhattan Bank, 559 F.3d 963 (9th Cir. 2009) (no implied duty of good faith where subject is expressly covered by contract or intentionally silent), *rev'd on other grounds*, 131 S. Ct. 871 (2011); Williams v. Washington Mut. Bank, 2008 WL 115097 (E.D. Cal. Jan. 11, 2008) (creditor-consumer relationship does not create special relationship necessary for claim of breach of good faith and fair dealing under Nevada law); Evans v. Chase Manhattan Bank, N.A., 2006 WL 213740 (N.D. Cal. Jan. 27, 2006) (when contract expressly permitted universal default, no breach of the implied covenant of good faith and fair dealing), *overruled on other grounds by* McCoy v. Chase Manhattan Bank, 559 F.3d 963 (9th Cir. 2009). *But cf.* Kent v. Bank of Am., 2003 WL 327465 (Cal. Ct. App. Feb. 11, 2003) (no duty to set reasonable charges under Arizona contract law; court need not consider contract law principles of unconscionability or bad faith when Arizona law permits bank to set charges at whatever bank desires).

557 United Kingdom Office of Fair Trading, Calculating Fair Default Charges in Credit Card Contracts 10 (Apr. 2006), *available at* www.oft.gov.uk/shared_oft/reports/financial_products/oft842.pdf.

558 *See, e.g.,* Sovereign Bank v. BJ's Wholesale Club, 395 F. Supp. 2d 183 (M.D. Pa. 2005) (collection of cases rejecting third-party beneficiary claims). This decision was reversed in part by 533 F.3d 162 (3d Cir. 2008), but the list of cases cited in the district court opinion is still useful.

559 *See generally* National Consumer Law Center, Unfair and Deceptive Acts and Practices (7th ed. 2008 and Supp.).

560 *See, e.g.,* Rubio v. Capital One Bank, 613 F.3d 1195 (9th Cir. 2010) (reversing dismissal of and allowing UDAP claims to go forward, but upholding dismissal of breach of contract claims); Arevalo v. Bank of America Corp., __ F. Supp. 2d __, 2011 WL 1195973 (N.D. Cal. Mar. 29, 2011) (declining to dismiss claims under California Consumer Legal Remedies Act and Unfair Competition Law over sale of debt protection products); Acosta v. Target, 728 F. Supp. 2d 968 (N.D. Ill. 2010) (declining to dismiss UDAP and breach of contract claims); Nobles v. MBNA Corp., 2009 WL 1854965 (N.D. Cal. June 29, 2009) (approving settlement of claims that convenience check practices violated state UDAP statute and breached duty of good faith or fail dealing); Van Slyke v. Capital One Bank, 503 F. Supp. 2d 1353 (N.D. Cal. 2007) (denying dismissal of challenge to subprime credit card abuses under California unfair competition law, despite contract's choice of Virginia law); Rubin v. MasterCard Int'l, L.L.C., 342 F. Supp. 2d 217 (S.D.N.Y. 2004); Landreneau v. Fleet Fin. Group, 197 F. Supp. 2d 551 (M.D. La. 2002); Bond v. Fleet Bank, 2002 WL 31500393 (D.R.I. Oct. 10, 2002); Sims v. First Consumers Nat'l Bank, 758 N.Y.S.2d 284 (N.Y. App. Div. 2003). *Cf.* Reeder v. HSBC USA, Inc., 2009 WL 4788488 (N.D. Ill. Dec. 8, 2009) (credit card lender promised to waive annual fee if plaintiff canceled within thirty days; when plaintiff did cancel, lender's failure to waive fee could constitute UDAP claim but plaintiff failed to adequately allege damages).

561 *See* § 8.5, *supra.*

562 Order to Cease and Desist, *In re* American Express Centurion Bank, Docket FDIC 09-251b (Dep't of the Treasury, Federal Deposit Insurance Corp. June 30, 2009), *available at* www.fdic.gov/news/news/press/2009/pr09108b.pdf.

563 National Consumer Law Center, Unfair and Deceptive Acts and Practices § 3.2.7 (7th 2008 and Supp.).

564 OCC Advisory Letter AL 2004-10 (Sept. 14, 2004), *available at* www.occ.gov/static/news-issuances/memos-advisory-letters/2004/advisory-letter-2004-10.pdf; OCC Advisory Letter AL 2004-4 (Apr. 28, 2004), *available at* www.occ.gov/static/news-issuances/memos-advisory-letters/2004/advisory-letter-2004-4.pdf. *See also* OCC Advisory Letter AL 2002-3 (Mar. 22, 2002), *available at* www.occ.gov/static/news-issuances/memos-advisory-letters/2002/advisory-letter-2002-3.pdf (discussing unfair or deceptive acts or practices with respect lending and marketing practices).

565 *See* National Consumer Law Center, Truth in Lending § 2.6.3 (7th ed. 2010 and Supp.); National Consumer Law Center Unfair and Deceptive Acts and Practices § 2.2.1 (7th ed. 2008 and Supp.).

566 National Consumer Law Center Unfair and Deceptive Acts and Practices § 5.6.5.1 (7th ed. 2008 and Supp.).

567 *See* §§ 3.2, 3.4, *supra.*

568 *Compare* Rose v. Chase Bank USA, N.A. 513 F.3d 1032 (9th Cir. 2008) (UDAP claim preempted where based on national bank's

preemption challenge by a national bank after July 1, 2011 must be analyzed under the Dodd-Frank Act's new preemption standard for these banks.[569]

In addition, some states exempt from UDAP coverage any practice permitted or regulated by statute or a regulatory body.[570] Another court oddly held that a credit card solicitation did not violate a state UDAP statute by stating that the consumer had been pre-approved for a credit limit "up to" $2,500 when most consumers received only $200 in credit, because the lender had not violated the Fair Credit Reporting Act's requirements for use of credit reports.[571]

Even if a lender is in compliance with the Truth in Lending Act, its advertisement may be deceptive in violation of a state UDAP statute.[572] For example, the Ninth Circuit held that a lender complied with TILA's disclosure requirements but could be found in violation of state UDAP law by deceptively offering an interest rate that the lender knew the consumer would not qualify for.[573] The Federal Reserve Board and FDIC have noted that "a transaction that is in technical compliance with [the Truth in Lending Act] or [the Truth in Savings Act] may nevertheless violate the FTC Act. For example, consumers could be misled by advertisements of 'guaranteed' or 'lifetime' interest rates when the creditor or depository institution intends to change the rates, whether or not the disclosures satisfy the technical requirements of TILA or TISA."[574] The OCC has made similar statements.[575]

## *8.11.4 Other Claims*

In addition to breach of contract and UDAP claims, there are potential claims available under a number of other statutes and common law theories, such as the Racketeer Influenced and Corrupt Organizations Act,[576] unconscionability,[577] breach of the duty of good faith and fair dealing,[578] breach of fiduciary duty,[579] and common law fraud.[580] The advantage of federal statutory and state common law claims is practitioners may be more able to avoid a preemption issue than for state statutory claims.

In contemplating state law claims against a credit card lender, practitioners should be wary of choice of law issues. For example, some credit card agreements state they are governed by Delaware law, which some courts have found to be very favorable for credit card lenders.[581] Practitioners have had mixed success avoiding these choice of law provisions.[582]

---

failure to make disclosures required by California law), *and* Kauinui v. Citibank (South Dakota), N.A., 2009 WL 3530373 (D. Haw. Oct. 28, 2009) (UDAP claim based on TILA violations and failure to make APR disclosures was preempted), *and* Augustine v. FIA Card Servs., N.A., 485 F. Supp. 2d 1172 (E.D. Cal. 2007) (UDAP claim for deception was preempted because it required bank to make disclosures in addition to those required by federal law), *with* Davis v. Chase Bank USA, N.A., 650 F. Supp. 2d 1073 (C.D. Cal. 2009) (plaintiff brought UDAP claims challenging payment allocation abuse; claims based on deceptiveness of lender's offer survived preemption, but unfair challenge to practice itself did not), *and* Parks v. MBNA Am. Bank, N.A., 109 Cal. Rptr. 3d 248 (Cal. Ct. App. 2010) (California law requiring disclosures for credit card "convenience checks" not preempted; disagreeing with Rose v. Chase Bank USA, N.A.), *review granted and op. superseded by* 238 P.3d 1251 (Cal. 2010).

569 *See* § 3.2, *supra.*

570 National Consumer Law Center, Unfair and Deceptive Acts and Practices § 2.3.3 (7th ed. 2008 and Supp.).

571 Jewett v. Capitol One Bank, 2006 WL 1085895 (Cal. Ct. App. Apr. 26, 2006).

572 People v. Applied Card Sys., 894 N.E.2d 1 (N.Y. 2008) (TILA does not preempt UDAP claim over deceptive credit card advertisement). *But see* Shah v. American Express Co., 2009 WL 3234594 (D.N.J. Sept. 30, 2009) (dismissing UDAP claim for failure to disclose amount of penalty fees in credit card solicitation, because plaintiffs did not apply for the credit card or use it and thus were not aggrieved consumers).

573 Hauk v. JP Morgan Chase, 552 F.3d 1114 (9th Cir. 2009).

574 Federal Reserve Board and Federal Deposit Insurance Corp., Unfair or Deceptive Acts or Practices by State-Chartered Banks (Mar. 11, 2004), *available at* www.federalreserve.gov/boardDocs/press/bcreg/2004/20040311/attachment.pdf.

575 OCC Advisory Letter AL 2002-3, at 6 (Mar. 22, 2002), *available at* www.occ.gov/static/news-issuances/memos-advisory-letters/2002/advisory-letter-2002-3.pdf.

576 *See* § 7.8.6.2, *supra.*

577 *See* § 2.4.7, *supra. See, e.g.,* Citibank v. DeCristoforo, 28 Mass. L. Rptr. 139 (Mass. Super. Ct. Jan. 4, 2011) (credit card rate was unconscionable, despite National Bank Act). *But see* Rockwell v. Chase Bank, 2011 WL 2292353 (W.D. Wash. June 7, 2011) (no claim for unconscionability when Delaware law permitted unilateral changes-in-terms contract provision); Jaffe v. Capital One Bank, 2010 WL 691639 (S.D.N.Y. Mar. 1, 2010) (consumer charged late fee despite electronic payment made one day prior to due date; consumer failed to adequately pleaded claims for fraud, conversion, or unjust enrichment); *In re* Chase Bank USA, N.A. "Check Loan" Contract Litig., 2009 WL 4063349 (N.D. Cal. Nov. 20, 2009); Williams v. Washington Mut. Bank, 2008 WL 115097 (E.D. Cal. Jan. 11, 2008) (rejecting claim that retroactive rate increases constituted an illegal penalty under Nevada law); Penner v. Chase Bank USA, N.A., 2006 WL 2192435 (W.D. Wash. Aug. 1, 2006) (universal default is specifically authorized by Delaware law and thus cannot be unconscionable); Citibank, S.D., N.A. v. Palma, 646 S.E.2d 635 (N.C. Ct. App. July 3, 2007) (doubling of interest rate was authorized by South Dakota law and thus cannot be unconscionable).

578 *See* § 2.4.10, *supra.*

579 *See* § 2.4.5, *supra. Cf.* Colorado Capital v. Owens, 227 F.R.D. 181 (E.D.N.Y. 2005) (credit card lender owes duty of reasonable care, different from fiduciary duty, to cardholder).

580 *See* § 2.4, *supra.*

581 For example, Delaware has an extremely expansive law permitting credit card lenders to unilaterally change the terms of an agreement. Del. Code. Ann. tit. 5, § 952(a). *See, e.g.,* McCoy v. Chase Manhattan Bank, 654 F.3d 971 (9th Cir. 2011), *on remand from,* 131 S. Ct. 871 (2011) (applying Delaware law, holding that rate increase was permitted under Delaware Banking Act); Shaner v. Chase Bank USA, N.A., 587 F.3d 488 (1st Cir. 2009) (concluding that Delaware law permits discretionary retroactive rate increase); Swanson v. Bank of Am., N.A., 559 F.3d 653 (7th Cir. 2009) (penalty rate increase was permissible under Delaware law); Penner v. Chase Bank USA, N.A., 2006 WL 2192435 (W.D. Wash. Aug. 1, 2006) (universal default is specifically authorized by Delaware law and thus cannot be unconscionable).

582 *Compare* Swanson v. Bank of Am., N.A., 559 F.3d 653 (7th Cir. 2009) (applying Delaware law over Illinois, finding penalty rates were permissible under Delaware law), *and* Cohen v. Chase Bank, N.A. 679 F. Supp. 2d 582 (D.N.J. 2010) (same as *Forness* but

## 8.11.5 Preemption and Credit Cards

### 8.11.5.1 General

The problems involved in analyzing an abusive credit card practice for legal violations is always complicated by the complex scheme of federal preemption of state law governing credit, because most credit card lenders are financial institutions who can avail themselves of the benefits of preemption.[583] Thus, it is rarely the substantive law of the state where the consumer lives that is applicable.[584] Practitioners cannot assume that a creditor has disclosed an illegal term simply by checking their own state's law.

Because of the doctrine of rate exportation, interest rates, as well as fees and charges, will certainly be governed by the law of the state where the lender is incorporated.[585] Other state laws governing credit cards, such as those mandating disclosures or prohibiting certain practices, may or may not be preempted by the National Bank Act and OCC regulations (for national banks).[586] Any preemption challenge after July 1, 2011 to the latter type of state law must be analyzed under the Dodd-Frank Act's new preemption standard for national banks.[587]

### 8.11.5.2 TILA Preemption

In contrast, the Truth in Lending Act (including the Credit CARD Act provisions) has a narrower scope of preemption.[588] Other than state laws relating to disclosures in credit applications, solicitations, or renewal notices, TILA does not preempt state laws governing credit cards (or open-end credit in general) as long as these laws are not inconsistent with TILA requirements. For example, a state law concerning periodic statements in general would not be preempted by TILA.[589] Neither is a claim for deceptive advertising in a credit card solicitation.[590]

Despite the fact that TILA itself has a narrow scope of preemption, the ability of states to require credit card disclosures is significantly constrained with respect to federally chartered financial institutions, which constitute the vast majority of credit card lenders. A federal court has held that the preemption provisions in the various banking statutes, and not TILA's preemption standard, control when analyzing whether state laws regarding credit card disclosures are preempted.[591]

## 8.12 Assisting Consumers Overwhelmed by Credit Card Debt

In many cases, consumers who come forward with problems concerning their credit card accounts are financially overwhelmed. Identifying state law or Truth in Lending violations may only partially resolve the consumers' needs. Consumers may be able to obtain relief by use of strategies such as debt prioritization, bankruptcy, and aggressive foreclosure defense. At the same time, practitioners should also consider educating consumers about careful use of available credit to avoid new problems in the future. Materials to educate consumers with credit card problems are available in National Consumer Law Center, *Guide to Surviving Debt* (2010 ed.).[592]

---

declining to enforce class action waiver as contrary to New Jersey public policy), *and* Forness v. Cross County Bank, 2006 WL 726233 (S.D. Ill. Mar. 20, 2006) (applying Delaware choice of law provision to compel arbitration), *and* Samadi v. MBNA Am. Bank, N.A. 2005 WL 6111467 (S.D. Ga. June 10, 2005), *adopted by* 2005 WL 6111614 (S.D. Ga. July 8, 2005), *and* Carroll v. MBNA Am. Bank, 220 P.3d 1080 (Idaho 2009), *and* Citibank, S.D., N.A. v. Palma, 646 S.E.2d 635 (N.C. Ct. App. 2007) (applying South Dakota law to find penalty rates not unconscionable), *with* Van Slyke v. Capital One Bank, 503 F. Supp. 2d 1353 (N.D. Cal. 2007) (permitting challenge to credit card abuses under California unfair competition law, despite contract's choice of Virginia law), *and* Coady v. Cross Country Bank, 729 N.W.2d 732 (Wis. Ct. App. 2007) (declining to apply Delaware law because of the important public policy embodied in Wisconsin Consumer Act). *See also* Brack v. Omni Loan Co., 80 Cal. Rptr. 3d 275 (Cal. Ct. App. 2008) (permitting challenge under California Finance Lenders Law to practices of Nevada consumer lender).

583 *See generally* Ch. 3, *supra*.

584 *See generally* § 3.4, *supra*.

585 *See* § 3.4, *supra*.

586 *See* § 3.2, *supra*.

587 *See* § 3.2.4, *supra*.

588 National Consumer Law Center, Truth in Lending §§ 2.6.3 (general TILA preemption), 6.5.6 (TILA preemption for credit card application and solicitation disclosures), 6.8.7.5 (change in insurance coverage disclosure), 7.9.10 (Fair Credit Billing Act preemption) (7th ed. 2010 and Supp.).

589 Reg. Z, Official Commentary to Reg. Z, 12 C.F.R. § 1026.28(d)-3 [§ 226.28(d)-3].

590 Acosta v. Target, 728 F. Supp. 2d 968 (N.D. Ill. 2010) (fraud and UDAP claims for misleading statements not preempted by TILA); People v. Applied Card Sys., 894 N.E.2d 1 (N.Y. 2008).

591 American Bankers Ass'n v. Lockyer, 239 F. Supp. 2d 1000 (E.D. Cal. 2002). *See also* Parks v. MBNA Am. Bank, N.A., 109 Cal. Rptr. 3d 248 (Cal. Ct. App. 2010) (agreeing with American Bankers Ass'n v. Lockyer, but requiring bank to make factual showing that California disclosure requirement imposed significant burdens), *review granted and op. superseded by* 238 P.3d 1251 (Cal. 2010).

592 Information about ordering is available on the NCLC website, www.nclc.org, or by contacting the Publications Department at 617-542-9595 or by faxing 617-542-8028.

# Chapter 9 Payday Loans

## 9.1 Background

### 9.1.1 Introduction

Payday lending has grown tremendously across the country over the past twenty years.[1] Marketed to those who have no savings but a steady income that is barely enough to make ends meet, these short-term, high-cost, unsecured loans are available from storefronts, banks, credit unions, and on the Internet. Payday lenders tout their loans as a quick fix for life's emergencies with fees that appear deceptively low compared to the cost of late fees on credit cards or bouncing a check. But in reality, payday loans have proven to be a costly trap for borrowers. When measured on an annual percentage rate basis, payday loans typically have triple-digit rates, making them one of the most expensive forms of credit available. Few borrowers can afford to repay their loans by the next payday, leading to multiple "rollovers" and additional fees.

There is no single federal regulatory scheme governing payday lending. Regulation is a patch work of federal and state laws with wide variation between states. A minority of states forbid payday lending entirely while others regulate small-dollar credit in a variety of ways. Some lenders go to great lengths to evade state laws. Some Internet lenders claim to be based in states with minimal regulation or a foreign country. Others claim to have sovereign immunity because they are allegedly owned by Native American Indian tribes. Some federally chartered banks offer their own version of payday loans and, by virtue of federal preemption, are able to ignore most state usury caps.

All lenders, however, are subject to a number of federal laws. The Truth in Lending Act imposes disclosure requirements.[2] The Equal Credit Opportunity Act bans discrimination and requires lenders to give borrowers important notices.[3] For military servicemembers and their families, the Military Lending Act may be the most important federal limit on payday lending because it imposes a 36% APR usury cap on some payday loans.[4]

1 *See* Gary Rivlin, Broke, USA: From Pawnshops to Poverty, Inc.—How the Working Poor Became Big Business (2010) (describing growth of payday lending industry).

2 *See* § 2.2.2, *supra*. *See generally* National Consumer Law Center, Truth in Lending (7th ed. 2010 and Supp.).

3 *See generally* National Consumer Law Center, Credit Discrimination (5th ed. 2009 and Supp.).

4 *See* § 2.2.5, *supra*.

The future of payday lending, however, is uncertain. The Consumer Financial Protection Bureau has jurisdiction over state and federal, bank and non-bank payday lenders. Though it has not issued any regulations governing lenders, in January 2012 it announced that that it would begin "giving payday lenders much more attention."[5]

### 9.1.2 How Payday Loans Work

A payday loan is a small, short-term cash loan. The typical loan matures in fourteen-days, usually coming due around the borrower's next payday. However, some payday lenders structure their products as longer term loans to avoid state payday loan definitions. A 2009 study found a median loan size of $350, though loans may range from $100 to $1,500 depending on the maximum allowed by state law.[6] Payday lenders do not charge interest but, instead, usually assess a fee per $100 borrowed. This fee is typically between $15 and $35 per $100 borrowed. The basic characteristics of a payday loan—a short repayment period and high fee (relative to the small amount borrowed)—combine to produce an obscenely high, triple-digit, annual percentage rate.[7] The problem of high rates is exacerbated when borrowers need to pay additional fees or borrow from other lenders to avoid default on loans they cannot afford to repay.

The overwhelming majority of payday loans are made by one of thousands of storefront lenders or Internet payday websites. Payday lenders emphasize the speed and simplicity of getting a loan and market themselves to borrowers with poor credit.[8] Consumers need only present identification and dem-

5 Press Release, Consumer Financial Protection Bureau, Consumer Financial Protection Bureau Examines Payday Lending (Jan. 19, 2012), *available at* www.consumerfinance.gov/pressreleases/consumer-financial-protection-bureau-examines-payday-lending/.

6 Uriah King & Leslie Parrish, Center for Responsible Lending, Phantom Demand: Short-Term Due Date Generates Need for Repeat Payday Loans, Accounting for 76% of Total Volume 15 (July 2009), *available at* www.responsiblelending.org/payday-lending/research-analysis/phantom-demand-short-term-due-date-generates-need-for-repeat-payday-loans-accounting-for-76-of-total-volume.html.

7 Robert W. Snarr, Jr., Fed. Reserve Bank of Phila., No Cash 'til Payday: The Payday Lending Industry, Compliance Corner (1st Q. 2002) *available at* www.philadelphiafed.org/bank-resources/publications/compliance-corner/2002/first-quarter/q1cc1_02.cfm.

8 *See, e.g.*, Personal Cash Advance, www.largecashloans.com (advertising "Get your money fast and easy from the privacy of your own home"); Payloan.com, www.paydayloan.com/new-b/ (advertising "No credit is required. Bad credit payday loans are our specialty.").

onstrate that they have a steady source of income—such as a job or Social Security benefits—and a bank account.[9] Lenders do not underwrite for ability to repay and do not use conventional credit checks or FICO scores. At most, they use specialized credit reporting services that track the subprime market and weed out only the very worst credit risks.[10] In some states they are also required to check a database of payday borrowers to comply with laws restricting the number of loans that may be extended to a borrower.[11]

The consumer's bank or prepaid card account is central to how payday lenders operate.[12] Lenders require the borrower to provide either a present or post-dated check for the amount borrowed plus the finance charge or authorize electronic payment from the borrower's bank account.[13] Sometimes lenders do both. Internet payday lenders dispense with the paper check, taking authorization for either a remotely-created check[14] and/or an electronic debit. Authorization for electronic access to the consumer's account enables payday lenders to avoid laws that permit borrowers to stop payment on checks.[15] Some lenders have gone a step further and use contracts authorizing access to *any* bank account the consumer has.

After approving a borrower and funding the loan, the lender holds the borrower's check or authorization until the next payday as security for repayment. When the loan comes due the borrower can pay it off in full. But many borrowers cannot afford to do so. Instead lenders encourage borrowers to "rollover" the loan (paying the loan fee again to extend the term for another pay-period)[16] or, where rollovers are prohibited, to repay one loan by taking out another. Some lenders also permit the consumer to pay down the loan principal in installments of a specified amount, with a new finance charge imposed each pay period.[17] These practices drive-up the advertised "low" cost of payday loans to amounts that can ultimately exceed the principal borrowed.[18]

In another variation found among those receiving government benefits, especially Social Security pensions and disability, the lender essentially hijacks the borrower's monthly benefit check by having the beneficiary sign documents authorizing the benefits to be deposited in a bank account under the lender's control.[19] The lender then deducts an amount sufficient to repay the loan and gives the borrower the remaining balance. What is left of the benefit payment is unlikely to be enough to meet the beneficiary's expenses, leading the beneficiary to take another loan and incur more fees. New rules governing the payment of federal benefits to accounts that are not in the name of the beneficiary should put an end to these practices.[20]

The payment mechanisms used by payday lenders are governed by an alphabet soup of rules. Payday lenders rely on paper checks and electronic authorizations to debit borrowers' accounts. The physical difference between these two payment methods is increasingly superficial. But there remain important substantive differences in the governing law and consumers' rights. Determining what law applies to a transaction is difficult. A full explanation of payment mechanisms and the relevant law can be found in another NCLC treatise, *Consumer Banking and Payments Law*.[21]

### 9.1.3 Description of the Borrowers

There have been a number of attempts to identify the typical payday borrower. While the results of studies have varied, a few common factors have become apparent.

- *Payday borrowers are disproportionately people of color.* While uniform, national data is not available, studies have shown that a disproportionate number of African Americans

9 Nathalie Martin, *1,000% Interest—Good While Supplies Last: A Study of Payday Loan Practices and Solutions*, Ariz. L. Rev. 563, 572 n.33 (Fall 2010) (discussing findings of Ronald Mann & James Hawkins, *Just Until Payday*, 54 UCLA L. Rev. 855 (2007)).

10 National Consumer Law Center, Stopping the Payday Loan Trap: Alternatives that Work, Ones that Don't 4 (June 2010), *available at* www.nclc.org/images/pdf/high_cost_small_loans/payday_loans/report-stopping-payday-trap.pdf; Fed. Reserve Bank of Phila., Robert W. Snarr, Jr., No Cash 'til Payday: The Payday Lending Industry, Compliance Corner (1st Q. 2002), *available at* www.philadelphiafed.org/bank-resources/publications/compliance-corner/2002/first-quarter/q1cc1_02.cfm.

11 *See, e.g.*, Ala. Code § 5-18A-13(o); Ind. Code § 24-4.5-7-404 (commercial database may be used to comply with restriction on number of loans). A number of states use Veritec Solutions, L.L.C. as a vendor.

12 Ohio Neighborhood Fin., Inc. v. Scott, No. 09CVF01488 (Elyria Mun. Ct., Lorain Cnty. Ohio Mar. 25, 2011) (appeal pending), *available at* www.nclc.org/unreported (describing history of payday lending in Ohio; observing "In the modern age, the ubiquitous checking account became the target.").

13 *See, e.g.*, Stone v. Advance Am., 2011 WL 5377638 (S.D. Cal. Nov. 7, 2011) ("On Oct. 21 Plaintiff gave defendants a check for $300. Defendants agreed not to cash it until Nov. 5 and immediately gave Plaintiff $255 in cash, retaining the $45 difference as a fee.").

14 A remotely created check, often called a demand draft, is a paper check that is created from the borrower's bank account information and does not contain the borrower's signature but may be negotiated just like a traditional paper check. *See* 12 C.F.R. pt. 229, app. E (commentary on § 229.2(fff)).

15 *See* § 9.2.8, *infra*.

16 The National Credit Union Administration has described rolling over a payday loan as a "situation[] in which a borrower is charged additional fees for extending or re-borrowing' funds to avoid delinquency." 75 Fed. Reg. 58,285, 58,286 (Sept. 24, 2010).

17 *See, e.g.*, Baillie v. Account Receivable Mgmt. of Florida, 2011 WL 566817 (N.D. Cal. Feb. 14, 2011) (quoting loan terms: "On your fifth renewal and every renewal thereafter, your loan will be paid down by $50. . . . [so] your account will be debited the finance charge plus $50 on the due date.").

18 *See, e.g.*, Ranzy v. Single N Corp., 2011 WL 864908 (S.D. Tex. Mar. 10, 2011) (describing loan for $500 with $125 fee; after multiple renewals borrower owed at least $650 in fees).

19 *See* Ellen E. Schultz And Theo Francis, *High-Interest Lenders Tap Elderly, Disabled*, Wall St. Journal, Feb. 12, 2008, *available at* http://online.wsj.com/article/SB120277630957260703.html. *See* Consumer Federation of America, Consumers Union et al., Comments to Dep't of Treasury Fin. Mgmt. Serv. (July 13, 2010) (extensively discussing these practices), *available at* www.nclc.org/images/pdf/public_benefits/comments-fiscal-fms-2010.pdf.

20 *See* National Consumer Law Center, Consumer Banking and Payments Law § 9.3.2A (4th ed. 2009 and Supp.).

21 (4th ed. 2009 and Supp.).

and, according to some studies, Latinos are payday loan borrowers.[22] There also appears to be a higher concentration of storefront payday lenders in African American and Latino neighborhoods in some parts of the country.[23]

- *Payday loan borrowers have regular incomes.* A long-term study of Colorado borrowers found a mean gross income of about $29,500 per year.[24] Another study of national data found similar results.[25] The average Colorado borrower had been at the same job for several years.[26]
- *Many payday loan borrowers are benefit recipients.* A survey commissioned by the California Department of Corporations found that 10.6% of payday loan users are public benefit recipients, plus another 4.9% listed disability and 2.9% listed retirement as their regular source of income.[27] Similarly, in Colorado one of the three most often cited occupations is benefit recipient.[28] In 2008, Social Security and Supplemental Security Income and other public benefit recipients were estimated to pay $860 million per year in payday loan finance charges.[29]
- *Payday borrowers may have access to other forms of credit.* Payday lenders often claim to be serving those who do not have credit files or cannot obtain credit. That is partly true, but many payday borrowers have credit cards and use other forms of credit.[30]
- *Borrowers use payday lenders because they are easy and fast.* The top reasons that consumers cite for taking out payday loans is that they are quick, easy to get approved, and convenient.[31] Though borrowers also cite the inability to get money at a bank or credit union and maxed out credit cards, those are not typically borrowers' top reasons.
- *Loans are often used to cover ordinary expenses, not emergencies.* Various studies have found that 40 to 60% of consumers take out payday loans to cover routine expenses like utility bills, rent or groceries, or nonessential items.[32] Much payday loan demand is also created by a prior payday loan.[33]

---

22 Wei Li et al., Ctr. for Responsible Lending, Predatory Profiling: The Role of Race and Ethnicity in the Location of Payday Lenders in California 4, n.5 (Mar. 26, 2009), *available at* www.responsiblelending.org/payday-lending/research-analysis/predatory-profiling.pdf.

The CRL report referred to similar findings from other studies: Paige Skiba and Jeremy Tobacman. Do Payday Loans Cause Bankruptcy? tbl.1 (Feb. 19, 2008) (showing African Americans and Latinos made up disproportionate percentage of borrowers in comparison to percentage of adult population from census); Payday Advance Customer Satisfaction Survey, Cypress Research Group (May 2004) (showing disproportionate share of African-American borrowers).

23 *See* National People's Action, Credit Segregation: Concentrations of Predatory Lenders in Communities of Color 4 (Feb. 2011) ("the report finds that black and Latino neighborhoods [in the Midwest] also have the highest concentration of payday lenders. In these communities . . . payday lenders are three times as concentrated as compared to other neighborhoods."); Robin A. Prager, *Determinants of the Locations of Payday Lenders, Pawnshops and Check-Cashing Outlets* 21 (Fed. Reserve Bd. Working Paper 2009-33) ("I find that [alternative financial services providers] are more prevalent in areas where a large percentage of the population is black or lacks a high school diploma. However, contrary to previous studies, I find that AFSPs generally avoid the poorest areas and areas with high concentrations of Hispanics"), *available at* www.federalreserve.gov/pubs/feds/2009/200933/200933pap.pdf; Sharon Hermanson & George Gaberlavage, AARP Pub. Policy Inst., The Alternative Financial Services Industry, Issue Brief 51, at 4, fig. 4 (2001) ("low-income and minority households are 'significantly more likely' to have payday-loan-service businesses located within one mile of their homes than higher-income, nonminority homes"), *available at* http://assets.aarp.org/rgcenter/consume/ib51_finance.pdf.

24 Colorado Attorney General, Payday Lending Demographic and Statistical Information for July 2000 through Dec. 2009 (Mar. 2010), *available at* www.coloradoattorneygeneral.gov/sites/default/files/uploads/DDLASummary2009corr.pdf.

25 Center for American Progress, Who Borrows from Payday Lenders? An Analysis of Newly Available Data 7 (Mar. 2009) (analyzing Federal Reserve Board's Survey of Consumer Finances and finding a median of $30,892 for 2007).

26 Colorado Attorney General, Payday Lending Demographic and Statistical Information for July 2000 through Dec. 2009 (Mar. 2010), *available at* www.coloradoattorneygeneral.gov/sites/default/files/uploads/DDLASummary2009corr.pdf.

27 California Budget Project, Payday Loans: Taking the Pay Out of Payday 31 (Sept. 2008) ("Cal. Budget Project") (reporting on study by Calif. Dep't of Corp.), *available at* www.cbp.org/pdfs/2008/080926_paydaychartbook.pdf.

28 Colorado Uniform Consumer Credit Code Administrator, Payday Lending Demographic and Statistical Information: July 2000 through Dec. 2008 (Mar. 1, 2010).

29 *Jean Ann Fox, Consumer Federation of America, Testimony on Protecting Social Security Beneficiaries from Predatory Lending and Other Harmful Financial Institution Practices, Subcommittee on Social Security, Committee on Ways & Means* (June 24, 2008).

30 Rebecca Blank & Michael Barr, Eds., Russell Sage Found., Insufficient Funds: Savings, Assets, Credit and Banking Among Low-Income Households 89 (2009) (43% of payday users had paid a late fee on a credit card); Cal. Budget Project 25–26 (54% of payday borrowers have a bank credit card and that 29% had home equity-lines of credit).

31 Federal Deposit Insurance Corp., National Survey of Unbanked and Underbanked Households 43 (Dec. 2009); Texas Appleseed, Short-Term Cash, Long-Term Debt: A Survey of Payday Borrowers at 9 (Apr. 2009).

32 Federal Deposit Insurance Corp., National Survey of Unbanked and Underbanked Households 42 (Dec. 2009) (38% of underbanked households that used some form of alternative financial service credit product did so to pay for basic living expenses, 6.2% did for special gifts or luxuries, 15.4% to make up for lost income, 7.4% for house repairs or to buy an appliance, 4.5% for car repairs, 2.3% for medical expenses, 1.6% for school or childcare expenses, and 24.9% for other reasons); Cal. Budget Project 25 (50% to pay bills; 22.3%, to buy groceries and other necessities; 10.3% for an emergency; 1.8% to repair a vehicle); Texas Appleseed, Short-Term Cash, Long-Term Debt: A Survey of Payday Borrowers 9 (Apr. 2009) (over half cited the need to pay routine utility bills, to buy groceries, gas or to pay rent; 38% had an emergency); Michael S. Barr, Payments, Federal Reserve Bank of Philadelphia, Credit and Savings Among Low- and Moderate-Income Households: Evidence from the Detroit Area Survey (May 22, 2007) (60% used payday loans to pay for everyday expenses; 11% paid credit card or bank debt).

33 Uriah King & Leslie Parrish, Center for Responsible Lending, Phantom Demand: Short-Term Due Date Generates Need for Repeat Payday Loans, Accounting for 76% of Total Volume 15 (July 2009), *available at* www.responsiblelending.org/payday-lending/research-analysis/phantom-demand-short-term-due-date-generates-need-for-repeat-payday-loans-accounting-for-76-of-total-volume.html.

### 9.1.4 Problems and Abuses

As payday lending has spread across the country, a growing body of independent academic research has documented the adverse impact on the consumers who use payday loans. Cash-strapped consumers rarely have the ability to repay the entire loan when their payday arrives because doing so would leave little or nothing on which to live until the next paycheck. Lenders encourage consumers repay one loan with another or to return for new credit a few days after paying off a previous loan.[34] The result is that the consumer pays another round of charges and fees and remains trapped in debt.

Payday lenders depend on this repeat borrowing despite their marketing messages that payday loans are for occasional, infrequent use. The CEO of Cash America noted that "you've got to get that customer in, work to turn him into a repetitive customer, long-term customer, because that's really where the profitability is."[35] A study by the Center for Responsible Lending found that 76% of payday loans are churned loans—ones that are made not because of a new need for credit, but because the borrower needs a new loan to pay off a previous, unaffordable payday loan.[36] This debt trap gives rise to numerous related problems:

- *Using payday loans increases the chance of losing a bank account.* Payday lenders often claim that payday loans are used to prevent bank overdrafts, but they actually may increase them and jeopardize the bank account. One study found that an increase in the number of payday loan outlets in a county is associated with an 11% increase in involuntary bank account closures, even when other variables such as income and poverty rate are taken into account.[37]
- *Using payday loans increases bankruptcy filings.* In a large Texas study, researchers found that payday borrowers were about 88% more likely to file for chapter 13 bankruptcy in the next two years than the rest of the Texas population.[38] Similarly, a Detroit area study found almost three times the rate of bankruptcy among payday loan users, compared to similar low to moderate-income households without payday loans.[39]
- *Using payday loans causes financial hardship for families.* A University of Chicago Business School doctoral student compared households in states with and without access to payday loans over a five-year period and found that access to payday loans increases the chances a family will face hardship, have difficulty paying bills, and have to delay medical care, dental care, and prescription drug purchases.[40] A Detroit area study found double the rate of evictions and phone cut-offs among payday borrowers and almost three times the rate of having utilities shut off.[41]
- *Payday loan users who also have credit cards are roughly twice as likely to become delinquent on the card.* In examining a large sample of payday loan users who also had a credit card from a major issuer, researchers found that credit card customers who took out a payday loan were almost twice as likely as other credit card customers to become seriously delinquent on their credit card during the next year.[42]
- *Half of payday borrowers default in the first year of use.* Researchers at Vanderbilt and the University of Pennsylvania examined a large sample of payday loan files at a Texas payday lender and found that over half (54%) of borrowers defaulted on their payday loans during the first year.[43]

Abusive contract provisions and debt collection efforts are also common in payday lending. Contracts may condition the loan on payment by repeated preauthorized electronic funds transfers, in violation of the Electronic Funds Transfer Act (EFTA).[44] Or they may include terms that violate the Federal Trade Commission's Credit Practices Rule,[45] such as an invalid

34 *See* Nathalie Martin, *1000% Interest—Good While Supplies Last: A Study of Payday Loan Practices and Solutions*, 52 Ariz. L. Rev. 563 (Fall 2010) (documenting payday lenders' business plan, including the importance of repeat borrowers).

35 Dan Feehan, CEO of Cash America, remarks made at Jefferies Financial Services Conference (June 20, 2007) (transcript on file with the Center for Responsible Lending).

36 Uriah King & Leslie Parrish, Center for Responsible Lending, Phantom Demand: Short-Term Due Date Generates Need for Repeat Payday Loans, Accounting for 76% of Total Volume 15 (July 2009), *available at* www.responsiblelending.org/payday-lending/research-analysis/phantom-demand-short-term-due-date-generates-need-for-repeat-payday-loans-accounting-for-76-of-total-volume.html.

37 Dennis Campbell et al., Bouncing Out of the Banking System: An Empirical Analysis of Involuntary Bank Account Closures (June 6, 2008) (paper presented at Boston Federal Reserve Board workshop on Consumer Behavior and Payment Choice).

38 Paige Marta Skiba and Jeremy Tobacman, Do Payday Loans Cause Bankruptcy? (Oct. 10, 2008), *available at* www.law.vanderbilt.edu/faculty/faculty-personal-sites/paige-skiba/publication/download.aspx?id=2221.

39 Michael S. Barr, Federal Trade Commission, Financial Services, Savings, & Borrowing Among LMI Households in the Mainstream Banking & Alternative Financial Services Sectors (Oct. 30, 2008).

40 Brian T. Melzer, The Real Costs of Credit Access: Evidence from the Payday Lending Market (Nov. 15, 2007), *available at* http://qje.oxfordjournals.org/content/126/1/517.full.

41 Michael S. Barr, Federal Trade Commission, Financial Services, Savings, & Borrowing Among LMI Households in the Mainstream Banking & Alternative Financial Services Sectors (Oct. 30, 2008).

42 Agarwal, Sumit, Skiba, Paige Marta and Tobacman, Jeremy Bruce, Payday Loans and Credit Cards: New Liquidity and Credit Scoring Puzzles? (Jan. 13, 2009), *available at* http://ssrn.com/abstract=1327125 (study by researchers at the Chicago Federal Reserve Bank, Vanderbilt University, and the University of Pennsylvania, concluding that for all credit card users, the seriously delinquent rate was 6%, while for payday loan borrowers in this sample the rate was around 11%).

43 Paige Marta et al., Payday Loans, Uncertainty, and Discounting: Explaining Patterns of Borrowing, Repayment, and Default (Aug. 21, 2008) (determining that by the time loans are written off by the lender, borrowers have repaid fees equaling about 90% of their initial loan principal but are counted as defaults for the full amount of the loan), *available at* www.law.vanderbilt.edu/faculty/faculty-personal-sites/paige-skiba/publication/download.aspx?id=1636.

44 *See* § 9.2.1, *infra*.

45 Credit Practices Rule, 16 C.F.R. pt. 444. *See* National Consumer Law Center, Unfair and Deceptive Acts and Practices § 6.11 (7th ed. 2008 and Supp.).

wage assignment or confession of judgment.[46] One lender included a clause saying loan agreements were only subject to the law and jurisdiction of a particular Indian tribe and then filed collection suits in a tribal court that had no jurisdiction over people who were neither members of the tribe nor residents of the reservation.[47] Some of these abuses are discussed in further detail elsewhere in this chapter.

## 9.2 Banking Law Applications to Payday Lending

### *9.2.1 Conditioning Payday Loan on EFT Repayment*

Since they cannot conveniently accept paper checks, Internet-based payday lenders commonly have the borrower authorize an electronic fund transfer to repay the loan.[48] The Electronic Funds Transfer Act (EFTA) prohibits any person from conditioning the extension of credit upon the consumer's repayment by means of a preauthorized electronic fund transfer.[49] But the definition of "preauthorized electronic fund transfer" leaves a loophole for one-time transfers. "Preauthorized electronic fund transfer" is defined as a transfer authorized in advance to recur at substantially regular intervals.[50] So payday lenders that withdraw the entire debt all at once will not be affected by this prohibition.

The repayment authorization should be examined carefully, however. Many Internet-based lenders structure loan agreements so the default option is for the debt to be repaid through several finance-charge only installments, over several paydays, before the creditor deducts the original loan principal.[51] Under some contracts, in order to pay off the loan, the borrower must separately contact the lender days before the due date and ask the lender to withdraw the full amount due.[52] This clearly shows an expectation that borrowers will rollover their loans multiple times rather than paying the loan off at the end of the initial two weeks.

Even if the contract only authorizes a single transfer, courts have found that a payday loans meets the definition of a preauthorized electronic fund transfer when the loan has rolled over repeatedly with recurring payments at regular intervals.[53] A payday lender that illegally requires a preauthorized electronic fund transfer may be liable for actual and statutory damages plus attorney fees.[54]

### *9.2.2 Repeated Presentment of Borrower's Check*

One of the worst problems for payday loan borrowers is the bounced check fees incurred if the lender presents the check when there are insufficient funds to cover it. The problem is most severe when the lender repeatedly re-presents the dishonored check, incurring more bounced check fees each time.

UCC Article 3 does not explicitly limit the number of times a check can be presented. But the UCC's general rules of good faith govern presentment of checks.[55] Good faith is defined as honesty in fact and the observance of reasonable commercial standards of fair dealing.[56] Repeated resubmission of an insufficient funds check may violate this standard.

If the payday lender presents the borrower's check electronically, rather than presenting the physical check, the rules of the National Automated Clearing House Association (NACHA)[57] prohibit more than the original presentment of the check plus two re-presentments.[58] NACHA also prohibits *any* re-presentment of "demand drafts" or "telechecks," which are paper checks that a lender or seller signs on behalf of the consumer, usually based on the consumer's telephone authorization.[59]

State law may impose additional restrictions. Virginia, for example, prohibits payday lenders from depositing or otherwise presenting a check more than two times, or recovering more than $25 in returned check fees for a single check.[60] Consumers

46 *See, e.g.,* Federal Trade Comm'n v. Loanpointe, L.L.C., 2011 WL 4348304 (D. Utah Sept. 16, 2011) (granting summary judgment on UDAP violations involving credit practices rule and contracts including illegal wage garnishment clause); Amended Complaint, Federal Trade Comm'n v. Payday Fin., L.L.C. et al., No. 11-3017, ¶ 22 (C.D. S. Dak., filed Mar. 1, 2012) (describing illegal use of wage assignment clause), *available at* http://ftc.gov/os/caselist/1123023/120307paydaycmpt.pdf.

47 Press Release, Federal Trade Comm'n, FTC Charges That Payday Lender Illegally Sued Debt-Burdened Consumers in South Dakota Tribal Court Without Jurisdiction (Mar. 7, 2012), *available at* www.ftc.gov/opa/2012/03/payday.shtm.

48 *See* Consumer Federation of America, Survey of Online Payday Loan Websites 7–8 (Aug. 2011) (discussing Internet lender access to consumer bank accounts), *available at* http://consumerfed.org/pdfs/CFAsurveyInternetPaydayLoanWebsites.pdf.

49 15 U.S.C. § 1693k. *See, e.g.,* O'Donovan v. Cashcall, Inc., 2009 WL 1833990 (N.D. Cal. June 24, 2009) (permitting most of plaintiffs' claims for EFTA violations in connection with high interest rate loans similar to payday products—including claim for conditioning extension of credit on repayment by electronic funds transfer—to go forward).

50 15 U.S.C. § 1693a(9).

51 Consumer Federation of America, Survey of Online Payday Loan Websites 9 (Aug. 2011), *available at* http://consumerfed.org/pdfs/CFAsurveyInternetPaydayLoanWebsites.pdf.

52 *Id.*

53 Mitchem v. GFG Loan Co., 2000 WL 294119, at *8 (N.D. Ill. Mar. 17, 2000) (denying motion to dismiss); Johnson v. Tele-Cash, Inc., 82 F. Supp. 2d 264 (D. Del. 1999), *rev'd in part on other grounds*, 225 F.3d 366 (3d Cir. 2000) (compelling arbitration). *But see* Mitchem v. Paycheck Advance Express, Inc., 2000 WL 419993 (N.D. Ill. Apr. 14, 2000).

54 15 U.S.C. § 1693m; National Consumer Law Center, Consumer Banking and Payments Law § 4.15.2 (4th ed. 2009 and Supp.) (liability for EFTA violations).

55 U.C.C. § 1-203.

56 U.C.C. §§ 3-103(a)(4), 4-104(c).

57 NACHA is a private organization that manages the primary electronic system for financial transactions in the United States.

58 NACHA's rules can be purchased from www.nacha.org. Whether there is a private right of action to enforce the rules is examined at National Consumer Law Center, Consumer Banking and Payments Law Ch. 1 (4th ed. 2009 and Supp.).

59 NACHA Rule 2.8.2 (2005).

60 10 Va. Admin. Code § 5-200-70(B).

may issue a stop-payment order to their bank,[61] but advocates have reported that creditors presenting checks electronically can easily defeat stop-payment orders and that banking institutions make little effort to prevent evasions. If a payday lender is prohibited from presenting a check additional times, it can still sue the borrower on the debt.

### 9.2.3 Bad Check Prosecutions

Another payday lending abuse occurs when a lender aggressively uses a state bad-check law to claim large penalties when a check is dishonored. The check in a payday loan serves a dual function—it is security for the loan and a method of repaying the debt at a later time.[62] As a result, any default will necessarily involve bouncing a check. The difference between a bad check given to a merchant, however, and a post-dated check given to a payday lender is that the borrower has no intent to deceive the lender, and the lender has no reason to believe the check is backed by adequate funds. A number of states limit the application of civil and criminal bad-check laws where the creditor knows there are insufficient funds in the account at the time he accepts the check.

Some payday lenders, however, have used state laws regarding bad checks as a collection tool against defaulting borrowers. For example, a Michigan statute provides that a check payee can sue for treble the face value of the check and $250 if the check is dishonored.[63] In other words, if a consumer's $100 check payment has insufficient funds to cover it, the payday lender can seek $550 in court.

When payday lenders began abusing this law, Michigan enacted a statute limiting payday lenders to recovery of the face amount of the check plus $25.[64] When the lenders continued to seek treble the face value and $250, the state agency licensing payday lenders issued an administrative order that the payday lenders cease the practice. When the payday lending industry challenged the order in court as limiting their access to the courts, a Michigan appellate court upheld the order as a correct interpretation of the statute limiting bad-check fees.[65]

In other states, courts have found that criminal and civil bad check laws do not apply to post-dated checks, electronic payments, and in certain other contexts.[66] These and other limits on civil and criminal prosecutions for dishonored checks are examined in another NCLC treatise, *Collection Actions*.[67]

### 9.2.4 Adding Fees to the Face Amount of a Check or Electronic Fund Transfer

A payday lender may claim that it is entitled to not only the face amount of the consumer's check, but also a dishonored check fee or some other charge. If the payday lender submits a paper check, no bank will negotiate that check for more than the amount of the check or pay the lender additional fees from the consumer's account. Payday lenders also sometimes, without authorization, generate a remotely created check in an amount slightly different than the original check or electronic fund transfer authorization in order to evade a stop payment order that describes a payment of a set amount.

If the lender re-presents a paper check electronically, NACHA rules prohibit asking for more than the face amount of the check.[68] However NACHA permits a separate electronic transfer for a return check fee, as long as the contract authorizes it, though only one fee is allowed per check.[69] The payday lender also may use an agreement in the contract to create a remotely created check (telecheck) for the new amount. Under the EFTA, the consumer is not liable for an unauthorized transfer,[70] so if the consumer did not authorize the payday lender to obtain an electronic transfer of the additional fee, the consumer's bank must re-credit the amount.

### 9.2.5 Early Presentation of Post-Dated Checks

Many storefront payday lenders require a post-dated check as security for a loan when permitted by state laws defining the payday loan product. But most consumers do not realize that,

61 *See* § 9.2.8, *infra* (discussing stop-payment orders); National Consumer Law Center, Consumer Banking and Payments Law § 2.8.2 (4th ed. 2009 and Supp.).

62 Iowa Dep't of Justice, Informal Advisory #87, Deferred Deposit Loans (Feb. 18, 1999) (extensively discussing relationship between criminal bad check laws and payday lending), *available at* www.iowa.gov/government/ag/protecting_consumers/ICCC_Opinions/87.pdf.

63 Mich. Comp. Laws § 600.2952(4).
Such statutes are examined at National Consumer Law Center, Collection Actions Ch. 8 (2d ed. 2011 and Supp.).

64 Mich. Comp. Laws § 487.2158.

65 Michigan Deferred Presentment Servs. Ass'n v. Commissioner of the Office of Fin. & Ins. Reg., 788 N.W.2d 842 (Mich. Ct. App. 2010).

66 *See, e.g.*, Payday Today, Inc. v. McCullough, 841 N.E.2d 638 (Ind. Ct. App. 2006) (statutory treble damages sought against payday borrower not triggered where there no evidence of fraud knowingly performed at the time the payday loans was signed even though the consumer subsequently placed a stop payment order on the check). *See also* National Consumer Law Center, Collection Actions § 8.2.3 (2d ed. 2011 and Supp.) ("Many courts have held that dishonored check laws do not apply to postdated checks."). *But see* Thompson v. Adcox, 63 S.W.3d 783 (Tenn. Ct. App. 2002) (post-dated check is not a "check" under the criminal worthless check statute at the time of its passing; however, borrower later committed fraud when he subsequently failed to pay check after notice of its nonpayment).

67 National Consumer Law Center, Collection Actions Ch. 8 (2d ed. 2011 and Supp.).

68 "Re-presented Check Entries may be originated only for the face amount of the check. No collection fees may be added to the amount of the item when it is transmitted as an ACH entry." NACHA Operating Guidelines 170 (2005). *See* National Consumer Law Center, Consumer Banking and Payments Law § 2.7.4 (4th ed. 2009 and Supp.) (electronic re-presentment of NSF checks).

69 *See* National Consumer Law Center, Consumer Banking and Payments Law § 4.11.7 (4th ed. 2009 and Supp.).

70 Reg. E, 12 C.F.R. § 1005.6(b) [§ 205.6(b)]. Note that the consumer must notify the bank within sixty days after the bank sends a statement showing the unauthorized debit. If the consumer does not, then the consumer may be stuck with any additional debits that occur after the sixty-day period.

under the UCC, a check is payable when it is presented to the bank, even if it is post-dated.[71] This means, if a payday lender attempts to present the consumer's check early, a bank will normally pay it regardless of the date. Consumers can only require their bank to wait until the date on the check by notifying the bank in advance of the post-dating and describing the check with reasonable certainty.[72] Regardless of whether the consumer has given notice to the bank, if a payday lender presents a post-dated check before its date, the consumer should be able to press UDAP and breach of contract claims against the lender.

### *9.2.6 Unauthorized Payments and Charges*

Another potential abuse is the presentation of a check or electronic debit that the consumer has not authorized. The UCC sets out rules for forged or altered checks. In general consumers are not liable for the payment of forged or altered checks under the UCC.[73] Similarly, the EFTA specifies that consumers have no liability for unauthorized electronic fund transfers or transfers made in the wrong amount. Where no debit card or other access device is involved, the only liability the consumer has under the EFTA arises if the unauthorized transfer appears on a monthly bank statement, and the consumer fails to report it for sixty days. Even then, the consumer's liability is limited just to any *new* unauthorized transfers occurring *after* that sixty-day period.[74]

In addition, under the EFTA, the consumer can require the bank to institute a procedure to resolve any error in the transfer. While the consumer is not entitled to an immediate re-credit, the bank must promptly re-credit the amount if its investigation discovers the transfer was unauthorized. If the bank does not complete its investigation within ten business days, it must provisionally re-credit the amount to the consumer.[75]

NACHA rules provide similar protections, but, if the consumer files an "Affidavit of Unauthorized ACH Withdrawal" form at their bank, the consumer's bank must promptly re-credit the disputed amount.[76] Under NACHA rules, consumers must report the error within fifteen days in writing and under penalty of perjury. But, even if the consumer does not comply with this NACHA requirement, the bank must still conduct the error resolution procedure required by the EFTA.

Consumers who discover unauthorized withdrawals from their account, whether made by check or electronic transfer, should ask the bank to file a suspicious activity report (an SAR) with the U.S. Treasury Department. Banks are required to file SARs for suspicious transactions related to potentially illegal activity involving at least $5,000. But Treasury Department regulations specifically permit banks to report suspicious activities even when a report is not required.[77]

71 U.C.C. § 4-401(c).
72 U.C.C. § 4-401(c).
73 *See* National Consumer Law Center, Consumer Banking and Payments Law Ch. 2 (4th ed. 2009 and Supp.).
74 Reg. E, 12 C.F.R. § 1005.6(b)(3) [§ 205.6(b)(3)].
75 Reg. E, 12 C.F.R. § 1005.11 [§ 205.11].
76 2005 NACHA Rule 8.6.1.
77 31 C.F.R. § 1020.320

### *9.2.7 Manipulating the Form of the Payment to Avoid Legal Protections*

State uniform commercial codes contain protections for payment by check,[78] and the Electronic Fund Transfer Act provides protections for electronic fund transfers (also known as automated clearinghouse transactions, or ACH).[79] These protections include the right to stop payment.[80]

However, most payday loan agreements include provisions intended to defeat these rights. When consumers provide a post-dated check to secure their loan, the agreement typically provides authority for the payday lender to use the check as a source document for information needed to create an ACH payment. Consequently, if the consumer attempts to stop payment on the check, the payday lender merely initiates an ACH. Bank payment systems set up to stop a check may not catch the payment if it is in the form of an ACH.

Similarly, when the payday loan agreement authorizes ACH withdrawals as the primary form of payment, as Internet payday loans typically do, the agreement will authorize the payday lender to generate a remotely created check in the event that the consumer stops payment on the ACH payments. Here again, a stop payment order on an ACH payment may not catch a paper check.

Complicating matters is the fact that the EFTA stop payment provisions apply only to electronic fund transfers that recur at regular intervals, not single ACH payments.[81] However, the rules of NACHA, the electronic payment association that processes most ACH payments, permit stop payment orders on single ACH payments.[82]

### *9.2.8 Stop Payment Orders*

If a consumer needs to stop a payday lender from withdrawing any additional money from the consumer's bank account, the consumer should notify both the bank and the payday lender in writing that she is withdrawing her previous authorization to withdraw funds. While many payday lenders will ignore such a notice, a stop payment order does, however, lay the groundwork for additional steps.[83]

Issuing a stop payment order on a paper check or electronic transfer is the easiest way to prevent the immediate transfer of funds to the payday lender, but it is not a complete solution either. Banks charge steep stop payment fees, which can be nearly as high as the payment the consumer is trying to stop,

78 *See* National Consumer Law Center, Consumer Banking and Payments Law Ch. 2 (4th ed. 2009 and Supp.).
79 *See* National Consumer Law Center, Consumer Banking and Payments Law Ch. 4 (4th ed. 2009 and Supp.).
80 *See* National Consumer Law Center, Consumer Banking and Payments Law §§ 2.8.2, 4.11.4 (4th ed. 2009 and Supp.).
81 *See* National Consumer Law Center, Consumer Banking and Payments Law §§ 4.11.1, 4.11.4 (4th ed. 2009 and Supp.).
82 *See* National Consumer Law Center, Consumer Banking and Payments Law § 4.10 (4th ed. 2009 and Supp.).
83 NACHA rules require notice to the lender.

particularly if the stop payment order is seeking to prevent the lender collecting the rollover fee and not the entire loan.

Some payday lenders have identified ways to evade stop payment orders, such as by illegally altering the check payment amount so that it no longer matches the check described in the stop-payment order. Furthermore, a stop payment order may prevent funds from being taken out of the consumer's account but will not resolve the consumer's underlying liability to repay the payday lender.

Under the UCC a consumer has the right to stop payment on a paper check or any other item payable by a bank and subject to the UCC.[84] A stop-payment order is valid for six months, if in writing, and for fourteen days if oral. Many banks charge for this service. To be effective, the consumer must describe the check to the consumer's bank with reasonable certainty and at a time and in a manner that affords the bank a reasonable opportunity to act on it.[85] There is no clear standard for what constitutes a sufficient description. If a bank pays a check contrary to a stop-payment order, the bank will be liable to the consumer for the amount paid and possibly additional damages arising any overdraft created by the wrongful payment.[86]

Similarly, consumers may also stop payment on electronic and telephone-initiated transfers orally or in writing.[87] For "preauthorized" electronic fund transfers, i.e., those authorized in advance to recur at substantially regular intervals, the consumer has the right under the EFTA to stop payment by notifying the financial institution where the account is located.[88] One example of a preauthorized electronic transfer to a payday lender is where the lender obtains the consumer's agreement to automatic renewal of the loan every two weeks, resulting in a series of interest-only debits to the consumer's account.[89] Under the EFTA either oral or written notice to the bank is effective to stop further debits, as long as it is given at least three business days before the scheduled date of the transfer.[90]

NACHA rules also allow the consumer to withdraw authorization for recurring debits to an account. The consumer must inform the payday lender directly as well as the financial institution where the account is maintained, and must sign a form under pain of perjury.[91] But the consumer still is protected if the consumer complies with the EFTA, and not with NACHA rules. A bank may also be liable for damages under the EFTA for failing to honor a valid stop-payment order.[92]

## 9.2.9 Closing Accounts

Because stop-payment orders are unlikely to permanently protect a consumer's assets from an aggressive payday lender, a consumer may be safer closing her bank account to prevent a payday lender from draining it. Closing an account, however, may not be as simple as it sounds. Consumers have reported that some banks will continue honoring creditors' electronic transfer authorizations even after the consumer has told the bank to close the account.

This is because some banks will leave an account open until the bank is certain that no more items will be presented for payment even though the accountholder has directed the bank to close the account. Or the bank will do a "soft close" and re-open the account to process a new item. Banks may also refuse to close an account if there are overdrafts or unpaid fees.

As a result, consumers may continue to incur overdraft charges or other fees when a payday lender attempts to debit what is, in effect, a "zombie" bank account. In addition, some banks report overdrafts and bounced checks to specialty reporting services, like ChexSystems, that are queried by other banks when reviewing account applications. This can prevent the consumer from opening a replacement account.

To avoid these problems, the consumer should first open a replacement account at a different banking institution, not just a different branch. The consumer should then switch any direct deposits, such as public benefits or their paycheck, to the new account.[93] It is also important to address any outstanding checks or valid electronic authorizations drawn on the old account, such as rent or mortgage payments, insurance premiums, student loans, or others.

Once the new account is ready and any valid debits from the old account have been paid or redirected to the new account, the consumer should visit the old bank in person and instruct the branch manager to permanently close the old account.[94] It is important to speak with a manager and to explain that the payday lender is expected to make unauthorized withdraws from the account, but that a stop-payment order will not be an acceptable solution. In addition, the consumer should:

- Opt-out of any overdraft protection on the account;
- Withdraw any remaining funds in the account; and
- Insist that the manager close the account immediately and permanently.

84 U.C.C. § 4-403(a), cmt. 3; National Consumer Law Center, Consumer Banking and Payments Law § 2.8.2 (4th ed. 2009 and Supp.) (discussing the right to stop payment).

85 U.C.C. § 4-403(a).

86 U.C.C. §§ 4-402, 4-403(c).

87 2005 NACHA Rule 8.4; National Consumer Law Center, Consumer Banking and Payments Law §§ 4.8.4, 4.9.1 (4th ed. 2009 and Supp.).

88 12 C.F.R. § 1005.10(c) [§ 205.10(c)]. National Consumer Law Center, Consumer Banking and Payments Law § 4.11.4 (4th ed. 2009 and Supp.).

89 *See* Consumer Federation of America, Survey of Online Payday Loan Websites 9 (Aug. 2011) (describing Internet lender contract terms), *available at* http://consumerfed.org/pdfs/CFAsurveyInternetPaydayLoanWebsites.pdf.

90 12 C.F.R. § 1005.10(c) [§ 205.10(c)].

91 NACHA 2005 Operating Guidelines 21–22, "Revocation of Authorization."

92 National Consumer Law Center, Consumer Banking and Payments Law § 4.15 (4th ed. 2009 and Supp.) (remedies for EFTA and NACHA rule violations).

93 *Consumer Reports'* blog, The Consumerist, has tips on switching to a new bank. Chris Morran, *7 Easy Steps To Safely Switching to a New Bank*, The Consumerist (Oct. 31, 2011), *available at* http://con.st/10024339.

94 Some banks refer to this as a "hard close."

The consumer should close all accounts at the bank, not just the checking account, and confirm all of these instructions in writing.

## 9.3 State Regulation of Payday Lending

### 9.3.1 General

States vary widely in how they approach payday loan regulation. Some states regulate payday lending directly. One state, Georgia, makes payday lending a RICO violation. Others have broader laws addressing small loans that include payday lending. Some states' usury laws preclude payday lending. The degree of regulation ranges from outright prohibitions to the virtual codification of *caveat emptor*. Such great variation means there can be little generalization about state regulation of payday lending. Instead, what follows is a summary of each state's approach.

### 9.3.2 Alabama

In Alabama, the Deferred Presentment Services Act[95] authorizes payday lending. The law places certain limitations on payday lenders. The maximum amount that may be advanced in any transaction is $500, and a lender is allowed to grant only one rollover of the loan.[96] In the event of a rollover, after two continuous transactions the lender must comply with a cooling off period by refraining from making another loan to the customer until the next business day after the transaction amount is paid in full.[97] Lenders must use a third-party, private sector database to ensure that customers do not have outstanding loans exceeding the $500 maximum.[98] The statute does not, however, establish a centralized database so each lender reportedly uses a different one, defeating the purpose of the database requirement.

Alabama law provides for both civil and criminal penalties[99] for lenders who violate the Deferred Presentment Services Act. In addition, the law authorizes the Supervisor of the Bureau of Loans to require the refund of fees collected in violation of the law.[100]

### 9.3.3 Alaska

Payday lending is authorized by statute in Alaska.[101] The law places several limitations on lenders. The maximum amount that may be advanced in any transaction is $500,[102] and the lender may not grant more than two rollovers of a loan.[103] In addition, the law provides that payday lenders must disclose to borrowers that criminal action may not be brought against them for failure to pay the amount advanced.[104]

### 9.3.4 Arizona

In July of 2010, Arizona allowed a law that formerly authorized payday lending to sunset, thus effectively ending the practice as it had existed in the state. The loans that were formerly covered under the statute now fall under the state's Consumer Lenders Act, which provides for no greater than a 36% rate of interest on loans of $1,000 or less.[105] This cap effectively prohibits the practice of payday lending in Arizona.

### 9.3.5 Arkansas

In 2008, the Check-Cashers Act, which had purported to authorize payday lending in Arkansas, was found to be unconstitutional by the state's Supreme Court.[106] Specifically, the court found that the law violated the usury cap of 17% provided in the state constitution[107] by attempting to circumvent the cap by designating as service "fees" what was actually interest. In the wake of this ruling, the practice of payday lending essentially came to an end in Arkansas. In 2011, the Arkansas legislature officially repealed the Check-Cashers Act[108] in order to protect consumers from unlawful consumer lending practices.

### 9.3.6 California

In California, the Deferred Deposit Transaction Law[109] authorizes payday lending. This law imposes certain restrictions on lenders. A payday lender may make only one loan at a time,[110] and that loan may not exceed $300.[111] The lender may not make a new loan to the borrower in order to pay off that borrower's existing loan.[112] However, nothing in the law prevents a *different* lender from making a loan to the borrower to pay off an existing loan that was made by the original lender. It is unlawful for a lender to threaten to prosecute a borrower in criminal court for insufficient funds.[113]

The Deferred Deposit Transaction Law provides that a payday loan transaction is void if a lender willfully exacts from a borrower fees or charges in excess of those permitted by law or if a lender willfully violates any provision of the statute. In both cases, the lender does not have the right to collect either the

95 Ala. Code §§ 5-18A-1 to 5-18A-22.
96 Ala. Code § 5-18A-12(a), (b).
97 Ala. Code § 5-18A-12(b).
98 Ala. Code § 5-18A-13(o).
99 Ala. Code §§ 5-18A-16, 5-18A-17, 5-18A-20.
100 Ala. Code § 5-18A-16(2).
101 Alaska Stat. §§ 06.50.010 to 06.50.900.
102 Alaska Stat. § 06.50.410.
103 Alaska Stat. § 06.50.470.
104 Alaska Stat. §§ 06.50.510(b)(9), 06.50.560.
105 Ariz. Rev. Stat. § 6-632.
106 McGhee v. Arkansas State Bd. of Collection Agencies, 289 S.W.3d 18, 23–28 (Ark. 2008).
107 Ark. Const. art. 19, § 13.
108 Ark. Code Ann. §§ 23-52-101 to 23-52-117, *repealed by* Acts of 2011, Act 720, § 2, eff. July 27, 2011.
109 Cal. Fin. Code §§ 23000 to 23106 (West).
110 Cal. Fin. Code § 23036(c) (West).
111 Cal. Fin. Code § 23035(a) (West).
112 Cal. Fin. Code § 23037(a) (West).
113 Cal. Fin. Code § 23035(e)(9) (West).

principal amount of the loan or any charges or fees connected with the transaction.[114] If an exaction of excess fees or a violation is not willful, the lender must forfeit any fees or charges, but may still collect the principal amount of the loan.[115] California law specifically authorizes a private right of action for damages and/or injunctive relief, in which a successful plaintiff may be awarded treble damages, reasonable attorney fees and costs, and punitive damages in the case of "clear and convincing evidence" of a willful breach.[116] The law also states that a plaintiff need not exhaust administrative remedies before pursuing a civil action.[117]

## 9.3.7 Colorado

In Colorado, payday lending is authorized by the Deferred Deposit Loan Act.[118] The statute provides that a loan may not be renewed more than once,[119] and a consumer is not subject to any criminal penalty for entering into a deferred deposit loan agreement unless the consumer's account on which a dishonored check was written is closed before the agreed on date of negotiation.[120]

In 2010, the payday lending law was amended and additional reforms and restrictions were put into place. Where no minimum loan period existed prior to the amendment, the law now provides for a six-month minimum term,[121] and allows consumers to prepay a loan without incurring any penalty for doing so.[122] The amendment also establishes a maximum 45% per annum interest rate, both for original loans and renewals.[123] In addition, the law permits a lender to make more than one loan at a time, but there must be at least a thirty-day waiting period between loans.[124]

## 9.3.8 Connecticut

Payday lending is not authorized by statute in Connecticut. Small loans are governed by a statute prescribing a rate cap of 17% for amounts under $600.[125] This cap effectively bans the practice of payday lending in Connecticut.

## 9.3.9 Delaware

In Delaware, payday lenders are authorized by statute to make short-term consumer loans,[126] for which they are permitted to charge any rate "as the agreement governing the loan provides." However, the law does impose several restrictions on lenders. They may not permit more than four rollovers[127] and may not pursue or threaten to pursue criminal action against a borrower in connection with the nonpayment of any amount due.[128]

## 9.3.10 District of Columbia

While the practice of payday lending was formerly permitted in the District of Columbia, the authorizing statute[129] was repealed in 2007. The law specifically provides that "no licensee shall at any time cash or advance any monies on a post dated check."[130] Small loans are governed by a statute prescribing a rate cap of 24%.[131]

## 9.3.11 Florida

Making payday loans, known as "deferred presentment transactions," is authorized by statute in Florida.[132] Several restrictions are imposed on lenders. Rollovers are prohibited,[133] and a lender may not make more than one loan at a time to a borrower who has taken out a loan either from that particular lender or from another lender.[134] The law also establishes a cooling off period of twenty-four hours between loans.[135] Before making a loan, lenders must check a centralized database to ensure compliance with these restrictions.[136] A lender may not pursue criminal prosecution of a borrower for activity relating to a payday loan.[137]

## 9.3.12 Georgia

By legislation enacted in 2004, Georgia has specifically prohibited payday lending[138] and declared any site or location of a place of business where payday lending takes place a public nuisance.[139] The law imposes monetary penalties on violators,[140] and it also criminalizes the practice.[141] If a payday loan is made in violation of the law, the transaction is void.[142] In addition, the lender is liable to the borrower for three times the amount of any interest or other charges, plus reasonable attorney fees and costs. A civil action may be brought on behalf of an individual borrower or on behalf of a class of borrowers.[143] This action may be

114 Cal. Fin. Code § 23060 (West).
115 Cal. Fin. Code §§ 23061, 23062 (West).
116 Cal. Fin. Code § 23064 (West).
117 Cal. Fin. Code § 23064.5 (West).
118 Colo. Rev. Stat. §§ 5-3.1-101 to 5-3.1-123.
119 Colo. Rev. Stat. § 5-3.1-108(a).
120 Colo. Rev. Stat. § 5-3.1-120.
121 Colo. Rev. Stat. § 5-3.1-103.
122 *Id.*
123 Colo. Rev. Stat. §§ 5-3.1-105, 5-3.1-108(2).
124 Colo. Rev. Stat. § 5-3.1-106(a).
125 Conn. Gen. Stat. § 36a-563.
126 Del. Code Ann. tit. 5, §§ 2227(7), 2235A.
127 Del. Code Ann. tit. 5, § 2235A(a)(1).
128 Del. Code Ann. tit. 5, § 2235A(a)(3).
129 D.C. Code Ann. § 26-319(c).
130 D.C. Code Ann. § 26-319(b).
131 D.C. Code Ann. § 28-3301(a).
132 Fla. Stat. §§ 560.402 to 560.408.
133 Fla. Stat. § 560.404(18).
134 Fla. Stat. § 560.404(19).
135 *Id.*
136 Fla. Stat. § 560.404(19), (23).
137 Fla. Stat. § 560.404(20).
138 Ga. Code Ann. §§ 16-7-1 to 16-7-97.
139 Ga. Code Ann. § 16-7-8.
140 Ga. Code Ann. § 16-7-2(a).
141 Ga. Code Ann. § 16-7-2(d).
142 Ga. Code. Ann. § 16-7-3.
143 *Id.*

brought by the attorney general, any district attorney, or a private party.[144]

## 9.3.13 Hawaii

Payday lending is legal in Hawaii.[145] While the law imposes some restrictions on lenders, there is no licensing requirement or supervision of payday lenders in Hawaii. A lender may not make more than one loan at a time, and rollovers are not allowed.[146] In addition, a lender may not pursue criminal penalties against a borrower for failure to comply with the terms of the loan unless the check is dishonored because the borrower closed the account or stopped payment on the check.[147]

A violation of the payday lending law is a UDAP violation in Hawaii, and borrowers may seek remedies accordingly.[148] Available remedies include treble damages, reasonable attorney fees, costs, and injunctive relief.[149]

## 9.3.14 Idaho

Payday lending is legal in Idaho,[150] yet certain restrictions are placed on the practice. While the law does not expressly restrict the lender from extending a certain number of loans at one time to a borrower, it does establish a limit of a $1,000 aggregate principal balance on all outstanding loans.[151] The law specifically prohibits a lender from making more than three renewals of a loan.[152] In addition, the law provides that a lender is not allowed to threaten a borrower with criminal action as a result of any payment deficit.[153]

In 2009, an amendment to the payday lending law provided that any loans made in Idaho by a payday lender that is not licensed by the state of Idaho are void, uncollectible, and unenforceable.[154] A borrower is not obligated to pay either the principal or any fees associated with the loan. If the borrower has paid any of the principal or associated fees, the law provides that the borrower has a "right to recover" such amounts from the unlicensed lender.[155]

## 9.3.15 Illinois

In Illinois, the Payday Loan Reform Act[156] has legalized payday lending. The statute does, however, impose some restrictions on the practice. A payday loan is defined in Illinois as "a loan with a finance charge exceeding an annual percentage rate of 36% and with a term that does not exceed 120 days." The law provides that if a borrower has or has had loans outstanding for over forty-five consecutive days, no payday lender may make a loan to that borrower for at least seven calendar days after the date on which the outstanding balance of all payday loans made during the forty-five consecutive day period is paid in full.[157] The law also states that no lender may make a payday loan to a borrower if the total of all payday loan payments coming due within the first month of the loan, when combined with the payment amount of all of the borrower's other outstanding payday loans coming due within the same month, exceeds the lesser of $1,000 or, in the case of one or more payday loans, 25% of the borrower's gross monthly income.[158] In addition, the law provides that rollovers are prohibited,[159] and a lender may not threaten to pursue a borrower in criminal court in connection with a payday loan.[160] Before making a payday loan, lenders must use a commercial database, if available, to verify that the loan would be permitted under the statute.[161]

In 2011, the statute was amended to include within its coverage an "installment payday loan," which is defined as any installment loan otherwise meeting the definition of a payday loan but having a term of between 112 and 180 days. By enacting the 2011 amendments, the Illinois legislature sought to close a loophole that had existed in the prior law that effectively allowed lenders to evade the cap on interest rates for payday loans with terms under 120 days[162] by making loans for one day over that limit.

Note that in certain respects, Illinois now has two different regulatory structures for "payday loans" and "installment payday loans." For instance, while rollovers of a payday loan are prohibited, the amendment states that an installment payday loan may be refinanced by a new installment payday loan one time during the term of the initial loan, but only if the total duration of indebtedness on the initial loan combined with the total term of indebtedness of the new loan refinancing that initial loan does not exceed 180 days.[163] The law also provides that no lender may make a payday loan to a borrower if the total of all payday loan payments coming due within the first month, when combined with the payment amount of all of the borrower's other outstanding payday loans coming due within the same month exceeds the lesser of $1,000 or, in the case of one or more installment payday loans, 22.5% of the borrower's gross monthly income.[164] The 22.5% figure differs from the 25% figure specified for regular payday loans noted above.

In Illinois, a "material" violation of the payday lending law is a UDAP violation.[165]

144 Ga. Code. Ann. § 16-7-4.
145 Haw. Rev. Stat. §§ 480F-1 to 480F-7.
146 Haw. Rev. Stat. § 480F-4(d).
147 Haw. Rev. Stat. § 480F-6(d).
148 Haw. Rev. Stat. §§ 480f-6(a).
149 Haw. Rev. Stat. § 480-13(b).
150 Idaho Code Ann. §§ 28-46-401 to 28-46-413.
151 Idaho Code Ann. § 28-46-413(1).
152 Idaho Code Ann. § 28-46-413(6).
153 Idaho Code Ann. § 28-46-413(4).
154 Idaho Code Ann. § 28-406-402(3).
155 *Id.*
156 815 Ill. Comp. Stat. §§ 122/1-1 to 122/99-99.
157 815 Ill. Comp. Stat. § 122/2-5(b).
158 815 Ill. Comp. Stat. § 122/2-5(e).
159 815 Ill. Comp. Stat. § 122/2-30.
160 815 Ill. Comp. Stat. § 122/4-5(1).
161 815 Ill. Comp. Stat. § 122/2-15.
162 815 Ill. Comp. Stat. § 122/1-10.
163 815 Ill. Comp. Stat. § 122/2-5(c)(ii).
164 815 Ill. Comp. Stat. § 122/2-5(e).
165 815 Ill. Comp. Stat. § 122/4-10(b).

### *9.3.16 Indiana*

Payday lending is authorized by statute in Indiana.[166] The law imposes several restrictions on lenders. Renewals of payday loans are prohibited.[167] Once a lender has made six consecutive payday loans to a borrower, the lender must observe a seven-day cooling off period after the sixth consecutive loan is paid in full before making another payday loan to that borrower.[168] A lender may not make more than one payday loan at a time with a particular borrower[169] and not make a payday loan to a borrower who has two or more payday loans outstanding with any lender, regardless of the total value of the loans.[170] In addition, a lender may not threaten to use or use the criminal process to collect on a payday loan.[171]

Indiana law provides that a lender that violates the payday lending statute has no right to collect, receive or retain any principal, interest, or other charges from a payday loan unless the violation is the result of an accident or bona fide error of computation. The lender is liable to the borrower for actual damages and statutory damages of $2,000 per violation, plus attorney fees and costs.[172]

### *9.3.17 Iowa*

Payday lending is authorized by statute in Iowa.[173] A lender is restricted from making more than two loans at a time, and the aggregate amount loaned at one time cannot be more than $500.[174] Rollovers are not permitted.[175]

### *9.3.18 Kansas*

Kansas law specifically authorizes payday lending,[176] but places a number of restrictions on the practice. A lender may not make more than two loans to the same borrower at any one time and may not make more than three loans to a borrower within a thirty-day period.[177] A lender may not extend a payday loan to repay another loan, and may not apply the proceeds from any payday loan to any other loan.[178] In addition, a lender is prohibited from using or threatening to use the criminal process to collect on a payday loan.[179]

### *9.3.19 Kentucky*

The Deferred Deposit Service Business and Check Cashing Act[180] authorizes payday lending in Kentucky. However, it does impose some restrictions on lenders. A lender may not make more than two payday loans from a borrower at a time and the aggregate of loans to a borrower may not exceed $500.[181] Further, the law specifies that a lender may not extend a loan to a borrower who has two open payday loans with any lender.[182] Lenders must query a centralized database to determine whether a prospective borrower has any loans outstanding.[183] A lender may not renew, roll over, or otherwise consolidate a payday loan.[184] Also, a lender is prohibited from prosecuting or threatening to prosecute a borrower in connection with a payday loan.[185]

Any loan made with an unlicensed lender is void, and the lender may not collect any principal, fee, interest, or charges.[186] In addition, if the commissioner of the Department of Financial Institutions determines that a lender has violated any provision of the payday loan law, the commissioner may void the loan. In such a case, the lender may recover the principal of the loan from the borrower, but may not recover any service fee or other charge related to the loan.[187]

### *9.3.20 Louisiana*

The Louisiana Deferred Presentment and Small Loan Act[188] governs payday loans. While the law appears to restrict lenders by stating that it does not allow rollovers or renewals, it contains the important caveat that a lender may accept a partial payment of 25% of the amount originally advanced, plus fees charged, and then enter into a new payday loan or renew the loan for the remaining balance.[189] As in a number of other states, a lender in Louisiana may not threaten any customer with prosecution in connection with a payday loan.[190]

### *9.3.21 Maine*

Maine law prohibits check cashers from advancing or cashing money on any post-dated check.[191] However, payday lending practices are not completely illegal in this state. Duly licensed "supervised lenders" may still offer short-term loans pursuant to Maine's Consumer Credit Code.[192] Under this statute, a lender making such loans is required to post a $50,000

166 Ind. Code Ann. §§ 24-4.5-7-101 to 24-4.5-7-414.
167 Ind. Code Ann. § 24-4.5-7-402(6).
168 Ind. Code Ann. § 24-4.5-7-401(2).
169 Ind. Code Ann. § 24-4.5-7-404(2).
170 Ind. Code Ann. § 24-4.5-7-404(3).
171 Ind. Code Ann. § 24-4.5-7-410(a).
172 Ind. Code Ann. § 24-4.5-7-409.
173 Iowa Code §§ 533D.1 to 533D.16.
174 Iowa Code § 533D.10(1)(a), (b).
175 Iowa Code § 533D.10(1)(e).
176 Kan. Stat. Ann. § 16a-2-404.
177 Kan. Stat. Ann. § 16a-2-404(3).
178 Kan. Stat. Ann. § 16a-2-404(6).
179 Kan. Stat. Ann. § 16a-2-404(10)(b).
180 Ky. Rev. Stat. Ann. §§ 286.9-010 to 286.9-991.
181 Ky. Rev. Stat. Ann. § 286.9-100(9).
182 Ky. Rev. Stat. Ann. § 286.9-100(18).
183 Ky. Rev. Stat. Ann. § 286.9-140.
184 Ky. Rev. Stat. Ann. § 286.9-100(14).
185 Ky. Rev. Stat. Ann. § 286.9-100(16).
186 Ky. Rev. Stat. Ann. § 286.9-035(1).
187 Ky. Rev. Stat. Ann. § 286.9-035(2).
188 La. Rev. Stat. Ann. §§ 9:3578.1 to 9:3578.8.
189 La. Rev. Stat. Ann. § 9:3578.6(7).
190 La. Rev. Stat. Ann. § 9:3578.6(5).
191 Me. Rev. Stat. tit. 32, § 6138.
192 Me. Rev. Stat. tit. 9-A, §§ 1-101 to 1-601.

consumer protection bond, and is limited to charging $15 on loans from $75 to $250, or $25 when the amount is $250 or more.[193]

## 9.3.22 Maryland

Payday lending is not authorized by statute in Maryland. Small loan transactions are governed by that state's Consumer Loan Act,[194] which prescribes an interest rate cap of 2.75% per month on that part of the principal balance not more than $500.[195] This 33% APR effectively prohibits the practice of payday lending in Maryland.

## 9.3.23 Massachusetts

Massachusetts law specifically prohibits check cashers from making small loans unless separately licensed under the state's small loan law.[196] The Small Loan Act prescribes a rate cap of 23% per year and allows an administrative fee of $20, which cannot be assessed more than once during any twelve-month period.[197] The rate cap effectively prohibits payday lending in Massachusetts.

## 9.3.24 Michigan

Payday lending is authorized in Michigan by the Deferred Presentment Service Transactions Act.[198] A payday loan lender may not make more than one loan at a time to a particular borrower and may not make a loan to a borrower if that borrower already has more than one outstanding loan in effect with any lender.[199] A lender is not allowed to renew a loan; however, a lender may extend a loan as long as no fee is charged for that extension, and the balance owed is equal to the amount owed on the original loan.[200] In addition, a lender may not pursue criminal penalties against a borrower in connection with a payday loan.[201]

Michigan law sets out a detailed procedure by which borrowers may complain about suspected violations of the payday loan law. A borrower who believes that a lender may have violated the law may so notify the lender in person before the end of the day on which the loan is made. The borrower must identify the nature of the violation and provide documentary or other evidence of the violation at that time. At any time before taking out a new loan, a borrower who believes a lender violated the law may deliver to the lender a written notice to this effect. Again, the borrower must identify the nature of the violation and include documentary or other evidence of the violation in the notice. In either if these scenarios, the lender must determine if it has violated the law as alleged.

If the lender determines that it has violated the law, it must return to the borrower the check it received along with any fees paid, and the borrower must return the amount advanced. In addition, the lender must make shall make restitution to the borrower for each violation in an amount equal to five times the amount of the fee charged, but not less than $15 or more than the face amount of the borrower's check. A lender that makes restitution in this fashion may still be subject to a civil action under the payday loan act.

If the lender determines that it did not violate the law, the lender must immediately notify the commissioner of the Office of Financial and Insurance Services and the borrower of that determination. A borrower who receives a notice of such a determination by the lender may then file a written complaint with the Office. The commissioner must promptly investigate a borrower's complaint. On a conclusion that the lender did indeed violate the statute, the commissioner may order the lender to make restitution in an amount equal to three times the amount provided for if the lender had made restitution of its own accord, as described above, but not less than $45 or more than three times the face amount of the borrower's check. A lender ordered to pay restitution by the commissioner is also subject to any other applicable penalties and remedies available under the statute.[202]

In addition to spelling out this procedure for making a complaint to the lender and/or commissioner, the Michigan statute also provides that a borrower may bring a civil cause of action against the lender and recover actual damages and fees, plus reasonable attorney fees.[203]

## 9.3.25 Minnesota

In Minnesota, payday lending is authorized by law[204] with several restrictions. A lender is not permitted to make a payday loan for more than $350.[205] No rollovers are allowed, as the statute provides that a loan must not be repaid by the proceeds of another loan made by the same lender.[206]

Minnesota law provides that a lender who violates the payday loan laws is subject to a private action by the borrower,[207] in which the borrower may recover actual damages, statutory damages of up to $1,000 per violation, and reasonable attorney fees and costs. The law also provides for injunctive relief. In addition, the statute states that a loan is void and the borrower is not obligated to pay any amounts owing on the agreement if a lender is unlicensed or has charged interest or fees in excess of those allowed by law.[208]

193 Me. Rev. Stat. tit. 9-A, § 2-401.
194 Md. Code Ann., Com. Law §§ 12-301 to 12-317.
195 Md. Code Ann., Com. Law §§ 12-306.
196 209 Mass. Regs. Code tit. 209, § 45:14(8); Mass. Gen. Laws ch. 140, § 96.
197 209 Mass. Regs. Code tit. 209, § 26.01.
198 Mich. Comp. Laws §§ 487.2121 to 487.2173.
199 Mich. Comp. Laws § 487.2153(2).
200 Mich. Comp. Laws § 487.2155(1).
201 Mich. Comp. Laws § 487.2158(4).
202 Mich. Comp. Laws § 487.2156.
203 Mich. Comp. Laws § 487.2173.
204 Minn. Stat. § 47.60.
205 Minn. Stat. § 47.60, subdiv. 1(a).
206 Minn. Stat. § 47.60, subdiv. 2(f).
207 Minn. Stat. §§ 47.60, subdiv. 6, 47.601, subdiv. 6.
208 Minn. Stat. § 47.601, subdiv. 6.

### 9.3.26 Mississippi

The Mississippi Check Cashers Act[209] authorizes payday lending. While this statute was previously scheduled to sunset in 2012, the date of repeal was extended by amendments enacted in 2011 until July 1, 2015.[210] The Check Cashers Act imposes certain restrictions on payday lenders. As of January 1, 2012, the maximum term of a loan of up to $250 is thirty days,[211] and a loan for between $251 and $500 must have a term of between twenty-eight and thirty days.[212] Although the statute does not specify a maximum number of loans allowed at one time, it does prescribe that in no event shall the amount of the checks cashed for any one borrower exceed $500, including the amount of the fee,[213] and it prohibits rollovers, renewals, and extensions.[214] A lender may not pursue criminal prosecution of a borrower in connection with a check returned for insufficient funds.[215]

The 2011 amendments to the Check Cashers Act also alter the rate structure for fees that a lender may charge for payday loans. While a lender was previously permitted to collect an 18% fee on the face amount of the check, the new law permits a fee of up to $20.00 per $100.00 advanced for amounts up to $250.00, and $21.95 per $100.00 for amounts between $250.00 and $500.00.[216] In addition, a new provision in the law directs that a payday lender must provide the borrower with a pamphlet containing general information about the customer's rights and responsibilities in the loan transaction, as well as the consumer hotline phone number for the Mississippi Department of Banking and Consumer Finance and the Mississippi Attorney General's office.[217]

Any payday loan made by an unlicensed lender is null and void under Mississippi law.[218]

### 9.3.27 Missouri

Missouri law authorizes payday lending.[219] A lender may make a payday loan of up to $500,[220] but may not have more than that aggregate amount in loans outstanding to the same borrower at any one time.[221] A lender is permitted to make up to six renewals of a payday loan and the finance charge is capped at 75% of the loan; however, on the first renewal of the loan and each subsequent renewal thereafter, the borrower must reduce the principal amount of the loan by not less than 5% of the original amount of the loan until the loan is paid in full.[222]

A borrower may not be subjected to criminal prosecution for passing a bad check in connection with a payday loan in Missouri unless the account on which the instrument was written was closed by the borrower before the agreed-on date of negotiation or the borrower stopped payment on the check.[223]

Missouri law also directs that payday lenders must "consider the financial ability of the borrower to reasonably repay the loan in the time and manner specified in the loan contract."[224] However, there is no case law to date that substantively discusses or analyzes this requirement.

### 9.3.28 Montana

Payday lending in Montana is authorized under the Deferred Deposit Loan Act.[225] In 2010, the statute was amended to cap the interest rate at 36%[226] after Montana voters approved a ballot initiative by a large margin. The statute contains other restrictions on lenders as well. The maximum amount of any loan is $300,[227] and a lender may not extend a deferred deposit loan to a consumer who has an outstanding payday loan[228] or accept payment of a payday loan through the proceeds of another.[229] In addition, a lender is prohibited from threatening to use or using the criminal process to collect on a payday loan.[230]

Any intentional violation of the payday lending law in Montana constitutes an unfair or deceptive trade practice.[231] A lender who intentionally violates the law is liable to the consumer for actual damages and statutory damages of $1,000 for each violation, plus attorney fees and costs.[232] A consumer may also bring an action for injunctive and other appropriate equitable relief to stop a lender from violating any provision of the law.[233] The statute authorizes class actions.[234]

### 9.3.29 Nebraska

Payday lending is legal in Nebraska, under the Delayed Deposit Services Licensing Act,[235] with some restrictions. A lender may not hold more than two checks from a borrower at one time, and the total aggregate face amount in outstanding loans from any one borrower may not exceed $500.[236] Also, a lender may not accept a check as repayment, refinancing, or any other consolidation of an outstanding payday loan,[237] and may not renew, roll over, defer, or in any way extend a payday loan by

209 Miss. Code Ann. §§ 75-67-501 to 75-67-539.
210 Miss. Code Ann. § 75-67-539.
211 Miss. Code Ann. § 75-67-519(1)(a).
212 Miss. Code Ann. § 75-67-519(1)(b).
213 Miss. Code Ann. § 75-67-519(4)(c).
214 Miss. Code Ann. § 75-67-519(5).
215 Miss. Code Ann. § 75-67-515(10).
216 Miss. Code Ann. § 75-67-519(4)(a), (b).
217 Miss. Code Ann. § 75-67-519(9).
218 Miss. Code Ann. § 75-67-505(1)(a).
219 Mo. Rev. Stat. §§ 408.500 to 408.510.
220 Mo. Rev. Stat. § 408.500(1).
221 Mo. Rev. Stat. § 408.505(5).
222 Mo. Rev. Stat. § 408.500(6).
223 Mo. Rev. Stat. § 408.505(8).
224 Mo. Rev. Stat. § 408.500(7).
225 Mont. Code Ann. §§ 31-1-701 to 31-1-729.
226 Mont. Code Ann. § 31-1-722.
227 Mont. Code Ann. § 31-1-715(2).
228 Mont. Code Ann. § 31-1-723(14).
229 Mont. Code Ann. § 31-1-723(13).
230 Mont. Code Ann. § 31-1-723(2).
231 Mont. Code Ann. § 31-1-724(2).
232 Mont. Code Ann. § 31-1-724(3).
233 Mont. Code Ann. § 31-1-724(4).
234 Mont. Code Ann. § 31-1-724(5).
235 Neb. Rev. Stat. §§ 45-901 to 45-929.
236 Neb. Rev. Stat. § 45-919(a), (b).
237 Neb. Rev. Stat. § 45-919(e).

allowing the borrower to pay less than the total amount of the loan and any fees or charges.[238] If a lender violates either of these last two restrictions, the director of banking and finance is authorized under the statute to order the lender to return to the borrower all fees collected plus "all or part of the amount of the check or checks" that the lender accepted from the borrower.[239]

### 9.3.30 Nevada

Payday lending is authorized by statute in Nevada,[240] but the practice is subject to a number of restrictions. While the law does not prescribe a maximum dollar amount on a payday loan, it does state that a lender may not make a loan for an amount that is greater than 25% of a borrower's expected gross monthly income.[241] A lender may not make more than one payday loan at a time to a particular borrower unless the aggregate amount of multiple loans does not exceed this 25% figure.[242] If a borrower agrees to extend the period for the repayment, renewal, refinancing, or consolidation of an outstanding payday loan by paying it off with the proceeds of a new payday loan, the lender may not extend the period beyond sixty days after the expiration of the initial loan period, and the lender may not add any unpaid interest or other charges accrued during the original term of the outstanding loan or any extension of the outstanding loan to the principal amount of the new payday loan.[243] In addition, a lender may not use or threaten to use the criminal process to collect on a payday loan[244] nor may the lender pursue criminal action against a borrower for insufficient funds, unless the borrower acted with criminal intent.[245]

If a lender willfully violates the payday lending law, the loan is void and the lender may not collect, receive or retain any principal, interest, or other charges or fees with respect to the loan unless the lender is able to establish that the violation was excused due to a bona fide error defense and the lender notifies the borrower within sixty days after discovering such error and makes the appropriate adjustments.[246] If an unlicensed lender makes a payday loan, that loan is voidable by the borrower. A borrower may also bring a civil action against the lender for making a loan without being properly licensed,[247] as well as for other violations of the payday lending law.[248] The statute provides that the borrower may sue for actual damages, punitive damages, reasonable attorney fees and costs, and any other legal or equitable relief that a court deems appropriate, and it also authorizes the recovery of statutory damages of up to $1,000 per violation for certain specified knowing violations.[249]

238 Neb. Rev. Stat. § 45-919(f).
239 Neb. Rev. Stat. § 45-925(2).
240 Nev. Rev. Stat. §§ 604A.010 to 604A.940.
241 Nev. Rev. Stat. § 604A.425(1).
242 Nev. Rev. Stat. § 604A.430.
243 Nev. Rev. Stat. § 604A.480.
244 Nev. Rev. Stat. § 604A.440(1).
245 Nev. Rev. Stat. § 604A.490(4).
246 Nev. Rev. Stat. § 604A.900.
247 Nev. Rev. Stat. § 604A.920.
248 Nev. Rev. Stat. § 604A.930.
249 *Id.*

### 9.3.31 New Hampshire

Payday lending is legal in New Hampshire.[250] The statute provides that a lender may not loan more than $500 to a given borrower,[251] and a lender may not make more than one loan at any time "for the purpose of increasing charges."[252] Additionally, a lender is not permitted to make a loan to a borrower who currently has, or has had within the previous sixty-day period, an outstanding payday or title loan.[253] Rollovers are not allowed, as a lender is not permitted to refinance, renew, or extend any loan.[254] In addition, the law states that a lender may not threaten or pursue criminal proceedings against a borrower if the borrower passes a bad check.[255]

If a payday lender in New Hampshire charges rates in excess of those permitted by the law, the payday loan is void and the lender then has "no right to collect or receive any principal, charges, or recompense whatsoever."[256]

As of 2008, the annual percentage rate cap on a payday loan in New Hampshire is 36%.[257] In January 2012, New Hampshire's governor vetoed legislation that would have established a new small loan product in the state and effectively eliminated the 36% cap by raising interest rates on payday loans to over 400% APR.

### 9.3.32 New Jersey

In New Jersey, a licensed check casher may not cash or advance money on a postdated check.[258] This limitation in and of itself does not prohibit payday loans in New Jersey, as lenders may still conceivably make loans in the state pursuant to the Consumer Loan Act. However, while this statute allows rates to be set according to the contract agreed on by the parties, New Jersey law also prescribes a criminal usury cap of 30%.[259] This cap expressly applies to payday loans in New Jersey,[260] and thereby effectively prohibits payday lending in the state.

### 9.3.33 New Mexico

Payday lending is authorized by statute in New Mexico.[261] The law imposes several restrictions on lenders. While the statute does not specify a particular dollar limit on the size of a payday loan, it states that no lender may make a payday loan if the total amount of principal and fees, when combined with the amount of principal and fees of all of the borrower's other

250 N.H. Rev. Stat. §§ 399-A:1 to 399-A:19.
251 N.H. Rev. Stat. § 399-A:13(VI).
252 N.H. Rev. Stat. § 399-A:13(VIII).
253 N.H. Rev. Stat. § 399-A:13(XIX).
254 N.H. Rev. Stat. § 399-A:13(VII).
255 N.H. Rev. Stat. § 399-A:13(X).
256 N.H. Rev. Stat. § 399-A:11.
257 N.H. Rev. Stat. § 399-A:13(XX).
258 N.J. Stat. Ann. § 17:15A-47.
259 N.J. Stat. Ann. § 2C:21-19.
260 N.J. Admin. Code § 3:24-1.3.
261 N.M. Stat. Ann. §§ 58-15-32 to 58-15-38.

outstanding payday loans, exceeds 25% percent of the borrower's gross monthly income.[262] Rollovers are prohibited.[263] While a cooling off period is not required for ordinary payday loans, the law provides that a lender must comply with a ten-day waiting period following the full payment of all outstanding payday loans before making a payday loan to a borrower who has entered into a payment plan.[264] In addition, a lender is prohibited from threatening a borrower with criminal action in order to collect on a payday loan.[265]

In order to evade the restrictions imposed by New Mexico's payday loan provisions, many lenders in the state offer loans of over thirty-five days, since the statute does not cover such loans. Rather, these loans, which lenders call "installment loans," are not regulated in the same way as payday loans.[266] While a lender is prohibited from charging more than $15.50 per $100 as an "administrative fee" for a payday loan, the other product, the "installment loan," is subject to no interest cap whatsoever. Similarly, many New Mexico lenders evade the payday loan statutory restrictions by offering short-term loans that do not involve post-dated checks or debit authorizations, since the law specifically defines payday loans as including one of those features.

### 9.3.34 New York

In New York, an individual licensed as a check casher may not make loans or cash or advance any moneys on a post-dated check unless it is a payroll check.[267] While a lender could conceivably make payday loans under the Licensed Lender law, which allows any interest rate agreed to by the parties, New York's criminal usury cap of 25%[268] effectively prohibits the practice of payday lending in the state.

### 9.3.35 North Carolina

In 2001, laws authorizing payday lending in North Carolina were allowed to sunset.[269] The loans that were formerly covered under the statute now fall under the state's consumer finance act, which sets an interest rate cap of 36%.[270]

### 9.3.36 North Dakota

Payday lending is legal in North Dakota under the Deferred Presentment Service Providers Act.[271] The statute imposes several restrictions on lenders. A lender may not make a loan of more than $500,[272] and while the statute does not impose a number limit on how many loans may be made to any one borrower at a time, it does provide that a lender may not loan to a borrower who has an aggregate of payday loans exceeding $600 payable to that lender or any other payday lenders.[273] The statute prescribes a cooling off period of three days between payday loans.[274] A lender is permitted to make one renewal of a payday loan,[275] but the total period of the deferral, including the initial deferral and one renewal, may not exceed sixty days, and an individual renewal period may not be fewer than fifteen days.[276] In addition, a lender may not subject a borrower to criminal prosecution for insufficient funds unless the customer's account was closed on the original date of the transaction.[277]

### 9.3.37 Ohio

Payday lending is legal in Ohio, with restrictions.[278] The maximum amount of a payday loan is $500,[279] and a lender may make only one loan at a time to a particular borrower.[280] Also, a lender may not make a payday loan to a borrower if doing so would obligate the borrower to repay a total amount of more than $500 to all payday lenders or put the borrower in debt to such lenders for an amount greater than 25% of the borrower's gross monthly salary.[281] Further, a lender may not make more than four payday loans to any one borrower during one year,[282] and may not make a loan to a borrower who has received two loans within the previous ninety days from any payday lenders unless the borrower has completed an approved financial literacy program during that period.[283] In addition, a lender is prohibited from bringing or threatening to pursue criminal action against a borrower due to insufficient funds unless the borrower has intentionally engaged in fraud by closing or using any closed or false account to evade payment.[284]

Although Ohio enacted legislation in 2008 that capped interest on all short-term loans at 28%, and also gave borrowers thirty-one days to pay off loans, some lenders in Ohio have taken advantage of a loophole in order to evade these restrictions. Specifically, some lenders have "simply switched their licenses so they can offer payday 'clones' under two parallel lending statutes, the Small Loan Act and the Mortgage Lending Act."[285] These "clones" have APRs ranging from 128% to

262 N.M. Stat. Ann. § 58-15-32(A).
263 N.M. Stat. Ann. § 58-15-34(A).
264 N.M. Stat. Ann. § 58-15-36.
265 N.M. Stat. Ann. § 58-15-34(C).
266 *See* Nathalie Martin, *1,000% Interest–Good While Supplies Last: A Study of Payday Loan Practices and Solutions*, 52 Ariz. L. Rev. 563, 585–86 (2010).
267 N.Y. Banking Law § 373 (McKinney).
268 N.Y. Penal Code § 190.40 (McKinney).
269 N.C. Gen. Stat. § 53-281 (McKinney).
270 N.C. Gen. Stat. § 53-173.
271 N.D. Cent. Code §§ 13-08-01 to 13-08-15.
272 N.D. Cent. Code § 13-08-12(3).
273 N.D. Cent. Code § 13-08-12(4).
274 *Id.*
275 N.D. Cent. Code § 13-08-12(12).
276 *Id.*
277 N.D. Cent. Code § 13-08-12(8).
278 Ohio Rev. Code Ann. §§ 1321.35 to 1321.48.
279 Ohio Rev. Code Ann. § 1321.39(A).
280 Ohio Rev. Code Ann. § 1321.41(E).
281 *Id.*
282 Ohio Rev. Code Ann. § 1321.41(R).
283 Ohio Rev. Code Ann. § 1321.41(N).
284 Ohio Rev. Code Ann. § 1321.41(F).
285 *See* Nathalie Martin, *1,000% Interest–Good While Supplies Last: A*

700%.[286] While legislation was introduced in 2010 to address this loophole, it has not yet been enacted. One trial court has found that payday loans may not be made under a Mortgage Lending Act license, however that decision was on appeal at the time this treatise went to press.[287]

In Ohio, a lender who commits a payday lending violation is deemed to have committed an unfair and deceptive practice[288] and therefore a borrower has a right of action pursuant to the UDAP law, which provides for the recovery of actual damages, "noneconomic damages," injunctive relief, and reasonable attorney fees.[289]

### 9.3.38 Oklahoma

Payday lending is legal in Oklahoma under the Deferred Deposit Lending Act.[290] A lender is restricted from making a loan for more than $500,[291] and may not make a loan if the borrower has more than one outstanding payday loan with any lender.[292] A lender is not allowed to renew a payday loan,[293] and any loan made within thirteen days after a previous loan is entered into is considered a renewal and "shall not be made."[294] After a lender has entered into a fifth consecutive payday loan with a particular borrower, the lender must respect a cooling off period, until 8:00 a.m. on the second business day after the fifth consecutive loan has been paid in full, before making another loan to that borrower.[295] In addition, Oklahoma law prohibits a lender from threatening or pursuing criminal action against a borrower due to a returned check or failure to repay the payday loan, or subjecting the borrower to any criminal penalty if a check is dishonored.[296]

### 9.3.39 Oregon

Payday lending is legal in Oregon. While the law does not specify either a maximum loan limit or the number of loans that may be made to a borrower at any one time, it does state that a lender may not grant more than two renewals,[297] and must comply with a cooling off period of seven days after the previous payday loan expires before making a new payday loan to a borrower.[298]

### 9.3.40 Pennsylvania

Pennsylvania has not legalized payday lending. Check cashers are specifically prohibited from making payday loans under the Check Cashing Licensing Act. Therefore, the Consumer Discount Company Act applies.[299] The interest rate cap prescribed under this statute effectively prohibits the practice of payday lending in the state.

In 2007, the Pennsylvania Department of Banking filed a civil action against a Delaware-based company that was engaging in payday lending at numerous locations in Pennsylvania. The company offered Pennsylvania consumers a "Choice Line of Credit" in which a $500 credit line was provided to qualifying borrowers at a simple daily periodic interest rate corresponding with an APR of 5.98%. The company also charged the consumer a "monthly participation fee" of $149.95, which was charged each month as long as the consumer had any outstanding principal, fees, and finance charges. This lending program was operated without the partnership of any bank and without the benefit of a license from the Secretary of Banking pursuant to the Consumer Discount Company Act.

A three-judge panel of the Commonwealth Court granted the Department of Banking's motion and issued a permanent injunction, finding that the monthly fee of $149.95 on a $500.00 line of credit, in addition to 5.98% interest, violated the statute. Using an APR rate calculator, the court determined that the $149.95 fee in combination with the 5.98% interest rate aggregated into an annual interest rate of approximately 368%, and that the company violated the statute because it was required to be licensed to charge interest in excess of the 6% rate authorized by the Loan Interest and Protection Law.[300]

### 9.3.41 Puerto Rico

Payday lending is not authorized by statute in Puerto Rico. Small loans are governed by the Small Personal Loan Act,[301] which provides that the maximum rate of interest is established by the Financial Board of the Financial Institutions Commissioner's Office.[302] This cap on rates effectively bans the practice of payday lending in Puerto Rico.

### 9.3.42 Rhode Island

Payday lending is legal in Rhode Island.[303] The law imposes several restrictions on lenders. The maximum loan amount a

---

*Study of Payday Loan Practices and Solutions*, 52 Ariz. L. Rev. 563, 590 (2010).

286 *Id.*

287 Ohio Neighborhood Fin., Inc. v. Scott, No. 09CVF01488 (Elyria Mun. Ct., Lorain Cnty., Ohio Mar. 25, 2011) (appeal pending), *available at* www.nclc.org/unreported.

288 Ohio Rev. Code Ann. § 1321.44(A).

289 Ohio Rev. Code Ann. § 1345.09.

290 Okla. Stat. tit. 59, §§ 3101 to 3119.

291 Okla. Stat. tit. 59, § 3106(7).

292 Okla. Stat. tit. 59, § 3109(B).

293 Okla. Stat. tit. 59, § 3109(A).

294 Okla. Stat. tit. 59, § 3109(C).

295 Okla. Stat. tit. 59, § 3110.

296 Okla. Stat. tit. 59, § 3107.

297 Or. Rev. Stat. § 21(6).

298 Or. Rev. Stat. § 21(7).

299 7 Pa. Cons. Stat. Ann. §§ 6201 to 6219.

300 *See* Pennsylvania Dep't of Banking v. NCAS of Delaware, L.L.C., 931 A.2d 771 (Pa. Commw. Ct. 2007), *aff'd* 948 A.2d 752, 761 (Pa. 2008) ("We conclude that Section 3.A of the CDCA prohibits unlicensed lenders of under $25,000 from charging interest and any type of other or additional charge or charges that aggregate in excess of six percent, the amount they would otherwise be permitted to charge on a loan under the LIPL.").

301 P.R. Laws Ann. tit. 10, §§ 941 to 959.

302 P.R. Laws Ann. tit. 10, § 954.

303 R.I. Gen. Laws. §§ 19-14.4-1 to 19-14.4-10.

payday lender may make is $500,[304] and that is also the maximum aggregate amount of concurrently outstanding checks a lender may hold from the same borrower.[305] A lender may hold a maximum number of three concurrently outstanding checks[306] and may make only one rollover.[307]

In 2010, the payday lending law was amended to change the percentage a lender may charge as a fee in connection with a payday loan from 15% to 10% of the amount of funds advanced.[308]

### 9.3.43 South Carolina

Payday lending is authorized in South Carolina under the Deferred Presentment Services Act,[309] but the statute imposes some restrictions on lenders. The total amount advanced by a payday lender to a borrower may not exceed $550,[310] and no rollovers are allowed.[311] A lender may not make a payday loan to a borrower who has an outstanding payday loan, has repaid a previous payday loan with any lender on the same business day as a new loan is requested, has repaid a payday loan with any lender on the same business day or the previous business day if the new loan requested would be the customer's borrower's eighth or more transaction within a calendar year, or has entered into an extended payment plan with any lender that has not been paid in full or terminated.[312] Also, the law provides that no eighth or subsequent loan within a calendar year may be made on the same or subsequent business day of the repayment of the previous payday loan.[313] In addition, a lender may not pursue criminal action against a borrower in connection with a payday loan.[314]

In order to evade the restrictions imposed by the payday lending provisions, many lenders have become licensed as supervised lenders and therefore follow another, more lenient set of rules.[315] In acknowledging this loophole in the law, legislators in South Carolina introduced a bill in 2010 that would change the definition of a supervised loan as having a minimum of 120 days, and that would specify that postdated checks may not secure supervised loans.[316] This bill has passed in the South Carolina Senate, but has not yet become law.

### 9.3.44 South Dakota

Payday lending is legal in South Dakota under the state's small loan law. While the law does not set any rate cap, it does impose a few restrictions on payday lenders. A lender may loan a borrower a maximum amount of $500, and a violation of this provision is a Class 1 misdemeanor.[317] In addition, a lender may make no more than four rollovers, and before any rollover may be made the borrower must pay the outstanding fee and reduce the principal amount by at least 10% of the original amount of the loan.[318]

### 9.3.45 Tennessee

Payday lending is authorized in Tennessee under the Deferred Presentment Services Act.[319] However, the practice is subject to certain restrictions. A lender may not have outstanding more than two checks from any one borrower at a time, and the aggregate face value of all outstanding checks from that customer may not exceed $500.[320] If a borrower has three outstanding checks from that lender and other lenders, or if the aggregate value of all of the borrower's outstanding payday loans exceeds $500, then the lender must not make another payday loan unless the borrower represents in writing that he or she qualifies to issue a new check for the amount requested.[321] Rollovers are not allowed, as the law specifies that a lender "shall not renew or otherwise consolidate a deferred presentment transaction with the proceeds of another deferred presentment transaction made by the same licensee," and any renewal or rollover that is made is void and unenforceable.[322] In addition, a lender may not pursue criminal action against a borrower in connection with a payday loan.[323]

### 9.3.46 Texas

Payday lenders do business in Texas under that state's Credit Services Organization Act.[324] That statute allows licensed credit services organizations to charge fees for arranging extensions of credit for consumers. The payday lender arranges for a short-term loan from an ostensibly independent lender. The lender charges just the legal rate of interest, but the payday lender that arranges the loan charges a large flat fee that brings the true APR to as much as 450%. In 2004, the Fifth Circuit interpreted the Texas Credit Services Organization Act to allow this arrangement.[325] In 2011, the Texas legislature amended the statute to codify the Fifth Circuit's decision.[326]

Payday loans are also made pursuant to the state's Consumer Loan Act.[327] Regulations enacted pursuant to that statute provide that a lender may renew a payday loan "where the effect of the

304 R.I. Gen. Laws § 19-14.4-5.1(a).
305 R.I. Gen. Laws § 19-14.4-5.1(e).
306 R.I. Gen. Laws § 19-14.4-5.1(f).
307 R.I. Gen. Laws § 19-14.4-5.1(g).
308 R.I. Gen. Laws § 19-14.4-4(4).
309 S.C. Code Ann. §§ 34-39-110 to 34-39-290.
310 S.C. Code Ann. § 34-39-180(B).
311 S.C. Code Ann. § 34-39-180(F).
312 S.C. Code Ann. § 34-39-270(A).
313 S.C. Code Ann. § 34-39-270(B).
314 S.C. Code Ann. § 34-39-180(G).
315 S.C. Code Ann. §§ 37-3-500 to 37-3-515.
316 *See* S. 1065, 2009-2010 Leg. Sess. (S.C. 2010).
317 S.D. Codified Laws § 54-4-66.
318 S.D. Codified Laws § 54-4-65.
319 Tenn. Code Ann. §§ 45-17-101 to 45-17-119.
320 Tenn. Code Ann. § 45-17-112(o).
321 Tenn. Code Ann. § 45-17-112(p).
322 Tenn. Code Ann. § 45-17-112(q).
323 Tenn. Code Ann. § 45-17-112(i).
324 Tex. Fin. Code Ann. §§ 393.001 to 393.003 (West). *See* § 9.6.5, *infra*.
325 *See* Lovick v. Ritemoney Ltd., 378 F.3d 433 (5th Cir. 2004).
326 Tex. Fin. Code §§ 393.601 to 393.628 (West).
327 Tex. Fin. Code §§ 342.201 to 342.259 (West).

total amount of the interest charge would not exceed the total amount authorized by [the] Texas Finance Code . . . having due regard for the amount of the cash advance and the time the cash advance is outstanding."[328] The regulations also provide that a lender must make a good faith effort to assess the borrower's ability to repay the payday loan under the loan terms.[329]

Under Texas law, a lender may not threaten or pursue criminal charges against a borrower related to a check or other debit authorization provided as security for a transaction in the absence of forgery, fraud, theft, or other criminal conduct.[330]

## *9.3.47 Utah*

Utah permits payday lending under its Check Cashing and Deferred Deposit Lending Registration Act.[331] This statute imposes several restrictions on lenders. A lender may not roll over a payday loan unless the borrower requests it, and may not roll over a loan if the rollover requires the borrower to pay the amount owed, in whole or in part, more than ten weeks from the day on which the loan is first executed.[332] A lender may not extend a new payday loan to a borrower on the same business day that the borrower makes a payment on another payday loan if the payment is made at least ten weeks after the day on which that loan is extended and results in the principal of that loan being paid in full.[333] In addition, a lender is not permitted to threaten to use or use the criminal process to collect on a payday loan.[334] A loan made by a person who is required to be registered but who is unregistered is void and uncollectible.[335]

## *9.3.48 Vermont*

Vermont does not authorize payday lending. Small loans are governed by the state's Small Loan Act, which prescribes a rate cap of 18%.[336] Consequently, payday lending is effectively prohibited in Vermont.

## *9.3.49 Virginia*

Payday lending is authorized by statute in Virginia.[337] The statute was most recently amended in 2010, and imposes a number of restrictions on lenders. A loan may not exceed $500,[338] and the loan term must be at least two times the borrower's pay cycle.[339] A lender may not make more than one loan at a time to a particular borrower,[340] and may not make a loan to a borrower if doing so would cause the borrower to have more than one payday loan from any lender outstanding at the same time.[341]

Rollovers are not allowed.[342] Lenders may not make a loan on the same day that the borrower pays a previous payday loan.[343] Also, a lender may not make a payday loan to a borrower within ninety days following the date on which the borrower paid a loan through an extended payment plan.[344] Nor may lenders make a loan within forty-five days following the date on which a borrower has paid a fifth payday loan made within a period of 180 days, or within ninety days following the date on which a has paid an extended term loan or 150 days following the date that the borrower enters into an extended term loan.[345] The fifth payday loan is made in the form of an extended term loan that is payable in four equal installments over a payment period of sixty days following the date the loan is made. Before making a loan, a lender must query a centralized database that tells the lender whether the borrower is eligible for a new loan and whether making loan is permissible under the provisions of state law.[346] In addition, a lender may not threaten or pursue criminal proceedings against a borrower if a check is dishonored.[347]

If a lender violates a provision of a payday loan agreement, then that provision is unenforceable against the borrower. Further, an injured borrower may bring a civil action to enforce any provision of the payday loan law and, if successful, the borrower is entitled to recover reasonable attorney fees, expert witness fees, and any court costs incurred by bringing such an action.[348] The statute also provides that a violation of the payday loan provisions is subject to the enforcement provisions of the Virginia Consumer Protection Act.[349]

## *9.3.50 Washington*

Payday lending is legal in Washington. In order to make payday loans, a lender must first obtain a small loan endorsement to its check casher license.[350] The maximum principal amount of any payday loan, or the aggregate amount of all outstanding payday loans made by all lenders to a single borrower at any one time, may not exceed $700 or 30% of the borrower's gross monthly income of the borrower, whichever is lower.[351] A lender may not make a payday loan to a borrower who is in default on another payday loan until after that loan is paid in full, or until two years have passed since the origination

328 7 Tex. Admin. Code § 83.604(f).
329 *Id.*
330 Tex. Fin. Code § 393.201(3).
331 Utah Code Ann. §§ 7-23-101 to 7-23-504.
332 Utah Code Ann. § 7-23-401(b), (c).
333 Utah Code Ann. § 7-23-401(d).
334 Utah Code Ann. § 7-23-401(e).
335 Utah Code Ann. § 7-23-201(7) (effective May 8, 2012).
336 Vt. Stat. Ann. tit. 9, § 41a.
337 Va. Code Ann. §§ 6.2-1800 to 6.2-1829.
338 Va. Code Ann. § 6.2-1816(5).
339 Va. Code Ann. § 6.2-1816(1).
340 Va. Code Ann. § 6.2-1816(7).
341 Va. Code Ann. § 6.2-1816(6).
342 *Id. See also* Ruby v. Cashnet, 708 S.E.2d 871 (Va. 2011) (lender's practice of making a loan to the borrower immediately after she repaid a previous loan was a refinancing or renewal under § 6.2-1816(6)(i) and, therefore, in violation of the Act).
343 *Id.*
344 *Id.*
345 Va. Code Ann. § 6.2-1816(27).
346 Va. Code Ann. § 6.2-1810.
347 Va. Code Ann. § 6.2-1816(9).
348 Va. Code Ann. § 6.2-1826.
349 Va. Code Ann. § 6.2-1829.
350 Wash. Rev. Code §§ 31.45.073(1), 31.45.079.
351 Wash. Rev. Code § 31.45.073(2).

date of the loan, whichever occurs first.[352] A lender may not make a payday loan to a borrower if doing so would result in the borrower receiving more than eight payday loans from all lenders in any twelve-month period.[353] Lenders must check a centralized database before making a loan to ensure that the loan is permissible under the limits imposed by state law.[354]

Lenders may not threaten criminal prosecution as a method of collecting a delinquent small loan.[355] A violation of the provisions governing payday loans is a UDAP under Washington law.[356]

### 9.3.51 West Virginia

Payday lending is not authorized by statute in West Virginia. Laws applying to check cashing specifically provide that merchants "may not, in connection with providing check cashing services, agree to hold checks submitted to them for deposit at a later date for the purpose of providing a loan of money and deriving profit therefrom."[357] Small loans are governed by the Small Loan Act, which establishes a rate cap of 31% per year on a loan of $2,000 or less.[358] This cap effectively prohibits the practice of payday lending in the state.

### 9.3.52 Wisconsin

As of 2011, Wisconsin has enacted a law specifically authorizing payday lending.[359] While this law specifically provides that it imposes no limit on the interest that a lender may charge before the maturity date of a payday loan,[360] it does impose other restrictions upon lenders. For payday loans not paid in full on or before the maturity date, a lender may charge, *after* the maturity date, interest at a rate not exceeding 2.75% per month, except that if a lender makes a subsequent payday loan to the borrower and the borrower does not pay the subsequent loan in full on or before the maturity date of the subsequent loan, the lender may charge, after the maturity date of the subsequent loan, interest at a rate not exceeding 2.75% per month on the subsequent loan and the lender may not charge any interest on the prior loan. A lender may not make a payday loan that results in the borrower having an outstanding aggregate liability in principal, interest, and all other fees and charges, to all lenders who have made payday loans to the borrower, of more than $1,500 or 35% of the borrower's gross monthly income, whichever is less.[361] A lender may not make more than one rollover of a payday loan.[362]

Lenders may not pursue criminal action against borrowers for dishonored checks or a denial of electronic funds.[363] Payday loans by unlicensed lenders are void. By statute, borrowers are not required to pay loans from unlicensed lenders and may recover from the lender all amounts paid.[364] A borrower injured by a violation of the payday loan law may bring an action against the lender for damages of $250 or the amount of the payday loan, whichever is greater, plus costs and reasonable attorney fees.[365]

### 9.3.53 Wyoming

Payday lending is legal in Wyoming.[366] The only restriction the law places on lenders, other than a maximum finance charge (the greater of $30 or 20% per month on the principal balance of the check[367]) is that no rollovers are permitted.[368]

## 9.4 Federal Regulation of Payday Lending

### 9.4.1 Talent-Nelson Military Lending Act

The Talent-Nelson Military Lending Act (MLA), described more thoroughly at § 2.2.5, *supra*, provides the most significant federal restriction on payday lending, however, it only applies to active duty servicemembers and their dependents. The MLA forbids making payday loans that meet the Department of Defense's definition of the term. The ban, however, is not explicit and is somewhat hampered by an unreasonably narrow definition.

The MLA regulations define a "payday loan" as a transaction meeting four conditions: 1) the loan is closed-end; 2) the term is ninety-one days or fewer; 3) the amount financed is $2,000 or less; and 4) the borrower provides a payment instrument or debit authorization that is deferred for more than one day.[369] Loans subject to the MLA, including payday loans as defined, may not require repayment through a payroll allotment or be secured with a check, title to a personal vehicle, or access to a financial account.[370] Because the definition of "payday loan" includes an element that is banned by the MLA—the deferred payment instrument or authorization—the MLA indirectly bans payday loans meeting the definition in the regulations.[371]

352 *Id.*
353 Wash. Rev. Code § 31.45.073(4).
354 Wash. Rev. Code § 31.45.093.
355 Wash. Rev. Code § 31.45.082(1).
356 Wash. Rev. Code § 31.45.190.
357 W. Va. Code § 32A-3-1(e).
358 W. Va. Code §§ 46A-4-107 to 46A-4-113.
359 Wis. Stat. § 138.14.
360 Wis. Stat. § 138.14(10).
361 Wis. Stat. § 138.14(12)(b).
362 Wis. Stat. § 138.14(12)(a).
363 Wis. Stat. § 138.14(12)(f).
364 Wis. Stat. § 138.14(15)(b). An action to recover such amounts must be brought within one year after the date of the last scheduled payment on the loan or it will be barred.
365 Wis. Stat. § 138.14(16).
366 Wyo. Stat. Ann. §§ 40-14-362 to 40-14-364.
367 Wyo. Stat. Ann. § 40-14-363.
368 Wyo. Stat. Ann. § 40-14-364.
369 Section 2.2.5, *supra*, describes the elements of this definition in greater detail.
370 § 2.2.5.7, *supra*.
371 *Compare* 32 C.F.R. § 232.3(i)(A) and (B) (defining payday loan), *with* 32 C.F.R. § 232.8(a)(5) (prohibitions).

While terms of the MLA would probably ensnare most traditional payday loans, the MLA does not reach bank payday loans structured as open-end credit,[372] or transactions not considered consumer credit under the Truth in Lending Act. In addition, an agreement allowing a depository institution to offset fees against deposited funds, consistent with the depository's legal offset rights, is not considered a deferred payment instrument.[373] Thus loans made as advances from bank accounts, such as direct deposit account advances or overdraft loans, are likely not covered, regardless of the interest rate. Loans otherwise meeting the MLA's definition of "consumer credit," must comply with the Department of Defense's restrictions.[374]

## *9.4.2 Federal Banking Agency Guidance on Payday Lending*

### 9.4.2.1 Introduction

This subsection considers Office of the Comptroller of the Currency (OCC) and Federal Deposit Insurance Corporation (FDIC) guidance on payday lending. Federal banking guidance applies not just to bank practices, but to situations where banks partner with traditional payday lenders, such as previously occurred with rent-a-bank arrangements.[375] The guidance also applies to the banks' relationships with payment processors. In addition, banks are beginning to make their own payday loans. Section 9.5, *infra*, specifically examines existing restrictions on banks and other financial institutions making their own payday loans.

### 9.4.2.2 OCC Guidance

In 2000, the Office of the Comptroller of the Currency (OCC), the regulator for national banks and (since 2011) federal savings associations, issued an advisory letter containing guidelines for banks involved in payday lending.[376] At the time the guidelines were issued, bank payday activity primarily took the form of relationships with non-bank partners, such as the rent-a-bank arrangements described at § 9.6.1, *infra*. In those arrangements, a non-bank would provide services in connection with the origination, servicing, and collection of payday loans ostensibly made by a national bank.

Though the OCC does not have regulatory authority over non-banks, the OCC asserted the right to examine the services performed by the non-bank "to the same extent as if the bank itself were performing these services on its own premises[,]" pursuant to the OCC's authority under Bank Service Company Act.[377]

The guidelines also include provisions applicable to banks' own payday lending activities, such as the deferred deposit advances described at § 9.5.1, *infra*. Overall, the OCC instructed banks involved in payday lending to "follow sound lending practices . . . and be mindful of the burden the loan will place on their customers."[378] One of the most important statements in the advisory letter discourages rollovers, referred to as "renewals":

> Unlimited renewals, multiple renewals without principal reduction, or renewals in which interest and fees are added to the principal balance are not consistent with safe and sound banking principles.

Elsewhere in the same letter, the OCC further cautions:

> Multiple renewals—particularly renewals without reduction in the principal balance, and renewals in which interest and fees are added to the principal balance, are an indication that a loan has been made without a reasonable expectation of repayment at maturity.[379]

Even though there is no private right of action for disregarding an advisory letter, this letter could be used to support a claim that the lender acted unfairly, deceptively, or unconscionably by rolling over loans despite knowing the consumer did not have the ability to repay at the time of each rollover.

In June 2011, the OCC proposed additional guidance for banks involved with payday lending.[380] The proposed guidance more directly addresses deferred deposit advances and articulates several principles, including credit based on ability to repay and prudent limitations on cost and usage. Nevertheless, the proposal is insufficient to protect bank customers from abusive practices.[381] As this treatise went to print, the proposal was still pending.

Arguably, OCC 2004 preemption regulations prevents national banks from engaging in payday lending directly. There, the OCC stated: "A national bank shall not make a consumer loan . . . based predominately on the bank's realization of the foreclosure or liquidation value of the borrower's collateral, without regard to the borrower's ability to repay the loan according to its terms."[382] Assuming the holding of a consumer's check or an electronic debit authorization rises to the level of "collateral" under state law,[383] traditional payday lending

372 *See* § 2.2.5.9, *supra*.

373 32 C.F.R. § 232.3(b)(1)(i)(B).

374 *See* § 2.2.5.3, *supra*.

375 *See* § 9.6.1, *infra*.

376 OCC Advisory Letter No. 2000-10 (Nov. 27, 2000), *available at* www.occ.gov/static/news-issuances/memos-advisory-letters/2000/advisory-letter-2000-10.pdf.

377 OCC Advisory Letter No. 2000-10 (Nov. 27, 2000), *available at* www.occ.gov/static/news-issuances/memos-advisory-letters/2000/advisory-letter-2000-10.pdf (citing 12 U.S.C. § 1867(c)).

378 OCC Advisory Letter No. 2000-10 (Nov. 27, 2000), *available at* www.occ.gov/static/news-issuances/memos-advisory-letters/2000/advisory-letter-2000-10.pdf.

379 OCC Advisory Letter No. AL 2000-10 (Nov. 27, 2000), *available at* www.occ.gov/static/news-issuances/memos-advisory-letters/2000/advisory-letter-2000-10.pdf.

380 76 Fed. Reg. 33,409 (June 8, 2011).

381 *See generally Comments of NCLC* et al. *to OCC on Docket ID OCC-2011-0012*, 76 Fed. Reg. 33,409 (filed Aug. 8, 2011), *available at* www.nclc.org/images/pdf/high_cost_small_loans/payday_loans/occ-comments-payday-overdraft.pdf.

382 12 C.F.R. § 7.4008(b).

383 In the Truth in Lending context, courts have uniformly held that the holding the consumer's check is security for the loan. *See* National

should be considered contrary to this rule because it does not involve a real assessment of ability to repay or debt-to-income ratios. Similarly, banks do not assess ability to repay or debt-to-income ratios when making deferred deposit advances.

### 9.4.2.3 FDIC Guidance

#### *9.4.2.3.1 2003 and 2005 guidance*

Certain state-chartered banks and savings associations come under the FDIC's jurisdiction if they are FDIC-insured banks. The FDIC issued Guidelines for Payday Lending in July 2003[384] and updated them in 2005.[385] The guidelines emphasize safety and soundness concerns, limit the volume of payday loans to less than 25% of the bank's Tier 1 capital, and called for up to 100% capitalization of loans outstanding.[386] The capitalization requirement is somewhat irrelevant, however, for banks that sell most of their loans or participation interests to their local storefront partners or others.

Examiners are to look at certain characteristics of their third-party lender programs but the FDIC did not create any firm prohibitions.[387] While the guidelines indicate that borrowers who request an extension, deferral, renewal, or rewrite should exhibit a renewed "willingness and ability to repay," they do not require banks to check credit history or debt-to-income ratios. Further, the guidelines only state that banks "should" limit the number and frequency of extensions, deferrals, renewals, or rewrites.

The guidelines also encourage banks to ensure that borrowers exhibit an ability to repay when they request an extension, deferral, renewal. For the FDIC, this exhortation translated into a bright-line rule that the bank offer the customer or refer the customer to an alternative longer-term credit product when the customer has used payday loans for more than three months in the past twelve months. This means that the customer could have six two-week loans in the past year before the bank has to refuse to renew or provide another payday loan. For example, if the loan cost $17 per $100, a customer will have paid more than she borrowed and still owe the principal ($\$17 \times 6 = \$102$).

The FDIC did not require its banks to determine ability to repay before making loans to consumers. Nor did it address the concern that renting a charter is an abuse of bank privileges which helps non-bank payday lenders evade state usury laws and consumer protections. Arguably, however, FDIC-insured state-chartered banks are prohibited from engaging in payday lending since national banks may not make loans based on the value of the collateral without consideration of the borrower's ability to repay and state banks may not engage in any type of activity that is not permissible for national bank.[388]

Like the OCC, the FDIC asserted that it may examine the non-bank payday firms associated with state banks pursuant to the Bank Service Company Act.[389] And the FDIC instructed its examiners to look at the "economic substance" of a transaction to determine the number of rollovers that have occurred.[390]

While the 2005 guidelines did not explicitly prevent state-chartered FDIC-insured banks from partnering with payday lenders, the issuance of these guidelines combined with subsequent examinations appears to have had the same effect. Within a few years after the 2005 guidelines had been issued all FDIC-insured banks had ended their payday partnerships.

#### *9.4.2.3.2 2007 guidance*

In 2007 the FDIC issued Affordable Small Loan Guidelines.[391] These guidelines encourage banks to develop affordable alternatives to payday loans. In doing so banks should:

- Collect fees that bear a direct relationship to origination costs and avoid charges such as annual fees, membership fees, advance fees, and prepayment penalties;
- Offer small loan credit with APRs of no greater than 36%;
- Encourage principal reduction by structuring closed-end loans to provide for affordable and amortizing payments; open-end loans should require minimum payments that pay off principal;
- Avoid excessive renewals or the prolonged failure to reduce the outstanding balance;
- Utilize sound underwriting that focuses on a borrower's history with the institution and ability to repay within an acceptable timeframe, though for small loans, documenting the borrower's ability to repay could be streamlined to include basic information, such as proof of recurring income.

#### *9.4.2.3.3 2012 guidance on payment processor relationships*

Another relevant FDIC pronouncement is its guidance on payment processor relationships.[392] Payment processors are third parties that handle payment transactions for other entities

---

Consumer Law Center, Truth in Lending § 7.8.2 (7th ed. 2010 and Supp.).

384 The FDIC appears to have removed this document from its website. The Press Release announcing its issuance is *available at* www.fdic.gov/news/news/press/2003/pr7003.html.

385 FDIC Guidelines for Payday Lending (2005), *available at* www.fdic.gov/news/news/financial/2005/fil1405a.html.

386 However, banks that sell 85% to 95% of their loans or participation interests to their local storefront partners have little to capitalize.

387 *See* Jean Ann Fox, Consumer Federation of America, Unsafe and Unsound: Payday Lenders Hide Behind FDIC Bank Charters to Peddle Usury 18–19 (Mar. 2004), *available at* www.consumerfed.org/pdfs/pdlrentabankreport.pdf.

388 *Compare* 12 U.S.C. § 1831a(a)(1), *with* 12 C.F.R. § 7.4008(b) (national bank regulation regarding ability to repay).

389 FDIC Guidelines for Payday Lending 2 (2005), *available at* www.fdic.gov/news/news/financial/2005/fil1405a.html.

390 *Id.* at 5. "Where the economic substance of consecutive advances is substantially similar to 'rollovers'—without appropriate intervening 'cooling off' or waiting periods—examiners should treat these loans as continuous advances and classify accordingly."

391 Fed. Deposit Ins. Corp., FIL 50-2007: Affordable Small-Dollar Loan Guidelines (June 19, 2007), *available on the companion website to this treatise.*

392 Fed. Deposit Ins. Corp., FIL-3-2012 (Jan. 31, 2012), *available at* www.fdic.gov/news/news/financial/2012/fil12003.pdf.

such as payday lenders or merchants. They typically do so by creating and depositing remotely created checks—often called "Demand Drafts"—or by originating Automated Clearing House (ACH) debits on behalf of their merchant customers. The processor may do so using its own deposit account at a bank to process such transactions, or it may establish deposit accounts for its clients at the bank.[393]

The FDIC expects banks to "understand, verify, and monitor" payment processor activities and the merchants they do business with.[394] This is because the FDIC has recognized a higher risk of fraud and other illegal activities among processors dealing with telemarketers and Internet merchants. The guidance specifically lists payday lenders as an example.[395] As a result, banks "that fail to adequately manage these relationships may be viewed as facilitating a payment processor's or merchant client's fraudulent or unlawful activity and, thus, may be liable for such acts or practices."[396] Notably, the FDIC warns banks that they should not rely on processors to do their own due diligence. Instead banks are, themselves, responsible for oversee all transactions and activities processed through the bank.

Banks are expected to promptly take measures to minimize possible consumer harm related to potentially fraudulent or improper activities involving payment processors and their clients. "Appropriate actions include filing a Suspicious Activity Report,[397] requiring the payment processor to cease processing for a specific merchant, freezing certain deposit account balances to cover anticipated charge backs, and/or terminating the financial institution's relationship with the payment processor."[398] As with the OCC's guidance, there is no private right of action for consumers harmed by banks that ignore the FDIC's guidelines. But the guidelines may be used as the basis for a RICO,[399] UDAP, or negligence claim by establishing the standards for reasonable conduct.

### *9.4.3 TILA and the ECOA*

The federal Truth in Lending Act imposes certain disclosure requirements on many forms of consumer credit, including payday loans, most significantly disclosure of the Annual Percentage Rate (APR).[400] TILA is summarized at 2.2.2, *supra,* and described extensively in National Consumer Law Center, *Truth in Lending* (7th ed. 2010 and Supp.). The federal Equal Credit Opportunity Act,[401] which prohibits discrimination in lending, also applies to payday loans. The ECOA is discussed in greater detail in National Consumer Law Center, *Credit Discrimination* (5th ed. 2009 and Supp.).

## 9.5 Financial Institution Payday Loans

### *9.5.1 Bank Payday Loans*

Banks, seeing a source of significant profit, have been increasingly offering their own version of payday loans, called a "checking account advance" or a "direct deposit advance."[402] Both large and small banks have begun offering payday loans.[403] Due to federal preemption, national banks making these loans are able to evade most state-level regulations applicable to other payday lenders.[404] And, because the transactions are usually structured as open-end credit, they are not subject to the Military Lending Act, which is limited to closed-end loans.[405] So, absent any other federal restrictions, national banks are essentially free to develop their own products.

Like other payday loans, these are small, short-term loans with high fees. Customers who sign up can take out advances by telephone or at ATMs. Eligibility requirements are minimal—often just having on file a regular, sufficiently-sized direct deposit, such as a paycheck or Social Security check. The funds are deposited into the consumer's bank account. The bank then repays itself in full for the advance, plus the fee, by taking some or all of the customer's next deposit, even if it comes the next day. If this deposit is insufficient to repay the bank in full, the bank keeps taking subsequent deposits. This continues automatically until the loan is repaid and in some circumstances regardless whether doing so overdraws the account or whether the funds in the account are public benefits exempt from garnishment.[406] If the borrower does not have sufficient funds

393 Fed. Deposit Ins. Corp., FIL-3-2012 (Jan. 31, 2012), *available at* www.fdic.gov/news/news/financial/2012/fil12003.pdf.

394 Fed. Deposit Ins. Corp., FIL-3-2012 (Jan. 31, 2012), *available at* www.fdic.gov/news/news/financial/2012/fil12003.pdf.

395 Fed. Deposit Ins. Corp., FIL-3-2012 n.1 (Jan. 31, 2012), *available at* www.fdic.gov/news/news/financial/2012/fil12003.pdf.

396 Fed. Deposit Ins. Corp., FIL-3-2012 (Jan. 31, 2012), *available at* www.fdic.gov/news/news/financial/2012/fil12003.pdf.

397 31 C.F.R. § 1020.320. *See* § 9.2.6, *supra* (describing suspicious activity reports).

398 Fed. Deposit Ins. Corp., FIL-3-2012 (Jan. 31, 2012), *available at* www.fdic.gov/news/news/financial/2012/fil12003.pdf.

399 *See* Reyes v. Zions First Nat'l Bank, Reyes v. Zion First N.A., 2012 U.S. Dist. LEXIS 38238 (E.D. Pa. Mar. 21, 2012) (refusing to dismiss claim against payment processors for facilitating fraudulent telemarketing schemes).

400 15 U.S.C. §§ 1601 to 1666j.

401 15 U.S.C. §§ 1691 to 1691f.

402 *See* Jim Puzzanghera, *Credit Unions, Banks Grabbing a Share of Payday Loan Dollars*, L.A. Times, Mar. 11, 2012, *available at* www.latimes.com/business/la-fi-banks-payday-loans-20120311,0,3076812.story; NCLC Issue Brief, 300% Bank Payday Loans Spreading: Regions Bank Joins Wells Fargo, U.S. Bank and Fifth Third in Predatory Lending (Aug. 2011), *available at* www.nclc.org/images/pdf/banking_and_payment_systems/ib_bank_payday_spreading.pdf.

403 *See* NCLC, Issue Brief: 300% Bank Payday Loans Spreading (Aug. 2011), *available at* www.nclc.org/images/pdf/banking_and_payment_systems/ib_bank_payday_spreading.pdf.

404 Ctr. for Responsible Lending, Predatory Payday Lending by Banks on the Rise, *available at* www.responsiblelending.org/payday-lending/policy-legislation/predatory-payday-lending-by-banks.html#_edn8.

405 *See* § 2.2.5.9, *supra.*

406 Leah Plunkett, Margot Saunders, National Consumer Law Center, Runaway Bandwagon: How the Government's Push for Direct Deposit of Social Security Exposes Seniors to Predatory Bank Loans 16 (July 2010), *available at* www.nclc.org/images/pdf/pr-reports/runaway-bandwagon.pdf; Ctr. for Responsible Lending, Predatory Payday Lending by Banks on the Rise n.8, *available at* www.responsiblelending.org/payday-lending/policy-legislation/

in the account, these withdraws are likely to result in overdraft charges as well as NSF fees if any checks are presented in the meantime.

While bank payday loans may appear slightly cheaper than traditional payday loans, they also carry additional fees, such as overdraft charges and late fees that traditional payday lenders do not have. Banks also receive very high interest rates on such loans, particularly considering the low risk and low transaction costs involved. A typical loan may cost $10 per $100 loaned.[407] If the borrower is paid biweekly and takes out a loan on payday, the loan must be repaid by the next paycheck in fourteen days, resulting in a 261% APR.

More likely, however, a borrower will become short of funds and take an advance between paydays. According to a 2011 study, the median loan length was only ten days.[408] When the bank repays itself from the borrower's next paycheck, this will yield an APR of 365%. An advance taken only three days before the borrower's next payday would yield an APR of 1217%. As a result, in practice, account advance loans can be much worse than payday loans. In one example, reported to NCLC by a disabled Army veteran:

> on several occasions I took a direct deposit advance on a Thursday, only to have the advance and fee taken out of the very next day's deposit. . . . I'm not good at math, but I began to suspect that a one-day loan of $500 with interest of $50 (the current maximum loan amount and the dollar interest amount) certainly exceeded the claimed APR rate."[409]

National banks, federal savings associations, and federally-insured state-chartered banks, savings associations, and credit unions need not comply with interest rate caps applicable to the consumer's home state. Instead, through rate exportation these depositories can comply with their home state interest rate caps.[410] They can often charge the rate allowed for the most favored lender in that state for that class of loans, but if they do use that cap, they must comply with all material state restrictions for that class of loans.[411]

## 9.5.2 *Prepaid Card Payday Loans*

In one of the newer forms of payday loan, payday lenders partner with a bank and a prepaid card program manager to offer payday loans on prepaid cards. A prepaid card is basically a debit card without the individual bank account.[412] Funds are typically held in a master account in the name of the program manager with subaccounts for individual consumers.

Prepaid card payday loans can take different forms.[413] The card may have an account advance feature similar to the bank payday loans described in § 9.5.1, *supra*. The card may be used to load a loan that purportedly comes from a third party lender, with load fees that add to any interest or fees charged by the lender. Or the card may have an overdraft feature that permits use of the card when it lacks funds, in exchange for a flat fee or a fee tied to the amount of the negative balance.[414]

Prepaid cards can be used to evade state usury and payday laws. Due to the type or structure of the fees, or the supposed separation between the lender and the prepaid card provider, the payday lender may claim that the fees are not imposed in connection with the credit and thus are outside of state fee or interest caps or federal annual percentage rate disclosure requirements. The lender may also claim that the bank's involvement with the product insulates it from state laws by virtue of preemption.

Advocates should closely examine the structure of the loan and the card and the relationship between the different parties involved. The companies may have related ownership, may purchase loans that they do not originate, or may have profit sharing arrangements that provide ground for attacking the compartmentalization of the charges. Both state laws and the federal Truth in Lending Act may cover fees charged by various parties if they are related to the extension of credit.[415] And even if the bank's conduct is beyond state laws due to federal preemption, the same may not be true for charges or practices of the nonbank lender or prepaid card program manager.[416]

predatory-payday-lending-by-banks.html#_edn8 (citing Wells Fargo terms and conditions).

407 Rebecca Borné et al., Ctr. for Responsible Lending, Big Bank Payday Loans: High-Interest Loans Through Checking Accounts Keep Customers in Long-Term Debt at 6 (July 2011), *available at* www.responsiblelending.org/payday-lending/research-analysis/big-bank-payday-loans.pdf.

408 *Id.*

409 Email from "Richard" to National Consumer Law Center (Apr. 21, 2010).

410 *See* § 3.4, *supra*.

411 *See* § 3.5.6, *supra*.

412 Prepaid cards are covered in National Consumer Law Center, Consumer Bankruptcy Law and Practice Ch. 7 (9th ed. 2009 and Supp.). Prepaid cards with credit features are discussed in National Consumer Law Center, Consumer Bankruptcy Law and Practice § 7.1.4 (9th ed. 2009 and Supp.).

413 Some of these forms of prepaid card payday loans and the legal issues associated with them are described in Letter from National Consumer Law Center et al. to the Comptroller of the Currency Regarding a CheckSmart Card Issued by Urban Trust Bank (May 3, 2012), *available at* www.nclc.org/images/pdf/high_cost_small_loans/ltr-urban-trust-occ.pdf.

414 The laws covering overdraft fees are discussed in National Consumer Law Center, Consumer Banking and Payments Law § 2a.4 (2011 Supp.). The Electronic Fund Transfer Act overdraft fee rules do not currently cover most prepaid cards, but that is likely to change in the near future and most prepaid cards voluntarily follow the EFTA rules.

415 *See* National Consumer Law Center, Truth in Lending § 3.7 (7th ed. 2010 and Supp.).

However, fees are included in annual percentage rate (APR) disclosure requirements only for closed-end credit. The APR calculation rules for open-end credit have been gutted and do not capture fees. *See id.* §§ 6.6.5, 6.6.6, 6.7.6.4.1.

416 Preemption is discussed at Ch. 3, *supra*.

## 9.5.3 Credit Unions and Payday Loans

### 9.5.3.1 General

Most credit unions in the United States are chartered either by the federal National Credit Union Administration (NCUA) or at the state level. The NCUA has regulatory authority over federal credit unions (FCUs). The NCUA also has some authority over state credit unions that are insured by the National Credit Union Share Insurance Fund. In theory credit unions should be less likely to be involved in abusive lending than other financial institutions because they are nonprofit entities intended to benefit their members.[417]

Federal credit unions are subject to statutory usury caps far lower than the rates typically charged on payday loans. In addition, all FCUs, and state credit unions insured by the Share Insurance Fund, must be organized "for the purpose of promoting thrift among [their] members and creating a source of credit for provident or productive purposes."[418] The Eighth Circuit Court of Appeals has stated that "[p]ayday loans are not 'credit for provident or productive purposes,' as they are not used for investment."[419] As a result, payday lending should be considered inconsistent with the purpose of credit unions generally. Nevertheless, a surprising number of credit unions offer payday loans with triple-digit APRs.[420]

### 9.5.3.2 FCU Interest Rate Caps

Unlike federally chartered banks and thrifts, federal credit unions are subject to a fairly clear and strict interest rate cap that is independent of state caps.[421] FCUs are chartered under the Federal Credit Union Act.[422] The statute sets a usury cap of 15% but allows the NCUA to authorize increases for as long as eighteen months at a time.[423] The NCUA has done so frequently, setting the cap at 18% since May 14, 1987.[424] The NCUA interprets the cap as including all finance charges, as defined by the Truth in Lending Act.[425] The 18% cap applies to all loans except those subject to the NCUA's more recent rule on "short-term, small amount loans" (STS loans), as discussed in the next subsection.[426]

Because of the relatively low interest cap, few federal credit unions make payday loans, though some have done so by exploiting loopholes in the APR calculation by charging high application or participation fees that they do not include in the finance charge. Others have taken broker fees for referrals to credit union subsidiaries.[427]

### 9.5.3.3 Higher Interest Cap for Short-Term, Small (STS) Loans

Effective October 25, 2010, FCUs may charge an interest rate on "short-term, small amount loans" (STS) that is up to 10 points higher than the rate allowed by the general rate cap (resulting, effectively, in a 28% cap), plus a single application fee up to \$20.[428] This rule is intended to give FCUs more latitude to make reasonably priced small loans as an alternative to high-priced payday loans.[429]

FCUs may charge the higher 28% rate on the following conditions:

- Loans must be between \$200 and \$1,000.
- The term must be between one and six months.
- No more than three STS loans can be made to a borrower, and no more than one at any given time, in any rolling six-month period.
- Loans cannot be rolled over.
- The loan must be fully amortizing, meaning it must be payable in installments.
- Borrowers must have been a credit union member for at least one month.
- Any application fee must meet Regulation Z requirements and be no more than \$20.[430]
- STS loans cannot exceed 20% of the FCU's net worth and the FCU must implement underwriting guidelines.[431]

417 *See* 12 U.S.C. § 1752(1); World Council of Credit Unions, What Is a Credit Union?, www.woccu.org/about/creditunion ("Members benefit from higher returns on savings, lower rates on loans and fewer fees on average.").

418 12 U.S.C. §§ 1752(1), 1781(c).

419 Oiciyapi Fed. Credit Union v. National Credit Union Admin., 936 F.2d 1007, 1011 (8th Cir. 1991) (affirming NCUA decision to dissolve credit union whose "primary activity" was "granting payday loans").

420 *See generally Comments of NCLC and Consumers Union on NCUA's Proposed Rule on Short-Term, Small Amount Loans*, 75 Fed. Reg. 24,497 (2010), *available at* www.nclc.org/images/pdf/high_cost_small_loans/payday_loans/comments-ncua-short-term-loan.pdf (July 6, 2010) (discussing abusive payday lending by credit unions); NCLC Stopping the Payday Loan Trap: Alternatives That Work, Ones That Don't (June 2010), *available at* www.nclc.org/images/pdf/high_cost_small_loans/payday_loans/report-stopping-payday-trap.pdf.

421 *See* § 3.3, *supra.*

422 12 U.S.C. §§ 1751 to 1795k.

423 12 U.S.C. § 1757(5)(A)(vi); 12 C.F.R. § 701.21(c)(7).

424 *See* § 3.3, *supra*; www.ncua.gov/Resources/Pages/LFCU2011-04.aspx (Apr. 2011) (renewing 18% rate cap through Sept. 10, 2012).

425 Payday Lending, NCUA Letter No. 09-FCU-05 at 2, *available at* www.ncua.gov/Resources/Documents/LFCU2009-05.pdf.

The Truth in Lending Act's definition of "finance charge" is explained in National Consumer Law Center, Truth in Lending Ch. 3 (7th ed. 2010 and Supp.).

426 75 Fed. Reg. 58,285 (Sept. 24, 2010) (codified at 12 C.F.R. § 701.21(c)(7)(iii)). *See* NCUA Regulatory Alert No.10-RA-13 (Oct. 2010) (announcing and describing short-term, small amount loans). *See generally* § 3.3, *supra* (discussing interest rate preemption and credit unions).

427 *Id.*

428 75 Fed. Reg. 58,285 (Sept. 24, 2010), *codified at* 12 C.F.R. § 701.21(c)(7)(iii). This assumes the application fee does not meet TILA's definition of a finance charge.

429 NCUA, Regulatory Alert on Final Rule—Part 701, Short-Term, Small Amount Loans, No. 10-RA-13, at 1 (Oct. 2010).

430 *See* National Consumer Law Center, Truth in Lending § 3.9.2 (7th ed. 2010 and Supp.).

431 12 C.F.R. § 701.21(c)(7)(iii)(1) to (8).

The rule also requires FCUs to implement "appropriate underwriting guidelines to minimize risk; for example, requiring a borrower to verify employment by producing at least two recent pay stubs."[432] This rule is amplified somewhat in a voluntary "best practices" portion of the rule. The best practices emphasize that "FCUs should be able to use a borrower's proof of recurring income as the key criterion in developing standards for maturity and lengths and loan amounts so a borrower can manage repayment of the loan."[433] Notably absent from this analysis is any evaluation of the borrower's other obligations, which could interfere with the ability to repay the loan.

### 9.5.3.4 Rollover Ban on STS Loans

NCUA expects FCUs "to set the term and amount of the loan in a way that allows borrowers to repay it within the term and avoid the need to extend a loan."[434] The rule states that an FCU "must not roll-over any STS loan."[435]

The rule does not define rollovers beyond stating that an FCU may extend the term of a loan, up to the maximum six-month term, as long as no additional fee (other than interest) is charged and no new credit is extended.[436] The explanatory information states that the rollover ban "applies to situations in which a borrower is charged additional fees for extending or 're-borrowing' funds to avoid delinquency."[437] The roll-over ban thus primarily applies in situations where the FCU charges an application fee.

A loan made quickly on the heels of repaying a previous loan, with a new application fee, is essentially "re-borrowing" and a prohibited rollover. The rule does not specify the amount of time that must elapse between the repayment and the new loan. The rollover ban should be interpreted to require a gap of at least one full month in order to ensure that the purpose of the new loan is not to cover the income gap caused by repayment of the first loan.

### 9.5.3.5 STS Loan Amortization Requirement and Fee Restriction

While the rule does not explicitly ban STS loans with single-payment or balloon payments, NCUA expects multiple, amortizing payments[438] rather than the single-payment loans many payday lenders make.[439] The rule states merely that the higher 28% rate may be charged on condition that the FCU "fully amortizes the loan."[440] The explanatory material adds NCUA's view that "balloon payments often create additional difficulty for borrowers trying to repay their loans, and requiring FCUs to fully amortize the loans will allow borrowers to make manageable payments over the term of the loan, *rather than trying to make one large payment*."[441]

FCUs may charge an application fee "that reflects the actual costs associated with processing the application, but not exceeding $20."[442] The connection between costs and the application fee is consistent with the admonition that "FCUs are still bound by the definition of application fee in Reg. Z [of the Truth in Lending Act]."[443] The Commentary to Regulation Z defines an application fee as a charge to recover the costs associated with processing loan applications.[444] In order to be excluded from calculation of a loan's APR, the creditor must charge all applicants for the application fee, not just those who actually get credit.[445] The rule puts no limit on how often borrowers may be charged an application fee each year. But NCUA emphasized that if "an FCU undertakes a more limited application process with repeat borrowers, there would be no justification for charging the same application fee each time."[446] NCUA also warned that "*FCUs cannot use the application fee to offset the higher degree of risk associated with this type of lending*."[447] Late fees are permitted but the NCUA's guidance cautions against setting loan terms that make late payments likely.[448] Other types of fees are presumably forbidden, though the rule does not address them.

### 9.5.3.6 Restrictions on STS Payment Method

As prohibited by the EFTA, FCUs cannot condition a loan on repayment by a preauthorized electronic fund transfer, such as a payroll deduction, except for single-payment loans.[449] FCUs

432 12 C.F.R. § 701.21(c)(7)(iii)(A)(8).

433 *Id.* § 701.21(c)(7)(iii)(B)(2).

434 75 Fed. Reg. at 58,286–58,287. *See* NCUA, Regulatory Alert on Final Rule—Part 701, Short-Term, Small Amount Loans, No. 10-RA-13, at 2 (Oct. 2010).

435 12 C.F.R. § 701.21(c)(7)(iii)(4).

436 *Id.* § 701.21(c)(7)(iii)(4)(A); NCUA, Regulatory Alert on Final Rule—Part 701, Short-Term, Small Amount Loans, No. 10-RA-13, at 2 (Oct. 2010).

437 75 Fed. Reg. at 58,286.

438 Amortization is the gradual reduction of a debt through regular payments. *See* § 5.3.1.1, *supra*.

439 *See* National Consumer Law Center, Stopping the Payday Loan Trap: Alternatives That Work, One That Don't at 31–43 (June 2010), *available at* www.nclc.org/images/pdf/high_cost_small_loans/payday_loans/report-stopping-payday-trap.pdf.

440 12 C.F.R. § 701.21(c)(7)(iii)(5). *See also* NCUA, Regulatory Alert on Final Rule—Part 701, Short-Term, Small Amount Loans, No. 10-RA-13, at 3 (Oct. 2010) ("FCUs must structure the payments so that the borrower is paying a portion of the principle and interest in equal or near-equal installments on a periodic basis over the course of the loan.").

441 75 Fed. Reg. at 58,287 (emphasis added).

442 12 C.F.R. § 701.21(c)(7)(iii)(7).

443 75 Fed. Reg. at 58,287. *See* Reg. Z, 12 C.F.R. § 1026.4(c)(1) [§ 226.4(c)(1)]; National Consumer Law Center, Truth in Lending § 3.9.2 (7th ed. 2010 and Supp.).

444 12 C.F.R. pt. 1026 [pt. 226]; Official Commentary to Reg. Z, 12 C.F.R. § 1026.4(c)(1)-1 [§ 226.4(c)(1)-1].

445 *Id.*

446 75 Fed. Reg. at 58,287.

447 NCUA, Regulatory Alert on Final Rule—Part 701, Short-Term, Small Amount Loans, No. 10-RA-13, at 3 (Oct. 2010) (original emphasis). *Accord* 75 Fed. Reg. 58,285, 58,287 (Sept. 24, 2010).

448 *See* NCUA, Regulatory Alert on Final Rule—Part 701, Short-Term, Small Amount Loans, No. 10-RA-13, at 4 (Oct. 2010).

449 NCUA, Regulatory Alert on Final Rule—Part 701, Short-Term, Small Amount Loans, No. 10-RA-13, at 4 (Oct. 2010); 75 Fed. Reg.

may, however, offer members incentives, such as a lower rate, if they authorize payment through payroll deductions.[450]

### 9.5.3.7 STS Loans and the MLA

In regulatory guidance sent to all FCUs, NCUA says credit unions will be able to make STS loans to servicemembers without complying with Department of Defense (DOD) regulations under the Military Lending Act, which caps the interest rate, including all fees, at 36%.[451] NCUA believes that most STS loans will not meet the DOD's definition of "covered payday loan" because FCUs will not require a post-dated payment instruction or obtain authorization to debit the borrower's account as security for STS loans under the new rule.[452] An NCLC survey, however, found that many credit unions' small loan programs—including both reasonably priced ones and high-priced loans—do require electronic security or electronic repayment of loans.[453] Doing so brings them within the scope of the MLA.[454]

An STS loan that qualifies as a covered loan could violate the MLA's usury cap. Depending on the size and term of the loan, an FCU that charges the full $20 application fee, on top of 28% annual interest, may exceed the 36% fee-inclusive "military annual percentage rate" (MAPR).[455] For example, a $200 one-month loan with a $20 application fee and a 28% annual interest rate carries a MAPR of 135%.

### 9.5.3.8 Other NCUA Guidance for All Credit Union Loans

The STS rule does not prevent credit unions from making payday loans outside the STS-loan criteria, though such loans must comply with the 18% rate cap, including any finance charges as defined by the Truth in Lending Act. Before creating the STS loan rule, the NCUA issued two guidance letters to FCUs discouraging them from engaging in payday lending.[456] Both letters remind credit unions of the risks posed by payday lending, including the risk of borrower default, transactional risk (fraud), damage to the credit union's reputation, and the risk of non-compliance with federal law.[457]

The 2001 letter emphasizes the importance of having loan guidelines that reduce the risk of borrowers getting trapped in a cycle of borrowing. According to NCUA the guidelines should include:

- Limits on rollovers;
- Limits on the number of loans a borrower may have per year;
- "Substantial waiting periods between loans;"
- A right to rescind without charge;
- Clear, understandable disclosures.[458]

The 2009 letter includes examples of permissible and impermissible lending programs. The permissible examples include small-dollar loans with terms of four to six months and no fees, other than interest below an 18% APR (which applies to all loans not meeting the STS requirements), and a program with low fees that required half the loan proceeds to be deposited in the borrower's savings account. The impermissible examples includes loans with higher rates and multiple fees. Though NCUA letters are non-binding, they may be persuasive to a court faced with an unfair credit union loan.

### 9.5.3.9 Credit Union Service Organizations

Despite the pro-consumer purpose of the credit union concept, some federal and state credit unions have developed ways to directly offer, or indirectly profit from, payday loans. They do so primarily in one of two ways (or both). They may put the bulk of their charges into application or participation fees that they claim are excluded from the finance charge used to calculate the APR under the Truth in Lending Act regulations.[459] Or the credit union collects a finder's or broker's fee for sending potential borrowers to a credit union service organization (CUSO) that the credit union has an arrangement with.[460]

CUSOs are subsidiaries formed to assist credit unions by providing legitimate services related to the routine operation of a credit union. Both state and federal credit unions use CUSOs. The NCUA bars FCUs from owning an interest in CUSOs engaged in certain activities.[461] The NCUA's 2009 letter spe-

58,285, 58,288 (Sept. 24, 2010). *See* Reg. E, 12 C.F.R. § 1005.10(e)(1) [§ 205.10(e)(1)].

450 *See* 75 Fed. Reg. 58,285, 58,288 (Sept. 24, 2010); 12 C.F.R. § 701.21(c)(7)(iii)(B)(1); NCUA, Regulatory Alert on Final Rule—Part 701, Short-Term, Small Amount Loans, No. 10-RA-13, at 4 (Oct. 2010).

451 *See* § 2.2.5.7, *supra*.

452 NCUA, Regulatory Alert on Final Rule—Part 701, Short-Term, Small Amount Loans, No. 10-RA-13, at 3 (Oct. 2010). *See* 32 C.F.R. § 232.3(b)(1)(i); § 2.2.5.3, *supra*.

453 National Consumer Law Center, Stopping the Payday Loan Trap 31–43 (June 2010), *available at* www.nclc.org/images/pdf/high_cost_small_loans/payday_loans/report-stopping-payday-trap.pdf.

454 *See* 32 C.F.R. § 232.3(b)(1)(i).

455 32 C.F.R. § 232.3(h); § 2.2.5.8, *supra*.

456 Payday Lending and Title Loans, NCUA Letter No. 01-FCU-03 (Apr. 2001), *available at* www.ncua.gov/Resources/Documents/LFCU2001-03.pdf; Payday Lending, NCUA Letter No. 09-FCU-05, *available at* www.ncua.gov/Resources/Documents/LFCU2009-05.pdf.

457 The letters specifically list compliance with the Equal Credit Opportunity Act, Truth in Lending Act, Truth in Savings Act, and the Electronic Funds Transfer Act. Payday Lending and Title Loans, NCUA Letter No. 01-FCU-03 (Apr. 2001); Payday Lending, NCUA Letter No. 09-FCU-05 (July 2009), *available at* www.ncua.gov.

458 Payday Lending and Title Loans, NCUA Letter No. 01-FCU-03 (Apr. 2001), *available at* www.ncua.gov.

459 The APR is calculated based on a loan's finance charge. The definition of finance charge is riddled with exceptions. *See* National Consumer Law Center, Truth in Lending Ch. 3 (7th ed. 2010 and Supp.).

460 *See* Letter from National Consumer Law Center to the National Credit Union Administration (Jan. 27, 2009) (describing these arrangements and shams and explaining why they are illegal), *available at* www.nclc.org/images/pdf/high_cost_small_loans/payday_loans/letter-ncua-payday-0109.pdf.

461 *See* 12 C.F.R. pt. 712; 12 C.F.R. § 712.5 ("What activities and

cifically notes that CUSOs are not approved to make payday loans. Accordingly, the NCUA says federal credit unions may not own an interest in any CUSO making payday loans.[462] This restriction does not affect state credit unions, nor does it prevent FCUs from collecting fees from making referrals to CUSOs.

Credit unions that act improperly may be sanctioned by the NCUA using its examination authority. The NCUA also has authority under the Federal Trade Commission Act to sanction unfair and deceptive acts and practices by state and federal credit unions.[463] Though the NCUA has not issued any guidance regarding state credit unions and CUSOs, the absence of adequate underwriting and other safety-and-soundness problems associated with payday lending suggest that state credit unions could jeopardize their relationship with the National Credit Union Share Insurance Fund by owning or investing in a CUSO that makes payday loans.

## 9.6 Attempts to Evade State Regulation

### *9.6.1 Rent-a-Bank*

In the early to mid-2000s a number of payday lenders attempted to evade state regulation by purporting to use national and state-chartered banks as conduits for their loans. They theorized that, by partnering with the banks, they could avail themselves of the banks' preemption[464] and rate-exportation privilege.[465] After briefly being adopted by several national payday lenders and being hotly litigated, the so-called "rent-a-bank" model was eventually abandoned after federal regulators began issuing and enforcing guidelines discouraging it.[466]

As discussed at § 3.4, *supra*, the exportation doctrine permits a bank chartered in a deregulated state to ignore the usury laws in the borrower's home state, undermining that state's ability to enforce its usury laws. Payday lenders attempted to take advantage of this by adopting an arrangement in which the payday lender would purport to make loans on the bank's behalf, then buy the loan from the bank. The bank would bear little or no risk of default and the payday lender would receive nearly all the profits from the transaction. If the borrower challenged the interest rate on the loan, the payday lender would assert the fiction that the bank had made the loan so the borrower's home state usury laws did not apply.[467]

These types of arrangements were very lucrative for payday lenders because they allowed the lender (unless challenged) to enter markets where payday lending was otherwise forbidden or heavily restricted. The profile of just one payday lender is instructive.[468] This lender partnered with four different banks to do business in five states, until a new law in Georgia froze its business there in 2004. Though it also maintained payday storefronts in twenty-nine other states, the revenues from the bank partnership states accounted for 24–30% of all revenues between 2003 and 2005. This lender and others using the rent-a-bank model were eventually forced to abandon the practice when the OCC and FDIC began to investigate and found the practices unsafe for the banks involved.

Though bank regulators, for the most part, put to an end to the rent-a-bank model, newer forms may be emerging. Payday lenders may claim preemption by making loans on prepaid cards.[469] Some payday lenders also continue to claim that the loan is actually originated by a bank. Such arrangements should be scrutinized closely to determine who the actual lender is and whether the payday lender insulates the bank from credit risk.

### *9.6.2 Internet Payday Loans*

Payday loans are, increasingly, being sold on the Internet by lenders that are not physically located in the consumer's home state. These loans present special problems and appear to have more abusive features than storefront loans. The lenders claim they are not subject to usury limits in the consumer's home state on the grounds that they have no physical presence there.[470] This argument should be rejected, however, as long as the lender is not entitled to invoke federal preemption or rate exportation.[471]

A state has the right to regulate lenders making loans within the state, even if the lender has no physical presence there.[472] Instead, it is the borrower's physical presence that matters.[473]

services are preapproved for CUSOs?").

462 NCUA Letter No. 09-FCU-05 (July 2009), *available at* www.ncua.gov.

463 *See* 15 U.S.C. § 57a(f)(4); 12 C.F.R. § 706.0(a).

464 *See* § 3.2, *supra*.

465 *See* § 3.4, *supra*.

466 *See* § 9.5.1, *supra*.

467 *See, e.g.*, New York *ex rel.* Spitzer v. County Bank of Rehoboth Beach, Index No. 6046-03; RJI No. 01-04-080549 (N.Y. Sup. Ct. Jan. 2, 2007), *available on the companion website to this treatise*. *See* descriptions of these arrangements and their variations in the following court decisions: BankWest Inc. v. Baker, 324 F. Supp. 2d 1333 (N.D. Ga. 2004), *aff'd*, 411 F.3d 1289 (2005), *reh'g granted, opinion vacated*, 433 F.3d 1344 (11th Cir. 2005), *opinion vacated due to mootness*, 446 F.3d 1358 (11th Cir. 2006); Flowers v. EZPawn Oklahoma, Inc., 307 F. Supp. 2d 1191 (N.D. Okla. 2004); BankWest Inc. v. Oxendine, 598 S.E.2d 343 (Ga. Ct. App. 2004).

468 The information in this paragraph is derived from Advance America, Cash Advance Centers, Inc.: Form S-1 SEC Registration Statement of Aug. 13, 2004, *available at* www.sec.gov/Archives/edgar/data/1299704/000104746904026511/a2141558zs-1.htm and Form 10-Q Filing of 3/31/05, *available at* www.sec.gov/Archives/edgar/data/1299704/000110465905023837/a05-9193_110q.htm.

469 *See* § 9.5.2, *supra*.

470 *See, e.g.*, Cash Am. Net of Nevada, L.L.C. v. Com., Dep't of Banking, 8 A.3d 282, 286 (Pa. Super. Ct. 2010).

471 *See* §§ 3.2, 3.4, *supra*.

472 Quik Payday, Inc. v. Stork, 549 F.3d 1302 (10th Cir. 2008) (finding Kansas may require out-of-state Internet lender to be licensed as condition of lending to state residents located in Kansas); Cash Am. Net of Nevada, L.L.C. v. Com., Dep't of Banking, 8 A.3d 282 (Pa. Super. Ct. 2010) (finding out-of-state Internet lender subject to state usury caps).

473 *See* Quik Payday, Inc. v. Stork, 549 F.3d 1302, 1308 (10th Cir. 2008) (finding reasonable state regulator's argument that Kansas credit code 'regulates the conduct of Internet payday lenders who choose to make payday loans with Kansas consumers *while they are in Kansas*.' ") (quoting Appellee's brief, emphasis in original).

For example, the Tenth Circuit rejected a Utah-based, Internet payday lender's argument that it did not need a Kansas license to make loans to Kansas residents when they were physically in Kansas.[474] In contrast, the Seventh Circuit found that an Illinois-based auto-pawn lender could *not* be compelled to obtain an Indiana license to do business in Illinois with Indiana residents who crossed the state line to visit the lender's Illinois locations.[475]

Internet payday lenders typically require electronic access to the borrower's account for both depositing the funds borrowed and to withdraw payments. A survey of Internet payday lenders found higher fees than storefront loans and a wide range of possible loan terms.[476] Permissible loan sizes ranged from $100 to $1,500 and maturities from five to thirty days.[477]

A particularly dangerous feature found in some Internet loans is an automated payment plan that withdraws only enough to pay the finance charge without reducing the loan principal. In order to repay the loan in full, the borrower must contact the lender in advance of the due date and ask the lender to withdraw the full amount due. Otherwise, the loan automatically rolls over, leading the borrower to incur additional fees. This type of arrangement for recurring payments should be found to violate the EFTA's ban on mandatory electronic repayment.[478]

Lead generators are also becoming a common feature on the Internet. A lead generator is a website that refers potential customers to vendors.[479] It may not be apparent from the website that it is operated by a lead generator rather than an actual lender.

Lead generators typically collect completed applications from site visitors, provide varying levels of data analysis, and sell applications to the highest bidders. Some lead generators are lenders themselves who make referrals when they do not lend in a consumer's jurisdiction or when the borrower does not fit the lender's requirements. Others are merely advertisers. A consumer visiting a lead generator's site is typically invited to enter their contact information (and usually banking details) into a form on the site. The site operator then sells the consumer's information to interested lenders. A 2011 survey found that leads are sometimes sold for over $100.[480]

Another dangerous aspect of Internet payday lending sites is the increased risk of identity theft and debt collection fraud. In one scam identified by the Federal Trade Commission, a company made threatening calls to consumers and demanded payment on phantom payday loan "debts" that consumers did not owe. The scammers are believed to have obtained the consumers' names and personal information from payday loan applications submitted online.[481]

### 9.6.3 *Tribal Payday Loans*

#### 9.6.3.1 General

Tribal payday lending is a version of Internet-based payday lending with an important difference: rather than claiming to be based in a state with permissive lending statutes or a foreign country, tribal payday lenders claim to be owned and operated by Native American Indian tribes. Using their tribal affiliation, these lenders then assert that they have sovereign immunity and, consequently, are not required to obey state laws.[482] Though this is somewhat a mischaracterization of how tribal sovereign immunity operates,[483] tribal payday lending nevertheless poses a significant challenge for regulators and consumer advocates.[484]

#### 9.6.3.2 Overview of Tribal Sovereign Immunity

State and federal law are presumed to apply to the activities of Indian tribes, both on and off their reservations, unless the law "would interfere with reservation self-government or would impair a right granted or reserved by federal law."[485] Tribal sovereign immunity, however, prohibits anyone but the federal government from suing a federally-recognized Indian tribe[486]

474 Quik Payday, Inc. v. Stork, 549 F.3d 1302 (10th Cir. 2008).

475 Midwest Title Loans, Inc. v. Mills, 593 F.3d 660 (7th Cir. 2010).

476 *See* Consumer Federation of America, Survey of Online Payday Loan Websites (Aug. 2011) (discussing Internet lender access to consumer bank accounts), *available at* http://consumerfed.org/pdfs/CFAsurveyInternetPaydayLoanWebsites.pdf.

477 *Id.*

478 *See* § 9.2.1, *supra.*

479 A "lead" is used in the sense of "information that directs a salesperson to a potential customer, a source of new business." Webster's New World College Dictionary (1999).

480 Consumer Federation of America, Survey of Online Payday Loan Websites 7 (Aug. 2011), *available at* http://consumerfed.org/pdfs/CFAsurveyInternetPaydayLoanWebsites.pdf.

481 Press Release, Federal Trade Comm'n, Court Halts Alleged Fake Debt Collector Calls from India, Grants FTC Request to Stop Defendants Who Posed as Law Enforcers (Apr. 11, 2012), *available at* www.ftc.gov/opa/2012/04/broadway.shtm. *See also* Federal Trade Comm'n v. Direct Benefits Group, L.L.C., 2011 WL 3654469 (M.D. Fla. Aug. 19, 2011) (granting preliminary injunction against defendants accused of UDAPs after acquiring consumers' bank account information when consumers applied for payday loans online).

482 *See* Western Sky Fin., L.L.C. v. Maryland Comm'r of Fin. Regulation, 2011 WL 4929485, at *1 (D. Md. Oct. 13, 2011) (describing loan contract that asserts agreement is not subject to any state law); Online Payday Loan Companies Ignoring Colorado Law, CBS4 News (Nov. 14, 2011), *available at* http://denver.cbslocal.com/2011/11/14/online-payday-loan-companies-ignoring-colorado-law/; Jessica Silver-Greenberg, *Payday Lenders Join With Indian Tribes*, Wall St. J. (Feb. 10, 2011), *available at* http://online.wsj.com/article/SB10001424052748703716904576134304155106320.html.

483 Tribes are required to obey the law, but they are immune from all but federal suits for violations. *See* § 9.6.3.2, *infra.*

484 *See* S. Unique, Ltd. v. Gila River Pima-Maricopa Indian Community, 674 P.2d 1376, 1384 (Ariz. Ct. App. 1984) (observing "businesses that deal with Indian tribes do so at great financial risk.").

485 Mescalero Apache Tribe v. Jones, 411 U.S. 145, 148 (1973); Florida Paraplegic, Ass'n, Inc. v. Miccosukee Tribe of Indians of Florida, 166 F.3d 1126, 1129 (11th Cir. 1999) ("a general statute applies to Indian tribes unless its application would (1) abrogate rights guaranteed under an Indian treaty, (2) interfere with purely intramural matters touching exclusive rights of self-government, or (3) contradict Congress's intent[.]").

486 "[A] group of Indians is a tribe—and therefore enjoys sovereign immunity—if it either 1) has been federally recognized by Congress or the [Bureau of Indian Affairs], or 2) meets the federal common law definition first articulated by the Supreme Court in *Montoya v. United States*, 180 U.S. at 266, 21 S. Ct. 358." Gristede's Foods,

for damages or injunctive relief.[487] This immunity from suit applies to tribal, state, and federal courts.[488] Consequently, sovereign immunity, where legitimately claimed, is a major threat to consumer protection and law-abiding competitors.[489]

Tribal immunity protects the tribe itself, tribal officers acting in their lawful authority,[490] tribal employees,[491] and arms of the tribe[492] from suit. Individual tribe members, non-members on a reservation, and corporate entities that are not sufficiently connected to the tribe are not protected.[493] Tribal immunity extends to a tribe's business activities, not just those activities considered traditionally governmental.[494] This means commercial ventures owned by a tribe may claim sovereign immunity to the same extent as the tribal government, even for business conducted off the reservation.[495] As a result, when a commercial entity asserts sovereign immunity, its relationship to the tribe must be closely examined to determine whether it is sufficiently related to be considered an arm of the tribe.

The concept of Indian tribes as sovereign is firmly grounded in history and has long been recognized, since well before the founding of the United States.[496] Recognition of tribal sovereign *immunity*, however, is comparatively recent and is based on little more than an "accident" of *stare decisis*.[497] The Supreme Court first mentioned it as minor *dicta*—only a few words—in an early twentieth century decision.[498] Two decades later it appeared in another case as the deciding factor, accepted as dogma without ever having been analyzed.[499] From there it was developed and expanded in subsequent Supreme Court decisions with little analysis until the Court finally admitted, in 1998 that it had come into existence "almost by accident"[500] and was based on little more than a "slender reed."[501] Nevertheless, the Court has firmly refused to reconsider it, deferring to Congress any change or restriction of the doctrine.[502]

### 9.6.3.3 Who Can Claim Tribal Sovereign Immunity

#### *9.6.3.3.1 Individuals*

Tribal immunity protects tribal officers and employees when they are acting within their lawful authority.[503] But it does not protect individual tribe members who are acting on their own behalf. In *West Virginia v. Payday Loan Resource Center, L.L.C.*, for example, a Native American who owned an Internet-based payday lending operation asserted sovereign immunity to rebuff the state's effort to enforce an investigative subpoena.[504] The court rejected his claim finding the business was operated for the benefit of its owner, who was a private individual rather than a tribe.

Courts have recognized *Ex parte Young*[505] as a limited exception to tribal sovereign immunity that permits suits against

---

Inc. v. Unkechuage Nation, 660 F. Supp. 2d 442, 465 (E.D.N.Y. 2009).

487 Kiowa Tribe of Oklahoma v. Manufacturing Technologies, Inc., 523 U.S. 751, 755 (1998) ("There is a difference between the right to demand compliance with state laws and the means available to enforce them."); Santa Clara Pueblo v. Martinez, 436 U.S. 49 (1978); Equal Employment Opportunity Comm'n v. Karuk Tribe, 260 F.3d 1071, 1075 (9th Cir. 2001); Imperial Granite Co. v. Pala Band of Mission Indians, 940 F.2d 1269, 1271 (9th Cir. 1991). *See* Native Am. Distrib. v. Seneca-Cayuga Tobacco Co., 546 F.3d 1288, 1292 (10th Cir. 2008) ("federally-recognized Indian tribes possess immunity from suit in federal court"); Nathalie Martin and Joshua Schwartz, The Alliance Between Payday Lenders and Tribes: Are Both Tribal Sovereignty and Consumer Protection at Risk?, __ Wash. & Lee L. Rev. __ (forthcoming) (describing tribal sovereign immunity). See also 25 C.F.R. § 83.2 (describing effect of federal recognition for tribes).

488 William V. Vetter, *Doing Business with Indians and the Three "S"es: Secretarial Approval, Sovereign Immunity, and Subject Matter Jurisdiction*, 36 Ariz. L. Rev. 169, 172 (1994).

489 *See* Kiowa Tribe of Oklahoma v. Manufacturing Technologies, Inc., 523 U.S. 751, 758 (1998) ("immunity can harm those who are unaware that they are dealing with a tribe, who do not know of tribal immunity, or who have no choice in the matter, as in the case of tort victims.").

490 Fletcher v. United States, 116 F.3d 1315, 1324 (10th Cir. 1999).

491 Kizis v. Morse Diesel Int'l, Inc., 794 A.2d 498 (Conn. 2002).

492 *See* § 9.6.3.3.2, *infra.*

493 Puyallup Tribe, Inc. v. State of Washington, 433 U.S. 165, 171–172 (1977).

494 Allen v. Gold Country Casino, 464 F.3d 1044, 1046 (9th Cir. 2006); Ameriloan v. Superior Ct. of Los Angeles Co., 86 Cal. Rptr. 3d 572 (Cal. Ct. App. 2008) (holding payday lender may claim sovereign immunity if facts show lender was acting on behalf of tribe). William V. Vetter, *Doing Business with Indians and the Three "S"es: Secretarial Approval, Sovereign Immunity, and Subject Matter Jurisdiction,* 36 Ariz. L. Rev. 169, 173 (1994).

495 Kiowa Tribe of Oklahoma v. Manufacturing Technologies, Inc., 523 U.S. 751 (1998); Jeff M. Kosseff, *Sovereignty for Profits: Courts' Expansion of Sovereign Immunity to Tribe-Owned Businesses*, 5 Fla. A&M U. L. Rev. 131, 138 (2009) (describing study of cases extending sovereign immunity to tribally-owned businesses).

496 *See* Cherokee Nation v. Georgia, 5 Pet. 1, 17, 8 L. Ed. 25 (1831); Felix Cohen, Handbook of Federal Indian Law § 4.01[1][a], at 204–206 (Matthew Bender 2005); Nathalie Martin and Joshua Schwartz, The Alliance Between Payday Lenders and Tribes: Are Both Tribal Sovereignty and Consumer Protection at Risk?, __ Wash. & Lee L. Rev. __ (forthcoming).

497 Kiowa Tribe of Oklahoma v. Manufacturing Technologies, Inc., 523 U.S. 751, 752 (1998). *See id.* at 760 (Stevens dissent) (describing and criticizing development of tribal sovereign immunity doctrine).

498 Turner v. United States, 248 U.S. 354, 358 (1919) ("The fundamental obstacle to recover is not the immunity of a sovereign to suit, but the lack of a substantive right to recover the damages. . . ."). The Court later said of this sentence: "The quoted language is the heart of *Turner.* It is, at best, an assumption of immunity for the sake of argument, not a reasoned statement of doctrine." Kiowa Tribe of Oklahoma v. Manufacturing Technologies, Inc., 523 U.S. 751, 757 (1998).

499 United States v. U.S. Fid. & Guar. Co., 309 U.S. 506, 512 (1940).

500 Kiowa Tribe of Oklahoma v. Manufacturing Technologies, Inc., 523 U.S. 751, 757 (1998).

501 Kiowa Tribe of Oklahoma v. Manufacturing Technologies, Inc., 523 U.S. 751, 757 (1998).

502 Kiowa Tribe of Oklahoma v. Manufacturing Technologies, Inc., 523 U.S. 751, 760 (1998).

503 Fletcher v. United States, 116 F.3d 1315, 1324 (10th Cir. 1997); Kizis v. Morse Diesel Int'l, Inc., 794 A.2d 498 (Conn. 2002).

504 No. 10-MISC-372 (W. Va. Cir. Ct. Oct. 24, 2011), *available at* www.nclc.org/unreported. *See also* W. Sky Fin., L.L.C. v. Maryland Comm'r of Fin. Regulation, 2011 WL 4929485 (D. Md. Oct. 13, 2011) (rejecting claim of sovereign immunity by same owner).

505 209 U.S. 123 (1908).

tribal officials for violating federal law. In *Ex parte Young,* the Supreme Court permitted a suit for equitable relief (not damages) against a state official to proceed in federal court, despite the Eleventh Amendment's ban on such suits under the doctrine of state sovereign immunity. The plaintiff sought to enjoin the official from enforcing an unconstitutional state law. The Court allowed the suit to proceed by adopting the fiction that, because the statute was unconstitutional, the official was exceeding his authority under state law and was, therefore, acting on his own behalf rather than as a representative of the state. Because he was acting on his own, the state's sovereign immunity did not apply. Courts have used the same fiction to permit suits against tribal officers to enjoin actions by tribes.[506] But courts have not yet allowed an equivalent exception to tribal immunity under state law.[507]

### *9.6.3.3.2 Arm of the tribe*

The question of whether an entity can claim immunity depends on how closely it is related to the tribal government.[508] This question is often phrased as whether the entity is an "arm"[509] or "subordinate economic unit"[510] of the tribe.

The Supreme Court has not addressed the standard for determining whether an entity other than the tribe itself is entitled to cloak itself in the tribe's sovereign immunity. But it has made clear that whether the entity carries out commercial or governmental functions on or off the reservation is irrelevant to whether the entity can claim immunity.[511] Other courts have considered a wide range of factors, some more easily evaluated than others:[512]

- *Whether the entity was formed under tribal, state, or federal law.* Many tribal governments have the authority to charter artificial entities. These may conduct a wide range of commercial or governmental activities on behalf of the tribe or for private individuals.[513] Being formed under tribal law should not automatically result in immunity. A prominent treatise on Indian Law observes that immunity "apparently does not cover tribally chartered corporations that are completely independent of the tribe."[514] While one state supreme court has observed that "[t]ribal law corporations are assumed to be a subdivision of the tribal government[,]"[515] courts generally consider this factor along with others.[516] At least one court has found incorporation under state law to be a major factor in deciding an entity was not an arm of the tribe.[517]

---

506 Santa Clara Pueblo v. Martinez, 436 U.S. 49, 59, 98 S. Ct. 1670, 56 L. Ed. 2d 106 (1978); Crowe & Dunlevy, P.C. v. Stidham, 640 F.3d 1140, 1154–1155 (10th Cir. 2011); Tamiami Partners, Ltd. *ex rel.* Tamiami Dev. Corp. v. Miccosukee Tribe of Indians, 177 F.3d 1212, 1225–1226 (11th Cir.1999); N. States Power Co. v. Prairie Island Mdewakanton Sioux Indian Cmty., 991 F.2d 458, 460 (8th Cir. 1993). *Cf.* Okla. Tax Comm'n v. Citizen Band Potawatomi Indian Tribe, 498 U.S. 505, 514 (1991) (leaving open *Ex parte* Young's applicability in tribal context).

507 *See* Frazier v. Turning Stone Casino, 254 F. Supp. 2d 295, 310 (N.D.N.Y.2003) (alleged violation of state law inadequate to demonstrate that tribal officers acted outside scope of their lawful authority); Bassett v. Mashantucket Pequot Museum & Research Ctr. Inc., 221 F. Supp. 2d 271, 280–281 (D. Conn.2002) (equating an allegation that tribal officers violated state law with a claim that they acted beyond the scope of their lawful authority "would be tantamount to eliminating tribal immunity"); Cash Advance v. Colorado, 242 P.3d 1099, 1112 (Colo. 2010) ("actions allegedly violating state law are not necessarily outside the scope of a tribal officer's lawful authority because that authority is defined by the sovereign tribe, not by state law").

508 Wright v. Colville Tribal Enter. Corp., 147 P.3d 1275, 1279 (Wash. 2006) ("Whether or not tribal sovereign immunity protects a particular tribal business enterprise depends on the nature of the enterprise and its relation to the tribe.").

509 Allen v. Gold Country Casino, 464 F.3d 1044, 1046 (9th Cir. 2006) (proper inquiry is "whether the entity acts as an arm of the tribe so that its activities are properly deemed to be those of the tribe").

510 White Mountain Apache Indian Tribe v. Shelley, 480 P.2d 654 (Ariz. 1971).

511 Kiowa Tribe of Oklahoma v. Manufacturing Technologies, Inc., 523 U.S. 751, 754–755 (1998); Ameriloan v. Superior Ct. of Los Angeles Co., 86 Cal. Rptr. 3d 572 (Cal. Ct. App. 2008) (reversing trial court's holding that doctrine of tribal sovereign immunity may not apply to off-reservation payday lending).

512 *See, e.g.*, Gristede's Foods, Inc. v. Unkechuage Nation, 660 F. Supp. 2d 442, 477–478 (E.D.N.Y. 2009) (eight factors); Cash Advance v. Colorado, 242 P.3d 1099, 1110 (Colo. 2010) (listing three factors); Wright v. Colville Tribal Enter. Corp., 147 P.3d 1275, 1288 (Wash. 2006) (dissent) (eleven factors). *See also* Nathalie Martin and Joshua Schwartz, The Alliance Between Payday Lenders and Tribes: Are Both Tribal Sovereignty and Consumer Protection at Risk?, __ Wash. & Lee L. Rev. __ (forthcoming) (discussing factors used to determine whether an entity is entitled to immunity); William V. Vetter, *Doing Business with Indians and the Three "S"es: Secretarial Approval, Sovereign Immunity, and Subject Matter Jurisdiction*, 36 Ariz. L. Rev. 169, 177 (1994).

513 *See* William V. Vetter, *Doing Business with Indians and the Three "S"es: Secretarial Approval, Sovereign Immunity, and Subject Matter Jurisdiction*, 36 Ariz. L. Rev. 169, 174–179 (1994) (discussing history and statutory basis for creation of tribal business entities).

514 Cohen, Handbook of Federal Indian Law § 7.05[1][a], at 636–637 (2005 ed.).

515 Wright v. Colville Tribal Enter. Corp., 147 P.3d 1275, 1279 (Wash. 2006) (quoting Dao Lee Bernardi-Boyle, State Corporations for Indian Reservations, 26 Am. Indian L .Rev. 41, 57 (2001)).

Despite noting this assumption, the court still considered other factors. *Id.* ("Whether or not tribal sovereign immunity protects a particular tribal business enterprise depends on the nature of the enterprise and its relation to the tribe.").

516 Breakthrough Mgmt. Group, Inc. v. Chukchansi Gold Casino & Resort, 629 F.3d 1173, 1187 (10th Cir. 2010) (noting relevance of "method of creation"); Gristede's Foods, Inc. v. Unkechuage Nation, 660 F. Supp. 2d 442, 477 (E.D.N.Y. 2009) (listing eight factors including whether "[t]he entity is organized under tribal constitution or laws (rather than federal law)."); Runyon *ex rel.* B.R. v. Ass'n of Vill. Council Presidents, 84 P.3d 437 (Alaska 2004) (no immunity for non-profit corporation formed by tribes under state law because members of corporation are not liable for corporation's obligations); Cash Advance v. Colorado, 242 P.3d 1099, 1110 (Colo. 2010) (listing three factors including "whether the tribes created the entities pursuant to tribal law"); Ransom v. St. Regis Mohawk Educ. & Cmty. Fund, Inc., 658 N.E.2d 989, 992 (N.Y. 1995) (describing multiple factors including whether entity is organized under tribal laws and constitution rather than federal law).

517 Runyon *ex rel.* B.R. v. Ass'n of Vill. Council Presidents, 84 P.3d 437 (Alaska 2004) (no immunity for non-profit corporation formed

- *Extent of tribal ownership and control.* How closely an entity is tied to the tribal government is relevant to whether it is an arm of the tribe.[518] This can be determined by examining details of the entity's governing structure, ownership of assets, and daily management. The more control the tribal government has over the entity, the more likely a court will be to allow the entity to claim the sovereign immunity. One court listed a number of factual issues to consider:
    - Is the organization's managing body required to be composed primarily of tribal officials?
    - Does the tribe's governing body have the unrestricted power to dismiss members of the organization's governing body?
    - Does the organization (and/or its governing body) "act for the tribe" in managing organization's activities?
    - Is the tribe the legal owner of property used by the organization, with title held in the tribe's name?
    - Are the organization's administrative or accounting activities are controlled or exercised by tribal officials?[519]
- *Whether immunity protects the tribe's sovereignty.* Sometimes this appears as a question of whether the tribe is the real party in interest.[520] However phrased, this factor goes to whether granting immunity will further the federal policy of protecting the tribe's assets, autonomy, and economic development.[521] The existence of liability insurance may indicate that immunity is not necessary to protect the tribe or that it is not the real party in interest.[522]
- *Does the economic benefit go to the tribe.* This factor overlaps somewhat with the question of who controls or owns the entity and whether the tribe is the real party in interest. This also involves considering the purpose of the entity—not whether it engages in commercial or governmental activities, but whether the entity was established to benefit the tribe.[523] As in much litigation, following the money trail is important but the degree of importance is not clear. In one case, the Ninth Circuit emphasized that a tribe would receive "all capital surplus" from a casino and would benefit as the sole shareholder.[524] But at the other extreme, a Colorado trial court found an Internet payday lender to be an arm of the tribe despite evidence that it only received 1% of the lender's revenue.[525] The latter decision is of dubious value, however, because the court disregarded evidence suggesting the tribes' involvement was a sham engineered by non-Indian business partners looking for a way to evade state law.[526]

---

by tribes under state law because members of corporation are not liable for corporation's obligations). *See* West Virginia v. Payday Loan Resource Center, L.L.C., No. 10-MISC-372 (W. Va. Cir. Ct. Oct. 24, 2011), *available at* www.nclc.org/unreported (payday lender formed under state law and owned by member of tribe not immune).

518 Breakthrough Mgmt. Group, Inc. v. Chukchansi Gold Casino & Resort, 629 F.3d 1173, 1187 (10th Cir. 2010) (relevant factors include "their structure, ownership, and management, including the amount of control the tribe has over the entities"); Cook v. AVI Casino Enters., Inc., 548 F.3d 718, 726 (9th Cir. 2008) ("tribal corporation is wholly owned and managed by the Tribe[;]" "[a] majority of ACE's board must be Tribe members, and the Tribe's council performs corporate shareholder functions for the benefit of the Tribe"); City of New York v. Golden Feather Smoke Shop, Inc., 2009 WL 705815, at *5–6 (E.D.N.Y. Mar. 16, 2009) (smoke shops owned by tribe members and licensed to operate on reservation not arm of tribe; tribe does not own or control and profits go to smoke shop's owners, not to tribe); Ameriloan v. Superior Ct., 86 Cal. Rptr. 3d 572, 586 (Cal. Ct. App. 2008) (instructing trial court to consider "whether the tribe and the entities are closely linked in governing structure and characteristics"); Cash Advance v. Colorado, 242 P.3d 1099, 1110 (Colo. 2010) (listing three relevant factors including "whether the tribes own and operate the entities"); Gavle v. Little Six, Inc., 555 N.W.2d 284, 294–295 (Minn. 1996) (discussing factors considered by other courts); Wright v. Colville Tribal Enter. Corp., 147 P.3d 1275, 1277–1279 (Wash. 2006) (discussing extent of tribal control over corporation). *Compare* Dixon v. Picopa Const. Co., 772 P.2d 1104, 1108 (Ariz. 1989) (construction company not subordinate economic unit [arm of tribe]), *with* White Mountain Apache Indian Tribe v. Shelley, 480 P.2d 654 (Ariz. 1971) (extensive tribal control indicates is arm of tribe).

519 Gristede's Foods, Inc. v. Unkechuage Nation, 660 F. Supp. 2d 442, 477 (E.D.N.Y. 2009).

520 *See, e.g.,* Runyon *ex. rel.* B.R. v. Ass'n of Vill. Council Presidents, 84 P.3d 437 (Alaska 2004).

521 Breakthough Mgmt. Grp., Inc. v. Chukchansi Gold Casino & Resort, 629 F.3d 1173, 1187 (10th Cir. 2010) (considering "the policies underlying tribal sovereign immunity and its connection to tribal economic development, and whether those policies are served by granting immunity to the economic entities"); Gavle v. Little Six, Inc., 555 N.W.2d 284, 294–95 (Minn. 1996) (considering whether federal policies intended to promote tribal autonomy are furthered by extension of immunity to organization); Ransom v. St. Regis Mohawk Educ. & Cmty. Fund, Inc. 658 N.W.2d 989, 993 (N.Y. 1995) ("The vulnerability of the tribe's coffers in defending a suit against the subentity indicates that the real party in interest is the tribe.").

522 Dixon v. Picopa Const. Co., 772 P.2d 1104, 1111 (Ariz. 1989) ("the presence of liability insurance is relevant to the question of whether an Indian commercial entity is a subordinate economic organization . . . [and] is some evidence that the Community expected its corporation to be liable for its torts."). *Cf.* Runyon *ex rel.* B.R. v. Ass'n of Vill. Council Presidents, 84 P.3d 437 (Alaska 2004) (regarding corporate structure that insulated tribe from liability, "if a judgment . . . will not reach the tribe's assets . . . it is unlikely that the tribe is the real party in interest.").

523 Allen v. Gold Country Casino, 464 F.3d 1044, 1047 (9th Cir. 2006) ("economic and other advantages inure to the benefit of the Tribe"). *Compare* Native Am. Distrib. v. Seneca-Cayuga Tobacco Co., 546 F.3d 1288, 1294 (10th Cir. 2008) (finding sovereign immunity for tobacco manufacturer in part because tribal "resolution expressly declares that the tobacco company will function as 'an economic development project to provide employment opportunities and revenue for the Tribe,' and states that the company and its activities are 'essential governmental functions of the Seneca-Cayuga Tribe' "), *with* Dixon v. Picopa Const. Co., 772 P.2d 1104, 1111 (Ariz. 1989) (rejecting claim of immunity citing "ordinance's express declaration that the Community formed Picopa solely for business purposes and without any declared objective of promoting the Community's general tribal or economic development further evidences Picopa's independence from the Community").

524 Cook v. AVI Casino Enters., Inc., 548 F.3d 718, 726 (9th Cir. 2008).

525 Colorado v. Cash Advance, Case No. 05CV1143, at 19–21 (Colo. Dist. Ct. Feb. 18, 2012), available at www.nclc.org/unreported.

526 The business had been owned and operated by non-Indians for several years before they solicited the tribes' involvement after state

A number of courts describe, as a common element among these factors, the concept that an arm of the tribe "operates 'not as a mere business,' but rather as an extension of the tribe's own economic activity, 'so that its activities are properly deemed to be those of the tribe' itself."[527]

### 9.6.3.4 Abrogating or Waiving Tribal Sovereign Immunity

Only Congress and the Supreme Court have the power to abrogate tribal sovereign immunity.[528] The Supreme Court has refused to do so.[529] If Congress chooses to do so, the abrogation must be "unequivocally expressed" and may not be implied.[530] A generally applicable statute that simply provides for federal jurisdiction will not be sufficient to create jurisdiction over a tribe. Even a statute specifically aimed at restricting tribal authority will not affect sovereign immunity unless the statute expressly subjects tribes to the jurisdiction of the federal courts.[531]

If an entity is an arm of a tribe and Congress has not abrogated immunity, the next question is whether the tribe has waived its immunity.[532] Tribes may waive their sovereign immunity but the standard for clarity is the same as for abrogation: the waiver must be clear and unequivocal.[533] Waivers are "strictly construed" and there is a "strong presumption against them."[534] Courts have refused to find implied waivers even under circumstances that would imply a waiver against non-Indian sovereigns.[535] Because a waiver is voluntary on the part of the tribe, the tribe may dictate the terms and limitations of a waiver.[536]

Waivers may be found in tribal charters, constitutions, ordinances, corporate charters, or contracts between the tribal entity and other parties. A significant number of tribes include a "sue and be sued" clause in their corporate charter.[537] Whether this waives immunity for litigation involving a payday loan will be a fact-intensive question.[538] A "sue and be sued" clause may be interpreted as a general waiver, allowing all suits.[539] However, these clauses often include limitations, such as on the assets subject to levy or requiring tribal officials to approve a waiver before it becomes effective.[540] Arbitration clauses in contracts have been found to constitute waivers, but only if they provide for judicial enforcement of the arbitration award.[541] Even then, the scope of the waiver may be limited by its terms.[542]

---

regulators initiated an investigation into unlicensed lending. *Id.* at 19–21. The court, nevertheless, observed that even if the arrangement was a sham, "that characterization would not displace their tribal immunity." *Id.* at 1 n.1.

527 Amerind Risk Mgmt. Corp. v. Malaterre, 633 F.3d 680, 685 (8th Cir. 2011), *cert. denied*, 132 S. Ct. 1094 (2012) ("Because Amerind is a § 477 corporation that administers a tribal self-insurance risk pool, we hold that Amerind "serves as an arm of the [Charter Tribes] and not as a mere business and is thus entitled to tribal sovereign immunity."); Pink v. Modoc Indian Health Project, Inc., 157 F.3d 1185, 1188 (9th Cir. 1998) ("a nonprofit corporation "organized to control a collective enterprise" of the Alturas and Cedarville Rancherias "served as an arm of the sovereign tribes, acting as more than a mere business," and therefore qualified for the exemption"); Gristede's Foods, Inc. v. Unkechuage Nation, 660 F. Supp. 2d 442, 478 (E.D.N.Y. 2009) (quoting Hagen v. Sisseton-Wahpeton Cmty. Coll., 205 F.3d 1040, 1043 (8th Cir.2000) and Allen, 464 F.3d at 1046).

528 *See* Kiowa Tribe of Oklahoma v. Manufacturing Technologies, Inc., 523 U.S. 751, 759 (1998).

529 Kiowa Tribe of Oklahoma v. Manufacturing Technologies, Inc., 523 U.S. 751, 760 (1998).

530 Santa Clara Pueblo v. Martinez, 436 U.S. 49, 58 (1978).

531 *See* Santa Clara Pueblo v. Martinez, 436 U.S. 49, 59 (1978).

532 State *ex rel.* Suthers v. Cash Advance & Preferred Cash Loans, 205 P.3d 389, 407 (Colo. App. 2008) *aff'd in part sub nom.* Cash Advance & Preferred Cash Loans v. State, 242 P.3d 1099 (Colo. 2010).

533 Okla. Tax Comm'n v. Citizen Band Potawatomi Indian Tribe, 498 U.S. 505, 509–510 (1991); Santa Clara Pueblo v. Martinez, 436 U.S. 49, 58 (1978), *quoting* United States v. Testan, 424 U.S. 392, 399 (1976); Bottomly v. Passamaquoddy Tribe, 599 F.2d 1061, 1066 (1st Cir. 1979) (applying Santa *Clara* standard to tribal waiver).

534 Ameriloan v. Superior Court, 86 Cal. Rptr. 3d 572, 582 (Cal. Ct. App. 2008).

535 William V. Vetter, *Doing Business with Indians and the Three "S"es: Secretarial Approval, Sovereign Immunity, and Subject Matter Jurisdiction*, 36 Ariz. L. Rev. 169, 174 (1994) (citing American Indian Agric. Credit Consortium v. Standing Rock Sioux Tribe, 780 F.2d 1374 (8th Cir. 1985) (signing promissory note providing for collection attorney's, mentioning remedies provided by law, and designating applicable law, not an express waiver of immunity)).

536 *See also* C&L Enters., Inc. v. Citizen Band Potawatomi, 532 U.S. 411, 419 (2001).

537 William V. Vetter, *Doing Business with Indians and the Three "S"es: Secretarial Approval, Sovereign Immunity, and Subject Matter Jurisdiction*, 36 Ariz. L. Rev. 169, 175 (1994).

538 Ameriloan v. Superior Ct. of Los Angeles Co., 86 Cal. Rptr. 3d 572 (Cal. Ct. App. 2008) (holding "sue or be sued" clause in Miami Tribe of Oklahoma resolution did not waive immunity to state agency's cease and desist order).

539 *See, e.g.*, Martinez v. S. Ute Tribe, 374 P.2d 691, 694 (Colo. 1962) ("by . . . consenting to sue and be sued in courts of competent jurisdiction within the United States, has rendered itself amenable to the courts of the State of Colorado in any action of which the state courts may take cognizance.").

540 *See, e.g.*, Memphis Biofuels, L.L.C. v. Chickasaw Nation Indus., Inc., 585 F.3d 917, 921–922 (6th Cir. 2009) (sue-and-be-sued clause limited to action approved by board of directors). Ameriloan v. Superior Ct. of Los Angeles Co., 86 Cal. Rptr. 3d 572 (Cal. Ct. App. 2008) ("sue or be sued" clause limited to terms of each contract entered by tribal entity; waiver created by clause may not be extended to unrelated claims). *See generally* William V. Vetter, *Doing Business with Indians and the Three "S"es: Secretarial Approval, Sovereign Immunity, and Subject Matter Jurisdiction*, 36 Ariz. L. Rev. 169, 179–185 (1994).

541 *See* William V. Vetter, *Doing Business with Indians and the Three "S"es: Secretarial Approval, Sovereign Immunity, and Subject Matter Jurisdiction*, 36 Ariz. L. Rev. 169, 183–184 (1994) (discussing cases). *Compare* Native Vill. of Eyak v. GC Contractors, 658 P.2d 756, 760 (Alaska 1983) (permitting judicial enforcement of award), *with* Pan Am. Co. v. Sycuan Band of Mission Indians, 884 F.2d 416 (9th Cir. 1989) (arbitration clause not mentioning judicial enforcement).

542 *See, e.g.,* Tamiami Partners, Ltd. *ex rel.* Tamiami Dev. Corp. v. Miccosukee Tribe of Indians of Fla., 177 F.3d 1212, 1225 (11th Cir. 1999) (interpreting arbitration clause as limiting waiver to enforcement of clause); Ameriloan v. Superior Ct. of Los Angeles Co., 86 Cal. Rptr. 3d 572, 583–584 (Cal. Ct. App. 2008) (arbitration clause in payday loan contracts was not general waiver of immunity).

A tribe may waive its immunity by filing a lawsuit.[543] Courts recognizing this form of waiver have derived it by analogy to common law limits on the federal government's sovereign immunity.[544] The waiver, however, will be limited to claims in recoupment and arising from the same transaction as the claims raised by the tribe.[545] In the payday lending context, this likely means that tribes filing suit to collect unpaid loans will waive their immunity to counterclaims based on the violation of state lending laws and UDAP claims. In practice, however, it appears that tribes generally do not file collection actions.[546]

### 9.6.3.5 Litigation Against Tribal Payday Lenders

When anyone other than the federal government initiates litigation against a purported tribal payday lender, one of the threshold questions will be whether the lender is truly an arm of the tribe that is entitled to immunity, or whether the tribe's involvement is a sham, sometimes called "rent-a-tribe."[547] Sovereign immunity is a barrier to litigation against Indian tribes because courts do not have subject matter jurisdiction over defendants with sovereign immunity.[548] Though sovereign immunity is generally asserted as an affirmative defense or in a motion to dismiss, it cannot be waived by failure to answer or failure to appear.[549] Instead, it can be raised at any time, even for the first time upon appeal.[550]

When a defendant asserts immunity, the plaintiff has the burden of proving jurisdiction by a preponderance of the evidence, either by showing waiver or that the defendant is not entitled to immunity.[551] The plaintiff should be allowed to conduct discovery into whether the defendant is an arm of the tribe and whether immunity has been waived.[552] Even when a defendant asserts immunity as a defense, a court will still have sufficient authority to order limited discovery for the purpose of evaluating the claim of immunity.[553] Refusal to allow discovery may be reversible error.[554]

Another issue is whether tribal courts have jurisdiction over non-tribe members who enter into loan contracts over the Internet with tribal lenders. There do not appear to be any decisions directly addressing this question. The FTC, however, has taken action against one payday lender that sued borrowers in a tribal court even though the court did not have jurisdiction over the borrowers.[555] As a general matter, tribal courts may have jurisdiction over "the activities of nonmembers who enter consensual relationships with the tribe or its members, through commercial dealing, contracts, leases, or other arrangements."[556] But tribes must follow the same basic rules of personal jurisdiction as federal courts, pursuant to the Indian Civil Rights Act,[557] such as the requirement for minimum contacts with the forum.[558]

## 9.6.4 Spurious Open-End Credit

Some lenders claim to structure their payday loans as lines of credit to avoid restrictions on closed-end credit, such as state small loan statutes, the Military Lending Act,[559] or the stricter disclosure rules and APR calculation for closed-end credit under the Truth in Lending Act. The MLA and most small loan laws only apply to closed-end credit.

---

543 Rosebud Sioux Tribe v. A & P Steel, Inc., 874 F.2d 550, 552 (8th Cir. 1989).

544 *See* Jicarilla Apache Tribe v. Andrus, 687 F.2d 1324, 1344 (10th Cir. 1982) ("Although the precise limits of this tribal immunity are not clear, . . . it is generally co-extensive with that of the United States.") (citations and footnote omitted).

545 Rosebud Sioux Tribe v. A & P Steel, Inc., 874 F.2d 550, 552–553 (8th Cir. 1989); Jicarilla Apache Tribe v. Andrus, 687 F.2d 1324, 1344 (10th Cir. 1982).

546 *But see* Press Release, Federal Trade Comm'n, FTC Charges That Payday Lender Illegally Sued Debt-Burdened Consumers in South Dakota Tribal Court Without Jurisdiction (Mar. 7, 2012), *available at* www.ftc.gov/opa/2012/03/payday.shtm.

547 *See Editorial: Consumers on Losing End of Payday Lending Decision*, The Denver Post (Feb. 26, 2012), *available at* www.denverpost.com/opinion/ci_20031374 (describing "online payday lenders associated with Native American tribes" as "so-called 'rent-a-tribe' operations").

548 Houghtaling v. Seminole Tribe of Florida, 611 So. 2d 1235, 1239 (Fla. 1993) (no subject matter jurisdiction absent where tribe immune).

549 Hagen v. Sisseton-Wahpeton Cmty. Coll., 205 F.3d 1040, 1043 (8th Cir. 2000) (failure to answer does not waive immunity because waiver must be explicit and unequivocal).

550 Hagen v. Sisseton-Wahpeton Cmty. Coll., 205 F.3d 1040, 1044 (8th Cir. 2000) ("because "[s]overeign immunity . . . is a jurisdictional threshold matter . . . [it] can be raised for the first time on appeal.").

551 Chayoon v. Chao, 355 F.3d 141, 143 (2d Cir. 2004); State *ex rel.* Suthers v. Cash Advance & Preferred Cash Loans, 205 P.3d 389, 409 (Colo. App. 2008), *aff'd sub nom.* Cash Advance & Preferred Cash Loans v. State, 242 P.3d 1099 (Colo. 2010).

552 Ameriloan v. Superior Ct. of Los Angeles County, 86 Cal. Rptr. 3d 572, 586 (Cal. Ct. App. 2008) (*dicta* suggesting discovery into jurisdiction over tribal payday lender should be permitted); State *ex rel.* Suthers v. Cash Advance & Preferred Cash Loans, 205 P.3d 389, 406 (Colo. App. 2008), *aff'd sub nom.* Cash Advance & Preferred Cash Loans v. State, 242 P.3d 1099 (Colo. 2010) (permitting discovery into immunity of tribal payday lender).

553 Lee v. Taipei Econ. & Cultural Representative Office, 716 F. Supp. 2d 626, 632 (S.D. Tex. 2009) (regarding claim of immunity under Foreign Sovereign Immunities Act, 28 U.S.C. §§ 1603 to 1611).

554 *See* Sizova v. Nat'l Inst. of Standards & Tech., 282 F.3d 1320, 1326 (10th Cir. 2002) ("Although a district court has discretion in the manner by which it resolves an issue of subject matter jurisdiction under Rule 12(b)(1), . . . a refusal to grant discovery constitutes an abuse of discretion if the denial results in prejudice to a litigant").

555 Press Release, Federal Trade Comm'n, FTC Charges That Payday Lender Illegally Sued Debt-Burdened Consumers in South Dakota Tribal Court Without Jurisdiction (Mar. 7, 2012), *available at* www.ftc.gov/opa/2012/03/payday.shtm.

556 Montana v. United States, 450 U.S. 544, 565 (1981).

557 25 U.S.C. §§ 1301 to1303.

558 Grant Christensen, *Creating Bright-Line Rules for Tribal Court Jurisdiction over Non-Indians: The Case of Trespass to Real Property*, 35 Am. Indian L. Rev. 527, 541 (2011).

559 *See, e.g.,* Military Financial Advertisement for Revolving Line of Credit, www.militaryfinancial.com/Faq.aspx (FAQ stating: "Is it illegal to charge more than 36% on a loan to the US Military? It is illegal to charge more than 36% for a closed end loan consumer loan that is less than 90 days for repayment. A Rapid Line of Credit is not a closed end loan. It is a revolving line of credit that allows you to access the available funds in your account at any time.").

Even when state usury caps apply to open-end credit, the usury caps may utilize TILA rules as to APR calculations. TILA applies to both open and closed-end credit, but applies weaker disclosure rules to open-end credit. For example, one reason the annual percentage rate on traditional payday loans is so high is that TILA requires lenders to include their fees and other finance charges in the APR for unsecured closed-end loans. For open-end loans, however, the APR is defined in a manner that excludes the fees and all other finance charges except interest. Because payday lenders charge fees rather than interest, an open-end payday line of credit may be disclosed with a 0% APR despite exorbitant fees.[560]

When examining an open-end credit product, it is important to look beyond the label to determine whether the product may actually be subject to the rules for closed-end credit. The MLA follows TILA's definitions for open- and closed-end credit. TILA defines closed-end credit as all credit that does not meet the definition of open-end credit. Open-end credit requires a plan that:

- Reasonably contemplates repeated transactions;
- Imposes a finance charge computed from time to time on an outstanding unpaid balance; and
- Provides a replenishable credit line that is reusable without further approvals.[561]

The label of a plan or account is not determinative,[562] and courts have sometimes found credit to be spurious open-end credit.[563] Most case law dealing with spurious open-end credit relates to purchase financing (excluded from the MLA) and may not be especially helpful. Nonetheless, analysis of a loan agreement or usage pattern may show that supposedly open-end payday loans do not meet the regulatory definition.[564]

Payday loans also typically require a fixed charge computed in advance, not one that is computed and fluctuates over time. Though the lender can be expected to argue that the charge is in fact computed each time a new advance is made, based on the amount of the advance.

The payment structure may make it unlikely that the credit line will be replenished, so that repeat transactions are not reasonably contemplated. Repayments must generally replenish the credit line for the plan to qualify as open-end credit.[565] The borrower may not have full access to the credit line initially or subsequently without new approvals. A credit line is reusable, and thus open-end credit, only if new approvals are not needed.[566] Or the loan may be due in full, or virtually in full, in a finite period of time, so that it is actually a closed-end loan and not a plan permitting a balance that fluctuates, can rise and fall, and can be carried over time.

Payday borrowers returning for new loans may not satisfy the "repeat transactions" requirement for open-end loans. New payday loans require new approvals and new fees not included in the original credit plan. Consequently they cannot be considered repeat transactions under an original open-end credit plan.

### 9.6.5 Brokers and Credit Service Organizations

Some payday lenders evade state lending regulations by positioning themselves as loan brokers, often by registering as a credit service organization (CSO) rather than as a lender. The so-called "CSO model" is an unintended consequence of state laws designed to protect the public from credit repair scams.[567] About three-quarters of states have adopted credit service organization acts modeled on the federal Credit Repair Organizations Act.[568] Generally these statutes impose restrictions on organizations that claim to help consumers improve their credit scores or credit reports.

The majority of states to enact credit service organization acts allow licensed CSOs to act as loan brokers by charging consumers a fee for obtaining credit from a third-party lender.[569] These acts are subject to abuse in states that lack adequate restrictions on the CSO's activities, such as limits on the CSO's fee or where the fee is not considered interest under the state's usury law. State CSO laws are summarized in an appendix to another NCLC treatise, *Fair Credit Reporting* (7th ed. 2010 and Supp.).

560 *See, e.g.,* Mobiloans Line of Credit, Agreement and Terms and Conditions (eff. Sept. 26, 2011), www.mobiloans.com/Home/TermsAndConditions (showing 0% APR, cash advance fee of $3 for every $20 advanced and a monthly finance charge ranging from $19, for balances up to $100, to $59 for balances over $400).

561 15 U.S.C. § 1602(i); Reg. Z, 12 C.F.R. § 1026.2(a)(20) [§ 226.2(a)(20)]; Official Commentary to Reg. Z, 12 C.F.R. § 1026.2(a)(20) [§ 226.2(a)(20)]; National Consumer Law Center, Truth in Lending § 6.2.2 (7th ed. 2010 and Supp.).

562 Official Commentary to Reg. Z, 12 C.F.R. § 1026.2(a)(20)-7 [§ 226.2(a)(20)-7].

563 National Consumer Law Center, Truth in Lending § 6.2.3 (7th ed. 2010 and Supp.) (discussing spurious open-end credit under the TILA). *See also* § 3.9.3, *supra* (discussing the distinction between open-end and closed-end credit under usury laws generally).

564 National Consumer Law Center, Truth in Lending § 6.2.2 (7th ed. 2010 and Supp.).

565 Official Commentary to Reg. Z, 12 C.F.R. § 1026.2(a)(20) [§ 226.2(a)(20)].

566 *See* National Consumer Law Center, Truth in Lending § 6.2.2.4 (7th ed. 2010 and Supp.).

567 Diane Standaert, Sara Weed, Ctr. for Responsible Lending, CRL Issue Brief: Payday Lenders Pose as Brokers to Evade Interest Rate Caps: The Next Chapter in Payday Lender Subterfuge 3 (July 2010), *available at* www.responsiblelending.org/payday-lending/policy-legislation/states/CRL-CSO-Issue-Brief-FINAL.pdf. Credit service organizations are sometimes referred to as "credit repair organizations."

568 15 U.S.C. §§ 1679–1679j. Pub. L. No. 104-208, 110 Stat. 3009 (Sept. 30., 1996). *See* National Consumer Law Center, Fair Credit Reporting Ch. 15 (7th ed. 2010 and Supp.) (regarding state and federal credit repair laws, including credit service organizations).

569 *See generally* Diane Standaert, Sara Weed, Ctr. for Responsible Lending, CRL Issue Brief: Payday Lenders Pose as Brokers to Evade Interest Rate Caps: The Next Chapter in Payday Lender Subterfuge (July 2010), *available at* www.responsiblelending.org/payday-lending/policy-legislation/states/CRL-CSO-Issue-Brief-FINAL.pdf (describing CSO model and state laws).

In a typical CSO/payday loan transaction, the CSO handles all contact with the borrower and arranges for a loan from a third-party lender. The lender will be subject to state lending regulations, including any usury cap. The CSO, however, will be free to charge any fee it desires in addition to the interest due on the loan. Fees are generally $20 to $30 per $100 borrowed and may also include an application fee.[570] Even where the CSO model allows the payday lender to evade state usury laws, the transaction will, nevertheless, be subject to the federal Truth in Lending Act. Under TILA, the broker's fee will be considered a finance charge. As a result, the loan may appear to have a relatively low interest rate but may have a triple-digit APR, and the disclosures should be examined.

The CSO model appears to be most widely used in Texas, where it was legitimized by the Fifth Circuit case of *Lovick v. Ritemoney Ltd.*[571] in 2004 and codified in state law in 2011.[572] In *Lovick* a CSO charged a $1,500 fee for obtaining a $2,000 loan secured by the borrower's car.[573] The loan carried a 10% interest rate, the maximum allowed under state law. But the APR on the loan was 131%, which the borrower argued violated Texas' 10% usury limit. The Fifth Circuit affirmed the trial court's dismissal on the grounds that the CSO's fee was not considered interest under Texas law. Although a matter of state law, the Fifth Circuit described some factors that may be relevant when challenging CSO fees in other states:

- Whether the broker and lender were truly independent entities;
- Whether the broker's fee was shared with the lender; and
- Whether the lender benefited from the broker's fee in another way that was more than incidental.

Texas has since codified the court's decision,[574] turning a loophole into an endorsement of this abusive practice. Other states, however, have taken a different approach. Some states have laws regulating payday lenders that trump the state's CSO law. A Michigan regulatory agency, for example, has prohibited use of the CSO model, finding it to be "a deceptive subterfuge designed to extract impermissible fees from a borrower" and an evasion of Michigan's law governing payday lenders.[575] Other states have amended their CSO laws to reduce or eliminate the problem. For example, Maryland has made the broker's fee subject to the state's interest rate cap,[576] and California restricts the ability of CSOs to broker loans.[577]

### 9.6.6 Other Attempts to Evade Regulation

Predatory lenders have been quite creative in trying to evade restrictions on small loans, like payday lending. Fortunately consumer advocates and regulators have been equally adept at protecting the public. This subsection describes a selection of shams and evasions.

- Charging a sham "monthly participation fee" to disguise an excessive interest charge in violation of a state UDAP law,[578] and potentially TILA.
- Evading rollover bans by making a "new" loan to pay off an old one. Experience has shown that rollover bans are easily evaded unless coupled with a cooling-off period between new loans.[579] Otherwise, consumers can simply bring in cash on payday, pay off the old loan, write a new check and sign a contract for a new loan (with a new finance charge), and then walk out the door deeper in debt. This practice should, however, be challengeable as a mere fiction. When the Virginia Supreme Court considered a borrower who had entered into a series of thirty-three consecutive loans from a payday lender, the court found that regardless of the lender's characterization, the transaction was a prohibited refinancing in substance.[580]
- Bogus sales or leases with cash back. Payday lenders in usury cap states have tried to disguise usurious loans as "sale-leaseback" transactions and "cash-back" sales of advertising space.[581] In the sale-leaseback scam, the lender

570 Trihouse Enters., Inc., A Discussion of the Texas CSO Model for Payday Loans, www.paydayloanindustry.com/texas-cso.html (website for loan industry consultant); Bill Analysis of Tex. S.B. 253 (Feb. 18, 2011), *available at* www.legis.state.tx.us/tlodocs/82R/analysis/html/SB00253I.htm (proposed amendment prohibiting CSOs from charging fees for brokering loans in Texas).

571 378 F.3d 433 (5th Cir. 2004).

572 Tex. Fin. Code §§ 393.601 to 393.628.

573 CSO fees are typically much lower. *See* Diane Standaert, Sara Weed, Ctr. for Responsible Lending, CRL Issue Brief: Payday Lenders Pose as Brokers to Evade Interest Rate Caps: The Next Chapter in Payday Lender Subterfuge 3 (July 2010), *available at* www.responsiblelending.org/payday-lending/policy-legislation/states/CRL-CSO-Issue-Brief-FINAL.pdf (noting fees of $20 to $25 per $100 borrowed).

574 Tex. Fin. Code §§ 393.601 to 393.628.

575 *In the Matter of* Credit Services Organizations, Regulatory Loan Act and Consumer Financial Services Act Licensees and Short-Term (Payday) Loans, Mich. Dep't of Labor and Economic Growth Bulletin 2006-06-CF (June 21, 2006), *available at* www.michigan.gov/documents/2006-06-CF_163413_7.pdf.

576 Md. Code Ann., Com. Law § 14-1902(7) ("A credit services business . . . shall not: . . . Charge or receive any money or other valuable consideration in connection with an extension of credit that, when combined with any interest charged on the extension of credit, would exceed the interest rate permitted for the extension of credit under the applicable title of this article.").

577 Cal. Civ. Code § 1789.13 (West 2007).

578 Pennsylvania Dep't of Banking v. NCAS of Del., L.L.C., 995 A.2d 422, 444 (Pa. Commw. Ct. 2010) (refusing to dismiss UDAP claim).

579 *See, e.g.*, Fla. Stat. § 560.404(19) (establishing twenty-four-hour cooling-off period between loans).

580 Ruby v. Cashnet, Inc., 281 S.E.2d 871 (Va. 2011).

581 *See, e.g.*, Upshaw v. Ga. Catalog Sales, 206 F.R.D. 694 (M.D. Ga. 2002) (class certification granted in catalog sales case); Henry v. Cash Today, Inc., 199 F.R.D. 566 (S.D. Tex. 2000) (class certification granted in cash back ad sale case on TILA, RICO, usury, UDAP, and civil conspiracy claims); SAL Leasing, Inc. v. Arizona *ex rel.* Napolitano, 10 P.3d 1221 (Ariz. Ct. App. 2000) (sale-leaseback in car context are loans); State *ex rel.* Salazar v. The Cash Now Store, Inc., 31 P.3d 161 (Colo. 2001) (tax refund assignments are loans); Clay v. Oxendine, 645 S.E.2d 553 (Ga. Ct. App. 2007) (affirming that sale-leaseback transactions constituted illegal payday loans); New York *ex rel.* Spitzer v. JAG NY, L.L.C., No. 5302 (N.Y. Sup. Ct. Jan. 20, 2005) (cash back catalog sale is sham), *aff'd in part and rev'd in part*, 794 N.Y.S.2d 488 (N.Y. App. Div. 2005). *See also*

"buys" an item of personal property from the consumer, for example, a television, and "leases" it back for a "rental payment" which is due in two weeks. The cash-back shams are even more transparent. The consumer must "buy" an advertisement of one line for every $100 borrowed and pay an "ad fee" of $33 per $100 (translating to an APR of 858%). In both scenarios, the lender requires a signed check just in case the consumer fails to make the payment in two weeks hence.

- Non-amortizing installment loans. Some payday lenders attempt to evade payday loan restrictions by offering bogus "installment" loans. For example, one product is a 140-day "look alike" loan requiring nine bi-weekly interest payments, with a final balloon payment of the entire principal amount. Because the installment payments do not reduce the principal balance, this loan is essentially a fourteen-day payday loan with ten built in rollovers.[582]
- Phony phone card clubs. In this scenario, a consumer signs an agreement to purchase a telephone card every two weeks for the next year for $25 per card.[583] The consumer is then given a "cash incentive" of $100. In two weeks, the consumer will owe $125. If the consumer cannot repay this amount, the check casher will debit the consumer's checking account or the consumer can pay another fee of $25. Meanwhile, the calling card cost the check casher only $4.
- Payday loans disguised as Internet service.[584] These "deals" advertise cash back for signing up for Internet access through in-store computers. Others offer cash back for joining a website at a cost of $6 per day or $180 per month.

## 9.7 Private Litigation Issues

Successful litigation against payday lending will often involve a combination of resources and will typically requiring overcoming some of the same obstacles found in other consumer protection litigation. Arbitration clauses and class action waivers are common in payday loan contracts but they should not be considered insurmountable barriers to helping borrowers. The Military Lending Act bans arbitration clauses in covered loans with active duty servicemembers and their families.[585] Otherwise, the enforceability of arbitration agreements found in payday lending transactions is discussed at § 7.4, *supra*, and is the focus of another treatise in this series—*Consumer Arbitration Agreements*.[586]

Two common tools for attacking payday loan terms are the doctrine of unconscionability and state laws prohibiting unfair and deceptive acts and practices (UDAP statutes). Courts have refused to dismiss substantive unconscionability claims in payday loan cases even in states where usury caps have been eliminated by the state legislatures.[587] Aggressive collection tactics, such as the improper use of criminal bad-check laws to collect a debt, may violate state UDAP statutes. A number of states limit the application of civil and criminal bad-check laws where the creditor knows there are insufficient funds in the account at the time he accepts the check. Case law on this issue is discussed in NCLC's *Collection Actions* Ch. 8 (2d ed. 2011 and Supp.). Other debt collection claims against debt collectors and creditors are discussed in more detail in another NCLC treatise, *Fair Debt Collection* (7th ed. 2011 and Supp.).

## 9.8 Local Ordinances

In states where payday lending is legal, local governments may have authority to regulate the location and operating hours of storefront payday lenders.[588] A significant number of cities

Consumers Union, A Usury Loophole—The Sale-Leaseback Arrangement (Jan. 2001), *available at* www.consumersunion.org/pdf/swro/ALLPapers.pdf.

582 Monsignor John Egan Campaign for Payday Loan Reform, Hunting Down the Payday Loan Customer: The Debt Collection Practices of Two Payday Loan Companies 4 (Sept. 2006), *available at* www.woodstockinst.org/publications/research_reports. *See also* Tom Feltner & Sarah Duda, Woodstock Institute, Beyond Payday Loans: Consumer Installment Lending in Illinois 7 (Mar. 2009) (survey of loans showing median interest rate on installment loans of 95% and range from 5% to 1,142% with median terms of nearly nine months).

583 *See, e.g.*, Austin v. Alabama Check Cashers Ass'n, 936 So. 2d 1014 (Ala. 2005).

584 Championcomm.net of Tuscaloosa, Inc. v. Morton, 12 So. 3d 1197 (Ala. 2009) (alleging lender attempted to circumvent Alabama's usury laws by setting up loans as cash rebates given to subscribers to "Internet service" on monthly basis); Dep't of Fin. Inst. v. Mega Net Servs., 833 N.E.2d 477 (Ind. Ct. App. 2005) (immediate cash rebate in exchange for a one-year commitment to purchase Internet service at a bi-weekly rate of $20 for $100 of "service").

585 § 2.2.5.7, *supra*.

586 National Consumer Law Center, Consumer Arbitration Agreements (6th ed. 2011).

587 *See, e.g.*, Van Jackson v. Check 'N Go of Ill., Inc., 193 F.R.D. 544 (N.D. Ill. 2000) (recognizing doctrine of unconscionability under Illinois law in the class certification context); Dienese v. McKenzie Cash Advance, 2000 WL 34511333 (E.D. Wis. Dec. 11, 2000) (granting class certification on unconscionability claim under Wisconsin law); Johnson v. Tele-Cash, Inc., 82 F. Supp. 2d 264 (D. Del. 1999), *rev'd on other grounds*, 225 F.3d 366 (3d Cir. 2000) (unconscionability can be the outer limit to interest charges in a state where there is no usury cap; denying motion to dismiss). *Cf.* Ferrell v. Express Check Advance of S.C., L.L.C., 591 F.3d 698 (4th Cir. 2010) (affirming remand to state court of plaintiffs' class action suit against lender alleging that loans were unconscionable under South Carolina law); Johnson v. Advance Am., 549 F.3d 932 (4th Cir. 2008) (affirming remand to state court of plaintiffs' class action suit against lender alleging that loans were unconscionable under South Carolina law); Smith v. Steinkamp, 318 F.3d 775, 778 (7th Cir. 2003) (upholding trial court's decision to deny in part defendant's motion to compel arbitration and noting that "[a] cynic might argue that, given the desperation of people who take out payday loans, these plaintiffs would have signed anything. . . . The defendants do not make this argument, however, perhaps fearing that it would invite a conclusion that payday loans are unconscionable and therefore unenforceable even in states that do not deem them usurious.").

588 *See also* Kelly Griffith, Linda Hilton & Lynn Drysdale, Controlling the Growth of Payday Lending Through Local Ordinances and Resolutions: A Guide for Advocacy Groups and Government Of-

and some counties have adopted ordinances restricting the density, business hours, and location of payday lenders.[589] Others have adopted temporary and permanent moratoriums on permits for new locations.[590] Land use regulations limiting density may be especially relevant for areas where payday lenders tend to cluster, such as low- and moderate-income neighborhoods and near military bases. New legislation may, however, need to grandfather existing businesses. Payday lenders are likely to challenge local restrictions their ability to operate. The success of challenges will depend on the type of restriction adopted and variations in the authority granted to local governments under state law.[591]

Local governments can also have an impact on payday lending by adopting resolutions urging state legislative reforms. City and county governments can adopt resolutions calling on the state legislature to repeal payday loan laws or enact rate caps to protect borrowers from triple-digit interest rates and to enact other consumer protections.[592] Local governments can also add payday loan reform to their legislative agenda for state-level lobbying.

## 9.9 Payday Lending and Bankruptcy

Bankruptcy can provide relief from unaffordable payday debt; conversely, it appears that payday loans drive borrowers into bankruptcy at much higher rate than non-payday borrowers. One study found that payday borrowers were about 88% more likely to file for chapter 13 bankruptcy in the next two years than the rest of the population.[593] Another found almost three times the rate of bankruptcy among payday loan users, compared to similar low- to moderate-income households without payday loans.[594]

Filing either a chapter 7 or chapter 13 bankruptcy petition initiates an automatic stay against most debt collection efforts.[595] Nevertheless, there is an exception for "the presentment of a negotiable instrument and the giving of notice of and protesting dishonor of such an instrument."[596] This means that a payday lender can negotiate the consumer's personal check even after the bankruptcy filing.[597] The same should not be the case for an electronic transfer because such a transfer does not involve a negotiable instrument.[598]

In addition, the post-petition negotiation of a check or an electronic transfer is an avoidable post-petition transfer.[599] The Bankruptcy Code allows the trustee to avoid a post-petition transfer of property[600] and, when the trustee has disclaimed an interest in the property, the property can be returned to the consumer. There is even an argument that a check cashed within ninety days prior to the bankruptcy filing can be avoided as a prepetition transfer. Bankruptcy is discussed in greater detail in another NCLC treatise, *Consumer Bankruptcy Law and Practice* (9th ed. 2009 and Supp.).

ficials (Nov. 2007), *available at* http://paydayloaninfo.org/pdfs/PDL%20Local%20Ordinance%20%20master%2011_08.pdf.

589 *See* Appendix 1 of Kelly Griffith, Linda Hilton & Lynn Drysdale, Controlling the Growth of Payday Lending Through Local Ordinances and Resolutions: A Guide for Advocacy Groups and Government Officials (Nov. 2007), *available at* http://paydayloaninfo.org/pdfs/PDL%20Local%20Ordinance%20%20master%2011_08.pdf.

590 *Id.*

591 *See, e.g.* The Payday Loan Store of Wisconsin v. Madison, 339 F. Supp. 2d 1058 (W.D. Wis. 2004) (city ordinance that required payday loan stores to close by 6:00 p.m. and prohibited stores from being within 5,000 feet of each other upheld); EZMONEY Wisconsin, Inc. v. City of Wauwatosa Bd. of Zoning Appeals, 774 N.W.2d 476 (Wis. Ct. App. 2009) (table) (upholding city's denial of zoning and occupancy permit to a payday lender on the grounds that its business fell under category of "check casher" which was prohibited in the trade district). *But see* Sunrise Check Cashing and Payroll Svcs., Inc. v. Town of Hempstead, 933 N.Y.S.2d 388 (N.Y. App. Div. 2011) (state law authorizing Banking Dep't Superintendent to determine appropriate location for check-cashers preempted local zoning law).

592 *See, e.g.,* Minutes of Decatur City, Ill. City Council Mtg. (Feb. 21, 2012), *available at* www.ci.decatur.il.us/council/2011/minutes.aspx?id=184 (passing Resolution R2012-27, asking state to enact additional consumer protection legislation regarding payday loans).

593 Paige Marta Skiba and Jeremy Tobacman, Do Payday Loans Cause Bankruptcy? (Oct. 10, 2008), *available at* www.law.vanderbilt.edu/faculty/faculty-personal-sites/paige-skiba/publication/download.aspx?id=2221 (examining Texas bankruptcy petitions).

594 Michael S. Barr, Federal Trade Commission, Financial Services, Savings, & Borrowing Among LMI Households in the Mainstream Banking & Alternative Financial Services Sectors (Oct. 30, 2008) (examining Detroit debtors).

595 National Consumer Law Center, Consumer Bankruptcy Law and Practice Ch. 9 (9th ed. 2009 and Supp.).

596 11 U.S.C. § 362(b)(11).

597 *See In re* Meadows, 396 B.R. 485 (B.A.P. 6th Cir. 2008); *In re* Kearns, 432 B.R. 276 (Bankr. D. Idaho 2010); *In re* Webb, 432 B.R. 234 (Bankr. N.D. Miss. 2010).

598 *In re* Snowden, 422 B.R. 737 (Bankr. W.D. Wash. 2009).

599 *See In re* Meadows, 396 B.R. 485 (B.A.P. 6th Cir. 2008); *In re* Webb, 432 B.R. 234 (Bankr. N.D. Miss. 2010).

600 11 U.S.C. § 549(a).

# Chapter 10 Motor Vehicle, Manufactured Home and Other Installment Sales

## 10.1 Getting Started

### 10.1.1 Organization of This Chapter

This chapter examines purchase financing of consumer goods primarily through retail installment sales contracts. Section 10.1.2, *infra*, reviews the different entities involved in these transactions and the roles they play and § 10.1.3 provides an overview of the applicable law. Section 10.2, *infra*, summarizes state retail installment sales act (RISA) substantive regulation of installment sales, § 10.3, *infra*, analyzes common abuses and special issues found in purchase money auto finance, and § 10.4, *infra*, examines other forms of motor vehicle financing. Section 10.5, *infra*, looks at special issues in the financing of manufactured homes, and the final section, § 10.6, *infra*, reviews the liability of the holder of the debt for the actions and inactions of the retail seller.

### 10.1.2 Who's Who in Retail Installment Sales

In order to understand installment sales financing, it is important to understand the different roles that retailers, assignees, and other parties play. The legal roles that different parties play may differ from their functional roles. Sometimes their legal rights and responsibilities are determined by their functional roles, and sometimes by their legal roles. This can create confusion for all concerned, including the creditors themselves.[1]

When a consumer buys financing along with the consumer good, most often the retail installment sales contract (RISC) will name the retailer as the "creditor-seller."[2] The contract commonly has an assignment printed on it, by which the "creditor/seller/dealer" assigns the contract to the lender. (Most retailers who enter into RISCs, including car dealers, do not keep the contracts in-house. An exception is the buy-here, pay-here used car lot.[3]) Technically, the assignment is a separate contractual arrangement between the retailer and the lender. In legal form, there are two two-party transactions: one between the consumer and the dealer (the retail installment contract), and a back-end commercial agreement between the dealer and the lender (the assignment). The consumer is a stranger to the second contract—the assignment.[4] Thus, in form, the lender and the consumer have a relationship only because the lender, as "assignee," has stepped into the shoes of the original creditor, the dealer.

However, the "assignee"-lender frequently takes a quite direct role behind the scenes from the outset, little different from that of an originating lender. Not only may it have furnished the forms to its dealer-partners, but it is likely to have called the shots on any given individual buyer's financing arrangement from the outset. The retailer employees (such as the employee at a car dealership responsible for finance and insurance (F&I)) typically fax or send electronically the prospective credit application to a lender. The lender makes the initial credit-granting decision and sets the credit terms for that consumer.

In these situations, the dealer functions more as a middleman, while the "assignee"-lender acts very much like an original creditor. Furthermore, the second contract, the assignment, may take place almost immediately upon the consumer signing the RISC. These two transactions almost seem to be one. This difference between form and function gives some retailers an identity crisis. They often view themselves as merely an "arranger" of a contract between the real creditor

1 It has caused some confusion in the courts, as well. In Riviere v. Banner Chevrolet, Inc., 158 F.3d 335 (5th Cir. 1998), the court held the dealer was not really a creditor, relying on case law interpreting a prior version of TILA's definition of creditor, since amended in relevant part. Upon rehearing, the court reversed itself and held that the dealer was a creditor and remanded as to whether the underlying transaction was a personal or commercial transaction. 184 F.3d 457 (5th Cir. 1999). The opinion was withdrawn, judgment vacated, and rehearing granted. 166 F.3d 727 (5th Cir. 1999). For non-TILA claims, however, looking at the substance, not the form, to argue that the dealer was not truly the lender, can expand the liability net.

2 Truth in Lending requires that the "creditor" be identified, 15 U.S.C. § 1638(a)(1); Reg. Z § 1026.18(a) [§ 226.18(a)].

3 *See* National Consumer Law Center, Unfair and Deceptive Acts and Practices § 7.4.14 (7th ed. 2008 and Supp.) (special problems at buy-here, pay-here lots).

4 As to the parties to the retail sales contract, see Walker Mobile Homes Sales, Inc. v. Walker, 965 S.W.2d 271 (Mo. Ct. App. 1998) (retail installment sales contract was a contract between the buyer and seller; not between the assignee and buyer).

As to the second contract, the assignment, see, e.g., Weatherman v. Gary-Wheaton Bank, 676 N.E.2d 206, 212 (Ill. App. Ct.) ("the assignment of a mortgage is a transaction as to which the borrower is completely passive, indeed a stranger"), *subsequent proceedings on procedural matters*, 683 N.E.2d 893, 689 N.E.2d 1147 (Ill. 1997); Broyles v. Iowa Dep't of Soc. Serv., 305 N.W.2d 718, 721 (Iowa 1981) ("An assignment is a contract between the assignor and assignee.").

(the indirect lender) and the consumer, which may lead them to ignore some basic obligations that their contract with the buyer imposes on them, most particularly in the spot delivery or conditional sale context.[5]

Despite the close relationship between the dealer and the assignee, courts tend not to find dealers to be agents of the assignee.[6] Even though the dealer may behave or see itself as a middleman in these transactions, in the auto area especially, there is a growing industry of third-party companies that are serve as middlemen between the dealer and the assignee.[7] These companies commonly provide assistance in obtaining credit reports and transmitting applications between dealer and assignee as well as perform other dealer services related to the F&I office.

In thinking about potential claims and allocating potential liability, remember that sometimes the legal role is determinative. In a spot delivery case, where the dealer attempts to make the vehicle's sale conditional upon the dealer finding financing for the transaction, the dealer is the creditor on a credit contract, not a mere arranger, and this defines its contractual obligation to the consumer. But for other claims, responsibility should follow function, not form.

With respect to statutory claims, the statutory definitions will be critical. For Truth in Lending Act purposes, the dealer, and *only* the dealer only, is a "creditor" if the dealer's name is the one on the contract.[8] But for purposes of the Equal Credit Opportunity Act, the statutory definition of "creditor" broadly encompasses arrangers and assignees, as well as those who extend credit, so that both the dealer and the lender are creditors.[9]

With the exception of TILA disclosure violations not apparent on the face of the contract, the assignee of a consumer car loan faces derivative liability for the seller's conduct under the FTC Holder Rule.[10] But if the lender was actively involved in the conduct being challenged, the evidence might warrant holding it jointly accountable with the dealer, primarily liable for its own wrong-doing. Some claims, such as UDAP, usury, common law misrepresentation or fraud, or RICO should permit going behind the contractual designations to look as a factual matter at each party's actual conduct, and each party's consequent liability.[11]

A good example of the need to match claims with both form and function can be found in the hidden interest and interest rate markup context discussed at §§ 10.3.5 and 10.3.6, *infra*. If a vehicle's cash price includes buried finance charges, the lender-assignee may avoid TILA liability, but the facts may establish a level of knowledge or culpability sufficient to find liability under other theories, such as UDAP, RICO, or state credit laws.[12]

Whether the consumer seeks to find the dealer or the lender liable, or both, the consumer's case will be bolstered by a close attention to the facts. Such facts might include: the "assignee" pays a large cut of the interest rate to the dealer; other potential assignees allow for less of a cut to the dealer but the dealer chooses the highest for itself (the reverse competition factor); the dealer makes representations to the consumer that it would find the best rate available; the dealer claims that the assignee is really the lender; direct bonus or other compensation sharing occurs with the employee (often the F&I (finance and insurance) person) who dealt directly with the consumer; the assignee represents that it is the lender; and a sympathetic client who thought that the assignee was the lender and that the dealer was trying to find the best rate. Pay attention also to whether the assignment is with recourse (the lender can sell the note back to the dealer). Joint advertising between the lender and dealer to promote special deals can help break through the usual roadblocks to holding the assignee primarily liable.

### 10.1.3 What Law Applies

Installment sales are subject to a variety of state and federal laws. Most states have retail installment sales acts (RISAs)

5 For a full discussion of spot delivery see National Consumer Law Center, Automobile Fraud Ch. 4 (4th ed. 2011).

6 Young v. Harbor Motor Works, Inc., 2009 WL 187793 (N.D. Ind. Jan. 27, 2009); Mardis v. Ford Motor Credit Co., 642 So. 2d 701 (Ala. 1994).

7 Dealertrack, one of the companies providing such services, indicates that it serves over 17,000 dealers and 950 lenders. Securities Exch. Comm'n, Dealertrack Holdings, Inc., Form 10-K Annual Report, File No. 000 51653 (for fiscal year ending Dec. 31, 2010).

8 The "creditor" is the person to whom the obligation is initially payable on its face, and there can be only one. Even if a bank has to approve the deal, and takes immediate assignment, the dealer is the sole creditor. Reg. Z § 1026.2(a)(17)(i)(B) [§ 226.2(a)(17)(i)(B)]; Reg. Z, Official Commentary § 1026.2(a)(17)(i)-2 [§ 226.2(a)(17)(i)-2]. *See generally* National Consumer Law Center, Truth in Lending § 2.3.5 (7th ed. 2010 and Supp.).

The lender, the "assignee" has limited TILA liability under 15 U.S.C. § 1641. *See generally* National Consumer Law Center, Truth in Lending § 12.3 (7th ed. 2010 and Supp.).

9 15 U.S.C. § 1691a(e); Reg. B § 202.2(*l*). *See generally* National Consumer Law Center, Credit Discrimination § 2.2.5 (5th ed. 2009 and Supp.).

10 Several circuits have held that the FTC holder provision on these contracts does not serve to expand TILA's limited assignee liability as to TILA claims. Ellis v. General Motors Acceptance Corp., 160 F.3d 703 (11th Cir. 1998); Taylor v. Quality Hyundai, Inc., 150 F.3d 689 (7th Cir. 1998); Schultz v. Burton-Moore Ford, Inc., 2008 WL 5111897 (E.D. Mich. Dec. 2, 2008).

But if the lender had actual responsibility for the TILA violations, it should be liable as a primary party under UDAP claims, or perhaps under a civil conspiracy or aiding and abetting theory. (Particularly if it is dealing with a small dealer, an indirect lender may actually do the calculations and prepare the TILA forms for the dealership.)

11 *See* § 2.4, *supra*; National Consumer Law Center, Unfair and Deceptive Acts and Practices § 11.6 (7th ed. 2008 and Supp.). *But see* Bell v. Muller, 118 P.3d 405 (Wash. Ct. App. 2005) (refusing to look behind the form when deciding which state usury law applied to this car financing deal due, in part, to legislative amendments exempting retail installment loans from usury caps).

12 *See, e.g.*, Wallace v. Walker Auto Sales, Inc., 155 F.3d 927 (7th Cir. 1998). For example, in an instance where the lender coached the dealers as to how much to mark up the cars' prices to recoup financing discounts, it would be hard, indeed, not to consider the lender liable as a primary party.

governing most or all retail installment sales; these laws are summarized at § 10.2, *infra* and at Appendix C, *infra*. Some states also have different laws dealing with motor vehicle sales or manufactured home sales, whether or not such sales are financed as installment sales. Information on these latter two types of statutes is provided at §§ 10.3 and 10.5, *infra*, respectively.

Most states address permissible interest rates either in their RISA or as a separate usury statute. Many states also have consumer lending acts which may apply. Most state UDAP statutes will apply as will state insurance regulation to the retailer's sale of credit insurance. A number of federal statutes and regulations also govern most installment sales to consumers, including the Truth in Lending Act, the FTC Holder Rule, the Equal Credit Opportunity Act, the Fair Credit Report Act. In limited circumstances, federal lending law and regulation may preempt state regulation of some aspects of retail financing products. These federal statutes and regulations will be addressed throughout this chapter.

## 10.2 State Retail Installment Sales Acts (RISAs)

### *10.2.1 Scope and Federal Preemption*

Most state retail installment sales acts (RISAs) include within their scope installment sales of good and services, and many also include various types of consumer leases and revolving credit. RISAs generally describe the goods and services covered as those "for personal, family or household use," and some add a specific exclusion for commercial, business, and/or agricultural use. A relatively small number of RISAs specify a minimum or maximum cash sale price or dollar amount that must be met in order for the statute to apply. Most motor vehicle retail installment acts (MVRISAs), but not all, also provide that they cover vehicles primarily "for personal, family, or household use," or "for use by the buyer or the buyer's benefit." Many MVRISAs also specify that the motor vehicles purchased shall not be principally for the purpose of resale by the buyer. RISAs typically specify that they apply only to credit sales with a certain minimum number of installment payments.[13] Nevertheless, a number of RISAs apply even if there is only one deferred installment. More detail about the scope of state RISAs may be found in Appendix C, *infra*.

Federal preemption is much less of an issue for RISAs than for other consumer credit legislation. By definition, the loan originator is the seller and not a financial institution. Thus rate exportation and the most favored lender status do not apply; in most cases, the applicable state law is the law of the state where the loan is made, not where the lender is chartered.

Moreover, with the exception of manufactured home loans, as discussed at § 10.5.5, *infra*, various federal statutes preempting mortgage loan interest rates do not apply to installment sales of cars or other goods. Nevertheless, one unresolved issue is the extent to which Office of the Comptroller of the Currency (OCC) regulation of national banks and federal savings associations preempts state law where an installment seller assigns the loan to a national bank or federal savings association. Although some older OCC letters suggest such preemption, the better view based on current federal legislation is that preemption does not apply where the federal depository is merely an assignee.[14]

### *10.2.2 Licensure*

In a number of states, RISAs or MVRISAs require that retail sellers or dealers be licensed, with a few specifying additionally that assignees acquiring retail installment contracts must be licensed as well. Many states require sales finance companies to be licensed, and some laws include within their statutory definition of "sales finance company" a retail seller that is engaged in the business of creating and holding retail installment contracts.[15] In states that have adopted the Uniform Consumer Credit Code, which governs retail installment contracts, the state UCCCs require that supervised lenders be licensed.

### *10.2.3 Limits on Interest*

All RISAs and MVRISAs permit sellers to impose a charge in connection with a retail installment agreement. These charges, which are termed variously "finance charges," credit service charges" and "time price differentials," differ from state to state. While many statutes provide that any charge or rate may be established by agreement of the parties, other statutes set forth formulas for figuring out the charge or, more commonly, they set maximum limits upon the rate that may be imposed.

MVRISAs often prescribe different rates depending upon the classification of the vehicle that is the subject of the sale. In these provisions, the rate for a Class 1, or new, vehicle is generally lower than the rate prescribed for other classes. Many statutes, both RISAs and MVRISA, permit a seller to impose a minimum charge, which is sometimes expressed as a flat amount[16] and other times varies according to the initial amount financed.[17] Some laws contain special provisions for sales pursuant to revolving credit that also impose maximum and minimum charges, although the rates often differ from the

13 *See, e.g.,* Ky. Rev. Stat. Ann. § 190.190(2) (installment sale defined as two or more installments); Wyo. Stat. § 40-14-140(a)(xiii) ("payable in installments" means payment required or permitted by written agreement of five or more installments).

14 National Consumer Law Center, Mortgage Lending § 5.9 (2012).

15 *See, e.g.,* Minn. Stat. § 53C.01 (definition of sales finance company includes "retail seller engaged, in whole or in part, in the business of creating and holding retail installment contracts"); Miss. Code Ann. § 63-19-7 (definition of sales finance company encompasses retail sellers holding retail installment contracts that exceed a total aggregate outstanding indebtedness of $500,000).

16 *See, e.g.,* Ga. Code Ann. § 10-1-33(b).

17 *See, e.g.,* Fla. Stat. § 520.34(6)(a); Ga. Code Ann. § 10-1-3(d)(2).

provisions addressing installment contracts. Appendix C, *infra*, summarizes the interest rate provision of each state's RISAs.

A number of laws, both RISAs and MVRISAs, contain special provisions for manufactured homes. These provisions often prescribe rates or limitations that are different from those that apply to other goods. While a few states' provisions applicable to manufactured homes state that the parties may agree to any finance charge, a greater number of laws prescribe a maximum rate or provide for a rate that is adjustable, subject to certain conditions. Nevertheless, federal law may preempt such interest limits for manufactured home sales.[18]

## *10.2.4 Limits on Points and Fees*

Only a handful of RISAs and MVRISAs place limitations upon points or prepaid interest. Similarly, only a few statutes limit documentary fees that may be charged by sellers in connection with retail installment sales. The most common limitation established is a maximum dollar cap on fees that, in some states, is subject to periodic adjustment based upon changes in the Consumer Price Index. Other limitations include requiring fees to be charged to both cash buyers and credit buyers, and, where no specific cap is set, requiring the fees to be reasonable in relation to the benefit conferred upon the consumer.

## *10.2.5 Schedule of Payments and Balloon Payments*

### 10.2.5.1 Limits on Term of Credit

A few RISAs provide a limit on a contract's term,[19] but the statutes that most commonly establish such a limitation are those that have adopted the Uniform Consumer Credit Code and the relevant provisions pertain to supervised loans. Generally speaking, these laws require that a loan shall be payable in a single installment or installments scheduled to be payable over a period of not more than thirty-seven months if the principal is more than a specified amount or over a period of not more than twenty-five months if the principal is that amount or less.[20]

### 10.2.5.2 Equal Installments and Balloon Payments

Although a small number of RISAs state that balloon note financing is permitted,[21] or only require that a contract disclose that an installment substantially exceeds a prior installment,[22] the majority of RISAs that address this subject limit the circumstances upon which unequal payments may be included in an agreement. These provisions are summarized in Appendix C, *infra*. Most of these laws state that the financed amount must be scheduled to be payable in substantially equal installments at equal periodic intervals except to the extent that the schedule of payments is adjusted to the seasonal or irregular income of the debtor, and they also provide that if any scheduled payment is more than twice as large as the average scheduled payment, than the consumer has the right to refinance that payment at the time it is due. Further, these laws generally state that the terms of the refinancing must be no less favorable that the terms of the original transaction.

## *10.2.6 Insurance*

In some states, the buyer in a retail installment contract may be required to insure the goods at the buyer's expense for the protection of the seller or subsequent holder. In addition to placing restrictions upon the amount and/or term of insurance a seller or lender may require, some RISAs also regulate the type of insurance that may be sold. A number of RISAs require that the sale of insurance be limited to insurance against a substantial risk of loss, damage, or destruction of the goods[23] or motor vehicle.[24]

In states that have adopted the Uniform Consumer Credit Code (UCCC), their statutes often include specific provisions applying to both property and liability insurance. With respect to property insurance, the UCCC requires that a creditor not contract for or receive a separate charge for insurance against loss of or damage to property unless the insurance covers a substantial risk of loss of or damage to property related to the credit transaction. In addition, the amount, terms, and conditions of the insurance must be reasonable in relation to the character and value of the property insured or to be insured, and the term of the insurance must be reasonable in relation to the terms of credit. The term of insurance is reasonable if it is customary and does not extend substantially beyond a scheduled maturity.[25] With respect to liability insurance, the UCCC states that a creditor may not contract for or receive a separate charge for insurance against liability unless the insurance covers a substantial risk of liability arising out of the ownership or use of property related to the credit transaction.[26]

18 *See* § 10.5.5, *infra*.

19 *See, e.g.*, Neb. Rev. Stat. § 45-335 (maximum term of 145 months, except that installment contracts for the purchase of mobile homes may exceed this limitation); N.J. § 17:16C-40.1 (sales finance company may loan up to a maximum of $10,000 secured by a purchase money security interest to finance the purchase of a passenger motor vehicle and principal amount may be repaid in not more than 48 substantially equal monthly installments).

20 *See, e.g.*, Ind. Code § 24-4.5-3-511 ($300).

21 *See, e.g.*, 815 Ill. Comp. Stat. Ann. §§ 405/6(b), 375/6.

22 *See, e.g.*, N.D. Cent. Code § 51-13-02 (contract must disclose that it is not payable in equal installments, as well as the amount of every larger installment and its due date and, if any payment is more than twice the amount of an otherwise regularly scheduled equal payment, seller must identify it by the term "balloon payment").

23 *See, e.g.*, Mont. Code Ann. § 31-1-233(3).

24 *See, e.g.*, Mo. Rev. Stat. § 365.070(1).

25 *See, e.g.*, Okla. Stat. tit. 14A, § 4-301.

26 *See, e.g.*, Okla. Stat. tit. 14A, § 4-303.

## 10.2.7 Deferral Charges

Many statutes authorize sellers or lenders to receive a deferral charge in the event that the parties agree, before or after default, to a deferral of all or part of one or more unpaid installments. Where some statutes state simply that the creditor may charge a rate not exceeding the one previously disclosed to the consumer,[27] a greater number of statutes provide specific methods to be used in the calculation. Depending on the state, the rate of interest on the amount extended or deferred for the period of extension or deferral may be the same as the finance charge originally disclosed in the contract,[28] it may be a different percentage,[29] or it may need to be calculated according to a particular formula dependent on certain factors or variables attendant to the contract or deferral.[30] Many RISAs also state that a deferral agreement may also provide for the buyer's payment of the additional insurance premiums to the holder of the contract for insurance coverage until the end of the period of extension or deferral as provided for in the contract. RISA provisions regarding deferral charges are summarized in more detail at Appendix C, *infra*.

## 10.2.8 Late Fees

A number of RISAs have limits on the fee or charge that a creditor may impose for a late payment. Often these are limited to the lesser of a percentage of the payment owed or a flat dollar amount such as $5 or $10 dollars.[31] A number of statutes also provide that if late fees are not assessed within a particular time period they are deemed to have been waived by the creditor.[32] Some RISAs are also specific that a late charge may only be assessed once on any delinquent payment so as to avoid cascading late fees.

## 10.2.9 Rebates of Unearned Interest

Some RISAs and MVRISAs provide that a consumer may prepay in full the unpaid balance of a credit sale without having to pay a penalty. When a consumer prepays a credit sale, the customer is generally entitled to a rebate of the unearned interest. Because the formula for calculating this rebate varies from state to state, the relevant state statute must be consulted in order to ascertain how to arrive at the correct figure. Some state statutes provide that the actuarial method should be used in calculating the rebate, while others prescribe the Rule of 78s.[33] Some RISAs and MVRISAs direct specifically that the Rule of 78s shall not be used.[34] A small number of RISAs provide a choice of alternative methods to calculate the rebate, depending on certain factors.[35] Certain RISAs also permit the seller to deduct an acquisition cost from the amount of the rebate. Almost all RISAs state that if the amount of the rebate is less than one dollar, no refund need be made.

Rebate calculations can be complex and are described in detail at § 5.8, *supra*. The rebate provisions of each state's RISA are summarized in Appendix C, *infra*.

## 10.2.10 Single Document Rule

Several RISAs require that a RISC be contained in a single document. While a few of these laws are absolute in this requirement, others allow for certain exceptions.[36] A number of other statutes provide specifically that a retail installment contract does not need to be contained in a single document.[37]

Whether the state's RISA includes a single document rule is listed in Appendix C, *infra*. A more through discussion of the single document rule found in both RISAs and motor vehicle finance acts and the significance of the these requirements is found at § 10.3.2.2, *infra*.

## 10.2.11 Remedies

RISA remedies vary significantly from state to state. For instance, some RISAs bar the seller's recovery of any finance charges, delinquency charges, or other similar fees, for a violation of *any* provision of the statute,[38] while other RISAs contain remedies that apply only to certain provisions[39] or willful violations.[40] Some RISAs provide different remedies for

27 *See, e.g.,* Colo. Rev. Stat. 5-2-204.

28 *See, e.g.,* 815 Ill. Comp. Stat. Ann. 405-20; Iowa Code § 322.20. *Cf.* Ky. Rev. Stat. Ann. § 190.130 (original finance charge plus a flat service fee).

29 *See, e.g.,* Md. Code Ann., Com. Law § 12-619(b) (extension or deferral charge may not exceed an amount equal to 1% per month of the amount extended or deferred for the period of extension or deferral).

30 *See, e.g.,* Mo. Rev. Stat. § 365.130.

31 *See, e.g.,* Ohio Rev. Code Ann. § 1317.06 (limiting late charges to delinquent payments more than ten days late and capping such fees at five cents for each dollar not to exceed three dollars).

32 *See, e.g.,* N.C. Gen Stat. § 25A-29 (late fee deemed to have been waived unless, within forty-five days following the default the charge is collected or written notice of the charge is sent to the buyer).

33 *See, e.g.,* Alaska Stat. § 45.10.070; Wash. Rev. Code § 63.14.080.

34 *See, e.g.,* Ariz. Rev. Stat. § 44-6602(a); S.D. Codified Laws Ann. 54-3A-9.

35 *See, e.g.,* S.C. Code Ann. § 37-2-210.

36 *See, e.g.,* Alaska Stat. § 45.10.010; Or. Rev. Stat. § 83.020(1).

37 *See, e.g.,* Ky. Rev. Stat. § 371.230; Mich. Comp. Laws § 445.854.

38 *See, e.g.,* Ariz. Rev. Stat. § 44-6006 (seller or holder who violates any provision of the statute is barred from recovery of any finance charge, official fees and delinquency charge under for as long as the violation continues); Cal. Civ. Code § 1812.7 (any person who fails to comply with Act is barred from recovery of any finance charge or of any delinquency, collection, extension, deferral or refinance and buyer has the right to recover an amount equal to any of such charges paid); 815 Ill. Comp. Stat. Ann. 405/31(b) (no person who violates Act, except as a result of an accident or bona fide error of computation, may recover any finance charge, delinquency or collection charge, or any refinance charge in connection with the related retail installment contract or retail charge agreement).

39 *See, e.g.,* Mass. Gen. Laws ch. 255B, § 22.

40 *See, e.g.,* Conn. Gen. Stat. § 36a-786 (willful violation of any provision other than a disclosure violation shall bar recovery of any finance, delinquency or collection charge provided owner or holder approved of or had knowledge of such violation and, after such approval or knowledge, retained the benefits accruing from the

willful and non-willful violations.[41] A handful of RISAs provide that when a seller has committed a willful violation of a consolidated total of two or more contracts, the seller is not only barred from recovery of finance and other charges, but the buyer may also recover three times the total of charges imposed.[42]

Even in states that have adopted the Uniform Consumer Credit Code, statutes differ with respect to remedy. For example, some UCCC states provide for a remedy in the event that only specified, enumerated provisions are violated, while others are more general in their application. Some UCCC statutes allow the barring of a seller's of recovery of finance and other charges, some allow the voiding of the contract under certain circumstances, and some provide for an action to recover actual damages plus penalties of not less than $100 but not more than $1,000 in certain situations.[43]

In most of the UCCC state statutes, if a creditor has contracted for or received a charge in excess of that allowed, or if a debtor is entitled to a refund and the person liable to the debtor refuses to make a refund within a reasonable time after demand, then the debtor is entitled to a penalty.[44] Some statutes even provide that if the creditor has made an excess charge in deliberate violation of or in reckless disregard for the statute, the penalty may be recovered even though the creditor has refunded the excess charge.[45]

Many UCCC and non-UCCC state statutes explicitly provide for the recovery of reasonable attorney fees and costs. In addition, many statutes provide for injunctive relief, usually in suits brought by the state attorney general or other authority, as well as civil and/or criminal penalties. A state-by-state summary of RISA remedies may be found in Appendix C, *infra*.

violation or otherwise ratified the violation); Del. Code Ann. tit. 6, § 2911(b) (willful violation of specified provisions shall bar recovery of any finance charge, delinquency or collection charge); Fla. Stat. § 520.39(2) (for willful violations, buyer may recover, or may set off or counterclaim in any action against the buyer, an amount equal to any finance charge and any delinquency fees, plus attorney fees and costs).

41 *See, e.g.,* Ga. Code Ann. § 10-1-15; Ga. Code Ann. § 10-1-38.

42 *See, e.g.,* Cal. Civ. Code § 1812.9; Del. Code Ann. tit. 6, § 4350.

43 *See, e.g.,* Colo. Rev. Stat. § 5-5-202 (violations of disclosure provisions are subject to twice the amount of the finance charge in connection with the transaction, but the liability shall be not less than $100 and nor more than $1,000, plus reasonable attorney fees); Idaho Code § 28-45-201(1) (if a creditor violates certain specified provisions of the Act, the debtor has a cause of action to recover actual damages and also a right in an action (other than a class action) to recover a penalty in an amount determined by the court not less than $100 and not more than $1,000).

44 *e.g.,* Idaho Code § 28-45-201(3) (a penalty in an amount determined by the court not less than $100 and not more than $1,000); Ind. Code § 24-4.5-5-202(3) (a penalty in an amount determined by a court not exceeding the greater of either the amount of the credit service or loan finance charge or 10 times the amount of the excess charge).

45 *See, e.g.,* Ind. Code § 24-4.5-5-202(3); Utah Code Ann. § 70C-7-201.

## *10.2.12 Assignee Liability*

Section 10.6, *infra*, examines assignee liability generally, and focuses in particular on the FTC Holder Rule. This subsection is limited to provisions dealing with assignee liability found in state RISAs. To a large extent, these RISA provisions are obsolete because a combination of the FTC Holder Rule and UCC Article 9 provides that assignees now are almost always liable for seller-related claims and defenses.[46]

Some RISAs provide that no provision of a RISC is valid by which the buyer agrees not to assert against the seller or assignee a claim or defense arising out of the sale.[47] Other RISAs go farther by affirmatively stating that an assignee shall be subject to all claims and defenses of the buyer arising from a specific consumer credit sale,[48] as long as the total of all claims and defenses that may be asserted against the assignee shall not exceed the amount owing to the assignee at the time of the assignment.[49] Some RISAs state that a claim may be asserted against the assignee only if the consumer has made a good faith attempt to obtain satisfaction from the seller.

Other RISAs, however, allow a RISC to contain a provision that the buyer will not assert against the assignee any claim or defense that he may have against the seller. As mentioned earlier, these provisions now are superseded by provisions in the FTC Holder Rule and UCC Article 9 that provide otherwise.[50]

Even RISAs that allow for waiver of assignee liability make exceptions, finding the assignee liable if the assignee or holder has actual knowledge, or has received notice before the contract or note is acquired, of repetitive complaints of a substantial nature by other buyers to any governmental agency. These complaints should allege that the seller has failed or refused to perform its agreements with such buyers, or the seller's failure to perform his agreements with such buyers within a reasonable time after the governmental agency has determined that the complaints are well-founded. In addition, the agreement will not be enforceable if the assignee or holder has actual knowledge, or has received notice from its course of dealing with the seller or from its own records, of substantial complaints by other buyers that the seller has failed or refused to perform his agreements with such buyers within a reasonable time after such complaints were made.[51]

Other statutes state that a buyer's agreement not to bring an action against an assignee is enforceable only if the assignee acquires the contract in good faith and for value, and if after the assignee gives the consumer notice of the assignment receives no written notice, within a prescribed number of days after the mailing of the notice, of the facts giving rise to a buyer's claim or defense. The agreement not to assert a claim or defense is not

46 *See* § 10.6, *infra.*

47 *See, e.g.,* Wash. Rev. Code § 63.14.150.

48 *See, e.g.,* Mass. Gen. Laws ch. 255D, § 25A.

49 *See, e.g.,* Cal. Civ. Code § 1804.2 (West); W. Va. Code § 46A-2-102.

50 *See* § 10.6, *infra.*

51 *See, e.g.,*815 Ill. Comp. Stat. Ann. § 405/17.

valid if the assignee receives such written notice from the consumer within the given period.[52]

Appendix C, *infra*, summarizes the assignee liability provisions of state RISAs. These statutes and their interplay with the FTC Holder Rule are also discussed in National Consumer Law Center, *Unfair and Deceptive Acts and Practices* § 11.6.5.2 (7th ed. 2008 and Supp.).

## 10.3 Motor Vehicle Finance

### *10.3.1 General*

#### 10.3.1.1 The Importance of Cars

For a majority of Americans, a car is a necessity. The design of most cities and suburbs, a lack of public transportation in both rural and urban areas, and numerous other factors make life without a car difficult if not impossible for many. A recent survey by the U.S. Department of Transportation found that 91.2% of adults commute to work using a personal vehicle.[53] While changes such as an ability to telecommute, improved public transportation alternatives, and smart planning may reduce the need for cars, for the foreseeable future many Americans will need a car to be productive, engaged members of society.

This is especially true for working families with low-incomes. Families with higher incomes may have the resources and opportunities to make choices, such as living close to their places of work, obtaining in-home child care or high-cost child care near their homes, working from home, and making other lifestyle changes. These options are typically not available to low-income families. And yet, households with incomes below $25,000 are nine times more likely to be without a car than households with incomes above $25,000.[54] This indicates that low-income families find it extremely difficult to buy and keep a reliable car. It also demonstrates that a family that does have a reliable car is much better poised to succeed economically than a family without a car.[55]

52 *See, e.g.*, Iowa Code § 537.3404; Okla. Stat. tit. 14A, § 2-404(1).

53 U.S. Department of Transportation, Bureau of Transportation Statistics, NHTS 2001 Highlights Report, BTS03-05 (Washington, DC: 2003).

54 U.S. Department of Transportation, Bureau of Transportation Statistics, NHTS 2001 Highlights Report, BTS03-05 (Washington, DC: 2003).

55 A study of one car ownership program, Good News Mountaineer Garage, implied that car ownership has a real impact on families' economic success. The families helped by the program all received Temporary Assistance for Needy Families (TANF) benefits. One year after receiving a vehicle, 70% of the families went off public assistance, 80% were working, and 13% were in job training. In another study of such a program the West Virginia the Department of Health and Human Services found that families receiving cars through a pilot program rather than a statewide leasing program had lower recidivism rates and used their car to become economically independent. *See* www.goodnewsmountaineergarage.com/about.html (discussing effects of car ownership).

#### 10.3.1.2 How Cars Are Financed and Common Abuses

Car dealers are generally thought of as selling cars, but generally one half or more of dealer's profits come not from the sale of cars, but from the sale of financing and related products.[56] About 80% of car purchases are financed at the dealership.[57] The vast majority of this financing is in the form of installment sales contracts in which the dealer is the original seller and lender. These contracts are generally quickly sold to lenders who have agreed to purchase the debt from the dealers.

The way in which cars are sold and financed is intentionally structured to be needlessly complicated and time consuming in order to confuse buyers and enable dealers to charge excessive prices and fees for both the car and financing. Dealers use psychological tactics to influence or coerce consumers. Often dealers force the consumer to stay at the dealership for long periods of time by keeping the potential trade-in, keeping the consumer's driver's license, or other ruses. The consumer is worn down and becomes much more susceptible to the dealer's efforts to extract excess profits from the transaction. Dealers mislead and simply lie to consumers.

Dealers also use tactics such as "yo-yo sales" to reduce any chance the consumer has of getting a fair deal. In a yo-yo sale the dealer sends the customer off the lot driving the newly purchased car only to call the customer back several days later to say that financing could not be arranged at the original terms and the consumer must sign new documents at a higher interest rate or other worse terms. Of course, if the consumer, rather than the dealer, had reconsidered the transaction and wished to back out, the dealer would be quick to tell the consumer that the deal is binding and the consumer may not cancel the transaction.

Sometimes the dealer is simply bringing the customer back in to get an even higher interest rate or add on more profitable items to the sale. These dealers realize that consumers are more likely to agree to these terms after they already feel so invested in the deal and are reluctant to see it undone. Often the consumer has already paid additional money to third parties for insurance or improvements to the newly purchased car. Indeed sometimes the consumer's trade in has already been sold. In such circumstances the consumer often believes there is no choice but to accept the new terms presented by the dealer.

Even if the dealer was unable to find a lender willing to purchase the debt at the terms the dealer would like, there are always entities that buy debt for less than its face value. The dealer has the option of selling the debt to such entities or keeping the contract. Instead the dealer will call the consumer

56 Glenn Roberts, *F&I Experts Discuss F&I Basics: The Art of the Deal*, F&I Magazine, February 2009, *available at* www.fi-magazine.com/Channel/F-I-Products/Article/Story/2009/02/The-Art-of-the-Deal.aspx.

57 *See* Raj Date and Brian Reed, Auto Race to the Bottom: Free Markets and Consumer Protection in Auto Finance (Nov. 16, 2009), *available at* http://cambridgewinter.org/Cambridge_Winter/Welcome_files/auto%20finance%20111609.pdf.

and inform them they must accept the new terms or walk away from a deal after investing substantial time and money. A more through discussion of yo-yo sales and how to address this abuse is found at § 10.3.7, *infra,* as well as in a different treatise in this series, National Consumer Law Center, *Automobile Fraud* Ch. 5 (4th ed. 2011).

Dealers often structure the negotiation for the sale of a car to obscure the costs and to prevent the consumer from understanding whether he or she is getting the car at a fair price. Excess dealer profits will be hidden in additions such as "window etching," service contracts, rust proofing, and vastly inflated document preparation fees. A more through discussion of add-on products is found at § 10.3.4, *infra.*

Financing markups by dealers create another opportunity for abuse. In most car purchase transactions in addition to selling the car, the dealer is the original lender and arranges with a lending company to buy the debt after the sale is completed. Dealers typically contact prospective lenders and present the consumer's financial information. Lenders then inform the dealer of the terms on which they will be willing to lend to that consumer, typically known as the buy rate. Often the dealer places the consumer in less favorable financing than the consumer qualifies for, and splits the extra profit with the lender. For example, if the lender was willing to lend to the consumer at an 8% interest rate, the dealer may place the consumer in a loan at 12% interest. The lender and dealer then split the extra money that will be paid by the consumer due to the higher interest charges.

An extremely troubling feature of dealer financing markups is their disparate racial impact. Information obtained through litigation mounted by NCLC and others has demonstrated that minority car buyers pay significantly higher dealer markups than non-minority car buyers *with the same credit scores*.[58] A more through discussion of dealer markups is found at § 10.3.5, *infra.*

The increasing length of used car loans, often five years or more, coupled with excessive interest rates that result from dealer markups, virtually ensure that the consumer will soon owe more than the car is worth. Many times potential car buyers will still owe more than the vehicle is worth when they must purchase a replacement. When such a customer comes in "upside down," dealers will often roll the excess amount still owed on the first vehicle into the deal for the next one and so make it even less likely that the consumer will ever have any equity in the car. A more through discussion of negative equity and its significance is found at § 10.3.3, *infra.*

58 *See, e.g.,* Ian Ayers, Expert Report (June 2004), *available at* www.nclc.org/images/pdf/litigation/closed/ahfc-ianayresreportexhibits.pdf; Cohen, Mark A. Imperfect Competition in Auto Lending: Subjective Markups, Racial Disparity, and Class Action Litigation, *available at* http://ssrn.com/abstract=951827.

## *10.3.2 Motor Vehicle Installment Sales Acts (MVISAs) and Motor Vehicle Finance Acts (MVFAs)*

### 10.3.2.1 General

While a state RISA may be the applicable statute in some states, other states have acts specific to the finance of motor vehicles often called motor vehicle installment sales acts (MVISAs) or motor vehicle finance acts (MVFAs). These acts often address the form of the contract and the substance of some of the contract terms. One important requirement regarding form is the single document rule, described at § 10.3.2.2, *infra.* Substantive rules addressed in MVISAs and MVFAs include permissible fees or charges, such as the limits on document fees discussed at § 10.3.2.3, *infra,* and caps on interest rates, discussed at § 10.3.2.4, *infra.*

### 10.3.2.2 Single Document Rule and Disclosure Requirements

Many states include a "single document rule" in certain consumer credit statutes, usually a retail installment sales act or a motor vehicle installment sales law. The single document rule is an important deterrent to shell games by dealers and financers. It prevents such ploys as side agreements making the deal contingent, requiring additional consideration, or containing additional promises on the part of the dealer. It prevents the dealer or creditor from taking a "mix and match" approach to the contract, having the consumer sign multiple documents containing contract clauses and later assembling selected clauses into a contract.

The single document rule statutes are of two general types. The first type states that the entire agreement must be contained in a single document.[59] The second type does not use words like

59 *See* Alaska Stat. § 45.10.010 (except for open-end credit, catalog sales, and consolidated contracts, retail installment contract must be single document); Cal. Civ. Code §§ 2981.9 (motor vehicle retail installment contracts must contain in a single document all of the agreements of the buyer and seller), 2985.8 (similar rule for vehicle leases); Nev. Rev. Stat. § 97; N.Y. Pers. Property Law § 337 (McKinney) (retail lease agreement must be a single document); N.D. Cent. Code § 51-13-02(1) (retail installment contract must be in writing and contain all the agreements of the parties); Or. Rev. Stat. § 83.020 (retail installment contract must be single document and must contain the entire agreement of the parties, except for open-end credit, mail order sales, and consolidated contracts; 69 Pa. Stat. Ann. § 1302 (West) (retail installment contract must be single document containing entire agreement of parties; note that this statute does not apply to motor vehicle installment sales); Wash. Rev. Code § 63.14.020 (retail installment contract must be single document containing parties' entire agreement; exceptions for open-end credit, catalog sales, and consolidated sales); Wis. Stat. § 422.303 (consumer credit sales other than open-end credit and in which finance charge is more than a discount for prompt payment). *See also* Mont. Code Ann. § 31-1-231(1) (by negative implication, retail installment contract must be single document if seller retains security interest); Wis. Stat. § 422.303 (in consumer credit sales other than open-end credit and contracts where only finance charge is a

"single document" but achieves the same result[60] by requiring the contract to contain all agreements of the parties.[61] The single document rule is by no means universal, however, and some states have statutes that say that a single document is *not* required.[62]

Many statutes that establish a single document rule also require disclosure in that document of a list of items, usually financial terms such as the amount of the down payment, the cash price, and the payment amount. Such a list is not an exclusive list because, otherwise, the single document rule would be mere surplusage.[63] Agreements of the parties that are not on the list of items that must be disclosed must still be included in the single document.[64]

Single document rules may make ineffective:

- An arbitration clause that is found in a buyer's order form but not in the installment sales contract;[65]
- A side agreement making an installment sales contract conditional on financing;[66] and
- Contracts that leave certain terms blank, to be filled in later once financing is arranged.[67]

It is a violation of the single document rule to have the buyer sign a separate agreement to roll negative equity into a new vehicle lease.[68] The agreement regarding the treatment of the negative equity must be included in the new lease.

Some single document rule statutes specify the consequences of a violation. In California[69] and Connecticut,[70] for example, the contract is unenforceable if it is not contained in a single document. In New York, a violation of the single document statute applicable to leases is also a UDAP violation.[71] In a number of states, the credit statute sets forth a penalty, typically denial of the right to collect finance charges, that applies not just to overcharges but also to violation of the single document rule and other procedural requirements.[72] Where the statute

---

discount for prompt payment, customer's obligation to pay the total of payments must be evidenced by a single document; statute specifies several other items that contract must include).

60 *See* Rugumbwa v. Betten Motor Sales, 136 F. Supp. 2d 729, 733 (W.D. Mich. 2001) ("the clear language of the MVISCA and the MFVSA envision the execution of a single, comprehensive installment contract containing all of the agreements made by the parties with regard to the subject matter of the retail installment sale"); Lozada v. Dale Baker Oldsmobile, Inc., 197 F.R.D. 321, 339 (W.D. Mich. 2000). *But see* Scott v. Forest Lake Chrysler-Plymouth-Dodge, 611 N.W.2d 346 (Minn. 2000) (interpreting Minnesota "all agreements" statute to require only that all credit terms be included).

61 *See, e.g.*, Conn. Gen. Stat. § 36a-771(a) (formerly § 42-84) (retail installment contracts must "contain all of the agreements of the parties" and must be completed as to all essential provisions before buyer signs); Fla. Stat. § 520.07(1)(a); Ky. Rev. Stat. Ann. § 190.100 (West) (motor vehicle installment sale contract); Mich. Comp. Laws §§ 492.112 (contract subject to Motor Vehicle Sales Finance Act must "contain all of the agreements between the buyer and the seller relating to the installment sale of the motor vehicle sold" and must be completed in all essential provisions before buyer signs), 566.302 (Motor Vehicle Installment Sales Contract Act); Minn. Stat. § 168.71 (motor vehicle retail installment contracts); Neb. Rev. Stat. §§ 37-1281 (motorboat sales), 60.1417 (vehicle sales); N.J. Rev. Stat. Ann. §§ 17:16C-21 (retail installment contracts), 17:16C-63 (home repair contracts); N.Y. Pers. Prop. Law § 302 (McKinney) (motor vehicle retail installment contracts); N.C. Gen. Stat. § 20-303 (motor vehicle installment sales); Ohio Rev. Code Ann. §§ 1317.02 (retail installment contracts), 4517.26 (motor vehicle sales); Or. Rev. Stat. § 83.520 (motor vehicle installment sales); 69 Pa. Stat. Ann. § 613 (West) (motor vehicle sales finance contracts); Va. Code Ann. § 29.1-826 (retail installment sales of boats); Wis. Stat. §§ 218.0142 (motor vehicle sales financing), 218.0144 (motor vehicle pre-lease agreements). *See* Martinez v. Rick Case Cars, Inc., 278 F. Supp. 2d 1371 (S.D. Fla. 2003) (dealer's motion to dismiss denied when consumer alleged that the dealer failed to fill in certain essential information on the contract and did not sign it). *See also* N.Y. Pers. Prop. Law § 402(7) (McKinney) (all terms of retail installment contract need not be included in single document, but if they are not then contract must be an open-end credit contract).

62 *See, e.g.*, Fla. Stat. § 520.34(f) (retail installment contract need not be contained in single document); Ga. Code Ann. § 10-1-3(c) (retail installment contracts); Mich. Comp. Laws § 445.854 (RISA); Mo. Rev. Stat. § 408.260 (retail installment contracts); N.M. Stat. Ann. § 56-1-2 (retail installment sales; contracts must be completed as to all essential provisions but need not be a single document); N.Y. Pers. Prop. Law § 402 (McKinney); Tenn. Code Ann. § 47-11-103 (retail installment contracts); Vt. Stat. Ann. tit. 9, § 2405(a) (retail installment contracts).

63 Kroupa v. Sunrise Ford, 92 Cal. Rptr. 2d 42 (Cal. Ct. App. 1999).

64 *But see* LaChappelle v. Toyota Motor Credit Corp., 126 Cal. Rptr. 2d 32 (Cal. Ct. App. 2002) (not a violation of the rule to fail to include terms of a trade-in agreement on the car lease unless the trade-in agreement is part of the lease agreement).

65 Rugumbwa v. Betten Motor Sales, 136 F. Supp. 2d 729, 733 (W.D. Mich. 2001).

66 Lozada v. Dale Baker Oldsmobile, Inc., 197 F.R.D. 321, 339 (W.D. Mich. 2000). *But see* Scott v. Forest Lake Chrysler-Plymouth-Dodge, 611 N.W.2d 346 (Minn. 2000). *See generally* National Consumer Law Center, Unfair and Deceptive Acts and Practices § 7.3.9 (7th ed. 2008 and Supp.) (discussing contract requirements for yo-yo sales; note that some states have rules or statutes that allow and regulate yo-yo sales despite single document rules); National Consumer Law Center, Automobile Fraud Ch. 4 (4th 2011).

67 Keyes v. Brown, 232 A.2d 486 (Conn. 1967); Weltchek v. Ford Motor Credit Co., 1982 Ohio App. LEXIS 15749 (July 30, 1982) (seller's assignee had no right to repossess vehicle when buyer's copy of contract did not include payment due date).

68 Kroupa v. Sunrise Ford, 92 Cal. Rptr. 2d 42 (Cal. Ct. App. 1999).

69 Cal. Civ. Code §§ 2983 (with some exceptions, motor vehicle retail installment contract is unenforceable if not contained in single document), 2988.7 (with some exceptions, lease is rescindable if not contained in single document). *See also* Angel v. YFB Hemet, Inc., 2004 WL 1058180 (Cal. Ct. App. Apr. 30, 2004) (upholding jury verdict that the single document rule was violated and the trial court's award of restitution).

70 Conn. Gen. Stat. §§ 36a-770 to 36a-788.

71 N.Y. Pers. Prop. Law § 346 (McKinney).

72 *See, e.g.*, Cal. Civ. Code § 1812.7 (West) (RISA); Conn. Gen. Stat. § 36a-786 (willful violations); N.Y. Pers. Prop. Law §§ 307 (uncorrected willful violations in motor vehicle retail installment contracts), 414 (uncorrected willful violations in retail installment contracts); N.D. Cent. Code 51-13-07; Or. Rev. Stat. § 83.170 (bars collection of service charges, official fees, delinquency, or collection charges for nonconforming contracts); 69 Pa. Stat. Ann. § 2202 (West) (installment sales of goods or services); Wash. Rev. Code § 63.14.180; Wis. Stat. §§ 425.304 (RISA), 218.0142(5) (MVRISA).

does not specify a penalty, or provides only a criminal penalty, a violation will be considered a UDAP violation in most states.[73]

In states that do not have a single document rule, state law requirements regarding disclosure, contract completion, and delivery may fill the gap to some extent. Many state installment credit statutes require that the contract be "completed as to all essential provisions" before the buyer signs and that an exact signed copy of the contract, containing certain specified terms, be delivered to the buyer.[74] These statutes may give the consumer a remedy against an installment seller who withholds the contract, planning to discard it if financing falls through.[75] In Minnesota, the consumer can recover the entire contract amount, plus attorney fees, if the seller intentionally fails to provide a signed copy of the contract.[76]

Usually, the state credit statute requires disclosures for all transactions that meet its definitions, even if the transaction is exempt from the disclosure requirements of the federal Truth in Lending Act.[77] But, for transactions that the Truth in Lending Act covers, the state law may allow the seller to give those disclosures in lieu of meeting the state law disclosure requirements.[78]

In some states, the contract is voidable at the buyer's election until an exact signed copy is delivered, although this right may not apply if the goods have been delivered.[79] Even where the statute did not explicitly make the contract voidable, the Connecticut Supreme Court found that the buyer had the right to rescind a contract that was not completely filled in and was not given to the buyer at the time of execution. The court stressed the mandatory language of the statute and that it was intended to protect buyers.[80] A federal court has construed a Michigan MVRISA to deny finance charges to a seller who did not give a copy of the contract to the buyer at the time of execution.[81] Other states specify another penalty, such as denial of finance charges.[82] An Illinois court has interpreted its MVRISA as denying any right to collect the finance charge to a seller who fails to fill in all the required information on the contract.[83] A UDAP claim may also be a possibility,[84] or the court may imply a private cause of action under the statute.[85]

---

*See also* Lozada v. Dale Baker Oldsmobile, Inc., 136 F. Supp. 2d 719 (W.D. Mich. 2001) (denying finance charge is penalty for violation of MVISCA single document rule, but not for denial of MVSFA requirement of delivery of contract), *later op. at* 145 F. Supp. 2d 878 (W.D. Mich. 2001); Cal. Civ. Code § 2988.5(a) (West) (statutory damages for vehicle leases); Kenworthy v. Bolen, 564 P.2d 835 (Wash. Ct. App. 1977).

73 *See* National Consumer Law Center, Unfair and Deceptive Acts and Practices § 3.2.7 (7th ed. 2008 and Supp.). *But see* Nigh v. Koons Buick Pontiac GMC, Inc., 143 F. Supp. 2d 535 (E.D. Va. 2001) (consumer cannot assert UDAP claim for violation of requirement of delivery of retail installment contract that was contained in statute that created comprehensive scheme of administrative enforcement).

74 *See, e.g.*, Ariz. Rev. Stat. Ann. § 44-286; 815 Ill. Comp. Stat. Ann. § 375/3 (motor vehicle installment sales); Mich. Comp. Laws §§ 492.112 (Motor Vehicle Sales Finance Act), 566.302 (Motor Vehicle Installment Sales Contract Act); Mont. Code Ann. § 31-1-231 (RISA); Ohio Rev. Code Ann. § 1317.2 (West) (RISA); Wis. Stat. §§ 218.0142 (motor vehicle installment sales), 218.0144 (motor vehicle pre-lease agreements). *See also* Lozada v. Dale Baker Oldsmobile, Inc., 136 F. Supp. 2d 719 (W.D. Mich. 2001) (finding statutory penalty of denial of finance charges to be available for violation of MVISCA but not MVSFA); Miranda v. AutoNation USA Corp. (Fla. Dist. Ct. Oct. 31, 2000), *available at* www.nclc.org/unreported (certifying class action), *aff'd in relevant part, rev'd in part on other grounds*, 789 So. 2d 1188 (Fla. Dist. Ct. App. 2001); Charley v. Franklin Capital Corp., 2010 WL 4162550 (N.M. Ct. App. June 17, 2010), *cert. granted*, 148 N.M. 943 (N.M. Aug. 30, 2010) (terms allowing use of Rule of 78s to refund unearned premiums for force-placed insurance not deemed essential, so failure to include such terms did not preclude assignee from utilizing this method). *Cf.* Cullen v. Art Goebel, Inc., 1997 U.S. Dist. LEXIS 23682 (D. Minn. July 23, 1997) (copy delivered to buyer upon execution need only have buyer's signature).

75 *See* Daenzer v. Wayland Ford, Inc., 193 F. Supp. 2d 1030 (W.D. Mich. 2002) (denying finance charges to seller who did not give copy of contract to buyer at time buyer signed it); Lozada v. Dale Baker Oldsmobile, Inc., 197 F.R.D. 321, 340, 341 (W.D. Mich. 2000).

76 Scott v. Forest Lake Chrysler-Plymouth Dodge, 637 N.W.2d 587 (Minn. Ct. App. 2002).

77 *See, e.g.*, Cal. Civ. Code § 2982 (West). *See also* Or. Rev. Stat. § 83.811 (making its disclosure requirements applicable only to transactions not covered by Truth in Lending Act); U.C.C.C. § 3-201.

78 *See, e.g.*, Minn. Stat. § 168.71(b); Mont. Code Ann. § 31-1-231(8). *See also* Cullen v. Art Goebel, Inc., 1997 U.S. Dist. LEXIS 23682 (D. Minn. July 23, 1997).

79 Mich. Comp. Laws § 445.853(b) (voidable unless buyer has received the goods or services); N.Y. Pers. Prop. Law § 302(3) (McKinney) (motor vehicle installment buyer can cancel contract unless vehicle has been delivered). *See also* Rulle v. Ivari Int'l, Inc., 746 N.Y.S.2d 338 (N.Y. App. Term 2002) (contract unenforceable if buyer cancelled before signed copy was mailed to her).

80 Keyes v. Brown, 232 A.2d 486 (Conn. 1967). *Accord* Barnes v. Holliday, 1990 Conn. Super. LEXIS 392 (June 5, 1990) (contract voidable at election of consumer). *But see* Rulle v. Ivari Int'l, Inc., 746 N.Y.S.2d 338 (N.Y. App. Term 2002) (failure to include required warnings on contract does not entitle buyer to cancel and obtain refund).

81 Daenzer v. Wayland Ford, Inc., 193 F. Supp. 2d 1030 (W.D. Mich. 2002).

82 *See, e.g.*, Mont. Code Ann. § 31-1-203; Wis. Stat. § 218.0142(5) (motor vehicle installment sales). *See also* Route 50 Auto Sales, Inc. v. Muncy, 771 N.E.2d 635 (Ill. App. Ct. 2002) (credit seller cannot collect interest and charges where contract did not include statutorily required terms).

83 Route 50 Auto Sales, Inc. v. Muncy, 771 N.E.2d 635 (Ill. App. Ct. 2002).

84 Lozada v. Dale Baker Oldsmobile, Inc., 197 F.R.D. 321, 340, 341 (W.D. Mich. 2000); Kleidon v. Rizza Chevrolet, Inc., 527 N.E.2d 374 (Ill. App. Ct. 1988) (omission of APR from contract, contrary to motor vehicle installment sales statute, was UDAP violation). *But see* Nigh v. Koons Buick Pontiac GMC, Inc., 143 F. Supp. 2d 535 (E.D. Va. 2001) (consumer cannot assert UDAP claim for violation of requirement of delivery of retail installment contract that was contained in statute that created comprehensive scheme of administrative enforcement). *See generally* National Consumer Law Center, Unfair and Deceptive Acts and Practices § 3.2.7 (7th ed. 2008 and Supp.).

85 *See, e.g.*, Couture v. G.W.M., Inc., 2002 WL 31962752 (N.H. Super. Ct. Dec. 3, 2002) (debtor has affirmative cause of action to recover finance charges paid). *But see* Forrest v. Simonds, 1997 WL 610761

#### 10.3.2.3 Limits on Document Fees

Car dealers often charge a document preparation fee, or "doc fee" in connection with car sales and financing. Generally these fees are entirely profit for the dealer. Since the spread of computers and the fact that almost all buyer's orders and RISCs are computer generated, there is typically no cost associated with the preparation of documents. Even if there were costs, there is really no other market where the retail seller charges the consumer for creating the documents that enables the retailer to sell to the consumer.

If the doc fee is for preparation of documents related to the financing of the vehicle, it should be categorized as part of the finance charge for purposes of the Truth in Lending Act. For a more thorough discussion of this issue see National Consumer Law Center, *Truth in Lending* §§ 3.6.2, 3.6.5 (7th ed. 2010 and Supp.).

Some states have specific restrictions on the amount of document fees, what fees may be charged, or the disclosure of doc fees. Many of these restrictions are found in state MVFAs or MVISAs.[86] Some are found elsewhere.

Arkansas limits service and handling fees, including document fees to $129.[87] California provides for a $55 limit on document fees.[88] Connecticut requires doc fee charges to be included in advertised prices. Illinois's statute provides for a $150 fee, adjusted annually for inflation that need not be included in the advertised price, but whose nature must be disclosed to the consumer.[89] Indiana's documentary fee statute requires that the fees reflect expenses actually incurred to prepare documents that are not incidental to the extension of credit, that the fee be both disclosed and negotiated, and that it not be preprinted on the sales documents.[90]

Louisiana's statute allows a $35 documentation fee.[91] Maryland permits a fee for dealer processing to include documents and limits this fee to $100.[92] Michigan limits document preparation fees to $160, or lesser amount of 5% of the cash price.[93] In New Mexico it is an unfair or deceptive trade practice for a dealer to use "documentary fee" or other similar term for any charges other than those actually required by law for processing of documents.[94] In New York dealers may charge a fee of not more than $45 for assisting in securing a registration and/or certificate of title.[95] Ohio law limits documentary fees to $250.[96]

Pennsylvania limits fees to the actual cost incurred by the dealer for fees associated with titling and registering the vehicle, including messenger fees, notary fees and electronic transaction fees and documentary preparation to $120.[97] In Texas the documentary fee is limited to $50.[98] In Washington dealers may charge documentary service fee not to exceed $50.[99]

In addition to the possibility that a dealer's doc fee may not be properly categorized in the Truth in Lending Act disclosures or may violate a state restriction on doc fees, a dealer that prepares legal documents related to the sale and financing of vehicle may be engaging in the unauthorized practice of law. A discussion of this issue can be found in another treatise in this series, National Consumer Law Center, *Unfair and Deceptive Acts and Practices* § 7.2.8.6 (7th ed. 2008 and Supp.).

#### 10.3.2.4 Limits on Interest Rates

While some MVRISA's provide that any charge or rate may be established by agreement of the parties, other statutes set forth formulas for figuring out the permissible charge or, more commonly, they set maximum limits upon the rate that may be imposed. MVRISAs often prescribe different rates depending upon the classification of the vehicle that is the subject of the sale. In these provisions, the rate for a class 1, or new, vehicle is generally lower than the rate prescribed for other classes. The classes may be based upon the age of the vehicle or sometimes upon the amount financed. Many statutes, both RISAs and MVRISA, permit a seller to impose a minimum charge, which is sometimes expressed as a flat amount[100] and other times varies according to the initial amount financed.[101]

### *10.3.3 Negative Equity-Driving "Upside Down"*

#### 10.3.3.1 Described

When a homeowner sells a home for less than the outstanding mortgage, a lender is unlikely to add the deficiency onto a new mortgage when the consumer purchases a new home. Yet this practice is becoming increasingly common in the case of auto financing. Given higher prices and the increasingly longer terms of car loans,[102] the rapid depreciation of cars, and the

(N.D.N.Y. Sept. 30, 1997) (no private cause of action for violating RISA disclosure requirements).

86 *See* Appx. C, *infra* (summarizing state RISAs and MVFAs).

87 Ark. Code Ann. § 23-112-317.

88 Cal. Veh. Code § 11713.1(b) (West) (sales).

89 *See* 815 Ill. Comp. Stat. § 375/11.1; Ill. Admin. Code tit. 14, § 475.310.

90 Ind. Code § 9-23-3-6.5.

91 La. Rev. Stat. Ann. § 6:969.18.

92 Md. Code Ann., Transp. § 15-311.1.

93 Mich. Comp. Laws § 492.113(2)(a).

94 N.M. Stat § 12.2.4.24.

95 N.Y. Comp. Codes R. & Regs. tit. 15, § 78.19(d).

96 Ohio Rev. Code § 1317.07; Ohio Admin. Code 109:4-3-16(B)(21).

97 63 Pa. Cons. Stat. § 818.27a.

98 Tex. Fin. Code Ann. § 348.006.

99 Wash. Rev. Code § 46.70.180.

100 *See, e.g.,* Ga. Code Ann. § 10-1-33(b).

101 *See, e.g.,* Fla. Stat. § 520.34(6)(a); Ga. Code Ann. § 10-1-3(d)(2).

102 In 1984, the average term for a new car loan was 48.3 months, and the average amount financed was $9,333. 73 Fed. Res. Bull. A41, tbl. 1.56 (June 1987). By 2009, the average term for a new car loan was 62 months, and the average amount financed was $28,272. Fed. Reserve Statistical Release G19, Consumer Credit (Apr. 7, 2010), *available at* www.federalreserve.gov/releases/g19/20100407. According to one court decision, data from General Motors Acceptance Corp. indicated that between 26% and 38% of car buyers have negative equity in their trade-in. *In re* Peaslee, 358 B.R. 545, 554

increasing frequency with which consumers want (or, in the case of consumers whose cars do not work, *need*) to obtain a different vehicle, it is not at all unusual for the outstanding balance on a car loan to exceed the car's value. When that car is traded in as part of a new purchase transaction, the deficit—the "negative equity"—is likely to be refinanced as part of the loan on the new car.

To illustrate: Harold wants to purchase a Honda, with a sticker price of $13,000. Harold has a Hyundai, with $8,000 left to pay. But his Hyundai has a fair market value of only $6,000, so Harold has $2,000 negative equity in the Hyundai he wants to trade-in for the Honda.

Dealer practices may vary as to how this $2,000 deficit is reflected on the new loan documents, but it appears to be common to hike the "cash price" of the newly purchased car to absorb—and disguise—the deficit on the trade-in.[103]

It works this way: on paper, the dealer gives a trade-in allowance value high enough to cover the payoff deficit (and perhaps a bit more.) In Harold's case, dealer might put down a paper allowance of $8,200, to cover the $2,000 deficit and make it look like Harold's still getting a net positive trade-in credit of $200. But if the dealer stopped with just an inflated trade-in allowance, it would have some real extra costs to absorb ($2,200 in this case). So the dealer then matches the inflated trade-in allowance with an upward ratchet on the cash price of the car being purchased. The $13,000 purchase price becomes $15,200 on paper. After this numbers game is done, the deficit on the trade-in is totally buried in the inflated trade-in allowance and cash price. The paper figures wrongly make it appear to the consumer[104] as though there is a *positive* net trade-in value, though in fact the trade-in added to the new debt rather than reducing it.

Here's a comparison of Harold's Honda deal, with and without finagling to bury the negative equity:[105]

| | Unfinagled Numbers | Finagled Numbers |
|---|---|---|
| Cash Price on Honda being purchased | $13,000 | $15,200 |
| Trade-in Allowance | $6,000 | $8,200 |
| less payoff balance | - $8,000 | - $8,000 |
| Net trade-in (+/-) | ($2,000) | $200 |
| Unpaid Balance of Cash Price | $13,000 | $15,000 |
| Add other charges | + $2,000 (payoff balance on trade-in) | none |
| Amount Financed | $15,000 | $15,000 |

### 10.3.3.2 Consumer Harm from Dealer's Hiding Negative Equity

#### *10.3.3.2.1 Introduction*

"So what's the problem?" some might say, "the bottom line for the consumer is the same." In Harold's case, the bottom line was indeed the same. Dealers and the finance industry argue that these are just consolidation loans—a service which simply helps consumers get the new car they want. That may be true for some buyers. But it is not always a case of "no harm, no foul."

#### *10.3.3.2.2 Hiding negative equity drives consumers deeper in debt*

The first possible foul is that the numbers-shuffle can present an impediment to informed decision-making about the second most expensive purchase most people make. While some consumers undoubtedly understand that they are refinancing debt on the car they traded in, it is probable that many do not. Many people think of trade-ins as reducing the cost of a new car purchase, not adding to it.

If the numbers explaining the refinanced debt are clearly and comprehensibly laid out in front of them, some consumers may well decide not to stack new debt on top of this old debt—especially as it means continuing to pay on a car they no longer own. Those who can afford it may wish to avoid this by making a larger down payment, or pay off the deficit from savings. Others may decide they must buy a cheaper new car, in order to leave room in their budget for refinancing the deficit on the trade. And others would probably decide to delay buying a car until the old one was paid for.

Lenders who finance transactions where the numbers are finagled by the dealer can be adversely affected as well. Assuming no collusion, these lenders cannot detect this fraud on the face of the paperwork and consequently may fund the sale of a car that is much less than the stated cash price. The loan is "under water" from the start, meaning that the loan amount is (much) greater than the fair market, making the loan riskier than the lender is led to believe. Further, honest dealers who quote a true trade-in value may be at a competitive disadvan-

(Bankr. W.D.N.Y. 2006), *rev'd on other grounds*, 373 B.R. 252 (W.D.N.Y. 2007), *aff'd*, 585 F.3d 53 (2d Cir. 2009). The court suggested that this situation is likely due to the fact that car loans often range in term from seven to eight years, resulting in a substantial number of trade-ins being upside-down. The court further observed that 15% to 25% of chapter 13 debtors "have significant loan deficiency obligations from the repossession and sale of previously owned vehicles." *Id.*

103 One bankruptcy trustee described three methods that he observed dealers using to manipulate the numbers when a trade-in results in negative equity: (1) marking up the price of the car being purchased over the dealer's sticker price or over the manufacturer's suggested retail price; (2) marking up the value of the trade-in over the average trade-in; or (3) creating or manipulating deposits and rebates in order to hide the rolled-in and refinanced negative equity. *In re* Peaslee, 358 B.R. 545, 550 (Bankr. W.D.N.Y. 2006), *rev'd on other grounds*, 373 B.R. 252 (W.D.N.Y. 2007), *aff'd*, 585 F.3d 53 (2d Cir. 2009).

104 While it would also appear in theory to conceal the negative equity from lenders, the apparent prevalence of the practice and resulting over-valuations which should be obvious to professionals invite questions as to whether they are in fact deceived.

105 *See* Thompson v. 10,000 RV Sales, Inc., 31 Cal. Rptr. 3d 18 (Cal. Ct. App. 2005) (real life example of this situation).

tage if lenders refuse to fund loans that actually show the negative equity in the trade-in.[106]

#### *10.3.3.2.3 Hiding negative equity increases opportunity for pricing deception*

It is easy for even educated consumers to lose track once the dealer employee called the "F&I" (finance and insurance) person starts shuffling numbers. The employee is playing a shell game with dollars, and in the process, it is not unheard of for a cash price to be inflated beyond the amount justified by the trade-in deficit.

Another way the shell game can be played is to "cover" the negative equity by reducing the value of the trade-in, which increases the amount of the negative equity. For example, if the trade-in is worth $8,800 but the balanced owed on it is $9,900, the trade-in is $1,100 "under water." The dealer may reduce the value of the trade-in, often unbeknownst to the consumer, to say $5,900 which jacks up the amount of the negative equity to $4,000 ($9,900 minus $5,900). The $4,000 (rather than the $1,100) is then added to the sales price to inflate the total cash price.

In addition, the dealer may also inflate the down payment amount if the lender demands that the consumer put down a certain percentage of the cash price and refuses to fund a deal with negative equity. For example, a car loan may show a down payment of $4,000 when the consumer will state that she only paid $2,500. The difference of $1,500 will be added to the cash price. The dealer file, including a recap sheet, an internal invoice, a finance disposition sheet and a trade-in valuation sheet help to show how the dealer inflated the numbers.

Understanding the transaction is a daunting task, given the many ways in which the dealer may alter the numbers. In one case, a new lease transaction did not reflect the negative equity resulting from the trade-in of two cars in the lease document itself.[107] By disclosing this information in a variety of places, the consumers, not surprisingly, did not understand the effect of the negative equity. The appellate court found that this behavior violated the single document rule.[108]

#### *10.3.3.2.4 Driving upside-down can have dramatic consequences*

Negative equity means the consumer is upside-down on the loan—the debt is greater than the value of the asset purchased from the first day the car is purchased. That leaves the consumer with a bigger deficiency after repossession or an insurance pay-out after an accident. Consequently, a used car loan inflated by negative equity may leave the consumer with a loan that outlives the second car, making it that much harder for the consumer to find needed replacement transportation. Or a consumer struggling to meet the payments cannot sell the second car for an amount sufficient to cover the debt.[109]

### 10.3.3.3 Consumer Remedies

#### *10.3.3.3.1 Introduction*

There has been little litigation addressing problems arising from negative equity financing.[110] Whether that is because most consumers do not perceive it as a problem, or because most consumers do not perceive it at all (which itself could be a problem) is unknown. Depending on the facts and circumstances, it might raise questions under a number of laws.

#### *10.3.3.3.2 Lemon law buy-backs*

To date, more of the debate about negative equity has been in the context of lemon law buy-backs than in the context of front-end purchases. If the manufacturer is required to buy back a lemon car for the "cash price," is it the "cash price" that represents the real price of the lemon, or the listed "cash price" which included the negative equity on the trade-in? The applicable statutory definition of cash price may point to the contract figures,[111] in which case that should be determinative.[112] Proper

106 *See* discussion in Thompson v. 10,000 RV Sales, Inc., 31 Cal. Rptr. 3d 18 (Cal. Ct. App. 2005).

107 Kroupa v. Sunrise Ford, 92 Cal. Rptr. 2d 42 (Cal. Ct. App. 1999).

108 *See* § 10.3.2.2, *supra*.

109 One bankruptcy judge fretted about how difficult this problem makes it for debtors to get and keep necessary transportation: "In this manner, the initial bad judgment becomes self-perpetuating, and has a continuing adverse impact upon debtors." *In re* Brown, 170 B.R. 362, 365 (Bankr. S.D. Ohio 1994).

110 *See* Thompson v. 10,000 RV Sales, Inc., 31 Cal. Rptr. 3d 18 (Cal. Ct. App. 2005) (affirming injunction issued prohibiting the dealer from raising the cash price of the RV by the amount of the over-allowance on the trade-in which results when the dealer hides the negative equity); State *ex rel.* Miller v. Dan Nelson Auto. Group, Inc., Equity No. CE 50210 (Dist. Ct. Polk County, Iowa filed Jan. 7, 2005) (complaint), *available at* www.state.ia.us/government/latest_news/releases/Jan_2005/dnelson.pdf.

In the private litigation context, negative equity may create some headaches in the context of determining damages, without being an issue itself. *Compare* Dyer v. Quality Car & Truck Leasing, 1990 Ohio App. LEXIS 2481 (Ohio Ct. App. June 18, 1990) (holding the dealer to its paper valuations as to a positive net equity; lease), *with* Meade v. Nelson Auto Group, 1997 WL 208685 (Ohio Ct. App. Mar. 31, 1997) (consumers granted rescission of lease under Ohio Consumer Sales Practices Act, but return of negative equity pay-off was required without discussion).

111 *E.g.*, Iowa Code § 322G.4(2) pegs the buyback amount to the purchase price, defined in turn as "cash price paid for the motor vehicle appearing in the sales agreement of contract, including any net allowance given for a trade-in vehicle." *See also* Iowa Code § 322G.2(17); DaimlerChrysler Corp. v. Victoria, 917 A.2d 209 (N.H. 2006) (noting the difference between the buyer's order cash price of $15,600 and the RISC price of $19,000, which was the result of inflating the price to hide negative equity, but holding that the New Motor Vehicle Arbitration Board exceeded its authority in awarding damages to the consumer based on the higher cash price listed in the RISC, relying on the state lemon law which uses the "full purchase price as indicated on the purchase contract").

112 *Cf.* Strachan v. Ford Motor Credit, 1997 WL 197301 (E.D. Pa. Apr. 17, 1997) (no documents in the lease transaction reflected negative equity, and they did show a trade-in allowance equal to the outstanding lien; defendant also unsuccessful in showing independent evidence of overvaluation on the trade-in).

disclosure of the negative equity deficit as a separate, identified component of the amount financed would avoid this issue.

### *10.3.3.3.3 Truth in Lending Act*

The Official Commentary to Regulation Z was amended in 1998 and 1999 to specifically address negative equity in credit sales. The primary purpose of the amendments was to provide instruction as to how to make disclosures relating to the down payment when there is negative equity.[113] How the down payment should have been disclosed in a negative equity situation presented genuinely unchartered territory prior to the 1998 Commentary amendment. However, even prior to the 1998 amendment there was no defensible ground for burying the deficit in an inflated cash price, given Regulation Z's definition of cash price.[114]

The supplementary information to the 1998 Commentary revision clarifies that the deficit "must appear in the itemization of the amount financed," and creditors are given leeway to add categories to the FRB model forms to explain that.[115] Improper disclosure of these items will not give rise to a claim for statutory damages under TILA.[116] Whether a claim might be made for actual damages would depend on the facts.[117] For example, what if Harold had bought his Hyundai under a special promotion, so the APR on the trade-in financing was 4.9%. If he did not understand that the $15,200 Honda price included a $2,000 refinance, and because of this inclusion his new rate is 12%, he might have actual damages flowing from the failure to properly disclose the deficit in the itemization.

Where the car dealer charges the sales tax on both the negative equity from the trade-in and on the price of the new car, the dealer should disclose the portion of the sales tax generated by the negative equity as a finance charge because it is only imposed on credit customers.[118]

### *10.3.3.3.4 State credit and UDAP statutes*

State credit and UDAP laws may raise questions similar to those under TILA, but definitions are likely to be important. For example, Ohio's retail installment sales act defines cash price as "the price, measured in dollars, agreed upon in good faith by the parties as the price at which the specific goods which are the subject matter of any retail installment sale would be sold if such sale were for cash. . . ."[119] The Ohio Supreme Court has said that, so long as the parties agree to it in good faith, negative equity can be included in "cash price" under that definition, which is a post-negotiation price.[120] But if the negative equity deficit is buried without good faith agreement, even under that definitional scheme there is arguably a RISA violation, as well as a potential UDAP violation.[121]

---

113 *See* Reg. Z, Official Commentary § 226.2(a)(18)-3 [§ 1026.2(a)(18)-3], *as amended* 63 Fed. Reg. 16,669, 16,674 (Apr. 6, 1998), and 64 Fed. Reg. 16,614 (Apr. 6, 1999). *See generally* National Consumer Law Center, Truth in Lending §§ 5.3.2.3, 5.6.2.3 (7th ed. 2010 and Supp.); K. Rojc & T. Juffernbruch, *The New Approach to Trade-In Vehicle Disclosures Under Regulation Z*, 54 Bus. Lawyer 1317 (May 1999).

The 1999 amendment addresses the issue of how to make the down payment disclosure when there is both negative equity in the trade-in and a cash down payment, a situation which also affects the disclosure of the "total sale price," Reg. Z § 226.18(j) [§ 1026.18(j)]. The 1999 Commentary amendment gives guidance for that disclosure, as well, Reg. Z, Official Commentary § 226.18(j)-3 [§ 1026.18(j)-3], *as amended by* 64 Fed. Reg. 16,614 (Apr. 6, 1999).

114 Reg. Z § 1026.2(a)(9) [§ 226.2(a)(9)]. While the definition lists some permissible optional additions, they all relate to "the property that is the subject of the transaction," such as accessories, taxes, license fees, service contracts, etc. To analogize to the lease context, the "agreed upon value" of a leased vehicle does not encompass negative equity on a trade-in. Reg. M, Official Commentary § 1013.4(f)(1)-1 [§ 213.4(f)(1)-1].

115 Supplementary Information, 63 Fed. Reg. at 16,673, regarding Reg. Z, Official Commentary § 226.18(c)-2(iii) [§ 1026.18(c)-2(iii)], *as amended* 63 Fed. Reg. at 16,677 (Apr. 6, 1998). *See, e.g.*, Slover-Becker v. Pitre Chrysler Plymouth Jeep of Scottsdale, Inc., 409 F. Supp. 2d 1158 (D. Ariz. 2005) (holding that negative equity must be included in the amount financed but found no violation where the parties agreed that the amount financed was correctly disclosed). *See also* K. Rojc & T. Juffernbruch, *The New Approach to Trade-In Vehicle Disclosures Under Regulation Z*, 54 Bus. Lawyer 1317, 1326–1328 (May 1999). *Cf.* Schultz v. Burton-Moore Ford, Inc., 2008 WL 5111897 (E.D. Mich. Dec. 2, 2008) (negative equity is properly included in amount financed rather than finance charge for purposes of determining whether amount financed exceeds TILA's $25,000 coverage limit). *But cf.* Fitts v. King Richard's Auto Ctr., Inc., 2009 WL 256379 (D.R.I. Feb. 3, 2009) (interpreting TILA to allow cash price to be inflated to include negative equity on trade-in without any additional disclosure).

116 The itemization of the amount financed, the cash price, the down payment, and the total sale price are not among the enumerated violations which trigger statutory damages. *See generally* National Consumer Law Center, Truth in Lending §§ 5.9.3, 5.9.5.1 (7th ed. 2010 and Supp.).

117 Actual damages are available for failure to comply with any disclosure requirement under Parts B (which includes the disclosure requirements), D, and E of TILA, except as specifically limited. 15 U.S.C. § 1640(a)(1).

While the standard for actual damages is difficult to meet, the increase in sales taxes and other fees and the interest on those amounts over the loan term should constitute actual damages under TILA. *See* National Consumer Law Center, Truth in Lending § 11.5 (7th ed. 2010 and Supp.).

118 Parra v. Borgman Ford Sales, 2001 U.S. Dist. LEXIS 16666 (W.D. Mich. Oct. 5, 2001); Thompson v. 10,000 RV Sales, Inc., 31 Cal. Rptr. 3d 18 (Cal. Ct. App. 2005).

119 Ohio Rev. Code Ann. § 1317.01(K).

120 Johns v. Ford Motor Credit, 551 N.E.2d 179 (Ohio 1990) (interpreting Ohio Rev. Code Ann. § 1317.01(K)).

Since the Reg. Z Commentary clarification that the negative equity should be a line item in the amount financed, state definitions of "cash price" which would seem to permit buried negative equity deficits might be inconsistent with TILA. *See* K. Rojc & T. Juffernbruch, *The New Approach to Trade-In Vehicle Disclosures Under Regulation Z*, 54 Bus. Lawyer 1317, 1324–1325 (May 1999).

121 *See also* Castro v. Union Nissan, Inc., 2002 WL 1466810 (N.D. Ill. July 8, 2002) (dealer liable under UDAP act for selling a car for $1,000 over the advertised price; the inflated price likely occurred as a result of the negative equity, though this is not clear from the decision). *Cf.* Motzer Dodge Jeep Eagle v. Ohio Att'y Gen., 642 N.E.2d 20 (Ohio Ct. App. 1994) (dealer violated UDAP regulations by failing to make car available at advertised price; dealer's attempted use of negative equity as justification failed).

Michigan amended its RISA law in 2005 to expressly permit the dealer to pay the balance due on a trade-in and finance it as part of the new deal.[122] Other states may have definitions of cash price more akin to the Truth in Lending Act's definition, setting a more objective standard. For example, Iowa's definition of cash price is the price at which goods are sold by the seller to cash buyers in the ordinary course of business.[123] The Iowa Consumer Credit Code defines "amount financed," as the "cash price of the goods *plus the amount actually paid or to be paid by the seller pursuant to an agreement with the buyer to discharge a security interest in, a lien on, or a debt with respect to property traded in*. . . ."[124] This statutory scheme, like TILA's, seems to preclude burying the trade-in's deficit in the new car's cash price, as well as requiring the consumer's actual agreement that the negative equity be refinanced.

#### *10.3.3.3.5 Other remedies*

Negative equity might also raise other issues. For example, there may be a question as to whether dealers should have lenders' licenses to make what is essentially a consolidation loan—financing more than just the purchase price of the new vehicle. However, in the wake of the greater attention focused on the issue of negative equity after the 1998 TILA Commentary amendments, there were efforts in several states to pass legislation to ensure that dealers could finance the negative equity on a trade-in.[125]

Another possible issue relates to GAP insurance. GAP coverage is sold to cover the deficiency between an outstanding loan balance and the amount paid out by a property insurer after a loss on the collateral. However, GAP products may limit the payout to a percentage of the collateral's value, such as 110 to 120%. With coverage so limited, dealers must be careful how they tout the benefits of GAP products to consumers who are upside down from the outset due to negative equity (or any other reason), lest they make deceptive representations to sell it.[126]

#### *10.3.3.3.6 Damage issues*

If the cash price was inflated to cover the negative equity, the sales tax on the purchase was calculated on an inflated sales price on the new purchase.[127] Depending on how sales taxes are calculated, an increase in the sale price of the car can result in the consumer paying more taxes. The difference in taxes is part of the damages incurred.

Where the consumer did not know about the negative equity and did not know that the sales price was raised to hide it, that consumer also did not know that she took out a direct loan from the dealer to pay down the negative equity. If the dealer charged an interest rate higher than the credit on the trade-in, the difference in the rates also constitute actual damages flowing from the nondisclosure.

## *10.3.4 Add-Ons and Loan Packing*

### 10.3.4.1 Introduction

Padding a loan with add-ons—particularly the high margin add-ons such as service contracts and various credit insurance products—gives the dealer considerably more income from a transaction. The lender also earns a higher yield from a higher principal balance. These benefits are evident to both the lender and the dealer. One subprime lender's sales representative excitedly explained at a dealer trade show that a service contract "can add six months to the [loan] term."[128]

---

122 Mich. Comp. Laws § 492.113a. *See* Schultz v. Burton-Moore Ford, Inc., 2008 WL 5111897 (E.D. Mich. Dec. 2, 2008) (Michigan RISA law requires itemization of cash price of the car and value of trade-in).

123 Iowa Code § 537.1301(8); Bledsoe Dodge, L.L.C. v. Kuberski, 279 S.W.3d 839 (Tex. App. 2009) ("cash price" under Tex. U.C.C. § 9.103 may include negative equity).

It goes on to permit incidental additions similar to TILA's. *See also In re* Sanders, 403 B.R. 435 (W.D. Tex. 2009) (interpreting § 348.006 and the Tex. U.C.C. § 9.103 to mean that the "cash price" may include negative equity, and prohibiting the bifurcation of the debt into a secured and unsecured portion in bankruptcy); *In re* Acaya, 369 B.R. 564 (Bankr. N.D. Cal. 2007) (relying upon the U.C.C. to decide that negative equity is not part of the cash price given to acquire rights in the collateral); Cal. Civ. Code §§ 2981 to 2984.5 (West) (the California Automobile Sales Finance Act); Tex. Fin. Code Ann. § 348.006 (West); Thompson v. 10,000 RV Sales, Inc., 31 Cal. Rptr. 3d 18 (Cal. Ct. App. 2005) (lengthy discussion of how one dealer violated this act when hiding the results of negative equity from consumers); K. Rojc & T. Juffernbruch, *The New Approach to Trade-In Vehicle Disclosures Under Regulation Z*, 54 Bus. Lawyer 1317 (May 1999). *But see In re* Graupner, 537 F.3d 1295 (11th Cir. 2008) (relying upon Georgia law to find that the definition of cash price includes negative equity); Gen. Motors Acceptance Corp. v. Peaslee (*In re* Peaslee), 373 B.R. 252 (W.D.N.Y. 2007) (the cash price can include negative equity when reading the U.C.C. and the New York motor vehicle retail installment act definitions together; therefore, the debtor could not bifurcate).

124 Iowa Code § 537.1301(4)(a).

125 The Michigan Financial Institutions Bureau has opined that the total cash price can include the negative equity but only if it is separately itemized. Michigan Department of Consumer and Industry Services, Financial Institutions Bureau, *Disclosure of Negative Equity on an Installment Sale Contract*, Motor Vehicle Bulletin 1999-1 (July 6, 1999), *available on the companion website to this treatise*. An example of the manner in which negative equity must be listed is attached to the Bulletin. *See also* K. Rojc & T. Juffernbruch, *The New Approach to Trade-In Vehicle Disclosures Under Regulation Z*, 54 Bus. Lawyer 1317 (May 1999).

126 *See generally* National Consumer Law Center, Truth in Lending § 3.9.4.7 (7th ed. 2010 and Supp.) (discussing 1996 amendments to Reg. Z §§ 226.4(b)(10), 226.4(d)(3) [§§ 1026.4(b)(10), 1026.4(d)(3)] concerning GAP insurance).

127 *See e.g.,* Schultz v. Burton-Moore Ford, Inc., 2008 WL 5111897 (E.D. Mich. Dec. 2, 2008) (dealer erroneously charged sales tax on amount financed including negative equity and not just the cash price of the vehicle).

128 The exchange was recorded by Dateline NBC for a segment on subprime lending which aired December 8, 1998. This particular exchange did not appear in the broadcast.

In some instances, either the dealer or the lender (or both) may also have an ownership interest in the company producing the

One way of reducing customer resistance to costly add-ons is "payment packing." While the salesperson and prospective buyer are chatting about the car, the salesperson talks about a monthly payment amount. The natural assumption for the consumer is that the figure is the price of the car at the interest rate the dealer offers. But that payment amount has "room to pack" built in. The amount may be, for example, $20 or $30 higher per month than necessary to buy that car. Then, when the salesperson sends the customer to the F&I (finance and insurance) employee, there is room in the payment to hike the cash price, to bump up the interest rate for a yield spread premium, or to pack in the add-ons like service contracts and insurance products.

The Washington Attorney General has attacked payment packing as an unfair and deceptive practice.[129] In an attempt to prevent packing, California now prohibits dealers from negotiating a sale or lease contract and then adding in the extra charges without first disclosing the goods and services to be purchased and obtaining the consumer's consent.[130] In addition, the law prohibits the dealers from inflating the amount of the installment payment or down payment or extending the maturity date of the contract for the purpose of disguising the fact that certain charges are added to the contract.[131]

An almost infinite number of products may be added on at the back end to car financing. Some of the most commonly seen products include window etching, rust proofing, stain proofing, paint sealant, lojack, and tire protection. The markup by the dealer on many of these items can be astronomical. While etching a VIN into a window may cost $10 to $15 dollars, dealers may charge a hundred dollars or more. In extreme cases, consumers have paid as much as $2,000 for a pen and key chain costing the dealership $15.[132] In some of the most egregious, but all too common abuses, dealers will charge outrageous prices for add-on products such as service contracts and then never actually pay the third-party provider to obtain the product, but instead pocket the payment financed by the consumer.

### 10.3.4.2 Service Contracts, Extended Warranties, and Breakdown Insurance

The sale of service contracts extended warranties and similar products represent a huge profit center for dealers. This subsection examines how these products are handled in the financing of vehicles and as part of the dealer's business plan. Other treatises in this series examine other aspects of these products. Coverage under these products, refunds for cancelation, and similar issues are addressed in National Consumer Law Center, *Consumer Warranty Law* Ch. 20 (4th ed. 2010 and Supp.). Abusive sales of these products and potential claims related to these sales practices are covered in National Consumer Law Center, *Unfair and Deceptive Acts and Practices* §§ 5.2.7.2, 5.4.3.6, and 5.4.3.7 (7th ed. 2008 and Supp.).

These products may be used in payment packing, and can also be a large source of dealer profits just from the mark up in the price of the products. (However, two courts have held that RISA statutes do not prohibit dealer markups on service contracts.[133]) Recently, more dealers have begun to examine creating their own service contract company. As described in an industry publication about how starting a dealer's own reinsurance company was a "no brainer," this can be a very profitable step to take: "Owning a reinsurance company is essential. Do the math: If you sell a service contact for $1,400 that cost $1,000, your dealership makes a $400 profit. If you own the service contract company, approximately $200 of that $1,000 goes to administer and insure. The remaining $800 goes into reserve. Loss ratios vary, but for this example let's say that $200 of every contract, on average, is used to pay claims. That leaves a $600 profit. The dealership made $400, your reinsurance company made $600. That's $1,000 profit on the same sale that used to net you $400. (No wonder your current warranty/service contract company loves you so much.) If you sold an average of 20 per month, that's $144,000 in additional profit per year."[134]

The return on investment described in this article, while astounding, is apparently just average for the industry. Even larger insurers tout how low their payments on claims actually are. A recent advertisement for Sureguard Products International, L.L.C., a company which claims to be the "#1 F&I product provider by volume," states that they have paid out $600 million in claims, and generated over $5 Billion in profits for their clients (the dealers).

Service contracts for purposes of TILA and state credit statutes are generally considered third-party charges that are applied to the amount financed. But if the dealer requires the consumer to purchase these products as a condition of financing the sale, then they should be treated as part of the finance charge and not the amount financed. This may result in TILA and/or state usury violations. The requirement may also be a state UDAP violation. If the vehicle is repossessed or sold, the contract should also be canceled with a refund to the consumer of the unearned portion of the contract.[135]

---

add-on products, or a reinsurance company, so that the financial rewards are greater than just commissions and mark-up.

129 Washington v. Resource Dealer Group, Inc. (Wash. Super. Ct. May 22, 1998), *available at* www.nclc.org/unreported. *See* National Consumer Law Center, Unfair and Deceptive Acts and Practices § 7.2.7 (7th ed. 2008 and Supp.). *See also* Ferrari v. Howard, 2002 WL 1500414 (Ohio Ct. App. July 11, 2002) (charging $19 extra for a filing fee is a UDAP violation).

130 Cal. Veh. Code § 11713.19 (West).

131 *Id.*

132 Gregory Arroyo, *Payment Packing in Los Angeles*, F&I Management & Technology Magazine, Feb. 2007.

133 King v. Ford Motor Credit Co., 668 N.W.2d 357 (Mich. Ct. App. 2003); Homziak v. Gen. Elec. Capital Warranty Corp., 839 A.2d 1076 (Pa. Super. Ct. 2003).

134 Timothy R. Byrd, It's a NO Brainer, Special Finance Insider, Oct. 12, 2011, *available at* www.specialfinanceinsider.com/19/468/ARTICLE/-It-s-a-NO-Brainer-.aspx.

135 *See* § 5.8, *supra*.

### 10.3.4.3 Insurance and Insurance-Like Products, Generally

A number of add-on products are either insurance, are regulated as insurance, or are very much like insurance. Whether a product is in fact insurance can have significance as to consumers' rights in the transaction. If the product is insurance the dealer may be required to be licensed in order to sell the product. But, if the product is regulated as insurance issues may be raised as to whether the Magnuson-Moss Warranty Act or even some state UDAP statutes apply. In some cases, federal statutes may not apply either if they conflict with state insurance regulation—the federal McCarran-Ferguson Act provides that certain federal laws are ousted by state insurance regulation.[136]

A number of state statutes recently have been enacted concerning whether certain add-on products should be treated as insurance. These statutes have largely been pushed by industry seeking to avoid requirements that dealers be licensed; the statutes also contain industry friendly rebate calculations and other benefits for lenders.[137]

One form of add-on is definitely regulated as insurance. Regulation of credit insurance—credit life, credit accident and health, and credit unemployment insurance—is examined in some detail at Chapter 6, *supra*.

### 10.3.4.4 Guaranteed Asset Protection (GAP) Products

Because of negative equity financing,[138] inflated cash sales prices,[139] and longer loan terms combined with vehicle depreciation, many consumers owe more than their car is worth. This is not only discouraging for consumers, but can be disastrous if the car is totaled or stolen. In such situations, the most the consumer's comprehensive insurance policy will pay will be the market value of the car. The consumer is left owing the remainder of the loan amount.

Guaranteed auto protection (GAP) products ostensibly offer protection for consumers who owe more than their car is worth. These products may be structured in different ways. Some are agreements between creditors and consumers, entered into at the time a consumer finances the purchase of a car, in which the creditor agrees to hold the consumer harmless for the difference between the balance on the debt and the amount paid under an automobile physical damage insurance policy in the event that the vehicle is totaled or stolen. Others are products offered by third parties which also claim to pay this difference which would otherwise be the responsibility of the consumer.

These products are often aggressively pushed by car dealers. Dealers are anxious to sell these products because they are greatly marked up, sometimes selling them for thousands of dollars, compared with the $135 flat fee that some credit unions and other lenders charge for the same protection.[140] Often a large portion of this inflated price goes directly to the dealer. In addition, because these GAP products are financed and dealers are commonly getting a portion of interest paid by the consumer on the loan,[141] they also profit from the larger loan amount that result from the expensive GAP policy.

Moreover, consumers often find these products fail to provide the touted benefits when something does in fact happen to the car. Most GAP products exclude cars that are uninsured or under insured, interest and fees accruing from the time the car was totaled or stolen until payment was made, add-ons such as service contracts, window etching, and sometimes even the GAP product itself, and negative equity from a trade-in that has been rolled into the loan for the covered car.

In order to determine what rules and laws apply to different GAP products, it is important to determine exactly what style of GAP product it is. A creditor can provide GAP protection to a consumer through a simple waiver provision in a loan contract, or through a separate agreement. That separate contract may be executed simply between the creditor and the consumer, where the creditor serves as the obligor, or may involve a third-party administrator or property insurer. The two-party agreement between the creditor and the consumer, whether part of the loan contract or provided for in a separate document, is generally not considered to be insurance. Where a third-party obligor is involved, the question of whether it is considered to be insurance (and thus whether it is regulated by state insurance rules) varies by state. While the bona fide insurance arrangement is subject to state insurance regulation, these arrangements are not as common as the two party arrangements.

Because the agreements between creditor and consumer that do not involve a third party generally are not subject to state insurance regulation, loss ratios—which indicate the ratio of premiums or GAP charges paid *in* to claims paid *out* (essentially the profit ratio)—are not publicly available. When they are available, for example through litigation, such ratios may not provide the full story because, at least in some cases, the

---

136 15 U.S.C. §§ 1011-1015. *See* § 6.5.6.2, *supra*.

137 Ala. Code § 8-33-2 (enacted in 2006); Ariz. Rev. Stat. § 20-1099.01 (enacted in 2004); Cal. Ins. Code § 116.6 (West) (enacted in 2002); Colo. Rev. Stat. § 42-9.5-106 (enacted in 2004); Fla. Stat. Ann. § 634.011(8) (enacted in 2003); Ga. Code Ann. § 33-34A-3(b) (enacted in 2003); Haw. Rev. Stat. § 481X-1(b) (enacted in 2000); 215 Ill. Stat. Ann. § 5/155.39 (enacted in 2003); Mass. Gen. Laws ch. 174C, § 2 (enacted in 2010); Mich. Comp. Laws § 257.1245(2) (enacted in 2006); Miss. Code Ann. § 63-29-5(2) (enacted in 2007); Mo. Stat. Ann. § 385.406(2) (enacted in 2009); Nev. Rev. Stat. § 690C.100 (enacted in 2007); N.J. Stat. Ann. § 17:18-22 (enacted in 2008); N.Y. Ins. Law § 7903 (McKinney) (enacted in 1997); Ohio Rev. Code § 3905.421(C)(2)(a) (enacted in 2003); Okla. Stat. Ann. tit. 36, § 6652(B) (enacted in 2009); Or. Rev. Stat. § 646A.432(3) (enacted in 2008); Tenn. Code Ann. § 56-55-103(b) (enacted in 2005); Tex. Code Ann. § 2306.004 (enacted in 2003); Wash. Rev. Code § 48.110.080(1) (enacted in 2006); Wis. Stat. Ann. § 100.203 (enacted in 2004).

138 *See* § 10.3.3, *supra*.

139 *See* § 10.3.4, *supra*.

140 *See, e.g.*, State Employees' Credit Union GAP Coverage, information available at www.ncsecu.org/AutoLoans/GAPCoverage.html.

141 *See* § 10.3.5, *infra*.

numbers are based upon the amount the finance company charged the dealer not the amount the dealer charged the consumer.

GAP waiver coverage remains in force for the entire term of the corresponding credit, since it is part of the credit obligation. GAP insurance may insure the entire credit term or may be limited to only the first few years of the loan term because of the fast depreciation of the secured asset (the car). Some states authorize GAP agreements independently, outside of insurance rules.

Importantly, a GAP waiver or agreement between the creditor and the consumer provides fewer benefits than actual GAP insurance. For example, many GAP insurance policies will cover the primary insurance company's deductible up to $1,000, while a GAP waiver or agreement often does not. Even where a consumer obtains the broader GAP insurance, the terms of the policy may not be provided to the consumer. Rather, the consumer's loan documents may simply summarize the terms of the GAP insurance coverage and identify the cost, while providing that any conflict between the summary and the actual policy will be resolved by the language in the policy.

### 10.3.4.5 Vendor Single Interest (VSI) Insurance

Vendor single interest insurance (VSI) may appear on many automobile retail installment contracts as an additional charge of $15 to $50 to sometimes hundreds of dollars. VSI often refers to two different insurance products. In this case, VSI is a relatively low-priced product that is assessed as a standard policy at the origination of a loan. VSI also refers to a form of force-placed insurance that can run into thousands of dollars and that is charged to the consumer after the auto loan is originated, if the consumer's own physical damage auto insurance lapses. Force-placed insurance is examined at § 10.3.8.3, *infra*. This subsection considers the VSI assessed at loan origination, whether or not the consumer purchases physical damage insurance on her own.

There is some variation as to what this form of VSI covers. It is compulsory and provides no benefit to the consumer and thus can cover whatever the dealer wants. One use of VSI is a payment toward an insurance policy that protects the lender where a loan goes into default and the consumer does not satisfy the deficiency. VSI coverage may only kick in where the vehicle is repossessed after an accident, or the vehicle is totaled or stolen. The VSI policy typically will be secondary insurance, covering all or part of an unpaid deficiency after recovering the sale price at a repossession sale price, payments from a claim under the consumer's individual physical damage insurance, any payment under a GAP policy, and the consumer's own payment on the deficiency. The VSI policy though could pay the lender where there is an unpaid deficiency not involving physical damage to a vehicle; in other words, it is merely deficiency insurance.

Some policies are purchased by the dealer on each individual vehicle sale. Other policies may cover a lender's complete book of auto loans with one policy paid by the lender and each individual VSI charge may go in whole or in part toward this premium. The consumer may have had no real "choice" about the charge because the business practice between the dealer and the assignee is that every retail installment contract must contain the charge in order to be assigned.

As a practical matter, the agreement between the dealer and the assignee should be reviewed. It may include provisions spelling out whether the VSI fee is a mandatory charge. The practice of the insurance company regarding premium pricing may be revealing. The charge may be higher on indirect loans, i.e., loans between the dealer and consumers, than on direct loans, i.e., loans between the lender and consumers. The difference may suggest that the dealer retains some of the charge.

The consumer is unlikely to receive any benefit from the coverage because the consumer's obligation to repay a deficiency will not be eliminated by the insurer's payment to the lender. One industry writer describes "blanket single interest insurance" as follows:

> Under [this type of] policy, a lender purchases coverage for all loans secured by property as collateral. A premium is paid monthly by the lender to the insurer. Rates are a flat premium per loan or a monthly outstanding balance premium per $1,000 of loan balances. Premiums are usually absorbed by the lender, although a charge may be passed on to the borrower in some states.
>
> Coverage protects only the lender. For benefits to be payable, the loan must be in default and the property repossessed. *The insurance covers only the difference between the value of the property at repossession and the loan balance at the time of repossession.* A benefit is paid only if the loss is caused by damage to the property. Perils covered are similar to standard collision and comprehensive coverage. The lender must require the borrower to carry insurance. (Emphasis added.)[142]

Since the lender must require the borrower to carry insurance on the collateral itself, and the covered risk is the gap between the property's value and the outstanding debt it is clear this insurance does *not* insure the *tangible property*, as contemplated for example by the TILA definition of VSI in Official Commentary to Regulation Z, 12 C.F.R. § 1026.4(d)-10 [§ 226.4(d)-10].

Some case law, in referring to single interest insurance, seems to be referring to a similar type of blanket single interest insurance. *Cordova & Simonpietri Ins. Agency v. Chase Manhattan Bank*,[143] describes "single interest" policies as insuring auto dealers against loss of the unpaid amount on each car sold.

> If, for example, a customer buys a $5,000 car, finances it with a $3,000 loan, *and then refuses to pay the loan*, the policy satisfies the dealer's obligation on the loan and would pay $3,000 directly to the bank

142 Fagg, Credit Life and Disability Insurance 523 (1986).

143 649 F.2d 36 (1st Cir. 1981). The case itself does not deal with the issues raised in this section.

that had financed the purchase of the car. (Emphasis added.)[144]

As described, neither of these insure the collateral, thus are not credit property insurance.[145] Rather they describe a type of default or "credit loss insurance," which under many state consumer financing laws may not be a permissible charge to separately pass on to borrowers. Many consumer financing laws define exclusively permissible charges, and credit loss insurance premiums are unlikely to be among them. A creditor may be required to disclose VSI charges as finance charges under the Truth in Lending Act if the disclosures and the policy itself do not meet the requirements for exemption from the finance charge under Regulation Z.[146]

An issue about the legality of the charge for VSI arises in those states whose retail installment acts, other applicable usury statutes, or credit insurance laws mandate clear and conspicuous disclosure to the borrower that a lender requires that VSI be purchased. If the lender fails to check a box indicating that such insurance is required or otherwise fails to clearly and conspicuously disclose this fact, the vendor may be vulnerable to a claim of usury or subject to a statutory penalty. Whether the insurance premium constitutes an "unauthorized charge" or usury will depend upon the language of the relevant acts.[147]

## *10.3.5 Dealer Markups*

Automobile lenders establish a "buy rate" at which they will lend to a particular consumer. The dealer is allowed to increase the financing rate beyond the buy rate, up to a maximum amount. The dealer and lender split the difference, often with the lion's share going to the dealer. Thus the dealer has unfettered discretion to charge very different interest rates to two consumers with identical credit risk. Moreover, since the dealer has little or no risk upon default, there is no possible argument that risk is a factor in the two consumers receiving different financing rates. The consumer is never informed of this arrangement or that the consumer is charged a higher interest rate than the buy rate—what the lender is willing to extend to a consumer of that particular risk.

The use of such mark-ups in the residential mortgage market (called yield spread premiums) have now been banned as unfair and deceptive.[148] No such ban applies to dealer markups in auto finance and there are fewer tools available to attack the practice. One successful approach has been class-wide Equal Credit Opportunity Act challenges to automobile lenders' pricing policies—not based upon individual dealer discrimination.[149] Statistical analysis has shown that the effect of giving dealers unfettered discretion to set interest rates for like credit risks is that minorities are more likely to have their interest rate jacked up beyond the buy rate, and to have that rate increased more than it is increased for whites. While the automobile lender may not be intentionally discriminating on the basis of race, its pricing policy has a disparate impact on minorities. The series of ECOA cases has, in almost every instance, resulted in significant settlements whereby the lenders agreed to cap the size of these finance upcharges.[150] All of the settlements have expired though, so advocates should remain alert for a revival of past abuses.

For an individual fraud or UDAP case challenging these finance upcharges, the fact pattern is very important. It will be best to have an unsophisticated borrower, a dealer that made representations about getting the buyer a good financing deal, and/or an agency relationship between the dealer and the consumer of which the lender was aware.[151]

## *10.3.6 Inflated Cash Price, Hidden Interest, and Finance Costs*

### 10.3.6.1 The Practices Described

Interest can be hidden in a vehicle's sale price as illustrated in the following example. Buyer A goes to a car dealer and expresses interest in a certain car. The dealer learns that Buyer A intends to pay cash and quotes a price of $5,000. Subsequently, Buyer B inquires about the same car. The dealer learns that Buyer B plans to buy on credit and offers him the identical car for $6,000 at the "low rate" of, say, 5% add-on interest over thirty months, with no down payment, total interest charges of $750, and an apparent APR of 9.33%. While the stated

144 *Id.* at 37.

145 *See also* §§ 6.6.4, 6.7.4, *supra* (discussing what can be the proper subject of credit property insurance); Iowa ICCC Informal Advisory #86 (Nov. 30, 1998), *available on the companion website to this treatise* (Iowa's Consumer Credit Code Commissioner clarified the difference between VSI and default insurance). *Cf.* Reg. Z, Official Commentary § 1026.4(d)-10 [§ 1026.4(d)-10] (VSI protects "tangible property").

146 Reg. Z § 1026.4(d)(2)(i), (ii) [§ 226.4(d)(2)(i), (ii)]. *See* Dixon v. World Fin. Corp. of Ga. (*In re* Dixon), 435 B.R. 768 (Bankr. N.D. Ga. 2010) (finding that insurer waived its right to subrogation as required under Truth in Lending and otherwise satisfied the requirements to permit disclosure in the amount financed instead of as a finance charge), *aff'd*, 2011 WL 1438995 (11th Cir. Apr. 14, 2011); North Shore Auto Fin. v. Block, 934 N.E.2d 381 (Ohio Ct. App. 2010) (disclosures required even where such insurance is not sold on the open market for consumers). *See generally* National Consumer Law Center, Truth in Lending § 3.9.4.8 (7th ed. 2010 and Supp.).

147 *Compare* Sunwest Bank of El Paso v. Gutierrez, 819 S.W.2d 673 (Tex. App. 1991) (unauthorized VSI premium did not constitute interest; rather it was assessed for separate and additional consideration), *with* Partridge v. Inv. Co. of the Southwest, BankTexas, N.A., 1996 WL 732469 (Tex. App. 1996) (agreeing with *Sunwest* as far as it went but indicating that the failure to check the box may not satisfy the clear and conspicuous disclosure required in Texas' MVRISA, thus subjecting the lender to the statutory penalty of twice the amount of the unauthorized charge; borrower, however, did not properly plead this violation).

148 *See* National Consumer Law Center, Mortgage Lending § 7.3.4.2 (2012).

149 *See* National Consumer Law Center, Credit Discrimination (5th ed. 2009 and Supp.).

150 *Id.*

151 *See* National Consumer Law Center, Unfair and Deceptive Acts and Practices § 7.2.4.4 (7th ed. 2008 and Supp.).

interest rate seems reasonable, if the true cash price of $5,000 is used as the amount financed, the total interest payments jump from $750 to $1,750 with an APR of almost 25%. Such a practice of hidden interest may lead to both TILA and usury violations, and at least one jury has treated it as outright fraud, warranting a punitive damage award of over $50 million.[152]

The financial arrangements by which an assignee pays the dealer for the retail installment contract vary. One method that creates considerable price distortion for the consumer is for the assignee to purchase the paper at a steep discount. This method is more common among assignees who specialize in subprime lending or those who purchase paper from "buy here pay here dealers." For example, a subprime lender may rate a buyer as a "B" credit risk, and only offer the dealer 75% of the amount financed to buy that consumer's paper. Alternatively, the lender may impose a large flat acquisition fee on the transaction, or some combination of the two.

It is not uncommon for the ultimate lender to pay a discounted price to a merchant for the consumer's obligation. For example, the price a credit card issuer pays a merchant may be a 2% to 3% discount. Merchants who let their customers use credit cards price their products accordingly. The customers at Store A may pay $40 for a widget because some of its customers will pay by credit card, though the widget might be priced at $39.20 at a store that does not take credit cards. Even though Store A took into account the credit card issuer's 2% discount in setting the widget's price, and hence is related to credit, the eighty cents differential is not a finance charge for purposes of the Truth in Lending Act, and would not be under most state credit regulatory statutes. Cash and credit customers pay the same amount; the differential is not passed onto individual credit card users.

With subprime auto financing, in contrast, the discounts are much greater, and they are individualized. This combination of facts makes it more likely that the loan may contain hidden finance charges as the law defines them. The amount of the discount at which subprime lenders purchase paper may be too great for dealers to absorb within a normal negotiating range for the price of the vehicle, creating an economic incentive for the dealer to pass it on to the buyer. Subprime lenders, for example, may pay only 60% to 80% of the amount financed on the paper. (Some have paid as little as 50%.)

Here's a basic example: The dealer acquires a used car at $3,700, puts $500 into fix-up, for a total acquisition cost of $4,200. If it wants to make $800 on the deal, it will price the car at $5,000. If customer A comes in, and has arranged the financing with her own bank, she walks out with the car for $5,000. But customer B is looking for financing as well as a car, so the dealer faxes a credit application off to Sublime Subprime Auto Finance. If the dealer gets approval from Sublime Subprime for a twenty-four month loan at 21% APR, a straightforward deal would give customer B monthly payments of $257 and a total cost of $6,168.

But if Sublime Subprime will pay the dealer only 75% of the amount financed to buy the contract, in this case, $3,750, the dealer will not make its profit and will lose $450.[153] Where no price was posted on the car, the dealer might be tempted to quote customer B a price that will mean the dealer still collects $5,000, in this case, a price of $6,700.[154] Here's how fudging the cash price changes the economics on this "21%" loan:

| | Straightforward deal | Fudged deal |
|---|---|---|
| Real cash price | $5,000 | $5,000 |
| Inflated cash price | NA | $6,700 |
| Disclosed rate | 21% | 21% |
| Real credit cost as rate | 21% | 53.7% |
| Monthly payments (24) | $ 257 | $ 344 |
| Total of payments | $6,128 | $8,256 |

See how well this subprime financing has worked for customer B. She gets the same car, nominally at the same APR, but her monthly payments are $87 higher and, at least economically, the real cost of credit is unquestionably nearly 54%, not 21%. The question is whether it is also legally considered a 54% rate.

There may be other reasons that dealers hide finance charges in the price of the car. In states that set limits on the permissible interest rates, even dealers that hold their own paper (such as many buy-here pay-here dealers) are constrained by the maximum interest rate they may change. Typically in these transactions the negotiation has been in regards to the monthly payment. If the dealer has successfully persuaded the consumer to accept a high monthly payment and there is a statutory cap on the maximum interest rate the dealer can charge, the dealer will often simply increase the price of the car to arrive at the high monthly payment. This is one reason that the price of the car, rather than the monthly payment, is rarely even discussed.

It is not only in the subprime market that finance charges are hidden in the cash price. Burying finance charge in the cash price is so openly practiced in the prime market too. For example, all the major American automobile manufacturers at times have offered supposedly below-market-rate financing for credit sales with advertised interest rates as low as 0.0%, while simultaneously offering rebates of as much as $1,000 to buyers who paid cash. Such sales gimmicks may well violate the Truth in Lending Act because of the misstatement of the amount financed (i.e., the sale price) in the credit purchases.[155] Indeed,

152 *See* Johnson v. Mercury Fin., Clearinghouse No. 50,407, Case No. CV 93-952 (Ala. Cir. Ct. Aug. 1994) (jury verdict).

153 Some lenders hold back a reserve, under which the dealer will get an additional portion back under specified conditions which indicate the contract will be performed. While some reserves actually pay out, others apparently are written with conditions which make it unlikely that the dealer will see any of the holdback.

154 $\$6,700 \times 0.75 = \$5,025$. Hiking the price to cover a flat acquisition fee works the same way. *N.B.*: Acquisition fees are also charged in leases, but the legal issues are not the same, as leases do not have to disclose the equivalent of an APR.

155 The only argument that might protect these financing arrangements from the TILA is the possibility that they are seller's points which, under the current TILA, may be excluded from the finance charge. *See* § 4.4.6, *supra*.

the practice of burying finance charges (i.e., interest) in the amount financed (i.e., sale price) has been noted by the U.S. Supreme Court,[156] and has been held to violate the TILA in several cases.[157]

### 10.3.6.2 Potential Claims

There are a variety of legal issues triggered when the car's cash price is inflated to cover finance-related costs—the most obvious claims involve Truth in Lending and usury. That the price of a car or the valuation of a trade-in is "negotiable" is not a license to violate the cardinal rule that the price of credit and the price of the product being sold on credit are supposed to be two distinct—and accurately disclosed—things. Whether a TILA finance charge is buried in an inflated cash price on a car is exclusively a factual question. If the dealer absorbs the lender's discount as part of the cost of doing business and takes it into account in pricing all cars, the discount is not a finance charge. Rather, the dealer is absorbing the discount as part of a cost of doing business—just like the widget-selling merchant.[158]

However, the discount that the lender charges the dealer for purchasing the paper *is* a finance charge "if the consumer is required to pay the charges in cash, *as an addition to the obligation*, or as a deduction from the proceeds of the obligation."[159] According to the Regulation Z Commentary, the distinction between the two is whether the charge is imposed *separately* on the borrower.[160] Note that just because it is not identified explicitly as a separate charge does not mean that it was not imposed separately, however denominated.[161] To think otherwise is to permit dishonesty in labeling to successfully circumvent Truth in Lending requirements.[162] The question then is the factual one of whether the dealer hikes the cash price on the cars purchased by customers like B, incident to their credit arrangements, or whether the dealer takes into account the fact that some will be financed at a discount when it prices

156 *See* Mourning v. Family Publications Serv., 411 U.S. 356, 93 S. Ct. 1652, 36 L. Ed. 2d 318 (1973).

157 *See generally* National Consumer Law Center, Truth in Lending §§ 3.6.3.4, 3.10 (7th ed. 2010 and Supp.).

158 If applicable alike to cash and credit customers, then it is a charge "payable in a comparable cash transaction" and is not a finance charge. 15 U.S.C. § 1605(a); Reg. Z § 1026.4(a) [§ 226.4(a)]; Reg. Z, Official Commentary § 1026.4(a)-1 [§ 226.4(a)-1].

159 Reg. Z § 1026.4(b)(6) [§ 226.4(b)(6)].

160 Reg. Z, Official Commentary § 1026.4(a)-2 [§ 226.4(a)-2]. *See generally* National Consumer Law Center, Truth in Lending § 3.7.8 (7th ed. 2010 and Supp.).

161 *See, e.g.*, Balderos v. City Chevrolet, 214 F.3d 849 (7th Cir. 2000) (even though car club membership fee was voluntary, part of it is a disguised finance charge if the consumer could prove that the excess part of the fee was imposed on buyers who did not purchase the membership and not imposed on those who did opt for it); Wallace v. Walker Auto Sales, Inc., 155 F.3d 927 (7th Cir. 1998); Knapp v. Americredit Fin. Serv., Inc., 245 F. Supp. 2d 841 (S.D. W. Va. 2003) (acquisition fee paid by dealer to lender based on the customer's creditworthiness may be a finance charge even though it was included in the cash price unbeknownst to the consumer and was charged only to "special" financing customers; dealer and lender motions for summary judgment denied on issue of whether the fee was "separately imposed"); Sampler v. City Chevrolet Buick Geo, Inc., 2000 U.S. Dist. LEXIS 2322 (N.D. Ill. Feb. 24, 2000), *rev'g* 10 F. Supp. 2d 934 (N.D. Ill. 1998), *in light of* Wallace v. Walker Auto Sales, Inc., 155 F.3d 927 (7th Cir. 1998) (denying summary judgment; grappling with the issue of the type of proof necessary to show that the cost of the discount is separately imposed; deciding that the borrower may prevail on this TILA claim if she can prove: (1) the dealer set the negotiated price of cars it anticipates will be purchased on credit high enough to cover the cost of discount; (2) the dealer does not similarly raise the prices of cars sold for cash; (3) the dealer does not disclose the discount to credit customers; (4) the dealer anticipated a discount when negotiating the price of the borrower's car; (5) the dealer did not disclose the discount to this particular borrower; as these elements are akin to proving discrimination; finding further that the borrower could prove by direct or indirect evidence that: (1) the dealer deducts the price of discounts from its profits on subprime cars but not on cash cars; (2) statistics demonstrate that the dealer's profits on cars bought with subprime credit are equal to or higher than the dealer's profits on cars bought with cash; (3) the dealer's sales managers knew that a particular customer is going to require subprime financing prior to setting a final price for the car. The proof presented by the consumer was sufficient to create a dispute of material fact, i.e., that discounts are listed on manager's sheets as a cost of subprime customers' cars and not on cash customers' cars shows that cost is imposed only on credit customers, profit margin is higher on subprime cars than on cash cars, the dealer knows the general rates of discount charged by subprime lenders and can reasonably approximate the amount to hold back in a particular transaction). *See also* Thompson v. 10,000 RV Sales, Inc., 31 Cal. Rptr. 3d 18, 30 (Cal. Ct. App. 2005) ("To the extent the case price in a credit transaction is increased above the cash price in a comparable cash transaction, the difference is a finance charge which must be disclosed."); Thomas B. Hudson, Michael A. Benoit & Joseph D. Looney, *Update on Indirect Auto Finance Dealer Compensation Litigation and Other Pertinent Litigation*, 56 Bus. Lawyer 1113 (May 2001); Thomas B. Hudson, Michael A. Benoit & Joseph D. Looney, *Update on Indirect Auto Finance Dealer Compensation Litigation and Other Pertinent Litigation*, 55 Bus. Lawyer 1281 (May 2000); Thomas B. Hudson, Michael A. Benoit, & Joseph D. Looney, *Indirect Auto Finance Dealer Compensation Litigation*, 54 Bus. Lawyer 1301 (May 1999) (industry representatives describe the difference between "dealer participation," discounted contracts, and upcharges and reviews some court decisions). *But see* Hoffman v. Grossinger Motor Corp., 218 F.3d 680 (7th Cir. 2000) (finding that consumer's general proof that a dealer, on average, charged subprime credit customers higher prices than it charged other customers was insufficient to survive a motion for summary judgment in light of dealer's proof that it used a unitary pricing system for its credit and cash customers which resulted in the salespeople trying to sucker everyone, even though a $400 holdback fee was imposed only in subprime financed transactions; while more general proof suffices at the motion to dismiss stage, not so for summary judgment); Slover-Becker v. Pitre Chrysler Plymouth Jeep of Scottsdale, Inc. 409 F. Supp. 2d 1158 (D. Ariz. 2005). *See generally* National Consumer Law Center, Truth in Lending §§ 3.6.5, 3.10 (7th ed. 2010 and Supp.).

162 *See* Wallace v. Walker Auto Sales, Inc., 155 F.3d 927, 934 n.9 (7th Cir. 1998); Sampler v. City Chevrolet Buick Geo, Inc., 2000 U.S. Dist. LEXIS 2322 (N.D. Ill. Feb. 24, 2000), *rev'd*, 10 F. Supp. 2d 934 (N.D. Ill. 1998).

In fact, many of the original cases challenging hidden finance charges in inflated cash prices were discount cases. *See generally* National Consumer Law Center, Truth in Lending § 3.10 (7th ed. 2010 and Supp.).

all its cars.[163] In the TILA context, practitioners should be aware of the question of assignee liability in this context. Assignees are liable for TILA violations that are apparent on the face of the document.[164] This standard has been strictly construed by the Seventh and Eleventh Circuits in hidden finance charge cases.[165]

The question of hidden interest in inflated finance charges can arise under state usury laws, as well. For both TILA and usury, the evidentiary issue is crucial. Checking the price at which the vehicle was advertised in the newspaper may help establish the regular cash price. Or investigation may show that the lender actually helps the dealer figure out how to price the car to a borrower to cover the lender's discount. (One subprime lender made a chart to explain to its dealers how to set the "cash price" of the car to recoup the lender's discount.)

Ask in discovery for all versions of the application and all correspondence between the dealer and the lender. In discovery it is important to obtain a clear, detailed record of what information passed between the dealer and the assignee. Try to obtain all versions of the application and all communication between the dealer and assignee. Considering the growing use of companies that offer electronic submission of applications, credit checks, and other services, it may also be necessary to subpoena records from third-party vendors used by the dealer or assignee.[166] One court denied summary judgment to the dealer after reviewing the discounts listed on the manager's sheets, the profit margin differential between subprime cars sold for cash and those sold on credit, and the dealer's knowledge of the general rates of discount charged by subprime lenders.[167]

Irrespective of whether a car has a posted price tag, a dealer might have listed a cash price in an advertisement. While that should be good evidence that the dealer imposed a higher cash price for a credit buyer, in and of itself the higher price also may raise a separate issue of deceptive advertising under a state UDAP statute.[168] It may also be deceptive for the dealer to fail to disclose its kickback from the assignee.[169]

### 10.3.6.3 "Time-Price Exception" and Usury Claims

A state that recognizes the "time-price exception" to state usury laws[170] has no usury ceiling for bona fide sales of goods, and a seller can charge whatever time-price it can extract, as long as it does not run afoul of an unconscionability claim. Sellers in such jurisdictions may still inflate their sales price so that the interest they charge appears to be low, and buyers may therefore have valid TILA claims. However, the time-price doctrine will preclude usury unless the purchaser can convince a court that the seller's failure to state an accurate cash price removes the transaction from the time-price usury exception.[171]

---

163 *See, e.g.*, Cornist v. B.J.T. Auto Sales, Inc., 272 F.3d 322 (6th Cir. 2001) (reversing summary judgment to the dealer and finance company; consumer presented evidence that the dealer markups on the cash price for credit customers was four to five times that of cash customers; court distinguished cases holding that evidence under TILA must show systemic disparity in prices; systematic disparity is but one type of proof); Balderos v. City Chevrolet, 214 F.3d 849 (7th Cir. 2000) (even though car club membership fee was voluntary, part of it is a disguised finance charge if the consumer could prove that the excess part of the fee was imposed on buyers who did not purchase the membership and not imposed on those who did opt for it); Diaz v. Paragon Motors of Woodside, Inc., 424 F. Supp. 2d 519 (E.D.N.Y. 2006) (granting summary judgment for the consumer who proved that advertised price of $13,495 was available only to prime credit or cash customers; rejecting the car dealer's claim that the price was simply the result of the consumer's bargaining with the salesman; hidden finance charge equaled the difference between the advertised price, $13,495, and the price the consumer actually paid, $16,590); Kilbourn v. Candy Ford-Mercury, Inc., 209 F.R.D. 121 (W.D. Mich. 2002) (summary judgment to dealer denied on issue of direct proof but granted as to indirect proof ). *Cf.* Hoffman v. Grossinger Motor Corp., 218 F.3d 680 (7th Cir. 2000) (finding that consumer's general proof that a dealer, on average, charged subprime credit customers higher prices than it charged other customers was insufficient to survive a motion for summary judgment in light of dealer's proof that it used a unitary pricing system for its credit and cash customers which resulted in the salespeople trying to sucker everyone, even though a $400 holdback fee was imposed only in subprime financed transactions).

For a discussion of the standard necessary to overcome a motion to dismiss, where less proof is required, see Wallace v. Walker Auto Sales, Inc., 155 F.3d 927 (7th Cir. 1998); Sampler v. City Chevrolet Buick Geo, Inc., 2000 U.S. Dist. LEXIS 2322 (N.D. Ill. Feb. 24, 2000), *rev'd* 10 F. Supp. 2d 934 (N.D. Ill. 1998); Cemail v. Viking Dodge, 982 F. Supp. 1296 (N.D. Ill. 1997); Chancellor v. Gateway Lincoln-Mercury, Inc., 502 S.E.2d 799 (Ga. Ct. App. 1998) (buyer failed to prove cash price was increased to recoup the fee).

164 15 U.S.C. § 1641(a). *See, e.g.*, Irby-Greene v. M.O.R., Inc., 79 F. Supp. 2d 630 (E.D. Va. 2000) (discount not apparent on face of documents; no assignee liability under TILA); Jackson v. South Holland Dodge, Inc., 755 N.E.2d 462 (Ill. 2001), (dealer practice of pocketing a portion of the service contract charge not apparent on the face; if no TILA liability, no Illinois UDAP liability against the assignee without specific knowledge).

165 *See* National Consumer Law Center, Truth in Lending § 12.3.2 (7th ed. 2010 and Supp.).

166 *See, e.g.*, www.dealertrack.com.

167 Sampler v. City Chevrolet Buick Geo, Inc., 2000 U.S. Dist. LEXIS 2322 (N.D. Ill. Feb. 24, 2000), *rev'd*, 10 F. Supp. 2d 934 (N.D. Ill. 1998).

168 *See, e.g.*, Ciampi v. Ogden Chrysler Plymouth, Inc., 634 N.E.2d 448 (Ill. App. Ct. 1994); Motzer Dodge Jeep-Eagle v. Ohio Atty. Gen., 642 N.E.2d 20 (Ohio Ct. App. 1994); Sanders v. Francis, 561 P.2d 1003 (Or. 1977); N.M. Code R. §§ 1.2.4.1–1.2.4.3.1 (LexisNexis). *See also* National Consumer Law Center, Unfair and Deceptive Acts and Practices § 5.3.7 (7th ed. 2008 and Supp.).

169 *See* National Consumer Law Center, Unfair and Deceptive Acts and Practices § 7.2.4 (7th ed. 2008 and Supp.).

170 *See* § 7.5.2.2, *supra* (discussing more completely the time-price doctrine).

171 Generally speaking, a transaction will not fall within the time-price doctrine if it looks too much like a loan. This may happen if the niceties of quoting separate cash and time prices are not observed. Daniel v. First Nat'l Bank of Birmingham, 227 F.2d 353 (5th Cir. 1955), *reh'g denied*, 228 F.2d 803 (5th Cir. 1956).

If the seller appears to be a mere front for a lender to whom the credit sale contract is immediately sold. Hare v. General Contract Purchase Corp., 249 S.W.2d 973 (Ark. 1952); Midland Guardian Co. v. Thacker, 314 S.E.2d 26 (S.C. Ct. App. 1984).

Or if the goods being sold are a sham. W.T. Grant Co. v. Walsh, 241 A.2d 46 (Middlesex Co. Ct. 1968) (coupons/script); Tuition

However, the time-price doctrine has been abolished in many states, to be replaced by RISAs or other statutes that limit the finance charge a seller can collect in a credit sale.[172] In such situations, the difference between the stated sale price and the actual value of the goods purchased is a clear example of hidden interest which, when included in the rate calculations, may cause usury. The difficulty here is proving the actual value of the goods.

### 10.3.6.4 Establishing Inflation of Price

Probably the best way to establish the true cash price of goods is to obtain an admission from the seller. Although unwary sellers may openly admit that they charge different cash and credit prices, or may stipulate to a maximum fair market value of the goods,[173] it may be both more realistic and more advantageous for a consumer to gain an admission by sending a credible third party to the seller's place of business to price the goods after letting the seller know that he or she will pay in cash.[174] Such a strategy should work if the goods that the buyer purchased are not unique and if the time of the third party's visit is not too distant from the time that the seller offered the higher credit price.[175]

A variety of other types of evidence have also been viewed by courts as convincing in establishing the true cash price.[176] The value of goods, such as used cars, that cannot be directly priced once they have been sold, may be established by comparison with the market price of comparable goods. This proof will probably require expert testimony. In the case of used cars, the National Automobile Dealers Association's *Official Used Car Guide* may establish an approximate market value, but the *Guide* may be inadmissible unless introduced into evidence through an expert who is familiar with the local car market, the accuracy of the *Guide*, and the effect of the car's condition on its precise price.[177] Such an expert might be a used car lot manager at another dealer, an insurance adjuster, a loan officer at a bank or finance company, or the dealer may in fact admit that it relies upon the guide.

---

Plan, Inc. v. Zicari, 335 N.Y.S.2d 95 (N.Y. Dist. Ct. 1972) (retail installment contract for tuition money was loan).

Also where a seller raises its sale price based on the reasonable assurance of discounting its credit contracts to a finance company, the transaction may be in substance a loan subject to usury laws rather than a bona fide credit sale. *See* Hare v. Gen. Contract Purchase Corp., 249 S.E.2d 973 (Ark. 1952). *See also* Butler v. Holt Machinery Co., 741 S.W.2d 169 (Tex. App. 1987), *corrected on denial of rehearing*, 739 S.W.2d 958 (1987) (where creditor added interest charges which were neither agreed to nor disclosed to the time-sale price in what was really a lending transaction rather than a credit sale, such charges should be deducted from the price).

It may also be fraud. *See* Johnson v. Mercury Fin., Clearinghouse No. 50,407, Case No. CV 93-952 (Ala. Cir. Ct. Aug. 1994) (jury verdict); § 2.4.3, *supra*.

172 *See* Appx. C, *infra* (summarizing each state RISA).

173 *See, e.g.*, Killings v. Jeff's Motors, Inc., 490 F.2d 865 (5th Cir. 1974).

174 This strategy was used by the buyer in Rowe Auto & Trailer Sales, Inc. v. King, 517 S.W.2d 946 (Ark. 1975), to demonstrate that the seller followed the general practice of hiding interest in the sale price.

175 *But cf.* Johns v. Ford Motor Credit Co., 551 N.E.2d 179 (Ohio 1990).

In *Johns* the Ohio Supreme Court defined "cash price" as the "bottom line" negotiated price, not the generally available starting price, such as the manufacturer's suggested retail price on a car. The court was interpreting the Ohio RISA provision prohibiting inclusion in a RISA contract indebtedness exceeding a specified amount tied to the "cash price." The court did limit its holding to the extent that the negotiated price must be agreed upon *in good faith*. (Case involved dealer's practice of raising the sale price to compensate for negative equity on trade-in, where buyer and seller both aware of practice and acting "in good faith.") *Cf.* Orosco v. Partyka Chevrolet, Inc., Clearinghouse No. 45,908, Civ. No. N-89-606 (D. Conn. July 18, 1990) (order on motions for summary judgment) (TILA case holding it was a question of fact whether dealer's practice of adding $800 to the sticker price occurred in both cash and credit transactions. *NB*: the TILA definition of cash price must be interpreted to require reference to the starting price, not the negotiated "bottom line" price. *See* Reg. Z, 12 C.F.R. § 1026.2(a)(9) [§ 226.2(a)(9)]: ". . . price at which a creditor, *in the ordinary course of business, offers to sell*. . . ." Emphasis added. The Ohio RISA definition of cash price, by contrast, referred to the price agreed upon in good faith by the parties.).

176 *See, e.g.*, *In re* Stewart, 93 B.R. 878 (Bankr. E.D. Pa. 1988) (creditor-seller sold goods on credit from the showroom of another retailer, who would have charged a cash price to its own customers for less than half of seller's "cash price," concealed a hidden finance charge of 80% instead of 18%; the actual value was established at the price available from the other retailer); Riley v. Red River Marine, Inc., 664 S.W.2d 200 (Ark. 1984) (car price raised by $200 from original price on bill of sale to price listed on subsequent retail installment sales agreement; court also noted the sales tax was still calculated on the original, lower figure). *See also* El Paso Dev. Co. v. Berryman, 729 S.W.2d 883 (Tex. App. 1987) (borrower's claim that inflated sales price of real estate constituted interest, instead of valid time-price differential, sufficiently established to warrant temporary injunction preventing foreclosure pending final resolution of usury claim; sale price in a cash contract for sale of property executed five months earlier than a renegotiated credit sales contract for purchase of same property should be considered in determining if a cash price existed, raised substantial questions of law and facts), *later proceeding*, 769 S.W.2d 584 (Tex. App. 1989) (found to be interest).

One legal services attorney, in challenging "0%" used car loans as containing a hidden finance charge for TILA purposes, established the actual value by showing what the dealer paid for it before selling it to the consumer, and what it got for it at a repossession sale.

Another possibility is to check newspaper ads for the advertised price for the vehicle. In addition to providing evidence that the vehicle was inflated to bury financing costs, it is also evidence of a UDAP violation in states where selling a vehicle above the advertised price violates UDAP. *See* Motzer Dodge Jeep-Eagle v. Ohio Atty. Gen, 642 N.E.2d 20 (Ohio Ct. App. 1994); Sanders v. Francis, 561 P.2d 1003 (Or. 1977); National Consumer Law Center, Unfair and Deceptive Acts and Practices §§ 5.3.5, 7.5.2 (7th ed. 2008 and Supp.).

177 *See* Vines v. Hodges, 422 F. Supp. 1292, 1300 (D.D.C. 1976); Rowe Auto & Trailer Sales, Inc. v. King, 517 S.W.2d 946 (Ark. 1975). *See generally* National Consumer Law Center, Automobile Fraud § 9.10.1.4 (4th ed. 2011) (discussing using guides as evidence of the true value of an automobile).

A final approach to proving the actual price of goods is to determine during discovery if the note that the credit purchaser signed was sold to a third party and, if so, the discount at which it was sold. Selling at a discount means that the assignee buys the paper from the original creditor for less than the face value of the debt, in effect imposing a cost on the original creditor. For example, if a credit contract for $2,500 with a stated interest rate of 0.0% is resold, immediately after signing, for $2,100, it is arguable that the true value of the goods is not $2,500, but only $2,100.[178] This theory was used to establish TILA violations in several cases[179] prior to a revision of Regulation Z which arbitrarily excluded discounts upon the resale of consumer credit contracts from the definition of "finance charge" unless the cost was separately imposed upon the borrower.[180] Despite the amendment of Regulation Z, these cases remain as authority for the proposition that discounts may constitute hidden finance charge in the absence of express statutory or regulatory statements to the contrary.

The discount paid by the assignee was at the crux of the fraud verdict awarded against the assignee-lender in *Johnson v. Mercury Finance*.[181] The car buyer in that case used evidence of the price for which the dealer bought the car ($1,900) and at which the dealer offered it for cash sale ($3,000). The credit price, hiked by a "dealer reserve," was almost $3,700. With insurance add-ons, the loan principal was over $4,000, written at 26.3%. The assignee paid the dealer only $2,700 for this note. The jury, as demonstrated by its sizeable punitive damage award, believed this arrangement fraudulently concealed an effective 50% return to the lender on the car loan.

Practitioners who are considering demonstrating usury through the existence of discounts should be aware that this is not an easy proposition. Courts generally hold that a seller or lender who has given value for a note may subsequently sell that note just like any other commodity for whatever price it can get, and that, for a discount to be usurious, the borrower must show that value was received before the note was discounted.[182] Unfortunately, the average purchaser has received some value for the note (i.e., the goods purchased), just not full value, and to prove that the purchaser did not get full value, the purchaser must arguably show that the price of the goods was inflated, which is what he or she had to prove in the first place.[183]

The existence of this legal Catch-22 suggests that the discounted resale of a consumer's note may be more useful in demonstrating the amount by which a sale price was inflated than in showing the initial fact that it was inflated. For example, the following strategy might be used. Two or more credible witnesses could be sent to a seller's place of business to obtain cash and credit prices for the goods being sold. If these prices were different, the fact that the seller generally inflated the sale price of goods sold on credit could be established.[184] At this point, the discount at which the consumer's particular contract was sold might be used to establish the amount of interest hidden in the price of the particular goods that a consumer had purchased. In the automobile financing context, if the lender pays a discount as a percentage of the amount financed, it may also cap the amount by which the dealer can recoup the discount in an inflated sale price. For example, the lender-dealer contract may cap the amount the financier will pay at 120% of NADA trade-in value. In that case, the dealer is likely to make up for the lender discount by packing add-ons, such as insurance and service contract charges, into the amount financed. Such practices raise issues of loan packing,[185] UDAP,[186] and fraud.[187]

---

178 Assuming a one-year contract, repayable in equal monthly installments of $208.33, with adjustment for odd cents in the final installment, the effective APR would be 33.48%.

179 *See* Joseph v. Norman's Health Club, Inc., 532 F.2d 86 (8th Cir. 1976); Schleimer v. McPherson, 400 N.Y.S.2d 566 (N.Y. App. Div. 1978). *But see* Jennings v. Edwards, 454 F. Supp. 770 (M.D.N.C. 1978), *aff'd*, 598 F.2d 614 (4th Cir. 1979) (table) (discount at which credit contract was purchased by bank did not have to be disclosed as a finance charge under TILA).

180 *See* Reg. Z, 12 C.F.R. § 1026.4(b)(6) [§ 226.4(b)(6)], *as interpreted in* Reg. Z, Official Commentary § 1026.4(a)-2 [§ 226.4(a)-2].

As subprime automobile financing has increased the size of these discounts, with increasingly distorted prices of both the vehicles and the credit pricing, this Truth in Lending Act provision is again the focus of litigation. *See generally* National Consumer Law Center, Truth in Lending §§ 3.7.8, 3.10 (7th ed. 2010 and Supp.).

181 Clearinghouse No. 50,407, Case No. CV 93-952 (Ala. Cir. Ct. jury verdict Aug. 1994).

182 *Compare* Baske v. Russell, 407 P.2d 434 (Wash. 1965) (note discounted through sham third-party lender was usurious), *with* Maynard v. England, 538 P.2d 551, 555 (Wash. Ct. App. 1975) (discount was not interest where credit purchasers receive value for their note), *and* Chancellor v. Gateway Lincoln-Mercury, 502 S.E.2d 799 (Ga. Ct. App. 1998) (discount not interest where consumers were obligated to repay same amount with or without the discount).

183 *See* Maynard v. England, 538 P.2d 551 (Wash. Ct. App. 1975) (purchaser fails to prove inflated price). *Cf.* April v. Union Mortgage, 709 F. Supp. 809 (N.D. Ill. 1989) (home improvement contract listed cash price as $20,000; that included a $3,300 discount, reflecting practice of selling commercial paper for less than face value, which did not constitute interest or TILA finance charge. *NB*: Some indication in opinion that ruling may have been otherwise had borrowers been able to establish that $20,000 was not the price charged in comparable cash transactions). *But cf.* Hare v. General Contract Purchase Corp., 249 S.W.2d 973 (Ark. 1952) (looking to seller's reasonable assurance that credit sale contract can be discounted).

184 *See* Rowe Auto & Trailer Sales, Inc. v. King, 517 S.W.2d 946 (Ark. 1975). *But see* Thrifty Oil Co. v. Superior Ct. of Los Angeles County, 111 Cal. Rptr. 2d 253 (Cal. Ct. App. 2001) (two-tier pricing at a gas station does not meet the definition of an illegal surcharge because the difference in the price for gas purchased with cash and gas purchased with a credit card was based on the additional cost to the merchant for credit card sales).

185 *See* discussion at § 10.3.4, *supra*.

186 *See* discussion at § 2.4.1, *supra*. *See generally* National Consumer Law Center, Unfair and Deceptive Acts and Practices (7th ed. 2008 and Supp.).

187 Johnson v. Mercury Fin., Clearinghouse No. 50,407, Case No. 93-952 (Ala. Cir. Ct. Jan. 1995).

### *10.3.7 Yo-Yo Sales, a.k.a. Spot Delivery*

A yo-yo sale involves a car dealer letting the consumer drive a vehicle off the lot after having signed a purchase agreement and a fully completed retail installment contract, but then contacting the consumer later that the deal has fallen through. Typically the dealer's stated justification for this action is that the dealer is unable to sell the loan to a lender. Yo-yo sales are examined in detail in National Consumer Law Center, *Automobile Fraud* Ch. 4 (4th ed. 2011) and will only be summarized here.

In a yo-yo transaction, the dealer considers that it has a right to back out of a deal even though it has represented the deal to the consumer as final and almost certainly will resist the consumer backing out of the deal. Dealers may want to back out because of their inability to sell the loan to a lender or it may just be a sales gimmick to squeeze more money out of the consumer. In a yo-yo sale, the dealer contacts the consumer and offers the consumer one or more options: bring the car back; find their own financing; or sign a new contract at different terms. In the latter case, it is usually at a higher rate, and perhaps requires an additional down payment.[188] The consumer is in a difficult situation. The car has likely already been shown proudly to family and friends. The consumer may already have incurred other costs, such as more expensive insurance on the new car. In the worst situations, the consumer's trade-in has already been sold. If the consumer does not return the car or sign the new, harsher terms, the dealer may repossess the newly purchased car, even though the consumer has not defaulted. Some contracts even purport to give the dealer the right to keep the trade-in if the financing falls through as "liquidated damages."

Yo-yo sales may involve a host of law violations. About a third of the states have a statute specifically regulating yo-yo transactions.[189] Moreover, as a matter of contract law, if the dealer has not inserted a valid contingency clause into the installment sales agreement, then the sale is final. The dealer is the original lender; there is an agreement as to the vehicle sale and financing; and whether or not the creditor can assign the paper is irrelevant to whether the deal is final. It would be a UDAP violation to represent otherwise.

The first step in a yo-yo case is to determine if there is a valid contingency clause allowing the dealer to back out of the sale.[190] The contingency clause should be in writing, agreed to by both parties, comply with state law, and, if there is a signal document rule,[191] be contained in the installment sales agreement itself and not in a separate rider. Also scrutinize the contingency clause language to see under what facts the dealer can cancel the sale. Also see if the dealer misrepresented the sale as final when it was in fact contingent.

The yo-yo sale may also run afoul of various federal statutes. Even if the dealer considers the sale contingent, the consumer should have received a copy of the TILA disclosure.[192] In addition, the Fair Credit Reporting Act and the Equal Credit Opportunity Act have notice requirements when a creditor takes an adverse action on a credit application, that are directly relevant to yo-yo transactions.[193]

A dealer's contingency clause, if valid, must either be a contingent precedent or subsequent. In a condition precedent sale, the sale is not yet final until the contingency is met. The consumer may be using the car, but the dealer still owns it. In a condition subsequent sale, ownership has passed to the consumer, but a subsequent condition will allow the sale to be canceled and ownership revert to the dealer.[194] As set out in detail in National Consumer Law Center, *Automobile Fraud* § 4.4 (4th ed. 2011), dealers often mix up the two and conduct a sale inconsistent with either type of contingency—such as selling a trade-in and charging interest from when the contract is signed (seemingly implying that the sale is a contingent subsequent) but also not handing over title or complying with UCC Article 9 after a repossession (seem to imply a condition precedent sale).

Yo-yo sales also may involve a host of other law violations, including the wrongful refusal to return a trade-in or down payment, threatening criminal action if the consumer does not return the car, and misrepresentations about the original transaction or a restructured deal after the yo-yo.[195]

The key to handling a yo-yo case is careful investigation and discovery of the facts.[196] This should involve scrutiny of all paperwork from the original transaction and any subsequent amendment of the original deal.[197]

---

188 Industry slang suggests that this may not always be done in the best of faith. "Gimme back," "yo-yo deal" and "bushing" (short for "ambushing," perhaps?) are some of the terms used to describe this practice. In one case, the lender played a shell game with a husband and wife, selling each a car, repossessing one after financing fell through, and then listing the repossessed car as a trade-in for the other car. Garcia v. Crabtree Imports, Inc., 2006 WL 1646158 (D. Conn. June 14, 2006) (car dealer's motion to dismiss denied).

189 National Consumer Law Center, Automobile Fraud § 4.1.4 (4th ed. 2011).

190 *Id.* § 4.2.

191 *See* § 10.3.2.2, *supra*.

192 National Consumer Law Center, Automobile Fraud § 4.3.2 (4th ed. 2011).

193 *Id.* § 4.3.3.

194 *See id.* § 4.4.

195 *Id.* §§ 4.5, 4.6.

196 *Id.* § 4.7.2.

197 Attorneys should discover all of the dealer files on the transaction with particular attention paid to getting the outside part of the "dealer's jacket." This may list the consumer's credit score which helps to determine if the dealer knew from the outset that the consumer would or would not obtain favorable financing or any financing at all. The jacket may also contain notes of relevant conversations. For an overview of the kinds of documents typically kept in car dealer files and what information they can provide, see National Consumer Law Center Automobile Fraud Ch. 2 (4th ed. 2011).

## 10.3.8 Motor Vehicle Loan Servicing

### 10.3.8.1 Introduction

Most car purchase loans are made by car dealers and then sold to lenders. Lenders that hold the loans typically service the loans themselves. However, a large percentage of auto loans are securitized. According to some industry data, car loan securitizations accounted for about 60% of all new asset-backed securities in 2010 and about 42% in 2009.[198] These loans, whether securitized or not, may experience many of the same issues in servicing that have so troubled the mortgage market.[199]

There are some servicing issues specific to the auto finance market. One very important servicing issue, repossession, is addressed in a different treatise in this series, National Consumer Law Center, *Repossessions* (7th ed. 2010 and Supp.). Two other servicing issues, "buy-here pay-here" dealerships and forced-placed insurance are addressed below.

### 10.3.8.2 Buy-Here Pay-Here

One specific subset of the cars sales and finance market is serviced differently than most car loans. Buy-here pay-here (BHPH) dealers, as the name implies, generally receive loan payments directly at the dealership. While the name might simply imply a different servicing model, the BHPH model differs from the more typical car dealer in several regards.[200]

BHPH dealers target consumers that are either unable to obtain credit from traditional dealers or lenders, or consumers who believe their credit problems may keep them from getting credit elsewhere. They typically advertise that they will finance anyone. Their business model generally involves selling cars at high prices and very high interest rates and obtaining a down payment sufficient cover all or most of their cost for the vehicle.

"Buy-here, pay-here" dealerships often require the consumer to stop by the dealership every pay day, so that payment may be required twice a month or even weekly. Missing just one weekly payment can lead to repossession. The use of electronic repossession devices is more common in this market than any other. These products are installed in the purchased car. Some require that each time a consumer makes a payment the dealer enters a new code. Without the new code, the vehicle will not start. Others permit the dealer to disable the car remotely or to set off an alarm or annoying noise "reminding" the consumer the payment is due. These electronic repossession devises are addressed in more detail in another treatise in this series, National Consumer Law Center, *Repossessions* § 6.6 (7th ed. 2010 and Supp.).

An important characteristic of a "buy-here pay-here" dealership is that the consumer is rarely told the vehicle's price. Its price is not disclosed in advertising, is not posted on the vehicle or elsewhere on the lot, and is not disclosed during sales negotiations. Consumer questions concerning price are defeated with a reference to the consumer's poor credit, and the opportunity to restore that credit through a purchase. The dealer instead concentrates on the consumer's ability to leave the lot with a car and the monthly payment. With a large enough down payment, the dealer profits even if the consumer never makes a payment. The importance of the down payment in this scheme is evidenced by the fact that the salesperson's commission may be based not on the car's selling price, but on the size of the down payment.

While stated interest rates will be high, the actual rate will be much higher because part of the financing costs will be hidden in the high sales price. A company, for example, may sell virtually the same car at another of its dealerships across town at a very different price. Pay special attention to who owns a BHPH dealership. Is the lot just a department of a larger dealership? Does the owner also own other dealerships? There may even be special salespeople that just sell BHPH at the same location where other consumers pay more standard prices.

It is also useful to investigate what the BHPH dealership does with the RISCs. While the dealer typically continues to receive payment at the dealership, the paper itself is often sold to another, often related entity. Typically, the paper is sold at a steep discount to the face value. This reflects the fact that the consumer has already paid an excessive down payment and now owes high payments on a car that very often has mechanical issues and so the likelihood of default is great. This discount is also necessary for dealers to avoid a heavy tax burden. Because they sell the cars at a price so much greater than what was paid for the vehicle when the BHPH dealer acquired it, they face a significant tax liability. By selling the paper at a discount the BHPH dealer attempts to avoid at least some of that tax liability.[201]

### 10.3.8.3 Force-Placed Insurance

One of the more common automobile loan servicing issues is forced-placed insurance. Auto RISCs almost universally require that insurance be maintained on the vehicle until the loan is completely repaid. Where the consumer does not maintain collision and theft coverage, the contract allows the lender to

198 *See* Auto Sector of Asset-Backed Market Revved Up, Dow Jones, January 26, 2011, *available at* www.dowjones.de/site/2011/01/auto-sector-of-asset-backed-market-revved-up.html.

199 *See generally Problems in Mortgage Servicing From Modification to Foreclosure, Written Testimony of Diane E. Thompson, National Consumer Law Center, Before the United States Senate Committee on Banking, Housing, & Urban Affairs* (Nov. 16, 2010), *available at* www.nclc.org/images/pdf/foreclosure_mortgage/mortgage_servicing/testimony-senate-banking.pdf (discussing problems in mortgage servicing).

200 For an enlightening explanation of the BHPH industry see Ken Bensinger, *A Vicious Cycle in the Used-Car Business Sign, Drive, Default, Repossess and Resell—That's the Game at Buy Here Pay Here Dealerships*, L.A. Times, Oct. 30, 2011, *available at* http://articles.latimes.com/2011/oct/30/business/la-fi-buy-here-pay-here-part1-storyb.

201 *See,* Internal Revenue Service, Retail Industry Audit Technique Guide (ATG) ch. 3, *available at* www.irs.gov/businesses/small/article/0,,id=141495,00.html (Examination Techniques for Specific Industries (Independent Used Automobile Dealerships)).

purchase the insurance coverage for the consumer and charge the insurance premium to the consumer. The premium is often added to the amount owing on the vehicle.

The sale of force-placed insurance in conjunction with car loans has special potential for unpleasant surprises for the borrower. Force-placed insurance can be either single interest or dual interest. If single-interest coverage is purchased, one such surprise is that the policy will only pay out to the lender and only up to the amount of the debt outstanding. If the car is stolen and even if the vehicle is worth more than the loan amount outstanding, the insurance will not pay the consumer anything for that lost value. The coverage will only pay off the loan. More expensive dual-interest coverage protects the value of the insured property, including the borrower's equity, and is not limited by the outstanding balance on the loan.

Consumers are sometimes confused if they realize that coverage is being purchased through the lender (often they do not even understand that there is any insurance at all), and assume that the insurance also includes personal injury and liability insurance. This is not the case.[202] The coverage only pays the lender for loss to the value of the collateral. The coverage may not even pay the consumer after a partial loss to repair the vehicle—the insurance payment for the partial loss goes to the lender, who may decide to use the payment to reduce the amount owed on the loan.

The consumer has no control over the size of the force-placed premium—the creditor selects the insurance and the insurer and adds the premium charge to the consumer's indebtedness. While the consumer can purchase insurance on her own and cancel the force-placed insurance, it is difficult for a consumer to accurately compare the cost of the force-placed insurance on a motor vehicle with ordinary auto insurance. The force-placed insurance typically offers far less coverage, and thus should be less expensive than a standard auto insurance policy. Considering the amount of coverage offered, force-placed insurance is very expensive. The same forces driving other credit insurance abuses drive this, too: the coverage is purchased from affiliated companies; large commissions and rebates are given to the creditors; the creditor has little incentive to shop for the best deal for the consumer instead of the highest commission for the lender.

Some of the additional expense of force-placed insurance may derive from purchasing default protection for the lender, in addition to insuring the collateral.[203] Nevertheless, if the contract does not authorize this purchase, consumers should have breach of contract, UDAP, and other claims if the lender seeks to charge for such coverage. The extra charge for this default insurance should also be treated as interest for usury purposes.[204]

A wide range of other abuses have made force-placed insurance the subject of litigation resulting in large settlements.[205] These include purchasing insurance even though standard auto insurance is in place (duplicate coverage) and failing to notify the consumer that coverage has been purchased and added to the consumer's obligation.

In those states that have adopted it, the UCCC requires that, within a reasonable time after advancing sums, a lender that obtains the insurance must send the borrower a written notice listing the amount advanced, any charges with respect to the advances, any revised payment schedules, and, in certain circumstances, a brief description of the insurance including the type and amount.[206] The failure to send this notice triggers a refund of the charge in excess of that allowed under the UCCC.[207] Consequently, the entire amount of the premium for the force-placed insurance can be forfeited where the entire fee was illegal.[208]

Review of the state's motor vehicle retail installment act, licensing laws, and applicable insurance statutes and regulations may also uncover requirements that the consumer be notified within a specified time of the purchase of the insurance and terms of coverage as well as other substantive obligations and prohibitions.[209]

The National Association of Insurance Commissioners (NAIC) drafted a "Creditor-Placed Insurance Model Act" which states are urged to adopt. Unfortunately, the NIAC model act legitimizes many of the consumer complaints raised in litigation. For example, while the model act prohibits tacking on certain types of excess coverages, it permits those not listed. Further, lenders are allowed to pass on certain incidental costs to borrowers as well as pay commissions and other compensation to an "insurance producer," i.e., lenders. Finally, the model act eliminates any private right of action consumers may have, and instead grants state insurance commissioners exclusive oversight and enforcement authority over claims against the insurers.[210] Versions of this model have been passed in some states.[211]

202 Some states now require a conspicuous disclaimer on credit property insurance disclosures that it does not provide liability coverage.

203 The less comprehensive coverage for typical property insurance risks may be supplemented by coverage for credit loss risks; e.g., repossession expenses, premium deficiency, etc. *See, e.g.*, Kenty v. Bank One, Columbus, N.A., 1992 WL 170605 (S.D. Ohio Apr. 23, 1992), *aff'd in part, rev'd in part*, 92 F.3d 384 (6th Cir. 1996); Kenty v. Transamerica Premium Ins. Co., 650 N.E.2d 863 (Ohio 1995). *See also* § 6.6.4, *supra* (discussing issues raised by such extraneous coverage).

204 *See* § 6.6.4, *supra*.

205 *See* Mark A. Chavez, *If You Can't Beat Them, Change the Rules: The Industry Response to Force-Placed Insurance Litigation*, The Consumer Advocate, vol. 3, issue 5 (Nov./Dec. 1997). *See also* LaBarre v. Credit Acceptance Corp., 175 F.3d 640 (8th Cir. 1999).

206 U.C.C.C. § 2-208(1) (1968); U.C.C.C. § 2-506 (1974).

207 U.C.C.C. § 5-202(3) (1968); U.C.C.C. § 5-201(2) (1974).

208 Bank of Oklahoma, N.A. v. Portis, 942 P.2d 249 (Okla. Civ. App. 1997).

209 Ortiz v. General Motors Acceptance Corp., 673 N.E.2d 424 (Ill. App. Ct. 1996) (while the court ultimately dismissed the consumer's claims for violation of Illinois' MVRISA and Sales Finance Agency Act, the scrutiny which the practitioners applied to these laws to find a cause of action is instructive).

210 For a longer discussion of this model act, see Mark A. Chavez, *If You Can't Beat Them, Change the Rules: The Industry Response to Forced-Place Insurance Litigation*, The Consumer Advocate, vol. 3, issue 5 (Nov./Dec. 1997).

211 *See, e.g.*, N.J. Stat. Ann. §§ 17:16V-1 to 17:16V-12; Tenn. Code Ann. §§ 56-49-101 to 56-49-115 (effective Oct. 2, 1999).

These cases are discussed in more detail in another treatise in this series,[212] and the widespread nature of the abuses suggests that any force-placed insurance on a credit contract warrants careful investigation.[213] Given the extensive litigation and the associated costs, some major automobile lenders have either eliminated or scaled back the program.[214]

## 10.4 Other Motor Vehicle Financing

### *10.4.1 Direct Financing*

In addition to the traditional RISC model, cars and other vehicles may be financed in a number of other ways. Consumers may finance the purchase of a car by obtaining financing elsewhere and using the loan proceeds to purchase the vehicle. This can be very helpful in aiding the consumer to get a better deal at the dealership. Not only does it remove the opportunity for the dealer to obtain excess profits from the consumer in the form of loan packing or interest rate markups, but it also allows the consumer to better focus on the price and condition of the car and the amount of the trade in. By removing financing from the list of things negotiated in the transaction, the consumer has at least a slightly greater ability to notice all the things the dealer is doing to the price of the car, the amount given for the trade-in, and the real price of any add-ons.

There is one, potential harm from obtaining financing elsewhere. When the consumer obtains financing directly, the lender will no longer be automatically subject to the claims and defenses the consumer might have had against the dealer,[215] unless the dealer has referred the consumer to the lender. In that case the dealer is required to arrange for a notice in the loan that the loan holder is subject to the consumer's seller-related claims and defenses.[216]

### *10.4.2 Auto Leasing*

Consumer leasing of motor vehicles is very cyclical in nature. At some times up to 30% of new cars sales are financed by leasing. Its prevalence can be driven by a number of factors.

212 *See* National Consumer Law Center, Unfair and Deceptive Acts and Practices § 10.5.10 (7th ed. 2008 and Supp.).

213 *See* Am. Bankers Ins. Co. of Florida v. Alexander, 818 So. 2d 1073 (Miss. 2001) (motion to dismiss misrepresentation claim denied; filed-rate doctrine does not prevent a consumer from bringing breach of good faith and fair dealing, breach of fiduciary duty, UDAP, and common law fraud claims based upon allegations that American Bankers consciously ignored its filed rates and that the manner in which the policies were force-placed was calculated to benefit the insurance company through a kickback scheme); Pitts v. Am. Sec. Ins. Co., 550 S.E.2d 179 (N.C. Ct. App. 2001) (class certification denial reversed on appeal), *aff'd*, 569 S.E.2d 647 (N.C. 2002). *See also* Kenty v. Bank One, Columbus, N.A., 92 F.3d 384 (6th Cir. 1996) (RICO, usury, antitrust); Ruiz v. Stewart Assocs., Inc., 171 F.R.D. 238 (N.D. Ill. 1997) (insurance company's motion for summary judgment on RICO claim denied; borrowers adequately pleaded misrepresentation and causation; class certified); Moore v. Fidelity Fin. Servs., Inc., 884 F. Supp. 288 (N.D. Ill. 1995) (RICO, TILA and state law challenges survived motion to dismiss. (But later the court dismissed the RICO count in *Moore*, 897 F. Supp. 378 (N.D. Ill. 1995) (failure to adequately plead an "enterprise") and dismissed RICO from the second amended complaint in Moore v. Fidelity Fin. Servs., Inc., 949 F. Supp. 673 (N.D. Ill. 1997) but granted class certification on the TILA, breach of contract and duty of good faith and fair dealing, and UDAP claims, 1998 WL 210941 (N.D. Ill. 1998).)); Dixon v. TCF Bank, 1995 WL 622409 (N.D. Ill. Oct. 23, 1995) (RICO challenge dismissed); Bermudez v. First of Am. Bank Champion, N.A., 860 F. Supp. 580 (N.D. Ill. 1994), *case subsequently withdrawn pursuant to settlement agreement*, 886 F. Supp. 643 (N.D. Ill. 1995) (RICO, TILA and state law challenges survived motion to dismiss); Gordon v. Ford Motor Credit Co., 868 F. Supp. 1191 (N.D. Cal. 1992) (RICO claim dismissed based on McCarran-Ferguson Act; *NB*: in so ruling, this decision is in the minority); Logan v. Norwest Bank Minnesota, N.A., 603 N.W.2d 659 (Minn. Ct. App. 1999) (summary judgment for lender on breach of contract claim for charging consumer for excessive coverage reversed; discussion of damages available to consumer); Kenty v. Transamerica Premium Ins. Co., 650 N.E.2d 863 (Ohio 1995) (tortious interference with a contractual relationship, civil conspiracy). *But see* Weathersby v. The Assocs. Fin. Servs. Co., 1999 U.S. Dist. LEXIS 6392 (E.D. La. Apr. 28, 1999) (RICO claim dismissed due to failure to allege injury related to the defendants' investment of racketeering proceeds or to RICO person gaining an interest in or control of the enterprise through a pattern of racketeering activity); Weinberger v. Mellon Mortgage Co., 1998 WL 599192 (E.D. Pa. 1998) (RICO claim against insurance company in this mortgage loan case dismissed because mortgage servicer had warned homeowner in writing that the forced-placed hazard insurance would cost substantially more and provide less coverage; therefore, no scheme to defraud even though the homeowner was not informed about the commissions paid by and between the insurer and servicer); Washington Mut. Bank, F.A. v. The Superior Court of Orange County, 15 P.3d 1071 (Cal. 2001) (nationwide class certification in a mortgage loan case reversed due to trial court's failure to adjudicate effect of choice of law provisions in the mortgages); Norwest Mortgage, Inc. v. The Superior Court of San Diego County, 85 Cal. Rptr. 2d 18 (Cal. Ct. App. 1999) (nationwide class certification denied where case was filed under the California unfair competition law which cannot apply to Norwest which, though incorporated in California, conducted all relevant business from other states in the making of mortgage loans to non-Californians; leave granted to amend class definition); General Motors Acceptance Corp. v. Baymon, 732 So. 2d 262 (Miss. 1999) (jury verdict for consumer for $35,000 in compensatory damages and $5 million in punitive damages reversed and remanded for new trial on issue of breach of contract claim; court finds that GMAC did not breach its duty of fair dealing and good faith, that no fraud occurred, and no fiduciary relationship existed between the creditor and debtor; court found that evidence of disproportionate impact on minorities from the purchase of force-placed insurance irrelevant and prejudicial; evidence of excessive profits, that rates amounted to "gouging" and that GMAC has manipulated the rate approval process held not relevant to issue of overcharging); Brannon v. Boatman's Nat'l Bank of Oklahoma, 976 P.2d 1077 (Okla. Civ. App. 1998) (claims of breach of contract, violations of state U.C.C.C., and unfair and deceptive acts based upon the purchase of more than "casualty" insurance, of insurance for periods of time exceeding than the uninsured period, and the payment of undisclosed commissions dismissed over strong dissent which lays out the telling facts).

214 *See* Mark A. Chavez, *If You Can't Beat Them, Change the Rules: The Industry Response to Force-Placed Insurance Litigation*, The Consumer Advocate, vol. 3, issue 5 (Nov./Dec. 1997).

215 *See* § 10.6, *infra* (discussing lender liability).

216 *Id.*

Manufacturers may guarantee inflated residual values to finance companies to persuade them to tout the leasing of their vehicles. Other market conditions in the credit market may also persuade finance companies to push leases. Dealers like leases because they know they will likely have the consumer back on their lot in two to three years to try to decide what to do with the car with the lease expiring.

Consumer car leases are regulated by the Federal Consumer Leasing Act and Regulation M, the Uniform Commercial Code Article 2A, as well as a number state leasing statutes. The Consumer Leasing Act is primarily a disclosure statute, but it does prohibit unreasonable early termination and default charges. UCC Article 2A and some state leasing statutes have more substantive requirements and prohibitions. Consumer leasing regulation is addressed in both National Consumer Law Center, *Truth in Lending* Ch. 13 (7th ed. 2010 and Supp.) and National Consumer Law Center, *Repossessions* § 14.2 (7th ed. 2010 and Supp.).

## *10.4.3 Auto Rent-to-Own*

A growing number of cars, especially at used car dealerships and buy-here-pay-here dealerships, are offered on a rent-to-own (RTO) basis, similar to a traditional appliance or electronics rent-to-own. They are marketed to those with poor credit or who believe they could not obtain reasonably priced credit elsewhere. The payments are typically very expensive relative to the value of the car. Title to the vehicle stays in the dealer's name and the dealers are typically quick to take the car back and feel they may do so more easily than repossessing a financed car.[217] While unlike a traditional lease the consumer may stop paying and return the car at any time, consumers are generally entering into these arrangements in hopes of paying for the car and keeping it. If the consumer stops paying, the consumer has no obligation but also loses any built up equity that the past payments have generated in the vehicle.

Depending on how the auto RTO transaction is structured, it may not fall within the scope of either TILA[218] or the Consumer Leasing Act.[219] RTO transactions are commonly found not to be subject to state RISAs either.[220] State UDAP statutes should still be applicable.

## *10.4.4 Credit Card Finance in Lieu of RISCs*

Another growing method for financing motorcycles, jet skis, boats, snowmobiles, even cars and other expensive items is credit cards opened at the dealership. Most of the larger captive finance companies for motorcycles and other sports and recreation machines tout credit card offers for financing purchases.

There are a number of reasons for the growth of this method of financing. Often these are touted at being 0% interest. In reality this credit is not offered at 0%. Rather interest is deferred for a period, generally six to eighteen months, and forgiven if all payments are made as scheduled. If a single payment is missed, the deferred interest is added to the outstanding balance.

Often, consumers who believe they are entering into a traditional RISC will instead be issued a credit card that has been charged for this large purchase. This open-end, rather than closed-end, credit will impact the disclosures and protections the consumer receives. A more detailed discussion of this issue can be found in another treatise in this series, National Consumer Law Center, *Truth in Lending* § 6.2.3 (7th ed. 2010 and Supp.). Credit cards are also examined at Chapter 8, *supra*.

## *10.4.5 Non-Purchase Auto Finance*

Most auto finance involves purchase money loans, whereby the loan is used to purchase the vehicle. One major exception is auto title lending where small loans are extended with the collateral being the title to the consumer's existing vehicle. Auto title lending is detailed at Chapter 11, *infra*.

A growing trend—as used vehicles increase in value—is for lenders (not dealers) to originate larger loans taking the consumer's existing vehicle as collateral. These loans are in all shapes and sizes. A bank may offer a "car equity" loan at 24% for amounts up to $10,000 and terms as long as five years.[221] Other lenders may offer what is in effect a high interest auto title loan (triple digit APR) but in much larger denominations than the traditional auto title loan.[222]

Since these loans are not originated by the dealer and are not used to purchase the vehicle, RISA and MVRISA statutes do not apply. Whether any state law limits interest rates or other terms of these loans is a matter of state law. Where the loan is originated by a national bank, federal savings association, or a federally-insured state-chartered bank, savings association, or credit union, the depository can export its home state interest limits and is not bound by the usury ceiling where the loan is extended.[223]

217 *See* BHPH and Rent-to-Own Pane, F&I Showroom, January 2009, *available at* www.fi-magazine.com/Channel/Special-Finance/Article/Story/2009/01/BHPH-and-Rent-to-Own-Panel.aspx.

218 National Consumer Law Center, Truth in Lending § 2.5.4 (7th ed. 2010 and Supp.).

219 National Consumer Law Center, Truth in Lending § 13.2.1 (7th ed. 2010 and Supp.).

220 *See, e.g.*, *In re* Williams, 2007 WL 1875652 (Bankr. W.D. Ky. June 25, 2007) (contract is an executory lease under the Bankruptcy Code).

221 *See, e.g.*, Helping Loans by Santander Consumer USA Inc., described as twelve to sixty month car equity loan from $1,000 to $10,000, at a 24% average APR. More information available at www.HelpingLoans.com.

222 *See, e.g.*, RPM car title loans, offering terms of up to thirty-six months at triple digit interest rates. *See also* David Lazarus, *Title loans' interest rates are literally out of control*, L.A. Times, Feb. 8, 2011, *available at* http://articles.latimes.com/2011/feb/08/business/la-fi-lazarus-20110208.

223 *See* § 3.4, *supra*.

## 10.5 Manufactured Home Finance

### *10.5.1 Background*

Manufactured housing is the largest source of unsubsidized, affordable housing in the United States.[224] The median household income of manufactured home residents was $30,000 in 2009, as compared with $60,000 for all households in owned units.[225] Many United States armed forces personnel live in manufactured home parks.[226] These homes often come with hidden costs, some revealing themselves at purchase, others going unnoticed until an owner occupies the home for some time, defaults on a payment, or decides to move. Manufactured homes often depreciate in value over time. They can also sustain serious damage in transit from the manufacturer to the home site and in inclement weather.[227] Manufactured homes are not very "mobile," even though they are often referred to as "mobile homes." Moving a manufactured home once it has been secured may be difficult, if not impossible. If a home is moved it often is expensive to do so and may cause damage to the home.

Some consumers who purchase manufactured homes also own the land on which the home is placed. In other cases the units are situated on rented land or in a leased manufactured home park space. The consumer may therefore be answerable to both the entity that financed the sale of the home as well as the land or park owner.

Because financing for manufactured home can be difficult to find outside of the initial sale of a new home, and because park owners frequently impose charges and restrictions (such as the right to refuse potential buyers), it may be hard for a consumer to sell a home for more than a fraction of its purchase price, which was often inflated above the home's value at the time of purchase. Furthermore, residents who lease space from park owners are vulnerable to sudden rent increases and charges for utilities and services formerly included in the base rent. The park may be poorly maintained and services may lapse. Finally, there is a critical shortage of park space. If a tenant wishes to leave a bad park rental situation, there may simply be no place else to go. Park owners therefore hold, and exercise, considerable leverage over their tenants.

Consumers usually lack real bargaining power when dealing with park owners. Some states and localities have restricted fees and rent increases, prohibited certain resale restrictions, and enacted disclosure requirements and rules governing evictions.[228] A majority of states have enacted legislation addressing at least some of the problems with parks,[229] but many abuses still are not prohibited. Even in states where protections have been enacted, enforcement of these laws may be sporadic at best, and tenants who cannot afford attorneys may have few means of curbing the abuses they encounter.

### *10.5.2 Classification of Homes As Real or Personal Property*

#### 10.5.2.1 Implications of Classification

In every state, manufactured homes are initially considered personal property. A manufactured home may cease to be personal property when certain conditions are met. When a manufactured home is classified as personal property it is bought and sold like other goods. In most states ownership is conveyed by certificate of title, similar to an automobile title, and security interests are noted on the title. In states that do not use a certificate of title, a security interest is typically perfected through a UCC filing. By contrast, if the home is classified as real property and state real property laws govern, then ownership is conveyed by deed or mortgage of the home if it is on leased land or often of both the home and the land on which it sits if it is on owned land.[230] If the home is real property, then security interests are recorded in the local land records.

And of course, different state and federal laws may apply depending on whether a manufactured home loan is considered a home loan or the installment sale of goods. Manufactured homes are sometimes financed through RISCs, especially those homes characterized as personal property. Other homes, especially those on owned land, are financed through a traditional mortgage.

Whether a home is classified as realty or personalty will affect the consumer and creditor's rights on default. If the home is considered personalty, UCC Article 9 repossession law applies. If realty, than home foreclosure laws typically apply. For more on post-default remedies, see National Consumer Law Center, *Repossessions* (7th ed. 2010 and Supp.) and National Consumer Law Center, *Foreclosures* Ch. 16 (4th ed. 2012).

---

224 CFED I'M Home: Innovations in Manufactured Housing, Facts About Manufactured Housing, *available at* http://cfed.org/programs/manufactured_housing_initiative/about_manufactured_housing/facts_about_manufactured_housing/.

225 American Housing Survey 2009, Table 2-12, Income Characteristics—Occupied Units, *available at* www.census.gov/housing/ahs/data/national.html.

226 Practice Note, 1997 Army Law. 29, 31.

227 *See Dream Home . . . or Nightmare?*, Consumer Rep., Feb. 1998, at 34. *See also* U.S. Dep't of Hous. & Urban Dev., An Assessment of Damage to Manufactured Homes Caused by Hurricane Charley (Mar. 31, 2005), *available at* www.huduser.org/Publications/pdf/HurricaneCharley04.pdf; David A. Jones & Brad German, *Blowout: South Florida Housing Damage Caused by Hurricane Andrew*, Builder, Feb. 1993, at 276 (noting that 97% of manufactured homes were destroyed in the hurricane, as compared to 10% of conventional single family homes); National Consumer Law Center, NCLC Guide to Mobile Homes (2002).

228 *See, e.g.*, Fla. Stat. § 723.037; Mobile Home Anti-Eviction Act, N.J. Stat. Ann. § 2A:18-61.1(f) (West) (unconscionable rent increases not permitted). *See also* Quinn v. Rent Control Bd., 698 N.E.2d 911 (Mass. App. Ct. 1998) (manufactured home rent control survives the abrogation act).

229 *See* National Consumer Law Center, Unfair and Deceptive Acts and Practices § 8.1.2.5.2 (7th ed. 2008 and Supp.).

230 *See In re* Claxton, 239 B.R. 598 (Bankr. N.D. Okla. 1999) (mortgage that bank took on real property after manufactured home had already been installed covered the home as well as the land).

A home's classification as either real or personal property will have a tremendous impact on what sort of financing is available to the homeowner. Manufactured homes have traditionally been financed by chattel loans as opposed to the real estate mortgages most home buyers use to purchase site-built homes. Chattel is simply the legal term for personal property or an interest in real property that is less than a freehold estate. Chattel loans can differ in many respects from real estate mortgages. Of great concern to consumers is the fact that the interest rates on chattel loans are generally 2 to 5% higher than comparable real estate mortgages.[231]

The number of lenders that make chattel loans on manufactured homes is much smaller than the many lenders who make traditional real estate mortgage loans. A problem that has been exacerbated in recent years is that a number of lenders have either stopped making chattel loans on manufactured homes or gone out of business. In addition, many lenders still making such loans are captive lenders affiliated with the manufacturers or are subsidiaries of the manufacturers. In either case, the lender is more likely to make loans as part of a sale from a dealer rather than a refinance or private sale. This limited number of lenders not only reduces consumers' opportunity to shop for competitive loans, but also has a damaging effect on resale prices and used home values, as potential buyers may have great difficulty in financing the purchase of a unit.

Permitting manufactured homes to be converted to real property can improve financing options. The mere fact that a manufactured home is considered real property will not automatically permit the owner or purchaser to obtain favorable home financing. However, designation as personal property will often preclude favorable financing terms.[232] There have been and continue to be efforts to develop more competitive loan products for manufactured homes on leased land. A common requirement of these products is that the home be real property.

At common law married couples are permitted to hold real property as tenants by the entireties. Often the ability to hold property by the entireties is limited to real property,[233] so that manufactured homes can only be held in a tenancy by the entirety if it is classified as realty. On the other hand, some states now allow both real and personal property to be held by the entireties. Some states have also enacted special statutes extending the right to hold property as tenants by the entireties to manufactured homes.[234]

Classification as realty or personalty even has an impact on the consumer's ability to obtain an appraisal on a manufactured home or to hire a real estate agent. In some states, licensed real estate appraisers are not permitted to appraise personal property or licensed real estate agents or brokers are prohibited from listing property that is not real property. Even where there are regulations in place allowing real estate appraisers to appraise manufactured housing considered personalty, the confusing status of such housing leads many appraisers to avoid appraising manufactured homes.[235]

The appraisers themselves often find it confusing to appraise a manufactured home, due to imprecise conversion statutes and the difficulty of trying to appraise a manufactured home as personalty when it is clearly being used in a manner more akin to realty. The *Uniform Standards of Professional Appraisal Practice* (USPAP) provides that only homes permanently affixed to land are considered real estate.[236] Nevertheless, "permanently affixed" is a term of art, and may only mean the owner of the home must have removed the wheels and tongue; tie downs must be installed; the owner must manifest an intent to have the property counted as real property, and have gone through the necessary channels to handle this legally, by surrendering the title to the tax assessor's office, and conforming with any other requirements. More difficult would be to treat homes as realty when they are sited on rented land.

### 10.5.2.2 Determining Proper Classification

To determine whether a manufactured home is personal property or real property, the first question is whether the state has a statute that governs this issue. There are several different types of state statutes. Many states have statutes that set forth a procedure for a manufactured home to become real property.[237] A few states also have statutes that specify whether a home is considered personalty or realty in a credit transaction.[238] Many states have a statutory scheme that establishes criteria for taxing the home as real property.[239] Some states have no statute at all. In many of the states that do have a statute detailing when a home is, or may become, real property, the statute is often unclear as to whether the home is to be real property for all

231 Ronald A. Wirtz, *Home, Sweet (Manufactured?) Home*, Fedgazette, July 1, 2005, *available at* www.minneapolisfed.org/pubs/fedgaz/05-07/cover.cfm.

232 *See, e.g.*, Fannie Mae Announcement 07-06, Manufactured Housing Requirements, Clarifications, and New Forms (June 15, 2007) *available at* www.efanniemae.com/sf/guides/ssg/annltrs/pdf/2007/0706.pdf (detailing Fannie Mae's standards for manufactured home loans and requiring that homes be classified as real property even though only loans secured by both the home and land are eligible for purchase by Fannie Mae).

233 *See, e.g.*, 735 Ill. Comp. Stat. Ann. 5/12-112 (real property held in tenancy by the entirety not subject to execution to satisfy debts of one spouse); Whitlock v. Public Serv. Co. of Indiana, 159 N.E.2d 280 (Ind. 1959) (with certain exceptions, such as profits from crops, personal property may not be held by the entireties); State, Dep't of Treasury v. Myndyllo, 542 A.2d 478 (N.J. Super. Ct. App. Div. 1988); Brown v. Havens, 85 A.2d 812 (N.J. Super. Ct. Ch. Div. 1952); N.Y. Est. Powers & Trusts Law § 6-2.1 (tenancy by the entireties applicable only to real property and shares of stock in a cooperative apartment); Stout v. Van Zante, 219 P. 804 (Or. 1923).

234 N.C. Gen. Stat. § 41-2.5.

235 Alabama Real Estate Appraisers Board, Appraisal of Manufactured Housing 1, *available at* http://reab.state.al.us/pdf/APPRAISAL_MANUFACTURED_HOUSING.pdf.

236 *Id.* at 2.

237 *See* National Consumer Law Center, Foreclosures § 12.2.3 (4th ed. 2012).

238 *See* National Consumer Law Center, Foreclosures § 12.2.3 (4th ed. 2012).

239 *See* National Consumer Law Center, Foreclosures § 12.2.4 (4th ed. 2012).

intents and purposes and whether the statutory method is the only way of converting the home to real property.

In states that do not have a definitive statute, courts generally refer to the law of fixtures and look to a series of factors to determine whether the home has become so attached to the land as to be considered part of the real property.[240] Even in states that have a conversion statute, courts may analyze these factors to buttress the conclusion that a home is or is not real property or the conversion process from the statute may not be the exclusive means of making the home real property and so meeting the fixture requirements may be another way to become real property.

## 10.5.3 What Law Applies

### 10.5.3.1 Overview

The sale and financing of manufactured homes can be incredibly confusing for consumers and its nature will differ widely from one retail provider to another. In some instances the sale may look, and in fact be, very much like the sale of a car. In these cases typically the home will be classified as personal property. Often financing will be accomplished by a retail installment sales contract that will immediately be assigned to a captive lender. Many of the abuses and issues described in the car financing section, § 10.3 *supra,* may apply to such loans.

These sales will often be made by a manufactured home dealer, but may also be made by the owner of a manufactured home park community, many of whom have found selling homes that are already in their community to be a very lucrative activity. Often these are homes that the community owner has acquired after evicting the previous owner. These homes are often lost because the homeowner cannot find another location willing or able to accept the home and may not be permitted to sell the home in place.[241] The community owner may also have acquired the home by repossessing it if they previously financed the home.

Other times the purchase financing of a home will be much more like the financing for a typical stick-built house. There will be a traditional mortgage loan for the final financing. There may be a construction loan during the period the home is being sited. This more traditional home financing may occur when a home is being placed on land already owned by the homebuyer. It may also occur when the retailer is selling or arranging to sell the land and the home together, often referred to as a "land-home package." This same phrase however may also be used to describe the sale of real property with a mortgage loan and the sale of a home as personal property with a more expensive chattel loan all in the same transaction. This more traditional financing arrangement may also occur when the home will be placed on leased property, but only in states where such homes may be classified as real property.

No matter how the sale and financing are structured, there are some consumer protection laws that will apply. Most recent federal laws applicable to mortgage loans are also applicable to the finance manufactured homes. They generally define residence broadly enough so as to cover homes that are titled as either real or personal property. Other lending or finance laws will only apply in specific situations. The determining factor in many instances will be the home's classification as real or personal property. Other federal and state consumer protection statutes apply only to transactions that involve real property, while others apply to transactions involving personal property.

### 10.5.3.2 State Installment Sales and Other Credit Statutes

Where a consumer purchases a manufactured home from a dealer, in most states, an installment sales act will apply—a RISA, an MVRISA, or a special manufactured home installment sales act.[242] In UCCC states, the credit code will apply. When the financing is not through a dealer, other state credit statutes may apply, but if the lender is a national bank, federal savings association, or a federally-insured state-chartered bank, savings association, or credit union, the depository need not comply with the interest rate ceiling or related limits on financing charges of the state where the sale is made.[243] Instead the lender can rely on its home state law. State interest rates are also generally preempted by loans made by federal credit unions, that have their own interest rate ceiling.[244]

### 10.5.3.3 Truth in Lending Act

Truth in Lending also has a number of substantive limits on residential mortgage transactions, and these limits generally apply to manufactured home loans, whether state law treats them as personalty or realty. Most TILA substantive provisions concerning mortgages apply to credit secured by the consumers' principal dwelling. Dwelling is defined as including a manufactured home.[245] In addition, TILA's definition of residential mortgage transaction also applies to manufactured homes: "a transaction in which a mortgage, deed of trust, purchase money security interest arising under an installment sales contract or equivalent consensual security interest is created or retained against the consumer's dwelling to finance the acquisition or initial construction of such dwelling."[246]

TILA does not apply to transactions in which the amount financed exceeds $50,000, unless the creditor takes a security interest in property used or expected to be used as the consum-

240 *See* National Consumer Law Center, Foreclosures § 12.2.5 (4th ed. 2012).

241 For more information about protections for homeowners, financing in communities, and other related issues see NCLC's issue page on manufactured home at www.nclc.org/issues/manufactured-housing.html.

242 *See* § 10.2, *supra*, Appx. C, *infra*.

243 *See* § 3.4, *supra*.

244 *See* § 3.3, *supra*.

245 15 U.S.C. § 1602(w).

246 15 U.S.C. § 1602(x).

er's principal dwelling.[247] Thus TILA applies to credit secured by a manufactured home that is the consumer's principal dwelling regardless of whether the home is considered real or personal property and regardless of whether the amount financed is over $50,000.

The following TILA substantive limits examined in NCLC's *Mortgage Lending* (2012) and in *Truth in Lending* (7th ed. 2010 and Supp.) apply to manufactured home loans, no matter how the manufactured home loan is structured:

- Limits on lender payments to brokers and other originators;[248]
- Limits on loan originators steering consumers to particular lenders;[249]
- Disclosure requirements where a loan is assigned;[250]
- Requirements as to the creditor's determination of the consumer's ability to repay the loan;[251]
- Standards as to appraisal independence[252] and property appraisal requirements;[253]
- Restrictions on prepayment penalties,[254] and requirements for accurate payoff statements;[255]
- Limits on pyramiding late fees;[256]
- Limits on sale of single premium credit insurance;[257]
- Limits on negative amortization;[258]
- Limits on escrow accounts;[259]
- For manufactured home loans meeting the "HOEPA" points and fees trigger,[260] numerous requirements concerning prepayment penalties, late fees, balloon payments, ability to repay, and refinancing.[261]

In addition, in any non-purchase money manufactured home loan, the consumer has a three-day right to rescind and an extended right to rescind for certain TILA violations. TILA remedies for many of the provisions described above include attorney fees, actual damages plus statutory damages as high as $4,000, or even higher in some cases.[262] For more on the substantive requirements, TILA remedies, and other TILA issues, see National Consumer Law Center, *Truth in Lending* (7th ed. 2010 and Supp.).

247 15 U.S.C. § 1603.
248 12 C.F.R. § 1026.36(d) [§ 226.36(d)].
249 12 C.F.R. § 1026.36(e) [§ 226.36(e)].
250 12 C.F.R. § 1026.39 [§ 226.39].
251 15 U.S.C. § 1639c(a). *See* National Consumer Law Center, Truth in Lending § 1.3 (7th ed. 2010 and Supp.) (concerning the effective date).
252 15 U.S.C. § 1639e.
253 15 U.S.C. § 1639h.
254 15 U.S.C. § 1639c(c).
255 12 C.F.R. § 1026.36(c)(1)(iii) [§ 226.36(c)(1)(iii)].
256 12 C.F.R. § 1026.36(c)(1)(ii) [§ 226.36(c)(1)(ii)].
257 15 U.S.C. § 1639c(d).
258 15 U.S.C. § 1639c(f).
259 15 U.S.C. § 1639d.
260 15 U.S.C. § 1602(bb).
261 15 U.S.C. § 1639.
262 *See* § 2.2.2.2, *supra*.

### 10.5.3.4 Real Estate Settlement and Procedures Act

The federal Real Estate Settlement Procedures Act (RESPA) provides some protection for consumers buying a home. RESPA applies to all loans secured by a first or subordinate lien on residential real property designed principally for the occupancy of one to four families.[263] When RESPA applies, it requires disclosures about closing costs both before and at the time of settlement, notices about escrow accounts and servicing transfers, and the right to obtain account information through a written request that meets certain requirements. RESPA also prohibits kickbacks and unearned fees for settlement services, charges for preparation of certain documents, and prohibits the steering of borrowers to a particular title insurance company. RESPA also regulates the handling of escrow accounts.

The Department of Housing and Urban Development regulations interpreting the Real Estate Settlement and Procedures Act state that the RESPA is limited to certain mortgage loans, which the regulations limit to loans involving real property.[264] While the regulations do not define real property and it may be assumed that determination is left to the states, the regulations do indicate that covered loans include those that are secured by a lien on residential real property upon which there is a manufactured home. The industry FAQ section of HUD's website states that RESPA covers manufactured homes only if the manufactured home is located on real property on which the lender has a lien or security interest.[265] While conversion to real property should provide the protections of RESPA, HUD should clarify that RESPA applies if the home itself is considered real property.

### 10.5.3.5 State UDAP Statutes

While state UDAP statutes are universally applicable to the sale of personalty, they are not always applicable to real property transactions. In some states real property is excluded because courts have ruled that real estate is not "goods or services," terminology used in many of the statutes.[266] In other states however, such language has been found to include real property.[267] Some statutes explicitly cover real property or all property.[268] In other states courts have found legislative intent to cover real property where the statute is silent about coverage real estate.[269] Even in states where the statute does not apply to

263 12 U.S.C. § 2602(1). The loan must also must be made by a federally insured lender or be federally related in one of the other ways spelled out in § 2602.
264 12 C.F.R. § 1024.2(b) [24 C.F.R. § 3500.2(b)].
265 Available at www.hud.gov/offices/hsg/sfh/res/resindus.cfm.
266 *See* State v. First Nat'l Bank of Anchorage, 660 P.2d 406 (Alaska 1982); McElhannon v. Ford, 73 P.3d 827 (N.M. Ct. App. 2003).
267 *See In re* Bryant, 111 B.R. 474 (E.D. Pa. 1990); People *ex rel.* MacFarlane v. Alpert Corp., 660 P.2d 464 (Ariz. 1986).
268 *See* Murphy v. Berlin Constr. Co., 1999 Del. Super. LEXIS 5 (Jan. 12, 1999) (Delaware defines "merchandise to include real estate); Ky. Rev. Stat. § 367.110 (statute covers "any property," however, a private right of action is only afforded in transactions involving "goods and services").
269 *See* Warren v. LeMay, 491 N.E.2d 464 (Ill. App. Ct. 1986).

the sale of real estate, services and personalty related to such transactions may be covered,[270] including loans taking the home as security.

Nevertheless, some UDAP statutes do not apply to credit at all,[271] in which case, the statute may not apply to manufactured homes, whether treated as loans secured by real estate or by personalty. But even in these states, services related to the loan may still be covered.[272]

### 10.5.3.6 FTC Credit Practices Rule

The Federal Trade Commission (FTC) Credit Practices Rule limits pyramiding of late charges, informs co-signors of their liability, and prohibits consumer credit contracts from containing confessions of judgment, wage assignments, and waivers of exemption.[273] The rule applies to consumers seeking to acquire "goods,"[274] so that it applies to manufactured homes when considered personalty, but not realty. FTC indicates in the "Statement of Basis and Purpose" when it promulgated the rule that it would not apply to credit involving the purchase of real property.[275] Similarly, when the FRB adopted a version of the Credit Practices Rule applicable to banks, its Staff Guidelines stated that "[t]he issue of whether purchases of mobile homes or houseboats are covered by the rule depends on how these dwellings are treated under state law. If the applicable state law considers them real property, as opposed to personal property, then transactions for their purchase would be exempt from the rule."[276]

## *10.5.5 Federal Preemption of State Interest Rate Caps*

### 10.5.5.1 Introduction

The most common form of federal preemption concerning state interest rate ceilings in non-mortgage transactions is "rate exportation" where federal law allows a lender to use its home state interest ceiling (often having no limit at all) instead of the consumer's state ceiling. Like other forms of credit analyzed in this treatise, rate exportation does not apply to manufactured home loans unless the loan is *originated* by a depository institution. Rate exportation does not apply to credit originated by the manufactured home dealer. Nevertheless, manufactured home credit and loans do present preemption issues not present for any other form of credit analyzed in this treatise.

Two federal statutes that preempt state law for mortgage loans extend their coverage to manufactured homes, even if the home is sold from a dealership and is not sited on real estate at the time of the loan. In addition, federal agencies insure manufactured home loans, and this also raises special preemption issues. The federal mortgage loan preemption statutes are discussed at § 3.7, *supra*, and in more detail in National Consumer Law Center, *Mortgage Lending* § 8.2.3 (2012).

### 10.5.5.2 DIDA Interest Rate Preemption

The Depository Institutions Deregulation and Monetary Control Act of 1980 (DIDA) preempts state laws limiting interest rates on *first* mortgage loans,[277] and this DIDA provision applies to manufactured home credit.[278] For preemption to be applicable, the manufactured home creditor must either be a "qualified lender" or the manufactured home creditor must sell the loan to a qualified lender, as described at § 3.7.2, *supra*. Most manufactured home loans meet this standard.

States can opt out of this DIDA preemption and opt-out states include Colorado, Georgia, Hawaii, Idaho, Iowa, Kansas, Maine, Massachusetts, Minnesota, Nebraska, North Carolina, Puerto Rico, South Carolina, and South Dakota, and to a lesser extent Nevada.[279] Special rules apply to non-purchase money first mortgages in Texas.[280]

DIDA first lien preemption only applies to a manufactured home loan or credit sale if it complies with certain federal consumer protection regulations.[281] These regulations govern the refund of pre-computed finance charges, prepayment penalties, late charges, deferral fees, balloon payments, and the consumer's right to notice before repossession, foreclosure, or acceleration.[282]

There is no direct remedy if a manufactured home lender fails to comply with the consumer protection regulations. Instead, DIDA first mortgage preemption is not applicable, and the lender is left to comply with any applicable state law. If the

270 *See* Deltona Corp. v. Jannetti, 392 So. 2d 976 (Fla. Dist. Ct. App. 1981) (UDAP statute applies to sale of carpeting and other accessories sold with the land); Woods v. Littleton, 554 S.W.2d 662 (Tex. 1977) (UDAP applicable when seller promises to make repairs on home if problems arise).

271 *See* § 2.4.1.2, *supra*.

272 *Id.*

273 16 C.F.R. pt. 444.

274 16 C.F.R. § 444.1(d).

275 *See also* Federal Trade Commission, Bureau of Consumer Protection, Business Center, Complying with the Credit Practices Rule, www.ftc.gov/bcp/conline/pubs/buspubs/complcred.shtm ("The Rule covers all consumer credit transactions, except those involving the purchase of real estate").

276 Federal Reserve Bd., Staff Guidelines on the Credit Practices Rule, Reg. AA, *available at* www.federalreserve.gov/Regulations/cg/crdtpracrul.htm. *But see* 12 C.F.R. § 706 (no exclusion for real property loans by federal credit unions).

277 U.S.C. § 1735f-7a.

278 12 U.S.C. § 1735f-7a(a)(1)(A), (B).

279 *See* § 3.7.2, *supra*.

280 *Id.*

281 DIDA § 501(c), 12 U.S.C. § 1735f-7a. *See also* Quiller v. Barclay's American/Credit, Inc.,764 F.2d 1400 (11th Cir. 1985), *reinstating* 727 F.2d 1067 (11th Cir. 1984); Livingston v. Vanguard Fed. Sav. Bank, 563 A.2d 175, 180 (Pa. Super. Ct. 1989) (DIDA does not apply where manufactured home lender's contract did not comply with applicable regulations). *But see* Nelson v. River Valley Bank & Trust, 971 S.W.2d 777 (Ark. 1998).

282 12 C.F.R. § 190.4 (OCC interim final rule, replacing 12 C.F.R. § 590.4 enacted by the OTS. *See* 76 Fed. Reg. 49,152 (Aug. 9, 2011)). *Cf.* Burris v. First Fin. Corp., 928 F.2d 797 (8th Cir. 1991) (holding an "acquisition charge" not refunded upon prepayment is not a prepayment penalty within 12 C.F.R. § 590.4).

remaining applicable state law is a usury cap, and the loan exceeds that cap, then failure to comply with the consumer protection regulations leads to *state* usury remedies.[283]

#### 10.5.5.3 AMTPA Preemption of State Restrictions on Loan Structure

The Alternative Mortgage Transaction Parity Act (AMTPA) preempts certain state restrictions *not* on interest rates, but on the *structure* of manufacture home credit sales and loans.[284] AMTPA is a complex statute summarized at § 3.7.3, *supra* and examined in more detail at National Consumer Law Center, *Mortgage Lending* § 8.6 (2012).

Effective for any loan made on or after July 21, 2011,[285] AMTPA only preempts any state law that limits a lender's ability "to make, purchase and enforce" adjustable rate mortgages.[286] State creditors who opt to avoid state law concerning adjustable rate mortgages must then comply with Consumer Financial Protection Bureau (CFPB) Regulation D.[287] AMTPA's preemptive reach was broader for manufactured home loans entered into prior to July 21, 2011.[288]

AMTPA does not apply where a state has opted out of AMTPA,[289] and Maine, Massachusetts, New York, South Carolina and Wisconsin have opted out.[290] In addition, by federal statute, AMTPA applies in Texas only to purchase money mortgages.[291]

#### 10.5.5.4 Manufactured Home Loans Insured by Federal Agencies

The Federal Housing Administration (FHA) and the Department of Veterans Affairs (VA) are authorized to insure loans for the purchase or improvement of manufactured homes,[292] and state interest ceilings are preempted for these loans.[293] Currently, both the VA[294] and the FHA[295] permit borrowers and lenders to agree to any interest rate. As a result, unless a state opts out of VA and FHA preemption, there is no interest ceiling on FHA-insured or VA-insured manufactured home loans. Section 3.7.4, *supra*, and in particular National Consumer Law Center, *Mortgage Lending* § 8.2.2 (2012) discuss state opt-out rights.

The Rural Housing Service (RHS), an agency of the United States Department of Agriculture, administers two different loan programs: direct loans and guaranteed loans. Both programs allow loans to purchase manufactured homes.

RHS sets the interest rate, term, and payment arrangements for section 502 direct single-family housing loans.[296] The section 502 guaranteed loan program regulations require that interest rates comply with state limits on interest rates and also be at or below the "Fannie Mae rate" as described in its regulations and as set out in RHS instructions.[297]

## 10.6 Raising Seller-Related Claims Against the Installment Sales Contract Holder

### *10.6.1 Holder-in-Due-Course Doctrine Inapplicable*

Assignees of an originating creditor are largely immune from the consumer's seller-related claims and defenses if the assignee qualifies under UCC Article 3 as a holder in due course or acquires the rights of a holder in due course from a prior assignor.[298] In installment sales, though, an assignee does not qualify as a holder in due course and does not acquire the rights of a holder in due course. This is because holder-in-due-course status is based upon transfer of a "negotiable instrument" and installment sales do not involve such instruments.

In order to be negotiable, an instrument must contain a written promise to pay money that is unconditional and there must be no other undertaking.[299] There must be a "naked promise to pay" or a "courier without baggage." In order to have an unconditional promise to pay, the note itself must not contain an express condition.[300] Additionally, the note cannot be subject to or governed by another document or obligation.[301]

A promise to pay that has an additional undertaking besides the promise to pay defeats negotiability and therefore elimi-

283 Quiller v. Barclay's American/Credit, Inc.,764 F.2d 1400 (11th Cir. 1985), *reinstating* 727 F.2d 1067 (11th Cir. 1984). *Cf.* Burris v. First Fin. Corp., 928 F.2d 797 (8th Cir. 1991) (no violation of consumer protection regulations, so not state usury claim); Atkinson v. General Elec. Credit Corp., 866 F.2d 396 (11th Cir. 1989); Moyer v. Citicorp Homeowners, *Inc.*,799 F.2d 1445 (11th Cir. 1986); Grant v. General Elec. Credit Corp.,764 F.2d 1404 (11th Cir. 1985); Chambliss v. Oakwood Acceptance Corp. (*In re* Chambliss), 315 B.R. 166 (Bankr. S.D. Ga. 2004).

284 12 U.S.C. §§ 3801–3806.

285 Dodd-Frank tit. X, § 1083(b), *codified at* 12 U.S.C. § 3802 note.

286 12 U.S.C. §§ 3802(1), 3803(a).

287 See 76 Fed. Reg. 44,226 (July 22, 2011), enacting interim final rule 12 C.F.R. § 1004, Alternative Mortgage Transaction Parity (Regulation D). *See also* 12 U.S.C. § 3802 note, 3803.

288 *See* § 3.7.3, *supra*.

289 *See* 12 U.S.C. § 3804.

290 Me. Rev. Stat. tit. 9A, § 1-110 (West); 1985 Mass. Acts 224; N.Y. Banking Law § 6-g (McKinney) (did not opt out with respect to residential manufactured homes); 1984 S.C. Acts 355, § 1 (not codified); 1983 Wis. Laws 389, § 11(1) (non-statutory).

291 12 U.S.C. § 1462a. *See also* H.R. Conf. Rep. No. 103-651, at 57 (1994), *reprinted in* 1994 U.S.C.C.A.N. 2068. *See* National Consumer Law Center, Mortgage Lending § 8.6.3 (2012).

292 *See* 12 U.S.C. § 1703; 38 U.S.C. § 3703.

293 *See* 12 U.S.C. § 1709-1a; 38 U.S.C. § 3728.

294 *See* 38 C.F.R. §§ 36.4311, 36.4312; 60 Fed. Reg. 38,256 (July 26, 1995).

295 12 U.S.C. § 1709(b)(5); 24 C.F.R. §§ 201, 203.20(a).

296 7 C.F.R. §§ 3550.66, 3550.67.

297 7 C.F.R. §§ 1980.320, 1980.321. *See also* 7 C.F.R. § 1980.302 (definition of "Fannie Mae rate").

298 U.C.C. § 3-305.

299 U.C.C. § 3-104(a).

300 U.C.C. § 3-106(a)(i).

301 U.C.C. § 3-106(a)(ii), (iii).

nates the possibility of holder-in-due-course status.[302] The only exceptions to this rule occur when a person promising to pay also: agrees to give, maintain or protect collateral to secure payment; authorizes the holder to confess judgment or dispose of collateral; or waives the benefit of any law intended for the advantage or protection of the obligor.[303] Any other undertaking does defeat negotiability.

Installment sales contracts clearly do not meet the requirement that there be no additional undertakings. The seller's performance will be part of the contract, for example, the delivery of the car or the performance of the home improvements. This "baggage" is sufficient in and of itself to prevent the contract from being a negotiable instrument. The drafters of the 1990 Article 3 stated:

> Article 3 is not meant to apply to contracts for the sale of goods or services or to the sale or lease of real property or similar writings that may contain a promise to pay money. The use of words of negotiability in such contracts would be an aberration.[304]

In addition, as described at § 10.6.4, *infra*, consumer installment sales almost always have the "FTC Holder Notice" either included in the agreement or implied into the agreement. UCC Article 3 states that where the notice is in the contract "there cannot be a holder in due course of [such an] instrument."[305]

## 10.6.2 Waiver of Defense Clause Generally Not Enforceable

Since an assignee of the installment sales contract is not a holder in due course, the general rule under the UCC is that the assignee stands in the shoes of the seller and is subject to seller-related *defenses*.[306] (Where the consumer wishes to bring an affirmative claim against the assignee for seller-related conduct, the consumer will have to find an alternative theory.[307]) Only if there is an enforceable waiver-of-defense clause can the creditor avoid the defenses that would be good against the seller.[308]

Installment sales contracts today typically do not contain waiver-of-defense clauses, and many states prohibit them in at least some types of transactions.[309] In addition, as described at § 10.6.4, *infra*, consumer installment sales almost always have the "FTC Holder Notice" either included in the agreement or implied into the agreement, that states that the assignee *is* subject to seller-related claims and defenses. A waiver of defenses provision in the contract should not have any effect where the same contract has another provision explicitly stating the opposite. As a result, under the UCC the assignee of an installment sales contract is subject to the defenses the consumer could raise against the seller.[310]

## 10.6.3 Critical Importance of FTC Holder Rule

The Federal Trade Commission Preservation of Consumer Claims and Defenses Rule (FTC Holder Rule) allows installment sale consumers to raise their seller-related *claims* and defenses against the party holding the installment sales agreement.[311] The prior two subsections mentioned that the FTC Holder Rule defeats any claimed holder in due course status and any claimed immunity based upon a waiver of defense clause. The rule goes further, not only allowing consumers to raise defenses but also to bring *affirmative seller-related claims* against the holder.

This means that the consumer may be able to cancel out existing indebtedness and also recover amounts already paid on the loan as an affirmative recovery. Moreover, the consumer can raise seller-related claims and defenses related not only to the sale or performance of the goods or services, but also related to the credit-seller's credit origination practices.

## 10.6.4 Operation of the FTC Holder Rule

### 10.6.4.1 General

The FTC Holder Rule requires credit sellers to place a notice in the installment sales agreement (FTC Holder Notice) that the holder is subject to all claims and defenses related to the seller.[312] Even where there is a direct loan from a lender to the consumer, the seller must still arrange for the notice to be included in the note where the seller refers the consumer to a lender or has a business relationship with that lender.[313] The FTC Holder Rule and state analogs are discussed in detail in National Consumer Law Center, *Unfair and Deceptive Acts and Practices* Ch. 11 (7th ed. 2008 and Supp.). This section provides a brief overview.

The rule operates under basic contract law principles. Because the installment sales agreement has a contract provision stating that holders are subject to seller-related claims and defenses, then as a matter of contract law, any entity taking

302 U.C.C. § 3-104(a)(3).
303 U.C.C. § 3-104(a)(3).
304 U.C.C. § 3-104 cmt. 2.
305 U.C.C. § 3-106(d);U.C.C. § 3-106 cmt. 3. *See also* Mitchell v. Church, 2006 WL 2194738 (Del. Super. Ct. July 31, 2006).
306 U.C.C. § 9-404(a).
307 McGinley v. Am. Home Mortgage Servicing, Inc., 2010 WL 4065826 (W.D. Wash. Oct. 15, 2010) (assignee of mortgage loan not liable for affirmative UDAP claims that were based on conduct of loan originator in which it was not involved); Novartis Animal Health US, Inc. v. Earle Palmer Brown, L.L.C., 424 F. Supp. 2d 1358 (N.D. Ga. 2006); Meyers v. Postal Fin. Co., 287 N.W.2d 614 (Minn. 1979). The most common alternative theory is examined at §§ 10.6.3 and 10.6.4, *infra*.
308 U.C.C. § 9-403.
309 *See* National Consumer Law Center, Unfair and Deceptive Acts and Practices § 11.6.5.2 (7th ed. 2008 and Supp.). *See also* § 2.4.1, *supra*.
310 *See* National Consumer Law Center, Unfair and Deceptive Acts and Practices § 11.7.3 (7th ed. 2008 and Supp.).
311 16 C.F.R. pt. 433.
312 16 C.F.R. § 433.2(a).
313 16 C.F.R. § 433.2(b).

assignment of the agreement is bound by those terms. Whether or not the rule requires the notice in a particular credit sale, if the notice is in the contract, it is enforceable as any other contract term, allowing the consumer to raise both defenses and claims against the holder.

On the other hand, if the notice is not in the contract, then the FTC Holder Rule does not directly create the derivative liability. Fortunately for consumers, in credit sales, UCC Article 9 is in effect in all fifty states and creates that liability whether or not the notice is in the contract, as long as the notice is required to be in the contract.[314] The consumer "may assert against an assignee those claims and defenses that would have been available" if the notice had been included,[315] and the contract has the same effect as if the contract included the notice.[316]

Matters get more complex where the seller refers the consumer to a lender for a direct loan to purchase the goods or service and the FTC Holder Notice is not included in the lender's documents. But even in this situation, the consumer has a number of possible approaches for recovery, as set out in another NCLC treatise in this series.[317]

### 10.6.4.2 The Notice

The notice that the seller must arrange to be placed in the installment credit document states "Any holder of this consumer credit contract is subject to all claims and defenses which the debtor could assert against the seller of the goods or services obtained pursuant hereto or with the proceeds hereof. Recovery hereunder by the debtor shall not exceed amounts paid by the debtor hereunder."[318] Where the seller arranges a direct loan for the consumer to purchase the goods or services, the notice is the same, only deleting the phrase "obtained pursuant hereto or."[319]

The notice applies to "any" holder, and the holder is subject to "all" claims and defenses that could be asserted against the "seller." The notice also sets out a cap for recovery, as examined in the next subsection.

### 10.6.4.3 The Consumer's Maximum Recovery

The consumer's claims and defenses can offset all remaining indebtedness and the consumer can also recover any amount paid in on the installment loan. This is a maximum amount that the consumer can recover from the assignee for the seller's misconduct. In addition, the consumer can recover amounts over and above the FTC Holder Rule maximum if the consumer has independent claims against the holder for the holder's own conduct (for example for collection abuse).

Even though the FTC Holder Notice speaks to the recovery being capped at the amount paid by the debtor, the consumer can also first offset claims and defenses against the remaining indebtedness.[320] Furthermore, the FTC has issued a formal advisory opinion that reaffirms that the consumer can obtain an affirmative recovery when the claims and defenses exceed the amount remaining on the debt.[321] This official opinion from the full Commission explicitly rejects a number of court decisions that had refused to allow the consumer an affirmative recovery unless the transaction could have been rescinded or nothing of value was received.[322]

The consumer's affirmative recovery in an installment sale is not limited to the amounts paid through monthly or other periodic payments. The consumer can also recover all down payments and the value of any trade-in.[323]

### 10.6.4.4 Remedies for Rule Violations

The FTC Act does not provide a private right of action and neither does the FTC Holder Rule. On the other hand, if the FTC Holder Notice is in the contract or implied there under UCC Article 9, then the consumer has a contract right to raise all seller-related claims and defenses against the holder.

The consumer should also have a deceptive practices act claim where a lender tells the consumer that any relief available for seller-related practices or problems with the goods or services must be directed to the seller—that the lender has no liability for the seller's actions. This is a misrepresentation of the consumer's rights under the FTC Holder Notice, and this refusal to acknowledge liability under the FTC Holder Rule may be a violation of the state's deceptive practices statute.[324]

---

314 U.C.C. §§ 9-403(d), 9-404(d).

315 U.C.C. § 9-403(d)(2).

316 U.C.C. § 9-403(d)(1).

317 National Consumer Law Center, Unfair and Deceptive Acts and Practices § 11.6.4 (7th ed. 2008 and Supp.).

318 16 C.F.R. § 433.2(a).

319 16 C.F.R. § 433.2(b).

320 *See* FTC Staff Guidelines, 41 Fed. Reg. 20,023 (May 14, 1976) and cases cited at National Consumer Law Center, Unfair and Deceptive Acts and Practices § 11.6.3.2 (7th ed. 2008 and Supp.).

321 FTC Advisory Opinion to Jonathan Sheldon and Carolyn Carter (May 3, 2012), *available at* www.nclc.org/holder.

322 *Id.*

323 National Consumer Law Center, Unfair and Deceptive Acts and Practices § 11.6.3.4.1 (7th ed. 2008 and Supp.).

324 Jaramillo v. Gonzales, 50 P.3d 554 (N.M. Ct. App. 2002).

# Chapter 11 Auto Title Loans

## 11.1 Overview

The use of car titles as collateral for non-purchase-money loans is not new. What is relatively new is the ability of a lender to charge triple-digit interest rates normally associated with pawn transactions. A loan product called an automobile "title loan" or "title pawn"[1] has grown tremendously in the last two decades.[2]

Title loans are marketed to consumers needing fast cash to meet emergent family needs such as paying rent to stop an eviction or repairing a vehicle to continue employment. Borrowers are required to sign a pawn ticket and leave the title and/or a set of keys with the lender. The borrower is customarily required to repay the loan in one lump sum at the end of the term, although weekly installment payments are sometimes permitted. The borrower keeps possession of the vehicle during the term of the loan, but the lender can repossess it if a default occurs.

These small loans are very expensive and have been seen with effective (and sometimes undisclosed) annual percentage rates (APRs) of as much as 900%. Most title loans are made for amounts far less than the value of the vehicle that secures the loan. Over-securing the loan allows the lender to make these high-cost loans without regard to the borrower's ability to repay—a hallmark of predatory lending.

In 2000, the Office of the Comptroller of the Currency (OCC) issued a warning to national banks about safety, soundness and other risks associated with this type of lending as some banks considered whether to partner with local entities to fund these loans.[3] The OCC's concerns included collection practices by local lenders which permitted them to repossess an automobile without providing the borrower an opportunity to cure the default or to share in the net proceeds upon the sale of the car, and some lenders' failure to treat the transactions as loans, thus running afoul of the Truth in Lending Act.[4]

The auto title loan industry continues to grow rapidly. For example, Mississippi had 360 licensed auto title lenders by the end of 2010, with nearly $25 million in loans outstanding.[5] There were 209,155 new agreements in Tennessee with $158,647,157 outstanding as of December 31, 2010.[6] Tennessee licensed 834 title pledge lender locations as of the end of 2011.[7]

Lenders have attempted to legitimize auto title lending transactions in a variety of ways requiring equally creative litigation strategies. Lenders have characterized the transactions as leaseback arrangements, pawn transactions, rent-to-own agreements and open-end lines of credit.

## 11.2 Leaseback Schemes

The first wave of auto title lending schemes attempted to disguise their nature as a loan and their high interest rates using a leaseback pretense. A good example of these schemes is described in *Pendleton v. American Title Brokers, Inc.*,[8] one of the first reported cases about these loans. American Title Brokers advertised "Pawn your title, keep your car." The borrower pledged the car in exchange for $100, with an interest charge of $3.50, repayable in ten weekly installments. (So far that is only about a 33% APR—not cheap, but within many states' small loan rate ceilings.) But simultaneously, the customer executed a separate leaseback for the car pledged (with a right of repossession in the event of a default). The lease payments for the ten-week period were $10. (The weekly rental was always set at 10% of the loan size.) Credit insurance and an undisclosed processing fee were also added. The total weekly pay-

1 In states in which they are not a creature of statute, creditors generally call these transactions pawns in an attempt to take advantage of the high interest rates that pawnshop laws allow, and to avoid the U.C.C.'s redemption and surplus requirements. However, in states in which these transactions are statutorily allowed, they are often called "title loans" as a result of pawnbroker lobbyists' efforts to avoid the sullying of their reputation by association with title lenders. *See, e.g.*, Fla. Stat. § 539.001(2)(*o*) (excluding title loans from the purview of the pawnbroker statute). Since both terms generally connote the same business model, they are used interchangeably in this section, unless otherwise specified.

2 *See* Amanda Quester & Jean Ann Fox, Center for Responsible Lending and Consumer Federation of America, Car Title Lending: Driving Borrowers to Financial Ruin 9 (Apr. 14, 2005), *available at* www.responsiblelending.org/issues/cartitle/reports/page.jsp?itemID=28012462.

3 OCC Advisory Letter, No. AL 2000-11 (Nov. 27, 2000), *available at* www.occ.treas.gov/advlst00.htm.

4 *Id.*

5 Mississippi Dep't of Banking & Consumer Fin., Annual Report 2010 *available at* www.dbcf.state.ms.us/documents/annualreport10.pdf.

6 *Id.* at 37.

7 Tennessee Dep't of Fin. Inst., 2011 Report on the Title Pledge Industry 1 (2011), *available at* http://state.tn.us/tdfi/annualreport/2011/2011finalrpt.html.

8 754 F. Supp. 860 (S.D. Ala. 1991). *See also* Quick Cash of Clearwater, Inc. v. State, Dep't of Agric., 605 So. 2d 898 (Fla. Dist. Ct. App. 1992) (describing the scheme and deciding the extent of regulatory authority), *additional proceedings*, 609 So. 2d 735 (Fla. Dist. Ct. App. 1992).

ments would have been $22.88, with a total pay-back of $228.80—an effective APR of 977%. A second, $400 advance, would have yielded a 903% APR. The court had little problem deciding that Alabama's consumer credit code applied to the transaction.

American Title Brokers, like many other auto title lenders, attempted to avoid small loan requirements by claiming it was exempt as a pawnbroker. The court found it was not a bona fide pawnbroker, because its practice of renting back the car was contrary to a traditional hallmark of the pawnbroking business—retaining possession of the collateral.[9] It was, in essence, an unlicensed small loan issued by a company operating as an unlicensed small loan lender.[10]

The court also found that the rental transaction was subject to the Truth in Lending Act (TILA), and the full amount of the "rental" payments a TILA finance charge—a cost imposed by the creditor *incident* to the extension of credit, even though the leaseback was not a mandatory condition of obtaining the pawn loan.[11] The same analysis should establish the cost as interest under state usury laws.[12]

Another sale and leaseback title loan scheme was analyzed by the Arizona Court of Appeals, which applied a six-factor test to determine whether the transaction was in essence a loan subject to the state's small loan law.[13] The factors included: the prior negotiations of the parties; the distress of the customer; whether the amount advanced was the amount the grantor needed; the disparity between the amount of cash received and the actual value of the property "leased" back; a contemporaneous agreement to repurchase; and whether the parties' subsequent acts shed light on the true nature of the transaction.[14] The scheme involved advertisements in local newspapers and the yellow pages which read "quick cash 4 your car/keep to drive." However, when consumers arrived at the storefront, they were required to sign a sale-leaseback agreement. The amount of cash the consumers received was close to the amount of their need and bore no relationship to the value of the car. The proceeds typically equaled only 18% of the car's retail value and no more than 30% of the low wholesale value. The "lease fees" translated to interest rates of 218% per year, with payments set at $5 to $12 per day. The company added $5 per day to the remaining lease payments together with a one-time charge of $25 for late payments, and required its customers to maintain their own car insurance during the lease term. Finally, the company repossessed about 18% of all vehicles "sold" and leased-back. The court ruled that the transactions were not sales, but rather disguised consumer loans.[15]

If a court determines that an auto leaseback scheme is in actuality a disguised loan to which the state small loan law applies, the court will refer to the small loan law for consumer remedies. These laws often offer a statutory penalty such as double the amount of illegal interest paid.[16] Some void the entire transaction if the lender charged more than the allowed interest rate.[17] If the lender was operating without a required license, it may also be possible to argue that failure to have such a license voids the transaction.[18]

## 11.3 Auto Title "Pawns"

As in *Pendelton v. American Title Brokers, Inc.*, many auto title lenders attempt to characterize their loans as pawns. A number of cases have found that auto title loans are not true pawns and therefore do not qualify for the special treatment allowed by state pawnbroker statutes.[19] However, a few

9 Pendleton v. American Title Brokers, Inc., 754 F. Supp. 860 (S.D. Ala. 1991). *See* § 11.3 *infra* (other cases in which courts have found that auto title loans are not true pawns).

10 *See also* Virginia v. Car Pawn of Virginia, Inc., No. HG-402-3 (Cir. Ct. Richmond, Va. Dec. 5, 1995), *available on the companion website to this treatise* (letter opinion).

11 *See also* Bumpus v. Vandeford, 2002 U.S. Dist. LEXIS 20062 (N.D. Miss. Mar. 27, 2002) (following Barlow v. Evans and Wiley v. Earl's Pawn); Barlow v. Evans, 992 F. Supp. 1299 (M.D. Ala. 1997) (holding that auto title pawnbroker (no leaseback) was a creditor under TILA); Wiley v. Earl's Pawn & Jewelry, Inc., 950 F. Supp. 1108 (S.D. Ala. 1997) (following Barlow v. Evans). *See generally* National Consumer Law Center, Truth in Lending §§ 3.6.4.2, 3.6.4.3 (7th ed. 2010 and Supp.).

12 *See, e.g.,* State v. R & A Inv. Co., 985 S.W.2d 299 (Ark. 1999) (auto title lender violated state usury cap of 17% contained in the state's constitution, rendering the transaction unconscionable and subject to usury remedies and UDAP enforcement by the attorney general; note that the court indicated that true annual interest rate on these transactions was 65% but that analysis was wrong; fees of 25% on amount of cash back yield an APR of 650%); Quick Cash of Clearwater, Inc. v. State, Dep't of Agric., 605 So. 2d 898 (Fla. Dist. Ct. App. 1992) (noting it did not decide whether consumers could bring action to void as unconscionable lease or for damages under other theories, or whether transactions were usurious, as question at issue is extent of department's regulatory authority; finding the pawn-loan agreement subject to usury law and UDAP statute so remanding to allow state to proceed to present its case), *additional proceedings*, 609 So. 2d 898 (Fla. Dist. Ct. App. 1992). *See also* Colorado Uniform Consumer Credit Administrator Letter (Mar. 20, 1999), *available on the companion website to this treatise* (proposed sale-leaseback scheme involving cars likely constitutes consumer loan subject to 12% usury cap).

13 Sal Leasing, Inc. v. State *ex rel.* Napolitano, 10 P.3d 1221 (Ariz. Ct. App. 2000).

14 *Id.*

15 *Id.*

16 *See* § 7.8.2.3, *supra.*

17 *See* § 7.8.2.2, *supra.*

18 *See* § 7.8.5.2, *supra.*

19 *See, e.g.,* Lynn v. Financial Solutions Corp. (*In re* Lynn), 173 B.R. 894 (Bankr. M.D. Tenn. 1994) (title pawn not true pawn and subject to Article 9 of U.C.C.; even if it were, violated pawnbroker statute's reasonableness limitation on supplemental fees; transaction void ab initio and matter referred to attorney general) (*Note: The decision in Lynn v. Financial Solutions Corp. was legislatively overruled.*); Commonwealth *ex rel.* Chandler v. Kentucky Title Loans, Inc., 16 S.W.3d 312 (Ky. Ct. App. 1999) (pawnbroker who held certificate of title and set of car keys not pawnbroker under state statute which required that loans be made on deposit of personal property); Commonwealth v. Car Pawn of Virginia, Inc., 37 Va. Cir. 412 (1995); State *ex rel.* McGraw v. Pawn Am., 518 S.E.2d 859 (W. Va. 1998) (pawnbroker who retains only title but not the car itself is not entitled to pawnbroker exception to consumer credit laws). *See also* Henley v. Cameron Auto Pawn (*In re* Henley), 228 B.R. 425 (Bankr.

states allow auto title lenders to take advantage of pawn statutes.[20]

Some auto title lenders omit the pretense of the leaseback, opting to assert that the transaction is a straight pawn.[21] These lenders use contractual language that gives the "pawnbroker" a security interest in the property or title and the borrower the option of keeping possession of the collateral or turning it over.[22] As with *Pendleton v. American Title Brokers*, the "interest" charge is comparable to small loan rates—2% per month (24% per year). However, an additional "service charge" is added to that, set at 40% of the principal, plus a fixed processing fee. Thus a ten-week repayment plan for a $500 auto pawn loan requires a total payback of $1,033, with $103.30 weekly payments. The APR on that transaction is 830%.

This seems plainly to be a loan secured by an Article 9 security interest, and thus an even easier case to make than in *Pendleton*, though that court's analysis is helpful both in establishing the "service charge" charge as interest and in distinguishing the transaction from a true pawn.[23] In an Alabama case, the court found that the pawn documents created an Article 9 security interest in both the title and the car, although only the security interest in the title documents in possession of the pawnbroker was perfected as of the date of the pawn transaction.[24]

Causes of action for unconscionability, usury fraud, misrepresentation, and unfair and/or deceptive acts should be pleaded to remedy overreaching or fraudulent conduct by such pawnbrokers.[25] If the interest charged exceeds twice that allowed under state law, the pawnbroker can also face RICO claims on the grounds that it is collecting an unlawful debt, as long as the pawnbroker is operating as an "enterprise."[26] These claims are strengthened when, as often is the case, the title lender is also a used car dealer.

An Alabama trial court tackled an interesting constitutional issue involving the conflict or interplay between two different usury laws. Specifically, the court addressed the question whether the state Pawn Shop Act, which permits pawn and auto title lenders to charge annual interest rates of 300%, violates the Equal Protection Clause, by favoring these lenders over other lenders who cannot charge more than 24%.[27] Applying a rational basis test, the court held that allowing pawnbrokers to charge 300% directly conflicts with the stated purpose and definitions of the small loan and consumer finance acts. In effect, the Pawn Shop Act creates a classification that is arbitrary and shields one class of lenders and burdens another. The Act also discriminates against borrowers who would otherwise enter into 24% loans. However, the trial court's decision did not survive appellate review. The Alabama Supreme Court held that the borrower lacked standing to raise the issue of equal protection.[28] While the opinion does not foreclose the possibility that another party could raise the issue successfully, it

E.D. Ark. 1998) (Tennessee auto title pawn law enacted in response to Lynn v. Financial Solutions Corp. permits lender to charge 2% interest plus "customary fee"; allowing this lender to charge "customary fee" of $432 per month on loan of $2,400).

20 *See, e.g.*, Floyd v. Title Exch. & Pawn of Anniston, Inc., 620 So. 2d 576 (Ala. 1993); Pattans Ventures, Inc. v. Williams, 959 So. 2d 115 (Ala. Civ. App. 2006) (Alabama Pawnshop Act applies to a pawned car title loan transaction and the provisions of that Act also govern the repossession, redemption, and transfer rights between the parties); Opinion of the Nevada Attorney General, No. 95-20 (Nov. 17, 1995), *available at* 1995 WL 737002 (opining that auto title pawn constitutes a "pawn" and the creditor is, therefore, not subject to licensing as an installment lender).

21 *See, e.g.,* State v. R & A Inv. Co., 985 S.W.2d 299 (Ark. 1999); Churchwell v. National Title Loan, Inc., Case No. 96-5098-CA (Cir. Ct. Duval County Fla. Dec. 2, 1997), *available at* www.nclc.org/unreported (order certifying class), (Cir. Ct. Duval County Oct. 23, 1998), *available at* www.nclc.org/unreported (granting summary judgment to consumer on TILA claim); Commonwealth *ex rel.* Chandler v. Kentucky Title Loans, Inc., 16 S.W.3d 312 (Ky. Ct. App. 1999).

22 The contract gives the pawnbroker the right to repossess, with a minimum repossession fee of $125, and includes boilerplate language purporting to waive the right to object to repossession. The preprinted contractual language may go on to say " . . . you have made a knowing choice to maintain possession."

23 *See, e.g.,* Lynn v. Financial Solutions Corp. (*In re* Lynn), 173 B.R. 894 (Bankr. M.D. Tenn. 1994) (title pawn not true pawn; contract called for security interest, so lender was subject to Article 9, which lender violated. *Note: The decision in Lynn v. Financial Solutions Corp. was legislatively overruled*). *See also* Henley v. Cameron Auto Pawn (*In re* Henley), 228 B.R. 425 (Bankr. E.D. Ark. 1998) (Tennessee auto title pawn law enacted in response to Lynn v. Financial Solutions Corp. permitted lender to charge 2% interest plus "customary fee"; in this case, lender permitted to charge "customary fee" of $432 per month on loan of $2,400).

24 Mattheiss v. Title Loan Express (*In re* Mattheiss), 214 B.R. 20 (Bankr. N.D. Ala. 1997) (addressing the implications of this holding in the bankruptcy context). *See* National Consumer Law Center, Consumer Bankruptcy Law and Practice §§ 11.6, 11.9 (9th ed. 2009 and Supp.) (bankruptcy implications of dealing with secured creditors in chapter 13 cases and the opportunity this presents to modify the creditor's rights).

25 *See* § 2.4, *supra*. *See also* Barlow v. Evans, 992 F. Supp. 1299 (M.D. Ala. 1997) (failure to disclose TILA-required costs of transaction states a claim of fraud by suppression under Alabama law); *Ex parte* Coleman (*In re* Coleman v. Higginbotham), 861 So. 2d 1080 (Ala. 2003) (consumer alleged that pawnbroker repossessed vehicle in violation of oral agreement; permitting consumer to bring claims for breach of contract and conversion, but not fraud or outrage); Sal Leasing, Inc. v. State *ex rel.* Napolitano, 10 P.3d 1221 (Ariz. 2000) (reversing dismissal of UDAP claims in light of holding that sale-leaseback auto scheme created loans which violated state usury law). *But see* Miller v. Pawn World, Inc., 705 So. 2d 467 (Ala. Civ. App. 1997) (dismissing fraud claims on ground that representations about selling the pawned property were part of the contract; borrower failed to read the contract and failed to meet his burden that the pawnbroker misrepresented that the loan would "roll over" more than once).

26 Sharp v. Easy Money Title Pawn, Inc., 128 Fed. Appx. 513 (6th Cir. 2005) (upholding summary judgment in favor of class on RICO claim). *See also* Markham v. Gibson, No. 97-01651 SPK (D. Haw. July 7, 1998), *available at* www.nclc.org/unreported.

27 Waites v. Express Enter., Inc., No. CV-00-165 (Ala. Cir. Ct., St. Clair County Aug. 25, 2006), *available at* www.nclc.org/unreported. *But cf.* Midwest Check Cashing, Inc. v. Richey, 728 N.W.2d 396 (Iowa 2007) (Iowa payday loan law is not unconstitutional under the equal protection and due process clauses, though not addressing the same issue as that raised in the *Waites* case; but where the payday law is silent, the UCCC applies; therefore, the right to cure provision of the UCCC applies).

28 Express Enter., Inc. v. Waites, 979 So. 2d 754 (Ala. 2007).

strongly suggests that this party would need to be a lender claiming discrimination rather than a consumer.

## 11.4 Other Schemes and Disguises

In a case from Oklahoma a lender claimed that its auto title loans were rent-to-own (RTO) transactions.[29] The Oklahoma Supreme Court disagreed, and applying the six-factor analysis from the Arizona Supreme Court in *Sal Leasing, Inc.*,[30] determined that the transactions were disguised loans. In this case, the auto title loans carried interest rates of 285%, 290%, and 484%. The court noted that a typical RTO business does not require the consumer to sell their property to the store at a significantly reduced price and then rent it back. The court also found significant the fact that the lender had no inventory and did not offer goods generally available to RTO customers.

In another case,[31] a $1,500 loan fee on a $2,000 title loan was disguised as a broker fee. The scheme involved two entities, one allegedly the broker, and the other the nominal lender. Unfortunately, the Fifth Circuit ruled that the Texas Credit Services Organization Act permitted such a brokerage arrangement.[32]

Some auto title lenders have also characterized auto title loans as open-end lines of credit.[33] This variation seeks to take advantage of state laws that permit lenders to contract for any rate of interest for open-end credit.[34] Also, Truth in Lending Act disclosures for open-end credit are much less informative than disclosures for closed-end credit.[35] Auto title "lines of credit" may be challenged as spurious open-end credit under the Truth in Lending Act[36] and state loan laws. Additionally, in states that have loopholes for open-end lines of credit, lenders are still vulnerable to suit if they fail to structure their loans properly as open-end credit within the meaning of state law or to comply with applicable licensing requirements.[37]

Auto title lenders have also attempted to increase loan fees by using questionable add-ons. Typical fees include late fees, repossession fees, and even fees to "call off" a repossession.[38] Other hidden loan fees are disguised in the form of charges for credit insurance, "auto club memberships," or other services.[39]

## 11.5 Auto Title Loan Statutes

### 11.5.1 Overview

Twenty-one states have enacted special automobile title pawn laws.[40] Some of the laws simply legalize high-rate title pawn

29 Aple Auto Cash Express, Inc. v. State *ex rel.* Oklahoma Dep't of Consumer Credit, 78 P.3d 1231 (Okla. 2003).

30 Sal Leasing, Inc. v. State *ex rel.* Napolitano, 10 P.3d 1221 (Ariz. Ct. App. 2000). *See* § 7.5.2.3.2, *infra*.

31 Lovick v. Ritemoney Ltd., 378 F.3d 433 (5th Cir. 2004).

32 *Id. See* § 4.5.3, *supra* (discussing challenging broker fees as disguised interest).

33 Amanda Quester & Jean Ann Fox, Center for Responsible Lending and Consumer Federation of America, Car Title Lending: Driving Borrowers to Financial Ruin (Apr. 14, 2005), *available at* www.responsiblelending.org/issues/cartitle/reports/page.jsp?itemID=28012462. *See also In re* Anderson Fin. Servs., L.L.C. & LoanSmart, L.L.C., Settlement Agreement in Commonwealth of Virginia *ex rel.* McDonnell (June 8, 2007), *available on the companion website to this treatise* (title lenders used the state's revolving credit law when making auto title loans; attorney general issued a violation notice because the lines of credit had not provided a grace period before imposing a finance charge and the lenders imposed a 25% fee at the time the account was opened; settlement agreement provided that the title lenders would provide restitution totaling approximately $205,000).

34 Va. Code Ann. § 6.1-330.78. *But see* Iowa Code § 537.2403 (expressly prohibiting interest in excess of 21% whether charged in a closed-end or open-end account).

The Iowa Supreme Court held that this cap—effective July 1, 2007—applies only prospectively. Title lenders offering open-end credit are thus permitted to charge rates in excess of 21% on advances made after July 1, 2007, as long as the rate was agreed upon in a pre-July 1, 2007 contract. Anderson Fin. Servs., L.L.C. v. Miller, 769 N.W.2d 575 (Iowa 2009).

35 *See generally* National Consumer Law Center, Truth in Lending Ch. 6 (7th ed. 2010 and Supp.).

36 *Id.* § 6.2.3.

37 *See, e.g.*, Tweedy v. RCAM Title Loans, L.L.C., 611 F. Supp. 2d 603 (W.D. Va. 2009) (granting default judgment against lender of motor vehicle line of credit secured by borrower's vehicle under Virginia Consumer Finance Act (VCFA) based on uncontested allegation that lender charged interest rate in excess of that permitted under VCFA without proper license).

38 *See* Marc Perrusquia, *Last-Resort Loans*, Memphis Commercial Appeal, July 11, 2004, at A1 (documenting illegal late fees, $175 repossession fee, and $75 "call off" fee charged by one auto title lender). *See generally* § 4.8.2, *supra* (discussing challenging late fees as hidden interest).

39 *See, e.g.*, Finch v. Wisconsin Auto Title Loans, Inc., 586 F. Supp. 2d 1070 (E.D. Wis. 2008) (granting borrower's motion to remand to state court her suit against title lender for requiring purchase of car-club membership as condition of title loan and allegedly disclosing membership cost as part of principal rather than finance charge); Low Cost Auto Pawn, Inc. v. Greco, 851 So. 2d 768 (Fla. Dist. Ct. App. 2003) (affirming summary judgment awarding borrower $32,656 against auto title lender who disguised loans as a "marketing agreement"); Tom Kertscher, *Car-Title Loan Company Takes Borrower for a Ride, Suit Says*, Milwaukee Journal Sentinel, July 13, 2002, at 1B. *See also* http://myfloridalegal.com/webfiles.nsf/WF/MRAY-6EPK3E/$file/FloridaAutoLoanSettlement.pdf (attorney general settlement with auto title lender requiring refunds to consumers who were required to buy travel club memberships and related products in order to obtain auto title loans).

40 *Alabama*: Ala. Code §§ 5-19A-1 to 5-19A-20 (general pawnshop law, interpreted by state supreme court to allow automobile title pawns). In Alabama, a court decision permits auto title lending given the broad interpretation it gave to the definition of a pawn transaction. Floyd v. Title Exch. and Pawn of Anniston, Inc., 620 So. 2d 576 (Ala. 1993) (interpreting Ala. Code §§ 5-19A-1 to 5-19A-20 to permit auto title lending).

*Delaware*: Del. Code Ann. tit. 5, §§ 2250 to 2261.

*Florida*: Fla. Stat. §§ 537.001 to 537.018.

*Georgia*: Ga. Code Ann. §§ 44-12-130 to 44-12-138.

*Idaho*: Idaho Code Ann. §§ 28-46-501 to 28-46-509; Idaho Department of Finance Enforcement Policy #2000-1, Fraudulent and Unconscionable Conduct in Title Loans, *available at* http://finance.idaho.gov/form/ConsumerLender/policy2000-1.pdf (defining what conduct relating to ability to repay, disclosures, and sale of the vehicles may be unconscionable).

*Illinois*: 205 Ill. Comp. Stat. Ann. § 670/15. *See also* Ill. Admin. Code tit. 38, §§ 110.300 to 110.410 (governing automobile title

lending while others either prohibit it or impose restrictions significant enough to dissuade title lenders from doing business in the state. Such statutes also often operate to trump otherwise applicable usury caps, even those found in criminal statutes.[41]

Title lenders in a few states have attempted to challenge title pawn laws. Illinois regulations withstood a challenge by title lenders who claimed that the law was unconstitutionally vague and an invalid delegation of legislative authority.[42] An Oregon regulation survived a challenge by a title lender because the lender failed to demonstrate irreparable harm.[43]

Some states have regulated title pawns by imposing rate caps. Montana passed a referendum that caps auto title pawn charges at 36%, effective January 1, 2011.[44] In other states where allowable interest rates for auto title loans are lower than for other types of small loans, the auto title lender may be able to license itself as a small loan lender and then charge the higher interest rate, even for auto title loans. But, in Montana, even these loans are capped at 36%.[45] Oregon caps auto title lending at 36% and requires lenders to consider a borrower's ability to repay the loan.[46] Wisconsin legislation, effective January 1, 2011, prohibits licensed lenders from making auto title loans.[47]

On the other hand, Texas legislation effective January 1, 2012 effectively endorses the Texas Credit Services Organization Act model,[48] while adding a few disclosure requirements.[49] Virginia's title pawn statute, enacted in 2010, limits interest rates, restricts the ability to renew or refinance an auto title loan, and regulates repossessions upon default.[50] However, the interest rate cap, while an improvement over the situation before the bill was enacted, is so high—as much as 240% per year—that it is not an effective limit. The Utah statute requires a pawnbroker that sells, exchanges, or pawns motor vehicles to be licensed as a motor vehicle dealer but exempts a title lender, check casher, or payday lender that sells cars *incident* to its business.[51]

New Hampshire capped interest rates for auto title loans at 36% per year in 2010 but the title lending industry quickly proposed legislation to reinstitute high-cost auto lending. Although this legislation was vetoed by the governor, the New Hampshire legislature overrode the veto. Consequently, legislation, effective March 4, 2012, allows auto title lenders to charge interest of 25% per month—an effective APR of 300%—and to pass along lender costs to the borrower.[52]

### 11.5.2 Potential Claims in States That Authorize High-Cost Auto Title Lending

Even in states that authorize auto title lending without placing effective limits on rates, lenders may cut corners and run afoul of the law. Where the applicable law allows only certain fees up to certain amounts or percentages of the loan, no other charges can be imposed.[53] Repossessing and selling the car and

---

loans; upheld in S. 51 Dev. Corp. v. Vega, 781 N.E.2d 528 (Ill. App. Ct. 2002)).

*Kentucky*: Ky. Rev. Stat. Ann. §§ 286.10-200 to 286.10-991 (West).

*Minnesota*: Minn. Stat. §§ 325J.01 to 325J.13.

*Mississippi*: Miss. Code Ann. §§ 75-67-401 to 75-67-449 (Mississippi Title Pledge Act).

*Missouri*: Mo. Rev. Stat. §§ 367.500 to 367.533 (pawnbrokers and small loans).

*Montana*: Mont. Code Ann. §§ 31-1-801 to 31-1-827 (Title Loan Act).

*Nevada*: Nev. Rev. Stat. §§ 604A.450, 604A.455 Opinion of the Nevada Attorney General, No. 95-20, 1995 WL 737002 (Nov. 17, 1995) (opining that auto title loan constitutes a "pawn" and the creditor is, therefore, not subject to licensing as an installment lender).

*New Hampshire*: N.H. Rev. Stat. Ann. §§ 398:1 to 398:14, 399-A:14.

*New Mexico*: *See also* N.M. Code R. §§ 12.18.4.1 to 12.18.4.8, 12.18.6.1 to 12.18.6.8 (LexisNexis) (regulating signs and requiring annual report).

*Ohio*: Ohio Rev. Code Ann. §§ 4505.102 (Certificate of Motor Vehicle Title Law; allows licensed pawnbrokers to make title pawn loans), 4727.01 to 4727.99 (pawnbrokers) (West).

*Oregon*: Or. Rev. Stat. Ann.§§ 1 to 27 (2010 Special Session Undesignated Enactment, *enacted by* 2010 Oregon Laws 1st Sp. Sess. Ch. 23 (S.B. 993)).

*South Carolina*: S.C. Code Ann. §§ 37-3-413, 36-9-201 (S.C. Code Ann. tit. 37 overrides Article 9 in case of conflict).

*South Dakota*: S.D. Codified Laws §§ 54-4-36(15), (16), 54-4-70 to 54-4-72.

*Tennessee*: Tenn. Code Ann. §§ 45-15-101 to 45-15-120 Tennessee Attorney Gen. Op. No. 05-11 (July 12, 2005), *available at* www.attorneygeneral.state.tn.us/op/2005/op/op111.pdf (finding that auto title lenders must comply with Article 9 of the U.C.C. unless it conflicts with provisions of the Title Pledge Statute).

*Texas*: Tex. Fin. Code §§ 393.221 to 393.224 (West).

*Utah*: Utah Code Ann. §§ 7-24-102 to 7-24-305.

*Virginia*: Va. Code Ann. §§ 6.2-2200 to 6.2-2227.

*Wisconsin*: *See also* Wis. Stat. § 138.16.

*See generally* Leah A. Plunkett and Ana Lucia Hurtado, *Small Dollar Loans, Big Problems: How States Protect Consumers from Abuses and How the Federal Government Can Help*, 44 Suffolk U.L. Rev. 31 (2011).

41 *See, e.g.,* Glinton v. And R, Inc., 524 S.E.2d 481 (Ga. 1999) (state pawnbroker law and criminal usury statute cannot be harmonized; the pawnbroker law prevails). *But see* Fryer v. Easy Money Title Pawn, Inc., 183 B.R. 322 (harmonizing these two statutes). *See generally* Leah A. Plunkett and Ana Lucia Hurtado, *Small Dollar Loans, Big Problems: How States Protect Consumers from Abuses and How the Federal Government Can Help*, 44 Suffolk U.L. Rev. 31 (2011) (providing detailed information about the applicability of state civil and criminal usury caps to auto title lending).

42 South 51 Dev. Corp. v. Vega, 781 N.E.2d 528 (Ill. Ct. App. 2002).

43 Northwestern Title Loans v. Division of Fin., 42 P.3d 313 (Or. Ct. App. 2002).

44 Mont. Code Ann. § 31-1-817.

45 Mont. Code Ann. § 32-5-301.

46 Or. Rev. Stat. Ann.§§ 1 to 27 (2010 Special Session Undesignated Enactment, enacted by 2010 Oregon Laws 1st Sp. Sess. Ch. 23 (S.B. 993)).

47 Wis. Stat. § 138.16.

48 Lovick v. Ritemoney Ltd., 378 F.3d 433 (5th Cir. 2004). *See* § 10.4, *supra*.

49 Tex. Fin. Code § 393.223 (West).

50 Va. Code Ann. § 6.2-2200 (effective Oct. 1, 2010).

51 Utah Code Ann. § 41-3-103.

52 N.H. Rev. Stat. Ann. § 399-A:14.

53 *See, e.g.,* Advisory Legal Opinion, Office of the Florida Attorney General, AGO 99-38 (June 14, 1999), *available on the companion website to this treatise* (repossession fee or other fee in excess of 22% per month allowable rate violates title loan cap). *See also* Press Release, Attorney General McDonnell Announces Settlement with

keeping the excess above the amount owed in violation of state law can also violate the fee or rate cap.[54]

The state title loan statute may not have an explicit private right of action, and at least two courts have refused to imply a private cause of action.[55] However, failure to comply with other requirements of a state pawnbroker law or auto title loan law may render the transaction voidable[56] or subject to a usury[57] or UDAP[58] claim.

### 11.5.3 Other State Statutory Limitations on Auto Title Lending

A few states have sought to limit auto title "pawns" by explicitly requiring that the "pawnbroker" take possession of the vehicle or by excluding pawns made solely against the title of a vehicle.[59] If the auto title pawn is not specifically authorized by the state's pawnbroking statute, mere possession of a title certificate does not create a valid security interest under the UCC.[60] Wrongful repossession of the car in this instance creates a wide range of claims.[61]

Some municipalities have responded to the growth of the auto title lending industry by enacting their own more protective regulation or through zoning actions.[62]

### 11.5.4 Interstate Title Pawn Lending

A significant issue is whether a state can regulate auto title loans when the consumer resides in that state, the vehicle is registered in that state, and any repossession is likely to occur in that state, but the loan transaction occurs in a neighboring state. For example, Indiana severely restricts auto title pawn, but Illinois does not. An Illinois auto title lender that primarily made loans to Illinois residents also advertised in Indiana but required the Indiana consumers to come to Illinois to take out the loan. The Seventh Circuit ruled that Indiana could not regulate that loan transaction.[63] Some language in the opinion suggests, however, that Indiana might have been allowed to apply its law if there had been evidence that the lender located near Indiana with the specific intent to evade Indiana law while lending to Indiana consumers.

---

Auto Title Lenders (Mar. 25, 2008), *available at* www.oag.state.va.us/PRESS_RELEASES/NewsArchive/032508_Auto.html (obtaining refunds to borrowers charged interest in excess of the limit).

54 *See, e.g.,* Advisory Legal Opinion, Office of the Florida Attorney General, AGO 99-38 (June 14, 1999), *available on the companion website to this treatise* (repossession fee or other fee in excess of 22% per month allowable rate violates title loan cap). *See also* Yazzie v. Ray Vicker's Special Cars, Inc., 12 F. Supp. 2d 1230 (D.N.M. 1998) (in this true pawn case (car was held, not merely the title), pawnbroker violated the state pawnbroker law by charging "pawn service" fees above the legal limit and by failing to provide a physical description of the consumer on the pawn tickets); Lynn v. Financial Solutions Corp. (*In re Lynn*), 173 B.R. 894 (Bankr. M.D. Tenn. 1994) (title pawn not true pawn, but in any event lender violated pawnbroker statute's reasonableness limitation on supplemental fees; transaction held void ab initio); Press Release, Attorney General McDonnell Announces Settlement with Auto Title Lenders (Mar. 25, 2008), *available at* www.oag.state.va.us/PRESS_RELEASES/NewsArchive/032508_Auto.html (obtaining refunds to borrowers charged interest in excess of the limit). *But see* Henley v. Cameron Auto Pawn (*In re* Henley), 228 B.R. 425 (Bankr. E.D. Ark. 1998) (construing Arkansas law and finding that a fee of 18% of the amount borrowed for thirty days did not violate the auto title act since the act only capped the interest rate (no discussion of when the size of a fee will cross an unconscionable line)).

55 Brown v. Tennessee Title Loans, Inc., 328 S.W.3d 850 (Tenn. 2010) (finding no private cause of action to enforce title pawn statute, but allowing consumers to proceed with claim that violation of title pawn statute was UDAP violation).

56 *See, e.g., In re* Jackson, 2007 WL 954751 (Bankr. E.D. Tenn. Mar. 29, 2007) (third extension of a car title loan which included a 25% fee, as opposed to a 12.5% fee, violated Georgia's auto title loan law; violation voids the loan but does not decide what "void" means under this law); Johnson v. Speedee Cash (*In re* Johnson), 289 B.R. 251 (Bankr. M.D. Ga. 2002) (auto title lender failed to include statutorily required terms in contract, such as thirty-day redemption period; loan voidable in bankruptcy). *See also* Brown v. Speedee Cash (*In re* Brown), 304 B.R. 544 (Bankr. M.D. Ga. 2004) (following Johnson v. Speedee Cash); Opinion of the Nevada Attorney General, No. 97-13 (Apr. 1, 1977), *available at* 1997 WL 169235 (if an auto title loan contains terms prohibited by state pawn statute, lender must comply with installment loan act).

57 Bumpus v. Vandeford, 2002 U.S. Dist. LEXIS 20062 (N.D. Miss. Mar. 27, 2002) (auto title lender failed to obtain license as a title-pledge creditor; loan subject to Mississippi usury cap of 10%).

58 Brown v. Tennessee Title Loans, Inc., 328 S.W.3d 850 (Tenn. 2010) (allowing consumers to proceed with claim that violation of title pawn statute was UDAP violation).

59 La. Rev. Stat. Ann. § 37:1801(D); Me. Rev. Stat. tit. 30-A, § 3960; Ohio Rev. Code Ann. §§ 4505.102, 4727.01(A), 4727.08(E) (West); S.C. Code Ann. § 40-39-10(3).

However, South Carolina permits auto title lending not structured as a pawn transaction. *See* S.C. Code Ann. § 37-3-413.

60 U.C.C. § 9-203. *See also In re* Schwalb, 347 B.R. 726 (Bankr. D. Nev. 2006) (Article 9 applies to pawn transaction in which the lender held endorsed auto title certificates and Nevada law did not explicitly exempt this type of transaction from the U.C.C.; a security interest attached because the consumer signed a pawn ticket granting a security interest but absent such an agreement, holding that mere possession of endorsed certificates of title did not create a security interest; offsetting the damages against the lender's bankruptcy claim since the lender violated various provisions of Article 9).

61 National Consumer Law Center, Repossessions § 3.10 (7th ed. 2010 and Supp.).

62 *See, e.g.,* Malish v. City of San Diego, 101 Cal. Rptr. 2d 18 (Cal. Ct. App. 2000) (upholding city's right to require pawnbroker to obtain local permit, but striking down parts of ordinance that were inconsistent with state pawnbroker licensing law); City of Bridgeton v. Titlemax of Missouri, Inc., 292 S.W.3d 530 (Mo. Ct. App. 2009) (lender's proposed use satisfies definition of "loan office" pursuant to city zoning ordinance); Missouri Title Loans v. City of St. Louis Bd. of Adjustment, 62 S.W.3d 408 (Mo. Ct. App. 2001) (zoning action); Circle D Pawn #2, Inc. v. Norman, 956 P.2d 931 (Okla. Civ. App. 1998) (local law did not conflict with the state act). *See also* Meredith Fischer and Paige Akin, *Board Rules Against Lender: Chesterfield Calls Store Site Wrong*, Richmond Times-Dispatch, Jan. 3, 2003, at A12; Dan Kulin, *City Considers Restrictions for Payday, Car Loan Firms*, Las Vegas Sun, Nov. 5, 2002, at 3.

63 Midwest Title Loans, Inc. v. Mills, 593 F.3d 660 (7th Cir. 2010).

## 11.6 The Military Lending Act

In 2006 Congress passed the Military Lending Act (MLA) as an amendment to a Department of Defense authorization bill.[64] The MLA was passed in response to numerous reports documenting predatory lending around military bases targeting servicemembers. The MLA imposes a 36% interest rate cap on "consumer credit" to military servicemembers and their dependents.[65] Additionally, the MLA preempts inconsistent state or federal laws which do not provide greater protections to borrowers.[66]

The MLA effectively bans auto title lending. It does this in two ways. First, it imposes a 36% interest rate cap. Auto title lenders generally decline to do business unless they can charge at least a rate five to ten times higher. Second, the MLA simply bans closed-end loans with terms of 181 days or less that are secured by the title to a personal vehicle, unless the credit is for the purchase of that vehicle.[67]

Since purchase money loans are excluded from coverage, vehicle title lenders may attempt to structure their loans using a "leaseback" pretense to fit within the purchase money loan exemption. However, if the consumer previously owned the vehicle, it should be fairly easy to demonstrate that the loan is not a purchase money loan as contemplated by the exemption.[68]

Lenders may also attempt to evade the MLA by structuring the transaction as open-end credit, which the regulations also exclude from coverage.[69] If the transaction does not truly have the characteristics of open-end credit—for example, if repeat transactions are not in fact contemplated, or if repayment is due in a finite period of time—it may be possible to show that it is actually closed-end credit subject to the MLA.[70]

The MLA is also inapplicable to an auto title loan that has a term of more than 181 days.[71] If a title loan purports to have a term greater than 181 days, but substantially all the payments are due within less than 181 days—for example, if repayment of all but $10 is required within 60 days, with the remaining $10 due on the 182nd day—a court may be willing to look at the substance rather than the form of the transaction, and conclude that the MLA applies.[72]

In dealing with transactions structured to evade the MLA, it should also be remembered that the MLA does not override state laws that protect borrowers.[73] If the MLA does not govern a transaction, a state law may still apply and provide protections for the borrower.

Both the MLA and the applicable regulations are discussed in more detail at § 2.2.6, *supra.*

64 Sen. John Warner National Defense Authorization Act (Talent/Nelson Amendment), Pub. L. No. 109-364, § 670, 120 Stat. 2266 (2006) (codified at 10 U.S.C. § 987).

65 10 U.S.C. § 987(b); 32 C.F.R.§ 232.4(b).

66 10 U.S.C. § 987(d)(1); 32 C.F.R. § 232.7.

67 10 U.S.C. § 987(i)(6); 32 C.F.R. § 232.3(b)(2)(ii).

68 32 C.F.R. § 232.3(b)(2)(ii).

69 32 C.F.R. § 232.3(b).

70 *See* § 2.2.5.9, *supra.*

71 32 C.F.R. § 232.3(b)(1)(ii).

72 *See* § 3.9.1, *supra.*

73 10 U.S.C. § 987(d)(1).

# Chapter 12 Rent-to-Own

## 12.1 Introduction to Rent-to-Own

Rent-to-own (RTO) businesses are essentially appliance, electronics, and furniture retailers that arrange lease agreements rather than typical installment sales contracts for customers who cannot purchase goods with cash. These lease agreements contain several special features. First, the typical lease agreement contains a purchase option allowing the lessee to obtain title to the goods by making a nominal payment at the end of a stated period, such as eighteen months.[1] Second, the typical lease is short term, so that "rental payments" are due weekly or monthly. Third, the lease is "at will." In other words, the lease theoretically need not be renewed at the end of each weekly or monthly term.[2]

The RTO industry aims its marketing efforts at low-income consumers by advertising in minority media, on buses, and in public housing projects, and by suggesting it has many features attractive to low-income consumers: quick delivery, weekly payments, no or small down payments, quick repair service, no credit checks, and no harm to one's credit rating if the transaction is canceled.[3]

As will be discussed in greater detail throughout this chapter, the chief problem with RTO contracts is that these sales are made at astronomic and undisclosed effective interest rates. Under most RTO contracts, the customer will pay between $1,000 and $2,400 for a television, stereo, or other major appliance worth as little as $200 retail, if used, and seldom more than $600 retail, if new. This means that a low-income RTO customer may pay 1.5 to 12 times what a cash customer would pay in a traditional retail store for the same appliance.[4]

Over the past thirty years, the RTO industry has been maneuvering its products and contracts just out of range of federal and state consumer protection laws bolstered by industry friendly legislation. Practitioners in this area must pay close attention to RTO statutes in their state and to the governing contracts. This chapter provides the practitioner with an overview of the RTO industry, common practices, and tools to assist consumers harmed by those RTO practices.

## 12.2 Evolution of the RTO Industry

As of the end of 2010, the Association of Progressive Rental Organizations (APRO), the RTO trade association, reports that RTO is a $7.6 billion a year industry serving about 4.1 million customers per year.[5] Thus, the average RTO customer is spend-

---

1 In at least one state—North Carolina—the transaction is considered a sale if the last payment is less than 10% of the total of payments, therefore all the RTO contracts in that state require a payment of more 10% of the total of payments in order to transfer ownership. N.C. Gen. Stat. § 25A-2(b).

2 For detailed descriptions of a rent-to-own contracts, see Sight & Sound of Ohio, Inc. v. Wright, 36 B.R. 885 (S.D. Ohio 1983); *In re* Williams, 2007 WL 1875652 (Bankr. W.D. Ky. June 25, 2007); *In re* Puckett, 60 B.R. 223 (Bankr. M.D. Tenn. 1986), *aff'd*, 838 F.2d 470 (6th Cir. 1988); Miller v. Colortyme, Inc., 518 N.W.2d 544 (Minn. 1994).

It is theoretically possible to structure rent-to-own contracts in other ways, such as an initial non-terminable term of five months which becomes terminable month-to-month thereafter, or as a fixed term, non-terminable lease with an option to purchase.

3 The Association of Progressive Rental Organizations (APRO), the RTO trade association, publishes information on RTO at its website. *See* www.aprovision.org.

It reports that more than half of RTO customers (72%) have annual incomes under $36,000 and nearly all (96%) have incomes under $50,000; over 58% are under the age of forty-five; over 61% have a high school education or less; and about 84% are Caucasian. *See* www.rtohq.org/apro-rto-industry-overview.html.

The Federal Trade Commission conducted a survey of 532 RTO customers and found that 79% of those customers who used RTO in the last year had incomes under $40,000 (over the last five years, about 70% of these customers had incomes under $40,000). James M. Lacko, Signe-Mary McKernan & Manoj Hastak, Federal Trade Commission, Survey of Rent-to-Own Customers (Apr. 2000), *available at* www.ftc.gov/reports/index.shtm (the survey also reports on other customer characteristics, such as, age, sex, race/ethnicity, education, employment, marital status, homeownership, geographical distribution, among other things). *See also* Creola Johnson, *Welfare Reform and Asset Accumulation: First We Need a Bed and a Car*, 2000 Wis. L. Rev. 1221, 1254 (2000) (citing an industry survey done in 1994 that revealed that 31% of RTO customers were on some form of public assistance); Warren B. Rudman, Market Survey Results and Economic Analysis 14 (Feb. 1994) (report to the Board of Directors of Thorn EMI PLC concerning the operations of the Rent-A-Center Division of Thorn Americas Inc.; report found that 61% of the respondents surveyed in 1994 had personal earnings less than $20,000 and 29% earned less than $10,000.).

4 *But see* Michael H. Anderson & Raymond Jackson, *A Reconsideration of Rent-to-Own*, 35 J. Cons. Affairs 295 (2001) (arguing that the total cost, potential lost equity, and the APR do not provide a good measure of the true value to the consumer of a RTO transaction; instead, the benefits to the consumer should be measured by the value of delivery, set up, maintenance, repair, immediate product availability without a formal credit check and without a security deposit or down payment, payments by cash or check on a weekly or monthly basis, ability to secure insurance against damage or theft, and termination of the agreement at any time without further financial liability or damage to credit history).

5 www.rtohq.org/apro-rto-industry-overview.html.

ing about $1,854 per year or $155 a month on RTO merchandise.

| Year | Total RTO revenues (in billions) | Total RTO customers (in millions) | Average RTO customer payment |
|---|---|---|---|
| 2010 | $7.60 | 4.10 | $1,854 |
| 2009 | $7.00 | 4.10 | $1,707 |
| 2008 | $6.60 | 3.60 | $1,833 |
| 2007 | $6.30 | 3.20 | $1,967 |
| 2006 | $6.80 | 3.00 | $2,266 |
| 2005 | $6.70 | 2.80 | $2,393 |
| 2004 | $6.60 | 2.70 | $2,444 |
| 2003 | $6.20 | 2.70 | $2,296 |
| 2002 | $6.00 | 2.90 | $2,069 |
| 2001 | $5.60 | 2.90 | $1,913 |
| 2000 | $5.30 | 3.10 | $1,710 |
| 1999 | $5.00 | 3.10 | $1,613 |
| 1996 | $3.98 | 2.85 | $1,396 |
| 1994 | $3.85 | 2.73 | $1,410 |
| 1993 | $4.49 | 3.43 | $1,282 |
| 1991 | $3.57 | 2.91 | $1,226 |

Source: APRO

With the enactment of protective state laws[6] and the resolution of IRS disputes,[7] banks and Wall Street have recognized the tremendous profit potential of RTO. The industry has consolidated into a few dominant national companies.[8]

In an attempt to expand its customer base, some companies have expanded their product offerings from basic consumer commodities to high-end items, such as big-screen televisions and flashy oversize chrome auto wheels aimed at young urban drivers.[9]

Other RTO companies have attempted to fill the void left by the departure of traditional credit card companies from the subprime finance market. In 2011, Rent-A-Center established "kiosks" in Best Buy, Ashley furniture, Conn's, and other retailers.[10] Under the arrangement, consumers who did not meet the retailer's credit standards had the option to enter into an RTO agreement. The retailer would then sell the merchandise to the RTO company. In turn, the RTO company would mark up the item by about two to three times the item's cost and lease it to the consumer under its standard RTO agreement. However, less than a year after announcing the program, Best Buy pulled the kiosks from its stores.[11]

Despite RTO successes in state legislatures, there have been problems for the industry. Industry giant Rentway was one of the companies caught in the accounting fraud scandals at the beginning of the decade.[12] Customer satisfaction is low, and the image of the industry is mostly negative.[13]

## 12.3 The Lease vs. Installment Contract Debate

### 12.3.1 How RTO Contracts Are Structured and Marketed

A common method of restructuring a credit transaction is to transform it into a lease. This is a common commercial prac-

6 *See* § 12.3.3, *infra*.

7 One of the most significant financial advantages enjoyed by RTO dealers that is not available to retail firms is the ability to depreciate household goods as rental merchandise. Retail merchants offering identical households goods cannot depreciate their inventory. For a discussion of the importance of the depreciation issue for RTO dealers, see Susan Lorde Martin & Nancy White Huckins, *Consumer Advocates v. The Rent-to-Own Industry: Reaching a Reasonable Accommodation*, 34 Am. Bus. L.J. 385, 416 (1997); Laura Saunders, *Taxing Matters*, Forbes, Mar. 10, 1997, at 84.

The RTO industry and the IRS have disputed the speed with which dealers can depreciate their merchandise. Dealers have argued that they should be able to depreciate very quickly since, on average, nearly all merchandise is disposed of in two to three years. In 1996, the industry prevailed on this issue in ABC Rentals & San Antonio Inc. v. Comm'r, 86 F.3d 392 (10th Cir. 1996). The court permitted RTO dealers to use a much faster depreciation methodology than the IRS argued was allowable. However, this decision was undermined by a change in the Code added by § 1086 of the Taxpayer Relief Act of 1997 which allows RTO dealers the ability to depreciate their goods over three years if they have "qualified rent-to-own property." Pub. L. No. 105-34 (1997), *codified at* 26 U.S.C. § 168(g)(14).

The impact of this tax provision on rent-to-own operations and customers may be profound since under the statute dealers are only entitled to use the three-year depreciation schedule "if a substantial portion of the rent-to-own contracts terminate and the property is returned." 26 U.S.C. § 168(i)(14)(B).

This provision provides an even greater financial motivation for RTO dealers to immediately repossess goods rather than refinance the contract, permit the customer to reinstate the contract with payment of a late fee or otherwise negotiate an extension for late payment. Previously, many RTO dealers permitted the customer to retain the goods in their home while a new contract was substituted for the prior one. This can no longer be done because the Code requires that the property must be returned to the dealer.

8 Phillip M. Perry and Julie Sherrier, *2005 Economic Forecast*, Progressive Rentals (Nov.–Dec. 2004) (describing RTO industry as consisting of national chains and single store "Mom & Pop" outlets.).

9 Chris Woodyard, *Spinning Wheels Got to Go Round for Hip Divers*, USA Today, Jan. 24, 2005 (noting one consumer who was paying $60 per week, or a total of more than $3,000, for a set of "bling-bling" rims retailing for $1,560).

10 Karen Talley, *Best Buy May Offer Rent-to-Own Option*, MarketWatch, Aug. 22, 2011.

11 Karen Talley, Dow Jones Newswires, *Best Buy Ceases Rent-to-Own Program with Rent-A-Center*, Wall Street Journal, Apr. 30, 2012.

12 Charles Duhigg, *3 Rent-Way Executives Plead Guilty*, Washington Post, July 23, 2003.

13 A survey commissioned by APRO revealed that 40% of RTO customers were unhappy with their experience and 24% felt they had been treated with disrespect by the RTO employees. Among non-RTO customers, 55% had a negative image of the industry, down from 64% in 1997. Ed Winn, *The RTO Customer Survey See-Saw*, Progressive Rentals (May–June 2004). *See, e.g.*, Alice Hines, *Rent-to-Own Industry, Long Criticized for Preying on Military, Pledges to Find Jobs for Vets*, Huffington Post, Apr. 20, 2012; Anya Schiffrin, *Pay Now, Pay Later*, Mother Jones, May/June 2005; David Abel, *Yours, For a Price*, Boston Globe, Feb. 17, 2003, at B1; *NBC Nightly News, The Fleecing of America* (NBC television broadcast Feb. 25, 1998).

| | | 52 Weeks | | 78 Weeks | | 104 Weeks | |
|---|---|---|---|---|---|---|---|
| Amount Financed | Weekly Payment | Finance Charge | APR | Finance Charge | APR | Finance Charge | APR |
| 200 | $16 | $632 | 408% | $1,048 | 415% | $1,464 | 416% |
| | $18 | $736 | 462% | $1,204 | 467% | $1,672 | 468% |
| 300 | $16 | $532 | 254% | $ 948 | 272% | $1,364 | 276% |
| | $18 | $636 | 294% | $1,104 | 309% | $1,572 | 311% |
| 400 | $16 | $432 | 68% | $ 848 | 197% | $1,264 | 204% |
| | $18 | $536 | 201% | $1,004 | 226% | $1,472 | 231% |
| 500 | $16 | $332 | 111% | $ 748 | 148% | $1,164 | 159% |
| | $18 | $436 | 140% | $ 904 | 173% | $1,372 | 182% |
| | $20 | $540 | 168% | $1,060 | 197% | $1,580 | 204% |
| 600 | $16 | $232 | 68% | $ 648 | 113% | $1,064 | 128% |
| | $18 | $336 | 95% | $ 804 | 135% | $1,272 | 147% |
| | $20 | $440 | 121% | $ 960 | 156% | $1,480 | 167% |
| 700 | $18 | $236 | 60% | $ 704 | 106% | $1,172 | 122% |
| | $20 | $340 | 84% | $ 860 | 125% | $1,380 | 139% |
| | $22 | $444 | 107% | $1,016 | 144% | $1,588 | 156% |

tice, and a vast body of case law considers whether business transactions are secured credit sales or true leases.[14] Numerous decisions have recognized that supposed leases may in fact be credit sales especially when the lessee holds an option to purchase the property at the end of the lease term for nominal additional consideration.[15] For example "leases" of manufactured homes have been held to be credit sales in several cases.[16]

In a consumer context, retailers have few reasons to structure credit sales as leases except to attempt to avoid the disclosures, interest ceilings, and repossession limitations imposed by the Truth in Lending Act, state retail installment sales acts, and the Uniform Commercial Code, respectively.[17]

Many consumer advocates have argued that RTO leases are used to mask installment sales in order to avoid consumer protections. If an RTO lease is treated as an installment sale, the finance charge and interest rate or annual percentage rate (APR) can be calculated by using the retail cash value of the appliance as the principal and then factoring in the timing, amount, and number of payments. The following chart illustrates the APR computations, assuming no payments in arrears.[18]

14 *See* National Consumer Law Center, Repossessions §§ 2.1.5, 14.1.1–14.1.3 (7th ed. 2010 and Supp.) (discussing leases as secured sales under the U.C.C.). *See also* Annotation, 4 A.L.R.4th 85 (1981) ("sale" within scope of U.C.C. Article 2).

15 *See, e.g.*, Davis v. Colonial Sec. Corp, 541 F. Supp. 302 (E.D. Pa. 1982), *appeal dismissed*, 720 F.2d 661 (3d Cir. 1983) (house lease actually a TILA credit sale); Hill v. Bentco Leasing Inc., 708 S.W.2d 608 (Ark. 1986) (purported lease was usurious despite absence of purchase option; no residual value in property at end of "lease"); Garrison Motor Freight v. Hammons, 628 S.W.2d 567 (Ark. 1982) (lease disguised as credit sale; free services to credit buyers held element of principal); Bell v. Itek Leasing Corp., 555 S.W.2d 1 (Ark. 1977) (purported lease was usurious loan); Barco Auto Leasing Corp. v. House, 520 A.2d 162 (Conn. 1987) (lease actually a credit sale subject to RISFA; little discussion of factors, but rider to lease had required lessee to purchase car at end of lease term); Halco Fin. Servs., Inc. v. Foster, 770 S.W.2d 554 (Tenn. Ct. App. 1989) (sale-leaseback of personal property with purchase option was disguised loan subject to usury laws); Vela v. Elberts Mobile Homes Inc., 630 S.W.2d 434 (Tex. App. 1982) (manufactured home credit sale disguised as lease); Rouse v. Peoples Leasing Co., 638 P.2d 1245 (Wash. 1982) (motor vehicle leases actually loans; lessor received fixed profit and lessee assumed risks). *Cf.* Wight v. Agristor Leasing, 652 F. Supp. 1000 (D. Kan. 1987) (true lease); *In re* Pellegrino, 205 B.R. 479 (Bankr. E.D. Pa. 1997) (true lease; no evidence presented to show "body-dragging" or gross overcharging and parties treated contract as a lease not a sale); Goodtimes v. IFG Leasing Co., 788 P.2d 853 (Idaho 1990) (true lease); State *ex rel.* Celebrezze v. Telecomms., Inc. 601 N.E.2d 234 (Ohio Ct. Cl. 1990) (true lease); Baldwin v. Liberty Leasing Co., 2000 Tex. App. LEXIS 4097 (Tex. App. June 20, 2000) (true lease in a commercial case); Potomac Leasing v. El Paso Hous. Auth., 743 S.W.2d 712 (Tex. App. 1988) (no usury where pure lease with no claim made of a lease-purchase agreement). *See generally* National Consumer Law Center, Repossessions § 14.1.2.3 (7th ed. 2010 and Supp.); Annotation, 94 A.L.R.3d 640 (1979) (application of usury law to "leases"); *Equipment Lease As Usurious Loan*, 25 Proof of Facts 2d 521 (1981).

16 Gulf Homes, Inc. v. Gonzales, 676 P.2d 635 (Ariz. Ct. App. 1983), *aff'd in part, rev'd in part on other grounds*, 676 P.2d 628 (Ariz. 1984); Vela v. Elberts Mobile Homes Inc., 630 S.W.2d 434 (Tex. App. 1982).

17 *See* National Consumer Law Center, Truth in Lending (7th ed. 2010 and Supp.); National Consumer Law Center, Repossessions Ch. 14 (7th ed. 2010 and Supp.).

18 Payments in advance are called "annuity due" transactions, as contrasted with "ordinary annuities" as used in Truth in Lending's Regulation Z, app. J. For example, the top line of the chart shows different APRs if RTO payments are made at the beginning of each week: 52 weeks at $16 bears an APR of 445%, 78 weeks at $16 amounts to 451% APR, and 104 weeks yields 452%, because the time value is different. The entire chart would show greater APRs for payments in advance. Because RTO dealers usually demand payments at the beginning of each week, the astronomic APRs in

For example, a brand new big-screen conventional television sells for about $1,000 from a leading electronics retailer. Therefore, if an RTO customer leases that big screen television (worth $1,000) for $37 per week for 52 weeks,[19] the APR would be about 192%. However, if the customer leased a *used* big screen television (worth about $700 or less) for the same payment terms, the APR could be 275% or more. This is because the RTO customer is typically required to pay the same weekly payment for the used goods, as she would for new ones. The only difference is that the number of payments is reduced slightly for the used goods.[20]

Unlike traditional leases, most RTO transactions are structured so that, customers obtain ownership of durable goods over time through periodic payments. In a credit sale ownership is transferred at the beginning of the transaction, but the creditor retains an interest in the property to secure payment of the purchase price plus the finance charge. An RTO customer only obtains legal title to the goods after successful completion of all the terms of the contract, an expensive and difficult process for many of these customers. Most RTO customers enter into these transactions with the expectation of buying an appliance and are seldom interested by the rental aspect of the contract.[21] This attitude is encouraged by RTO dealers who emphasize the purchase option in their marketing even while they are minimizing its importance in the written contract. If a transaction is challenged in court, the RTO dealer will point to the rental provisions of the contract and claim that statutes which control traditional retail installment sales are irrelevant to RTO agreements.[22]

## *12.3.2 Legal Challenges Based on Treating RTO Contracts As Installment Sales*

### 12.3.2.1 Introduction

If RTO contracts are in fact installment sales, then a number of consumer protection statutes apply to them. This subsection reviews the litigation on these issues. However, the passage of industry-sponsored RTO statutes in almost all states has undermined this approach in most states.

### 12.3.2.2 Application of State Retail Installment Sales Acts

If RTO agreements are disguised credit sales, then state retail installment sales acts (RISAs)[23] should apply to them.[24] A number of decisions over the years have found RTO contracts to be subject to the interest rate ceilings and other requirements of state RISAs.[25] However, the industry-friendly RTO statutes

this chart are probably understated.

19 This was the weekly rental fee reported for a big screen television in Rent-A-Center v. Duron, 2004 WL 2403571 (Tex. App. Oct. 28, 2004).

20 The effective APR for used goods is much higher because the total of payments is only slightly decreased, while the amount financed—the cash price in an RTO transaction—is significantly decreased.

21 A telephone survey of RTO customers that was commissioned by APRO found that 90% of customers intended to own the product they were renting, but only 40% managed to keep the product. Ed Winn, *The RTO Customer Survey See-Saw*, Progressive Rentals, May–June 2004.

APRO claims on its website that less than one-quarter of its customers rent long enough to own the "rented" goods. *See* www.rtohq.org/apro-rto-industry-overview.html.

However, according to testimony by Rent-A-Center's experts in one case, 64% of that company's inventory was sold to its customers. Perez v. Rent-A-Center, Inc., 892 A.2d 1255 (N.J. 2006).

The Federal Trade Commission conducted a survey of 532 RTO customers and found that 70% of RTO merchandise was purchased by the customer. Furthermore, 90% of the merchandise on which customers had made substantial payments (of six months or more) was purchased. James M. Lacko, Signe-Mary McKernan & Manoj Hastak, Federal Trade Commission, Survey of Rent-to-Own Customers (Apr. 2000), *available at* http://www.ftc.gov/reports/index.shtm.

One conclusion to draw from this latter statistic is that if the RTO contract fails, this most often occurs within the first six months. *See also* Creola Johnson, *Welfare Reform and Asset Accumulation: First We Need a Bed and a Car*, 2000 Wis. L. Rev. 1221, 1259–1270 (2000) (arguing that most customers intend to purchase the items leased but fail to do so, citing an industry source; the author posits several reasons why low-income consumers had difficulty saving, or in utilizing alternatives to RTO.).

Discovery obtained in one class action against a major RTO company showed that 66% of one year's inventory was sold, and between 73% and 77% of the company's revenues came from sales, not rentals. *See* Ramp, *Renting-to-Own in the United States*, 24 Clearinghouse Rev. 797 (Dec. 1990).

All of these statistics can be reconciled by realizing that the majority of RTO customers enter into the transaction to purchase items, yet the majority of the transactions are unsuccessful. However, the customers persist, and enter into multiple transactions, accomplishing the original goal of ownership after multiple attempts.

22 *See* § 12.3.2.2, *infra.*

23 *See* Appx. C, *infra* (summarizing state RISAs).

24 Susan Lorde Martin & Nancy White Huckins, *Consumer Advocates v. The Rent-to-Own Industry: Reaching a Reasonable Accommodation*, 34 Am. Bus. L.J. 385, 389 (1997); James Nehf, *Effective Regulation of Rent-to-Own Contracts*, 42 Ohio St. L.J. 751, 758 (1991); Scott J. Burnham, *The Regulation of Rent-to-Own Transactions*, 3 Loy. Consumer L. Rep. 40, 41 (1991); David L. Ramp, *Renting to Own in the U.S.*, 24 Clearinghouse Rev. 797 (1990); Karen F. Meenan, Note, *The Applicability of the Federal Truth in Lending Act to Rental Purchase Contracts*, Cornell L. Rev. 118, 132–133 (1980).

25 *See, e.g.,* Burney v. Thorn Americas, Inc., 944 F. Supp. 762 (D. Minn. 1996) (measure of damages is the difference between the finance charge and a 5% interest rate; finance charge includes everything except the retail price); Fogie v. Rent-A-Center, Inc., 1995 WL 649575 (D. Minn. Sept. 28, 1995) (RTO contracts are credit sales for all purposes, and are subject to general contract usury ceiling), *aff'd sub nom.* Fogie v. Thorn Americas, Inc., 95 F.3d 645 (8th Cir. 1996), *subsequent appeal on different grounds*, 190 F.3d 889 (8th Cir. 1999) (RICO claim dismissed); *In re* Rose, 94 B.R. 103 (Bankr. S.D. Ohio 1988); Murphy v. McNamara, 416 A.2d 170 (Conn. Super. Ct. 1979); Miller v. Colortyme, Inc., 518 N.W.2d 544 (Minn. 1994); Starks v. Rent-A-Center, Clearinghouse No. 45,215 (Minn. Dist. Ct. 1990); Robinson v. Thorn Americas, Inc., #L-003697-94 (N.J. Super. Ct. Dec. 19, 1997), *available on the companion website to this treatise*; Green v. Continental Rentals, Clearinghouse No. 50,403 (N.J. Super. Ct. Law Div., Passaic Cty. Mar. 25, 1994); Commonwealth of Pennsylvania v. Riverview

that most states have adopted exclude RTO transactions from the state RISA.[26]

Three states—New Jersey,[27] Minnesota,[28] and Wisconsin[29]—are exceptions and continue to apply their RISAs to RTO transactions. Most recently, the Supreme Court of New Jersey affirmed that rent-to-own contracts as structured were closer to sales and violated that state's Retail Installment Sales Act.[30] However, RTO dealers are likely to attempt to avoid these decisions by structuring the payment schedule or other features of their RTO contracts to disguise their nature.

Leasing, Inc., Clearinghouse No. 50,401, No. 325 M.D. 1993 (Pa. Commw. Ct. Aug. 5, 1994); Chandler v. Riverview Leasing, Inc., Clearinghouse No. 40,628 (Pa. C.P. Northampton Cty. May 15, 1986); State v. Rentavision Corp. of Am., Clearinghouse No. 35,731 (Tenn. Chanc. Ct. 1983); LeBakken Rent-to-Own v. Warnell, 589 N.W.2d 425 (Wis. Ct. App. 1998); Rent-A-Center, Inc. v. Hall, 510 N.W.2d 789 (Wis. Ct. App. 1993); Palacios v. ABC TV & Stereo Retail, 365 N.W.2d 882 (Wis. Ct. App. 1985). *See also* Remco Enters., Inc. v. Houston, 677 P.2d 567 (Kan. Ct. App. 1984) (RTO contract not unconscionable); Anoushian v. Rent-Rite, 2002 WL 1023438 (Pa. Commw. Ct. May 10, 2002) (Pennsylvania Retail Installment Sales Act, not RTO statute, governed lease agreement with option to purchase) (*Anoushian* was legislatively overruled in 2003, see KFJ Enters., Ltd. Liab. Co. v. Rembert (*In re* Rembert), 293 B.R. 664 (Bankr. M.D. Pa. 2003), and abrogated by Griffin v. Rent-A-Center, 843 A.2d 393 (Pa. Super. Ct. 2004) (2003 amendments were a clarification, which the court applied retroactively)). *But see* Givens v. Rent-A-Center, Inc., 720 F. Supp. 160 (S.D. Ala. 1988), *aff'd mem.*, 885 F.2d 879 (11th Cir. 1989) (rental agreement not credit sale under Alabama Consumer Fin. Act); State v. Action TV Rentals, Inc., 467 A.2d 1000 (Md. 1983); Hawkes Television Inc. v. Maine Bureau of Consumer Credit Prot., 462 A.2d 1167 (Me. 1983).

26 *See* § 12.3.3, *infra*.

27 The New Jersey cases successfully challenging RTO practices include: Perez v. Rent-A-Center, Inc., 892 A.2d 1255 (N.J. 2006); Robinson v. Thorn Americas, Inc., #L-003697-94 (N.J. Super. Ct. Dec. 19, 1997), *available on the companion website to this treatise* (after plaintiffs won summary judgment on the merits, the damage portion of the case (and two other related suits) was settled for almost $60 million); Green v. Continental Rentals, 678 A.2d 759 (N.J. Super. Ct. Law. Div. 1994).

28 The Minnesota cases include Starks v. Rent-A-Center, Clearinghouse No. 45,215 (Minn. Dist. Ct. 1990), which involved a statute that included terminable leases within the definition of credit sale in certain circumstances. This statute was superseded by Minn. Stat. §§ 325F.82 to 325F.95, which in turn was interpreted in Miller v. Colortyme, Inc., 518 N.W.2d 544 (Minn. 1994) and Fogie v. Rent-A-Center, Inc., 1995 WL 649575 (D. Minn. 1995) (RTO contracts are credit sales for all purposes; thus are subject to general contract usury ceiling), *aff'd sub nom.* Fogie v. Thorn Americas, Inc., 95 F.3d 645 (8th Cir. 1996), *subsequent appeal on different grounds*, 190 F.3d 889 (8th Cir. 1999) (RICO claim dismissed).

29 The Wisconsin cases include Rent-A-Center, Inc. v. Hall, 510 N.W.2d 789 (Wis. Ct. App. 1993) (rent-to-own transaction covered by the Wisconsin Consumer Act, Wis. Stat. §§ 421.101 to 421.401 and violated that Act). In addition, the Wisconsin attorney general reached settlements with several RTO companies over their failure to make finance charge and rate disclosures. Press Release, Wisconsin Attorney General's Office, State Reaches Major Settlement with Rent-to-Own Company (Nov. 12, 2002) (noting this was the Wisconsin attorney general's fifth settlement with an RTO company over violations of the Wisconsin Consumer Act).

30 Perez v. Rent-A-Center, Inc., 892 A.2d 1255 (N.J. 2006).

#### 12.3.2.3 Truth in Lending Disclosure Requirements for Credit Sales

Several early decisions held that RTO transactions were credit sales under the Truth in Lending Act (TILA).[31] TILA defines "credit sale" to include a lease under which the lessee agrees to pay a sum equal to or exceeding the value of goods, and under which the lessee acquires an option to purchase for nominal consideration.[32] However, in 1981, Regulation Z, which implements TILA, was amended to exclude from its coverage leases that are "terminable without penalty or at any time by the customer."[33] Although there are arguments to the contrary,[34] courts have held that TILA's credit sale rules do not apply to the typical RTO contract, which is drafted to fall into this loophole.[35]

#### 12.3.2.4 UCC Article 9

If an RTO contract is treated as a credit sale, then the seller's interest in the goods is a security interest and is governed by the repossession rules of Article 9 of the Uniform Commercial Code (UCC).[36] If an RTO transactions is a security agreement rather than a true lease, then consumers who file bankruptcy also have greater rights under the Bankruptcy Code.[37]

Prior to 1987, the UCC focused on the parties' intent to differentiate between true leases and security agreements, thereby leaving room to show that the consumer intended to purchase the "rented" goods.[38] The UCC was amended in 1987 to base this determination on a series of objective factors that RTO leases are structured to avoid.[39] In addition, many state RTO statutes now explicitly exempt RTOs from Article 9.[40]

31 *See* Clark v. Rent-It Corp., 685 F.2d 245 (8th Cir. 1982); Green v. Continental Rentals, Clearinghouse No. 50,403 (N.J. Super. Ct. Law Div., Passaic County Mar. 25, 1994) (RTO agreement a credit sale subject to TILA). *But see* Smith v. ABC Rental Sys., 491 F. Supp. 127 (E.D. La. 1978), *aff'd*, 618 F.2d 397 (5th Cir. 1982). *See generally* Annotation, 59 A.L.R. Fed. 929 (1982) (leases as TILA credit sales).

32 15 U.S.C. § 1602(h) (formerly § 1602(g)).

33 *See* Reg. Z, 12 C.F.R. § 1026.2(a)(16) [§ 226.2(a)(16)].

34 *See* National Consumer Law Center Truth in Lending § 2.5.4 (7th ed. 2010 and Supp.).

35 *See, e.g.*, Ortiz v. Rental Mgmt., Inc., 65 F.3d 335 (3d Cir. 1995).

36 *See, e.g.*, Sight & Sound of Ohio, Inc. v. Wright, 36 B.R. 885 (S.D. Ohio 1983); Murphy v. McNamara, 416 A.2d 170 (Conn. Super. Ct. 1979) (RTO agreement was unconscionable sale); Broad v. Curtis Mathes Sales Co., Clearinghouse No. 36,376, CV-82-1254 (Me. Sup. Ct. Feb. 6, 1984). *See generally* National Consumer Law Center, Repossessions § 14.3 (7th ed. 2010 and Supp.).

37 *See, e.g.*, *In re* Puckett, 60 B.R. 223 (Bankr. M.D. Tenn. 1986), *aff'd*, 838 F.2d 470 (6th Cir. 1988). *See generally* National Consumer Law Center, Consumer Bankruptcy Law and Practice § 11.8 (9th ed. 2009 and Supp.).

38 *See* National Consumer Law Center, Repossessions § 14.1.2.2 (7th ed. 2010 and Supp.).

39 U.C.C. § 1-201(37) (revised again in 2001 and renumbered as U.C.C. § 1-203).

40 *See* National Consumer Law Center, Repossessions § 14.3.2.1 (7th ed. 2010 and Supp.).

### 12.3.3 Industry-Friendly RTO Legislation

While practitioners have challenged RTO transactions in court, the RTO industry aggressively (and successfully in most cases) lobbied state legislatures for a statutory exemption from consumer protection statutes, from annual percentage rate disclosure requirements, and from usury rate limitations.[41] The industry has also lobbied Congress for legislation that would eliminate the consumer protections that a few states have retained.[42]

In nearly every state there are now RTO statutes that were carefully drafted by the industry to insulate dealers from claims of consumer abuse.[43] Practitioners must acknowledge the current state of the law when looking for ways to seek redress for their clients' RTO problems.

The specific exemption of RTO transactions from other state and federal laws is the essential feature of these RTO statutes. All of the RTO laws provide that transactions that comply with their provisions are not "credit sales." Many statutes explicitly exempt RTOs from the state's home solicitation sales laws and from UCC Article 9 security interest definitions.[44] It is evident that the RTO statutes were intended to insulate dealers from consumer claims that the transactions are disguised credit sales.

## 12.4 Challenging Current Practices

### 12.4.1 Laws That Apply to RTO Transactions

Although most RTO transactions are designed to circumvent numerous consumer protection statutes, a number of claims are still available.[45] On the state level, most common law claims are still available, and Article 2A of the UCC specifically applies to consumer leases in most states.

In addition, RTO practices are almost always within the scope of a state UDAP statute. UDAP statutes can effectively address a wide range of abuses, including false or deceptive advertising; bait-and-switch practices; misrepresentation of the terms of the RTO contract; failure to disclose material facts about the transaction; padding the retail value of the goods being leased with unjustifiable and sometimes phantom costs of lease services; renting used appliances as new; delivering defective goods; failing to repair as promised; and utilizing misrepresentations, deceptions, or illegal tactics to repossess the goods.[46] A more detailed discussion of how UDAP statutes can provide an effective remedy against RTO abuses can be found in NCLC's *Unfair and Deceptive Acts and Practices*.[47]

Despite their weaknesses, all RTO statutes contain "consumer remedy" provisions but these must be read carefully. For example, Florida provides for statutory damages with attorney fees and costs. Dealers, however, are only liable if they were notified of the violation in writing and failed to correct it within thirty days.[48] Some states provide for a mandatory minimum recovery of, say, $100 which is not permitted if the case is filed as a class action.[49] Other states statutes do not include a minimum statutory award.

The subsections that follow describe some of the most common abuses by the RTO industry and suggest potential remedies for consumers.

---

41 *See* James Nehf, *Effective Regulation of Rent-to-Own Contracts*, 42 Ohio State L.J. 751, 821 (1991) (discussion of the RTO industry's legislative efforts between 1983–1991).

42 *See Margot Freeman Saunders, Testimony before the House Committee on Financial Services, Subcommittee on Financial Institutions and Consumer Credit, "Examining Rental Purchase Agreements and the Potential Role for Federal Regulation"* (July 26, 2011) *available at* financialservices.house.gov/UploadedFiles/072611saunders2.pdf.

43 Ala. Code §§ 8-25-1 to 8-25-6; Alaska Stat. §§ 45.35.010 to 45.35.099; Ariz. Rev. Stat. Ann. §§ 44-6801 to 44-6814; Ark. Code Ann. §§ 4-92-101 to 4-92-107; Cal. Civ. Code §§ 1812.620 to 1812.649 (West); Colo. Rev. Stat. §§ 5-10-101 to 5-10-1001; Conn. Gen. Stat. §§ 42-240 to 42-253; D.C. Code Mun. Regs., tit. 16 §§ 1000 to 1013; Del. Code Ann. tit. 6, §§ 7601 to 7616; Fla. Stat. §§ 559.9231 to 559.9241; Ga. Code Ann. §§ 10-1-680 to 10-1-689; Haw. Rev. Stat. §§ 481M-1 to 481M-18; Idaho Code Ann. §§ 28-36-101 to 28-36-111; 815 Ill. Comp. Stat. §§ 655/0.01 to 655/5; Ind. Code §§ 24-7-1-1 to 24-7-9-7; Iowa Code §§ 537.3601 to 537.3624; Kan. Stat. Ann. §§ 50-680 to 560-690; Ky. Rev. Stat. Ann. §§ 367.976 to 367.985 (West); La. Rev. Stat. Ann. §§ 9:3351 to 9:3362; Me. Rev. Stat. tit. 9-A, §§ 11-101 to 11-122; Md. Code Ann., Com. Law, §§ 12-1101 to 12-1112; Mass. Gen. Laws. ch. 93, §§ 90 to 93; Mich. Comp. Laws §§ 445.951 to 445.970; Miss. Code Ann. §§ 75-24-151 to 75-24-175; Mo. Rev. Stat. §§ 407.660 to 407.665; Mont. Code Ann. §§ 30-19-101 to 30-19-116; Neb. Rev. Stat. §§ 69-2101 to 69-2119; Nev. Rev. Stat. §§ 597.010 to 597.110; N.H. Rev. Stat. Ann. §§ 358-P:1 to 358-P:12; N.M. Stat. Ann. §§ 57-26-1 to 57-26-12; N.Y. Pers. Prop. Law §§ 500 to 507 (McKinney); N.D. Cent. Code §§ 47-15.1-01 to 47-15.1-08; Ohio Rev. Code Ann. §§ 1351.01 to 1351.09 (West); Okla. Stat. tit. 59, §§ 1950 to 1957; Or. Rev. Stat. §§ 646A.120 to 646A.134; 42 Pa. Cons. Stat. §§ 6901 to 6911; P.R. Laws Ann. tit. 10, §§ 2451 to 2466; R.I. Gen. Laws §§ 6-44-1 to 6-44-10; S.C. Code Ann. §§ 37-2-701 to 37-2-714; S.D. Codified Laws §§ 54-6A-1 to 54-6A-10; Tenn. Code Ann. §§ 47-18-601 to 47-18-614; Tex. Bus. & Com. Code Ann. ch. 92 (West); Utah Code Ann. §§ 15-8-1 to 15-8-12; Vt. Stat. Ann. tit. 9, §§ 41b to 50 (defining RTO transactions not to be retail installment sales, but requiring AG to adopt disclosure rules); 06 031 015 Vt. Code R. §§ 115.01 to 115.10 (requiring disclosure of effective APR); Va. Code Ann. §§ 59.1-207.17 to 59.1-207.27; Wash. Rev. Code §§ 63.19.010 to 63.19.901; W. Va. Code §§ 46B-1-1 to 46B-1-5; Wyo. Stat. Ann. §§ 40-19-101 to 40-19-120. *See also* Minn. Stat. §§ 325F.84 to 325F.97 (RTO statute; construed by Miller v. Colortyme, Inc., 518 N.W.2d 544 (Minn. 1994) not to have superseded state RISA).

44 *See, e.g., In re Mitchell*, 108 B.R. 166 (Bankr. S.D. Ohio 1989). *See generally* National Consumer Law Center, Repossessions § 14.3.2.1 (7th ed. 2010 and Supp.).

45 *See* National Consumer Law Center, Consumer Law Pleadings No. 2, Ch. 8 (Index Guide with Companion Website) (pleadings in RTO case).

46 For example, one court denied summary judgment to the RTO company and sent the case to the jury on the issue of whether the state's UDAP statute was violated due to an overly inflated cash price. Colon v. Rent-A-Center, Inc., 716 N.Y.S.2d 7 (N.Y. App. Div. 2000). *See also* Perez v. Rent-A-Center, Inc., 892 A.2d 1255 (N.J. 2006) (UDAP act applied to RTO contracts even though the retail installment sales act covered the transaction).

47 *See* National Consumer Law Center, Unfair and Deceptive Acts and Practices § 8.8 (7th ed. 2008 and Supp.).

48 Fla. Stat. § 559.9239.

49 *See, e.g.*, Ky. Rev. Stat. Ann. § 367.983(c) (West).

## 12.4.2 Pricing and Fees

### 12.4.2.1 Industry Practices

RTO dealers usually charge the same periodic payment whether the item is used or new, but adjust the total number of weekly or monthly payments required to achieve ownership of the used item. This means that the rental consumers are paying is the same for used goods as for new. For example, a low-end new stereo may be priced at $15.99 a week for seventy-eight weeks for a total of $1,247.22, while a low-end used stereo may also be $15.99 a week but only for sixty weeks, for a total of $959.40. A consumer who does not succeed in making all the payments to acquire ownership of the item ends up paying a new-goods rental amount for lower-value used goods. The result is that the unsuccessful consumers pay far more than the rental value of used goods.

Another common industry practice is to set the cash price (the price at which the dealer would offer the property for cash on the date of the rent-to-own agreement) as a percentage of the total RTO price. This percentage varies, but typically the cash price is an amount equal to 55–60% of the total rent-to-own price, although it may be as low as 30% of the total RTO price.[50] Some states require disclosure of the balance of the total rent-to-own price less the cash price as the "cost of lease services."[51] Using the example set forth above, the cash price for the stereo might be set as 60% of $1,247.22 or $748.33. The cost of lease services would be $498.88, 40% of $1,247.22.

### 12.4.2.2 Unconscionability and Unfairness

An early RTO decision held that a RTO contract was unconscionable, in violation of the Uniform Commercial Code and the state UDAP statute, because of the grossly excessive price and the consumer's lack of bargaining power.[52] The argument centered around the idea that the padding in the total rent-to-own price above the value of the goods themselves constituted interest and, was thus, unconscionable. For example, if an RTO customer leases a new 27-inch color television (worth $300) for $16 per week for fifty-two weeks, the customer would pay a total of $832. The APR would be about 254%, arguably unconscionable.

Traditionally, common law unconscionability claims could only be raised defensively.[53] Since all RTO leases are terminable and because RTO dealers repossess and re-sell the goods (and do not sue to collect any unpaid "rent"), consumers rarely find themselves in a defensive posture. However, a number of state UDAP statutes prohibit unconscionable practices.[54] In addition, in those states that have adopted Article 2A of the UCC governing leases,[55] practitioners can seek affirmative relief from an unconscionable RTO transaction under UCC § 2A-108.[56]

It is important to note that many state UDAP statutes prohibit "unfair" practices. Arguably, the notion of unfairness is broader than that of unconscionability since unconscionability implies "shocking the conscience of the court." Given the unjustified overpricing in RTO transactions, as discussed above, raising claims based on unfairness under the state UDAP statute may succeed where unconscionability may not.

An argument that the transaction is unconscionable must include an analysis of whether the cash price is excessive in relation to the actual cost to purchase the item in a retail store and whether the remainder of the total RTO price is justifiable. The industry has claimed that the difference between the value of the goods and the total rent-to-own price consists of the "cost of lease services." When the industry raises this argument, however, it has been required to justify the cost of providing these services and, even more intangibly, the dollar value of these services to the customer.[57]

Most RTO contracts in the United States disclose the cost of lease services as a single, undifferentiated number, if it is disclosed at all. Dealers argue that there are many components to the cost of lease services, most notably the right to return the goods and the servicing of merchandise. Because the RTO contract does not itemize these charges, dealers are compelled to justify these charges after the fact. Dealers and the experts they hire have used many approaches to try and justify these charges. In several cases, these arguments have not been accepted by the courts.[58]

---

50 California requires the RTO company to establish its costs for each item of personal property and sets maximum cash prices for the first and subsequent rental of 1.65 times (or 65% higher than) the cost of computer systems and appliances, 1.7 times (or 70% higher than) the cost for electronic sets, 1.9 times (or 90% higher than) the cost for automotive accessories, furniture, jewelry, and musical instruments, and 1.65 times (or 65% higher than) the cost for all other items. Cal. Civ. Code § 1812.644(b)–(e) (West). The maximum total of payments may not exceed 2.25 times the maximum cash price for the first rental. These figures are higher than the general markup used by the industry in the past.

51 *See, e.g.*, Ga. Code Ann. § 10-1-682(a)(13); Minn. Stat. § 325F.86(c); 42 Pa. Cons. Stat. § 6903(a)(12); W. Va. Code § 46B-3-7 (requiring disclosure of "rent-to-own charge," defined at § 46B-1-5(19)).

52 Murphy v. McNamara, 416 A.2d 170 (Conn. Super. Ct. 1979).

53 *See* § 2.4.7, *supra*.

54 *See* National Consumer Law Center, Unfair and Deceptive Acts and Practices § 4.4 (7th ed. 2008 and Supp.).

55 At least forty-five states and the District of Columbia have adopted some form of Article 2A. *See* National Consumer Law Center, Consumer Warranty Law § 21.2.1 (4th ed. 2010 and Supp.).

56 *Id.* § 18.4. Further, virtually none of the RTO statutes contain a specific exemption from Article 2A coverage.

57 Fogie v. Rent-A-Center, Inc., 1995 WL 649575 (D. Minn. 1995) (noting that the cost of lease services was disclosed as one charge; the lack of itemization of the services allegedly provided to customers made it impossible to find that the services were bona fide and/or reasonable), *aff'd sub nom.* Fogie v. Thorn Americas, Inc., 95 F.3d 645 (8th Cir. 1996), *subsequent appeal on different grounds*, 190 F.3d 889 (8th Cir. 1999) (RICO claim dismissed); Miller v. Colortyme, Inc., 518 N.W.2d 544 (Minn. 1994); Robinson v. Thorn Americas, Inc., #L-003697-94 (N.J. Super. Ct. Dec. 19, 1997), *available on the companion website to this treatise*.

58 Fogie v. Rent-A-Center, Inc., 1995 WL 649575 (D. Minn. 1995), *aff'd sub nom.* Fogie v. Thorn Americas, Inc., 95 F.3d 645 (8th Cir. 1996) (in the district court noting that the cost of lease services was

RTO dealers have argued that the interest rate implicit in rent-to-own transactions is very low or non-existent. This assertion depends upon attaching high values for services and costs.[59] RTO dealers also claim an extraordinary cost for providing terminability. This assertion is unjustified because RTO dealers frequently receive more money for the same goods after repossession than they would have received had the first customer been able to pay in full.[60] RTO dealer experts have also asserted that terminability is extraordinarily valuable to the customer. The industry has funded a number of market surveys in an attempt to justify this claim.[61] These surveys are highly questionable.[62] There is no support in any of the industry surveys to suggest that people understand that nearly 40% of the RTO payment is being charged for the right to terminate the contract.

Finally, charges added into the cost of lease services for delivery and maintenance are problematic because many dealers advertise these charges as "free." Challenging the cost of lease services added to the already arbitrary method by which the RTO cash price is determined (i.e., a percentage of the total RTO cost) can significantly increase the likelihood of success of an unconscionability claim even in the current deregulated climate.

---

disclosed as one charge; the lack of itemization of the services allegedly provided making it impossible to find that the services were bona fide and/or reasonable), *subsequent appeal on different grounds*, 190 F.3d 889 (8th Cir. 1999) (RICO claim dismissed); Miller v. Colortyme, Inc., 518 N.W.2d 544 (Minn. 1994); Robinson v. Thorn Americas, Inc., #L-003697-94 (N.J. Super. Ct. Dec. 19, 1997), *available on the companion website to this treatise*; Rent-A-Center, Inc. v. Hall, 510 N.W.2d 789 (Wis. Ct. App. 1993). *Cf.* Lessard v. Rent-A-Center East, Inc., 250 F.R.D. 103 (D. Conn. 2008) (certifying class and approving settlement in case challenging, among other things, the overstatement of the cost of lease services).

59 For a lengthy discussion of the impact of the cost of lease services on the interest rate, see Michael Walden, *The Economics of Rent-to-Own Contracts*, 24 J. of Consumer of Affairs No. 2, at 326 (1990). Professor Walden developed an economical model to determine implicit interest rates in RTO transactions. According to Walden, previous attempts treated RTO transactions as purchases, a shortcoming which created uncertainty in results and left allegations of high interest rates open to attack. Using industry estimates, Walden builds four cost factors into his calculations in order to address the specificity of the RTO transactions: the cost of depreciation; the cost of maintenance and repair; the cost of servicing the RTO contract (which includes collecting and processing payments); and opportunity cost. *Id.* at 327.

In most cases, Professor Walden's calculations yield lower implied interest rates than those that treated RTO transactions as sales. Implied interest on a twenty-inch television, for example, was 71.5% calculated as a sale; calculated according to Walden's model, that rate drops to 60%. Overall, implicit interest rates in Walden's empirical study ranged from about 33% to 125%, with the lion's share above 60%. *Id.* at 330–331. Interestingly, Walden was able to account for some of that variation based on demographics, concluding that implied interest rates were inversely proportional to average income in the tract where the RTO dealer was located. *Id.* 334–335. This may support a claim of discrimination under the Equal Credit Opportunity Act if the census tracts with the lowest incomes served by the dealer also include large numbers of minority customers. *See* National Consumer Law Center, Credit Discrimination (5th ed. 2009 and Supp.).

Although Walden's model improves previous calculations of interest for RTO transactions—and makes allegations of usurious rates more defensible—some aspects of his paper pose problems. First, Walden uses industry estimates for costs and keep rates that are disputed both inside and outside the industry. (The keep rate is the ratio of number of contracts that result in a purchase compared to the number of contracts that do not result in a sale.) As Walden notes, it is likely that industry estimates would bias interest rates downward by overestimating dealer costs. Second, although Walden finds significant variation in interest rates among different products, his study does not include all of the kinds of products rented by typical RTO dealers. Furniture, which may be the product class with the highest interest rates, is conspicuously absent in the study. Third, Walden does not consider the value of terminability, the customer's right to end the RTO agreement at any time. If terminability were included, his interest rates might have to be adjusted downward. But recent attempts at calculating this intangible have been inconclusive, and in many cases, amount to little more than an attempt on the part of the industry to disguise interest. Finally, Walden does not balance out RTO dealers' depreciation costs with the enormous tax shields, to which they are now entitled.

60 Michael Walden, *The Economics of Rent-to-Own Contracts*, 24 J. of Consumer of Affairs No. 2, at 415 (1990). *But see* Michael H. Anderson & Raymond Jackson, *A Reconsideration of Rent-to-Own*, 35 J. Cons. Affairs 295 (2001) (challenging Walden's assessment).

61 *See, e.g.*, Warren B. Rudman, Market Survey Results and Economic Analysis 14 (Feb. 1994) (report to the Board of Directors of Thorn EMI PLC concerning the operations of the Rent-A-Center Division of Thorn Americas Inc.).

62 For example, a large CPA firm compared the cost of short term and long-term rentals, asserting that the difference between the two prices represented the value of terminability. Among the items surveyed were sports cars and construction equipment. Short term and long-term rental prices were significantly different for these items, whereas short and long-term rates for rentals of household goods did not show a wide price spread. The CPA firm averaged the difference of the total price paid for both types of rentals (short and long) for all items, including sports cars and construction equipment, to justify a very high price for terminability for RTO. *See* Coopers & Lybrand Study, *available on the companion website to this treatise* (performed in connection with litigation in Burney v. Thorn Americas, Inc.).

This study is problematic for a variety of reasons: First, the markets chosen for comparisons are not comparable. Some of the comparisons include high-end automobiles, and most of them include office equipment, which has a higher rate of obsolescence than the majority of the products (furniture, appliances) offered by an RTO dealer. Higher obsolescence means higher terminability values. No market this second account firm considered is parallel to the RTO furniture market, where both maintenance and obsolescence are low. Second, the analysis only considers value to the consumer, not cost to the service provider; yet the accountant did not survey any customers to find out how much they value a particular service. Since the services are advertised as "included," consumers have no opportunity to evaluate the costs of these services or the terminability provision in order to comparison shop. Finally, many of these values (services or terminability) vary from item to item, yet the only differentiation provided for in this instance was between small and large items in delivery. The analysis does not take into account customers who do not use the delivery service or customers whose merchandise has low obsolescence rates or low maintenance costs.

#### 12.4.2.3 State Price Controls

Five states—California, Hawaii, Maine, New York, and West Virginia—have enacted legislation that fixes *both* the cash price and the total price for RTO transactions.[63] In these states, the maximum cash price that a RTO dealer can charge is fixed as a multiplier of the wholesale cost of the item. With the exception of Hawaii, the specific multiplier varies by the product category (e.g., appliances, electronics, computers, furniture, jewelry, etc.). The total rental price, in those states, is set as a multiplier of the cash price.

Several other states also have a cap on the total price in relationship to the cash price; however, those statutes do not limit the "cash price."[64] Therefore, RTO dealers in those states are able to set the cash price at a much higher amount than other retail stores would charge for the same item.

Some RTO statutes prohibit certain types of fees. For example, Connecticut prohibits fees for early termination or return of the property; fees for pick-up of the rental property; any additional payment for ownership; and application or processing fees.[65] It also caps late charges.[66] Pennsylvania caps late fees and prohibits fees for returning the rental property or terminating the agreement.[67] When addressing fees that the dealer imposed, advocates should check their state RTO statute carefully to determine if it places any restrictions on the amount of fees or the circumstances in which they can be imposed.

#### 12.4.2.4 Liability Damage Waivers

A widespread abuse involves the inclusion of so-called "optional fees," such as liability damage waivers (LDW). LDW programs purport to relieve customers of any further responsibility for the fair market value of the property if the property is stolen or destroyed by certain specified acts.

The value of LDW is highly questionable.[68] RTO dealers rarely if ever sue customers. They expect their customers to be judgment proof. Further, many RTO dealers report that 95% or more of contracts include so called "optional" fees. In fact, it appears that the fee in many cases is not truly optional but mandatory. RTO contracts are frequently prepared at the store and taken to the customer's home with the goods. The contract may have the liability damage waiver fee already added to the rental rate. If the customer objects to the fee, the delivery person may state that the contract will have to be rewritten and threatens that the goods cannot delivered. Faced with this alternative the customer may elect to sign the contract with the optional fee included.

RTO companies argue that LDW is not insurance because the plan does not offer to replace the lost property. This fact may not be dispositive of whether this product is insurance. The analysis depends upon state insurance law. Generally, a contract for insurance is created where there is a risk of loss to which one party is subject based on contingent or future events and the contract shifts that risk to another.[69] To the extent that the purchase of LDW shifts the risk of loss to another party in the event of theft or destruction of the property in certain circumstances, it certainly looks and smells like insurance. If so, claims of coercion in the sale of LDW can be attacked in the same ways that allegations of coercion in the sale of credit insurance are addressed. Causes of action could include usury, UDAP, fraud, and misrepresentation.[70] These issues are discussed in detail at § 8.5, *infra*. Further, if the product is insurance, practitioners should determine if the "insurer" complied with the state insurance code in all respects.[71]

### 12.4.3 Disclosures

#### 12.4.3.1 Consumer Leasing Act

The Consumer Leasing Act (CLA) is one of five "parts" of the Truth in Lending Act,[72] which in turn is the first of six "subchapters" of the Consumer Credit Protection Act.[73] The CLA and Regulation M specify approximately thirty terms that must be disclosed to lessees, and require that charges on default or early termination be reasonable. Failure to comply with any disclosure requirement or the reasonableness requirement can lead to a statutory damages award plus actual damages and

63 Civ. Code § 1812.644 (West); Haw. Rev. Stat. Ann. §§ 481M-1, 481M-5; Me. Rev. Stat. tit. 9-A, § 11-105; N.Y. Pers. Prop. Law § 503; W. Va. Code R. § 142-22-3.

64 Conn. Gen. Stat. Ann. § 42-240; Iowa Code §§ 537.3601–537.3624; Mich. Comp. Laws §§ 445.951-445.970; Ohio Rev. Code Ann. §§ 1351.01–1351.09 (West); 42 Pa. Cons. Stat. §§ 6901–6911; S.C. Code Ann. §§ 37-2-701–37-2-714.

65 Conn. Gen. Stat. § 42-243.

66 *Id.*

67 42 Pa. Cons. Stat. § 6904.

68 *See* James Nehf, *Effective Regulation of Rent-to-Own Contract*, 42 Ohio St. L.J. 751, 824 (1991) (detailed discussion of LDW and other miscellaneous charges such as processing fees and reinstatement fees; recognizing that these miscellaneous charges can present some of the most offensive aspects of RTO contracts because even a capable customer who has read the contract will have difficulty understanding these fees).

69 *See, e.g.*, Hertz Corp. v. Home Ins. Co., 18 Cal. Rptr. 267 (Cal. Ct. App. 1993) (compiling cases regarding LDW in the car rental context); Norwest Corp. v. State Dep't of Ins., 571 N.W.2d 628 (Neb. 1997) (finding title product to be insurance); Lawyers Title Ins. Corp. v. Norwest Corp., 493 S.E.2d 114 (Va. 1997) (finding title product not to be insurance).

70 *See* Ed Winn, *Risk of Option Fees*, Progressive Rentals 14 (Dec. 1996/Jan. 1997). *But see* South Carolina Dep't of Consumer Affairs v. Rent-A-Center, Inc., 547 S.E.2d 881 (S.C. Ct. App. 2001) (state RTO law does not expressly limit allowable fees to those included in the statute; therefore, LDW is a permissible charge; no allegation that the fee was unconscionable).

71 *See, e.g.*, Norwest Corp. v. State Dep't of Ins., 571 N.W.2d 628 (Neb. 1997) (affirming issuance of issued a cease and desist order by Nebraska Department of Insurance, finding that Norwest had engaged in the unauthorized business of insurance).

72 Part A is General Provisions; Part B is Credit Transactions; Part C is Credit Advertising; Part D is Credit Billing; and Part E is Consumer Leases.

73 Truth in Lending, Restrictions on Garnishment, Fair Credit Reporting Act, Equal Credit Opportunity Act, the Fair Debt Collection Practices Act, and Electronic Fund Transfers.

attorney fees. There are also a number of CLA lease advertising requirements, with private remedies if the consumer is damaged.

However, the CLA only applies to leases greater than four months in duration.[74] The CLA does not apply to a lease that is terminable without penalty during its first four months.[75] Similarly, the CLA does not apply to a four-month lease with an option to extend, if there is no penalty for termination at the end of four months. The CFPB's board's official commentary to Regulation M, states that a three-month lease, extended on a month-to-month basis, is not covered by the CLA, because the federal act only applies to leases with a term of "more than four months."[76] In other words, the CLA does not apply to week-to-week, or month-to-month, agreements, even though such consumers have the right (but not the obligation) to extend such agreements to four months or more. The CLA does apply if there is a penalty for canceling in the first four months.[77] A majority of courts have held that the CLA does not apply to RTO leases because they are terminable at will without penalty.[78]

#### 12.4.3.2 State Laws

Although there are variations, nearly all RTO statutes require certain disclosures in the contract including: the number and timing of the payments necessary to acquire ownership of the property; a statement declaring that the consumer will not own the property until the consumer has made the total payment necessary to acquire ownership; the cash price of the property (most commonly defined as whatever price the lessor sets); and a statement as to whether the property is new or used.[79] Although many state statutes provide that these disclosures must be made clearly and conspicuously, none require that the information be given on a separate document or separately segregated. The mandated disclosures, therefore, often appear scattered throughout the contract.

Some states mandate in-store price tag disclosures.[80] Vermont is unique in requiring a disclosure of the effective APR.[81]

### 12.4.4 *Loss of Equity*

In the typical RTO transaction, a consumer does not obtain any ownership rights in the item until he or she completes the RTO contract. Regardless of whether the customer has made payment for one week or for seventy weeks, the customer has the exact same ownership interest in the goods: none. The income levels of most RTO customers create ample opportunity for bumps in the customer's economic road that adversely affect the ability to consistently pay $19.99 a week to a RTO dealer over a period of eighteen to twenty-one months. As the industry statistics show, the ultimate purchase will frequently not occur until the customer has entered into two or three RTO contracts for the same or a similar item.[82]

Most state RTO statutes provide some reinstatement protections.[83] Reinstatement allows a consumer who has terminated or defaulted on an RTO contract to restore the contract and apply some of the past payments toward the purchase of the item. However, these statutes must be read very carefully. Most of these statutes only apply if the item is returned to the dealer and any fees or past due amounts are paid within a short time frame. Also, the consumer has a short amount of time (as little as twenty-one days) to implement this reinstatement right. California has the most generous reinstatement rights of any state. If the property is returned to the dealer within seven days for weekly contracts and ten days for monthly contracts, the consumer has one year to have payments made on previous contracts applied to new contracts for the same types of items.[84]

The reinstatement provisions are often touted to customers and legislators as significant consumer protections. Unfortunately, because of the strict requirements and the short time periods, few customers appear able to take advantage of them.

### 12.4.5 *Repossession*

RTO companies are known to use aggressive repossession tactics. Even if the state RTO statute exempts the transaction

74 15 U.S.C. § 1667(1).

75 15 U.S.C. § 1667(1).

76 Reg. M, Official Commentary § 1013.22(e)-2 [§ 213.22(e)-2].

77 Reg. M, Official Commentary § 1013.2(e)-2(ii) [§ 213.2(e)-2(ii)].

78 *See, e.g.*, Smith v. ABC Rental Sys. of New Orleans, Inc., 618 F.2d 397 (5th Cir. 1980), *aff'g* 491 F. Supp. 127 (E.D. La. 1978); Givens v. Rent-A-Center, Inc., 720 F. Supp. 160 (S.D. Ala. 1988), *aff'd without op.*, 885 F.2d 879 (11th Cir. 1989); Lemay v. Stroman's Inc., 510 F. Supp. 921 (E.D. Ark. 1981); Stewart v. Remco Enterp., 487 F. Supp. 361 (D. Neb. 1980); Dodson v. Remco Enterp., Inc., 504 F. Supp. 540 (E.D. Va. 1980); *In re* Hanley, 105 B.R. 458 (Bankr. C.D. Ill. 1989), *rev'd on other grounds*, 135 B.R. 311 (C.D. Ill. 1990). *Cf. In re* Hanley, 111 B.R. 709 (Bankr. C.D. Ill. 1990). *But see* Rentacolor, Inc., 103 F.T.C. 400 (1984) (ambiguous contract, lessor's advertising, and parties' intent indicate that lease is year to year). *See generally* National Consumer Law Center, Truth in Lending §§ 13.2.1, 13.2.3 (7th ed. 2010 and Supp.).

79 The disclosure of an effective interest rate is never required, although consumers tried to convince a court that it should be disclosed under New York law, despite its silence. Colon v. Rent-A-Center, Inc., 716 N.Y.S.2d 7 (N.Y. App. Div. 2000).

80 *See, e.g.*, W. Va. Code § 46B-3-7; 06 031 015 Vt. Code R. §§ 115.01 to 115.10.

81 Vt. Stat. Ann. tit. 9, §§ 41b to 50 (defining RTO transactions not to be retail installment sales, but requiring AG to adopt disclosure rules); 06 031 015 Vt. Code R. §§ 115.01 to 115.10 (requiring disclosure of effective APR). *See also* Thorn Americas, Inc. v. Vermont Attorney General (Vt. Super. Ct. Mar. 7, 1997), *available at* www.nclc.org/unreported (upholding the disclosure rule).

82 While the industry attempts to claim that the majority of these transactions are rentals, this is belied by the information provided to the IRS and in litigation. On average the RTO stores dispose of rental units within two years of their purchase of inventory and dispose of about 90% of all rental units with 3.5 years of purchase. In other words, everything is sold to the RTO customer base in two to three years. *See* ABC Rentals v. Internal Revenue Serv., 142 F.3d 1200, 1202–1203 (10th Cir. 1998).

83 § 12.3.3, *supra*.

84 Cal. Civ. Code § 1812 (West).

from UCC Article 9, abusive repossession tactics may be actionable under Article 2A of the Uniform Commercial Code or state tort law.

Article 2A of the Uniform Commercial Code, governing lease transactions, will generally be applicable to RTO contracts. It prohibits seizures that breach the peace.[85] Article 2A affords consumers a private cause of action for unconscionable conduct, including unconscionable conduct in collection of a claim under the contract[86]—its only private remedy. Consumers may recover "appropriate relief" and attorney fees in such cases.[87]

In a few states such as Michigan and Illinois, the RTO statute does not specifically exclude the transactions from Article 9. In those states, practitioners can raise Article 9 claims regarding wrongful repossession.

Tort claims such as assault, battery, conversion, and trespass are also available against dealers for wrongful or abusive repossession.[88] For example:

- In Washington state, the attorney general sued Rent-A-Center for engaging in unfair and deceptive collection practices. It included affidavits from customers who had been physically intimidated and from one customer whose door was kicked so hard by Rent-A-Center employees, that it had a large crack and footprint on it. In addition to UDAP claims, these customers would likely have claims assault and trespass.[89]
- In one case in Mississippi, two RTO employees broke into and entered a customer's home, and not only repossessed the RTO merchandise but also stole some of the customer's other possessions. The customer sued the RTO company and its employees. The appellate court held that a question for the jury existed to determine whether the employees were acting within the scope of their employment.[90]
- Another collection tactic used by RTO companies is filing criminal charges when the customer does not return RTO merchandise. In Georgia, one customer sued an RTO company for malicious prosecution and intentional infliction of emotional distress in obtaining an arrest warrant against him. The tort claims were permitted to go to trial but trial court then directed verdict for the RTO company on the basis that the company was not responsible for actions of employee.[91]

Many RTO dealers when faced with an incident of wrongful repossession will attempt to accuse the employee of unforeseen misconduct.[92] The general rule, however, is that care in repossession is a non-delegable duty, so a dealer cannot avoid liability for the acts of a repossession agent.[93] To hold the dealer liable for punitive damages, the consumer may have to show authorization, approval, or recklessness on the part of the dealer, or that the repossession agent was employed in a managerial capacity and was acting within the scope of employment.[94] While most RTO companies are going to have written policies that prohibit the use of force during a repossession, it should be possible in most cases to prove that the employer knew or should have known that force and threats of force are commonly used and approved during repossessions. Many RTO contracts have clauses which attempt to sanction entry into the customer's residence even when the customer is not home.[95] The use of such clauses should be construed as evidence that dealers know, anticipate and even sanction wrongful repossessions despite company manual language to the contrary.[96]

### *12.4.6 Discrimination*

There is some evidence that RTO dealers treat delinquent customers differently based on their race.[97] African-American

85 U.C.C. § 2A-525(3).

86 U.C.C. § 2A-108.

87 *See* National Consumer Law Center, Repossessions §§ 14.3.6.1–14.3.6.6 (7th ed. 2010 and Supp.) (discussing more fully limitations on the seizure of RTO goods).

88 *See, e.g.*, Botello v. Remco, No. 300,458 (Tex. Dist. Ct. 1985) (verdict for nearly $130,000 against a rental company for injuries to a customer which occurred during an attempted repossession).

89 Settlement Agreement, Rent-A-Center West, Inc. v. State of Washington et al., Case No. 08-2-32502-4 SEA (Superior Ct. State of Washington, King County, 2010). Court documents available at: www.atg.wa.gov/pressrelease.aspx?&id=23480.

90 Partridge v. Harvey, 805 So. 2d 668 (Miss. Ct. App. 2002).

91 Bragg v. Rent to Own, 570 S.E.2d 671 (Ga. Ct. App. 2002). *See also* State v. Cox, 2002 WL 1083897 (Ohio Ct. App. May 14, 2002).

92 *See, e.g.*, Partridge v. Harvey, 805 So. 2d 668 (Miss. Ct. App. 2002).

93 *See* National Consumer Law Center, Repossessions § 13.10.4 (7th ed. 2010 and Supp.).

94 *Id.* § 13.10.4.1.

95 The contract used by one large company contained the following provision: "Lessor shall have the right forthwith and without prior notice to enter any premises where said property is located and take immediate possession of said property without the necessity of any legal or judicial process and the Lessee shall be obligated to reimburse Lessor for any and all expenses related to any reasonable effort to repossess its property including reasonable attorneys fees." Similar contract language was in the RTO contract in Kimble v. Universal TV Rental, Inc., 417 N.E.2d 597 (Ohio Mun. Ct. 1980). Despite the contract language, the court rejected the argument that the repossession was in fact peaceful since the customer was not home at the time and concluded that the entry of locked premises constituted a trespass. Other courts have similarly found a dealer's attempt to use right of entry clauses in a contract as not a defense to wrongful repossession claims. In Fassitt v. United TV Rental, Inc., 297 So. 2d 283 (La. Ct. App. 1974), the RTO contract had similar reentry language. The dealer entered the house and repossessed a stereo when the only person in the house was the customer's eleven-year-old daughter. The court in *Fassitt* held that the reentry language was void as against public policy.

96 The industry often incorporates each individual store as a separate entity which may have no assets to pay a judgment. The parent corporation will deny responsibility for the misconduct of its subsidiaries. Practitioners faced with this situation should review their state law regarding piercing the corporate veil.

97 *See Testimony of David Ramp Regarding S.R. 1566, 1956, United States Senate Banking Committee*, Clearinghouse No. 49,965 (May 13, 1994). *See also* Walker v. Rent-A-Center, 2007 WL 3071806 (N.D. Ohio Oct. 19, 2007) (African American alleging inappropriate remarks by RTO employee during a conversation about the delinquent amount on one account; court dismissed the 42 U.S.C.

customers may experience more rapid repossession and may be less likely to have late fees waived than white customers.[98] The Equal Credit Opportunity Act (ECOA) arguably applies to RTO transactions.[99] If so, RTO dealers cannot treat customers differently post-default based on prohibited reasons.[100] Actual and punitive damages are available under the ECOA as well as attorney fees and costs.[101]

### 12.4.7 Arbitration

Large RTO companies responded to attempts to enforce state RTO statutes by placing mandatory arbitration clauses in their contracts, eliminating judicial review. Like other corporations, the main reason RTO dealers want to arbitrate disputes is that arbitration often dramatically reduces companies' exposure to large damage awards, even when the companies engage in widespread patterns of egregious wrongdoing. As discussed at § 7.4.3.7, *supra*, unconscionability is an extremely fertile issue for challenging one-sided or unfair arbitration clauses.

## 12.5 Other High-Cost Credit Disguised As RTOs

Because of lenient RTO statutes in almost all states, other high-cost creditors have attempted to disguise their loans as rent-to-own transactions. There is some indication that automobile dealers may structure car sales as rent-to-own deals. In this instance, the state RTO act and the motor vehicle retail installment sales act (MVRISA) should be carefully reviewed. States may not have specifically exempted RTO deals from their MVRISAs, which often cover leases. In those instances, it is likely that the MVRISA applies and was violated. These issues are discussed in greater detail at § 10.4.3, *supra*.

Auto title pawn lenders have also attempted to structure their loans as rent-to-own transactions. One court has rejected such an attempt, noting that a typical RTO business does not require the consumer to sell her property to the store at a significantly reduced price and then rent it back.[102] The court also noted that the lender had no inventory and did not offer goods generally available to RTO customers.

With the declining housing market and tougher lending standards, rent-to-own real estate schemes are also becoming more common. In these deals, renters may pay an up-front fee and then pay above market rent for a set period of time. A portion of the rent payments are to be applied towards an eventual down payment. However, like traditional RTO contracts, the renter does not build any equity nor have any ownership interest in the property. Therefore, if something goes wrong with the contract, the renter is has no rights to the property and loses any amount paid toward the down payment.[103] Rent-to-own real estate scams are discussed in greater detail in National Consumer Law Center, *Mortgage Lending* § 2.3.5.3 (2012).

§ 1981 claim because the plaintiff was not a party to the particular rental contract at issue in the conversation), *aff'd*, 301 Fed. Appx. 490 (6th Cir. 2008).

98 *Testimony of David Ramp Regarding S.R. 1566, 1956, United States Senate Banking Committee*, Clearinghouse No. 49,965 (May 13, 1994).

99 *See* National Consumer Law Center, Credit Discrimination § 2.2.2.2.5 (5th ed. 2009 and Supp.).

100 *Id.* § 9.2.4.

101 *Id.* at Ch. 11.

102 Aple Auto Cash Express, Inc. of Okla. v. State *ex rel.* Oklahoma Dep't of Consumer Credit, 78 P.3d 1231 (Okla. 2003).

103 *See, e.g., In re* Garcia, 2012 WL 37640 (Bankr. D. Idaho 2012).

# Chapter 13 "Sale" of Future Payment Streams

## 13.1 Introduction

This chapter discusses various schemes by which a lender provides a lump sum in exchange for an interest in a future stream of income, such as wages, pensions, government benefits, or structured settlements. Lenders may characterize these transactions as assignments, sales of income, advances, or similar names.[1] In some cases, these transactions are treated as valid sales or assignments, but they are often disguised high-cost loans. The annualized interest rates on these transactions have been reported to be as high as 280%.[2] For convenience, this chapter will generally refer to borrowers and lenders or creditors, rather than assignors and assignees or sellers and purchasers.

Section 13.2, infra, considers the legal implications of characterizing the "sale" as a loan and § 13.3 examines factors that lead courts to decide whether to treat the transaction as a loan. Sections 13.4–13.6 then examine the applicable law where cash payments are given to the consumer in exchange for three specific forms of future income streams:

- Military pensions and benefits;
- Settlements or judgments (factoring);
- Causes of actions (litigation financing).

These sections consider not only whether these transactions should be treated as loans, but also detail other federal and state limits on such transactions. Finally, a number of other restrictions on assignment of income are listed in § 13.7, infra.

1 *See, e.g.*, Structured Invs. Co. v. Price (*In re* Price), 313 B.R. 805 (Bankr. E.D. Ark. 2004) (lender claimed that loan was a "sale of income stream"); Stone Street Capital v. Granati (*In re* Granati), 270 B.R. 575 (Bankr. E.D. Va. 2001) (agreeing with lender that it had a nondischargeable property interest in the income stream; lender characterized its purchase of an income stream as an assignment not a loan), *aff'd*, 63 Fed. Appx. 741 (4th Cir. 2003); Decision Point, Inc. v. Reece & Nichols Realtor, Inc., 144 P.3d 706 (Kan. 2006) (discounted cash advance subject to percentage-based fees made to real estate agents in exchange for the assignments of their commissions were consumer loans and subject to the state's usury laws (the U.C.C.C.) and were not the purchase of the agents' accounts for a discount subject to the U.C.C.; the transactions included the assignment of wages in violation of the U.C.C.C. and were unenforceable); Rancman v. Interim Settlement Funding Corp., 2001 WL 1339487 (Ohio Ct. App. Oct. 31, 2001) (lender characterized payment collateralized by possible settlement a "contingent cash advance" not a loan; court disagreed), *aff'd on other grounds*, 789 N.E.2d 217 (Ohio 2003).

2 *See, e.g.*, Rancman v. Interim Settlement Funding Corp., 2001 WL 1339487 (Ohio Ct. App. Oct. 31, 2001), *aff'd on other grounds*, 789 N.E.2d 217 (Ohio 2003).

## 13.2 Legal Consequences of Characterizing the Transaction As a Loan or Assignment

If the transaction is a loan but was disguised as something else, the lender may be liable for violations of a state credit statute,[3] state licensing statutes[4] and the Truth in Lending Act.[5] A UDAP claim may also be available for a transaction which is not what it claims to be.[6] A business which makes disguised high-cost loans to consumers is likely to use uniform contracts and other consistent practices. Where the transaction should be treated as a loan, and thus violates state credit legislation, there is a potential for class-wide relief.[7]

Even if a transaction involving a future income stream is found to be a sale or assignment and not a loan, federal and state law apply a number of restrictions on the alienation of pension or other benefits and the "factoring" of structured settlements.[8]

Whether a transaction is characterized as a loan or as a sale or assignment may have a significant impact on the treatment of the obligation if the borrower files for bankruptcy. A transaction treated as a loan may be dischargeable in the bankruptcy. In contrast, where a true assignment or sale has taken place, the purchaser may have a property interest in the income stream that is unaffected by the bankruptcy; in other words, the obligation effectively cannot be discharged. Depending on the nature of the interest purportedly assigned, it may be only an equitable, rather than a legal assignment.[9] The former should arguably be dischargeable as a "claim," but bankruptcy courts

3 *See* § 2.3, *supra.*

4 *See* § 7.8.5, *supra.*

5 *See* § 2.2.2, *supra*; National Consumer Law Center, Truth in Lending (7th ed. 2010 and Supp.).

6 *See* § 2.4.1, *supra;* National Consumer Law Center, Unfair and Deceptive Acts and Practices (7th ed. 2008 and Supp.). *Cf.* Chroniak v. Golden Inv. Corp., 983 F.2d 1140 (1st Cir. 1993) (where statute required disclosure of rate of interest and set cap at agreed upon rate, specifying only dollar amount was both a violation of that statute and a UDAP violation).

7 *See* § 7.8.7, *supra.*

8 *See* §§ 13.4–13.7, *infra.*

9 *See, e.g.*, A. Unruh Chiropractic Clinic v. De Smet Ins. Co., 782 N.W.2d 367 (S.D. 2010) (discussing the difference between legal and equitable assignments in the context of a purported assignment of proceeds of a personal injury claim that had not yet commenced); W. Broad Chiropractic v. Am. Family Ins., 912 N.E.2d 1093, 1097–1098 (Ohio 2009).

have nevertheless held otherwise.[10]

## 13.3 Determining the True Nature of an Income Purchase Transaction

### *13.3.1 Substance, Not Form, Dictates*

The creditor's characterization of a transaction does not control whether it is a loan. Courts look behind the face of documents to ascertain the actual nature of the transaction; substance, not form dictates what law will govern.[11] As one judge put it:

> No disguise of language can avail for covering up usury. . . . The theory that a contract will be usurious or not, according to the kind of paper bag it is put up in, or according to the more or less ingenious phrases made use of in negotiating it, is altogether erroneous.[12]

This rule should apply not only when a court is considering the application of a traditional usury statute, but also when considering the application of other types of credit-related consumer protection statutes.[13]

---

10 *See In re Granati*, 270 B.R. 575, 586 (Bankr. E.D. Va. 2001), *aff'd*, 307 B.R. 827 (E.D. Va. 2002), *aff'd*, 63 Fed. Appx. 741 (4th Cir. 2003) (discussing why an equitable assignment should be dischargeable as a "claim," but nevertheless following other bankruptcy decisions that "seem to have uniformly treated equitable assignments of personal injury proceeds and structured settlements not as dischargeable claims but rather as property interests" and therefore not dischargeable).

11 *See, e.g.*, Easter v. Am. West Fin., 381 F.3d 948 (9th Cir. 2004); ECE Technologies, Inc. v. Cherrington Corp., 168 F.3d 201 (5th Cir. 1999) (commercial case applying substance over form doctrine); Aaron v. Mattikow, 146 F. Supp. 2d 263 (E.D.N.Y. 2001), *aff'd*, 2003 WL 1973353 (2d Cir. Apr. 22, 2003); Cashback Catalog Sales v. Price, 102 F. Supp. 2d 1375 (S.D. Ga. 2000) (declining to accept payday lender's attempt to disguise finance charges as the consumer's payment for catalog gift certificates); Hamilton v. York, 987 F. Supp. 953 (E.D. Ky. 1997) (alleged "deferred" presentment of a check really a loan); Khalif v. Khalif, 308 B.R. 614 (Bankr. N.D. Ga. 2004) (use of terms like "guarantor" and "investors" was contrivance); Brown v. Courtesy Consumer Discount Co., 134 B.R. 134 (Bankr. E.D. Pa. 1991) ("[b]ecause of the fertility of the minds of those who would devise schemes to circumvent remedial consumer protection laws, these laws must be interpreted with a flexibility necessary to preserve their spirit"; RISA disguised as direct loan in order to charge a higher rate in a "body-dragging" case); Carter v. Four Seasons Funding Corp., 97 S.W.3d 387, 395 (Ark. 2003); Luebbers v. Money Store, Inc., 40 S.W.3d 745 (Ark. 2001); McElroy v. Grisham, 810 S.W.2d 933 (Ark. 1991) (sale-repurchase); Smith v. Eisen, 245 S.W.3d 160 (Ark. Ct. App. 2006) (sale-repurchase agreement for home was loan); Ghirardo v. Antonioli, 883 P.2d 960 (Cal. 1994) (trier of fact must look to substance, not form; "sensitive to the ingenuity and creativity of those entrepreneurs willing to engage in legal brinkmanship to maximize profits, courts have scrutinized the form of seemingly innocuous commercial transactions to determine whether the substance amounts to a usurious arrangement"; but settlement notes executed by sophisticated real estate purchasers at issue were exempt credit sale, not loan or forbearance); Sheehy v. Franchise Tax Bd., 100 Cal. Rptr. 2d 760 (Cal Ct. App. 2000) (substance prevails over form, but delay in recovering taxes is neither a loan nor a forbearance); Hernandez v. Atlantic Fin., 164 Cal. Rptr. 279 (Cal Ct. App. 1980) (in determining the applicability of consumer protection laws to particular transactions, substance, not form, dictates the results); Browner v. District of Columbia, 549 A.2d 1107, 1114 (D.C. App. Ct. 1988) (sale-leaseback was "transparent sham which masked an unlawful loan"); Pinchuck v. Canzoneri, 920 So. 2d 713 (Fla. Dist. Ct. App. 2006); Oregrund Ltd. P'ship v. Sheive, 873 So. 2d 451, 457 (Fla. Dist. Ct. App. 2004); Low Cost Auto Pawn, Inc. v. Greco, 851 So. 2d 768 (Fla. Dist. Ct. App. 2003) (affirming judgment that vehicle marketing agreement was disguised title pawn loan); Party Yards, Inc. v. Templeton, 751 So. 2d 121 (Fla. Dist. Ct. App. 2000) (commissions in addition to interest may make loan usurious); Antonelli v. Neumann, 537 So. 2d 1027 (Fla. Dist. Ct. App. 1988); Bankwest, Inc. v. Oxendine, 598 S.E.2d 343 (Ga. Ct. App. 2004) (substance, not form, controls question whether payday lender or its rent-a-bank partner is the real lender); Williams v. Powell, 447 S.E.2d 45 (Ga. Ct. App. 1994); Jackson v. Commercial Credit Corp., 83 S.E.2d 76 (Ga. Ct. App. 1954); Bednar v. Provident Bank, 937 A.2d 210 (Md. 2007) (creditor cannot evade usury statutes by labeling a charge as something other than a prepayment penalty); Wilcox v. Moore, 93 N.W.2d 288 (Mich. 1958) ("court must look squarely at the real nature of the transaction, thus avoiding . . . the betrayal of justice by the cloak of words, the contrivances of form, or the paper tigers of the crafty."); Aple Auto Cash Express of Okla., Inc. v. State *ex rel.* Oklahoma Dep't of Consumer Credit, 78 P.3d 1231 (Okla. 2003) (sale-leaseback was loan); Income Tax Buyers, Inc. v. Hamm, 1992 WL 12092431 (S.C. Com. Pleas Jan. 14, 1992) (sale of right to receive tax refund was loan); Pacific E. Corp. v. Gulf Life Holding Co., 902 S.W.2d 946 (Tenn. Ct. App. 1995); Sturm v. Muens, 224 S.W.3d 758, 764 (Tex. App. 2007); Swank v. Sverdlin, 121 S.W.3d 785 (Tex. App. 2003); Bantuelle v. Williams, 667 S.W.2d 810 (Tex. App. 1983); Zachman v. Whirlpool Acceptance Corp., 841 P.2d 27 (Wash. 1992). *See also* Adams v. Plaza Fin. Co., 168 F.3d 932 (7th Cir. 1999) (must look to substance of purported "non-filing" insurance, not form, to determine whether the premium is a hidden finance charge under TILA); Edwards v. Your Credit, Inc., 148 F.3d 427 (5th Cir. 1998); McGhee v. Ark. State Bd. of Collection Agencies, 289 S.W.3d 18 (Ark. 2008) (whether a fee constitutes interest is determined by the facts, not by labels); Kjar v. Brimley, 497 P.2d 23, 25 (Utah 1972) (whether lease-purchase is in fact a sale, or is "a loan disguised as a sale to cover up a scheme to collect usurious interest" is a question of fact). *Cf.* First USA Mgmt., Inc. v. Esmond, 960 S.W.2d 625 (Tex. 1997) (substance rather than form controls, but arrangement here did not create usurious interest). *But cf.* Jones v. Wells Fargo Bank, 5 Cal. Rptr. 3d 835 (Cal. Ct. App. 2003) (no sham when defendant intended to and did fit loan into exception to general usury law); Bell v. Muller, 118 P.3d 405 (Wash. Ct. App. 2005) (transaction was retail installment transaction regardless of level of involvement by assignee financial institution; statute prevents court from looking beyond form of transaction). *See generally Creola Johnson, Payday Loans: Shrewd Business or Predatory Lending?*, 87 Minn. L. Rev. 1, 18–26 (Nov. 2002) (documenting ways in which payday lenders disguise their loans); Singer, 3A Sutherland Statutory Construction § 70.7 (6th ed. 2003); 44B Am. Jur. 2d *Interest and Usury* § 84 (2007); 47 C.J.S. *Interest and Usury* § 144 (2005).

12 Pope v. Marshall, 4 S.E. 116, 118–119 (Ga. 1887).

13 *See, e.g.*, Burnett v. Ala Moana Pawn Shop, 3 F.3d 1261, 1262 (9th Cir. 1993) ("Because the Truth in Lending Act is liberally construed to protect consumers," lower court was correct in "looking past the form of the [pawn] transactions to their economic substance in deciding whether the Act applied."); Thompson v. 10,000 RV Sales, Inc., 31 Cal. Rptr. 3d 18, 27–28 (Cal. Ct. App. 2005) ("[I]n determining whether consumer protection laws such as the ASFA

One should not take the creditor's description of the transaction at face value. There may be alternate ways of characterizing the transaction, and one may be more favorable to the consumer than another, either because of available state laws or because of the consumer's situation (defending a collection action, filing for bankruptcy, etc.). Creditors have been known to characterize identical transactions in different ways in different contexts.[14] Attorneys for debtors should be no less aggressive in seeking and using alternate theories on behalf of their clients.

## 13.3.2 Features of a Loan As Distinct from a Sale or Assignment

One commonly cited definition of a loan comes from a Second Circuit case, *In re Grand Union Co.*:

> A loan of money is a contract by which one delivers a sum of money to another and the latter agrees to return at a future time a sum equivalent to that which he borrows. In order to constitute a loan there must be a contract whereby, in substance one party transfers to the other a sum of money which that other agrees to repay absolutely, together with such additional sums as may be agreed upon for its use. If such be the intent of the parties, the transaction will be considered a loan without regard to its form.[15]

The *Grand Union* court contrasts loans to sales, which it defines as:

> [T]he transfer of property in a thing for a price in money. The transfer of the property in a thing sold from a buyer to a seller for a price is the essence of the transaction. And the transfer is a transfer of the general or absolute property as distinguished from a special property.[16]

The Grand Union Company sold pianos on a rent-to-own basis. Grand Union entered into a contract by which it purportedly "sold" its piano leases to an investment company at a discount. However, Grand Union continued to collect all payments under the leases and made aggregate payments to the investment company. Grand Union's customers were never notified of the supposed assignment of the leases. Furthermore, if a particular lease became non-performing, Grand Union took it back and substituted a different one. The court considered these features of the transaction and examined the contract to determine the intent of the parties and concluded that the transaction was a loan, not a sale.

Although it is not a consumer case, the Second Circuit's approach in *Grand Union* provides a roadmap of many of the factors courts take into account in distinguishing between loans and bona fide sales or assignments.[17] These factors include: whether the lender receives the funds directly from the original source or through the borrower; whether notice of the sale or assignment is provided to the original source of the funds; whether the borrower has an obligation to repay the principal amount if the assigned income stream fails or ceases; the intention of the parties; and the presence of other 'loan-like' features. Some courts also discuss the relative wealth, sophistication and bargaining power of the parties and the public policy considerations supporting credit regulation.[18] However,

---

apply to a particular transaction, we look to the substance of the transaction and do not allow mere form to dictate the result."); Berg v. Midwest Laundry Equip. Corp., 122 N.W.2d 250, 252–253, *reh'g denied and opinion modified,* 124 N.W.2d 699 (Neb. 1963) (transaction to sell laundry equipment was not a time sale; "[i]n determining whether a transaction is a bona fide time sale or a loan, the court will look through the form of the transaction and examine its substance.").

14 *See, e.g., In re* Dunlap, 458 B.R. 301 (Bankr. E.D. Va. 2011) (another Structured Investments Co. case, in which SICO unsuccessfully claimed that the transaction created a "constructive trust"); Henry v. Structured Invs. Co., L.L.C., Statement of Decision on Trial Phases 2 and 3, Case No. 05CC00167 (Cal. Sup. Ct. Orange Cty. Sept. 17, 2011), *available at* www.nclc.org/unreported ("Sometimes the defendants called the Agreements [to provide lump sums in exchange for military pensions] assignments, other times they called them loans, and, most recently, the defendants called them "purchases" depending upon whatever suited their purpose at the time").

In some jurisdictions, it may be possible to argue that the doctrine of judicial estoppel prevents a lender from taking inconsistent positions as to the nature of the agreement. *See* New Hampshire v. Maine, 532 U.S. 742 (2001) (general outline of the doctrine).

15 *In re* Grand Union Co., 219 F. 353, 356 (2d Cir. 1914). *See also* 44B Am. Jur. 2d *Interest and Usury* § 87 (2012) ("For purposes of usury law, a 'loan' is an advancement of money or other personal property under a contract or stipulation, express or implied, whereby the person to whom the advancement is made binds himself or herself to repay it at some future time, together with such other sum as may be agreed upon for the use of the money or thing advanced. If such is the intent of the parties, a transaction will be deemed a loan regardless of its form.").

16 *In re* Grand Union Co., 219 F. 353, 356 (2d Cir. 1914). *See also* 44B Am. Jur. 2d *Interest and Usury* § 87 (2012) ("For purposes of usury law, a 'loan' is an advancement of money or other personal property under a contract or stipulation, express or implied, whereby the person to whom the advancement is made binds himself or herself to repay it at some future time, together with such other sum as may be agreed upon for the use of the money or thing advanced. If such is the intent of the parties, a transaction will be deemed a loan regardless of its form.").

17 There are a number of cases involving very similar facts (working capital provided to a retailer through the mechanism of "assignment" of leases or installment sales agreements) and parallel analysis of the loan vs. assignment or sale question. *See, e.g.,* W. Pico Furniture Co. v. Pac. Fin. Loans, 86 Cal. Rptr. 793 (Cal. 1970); B & D, Inc. of Miami v. E-Z Acceptance Corp., 186 So. 2d 29 (Fla. Dist. Ct. App. 1966); Starker v. Heckart, 267 P.2d 219 (Or. 1954).

18 *See, e.g.,* Provident Life & Trust Co. v. Fletcher, 237 F. 104, 111 (S.D.N.Y. 1916) *aff'd,* 258 F. 583 (2d Cir. 1919) (Judge Learned Hand) (finding that the assignment of an inheritance was not a disguised loan and noting "[a] hard bargain with a hard-pressed man is one thing; we do not allow a workman to barter away his protection from injury. But a hard bargain with a well-furnished spendthrift is another; I can see no social purpose in giving such a one an immunity which the community at large does not enjoy."); State, on Inf. of Taylor v. Salary Purchasing Co., 218 S.W.2d 571, 572 (Mo. 1949) (concluding that a series of purported assignments wages was really a high interest loan and noting that "[r]espondent's customers were persons of low income, unable to procure credit

courts engage in a fact-specific inquiry,[19] and none of these factors is an absolute test for whether a transaction is a disguised loan.

Some cases emphasize that determining the nature of the transaction requires a factual inquiry into the intent of the parties.[20] While technically focused on the question of whether the parties intended a loan (characterized by the return of the money) or a sale or assignment (characterized by the transfer of a property interest),[21] the inquiry into intent often shades into determining intent as an element of usury.[22] As discussed elsewhere in this treatise, courts take differing approaches in how they apply that element of a traditional usury case.[23]

Another factor will be the statutory definition of a loan for purposes of applying a particular state credit statute. Some usury statutes cover forbearances and advances, as well as loans, so it will be important to know the details of the applicable state law.[24]

### *13.3.3 Relationship Between Lender and the Original Obligor*

Some courts find persuasive evidence that a transaction is actually a disguised loan where the lender collects payments from the borrower, rather than directly collecting the income stream supposedly purchased. The "salary buyers" of the early 20th century often structured transactions in this way; they would "purchase" a borrower's next pay packet at a discount and have the borrower execute documents purporting to assign the right to collect the wages.[25]

However, in most cases, the salary buyer made no effort to collect the wages directly. Instead, the borrower collected his wages as usual and returned on payday either to pay off the loan or to pay fees and interest and roll over the principal by executing a new assignment for the next pay period. A number of courts considered this factor relevant in determining that the salary transactions were disguised loans (and therefore subject to usury laws).[26]

Related to the question of who collects payments is whether any notice of the sale or assignment is given to the original obligor. Again, this was a factor in "salary buyer" cases. As one court put it:

> It is usual experience that, when a buyer buys an article, he proceeds to possess himself of it or arrange to insure its possession. Whether the subject-matter be a horse or promissory note or account or what not, that is the usual procedure. If A for some reason satisfactory to himself desires to be the owner of an account due by X to a certain person, and goes to the creditor and buys the account and has it transferred to him, in the nature of the case he will notify X that he is now the owner of the account. That is the only thing he can do for his full protection.[27]

As with other factors, the issues of notice and mechanism of collections are not necessarily dispositive. In cases similar to *Grand Union*, where a business sells or assigns its customer accounts to get operating capital, courts have found loans even where notice was given to the customers and the lender collected directly.[28]

Likewise, in at least one "salary buyer" case, the fact that the lender *did* occasionally enforce its rights as assignee by filing the assignment with the employer and attempting to collect (when the borrower failed to pay) was not enough to persuade the court that the transaction was a true assignment.[29] Instead, it was "clearly an extension of credit, an advance, or loan . . . with the assignment held over the employee as a sort of club or collateral security."[30]

In contrast, the lack of any notice to the government regarding the purported sale of military pension payments or any attempt at direct collection did not dissuade one court from concluding that the transactions were assignments (and therefore void under federal law).[31] The court acknowledged the

from banks and other conservative money lenders. They were attracted to respondent's office by alluring advertisements and solicitation through the mail.").

19 Courts may look beyond the contract to the facts and circumstances of the transaction; the parol evidence rule should not operate to exclude evidence of usury. *See* § 7.5.1.4, *supra.*

20 *See, e.g.,* Ghirardo v. Antonioli, 8 Cal. 4th 791 (Cal. 1994); Kunert v. Mission Fin. Servs. Corp., 1 Cal. Rptr. 3d 589 (Cal. Ct. App. 2003); Bullock v. Becker, 276 N.Y.S.2d 213 (N.Y. Sup. Ct. 1965). *But see* Anglo-Dutch Petroleum Int'l, Inc. v. Haskell, 193 S.W.3d 87, 98 (Tex. App. 2006) (borrower's "subjective intent" to repay did not trump the lack of absolute obligation in the agreement).

21 Bullock v. Becker, 276 N.Y.S.2d 213 (N.Y. Sup. Ct. 1965).

22 *See, e.g., In re* Bechtoldt's Estate, 289 N.Y.S. 838 (N.Y. Sur. Ct. 1936).

23 *See* § 7.5.5, *supra.*

24 *See* § 7.5.2, *supra.*

25 *See* Lynn Drysdale, Kathleen E. Keest, *The Two-Tiered Consumer Financial Services Marketplace: The Fringe Banking System and Its Challenge to Current Thinking About the Role of Usury Laws in Today's Society*, 51 S.C. L. Rev. 589 (2000). *See generally* § 1.2.2, *supra* (discussing of salary buyers and other precursors of modern payday lending).

26 *See, e.g.,* State, on Inf. of Taylor v. Salary Purchasing Co., 218 S.W.2d 571 (Mo. 1949); Parsons v. Fox, 176 S.E. 642 (Ga. 1934); Cotton v. Thompson, 159 S.W. 455 (Tex. Civ. App. 1913). *See also* McWhite v. State, 226 S.W. 542 (Tenn. 1921) (although company that supposedly purchased wages did "rarely" enforce its rights as assignee court still determined that transaction was a loan, with assignment "held over the employee as a sort of club or collateral security.").

27 Parsons v. Fox, 176 S.E. 642 (Ga. 1934) (concluding that "the continued failure of Henry & Co. to serve notice on the railroad company, and its continued acquiescence in the collections by Fox which it claimed belonged to it" lent weight to conclusion that transaction was actually a loan). *See also*, State, on Inf. of Taylor v. Salary Purchasing Co., 218 S.W.2d 571 (Mo. 1949) (noting that although agreement authorized lender to notify borrower's employer and to collect directly, this was never done).

28 Milana v. Credit Disc. Co., 163 P.2d 869 (Cal. 1945).

29 McWhite v. State, 226 S.W. 542 (Tenn. 1921).

30 *Id.*

31 Henry v. Structured Invs. Co., L.L.C., Statement of Decision on Trial Phases 2 and 3, Case No. 05CC00167 (Cal. Sup. Ct. Orange Cty. Sept. 17, 2011), *available at* www.nclc.org/images/pdf/litigation/

lack of some traditional features of assignments, but reached its conclusion on the basis of other features (such as the purported purchaser's power of attorney) and the remedial nature of the federal statutes.[32]

### 13.3.4 Borrower's Obligation to Repay; Other Features Minimizing Lender's Risk

Another feature which may distinguish disguised loans from other types of transactions is whether the principal must be repaid or otherwise returned to the lender. Of course, every loan carries some risk of non-payment. The question is not level of risk (with exceptions discussed below), but rather legal obligation.

If there is a contingency that would terminate the borrower's obligation, the transaction may not be a loan. The obligation will not be considered contingent unless the lender, by the terms of the loan, is subjected to some greater hazard than that the borrower will fail to repay or that the security will depreciate in value.[33]

In contrast, transactions in which money is provided in exchange for a share of future profits, with no guarantee of repayment, may be bona fide investments or joint ventures, not loans. In such cases, the return of the principal is contingent on the success of the enterprise.[34] The investor's return may be very large, but if it is contingent on the success of the enterprise and is thus a true joint venture, it is exempt from usury law.[35]

Similarly, some courts have held that purchase of a stake in litigation does not involve usury where there is no repayment obligation if the suit is unsuccessful.[36]

In addition to being relevant to whether a transaction is a loan in the first place, existence of an obligation to repay is an element of a traditional usury case.[37] In the average consumer credit case, proving the existence of an absolute obligation to repay principal is not a problem; the obligation is stated on the face of the note or credit contract. However, in the transactions discussed in this chapter, which involve purported assignments or purchases of future income streams, the obligation to repay may not be apparent on the face of the agreement. Whether there is an absolute obligation to repay is also occasionally an issue in complex business transactions.[38]

---

Henry.pdf. *See* § 13.4, *infra* (additional discussion of military pension cases).

32 Henry v. Structured Invs. Co., L.L.C., Statement of Decision on Trial Phases 2 and 3, Case No. 05CC00167 (Cal. Sup. Ct. Orange Cty. Sept. 17, 2011), *available at* www.nclc.org/images/pdf/litigation/Henry.pdf. *See* § 13.4, *infra* (additional discussion of military pension cases).

The power of attorney appears to have been used by SICO to redirect pension payments in at least some cases, without the permission of the veteran. *See In re* Bowden, 315 B.R. 903 (Bankr. W.D. Wash. 2004) (allotment to SICO reinstated without borrower's instructions).

33 Britz v. Kinsvater, 351 P.2d 986 (Ariz. 1960). *See also* Brown v. Fletcher, 253 F. 15, 18 (2d Cir. 1918) (distinguishing "legal" and "natural" contingencies; mere inability to collect is the latter and is not a genuine hazard).

34 *See, e.g.*, Burge v. Pack, 785 S.W.2d 207 (Ark. 1990) (discussing evidence necessary to establish a joint venture). *See generally Existence of Joint Venture*, 12 Proof of Facts 2d 295 (1977).

35 Securities & Exch. Comm'n v. First Sec. Co., 507 F.2d 417 (7th Cir. 1974); L'Arbalete, Inc. v. Zaczac, 474 F. Supp. 2d 1314 (S.D. Fla. 2007) (investment interest not a loan as it was a substantial risk); *In re* York Furniture Co., 32 B.R. 211 (Bankr. S.D.N.Y. 1983) (transaction constituted joint venture, not loan); Donatelli v. Siskind, 565 N.Y.S.2d 224 (N.Y. App. Div. 1991) (arrangement found to be joint venture, not loan). *Cf.* D-Beam Ltd. P'ship v. Roller Derby Skates, 366 F.3d 972 (9th Cir. 2004) (when promissory notes limited repayment to borrower's interest in royalty payments, loans were not usurious because of contingency); Concord Realty Co. v. Continental Funding Corp., 776 P.2d 1114 (Colo. 1989) (en banc) (usury law does not apply if return of principal is guaranteed but profit is uncertain). *See generally* § 7.5.3, *supra* (regarding whether a loan is usurious when part of the compensation is a contingent share of profits).

36 *See* § 13.6, *infra* (discussion and contrary decisions); Dopp v. Yari, 927 F. Supp. 814 (D.N.J. 1996); *In re* Transcapital Fin. Corp., 433 B.R. 900, 907 (Bankr. S.D. Fla. 2010) (financing provided to company to enable it to continue litigation was not loan because repayment contingent on success); Anglo-Dutch Petroleum Int'l, Inc. v. Haskell, 193 S.W.3d 87 (Tex. App. 2006). *See also* Kraft v. Mason, 668 So. 2d 679 (Fla. Dist. Ct. App. 1996) (no usury where borrower had duty to repay principal, but the usurious interest was contingent on litigation success); Anglo-Dutch Petroleum Int'l, Inc. v. Haskell, 193 S.W.3d 87 (Tex. App. 2006) (loan that was only to be paid back at the successful completion of litigation created no absolute obligation to repay and was not therefore usurious); Goffney v. O'Quinn, 2004 WL 2415067 (Tex. App. Oct. 28, 2004) (contingency contracts between attorneys and clients for repayment of litigation expenses upon successful completion of case do not create an absolute obligation to repay and so are not usurious). *But cf.* Lawsuit Fin., L.L.C. v. Curry, 683 N.W.2d 233 (Mich. Ct. App. 2004) (repayment obligation was not contingent where borrower signed agreement after tortfeasor had admitted liability and jury had returned $27 million verdict); Rancman v. Interim Settlement Funding Corp., 789 N.E.2d 217 (Ohio 2003) (declining to decide whether nonrecourse advance of funds secured solely by interest in a pending lawsuit and at 180% interest is a loan; contract is void as champerty and maintenance). *See generally* § 7.5.3, *supra*.

37 *See* § 7.5.3, *supra*.

38 *See* D-Beam Ltd. P'ship v. Roller Derby Skates, Inc., 366 F.3d 972 (9th Cir. 2004) (repayment obligation was contingent where it was to come from royalty payments); Valliappan v. Cruz, 917 So. 2d 257 (Fla. Dist. Ct. App. 2005) (loan not usurious where obligation to repay more than principal was contingent upon outcome of business negotiation); Dublin v. Veal, 341 S.W.2d 776 (Ky. 1960) (usury laws inapplicable to transaction that obliged obligor to repay principal amount invested in business plus portion of profits); Meklir v. J.C. Penney Co., 2005 WL 1579658 (Mich. Ct. App. July 5, 2005) (investment transaction was loan because contract created absolute obligation to repay principal); Olson v. Froslee, 2000 Minn. App. LEXIS 795 (Aug. 1, 2000) (lease of equipment with option to buy was not loan because no absolute obligation to pay option price); Transmedia Restaurant Co. v. 33 East 61st St. Restaurant Corp., 710 N.Y.S.2d 756 (N.Y. Sup. Ct. 2000) (money that network gave to restaurant would be repaid only if and when cardholders bought meals at restaurant; since network bore risk of loss, transaction was not a loan). *See also* Zoo Holdings, L.L.C. v. Clinton, 814 N.Y.S.2d 893 (N.Y. Sup. Ct. 2006) (table; unpublished). *Cf.* WRI Opportunity Loans II L.L.C. v. Cooper, 65 Cal. Rptr. 3d 205 (Cal. Ct. App. 2007) (interest contingency and shared appreciation exceptions inapplicable when repayment of loan to develop condos was not subject to any significant risk).

Fortunately, most courts recognize that, as with other aspects of potentially usurious transactions, they must look to the substance of the transaction rather than the form.[39] The Supreme Court has recognized that usury statutes would be defeated otherwise. "If an express stipulation for the repayment of the sum advanced be indispensable to the existence of usury, he must be a bungler indeed, who frames his contract on such terms as to expose himself to the penalties of the law.[40] Courts have found various substitutes for an express obligation to repay principal to be sufficient to qualify the transaction as a loan. The crux of the inquiry is "whether the principal is put at any genuine hazard."[41]

The inquiry is necessarily fact-specific. However, some examples where courts have found that the transaction is a loan[42] include:

- Where payment is contingent on the borrower remaining alive (to receive an annuity, pension or inheritance for example), but the transaction includes provision of a life insurance policy at the borrower's expense, payable to the lender;[43]
- Where the transaction is structured as a sale with option to repurchase, but the value of the object allegedly sold is so much higher than the sale price that the borrower must repurchase it (*i.e.* repay the principal) or face a huge loss;[44]
- Where the transaction is structured as a sale of an account, but the seller (borrower) guarantees payment of the account;[45]
- Where the contingency is effectively impossible;[46] and
- Where the success of the 'investment' is guaranteed by the contract[47] or otherwise nearly certain.[48]

39 *See* § 13.3.1, *supra.*

40 Scott v. Lloyd, 34 U.S. 418, 448 (1835). In the transactions discussed in Scott v. Lloyd, lenders sought to avoid usury by structuring the transactions as purchases of annuities or rental income. In that case, the lender paid $5000 in exchange for $500 per year of the rental income of borrower's property "forever," but the borrower had the option after five years to pay $5000 to extinguish the obligation. It was up to the jury, considering all the circumstances, to determine whether the contract was a bona fide purchase of an annuity or a disguised loan.

41 Provident Life & Trust Co. v. Fletcher, 237 F. 104, 108 (S.D.N.Y. 1916) *aff'd,* 258 F. 583 (2d Cir. 1919) (Judge Learned Hand) (rejecting view that borrower must be bound to pay principal in order to constitute usury and recognizing that other features, in particular life insurance payable to lender, might achieve the same end).

42 One additional potential complication is that the transaction may be found to be a loan because repayment of principal is guaranteed, but may not be usurious if some or all of the "interest" is contingent. *See generally* § 7.5.3, *supra.*

43 *See, e.g.,* DeKorwin v. First Nat'l Bank of Chicago, 318 F.2d 176, 178 (7th Cir. 1963) ("The insurance requirements by Levy on the life of Brill is substantially relevant to the test of whether the transaction was a loan or a sale."); Brown v. Fletcher, 253 F. 15, 18 (2d Cir. 1918) (life insurance eliminated hazard of borrower dying before his interest in trust funds vested (at age 55), and finding no difference between borrower directly paying life insurance premiums or having them deducted from the amount advanced); Provident Life & Trust Co. v. Fletcher, 237 F. 104 (S.D.N.Y. 1916) *aff'd,* 258 F. 583 (2d Cir. 1919). *See also In re* Price, 313 B.R. 805 (Bankr. E.D. Ark. 2004) (noting that borrower was required to pay for life insurance, describing military pension transaction as a loan secured by an assignment of pension benefits).

44 *See, e.g.,* Oregrund Ltd. P'ship v. Sheive, 873 So. 2d 451 (Fla. Dist. Ct. App. 2004) (fact that value of land to lender was three to five times the amount of its "investment," could support finding that borrower was "economically bound" to repurchase the property); SAL Leasing, Inc. v. State *ex rel.* Napolitano, 10 P.3d 1221 (Ariz. Ct. App. 2000) (disparity between value of vehicles and "purchase" price; one of six factors considered in concluding that auto sale and leaseback transactions were really loans). *See generally* Ch. 11, *supra* (discussing generally auto title lending).

45 *See, e.g., In re* Grand Union Co., 219 F. 353 (2d Cir. 1914) (considering fact that Grand Union would replace any non-performing leases that were allegedly "sold" to secure operating capital); Decision Point, Inc. v. Reece & Nichols Realtors, Inc., 144 P.3d 706 (Kan. 2006) (applying U.C.C.C. definition of loan as "creation of debt by the lender's payment of or agreement to pay money to the debtor"; advancing money to real estate agents in return for their agreement to repay it either through assignment of specific anticipated commissions or repurchase of the account creates loans); Baxter v. Stevens, 773 P.2d 890 (Wash. Ct. App. 1989) (sale of payment obligation, a promissory note, for an amount less than its face value was loan where transferor had absolute obligation of repayment if the obligor on the note defaulted). *But see* Berger v. State, Dep't of Revenue, 910 P.2d 581 (Alaska 1996) (concluding that transactions involving Alaskan permanent fund dividends were not loans because repayment obligation was conditional on the state refusing to honor the transactions; two justices dissented); Carter v. Four Seasons Funding Corp., 97 S.W.3d 387 (Ark. 2003) (sale of accounts receivable by sophisticated business entity not a loan even though buyer had recourse against seller if accounts proved uncollectible); Coast Fin. Corp. v. Ira F. Powers Furniture Co., 209 P. 614 (Or. 1922) (indorsement or guarantee of seller of conditional sales contract making him liable to purchaser does not transform valid sale into usurious loan); Ravkind v. Mortgage Funding Corp., 881 S.W.2d 203 (Tex. App. 1994) (assignment of payments due on contract for deed not a loan even though assignee had recourse against assignor).

46 *See, e.g.,* Schwartz v. Lincoln Constr. & Dev. Corp., 455 So. 2d 612 (Fla. Dist. Ct. App. 1984) (although part of repayment was contingent on failure to complete construction of a condominium development in twenty months, transaction was disguised usurious mortgage because construction could not have been done in that time frame).

47 Najarro v. SASI Int'l Ltd., 904 F.2d 1002, 1007 (5th Cir. 1990) (Tex. law) (advance of money with absolute obligation to repay was loan, not investment, regardless of parties' intent); Beausejour Corp., N.V. v. Offshore Dev. Co., 802 F.2d 1319 (11th Cir. 1986) (Fla. law) (loan was usurious where absolute repayment obligation was evidenced by mortgage note); Hufnagel v. George, 121 F. Supp. 2d 305 (S.D.N.Y. 2000) (agreement creates a loan, not a joint venture, where advanced money was repayable on a date certain; no profits existed to pay the interest or return on the investment), *subsequent proceeding at* 135 F. Supp. 2d 406 (S.D.N.Y. 2001) (affirming that agreement creates a loan and voiding loan for violation of N.Y. criminal usury statute); Peterson v. Harville, 455 F. Supp. 16 (D. Or. 1977), *aff'd,* 623 F.2d 611 (9th Cir. 1980) (also emphasizing intent of parties); Dennis v. Bradbury, 236 F. Supp. 683 (D. Colo. 1964), *aff'd,* 368 F.2d 905 (10th Cir. 1966); Maze v. Sycamore Homes, Inc., 41 Cal. Rptr. 338 (Cal. Ct. App. 1964); Whittemore Homes, Inc. v. Fleishman, 12 Cal. Rptr. 235 (Cal. Ct. App. 1961); Dang v. F & S Land Dev. Corp., 618 P.2d 276 (Haw. 1980); Grotjohn Precise Connexiones Int'l, S.A. v. JEM Fin., Inc., 12 S.W.3d 859 (Tex. App. 2000); Johns v. Jaeb, 518 S.W.2d 857 (Tex. Civ. App. 1974). *See also In re* Venture Mortgage Fund, Ltd. P'ship, 245 B.R. 460 (Bankr. S.D.N.Y. 2000) (religious document

When dealing with an arguably non-absolute repayment obligation, it is important to check the exact language of the usury statute. If the statute extends to "advances" as well as loans, for example, it may cover transactions where the repayment obligation is not absolute.[49]

## 13.4 Military Pensions and Benefits

A few companies specialize in providing lumps sums in exchange for military veterans' promises to redirect their monthly pension or disability benefits directly to the lender for a number of years. Typically, prospective borrowers contact the lender in response to advertisements placed in military newspapers or magazines or internet sites giving the appearance of military approval. The veteran must send a DD Form 214 (an official discharge document), a copy of his or her Retiree Account Statement, income tax returns, pay checks, and evidence of other income and financial status in order to obtain a loan approval. The company quotes the potential borrower a cash amount and repayment period based on the amount of the pension payments that will be redirected to the lender.

Prior to forwarding the loan proceeds to the borrower, the lender subtracts administrative fees and an amount equivalent to an annual life insurance premium for each year of the repayment period. These loan agreements are normally over a dozen pages couching the transaction in terms of the "sale" or "assignment" of the veterans' benefit payment. No interest rate information is calculated or provided and the rates usually exceed a state's usury limitations. Lenders do not provide Truth in Lending Act disclosures. Loans also contain clauses threatening borrowers with criminal fines and imprisonment for failure to repay the loan.[50]

The sale or assignment of a veteran's retirement or disability benefits is prohibited by federal law.[51] Typically, courts will invalidate these transactions.[52] However, the decisions have not been consistent in determining whether the transactions are loans, assignments, or loans secured by assignments.[53] Arguably, the transactions should be invalidated as assignments forbidden by federal law, but also be subject to usury, Truth in Lending and other remedies associated with loan statutes.

creating a joint venture to avoid a religious ban on charging interest has no effect on whether the transaction is a usurious loan; finding business loan violated the New York criminal usury law), *aff'd*, 282 F.3d 185 (2d Cir. 2002). *Cf.* Jones v. Wells Fargo Bank, 5 Cal. Rptr. 3d 835 (Cal. Ct. App. 2003) (holding no usury because California law exempted national banks acting as a fiduciary for a trust from usury cap where the parties did not dispute that shared appreciation mortgage arrangement was a loan). *But see* Florida Trading & Inv. Co. v. River Constr. Servs., 537 So. 2d 600 (Fla. Dist. Ct. App. 1988) (fact that agreement did not explicitly provide for sharing losses does not preclude its characterization as investment, where entity supplying capital was fully integrated into the operation).

48 *See, e.g.*, WRI Opportunity Loans II L.L.C. v. Cooper, 65 Cal. Rptr. 3d 205 (Cal. Ct. App. 2007) (finding that the shared appreciation provisions did not subject the plaintiff to any real risk and, thus, did not fall within the statutory exemption from the usury law); Lawsuit Fin., L.L.C. v. Curry, 683 N.W.2d 233 (Mich. Ct. App. 2004) (there was no contingency and settlement advance was a loan where the borrower had already obtained a jury verdict, even though the award might be reduced as excessive.); Echeverria v. Estate of Lindner, 801 N.Y.S.2d 233, (N.Y. Sup. Ct. 2005) (litigation finance agreement in a labor law action where there was strict liability "is not a gamble, but a 'sure thing,' therefore, it is a loan, not an investment.").

49 Odell v. Legal Bucks, L.L.C., 665 S.E.2d 767 (N.C. Ct. App. 2008).

50 *See* Steve Tripoli & Amy Mix, In Harm's Way—At Home: Consumer Scams and the Targeting of America's Military and Veterans 25–28 (May 2003), *available at* www.nclc.org/images/pdf/special_projects/military/report-scams-facing-military.pdf (discussing these scams).

51 37 U.S.C. § 701(c) (prohibits the assignment of the pay of an enlisted member of the Army, Navy, Air Force, or Marine Corps, and if the member does so, the assignment is void; retired pay is included in the definition of "pay" in 37 U.S.C. § 101); 38 U.S.C. § 5301(a)(1) (prohibits the assignment of benefits payments due or to become due under any law administered by the Secretary of Veterans Affairs); 10 U.S.C. § 1175(f) (prohibits the transfer of VSI benefits); 16 C.F.R. § 444.2(a)(3) (prohibits assignment of wages or other earnings unless: (a) the assignment by its terms is revocable at the will of the debtor; (b) the assignment is a payroll deduction plan or preauthorized payment plan, commencing at the time of the transaction, in which the consumer authorizes a series of wage deductions as a method of making each payment; or, (c) the assignment applies only to wages or other earnings already earned by the time of the assignment).

52 Dorfman v. Moorhous (*In re* Moorhous), 108 F.3d 51 (4th Cir. 1997) (debtor could not assign any retired pay that was not yet due and payable under 37 U.S.C. § 701 and, consequently, creditors acquired no ownership interest in that pay that could be enforced through equitable remedies); *In re* Dunlap, 458 B.R. 301 (Bankr. E.D. Va. 2011); *In re* Webb, 376 B.R. 765 (Bankr. W.D. Okla. 2007); Bowden v. Structured Inv. Co. (*In re* Bowden), 315 B.R. 903 (Bankr. W.D. Wash 2004) (creditor argued that pension loan agreement created an enforceable trust and, therefore, debtor's ongoing military retirement and disability pay were not property of estate; purported trust failed because there was no trust *res*, i.e., rights to military retired pay and veterans' disability benefits were neither entitlements nor vested rights); Structured Inv. Co. v. Price (*In re* Price), 313 B.R. 805 (Bankr. E.D. Ark. 2004) (sale or assignment of future pension rights is unenforceable; debtor had not waived defense of illegality; agreement was unconscionable); Henry v. Structured Invs. Co., L.L.C., Statement of Decision on Trial Phases 2 and 3, Case No. 05CC00167 (Cal. Sup. Ct. Orange Cty. Sept. 17, 2011), *available at* www.nclc.org/images/pdf/litigation/Henry.pdf (finding that the agreements were illegal assignments); C & A Fin. Programs, Inc. vs. Amos, Case No.: 04-377-CA (Fla. Cir. Ct. Martin Cty. Jan. 10, 2006), *available at* www.nclc.org/unreported (granting veteran's motion for summary judgment and determining that the "sale" of his right to seek pension benefits was really an illegal assignment of these benefits and, therefore, void ab initio). *But see* *In re* Weber, 2009 WL 983311 (Bankr. D. Neb. Apr. 10, 2009) (denying debtor's summary judgment motion, because it was "not clear that the payment arrangement is an assignment.").

53 *Compare* Henry v. Structured Invs. Co., L.L.C., Statement of Decision on Trial Phases 2 and 3, Case No. 05CC00167 (Cal. Sup. Ct. Orange Cty. Sept. 17, 2011), *available at* www.nclc.org/images/pdf/litigation/Henry.pdf (finding that the agreements could not be both assignment and loans), *with In re* Price, 313 B.R. 805 (Bankr. E.D. Ark. 2004) (describing transaction as a loan secured by an assignment of pension benefits).

## 13.5 Settlements or Judgments ("Factoring")

Tort or other legal settlements are often structured to provide payment over a period of years. A number of companies offer to pay the consumer cash up front to transfer the right to receive those payments over time.[54] Challenging these transactions as loans may be tricky, especially in states that have a statutory framework by which courts approve the transfer of structured settlement rights from the recipient to an entity that in turn disburses lump sum amounts to him or her. The majority of states have such laws, which typically condition the assignment of structured settlements on the presence of protections including disclosures, independent counsel or court approval.[55]

New York has a Structured Settlement Protection Act (SSPA), which requires court approval of such transfers.[56] In 2009, the United States District Court for the Eastern District of New York addressed the issue of whether such a transaction approved by a state court under the SSPA was a loan subject to Truth in Lending Act (TILA) disclosures.[57] The court asserted that it had not uncovered any other federal court opinions directly on point, making its decision potentially the only federal authority on the issue of "whether assignment of structured settlement rights should be subject to TIL requirements."[58] The court answered the question in the negative; in addition, it dismissed the plaintiff's claim under New York's UDAP law and held that the entire complaint was subject to claim preclusion due to the prior state court proceeding.[59] In an unreported decision, a California appellate court reached a similar conclusion in a class action seeking to collaterally attack a series of court-approved transfers where the factoring company failed to comply with the terms of the statute (by failing to provide and pay for independent advisors, among other things).[60]

However, at least one state court has held a settlement advance to be a usurious loan,[61] and some claims under state UDAP statutes have also been successful.[62] The terms of the settlement income source may prohibit assignment, which may provide a means of invalidating these agreements.[63] Like many consumer contracts, settlement factoring agreements often contain pre-dispute arbitration clauses, further restricting the ability of consumers to attack unlawful or unfair terms.[64]

## 13.6 Causes of Action (Litigation Financing)

An entire industry has developed around the concept of "litigation finance."[65] These transactions purport to provide a cash payment in exchange for a share of the potential judgment or settlement of legal actions.[66] They differ from settlement

54 *See, e.g.*, *In re* Wiggins, 273 B.R. 839 (Bankr. D. Idaho 2001) (loan in which young accident victim suffering from brain injuries sold his rights to a structured annuity).

55 *See e.g.* Cal. Ins. Code §§ 10134 to 10139.5 (West); Ga. Code Ann. §§ 51-12-70 to 51-12-77 (West); 215 Ill. Comp. Stat. §§ 153/1 to 153/35; N.Y. Gen. Oblig. Law § 5-1701(f) (McKinney). *See also* Symetra Life Ins. Co. v. Rapid Settlements, Ltd., 2011 WL 4807901 (S.D. Tex. Oct. 11, 2011) (noting that forty-seven states have structured settlement protection acts).

56 *See* N.Y. Gen. Oblig. Law § 5-1701(f) (McKinney).

57 Capela v. J.G. Wentworth, L.L.C., 2009 WL 3128003 (E.D.N.Y. Sept. 24, 2009).

58 *Id.*

59 *Id.*

60 Ceron v. 321 Henderson Receivables, 2011 WL 240243 (Cal. Ct. App. Jan. 26, 2011).

61 Lawsuit Fin., L.L.C. v. Curry, 683 N.W.2d 233 (Mich. Ct. App. 2004) (settlement advances were loans when borrower had already obtained jury verdict; loans were usurious where agreement required borrower to pay $887,500 for principal advances totaling $177,500). *But see In re* Jack, 390 B.R. 307 (Bankr. S.D. Tex. 2008) (never considering whether purported assignment of structured settlement payments was a loan).

62 *See, e.g.*, *In re* Wiggins, 273 B.R. 839 (Bankr. D. Idaho 2001) (income buyer violated Idaho UDAP statute in convincing young accident victim suffering from brain injuries to sell his rights to a structured annuity).

63 *See, e.g.*, Singer Asset Fin. Co. v. Gallagher (*In re* Gallagher), 331 B.R. 895 (B.A.P. 9th Cir. 2005) (anti-assignment provision upheld), *opinion vacated due to minor changes*, 2005 Bankr. LEXIS 1967 (Oct. 14, 2005); Liberty Life Assurance Co. v. Stone Street Capital, 93 F. Supp. 2d 630 (D. Md. 2000) (anti-assignment clause of structured settlement was enforceable by insurer that paid annuity); Grieve v. General Am. Life Ins., 58 F. Supp. 2d 319 (D. Vt. 1999); First Providian, Ltd. Liab. Co. v. Evans, 852 So. 2d 908 (Fla. Dist. Ct. App. 2003). *But see In re* Jack, 390 B.R. 307 (Bankr. S.D. Tex. 2008) (finding that borrower's first three purported assignments of payments under a structured personal injury settlement were not valid, but the fourth—to same lender, and for no additional consideration—was valid because, *inter alia*, it contained language effective to waive anti-assignment provision of settlement agreement).

64 *See, e.g.*, Sparks v. Stone Street Capital, 2002 WL 1575404 (N.D. Tex. July 15, 2002) (class action on behalf of consumers who transferred their interests in structured settlement payments in exchange for money; granting motion to compel arbitration). *See also* Symetra Life Ins. Co. v. Rapid Settlements, Ltd., 599 F. Supp. 2d 809 (S.D. Tex. 2008), *aff'd*, 567 F.3d 754 (5th Cir. 2009) (granting injunction preventing factoring company from using arbitration to circumvent the requirements of the state structured settlement protection statutes), *later decision*, 2011 WL 4807901 (S.D. Tex. Oct. 11, 2011) (extensive discussion of state settlement protection statutes; granting summary judgment for insurer on tortious interference claim; provisions of statutes were so clear that settlement purchaser could not have had good faith belief in rights it asserted).

65 This industry grew quickly in the early 2000s. For example, the chair of the American Legal Fin. Association, which is the trade association for this industry, started making loans in 2000. By 2005, his company, LawCash, had made 3000 loans with $25 million in loan volume. Joseph Fried, *Wanting to Settle a Lawsuit? Beware of Cash Advances*, New York Times, Apr. 4, 2005. For an example of a case where an investor in a litigation finance company sued the owners and aired the dirty laundry, see Douglas v. Bigley, 628 S.E.2d 199 (Ga. Ct. App. 2006).

66 *See, e.g.*, Advocate Fin., L.L.C. v. Longenecker & Assocs., Ltd., 3 So. 3d 1 (La. Ct. App. 2008) (successful suit by lender against insurance company for tortfeasor in personal injury case for paying litigation proceeds directly to victorious personal injury plaintiff and her attorney when both plaintiff and attorney had pledged these proceeds to lender as security for loans issued during course of litigation); Rancman v. Interim Settlement Funding Corp., 2001 WL 1339487 (Ohio Ct. App. Oct. 31, 2001) (payment collateralized by

factoring, described in the preceding section, because the judgment or settlement does not yet exist. These transactions have been justified as a way to provide injured plaintiffs, who may be in dire financial straits due to their injury or unemployment, with funds while they pursue a lawsuit.

Some states prohibit assignment of certain causes of action, particularly personal injury, either by statute or common law.[67] Some commentators have suggested legalizing litigation funding, but setting up a regulatory structure to govern these transactions[68] and some states are indeed taking steps to regulate these transactions.[69]

Litigation finance companies have also attracted regulatory scrutiny. The New York Attorney General reached settlements with a number of litigation finance companies requiring them to make better disclosures of the cost of the advance and the total amount to be repaid.[70]

Challenging litigation finance as a disguised loan may be difficult because repayment is contingent upon the successful settlement of a lawsuit.[71] However, if the likelihood of winning the case is very high, or payment is otherwise assured, courts are more likely to find that the arrangement is a loan.

A settlement advance was held to be a loan where the borrower had already obtained a $27 million jury verdict in a case, but there was an issue as to whether the award would be reduced as excessive.[72] An Ohio intermediate appellate court was willing to hold that a litigation finance arrangement was really a usurious loan, noting there was ample evidence to support the trial court's determination that no real risk of nonpayment existed,[73] but the Ohio Supreme Court affirmed this decision on the basis that the arrangement was void as champerty, without considering the usury issue.[74] In contrast, the North Carolina intermediate appellate court rejected a champerty claim in a similar case, instead squarely ruling that the litigation "advance" was a usurious loan.[75]

Not all litigation funding is contingent. Some agreements require a minimum specific repayment regardless of the outcome of the borrower's lawsuit.[76] However, the fact that principal must be repaid, but the amount of interest being charged is contingent upon success of the lawsuit, may insulate the lender from a usury claim.[77]

Of course, practitioners should be aware of state attorney ethics rules and opinions on the issue of litigation financing.[78]

## 13.7 Other Limits on Assignment of Future Income

Whether or not the transaction qualifies as a loan and runs afoul of any usury or other cost-of-credit laws, it may violate or be voidable under other laws or regulations designed to protect specific sources of funds or vulnerable groups. The following is a (non-exhaustive) list of such restrictions.

- Federal Old-Age, Survivors, and Disability Insurance Benefits (Social Security) are protected from assignment, gar-

possible settlement in personal injury litigation), *aff'd on other grounds*, 789 N.E.2d 217 (Ohio 2003).

67 *See, e.g.*, Ga. Code § 44-12-24; N.Y. Gen. Oblig. Law § 13-101; Gurski v. Rosenblum & Filan, L.L.C., 885 A.2d 163 (Conn. 2005) (Connecticut common law forbids assignment of personal injury tort claims; recognizing as "meaningless" distinction between assignment of a cause of action and assignment of the recovery from the action.).

68 *See* Yifat Shaltiel, John Cofresi, *Litigation Lending for Personal Needs Act: A Regulatory Framework to Legitimize Third Party Litigation Fin.*, 58 Consumer Fin. L. Q. Rep. 347 (Winter 2004) (suggesting that fees be limited to the state usury cap or 25% of the amount loaned).

69 *See, e.g.*, Me. Rev. Stat. tit. 9-A, §§ 12-101 to 12-107 (regulating loans secured by potential settlement of civil actions).

70 John Caher, *State, Legal Settlement Advance Business Agree on Measures to Protect Consumers*, N.Y. L.J., June 29, 2004, at 1. *See also Interest Rate Charged by Litigation Finance Company is Deemed Usurious*, 231 N.Y. L.J. 23, Apr. 1, 2005 (agreement to advance money to a litigant and to charge 3.85% per month (or 46.2% per annum) does not constitute champerty but does create a usurious loan; court reformed the interest rate to 16% per annum).

71 *See, e.g.*, Dopp v. Yari, 927 F. Supp. 814 (D.N.J. 1996); *In re* Transcapital Fin. Corp., 433 B.R. 900, 907 (Bankr. S.D. Fla. 2010) (financing provided to company to enable it to continue litigation was not loan because repayment contingent on success); Anglo-Dutch Petroleum Int'l, Inc. v. Smith, 243 S.W.3d 776 (Tex. App. 2007) (affirming finding of no loan because the agreements in this commercial case contained no absolute obligation to repay any amount of money); Anglo-Dutch Petroleum Int'l, Inc. v. Haskell, 193 S.W.3d 87 (Tex. App. 2006) (loan that was only to be paid back at the successful completion of litigation created no absolute obligation to repay and was not therefore usurious).

72 Lawsuit Fin., L.L.C. v. Curry, 683 N.W.2d 233 (Mich. Ct. App. 2004). *See also* Echeverria v. Estate of Lindner, 801 N.Y.S.2d 233, (N.Y. Sup. Ct. 2005) (litigation finance agreement in a labor law action where there was strict liability "is not a gamble, but a 'sure thing,' therefore, it is a loan, not an investment.").

73 Rancman v. Interim Settlement Funding Corp., 2001 WL 1339487 (Ohio Ct. App. Oct. 31, 2001). *But cf.* Anglo-Dutch Petroleum Int'l, Inc. v. Haskell, 193 S.W.3d 87 (Tex. App. 2006) (investment to a company to help it finance commercial litigation in exchange for a sizeable return if the lawsuit succeeded or was settled, is not a loan since repayment was contingent).

74 Rancman v. Interim Settlement Funding Corp., 789 N.E.2d 217 (Ohio 2003).

75 Odell v. Legal Bucks, L.L.C., 665 S.E.2d 767 (N.C. Ct. App. 2008).

76 *See, e.g.*, Houston v. Cohen (*In re* Cohen), 305 B.R. 886 (B.A.P. 9th Cir. 2004) (debtor's assignment of anticipated settlement proceeds was a loan because debtor obligated to pay off "promissory note" whether or not lawsuit was successful).

77 *See* Dopp v. Yari, 927 F. Supp. 814 (D.N.J. 1996) (following Kraft v. Mason; note this was a commercial case); Kraft v. Mason, 668 So. 2d 679 (Fla. Dist. Ct. App. 1996) (fact that payment of interest depended on contingency of successful lawsuit, and that the lender was an unsophisticated party, showed lack of corrupt intent to render loan usurious). *See generally* § 7.5.3, *supra* (regarding whether a loan is usurious when part of the compensation is a contingent share of profits).

78 *See, e.g.*, N.Y. City Bar Ass'n, Formal Opinion 2011-2: Third Party Litigation Financing, *available at* www.nycbar.org/ethics/ethics-opinions-local; ABA Comm. on Ethics, Issues Paper Concerning Lawyer's Involvement in Alternative Litigation Financing (Nov. 23, 2010), *available at* www.americanbar.org/content/dam/aba/migrated/2011_build/ethics_2020/altl_lit_financing_issuespaper.authcheckdam.pdf.

nishment and other legal process.[79] Other public benefits may also be protected.[80]

- Benefits administered by the Secretary of Veterans Affairs (generally for disabled veterans) are protected from assignment, garnishment and other legal process "either before or after receipt by the beneficiary."[81]
- Pay[82] of enlisted members (as opposed to officers) of the armed forces cannot be assigned and purported assignments are void.[83]
- ERISA (the Employee Retirement Income Security Act) requires that covered pension plans include provisions restricting the assignment or alienation of plan benefits.[84] Courts differ on whether the anti-assignment and anti-alienation provisions continue to protect pension benefits after they are received by the beneficiary.[85]
- State and local government pensions may have anti-assignment and anti-alienation provisions.[86]
- Tribal Per Capita gaming revenue payments may be protected from alienation by the terms of the tribal Ordinance governing allocation of the revenue to tribe members.[87]
- State lottery statutes may prohibit or condition assignment of lottery winnings (which are typically paid out over time).[88]

In addition to statutory and common law protections, the agreement creating the original payment obligation (a settlement or annuity, for example) may contain restrictions on assignment or other transfers.[89] However, these restrictions may not be binding in all circumstances.[90] Companies that buy annuities and structured settlements have argued that such clauses are invalidated by U.C.C. Article 9, which nullifies any contract term that prohibits assignment of an account.[91]

---

79 42 U.S.C. § 407(a). *See also* Stewart v. Favors, 590 S.E.2d 186 (Ga. Ct. App. 2003) (lawsuit challenging loan arrangement that required borrowers to deposit their Social Security or SSI payments into bank accounts controlled by the lender; motion to compel arbitration denied). *See generally* National Consumer Law Center, Collection Actions § 12.5.5 (2d ed. 2011 and Supp.).

80 *See, e.g.,* Florida Asset Fin. v. Utah Labor Comm'n, 98 P.3d 436 (Utah Ct. App. 2004) (Utah law does not prohibit assignment of workers' compensation benefits, but state commission must comply with beneficiary's instruction to redirect payments from lender to beneficiary), *aff'd*, 147 P.3d 1189 (Utah 2006).

81 38 U.S.C. § 5301(a)(1).

82 Military retirement payments are "pay" within the meaning of this statutory provision. Structured Inv. Co. v. Webb (*In re* Webb), 376 B.R. 765 (W.D. Ark. 2007).

83 37 U.S.C. § 701(c).

84 29 U.S.C. § 1056(d).

85 *Compare* Hoult v. Hoult, 373 F.3d 47 (1st Cir. 2004) (once benefits are disbursed to beneficiary, restriction on alienation or assignment no longer applies), *with* United States v. Smith, 47 F.3d 681 (4th Cir. 1995) (benefits are protected after disbursement).

86 *See, e.g. In re* Bechtel, 2011 WL 976560 (Bankr. M.D.N.C. Mar. 15, 2011) (anti-alienation clause in statute authorizing local government retirement benefits bars voluntary assignments, here as security for business loan; only exceptions are family support and property division at divorce); Prince George's County Police Pension Plan v. Burke, 584 A.2d 702 (Md. 1991).

Many cases arise in the context of divorce, where courts are apt to find an exception to the rules against alienation for former spouses entitled to a share of the pension as marital property. *Id.*

87 *See In re* Brown, BAP Nos. 2006 WL 6810938 (B.A.P. 9th Cir. Sept. 28, 2006).

88 *See, e.g.,* Singer Asset Fin. v. Duboff Family Invs. (*In re* Duboff), 290 B.R. 652 (Bankr. C.D. Ill. 2003) (assignment of Illinois lottery prize payments violated Illinois lottery law and was void); Cal. Gov't Code § 8880.325 (West); N.J. Stat. Ann. § 5:9-13 (West).

However, these restrictions may be invalidated by U.C.C. Article 9, which nullifies any contract term that prohibits assignment of an account. *See* Texas Lottery Comm'n v. First State Bank, 325 S.W.3d 628 (Tex. 2010). *But see* Stone Street Capital, L.L.C. v. Cal. State Lottery Comm'n, 80 Cal. Rptr. 3d 326 (Ct. App. 2008).

89 *See, e.g.,* Singer Asset Fin. Co. v. Gallagher (*In re* Gallagher), 331 B.R. 895 (B.A.P. 9th Cir. 2005) (anti-assignment provision upheld), *opinion vacated due to minor changes*, 2005 Bankr. LEXIS 1967 (Oct. 14, 2005); Liberty Life Assurance Co. v. Stone Street Capital, 93 F. Supp. 2d 630 (D. Md. 2000) (anti-assignment clause of structured settlement was enforceable by insurer that paid annuity); Grieve v. General Am. Life Ins., 58 F. Supp. 2d 319 (D. Vt. 1999); First Providian, Ltd. Liab. Co. v. Evans, 852 So. 2d 908 (Fla. Dist. Ct. App. 2003).

90 *See, e.g., In re* Jack, 390 B.R. 307 (Bankr. S.D. Tex. 2008) (finding that borrower's first three purported assignments of payments under a structured personal injury settlement were not valid, but the fourth—to same lender, and for no additional consideration—was valid because, *inter alia*, it contained language effective to waive anti-assignment provision of settlement agreement).

91 U.C.C. §§ 9-406(d), 9-408 [formerly U.C.C. § 9-318(4)].

Many states have adopted non-uniform amendments to revised Article 9 which exempt structured settlements, annuities, special needs trusts, or certain claims or rights to receive compensation for injuries or sickness. *See* National Consumer Law Center, Repossessions § 2.2.8.2 (7th ed. 2010 and Supp.).

# Chapter 14 Refund Anticipation Loans (RALs) and Tax Refund Schemes

## 14.1 Overview of RALs and Tax Refund Schemes

### 14.1.1 Introduction

Refund anticipation loans (RALs) are high-cost, short-term loans secured by a taxpayer's expected refund.[1] They are made by banks with the assistance of commercial tax preparers, who broker or "facilitate" the RAL. RALs were prevalent during the 1990s and 2000s, but after 2012, all of the banks that made RALs will have stopped doing so.[2]

Another form of tax-refund-based lending is the assignment of a taxpayer's expected tax refund in return for an immediate cash payment. These are actually disguised loans containing hidden interest in the form of a "discount" from the full value of the refund.

### 14.1.2 How RALs Work

A RAL puts cash into the consumer's hand in one or two days, or even on the same day for an extra fee. However, these loans only lasted about a week or two, because the IRS usually issues a refund within eight to fifteen days if the tax return is filed electronically and the refund is direct deposited into a bank account.[3]

With RALs, the lending bank sets up at temporary or "disposable" bank account and the IRS is instructed to send the refund to that account. The loans are repaid when the consumer's refund is direct deposited. Thus, RALs were extremely short-term loans of only one to two weeks.

A product related to RALs is the "refund anticipation check" (RAC). With a RAC, the bank allegedly does not make a loan but waits until the IRS direct deposits the refund into the disposable bank account. After the refund is deposited, the bank issues the consumer a check or prepaid card, or makes a direct deposit into the consumer's own account, then closes the disposable account. A RAC does not provide the refund monies any faster than if the consumer elects e-filing and direct deposit, but it does allow the consumer to pay for tax preparation fees out of the refund at an additional cost of $30 to $35.[4]

For many years, banks made RALs for the full amount of the refund minus the loan and tax preparation fees, with loan

1 NCLC and the Consumer Federation of America have issued annual reports focusing on the RAL industry, the cost to consumers, the effect upon the Earned Income Tax Credit, and RAL litigation. For the first and most comprehensive of these reports, see Chi Chi Wu, Jean Ann Fox & Elizabeth Renuart, National Consumer Law Center & Consumer Fed'n of Am., Tax Preparers Peddle High Cost Tax Refund Loans: Millions Skimmed from the Working Poor and the U.S. Treasury (Jan. 31, 2002).

The other annual RAL reports are: Chi Chi Wu & Jean Ann Fox, National Consumer Law Center & Consumer Fed'n of Am., The Party's Over for Quickie Tax Loans: But Traps Remain for Unwary Taxpayers (Feb. 2012), *available at* www.nclc.org/images/pdf/pr-reports/report-ral-2012.pdf; Chi Chi Wu & Jean Ann Fox, National Consumer Law Center & Consumer Fed'n of Am., End of the Rapid Rip-Off: An Epilogue for Quickie Tax Loans (Feb. 2011); Chi Chi Wu & Jean Ann Fox, National Consumer Law Center & Consumer Fed'n of Am., Major Changes in the Quick Tax Refund Loan Industry (Feb. 2010), *available at* www.nclc.org/images/pdf/high_cost_small_loans/report-ral-2010.pdf; Chi Chi Wu & Jean Ann Fox, National Consumer Law Ctr. & Consumer Fed'n of Am., Big Business, Big Bucks: Quickie Tax Loans Generate Profits for Banks and Tax Preparers While Putting Low-Income Taxpayers At Risk (Feb. 2009); Chi Chi Wu & Jean Ann Fox, National Consumer Law Center & Consumer Fed'n of Am., Coming Down: Fewer Refund Anticipation Loans, Lower Prices from Some Providers, but Quickie Tax Refund Loans Still Burden the Working Poor (Mar. 2008); Chi Chi Wu & Jean Ann Fox, National Consumer Law Center & Consumer Fed'n of Am., Another Year of Losses: High-Priced Refund Anticipation Loans Continue to Take a Chunk Out of Americans' Tax Refunds (Jan. 2006); Chi Chi Wu & Jean Ann Fox, National Consumer Law Center & Consumer Fed'n of Am., Picking Taxpayers' Pockets, Draining Tax Relief Dollars: Refund Anticipation Loans Still Slicing into Low-Income Americans' Hard-Earned Tax Refunds (Jan. 2005); Chi Chi Wu & Jean Ann Fox, National Consumer Law Center & Consumer Fed'n of Am., All Drain, No Gain: Refund Anticipation Loans Continue to Sap the Hard-Earned Tax Dollars of Low-Income Americans (Jan. 2004); Chi Chi Wu & Jean Ann Fox, National Consumer Law Center & Consumer Fed'n of Am., The High Cost of Quick Tax Money: Tax Preparation, "Instant Refund" Loans, and Check Cashing Fees Target the Working Poor (Jan. 30, 2003). All of these reports are available at www.nclc.org/issues/refund-anticipation-loans.html.

2 Chi Chi Wu & Jean Ann Fox, National Consumer Law Center & Consumer Fed'n of Am., The Party's Over for Quickie Tax Loans: But Traps Remain for Unwary Taxpayers 5 (Feb. 2012), *available at* http://www.nclc.org/images/pdf/pr-reports/report-ral-2012.pdf.

3 IRS Publication 2043, 2012 IRS e-file Refund Cycle Chart (Nov. 2011), *available at* www.irs.gov/pub/irs-pdf/p2043.pdf.

4 Chi Chi Wu & Jean Ann Fox, National Consumer Law Center & Consumer Fed'n of Am., The Party's Over for Quickie Tax Loans: But Traps Remain for Unwary Taxpayers 10-11 (Feb. 2012), *available at* www.nclc.org/images/pdf/pr-reports/report-ral-2012.pdf.

amounts ranging from $500 to $9,999.[5] For those loans, the banks would charge loan fees ranging from $34 to $140.[6] Commonly, the note was formally designated a demand note. Because of the short time period for which RALs were made, the APRs on these loans ranged from 50% to almost 500%.[7]

In 2011 and 2012, only one bank made RALs, and its loans were limited to an amount of $1,500.[8] This bank, Republic Bank & Trust, charged a fee of $61.22 for this RAL, which represents an APR of 149%.[9] If the refund was greater than $1,500 plus fees, the bank would deliver the rest of it in the form of a RAC, at a cost of $30.[10]

Since RALs were made through tax preparers, consumers were also required to pay a tax preparation fee. In some cases, tax preparers charged additional "add-on" fees using different names such as "application," "administrative," "e-filing," "service bureau," "transmission," or "processing" fees.[11] These fees ranged from $25 to several hundred dollars.[12] Some consumers might also pay a separate fee to cash the RAL checks.

### *14.1.3 RALs As Big Business*

In 2010, taxpayers paid approximately $338 million in RAL fees alone and another $48 million for add-on fees.[13] Consumers took out approximately 5 million RALs during the 2010 tax-filing season, which is significantly lower than the high of 12.4 million (at a cost of $1.24 billion) in 2004.[14]

The following is a chart of RAL volume and an estimate of their costs to consumers since 2000:[15]

| **Filing Year** | **No. of RAL applications** | **Increase/ decrease from prior year** | **No. of RALs made** | **RAL loan fees** |
|---|---|---|---|---|
| 2010 | 6.85 million | (-18.5%) | 5 million | $338 million |
| 2009 | 8.4 million | (-14%) | 7.2 million | $606 million |
| 2008 | 9.9 million | (- 3%) | 8.4 million | $738 million |
| 2007 | 10.2 million | 2% | 8.67 million | $833 million |
| 2006 | 10 million | (- 7%) | 9 million | $900 million |
| 2005 | 10.7 million | (-22%) | 9.60 million | $960 million |
| 2004 | 13.8 million | 2% | 12.38 million | $1.24 billion |
| 2003 | 13.5 million | (- 4%) | 12.15 million | $1.1 billion |
| 2002 | 14.1 million | 5% | 12.7 million | $1.1 billion |
| 2001 | 13.4 million | 12% | 12.1 million | $907 million |
| 2000 | 12 million | — | 10.8 million | $810 million |

## 14.2 Regulation of RALs

### *14.2.1 Truth in Lending Act*

Bank RALs are clearly credit that requires disclosures under the Truth in Lending Act. Until 2010, the APRs on RALs generally ranged from 50% to almost 500%.[16] However, RAL lenders usually reported lower APRs because they subtracted out or "unbundled" a fee that was supposedly for the disposal account into which the taxpayer's refund was deposited to repay the RAL.[17]

Previously, some RAL lenders reported even lower APRs because they characterized the loans as a "demand obligation," for which lenders are permitted to use a one-year repayment period.[18] However, the Official Commentary to Regulation Z

5 *See, e.g.*, Chi Chi Wu & Jean Ann Fox, National Consumer Law Center & Consumer Fed'n of Am., Major Changes in the Quick Tax Refund Loan Industry 7–8 (Feb. 2010), *available at* www.nclc.org/images/pdf/high_cost_small_loans/report-ral-2010.pdf.
For pricing from 2002 to 2009, see the annual RAL reports list in note 1, *supra*.

6 *See, e.g.*, Chi Chi Wu & Jean Ann Fox, National Consumer Law Center & Consumer Fed'n of Am., Major Changes in the Quick Tax Refund Loan Industry 7–8 (Feb. 2010), *available at* www.nclc.org/images/pdf/high_cost_small_loans/report-ral-2010.pdf.
For pricing from 2002 to 2009, see the annual RAL reports list in note 1, *supra*.

7 Chi Chi Wu & Jean Ann Fox, National Consumer Law Center & Consumer Fed'n of Am., Major Changes in the Quick Tax Refund Loan Industry 11 (Feb. 2010), *available at* www.nclc.org/images/pdf/high_cost_small_loans/report-ral-2010.pdf. *See also* United States Gen. Accounting Office, Pub. No. GAO-04-70, Tax Administration: Most Taxpayers Believe They Benefit from Paid Tax Preparers, but Oversight for IRS Is a Challenge 10 (Oct. 31, 2003), *available at* www.gao.gov/cgi-bin/getrpt?GAO-04-70 (findings include fact that GAO investigators were quoted loan fees ranging from $130 on a $1,200 refund—or 400% APR—to $174 on a $700 refund—or 900% APR).

8 Chi Chi Wu & Jean Ann Fox, National Consumer Law Center & Consumer Fed'n of Am., The Party's Over for Quickie Tax Loans: But Traps Remain for Unwary Taxpayers 10 (Feb. 2012), *available at* www.nclc.org/images/pdf/pr-reports/report-ral-2012.pdf.

9 *Id.*

10 *Id.*

11 *Id.* at 13–14.

12 *Id.*

13 *Id.* at 6–7.

14 *Id.*

15 *Id.* at 6. *See also* Annual RAL reports issued by NCLC and Consumer Federation of America, *supra* note 1; Neighborhood Economic Development Advocacy Project, Rapid Rip-Offs: Tax Refund Anticipation Lending in New York City (Mar. 2006), *available at* www.nedap.org (New Yorkers paid more than $43 million in RAL fees in 2004); Children's Defense Fund, Keeping What They've Earned: Tax Credit for Working Families (Feb. 2006), *available at* www.childrensdefense.org (this organization broke out the cost of RAL fees for taxpayers in: Cal. ($65.7 million); D.C. ($2.64 million); Miss. ($25 million); Ohio ($35 million); S.C. ($26 million); Tenn. ($29.4 million); Texas ($111 million)); Alan Berube, Anne Kim, Benjamin Foman, & Megan Burns, Brookings Institution and Progressive Policy Institute, The Price of Paying Taxes: How Tax Preparation and Refund Loan Fees Erode the Benefits of the EITC (May 2002), *available at* www.brookings.org (estimated $1.75 billion diverted from the Earned Income Tax Credit to pay for RALs plus tax preparation and electronic filing).

16 *See* § 14.1.2, *supra*.

17 Chi Chi Wu & Jean Ann Fox, National Consumer Law Center & Consumer Fed'n of Am., All Drain, No Gain: Refund Anticipation Loans Continue to Sap the Hard-Earned Tax Dollars of Low-Income Americans 5 (Jan. 2004), *available at* www.nclc.org/images/pdf/high_cost_small_loans/ral/2004-ral-report.pdf.

18 Reg. Z § 1026.17(c)(5) [§ 226.17(c)(5)].

now has specific provisions governing RALs. The Commentary provides that, when repayment of a RAL is required when the refund is received, including repayment by deposit into the consumer's account, the APR disclosures should be based on the creditor's estimate of the time the refund will be delivered, even if the loan also contains a demand clause.[19]

## 14.2.2 State Usury Laws

Despite the high APRs on RALs, state usury claims often ran into the issue of federal preemption/exportation.[20] All of the major RAL lenders were federally chartered banks or federally insured state banks chartered in states without usury caps. In 1994, the Fourth Circuit upheld the right of the then-largest RAL lender, Beneficial National Bank (now HSBC Bank) to export Delaware law (which permits any rate of interest agreed to by a lender and borrower) to wherever the RALs were written, at least in states where Beneficial had no branch offices.[21] At the time the Fourth Circuit issued this decision, H&R Block had no ownership interest in the loans. From 1996 to 2010, however, Block bought back a 49.9% interest in each loan it processes with HSBC (formerly Beneficial Bank/Household Bank).[22]

Refund anticipation checks (RACs)[23] present another TILA issue. Banks claim that RACs are a non-loan product, because the payment of refund monies is not made until the refund is actually received by the bank. However, in many cases, consumers will purchase a RAC solely for the purpose of deferring payment of the tax preparation fee until the refund arrives. In that case, the RAC really represents a loan of the tax preparation fee, and TILA disclosures should be made. This is especially true if the consumer receives a direct deposit of the RAC into his or her own bank account, or onto a prepaid card. In such cases, the RAC does not provide the refund monies any faster, and the only reason to use it is to pay for the tax preparation fee. The California Attorney General's office obtained a judgment against one commercial preparation chain that found, *inter alia*, that the chain violated TILA for failing to disclose that RACs are actually loans for the tax preparation fee, and that the RAC fee is a finance charge.[24]

## 14.2.3 State Laws Governing RALs

Twenty states[25] and one municipality[26] have passed RAL legislation. Most of these states have addressed tax refund loans through disclosures, but a few states have gone further.

North Carolina focused on regulating the RALs facilitator (i.e., those who broker or process RALs), rather than on the lender. The law also allows the North Carolina Commissioner of Banks to review RALs for "unconscionable fees."[27]

Connecticut prohibits RAL facilitators from facilitating a RAL over 60% APR and imposes a fine of $500 per violation.[28] However, the Second Circuit held that this rate cap is preempted by the National Bank Act.[29]

New Jersey enacted a law requiring facilitators to comply with the New Jersey Licensed Lenders Act, its criminal usury cap, and general usury law. As these laws limit the interest rate on small loans to 30% APR, it prohibits tax preparers from facilitating RALs over that limit.[30] However, immediately after the governor of New Jersey signed the law, a RAL lending bank challenged the rate cap and the criminal liability provisions, successfully arguing federal law preempted these protections.[31]

---

19 Official Commentary to Reg. Z § 1026.17(c)(1)-17 [§ 226.17(c)(1)-17]. *See generally* National Consumer Law Center, Truth in Lending § 4.5.10.2 (7th ed. 2010 and Supp.) (discussing TILA implications for RALs).

20 *See* § 3.4, *supra*.

21 Cades v. H&R Block, Inc., 43 F.3d 869 (4th Cir. 1994) (H&R Block office itself did not constitute a "branch" office). *See also* Christiansen v. Beneficial Nat'l Bank, 972 F. Supp. 681 (S.D. Ga. 1997) (relying upon *Cades* decision).

The OCC issued an amendment to Interpretive Ruling 7.1012 addressing "messenger services." 64 Fed. Reg. 60,092 (Nov. 4, 1999). The supplementary information clearly shows that the OCC intended to incorporate the more lax standard enunciated in *Cades* and *Christiansen* in determining under what circumstances the H&R Block office does not constitute a branch of the bank itself. *See* discussion at § 3.4.4.3, *supra*.

A preemption issue in a RAL case that reached the Supreme Court is the scope of the National Bank Act's preemption for state usury claims, that is, whether such claims are subject to conflict preemption or complete preemption. The Supreme Court held that the NBA did completely preempt any usury claims against H&R Block and Household concerning RALs. Beneficial Nat'l Bank v. Anderson, 539 U.S. 1, 123 S. Ct. 2058, 156 L. Ed. 2d 1 (2003). *See* § 7.9.1.3, *supra*.

22 *See* Chi Chi Wu, Jean Ann Fox & Elizabeth Renuart, National Consumer Law Center & Consumer Federation of America, Tax Preparers Peddle High Cost Tax Refund Loans: Millions Skimmed from the Working Poor and the U.S. Treasury 12 n.53 (Jan. 31, 2002), *available at* www.nclc.org/images/pdf/high_cost_small_loans/ral/2002-ral-report.pdf.

23 *See* § 14.1.2, *supra* (description of RACs).

24 Statement of Decision, People v. JTH Tax, Inc., Case No. CGC-07-460778 (Cal. Super. Ct. June 15, 2009), *available at* www.nclc.org/unreported.

25 *See* Appx. B, *infra*. *See also* Chi Chi Wu & Jean Ann Fox, National Consumer Law Center & Consumer Fed'n of Am., End of the Rapid Rip-Off: An Epilogue for Quickie Tax Loans 27–29 (Feb. 2011), *available at* www.nclc.org/images/pdf/high_cost_small_loans/ral/report-ral-2011.pdf (summary of Colorado, Louisiana, and Maryland RAL laws); Chi Chi Wu & Jean Ann Fox, National Consumer Law Center & Consumer Fed'n of Am., Major Changes in the Quick Tax Refund Loan Industry 27–29 (Feb. 2010), *available at* www.nclc.org/images/pdf/high_cost_small_loans/report-ral-2010.pdf (summary of Arkansas, Maine, Michigan, and New York RAL laws); National Consumer Law Center, Appendix A to Model Refund Anticipation Loan Act (Dec. 2008), *available at* www.nclc.org/images/pdf/high_cost_small_loans/ral/model-refund-anticipation-loan-act.pdf.

26 New York City Admin. Code §§ 20-739 to 20-741.1.

27 N.C. Gen. Stat. §§ 53-245 to 53-254. This statute has withstood a federal preemption challenge. North Carolina Ass'n of Elec. Tax Filers, Inc. v. Graham, 429 S.E.2d 544 (N.C. 1993).

28 Conn. Gen. Stat. § 42-480(d), (e).

29 Pacific Capital Bank, N.A. v. Conn., 542 F.3d 341 (2d Cir. 2008).

30 N.J. Stat. Ann. §§ 17:11D-1 to 17:11D-7 (West).

31 Pac. Capital Bank, N.A. v. Milgram, 2008 WL 700180 (D.N.J. Mar. 13, 2008).

The remaining provisions, including a mandatory warning about RALs in fourteen-point type and various prohibitions for RAL facilitators in their role as tax preparers, remain in effect.

A few states require registration of RAL facilitators.[32] Texas and Colorado require a RAL facilitator to be primarily involved in tax preparation or financial services and be authorized as an e-file provider with the IRS.[33] Texas law also requires that a facilitator who advertises RALs in Spanish must offer Spanish-language disclosures and loan documents.[34]

Several states, including Arkansas, Maine, Maryland, and New York, prohibit facilitators from charging a fee for a RAL except for the fee charged by the creditor, i.e., these laws ban preparer "add-on" fees.[35] These states also require oral disclosures.[36] The New York and Maine laws also contain prohibitions for RAL facilitators against: (1) engaging in collection of a delinquent RAL debt; (2) arranging for check cashers or other third parties to charge a fee or referring the consumer to a check casher; (3) engaging in any unfair or deceptive acts; and (4) including certain abusive clauses in a RAL contract.[37]

### *14.2.4 Military Lending Act*

One population that is protected from the high cost of RALs is active duty servicemembers and their families. The John Warner Defense Authorization Act of 2007, also known as the Military Lending Act (MLA), caps rates for loans to the military at 36% APR, including fees and insurance premiums.[38] The Department of Defense issued regulations that include RALs as one of three loan products covered by the MLA protections. The regulations define a "refund anticipation loan" as:

- Closed-end credit
- That is "expressly" repaid with a tax refund.[39]

This definition excludes loans made by tax preparers if the terms of the agreement do not expressly require it to be repaid by the anticipated tax refund. The supplemental information to the regulation explains that loans are not covered if the borrower merely notes that the source of the repayment is the tax refund.[40]

The MLA regulations cap interest rates for loans secured by expected tax refunds at 36% annual interest, which includes all fees associated with extending credit ("military APR"). Thus, the fee charged by RAL lenders for the disposable account used to repay a RAL—which was usually excluded by RAL banks from their APR calculations[41]—must be included in the military APR.

The MLA is discussed in greater detail elsewhere in this treatise.[42]

### *14.2.5 OCC Policy Statements*

The three largest RAL lending banks during the 2000s—HBSC (formerly known as Household Bank), JPMorgan Chase, and Pacific Capital Bancorp/Santa Barbara Bank & Trust—are all national banks regulated by the Office of Comptroller of Currency (OCC). In 2010, the OCC issued a policy statement setting forth its expectations for national banks that make RALs.[43] The policy statement requires RAL-lending national banks to monitor and oversee the activities of third-party tax preparers when these preparers facilitate RALs.[44] The policy statement requires the national banks to:

- Make certain disclosures to RAL borrowers;
- Review and approve RAL advertising by third-party preparers;
- Perform due diligence checks of third-party preparers (including conducting background checks and assessing general competence);
- Maintain an oversight program during tax season;
- Monitor practices of third-party preparers, including designing a mystery shopper program;
- Provide training and an annual certification process for third-party preparers.[45]

The policy statement also requires national banks to treat a RAL as delinquent for loss recognition purposes no more than

32 N.Y. Tax Law § 32 (McKinney); N.C. Gen. Stat. § 53-247.
Other states with registration requirements include Texas (Tex. Fin. Code § 350.003 (West)) and Washington State (Wash. Rev. Code § 19.265.020).

33 Tex. Fin. Code § 350.002(a) (West); Colo. Rev. Stat. § 5-9.5-104.
Washington State requires the facilitator to be a tax preparer. Wash. Rev. Code § 19.265.020(1)(a).

34 Tex. Fin. Code § 350.002(a) (West).

35 Ark. Code Ann. §§ 4-116-101 to 4-116-108; Me. Rev. Stat. tit. 9-A, §§ 10-102, 10-310; Md. Code Ann., Com. Law §§ 14-801 to 14-3807 (West); N.Y. Tax Law § 32 (McKinney); N.Y. Gen. Bus. Law § 372 (McKinney). *See* § 14.1.2, *supra* (description of "add-on" fees).

36 Ark. Code Ann. §§ 4-116-101 to 4-116-108; Me. Rev. Stat. tit. 9-A, §§ 10-102, 10-310; Md. Code Ann., Com. Law §§ 14-801 to 14-3807 (West); N.Y. Tax Law § 32 (McKinney); N.Y. Gen. Bus. Law § 372 (McKinney).

37 Me. Rev. Stat. tit. 9-A, §§ 10-102, 10-310; N.Y. Tax Law § 32 (McKinney); N.Y. Gen. Bus. Law § 372 (McKinney).

38 *See* § 2.2.5, *supra* (discussing fully this Act and its implementing regulations).

39 32 C.F.R. § 232.3(b)(1)(iii).

40 72 Fed. Reg. 50,580, 50,586 (Aug. 31, 2007).

41 *See* § 14.2.1, *supra.*

42 *See* § 2.2.5, *supra.*

43 Ann F. Jaedicke, Deputy Comptroller—Compliance Policy, Office of the Comptroller of Currency, Tax Refund Anticipation Loans—Guidance on Consumer Protection and Safety and Soundness, OCC Bulletin 2010-7 (Feb. 18, 2010), *available at* www.occ.treas.gov/ftp/bulletin/2010-7.html.

44 *Id.*
Earlier, the OCC refused to hold up a bank's request to merge on the basis of a bank's participation in RALs with a third-party vendor. OCC Corporate Decision No. 2005-11 (Aug. 2005), *available at* www.occ.gov/static/interpretations-and-precedents/aug05/cd05-11.pdf. Nor did the OCC downgrade the bank's CRA lending score based on making RALs.

45 Ann F. Jaedicke, Deputy Comptroller—Compliance Policy, Office of the Comptroller of Currency, Tax Refund Anticipation Loans—Guidance on Consumer Protection and Safety and Soundness, OCC Bulletin 2010-7 (Feb. 18, 2010), *available at* www.occ.treas.gov/ftp/bulletin/2010-7.html.

three e-file refund cycles after the tax return is submitted to the IRS.[46]

Previously, the OCC had issued an interpretative letter requiring RALs to be subject to a 100% risk weight, instead of the lower 20% risk weight for loans guaranteed by the federal government.[47] Pacific Capital Bancorp had requested to carry the loans at the 20% risk weight, arguing that RALs should be considered low-risk loans because they are effectively collateralized by a direct obligation of the U.S. government. The OCC disagreed, noting that the bank's actual loss experience (1.5% of RAL borrowers) suggests that RALs do not perform as if the federal government guarantees them.[48]

### *14.2.6 IRS Rules on RALs*

The IRS has issued a handful of rules governing RALs in IRS Publication 1345, an IRS document that governs providers of electronic tax return filing or "e-file providers," including the vast majority of tax preparers who facilitate RALs. The IRS requires e-file providers to disclose that: a RAL is an interest bearing loan; a RAL is not a substitute for or faster way to receive a refund; and if the refund is not received by the RAL lender within the expected time frame, the taxpayer may be liable for additional interest on the RAL.[49]

The IRS allows an e-file provider to charge a fee for RALs, but requires that it be a flat fee and be identical for all customers.[50] It forbids an e-file provider who is also a tax preparer from acting as the lender who makes the tax refund loan.[51] It also requires that the e-file provider disclose the existence of a RAL to the IRS, by requiring providers to include "RAL indicators" in the electronic return.[52]

Previously, the IRS had supported RAL lending with the debt indicator, a service that helped tax preparers and banks make RALs by acting as a form of credit check.[53] The debt indicator revealed whether a taxpayer's refund would be paid or would be intercepted for certain debts, such as child support, defaulted student loans, and debts owed to the federal government.[54] In 2010, the IRS stopped providing the debt indicator.[55] Without the debt indicator, RAL lending became much riskier. The OCC and FDIC essentially ordered the banks under their supervision to stop making RALs based on the IRS's termination of the debt indicator.[56]

## 14.3 RAL Litigation

### *14.3.1 Private Litigation*

#### 14.3.1.1 General

There have been a number of class action lawsuits filed against RAL providers over the years. National banks can export their home state usury cap, which eliminates usury claims based upon the consumer's home state usury ceiling. Nevertheless, borrowers can raise a myriad of other state law claims, particularly against the tax preparer. Examples are breach of fiduciary duty, fraud, negligent misrepresentation, UDAP, breach of duty of good faith and fair dealing, civil conspiracy, and RICO.[57] These claims often arise if the tax preparer receives an undisclosed kickback from the lender to make the loan and when the tax preparer advertises the loans as "advances."[58] They may also arise when preparers charge extra hidden fees for RALs.[59] One court held that a tax preparation company that continued to advertise RALs as "advances" and not as "loans" in the face of numerous consent orders and enforcement actions operated in bad faith and issued a nationwide injunction.[60]

46 *Id.*

47 Tommy Snow, Director of Capital Policy, Office of the Comptroller of the Currency, Interpretive Letter No. 959 (Feb. 13, 2003), *available at* www.occ.treas.gov/interp/mar03/int959.pdf.

48 *Id.*

49 IRS, Handbook for Authorized IRS e-File Providers of Individual Income Tax Returns Publication 1345, at 47 (rev. Nov. 2009), *available at* www.irs.gov/pub/irs-pdf/p1345.pdf.

50 *Id.* at 48.

51 *Id.* at 47.

52 *Id.* at 44.

53 Chi Chi Wu, National Consumer Law Center, Corporate Welfare for the RAL Industry: the Debt Indicator, IRS Subsidy, and Tax Fraud (July 2005), *available at* www.nclc.org/images/pdf/high_cost_small_loans/ral/debt_indicator_white_paper.pdf.

54 *Id.*

55 Press Release, Internal Revenue Serv., IRS Removes Debt Indicator for 2011 Tax Filing Season (Aug. 5, 2010), *available at* www.irs.gov/newsroom/article/0,,id=226310,00.html.

56 *See* § 14.3.2, *infra.*

57 *See, e.g.*, Peterson v. H&R Block Tax Servs., 22 F. Supp. 2d 795 (N.D. Ill. 1998); Affafato v. Beneficial, 1998 U.S. Dist. LEXIS 12447 (E.D.N.Y. Aug. 7, 1998); Green v. H&R Block, 735 A.2d 1039 (Md. 1999); Basile v. H&R Block, Inc., 761 A.2d 1115 (Pa. 2000) (holding no fiduciary relationship on the basis of an agency relationship, but remanding for findings on the basis of a confidential relationship), *subsequent proceeding at* 777 A.2d 95 (Pa. Super. Ct. 2001) (finding confidential relationship), 894 A.2d 786 (Pa. Super. Ct. 2006) (trial court's order de-certifying the class reversed due to the defendant's failure to appeal the certification order in 1997), *vacated and remanded*, 909 A.2d 298 (Pa. 2006), *upon reconsideration*, 926 A.2d 493 (Pa. Super. Ct. 2007) (after reviewing pertinent law, court found defendant failed to timely appeal class certification), *rev'd*, 973 A.2d 417 (Pa. 2009) (holding defendant did not waive appellate review of class certification order); H&R Block v. Haese, 976 S.W.2d 237 (Tex. App. 1998). *See also* Ch. 2, *supra* (discussing these claims more broadly).

58 *See* Chi Chi Wu, Jean Ann Fox & Elizabeth Renuart, National Consumer Law Center & Consumer Federation of America, Tax Preparers Peddle High Cost Tax Refund Loans: Millions Skimmed from the Working Poor and the U.S. Treasury (Jan. 31, 2002), *available at* www.nclc.org (discussing fees and advertising practices).

59 Watts v. Jackson Hewitt Tax Serv., 579 F. Supp. 2d 334 (E.D.N.Y. 2008) (denying motion to dismiss claim that Jackson Hewitt franchisee charged a hidden $25 fee for RALs, on top of a disclosed $75 application fee and the RAL loan fee).

60 JTH Tax v. H&R Block, 128 F. Supp. 2d 926, 938 (E.D. Va. 2001), *aff'd in part, vacated in part, and remanded in part*, 28 Fed. Appx. 207 (4th Cir. 2002) (appellate court upheld the finding of bad faith, though it modified the scope of the injunction) (in determining whether the various advertisements were misleading, the district

In other decisions, courts have split on whether to dismiss or grant summary judgment on claims alleging breach of fiduciary duty and breach of duty of good faith and fair dealing.[61] One barrier to RAL litigation is the prevalence of mandatory arbitration clauses in RAL contracts.[62]

A series of class actions against the largest tax preparation chain, H&R Block, and its lending partner, Beneficial Bank (now HSBC Bank) were at risk of being snuffed out by a controversial $25 million global settlement.[63] The Seventh Circuit, however, overturned the approval of the settlement and sent the case back to the district court with the requirement that the case be assigned to a different judge.[64] On remand, the district court rejected the settlement on the basis that the class counsel who negotiated the settlement were inadequate representatives for the plaintiff class.[65] Subsequently, the district court permitted a nationwide class action to go forward on a RICO claim, plus a breach of contract claim against HSBC alone.[66] In 2005, the district court refused to proceed to a fairness hearing regarding another weak settlement proposal and refused to enjoin lawsuits proceeding in other courts.[67] In

court relied upon survey evidence showing that 22% of the surveyed consumers believed the poster advertisement was deceptive; the court found this degree of deception to be substantial; interestingly, H&R Block's own research indicated that most consumers would not associate an "advance" with a loan). *See also* California v. Jackson Hewitt Inc., Case No. 070304558 (Cal. Super. Ct., Alameda filed Jan. 3, 2007), *available at* http://ag.ca.gov/newsalerts/release.php?id=1405&year=2007&month=1 (complaint and judgment) (permanent injunction, restitution of $4 million, civil penalties and fees of $1 million assessed against a tax preparer based in part on how it advertised and disclosed its "Money Now" and "Super Fast Refund" products).

61 *See* Basile v. H&R Block, Inc., 761 A.2d 1115 (Pa. 2000) (holding no fiduciary relationship on the basis of an agency relationship, but remanding for findings on the basis of a confidential relationship), *subsequent proceeding at* 777 A.2d 95 (Pa. Super. Ct. 2001) (finding confidential relationship), 894 A.2d 786 (Pa. Super. Ct. 2006) (trial court's order to de-certifying the class reversed due to the defendant's failure to appeal the certification order in 1997), *vacated and remanded,* 909 A.2d 298 (Pa. 2006). *Cf.* Kleven v. Household Bank, 334 F.3d 638 (7th Cir. 2003) (trustee could not set aside repayment of RALs by taxpayers who filed for bankruptcy shortly after receiving a RAL; however, court remarks on the predatory nature of RALs, noting: "an attack on RALs based on fairness and equity would certainly have some appeal"). *Compare* Peterson v. H&R Block Tax Servs., Inc., 971 F. Supp. 1204 (N.D. Ill. 1997) (motion to dismiss on breach of duty of good faith and fair dealing denied; granted as to breach of fiduciary duty), 174 F.R.D. 78 (N.D. Ill. 1997) (class certification granted on RICO and UDAP claim), 22 F. Supp. 2d 795 (N.D. Ill. 1998) (RICO claim dismissed due to inability to show H&R Block's deliberate fraud in failing to advise customers that tax refunds where the earned income tax credit is sought may be delayed beyond three weeks; state law claim remanded to state court), *and* Green v. H&R Block, Inc., 735 A.2d 1039 (Md. 1999) (tax preparer found to be agent of consumer thus creating fiduciary duty to advise the consumer that it receives payments and other benefits from the lender for facilitating the making of the loan), *and* Haese v. H&R Block, Clearinghouse No. 54586 (Tex. Dist. Ct. 105th Jud. Nov. 6, 2002) (one-page letter ruling in which court held that tax preparer owed fiduciary duty to consumers; court found that H&R Block had violated that duty and assessed a forfeiture of all of the company's tax preparation fees in Texas for a five-year period), *with* Beckett v. H&R Block, Inc., 714 N.E.2d 1033 (Ill. App. Ct. 1999) (tax preparer not an agent; no duty to disclose secret profit to consumer). *But cf.* Sorenson v. H&R Block, 107 Fed. Appx. 227 (1st Cir. 2004) (holding in this non-RAL case that, under Massachusetts law, a tax preparer does not owe per se fiduciary duty to client).

62 *See, e.g.,* Carbajal v. Household Bank, Fed. Sav. Bank, 372 F.3d 903 (7th Cir. 2004) (affirming order compelling arbitration of claims against Household, H&R Block, and other RAL lenders.).

In *Carbajal*, the Seventh Circuit made some astounding assumptions about the RAL business. The court stated its belief that one-sided form contracts are beneficial because "[f]orms reduce transaction costs and benefit consumers because, in competition, reductions in the cost of doing business show up as lower prices (here, a slightly lower rate of interest on the loan)." The court apparently had not seen the astronomical prices of RALs, nor read its own prior opinions discussing the predatory nature of RALs in Kleven v. Household Bank, 334 F.3d 638,640 (7th Cir. 2003), which noted that "[t]he bargain struck [for a RAL] is a good one for only one of the two parties. Guess which one?"). The court also apparently had not noticed there was little competition or "shopping around" for RAL prices, which at that time differed between the handful of RAL lenders by only a few dollars.

In contrast, the Pennsylvania Supreme Court denied a motion to compel arbitration in part on the basis that the arbitration clause in the RAL agreement was unconscionable towards consumers. McNulty v. H&R Block, 843 A.2d 1267 (Pa. Super. Ct. 2004). The Pennsylvania court noted that the RAL Agreement is a contract of "adhesion," and that the arbitration provision unreasonably favors H&R Block, in that it required the consumer to pay a $50 fee that exceeded the $37 e-filing fee at issue in the case. *See also* Cummins v. H&R Block, Civil Action No. 03-C-134 (Cir. Ct. of Kanawha Cnty., W. Va. June 1, 2004) (order denying defendants' motion to compel arbitration in case challenging H&R Block's brokering of RALs under West Virginia Credit Services Organization Act), *available on the companion website to this treatise.*

63 Zawikowski v. Beneficial Nat'l Bank, 2000 WL 1051879 (N.D. Ill. July 28, 2000) (objections to the settlement included allegations that it would only pay pennies on the dollar and that it was a product of collusion between H&R Block, Beneficial, and some "friendly" plaintiffs' attorneys).

Following the settlement, Household and H&R Block filed actions seeking to enforce arbitration clauses against any class members who opted out of the *Zawikowski* settlement (and there were about 2,100 such consumers). Household Bank, F.S.B. v. JFS Group, 320 F.3d 1249 (11th Cir. 2003); Household Bank, F.S.B. v. Allen, 2001 WL 737532 (S.D. Miss. May 25, 2001).

64 Reynolds v. Beneficial Nat'l Bank, 288 F.3d 277 (7th Cir. 2002).

65 Reynolds v. Beneficial Nat'l Bank, 260 F. Supp. 2d 680 (N.D. Ill. 2003).

66 Carnegie v. Household Int'l, Inc., 220 F.R.D. 542 (N.D. Ill. 2004) (dismissing in addition, the breach of contract claim as to H&R Block, and withdrawing class certification for several state claims on the basis that a fifty state legal analysis would be required to resolve them, presenting an intractable class manageability problem; also reaffirming a ruling by prior judge enforcing mandatory arbitration clauses against those RAL customers whose contracts included them), *aff'd*, 376 F.3d 656 (7th Cir. 2004).

67 Carnegie v. Household Int'l, Inc., 371 F. Supp. 2d 954 (N.D. Ill. 2005). *See also* Turner v. Beneficial Nat'l Bank, 405 F. Supp. 2d 929 (N.D. Ill. 2005) (approving only a fraction of the fee sought by a named plaintiff in the large class case who decided to pursue her own individual case; court had previously determined that the attorney had not adequately represented the class).

2006, the saga of this case came to a conclusion, as the district court finally approved a settlement that paid approximately $30 million or up to $80 to each class member.[68]

#### 14.3.1.2 Loan Broker and Credit Service Organization Statutes

Tax preparers who facilitate RALs may also run afoul of state laws governing loan brokers or credit services organizations.[69] These laws require the broker or credit services organization to register with a state regulator and provide certain disclosures. Some of these laws may also cap the rate of loans that the broker or credit services organization can arrange; however, these rate caps are preempted by federal banking laws.[70] State regulators have issued warning letters to tax preparers that they must comply with state credit services organization acts (CSOAs).[71]

#### 14.3.1.3 Cross-Lender Debt Collection

A significant risk to RAL consumers had been the practice of cross-lender debt collection, by which all of the RAL lenders have included a provision in their RAL agreements allowing them to take a consumer's tax refund and use it to pay back any prior RAL debts for any other RAL lender.[72] There were several lawsuits filed against RAL lenders and tax preparers over these cross-lender debt collection provisions.[73] The California Attorney General's enforcement actions against the three major tax preparers included claims for failure to inform consumers that they could be subject to cross-collection.[74]

### *14.3.2 Federal Enforcement*

#### 14.3.2.1 FDIC and OCC 2009 Actions

The Federal Trade Commission was one of the first federal regulators take enforcement action over deceptive advertising of RALs in the mid-1970s.[75] However, federal regulators did not address RALs for over three decades after that.

In 2009, the FDIC issued a cease and desist order against Republic Bank & Trust, a RAL lending bank, over unspecified consumer protection law violations and unsafe and unsound banking practices.[76] The order required the bank to develop a compliance plan for its RAL business, including establishing a training program for all tax preparers who offer its RALs about relevant consumer protection laws, and to audit compliance by tax preparers.[77]

In December 2009, the Office of Comptroller of Currency (OCC) forced Jackson Hewitt's main RAL partner—Pacific Capital Bancorp, also known as Santa Barbara Bank and

---

68 Carnegie v. Household Int'l, Inc., 445 F. Supp. 2d 1032 (N.D. Ill. 2006).

69 *E.g.,* H&R Block Eastern Enters., Inc. v. Raskin, 591 F.3d 718 (4th Cir. 2010) (remanding case; requiring district court to address the issue of whether tax preparers who make RALs are covered as "credit services organizations" under Maryland CSO law); Hunter v. Jackson Hewitt, Inc., 2008 WL 706788 (S.D. W. Va. Mar. 13, 2008) (granting summary judgment on consumer's claim for breach of contract); Brown v. Jackson Hewitt, Inc., 2007 WL 642011 (N.D. Ohio Feb. 27, 2007) (granting motion to remand case from federal court to state court); Fugate v. Jackson Hewitt, Inc., 347 S.W.3d 81 (Mo. Ct. App. 2011) (reversing dismissal, tax preparer could be credit services organization even though consumer did not make payment directly to preparer); Harper v. Jackson Hewitt, 706 S.E.2d 63 (W. Va. 2010) (tax preparer who receives compensation, either from borrower or lending bank, for helping borrower obtain a RAL meets the definition of "credit services organization" under West Virginia law); Cummins v. H&R Block, Civil Action No. 03-C-134 (Cir. Ct. of Kanawha Cnty., W. Va. Dec. 30, 2004), *available at* www.nclc.org/unreported (order granting plaintiffs' motion for class certification in case challenging H&R Block's brokering of RALs under West Virginia Credit Services Organization Act).

For a discussion of how state credit services organization laws may apply to credit arrangers, see National Consumer Law Center, Fair Credit Reporting § 15.3.4 (7th ed. 2010 and Supp.). *But see* Norris v. Jackson Hewitt, Inc., 2010 WL 2629723 (S.D. Ind. June 28, 2010) (dismissing case on basis that plaintiff failed to sufficiently allege that she had been damaged by Hewitt's violation of Indiana Credit Services Organization Act); Gomez v. Jackson Hewitt, Inc., 16 A.3d 261 (Md. Ct. Spec. App. 2011) (tax preparer that facilitated RALs was not a credit service organization because customer paid preparer for RAL facilitation only indirectly; court relied, ironically, in part on the fact that Maryland specifically passed a law governing RAL facilitators); Thomas v. Jackson Hewitt, Inc., 950 N.E.2d 578 (Ohio Ct. App. 2011) (affirming dismissal based on failure to sufficiently allege damages from Hewitt's violation of state credit services organization act).

70 H&R Block E. Enters., Inc. v. Turnbaugh, Civ. Ac. No. 07-1822 (D. Md. July 30, 2008), *available on the companion website to this treatise, remanded sub. nom,* H&R Block E. Enters. v. Raskin, 591 F.3d 718 (4th Cir. 2010) (remanding case on the basis that district court should have first addressed the issue of whether tax preparers who make RALs are covered as "credit services organizations" under Maryland CSO law). *See also* § 3.4, *supra.*

71 *See* § 14.3.3, *infra.*

72 Thus, if a taxpayer owes money to one RAL lender from a prior year and applies for a RAL from a different lender, her RAL will be denied and her refund will be gone. The second lender will take her refund and use it to repay the prior RAL debt to the first lender.

73 Carbajal v. Household Bank, Fed. Sav. Bank, 372 F.3d 903 (7th Cir. 2004) (affirming order compelling arbitration of claims against Household, H&R Block, and other RAL lenders for violation of Fair Debt Collection Practices Act, the Equal Credit Opportunity Act, and Illinois consumer protection laws); Hood v. Santa Barbara Bank & Trust, 49 Cal. Rptr. 3d 369 (Cal. Ct. App. 2006) (reversing the dismissal of the plaintiffs' claims against SBBT on the basis of federal preemption under the National Bank Act).

The latter case resulted in a settlement in which the lender agreed to cease cross-collection for one year and in subsequent years to provide notices informing consumers before they apply for RALs, if they have an outstanding RAL debt which will result in cross-collection. Preliminary Approval of Class Settlement, Hood v. Santa Barbara Bank & Trust, Case No. 1156354 (Cal. Super. Ct. County of Santa Barbara Jan. 7, 2009), *available at* www.nclc.org/images/pdf/litigation/closed/hood-settlement-agreement.pdf.

74 *See* § 14.3.3, *infra.*

75 *See, e.g.,* Beneficial Corp. v. Federal Trade Comm'n, 542 F.2d 611 (3d Cir. 1976).

76 Order to Cease And Desist, In the Matter of Republic Bank & Trust Company, Louisville, Kentucky, FDIC-08-308b (Dep't of Treas. FDIC Feb. 27, 2009), *available at* www.fdic.gov/bank/individual/enforcement/2009-02-10.pdf.

77 *Id.*

Trust—to exit the RAL business.[78] In December 2010, the OCC issued an order forcing HSBC to exit the RAL business.[79] This OCC order may have been a "friendly" order, as HSBC had shown signs it was unwilling to continue to make RALs. H&R Block actually sued HSBC in October 2010 to force the bank to make preparations for RAL lending in the 2011 tax season.[80]

#### 14.3.2.2 FDIC's 2011 Action Against Republic Bank

In February 2011, the FDIC notified Republic Bank that the practice of originating RALs was unsafe and unsound.[81] The FDIC's action was based on the IRS's decision to stop providing the debt indicator, a service that helped tax preparers and banks make RALs by acting as a form of credit check.[82] In response, Republic announced its plans to appeal the FDIC's decision[83] and filed a lawsuit against the FDIC.[84] The FDIC sent similar notices about ending RAL lending to two other banks under its supervision, both of which acquiesced in the decision.[85]

Subsequently, the FDIC issued an amended complaint detailing the widespread legal violations in Republic's RAL program and proposed a $2 million civil penalty.[86] These violations included:[87]

- *Truth-in-Lending Act (TILA):* Copies of TILA disclosures were regularly absent from loan files. Nearly 88% of the tax preparers that FDIC investigators called failed to make an oral disclosure of the APR when requested.
- *Gramm-Leach-Bliley Act*: Tax preparers did not have proper physical and electronic safeguards for the protection of confidential consumer information, such as shredders or locked dumpsters. Half of the tax preparer offices had no alarm system, even though the stores had bank checks inside.
- *Federal Trade Commission Act*: The FDIC alleged that Republic engaged in unfair and deceptive actions, such as implying that customers would receive the full amount of their refunds minus fees in one or two days by getting a RAL, despite the fact that the RAL amounts were limited by Republic to $1,500.
- *Equal Credit Opportunity Act (ECOA)*: The FDIC found tax preparers refused to process a RAL application when only one spouse applied for the loan, in violation of the ECOA.

According to the FDIC, 46.5% of tax preparers who made Republic RALs were in violation of at least three different laws. The FDIC found that Republic failed to properly train tax preparers to comply with consumer protection laws. In particular, Republic tested preparers' knowledge of consumer laws by giving them an online quiz that permitted the preparers to keep guessing until they passed the test. In addition, the FDIC alleged that Republic attempted to interfere with its investigation by setting up an Internet webpage of "Frequently Asked Questions" to coach tax preparers during the day when the FDIC tested the preparers.[88]

Ultimately, the FDIC reached a settlement with Republic in which the bank agreed to cease making RALs after April 2012, and to pay a $900,000 civil penalty.[89]

#### 14.3.2.3 IRS Rulemaking

RALs sometimes become the issue of regulatory action because they are often involved in tax fraud cases. There is significant evidence that RALs promote tax fraud by preparers.[90] In fact, these concerns were significant enough for the IRS to open a rulemaking proceeding in 2008 asking whether the agency should develop rules restricting the sharing of tax return information to market RALs and other financial products because they provide preparers with a financial incentive to inflate refund claims inappropriately.[91]

### *14.3.3 State Enforcement Actions*

Over the decades, state regulators, enforcement agencies, and municipal regulators have all taken actions against tax preparers over RALs. In the 1990s, state attorneys general sued preparers over deceptive advertising of RALs.[92]

78 Press Release, Pacific Capital Bancorp, Pacific Capital Bancorp Announces Planned Sale of Refund Anticipation Loan and Refund Transfer Businesses (Dec. 24, 2010), *available at* www.snl.com/irweblinkx/file.aspx?IID=100652&FID=8796232.

79 Press Release, H&R Block, HSBC Terminates Agreement to Provide RALs at Direction of OCC (Dec. 24, 2010).

80 *See* Complaint, HRB Tax Group, Inc. v. HSBC Bank USA, N.A., Case 4:10-cv-01946 (E.D. Mo. Oct. 15, 2010).

81 Republic Bank & Trust, Form 8-K, Other Events, Financial Statements and Exhibits (Feb. 10, 2011).

82 *See* § 14.2.6, *supra*.

83 Robert Barba, *Republic, a Holdout in Refund-Anticipation Loans, Challenges FDIC Order*, Am. Banker, Feb. 16, 2011; Republic Bank & Trust, Form 8-K, Other Events, Financial Statements and Exhibits (Feb. 10, 2011).

84 Complaint, Republic Bank v. Federal Deposit Ins. Corp., No. 3:11-cv-00119-CRS (W.D. Ky. Feb. 28, 2011), *available on the companion website to this treatise*.

85 Ohio Valley Banc Corp., Form 8-K, Current Report Pursuant to Section 13 or 15(d) of the Securities Exchange Act of 1934 (Feb. 11, 2011); Press Release, River City Bank, River City Bank Exits Refund Anticipation Loan Business (Feb. 16, 2011), *available at* www.rcbral.com.

86 Amended Notice of Charges for an Order to Cease and Desist, In the Matter of Republic Bank & Trust Co., FDIC-10-079b and FDIC-10-216k, May 3, 2011, *available on the companion website to this treatise*.

87 *Id.*

88 *Id.*

89 Consent Order, In the Matter of Republic Bank & Trust Co., FDIC-10-079b and FDIC-10-216k, Dec. 8, 2011, *available on the companion website to this treatise*.

90 *See* Chi Chi Wu and Jean Ann Fox, National Consumer Law Center & Consumer Fed'n of Am., RAL, Tax Fraud, and Fringe Preparers (Feb. 2009), *available at* www.nclc.org/images/pdf/high_cost_small_loans/ral/2009-ral-appendix.pdf.

91 73 Fed. Reg. 1131 (Jan. 7, 2008).

92 These state enforcement actions are discussed in JTH Tax v. H&R

The New York City Department of Consumer Affairs (DCA) filed a lawsuit against H&R Block over the company's allegedly deceptive advertising. As a result of its investigation, DCA found that 86% of the company's branches in the city failed to differentiate between true refunds and RALs.[93] In addition, DCA reached an agreement with Jackson Hewitt over charges of deceptive promotion of RALs.[94]

The California Attorney General filed enforcement actions against all three of the national tax preparation chains. The lawsuits alleged violation of that state's credit services organization act (CSOA) because the chains received a fee for obtaining RALs without complying with that law, failed to inform consumers that they could be subject to cross-lender debt collection, and engaged in deceptive advertising.[95] Two of the three national chains reached settlements with the California Attorney General.[96]

The California Attorney General's office obtained a judgment against the third chain, Liberty Tax Service.[97] The judgment found that Liberty: (1) engaged in deceptive marketing, including ads that promoted "refunds in one day" or "refunds in only 24 hours"; (2) violated the Fair Debt Collection Practices Act by assisting Santa Barbara Bank and Trust in cross-lender debt collection; and (3) violated the Truth in Lending Act for failing to disclose that refund anticipation checks (RACs)[98] are actually loans for the tax preparation fee, and that the RAC fee is a finance charge.[99] Liberty Tax Service was ordered to pay $1.16 million in civil penalties and $135,886 in restitution to consumers.[100]

The New Jersey Attorney General's office sued a local tax preparation chain for deceptive advertisement of RALs, alleging that the chain misrepresented RALs as tax refunds, and did not disclose that they were loans.[101] The New Jersey Attorney General's office won that case, obtaining a judgment finding that the tax preparation chain was liable for hundreds of Consumer Fraud Act violations.[102] The preparer was ordered to pay $1.86 million in penalties and to repay $1.64 million to RAL borrowers.[103] That office also cited thirty-eight tax preparers for deceptive marketing of RALs, such as advertisements of RALs as "instant," "same day," or day-specific ("1 Day" or "2 Day") refunds without disclosing that they were loans.[104]

The New York State Division of Human Rights sued both Jackson Hewitt and Liberty Tax Service for discriminatory targeting of minorities for RALs, in violation of that state's human rights law.[105] The same agency investigated H&R Block for similar violations, but H&R Block struck back preemptively by seeking to stop the investigation. That effort failed, with a court holding that federal law did not prohibit the New York agency from investigating H&R Block.[106] Similarly, a federal district court held that the New York agency's enforcement action against Jackson Hewitt was not preempted by the National Bank Act.[107]

The North Carolina Commissioner of Banks took action against Mo' Money Taxes, a small tax preparation chain, for its failure to comply with the North Carolina RAL law. Mo' Money Taxes had failed to register its thirteen offices in North

Block, 128 F. Supp. 2d 926 (E.D. Va. 2001) (citing *In re* H&R Block, No. 93-198 (Conn. Comm'r Consumer Prot. July 27, 1993); *In re* H&R Block E. Tax Servs., No. 93-410039 (Fla. Office A.G. Jan. 6, 1994) (assurance of voluntary compliance); Cerullo v. H&R Block, No. 95-409497 (N.Y. Gen. Term) (consent order)), *aff'd in part, vacated in part, and remanded in part*, 28 Fed. Appx. 207 (4th Cir. 2002).

93 Dykstra v. H&R Block, Clearinghouse No. 54587A (N.Y. Sup. Ct. Mar. 12, 2002) (complaint).

94 Press Release, New York City Department of Consumer Affairs, Consumer Affairs Releases Preliminary Results of Tax Preparer Enforcement and Monitoring for 2004 Season (Apr. 5, 2004), *available at* www.ci.nyc.ny.us/html/dca/pdf/pr40504.pdf.

95 Complaint, California v. JTH Tax, Inc., Case No. CGC-07-460778 (Cal. Super. Ct. Feb. 26, 2007), *available at* http://ag.ca.gov/cms_attachments/press/pdfs/n1531_liberty_complaint_022607_(final).pdf; California v. Jackson Hewitt Inc., Case No. 070304558 (Cal. Super. Ct., Alameda filed Jan. 3, 2007), *available at* http://ag.ca.gov/newsalerts/release.php?id=1405&year=2007&month=1 (complaint and judgment) (permanent injunction, restitution of $4 million, civil penalties and fees of $1 million); People of California v. H&R Block, 2006 WL 2669045 (N.D. Cal. Sep. 18, 2006).

96 Judgment, People of the State of California v. H&R Block, Case No. 06-449461 (Cal. Sup. Ct. Dec. 31, 2008), *available at* http://ag.ca.gov/cms_attachments/press/pdfs/n1645_block_judgment.pdf (permanent injunction, restitution of $2.45 million, civil penalties and fees of $2.4 million); California v. Jackson Hewitt Inc., Case No. 070304558 (Cal. Super. Ct., Alameda filed Jan. 3, 2007), *available at* http://ag.ca.gov/newsalerts/release.php?id=1405&year=2007&month=1 (complaint and judgment) (permanent injunction, restitution of $4 million, civil penalties and fees of $1 million).

97 Statement of Decision, People v. JTH Tax, Inc., Case No. CGC-07-460778 (Cal. Super. Ct. June 15, 2009), *available at* www.nclc.org/unreported.

98 *See* § 14.1.2, *supra* (description of RACs).

99 Statement of Decision, People v. JTH Tax, Inc., Case No. CGC-07-460778 (Cal. Super. Ct. June 15, 2009), *available at* www.nclc.org/unreported.

100 *Id.*

101 Press Release, New Jersey Attorney General's Office, State Sues Tax Preparation Firm Over Deceptive "Fast Refund" Offers (Mar. 5, 2007).

102 Press Release, Office of the New Jersey Attorney General, Tax Preparation Firm Ordered to Pay $3.5 Million for Deceptive Sales of "Refund Anticipation Loans" (Apr. 14, 2009), *available at* www.nj.gov/oag/newsreleases09/pr20090414a.html.

103 *Id.*

104 Press Release, Office of the New Jersey Attorney General, Attorney General Anne Milgram Charges Tax Preparers Falsely Advertised "Same Day" Tax Refunds (Feb. 5, 2009), *available at* www.nj.gov/oag/newsreleases09/pr20090205d.html.

105 Complaint, New York State Division of Human Rights v. Jackson Hewitt (Jan. 17, 2008), *available at* www.dhr.state.ny.us/pdf/Division%20vs.%20Jackson%20Hewitt_Complaint.pdf; Complaint, New York State Div. of Human Rights v. JTH Tax, Inc. (Jan. 17, 2008), *available at* www.dhr.state.ny.us/pdf/Division%20vs.%20Liberty%20Financial_Complaint.pdf.

106 New York State Div. of Human Rights v. H&R Block Tax Servs., 897 N.Y.S.2d 75 (N.Y. App. Div. 2010) (upholding trial court's denial of motion to quash subpoena, compelling H&R Block to produce documents, and holding that investigation was not preempted by the National Bank Act).

107 Jackson Hewitt Tax Serv. v. Kirkland, 735 F. Supp. 2d 91 (S.D.N.Y. 2010).

Carolina with the commissioner, as required by North Carolina's law.[108] Mo' Money Taxes agreed to pay a civil penalty of $13,000 and to properly register as a RAL facilitator.[109]

The Arkansas Attorney General also filed a lawsuit against Mo' Money Taxes for violations of the Arkansas RAL Act. The complaint alleged that Mo' Money Taxes violated the statute by charging add-on fees, which are prohibited by the Arkansas RAL Act.[110] The complaint also alleged that Mo' Money Taxes failed to provide required written and oral disclosures and failed to post a mandatory warning and schedule of RAL fees in its offices.[111] The Arkansas Attorney General obtained a consent judgment in which Mo' Money agreed to comply with the Arkansas RAL Act and to pay a fine of $25,000.[112]

State regulators also have directed warning letters to tax preparers that they must comply with state loan broker or credit services organization acts. The Massachusetts Commissioner of Banks issued a warning letter to tax preparers that they would be required to obtain a small loan company license under Massachusetts law if they were offering RALs, regardless of whether the preparer originated the loan.[113] The Mississippi Commissioner of Banking and Consumer Finance issued a similar letter.[114] The Illinois Division of Finance and Professional Regulation issued an order prohibiting consumer installment lenders in that state from facilitating RALs. The division sent notices to 128 consumer installment lenders that offered RALs and tax preparation services.[115]

The Maryland Commissioner of Financial Institutions released an advisory that warned tax preparers who assisted Maryland taxpayers in obtaining RALs that they were operating as a credit services organization, and that they must be licensed and comply with Maryland's CSOA.[116] In response, H&R Block sued the commissioner alleging that it did not need to comply with Maryland's CSOA because the company, when it facilitates RALs, is serving as an agent of a national bank and is thus exempt from state regulation under the National Bank Act. A federal court ruled partly in H&R Block's favor, holding that federal law did preempt the fee caps and contract requirements of Maryland's CSOA, but not the licensing, bonding, and disclosure provisions.[117] This decision was appealed to the Fourth Circuit Court of Appeals, which remanded the case back to the district court, holding that the lower court should have first addressed the issue of whether tax preparers who make RALs are covered as "credit services organizations" under Maryland's CSOA.[118]

## 14.4 Pay Stub RALs

A "pay stub RAL" or "pre-season loan" is a variation on a traditional RAL. Pay stub RALs differ from traditional RALs in that they are offered earlier in the year, even before a taxpayer receives an IRS Form W-2. Since a taxpayer cannot file a tax return without a W-2 form, this loan is made prior to the filing of the return and before the tax season officially starts. In some cases, the loan is based on an estimate of the expected tax refund calculated from the taxpayer's "pay stub"—hence the name.

What the pay stub RALs have in common with traditional RALs is that they are risky loans repaid from the proceeds of the consumer's tax refund. With some pay stub RALs, the loan is secured by the tax refund, while other variations merely carry an expectation that the loans will be repaid from the refund.

Some pay stub RALs are structured as open-end lines of credit. In late 2008/early 2009, Jackson Hewitt offered the ipower Line of Credit, up to $500, issued by MetaBank. Subsequently, the Office of Thrift Supervision, which was the then-regulator for MetaBank, issued a directive terminating this program, citing "unfair or deceptive acts or practices," as well as prohibiting MetaBank making from traditional RALs.[119]

H&R Block offers the Emerald Advance Line of Credit, up to $1,000.[120] Using a line of credit to make pay stub RALs raises the question as to whether these are really closed-end loans offered as "spurious" open-end credit.[121] However, the Block Emerald Advance can be kept open after tax season, if the consumer either has his or her payroll directly deposited to Block's Emerald Card or has a savings account linked to the card.[122]

108 Consent Order, *In re* Application of Mo Money of North Carolina, Inc., No. 10:036:RAL (N.C. Comm'r Banks Feb. 8, 2010), *available on the companion website to this treatise*.

109 *Id.*

110 Complaint, State v. Mo' Money Tax Serv., No. CV 2010 6958 (Ark Cir. Ct. Pulaski Cty. Dec. 6, 2010), *available on the companion website to this treatise*.

111 *Id.*

112 Consent Judgment, State v. Mo' Money Tax Serv., Case No. 10-6958 (Ark. Cir. Ct. Pulaski Cty. Nov. 22, 2011), *available on the companion website to this treatise*.

113 Letter from Thomas J. Curry, Mass. Commissioner of Banks, Division of Banks Warns Tax Preparers That They Must Be Licensed to Provide Refund Anticipation Loan (Mar. 5, 2003), *available at* www.state.ma.us/dob/taxprep.htm.

114 Memorandum from Commissioner John Allison re: Department Warns Mississippi Tax Preparers They May Have to Obtain a License to Provide Refund Anticipation Loans (Aug. 19, 2003), *available at* www.dbcf.state.ms.us/documents/cons_finance/tax-preparers-1st-memo.pdf.

115 Press Release, Governor Quinn Cracks Down on Predatory Refund Anticipation Loans (Nov. 23, 2009).

116 Maryland Commissioner of Financial Regulation, Refund Anticipation Loans/Rapid Refund Program Advisory 05-01 (Jan. 24, 2005), *available at* www.dllr.md.gov/finance/advisories/advisory05-01.htm.

117 H&R Block E. Enters., Inc. v. Turnbaugh, Civ. Ac. No. 07-1822 (D. Md. July 30, 2008), *available on the companion website to this treatise*.

118 H&R Block E. Enters. v. Raskin, 591 F.3d 718 (4th Cir. 2010).

119 MetaBank, Form 8-K, Current Report Pursuant to Section 13 or 15(d) of the Securities Exchange Act of 1934 (Oct. 6, 2010).

120 H&R Block, Emerald Advance Overview 3 (Jan. 14, 2009), *available on the companion website to this treatise*.

121 *See* National Consumer Law Center, Truth in Lending § 6.2.3 (7th ed. 2010 and Supp.).

122 H&R Block, Emerald Advance Overview 3 (Jan. 14, 2009), *available on the companion website to this treatise*; H&R Block, Inc. F2Q09 (Qtr. End 10/31/08) Earnings Call Transcript, Dec. 8, 2008, from Seeking Alpha, *available at* http://seekingalpha.com/article/

The charge for a pay stub RAL varies by the tax preparer and lender offering it. For the ipower Line of Credit, MetaBank charged a 1.5% fee for the first advance from the line, and a 10% charge per advance thereafter, plus 18% periodic interest.[123] A taxpayer who borrowed the entire $500 in the first advance would be charged a $57.65 fee. If the ipower loan was repaid in one month, the total fee would be $65.15. A one-month, closed-end loan with the same loan amount and fee would have an APR of 177%. The Emerald Line of Credit carries an interest rate of 36% plus an annual fee of $45.[124] For a $500 advance repaid in one month, the total fee is $60. A one-month, closed-end loan with the same loan amount and fee would have an APR of 158%, if the annual fee were to be included in the finance charge.[125]

Closed-end pay stub RALs also present Truth in Lending Act issues.[126] Critical to a computation of an annual percentage rate (APR) is the date of repayment. The loan contract for one pay stub RAL in 2006 stated that the loan was due on February 17. However, the loan contracts also provided that the loan could be paid off earlier if the taxpayer returned to the tax preparer earlier.[127] Thus, the APR disclosure could vary widely because the loan period could be as little as a few days (if the taxpayer took out the pay stub loan in mid-January, received her W-2 form, and filed her taxes a few days later) to forty-six days (from January 2 to February 17). Thus, the APR for a Jackson Hewitt pay stub RAL of $488.50 (finance charge of $61) could vary from 651% (seven days) to 99% (forty-six days).

To avoid this problem as to the APR disclosure, lenders structured the closed-end pay stub RAL as a "demand note," attempting to use a loophole in the Official Commentary to Regulation Z that permits APRs for demand notes to be disclosed based on a one-year period.[128] But there are serious questions as to whether this practice in fact complied with TILA.

The failure of a lender to rebate a portion of the loan fee if the loan was repaid earlier was challenged as a violation of the Federal Rebate Act.[129] However, the Ninth Circuit Court of Appeals rejected that theory, holding that a flat-fee finance charge was not "interest" under the Federal Rebate Act.[130]

## 14.5 Assignment of Tax Refunds As Disguised Credit

### *14.5.1 Background*

The disguised credit version of refund lending is the "tax refund assignment." It is sometimes characterized as the sale of a chose in action, in which the lenders claim that they are buying the borrower's right to receive the refund. As with other disguised credit transactions, these loans frequently conceal extremely high rates of interest. For example, the assignment of a $100 tax refund for a $60 cash payment produces a $40 profit in a relatively short period of time. Depending upon the precise length of time between the $60 payment and the lender's receipt of the refund, the effective annual interest rate may reach 1,700%.

### *14.5.2 Sale of Chose in Action vs. Loan*

Whether such a transaction is subject to usury law depends on whether a court is willing to accept the transaction as the sale of a chose in action. Generally, it is permissible to sell notes or other obligations at a discount without the interference of usury ceilings,[131] so long as the seller is not the maker of the note.[132] At least one court has held that the assignment of a tax refund falls within this exception to usury law, and that the assignment is not a loan because the taxpayer is never obligated to repay anything to the assignee.[133]

The problem with this analysis is that it ignores the basic obligation of a court in a usury case to look beyond the legal formalities of a transaction and to examine its substance.[134] The substance of the tax refund transaction is that the taxpayer, who needs money immediately, obtains that money from another party such as a tax return preparer, and that the other party receives in return a larger payment at a later date. If that larger payment were made directly by the taxpayer, the transaction would be a textbook loan. To say that the transaction is not a loan because the later payment does not literally come from the taxpayer's pocket is to ignore the reality of the transaction.

---

109760-h-amp-r-block-inc-f2q09-qtr-end-10-31-08-earnings-call-transcript.

123 Metabank, ipower® Plus Line of Credit Terms and Conditions (2008) (on file with NCLC).

124 H&R Block, Emerald Advance Overview 3 (Jan. 14, 2009), *available on the companion website to this treatise.*

125 Regulation Z excludes annual fees from the finance charge. Reg. Z, 12 C.F.R. § 1026.4(b)(2) [§ 226.4(b)(2)].

126 In the spring of 2007, the three largest RAL lenders, Santa Barbara Bank & Trust, HSBC, and JPMorgan Chase announced that they would stop offering this type of pay stub RAL. *End to Pay Stub and Holiday RALs*, 25 NCLC REPORTS, *Consumer Credit & Usury Ed.* 20 (Mar./Apr. 2007).

127 Pay Stub RAL Loan Agreement from HSBC (on file with the NCLC); Pay Stub RAL loan Agreement from Santa Barbara Bank & Trust (on file with NCLC).

128 Reg. Z § 1026.17(c)(5) [§ 226.17(c)(5)]. *See generally* National Consumer Law Center, Truth in Lending § 4.5.10 (7th ed. 2010 and Supp.).

129 15 U.S.C. § 1615. *See Pay Stub RALs: Potential Violations of Truth in Lending and the Federal Rebate Statute*, NCLC REPORTS, *Consumer Credit and Usury Ed.* 9 (Nov./Dec. 2006).

130 Davis v. Pacific Capital Bank, 550 F.3d 915 (9th Cir. 2008).

131 This rule comes from the longstanding usury distinction between sales and loans and is a good example of the illogic of the distinction.

132 The use of a sham intermediary will not prevent the application of usury laws. *See, e.g.*, Graham & Locke Inv. v. Madison, 295 S.W.2d 234 (Tex. 1956); Baske v. Russell, 407 P.2d 434 (Wash. 1965).

The argument can be made in the tax refund context that the IRS is merely a sham intermediary for the borrower-assignor's payment to the lender-assignee since the refund is technically the borrower's money. *See* Opinion of the Attorney General of Kentucky, Clearinghouse No. 41,261 (May 3, 1982).

133 *See* Cullen v. Bragg, 350 S.E.2d 798 (Ga. Ct. App. 1986).

134 *See* § 3.9.1, *supra*.

### 14.5.3 Precedent That Assignments Are Disguised Loans

Some courts and authorities have been willing to look at the substance of tax refund assignments, and have concluded that the transactions are loans that may violate usury laws. A New York court held that an individual who paid $5,500 for an assignment of a $7,500 interest in an estate was guilty of usury.[135] An opinion of the Attorney General of Kentucky determined that tax refund assignments in that state were loans that could violate that state's usury law.[136] Similarly, a scheme whereby tax refunds were "purchased" at deep discounts from the taxpayer was found to constitute the lending of money; the regulator considered a provision in the contract that required repayment of the *full* refund amount after six weeks if the refund has not been paid by the government to be a significant factor.[137]

In Colorado, a lender claimed that the transaction was not a loan because it did not require the borrower to repay the advance unless the amount of the refund received was less than anticipated.[138] The Colorado Supreme Court in *Cash Now Store* rejected this argument, holding that the borrower's obligation to repay if the expected tax refund did not come through was sufficient to make the transaction a loan under the UCCC.[139] While the court stressed the differences between the UCCC and other states' definitions of "loan," its reasoning should be persuasive in other states, as the court debunked the claim that the transaction was merely the sale of a chose in action.[140]

### 14.5.4 Assignments Are Not Contingent

As *Cash Now Store*, discussed at § 14.5.3, *supra*, demonstrates, terming the obligation to repay a tax refund assignment as contingent is unjustified in many cases, because the agreement will require the consumer to repay the lender if the government fails to pay the full refund. Either the lender will be paid the principal plus interest by IRS's payment of the refund or the borrower will pay that exact same amount. There is no uncertainty in the amount of the payment. Neither the repayment itself nor the amount of the repayment is contingent upon a future event. The lender has not accepted any risk or uncertainty beyond those present in a typical consumer loan.

Since the money from the IRS is the taxpayer's money in the first place, which is being temporarily held by the government, the only uncertainty is how the borrower pays—directly, or through the IRS as an intermediary. Repayment is no more contingent than when a borrower gives a post-dated check for the principal plus interest and remains liable for repayment if the check does not clear. In both cases, there are two routes by which the borrower's money will reach the lender, but the borrower's obligation to repay the principal plus the interest is not subject to any contingency. Other courts have followed the maxim that substance prevails over form and have seen through alleged contingencies to recognize the underlying absolute obligation of the borrower to repay.[141]

Some courts have found that, when a person transfers a note or account to another at a discount, and guarantees payment, the guarantee makes the transaction a loan.[142] The more generally accepted holding, however, is that there is no per se rule, but a guarantee is one factor in determining whether the transaction is a disguised loan.[143] Thus, the borrower's guarantee of pay-

135 *See* Leavitt v. Enos, 140 N.Y.S. 862 (1913).

136 Opinion of the Attorney General of Kentucky, Clearinghouse No. 41,261 (May 3, 1982).

137 *In re* Income Tax Buyers, S.C. Dep't of Consumer Affairs, Docket No. 9004 (order Feb. 5, 1991), *on rehearing*, (June 19, 1991), Clearinghouse No. 46,756, *aff'd*, Income Tax Buyers, Inc. v. Hamm, 1992 WL 12092431 (S.C. Ct. Common. Pleas 1992) (company giving consumers advances on their tax refunds, discounted by 20%–40%, in exchange for their full refunds (equivalent to 200% APRs) were engaged in loaning money and required to be licensed; administrator rejected Cullen v. Bragg, 350 S.E.2d 798 (Ga. Ct. App. 1986), and the argument that these were sales of chose in action).

The regulator also noted that the assignment of the right to a tax refund before it is processed and issued runs afoul of the Assignment Act, 31 U.S.C. § 3727, and that IRS rules make clear that advertisements for these anticipated refunds must be described as loans. *See* IRS Publication 1345, Revenue Procedures for Electronic Filing of Individual Income Tax Returns 47 (2009).

138 State *ex rel.* Salazar v. The Cash Now Store, Inc., 31 P.3d 161 (Colo. 2001). On remand, the attorney general obtained a final judgment in excess of $49 million in damages and penalties. State *ex rel.* Salazar v. The Cash Now Store, Inc., Clearinghouse No. 55,601 (Colo. Dist. Ct. Mar. 8, 2004) (order and final judgment).

139 State *ex rel.* Salazar v. Cash Now Store, Inc., 31 P.3d 161 (Colo. 2001).

140 *Id.* at 167 (noting that the lender demonstrates that it does not view the refund as a chose in action because the borrower owes it a sum of money whether the refund or "chose" is valuable to the lender or not). *See also* Income Tax Buyers, Inc. v. Hamm, 1992 WL 12092431 (S.C. Ct. Com. Pleas Jan. 14, 1992) (discounted sale of right to receive income tax refund is loan because contract obliges borrower to pay the amount of the refund if IRS does not).

141 *See, e.g.*, Tiffany v. Boatman's Sav. Inst., 85 U.S. 375, 18 Wall. 375, 21 L. Ed. 868, 870 (1873); Britz v. Kinsvater, 351 P.2d 986 (Ariz. 1960); Seargeant v. Smith, 163 P.2d 680 (Ariz. 1945). *Cf.* Baxter v. Stevens, 773 P.2d 890 (Wash. Ct. App. 1989) ("sale" of promissory note with recourse guarantee was a loan). *But see* Berger v. State, 910 P.2d 581 (Alaska 1996) (assignments of anticipated distributions of oil "manna" (called "permanent fund dividends") to Alaskans not a disguised loan; case distinguishable because the assignment did not involve one's own money, as tax refunds do; further, court erroneously found that the assignors did not have an unconditional obligation to repay).

142 Western Auto Supply Co. v. Vick, 277 S.E.2d 360 (N.C. 1981) (seller transferred rights under chattel paper to lender, with a guarantee of payment; seller then collected the money from the account debtors and transmitted it to lender); Baxter v. Stevens, 773 P.2d 890 (Wash. Ct. App. 1989). *See generally* 45 Am. Jur. 2d *Interest and Usury* § 127 (1999).

143 *See, e.g.*, Berger v. State, 910 P.2d 581 (Alaska 1996) (repayment guarantees do not necessarily turn sales into loans; sale of rights to Alaska permanent fund distributions was not a loan even though borrower guaranteed payment); Carter v. Four Seasons Funding Corp., 97 S.W.3d 387 (Ark. 2003) (warranty that accounts would be collectable within ninety days and agreement to repurchase uncollectible accounts did not make sale of accounts receivable a loan); Investors Thrift v. AMA Corp., 63 Cal. Rptr. 157 (Cal. Ct. App. 1967) (agreement to repurchase uncollectible or disputed accounts did not make transaction a loan, but court suggests that it might

ment in a refund anticipation transaction may be insufficient in and of itself to persuade the court that the transaction is a loan. But tax refund assignment cases are significantly more clear-cut, because the tax refund represents the consumer's own money.

Thus, practitioners whose clients have been the victims of tax refund assignment schemes should closely examine the transaction for terms that reveal the true extension of credit. For example, if the taxpayer is in any way liable to the "assignee" where the refund is smaller than expected, the argument that the transaction is merely a sale of a chose in action would be rebutted. Practitioners should also consider potential liability under disclosure statutes[144] or under statutes forbidding deceptive trade practices if the purported assignee in any way conceals the nature or terms of the transaction.[145]

have ruled differently if more indicia of a loan had been present). *See also* Ravkind v. Mortgage Funding Corp., 881 S.W.2d 203 (Tex. App. 1994) (assignment of payments due on contract for deed not a loan even though assignee had recourse against assignor); § 7.5.3, *supra*.

144 *But see* Cullen v. Bragg, 350 S.E.2d 798 (Ga. Ct. App. 1986) (neither state usury law nor the TILA applied to refund assignment). *See generally* National Consumer Law Center, Truth in Lending § 4.5.10.2 (7th ed. 2010 and Supp.) (discussing Truth in Lending rules on tax refund anticipation loans).

145 *See* Consent Order, 94 F.T.C. 425 (Sept. 12, 1979) *modified* 51 Fed. Reg. 43,587 (Dec. 3, 1986) (Beneficial Fin. precluded from using the terms "instant tax refund" or "immediate tax refund" except in immediate conjunction with the word "loan.").

For a compilation of enforcement actions filed by state attorney generals based upon this mischaracterization, see JTH Tax v. H&R Block, 128 F. Supp. 2d 926, 938 (E.D. Va. 2001), *aff'd in part, vacated in part, and remanded in part*, 28 Fed. Appx. 207 (4th Cir. 2002).

# Appendix A Federal Credit Regulation

## A.1 Military Lending Act

### *A.1.1 The Act*

**TITLE 10—ARMED FORCES**

**SUBTITLE A—GENERAL MILITARY LAW**

* * *

**PART II—PERSONNEL**

* * *

**CHAPTER 49—MISCELLANEOUS PROHIBITIONS AND PENALTIES**

* * *

#### 10 U.S.C. § 987. Terms of consumer credit extended to members and dependents: limitations

**(a) Interest**

A creditor who extends consumer credit to a covered member of the armed forces or a dependent of such a member shall not require the member or dependent to pay interest with respect to the extension of such credit, except as—

**(1)** agreed to under the terms of the credit agreement or promissory note;

**(2)** authorized by applicable State or Federal law; and

**(3)** not specifically prohibited by this section.

**(b) Annual percentage rate**

A creditor described in subsection (a) may not impose an annual percentage rate of interest greater than 36 percent with respect to the consumer credit extended to a covered member or a dependent of a covered member.

**(c) Mandatory loan disclosures**

**(1) Information required**

With respect to any extension of consumer credit (including any consumer credit originated or extended through the internet) to a covered member or a dependent of a covered member, a creditor shall provide to the member or dependent the following information orally and in writing before the issuance of the credit:

**(A)** A statement of the annual percentage rate of interest applicable to the extension of credit.

**(B)** Any disclosures required under the Truth in Lending Act (15 U.S.C. 1601 et seq.).

**(C)** A clear description of the payment obligations of the member or dependent, as applicable.

**(2) Terms**

Such disclosures shall be presented in accordance with terms prescribed by the regulations issued by the Board of Governors of the Federal Reserve System to implement the Truth in Lending Act (15 U.S.C. 1601 et seq.).

**(d) Preemption**

**(1) Inconsistent laws**

Except as provided in subsection (f)(2), this section preempts any State or Federal law, rule, or regulation, including any State usury law, to the extent that such law, rule, or regulation is inconsistent with this section, except that this section shall not preempt any such law, rule, or regulation that provides protection to a covered member or a dependent of such a member in addition to the protection provided by this section.

**(2) Different treatment under State law of members and dependents prohibited**

States shall not—

**(A)** authorize creditors to charge covered members and their dependents annual percentage rates of interest for loans higher than the legal limit for residents of the State; or

**(B)** permit violation or waiver of any State consumer lending protections for the benefit of residents of the State on the basis of nonresident or military status of a covered member or dependent of such a member, regardless of the member's or dependent's domicile or permanent home of record.

**(e) Limitations**

It shall be unlawful for any creditor to extend consumer credit to a covered member or a dependent of such a member with respect to which—

**(1)** the creditor rolls over, renews, repays, refinances, or consolidates any consumer credit extended to the borrower by the same creditor with the proceeds of other credit extended to the same covered member or a dependent;

**(2)** the borrower is required to waive the borrower's right to legal recourse under any otherwise applicable provision of State or Federal law, including any provision of the Servicemembers Civil Relief Act;

**(3)** the creditor requires the borrower to submit to arbitration or imposes onerous legal notice provisions in the case of a dispute;

**(4)** the creditor demands unreasonable notice from the borrower as a condition for legal action;

**(5)** the creditor uses a check or other method of access to a deposit, savings, or other financial account maintained by the borrower, or the title of a vehicle as security for the obligation;

**(6)** the creditor requires as a condition for the extension of credit that the borrower establish an allotment to repay an obligation; or

**(7)** the borrower is prohibited from prepaying the loan or is charged a penalty or fee for prepaying all or part of the loan.

**(f) Penalties and remedies**

**(1) Misdemeanor**

A creditor who knowingly violates this section shall be fined as provided in title 18, or imprisoned for not more than one year, or both.

**(2) Preservation of other remedies**

The remedies and rights provided under this section are in addition to and do not preclude any remedy otherwise available under law to the person claiming relief under this section, including any award for consequential and punitive damages.

**(3) Contract void**

Any credit agreement, promissory note, or other contract prohibited under this section is void from the inception of such contract.

**(4) Arbitration**

Notwithstanding section 2 of title 9, or any other Federal or State law, rule, or regulation, no agreement to arbitrate any dispute involving the extension of consumer credit shall be enforceable against any covered member or dependent of such a member, or any person who was a covered member or dependent of that member when the agreement was made.

**(g) Servicemembers Civil Relief Act protections unaffected**

Nothing in this section may be construed to limit or otherwise affect the applicability of section 207 of the Servicemembers Civil Relief Act (50 U.S.C. App. 527).

**(h) Regulations**

**(1)** The Secretary of Defense shall prescribe regulations to carry out this section.

**(2)** Such regulations shall establish the following:

**(A)** Disclosures required of any creditor that extends consumer credit to a covered member or dependent of such a member.

**(B)** The method for calculating the applicable annual percentage rate of interest on such obligations, in accordance with the limit established under this section.

**(C)** A maximum allowable amount of all fees, and the types of fees, associated with any such extension of credit, to be expressed and disclosed to the borrower as a total amount and as a percentage of the principal amount of the obligation, at the time at which the transaction is entered into.

**(D)** Definitions of "creditor" under paragraph (5) and "consumer credit" under paragraph (6) of subsection (i), consistent with the provisions of this section.

**(E)** Such other criteria or limitations as the Secretary of Defense determines appropriate, consistent with the provisions of this section.

**(3)** In prescribing regulations under this subsection, the Secretary of Defense shall consult with the following:

**(A)** The Federal Trade Commission.

**(B)** The Board of Governors of the Federal Reserve System.

**(C)** The Office of the Comptroller of the Currency.

**(D)** The Federal Deposit Insurance Corporation.

**(E)** The Office of Thrift Supervision.

**(F)** The National Credit Union Administration.

**(G)** The Treasury Department.

**(*i*) Definitions**

In this section:

**(1) Covered member**

The term "covered member" means a member of the armed forces who is—

**(A)** on active duty under a call or order that does not specify a period of 30 days or less; or

**(B)** on active Guard and Reserve Duty.

**(2) Dependent**

The term "dependent," with respect to a covered member, means—

**(A)** the member's spouse;

**(B)** the member's child (as defined in section 101(4) of title 38); or

**(C)** an individual for whom the member provided more than one-half of the individual's support for 180 days immediately preceding an extension of consumer credit covered by this section.

**(3) Interest**

The term "interest" includes all cost elements associated with the extension of credit, including fees, service charges, renewal charges, credit insurance premiums, any ancillary product sold with any extension of credit to a servicemember or the servicemember's dependent, as applicable, and any other charge or premium with respect to the extension of consumer credit.

**(4) Annual percentage rate**

The term "annual percentage rate" has the same meaning as in section 107 of the Truth and Lending Act (15 U.S.C. 1606), as implemented by regulations of the Board of Governors of the Federal Reserve System. For purposes of this section, such term includes all fees and charges, including charges and fees for single premium credit insurance and other ancillary products sold in connection with the credit transaction, and such fees and charges shall be included in the calculation of the annual percentage rate.

**(5) Creditor**

The term "creditor" means a person—

**(A)** who—

**(i)** is engaged in the business of extending consumer credit; and

**(ii)** meets such additional criteria as are specified for such purpose in regulations prescribed under this section; or

**(B)** who is an assignee of a person described in subparagraph (A) with respect to any consumer credit extended.

**(6) Consumer credit**

The term "consumer credit" has the meaning provided for such term in regulations prescribed under this section, except that such term does not include (A) a residential mortgage, or (B) a loan procured in the course of purchasing a car or other personal property, when that loan is offered for the express purpose of financing the purchase and is secured by the car or personal property procured.

[Pub. L. No. 109-364, div. A, tit. VI, § 670(a), 120 Stat. 2266 (Oct. 17, 2006) (*Effective Date*: Oct. 1, 2007 or on such earlier date as may be prescribed by the Secretary of Defense and shall apply with respect to extensions of consumer credit on or after such effective date. Subsection (h) is effective as of Oct. 17, 2006.)]

## *A.1.2 Department of Defense Regulations*

### 32 C.F.R. Part 232—Limitations on Terms of Consumer Credit Extended to Service Members and Dependents

SOURCE: 72 Fed. Reg. 50,591 (Aug. 31, 2007), unless otherwise noted.

AUTHORITY: 10 U.S.C. § 987.

## 32 C.F.R. § 232.1 Authority, purpose, and coverage.

(a) *Authority*. This part is issued by the Department of Defense to implement 10 U.S.C. 987.

(b) *Purpose*. The purpose of this part is to impose limitations on the cost and terms of certain defined extensions of consumer credit to Service members and their dependents, and to provide additional consumer disclosures for such transactions.

(c) *Coverage*. This part defines the types of consumer credit transactions, creditors, and borrowers covered by the regulation, consistent with the provisions of 10 U.S.C. 987. In addition, the regulation:

(1) Provides the maximum allowable amount of all charges, and the types of charges, that may be associated with a covered extension of consumer credit;

(2) Requires creditors to disclose to covered borrowers the cost of the transaction as a total dollar amount and as an annualized percentage rate referred to as the Military Annual Percentage Rate or MAPR, which must be disclosed before the borrower becomes obligated on the transaction. The disclosures required by this regulation differ from and are in addition to the disclosures that must be provided to consumers under the Federal Truth in Lending Act;

(3) Provides for the method creditors shall use in calculating the MAPR, and;

(4) Contains such other criteria and limitations as the Secretary of Defense has determined appropriate, consistent with the provisions of 10 U.S.C. 987.

## 32 C.F.R. § 232.2 Applicability.

This part applies to consumer credit extended by creditors to a covered borrower, as those terms are defined in this part.

## 32 C.F.R. § 232.3 Definitions.

Terms used in this part are defined as follows:

(a) *Closed-end credit* means consumer credit other than "open-end credit" as that term is defined in Regulation Z (Truth in Lending), 12 CFR part 226.

(b) *Consumer credit* means closed-end credit offered or extended to a covered borrower primarily for personal, family or household purposes, as described in paragraph (b)(1) of this section.

(1) Except as provided in paragraph (b)(2) of this section, consumer credit means the following transactions:

(i) *Payday loans*. Closed-end credit with a term of 91 days or fewer in which the amount financed does not exceed $2,000 and the covered borrower:

(A) Receives funds from and incurs interest and/or is charged a fee by a creditor, and contemporaneously with the receipt of funds, provides a check or other payment instrument to the creditor who agrees with the covered borrower not to deposit or present the check or payment instrument for more than one day, or;

(B) Receives funds from and incurs interest and/or is charged a fee by a creditor, and contemporaneously with the receipt of funds, authorizes the creditor to initiate a debit or debits to the covered borrower's deposit account (by electronic fund transfer or remotely created check) after one or more days. This provision does not apply to any right of a depository institution under statute or common law to offset indebtedness against funds on deposit in the event of the covered borrower's delinquency or default.

(ii) *Vehicle title loans*. Closed-end credit with a term of 181 days or fewer that is secured by the title to a motor vehicle, that has been registered for use on public roads and owned by a covered borrower, other than a purchase money transaction described in paragraph (b)(2)(ii) of this section.

(iii) *Tax refund anticipation loans*. Closed-end credit in which the covered borrower expressly grants the creditor the right to receive all or part of the borrower's income tax refund or expressly agrees to repay the loan with the proceeds of the borrower's refund.

(2) For purposes of this part, consumer credit does not mean:

(i) Residential mortgages, which are any credit transactions secured by an interest in the covered borrower's dwelling, including transactions to finance the purchase or initial construction of a dwelling, refinance transactions, home equity loans or lines of credit, and reverse mortgages;

(ii) Any credit transaction to finance the purchase or lease of a motor vehicle when the credit is secured by the vehicle being purchased or leased;

(iii) Any credit transaction to finance the purchase of personal property when the credit is secured by the property being purchased;

(iv) Credit secured by a qualified retirement account as defined in the Internal Revenue Code; and

(v) Any other credit transaction that is not consumer credit extended by a creditor, is an exempt transaction, or is not otherwise subject to disclosure requirements for purposes of Regulation Z (Truth in Lending), 12 CFR part 226.

(c) *Covered borrower* means a person with the following status at the time he or she becomes obligated on a consumer credit transaction covered by this part:

(1) A regular or reserve member of the Army, Navy, Marine Corps, Air Force, or Coast Guard, serving on active duty under a call or order that does not specify a period of 30 days or fewer, or such a member serving on Active Guard and Reserve duty as that term is defined in 10 U.S.C. 101(d)(6), or

(2) The member's spouse, the member's child defined in 38 U.S.C. 101(4), or an individual for whom the member provided more than one-half of the individual's support for 180 days immediately preceding an extension of consumer credit covered by this part.

(d) *Credit* means the right granted by a creditor to a debtor to defer payment of debt or to incur debt and defer its payment.

(e) *Creditor* means a person who is engaged in the business of extending consumer credit with respect to a consumer credit transaction covered by this part. For the purposes of this section, "person" includes a natural person, organization, corporation, partnership, proprietorship, association, cooperation, estate, trust, and any other business entity and who otherwise meets the definition of "creditor" for purposes of Regulation Z.

(f) *Dwelling* means a residential structure that contains one to four units, whether or not the structure is attached to real property. The term includes an individual condominium unit, cooperative unit, mobile home, and manufactured home.

(g) *Electronic fund transfer* (EFT) has the same meaning for purposes of this part as in Regulation E (Electronic Fund Transfers) issued by the Board of Governors of the Federal Reserve System, 12 CFR part 205.

(h) *Military annual percentage rate* (MAPR). The MAPR is the cost of the consumer credit transaction expressed as an annual rate. The MAPR shall be calculated based on the costs in this definition but in all other respects it shall be calculated and disclosed following the rules used for calculating the Annual Percentage Rate (APR) for closed-end credit transactions under Regulation Z (Truth in Lending), 12 CFR part 226.

(1) The MAPR includes the following cost elements associated with the extension of consumer credit to a covered borrower if they are financed, deducted from the proceeds of the consumer credit, or otherwise required to be paid as a condition of the credit:

(i) Interest, fees, credit service charges, credit renewal charges;

(ii) Credit insurance premiums including charges for single premium credit insurance, fees for debt cancellation or debt suspension agreements; and

(iii) Fees for credit-related ancillary products sold in connection with and either at or before consummation of the credit transaction.

(2) The MAPR does not include:

(i) Fees or charges imposed for actual unanticipated late payments, default, delinquency, or similar occurrence;

(ii) Taxes or fees prescribed by law that actually are or will be paid to public officials for determining the existence of, or for perfecting, releasing, or satisfying a security interest;

(iii) Any tax levied on security instruments or documents evidencing indebtedness if the payment of such taxes is a requirement for recording the instrument securing the evidence of indebtedness; and

(iv) Tax return preparation fees associated with a tax refund anticipation loan, whether or not the fees are deducted from the loan proceeds.

(*i*) *Regulation Z* means any of the rules, regulations, or interpretations thereof, issued by the Board of Governors of the Federal Reserve System to implement the Truth in Lending Act, as amended, from time to time, including any interpretation or approval issued by an official or employee duly authorized by the Board of Governors of the Federal Reserve System to issue such interpretations or approvals. Words that are not defined in this regulation have the meanings given to them in Regulation Z (12 CFR part 226) issued by the Board of Governors of the Federal Reserve System (the "Board"), as amended from time to time, including any interpretation thereof by the Board or an official or employee of the Federal Reserve System duly authorized by the Board to issue such interpretations. Words that are not defined in this regulation or Regulation Z, or any interpretation thereof, have the meanings given to them by State or Federal law, or contract.

## 32 C.F.R. § 232.4 Terms of consumer credit extended to covered borrowers.

(a) Neither a creditor who extends consumer credit to a covered borrower nor an assignee of the creditor shall require the member or dependent to pay a military annual percentage rate (MAPR) with respect to such extension of credit, except as—

(1) Agreed to under the terms of the credit agreement or promissory note;

(2) Authorized by applicable State or Federal law; and

(3) Not specifically prohibited by this part.

(b) A creditor described in paragraph (a) of this section or an assignee may not impose an MAPR greater than 36 percent in connection with an extension of consumer credit to a covered borrower.

## 32 C.F.R. § 232.5 Identification of covered borrower.

(a) This part shall not apply to a consumer credit transaction if the conditions described in paragraphs (a)(1) and (a)(2) of this section are met:

(1) Prior to becoming obligated on the transaction, each applicant is provided with a clear and conspicuous "covered borrower identification statement" substantially similar to the following statement and each applicant signs the statement indicating that he or she is or is not a covered borrower:

> Federal law provides important protections to active duty members of the Armed Forces and their dependents. To ensure that these protections are provided to eligible applicants, we require you to sign one of the following statements as applicable:
>
> I AM a regular or reserve member of the Army, Navy, Marine Corps, Air Force, or Coast Guard, serving on active duty under a call or order that does not specify a period of 30 days or fewer.
>
> ______________________
>
> I AM a dependent of a member of the Armed Forces on active duty as described above, because I am the member's spouse, the member's child under the age of eighteen years old, or I am an individual for whom the member provided more than one-half of my financial support for 180 days immediately preceding today's date.
>
> ______________________
>
> —OR—
>
> I AM NOT a regular or reserve member of the Army, Navy, Marine Corps, Air Force, or Coast Guard, serving on active duty under a call or order that does not specify a period of 30 days or fewer (or a dependent of such a member).
>
> ______________________
>
> Warning: It is important to fill out this form accurately. Knowingly making a false statement on a credit application is a crime.

(2) The creditor has not determined, pursuant to the optional verification procedures in paragraphs (b) or (c) of this section, that any such applicant is a covered borrower.

(b) The creditor may, but is not required to, verify the status of an applicant as a covered borrower by requesting the applicant to provide a current (previous month) military leave and earning statement, or a military identification card (DD Form 2 for members, DD Form 1173 for dependents), as described in DoD Instruction 1003.1, *Identification (ID) Cards for Members of the Uniformed Services, Their Dependents, and Other Eligible Individuals*, December 5, 1997. Upon such request, activated members of the National Guard or Reserves shall also provide a copy of the military orders calling the covered member to military service and any orders further extending military service.

(c) The creditor may, but is not required to, verify the status of an applicant as a covered borrower by accessing the information available at *http://www.dmdc.osd.mil/mla/owa/home*. Searches require the service member's full name, Social Security number, and date of birth.

(d) This part shall not apply to a consumer credit transaction in which the creditor rolls over, renews, repays, refinances, or consolidates consumer credit in accordance with § 232.8(a)(1) if § 232.5(a)(1) and § 232.5(a)(2) applied to the previous transaction.

## 32 C.F.R. § 232.6 Mandatory loan disclosures.

(a) *Required information.* With respect to any extension of consumer credit (including any consumer credit originated or extended through the internet) to a covered borrower, a creditor shall provide to the member or dependent the following information clearly and conspicuously before consummation of the consumer credit transaction:

(1) The MAPR applicable to the extension of consumer credit, and the total dollar amount of all charges included in the MAPR.

(2) Any disclosures required by Regulation Z (Truth in Lending), 12 CFR part 226.

(3) A clear description of the payment obligation of the covered borrower, as applicable. A payment schedule provided pursuant to paragraph (a)(2) of this section satisfies this requirement.

(4) A statement that "Federal law provides important protections to regular or reserve members of the Army, Navy, Marine Corps, Air Force, or Coast Guard, serving on active duty under a call or order that does not specify a period of 30 days or fewer, and their dependents. Members of the Armed Forces and their dependents may be able to obtain financial assistance from Army Emergency Relief, Navy and Marine Corps Relief Society, the Air Force Aid Society, or Coast Guard Mutual Aid. Members of the Armed Forces and their dependents may request free legal advice regarding an application for credit from a service legal assistance office or financial counseling from a consumer credit counselor."

(b) *Method of disclosure.*

(1) *Written disclosures.* The creditor shall provide the disclosures required by paragraph (a) in writing in a form the covered borrower can keep.

(2) *Oral disclosures.* The creditor also shall provide the disclosures required by paragraphs (a)(1), (a)(3) and (a)(4) of this section orally before consummation. In mail and internet transactions, the creditor satisfies this requirement if it provides a toll-free telephone number on or with the written disclosures that consumers may use to obtain oral disclosures and the creditor provides oral disclosures when the covered borrower contacts the creditor for this purpose.

(c) *When disclosures are required for refinancing or renewal of covered loan.* The refinancing or renewal of a covered loan requires new disclosures under § 232.6 only when the transaction would be considered a new transaction that requires disclosures under the Truth in Lending Act, as implemented by the Federal Reserve Board's Regulation Z, 12 CFR part 226.

## 32 C.F.R. § 232.7 Preemption.

(a) *Inconsistent laws.* 10 U.S.C. 987 as implemented by this part preempts any State or Federal law, rule or regulation, including any State usury law, to the extent such law, rule or regulation is inconsistent with this part, except that any such law, rule or regulation is not preempted by this part to the extent that it provides protection to a covered borrower greater than those protections provided by 10 U.S.C. 987 and this part.

(b) Different treatment under State law of covered borrowers is prohibited. States may not:

(1) Authorize creditors to charge covered borrowers rates of interest that are higher than the legal limit for residents of the State, or

(2) Permit the violation or waiver of any State consumer lending protection that is for the benefit of residents of the State on the basis of the covered borrower's nonresident or military status, regardless of the covered borrower's domicile or permanent home of record, provided that the protection would otherwise apply to the covered borrower.

## 32 C.F.R. § 232.8 Limitations.

(a) 10 U.S.C. 987 makes it unlawful for any creditor to extend consumer credit to a covered borrower with respect to which:

(1) The creditor rolls over, renews, repays, refinances, or consolidates any consumer credit extended to the covered borrower by the same creditor with the proceeds of other consumer credit extended by that creditor to the same covered borrower, unless the new transaction results in more favorable terms to the covered borrower, such as a lower MAPR. This part shall not apply to a transaction permitted by this paragraph when the same creditor extends consumer credit to a covered borrower to refinance or renew an extension of credit that was not covered by this part because the consumer was not a covered borrower at the time of the original transaction.

(2) The covered borrower is required to waive the covered borrower's right to legal recourse under any otherwise applicable provision of State or Federal law, including any provision of the Servicemembers Civil Relief Act (50 U.S.C. App. 10 U.S.C. 527 *et seq.*).

(3) The creditor requires the covered borrower to submit to arbitration or imposes other onerous legal notice provisions in the case of a dispute.

(4) The creditor demands unreasonable notice from the covered borrower as a condition for legal action.

(5) The creditor uses a check or other method of access to a deposit, savings, or other financial account maintained by the covered borrower, except that, in connection with a consumer credit transaction with an MAPR consistent with § 232.4(b):

(i) The creditor may require an electronic fund transfer to repay a consumer credit transaction, unless otherwise prohibited by Regulation E (Electronic Fund Transfers) 12 CFR part 205;

(ii) The creditor may require direct deposit of the consumer's salary as a condition of eligibility for consumer credit, unless otherwise prohibited by law; or

(iii) The creditor may, if not otherwise prohibited by applicable law, take a security interest in funds deposited after the extension of credit in an account established in connection with the consumer credit transaction.

(6) The creditor requires as a condition for the extension of consumer credit that the covered borrower establish an allotment to repay the obligation.

(7) The covered borrower is prohibited from prepaying the consumer credit or is charged a penalty fee for prepaying all or part of the consumer credit.

(b) For purposes of this section, an assignee may not engage in any transaction or take any action that would be prohibited for the creditor.

## 32 C.F.R. § 232.9 Penalties and remedies.

(a) *Misdemeanor.* A creditor or assignee who knowingly violates 10 U.S.C. 987 as implemented by this part shall be fined as provided in title 18, United States Code, or imprisoned for not more than one year, or both.

(b) *Preservation of other remedies.* The remedies and rights provided under 10 U.S.C. 987 as implemented by this part are in addition to and do not preclude any remedy otherwise available under State or Federal law or regulation to the person claiming relief under the statute, including any award for consequential damages and punitive damages.

(c) *Contract void.* Any credit agreement, promissory note, or other contract with a covered borrower that fails to comply with 10 U.S.C. 987 as implemented by this regulation or which contains one or more provisions prohibited under 10 U.S.C. 987 as implemented by this regulation is void from the inception of the contract.

(d) *Arbitration.* Notwithstanding 9 U.S.C. 2, or any other Federal or State law, rule, or regulation, no agreement to arbitrate any dispute involving the extension of consumer credit to a covered borrower pursuant to this part shall be enforceable against any covered borrower, or any person who was a covered borrower when the agreement was made.

### 32 C.F.R. § 232.10 Servicemembers Civil Relief Act protections unaffected.

Nothing in this part may be construed to limit or otherwise affect the applicability of Section 207 and any other provisions of the Servicemembers Civil Relief Act (50 U.S.C. App. 527).

### 32 C.F.R. § 232.11 Effective date and transition.

Applicable consumer credit—This part shall only apply to consumer credit that is extended to a covered borrower and consummated on or after October 1, 2007.

## A.2 Servicemembers Civil Relief Act—Selected Provisions

### TITLE 50 APPENDIX—WAR AND NATIONAL DEFENSE

### SERVICEMEMBERS CIVIL RELIEF ACT

### TITLE I—GENERAL PROVISIONS

* * *

### 50 U.S.C. app. § 511. Definitions

For the purposes of this Act [sections 501 to 596 of this Appendix]:

**(1) Servicemember**

The term "servicemember" means a member of the uniformed services, as that term is defined in section 101(a)(5) of title 10, United States Code.

**(2) Military service**

The term "military service" means—

**(A)** in the case of a servicemember who is a member of the Army, Navy, Air Force, Marine Corps, or Coast Guard—

**(i)** active duty, as defined in section 101(d)(1) of title 10, United States Code, and

**(ii)** in the case of a member of the National Guard, includes service under a call to active service authorized by the President or the Secretary of Defense for a period of more than 30 consecutive days under section 502(f) of title 32, United States Code, for purposes of responding to a national emergency declared by the President and supported by Federal funds;

**(B)** in the case of a servicemember who is a commissioned officer of the Public Health Service or the National Oceanic and Atmospheric Administration, active service; and

**(C)** any period during which a servicemember is absent from duty on account of sickness, wounds, leave, or other lawful cause.

**(3) Period of military service**

The term "period of military service" means the period beginning on the date on which a servicemember enters military service and ending on the date on which the servicemember is released from military service or dies while in military service.

**(4) Dependent**

The term "dependent", with respect to a servicemember, means—

**(A)** the servicemember's spouse;

**(B)** the servicemember's child (as defined in section 101(4) of title 38, United States Code); or

**(C)** an individual for whom the servicemember provided more than one-half of the individual's support for 180 days immediately preceding an application for relief under this Act [sections 501 to 596 of this Appendix].

**(5) Court**

The term "court" means a court or an administrative agency of the United States or of any State (including any political subdivision of a State), whether or not a court or administrative agency of record.

**(6) State**

The term "State" includes—

**(A)** a commonwealth, territory, or possession of the United States; and

**(B)** the District of Columbia.

**(7) Secretary concerned**

The term "Secretary concerned"—

**(A)** with respect to a member of the armed forces, has the meaning given that term in section 101(a)(9) of title 10, United States Code;

**(B)** with respect to a commissioned officer of the Public Health Service, means the Secretary of Health and Human Services; and

**(C)** with respect to a commissioned officer of the National Oceanic and Atmospheric Administration, means the Secretary of Commerce.

**(8) Motor vehicle**

The term "motor vehicle" has the meaning given that term in section 30102(a)(6) of title 49, United States Code.

**(9) Judgment**

The term "judgment" means any judgment, decree, order, or ruling, final or temporary.

[Oct. 17, 1940, ch. 888, § 101, *as added* Pub. L. No. 108-189, § 1, 117 Stat. 2836 (Dec. 19, 2003); Pub. L. No. 108-454, tit. VII, § 701, 118 Stat. 3624 (Dec. 10, 2004)]

* * *

### TITLE II—GENERAL RELIEF

* * *

### 50 U.S.C. app. § 527. Maximum rate of interest on debts incurred before military service

**(a) Interest rate limitation**

**(1) Limitation to 6 percent**

An obligation or liability bearing interest at a rate in excess of 6 percent per year that is incurred by a servicemember, or the servicemember and the servicemember's spouse jointly, before the servicemember enters military service shall not bear interest at a rate in excess of 6 percent—

**(A)** during the period of military service and one year thereafter, in the case of an obligation or liability consisting of a mortgage, trust deed, or other security in the nature of a mortgage; or

**(B)** during the period of military service, in the case of any other obligation or liability.

**(2) Forgiveness of interest in excess of 6 percent**

Interest at a rate in excess of 6 percent per year that would otherwise be incurred but for the prohibition in paragraph (1) is forgiven.

**(3) Prevention of acceleration of principal**

The amount of any periodic payment due from a servicemember under the terms of the instrument that created an obligation or liability covered by this section shall be reduced by the amount of the interest forgiven under paragraph (2) that is allocable to the period for which such payment is made.

**(b) Implementation of limitation**

**(1) Written notice to creditor**

In order for an obligation or liability of a servicemember to be subject to the interest rate limitation in subsection (a), the servicemember shall provide to the creditor written notice and a copy of the military orders calling the servicemember to military service and any orders further extending military service, not later than 180 days after the date of the servicemember's termination or release from military service.

**(2) Limitation effective as of date of order to active duty**

Upon receipt of written notice and a copy of orders calling a servicemember to military service, the creditor shall treat the debt in accordance with subsection (a), effective as of the date on which the servicemember is called to military service.

**(c) Creditor protection**

A court may grant a creditor relief from the limitations of this section if, in the opinion of the court, the ability of the servicemember to pay interest upon the obligation or liability at a rate in excess of 6 percent per year is not materially affected by reason of the servicemember's military service.

**(d) Definitions**

In this section:

**(1) Interest**

The term "interest" includes service charges, renewal charges, fees, or any other charges (except bona fide insurance) with respect to an obligation or liability.

**(2) Obligation or liability**

The term "obligation or liability" includes an obligation or liability consisting of a mortgage, trust deed, or other security in the nature of a mortgage.

**(e) Penalty**

Whoever knowingly violates subsection (a) shall be fined as provided in title 18, United States Code, imprisoned for not more than one year, or both.

[Oct. 17, 1940, ch. 888, § 207, *as added* Pub. L. No. 108-189, § 1, 117 Stat. 2844 (Dec. 19, 2003); Pub. L. No. 110-289, div. B, tit. II, § 2203(b), 122 Stat. 2849 (July 30, 2008); Pub. Law No. 110-389, tit. VIII, § 807, 122 Stat. 4189 (Oct. 10, 2008); Pub. L. No. 111-275, tit. III, § 303(b)(1), 124 Stat. 2877 (Oct. 13, 2010)]

## A.3 Federal Rebate Statute

Housing and Community Development Act of 1992, 15 U.S.C. § 1615, Pub. L. No. 102-550, 106 Stat. 3891, tit. IX, § 933 (Oct. 28, 1992).

*Though codified within the Truth in Lending Act, this statute was not enacted as part of that Act.*

### TITLE 15—COMMERCE AND TRADE

### CHAPTER 41—CONSUMER CREDIT PROTECTION

### SUBCHAPTER I—CONSUMER CREDIT COST DISCLOSURE

### PART A—GENERAL PROVISIONS

### 15 U.S.C. § 1615. Prohibition on use of "Rule of 78's" in connection with mortgage refinancings and other consumer loans

**(a) Prompt refund of unearned interest required**

**(1) In general**

If a consumer prepays in full the financed amount under any consumer credit transaction, the creditor shall promptly refund any unearned portion of the interest charge to the consumer.

**(2) Exception for refund of de minimis amount**

No refund shall be required under paragraph (1) with respect to the prepayment of any consumer credit transaction if the total amount of the refund would be less than $1.

**(3) Applicability to refinanced transactions and acceleration by the creditor**

This subsection shall apply with respect to any prepayment of a consumer credit transaction described in paragraph (1) without regard to the manner or the reason for the prepayment, including—

**(A)** any prepayment made in connection with the refinancing, consolidation, or restructuring of the transaction; and

**(B)** any prepayment made as a result of the acceleration of the obligation to repay the amount due with respect to the transaction.

**(b) Use of "Rule of 78's" prohibited**

For the purpose of calculating any refund of interest required under subsection (a) of this section for any precomputed consumer credit transaction of a term exceeding 61 months which is consummated after September 30, 1993, the creditor shall compute the refund based on a method which is at least as favorable to the consumer as the actuarial method.

**(c) Statement of prepayment amount**

**(1) In general**

Before the end of the 5-day period beginning on the date an oral or written request is received by a creditor from a consumer for the disclosure of the amount due on any precomputed consumer credit account, the creditor or assignee shall provide the consumer with a statement of—

**(A)** the amount necessary to prepay the account in full; and

**(B)** if the amount disclosed pursuant to subparagraph (A) includes an amount which is required to be refunded under this section with respect to such prepayment, the amount of such refund.

**(2) Written statement required if request is in writing**

If the customer's request is in writing, the statement under paragraph (1) shall be in writing.

**(3) 1 free annual statement**

A consumer shall be entitled to obtain 1 statement under paragraph (1) each year without charge.

**(4) Additional statements subject to reasonable fees**

Any creditor may impose a reasonable fee to cover the cost of providing any statement under paragraph (1) to any consumer in addition to the 1 free annual statement required under paragraph (3) if the amount of the charge for such additional statement is disclosed to the consumer before furnishing such statement.

**(d) Definitions**

For the purpose of this section—

**(1) Actuarial method**

The term "actuarial method" means the method of allocating payments made on a debt between the amount financed and the finance charge pursuant to which a payment is applied first to the accumulated finance charge and any remainder is subtracted from, or any deficiency is added to, the unpaid balance of the amount financed.

**(2) Consumer, credit**

The terms "consumer" and "creditor" have the meanings given to such terms in section 1602 of this title.

**(3) Creditor**

The term "creditor"—

**(A)** has the meaning given to such term in section 1602 of this title; and

**(B)** includes any assignee of any creditor with respect to credit extended in connection with any consumer credit transaction and any subsequent assignee with respect to such credit.

[Pub. L. No. 102-550, tit. IX, § 933, 106 Stat. 3891 (Oct. 28, 1992)]

# A.4 Credit Practices Rule, Unfair Late Charges

TITLE 16—COMMERCIAL PRACTICES

CHAPTER I—FEDERAL TRADE COMMISSION

SUBCHAPTER D—TRADE REGULATION RULES

PART 444—CREDIT PRACTICES

## 16 C.F.R. § 444.1 Definitions.

(a) *Lender.* A person who engages in the business of lending money to consumers within the jurisdiction of the Federal Trade Commission.

(b) *Retail installment seller.* A person who sells goods or services to consumers on a deferred payment basis or pursuant to a lease-purchase arrangement within the jurisdiction of the Federal Trade Commission.

* * *

(d) *Consumer.* A natural person who seeks or acquires goods, services, or money for personal, family, or household use.

(e) *Obligation.* An agreement between a consumer and a lender or retail installment seller.

(f) *Creditor.* A lender or a retail installment seller.

(g) *Debt.* Money that is due or alleged to be due from one to another.

* * *

## 16 C.F.R. § 444.4 Late charges.

(a) In connection with collecting a debt arising out of an extension of credit to a consumer in or affecting commerce, as commerce is defined in the Federal Trade Commission Act, it is an unfair act or practice within the meaning of section 5 of that Act for a creditor, directly or indirectly, to levy or collect any delinquency charge on a payment, which payment is otherwise a full payment for the applicable period and is paid on its due date or within an applicable grace period, when the only delinquency is attributable to late fee(s) or delinquency charge(s) assessed on earlier installment(s).

(b) For purposes of this section, collecting a debt means any activity other than the use of judicial process that is intended to bring about or does bring about repayment of all or part of a consumer debt.

# A.5 TILA Credit Card Provisions

## *A.5.1 Selected Statutory Provisions*

PART A—GENERAL PROVISIONS

* * *

## 15 U.S.C. § 1602. Definitions and rules of construction [TILA § 103]

* * *

**(g)** The term "creditor" refers only to a person who both (1) regularly extends, whether in connection with loans, sales of property or services, or otherwise, consumer credit which is payable by agreement in more than four installments or for which the payment of a finance charge is or may be required, and (2) is the person to whom the debt arising from the consumer credit transaction is initially payable on the face of the evidence of indebtedness or, if there is no such evidence of indebtedness, by agreement. Notwithstanding the preceding sentence, in the case of an open-end credit plan involving a credit card, the card issuer and any person who honors the credit card and offers a discount which is a finance charge are creditors. For the purpose of the requirements imposed under part D of this subchapter and sections 1637(a)(5), 1637(a)(6), 1637(a)(7), 1637(b)(1), 1637(b)(2), 1637(b)(3), 1637(b)(8), and 1637(b)(10) of this title, the term "creditor" shall also include card issuers whether or not the amount due is payable by agreement in more than four installments or the payment of a finance charge is or may be required, and the Bureau shall, by regulation, apply these requirements to such card issuers, to the extent appropriate, even though the requirements are by their terms applicable only to creditors offering open-end credit plans. ****

* * *

**(j)** The term "open end credit plan" and "open end consumer credit plan" mean a plan under which the creditor reasonably contemplates repeated transactions, which prescribes the terms of such transactions, and which provides for a finance charge which may be computed from time to time on the outstanding unpaid balance. A credit plan terms "open end credit plan" and "open end consumer credit plan" mean which is an open end credit plan or open end consumer credit plan within the meaning of the preceding sentence is an open end credit plan or open end consumer credit plan even if credit information is verified from time to time.

* * *

**(*l*)** The term "credit card" means any card, plate, coupon book or other credit device existing for the purpose of obtaining money, property, labor, or services on credit.

**(m)** The term "accepted credit card" means any credit card which the cardholder has requested and received or has signed or has used, or authorized another to use, for the purpose of obtaining money, property, labor, or services on credit.

**(n)** The term "cardholder" means any person to whom a credit card is issued or any person who has agreed with the card issuer to pay obligations arising from the issuance of a credit card to another person.

**(*o*)** The term "card issuer" means any person who issues a credit card, or the agent of such person with respect to such card.

**(p)** The term "unauthorized use," as used in section 1643 of this title, means a use of a credit card by a person other than the cardholder who does not have actual, implied, or apparent authority for such use and from which the cardholder receives no benefit.

**(q)** The term "discount" as used in section 1666f of this title means a reduction made from the regular price. The term "discount" as used in section 1666f of this title shall not mean a surcharge.

[Pub. L. No. 90-321, 82 Stat. 147 (May 29, 1968); Pub. L. No. 91-508, 84 Stat. 1126 (Oct. 26, 1970); Pub. L. No. 93-495, 88 Stat. 1511 (Oct. 28, 1974); Pub. L. No. 94-222, 90 Stat. 197 (Feb. 27, 1976); Pub. L. No. 96-221, 94 Stat. 168 (Mar. 31, 1980); Pub. L. No. 97-25, 95 Stat. 144 (July 27, 1981); Pub. L. No. 97-320, 96 Stat. 1538 (Oct. 15, 1982); Pub. L. No. 103-325, 108 Stat. 2190 (Sept. 23, 1994); Pub. L. No. 110-315, tit. X, 122 Stat 3078 (Aug. 14, 2008); Pub. L. No. 111-24, tit. I, § 108, 123 Stat. 1743 (May 22, 2009); Pub. L. No. 111-203, §§ 1100A, 1401, 1431, 124 Stat. 1376, 2107, 2137, 2157–2159 (July 21, 2010)]

* * *

### PART B—CREDIT TRANSACTIONS

* * *

## 15 U.S.C. § 1637. Open end consumer credit plans [TILA § 127]

* * *

**(c) Disclosure in credit and charge card applications and solicitations**

* * *

**(8) Applications from underage consumers**

**(A) Prohibition on issuance**

No credit card may be issued to, or open end consumer credit plan established by or on behalf of, a consumer who has not attained the age of 21, unless the consumer has submitted a written application to the card issuer that meets the requirements of subparagraph (B).

**(B) Application requirements**

An application to open a credit card account by a consumer who has not attained the age of 21 as of the date of submission of the application shall require—

**(i)** the signature of a cosigner, including the parent, legal guardian, spouse, or any other individual who has attained the age of 21 having a means to repay debts incurred by the consumer in connection with the account, indicating joint liability for debts incurred by the consumer in connection with the account before the consumer has attained the age of 21; or

**(ii)** submission by the consumer of financial information, including through an application, indicating an independent means of repaying any obligation arising from the proposed extension of credit in connection with the account.

**(C) Safe harbor**

The Bureau shall promulgate regulations providing standards that, if met, would satisfy the requirements of subparagraph (B)(ii).

* * *

**(h) Prohibition on certain actions for failure to incur finance charges**

A creditor of an account under an open end consumer credit plan may not terminate an account prior to its expiration date solely because the consumer has not incurred finance charges on the account. Nothing in this subsection shall prohibit a creditor from terminating an account for inactivity in 3 or more consecutive months.

**(i) Advance notice of rate increase and other changes required**

**(1) Advance notice of increase in interest rate required**

In the case of any credit card account under an open end consumer credit plan, a creditor shall provide a written notice of an increase in an annual percentage rate (except in the case of an increase described in paragraph (1), (2), or (3) of section 1666i-1(b)) not later than 45 days prior to the effective date of the increase.

**(2) Advance notice of other significant changes required**

In the case of any credit card account under an open end consumer credit plan, a creditor shall provide a written notice of any significant change, as determined by rule of the Bureau, in the terms (including an increase in any fee or finance charge, other than as provided in paragraph (1)) of the cardholder agreement between the creditor and the obligor, not later than 45 days prior to the effective date of the change.

**(3) Notice of right to cancel**

Each notice required by paragraph (1) or (2) shall be made in a clear and conspicuous manner, and shall contain a brief statement of the right of the obligor to cancel the account pursuant to rules established by the Bureau before the effective date of the subject rate increase or other change.

**(4) Rule of construction**

Closure or cancellation of an account by the obligor shall not constitute a default under an existing cardholder agreement, and shall not trigger an obligation to immediately repay the obligation in full or through a method that is less beneficial to the obligor than one of the methods described in section 1666i-1(c)(2), or the imposition of any other penalty or fee.

**(j) Prohibition on penalties for on-time payments**

**(1) Prohibition on double-cycle billing and penalties for on-time payments**

Except as provided in paragraph (2), a creditor may not impose any finance charge on a credit card account under an open end consumer credit plan as a result of the loss of any time period provided by the creditor within which the obligor may repay any portion of the credit extended without incurring a finance charge, with respect to—

**(A)** any balances for days in billing cycles that precede the most recent billing cycle; or

**(B)** any balances or portions thereof in the current billing cycle that were repaid within such time period.

**(2) Exceptions**

Paragraph (1) does not apply to—

**(A)** any adjustment to a finance charge as a result of the resolution of a dispute; or

**(B)** any adjustment to a finance charge as a result of the return of a payment for insufficient funds.

**(k) Opt-in required for over-the-limit transactions if fees are imposed**

**(1) In general**

In the case of any credit card account under an open end consumer credit plan under which an over-the-limit fee may be imposed by the creditor for any extension of credit in excess of the amount of credit authorized to be extended under such account, no such fee shall be charged, unless the consumer has expressly elected to permit the creditor, with respect to such account, to complete transactions involving the extension of credit under such account in excess of the amount of credit authorized.

**(2) Disclosure by creditor**

No election by a consumer under paragraph (1) shall take effect unless the consumer, before making such election, received a notice from the creditor of any over-the-limit fee in the form and manner, and at the time, determined by the Bureau. If the consumer makes the election referred to in paragraph (1), the creditor shall provide notice to the consumer of the right to revoke the election, in the form prescribed by the Bureau, in any periodic statement that includes notice of the imposition of an over-the-limit fee during the period covered by the statement.

**(3) Form of election**

A consumer may make or revoke the election referred to in paragraph (1) orally, electronically, or in writing, pursuant to regulations prescribed by the Bureau. The Bureau shall prescribe regulations to ensure that the same options are available for both making and revoking such election.

**(4) Time of election**

A consumer may make the election referred to in paragraph (1) at any time, and such election shall be effective until the election is revoked in the manner prescribed under paragraph (3).

**(5) Regulations**

The shall prescribe regulations—

**(A)** governing disclosures under this subsection; and

**(B)** that prevent unfair or deceptive acts or practices in connection with the manipulation of credit limits designed to increase over-the-limit fees or other penalty fees.

**(6) Rule of construction**

Nothing in this subsection shall be construed to prohibit a creditor from completing an over-the-limit transaction, provided that a consumer who has not made a valid election under paragraph

(1) is not charged an over-the-limit fee for such transaction.

**(7) Restriction on fees charged for an over-the-limit transaction**

With respect to a credit card account under an open end consumer credit plan, an over-the-limit fee may be imposed only once during a billing cycle if the credit limit on the account is exceeded, and an over-the-limit fee, with respect to such excess credit, may be imposed only once in each of the 2 subsequent billing cycles, unless the consumer has obtained an additional extension of credit in excess of such credit limit during any such subsequent cycle or the consumer reduces the outstanding balance below the credit limit as of the end of such billing cycle.

**(*l*) Limit on fees related to method of payment**

With respect to a credit card account under an open end consumer credit plan, the creditor may not impose a separate fee to allow the obligor to repay an extension of credit or finance charge, whether such repayment is made by mail, electronic transfer, telephone authorization, or other means, unless such payment involves an expedited service by a service representative of the creditor.

**(m) Use of term "fixed rate"**

With respect to the terms of any credit card account under an open end consumer credit plan, the term "fixed", when appearing in conjunction with a reference to the annual percentage rate or interest rate applicable with respect to such account, may only be used to refer to an annual percentage rate or interest rate that will not change or vary for any reason over the period specified clearly and conspicuously in the terms of the account.

**(n) Standards applicable to initial issuance of subprime or "fee harvester" cards**

**(1) In general**

If the terms of a credit card account under an open end consumer credit plan require the payment of any fees (other than any late fee, over-the-limit fee, or fee for a payment returned for insufficient funds) by the consumer in the first year during which the account is opened in an aggregate amount in excess of 25 percent of the total amount of credit authorized under the account when the account is opened, no payment of any fees (other than any late fee, over-the-limit fee, or fee for a payment returned for insufficient funds) may be made from the credit made available under the terms of the account.

**(2) Rule of construction**

No provision of this subsection may be construed as authorizing any imposition or payment of advance fees otherwise prohibited by any provision of law.

**(*o*) Due dates for credit card accounts**

**(1) In general**

The payment due date for a credit card account under an open end consumer credit plan shall be the same day each month.

**(2) Weekend or holiday due dates**

If the payment due date for a credit card account under an open end consumer credit plan is a day on which the creditor does not receive or accept payments by mail (including weekends and holidays), the creditor may not treat a payment received on the next business day as late for any purpose.

**(p) Parental approval required to increase credit lines for accounts for which parent is jointly liable**

No increase may be made in the amount of credit authorized to be extended under a credit card account for which a parent, legal guardian, or spouse of the consumer, or any other individual has assumed joint liability for debts incurred by the consumer in connection with the account before the consumer attains the age of 21, unless that parent, guardian, or spouse approves in writing, and assumes joint liability for, such increase.

[Pub. L. No. 90-321, 82 Stat. 153 (May 29, 1968); Pub. L. No. 93-495, 88 Stat. 1511 (Oct. 28, 1974); Pub. L. No. 96-221, 94 Stat. 176 (Mar. 31, 1980); Pub. L. No. 100-583, 102 Stat. 2960 (Nov. 3, 1988); Pub. L. No. 100-709, 102 Stat. 4729. (Nov. 23, 1988); Pub. L. No. 109-8, 119 Stat. 204, 209, 211, 212 (Apr. 20, 2005); Pub. L. No. 111-24, tits. I–V, 123 Stat. 1735–1752 (May 22, 2009); Pub. L. No. 111-203, § 1100A, 124 Stat. 1376, 2107 (July 21, 2010)]

* * *

## 15 U.S.C. § 1640. Civil liability [TILA § 130]

**(a) Individual or class action for damages; amount of award; factors determining amount of award**

Except as otherwise provided in this section, any creditor who fails to comply with any requirement imposed under this part, including any requirement under section 1635 of this title, subsection (f) or (g) of section 1641 of this title, or part D or E of this subchapter with respect to any person is liable to such person in an amount equal to the sum of—

**(1)** any actual damage sustained by such person as a result of the failure;

**(2)(A)** (i) in the case of an individual action twice the amount of any finance charge in connection with the transaction, (ii) in the case of an individual action relating to a consumer lease under part E of this subchapter, 25 per centum of the total amount of monthly payments under the lease, except that the liability under this subparagraph shall not be less than $200 nor greater than $2,000, (iii) in the case of an individual action relating to an open end consumer credit plan that is not secured by real property or a dwelling, twice the amount of any finance charge in connection with the transaction, with a minimum of $500 and a maximum of $5,000, or such higher amount as may be appropriate in the case of an established pattern or practice of such failures; or (iv) in the case of an individual action relating to a credit transaction not under an open end credit plan that is secured by real property or a dwelling, not less than $400 or greater than $4,000;

**(B)** in the case of a class action, such amount as the court may allow, except that as to each member of the class no minimum recovery shall be applicable, and the total recovery under this subparagraph in any class action or series of class actions arising out of the same failure to comply by the same creditor shall not be more than the lesser of $1,000,000 or 1 per centum of the net worth of the creditor;

**(3)** in the case of any successful action to enforce the foregoing liability or in any action in which a person is determined to have a right of rescission under section 1635 or 1638(e)(7) of this title, the costs of the action, together with a reasonable attorney's fee as determined by the court; and

**(4)** in the case of a failure to comply with any requirement under section 1639 of this title, paragraph (1) or (2) of section 1639b(c), or section 1639c(a), an amount equal to the sum of all finance charges and fees paid by the consumer, unless the creditor demonstrates that the failure to comply is not material.

In determining the amount of award in any class action, the court shall consider, among other relevant factors, the amount of any actual damages awarded, the frequency and persistence of failures of compliance by the creditor, the resources of the creditor, the number of persons adversely affected, and the extent to which the creditor's failure of compliance was intentional. In connection with the disclosures referred to in subsections (a) and (b) of section 1637 of this title, a creditor shall have a liability determined under paragraph (2) only for failing to comply with the requirements of section 1635, 1637(a) of this title, or any of paragraphs (4) through (13) of section 1637(b) of this title, or for failing to comply with disclosure requirements under State law for any term or item that the Bureau has determined to be substantially the same in meaning under section 1610(a)(2) of this title as any of the terms or items referred to in section 1637(a) of this title, or any of paragraphs (4) through (13) of section 1637(b) of this title. In connection with the disclosures referred to in subsection (c) or (d) of section 1637 of this title, a card issuer shall have a liability under this section only to a cardholder who pays a fee described in section 1637(c)(1)(A)(ii)(I) or section 1637(c)(4)(A)(i) of this title or who uses the credit card or charge card. In connection with the disclosures referred to in section 1638 of this title, a creditor shall have a liability determined under paragraph (2) only for failing to comply with the requirements of section 1635 of this title or of paragraph (2) (insofar as it requires a disclosure of the "amount financed"), (3), (4), (5), (6), or (9) of section 1638(a) or section 1638(b)(2)(C)(ii) of this title, of subparagraphs (A), (B), (D), (F), or (J) of section 1638(e)(2) of this title (for purposes of paragraph (2) or (4) of section

1638(e) of this title), or paragraph (4)(C), (6), (7), or (8) of section 1638(e) of this title or for failing to comply with disclosure requirements under State law for any term which the Bureau has determined to be substantially the same in meaning under section 1610(a)(2) of this title as any of the terms referred to in any of those paragraphs of section 1638(a) or section 1638(b)(2)(C)(ii) of this title. With respect to any failure to make disclosures required under this part or part D or E of this subchapter, liability shall be imposed only upon the creditor required to make disclosure, except as provided in section 1641 of this title. * * * *

* * *

## 15 U.S.C. § 1650. Preventing unfair and deceptive private educational lending practices and eliminating conflicts of interest [TILA § 140]

* * *

**(f) Credit card protections for college students**

**(1) Disclosure required**

An institution of higher education shall publicly disclose any contract or other agreement made with a card issuer or creditor for the purpose of marketing a credit card.

**(2) Inducements prohibited**

No card issuer or creditor may offer to a student at an institution of higher education any tangible item to induce such student to apply for or participate in an open end consumer credit plan offered by such card issuer or creditor, if such offer is made—

**(A)** on the campus of an institution of higher education;

**(B)** near the campus of an institution of higher education, as determined by rule of the Bureau; or

**(C)** at an event sponsored by or related to an institution of higher education.

**(3) Sense of the Congress**

It is the sense of the Congress that each institution of higher education should consider adopting the following policies relating to credit cards:

**(A)** That any card issuer that markets a credit card on the campus of such institution notify the institution of the location at which such marketing will take place.

**(B)** That the number of locations on the campus of such institution at which the marketing of credit cards takes place be limited.

**(C)** That credit card and debt education and counseling sessions be offered as a regular part of any orientation program for new students of such institution.

[Pub. L. No. 110-315, tit. X, 122 Stat 3078 (Aug. 14, 2008); Pub. L. No. 111-24, tit. 3, § 304, 123 Stat. 1749 (May 22, 2009); Pub. L. No. 111-203, § 1100A, 124 Stat. 1376, 2107 (July 21, 2010)]

* * *

**PART C—CREDIT ADVERTISING AND LIMITS ON CREDIT CARD FEES**

* * *

## 15 U.S.C. § 1665c. Interest rate reduction on open end consumer credit plans

**(a) In general**

If a creditor increases the annual percentage rate applicable to a credit card account under an open end consumer credit plan, based on factors including the credit risk of the obligor, market conditions, or other factors, the creditor shall consider changes in such factors in subsequently determining whether to reduce the annual percentage rate for such obligor.

**(b) Requirements**

With respect to any credit card account under an open end consumer credit plan, the creditor shall—

**(1)** maintain reasonable methodologies for assessing the factors described in subsection (a);

**(2)** not less frequently than once every 6 months, review accounts as to which the annual percentage rate has been increased since January 1, 2009, to assess whether such factors have changed (including whether any risk has declined);

**(3)** reduce the annual percentage rate previously increased when a reduction is indicated by the review; and

**(4)** in the event of an increase in the annual percentage rate, provide in the written notice required under section 1637(i) a statement of the reasons for the increase.

**(c) Rule of construction**

This section shall not be construed to require a reduction in any specific amount.

**(d) Rulemaking**

The Bureau shall issue final rules not later than 9 months after the date of enactment of this section to implement the requirements of and evaluate compliance with this section, and subsections (a), (b), and (c) shall become effective 15 months after that date of enactment.

[Pub. L. No. 111-24, tit. I, § 171(c), 123 Stat. 1737 (May 22, 2009); Pub. L. No. 111-203, § 1100A, 124 Stat. 1376, 2107 (July 21, 2010)]

## 15 U.S.C. § 1665d. Reasonable penalty fees on open end consumer credit plans

**(a) In general**

The amount of any penalty fee or charge that a card issuer may impose with respect to a credit card account under an open end consumer credit plan in connection with any omission with respect to, or violation of, the cardholder agreement, including any late payment fee, over-the-limit fee, or any other penalty fee or charge, shall be reasonable and proportional to such omission or violation.

**(b) Rulemaking required**

The Bureau, in consultation with the Comptroller of the Currency, the Bureau of Directors of the Federal Deposit Insurance Corporation, the Director of the Office of Thrift Supervision, and the National Credit Union Administration Bureau, shall issue final rules not later than 9 months after the date of enactment of this section, to establish standards for assessing whether the amount of any penalty fee or charge described under subsection (a) is reasonable and proportional to the omission or violation to which the fee or charge relates. Subsection (a) shall become effective 15 months after the date of enactment of this section.

**(c) Considerations**

In issuing rules required by this section, the Bureau shall consider—

**(1)** the cost incurred by the creditor from such omission or violation;

**(2)** the deterrence of such omission or violation by the cardholder;

**(3)** the conduct of the cardholder; and

**(4)** such other factors as the Bureau may deem necessary or appropriate.

**(d) Differentiation permitted**

In issuing rules required by this subsection, the Bureau may establish different standards for different types of fees and charges, as appropriate.

**(e) Safe harbor rule authorized**

The Bureau, in consultation with the Comptroller of the Currency, the Bureau of Directors of the Federal Deposit Insurance Corporation, the Director of the Office of Thrift Supervision, and the National Credit Union Administration Bureau, may issue rules to provide an amount for any penalty fee or charge described under subsection (a) that is presumed to be reasonable and proportional to the omission or violation to which the fee or charge relates.

[Pub. L. No. 111-24, tit. I, § 102(b)(1), 123 Stat. 1740 (May 22, 2009); Pub. L. No. 111-203, § 1100A, 124 Stat. 1376, 2107 (July 21, 2010)]

## 15 U.S.C. § 1665e. Consideration of ability to repay

A card issuer may not open any credit card account for any consumer under an open end consumer credit plan, or increase any credit limit applicable to such account, unless the card issuer considers the ability of the consumer to make the required payments under the terms of such account.

[Pub. L. No. 111-24, tit. I, § 109, 123 Stat. 1743 (May 22, 2009)]

PART D—CREDIT BILLING

* * *

## 15 U.S.C. § 1666b. Timing of payments [TILA § 163]

**(a) Time to make payments**

A creditor may not treat a payment on a credit card account under an open end consumer credit plan as late for any purpose, unless the creditor has adopted reasonable procedures designed to ensure that each periodic statement including the information required by section 1637(b) is mailed or delivered to the consumer not later than 21 days before the payment due date.

**(b) Grace period**

If an open end consumer credit plan provides a time period within which an obligor may repay any portion of the credit extended without incurring an additional finance charge, such additional finance charge may not be imposed with respect to such portion of the credit extended for the billing cycle of which such period is a part, unless a statement which includes the amount upon which the finance charge for the period is based was mailed or delivered to the consumer not later than 21 days before the date specified in the statement by which payment must be made in order to avoid imposition of that finance charge.

[Pub. L. No. 90-321, *as added* Pub. L. No. 93-495, 88 Stat. 1514 (Oct. 28, 1974); Pub. L. No. 111-24, tit. I, § 106(b)(1), 123 Stat. 1742 (May 22, 2009); Pub. L. No. 111-93, § 2, 123 Stat. 2998 (Nov. 6, 2009)]

## 15 U.S.C. § 1666c. Prompt and fair crediting of payments [TILA § 164]

**(a) In general**

Payments received from an obligor under an open end consumer credit plan by the creditor shall be posted promptly to the obligor's account as specified in regulations of the Bureau. Such regulations shall prevent a finance charge from being imposed on any obligor if the creditor has received the obligor's payment in readily identifiable form, by 5:00 p.m. on the date on which such payment is due in the amount, manner, location, and time indicated by the creditor to avoid the imposition thereof.

**(b) Application of payments**

**(1) In general**

Upon receipt of a payment from a cardholder, the card issuer shall apply amounts in excess of the minimum payment amount first to the card balance bearing the highest rate of interest, and then to each successive balance bearing the next highest rate of interest, until the payment is exhausted.

**(2) Clarification relating to certain deferred interest arrangements**

A creditor shall allocate the entire amount paid by the consumer in excess of the minimum payment amount to a balance on which interest is deferred during the last 2 billing cycles immediately preceding the expiration of the period during which interest is deferred.

**(c) Changes by card issuer**

If a card issuer makes a material change in the mailing address, office, or procedures for handling cardholder payments, and such change causes a material delay in the crediting of a cardholder payment made during the 60-day period following the date on which such change took effect, the card issuer may not impose any late fee or finance charge for a late payment on the credit card account to which such payment was credited.

[Pub. L. No. 90-321, *as added* Pub. L. No. 93-495, 88 Stat. 1514 (Oct. 28, 1974); Pub. L. No. 111-24, tit. I, § 104, 123 Stat. 1741 (May 22, 2009); Pub. L. No. 111-203, §§ 1087, 1100A, 124 Stat. 1376, 2086, 2107 (July 21, 2010)]

## 15 U.S.C. § 1666f. Inducements to cardholders by sellers of cash discounts for payments by cash, check or similar means; credit card surcharge prohibition; finance charge for sales transactions involving cash discounts [TILA § 167]

* * *

**(b) Finance charge**

With respect to any sales transaction, any discount from the regular price offered by the seller for the purpose of inducing payment by cash, checks, or other means not involving the use of an open-end credit plan or a credit card shall not constitute a finance charge as determined under section 1605 of this title if such discount is offered to all prospective buyers and its availability is disclosed clearly and conspicuously.

[Pub. L. No. 90-321, *as added* Pub. L. No. 93-495, 88 Stat. 1515 (Oct. 28, 1974) *and amended* Pub. L. No. 94-222, 90 Stat. 197 (Feb. 27, 1976); Pub. L. No. 97-25, 95 Stat. 144 (July 27, 1981)]

## 15 U.S.C. § 1666g. Tie-in services prohibited for issuance of credit card [TILA § 168]

Notwithstanding any agreement to the contrary, a card issuer may not require a seller, as a condition to participating in a credit card plan, to open an account with or procure any other service from the card issuer or its subsidiary or agent.

[Pub. L. No. 90-321, *as added* Pub. L. No. 93-495, 88 Stat. 1515 (Oct. 28, 1974)]

* * *

## 15 U.S.C. § 1666i-1. Limits on interest rate, fee, and finance charge increases applicable to outstanding balances [TILA § 171]

**(a) In general**

In the case of any credit card account under an open end consumer credit plan, no creditor may increase any annual percentage rate, fee, or finance charge applicable to any outstanding balance, except as permitted under subsection (b).

**(b) Exceptions**

The prohibition under subsection (a) shall not apply to—

**(1)** an increase in an annual percentage rate upon the expiration of a specified period of time, provided that—

**(A)** prior to commencement of that period, the creditor disclosed to the consumer, in a clear and conspicuous manner, the length of the period and the annual percentage rate that would apply after expiration of the period;

**(B)** the increased annual percentage rate does not exceed the rate disclosed pursuant to subparagraph (A); and

**(C)** the increased annual percentage rate is not applied to transactions that occurred prior to commencement of the period;

**(2)** an increase in a variable annual percentage rate in accordance with a credit card agreement that provides for changes in the rate according to operation of an index that is not under the control of the creditor and is available to the general public;

**(3)** an increase due to the completion of a workout or temporary hardship arrangement by the obligor or the failure of the obligor to comply with the terms of a workout or temporary hardship arrangement, provided that—

**(A)** the annual percentage rate, fee, or finance charge applicable to a category of transactions following any such increase does not exceed the rate, fee, or finance charge that applied to that category of transactions prior to commencement of the arrangement; and

**(B)** the creditor has provided the obligor, prior to the commencement of such arrangement, with clear and conspicuous disclosure of the terms of the arrangement (including any increases due to such completion or failure); or

**(4)** an increase due solely to the fact that a minimum payment by the obligor has not been received by the creditor within 60 days after the due date for such payment, provided that the creditor shall—

**(A)** include, together with the notice of such increase required under section 1637(i), a clear and conspicuous written statement of the reason for the increase and that the increase will terminate not later than 6 months after the date on which it is imposed, if the creditor receives the required minimum payments on time from the obligor during that period; and

**(B)** terminate such increase not later than 6 months after the date on which it is imposed, if the creditor receives the required minimum payments on time during that period.

**(c) Repayment of outstanding balance**

**(1) In general**

The creditor shall not change the terms governing the repayment of any outstanding balance, except that the creditor may provide the obligor with one of the methods described in paragraph (2) of repaying any outstanding balance, or a method that is no less beneficial to the obligor than one of those methods.

**(2) Methods**

The methods described in this paragraph are—

**(A)** an amortization period of not less than 5 years, beginning on the effective date of the increase set forth in the notice required under section 1637(i); or

**(B)** a required minimum periodic payment that includes a percentage of the outstanding balance that is equal to not more than twice the percentage required before the effective date of the increase set forth in the notice required under section 1637(i).

**(d) Outstanding balance defined**

For purposes of this section, the term "outstanding balance" means the amount owed on a credit card account under an open end consumer credit plan as of the end of the 14th day after the date on which the creditor provides notice of an increase in the annual percentage rate, fee, or finance charge in accordance with section 1637(i).

[Pub. L. No. 111-24, tit. I, § 101(b)(2), 123 Stat. 1736 (May 22, 2009)]

## 15 U.S.C. § 1666i-2. Additional limits on interest rate increases [TILA § 172]

**(a) Limitation on increases within first year**

Except in the case of an increase described in paragraph (1), (2), (3), or (4) of section 1666i-1(b), no increase in any annual percentage rate, fee, or finance charge on any credit card account under an open end consumer credit plan shall be effective before the end of the 1-year period beginning on the date on which the account is opened.

**(b) Promotional rate minimum term**

No increase in any annual percentage rate applicable to a credit card account under an open end consumer credit plan that is a promotional rate (as that term is defined by the Bureau) shall be effective before the end of the 6-month period beginning on the date on which the promotional rate takes effect, subject to such reasonable exceptions as the Bureau may establish, by rule.

[Pub. L. No. 111-24, tit. I, § 101(d), 123 Stat. 1738 (May 22, 2009); Pub. L. No. 111-203, § 1100A, 124 Stat. 1376, 2107 (July 21, 2010)]

## 15 U.S.C. § 1666j. Applicability of State laws [TILA § 173]

**(a) Consistency of provisions**

This part does not annul, alter, or affect, or exempt any person subject to the provisions of this part from complying with, the laws of any State with respect to credit billing practices, except to the extent that those laws are inconsistent with any provision of this part, and then only to the extent of the inconsistency. The Bureau is authorized to determine whether such inconsistencies exist. The Bureau may not determine that any State law is inconsistent with any provision of this part if the Bureau determines that such law gives greater protection to the consumer.

**(b) Exemptions by Bureau from credit billing requirements**

The Bureau shall by regulation exempt from the requirements of this part any class of credit transactions within any State if it determines that under the law of that State that class of transactions is subject to requirements substantially similar to those imposed under this part or that such law gives greater protection to the consumer, and that there is adequate provision for enforcement.

**(c) Finance charge or other charge for credit for sales transactions involving cash discounts**

Notwithstanding any other provisions of this subchapter, any discount offered under section 1666f(b) of this title shall not be considered a finance charge or other charge for credit under the usury laws of any State or under the laws of any State relating to disclosure of information in connection with credit transactions, or relating to the types, amounts or rates of charges, or to any element or elements of charges permissible under such laws in connection with the extension or use of credit.

[Pub. L. No. 90-321, *as added* Pub. L. No. 93-495, 88 Stat. 1516 (Oct. 28, 1974) *and amended* Pub. L. No. 94-222, 90 Stat. 198 (Feb. 27, 1976); Pub. L. No. 111-203, §§ 1087, 1100A, 124 Stat. 1376, 2086, 2107 (July 21, 2010)]

# *A.5.2 Selected Regulation Z Provisions*

Citations are to the CFPB regulation, 12 C.F.R. pt. 1026, with citations to the FRB regulation, 12 C.F.R. pt. 226, in brackets, e.g., 1026.2 [226.2].

Section

**SUBPART A—GENERAL**

* * *

| | |
|---|---|
| 1026.2 [226.2] | Definitions and Rules of Construction |

* * *

**SUBPART B—OPEN-END CREDIT**

* * *

| | |
|---|---|
| 1026.9 [226.9] | Subsequent Disclosure Requirements |
| 1026.10 [226.10] | Payments |

* * *

**SUBPART G—SPECIAL RULES APPLICABLE TO CREDIT CARD ACCOUNTS AND OPEN-END CREDIT OFFERED TO COLLEGE STUDENTS**

| | |
|---|---|
| 1026.51 [226.51] | Ability to Pay |
| 1026.52 [226.52] | Limitations on Fees |
| 1026.53 [226.53] | Allocation of Payments |
| 1026.54 [226.54] | Limitations on the Imposition of Finance Charges |
| 1026.55 [226.55] | Limitations on Increasing Annual Percentage Rates, Fees, and Charges |
| 1026.56 [226.56] | Requirements for Over-the-Limit Transactions |
| 1026.57 [226.57] | Reporting and Marketing Rules for College Student Open-End Credit |

* * *

| | |
|---|---|
| 1026.59 [226.59] | Reevaluation of Rate Increases |
| 1026.60 [226.5a] | Credit and Charge Card Applications and Solicitations |

* * *

**SUBPART A—GENERAL**

* * *

## 12 C.F.R. § 1026.2 Definitions and Rules of Construction [§ 226.2]

(a) *Definitions.* For purposes of this part, the following definitions apply:

* * *

(4) *Billing cycle* or *cycle* means the interval between the days or dates of regular periodic statements. These intervals shall be equal and no longer than a quarter of a year. An interval will be considered equal if the number of days in the cycle does not vary more than four days from the regular day or date of the periodic statement.

* * *

(6) *Business day* means a day on which the creditor's offices are open to the public for carrying on substantially all of its business functions. However, for purposes of rescission under §§ 1026.15 and 1026.23, and for purposes of §§ 1026.19(a)(1)(ii), 1026.19(a)(2), 1026.31, and 1026.46(d)(4), the term means all calendar days except Sundays and the legal public holidays specified in 5 U.S.C. 6103(a), such as New Year's Day, the Birthday of Martin Luther King, Jr., Washington's Birthday, Memorial Day, Independence Day, Labor Day, Columbus Day, Veterans Day, Thanksgiving Day, and Christmas Day.

(7) *Card issuer* means a person that issues a credit card or that person's agent with respect to the card.

(8) *Cardholder* means a natural person to whom a credit card is issued for consumer credit purposes, or a natural person who has agreed with the card issuer to pay consumer credit obligations arising from the issuance of a credit card to another natural person. For purposes of § 1026.12(a) and (b), the term includes any person to whom a credit card is issued for any purpose, including business, commercial or agricultural use, or a person who has agreéd with the card issuer to pay obligations arising from the issuance of such a credit card to another person.

* * *

(14) *Credit* means the right to defer payment of debt or to incur debt and defer its payment.

(15)(i) *Credit card* means any card, plate, or other single credit device that may be used from time to time to obtain credit.

(ii) Credit card account under an open-end (not home-secured) consumer credit plan means any open-end credit account that is accessed by a credit card, except:

(A) A home-equity plan subject to the requirements of § 1026.40 that is accessed by a credit card; or

(B) An overdraft line of credit that is accessed by a debit card or an account number.

(iii) *Charge card* means a credit card on an account for which no periodic rate is used to compute a finance charge.

* * *

(17) *Creditor* means:

(i) A person who regularly extends consumer credit that is subject to a finance charge or is payable by written agreement in more than four installments (not including a down payment), and to whom the obligation is initially payable, either on the face of the note or contract, or by agreement when there is no note or contract.

(ii) For purposes of §§ 1026.4(c)(8) (Discounts), 1026.9(d) (Finance charge imposed at time of transaction), and 1026.12(e) (Prompt notification of returns and crediting of refunds), a person that honors a credit card.

(iii) For purposes of subpart B, any card issuer that extends either open-end credit or credit that is not subject to a finance charge and is not payable by written agreement in more than four installments.

* * *

(v) A person regularly extends consumer credit only if it extended credit (other than credit subject to the requirements of § 1026.32) more than 25 times (or more than 5 times for transactions secured by a dwelling) in the preceding calendar year. If a person did not meet these numerical standards in the preceding calendar year, the numerical standards shall be applied to the current calendar year. A person regularly extends consumer credit if, in any 12-month period, the person originates more than one credit extension that is subject to the requirements of § 1026.32 or one or more such credit extensions through a mortgage broker.

* * *

(21) *Periodic rate* means a rate of finance charge that is or may be imposed by a creditor on a balance for a day, week, month, or other subdivision of a year.

* * *

**SUBPART B—OPEN-END CREDIT**

* * *

## 12 C.F.R. § 1026.9 Subsequent Disclosure Requirements [§ 226.9]

* * *

(c) *Change in terms.*

* * *

(2) *Rules affecting open-end (not home-secured) plans*

(i) *Changes where written advance notice is required*

(A) *General.* For plans other than home-equity plans subject to the requirements of § 1026.40, except as provided in paragraphs (c)(2)(i)(B), (c)(2)(iii) and (c)(2)(v) of this section, when a significant change in account terms as described in paragraph (c)(2)(ii) of this section is made, a creditor must provide a written notice of the change at least 45 days prior to the effective date of the change to each consumer who may be affected. The 45-day timing requirement does not apply if the consumer has agreed to a particular change as described in paragraph (c)(2)(i)(B) of this section; for such changes, notice must be given in accordance with the timing requirements of paragraph (c)(2)(i)(B) of this section. Increases in the rate applicable to a consumer's account due to delinquency, default or as a penalty described in paragraph (g) of this section that are not due to a change in the contractual terms of the consumer's account must be disclosed pursuant to paragraph (g) of this section instead of paragraph (c)(2) of this section.

(B) *Changes agreed to by the consumer.* A notice of change in terms is required, but it may be mailed or delivered as late as the effective date of the change if the consumer agrees to the particular change. This paragraph (c)(2)(i)(B) applies only when a consumer substitutes collateral or when the creditor can advance additional credit only if a change relatively unique to that consumer is made, such as the consumer's providing additional security or paying an increased minimum payment amount. The following are not considered agreements between the consumer and the creditor for purposes of this paragraph (c)(2)(i)(B): The consumer's general acceptance of the creditor's contract reservation of the right to change terms; the consumer's use of the account (which might imply acceptance of its terms under state law); the consumer's acceptance of a unilateral term change that is not particular to that consumer, but rather is of general applicability to consumers with that type of account; and the consumer's request to reopen a closed account or to upgrade an existing account to another account offered by the creditor with different credit or other features.

(ii) *Significant changes in account terms.* For purposes of this section, a "significant change in account terms" means a change to a term required to be disclosed under § 1026.6(b)(1) and (b)(2), an increase in the required minimum periodic payment, a change to a term required to be disclosed under § 1026.6(b)(4), or the acquisition of a security interest.

(iii) *Charges not covered by § 1026.6(b)(1) and (b)(2).* Except as provided in paragraph (c)(2)(vi) of this section, if a creditor increases any component of a charge, or introduces a new charge, required to be disclosed under § 1026.6(b)(3) that is not a significant change in account terms as described in paragraph (c)(2)(ii) of this section, a creditor must either, at its option:

(A) Comply with the requirements of paragraph (c)(2)(i) of this section; or

(B) Provide notice of the amount of the charge before the consumer agrees to or becomes obligated to pay the charge, at a time and in a manner that a consumer would be likely to notice the disclosure of the charge. The notice may be provided orally or in writing.

(iv) *Disclosure requirements.*

(A) *Significant changes in account terms.* If a creditor makes a significant change in account terms as described in paragraph (c)(2)(ii) of this section, the notice provided pursuant to paragraph (c)(2)(i) of this section must provide the following information:

(*1*) A summary of the changes made to terms required by § 1026.6(b)(1) and (b)(2) or § 1026.6(b)(4), a description of any increase in the required minimum periodic payment, and a description of any security interest being acquired by the creditor;

(*2*) A statement that changes are being made to the account;

(*3*) For accounts other than credit card accounts under an open-end (not home-secured) consumer credit plan subject to § 1026.9(c)(2)(iv)(B), a statement indicating the consumer has the right to opt out of these changes, if applicable, and a reference to additional information describing the opt-out right provided in the notice, if applicable;

(*4*) The date the changes will become effective;

(*5*) If applicable, a statement that the consumer may find additional information about the summarized changes, and other changes to the account, in the notice;

(*6*) If the creditor is changing a rate on the account, other than a penalty rate, a statement that if a penalty rate currently applies to the consumer's account, the new rate described in the notice will not apply to the consumer's account until the consumer's account balances are no longer subject to the penalty rate;

(*7*) If the change in terms being disclosed is an increase in an annual percentage rate, the balances to which the increased rate will be applied. If applicable, a statement identifying the balances to which the current rate will continue to apply as of the effective date of the change in terms; and

(*8*) If the change in terms being disclosed is an increase in an annual percentage rate for a credit card account under an open-end (not home-secured) consumer credit plan, a statement of no more than four principal reasons for the rate increase, listed in their order of importance.

(B) *Right to reject for credit card accounts under an open-end (not home-secured) consumer credit plan.* In addition to the disclosures in paragraph (c)(2)(iv)(A) of this section, if a card issuer makes a significant change in account terms on a credit card account under an open-end (not home-secured) consumer credit plan, the creditor must generally provide the following information on the notice provided pursuant to paragraph (c)(2)(i) of this section. This information is not required to be provided in the case of an increase in the required minimum periodic payment, an increase in a fee as a result of a reevaluation of a determination made under § 1026.52(b)(1)(i) or an adjustment to the safe harbors in § 1026.52(b)(1)(ii) to reflect changes in the Consumer Price Index, a change in an annual percentage rate applicable to a consumer's account, an increase in a fee previously reduced consistent with 50 U.S.C. app. 527 or a similar Federal or state statute or regulation if the amount of the increased fee does not exceed the amount of that fee prior to the reduction, or when the change results from the creditor not receiving the consumer's required minimum periodic payment within 60 days after the due date for that payment:

(*1*) A statement that the consumer has the right to reject the change or changes prior to the effective date of the changes, unless the consumer fails to make a required minimum periodic payment within 60 days after the due date for that payment;

(*2*) Instructions for rejecting the change or changes, and a toll-free telephone number that the consumer may use to notify the creditor of the rejection; and

(*3*) If applicable, a statement that if the consumer rejects the change or changes, the consumer's ability to use the account for further advances will be terminated or suspended.

(C) *Changes resulting from failure to make minimum periodic payment within 60 days from due date for credit card accounts under an open-end (not home-secured) consumer credit plan.* For a credit card account under an open-end (not home-secured) consumer credit plan:

(*1*) If the significant change required to be disclosed pursuant to paragraph (c)(2)(i) of this section is an increase in an annual percentage rate or a fee or charge required to be disclosed under § 1026.6(b)(2)(ii), (b)(2)(iii), or (b)(2)(xii) based on the consumer's failure to make a minimum periodic payment within 60 days from the due date for that payment, the notice provided pursuant to paragraph (c)(2)(i) of this section must state that the increase will cease to apply to transactions that occurred prior to or within 14 days of provision of the notice, if the creditor receives six consecutive required minimum periodic payments on or before the payment due date, beginning with the first payment due following the effective date of the increase.

(*2*) If the significant change required to be disclosed pursuant to paragraph (c)(2)(i) of this section is an increase in a fee or charge required to be disclosed under § 1026.6(b)(2)(ii), (b)(2)(iii), or (b)(2)(xii) based on the consumer's failure to make a minimum periodic payment within 60 days from the due date for that payment, the notice provided pursuant to paragraph (c)(2)(i) of this section must also state the reason for the increase.

(D) *Format requirements.*

(*1*) *Tabular format.* The summary of changes described in paragraph (c)(2)(iv)(A)(1) of this section must be in a tabular format (except for a summary of any increase in the required minimum periodic payment, a summary of a term required to be disclosed under § 1026.6(b)(4) that is not required to be disclosed under § 1026.6(b)(1) and (b)(2), or a description of any security interest being acquired by the creditor), with headings and format substantially similar to any of the account-opening tables found in G-17 in Appendix G to this part. The table must disclose the changed term and information relevant to the change, if that relevant information is required by § 1026.6(b)(1) and (b)(2). The new terms shall be described in the same level of detail as required when disclosing the terms under § 1026.6(b)(2).

(*2*) *Notice included with periodic statement.* If a notice required by paragraph (c)(2)(i) of this section is included on or with a periodic statement, the information described in paragraph (c)(2)(iv)(A)(1) of this section must be disclosed on the front of any page of the statement. The summary of changes described in paragraph (c)(2)(iv)(A)(1) of this section must immediately follow the information described in paragraph (c)(2)(iv)(A)(2) through (c)(2)(iv)(A)(7) and, if applicable, paragraphs (c)(2)(iv)(A)(8), (c)(2)(iv)(B), and (c)(2)(iv)(C) of this section, and be substantially similar to the format shown in Sample G-20 or G-21 in Appendix G to this part.

(*3*) *Notice provided separately from periodic statement.* If a notice required by paragraph (c)(2)(i) of this section is not included on or with a periodic statement, the information described in paragraph (c)(2)(iv)(A)(1) of this section must, at the creditor's option, be disclosed on the front of the first page of the notice or segregated on a separate page from other information given with the notice. The summary of changes required to be in a table pursuant to paragraph (c)(2)(iv)(A)(1) of this section may be on more than one page, and may use both the front and reverse sides, so long as the table begins on the front of the first page of the notice and there is a reference on the first page indicating that the table continues on the following page. The summary of changes described in paragraph (c)(2)(iv)(A)(1) of this section must immediately follow the information described in paragraph (c)(2)(iv)(A)(2) through (c)(2)(iv)(A)(7) and, if applicable, paragraphs (c)(2)(iv)(A)(8), (c)(2)(iv)(B), and (c)(2)(iv)(C), of this section, substantially similar to the format shown in Sample G-20 or G-21 in Appendix G to this part.

(v) *Notice not required.* For open-end plans (other than home equity plans subject to the requirements of § 1026.40) a creditor is not required to provide notice under this section:

(A) When the change involves charges for documentary evidence; a reduction of any component of a finance or other charge; suspension of future credit privileges (except as provided in paragraph (c)(2)(vi) of this section) or termination of an account or plan; when the change results from an agreement involving a court proceeding; when the change is an extension of the grace period; or if the change is applicable only to checks that access a credit card account and the changed terms are disclosed on or with the checks in accordance with paragraph (b)(3) of this section;

(B) When the change is an increase in an annual percentage rate or fee upon the expiration of a specified period of time, provided that:

(*1*) Prior to commencement of that period, the creditor disclosed in writing to the consumer, in a clear and conspicuous manner, the length of the period and the annual percentage rate or fee that would apply after expiration of the period;

(*2*) The disclosure of the length of the period and the annual percentage rate or fee that would apply after expiration of the period are set forth in close proximity and in equal prominence to the first listing of the disclosure of the rate or fee that applies during the specified period of time; and

(*3*) The annual percentage rate or fee that applies after that period does not exceed the rate or fee disclosed pursuant to paragraph (c)(2)(v)(B)(1) of this paragraph or, if the rate disclosed pursuant to paragraph (c)(2)(v)(B)(1) of this section was a variable rate, the rate following any such increase is a variable rate determined by the same formula (index and margin) that was used to calculate the variable rate disclosed pursuant to paragraph (c)(2)(v)(B)(1);

(C) When the change is an increase in a variable annual percentage rate in accordance with a credit card or other account agreement that provides for changes in the rate according to operation of an index that is not under the control of the creditor and is available to the general public; or

(D) When the change is an increase in an annual percentage rate, a fee or charge required to be disclosed under § 1026.6(b)(2)(ii), (b)(2)(iii), (b)(2)(viii), (b)(2)(ix), (b)(2)(ix) or (b)(2)(xii), or the required minimum periodic payment due to the completion of a workout or temporary hardship arrangement by the consumer or the consumer's failure to comply with the terms of such an arrangement, provided that:

(*1*) The annual percentage rate or fee or charge applicable to a category of transactions or the required minimum periodic payment following any such increase does not exceed the rate or fee or charge or required minimum periodic payment that applied to that category of transactions prior to commencement of the arrangement or, if the rate that applied to a category of transactions prior to the commencement of the workout or temporary hardship arrangement was a variable rate, the rate following any such increase is a variable rate determined by the same formula (index and margin) that applied to the category of transactions prior to commencement of the workout or temporary hardship arrangement; and

(*2*) The creditor has provided the consumer, prior to the commencement of such arrangement, with a clear and conspicuous disclosure of the terms of the arrangement (including any increases due to such completion or failure). This disclosure must generally be provided in writing. However, a creditor may provide the disclosure of the terms of the arrangement orally by telephone, provided that the creditor mails or delivers a written disclosure of the terms of the arrangement to the consumer as soon as reasonably practicable after the oral disclosure is provided.

(vi) *Reduction of the credit limit.* For open-end plans that are not subject to the requirements of § 1026.40, if a creditor decreases the credit limit on an account, advance notice of the decrease must be provided before an over-the-limit fee or a penalty rate can be imposed solely as a result of the consumer exceeding the newly decreased credit limit. Notice shall be provided in writing or orally at least 45 days prior to imposing the over-the-limit fee or penalty rate and shall state that the credit limit on the account has been or will be decreased.

* * *

[Reg. Z, 34 Fed. Reg. 2,002 (Feb. 11, 1969); 34 Fed. Reg. 5,327 (Mar. 18, 1969), *as amended at* 34 Fed. Reg. 18,242 (Nov. 14, 1969); 36 Fed. Reg. 4,113 (Mar. 4, 1971); 36 Fed. Reg. 19,671 (Oct. 9, 1971); 40 Fed. Reg. 30,086 (July 17, 1975); 43 Fed. Reg. 34,113 (Aug. 3, 1978); 46 Fed. Reg. 20,892 (Apr. 7, 1981); 46 Fed. Reg. 29,246 (June 1, 1981); 54 Fed. Reg. 13,867 (Apr. 6, 1989); 54 Fed. Reg. 24,688 (June 9, 1989); 54 Fed. Reg. 32,954 (Aug. 11, 1989); 55 Fed. Reg. 38,312 (Sept. 18, 1990); 55 Fed. Reg. 39,538 (Sept. 27, 1990); 55 Fed. Reg. 42,148 (Oct. 17, 1990); 74 Fed. Reg. 36,094 (July 22, 2009) (interim final rule); 75 Fed. Reg. 7807 (Feb. 22, 2010); 75 Fed. Reg. 37,568 (June 29, 2010); 76 Fed. Reg. 23,000, 23,001 (Apr. 25, 2011)]

## 12 C.F.R. § 1026.10 Payments [§ 226.10]

(a) *General rule.* A creditor shall credit a payment to the consumer's account as of the date of receipt, except when a delay in crediting does not result in a finance or other charge or except as provided in paragraph (b) of this section.

(b) *Specific requirements for payments.*

(1) *General rule.* A creditor may specify reasonable requirements for payments that enable most consumers to make conforming payments.

(2) *Examples of reasonable requirements for payments.* Reasonable requirements for making payment may include:

(i) Requiring that payments be accompanied by the account number or payment stub;

(ii) Setting reasonable cut-off times for payments to be received by mail, by electronic means, by telephone, and in person (except as provided in paragraph (b)(3) of this section), provided that such cut-off times shall be no earlier than 5 p.m. on the payment due date at the location specified by the creditor for the receipt of such payments;

(iii) Specifying that only checks or money orders should be sent by mail;

(iv) Specifying that payment is to be made in U.S. dollars; or

(v) Specifying one particular address for receiving payments, such as a post office box.

(3) *In-person payments on credit card accounts.*

(i) *General.* Notwithstanding § 1026.10(b), payments on a credit card account under an open-end (not home-secured) consumer credit plan made in person at a branch or office of a card issuer that is a financial institution prior to the close of business of that branch or office shall be considered received on the date on which the consumer makes the payment. A card issuer that is a financial institution shall not impose a cut-off time earlier than the close of business for any such payments made in person at any branch or office of the card issuer at which such payments are accepted. Notwithstanding § 1026.10(b)(2)(ii), a card issuer may impose a cut-off time earlier than 5 p.m. for such payments, if the close of business of the branch or office is earlier than 5 p.m.

(ii) *Financial institution.* For purposes of paragraph (b)(3) of this section, "financial institution" shall mean a bank, savings association, or credit union.

(4) *Nonconforming payments.*

(i) *In general.* Except as provided in paragraph (b)(4)(ii) of this section, if a creditor specifies, on or with the periodic statement, requirements for the consumer to follow in making payments as permitted under this § 1026.10, but accepts a payment that does not conform to the requirements, the creditor shall credit the payment within five days of receipt.

(ii) *Payment methods promoted by creditor.* If a creditor promotes a method for making payments, such payments shall be considered conforming payments in accordance with this paragraph (b) and shall be credited to the consumer's account as of the date of receipt, except when a delay in crediting does not result in a finance or other charge.

(c) *Adjustment of account.* If a creditor fails to credit a payment, as required by paragraphs (a) or (b) of this section, in time to avoid the imposition of finance or other charges, the creditor shall adjust the consumer's account so that the charges imposed are credited to the consumer's account during the next billing cycle.

(d) *Crediting of payments when creditor does not receive or accept payments on due date.*

(1) *General.* Except as provided in paragraph (d)(2) of this section, if a creditor does not receive or accept payments by mail on the due date for payments, the creditor may generally not treat a payment received the next business day as late for any purpose. For purposes of this paragraph (d), the "next business day" means the next day on which the creditor accepts or receives payments by mail.

(2) *Payments accepted or received other than by mail.* If a creditor accepts or receives payments made on the due date by a method other than mail, such as electronic or telephone payments, the creditor is not required to treat a payment made by that method on the next business day as timely, even if it does not accept mailed payments on the due date.

(e) *Limitations on fees related to method of payment.* For credit card accounts under an open-end (not home-secured) consumer credit plan, a creditor may not impose a separate fee to allow consumers to make a payment by any method, such as mail, electronic, or telephone payments, unless such payment method involves an expedited service by a customer service representative of the creditor. For purposes of paragraph (e) of this section, the term "creditor" includes a third party that collects, receives, or processes payments on behalf of a creditor.

(f) *Changes by card issuer.* If a card issuer makes a material change in the address for receiving payments or procedures for handling payments, and such change causes a material delay in the crediting of a payment to the consumer's account during the 60-day period following the date on which such change took effect, the card issuer may not impose any late fee or finance charge for a late payment on the credit card account during the 60-day period following the date on which the change took effect.

[Reg. Z, 34 Fed. Reg. 2,002 (Feb. 11, 1969); 34 Fed. Reg. 5,327 (Mar. 18, 1969), *as amended at* 36 Fed. Reg. 4,113 (Mar. 4, 1971); 38 Fed. Reg. 18,457 (July 11, 1973); 40 Fed. Reg. 30,085 (July 17, 1975); 41 Fed. Reg. 45,539 (Oct. 15, 1976); 42 Fed. Reg. 3 (Jan. 3, 1977); 75 Fed. Reg. 7811 (Feb. 22, 2010); 76 Fed. Reg. 23,002 (Apr. 25, 2011)]

* * *

**SUBPART G—SPECIAL RULES APPLICABLE TO CREDIT CARD ACCOUNTS AND OPEN-END CREDIT OFFERED TO COLLEGE STUDENTS**

## 12 C.F.R. § 1026.51 Ability to Pay [§ 226.51]

(a) *General rule.*

(1)(i) *Consideration of ability to pay.* A card issuer must not open a credit card account for a consumer under an open-end (not home-secured) consumer credit plan, or increase any credit limit applicable to such account, unless the card issuer considers the consumer's independent ability to make the required minimum periodic payments under the terms of the account based on the consumer's income or assets and current obligations.

(ii) *Reasonable policies and procedures.* Card issuers must establish and maintain reasonable written policies and procedures to consider a consumer's independent income or assets and current obligations. Reasonable policies and procedures to consider a consumer's independent ability to make the required payments include the consideration of at least one of the following: The ratio of debt obligations to income; the ratio of debt obligations to assets; or the income the consumer will have after paying debt obligations. It would be unreasonable for a card issuer to not review any information about a consumer's income, assets, or current obligations, or to issue a credit card to a consumer who does not have any independent income or assets.

(2) *Minimum periodic payments.*

(i) *Reasonable method.* For purposes of paragraph (a)(1) of this section, a card issuer must use a reasonable method for estimating the minimum periodic payments the consumer would be required to pay under the terms of the account.

(ii) *Safe harbor.* A card issuer complies with paragraph (a)(2)(i) of this section if it estimates required minimum periodic payments using the following method:

(A) The card issuer assumes utilization, from the first day of the billing cycle, of the full credit line that the issuer is considering offering to the consumer; and

(B) The card issuer uses a minimum payment formula employed by the issuer for the product the issuer is considering offering to the consumer or, in the case of an existing account, the minimum payment formula that currently applies to that account, provided that:

(*1*) If the applicable minimum payment formula includes interest charges, the card issuer estimates those charges using an interest rate that the issuer is considering offering to the consumer for purchases or, in the case of an existing account, the interest rate that currently applies to purchases; and

(*2*) If the applicable minimum payment formula includes mandatory fees, the card issuer must assume that such fees have been charged to the account.

(b) *Rules affecting young consumers.*

(1) *Applications from young consumers.* A card issuer may not open a credit card account under an open-end (not home-secured) consumer credit plan for a consumer less than 21 years old, unless the consumer has submitted a written application and the card issuer has:

(i) Financial information indicating the consumer has an independent ability to make the required minimum periodic payments on the proposed extension of credit in connection with the account, consistent with paragraph (a) of this section; or

(ii)(A) A signed agreement of a cosigner, guarantor, or joint applicant who is at least 21 years old to be either secondarily liable for any debt on the account incurred by the consumer before the consumer has attained the age of 21 or jointly liable with the consumer for any debt on the account, and

(B) Financial information indicating such cosigner, guarantor, or joint applicant has the independent ability to make the required minimum periodic payments on such debts, consistent with paragraph (a) of this section.

(2) *Credit line increases for young consumers.* If a credit card account has been opened pursuant to paragraph (b)(1)(ii) of this section, no increase in the credit limit may be made on such account before the consumer attains the age of 21 unless the cosigner, guarantor, or joint accountholder who assumed liability at account opening agrees in writing to assume liability on the increase.

[75 Fed. Reg. 7818 (Feb. 22, 2010); 76 Fed. Reg. 23,002 (Apr. 25, 2011)]

## 12 C.F.R. § 1026.52 Limitations on Fees [§ 226.52]

(a) *Limitations prior to account opening and during first year after account opening.*

(1) *General rule.* Except as provided in paragraph (a)(2) of this section, the total amount of fees a consumer is required to pay with respect to a credit card account under an open-end (not home-secured) consumer credit plan prior to account opening and during the first year after account opening must not exceed 25 percent of the credit limit in effect when the account is opened. For purposes of this paragraph, an account is considered open no earlier than the date on which the account may first be used by the consumer to engage in transactions.

(2) *Fees not subject to limitations.* Paragraph (a) of this section does not apply to:

(i) Late payment fees, over-the-limit fees, and returned-payment fees; or

(ii) Fees that the consumer is not required to pay with respect to the account.

(3) *Rule of construction.* Paragraph (a) of this section does not authorize the imposition or payment of fees or charges otherwise prohibited by law.

(b) *Limitations on penalty fees.* A card issuer must not impose a fee for violating the terms or other requirements of a credit card account under an open-end (not home-secured) consumer credit plan unless the dollar amount of the fee is consistent with paragraphs (b)(1) and (b)(2) of this section.

(1) *General rule.* Except as provided in paragraph (b)(2) of this section, a card issuer may impose a fee for violating the terms or other requirements of a credit card account under an

open-end (not home-secured) consumer credit plan if the dollar amount of the fee is consistent with either paragraph (b)(1)(i) or (b)(1)(ii) of this section.

(i) *Fees based on costs.* A card issuer may impose a fee for violating the terms or other requirements of an account if the card issuer has determined that the dollar amount of the fee represents a reasonable proportion of the total costs incurred by the card issuer as a result of that type of violation. A card issuer must reevaluate this determination at least once every twelve months. If as a result of the reevaluation the card issuer determines that a lower fee represents a reasonable proportion of the total costs incurred by the card issuer as a result of that type of violation, the card issuer must begin imposing the lower fee within 45 days after completing the reevaluation. If as a result of the reevaluation the card issuer determines that a higher fee represents a reasonable proportion of the total costs incurred by the card issuer as a result of that type of violation, the card issuer may begin imposing the higher fee after complying with the notice requirements in § 1026.9.

(ii) *Safe harbors.* A card issuer may impose a fee for violating the terms or other requirements of an account if the dollar amount of the fee does not exceed, as applicable:

(A) $25.00;

(B) $35.00 if the card issuer previously imposed a fee pursuant to paragraph (b)(1)(ii)(A) of this section for a violation of the same type that occurred during the same billing cycle or one of the next six billing cycles; or

(C) Three percent of the delinquent balance on a charge card account that requires payment of outstanding balances in full at the end of each billing cycle if the card issuer has not received the required payment for two or more consecutive billing cycles.

(D) The amounts in paragraphs (b)(1)(ii)(A) and (b)(1)(ii)(B) of this section will be adjusted annually by the Bureau to reflect changes in the Consumer Price Index.

(2) *Prohibited fees.*

(i) *Fees that exceed dollar amount associated with violation.*

(A) *Generally.* A card issuer must not impose a fee for violating the terms or other requirements of a credit card account under an open-end (not home-secured) consumer credit plan that exceeds the dollar amount associated with the violation.

(B) *No dollar amount associated with violation.* A card issuer must not impose a fee for violating the terms or other requirements of a credit card account under an open-end (not home-secured) consumer credit plan when there is no dollar amount associated with the violation. For purposes of paragraph (b)(2)(i) of this section, there is no dollar amount associated with the following violations:

(*1*) Transactions that the card issuer declines to authorize;

(*2*) Account inactivity; and

(*3*) The closure or termination of an account.

(ii) *Multiple fees based on a single event or transaction.* A card issuer must not impose more than one fee for violating the terms or other requirements of a credit card account under an open-end (not home-secured) consumer credit plan based on a single event or transaction. A card issuer may, at its option, comply with this prohibition by imposing no more than one fee for violating the terms or other requirements of an account during a billing cycle.

[75 Fed. Reg. 7819 (Feb. 22, 2010); 75 Fed. Reg. 37,571 (June 29, 2010); 76 Fed. Reg. 23,002, 23,003 (Apr. 25, 2011)]

## 12 C.F.R. § 1026.53 Allocation of Payments [§ 226.53]

(a) *General rule.* Except as provided in paragraph (b) of this section, when a consumer makes a payment in excess of the required minimum periodic payment for a credit card account under an open-end (not home-secured) consumer credit plan, the card issuer must allocate the excess amount first to the balance with the highest annual percentage rate and any remaining portion to the other balances in descending order based on the applicable annual percentage rate.

(b) *Special rules.*

(1) *Accounts with balances subject to deferred interest or similar program.* When a balance on a credit card account under an open-end (not home-secured) consumer credit plan is subject to a deferred interest or similar program that provides that a consumer will not be obligated to pay interest that accrues on the balance if the balance is paid in full prior to the expiration of a specified period of time:

(i) *Last two billing cycles.* The card issuer must allocate any amount paid by the consumer in excess of the required minimum periodic payment consistent with paragraph (a) of this section, except that, during the two billing cycles immediately preceding expiration of the specified period, the excess amount must be allocated first to the balance subject to the deferred interest or similar program and any remaining portion allocated to any other balances consistent with paragraph (a) of this section; or

(ii) *Consumer request.* The card issuer may at its option allocate any amount paid by the consumer in excess of the required minimum periodic payment among the balances on the account in the manner requested by the consumer.

(2) *Accounts with secured balances.* When a balance on a credit card account under an open-end (not home-secured) consumer credit plan is secured, the card issuer may at its option allocate any amount paid by the consumer in excess of the required minimum periodic payment to that balance if requested by the consumer.

[75 Fed. Reg. 7819 (Feb. 22, 2010); 76 Fed. Reg. 23,003 (Apr. 25, 2011)]

## 12 C.F.R. § 1026.54 Limitations on the Imposition of Finance Charges [§ 226.54]

(a) *Limitations on imposing finance charges as a result of the loss of a grace period.*

(1) *General rule.* Except as provided in paragraph (b) of this section, a card issuer must not impose finance charges as a result of the loss of a grace period on a credit card account under an open-end (not home-secured) consumer credit plan if those finance charges are based on:

(i) Balances for days in billing cycles that precede the most recent billing cycle; or

(ii) Any portion of a balance subject to a grace period that was repaid prior to the expiration of the grace period.

(2) *Definition of grace period.* For purposes of paragraph (a)(1) of this section, "grace period" has the same meaning as in § 1026.5(b)(2)(ii)(B)(3).

(b) *Exceptions.* Paragraph (a) of this section does not apply to:

(1) Adjustments to finance charges as a result of the resolution of a dispute under § 1026.12 or § 1026.13; or

(2) Adjustments to finance charges as a result of the return of a payment.

[75 Fed. Reg. 7819 (Feb. 22, 2010)]

## 12 C.F.R. § 1026.55 Limitations on Increasing Annual Percentage Rates, Fees, and Charges [§ 226.55]

(a) *General rule.* Except as provided in paragraph (b) of this section, a card issuer must not increase an annual percentage rate or a fee or charge required to be disclosed under § 1026.6(b)(2)(ii), (b)(2)(iii), or (b)(2)(xii) on a credit card account under an open-end (not home-secured) consumer credit plan.

(b) *Exceptions.* A card issuer may increase an annual percentage rate or a fee or charge required to be disclosed under § 1026.6(b)(2)(ii), (b)(2)(iii), or (b)(2)(xii) pursuant to an exception set forth in this paragraph even if that increase would not be permitted under a different exception.

(1) *Temporary rate, fee, or charge exception.* A card issuer may increase an annual percentage rate or a fee or charge required to be disclosed under § 1026.6(b)(2)(ii), (b)(2)(iii), or (b)(2)(xii) upon the expiration of a specified period of six months or longer, provided that:

(i) Prior to the commencement of that period, the card issuer disclosed in writing to the consumer, in a clear and conspicuous manner, the length of the period and the annual percentage rate, fee, or charge that would apply after expiration of the period; and

(ii) Upon expiration of the specified period:

(A) The card issuer must not apply an annual percentage rate, fee, or charge to transactions that occurred prior to the period that exceeds the annual percentage rate, fee, or charge that applied to those transactions prior to the period;

(B) If the disclosures required by paragraph (b)(1)(i) of this section are provided pursuant to § 1026.9(c), the card issuer must not apply an annual percentage rate, fee, or charge to transactions that occurred within 14 days after provision of the notice that exceeds the annual percentage rate, fee, or charge that applied to that category of transactions prior to provision of the notice; and

(C) The card issuer must not apply an annual percentage rate, fee, or charge to transactions that occurred during the period that exceeds the increased annual percentage rate, fee, or charge disclosed pursuant to paragraph (b)(1)(i) of this section.

(2) *Variable rate exception.* A card issuer may increase an annual percentage rate when:

(i) The annual percentage rate varies according to an index that is not under the card issuer's control and is available to the general public; and

(ii) The increase in the annual percentage rate is due to an increase in the index.

(3) *Advance notice exception.* A card issuer may increase an annual percentage rate or a fee or charge required to be disclosed under § 1026.6(b)(2)(ii), (b)(2)(iii), or (b)(2)(xii) after complying with the applicable notice requirements in § 1026.9(b), (c), or (g), provided that:

(i) If a card issuer discloses an increased annual percentage rate, fee, or charge pursuant to § 1026.9(b), the card issuer must not apply that rate, fee, or charge to transactions that occurred prior to provision of the notice;

(ii) If a card issuer discloses an increased annual percentage rate, fee, or charge pursuant to § 1026.9(c) or (g), the card issuer must not apply that rate, fee, or charge to transactions that occurred prior to or within 14 days after provision of the notice; and

(iii) This exception does not permit a card issuer to increase an annual percentage rate or a fee or charge required to be disclosed under § 1026.6(b)(2)(ii), (iii), or (xii) during the first year after the account is opened, while the account is closed, or while the card issuer does not permit the consumer to use the account for new transactions. For purposes of this paragraph, an account is considered open no earlier than the date on which the account may first be used by the consumer to engage in transactions.

(4) *Delinquency exception.* A card issuer may increase an annual percentage rate or a fee or charge required to be disclosed under § 1026.6(b)(2)(ii), (b)(2)(iii), or (b)(2)(xii) due to the card issuer not receiving the consumer's required minimum periodic payment within 60 days after the due date for that payment, provided that:

(i) The card issuer must disclose in a clear and conspicuous manner in the notice of the increase pursuant to § 1026.9(c) or (g):

(A) A statement of the reason for the increase; and

(B) That the increased annual percentage rate, fee, or charge will cease to apply if the card issuer receives six consecutive required minimum periodic payments on or before the payment due date beginning with the first payment due following the effective date of the increase; and

(ii) If the card issuer receives six consecutive required minimum periodic payments on or before the payment due date beginning with the first payment due following the effective date of the increase, the card issuer must reduce any annual percentage rate, fee, or charge increased pursuant to this exception to the annual percentage rate, fee, or charge that applied prior to the increase with respect to transactions that occurred prior to or within 14 days after provision of the § 1026.9(c) or (g) notice.

(5) *Workout and temporary hardship arrangement exception.* A card issuer may increase an annual percentage rate or a fee or charge required to be disclosed under § 1026.6(b)(2)(ii), (b)(2)(iii), or (b)(2)(xii) due to the consumer's completion of a workout or temporary hardship arrangement or the consumer's failure to comply with the terms of such an arrangement, provided that:

(i) Prior to commencement of the arrangement (except as provided in § 1026.9(c)(2)(v)(D)), the card issuer has provided the consumer with a clear and conspicuous written disclosure of the terms of the arrangement (including any increases due to the completion or failure of the arrangement); and

(ii) Upon the completion or failure of the arrangement, the card issuer must not apply to any transactions that occurred prior to commencement of the arrangement an annual percentage rate, fee, or charge that exceeds the annual percentage rate, fee, or charge that applied to those transactions prior to commencement of the arrangement.

(6) *Servicemembers Civil Relief Act exception.* If an annual percentage rate or a fee or charge required to be disclosed under § 1026.6(b)(2)(ii), (iii), or (xii) has been decreased pursuant to 50 U.S.C. app. 527 or a similar Federal or state statute or regulation, a card issuer may increase that annual percentage rate, fee, or charge once 50 U.S.C. app. 527 or the similar statute or regulation no longer applies, provided that the card issuer must not apply to any transactions that occurred prior to the decrease an annual percentage rate, fee, or charge that exceeds the annual percentage rate, fee, or charge that applied to those transactions prior to the decrease.

(c) *Treatment of protected balances.*

(1) *Definition of protected balance.* For purposes of this paragraph, "protected balance" means the amount owed for a category of transactions to which an increased annual percentage rate or an increased fee or charge required to be disclosed under § 1026.6(b)(2)(ii), (b)(2)(iii), or (b)(2)(xii) cannot be applied after the annual percentage rate, fee, or charge for that category of transactions has been increased pursuant to paragraph (b)(3) of this section.

(2) *Repayment of protected balance.* The card issuer must not require repayment of the protected balance using a method that is less beneficial to the consumer than one of the following methods:

(i) The method of repayment for the account before the effective date of the increase;

(ii) An amortization period of not less than five years, beginning no earlier than the effective date of the increase; or

(iii) A required minimum periodic payment that includes a percentage of the balance that is equal to no more than twice the percentage required before the effective date of the increase.

(d) *Continuing application.* This section continues to apply to a balance on a credit card account under an open-end (not home-secured) consumer credit plan after:

(1) The account is closed or acquired by another creditor; or

(2) The balance is transferred from a credit card account under an open-end (not home-secured) consumer credit plan issued by a creditor to another credit account issued by the same creditor or its affiliate or subsidiary (unless the account to which the balance is transferred is subject to § 1026.40).

(e) *Promotional waivers or rebates of interest, fees, and other charges.* If a card issuer promotes the waiver or rebate of finance charges due to a periodic interest rate or fees or charges required to be disclosed under § 1026.6(b)(2)(ii), (iii), or (xii) and applies the waiver or rebate to a credit card account under an open-end (not home-secured) consumer credit plan, any cessation of the waiver or rebate on that account constitutes an increase in an annual percentage rate, fee, or charge for purposes of this section.

[75 Fed. Reg. 7819 (Feb. 22, 2010); 76 Fed. Reg. 23,003 (Apr. 25, 2011)]

## 12 C.F.R. § 1026.56 Requirements for Over-the-Limit Transactions [§ 226.56]

(a) *Definition.* For purposes of this section, the term *over-the-limit transaction* means any extension of credit by a card issuer to complete a transaction that causes a consumer's credit card account balance to exceed the credit limit.

(b) *Opt-in requirement.*

(1) *General.* A card issuer shall not assess a fee or charge on a consumer's credit card account under an open-end (not home-secured) con-

sumer credit plan for an over-the-limit transaction unless the card issuer:

(i) Provides the consumer with an oral, written or electronic notice, segregated from all other information, describing the consumer's right to affirmatively consent, or opt in, to the card issuer's payment of an over-the-limit transaction;

(ii) Provides a reasonable opportunity for the consumer to affirmatively consent, or opt in, to the card issuer's payment of over-the-limit transactions;

(iii) Obtains the consumer's affirmative consent, or opt-in, to the card issuer's payment of such transactions;

(iv) Provides the consumer with confirmation of the consumer's consent in writing, or if the consumer agrees, electronically; and

(v) Provides the consumer notice in writing of the right to revoke that consent following the assessment of an over-the-limit fee or charge.

(2) *Completion of over-the-limit transactions without consumer consent.* Notwithstanding the absence of a consumer's affirmative consent under paragraph (b)(1)(iii) of this section, a card issuer may pay any over-the-limit transaction on a consumer's account provided that the card issuer does not impose any fee or charge on the account for paying that over-the-limit transaction.

(c) *Method of election.* A card issuer may permit a consumer to consent to the card issuer's payment of any over-the-limit transaction in writing, orally, or electronically, at the card issuer's option. The card issuer must also permit the consumer to revoke his or her consent using the same methods available to the consumer for providing consent.

(d) *Timing and placement of notices.*

(1) *Initial notice.*

(i) *General.* The notice required by paragraph (b)(1)(i) of this section shall be provided prior to the assessment of any over-the-limit fee or charge on a consumer's account.

(ii) *Oral or electronic consent.* If a consumer consents to the card issuer's payment of any over-the-limit transaction by oral or electronic means, the card issuer must provide the notice required by paragraph (b)(1)(i) of this section immediately prior to obtaining that consent.

(2) *Confirmation of opt-in.* The notice required by paragraph (b)(1)(iv) of this section may be provided no later than the first periodic statement sent after the consumer has consented to the card issuer's payment of over-the-limit transactions.

(3) *Notice of right of revocation.* The notice required by paragraph (b)(1)(v) of this section shall be provided on the front of any page of each periodic statement that reflects the assessment of an over-the-limit fee or charge on a consumer's account.

(e) *Content.*

(1) *Initial notice.* The notice required by paragraph (b)(1)(i) of this section shall include all applicable items in this paragraph (e)(1) and may not contain any information not specified in or otherwise permitted by this paragraph.

(i) *Fees.* The dollar amount of any fees or charges assessed by the card issuer on a consumer's account for an over-the-limit transaction;

(ii) *APRs.* Any increased periodic rate(s) (expressed as an annual percentage rate(s)) that may be imposed on the account as a result of an over-the-limit transaction; and

(iii) *Disclosure of opt-in right.* An explanation of the consumer's right to affirmatively consent to the card issuer's payment of over-the-limit transactions, including the method(s) by which the consumer may consent.

(2) *Subsequent notice.* The notice required by paragraph (b)(1)(v) of this section shall describe the consumer's right to revoke any consent provided under paragraph (b)(1)(iii) of this section, including the method(s) by which the consumer may revoke.

(3) *Safe harbor.* Use of Model Forms G-25(A) or G-25(B) of Appendix G to this part, or substantially similar notices, constitutes compliance with the notice content requirements of paragraph (e) of this section.

(f) *Joint relationships.* If two or more consumers are jointly liable on a credit card account under an open-end (not home-secured) consumer credit plan, the card issuer shall treat the affirmative consent of any of the joint consumers as affirmative consent for that account. Similarly, the card issuer shall treat a revocation of consent by any of the joint consumers as revocation of consent for that account.

(g) *Continuing right to opt in or revoke opt-in.* A consumer may affirmatively consent to the card issuer's payment of over-the-limit transactions at any time in the manner described in the notice required by paragraph (b)(1)(i) of this section. Similarly, the consumer may revoke the consent at any time in the manner described in the notice required by paragraph (b)(1)(v) of this section.

(h) *Duration of opt-in.* A consumer's affirmative consent to the card issuer's payment of over-the-limit transactions is effective until revoked by the consumer, or until the card issuer decides for any reason to cease paying over-the-limit transactions for the consumer.

(i) *Time to comply with revocation request.* A card issuer must comply with a consumer's revocation request as soon as reasonably practicable after the card issuer receives it.

(j) *Prohibited practices.* Notwithstanding a consumer's affirmative consent to a card issuer's payment of over-the-limit transactions, a card issuer is prohibited from engaging in the following practices:

(1) *Fees or charges imposed per cycle.*

(i) *General rule.* A card issuer may not impose more than one over-the-limit fee or charge on a consumer's credit card account per billing cycle, and, in any event, only if the credit limit was exceeded during the billing cycle. In addition, except as provided in paragraph (j)(1)(ii) of this section, a card issuer may not impose an over-the-limit fee or charge on the consumer's credit card account for more than three billing cycles for the same over-the-limit transaction where the consumer has not reduced the account balance below the credit limit by the payment due date for either of the last two billing cycles.

(ii) *Exception.* The prohibition in paragraph (j)(1)(i) of this section on imposing an over-the-limit fee or charge in more than three billing cycles for the same over-the-limit transaction(s) does not apply if another over-the-limit transaction occurs during either of the last two billing cycles.

(2) *Failure to promptly replenish.* A card issuer may not impose an over-the-limit fee or charge solely because of the card issuer's failure to promptly replenish the consumer's available credit following the crediting of the consumer's payment under § 1026.10.

(3) *Conditioning.* A card issuer may not condition the amount of a consumer's credit limit on the consumer affirmatively consenting to the card issuer's payment of over-the-limit transactions if the card issuer assesses a fee or charge for such service.

(4) *Over-the-limit fees attributed to fees or interest.* A card issuer may not impose an over-the-limit fee or charge for a billing cycle if a consumer exceeds a credit limit solely because of fees or interest charged by the card issuer to the consumer's account during that billing cycle. For purposes of this paragraph (j)(4), the relevant fees or interest charges are charges imposed as part of the plan under § 1026.6(b)(3).

[75 Fed. Reg. 7820 (Feb. 22, 2010)]

## 12 C.F.R. § 1026.57 Reporting and Marketing Rules for College Student Open-End Credit [§ 226.57]

(a) *Definitions.*

(1) *College student credit card.* The term *college student credit card* as used in this section means a credit card issued under a credit card account under an open-end (not home-secured) consumer credit plan to any college student.

(2) *College student.* The term *college student* as used in this section means a consumer who is a full-time or part-time student of an institution of higher education.

(3) *Institution of higher education.* The term *institution of higher education* as used in this section has the same meaning as in sections 101 and 102 of the Higher Education Act of 1965 (20 U.S.C. 1001 and 1002).

(4) *Affiliated organization.* The term *affiliated organization* as used in this section means an alumni organization or foundation affiliated with or related to an institution of higher education.

(5) *College credit card agreement.* The term *college credit card agreement* as used in this section means any business, marketing or pro-

motional agreement between a card issuer and an institution of higher education or an affiliated organization in connection with which college student credit cards are issued to college students currently enrolled at that institution.

(b) *Public disclosure of agreements*. An institution of higher education shall publicly disclose any contract or other agreement made with a card issuer or creditor for the purpose of marketing a credit card.

(c) *Prohibited inducements*. No card issuer or creditor may offer a college student any tangible item to induce such student to apply for or open an open-end consumer credit plan offered by such card issuer or creditor, if such offer is made:

(1) On the campus of an institution of higher education;

(2) Near the campus of an institution of higher education; or

(3) At an event sponsored by or related to an institution of higher education.

(d) *Annual report to the Bureau*.

(1) *Requirement to report*. Any card issuer that was a party to one or more college credit card agreements in effect at any time during a calendar year must submit to the Bureau an annual report regarding those agreements in the form and manner prescribed by the Bureau.

(2) *Contents of report*. The annual report to the Bureau must include the following:

(i) Identifying information about the card issuer and the agreements submitted, including the issuer's name, address, and identifying number (such as an RSSD ID number or tax identification number);

(ii) A copy of any college credit card agreement to which the card issuer was a party that was in effect at any time during the period covered by the report;

(iii) A copy of any memorandum of understanding in effect at any time during the period covered by the report between the card issuer and an institution of higher education or affiliated organization that directly or indirectly relates to the college credit card agreement or that controls or directs any obligations or distribution of benefits between any such entities;

(iv) The total dollar amount of any payments pursuant to a college credit card agreement from the card issuer to an institution of higher education or affiliated organization during the period covered by the report, and the method or formula used to determine such amounts;

(v) The total number of credit card accounts opened pursuant to any college credit card agreement during the period covered by the report; and

(vi) The total number of credit card accounts opened pursuant to any such agreement that were open at the end of the period covered by the report.

(3) *Timing of reports*. Except for the initial report described in this paragraph (d)(3), a card issuer must submit its annual report for each calendar year to the Bureau by the first business day on or after March 31 of the following calendar year.

[75 Fed. Reg. 7821 (Feb. 22, 2010)]

* * *

## 12 C.F.R. § 1026.59 Reevaluation of Rate Increases [§ 226.59]

(a) *General rule*.

(1) *Evaluation of increased rate*. If a card issuer increases an annual percentage rate that applies to a credit card account under an open-end (not home-secured) consumer credit plan, based on the credit risk of the consumer, market conditions, or other factors, or increased such a rate on or after January 1, 2009, and 45 days' advance notice of the rate increase is required pursuant to § 1026.9(c)(2) or (g), the card issuer must:

(i) Evaluate the factors described in paragraph (d) of this section; and

(ii) Based on its review of such factors, reduce the annual percentage rate applicable to the consumer's account, as appropriate.

(2) *Rate reductions*.

(i) *Timing*. If a card issuer is required to reduce the rate applicable to an account pursuant to paragraph (a)(1) of this section, the card issuer must reduce the rate not later than 45 days after completion of the evaluation described in paragraph (a)(1).

(ii) *Applicability of rate reduction*. Any reduction in an annual percentage rate required pursuant to paragraph (a)(1) of this section shall apply to:

(A) Any outstanding balances to which the increased rate described in paragraph (a)(1) of this section has been applied; and

(B) New transactions that occur after the effective date of the rate reduction that would otherwise have been subject to the increased rate.

(b) *Policies and procedures*. A card issuer must have reasonable written policies and procedures in place to conduct the review described in paragraph (a) of this section.

(c) *Timing*. A card issuer that is subject to paragraph (a) of this section must conduct the review described in paragraph (a)(1) of this section not less frequently than once every six months after the rate increase.

(d) *Factors*.

(1) *In general*. Except as provided in paragraph (d)(2) of this section, a card issuer must review either:

(i) The factors on which the increase in an annual percentage rate was originally based; or

(ii) The factors that the card issuer currently considers when determining the annual percentage rates applicable to similar new credit card accounts under an open-end (not home-secured) consumer credit plan.

(2) *Rate increases imposed between January 1, 2009 and February 21, 2010*. For rate increases imposed between January 1, 2009 and February 21, 2010, an issuer must consider the factors described in paragraph (d)(1)(ii) when conducting the first two reviews required under paragraph (a) of this section, unless the rate increase subject to paragraph (a) of this section was based solely upon factors specific to the consumer, such as a decline in the consumer's credit risk, the consumer's delinquency or default, or a violation of the terms of the account.

(e) *Rate increases due to delinquency*. If an issuer increases a rate applicable to a consumer's account pursuant to § 1026.55(b)(4) based on the card issuer not receiving the consumer's required minimum periodic payment within 60 days after the due date, the issuer is not required to perform the review described in paragraph (a) of this section prior to the sixth payment due date after the effective date of the increase. However, if the annual percentage rate applicable to the consumer's account is not reduced pursuant to § 1026.55(b)(4)(ii), the card issuer must perform the review described in paragraph (a) of this section. The first such review must occur no later than six months after the sixth payment due following the effective date of the rate increase.

(f) *Termination of obligation to review factors*. The obligation to review factors described in paragraph (a) and (d) of this section ceases to apply:

(1) If the issuer reduces the annual percentage rate applicable to a credit card account under an open-end (not home-secured) consumer credit plan to the rate applicable immediately prior to the increase, or, if the rate applicable immediately prior to the increase was a variable rate, to a variable rate determined by the same formula (index and margin) that was used to calculate the rate applicable immediately prior to the increase; or

(2) If the issuer reduces the annual percentage rate to a rate that is lower than the rate described in paragraph (f)(1) of this section.

(g) *Acquired accounts*.

(1) *General*. Except as provided in paragraph (g)(2) of this section, this section applies to credit card accounts that have been acquired by the card issuer from another card issuer. A card issuer that complies with this section by reviewing the factors described in paragraph (d)(1)(i) must review the factors considered by the card issuer from which it acquired the accounts in connection with the rate increase.

(2) *Review of acquired portfolio*. If, not later than six months after the acquisition of such accounts, a card issuer reviews all of the credit card accounts it acquires in accordance with the factors that it currently considers in determining the rates applicable to its similar new credit card accounts:

(i) Except as provided in paragraph (g)(2)(iii), the card issuer is required to conduct reviews described in paragraph (a) of this section only for rate increases that are imposed as a result of its review under this paragraph. See §§ 1026.9

and 1026.55 for additional requirements regarding rate increases on acquired accounts.

(ii) Except as provided in paragraph (g)(2)(iii) of this section, the card issuer is not required to conduct reviews in accordance with paragraph (a) of this section for any rate increases made prior to the card issuer's acquisition of such accounts.

(iii) If as a result of the card issuer's review, an account is subject to, or continues to be subject to, an increased rate as a penalty, or due to the consumer's delinquency or default, the requirements of paragraph (a) of this section apply.

(h) *Exceptions.*

(1) *Servicemembers Civil Relief Act exception.* The requirements of this section do not apply to increases in an annual percentage rate that was previously decreased pursuant to 50 U.S.C. app. 527, provided that such a rate increase is made in accordance with § 1026.55(b)(6).

(2) *Charged off accounts.* The requirements of this section do not apply to accounts that the card issuer has charged off in accordance with loan-loss provisions.

[75 Fed. Reg. 37,572 (June 29, 2010)]

## 12 C.F.R. § 1026.60 Credit and Charge Card Applications and Solicitations [§ 226.5a]

(a) *General rules.* The card issuer shall provide the disclosures required under this section on or with a solicitation or an application to open a credit or charge card account.

(1) *Definition of solicitation.* For purposes of this section, the term *solicitation* means an offer by the card issuer to open a credit or charge card account that does not require the consumer to complete an application. A "firm offer of credit" as defined in section 603(l) of the Fair Credit Reporting Act (15 U.S.C. 1681a(l)) for a credit or charge card is a solicitation for purposes of this section.

(2) *Form of disclosures; tabular format.*

(i) The disclosures in paragraphs (b)(1) through (5) (except for (b)(1)(iv)(B)) and (b)(7) through (15) of this section made pursuant to paragraph (c), (d)(2), (e)(1) or (f) of this section generally shall be in the form of a table with headings, content, and format substantially similar to any of the applicable tables found in G-10 in appendix G to this part.

(ii) The table described in paragraph (a)(2)(i) of this section shall contain only the information required or permitted by this section. Other information may be presented on or with an application or solicitation, provided such information appears outside the required table.

(iii) Disclosures required by paragraphs (b)(1)(iv)(B), (b)(1)(iv)(C) and (b)(6) of this section must be placed directly beneath the table.

(iv) When a tabular format is required, any annual percentage rate required to be disclosed pursuant to paragraph (b)(1) of this section, any introductory rate required to be disclosed pursuant to paragraph (b)(1)(ii) of this section, any rate that will apply after a premium initial rate expires required to be disclosed under paragraph (b)(1)(iii) of this section, and any fee or percentage amounts or maximum limits on fee amounts disclosed pursuant to paragraphs (b)(2), (b)(4), (b)(8) through (b)(13) of this section must be disclosed in bold text. However, bold text shall not be used for: The amount of any periodic fee disclosed pursuant to paragraph (b)(2) of this section that is not an annualized amount; and other annual percentage rates or fee amounts disclosed in the table.

(v) For an application or a solicitation that is accessed by the consumer in electronic form, the disclosures required under this section may be provided to the consumer in electronic form on or with the application or solicitation.

(vi)(A) Except as provided in paragraph (a)(2)(vi)(B) of this section, the table described in paragraph (a)(2)(i) of this section must be provided in a prominent location on or with an application or a solicitation.

(B) If the table described in paragraph (a)(2)(i) of this section is provided electronically, it must be provided in close proximity to the application or solicitation.

(3) *Fees based on a percentage.* If the amount of any fee required to be disclosed under this section is determined on the basis of a percentage of another amount, the percentage used and the identification of the amount against which the percentage is applied may be disclosed instead of the amount of the fee.

(4) *Fees that vary by state.* Card issuers that impose fees referred to in paragraphs (b)(8) through (12) of this section that vary by state may, at the issuer's option, disclose in the table required by paragraph (a)(2)(i) of this section: The specific fee applicable to the consumer's account; or the range of the fees, if the disclosure includes a statement that the amount of the fee varies by state and refers the consumer to a disclosure provided with the table where the amount of the fee applicable to the consumer's account is disclosed. A card issuer may not list fees for multiple states in the table.

(5) *Exceptions.* This section does not apply to:

(i) Home-equity plans accessible by a credit or charge card that are subject to the requirements of § 1026.40;

(ii) Overdraft lines of credit tied to asset accounts accessed by check-guarantee cards or by debit cards;

(iii) Lines of credit accessed by check-guarantee cards or by debit cards that can be used only at automated teller machines;

(iv) Lines of credit accessed solely by account numbers;

(v) Additions of a credit or charge card to an existing open-end plan;

(vi) General purpose applications unless the application, or material accompanying it, indicates that it can be used to open a credit or charge card account; or

(vii) Consumer-initiated requests for applications.

(b) *Required disclosures.* The card issuer shall disclose the items in this paragraph on or with an application or a solicitation in accordance with the requirements of paragraphs (c), (d), (e)(1) or (f) of this section. A credit card issuer shall disclose all applicable items in this paragraph except for paragraph (b)(7) of this section. A charge card issuer shall disclose the applicable items in paragraphs (b)(2), (4), (7) through (12), and (15) of this section.

(1) *Annual percentage rate.* Each periodic rate that may be used to compute the finance charge on an outstanding balance for purchases, a cash advance, or a balance transfer, expressed as an annual percentage rate (as determined by § 1026.14(b)). When more than one rate applies for a category of transactions, the range of balances to which each rate is applicable shall also be disclosed. The annual percentage rate for purchases disclosed pursuant to this paragraph shall be in at least 16-point type, except for the following: Oral disclosures of the annual percentage rate for purchases; or a penalty rate that may apply upon the occurrence of one or more specific events.

(i) *Variable rate information.* If a rate disclosed under paragraph (b)(1) of this section is a variable rate, the card issuer shall also disclose the fact that the rate may vary and how the rate is determined. In describing how the applicable rate will be determined, the card issuer must identify the type of index or formula that is used in setting the rate. The value of the index and the amount of the margin that are used to calculate the variable rate shall not be disclosed in the table. A disclosure of any applicable limitations on rate increases shall not be included in the table.

(ii) *Discounted initial rate.* If the initial rate is an introductory rate, as that term is defined in § 1026.16(g)(2)(ii), the card issuer must disclose in the table the introductory rate, the time period during which the introductory rate will remain in effect, and must use the term "introductory" or "intro" in immediate proximity to the introductory rate. The card issuer also must disclose the rate that would otherwise apply to the account pursuant to paragraph (b)(1) of this section. Where the rate is not tied to an index or formula, the card issuer must disclose the rate that will apply after the introductory rate expires. In a variable-rate account, the card issuer must disclose a rate based on the applicable index or formula in accordance with the accuracy requirements set forth in paragraphs (c)(2), (d)(3), or (e)(4) of this section, as applicable.

(iii) *Premium initial rate.* If the initial rate is temporary and is higher than the rate that will apply after the temporary rate expires, the card issuer must disclose the premium initial rate pursuant to paragraph (b)(1) of this section and the time period during which the premium initial rate will remain in effect. Consistent with paragraph (b)(1) of this section, the premium initial rate for purchases must be in at least 16-point type. The issuer must also disclose in the table the rate that will apply after the premium initial rate expires, in at least 16-point type.

(iv) *Penalty rates.*

(A) *In general.* Except as provided in paragraph (b)(1)(iv)(B) and (C) of this section, if a rate may increase as a penalty for one or more events specified in the account agreement, such as a late payment or an extension of credit that exceeds the credit limit, the card issuer must disclose pursuant to this paragraph (b)(1) the increased rate that may apply, a brief description of the event or events that may result in the increased rate, and a brief description of how long the increased rate will remain in effect.

(B) *Introductory rates.* If the issuer discloses an introductory rate, as that term is defined in § 1026.16(g)(2)(ii), in the table or in any written or electronic promotional materials accompanying applications or solicitations subject to paragraph (c) or (e) of this section, the issuer must briefly disclose directly beneath the table the circumstances, if any, under which the introductory rate may be revoked, and the type of rate that will apply after the introductory rate is revoked.

(C) *Employee preferential rates.* If a card issuer discloses in the table a preferential annual percentage rate for which only employees of the card issuer, employees of a third party, or other individuals with similar affiliations with the card issuer or third party, such as executive officers, directors, or principal shareholders are eligible, the card issuer must briefly disclose directly beneath the table the circumstances under which such preferential rate may be revoked, and the rate that will apply after such preferential rate is revoked.

(v) *Rates that depend on consumer's creditworthiness.* If a rate cannot be determined at the time disclosures are given because the rate depends, at least in part, on a later determination of the consumer's creditworthiness, the card issuer must disclose the specific rates or the range of rates that could apply and a statement that the rate for which the consumer may qualify at account opening will depend on the consumer's creditworthiness, and other factors if applicable. If the rate that depends, at least in part, on a later determination of the consumer's creditworthiness is a penalty rate, as described in paragraph (b)(1)(iv) of this section, the card issuer at its option may disclose the highest rate that could apply, instead of disclosing the specific rates or the range of rates that could apply.

(vi) *APRs that vary by state.* Issuers imposing annual percentage rates that vary by state may, at the issuer's option, disclose in the table: the specific annual percentage rate applicable to the consumer's account; or the range of the annual percentage rates, if the disclosure includes a statement that the annual percentage rate varies by state and refers the consumer to a disclosure provided with the table where the annual percentage rate applicable to the consumer's account is disclosed. A card issuer may not list annual percentage rates for multiple states in the table.

(2) *Fees for issuance or availability.*

(i) Any annual or other periodic fee that may be imposed for the issuance or availability of a credit or charge card, including any fee based on account activity or inactivity; how frequently it will be imposed; and the annualized amount of the fee.

(ii) Any non-periodic fee that relates to opening an account. A card issuer must disclose that the fee is a one-time fee.

(3) *Fixed finance charge; minimum interest charge.* Any fixed finance charge and a brief description of the charge. Any minimum interest charge if it exceeds $1.00 that could be imposed during a billing cycle, and a brief description of the charge. The $1.00 threshold amount shall be adjusted periodically by the Bureau to reflect changes in the Consumer Price Index. The Bureau shall calculate each year a price level adjusted minimum interest charge using the Consumer Price Index in effect on June 1 of that year. When the cumulative change in the adjusted minimum value derived from applying the annual Consumer Price level to the current minimum interest charge threshold has risen by a whole dollar, the minimum interest charge will be increased by $1.00. The issuer may, at its option, disclose in the table minimum interest charges below this threshold.

(4) *Transaction charges.* Any transaction charge imposed by the card issuer for the use of the card for purchases.

(5) *Grace period.* The date by which or the period within which any credit extended for purchases may be repaid without incurring a finance charge due to a periodic interest rate and any conditions on the availability of the grace period. If no grace period is provided, that fact must be disclosed. If the length of the grace period varies, the card issuer may disclose the range of days, the minimum number of days, or the average number of days in the grace period, if the disclosure is identified as a range, minimum, or average. In disclosing in the tabular format a grace period that applies to all types of purchases, the phrase "How to Avoid Paying Interest on Purchases" shall be used as the heading for the row describing the grace period. If a grace period is not offered on all types of purchases, in disclosing this fact in the tabular format, the phrase "Paying Interest" shall be used as the heading for the row describing this fact.

(6) *Balance computation method.* The name of the balance computation method listed in paragraph (g) of this section that is used to determine the balance for purchases on which the finance charge is computed, or an explanation of the method used if it is not listed. In determining which balance computation method to disclose, the card issuer shall assume that credit extended for purchases will not be repaid within the grace period, if any.

(7) *Statement on charge card payments.* A statement that charges incurred by use of the charge card are due when the periodic statement is received.

(8) *Cash advance fee.* Any fee imposed for an extension of credit in the form of cash or its equivalent.

(9) *Late payment fee.* Any fee imposed for a late payment.

(10) *Over-the-limit fee.* Any fee imposed for exceeding a credit limit.

(11) *Balance transfer fee.* Any fee imposed to transfer an outstanding balance.

(12) *Returned-payment fee.* Any fee imposed by the card issuer for a returned payment.

(13) *Required insurance, debt cancellation or debt suspension coverage.*

(i) A fee for insurance described in § 1026.4(b)(7) or debt cancellation or suspension coverage described in § 1026.4(b)(10), if the insurance or debt cancellation or suspension coverage is required as part of the plan; and

(ii) A cross reference to any additional information provided about the insurance or coverage accompanying the application or solicitation, as applicable.

(14) *Available credit.* If a card issuer requires fees for the issuance or availability of credit described in paragraph (b)(2) of this section, or requires a security deposit for such credit, and the total amount of those required fees and/or security deposit that will be imposed and charged to the account when the account is opened is 15 percent or more of the minimum credit limit for the card, a card issuer must disclose the available credit remaining after these fees or security deposit are debited to the account, assuming that the consumer receives the minimum credit limit. In determining whether the 15 percent threshold test is met, the issuer must only consider fees for issuance or availability of credit, or a security deposit, that are required. If fees for issuance or availability are optional, these fees should not be considered in determining whether the disclosure must be given. Nonetheless, if the 15 percent threshold test is met, the issuer in providing the disclosure must disclose the amount of available credit calculated by excluding those optional fees, and the available credit including those optional fees. This paragraph does not

apply with respect to fees or security deposits that are not debited to the account.

(15) *Web site reference*. A reference to the Web site established by the Bureau and a statement that consumers may obtain on the Web site information about shopping for and using credit cards. Until January 1, 2013, issuers may substitute for this reference a reference to the Web site established by the Board of Governors of the Federal Reserve System.

(c) *Direct mail and electronic applications and solicitations*.

(1) *General*. The card issuer shall disclose the applicable items in paragraph (b) of this section on or with an application or solicitation that is mailed to consumers or provided to consumers in electronic form.

(2) *Accuracy*.

(i) Disclosures in direct mail applications and solicitations must be accurate as of the time the disclosures are mailed. An accurate variable annual percentage rate is one in effect within 60 days before mailing.

(ii) Disclosures provided in electronic form must be accurate as of the time they are sent, in the case of disclosures sent to a consumer's email address, or as of the time they are viewed by the public, in the case of disclosures made available at a location such as a card issuer's Web site. An accurate variable annual percentage rate provided in electronic form is one in effect within 30 days before it is sent to a consumer's email address, or viewed by the public, as applicable.

(d) *Telephone applications and solicitations*.

(1) *Oral disclosure*. The card issuer shall disclose orally the information in paragraphs (b)(1) through (7) and (b)(14) of this section, to the extent applicable, in a telephone application or solicitation initiated by the card issuer.

(2) *Alternative disclosure*. The oral disclosure under paragraph (d)(1) of this section need not be given if the card issuer either:

(i)(A) Does not impose a fee described in paragraph (b)(2) of this section; or

(B) Imposes such a fee but provides the consumer with a right to reject the plan consistent with § 1026.5(b)(1)(iv); and

(ii) The card issuer discloses in writing within 30 days after the consumer requests the card (but in no event later than the delivery of the card) the following:

(A) The applicable information in paragraph (b) of this section; and

(B) As applicable, the fact that the consumer has the right to reject the plan and not be obligated to pay fees described in paragraph (b)(2) or any other fees or charges until the consumer has used the account or made a payment on the account after receiving a billing statement.

(3) *Accuracy*.

(i) The oral disclosures under paragraph (d)(1) of this section must be accurate as of the time they are given.

(ii) The alternative disclosures under paragraph (d)(2) of this section generally must be accurate as of the time they are mailed or delivered. A variable annual percentage rate is one that is accurate if it was:

(A) In effect at the time the disclosures are mailed or delivered; or

(B) In effect as of a specified date (which rate is then updated from time to time, but no less frequently than each calendar month).

(e) *Applications and solicitations made available to general public*. The card issuer shall provide disclosures, to the extent applicable, on or with an application or solicitation that is made available to the general public, including one contained in a catalog, magazine, or other generally available publication. The disclosures shall be provided in accordance with paragraph (e)(1) or (e)(2) of this section.

(1) *Disclosure of required credit information*. The card issuer may disclose in a prominent location on the application or solicitation the following:

(i) The applicable information in paragraph (b) of this section;

(ii) The date the required information was printed, including a statement that the required information was accurate as of that date and is subject to change after that date; and

(iii) A statement that the consumer should contact the card issuer for any change in the required information since it was printed, and a toll-free telephone number or a mailing address for that purpose.

(2) No disclosure of credit information. If none of the items in paragraph (b) of this section is provided on or with the application or solicitation, the card issuer may state in a prominent location on the application or solicitation the following:

(i) There are costs associated with the use of the card; and

(ii) The consumer may contact the card issuer to request specific information about the costs, along with a toll-free telephone number and a mailing address for that purpose.

(3) *Prompt response to requests for information*. Upon receiving a request for any of the information referred to in this paragraph, the card issuer shall promptly and fully disclose the information requested.

(4) *Accuracy*. The disclosures given pursuant to paragraph (e)(1) of this section must be accurate as of the date of printing. A variable annual percentage rate is accurate if it was in effect within 30 days before printing.

(f) *In-person applications and solicitations*. A card issuer shall disclose the information in paragraph (b) of this section, to the extent applicable, on or with an application or solicitation that is initiated by the card issuer and given to the consumer in person. A card issuer complies with the requirements of this paragraph if the issuer provides disclosures in accordance with paragraph (c)(1) or (e)(1) of this section.

(g) *Balance computation methods defined*. The following methods may be described by name. Methods that differ due to variations such as the allocation of payments, whether the finance charge begins to accrue on the transaction date or the date of posting the transaction, the existence or length of a grace period, and whether the balance is adjusted by charges such as late payment fees, annual fees and unpaid finance charges do not constitute separate balance computation methods.

(1)(i) *Average daily balance (including new purchases)*. This balance is figured by adding the outstanding balance (including new purchases and deducting payments and credits) for each day in the billing cycle, and then dividing by the number of days in the billing cycle.

(ii) *Average daily balance (excluding new purchases)*. This balance is figured by adding the outstanding balance (excluding new purchases and deducting payments and credits) for each day in the billing cycle, and then dividing by the number of days in the billing cycle.

(2) *Adjusted balance*. This balance is figured by deducting payments and credits made during the billing cycle from the outstanding balance at the beginning of the billing cycle.

(3) *Previous balance*. This balance is the outstanding balance at the beginning of the billing cycle.

(4) *Daily balance*. For each day in the billing cycle, this balance is figured by taking the beginning balance each day, adding any new purchases, and subtracting any payment and credits.

[54 Fed. Reg. 13,865 (Apr. 6, 1989); 54 Fed. Reg. 24,686 (June 9, 1989); 54 Fed. Reg. 32,954 (Aug. 11, 1989); 65 Fed. Reg. 17,131 (Mar. 31, 2000); 65 Fed. Reg. 58,908 (Oct. 3, 2000); 66 Fed. Reg. 17,338 (Mar. 30, 2001); 66 Fed. Reg. 41,440 (Aug. 8, 2001) (*COMPLIANCE DATE NOTE*: At 66 Fed. Reg. 41,440 (Aug. 8, 2001) the Oct. 1, 2001, mandatory compliance date for the interim final rules published at 66 Fed. Reg. 17,311 (Mar. 30, 2001) was lifted.); 72 Fed. Reg. 63,473 (Nov. 9, 2007); 75 Fed. Reg. 7798 (Feb. 22, 2010); 75 Fed. Reg. 37,568 (June 29, 2010); 76 Fed. Reg. 22,999 (Apr. 25, 2011)]

## A.5.3 Selected Official Staff Commentary Provisions

Citations are to the CFPB commentary, 12 C.F.R. pt. 1026, supp. I with citations to the FRB commentary, 12 C.F.R. pt. 226, supp. I in brackets, e.g., 1026.2 [226.2].

### SUPPLEMENT I TO PART 1026—OFFICIAL INTERPRETATIONS

### SUBPART A GENERAL

* * *

## SECTION 1026.2 Definitions and Rules of Construction [§ 226.2]

### *2(a)(2) Advertisement*

* * *

### *2(a)(4) Billing Cycle or Cycle*

1. *Intervals*. In open-end credit plans, the billing cycle determines the intervals for which periodic disclosure statements are required; these intervals are also used as measuring points for other duties of the creditor. Typically, billing cycles are monthly, but they may be more frequent or less frequent (but not less frequent than quarterly).

2. *Creditors that do not bill*. The term *cycle* is interchangeable with *billing cycle* for definitional purposes, since some creditors' cycles do not involve the sending of bills in the traditional sense but only statements of account activity. This is commonly the case with financial institutions when periodic payments are made through payroll deduction or through automatic debit of the consumer's asset account.

3. *Equal cycles*. Although cycles must be equal, there is a permissible variance to account for weekends, holidays, and differences in the number of days in months. If the actual date of each statement does not vary by more than four days from a fixed *day* (for example, the third Thursday of each month) or *date* (for example, the 15th of each month) that the creditor regularly uses, the intervals between statements are considered equal. The requirement that cycles be equal applies even if the creditor applies a daily periodic rate to determine the finance charge. The requirement that intervals be equal does not apply to the first billing cycle on an open-end account (i.e., the time period between account opening and the generation of the first periodic statement) or to a transitional billing cycle that can occur if the creditor occasionally changes its billing cycles so as to establish a new statement day or date. (See comments 9(c)(1)-3 and 9(c)(2)-3.)

4. *Payment reminder*. The sending of a regular payment reminder (rather than a late payment notice) establishes a cycle for which the creditor must send periodic statements.

### *2(a)(6) Business Day*

1. *Business function test*. Activities that indicate that the creditor is open for substantially all of its business functions include the availability of personnel to make loan disbursements, to open new accounts, and to handle credit transaction inquiries. Activities that indicate that the creditor is not open for substantially all of its business functions include a retailer's merely accepting credit cards for purchases or a bank's having its customer-service windows open only for limited purposes such as deposits and withdrawals, bill paying, and related services.

2. *Rule for rescission, disclosures for certain mortgage transactions, and private education loans*. A more precise rule for what is a business day (all calendar days except Sundays and the Federal legal holidays specified in 5 U.S.C. 6103(a)) applies when the right of rescission, the receipt of disclosures for certain dwelling-secured mortgage transactions under §§ 1026.19(a)(1)(ii), 1026.19(a)(2), 1026.31(c), or the receipt of disclosures for private education loans under § 1026.46(d)(4) is involved. Four Federal legal holidays are identified in 5 U.S.C. 6103(a) by a specific date: New Year's Day, January 1; Independence Day, July 4; Veterans Day, November 11; and Christmas Day, December 25. When one of these holidays (July 4, for example) falls on a Saturday, Federal offices and other entities might observe the holiday on the preceding Friday (July 3). In cases where the more precise rule applies, the observed holiday (in the example, July 3) is a business day.

### *2(a)(7) Card Issuer*

1. *Agent*. An agent of a card issuer is considered a card issuer. Because agency relationships are traditionally defined by contract and by state or other applicable law, the regulation does not define agent. Merely providing services relating to the production of credit cards or data processing for others, however, does not make one the agent of the card issuer. In contrast, a financial institution may become the agent of the card issuer if an agreement between the institution and the card issuer provides that the cardholder may use a line of credit with the financial institution to pay obligations incurred by use of the credit card.

### *2(a)(8) Cardholder*

1. *General rule*. A cardholder is a natural person at whose request a card is issued for consumer credit purposes or who is a co-obligor or guarantor for such a card issued to another. The second category does not include an employee who is a co-obligor or guarantor on a card issued to the employer for business purposes, nor does it include a person who is merely the authorized user of a card issued to another.

2. *Limited application of regulation*. For the limited purposes of the rules on issuance of credit cards and liability for unauthorized use, a cardholder includes *any* person, including an organization, to whom a card is issued for *any* purpose—including a business, agricultural, or commercial purpose.

3. *Issuance*. See the commentary to § 1026.12(a).

4. *Dual-purpose cards and dual-card systems*. Some card issuers offer dual-purpose cards that are for business as well as consumer purposes. If a card is issued to an individual for consumer purposes, the fact that an organization has guaranteed to pay the debt does not make it business credit. On the other hand, if a card is issued for business purposes, the fact that an individual sometimes uses it for consumer purchases does not subject the card issuer to the provisions on periodic statements, billing-error resolution, and other protections afforded to consumer credit. Some card issuers offer dual-card systems—that is, they issue two cards to the same individual, one intended for business use, the other for consumer or personal use. With such a system, the same person may be a cardholder for general purposes when using the card issued for consumer use, and a cardholder only for the limited purposes of the restrictions on issuance and liability when using the card issued for business purposes.

### *2(a)(9) Cash Price*

1. *Components*. This amount is a starting point in computing the amount financed and the total sale price under § 1026.18 for credit sales. Any charges imposed equally in cash and credit transactions may be included in the cash price, or they may be treated as other amounts financed under § 1026.18(b)(2).

2. *Service contracts*. Service contracts include contracts for the repair or the servicing of goods, such as mechanical breakdown coverage, even if such a contract is characterized as insurance under state law.

3. *Rebates*. The creditor has complete flexibility in the way it treats rebates for purposes of disclosure and calculation. (See the commentary to § 1026.18(b).)

* * *

Paragraph 2(a)(15)

1. *Usable from time to time*. A credit card must be usable from time to time. Since this involves the possibility of repeated use of a single device, checks and similar instruments that can be used only once to obtain a single credit extension are not credit cards.

2. *Examples*.

i. Examples of credit cards include:

A. A card that guarantees checks or similar instruments, if the asset account is also tied to an overdraft line or if the instrument directly accesses a line of credit.

B. A card that accesses both a credit and an asset account (that is, a debit-credit card).

C. An identification card that permits the consumer to defer payment on a purchase.

D. An identification card indicating loan approval that is presented to a merchant or to a lender, whether or not the consumer signs a separate promissory note for each credit extension.

E. A card or device that can be activated upon receipt to access credit, even if the card has a substantive use other than credit, such as a purchase-price discount card. Such a card or device is a credit card notwithstanding the fact that the recipient must first contact the card issuer to access or activate the credit feature.

ii. In contrast, credit card does not include, for example:

A. A check-guarantee or debit card with no credit feature or agreement, even if the creditor occasionally honors an inadvertent overdraft.

B. Any card, key, plate, or other device that is used in order to obtain petroleum products for business purposes from a wholesale distribution facility or to gain access to that facility, and that is required to be used without regard to payment terms.

C. An account number that accesses a credit account, unless the account number can access an open-end line of credit to purchase goods or services. For example, if a creditor provides a consumer with an open-end line of credit that can be accessed by an account number in order to transfer funds into another account (such as an asset account with the same creditor), the account number is not a credit card for purposes of § 1026.2(a)(15)(i). However, if the account number can also access the line of credit to purchase goods or services (such as an account number that can be used to purchase goods or services on the Internet), the account number is a credit card for purposes of § 1026.2(a)(15)(i), regardless of whether the creditor treats such transactions as purchases, cash advances, or some other type of transaction. Furthermore, if the line of credit can also be accessed by a card (such as a debit card), that card is a credit card for purposes of § 1026.2(a)(15)(i).

3. *Charge card.* Generally, charge cards are cards used in connection with an account on which outstanding balances cannot be carried from one billing cycle to another and are payable when a periodic statement is received. Under the regulation, a reference to credit cards generally includes charge cards. In particular, references to credit card accounts under an open-end (not home-secured) consumer credit plan in Subparts B and G generally include charge cards. The term charge card is, however, distinguished from credit card or credit card account under an open-end (not home-secured) consumer credit plan in §§ 1026.60, 1026.6(b)(2)(xiv), 1026.7(b)(11), 1026.7(b)(12), 1026.9(e), 1026.9(f), 1026.28(d), 1026.52(b)(1)(ii)(C), and Appendices G-10 through G-13.

4. *Credit card account under an open-end (not home-secured) consumer credit plan.* An open-end consumer credit account is a credit card account under an open-end (not home-secured) consumer credit plan for purposes of § 1026.2(a)(15)(ii) if:

i. The account is accessed by a credit card, as defined in § 1026.2(a)(15)(i); and

ii. The account is not excluded under § 1026.2(a)(15)(ii)(A) or (a)(15)(ii)(B).

* * *

### 2(a)(17) Creditor

* * *

*Paragraph 2(a)(17)(iii)*

1. *Card issuers subject to Subpart B.* Section 1026.2(a)(17)(iii) makes certain card issuers creditors for purposes of the open-end credit provisions of the regulation. This includes, for example, the issuers of so-called travel and entertainment cards that expect repayment at the first billing and do not impose a finance charge. Since all disclosures are to be made only as applicable, such card issuers would omit finance charge disclosures. Other provisions of the regulation regarding such areas as scope, definitions, determination of which charges are finance charges, Spanish language disclosures, record retention, and use of model forms, also apply to such card issuers.

*Paragraph 2(a)(17)(iv)*

1. *Card issuers subject to Subparts B and C.* Section 1026.2(a)(17)(iv) includes as creditors card issuers extending closed-end credit in which there is a finance charge or an agreement to pay in more than four installments. These card issuers are subject to the appropriate provisions of Subparts B and C, as well as to the general provisions.

* * *

## SUBPART B OPEN-END CREDIT

* * *

## SECTION 1026.9 Subsequent Disclosure Requirements [§ 226.9]

### 9(c) Change in Terms

* * *

### 9(c)(2) Rules Affecting Open-End (Not Home-Secured) Plans

1. *Changes initially disclosed.* Except as provided in § 1026.9(g)(1), no notice of a change in terms need be given if the specific change is set forth initially consistent with any applicable requirements, such as rate or fee increases upon expiration of a specific period of time that were disclosed in accordance with § 1026.9(c)(2)(v)(B) or rate increases under a properly disclosed variable-rate plan in accordance with § 1026.9(c)(2)(v)(C). In contrast, notice must be given if the contract allows the creditor to increase a rate or fee at its discretion.

2. *State law issues.* Some issues are not addressed by § 1026.9(c)(2) because they are controlled by state or other applicable laws. These issues include the types of changes a creditor may make, to the extent otherwise permitted by this part.

3. *Change in billing cycle.* Whenever the creditor changes the consumer's billing cycle, it must give a change-in-terms notice if the change affects any of the terms described in § 1026.9(c)(2)(i), unless an exception under § 1026.9(c)(2)(v) applies; for example, the creditor must give advance notice if the creditor initially disclosed a 28-day grace period on purchases and the consumer will have fewer days during the billing cycle change. *See also* § 1026.7(b)(11)(i)(A) regarding the general requirement that the payment due date for a credit card account under an open-end (not home-secured) consumer credit plan must be the same day each month.

4. *Relationship to § 1026.9(b).* If a creditor adds a feature to the account on the type of terms otherwise required to be disclosed under § 1026.6, the creditor must satisfy: The requirement to provide the finance charge disclosures for the added feature under § 1026.9(b); and any applicable requirement to provide a change-in-terms notice under § 1026.9(c), including any advance notice that must be provided. For example, if a creditor adds a balance transfer feature to an account more than 30 days after account-opening disclosures are provided, it must give the finance charge disclosures for the balance transfer feature under § 1026.9(b) as well as comply with the change-in-terms notice requirements under § 1026.9(c), including providing notice of the change at least 45 days prior to the effective date of the change. Similarly, if a creditor makes a balance transfer offer on finance charge terms that are higher than those previously disclosed for balance transfers, it would also generally be required to provide a change-in-terms notice at least 45 days in advance of the effective date of the change. A creditor may provide a single notice under § 1026.9(c) to satisfy the notice requirements of both paragraphs (b) and (c) of § 1026.9. For checks that access a credit card account subject to the disclosure requirements in § 1026.9(b)(3), a creditor is not subject to the notice requirements under § 1026.9(c) even if the applicable rate or fee is higher than those previously disclosed for such checks. Thus, for example, the creditor need not wait 45 days before applying the new rate or fee for transactions made using such checks, but the creditor must make the required disclosures on or with the checks in accordance with § 1026.9(b)(3).

### 9(c)(2)(i) Changes Where Written Advance Notice is Required

1. *Affected consumers.* Change-in-terms notices need only go to those consumers who may be affected by the change. For example, a change in the periodic rate for check overdraft credit need not be disclosed to consumers who do not have that feature on their accounts. If a single credit account involves multiple consumers that may be affected by the change, the creditor should refer to § 1026.5(d) to determine the number of notices that must be given.

2. *Timing—effective date of change.* The rule that the notice of the change in terms be provided at least 45 days before the change takes effect permits mid-cycle changes when there is clearly no retroactive effect, such as the imposition of a transaction fee. Any change in the balance computation method, in contrast, would need to be disclosed at least 45 days prior to the billing cycle in which the change is to be implemented.

3. *Changes agreed to by the consumer. See also* comment 5(b)(1)(i)-6.

4. *Form of change-in-terms notice.* Except if § 1026.9(c)(2)(iv) applies, a complete new set of the initial disclosures containing the changed term

complies with § 1026.9(c)(2)(i) if the change is highlighted on the disclosure statement, or if the disclosure statement is accompanied by a letter or some other insert that indicates or draws attention to the term being changed.

5. *Security interest change—form of notice.* A creditor must provide a description of any security interest it is acquiring under § 1026.9(c)(2)(iv). A copy of the security agreement that describes the collateral securing the consumer's account may also be used as the notice, when the term change is the addition of a security interest or the addition or substitution of collateral.

6. *Examples. See* comment 55(a)-1 and 55(b)-3 for examples of how a card issuer that is subject to § 1026.55 may comply with the timing requirements for notices required by § 1026.9(c)(2)(i).

### *9(c)(2)(iii) Charges not Covered by § 1026.6(b)(1) and (b)(2)*

1. *Applicability.* Generally, if a creditor increases any component of a charge, or introduces a new charge, that is imposed as part of the plan under § 1026.6(b)(3) but is not required to be disclosed as part of the account-opening summary table under § 1026.6(b)(1) and (b)(2), the creditor must either, at its option (i) provide at least 45 days' written advance notice before the change becomes effective to comply with the requirements of § 1026.9(c)(2)(i), or (ii) provide notice orally or in writing, or electronically if the consumer requests the service electronically, of the amount of the charge to an affected consumer before the consumer agrees to or becomes obligated to pay the charge, at a time and in a manner that a consumer would be likely to notice the disclosure. (*See* the commentary under § 1026.5(a)(1)(iii) regarding disclosure of such changes in electronic form.) For example, a fee for expedited delivery of a credit card is a charge imposed as part of the plan under § 1026.6(b)(3) but is not required to be disclosed in the account-opening summary table under § 1026.6(b)(1) and (b)(2). If a creditor changes the amount of that expedited delivery fee, the creditor may provide written advance notice of the change to affected consumers at least 45 days before the change becomes effective. Alternatively, the creditor may provide oral or written notice, or electronic notice if the consumer requests the service electronically, of the amount of the charge to an affected consumer before the consumer agrees to or becomes obligated to pay the charge, at a time and in a manner that the consumer would be likely to notice the disclosure. (*See* comment 5(b)(1)(ii)-1 for examples of disclosures given at a time and in a manner that the consumer would be likely to notice them.)

### *9(c)(2)(iv) Disclosure Requirements*

1. *Changing margin for calculating a variable rate.* If a creditor is changing a margin used to calculate a variable rate, the creditor must disclose the amount of the new rate (as calculated using the new margin) in the table described in § 1026.9(c)(2)(iv), and include a reminder that the rate is a variable rate. For example, if a creditor is changing the margin for a variable rate that uses the prime rate as an index, the creditor must disclose in the table the new rate (as calculated using the new margin) and indicate that the rate varies with the market based on the prime rate.

2. *Changing index for calculating a variable rate.* If a creditor is changing the index used to calculate a variable rate, the creditor must disclose the amount of the new rate (as calculated using the new index) and indicate that the rate varies and how the rate is determined, as explained in § 1026.6(b)(2)(i)(A). For example, if a creditor is changing from using a prime rate to using the LIBOR in calculating a variable rate, the creditor would disclose in the table the new rate (using the new index) and indicate that the rate varies with the market based on the LIBOR.

3. *Changing from a variable rate to a non-variable rate.* If a creditor is changing a rate applicable to a consumer's account from a variable rate to a non-variable rate, the creditor generally must provide a notice as otherwise required under § 1026.9(c) even if the variable rate at the time of the change is higher than the non-variable rate. However, a creditor is not required to provide a notice under § 1026.9(c) if the creditor provides the disclosures required by § 1026.9(c)(2)(v)(B) or (c)(2)(v)(D) in connection with changing a variable rate to a lower non-variable rate. Similarly, a creditor is not required to provide a notice under § 1026.9(c) when changing a variable rate to a lower non-variable rate in order to comply with 50 U.S.C. app. 527 or a similar Federal or state statute or regulation. Finally, a creditor is not required to provide a notice under § 1026.9(c) when changing a variable rate to a lower non-variable rate in order to comply with § 1026.55(b)(4).

4. *Changing from a non-variable rate to a variable rate.* If a creditor is changing a rate applicable to a consumer's account from a non-variable rate to a variable rate, the creditor generally must provide a notice as otherwise required under § 1026.9(c) even if the non-variable rate is higher than the variable rate at the time of the change. However, a creditor is not required to provide a notice under § 1026.9(c) if the creditor provides the disclosures required by § 1026.9(c)(2)(v)(B) or (c)(2)(v)(D) in connection with changing a non-variable rate to a lower variable rate. Similarly, a creditor is not required to provide a notice under § 1026.9(c) when changing a non-variable rate to a lower variable rate in order to comply with 50 U.S.C. app. 527 or a similar Federal or state statute or regulation. Finally, a creditor is not required to provide a notice under § 1026.9(c) when changing a non-variable rate to a lower variable rate in order to comply with § 1026.55(b)(4). *See* comment 55(b)(2)-4 regarding the limitations in § 1026.55(b)(2) on changing the rate that applies to a protected balance from a non-variable rate to a variable rate.

5. *Changes in the penalty rate, the triggers for the penalty rate, or how long the penalty rate applies.* If a creditor is changing the amount of the penalty rate, the creditor must also redisclose the triggers for the penalty rate and the information about how long the penalty rate applies even if those terms are not changing. Likewise, if a creditor is changing the triggers for the penalty rate, the creditor must redisclose the amount of the penalty rate and information about how long the penalty rate applies. If a creditor is changing how long the penalty rate applies, the creditor must redisclose the amount of the penalty rate and the triggers for the penalty rate, even if they are not changing.

6. *Changes in fees.* If a creditor is changing part of how a fee that is disclosed in a tabular format under § 1026.6(b)(1) and (b)(2) is determined, the creditor must redisclose all relevant information related to that fee regardless of whether this other information is changing. For example, if a creditor currently charges a cash advance fee of "Either $5 or 3% of the transaction amount, whichever is greater (Max: $100)," and the creditor is only changing the minimum dollar amount from $5 to $10, the issuer must redisclose the other information related to how the fee is determined. For example, the creditor in this example would disclose the following: "Either $10 or 3% of the transaction amount, whichever is greater (Max: $100)."

7. *Combining a notice described in § 1026.9(c)(2)(iv) with a notice described in § 1026.9(g)(3).* If a creditor is required to provide a notice described in § 1026.9(c)(2)(iv) and a notice described in § 1026.9(g)(3) to a consumer, the creditor may combine the two notices. This would occur if penalty pricing has been triggered, and other terms are changing on the consumer's account at the same time.

8. *Content.* Sample G-20 contains an example of how to comply with the requirements in § 1026.9(c)(2)(iv) when a variable rate is being changed to a non-variable rate on a credit card account. The sample explains when the new rate will apply to new transactions and to which balances the current rate will continue to apply. Sample G-21 contains an example of how to comply with the requirements in § 1026.9(c)(2)(iv) when the late payment fee on a credit card account is being increased, and the returned payment fee is also being increased. The sample discloses the consumer's right to reject the changes in accordance with § 1026.9(h).

9. *Clear and conspicuous standard. See* comment 5(a)(1)-1 for the clear and conspicuous standard applicable to disclosures required under § 1026.9(c)(2)(iv)(A)(1).

10. *Terminology. See* § 1026.5(a)(2) for terminology requirements applicable to disclosures required under § 1026.9(c)(2)(iv)(A)(1).

11. *Reasons for increase.*

i. *In general.* Section 1026.9(c)(2)(iv)(A)(8) requires card issuers to disclose the principal reason(s) for increasing an annual percentage rate applicable to a credit card account under an open-end (not home-secured) consumer credit plan. The regulation does not mandate a minimum number of reasons that must be disclosed. However, the specific reasons disclosed under § 1026.9(c)(2)(iv)(A)(8) are required to relate to and accurately describe the principal factors actually considered by the card issuer in increasing the rate. A card issuer may describe the reasons for the increase in general terms. For example, the notice of a rate increase triggered by a decrease of 100 points in a consumer's credit score may state that the increase is due to "a decline in your creditworthiness" or "a decline in your credit score." Similarly, a notice of a rate increase triggered by a 10% increase in the card issuer's cost of funds may be disclosed as "a change in market conditions." In some circumstances, it may be appropriate for a card issuer to combine the disclosure of several reasons in one statement. However, § 1026.9(c)(2)(iv)(A)(8) requires that the notice specifically disclose any violation of the terms of the account on which the rate is being increased, such as a late payment or a returned payment, if such violation of the account terms is one of the four principal reasons for the rate increase.

ii. *Example.* Assume that a consumer made a late payment on the credit card account on which the rate increase is being imposed, made a late payment on a credit card account with another card issuer, and the consumer's credit score decreased, in part due to such late payments. The card issuer may disclose the reasons for the rate increase as a decline in the consumer's credit score and the consumer's late payment on the account subject to the increase. Because the late payment on the credit card account with the other issuer also likely contributed to the decline in the consumer's credit score, it is not required to be separately disclosed. However, the late payment on the credit card account on which the rate increase is being imposed must be specifically disclosed even if that late payment also contributed to the decline in the consumer's credit score.

## *9(c)(2)(v) Notice not Required*

1. *Changes not requiring notice.* The following are examples of changes that do not require a change-in-terms notice:

i. A change in the consumer's credit limit except as otherwise required by § 1026.9(c)(2)(vi).

ii. A change in the name of the credit card or credit card plan.

iii. The substitution of one insurer for another.

iv. A termination or suspension of credit privileges.

v. Changes arising merely by operation of law; for example, if the creditor's security interest in a consumer's car automatically extends to the proceeds when the consumer sells the car.

2. *Skip features.*

i. *Skipped or reduced payments.* If a credit program allows consumers to skip or reduce one or more payments during the year, no notice of the change in terms is required either prior to the reduction in payments or upon resumption of the higher payments if these features are explained on the account-opening disclosure statement (including an explanation of the terms upon resumption). For example, a merchant may allow consumers to skip the December payment to encourage holiday shopping, or a teacher's credit union may not require payments during summer vacation. Otherwise, the creditor must give notice prior to resuming the original payment schedule, even though no notice is required prior to the reduction. The change-in-terms notice may be combined with the notice offering the reduction. For example, the periodic statement reflecting the skip feature may also be used to notify the consumer of the resumption of the original payment schedule, either by stating explicitly when the higher resumes or by indicating the duration of the skip option. Language such as "You may skip your October payment" may serve as the change-in-terms notice.

ii. *Temporary reductions in interest rates or fees.* If a credit program involves temporary reductions in an interest rate or fee, no notice of the change in terms is required either prior to the reduction or upon resumption of the original rate or fee if these features are disclosed in advance in accordance with the requirements of § 1026.9(c)(2)(v)(B). Otherwise, the creditor must give notice prior to resuming the original rate or fee, even though no notice is required prior to the reduction. The notice provided prior to resuming the original rate or fee must comply with the timing requirements of § 1026.9(c)(2)(i) and the content and format requirements of § 1026.9(c)(2)(iv)(A), (B) (if applicable), (C) (if applicable), and (D). *See* comment 55(b)-3 for guidance regarding the application of § 1026.55 in these circumstances.

3. *Changing from a variable rate to a non-variable rate. See* comment 9(c)(2)(iv)-3.

4. *Changing from a non-variable rate to a variable rate. See* comment 9(c)(2)(iv)-4.

5. *Temporary rate or fee reductions offered by telephone.* The timing requirements of § 1026.9(c)(2)(v)(B) are deemed to have been met, and written disclosures required by § 1026.9(c)(2)(v)(B) may be provided as soon as reasonably practicable after the first transaction subject to a rate that will be in effect for a specified period of time (a temporary rate) or the imposition of a fee that will be in effect for a specified period of time (a temporary fee) if:

i. The consumer accepts the offer of the temporary rate or temporary fee by telephone;

ii. The creditor permits the consumer to reject the temporary rate or temporary fee offer and have the rate or rates or fee that previously applied to the consumer's balances reinstated for 45 days after the creditor mails or delivers the written disclosures required by § 1026.9(c)(2)(v)(B), except that the creditor need not permit the consumer to reject a temporary rate or temporary fee offer if the rate or rates or fee that will apply following expiration of the temporary rate do not exceed the rate or rates or fee that applied immediately prior to commencement of the temporary rate or temporary fee; and

iii. The disclosures required by § 1026.9(c)(2)(v)(B) and the consumer's right to reject the temporary rate or temporary fee offer and have the rate or rates or fee that previously applied to the consumer's account reinstated, if applicable, are disclosed to the consumer as part of the temporary rate or temporary fee offer.

6. *First listing.* The disclosures required by § 1026.9(c)(2)(v)(B)(1) are only required to be provided in close proximity and in equal prominence to the first listing of the temporary rate or fee in the disclosure provided to the consumer. For purposes of § 1026.9(c)(2)(v)(B), the first statement of the temporary rate or fee is the most prominent listing on the front side of the first page of the disclosure. If the temporary rate or fee does not appear on the front side of the first page of the disclosure, then the first listing of the temporary rate or fee is the most prominent listing of the temporary rate on the subsequent pages of the disclosure. For advertising requirements for promotional rates, see § 1026.16(g).

7. *Close proximity—point of sale.* Creditors providing the disclosures required by § 1026.9(c)(2)(v)(B) of this section in person in connection with financing the purchase of goods or services may, at the creditor's option, disclose the annual percentage rate or fee that would apply after expiration of the period on a separate page or document from the temporary rate or fee and the length of the period, provided that the disclosure of the annual percentage rate or fee that would apply after the expiration of the period is equally prominent to, and is provided at the same time as, the disclosure of the temporary rate or fee and length of the period.

8. *Disclosure of annual percentage rates.* If a rate disclosed pursuant to § 1026.9(c)(2)(v)(B) or (c)(2)(v)(D) is a variable rate, the creditor must disclose the fact that the rate may vary and how the rate is determined. For example, a creditor could state "After October 1, 2009, your APR will be 14.99%. This APR will vary with the market based on the Prime Rate."

9. *Deferred interest or similar programs.* If the applicable conditions are met, the exception in § 1026.9(c)(2)(v)(B) applies to deferred interest or similar promotional programs under which the consumer is not obligated to pay interest that accrues on a balance if that balance is paid in full prior to the expiration of a specified period of time. For purposes of this comment and § 1026.9(c)(2)(v)(B), "deferred interest" has the same meaning as in § 1026.16(h)(2) and associated commentary. For such programs, a creditor must disclose pursuant to § 1026.9(c)(2)(v)(B)(1) the length of the deferred interest period and the rate that will apply to the balance subject to the deferred interest program if that balance is not paid in full prior to expiration of the deferred interest period. Examples of language that a creditor may use to make the required disclosures under § 1026.9(c)(2)(v)(B)(1) include:

i. "No interest if paid in full in 6 months. If the balance is not paid in full in 6 months, interest will be imposed from the date of purchase at a rate of 15.99%."

ii. "No interest if paid in full by December 31, 2010. If the balance is not paid in full by that date, interest will be imposed from the transaction date at a rate of 15%."

10. *Relationship between §§ 1026.9(c)(2)(v)(B) and 1026.6(b).* A disclosure of the information described in § 1026.9(c)(2)(v)(B)(1) provided in the account-opening table in accordance with § 1026.6(b) complies with the requirements of § 1026.9(c)(2)(v)(B)(2), if the listing of the introductory rate in such tabular disclosure also is the first listing as described in comment 9(c)(2)(v)-6.

11. *Disclosure of the terms of a workout or temporary hardship arrangement.* In order for the exception in § 1026.9(c)(2)(v)(D) to apply, the disclosure provided to the consumer pursuant to § 1026.9(c)(2)(v)(D)(2) must set forth:

i. The annual percentage rate that will apply to balances subject to the workout or temporary hardship arrangement;

ii. The annual percentage rate that will apply to such balances if the consumer completes or fails to comply with the terms of, the workout or temporary hardship arrangement;

iii. Any reduced fee or charge of a type required to be disclosed under § 1026.6(b)(2)(ii), (b)(2)(iii), (b)(2)(viii), (b)(2)(ix), (b)(2)(xi), or (b)(2)(xii) that will apply to balances subject to the workout or temporary hardship arrangement, as well as the fee or charge that will apply if the consumer completes or fails to comply with the terms of the workout or temporary hardship arrangement;

iv. Any reduced minimum periodic payment that will apply to balances subject to the workout or temporary hardship arrangement, as well as the minimum periodic payment that will apply if the consumer completes or fails to comply with the terms of the workout or temporary hardship arrangement; and

v. If applicable, that the consumer must make timely minimum payments in order to remain eligible for the workout or temporary hardship arrangement.

12. *Index not under creditor's control. See* comment 55(b)(2)-2 for guidance on when an index is deemed to be under a creditor's control.

13. *Temporary rates—relationship to § 1026.59.*

i. *General.* Section 1026.59 requires a card issuer to review rate increases imposed due to the revocation of a temporary rate. In some circumstances, § 1026.59 may require an issuer to reinstate a reduced temporary rate based on that review. If, based on a review required by § 1026.59, a creditor reinstates a temporary rate that had been revoked, the card issuer is not required to provide an additional notice to the consumer when the reinstated temporary rate expires, if the card issuer provided the disclosures required by § 1026.9(c)(2)(v)(B) prior to the original commencement of the temporary rate. *See* § 1026.55 and the associated commentary for guidance on the permissibility and applicability of rate increases.

ii. *Example.* A consumer opens a new credit card account under an open-end (not home-secured) consumer credit plan on January 1, 2011. The annual percentage rate applicable to purchases is 18%. The card issuer offers the consumer a 15% rate on purchases made between January 1, 2012 and January 1, 2014. Prior to January 1, 2012, the card issuer discloses, in accordance with § 1026.9(c)(2)(v)(B), that the rate on purchases made during that period will increase to the standard 18% rate on January 1, 2014. In March 2012, the consumer makes a payment that is ten days late. The card issuer, upon providing 45 days' advance notice of the change under § 1026.9(g), increases the rate on new purchases to 18% effective as of June 1, 2012. On December 1, 2012, the issuer performs a review of the consumer's account in accordance with § 1026.59. Based on that review, the card issuer is required to reduce the rate to the original 15% temporary rate as of January 15, 2013. On January 1, 2014, the card issuer may increase the rate on purchases to 18%, as previously disclosed prior to January 1, 2012, without providing an additional notice to the consumer.

* * *

[74 Fed. Reg. 5244 (Jan. 29, 2009); 74 Fed. Reg. 36,097 (July 22, 2009) (interim final rule); 75 Fed. Reg. 7848 (Feb. 22, 2010); 75 Fed. Reg. 7925 (Feb. 22, 2010); 75 Fed. Reg. 37,583 (June 29, 2010); 76 Fed. Reg. 23,015, 23,016, 23,018 (Apr. 25, 2011)]

## SECTION 1026.10 Payments [§ 226.10]

### *10(a) General Rule.*

1. *Crediting date.* Section 1026.10(a) does not require the creditor to post the payment to the consumer's account on a particular date; the creditor is only required to credit the payment *as of* the date of receipt.

2. *Date of receipt.* The "date of receipt" is the date that the payment instrument or other means of completing the payment reaches the creditor. For example:

i. Payment by check is received when the creditor gets it, not when the funds are collected.

ii. In a payroll deduction plan in which funds are deposited to an asset account held by the creditor, and from which payments are made periodically to an open-end credit account, payment is received on the date when it is debited to the asset account (rather than on the date of the deposit), provided the payroll deduction method is voluntary and the consumer retains use of the funds until the contractual payment date.

iii. If the consumer elects to have payment made by a third party payor such as a financial institution, through a preauthorized payment or telephone bill-payment arrangement, payment is received when the creditor gets the third party payor's check or other transfer medium, such as an electronic fund transfer, as long as the payment meets the creditor's requirements as specified under § 1026.10(b).

iv. Payment made via the creditor's Web site is received on the date on which the consumer authorizes the creditor to effect the payment, even if the consumer gives the instruction authorizing that payment in advance of the date on which the creditor is authorized to effect the payment. If the consumer authorizes the creditor to effect the payment immediately, but the consumer's instruction is received after 5 p.m. or any later cut-off time specified by the creditor, the date on which the consumer authorizes the creditor to effect the payment is deemed to be the next business day.

### *10(b) Specific Requirements for Payments*

1. *Payment by electronic fund transfer.* A creditor may be prohibited from specifying payment by preauthorized electronic fund transfer. (See Section 913 of the Electronic Fund Transfer Act.)

2. *Payment methods promoted by creditor.* If a creditor promotes a specific payment method, any payments made via that method (prior to any cut-off time specified by the creditor, to the extent permitted by § 1026.10(b)(2)) are generally conforming payments for purposes of § 1026.10(b). For example:

i. If a creditor promotes electronic payment via its Web site (such as by disclosing on the Web site itself that payments may be made via the Web site), any payments made via the creditor's Web site prior to the creditor's specified cut-off time, if any, would generally be conforming payments for purposes of § 1026.10(b).

ii. If a creditor promotes payment by telephone (for example, by including the option to pay by telephone in a menu of options provided to consumers at a toll-free number disclosed on its periodic statement), payments made by telephone would generally be conforming payments for purposes of § 1026.10(b).

iii. If a creditor promotes in-person payments, for example by stating in an advertisement that payments may be made in person at its branch locations, such in-person payments made at a branch or office of the creditor generally would be conforming payments for purposes of § 1026.10(b).

iv. If a creditor promotes that payments may be made through an unaffiliated third party, such as by disclosing the Web site address of that third party on the periodic statement, payments made via that third party's Web site generally would be conforming payments for purposes of § 1026.10(b). In contrast, if a customer service representative of the creditor confirms to a consumer that payments may be made via an unaffiliated third party, but the creditor does not otherwise promote that method of payment, § 1026.10(b) permits the creditor to treat payments made via such third party as nonconforming payments in accordance with § 1026.10(b)(4).

3. *Acceptance of nonconforming payments.* If the creditor accepts a nonconforming payment (for example, payment mailed to a branch office, when the creditor had specified that payment be sent to a different location), finance charges may accrue for the period between receipt and crediting of payments.

4. *Implied guidelines for payments.* In the absence of specified requirements for making payments (see § 1026.10(b)):

i. Payments may be made at any location where the creditor conducts business.

ii. Payments may be made any time during the creditor's normal business hours.

iii. Payment may be by cash, money order, draft, or other similar instrument in properly negotiable form, or by electronic fund transfer if the creditor and consumer have so agreed.

5. *Payments made at point of sale.* If a card issuer that is a financial institution issues a credit card under an open-end (not home-secured) consumer credit plan that can be used only for transactions with a particular merchant or merchants or a credit card that is cobranded with the name of a particular merchant or merchants, and a consumer is able to make a payment on that credit card account at a retail location maintained by such a merchant, that retail location is not considered to be a branch or office of the card issuer for purposes of § 1026.10(b)(3).

6. *In-person payments on credit card accounts.* For purposes of § 1026.10(b)(3), payments made in person at a branch or office of a financial institution include payments made with the direct assistance of, or to, a branch or office employee, for example a teller at a bank branch. A payment made at the bank branch without the direct assistance of a branch or office employee, for example a payment placed in a branch or office mail slot, is not a payment made in person for purposes of § 1026.10(b)(3).

7. *In-person payments at affiliate of card issuer.* If an affiliate of a card issuer that is a financial institution shares a name with the card issuer, such as "ABC," and accepts in-person payments on the card issuer's credit card accounts, those payments are subject to the requirements of § 1026.10(b)(3).

## *10(d) Crediting of Payments When Creditor Does Not Receive or Accept Payments on Due Date*

1. *Example.* A day on which the creditor does not receive or accept payments by mail may occur, for example, if the U.S. Postal Service does not deliver mail on that date.

2. *Treating a payment as late for any purpose.* See comment 5(b)(2)(ii)-2 for guidance on treating a payment as late for any purpose. When an account is not eligible for a grace period, imposing a finance charge due to a periodic interest rate does not constitute treating a payment as late.

## *10(e) Limitations on Fees Related to Method of Payment*

1. *Separate fee to allow consumers to make a payment.* For purposes of § 1026.10(e), the term "separate fee" means a fee imposed on a consumer for making a payment to the consumer's account. A fee or other charge imposed if payment is made after the due date, such as a late fee or finance charge, is not a separate fee to allow consumers to make a payment for purposes of § 1026.10(e).

2. *Expedited.* For purposes of § 1026.10(e), the term "expedited" means crediting a payment the same day or, if the payment is received after any cut-off time established by the creditor, the next business day.

3. *Service by a customer service representative.* Service by a customer service representative of a creditor means any payment made to the consumer's account with the assistance of a live representative or agent of the creditor, including those made in person, on the telephone, or by electronic means. A customer service representative does not include automated means of making payment that do not involve a live representative or agent of the creditor, such as a voice response unit or interactive voice response system. Service by a customer service representative includes any payment transaction which involves the assistance of a live representative or agent of the creditor, even if an automated system is required for a portion of the transaction.

4. *Creditor.* For purposes of § 1026.10(e), the term "creditor" includes a third party that collects, receives, or processes payments on behalf of a creditor. For example:

i. Assume that a creditor uses a service provider to receive, collect, or process on the creditor's behalf payments made through the creditor's Web site or made through an automated telephone payment service. In these circumstances, the service provider would be considered a creditor for purposes of paragraph (e).

ii. Assume that a consumer pays a fee to a money transfer or payment service in order to transmit a payment to the creditor on the consumer's behalf. In these circumstances, the money transfer or payment service would not be considered a creditor for purposes of paragraph (e).

iii. Assume that a consumer has a checking account at a depository institution. The consumer makes a payment to the creditor from the checking account using a bill payment service provided by the depository institution. In these circumstances, the depository institution would not be considered a creditor for purposes of paragraph (e).

## *10(f) Changes by Card Issuer*

1. *Address for receiving payment.* For purposes of § 1026.10(f), "address for receiving payment" means a mailing address for receiving payment, such as a post office box, or the address of a branch or office at which payments on credit card accounts are accepted.

2. *Materiality.* For purposes of § 1026.10(f), a "material change" means any change in the address for receiving payment or procedures for handling cardholder payments which causes a material delay in the crediting of a payment. "Material delay" means any delay in crediting payment to a consumer's account which would result in a late payment and the imposition of a late fee or finance charge. A delay in crediting a payment which does not result in a late fee or finance charge would be immaterial.

3. *Safe harbor.*

i. *General.* A card issuer may elect not to impose a late fee or finance charge on a consumer's account for the 60-day period following a change in address for receiving payment or procedures for handling cardholder payments which could reasonably be expected to cause a material delay in crediting of a payment to the consumer's account. For purposes of § 1026.10(f), a late fee or finance charge is not imposed if the fee or charge is waived or removed, or an amount equal to the fee or charge is credited to the account.

ii. *Retail location.* For a material change in the address of a retail location or procedures for handling cardholder payments at a retail location, a card issuer may impose a late fee or finance charge on a consumer's account for a late payment during the 60-day period following the date on which the change took effect. However, if a card issuer is notified by a consumer no later than 60 days after the card issuer transmitted the first periodic statement that reflects the late fee or finance charge for a late payment that the late payment was caused by such change, the card issuer must waive or remove any late fee or finance charge, or credit an amount equal to any late fee or finance charge, imposed on the account during the 60-day period following the date on which the change took effect.

4. *Examples.*

i. A card issuer changes the mailing address for receiving payments by mail from a five-digit postal zip code to a nine-digit postal zip code. A consumer mails a payment using the five-digit postal zip code. The change in mailing address is immaterial and it does not cause a delay. Therefore, a card issuer may impose a late fee or finance charge for a late payment on the account.

ii. A card issuer changes the mailing address for receiving payments by mail from one post office box number to another post office box number. For a 60-day period following the change, the card issuer continues to use both post office box numbers for the collection of payments received by mail. The change in mailing address would not cause a material delay in crediting a payment because payments would be received and credited at both addresses. Therefore, a card issuer may impose a late fee or finance charge for a late payment on the account during the 60-day period following the date on which the change took effect.

iii. Same facts as paragraph ii above, except the prior post office box number is no longer valid and mail sent to that address during the 60-day period following the change would be returned to sender. The change in mailing address is material and the change could cause a material delay in the crediting of a payment because a payment sent to the old address could be delayed past the due date. If, as a result, a consumer makes a late payment on the account during the 60-day period following the date on which the change took effect, a card issuer may not impose any late fee or finance charge for the late payment.

iv. A card issuer permanently closes a local branch office at which payments are accepted on credit card accounts. The permanent closing of the local branch office is a material change in address for receiving payment. Relying on the safe harbor, the card issuer elects not to impose a late fee or finance charge for the 60-day period following the local branch closing for late payments on consumer accounts which the issuer reasonably determines are associated with the local branch and which could reasonably be expected to have been caused by the branch closing.

v. A consumer has elected to make payments automatically to a credit card account, such as through a payroll deduction plan or a third party payor's preauthorized payment arrangement. A card issuer changes the procedures for handling such payments and as a result, a payment is delayed and not credited to the consumer's account before the due date. In these circumstances, a card issuer may not impose any late fee or finance charge during the 60-day period following the date on which the change took effect for a late payment on the account.

vi. A card issuer no longer accepts payments in person at a retail location as a conforming method of payment, which is a material change in the procedures for handling cardholder payment. In the 60-day period following the date on which the change took effect, a consumer attempts to make a payment in person at a retail location of a card issuer. As a result, the consumer makes a late payment and the issuer charges a late fee on the consumer's account. The consumer notifies the card issuer of the late fee for the late payment which was caused by the material change. In order to comply with § 1026.10(f), the card issuer must waive or remove the late fee or finance charge, or credit the consumer's account in an amount equal to the late fee or finance charge.

5. *Finance charge due to periodic interest rate.* When an account is not eligible for a grace period, imposing a finance charge due to a periodic interest rate does not constitute imposition of a finance charge for a late payment for purposes of § 1026.10(f).

[74 Fed. Reg. 5244 (Jan. 29, 2009); 75 Fed. Reg. 7848 (Feb. 22, 2010); 75 Fed. Reg. 7925 (Feb. 22, 2010); 76 Fed. Reg. 23,018, 23,019 (Apr. 25, 2011)]

* * *

# SUBPART G SPECIAL RULES APPLICABLE TO CREDIT CARD ACCOUNTS AND OPEN-END CREDIT OFFERED TO COLLEGE STUDENTS

## SECTION 1026.51 Ability To Pay [§ 226.51]

### *51(a) General Rule*

### *51(a)(1)(i) Consideration of Ability to Pay*

1. *Consideration of additional factors.* Section 1026.51(a) requires a card issuer to consider a consumer's independent ability to make the required minimum periodic payments under the terms of an account based on the consumer's independent income or assets and current obligations. The card issuer may also consider consumer reports, credit scores, and other factors, consistent with Regulation B (12 CFR part 1002).

2. *Ability to pay as of application or consideration of increase.* A card issuer complies with § 1026.51(a) if it bases its determination regarding a consumer's independent ability to make the required minimum periodic payments on the facts and circumstances known to the card issuer at the time the consumer applies to open the credit card account or when the card issuer considers increasing the credit line on an existing account.

3. *Credit line increase.* When a card issuer considers increasing the credit line on an existing account, § 1026.51(a) applies whether the consideration is based upon a request of the consumer or is initiated by the card issuer.

4. *Income and assets.*

i. *Sources of information.* For purposes of § 1026.51(a), a card issuer may consider the consumer's income and assets based on:

A. Information provided by the consumer in connection with the credit card account under an open-end (not home-secured) consumer credit plan;

B. Information provided by the consumer in connection with any other financial relationship the card issuer or its affiliates have with the consumer (subject to any applicable information-sharing rules);

C. Information obtained through third parties (subject to any applicable information-sharing rules); and

D. Information obtained through any empirically derived, demonstrably and statistically sound model that reasonably estimates a consumer's income and assets.

ii. *Income and assets of persons liable for debts incurred on account.* For purposes of § 1026.51(a), a card issuer may consider any current or reasonably expected income and assets of the consumer or consumers who are applying for a new account and will be liable for debts incurred on that account. Similarly, when a card issuer is considering whether to increase the credit limit on an existing account, the card issuer may consider any current or reasonably expected income and assets of the consumer or consumers who are accountholders and are liable for debts incurred on that account. A card issuer may also consider any current or reasonably expected income and assets of a cosigner or guarantor who is or will be liable for debts incurred on the account. However, a card issuer may not use the income and assets of an authorized user or other person who is not liable for debts incurred on the account to satisfy the requirements of § 1026.51, unless a Federal or state statute or regulation grants a consumer who is liable for debts incurred on the account an ownership interest in such income and assets. Information about current or reasonably expected income and assets includes, for example, information about current or expected salary, wages, bonus pay, tips, and commissions. Employment may be full-time, part-time, seasonal, irregular, military, or self-employment. Other sources of income could include interest or dividends, retirement benefits, public assistance, alimony, child support, or separate maintenance payments. A card issuer may also take into account assets such as savings accounts or investments.

iii. *Household income and assets.* Consideration of information regarding a consumer's household income does not by itself satisfy the requirement in § 1026.51(a) to consider the consumer's independent ability to pay. For example, if a card issuer requests on its application forms that applicants provide their "household income," the card issuer may not rely solely on the information provided by applicants to satisfy the requirements of § 1026.51(a). Instead, the card issuer would need to obtain additional information about an applicant's independent income (such as by contacting the applicant). However, if a card issuer requests on its application forms that applicants provide their income without reference to household income (such as by requesting "income" or "salary"), the card issuer may rely on the information provided by applicants to satisfy the requirements of § 1026.51(a).

5. *Current obligations.* A card issuer may consider the consumer's current obligations based on information provided by the consumer or in a consumer report. In evaluating a consumer's current obligations, a card issuer need not assume that credit lines for other obligations are fully utilized.

6. *Joint applicants and joint accountholders.* With respect to the opening of a joint account for two or more consumers or a credit line increase on such an account, the card issuer may consider the collective ability of all persons who are or will be liable for debts incurred on the account to make the required payments.

### *51(a)(2) Minimum Periodic Payments*

1. *Applicable minimum payment formula.* For purposes of estimating required minimum periodic

payments under the safe harbor set forth in § 1026.51(a)(2)(ii), if the account has or may have a promotional program, such as a deferred payment or similar program, where there is no applicable minimum payment formula during the promotional period, the issuer must estimate the required minimum periodic payment based on the minimum payment formula that will apply when the promotion ends.

2. *Interest rate for purchases.* For purposes of estimating required minimum periodic payments under the safe harbor set forth in § 1026.51(a)(2)(ii), if the interest rate for purchases is or may be a promotional rate, the issuer must use the post-promotional rate to estimate interest charges.

3. *Mandatory fees.* For purposes of estimating required minimum periodic payments under the safe harbor set forth in § 1026.51(a)(2)(ii), mandatory fees that must be assumed to be charged include those fees the card issuer knows the consumer will be required to pay under the terms of the account if the account is opened, such as an annual fee. If a mandatory fee is a promotional fee (as defined in § 1026.16(g)), the issuer must use the post-promotional fee amount for purposes of § 1026.51(a)(2)(ii).

### 51(b) Rules Affecting Young Consumers

1. *Age as of date of application or consideration of credit line increase.* Sections 1026.51(b)(1) and (b)(2) apply only to a consumer who has not attained the age of 21 as of the date of submission of the application under § 1026.51(b)(1) or the date the credit line increase is requested by the consumer (or if no request has been made, the date the credit line increase is considered by the card issuer) under § 1026.51(b)(2).

2. *Liability of cosigner, guarantor, or joint accountholder.* Sections 1026.51(b)(1)(ii) and (b)(2) require the signature or written consent of a cosigner, guarantor, or joint accountholder agreeing either to be secondarily liable for any debt on the account incurred by the consumer before the consumer has attained the age of 21 or to be jointly liable with the consumer for any debt on the account. Sections 1026.51(b)(1)(ii) and (b)(2) do not prohibit a card issuer from also requiring the cosigner, guarantor, or joint accountholder to assume liability for debts incurred after the consumer has attained the age of 21, consistent with any agreement made between the parties.

3. *Authorized users exempt.* If a consumer who has not attained the age of 21 is being added to another person's account as an authorized user and has no liability for debts incurred on the account, § 1026.51(b)(1) and (b)(2) do not apply.

4. *Electronic application.* Consistent with § 1026.5(a)(1)(iii), an application may be provided to the consumer in electronic form without regard to the consumer consent or other provisions of the Electronic Signatures in Global and National Commerce Act (E-Sign Act) (15 U.S.C. 7001 *et seq.*) in the circumstances set forth in § 1026.60. The electronic submission of an application from a consumer or a consent to a credit line increase from a cosigner, guarantor, or joint accountholder to a card issuer would constitute a written application or consent for purposes of § 1026.51(b) and would not be considered a consumer disclosure for purposes of the E-Sign Act.

### 51(b)(1) Applications from young consumers

1. *Relation to Regulation B.* In considering an application or credit line increase on the credit card account of a consumer who is less than 21 years old, creditors must comply with the applicable rules in Regulation B (12 CFR part 1002).

2. *Financial information.* Information regarding income and assets that satisfies the requirements of § 1026.51(a) also satisfies the requirements of § 1026.51(b)(1). *See* comment 51(a)(1)-4.

### 51(b)(2) Credit line increases for young consumers

1. *Credit line request by joint accountholder aged 21 or older.* The requirement under § 1026.51(b)(2) that a cosigner, guarantor, or joint accountholder for a credit card account opened pursuant to § 1026.51(b)(1)(ii) must agree in writing to assume liability for the increase before a credit line is increased, does not apply if the cosigner, guarantor or joint accountholder who is at least 21 years old initiates the request for the increase.

[75 Fed. Reg. 7848 (Feb. 22, 2010); 76 Fed. Reg. 23,020 (Apr. 25, 2011); 76 Fed. Reg. 31,221 (May 31, 2011)]

## SECTION 1026.52 Limitations on Fees [§ 226.52]

### 52(a) Limitations prior to account opening and during first year after account opening

### 52(a)(1) General rule

1. *Application.* The 25 percent limit in § 1026.52(a)(1) applies to fees that the card issuer charges to the account as well as to fees that the card issuer requires the consumer to pay with respect to the account through other means (such as through a payment from the consumer's asset account to the card issuer or from another credit account provided by the card issuer). For example:

i. Assume that, under the terms of a credit card account, a consumer is required to pay $120 in fees for the issuance or availability of credit at account opening. The consumer is also required to pay a cash advance fee that is equal to five percent of the cash advance and a late payment fee of $15 if the required minimum periodic payment is not received by the payment due date (which is the twenty-fifth of the month). At account opening on January 1 of year one, the credit limit for the account is $500. Section 1026.52(a)(1) permits the card issuer to charge to the account the $120 in fees for the issuance or availability of credit at account opening. On February 1 of year one, the consumer uses the account for a $100 cash advance. Section 1026.52(a)(1) permits the card issuer to charge a $5 cash-advance fee to the account. On March 26 of year one, the card issuer has not received the consumer's required minimum periodic payment. Section 1026.52(a)(2) permits the card issuer to charge a $15 late payment fee to the account. On July 15 of year one, the consumer uses the account for a $50 cash advance. Section 1026.52(a)(1) does not permit the card issuer to charge a $2.50 cash advance fee to the account. Furthermore, § 1026.52(a)(1) prohibits the card issuer from collecting the $2.50 cash advance fee from the consumer by other means.

ii. Assume that, under the terms of a credit card account, a consumer is required to pay $125 in fees for the issuance or availability of credit during the first year after account opening. At account opening on January 1 of year one, the credit limit for the account is $500. Section 1026.52(a)(1) permits the card issuer to charge the $125 in fees to the account. However, § 1026.52(a)(1) prohibits the card issuer from requiring the consumer to make payments to the card issuer for additional non-exempt fees with respect to the account prior to account opening or during the first year after account opening. Section 1026.52(a)(1) also prohibits the card issuer from requiring the consumer to open a separate credit account with the card issuer to fund the payment of additional non-exempt fees prior to the opening of the credit card account or during the first year after the credit card account is opened.

iii. Assume that, on January 1 of year one, a consumer is required to pay a $100 fee in order to apply for a credit card account. On January 5, the card issuer approves the consumer's application, assigns the account a credit limit of $1,000, and provides the consumer with account-opening disclosures consistent with § 1026.6. The date on which the account may first be used by the consumer to engage in transactions is January 5. The consumer is required to pay $150 in fees for the issuance or availability of credit, which § 1026.52(a)(1) permits the card issuer to charge to the account on January 5. However, because the $100 application fee is subject to the 25 percent limit in § 1026.52(a)(1), the card issuer is prohibited from requiring the consumer to pay any additional non-exempt fees with respect to the account until January 5 of year two.

2. *Fees that exceed 25 percent limit.* A card issuer that charges a fee to a credit card account that exceeds the 25 percent limit complies with § 1026.52(a)(1) if the card issuer waives or removes the fee and any associated interest charges or credits the account for an amount equal to the fee

and any associated interest charges within a reasonable amount of time but no later than the end of the billing cycle following the billing cycle during which the fee was charged. For example, assuming the facts in the example in comment 52(a)(1)-1.i above, the card issuer complies with § 1026.52(a)(1) if the card issuer charged the $2.50 cash advance fee to the account on July 15 of year one but waived or removed the fee or credited the account for $2.50 (plus any interest charges on that $2.50) at the end of the billing cycle.

3. *Changes in credit limit during first year.*

i. *Increases in credit limit.* If a card issuer increases the credit limit during the first year after the account is opened, § 1026.52(a)(1) does not permit the card issuer to require the consumer to pay additional fees that would otherwise be prohibited (such as a fee for increasing the credit limit). For example, assume that, at account opening on January 1, the credit limit for a credit card account is $400 and the consumer is required to pay $100 in fees for the issuance or availability of credit. On July 1, the card issuer increases the credit limit for the account to $600. Section 1026.52(a)(1) does not permit the card issuer to require the consumer to pay additional fees based on the increased credit limit.

ii. *Decreases in credit limit.* If a card issuer decreases the credit limit during the first year after the account is opened, § 1026.52(a)(1) requires the card issuer to waive or remove any fees charged to the account that exceed 25 percent of the reduced credit limit or to credit the account for an amount equal to any fees the consumer was required to pay with respect to the account that exceed 25 percent of the reduced credit limit within a reasonable amount of time but no later than the end of the billing cycle following the billing cycle during which the credit limit was reduced. For example:

A. Assume that, at account opening on January 1, the credit limit for a credit card account is $1,000 and the consumer is required to pay $250 in fees for the issuance or availability of credit. The billing cycles for the account begin on the first day of the month and end on the last day of the month. On July 30, the card issuer decreases the credit limit for the account to $500. Section 1026.52(a)(1) requires the card issuer to waive or remove $175 in fees from the account or to credit the account for an amount equal to $175 within a reasonable amount of time but no later than August 31.

B. Assume that, on June 25 of year one, a consumer is required to pay a $75 fee in order to apply for a credit card account. At account opening on July 1 of year one, the credit limit for the account is $500 and the consumer is required to pay $50 in fees for the issuance or availability of credit. The billing cycles for the account begin on the first day of the month and end on the last day of the month. On February 15 of year two, the card issuer decreases the credit limit for the account to $250. Section 1026.52(a)(1) requires the card issuer to waive or remove fees from the account or to credit the account for an amount equal to $62.50 within a reasonable amount of time but no later than March 31 of year two.

4. *Date on which account may first be used by consumer to engage in transactions.*

i. *Methods of compliance.* For purposes of § 1026.52(a)(1), an account is considered open no earlier than the date on which the account may first be used by the consumer to engage in transactions. A card issuer may consider an account open for purposes of § 1026.52(a)(1) on any of the following dates:

A. The date the account is first used by the consumer for a transaction (such as when an account is established in connection with financing the purchase of goods or services).

B. The date the consumer complies with any reasonable activation procedures imposed by the card issuer for preventing fraud or unauthorized use of a new account (such as requiring the consumer to provide information that verifies his or her identity), provided that the account may be used for transactions on that date.

C. The date that is seven days after the card issuer mails or delivers to the consumer account-opening disclosures that comply with § 1026.6, provided that the consumer may use the account for transactions after complying with any reasonable activation procedures imposed by the card issuer for preventing fraud or unauthorized use of the new account (such as requiring the consumer to provide information that verifies his or her identity). If a card issuer has reasonable procedures designed to ensure that account-opening disclosures that comply with § 1026.6 are mailed or delivered to consumers no later than a certain number of days after the card issuer establishes the account, the card issuer may add that number of days to the seven-day period for purposes of determining the date on which the account was opened.

ii. *Examples.*

A. Assume that, on July 1 of year one, a credit card account under an open-end (not home-secured) consumer credit plan is established in connection with financing the purchase of goods or services and a $500 transaction is charged to the account by the consumer. The card issuer may consider the account open on July 1 of year one for purposes of § 1026.52(a)(1). Accordingly, § 1026.52(a)(1) ceases to apply to the account on July 1 of year two.

B. Assume that, on July 1 of year one, a card issuer approves a consumer's application for a credit card account under an open-end (not home-secured) consumer credit plan and establishes the account on its internal systems. On July 5, the card issuer mails or delivers to the consumer account-opening disclosures that comply with § 1026.6. If the consumer may use the account for transactions on the date the consumer complies with any reasonable procedures imposed by the card issuer for preventing fraud or unauthorized use, the card issuer may consider the account open on July 12 of year one for purposes of § 1026.52(a)(1). Accordingly, § 1026.52(a)(1) ceases to apply to the account on July 12 of year two.

C. Same facts as in paragraph B above except that the card issuer has adopted reasonable procedures designed to ensure that account-opening disclosures that comply with § 1026.6 are mailed or delivered to consumers no later than three days after an account is established on its systems. If the consumer may use the account for transactions on the date the consumer complies with any reasonable procedures imposed by the card issuer for preventing fraud or unauthorized use, the card issuer may consider the account open on July 11 of year one for purposes of § 1026.52(a)(1). Accordingly, § 1026.52(a)(1) ceases to apply to the account on July 11 of year two. However, if the consumer uses the account for a transaction or complies with the card issuer's reasonable procedures for preventing fraud or unauthorized use on July 8 of year one, the card issuer may, at its option, consider the account open on that date for purposes of § 1026.52(a)(1) and § 1026.52(a)(1) therefore ceases to apply to the account on July 8 of year two.

### *52(a)(2) Fees Not Subject to Limitations*

1. *Covered fees.* Except as provided in § 1026.52(a)(2), § 1026.52(a) applies to any fees or other charges that a card issuer will or may require the consumer to pay with respect to a credit card account prior to account opening and during the first year after account opening, other than charges attributable to periodic interest rates. For example, § 1026.52(a) applies to:

i. Fees that the consumer is required to pay for the issuance or availability of credit described in § 1026.60(b)(2), including any fee based on account activity or inactivity and any fee that a consumer is required to pay in order to receive a particular credit limit;

ii. Fees for insurance described in § 1026.4(b)(7) or debt cancellation or debt suspension coverage described in § 1026.4(b)(10) written in connection with a credit transaction, if the insurance or debt cancellation or debt suspension coverage is required by the terms of the account;

iii. Fees that the consumer is required to pay in order to engage in transactions using the account (such as cash advance fees, balance transfer fees, foreign transaction fees, and fees for using the account for purchases);

iv. Fees that the consumer is required to pay for violating the terms of the account (except to the extent specifically excluded by § 1026.52(a)(2)(i));

v. Fixed finance charges; and

vi. Minimum charges imposed if a charge would otherwise have been determined by applying a periodic interest rate to a balance except for the fact that such charge is smaller than the minimum.

2. *Fees the consumer is not required to pay.* Section 1026.52(a)(2)(ii) provides that § 1026.52(a) does not apply to fees that the consumer is not required to pay with respect to the account. For example, § 1026.52(a) generally does not apply to fees for making an expedited payment (to the extent permitted by § 1026.10(e)), fees for optional services (such as travel insurance), fees for reissuing a lost or stolen card, or statement reproduction fees.

3. *Security deposits.* A security deposit that is charged to a credit card account is a fee for purposes of § 1026.52(a). In contrast, however, a security deposit is not subject to the 25 percent limit in § 1026.52(a)(1) if it is not charged to the account. For example, § 1026.52(a)(1) does not prohibit a card issuer from requiring a consumer to provide funds at account opening pledged as security for the account that exceed 25 percent of the credit limit at account opening so long as those funds are not obtained from the account.

## *52(a)(3) Rule of Construction*

1. *Fees or charges otherwise prohibited by law.* Section 1026.52(a) does not authorize the imposition or payment of fees or charges otherwise prohibited by law. For example, see 16 CFR 310.4(a)(4).

## *52(b) Limitations on Penalty Fees*

1. *Fees for violating the account terms or other requirements.* For purposes of § 1026.52(b), a fee includes any charge imposed by a card issuer based on an act or omission that violates the terms of the account or any other requirements imposed by the card issuer with respect to the account, other than charges attributable to periodic interest rates. Accordingly, for purposes of § 1026.52(b), a fee does not include charges attributable to an increase in an annual percentage rate based on an act or omission that violates the terms or other requirements of an account.

i. The following are examples of fees that are subject to the limitations in § 1026.52(b) or are prohibited by § 1026.52(b):

A. Late payment fees and any other fees imposed by a card issuer if an account becomes delinquent or if a payment is not received by a particular date.

B. Returned payment fees and any other fees imposed by a card issuer if a payment received via check, automated clearing house, or other payment method is returned.

C. Any fee or charge for an over-the-limit transaction as defined in § 1026.56(a), to the extent the imposition of such a fee or charge is permitted by § 1026.56.

D. Any fee imposed by a card issuer if payment on a check that accesses a credit card account is declined.

E. Any fee or charge for a transaction that the card issuer declines to authorize. *See* § 1026.52(b)(2)(i)(B).

F. Any fee imposed by a card issuer based on account inactivity (including the consumer's failure to use the account for a particular number or dollar amount of transactions or a particular type of transaction). *See* § 1026.52(b)(2)(i)(B).

G. Any fee imposed by a card issuer based on the closure or termination of an account. *See* § 1026.52(b)(2)(i)(B).

ii. The following are examples of fees to which § 1026.52(b) does not apply:

A. Balance transfer fees.

B. Cash advance fees.

C. Foreign transaction fees.

D. Annual fees and other fees for the issuance or availability of credit described in § 1026.60(b)(2), except to the extent that such fees are based on account inactivity. *See* § 1026.52(b)(2)(i)(B).

E. Fees for insurance described in § 1026.4(b)(7) or debt cancellation or debt suspension coverage described in § 1026.4(b)(10) written in connection with a credit transaction, provided that such fees are not imposed as a result of a violation of the account terms or other requirements of an account.

F. Fees for making an expedited payment (to the extent permitted by § 1026.10(e)).

G. Fees for optional services (such as travel insurance).

H. Fees for reissuing a lost or stolen card.

2. *Rounding to nearest whole dollar.* A card issuer may round any fee that complies with § 1026.52(b) to the nearest whole dollar. For example, if § 1026.52(b) permits a card issuer to impose a late payment fee of $21.50, the card issuer may round that amount up to the nearest whole dollar and impose a late payment fee of $22. However, if the late payment fee permitted by § 1026.52(b) were $21.49, the card issuer would not be permitted to round that amount up to $22, although the card issuer could round that amount down and impose a late payment fee of $21.

## *52(b)(1) General Rule*

1. *Relationship between § 1026.52(b)(1)(i), (b)(1)(ii), and (b)(2).*

i. *Relationship between § 1026.52(b)(1)(i) and (b)(1)(ii).* A card issuer may impose a fee for violating the terms or other requirements of an account pursuant to either § 1026.52(b)(1)(i) or (b)(1)(ii).

A. A card issuer that complies with the safe harbors in § 1026.52(b)(1)(ii) is not required to determine that its fees represent a reasonable proportion of the total costs incurred by the card issuer as a result of a type of violation under § 1026.52(b)(1)(i).

B. A card issuer may impose a fee for one type of violation pursuant to § 1026.52(b)(1)(i) and may impose a fee for a different type of violation pursuant to § 1026.52(b)(1)(ii). For example, a card issuer may impose a late payment fee of $30 based on a cost determination pursuant to § 1026.52(b)(1)(i) but impose returned payment and over-the-limit fees of $25 or $35 pursuant to the safe harbors in § 1026.52(b)(1)(ii).

C. A card issuer that previously based the amount of a penalty fee for a particular type of violation on a cost determination pursuant to § 1026.52(b)(1)(i) may begin to impose a penalty fee for that type of violation that is consistent with § 1026.52(b)(1)(ii) at any time (subject to the notice requirements in § 1026.9), provided that the first fee imposed pursuant to § 1026.52(b)(1)(ii) is consistent with § 1026.52(b)(1)(ii)(A). For example, assume that a late payment occurs on January 15 and that, based on a cost determination pursuant to § 1026.52(b)(1)(i), the card issuer imposes a $30 late payment fee. Another late payment occurs on July 15. The card issuer may impose another $30 late payment fee pursuant to § 1026.52(b)(1)(i) or may impose a $25 late payment fee pursuant to § 1026.52(b)(1)(ii)(A). However, the card issuer may not impose a $35 late payment fee pursuant to § 1026.52(b)(1)(ii)(B). If the card issuer imposes a $25 fee pursuant to § 1026.52(b)(1)(ii)(A) for the July 15 late payment and another late payment occurs on September 15, the card issuer may impose a $35 fee for the September 15 late payment pursuant to § 1026.52(b)(1)(ii)(B).

ii. *Relationship between § 1026.52(b)(1) and (b)(2).* Section 1026.52(b)(1) does not permit a card issuer to impose a fee that is inconsistent with the prohibitions in § 1026.52(b)(2). For example, if § 1026.52(b)(2)(i) prohibits the card issuer from imposing a late payment fee that exceeds $15, § 1026.52(b)(1)(ii) does not permit the card issuer to impose a higher late payment fee.

## *52(b)(1)(i) Fees Based on Costs*

1. *Costs incurred as a result of violations.* Section 1026.52(b)(1)(i) does not require a card issuer to base a fee on the costs incurred as a result of a specific violation of the terms or other requirements of an account. Instead, for purposes of § 1026.52(b)(1)(i), a card issuer must have determined that a fee for violating the terms or other requirements of an account represents a reasonable proportion of the costs incurred by the card issuer as a result of that type of violation. A card issuer may make a single determination for all of its credit card portfolios or may make separate determinations for each portfolio. The factors relevant to this determination include:

i. The number of violations of a particular type experienced by the card issuer during a prior period of reasonable length (for example, a period of twelve months).

ii. The costs incurred by the card issuer during that period as a result of those violations.

iii. At the card issuer's option, the number of fees imposed by the card issuer as a result of those violations during that period that the card issuer reasonably estimates it will be unable to collect. *See* comment 52(b)(1)(i)-5.

iv. At the card issuer's option, reasonable estimates for an upcoming period of changes in the number of violations of that type, the resulting costs, and the number of fees that the card issuer will be unable to collect. *See* illustrative examples in comments 52(b)(1)(i)-6 through -9.

2. *Amounts excluded from cost analysis.* The following amounts are not costs incurred by a card issuer as a result of violations of the terms or other requirements of an account for purposes of § 1026.52(b)(1)(i):

i. Losses and associated costs (including the cost of holding reserves against potential losses and the cost of funding delinquent accounts).

ii. Costs associated with evaluating whether consumers who have not violated the terms or other requirements of an account are likely to do so in the future (such as the costs associated with underwriting new accounts). However, once a violation of the terms or other requirements of an account has occurred, the costs associated with preventing additional violations for a reasonable period of time are costs incurred by a card issuer as a result of violations of the terms or other requirements of an account for purposes of § 1026.52(b)(1)(i).

3. *Third party charges.* As a general matter, amounts charged to the card issuer by a third party as a result of a violation of the terms or other requirements of an account are costs incurred by the card issuer for purposes of § 1026.52(b)(1)(i). For example, if a card issuer is charged a specific amount by a third party for each returned payment, that amount is a cost incurred by the card issuer as a result of returned payments. However, if the amount is charged to the card issuer by an affiliate or subsidiary of the card issuer, the card issuer must have determined that the charge represents a reasonable proportion of the costs incurred by the affiliate or subsidiary as a result of the type of violation. For example, if an affiliate of a card issuer provides collection services to the card issuer on delinquent accounts, the card issuer must have determined that the amounts charged to the card issuer by the affiliate for such services represent a reasonable proportion of the costs incurred by the affiliate as a result of late payments.

4. *Amounts charged by other card issuers.* The fact that a card issuer's fees for violating the terms or other requirements of an account are comparable to fees assessed by other card issuers does not satisfy the requirements of § 1026.52(b)(1)(i).

5. *Uncollected fees.* For purposes of § 1026.52(b)(1)(i), a card issuer may consider fees that it is unable to collect when determining the appropriate fee amount. Fees that the card issuer is unable to collect include fees imposed on accounts that have been charged off by the card issuer, fees that have been discharged in bankruptcy, and fees that the card issuer is required to waive in order to comply with a legal requirement (such as a requirement imposed by 12 CFR Part 1026 or 50 U.S.C. app. 527). However, fees that the card issuer chooses not to impose or chooses not to collect (such as fees the card issuer chooses to waive at the request of the consumer or under a workout or temporary hardship arrangement) are not relevant for purposes of this determination. *See* illustrative examples in comments 52(b)(2)(i)-6 through -9.

6. *Late payment fees.*

i. *Costs incurred as a result of late payments.* For purposes of § 1026.52(b)(1)(i), the costs incurred by a card issuer as a result of late payments include the costs associated with the collection of late payments, such as the costs associated with notifying consumers of delinquencies and resolving delinquencies (including the establishment of workout and temporary hardship arrangements).

ii. *Examples.*

A. *Late payment fee based on past delinquencies and costs.* Assume that, during year one, a card issuer experienced 1 million delinquencies and incurred $26 million in costs as a result of those delinquencies. For purposes of § 1026.52(b)(1)(i), a $26 late payment fee would represent a reasonable proportion of the total costs incurred by the card issuer as a result of late payments during year two.

B. *Adjustment based on fees card issuer is unable to collect.* Same facts as above except that the card issuer imposed a late payment fee for each of the 1 million delinquencies experienced during year one but was unable to collect 25% of those fees (in other words, the card issuer was unable to collect 250,000 fees, leaving a total of 750,000 late payments for which the card issuer did collect or could have collected a fee). For purposes of § 1026.52(b)(2)(i), a late payment fee of $35 would represent a reasonable proportion of the total costs incurred by the card issuer as a result of late payments during year two.

C. *Adjustment based on reasonable estimate of future changes.* Same facts as paragraphs A and B above except the card issuer reasonably estimates that—based on past delinquency rates and other factors relevant to potential delinquency rates for year two—it will experience a 2% decrease in delinquencies during year two (in other words, 20,000 fewer delinquencies for a total of 980,000). The card issuer also reasonably estimates that it will be unable to collect the same percentage of fees (25%) during year two as during year one (in other words, the card issuer will be unable to collect 245,000 fees, leaving a total of 735,000 late payments for which the card issuer will be able to collect a fee). The card issuer also reasonably estimates that—based on past changes in costs incurred as a result of delinquencies and other factors relevant to potential costs for year two—it will experience a 5% increase in costs during year two (in other words, $1.3 million in additional costs for a total of $27.3 million). For purposes of § 1026.52(b)(1)(i), a $37 late payment fee would represent a reasonable proportion of the total costs incurred by the card issuer as a result of late payments during year two.

7. *Returned payment fees.*

i. *Costs incurred as a result of returned payments.* For purposes of § 1026.52(b)(1)(i), the costs incurred by a card issuer as a result of returned payments include:

A. Costs associated with processing returned payments and reconciling the card issuer's systems and accounts to reflect returned payments;

B. Costs associated with investigating potential fraud with respect to returned payments; and

C. Costs associated with notifying the consumer of the returned payment and arranging for a new payment.

ii. *Examples.*

A. *Returned payment fee based on past returns and costs.* Assume that, during year one, a card issuer experienced 150,000 returned payments and incurred $3.1 million in costs as a result of those returned payments. For purposes of § 1026.52(b)(1)(i), a $21 returned payment fee would represent a reasonable proportion of the total costs incurred by the card issuer as a result of returned payments during year two.

B. *Adjustment based on fees card issuer is unable to collect.* Same facts as above except that the card issuer imposed a returned payment fee for each of the 150,000 returned payments experienced during year one but was unable to collect 15% of those fees (in other words, the card issuer was unable to collect 22,500 fees, leaving a total of 127,500 returned payments for which the card issuer did collect or could have collected a fee). For purposes of § 1026.52(b)(2)(i), a returned payment fee of $24 would represent a reasonable proportion of the total costs incurred by the card issuer as a result of returned payments during year two.

C. *Adjustment based on reasonable estimate of future changes.* Same facts as paragraphs A and B above except the card issuer reasonably estimates that—based on past returned payment rates and other factors relevant to potential returned payment rates for year two—it will experience a 2% increase in returned payments during year two (in other words, 3,000 additional returned payments for a total of 153,000). The card issuer also reasonably estimates that it will be unable to collect 25% of returned payment fees during year two (in other words, the card issuer will be unable to collect 38,250 fees, leaving a total of 114,750 returned payments for which the card issuer will be able to collect a fee). The card issuer also reasonably estimates that—based on past changes in costs incurred as a result of returned payments and other factors relevant to potential costs for year two—it will experience a 1% decrease in costs during year two (in other words, a $31,000 reduction in costs for a total of $3.069 million). For purposes of

§ 1026.52(b)(1)(i), a $27 returned payment fee would represent a reasonable proportion of the total costs incurred by the card issuer as a result of returned payments during year two.

8. *Over-the-limit fees.*

i. *Costs incurred as a result of over-the-limit transactions.* For purposes of § 1026.52(b)(1)(i), the costs incurred by a card issuer as a result of over-the-limit transactions include:

A. Costs associated with determining whether to authorize over-the-limit transactions; and

B. Costs associated with notifying the consumer that the credit limit has been exceeded and arranging for payments to reduce the balance below the credit limit.

ii. *Costs not incurred as a result of over-the-limit transactions.* For purposes of § 1026.52(b)(1)(i), costs associated with obtaining the affirmative consent of consumers to the card issuer's payment of transactions that exceed the credit limit consistent with § 1026.56 are not costs incurred by a card issuer as a result of over-the-limit transactions.

iii. *Examples.*

A. *Over-the-limit fee based on past fees and costs.* Assume that, during year one, a card issuer authorized 600,000 over-the-limit transactions and incurred $4.5 million in costs as a result of those over-the-limit transactions. However, because of the affirmative consent requirements in § 1026.56, the card issuer was only permitted to impose 200,000 over-the-limit fees during year one. For purposes of § 1026.52(b)(1)(i), a $23 over-the-limit fee would represent a reasonable proportion of the total costs incurred by the card issuer as a result of over-the-limit transactions during year two.

B. *Adjustment based on fees card issuer is unable to collect.* Same facts as above except that the card issuer was unable to collect 30% of the 200,000 over-the-limit fees imposed during year one (in other words, the card issuer was unable to collect 60,000 fees, leaving a total of 140,000 over-the-limit transactions for which the card issuer did collect or could have collected a fee). For purposes of § 1026.52(b)(2)(i), an over-the-limit fee of $32 would represent a reasonable proportion of the total costs incurred by the card issuer as a result of over-the-limit transactions during year two.

C. *Adjustment based on reasonable estimate of future changes.* Same facts as paragraphs A and B above except the card issuer reasonably estimates that—based on past over-the-limit transaction rates, the percentages of over-the-limit transactions that resulted in an over-the-limit fee in the past (consistent with § 1026.56), and factors relevant to potential changes in those rates and percentages for year two—it will authorize approximately the same number of over-the-limit transactions during year two (600,000) and impose approximately the same number of over-the-limit fees (200,000). The card issuer also reasonably estimates that it will be unable to collect the same percentage of fees (30%) during year two as during year one (in other words, the card issuer was unable to collect 60,000 fees, leaving a total of 140,000 over-the-limit transactions for which the card issuer will be able to collect a fee). The card issuer also reasonably estimates that—based on past changes in costs incurred as a result of over-the-limit transactions and other factors relevant to potential costs for year two—it will experience a 6% decrease in costs during year two (in other words, a $270,000 reduction in costs for a total of $4.23 million). For purposes of § 1026.52(b)(1)(i), a $30 over-the-limit fee would represent a reasonable proportion of the total costs incurred by the card issuer as a result of over-the-limit transactions during year two.

9. *Declined access check fees.*

i. *Costs incurred as a result of declined access checks.* For purposes of § 1026.52(b)(1)(i), the costs incurred by a card issuer as a result of declining payment on a check that accesses a credit card account include:

A. Costs associated with determining whether to decline payment on access checks;

B. Costs associated with processing declined access checks and reconciling the card issuer's systems and accounts to reflect declined access checks;

C. Costs associated with investigating potential fraud with respect to declined access checks; and

D. Costs associated with notifying the consumer and the merchant or other party that accepted the access check that payment on the check has been declined.

ii. *Example.* Assume that, during year one, a card issuer declined 100,000 access checks and incurred $2 million in costs as a result of those declined checks. The card issuer imposed a fee for each declined access check but was unable to collect 10% of those fees (in other words, the card issuer was unable to collect 10,000 fees, leaving a total of 90,000 declined access checks for which the card issuer did collect or could have collected a fee). For purposes of § 1026.52(b)(1)(i), a $22 declined access check fee would represent a reasonable proportion of the total costs incurred by the card issuer as a result of declined access checks during year two.

## *52(b)(1)(ii) Safe harbors*

1. *Multiple violations of same type.*

i. *Same billing cycle or next six billing cycles.* A card issuer cannot impose a fee for a violation pursuant to § 1026.52(b)(1)(ii)(B) unless a fee has previously been imposed for the same type of violation pursuant to § 1026.52(b)(1)(ii)(A). Once a fee has been imposed for a violation pursuant to § 1026.52(b)(1)(ii)(A), the card issuer may impose a fee pursuant to § 1026.52(b)(1)(ii)(B) for any subsequent violation of the same type until that type of violation has not occurred for a period of six consecutive complete billing cycles. A fee has been imposed for purposes of § 1026.52(b)(1)(ii) even if the card issuer waives or rebates all or part of the fee.

A. *Late payments.* For purposes of § 1026.52(b)(1)(ii), a late payment occurs during the billing cycle in which the payment may first be treated as late consistent with the requirements of this part and the terms or other requirements of the account.

B. *Returned payments.* For purposes of § 1026.52(b)(1)(ii), a returned payment occurs during the billing cycle in which the payment is returned to the card issuer.

C. *Transactions that exceed the credit limit.* For purposes of § 1026.52(b)(1)(ii), a transaction that exceeds the credit limit for an account occurs during the billing cycle in which the transaction occurs or is authorized by the card issuer.

D. *Declined access checks.* For purposes of § 1026.52(b)(1)(ii), a check that accesses a credit card account is declined during the billing cycle in which the card issuer declines payment on the check.

ii. *Relationship to §§ 1026.52(b)(2)(ii) and 1026.56(j)(1).* If multiple violations are based on the same event or transaction such that § 1026.52(b)(2)(ii) prohibits the card issuer from imposing more than one fee, the event or transaction constitutes a single violation for purposes of § 1026.52(b)(1)(ii). Furthermore, consistent with § 1026.56(j)(1)(i), no more than one violation for exceeding an account's credit limit can occur during a single billing cycle for purposes of § 1026.52(b)(1)(ii). However, § 1026.52(b)(2)(ii) does not prohibit a card issuer from imposing fees for exceeding the credit limit in consecutive billing cycles based on the same over-the-limit transaction to the extent permitted by § 1026.56(j)(1). In these circumstances, the second and third over-the-limit fees permitted by § 1026.56(j)(1) may be imposed pursuant to § 1026.52(b)(1)(ii)(B). *See* comment 52(b)(2)(ii)-1.

iii. *Examples.* The following examples illustrate the application of § 1026.52(b)(1)(ii)(A) and (b)(1)(ii)(B) with respect to credit card accounts under an open-end (not home-secured) consumer credit plan that are not charge card accounts. For purposes of these examples, assume that the billing cycles for the account begin on the first day of the month and end on the last day of the month and that the payment due date for the account is the twenty-fifth day of the month.

A. *Violations of same type (late payments).* A required minimum periodic payment of $50 is due on March 25. On March 26, a late payment has occurred because no payment has been received. Accordingly, consistent with § 1026.52(b)(1)(ii)(A), the card issuer imposes a $25 late payment fee on March 26. In order for the card issuer to impose a $35 late payment fee pursuant to § 1026.52(b)(1)(ii)(B), a second late payment must occur during the April, May, June, July, August, or September billing cycles.

1. The card issuer does not receive any payment during the March billing cycle. A required minimum periodic payment of $100 is due on April 25. On April 20, the card issuer receives a $50 payment. No further payment is received during the April billing cycle. Accordingly, consistent with § 1026.52(b)(1)(ii)(B), the card issuer may impose a $35 late payment fee on April 26. Furthermore, the card issuer may impose a $35 late payment fee for any late payment that occurs during the May, June, July, August, September, or October billing cycles.

2. Same facts as in paragraph A above. On March 30, the card issuer receives a $50 payment and the required minimum periodic payments for the April, May, June, July, August, and September billing cycles are received on or before the payment due date. A required minimum periodic payment of $60 is due on October 25. On October 26, a late payment has occurred because the required minimum periodic payment due on October 25 has not been received. However, because this late payment did not occur during the six billing cycles following the March billing cycle, § 1026.52(b)(1)(ii) only permits the card issuer to impose a late payment fee of $25.

B. *Violations of different types (late payment and over the credit limit).* The credit limit for an account is $1,000. Consistent with § 1026.56, the consumer has affirmatively consented to the payment of transactions that exceed the credit limit. A required minimum periodic payment of $30 is due on August 25. On August 26, a late payment has occurred because no payment has been received. Accordingly, consistent with § 1026.52(b)(1)(ii)(A), the card issuer imposes a $25 late payment fee on August 26. On August 30, the card issuer receives a $30 payment. On September 10, a transaction causes the account balance to increase to $1,150, which exceeds the account's $1,000 credit limit. On September 11, a second transaction increases the account balance to $1,350. On September 23, the card issuer receives the $50 required minimum periodic payment due on September 25, which reduces the account balance to $1,300. On September 30, the card issuer imposes a $25 over-the-limit fee, consistent with § 1026.52(b)(1)(ii)(A). On October 26, a late payment has occurred because the $60 required minimum periodic payment due on October 25 has not been received. Accordingly, consistent with § 1026.52(b)(1)(ii)(B), the card issuer imposes a $35 late payment fee on October 26.

C. *Violations of different types (late payment and returned payment).* A required minimum periodic payment of $50 is due on July 25. On July 26, a late payment has occurred because no payment has been received. Accordingly, consistent with § 1026.52(b)(1)(ii)(A), the card issuer imposes a $25 late payment fee on July 26. On July 30, the card issuer receives a $50 payment. A required minimum periodic payment of $50 is due on August 25. On August 24, a $50 payment is received. On August 27, the $50 payment is returned to the card issuer for insufficient funds. In these circumstances, § 1026.52(b)(2)(ii) permits the card issuer to impose either a late payment fee or a returned payment fee but not both because the late payment and the returned payment result from the same event or transaction. Accordingly, for purposes of § 1026.52(b)(1)(ii), the event or transaction constitutes a single violation. However, if the card issuer imposes a late payment fee, § 1026.52(b)(1)(ii)(B) permits the issuer to impose a fee of $35 because the late payment occurred during the six billing cycles following the July billing cycle. In contrast, if the card issuer imposes a returned payment fee, the amount of the fee may be no more than $25 pursuant to § 1026.52(b)(1)(ii)(A).

2. *Adjustments based on Consumer Price Index.* For purposes of § 1026.52(b)(1)(ii)(A) and (b)(1)(ii)(B), the Bureau shall calculate each year price level adjusted amounts using the Consumer Price Index in effect on June 1 of that year. When the cumulative change in the adjusted minimum value derived from applying the annual Consumer Price level to the current amounts in § 1026.52(b)(1)(ii)(A) and (b)(1)(ii)(B) has risen by a whole dollar, those amounts will be increased by $1.00. Similarly, when the cumulative change in the adjusted minimum value derived from applying the annual Consumer Price level to the current amounts in § 1026.52(b)(1)(ii)(A) and (b)(1)(ii)(B) has decreased by a whole dollar, those amounts will be decreased by $1.00. The Bureau will publish adjustments to the amounts in § 1026.52(b)(1)(ii)(A) and (b)(1)(ii)(B).

3. *Delinquent balance for charge card accounts.* Section 1026.52(b)(1)(ii)(C) provides that, when a charge card issuer that requires payment of outstanding balances in full at the end of each billing cycle has not received the required payment for two or more consecutive billing cycles, the card issuer may impose a late payment fee that does not exceed three percent of the delinquent balance. For purposes of § 1026.52(b)(1)(ii)(C), the delinquent balance is any previously billed amount that remains unpaid at the time the late payment fee is imposed pursuant to § 1026.52(b)(1)(ii)(C). Consistent with § 1026.52(b)(2)(ii), a charge card issuer that imposes a fee pursuant to § 1026.52(b)(1)(ii)(C) with respect to a late payment may not impose a fee pursuant to § 1026.52(b)(1)(ii)(B) with respect to the same late payment. The following examples illustrate the application of § 1026.52(b)(1)(ii)(C):

i. Assume that a charge card issuer requires payment of outstanding balances in full at the end of each billing cycle and that the billing cycles for the account begin on the first day of the month and end on the last day of the month. At the end of the June billing cycle, the account has a balance of $1,000. On July 5, the card issuer provides a periodic statement disclosing the $1,000 balance consistent with § 1026.7. During the July billing cycle, the account is used for $300 in transactions, increasing the balance to $1,300. At the end of the July billing cycle, no payment has been received and the card issuer imposes a $25 late payment fee consistent with § 1026.52(b)(1)(ii)(A). On August 5, the card issuer provides a periodic statement disclosing the $1,325 balance consistent with § 1026.7. During the August billing cycle, the account is used for $200 in transactions, increasing the balance to $1,525. At the end of the August billing cycle, no payment has been received. Consistent with § 1026.52(b)(1)(ii)(C), the card issuer may impose a late payment fee of $40, which is 3% of the $1,325 balance that was due at the end of the August billing cycle. Section 1026.52(b)(1)(ii)(C) does not permit the card issuer to include the $200 in transactions that occurred during the August billing cycle.

ii. Same facts as above except that, on August 25, a $100 payment is received. Consistent with § 1026.52(b)(1)(ii)(C), the card issuer may impose a late payment fee of $37, which is 3% of the unpaid portion of the $1,325 balance that was due at the end of the August billing cycle ($1,225).

iii. Same facts as in paragraph A above except that, on August 25, a $200 payment is received. Consistent with § 1026.52(b)(1)(ii)(C), the card issuer may impose a late payment fee of $34, which is 3% of the unpaid portion of the $1,325 balance that was due at the end of the August billing cycle ($1,125). In the alternative, the card issuer may impose a late payment fee of $35 consistent with § 1026.52(b)(1)(ii)(B). However, § 1026.52(b)(2)(ii) prohibits the card issuer from imposing both fees.

## 52(b)(2) Prohibited fees

1. *Relationship to § 1026.52(b)(1).* A card issuer does not comply with § 1026.52(b) if it imposes a fee that is inconsistent with the prohibitions in § 1026.52(b)(2). Thus, the prohibitions in § 1026.52(b)(2) apply even if a fee is consistent with § 1026.52(b)(1)(i) or (b)(1)(ii). For example, even if a card issuer has determined for purposes of § 1026.52(b)(1)(i) that a $27 fee represents a reasonable proportion of the total costs incurred by the card issuer as a result of a particular type of violation, § 1026.52(b)(2)(i) prohibits the card issuer from imposing that fee if the dollar amount associated with the violation is less than $27. Similarly, even if § 1026.52(b)(1)(ii) permits a card issuer to impose a $25 fee, § 1026.52(b)(2)(i) prohibits the card issuer from imposing that fee if the dollar amount associated with the violation is less than $25.

## 52(b)(2)(i) Fees That Exceed Dollar Amount Associated With Violation

1. *Late payment fees.* For purposes of § 1026.52(b)(2)(i), the dollar amount associated with a late payment is the amount of the required minimum

periodic payment due immediately prior to assessment of the late payment fee. Thus, § 1026.52(b)(2)(i)(A) prohibits a card issuer from imposing a late payment fee that exceeds the amount of that required minimum periodic payment. For example:

i. Assume that a $15 required minimum periodic payment is due on September 25. The card issuer does not receive any payment on or before September 25. On September 26, the card issuer imposes a late payment fee. For purposes of § 1026.52(b)(2)(i), the dollar amount associated with the late payment is the amount of the required minimum periodic payment due on September 25 ($15). Thus, under § 1026.52(b)(2)(i)(A), the amount of that fee cannot exceed $15 (even if a higher fee would be permitted under § 1026.52(b)(1)).

ii. Same facts as above except that, on September 25, the card issuer receives a $10 payment. No further payments are received. On September 26, the card issuer imposes a late payment fee. For purposes of § 1026.52(b)(2)(i), the dollar amount associated with the late payment is the full amount of the required minimum periodic payment due on September 25 ($15), rather than the unpaid portion of that payment ($5). Thus, under § 1026.52(b)(2)(i)(A), the amount of the late payment fee cannot exceed $15 (even if a higher fee would be permitted under § 1026.52(b)(1)).

iii. Assume that a $15 required minimum periodic payment is due on October 28 and the billing cycle for the account closes on October 31. The card issuer does not receive any payment on or before November 3. On November 3, the card issuer determines that the required minimum periodic payment due on November 28 is $50. On November 5, the card issuer imposes a late payment fee. For purposes of § 1026.52(b)(2)(i), the dollar amount associated with the late payment is the amount of the required minimum periodic payment due on October 28 ($15), rather than the amount of the required minimum periodic payment due on November 28 ($50). Thus, under § 1026.52(b)(2)(i)(A), the amount of that fee cannot exceed $15 (even if a higher fee would be permitted under § 1026.52(b)(1)).

2. *Returned payment fees.* For purposes of § 1026.52(b)(2)(i), the dollar amount associated with a returned payment is the amount of the required minimum periodic payment due immediately prior to the date on which the payment is returned to the card issuer. Thus, § 1026.52(b)(2)(i)(A) prohibits a card issuer from imposing a returned payment fee that exceeds the amount of that required minimum periodic payment. However, if a payment has been returned and is submitted again for payment by the card issuer, there is no additional dollar amount associated with a subsequent return of that payment and § 1026.52(b)(2)(i)(B) prohibits the card issuer from imposing an additional returned payment fee. For example:

i. Assume that the billing cycles for an account begin on the first day of the month and end on the last day of the month and that the payment due date is the twenty-fifth day of the month. A minimum payment of $15 is due on March 25. The card issuer receives a check for $100 on March 23, which is returned to the card issuer for insufficient funds on March 26. For purposes of § 1026.52(b)(2)(i), the dollar amount associated with the returned payment is the amount of the required minimum periodic payment due on March 25 ($15). Thus, § 1026.52(b)(2)(i)(A) prohibits the card issuer from imposing a returned payment fee that exceeds $15 (even if a higher fee would be permitted under § 1026.52(b)(1)). Furthermore, § 1026.52(b)(2)(ii) prohibits the card issuer from assessing both a late payment fee and a returned payment fee in these circumstances. *See* comment 52(b)(2)(ii)-1.

ii. Same facts as above except that the card issuer receives the $100 check on March 31 and the check is returned for insufficient funds on April 2. The minimum payment due on April 25 is $30. For purposes of § 1026.52(b)(2)(i), the dollar amount associated with the returned payment is the amount of the required minimum periodic payment due on March 25 ($15), rather than the amount of the required minimum periodic payment due on April 25 ($30). Thus, § 1026.52(b)(2)(i)(A) prohibits the card issuer from imposing a returned payment fee that exceeds $15 (even if a higher fee would be permitted under § 1026.52(b)(1)). Furthermore, § 1026.52(b)(2)(ii) prohibits the card issuer from assessing both a late payment fee and a returned payment fee in these circumstances. *See* comment 52(b)(2)(ii)-1.

iii. Same facts as paragraph i above except that, on March 28, the card issuer presents the $100 check for payment a second time. On April 1, the check is again returned for insufficient funds. Section 1026.52(b)(2)(i)(B) prohibits the card issuer from imposing a returned payment fee based on the return of the payment on April 1.

iv. Assume that the billing cycles for an account begin on the first day of the month and end on the last day of the month and that the payment due date is the twenty-fifth day of the month. A minimum payment of $15 is due on August 25. The card issuer receives a check for $15 on August 23, which is not returned. The card issuer receives a check for $50 on September 5, which is returned to the card issuer for insufficient funds on September 7. Section 1026.52(b)(2)(i)(B) does not prohibit the card issuer from imposing a returned payment fee in these circumstances. Instead, for purposes of § 1026.52(b)(2)(i), the dollar amount associated with the returned payment is the amount of the required minimum periodic payment due on August 25 ($15). Thus, § 1026.52(b)(2)(i)(A) prohibits the card issuer from imposing a returned payment fee that exceeds $15 (even if a higher fee would be permitted under § 1026.52(b)(1)).

3. *Over-the-limit fees.* For purposes of § 1026.52(b)(2)(i), the dollar amount associated with extensions of credit in excess of the credit limit for an account is the total amount of credit extended by the card issuer in excess of the credit limit during the billing cycle in which the over-the-limit fee is imposed. Thus, § 1026.52(b)(2)(i)(A) prohibits a card issuer from imposing an over-the-limit fee that exceeds that amount. Nothing in § 1026.52(b) permits a card issuer to impose an over-the-limit fee if imposition of the fee is inconsistent with § 1026.56. The following examples illustrate the application of § 1026.52(b)(2)(i)(A) to over-the-limit fees:

i. Assume that the billing cycles for a credit card account with a credit limit of $5,000 begin on the first day of the month and end on the last day of the month. Assume also that, consistent with § 1026.56, the consumer has affirmatively consented to the payment of transactions that exceed the credit limit. On March 1, the account has a $4,950 balance. On March 6, a $60 transaction is charged to the account, increasing the balance to $5,010. On March 25, a $5 transaction is charged to the account, increasing the balance to $5,015. On the last day of the billing cycle (March 31), the card issuer imposes an over-the-limit fee. For purposes of § 1026.52(b)(2)(i), the dollar amount associated with the extensions of credit in excess of the credit limit is the total amount of credit extended by the card issuer in excess of the credit limit during the March billing cycle ($15). Thus, § 1026.52(b)(2)(i)(A) prohibits the card issuer from imposing an over-the-limit fee that exceeds $15 (even if a higher fee would be permitted under § 1026.52(b)(1)).

ii. Same facts as above except that, on March 26, the card issuer receives a payment of $20, reducing the balance below the credit limit to $4,995. Nevertheless, for purposes of § 1026.52(b)(2)(i), the dollar amount associated with the extensions of credit in excess of the credit limit is the total amount of credit extended by the card issuer in excess of the credit limit during the March billing cycle ($15). Thus, consistent with § 1026.52(b)(2)(i)(A), the card issuer may impose an over-the-limit fee of $15.

4. *Declined access check fees.* For purposes of § 1026.52(b)(2)(i), the dollar amount associated with declining payment on a check that accesses a credit card account is the amount of the check. Thus, when a check that accesses a credit card account is declined, § 1026.52(b)(2)(i)(A) prohibits a card issuer from imposing a fee that exceeds the amount of that check. For example, assume that a check that accesses a credit card account is used as payment for a $50 transaction, but payment on the check is declined by the card issuer because the transaction would have exceeded the credit limit for the account. For purposes of § 1026.52(b)(2)(i), the dollar amount associated with the declined check is the amount of the check ($50). Thus, § 1026.52(b)(2)(i)(A) prohibits the card issuer from imposing a fee that exceeds $50. However, the amount of this fee must also comply with § 1026.52(b)(1)(i) or (b)(1)(ii).

5. *Inactivity fees.* Section 1026.52(b)(2)(i)(B)(2) prohibits a card issuer from imposing a fee with respect to a credit card account under an open-end (not home-secured) consumer credit plan based on inactivity on that account (including the consumer's failure to use the account for a particular number or

dollar amount of transactions or a particular type of transaction). For example, § 1026.52(b)(2)(i)(B)(2) prohibits a card issuer from imposing a $50 fee when a credit card account under an open-end (not home-secured) consumer credit plan is not used for at least $2,000 in purchases over the course of a year. Similarly, § 1026.52(b)(2)(i)(B)(2) prohibits a card issuer from imposing a $50 annual fee on all accounts of a particular type but waiving the fee on any account that is used for at least $2,000 in purchases over the course of a year if the card issuer promotes the waiver or rebate of the annual fee for purposes of § 1026.55(e). However, if the card issuer does not promote the waiver or rebate of the annual fee for purposes of § 1026.55(e), § 1026.52(b)(2)(i)(B)(2) does not prohibit a card issuer from considering account activity along with other factors when deciding whether to waive or rebate annual fees on individual accounts (such as in response to a consumer's request).

6. *Closed account fees.* Section 1026.52(b)(2)(i)(B)(3) prohibits a card issuer from imposing a fee based on the closure or termination of an account. For example, 1026.52(b)(2)(i)(B)(3) prohibits a card issuer from:

i. Imposing a one-time fee to consumers who close their accounts.

ii. Imposing a periodic fee (such as an annual fee, a monthly maintenance fee, or a closed account fee) after an account is closed or terminated if that fee was not imposed prior to closure or termination. This prohibition applies even if the fee was disclosed prior to closure or termination. *See also* comment 55(d)-1.

iii. Increasing a periodic fee (such as an annual fee or a monthly maintenance fee) after an account is closed or terminated. However, a card issuer is not prohibited from continuing to impose a periodic fee that was imposed before the account was closed or terminated.

### *52(b)(2)(ii) Multiple Fees Based on a Single Event or Transaction*

1. *Single event or transaction.* Section 1026.52(b)(2)(ii) prohibits a card issuer from imposing more than one fee for violating the terms or other requirements of an account based on a single event or transaction. If § 1026.56(j)(1) permits a card issuer to impose fees for exceeding the credit limit in consecutive billing cycles based on the same over-the-limit transaction, those fees are not based on a single event or transaction for purposes of § 1026.52(b)(2)(ii). The following examples illustrate the application of § 1026.52(b)(2)(ii). Assume for purposes of these examples that the billing cycles for a credit card account begin on the first day of the month and end on the last day of the month and that the payment due date for the account is the twenty-fifth day of the month.

i. Assume that the required minimum periodic payment due on March 25 is $20. On March 26, the card issuer has not received any payment and imposes a late payment fee. Consistent with §§ 1026.52(b)(1)(ii)(A) and (b)(2)(i), the card issuer may impose a $20 late payment fee on March 26. However, § 1026.52(b)(2)(ii) prohibits the card issuer from imposing an additional late payment fee if the $20 minimum payment has not been received by a subsequent date (such as March 31).

A. On April 3, the card issuer provides a periodic statement disclosing that a $70 required minimum periodic payment is due on April 25. This minimum payment includes the $20 minimum payment due on March 25 and the $20 late payment fee imposed on March 26. On April 20, the card issuer receives a $20 payment. No additional payments are received during the April billing cycle. Section 1026.52(b)(2)(ii) does not prohibit the card issuer from imposing a late payment fee based on the consumer's failure to make the $70 required minimum periodic payment on or before April 25. Accordingly, consistent with § 1026.52(b)(1)(ii)(B) and (b)(2)(i), the card issuer may impose a $35 late payment fee on April 26.

B. On April 3, the card issuer provides a periodic statement disclosing that a $20 required minimum periodic payment is due on April 25. This minimum payment does not include the $20 minimum payment due on March 25 or the $20 late payment fee imposed on March 26. On April 20, the card issuer receives a $20 payment. No additional payments are received during the April billing cycle. Because the card issuer has received the required minimum periodic payment due on April 25 and because § 1026.52(b)(2)(ii) prohibits the card issuer from imposing a second late payment fee based on the consumer's failure to make the $20 minimum payment due on March 25, the card issuer cannot impose a late payment fee in these circumstances.

ii. Assume that the required minimum periodic payment due on March 25 is $30.

A. On March 25, the card issuer receives a check for $50, but the check is returned for insufficient funds on March 27. Consistent with §§ 1026.52(b)(1)(ii)(A) and (b)(2)(i)(A), the card issuer may impose a late payment fee of $25 or a returned payment fee of $25. However, § 1026.52(b)(2)(ii) prohibits the card issuer from imposing both fees because those fees would be based on a single event or transaction.

B. Same facts as paragraph ii.A above except that that card issuer receives the $50 check on March 27 and the check is returned for insufficient funds on March 29. Consistent with §§ 1026.52(b)(1)(ii)(A) and (b)(2)(i)(A), the card issuer may impose a late payment fee of $25 or a returned payment fee of $25. However, § 1026.52(b)(2)(ii) prohibits the card issuer from imposing both fees because those fees would be based on a single event or transaction. If no payment is received on or before the next payment due date (April 25), § 1026.52(b)(2)(ii) does not prohibit the card issuer from imposing a late payment fee.

iii. Assume that the required minimum periodic payment due on July 25 is $30. On July 10, the card issuer receives a $50 payment, which is not returned. On July 20, the card issuer receives a $100 payment, which is returned for insufficient funds on July 24. Consistent with § 1026.52(b)(1)(ii)(A) and (b)(2)(i)(A), the card issuer may impose a returned payment fee of $25. Nothing in § 1026.52(b)(2)(ii) prohibits the imposition of this fee.

iv. Assume that the credit limit for an account is $1,000 and that, consistent with § 1026.56, the consumer has affirmatively consented to the payment of transactions that exceed the credit limit. On March 31, the balance on the account is $970 and the card issuer has not received the $35 required minimum periodic payment due on March 25. On that same date (March 31), a $70 transaction is charged to the account, which increases the balance to $1,040. Consistent with § 1026.52(b)(1)(ii)(A) and (b)(2)(i)(A), the card issuer may impose a late payment fee of $25 and an over-the-limit fee of $25. Section 1026.52(b)(2)(ii) does not prohibit the imposition of both fees because those fees are based on different events or transactions. No additional transactions are charged to the account during the March, April, or May billing cycles. If the account balance remains more than $35 above the credit limit on April 26, the card issuer may impose an over-the-limit fee of $35 pursuant to § 1026.52(b)(1)(ii)(B), to the extent consistent with § 1026.56(j)(1). Furthermore, if the account balance remains more than $35 above the credit limit on May 26, the card issuer may again impose an over-the-limit fee of $35 pursuant to § 1026.52(b)(1)(ii)(B), to the extent consistent with § 1026.56(j)(1). Thereafter, § 1026.56(j)(1) does not permit the card issuer to impose additional over-the-limit fees unless another over-the-limit transaction occurs. However, if an over-the-limit transaction occurs during the six billing cycles following the May billing cycle, the card issuer may impose an over-the-limit fee of $35 pursuant to § 1026.52(b)(1)(ii)(B).

v. Assume that the credit limit for an account is $5,000 and that, consistent with § 1026.56, the consumer has affirmatively consented to the payment of transactions that exceed the credit limit. On July 23, the balance on the account is $4,950. On July 24, the card issuer receives the $100 required minimum periodic payment due on July 25, reducing the balance to $4,850. On July 26, a $75 transaction is charged to the account, which increases the balance to $4,925. On July 27, the $100 payment is returned for insufficient funds, increasing the balance to $5,025. Consistent with §§ 1026.52(b)(1)(ii)(A) and (b)(2)(i)(A), the card issuer may impose a returned payment fee of $25 or an over-the-limit fee of $25. However, § 1026.52(b)(2)(ii) prohibits the card issuer from imposing both fees because those fees would be based on a single event or transaction.

vi. Assume that the required minimum periodic payment due on March 25 is $50. On March 20, the card issuer receives a check for $50, but the check is returned for insufficient funds on March 22. Consistent with §§ 1026.52(b)(1)(ii)(A) and (b)(2)(i)(A), the card issuer may impose a returned payment fee of $25. On March 25, the card issuer receives a second check for $50, but the check is returned for insufficient funds on March 27. Consistent with §§ 1026.52(b)(1)(ii)(A), (b)(1)(ii)(B), and (b)(2)(i)(A), the card issuer may impose a late payment fee of $25 or a returned payment fee of $35. However, § 1026.52(b)(2)(ii) prohibits the card issuer from imposing both fees because those fees would be based on a single event or transaction.

vii. Assume that the required minimum periodic payment due on February 25 is $100. On February 25, the card issuer receives a check for $100. On March 3, the card issuer provides a periodic statement disclosing that a $120 required minimum periodic payment is due on March 25. On March 4, the $100 check is returned to the card issuer for insufficient funds. Consistent with §§ 1026.52(b)(1)(ii)(A) and (b)(2)(i)(A), the card issuer may impose a late payment fee of $25 or a returned payment fee of $25 with respect to the $100 payment. However, § 1026.52(b)(2)(ii) prohibits the card issuer from imposing both fees because those fees would be based on a single event or transaction. On March 20, the card issuer receives a $120 check, which is not returned. No additional payments are received during the March billing cycle. Because the card issuer has received the required minimum periodic payment due on March 25 and because § 1026.52(b)(2)(ii) prohibits the card issuer from imposing a second fee based on the $100 payment that was returned for insufficient funds, the card issuer cannot impose a late payment fee in these circumstances.

[75 Fed. Reg. 7848 (Feb. 22, 2010); 75 Fed. Reg. 37,583 (June 29, 2010); 76 Fed. Reg. 23,021 (Apr. 25, 2011)]

## SECTION 1026.53 Allocation of Payments [§ 226.53]

1. *Required minimum periodic payment.* Section 1026.53 addresses the allocation of amounts paid by the consumer in excess of the minimum periodic payment required by the card issuer. Section 1026.53 does not limit or otherwise address the card issuer's ability to determine, consistent with applicable law and regulatory guidance, the amount of the required minimum periodic payment or how that payment is allocated. A card issuer may, but is not required to, allocate the required minimum periodic payment consistent with the requirements in § 1026.53 to the extent consistent with other applicable law or regulatory guidance.

2. *Applicable rates and balances.* Section 1026.53 permits a card issuer to allocate an amount paid by the consumer in excess of the required minimum periodic payment based on the annual percentage rates and balances on the day the preceding billing cycle ends, on the day the payment is credited to the account, or on any day in between those two dates. The day used by the card issuer to determine the applicable annual percentage rates and balances for purposes of § 1026.53 generally must be consistent from billing cycle to billing cycle, although the card issuer may adjust this day from time to time. For example:

i. Assume that the billing cycles for a credit card account start on the first day of the month and end on the last day of the month. On the date the March billing cycle ends (March 31), the account has a purchase balance of $500 at a promotional annual percentage rate of 5% and another purchase balance of $200 at a non-promotional annual percentage rate of 15%. On April 5, a $100 purchase to which the 15% rate applies is charged to the account. On April 15, the promotional rate expires and § 1026.55(b)(1) permits the card issuer to increase the rate that applies to the $500 balance from 5% to 18%. On April 25, the card issuer credits to the account $400 paid by the consumer in excess of the required minimum periodic payment. If the card issuer's practice is to allocate payments based on the rates and balances on the last day of the prior billing cycle, the card issuer would allocate the $400 payment to pay in full the $200 balance to which the 15% rate applied on March 31 and then allocate the remaining $200 to the $500 balance to which the 5% rate applied on March 31. In the alternative, if the card issuer's practice is to allocate payments based on the rates and balances on the day a payment is credited to the account, the card issuer would allocate the $400 payment to the $500 balance to which the 18% rate applied on April 25.

ii. Same facts as above except that, on April 25, the card issuer credits to the account $750 paid by the consumer in excess of the required minimum periodic payment. If the card issuer's practice is to allocate payments based on the rates and balances on the last day of the prior billing cycle, the card issuer would allocate the $750 payment to pay in full the $200 balance to which the 15% rate applied on March 31 and the $500 balance to which the 5% rate applied on March 31 and then allocate the remaining $50 to the $100 purchase made on April 5. In the alternative, if the card issuer's practice is to allocate payments based on the rates and balances on the day a payment is credited to the account, the card issuer would allocate the $750 payment to pay in full the $500 balance to which the 18% rate applied on April 25 and then allocate the remaining $250 to the $300 balance to which the 15% rate applied on April 25.

3. *Claims or defenses under § 1026.12(c) and billing error disputes under § 1026.13.* When a consumer has asserted a claim or defense against the card issuer pursuant to § 1026.12(c) or alleged a billing error under § 1026.13, the card issuer must apply the consumer's payment in a manner that avoids or minimizes any reduction in the amount subject to that claim, defense, or dispute. For example:

i. Assume that a credit card account has a $500 cash advance balance at an annual percentage rate of 25% and a $1,000 purchase balance at an annual percentage rate of 17%. Assume also that $200 of the cash advance balance is subject to a claim or defense under § 1026.12(c) or a billing error dispute under § 1026.13. If the consumer pays $900 in excess of the required minimum periodic payment, the card issuer must allocate $300 of the excess payment to pay in full the portion of the cash advance balance that is not subject to the claim, defense, or dispute and then allocate the remaining $600 to the $1,000 purchase balance.

ii. Same facts as above except that the consumer pays $1,400 in excess of the required minimum periodic payment. The card issuer must allocate $1,300 of the excess payment to pay in full the $300 cash advance balance that is not subject to the claim, defense, or dispute and the $1,000 purchase balance. If there are no new transactions or other amounts to which the remaining $100 can be allocated, the card issuer may apply that amount to the $200 cash advance balance that is subject to the claim, defense, or dispute. However, if the card issuer subsequently determines that a billing error occurred as asserted by the consumer, the card issuer must credit the account for the disputed amount and any related finance or other charges and send a correction notice consistent with § 1026.13(e).

4. *Balances with the same rate.* When the same annual percentage rate applies to more than one balance on an account and a different annual percentage rate applies to at least one other balance on that account, § 1026.53 generally does not require that any particular method be used when allocating among the balances with the same annual percentage rate. Under these circumstances, a card issuer may treat the balances with the same rate as a single balance or separate balances. *See* example in comment 53-5.iv. However, when a balance on a credit card account is subject to a deferred interest or similar program that provides that a consumer will not be obligated to pay interest that accrues on the balance if the balance is paid in full prior to the expiration of a specified period of time, that balance must be treated as a balance with an annual percentage rate of zero for purposes of § 1026.53 during that period of time. For example, if an account has a $1,000 purchase balance and a $2,000 balance that is subject to a deferred interest program that expires on July 1 and a 15% annual percentage rate applies to both, the balances must be treated as balances with different rates for purposes of § 1026.53 until July 1. In addition, unless the card issuer allocates amounts paid by the consumer in excess of the required minimum periodic payment in the manner requested by the consumer pursuant to § 1026.53(b)(1)(ii), § 1026.53(b)(1)(i) requires the card issuer to apply any excess payments first to the $1,000 purchase balance except during the last two billing cycles of the deferred interest period (when it must be applied first to any remaining portion of the $2,000 balance). *See* example in comment 53-5.v.

5. *Examples.* For purposes of the following examples, assume that none of the required minimum periodic payment is allocated to the balances discussed (unless otherwise stated).

i. Assume that a credit card account has a cash advance balance of $500 at an annual percentage rate of 20% and a purchase balance of $1,500 at an annual percentage rate of 15% and that the consumer pays $800 in excess of the required minimum periodic payment. Under § 1026.53(a), the card issuer must allocate $500 to pay off the cash advance balance and then allocate the remaining $300 to the purchase balance.

ii. Assume that a credit card account has a cash advance balance of $500 at an annual percentage rate of 20% and a purchase balance of $1,500 at an annual percentage rate of 15% and that the consumer pays $400 in excess of the required minimum periodic payment. Under § 1026.53(a), the card issuer must allocate the entire $400 to the cash advance balance.

iii. Assume that a credit card account has a cash advance balance of $100 at an annual percentage rate of 20%, a purchase balance of $300 at an annual percentage rate of 18%, and a $600 protected balance on which the 12% annual percentage rate cannot be increased pursuant to § 1026.55. If the consumer pays $500 in excess of the required minimum periodic payment, § 1026.53(a) requires the card issuer to allocate $100 to pay off the cash advance balance, $300 to pay off the purchase balance, and $100 to the protected balance.

iv. Assume that a credit card account has a cash advance balance of $500 at an annual percentage rate of 20%, a purchase balance of $1,000 at an annual percentage rate of 15%, and a transferred balance of $2,000 that was previously at a discounted annual percentage rate of 5% but is now at an annual percentage rate of 15%. Assume also that the consumer pays $800 in excess of the required minimum periodic payment. Under § 1026.53(a), the card issuer must allocate $500 to pay off the cash advance balance and allocate the remaining $300 among the purchase balance and the transferred balance in the manner the card issuer deems appropriate.

v. Assume that on January 1 a consumer uses a credit card account to make a $1,200 purchase subject to a deferred interest program under which interest accrues at an annual percentage rate of 15% but the consumer will not be obligated to pay that interest if the balance is paid in full on or before June 30. The billing cycles for this account begin on the first day of the month and end on the last day of the month. Each month from January through June, the consumer uses the account to make $200 in purchases that are not subject to the deferred interest program but are subject to the 15% rate.

A. Each month from February through June, the consumer pays $400 in excess of the required minimum periodic payment on the payment due date, which is the twenty-fifth of the month. Any interest that accrues on the purchases not subject to the deferred interest program is paid by the required minimum periodic payment. The card issuer does not accept requests from consumers regarding the allocation of excess payments pursuant to § 1026.53(b)(1)(ii). Thus, § 1026.53(b)(1)(i) requires the card issuer to allocate the $400 excess payments received on February 25, March 25, and April 25 consistent with § 1026.53(a). In other words, the card issuer must allocate those payments as follows: $200 to pay off the balance not subject to the deferred interest program (which is subject to the 15% rate) and the remaining $200 to the deferred interest balance (which is treated as a balance with a rate of zero). However, § 1026.53(b)(1)(i) requires the card issuer to allocate the entire $400 excess payment received on May 25 to the deferred interest balance. Similarly, § 1026.53(b)(1)(i) requires the card issuer to allocate the $400 excess payment received on June 25 as follows: $200 to the deferred interest balance (which pays that balance in full) and the remaining $200 to the balance not subject to the deferred interest program.

B. Same facts as above, except that the card issuer does accept requests from consumers regarding the allocation of excess payments pursuant to § 1026.53(b)(1)(ii). In addition, on April 25, the card issuer receives an excess payment of $800, which the consumer requests be allocated to pay off the $800 balance subject to the deferred interest program. Section 1026.53(b)(1)(ii) permits the card issuer to allocate the $800 excess payment in the manner requested by the consumer.

## *53(b) Special Rules*

1. *Deferred interest and similar programs.* Section 1026.53(b)(1) applies to deferred interest or similar programs under which the consumer is not obligated to pay interest that accrues on a balance if that balance is paid in full prior to the expiration of a specified period of time. For purposes of § 1026.53(b)(1), "deferred interest" has the same meaning as in § 1026.16(h)(2) and associated commentary. Section 1026.53(b)(1) applies regardless of whether the consumer is required to make payments with respect to that balance during the specified period. However, a grace period during which any credit extended may be repaid without incurring a finance charge due to a periodic interest rate is not a deferred interest or similar program for purposes of § 1026.53(b)(1). Similarly, a temporary annual percentage rate of zero percent that applies for a specified period of time consistent with § 1026.55(b)(1) is not a deferred interest or similar program for purposes of § 1026.53(b)(1) unless the consumer may be obligated to pay interest that accrues during the period if a balance is not paid in full prior to expiration of the period.

2. *Expiration of deferred interest or similar program during billing cycle.* For purposes of § 1026.53(b)(1)(i), a billing cycle does not constitute one of the two billing cycles immediately preceding expiration of a deferred interest or similar program if the expiration date for the program precedes the payment due date in that billing cycle. For example, assume that a credit card account has a balance subject to a deferred interest program that expires on June 15. Assume also that the billing cycles for the account begin on the first day of the month and end on the last day of the month and that the required minimum periodic payment is due on the twenty-fifth day of the month. The card issuer does not accept requests from consumers regarding the allocation of excess payments pursuant to § 1026.53(b)(1)(ii). Because the expiration date for the deferred interest program (June 15) precedes the due date in the June billing cycle (June 25), § 1026.53(b)(1)(i) requires the card issuer to allocate first to the deferred interest balance any amount paid by the consumer in excess of the required minimum periodic payment during the April and May billing cycles (as well as any amount paid by the consumer before June 15). However, if the deferred interest program expired on June 25 or on June 30 (or on any day in between), § 1026.53(b)(1)(i) would apply only to the May and June billing cycles.

3. *Consumer requests.*

i. *Generally.* Section 1026.53(b) does not require a card issuer to allocate amounts paid by the consumer in excess of the required minimum periodic payment in the manner requested by the consumer, provided that the card issuer instead allocates such amounts consistent with § 1026.53(a) or (b)(1)(i), as applicable. For example, a card issuer may decline consumer requests regarding payment allocation as a general matter or may decline such requests when a consumer does not comply with requirements set by the card issuer (such as submitting the request in writing or submitting the request prior to or contemporaneously with submission of the payment), provided that amounts paid by the consumer in excess of the required minimum periodic payment are allocated consistent with § 1026.53(a) or (b)(1)(i), as applicable. Similarly, a card issuer that accepts requests pursuant to § 1026.53(b)(1)(ii) or (b)(2) must allocate amounts paid by a consumer in excess of the required minimum periodic payment consistent with § 1026.53(a) or (b)(1)(i), as applicable, if the consumer does not submit a request. Furthermore, a card issuer that accepts requests pursuant to § 1026.53(b)(1)(ii) or (b)(2) must allocate consistent with § 1026.53(a) or (b)(1)(i), as applicable, if the consumer submits a request with which the card issuer cannot comply (such as a request that contains a mathematical error), unless the consumer submits an additional request with which the card issuer can comply.

ii. *Examples of consumer requests that satisfy § 1026.53(b)(1)(ii) or (b)(2).* A consumer has made a request for purposes of § 1026.53(b)(1)(ii) or (b)(2) if:

A. The consumer contacts the card issuer orally, electronically, or in writing and specifically requests that a payment or payments be allocated in a particular manner during the period of time that the deferred interest or similar program applies to a balance on the account or the period of time that a balance on the account is secured.

B. The consumer completes and submits to the card issuer a form or payment coupon provided by the card issuer for the purpose of requesting that a payment or payments be allocated in a particular manner during the period of time that the deferred interest or similar program applies to a balance on the account or the period of time that a balance on the account is secured.

C. The consumer contacts the card issuer orally, electronically, or in writing and specifically requests that a payment that the card issuer has previously allocated consistent with § 1026.53(a) or (b)(1)(i), as applicable, instead be allocated in a different manner.

iii. *Examples of consumer requests that do not satisfy § 1026.53(b)(1)(ii) or (b)(2).* A consumer has not made a request for purposes of § 1026.53(b)(1)(ii) or (b)(2) if:

A. The terms and conditions of the account agreement contain preprinted language stating that by applying to open an account, by using that account for transactions subject to a deferred interest or similar program, or by using the account to purchase property in which the card issuer holds a security interest the consumer requests that payments be allocated in a particular manner.

B. The card issuer's online application contains a preselected check box indicating that the consumer requests that payments be allocated in a particular manner and the consumer does not deselect the box.

C. The payment coupon provided by the card issuer contains preprinted language or a preselected check box stating that by submitting a payment the consumer requests that the payment be allocated in a particular manner.

D. The card issuer requires a consumer to accept a particular payment allocation method as a condition of using a deferred interest or similar program, purchasing property in which the card issuer holds a security interest, making a payment, or receiving account services or features.

[75 Fed. Reg. 7848 (Feb. 22, 2010); 76 Fed. Reg. 23,028, 23,029 (Apr. 25, 2011)]

## SECTION 1026.54 Limitations on the Imposition of Finance Charges [§ 226.54]

### *54(a) Limitations on imposing finance charges as a result of the loss of a grace period*

### *54(a)(1) General Rule*

1. *Eligibility for grace period.* Section 1026.54 prohibits the imposition of finance charges as a result of the loss of a grace period in certain specified circumstances. Section 1026.54 does not require the card issuer to provide a grace period. Furthermore, § 1026.54 does not prohibit the card issuer from placing limitations and conditions on a grace period (such as limiting application of the grace period to certain types of transactions or conditioning eligibility for the grace period on certain transactions being paid in full by a particular date), provided that such limitations and conditions are consistent with § 1026.5(b)(2)(ii)(B) and § 1026.54. Finally, § 1026.54 does not limit the imposition of finance charges with respect to a transaction when the consumer is not eligible for a grace period on that transaction at the end of the billing cycle in which the transaction occurred. For example:

i. Assume that the billing cycles for a credit card account begin on the first day of the month and end on the last day of the month and that the payment due date is the twenty-fifth day of the month. Assume also that, for purchases made during the current billing cycle (for purposes of this example, the June billing cycle), the grace period applies from the date of the purchase until the payment due date in the following billing cycle (July 25), subject to two conditions. First, the purchase balance at the end of the preceding billing cycle (the May billing cycle) must have been paid in full by the payment due date in the current billing cycle (June 25). Second, the purchase balance at the end of the current billing cycle (the June billing cycle) must be paid in full by the following payment due date (July 25). Finally, assume that the consumer was eligible for a grace period at the start of the June billing cycle (in other words, assume that the purchase balance for the April billing cycle was paid in full by May 25).

A. If the consumer pays the purchase balance for the May billing cycle in full by June 25, then at the end of the June billing cycle the consumer is eligible for a grace period with respect to purchases made during that billing cycle. Therefore, § 1026.54 limits the imposition of finance charges with respect to purchases made during the June billing cycle if the consumer does not pay the purchase balance for the June billing cycle in full by July 25. Specifically, § 1026.54(a)(1)(i) prohibits the card issuer from imposing finance charges based on the purchase balance at the end of the June billing cycle for days that precede the July billing cycle. Furthermore, § 1026.54(a)(1)(ii) prohibits the card issuer from imposing finance charges based on any portion of the balance at the end of the June billing cycle that was paid on or before July 25.

B. If the consumer does not pay the purchase balance for the May billing cycle in full by June 25, then the consumer is not eligible for a grace period with respect to purchases made during the June billing cycle at the end of that cycle. Therefore, § 1026.54 does not limit the imposition of finance charges with respect to purchases made during the June billing cycle regardless of whether the consumer pays the purchase balance for the June billing cycle in full by July 25.

ii. Same facts as above except that the card issuer places only one condition on the provision of a grace period for purchases made during the current billing cycle (the June billing cycle): that the purchase balance at the end of the current billing cycle (the June billing cycle) be paid in full by the following payment due date (July 25). In these circumstances, § 1026.54 applies to the same extent as discussed in paragraphs i.A and i.B above regardless of whether the purchase balance for the April billing cycle was paid in full by May 25.

2. *Definition of grace period.* For purposes of §§ 1026.5(b)(2)(ii)(B) and 1026.54, a grace period is a period within which any credit extended may be repaid without incurring a finance charge due to a periodic interest rate. The following are not grace periods for purposes of § 1026.54:

i. *Deferred interest and similar programs.* A deferred interest or similar promotional program under which a consumer will not be obligated to pay interest that accrues on a balance if that balance is paid in full prior to the expiration of a specified period of time is not a grace period for purposes of § 1026.54. Thus, § 1026.54 does not prohibit the card issuer from charging accrued interest to an account upon expiration of a deferred interest or similar program if the balance was not paid in full prior to expiration (to the extent consistent with § 1026.55 and other applicable law and regulatory guidance).

ii. *Waivers or rebates of interest.* As a general matter, a card issuer has not provided a grace period with respect to transactions for purposes of § 1026.54 if, on an individualized basis (such as in response to a consumer's request), the card issuer waives or rebates finance charges that have accrued on transactions. In addition, when a balance at the end of the preceding billing cycle is paid in full on or before the payment due date in the current billing cycle, a card issuer that waives or rebates trailing or residual interest accrued on that balance or any other transactions during the current billing cycle has not provided a grace period with respect to that balance or any other transactions for purposes of § 1026.54. However, if the terms of the account provide that all interest accrued on transactions will be waived or rebated if the balance for those transactions at the end of the billing cycle during which the transactions occurred is paid in full by the following payment due date, the card issuer is providing a grace period with respect to those transactions for purposes of § 1026.54. For example:

A. Assume that the billing cycles for a credit card account begin on the first day of the month and end on the last day of the month and that the payment due date is the twenty-fifth day of the month. On March 31, the balance on the account is $1,000 and the consumer is not eligible for a grace period with respect to that balance because the balance at the end of the prior billing cycle was not paid in full on March 25. On April 15, the consumer uses the account for a $500 purchase. On April 25, the card issuer receives a payment of $1,000. On May 3, the card issuer mails or delivers a periodic statement reflecting trailing or residual interest that accrued on the $1,000 balance from April 1 through April 24 as well as interest that accrued on the $500 purchase from April 15 through April 30. On May 10, the consumer requests that the trailing or residual interest charges be waived and the card issuer complies. By waiving these interest charges, the card issuer has not provided a grace period with respect to the $1,000 balance or the $500 purchase.

B. Same facts as in paragraph ii.A above except that the terms of the account state that trailing or residual interest will be waived in these circumstances or it is the card issuer's practice to waive trailing or residual interest in these circumstances. By waiving these interest charges, the card issuer has not provided a grace period with respect to the $1,000 balance or the $500 purchase.

C. Assume that the billing cycles for a credit card account begin on the first day of the month and end on the last day of the month and that the payment due date is the twenty-fifth day of the month. Assume also that, for purchases made during the current billing cycle (for purposes of this example, the June billing cycle), the terms of the account provide that interest accrued on those purchases from the date of the purchase until the payment due date in the following billing cycle (July 25) will be waived or rebated, subject to two conditions. First, the purchase balance at the end of the preceding billing cycle (the May billing cycle) must have been paid in full by the payment due date in the current billing cycle (June 25). Second, the purchase balance at the end of the current billing cycle (the June billing cycle) must be paid in full by the following payment due date (July 25). Under these circumstances, the card issuer is providing a grace period on purchases for purposes of § 1026.54. Therefore, assuming that the consumer was eligible for this grace period at the start of the June billing cycle (in other words, assuming that the purchase balance for the April billing cycle was paid in full by May 25) and assuming that the consumer pays the purchase balance for the May billing cycle in full by June 25, § 1026.54 applies to the imposition of finance charges with respect to purchases made during the June billing cycle. Specifically, § 1026.54(a)(1)(i) prohibits the card issuer from imposing finance charges based on the purchase balance at the end of the June billing cycle for days that precede the July billing cycle. Furthermore, § 1026.54(a)(1)(ii) prohibits the card issuer from imposing finance charges based on any portion of the balance at the end of the June billing cycle that was paid on or before July 25.

3. *Relationship to payment allocation requirements in § 1026.53.* Card issuers must comply with the payment allocation requirements in § 1026.53 even if doing so will result in the loss of a grace period.

4. *Prohibition on two-cycle balance computation method.* When a consumer ceases to be eligible for a grace period, § 1026.54(a)(1)(i) prohibits the card issuer from computing the finance charge using the two-cycle average daily balance computation method. This method calculates the finance charge using a balance that is the sum of the average daily balances for two billing cycles. The first balance is for the current billing cycle, and is calculated by adding the total balance (including or excluding new purchases and deducting payments and credits) for each day in the billing cycle, and then dividing by the number of days in the billing cycle. The second balance is for the preceding billing cycle.

5. *Prohibition on imposing finance charges on amounts paid within grace period.* When a balance on a credit card account is eligible for a grace period and the card issuer receives payment for some but not all of that balance prior to the expiration of the grace period, § 1026.54(a)(1)(ii) prohibits the card issuer from imposing finance charges on the portion of the balance paid. Card issuers are not required to use a particular method to comply with § 1026.54(a)(1)(ii). However, when § 1026.54(a)(1)(ii) applies, a card issuer is in compliance if, for example, it applies the consumer's payment to the balance subject to the grace period at the end of the preceding billing cycle (in a manner consistent with the payment allocation requirements in § 1026.53) and then calculates interest charges based on the amount of the balance that remains unpaid.

6. *Examples.* Assume that the annual percentage rate for purchases on a credit card account is 15%. The billing cycle starts on the first day of the month and ends on the last day of the month. The payment due date for the account is the twenty-fifth day of the month. For purchases made during the current billing cycle, the card issuer provides a grace period from the date of the purchase until the payment due date in the following billing cycle, provided that the purchase balance at the end of the current billing cycle is paid in full by the following payment due date. For purposes of this example, assume that none of the required minimum periodic payment is allocated to the balances discussed. During the March billing cycle, the following transactions are charged to the account: A $100 purchase on March 10, a $200 purchase on March 15, and a $300 purchase on March 20. On March 25, the purchase balance for the February billing cycle is paid in full. Thus, for purposes of § 1026.54, the consumer is eligible for a grace period on the March purchases. At the end of the March billing cycle (March 31), the consumer's total purchase balance is $600 and the consumer will not be charged interest on that balance if it is paid in full by the following due date (April 25).

i. On April 10, a $150 purchase is charged to the account. On April 25, the card issuer receives $500 in excess of the required minimum periodic payment. Section 1026.54(a)(1)(i) prohibits the card issuer from reaching back and charging interest on any of the March transactions from the date of the transaction through the end of the March billing cycle (March 31). In these circumstances, the card issuer may comply with § 1026.54(a)(1)(ii) by applying the $500 excess payment to the $600 purchase balance and then charging interest only on the portion of the $600 purchase balance that remains unpaid ($100) from the start of the April billing cycle (April 1) through the end of the April billing cycle (April 30). In addition, the card issuer may charge interest on the $150 purchase from the date of the transaction (April 10) through the end of the April billing cycle (April 31).

ii. Same facts as in paragraph 6 above except that, on March 18, a $250 cash advance is charged to the account at an annual percentage rate of 25%. The card issuer's grace period does not apply to cash advances, but the card issuer does provide a grace period on the March purchases because the purchase balance for the February billing cycle is paid in full on March 25. On April 25, the card issuer receives $600 in excess of the required minimum periodic payment. As required by § 1026.53, the card issuer allocates the $600 excess payment first to the balance with the highest annual percentage rate (the $250 cash advance balance). Although § 1026.54(a)(1)(i) prohibits the card issuer from charging interest on the March purchases based on days in the March billing cycle, the card issuer may charge interest on the $250 cash advance from the date of the transaction (March 18) through April 24. In these circumstances, the card issuer may comply with § 1026.54(a)(1)(ii) by applying the remainder of the excess payment ($350) to the $600 purchase balance and then charging interest only on the portion of the $600 purchase balance that remains unpaid ($250) from the start of the April billing cycle (April 1) through the end of the April billing cycle (April 30).

iii. Same facts as in paragraph 6 above except that the consumer does not pay the balance for the February billing cycle in full on March 25 and therefore is not eligible for a grace period on the March purchases. Under these circumstances, § 1026.54 does not apply and the card issuer may charge interest from the date of each transaction through April 24 and interest on the remaining $100 from April 25 through the end of the April billing cycle (April 25).

[75 Fed. Reg. 7848 (Feb. 22, 2010)]

## SECTION 1026.55 Limitations on Increasing Annual Percentage Rates, Fees, and Charges [§ 226.55]

### *55(a) General Rule*

1. *Increase in rate, fee, or charge.* Section 1026.55(a) prohibits card issuers from increasing an annual percentage rate or any fee or charge required to be disclosed under § 1026.6(b)(2)(ii),

(b)(2)(iii), or (b)(2)(xii) on a credit card account unless specifically permitted by one of the exceptions in § 1026.55(b). Except as specifically provided in § 1026.55(b), this prohibition applies even if the circumstances under which an increase will occur are disclosed in advance. The following examples illustrate the general application of § 1026.55(a) and (b). Additional examples illustrating specific aspects of the exceptions in § 1026.55(b) are provided in the commentary to those exceptions.

i. *Account-opening disclosure of non-variable rate for six months, then variable rate.* Assume that, at account opening on January 1 of year one, a card issuer discloses that the annual percentage rate for purchases is a non-variable rate of 15% and will apply for six months. The card issuer also discloses that, after six months, the annual percentage rate for purchases will be a variable rate that is currently 18% and will be adjusted quarterly by adding a margin of 8 percentage points to a publicly-available index not under the card issuer's control. Furthermore, the card issuer discloses that the annual percentage rate for cash advances is the same variable rate that will apply to purchases after six months. Finally, the card issuer discloses that, to the extent consistent with § 1026.55 and other applicable law, a non-variable penalty rate of 30% may apply if the consumer makes a late payment. The payment due date for the account is the twenty-fifth day of the month and the required minimum periodic payments are applied to accrued interest and fees but do not reduce the purchase and cash advance balances.

A. *Change-in-terms rate increase for new transactions after first year.* On January 15 of year one, the consumer uses the account to make a $2,000 purchase and a $500 cash advance. No other transactions are made on the account. At the start of each quarter, the card issuer may adjust the variable rate that applies to the $500 cash advance consistent with changes in the index (pursuant to § 1026.55(b)(2)). All required minimum periodic payments are received on or before the payment due date until May of year one, when the payment due on May 25 is received by the creditor on May 28. At this time, the card issuer is prohibited by § 1026.55 from increasing the rates that apply to the $2,000 purchase, the $500 cash advance, or future purchases and cash advances. Six months after account opening (July 1), the card issuer may begin to accrue interest on the $2,000 purchase at the previously-disclosed variable rate determined using an 8-point margin (pursuant to § 1026.55(b)(1)). Because no other increases in rate were disclosed at account opening, the card issuer may not subsequently increase the variable rate that applies to the $2,000 purchase and the $500 cash advance (except due to increases in the index pursuant to § 1026.55(b)(2)). On November 16, the card issuer provides a notice pursuant to § 1026.9(c) informing the consumer of a new variable rate that will apply on January 1 of year two (calculated using the same index and an increased margin of 12 percentage points). On December 15, the consumer makes a $100 purchase. On January 1 of year two, the card issuer may increase the margin used to determine the variable rate that applies to new purchases to 12 percentage points (pursuant to § 1026.55(b)(3)). However, § 1026.55(b)(3)(ii) does not permit the card issuer to apply the variable rate determined using the 12-point margin to the $2,000 purchase balance. Furthermore, although the $100 purchase occurred more than 14 days after provision of the § 1026.9(c) notice, § 1026.55(b)(3)(iii) does not permit the card issuer to apply the variable rate determined using the 12-point margin to that purchase because it occurred during the first year after account opening. On January 15 of year two, the consumer makes a $300 purchase. The card issuer may apply the variable rate determined using the 12-point margin to the $300 purchase.

B. *Account becomes more than 60 days delinquent during first year.* Same facts as above except that the required minimum periodic payment due on May 25 of year one is not received by the card issuer until July 30 of year one. Because the card issuer received the required minimum periodic payment more than 60 days after the payment due date, § 1026.55(b)(4) permits the card issuer to increase the annual percentage rate applicable to the $2,000 purchase, the $500 cash advance, and future purchases and cash advances. However, § 1026.55(b)(4)(i) requires the card issuer to first comply with the notice requirements in § 1026.9(g). Thus, if the card issuer provided a § 1026.9(g) notice on July 25 stating that all rates on the account would be increased to the 30% penalty rate, the card issuer could apply that rate beginning on September 8 to all balances and to future transactions.

ii. *Account-opening disclosure of non-variable rate for six months, then increased non-variable rate for six months, then variable rate; change-in-terms rate increase for new transactions after first year.* Assume that, at account opening on January 1 of year one, a card issuer discloses that the annual percentage rate for purchases will increase as follows: A non-variable rate of 5% for six months; a non-variable rate of 10% for an additional six months; and thereafter a variable rate that is currently 15% and will be adjusted monthly by adding a margin of 5 percentage points to a publicly-available index not under the card issuer's control. The payment due date for the account is the fifteenth day of the month and the required minimum periodic payments are applied to accrued interest and fees but do not reduce the purchase balance. On January 15 of year one, the consumer uses the account to make a $1,500 purchase. Six months after account opening (July 1), the card issuer may begin to accrue interest on the $1,500 purchase at the previously-disclosed 10% non-variable rate (pursuant to § 1026.55(b)(1)). On September 15, the consumer uses the account for a $700 purchase. On November 16, the card issuer provides a notice pursuant to § 1026.9(c) informing the consumer of a new variable rate that will apply on January 1 of year two (calculated using the same index and an increased margin of 8 percentage points). One year after account opening (January 1 of year two), the card issuer may begin accruing interest on the $2,200 purchase balance at the previously-disclosed variable rate determined using a 5-point margin (pursuant to § 1026.55(b)(1)). Section 1026.55 does not permit the card issuer to apply the variable rate determined using the 8-point margin to the $2,200 purchase balance. Furthermore, § 1026.55 does not permit the card issuer to subsequently increase the variable rate determined using the 5-point margin that applies to the $2,200 purchase balance (except due to increases in the index pursuant to § 1026.55(b)(2)). The card issuer may, however, apply the variable rate determined using the 8-point margin to purchases made on or after January 1 of year two (pursuant to § 1026.55(b)(3)).

iii. *Change-in-terms rate increase for new transactions after first year; penalty rate increase after first year.* Assume that, at account opening on January 1 of year one, a card issuer discloses that the annual percentage rate for purchases is a variable rate determined by adding a margin of 6 percentage points to a publicly-available index outside of the card issuer's control. The card issuer also discloses that, to the extent consistent with § 1026.55 and other applicable law, a non-variable penalty rate of 28% may apply if the consumer makes a late payment. The due date for the account is the fifteenth of the month. On May 30 of year two, the account has a purchase balance of $1,000. On May 31, the card issuer provides a notice pursuant to § 1026.9(c) informing the consumer of a new variable rate that will apply on July 16 for all purchases made on or after June 15 (calculated by using the same index and an increased margin of 8 percentage points). On June 14, the consumer makes a $500 purchase. On June 15, the consumer makes a $200 purchase. On July 1, the card issuer has not received the payment due on June 15 and provides the consumer with a notice pursuant to § 1026.9(g) stating that the 28% penalty rate will apply as of August 15 to all transactions made on or after July 16 and that, if the consumer becomes more than 60 days late, the penalty rate will apply to all balances on the account. On July 17, the consumer makes a $300 purchase.

A. *Account does not become more than 60 days delinquent.* The payment due on June 15 of year two is received on July 2. On July 16, § 1026.55(b)(3)(ii) permits the card issuer to apply the variable rate determined using the 8-point margin disclosed in the § 1026.9(c) notice to the $200 purchase made on June 15 but does not permit the card issuer to apply this rate to the $1,500 purchase balance. On August 15, § 1026.55(b)(3)(ii) permits the card issuer to apply the 28% penalty rate disclosed at account opening and in the § 1026.9(g) notice to the $300 purchase made on July 17 but does not permit the card issuer to apply this rate to the $1,500 purchase balance (which remains at the variable rate determined using the 6-point margin) or the $200 purchase (which remains at the variable rate determined using the 8-point margin).

B. *Account becomes more than 60 days delinquent after provision of § 1026.9(g) notice.* Same facts as above except the payment due on June 15 of year two has not been received by August 15. Section 1026.55(b)(4) permits the card issuer to apply the 28% penalty rate to the $1,500 purchase balance and the $200 purchase because it has not received the June 15 payment within 60 days after the due date. However, in order to do so, § 1026.55(b)(4)(i) requires the card issuer to first provide an additional notice pursuant to § 1026.9(g). This notice must be sent no earlier than August 15, which is the first day the account became more than 60 days' delinquent. If the notice is sent on August 15, the card issuer may begin accruing interest on the $1,500 purchase balance and the $200 purchase at the 28% penalty rate beginning on September 29.

2. *Relationship to grace period.* Nothing in § 1026.55 prohibits a card issuer from assessing interest due to the loss of a grace period to the extent consistent with § 1026.5(b)(2)(ii)(B) and § 1026.54. In addition, a card issuer has not reduced an annual percentage rate on a credit card account for purposes of § 1026.55 if the card issuer does not charge interest on a balance or a portion thereof based on a payment received prior to the expiration of a grace period. For example, if the annual percentage rate for purchases on an account is 15% but the card issuer does not charge any interest on a $500 purchase balance because that balance was paid in full prior to the expiration of the grace period, the card issuer has not reduced the 15% purchase rate to 0% for purposes of § 1026.55.

## *55(b) Exceptions*

1. *Exceptions not mutually exclusive.* A card issuer generally may increase an annual percentage rate or a fee or charge required to be disclosed under § 1026.6(b)(2)(ii), (b)(2)(iii), or (b)(2)(xii) pursuant to an exception set forth in § 1026.55(b) even if that increase would not be permitted under a different exception. For example, although a card issuer cannot increase an annual percentage rate pursuant to § 1026.55(b)(1) unless that rate is provided for a specified period of at least six months, the card issuer may increase an annual percentage rate during a specified period due to an increase in an index consistent with § 1026.55(b)(2). Similarly, although § 1026.55(b)(3) does not permit a card issuer to increase an annual percentage rate during the first year after account opening, the card issuer may increase the rate during the first year after account opening pursuant to § 1026.55(b)(4) if the required minimum periodic payment is not received within 60 days after the due date. However, if § 1026.55(b)(4)(ii) requires a card issuer to decrease the rate, fee, or charge that applies to a balance while the account is subject to a workout or temporary hardship arrangement or subject to 50 U.S.C. app. 527 or a similar Federal or state statute or regulation, the card issuer may not impose a higher rate, fee, or charge on that balance pursuant to § 1026.55(b)(5) or (b)(6) upon completion or failure of the arrangement or once 50 U.S.C. app. 527 or the similar Federal or state statute or regulation no longer applies. For example, assume that, on January 1, the annual percentage rate that applies to a $1,000 balance is increased from 12% to 30% pursuant to § 1026.55(b)(4). On February 1, the rate on that balance is decreased from 30% to 15% consistent with § 1026.55(b)(5) as a part of a workout or temporary hardship arrangement. On July 1, § 1026.55(b)(4)(ii) requires the card issuer to reduce the rate that applies to any remaining portion of the $1,000 balance from 15% to 12%. If the consumer subsequently completes or fails to comply with the terms of the workout or temporary hardship arrangement, the card issuer may not increase the 12% rate that applies to any remaining portion of the $1,000 balance pursuant to § 1026.55(b)(5).

2. *Relationship between exceptions in § 1026.55(b) and notice requirements in § 1026.9.* Nothing in § 1026.55 alters the requirements in § 1026.9(c) and (g) that creditors provide written notice at least 45 days prior to the effective date of certain increases in annual percentage rates, fees, and charges.

i. *14-day rule in § 1026.55(b)(3)(ii).* Although § 1026.55(b)(3)(ii) permits a card issuer that discloses an increased rate pursuant to § 1026.9(c) or (g) to apply that rate to transactions that occur more than 14 days after provision of the notice, the card issuer cannot begin to accrue interest at the increased rate until that increase goes into effect, consistent with § 1026.9(c) or (g). For example, if on May 1 a card issuer provides a notice pursuant to § 1026.9(c) stating that a rate will increase from 15% to 18% on June 15, § 1026.55(b)(3)(ii) permits the card issuer to apply the 18% rate to transactions that occur on or after May 16. However, neither § 1026.55 nor § 1026.9(c) permits the card issuer to begin accruing interest at the 18% rate on those transactions until June 15. See additional examples in comment 55(b)(3)-4.

ii. *Mid-cycle increases; application of balance computation methods.* Once an increased rate has gone into effect, the card issuer cannot calculate interest charges based on that increased rate for days prior to the effective date. Assume that, in the example in paragraph i above, the billing cycles for the account begin on the first day of the month and end on the last day of the month. If, for example, the card issuer uses the average daily balance computation method, it cannot apply the 18% rate to the average daily balance for the entire June billing cycle because that rate did not become effective until June 15. However, the card issuer could apply the 15% rate to the average daily balance from June 1 through June 14 and the 18% rate to the average daily balance from June 15 through June 30. Similarly, if the card issuer that uses the daily balance computation method, it could apply the 15% rate to the daily balance for each day from June 1 through June 14 and the 18% rate to the daily balance for each day from June 15 through June 30.

iii. *Mid-cycle increases; delayed implementation of increase.* If § 1026.55(b) and § 1026.9(b), (c), or (g) permit a card issuer to apply an increased annual percentage rate, fee, or charge on a date that is not the first day of a billing cycle, the card issuer may delay application of the increased rate, fee, or charge until the first day of the following billing cycle without relinquishing the ability to apply that rate, fee, or charge. Thus, in the example in paragraphs i and ii above, the card issuer could delay application of the 18% rate until the start of the next billing cycle (April 1) without relinquishing its ability to apply that rate under § 1026.55(b)(3). Similarly, assume that, at account opening on January 1, a card issuer discloses that a non-variable annual percentage rate of 10% will apply to purchases for six months and a non-variable rate of 15% will apply thereafter. The first day of each billing cycle for the account is the fifteenth of the month. If the six-month period expires on July 1, the card issuer may delay application of the 15% rate until the start of the next billing cycle (July 15) without relinquishing its ability to apply that rate under § 1026.55(b)(1).

3. *Application of a lower rate, fee, or charge.* Nothing in § 1026.55 prohibits a card issuer from lowering an annual percentage rate or a fee or charge required to be disclosed under § 1026.6(b)(2)(ii), (b)(2)(iii), or (b)(2)(xii). However, a card issuer that does so cannot subsequently increase the rate, fee, or charge unless permitted by one of the exceptions in § 1026.55(b). The following examples illustrate the application of the rule:

i. *Application of lower rate during first year.* Assume that a card issuer discloses at account opening on January 1 of year one that a non-variable annual percentage rate of 15% will apply to purchases. The card issuer also discloses that, to the extent consistent with § 1026.55 and other applicable law, a non-variable penalty rate of 30% may apply if the consumer's required minimum periodic payment is received after the payment due date, which is the tenth of the month. The required minimum periodic payments are applied to accrued interest and fees but do not reduce the purchase balance.

A. *Temporary rate returns to standard rate at expiration.* On September 30 of year one, the account has a purchase balance of $1,400 at the 15% rate. On October 1, the card issuer provides a notice pursuant to § 1026.9(c) informing the consumer that the rate for new purchases will decrease to a non-variable rate of 5% for six months (from October 1 through March 31 of year two) and that, beginning on April 1 of year two, the rate for purchases will increase to the 15% non-variable rate disclosed at account opening. The card issuer does not apply the 5% rate to the $1,400 purchase balance. On October 14 of year one, the consumer makes a $300 purchase at the 5% rate. On January 15 of year two, the consumer makes a $150 purchase at the 5% rate. On April 1 of year two, the card issuer may begin accruing interest on the $300 purchase and the $150 purchase at 15% as disclosed in the § 1026.9(c) notice (pursuant to § 1026.55(b)(1)).

B. *Penalty rate increase.* Same facts as above except that the required minimum periodic payment due on November 10 of year one is not received until November 15. Section 1026.55 does not permit the card issuer to increase any annual percentage rate on the account at this time. The card issuer may apply the 30% penalty rate to new transactions beginning on April 1 of year two pursuant to § 1026.55(b)(3) by providing a § 1026.9(g) notice informing the consumer of this increase no later than February 14 of year two. The card issuer may not, however, apply the 30% penalty rate to the $1,400 purchase balance as of September 30 of year one, the $300 purchase on October 15 of year one, or the $150 purchase on January 15 of year two.

ii. *Application of lower rate at end of first year.* Assume that, at account opening on January 1 of year one, a card issuer discloses that a non-variable annual percentage rate of 15% will apply to purchases for one year and discloses that, after the first year, the card issuer will apply a variable rate that is currently 20% and is determined by adding a margin of 10 percentage points to a publicly-available index not under the card issuer's control. On December 31 of year one, the account has a purchase balance of $3,000.

A. *Notice of extension of existing temporary rate provided consistent with § 1026.55(b)(1)(i).* On December 15 of year one, the card issuer provides a notice pursuant to § 1026.9(c) informing the consumer that the existing 15% rate will continue to apply until July 1 of year two. The notice further states that, on July 1 of year two, the variable rate disclosed at account opening will apply. On July 1 of year two, § 1026.55(b)(1) permits the card issuer to apply that variable rate to any remaining portion of the $3,000 balance and to new transactions.

B. *Notice of new temporary rate provided consistent with § 1026.55(b)(1)(i).* On December 15 of year one, the card issuer provides a notice pursuant to § 1026.9(c) informing the consumer of a new variable rate that will apply on January 1 of year two that is lower than the variable rate disclosed at account opening. The new variable rate is calculated using the same index and a reduced margin of 8 percentage points. The notice further states that, on July 1 of year two, the margin will increase to the margin disclosed at account opening (10 percentage points). On July 1 of year two, § 1026.55(b)(1) permits the card issuer to increase the margin used to determine the variable rate that applies to new purchases to 10 percentage points and to apply that rate to any remaining portion of the $3,000 purchase balance.

C. *No notice provided.* Same facts as in paragraph ii.B above except that the card issuer does not send a notice on December 15 of year one. Instead, on January 1 of year two, the card issuer lowers the margin used to determine the variable rate to 8 percentage points and applies that rate to the $3,000 purchase balance and to new purchases. Section 1026.9 does not require advance notice in these circumstances. However, unless the account becomes more than 60 days' delinquent, § 1026.55 does not permit the card issuer to subsequently increase the rate that applies to the $3,000 purchase balance except due to increases in the index (pursuant to § 1026.55(b)(2)).

iii. *Application of lower rate after first year.* Assume that a card issuer discloses at account opening on January 1 of year one that a non-variable annual percentage rate of 10% will apply to purchases for one year, after which that rate will increase to a non-variable rate of 15%. The card issuer also discloses that, to the extent consistent with § 1026.55 and other applicable law, a non-variable penalty rate of 30% may apply if the consumer's required minimum periodic payment is received after the payment due date, which is the tenth of the month. The required minimum periodic payments are applied to accrued interest and fees but do not reduce the purchase balance.

A. *Effect of 14-day period.* On June 30 of year two, the account has a purchase balance of $1,000 at the 15% rate. On July 1, the card issuer provides a notice pursuant to § 1026.9(c) informing the consumer that the rate for new purchases will decrease to a non-variable rate of 5% for six months (from July 1 through December 31 of year two) and that, beginning on January 1 of year three, the rate for purchases will increase to a non-variable rate of 17%. On July 15 of year two, the consumer makes a $200 purchase. On July 16, the consumer makes a $100 purchase. On January 1 of year three, the card issuer may begin accruing interest on the $100 purchase at 17% (pursuant to § 1026.55(b)(1)). However, § 1026.55(b)(1)(ii)(B) does not permit the card issuer to apply the 17% rate to the $200 purchase because that transaction occurred within 14 days after provision of the § 1026.9(c) notice. Instead, the card issuer may apply the 15% rate that applied to purchases prior to provision of the § 1026.9(c) notice. In addition, if the card issuer applied the 5% rate to the $1,000 purchase balance, § 1026.55(b)(ii)(A) would not permit the card issuer to increase the rate that applies to that balance on January 1 of year three to a rate that is higher than 15% that previously applied to the balance.

B. *Penalty rate increase.* Same facts as above except that the required minimum periodic payment due on August 25 is received on August 30. At this time, § 1026.55 does not permit the card issuer to increase the annual percentage rates that apply to the $1,000 purchase balance, the $200 purchase, or the $100 purchase. Instead, those rates can only be increased as discussed in paragraph iii.A above. However, if the card issuer provides a notice pursuant to § 1026.9(c) or (g) on September 1, § 1026.55(b)(3) permits the card issuer to apply an increased rate (such as the 17% purchase rate or the 30% penalty rate) to transactions that occur on or after September 16 beginning on October 16.

C. *Application of lower temporary rate during specified period.* Same facts as in paragraph iii above. On June 30 of year two, the account has a purchase balance of $1,000 at the 15% non-variable rate. On July 1, the card issuer provides a notice pursuant to § 1026.9(c) informing the consumer that the rate for the $1,000 balance and new purchases will decrease to a non-variable rate of 12% for six months (from July 1 through December 31 of year two) and that, beginning on January 1 of year three, the rate for purchases will increase to a variable rate that is currently 20% and is determined by adding a margin of 10 percentage points to a publicly-available index not under the card issuer's control. On August 15 of year two, the consumer makes a $500 purchase. On October 1, the card issuer provides another notice pursuant to § 1026.9(c) informing the consumer that the rate for the $1,000 balance, the $500 purchase, and new purchases will decrease to a non-variable rate of 5% for six months (from October 1 of year two through March 31 of year three) and that, beginning on April 1 of year three, the rate for purchases will increase to a variable rate that is currently 23% and is determined by adding a margin of 13 percentage points to the previously-disclosed index. On November 15 of year two, the consumer makes a $300 purchase. On April 1 of year three, § 1026.55 permits the card issuer to begin accruing interest using the following rates for any remaining portion of the following balances: The 15% non-variable rate for the $1,000 balance; the variable rate determined using the 10-point margin for the $500 purchase; and the variable rate determined using the 13-point margin for the $300 purchase.

4. *Date on which transaction occurred.* When a transaction occurred for purposes of § 1026.55 is generally determined by the date of the transaction. However, if a transaction that occurred within 14 days after provision of a § 1026.9(c) or (g) notice is

not charged to the account prior to the effective date of the change or increase, the card issuer may treat the transaction as occurring more than 14 days after provision of the notice for purposes of § 1026.55. See example in comment 55(b)(3)-4.iii.B. In addition, when a merchant places a "hold" on the available credit on an account for an estimated transaction amount because the actual transaction amount will not be known until a later date, the date of the transaction for purposes of § 1026.55 is the date on which the card issuer receives the actual transaction amount from the merchant. See example in comment 55(b)(3)-4.iii.A.

5. *Category of transactions.* For purposes of § 1026.55, a "category of transactions" is a type or group of transactions to which an annual percentage rate applies that is different than the annual percentage rate that applies to other transactions. Similarly, a type or group of transactions is a "category of transactions" for purposes of § 1026.55 if a fee or charge required to be disclosed under § 1026.6(b)(2)(ii), (b)(2)(iii), or (b)(2)(xii) applies to those transactions that is different than the fee or charge that applies to other transactions. For example, purchase transactions, cash advance transactions, and balance transfer transactions are separate categories of transactions for purposes of § 1026.55 if a card issuer applies different annual percentage rates to each. Furthermore, if, for example, the card issuer applies different annual percentage rates to different types of purchase transactions (such as one rate for purchases of gasoline or purchases over $100 and a different rate for all other purchases), each type constitutes a separate category of transactions for purposes of § 1026.55.

## 55(b)(1) Temporary rate, fee, or charge exception

1. *Relationship to § 1026.9(c)(2)(v)(B).* A card issuer that has complied with the disclosure requirements in § 1026.9(c)(2)(v)(B) has also complied with the disclosure requirements in § 1026.55(b)(1)(i).

2. *Period of six months or longer.* A temporary annual percentage rate, fee, or charge must apply for a specified period of six months or longer before a card issuer can increase that rate, fee, or charge pursuant to § 1026.55(b)(1). The specified period must expire no less than six months after the date on which the card issuer provides the consumer with the disclosures required by § 1026.55(b)(1)(i) or, if later, the date on which the account can be used for transactions to which the temporary rate, fee, or charge applies. Section 1026.55(b)(1) does not prohibit a card issuer from limiting the application of a temporary annual percentage rate, fee, or charge to a particular category of transactions (such as to balance transfers or to purchases over $100). However, in circumstances where the card issuer limits application of the temporary rate, fee, or charge to a single transaction, the specified period must expire no less than six months after the date on which that transaction occurred. The following examples illustrate the application of § 1026.55(b)(1):

i. Assume that on January 1 a card issuer offers a consumer a 5% annual percentage rate on purchases made during the months of January through June. A 15% rate will apply thereafter. On February 15, a $500 purchase is charged to the account. On June 15, a $200 purchase is charged to the account. On July 1, the card issuer may begin accruing interest at the 15% rate on the $500 purchase and the $200 purchase (pursuant to § 1026.55(b)(1)).

ii. Same facts as above except that on January 1 the card issuer offered the 5% rate on purchases beginning in the month of February. Section 1026.55(b)(1) would not permit the card issuer to begin accruing interest at the 15% rate on the $500 purchase and the $200 purchase until August 1.

iii. Assume that on October 31 of year one the annual percentage rate for purchases is 17%. On November 1, the card issuer offers the consumer a 0% rate for six months on purchases made during the months of November and December. The 17% rate will apply thereafter. On November 15, a $500 purchase is charged to the account. On December 15, a $300 purchase is charged to the account. On January 15 of year two, a $150 purchase is charged to the account. Section 1026.55(b)(1) would not permit the card issuer to begin accruing interest at the 17% rate on the $500 purchase and the $300 purchase until May 1 of year two. However, the card issuer may accrue interest at the 17% rate on the $150 purchase beginning on January 15 of year two.

iv. Assume that on June 1 of year one a card issuer offers a consumer a 0% annual percentage rate for six months on the purchase of an appliance. An 18% rate will apply thereafter. On September 1, a $5,000 transaction is charged to the account for the purchase of an appliance. Section 1026.55(b)(1) would not permit the card issuer to begin accruing interest at the 18% rate on the $5,000 transaction until March 1 of year two.

v. Assume that on May 31 of year one the annual percentage rate for purchases is 15%. On June 1, the card issuer offers the consumer a 5% rate for six months on a balance transfer of at least $1,000. The 15% rate will apply thereafter. On June 15, a $3,000 balance is transferred to the account. On July 15, a $200 purchase is charged to the account. Section 1026.55(b)(1) would not permit the card issuer to begin accruing interest at the 15% rate on the $3,000 transferred balance until December 15. However, the card issuer may accrue interest at the 15% rate on the $200 purchase beginning on July 15.

vi. Same facts as in paragraph v above except that the card issuer offers the 5% rate for six months on all balance transfers of at least $1,000 during the month of June and a $2,000 balance is transferred to the account on June 30 (in addition to the $3,000 balance transfer on June 15). Because the 5% rate is not limited to a particular transaction, § 1026.55(b)(1) permits the card issuer to begin accruing interest on the $3,000 and $2,000 transferred balances on December 1.

vii. Assume that a card issuer discloses at account opening on January 1 of year one that the annual fee for the account is $0 until January 1 of year two, when the fee will increase to $50. On January 1 of year two, the card issuer may impose the $50 annual fee. However, the issuer must also comply with the notice requirements in § 1026.9(e).

viii. Assume that a card issuer discloses at account opening on January 1 of year one that the monthly maintenance fee for the account is $0 until July 1 of year one, when the fee will increase to $10. Beginning on July 1 of year one, the card issuer may impose the $10 monthly maintenance fee (to the extent consistent with § 1026.52(a)).

3. *Deferred interest and similar promotional programs.*

i. *Application of § 1026.55.* The general prohibition in § 1026.55(a) applies to the imposition of accrued interest upon the expiration of a deferred interest or similar promotional program under which the consumer is not obligated to pay interest that accrues on a balance if that balance is paid in full prior to the expiration of a specified period of time. However, the exception in § 1026.55(b)(1) also applies to these programs, provided that the specified period is six months or longer and that, prior to the commencement of the period, the card issuer discloses the length of the period and the rate at which interest will accrue on the balance subject to the deferred interest or similar program if that balance is not paid in full prior to expiration of the period. *See* comment 9(c)(2)(v)-9. For purposes of § 1026.55, "deferred interest" has the same meaning as in § 1026.16(h)(2) and associated commentary.

ii. *Examples.*

A. *Deferred interest offer at account opening.* Assume that, at account opening on January 1 of year one, the card issuer discloses the following with respect to a deferred interest program: "No interest on purchases made in January of year one if paid in full by December 31 of year one. If the balance is not paid in full by that date, interest will be imposed from the transaction date at a rate of 20%." On January 15 of year one, the consumer makes a purchase of $2,000. No other transactions are made on the account. The terms of the deferred interest program require the consumer to make minimum periodic payments with respect to the deferred interest balance, and the payment due on April 1 is not received until April 10. Section 1026.55 does not permit the card issuer to charge to the account interest that has accrued on the $2,000 purchase at this time. Furthermore, if the consumer pays the $2,000 purchase in full on or before December 31 of year one, § 1026.55 does not permit the card issuer to charge to the account any interest that has accrued on that purchase. If, however, the $2,000 purchase has not been paid in full by January 1 of year two, § 1026.55(b)(1) permits the card issuer to charge to the account the interest accrued on that purchase at the 20% rate during year one (to the extent consistent with other applicable law).

B. *Deferred interest offer after account opening.* Assume that a card issuer discloses at account opening on January 1 of year one that the rate that applies to purchases is a variable annual percentage rate that is currently 18% and will be adjusted quarterly by adding a margin of 8 percentage points to a publicly-available index not under the card issuer's control. The card issuer also discloses that, to the extent consistent with § 1026.55 and other applicable law, a non-variable penalty rate of 30% may apply if the consumer's required minimum periodic payment is received after the payment due date, which is the first of the month. On June 30 of year two, the consumer uses the account for a $1,000 purchase in response to an offer of a deferred interest program. Under the terms of this program, interest on the purchase will accrue at the variable rate for purchases but the consumer will not be obligated to pay that interest if the purchase is paid in full by December 31 of year three. The terms of the deferred interest program require the consumer to make minimum periodic payments with respect to the deferred interest balance, and the payment due on September 1 of year two is not received until September 6. Section 1026.55 does not permit the card issuer to charge to the account interest that has accrued on the $1,000 purchase at this time. Furthermore, if the consumer pays the $1,000 purchase in full on or before December 31 of year three, § 1026.55 does not permit the card issuer to charge to the account any interest that has accrued on that purchase. On December 31 of year three, the $1,000 purchase has been paid in full. Under these circumstances, the card issuer may not charge any interest accrued on the $1,000 purchase.

C. *Application of § 1026.55(b)(4) to deferred interest programs.* Same facts as in paragraph ii.B above except that, on November 2 of year two, the card issuer has not received the required minimum periodic payments due on September 1, October 1, or November 1 of year two and sends a § 1026.9(c) or (g) notice stating that interest accrued on the $1,000 purchase since June 30 of year two will be charged to the account on December 17 of year two and thereafter interest will be charged on the $1,000 purchase consistent with the variable rate for purchases. On December 17 of year two, § 1026.55(b)(4) permits the card issuer to charge to the account interest accrued on the $1,000 purchase since June 30 of year two and § 1026.55(b)(3) permits the card issuer to begin charging interest on the $1,000 purchase consistent with the variable rate for purchases. However, if the card issuer receives the required minimum periodic payments due on January 1, February 1, March 1, April 1, May 1, and June 1 of year three, § 1026.55(b)(4)(ii) requires the card issuer to cease charging the account for interest on the $1,000 purchase no later than the first day of the next billing cycle. *See* comment 55(b)(4)-3.iii. However, § 1026.55(b)(4)(ii) does not require the card issuer to waive or credit the account for interest accrued on the $1,000 purchase since June 30 of year two. If the $1,000 purchase is paid in full on December 31 of year three, the card issuer is not permitted to charge to the account interest accrued on the $1,000 purchase after June 1 of year three.

4. *Contingent or discretionary increases.* Section 1026.55(b)(1) permits a card issuer to increase a temporary annual percentage rate, fee, or charge upon the expiration of a specified period of time. However, § 1026.55(b)(1) does not permit a card issuer to apply an increased rate, fee, or charge that is contingent on a particular event or occurrence or that may be applied at the card issuer's discretion. The following examples illustrate rate increases that are not permitted by § 1026.55:

i. Assume that a card issuer discloses at account opening on January 1 of year one that a non-variable annual percentage rate of 15% applies to purchases but that all rates on an account may be increased to a non-variable penalty rate of 30% if a consumer's required minimum periodic payment is received after the payment due date, which is the fifteenth of the month. On March 1, the account has a $2,000 purchase balance. The payment due on March 15 is not received until March 20. Section 1026.55 does not permit the card issuer to apply the 30% penalty rate to the $2,000 purchase balance. However, pursuant to § 1026.55(b)(3), the card issuer could provide a § 1026.9(c) or (g) notice on or before November 16 informing the consumer that, on January 1 of year two, the 30% rate (or a different rate) will apply to new transactions.

ii. Assume that a card issuer discloses at account opening on January 1 of year one that a non-variable annual percentage rate of 5% applies to transferred balances but that this rate will increase to a non-variable rate of 18% if the consumer does not use the account for at least $200 in purchases each billing cycle. On July 1, the consumer transfers a balance of $4,000 to the account. During the October billing cycle, the consumer uses the account for $150 in purchases. Section 1026.55 does not permit the card issuer to apply the 18% rate to the $4,000 transferred balance or the $150 in purchases. However, pursuant to § 1026.55(b)(3), the card issuer could provide a § 1026.9(c) or (g) notice on or before November 16 informing the consumer that, on January 1 of year two, the 18% rate (or a different rate) will apply to new transactions.

iii. Assume that a card issuer discloses at account opening on January 1 of year one that the annual fee for the account is $10 but may be increased to $50 if a consumer's required minimum periodic payment is received after the payment due date, which is the fifteenth of the month. The payment due on July 15 is not received until July 23. Section 1026.55 does not permit the card issuer to impose the $50 annual fee at this time. Furthermore, § 1026.55(b)(3) does not permit the card issuer to increase the $10 annual fee during the first year after account opening. However, § 1026.55(b)(3) does permit the card issuer to impose the $50 fee (or a different fee) on January 1 of year two if, on or before November 16 of year one, the issuer informs the consumer of the increased fee consistent with § 1026.9(c) and the consumer does not reject that increase pursuant to § 1026.9(h).

iv. Assume that a card issuer discloses at account opening on January 1 of year one that the annual fee for a credit card account under an open-end (not home-secured) consumer credit plan is $0 but may be increased to $100 if the consumer's balance in a deposit account provided by the card issuer or its affiliate or subsidiary falls below $5,000. On June 1 of year one, the balance on the deposit account is $4,500. Section 1026.55 does not permit the card issuer to impose the $100 annual fee at this time. Furthermore, § 1026.55(b)(3) does not permit the card issuer to increase the $0 annual fee during the first year after account opening. However, § 1026.55(b)(3) does permit the card issuer to impose the $100 fee (or a different fee) on January 1 of year two if, on or before November 16 of year one, the issuer informs the consumer of the increased fee consistent with § 1026.9(c) and the consumer does not reject that increase pursuant to § 1026.9(h).

5. *Application of increased fees and charges.* Section 1026.55(b)(1)(ii) limits the ability of a card issuer to apply an increased fee or charge to certain transactions. However, to the extent consistent with § 1026.55(b)(3), (c), and (d), a card issuer generally is not prohibited from increasing a fee or charge that applies to the account as a whole. *See* comments 55(c)(1)-3 and 55(d)-1.

### *55(b)(2) Variable rate exception*

1. *Increases due to increase in index.* Section 1026.55(b)(2) provides that an annual percentage rate that varies according to an index that is not under the card issuer's control and is available to the general public may be increased due to an increase in the index. This section does not permit a card issuer to increase the rate by changing the method used to determine a rate that varies with an index (such as by increasing the margin), even if that change will not result in an immediate increase. However, from time to time, a card issuer may change the day on which index values are measured to determine changes to the rate.

2. *Index not under card issuer's control.* A card issuer may increase a variable annual percentage rate pursuant to § 1026.55(b)(2) only if the increase

is based on an index or indices outside the card issuer's control. For purposes of § 1026.55(b)(2), an index is under the card issuer's control if:

i. *The index is the card issuer's own prime rate or cost of funds.* A card issuer is permitted, however, to use a published prime rate, such as that in the *Wall Street Journal*, even if the card issuer's own prime rate is one of several rates used to establish the published rate.

ii. *The variable rate is subject to a fixed minimum rate or similar requirement that does not permit the variable rate to decrease consistent with reductions in the index.* A card issuer is permitted, however, to establish a fixed maximum rate that does not permit the variable rate to increase consistent with increases in an index. For example, assume that, under the terms of an account, a variable rate will be adjusted monthly by adding a margin of 5 percentage points to a publicly-available index. When the account is opened, the index is 10% and therefore the variable rate is 15%. If the terms of the account provide that the variable rate will not decrease below 15% even if the index decreases below 10%, the card issuer cannot increase that rate pursuant to § 1026.55(b)(2). However, § 1026.55(b)(2) does not prohibit the card issuer from providing in the terms of the account that the variable rate will not increase above a certain amount (such as 20%).

iii. *The variable rate can be calculated based on any index value during a period of time (such as the 90 days preceding the last day of a billing cycle).* A card issuer is permitted, however, to provide in the terms of the account that the variable rate will be calculated based on the average index value during a specified period. In the alternative, the card issuer is permitted to provide in the terms of the account that the variable rate will be calculated based on the index value on a specific day (such as the last day of a billing cycle). For example, assume that the terms of an account provide that a variable rate will be adjusted at the beginning of each quarter by adding a margin of 7 percentage points to a publicly-available index. At account opening at the beginning of the first quarter, the variable rate is 17% (based on an index value of 10%). During the first quarter, the index varies between 9.8% and 10.5% with an average value of 10.1%. On the last day of the first quarter, the index value is 10.2%. At the beginning of the second quarter, § 1026.55(b)(2) does not permit the card issuer to increase the variable rate to 17.5% based on the first quarter's maximum index value of 10.5%. However, if the terms of the account provide that the variable rate will be calculated based on the average index value during the prior quarter, § 1026.55(b)(2) permits the card issuer to increase the variable rate to 17.1% (based on the average index value of 10.1% during the first quarter). In the alternative, if the terms of the account provide that the variable rate will be calculated based on the index value on the last day of the prior quarter, § 1026.55(b)(2) permits the card issuer to increase the variable rate to 17.2% (based on the index value of 10.2% on the last day of the first quarter).

3. *Publicly available.* The index or indices must be available to the public. A publicly-available index need not be published in a newspaper, but it must be one the consumer can independently obtain (by telephone, for example) and use to verify the annual percentage rate applied to the account.

4. *Changing a non-variable rate to a variable rate.* Section 1026.55 generally prohibits a card issuer from changing a non-variable annual percentage rate to a variable annual percentage rate because such a change can result in an increase. However, a card issuer may change a non-variable rate to a variable rate to the extent permitted by one of the exceptions in § 1026.55(b). For example, § 1026.55(b)(1) permits a card issuer to change a non-variable rate to a variable rate upon expiration of a specified period of time. Similarly, following the first year after the account is opened, § 1026.55(b)(3) permits a card issuer to change a non-variable rate to a variable rate with respect to new transactions (after complying with the notice requirements in § 1026.9(b), (c) or (g)).

5. *Changing a variable rate to a non-variable rate.* Nothing in § 1026.55 prohibits a card issuer from changing a variable annual percentage rate to an equal or lower non-variable rate. Whether the non-variable rate is equal to or lower than the variable rate is determined at the time the card issuer provides the notice required by § 1026.9(c). For example, assume that on March 1 a variable annual percentage rate that is currently 15% applies to a balance of $2,000 and the card issuer sends a notice pursuant to § 1026.9(c) informing the consumer that the variable rate will be converted to a non-variable rate of 14% effective April 15. On April 15, the card issuer may apply the 14% non-variable rate to the $2,000 balance and to new transactions even if the variable rate on March 2 or a later date was less than 14%.

6. *Substitution of index.* A card issuer may change the index and margin used to determine the annual percentage rate under § 1026.55(b)(2) if the original index becomes unavailable, as long as historical fluctuations in the original and replacement indices were substantially similar, and as long as the replacement index and margin will produce a rate similar to the rate that was in effect at the time the original index became unavailable. If the replacement index is newly established and therefore does not have any rate history, it may be used if it produces a rate substantially similar to the rate in effect when the original index became unavailable.

### *55(b)(3) Advance notice exception*

1. *Relationship to § 1026.9(h).* A card issuer may not increase a fee or charge required to be disclosed under § 1026.6(b)(2)(ii), (b)(2)(iii), or (b)(2)(xii) pursuant to § 1026.55(b)(3) if the consumer has rejected the increased fee or charge pursuant to § 1026.9(h).

2. *Notice provided pursuant to § 1026.9(b) and (c).* If an increased annual percentage rate, fee, or charge is disclosed pursuant to both § 1026.9(b) and (c), that rate, fee, or charge may only be applied to transactions that occur more than 14 days after provision of the § 1026.9(c) notice as provided in § 1026.55(b)(3)(ii).

3. *Account opening.*

i. *Multiple accounts with same card issuer.* When a consumer has a credit card account with a card issuer and the consumer opens a new credit card account with the same card issuer (or its affiliate or subsidiary), the opening of the new account constitutes the opening of a credit card account for purposes of § 1026.55(b)(3)(iii) if, more than 30 days after the new account is opened, the consumer has the option to obtain additional extensions of credit on each account. For example, assume that, on January 1 of year one, a consumer opens a credit card account with a card issuer. On July 1 of year one, the consumer opens a second credit card account with that card issuer. On July 15, a $1,000 balance is transferred from the first account to the second account. The opening of the second account constitutes the opening of a credit card account for purposes of § 1026.55(b)(3)(iii) so long as, on August 1, the consumer has the option to engage in transactions using either account. Under these circumstances, the card issuer could not increase an annual percentage rate or a fee or charge required to be disclosed under § 1026.6(b)(2)(ii), (b)(2)(iii), or (b)(2)(xii) on the second account pursuant to § 1026.55(b)(3) until July 1 of year two (which is one year after the second account was opened).

ii. *Substitution, replacement or consolidation.*

A. *Generally.* A credit card account has not been opened for purposes of § 1026.55(b)(3)(iii) when a credit card account issued by a card issuer is substituted, replaced, or consolidated with another credit card account issued by the same card issuer (or its affiliate or subsidiary). Circumstances in which a credit card account has not been opened for purposes of § 1026.55(b)(3)(iii) include when:

*1.* A retail credit card account is replaced with a cobranded general purpose credit card account that can be used at a wider number of merchants;

*2.* A credit card account is replaced with another credit card account offering different features;

*3.* A credit card account is consolidated or combined with one or more other credit card accounts into a single credit card account; or

*4.* A credit card account acquired through merger or acquisition is replaced with a credit card account issued by the acquiring card issuer.

B. *Limitation.* A card issuer that replaces or consolidates a credit card account with another credit card account issued by the card issuer (or its affiliate or subsidiary) may not increase an annual percentage rate or a fee or charge required to be disclosed under § 1026.6(b)(2)(ii), (b)(2)(iii), or (b)(2)(xii) in a manner otherwise prohibited by § 1026.55. For example, assume that, on January 1 of year one, a consumer opens a credit card account with an annual percentage rate of 15% for purchases. On July 1 of year one, the account is replaced with a credit card account that offers different features (such as rewards on purchases). Under these circumstances, § 1026.55(b)(3)(iii) prohibits the card issuer from increasing the annual percentage rate for new purchases to a rate that is higher than 15% pursuant to § 1026.55(b)(3) until January 1 of year two (which is one year after the first account was opened).

4. *Examples.*

i. *Change-in-terms rate increase; temporary rate increase; 14-day period.* Assume that an account is opened on January 1 of year one. On March 14 of year two, the account has a purchase balance of $2,000 at a non-variable annual percentage rate of 15%. On March 15, the card issuer provides a notice pursuant to § 1026.9(c) informing the consumer that the rate for new purchases will increase to a non-variable rate of 18% on May 1. The notice further states that the 18% rate will apply for six months (until November 1) and that thereafter the card issuer will apply a variable rate that is currently 22% and is determined by adding a margin of 12 percentage points to a publicly-available index that is not under the card issuer's control. The fourteenth day after provision of the notice is March 29 and, on that date, the consumer makes a $200 purchase. On March 30, the consumer makes a $1,000 purchase. On May 1, the card issuer may begin accruing interest at 18% on the $1,000 purchase made on March 30 (pursuant to § 1026.55(b)(3)). Section 1026.55(b)(3)(ii) does not permit the card issuer to apply the 18% rate to the $2,200 purchase balance as of March 29 because that balance reflects transactions that occurred prior to or within 14 days after the provision of the § 1026.9(c) notice. After six months (November 2), the card issuer may begin accruing interest on any remaining portion of the $1,000 purchase at the previously-disclosed variable rate determined using the 12-point margin (pursuant to § 1026.55(b)(1) and (b)(3)).

ii. *Checks that access an account.* Assume that a card issuer discloses at account opening on January 1 of year one that the annual percentage rate that applies to cash advances is a variable rate that is currently 24% and will be adjusted quarterly by adding a margin of 14 percentage points to a publicly available index not under the card issuer's control. On July 1 of year two, the card issuer provides checks that access the account and, pursuant to § 1026.9(b)(3)(i)(A), discloses that a promotional rate of 15% will apply to credit extended by use of the checks until January 1 of year three, after which the cash advance rate determined using the 14-point margin will apply. On July 9 of year two, the consumer uses one of the checks to pay for a $500 transaction. Beginning on January 1 of year three, the card issuer may apply the cash advance rate determined using the 14-point margin to any remaining portion of the $500 transaction (pursuant to § 1026.55(b)(1) and (b)(3)).

iii. *Hold on available credit; 14-day period.* Assume that an account is opened on January 1 of year one. On September 14 of year two, the account has a purchase balance of $2,000 at a non-variable annual percentage rate of 17%. On September 15, the card issuer provides a notice pursuant to § 1026.9(c) informing the consumer that the rate for new purchases will increase to a non-variable rate of 20% on October 30. The fourteenth day after provision of the notice is September 29. On September 28, the consumer uses the credit card to check into a hotel and the hotel obtains authorization for a $1,000 hold on the account to ensure there is adequate available credit to cover the anticipated cost of the stay.

A. The consumer checks out of the hotel on October 2. The actual cost of the stay is $1,100 because of additional incidental costs. On October 2, the hotel charges the $1,100 transaction to the account. For purposes of § 1026.55(b)(3), the transaction occurred on October 2. Therefore, on October 30, § 1026.55(b)(3) permits the card issuer to apply the 20% rate to new purchases and to the $1,100 transaction. However, § 1026.55(b)(3)(ii) does not permit the card issuer to apply the 20% rate to any remaining portion of the $2,000 purchase balance.

B. Same facts as above except that the consumer checks out of the hotel on September 29. The actual cost of the stay is $250, but the hotel does not charge this amount to the account until November 1. For purposes of § 1026.55(b)(3), the card issuer may treat the transaction as occurring more than 14 days after provision of the § 1026.9(c) notice (*i.e.*, after September 29). Accordingly, the card issuer may apply the 20% rate to the $250 transaction.

5. *Application of increased fees and charges. See* comment 55(c)(1)-3.

6. *Delayed implementation of increase.* Section 1026.55(b)(3)(iii) does not prohibit a card issuer from notifying a consumer of an increase in an annual percentage rate, fee, or charge consistent with § 1026.9(b), (c), or (g). However, § 1026.55(b)(3)(iii) does prohibit application of an increased rate, fee, or charge during the first year after the account is opened, while the account is closed, or while the card issuer does not permit the consumer to use the account for new transactions. If § 1026.9(b), (c), or (g) permits a card issuer to apply an increased rate, fee, or charge on a particular date and the account is closed on that date or the card issuer does not permit the consumer to use the account for new transactions on that date, the card issuer may delay application of the increased rate, fee, or charge until the first day of the following billing cycle without relinquishing the ability to apply that rate, fee, or charge (assuming the increase is otherwise consistent with § 1026.55). *See* examples in comment 55(b)-2.iii. However, if the account is closed or the card issuer does not permit the consumer to use the account for new transactions on the first day of the following billing cycle, then the card issuer must provide a new notice of the increased rate, fee, or charge consistent with § 1026.9(b), (c), or (g).

7. *Date on which account may first be used by consumer to engage in transactions.* For purposes of § 1026.55(b)(3)(iii), an account is considered open no earlier than the date on which the account may first be used by the consumer to engage in transactions. An account is considered open for purposes of § 1026.55(b)(3)(iii) on any date that the card issuer may consider the account open for purposes of § 1026.52(a)(1). *See* comment 52(a)(1)-4.

## *55(b)(4) Delinquency exception*

1. *Receipt of required minimum periodic payment within 60 days of due date.* Section 1026.55(b)(4) applies when a card issuer has not received the consumer's required minimum periodic payment within 60 days after the due date for that payment. In order to satisfy this condition, a card issuer that requires monthly minimum payments generally must not have received two consecutive required minimum periodic payments. Whether a required minimum periodic payment has been received for purposes of § 1026.55(b)(4) depends on whether the amount received is equal to or more than the first outstanding required minimum periodic payment. For example, assume that the required minimum periodic payments for a credit card account are due on the fifteenth day of the month. On May 13, the card issuer has not received the $50 required minimum periodic payment due on March 15 or the $150 required minimum periodic payment due on April 15. The sixtieth day after the March 15 payment due date is May 14. If the card issuer receives a $50 payment on May 14, § 1026.55(b)(4) does not apply because the payment is equal to the required minimum periodic payment due on March 15 and therefore the account is not more than 60 days delinquent. However, if the card issuer instead received a $40 payment on May 14, § 1026.55(b)(4) would apply beginning on May 15 because the payment is less than the required minimum periodic payment due on March 15. Furthermore, if the card issuer received the $50 payment on May 15, § 1026.55(b)(4) would apply because the card issuer did not receive the required minimum periodic payment due on March 15 within 60 days after the due date for that payment.

2. *Relationship to § 1026.9(g)(3)(i)(B).* A card issuer that has complied with the disclosure requirements in § 1026.9(g)(3)(i)(B) has also complied with the disclosure requirements in § 1026.55(b)(4)(i).

3. *Reduction in rate pursuant to § 1026.55(b)(4)(ii).* Section 1026.55(b)(4)(ii) provides that, if the card issuer receives six consecutive required mini-

mum periodic payments on or before the payment due date beginning with the first payment due following the effective date of the increase, the card issuer must reduce any annual percentage rate, fee, or charge increased pursuant to § 1026.55(b)(4) to the annual percentage rate, fee, or charge that applied prior to the increase with respect to transactions that occurred prior to or within 14 days after provision of the § 1026.9(c) or (g) notice.

i. *Six consecutive payments immediately following effective date of increase.* Section 1026.55(b)(4)(ii) does not apply if the card issuer does not receive six consecutive required minimum periodic payments on or before the payment due date beginning with the payment due immediately following the effective date of the increase, even if, at some later point in time, the card issuer receives six consecutive required minimum periodic payments on or before the payment due date.

ii. *Rate, fee, or charge that does not exceed rate, fee, or charge that applied before increase.* Although § 1026.55(b)(4)(ii) requires the card issuer to reduce an annual percentage rate, fee, or charge increased pursuant to § 1026.55(b)(4) to the annual percentage rate, fee, or charge that applied prior to the increase, this provision does not prohibit the card issuer from applying an increased annual percentage rate, fee, or charge consistent with any of the other exceptions in § 1026.55(b). For example, if a temporary rate applied prior to the § 1026.55(b)(4) increase and the temporary rate expired before a reduction in rate pursuant to § 1026.55(b)(4)(ii), the card issuer may apply an increased rate to the extent consistent with § 1026.55(b)(1). Similarly, if a variable rate applied prior to the § 1026.55(b)(4) increase, the card issuer may apply any increase in that variable rate to the extent consistent with § 1026.55(b)(2).

iii. *Delayed implementation of reduction.* If § 1026.55(b)(4)(ii) requires a card issuer to reduce an annual percentage rate, fee, or charge on a date that is not the first day of a billing cycle, the card issuer may delay application of the reduced rate, fee, or charge until the first day of the following billing cycle.

iv. *Examples.* The following examples illustrate the application of § 1026.55(b)(4)(ii):

A. Assume that the billing cycles for an account begin on the first day of the month and end on the last day of the month and that the required minimum periodic payments are due on the fifteenth day of the month. Assume also that the account has a $5,000 purchase balance to which a non-variable annual percentage rate of 15% applies. On May 16 of year one, the card issuer has not received the required minimum periodic payments due on the fifteenth day of March, April, or May and sends a § 1026.9(c) or (g) notice stating that the annual percentage rate applicable to the $5,000 balance and to new transactions will increase to 28% effective July 1. On July 1, § 1026.55(b)(4) permits the card issuer to apply the 28% rate to the $5,000 balance and to new transactions. The card issuer receives the required minimum periodic payments due on the fifteenth day of July, August, September, October, November, and December. On January 1 of year two, § 1026.55(b)(4)(ii) requires the card issuer to reduce the rate that applies to any remaining portion of the $5,000 balance to 15%. The card issuer is not required to reduce the rate that applies to any transactions that occurred on or after May 31 (which is the fifteenth day after provision of the § 1026.9(c) or (g) notice).

B. Same facts as paragraph iv.A above except that the 15% rate that applied to the $5,000 balance prior to the § 1026.55(b)(4) increase was scheduled to increase to 20% on August 1 of year one (pursuant to § 1026.55(b)(1)). On January 1 of year two, § 1026.55(b)(4)(ii) requires the card issuer to reduce the rate that applies to any remaining portion of the $5,000 balance to 20%.

C. Same facts as paragraph iv.A above except that the 15% rate that applied to the $5,000 balance prior to the § 1026.55(b)(4) increase was scheduled to increase to 20% on March 1 of year two (pursuant to § 1026.55(b)(1)). On January 1 of year two, § 1026.55(b)(4)(ii) requires the card issuer to reduce the rate that applies to any remaining portion of the $5,000 balance to 15%.

D. Same facts as paragraph iv.A above except that the 15% rate that applied to the $5,000 balance prior to the § 1026.55(b)(4) increase was a variable rate that was determined by adding a margin of 10 percentage points to a publicly-available index not under the card issuer's control (consistent with § 1026.55(b)(2)). On January 1 of year two, § 1026.55(b)(4)(ii) requires the card issuer to reduce the rate that applies to any remaining portion of the $5,000 balance to the variable rate determined using the 10-point margin.

E. For an example of the application of § 1026.55(b)(4)(ii) to deferred interest or similar programs, see comment 55(b)(1)-3.ii.C.

### *55(b)(5) Workout and temporary hardship arrangement exception*

1. *Scope of exception.* Nothing in § 1026.55(b)(5) permits a card issuer to alter the requirements of § 1026.55 pursuant to a workout or temporary hardship arrangement. For example, a card issuer cannot increase an annual percentage rate or a fee or charge required to be disclosed under § 1026.6(b)(2)(ii), (b)(2)(iii), or (b)(2)(xii) pursuant to a workout or temporary hardship arrangement unless otherwise permitted by § 1026.55. In addition, a card issuer cannot require the consumer to make payments with respect to a protected balance that exceed the payments permitted under § 1026.55(c).

2. *Relationship to § 1026.9(c)(2)(v)(D).* A card issuer that has complied with the disclosure requirements in § 1026.9(c)(2)(v)(D) has also complied with the disclosure requirements in § 1026.55(b)(5)(i). See comment 9(c)(2)(v)-10. Thus, although the disclosures required by § 1026.55(b)(5)(i) must generally be provided in writing prior to commencement of the arrangement, a card issuer may comply with § 1026.55(b)(5)(i) by complying with § 1026.9(c)(2)(v)(D), which states that the disclosure of the terms of the arrangement may be made orally by telephone, provided that the card issuer mails or delivers a written disclosure of the terms of the arrangement to the consumer as soon as reasonably practicable after the oral disclosure is provided.

3. *Rate, fee, or charge that does not exceed rate, fee, or charge that applied before workout or temporary hardship arrangement.* Upon the completion or failure of a workout or temporary hardship arrangement, § 1026.55(b)(5)(ii) prohibits the card issuer from applying to any transactions that occurred prior to commencement of the arrangement an annual percentage rate, fee, or charge that exceeds the annual percentage rate, fee, or charge that applied to those transactions prior to commencement of the arrangement. However, this provision does not prohibit the card issuer from applying an increased annual percentage rate, fee, or charge upon completion or failure of the arrangement, to the extent consistent with any of the other exceptions in § 1026.55(b). For example, if a temporary rate applied prior to the arrangement and that rate expired during the arrangement, the card issuer may apply an increased rate upon completion or failure of the arrangement to the extent consistent with § 1026.55(b)(1). Similarly, if a variable rate applied prior to the arrangement, the card issuer may apply any increase in that variable rate upon completion or failure of the arrangement to the extent consistent with § 1026.55(b)(2).

4. *Examples.*

i. Assume that an account is subject to a $50 annual fee and that, consistent with § 1026.55(b)(4), the margin used to determine a variable annual percentage rate that applies to a $5,000 balance is increased from 5 percentage points to 15 percentage points. Assume also that the card issuer and the consumer subsequently agree to a workout arrangement that reduces the annual fee to $0 and reduces the margin back to 5 points on the condition that the consumer pay a specified amount by the payment due date each month. If the consumer does not pay the agreed-upon amount by the payment due date, § 1026.55(b)(5) permits the card issuer to increase the annual fee to $50 and increase the margin for the variable rate that applies to the $5,000 balance up to 15 percentage points.

ii. Assume that a consumer fails to make four consecutive monthly minimum payments totaling $480 on a consumer credit card account with a balance of $6,000 and that, consistent with § 1026.55(b)(4), the annual percentage rate that applies to that balance is increased from a non-variable rate of 15% to a non-variable penalty rate of 30%. Assume also that the card issuer and the consumer subsequently agree to a temporary hardship arrangement that reduces all rates on the account to 0% on the condition that the consumer pay an amount by the payment due date each month that is sufficient to cure the $480 delinquency within six months. If the consumer pays the agreed-upon amount by the payment due date during the six-month period and cures the delinquency, § 1026.55(b)(5) permits the card issuer to increase the rate that applies to any remaining portion of the $6,000 balance to 15% or any other rate up to the 30% penalty rate.

### *55(b)(6) Servicemembers Civil Relief Act exception*

1. *Rate, fee, or charge that does not exceed rate, fee, or charge that applied before decrease.* When a rate or a fee or charge subject to § 1026.55 has been decreased pursuant to 50 U.S.C. app. 527 or a similar Federal or state statute or regulation, § 1026.55(b)(6) permits the card issuer to increase the rate, fee, or charge once 50 U.S.C. app. 527 or the similar statute or regulation no longer applies. However, § 1026.55(b)(6) prohibits the card issuer from applying to any transactions that occurred prior to the decrease a rate, fee, or charge that exceeds the rate, fee, or charge that applied to those transactions prior to the decrease (except to the extent permitted by one of the other exceptions in § 1026.55(b)). For example, if a temporary rate applied prior to a decrease in rate pursuant to 50 U.S.C. app. 527 and the temporary rate expired during the period that 50 U.S.C. app. 527 applied to the account, the card issuer may apply an increased rate once 50 U.S.C. app. 527 no longer applies to the extent consistent with § 1026.55(b)(1). Similarly, if a variable rate applied prior to a decrease in rate pursuant to 50 U.S.C. app. 527, the card issuer may apply any increase in that variable rate once 50 U.S.C. app. 527 no longer applies to the extent consistent with § 1026.55(b)(2).

2. *Decreases in rates, fees, and charges to amounts consistent with 50 U.S.C. app. 527 or similar statute or regulation.* If a card issuer deceases an annual percentage rate or a fee or charge subject to § 1026.55 pursuant to 50 U.S.C. app. 527 or a similar Federal or state statute or regulation and if the card issuer also decreases other rates, fees, or charges (such as the rate that applies to new transactions) to amounts that are consistent with 50 U.S.C. app. 527 or a similar Federal or state statute or regulation, the card issuer may increase those rates, fees, and charges consistent with § 1026.55(b)(6).

3. *Example.* Assume that on December 31 of year one the annual percentage rate that applies to a $5,000 balance on a credit card account is a variable rate that is determined by adding a margin of 10 percentage points to a publicly-available index that is not under the card issuer's control. The account is also subject to a monthly maintenance fee of $10. On January 1 of year two, the card issuer reduces the rate that applies to the $5,000 balance to a non-variable rate of 6% and ceases to impose the $10 monthly maintenance fee and other fees (including late payment fees) pursuant to 50 U.S.C. app. 527. The card issuer also decreases the rate that applies to new transactions to 6%. During year two, the consumer uses the account for $1,000 in new transactions. On January 1 of year three, 50 U.S.C. app. 527 ceases to apply and the card issuer provides a notice pursuant to § 1026.9(c) informing the consumer that on February 15 of year three the variable rate determined using the 10-point margin will apply to any remaining portion of the $5,000 balance and to any remaining portion of the $1,000 balance. The notice also states that the $10 monthly maintenance fee and other fees (including late payment fees) will resume on February 15 of year three. Consistent with § 1026.9(c)(2)(iv)(B), the card issuer is not required to provide a right to reject in these circumstances. On February 15 of year three, § 1026.55(b)(6) permits the card issuer to begin accruing interest on any remaining portion of the $5,000 and $1,000 balances at the variable rate determined using the 10-point margin and to resume imposing the $10 monthly maintenance fee and other fees (including late payment fees).

## *55(c) Treatment of protected balances*

### *55(c)(1) Definition of protected balance*

1. *Example of protected balance.* Assume that, on March 15 of year two, an account has a purchase balance of $1,000 at a non-variable annual percentage rate of 12% and that, on March 16, the card issuer sends a notice pursuant to § 1026.9(c) informing the consumer that the annual percentage rate for new purchases will increase to a non-variable rate of 15% on May 1. The fourteenth day after provision of the notice is March 29. On March 29, the consumer makes a $100 purchase. On March 30, the consumer makes a $150 purchase. On May 1, § 1026.55(b)(3)(ii) permits the card issuer to begin accruing interest at 15% on the $150 purchase made on March 30 but does not permit the card issuer to apply that 15% rate to the $1,100 purchase balance as of March 29. Accordingly, the protected balance for purposes of § 1026.55(c) is the $1,100 purchase balance as of March 29. The $150 purchase made on March 30 is not part of the protected balance.

2. *First year after account opening.* Section 1026.55(c) applies to amounts owed for a category of transactions to which an increased annual percentage rate or an increased fee or charge cannot be applied after the rate, fee, or charge for that category of transactions has been increased pursuant to § 1026.55(b)(3). Because § 1026.55(b)(3)(iii) does not permit a card issuer to increase an annual percentage rate or a fee or charge required to be disclosed under § 1026.6(b)(2)(ii), (b)(2)(iii), or (b)(2)(xii) during the first year after account opening, § 1026.55(c) does not apply to balances during the first year after account opening.

3. *Increased fees and charges.* Except as provided in § 1026.55(b)(3)(iii), § 1026.55(b)(3) permits a card issuer to increase a fee or charge required to be disclosed under § 1026.6(b)(2)(ii), (b)(2)(iii), or (b)(2)(xii) after complying with the applicable notice requirements in § 1026.9(b) or (c), provided that the increased fee or charge is not applied to a protected balance. To the extent consistent with § 1026.55(b)(3)(iii), a card issuer is not prohibited from increasing a fee or charge that applies to the account as a whole or to balances other than the protected balance. For example, after the first year following account opening, a card issuer generally may add or increase an annual or a monthly maintenance fee for an account after complying with the notice requirements in § 1026.9(c), including notifying the consumer of the right to reject the new or increased fee under § 1026.9(h). However, except as otherwise provided in § 1026.55(b), an increased fee or charge cannot be applied to an account while the account is closed or while the card issuer does not permit the consumer to use the account for new transactions. *See* § 1026.55(b)(3)(iii); *see also* §§ 1026.52(b)(2)(i)(B)(3) and 1026.55(d)(1). Furthermore, if the consumer rejects an increase in a fee or charge pursuant to § 1026.9(h), the card issuer is prohibited from applying the increased fee or charge to the account and from imposing any other fee or charge solely as a result of the rejection. *See* § 1026.9(h)(2)(i) and (ii); comment 9(h)(2)(ii)-2.

4. *Changing balance computation method.* Nothing in § 1026.55 prohibits a card issuer from changing the balance computation method that applies to new transactions as well as protected balances.

### *55(c)(2) Repayment of protected balance*

1. *No less beneficial to the consumer.* A card issuer may provide a method of repaying the protected balance that is different from the methods listed in § 1026.55(c)(2) so long as the method used is no less beneficial to the consumer than one of the listed methods. A method is no less beneficial to the consumer if the method results in a required minimum periodic payment that is equal to or less than a minimum payment calculated using the method for the account before the effective date of the increase. Similarly, a method is no less beneficial to the consumer if the method amortizes the balance in five years or longer or if the method results in a required minimum periodic payment that is equal to or less than a minimum payment calculated consistent with § 1026.55(c)(2)(iii). For example:

i. If at account opening the cardholder agreement stated that the required minimum periodic payment would be either the total of fees and interest charges plus 1% of the total amount owed or $20 (whichever is greater), the card issuer may require the consumer to make a minimum payment of $20 even if doing so would pay off the balance in less than five years or constitute more than 2% of the balance plus fees and interest charges.

ii. A card issuer could increase the percentage of the balance included in the required minimum periodic payment from 2% to 5% so long as doing so would not result in amortization of the balance in less than five years.

iii. A card issuer could require the consumer to make a required minimum periodic payment that amortizes the balance in four years so long as doing so would not more than double the percentage of the balance included in the minimum payment prior to the date on which the increased annual percentage rate, fee, or charge became effective.

*Paragraph 55(c)(2)(ii)*

1. *Amortization period starting from effective date of increase.* Section 1026.55(c)(2)(ii) provides for an amortization period for the protected balance of no less than five years, starting from the date on which the increased annual percentage rate or fee or charge required to be disclosed under § 1026.6(b)(2)(ii), (b)(2)(iii), or (b)(2)(xii) became effective. A card issuer is not required to recalculate the required minimum periodic payment for the protected balance if, during the amortization period, that balance is reduced as a result of the allocation of payments by the consumer in excess of that minimum payment consistent with § 1026.53 or any other practice permitted by these rules and other applicable law.

2. *Amortization when applicable rate is variable.* If the annual percentage rate that applies to the protected balance varies with an index, the card issuer may adjust the interest charges included in the required minimum periodic payment for that balance accordingly in order to ensure that the balance is amortized in five years. For example, assume that a variable rate that is currently 15% applies to a protected balance and that, in order to amortize that balance in five years, the required minimum periodic payment must include a specific amount of principal plus all accrued interest charges. If the 15% variable rate increases due to an increase in the index, the creditor may increase the required minimum periodic payment to include the additional interest charges.

*Paragraph 55(c)(2)(iii)*

1. *Portion of required minimum periodic payment on other balances.* Section 1026.55(c)(2)(iii) addresses the portion of the required minimum periodic payment based on the protected balance. Section 1026.55(c)(2)(iii) does not limit or otherwise address the card issuer's ability to determine the portion of the required minimum periodic payment based on other balances on the account or the card issuer's ability to apply that portion of the minimum payment to the balances on the account.

2. *Example.* Assume that the method used by a card issuer to calculate the required minimum periodic payment for a credit card account requires the consumer to pay either the total of fees and accrued interest charges plus 2% of the total amount owed or $50, whichever is greater. Assume also that the account has a purchase balance of $2,000 at an annual percentage rate of 15% and a cash advance balance of $500 at an annual percentage rate of 20% and that the card issuer increases the rate for purchases to 18% but does not increase the rate for cash advances. Under § 1026.55(c)(2)(iii), the card issuer may require the consumer to pay fees and interest plus 4% of the $2,000 purchase balance. Section 1026.55(c)(2)(iii) does not limit the card issuer's ability to increase the portion of the required minimum periodic payment that is based on the cash advance balance.

## *55(d) Continuing application*

1. *Closed accounts.* If a credit card account under an open-end (not home-secured) consumer credit plan with a balance is closed, § 1026.55 continues to apply to that balance. For example, if a card issuer or a consumer closes a credit card account with a balance, § 1026.55(d)(1) prohibits the card issuer from increasing the annual percentage rate that applies to that balance or imposing a periodic fee based solely on that balance that was not charged before the account was closed (such as a closed account fee) unless permitted by one of the exceptions in § 1026.55(b).

2. *Acquired accounts.* If, through merger or acquisition (for example), a card issuer acquires a credit card account under an open-end (not home-secured) consumer credit plan with a balance, § 1026.55 continues to apply to that balance. For example, if a credit card account has a $1,000 purchase balance with an annual percentage rate of 15% and the card issuer that acquires that account applies an 18% rate to purchases, § 1026.55(d)(1) prohibits the card issuer from applying the 18% rate to the $1,000 balance unless permitted by one of the exceptions in § 1026.55(b).

3. *Balance transfers.*

i. *Between accounts issued by the same creditor.* If a balance is transferred from a credit card account under an open-end (not home-secured) consumer credit plan issued by a creditor to another credit account issued by the same creditor or its affiliate or subsidiary, § 1026.55 continues to apply to that balance. For example, if a credit card account has a $2,000 purchase balance with an annual percentage rate of 15% and that balance is transferred to another credit card account issued by the same creditor that applies an 18% rate to purchases, § 1026.55(d)(2) prohibits the creditor from applying the 18% rate to the $2,000 balance unless permitted by one of the exceptions in § 1026.55(b). However, the creditor would not generally be prohibited from charging a new periodic fee (such as an annual fee) on the second account so long as the fee is not based solely on the $2,000 balance and the creditor has notified the consumer of the fee either by providing written notice 45 days before imposing the fee pursuant to § 1026.9(c) or by providing account-opening disclosures pursuant to § 1026.6(b). See also § 1026.55(b)(3)(iii); comment 55(b)(3)-3; comment 5(b)(1)(i)-6. Additional circumstances in which a balance is considered transferred for purposes of § 1026.55(d)(2) include when:

A. A retail credit card account with a balance is replaced or substituted with a cobranded general purpose credit card account that can be used with a broader merchant base;

B. A credit card account with a balance is replaced or substituted with another credit card account offering different features;

C. A credit card account with a balance is consolidated or combined with one or more other credit card accounts into a single credit card account; and

D. A credit card account is replaced or substituted with a line of credit that can be accessed solely by an account number.

ii. *Between accounts issued by different creditors.* If a balance is transferred to a credit card account under an open-end (not home-secured) consumer credit plan issued by a creditor from a credit card account issued by a different creditor or an institution that is not an affiliate or subsidiary of the creditor that issued the account to which the balance is transferred, § 1026.55(d)(2) does not prohibit the creditor to which the balance is transferred from applying its account terms to that balance, provided that those terms comply with this part. For example, if a credit card account issued by creditor A has a $1,000 purchase balance at an annual percentage rate of 15% and the consumer transfers that balance to a credit card account with a purchase rate of 17% issued by creditor B, creditor B may apply the 17% rate to the $1,000 balance. However, creditor B may not subsequently increase the rate on that balance unless permitted by one of the exceptions in § 1026.55(b).

## *55(e) Promotional waivers or rebates of interest, fees, and other charges*

1. *Generally.* Nothing in § 1026.55 prohibits a card issuer from waiving or rebating finance charges due to a periodic interest rate or a fee or charge required to be disclosed under § 1026.6(b)(2)(ii), (b)(2)(iii), or (b)(2)(xii). However, if a card issuer promotes and applies the waiver or rebate to an account, the card issuer cannot temporarily or permanently cease or terminate any portion of the waiver or rebate on that account unless permitted by one of the exceptions in § 1026.55(b). For example:

i. A card issuer applies an annual percentage rate of 15% to balance transfers but promotes a program under which all of the interest accrued on transferred balances will be waived or rebated for one year. If, prior to the commencement of the one-year period, the card issuer discloses the length of the period and the annual percentage rate that will apply to transferred balances after expiration of that period consistent with § 1026.55(b)(1)(i), § 1026.55(b)(1) permits the card issuer to begin imposing interest charges on transferred balances after one year. Furthermore, if, during the one-year period, a required minimum periodic payment is not received within 60 days of the payment due date, § 1026.55(b)(4) permits the card issuer to begin imposing interest charges on transferred balances (after providing a notice consistent with § 1026.9(g) and § 1026.55(b)(4)(i)). However, if a required minimum periodic payment is not more than 60 days delinquent or if the consumer otherwise violates the terms or other requirements of the account, § 1026.55 does not permit the card issuer to begin imposing interest charges on transferred balances until the expiration of the one-year period.

ii. A card issuer imposes a monthly maintenance fee of $10 but promotes a program under which the fee will be waived or rebated for the six months following account opening. If, prior to account opening, the card issuer discloses the length of the period and the monthly maintenance fee that will be imposed after expiration of that period consistent with § 1026.55(b)(1)(i), § 1026.55(b)(1) permits the card issuer to begin imposing the monthly maintenance fee six months after account opening. Furthermore, if, during the six-month period, a required minimum periodic payment is not received within 60 days of the payment due date, § 1026.55(b)(4) permits the card issuer to begin imposing the monthly maintenance fee (after providing a notice consistent with § 1026.9(c) and § 1026.55(b)(4)(i)). However, if a required minimum periodic payment is not more than 60 days delinquent or if the consumer otherwise violates the terms or other requirements of the account, § 1026.55 does not permit the card issuer to begin imposing the monthly maintenance fee until the expiration of the six-month period.

2. *Promotion of waiver or rebate.* For purposes of § 1026.55(e), a card issuer generally promotes a waiver or rebate if the card issuer discloses the waiver or rebate in an advertisement (as defined in § 1026.2(a)(2)). *See* comment 2(a)(2)-1. In addition, a card issuer generally promotes a waiver or rebate for purposes of § 1026.55(e) if the card issuer discloses the waiver or rebate in communications regarding existing accounts (such as communications regarding a promotion that encourages additional or different uses of an existing account). However, a card issuer does not promote a waiver or rebate for purposes of § 1026.55(e) if the advertisement or communication relates to an inquiry or dispute about a specific charge or to interest, fees, or charges that have already been waived or rebated.

i. *Examples of promotional communications.* The following are examples of circumstances in which a card issuer is promoting a waiver or rebate for purposes of § 1026.55(e):

A. A card issuer discloses the waiver or rebate in a newspaper, magazine, leaflet, promotional flyer, catalog, sign, or point-of-sale display, unless the disclosure relates to interest, fees, or charges that have already been waived.

B. A card issuer discloses the waiver or rebate on radio or television or through electronic advertisements (such as on the Internet), unless the disclosure relates to interest, fees, or charges that have already been waived or rebated.

C. A card issuer discloses a waiver or rebate to individual consumers, such as by telephone, letter, or electronic communication, through direct mail literature, or on or with account statements, unless the disclosure relates to an inquiry or dispute about a specific charge or to interest, fees, or charges that have already been waived or rebated.

ii. *Examples of non-promotional communications.* The following are examples of circumstances in which a card issuer is not promoting a waiver or rebate for purposes of § 1026.55(e):

A. After a card issuer has waived or rebated interest, fees, or other charges subject to § 1026.55 with respect to an account, the issuer discloses the waiver or rebate to the accountholder on the periodic statement or by telephone, letter, or electronic communication. However, if the card issuer also discloses prospective waivers or rebates in the same communication, the issuer is promoting a waiver or rebate for purposes of § 1026.55(e).

B. A card issuer communicates with a consumer about a waiver or rebate of interest, fees, or other charges subject to § 1026.55 in relation to an inquiry or dispute about a specific charge, including a dispute under §§ 1026.12 or 1026.13.

C. A card issuer waives or rebates interest, fees, or other charges subject to § 1026.55 in order to comply with a legal requirement (such as the limitations in § 1026.52(a)).

D. A card issuer discloses a grace period, as defined in § 1026.5(b)(2)(ii)(3).

E. A card issuer provides a period after the payment due date during which interest, fees, or other charges subject to § 1026.55 are waived or rebated even if a payment has not been received.

F. A card issuer provides benefits (such as rewards points or cash back on purchases or finance charges) that can be applied to the account as credits, provided that the benefits are not promoted as reducing interest, fees, or other charges subject to § 1026.55.

3. *Relationship of § 1026.55(e) to grace period.* Section 1026.55(e) does not apply to the waiver of finance charges due to a periodic rate consistent with a grace period, as defined in § 1026.5(b)(2)(ii)(3).

[75 Fed. Reg. 7848 (Feb. 22, 2010); 76 Fed. Reg. 23,029, 23,031–23,034 (Apr. 25, 2011); 76 Fed. Reg. 31,221 (May 31, 2011)]

## SECTION 1026.56 Requirements for Over-the-Limit Transactions [§ 226.56]

### *56(b) Opt-in requirement*

1. *Policy and practice of declining over-the-limit transactions.* Section 1026.56(b)(1)(i)-(v), including the requirements to provide notice and obtain consumer consent, do not apply to any card issuer that has a policy and practice of declining to pay any over-the-limit transactions for the consumer's credit card account when the card issuer has a reasonable belief that completing a transaction will cause the consumer to exceed the consumer's credit limit for that account. For example, if a card issuer only authorizes those transactions which, at the time of authorization, would not cause the consumer to exceed a credit limit, it is not subject to the requirement to provide consumers notice and an opportunity to affirmatively consent to the card issuer's payment of over-the-limit transactions. However, if an over-the-limit transaction is paid without the consumer providing affirmative consent, the card issuer may not charge a fee for paying the transaction.

2. *Over-the-limit transactions not required to be authorized or paid.* Section 1026.56 does not require a card issuer to authorize or pay an over-the-limit transaction even if the consumer has affirmatively consented to the card issuer's over-the-limit service.

3. *Examples of reasonable opportunity to provide affirmative consent.* A card issuer provides a reasonable opportunity for the consumer to provide affirmative consent to the card issuer's payment of over-the-limit transactions when, among other things, it provides reasonable methods by which the consumer may affirmatively consent. A card issuer provides such reasonable methods if:

i. *On the application.* The card issuer provides the notice on the application form that the consumer can fill out to request the service as part of the application;

ii. *By mail.* The card issuer provides a form with the account-opening disclosures or the periodic statement for the consumer to fill out and mail to affirmatively request the service;

iii. *By telephone.* The card issuer provides a readily available telephone line that consumers may call to provide affirmative consent.

iv. *By electronic means.* The card issuer provides an electronic means for the consumer to affirmatively consent. For example, a card issuer could provide a form that can be accessed and processed at its Web site, where the consumer can check a box to opt in and confirm that choice by clicking on a button that affirms the consumer's consent.

4. *Separate consent required.* A consumer's affirmative consent, or opt-in, to a card issuer's payment of over-the-limit transactions must be obtained separately from other consents or acknowledgments obtained by the card issuer. For example, a consumer's signature on a credit application to request a credit card would not by itself sufficiently evidence the consumer's consent to the card issuer's payment of over-the-limit transactions. However, a card issuer may obtain a consumer's affirmative consent by providing a blank signature line or a check box on the application that the consumer can sign or select to request the over-the-limit service, provided that the signature line or check box is used solely for purposes of evidencing the choice and not for any other pur-

pose, such as to also obtain consumer consents for other account services or features or to receive disclosures electronically.

5. *Written confirmation.* A card issuer may comply with the requirement in § 1026.56(b)(1)(iv) to provide written confirmation of the consumer's decision to affirmatively consent, or opt in, to the card issuer's payment of over-the-limit transactions by providing the consumer a copy of the consumer's completed opt-in form or by sending a letter or notice to the consumer acknowledging that the consumer has elected to opt into the card issuer's service. A card issuer may also satisfy the written confirmation requirement by providing the confirmation on the first periodic statement sent after the consumer has opted in. For example, a card issuer could provide a written notice consistent with § 1026.56(e)(2) on the periodic statement. A card issuer may not, however, assess any over-the-limit fees or charges on the consumer's credit card account unless and until the card issuer has sent the written confirmation. Thus, if a card issuer elects to provide written confirmation on the first periodic statement after the consumer has opted in, it would not be permitted to assess any over-the-limit fees or charges until the next statement cycle.

## 56(b)(2) Completion of over-the-limit transactions without consumer consent

1. *Examples of over-the-limit transactions paid without consumer consent.* Section 1026.56(b)(2) provides that a card issuer may pay an over-the-limit transaction even if the consumer has not provided affirmative consent, so long as the card issuer does not impose a fee or charge for paying the transaction. The prohibition on imposing fees for paying an over-the-limit transaction applies even in circumstances where the card issuer is unable to avoid paying a transaction that exceeds the consumer's credit limit.

i. *Transactions not submitted for authorization.* A consumer has not affirmatively consented to a card issuer's payment of over-the-limit transactions. The consumer purchases a $3 cup of coffee using his credit card. Because of the small dollar amount of the transaction, the merchant does not submit the transaction to the card issuer for authorization. The transaction causes the consumer to exceed the credit limit. Under these circumstances, the card issuer is prohibited from imposing a fee or charge on the consumer's credit card account for paying the over-the-limit transaction because the consumer has not opted in to the card issuer's over-the-limit service.

ii. *Settlement amount exceeds authorization amount.* A consumer has not affirmatively consented to a card issuer's payment of over-the-limit transactions. The consumer uses his credit card at a pay-at-the-pump fuel dispenser to purchase $50 of fuel. Before permitting the consumer to use the fuel pump, the merchant verifies the validity of the card by requesting an authorization hold of $1. The subsequent $50 transaction amount causes the consumer to exceed his credit limit. Under these circumstances, the card issuer is prohibited from imposing a fee or charge on the consumer's credit card account for paying the over-the-limit transaction because the consumer has not opted in to the card issuer's over-the-limit service.

iii. *Intervening charges.* A consumer has not affirmatively consented to a card issuer's payment of over-the-limit transactions. The consumer makes a $50 purchase using his credit card. However, before the $50 transaction is charged to the consumer's account, a separate recurring charge is posted to the account. The $50 purchase then causes the consumer to exceed his credit limit. Under these circumstances, the card issuer is prohibited from imposing a fee or charge on the consumer's credit card account for paying the over-the-limit transaction because the consumer has not opted in to the card issuer's over-the-limit service.

2. *Permissible fees or charges when a consumer has not consented.* Section 1026.56(b)(2) does not preclude a card issuer from assessing fees or charges other than over-the-limit fees when an over-the-limit transaction is completed. For example, if a consumer has not opted in, the card issuer may assess a balance transfer fee in connection with a balance transfer, provided such a fee is assessed whether or not the transfer exceeds the credit limit. Section 1026.56(b)(2) does not limit the card issuer's ability to debit the consumer's account for the amount of the over-the-limit transaction if the card issuer is permitted to do so under applicable law. The card issuer may also assess interest charges in connection with the over-the-limit transaction.

## 56(c) Method of election

1. *Card issuer-determined methods.* A card issuer may determine the means available to consumers to affirmatively consent, or opt in, to the card issuer's payment of over-the-limit transactions. For example, a card issuer may decide to obtain consents in writing, electronically, or orally, or through some combination of these methods. Section 1026.56(c) further requires, however, that such methods must be made equally available for consumers to revoke a prior consent. Thus, for example, if a card issuer allows a consumer to consent in writing or electronically, it must also allow the consumer to revoke that consent in writing or electronically.

2. *Electronic requests.* A consumer consent or revocation request submitted electronically is not considered a consumer disclosure for purposes of the E-Sign Act.

## 56(d) Timing and placement of notices

1. *Contemporaneous notice for oral or electronic consent.* Under § 1026.56(d)(1)(ii), if a card issuer seeks to obtain consent from the consumer orally or by electronic means, the card issuer must provide a notice containing the disclosures in § 1026.56(e)(1) prior to and as part of the process of obtaining the consumer's consent.

## 56(e) Content

1. *Amount of over-the-limit fee.* See Model Forms G-25(A) and G-25(B) for guidance on how to disclose the amount of the over-the-limit fee.

2. *Notice content.* In describing the consumer's right to affirmatively consent to a card issuer's payment of over-the-limit transactions, the card issuer may explain that any transactions that exceed the consumer's credit limit will be declined if the consumer does not consent to the service. In addition, the card issuer should explain that even if a consumer consents, the payment of over-the-limit transactions is at the discretion of the card issuer. For example, the card issuer may indicate that it may decline a transaction for any reason, such as if the consumer is past due or significantly over the limit. The card issuer may also disclose the consumer's right to revoke consent.

## 56(f) Joint relationships

1. *Authorized users.* Section 1026.56(f) does not permit a card issuer to treat a request to opt in to or to revoke a prior request for the card issuer's payment of over-the-limit transactions from an authorized user that is not jointly liable on a credit card account as a consent or revocation request for that account.

## 56(g) Continuing right to opt in or revoke opt-in

1. *Fees or charges for over-the-limit transactions incurred prior to revocation.* Section 1026.56(g) provides that a consumer may revoke his or her prior consent at any time. If a consumer does so, this provision does not require the card issuer to waive or reverse any over-the-limit fees or charges assessed to the consumer's account for transactions that occurred prior to the card issuer's implementation of the consumer's revocation request. Nor does this requirement prevent the card issuer from assessing over-the-limit fees in subsequent cycles if the consumer's account balance continues to exceed the credit limit after the payment due date as a result of an over-the-limit transaction that occurred prior to the consumer's revocation of consent.

## 56(h) Duration of opt-in

1. *Card issuer ability to stop paying over-the-limit transactions after consumer consent.* A card issuer may cease paying over-the-limit transactions for consumers that have previously opted in at any time and for any reason. For example, a card issuer may stop paying over-the-limit transactions for a consumer to respond to changes in the credit risk presented by the consumer.

### *56(j) Prohibited practices*

1. *Periodic fees or charges.* A card issuer may charge an over-the-limit fee or charge only if the consumer has exceeded the credit limit during the billing cycle. Thus, a card issuer may not impose any recurring or periodic fees for paying over-the-limit transactions (for example, a monthly "over-the-limit protection" service fee), even if the consumer has affirmatively consented to or opted in to the service, unless the consumer has in fact exceeded the credit limit during that cycle.

2. *Examples of limits on fees or charges imposed per billing cycle.* Section 1026.56(j)(1) generally prohibits a card issuer from assessing a fee or charge due to the same over-the-limit transaction for more than three billing cycles. The following examples illustrate the prohibition.

i. Assume that a consumer has opted into a card issuer's payment of over-the-limit transactions. The consumer exceeds the credit limit during the December billing cycle and does not make sufficient payment to bring the account balance back under the limit for four consecutive cycles. The consumer does not engage in any additional transactions during this period. In this case, § 1026.56(j)(1) would permit the card issuer to charge a maximum of three over-the-limit fees for the December over-the-limit transaction.

ii. Assume the same facts as above except that the consumer makes sufficient payment to reduce his account balance by the payment due date during the February billing cycle. The card issuer may charge over-the-limit fees for the December and January billing cycles. However, because the consumer's account balance was below the credit limit by the payment due date for the February billing cycle, the card issuer may not charge an over-the-limit fee for the February billing cycle.

iii. Assume the same facts as in paragraph i, except that the consumer engages in another over-the-limit transaction during the February billing cycle. Because the consumer has obtained an additional extension of credit which causes the consumer to exceed his credit limit, the card issuer may charge over-the-limit fees for the December transaction on the January, February and March billing statements, and additional over-the-limit fees for the February transaction on the April and May billing statements. The card issuer may not charge an over-the-limit fee for each of the December and the February transactions on the March billing statement because it is prohibited from imposing more than one over-the-limit fee during a billing cycle.

3. *Replenishment of credit line.* Section 1026.56(j)(2) does not prevent a card issuer from delaying replenishment of a consumer's available credit where appropriate, for example, where the card issuer may suspect fraud on the credit card account. However, a card issuer may not assess an over-the-limit fee or charge if the over-the-limit transaction is caused by the card issuer's decision not to promptly replenish the available credit after the consumer's payment is credited to the consumer's account.

4. *Examples of conditioning.* Section 1026.56(j)(3) prohibits a card issuer from conditioning or otherwise tying the amount of a consumer's credit limit on the consumer affirmatively consenting to the card issuer's payment of over-the-limit transactions where the card issuer assesses an over-the-limit fee for the transaction. The following examples illustrate the prohibition.

i. *Amount of credit limit.* Assume that a card issuer offers a credit card with a credit limit of $1,000. The consumer is informed that if the consumer opts in to the payment of the card issuer's payment of over-the-limit transactions, the initial credit limit would be increased to $1,300. If the card issuer would have offered the credit card with the $1,300 credit limit but for the fact that the consumer did not consent to the card issuer's payment of over-the-limit transactions, the card issuer would not be in compliance with § 1026.56(j)(3). Section 1026.56(j)(3) prohibits the card issuer from tying the consumer's opt-in to the card issuer's payment of over-the-limit transactions as a condition of obtaining the credit card with the $1,300 credit limit.

ii. *Access to credit.* Assume the same facts as above, except that the card issuer declines the consumer's application altogether because the consumer has not affirmatively consented or opted in to the card issuer's payment of over-the-limit transactions. The card issuer is not in compliance with § 1026.56(j)(3) because the card issuer has required the consumer's consent as a condition of obtaining credit.

5. *Over-the-limit fees caused by accrued fees or interest.* Section 1026.56(j)(4) prohibits a card issuer from imposing any over-the-limit fees or charges on a consumer's account if the consumer has exceeded the credit limit solely because charges imposed as part of the plan as described in § 1026.6(b)(3) were charged to the consumer's account during the billing cycle. For example, a card issuer may not assess an over-the-limit fee or charge even if the credit limit was exceeded due to fees for services requested by the consumer if such fees would constitute charges imposed as part of the plan (such as fees for voluntary debt cancellation or suspension coverage). Section 1026.56(j)(4) does not, however, restrict card issuers from assessing over-the-limit fees or charges due to accrued finance charges or fees from prior cycles that have subsequently been added to the account balance. The following examples illustrate the prohibition.

i. Assume that a consumer has opted in to a card issuer's payment of over-the-limit transactions. The consumer's account has a credit limit of $500. The billing cycles for the account begin on the first day of the month and end on the last day of the month. The account is not eligible for a grace period as defined in § 1026.5(b)(2)(ii)(B)(3). On December 31, the only balance on the account is a purchase balance of $475. On that same date, $50 in fees charged as part of the plan under § 1026.6(b)(3)(i) and interest charges are imposed on the account, increasing the total balance at the end of the December billing cycle to $525. Although the total balance exceeds the $500 credit limit, § 1026.56(j)(4) prohibits the card issuer from imposing an over-the-limit fee or charge for the December billing cycle in these circumstances because the consumer's credit limit was exceeded solely because of the imposition of fees and interest charges during that cycle.

ii. Same facts as above except that, on December 31, the only balance on the account is a purchase balance of $400. On that same date, $50 in fees imposed as part of the plan under § 1026.6(b)(3)(i), including interest charges, are imposed on the account, increasing the total balance at the end of the December billing cycle to $450. The consumer makes a $25 payment by the January payment due date and the remaining $25 in fees imposed as part of the plan in December is added to the outstanding balance. On January 25, an $80 purchase is charged to the account. At the close of the cycle on January 31, an additional $20 in fees imposed as part of the plan are imposed on the account, increasing the total balance to $525. Because § 1026.56(j)(4) does not require the issuer to consider fees imposed as part of the plan for the prior cycle in determining whether an over-the-limit fee may be properly assessed for the current cycle, the issuer need not take into account the remaining $25 in fees and interest charges from the December cycle in determining whether fees imposed as part of the plan caused the consumer to exceed the credit limit during the January cycle. Thus, under these circumstances, § 1026.56(j)(4) does not prohibit the card issuer from imposing an over-the-limit fee or charge for the January billing cycle because the $20 in fees imposed as part of the plan for the January billing cycle did not cause the consumer to exceed the credit limit during that cycle.

6. *Additional restrictions on over-the-limit fees.* See § 1026.52(b).

[75 Fed. Reg. 7848 (Feb. 22, 2010); 75 Fed. Reg. 37,583 (June 29, 2010)]

## SECTION 1026.57 Reporting and Marketing Rules for College Student Open-End Credit [§ 226.57]

### *57(a) Definitions*

### *57(a)(1) College student credit card*

1. *Definition.* The definition of college student credit card excludes home-equity lines of credit accessed by credit cards and overdraft lines of credit accessed by debit cards. A college student credit card includes a college affinity card within the meaning of TILA section 127(r)(1)(A). In addition, a card may fall within the scope of the definition regardless of the fact that it is not intentionally targeted at

or marketed to college students. For example, an agreement between a college and a card issuer may provide for marketing of credit cards to alumni, faculty, staff, and other non-student consumers who have a relationship with the college, but also contain provisions that contemplate the issuance of cards to students. A credit card issued to a student at the college in connection with such an agreement qualifies as a college student credit card.

### *57(a)(5) College credit card agreement*

1. *Definition.* Section 1026.57(a)(5) defines "college credit card agreement" to include any business, marketing or promotional agreement between a card issuer and a college or university (or an affiliated organization, such as an alumni club or a foundation) if the agreement provides for the issuance of credit cards to full-time or part-time students. Business, marketing or promotional agreements may include a broad range of arrangements between a card issuer and an institution of higher education or affiliated organization, including arrangements that do not meet the criteria to be considered college affinity card agreements as discussed in TILA section 127(r)(1)(A). For example, TILA section 127(r)(1)(A) specifies that under a college affinity card agreement, the card issuer has agreed to make a donation to the institution or affiliated organization, the card issuer has agreed to offer discounted terms to the consumer, or the credit card will display pictures, symbols, or words identified with the institution or affiliated organization; even if these conditions are not met, an agreement may qualify as a college credit card agreement, if the agreement is a business, marketing or promotional agreement that contemplates the issuance of college student credit cards to college students currently enrolled (either full-time or part-time) at the institution. An agreement may qualify as a college credit card agreement even if marketing of cards under the agreement is targeted at alumni, faculty, staff, and other non-student consumers, as long as cards may also be issued to students in connection with the agreement.

### *57(b) Public disclosure of agreements*

1. *Public disclosure.* Section 1026.57(b) requires an institution of higher education to publicly disclose any contract or other agreement made with a card issuer or creditor for the purpose of marketing a credit card. Examples of publicly disclosing such contracts or agreements include, but are not limited to, posting such contracts or agreements on the institution's Web site or making such contracts or agreements available upon request, provided the procedures for requesting the documents are reasonable and free of cost to the requestor, and the requested contracts or agreements are provided within a reasonable time frame.

2. *Redaction prohibited.* An institution of higher education must publicly disclose any contract or other agreement made with a card issuer for the purpose of marketing a credit card in its entirety and may not redact any portion of such contract or agreement. Any clause existing in such contracts or agreements, providing for the confidentiality of any portion of the contract or agreement, would be invalid to the extent it restricts the ability of the institution of higher education to publicly disclose the contract or agreement in its entirety.

### *57(c) Prohibited inducements*

1. *Tangible item clarified.* A tangible item includes any physical item, such as a gift card, a t-shirt, or a magazine subscription, that a card issuer or creditor offers to induce a college student to apply for or open an open-end consumer credit plan offered by such card issuer or creditor. Tangible items do not include non-physical inducements such as discounts, rewards points, or promotional credit terms.

2. *Inducement clarified.* If a tangible item is offered to a person whether or not that person applies for or opens an open-end consumer credit plan, the tangible item has not been offered to induce the person to apply for or open the plan. For example, refreshments offered to a college student on campus that are not conditioned on whether the student has applied for or agreed to open an open-end consumer credit plan would not violate § 1026.57(c).

3. *Near campus clarified.* A location that is within 1,000 feet of the border of the campus of an institution of higher education, as defined by the institution of higher education, is considered near the campus of an institution of higher education.

4. *Mailings included.* The prohibition in § 1026.57(c) on offering a tangible item to a college student to induce such student to apply for or open an open-end consumer credit plan offered by such card issuer or creditor applies to any solicitation or application mailed to a college student at an address on or near the campus of an institution of higher education.

5. *Related event clarified.* An event is related to an institution of higher education if the marketing of such event uses the name, emblem, mascot, or logo of an institution of higher education, or other words, pictures, symbols identified with an institution of higher education in a way that implies that the institution of higher education endorses or otherwise sponsors the event.

6. *Reasonable procedures for determining if applicant is a student.* Section 1026.57(c) applies solely to offering a tangible item to a college student. Therefore, a card issuer or creditor may offer any person who is not a college student a tangible item to induce such person to apply for or open an open-end consumer credit plan offered by such card issuer or creditor, on campus, near campus, or at an event sponsored by or related to an institution of higher education. The card issuer or creditor must have reasonable procedures for determining whether an applicant is a college student before giving the applicant the tangible item. For example, a card issuer or creditor may ask whether the applicant is a college student as part of the application process. The card issuer or creditor may rely on the representations made by the applicant.

### *57(d) Annual report to the Bureau*

### *57(d)(2) Contents of report*

1. *Memorandum of understanding.* Section 1026.57(d)(2) requires that the report to the Bureau include, among other items, a copy of any memorandum of understanding between the card issuer and the institution (or affiliated organization) that "directly or indirectly relates to the college credit card agreement or that controls or directs any obligations or distribution of benefits between any such entities." Such a memorandum of understanding includes any document that amends the college credit card agreement, or that constitutes a further agreement between the parties as to the interpretation or administration of the agreement. For example, a memorandum of understanding required to be included in the report would include a document that provides details on the dollar amounts of payments from the card issuer to the university, to supplement the original agreement which only provided for payments in general terms (e.g., as a percentage). A memorandum of understanding for these purposes would not include email (or other) messages that merely discuss matters such as the addresses to which payments should be sent or the names of contact persons for carrying out the agreement.

[75 Fed. Reg. 7848 (Feb. 22, 2010)]

* * *

## SECTION 1026.59 Reevaluation of Rate Increases [§ 226.59]

### *59(a) General Rule*

### *59(a)(1) Evaluation of Increased Rate*

1. *Types of rate increases covered.* Section 1026.59(a) applies both to increases in annual percentage rates imposed on a consumer's account based on that consumer's credit risk or other circumstances specific to that consumer and to increases in annual percentage rates imposed based on factors that are not specific to the consumer, such as changes in market conditions or the issuer's cost of funds.

2. *Rate increases actually imposed.* Under § 1026.59(a), a card issuer must review changes in factors only if the increased rate is actually imposed on the consumer's account. For example, if a card issuer increases the penalty rate for a credit card account under an open-end (not home-secured) consumer credit plan and the consumer's account has no balances that are currently subject to the penalty rate, the card issuer is required to provide a notice pursuant to § 1026.9(c) of the change in terms, but the requirements of § 1026.59 do not apply. However, if the consumer's account later becomes subject to the penalty rate, the card issuer is required to

provide a notice pursuant to § 1026.9(g) and the requirements of § 1026.59 begin to apply upon imposition of the penalty rate. Similarly, if a card issuer raises the cash advance rate applicable to a consumer's account but the consumer engages in no cash advance transactions to which that increased rate is applied, the card issuer is required to provide a notice pursuant to § 1026.9(c) of the change in terms, but the requirements of § 1026.59 do not apply. If the consumer subsequently engages in a cash advance transaction, the requirements of § 1026.59 begin to apply at that time.

3. *Change in type of rate.*

i. *Generally.* A change from a variable rate to a non-variable rate or from a non-variable rate to a variable rate is not a rate increase for purposes of § 1026.59, if the rate in effect immediately prior to the change in type of rate is equal to or greater than the rate in effect immediately after the change. For example, a change from a variable rate of 15.99% to a non-variable rate of 15.99% is not a rate increase for purposes of § 1026.59 at the time of the change. *See* § 1026.55 for limitations on the permissibility of changing from a non-variable rate to a variable rate.

ii. *Change from non-variable rate to variable rate.* A change from a non-variable to a variable rate constitutes a rate increase for purposes of § 1026.59 if the variable rate exceeds the non-variable rate that would have applied if the change in type of rate had not occurred. For example, assume a new credit card account under an open-end (not home-secured) consumer credit plan is opened on January 1 of year 1 and that a non-variable annual percentage rate of 12% applies to all transactions on the account. On January 1 of year 2, upon 45 days' advance notice pursuant to § 1026.9(c)(2), the rate on all new transactions is changed to a variable rate that is currently 12% and is determined by adding a margin of 10 percentage points to a publicly-available index not under the card issuer's control. The change from the 12% non-variable rate to the 12% variable rate on January 1 of year 2 is not a rate increase for purposes of § 1026.59(a). On April 1 of year 2, the value of the variable rate increases to 12.5%. The increase in the rate from 12% to 12.5% is a rate increase for purposes of § 1026.59, and the card issuer must begin periodically conducting reviews of the account pursuant to § 1026.59. The increase that must be evaluated for purposes of § 1026.59 is the increase from a non-variable rate of 12% to a variable rate of 12.5%.

iii. *Change from variable rate to non-variable rate.* A change from a variable to a non-variable rate constitutes a rate increase for purposes of § 1026.59 if the non-variable rate exceeds the variable rate that would have applied if the change in type of rate had not occurred. For example, assume a new credit card account under an open-end (not home-secured) consumer credit plan is opened on January 1 of year 1 and that a variable annual percentage rate that is currently 15% and is determined by adding a margin of 10 percentage points to a publicly-available index not under the card issuer's control applies to all transactions on the account. On January 1 of year 2, upon 45 days' advance notice pursuant to § 1026.9(c)(2), the rate on all existing balances and new transactions is changed to a non-variable rate that is currently 15%. The change from the 15% variable rate to the 15% non-variable rate on January 1 of year 2 is not a rate increase for purposes of § 1026.59(a). On April 1 of year 2, the value of the variable rate that would have applied to the account decreases to 12.5%. Accordingly, on April 1 of year 2, the non-variable rate of 15% exceeds the 12.5% variable rate that would have applied but for the change in type of rate. At this time, the change to the non-variable rate of 15% constitutes a rate increase for purposes of § 1026.59, and the card issuer must begin periodically conducting reviews of the account pursuant to § 1026.59. The increase that must be evaluated for purposes of § 1026.59 is the increase from a variable rate of 12.5% to a non-variable rate of 15%.

4. *Rate increases prior to effective date of rule.* For increases in annual percentage rates made on or after January 1, 2009, and prior to August 22, 2010, § 1026.59(a) requires the card issuer to review the factors described in § 1026.59(d) and reduce the rate, as appropriate, if the rate increase is of a type for which 45 days' advance notice would currently be required under § 1026.9(c)(2) or (g). For example, 45 days' notice is not required under § 1026.9(c)(2) if the rate increase results from the increase in the index by which a properly-disclosed variable rate is determined in accordance with § 1026.9(c)(2)(v)(C) or if the increase occurs upon expiration of a specified period of time and disclosures complying with § 1026.9(c)(2)(v)(B) have been provided. The requirements of § 1026.59 do not apply to such rate increases.

5. *Amount of rate decrease.*

i. *General.* Even in circumstances where a rate reduction is required, § 1026.59 does not require that a card issuer decrease the rate that applies to a credit card account to the rate that was in effect prior to the rate increase subject to § 1026.59(a). The amount of the rate decrease that is required must be determined based upon the card issuer's reasonable policies and procedures under § 1026.59(b) for consideration of factors described in § 1026.59(a) and (d). For example, assume a consumer's rate on new purchases is increased from a variable rate of 15.99% to a variable rate of 23.99% based on the consumer's making a required minimum periodic payment five days late. The consumer makes all of the payments required on the account on time for the six months following the rate increase. Assume that the card issuer evaluates the account by reviewing the factors on which the increase in an annual percentage rate was originally based, in accordance with § 1026.59(d)(1)(i). The card issuer is not required to decrease the consumer's rate to the 15.99% that applied prior to the rate increase. However, the card issuer's policies and procedures for performing the review required by § 1026.59(a) must be reasonable, as required by § 1026.59(b), and must take into account any reduction in the consumer's credit risk based upon the consumer's timely payments.

ii. *Change in type of rate.* If the rate increase subject to § 1026.59 involves a change from a variable rate to a non-variable rate or from a non-variable rate to a variable rate, § 1026.59 does not require that the issuer reinstate the same type of rate that applied prior to the change. However, the amount of any rate decrease that is required must be determined based upon the card issuer's reasonable policies and procedures under § 1026.59(b) for consideration of factors described in § 1026.59(a) and (d).

## *59(a)(2) Rate Reductions*

## *59(a)(2)(ii) Applicability of Rate Reduction*

1. *Applicability of reduced rate to new transactions.* Section 1026.59(a)(2)(ii) requires, in part, that any reduction in rate required pursuant to § 1026.59(a)(1) must apply to new transactions that occur after the effective date of the rate reduction, if those transactions would otherwise have been subject to the increased rate described in § 1026.59(a)(1). A credit card account may have multiple types of balances, for example, purchases, cash advances, and balance transfers, to which different rates apply. For example, assume a new credit card account opened on January 1 of year one has a rate applicable to purchases of 15% and a rate applicable to cash advances and balance transfers of 20%. Effective March 1 of year two, consistent with the limitations in § 1026.55 and upon giving notice required by § 1026.9(c)(2), the card issuer raises the rate applicable to new purchases to 18% based on market conditions. The only transaction in which the consumer engages in year two is a $1,000 purchase made on July 1. The rate for cash advances and balance transfers remains at 20%. Based on a subsequent review required by § 1026.59(a)(1), the card issuer determines that the rate on purchases must be reduced to 16%. Section 1026.59(a)(2)(ii) requires that the 16% rate be applied to the $1,000 purchase made on July 1 and to all new purchases. The rate for new cash advances and balance transfers may remain at 20%, because there was no rate increase applicable to those types of transactions and, therefore, the requirements of § 1026.59(a) do not apply.

## *59(c) Timing*

1. *In general.* The issuer may review all of its accounts subject to § 1026.59(a) at the same time once every six months, may review each account once each six months on a rolling basis based on the date on which the rate was increased for that account, or may otherwise review each account not less frequently than once every six months.

2. *Example.* A card issuer increases the rates applicable to one half of its credit card accounts on June 1, 2011. The card issuer increases the rates applicable to the other half of its credit card accounts on September 1, 2011. The card issuer may review the rate increases for all of its credit card accounts on or before December 1, 2011, and at least every six months thereafter. In the alternative, the card issuer may first review the rate increases for the accounts that were repriced on June 1, 2011 on or before December 1, 2011, and may first review the rate increases for the accounts that were repriced on September 1, 2011 on or before March 1, 2012.

3. *Rate increases prior to effective date of rule.* For increases in annual percentage rates applicable to a credit card account under an open-end (not home-secured) consumer credit plan on or after January 1, 2009 and prior to August 22, 2010, § 1026.59(c) requires that the first review for such rate increases be conducted prior to February 22, 2011.

## *59(d) Factors*

1. *Change in factors.* A creditor that complies with § 1026.59(a) by reviewing the factors it currently considers in determining the annual percentage rates applicable to similar new credit card accounts may change those factors from time to time. When a creditor changes the factors it considers in determining the annual percentage rates applicable to similar new credit card accounts from time to time, it may comply with § 1026.59(a) by reviewing the set of factors it considered immediately prior to the change in factors for a brief transition period, or may consider the new factors. For example, a creditor changes the factors it uses to determine the rates applicable to similar new credit card accounts on January 1, 2012. The creditor reviews the rates applicable to its existing accounts that have been subject to a rate increase pursuant to § 1026.59(a) on January 25, 2012. The creditor complies with § 1026.59(a) by reviewing, at its option, either the factors that it considered on December 31, 2011 when determining the rates applicable to similar new credit card accounts or the factors that it considers as of January 25, 2012. For purposes of compliance with § 1026.59(d), a transition period of 60 days from the change of factors constitutes a brief transition period.

2. *Comparison of existing account to factors used for similar new accounts.* Under § 1026.59(a), if a creditor evaluates an existing account using the same factors that it considers in determining the rates applicable to similar new accounts, the review of factors need not result in existing accounts being subject to exactly the same rates and rate structure as a creditor imposes on similar new accounts. For example, a creditor may offer variable rates on similar new accounts that are computed by adding a margin that depends on various factors to the value of the LIBOR index. The account that the creditor is required to review pursuant to § 1026.59(a) may have variable rates that were determined by adding a different margin, depending on different factors, to a published prime rate. In performing the review required by § 1026.59(a), the creditor may review the factors it uses to determine the rates applicable to similar new accounts. If a rate reduction is required, however, the creditor need not base the variable rate for the existing account on the LIBOR index but may continue to use the published prime rate. Section 1026.59(a) requires, however, that the rate on the existing account after the reduction, as determined by adding the published prime rate and margin, be comparable to the rate, as determined by adding the margin and LIBOR, charged on a new account for which the factors are comparable.

3. *Similar new credit card accounts.* A card issuer complying with § 1026.59(d)(1)(ii) is required to consider the factors that the card issuer currently considers when determining the annual percentage rates applicable to similar new credit card accounts under an open-end (not home-secured) consumer credit plan. For example, a card issuer may review different factors in determining the annual percentage rate that applies to credit card plans for which the consumer pays an annual fee and receives rewards points than it reviews in determining the rates for credit card plans with no annual fee and no rewards points. Similarly, a card issuer may review different factors in determining the annual percentage rate that applies to private label credit cards than it reviews in determining the rates applicable to credit cards that can be used at a wider variety of merchants. In addition, a card issuer may review different factors in determining the annual percentage rate that applies to private label credit cards usable only at Merchant A than it may review for private label credit cards usable only at Merchant B. However, § 1026.59(d)(1)(ii) requires a card issuer to review the factors it considers when determining the rates for new credit card accounts with similar features that are offered for similar purposes.

4. *No similar new credit card accounts.* In some circumstances, a card issuer that complies with § 1026.59(a) by reviewing the factors that it currently considers in determining the annual percentage rates applicable to similar new accounts may not be able to identify a class of new accounts that are similar to the existing accounts on which a rate increase has been imposed. For example, consumers may have existing credit card accounts under an open-end (not home-secured) consumer credit plan but the card issuer may no longer offer a product to new consumers with similar characteristics, such as the availability of rewards, size of credit line, or other features. Similarly, some consumers' accounts may have been closed and therefore cannot be used for new transactions, while all new accounts can be used for new transactions. In those circumstances, § 1026.59 requires that the card issuer nonetheless perform a review of the rate increase on the existing customers' accounts. A card issuer does not comply with § 1026.59 by maintaining an increased rate without performing such an evaluation. In such circumstances, § 1026.59(d)(1)(ii) requires that the card issuer compare the existing accounts to the most closely comparable new accounts that it offers.

5. *Consideration of consumer's conduct on existing account.* A card issuer that complies with § 1026.59(a) by reviewing the factors that it currently considers in determining the annual percentage rates applicable to similar new accounts may consider the consumer's payment or other account behavior on the existing account only to the same extent and in the same manner that the issuer considers such information when one of its current cardholders applies for a new account with the card issuer. For example, a card issuer might obtain consumer reports for all of its applicants. The consumer reports contain certain information regarding the applicant's past performance on existing credit card accounts. However, the card issuer may have additional information about an existing cardholder's payment history or account usage that does not appear in the consumer report and that, accordingly, it would not generally have for all new applicants. For example, a consumer may have made a payment that is five days late on his or her account with the card issuer, but this information does not appear on the consumer report. The card issuer may consider this additional information in performing its review under § 1026.59(a), but only to the extent and in the manner that it considers such information if a current cardholder applies for a new account with the issuer.

6. *Multiple rate increases between January 1, 2009 and February 21, 2010.*

i. *General.* Section 1026.59(d)(2) applies if an issuer increased the rate applicable to a credit card account under an open-end (not home-secured) consumer credit plan between January 1, 2009 and February 21, 2010, and the increase was not based solely upon factors specific to the consumer. In some cases, a credit card account may have been subject to multiple rate increases during the period from January 1, 2009 to February 21, 2010. Some such rate increases may have been based solely upon factors specific to the consumer, while others may have been based on factors not specific to the consumer, such as the issuer's cost of funds or market conditions. In such circumstances, when conducting the first two reviews required under § 1026.59, the card issuer may separately review: (i) Rate increases imposed based on factors not specific to the consumer, using the factors described in § 1026.59(d)(1)(ii) (as required by § 1026.59(d)(2)); and (ii) rate increases imposed based on consumer-specific factors, using the factors described in § 1026.59(d)(1)(i). If the review of factors described in § 1026.59(d)(1)(i) indicates that it is appropriate to continue to apply a penalty or other increased rate to the account as a result of the consumer's payment history or other factors specific to the consumer, § 1026.59 permits the card issuer to continue to impose the penalty or other increased rate, even if the review of the factors described in § 1026.59(d)(1)(ii) would otherwise require a rate decrease.

ii. *Example.* Assume a credit card account was subject to a rate of 15% on all transactions as of January 1, 2009. On May 1, 2009, the issuer increased the rate on existing balances and new transactions to 18%, based upon market conditions or other factors not specific to the consumer or the consumer's account. Subsequently, on September 1, 2009, based on a payment that was received five days after the due date, the issuer increased the applicable rate on existing balances and new transactions from 18% to a penalty rate of 25%. When conducting the first review required under § 1026.59, the card issuer reviews the rate increase from 15% to 18% using the factors described in § 1026.59(d)(1)(ii) (as required by § 1026.59(d)(2)), and separately but concurrently reviews the rate increase from 18% to 25% using the factors described in paragraph § 1026.59(d)(1)(i). The review of the rate increase from 15% to 18% based upon the factors described in § 1026.59(d)(1)(ii) indicates that a similarly situated new consumer would receive a rate of 17%. The review of the rate increase from 18% to 25% based upon the factors described in § 1026.59(d)(1)(i) indicates that it is appropriate to continue to apply the 25% penalty rate based upon the consumer's late payment. Section 1026.59 permits the rate on the account to remain at 25%.

## 59(f) Termination of Obligation to Review Factors

1. *Revocation of temporary rates.*

i. *In general.* If an annual percentage rate is increased due to revocation of a temporary rate, § 1026.59(a) requires that the card issuer periodically review the increased rate. In contrast, if the rate increase results from the expiration of a temporary rate previously disclosed in accordance with § 1026.9(c)(2)(v)(B), the review requirements in § 1026.59(a) do not apply. If a temporary rate is revoked such that the requirements of § 1026.59(a) apply, § 1026.59(f) permits an issuer to terminate the review of the rate increase if and when the applicable rate is the same as the rate that would have applied if the increase had not occurred.

ii. *Examples.* Assume that on January 1, 2011, a consumer opens a new credit card account under an open-end (not home-secured) consumer credit plan. The annual percentage rate applicable to purchases is 15%. The card issuer offers the consumer a 10% rate on purchases made between February 1, 2012 and August 1, 2013 and discloses pursuant to § 1026.9(c)(2)(v)(B) that on August 1, 2013 the rate on purchases will revert to the original 15% rate. The consumer makes a payment that is five days late in July 2012.

A. Upon providing 45 days' advance notice and to the extent permitted under § 1026.55, the card issuer increases the rate applicable to new purchases to 15%, effective on September 1, 2012. The card issuer must review that rate increase under § 1026.59(a) at least once each six months during the period from September 1, 2012 to August 1, 2013, unless and until the card issuer reduces the rate to 10%. The card issuer performs reviews of the rate increase on January 1, 2013 and July 1, 2013. Based on those reviews, the rate applicable to purchases remains at 15%. Beginning on August 1, 2013, the card issuer is not required to continue periodically reviewing the rate increase, because if the temporary rate had expired in accordance with its previously disclosed terms, the 15% rate would have applied to purchase balances as of August 1, 2013 even if the rate increase had not occurred on September 1, 2012.

B. Same facts as above except that the review conducted on July 1, 2013 indicates that a reduction to the original temporary rate of 10% is appropriate. Section 1026.59(a)(2)(i) requires that the rate be reduced no later than 45 days after completion of the review, or no later than August 15, 2013. Because the temporary rate would have expired prior to the date on which the rate decrease is required to take effect, the card issuer may, at its option, reduce the rate to 10% for any portion of the period from July 1, 2013, to August 1, 2013, or may continue to impose the 15% rate for that entire period. The card issuer is not required to conduct further reviews of the 15% rate on purchases.

C. Same facts as above except that on September 1, 2012 the card issuer increases the rate applicable to new purchases to the penalty rate on the consumer's account, which is 25%. The card issuer conducts reviews of the increased rate in accordance with § 1026.59 on January 1, 2013 and July 1, 2013. Based on those reviews, the rate applicable to purchases remains at 25%. The card issuer's obligation to review the rate increase continues to apply after August 1, 2013, because the 25% penalty rate exceeds the 15% rate that would have applied if the temporary rate expired in accordance with its previously disclosed terms. The card issuer's obligation to review the rate terminates if and when the annual percentage rate applicable to purchases is reduced to the 15% rate.

2. *Example—relationship to § 1026.59(a).* Assume that on January 1, 2011, a consumer opens a new credit card account under an open-end (not home-secured) consumer credit plan. The annual percentage rate applicable to purchases is 15%. Upon providing 45 days' advance notice and to the extent permitted under § 1026.55, the card issuer increases the rate applicable to new purchases to 18%, effective on September 1, 2012. The card issuer conducts reviews of the increased rate in accordance with § 1026.59 on January 1, 2013 and July 1, 2013, based on the factors described in § 1026.59(d)(1)(ii). Based on the January 1, 2013 review, the rate applicable to purchases remains at 18%. In the review conducted on July 1, 2013, the card issuer determines that, based on the relevant factors, the rate it would offer on a comparable new account would be 14%. Consistent with § 1026.59(f), § 1026.59(a) requires that the card issuer reduce the rate on the existing account to the 15% rate that was in effect prior to the September 1, 2012 rate increase.

## 59(g) Acquired Accounts

## 59(g)(1) General

1. *Relationship to § 1026.59(d)(2) for rate increases imposed between January 1, 2009 and February 21, 2010.* Section 1026.59(d)(2) applies to acquired accounts. Accordingly, if a card issuer acquires accounts on which a rate increase was imposed between January 1, 2009 and February 21, 2010 that was not based solely upon consumer-specific factors, that acquiring card issuer must consider the factors that it currently considers when determining the annual percentage rates applicable to similar new credit card accounts, if it conducts either or both of the first two reviews of such accounts that are required after August 22, 2010 under § 1026.59(a).

## 59(g)(2) Review of Acquired Portfolio

1. *Example—general.* A card issuer acquires a portfolio of accounts that currently are subject to annual percentage rates of 12%, 15%, and 18%. Not later than six months after the acquisition of such accounts, the card issuer reviews all of these accounts in accordance with the factors that it currently uses in determining the rates applicable to similar new credit card accounts. As a result of that review, the card issuer decreases the rate on the accounts that are currently subject to a 12% annual percentage rate to 10%, leaves the rate applicable to the accounts currently subject to a 15% annual percentage rate at 15%, and increases the rate applicable to the accounts currently subject to a rate of 18% to 20%. Section 1026.59(g)(2) requires the card issuer to review, no less frequently than once every six months, the accounts for which the rate has been increased to 20%. The card issuer is not required to review the accounts subject to 10% and 15% rates pursuant to § 1026.59(a), unless and until the card issuer makes a subsequent rate increase applicable to those accounts.

2. *Example—penalty rates.* A card issuer acquires a portfolio of accounts that currently are subject to standard annual percentage rates of 12% and 15%. In addition, several acquired accounts are subject to a penalty rate of 24%. Not later than six months after the acquisition of such accounts, the card issuer reviews all of these accounts in accordance with the factors that it currently uses in determining the rates applicable to similar new credit card accounts. As a result of that review, the card issuer leaves the standard rates applicable to the accounts at 12% and 15%, respectively. The card issuer decreases the rate applicable to the accounts currently at 24% to its penalty rate of 23%. Section 1026.59(g)(2) requires the card issuer to review, no less frequently than once every six months, the accounts that are subject to a penalty rate of 23%. The card issuer is not required to review the accounts subject to 12% and 15% rates pursuant to § 1026.59(a), unless and until the card issuer makes a subsequent rate increase applicable to those accounts.

[75 Fed. Reg. 37,583 (June 29, 2010); 76 Fed. Reg. 23,038, 23,039 (Apr. 25, 2011)]

## SECTION 1026.60 Credit and Charge Card Applications and Solicitations [§ 226.5a]

1. *General.* Section 1026.60 generally requires that credit disclosures be contained in application forms and solicitations initiated by a card issuer to open a credit or charge card account. (See § 1026.60(a)(5) and (e)(2) for exceptions; see § 1026.60(a)(1) and accompanying commentary for the definition of solicitation; see also § 1026.2(a)(15) and accompanying commentary for the definition of charge card.)

2. *Substitution of account-opening summary table for the disclosures required by § 1026.60.* In complying with § 1026.60(c), (e)(1) or (f), a card issuer may provide the account-opening summary table described in § 1026.6(b)(1) in lieu of the disclosures required by § 1026.60, if the issuer provides the disclosures required by § 1026.6 on or with the application or solicitation.

3. *Clear and conspicuous standard.* See comment 5(a)(1)-1 for the clear and conspicuous standard applicable to § 1026.60 disclosures.

### *60(a) General Rules*

### *60(a)(1) Definition of Solicitation*

1. *Invitations to apply.* A card issuer may contact a consumer who has not been preapproved for a card account about opening an account (whether by direct mail, telephone, or other means) and invite the consumer to complete an application. Such a contact does not meet the definition of *solicitation*, nor is it covered by this section, unless the contact itself includes an application form in a direct mailing, electronic communication or "take-one"; an oral application in a telephone contact initiated by the card issuer; or an application in an in-person contact initiated by the card issuer.

### *60(a)(2) Form of Disclosures; Tabular Format*

1. *Location of table.*

i. *General.* Except for disclosures given electronically, disclosures in § 1026.60(b) that are required to be provided in a table must be prominently located on or with the application or solicitation. Disclosures are deemed to be prominently located, for example, if the disclosures are on the same page as an application or solicitation reply form. If the disclosures appear elsewhere, they are deemed to be prominently located if the application or solicitation reply form contains a clear and conspicuous reference to the location of the disclosures and indicates that they contain rate, fee, and other cost information, as applicable.

ii. *Electronic disclosures.* If the table is provided electronically, the table must be provided in close proximity to the application or solicitation. Card issuers have flexibility in satisfying this requirement. Methods card issuers could use to satisfy the requirement include, but are not limited to, the following examples (whatever method is used, a card issuer need not confirm that the consumer has read the disclosures):

A. The disclosures could automatically appear on the screen when the application or reply form appears;

B. The disclosures could be located on the same Web page as the application or reply form (whether or not they appear on the initial screen), if the application or reply form contains a clear and conspicuous reference to the location of the disclosures and indicates that the disclosures contain rate, fee, and other cost information, as applicable;

C. Card issuers could provide a link to the electronic disclosures on or with the application (or reply form) as long as consumers cannot bypass the disclosures before submitting the application or reply form. The link would take the consumer to the disclosures, but the consumer need not be required to scroll completely through the disclosures; or

D. The disclosures could be located on the same Web page as the application or reply form without necessarily appearing on the initial screen, immediately preceding the button that the consumer will click to submit the application or reply.

2. *Multiple accounts.* If a tabular format is required to be used, card issuers offering several types of accounts may disclose the various terms for the accounts in a single table or may provide a separate table for each account.

3. *Information permitted in the table. See* the commentary to § 1026.60(b), (d), and (e)(1) for guidance on additional information permitted in the table.

4. *Deletion of inapplicable disclosures.* Generally, disclosures need only be given as applicable. Card issuers may, therefore, omit inapplicable headings and their corresponding boxes in the table. For example, if no foreign transaction fee is imposed on the account, the heading *Foreign transaction* and disclosure may be deleted from the table or the disclosure form may contain the heading *Foreign transaction* and a disclosure showing *none*. There is an exception for the grace period disclosure; even if no grace period exists, that fact must be stated.

5. *Highlighting of annual percentage rates and fee amounts.*

i. *In general.* See Samples G-10(B) and G-10(C) for guidance on providing the disclosures described in § 1026.60(a)(2)(iv) in bold text. Other annual percentage rates or fee amounts disclosed in the table may not be in bold text. Samples G-10(B) and G-10(C) also provide guidance to issuers on how to disclose the rates and fees described in § 1026.60(a)(2)(iv) in a clear and conspicuous manner, by including these rates and fees generally as the first text in the applicable rows of the table so that the highlighted rates and fees generally are aligned vertically in the table.

ii. *Maximum limits on fees.* Section 1026.60(a)(2)(iv) provides that any maximum limits on fee amounts must be disclosed in bold text. For example, assume that, consistent with § 1026.52(b)(1)(ii), a card issuer's late payment fee will not exceed $35. The maximum limit of $35 for the late payment fee must be highlighted in bold. Similarly, assume an issuer will charge a cash advance fee of $5 or 3 percent of the cash advance transaction amount, whichever is greater, but the fee will not exceed $100. The maximum limit of $100 for the cash advance fee must be highlighted in bold.

iii. *Periodic fees.* Section 1026.60(a)(2)(iv) provides that any periodic fee disclosed pursuant to § 1026.60(b)(2) that is not an annualized amount must not be disclosed in bold. For example, if an issuer imposes a $10 monthly maintenance fee for a card account, the issuer must disclose in the table that there is a $10 monthly maintenance fee, and that the fee is $120 on an annual basis. In this example, the $10 fee disclosure would not be disclosed in bold, but the $120 annualized amount must be disclosed in bold. In addition, if an issuer must disclose any annual fee in the table, the amount of the annual fee must be disclosed in bold.

6. *Form of disclosures.* Whether disclosures must be in electronic form depends upon the following:

i. If a consumer accesses a credit card application or solicitation electronically (other than as described under ii. below), such as online at a home computer, the card issuer must provide the disclosures in electronic form (such as with the application or solicitation on its Web site) in order to meet the requirement to provide disclosures in a timely manner on or with the application or solicitation. If the issuer instead mailed paper disclosures to the consumer, this requirement would not be met.

ii. In contrast, if a consumer is physically present in the card issuer's office, and accesses a credit card application or solicitation electronically, such as via a terminal or kiosk (or if the consumer uses a terminal or kiosk located on the premises of an affiliate or third party that has arranged with the card issuer to provide applications or solicitations to consumers), the issuer may provide disclosures in either electronic or paper form, provided the issuer complies with the timing and delivery ("on or with") requirements of the regulation.

7. *Terminology.* Section 1026.60(a)(2)(i) generally requires that the headings, content and format of the tabular disclosures be substantially similar, but need not be identical, to the applicable tables in Appendix G-10 to part 1026; but *see* § 1026.5(a)(2) for terminology requirements applicable to § 1026.60 disclosures.

### *60(a)(4) Fees That Vary by State*

1. *Manner of disclosing range.* If the card issuer discloses a range of fees instead of disclosing the amount of the specific fee applicable to the con-

sumer's account, the range may be stated as the lowest authorized fee (zero, if there are one or more states where no fee applies) to the highest authorized fee.

### 60(a)(5) Exceptions

1. *Noncoverage of consumer-initiated requests.* Applications provided to a consumer upon request are not covered by § 1026.60, even if the request is made in response to the card issuer's invitation to apply for a card account. To illustrate, if a card issuer invites consumers to call a toll-free number or to return a response card to obtain an application, the application sent in response to the consumer's request need not contain the disclosures required under § 1026.60. Similarly, if the card issuer invites consumers to call and make an oral application on the telephone, § 1026.60 does not apply to the application made by the consumer. If, however, the card issuer calls a consumer or initiates a telephone discussion with a consumer about opening a card account and contemporaneously takes an oral application, such applications are subject to § 1026.60, specifically § 1026.60(d). Likewise, if the card issuer initiates an in-person discussion with a consumer about opening a card account and contemporaneously takes an application, such applications are subject to § 1026.60, specifically § 1026.60(f).

### 60(b) Required Disclosures

1. *Tabular format.* Provisions in § 1026.60(b) and its commentary provide that certain information must appear or is permitted to appear in a table. The tabular format is required for § 1026.60(b) disclosures given pursuant to § 1026.60(c), (d)(2), (e)(1) and (f). The tabular format does not apply to oral disclosures given pursuant to § 1026.60(d)(1). (*See* § 1026.60(a)(2).)

2. *Accuracy.* Rules concerning accuracy of the disclosures required by § 1026.60(b), including variable rate disclosures, are stated in § 1026.60(c)(2), (d)(3), and (e)(4), as applicable.

### 60(b)(1) Annual Percentage Rate

1. *Variable-rate accounts—definition.* For purposes of § 1026.60(b)(1), a variable-rate account exists when rate changes are part of the plan and are tied to an index or formula. (*See* the commentary to § 1026.6(b)(4)(ii) for examples of variable-rate plans.)

2. *Variable-rate accounts—fact that rate varies and how the rate will be determined.* In describing how the applicable rate will be determined, the card issuer must identify in the table the type of index or formula used, such as the prime rate. In describing the index, the issuer may not include in the table details about the index. For example, if the issuer uses a prime rate, the issuer must disclose the rate as a "prime rate" and may not disclose in the table other details about the prime rate, such as the fact that it is the highest prime rate published in the *Wall Street Journal* two business days before the closing date of the statement for each billing period. The issuer may not disclose in the table the current value of the index (such as that the prime rate is currently 7.5 percent) or the amount of the margin or spread added to the index or formula in setting the applicable rate. A card issuer may not disclose any applicable limitations on rate increases or decreases in the table, such as describing that the rate will not go below a certain rate or higher than a certain rate. (*See* Samples G-10(B) and G-10(C) for guidance on how to disclose the fact that the applicable rate varies and how it is determined.)

3. *Discounted initial rates.*

i. *Immediate proximity.* If the term "introductory" is in the same phrase as the introductory rate, as that term is defined in § 1026.16(g)(2)(ii), it will be deemed to be in immediate proximity of the listing. For example, an issuer that uses the phrase "introductory balance transfer APR X percent" has used the word "introductory" within the same phrase as the rate. (*See* Sample G-10(C) for guidance on how to disclose clearly and conspicuously the expiration date of the introductory rate and the rate that will apply after the introductory rate expires, if an introductory rate is disclosed in the table.)

ii. *Subsequent changes in terms.* The fact that an issuer may reserve the right to change a rate subsequent to account opening, pursuant to the notice requirements of § 1026.9(c) and the limitations in § 1026.55, does not, by itself, make that rate an introductory rate. For example, assume an issuer discloses an annual percentage rate for purchases of 12.99% but does not specify a time period during which that rate will be in effect. Even if that issuer subsequently increases the annual percentage rate for purchases to 15.99%, pursuant to a change-in-terms notice provided under § 1026.9(c), the 12.99% is not an introductory rate.

iii. *More than one introductory rate.* If more than one introductory rate may apply to a particular balance in succeeding periods, the term "introductory" need only be used to describe the first introductory rate. For example, if an issuer offers a rate of 8.99% on purchases for six months, 10.99% on purchases for the following six months, and 14.99% on purchases after the first year, the term "introductory" need only be used to describe the 8.99% rate.

4. *Premium initial rates—subsequent changes in terms.* The fact that an issuer may reserve the right to change a rate subsequent to account opening, pursuant to the notice requirements of § 1026.9(c) and the limitations in § 1026.55 (as applicable), does not, by itself, make that rate a premium initial rate. For example, assume an issuer discloses an annual percentage rate for purchases of 18.99% but does not specify a time period during which that rate will be in effect. Even if that issuer subsequently reduces the annual percentage rate for purchases to 15.99%, the 18.99% is not a premium initial rate. If the rate decrease is the result of a change from a non-variable rate to a variable rate or from a variable rate to a non-variable rate, see comments 9(c)(2)(v)-3 and 9(c)(2)(v)-4 for guidance on the notice requirements under § 1026.9(c).

5. *Increased penalty rates.*

i. *In general.* For rates that are not introductory rates or employee preferential rates, if a rate may increase as a penalty for one or more events specified in the account agreement, such as a late payment or an extension of credit that exceeds the credit limit, the card issuer must disclose the increased rate that would apply, a brief description of the event or events that may result in the increased rate, and a brief description of how long the increased rate will remain in effect. The description of the specific event or events that may result in an increased rate should be brief. For example, if an issuer may increase a rate to the penalty rate because the consumer does not make the minimum payment by 5 p.m., Eastern Time, on its payment due date, the issuer should describe this circumstance in the table as "make a late payment." Similarly, if an issuer may increase a rate that applies to a particular balance because the account is more than 60 days late, the issuer should describe this circumstance in the table as "make a late payment." An issuer may not distinguish between the events that may result in an increased rate for existing balances and the events that may result in an increased rate for new transactions. (*See* Samples G-10(B) and G-10(C) (in the row labeled "Penalty APR and When it Applies") for additional guidance on the level of detail in which the specific event or events should be described.) The description of how long the increased rate will remain in effect also should be brief. If a card issuer reserves the right to apply the increased rate to any balances indefinitely, to the extent permitted by §§ 1026.55(b)(4) and 1026.59, the issuer should disclose that the penalty rate may apply indefinitely. The card issuer may not disclose in the table any limitations imposed by §§ 1026.55(b)(4) and 1026.59 on the duration of increased rates. For example, if the issuer generally provides that the increased rate will apply until the consumer makes twelve timely consecutive required minimum periodic payments, except to the extent that §§ 1026.55(b)(4) and 1026.59 apply, the issuer should disclose that the penalty rate will apply until the consumer makes twelve consecutive timely minimum payments. (*See* Samples G-10(B) and G-10(C) (in the row labeled "Penalty APR and When it Applies") for additional guidance on the level of detail which the issuer should use to describe how long the increased rate will remain in effect.) A card issuer will be deemed to meet the standard to clearly and conspicuously disclose the information required by § 1026.60(b)(1)(iv)(A) if the issuer uses the format shown in Samples G-10(B) and G-10(C) (in the row labeled "Penalty APR and When it Applies") to disclose this information.

ii. *Introductory rates—general.* An issuer is required to disclose directly beneath the table the circumstances under which an introductory rate, as that term is defined in § 1026.16(g)(2)(ii), may be revoked, and the rate that will apply after the revocation. This information about revocation of an introductory rate and the rate that will apply after revocation must be provided even if the rate that will apply after the introductory rate is revoked is the rate that would have applied at the end of the promotional period. In a variable-rate account, the rate that would have applied at the end of the promotional period is a rate based on the applicable index or formula in accordance with the accuracy requirements set forth in § 1026.60(c)(2) or (e)(4). In describing the rate that will apply after revocation of the introductory rate, if the rate that will apply after revocation of the introductory rate is already disclosed in the table, the issuer is not required to repeat the rate, but may refer to that rate in a clear and conspicuous manner. For example, if the rate that will apply after revocation of an introductory rate is the standard rate that applies to that type of transaction (such as a purchase or balance transfer transaction), and the standard rates are labeled in the table as "standard APRs," the issuer may refer to the "standard APR" when describing the rate that will apply after revocation of an introductory rate. (*See* Sample G-10(C) in the disclosure labeled "Loss of Introductory APR" directly beneath the table.) The description of the circumstances in which an introductory rate could be revoked should be brief. For example, if an issuer may increase an introductory rate because the account is more than 60 days late, the issuer should describe this circumstance directly beneath the table as "make a late payment." In addition, if the circumstances in which an introductory rate could be revoked are already listed elsewhere in the table, the issuer is not required to repeat the circumstances again, but may refer to those circumstances in a clear and conspicuous manner. For example, if the circumstances in which an introductory rate could be revoked are the same as the event or events that may trigger a "penalty rate" as described in § 1026.60(b)(1)(iv)(A), the issuer may refer to the actions listed in the Penalty APR row, in describing the circumstances in which the introductory rate could be revoked. (*See* Sample G-10(C) in the disclosure labeled "Loss of Introductory APR" directly beneath the table for additional guidance on the level of detail in which to describe the circumstances in which an introductory rate could be revoked.) A card issuer will be deemed to meet the standard to clearly and conspicuously disclose the information required by § 1026.60(b)(1)(iv)(B) if the issuer uses the format shown in Sample G-10(C) to disclose this information.

iii. *Introductory rates—limitations on revocation.* Issuers that are disclosing an introductory rate are prohibited by § 1026.55 from increasing or revoking the introductory rate before it expires unless the consumer fails to make a required minimum periodic payment within 60 days after the due date for the payment. In making the required disclosure pursuant to § 1026.60(b)(1)(iv)(B), issuers should describe this circumstance directly beneath the table as "make a late payment."

iv. *Employee preferential rates.* An issuer is required to disclose directly beneath the table the circumstances under which an employee preferential rate may be revoked, and the rate that will apply after the revocation. In describing the rate that will apply after revocation of the employee preferential rate, if the rate that will apply after revocation of the employee preferential rate is already disclosed in the table, the issuer is not required to repeat the rate, but may refer to that rate in a clear and conspicuous manner. For example, if the rate that will apply after revocation of an employee preferential rate is the standard rate that applies to that type of transaction (such as a purchase or balance transfer transaction), and the standard rates are labeled in the table as "standard APRs," the issuer may refer to the "standard APR" when describing the rate that will apply after revocation of an employee preferential rate. The description of the circumstances in which an employee preferential rate could be revoked should be brief. For example, if an issuer may increase an employee preferential rate based upon termination of the employee's employment relationship with the issuer or a third party, issuers may describe this circumstance as "if your employment with [issuer or third party] ends."

6. *Rates that depend on consumer's creditworthiness.*

i. *In general.* The card issuer, at its option, may disclose the possible rates that may apply as either specific rates, or a range of rates. For example, if there are three possible rates that may apply (9.99, 12.99 or 17.99 percent), an issuer may disclose specific rates (9.99, 12.99 or 17.99 percent) or a range of rates (9.99 to 17.99 percent). The card issuer may not disclose only the lowest, highest or median rate that could apply. (*See* Samples G-10(B) and G-10(C) for guidance on how to disclose a range of rates.)

ii. *Penalty rates.* If the rate is a penalty rate, as described in § 1026.60(b)(1)(iv), the card issuer at its option may disclose the highest rate that could apply, instead of disclosing the specific rates or the range of rates that could apply. For example, if the penalty rate could be up to 28.99 percent, but the issuer may impose a penalty rate that is less than that rate depending on factors at the time the penalty rate is imposed, the issuer may disclose the penalty rate as "up to" 28.99 percent. The issuer also must include a statement that the penalty rate for which the consumer may qualify will depend on the consumer's creditworthiness, and other factors if applicable.

iii. *Other factors.* Section 1026.60(b)(1)(v) applies even if other factors are used in combination with a consumer's creditworthiness to determine the rate for which a consumer may qualify at account opening. For example, § 1026.60(b)(1)(v) would apply if the issuer considers the type of purchase the consumer is making at the time the consumer opens the account, in combination with the consumer's creditworthiness, to determine the rate for which the consumer may qualify at account opening. If other factors are considered, the issuer should amend the statement about creditworthiness, to indicate that the rate for which the consumer may qualify at account opening will depend on the consumer's creditworthiness and other factors. Nonetheless, § 1026.60(b)(1)(v) does not apply if a consumer's creditworthiness is not one of the factors that will determine the rate for which the consumer may qualify at account opening (for example, if the rate is based solely on the type of purchase that the consumer is making at the time the consumer opens the account, or is based solely on whether the consumer has other banking relationships with the card issuer).

7. *Rate based on another rate on the account.* In some cases, one rate may be based on another rate on the account. For example, assume that a penalty rate as described in § 1026.60(b)(1)(iv)(A) is determined by adding 5 percentage points to the current purchase rate, which is 10 percent. In this example, the card issuer in disclosing the penalty rate must disclose 15 percent as the current penalty rate. If the purchase rate is a variable rate, then the penalty rate also is a variable rate. In that case, the card issuer also must disclose the fact that the penalty rate may vary and how the rate is determined, such as "This APR may vary with the market based on the Prime Rate." In describing the penalty rate, the issuer shall not disclose in the table the amount of the margin or spread added to the current purchase rate to determine the penalty rate, such as describing that the penalty rate is determined by adding 5 percentage points to the purchase rate. (*See* § 1026.60(b)(1)(i) and comment 60(b)(1)-2 for further guidance on describing a variable rate.)

8. *Rates.* The only rates that shall be disclosed in the table are annual percentage rates determined under § 1026.14(b). Periodic rates shall not be disclosed in the table.

9. *Deferred interest or similar transactions.* An issuer offering a deferred interest or similar plan, such as a promotional program that provides that a consumer will not be obligated to pay interest that accrues on a balance if that balance is paid in full prior to the expiration of a specified period of time, may not disclose a 0% rate as the rate applicable to deferred interest or similar transactions if there are any circumstances under which the consumer will be obligated for interest on such transactions for the deferred interest or similar period.

### *60(b)(2) Fees for Issuance or Availability*

1. *Membership fees.* Membership fees for opening an account must be disclosed under this paragraph. A membership fee to join an organization that provides a credit or charge card as a privilege of

membership must be disclosed only if the card is issued automatically upon membership. Such a fee shall not be disclosed in the table if membership results merely in eligibility to apply for an account.

2. *Enhancements.* Fees for optional services in addition to basic membership privileges in a credit or charge card account (for example, travel insurance or card-registration services) shall not be disclosed in the table if the basic account may be opened without paying such fees. Issuing a card to each primary cardholder (not authorized users) is considered a basic membership privilege and fees for additional cards, beyond the first card on the account, must be disclosed as a fee for issuance or availability. Thus, a fee to obtain an additional card on the account beyond the first card (so that each cardholder would have his or her own card) must be disclosed in the table as a fee for issuance or availability under § 1026.60(b)(2). This fee must be disclosed even if the fee is optional; that is, if the fee is charged only if the cardholder requests one or more additional cards. (*See* the available credit disclosure in § 1026.60(b)(14).)

3. *One-time fees.* Disclosure of non-periodic fees is limited to fees related to opening the account, such as one-time membership or participation fees, or an application fee that is excludable from the finance charge under § 1026.4(c)(1). The following are examples of fees that shall not be disclosed in the table:

i. Fees for reissuing a lost or stolen card.

ii. Statement reproduction fees.

4. *Waived or reduced fees.* If fees required to be disclosed are waived or reduced for a limited time, the introductory fees or the fact of fee waivers may be disclosed in the table in addition to the required fees if the card issuer also discloses how long the reduced fees or waivers will remain in effect in accordance with the requirements of §§ 1026.9(c)(2)(v)(B) and 1026.55(b)(1).

5. *Periodic fees and one-time fees.* A card issuer disclosing a periodic fee must disclose the amount of the fee, how frequently it will be imposed, and the annualized amount of the fee. A card issuer disclosing a non-periodic fee must disclose that the fee is a one-time fee. (*See* Sample G-10(C) for guidance on how to meet these requirements.)

### *60(b)(3) Fixed Finance Charge; Minimum Interest Charge*

1. *Example of brief statement. See* Samples G-10(B) and G-10(C) for guidance on how to provide a brief description of a minimum interest charge.

2. *Adjustment of $1.00 threshold amount.* Consistent with § 1026.60(b)(3), the Bureau will publish adjustments to the $1.00 threshold amount, as appropriate.

### *60(b)(4) Transaction Charges*

1. *Charges imposed by person other than card issuer.* Charges imposed by a third party, such as a seller of goods, shall not be disclosed in the table under this section; the third party would be responsible for disclosing the charge under § 1026.9(d)(1).

2. *Foreign transaction fees.* A transaction charge imposed by the card issuer for the use of the card for purchases includes any fee imposed by the issuer for purchases in a foreign currency or that take place outside the United States or with a foreign merchant. (*See* comment 4(a)-4 for guidance on when a foreign transaction fee is considered charged by the card issuer.) If an issuer charges the same foreign transaction fee for purchases and cash advances in a foreign currency, or that take place outside the United States or with a foreign merchant, the issuer may disclose this foreign transaction fee as shown in Samples G-10(B) and G-10(C). Otherwise, the issuer must revise the foreign transaction fee language shown in Samples G-10(B) and G-10(C) to disclose clearly and conspicuously the amount of the foreign transaction fee that applies to purchases and the amount of the foreign transaction fee that applies to cash advances.

### *60(b)(5) Grace Period*

1. *How grace period disclosure is made.* The card issuer must state any conditions on the applicability of the grace period. An issuer, however, may not disclose under § 1026.60(b)(5) the limitations on the imposition of finance charges as a result of a loss of a grace period in § 1026.54, or the impact of payment allocation on whether interest is charged on purchases as a result of a loss of a grace period. Some issuers may offer a grace period on all purchases under which interest will not be charged on purchases if the consumer pays the outstanding balance shown on a periodic statement in full by the due date shown on that statement for one or more billing cycles. In these circumstances, § 1026.60(b)(5) requires that the issuer disclose the grace period and the conditions for its applicability using the following language, or substantially similar language, as applicable: "Your due date is [at least]——days after the close of each billing cycle. We will not charge you any interest on purchases if you pay your entire balance by the due date each month." However, other issuers may offer a grace period on all purchases under which interest may be charged on purchases even if the consumer pays the outstanding balance shown on a periodic statement in full by the due date shown on that statement each billing cycle. In these circumstances, § 1026.60(b)(5) requires the issuer to amend the above disclosure language to describe accurately the conditions on the applicability of the grace period.

2. *No grace period.* The issuer may use the following language to describe that no grace period on any purchases is offered, as applicable: "We will begin charging interest on purchases on the transaction date."

3. *Grace period on some purchases.* If the issuer provides a grace period on some types of purchases but no grace period on others, the issuer may combine and revise the language in comments 60(b)(5)-1 and -2 as appropriate to describe to which types of purchases a grace period applies and to which types of purchases no grace period is offered.

### *60(b)(6) Balance Computation Method*

1. *Form of disclosure.* In cases where the card issuer uses a balance computation method that is identified by name in § 1026.60(g), the card issuer must disclose below the table only the name of the method. In cases where the card issuer uses a balance computation method that is not identified by name in § 1026.60(g), the disclosure below the table must clearly explain the method in as much detail as set forth in the descriptions of balance methods in § 1026.60(g). The explanation need not be as detailed as that required for the disclosures under § 1026.6(b)(4)(i)(D).

2. *Determining the method.* In determining which balance computation method to disclose for purchases, the card issuer must assume that a purchase balance will exist at the end of any grace period. Thus, for example, if the average daily balance method will include new purchases only if purchase balances are not paid within the grace period, the card issuer would disclose the name of the average daily balance method that includes new purchases. The card issuer must not assume the existence of a purchase balance, however, in making other disclosures under § 1026.60(b).

### *60(b)(7) Statement on Charge Card Payments*

1. *Applicability and content.* The disclosure that charges are payable upon receipt of the periodic statement is applicable only to charge card accounts. In making this disclosure, the card issuer may make such modifications as are necessary to more accurately reflect the circumstances of repayment under the account. For example, the disclosure might read, "Charges are due and payable upon receipt of the periodic statement and must be paid no later than 15 days after receipt of such statement."

### *60(b)(8) Cash Advance Fee*

1. *Content. See* Samples G-10(B) and G-10(C) for guidance on how to disclose clearly and conspicuously the cash advance fee.

2. *Foreign cash advances.* Cash advance fees required to be disclosed under § 1026.60(b)(8) include any charge imposed by the card issuer for cash advances in a foreign currency or that take place outside the United States or with a foreign merchant. (*See* comment 4(a)-4 for guidance on when a foreign transaction fee is considered charged by the card issuer.) If an issuer charges the same foreign transaction fee for purchases and cash advances in a foreign currency or that take place outside the United States or with a foreign merchant, the issuer may disclose this foreign transaction fee as shown in Samples G-10(B) and (C).

Otherwise, the issuer must revise the foreign transaction fee language shown in Samples G-10(B) and (C) to disclose clearly and conspicuously the amount of the foreign transaction fee that applies to purchases and the amount of the foreign transaction fee that applies to cash advances.

3. *ATM fees.* An issuer is not required to disclose pursuant to § 1026.60(b)(8) any charges imposed on a cardholder by an institution other than the card issuer for the use of the other institution's ATM in a shared or interchange system.

### 60(b)(9) Late Payment Fee

1. *Applicability.* The disclosure of the fee for a late payment includes only those fees that will be imposed for actual, unanticipated late payments. (*See* the commentary to § 1026.4(c)(2) for additional guidance on late payment fees. *See* Samples G-10(B) and G-10(C) for guidance on how to disclose clearly and conspicuously the late payment fee.)

### 60(b)(10) Over-the-Limit Fee

1. *Applicability.* The disclosure of fees for exceeding a credit limit does not include fees for other types of default or for services related to exceeding the limit. For example, no disclosure is required of fees for reinstating credit privileges or fees for the dishonor of checks on an account that, if paid, would cause the credit limit to be exceeded. (*See* Samples G-10(B) and G-10(C) for guidance on how to disclose clearly and conspicuously the over-the-limit fee.)

### 60(b)(13) Required Insurance, Debt Cancellation or Debt Suspension Coverage

1. *Content. See* Sample G-10(B) for guidance on how to comply with the requirements in § 1026.60(b)(13).

### 60(b)(14) Available Credit

1. *Calculating available credit.* If the 15 percent threshold test is met, the issuer must disclose the available credit excluding optional fees, and the available credit including optional fees. In calculating the available credit to disclose in the table, the issuer must consider all fees for the issuance or availability of credit described in § 1026.60(b)(2), and any security deposit, that will be imposed and charged to the account when the account is opened, such as one-time issuance and set-up fees. For example, in calculating the available credit, issuers must consider the first year's annual fee and the first month's maintenance fee (as applicable) if they are charged to the account on the first billing statement. In calculating the amount of the available credit including optional fees, if optional fees could be charged multiple times, the issuer shall assume that the optional fee is only imposed once. For example, if an issuer charges a fee for each additional card issued on the account, the issuer in calculating the amount of the available credit including optional fees may assume that the cardholder requests only one additional card. In disclosing the available credit, the issuer shall round down the available credit amount to the nearest whole dollar.

2. *Content. See* Sample G-10(C) for guidance on how to provide the disclosure required by § 1026.60(b)(14) clearly and conspicuously.

### 60(b)(15) Web Site Reference

1. *Content. See* Samples G-10(B) and G-10(C) for guidance on disclosing a reference to the Web site established by the Bureau and a statement that consumers may obtain on the Web site information about shopping for and using credit card accounts.

### 60(c) Direct Mail and Electronic Applications and Solicitations

1. *Mailed publications.* Applications or solicitations contained in generally available publications mailed to consumers (such as subscription magazines) are subject to the requirements applicable to *take-ones* in § 1026.60(e), rather than the direct mail requirements of § 1026.60(c). However, if a primary purpose of a card issuer's mailing is to offer credit or charge card accounts—for example, where a card issuer "prescreens" a list of potential cardholders using credit criteria, and then mails to the targeted group its catalog containing an application or a solicitation for a card account—the direct mail rules apply. In addition, a card issuer may use a single application form as a *take-one* (in racks in public locations, for example) and for direct mailings, if the card issuer complies with the requirements of § 1026.60(c) even when the form is used as a *take-one*—that is, by presenting the required § 1026.60 disclosures in a tabular format. When used in a direct mailing, the credit term disclosures must be accurate as of the mailing date whether or not the § 1026.60(e)(1)(ii) and (e)(1)(iii) disclosures are included; when used in a *take-one*, the disclosures must be accurate for as long as the *take-one* forms remain available to the public if the § 1026.60(e)(1)(ii) and (e)(1)(iii) disclosures are omitted. (If those disclosures are included in the take-one, the credit term disclosures need only be accurate as of the printing date.)

### 60(d) Telephone Applications and Solicitations

1. *Coverage.*
   i. This paragraph applies if:
      A. A telephone conversation between a card issuer and consumer may result in the issuance of a card as a consequence of an issuer-initiated offer to open an account for which the issuer does not require any application (that is, a *prescreened* telephone solicitation).
      B. The card issuer initiates the contact and at the same time takes application information over the telephone.
   ii. This paragraph does not apply to:
      A. Telephone applications initiated by the consumer.
      B. Situations where no card will be issued—because, for example, the consumer indicates that he or she does not want the card, or the card issuer decides either during the telephone conversation or later not to issue the card.

2. *Right to reject the plan.* The right to reject the plan referenced in this paragraph is the same as the right to reject the plan described in § 1026.5(b)(1)(iv). If an issuer substitutes the account-opening summary table described in § 1026.6(b)(1) in lieu of the disclosures specified in § 1026.60(d)(2)(ii), the disclosure specified in § 1026.60(d)(2)(ii)(B) must appear in the table, if the issuer is required to do so pursuant to § 1026.6(b)(2)(xiii). Otherwise, the disclosure specified in § 1026.60(d)(2)(ii)(B) may appear either in or outside the table containing the required credit disclosures.

3. *Substituting account-opening table for alternative written disclosures.* An issuer may substitute the account-opening summary table described in § 1026.6(b)(1) in lieu of the disclosures specified in § 1026.60(d)(2)(ii).

### 60(e) Applications and Solicitations Made Available to General Public

1. *Coverage.* Applications and solicitations made available to the general public include what are commonly referred to as *take-one* applications typically found at counters in banks and retail establishments, as well as applications contained in catalogs, magazines and other generally available publications. In the case of credit unions, this paragraph applies to applications and solicitations to open card accounts made available to those in the general field of membership.

2. *In-person applications and solicitations.* In-person applications and solicitations initiated by a card issuer are subject to § 1026.60(f), not § 1026.60(e). (*See* § 1026.60(f) and accompanying commentary for rules relating to in-person applications and solicitations.)

3. *Toll-free telephone number.* If a card issuer, in complying with any of the disclosure options of § 1026.60(e), provides a telephone number for consumers to call to obtain credit information, the number must be toll-free for nonlocal calls made from an area code other than the one used in the card issuer's dialing area. Alternatively, a card issuer may provide any telephone number that allows a consumer to call for information and reverse the telephone charges.

### 60(e)(1) Disclosure of Required Credit Information

1. *Date of printing.* Disclosure of the month and year fulfills the requirement to disclose the date an application was printed.

2. *Form of disclosures.* The disclosures specified in § 1026.60(e)(1)(ii) and (e)(1)(iii) may appear either

in or outside the table containing the required credit disclosures.

### *60(e)(2) No Disclosure of Credit Information*

1. *When disclosure option available.* A card issuer may use this option only if the issuer does not include on or with the application or solicitation any statement that refers to the credit disclosures required by § 1026.60(b). Statements such as *no annual fee, low interest rate, favorable rates,* and *low costs* are deemed to refer to the required credit disclosures and, therefore, may not be included on or with the solicitation or application, if the card issuer chooses to use this option.

### *60(e)(3) Prompt Response to Requests for Information*

1. *Prompt disclosure.* Information is promptly disclosed if it is given within 30 days of a consumer's request for information but in no event later than delivery of the credit or charge card.

2. *Information disclosed.* When a consumer requests credit information, card issuers need not provide all the required credit disclosures in all instances. For example, if disclosures have been provided in accordance with § 1026.60(e)(1) and a consumer calls or writes a card issuer to obtain information about changes in the disclosures, the issuer need only provide the items of information that have changed from those previously disclosed on or with the application or solicitation. If a consumer requests information about particular items, the card issuer need only provide the requested information. If, however, the card issuer has made disclosures in accordance with the option in § 1026.60(e)(2) and a consumer calls or writes the card issuer requesting information about costs, all the required disclosure information must be given.

3. *Manner of response.* A card issuer's response to a consumer's request for credit information may be provided orally or in writing, regardless of the manner in which the consumer's request is received by the issuer. Furthermore, the card issuer must provide the information listed in § 1026.60(e)(1). Information provided in writing need not be in a tabular format.

### *60(f) In-Person Applications and Solicitations*

1. *Coverage.*

i. This paragraph applies if:

A. An in-person conversation between a card issuer and a consumer may result in the issuance of a card as a consequence of an issuer-initiated offer to open an account for which the issuer does not require any application (that is, a *preapproved* in-person solicitation).

B. The card issuer initiates the contact and at the same time takes application information in person. For example, the following are covered:

*1.* A consumer applies in person for a car loan at a financial institution and the loan officer invites the consumer to apply for a credit or charge card account; the consumer accepts the invitation and submits an application.

*2.* An employee of a retail establishment, in the course of processing a sales transaction using a bank credit card, asks a customer if he or she would like to apply for the retailer's credit or charge card; the customer responds affirmatively and submits an application.

ii. This paragraph does not apply to:

A. In-person applications initiated by the consumer.

B. Situations where no card will be issued—because, for example, the consumer indicates that he or she does not want the card, or the card issuer decides during the in-person conversation not to issue the card.

[65 Fed. Reg. 58,911 (Oct. 3, 2000); 66 Fed. Reg. 17,339 (Mar. 30, 2001); 72 Fed. Reg. 63,475 (Nov. 9, 2007); 72 Fed. Reg. 71,059 (Dec. 14, 2007); 74 Fed. Reg. 5244 (Jan. 29, 2009); 75 Fed. Reg. 7848 (Feb. 22, 2010); 75 Fed. Reg. 7925 (Feb. 22, 2010); 75 Fed. Reg. 37,583 (June 29, 2010); 76 Fed. Reg. 23,007 (Apr. 25, 2011)]

* * *

# A.6 OCC Regulation on Debt Cancellation and Suspension Agreements

**Title 12—Banks and Banking**
**Chapter I-Comptroller of the Currency, Department of the Treasury**
**Part 37—Debt Cancellation Contracts and Debt Suspension Agreements**



SOURCE: 67 Fed. Reg. 58,976 (Sept. 19, 2002), unless otherwise noted.

AUTHORITY: 12 U.S.C. 1 *et seq.*, 24 (Seventh), 93a, 1818.

**Title 12—Banks and Banking**
**Chapter I-Comptroller of the Currency, Department of the Treasury**
**Part 37—Debt Cancellation Contracts and Debt Suspension Agreements**

## 12 C.F.R. § 37.1 Authority, purpose, and scope.

(a) *Authority.* A national bank is authorized to enter into debt cancellation contracts and debt suspension agreements and charge a fee therefor, in connection with extensions of credit that it makes, pursuant to 12 U.S.C. 24 (Seventh).

(b) *Purpose.* This part sets forth the standards that apply to debt cancellation contracts and debt suspension agreements entered into by national banks. The purpose of these standards is to ensure that national banks offer and implement such contracts and agreements consistent with safe and sound banking practices, and subject to appropriate consumer protections.

(c) *Scope.* This part applies to debt cancellation contracts and debt suspension agreements entered into by national banks in connection with extensions of credit they make. National banks' debt cancellation contracts and debt suspension agreements are governed by this part and applicable Federal law and regulations, and not by part 14 of this chapter or by State law.

## 12 C.F.R. § 37.2 Definitions.

For purposes of this part:

(a) *Actuarial method* means the method of allocating payments made on a debt between the amount financed and the finance charge pursuant to which a payment is applied first to the accumulated finance charge and any remainder is subtracted from, or any deficiency is added to, the unpaid balance of the amount financed.

(b) *Bank* means a national bank and a Federal branch or Federal agency of a foreign bank as those terms are defined in part 28 of this chapter.

(c) *Closed-end credit* means consumer credit other than open-end credit as defined in this section.

(d) *Contract* means a debt cancellation contract or a debt suspension agreement.

(e) *Customer* means an individual who obtains an extension of credit from a bank primarily for personal, family or household purposes.

(f) *Debt cancellation contract* means a loan term or contractual arrangement modifying loan terms under which a bank agrees to cancel all or part of a customer's obligation to repay an extension of credit from that bank upon the occurrence of a specified event. The agreement may be separate from or a part of other loan documents.

(g) *Debt suspension agreement* means a loan term or contractual arrangement modifying loan terms under which a bank agrees to suspend all or part of a customer's obligation to repay an extension of credit from that bank upon the occurrence of a specified event. The agreement may be separate from or a part of other loan documents. The term debt suspension agreement does not include loan payment deferral arrangements in which the triggering event is the borrower's unilateral election to defer repayment, or the bank's unilateral decision to allow a deferral of repayment.

(h) *Open-end credit* means consumer credit extended by a bank under a plan in which:

(1) The bank reasonably contemplates repeated transactions;

(2) The bank may impose a finance charge from time to time on an outstanding unpaid balance; and

(3) The amount of credit that may be extended to the customer during the term of the plan (up to any limit set by the bank) is generally made available to the extent that any outstanding balance is repaid.

(*i*) *Residential mortgage loan* means a loan secured by 1–4 family, residential real property.

## 12 C.F.R. § 37.3 Prohibited practices.

(a) *Anti-tying.* A national bank may not extend credit nor alter the terms or conditions of an extension of credit conditioned upon the customer entering into a debt cancellation contract or debt suspension agreement with the bank.

(b) *Misrepresentations generally.* A national bank may not engage in any practice or use any advertisement that could mislead or otherwise cause a reasonable person to reach an erroneous belief with respect to information that must be disclosed under this part.

(c) *Prohibited contract terms.* A national bank may not offer debt cancellation contracts or debt suspension agreements that contain terms:

(1) Giving the bank the right unilaterally to modify the contract unless:

(i) The modification is favorable to the customer and is made without additional charge to the customer; or

(ii) The customer is notified of any proposed change and is provided a reasonable opportunity to cancel the contract without penalty before the change goes into effect; or

(2) Requiring a lump sum, single payment for the contract payable at the outset of the contract, where the debt subject to the contract is a residential mortgage loan.

## 12 C.F.R. § 37.4 Refunds of fees in the event of termination or prepayment of the covered loan.

(a) *Refunds.* If a debt cancellation contract or debt suspension agreement is terminated (including, for example, when the customer prepays the covered loan), the bank shall refund to the customer any unearned fees paid for the contract unless the contract provides otherwise. A bank may offer a customer a contract that does not provide for a refund only if the bank also offers that customer a bona fide option to purchase a comparable contract that provides for a refund.

(b) *Method of calculating refund.* The bank shall calculate the amount of a refund using a method at least as favorable to the customer as the actuarial method.

## 12 C.F.R. § 37.5 Method of payment of fees.

Except as provided in § 37.3(c)(2), a bank may offer a customer the option of paying the fee for a contract in a single payment, provided the bank also offers the customer a bona fide option of paying the fee for that contract in monthly or other periodic payments. If the bank offers the customer the option to finance the single payment by adding it to the amount the customer is borrowing, the bank must also disclose to the customer, in accordance with § 37.6, whether and, if so, the time period during which, the customer may cancel the agreement and receive a refund.

## 12 C.F.R. § 37.6 Disclosures.

(a) *Content of short form of disclosures.* The short form of disclosures required by this part must include the information described in appendix A to this part that is appropriate to the product offered. Short form disclosures made in a form that is substantially similar to the disclosures in appendix A to this part will satisfy the short form disclosure requirements of this section.

(b) *Content of long form of disclosures.* The long form of disclosures required by this part must include the information described in appendix B to this part that is appropriate to the product offered. Long form disclosures made in a form that is substantially similar to the disclosures in appendix B to this part will satisfy the long form disclosure requirements of this section.

(c) Disclosure requirements; timing and method of disclosures—

(1) *Short form disclosures.* The bank shall make the short form disclosures orally at the time the bank first solicits the purchase of a contract.

(2) *Long form disclosures.* The bank shall make the long form disclosures in writing before the customer completes the purchase of the contract. If the initial solicitation occurs in person, then the bank shall provide the long form disclosures in writing at that time.

(3) *Special rule for transactions by telephone.* If the contract is solicited by telephone, the bank shall provide the short form disclosures orally and shall mail the long form disclosures, and, if appropriate, a copy of the contract to the customer within 3 business days, beginning on the first business day after the telephone solicitation.

(4) *Special rule for solicitations using written mail inserts or "take one" applications.* If the contract is solicited through written materials such as mail inserts or "take one" applications, the bank may provide only the short form disclosures in the written materials if the bank mails the long form disclosures to the customer within 3 business days, beginning on the first business day after the customer contacts the bank to respond to the solicitation, subject to the requirements of § 37.7(c).

(5) *Special rule for electronic transactions.* The disclosures described in this section may be provided through electronic media in a manner consistent with the requirements of the Electronic Signatures in Global and National Commerce Act, 15 U.S.C. 7001 *et seq.*

(d) *Form of disclosures*—

(1) *Disclosures must be readily understandable.* The disclosures required by this section must be conspicuous, simple, direct, readily understandable, and designed to call attention to the nature and significance of the information provided.

(2) *Disclosures must be meaningful.* The disclosures required by this section must be in a meaningful form. Examples of methods that could call attention to the nature and significance of the information provided include:

(i) A plain-language heading to call attention to the disclosures;

(ii) A typeface and type size that are easy to read;

(iii) Wide margins and ample line spacing;

(iv) Boldface or italics for key words; and

(v) Distinctive type style, and graphic devices, such as shading or sidebars, when the disclosures are combined with other information.

(e) *Advertisements and other promotional material for debt cancellation contracts and debt suspension agreements.* The short form disclosures are required in advertisements and promotional material for contracts unless the advertisements and promotional materials are of a general nature describing or listing the services or products offered by the bank.

## 12 C.F.R. § 37.7 Affirmative election to purchase and acknowledgment of receipt of disclosures required.

(a) *Affirmative election and acknowledgment of receipt of disclosures.* Before entering into a contract the bank must obtain a customer's written affirmative election to purchase a contract and written acknowledgment of receipt of the disclosures required by § 37.6(b). The election and acknowledgment information must be conspicuous, simple, direct, readily understandable, and designed to call attention to their significance. The election and acknowledgment satisfy these standards if they conform with the requirements in § 37.6(d) of this part.

(b) *Special rule for telephone solicitations.* If the sale of a contract occurs by telephone, the customer's affirmative election to purchase may be made orally, provided the bank:

(1) Maintains sufficient documentation to show that the customer received the short form disclosures and then affirmatively elected to purchase the contract;

(2) Mails the affirmative written election and written acknowledgment, together with the long form disclosures required by § 37.6 of this part, to the customer within 3 business days after the tele-

phone solicitation, and maintains sufficient documentation to show it made reasonable efforts to obtain the documents from the customer; and

(3) Permits the customer to cancel the purchase of the contract without penalty within 30 days after the bank has mailed the long form disclosures to the customer.

(c) *Special rule for solicitations using written mail inserts or "take one" applications.* If the contract is solicited through written materials such as mail inserts or "take one" applications and the bank provides only the short form disclosures in the written materials, then the bank shall mail the acknowledgment of receipt of disclosures, together with the long form disclosures required by § 37.6 of this part, to the customer within 3 business days, beginning on the first business day after the customer contacts the bank or otherwise responds to the solicitation. The bank may not obligate the customer to pay for the contract until after the bank has received the customer's written acknowledgment of receipt of disclosures unless the bank:

(1) Maintains sufficient documentation to show that the bank provided the acknowledgment of receipt of disclosures to the customer as required by this section;

(2) Maintains sufficient documentation to show that the bank made reasonable efforts to obtain from the customer a written acknowledgment of receipt of the long form disclosures; and

(3) Permits the customer to cancel the purchase of the contract without penalty within 30 days after the bank has mailed the long form disclosures to the customer.

(d) *Special rule for electronic election.* The affirmative election and acknowledgment may be made electronically in a manner consistent with the requirements of the Electronic Signatures in Global and National Commerce Act, 15 U.S.C. 7001 et seq.

[73 Fed. Reg. 22252 (Apr. 24, 2008)]

## 12 C.F.R. § 37.8 Safety and soundness requirements.

A national bank must manage the risks associated with debt cancellation contracts and debt suspension agreements in accordance with safe and sound banking principles. Accordingly, a national bank must establish and maintain effective risk management and control processes over its debt cancellation contracts and debt suspension agreements. Such processes include appropriate recognition and financial reporting of income, expenses, assets and liabilities, and appropriate treatment of all expected and unexpected losses associated with the products. A bank also should assess the adequacy of its internal control and risk mitigation activities in view of the nature and scope of its debt cancellation contract and debt suspension agreement programs.

## APPENDIX A TO PART 37—SHORT FORM DISCLOSURES

• This product is optional

Your purchase of [PRODUCT NAME] is optional. Whether or not you purchase [PRODUCT NAME] will not affect your application for credit or the terms of any existing credit agreement you have with the bank.

• Lump sum payment of fee

[Applicable if a bank offers the option to pay the fee in a single payment]

[Prohibited where the debt subject to the contract is a residential mortgage loan]

You may choose to pay the fee in a single lump sum or in [monthly/quarterly] payments. Adding the lump sum of the fee to the amount you borrow will increase the cost of [PRODUCT NAME].

• Lump sum payment of fee with no refund

[Applicable if a bank offers the option to pay the fee in a single payment for a no-refund DCC]

[Prohibited where the debt subject to the contract is a residential mortgage loan]

You may choose [PRODUCT NAME] with a refund provision or without a refund provision. Prices of refund and no-refund products are likely to differ.

• Refund of fee paid in lump sum

[Applicable where the customer pays the fee in a single payment and the fee is added to the amount borrowed]

[Prohibited where the debt subject to the contract is a residential mortgage loan]

[Either:] (1) You may cancel [PRODUCT NAME] at any time and receive a refund; or (2) You may cancel [PRODUCT NAME] within______________ days and receive a full refund; or (3) If you cancel [PRODUCT NAME] you will not receive a refund.

• Additional disclosures

We will give you additional information before you are required to pay for [PRODUCT NAME]. [If applicable]: This information will include a copy of the contract containing the terms of [PRODUCT NAME].

Eligibility requirements, conditions, and exclusions

There are eligibility requirements, conditions, and exclusions that could prevent you from receiving benefits under [PRODUCT NAME].

[Either:] You should carefully read our additional information for a full explanation of the terms of [PRODUCT NAME] or You should carefully read the contract for a full explanation of the terms of [PRODUCT NAME].

## APPENDIX B TO PART 37—LONG FORM DISCLOSURES

• This product is optional

Your purchase of [PRODUCT NAME] is optional. Whether or not you purchase [PRODUCT NAME] will not affect your application for credit or the terms of any existing credit agreement you have with the bank.

• Explanation of debt suspension agreement

[Applicable if the contract has a debt suspension feature]

If [PRODUCT NAME] is activated, your duty to pay the loan principal and interest to the bank is only suspended. You must fully repay the loan after the period of suspension has expired. [If applicable]: This includes interest accumulated during the period of suspension.

• Amount of fee

[For closed-end credit]: The total fee for [PRODUCT NAME] is ______________.

[For open-end credit, either:] (1) The monthly fee for [PRODUCT NAME] is based on your account balance each month multiplied by the unit-cost, which is ______________; or (2) The formula used to compute the fee is ______________].

• Lump sum payment of fee

[Applicable if a bank offers the option to pay the fee in a single payment]

[Prohibited where the debt subject to the contract is a residential mortgage loan]

You may choose to pay the fee in a single lump sum or in [monthly/quarterly] payments. Adding the lump sum of the fee to the amount you borrow will increase the cost of [PRODUCT NAME].

• Lump sum payment of fee with no refund

[Applicable if a bank offers the option to pay the fee in a single payment for a no-refund DCC]

[Prohibited where the debt subject to the contract is a residential mortgage loan]

You have the option to purchase [PRODUCT NAME] that includes a refund of the unearned portion of the fee if you terminate the contract or prepay the loan in full prior to the scheduled termination date. Prices of refund and no-refund products may differ.

• Refund of fee paid in lump sum

[Applicable where the customer pays the fee in a single payment and the fee is added to the amount borrowed]

[Prohibited where the debt subject to the contract is a residential mortgage loan]

[Either:] (1) You may cancel [PRODUCT NAME] at any time and receive a refund; or (2) You may cancel [PRODUCT NAME] within_______________ days and receive a full refund; or (3) If you cancel [PRODUCT NAME] you will not receive a refund.

- Use of card or credit line restricted

[Applicable if the contract restricts use of card or credit line when customer activates protection]

If [PRODUCT NAME] is activated, you will be unable to incur additional charges on the credit card or use the credit line.

- Termination of [PRODUCT NAME]

[Either]: (1) You have no right to cancel [PRODUCT NAME]; or (2) You have the right to cancel [PRODUCT NAME] in the following circumstances: _______________.

[And either]: (1) The bank has no right to cancel [PRODUCT NAME]; or (2)The bank has the right to cancel [PRODUCT NAME] in the following circumstances: _______________.

- Eligibility requirements, conditions, and exclusions

There are eligibility requirements, conditions, and exclusions that could prevent you from receiving benefits under [PRODUCT NAME].

[Either]: (1) The following is a summary of the eligibility requirements, conditions, and exclusions. [The bank provides a summary of any eligibility requirements, conditions, and exclusions]; or (2) You may find a complete explanation of the eligibility requirements, conditions, and exclusions in paragraphs _______________ of the [PRODUCT NAME] agreement.

# Appendix B State Lending Statutes

This appendix compiles citations to state statutes that regulate non-mortgage consumer credit. A citation appearing in parentheses represents the specific section of the law that addresses caps on interest, fees, or finance charges, but different caps may well apply to different types of lending arrangements within the same state.

This appendix uses the term "payday loans" for statues permitting very high rate loans variously called "payday loans," "cash advance loans," or "delayed deposit check loans." For more details about the interest rates allowed by states for payday, auto title, and short-term installment loans, see NCLC's Small Dollar Loan Scorecard, *available at* www.nclc.org.[1]

### Alabama

*Legal Interest Rate*: Ala. Code § 8-8-1
*Contract*: Ala. Code § 8-8-1 *or* Ala. Code § 8-8-14 *or* Ala. Code § 8-8-5
*Judgment*: Ala. Code § 8-8-10
*Small Loans*: Ala. Code §§ 5-18-1 to 5-18-23 (§ 5-18-15), Small Loan Act
*Installment Loans & Credit*: Ala. Code §§ 5-19-1 to 5-19-33 (§ 5-19-3), Consumer Finance
*Insurance Premium Finance*: Ala. Code §§ 27-40-1 to 27-40-18 (§ 27-40-9)
*Revolving Charge*: Ala. Code § 8-8-14; Ala. Code § 5-19-3, Consumer Finance; Ala. Code § 5-20-5 (credit cards)
*Life Insurance and Annuity Policy Loans*: Ala. Code § 27-15-8.1
*Auto Title Loans*: Ala. Code §§ 5-19A-1 to 5-19A-20 (interpreted in *Floyd v. Title Exch. & Pawn of Anniston, Inc.*, 620 So. 2d 576 (Ala. 1993) to permit auto title lending)
*Payday Loans*: Ala. Code §§ 5-18A-1 to 5-18A-22 (§ 5-18A-12(a)), Deferred Presentment Services Act

### Alaska

*Legal Interest Rate*: Alaska Stat. § 45.45.010
*Contract*: Alaska Stat. § 45.45.010
*Judgment*: Alaska Stat. § 09.30.070
*Small Loans*: Alaska Stat. §§ 06.20.010 to 06.20.920
*Installment Loan Law*: Alaska Stat. § 45.45.080
*Sales Finance Act*: Alaska Stat. §§ 45.10.010 to 45.10.230 (§ 45.10.120), Retail Installment Sales Act
*Insurance Premium Finance*: Alaska Stat. §§ 06.40.010 to 06.40.190 (§ 06.40.120), Premium Financing Act
*Revolving Credit*: Alaska Stat. § 45.10.120, Retail Installment Sales Act
*Bank Credit Cards*: Alaska Stat. §§ 45.10.010 to 45.10.230 (§ 45.10.120), Retail Installment Sales Act; Alaska Stat. § 06.05.209
*Open-End Loans*: Alaska Stat. § 06.20.285 (open-end loans); Alaska Stat. § 06.20.230, Small Loans Act
*Life Insurance and Annuity Policy Loans*: Alaska Stat. § 21.45.080
*Payday Loans*: Alaska Stat. §§ 06.50.010 to 06.50.900 (§ 06.50.460) (deferred deposit advances)

### Arizona

*Legal Interest Rate*: Ariz. Rev. Stat. Ann. § 44-1201
*Contract*: Ariz. Rev. Stat. Ann. § 44-1201
*Judgment*: Ariz. Rev. Stat. Ann. § 44-1201, except on a condemnation, then interest, including interest payable pursuant to § 12-1123 (sub. B) is payable at rate prescribed by § 9-409 (if instituted by city or town), § 11-269.04 (if instituted by a county), § 28-7101 (if instituted by the department of transportation) and § 48-3628 (if instituted by county flood control district, power district, or agricultural improvement district)
*Criminal Usury Cap*: Ariz. Rev. Stat. Ann. § 13-2208
*Small Loans*: Ariz. Rev. Stat. Ann. §§ 6-601 to 6-638 (§§ 6-632), Consumer Loans Act
*Installment Loan Act*: Ariz. Rev. Stat. Ann. § 44-1205
*Insurance Premium Finance*: Ariz. Rev. Stat. Ann. § 6-1412
*Auto Finance*: Ariz. Rev. Stat. Ann. §§ 44-281 to 295 (§ 44-291), Motor Vehicle Time Sales Disclosure Act
*Other Goods Finance*: Ariz. Rev. Stat. Ann. § 44-6001 to 44-6006 (retail installment sales transactions)
*Revolving Loan Credit*: Ariz. Rev. Stat. Ann. § 44-1205, Interest Usury for closed-end loans up to $5,000 and revolving loans up to $10,000 provided the loans are not subject to the Small Loans provisions; if both Revolving Loan and Retail Installment Sales statutes apply, then the parties may agree which statute governs
*Life Insurance and Annuity Policy Loans*: Ariz. Rev. Stat. Ann. §§ 20-1208, 20-1209, 20-1209.01
*Auto Title Loans*: Ariz. Rev. Stat. Ann. §§ 44-281, 44-291
*Payday Loans*: Ariz. Rev. Stat. Ann. §§ 6-1251 to 6-1263 (§ 6-1260) (licensing of payday lenders pursuant to these statutory provisions ends July 1, 2010)
*Revolving Sales Credit*: Ariz. Rev. Stat. Ann. §§ 44-6001 to 44-6006 (retail installment sales transactions)

### Arkansas

*Legal Interest Rate*: Repealed effective Jan. 1, 2011.
*Contract*: Ark. Code Ann. §§ 4-57-101 to 4-57-108
*Judgment*: Ark. Code Ann. § 16-65-114
*Consumer Loans & Credit Sales*: Ark. Code Ann. §§ 4-57-101 to 4-57-108
*Life Insurance and Annuity Policy Loans*: Ark. Code Ann. § 23-81-109
*Industrial Loans*: Ark Code Ann. §§ 23-36-101 to 23-36-117
*Payday Loans*: Ark. Code. Ann. §§ 23-52-101 to 23-52-117, Check Cashers Act (held unconstitutional by *McGhee v. Arkansas State Bd. of Collection Agencies*, 289 S.W.3d 18 (Ark. 2008))

1 The scorecard is also published at Leah A. Plunkett and Ana Lucia Hurtado, *Small Dollar Loans, Big Problems: How States Protect Consumers from Abuses and How the Federal Government Can Help*, 44 Suffolk U. L. Rev. 31 (2011).

*Attorney General Opinions*: Op. No. 99-074, 1999 Ark. AG LEXIS 105 (May 7, 1999)
*Anti-Predatory Mortgage Lending Laws*: Ark. Code Ann. §§ 23-53-101 to 23-53-106
*Refund Anticipation Loans*: Ark. Code Ann. §§ 4-116-101 to 4-116-108

**California**

*Legal Interest Rate*: Cal. Const. art. XV, § 1; Cal. Civ. Code § 1916-1
*Contract*: Cal. Const. art. XV, § 1; Usury Law of 1919: Cal. Uncodified Initiative Measures and Statutes 1919-1 Ann. § 2 (Deering); Cal. Civ. Code § 1916-1 (West)
*Usury Law of 1919*: Cal. Gen. Laws Ann. act 3757, § 2 (Deering) (uncodified); Cal. Civ. Code §§ 1916-1 to 1916-5 (West)
*Judgment*: Cal. Const. art. XV, § 1; Cal. Civ. Proc. Code § 685.010 (West)
*Consumer Loans*: Cal. Fin. Code §§ 22000 to 22754 (§§ 22303–22305) (West), California Finance Lenders Law
*Personal Property Brokers*: Cal. Fin. Code §§ 22000 to 22754 (§§ 22009, 22303 and 22304) (West), California Finance Lenders Law
*Industrial Loan Companies*: Cal. Fin. Code §§ 18212 to 18212.1 (West), Industrial Loan Law
*Insurance Premium Finance*: Cal. Fin. Code §§ 18560 to 18643 (§ 18626) (West) (insurance premium financing)
*Auto Finance*: Cal. Civil Code §§ 2981 to 2984.6 (§ 2982(j)) (West), Automobile Sales Finance Act
*Other Goods Finance*: Cal. Civ. Code §§ 1801 to 1812.20 (§ 1805.1) (West), "Unruh Act" (retail installment sales)
*Revolving Sales Credit*: Cal. Civ. Code §§ 1801 to 1812.20 (§ 1810.2) (West), "Unruh Act" (retail installment sales)
*Revolving Loan Credit*: Cal. Fin. Code §§ 22450 to 22467 (West) (open-end loans); Cal. Fin. Code §§ 22300 to 22341 (West) (loan regulations and retail installment contracts)
*Payday Loans*: Cal. Fin. Code §§ 23000 to 23106 (§ 23036) (West), California Deferred Deposit Transaction Law
*Attorney General Opinions*: 78 Op. Atty. Gen. Cal. 101, 1995 WL 265366 (Cal. A.G. May 9, 1995)
*Refund Anticipation Loans*: Cal. Bus. & Prof. Code §§ 22251–22259 (West)

**Colorado**

*Legal Interest Rate*: Colo. Rev. Stat. § 5-12-101
*Contract*: Colo. Rev. Stat. § 5-12-103
*Judgment*: Colo. Rev. Stat. § 5-12-102
*Criminal Usury Cap*: Colo. Rev. Stat. §§ 18-15-101, 18-15-104
*Personal Injury Judgments*: Colo. Rev. Stat. § 13-21-101
*Appealed Judgments*: Colo. Rev. Stat. § 5-12-106
*Consumer Supervised Loans—Licensed Lenders*: Colo. Rev. Stat. § 5-2-201(2). Colo. UCCC also includes revolving loan provision
*Consumer Loans in General*: Colo. Rev. Stat. §§ 5-1-301(15)(a), (b), 5-2-201, 5-2-214 (includes revolving loan provision)
*Non-Consumer Loans*: Colo. Rev. Stat. §§ 5-1-301(15), 5-2-502, Colo. UCCC
*Consumer Credit Sales*: Colo. Rev. Stat. § 5-2-201, Colo. UCCC
*Insurance Premium Finance*: Colo. Rev. Stat. §§ 5-2-201(8), 5-3-502, Colo. UCCC
*Revolving Charge Accounts*: Colo. Rev. Stat. § 5-2-213, Colo. UCCC
*Payday Loans*: Colo. Rev. Stat. §§ 5-3.1-101 to 5-3.1-123 (§ 5-3.1-105), Deferred Deposit Loan Act
*Refund Anticipation Loans*: Colo. Rev. Stat. §§ 5-9.5-101 to 5-9.5-109

**Connecticut**

*Legal Interest Rate*: Conn. Gen. Stat. § 37-1
*Contract*: Conn. Gen. Stat. § 37-4
*Judgment*: Conn. Gen. Stat. §§ 37-3a and 37-3b
*Criminal Usury Cap*: Conn. Gen. Stat. §§ 37-4, 37-7
*Small Loans*: Conn. Gen. Stat. §§ 36a-555 to 573, Small Loan Law
*Auto Finance*: Conn. Gen. Stat. §§ 36a-770 to 36a-788 (§ 36a-772) (retail installment sales financing)
*Retail Installment Sales (Other Goods)*: Conn. Gen. Stat. §§ 36a-770 to 36a-788 (§ 36a-772) (retail installment sales financing)
*Retail Credit Transaction Statement Errors*: Conn. Gen. Stat. §§ 42-100b, 42-100c
*Insurance Premium Finance*: Conn. Gen. Stat. §§ 38a-160 to 38a-170 (§ 38a-168) (insurance premium finance companies)
*Revolving Credit*: Conn. Gen. Stat. § 42-133c (open-end credit)
*Life Insurance and Annuity Policy Loans*: Conn. Gen. Stat. § 38a-444
*Refund Anticipation Loans*: Conn. Gen. Stat. § 42-480

**Delaware**

*Legal Interest Rate*: Del. Code Ann. tit. 6, § 2301
*Contract*: Del. Code Ann. tit. 6, § 2301
*Judgment*: Del. Code Ann. tit. 6, § 2301
*Auto Finance*: Del. Code Ann. tit. 5, §§ 2901-2914 (§ 2908), Motor Vehicle Sales Finance Act
*Other Goods*: Del. Code Ann. tit. 6, §§ 4301–4351 (§ 4315), Retail Installment Sales Law
*Insurance Premium Finance*: Del. Code Ann. tit. 18, §§ 4801-4812 (§ 4807)
*Revolving Sales Credit*: Del. Code Ann. tit. 5, §§ 2214–2226 (licensed lenders)
*Bank Revolving Credit*: Del. Code Ann. tit. 5, §§ 941–956 (§§ 943 and 945)
*Regulated Closed-End Credit*: Del. Code Ann. tit. 5, §§ 961 to 978 (banks), §§ 2227 to 2238 (§ 2229) (licensed lenders)
*Life Insurance and Annuity Policy Loans*: Del. Code Ann. tit. 18, § 2911
*Auto Title Loans*: Del. Code Ann. tit. 5, §§ 2250 to 2261
*Payday Loans*: Del. Code Ann. tit. 5, §§ 2227 to 2238 (§ 2229 (lender can charge any rate that "the agreement governing the loan provides")), § 2744 (check cashers prohibited from making payday loans)

**District of Columbia**

*Legal Interest Rate*: D.C. Code § 28-3302(a)
*Contract*: D.C. Code § 28-3301
*Judgment*: D.C. Code §§ 28-3302(b), (c), 15-108 (liquidated debts), 15-109 (other contracts), 15-110 (foreign contracts)
*Small Loans*: §§ 26-901 to 26-912 (§ 26-905), 28-3301
*Auto Finance*: §§ 50-601 to 50-610 (§ 50-602); D.C. Code §§ 28-3601 to 28-3603 (§ 28-3602) (direct motor vehicle installment loans)
*Installment Loans*: D.C. Code § 28-3308 (direct installment loans)
*Revolving Charge*: D.C. Code §§ 28-3701 and 28-3702 (§ 28-3702) (revolving credit accounts)
*Insurance Premium Finance*: D.C. Code §§ 31-1101 to 31-1112 (§ 31-1109) (insurance premium finance companies)
*Payday Loans*: D.C. Code §§ 26-301 to 26-323

**Florida**

*Legal Interest Rate*: Fla. Stat. § 687.01
*Contract*: Fla. Stat. § 687.01, 687.02
*Judgment*: Fla. Stat. § 55.03

*Criminal Usury Cap*: Fla. Stat. §§ 687.03, 687.031, 687.071, 687.146
*Small Loans*: Fla. Stat. §§ 516.001 to 516.36 (§§ 516.031 and 516.035), Consumer Finance Act
*Bank Installment Loans*: Fla. Stat. § 658.49
*Insurance Premium Finance*: Fla. Stat. §§ 627.826 to 627.849 (§ 627.840)
*Auto Finance*: Fla. Stat. §§ 520.01 to 520.13 (§ 520.08), Motor Vehicle Retail Sales Finance Act
*Other Goods Finance*: Fla. Stat. §§ 520.30 to 520.42 (§ 520.34), Retail Installment Sales Act
*Home Improvements*: Fla. Stat. §§ 520.60 to 520.98 (§ 520.78), Home Improvement Sales and Finance Act
*Revolving Credit*: Fla. Stat. §§ 520.30 to 520.42 (§ 520.35), Retail Installment Sales Act
*Life Insurance and Annuity Policy Loans*: Fla. Stat. §§ 627.458 and 627.4585
*Auto Title Loans*: Fla. Stat. Ann. §§ 537.001 to 537.018 (§ 537.011)
*Payday Loans*: Fla. Stat. §§ 560.402 to 560.408 (§ 560.404(6)), 560.408; Fla. Admin. Code. Ann. r. 69V-560.707, 69V-560.801, 69V-560.901 to 69V-560.1000

**Georgia**

*Legal Interest Rate*: Ga. Code Ann. § 7-4-2
*Contract*: Ga. Code Ann. § 7-4-2
*Judgment*: Ga. Code Ann. § 7-4-12
*Criminal Usury Cap*: Ga. Code Ann. § 7-4-18
*Small Loans*: Ga. Code Ann. §§ 7-3-1 to 7-3-29 (§ 7-3-14), Industrial Loan Act
*Auto Finance*: Ga. Code Ann. §§ 10-1-30 to 10-1-42 (§ 10-1-33), Motor Vehicle Sales Finance Act; Ga. Code Ann. § 7-4-3 (retail installment contracts and mobile homes and motor vehicles)
*Other Goods Finance*: Ga. Code Ann. §§ 10-1-1 to 10-1-16 (§§ 10-1-3 and 10-1-4), Retail Installment & Home Solicitation Sales Act
*Insurance Premium Finance*: Ga. Code Ann. §§ 33-22-1 to 33-22-16 (§ 33-22-9), Insurance Premium Finance Company Act
*Revolving Loans*: Ga. Code Ann. §§ 7-5-1 to 7-5-6 (§ 7-5-4), Credit Card and Credit Card Bank Act
*Revolving Sales Credit*: Ga. Code Ann. § 10-1-4
*Life Insurance and Annuity Policy Loans*: Ga. Code Ann. § 33-25-3.1
*Auto Title Loans*: Ga. Code Ann. §§ 44-12-130 to 44-12-138 (§ 44-12-131)
*Payday Loans*: Ga. Code Ann. §§ 16-17-1 to 16-17-10 (payday lending specifically prohibited)

**Hawaii**

*Legal Interest Rate*: Haw. Rev. Stat. § 478-2
*Contract*: Haw. Rev. Stat. § 478-4
*Judgment*: Haw. Rev. Stat. § 478-3
*Criminal Usury Cap*: Haw. Rev. Stat. § 478-6
*Consumer Loans in General*: Haw. Rev. Stat. §§ 412:9-100 to 412:9-500 (§ 412:9-302) (financial services loan companies)
*Consumer Sales Credit*: Haw. Rev. Stat. §§ 476-1 to 476-32 (§ 476-28), Credit Sales Act
*Open-End Consumer Loans*: Haw. Rev. Stat. §§ 412:9-302, 412:9-305 (financial services loan companies)
*Open-End Credit*: Haw. Rev. Stat. § 478-11.5 (credit cards)
*Life Insurance and Annuity Policy Loans*: Haw. Rev. Stat. § 431:10D-103
*Payday Loans*: Haw. Rev. Stat. §§ 480F-1 to 480F-7 (§ 480F-4(c))

**Idaho**

*Legal Interest Rate*: Idaho Code Ann. § 28-22-104(1)
*Contract*: Idaho Code Ann. § 28-42-201
*Judgment*: Idaho Code Ann. § 28-22-104(2)
*Consumer Sales Credit*: Idaho Code Ann. §§ 28-41-101 to 28-49-107 (§ 28-42-201), Idaho UCCC
*Life Insurance and Annuity Policy Loans*: Idaho Code Ann. §§ 41-1901 to 41-1940 (§ 41-1909)
*Auto Title Loans:* Idaho Code Ann. §§ 28-46-501 to 28-46-509, Title Loan Act
*Payday Loans*: Idaho Code Ann. §§ 28-46-401 to 28-46-413 (§ 28-46-412, lender can charge any fee per $100 that borrower agrees to pay)

**Illinois**

*Legal Interest Rate*: 815 Ill. Comp. Stat. Ann. 205/1
*Contract*: 815 Ill. Comp. Stat. Ann. 205/4
*Judgment*: 735 Ill. Comp. Stat. Ann. 5/2-1303
*Criminal Usury Cap*: 720 Ill. Comp. Stat. Ann. 5/17-59
*Small Loans*: 815 Ill. Comp. Stat. Ann. 205/4a, Interest Act; 205 Ill. Comp. Stat. Ann. 670/1 to 670/27 (670/15), Consumer Installment Loan Act
*Revolving Loans*: 815 Ill. Comp. Stat. Ann. 205/4.2
*Revolving Sales Credit*: 815 Ill. Comp. Stat. Ann. 405/1 to 405/33 (405/27 and 405/28), Retail Installment Sales Act
*Auto Finance*: 815 Ill. Comp. Stat. Ann. 375/1 to 375/26, Motor Vehicle Retail Installment Sales Act
*Insurance Premium Finance*: 215 Ill. Comp. Stat. Ann. 5/513a1 to 5/513a12 (5/513a10) (premium finance regulation)
*Life Insurance and Annuity Policy Loans*: 215 Ill. Comp. Stat. Ann. 5/229.5
*Auto Title Loans*: Ill. Admin. Code tit. 38, 110.300 to 110.430
*Payday Loans*: 815 Ill. Comp. Stat. Ann. 122/1-1 to 122/99-99 (122/2-5), Payday Loan Reform Act; Ill. Admin. Code tit. 38, §§ 190.600 to 190.610, 210, 365, 1000.5000 to 1000.5030, 1075.5000 to 1075.5030
*Refund Anticipation Loans*: 815 Ill. Comp. Stat. Ann. 177/1 to 177/99

**Indiana**

*Legal Interest Rate*: Ind. Code § 24-4.6-1-102
*Contract*: See rates specified in consumer sections of UCCC. *See* Ind. Code §§ 24-4.5-3-601 to 24-4.5-3-605.
*Judgment*: Ind. Code § 24-4.6-1-101
*Criminal Usury Cap*: Ind. Code §§ 24-4.5-5-107, 35-45-7-2
*Consumer Supervised Loans—Licensed Lenders*: Ind. Code § 24-4.5-3-508, Ind. UCCC
*Consumer Loans In General*: Ind. Code § 24-4.5-3-201, Ind. UCCC
*Revolving Loan Accounts*: Ind. Code § 24-4.5-3-201(4), Ind. UCCC
*Small Loans Other than "Consumer Loans"*: Ind. Code §§ 24-4.5-3-601 to 24-4.5-3-606 (§ 24-4.5-3-605), Ind. UCCC
*Consumer Sales Credit*: Ind. Code § 24-4.5-2-201, Ind. UCCC
*Life Insurance and Annuity Policy Loans*: Ind. Code §§ 27-1-12.3-1 to 27-1-12.3-6 (§ 27-1-12.3-2) (interest rates on insurance policy loans)
*Payday Loans*: Ind. Code §§ 24-4.5-7-101 to 24-4.5-7-414 (§ 24-4.5-7-201), UCCC (small loans)
*Anti-Predatory Mortgage Lending Laws*: Ind. Code §§ 24-9-1-1 to 24-9-9-4

### Iowa

*Legal Interest Rate*: Iowa Code § 535.2
*Contract*: Iowa Code § 535.2
*Judgment*: Iowa Code § 535.3
*Small Loans*: Iowa Code §§ 536.1 to 536.30 (§ 536.13), Iowa Regulated Loan Act
*Industrial Loans*: Iowa Code §§ 536A.1 to 536A.32 (§ 536A.23), Iowa Industrial Loan Law, Iowa Code §§ 537.1101 to 537.8101, Iowa UCCC
*Consumer Credit Sales*: Iowa Code §§ 537.2101 to 537.2601 (§ 537.2201), Iowa UCCC
*Revolving Sales Accounts*: Iowa Code §§ 537.2101 to 537.2601 (§ 537.2202), Iowa UCCC
*Consumer Loans In General*: Iowa Code §§ 537.2101 to 537.2601 (§ 537.2401, finance charges), (§ 537.1301, definition), (§ 537.2301, consumer loan licensees), Iowa UCCC
*Consumer Revolving Loans*: Iowa Code §§ 537.2101 to 537.2601 (§ 537.2402), Iowa UCCC
*Manufactured Home Loans*: Iowa Code § 103A.58
*Auto Finance*: Iowa Code §§ 322.1 to 322.35 (§§ 322.3, 322.19, & 322.33), Motor Vehicle Dealer's Licensing Act (requires compliance with Iowa UCCC); Iowa Code § 537.2201 (Iowa UCCC)
*Life Insurance and Annuity Policy Loans*: Iowa Code § 511.36
*Auto Title Loans*: Iowa Code § 537.2403
*Payday Loans*: Iowa Code §§ 533D.1 to 533D.16 (§ 533D.9), Delayed Deposit Services Licensing Act

### Kansas

*Legal Interest Rate*: Kan. Stat. Ann. § 16-201 (West)
*Contract*: Kan. Stat. Ann. § 16-207 (West)
*Judgment*: Kan. Stat. Ann. § 16-204 (West)
*Consumer Loans*: Kan. Stat. Ann. §§ 16a-2-101 to 16a-2-510 (§ 16a-2-401, finance charges), (§ 16a-2-301, consumer loan licensees) (West), Kan. UCCC
*Consumer Credit Sales*: Kan. Stat. Ann. §§ 16a-2-101 to 16a-2-510 (§ 16a-2-201) (West), Kan. UCCC
*Revolving Sales Accounts*: Kan. Stat. Ann. §§ 16a-2-101 to 16a-2-510 (§ 16a-2-202) (West), Kan. UCCC
*Insurance Premium Finance*: Kan. Stat Ann. §§ 40-2601 to 40-2613 (§ 40-2610) (West), Insurance Premium Finance Company Act
*Life Insurance Policy Loans*: Kan. Stat. Ann. §§ 40-420a to 40-420d (West)
*Payday Loans*: Kan. Stat. Ann. § 16a-2-404 (§ 16a-2-404(1)(c)) (West)
*Attorney General Opinions*: Att'y Gen. Op. 97-99, 1997 WL 808540 (Kan. A.G. Dec. 19, 1997)

### Kentucky

*Legal Interest Rate*: Ky. Rev. Stat. Ann. § 360.010 (West)
*Contract*: Ky. Rev. Stat. Ann. § 360.010 (West)
*Judgment*: Ky. Rev. Stat. Ann. § 360.040 (West)
*Small Loans*: Ky. Rev. Stat. Ann. §§ 286.4-410 to 286.4-991 (§ 286.4-530) (West)
*Industrial Loans*: Ky. Rev. Stat. Ann. §§ 286.7-410 to 286.7-990 (§ 286.7-460) (West)
*Bank Installment Loans*: Ky. Rev. Stat. Ann. § 286.3-215 (West)
*Auto Finance*: Ky. Rev. Stat. Ann. §§ 190.090 to 190.140 (§ 190.110) (West), Motor Vehicle Retail Installment Sales Act
*Other Goods Finance*: Ky. Rev. Stat. Ann. §§ 371.210 to 371.330 (West) (retail installment sales and credit)
*Insurance Premium Finance*: Ky. Rev. Stat. Ann. §§ 304.30-010 to 304.30-120 (§ 304.30-090) (West), Insurance Premium Finance Companies
*Bank Revolving Credit*: Ky. Rev. Stat. Ann. §§ 286.3-710 to 286.3-770 (West)
*Life Insurance and Annuity Policy Loans*: Ky. Rev. Stat. Ann. § 304.15-115 (West)
*Auto Title Loans*: Ky. Rev. Stat. Ann. §§ 286.10-200 to 286.10-285, 286.10-991 (West), Title Pledge Act
*Payday Loans*: Ky. Rev. Stat. Ann. §§ 286.9-010 to 286.9-140 (§ 286.9-100), 286.9-990, 286.9-991 (West)
*Attorney General Opinions*: OAG 92-41, 1992 WL 540962 (Ky. A.G. Mar. 17, 1992)

### Louisiana

*Legal Interest Rate*: La. Rev. Stat. Ann. § 9:3500
*Contract*: La. Rev. Stat. Ann. § 9:3500
*Judgment*: La. Rev. Stat. Ann. §§ 9:3500, 13:4202
*Consumer Loans*: La. Rev. Stat. Ann. §§ 9:3510 to 9:3568 (§ 9:3519), Louisiana Consumer Credit Law
*Consumer Credit Sales*: La. Rev. Stat. Ann. §§ 9:3510 to 9:3568 (§ 9:3520), Louisiana Consumer Credit Law
*Auto Finance*: La. Rev. Stat. Ann. §§ 6:969.1 to 6:969.54 (§§ 6:969.9 to 6:969.14), Motor Vehicle Sales Finance Act
*Revolving Charge Accounts*: La. Rev. Stat. Ann. §§ 9:3510 to 9:3568 (§ 9:3523), Louisiana Consumer Credit Law
*Revolving Loan Accounts*: La. Rev. Stat. Ann. §§ 9:3510 to 9:3568 (§ 9:3519), Louisiana Consumer Credit Law
*Lender Credit Cards*: La. Rev. Stat. Ann. §§ 9:3510 to 9:3568 (§ 9:3524), Louisiana Consumer Credit Law
*Insurance Premium Finance*: La. Rev. Stat. Ann. §§ 9.3510 to 9:3568 (§ 9:3550), Louisiana Consumer Credit Law
*Life Insurance and Annuity Policy Loans*: La. Rev. Stat. Ann. § 22:932
*Auto Title Loans*: La. Rev. Stat. Ann. § 37:1801(D) (prohibiting title loans)
*Payday Loans*: La. Rev. Stat. Ann. §§ 9:3578.1 to 9:3578.8 (§ 9:3578.4), Louisiana Deferred Presentment and Small Loan Act
*Attorney General Opinions*: Op. No. 98-88, 1998 WL 651149 (La. A.G. Mar. 12, 1998); Op. No. 94-297, 1994 WL 440575 (La. A.G. July 21, 1994)
*Refund Anticipation Loans*: La. Rev. Stat. Ann. §§ 6:242, 9:3579.1 to 9:3579.4

### Maine

*Legal Interest Rate*: Me. Rev. Stat. Ann. tit. 9-B, § 432
*Contract*: Me. Rev. Stat. Ann. tit. 9-B, § 432
*Judgment*: Me. Rev. Stat. Ann. tit. 14, §§ 1602-B, 1602-C
*Consumer Supervised Loans—Licensed Lenders*: Me. Rev. Stat. Ann. tit. 9-A, §§ 1-301, 2-101 to 2-601 (§ 2-301), Maine UCCC
*Consumer Credit Sales*: Me. Rev. Stat. Ann. tit. 9-A, §§ 2-101 to 2-601 (§ 2-201), Maine UCCC
*Revolving Charge Accounts*: Me. Rev. Stat. Ann. tit. 9-A, §§ 2-101 to 2-601 (§ 2-202), Maine UCCC
*Consumer Loans*: Me. Rev. Stat. Ann. tit. 9-A, §§ 2-101 to 2-601 (§ 2-401), Maine UCCC
*Revolving Loans*: Me. Rev. Stat. Ann. tit. 9-A, §§ 2-101 to 2-601 (§ 2-402), Maine UCCC
*Auto Finance*: Me. Rev. Stat. Ann. tit. 9-A, § 2-201(9-A), Maine UCCC
*Industrial Banks*: Me. Rev. Stat. Ann. tit. 9-B, § 917

*Insurance Premium Finance*: Me. Rev. Stat. Ann. tit. 9-A, § 2-401(9)
*Life Insurance and Annuity Policy Loans*: Me. Rev. Stat. Ann. tit. 24-A, § 2553
*Auto Title Loans*: Me. Rev. Stat. Ann. tit. 30-A, § 3960 (prohibiting title loans)
*Payday Loans*: Me. Rev. Stat. Ann. tit. 9-A, §§ 1-301(28-A), 2-401 (§ 2-401); Me. Rev. Stat. Ann. tit. 32, § 6138(4)(D) (check cashers cannot make payday loans unless they are supervised lenders)
*Refund Anticipation Loans*: Me. Rev. Stat. Ann. tit. 9-A, §§ 10-102, 10-310

### Maryland

*Legal Interest Rate*: Md. Const. art. III, § 57; Md. Code Ann., Com. Law § 12-102 (West)
*Contract*: Md. Code Ann., Com. Law § 12-103 (West)
*Judgment*: Md. Code Ann., Cts. & Jud. Proc. §§ 11-106, 11-107 (West)
*Consumer Loans*: Md. Code Ann., Com. Law §§ 12-301 to 12-317 (§ 12-306) (West), Maryland Consumer Loan Law (credit provisions)
*Auto Finance*: Md. Code Ann., Com. Law §§ 12-601 to 12-636 (§ 12-609) (West), Retail Installment Sales Act
*Other Goods Finance*: Md. Code Ann., Com. Law §§ 12-601 to 12-636 (§ 12-610) (West), Retail Installment Sales Act
*Insurance Premium Finance*: Md. Code Ann., Ins. §§ 23-303, 23-304, 23-305 (West) (Oct. 1, 1997) (replaced Md. Ann. Code art. 48A, §§ 486D, 486E)
*Retail Credit*: Md. Code Ann., Com. Law §§ 12-501 to 12-515 (§ 12-505, closed-end; § 12-506, open-end) (West)
*Revolving Loans*: Md. Code Ann., Com. Law § 12-903 (West)
*Closed-End Credit*: Md. Code Ann., Com. Law §§ 12-1001 to 12-1029 (West)
*Life Insurance and Annuity Policy Loans*: Md. Code Ann., Ins. §§ 16-207 to 16-208 (West) (Oct. 1, 1997) (replaced Md. Ann. Code art. 48A, §§ 394 and 394A)
*Refund Anticipation Loans*: Md. Code Ann., Com. Law §§ 14-801 to 14-3807 (West)

### Massachusetts

*Legal Interest Rate*: Mass. Gen. Laws ch. 107, § 3
*Contract*: Mass. Gen. Laws ch. 107, § 3
*Judgment*: Mass. Gen. Laws ch. 231, §§ 6B, 6C, 6H
*Criminal Usury Cap*: Mass. Gen. Laws ch. 271, § 49
*Small Loans*: Mass. Gen. Laws ch. 140, §§ 90 and 96; 209 Mass. Code Regs. 26.01
*Industrial Banks*: Mass. Gen. Laws. ch. 172A, §§ 1 to 15 (§ 9), Banking Company Act (*repealed effective March 30, 2005)*
*Insurance Premium Finance*: Mass. Gen. Laws. ch. 255C, § 14
*Auto Finance*: Mass. Gen. Laws. ch. 255B, §§ 1 to 25 (§ 14) (motor vehicle retail installment sales)
*Other Goods Finance*: Mass. Gen. Laws. ch. 255D, §§ 1 to 32 (§ 11) (retail installment sales and services)
*Revolving Sales Credit*: Mass. Gen. Laws. ch. 255D, §§ 1 to 32 (§ 27) (retail installment sales and services)
*Open-End Credit Loans*: Mass. Gen. Laws. ch. 140, § 114B
*Life Insurance and Annuity Policy Loans*: Mass. Gen. Laws ch. 175, § 142

### Michigan

*Legal Interest Rate*: Mich. Comp. Laws § 438.31
*Contract*: Mich. Comp. Laws § 438.31
*Judgment*: Mich. Comp. Laws § 600.6013
*Criminal Usury Cap*: Mich. Comp. Laws § 438.41
*Small Loans*: Mich. Comp. Laws §§ 493.1 to 493.24 (§ 493.13), Regulatory Loan Act
*Regulated Loans*: Mich. Comp. Laws §§ 445.1851 to 445.1864, Credit Reform Act
*Bank Installment and Credit Card Loans*: Mich. Comp. Laws §§ 445.1851 to 445.1864, Credit Reform Act
*Auto Finance*: Mich. Comp. Laws §§ 492.101 to 492.151 (§ 492.118), Motor Vehicle Sales Finance Act
*Other Goods Finance*: Mich. Comp. Laws §§ 445.851 to 445.873 (§ 445.857), Retail Installment Sales Act
*Home Improvement Loans*: Mich. Comp. Laws §§ 445.1101 to 445.1431 (§§ 445.1204b and 445.1301), Home Improvement Finance Act
*Insurance Premium Finance*: Mich. Comp. Laws §§ 500.1501 to 500.1514 (§ 500.1509) (insurance premium finance companies)
*Revolving Credit*: Mich. Comp. Laws §§ 445.851 to 445.873 (§ 445.862), Retail Installment Sales Act
*Life Insurance and Annuity Policy Loans*: Mich. Comp. Laws §§ 500.4022 and 500.4023
*Credit Cards*: Mich. Comp. Laws § 493.101 to 493.114 (§ 493.110)
*Payday Loans*: Mich. Comp. Laws §§ 487.2121 to 487.2173 (§ 487.2153), Deferred Presentment Service Transactions Act; Mich. Admin. Code r. 487.2121 to 487.2123
*Refund Anticipation Loans*: Mich. Comp. Laws §§ 446.111 to 446.121

### Minnesota

*Legal Interest Rate*: Minn. Stat. § 334.01
*Contract*: Minn. Stat. §§ 47.59 subdivs. 2, 3, 334.01
*Judgment*: Minn. Stat. § 549.09
*Small Loans*: Minn. Stat. §§ 56.0001 to 56.26 (§ 56.125, open-end; § 56.131), Minn. Regulated Loan Act
*Industrial Loans*: Minn. Stat. § 53.04, Industrial Loan & Thrift Company Law
*Bank and Savings Bank Loans*: Minn. Stat. § 48.195, § 47.59
*Auto Finance*: Minn. Stat. §§ 53C.01 to 53C.14 (53C.09), Motor Vehicle Retail Installment Sales Act; Minn. Stat. § 47.59(4a)
*Insurance Premium Finance*: Minn. Stat. §§ 59A.01 to 59A.15 (§ 59A.09), Insurance Premium Finance Company Act; Minn. Stat. § 47.59(2), (3)
*Revolving Credit*: Minn. Stat. § 334.16 (finance charges for open-end credit sales)
*Revolving Loans*: Minn. Stat. § 48.185 (open-end loan account arrangements); § 47.59, subdivs. 2, 3
*Consumer Credit Sales*: Minn. Stat. §§ 325G.15 and 325G.16, 334.16
*Consumer Loans*: Minn. Stat. §§ 47.59, subdivs. 2, 3, 47.60, 47.601 (consumer short-term loans)
*Life Insurance and Annuity Policy Loans*: Minn. Stat. § 61A.03
*Auto Title Loans*: Minn. Stat. §§ 325J.01 to 325J.13 (§§ 325J.07, 325J.095)
*Payday Loans*: Minn. Stat. § 47.60 (§ 47.60, subdiv. 2)
*Refund Anticipation Loans*: Minn. Stat. § 270C.445 [Minn. Stat. § 270.30 repealed effective Aug. 1, 2005]

### Mississippi

*Legal Interest Rate*: Miss. Code § 75-17-1
*Contract*: Miss. Code § 75-17-1 (§ 75-17-25, finance charge defined)
*Judgment*: Miss. Code § 75-17-7
*Small Loans*: Miss. Code § 75-17-21 and Miss. Code §§ 75-67-101 to 75-67-139, Small Loan Regulatory Law
*Bank & Trust Company Installment Loans*: Miss. Code § 81-5-79

*Insurance Premium Finance*: Miss. Code §§ 81-21-1 to 81-21-27 (§ 81-21-15) (insurance premium finance companies)
*Other Installment Loans*: Miss. Code § 75-67-39
*Manufactured Home Loans*: Miss. Code § 75-17-23
*Auto Finance*: Miss. Code § 63-19-43, Motor Vehicle Sales Finance Law
*Retail Closed-End Credit*: Miss. Code § 75-17-19(5)
*Revolving Credit*: Miss. Code § 75-17-19
*Revolving Loans*: Miss. Code § 75-17-1
*Life Insurance and Annuity Policy Loans*: Miss. Code § 83-7-26
*Auto Title Loans*: Miss. Code §§ 75-67-401 to 75-67-449, Mississippi Title Pledge Act
*Payday Loans*: Miss. Code §§ 75-67-501 to 75-67-539 (§ 75-67-519), Mississippi Check Cashers Act (repealed effective July 1, 2012)

**Missouri**

*Legal Interest Rate*: Mo. Rev. Stat. § 408.020, *see* Mo. Const. art. III, § 44
*Contract*: Mo. Rev. Stat. §§ 408.030, 408.035, 408.080, 408.455
*Judgment*: Mo. Rev. Stat. § 408.040
*Criminal Usury Cap*: Mo. Rev. Stat. § 408.095
*Small Loans*: Mo. Rev. Stat. §§ 408.100 to 408.213 (§§ 408.100, 408.120, 408.140)
*Auto Finance*: Mo. Rev. Stat. §§ 365.010 to 365.200 (§§ 365.120 and 365.125), Motor Vehicle Time Sales Law
*Other Goods Finance*: Mo. Rev. Stat. §§ 408.250 to 408.375 (§ 408.300) (retail credit sales)
*Consumer Installment Loans*: Mo. Rev. Stat. § 408.510
*Insurance Premium Finance*: Mo. Rev. Stat. §§ 364.100 to 364.160 (§ 364.120)
*Loan and Investment Companies*: Mo. Rev. Stat. § 368.040
*Revolving Loans (and Credit Cards)*: Mo. Rev. Stat. § 408.140, 408.145, 408.232(3), 408.455
*Life Insurance Policy Loans*: Mo. Rev. Stat. §§ 375.298, 376.295, 376.306
*Auto Title Loans*: Mo. Rev. Stat. §§ 367.500 to 367.533 (pawnbrokers and small loans)
*Payday Loans*: Mo. Rev. Stat. §§ 408.500, 408.505 (§ 408.505(3))

**Montana**

*Legal Interest Rate*: Mont. Code Ann. § 31-1-106
*Contract*: Mont. Code Ann. § 31-1-107
*Judgment*: Mont. Code Ann. § 25-9-205
*Small Loans*: Mont. Code Ann. §§ 32-5-101 to 32-5-409 (§ 32-5-301), Consumer Loan Act
*Credit Sales*: Mont. Code Ann. §§ 31-1-201 to 31-1-243 (§ 31-1-241), Retail Installment Sales Act
*Revolving Credit*: Mont. Code Ann. §§ 31-1-201 to 31-1-243 (§ 31-1-241), Retail Installment Sales Act
*Installment Loans By Regulated Lenders*: Mont. Code Ann. § 31-1-112
*Insurance Premium Finance*: Mont. Code. Ann. §§ 33-14-101 to 33-14-307 (§ 33-14-302)
*Life Insurance and Annuity Policy Loans*: Mont. Code Ann. §§ 33-20-131 and 33-20-135
*Auto Title Loans*: Mont. Code Ann. §§ 31-1-801 to 31-1-842, Title Loan Act
*Payday Loans*: Mont. Code Ann. §§ 31-1-701 to 31-1-729 (§ 31-1-722), Montana Deferred Deposit Loan Act

**Nebraska**

*Legal Interest Rate*: Neb. Rev. Stat. § 45-102
*Contract*: Neb. Rev. Stat. §§ 45-101.03 and 45-101.04
*Judgment*: Neb. Rev. Stat. § 45-103
*Small Loans*: Neb. Rev. Stat. §§ 45-1001 to 45-1069 (§§ 45-1024, 45-1025), Installment Loan Act
*Bank Installment Loans and Credit Cards*: Neb. Rev. Stat. § 8-820
*Installment Sales, All Goods*: Neb. Rev. Stat. §§ 45-334 to 45-353 (§ 45-338), Installment Sales Act
*Revolving Credit*: Neb. Rev. Stat. §§ 45-204 to 45-209 (§ 45-207) (revolving charge agreements)
*Life Insurance and Annuity Policy Loans*: Neb. Rev. Stat. § 44-502.03
*Payday Loans*: Neb. Rev. Stat. Ann. §§ 45-901 to 45-929 (§ 45-918), Delayed Deposit Services Licensing Act

**Nevada**

*Legal Interest Rate*: Nev. Rev. Stat. § 99.040
*Contract*: Nev. Rev. Stat. § 99.050
*Judgment*: Nev. Rev. Stat. § 17.130
*Small Loans*: Nev. Rev. Stat. §§ 675.010 to 675.490 (§ 675.363), Installment Loan and Finance Act
*Thrift Company Loans*: Nev. Rev. Stat. § 677.730
*Installment Sales, All Goods*: Nev. Rev. Stat. §§ 97.015 to 97.335 (§ 97.195) (retail installment sales of goods and services)
*Revolving Credit*: Nev. Rev. Stat. §§ 97.015 to 97.335 (§ 97.245) (retail installment sales of goods and services); Nev. Rev. Stat. §§ 97A.010 to 97A.210 (debt evidenced by credit card)
*Insurance Premium Finance*: Nev. Rev. Stat. § 686A.440
*Life Insurance & Annuity Policy Loans*: Nev. Rev. Stat. 688A.110
*Auto Title Loans*: Nev. Rev. Stat. §§ 604A.010 to 604A.940; 1995 Nev. Op. Atty. Gen. No. 20, 1995 WL 737002 (Nov. 17, 1995) (persons making title loans are pawnbrokers)
*Payday Loans*: Nev. Rev. Stat. §§ 604A.010 to 604A.940
*Attorney General Opinions*: Op. No. 99-04, 1999 WL 51658 (Nev. A.G. Feb. 1, 1999)
*Refund Anticipation Loans*: Nev. Rev. Stat. §§ 604B.010 to 604B.910

**New Hampshire**

*Legal Interest Rate*: N.H. Rev. Stat. Ann. § 336:1 (consumer loans, N.H. Rev. Stat. Ann. §§ 358-K:1 to 358K:6, exempted)
*Contract*: N.H. Rev. Stat. Ann. § 336:1 (consumer loans, N.H. Rev. Stat. Ann. §§ 358-K:1 to 358-K:6, exempted)
*Judgment*: N.H. Rev. Stat. Ann. § 336:1
*Small Loans*: N.H. Rev. Stat. Ann. §§ 399-A:1 to 399-A:19 (§ 399-A:12), Small Loan Law
*Insurance Premium Finance*: N.H. Rev. Stat. Ann. §§ 415-B:1 to 415-B:13 (§ 415-B:7) (premium finance companies)
*Auto Finance*: N.H. Rev. Stat. Ann. §§ 361-A:1 to 361-A:13 (§ 361-A:8) (retail installment sales of motor vehicles)
*Other Consumer Credit*: N.H. Rev. Stat. Ann. §§ 358-K:1 to 358K:6 (regulation of consumer credit transactions)
*Auto Title Loans*: N.H. Rev. Stat. Ann. §§ 398:1 to 398:14, Pawnbrokers; N.H. Rev. Stat. Ann. §§ 399-A:1 to 399-A:19 (§ 399-A:14)
*Payday Loans*: N.H. Rev. Stat. Ann. § 399-A:1 to 399-A:19 (§ 399-A:13)

**New Jersey**

*Legal Interest Rate*: N.J. Stat. Ann. § 31:1-1 (West)
*Contract*: N.J. Stat. Ann. §§ 31:1-1 and 31:1-1.1 (West)

*Criminal Usury Cap*: N.J. Stat. Ann. § 2C:21-19 (West)
*Judgment*: No statutory provision; N.J. Superior, Tax & Surrogate Courts Civ. Rule 4:42-11
*Small Loans*: N.J. Stat. Ann. §§ 17:11C-1 to 17:11C-49 (§ 17:11C-32) (West) (licensed lenders)
*Bank Installment Loans*: N.J. Stat. Ann. § 17:9A-54 (West)
*Installment Sales Including Auto Finance*: N.J. Stat. Ann. §§ 17:16C-1 to 17:16C-61 (§ 17:16C-41) (West), Retail Installment Sales Act
*Home Repair*: N.J. Stat. Ann. §§ 17:16C-62 to 17:16C-94 (§ 17:16C-69) (West), Home Repair Financing Act
*Insurance Premium Finance*: N.J. Stat. Ann. §§ 17:16D-1 to 17:16D-16 (§ 17:16D-10) (West), Insurance Premium Financing Company Act
*Bank Revolving Loan Credit*: N.J. Stat. Ann. §§ 17:3B-4 to 17:3B-46 (§§ 17:3B-7, 17:3B-8) (West), Market Rate Consumer Loan Act
*Bank Closed-End Credit*: N.J. Stat. Ann. §§ 17:3B-4 to 17:3B-46 (§§ 17:3B-17, 17:3B-18) (West), Market Rate Consumer Loan Act
*Market Rate Consumer Loan Act*: N.J. Stat. Ann. §§ 17:3B-4 to 17:3B-46 (West)
*Revolving Retail Charge*: N.J. Stat. Ann. § 17:16C-44.1 (West)
*Title Loans*: N.J. Admin. Code §§ 3:24-1.1 to 3:24-6.2
*Payday Loans*: N.J. Admin. Code §§ 3:24-1.1 to 3:24-6.2
*Refund Anticipation Loans*: N.J. Stat. Ann. §§ 17:11D-1 to 17:11D-7 (West); N.J. Admin. Code §§ 3:24-1.1 to 3:24-6.2

**New Mexico**

*Legal Interest Rate*: N.M. Stat. § 56-8-3
*Contract*: N.M. Stat. § 56-8-9
*Judgment*: N.M. Stat. § 56-8-4
*Criminal Usury Cap*: N.M. Stat. §§ 56-8-9, 56-8-14
*Small Loans*: N.M. Stat. §§ 58-15-1 to 58-15-39 (§ 58-15-23), Small Loan Act
*Bank Installment Loans*: N.M. Stat. §§ 58-7-1 to 58-7-9, Bank Installment Loan Act
*Auto Finance*: N.M. Stat. §§ 58-19-1 to 58-19-14, Motor Vehicle Sales Finance Act
*Other Goods Finance*: N.M. Stat. §§ 56-1-1 to 56-1-16 (retail installment and credit sales)
*Insurance Premium Finance*: N.M. Stat. §§ 59A-45-1 to 59A-45-16, Insurance Premium Financing Law
*Life Insurance and Annuity Policy Loans*: N.M. Stat. § 59A-20-10
*Auto Title Loans*: N.M. Code Admin. R. §§ 12.18.4 and 12.18.6
*Payday Loans*: N.M. Stat. §§ 58-15-32 to 58-15-39 (§ 58-15-33)
*Attorney General Opinions*: Op. No. 85.1, 1985 WL 190664 (N.M. A.G. Feb. 2, 1985)

**New York**

*Legal Interest Rate*: N.Y. Gen. Oblig. Law § 5-501; N.Y. Banking Law § 14-a (McKinney); N.Y. Comp. Codes R. & Regs. tit. 3, §§ 4.1 to 4.7 (banking board regulations—interest rates)
*Criminal Usury Cap*: N.Y. Penal Law §§ 190.40 (McKinney)
*Contract*: N.Y. Gen. Oblig. Law § 5-501 (McKinney); N.Y. Banking Law § 108 (McKinney)
*Judgment*: N.Y. Civ. Prac. L. & R. § 5004
*Small Loans*: N.Y. Banking Law §§ 340 to 361 (§ 351) (McKinney), Licensed Lender Law
*Bank Installment Loans*: N.Y. Banking Law § 108 (McKinney)
*Auto Finance*: N.Y. Pers. Prop. Law §§ 301 to 316 (§ 303) (McKinney), Motor Vehicle Retail Installment Sales Act
*Other Goods Finance*: N.Y. Pers. Prop. Law §§ 401 to 422 (§ 404) (McKinney), Retail Installment Sales Act
*Insurance Premium Finance*: N.Y. Banking Law §§ 554 to 578 (§ 568) (McKinney) (insurance premium finance agencies)
*Revolving Credit*: N.Y. Pers. Prop. Law §§ 401 to 422 (§ 413) (McKinney), Retail Installment Sales Act
*Life Insurance and Annuity Policy Loans*: N.Y. Ins. Law § 3206 (McKinney)
*Payday Loans*: New York City Admin. Code §§ 20-780 to 20-784
*Refund Anticipation Loans*: N.Y. Gen. Bus. Law §§ 371 to 373 (McKinney); N.Y. Tax Law § 32 (McKinney); New York City Admin. Code §§ 20-739 to 20-743.1

**North Carolina**

*Legal Interest Rate*: N.C. Gen. Stat. § 24-1
*Contract*: N.C. Gen. Stat. § 24-1.1
*Judgment*: N.C. Gen. Stat. §§ 24-5, 53-173(c)
*Small Loans*: N.C. Gen. Stat. §§ 53-164 to 53-191 (§§ 53-173 and 53-176), Consumer Finance Act
*Industrial Bank Loans*: N.C. Gen. Stat. § 53-141 (industrial banks)
*Bank Installment Loans*: N.C. Gen. Stat. § 53-43(1)
*Installment Sales Including Auto Finance*: N.C. Gen. Stat. §§ 25A-1 to 25A-45 (§ 25A-15), Retail Installment Sales Act
*Insurance Premium Finance*: N.C. Gen. Stat. §§ 58-35-1 to 58-35-100 (§ 58-35-55) (insurance premium financing)
*Revolving Charge*: N.C. Gen. Stat. § 25A-14 and § 24-11
*Open-End Loans*: N.C. Gen. Stat. § 24-11
*Home Equity Loans*: N.C. Gen. Stat. § 24-1.2A
*Life Insurance and Annuity Policy Loans*: N.C. Gen. Stat. §§ 58-61-1 to 58-61-15 (§ 58-61-10) (regulation of interest rates on life insurance policy loans)
*Refund Anticipation Loans*: N.C. Gen. Stat. §§ 53-245 to 53-254

**North Dakota**

*Legal Interest Rate*: N.D. Cent. Code § 47-14-05
*Contract*: N.D. Cent. Code § 47-14-09
*Judgment*: N.D. Cent. Code § 28-20-34
*Criminal Usury Cap*: N.D. Cent. Code §§ 47-14-09, 47-14-11 (*cf.* 12.1-31-02)
*Installment Sales, All Goods*: N.D. Cent. Code §§ 51-13-01 to 51-13-08 (§ 51-13-03), Retail Installment Sales Act
*Insurance Premium Finance*: N.D. Cent. Code § 26.1-20.1-07
*Revolving Credit*: N.D. Cent. Code §§ 51-14-01 to 51-14-05 (§ 51-14-03) (revolving charge accounts)
*Payday Loans*: N.D. Cent. Code §§ 13-08-01 to 13-08-15 (§ 13-08-12)
*Attorney General Opinions*: 1997 Op. Atty. Gen. N.D. L-56, 1997 WL 930120 (N.D. A.G. May 27, 1997)

**Ohio**

*Legal Interest Rate*: Ohio Rev. Code Ann. §§ 1343.01, 1343.03 (West)
*Contract*: Ohio Rev. Code Ann. §§ 1343.01, 1343.03 (West)
*Judgment*: Ohio Rev. Code Ann. § 1343.03 (West)
*Criminal Usury Cap*: Ohio Rev. Code Ann. §§ 2905.21, 2905.22 (West)
*Small Loans Including Open-End Loans*: Ohio Rev. Code Ann. §§ 1321.01 to 1321.20 (§§ 1321.13, 1321.131 and 1321.16) (West), Small Loan Law
*Installment Sales, All Goods*: Ohio Rev. Code Ann. §§ 1317.01 to 1317.99 (§§ 1317.06 and 1317.061) (West) (retail installment sales)
*Bank Installment Loans*: Ohio Rev. Code Ann. § 1109.20 (West)
*Insurance Premium Finance*: Ohio Rev. Code Ann. §§ 1321.71 to 1321.99 (§§ 1321.79 and 1321.791) (West) (insurance premium finance companies)

*Revolving Credit*: Ohio Rev. Code Ann. §§ 1317.01 to 1317.99 (§ 1317.11) (West) (retail installment sales)
*Bank Revolving Credit*: Ohio Rev. Code Ann. § 1109.20 (West)
*Life Insurance and Annuity Policy Loans*: Ohio Rev. Code Ann. § 3915.051 (West)
*Auto Title Loans*: Ohio Rev. Code Ann. § 4505.102 (West), Certificate of Motor Vehicle Title Law; Ohio Rev. Code Ann. §§ 4727.01 to 4727.99 (§ 4727.06) (West) (pawnbrokers)
*Payday Loans*: Ohio Rev. Code Ann. §§ 1321.35 to 1321.48 (§ 1321.40) (West)

**Oklahoma**

*Legal Interest Rate*: Okla. Const. art. 14, § 2; Okla. Stat. tit. 15, § 266
*Contract*: Okla. Const. art. 14, § 2; Okla. Stat. tit. 15, § 266 (see rates specified in consumer sections of Okla. UCCC)
*Judgment*: Okla. Stat. tit. 12, §§ 727, 727.1
*Criminal Usury Cap*: Okla. Stat. tit. 14A, §§ 5-107, 5-301
*Supervised Loans*: Okla. Stat. tit. 14A, §§ 3-508A and 3-508B, Okla. UCCC
*Unsupervised Consumer Loans*: Okla. Stat. tit. 14A, § 3-201, Okla. UCCC
*Non-Consumer Loans*: Okla. Stat. tit. 14A, §§ 3-601, 3-605 and 5-107(2), Okla. UCCC
*Consumer Sales Finance Including Auto Finance*: Okla. Stat. tit. 14A, § 2-201, Okla. UCCC
*Revolving Credit*: Okla. Stat. tit. 14A, § 2-207, Okla. UCCC
*Banks*: Okla. Stat. tit. 15, § 272
*Life Insurance and Annuity Policy Loans*: Okla. Stat. tit. 36, § 4008
*Payday Loans*: Okla. Stat. tit. 59, §§ 3101 to 3119 (§§ 3108, 3109), Deferred Deposit Lending Act
*Attorney General Opinions*: 1997 Op. Okla. Att'y Gen. No. 96-84, 1997 WL 130728 (Okla. A.G. Feb. 20, 1997) (regarding Okla. Stat. tit. 14A, §§ 3-508A, 3-508B)

**Oregon**

*Legal Interest Rate*: Or. Rev. Stat. § 82.010
*Contract*: Or. Rev. Stat. §§ 82.010, 82.025
*Judgment*: Or. Rev. Stat. § 82.010
*Small Loans*: Or. Rev. Stat. §§ 725.010 to 725.910 (§§ 725.340, 725.345), Consumer Finance Act
*Bank Installment Loans*: Or. Rev. Stat. § 708A.255
*Auto Finance*: Or. Rev. Stat. §§ 83.510 to 83.680 (§§ 83.095, 83.560, 83.565), Motor Vehicle Retail Installment Sales Act
*Other Goods Finance*: Or. Rev. Stat. §§ 83.010 to 83.190 (§ 83.095) (retail installment sales)
*Insurance Premium Finance*: Or. Rev. Stat. § 746.405 to 746.530 (§ 746.485) (premium financing)
*Life Insurance Policy Loans*: Or. Rev. Stat. § 743.187
*Auto Title Loans*: 2010 Special Session Undesignated Enactments, Laws 2010, ch. 23, §§ 1 to 28 (eff. June 1, 2010); Or. Admin. R. §§ 44-735-0000 to 441-735-0320
*Payday Loans*: 2010 Special Session Undesignated Enactments, Laws 2010, ch. 23, §§ 1 to 28 (eff. June 1, 2010); Or. Admin. R. §§ 44-735-0000 to 441-735-0320
*Refund Anticipation Loans*: Or. Rev. Stat. §§ 673.605 to 673.990

**Pennsylvania**

*Legal Interest Rate*: 41 Pa. Stat. Ann. §§ 201, 202 (West)
*Contract*: 41 Pa. Stat. Ann § 201 (West)
*Judgment*: 42 Pa. Cons. Stat. Ann. § 8101 (West)
*Criminal Usury Cap*: 41 Pa. Stat. Ann. §§ 501, 505 (West); 18 Pa. Stat. Ann. §§ 4806.1 to 4806.3 (West)
*Small Loans*: 7 Pa. Stat. Ann. §§ 6201 to 6219 (§ 6213) (West), Consumer Discount Company Act
*Bank Installment Loans*: 7 Pa. Stat. Ann. §§ 309 and 318 (West)
*Auto Finance*: 69 Pa. Stat. Ann. §§ 601 to 637.1 (§ 619) (West), Motor Vehicle Sales Finance Act
*Other Goods*: 69 Pa. Stat. Ann. §§ 1101 to 2303 (§ 1501) (West), Goods and Services Installment Sales Act
*Improvement Loans*: 73 Pa. Stat. Ann. §§ 500-101 to 500-602 (§ 500-301) (West), Home Improvement Finance Act
*Revolving Loan Credit*: 7 Pa. Stat. Ann. §§ 6201 to 6219 (§ 6217.1) (West), Consumer Discount Company Act
*Revolving Charge Credit*: 69 Pa. Stat. Ann. §§ 1101 to 2303 (§ 1904) (West), Goods and Services Installment Sales Act
*Bank Revolving Loans*: 7 Pa. Stat. Ann. § 309 (West)
*Insurance Premium Finance*: 40 Pa. Stat. Ann. §§ 3301 to 3314 (§ 3308) (West)
*Life Insurance and Annuity Policy Loans*: 40 Pa. Stat. Ann. § 510e (West)

**Puerto Rico**

*Legal Interest Rate*: P.R. Laws Ann. tit. 31, § 4591
*Contract*: P.R. Laws Ann. tit. 10, §§ 998, 998n; P.R. Laws Ann. tit. 31, § 4591
*Judgment*: P.R. Laws Ann. tit. 32, app. III, R. Civ. P. 44.3
*Small Loans*: P.R. Laws Ann. tit. 10, §§ 941 to 959 (§ 954), Small Personal Loan Act; Office of the Comm'r of Fin. Inst., Art. 4, Reg. No. 5782 (Apr. 14, 1998) (lifts interest rate caps)
*Retail Installment Sales*: P.R. Laws Ann. tit. 10, §§ 731 to 793 (§ 750)
*Loans*: 10 P.R. Laws. Ann. §§ 998, 998n
*Life Insurance and Annuity Policy Loans*: P.R. Laws Ann. tit. 26, § 1346
*Revolving Credit*: P.R. Laws Ann. tit. 10, §§ 731 to 793 (§ 750)

**Rhode Island**

*Legal Interest Rate*: R.I. Gen. Laws § 6-26-1
*Contract*: R.I. Gen. Laws § 6-26-2
*Judgment*: R.I. Gen. Laws § 6-26-1
*Criminal Usury Cap*: R.I. Gen. Laws §§ 6-26-2, 6-26-3
*Small Loans*: R.I. Gen. Laws §§ 19-14.2-1 to 19-14.2-16 (§§ 19-14.2-8 and 19-14.2-10), Small Loan Lenders Act
*Loan and Investment Company Loans*: R.I. Gen. Laws §§ 19-14.1-1 to 19-14.1-12 (§ 19-14.1-2) (lenders and loan brokers)
*Installment Sales Finance*: R.I. Gen. Laws §§ 6-27-1 to 6-27-11 (§ 6-27-4), Truth-in-Lending and Retail Selling Act
*Revolving Credit*: R.I. Gen. Laws §§ 6-27-1 to 6-27-11 (§ 6-27-4), Truth-in-Lending and Retail Selling Act
*Credit Cards*: R.I. Gen. Laws §§ 6-26.1-1 to 6-26.1-13 (§§ 6-26.1-4, 6-26.1-5)
*Insurance Premium Financing*: R.I. Gen. Laws §§ 19-14.6-1 to 19-14.6-7 (§ 19-14.6-2), Insurance Premium Finance Act
*Life Insurance and Annuity Policy Loans*: R.I. Gen. Laws § 27-4-13.1
*Payday Loans*: R.I. Gen. Laws §§ 19-14.4-1 to 19-14.4-10 (§ 19-14.4-4(4))

**South Carolina**

*Legal Interest Rate*: S.C. Code Ann. § 37-10-106(1)
*Contract*: S.C. Code Ann. §§ 37-10-106(1) and 34-31-20
*Judgment*: S.C. Code Ann. § 34-31-20
*"Restricted" Loans*: S.C. Code Ann. §§ 34-29-10 to 34-29-260 (§ 34-

29-140), Consumer Finance Law
*"Supervised" Loans*: S.C. Code Ann. §§ 37-3-500 to 37-3-515 (§ 37-3-501), Consumer Protection Code
*Consumer Credit Sales*: S.C. Code Ann. §§ 37-2-101 to 37-2-714 (§ 37-2-201), Consumer Protection Code
*Consumer Loans in General*: S.C. Code Ann. §§ 37-3-101 to 37-3-413 (§ 37-3-201), Consumer Protection Code
*Non-Consumer Loans*: S.C. Code Ann. §§ 37-3-601, 37-3-605, Consumer Protection Code
*Insurance Premium Finance*: S.C. Code Ann. §§ 38-39-10 to 38-39-110 (§ 38-39-80) (insurance premium service companies)
*Revolving Charge*: S.C. Code Ann. §§ 37-2-101 to 37-2-714 (§ 37-2-207), Consumer Protection Code
*Revolving Loans*: S.C. Code Ann. §§ 37-3-101 to 37-3-408 (§ 37-3-201), Consumer Protection Code
*Life Insurance and Annuity Policy Loans*: S.C. Code Ann. §§ 38-63-240 and 38-63-250
*Auto Title Loans*: S.C. Code Ann. §§ 37-3-413, 40-39-10(3)
*Payday Loans*: S.C. Code Ann. §§ 34-39-110 to 34-39-290 (§ 34-39-180), South Carolina Deferred Presentment Services Act

**South Dakota**

*Legal Interest Rate*: S.D. Codified Laws Ann. § 54-3-16
*Contract*: S.D. Codified Laws Ann. § 54-3-1.1
*Judgment*: S.D. Codified Laws Ann. § 54-3-5.1
*Installment Sales*: S.D. Codified Laws Ann. §§ 54-3A-1 to 54-3A-25 (§ 54-3A-3) (consumer installment sales contracts)
*Bank Revolving Loan Credit*: S.D. Codified Laws §§ 51A-12-12, 51A-12-13
*Revolving Charge*: S.D. Codified Laws Ann. §§ 54-11-1 to 54-11-11 (§ 54-11-6.1) (credit cards and revolving charge accounts)
*Life Insurance and Annuity Policy Loans*: S.D. Codified Laws Ann. §§ 58-15-15.4 to 58-15-15.12
*Auto Title Loans*: S.D. Codified Laws §§ 54-4-36 to 54-4-72
*Payday Loans*: S.D. Codified Laws §§ 54-4-36 to 54-4-72

**Tennessee**

*Legal Interest Rate*: Tenn. Const. art XI, § 7; Tenn. Code Ann. § 47-14-103
*Contract*: Tenn. Code Ann. § 47-14-103 (formula rate defined in § 47-14-102(7) and § 47-14-106)
*Judgment*: Tenn. Code Ann. § 47-14-121
*Industrial Loans*: Tenn. Code Ann. §§ 45-5-101 to 45-5-612 (§ 45-5-301) (industrial loan and thrift companies)
*Bank Installment Loans*: Tenn. Code Ann. § 45-2-1106
*Revolving Credit*: Tenn. Code Ann. §§ 47-11-101 to 47-11-111 (§ 47-11-104), Retail Installment Sales Act
*Home Loans*: Tenn. Code Ann. §§ 47-15-101 to 47-15-104 (§§ 47-15-102 and 47-15-104) (interest on home loans)
*Goods Finance*: Tenn. Code Ann. §§ 47-11-101 to 47-11-111 (§ 47-11-103), Retail Installment Sales Act
*Insurance Premium Finance*: Tenn. Code Ann. §§ 56-6-301, 56-37-108
*Installment Loans*: Tenn. Code Ann. § 47-14-107
*Home Improvement Loans*: Tenn. Code Ann. § 45-3-705
*Life Insurance and Annuity Policy Loans*: Tenn. Code Ann. § 56-7-2307
*Auto Title Loans*: Tenn. Code Ann. §§ 45-15-101 to 45-15-120 (§ 45-15-111)
*Payday Loans*: Tenn. Code Ann. §§ 45-17-101 to 45-17-119 (§ 45-17-112(b)), Deferred Presentment Services Act
*Attorney General Opinions*: Op. No. 90-79, 1990 WL 513057 (Tenn. A.G. Aug. 17, 1990); Op. No. 06-068, 2006 WL 1197462 (Tenn. A.G. Apr. 12, 2006)
*Refund Anticipation Loans*: Tenn. Code Ann. §§ 62-29-201 to 62-29-205

**Texas**

*Legal Interest Rate*: Tex. Const. art. 16, § 11; Tex. Fin. Code Ann. § 302.001 (West)
*Contract*: Tex. Const. art. 16, § 11; Tex. Fin. Code Ann. §§ 302.001, 302.002, 303.001 to 303.502 (West)
*Judgment*: Tex. Fin. Code Ann. §§ 304.001 to 304.007 (West)
*Consumer Loans*: Tex. Fin. Code Ann. §§ 342.051 to 342.560 (§ 342.201) (West)
*Installment Sales*: Tex. Fin. Code Ann. §§ 345.001 to 345.357 (West) (retail installment sales)
*Auto Finance*: Tex. Fin. Code Ann. §§ 348.001 to 348.413 (West) (motor vehicle installment sales)
*Other Goods Finance*: Tex. Fin. Code Ann. §§ 345.001 to 345.357 (West) (retail installment sales)
*Manufactured Homes*: Tex. Fin. Code Ann. §§ 347.001 to 347.403 (West) (manufactured home credit transactions)
*Insurance Premium Finance*: Tex. Ins. Code Ann. §§ 651.001 to 651.209 (§ 651.109) (West)
*Revolving Loans & Credit Cards*: Tex. Fin. Code Ann. §§ 346.001 to 346.206 (West) (revolving credit accounts)
*Revolving Credit*: Tex. Fin. Code Ann. §§ 345.001 to 345.357 (West) (retail installment sales)
*Life Insurance and Annuity Policy Loans*: Tex. Ins. Code. Ann. §§ 1110.001 to 1110.008 (§ 1110.004) (West)
*Payday Loans*: Tex. Fin. Code Ann. §§ 341.001, 342.051 to 342.259 (§§ 342.252, 342.253), 342.601 to 342.605 (West); 7 Tex. Admin. Code § 83.604
*Refund Anticipation Loans*: Tex. Fin. Code Ann. §§ 352.001 to 352.008 (West)

**Utah**

*Legal Interest Rate*: Utah Code Ann. § 15-1-1
*Contract*: Utah Code Ann. §§ 15-1-1 and 70C-2-101
*Judgment*: Utah Code Ann. § 15-1-4
*Criminal Usury Cap*: Utah Code Ann. § 76-6-520
*Consumer Credit*: Utah Code Ann. §§ 70C-1-101 to 70C-8-203 (§ 70C-2-101), Utah UCCC
*Life Insurance and Annuity Policy Loans*: Utah Code Ann. § 31A-22-420
*Auto Title Loans*: Utah Code Ann. §§ 7-24-101 to 7-24-305
*Payday Loans*: Utah Code Ann. §§ 7-23-101 to 7-23-504, Check Cashing and Deferred Deposit Lending Registration Act

**Vermont**

*Legal Interest Rate*: Vt. Stat. Ann. tit. 9, § 41a
*Contract*: Vt. Stat. Ann. tit. 9, § 41a
*Judgment*: Vt. R. App. P. 37; Vt. R. Civ. P. 69
*Criminal Usury Cap*: Vt. Stat. Ann. tit. 9, § 50
*Small Loans*: *See* Licensed Lender Act, below
*Financial Institutions*: Vt. Stat. Ann. tit. 8, §§ 10101 to 20106 (§ 14301(c))
*Installment Loans*: Vt. Stat. Ann. tit. 9, §§ 41a(b)(2), (5)
*Auto Finance*: Vt. Stat. Ann. tit. 9, §§ 2351 to 2362 (§ 2356a) (motor vehicle retail installment sales financing); Vt. Stat. Ann. tit. 9, § 41a(b)(4)

*Other Goods Finance*: Vt. Stat. Ann. tit. 9, §§ 2401 to 2410 (§ 2405) (retail installment sales); Vt. Stat. Ann. tit. 9, § 41a(b)(2)
*Revolving Credit*: Vt. Stat. Ann. tit. 9, §§ 2401 to 2410 (§ 2406) (retail installment sales); Vt. Stat. Ann. tit. 9, § 41a(b)(3), (9)
*Insurance Premium Finance*: Vt. Stat. Ann. tit. 8, §§ 7001 to 7011 (§ 7007) (insurance premium finance companies)
*Life Insurance and Annuity Policy Loans*: Vt. Stat. Ann. tit. 8, § 3731
*Licensed Lender Act*: Vt. Stat. Ann. tit. 8, §§ 2200 to 2244 (§ 2230)

### Virginia

*Legal Interest Rate*: Va. Code Ann. § 6.2-301
*Contract*: Va. Code Ann. § 6.2-303
*Judgment*: Va. Code Ann. § 6.2-302; Va. Code Ann. § 8.01-382 (prejudgment and postjudgment interest).
*Small Loans*: Va. Code Ann. §§ 6.2-1500 to 6.2-1543 (§ 6.2-1520) (consumer finance companies)
*Industrial Loans*: Va. Code Ann. § 6.2-320
*Bank Installment Loans*: Va. Code Ann. § 6.2-309
*Installment Sales*: Va. Code Ann. §§ 6.2-309, 6.2-311, 6.2-314
*Insurance Premium Financing*: Va. Code Ann. §§ 38.2-4700 to 38.2-4712 (§ 38.2-4705) (insurance premium finance companies)
*Bank Revolving Credit*: Va. Code Ann. § 6.2-313
*Credit Union Loans*: Va. Code Ann. § 6.2-318
*Other Revolving Loan or Charge Credit*: Va. Code Ann. § 6.2-312
*Open Accounts*: Va. Code Ann. § 6.2-301(C)
*Life Insurance and Annuity Policy Loans*: Va. Code Ann. § 38.2-3308
*Auto Title Loans*: Va. Code Ann. §§ 6.2-2200 to 6.2-2227 (§ 6.2-2216); 10 Va. Admin. Code §§ 5-210-10 to 5-210-110
*Payday Loans*: Va. Code Ann. §§ 6.2-1800 to 6.2-1829 (§ 6.2-1817); 10 Va. Admin. Code §§ 5-200-10 to 5-200-130
*Refund Anticipation Loans*: Va. Code Ann. §§ 6.2-2500 to 6.2-2505

### Virgin Islands

*Legal Interest Rate*: V.I. Code Ann. tit. 11, § 951
*Contract*: V.I. Code Ann. tit. 11, § 951
*Judgment*: V.I. Code Ann. tit. 5, § 426
*Small Loans*: V.I. Code Ann. tit. 9, §§ 181 to 204 (§ 183) (small loan law)
*Credit Cards*: V.I. Code Ann. tit. 11, § 957
*Life Insurance Policy Loans*: V.I. Code Ann. tit. 22, § 958
*Insurance Premium Finance*: V.I. Code Ann. tit. 22, § 1634

### Washington

*Legal Interest Rate*: Wash. Rev. Code § 19.52.010
*Contract*: Wash. Rev. Code § 19.52.010, 19.52.020
*Judgment*: Wash. Rev. Code § 4.56.110
*Consumer Open- and Closed-End Loans*: Wash. Rev. Code §§ 31.04.015 to 31.04.903 (§§ 31.04.015, 31.04.105, 31.04.115), Consumer Loan Act
*Installment Finance—All Goods*: Wash. Rev. Code §§ 63.14.010 to 63.14.926 (§ 63.14.130) (retail installment sales of goods and services)
*Insurance Premium Finance*: Wash. Rev. Code §§ 48.56.010 to 48.56.900 (§ 48.56.090), Insurance Premium Finance Company Act
*Revolving Credit*: Wash. Rev. Code §§ 63.14.010 to 63.14.926 (§ 63.14.130) (retail installment sales of goods and services)
*Life Insurance and Annuity Policy Loans*: Wash. Rev. Code §§ 48.23.080 and 48.23.085
*Payday Loans*: Wash. Rev. Code Ann. §§ 31.45.010 to 31-45-901 (§ 31.45.073)
*Refund Anticipation Loans*: Wash. Rev. Code §§ 19.265.010 to 19.265.900

### West Virginia

*Legal Interest Rate*: W. Va. Code §§ 47-6-5 to 47-6-5c
*Contract*: W. Va. Code § 47-6-5. Alternative rates for loans and credit sales set by Lending and Credit Rate Board under W. Va. Code § 47A-1-1. Alternative bank rate set by Commissioner of Banking under W. Va. Code § 31A-4-30a
*Judgment*: W. Va. Code §§ 56-6-31 and 46A-3-111(4)
*Criminal Usury Cap*: W. Va. Code § 46A-5-103
*Small Loans*: W. Va. Code §§ 46A-1-101 to 46A-8-102 (§ 46A-4-107), Consumer Credit and Protection Act
*Bank and Other Installment Loans*: W. Va. Code §§ 31A-4-30, 31A-4-30a, 47-6-5a
*Auto Finance*: W. Va. Code §§ 46A-1-101 to 46A-8-102 (§ 46A-3-101(6)), Consumer Credit and Protection Act
*Installment Sales—Other Goods*: W. Va. Code § 47-6-5a and §§ 46A-1-101 to 46A-8-102 (§§ 46A-3-101 and 46A-3-104), Consumer Credit and Protection Act
*Revolving Charge Accounts*: W. Va. Code §§ 46A-1-101 to 46A-8-102 (§ 46A-3-103), Consumer Credit and Protection Act
*Revolving Loans*: W. Va. Code §§ 46A-1-101 to 46A-8-102 (§ 46A-3-106), Consumer Credit and Protection Act
*Life Insurance and Annuity Policy Loans*: W. Va. Code §§ 33-13-8 and 33-13-8a

### Wisconsin

*Legal Interest Rate*: Wis. Stat. §§ 138.04, 138.05
*Contract*: Wis. Stat. §§ 138.04, 138.05
*Judgment*: Wis. Stat. §§ 814.04 and 815.05
*Criminal Usury Cap*: Wis. Stat. § 943.27
*State Bank Loans*: Wis. Stat. § 138.041
*Small Loans*: Wis. Stat. § 138.09, Precomputed Loan Law; Wis. Stat. §§ 421.101 to 427.105 (§ 422.201), Wis. UCCC
*Credit Sales*: Wis. Stat. §§ 421.101 to 427.105 (§ 422.201), Wis. UCCC
*Installment Loans*: Wis. Stat. § 138.05
*Insurance Premium Finance*: Wis. Stat. § 138.12 (insurance premium finance companies)
*Auto Finance*: Wis. Stat. §§ 218.0142, 422.201(3)
*Revolving Credit*: Wis. Stat. §§ 421.101 to 427.105 (§ 422.201(10s)), Wis. UCCC
*Life Insurance and Annuity Policy Loans*: Wis. Stat. § 632.475
*Auto Title Loans*: Wis. Stat. § 138.16 (eff. Jan. 1, 2011)
*Payday Loans*: Wis. Stat. § 138.14 (eff. Jan. 1, 2011)
*Refund Anticipation Loans*: Wis. Stat. §§ 421.301, 422.310

### Wyoming

*Legal Interest Rate*: Wyo. Stat. Ann. § 40-14-106
*Contract*: See rates specified in consumer sections of Wyo. UCCC (Wyo. Stat. Ann. §§ 40-14-101 to 40-14-702)
*Judgment*: Wyo. Stat. Ann. § 1-16-102
*Consumer Supervised Loans; Licensed Lenders*: Wyo. Stat. Ann. §§ 40-14-101 to 40-14-702 (§ 40-14-348) (includes revolving loans), Wyoming UCCC
*Consumer Loans in General*: Wyo. Stat. Ann. §§ 40-14-101 to 40-14-702 (§ 40-14-310), Wyo. UCCC
*Non-Consumer & Non-Consumer Related Loans*: Wyo. Stat. Ann. §§ 40-14-101 to 40-14-702 (§ 40-14-358), Wyo. UCCC

*Consumer Credit Sales*: Wyo. Stat. Ann. §§ 40-14-101 to 40-14-702 (§ 40-14-212), Wyo. UCCC
*Non-Consumer Related Credit Sales*: Wyo. Stat. Ann. §§ 40-14-101 to 40-14-702 (§ 40-14-260), Wyo. UCCC
*Revolving Charge Accounts*: Wyo. Stat. Ann. §§ 40-14-101 to 40-14-702 (§ 40-14-218), Wyo. UCCC
*Life Insurance and Annuity Policy Loans*: Wyo. Stat. Ann. § 26-16-108
*Payday Loans*: Wyo. Stat. Ann. §§ 40-14-362 to 40-14-364 (§ 40-14-363)

# Appendix C Summaries of State Retail Installment Sales Acts

This appendix summarizes state Retail Installment Sales Acts (RISAs). These statutes typically cover installment sales of goods and services, but some regulate certain purchase-money consumer loans as well. Some states have a RISA that applies exclusively to installment sales contracts for motor vehicles or manufactured homes, and some have more than one RISA. Many RISAs include provisions for retail charge accounts. All these types of RISAs, for each state, are included in this appendix.

Most RISAs cap finance charges (often referred to in the statute as a "service charge" or a "time-price differential"). However, a number of states removed these caps in the 1980s and 1990s, and now allow any finance charges agreed upon by the parties. RISAs often regulate late charges, prepayment penalties and rebates of unearned interest, deferral charges, and document preparation fees.

Many RISAs also prohibit balloon payments or require the obligation to be repayable in substantially equal installments. They may limit the length of the term of the installment contract, and restrict the types of insurance that can be sold in connection with the transaction. Some include special provisions preserving the liability of assignees. RISA restrictions on default and repossession are not included in this appendix, but are discussed in National Consumer Law Center, *Repossessions* (7th ed. 2010 and Supp.).

This appendix summarizes key provisions of state RISAs. The summaries do not include all details of these statutes, however. For example, RISAs provisions regarding rebates of unearned interest often specify how to count the number of months for which interest is unearned, or whether the creditor must rebate any deferral charges that have been imposed. The summaries in this appendix exclude these details.

**Ala. Code §§ 5-19-1 to 5-19-33 (Consumer Credit Transactions Law "Mini-Code").**

*Scope*: Credit transactions in which the party to whom credit is extended is a natural person and the money, property, or services are primarily for personal, family, or household purposes. Some lease transactions. Non-consumer transactions of less than $2,000 are subject to Act's finance charge limits only. § 5-19-1. *Note that the Mini-Code is broader in scope than most state RISAs and is applicable to a wide range of consumer credit transactions.*

*Licensure requirements*: Creditors making consumer loans, making consumer loans originated by a mortgage loan originator, and taking assignments of consumer credit contracts must obtain licenses. A seller, with respect to consumer credit sale transactions and the financing of permitted charges, is not required to be licensed under the provision. § 5-19-22(a).

*Credit terms*: Except under open-end credit plans, the maximum finance charge for any credit transaction where the original amount financed is less than $2,000 may equal but may not exceed the total of the following: (1) $15 per $100 per year for the first $750 of the original amount financed; and (2) $10 per $100 per year for that portion of the original amount financed exceeding $750 and less than $2,000. The maximum finance charge shall be determined by computing the maximum authorized rates on the original amount financed for the full term of the contract without regard to scheduled payments and the maximum finance charge so determined, or any lesser amount, may be added to the original amount financed. The finance charge may be calculated and expressed as a simple interest charge or by any method that does not result in a finance charge yield greater than the yield permitted. § 5-19-3(a). A creditor, in connection with any credit sale other than a sale made under an open-end credit plan, may contract for and receive a minimum finance charge not in excess of the following amounts: (1) $4 on any credit sale in which the amount financed is $25 or less; and (2) $6 on any credit sale in which the amount financed is more than $25. § 5-19-3(b). In an open-end credit plan, if there is an unpaid balance on the date as of which the finance charge is applied, a creditor may contract for and receive a minimum finance charge in an amount not exceeding fifty cents ($.50) per month. § 5-19-3(c). The finance charge for any credit transaction with an original amount financed or original principal balance not less than $2,000 and for any open-end credit plan with a credit limit not less than $2,000 shall be subject to the provisions of §§ 8-8-5 to 8-8-15, or §§ 5-20-2 to 5-20-10, as applicable. The maximum finance charge for any open-end credit plan with a credit limit of less than $2,000 shall be determined by § 8-8-14, or §§ 5-20-2 to 5-20-10, as applicable. § 5-19-3(e). In addition to other lawful charges, except under open-end credit plans, a creditor may, if provided in the contract, charge an account maintenance fee of not more than $3 for each month of the scheduled period of repayment of the credit transaction. § 5-19-33.

*Restrictions on points or prepaid interest*: For a consumer credit transaction contract secured by an interest in real property, a creditor may charge points in an amount not to exceed 5% of the original principal balance in the case of a closed-end consumer credit transaction, or 5% of the total line of credit in the case of an open-end credit plan. Points shall be in addition to all other charges, are fully earned on the date of the consumer credit transaction, and may be excluded from the finance charge for the purpose of computing any finance charge credit or refund. § 5-19-4(g). Except for permissible prepaid finance charges, the finance charge shall not be payable in advance, or compounded; however, if part or all of the consideration for a new credit transaction contract is the unpaid amount financed and unpaid accrued charges of a prior credit transaction, then the amount financed under the new credit transaction contract may include any unpaid accrued charges. The resulting credit transaction contract shall be deemed a new and separate credit transaction for all purposes. § 5-19-3(d).

*Permissible length of term*: None.

*Restrictions on prepayment penalties*: Debtors may pay in advance the unpaid balance of the amount financed and all accrued finance charges without penalty. § 5-19-3(d).

*Requirement of substantially equal installments or limits on balloon payments*: With respect to a consumer credit transaction, if any scheduled payment is more than one and one-half times as large as the average of earlier scheduled payments, the debtor has the right to refinance the amount of that payment at the time it is due without penalty. The terms of the refinancing shall be no less favorable than the terms of the original transaction. This provision does not apply if the payment schedule has been adjusted to conform with the seasonal or irregular income of the debtor, or if a consumer credit transaction is repayable in a single principal payment irrespective of the scheduled interest payments. § 5-19-7. With respect to consumer credit transactions, where the debt is payable in installments, not made pursuant to an open-end credit plan and in which the original amount financed is $1,000 or less, the debt shall be scheduled to be payable in substantially equal installments at equal periodic intervals, except to the extent that the schedule of payments is adjusted to the seasonal or irregular income of the debtor or when the transaction is a single principal payment obligation irrespective of the scheduled interest payments, and: (1) over a period of not more than 36 months and 15 days if the original amount financed is more than $300; or (2) over a period of not more than 24 months and 15 days if the original amount financed is $300 or less. § 5-19-18.

*Formula for rebate of unearned interest*: For transaction with original term of 61 months or less, calculated by Rule of 78s (sum of the balances method); otherwise, by actuarial method. No refund of less than $1 need be made. § 5-19-4(c).

*Deferral charges*: With respect to the deferral of one or more wholly unpaid scheduled payments in a consumer credit transaction, in which the finance charge was determined by the precomputed method, the creditor may collect, by agreement with the debtor either before or after default, an additional charge for each full month that any wholly unpaid scheduled payments are outstanding after the due date of each scheduled payment equal to that proportion of the finance charge which the amount of the deferred monthly scheduled payment bears to the sum of all monthly balances originally scheduled. § 5-19-4(b).

*Limits on document fees*: A creditor may charge in a transaction secured by real property certain fees and charges if "bona fide and reasonable in amount." § 5-19-4(f).

*Restrictions on types of insurance that can be sold*: With respect to any consumer credit transaction, the creditor shall not require any insurance other than insurance against loss of or damage to any property in which the creditor is given a security interest and insurance insuring the lien of the creditor on the property which is collateral for the transaction. § 5-19-20(a).

*Single document rule?*: None.

*Assignee liability provision*: With respect to a consumer credit sale, an assignee of the rights of the seller is subject to all claims and defenses of the buyer against the seller arising out of the sale, notwithstanding an agreement to the contrary, but the assignee's liability may not exceed the amount owing to the assignee at the time the claim or defense is asserted against the assignee. Rights of the buyer can be asserted only as a matter of defense to or setoff against a claim by the assignee. § 5-19-8.

*Special provisions for manufactured homes*: None.

*Revolving credit*: In an open-end credit plan, if there is an unpaid balance on the date as of which the finance charge is applied, a creditor may contract for and receive a minimum finance charge in an amount not exceeding fifty cents ($.50) per month. § 5-19-3(c).

*Other noteworthy provisions*: Other than under an open-end credit plan, in any credit transaction where the finance charge is computed on the unpaid balance of the amount financed outstanding from time to time, for the actual time outstanding: Each payment shall be applied first to accrued charges and the remainder of the payment applied to the unpaid balance of the amount financed, except that if the amount of the payment is insufficient to pay the accumulated charges, unpaid charges continue to accumulate to be paid from the proceeds of subsequent payments and are not added to the unpaid amount financed. § 5-19-3(d).

*Remedies*: Any creditor charging a finance charge in excess of the authorized amount shall forfeit actual economic damages not to exceed the finance charge, and shall refund to the debtor such amount, which may be done by reducing the amount of the debtor's obligation. If the debtor is entitled to a refund and the creditor refuses to refund within a reasonable time, not to exceed 60 days, after written demand, including the filing of a legal action, the debtor shall recover a penalty of five times the amount of the actual economic damages not to exceed the finance charge, but in any event not less than $100. Any creditor that has made an excess finance charge in deliberate violation of or in reckless disregard for the statute is liable shall forfeit the greater of the entire finance charge imposed or five times the amount of the actual economic damages, but not less than $100. § 5-19-19(a). Other violations are subject to actual economic damages sustained by the person as the result of the failure to comply. § 5-19-19(c). Injunctive relief in an action brought by the administrator is authorized under § 5-19-29.

**Alaska Stat. §§ 45.10.010 to 45.10.230 (Retail Installment Sales Act).**

*Scope*: Installment sales of goods or services for personal use from a retail seller under an installment contract or charge agreement including repairs or improvements of real property, but not services of a professional licensed by the state, or some services for which the price is determined or approved by a governmental entity. § 45.10.220

*Licensure requirements*: None.

*Credit terms*: The rate agreed upon by the retail seller and the buyer. § 45.10.120.

*Restrictions on points or prepaid interest*: None.

*Restrictions on length of term*: None.

*Restrictions on prepayment penalties*: None.

*Requirement of substantially equal installments or limits on balloon payments*: None.

*Formula for rebate of unearned interest*: Rebate calculation based on Rule of 78s (sum of the balances method). § 45.10.070.

*Restrictions on deferral charges*: None.

*Limits on document fees*: None.

*Restrictions on types of insurance that can be sold*: None.

*Single document rule?*: A retail installment contract must be contained in a single document with some exceptions (*see* §§ 45.10.040, 45.10.050 and 45.10.100). § 45.10.010.

*Assignee liability provision*: None.

*Special provisions for manufactured homes*: None.

*Special provisions for revolving credit*: None.

*Other noteworthy provisions*: None.

*Remedies*: The attorney general may bring an action in the name of the state against a person to restrain and prevent a violation. § 45.10.170.

**Ariz. Rev. Stat. Ann. §§ 44-6001 to 44-6006 (Retail Installment Sales Transactions).**

*Scope*: Installment sales of tangible chattels, except motor vehicles, money, things in action, or intangible personal property. Includes fixtures and merchandise certificates or coupons issued by a retail

seller that are not redeemable in cash and to be used in the face amount instead of cash for goods or services sold by such seller. Revolving credit. Services. § 44-6001.
*Licensure requirements*: None.
*Credit terms*: Rate set by contract. § 44-6002.
*Restrictions on points or prepaid interest*: None.
*Restrictions on length of term*: None.
*Restrictions on prepayment penalties*: None.
*Requirement of substantially equal installments or limits on balloon payments*: None.
*Formula for rebate of unearned interest*: Prohibits use of Rule of 78s. Calculation of earned finance charge can be based on 360-, 365-, or 366-day year. § 44-6602(A).
*Restrictions on deferral charges*: None.
*Limits on document fees*: None.
*Restrictions on types of insurance that can be sold*: None.
*Single document rule?*: None.
*Assignee liability provision*: None.
*Special provisions for manufactured homes*: None.
*Special provisions for revolving credit*: None.
*Other noteworthy provisions*: None.
*Remedies*: A seller or holder who violates any provision of the statute is barred from recovery of any finance charge, official fees, and delinquency charge under or in connection with the related retail installment contract or the related retail charge account agreement for as long as the violation continues. § 44-6006.

**Ariz. Rev. Stat. Ann. §§ 44-281 to 44-295 (Motor Vehicle Time Sales Disclosure Act).**

*Scope*: Motor vehicle sales. § 44-281.
*Licensure requirements*: License required by dealer and any persons to whom dealer sells or transfers any contract. § 44-282(A).
*Credit terms*: Rate set by contract. § 44-291(A). However, maximum finance rates apply for secondary (non-purchase money) motor vehicle retail installment contracts. § 44-291(G).
*Restrictions on points or prepaid interest*: None.
*Restrictions on length of term*: None.
*Restrictions on prepayment penalties*: None.
*Requirement of substantially equal installments or limits on balloon payments*: None.
*Formula for rebate of unearned interest*: Prohibits use of Rule of 78s. Calculation of earned finance charge can be based on 360-, 365-, or 366-day year. § 44-291(B).
*Restrictions on deferral charges*: No special provisions of deferral charges. Statute requires creditor to calculate charges for a deferral the same as for a refinancing, by rebating unearned changes and adding and additional costs for insurance and other benefits incidental to the refinancing. Accrued delinquency and collateral charges may be included in the unpaid balance. The vehicle may be reclassified based on its model year. § 44-293(B).
*Limits on document fees*: None.
*Restrictions on types of insurance that can be sold*: None.
*Single document rule?*: None.
*Assignee liability provision*: None.
*Special provisions for manufactured homes*: None.
*Special provisions for revolving credit*: None.
*Other noteworthy provisions*: None.
*Remedies*: Any person who willfully violates any provision of the Act relating to the provisions of a contract shall not receive or retain any finance, delinquency, or collection charge on the contract. § 44-295.

**Cal. Civ. Code §§ 1801 to 1812.20 (West) (Retail Installment Sales "Unruh" Act).**

*Scope*: Installment sales of goods for personal use other than motor vehicles. including goods which, at the time of the sale or subsequently, are to be so affixed to real property as to become a part of such real property whether or not severable therefrom. § 1802.1. Services for other than a commercial or business use, including services furnished in connection with the sale or repair of goods or furnished in connection with the repair of motor vehicles or in connection with the improvement of real property or the providing of insurance, but does not include the services of physicians or dentists, or some services for which rates are required by law to be filed with a governmental entity. § 1802.2.
*Licensure requirements*: None.
*Credit terms*: No annual fee or charge shall be made in any retail installment contract. § 1805.1.
*Restrictions on points or prepaid interest*: None.
*Restrictions on length of term*: None.
*Restrictions on prepayment penalties*: The buyer may pay at any time before maturity the entire indebtedness evidenced by the contract without penalty. § 1806.3(a).
*Requirement of substantially equal installments or limits on balloon payments*: If any payment, other than a deferred down payment, is more than twice the amount of an otherwise regularly scheduled equal payment, the contract must include language to notify the buyer of the right to obtain a new payment schedule. Unless agreed to by the buyer, the periodic payments under the new schedule shall not be substantially greater than the average of the preceding installments. § 1807.3.
*Formula for rebate of unearned interest*: Calculated based on Rule of 78s (sum of the balances method), but refund of less than $1 need not be made. § 1806.3(a)(1).
*Restrictions on deferral charges*: No charge shall be made for any of extension of the scheduled due date or deferment of the scheduled payment of all or of any part of any installment or installments unless the agreement for such extension or deferment is in writing and signed by the parties. § 1807.1(a). Where the contract includes a finance charge determined on the precomputed basis, the holder may charge and contract for the payment of an extension or deferral agreement charge, but such charge may not exceed an amount equal to 1% per month simple interest on the amount of the installment or installments, or part thereof, extended or deferred for the period of extension or deferral. Such period shall not exceed the period from the date when such extended or deferred installment or installments, or part thereof, would have been payable in the absence of such extension or deferral, to the date when such installment or installments, or part thereof, are made payable under the agreement of extension or deferment; except that a minimum charge of $1 for the period of extension or deferral may be made in any case where the extension or deferral agreement charge, when computed at such rate, amounts to less than $1. § 1807.1(b). Where the contract includes a finance charge determined on the simple-interest basis, the holder may charge and contract for the payment of an extension or deferral agreement charge by the buyer, but the charge for the extension or deferral agreement may not exceed the lesser of $25 or 10% of the then unpaid balance of the contract. Such charge shall be in addition to any finance charges that accrue because such extended or deferred payments are received at a time other than as originally scheduled. § 1807.1(c).
*Limits on document fees*: None.

*Restrictions on types of insurance that can be sold*: None.
*Single document rule?*: Every retail installment contract shall be contained in a single document. § 1803.2.
*Assignee liability provision*: An assignee of the seller is subject to all equities and defenses of the buyer against the seller arising out of the sale, notwithstanding an agreement to the contrary, but the assignee's liability may not exceed the amount of the debt owing to the assignee at the time of the assignment. § 1804.2.
*Special provisions for manufactured homes*: None.
*Special provisions for revolving credit*: None.
*Other noteworthy provisions*: None.
*Remedies*: If any person fails to comply with the Act, such person, or any person who acquires a contract or installment account with knowledge of such noncompliance, is barred from recovery of any finance charge or of any delinquency, collection, extension, deferral, or refinance charge imposed in connection with such contract or installment account, and the buyer has the right to recover an amount equal to any of such charges paid. § 1812.7. If a person willfully violates any provision of the Act in connection with the imposition, computation, or disclosures of or relating to a finance charge on a consolidated total of two or more contracts the buyer may recover an amount equal to three times the total of the finance charges and any delinquency, collection, extension, deferral, or refinance charges imposed, contracted for, or received on all contracts included in the consolidated total and the seller shall be barred from the recovery of any such charges. § 1812.9.

**Cal. Civ. Code §§ 2981 to 2984.6 (West) (Automobile Sales Finance Act).**

*Scope*: Sales of motor vehicles required to be registered that are bought for use primarily for personal or family purposes. Excludes mobile homes and any vehicles bought for use primarily for business or commercial purposes. § 2981.
*Licensure requirements*: None.
*Credit terms*: Except for contracts in which the finance charge or a portion of the finance charge is determined by the simple-interest basis and the amount financed is more than $2,500, the dollar amount of the finance charge may not exceed the greater of: 1% on entire unpaid balance or 1.5% on the unpaid balance up to $225, 1 1/6% on the unpaid balance over $225 but less than $900, and five-sixths of 1% on the unpaid balance over $900 but less than $2,500. If the finance charge is determined by the precomputed basis, $25. If the finance charge or a portion thereof is determined by the simple-interest basis: $25 if the unpaid balance does not exceed $1,000, $50 if the unpaid balance exceeds $1,000 but does not exceed $2,000, $75 if the unpaid balance exceeds two thousand dollars $2,000. § 2982(j)(1). If the finance charge or a portion thereof is determined by the simple-interest basis and the amount of the unpaid balance exceeds $5,000, the holder of the contract may, in lieu of its right to a minimum finance charge, charge on the date of the contract an administrative finance charge not to exceed $75, provided that the sum of the administrative finance charge and the portion of the finance charge determined by the simple-interest basis shall not exceed the maximum total finance charge permitted by the Act. § 2982(j)(3).

*Restrictions on points or prepaid interest*: None.
*Restrictions on length of term*: None.
*Restrictions on prepayment penalties*: The buyer may pay at any time before maturity the entire indebtedness without penalty. § 2981(l).
*Requirement of substantially equal installments or limits on balloon payments*: If a contract provides for unequal or irregular payments, or payments on other than a monthly basis, the maximum finance charge shall be at the effective rate provided for according to the method described in § 2981(j)(1) (see *Credit terms*, above). § 2981(j)(4).
*Formula for rebate of unearned interest*: Calculated based on Rule of 78s (sum of the balances method), but refund of less than $1 need not be made. § 2981(l)(1).
*Restrictions on deferral charges*: No charge shall be made for any such extension of the scheduled due date or deferment of scheduled payment of any installment or installments unless the agreement for such extension or deferment is in writing and signed by the parties thereto. If the finance charge is determined on the precomputed basis, the holder may charge for the payment of an extension or deferral agreement charge, but such charge may not exceed an amount equal to 1% per month simple interest on the amount of the installment or installments, or part thereof, extended or deferred for the period of extension or deferral. Such period shall not exceed the period from the date when such extended or deferred installment or installments, or part thereof, would have been payable in the absence of such extension or deferral to the date when such installment or installments, or part thereof, are made payable under the agreement of extension or deferment; except that a minimum charge of $1 for the period of extension or deferral may be made in any case where the extension or deferral agreement charge, when computed at such rate, amounts to less than $1. If finance charge is determined on the simple-interest basis, the holder may charge for the payment of an extension or deferral agreement charge, but may not exceed the lesser of $25 or 10% of the then outstanding principal balance of the contract. Such charge shall be in addition to any finance charges that accrue because such extended or deferred payments are received at a time other than as originally scheduled. § 2982.3.

*Limits on document fees*: If the seller imposes a fee for document preparation, the contract shall contain a disclosure that the fee is not a governmental fee. § 2981(n). A seller shall not impose an application fee for a transaction governed by the Act. § 2981(o).
*Restrictions on types of insurance that can be sold*: None.
*Single document rule?*: Every conditional sale contract subject to the Act shall contain in a single document all of the agreements of the buyer and seller with respect to the total cost and the terms of payment for the motor vehicle, including any promissory notes or any other evidences of indebtedness. § 2981.9.
*Assignee liability provision*: An assignee of the seller is subject to all equities and defenses of the buyer against the seller, notwithstanding an agreement to the contrary, but the assignee's liability may not exceed the amount of the debt owing to the assignee at the time of the assignment. § 2983.5.
*Special provisions for manufactured homes*: None.
*Special provisions for revolving credit*: None.
*Other noteworthy provisions*: None.
*Remedies*: If the seller, except as the result of an accidental or bona fide error in computation, violates certain specified provisions of the Act, the conditional sale contract shall not be enforceable, except by a bona fide purchaser, assignee or pledgee for value or until after the violation is corrected and, if the violation is not corrected, the buyer may recover from the seller the total amount paid, pursuant to the terms of the contract, by the buyer to the seller or his assignee. The amount recoverable for property traded in as all or part of the down payment shall be equal to the greater of the agreed cash value of such property as the value appears on the conditional sale contract or the fair market value of such property as of the time the contract is made. However, a conditional

sale contract executed or entered into on or after January 1, 2012 shall not be made unenforceable solely because of a violation by the seller of certain specified violations. In addition to any other remedies that may be available, the buyer is entitled to any actual damages sustained as a result of a violation of those provisions. § 2983(a). If the seller or holder of a conditional sale contract, except as the result of an accidental or bona fide error of computation, violates any provision of § 2982(l) (the provision regarding the rebate of unearned interest), the buyer may recover three times the amount of any finance charge paid. § 2983.1(a). If a holder acquires a conditional sale contract without actual knowledge of the violation by the seller of certain specified provisions, the contract shall be valid and enforceable by the holder, but the buyer is excused from payment of the unpaid finance charge, unless the violation is corrected according to the method prescribed by the statute. § 2983.1(b). However, if a holder acquires a conditional sale contract with knowledge of a violation of those same specified sections, the conditional sale contract shall not be enforceable except by a bona fide purchaser, assignee, or pledgee for value, or unless the violation is corrected as provided by the method prescribed by the statute, and if the violation is not corrected, the buyer may recover the amounts specified in § 2983 from the person to whom payment was made. § 2983.1(c). When a conditional sale contract is not enforceable under the Act, the buyer may elect to retain the motor vehicle and continue the contract in force, or may, with reasonable diligence, elect to rescind the contract and return the motor vehicle. The value of the motor vehicle returned shall be credited as restitution by the buyer without any decrease that results from the passage of time in the cash price of the motor vehicle as the price appears on the conditional sale contract. § 2983.1(d). Reasonable attorney fees and costs shall be awarded to the prevailing party in any action regardless of whether the action is instituted by the seller, holder or buyer. § 2983.4.

**Colo. Rev. Stat. §§ 5-1-101 to 5-9.5-109 (Colorado Uniform Consumer Credit Code).**

*Scope*: All creditors extending consumer credit except lessors and specified exclusions. § 5-1-107.

*Licensure requirements*: Supervised lenders must be licensed. § 5-2-301.

*Credit terms*: With respect to a consumer loan other than a supervised loan, including a revolving loan, a finance charge may not exceed 12% per year. With respect to a supervised loan or a consumer credit sale, except for a loan or sale pursuant to a revolving account, a finance charge may not exceed the greater of: 36% per year on the amount financed that is $1,000 or less; 21% per year on the amount financed that is more than $1,000 but less than $3,000; 15% per year on the amount financed that is more than $3,000; or 21% per year on the amount financed. § 5-2-201. *OR*: For a consumer loan where the amount financed is not more than $1,000, a supervised lender may charge, in lieu of the loan finance charges permitted by § 5-2-201, the following finance charges: (1) An acquisition charge for making the original loan, not to exceed 10% of the amount financed; (2) An acquisition charge for making any refinanced loan, not to exceed 7.5% of the amount financed; and (3) a monthly installment account handling charge, not to exceed the following per month amounts: $100.00–$300.00, $12.50;$300.01–$500.00, $15.00; $500.01–$750.00, $17.50; $750.01–$1,000.00, $20.00.The minimum term of a loan made pursuant to this section shall be 90 days. The maximum term of a loan made pursuant to this section shall be 12 months. § 5-2-214.

*Restrictions on points or prepaid interest*: The prepaid finance charge shall not exceed that permitted for consumer credit transactions. § 5-2-207(1).

*Restrictions on length of term*: Supervised loans not made pursuant to a revolving credit account and in which the principal is $3,000 or less shall be scheduled to be payable in substantially equal installments at equal periodic intervals except to the extent that the schedule of payments is adjusted to the seasonal or irregular income of the debtor and: over a period of not more than 37 months if the principal is more than $1,000; or over a period of not more than 25 months if the principal is $1,000 or less. § 5-2-308.

*Restrictions on prepayment penalties*: The consumer may prepay in full, or in part if payment is no less than $5, the unpaid balance of a consumer credit transaction at any time without penalty. § 5-2-210.

*Requirement of substantially equal installments or limits on balloon payments*: For closed-end consumer credit transactions if any scheduled payment is more than twice as large as the average scheduled payment, the consumer has the right to refinance that payment at the time it is due at the creditor's prevailing rates. The creditor shall disclose this right in writing to the consumer at the time the transaction is entered into. These provisions do not apply to the extent that the payment schedule is adjusted to the seasonal or irregular income of the consumer. § 5-3-208.

*Formula for rebate of unearned interest*: Calculated based on actuarial method, with minimum charge of up to $25. § 5-2-211.

*Restrictions on deferral charges*: With respect to a precomputed consumer credit transaction, the parties before or after default may agree in writing to a deferral of all or part of one or more unpaid installments, and the creditor may charge a rate not exceeding the one previously disclosed to the consumer. § 5-2-204.

*Limits on document fees*: None.

*Restrictions on types of insurance that can be sold*: A creditor may not contract for or receive a separate charge for insurance against loss of or damage to property unless the insurance covers a substantial risk of loss of or damage to property related to the credit transaction. In addition, the amount, terms and conditions must be reasonable in relation to the character and value of the property insured or to be insured, and the term of the insurance must be reasonable in relation to the terms of credit. The term of the insurance is reasonable if it is customary and does not extend substantially beyond a scheduled maturity. A creditor may not contract for a separate charge for insurance against loss of or damage to property unless the amount financed exclusive of charges for the insurance is $1,000 or more and the value of the property is $1,000 or more. § 5-4-301. A creditor may not contract for or receive a separate charge for insurance against liability unless the insurance covers a substantial risk of liability arising out of the ownership or use of property related to the credit transaction. § 5-4-303.

*Single document rule?*: None.

*Assignee liability provision*: With respect to a consumer credit sale or consumer lease, an assignee of the rights of the seller or lessor is subject to all claims and defenses of the buyer against the seller or lessor arising from the sale or lease. A claim or defense may be asserted against the assignee only to the extent of the amount owing to the assignee with respect to the sale or lease as to which the claim or defense arose at the time the assignee has written notice of the claim or defense. An agreement may not limit or waive the claims or defenses of a consumer. § 5-3-303.

*Special provisions for manufactured homes*: None.

*Special provisions for revolving credit*: None.

*Other noteworthy provisions*: None.

*Remedies*: If a creditor violates the provisions of the Act applying to limitations on the schedule of payments or loan term for supervised loans or the authority to make supervised loans, the consumer is not obligated to pay the finance charge and has a right to recover from the person violating this code or from an assignee of that person's rights a penalty in an amount determined by the court not in excess of three times the amount of the finance charge. A consumer is not obligated to pay a charge in excess of that allowed by the Act, and if a consumer has paid an excess charge he or she has a right to a refund. If the consumer has paid an amount in excess of the lawful obligation, the consumer may recover the excess amount from the person who made the excess charge or from an assignee of that person. If a consumer is entitled to a refund and a person liable to the consumer refuses to make a refund within a reasonable time after demand, the consumer may recover a penalty in an amount determined by a court not exceeding the greater of either the amount of the finance charge or ten times the amount of the excess charge. If the creditor has made an excess charge in deliberate violation of or in reckless disregard for the Act, the penalty may be recovered even though the creditor has refunded the excess charge. § 5-5-201. Violations of disclosure provisions are subject to twice the amount of the finance charge in connection with the transaction, but the liability shall be not less than $100 and nor more than $1,000, plus reasonable attorney fees. § 5-5-202.

**Conn. Gen. Stat. §§ 36a-770 to 36a-788 (Retail Installment Sales Financing).**

*Scope*: Installment sales of consumer goods and motor vehicles (having an aggregate cash price of $50,000 or less) and equipment. § 36a-770.
*Licensure requirements*: None.
*Credit terms*: For sales made on or after October 1, 1987: For new motor vehicles, 15%; For used motor vehicles of a model designated by the manufacturer by a year not more than 2 years prior to the year in which the sale is made, 17%; For used motor vehicles of a model designated by the manufacturer by a year more than 2 years prior to the year in which the sale is made, 19%. § 36a-772(a). The finance charge in a contract for goods other than motor vehicles may not exceed 18%. § 36a-772(b). For sales made before 1987, different rules apply.
*Restrictions on points or prepaid interest*: None.
*Restrictions on length of term*: None.
*Restrictions on prepayment penalties*: None.
*Requirement of substantially equal installments or limits on balloon payments*: None.
*Formula for rebate of unearned interest*: Rebate is calculated by applying Rule of 78s (sum of the balances method) to original finance charge minus $15. No rebate of less than $1 need be made. Calculation rules are different if retail installment contract is for a commercial vehicle. § 36a-783.
*Restrictions on deferral charges*: Whenever any sales finance company or retail seller renews or extends the installments remaining unpaid so that the contract is both extended beyond its original date of final payment and the installments are reduced or increased in amount, the sales finance company or retail seller may collect an additional charge not exceeding 12% per annum on the respective descending balances computed from the date of the oldest unpaid installment existing prior to such renewal or extension. When the renewal or extension does not include both an extension beyond the original date of final payment and a reduction or increase in the amount of the installments, the sales finance company or retail seller may make charge up to 12% per annum on the payment or payments extended for the period or periods of the extension. § 36a-784.
*Limits on document fees*: None.
*Restrictions on types of insurance that can be sold*: None.
*Single document rule?*: None.
*Assignee liability provision*: None.
*Special provisions for manufactured homes*: None.
*Special provisions for revolving credit*: A retail seller under an open-end credit plan in connection with a transaction arising out of the retail sale of consumer goods or services on sales made on or after October 1, 1993 may contract for a finance charge at the rate agreed to by the retail buyer. The maximum finance charge shall not exceed 1.5% per month on the average daily balance of the account or the unpaid balance outstanding as of the end of the current billing cycle. § 42-133c.
*Other noteworthy provisions*: None.
*Remedies*: A willful violation of any provision of the Act other than a disclosure violation shall bar recovery of any finance, delinquency or collection charge by the owner or holder of the contract provided such owner or holder approved of or had knowledge of such violation and, after such approval or knowledge, retained the benefits accruing from the violation or otherwise ratified the violation. § 36a-786.

**Del. Code Ann. tit. 6, §§ 4301 to 4351 (Retail Installment Sales Act).**

*Scope*: Installment sales of goods for personal, family, or household use or furnishing of services (not commercial or business use). Revolving credit. § 4301. Act does not apply to any retail installment sale made for a cash sale price of $75 or less where no title, lien, or other security interest is taken by the seller. § 4302.
*Licensure requirements*: None.
*Credit terms*: Rate established by contract. § 4315.
*Restrictions on points or prepaid interest*: None.
*Restrictions on length of term*: None.
*Restrictions on prepayment penalties*: A holder may not impose any prepayment charge in connection with any prepayment of a debt due under a retail installment contract. § 4322(e).
*Requirement of substantially equal installments or limits on balloon payments*: If a contract provides for the payment of any installment that is more than double the amount of the average of the preceding installments, the buyer, upon default of this installment, shall be given an absolute right to obtain a new payment schedule. Unless agreed to by the buyer, the periodic payments under the new schedule shall not be substantially greater than the average of the preceding installments. § 4326.
*Formula for rebate of unearned interest*: Calculated by actuarial method, but no refund of less than $1 need be made. § 4322(b).
*Restrictions on deferral charges*: In connection with the deferral of installment payments, a holder may collect deferral charges and may also require payment by the buyer of the additional cost to the holder of premiums for continuing in force until the end of such period of deferral, any insurance coverage provided in connection with the contract. § 4324.
*Limits on document fees*: None.
*Restrictions on types of insurance that can be sold*: None.
*Single document rule?*: None.
*Assignee liability provision*: No right of action or defense arising out of a retail installment sale that the buyer has against the seller, which would be cut off by assignment, shall be cut off by assignment of the contract to any third party whether or not the third party acquires the contract in good faith and for value unless the assignee given notice of the assignment to the buyer and, within 15 days of the mailing of such notice, receives no written notice of the facts giving rise to the claim

or defense of the buyer, or unless the assignee acquires the contract or evidence of indebtedness relying in good faith upon a certificate of completion or certificate of satisfaction signed by the buyer. § 4312.
*Special provisions for manufactured homes*: None.
*Special provisions for revolving credit*: Rate established by contract. Del. Code Ann. tit. 5, § 2216.
*Other noteworthy provisions*: None.
*Remedies*: If any person willfully violates any provision of the Act in connection with the imposition, computation or disclosures of or relating to a time price differential or service charge on a consolidated total of two or more contracts under enumerated provisions of the Act, the buyer may recover three times the total of the time price differentials or service charges, plus any delinquency, collection, extension, deferral, or refinance charges on all contracts included in the consolidated total, and the seller shall be barred from the recovery of any such charges. § 4350. Reasonable attorney fees and costs shall be awarded to the prevailing party regardless of whether the action is instituted by the seller, holder or buyer. § 4344.

**Del. Code Ann. tit. 5, §§ 2901 to 2914 (Motor Vehicle Sales Finance Act).**

*Scope*: Installment sales of motor vehicles. § 2901.
*Licensure requirements*: Sales finance companies must be licensed. § 2902.
*Credit terms*: Rate established by contract. § 2908.
*Restrictions on points or prepaid interest*: None.
*Restrictions on length of term*: None.
*Restrictions on prepayment penalties*: The holder may not impose any prepayment charge in connection with the prepayment of a debt under a retail installment contract. § 2909(e).
*Requirement of substantially equal installments or limits on balloon payments*: None.
*Formula for rebate of unearned interest*: Calculated based on actuarial method, but creditor is entitled to retain a finance charge of at least $25, and no refund of less than $1 need be made. § 2909(b).
*Restrictions on deferral charges*: A holder may collect deferral charges and may also require payment by the buyer of the additional cost to the holder of premiums for continuing in force, until the end of such period of deferral, any insurance coverage provided in connection with the contract. § 2910.
*Limits on document fees*: None.
*Restrictions on types of insurance that can be sold*: None.
*Single document rule?*: None.
*Assignee liability provision*: None.
*Special provisions for manufactured homes*: None.
*Special provisions for revolving credit*: Rate established by contract. Del. Code Ann. tit. 5, § 2216.
*Other noteworthy provisions*: None.
*Remedies*: A seller's or holder's willful violation of specified provisions shall bar recovery of any finance charge, delinquency or collection charge on the contract. § 2911(b).

**D.C. Code §§ 50-601 to 50-610 (Installment Sales of Motor Vehicles Act).**

*Scope*: Installment sales of motor vehicles (automobile, mobile home, motorcycle, truck, truck tractor, trailer, semi-trailer or bus). § 50-601.
*Licensure requirements*: According to D.C. Code § 47-2851.03a(j), there is no longer a separate licensure category for motor vehicle dealers. § 50-603 gives the D.C. Council the authority to require licensed dealers and persons licensed to purchase vehicle installment contracts to be bonded.
*Credit terms*: The larger of $25 or an amount determined under the following schedule: for Class 1 vehicles (Any new domestic motor vehicle designated by the manufacturer by a year model not earlier than the year in which the sale is made and any new foreign motor vehicle), 21.5% APR; for Class 2 (any new domestic motor vehicle not in Class 1 and any used domestic motor vehicle designated by the manufacturer by a year model of the same or not more than 2 years prior to the year in which the sale is made and any used foreign motor vehicle not more than 2 years old), 23.5% APR; for Class 3 (any used motor vehicle not in Class 2, and, if a domestic motor vehicle, designated by the manufacturer by a year model not more than 4 years prior to the year in which the sale is made, and, if a foreign motor vehicle, not more than 4 years old), 27% APR; for Class 4 (any used motor vehicle not in Class 2 or 3), 28.33% APR. § 50-602.
*Restrictions on points or prepaid interest*: None.
*Restrictions on length of term*: None.
*Restrictions on prepayment penalties*: None.
*Requirement of substantially equal installments or limits on balloon payments*: None.
*Formula for rebate of unearned interest*: None.
*Restrictions on deferral charges*: None.
*Limits on document fees*: None.
*Restrictions on types of insurance that can be sold*: None.
*Single document rule?*: None.
*Assignee liability provision*: None.
*Special provisions for manufactured homes*: None.
*Revolving credit*: A credit service charge may be made in each billing cycle. For the purpose of computing the outstanding balance subject to the credit service charge (1) the outstanding balance on any day shall consist of an amount which shall not exceed the sum of the total charges to the account less the amounts paid or credited to the account prior to such day, or (2) the outstanding balance may be computed by the average daily balance method. The credit service charge may also be computed for all outstanding balances within a range of not in excess of $10 on the basis of the median amount within such range if as so computed such credit service charge is applied to all outstanding balance within such range. If the billing cycle is monthly, a credit service charge may be imposed in the maximum amount of 2%. If the billing cycle is not monthly, the maximum charge is that percentage that bears the relation to the applicable monthly percentage as the number of days in the billing cycle bears to 30. A variation of not more than 4 days from month to month is "the same day of the billing cycle." D.C. Code Ann. § 28-3702.
*Other noteworthy provisions*: None.
*Remedies*: None.

**Fla. Stat. §§ 520.30 to 520.42 (Retail Installment Sales Act).**

*Scope*: Goods purchased primarily for personal, family, or household use, but not including motor vehicles, and services for personal, family, or household use on goods and real property. Revolving credit. § 520.31.
*Licensure requirements*: Retail sellers must be licensed. § 520.32.
*Credit terms*: The seller may collect a finance charge that may not exceed $12 per $100 per year. A minimum finance charge not in excess of the following amounts may be charged on any retail installment contract: $12 on a contract involving an initial amount financed of $50 or more; $7.50 on a contract involving an initial amount financed of more than $25 and less than $50; and $5 on a contract

involving an initial amount financed of $25 or less. § 520.34(6)(a). The seller under a retail installment contract may collect a $10 processing fee for each contract that is approved and activated. § 520.34(14). The Act also states that a retail installment contract may provide that the rate of finance charge be calculated on a simple interest basis subject to certain specified provisions. § 520.345.

*Restrictions on points or prepaid interest*: None.

*Restrictions on length of term*: None.

*Restrictions on prepayment penalties*: None.

*Requirement of substantially equal installments or limits on balloon payments*: None.

*Formula for rebate of unearned interest*: Rebate is calculated by applying Rule of 78s (sum of the balances method) to original finance charge minus $15, but no rebate of less than $1 need be made. § 520.34(11). Note that these provisions shall not be applicable to a simple interest contract. § 520.345(3).

*Restrictions on deferral charges*: If the unpaid time balance of the contract is extended, the holder may charge for each 30 days' extension an amount not to exceed 1/12 of the maximum allowable rate per annum of the unpaid balance at the time of extension. § 520.34(6)(b). The Act also provides that in the event the unpaid balance of a retail installment contract is extended, deferred, renewed or restated, the holder may compute the refinance charge in accordance with the provisions of § 520.345 (provision on simple interest contracts). § 520.345(4).

*Limits on document fees*: None.

*Restrictions on types of insurance that can be sold*: None.

*Single document rule?*: A retail installment contract need not be contained in a single document. § 520.34(5).

*Assignee liability provision*: None.

*Special provisions for manufactured homes*: None.

*Special provisions for revolving credit*: The seller under a revolving account may charge, receive, and collect a finance charge of $0.15 per $10 per month, computed on all amounts unpaid under the revolving account from month to month or other regular period, and a delinquency charge of $10 for each payment in default for a period of not less than 10 days, if the charge is agreed upon, in writing, between the parties before imposing any charge. If the amount of the finance charge is less than $1 for any such month, a finance charge of $1 for any such month may be charged. If the regular period is other than such monthly period or if the unpaid amount is less than or greater than $5, the permitted finance charge shall be computed proportionately. Such finance charge may be computed for all unpaid balances within a range of not in excess of $10 on the basis of the median amount within such range, if such finance charge is applied to all unpaid balances within such range. § 520.35(3).

*Other noteworthy provisions*: None.

*Remedies*: In the case of a willful violation with respect to any retail installment transaction, the buyer may recover from the person committing such violation, or may set off or counterclaim in any action against the buyer by such person, an amount equal to any finance charge and any delinquency fees, plus attorney fees and costs. § 520.39(2).

**Fla. Stat. §§ 520.01 to 520.14 (Motor Vehicle Retail Sales Finance Act).**

*Scope*: Installment sales of motor vehicles. § 520.02.

*Licensure requirements*: Retail sellers must be licensed. § 520.03.

*Credit terms*: $10 per $100 per year for Class 1 vehicles (any new motor vehicle designated by the manufacturer by a year model not earlier than the year in which the sale is made); $11 per $100 per year for Class 2 (any new motor vehicle not in Class 1 and any used motor vehicle designated by the manufacturer by a year model of the same or not more than 2 years prior to the year in which the sale is made); $15 per $100 per year for Class 3 (any used motor vehicle not in Class 2 and designated by the manufacturer by a year model not more than 4 years prior to the year in which the sale is made); $17 per $100 per year for Class 4 (any used motor vehicle not in Class 2 or 3 and designated by the manufacturer by a year model more than 4 years prior to the year in which the sale is made). § 520.08(1). The Act also states that a retail installment contract may provide that the rate of finance charge be calculated on a simple interest basis subject to certain specified provisions. § 520.085.

*Restrictions on points or prepaid interest*: None.

*Restrictions on length of term*: None.

*Restrictions on prepayment penalties*: None.

*Requirement of substantially equal installments or limits on balloon payments*: None.

*Formula for rebate of unearned interest*: Rebate is calculated by applying Rule of 78s (sum of the balances method) to original finance charge minus $25, but no rebate of less than $1 need be made. § 520.09. Note that the provisions of § 520.09 shall not be applicable to a simple interest contract. However, the lender may impose an acquisition charge, not to exceed $75, for services performed on behalf of the borrower for processing the retail installment contract if the contract is paid in full within 6 months after the contract's effective date. § 520.085(1)(c).

*Restrictions on deferral charges*: In the event the unpaid balance of the contract is extended, deferred, renewed or restated, the holder may compute the refinance charge on such amount by adding to the unpaid balance the cost for insurance and other benefits incidental to the refinancing plus any accrued delinquency and collection charges after deducting any refund that may be due the buyer at the time of the renewal or restatement by prepayment and by reclassifying the motor vehicle by its then year model for the term of the refinancing agreement, but otherwise subject to the provisions of this act governing computation of the original finance charge. The provisions of the Act relating to minimum finance charges and acquisition costs under the refund schedule in § 520.09 (rebate of unearned interest provision) shall not apply in calculating refinance charges on the contract extended, deferred, renewed or restated. If all unpaid installments are deferred, the holder may, at her or his election, charge for such deferment an amount equal to the difference between the refund required for prepayment in full under § 520.09 as of the scheduled due date of the first deferred installment and the refund required for prepayment in full as of one month prior to said date times the number of months in which no scheduled payment is made. § 520.10. The Act also provides that if the unpaid balance of a contract is extended, deferred, renewed or restated, the holder may compute the refinance charge in accordance with the provisions of § 520.085 (provision on simple interest contracts). § 520.085(1)(d).

*Limits on document fees*: None.

*Restrictions on types of insurance that can be sold*: None.

*Single document rule?*: None.

*Assignee liability provision*: None.

*Special provisions for manufactured homes*: A retail installment contract for the purchase of a mobile home may provide that the finance charge may be adjusted at stated regular intervals, in which case the contract shall be subject to the following provisions: The seller may compute the finance charge on the unpaid balance as it changes from time to time or by any other method. Adjustments to the finance charge shall be based on changes in the monthly average yield on U.S. Treasury securities adjusted to a constant maturity of 5 years as published in the Federal Reserve Bulletin, multiplied by 2.0, or "index value." Adjustments to the finance charge may not exceed 0.5% a year for any 6-month period. The maximum net adjustment over the term of the contract shall not exceed 5 percentage points. The finance charge shall not increase or decrease during the 6-month period beginning with the date of execution of the contract, and at least 6 months shall elapse between changes. Subject to the limitations prescribed, the adjustments, either up or down, to the rate of finance charge on each rate adjustment date shall be equal: (a) for an initial adjustment, to the difference between the index value for the third calendar month preceding the month in which the rate adjustment date falls and the index value for the month of execution of the retail installment contract; (b) for an adjustment after the initial adjustment, to the difference between the index value for the third calendar month preceding the month in which the rate adjustment date falls and the index value for the third calendar month preceding the month in which the immediately preceding rate adjustment date fell. Any increase in the finance charge may be waived at the option of the seller. Subject to the limitations described, decreases in the finance charge are mandatory in the event of any decrease in the index value exceeding one-tenth of 1 percentage point in any 6-month period. If the parties agree in writing to impose limitations on the frequency or amount of increases in the finance charge that are less than the limitations permitted, those limitations shall also apply to decreases in the finance charge. Changes in the index value that are not taken may be accumulated by the seller in the case of an increase, and shall be accumulated in the case of a decrease, and taken at a later time or used to offset other changes. Such changes shall not exceed the maximum provided in the statute. By written agreement of the parties, adjustments to the finance charge may result in changes in the amount of any installment payment due, changes in the term of the contract, or a combination of such changes. The parties may agree in writing that any change in the amount of any installment payment that results from an adjustment to the finance charge may be applied to any subsequent installment payments. Adjustments to the amount of the installment payments may be made less frequently than adjustments to the finance charge. § 520.125.

*Special provisions for revolving credit*: None.

*Other noteworthy provisions*: None.

*Remedies*: For willful violations, the buyer may recover, or may set off or counterclaim in any action against the buyer, an amount equal to any finance charge and any delinquency fees, plus attorney fees and costs. § 520.12(2).

**Ga. Code Ann. §§ 10-1-1 to 10-1-16 (Retail Installment and Home Solicitation Sales Act).**

*Scope*: Installment sales of goods (other than motor vehicles) and services for personal, family, or household use on goods, including delivery, installation, and repair. Revolving credit. § 10-1-2.

*Licensure requirements*: None.

*Credit terms*: The seller under a retail installment contract may charge a time price differential not exceeding $0.13 per $1 per year. § 10-1-3(d)(1). A minimum time price differential not in excess of the following amounts may be charged on any retail installment contract: $12 on any contract with an initial unpaid balance of $50 or more, $7.50 on a contract with an initial unpaid balance of more than $25 and less than $50, and $5 on a contract with an initial unpaid balance of $25 or less. § 10-1-3(d)(2).

*Restrictions on points or prepaid interest*: None.

*Restrictions on length of term*: None.

*Restrictions on prepayment penalties*: None.

*Requirement of substantially equal installments or limits on balloon payments*: None.

*Formula for rebate of unearned interest*: Rebate is calculated by applying Rule of 78s (sum of the balances method) to original finance charge minus $20, but no rebate of less than $1 need be made. § 10-1-3(i).

*Restrictions on deferral charges*: None.

*Limits on document fees*: None.

*Restrictions on types of insurance that can be sold*: None.

*Single document rule?*: A retail installment contract need not be contained in a single document. § 10-1-3(c).

*Assignee liability provision:* An assignment may not bar any right of action against the seller nor bar any defense against the sales finance company or other assignee. § 10-1-9.

*Special provisions for manufactured homes*: None.

*Special provisions for revolving credit*: The seller under a revolving account may charge a time price differential not exceeding 17.5¢ per $10 per month computed on all amounts unpaid from month to month or other regular period. If the amount of time price differential is less than $1 for any month, a time price differential of $1 may be charged. If the regular period is other than a monthly period or if the unpaid amount is less than or greater than $1, the permitted time price differential shall be computed proportionately. Such time price differential may be computed for all unpaid balances within a range of not in excess of $10 on the basis of the median amount within such range if the time price differential is applied to all unpaid balances within such range. § 10-1-4(b).

*Other noteworthy provisions*: None.

*Remedies*: A violation with respect to the finance charge on a retail installment contract shall bar recovery of any finance charge, delinquency or collection charge on the contract. A violation with respect to the finance charge on a revolving account shall bar recovery of any finance charge, delinquency or collection charge stated on or collected in connection with the affected statement. § 10-1-15(b). For willful violations of any provision, with respect to any transaction, the buyer may recover (or set off or counterclaim in any action) a minimum of $100 or double the time price differential and any delinquency charge and any attorney fees and court costs. However, the seller may recover from the buyer the cash price of the goods or services and the cost of any insurance purchased by the seller for the buyer in connection with the transaction. § 10-1-15(c). The penalties under the statute shall be the sole remedy for violations and a claim may be asserted in an individual action only. § 10-1-15(f).

**Ga. Code Ann. §§ 10-1-30 to 10-1-42 (Motor Vehicle Sales Finance Act).**

*Scope*: Installment sales of motor vehicles not principally for the purpose of resale. § 10-1-31.

*Licensure requirements*: None.

*Credit terms*: The finance charge shall not exceed the following rates: $10 per $100 per year on Class 1 vehicles (any new motor vehicle designated by the manufacturer by a year model not earlier than the year in which the sale is made and all vehicles not previously titled); $13 per $100 per year for Class 2 (any new motor vehicle not in Class 1 and any used motor vehicle designated by the manufacturer by a year model of the same or not more than 2 years prior to the year in which the sale is made); $15 per $100 per year for Class 3 (any used motor vehicle not in Class 2 and designated by the manufacturer by a year model not more than 4 years prior to the year in which the sale is made); $17 per $100 per year for Class 4 (any used motor vehicle not in Class 2 or 3 and designated by the manufacturer by a year model more than 4 years prior to the year in which the sale is made). A seller who computes a finance charge on an actuarial basis may charge a finance charge, which, when calculated according to the actuarial method, does not exceed the yield that would have been otherwise permitted on monthly contracts, having due regard for the schedule of payments. However, when a seller computes the finance charge according to the actuarial method, then the entire term of the contract shall be considered to be the number of whole months within the scheduled payment period, disregarding any odd days. § 10-1-33(c). A minimum finance charge of $25 may be charged on any retail installment transaction. § 10-1-33(b). The Act also provides that a buyer and seller may establish any finance charge agreed upon in writing in a retail installment contract for a motor vehicle where the amount financed is more than $5,000 (§ 7-4-3(a)(2); § 10-1-33(d)) and for any manufactured home with a cash sale price of more than $3,000 (§ 7-4-3(a)(2)).

*Restrictions on points or prepaid interest*: None.

*Restrictions on length of term*: None.

*Restrictions on prepayment penalties*: None.

*Requirement of substantially equal installments or limits on balloon payments*: None.

*Formula for rebate of unearned interest*: Calculated by Rule of 78s (sum of the balances method), but refund of less than $1 need not be made. § 10-1-34.

*Restrictions on deferral charges*: In the event the unpaid time balance of the contract is extended, deferred, renewed or restated, the holder may compute a refinance charge on such amount by adding to the unpaid time balance the cost for insurance and other benefits incidental to the refinancing, plus any accrued delinquency and collection charges after deducting any refund credit for prepayment at the rate of the finance charge specified in the statute, and by reclassifying the motor vehicle by its then year model for the term of the refinancing agreement, but otherwise subject to the provisions of this article governing computation of the original finance charge. If all unpaid installments are deferred for not more than 2 months, the holder may charge for such deferment an amount equal to the difference between the refund required for prepayment in full as of the scheduled due date of the first deferred installment and the refund required for prepayment in full as of 1 month prior to said date times the number of months in which no scheduled payment is made. § 10-1-35.

*Limits on document fees*: None.

*Restrictions on types of insurance that can be sold*: None.

*Single document rule?*: None.

*Assignee liability provision*: An assignment may not bar any right of action against the seller nor bar any defense against the sales finance company or other assignee. § 10-1-33(f).

*Special provisions for manufactured homes*: A buyer and seller may establish any finance charge agreed upon in writing in a retail installment contract for a manufactured home with a cash sale price of more than $3,000. "Manufactured home" means a structure, transportable in one or more sections, which, in the traveling mode, is eight body feet or more in width, or 40 body feet or more in length, or, when erected on site, is 320 or more square feet and which is built on a permanent chassis and designed to be used as a dwelling with or without a permanent foundation when connected to the required utilities and includes the plumbing, heating, air-conditioning, and electrical systems contained therein; except that such term shall include any structure which meets all the requirements of this paragraph except the size requirements and with respect to which the manufacturer voluntarily files a certification required by the secretary of Housing and Urban Development and complies with the standards established under The National Mobile Home Construction and Safety Standards Act of 1974, 42 U.S.C. §§ 5401 to 5426. § 7-4-3.

*Special provisions for revolving credit*: None.

*Other noteworthy provisions*: None.

*Remedies*: A violation with respect to a finance charge shall bar recovery of any finance charge, delinquency or collection charge on the contract. § 10-1-38(b). For willful violations, with respect to any transaction, the buyer may recover (or may set off or counterclaim in any action) a minimum of $100 or double the time price differential and any delinquency charge and attorney fees and court costs. However, the seller may recover from the buyer the cash price of the goods or services and the cost of any insurance purchased by the seller for the buyer in connection with the transaction. § 10-1-38(c). A claim may be asserted in an individual action only and may not be the subject of a class action. § 10-1-36.1.

**Haw. Rev. Stat. §§ 476-1 to 476-32 (Credit Sales Act).**

*Scope*: Any agreement, including a conditional sale contract, a retail installment contract, or any other form of instrument evidencing an obligation to pay the price of goods (personal and not for resale), services (personal), or both, purchased in a credit sale. Act does not apply to any sale to other than a natural person, including a sale to government entity, or any sale not secured by real property or by personal property used or expected to be used as the principal dwelling of the consumer, in which the principal balance, less any prepaid finance charge, exceeds $25,000 or in which there is an express written commitment to extend credit in excess of $25,000. § 476-1.

*Licensure requirements*: None.

*Credit terms*: If the finance charge is stated as a dollar amount and is added on or deducted in advance, and the buyer promises to pay a fixed total of payments, the finance charge shall not exceed the amount of interest or discount which could lawfully be added on or deducted in advance by a financial services loan company under § 412:9-302 (provision on interest rates charged by financial services loan companies): 14% a year for the first 18 months or portion thereof, plus 10.5% a year for the next 12 months or portion thereof, plus 7% a year for the next 12 months or portion thereof, plus 4% a year for the last 6 months or portion thereof. The maximum term of a precomputed loan where the preceding rates are charged will be 48 months. If the term of a precomputed loan exceeds 48 months, the financial services loan company may charge a finance charge in any form or forms at an annual percentage rate not to exceed 24% a year, together with any other charges that are excluded or excludable from the determination of finance charge under the Truth in Lending Act. As an alternative to this finance charge, a seller may receive a finance charge of 24% a year on the principal balance remaining unpaid from time to time under the contract, whether or not the rate of the finance charge under the contract is fixed or variable. Upon maturity of a contract, the rate of finance charge on the unpaid principal balance of the contract may be 12% a year, the original contract rate of finance charge or, in the case of any extension or deferral, the rate of finance charge permitted by this chapter on the amount extended or deferred, whichever is greatest. § 476-28.

*Restrictions on points or prepaid interest*: None.

*Restrictions on length of term*: The maximum term of a precomputed loan where the rates described in § 412:9-302 (and described above, in *Credit Terms*) are charged will be 48 months. § 412:9-302.

*Restrictions on prepayment penalties*: None.

*Requirement of substantially equal installments or limits on balloon payments*: If any scheduled payment is more than twice as large as the average of earlier scheduled payments, the buyer has the right to refinance that payment at the time it is due without penalty. If the principal balance of the original contract is less than $10,000, and the finance charge either is stated as a dollar amount and added on or deducted in advance or is computed at a fixed rate, all the terms of the refinancing shall be no less favorable to the buyer than the terms of the original sale, except that the payment schedule may be modified so as to effect the amortization of the total amount refinanced over the period for which it is refinanced, which shall not be less than the term of the original contract, or that no scheduled payment required upon refinancing shall be greater than the amount of the average scheduled payment required by the original contract. These provisions do not apply to the extent that the payment schedule is adjusted to the seasonal or irregular income of the buyer. § 476-5.

*Formula for rebate of unearned interest*: Rebate is calculated by applying Rule of 78s (sum of the balances method) to original finance charge minus $10, but no rebate of less than $1 need be made. § 476-23.

*Restrictions on deferral charges*: A finance charge not exceeding that permitted by the Act (§ 476-28) upon an original contract in the amount of the principal balance payment, for the actual period of the extension or deferment, may be charged in advance at the commencement of the period of extension or deferment or thereafter; provided that the term and conditions of the extension or deferment, including the amount of the principal balance extended or deferred, and the period of and charge for the extension or deferment, shall be in writing and signed in duplicate by the parties. § 476-6.

*Limits on document fees*: None.

*Restrictions on types of insurance that can be sold*: None.

*Single document rule?*: None.

*Assignee liability provision*: A contract may not contain any provision by which a buyer agrees not to assert against an assignee a claim or defense arising out of the sale An assignment shall not cut off any rights of action or defense arising out of a credit sale that the buyer has against the seller; however, any recovery by the buyer shall not exceed amounts paid and to be paid by the buyer on the contract and may be set off against any amount to be paid. When an assignee asserts its rights against a buyer, the buyer may assert any available defense against the assignee as if the assignee were the seller. § 476-19.

*Special provisions for manufactured homes*: None.

*Special provisions for revolving credit*: None.

*Other noteworthy provisions*: None.

*Remedies*: If a seller or holder violates certain specified provisions, the buyer may recover from the seller or holder the finance charge or 10% of the cash price if no finance charge is specified in the contract, and the seller is barred from recovery of any finance charge, late fee, collection charge or refinancing charge on the contract. In any successful action, the buyer shall be entitled to the reasonable attorney fees and costs. § 476-21.

**Idaho Code Ann. §§ 28-41-101 to 28-49-107 (Credit Code).**

*Scope*: Sellers of goods or services, small loan companies, licensed lenders, finance companies, sales finance companies, industrial banks and loan companies, and commercial banks. § 28-41-107.

*Licensure requirements*: A license is required to make regulated consumer loans under the Act. § 28-46-301.

*Credit terms*: Rate established by agreement of the parties. § 28-42-201.

*Restrictions on points or prepaid interest*: None.

*Restrictions on length of term*: Regulated consumer loans that are not made pursuant to open-end credit and in which the principal is $1,000 or less shall be scheduled to be payable in substantially equal installments at equal periodic intervals except to the extent that the schedule of payments is adjusted to the seasonal or irregular income of the debtor, and: (1) over a period of not more than 37 months if the principal is more than $300, or (2) over a period of not more than 25 months if the principal is $300 or less. § 28-43-310.

*Restrictions on prepayment penalties*: The debtor may prepay in full the unpaid balance of a regulated consumer credit transaction at any time without penalty. § 28-42-306(1).

*Requirement of substantially equal installments or limits on balloon payments*: Regulated consumer loans not made pursuant to open-end credit and in which the principal is $1,000 or less shall be scheduled to be payable in substantially equal installments at equal periodic intervals except to the extent that the schedule of payments is adjusted to the seasonal or irregular income of the debtor. § 28-43-310. If any scheduled payment of a regulated consumer credit transaction is more than twice as large as the average scheduled payment, the debtor has the right to refinance, without penalty, that payment at the time it is due. The terms of the refinancing shall be no less favorable to the debtor than the terms of the original transaction. However, this provision does not apply to a transaction pursuant to open-end credit, a transaction in which the payment schedule is adjusted to the seasonal or irregular income or scheduled payments or obligations of the debtor, a transaction of a class defined by rule of the administrator as not requiring for the protection of the debtor the right to refinance, or a transaction secured by a second deed of trust or mortgage on a one to four family dwelling occupied by the debtor. § 28-43-307.

*Formula for rebate of unearned interest*: Calculated by Rule of 78s (sum of the balances method), but actuarial method must be used for transactions of more than 61 installments entered into on or after July 1, 1978. § 28-42-307.

*Restrictions on deferral charges*: The creditor may collect a charge not exceeding the rate previously stated to the debtor and apply it to the amount deferred. This charge may be collected at the time it is assessed or at any time after that. The parties may agree in writing at the time of a precomputed regulated consumer credit transaction, refinancing, or consolidation that if an installment is not paid within 10 days after its due date, the creditor may unilaterally grant a deferral and make charges accordingly. No deferral charge may be made for a period after the date that the creditor elects to accelerate the maturity of the agreement. A delinquency charge made by the creditor on an installment may not be retained if a deferral charge is made with respect to the period of delinquency. § 28-42-302.

*Limits on document fees*: None.

*Restrictions on types of insurance that can be sold*: A creditor may not contract for or receive a separate charge for insurance against loss of or damage to property unless the creditor qualifies under chapter 9 (insurance administrators), title 41 (insurance) or rule or regulation prescribed by the director of the department of insurance, and the insurance covers a substantial risk of loss of or damage to property related to the credit transaction, the amount, terms, and conditions of the insurance are reasonable in relation to the character and value of the property insured or to be insured, and the term of the insurance is reasonable in relation to the terms of credit. The term of the insurance is reasonable if it is customary and does not extend substantially beyond a scheduled maturity. A creditor may not contract for or receive a separate charge for insurance against loss of or damage to property unless the amount financed or principal exclusive of charges for the insurance is $500 or more and the value of the property is $500 or more. § 28-44-301. A creditor may not contract for or receive a separate charge for insurance against liability unless the insurance covers a substantial risk of liability arising out of the ownership or use of property related to the credit transaction. § 28-44-303.

*Single document rule?*: None.

*Assignee liability provision*: A seller's assignee is subject to all claims and defenses of the debtor against the seller. § 28-45-302(1). The assignee's liability may not exceed the amount owing to the assignee with respect to the sale at the time the assignee has notice of a claim or defense of the buyer. § 28-45-302(2).

*Special provisions for manufactured homes*: None.

*Special provisions for revolving credit*: None.

*Other noteworthy provisions*: None.

*Remedies*: If a creditor violates certain specified provisions of the Act, the debtor has a cause of action to recover actual damages and also a right in an action (other than a class action) to recover a penalty in an amount determined by the court not less than $100 and not more than $1,000. § 28-45-201(1). A debtor is not obligated to pay a charge in excess of that allowed by the Act and has a right of refund of any excess charge paid. If the debtor has paid an amount in excess of the lawful obligation, the debtor may recover the excess amount from the person who made the excess charge or from an assignee of that person's rights. § 28-45-201(2). If a creditor has contracted for or received a charge in excess of that allowed, or if a debtor is entitled to a refund and a person liable to the debtor refuses to make a refund within a reasonable time after demand, the debtor may recover from the creditor or the person liable in an action (other than a class action) a penalty in an amount determined by the court not less than $100 and not more than $1,000. § 28-45-201(3). In a successful action, the debtor is entitled to attorney fees and costs. In determining the attorney fees, the amount of the debtor's recovery is not controlling. § 28-45-201(8).

**815 Ill. Comp. Stat. 405/1 to 405/33 (Retail Installment Sales Act).**

*Scope*: Installment sales of goods (other than motor vehicles) used or purchased primarily for personal purposes and services of any kind rendered or furnished by a retail seller for a use other than in business (including farming or a profession) under an installment sales contract or charge agreement. 405/2.1 and 405/2.2.

*Licensure requirements*: None.

*Credit terms*: No limit on the finance charges that may be charged, collected, and received. 405/27 and 405/28.

*Restrictions on points or prepaid interest*: None.

*Restrictions on length of term*: None.

*Restrictions on prepayment penalties*: None.

*Requirement of substantially equal installments or limits on balloon payments*: Retail installment contracts may provide for balloon note financing. 405/6(b).

*Formula for rebate of unearned interest*: Rebate is calculated by applying Rule of 78s (sum of the balances method) to original finance charge minus $25, but no rebate of less than $1 (or $5 if creditor issues a negotiable instrument to make the rebate) need be made. 405/7.

*Restrictions on deferral charges*: Fifteen days after the final installment is due as originally scheduled or deferred, the holder may charge interest on any unpaid, including unpaid default or deferment charges, at the annual percentage rate stated in the contract until fully paid or reduced to judgment. 405/12.1. If the unpaid time balance of a contract is extended, renewed or restated, the holder may compute the refinance charge on an amount determined by adding to the unpaid balance the cost to the holder for insurance and official fees incidental to the refinancing and accrued delinquency and collection charges and deducting any refund credit which may be due the buyer for prepayment under the Act. 405/20.

*Limits on document fees*: None.

*Restrictions on types of insurance that can be sold*: No charge may be made to a buyer under an installment contract or charge agreement for insurance against loss or damage to the goods, for insurance against liability for personal injury or property damage caused to others by reason of ownership or operation of the goods, for credit life insurance, for credit health and accident insurance or for any other kind of insurance, unless the installment contract or charge agreement separately specifies for each kind of insurance the type of coverage, the term of coverage and the separate, identified charge made therefor. However, a single charge may be made for credit life, credit health and accident insurance whose issuance in a single form or package has been authorized by the Director of Insurance and whose charges for its various parts cannot be separately stated, and, in the case of contracts or charge agreements negotiated and entered into by mail or telephone, in which the kind of insurance, type of coverage, the term of coverage and the charge to be made therefor is clearly set forth in a catalog or other printed solicitation of the seller, disclosure shall be made in the manner required by law. 405/4. A seller under a retail installment contract or retail charge agreement may require insurance against substantial risk of loss of or damage to the goods protecting the seller or holder, as well as the buyer, and may, if the buyer elects, include in the contract an amount not exceeding the premiums chargeable for similar insurance in accordance with rate filings made with the Director of Insurance. No seller or holder may require, as a condition precedent to or as a part of a retail installment transaction, that such insurance be purchased from or through the seller or holder, or any employee, affiliate, or associate of seller or holder. A seller under a retail installment contract may not require other insurance, but if the buyer voluntarily contracts for other insurance, the seller may then include in the contract an amount for that insurance not exceeding the premiums paid or payable by the seller or holder. 405/8.

*Single document rule?*: None.

*Assignee liability provision*: An agreement by a buyer that he will not assert against the assignee or the holder of a retail installment contract executed by the buyer any claim or defense which he may have against the seller and the rights of a holder in due course of any negotiable note executed in connection with a retail installment contract are enforceable by an assignee or holder who takes his assignment for value in good faith and without notice of a claim or defense unless: (a) the assignee or holder is an affiliate of the seller; (b) the assignee or the holder has actual knowledge or has received notice before the contract or note is acquired of repetitive complaints of a substantial nature by other buyers to any governmental agency that the seller has failed or refused to perform his agreements with such buyer and of the failure of the seller to perform his agreements with such buyers within a reasonable time after the governmental agency has determined that the complaints are well-founded and has notified seller thereof, and the assignee, if known; or (c) the assignee or the holder has actual knowledge or has received notice from its course of dealing with the seller or from its own records of substantial complaints by other buyers

that seller has failed or refused to perform his agreements with such buyers within a reasonable time after such complaints are made. 405/17.
*Special provisions for manufactured homes*: None.
*Special provisions for revolving credit*: None.
*Other noteworthy provisions*: None.
*Remedies*: No person who violates the Act, except as a result of an accident or bona fide error of computation, may recover any finance charge, delinquency or collection charge, or any refinance charge in connection with the related retail installment contract or retail charge agreement. 405/31(b).

**815 Ill. Comp. Stat. 375/1 to 375/26 (Motor Vehicle Retail Installment Sales Act).**

*Scope*: Installment sales of motor vehicles by retail sellers to retail buyers primarily for personal, family, household or agricultural purposes, but not for use in business (not including farming or a profession). 375/2.1 and 375/2.2.
*Licensure requirements*: None.
*Credit terms*: No limit on the finance charges that may be charged, collected, and received. 375/21.

*Restrictions on points or prepaid interest*: None.
*Restrictions on length of term*: None.
*Restrictions on prepayment penalties*: None.
*Requirement of substantially equal installments or limits on balloon payments*: Retail installment contracts may provide for balloon note financing. 375/6.
*Formula for rebate of unearned interest*: Rebate is calculated by applying Rule of 78s (sum of the balances method) to original finance charge minus $15, but no rebate of less than $1 need be made. 375/7.
*Restrictions on deferral charges*: Fifteen days after the final installment is due as originally scheduled or deferred, the holder may charge interest on any unpaid balance, including unpaid default or deferment charges, at the annual percentage rate stated in the contract until fully paid or reduced to judgment. 375/11.2. If the unpaid time balance of the contract is extended, renewed or restated, the holder may compute the refinance charge on an amount determined by adding to the unpaid balance the cost to the holder for insurance and official fees incidental to the refinancing, and accrued delinquency and collection charges and deducting any refund credit which may be due the buyer for prepayment. 375/19

*Limits on document fees*: A seller may add a "documentary fee" for processing documents and performing services related to closing of a sale. The maximum amount that may be charged is the base documentary fee of $150, which shall be subject to an annual rate adjustment equal to the percentage of change in the Bureau of Labor Statistics Consumer Price Index. 375/11.1.
*Restrictions on types of insurance that can be sold*: A seller under a retail installment contract may require insurance against substantial risk of loss of or damage to the motor vehicle, protecting the seller or holder as well as the buyer, and may, if the buyer elects, include in the contract an amount not exceeding the premiums chargeable for such insurance in accordance with rate filings made with the Director of Insurance. No seller or holder may require as a condition precedent to, or as a part of, a retail installment transaction that such insurance be purchased from or through the seller or holder, or any employee, affiliate, or associate of seller or holder. A seller under a retail installment contract may not require other insurance, but if the buyer voluntarily contracts for other insurance, the seller may then include in the contract an amount for that insurance not exceeding the premiums paid or payable by the seller or holder. In those transactions where the buyer elects to select the insurance company, broker or agent for the purpose of obtaining insurance required by the holder under the Act, the buyer must, on or before the date when buyer takes possession of the motor vehicle, furnish the holder with satisfactory evidence of insurance in a company acceptable to the seller or holder. 375/8.
*Single document rule?*: None.
*Assignee liability provision*: An agreement by a buyer that he will not assert against the assignee or the holder of a retail installment contract executed by the buyer any claim or defense that he may have against the seller and the rights of a holder in due course of any negotiable note executed in connection with a retail installment contract are enforceable by an assignee or holder who takes his assignment for value in good faith and without notice of a claim or defense unless: (a) the assignee or holder is an affiliate of the seller; (b) the assignee or holder has actual knowledge or has received notice before the contract or note is acquired (1) of repetitive complaints of a substantial nature by other buyers to any governmental agency that the seller has failed or refused to perform his agreements with such buyers and (2) of the failure of the seller to perform his agreements with such buyers within a reasonable time after the governmental agency has determined that the complaints are well-founded and has notified seller thereof, and the assignee, if known; or (c) the assignee or holder has actual knowledge or has received notice from its course of dealing with the seller or from its own records of substantial complaints by other buyers that the seller has failed or refused to perform his agreements with such buyers within a reasonable time after such complaints are made. 375/16.
*Special provisions for manufactured homes*: None.
*Special provisions for revolving* credit: None.
*Other noteworthy provisions*: None.
*Remedies*: No person who violates the Act, except as a result of an accident or bona fide error of computation, may recover any unpaid finance charge, delinquency or collection charge, or refinance charge in connection with the related retail installment contract. 375/24(b).

**Ind. Code §§ 24-4.5-1-101 to 24-4.5-7-414 (Indiana Uniform Consumer Credit Code).**

*Scope*: Retail installment sales (other than sales of goods, services or an interest in land in which they are purchased primarily for a purpose other than a personal, family, or household purpose), consumer credit, small loans. §§ 24-4.5-1-202.
*Licensure requirements*: Licenses to make consumer loans are required. § 24-4.5-3-503.
*Credit terms*: In a consumer credit sale, other than a sale pursuant to a revolving charge account, a seller may charge: 36% per year on that part of the unpaid balance that is $300 or less; 21% per year on that part of the unpaid balance that is more than $300 but not over $1,000; 15% per year on that part of the unpaid balance that is more than $1,000; or 21% per year on the unpaid balance of the amount financed. § 24-4.5-2-201.

*Restrictions on points or prepaid interest*: None.
*Restrictions on length of term*: Supervised loans not made pursuant to a revolving loan account and in which the principal is $1,000 or less shall be payable in a single installment or shall be scheduled to be payable in substantially equal installments that shall be payable at equal periodic intervals except to the extent that the schedule of payments is adjusted to the seasonal or irregular income of the debtor and (a) over a period of not more than 37 months if the

principal is more than $300, or (b) over a period of not more than 25 months if the principal is $300 or less. § 24-4.5-3-511.

*Restrictions on prepayment penalties*: The buyer may prepay in full the unpaid balance of a consumer credit sale, refinancing or consolidation at any time without penalty. § 24-4.5-2-209(1).

*Requirement of substantially equal installments or limits on balloon payments*: With respect to a consumer credit sale, other than one pursuant to a revolving charge account or one on which only credit service charges are payable before the time the final payment is due, if any scheduled payment is more than twice as large as the average scheduled payment, the buyer has the right to refinance that payment at the time it is due without penalty. The terms of the refinancing shall be no less favorable to the buyer than the terms of the original sale. This provision does not apply where the payment schedule is adjusted to the seasonal or irregular income of the buyer. § 24-4.5-2-405.

*Formula for rebate of unearned interest*: Calculated by Rule of 78s (sum of the balances method), but creditor may retain any permitted minimum finance charge and need not make refund of less than $1. § 24-4.5-2-210.

*Restrictions on deferral charges*: With respect to a precomputed consumer credit sale, refinancing or consolidation, the parties before or after default may agree in writing to a deferral of all or part of one or more unpaid installments, and the seller may make and collect a charge not exceeding the rate previously stated to the buyer pursuant to the statutory provisions on disclosure applied to the amount or amounts deferred for the period of deferral calculated without regard to differences in lengths of months, but proportionately for a part of a month. § 24-4.5-2.204.

*Limits on document fees*: None.

*Restrictions on types of insurance that can be sold*: A creditor may not contract for or receive a separate charge for insurance against loss of or damage to property unless the insurance covers a substantial risk of loss of or damage to property related to the credit transaction, the amount, terms, and conditions of the insurance are reasonable in relation to the character and value of the property insured or to be insured, and the term of the insurance is reasonable in relation to the terms of credit. The term of the insurance is reasonable if it is customary and does not extend substantially beyond a scheduled maturity. A creditor may not contract for or receive a separate charge for insurance against loss of or damage to property unless the amount financed or principal exclusive of charges for the insurance is $300 or more and the value of the property is $300 or more. § 24-4.5-4-301. A creditor may not contract for or receive a separate charge for insurance against liability unless the insurance covers a substantial risk of liability arising out of the ownership or use of property related to the credit transaction. 24-4.5-4-303.

*Single document rule?*: None.

*Assignee liability provision*: None.

*Special provisions for manufactured homes*: None.

*Special provisions for revolving credit*: With respect to a consumer credit sale made pursuant to a revolving charge account, the parties may contract for the payment of a service charge that is no greater than: (a) the average daily balance of the account; (b) the unpaid balance of the account on the same day of the billing cycle; or (c) the median amount within a specified range within which the average daily balance of the account or the unpaid balance of the account on the same day of the billing cycle is included. A charge may be made pursuant to this paragraph only if the seller, subject to classification and differentiations he may reasonably establish, makes the same charge on all balances within the specified range and if the percentage when applied to the median amount within the range does not produce a charge exceeding the charge resulting from applying that percentage to the lowest amount within the range by more than 8% of the charge on the median amount. If the billing cycle is monthly, the charge may not exceed 1.75% of the amount. If the billing cycle is not monthly, the maximum charge is that percentage which bears the same relation to the applicable monthly percentage as the number of days in the billing cycle bears to thirty. If there is an unpaid balance on the date as of which the credit service charge is applied, the seller may receive a charge not exceeding $0.50, if the billing cycle is monthly or longer, or the pro rata part of $0.50 that bears the same relation to $0.50 as the number of days in the billing cycle bears to thirty if the billing cycle is shorter than monthly. § 24-4.5-2-5-207.

*Other noteworthy provisions*: None.

*Remedies*: If a creditor violates the provision of the Act applying to limitations on the schedule of payments or loan term for supervised loans (§ 24-4.5-3-511), the debtor is not obligated to pay the loan finance charge and has a right to recover from the person or from an assignee of that person's rights who undertakes direct collection of payments or enforcement of rights arising from the debt a penalty in an amount determined by the court not in excess of three times the amount of the loan finance charge. § 24-4.5-5-202(1). If a creditor violates the provisions of the Act applying to authority to make consumer loans (§ 24-4.5-3-502), the loan is void and the debtor is not obligated to pay either the principal or loan finance charge. If the debtor has paid any part of the principal or of the loan finance charge, the debtor has a right to recover the payment from the person or from an assignee of that person's rights who undertakes direct collection of payments or enforcement of rights arising from the debt. § 24-4.5-5-202(2). A debtor is not obligated to pay a charge in excess of that allowed by the Act, and a debtor who has paid an excess charge has a right to a refund. If the debtor has paid an amount in excess of the lawful obligation, the debtor may recover the excess amount from the person who made the excess charge or from an assignee of that person's rights. If a debtor is entitled to a refund and a person liable to the debtor refuses to make a refund within a reasonable time after demand, the debtor may recover a penalty in an amount determined by a court not exceeding the greater of either the amount of the credit service or loan finance charge or 10 times the amount of the excess charge. If the creditor has made an excess charge in deliberate violation of or in reckless disregard for the Act, the penalty may be recovered even though the creditor has refunded the excess charge. § 24-4.5-5-202(3). If it is found that a creditor has violated the Act, the court may award reasonable attorney fees incurred by the debtor. § 24-4.5-5-202(8). A creditor who, in violation of the provisions on disclosure of the Chapter on Credit Sales and the Chapter on Loans, fails to disclose information to a person entitled to the information is liable to that person in an amount equal to the sum of the following: (1) in the case of an individual action, twice the amount of the credit service or loan finance charge in connection with the transaction, but the liability shall be not less than $100 nor more than $1,000; or (2) in the case of a class action, an amount the court allows, except that as to each member of the class no minimum recovery is applicable, and the total recovery in any class action or series of class actions arising out of the same failure to comply by the same creditor may not be more than the lesser of: (i) $500,000; or (ii) 1% of the net worth of the creditor. In the case of a successful action to enforce liability, attorney fees and costs may be recovered. § 24-4.5-5-203.

**Iowa Code §§ 537.2101 to 537.8101 (Iowa Consumer Credit Code).**

*Scope*: Consumer credit transactions, including sales and loans. § 537.2102.

*Licensure requirements*: A license is required to make supervised loans. § 537.2301.

*Credit terms*: With respect to a consumer credit sale, other than a sale pursuant to open-end credit, the finance charge may not exceed 21% per year on the unpaid balance. § 537.2201(2). The seller may receive a minimum finance charge of not more than $5 when the amount financed does not exceed $75, or $7.50 when the amount financed exceeds $75. § 537.2201(6). For a sale made pursuant to open-end credit, a creditor may receive a finance charge. For each billing cycle, a charge may be made that is a percentage of an amount not exceeding the greatest of the following: (a) the average daily balance of the open-end account in the billing cycle for which the charge is made, which is the sum of the amount unpaid each day during that cycle, divided by the number of days in that cycle; (b) the balance of the open-end account at the beginning of the first day of the billing cycle, after deducting all payments and credits made in the cycle except credits attributable to purchases charged to the account during the cycle; (c) the median amount within a specified range including the balance of the open-end account not exceeding that permitted by paragraph (a) or (b). A charge may be made only if the creditor, subject to classifications and differentiations the creditor may reasonably establish, makes the same charge on all balances within the specified range and if the percentage when applied to the median amount within the range does not produce a charge exceeding the charge resulting from applying that percentage to the lowest amount within the range by more than 8% of the charge on the median amount. § 537.2202.

*Restrictions on points or prepaid interest*: None.

*Restrictions on length of term*: Supervised loans, not made pursuant to open-end credit and in which the amount financed is $1,000 or less, shall be scheduled to be payable in substantially equal installments at substantially equal periodic intervals except to the extent that the schedule of payments is adjusted to the seasonal or irregular income of the debtor, and over a period of not more than 37 months if the amount financed is more than $300, or over a period of not more than 25 months if the amount financed is $300 or less. However, a lender may make a loan not pursuant to open-end credit that is repayable in a single payment if the amount financed does not exceed $1,000 and if the finance charge does not exceed the rate permitted by law. § 537.2308.

*Restrictions on prepayment penalties*: None.

*Requirement of substantially equal installments or limits on balloon payments*: If any scheduled payment of a consumer credit transaction is more than twice as large as the average scheduled payment, the consumer has the right to refinance that payment at the time it is due without penalty. The terms of the refinancing shall be no less favorable to the consumer than the terms of the original transaction. However, this provision does not apply to the following: (a) a consumer lease; (b) a transaction pursuant to open-end credit; (c) a transaction to the extent that the payment schedule is adjusted to the seasonal or irregular income or scheduled payments of obligations of the consumer; (d) a transaction of a class defined by rule of the administrator as not requiring for the protection of the consumer a right to refinance as provided in this section; (e) a consumer loan in which the amount financed exceeds five thousand dollars and is secured by an interest in land; (f) a consumer rental purchase agreement; (g) a consumer loan secured by a certificate of title in a motor vehicle. § 537.3308.

*Formula for rebate of unearned interest*: Rebate calculated by actuarial method, according to detailed statutory rules, with minimum charge of $5 to $7.50. § 537.2510.

*Restrictions on deferral charges*: A creditor may receive a deferral charge that is not in excess of 1.5% per month for the period of time for which it is deferred, but not to exceed the rate of finance charge that was required to be disclosed in the transaction to the consumer applied to each amount deferred for the period for which it is deferred. § 537.2503.

*Limits on document fees*: None.

*Restrictions on types of insurance that can be sold*: None.

*Single document rule?*: None.

*Assignee liability provision*: With respect to a consumer credit sale or consumer lease, an assignee of the seller's or lessor's rights is subject to all claims and defenses of the consumer against the seller or lessor arising from the sale or lease of property or services unless the consumer has agreed in writing not to assert against an assignee a claim or defense arising out of such sale, and the consumer's contract has been assigned to an assignee not related to the seller who acquired the consumer's contract in good faith and for value and who gives the consumer notice of the assignment and who, within 30 days after the mailing of the notice, receives no written notice of the facts giving rise to the consumer's claim or defense. Such agreement not to assert a claim or defense is not valid if the assignee receives such written notice from the consumer within such 30-day period. A claim or defense of a consumer may be asserted against the assignee only if the consumer has made a good faith attempt to obtain satisfaction from the seller or lessor with respect to the claim or defense, and only to the extent of the amount owing to the assignee with respect to the sale or lease of the property or services as to which the claim or defense arose, at the time the assignee has notice of the claim or defense. § 537.3404.

*Special provisions for manufactured homes*: A retail installment contract or agreement for the sale of a manufactured home, mobile home or modular home may include a finance charge of not more than 1.75% per month simple interest on the declining balance of the amount financed. § 103A.58.

*Special provisions for revolving credit*: None.

*Other noteworthy provisions*: None.

*Remedies*: The consumer, other than a lessee in a consumer rental purchase agreement, has a cause of action to recover actual damages and a right in an action (other than a class action) to recover a penalty in an amount determined by the court, but not less than $100 nor more than $1,000, if a person has violated certain specified provisions of the Act. § 537.5201(1). A consumer is not obligated to pay a charge in excess of that allowed by the Act and has a right of refund of any excess charge paid. A refund may not be made by reducing the consumer's obligation by the amount of the excess charge unless the creditor has notified the consumer that the consumer may request a refund and the consumer has not so requested within 30 days thereafter. If the consumer has paid an amount in excess of the lawful obligation, the consumer may recover the excess amount either from the person who made the excess charge or from an assignee. § 537.5201(2). If a creditor has contracted for or received a charge in excess of that allowed by the Act, or if a consumer is entitled to a refund and a person liable to the consumer refuses to make a refund within a reasonable time after demand, the consumer may recover, in an action other than a class action, the excess charge or refund and a penalty in an amount determined by the court not less than $100 nor more than $1,000. § 537.5201(3). In an action in which liability is found, the court shall award to the consumer the costs of the action and attorney fees. Reasonable attorney fees shall be determined by the value of the time reasonably expended by the attorney and not by the amount of the recovery on behalf of the consumer. § 537.5201(8).

**Iowa Code §§ 322.1 to 322.36 (Motor Vehicle Manufacturers, Distributors, Wholesalers, and Dealers Law).**

*Scope*: Licensing of motor vehicle manufacturers, distributors, wholesalers and dealers; retail sales of motor vehicles.
*Licensure requirements*: Dealers must be licensed. § 322.3(1).
*Credit terms*: A retail installment transaction may include a finance charge not in excess of the following rates: (a) for Class 1 vehicles (any new motor vehicle designated by the manufacturer by a year model not earlier than the year in which the sale is made), 1.75% per month simple interest on the declining balance of the amount financed; (b) for Class 2 (any new motor vehicle not in Class 1 and any used motor vehicle designated by the manufacturer by a year model of the same or not more than 2 years prior to the year in which the sale is made), 2% per month simple interest on the declining balance of the amount financed; (c) for Class 3 (any used motor vehicle not in Class 2 and designated by the manufacturer by a year model more than 2 years prior to the year in which the sale is made), 2.25% simple interest on the declining balance of the amount financed. § 322.19. The contract shall comply with the Iowa Consumer Credit Code where applicable. § 322.3(6)(b).

*Restrictions on points or prepaid interest*: None.
*Restrictions on length of term*: None.
*Restrictions on prepayment penalties*: None.
*Requirement of substantially equal installments or limits on balloon payments*: None.
*Formula for rebate of unearned interest*: None.
*Restrictions on deferral charges*: If the holder of a retail installment contract in connection with the purchase or sale of a vehicle renews the loan or extends the scheduled due date of all or any part of an installment or installments, the holder may collect a finance charge on the outstanding declining balance of the amount financed for the period of the extension or renewal. The finance charge on a renewal or extension shall not exceed the rate on the original retail installment contract. § 322.20

*Limits on document fees*: None.
*Restrictions on types of insurance that can be sold*: None.
*Single document rule?*: None.
*Assignee liability provision*: None.
*Special provisions for manufactured homes*: A retail installment contract or agreement for the sale of a manufactured home, mobile home or modular home may include a finance charge of not more than 1.75% per month simple interest on the declining balance of the amount financed. § 103A.58.
*Special provisions for revolving credit*: None.
*Other noteworthy provisions*: None.
*Remedies*: The provisions of the Iowa Consumer Credit Code apply to a consumer credit sale in which a licensed motor vehicle dealer participates or engages, and any violation of that Code is a violation of this Act. § 322.33.

**Kan. Stat. Ann. §§ 16a-2-101 to 16a-9-102 (Kansas Uniform Consumer Credit Code).**

*Scope*: Consumer credit transactions, including sales and loans. § 16a-2-102.
*Licensure requirements*: Supervised lenders must be licensed. § 16a-2-302.
*Credit terms*: In a closed-end consumer credit sale, a seller may charge a finance charge at any rate agreed to by the parties. § 16a-2-201(2). In a consumer credit sale made pursuant to open-end credit, a seller may charge a finance charge at any rate agreed to by the parties. § 16a-2-202(1).

*Restrictions on points or prepaid interest*: A seller may charge a prepaid finance charge for a consumer credit sale secured by a security interest in a manufactured home as defined by 42 U.S.C. § 5402(6) in an amount not to exceed 5% of the amount financed for the sole purpose of reducing the interest rate of the consumer credit sale, or for any other consumer credit sale, an amount not to exceed the lesser of 2% of the amount financed or $100. § 16a-2-201(3).
*Restrictions on length of term*: If consumer loans in which the finance charge exceeds 12%, not made pursuant to open-end credit or lender credit cards issued by a licensed lender, and in which the amount financed is $1,000 or less are payable in installments, they shall be scheduled to be payable in substantially equal installments at substantially equal periodic intervals except to the extent that the schedule of payments is adjusted to the seasonal or irregular income of the debtor, and (a) over a period of not more than 37 calendar months if the amount financed is more than $300 or (b) over a period of not more than 25 calendar months if the amount financed is $300 or less. § 16a-2-308.
*Restrictions on prepayment penalties*: The consumer may prepay in full the unpaid balance of a consumer credit transaction at any time without penalty. § 16a-2-509.
*Requirement of substantially equal installments or limits on balloon payments*: For closed-end consumer credit transactions, if any scheduled payment is more than twice as large as the average scheduled payment, the consumer has the right to refinance that payment at the time it is due without penalty. The terms of the refinancing shall be no less favorable to the consumer than the terms of the original transaction. These provisions do not apply to the extent that the payment schedule is adjusted to the seasonal or irregular income of the consumer or to a note secured by a real estate mortgage. § 16a-3-308.
*Formula for rebate of unearned interest*: Rebate calculated by actuarial method, according to detailed statutory rules, with minimum charge of $5 to $7.50. § 16a-2-201(5).
*Restrictions on deferral charges*: None.

*Limits on document fees*: None.
*Restrictions on types of insurance that can be sold*: A creditor may not contract for or receive a separate charge for insurance against loss of or damage to property unless the insurance covers a substantial risk of loss of or damage to property related to the credit transaction, the amount, terms, and conditions of the insurance are reasonable in relation to the character and value of the property insured or to be insured, and the term of the insurance is reasonable in relation to the terms of credit. The term of the insurance is reasonable if it is customary and does not extend substantially beyond a scheduled maturity. A creditor may not contract for or receive a separate charge for insurance against loss of or damage to property unless property is purchased pursuant to a credit card or in a transaction pursuant to open-end credit, or unless the amount financed exclusive of charges for the insurance is $900 or more and the value of the property is $900 or more. § 16a-4-301. A creditor may not contract for or receive a separate charge for insurance against liability unless the insurance covers a substantial risk of liability arising out of the ownership or use of property related to the credit transaction. § 16a-4-303.
*Single document rule?*: None.

*Assignee liability provision*: An assignee of the seller's or lessor's rights under a consumer credit sale or consumer lease is subject to all claims and defenses of the buyer or lessee against the seller or lessor arising out of the sale or lease, notwithstanding: (a) there is an agreement to the contrary, or (b) the assignee is a holder in due course of a negotiable instrument issued in violation of the Act's provisions prohibiting certain negotiable instruments. Claims or defenses of a buyer or lessee may be asserted against the assignee only: (a) if the buyer or lessee has attempted in good faith to obtain reasonable satisfaction from the seller or lessor with respect to claims or defenses; (b) if the buyer or lessee, when requested in writing to do so by the seller, lessor or the assignee, has given notice in writing to the seller or lessee and the assignee stating the claims or defenses; (c) to the extent of the amount owing to the assignee with respect to the sale or lease at the time the assignee has notice of such claims or defenses; (d) as a matter of defense to or setoff against claims by the assignee except that the buyer or lessee shall not be prohibited from bringing an action to rescind an obligation against which it has a defense or setoff. § 16a-3-404.

*Special provisions for manufactured homes*: A seller may charge a prepaid finance charge for a consumer credit sale secured by a security interest in a manufactured home as defined by 42 U.S.C. § 5402(6) in an amount not to exceed 5% of the amount financed for the sole purpose of reducing the interest rate of the consumer credit sale. § 16a-2-201(3)(a).

*Special provisions for revolving credit*: None.

*Other noteworthy provisions*: None.

*Remedies*: If a creditor violates certain specified provisions of the Act, the consumer has a cause of action to recover actual damages and a right in an action (other than a class action) to recover a penalty of not less than $100 and not more than $1,000. § 16a-5-201(1). If a creditor violates the provisions of the Act applying to authority to make supervised loans (§ 16a-2-301), the loan is void and the consumer is not obligated to pay either the amount financed or finance charge. If the consumer has paid any part of the amount financed or of the finance charge, the consumer has a right to recover the payment from the person or from an assignee of that person's rights who undertakes direct collection of payments or enforcement of rights arising from the debt. § 16a-5-201(2). A consumer is not obligated to pay a charge in excess of that allowed by the Act, and a consumer who has paid an excess charge has a right to a refund of twice the excess charge. If the consumer has paid an amount in excess of the lawful obligation, the consumer may recover twice the excess amount from the person who made the excess charge or from an assignee. § 16a-5-201(3). If a creditor has contracted for or received a charge in excess of that allowed by the Act, or if a consumer is entitled to a refund and a person liable to the consumer refuses to make a refund within a reasonable time after demand, the consumer may recover in an action (other than a class action) a penalty of not less than $100 nor more than $1,000. § 16a-5-201(4). If a creditor is found liable for a violation of the Act, the court shall award to the consumer reasonable attorney fees and costs. Reasonable attorney fees shall be determined by the value of the time reasonably expended by the attorney and not by the amount of the recovery on behalf of the consumer. § 16a-5-201(8).

**Ky. Rev. Stat. Ann. §§ 371.210 to 371.330 (West) (Installment Sales Contracts).**

*Scope*: Installment sales of goods (not including motor vehicles) and services purchased primarily for personal use pursuant to retail installment contract or retail charge agreement. § 371.210.

*Licensure requirements*: None.

*Credit terms*: A retail charge agreement may charge a time price differential for the privilege of paying in installments. § 371.300(3).

*Restrictions on points or prepaid interest*: None.

*Restrictions on length of term*: None.

*Restrictions on prepayment penalties*: None.

*Requirement of substantially equal installments or limits on balloon payments*: None.

*Formula for rebate of unearned interest*: Rebate is calculated by applying Rule of 78s (sum of the balances method) to original finance charge minus $20, but no rebate of less than $1 need be made. § 371.260.

*Restrictions on deferral charges*: The holder of a retail installment contract, upon request by the buyer, may agree to extend or defer the scheduled due date of all or any part of any installment or installments or to renew, restate or reschedule the unpaid balance of the contract, and may collect a refinance charge not to exceed an amount ascertained as provided under either of the following optional methods of computation: Option I. The refinance charge may be computed on the amount of the scheduled installment or installments extended or deferred for the period of extension or deferment at the rate of 1.5%) per month; provided that a minimum deferment charge of $1 shall be permitted; Option II. The refinance charge may be computed as follows: The sum of the unpaid balance as of the refinancing date and the cost for any insurance and other benefits incidental to the refinancing, and for any additional necessary official fees and any accrued delinquency and collection charges, after deducting a refund credit, shall constitute a principal balance for such refinancing on which the refinance charge may be computed for the term of the refinanced contract at the applicable rate for finance charges. Acquisition costs under the refund schedule shall not apply in calculating refinance charges. § 371.270.

*Limits on document fees*: None.

*Restrictions on types of insurance that can be sold*: None.

*Single document rule?*: A retail installment contract need not be contained in a single document. § 371.230.

*Assignee liability provision*: Except in the case of negotiable instruments, the assignment shall not impair the right to any defense, discount or set-off that the defendant has and might have used against the original obligee, or any intermediate assignor, before the defendant received notice of the assignment. § 371.040.

*Special provisions for manufactured homes*: None.

*Special provisions for revolving credit*: § 371.300 regulates retail charge accounts. It requires a written agreement and monthly statements. It allows creditors to charge a time-price differential but does not specify limits on the amount. It allows a delinquency charge of 5% of the payment or $10, whichever is greater, if payment is more than 10 days late. In addition, § 286.3-740 regulates bank revolving credit. It allows a bank to collect a finance charge pursuant to a revolving credit plan in an amount not in excess of 1.75% per month of either the average daily unpaid balance of the debtor's account under such plan during the billing cycle or of the unpaid balance of such account on the same day of each billing cycle. § 286.3-740.

*Other noteworthy provisions*: None.

*Remedies*: None.

**Ky. Rev. Stat. Ann. §§ 190.090 to 190.140 (West) (Motor Vehicle Retail Installment Sales Act).**

*Scope*: Sales of motor vehicles for other than business or commercial use. § 190.090.

*Licensure requirements*: None.

*Credit terms*: The finance charge in a retail installment sale shall not exceed the following rates: for Class 1 vehicles (any new or used motor vehicle designated by the manufacturer by a year model not earlier than the year in which the sale is made), $11 per $100; for Class 2 (any new motor vehicle not in Class 1 and any used motor vehicle designated by the manufacturer by a year model of one or 2 years prior to the year in which the sale is made), $13 per $100; for Class 3 (all other motor vehicles not in Class 1 or 2), $15 per $100. § 190.110.

*Restrictions on points or prepaid interest*: None.

*Restrictions on length of term*: Installment sales defined as two or more installments. § 190.190(2).

*Restrictions on prepayment penalties*: If the finance charge applicable to the retail installment contract is determined by a simple interest method, the retail buyer may pay in full at any time before the stated maturity date without penalty, except that the holder may collect and receive a minimum finance charge of $25 in any event. § 190.120.

*Requirement of substantially equal installments or limits on balloon payments*: None.

*Formula for rebate of unearned interest*: Rebate is calculated by applying Rule of 78s (sum of the balances method) to original finance charge minus $25, but no rebate of less than $1 need be made. § 190.120.

*Restrictions on deferral charges*: If the holder of a retail installment contract extends the scheduled due date, defers the scheduled payment of all or part of any installment payment or payments, or renews the balance of such contract, the holder may collect as a refinance charge for such extension, deferment or renewal a flat service fee not to exceed $5 and an additional finance charge computed at the same rate and by the same method as originally set out in the contract computed from the date of such extension, deferment or renewal. § 190.130.

*Limits on document fees*: None.

*Restrictions on types of insurance that can be sold*: None.

*Single document rule?*: None.

*Assignee liability provision*: None.

*Special provisions for manufactured homes*: None.

*Special provisions for revolving credit*: None.

*Other noteworthy provisions*: None.

*Remedies*: None.

**La. Rev. Stat. Ann. §§ 6:969.1 to 6:969.51 (Motor Vehicle Sales Finance Act).**

*Scope*: Motor vehicle credit transactions. Excludes extensions of credit to business entities, including government or governmental agencies or instrumentalities, extensions of credit primarily for business, commercial or agricultural purposes, and open-end credit transactions, including revolving loan and lender credit card transactions that may involve the secured purchase money financing of a motor vehicle. § 6:969.3.

*Licensure requirements*: A person who has not first obtained a license from the commission or is otherwise exempt shall not engage in the business of making consumer loans or the origination of consumer credit sales subject to the Act. An assignee may not take assignments of and undertake direct collection of payments from or enforce rights against consumers under a consumer loan or consumer credit sale subject to the Act without first having obtained a license from the commission. § 6:969.35.

*Credit terms*: The maximum credit service charge for any consumer credit sale that may be charged may not exceed: for Class 1 vehicles (any new motor vehicle designated by the manufacturer by a year model not earlier than the year in which the sale is made), 18% per year; for Class 2 (any new motor vehicle not in Class 1, and any used motor vehicle designated by the manufacturer by year model of the same or not more than 2 years prior to the year in which the sale is made), 24% per year; for Class 3 (any used motor vehicle not in Class 2 and designated by the manufacturer by year model not more than 4 years prior to the year in which the sale is made), 27% per year; for Class 4 (any used motor vehicle not in Class 2 or 3 and designated by the manufacturer by year model more than 4 years prior to the year in which the sale is made), 33% per year. § 6:969.10(A). The extender of credit may receive a minimum credit service charge of not more than $15 when the amount deferred does not exceed $200, or $25 when the amount deferred exceeds $200. § 6:969.10(D).

*Restrictions on points or prepaid interest*: None.

*Restrictions on length of term*: None.

*Restrictions on prepayment penalties*: None.

*Requirement of substantially equal installments or limits on balloon payments*: None.

*Formula for rebate of unearned interest*: Rebate must be at least 90% of the amount calculated by applying the Rule of 78s (sum of the balances method) to the original finance charge, but may first deduct $25 from the finance charge if one-half or less of the term has elapsed. No rebate of less than $1 need be made. For simple interest transactions, creditor may charge $25 prepayment charge, and statute specifies when prepaid finance charges need not be rebated. § 6:969.20.

*Restrictions on deferral charges*: The extender of credit may collect a deferral charge not exceeding the contract rate previously stated to the consumer calculated without regard to differences in the lengths of months, but proportionately for a part of a month, counting each day as one-thirtieth of a month. A deferral charge may be collected at the time it is assessed or at any time thereafter. Deferral charges on a precomputed transaction may be computed on a pro rata basis or any other method of calculation that does not yield a greater sum than the maximum rates permitted. In lieu of the above, the entire unpaid balance of the transaction may be deferred by charging an amount equal to the contract rate of interest under the transaction times the balance at the time of deferral for the period of deferral. In such a case, the transaction maturity date will be extended by the number of months that the balance is deferred. The parties may agree in writing at the time of a precomputed transaction that if an installment is not paid within 10 days after its due date, the extender of credit may unilaterally grant a deferral and make charges accordingly. No deferral charge may be made for a period after the date that the extender of credit elects to accelerate the maturity of the agreement. In addition to the continued assessment of loan finance charges or credit service charges that may be assessed on the outstanding balance of a simple interest transaction, the parties may before or after default agree in writing to a deferral of all or part of one or more unpaid installments, and the extender of credit may make and collect an additional deferral charge in an amount not to exceed $25. § 6:969.16.

*Limits on document fees*: Up to a $35 documentation fee for services performed in documenting a motor vehicle credit transaction allowed. § 6:969.18(A)(1). Maximum fee of $100 for credit investigation, compliance with federal and state law, preparation of the documents necessary to perfect or satisfy a lien upon the objects sold, and any other functions incidental to the titling of the retail sale. § 6:969.18(A)(2). Seller or extender of credit may charge a $15 fee for notarizing

acts of sale, applications for license and title, and other documents that are required to be notarized, but amount of notary fees charged in a single transaction may not exceed $15 in the aggregate. § 6:969.18(A)(7)(B).
*Restrictions on types of insurance that can be sold*: No policy of credit health and accident insurance may be issued pursuant to a motor vehicle credit transaction other than 7-day, 14-day, or 30-day retroactive health and accident insurance. § 6:969.25(E).
*Single document rule?*: None.
*Assignee liability provision*: None.
*Special provisions for manufactured homes*: None.
*Special provisions for revolving credit*: None.
*Other noteworthy provisions*: None.
*Remedies*: If an extender of credit intentionally or as a result of error not in good faith violates the provisions of the Act regulating loan finance charges, credit service charges, and other fees and charges, the consumer is entitled to a refund of all loan finance charges or credit service charges and has the right to recover three times the amount of such charge together with reasonable attorney fees. Right to civil penalty accrues only if specified circumstances are met. § 6:969.33(A).

**Me. Rev. Stat. tit. 9-A, §§ 2-201 to 2-601 (Maine Consumer Credit Code).**

*Scope*: Consumer credit sales, including sales and loans. § 2-102.
*Licensure requirements*: Supervised lenders must be licensed. § 2-301.
*Credit terms*: The finance charge on a consumer credit sale of a motor vehicle that is sold on or after January 1, 1994 may not exceed 18% per year on the amount financed. For sales made before 1994, different rules apply. "Motor vehicle" means any self-propelled vehicle not operated exclusively on tracks, except agricultural machinery and any other devices that do not constitute consumer goods, as defined in the statute. § 2-201(9-A). For an open-end consumer credit sale, a creditor may receive a charge made in each billing cycle that is a percentage of an amount not exceeding the greater of: (A) the average daily balance in the billing cycle for which the charge is made, which is the sum of the amount unpaid each day during that cycle, divided by the number of days in that cycle; or (B) the unpaid balance at the beginning of the first day of the billing cycle after all payments on account, returns and other credits made or given during the first 25 days of the billing cycle, if the billing cycle is monthly, shall have been first deducted; provided that returns and other credits may be deducted only to the extent that the purchase to which the credit or return relates has been reflected in the previous balance. § 2-202.

*Restrictions on points or prepaid interest*: None.

*Restrictions on length of term*: Supervised loans, not made pursuant to open-end credit and in which the amount financed is $1,000 or less and the principal of which is payable in more than a single payment must be scheduled to be payable in substantially equal installments at equal periodic intervals except to the extent that the schedule of payments is adjusted to the seasonal or irregular income of the debtor and over a period of not more than 25 months. § 2-308.

*Restrictions on prepayment penalties*: Subject to the provisions on rebate upon prepayment, the consumer may prepay the unpaid balance of a consumer credit transaction at any time without penalty, except for minimum charges as permitted by law. § 2-509.

*Requirement of substantially equal installments or limits on balloon payments*: For closed-end consumer credit transactions having a schedule of payments requiring more than one payment of principal, no creditor may contract for payments of principal and interest pursuant to a schedule of payments under which payments are not substantially equal, other than the down payment. However, when a consumer's livelihood is dependent upon seasonal or intermittent income, the parties may agree in a separate writing that one or more payments or the intervals between one or more payments may be reduced or expanded in accordance with the consumer's needs if the payments or intervals are expressly related to expected income. A schedule of payments may provide for the deferral of the first periodic payment subsequent to any down payment for a period of not more than 12 months, except that interest or costs may not accrue in connection with the deferral of the first periodic payment if the deferral is for a period of time in excess of 120 days. A schedule of payments may require a final payment not substantially equal to all other periodic payments if the transaction is made for a term of not fewer than 4 years and if the contract gives the consumer the right to refinance the amount of the final payment in order to amortize the obligation on terms then generally offered by the creditor, if the consumer satisfies reasonable credit standards, and if the property satisfies reasonable loan-to-value standards. The 4-year limitation does not apply to a consumer credit transaction secured by a motor vehicle if the contract otherwise conforms to the statute's requirements and also permits the consumer to transfer the motor vehicle to the creditor in lieu of making the final payment without further liability, except that the contract may provide for the assessment against the consumer of one or more of the following: (A) a reasonable disposition fee; (B) reasonable charges for excess mileage; (C) reasonable charges for excess wear and tear; and (D) reasonable charges for damage to the motor vehicle. § 3-308.
*Formula for rebate of unearned interest*: Rebate calculated by actuarial method, but creditor may contract for and retain the minimum charge allowed by § 2-201, which varies from $5 to $25 depending on the amount and terms of the credit. § 2-510.
*Restrictions on deferral charges*: The deferral charge for a standard deferral may equal but not exceed the portion of the finance charge attributable to the computational period immediately preceding the due date of the earliest maturing installment deferred as determined according to the sum of the balances method multiplied by the whole or fractional number of computational periods in the deferral period, counting each day as 1/30th of a month without regard to differences in lengths of months when the computational period is one month or as 1/7 of a week when the computational period is one week. A deferral charge computed according to this method is earned pro rata during the deferral period and is fully earned on the last day of the deferral period. With respect to a transaction as to which a creditor does not make a standard deferral or a deferral charge for a standard deferral, a deferral charge may be made as of the due date of an installment with respect to which no delinquency charge has been made or, if made, is deducted from the deferral charge. A deferral charge may equal but not exceed the rate of finance charge required to be disclosed pursuant to law applied to each amount deferred for the period for which it is deferred computed without regard to differences in lengths of months, but proportionately for a part of a month, counting each day as 1/30 of a month or as 1/7 of a week. A deferral charge computed according to this method is earned pro rata with respect to each amount deferred during the period for which it is deferred. In addition to the deferral charge permitted, a creditor may receive appropriate additional charges, and any amount of these charges which is not paid may be added to the deferral charge computed or to the amount deferred for the purpose of computing the deferral charge com-

puted. The parties may agree in writing at the time of a transaction that, if an installment is not paid within 10 days after its due date, the creditor may unilaterally grant a deferral and make charges accordingly. A deferral charge may not be made for a period after the date that the creditor elects to accelerate the maturity of the transaction. § 2-503.

*Limits on document fees*: None.

*Restrictions on types of insurance that can be sold*: A creditor may not contract for or receive a separate charge for insurance against loss of or damage to property unless the insurance covers a substantial risk of loss of or damage to property related to the credit transaction, the amount, terms and conditions of the insurance are reasonable in relation to the character and value of the property insured or to be insured, and the term of the insurance is reasonable in relation to the term of credit. The term of the insurance is reasonable if it is customary and does not extend substantially beyond a scheduled maturity. With respect to a transaction, except pursuant to open-end credit, a creditor may not contract for or receive a separate charge for insurance against loss of or damage to property unless the amount financed exclusive of charges for the insurance is $1,400 or more and the cash price of the item or property is $1,400 or more. § 4-301.

*Single document rule?*: None.

*Assignee liability provision*: With respect to a consumer credit sale or consumer lease, an assignee of the rights of the seller or lessor is subject to all claims and defenses of the buyer or lessee against the seller or lessor arising out of the sale or lease notwithstanding that there is an agreement to the contrary or the assignee is a holder in due course of a negotiable instrument issued in violation of the provisions on prohibition of certain negotiable instruments. The assignee's liability may not exceed the amount owing to the assignee with respect to the sale or lease at the time the assignee has notice of a claim or defense of the buyer or lessee. § 3-403.

*Special provisions for manufactured homes*: The finance charge on a transaction to finance or refinance the acquisition of, or secured by, manufactured housing, not involving a security interest in real estate, may not exceed the greater of the following: A rate 2% greater than the maximum rate established by federal regulations pursuant to the Veterans Housing Act of 1970; or 18% per year. § 2-201(10). "Manufactured housing" means a structural unit or units designed to be used as a dwelling or dwellings and constructed in a manufacturing facility and then transported by the use of its own chassis or placement on an independent chassis to a building site. The term includes any type of building that is constructed at a manufacturing facility and then transported to a building site where it is utilized for housing and that may be purchased, sold, offered for sale or brokered by a licensee in the interim. Me. Rev. Stat. Ann. tit. 10, § 9002(7).

*Special provisions for revolving credit*: None.

*Other noteworthy provisions*: None.

*Remedies*: If a creditor violates certain specified provisions of the Act, a consumer has a right to recover actual damages an amount determined by the court not less than $250 nor more than $1,000. § 5-201(1). A debtor is not obligated to pay a charge in excess of that allowed by the Act, and has a right to a refund if he has paid an excess charge from the person who made the excess charge or from an assignee. § 5-201(3). If a creditor has contracted for or received a charge in excess of that allowed, or if a debtor is entitled to a refund and a person liable to the debtor refuses to make a refund within a reasonable time after demand, the debtor may recover an amount determined by the court not less than $250 nor more than $1,000. § 5-201(4). If it is found that a creditor has violated the Act, the court shall award the debtor reasonable attorney fees and costs. Reasonable attorney fees shall be determined by the value of the time reasonably expended by the attorney and not by the amount of the recovery on behalf of the debtor. § 5-201(9).

**Md. Code Ann., Com. Law §§ 12-601 to 12-636 (West) (Retail Installment Sales Act).**

*Scope*: Sales of goods (all tangible personal property that has a cash price of $25,000 or less) for use or consumption by the buyer, or for the benefit or satisfaction that the buyer may derive from the use or consumption of the goods by another, but not for resale by the buyer. § 12-601.

*Licensure requirements*: None.

*Credit terms*: The finance charge for the sale of a motor vehicle may not exceed the following annual simple interest rates: (1) for Class 1 vehicles (new), 16.5% on the outstanding balance; (2) for Class 2 (used motor vehicle designated by the manufacturer by a model year not more than 2 years before the year in which the sale is made), 22%; (3) for Class 3 (used motor vehicle designated by the manufacturer by a model year more than 2 years before the year in which the sale is made), 27%. § 12-609(a). Notwithstanding the foregoing, the finance charge on a motor vehicle sold under a contract may not exceed the following annual simple interest rates of finance charge: for Class 1 vehicles, 24%; for Class 2, 24 %. § 12-609(f). The finance charge for the retail sale of consumer goods (but not motor vehicles) bought under an installment sale agreement may not exceed the greater of: 22% on that part of the outstanding balance not exceeding $1,000; and 18% on that part of the outstanding balance exceeding $1,000; or a minimum charge of $10 or, if the date of the last installment is 8 months or less after the effective date of the installment sale agreement, $8. Notwithstanding the foregoing, a seller may charge a finance charge at a rate not in excess of 24% per year simple interest on the outstanding balance under an installment sale agreement made on or after July 1, 1982. § 12-610.

*Restrictions on points or prepaid interest*: None.

*Restrictions on length of term*: None.

*Restrictions on prepayment penalties*: A buyer may prepay at any time, without penalty, all or part of the outstanding balance payable under an installment sale agreement relating to consumer goods. § 12-612(b). A buyer may prepay at any time, without penalty, all or any part of the unpaid time balance payable under the installment sale agreement if such agreement is for the retail sale of personal property purchased primarily for personal, family, or household purposes, regardless of the original price of that personal property. § 12-620(a).

*Requirement of substantially equal installments or limits on balloon payments*: Agreement may not contain a schedule of payments under which any installment, except the down payment, is more than double the average of all other installments, or under which the interval between any consecutive installments is less than one half the average of all other intervals, unless the buyer is given an absolute right, on default in any of the excess or irregular installments, to have the schedule of unpaid installments revised to conform in both amounts and intervals to the average of all preceding installments and intervals. § 12-607(a)(3).

*Formula for rebate of unearned interest*: §§ 12-612 and 12-620 are overlapping sections that appear to have the same scope. Both require an actuarial rebate upon prepayment of an installment sale agreement relating to consumer goods, and both provide that a rebate of less than $1 need not be made. In addition § 12-612 provides that the seller is entitled to retain a finance charge of at least $6, and that the rebate applies not just to interest but also to the $8-$10 minimum charge allowed by § 12-610(2). § 12-620(b).

*Restrictions on deferral charges*: An extension or deferral charge may not exceed an amount equal to 1% per month of the amount extended or deferred for the period of extension or deferral. § 12-619(b).

*Limits on document fees*: None.

*Restrictions on types of insurance that can be sold*: A holder may not collect from the buyer a greater amount for insurance than that allowed by the State Insurance Department for the insurer carrying the risk. The insurance for which the holder may collect from the buyer is limited to automobile bodily injury and property damage liability, automobile physical damage, life and accident, medical reimbursement, and nonfiling insurance. § 12-609(d).

*Single document rule?*: None.

*Assignee liability provision*: If a promissory note taken by a seller or sales finance company is assigned, it is subject to all defenses that the buyer might have asserted against the seller or sales finance company, except that an acknowledgment by the buyer of delivery of a copy of the agreement is conclusive proof of the delivery in favor of an assignee of the note without actual knowledge to the contrary. § 12-628.

*Special provisions for manufactured homes*: None.

*Special provisions for revolving credit*: In an open-end account, the finance charge may not exceed: 1.5% a month on that part of the outstanding balance not exceeding $700; 1% per month on that part of the outstanding balance exceeding $700. Notwithstanding the foregoing, the finance charge may not exceed 2% per month on that part of the outstanding balance originating on or after July 1, 1982. Including a credit card plan that provides for sales, cash advances, or both, the buyer or borrower may not be required to pay a membership fee for the privilege of participating in the plan. If interest is at a rate of 2%, the seller or holder may not receive any compounded interest or compounded finance charge. A seller or financial institution may assess either, but not both: (i) a finance charge equal to the rate of interest charged on past due accounts as provided in the agreement; or (ii) a late payment charge. In an open-end account, if a finance charge is applied to all outstanding balances within a range not exceeding $10, the finance charge may be computed on the basis of the median amount within the range. § 12-506.

*Other noteworthy provisions*: None.

*Remedies*: Except for an overcharge resulting from a bona fide error that is corrected within 60 days from the date of the agreement, if a holder collects a charge greater in amount than the maximum permitted for motor vehicles, he shall forfeit to the buyer all finance charges paid or payable under the agreement. § 12-609(c). Except for an overcharge resulting from a bona fide error in computation that is corrected within 60 days from the date of the agreement, if a holder collects from the buyer a charge for insurance greater than that permitted, he shall pay to the buyer a sum equal to ten times the amount of the overcharge. § 12-609(d). A holder may not collect or receive any finance, delinquency or collection charge from the buyer if the agreement does not contain the required information and disclosures, the seller fails to deliver to the buyer a required copy of the agreement, or the agreement contains a finance charge in excess of the applicable permitted charges. If a contract contains any provision prohibited by the statute (as described in § 12-607), that provision is void and the holder may not collect or receive from the buyer any finance, delinquency or collection charge. § 12-630.

**Mass. Gen. Laws ch. 255D, §§ 1 to 32 (Retail Installment Sales and Services).**

*Scope*: Installment sales of all things movable purchased primarily for personal, family, or household purposes (excluding motor vehicles), including fixtures and gift certificates, and services purchased primarily for personal, family, or household purposes, including alterations or improvements upon or in connection with real property, but excluding insurance of all types. A retail installment sale agreement shall not include an agreement that provides (a) for the payment of the total sale price in no more than 3 monthly installments and (b) a finance charge not in excess of $1 and (c) no collateral security for the seller. § 1.

*Licensure requirements*: Sales finance companies must be licensed. § 2.

*Credit terms*: An installment seller may charge an annual percentage rate of 21%. § 11(B).

*Restrictions on points or prepaid interest*: None.

*Restrictions on length of term*: Installment sale defined as more than one payment and finance charge or over five installments and no finance charge. § 1.

*Restrictions on prepayment penalties*: None.

*Requirement of substantially equal installments or limits on balloon payments*: No retail installment sale agreement may contain any schedule of payments under which any one installment, except the down payment, is not equal or substantially equal to all other installments, or under which the intervals between any consecutive installments except the down payment differ substantially, unless (a) the buyer is given an absolute right upon default in any such excess or irregular installments to have the schedule of unpaid installments, including that in default, revised to conform in both amounts and intervals to the average of all preceding installments and intervals, or (b) unless the time and amounts of installments relate to the uneven seasonal income of the buyer and a statement appears in the contract to that effect. § 10(3).

*Formula for rebate of unearned interest*: Calculated by actuarial method, but no refund of less than $1 need be made. § 13.

*Restrictions on deferral charges*: An extension agreement may provide for an extension charge not to exceed 1% of each installment for each month from the date when such installment or part thereof would otherwise have been payable to the date when such installment or part thereof is made payable under the extension agreement However, when any such charge is made, no delinquency charge shall be charged unless an installment as extended is not paid by the end of the grace period beyond the extended due date. An extension agreement may also provide that the buyer shall pay the additional cost, if any, for insurance coverage provided in the extension. § 16.

*Limits on document fees*: None.

*Restrictions on types of insurance that can be sold*: None.

*Single document rule?*: None.

*Assignee liability provision*: The holder of a retail installment sale agreement, or other person acting in his behalf, shall be subject to all defenses, real and personal, which the installment buyer may have against the installment seller. § 25A.

*Special provisions for manufactured homes*: None.

*Special provisions for revolving credit*: An installment seller under a revolving credit agreement may assess a finance charge that shall not exceed 1.5% per month computed upon the outstanding unpaid balance from month to month. If the amount of any finance charge is less than $0.50 for any month, $0.50 may be assessed, provided that no finance is assessed for a zero balance. Finance charges may be computed under revolving credit agreements within a range of not in excess of $10 on the basis of the median amount within the selected range, provided that such finance charge is applied to all unpaid balances within such range. In the event that a finance charge is imposed, it shall be computed upon (i) the previous balance after all payments on account, returns, and other credits made or given during the billing cycle shall have been first deducted; provided, however, that returns and other credits may be deducted only to the extent that the purchase to which the credit or return relates has been reflected in the previous balance; or (ii) the average daily balance determined by adding the daily balances on the account for each day in the billing cycle, and dividing this total by the number of days in the billing cycle. § 27.

*Other noteworthy provisions*: None.

*Remedies*: The violation of certain specified provisions will bar recovery of any finance charge, delinquency or collection charge or refinancing charge on the retail installment sale agreement or on the revolving credit agreement, or on the sale pursuant to a revolving credit agreement. However, such violation shall not bar the seller's right to recover from the buyer an amount equal to the unpaid principal balance or repossess the goods and recover from the buyer an amount equal to the unpaid balance less the proceeds of any disposition of the goods. § 29(A). Any agreement that violates the provisions of the Act may be declared void by the supreme judicial or superior court upon a civil action brought by the buyer. § 29(C).

**Mass. Gen. Laws ch. 255B, §§ 1 to 25 (Retail Installment Sales of Motor Vehicles).**

*Scope*: Installment sales of motor vehicles upon or by which any person may be transported or drawn upon a highway and which is used or bought for use primarily for personal, family, or household purposes. § 1.

*Licensure requirements*: Sales finance companies must be licensed. Includes retail sellers holding contracts. § 2.

*Credit terms*: A retail seller may charge for any new or used motor vehicle a finance charge not in excess of an annual percentage rate of 21%. § 14.

*Restrictions on points or prepaid interest*: None.

*Restrictions on length of term: None.*

*Restrictions on prepayment penalties*: None.

*Requirement of substantially equal installments or limits on balloon payments*: None.

*Formula for rebate of unearned interest*: Calculated by actuarial method, but no refund of less than $1 need be made. § 16.

*Restrictions on deferral charges:* A deferment charge shall not exceed an amount equal to 1% per month simple interest on the amount of the installment or installments, or part thereof, deferred for the period of deferment. Such period shall not exceed the period from the date when such deferred installment or installments, or part thereof, would have been payable in the absence of such deferment, to the date when such installment or installments, or part thereof, are made payable under the agreement for deferment; except that a minimum charge of $1 for the period of deferment may be made in any case where the deferment charge, when computed at such rate, amounts to less than $1. Such agreement may also provide for the payment by the buyer of the additional cost to the holder of the contract of premiums for continuing in force, until the end of such period of deferment, any insurance coverage provided for in the contract. No deferment charge shall be made on any installment for which a default charge has been made unless the default charge on such installment is rebated in full. If a contract is prepaid in full during a deferment period the buyer shall receive, in addition to the refund credit, the refund of that portion of the deferment charge applicable to any unexpired months of the deferment period. § 17.

*Limits on document fees*: None.

*Restrictions on types of insurance that can be sold*: None.

*Single document rule?*: None.

*Assignee liability provision*: The holder of a retail installment contract or other person acting in his behalf shall be subject to all defenses, real and personal, which the retail buyer may have against the retail seller. § 19A.

*Special provisions for manufactured homes*: None.

*Special provisions for revolving credit*: None.

*Other noteworthy provisions*: None.

*Remedies*: A violation of certain specified provisions of the Act shall bar the recovery of any finance charge, delinquency or collection charge or refinancing charge on the contract involved. § 22.

**Mich. Comp. Laws §§ 445.851 to 445.873 (Retail Installment Sales Act).**

*Scope*: Installment sales of goods purchased primarily for personal, family, or household use, excluding motor vehicles, and services for personal, family, or household use. § 445.852.

*Licensure requirements*: None.

*Credit terms*: A retail installment contract may provide for a time price differential that does not exceed the rate of interest permitted a regulated lender by the credit reform act (25% per year—§ 445.1854). A minimum time price differential of not more than $10 may be charged on each contract, whether or not the contract is prepaid. § 445.857. Instead of a time price differential computed on the original principal balance, the seller may charge from time to time a time price differential consisting of interest on the amount of the unpaid principal balance of the contract. The transaction is subject to the following provisions: (a) the number and amount of installment payments required to be stated may be estimated assuming that each scheduled payment is made on the date it is due and in the scheduled amount; (b) the holder of the contract has the option of deferring interest charges that accrue due to installment payments being received later than the periodic installment due date. The deferred interest charge shall be computed on the basis of additional interest charges accruing for late installment payments and appropriate interest reductions for installment payments made before the due date. On contracts providing for equal monthly installments, if the final installment is more than 105% of a previous installment as a result of the deferred interest charges, the installment buyer shall be given the option to pay the deferred interest charges not less than 25 days after the date the last installment payment is due; (c) if the entire principal balance is prepaid in full, together with all interest incurred to the date of prepayment, the balance of the original time price differential shall be canceled and the provisions concerning a refund credit shall not be applicable. § 445.873.

*Restrictions on points or prepaid interest*: None.

*Restrictions on length of term*: None.

*Restrictions on prepayment penalties*: None.

*Requirement of substantially equal installments or limits on balloon payments*: None.

*Formula for rebate of unearned interest*: Calculated by actuarial method, but no refund of less than $1 need be made. § 445.858.

*Restrictions on deferral charges*: A minimum charge of $1 for the period of extension or deferral may be made in any case where the extension or deferral charge, when computed at the rate permitted a regulated lender by the credit reform act, amounts to less than $1. The agreement may also provide for the buyer's payment of the additional cost to the holder of the contract of premiums for continuing in force until the end of the period of extension or deferral any insurance coverage provided for in the contract. § 445.861(d)(1).

*Limits on document fees*: None.

*Restrictions on types of insurance that can be sold*: None.

*Single document rule?*: A retail installment contract need not be contained in a single document. § 445.854.

*Assignee liability provision*: A holder of a retail installment contract is subject to all the claims and defenses of the buyer arising out of the retail installment transaction, but the buyer's recovery shall not exceed the amount paid to the holder thereunder. § 445.865(d).

*Special provisions for manufactured homes*: None.

*Special provisions for revolving credit*: A retail charge agreement may provide for a time price differential for the privilege of paying in installments under the agreement at a rate not greater than the rate permitted a regulated lender by the credit reform act. The time price differential shall be computed on all amounts unpaid under the agreement from month to month or other regular periods. If the regular period is other than a monthly period, the time price differential may be computed proportionately. The time price differential may be computed for all unpaid balances within a range of $10 or less on the basis of the median amount within that range if as so computed the time price differential is applied to all unpaid balances within that range. A minimum time price differential of not more than $0.70 per month may be charged. § 445.862.

*Other noteworthy provisions*: None.

*Remedies*: Any seller who enters into any contract that does not comply with the provisions of the Act or who violates any provision of the Act, except as a result of accidental or bona fide error, is barred from the recovery of any time price differential, any official fees, delinquency or collection charge, attorney fees or court costs. The buyer shall be entitled to recover reasonable attorney fees and costs from the seller or assignee. § 445.868. The attorney general, the prosecuting attorney for the county where an alleged violation occurred, or a borrower may bring an action against a retail seller to do one or more of the following: (a) obtain a declaratory judgment that a method, act or practice of a retail seller is a violation of the Act; (b) enjoin a retail seller who is engaging or about to engage in a method, act or practice that is a violation of the Act; (c) recover $1,000 and actual damages if the alleged violation was committed by a retail seller for a non-credit card arrangement or $1,500 and actual damages if the alleged violation involved any other credit arrangements; (d) recover reasonable attorney fees and costs if the seller is found to have violated the Act; (e) in an action brought by the attorney general or a county prosecutor, recover a civil fine of not more than $10,000 if the retail seller is found to have willfully and knowingly violated the Act and $20,000 if the seller is found to have persistently violated the Act. Except for a violation described in the Act's provision concerning a retail charge agreement, a seller who violates the Act in the extension of credit to a borrower or buyer shall not recover any interest or other charges in connection with the extension of credit. The borrower or buyer may recover reasonable attorney fees and costs for bringing a cause of action or defending against one brought by a seller who has violated the Act. The attorney general or a borrower may bring a class action on behalf of persons injured by a violation. § 445.869.

**Mich. Comp. Laws §§ 492.101 to 492.151 (Motor Vehicle Sales Finance Act).**

*Scope*: Installment sales of motor vehicles for use by buyer or for buyer's benefit. § 492.102.

*Licensure requirements*: Installment sellers and sales finance companies must be licensed. § 492.103. No installment sales contract shall be sold to any person doing business in the state who is not licensed under the provisions of the Act. § 492.115(a).

*Credit terms*: A seller may charge a finance charge on any installment sale contract not exceeding the rate permitted by the credit reform act (25% per year—§ 445.1854). § 492.118(1). A seller may charge a minimum finance charge of $15 where the finance charge, when computed at the permitted rate, results in a total charge of less than $15. § 492.118(5). Instead of a finance charge computed on the principal amount financed, the seller may charge from time to time a finance charge consisting of interest on the amount of the unpaid principal balance of the contract. In this event, the transaction is subject to the following provisions: (a) the number and amount of installment payments required to be stated may be estimated for purposes of assuming that each scheduled payment is made on the date it is due and in the scheduled amount; (b) the holder of the contract has the option of deferring interest charges that accrue due to installment payments being received later than the periodic installment due date. The deferred interest charge shall be computed on the basis of additional interest charges accruing for late installment payments and appropriate interest reductions for installment payments made before the due date. On contracts providing for equal monthly installments, if the final installment is more than 105% of a previous installment as a result of the deferred interest charges, the installment buyer shall be given the option to pay the deferred interest charges not less than 25 days after the date the last installment payment is due; (c) if the unpaid time balance is prepaid in full, together with all interest incurred to the date of prepayment, the balance of the original finance charge shall be canceled and the finance charge rebate provisions of the Act do not apply. § 497.141.

*Restrictions on points or prepaid interest*: None.

*Restrictions on length of term*: Installment sale defined as two or more scheduled payments. § 492.102(9).

*Restrictions on prepayment penalties*: None.

*Requirement of substantially equal installments or limits on balloon payments*: Contract shall provide for payments in substantially equal periods and amounts. However, this requirement does not apply to contracts made between an installment seller and buyer who is an employee of the installment seller, nor does it prohibit contracts that extend the time for making installment payments for a period not to exceed 3 months. § 492.112(f). An installment sale contract may provide for a series of payments in substantially equal periods and amounts followed by a single larger payment of the unpaid balance, in which event the buyer shall have the right to an option, at the time the larger payment becomes due, to make such payment or to enter into a second contract charging the same finance charge as the first contract. § 492.122.

*Formula for rebate of unearned interest*: Calculated by actuarial method, seller may retain a net finance charge of $15, and no refund of less than $1 need be made. § 492.121(3).

*Restrictions on deferral charges*: The holder may collect a refinance charge for extension, deferment or renewal. The refinance charge shall not exceed the amount ascertained under the permitted rate. If one or more installment payments are extended or deferred, computing the refinance charge on the amount of the installment payment or payments or part of a payment that is refinanced, for the period of time for which each payment or part of a payment is extended or deferred, shall not exceed the permitted rate. § 492.119(b), (c).

*Limits on document fees*: The documentary preparation fee shall not exceed the lesser of 5% of the cash price of the motor vehicle or $60. The maximum amount is adjusted every 2 years to reflect the cumulative percentage change in the consumer price index for the two immediately preceding calendar years, as determined by the administrator. § 492.113(2)(a).

*Restrictions on types of insurance that can be sold*: The buyer of a motor vehicle under an installment sale contract may be required to provide insurance on the vehicle at the buyer's expense for the protection of the seller or subsequent holder. Such insurance shall be limited to insurance against substantial risk of damage, destruction, or theft of the vehicle. § 492.116(a).

*Single document rule?*: None.

*Assignee liability provision*: Contract shall contain the following provision: "Any holder of this consumer credit contract is subject to all claims and defenses which the debtor could assert against the seller of goods or services obtained pursuant hereto or with the proceeds hereof. Recovery hereunder by the debtor shall not exceed amounts paid by the debtor hereunder." § 492.114a(c).

*Special provisions for manufactured homes*: None.

*Special provisions for revolving credit*: None.

*Other noteworthy provisions*: None.

*Remedies*: None.

**Minn. Stat. §§ 53C.01 to 53C.14 (Motor Vehicle Retail Installment Sales Act).**

*Scope*: Installment sales of motor vehicles not for resale and purchased primarily for personal, family, or household use. § 53C.01.

*Licensure requirements*: Sales finance companies must be licensed. Includes retail sellers holding contracts. § 53C.02.

*Credit terms*: The finance charge may not exceed the following simple interest annual percentage rates: for Class 1 vehicles (any motor vehicle designated by the manufacturer by a year model of the same or not more than 1 year prior to the year in which the sale is made), 18% per year; for Class 2 (any motor vehicle designated by the manufacturer by a year model of two or 3 years prior to the year in which the sale is made), 19.75% per year; for Class 3 (any motor vehicle not in Class 1 or 2), 23.25% per year. § 53C.09, subdiv. 1.

*Restrictions on points or prepaid interest*: None.

*Restrictions on length of term*: None.

*Restrictions on prepayment penalties*: Any retail buyer may pay in full at any time before maturity without penalty. § 53C.10, subdiv. 1.

*Requirement of substantially equal installments or limits on balloon payments*: None.

*Formula for rebate of unearned interest*: Calculated by actuarial method, less an acquisition cost of $15, but no rebate of less than $1 need be made. § 53C.10, subdiv. 1.

*Restrictions on deferral charges*: Where the holder defers the scheduled payment of all or part of any installment payment or payments, the holder may restate the amount of the installments and the time schedule, and collect a flat service fee not to exceed $5 plus a total additional charge not exceeding the simple interest annual percentage rate under the original contract calculated on the respective descending balances computed from the date of such deferment. § 53C.11.

*Limits on document fees*: None.

*Restrictions on types of insurance that can be sold*: None.

*Single document rule?*: None.

*Assignee liability provision*: None.

*Special provisions for manufactured homes*: The finance charge in a sale of a manufactured home is governed by the same provisions as motor vehicles (see *Credit terms,* above) except that the maximum finance charge for a Class I manufactured home may not exceed 14.5% per year. § 53C.09, subdiv. 3.

*Special provisions for revolving credit*: With respect to finance charges for open-end credit sales, the collection of a finance charge upon an account balance by a seller of goods, services or both shall be lawful, provided that the charge that does not exceed 1.5% per month computed on an amount no greater than the average daily balance of the account during each monthly billing cycle, provided a minimum finance charge not in excess of $0.50 cents per month may be collected. In addition, no finance charge in excess of 1 1/3% per month shall be imposed on an open-end and consumer credit account by any issuer whose credit card is issued primarily for the purpose of purchasing motor fuels and related products and whose gross annual national sales exceed $10 billion. Retailers must give adequate notice to open-end consumer credit customers before any higher interest rate is applied. Accompanying credit statements must not suggest that the Minnesota legislature required retailers to raise interest rates. The accompanying material must make clear that the increase affects only the maximum allowable interest rate. § 334.16.

*Other noteworthy provisions*: None.

*Remedies*: In case of a fraudulent violation of any provision of the Act, the buyer has a right to recover from the person committing such violation, to set off or counterclaim in any action by such person to enforce such contract an amount as liquidated damages, the whole of the contract due and payable, plus reasonable attorney fees. § 53C.12, subdiv. 2. In case of a failure to comply with any provision of the Act, but other than a fraudulent violation, the buyer shall have a right to recover from the person committing such violation, to set off or counterclaim in any action by such person to enforce such contract an amount as liquidated damages equal to three times the amount of any time price differential charged in excess of the authorized amount or $50, whichever is greater, plus reasonable attorney fees. § 53C.12, subdiv. 3.

**Miss. Code Ann. §§ 63-19-1 to 63-19-57 (Motor Vehicle Sales Finance Law).**

*Scope*: Sales of motor vehicles and commercial vehicles not for resale. § 63-19-3.

*Licensure requirements*: Sales finance companies must be licensed. Includes retail sellers holding retail installment contracts that exceed a total aggregate outstanding indebtedness of $500,000. § 63-19-7.

*Credit terms*: The maximum finance charge that may be charged in connection with sales or financing of motor vehicles and commercial vehicles may result in a yield not to exceed the following annual percentage rates calculated according to the actuarial method: for Class 1 vehicles (any new motor vehicle manufactured in the same year or the year immediately prior to the year in which the sale is made), 18% per year; (b) for Class 2 (any new motor vehicle not in Class 1, any used motor vehicle manufactured not more than 2 years prior to the year in which the sale is made, and any new commercial vehicle or used commercial vehicle manufactured not more than 1 year prior to the year in which the sale is made), 21%; for Class 3 (any used motor vehicle not in Class 2 and manufactured not more than 4 years prior to the year in which the sale is made and any used commercial vehicle not in Class 2), 26.75%; for Class 4 (any used motor vehicle not in Class 2 or 3 and manufactured more than 4 years prior to the year in which the sale is made), 28.75%. § 63-19-43.

*Restrictions on points or prepaid interest*: In the event the finance charge on a contract regarding the sale of a commercial vehicle is not precomputed, any buyer may pay in full at any time before maturity the unpaid balance and shall pay a penalty not to exceed $50. § 63-19-47.

*Restrictions on length of term*: None.

*Restrictions on prepayment penalties*: None.

*Requirement of substantially equal installments or limits on balloon payments*: None.

*Formula for rebate of unearned interest*: Calculated by Rule of 78s, but creditor may deduct $10 acquisition cost from refund, and no refund of less than $1 need be made. § 63-19-47.

*Restrictions on deferral charges*: None.

*Limits on document fees*: None.

*Restrictions on types of insurance that can be sold*: None.

*Single document rule?*: None.

*Assignee liability provision*: None.

*Special provisions for manufactured homes*: The maximum finance charge that may be received for any loan or extension of credit made by any lender or by any retail seller in connection with sales of manufactured homes may result in a yield not to exceed the following annual percentage rates calculated according to the actuarial method: (a) 25% per year on that part of the unpaid balance that does not exceed $1,000; (b) 18% per year on that part of the unpaid balance that is more than $1,000 but does not exceed $2,500; (c) the greater of 15% per year or 5% per year above the discount rate, excluding any surcharge thereon, on 90-day commercial paper in effect at the Federal Reserve bank in the Federal Reserve district where the lender or retail seller is located, on that part of the unpaid balance of the amount financed that is more than $2,500. § 75-17-23.

*Special provisions for revolving credit*: None.

*Other noteworthy provisions*: None.

*Remedies*: Any person willfully violating specified provisions of the Act shall be barred from recovery of any finance charge, delinquency or collection charge on the contract. § 63-19-55(4).

**Mo. Rev. Stat. §§ 408.250 to 408.380 (Retail Credit Sales Law).**

*Scope*: Sales of goods, excluding motor vehicles, and services to be used primarily for personal, family, or household purposes and not primarily for business, commercial or agricultural purposes. § 408.250.

*Licensure requirements*: None.

*Credit terms*: The amount agreed to by the parties to the retail time contract or retail charge agreement. § 408.300.

*Restrictions on points or prepaid interest*: None.

*Restrictions on length of term*: Installment sales defined as one or more deferred payments. § 408.250(14).

*Restrictions on prepayment penalties*: None.

*Requirement of substantially equal installments or limits on balloon payments*: None.

*Formula for rebate of unearned interest*: Actuarial method. § 408.320.

*Restrictions on deferral charges*: None.

*Limits on document fees*: None.

*Restrictions on types of insurance that can be sold*: A buyer may be required to provide insurance on the goods at his own cost for the protection of the seller or other person holding a retail time contract or account under a retail charge agreement, as well as the buyer, but such insurance shall be subject to limitations provided for in regulations referenced in the Act. § 408.280(1).

*Single document rule?*: A retail time contract need not be contained in a single document. § 408.260(6).

*Assignee liability provision*: No retail time contract shall contain any provision by which the buyer agrees to relieve the seller, assignee or holder of any liabilities, or whereby the buyer agrees to waive any claim, rights or legal remedies that the buyer may have against the seller, assignee, or holder under the contract. § 408.260(11).

*Special provisions for manufactured homes*: None.

*Special provisions for revolving credit*: None.

*Other noteworthy provisions*: None.

*Remedies*: Any person violating certain specified provisions, except as the result of an accidental and bona fide error of computation, shall be barred from recovery of any time charge, delinquency or collection charge on the contract. § 408.370(2). Any buyer who suffers an ascertainable loss of money or property, real or personal, as a result of any method, act or practice in violation of specified provisions that is not corrected according to the Act may bring a private cause of action. § 408.370(4).

**Mo. Rev. Stat. §§ 365.010 to 365.200 (Motor Vehicle Time Sales Law).**

*Scope*: Installment sales of motor vehicles, excluding manufactured homes. § 365.020.

*Licensure requirements*: Sales finance companies must be licensed. § 365.030.

*Credit terms*: A retail seller may charge any time price differential agreed to by the buyer. A minimum time price differential of $25 may be charged on any retail installment transaction. § 365.120.

*Restrictions on points or prepaid interest*: None.

*Restrictions on length of term*: None.

*Restrictions on prepayment penalties*: None.

*Requirement of substantially equal installments or limits on balloon payments*: None.

*Formula for rebate of unearned interest*: Actuarial method. § 365.140.

*Restrictions on deferral charges*: If all or any part of any installment or installments is deferred for not more than 2 months, the holder may charge a refinance charge computed at a rate permitted on monthly payment contracts, provided that the minimum deferment charge shall be $1. The buyer may also be required to pay the additional cost to the holder of premiums for continuing in force any insurance coverage provided for in the contract and any additional necessary official fees. In any other extension, renewal, restatement or rescheduling of the unpaid balance, the refinance charge may be computed as follows: the sum of the unpaid balance as of the refinancing date and the cost for any insurance and other benefits incidental to the refinancing, any additional necessary official fees, and any accrued delinquency and collection charges, after deducting a refund credit for prepayment, shall constitute a principal balance, the refinance charge may be computed for the term of the refinanced contract at the applicable rate obtained by reclassifying the motor vehicle by its year model at the time of the refinancing. In an agreement to extend or defer the scheduled due dates on a contract with an original amount of $600 or more, and provided the debtor agrees in writing, the holder may collect a fee in advance for allowing the debtor to defer monthly payments as long as the fee on each deferred period is no more than the lesser of $50 or 10% of the payments deferred. However, a minimum fee of $25 is permitted. § 365.130.

*Limits on document fees*: None.

*Restrictions on types of insurance that can be sold*: A buyer may be

required to provide insurance on the motor vehicle at his own cost for the protection of the seller or holder, as well as the buyer, but the insurance shall be limited to insurance against substantial risk of loss, damage or destruction of the motor vehicle. § 365.080(1).
*Single document rule?*: None.
*Assignee liability provision*: None.
*Special provisions for manufactured homes*: None.
*Special provisions for revolving credit*: None.
*Other noteworthy provisions*: None.
*Remedies*: Any person violating specified provisions of the Act shall be barred from recovery of any time price differential, delinquency or collection charge on the contract. § 365.150(2).

**Mont. Code Ann. §§ 31-1-201 to 31-1-243 (Retail Installment Sales Act).**

*Scope*: Installment sales of goods or services by a retail seller to a retail buyer pursuant to a retail charge account agreement or under a retail installment contract. Includes motor vehicles and mobile homes. § 31-1-202.
*Licensure requirements*: Sales finance companies must be licensed. § 31-1-221.
*Credit terms*: The finance charge included in a retail installment contract or a retail charge account agreement must be at a rate agreed upon by the parties, but the finance charge may not exceed 36% per year. § 31-1-241.
*Restrictions on points or prepaid interest*: None.
*Restrictions on length of term*: None.
*Restrictions on prepayment penalties*: None.
*Requirement of substantially equal installments or limits on balloon payments*: None.
*Formula for rebate of unearned interest*: Calculated by Rule of 78s (sum of the balances) method, but no refund of less than $1 need be made, and actuarial method is required if contract term exceeds 61 months. § 31-1-242(3).
*Restrictions on deferral charges*: The holder may compute the charge on the unpaid time balance to be extended, deferred, renewed or restated by adding to the unpaid time balance the cost for any insurance and other benefits incidental to the refinancing plus any accrued delinquency and collection charges, after deducting any refund that may be due the buyer at the rate of the specified finance charge. If all unpaid installments are deferred for not more than 2 months, the holder may charge and collect for the deferment an amount equal to the difference between the refund required for prepayment in full as of the scheduled due date of the first deferred installment and the refund required for prepayment in full as of 1 month prior to the date, times the number of months in which a scheduled payment is not made. § 31-1-243.
*Limits on document fees*: None.
*Restrictions on types of insurance that can be sold*: A buyer may be required to provide insurance on the goods at the buyer's own cost for the protection of the seller or holder as well as the buyer, but the insurance is limited to insurance against substantial risk of loss, damage, or destruction of the goods. § 31-1-233(3).
*Single document rule?*: Each retail installment contract must be in writing, signed by both the buyer and the seller, and completed as to all essential provisions prior to the signing of the contract by the buyer. However, if a retail installment transaction is a sale of goods other than a motor vehicle where title, lien, or other security interest is not retained or taken by the seller, then the retail installment contract is not required to be contained in a single document. § 31-1-231(1).
*Assignee liability provision*: None.
*Special provisions for manufactured homes*: None.
*Special provisions for revolving credit*: None.
*Other noteworthy provisions*: None.
*Remedies*: Any person violating certain specified provisions, except as the result of an accidental and bona fide error of computation, shall be barred from recovery of any finance, delinquency or collection charge on the contract. In addition to other penalties provided by law, a contract made in violation of the finance charge limitations imposed by the Act is a violation of the Consumer Protection Act. § 31-1-203.

**Neb. Rev. Stat. §§ 45-334 to 45-353 (Installment Sales Act).**

*Scope:* Installment sales in which a buyer acquires goods or services from a seller pursuant to an agreement that provides for a time price differential and under which the buyer agrees to pay all or part of the price in one or more installments and within 145 months, except that installment contracts for the purchase of mobile homes may exceed this 145-month limitation. § 45-335.
*Licensure requirements*: Sales finance companies must be licensed. § 45-345(1) A seller that does not otherwise act as a sales finance company is not required to obtain a license, but shall comply with all of the other provisions of the Act in order to charge the authorized time price differential. § 45-345(3).
*Credit terms*: The rate may not exceed 18% per year, except that a minimum time price differential of $10 may be charged on any installment contract. § 45-338.
*Restrictions on points or prepaid interest*: None.
*Restrictions on length of term*: Installment sale defined as one or more installments and within 145 months, except contracts for mobile homes may exceed this 145-month limitation. § 45-335(5).
*Restrictions on prepayment penalties*: None.
*Requirement of substantially equal installments or limits on balloon payments*: None.
*Formula for rebate of unearned interest*: actuarial method, but no rebate of less than $1 need be made. § 45-342.
*Restrictions on deferral charges*: A holder that defers the scheduled payment of any installment payment under the contract may charge a reasonable flat service fee for such deferment in addition to the time price differential calculated for the period of such deferment at the rate originally agreed upon in the contract on the outstanding balance. § 45-351.01.
*Limits on document fees*: None.
*Restrictions on types of insurance that can be sold*: None.
*Single document rule?*: None.
*Assignee liability provision*: None.
*Special provisions for manufactured homes*: None.
*Special provisions for revolving credit*: The seller or assignee under a revolving charge agreement may charge a time price differential that shall not exceed the following rate: 1.75% per month on amounts less than $500, and 1.5% per month on amounts of $500 or more. § 45-207.
*Other noteworthy provisions*: None.
*Remedies*: If any seller or sales finance company contracts for or receives charges in excess of those authorized by the Act except as a result of an accidental and bona fide error, the contract shall be void and uncollectible as to all of the excessive portion of the time price differential, the first $1,000 of the time price differential, and the first $4,000 of the principal of the contract. If any seller or sales finance company violates any provision of the Act, other than the one relating to finance charges, except as a result of an accidental and bona fide error, the contract shall be void and uncollectible as to the first $500 of the time

price differential and the first $1,000 of the principal of the contract. § 45-344.

**Nev. Rev. Stat. §§ 97.015 to 97.335 (Retail Installment Sales of Goods and Services).**

*Scope*: Installment sales of goods for use primarily for personal, family, or household purposes and services of any kind when purchased primarily for personal, family, or household use (other than services for which the price charged is required by law to be determined or approved by a governmental entity). §§ 97.035, 97.135.

*Licensure requirements*: None.

*Credit terms*: For both retail installment contracts and retail charge agreements, the finance charge may be any amount agreed upon by the parties. §§ 97.195, 97.245.

*Restrictions on points or prepaid interest*: None.

*Restrictions on length of term*: Installment sale defined as one or more installments. § 97.115.

*Restrictions on prepayment penalties*: None.

*Requirement of substantially equal installments or limits on balloon payments*: None.

*Formula for rebate of unearned interest*: Appears to be actuarial method. § 97.225.

*Restrictions on deferral charges*: None.

*Limits on document fees*: None.

*Restrictions on types of insurance that can be sold*: None.

*Single document rule?*: Every retail installment contract must be contained in a single document that must contain the entire agreement of the parties, including any promissory notes or other evidences of indebtedness between the parties relating to the transaction, with some exceptions (*see* §§ 97.205 and 97.235). § 97.165.

*Assignee liability provision*: No provision of a retail installment contract or retail charge agreement shall be valid by which the buyer agrees not to assert against the seller or against an assignee a claim or defense arising out of the sale. § 97.275(1).

*Special provisions for manufactured homes*: None.

*Special provisions for revolving credit*: None.

*Other noteworthy provisions*: None.

*Remedies*: A seller who enters into a contract that does not comply with the provisions of the Act or who violates any provision of the Act, except as a result of an accidental or bona fide error, is barred from the recovery of any finance charge, official fees, or any charge for delinquency or collection under or in connection with the related retail installment contract or purchase under a retail charge agreement. However, the seller may nevertheless recover from the buyer an amount equal to the cash price of the goods or services and the cost to the seller of any insurance included in the transaction. § 97.305.

**N.H. Rev. Stat. Ann. §§ 361-A:1 to 361-A:13 (Retail Installment Sales of Motor Vehicles).**

*Scope*: Installment sales of motor vehicles. § 361-A:1.

*Licensure requirements*: Sales finance companies and retail sellers must be licensed. § 361-A:2.

*Credit terms*: The finance charge on any retail installment contract is any amount agreed upon by the buyer and the seller or sales finance company. A minimum finance charge of $25 may be charged on any retail installment transaction. § 361-A:8.

*Restrictions on points or prepaid interest*: None.

*Restrictions on length of term*: Installment sale defined as one or more deferred installments. § 361-A:1(XI).

*Restrictions on prepayment penalties*: A provision that assesses a prepayment penalty on a contract with a term of fewer than 6 years is prohibited and unenforceable. § 361-A:7(IX)(c)(3).

*Requirement of substantially equal installments or limits on balloon payments*: Balloon contracts shall contain a provision requiring the lienholder to accept return of the motor vehicle that secures the balloon loan, without penalty or additional cost, payment, or expense to the buyer in satisfaction of the balloon payment due under the contract. § 361-A:8-a(III)(a). Balloon retail installment contracts shall contain a provision that affords buyers the option to refinance the balloon payment at an annual percentage rate no greater than that under the balloon contract. The creditor's underwriting standards for refinancing a balloon payment shall be substantially identical to those used when the creditor issued a commitment to the borrower to fund the original balloon contract. § 361-A:8-a(V).

*Formula for rebate of unearned interest*: None.

*Restrictions on deferral charges*: None.

*Limits on document fees*: None.

*Restrictions on types of insurance that can be sold*: None.

*Single document rule?*: None.

*Assignee liability provision*: None.

*Special provisions for manufactured homes*: None.

*Special provisions for revolving credit*: None.

*Other noteworthy provisions*: None.

*Remedies*: Any person violating specified provisions or engaging in the business of a sales finance company without a license if a license is required under the Act shall be barred from recovering any finance charge, delinquency or collection charge on the contract. § 361-A:11(III).

**N.J. Stat. Ann. §§ 17:16C-1 to 17:16C-61 (West) (Retail Installment Sales Act).**

*Scope*: Installment sales contracts, other than retail charge accounts, entered into between a retail seller and a retail buyer evidencing an agreement to pay the retail purchase price of goods (having a cash price of $10,000 or less) or services (other than services subject to the Home Repair Financing Act and insurance premiums financing subject to the Insurance Premium Finance Company Act) that are primarily for personal, family, or household purposes. Includes sales of motor vehicles. § 17:16C-1.

*Licensure requirements*: Sales finance companies and motor vehicle installment sellers must be licensed. § 17:16C-2. No retail seller under a contract executed in the state, shall sell, transfer or assign the obligation to any person who is not authorized as a sales finance company pursuant to the provisions of the Act, except that such obligation may be sold, transferred or assigned to a state or national bank outside of the state if the contract is retained by the seller or sales finance company and collection of payments is made to retail seller or sales finance company. § 17:16C-45.

*Credit terms*: Any rate agreed to by the sales finance company and the borrower. § 17:16C-40.1 (loan to purchase motor vehicle). Any rate agreed to by the seller and the buyer. The contract may provide for an increase or decrease in the time price differential. No increase during the entire loan term shall result in an interest rate of more than 6% per year over the rate applicable initially, nor shall the rate be raised more than 3% per year during any 12-month period. The lender shall not be obligated to decrease the interest rate more than 6% over the term of the loan, nor more than 3% per year during any 12-month period. If the time price differential is less than $12, and if the due date of the last installment of the contract is more than 8 months after the contract date, a charge of not more than $12 may be made in lieu of the time price differential. If the time price differential is less than $10, and if the due date of the last installment of the contract is 8 months or less after the contract date, a charge of not more than $10 may be made in lieu of the time price differential. § 17:16C-41 (motor vehicles and on all other goods or services).

*Restrictions on points or prepaid interest*: None.

*Restrictions on length of term*: Installment sale defined as two or more installments. § 17:16C-1(b). A sales finance company may loan to any one person any sum of money up to a maximum of $10,000 secured by a purchase money security interest to finance the purchase of a passenger motor vehicle not intended to be used for the transportation of passengers for hire or upon a contract basis. The principal amount of such loan may be repaid in not more than 48 substantially equal monthly installments. § 17:16C-40.1.

*Restrictions on prepayment penalties*: If the retail installment contract provides that the time price differential may be increased then, when the unpaid balance is paid in full or the maturity of the unpaid balance is accelerated before the date scheduled for the payment of the final installment, the holder shall allow a credit on account of the precomputed time price differential, but a holder may charge a prepayment penalty of not more than $20 on any contract up to and including $2,000, an amount equal to 1% of the loan on any contract greater than $2,000 and up to and including $5,000, and $100 on any contract exceeding $5,000. § 17:16C-41.When the unpaid balance owing upon a precomputed loan to purchase a motor vehicle is repaid in full or the maturity of the unpaid balance of a loan to purchase a motor vehicle is accelerated before the date scheduled for the payment of the final installment, the association shall allow a credit on account of the precomputed interest but if the loan is prepaid within 12 months after the first payment is due, an association may charge a prepayment penalty of not more than $20 on any loan up to and including $2,000, an amount equal to 1% of the loan on any loan greater than $2,000 and up to and including $5,000, and $100 on any loan exceeding $5,000. § 17:16C-40.1 (loan to purchase motor vehicle).

*Requirement of substantially equal installments or limits on balloon payments*: Every retail installment contract shall provide for the payment of the time balance in substantially equal amounts on dates separated by substantially equal payment periods, except that the seller may defer the initial installment for any period of time up to 1 year from the date of the execution of the contract. Also, when appropriate for the purpose of facilitating payment, in accordance with a buyer's intermittent income, a contract may provide for payment on a schedule that reduces or omits payments over a period not in excess of 93 days in any 12-month period or a contract may provide an installment schedule that reduces or omits payments over any period of time during which period or periods the buyer's income is reduced or suspended. § 17:16C-26.

*Formula for rebate of unearned interest*: § 17:16C-43 provides that the rebate upon prepayment of a retail installment contract is to be calculated by the Rule of 78s, but no rebate of less than $1 need be made. However, § 17:16C-41 provides that, starting a year after its enactment in 1981, rebates must be calculated by the actuarial method, but the creditor may charge a prepayment penalty ranging from $20 to $100 depending on the amount of the loan. This same rebate calculation method applies if the contract has an adjustable rate provision. Section 17:16C-40.1 also applies this rebate calculation method to loans to purchase motor vehicles.

*Restrictions on deferral charges*: The holder of a retail installment contract may extend the scheduled due date of a contract and defer the scheduled due date of any or all installment payments, or reduce the amount of any or all installments, and may impose an additional charge. Option 1: The additional charge shall be computed on the amount of the scheduled installment on installments extended, deferred or reduced for the period or periods for which each installment or part thereof is extended, deferred or reduced at the following rates on contracts originally in the respective classifications set forth in § 41 of the Act: Class I—1% per month; Class II—1 1/2 % per month; Class III—2% per month; Class IV—2% per month. Option 2: The holder may renew the entire unpaid balance on any retail installment contract and may make a charge at the rates charged in the original contract from the date of renewal to the maturity of the final installment. The amount of the balance to be renewed shall be obtained by adding to the existing unpaid balance on the original contract the cost of any insurance or other benefits for the period of the extension and any accrued default charges and refunding the unearned portion of the time price differential charged according to the formula provided in the Act, provided that in computing the unearned time price differential charge no allowance shall be taken for the amount of the acquisition cost permitted. § 17:16C-44.

*Limits on document fees*: None.

*Restrictions on types of insurance that can be sold*: Where title to or a lien upon goods sold by the seller is retained or taken by the seller, the buyer may be required to insure the goods at the buyer's expense for the protection of the seller or subsequent holder, and that insurance may be purchased by the holder. Such insurance shall be written for the dual protection of the buyer and the seller or subsequent holder to the extent of his interest in the goods and shall be limited to insurance against substantial risk of damage, destruction, or theft of such goods and shall be upon terms and conditions, which are reasonable and appropriate, considering the type and conditions of such goods. When the buyer fails or is unable to acquire insurance or the seller or subsequent holder is unable to purchase insurance covering the dual protection of the buyer and seller or subsequent holder, the seller or holder may purchase a single interest insurance policy on the goods and may collect the premium from the buyer. § 17:16C-30.

*Single document rule?*: None.

*Assignee liability provision*: No retail installment contract shall contain any provision relieving the holder or other assignee from liability for any civil remedy that the buyer has against the seller. § 17:16C-38.1. Any subsequent holder of a consumer note shall be subject to all claims and defenses of the buyer against the seller arising out of the transaction but no such claim or defense may be asserted against such holder in excess of the time sales price under the contract for any sale, except that, in the case of the sale of a new motor vehicle, no claim or defense may be asserted against such holder in excess of the time balance under the contract. § 17:16C-38.2.

*Special provisions for manufactured homes*: None.

*Special provisions for revolving credit*: Any amount agreed upon by the retail seller, sales finance company, banking institution, or other holder and the buyer. § 17:16C-44.1.

*Other noteworthy provisions*: None.

*Remedies*: Whenever the retail seller, sales finance company or holder has knowingly charged any costs or charges not authorized by the Act, all costs and charges in connection with such contract or account, other than for insurance authorized by the Act, shall be void and unenforceable, and any such costs or charges other than for insurance shall be applied to the unpaid balance or, if the account has been fully paid, remitted to the buyer, who shall be entitled to recover all such costs or charges. § 17:16C-54.

**N.M. Stat. Ann. §§ 56-1-1 to 56-1-16 (Retail Installment Sales).**

*Scope*: Installment sales of goods or services purchased primarily for personal, family, or household use. Includes mobile homes. Does not include motor vehicles. § 56-1-1.
*Licensure requirements*: None.
*Credit terms*: A retail installment contract may provide for a time price differential. No maximum rate specified. § 56-1-2(I). A retail charge agreement may provide for a time price differential for the privilege of paying in installments. No maximum rate specified. § 56-1-3(C).
*Restrictions on points or prepaid interest*: None.
*Restrictions on length of term*: Installment sale defined as one or more installments. § 56-1-1.
*Restrictions on prepayment penalties*: None.
*Requirement of substantially equal installments or limits on balloon payments*: If any installment (except the down payment) is more than double the average of all other installments (except the down payment), the contract must disclose that it is not payable in installments of equal amounts, as well as the amount of every such larger installment and its due date. § 56-1-2(E)(11).
*Formula for rebate of unearned interest*: Rebate is calculated by applying Rule of 78s (sum of the balances method) to original finance charge minus $10, but no rebate of less than $1 need be made. § 56-1-2(J).
*Restrictions on deferral charges*: None.
*Limits on document fees*: None.
*Restrictions on types of insurance that can be sold*: None.
*Single document rule?*: A retail installment contract need not be contained in a single document. § 56-1-2(F).
*Assignee liability provision*: No retail installment contract or retail charge agreement shall contain any provision by which the buyer agrees not to assert against the seller or assignee a claim or defense arising out of the sale. § 56-1-5(F).
*Special provisions for manufactured homes*: "Mobile home" means a structure transportable in one or more sections which is at least eight body feet wide, thirty-two body feet long and which is built on a permanent chassis and designed to be used as a dwelling, with or without a permanent foundation, when connected to the required utilities, and includes the plumbing, heating, air-conditioning, and electrical systems contained in the structure. § 56-1-1(D). A retail installment contract for the purchase of a mobile home may provide that the rate of time price differential may be adjusted at stated intervals, in which case the retail installment contract shall be subject to the following provisions: (A) adjustments in the rate charged shall be based on changes in a specific index, as set forth in the retail installment contract, with the index base being fixed by the index value in effect on the first day of the month in which the retail installment contract is dated. The index may be only an index approved by the federal home loan bank board or by the office of the comptroller of the currency of the department of the treasury for adjustable or variable interest rates on residential mortgage loans; (B) subject to the limitations prescribed by this section, the adjustments to the rate of time price differential on each rate adjustment date, either up or down, shall be equal to the difference between the index value in effect on the first day of the second calendar month preceding the month in which the rate adjustment falls and the index value in effect on the first day of the month in which the retail installment contract is executed; or, for adjustments after the initial adjustment, the adjustment shall be equal to the difference between the index value in effect on the first day of the second calendar month preceding the adjustment date and the index value in effect on the first day of the second calendar month preceding the date of the immediately preceding rate adjustment; (C) for any 6-month period, no rate adjustment may result in a rate of time price differential which is more than one percentage point greater or less than the rate of time price differential in effect in the preceding 6-month period. At no point in time shall the rate of time price differential after adjustment be more than ten percentage points more or less than the rate of time price differential in effect when the retail installment contract was dated; (D) any increase in the rate permitted by this section may be waived at the option of the seller. Any decrease in the rate warranted by decreases in the index is mandatory, subject to the limitations prescribed by this section and by the provisions of Subsection E. If the seller agrees to impose a periodic or aggregate limitation on rate adjustments that is smaller or more restrictive than the limitations prescribed by this section, such limitation shall apply both to increases and decreases; (E) any changes in the index not reflected in adjustments to the rate of time price differential shall be carried over to succeeding rate adjustment periods and be implemented to the extent they are not offset by opposite movements in the index; and (F) adjustments to the rate of time price differential may result in changes in the amount of any installment payment due under the retail installment contract or in changes in the term of the retail installment contract or in a combination of such changes in amount and term. Adjustments to the amount of installment payments may be made less frequently than adjustments to the rate of time price differential. § 56-1-16.
*Special provisions for revolving credit*: A retail charge agreement may provide for a time price differential for the privilege of paying in installments. No maximum rate specified. § 56-1-3(C). The time price differential on a retail charge agreement shall be computed from month to month, or other regular period, on all amounts unpaid under the agreement at the beginning of each such period. The time price differential may be computed for all unpaid balances within a range of not in excess of $10 on the basis of the median amount within such range, if as so computed such time price differential is applied to all unpaid balances within such range. § 56-1-3.
*Other noteworthy provisions*: Payments made on retail charge agreements, open-end contracts or similar types of add-on retail sales agreements shall be first applied to the purchases earliest in time. The payments shall be credited first to the current interest or carrying charges and then in reduction of the purchase price of merchandise in the order in which it was purchased. § 56-1-14.
*Remedies*: Any seller who enters into any contract or agreement that does not comply with the provisions of the Act or who violates any provision of the Act, except as a result of an accidental or bona fide error, shall be barred from the recovery of any time price differential, official fees, or any delinquency or collection charge under or in connection with the agreement. However, the seller may nevertheless recover from the buyer an amount equal to the cash price of the goods or services and the cost to the seller of any insurance included in the transaction. § 56-1-9.

**N.M. Stat. Ann. §§ 58-19-1 to 58-19-14 (Motor Vehicle Sales Finance Act).**

*Scope*: Installment sales of motor vehicles for personal, family, or household purposes, and not for resale. Does not include any motor vehicle having a gross vehicle weight of 10,000 pounds or more purchased primarily for business or commercial purposes. § 58-19-2.
*Licensure requirements*: Sales finance companies must be licensed.

§ 58-19-3. Includes retail sellers engaged in whole or in part in the business of creating and holding retail installment contracts that exceed a total aggregate outstanding indebtedness of $100,000. § 58-19-2(K).

*Credit terms*: No maximum rate specified.

*Restrictions on points or prepaid interest*: None.

*Restrictions on length of term*: Installment sale defined as one or more deferred installments. § 58-19-2.

*Restrictions on prepayment penalties*: None.

*Requirement of substantially equal installments or limits on balloon payments*: None.

*Formula for rebate of unearned interest*: Rebate is calculated by applying Rule of 78s (sum of the balances method), but creditor may retain minimum charge of $25, and no rebate of less than $1 need be made. § 58-19-9.

*Restrictions on deferral charges*: A holder may collect for such extension, deferment, renewal or restatement a refinance charge under either of the following optional methods of computation at the rates indicated as follows: Option 1. In the event one or more installments are extended, deferred or restated, the holder may compute an extension charge on the amount of the installment payment or payments or part thereof which is extended, for the period of time for which each payment, or part thereof is extended, deferred or restated, at the following rates on contracts originally in the respective classification of motor vehicles set forth in the Act: Class 1—1% per month; Class 2—1.5 % per month; Class 3 and 4—2% per month. Option 2. In the event the unpaid time balance of the contract is extended, deferred, renewed or restated, the holder may compute a refinance charge on such amount by adding to the unpaid time balance the cost for insurance and other benefits incidental to the refinancing plus any accrued delinquency and collection charges, and deducting any refund that may be due the buyer by prepayment at the rate of the finance charge specified in the Act and by reclassifying the motor vehicle by its then year model for the term of the refinancing agreement, but otherwise subject to the provisions of the Act governing computation of the original finance charge. The provisions of the Act governing minimum finance charges and acquisition costs under the refund schedule shall not apply in calculating refinance charges on the contract renewed under this method of computation. § 58-19-10.

*Limits on document fees*: None.

*Restrictions on types of insurance that can be sold*: None.

*Single document rule?*: None.

*Assignee liability provision*: None.

*Special provisions for manufactured homes*: None.

*Special provisions for revolving credit*: None.

*Other noteworthy provisions*: None.

*Remedies*: A willful violation of the Act by any person or individual shall bar recovery of the finance charge, delinquency and collection or other charges by the owner or holder of the retail installment contract involved. § 58-19-11.

**N.Y. Pers. Prop. Law §§ 401 to 422 (McKinney) (Retail Installment Sales Act).**

*Scope*: Installment sales of goods (but not motor vehicles) for other than a commercial or business use or for purpose of resale, and services for other than a commercial or business use and other than services for which tariffs or rates are required by law to be filed with or determined or approved by a governmental entity. Revolving credit. § 401.

*Licensure requirements*: None.

*Credit terms*: Rate agreed to by the buyer. § 404(1).

*Restrictions on points or prepaid interest*: None.

*Restrictions on length of term*: None.

*Restrictions on prepayment penalties*: If the credit service charge imposed on the contract or obligation is computed pursuant to § 404(4) (described below), the contract or obligation may be prepaid in full without penalty. § 408(2). Section 404(4) provides that a credit service charge may be calculated on the unpaid principal balances of the contract for the time each is outstanding according to a generally accepted actuarial method at rates that may vary from time to time and in accordance with the provisions of the contract or obligation. On any contract or obligation with a variable rate credit service charge made pursuant to this subdivision, each rate shall be determined at regular intervals as set forth in the contract or obligation and in accordance with such regulations as the superintendent of financial services shall prescribe but said rate shall not vary more often than once in any 3-month period and shall be based on a published index that is (a) readily available, (b) independently verifiable, (c) beyond the control of the holder, and (d) approved by the superintendent. § 404(4).

*Requirement of substantially equal installments or limits on balloon payments*: If any installment substantially exceeds any prior installment other than the down payment, the contract must disclose that it is not payable in equal installments, as well as the amount of every larger installment and its due date. § 402(3)(b)(2).

*Formula for rebate of unearned interest*: The amount of the refund credit shall be determined according to a generally acceptable actuarial method. If the credit service charge imposed on the contract or obligation is computed pursuant to § 404(4) (actuarial rates), the contract or obligation may be prepaid in full without penalty. § 408(2). Where the amount of the credit is less than $1, no refund need be made. The statute provides that the seller may retain at least the minimum credit service charge applicable, but it appears that the act no longer addresses minimum service charges. § 408(3).

*Restrictions on deferral charges*: The holder may contract for the payment of an extension or deferral charge by the buyer at the rate agreed to by the parties on the amount of the installment or installments, or part thereof, extended or deferred for the period of extension or deferral. Such period shall not exceed the period from the date when such extended or deferred installment or installments, or part thereof, would have been payable in the absence of such extension or deferral, to the date when such installment or installments, or part thereof, are made payable under the agreement of extension or deferment; except that a minimum charge of $1 for the period of extension or deferral may be made in any case where the extension or deferral charge amounts to less than $1. Such agreement may also provide for the payment by the buyer of the additional cost to the holder of premiums for continuing in force, until the end of such period of extension or deferral, any insurance coverage provided for in the contract or obligation. § 409(1).

*Limits on document fees*: None.

*Restrictions on types of insurance that can be sold*: None.

*Single document rule?*: All terms need not be contained in a single document, but if they are not then there shall be an original document executed by the parties containing provisions making it applicable to purchases of goods or services, which may not exceed a cash sale price of $175 on each purchase, to be made by the buyer from time to time from a retail seller. This document, together with other written statements relating to the sale of goods or services, shall constitute a retail installment obligation and shall contain the entire agreement of the parties. § 402(7).

*Assignee liability provision*: No contract or obligation shall contain any provision by which the buyer agrees not to assert against an assignee a claim or defense arising out of the sale, but it may contain such a provision as to an assignee who acquires the contract or obligation on the sale of a boat where the principal balance at the time of sale exceeds $5,000, and to whom the buyer has not mailed written notice of the facts giving rise to the claim or defense within 10 days after such assignee mails to the buyer notice of the assignment. § 403(2)(a). Except as provided in the foregoing, the assignee shall be subject to all claims and defenses of the buyer against the seller arising from the sale notwithstanding any agreement to the contrary, but the assignee's liability shall not exceed the amount owing to the assignee at the time the claim or defense is asserted against the assignee. § 403(4).
*Special provisions for manufactured homes*: None.
*Special provisions for revolving credit*: A seller may, in a retail installment credit agreement, collect a service charge that shall not exceed the rate agreed upon by the seller and the buyer, including rates that may vary, from time to time computed on the outstanding indebtedness from month to month, or if the service charge is less than $0.70 for any month, $0.70. If the credit agreement provides for a variable rate of service charge, such rate shall be determined at regular intervals as set forth in the credit agreement and in accordance with such regulations as the superintendent of financial services shall prescribe, but said rate shall not vary more often than once in any 3-month period and shall be based on a published index that is (a) readily available, (b) independently verifiable, (c) beyond the control of the seller, and (d) approved by the superintendent, (e) such charges in credit agreements shall be based on the index values, or the index numbers plus or minus additional percentage points provided, however, that variations in the charge must correspond directly to the movements of the index values plus or minus additional percentage points only. If the credit agreement so provides, the service charge may be computed on a schedule of fixed amounts if as so computed it is applied to all amounts of outstanding balances equal to the fixed amount minus a differential of not more than $5, provided that it is also applied to all amounts of outstanding balances equal to the fixed amount plus at least the same differential. § 413
*Other noteworthy provisions*: None.
*Remedies*: In case of failure by any person to comply with the provisions of the Act, the buyer shall have the right to recover an amount equal to the credit service charge or service charge imposed and the amount of any delinquency, collection, extension, deferral, or refinance charge imposed. § 414(2).

**N.Y. Pers. Prop. Law §§ 301 to 316 (McKinney) (Motor Vehicle Retail Installment Sales Act).**

*Scope*: Installment sales, other than for a commercial or business use or for the purpose of resale, of a motor vehicle by a retail seller to a retail buyer. Includes "mobile home" or "manufactured home." § 301.
*Licensure requirements*: None.
*Credit terms*: Rate agreed to by the seller and buyer. § 303(1).
*Restrictions on points or prepaid interest*: None.
*Restrictions on length of term*: Installment sale defined as two or more installments. § 301.
*Restrictions on prepayment penalties*: If the service charge imposed on the contract is computed pursuant to § 303(4) (described below), the contract may, after deduction of the acquisition cost of $15, be prepaid in full without penalty. § 305(1). Section 303(4) provides that a seller may collect a service charge calculated on the unpaid balances for the time outstanding according to a generally accepted actuarial method at rates that may vary from time to time and in accordance with the provisions of the contract. On any contract with a variable rate credit service charge made pursuant to this subdivision the rate shall be determined at regular intervals as set forth in the contract and in accordance with such regulations as the superintendent of financial services shall prescribe but said rate shall not vary more often than once in any 3-month period and shall be based on a published index that is (a) readily available, (b) independently verifiable, (c) beyond the control of the retail seller and (d) approved by the superintendent. § 303(4).
*Requirement of substantially equal installments or limits on balloon payments*: None.
*Formula for rebate of unearned interest*: Calculated by applying actuarial method to original finance charge, but creditor may retain an acquisition charge of $15 and no refund of less than $1 need be made. Interest bearing contracts may be prepaid in full without penalty, after deducting an acquisition charge of $15. § 305(1).
*Restrictions on deferral charges*: The holder may contract for the payment of an extension or deferred charge at the rate agreed to by the parties on the amount of the installment or installments, or part thereof, extended or deferred for the period of extension or deferral. Such period shall not exceed the period from the date when such extended or deferred installment or installments, or part thereof, would have been payable in the absence of such extension or deferral, to the date when such installment or installments, or part thereof, are made payable under the agreement of extension or deferment; except that a minimum charge of $1 for the period of extension or deferral may be made in any case where the extension or deferral charge amounts to less than $1. Such agreement may also provide for the payment by the buyer of the additional cost to the holder of the contract of premiums for continuing in force, until the end of such period of extension or deferral, any insurance coverage provided for in the contract. § 306(1).
*Limits on document fees*: None.
*Restrictions on types of insurance that can be sold*: None.
*Single document rule?*: None.
*Assignee liability provision*: No retail installment contract shall contain any provision by which the buyer agrees not to assert against an assignee a claim or defense arising out of the sale, or require the execution of any note that would will cut off as to third parties any right of action or defense that the buyer may have against the seller. The assignee of a retail installment contract or obligation shall be subject to all claims and defenses of the buyer against the seller arising from the sale notwithstanding any agreement to the contrary, but the assignee's liability shall not exceed the amount owing to the assignee at the time the claim or defense is asserted against the assignee. § 302(9).
*Special provisions for manufactured homes*: None.
*Special provisions for revolving credit*: None.
*Other noteworthy provisions*: None.
*Remedies*: A willful violation of certain specified provisions of the Act by any person shall bar his recovery of any credit service charge, delinquency or collection charge or refinancing charge on the contract involved. § 307(2).

**N.C. Gen. Stat. §§ 25A-1 to 25A-45 (Retail Installment Sales Act).**

*Scope*: Consumer credit sales of goods and services (but not those for which the cost is by law fixed, approved by or filed with a governmental entity) purchased primarily for a personal, family, household or agricultural purpose. The amount financed may not exceed $75,000, except that there is no maximum limit for manufactured homes. §§ 25A-1, 25A-2.

*Licensure requirements*: None.

*Credit terms*: The finance charge rate for a consumer credit installment sales contract may not exceed: 24% per year where the amount financed is less than $1,500; 22% where the amount financed is $1,500 or greater but less than $2,000; 20% where the amount financed is $2,000 or greater but less than $3,000; 18% where the amount financed is $3,000 or greater. A minimum finance charge of $5 may be imposed. § 25A-15(b). For installment sales of motor vehicles, a finance charge rate not to exceed the higher of the rate established above or the rate set forth below may be imposed in a contract repayable in six or more installments: 18% per year for vehicles one and two model years old; 20% per year for vehicles three model years old; 22% for vehicles four model years old; and 29% for vehicles five model years old and older. § 25A-15(c). If the amount financed in a consumer credit sale contract is secured in whole or in part by a security interest in real property, the finance charge rate may not exceed 16%. § 25A-15(d). With respect to installment sales of manufactured homes, a finance charge may be imposed as agreed upon by the parties. § 25A-15(f). A "manufactured home" is a structure, transportable in one or more sections, which in the traveling mode is eight body feet or more in width, or 40 body feet or more in length, or, when erected on site, is 320 or more square feet; and which is built on a permanent chassis and designed to be used as a dwelling, with or without permanent foundation when connected to the required utilities, including the plumbing, heating, air conditioning, and electrical systems contained therein. "Manufactured home" also includes any structure that meets all of these requirements except the size requirements and with respect to which the manufacturer voluntarily files a certification required by the Secretary of HUD and complies with the standards established under the Act. § 143-145(7).

*Restrictions on points or prepaid interest*: None.

*Restrictions on length of term*: Debt payable in installments is defined as more than four installments, excluding a down payment. § 25A-3. A consumer credit installment sale contract shall provide for complete payment of all charges due under the contract within a period from the time of the sale of: 42 months, if the amount financed is less than $1,500; 64 months, if the amount financed is $1,500 or greater but less than $2,500; 122 months, if the amount financed is $2,500 or greater but less than $5,000; 182 months, if the amount financed is $5,000 or greater but less than $10,000; or as the contract provides, if the amount financed is $10,000 or greater. § 25A-33.

*Restrictions on prepayment penalties*: None.

*Requirement of substantially equal installments or limits on balloon payments*: For a consumer credit sale, other than one pursuant to a revolving charge account, no scheduled payment may be more than 10% (except the final payment may be 25%) larger than the average payments. This restriction does not apply when the payment schedule is adjusted to the seasonal or irregular income of the buyer. § 25A-34.

*Formula for rebate of unearned interest*: Calculated by Rule of 78s (sum of the balances method), but no refund of less than $1 need be made. § 25A-32. Actuarial method is required for installment sale contract of $5000 or more secured by real estate or a residential manufactured home. § 25A-32.1.

*Restrictions on deferral charges*: A deferral agreement may provide for a deferral charge not to exceed the rate of 1.5% of each installment for each month from the date that such installment or part thereof would otherwise have been payable to the date when such installment or part thereof is made payable under the deferral agreement. § 25A-30(c).

*Limits on document fees*: None.

*Restrictions on types of insurance that can be sold*: For consumer credit installment sale contracts, a seller may contract for additional charges or premiums (i) for insurance written in connection with any consumer credit sale, for loss of or damage to property or against liability arising out of the ownership or use of property, provided a clear, conspicuous, and specific statement in writing is furnished by the seller setting forth the cost of the insurance if obtained from or through the seller and stating that the buyer may choose the person through which the insurance is to be obtained; (ii) for credit life, credit accident and health, or credit unemployment insurance, written in connection with any consumer credit sale, provided the insurance coverage is not required by the seller and this fact is clearly and conspicuously disclosed in writing to the buyer; and any buyer desiring such insurance coverage gives specific dated and separately signed affirmative written indication of such desire after receiving written disclosure of the cost of such insurance. § 25A-17(3). For revolving charge account contracts, a seller may contract for additional charges or premiums (i) for insurance written in connection with any consumer credit sale, against loss of or damage to property securing the debt, provided a clear, conspicuous, and specific statement in writing is furnished by the seller to the buyer setting forth the cost of the insurance if obtained from or through the seller and stating that the buyer may choose the insurer through which the insurance is obtained; (ii) for credit life, credit accident and health, or credit unemployment insurance, written in connection with any consumer credit sale, provided the insurance coverage is not required by the seller and this fact is clearly disclosed to the buyer, and any buyer desiring such insurance coverage gives affirmative indication of such desire after disclosure of the cost of such insurance. § 25A-17(a).

*Single document rule?*: None.

*Assignee liability provision*: In a consumer credit sale, a buyer may assert against the seller, assignee or other holder any claims or defenses available against the original seller, and the buyer may not waive the right to assert these claims or defenses in connection with a transaction. Affirmative recovery by the buyer on a claim asserted against an assignee or other holder shall not exceed amounts paid by the buyer under the contract. Every consumer credit sale contract shall contain a notice to this effect. § 25A-25.

*Special provisions for manufactured homes*: With respect to installment sales of manufactured homes, a finance charge may be imposed as agreed upon by the parties. § 25A-15(f). A "manufactured home" is a structure, transportable in one or more sections, which in the traveling mode is eight body feet or more in width, or 40 body feet or more in length, or, when erected on site, is 320 or more square feet; and which is built on a permanent chassis and designed to be used as a dwelling, with or without permanent foundation when connected to the required utilities, including the plumbing, heating, air conditioning, and electrical systems contained therein. "Manufactured home" also includes any structure that meets all of these requirements except the size requirements and with respect to which the manufacturer voluntarily files a certification required by the Secretary of HUD and complies with the standards established under the Act. § 143-145(7).

*Special provisions for revolving credit*: On the extension of credit under an open-end credit or similar plan under which no service charge shall be imposed upon the consumer or debtor if the account is paid in full within 25 days from the billing date, but upon which there may be imposed an annual charge not to exceed $24, there may be charged and collected interest, finance charges, or other fees at a rate in the aggregate not to exceed 1.5% per month computed on the unpaid portion of the balance of the previous month. If the lender chooses not to impose an annual charge, the lender may impose a service charge not to exceed $2 per month on the balance of any account not paid in full within 25 days from the billing date. No entity may charge a discount or fee in excess of 6% of the principal amount of the accounts acquired from or through any vendors or others providing services who participate in such plan. §§ 25A-14 and 24-11.

*Other noteworthy provisions*: None.

*Remedies*: If a consumer credit sale contract requires the payment of a finance charge not more than two times in excess of that permitted by the Act, the seller or an assignee shall not be permitted to recover any finance charge and, in addition, the seller shall be liable to the buyer in an amount that is two times the amount of any finance charge that has been received by the seller, plus reasonable attorney fees. However, if the requirement of an excess charge results from an accidental or good faith error, the seller shall be liable only for the amount by which the finance charge exceeds the permitted rates. § 25A-44(1). If a consumer credit sale contract requires the payment of a finance charge more than two times that permitted by the Act, the contract shall be void. The buyer may, at his option, retain without any liability any goods delivered under such a contract and the seller or assignee shall not be entitled to recover anything. § 25A-44(2). If the seller or assignee fails to make any required rebates, or charges fees in excess of those specifically authorized by the Act, the buyer shall be entitled to demand and receive the rebate due and excessive or unauthorized charges. If the seller does not provide the rebate or refund within the 10-day period, the seller shall be liable to the buyer for an amount equal to three times the sum of any rebate due and all improper charges that have not been rebated or refunded. § 25A-44(3). A knowing and willful violation of any provision of the Act is a UDAP violation. § 25A-44(4).

**N.D. Cent. Code §§ 51-13-01 to 51-13-08 (Retail Installment Sales Act).**

*Scope*: Installment sales of personal property not for purpose of resale by a retail seller to a retail buyer. § 51-13-01. The Act does not apply if the cash price of the personal property exceeds $25,000 or if the personal property is to be used primarily for a business, commercial or agricultural purpose rather than a personal, family, or household purpose. § 51-13-06.2.

*Licensure requirements*: None.

*Credit terms*: Mo maximum rate specified. § 51-13-03.

*Restrictions on points or prepaid interest*: None.

*Restrictions on length of term*: Installment sale defined as one or more deferred payments. § 51-13-01.

*Restrictions on prepayment penalties*: None.

*Requirement of substantially equal installments or limits on balloon payments*: If any installment substantially exceeds any prior installment other than the down payment, the contract must disclose that it is not payable in equal installments, as well as the amount of every larger installment and its due date. § 51-13-02(11). If any payment under a contract is more than twice the amount of an otherwise regularly scheduled equal payment, the seller shall identify it by the term "balloon payment." § 51-13-02(12).

*Formula for rebate of unearned interest*: Calculated by simple interest method, using the annual percentage rate disclosed under federal law to the nearest 0.25%. For a contract in which the amount financed is not more than $10,000, an acquisition cost of $15 may be deducted from the refund. A refund is not required if it is less than $1. § 51-13-05.

*Restrictions on deferral charges*: None.

*Limits on document fees*: None.

*Restrictions on types of insurance that can be sold*: None.

*Single document rule?*: None.

*Assignee liability provision*: None.

*Special provisions for manufactured homes*: None.

*Special provisions for revolving credit*: Rate agreed to by the parties. § 51-14-03 (revolving charge accounts).

*Other noteworthy provisions*: None.

*Remedies*: A willful violation of specified provisions of the Act by any person bars that person's recovery of any finance, delinquency or collection charge on the contract. § 51-13-07.

**Ohio Rev. Code Ann. §§ 1317.01 to 1317.99 (West) (Retail Installment Sales).**

*Scope*: Installment sales of goods purchased primarily for personal, family, or household purposes and not for resale. § 1317.01. The base finance and service charge must exceed the sum of $15. § 1317.06(A)(2).

*Licensure requirements*: None.

*Credit terms*: A seller may charge a finance charge that shall not exceed the greater of the following: (1) a base finance charge at the rate of $8 per $100 per year on the principal balance. In addition to the base finance charge, the seller may charge a service charge of $0.50 per month for the first fifty dollar unit or fraction thereof, of the principal balance for each month of the term, plus an additional service charge of $0.25 per month for each of the next five fifty dollar units or fraction thereof of the principal balance for each month of the contract's term. This provision applies only to contracts with a principal balance of $700 or less. OR (2) a pre-computed base finance charge not in excess of the amount obtained by applying the rate of 1.5% per month to the unpaid portion of the unpaid principal balance from time to time according to the terms and schedule of payments of the contract. § 1317.06(A)(1). Alternatively, a seller may charge any rate or rates agreed to by the parties, but not exceeding an annual percentage rate of 25%. § 1317.061.

*Restrictions on points or prepaid interest*: None.

*Restrictions on length of term*: None.

*Restrictions on prepayment penalties*: None.

*Requirement of substantially equal installments or limits on balloon payments*: None.

*Formula for rebate of unearned interest*: Rebate is calculated by applying Rule of 78s (sum of the balances method) to original finance charge minus $10, but no rebate of less than $1 need be made § 1317.09.

*Restrictions on deferral charges*: None.

*Limits on document fees*: None.

*Restrictions on types of insurance that can be sold*: None.

*Single document rule?*: None.

*Assignee liability provision*: A buyer may assert against any holder, assignee or transferee, specifically including any holder in due course, any defense that the buyer may assert against the seller that is authorized by the Act. § 1317.031.

*Special provisions for manufactured homes*: None.

*Special provisions for revolving credit*: A seller or holder under a revolving budget agreement may charge a finance charge that shall not exceed the sum obtained by applying to the unpaid balance, including any arrearages of finance charges, at the beginning or end of each period, or upon the average daily balance during each period, a finance charge at a rate not exceeding 1.5% per month. If the finance charge is less than $1 for any such monthly period, the seller or holder may nevertheless charge $1 for such month's charges. § 1317.11.

*Other noteworthy provisions*: Payments received by the seller upon a revolving charge account are deemed, for the purpose of determining the amount of the debt secured by the various security interests, to have been applied first to the payment of credit service charges in the order of their entry to the account and then to the payment of debts in the order in which the entries to the account showing the debts were made. § 1317.071.

*Remedies*: If charges greater in amount than those provided for in Act are contracted for or received by the seller, assignee or successor in interest, the buyer may recover the total amount of finance charges paid in excess of the interest rate that otherwise would apply under § 1343.01 (maximum rate of interest provision). § 1317.08(D).

**Okla. Stat. tit. 14A, §§ 2-201 to 9-101 (Oklahoma Uniform Consumer Credit Code).**

*Scope*: Consumer credit sales, including home solicitation sales, consumer leases, and consumer loans. § 2-102. "Consumer credit sale" is a sale of goods, services or an interest in land in which the goods, services or interest in land are purchased primarily for a personal, family, or household purpose, either the debt is payable in installments or a credit service charge is made, and the amount financed in a sale of goods or services does not exceed $45,000. § 2-104.

*Licensure requirements*: Supervised lenders must be licensed. § 3-502.

*Credit terms*: For consumer credit sales, other than pursuant to a revolving charge account, a seller may receive a credit service charge, calculated according to the actuarial method, not exceeding the equivalent of the greater of either of the following:(a) the total of 30% per year on that part of the unpaid balance that is $300 or less, 21% per year on that part of the unpaid balance that is more than $300 but does not exceed $1,000, and 15% per year on that part of the unpaid balance that is more than $1,000, or the seller may charge 21% per year on the unpaid balance of the amount financed. § 2-201(2). The seller may receive a minimum credit service charge of not more than $5 when the amount financed does not exceed $75 or not more than $7.50 when the amount financed exceeds $75. § 2-201(6).

*Restrictions on points or prepaid interest*: None.

*Restrictions on length of term*: Supervised loans, not made pursuant to a revolving loan account, in which the principal is $1,000 or less and the rate of the loan finance charge calculated according to the actuarial method exceeds 18% on the unpaid balances of the principal shall be scheduled to be payable in substantially equal installments at equal periodic intervals except to the extent that the schedule of payments is adjusted to the seasonal or irregular income of the debtor, and (a) over a period of not more than 49 months if the principal is more than $300; or (b) over a period of not more than 37 months if the principal is $300 or less. § 3-511.

*Restrictions on prepayment penalties*: The buyer may prepay in full the unpaid balance of a consumer credit sale, refinancing or consolidation at any time without penalty. § 2-209.

*Requirement of substantially equal installments or limits on balloon payments*: For a consumer credit sale, other than one pursuant to a revolving charge account, if any scheduled payment is more than twice as large as the average scheduled payment, the buyer has the right to refinance that payment at the time it is due without penalty. The terms of the refinancing shall be no less favorable to the buyer than the terms of the original sale. These provisions do not apply to the extent that the payment schedule is adjusted to the seasonal or irregular income of the buyer. § 2-405.

*Formula for rebate of unearned interest*: For contracts of more than 61 months, calculated by actuarial method. Otherwise, calculated by Rule of 78s (sum of the balances method), but no portion of closing costs paid to third parties in connection with the sale of land or a credit sale secured by land need be rebated, and creditor may retain any permitted minimum finance charge contracted for. § 2-210.

*Restrictions on deferral charges*: With respect to a precomputed consumer credit sale, refinancing or consolidation, the seller may collect a charge not exceeding the rate previously stated to the buyer applied to the amount or amounts deferred for the period of deferral calculated without regard to differences in lengths of months, but proportionally for a part of a month, counting each day as 1/30 of a month. § 2-204(3).

*Limits on document fees*: None.

*Restrictions on types of insurance that can be sold*: A creditor may not contract for or receive a separate charge for insurance against loss of or damage to property unless the insurance covers a substantial risk of loss of or damage to property related to the credit transaction, the amount, terms, and conditions of the insurance are reasonable in relation to the character and value of the property insured or to be insured, and the term of the insurance is reasonable in relation to the terms of credit. The term of insurance is reasonable if it is customary and does not extend substantially beyond a scheduled maturity. § 4-301. A creditor may not contract for or receive a separate charge for insurance against liability unless the insurance covers a substantial risk of liability arising out of the ownership or use of property related to the credit transaction. § 4-303.

*Single document rule?*: None.

*Assignee liability provision*: An agreement by the buyer not to assert against an assignee a claim or defense arising out of the sale is enforceable only by an assignee not related to the seller who acquires the buyer's contract in good faith and for value, who gives the buyer notice of the assignment as provided in the statute, and who, within 30 days after the mailing of the notice of assignment, receives no written notice of the facts giving rise to the buyer's claim or defense. This agreement is enforceable only with respect to claims or defenses that have arisen before the end of the 30-day period after notice was mailed. The notice of assignment shall be in writing and must contain a conspicuous notice to the buyer that he has 30 days within which to notify the assignee in writing of any complaints, claims or defenses he may have against the seller and that if written notification of the complaints, claims or defenses is not received by the assignee within the 30-day period, the assignee will have the right to enforce the contract free of any claims or defenses the buyer may have against the seller that have arisen before the end of the 30-day period after notice was mailed. § 2-404(1). An assignee does not acquire a buyer's contract in good faith if the assignee has knowledge or, from his course of dealing with the seller or his records, notice of substantial complaints by other buyers of the seller's failure or refusal to perform his contracts with them and of the seller's failure to remedy his defaults within a reasonable time after the assignee notifies him of the complaints. § 2-404(2). To the extent that an assignee is subject to claims or defenses of the buyer against the seller, the assignee's liability may not exceed the amount owing to the assignee at the time the claim or defense is asserted against the assignee, and rights of the buyer under this section can only be asserted as a matter of defense to or setoff against a claim by the assignee. § 2-404(3).

*Special provisions for manufactured homes*: None.

*Special provisions for revolving credit*: A charge may be made in each billing cycle that is a percentage of an amount no greater than: (a) the average daily balance of the account; (b) the unpaid balance of the account on the same day of the billing cycle; or (c) the median amount within a specified range within which the average daily balance of the account or the unpaid balance of the account on the same day of the billing cycle is included. A charge may be made pursuant to this paragraph only if the seller makes the same charge on all balances within the specified range and if the percentage when applied to the median amount within the range does not produce a charge exceeding the charge resulting from applying that percentage to the lowest amount within the range by more than 8% of the charge on the median amount. § 2-207(2) If the billing cycle is monthly, the charge may not exceed 1.75%. If the billing cycle is not monthly, the maximum charge is that percentage that bears the same relation to the applicable monthly percentage as the number of days in the billing cycle bears to thirty. § 2-207(3). Notwithstanding the foregoing, if there is an unpaid balance on the date as of which the credit service charge is applied, the seller may receive a charge not exceeding $0.50, if the billing cycle is monthly or longer, or the pro rata part of $0.50 that bears the same relation to $0.50 as the number of days in the billing cycle bears to thirty if the billing cycle is shorter than monthly. § 2-207(4).

*Other noteworthy provisions*: None.

*Remedies*: If a creditor violates the provisions of the Act relating to limitations on the schedule of payments or loan term for supervised loans (§ 3-512), the debtor is not obligated to pay the credit service charge or loan finance charge and has a right to recover from the person or from an assignee of that person's rights who undertakes direct collection of payments or enforcement of rights arising from the debt a penalty in an amount determined by the court not in excess of three times the amount of the credit service charge or loan finance charge. § 5-202(1). If a creditor violates the provisions of the Act relating to authority to make supervised loans (§ 3-502), the loan is void and the debtor is not obligated to pay either the principal or loan finance charge. If the buyer has paid any part of the principal or of the loan finance charge, he has a right to recover the payment from the person or from an assignee of that person's rights who undertakes direct collection of payments or enforcement of rights arising from the debt. § 5-202(2). A debtor is not obligated to pay a charge in excess of that allowed by the Act, and a debtor who has paid an excess charge has a right to a refund. If the debtor has paid an amount in excess of the lawful obligation, the debtor may recover the excess amount from the person who made the excess charge or from an assignee. § 5-202(4). If a debtor is entitled to a refund and a person liable to the debtor refuses to make a refund within a reasonable time after demand, the debtor may recover a penalty in an amount determined by a court not exceeding the greater of either the amount of the credit service charge or ten times the amount of the excess charge. If the creditor has made an excess charge in deliberate violation of or in reckless disregard for the Act, the penalty may be recovered even though the creditor has refunded the excess charge. § 5-202(5). In any case in which it is found that a creditor has violated the Act, the court may award reasonable attorney fees. § 5-202(9).

**Or. Rev. Stat. §§ 83.010 to 83.190 (Retail Installment Contracts).**

*Scope*: Installment sales of goods, other than motor vehicles, for personal, family, or household use, and services purchased primarily for personal, family, or household use but not including services for which the price charged is required by law to be determined, approved by or filed with a governmental entity. Revolving credit. § 83.010.

*Licensure requirements*: None.

*Credit terms*: A retail seller in a retail installment contract may contract for a service charge computed by the actuarial method. No maximum rate specified. § 83.095.

*Restrictions on points or prepaid interest*: None.

*Restrictions on length of term*: Installment sale defined as one or more installments. § 53.010(9).

*Restrictions on prepayment penalties*: None.

*Requirement of substantially equal installments or limits on balloon payments*: None.

*Formula for rebate of unearned interest*: Actuarial method. However, creditor may retain 10% of amount financed or $75, whichever is less, and no rebate of less than $2 need be made. § 83.130.

*Restrictions on deferral charges*: None.

*Limits on document fees*: None.

*Restrictions on types of insurance that can be sold*: None.

*Single document rule?*: Every retail installment contract shall be contained in a single document that shall contain the entire agreement of the parties including any promissory notes or other evidences of indebtedness between the parties relating to the transaction, with some exceptions (*see* §§ 83.040, 83.050 and 83.140). § 83.020(1).

*Assignee liability provision*: No provision of a retail installment contract or retail charge agreement shall be valid by which the buyer agrees not to assert against the seller or against an assignee a claim or defense arising out of the sale. § 83.150.

*Special provisions for manufactured homes*: None.

*Special provisions for revolving credit*: None.

*Other noteworthy provisions*: None.

*Remedies*: Any seller who enters into any contract or agreement that does not comply with the provisions of the Act or who violates any provision of the Act except as a result of an accidental or bona fide error shall be barred from the recovery of any service charge, official fees or any delinquency or collection charge in connection with the related installment contract or purchases under a retail charge agreement. However, the seller may nevertheless recover from the buyer an amount equal to the cash price of the goods or services and the cost to the seller of any insurance included in the transaction. § 83.170.

**Or. Rev. Stat. §§ 83.510 to 83.680 (Retail Installment Contracts—Motor Vehicles; Mobile Homes).**

*Scope*: Installment sales of motor vehicles not for resale. § 83.510.

*Licensure requirements*: None.

*Credit terms*: A dealer may contract for a finance charge agreed upon by the parties. No maximum rate specified. § 83.560.

*Restrictions on points or prepaid interest*: None.

*Restrictions on length of term*: Installment sale defined as one or more installments. § 83.510(12)(a).

*Restrictions on prepayment penalties*: None.

*Requirement of substantially equal installments or limits on balloon payments*: None.

*Formula for rebate of unearned interest*: Actuarial method. However, creditor may retain 10% of amount financed or $75, whichever is less, and no rebate of less than $2 need be made. § 83.620.

*Restrictions on deferral charges*: In the case of an extension of the due date or a deferral of the scheduled payment of all or part of any installment or installments, the holder may restate the amount of the installments and the time schedule, and collect as a refinance charge a flat service fee not to exceed $15 and a total additional charge on the balance being extended not exceeding an amount equal to 1/12 of the annual percentage rate originally charged on the agreement for each month the payments on the agreement are being extended or deferred. § 83.630.

*Limits on document fees*: None.
*Restrictions on types of insurance that can be sold*: None.
*Single document rule?*: None.
*Assignee liability provision*: No retail installment contract shall require or entail the execution by the buyer of any note or series of notes that will cut off as against third parties any right of action or defense that the buyer may have against the dealer. § 83.650.
*Special provisions for manufactured homes*: None.
*Special provisions for revolving credit*: None.
*Other noteworthy provisions*: None.
*Remedies*: None.

**69 Pa. Stat. Ann. §§ 1101 to 2303 (West) (Goods and Services Installment Sales Act).**

*Scope*: Installment contracts for all goods purchased for personal, family, or household use, except motor vehicles and home improvement goods, and services or other than a commercial or business use. Revolving credit. § 1201.
*Licensure requirements*: None.
*Credit terms*: Rate agreed upon by seller or holder and buyer, except for gasoline credit card issuers, who may charge no more than 15% simple interest per year. A minimum service charge of $0.50 per month may be made for each month if the service charge is less than that amount; minimum service charge may be imposed for a minimum period of 6 months. § 1501.

*Restrictions on points or prepaid interest*: None.
*Restrictions on length of term*: None.
*Restrictions on prepayment penalties*: None.
*Requirement of substantially equal installments or limits on balloon payments*: If a contract provides for the payment of any installment that is more than double the amount of the average of the preceding installments, the buyer, upon default of this installment, shall be given an absolute right to obtain a new payment schedule. Unless agreed to by the buyer, the periodic payments under the new schedule shall not be greater than the average of the preceding installments. § 1703.
*Formula for rebate of unearned interest*: Actuarial method, but creditor may retain at least the minimum charge allowed by statute, and no rebate of less than $1 need be made. § 1603.
*Restrictions on deferral charges*: The charge may not exceed 1% per month simple interest on the amount of the installment or installments, or part thereof, extended or deferred for the period of extension or deferral. Such period shall not exceed the period from the date when such extended or deferred installment or installments, or part thereof, would have been payable in the absence of such extension or deferral, to the date when such installment or installments, or part thereof, are made payable under the agreement of extension or deferment A minimum charge of $1 for the period of extension or deferral may be made in any case where the extension or deferral charge amounts to less than $1. Agreement may also provide for the payment of the additional cost to the holder of the contract or premiums for continuing in force, until the end of such period of extension or deferral, any insurance coverage provided for in the contract, § 1701.

*Limits on document fees*: None.
*Restrictions on types of insurance that can be sold*: None.
*Single document rule?*: If a retail installment sale has a cash sale price of $50 or less, then the contract need not be contained in a single document. § 1309.
*Assignee liability provision*: The following provision in at least ten-point, boldface type must be included in the contract: "Any holder of this consumer credit contract is subject to all claims and defenses which the debtor could assert against the seller of goods or services obtained pursuant hereto or with the proceeds hereof. Recovery hereunder by the debtor shall not exceed amount paid by the debtor hereunder." § 1303(k). No right of action or defense arising out of a sale that the buyer has against the seller shall be cut off by assignment of the contract to any third party whether or not he acquires the contract in good faith and for value. § 1402.
*Special provisions for manufactured homes*: None.
*Special provisions for revolving credit*: Rate agreed upon by seller or holder and buyer, except for gasoline credit card issuers, who may charge no more than 15% simple interest per year. A minimum service charge of $0.50 per month may be made if the service charge is less than that amount; such minimum service charge may be imposed for a minimum period of 6 months. § 1904.
*Other noteworthy provisions*: None.
*Remedies*: If any person fails to comply with the provisions of the Act, such person, or any person who acquires a contract or installment account with knowledge of such noncompliance, is barred from recovery of any time price differential or service charge or of any delinquency, collection, extension, deferral, or refinance charge imposed in connection with such contract or account, and the buyer shall have the right to recover an amount equal to any of such charges paid. § 2202. Reasonable attorney fees and costs shall be awarded to the prevailing party in any action on a contract or installment account regardless of whether action is instituted by the seller, holder or buyer. § 2001. If a person willfully violates any provision of the Act in connection with the imposition, computation, or disclosures of or relating to a time price differential or service charge on a consolidated total of two or more contracts, the buyer may recover an amount equal to three times the total of the time price differentials or service charges and any delinquency, collection, extension, deferral, or refinance charges imposed on all contracts included in the consolidated total, and the seller shall be barred from the recovery of any such charges. § 2204.

**69 Pa. Stat. Ann. §§ 601 to 637 (West) (Motor Vehicle Sales Finance Act).**

*Scope*: Installment sales of motor vehicles for use by the buyer, or for the benefit or satisfaction that the buyer may derive from the use of the motor vehicle by another. § 603.
*Licensure requirements*: Installment sellers and sales finance companies must be licensed. § 604. The seller of a motor vehicle under an installment sale contract, executed in Pennsylvania, shall not sell, transfer or assign the obligation represented by such contract to any person in Pennsylvania or elsewhere who is not licensed as a sales finance company pursuant to the Act. A licensed sales finance company shall not sell, transfer or assign the obligation represented by the contract, executed in Pennsylvania, to any other person in Pennsylvania or elsewhere who is not licensed as a sales finance company pursuant to the Act. § 616.
*Credit terms*: for Class I vehicles (new motor vehicles, except those having a cash price of $10,000 or more and used primarily for commercial purposes, and except mobile homes and new trucks or

truck tractors having a manufacturer's gross vehicular weight of 15,000 pounds or more and new semitrailers or trailers designed for use in combination with truck tractors), 18% simple interest per year; for Class II (used motor vehicles of a model designated by the manufacturer by a year not more than 2 years prior to the year in which the sale is made), 18% per year; for Class III (older used motor vehicles of a model designated by the manufacturer by a year more than 2 years prior to the year in which the sale is made), 21% per year; for Class IV (new motor vehicles having a cash price of $10,000 or more and used primarily for commercial purposes, and except new trucks or truck tractors having a manufacturer's gross vehicular weight of 15,000 pounds or more and new semitrailers or trailers designed for use in combination with truck tractors), 7.5% per year; for Class V (new mobile homes), such percent established as a maximum finance charge for mobile homes by regulation of the FHA whether or not the mobile home is subject to a sale on credit or loan insured or guaranteed in whole or in part by such administration; for Class VI (new trucks and truck tractors having a manufacturer's gross vehicular weight of 15,000 pounds or more and new semitrailers and trailers designed for use in combination with truck tractors), 10% per year. § 619(A). A minimum finance charge of $10 may be charged on any contract in which the finance charge results in a total charge of less than $10. § 619(E).

*Restrictions on points or prepaid interest*: None.

*Restrictions on length of term*: Installment sale defined as two or more scheduled payments subsequent to the making of the contract, § 603(10).

*Restrictions on prepayment penalties*: None.

*Requirement of substantially equal installments or limits on balloon payments*: Every installment sale contract shall provide for payment substantially equal periods and in substantially equal amounts except that when the buyer expects income to vary because of seasonal employment, seasonal sales, use of accelerated depreciation for tax purposes or other known cause, the contract may provide for payment in varying amounts. A contract for the sale of a heavy commercial motor vehicle is exempt from the requirement. Also, an installment sale of a new motor vehicle to a bona fide salesman or of motor vehicles to be used by him principally as a demonstrator is exempt from the requirement. § 613(F).

*Formula for rebate of unearned interest*: Calculated by Rule of 78s (sum of the balances method), but creditor is entitled to net minimum finance charge of no less than $10, and need not make rebate of less than $1. § 622(C).

*Restrictions on deferral charges*: The charge for extension, deferment or renewal shall not exceed the amount ascertained under either of the following methods of computation at the respective rates indicated by: Option 1. Computing the refinance charge on the amount of the installment payment or payments that is refinanced for the period of time for which each payment or part thereof is extended or deferred at the following rates on contracts originally in the respective classification of motor vehicles set forth in the Act, namely Class I—1% per month; Class II—1.5% per month; Class III—2% per month. OR Option 2: Computing the refinance charge on the amount obtained by adding to the unpaid balance of the contract charges for insurance and other charges incidental to refinancing, by adding unpaid default charges, which may be accrued, and by deducting any rebate that may be due to the buyer for prepayment incidental to refinancing, at the rate of the finance charge in the original contract, for the term of the renewal contract, and subject to the provisions of the Act governing computation of the original finance charge. However, the provisions of the Act governing minimum finance charges and minimum prepayment rebate shall not apply in calculating refinance charges on the contract renewed under Option 2. § 620.

*Limits on document fees*: Unless otherwise permitted by law, certain costs and document fees that are paid or payable by the buyer shall not exceed the amount the seller expends or intends to expend for them Any costs the seller has collected from the buyer, or which have been included in the buyer's obligation under the contract that are not disbursed by the seller as contemplated, shall be immediately refunded or credited to the buyer. § 618(D).

*Restrictions on types of insurance that can be sold*: The buyer may be required to provide insurance on at the buyer's expense for the protection of the seller or subsequent holder. Such insurance shall be limited to insurance against substantial risk of damage, destruction, or theft of such motor vehicle. § 617(A).

*Single document rule?*: None.

*Assignee liability provision*: Contract may not contain any provision relieving the holder, or other assignee from liability for any legal remedies that the buyer may have had against the seller under the contract or under any separate instrument executed in connection with the contract. § 615(F).

*Special provisions for manufactured homes*: for Class V vehicles (new mobile homes), the finance charge is such percent established as a maximum finance charge for mobile homes by regulation of the FHA whether or not the mobile home is subject to a sale on credit or loan insured or guaranteed in whole or in part by such administration. § 619(A).

*Special provisions for revolving credit*: None.

*Other noteworthy provisions*: None.

*Remedies*: A contract that contains prohibited charges shall be unenforceable as to such charges. § 631(C).

**P.R. Laws Ann. tit. 10, §§ 731 to 793 (Retail Installment Sales of Goods and Services).**

*Scope*: Installment sales of goods and services. Revolving credit. § 731.

*Licensure requirements*: Finance companies must be licensed. § 761.

*Credit terms*: Contract or revolving account plan may not include financing charges in excess of those allowed by the regulations approved by the Board of the Office of Commissioner of Financial Institutions. § 750.

*Restrictions on points or prepaid interest*: None.

*Restrictions on length of term*: None.

*Restrictions on prepayment penalties*: None.

*Requirement of substantially equal installments or limits on balloon payments*: None.

*Formula for rebate of unearned interest*: "The procedure for computing the refunds or credits shall be established through regulations approved by the Board. Unearned interest shall not be collected or withheld." § 754.

*Restrictions on deferral charges:* "The extension or deferral agreement shall meet the requirements, if any, provided by the Board [of Office of Commissioner of Financial Institutions] through regulations." § 755.

*Limits on document fees*: None.

*Restrictions on types of insurance that can be sold*: None.

*Single document rule?*: None.

*Assignee liability provision*: Any contract shall contain the following notice: "Notice to the Assignee—The assignee receiving or acquiring

this retail installment contract or a promissory note related thereto, shall be subject, under equal conditions, to any claim or defense that the buyer may initiate against the seller. The assignee of the contract shall be entitled to file against the seller all the claims and defenses that the buyer may raise against the seller of the goods and the services." § 742(4). Contract may not contain a provision stating that the buyer agrees not to assert against an assignee a claim or defense arising out of the sale. § 749.
*Special provisions for manufactured homes*: None.
*Special provisions for revolving credit*: None.
*Other noteworthy provisions*: None.
*Remedies*: None.

**R.I. Gen. Laws §§ 6-27-1 to 6-27-11 (Truth in Lending and Retail Selling Act).**

*Scope*: Sales of property or services involving credit. Revolving credit. § 6-27-3.
*Licensure requirements*: None.
*Credit terms*: 18% simple interest per year. Does not apply to transactions in which the finance charge does not exceed $10. § 6-27-4(a).
*Restrictions on points or prepaid interest*: None.
*Restrictions on length of term*: None.
*Restrictions on prepayment penalties*: None.
*Requirement of substantially equal installments or limits on balloon payments*: None.
*Formula for rebate of unearned interest*: Calculated by Rule of 78s if term is 60 months or less, but by "rule of anticipation," a term not defined by the statute, if the term exceeds 60 months. Refund of less than $1 need not be made. § 6-27-4.
*Restrictions on deferral charges*: None.
*Limits on document fees*: None.
*Restrictions on types of insurance that can be sold*: None.
*Single document rule?*: None.
*Assignee liability provision*: None.
*Special provisions for manufactured homes*: None.
*Special provisions for revolving credit*: The maximum finance charge for revolving or open-end credit in connection with a transaction arising out of a retail sale of consumer goods, including gasoline, or services shall not exceed the rate agreed to by the creditor and buyer compared on the average daily balance of the open-end or revolving account or the unpaid balance of the open-end or revolving account outstanding as of the end of the current billing cycle. § 6-27-4(c).
*Other noteworthy provisions*: None.
*Remedies*: Any creditor who willfully imposes a finance charge in violation of the Act shall be liable to the person for the greater of $100 or twice the finance charge required by the creditor. The liabilities shall not exceed $2,000 on any credit transaction. Buyer may also recover reasonable attorney fees and costs. § 6-27-7(a).

**S.C. Code Ann. 37-1-101 to 37-15-100 (South Carolina Consumer Protection Code).**

*Scope*: Retail installment sales and consumer credit sales (including home solicitation sales and consumer leases of goods), services and interests in land purchased primarily for a personal, family, or household purposes. With respect to a sale of goods or services, the amount financed may not exceed $25,000. § 37-2-104.
*Licensure requirements*: Supervised lenders must be licensed. § 37-3-503.
*Credit terms*: The credit service charge, calculated according to the actuarial method, may not exceed the greater of either of the following:(a) any rate filed and posted pursuant to § 37-2-305 (provision requiring creditors intending to impose a credit service charge in excess of 18% to file with the Department of Consumer Affairs and post in one conspicuous place in every place of business in the state a maximum rate schedule; (b) 18% per year on the unpaid balance. § 37-2-201(2). The seller may receive a minimum credit service charge of not more than $5 when the amount financed does not exceed $75, or $7.50 when the amount financed exceeds $75. § 37-2-201(6).
*Restrictions on points or prepaid interest*: None.
*Restrictions on length of term*: "Payable in installments" defined as: two or more periodic payments, excluding a down payment, with respect to a debt arising from a consumer credit sale pursuant to which a credit service charge is made; four or more periodic payments, excluding a down payment, with respect to a debt arising from a consumer credit sale pursuant to which no credit service charge is made, or two or more periodic payments with respect to a debt arising from a consumer loan. § 37-1-301(19).
*Restrictions on prepayment penalties*: The buyer may prepay in full the unpaid balance of a consumer credit sale, refinancing or consolidation at any time without penalty. § 37-2-209.
*Requirement of substantially equal installments or limits on balloon payments*: If any scheduled payment of a consumer credit sale is more than twice as large as the average scheduled payment, the consumer has the right to refinance, without penalty, that payment at the time it is due. The terms of the refinancing shall be no less favorable to the consumer than the terms of the original transaction. This provision does not apply to: (a) a transaction pursuant to a revolving charge account; (b) a transaction to the extent that the payment schedule is adjusted to the seasonal or irregular income or scheduled payments or obligations of the consumer; (c) a credit transaction to the extent a formula for determining the rate of the credit service charge and any change in the amount of payment upon renegotiation or refinancing is specified in the agreement between the parties or is an alternative mortgage instrument; or (d) a transaction of a class defined by the Administrator as not requiring for the protection of the consumer the right to refinance. § 37-2-405.
*Formula for rebate of unearned interest*: Calculated by Rule of 78s (sum of the balances method), but creditor may retain a minimum charge of $15 if contracted for. Creditor has option of using actuarial method, and must do so if transaction was payable by its original terms in more than 61 months (or in some cases where the original term has been extended by deferring payments). No refund of less than $1 need be made. § 37-2-210.
*Limits on document fees*: None.
*Restrictions on types of insurance that can be sold*: A creditor may not contract for or receive a separate charge for insurance against loss of or damage to property unless the insurance covers a substantial risk of loss or damage to property, all or part of which is related to the credit transaction, the amount, terms and conditions of the insurance are reasonable in relation to the character and value of the property insured or to be insured, and the term of the insurance is reasonable in relation to the terms of credit. The term of the insurance is reasonable if it is customary and does not extend substantially beyond a scheduled maturity. § 37-4-301. A creditor may not contract for or receive a separate charge for insurance against liability unless the insurance covers a substantial risk of liability arising out of the ownership or use of property related to the credit transaction. § 37-4-303.
*Single document rule?*: None.
*Assignee liability provision*: With respect to a consumer credit sale or consumer lease, an assignee of the rights of the seller or lessor is

subject to all claims and defenses of the consumer against the seller or lessor arising from the sale or lease of property or services, notwithstanding that the assignee is a holder in due course of a negotiable instrument issued in violation of the provisions prohibiting certain negotiable instruments. § 37-2-404(1). A claim or defense may be asserted against the assignee only if the consumer has made a good faith attempt to obtain satisfaction from the seller or lessor and then only to the extent of the amount owing to the assignee with respect to the sale or lease of the property or services as to which the claim or defense arose at the time the assignee has written notice of the claim or defense. § 37-2-404(2).

*Special provisions for manufactured homes*: Section 37-2-309 provides requirements for manufactured home credit disclosure of material terms. § 37-2-309.

*Special provisions for revolving credit*: A charge may be made in each billing cycle that is a percentage of an amount no greater than: (a) the average daily balance of the account, (b) the unpaid balance of the account on the same day of the billing cycle, or (c) the median amount within a specified range within which the average daily balance of the account or the unpaid balance of the account on the same day of the billing cycle is included. A charge may be made pursuant to this paragraph only if the seller, subject to classifications and differentiations he may reasonably establish, makes the same charge on all balances within the specified range and if the percentage when applied to the median amount within the range does not produce a charge exceeding the charge resulting from applying that percentage to the lowest amount within the range by more than 8% of the charge on the median amount. § 37-2-207(2). If the billing cycle is monthly, the charge may not exceed that authorized by § 37-2-201 (the provision on permitted credit service charges) on the amount specified above. If the billing cycle is not monthly, the maximum charge is the percentage that bears the same relation to the applicable monthly percentage as the number of days in the billing cycle bears to thirty. § 37-2-207(3). If there is an unpaid balance on the same date as of which the credit service charge is applied, the seller may contract for and receive a charge not exceeding $0.50 if the billing cycle is monthly or longer, or the pro rata part of $0.50 that bears the same relation to $0.50 as the number of days in the billing cycle bears to thirty if the billing cycle is shorter than monthly. § 37-2-207(4).

*Other noteworthy provisions*: None.

*Remedies*: If a creditor violates certain specified provisions of the Act, the consumer has a cause of action to recover actual damages and also a right in an action (other than a class action) to recover a penalty in an amount determined by the court not less than $100 but not more than $1,000. § 37-5-202(1). A consumer is not obligated to pay a charge in excess of that allowed by this title and has a right of refund of any excess charge paid. § 37-5-202(2). If a creditor has contracted for or received a charge in excess of that allowed, or if a consumer is entitled to a refund and a person liable to the consumer refuses to make a refund within a reasonable time after demand, the consumer may recover in an action other than a class action a penalty in an amount determined by the court not less than $100 nor more than $1,000. A reasonable time is presumed to be 30 days. § 37-5-202(3). If it is found that a creditor has violated the Act, the court shall award to the consumer reasonable attorney fees and costs. In determining attorney fees, the amount of the recovery on behalf of the consumer is not controlling. § 37-5-202(8). A creditor who, in violation of the provisions of the Federal Truth in Lending Act or certain specified sections, fails to disclose required information is liable in an amount equal to the sum of twice the amount of the finance charge in connection with the transaction, but the liability pursuant to this item must be not less than $100 or more than $1,000, and reasonable attorney fees and costs. § 37-5-203(1). The administrator may bring a civil action against a creditor or a person subject to the Act to recover actual damages and excess charges paid by one or more consumers who have a right to recover explicitly granted by the Act. § 37-6-113.

**S.D. Codified Laws §§ 54-3A-1 to 54-3A-25 (Consumer Installment Sales Contracts).**

*Scope*: Installment sales of goods or services for personal, family, or household use. § 54-3A-1.

*Licensure requirements*: None.

*Credit terms*: Rate agreed upon by the creditor and the consumer by written agreement. The finance charge is expressed and compounded in the same manner as an interest rate. § 54-3A-3.

*Restrictions on points or prepaid interest*: None.

*Restrictions on length of term*: Installment sale defined as one or more installments. § 54-3A-1(6).

*Restrictions on prepayment penalties*: None.

*Requirement of substantially equal installments or limits on balloon payments*: None.

*Formula for rebate of unearned interest*: The Rule of 78 may not be used in any consumer installment sales contract, but may be used to compute the unearned premium on insurance. § 54-3A-8.1. Upon prepayment in full of the unpaid balance of an installment sales contract, or upon a refinancing or consolidation thereof, an amount equal to the total finance charge contracted for, less the finance charge earned, shall be rebated to the buyer. If the total of all rebates, refunds and credits to be paid to the buyer under the Act is less than $1, no rebate need be made. § 54-3A-9.

*Restrictions on deferral charges*: A deferral agreement must provide the amount of the deferral charge. § 54-3A-15. A charge may not be collected for the deferral of an installment payment or any part thereof if the unpaid balance is refinanced. § 54-3A-16.

*Limits on document fees*: None.

*Restrictions on types of insurance that can be sold*: None.

*Single document rule?*: None.

*Assignee liability provision*: None.

*Special provisions for manufactured homes*: None.

*Special provisions for revolving credit*: A charge may be made in each billing cycle that is a percentage of an amount no greater than the average daily balance of the account, the unpaid balance of the account on approximately the same day of the billing cycle or the median amount within a specified range within which the average daily balance or the unpaid balance of the account, on approximately the same day of the billing cycle, is included. A charge may be made only if the same charge is applied to all balances within the specified range and if the percentage when applied to the median amount within the range does not produce a charge exceeding the charge resulting from applying that percentage to the lowest amount within the range by more than 8% of the charge on the median amount. This charge may be compounded. § 54-11-6.2. The charge shall be at a rate or amount agreed upon by the parties. If the billing cycle is not monthly, the maximum charge is that percentage that bears the same relation to the agreed upon rate as the number of days in the billing cycle bears to thirty. § 54-11-6.3. If there is an unpaid balance on the date of which the credit service charge is applied and the credit service charge is less than the minimum charge, a minimum charge not exceeding $0.50 may be made if the billing cycle is monthly. If the billing cycle is not monthly, a minimum charge may be made that bears the same relation

to $0.50 as the number of days in the billing cycle bears to thirty. § 54-11-6.4.
*Other noteworthy provisions*: None.
*Remedies*: If any amount in excess of the charges permitted is contracted for or received, or if any other provision of the Act is violated that is not a result of an unintentional or bona fide error of computation, the consumer shall not be liable for any part of the principal, interest or any other charges, and shall be allowed to recover reasonable attorney fees and costs. § 54-3A-20.

**Tenn. Code Ann. §§ 47-11-101 to 47-11-111 (Retail Installment Sales Act).**

*Scope*: Installment sales of goods and services, whether or not purchased for commercial or industrial use, not principally for the purpose of resale. Revolving credit. § 47-11-102.
*Licensure requirements*: None.
*Credit terms*: The seller or other holder under a retail installment contract may charge a time price differential that shall not exceed $11.75 per $100 per year on the principal balance. § 47-11-103(d).
*Restrictions on points or prepaid interest*: None.
*Restrictions on length of term*: None.
*Restrictions on prepayment penalties*: None.
*Requirement of substantially equal installments or limits on balloon payments*: None.
*Formula for rebate of unearned interest*: Rebate is calculated by applying Rule of 78s (sum of the balances method) to original finance charge minus $15, but no rebate of less than $1 need be made. § 47-11-103(h).
*Restrictions on deferral charges*: None.
*Limits on document fees*: None.
*Restrictions on types of insurance that can be sold*: The seller under any retail installment contract shall have no authority to collect any fees or charges for a policy of credit life insurance issued in connection with property purchased under the contract unless the consumer has specifically elected, in writing, to authorize the addition of the policy. § 47-11-111(a).
*Single document rule?*: A retail installment contract need not be contained in a single document. § 47-11-103(c).
*Assignee liability provision*: None.
*Special provisions for manufactured homes*: None.
*Special provisions for revolving credit*: The seller and assignee under a retail charge agreement may charge a time price differential that shall not exceed 17 1/2 ¢ per $10 per month, computed from month to month or other regular period, on all amounts unpaid from time to time under the agreement. The time price differential may be computed for all unpaid balances within a range of not more than $10 on the basis of the median amount within such range, if as so computed such time price differential is applied to all unpaid balances within such range. A minimum time price differential not in excess of $0.70 per month may be charged under each such agreement. § 47-11-104(c).
*Other noteworthy provisions*: None.
*Remedies*: In case of an intentional failure to comply with the provisions of the Act, or if the seller permits the buyer to sign a contract containing blank spaces not permitted by the Act, the buyer shall have a right to recover from the person, or to set off or counterclaim in any action by such person, as liquidated damages, an amount equal to the whole of the original time balance in a contract, and all amounts payable under an agreement with respect to the transaction to which such violation pertains, plus reasonable attorney fees. § 47-11-107(b). For other violations, the buyer shall have a right to recover from the person committing such violation, or to set off or counterclaim in any action by such person, as liquidated damages, an amount equal to two times the time price differential charged to the buyer, plus reasonable attorney fees. § 47-11-107(c).

**Tex. Fin. Code Ann. §§ 354.001 to 345.357 (West) (Retail Installment Sales).**

*Scope*: Installment sales of goods (but not motor vehicles) and services purchased for personal, family, or household use. Revolving credit. §§ 345.001, 345.002 and 345.003.
*Licensure requirements*: Each holder must pay $10 annual fee per location at which a retail installment transaction is originated, serviced or collected. § 345.351.
*Credit terms*: A retail installment contract that is payable in substantially equal monthly payments beginning one month after the date of the contract may provide for a time price differential that does not exceed a charge equal to: (1) $12 per $100 per year on the part of the principal balance that is less than or equal to the amount computed under subchapter C, chapter 341, using the reference amount of $500; (2) $10 per $100 per year on the part of the principal balance that is more than the amount computed for subdivision (1) but less than or equal to the amount computed under subchapter C, chapter 341, using the reference amount of $1,000; and (3) $8 per $100 per year on the part of the principal balance that is more than the amount computed for subdivision (2). § 345.055. Alternatively, a retail installment contract may provide for a rate or amount of time price differential that does not exceed the rate or amount authorized by chapter 303 (authorizing annualized or quarterly rate). § 345.056. A retail installment contract with an initial principal balance of $75 or more may provide for a minimum time price differential that does not exceed $12; a retail installment contract with an initial principal balance of more than $25 and less than $75 may provide for a minimum time price differential that does not exceed $9; and a retail installment contract with an initial principal balance of $25 or less may provide for a minimum time price differential that does not exceed $6. § 345.058. A retail charge agreement may provide for a time price differential for the payment that may not be more than the amount computed on the unpaid amount under the retail charge agreement at a rate equal to: (1) $0.15 per $10 per month on the part of the unpaid balance that is equal to or less than the amount computed under subchapter C, chapter 341, using the reference amount of $500; and (2) $0.10 per $10 per month on the part of the unpaid balance that is more than the amount computed for subdivision (1). § 345.103. Alternatively, a retail charge agreement may provide for a rate or amount of time price differential that does not exceed the rate or amount authorized by chapter 303(authorizing annualized or quarterly rate). § 345.104.
*Restrictions on points or prepaid interest*: None.
*Restrictions on length of term*: None.
*Restrictions on prepayment penalties*: None.
*Requirement of substantially equal installments or limits on balloon payments*: None.
*Formula for rebate of unearned interest*: Rebate is calculated by applying Rule of 78s (sum of the balances method) to original finance charge minus the minimum charge authorized by statute, but no rebate of less than $1 need be made. § 345.075.
*Restrictions on deferral charges*: A holder may a charge that is a part of the time price differential and computed on the amount deferred for the period of deferment at the monthly rate of $0.15 for each $10, plus the amount of the additional cost to the holder for premiums for continuing in force any insurance provided for by the

contract and additional necessary official fees. § 345.069(b). The minimum deferral charge is $1. § 345.069(c).

*Limits on document fees*: A retail seller may charge a documentary fee for services rendered in preparing, handling, and processing documents relating to a transaction involving a motorcycle, motor-driven cycle, moped, all-terrain vehicle, boat, boat motor, boat trailer, or towable recreational vehicle. Such document fee: must be charged to cash buyers and credit buyers, may not exceed $50 and must be disclosed on the contract as a separate itemized charge. § 345.251.

*Restrictions on types of insurance that can be sold*: A holder may request or require a retail buyer to insure the property purchased or improved under a retail installment transaction, including the purchase of title insurance on real property that is involved in the retail installment contract or retail charge agreement and that is subject to a security interest of the holder, including a lien. The insurance and the premiums or charges for the insurance must bear a reasonable relationship to the amount, term, and conditions of the retail installment contract or retail charge agreement, the existing hazards or risk of loss, damage, or destruction, or the potential liability. The insurance may not cover unusual or exceptional risks, or provide coverage not ordinarily included in policies issued to the public. § 345.201.

*Single document rule?*: A retail installment contract may be more than one document. § 345.063.

*Assignee liability provision*: A right of action or defense of a buyer is not affected by the negotiation of the retail installment contract or retail charge agreement to a third party except as authorized by law and the third party acquires the contract relying in good faith on a certificate of completion or certificate of satisfaction, if required by law, gives notice of the negotiation to the buyer, and does not receive from the buyer, before the 31st day after the day on which that notice is mailed, written notice of a fact that gives rise to a claim or defense of the buyer. § 345.304.

*Special provisions for manufactured homes*: chapter 347 deals with manufactured home credit transactions. A credit transaction may provide for an adjustable interest rate or time price differential. § 347.101. The amount of a rate adjustment is computed by subtracting the index base or, for a change after the initial change, the index value used for the preceding rate adjustment from the index value on the first day of a month that precedes the 50th day before the date on which the adjustment is to take effect. The amount is applied to the rate applicable to the credit transaction. The rate in a credit transaction may be adjusted only if the adjustment results in a change of at least one-eighth of 1% a year. § 347.104. The total of the rate adjustments for any 6-month period may not exceed 0.50% a year. If the stated interval for rate adjustments is a 12-month period or longer, a rate adjustment may not exceed 1% a year. The total of all rate adjustments over the term of the credit transaction may not exceed the least of: (1) one-half of the initial rate; (2) 8%; or (3) a rate, expressed as a percentage, computed by dividing the term of the loan in years by two. § 347.105. A creditor may collect a charge that does not exceed the amount computed by applying the credit transaction's interest rate or time price differential applicable on the date of adjustment to the remaining amount of the unpaid balance for the period that the amount is extended or deferred. § 347.151(b). On prepayment, after deduction of an acquisition charge that does not exceed $50, the consumer is entitled to a refund credit of the time price differential or interest. The amount of the credit is computed on an actuarial basis in accordance with regulations of the Office of Thrift Supervision adopted under the Depository Institutions Deregulation and Monetary Control Act of 1980 for the prepayment of a mortgage loan that is secured by a first lien on a residential manufactured home. § 347.155(b). A creditor may require a consumer to insure the property involved in a credit transaction with coverage designated by the creditor. Insurance required may include federal flood coverage. § 347.201.

*Special provisions for revolving credit*: A revolving credit account may provide for interest on an account at an annual rate that does not exceed the greater of: (1) 18% per year; or (2) the applicable alternative rate ceiling under chapter 303 (authorizing annualized or quarterly rate). A revolving credit account may provide for interest computed under a method other than the average daily balance method if the amount of interest computed under that method does not exceed the amount of interest computed under the average daily balance method. § 346.101. Section 346.103 limits fees that may be imposed.

*Other noteworthy provisions*: None.

*Remedies*: None.

**Tex. Fin. Code Ann. §§ 348.001 to 348.606 (West) (Motor Vehicle Installment Sales).**

*Scope*: Installment sales of motor vehicles. The term "motor vehicles" includes automobile, motor home, truck, truck tractor, trailer, semitrailer, or bus designed, and used primarily to transport persons or property on a highway, as well as a commercial vehicle or heavy commercial vehicle. § 348.001(4).

*Licensure requirements*: A person may not act as a holder unless the person is an authorized lender or a credit union or holds a license issued under the Act. A person who is required to hold a license under the Act must ensure that each office at which retail installment transactions are made, serviced, held or collected is licensed or otherwise authorized to make, service, hold or collect retail installment transactions in accordance with the Act. § 348.501(a).

*Credit terms*: A retail installment contract payable in substantially equal successive monthly installments beginning 1 month after the date of the contract may provide for a time price differential that does not exceed the greater of $25 or: $7.50 per $100 per year on the principal balance for a new motor vehicle designated by the manufacturer by a model year that is not earlier than the year in which the sale is made; $10 per $100 per year for a new motor vehicle not covered by the previous category or a used motor vehicle designated by the manufacturer by a model year that is not more than two years before the year in which the sale is made; $12.50 per $100 per year for a used motor vehicle that is a motor vehicle designated by the manufacturer by a model year that is not more than 4 years before the year in which the sale is made; $15 per $100 per year for a used motor vehicle not covered by the previous two categories or $18 per $100 per year if the principal balance under the contract does not exceed $300. § 348.104. Alternatively, the contract may provide for a rate or amount of time price differential that does not exceed the rate or amount authorized by chapter 303 (authorizing annualized or quarterly rate). § 348.105.

*Restrictions on points or prepaid interest*: None.

*Restrictions on length of term*: None.

*Restrictions on prepayment penalties*: None.

*Requirement of substantially equal installments or limits on balloon payments*: If a scheduled installment is more than an amount equal to twice the average of all installments scheduled before that installment, other than the down payment, the retail buyer is entitled to refinance that installment when the installment is due, without an acquisition cost, in installments that are not greater or more frequent than the average amount and frequency of previous installments, and at a rate of time price differential that does not exceed the rate applicable to the original contract. Note that this requirement does not apply to: (1) a lease; (2) a retail installment transaction for a vehicle that is to be used primarily for a purpose other than personal, family, or household use; (3) a transaction for which the payment schedule is adjusted to the seasonal or irregular income or scheduled payments or obligations of the buyer; (4) a transaction of a type that the commissioner determines does not require the protection for the buyer provided by this provision; or (5) a retail installment transaction in which the seller is a franchised, licensed dealer and the buyer is entitled, at the end of the term of the retail installment contract, to sell the vehicle back to the holder according to a written agreement entered into between the buyer and holder concurrently with or as a part of the transaction and under which the buyer will be released from liability or obligation for the final scheduled payment, pay the final scheduled payment under the contract, or, if the buyer is not in default under the contract, refinance the final scheduled payment with the holder for repayment in not fewer than 24 equal monthly installments or on other terms agreed to by the buyer and holder at the time of refinancing and at a rate of time price differential not to exceed the lesser of a rate equal to the maximum authorized rate or an annual percentage rate of 5% a year more than the annual percentage rate of the original contract. § 348.123.

*Formula for rebate of unearned interest*: Rebate is calculated by applying Rule of 78s (sum of the balances method) to original finance charge minus $25, but no rebate of less than $1 need be made. § 348.120.

*Restrictions on deferral charges*: If a retail installment contract is amended to defer all or a part of one or more installments for not longer than 3 months, the holder may collect from the retail buyer an amount computed on the amount deferred for the period of deferment at a rate that does not exceed the effective return for time price differential permitted for a monthly payment retail installment contract, and the amount of the additional cost to the holder for premiums for continuing in force any insurance coverage provided for by the contract any additional necessary official fees. The minimum charge is $1. § 348.114.

*Limits on document fees*: For a documentary fee to be included in the principal balance of a, the seller must charge the documentary fee to cash buyers and credit buyers, the fee may not exceed a reasonable amount agreed to by the parties for the services, and the buyer's order and the retail installment contract must include a statement of the amount of the fee. Also, the following notice must be included: "A DOCUMENTARY FEE IS NOT AN OFFICIAL FEE. A DOCUMENTARY FEE IS NOT REQUIRED BY LAW, BUT MAY BE CHARGED TO BUYERS FOR HANDLING DOCUMENTS RELATING TO THE SALE. A DOCUMENTARY FEE MAY NOT EXCEED A REASONABLE AMOUNT AGREED TO BY THE PARTIES. THIS NOTICE IS REQUIRED BY LAW." Prior to increasing the maximum amount of the documentary fee, a seller shall provide written notice to the commissioner of the maximum amount of the documentary fee the retail seller intends to charge. The commissioner may review the amount of a documentary fee for reasonableness. In determining whether a fee charged by a retail seller is reasonable, the commissioner may consider the resources required by the retail seller to perform the retail seller's duties under state and federal law with respect to the handling and processing of documents relating to the sale and financing of a motor vehicle. If the commissioner determines that a documentary fee charged is not reasonable, the commissioner may require that the documentary fee charged be reduced or suspended. § 348.006.

*Restrictions on types of insurance that can be sold*: A holder may request or require a retail buyer to insure the motor vehicle purchased under a retail installment transaction and accessories and related goods subject to the holder's security interest. The insurance and the premiums or charges for the insurance must bear a reasonable relationship to the amount, term, and conditions of the contract and the existing hazards or risk of loss, damage or destruction. The insurance may not cover unusual or exceptional risks or provide coverage not ordinarily included in policies issued to the public. § 348.201. A retail buyer and retail seller may agree to include a charge for insurance coverage that is for a risk of loss or liability reasonably related to: (A) the motor vehicle; (B) the use of the motor vehicle; or (C) goods or services that are related to the motor vehicle and may ordinarily be insured with a motor vehicle. § 348.208.

*Single document rule?*: A retail installment contract may be more than one document. § 348.101(a).

*Assignee liability provision*: None.

*Special provisions for revolving credit*: None.

*Other noteworthy provisions*: None.

*Remedies*: A holder who violates § 348.408 (provision on outstanding balance information) is liable to the buyer in an amount computed by adding three times the difference between the amount tendered and the amount sought by the holder at the time of tender, plus interest, reasonable attorney fees, and costs. § 348.409.

**Utah Code Ann. §§ 70C-1-101 to 70C-8-203 (West) (Utah Consumer Credit Code).**

*Scope*: All credit offered or extended by a creditor to an individual person primarily for personal, family, or household purposes. Does not include any extension of credit primarily for business, commercial or agricultural purposes and does not apply to any extension of credit in which amount financed exceeds $25,000. §§ 70C-1-201, 70C-1-202.

*Licensure requirements*: None.

*Credit terms*: Any finance charge and other charges and fees. § 70C-2-101. With respect to an open-end consumer credit contract, a finance charge may only be calculated during any particular billing cycle on the basis of either: (1) the average or actual daily balance of the account; or (2) the unpaid balance of the account on the last day of the billing cycle after deducting payments and credits received during the same cycle. § 70C-4-103.

*Restrictions on points or prepaid interest*: None.

*Restrictions on length of term*: None.

*Restrictions on prepayment penalties*: Subject to the exceptions described in the provision, a debtor may prepay the unpaid balance of a closed-end consumer credit debt at any time without penalty. § 70C-3-101.

*Requirement of substantially equal installments or limits on balloon payments*: If any scheduled payment of a closed-end consumer credit debt is more than twice as large as the average scheduled payment, the debtor has the right to refinance that payment at the time it is due. Credit terms may be no less favorable than those offered to the general public by the creditor for the same type of credit at the time a request for refinancing is accepted. § 70C-3-102.

*Formula for rebate of unearned interest*: Actuarial method, but creditor may retain a prepaid finance charge of up to 5% of the original principal amount if so agreed; pro rata rebate of any additional prepaid finance charge. Fees paid to third parties need not be rebated except to extent that they are rebated to the creditor. § 70C-3-101.

*Restrictions on deferral charges*: The creditor may collect a reasonable charge that the debtor expressly agrees to pay as consideration for a deferral. § 70C-2-103.

*Limits on document fees*: None.

*Restrictions on types of insurance that can be sold*: A creditor may not contract for or receive a separate charge for insurance against loss of or damage to property related to the credit transaction unless the insurance covers a significant risk of loss of or damage to the property, the amount, terms, and conditions of the insurance are reasonable in relation to the character and value of the property insured, and the term of the insurance is reasonable in relation to the terms of credit. § 70C-6-301. A creditor may not contract for or receive a separate charge for insurance against liability arising out of the ownership or use of property related to the credit transaction unless the insurance covers a significant risk of liability. § 70C-6-303.

*Single document rule?*: None.

*Assignee liability provision*: With respect to a consumer credit sale, a seller's assignee is subject to all defenses of the buyer against the seller arising out of the sale, but the liability may not exceed the amount owing to the assignee at the time the defense is asserted, and the rights of the buyer may be asserted only as a matter of defense to or setoff against a claim by the assignee. § 70C-2-205. Except as otherwise specifically provided in the Act, or unless the assignment is involuntary, any civil action for a violation that may be brought against the original creditor in any consumer credit transaction may be maintained against any subsequent assignee where the violation from which the alleged liability arose is apparent on the face of the instrument assigned. § 70C-7-202.

*Special provisions for manufactured homes*: None.

*Special provisions for revolving credit*: None.

*Other noteworthy provisions*: None.

*Remedies*: A debtor is not obligated to pay a charge in excess of that allowed by the Act and has a right to a refund of excess charges. If the debtor has paid an amount in excess of the lawful obligation, the debtor may recover the excess amount from the party who made the excess charge or from an assignee of the creditor's rights who undertakes direct collection of payments from or enforcement of rights against the debtor with respect to the debt. If a debtor is entitled to a refund and a party liable to the debtor in bad faith refuses to make a refund within a reasonable time after demand, the debtor may recover a penalty in an amount to be determined by a court not exceeding the greater of either the amount of the finance charge or 10 times the amount of the excess charge. If the creditor has made an excess charge in deliberate violation of or in reckless disregard for the Act, the penalty may be recovered even though the creditor has refunded the excess charge. § 70C-7-201. If it is found that a creditor has violated the Act or its agreement with the debtor, the court may award reasonable attorney fees to the debtor. § 70C-7-204.

**Vt. Stat. Ann. tit. 9, §§ 2401 to 2410 (Retail Installment Sales).**

*Scope*: Installment sales of goods (but not motor vehicles or mobile homes) and services purchased primarily for personal, family, or household use. § 2401.

*Licensure requirements*: Sales finance companies must be licensed. Vt. Stat. Ann. tit. 8 § 2201(a).

*Credit terms*: For a retail installment contract, the finance charge shall not exceed 18% per year of the first $500 of the balance and 15% on the balance in excess of $500. §§ 2405(k) and 41a(b)(2).

*Restrictions on points or prepaid interest*: None.

*Restrictions on length of term*: For retail installment contract: installment sale defined as two or more installments. For retail charge agreement: one or more installments. § 2401.

*Restrictions on prepayment penalties*: Any buyer may prepay the contract in full at any time before maturity without penalty. § 2405(p)(1).

*Requirement of substantially equal installments or limits on balloon payments*: None.

*Formula for rebate of unearned interest*: None.

*Restrictions on deferral charges*: None.

*Limits on document fees*: None.

*Restrictions on types of insurance that can be sold*: None.

*Single document rule?*: A retail installment contract need not be contained in a single document. § 2405(a).

*Assignee liability provision*: None.

*Special provisions for manufactured homes*: None.

*Special provisions for revolving credit*: For a bank credit card account or revolving line of credit the rate shall be the rate agreed upon by the lender and the borrower. However, except for cash advances, no finance charge may be imposed for any monthly billing period in which there is no previous balance, or during which the sum of the payments received and other credits issued are equal to or exceed the amount of the previous balance. §§ 2406(c) and 41a(b)(3). For a retail charge agreement, the finance charge shall be the rate or rates agreed upon by the parties but not to exceed 21% per year. However, no finance charge may be imposed for any monthly billing period in which there is no previous balance, or during which the sum of the payments received and other credits issued are equal to or exceed the amount of the previous balance. §§ 2406(c) and 41a(b)(9). If the amount of the finance charge is less than $0.50 for any month or longer regular period, $0.50 may nevertheless be charged. § 2406(c)

*Other noteworthy provisions*: No seller shall discriminate against any buyer or prospective buyer who desires to establish a retail installment contract or retail charge agreement because of the sex, sexual orientation, gender identity, marital status, race, color, religion, national origin, age, or handicapping condition of the buyer. § 2410.

*Remedies*: If any person fails to comply with any of the provisions of the Act, such person, or any person who acquires a contract or installment account with knowledge of such noncompliance, is barred from recovery of any finance charge or of any delinquency, collection, deferral, or refinance charge imposed in connection with such contract or account and the buyer shall have the right to recover in a civil action an amount equal to any charges paid by the buyer with interest thereon from the time of payment and all expenses of collection including a reasonable attorney fee. If the violation is willful, the buyer may recover an amount equal to two times the total of the finance charges and any delinquency, collection, extension, deferral, or refinance charges imposed and the seller shall be barred from the recovery of any such charges. The buyer shall also recover reasonable attorney fees. § 2409(a), (b).

**Vt. Stat. Ann. tit. 9, §§ 2351 to 2362 (Motor Vehicle Installment Sales Financing).**

*Scope*: Installment sales of motor vehicles not for resale. § 2351.

*Licensure requirements*: Sales finance companies must be licensed. Vt. Stat. Ann. tit. 8 § 2201(a).

*Credit terms*: For a loan or extension of credit secured by motor vehicles, mobile homes, travel trailers, aircraft, watercraft, and farm equipment, of the current and previous model year, the interest rate shall not exceed 18% per year. For a loan or extension of credit secured by such collateral older than the current or previous model year, the interest rate shall not exceed 20% per year. §§ 2356a and 41a(b)(4).

*Restrictions on points or prepaid interest*: None.

*Restrictions on length of term*: Installment sale defined as one or more installments. § 2351(4).

*Restrictions on prepayment penalties*: Any buyer may prepay it in full at any time before maturity without penalty. § 2357.

*Requirement of substantially equal installments or limits on balloon payments*: None.

*Formula for rebate of unearned interest*: None.

*Restrictions on deferral charges*: None.

*Limits on document fees*: None.

*Restrictions on types of insurance that can be sold*: None.

*Single document rule?*: A retail installment contract need not be contained in a single document. § 2355(a).

*Assignee liability provision*: None.

*Special provisions for manufactured homes*: None.

*Special provisions for revolving credit*: None.

*Other noteworthy provisions*: No seller shall discriminate against any buyer or prospective buyer who desires to establish a retail installment contract because of the sex, sexual orientation, gender identity, marital status, race, color, religion, national origin, age, or handicapping condition of the buyer. § 2362.

*Remedies*: If any person fails to comply with any of the provisions of the Act, such person or any person who acquires a contract or installment account with knowledge of such noncompliance is barred from recovery of any finance charge or of any delinquency, collection, deferral, or refinance charge imposed in connection with such contract or account and the buyer shall have the right to recover in a civil action an amount equal to any charges paid by the buyer with interest thereon from the time of payment and all expenses of collection including a reasonable attorney fee. If the violation is willful, the buyer may recover an amount equal to two times the total of the estimated finance charges and any delinquency, collection, extension, deferral, or refinance charges imposed, and the seller shall be barred from the recovery of any such charges. The buyer shall also recover reasonable attorney fees. § 2361(a), (b).

**Wash. Rev. Code §§ 63.14.010 to 63.14.926 (Retail Installment Sales of Goods and Services).**

*Scope*: Installment sales of goods and services purchased for personal, family, or household use. Revolving credit. § 63.14.010.

*Licensure requirements*: None.

*Credit terms*: The dollar amount or rate agreed to by contract. § 63.14.130.

*Restrictions on points or prepaid interest*: None.

*Restrictions on length of term*: None.

*Restrictions on prepayment penalties*: None.

*Requirement of substantially equal installments or limits on balloon payments*: If a contract provides for the payment of any installment that is more than double the amount of the average of the preceding installments, the buyer, upon default of this installment, shall be given an absolute right to obtain a new payment schedule. Unless agreed to by the buyer, the periodic payments under the new schedule shall not be substantially greater than the average preceding installment. This provision shall not apply if the payment schedule is adjusted to the seasonal or irregular income of the buyer or to accommodate the nature of the buyer's employment. § 63.14.159.

*Formula for rebate of unearned interest*: Calculated by Rule of 78s, but creditor is entitled to a minimum charge of $15 to $50 depending on amount of original obligation, and no refund of less than $1 need be made. § 63.14.080.

*Restrictions on deferral charges*: No charge shall be made for extension or deferment unless a written acknowledgment of such extension or deferment is sent or delivered to the buyer. The holder may charge an extension or deferral charge, but such charge may not exceed that permitted by the Act (§ 63.14.130) on the amount of the installment or installments, or part thereof, extended or deferred for the period of extension or deferral. Such period shall not exceed the period from the date when such extended or deferred installment or installments would have been payable in the absence of such extension or deferral, to the date when such installment or installments are made payable under the agreement of extension or deferment; except that a minimum charge of $1 for the period of extension or deferral may be where the charge is less than $1. Such agreement may also provide for the payment of the additional cost to the holder of the contract of premiums for continuing in force until the end of such period of extension or deferral any insurance coverage provided for in the contract. § 63.14.156.

*Limits on document fees*: None.

*Restrictions on types of insurance that can be sold*: None.

*Single document rule?*: Every retail installment contract shall be contained in a single document that shall contain the entire agreement of the parties including any promissory notes or other evidences of indebtedness between the parties, with some exceptions (*see* §§ 63.14.050, 63.14.060 and 63.14.110). § 63.14.020.

*Assignee liability provision*: No provision of a retail installment contract, retail charge agreement, or lender credit card agreement is valid by which the buyer agrees not to assert against the seller or assignee a claim or defense arising out of the sale. § 63.14.150.

*Special provisions for manufactured homes*: None.

*Special provisions for revolving credit*: The service charge in a retail charge agreement, revolving charge agreement, lender credit card agreement, or charge agreement shall not exceed the schedule or rate agreed to by contract. If the service charge is less than $1 for any month, then $1 may be charged. § 63.14.130(2).

*Other noteworthy provisions*: None.

*Remedies*: Any person who enters into a retail installment contract, charge agreement, or lender credit card agreement that does not comply with the provisions of the Act or who violates any provision except as a result of an accidental or bona fide error shall be barred from the recovery of any service charge, official fees, or any delinquency or collection charge under or in connection with the contract or agreement, but such person may nevertheless recover from the buyer an amount equal to the cash price of the goods or services and the cost to such person of any insurance included in the transaction. If the service charge is in excess of that allowed by law, the buyer shall be entitled to an amount equal to the total of twice the amount of the service charge paid and the amount of the service charge contracted for and not paid, plus reasonable attorney fees and costs. § 63.14.180.

**W. Va. Code §§ 46A-1-101 to 46A-8-102 (Consumer Credit and Protection Act).**

*Scope*: Sales of goods, services or interest in land purchased primarily for personal, family, household or agricultural purpose. With respect to a sale of goods or services, the amount financed may not exceed $45,000. However, the sale of a factory-built home is not subject to this dollar limit. § 46A-1-102(13).

*Licensure requirements*: A license is required to make regulated consumer loans. § 46A-1-101.

*Credit terms*: With respect to a consumer credit sale, other than a sale of real estate or a sale pursuant to a revolving charge account, a seller may contract for a finance charge not exceeding 18% per year on the unpaid balance that is $1,500 or less and 12% per year on the unpaid balance that is more than $1,500. § 46A-3-101(1). Alternatively, a seller may contract for a finance charge not exceeding 18% on the unpaid balance of the amount financed calculated according to the actuarial method. § 46A-3-101(7). The seller may contract for a minimum finance charge of not more than $5 when the amount financed is not more than $75, or $7.50 when the amount financed is more than $75. § 46A-3-101(5). In the alternative, seller may charge a sales finance charge or rate of interest as permitted by § 31a-4-30a, § 47-6-5b, or 47-6-5c. § 46A-3-117. With respect to a consumer credit sale involving a motor vehicle or a mobile home or a consumer credit sale from the same seller of both a mobile home and the real estate upon which such mobile home is located, or a consumer credit sale of a mobile home where a security interest in real estate owned by the buyer is given to the seller as collateral, a seller may contract for a finance charge not exceeding 18% per year on the unpaid balance calculated according to the actuarial method. Note that the quantity of real estate involved with the consumer credit sale of a mobile home upon which such finance charge is contracted for and received shall not exceed one acre. § 46A-3-101(6).

*Restrictions on points or prepaid interest*: None.

*Restrictions on length of term*: Installment sale defined as two or more periodic payments, excluding a down payment, for a debt arising from a consumer credit sale where a sales finance charge is made; four or more periodic payments, excluding a down payment, for a debt arising from a consumer credit sale where no sales finance charge is made, or two or more periodic payments with respect to a debt arising from a consumer loan. § 46A-1-102(30).

*Restrictions on prepayment penalties*: The consumer may repay in full the unpaid balance of a consumer credit sale at any time without penalty. However, it is permissible within the first 3 years of a credit extension or loan to charge a prepayment penalty of up to 1% of the original principal amount in a consumer credit sale or on a consumer loan secured by an interest in land. Such penalty may not be imposed as part of any industrial loan company licensee or secondary mortgage lender licensee contract, and in no event can a prepayment penalty be assessed on a refinancing within 1 year from the date of the prior loan. § 46A-3-110.

*Requirement of substantially equal installments or limits on balloon payments*: For a consumer credit sale or loan in which the initial total amount payable is less than $1,500, other than one primarily for an agricultural purpose or one pursuant to a revolving charge or revolving loan account, if any scheduled payment is more than twice as large as the average scheduled payment, the consumer has the right to refinance that payment at the time it is due without penalty. § 46A-2-105(1). For a sale or loan whenever any scheduled payment is at least twice as large as the smallest of all earlier scheduled payments other than any down payment, any agreement shall contain a disclosure that the contract is not payable in equal installments § 46A-2-105(2). These requirements do not apply to the extent that the payment schedule is adjusted to the seasonal or irregular income of the consumer. § 46A-2-105(3).

*Formula for rebate of unearned interest*: For transaction with original term of 36 months or less, rebate is calculated by Rule of 78s (sum of the balances method), but state agency is to prescribe an equivalent calculation if transaction is not repayable in substantially equal installments. Otherwise, actuarial method must be used. The appropriate portion of any prepaid finance charges, credit investigation fee, origination fee, or points must be rebated except where the transaction is a purchase money loan secured by a first lien mortgage on residential property, or is made by a federally-insured depository institution. No rebate of less than $1 need be made. §§ 46A-3-111; 47-6-5d.

*Restrictions on deferral charges*: With respect to a precomputed consumer credit sale or consumer loan, refinancing or consolidation, the parties before or after default may agree in writing to a deferral of all or part of one or more unpaid installments, and the seller or lender may collect a deferral charge not exceeding the amount of the sales finance charge or loan finance charge attributable to the first of the deferred monthly installment periods multiplied by number of months in the deferral period. No installment on which a delinquency charge has been collected or partial payment made shall be deferred unless the amount of the delinquency charge or partial payment is first applied to the deferral charge. If prepayment in full occurs during a deferral period, the portion of the deferral charge attributable to the unexpired full months in the deferral period shall also be rebated. § 46A-3-114(1).

*Limits on document fees*: In connection with a consumer credit sale, a creditor may contract for a documentary charge or any other similar charge for documentary services in relation to securing a title as long as the charge is applied equally to cash customers and credit customers and there is a reasonable relationship between the charge and the benefit conferred. § 46A-3-109(6).

*Restrictions on types of insurance that can be sold*: A creditor may obtain or provide reasonable insurance on the life and earning capacity of any consumer obligated on a consumer credit sale. Only one policy of life insurance and/or one policy of health and accident insurance and/or one policy of accident insurance and/or one policy of loss of income insurance on any one consumer may be in force with respect to any one contract or agreement at any one time, but one policy may cover both a consumer and his or her spouse. The amount, terms and conditions of property insurance shall have a reasonable relation to the existing hazards or risk of loss, damage or destruction and be reasonable in relation to the character and value of the property insured, and the term of the insurance shall be reasonable in relation to the terms of credit: Life insurance shall be in an initial amount not to exceed the total amount repayable under the consumer credit agreement, and where a consumer credit sale is repayable in installments, such insurance may at no time exceed the scheduled or actual amount of unpaid indebtedness, whichever is greater. § 46A-3-109(6)(b).

*Single document rule?*: No.

*Assignee liability provision*: An assignee shall be subject to all claims and defenses of the buyer or lessee against the seller or lessor arising from a specific consumer credit sale or lease of goods or services, but the total of all claims and defenses that may be asserted against the assignee shall not exceed the amount owing to the assignee at the time of such assignment except as to any claim or defense founded in fraud. As to any claim or defense founded in fraud, the total sought shall not exceed the amount of the original obligation plus any excess charges and penalties recoverable under the Act. § 46A-2-102.

*Special provisions for manufactured homes*: With respect to a consumer credit sale involving a motor vehicle or a mobile home or a consumer credit sale from the same seller of both a mobile home and the real estate upon which such mobile home is located, or a consumer credit sale of a mobile home where a security interest in real estate owned by the buyer is given to the seller as collateral, a seller may contract for a finance charge not exceeding 18% per year on the unpaid balance calculated according to the actuarial method. Note that the quantity of real estate involved with the consumer credit sale of a mobile home upon which such finance charge is contracted for and received shall not exceed one acre. § 46A-3-101(6).

*Special provisions for revolving credit*: With respect to a consumer credit sale made pursuant to a revolving charge account, other than sales of real estate, the parties may contract for the payment of a finance charge not exceeding a percentage of an amount not exceeding the greatest of: (a) the average daily balance of the account; (b) the balance of the account at the beginning of the first day of the billing cycle, less all payments on and credits to such account during such billing cycle and excluding all charges to such account during such billing cycle; or (c) the median amount within a specified range within which the average daily balance of the account or the balance of the account at the beginning of the first day of the billing cycle, less all payments on and credits to such account during such billing cycle and excluding all charges to such account during such billing cycle, is included. A charge may be made only if the seller, subject to classifications and differentiations he may reasonably establish, makes the same charge on all balances within the specified range and if the percentage, when applied to the median amount within the range, does not produce a charge exceeding the charge resulting from applying that percentage to the lowest amount within the range by more than 8% of the charge on the median amount. If the billing cycle is monthly, the finance charge may not exceed 1.5% on the first $750 of unpaid balance and 1% on the unpaid balance in excess of $750. If there is an unpaid balance on the date as of which the finance charge is applied, the seller may contract for a charge not exceeding $0.50 if the billing cycle is monthly or longer, or the pro rata part of $0.50 that bears the same relation to $0.50 as the number of days in the billing cycle bears to thirty if the billing cycle is shorter than monthly. Alternatively, if the billing cycle is monthly, the finance charge may not exceed 1.5% on the unpaid principal balance. § 46A-3-103.

*Other noteworthy provisions*: None.

*Remedies*: If a creditor violates the Act with respect to specified actions, including the collection of excess charges, the consumer has a cause of action to recover actual damages and a penalty in an amount determined by the court not less than $100 nor more than one $1,000. § 46A-5-101(1). A consumer is not obligated to pay a charge in excess of that allowed, and if he has paid an excess charge he has a right to a refund. A refund may be made by reducing the obligation by the amount of the excess charge. A consumer who has paid an amount in excess of the lawful obligation may recover in an action the excess amount from the person who made the excess charge or from an assignee of that person's rights who undertakes direct collection of payments from or enforcement of rights against the consumer arising from the debt. § 46A-5-101(3). In any claim applying to illegal, fraudulent or unconscionable conduct or any prohibited debt collection practice, the court may award all or a portion of the costs of litigation, including reasonable attorney fees and costs. On a finding by the court that a claim applying to illegal, fraudulent or unconscionable conduct or any prohibited debt collection practice was brought in bad faith and for the purposes of harassment, the court may award to the defendant reasonable attorney fees. § 46A-5-104.

**Wis. Stat. §§ 421.101 to 427.105 (Wisconsin Consumer Act).**

*Scope*: Consumer credit transactions, including sales of goods, services (but not of common carriers if the tariffs, rates, charges, costs or expenses are required by law to be filed with or approved by governmental entity) or interest in land purchased for personal, family, household or agricultural purposes. Consumer leases. Open-end credit plans. § 421.102. Act does not apply to consumer credit transactions in which the amount financed exceeds $25,000, motor vehicle consumer leases in which the total lease obligation exceeds $25,000, or other consumer transactions in which the cash price exceeds $25,000. § 421.202(6).

*Licensure requirements*: Persons who make or solicit consumer credit transactions and directly collect payments from or enforce rights against customers arising from such transactions are subject to registration requirements. § 426.201.

*Credit terms*: A consumer credit transaction entered into after October 31, 1984 is not subject to any maximum limit on finance charges. § 422.201(3). *See also* § 218.0142(3) (no maximum finance charge in motor vehicle retail installment sales). A merchant may contract for a minimum finance charge with respect to a transaction other than one pursuant to an open-end credit plan of not more than $5 when the amount financed does not exceed $75, or $7.50 when the amount financed exceeds $75. § 422.201(9). Note that the provision on finance charges for consumer credit transactions does not apply to consumer credit sales of or consumer loans secured by a first lien on or equivalent security interest in mobile homes or manufactured homes if the sales or loans are made on or after November 1, 1981. § 422.201(12m).

*Restrictions on points or prepaid interest*: None.

*Restrictions on length of term*: Installment sale defined as two or more installments, excluding the down payment in a consumer credit sale, with respect to an obligation arising from a consumer credit transaction for which a finance charge is imposed; more than four installments, excluding the down payment in a consumer credit sale, in any other consumer credit transaction; two or more installments if any installment other than the down payment is more than twice the amount of any other installment, excluding the down payment. § 421.102(30). Consumer lease is a lease of goods that a merchant makes to a customer for a term exceeding 4 months. § 421.102(11). For a consumer credit transaction other than one pursuant to an open-end credit plan or one pursuant to § 138.09 (provision governing licensed lenders), no merchant shall initially schedule payments to be paid in full: (a) over a period of more than 25 months if the total of payments is $700 or less; (b) over a period of more than 37 months if the total of payments is more than $700 but does not exceed $1,400; or (c) over a period of more than 49 months if the total of payments is more than $1,400 but does not exceed $2,000, unless the transaction is for the acquisition of or substantial improvement to real property, in which case such period shall not exceed 61 months. For a consumer credit transaction other than one pursuant to an open-end credit plan or one pursuant to § 138.09 (provision governing licensed lenders), which is for the purpose of an improvement to real property and in which the annual percentage rate is 15% or less, no merchant may initially schedule payments to be paid in full: (a) over a period of more than 25 months if the total of payments is $300 or less; (b) over a period of more than 48 months if the total of payments is more than $300 but does not exceed $1,000; or (c) over a period of more than 60 months if the total of payments is more than $1,000 but does not exceed $2,000. § 422.403.

*Restrictions on prepayment penalties*: The customer may prepay in full or in any part at any time without penalty the unpaid balance of any consumer credit transaction other than a transaction secured by a first lien mortgage or equivalent security interest on real estate with an original term of 10 years or more and on which the annual percentage rate is 10% or less. § 422.208.

*Requirement of substantially equal installments or limits on balloon payments*: Restrictions apply only to transactions entered into prior to November 1, 1984. § 422.402.

*Formula for rebate of unearned interest*: For consumer credit transactions entered into before November 1, 1981, consumer credit transactions having initial terms of less than 49 months entered into on or after November 1, 1981 and before August 1, 1987, and consumer credit transactions in which the amount financed is less than $5,000, which have initial terms of less than 37 months and which are entered into on or after August 1, 1987, rebate is calculated by Rule of 78s (sum of the balances method); otherwise by actuarial method. No rebate of less than $1 need be made. § 422.209.

*Restrictions on deferral charges*: For a precomputed transaction scheduled to be repaid in substantially equal successive installments at approximately equal intervals, if the deferral is made as of an installment due date and the payment dates for all wholly unpaid installments are deferred for one or more full installment periods and the maturity is extended for a corresponding period, the deferral charge shall not exceed the portion of the precomputed finance charge attributable to the final installment of the original schedule of payments multiplied by the total number of installments to be deferred and by the number of full installment periods in the deferment period. If the deferral is not made pursuant to this method, the deferral charge shall not exceed the rate previously disclosed to the customer applied to the amount or amounts deferred for the period of deferral calculated without regard to differences in the lengths of months, but proportionally for a part of a month, counting each day as 1/30 of a month. § 422.204(1).

*Limits on document fees*: None.

*Restrictions on types of insurance that can be sold*: A creditor may not contract for a separate charge or receive a separate charge for insurance against loss of or damage to property in which the creditor holds a security interest or to property leased under a motor vehicle consumer lease unless all of the following conditions are met: (a) the insurance covers a substantial risk of loss or damage to property which is allowable collateral for the credit transaction; (b) the amount of the insurance does not exceed any of the following: (1) the actual cash value or stated value of any motor vehicle, manufactured home, or mobile home in which the creditor holds a security interest; (2) the cash value or replacement value of any property in which the creditor holds a purchase money security interest; (3) the stated amount of the customer's credit line if the purchase money security interest secures transactions pursuant to an open-end credit plan. In any other transaction, the total payments or, if the transaction is for a term of 49 months or more, the amount financed; (c) the term of the insurance is reasonable in relation to the terms of credit. § 424.301.

*Single document rule?*: Disclosures need not be contained in a single writing. § 422.302(1)(c).

*Assignee liability provision*: In a consumer credit transaction other than a consumer loan that is not an interlocking consumer loan, a creditor's assignee is subject to all claims and defenses of the customer against the assignor arising out of the transaction notwithstanding an agreement to the contrary. An agreement by the customer not to assert against an assignee a claim or defense arising from a consumer credit transaction is enforceable only by an assignee not related to the assignor who acquires the customer's contract in good faith and for value, who gives the customer notice of the assignment as provided in the Act, and who, within 12 months after the mailing of the notice of assignment, has not received notice of the customer's claim or defense. Such good faith assignee's liability under this section is limited to: (a) the amount owing to the assignee with respect to the transaction at the time the assignee received notice of a claim or defense; plus (b) if the customer has obtained a judgment against the assignor and execution with bond is issued within 1 year after judgment and is returned unsatisfied, the amount paid by the customer to the assignee before the assignee received notice of the claim or defense of the customer, if such claim is made against the assignee within 2 years after execution is returned unsatisfied. An assignee does not acquire a contract in good faith if the assignee has knowledge, including knowledge from his or her course of dealing with other customers of the assignor or from the assignor or the assignee's records, or written notice of specified violations or of substantial complaints by such other customers that such assignor fails or refuses to perform his or her contracts with such customers and fails to remedy their complaints. § 422.407.

*Special provisions for manufactured homes*: None.

*Special provisions for revolving credit*: The parties may agree to the payment by the customer of a finance charge at any periodic rate. § 422.201(10s).

*Other noteworthy provisions*: None.

*Remedies*: For violations relating to finance charges, the customer shall be entitled to retain the goods, services or money received pursuant to the transaction without obligation to pay any amount, and shall be entitled to recover any sums paid to the merchant. § 425.305. For other violations, including those related to deferral charges, prepayment rebates, maximum periods of repayment, and limitations on default charges, a person is liable to the customer in an amount equal to the greater of twice the amount of the finance charge in connection with the transaction, except that the liability shall not be less than $100 nor greater than $1,000. Actual damages. § 425.304. A customer who prevails in an action shall recover reasonable attorney fees and costs. § 425.308.

**Wyo. Stat. Ann. §§ 40-14-101 to 40-14-702 (Wyoming Uniform Consumer Credit Code).**

*Scope*: Sales of goods, services or an interest in land purchased primarily for a personal, family, or household purpose where either the debt is payable in installments or a credit service charge is made, and, with respect to a sale of goods or services, the amount financed does not exceed $50,000 or the debt is secured by a dwelling. Includes home solicitation sales and consumer leases. "Consumer lease" means a lease of goods in which the amount payable under the lease does not exceed $25,000 and which is for a term exceeding 4 months. Includes consumer loans. § 40-14-204.

*Licensure requirements*: Unless a person has first obtained a license from the administrator authorizing him to take assignments of and undertake direct collection of payments from or enforcement of rights against debtors arising from sales and leases, not in default at time of assignment, he shall not engage in the business of taking such assignments. § 40-14-261(c). Supervised lenders must be licensed. § 40-14-342.

*Credit terms*: With respect to a consumer credit sale other than a sale pursuant to a revolving charge account, a seller may contract for a credit service charge not exceeding, where the amount financed does not exceed $50,000, the equivalent of the greater of either of the following: (A) 36% per year on that part of the unpaid balances of the amount financed that is $1,000 or less and 21% per year on that part of the unpaid balances of the amount financed that is more than $1,000; or (B) 21% per year on that part of the unpaid balances of the amount financed. Where the amount financed exceeds $50,000, any credit service charge specified in the buyer's sale agreement is permitted. § 40-14-212(b). The seller may contract for a minimum credit service charge of not more than $30. § 40-14-212(f).

*Restrictions on points or prepaid interest*: None.

*Restrictions on length of term*: "Payable in installments" means that payment is required or permitted by a written agreement in five or more installments. § 40-14-140(a)(xiii). Supervised loans, not made pursuant to a revolving loan account and in which the principal is $1,000 or less, shall be scheduled to be payable in substantially equal installments at equal periodic intervals except to the extent that the schedule of payments is adjusted to the seasonal or irregular income of the debtor, and over a period of not more than 37 months if the principal is more than $300 or over a period of not more than 25 months if the principal is $300 or less. § 40-14-351.

*Restrictions on prepayment penalties:* The buyer may prepay in full the unpaid balance of a consumer credit sale, refinancing or consolidation at any time without penalty. § 40-14-220.

*Requirement of substantially equal installments or limits on balloon payments*: For a consumer credit sale other than one pursuant to a revolving charge account, if any scheduled payment is more than twice as large as the average scheduled payment, the buyer has the right to refinance that payment at the time it is due at the seller's prevailing rates. These provisions do not apply to the extent that the payment schedule is adjusted to the seasonal or irregular income of the buyer. § 40-14-239.

*Formula for rebate of unearned interest*: Rule of 78s if original term is less than 61 months; otherwise, actuarial method. Agency may prescribe rule for irregular payment transactions. No rebate of less than $1 need be made. § 40-14-221.

*Restrictions on deferral charges*: The seller may collect a charge that the buyer expressly agrees to pay as consideration for the deferral. No specific amount or formula specified. § 40-14-215(a).

*Limits on document fees*: None.

*Restrictions on types of insurance that can be sold*: A creditor may not contract for or receive a separate charge for insurance against loss of or damage to property unless the insurance covers a substantial risk of loss of or damage to property related to the credit transaction, the amount, terms, and conditions of the insurance are reasonable in relation to the character and value of the property insured or to be insured, and the term of the insurance is reasonable in relation to the terms of credit. The term of the insurance is reasonable if it is customary and does not extend substantially beyond a scheduled maturity. A creditor may not contract for or receive a separate charge for insurance against loss of or damage to property unless the amount financed or principal exclusive of changes for the insurance is $300 or more, and the value of the property is $300 or more. § 40-14-450. A creditor may not contract for or receive a separate charge for insurance against liability unless the insurance covers a substantial risk of liability arising out of the ownership or use of property related to the credit transaction. § 40-14-452.

*Single document rule?*: None.

*Assignee liability provision*: In consumer credit sales or leases, an agreement by the buyer or lessee not to assert against an assignee a claim or defense arising out of the sale or lease is enforceable only by an assignee not related to the seller or lessor who acquires the contract in good faith and for value, and who gives the buyer or lessee notice of the assignment and within 45 days after the mailing of the notice receives no written notice of the facts giving rise to the claim or defense. This agreement is enforceable only with respect to claims or defenses that have arisen before the end of the 45-day period after notice was mailed. An assignee does not acquire a contract in good faith if the assignee has knowledge or, from his course of dealing with the seller or lessor, notice of substantial complaints by other buyers or lessees of the seller's or lessor's failure or refusal to perform his contracts with them and of the seller's or lessor's failure to remedy his defaults within a reasonable time after the assignee notifies him of the complaints. If an assignee is subject to claims or defenses of the buyer or lessee against the seller or lessor, the liability may not exceed the amount owing to the assignee at the time the claim or defense is asserted against the assignee and rights of the buyer or lessee can only be asserted as a matter of defense to or setoff against a claim by the assignee. § 40-14-238.

*Special provisions for manufactured homes*: None.

*Special provisions for revolving credit*: A charge may be made in each billing cycle that is a percentage of an amount no greater than: (i) the average daily balance of the account; (ii) the unpaid balance of the account on the same day of the billing cycle; or (iii) the median amount within a specified range within which the average daily balance of the account or the unpaid balance of the account on the same day of the billing cycle is included. A charge may be made pursuant to this paragraph only if the seller, subject to classifications and differentiations he may reasonably establish, makes the same charge on all balances within the specified range, and if the percentage when applied to the median amount within the range does not produce a charge exceeding the charge resulting from applying that percentage to the lowest amount within the range by more than 8% of the charge on the median amount. If the billing cycle is monthly, the charge may not exceed 1.75% of the amount pursuant to the paragraph above; or if the billing cycle is not monthly, the maximum charge is that percentage that bears the same relation to the applicable monthly percentage as the number of days in the billing cycle bears to thirty. If there is an unpaid balance on the date as of which the credit service charge is applied, the seller may contract for a charge not exceeding $0.50 if the billing cycle is monthly or longer, or the pro rata part of $0.50 that bears the same relation to $0.50 as the number of days in the billing cycle bears to thirty if the billing cycle is shorter than monthly. § 40-14-218.

*Other noteworthy provisions*: None.

*Remedies*: If a creditor violates the provisions of the Act relating to limitations on the schedule of payments or loan term for supervised loans, the debtor is not obligated to pay the credit service charge or loan finance charge, and has a right to recover from the person or from an assignee of that person's rights who undertakes direct collection of payments or enforcement of rights arising from the debt a penalty in an amount determined by the court not in excess of three times the amount of the credit service charge or loan finance charge. § 40-14-521(a). If a creditor violates the provisions relating to authority to make supervised loans, the loan is void and the debtor is not obligated to pay either the principal or loan finance charge. If he has paid any part of the principal or of the loan finance charge, he has a right to recover the payment from the person or from an assignee. § 40-14-521(b). A debtor is not obligated to pay a charge in excess of that allowed by the Act, and if he has paid an excess charge he has a right to a refund. If the debtor has paid an amount in excess of the lawful obligation, the debtor may recover the excess amount from the person who made the excess charge or from an assignee who undertakes direct collection of payments from or enforcement of rights against debtors arising from the debt. § 40-14-521(c). If a debtor is entitled to a refund and a person refuses to make a refund within a reasonable time after demand, the debtor may recover a penalty in an amount determined by a court not exceeding the greater of either the amount of the credit service charge or ten times the amount of the excess charge. If the creditor has made an excess charge in deliberate violation of or in reckless disregard for the Act, the penalty may be recovered even though the creditor has refunded the excess charge. § 40-14-521(d). If it is found that a creditor has violated the Act, the court may award reasonable attorney fees to the debtor. § 40-14-521(h). A creditor who violates the laws relating to disclosure, other than the provisions on advertising, applicable to credit sales and loans is liable in an amount equal to the sum of twice the amount of the credit service or loan finance charge in connection with the transaction, but the liability shall be not less than $100 or more than $1,000. Reasonable attorney fees and costs are recoverable. § 40-14-522.

Appendix D Rate Exportation

# D.1 National Banks

## D.1.1 Statutory Provisions

### TITLE 12—BANKS AND BANKING

### CHAPTER 2—NATIONAL BANKS

### SUBCHAPTER I—ORGANIZATION AND GENERAL PROVISIONS

* * *

### 12 U.S.C. § 25b. State law preemption standards for national banks and subsidiaries clarified

**(a) Definitions**

For purposes of this section, the following definitions shall apply:

* * *

**(2) State consumer financial laws**

The term "State consumer financial law" means a State law that does not directly or indirectly discriminate against national banks and that directly and specifically regulates the manner, content, or terms and conditions of any financial transaction (as may be authorized for national banks to engage in), or any account related thereto, with respect to a consumer.

* * *

**(e) Application of State consumer financial law to subsidiaries and affiliates**

Notwithstanding any provision of title 62 of the Revised Statutes or section 371 of this title, a State consumer financial law shall apply to a subsidiary or affiliate of a national bank (other than a subsidiary or affiliate that is chartered as a national bank) to the same extent that the State consumer financial law applies to any person, corporation, or other entity subject to such State law.

[R.S. § 5136C, *as added and amended by* Pub. L. No. 111–203, tit. X, §§ 1044(a), 1045, 1047(a), 124 Stat. 2014, 2017, 2018 (July 21, 2010)]

### 12 U.S.C. § 36. Branch banks

* * *

**(f) Law applicable to interstate branching operations**

* * *

**(2) Treatment of branch as bank**

All laws of a host State, other than the laws regarding community reinvestment, consumer protection, fair lending, establishment of intrastate branches, and the application or administration of any tax or method of taxation, shall apply to a branch (in such State) of an out-of-State national bank to the same extent as such laws would apply if the branch were a national bank the main office of which is in such State.

* * *

**(j) "Branch" defined**

The term "branch" as used in this section shall be held to include any branch bank, branch office, branch agency, additional office, or any branch place of business located in any State or Territory of the United States or in the District of Columbia at which deposits are received, or checks paid, or money lent. The term "branch", as used in this section, does not include an automated teller machine or a remote service unit.

* * *

[R.S. § 5155; Feb. 25, 1927, ch. 191, § 7, 44 Stat. 1228; June 16, 1933, ch. 89, § 23,48 Stat. 189; Aug. 23, 1935, ch. 614, tit. III, § 305,49 Stat. 708; July 15, 1952, ch. 753, § 2(b), 66 Stat. 633; Pub. L. No. 87–721, 1962, 76 Stat. 667 (Sept. 28); Pub. L. No. 103–328, tit. I, §§ 102(b)(1), 103(a), 108 Stat. 2349, 2352 (Sept. 29, 1994); Pub. L. No. 104–208, div. A, tit. II, §§ 2204, 2205(a), 110 Stat. 3009–405 (Sept. 30, 1996); Pub. L. No. 105–24, § 2(b), 111 Stat. 239 (July 3, 1997); Pub. L. No. 111–203, tit. VI, § 613(a), 124 Stat. 1614 (July 21, 2010)]

### SUBCHAPTER IV—REGULATION OF THE BANKING BUSINESS; POWERS AND DUTIES OF NATIONAL BANKS

* * *

### 12 U.S.C. § 85. Rate of interest on loans, discounts and purchases

Any association may take, receive, reserve, and charge on any loan or discount made, or upon any notes, bills of exchange, or other evidences of debt, interest at the rate allowed by the laws of the State, Territory, or District where the bank is located, or at a rate of 1 per centum in excess of the discount rate on ninety-day commercial paper in effect at the Federal reserve bank in the Federal reserve district where the bank is located, whichever may be the greater, and no more, except that where by the laws of any State a different rate is limited for banks organized under State laws, the rate so limited shall be allowed for associations organized or existing in any such State under title 62 of the Revised Statutes. When no rate is fixed by the laws of the State, or Territory, or District, the bank may take, receive, reserve, or charge a rate not exceeding 7 per centum, or 1 per centum in excess of the discount rate on ninety-day commercial paper in effect at the Federal reserve bank in the Federal reserve district where the bank is located, whichever may be the greater, and such interest may be taken in advance, reckoning the days for which the note, bill, or other evidence of debt has to run. The maximum amount of interest or discount to be charged at a branch of an association located outside of the States of the United States and the District of Columbia shall be at the rate allowed by the laws of the country, territory, dependency, province, dominion, insular possession, or other political subdivision where the branch is located. And the purchase, discount, or sale of a bona fide bill of exchange, payable at another place than the place of such purchase, discount, or sale, at not more than the current rate of exchange for sight drafts in addition to the interest, shall not be considered as taking or receiving a greater rate of interest.

[R.S. § 5197; June 16, 1933, c. 89, § 25, 48 Stat. 191; Aug. 23, 1935, c. 614, tit. III, § 314, 49 Stat. 711; Pub. L. No. 93-501, tit. II, § 201, 88 Stat. 1558 (Oct. 29, 1974); Pub. L. No. 96-104, tit. I, § 101, 93 Stat. 789 (Nov. 5, 1979); Pub. L. No. 96-161, tit. II, § 201, 93 Stat. 1235 (Dec. 28, 1979); Pub. L. No. 96-221, tit. V, § 529, 94 Stat. 168 (Mar. 31, 1980)]

## 12 U.S.C. § 86. Usurious interest; penalty for taking; limitations

The taking, receiving, reserving, or charging a rate of interest greater than is allowed by section 85 of this title, when knowingly done, shall be deemed a forfeiture of the entire interest which the note, bill, or other evidence of debt carries with it, or which has been agreed to be paid thereon. In case the greater rate of interest has been paid, the person by whom it has been paid, or his legal representatives, may recover back, in an action in the nature of an action of debt, twice the amount of the interest thus paid from the association taking or receiving the same: *Provided,* That such action is commenced within two years from the time the usurious transaction occurred.

[R.S. § 5198]

## CHAPTER 16—FEDERAL DEPOSIT INSURANCE CORPORATION

* * *

## 12 U.S.C. § 1831a. Activities of insured State banks

* * *

**(j) Activities of branches of out-of-State banks**

**(1) Application of host State law**

The laws of a host State, including laws regarding community reinvestment, consumer protection, fair lending, and establishment of intrastate branches, shall apply to any branch in the host State of an out-of-State State bank to the same extent as such State laws apply to a branch in the host State of an out-of-State national bank. To the extent host State law is inapplicable to a branch of an out-of-State State bank in such host State pursuant to the preceding sentence, home State law shall apply to such branch.

**(2) Activities of branches**

An insured State bank that establishes a branch in a host State may conduct any activity at such branch that is permissible under the laws of the home State of such bank, to the extent such activity is permissible either for a bank chartered by the host State (subject to the restrictions in this section) or for a branch in the host State of an out-of-State national bank.

**(3) Savings provision**

No provision of this subsection shall be construed as affecting the applicability of—

**(A)** any State law of any home State under subsection (b), (c), or (d) of section 1831u of this title; or

**(B)** Federal law to State banks and State bank branches in the home State or the host State.

**(4) Definitions**

The terms "host State", "home State", and "out-of-State bank" have the same meanings as in section 1831u(f)[1] of this title.

[Sept. 21, 1950, ch. 967, § 2[24], *as added by* Pub. L. No. 102–242, tit. III, § 303(a), 105 Stat. 2349 (Dec. 19, 1991); *amended by* Pub. L. No. 102–550, tit. XVI, § 1605(a)(8), 106 Stat. 4086 (Oct. 28, 1992); Pub. L. No. 103–328, tit. I, § 102(b)(3)(B), 108 Stat. 2351 (Sept. 29, 1994); Pub. L. No. 104–208, div. A, tit. II, §§ 2217, 2704(d)(14)(W), 110 Stat. 3009–414, 3009–494 (Sept. 30, 1996); Pub. L. No. 105–24, § 2(a), 111 Stat. 238 (July 3, 1997); Pub. L. No. 109–171, tit. II, § 2102(b), 120 Stat. 9 (Feb. 8, 2006); Pub. L. No. 109–173, § 8(a)(31), 119 Stat. 3615 (Feb. 15, 2006)]

1 Section 1831u(f) no longer defines the terms "host State", "home State", and "out-of-State bank". However, such terms are defined elsewhere in that section.

# *D.1.2 Regulations*

## TITLE 12—BANKS AND BANKING

## CHAPTER I—COMPTROLLER OF THE CURRENCY, DEPARTMENT OF THE TREASURY

## PART 7—BANK ACTIVITIES AND OPERATIONS

## SUBPART D—PREEMPTION

* * *

## 12 C.F.R. § 7.5001 Charging interest at rates permitted competing institutions; charging interest to corporate borrowers.

(a) *Definition.* The term "interest" as used in 12 U.S.C. 85 includes any payment compensating a creditor or prospective creditor for an extension of credit, making available of a line of credit, or any default or breach by a borrower of a condition upon which credit was extended. It includes, among other things, the following fees connected with credit extension or availability: numerical periodic rates, late fees, creditor-imposed not sufficient funds (NSF) fees charged when a borrower tenders payment on a debt with a check drawn on insufficient funds, overlimit fees, annual fees, cash advance fees, and membership fees. It does not ordinarily include appraisal fees, premiums and commissions attributable to insurance guaranteeing repayment of any extension of credit, finders' fees, fees for document preparation or notarization, or fees incurred to obtain credit reports.

(b) *Authority.* A national bank located in a state may charge interest at the maximum rate permitted to any state-chartered or licensed lending institution by the law of that state. If state law permits different interest charges on specified classes of loans, a national bank making such loans is subject only to the provisions of state law relating to that class of loans that are material to the determination of the permitted interest. For example, a national bank may lawfully charge the highest rate permitted to be charged by a state-licensed small loan company, without being so licensed, but subject to state law limitations on the size of loans made by small loan companies.

(c) *Effect on state definitions of interest.* The Federal definition of the term "interest" in paragraph (a) of this section does not change how interest is defined by the individual states (nor how the state definition of interest is used) solely for purposes of state law. For example, if late fees are not "interest" under state law where a national bank is located but state law permits its most favored lender to charge late fees, then a national bank located in that state may charge late fees to its intrastate customers. The national bank may also charge late fees to its interstate customers because the fees are interest under the Federal definition of interest and an allowable charge under state law where the national bank is located. However, the late fees would not be treated as interest for purposes of evaluating compliance with state usury limitations because state law excludes late fees when calculating the maximum interest that lending institutions may charge under those limitations.

(d) *Usury.* A national bank located in a state the law of which denies the defense of usury to a corporate borrower may charge a corporate borrower any rate of interest agreed upon by a corporate borrower.

[66 Fed. Reg. 34791 (July 2, 2001)]

* * *

### SUBPART E—ELECTRONIC ACTIVITIES

* * *

### 12 C.F.R.§ 7.5008 Location of a national bank conducting electronic activities.

A national bank shall not be considered located in a State solely because it physically maintains technology, such as a server or automated loan center, in that state, or because the bank's products or services are accessed through electronic means by customers located in the state.

### 12 C.F.R.§ 7.5009 Location under 12 U.S.C. 85 of national banks operating exclusively through the Internet.

For purposes of 12 U.S.C. 85, the main office of a national bank that operates exclusively through the Internet is the office identified by the bank under 12 U.S.C. 22(Second) or as relocated under 12 U.S.C. 30 or other appropriate authority.

* * *

## *D.1.3 Summary of OCC Interpretative Letters*

The full text of these letters is found on the companion website to this treatise.

*Interpretative Letter No. 1100 (May 5, 2008).* An operating subsidiary is entitled to use the interest rate permitted by its parent bank's home state where the subsidiary does not conduct any business in that home state and where approval of the loans does not occur at any branch of the bank.

*Interpretative Letter No. 1036 (Aug. 10, 2005).* A check scanning device located in a customer's office, even if owned by a bank, whereby the customer can effect a deposit, is not a "branch."

*Interpretive Letter No. 1004 (Aug. 4, 2004).* Broad state parity act may be read to allow national banks to charge prepayment fees because it permits banks to charge "interest" on loans as permitted by federal law and federal law allows federal savings associations to collect prepayment fees.

*Interpretive Letter No. 974 (July 21, 2003).* Operating subsidiary may originate loans and charge interest as authorized under § 85 and applicable Indiana law to borrowers residing in all states without regard to the location of the property securing the loan.

*Interpretive Letter No. 968 (Feb. 12, 2003).* A holding company affiliate of a national bank may become an operating subsidiary of the bank. After this occurs, the operating subsidiary may impose and export interest charges under the same terms and conditions as the bank.

*Interpretive Letter No. 952 (Oct. 23, 2002).* For purposes of the applicability of substantive state and federal laws, the corporate location of a national bank is where the bank currently maintains its main office. For purposes of diversity jurisdiction, the bank is a citizen of the state in which its principal place of business is located and of the state that was originally designated in its organization certificate and articles of association, or, if applicable, to the state which that designation has changed under other authority (i.e., the state in which its main office is currently located).

*Interpretive Letter No. 822 (Feb. 17, 1998).* Letter addresses use of home state and host state interest rates by interstate national banks. National banks may be located in both its home and host (branch) states and may charge the interest allowed in its home state unless certain functions are performed in the host state.

*Interpretive Letter No. 817 (Jan. 7, 1998).* Letter clarifies status of certain fees as "interest" following termination of credit card account where outstanding balance remains on the account.

*Interpretive Letter No. 803 (Oct. 7, 1997).* Letter opines on whether certain fees, such as account opening fees, fixed rate option fees, prepayment of a fixed rate option fees, early account closure fees, are interest under 12 U.S.C. § 85 and 12 CFR § 7.4001(a).

*Interpretive Letter No. 776 (Mar. 18, 1997).* Letter concerns the exportation of main office state credit card rates by interstate national bank when it intended to merge with an affiliated bank in the consumer's state.

*Interpretive Letter No. 772 (Mar. 6, 1997).* Automated loan machines are not branches under 12 U.S.C. § 36(J). The recently amended definition in 36(J) excludes ATMs and remote service units, which are unstaffed electronic devices that accept deposits, dispense withdrawals or make loans. Deposit boxes are (still) branches, and are not remote service units.

*Interpretive Letter No. 744 (Aug. 21, 1996).* Prepayment fees constitute interest for purposes of section 85; bank chartered and located solely in a state which permits prepayment penalties may charge prepayment penalties in loans made to out-of-state residents.

# D.2 Federal Savings Associations

## *D.2.1 Statutory Provisions*

### TITLE 12—BANKS AND BANKING

### CHAPTER 12—SAVINGS ASSOCIATIONS

* * *

### 12 U.S.C. § 1463. Supervision of savings associations

* * *

**(g) Preemption of State usury laws**

**(1)** Notwithstanding any State law, a savings association may charge interest on any extension of credit at a rate of not more than 1 percent in excess of the discount rate on 90-day commercial paper in effect at the Federal Reserve bank in the Federal Reserve district in which such savings association is located or at the rate allowed by the laws of the State in which such savings association is located, whichever is greater.

**(2)** If the rate prescribed in paragraph (1) exceeds the rate such savings association would be permitted to charge in the absence of this subsection, the receiving or charging a greater rate of interest than that prescribed by paragraph (1), when knowingly done, shall be deemed a forfeiture of the entire interest which the extension of credit carries with it, or which has been agreed to be paid thereon. If such greater rate of interest has been paid, the person who paid it may recover, in a civil action commenced in a court of appropriate jurisdiction not later than 2 years after the date of such payment, an amount equal to twice the amount of the interest paid from the savings association taking or receiving such interest.

[June 13, 1933, ch. 64, § 4, *as added by* Pub. L. No. 101–73, tit. III, § 301, 103 Stat. 280 (Aug. 9, 1989), *and amended by* Pub. L. No. 111–203, tit. III, § 369(4), 124 Stat. 1558 (July 21, 2010)]

* * *

## 12 U.S.C. § 1464. Federal savings associations

* * *

**(m) Branching**

* * *

**(2) "Branch" defined**

For purposes of this subsection the term "branch" means any office, place of business, or facility, other than the principal office as defined by the Comptroller, of a savings association at which accounts are opened or payments are received or withdrawals are made, or any other office, place of business, or facility of a savings association defined by the Comptroller as a branch within the meaning of such sentence.

[Prior citations omitted. As amended by Pub. L. No. 111–203, tit. III, § 369(5), tit. VI, §§ 610(b), 612(c), 627(a)(2), 124 Stat. 1559, 1612, 1613, 1640 (July 21, 2010)]

* * *

## 12 U.S.C. § 1465. State law preemption standards for Federal savings associations clarified

**(a) In general**

Any determination by a court or by the Director or any successor officer or agency regarding the relation of State law to a provision of this chapter or any regulation or order prescribed under this chapter shall be made in accordance with the laws and legal standards applicable to national banks regarding the preemption of State law.

* * *

[June 13, 1933, ch. 64, § 6, *as added and amended by* Pub. L. No. 111–203, tit. X, §§ 1046(a), 1047(b), 124 Stat. 2017, 2018 (July 21, 2010)]

# *D.2.2 Regulations*

## TITLE 12—BANKS AND BANKING

## PART 560—LENDING AND INVESTMENT

## SUBPART B—LENDING AND INVESTMENT PROVISIONS APPLICABLE TO ALL SAVINGS ASSOCIATIONS

* * *

## 12 C.F.R. § 560.110 Most favored lender usury preemption.

(a) *Definition.* The term "interest" as used in 12 U.S.C. 1463(g) includes any payment compensating a creditor or prospective creditor for an extension of credit, making available of a line of credit, or any default or breach by a borrower of a condition upon which credit was extended. It includes, among other things, the following fees connected with credit extension or availability: numerical periodic rates, late fees, not sufficient funds (NSF) fees, overlimit fees, annual fees, cash advance fees, and membership fees. It does not ordinarily include appraisal fees, premiums and commissions attributable to insurance guaranteeing repayment of any extension of credit, finders' fees, fees for document preparation or notarization, or fees incurred to obtain credit reports.

(b) *Authority.* A savings association located in a state may charge interest at the maximum rate permitted to any state-chartered or licensed lending institution by the law of that state. If state law permits different interest charges on specified classes of loans, a federal savings association making such loans is subject only to the provisions of state law relating to that class of loans that are material to the determination of the permitted interest. For example, a federal savings association may lawfully charge the highest rate permitted to be charged by a state-licensed small loan company, without being so licensed, but subject to state law limitations on the size of loans made by small loan companies. Except as provided in this paragraph, the applicability of state law to Federal savings associations shall be determined in accordance with §560.2 of this part. State supervisors determine the degree to which state-chartered savings associations must comply with state laws other than those imposing restrictions on interest, as defined in paragraph (a) of this section.

(c) *Effect on state definitions of interest.* The Federal definition of the term "interest" in paragraph (a) of this section does not change how interest is defined by the individual states (nor how the state definition of interest is used) solely for purposes of state law. For example, if late fees are not "interest" under state law where a savings association is located but state law permits its most favored lender to charge late fees, then a savings association located in that state may charge late fees to its intrastate customers. The savings association may also charge late fees to its interstate customers because the fees are interest under the Federal definition of interest and an allowable charge under state law where the savings association is located. However, the late fees would not be treated as interest for purposes of evaluating compliance with state usury limitations because state law excludes late fees when calculating the maximum interest that lending institutions may charge under those limitations.

* * *

## D.2.3 *Summary of OTS Interpretative Letters*

The full text of these letters is found on the companion website to this treatise.

*OTS Interpretive Letter P-2006-6 (July 20, 2006).* Subsidiary of an operating subsidiary of a savings association is entitled to the same preemption rights as the association. Regarding the exportation of interest rates, the subsidiary of the operating subsidiary (located in Fla.) can export the rate of its home state or the rate of the home state of its grandparent FSB, in this case, N.Y.

*OTS Interpretive Letter P-2004-8 (Sept. 17, 2004).* OTS confirms that savings associations may charge the interest rate allowed by its home state regardless of where the loan is "made" or "booked"; or the state in which a branch exists, if the loan is "booked" in the branch's state. OTS distinguishes the more restrictive standards set forth in OCC and FDIC letters on this issue.

# D.3 State Banks and Savings Associations

## D.3.1 *Statutory Provisions*

### TITLE 12—BANKS AND BANKING

### CHAPTER 16—FEDERAL DEPOSIT INSURANCE CORPORATION

* * *

### 12 U.S.C. § 1813. Definitions

As used in this chapter—

**(a) Definitions of bank and related terms**

**(1) Bank**

The term "bank"—

**(A)** means any national bank and State bank, and any Federal branch and insured branch;

**(B)** includes any former savings association.

**(2) State bank**

The term "State bank" means any bank, banking association, trust company, savings bank, industrial bank (or similar depository institution which the Board of Directors finds to be operating substantially in the same manner as an industrial bank), or other banking institution which—

**(A)** is engaged in the business of receiving deposits, other than trust funds (as defined in this section); and

**(B)** is incorporated under the laws of any State or which is operating under the Code of Law for the District of Columbia,

including any cooperative bank or other unincorporated bank the deposits of which were insured by the Corporation on the day before August 9, 1989.

**(3) State**

The term "State" means any State of the United States, the District of Columbia, any territory of the United States, Puerto Rico, Guam, American Samoa, the Trust Territory of the Pacific Islands, the Virgin Islands, and the Northern Mariana Islands.

* * *

[Prior citations omitted. As amended by Pub. L. No. 111-203, tit. III, §§ 312(c), 334(b), 363(1), 124 Stat. 1522, 1539, 1550 (July 21, 2010)]

* * *

### 12 U.S.C. § 1831d. State-chartered insured depository institutions and insured branches of foreign banks

**(a) Interest rates**

In order to prevent discrimination against State-chartered insured depository institutions, including insured savings banks, or insured branches of foreign banks with respect to interest rates, if the applicable rate prescribed in this subsection exceeds the rate such State bank or insured branch of a foreign bank would be permitted to charge in the absence of this subsection, such State bank or such insured branch of a foreign bank may, notwithstanding any State constitution or statute which is hereby preempted for the purposes of this section, take, receive, reserve, and charge on any loan or discount made, or upon any note, bill of exchange, or other evidence of debt, interest at a rate of not more than 1 per centum in excess of the discount rate on ninety-day commercial paper in effect at the Federal Reserve bank in the Federal Reserve district where such State bank or such insured branch of a foreign bank is located or at the rate allowed by the laws of the State, territory, or district where the bank is located, whichever may be greater.

**(b) Interest overcharge; forfeiture; interest payment recovery**

If the rate prescribed in subsection (a) of this section exceeds the rate such State bank or such insured branch of a foreign bank would be permitted to charge in the absence of this section, and such State fixed rate is thereby preempted by the rate described in subsection (a) of this section, the taking, receiving, reserving, or charging a greater rate of interest than is allowed by subsection (a) of this section, when knowingly done, shall be deemed a forfeiture of the entire interest which the note, bill, or other evidence of debt carries with it, or which has been agreed to be paid thereon. If such greater rate of interest has been paid, the person who paid it may recover in a civil action commenced in a court of appropriate jurisdiction not later than two years after the date of such payment, an amount equal to twice the amount of the interest paid from such State bank or such insured branch of a foreign bank taking, receiving, reserving, or charging such interest.

**[State Opt-Out Provision]**

* * *

Section 525 of Pub. L. No. 96-221 provides that: "The amendments made by sections 521 through 523 of this title [applicable to now codified 12 U.S.C. § 1831d] shall apply only with respect to loans made in any State during the period beginning on April 1, 1980, and ending on the date, on or after April 1, 1980, on which such State adopts a law or certifies that the voters of such State have voted in favor of any provision, constitutional or otherwise, which states explicitly and by its terms that such State does not want the amendments made by such sections to apply with respect to loans made in such State, except that such amendments shall apply to a loan made on or after the date such law is adopted or such certification is made if such loan is made pursuant to a commitment to make such loan which was entered into on or after April 1, 1980, and prior to the date on which such law is adopted or such certification is made."

[Sept. 21, 1950, c. 967, § 2[27], *as added by* Pub. L. No. 96-221, tit. V, § 521, 94 Stat. 164 (Mar. 31, 1980); *amended by* Pub. L. No. 100-86, tit. I, § 101(g)(2), 101 Stat. 563 (Aug. 10, 1987); Pub. L. No. 101-73, tit. II, § 201(a)(1), 103 Stat. 187 (Aug. 9, 1989)]

* * *

## 12 U.S.C. § 1831u. Interstate bank mergers

* * *

**(f) Applicable rate and other charge limitations**

**(1) In general**

In the case of any State that has a constitutional provision that sets a maximum lawful annual percentage rate of interest on any contract at not more than 5 percent above the discount rate for 90-day commercial paper in effect at the Federal reserve bank for the Federal reserve district in which such State is located, except as provided in paragraph (2), upon the establishment in such State of a branch of any out-of-State insured depository institution in such State under this section, the maximum interest rate or amount of interest, discount points, finance charges, or other similar charges that may be charged, taken, received, or reserved (or in the case of a governmental entity located in such State, paid) from time to time in any loan or discount made or upon any note, bill of exchange, financing transaction, or other evidence of debt by—

**(A)** any insured depository institution whose home State is such State shall be equal to not more than the greater of—

**(i)** the maximum interest rate or amount of interest, discount points, finance charges, or other similar charges that may be charged, taken, received, or reserved in a similar transaction under the constitution or any statute or other law of the home State of the out-of-State insured depository institution establishing any such branch, without reference to this section, as such maximum interest rate or amount of interest may change from time to time; or

**(ii)** the maximum rate or amount of interest, discount points, finance charges, or other similar charges that may be charged, taken, received, or reserved in a similar transaction by a State insured depository institution chartered under the laws of such State or a national bank or Federal savings association whose main office is located in such State without reference to this section; * * * *

* * *

**(2) Rule of construction**

**(A) In general**

No provision of this subsection shall be construed as superseding or affecting—

**(i)** the authority of any insured depository institution to take, receive, reserve, and charge interest on any loan made in any State other than the State referred to in paragraph (1); or

**(ii)** the applicability of section 1735f–7a of this title, section 85 of this title, or section 1831d of this title.

**(B) Applicability**

This subsection shall be construed to apply to any loan or discount made, or note, bill of exchange, financing transaction, or other evidence of debt, originated by an insured depository institution, a governmental entity located in such State, or a person that is not a depository institution described in subparagraph (A) doing business in such State.

* * *

[Sept. 21, 1950, ch. 967, § 2[44], *as added by* Pub. L. No. 103–328, tit. I, § 102(a), 108 Stat. 2343 (Sept. 29, 1994); *amended by* Pub. L. No. 106–102, tit. VII, § 731, 113 Stat. 1477 (Nov. 12, 1999); Pub. L. No. 111–32, tit. V, § 504(a), 123 Stat. 1880 (June 24, 2009); Pub. L. No. 111–83, tit. V, § 563(a), (b), 123 Stat. 2183 (Oct. 28, 2009); Pub. L. No. 111–203, tit. VI, § 607(b), 124 Stat. 1608 (July 21, 2010)]

## D.3.2 *Summary of FDIC Interpretation Letters*

The full text of these letters is found on the companion website to this treatise.

*Interpretive Letter No. FDIC-02-06 (Dec. 19, 2002).*
The Michigan motor vehicle retail installment sales act is preempted by § 521 for insured state-chartered banks only to the extent that the state law is interpreted to require an out-of-state bank to comply, directly or through its agent, with the law's interest rate and remedy provisions when making loans through car dealers acting as the bank's agents. Other parts of the act are not preempted, however. Section 85 of the National Bank Act and § 521 of DIDA should be construed the same. The state's ruling affects the lending of out-of-state banks by implication (even if not directly since the ruling was directed to policing the actions of bank agents, not the banks themselves) because it specifically provides that the lender's status as a bank does not mean that entities entering into agency arrangements with a bank may do so without complying with the licensing requirements of the act and imposes compliance obligations.

*FDIC General Counsel's Opinion No. 12 (Mar. 17, 2000), available at* 65 Fed. Reg. 14,568. "Engaged in the business of receiving deposits" includes the holding by a depository institution of one or more non-trust deposits in the aggregate of $500,000.

*FDIC General Counsel's Opinion No. 11 (May 18, 1998), available at* 63 Fed. Reg. 27,282. The lengthy opinion analyzes § 1831d of the FDI Act regarding the issue of which state's law applies for the most favored lender doctrine and exportation purposes, i.e., the "location" of the bank for exportation purposes. The FDIC adopts OCC Interpretive Letter No. 822. Therefore, an insured state-chartered bank can be located for purposes of § 1831d in the state in which it is chartered as well as where the branches are located, under certain circumstances. State banks should make an appropriate disclosure to the customer of the relevant state which will govern the transaction.

*FDIC General Counsel Opinion No. 10 (Apr. 17, 1998), available at* 63 Fed. Reg. 19,258. The definition of interest for § 521 purposes is the same for national banks and savings associations. Therefore, one looks to the OCC regulation on this point, 12 C.F.R. § 7.4001.

*Interpretive Letter No. FDIC-97-05 (July 8, 1997).* An automated loan machine is not a branch even if it approves the loan and disburses the loan proceeds due to an amendment to the FDIA in 1996.

*Interpretive Letter No. FDIC-95-28 (Oct. 4, 1995).* Soliciting borrowers, accepting loan applications, reviewing and processing loan applications, and forwarding the applications to an out-of-state bank does not turn a "loan production office" into a bank branch; however, the office becomes a branch if it approves loans and funds the loans.

*Interpretive Letter No. FDIC-93-27 (July 12, 1993).* The FDIC interprets § 521 to include the preemption of common law restrictions as well as statutory and constitutional restrictions on interest rates. In a lengthy letter, the FDIC reviewed court decisions and legislative history in interpreting the scope of § 521.

*Interpretive Letter No. FDIC-92-47 (July 8, 1992).* Section 521 of DIDA authorizes insured state-chartered banks to export the same fees and charges that are a component of interest or material to the determination of interest on interstate loans as national banks may export under the NBA. Purposes of § 501 and § 521 of DIDA are different and cases interpreting one section are not necessarily applicable to the other.

*Interpretive Letter No. FDIC-88-45 (June 29, 1988).* If the state where the loan is made opted out of § 521 of DIDA, then the usury law of that state applies. Where a loan is made is a factual determination. The letter does not list any determinative factors other than the contract terms and all facts. Rejects the proposition that the only a bank's home state has the right to countermand preemption regarding loans made by that bank.

*FDIC Interpretive Letter (Oct. 20, 1983).* The analysis under § 85 of the National Bank Act applies with equal force to § 521 of DIDA regarding a state bank making a loan to a borrower in another state that opted out of § 521. The bank may rely on the interest rate provisions of the state where the bank is located in extending credit to the residents of its state and of other states.

*FDIC Interpretive Letter (Mar. 17, 1981).* A state bank, making an interstate loan, would determine the permissible interest rates by referring only to the laws of the state in which it is located (i.e., chartered), and not to the state in which the borrower resides or any other state.

# D.4 State Credit Unions

## *D.4.1 Statutory Provisions*

### TITLE 12—BANKS AND BANKING

### CHAPTER 14—FEDERAL CREDIT UNIONS

### SUBCHAPTER II—SHARE INSURANCE

* * *

### 12 U.S.C. § 1785. Requirements governing insured credit unions

* * *

**(g) Interest rates**

**(1)** If the applicable rate prescribed in this subsection exceeds the rate an insured credit union would be permitted to charge in the absence of this subsection, such credit union may, notwithstanding any State constitution or statute which is hereby preempted for the purposes of this subsection, take, receive, reserve, and charge on any loan, interest at a rate of not more than 1 per centum in excess of the discount rate on ninety-day commercial paper in effect at the Federal Reserve bank in the Federal Reserve district where such insured credit union is located or at the rate allowed by the laws of the State, territory, or district where such credit union is located, whichever may be greater.

**(2)** If the rate prescribed in paragraph (1) exceeds the rate such credit union would be permitted to charge in the absence of this subsection, and such State fixed rate is thereby preempted by the rate described in paragraph (1), the taking, receiving, reserving, or charging a greater rate than is allowed by paragraph (1), when knowingly done, shall be deemed a forfeiture of the entire interest which the loan carries with it, or which has been agreed to be paid thereon. If such greater rate of interest has been paid, the person who paid it may recover, in a civil action commenced in a court of appropriate jurisdiction not later than two years after the date of such payment, an amount equal to twice the amount of interest paid from the credit union taking or receiving such interest.

* * *

**[State Opt-Out Provision]**

* * *

Section 525 of Pub. L. No. 96-221 provides that: "The amendments made by sections 521 through 523 of this title [applicable to now codified 12 U.S.C. § 1785(g)] shall apply only with respect to loans made in any State during the period beginning on April 1, 1980, and ending on the date, on or after April 1, 1980, on which such State adopts a law or certifies that the voters of such State have voted in favor of any provision, constitutional or otherwise, which states explicitly and by its terms that such State does not want the amendments made by such sections to apply with respect to loans made in such State, except that such amendments shall apply to a loan made on or after the date such law is adopted or such certification is made if such loan is made pursuant to a commitment to make such loan which was entered into on or after April 1, 1980, and prior to the date on which such law is adopted or such certification is made."

* * *

[June 26, 1934, c. 750, tit. II, § 205, *as added by* Pub. L. No. 91-468, § 1(3), 84 Stat. 1002 (Oct. 19, 1970); *amended by* Pub. L. No. 95-630, tit. V, § 502(b), 92 Stat. 3681 (Nov. 10, 1978); Pub. L. No. 96-221, tit. III, § 305(d), tit. V, § 523, 94 Stat. 147, 166 (Mar. 31, 1980); Pub. L. No. 97-320, tit. I, §§ 131, 141(a)(8), tit. VII, § 706(b), 96 Stat. 1486, 1489, 1540 (Oct. 15, 1982); Pub. L. No. 100-86, tit. V, § 509(a), 101 Stat. 635 (Aug. 10, 1987); Pub. L. No. 101-73, tit. IX, § 910(b), 103 Stat. 478 (Aug. 9, 1989); Pub. L. No. 103-322, tit. XXXII, § 320606, 108 Stat. 2119 (Sept. 13, 1994); Pub. L. No. 105-219, tit. II, § 202, 112 Stat. 919 (Aug. 7, 1998); Pub. L. No. 109-173, § 2(d)(3), 119 Stat. 3604 (Feb. 15, 2006); Pub. L. No. 109-351, tit. VI, § 607(b), 120 Stat. 1982 (Oct. 13, 2006); Pub. L. No. 111-203, tit. III, § 362(2), 124 Stat. 1549 (July 21, 2010)]

## *D.4.2 Summary of NCUA Formal Statement of Interpretation and Policy*

The full text of this formal statement is available on the companion website to this treatise.

**State Chartered Federally Insured Credit Unions as "Most Favored Lenders," IRPS 81-3, 46 Fed. Reg. 24,153 (Apr. 10, 1981).** NCUA interprets 12 U.S.C. § 1785(g) to mean that state chartered federally insured credit unions may charge the federal interest rate or the rate allowed to the most favored lender on the particular class of loans under state law, if either of these rates exceeds the rate the state chartered credit unions are normally permitted to charge under state law.

# Appendix E Preemption Based on OCC Regulation of Federal Depositories

This appendix includes materials relevant to federal preemption of state law as applicable to national banks and federal savings associations, based upon Office of the Comptroller of Currency (OCC) regulation of those federal depositories.

## E.1 Dodd-Frank Standards for Preemption Determinations

These provisions were enacted as part of the Dodd-Frank Wall Street Reform and Consumer Protection Act, Pub. L. No. 111-203, tit. X, §§ 1044(a), 1045, 1047(a), 1048, 124 Stat. 2014, 2017, 2018 (July 21, 2010).

### TITLE 12—BANKS AND BANKING

### CHAPTER 2—NATIONAL BANKS

### SUBCHAPTER I—ORGANIZATION AND GENERAL PROVISIONS

* * *

### 12 U.S.C. § 25b. State law preemption standards for national banks and subsidiaries clarified

**(a) Definitions**

For purposes of this section, the following definitions shall apply:

**(1) National bank**

The term "national bank" includes—

**(A)** any bank organized under the laws of the United States; and

**(B)** any Federal branch established in accordance with the International Banking Act of 1978.

**(2) State consumer financial laws**

The term "State consumer financial law" means a State law that does not directly or indirectly discriminate against national banks and that directly and specifically regulates the manner, content, or terms and conditions of any financial transaction (as may be authorized for national banks to engage in), or any account related thereto, with respect to a consumer.

**(3) Other definitions**

The terms "affiliate", "subsidiary", "includes" , and "including" have the same meanings as in section 3 of the Federal Deposit Insurance Act [12 U.S.C. § 1813].

**(b) Preemption standard**

**(1) In general**

State consumer financial laws are preempted, only if—

**(A)** application of a State consumer financial law would have a discriminatory effect on national banks, in comparison with the effect of the law on a bank chartered by that State;

**(B)** in accordance with the legal standard for preemption in the decision of the Supreme Court of the United States in Barnett Bank of Marion County, N. A. v. Nelson, Florida Insurance Commissioner, et al., 517 U.S. 25 (1996), the State consumer financial law prevents or significantly interferes with the exercise by the national bank of its powers; and any preemption determination under this subparagraph may be made by a court, or by regulation or order of the Comptroller of the Currency on a case-by-case basis, in accordance with applicable law; or

**(C)** the State consumer financial law is preempted by a provision of Federal law other than this title [Title 62 of the Revised Statutes].

**(2) Savings clause**

This title [Title 62 of the Revised Statutes] and section 24 of the Federal Reserve Act [12 U.S.C. § 371] do not preempt, annul, or affect the applicability of any State law to any subsidiary or affiliate of a national bank (other than a subsidiary or affiliate that is chartered as a national bank).

**(3) Case-by-case basis**

**(A) Definition**

As used in this section the term "case-by-case basis" refers to a determination pursuant to this section made by the Comptroller concerning the impact of a particular State consumer financial law on any national bank that is subject to that law, or the law of any other State with substantively equivalent terms.

**(B) Consultation**

When making a determination on a case-by-case basis that a State consumer financial law of another State has substantively equivalent terms as one that the Comptroller is preempting, the Comptroller shall first consult with the Bureau of Consumer Financial Protection and shall take the views of the Bureau into account when making the determination.

**(4) Rule of construction**

This title [Title 62 of the Revised Statutes] does not occupy the field in any area of State law.

**(5) Standards of review**

**(A) Preemption**

A court reviewing any determinations made by the Comptroller regarding preemption of a State law by this title [Title 62 of the Revised Statutes] or section 24 of the Federal Reserve Act [12 U.S.C. § 371] shall assess the validity of such determinations, depending upon the thoroughness evident in the consideration of the agency, the validity of the reasoning of the agency, the consistency with other valid determinations made by the agency, and other factors which the court finds persuasive and relevant to its decision.

**(B) Savings clause**

Except as provided in subparagraph (A), nothing in this section shall affect the deference that a court may afford to the Comptroller in making determinations regarding the meaning or interpretation of title LXII of the Revised Statutes of the United States or other Federal laws [12 U.S.C. §§ 21–43].

**(6) Comptroller determination not delegable**

Any regulation, order, or determination made by the Comptroller of the Currency under paragraph (1)(B) shall be made by the Comptroller, and shall not be delegable to another officer or employee of the Comptroller of the Currency.

**(c) Substantial evidence**

No regulation or order of the Comptroller of the Currency prescribed under subsection (b)(1)(B), shall be interpreted or applied so as to invalidate, or otherwise declare inapplicable to a national bank, the provision of the State consumer financial law, unless substantial evidence, made on the record of the proceeding, supports the specific finding regarding the preemption of such provision in accordance with the legal standard of the decision of the Supreme Court of the United States in Barnett Bank of Marion County, N.A. v. Nelson, Florida Insurance Commissioner, et al., 517 U.S. 25 (1996).

**(d) Periodic review of preemption determinations**

**(1) In general**

The Comptroller of the Currency shall periodically conduct a review, through notice and public comment, of each determination that a provision of Federal law preempts a State consumer financial law. The agency shall conduct such review within the 5-year period after prescribing or otherwise issuing such determination, and at least once during each 5-year period thereafter. After conducting the review of, and inspecting the comments made on, the determination, the agency shall publish a notice in the Federal Register announcing the decision to continue or rescind the determination or a proposal to amend the determination. Any such notice of a proposal to amend a determination and the subsequent resolution of such proposal shall comply with the procedures set forth in subsections (a) and (b) of section 5244 of the Revised Statutes of the United States [12 U.S.C. § 43(a), (b)].

**(2) Reports to Congress**

At the time of issuing a review conducted under paragraph (1), the Comptroller of the Currency shall submit a report regarding such review to the Committee on Financial Services of the House of Representatives and the Committee on Banking, Housing, and Urban Affairs of the Senate. The report submitted to the respective committees shall address whether the agency intends to continue, rescind, or propose to amend any determination that a provision of Federal law preempts a State consumer financial law, and the reasons therefor.

**(e) Application of State consumer financial law to subsidiaries and affiliates**

Notwithstanding any provision of this title [Title 62 of the Revised Statutes] or section 24 of the Federal Reserve Act [12 U.S.C. § 371], a State consumer financial law shall apply to a subsidiary or affiliate of a national bank (other than a subsidiary or affiliate that is chartered as a national bank) to the same extent that the State consumer financial law applies to any person, corporation, or other entity subject to such State law.

**(f) Preservation of powers related to charging interest**

No provision of this title [Title 62 of the Revised Statutes] shall be construed as altering or otherwise affecting the authority conferred by section 5197 of the Revised Statutes of the United States [12 U.S.C. § 85] for the charging of interest by a national bank at the rate allowed by the laws of the State, territory, or district where the bank is located, including with respect to the meaning of "interest" under such provision.

**(g) Transparency of OCC preemption determinations**

The Comptroller of the Currency shall publish and update no less frequently than quarterly, a list of preemption determinations by the Comptroller of the Currency then in effect that identifies the activities and practices covered by each determination and the requirements and constraints determined to be preempted.

**(h) Clarification of law applicable to nondepository institution subsidiaries and affiliates of national banks**

**(1) Definitions**

For purposes of this subsection, the terms "depository institution", "subsidiary", and "affiliate" have the same meanings as in section 3 of the Federal Deposit Insurance Act [12 U.S.C. § 1813].

**(2) Rule of construction**

No provision of this title [Title 62 of the Revised Statutes] or section 24 of the Federal Reserve Act [12 U.S.C. § 371] shall be construed as preempting, annulling, or affecting the applicability of State law to any subsidiary, affiliate, or agent of a national bank (other than a subsidiary, affiliate, or agent that is chartered as a national bank).

**(*i*) Visitorial powers**

**(1) In general**

In accordance with the decision of the Supreme Court of the United States in Cuomo v. Clearing House Assn., L. L. C. (129 S. Ct. 2710 (2009)), no provision of title 62 of the Revised Statutes which relates to visitorial powers or otherwise limits or restricts the visitorial authority to which any national bank is subject shall be construed as limiting or restricting the authority of any attorney general (or other chief law enforcement officer) of any State to bring an action against a national bank in a court of appropriate jurisdiction to enforce an applicable law and to seek relief as authorized by such law.

**(j) Enforcement actions**

The ability of the Comptroller of the Currency to bring an enforcement action under this title [Title 62 of the Revised Statutes] or section 5 of the Federal Trade Commission Act [15 U.S.C. § 45] does not preclude any private party from enforcing rights granted under Federal or State law in the courts.

Pub. L. No. 111-203, tit. X, §§ 1044(a), 1045, 1047(a), 1048, 124 Stat. 2014, 2017, 2018 (July 21, 2010)]

* * *

## Chapter 12—SAVINGS ASSOCIATIONS

* * *

## 12 U.S.C. § 1465. State law preemption standards for Federal savings associations clarified

**(a) In general**

Any determination by a court or by the Director or any successor officer or agency regarding the relation of State law to a provision of this chapter or any regulation or order prescribed under this chapter shall be made in accordance with the laws and legal standards applicable to national banks regarding the preemption of State law.

**(b) Principles of conflict preemption applicable**

Notwithstanding the authorities granted under sections 4 and 5 [12 U.S.C. §§ 1463 and 1464], this chapter does not occupy the field in any area of State law.

**(c) Visitorial powers**

The provisions of sections 5136C(i) of the Revised Statutes of the United States [12 U.S.C. § 25b(i)] shall apply to Federal savings associations, and any subsidiary thereof, to the same extent and in the same manner as if such savings associations, or subsidiaries thereof, were national banks or subsidiaries of national banks, respectively.

**(d) Enforcement actions**

The ability of the Comptroller of the Currency to bring an enforcement action under this chapter or section 5 of the Federal Trade Commission Act [15 U.S.C. § 45] does not preclude any private party from enforcing rights granted under Federal or State law in the courts.

[Pub. L. No. 111-203, tit. X, §§ 1046(a), 1047(b), 1048, 124 Stat. 2017, 2018 (July 21, 2010)]

* * *

# CHAPTER 53—WALL STREET REFORM AND CONSUMER PROTECTION

## SUBCHAPTER V—BUREAU OF CONSUMER FINANCIAL PROTECTION

## PART D—PRESERVATION OF STATE LAW

### 12 U.S.C. § 5551. Relation to State law

**(a) In general**

**(1) Rule of construction**

This subchapter, other than sections 1044 through 1048,[3] may not be construed as annulling, altering, or affecting, or exempting any person subject to the provisions of this subchapter from complying with, the statutes, regulations, orders, or interpretations in effect in any State, except to the extent that any such provision of law is inconsistent with the provisions of this subchapter, and then only to the extent of the inconsistency.

**(2) Greater protection under State law**

For purposes of this subsection, a statute, regulation, order, or interpretation in effect in any State is not inconsistent with the provisions of this subchapter if the protection that such statute, regulation, order, or interpretation affords to consumers is greater than the protection provided under this subchapter. A determination regarding whether a statute, regulation, order, or interpretation in effect in any State is inconsistent with the provisions of this subchapter may be made by the Bureau on its own motion or in response to a nonfrivolous petition initiated by any interested person.

**(b) Relation to other provisions of enumerated consumer laws that relate to State law**

No provision of this subchapter, except as provided in section 1083,[4] shall be construed as modifying, limiting, or superseding the operation of any provision of an enumerated consumer law that relates to the application of a law in effect in any State with respect to such Federal law.

* * *

[Pub. L. No. 111-203, tit. X, §§ 1041, 1048, 124 Stat. 2011, 2018 (July 21, 2010)]

* * *

### 12 U.S.C. § 5553. Preservation of existing contracts

This subchapter, and regulations, orders, guidance, and interpretations prescribed, issued, or established by the Bureau, shall not be construed to alter or affect the applicability of any regulation, order, guidance, or interpretation prescribed, issued, and established by the Comptroller of the Currency or the Director of the Office of Thrift Supervision regarding the applicability of State law under Federal banking law to any contract entered into on or before July 21, 2010, by national banks, Federal savings associations, or subsidiaries thereof that are regulated and supervised by the Comptroller of the Currency or the Director of the Office of Thrift Supervision, respectively.

[Pub. L. No. 111-203, tit. X, §§ 1043, 1048, 124 Stat. 2014, 2018 (July 21, 2010)]

3 Sections 1044–1048 of Title X of the Dodd-Frank Act added 12 U.S.C. §§ 25b and 1465. Pub. L. No. 111-203, tit. X, §§ 1044–1048, 124 Stat. 2014–2018 (July 21, 2010).

4 Section 1083 of Title X of the Dodd-Frank Act amended portions of Alternative Mortgage Transaction Parity Act. Pub. L. No. 111-203, tit. X, § 1083, 124 Stat. 2080 (July 21, 2010).

## E.2 OCC Regulations

### TITLE 12—BANKS AND BANKING

### CHAPTER I—COMPTROLLER OF THE CURRENCY, DEPARTMENT OF THE TREASURY

### PART 7—BANK ACTIVITIES AND OPERATIONS

### SUBPART D—PREEMPTION

* * *

### 12 C.F.R. § 7.4008 Lending.

(a) *Authority of national banks.* A national bank may make, sell, purchase, participate in, or otherwise deal in loans and interests in loans that are not secured by liens on, or interests in, real estate, subject to such terms, conditions, and limitations prescribed by the Comptroller of the Currency and any other applicable Federal law.

(b) *Standards for loans.* A national bank shall not make a consumer loan subject to this § 7.4008 based predominantly on the bank's realization of the foreclosure or liquidation value of the borrower's collateral, without regard to the borrower's ability to repay the loan according to its terms. A bank may use any reasonable method to determine a borrower's ability to repay, including, for example, the borrower's current and expected income, current and expected cash flows, net worth, other relevant financial resources, current financial obligations, employment status, credit history, or other relevant factors.

(c) *Unfair and deceptive practices.* A national bank shall not engage in unfair or deceptive practices within the meaning of section 5 of the Federal Trade Commission Act, 15 U.S.C. 45(a)(1), and regulations promulgated thereunder in connection with loans made under this § 7.4008.

(d) A national bank may make non-real estate loans without regard to state law limitations concerning:

(1) Licensing, registration (except for purposes of service of process), filings, or reports by creditors;

(2) The ability of a creditor to require or obtain insurance for collateral or other credit enhancements or risk mitigants, in furtherance of safe and sound banking practices;

(3) Loan-to-value ratios;

(4) The terms of credit, including the schedule for repayment of principal and interest, amortization of loans, balance, payments due, minimum payments, or term to maturity of the loan, including the circumstances under which a loan may be called due and payable upon the passage of time or a specified event external to the loan;

(5) Escrow accounts, impound accounts, and similar accounts;

(6) Security property, including leaseholds;

(7) Access to, and use of, credit reports;

(8) Disclosure and advertising, including laws requiring specific statements, information, or other content to be included in credit application forms, credit solicitations, billing statements, credit contracts, or other credit-related documents;

(9) Disbursements and repayments; and

(10) Rates of interest on loans.[1]

(e) *State laws that are not preempted.* State laws on the following subjects are not inconsistent with the non-real estate lending powers of national banks and apply to national banks to the extent consistent with the decision of the Supreme Court in Barnett Bank of Marion County, N.A. v. Nelson, Florida Insurance Commissioner, et al., 517 U.S. 25 (1996):

(1) Contracts;

(2) Torts;

(3) Criminal law;[2]

(4) Rights to collect debts;

(5) Acquisition and transfer of property;

(6) Taxation;

(7) Zoning; and

(8) Any other law that the OCC determines to be applicable to national banks in accordance with the decision of the Supreme Court in Barnett Bank of Marion County, N.A. v. Nelson, Florida Insurance Commissioner, et al., 517 U.S. 25 (1996) or that is made applicable by Federal law.

[69 Fed. Reg. 1916 (Jan. 13, 2004); 76 Fed. Reg. 43,565 (July 21, 2011)]

* * *

1 The limitations on charges that comprise rates of interest on loans by national banks are determined under Federal law. See 12 U.S.C. 85; 12 CFR 7.4001. State laws purporting to regulate national bank fees and charges that do not constitute interest are addressed in 12 CFR 7.4002.

2 See *supra* note 5 regarding the distinction drawn by the Supreme Court in Easton v. Iowa, 188 U.S. 220, 238 (1903). [*Editor's note:* Note 5 is found in § 7.4007.]

### PART 34—REAL ESTATE LENDING AND APPRAISALS

### SUBPART A—GENERAL

* * *

### 12 C.F.R. § 34.6 Applicability of state law to Federal savings associations and subsidiaries.

In accordance with section 1046 of the Dodd–Frank Wall Street Reform and Consumer Protection Act (12 U.S.C. 25b), Federal savings associations and their subsidiaries shall be subject to the same laws and legal standards, including regulations of the OCC, as are applicable to national banks and their subsidiaries, regarding the preemption of state law.

[76 Fed. Reg. 43,569 (July 21, 2011)]

* * *

## E.3 OCC/OTS Interpretations

The Office of the Comptroller of the Currency and the former Office of Thrift Supervision have issued a large number of interpretive and advisory letters concerning preemption of state law. The full text and summaries of these letters are found on the companion website. Because the Dodd-Frank Act has so thoroughly changed preemption standards (*see* Appx. E.1, *supra*), these letters now have less value in analyzing the applicability of state law to credit transactions.

Appendix F

# Preemption of Manufactured Home Loan Interest Rates

## F.1 Depository Institutions Deregulation and Monetary Control Act (DIDA)

### TITLE 12. BANKS AND BANKING

### CHAPTER 13. NATIONAL HOUSING

### SUBCHAPTER V. MISCELLANEOUS

* * *

### 12 U.S.C. § 1735f-7a. State constitution or laws limiting mortgage interest, discount points, and finance or other charges; exemption for obligations made after March 31, 1980

**(a) Applicability to loan, mortgage, credit sale, or advance; applicability to deposit, account, or obligation**

**(1)** The provisions of the constitution or the laws of any State expressly limiting the rate or amount of interest, discount points, finance charges, or other charges which may be charged, taken, received, or reserved shall not apply to any loan, mortgage, credit sale, or advance which is—

**(A)** secured by a first lien on residential real property, by a first lien on all stock allocated to a dwelling unit in a residential cooperative housing corporation, or by a first lien on a residential manufactured home;

**(B)** made after March 31, 1980; and

**(C)** described in section 527(b) of the National Housing Act (12 U.S.C. 1735f–5(b)), except that for the purpose of this section—

**(i)** the limitation described in section 527(b)(1) of such Act that the property must be designed principally for the occupancy of from one to four families shall not apply;

**(ii)** the requirement contained in section 527(b)(1) of such Act that the loan be secured by residential real property shall not apply to a loan secured by stock in a residential cooperative housing corporation or to a loan or credit sale secured by a first lien on a residential manufactured home;

**(iii)** the term "federally related mortgage loan" in section 527(b) of such Act shall include a credit sale which is secured by a first lien on a residential manufactured home and which otherwise meets the definitional requirements of section 527(b) of such Act, as those requirements are modified by this section;

**(iv)** the term "residential loans" in section 527(b)(2)(D) of such Act shall also include loans or credit sales secured by a first lien on a residential manufactured home;

**(v)** the requirement contained in section 527(b)(2)(D) of such Act that a creditor make or invest in loans aggregating more than $1,000,000 per year shall not apply to a creditor selling residential manufactured homes financed by loans or credit sales secured by first liens on residential manufactured homes if the creditor has an arrangement to sell such loans or credit sales in whole or in part, or if such loans or credit sales are sold in whole or in part to a lender, institution, or creditor described in section 527(b) of such Act or in this section or a creditor, as defined in section 103(f) of the Truth in Lending Act [15 U.S.C. 1602(f)], as such section was in effect on the day preceding March 31, 1980, if such creditor makes or invests in residential real estate loans or loans or credit sales secured by first liens on residential manufactured homes aggregating more than $1,000,000 per year; and

**(vi)** the term "lender" in section 527(b)(2)(A) of such Act shall also be deemed to include any lender approved by the Secretary of Housing and Urban Development for participation in any mortgage insurance program under the National Housing Act [12 U.S.C. 1701 et seq.], and any individual who finances the sale or exchange of residential real property or a residential manufactured home which such individual owns and which such individual occupies or has occupied as his principal residence.

**(2)** The provisions of the constitution or law of any State expressly limiting the rate or amount of interest which may be charged, taken, received, or reserved shall not apply to any deposit or account held by, or other obligation of a depository institution. For purposes of this paragraph, the term "depository institution" means—

**(i)** any insured bank as defined in section 3 of the Federal Deposit Insurance Act (12 U.S.C. 1813);

**(ii)** any mutual savings bank as defined in section 3 of the Federal Deposit Insurance Act (12 U.S.C. 1813);

**(iii)** any savings bank as defined in section 3 of the Federal Deposit Insurance Act (12 U.S.C. 1813);

**(iv)** any insured credit union as defined in section 101 of the Federal Credit Union Act (12 U.S.C. 1752);

**(v)** any member as defined in section 2 of the Federal Home Loan Bank Act (12 U.S.C. 1422); and

**(vi)** any insured institution as defined in section 408[1] of the National Housing Act (12 U.S.C. 1730a).

**(b) Applicability to loan, mortgage, credit sale, or advance made in any State after April 1, 1980**

**(1)** Except as provided in paragraphs (2) and (3), the provisions of subsection (a)(1) of this section shall apply to any loan, mortgage, credit sale, or advance made in any State on or after April 1, 1980.

**(2)** Except as provided in paragraph (3), the provisions of subsection (a)(1) of this section shall not apply to any loan, mortgage, credit sale, or advance made in any State after the date (on or after April 1, 1980, and before April 1, 1983) on which such State adopts a law or certifies that the voters of such State have voted in favor of any provision, constitutional or otherwise, which states explicitly and by its terms that such State does not want the provisions of subsection (a)(1) of this section to apply with respect to loans, mortgages, credit sales, and advances made in such State.

**(3)** In any case in which a State takes an action described in paragraph (2), the provisions of subsection (a)(1) of this section shall continue to apply to—

**(A)** any loan, mortgage, credit sale, or advance which is made after the date such action was taken pursuant to a commitment therefor which was entered during the period beginning on April 1, 1980, and ending on the date on which such State takes such action; and

**(B)** any loan, mortgage, or advance which is a rollover of a loan, mortgage, or advance, as described in regulations of the Federal Home Loan Bank Board, which was made or committed to be made during the period beginning on April 1, 1980, and ending on the date on which such State takes any action described in paragraph (2).

**(4)** At any time after March 31, 1980, any State may adopt a provision of law placing limitations on discount points or such other charges on any loan, mortgage, credit sale, or advance described in subsection (a)(1) of this section.

**(c) Applicability to loan, mortgage, credit sale, or advance secured by first lien on residential manufactured home**

The provisions of subsection (a)(1) of this section shall not apply to a loan, mortgage, credit sale, or advance which is secured by a first lien on a residential manufactured home unless the terms and conditions relating to such loan, mortgage, credit sale, or advance comply with consumer protection provisions specified in regulations prescribed by the Federal Home Loan Bank Board. Such regulations shall—

**(1)** include consumer protection provisions with respect to balloon payments, prepayment penalties, late charges, and deferral fees;

**(2)** require a 30-day notice prior to instituting any action leading to repossession or foreclosure (except in the case of abandonment or other extreme circumstances);

**(3)** require that upon prepayment in full, the debtor shall be entitled to a refund of the unearned portion of the precomputed finance charge in an amount not less than the amount which would be calculated by the actuarial method, except that the debtor shall not be entitled to a refund which is less than $1; and

**(4)** include such other provisions as the Federal Home Loan Bank Board may prescribe after a finding that additional protections are required.

**(d) Implementation of provisions applicable to residential manufactured home**

The provisions of subsection (c) of this section shall not apply to a loan, mortgage, credit sale, or advance secured by a first lien on a residential manufactured home until regulations required to be issued pursuant to paragraphs (1), (2), and (3) of subsection (c) of this section take effect, except that the provisions of subsection (c) of this section shall apply in the case of such a loan, mortgage, credit sale, or advance made prior to the date on which such regulations take effect if the loan, mortgage, credit sale, or advance includes a precomputed finance charge and does not provide that, upon prepayment in full, the refund of the unearned portion of the precomputed finance charge is in an amount not less the amount which would be calculated by the actuarial method, except that the debtor shall not be entitled to a refund which is less than $1. The Federal Home Loan Bank Board shall issue regulations pursuant to the provisions of paragraphs (1), (2), and (3) of subsection (c) of this section that shall take effect prospectively not less than 30 days after publication in the Federal Register and not later than 120 days from March 31, 1980.

**(e) Definitions**

For the purpose of this section—

**(1)** a "prepayment" occurs upon—

**(A)** the refinancing or consolidation of the indebtedness;

**(B)** the actual prepayment of the indebtedness by the consumer whether voluntarily or following acceleration of the payment obligation by the creditor; or

**(C)** the entry of a judgment for the indebtedness in favor of the creditor;

**(2)** the term "actuarial method" means the method of allocating payments made on a debt between the outstanding balance of the obligation and the precomputed finance charge pursuant to which a payment is applied first to the accrued precomputed finance charge and any remainder is subtracted from, or any deficiency is added to, the outstanding balance of the obligation;

**(3)** the term "precomputed finance charge" means interest or a time price differential within the meaning of sections 106(a)(1) and (2) of the Truth in Lending Act (15 U.S.C. 1605(a)(1) and (2)) as computed by an add-on or discount method; and

**(4)** the term "residential manufactured home" means a manufactured home as defined in section 603(6) of the National Mobile Home Construction and Safety Standards Act of 1974 [42 U.S.C. 5402(6)] which is used as a residence.

**(f) Rules, regulations, and interpretations**

The Federal Home Loan Bank Board is authorized to issue rules and regulations and to publish interpretations governing the implementation of this section.

**(g) Effective date**

This section takes effect on April 1, 1980.

[Pub. L. No. 96–221, tit. V, § 501, 94 Stat. 161 (Mar. 31, 1980); Pub. L. No. 96–221, tit. II, § 207(b)(11), 94 Stat. 144 (Mar. 31, 1980); Pub. L. No. 96–399, tit. III, §§ 308(c)(6), 324(a), (e), 94 Stat. 1641, 1647, 1648 (Oct. 8, 1980); Pub. L. No. 97–35, tit. III, § 384, 95 Stat. 432 (Aug. 13, 1981)]

* * *

# F.2 DIDA Regulations

These regulations were initially promulgated by the Federal Home Loan Bank Board, but its authority was later transferred to the Office of Thrift Supervision, which effective July 21, 2011 has transferred its authority to the Office of the Comptroller of the Currency.

## TITLE 12. BANKS AND BANKING

## CHAPTER V. OFFICE OF THRIFT SUPERVISION, DEPARTMENT OF THE TREASURY

## PART 590. PREEMPTION OF STATE USURY LAWS

### 12 C.F.R. § 590.1 Authority, purpose, and scope.

(a) *Authority.* This part contains regulations issued under section 501 of the Depository Institutions Deregulation and Monetary Control Act of 1980, Pub. L. 96–221, 94 Stat. 161.

(b) *Purpose and scope.* The purpose of this permanent preemption of state interest-rate ceilings applicable to Federally-related residential mortgage loans is to ensure that the availability of such loans is not impeded in states having restrictive interest limitations. This part applies to loans, mortgages, credit sales, and advances, secured by first liens on residential real property, stock in residential cooperative housing corporations, or residential manufactured homes as defined in §590.2 of this part.

### 12 C.F.R. § 590.2 Definitions.

For the purposes of this part, the following definitions apply:

(a) *Loans* mean any loans, mortgages, credit sales, or advances.

(b) *Federally-related loans* include any loan:

(1) Made by any lender whose deposits or accounts are insured by any agency of the Federal government;

(2) Made by any lender regulated by any agency of the Federal government;

(3) Made by any lender approved by the Secretary of Housing and Urban Development for participation in any mortgage insurance program under the National Housing Act;

(4) Made in whole or in part by the Secretary of Housing and Urban Development; insured, guaranteed, supplemented, or assisted in any way by the Secretary or any officer or agency of the Federal government, or made under or in connection with a housing or urban development program administered by the Secretary, or a housing or related program administered by any other such officer or agency;

(5) Eligible for purchase by the Federal National Mortgage Association, the Government National Mortgage Association, or the Federal Home Loan Mortgage Corporation, or made by any financial institution from which the loan could be purchased by the Federal Home Loan Mortgage Corporation; or

(6) Made in whole or in part by any entity which:

(i) Regularly extends, or arranges for the extension of, credit payable by agreement in more than four installments or for which the payment of a finance charge is or may be required; and

(ii) Makes or invests in residential real property loans, including loans secured by first liens on residential manufactured homes that aggregate more than $1,000,000 per year; except that the latter requirement shall not apply to such an entity selling residential manufactured homes and providing financing for such sales through loans or credit sales secured by first liens on residential manufactured homes, if the entity has an arrangement to sell such loans or credit sales in whole or in part, or where such loans or credit sales are sold in whole or in part, to a lender or other institution otherwise included in this section.

(c) *Loans which are secured by first liens on real estate* means loans on the security of any instrument (whether a mortgage, deed of trust, or land contract) which makes the interest in real estate (whether in fee, or in a leasehold or subleasehold extending, or renewable, automatically or at the option of the holder or the lender, for a period of at least 5 years beyond the maturity of the loan) specific security for the payment of the obligation secured by the instrument: *Provided,* That the instrument is of such a nature that, in the event of default, the real estate described in the instrument could be subjected to the satisfaction of the obligation with the same priority as a first mortgage of a first deed of trust in the jurisdiction where the real estate is located.

(d) *Loans secured by first liens on stock in a residential cooperative housing corporation* means loans on the security of:

(1) A first security interest in stock or a membership certificate issued to a tenant stockholder or resident member by a cooperative housing organization; and

(2) An assignment of the borrower's interest in the proprietary lease or occupancy agreement issued by such organization.

(e) *Loans secured by first liens on residential manufactured homes* means a loan made pursuant to an agreement by which the party extending the credit acquires a security interest in the residential manufactured home which will have priority over any conflicting security interest.

(f) *Residential real property* means real estate improved or to be improved by a structure or structures designed primarily for dwelling, as opposed to commercial use.

(g) *Residential manufactured home* shall mean a manufactured home as defined in the National Manufactured Home Construction and Safety Standards Act, 42 U.S.C. 5402(6), which is or will be used as a residence.

(h) *State* means the several states, Puerto Rico, the District of Columbia, Guam, the Trust Territories of the Pacific Islands, the Northern Mariana Islands, and the Virgin Islands, except as provided in section 501(a)(2)(B) of the Depository Institutions Deregulation and Monetary Control Act of 1980, Pub. L. 96–221, 94 Stat. 161.

### 12 C.F.R. § 590.3 Operation.

(a) The provisions of the constitution or law of any state expressly limiting the rate or amount of interest, discount points, finance charges, or other charges which may be charged, taken, received, or reserved shall not apply to any Federally-related loan:

(1) Made after March 31, 1980; and

(2) Secured by a first lien on:

(i) Residential real property;

(ii) Stock in a residential cooperative housing corporation when the loan is used to finance the acquisition of such stock; or

(iii) A residential manufactured home: *Provided,* That the loan so secured contains the consumer safeguards required by §590.4 of this part;

(b) The provisions of paragraph (a) of this section shall apply to loans made in any state on or before the date (after April 1, 1980 and prior to April 1, 1983) on which the state adopts a law or certifies that the voters of such state have voted in favor of any law, constitutional or otherwise, which states explicitly and by its terms that such state does not want the provisions of paragraph (a) of this section to apply with respect to loans made in such state, except that—

(1) The provisions of paragraph (a) of this section shall apply to any loan which is made after such date pursuant to a commitment therefore which was entered into during the period beginning on April 1, 1980, and ending on the date the state takes such action;

(2) The provisions of paragraph (a) of this section shall apply to any rollover of a loan which loan was made, or committed to be made, during the period beginning on April 1, 1980, and ending on the date the state takes such action, if the mortgage document or loan note provided that the interest rate to the original borrower could be changed through the use of such a rollover; and

(3) At any time after the date of adoption of these regulations, any state may adopt a provision of law placing limitations on discount points or such other charges on any loan described in this part.

(c) Nothing in this section preempts limitations in state laws on prepayment charges, attorneys' fees, late charges or other provisions designed to protect borrowers.

[54 Fed. Reg. 49715 (Nov. 30, 1989), *as amended by* 66 Fed. Reg. 65822 (Dec. 21, 2001)]

## 12 C.F.R. § 590.4 Federally-related residential manufactured housing loans—consumer protection provisions.

(a) *Definitions.* As used in this section:

(1) *Prepayment.* A "prepayment" occurs upon—

(i) Refinancing or consolidation of the indebtedness;

(ii) Actual prepayment of the indebtedness by the debtor, whether voluntarily or following acceleration of the payment obligation by the creditor; or

(iii) The entry of a judgment for the indebtedness in favor of the creditor.

(2) *Actuarial method.* The term *actuarial method* means the method of allocating payments made on a debt between the outstanding balance of the obligation and the finance charge pursuant to which a payment is applied first to the accumulated finance charge and any remainder is subtracted from, or any deficiency is added to, the outstanding balance of the obligation.

(3) *Precomputed Finance Charge.* The term *precomputed finance charge* means interest or a time/price differential as computed by the add-on or discount method. Precomputed finance charges do not include loan fees, points, finder's fees, or similar charges.

(4) *Creditor.* The term *creditor* means any entity covered by this part, including those which regularly extend or arrange for the extension of credit and assignees that are creditors under section 501(a)(1)(C)(v) of the Depository Institutions Deregulation and Monetary Control Act of 1980.

(b) *General.*

(1) The provisions of the constitution or the laws of any state expressly limiting the rate or amount of interest, discount points, finance charges, or other charges which may be charged, taken, received, or reserved shall not apply to any loan, mortgage, credit sale, or advance which is secured by a first lien on a residential mobile home if a creditor covered by this part complies with the consumer protection regulations of this section.

(2) *Relation to state law.*

(i) In making loans or credit sales subject to this section, creditors shall comply with state and Federal law in accordance with the following:

(A) *State law regulating matters not covered by this section.* When state law regulating matters not covered by this section is otherwise applicable to a loan or credit sale subject to this section, creditors shall comply with such state law provisions.

(B) *State law regulating matters covered by this section.* Creditors need comply only with the provisions of this section, unless the Office determines that an otherwise applicable state law regulating matters covered by this section provides greater protection to consumers. Such determinations shall be published in the Federal Register and shall operate prospectively.

(ii) Any interested party may petition the Office for a determination that state law requirements are more protective of consumers than the provisions of this section. Petitions shall be sent to: Secretary to the Office of Thrift Supervision, 1700 G Street, NW., Washington, DC 20552, and shall include:

(A) A copy of the state law to be considered;

(B) Copies of any relevant judicial, regulatory, or administrative interpretations of the state law; and

(C) An opinion or memorandum from the state Attorney General or other appropriate state official having primary enforcement responsibilities for the subject state law provision, indicating how the state law to be considered offers greater protection to consumers than the Office's regulation.

(c) *Refund of precomputed finance charge.* In the event the entire indebtedness is prepaid, the unearned portion of the precomputed finance charge shall be refunded to the debtor. This refund shall be in an amount not less than the amount which would be refunded if the unearned precomputed finance charge were calculated in accordance with the actuarial method, except that the debtor shall not be entitled to a refund which, is less than one dollar. The unearned portion of the precomputed finance charge is, at the option of the creditor, either:

(1) That portion of the precomputed finance charge which is allocable to all unexpired payment periods as originally scheduled, or if deferred, as deferred. A payment period shall be deemed unexpired if prepayment is made within 15 days after the payment period's scheduled due date. The unearned precomputed finance charge is the total of that which would have been earned for each such period had the loan not been precomputed, by applying to unpaid balances of principal, according to the actuarial method, an annual percentage rate based on those charges which are considered precomputed finance charges in this section, assuming that all payments were made as originally scheduled, or as deferred, if deferred. The creditor, at its option, may round this annual percentage rate to the nearest one-quarter of one percent; or

(2) The total precomputed finance charge less the earned precomputed finance charge. The earned precomputed finance charge shall be determined by applying an annual percentage rate based on the total precomputed finance charge (as that term is defined in this section), under the actuarial method, to the unpaid balances for the actual time those balances were unpaid up to the date of prepayment. If a late charge or deferral fee has been collected, it shall be treated as a payment.

(d) *Prepayment penalties.* A debtor may prepay in full or in part the unpaid balance of the loan at any time without penalty. The right to prepay shall be disclosed in the loan contract in type larger than that used for the body of the document.

(e) *Balloon payments.*

(1) *Federal savings associations.* Federal savings association creditors may enter into agreements with debtors which provide for non-amortized and partially-amortized loans on residential manufactured homes, and such loans shall be governed by the provisions of this section and §560.220 of this chapter.

(2) *Other creditors.* All other creditors may enter into agreements with debtors which provide for non-amortized and partially-amortized loans on residential manufactured homes to the extent authorized by applicable Federal or state law or regulation.

(f) *Late charges.*

(1) No late charge may be assessed, imposed, or collected unless provided for by written contract between the creditor and debtor.

(2) To the extent that applicable state law does not provide for a longer period of time, no late charge may be collected on an installment which is paid in full on or before the 15th day after its scheduled or deferred due date even though an earlier maturing installment or a late charge on an earlier installment may not have been paid in full. For purposes of assessing late charges, payments received are deemed to be applied first to current installments.

(3) A late charge may be imposed only once on an installment; however, no such charge may be collected for a late installment which has been deferred.

(4) To the extent that applicable state law does not provide for a lower charge or a longer grace period, a late charge on any installment not paid in full on or before the 15th day after its scheduled or deferred due date may not exceed five percent of the unpaid amount of the installment.

(5) If, at any time after imposition of a late charge, the lender provides the borrower with written notice regarding amounts claimed to be due but unpaid, the notice shall separately state the total of all late charges claimed.

(6) Interest after the final scheduled maturity date may not exceed the maximum rate otherwise allowable under State law for such contracts, and if such interest is charged, no separate late charge may be made on the final scheduled installment.

(g) *Deferral fees.*

(1) With respect to mobile home credit transactions containing precomputed finance charges, agreements providing for deferral of all or part of one or more installments shall be in writing, signed by the parties, and

(i) Provide, to the extent that applicable state law does not provide for a lower charge, for a charge not exceeding one percent of each installment or part thereof for each month from the date when such installment was due to the date when it is agreed to become payable and proportionately for a part of each month, counting each day as 1/30th of a month;

(ii) Incorporate by reference the transaction to which the deferral applied;

(iii) Disclose each installment or part thereof in the amount to be deferred, the date or dates originally payable, and the date or dates agreed to become payable: and

(iv) Set forth the fact of the deferral charge, the dollar amount of the charge for each installment to be deferred, and the total dollar amount to be paid by the debtor for the privilege of deferring payment.

(2) No term of a writing executed by the debtor shall constitute authority for a creditor unilaterally to grant a deferral with respect to which a charge is to be imposed or collected.

(3) The deferral period is that period of time in which no payment is required or made by reason of the deferral.

(4) Payments received with respect to deferred installments shall be deemed to be applied first to deferred installments.

(5) A charge may not be collected for the deferral of an installment or any part thereof if, with respect to that installment, a refinancing or consolidation agreement is concluded by the parties, or a late charge has been imposed or collected, unless such late charge is refunded to the borrower or credited to the deferral charge.

(h) *Notice before repossession, foreclosure, or acceleration.*

(1) Except in the case of abandonment or other extreme circumstances, no action to repossess or foreclose, or to accelerate payment of the entire outstanding balance of the obligation, may be taken against the debtor until 30 days after the creditor sends the debtor a notice of default in the form set forth in paragraph (h)(2) of this section. Such notice shall be sent by registered or certified mail with return receipt requested. In the case of default on payments, the sum stated in the notice may only include payments in default and applicable late or deferral charges. If the debtor cures the default within 30 days of the postmark of the notice and subsequently defaults a second time, the creditor shall again give notice as described in this paragraph (h)(1). The debtor is not entitled to notice of default more than twice in any one-year period.

(2) The notice in the following form shall state the nature of the default, the action the debtor must take to cure the default, the creditor's intended actions upon failure of the debtor to cure the default, and the debtor's right to redeem under state law.

To:

Date: , 19

Notice of Default and Right To Cure Default

Name, address, and telephone number of creditor

Account number, if any

Brief identification of credit transaction

You are now in default on this credit transaction. You have a right to correct this default within 30 days from the postmarked date of this notice.

If you correct the default, you may continue with the contract as though you did not default. Your default consists of:

Describe default alleged

*Cure of default:* Within 30 days from the postmarked date of this notice, you may cure your default by (describe the acts necessary for cure, including, if applicable, the amount of payment required, including itemized delinquency or deferral charges).

Creditor's rights: If you do not correct your default in the time allowed, we may exercise our rights against you under the law by (describe action creditor intends to take).

If you have any questions, write (the creditor) at the above address or call (creditor's designated employee) at (telephone number) between the hours of and on (state days of week).

If this default was caused by your failure to make a payment or payments, and you want to pay by mail, please send a check or money order; do not send cash.

[54 Fed. Reg. 49715 (Nov. 30, 1989), *as amended by* 61 Fed. Reg. 50984 (Sept. 30, 1996); 67 Fed. Reg. 60554 (Sept. 26, 2002)]

* * *

## 12 C.F.R. § 590.101 State criminal usury statutes.

(a) Section 501 provides that "the provisions of the constitution or laws of any state expressly limiting the rate or amount of interest, discount points, finance charges, or other charges shall not apply to any" federally-related loan secured by a first lien on residential real property, a residential manufactured home, or all the stock allocated to a dwelling unit in a residential housing cooperative. 12 U.S.C. 1735f–7 note (Supp. IV 1980). The question has arisen as to whether the federal statute preempts a state law which deems it a criminal offense to charge interest at a rate in excess of that specified in the state law.

(b) In the Office's view, section 501 preempts all state laws which expressly limit the rate or amount of interest chargeable on a federally-related residential first mortgage. It does not matter whether the statute in question imposes criminal or civil sanctions; section 501, by its terms, preempts "any" state law which imposes a ceiling on interest rates. The wording of the federal statute clearly expresses an intent to displace all direct state law restraints on interest. Any state law that conflicts with this Congressional purpose must yield.

# Appendix G Federal Credit Unions

## G.1 Federal Credit Union Act

### TITLE 12—BANKS AND BANKING

### CHAPTER 14—FEDERAL CREDIT UNIONS

### SUBCHAPTER I—GENERAL PROVISIONS

* * *

### 12 U.S.C. § 1757. Powers

A Federal credit union shall have succession in its corporate name during its existence and shall have power—

* * *

**(5)** to make loans, the maturities of which shall not exceed 15 years, except as otherwise provided herein, and extend lines of credit to its members, to other credit unions, and to credit union organizations and to participate with other credit unions, credit union organizations, or financial organizations in making loans to credit union members in accordance with the following:

**(A)** Loans to members shall be made in conformity with criteria established by the board of directors: Provided, That—

**(i)** a residential real estate loan on a one-to-four-family dwelling, including an individual cooperative unit, that is or will be the principal residence of a credit union member, and which is secured by a first lien upon such dwelling, may have a maturity not exceeding thirty years or such other limits as shall be set by the National Credit Union Administration Board (except that a loan on an individual cooperative unit shall be adequately secured as defined by the Board), subject to the rules and regulations of the Board;

**(ii)** a loan to finance the purchase of a mobile home, which shall be secured by a first lien on such mobile home, to be used by the credit union member as his residence, a loan for the repair, alteration, or improvement of a residential dwelling which is the residence of a credit union member, or a second mortgage loan secured by a residential dwelling which is the residence of a credit union member, shall have a maturity not to exceed 15 years or any longer term which the Board may allow;

**(iii)** a loan secured by the insurance or guarantee of, or with advance commitment to purchase the loan by, the Federal Government, a State government, or any agency of either may be made for the maturity and under the terms and conditions specified in the law under which such insurance, guarantee, or commitment is provided;

**(iv)** a loan or aggregate of loans to a director or member of the supervisory or credit committee of the credit union making the loanwhich exceeds $20,000 plus pledged shares, be approved by the board of directors;

**(v)** loans to other members for which directors or members of the supervisory or credit committee act as guarantor or endorser be approved by the board of directors when such loans standing alone or when added to any outstanding loan or loans of the guarantor or endorser exceeds $20,000;

**(vi)** the rate of interest may not exceed 15 per centum per annum on the unpaid balance inclusive of all finance charges, except that the Board may establish—

**(I)** after consultation with the appropriate committees of the Congress, the Department of Treasury, and the Federal financial institution regulatory agencies, an interest rate ceiling exceeding such 15 per centum per annum rate, for periods not to exceed 18 months, if it determines that money market interest rates have risen over the preceding six-month period and that prevailing interest rate levels threaten the safety and soundness of individual credit unions as evidenced by adverse trends in liquidity, capital, earnings, and growth; and

**(II)** a higher interest rate ceiling for Agent members for the Central Liquidity Facility in carrying out the provisions of subchapter III of this chapter for such periods as the Board may authorize;

**(vii)** the taking, receiving, reserving, or charging of a rate of interest greater than is allowed by this paragraph, when knowingly done, shall be deemed a forfeiture of the entire interest which the note, bill, or other evidence of debt carries with it, or which has been agreed to be paid thereon. If such greater rate of interest has been paid, the person by whom it has been paid, or his legal representatives, may recover back from the credit union taking or receiving the same, in an action in the nature of an action of debt, the entire amount of interest paid; but such action must be commenced within two years from the time the usurious collection was made;

**(viii)** a borrower may repay his loan, prior to maturity in whole or in part on any business day without penalty, except that on a first or second mortgage loan a Federal credit union may require that any partial prepayments

**(I)** be made on the date monthly installments are due, and

**(II)** be in the amount of that part of one or more monthly installments which would be applicable to principal;

**(ix)** loans shall be paid or amortized in accordance with rules and regulations prescribed by the Board after taking into account the needs or conditions of the borrowers, the amounts and duration of the loans, the interests of the members and the credit unions, and such other factors as the Board deems relevant;

**(x)** loans must be approved by the credit committee or a loan officer, but no loan may be made to any member if, upon the making of that loan, the member would be indebted to the Federal credit union upon loans made to him in an aggregate amount which would exceed 10 per centum of the credit union's unimpaired capital and surplus.

* * *

(10) to levy late charges, in accordance with the bylaws, for failure of members to meet promptly their obligations to the Federal credit union;

* * *

[Prior citations omitted. As amended by Pub. L. No. 111–203, tit. III, § 362(1), tit. X, § 1073(d), 124 Stat. 1549, 2066 (July 21, 2010)]

* * *

# G.2 NCUA Regulations

## TITLE 12—BANKS AND BANKING

## CHAPTER VII—NATIONAL CREDIT UNION ADMINISTRATION

## SUBCHAPTER A—REGULATIONS AFFECTING CREDIT UNIONS

## PART 701—ORGANIZATION AND OPERATION OF FEDERAL CREDIT UNIONS

* * *

### 12 C.F.R. § 701.21 Loans to members and lines of credit to members.

* * *

(b) *Relation to other laws*—

(1) *Preemption of state laws.* Section 701.21 is promulgated pursuant to the NCUA Board's exclusive authority as set forth in section 107(5) of the Federal Credit Union Act (12 U.S.C. 1757(5)) to regulate the rates, terms of repayment and other conditions of Federal credit union loans and lines of credit (including credit cards) to members. This exercise of the Board's authority preempts any state law purporting to limit or affect:

(i)(A) Rates of interest and amounts of finance charges, including:

(*1*) The frequency or the increments by which a variable interest rate may be changed;

(*2*) The index to which a variable interest rate may be tied;

(*3*) The manner or timing of notifying the borrower of a change in interest rate;

(*4*) The authority to increase the interest rate on an existing balance;

(B) Late charges; and

(C) Closing costs, application, origination, or other fees;

(ii) Terms of repayment, including:

(A) The maturity of loans and lines of credit;

(B) The amount, uniformity, and frequency of payments, including the accrual of unpaid interest if payments are insufficient to pay all interest due;

(C) Balloon payments; and

(D) Prepayment limits;

(iii) Conditions related to:

(A) The amount of the loan or line of credit;

(B) The purpose of the loan or line of credit;

(C) The type or amount of security and the relation of the value of the security to the amount of the loan or line of credit;

(D) Eligible borrowers; and

(E) The imposition and enforcement of liens on the shares of borrowers and accommodation parties.

(2) *Matters not preempted.* Except as provided by paragraph (b)(1) of this section, it is not the Board's intent to preempt state laws that do not affect rates, terms of repayment and other conditions described above concerning loans and lines of credit, for example:

(i) Insurance laws;

(ii) Laws related to transfer of and security interests in real and personal property (see, however, paragraph (g)(6) of this section concerning the use and exercise of due-on-sale clauses);

(iii) Conditions related to:

(A) Collection costs and attorneys' fees;

(B) Requirements that consumer lending documents be in "plain language;" and

(C) The circumstances in which a borrower may be declared in default and may cure default.

(3) *Other Federal law.* Except as provided by paragraph (b)(1) of this section, it is not the Board's intent to preempt state laws affecting aspects of credit transactions that are primarily regulated by Federal law other than the Federal Credit Union Act, for example, state laws concerning credit cost disclosure requirements, credit discrimination, credit reporting practices, unfair credit practices, and debt collection practices. Applicability of state law in these instances should be determined pursuant to the preemption standards of the relevant Federal law and regulations.

(4) *Examination and enforcement.* Except as otherwise agreed by the NCUA Board, the Board retains exclusive examination and administrative enforcement jurisdiction over Federal credit unions. Violations of Federal or applicable state laws related to the lending activities of a Federal credit union should be referred to the appropriate NCUA regional office.

(5) *Definition of State law.* For purposes of paragraph (b) of this section "state law" means the constitution, laws, regulations and judicial decisions of any state, the District of Columbia, the several territories and possessions of the United States, and the Commonwealth of Puerto Rico.

(c) *General rules*—

(1) *Scope.* The following general rules apply to all loans to members and, where indicated, all lines of credit (including credit cards) to members, except as otherwise provided in the remaining provisions of §701.21.

(2) *Written policies.* The board of directors of each Federal credit union shall establish written policies for loans and lines of credit consistent with the relevant provisions of the Act, NCUA's regulations, and other applicable laws and regulations.

(3) *Credit applications and overdrafts.* Consistent with policies established by the board of directors, the credit committee or loan officer shall ensure that a credit application is kept on file for each borrower supporting the decision to make a loan or establish a line of credit. A credit union may advance money to a member to cover an account deficit without having a credit application from the borrower on file if the credit union has a written overdraft policy. The policy must: set a cap on the total dollar amount of all overdrafts the credit union will honor consistent with the credit union's ability to absorb losses; establish a time limit not to exceed forty-five calendar days for a member either to deposit funds or obtain an approved loan from the credit union to cover each overdraft; limit the dollar amount of overdrafts the credit union will honor per member; and establish the fee and interest rate, if any, the credit union will charge members for honoring overdrafts.

(4) *Maturity.* The maturity of a loan to a member may not exceed 15 years. Lines of credit are not subject to a statutory or regulatory maturity limit. Amortization of line of credit balances and the type and amount of security on any line of credit shall be as determined by contract between the Federal credit union and the member/borrower.

(5) *Ten percent limit.* No loan or line of credit advance may be made to any member if such loan or advance would cause that member to be indebted to the Federal credit union upon loans and advances made to the member in an aggregate amount exceeding 10% of the credit union's total unimpaired capital and surplus. In the case of member business loans as defined in § 723.1 of this chapter, additional limitations apply as set forth in §§ 723.8 and 723.9 of this chapter.

(6) *Early payment.* A member may repay a loan, or outstanding balance on a line of credit, prior to maturity in whole or in part on any business day without penalty.

(7) *Loan interest rates*—

(i) *General.* Except when the Board establishes a higher maximum rate, federal credit unions may not extend credit to members at rates exceeding 15 percent per year on the unpaid balance inclusive of all finance charges. Federal credit unions may use variable rates of interest but only if the effective rate over the term of a loan or line of credit does not exceed the maximum permissible rate.

(ii) *Temporary rates.*

(A) At least every 18 months, the Board will determine if federal credit unions may extend credit to members at an interest rate exceeding 15 percent. After consultation with appropriate congressional committees, the Department of Treasury, and other federal financial institution regulatory agencies, the Board may establish a rate exceeding the 15 percent per year rate, if it determines money market interest rates have risen over the preceding six-month period and prevailing interest rate levels threaten the safety and soundness of individual federal credit unions as evidenced by adverse trends in liquidity, capital, earnings, and growth.

(B) When the Board establishes a higher maximum rate, the Board will provide notice to federal credit unions of the adjusted rate by issuing a *Letter to Federal Credit Unions* , as well as providing information in other NCUA publications and in a statement for the press.

(C) Federal credit unions may continue to charge rates exceeding the established maximum rate only on existing loans or lines of credit made before the effective date of any lowering of the maximum rate.

(iii) *Short-term, small amount Loans (STS loans).*

(A) Notwithstanding the provisions in §701.21(c)(7)(ii), a Federal credit union may charge an interest rate of 1000 basis points above the maximum interest rate as established by the Board, provided the Federal credit union is making a closed-end loan in accordance with the following conditions:

(*1*) The principal of the loan is not less than $200 or more than $1000;

(*2*) The loan has a minimum maturity term of one month and a maximum maturity term of six months;

(*3*) The Federal credit union does not make more than three STS loans in any rolling six-month period to any one borrower and makes no more than one short-term, small amount loan at a time to a borrower;

(*4*) The Federal credit union must not roll-over any STS loan;

(A) The prohibition against roll-overs does not apply to an extension of the loan term within the maximum loan terms in paragraph (c)(7)(iii)(*3*) provided the Federal credit union does not charge any additional fees or extend any new credit.

(B) [Reserved]

(*5*) The Federal credit union fully amortizes the loan;

(*6*) The Federal credit union sets a minimum length of membership requirement of at least one month;

(*7*) The Federal credit union charges an application fee to all members applying for a new loan that reflects the actual costs associated with processing the application, but in no case may the application fee exceed $20; and

(*8*) The Federal credit union includes, in its written lending policies, a limit on the aggregate dollar amount of loans made under this section of a maximum of 20% of net worth and implements appropriate underwriting guidelines to minimize risk; for example, requiring a borrower to verify employment by producing at least two recent pay stubs.

(B) *STS Loan Program Guidance and Best Practices.* In developing a successful STS loan program, a Federal credit union should consider how the program will help benefit a member's financial well-being while considering the higher degree of risk associated with this type of lending. The guidance and best practices are intended to help Federal credit unions minimize risk and develop a successful program, but are not an exhaustive checklist and do not guarantee a successful program with a low degree of risk.

(*1*) *Program Features.* Several features that may increase the success of an STS loan program and enhance member benefit include adding a savings component, financial education, reporting of members' payment of STS loans to credit bureaus, or electronic loan transactions as part of an STS program. In addition, although a Federal credit union cannot require members to authorize a payroll deduction, a Federal credit union should encourage or incentivize members to utilize payroll deduction.

(*2*) *Underwriting.* Federal credit unions need to develop minimum underwriting standards that account for a member's need for quickly available funds, while adhering to principles of responsible lending. Underwriting standards should address required documentation for proof of employment or income, including at least two recent paycheck stubs. FCUs should be able to use a borrower's proof of recurring income as the key criterion in developing standards for maturity lengths and loan amounts so a borrower can manage repayment of the loan. For members with established accounts, FCUs should only need to review a member's account records and proof of recurring income or employment.

(*3*) *Risk Avoidance.* Federal credit unions need to consider risk avoidance strategies, including: requiring members to participate in direct deposit and conducting a thorough evaluation of the Federal credit union's resources and ability to engage in an STS loan program.

(8)(i) Except as otherwise provided herein, no official or employee of a Federal credit union, or immediate family member of an official or employee of a Federal credit union, may receive, directly or indirectly, any commission, fee, or other compensation in connection with any loan made by the credit union.

(ii) For the purposes of this section:

*Compensation* includes non-monetary items, except those of nominal value.

*Immediate family member* means a spouse or other family member living in the same household.

*Loan* includes line of credit.

*Official* means any member of the board of directors or a volunteer committee.

*Person* means an individual or an organization.

*Senior management employee* means the credit union's chief executive officer (typically, this individual holds the title of President or Treasurer/Manager), any assistant chief executive officers (e.g., Assistant President, Vice President, or Assistant Treasurer/Manager), and the chief financial officer (Comptroller).

*Volunteer official* means an official of a credit union who does not receive compensation from the credit union solely for his or her service as an official.

(iii) This section does not prohibit:

(A) Payment, by a Federal credit union, of salary to employees;

(B) Payment, by a Federal credit union, of an incentive or bonus to an employee based on the credit union's overall financial performance;

(C) Payment, by a Federal credit union, of an incentive or bonus to an employee, other than a senior management employee, in connection with a loan or loans made by the credit union, provided that the board of directors of the credit union establishes written policies and internal controls in connection with such incentive or bonus and monitors compliance with such policies and controls at least annually.

(D) Receipt of compensation from a person outside a Federal credit union by a volunteer official or non-senior-management employee of the credit union, or an immediate family member of a volunteer official or employee of the credit union, for a service or activity performed outside the credit union, provided that no referral has been made by the credit union or the official, employee, or family member.

* * *

[49 Fed. Reg. 30685 (Aug. 1, 1984); 49 Fed. Reg. 46105 (Nov. 23, 1984); 49 Fed. Reg. 46541 (Nov. 27, 1984); 50 Fed. Reg. 48077 (Nov. 21, 1985); 52 Fed. Reg. 8061 (Mar. 16, 1987); 52 Fed. Reg. 12368 (Apr. 16, 1987); 53 Fed. Reg. 19751 (May 31, 1988); 53 Fed. Reg. 29645 (Aug. 8, 1988); 54 Fed. Reg. 18472 (May 1, 1989); 54 Fed. Reg. 43278 (Oct. 24, 1989); 55 Fed. Reg. 1797 (Jan. 19, 1990); 55 Fed. Reg. 30207 (July 25, 1990); 56 Fed. Reg. 37831 (Aug. 9, 1991); 56 Fed. Reg. 48425 (Sept. 25, 1991); 57 Fed. Reg. 42488 (Sept. 15, 1992); 58 Fed. Reg. 6077 (Jan. 26, 1993); 58 Fed. Reg. 40043 (July 27, 1993); 59 Fed. Reg. 39425 (Aug. 1, 1994); 60 Fed. Reg. 51889 (Oct. 4, 1995); 60 Fed. Reg. 58504 (Nov. 28, 1995); 61 Fed. Reg. 4214 (Feb. 5, 1996); 61 Fed. Reg. 68128 (Dec. 27, 1996); 62 Fed. Reg. 40930 (July 31, 1997); 63 Fed. Reg. 51799 (Sept. 29, 1998); 63 Fed. Reg. 71214 (Dec. 24, 1998); 64 Fed. Reg. 5929 (Feb. 8, 1999); 64 Fed. Reg. 28729 (May 27, 1999); 64 Fed. Reg. 57365 (Oct. 25, 1999); 65 Fed. Reg. 15226 (Mar. 22, 2000); 65 Fed. Reg. 44977 (July 20, 2000); 67 Fed. Reg. 7059 (Feb. 15, 2002); 68 Fed. Reg. 46441 (Aug. 6, 2003); 69 Fed. Reg. 27828 (May 17, 2004); 70 Fed. Reg. 3863 (Jan. 27, 2005); 70 Fed. Reg. 8923 (Feb. 24, 2005); 71 Fed. Reg. 36666 (June 28, 2006); 71 Fed. Reg. 42251 (July 26, 2006); 71 Fed. Reg. 62876 (Oct. 27, 2006); 72 Fed. Reg. 7928 (Feb. 22, 2007); 72 Fed. Reg. 30246 (May 31, 2007); 74 Fed. Reg. 29934 (June 24, 2009); 74 Fed. Reg. 68370 (Dec. 24, 2009); 75 Fed. Reg. 34620 (June 18, 2010); 75 Fed. Reg. 58289 (Sept. 24, 2010); 76 Fed. Reg. 60366 (Sept. 29, 2011)]

## G.3 NCUA Interpretative Letters

This section summarizes NCUA interpretative letters and releases relating to the preemption of state laws by federal credit unions issued from 1992 forward. The full text of these letters is located on NCLC's website at www.nclc.org/webaccess. Archived and recently released letters and opinions can be obtained from NCUA's website: www.ncua.gov. Under "Resources for Credit Unions," click on "Legal Opinion Letters." Then search by year. Guidance and letter to credit unions can be found under "Resources for Credit Union" by clicking on "Letters to Credit Unions" and "Regulatory Alerts." These latter two categories of information directed to credit unions are not summarized here.

*Interpretive Letter No. NCUA-09-1018 (Dec. 9, 2009)* (State Affected: North Carolina). Federal SAFE Act preempts provision of state SAFE Act requiring federal credit unions to file a notice of exemption from state licensing requirements. The NCUA also opined that the state should change the way it administered a database required by lenders so FCUs could access it without filing the preempted notice. *See* www.ncua.gov/Resources/RegulationsOpinionsLaws/OpinionLetters/2009/09-1018.pdf.

*Interpretive Letter No. NCUA-09-0218 (Feb. 24, 2009)* (State Affected: New York). Credit unions may offer GAP waivers on loans regardless of state law categorizing them as an insurance business because they are a permissible loan-related activity for FCUs under NCUA's incidental powers rule. *See* www.ncua.gov/Resources/RegulationsOpinionsLaws/OpinionLetters/2009/09-0218.pdf.

*Interpretive Letter No. NCUA-08-0735 (Oct. 3, 2008)* (State Affected: All). Credit union service organizations (CUSOs) do not operate under the authority and regulation of the NCUA and are not exempt from applicable state licensing laws. Regarding the new SAFE Licensing Act of 2008, the NCUA opines that it applies to all residential mortgage loans, including subordinate lien mortgages and home equity lines of credit; only certain staff must be licensed or registered—those who negotiate terms, discuss and counsel about various options, and provide and explain legally required disclosures; employees of state credit unions need only be registered, not licensed, if they perform these activities.

*Interpretive Letter No. NCUA-08-0120 (July 14, 2008)* (State Affected: Massachusetts). State unfair and deceptive acts or practices act is not applicable to federal credit unions by its own terms because it does not apply to transactions otherwise permitted under laws administered by any regulatory board or officer acting under the authority of the United States.

*Interpretive Letter No. NCUA-08-0121 (June 10, 2008)* (State Affected: All). University-related credit union may accept payments for gift cards issued by the university and track debits, though the university or a subdivision must be a member of the credit union.

*Interpretive Letter No. NCUA-07-0562A (Dec. 21, 2007)* (State Affected: California). State law that requires a notice of the right to redeem a repossessed car within a certain time and of the consumer's potential liability for a deficiency creates a conditional right to reinstate, allows a ten-day extension of the redemption period upon written request, and allows for an accounting, is preempted under the "laws affecting the terms of repayment" provision of 12 C.F.R. § 701.21. NCUA claims "cradle to grave" supervision of federal credit unions.

*Interpretive Letter No. NCUA-07-0633 (Nov. 19, 2007)* (State Affected: All). Federal credit unions may not force-place collateral protection with an internal program as that constitutes insurance and FCUs may not engage in the business of insurance. Proposed program to replace PMI with an internal program is also impermissible.

*Interpretive Letter No. NCUA-07-0745 (Sept. 6, 2007)* (State Affected: Hawaii). Hawaii law requiring federal credit unions to report suspected financial abuse of elders not preempted.

*Interpretive Letter No. NCUA-07-0743 (Aug. 7, 2007)* (State Affected: Georgia). Georgia statute prohibiting financial institutions from charging fees for cashing checks for non-account holders is preempted.

*Interpretive Letter No. 06-FCU-03 (July 2006)* (State Affected: All). The NCUA Board extended the 18% interest rate cap set to expire on September 8, 2006 to March 9, 2008.

*Interpretive Letter No. NCUA-05-0423 (May 3, 2005)* (State Affected: Texas). Proposed state law providing debt relief on loans owed by the military on active duty would be preempted to the extent it is broader than the Servicemember Civil Relief Act (SCRA). Credit unions must comply with the SCRA.

*Interpretive Letter No. NCUA-04-0727 (Feb. 11, 2005)* (State Affected: Puerto Rico). Puerto Rico law can be preempted by the NCUA even though it is not a state. The Puerto Rico Retail Installment Sales and Financing Act is preempted to the extent that it prohibits the use of open-end credit to finance the purchase of a car even though credit unions are unlikely to finance the purchase of cars in this way. The law generally is not applicable to credit unions, regardless of preemption, to the extent that it covers credit transactions financing the sale of goods, since credit unions do not sell goods.

*Interpretive Letter No. NCUA-04-0606 (July 28, 2004)* (State Affected: Wisconsin). This state's anti-predatory lending law is preempted in its entirety in light of NCUA's "long-standing" position that state laws affecting rates, repayment terms, or lending conditions are preempted. NCUA also states that it alone can initiate enforcement actions against federal credit unions, citing to its Nov. 10, 2003 and Jan. 28, 2004 letters.

*Interpretive Letter No. NCUA-03-1242 (Mar. 12, 2004)* (State Affected: Georgia). Further explanation of NCUA's change in its position regarding how it evaluates state laws generally and anti-predatory lending laws in particular regarding preemption.

*Interpretive Letter No. NCUA-04-0147 (Feb. 10, 2004)* (State Affected: New Mexico). State anti-predatory lending law is preempted, relying on the analysis in the November 10, 2003 letter regarding Georgia's law.

*Interpretive Letter No. NCUA-03-1020 (Jan. 28, 2004)* (State Affected: General). State laws that limit or prohibit charges related to debt cancellation or suspension agreements are preempted.

*Interpretive Letter No. NCUA-03-1039 (Jan. 28, 2004)* (State Affected: General). Federal credit unions may offer debt cancellation agreements to its members as an exercise of incidental powers without having to comply with state insurance licensing laws. NCUA does not believe that a federal credit union that offers debt cancellation agreements is engaging in the business of insurance.

*Interpretive Letter No. NCUA-03-1106 (Jan. 28, 2004)* (State Affected: New Jersey). State Homeownership Security Act (anti-predatory lending law) is preempted.

*Interpretive Letter No. NCUA-03-0905A (Dec. 14, 2003)* (State Affected: Texas). State debt collection act that is amended and only applies to third party collectors and will, therefore, not apply to federal credit unions. See earlier letter of November 26, 2003.

*Interpretive Letter No. NCUA-03-0905 (Nov. 26, 2003)* (State Affected: Texas). State debt collection act is not preempted for federal credit union members in that state. Some federal laws permit states to regulate in the same area. State laws of this sort normally apply to federal credit unions. The relevant federal law's preemption standards determine whether a state law is preempted. Further, the state FDCPA does not regulate the terms of lending.

*Interpretive Letter No. NCUA-03-0412 (Nov. 10, 2003)* (State Affected: Georgia). Amended Georgia Fair Lending Act is preempted. NCUA amends its position and states that any state law that affects the rates, terms, and conditions of the loan is preempted regardless of whether another federal law permits the state to enact it.

*Interpretive Letter No. NCUA-03-0165 (May 23, 2003)* (State Affected: District of Columbia). D.C.'s Home Loan Protection Act is preempted even though it is a state law more protective than the federal Homeownership Equity Protection Act.

*Interpretive Letter No. NCUA-02-1074 (Dec. 23, 2002)* (State Affected: General). Credit unions need not obtain stop-loss insurance coverage if it institutes a debt cancellation or suspension program. NCUA argues that these products are not insurance.

*Interpretive Letter No. NCUA-02-0566 (Oct. 4, 2002)* (State Affected: North Carolina). North Carolina's Mortgage Lending Act that requires financial institutions to file for an exemption from licensing requirements and that imposes a penalty if they fail to file for an exemption is preempted. HOEPA-like provisions are preempted to the extent of loans not covered by HOEPA and then to the extent that it limits or affects rates of interest, finance charges, late fees, closing costs, terms or repayment, and loan conditions.

*Interpretive Letter No. NCUA-02-0827 (Oct. 3, 2002)* (State Affected: Connecticut). Connecticut law that bars financial institutions from permitting borrowers to use credit cards to access a home equity line of credit is preempted.

*Interpretive Letter No. NCUA-02-0649 (July 29, 2002)* (State Affected: Georgia). Georgia's Fair Lending Act is preempted in part. For loans covered by the Act and covered under the HOEPA, the Act is generally not preempted. For covered loans below the HOEPA triggers, the Act is preempted to the extent it limits or affects rates of interest, finance charges, late fees, closing costs, terms or repayment, and loan conditions.

*Interpretive Letter No. NCUA-02-0638 (June 26, 2002)* (State Affected: California). California's minimum payment credit card disclosure act is preempted as it affects the terms of repayment.

*Interpretive Letter No. NCUA-00-08027 (Mar. 2, 2001)* (State Affected: New York HOEPA-like regulations). NCUA's lending regulation does not preempt state laws that affect aspects of credit transactions that are primarily regulated by other federal laws or regulations. In these cases, preemption is defined under the standards in those other federal laws. NCUA's regulations preempt some but not all of New York's HOEPA-like regulations.

*Interpretive Letter No. NCUA-98-0961 (Feb. 1, 1999)* (State Affected: Connecticut). State law limiting finance charges on retail installment contracts does not apply to federal credit unions that buy loans from dealers that the federal credit unions approved before the financing was granted to the consumer. These are so-called "indirect" loans. Opinion expressly declines to discuss legality of the car dealer's role under state law. Opinion conflicts with the letter of June 24, 1992.

*Interpretive Letter No. NCUA-98-0926 (Dec. 9, 1998)* (State Affected: Wyoming). State law prohibiting a federal credit union from establishing an ATM unless it has a place of business in that state is preempted.

*Interpretive Letter No. NCUA-98-0329 (Apr. 21, 1998)* (State Affected: Maryland). Federal Credit Union Act does not regulate in the area of electronic branching; therefore, state law prohibiting federal credit unions from charging a fee to non-members who use their ATMs is not preempted.

*Interpretive Letter (Sept. 4, 1997)* (State Affected: Indiana). State law permitting consumers to refinance a balloon payment loan on the same terms and conditions as the original loan at maturity is preempted.

*Interpretive Letter No. NCUA-97-0633 (July 31, 1997)* (State Affected: North Carolina). State law regarding late charges is preempted. The fact that North Carolina opted out of the National Housing Act preemption of interest rates is not relevant to FCU Act preemption.

*Interpretive Letter No. NCUA-97-0225 (Apr. 14, 1997)* (State Affected: Maine). State law restricting the finance charge that can be collected on open-end credit is preempted.

*Interpretive Letter No. NCUA-96-1132 (Dec. 30, 1996)* (State Affected: Arizona). Whether a federal credit union is exempt from state transaction privilege tax will be referred to the United States Attorney as NCUA does not have direct authority to enforce § 122 of the FCU Act.

*Interpretive Letter No. NCUA-95-0106 (Jan. 29, 1996)* (State Affected: Wisconsin). State law regarding the advertising of loans is not preempted, if not specifically addressed by NCUA regulations; state law one-year notice rule for any change in terms and conditions of an open-end credit plan is preempted; state law collection requirements are not preempted.

*Interpretive Letter No. NCUA-0404 (Apr. 26, 1995)* (State Affected: General). State usury laws are preempted. The federal 18% cap applies.

*Interpretive Letter No. NCUA-92-1131 (Jan. 21, 1993)* (State Affected: Pennsylvania). If the state law restricts fees for the recordation of the satisfaction of a mortgage or for the federal credit union's preparation of a satisfaction, it is preempted.

*Interpretive Letter No. NCUA-92-0639 (July 7, 1992)* (State Affected: South Dakota). State law affecting the disposition of funds in a decedent's accounts is not preempted because it does not affect the opening, maintaining, or closing of an account.

*Interpretive Letter No. NCUA-92-0612 (June 24, 1992)* (State Affected: Texas). State motor vehicle retail installment sales law applies to loan originated by car dealers and purchased or assigned to a federal credit union. FCU Act preemption only applies to loans originated by federal credit unions regardless of the fact that all parties contemplate that the loan will be assigned immediately to the federal credit union.

*Interpretive Letter No. NCUA-92-0123 (June 11, 1992)* (State Affected: Iowa). State law requiring credit card issuers whose principal place of business is not in Iowa to register and provide certain information is not preempted as it does not conflict with the FCU Act or frustrate the federal credit union's ability to carry out its regulatory duties. Only the NCUA can enforce state law against a federal credit union, however. Letter affirms the April 25, 1992 letter regarding the preemption of restrictions on security and balloon payments.

*Interpretive Letter No. NCUA-92-0332 (June 1, 1992)* (State Affected: New York). Assuming the state's motor vehicle retail installment loan law applied to a federal credit union, then a limit on a grace period is preempted.

*Interpretive Letter No. NCUA-92-0335 (May 18, 1992)* (State Affected: Massachusetts). Massachusetts law prohibiting the charging of a late fee unless the mortgage payment is at least 15 days late is preempted; state law stating that payments due on a Saturday or holiday may be made on the next business day is not preempted since it is a matter of statutory contract law.

*Interpretive Letter No. NCUA-92-0316 (Apr. 25, 1992)* (State Affected: Iowa). State credit card law, for the most part, is not preempted. The sections that impose limitations on the use of security for loans and balloon payments are preempted.

## G.4 Formal Statements of Interpretation and Policy

This section summarizes NCUA formal interpretations of policy relating to preemption that the agency published in the *Federal Register*. The list of all such formal interpretations can be found at www.ncua.gov. Once at the NCUA's homepage, click the link for "Resources & Publications." Then select "Legal," followed by "Regulations, Legal Opinions and Laws" from the menus. Last, click the link for "Interpretive Rulings and Policy Statements."

*Examination for Compliance with State Unclaimed Property Laws, IRPS 82-4, 47 Fed. Reg. 53,325 (Nov. 26, 1982).* The NCUA's Ruling and Policy Statement designating certain state authorities to inspection federal credit unions for compliance with state unclaimed property laws was not intended to preempt states law prerequisites for an inspection of records.

*State Chartered Federally Insured Credit Unions as "Most Favored Lenders," IRPS 81-3, 46 Fed. Reg. 24,153 (Apr. 10, 1981).* NCUA interprets 12 U.S.C. § 1785(g) to mean that state chartered federally insured credit unions may charge the federal interest rate or the rate allowed to the most favored lender on the particular class of loans under state law, if either of these rates exceeds the rate the state chartered credit unions are normally permitted to charge under state law.

Appendix H

# Finding Pleadings and Primary Sources on the Companion Website

## H.1 Introduction

*Consumer Credit Regulation* includes free access to its companion website, which remains free with continued subscription to this title. The companion website includes all appendices found in *Consumer Credit Regulation* plus sample pleadings and dozens of other primary source documents—statutes, regulations, federal and state agency interpretations, and practice aids—all easily located with flexible, powerful search tools. Documents are available in Adobe Acrobat (PDF) format while pleadings are also available in Microsoft Word format.

This appendix describes the documents found on the companion website, how to access and print them, and how to download them to your computer or copy and paste them into a word processing file. Note that the actual site may differ slightly in appearance from the screenshots below.

## H.2 Pleadings and Primary Sources Found on the Companion Website

The companion website to *Consumer Credit Regulation* includes a guide to analyzing a loan flipping case, a large number of sample complaints and discovery requests, and sample affidavits and expert witness testimony. Other pleadings include sample briefs, class certification materials, settlements, injunctive orders, jury instructions, and judgments.

The website also includes key federal statutes with updates, retail installment sales acts summarized and citations to other state lending statutes. Also included are federal agency regulations with recent updates, the full text of numerous other hard-to-find statements of policy, interpretation letters, opinion letters, and guidelines from HUD, NCUA, OCC, OTS, and FDIC.

The website does *not* contain the full text of this treatise's chapters. See Appx. H.6, *infra*, for instructions on how to use Internet-based keyword searches to pinpoint page numbers in the treatise where particular topics are discussed.

## H.3 How to Access the Website

One-time registration is required to access the companion website. Once registered, a user subsequently logging in will be granted immediate access to all the companion websites he or she is authorized to use. For example, one user name and password allows a subscriber to four NCLC titles to access all four related companion websites.

To register for the first time, go to **www.nclc.org/webaccess** and click on the "New users click here to register" link. Enter the Companion Website Registration Number found on the packing statement or invoice accompanying this publication. Then enter the requested information and click on "Login." An e-mail address may be used for the user name, or a different user name may be chosen.

**Subscribers do *not* need to register more than once.** If subscribers subsequently purchase additional NCLC titles, they will automatically be given access to the corresponding companion websites. Registering a second time with the same registration number overrides a prior user name and password. (Note that if users allow all their subscriptions to lapse and then subsequently purchase a manual they will have to register again.)

Once registered, click on the log-in link at **www.nclc.org/webaccess**, enter the user name and password, and select the *Consumer Credit Regulation* website from the list of authorized websites.

An alternative log-in method may be particularly useful for libraries, legal aid offices, or law firms that subscribe to the entire set of NCLC treatises. Simply send an e-mail to publications@nclc.org with a list or range of static IP addresses for which access should be permitted. Users from those addresses can then go to www.nclc.org/ipaccess to be granted access *without* entering a user name and password.

Once logged in, users can click the "My Account" link located on the toolbar to change their personal information.

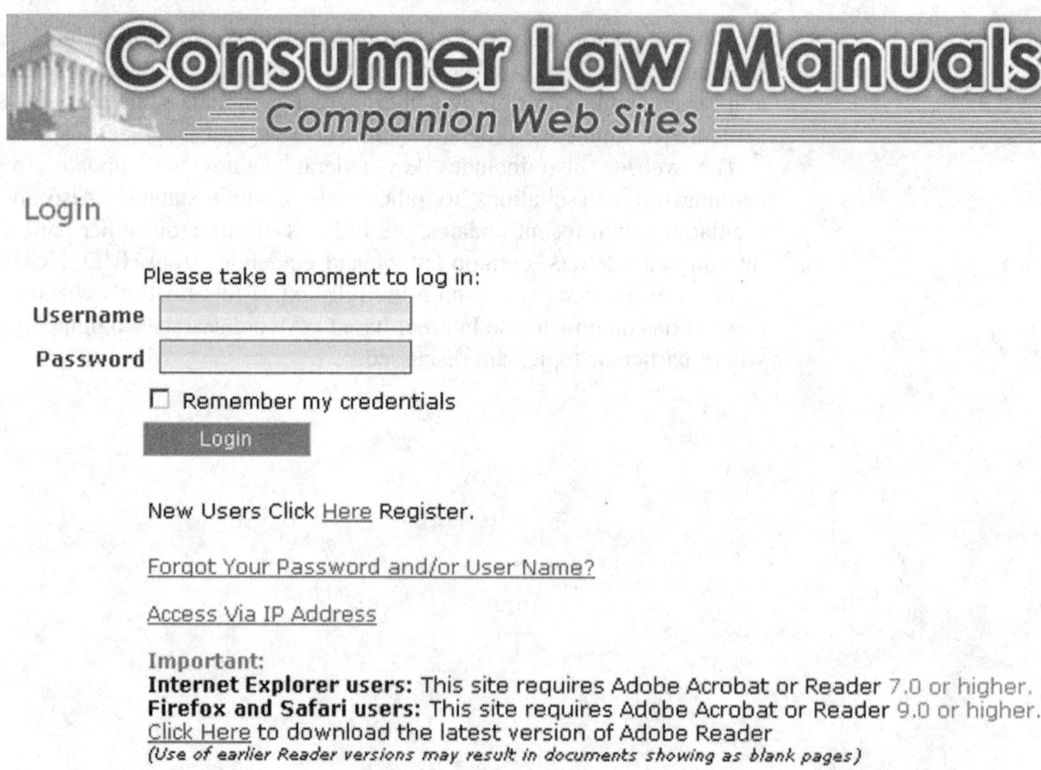

# H.4 Locating Documents on the Website

The companion website provides three ways to locate documents:

**1. The search page** (the home page) uses keyword searches to find documents—full text searches of all documents on the website or searches of just the documents' titles. Enter text in the appropriate field and click the **Search Database** button.

- Narrow the search to documents of a certain type (for example, federal regulations or pleadings) by making a selection from the "Document Type" menu, and then perform a full text or document title search.
- To locate a specific appendix section, select the appendix section number (for example, A.2.3) or a partial identifier (for example, A) in the search page's "Appendix" drop-down fields.
- Click on the "Search Hints" link for a quick reference to special search operators, wildcards, shortcuts, and complex searches. Read this information closely, as syntax and search operators may be slightly different from those used by other websites.

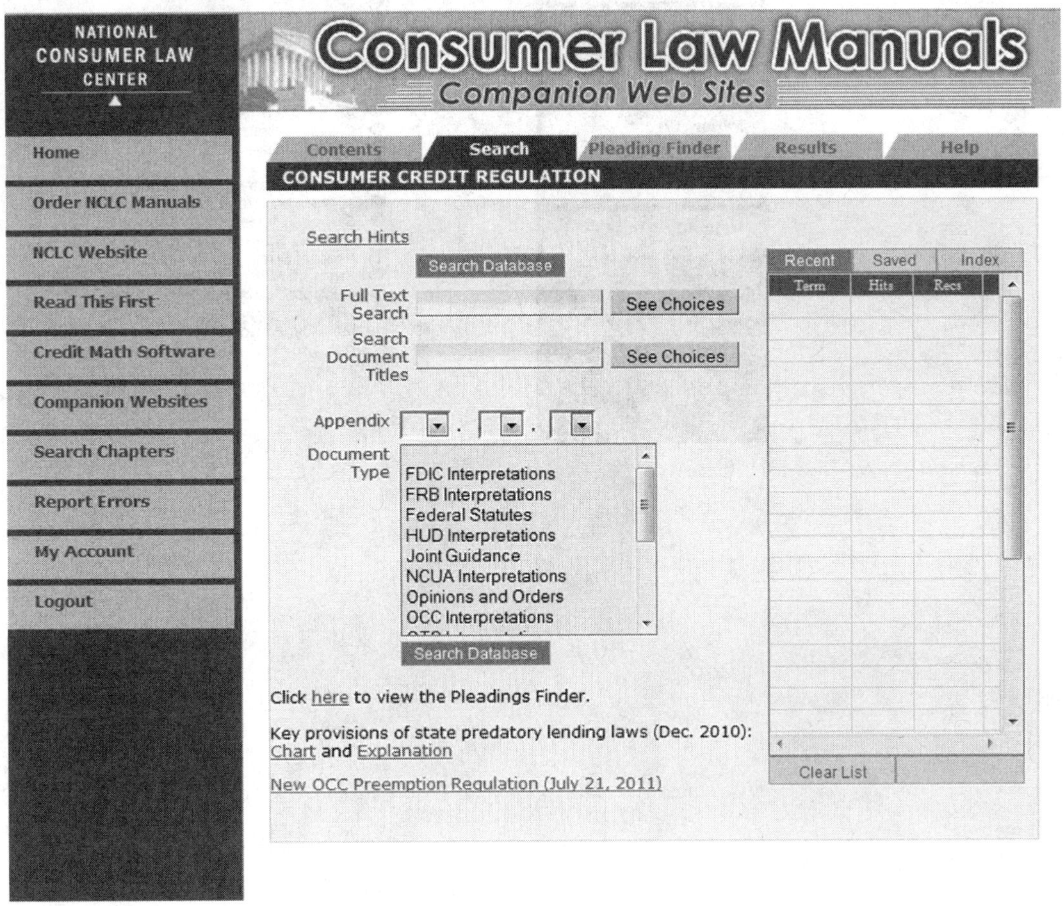

• **2. The contents page** (click on the "Contents" tab at the top of the page) is a traditional nested table of contents. Click a branch to expand it into a list of sub-branches or documents. Each document appears once in this contents tree.

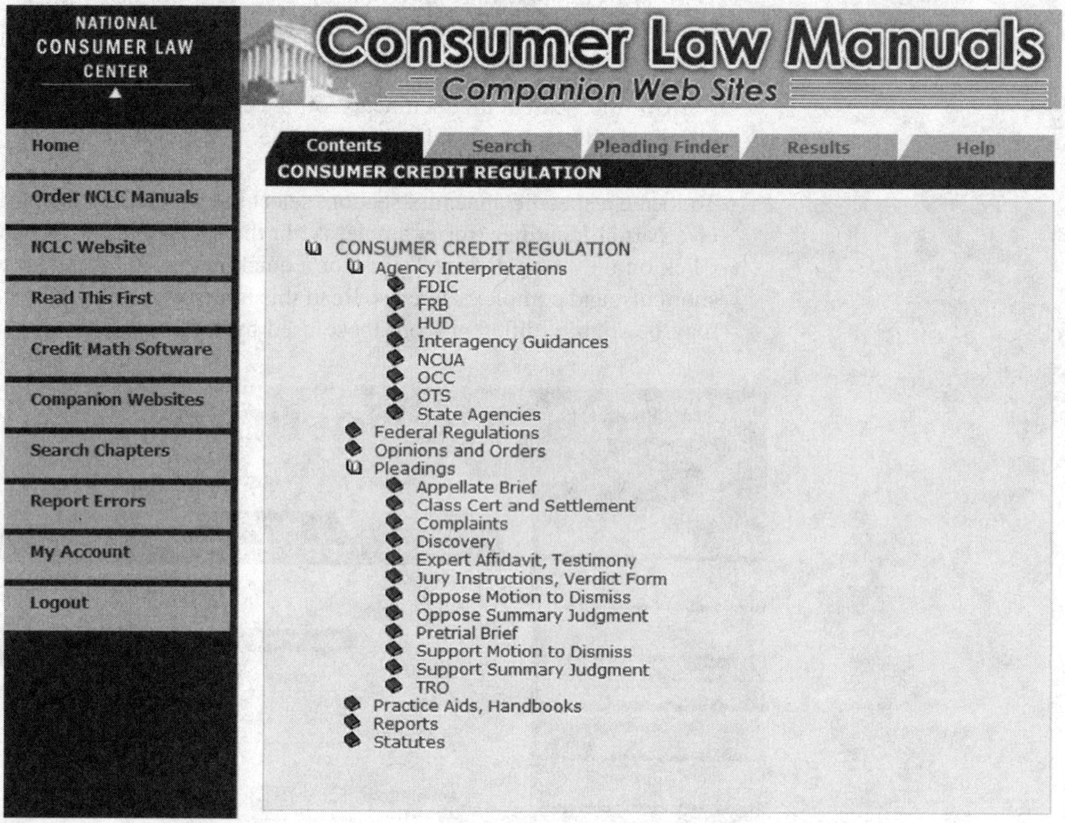

- **3. The pleading finder page** (click on the "Pleading Finder" tab at the top of the page) allows pleadings to be located using one or more menus (for example, "Type of Pleading—General" or "Subject"). For many users, this method will be the preferred way to find a pleading. More than one item can be selected from a menu by using the Ctrl key. For example, make one selection from "Type of Pleading—General," one from "Subject," and three from "Legal Claim" to locate all pleadings of that type and subject that contain one or more of the three legal claims selected. If this search produces insufficient results, deselect "Subject" or "Legal Claim" to find pleadings of that type in any subject area or based upon any legal claim.

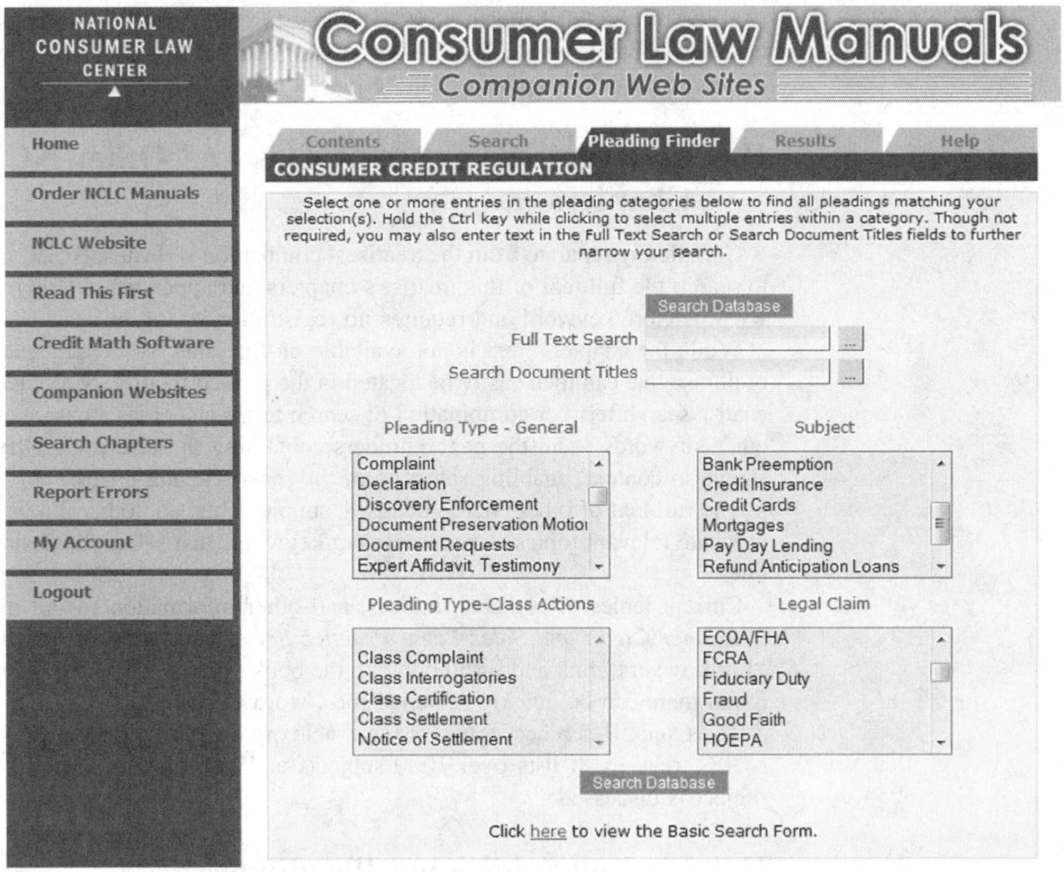

## H.5 How to Use the Documents, Find Microsoft Word Versions, and Locate Additional Features

Click a document title in your search results or on the contents page to view the document in your web browser. Text may be copy-pasted directly from the page or the full document may be downloaded as a PDF file. (You will need a PDF reader to open PDF documents; the free Adobe Reader is available at www.adobe.com.) Additionally, pleadings and certain other documents can be downloaded in Microsoft Word format, enabling the opening of entire documents in a word processing program. Icons to download PDF and Word versions are found at the top of the page.

Links on the left-hand toolbar bring you to credit math software, search tips, other websites, tables of contents and indices of all NCLC treatises, and other practice aids. Links to especially important new developments will be placed toward the bottom of the "Search" page.

## H.6 Electronic Searches of This and Other NCLC Titles' Chapters

Completely separate from the treatises' companion websites, NCLC offers a handy on-line utility to search the full text of this treatise's chapters and appendices. This free search utility is found at www.nclc.org/keyword and requires no registration or log-in.

While the chapters' text is not available on-line, this web-based search engine will find a word or phrase that can then easily be located in the printed treatise. Select *Consumer Credit Regulation*, enter a search term or combination of search terms—such as a case name, a regulation citation, or other keywords—and the page numbers containing those terms will be listed. Search results are shown in context, enabling selection of the most relevant pages.

The full text of other NCLC treatises, supplements, and other publications can also be searched to locate relevant topics at www.nclc.org/keyword. Just select the desired title or search all NCLC titles.

Current tables of contents, indices, and other information for all nineteen titles in the NCLC *Consumer Credit and Sales Legal Practice Series* can be found at www.nclc.org/shop. Click the "For Lawyers" link and scroll down to the book you are interested in. The PDF-format documents found there can be quickly searched for a word or phrase.

The Quick Reference, found at www.nclc.org/qr, is an alphabetical index spanning all nineteen NCLC treatises. It lists over 1000 subjects and indicates the book(s) and section(s) where each subject is discussed.

## H.7 Finding Additional Pleadings

Pleadings specifically relating to this title are found in Adobe Acrobat (PDF) and Microsoft Word format on the companion website. Over 2000 other pleadings are available in NCLC's *Consumer Law Pleadings* and can be found on the *Consumer Law Pleadings* companion website using the same search techniques discussed above. These 2000 pleadings can also be located using the *Consumer Law Pleadings* index guide, which organizes pleadings by type, subject area, legal claim, title, and other categories identical to those used on the website.

# Index and Quick Reference

## Quick Reference to the Consumer Law Practice Series

The Quick Reference to the Consumer Law Practice Series pinpoints where to find specific topics analyzed in any of the nineteen NCLC treatises. The Quick Reference is now available at www.nclc.org/qr. Placing the Quick Reference on a website ensures that readers have the most up-to-date version, including any revised section numbering.

Another way to locate topics is to go to www.nclc.org/keyword and perform keyword searches on individual treatises or across all NCLC publications. This function allows for compound searches such as "identity theft (near) punitive damages," and shows results in context, with the appropriate book title and page number where the reference is found.

Pleadings related just to *Consumer Credit Regulation* can be found on the companion website to this title and can be located using different search functions, including the "Pleading Finder." For more information, see page ix, *supra*.

NCLC also has over 2000 additional sample pleadings on websites accompanying our other titles. The best way to locate and access a pleading among this broader group is to use NCLC's *Consumer Law Pleadings Index Guide* or the finding aids on its website.

More information on individual treatises in this series is available at What Your Library Should Contain on page v, *supra,* or by going to www.nclc.org/shop.

## Index

References are to sections

References are to sections

**References are to sections**

References are to sections

References are to sections

*NOTES*

*NOTES*

# *NOTES*